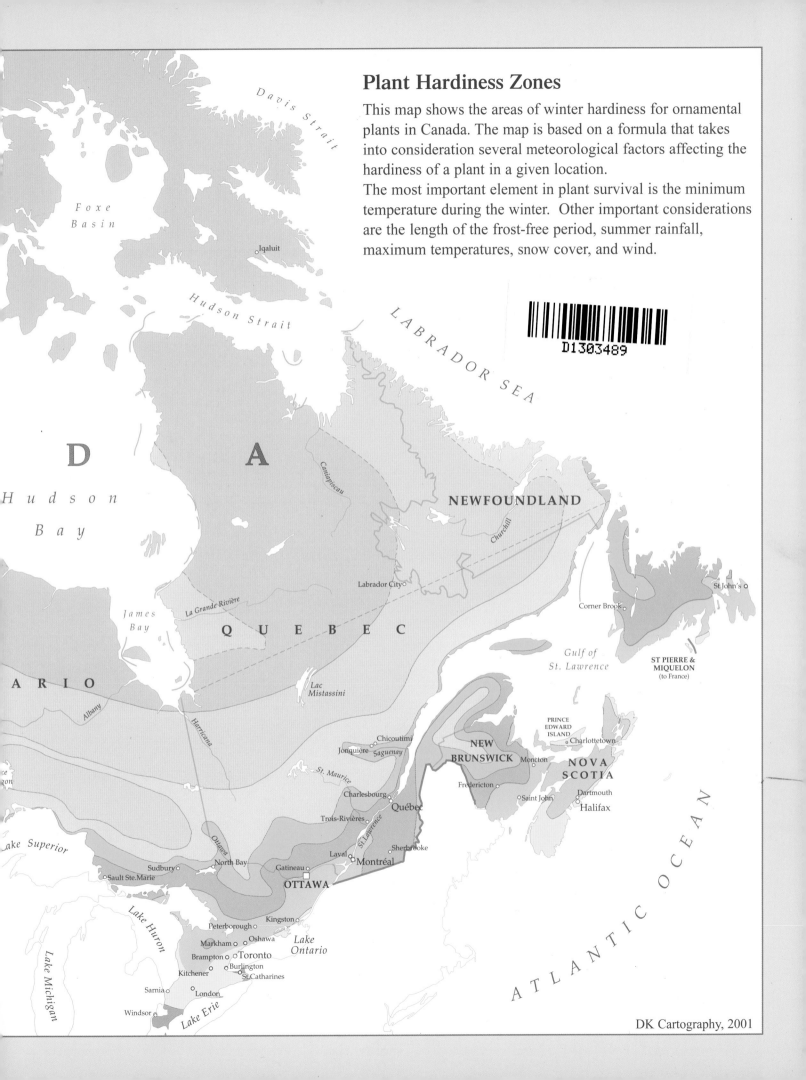

Plant Hardiness Zones

This map shows the areas of winter hardiness for ornamental plants in Canada. The map is based on a formula that takes into consideration several meteorological factors affecting the hardiness of a plant in a given location.

The most important element in plant survival is the minimum temperature during the winter. Other important considerations are the length of the frost-free period, summer rainfall, maximum temperatures, snow cover, and wind.

D1303489

DK Cartography, 2001

DORLING KINDERSLEY

CANADIAN
ENCYCLOPEDIA *of*
PLANTS
AND
FLOWERS

DORLING KINDERSLEY

CANADIAN
ENCYCLOPEDIA *of*
PLANTS
AND
FLOWERS

Editor-in-chief for Canada

TREVOR COLE

DORLING KINDERSLEY
www.dk.com

London, New York, Munich, Melbourne, Delhi

Senior Editor Joanna Chisholm
Project Editors Alison Copland, Marion Dent, Angeles Gavira,
Jacqueline Jackson, Stella Martin, Lesley Riley
Additional editorial assistance from Polly Boyd, Lynn Bresler,
Michèle Clarke, Peter Kirkham, Maggie O'Hanlon, Jane Parker,
Nichola Thomasson, Sarah Widdicombe

Senior Art Editor Ina Stradins
DTP Project Manager Robert Campbell
Picture Research Neale Chamberlaine, Sue Hadley, Sean Hunter,
Hugh Thompson

Senior Managing Editor Jonathan Metcalf
Senior Managing Art Editor Bryn Walls

Design and page make-up Schermuly Design Co.
(Jenny Buzzard, Nick Buzzard, Masumi Higo, Hugh Schermuly)

Photographers Clive Boursnell, Deni Bown, Jonathan Buckley,
Andrew Butler, Eric Crichton, Christine M. Douglas, John Fielding,
Neil Fletcher, Nancy Gardiner, John Glover, Jerry Harpur, Sunniva Harte,
Neil Holmes, Jacqui Hurst, Andrew Lawson, Andrew de Lory,
Howard Rice, Matthew Ward, Steve Wooster
Illustrators Vanessa Luff, Amanda Lunn, Eric Thomas, Janos Marffy

Advisors and consultants In addition to the contributors listed on the
Contents page, Dorling Kindersley would like to thank Barry Ambrose,
John Bond, Tony Clements, Steven Davis, Sheila Ecklin, Barbara Ellis,
the late Thomas Everett, Jim Gardiner, Ralph Gould, David Kerly,
David Pycraft, Piers Trehane, Dr Simon Thornton-Wood, Adrian
Whiteley, and the staff of the Royal Horticultural Society at
Vincent Square and Wisley Garden.

First Canadian Edition
Published in Canada in 2001 by Dorling Kindersley Limited
Represented in Canada by Tourmaline Editions Inc., 27 Davies Avenue, Suite 101,
Toronto, Ontario M4M 2A9
Canadian edition copyright © 2001 Dorling Kindersley Limited, London

British edition, entitled The Royal Horticultural Society New Encyclopedia of Plants
and Flowers, first published in Great Britain in 1989 by Dorling Kindersley Limited,
80 Strand, London WC2R 0RL

A Penguin Company

Canadian Cataloging-in-Publication Data
Main entry under title:
Canadian encyclopedia of plants and flowers
1st Canadian ed.
Includes index.
ISBN 1-55363-006-8
1. Plants, Ornamental--Encyclopedias. 2. Flowers--Encyclopedias.
I.Brickell, Christopher. II. Cole, Trevor J.
SB403.2.C35 2001   635.9'03   C2001-900647-0

Reproduced by Colourscan, Singapore
Printed and bound in Germany by Mohndruck GmbH, Gütersloh
01 02 03 04 / 4 3 2 1

www.dk.com

Preface

Originally published in Canada as *The Gardener's Encyclopedia of Plants and Flowers*, this new issue is the first truly Canadian edition. Extensively adapted for Canadian gardeners, the *Encyclopedia* includes new and updated material, hardiness zones for woody plants, new introductions, and plants commonly grown in Canada.

The format is unique in assisting the gardener to select plants by size, colour, and season of interest. The Plant Selector lists plants for a variety of locations and categories, such as sandy soil, dry shade, deer-resistance, and aromatic foliage. Each list is divided into plant types, for example trees, shrubs, perennials, or annuals, with a cross-reference to illustrations, making it easy to find the ideal plant for your garden.

The photographic Plant Catalogue has more than 4,000 colour illustrations arranged in 10 main divisions, like trees, climbers, and water plants, and 27 subdivisions. It includes many single and double pages of photographs of individual plants: clematis, daylilies, and daffodils to name a few. Whether you are just browsing for possible plants for your garden or looking for a specific type of plant for a certain location, this is the place to start. In addition to the superb photographs, each page cross-references other suitable plants that are illustrated elsewhere or are in the Dictionary. It is also invaluable for identifying unknown plants you may already have. Each entry gives a brief description, size, and ideal growing conditions in an easy-to-read format.

The Plant Dictionary is an alphabetical listing of more than 8,000 plants, cross indexed both to the photographs and to common names, eliminating the need to check on common names in a separate index. The botanical nomenclature has been revised to reflect modern practices, with older names given for reference. Use this section to supplement the plants illustrated in the Plant Catalogue and discover other plants you could grow in your garden.

TREVOR COLE
Editor-in-Chief for Canada
Ottawa, Ontario

Contributors

Contents

CREATING A GARDEN

14

THE PLANT SELECTOR

34

THE PLANT CATALOGUE

THE PLANT DICTIONARY

including Common Names

481

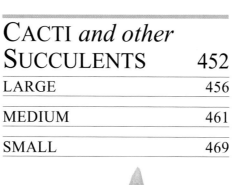

How to Use this Book

The Canadian Encyclopedia of Plants and Flowers is the ideal reference when planning a garden, selecting plants or identifying specimens; it provides a wealth of information on the appearance and cultivation of thousands of individual plants.

The Encyclopedia is divided into several sections. Plant Names and Origins explains the international system for classifying and naming plants, while Creating a Garden offers advice on garden styles, how to position and group plants, and the use of colour and texture. The Plant Selector helps you select suitable species and varieties, while the heart of the book, The Plant Catalogue and The Plant Dictionary, provide detailed photographs, descriptions and cultivation information.

Size categories

Within most groups in The Plant Catalogue, plants are arranged by size (then subsequently by season of interest). Size categories range from large to small, but are defined differently from group to group. Sizes are based on plant heights. The specific height ranges for large, medium, and small can be found in the introductory section for the relevant plant group.

The colour order

Within each group, plants are arranged by the colour of their main feature. Colours are arranged in the same order: from white through reds, purples and blues to greens, yellows and oranges.

Variegated plants are categorized by the colour of their foliage variegation (i.e. white or yellow); succulents are arranged by the colour of their flowers, if produced.

The symbols

- ☀ Prefers sun
- ◐ Prefers partial shade
- ☀ Tolerates full shade
- pH Needs acid soil

- ◌ Prefers well-drained soil
- ◐ Prefers moist soil
- ● Prefers wet soil
- ⨀ Toxic plant

Canadian hardiness zone

This indicates the coldest zone in which this plant can be expected to survive (see Hardiness map on endpapers)

The Plant Selector

The Plant Selector recommends plants for a particular site, soil or purpose, making it easy to find one to suit your needs. The list is divided into 24 useful categories, ranging from plants for hedges and windbreaks to those suitable for containers. Cross-references to The Plant Catalogue lead you to a photograph and description of the plant you choose.

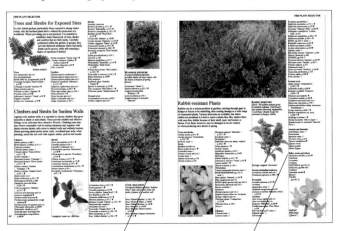

PHOTOGRAPHIC REFERENCE
Garden themes and uses are illustrated, together with photographs of selected plants.

TOP CHOICES
Recommended plants are arranged by group, then listed alphabetically.

The Plant Catalogue

This section brings together plant portraits and descriptions in a colourful catalogue that is divided into groups: Trees (including conifers), Shrubs, Roses, Climbers, Perennials (including grasses, bamboos, rushes, sedges and ferns), Annuals and Biennials, Rock plants, Bulbs, Water plants, and Cacti and other succulents.

Each group is introduced by a four-page section that provides valuable information for growing and designing with plants in the group. This is followed by a catalogue of plants arranged by size, season of interest and colour. Also included are a number of feature panels on plants of special interest, such as camellias, hollies and African violets.

CATALOGUE PAGE ▼

If you know a plant but cannot recall its name, have a specimen that you want to identify, or simply wish to choose plants for your garden based on their size or colouring, The Plant Catalogue will provide the answer.

PAGE HEADINGS
The headings on each page reflect the way in which each plant group is subdivided – usually by size and main season of interest. (See also Size categories, left.)

PLANT PORTRAITS
Colour photographs assist in the identification and selection of plants.

PLANT NAMES
The botanical name is given for each plant, along with synonyms (syn.) and common names where appropriate.

CAPTIONS
Captions describe the plants in detail and draw attention to any special uses they may have.

SIZE AND SHAPE
For most plants the approximate height (H) and spread (S) are given at the end of each caption. (The 'height' of a trailing plant is the length of its stems, either hanging or spreading.) For Trees, Conifers and Shrubs a scale drawing shows the size and shape of each plant at maturity.

CULTIVATION AND HARDINESS
Symbols show the plant's preferred growing conditions and hardiness. For frost tender plants the minimum temperature required for its cultivation is stated. However, the climatic and soil conditions of your particular site should also be taken into account as they may affect a plant's growth. (See also key, left.)

COLOUR BOXES
These show the colour range of plants featured on each page. (See also chart, left.)

Cotoneaster simonsii
Deciduous or semi-evergreen, upright shrub, suitable for hedging. Has oval, glossy, dark green leaves, shallowly cup-shaped, white flowers in early summer and long-lasting, orange-red fruits in autumn.

☀ ◌ ⨀ Zone 7

TOXIC PLANTS
This symbol indicates that the plant can be toxic. Details are given in the genus introductions in The Plant Dictionary.

◀ **GROUP OPENER**
Each new group begins with a photograph
featuring an inspirational display of plants
in the group.

▼ **DESIGN ADVICE**
Group openers are followed by more detailed
descriptions of the characteristics of plants in the
group, together with ideas for how to use these
plants to best effect in the garden.

TABS
Colour-coded tabs make
it easy to find each plant
group.

CROSS-REFERENCES ▼
Plants featured elsewhere
in the book but similar in
type, size, season of
interest and colour to
those illustrated are listed
for consideration.

Chaenomeles speciosa
HEATHERS, illus. pp.178–9
HOLLIES, illus. pp.98–9
Nicotiana glauca

FEATURE PANELS ▶
Plant types or genera of special
interest to the gardener are
presented in separate feature panels
within the appropriate group.

KEY CHARACTERISTICS
The introduction outlines the features
of that type of plant and gives
guidance on cultivation and planting.

FLOWER FORMS
Detailed descriptions of forms and
horticultural classifications within a
genus are given where appropriate
and often supported by line drawings.

PLANT NAMES
The botanical name is given and
the Group or classification where
appropriate. Plant descriptions
appear in The Plant Dictionary.

PLANT PORTRAITS
Close-up photographs of individual
flowers or plants allow quick
identification or selection.

The Plant Dictionary

The Plant Dictionary contains entries
for every genus in the Encyclopedia
and includes over 4,000 recommended
plants not featured in The Plant
Catalogue. It also functions as the
index to The Plant Catalogue.

GENUS NAMES
The genus name is followed
by common names, where
appropriate, and family names.

GENUS ENTRIES
A concise introduction covers
the distinctive characteristics
and hardiness range of plants in
the genus, as well as advice on
siting, cultivation, propagation,
and, if relevant, pruning, pests
and diseases, and toxicity.

SYNONYMS
Synonyms cross-refer to the
correct botanical name.

ILLUSTRATED PLANTS
Descriptions for illustrated
plants appear in The Plant
Catalogue, unless part of a
feature panel (see below left).

PLANT NAMES
Botanical names, synonyms
and common names are given
as appropriate. The genus
name is abbreviated; specific
epithets (e.g. *sagittifolia*) are
abbreviated only if previously
given in full.

PLANT DESCRIPTIONS
Key characteristics of the plant
are described. Hardiness and
cultivation needs are included
only if specific to the plant. Cultivar
entries run on from the species entry,
with the binomial omitted.

SAGITTARIA
Arrowhead

ALISMATACEAE

Genus of deciduous, perennial,
submerged and marginal water plants,
grown for their foliage and flowers.
Species are hardy to tender, min. 5°C
(41°F). Some species are suitable for
pools, others for aquariums. All require
full sun. Remove fading foliage as
necessary. Propagate by division in
spring or summer or by breaking off
turions (scaly, young shoots) in spring.
S. japonica. See *S. sagittifolia*
'Flore Pleno'.
S. latifolia illus. p.446.
S. sagittifolia (Common arrowhead).
Deciduous, perennial, marginal water
plant. H 45cm (18in), S 30cm (12in).
Fully hardy. Upright, mid-green leaves
are acutely arrow-shaped. In summer
produces 3-petalled, white flowers with
dark purple centres. May be grown in
up to 23cm (9in) depth of water. **'Flore
Pleno'** (syn. *S. japonica*; Japanese
arrowhead) has double flowers.

Saguaro. See *Carnegiea gigantea*,
illus. p.456.
St Augustine grass. See *Stenotaphrum
secundatum*.

CROSS-REFERENCES
Common name and synonym cross-
references are listed alphabetically.

Abbreviations

cv(s)	cultivar(s)	illus.	illustrated	subsp.	subspecies
f.	forma	min.	minimum	subspp.	subspecies
H	height	p(p).	page(s)		(pl.)
	(or length of	pl.	plural	syn.	synonym(s)
	trailing stems)	S	spread	var.	varietas

Plant Hardiness Zones

The survival of woody plants has
been determined and plotted in the
Canadian Plant Hardiness Zone
Map. This divides the country into
nine zones, most of which can be
subdivided into warmer and cooler
regions (a) and (b). These zones are
only a guide and within each zone
there will be areas that are warmer
or cooler than the norm.

A garden surrounded by hedges
where snow collects could be a
half zone warmer, while one at the
base of a slope, where frost
collects, would be colder than
average. Within the garden
microclimates exist and a plant may
survive in one place and die a little

way away. Some of the plants listed
are at the very limits of hardiness,
they may survive in a sheltered
garden in zone 9 and have been
listed as zone 9?.

Most perennial plants die down
to ground level in the fall and are
not as influenced by winter
temperatures as woody plants.
Their survival depends much more
on snow depth and persistence.
A region with little snow or regular
mid-winter thaws may not be able
to grow as wide a range as
somewhere colder that had a good
snowfall. For these reasons,
hardiness zones have not been given
for non-woody plants.

Plant Names and Origins

People have always given names to plants, but once they began to travel extensively they discovered that the same plant was often called by a different name in various parts of the world. To overcome this problem, a common naming system was devised.

THE BINOMIAL SYSTEM

Greek and Roman scholars laid the foundations of our method of naming plants, and their practice of observing and describing nature in detail was continued in the monasteries and universities of Europe, where classical Latin remained the common language. However, the binomial system in use today was established largely under the influence of the famous eighteenth-century Swedish botanist, Carl Linnaeus (1707–78). In his definitive works *Genera plantarum* and *Species plantarum*, Linnaeus classified each

CARL LINNAEUS
The father of plant classification, Carl Linnaeus, in Lapp costume; this engraving is from a portrait by M. Hoffman, c.1737.

WILD ORIGINS
Below: Rhododendron rupicola *var.* chryseum *grows wild in north-western Yunnan, China, from where it was introduced into British gardens early in the nineteenth century.*

plant by using two words in Latin form, instead of adopting the descriptive phrases that had been in common usage among the botanists and herbalists of his day. The first word was the name of the genus (e.g. *Ilex*) and the second the specific epithet (e.g. *aquifolium*). Together they provided a name by which a particular plant (species) could be universally known (*Ilex aquifolium*, English or common holly). Other species in the same genus were then given different epithets (*Ilex crenata*, *Ilex pernyi*, *Ilex serrata* and so on).

THE MEANING OF PLANT NAMES

A greater appreciation of botanical names may be gained by knowing something of their meaning. A name may be commemorative: the *Fuchsia* is a tribute to Leonhart Fuchs, a German physician and herbalist. It may tell us where a plant comes from, as with *Parrotia persica* (of Persia, now Iran). A plant may bear the name of the collector who introduced it: *Primula forrestii* was brought into cultivation by George Forrest. Or the name may tell us something about its physical character: *Pelargonium* derives from the Greek word *pelargos* (a stork), an appropriate description of the fruits of these plants, which resemble storks' bills; *quinquefolia*, the epithet of *Parthenocissus quinquefolia*, means with foliage made up of five leaflets, from the Latin *quinque* ('five') and *folium* ('leaf').

COMMON NAMES

Although many have familiar common names, plants are usually listed under their botanical names. There are a number of reasons for this. Many plants either do not possess a common name, or they share a common name with others. Even more confusingly, the same common name may be used in different regions to describe different plants: in Scotland 'plane' refers to Acer *pseudoplatanus* (sycamore), in England to the London plane (*Platanus* x *hispanica*), while in North America the native plane (*Platanus occidentalis*) may be called plane or sycamore. Unlike botanical names, which bring related plants together by grouping them in a genus (all true hollies belong to the genus *Ilex*), with common names the same word is often used for quite unrelated plants, such as sea holly (*Eryngium*), hollyhock (*Alcea*) and summer holly (Arctostaphylos *diversifolia*), none of which is related to the true holly. Conversely, one plant may have several common names: heartsease, love-in-idleness and Johnny-jump-up are all charming titles for *Viola tricolor*. Even greater confusion arises when a vernacular common name is in Malay, Chinese or Arabic. In botany, as in other scientific disciplines, the universal use of Latin has therefore been found to be a convenient and precise basis for the naming of plants.

INTERNATIONAL CODES

Since its instigation the Linnaean system of plant classification has been developed by scientists so that the entire plant kingdom is divided into a multi-branched 'family tree' (see p.13). International co-operation has been essential to ensure that the system is reliable for scientific, commercial and horticultural use. To this end, there are now rules laid down in the *International Code of Nomenclature for Cultivated Plants* (1995) and the *International Code of Botanical Nomenclature* (1994).

PLANT INTRODUCTIONS

Just as the origins of plant names may be traced to Classical civilization, so can the first plant introductions. The Roman Empire at its peak covered a vast area, from western Europe to Asia, and as the Romans travelled they brought with them plants they used for food or ornament, such as the Spanish chestnut, peach, fig and many herbs. During the thirteenth century, returning Crusaders brought the Damask rose from Damascus. Centuries later, cultivated plants such as Persian lilac and the apricot were brought home from the sophisticated Turkish and Moorish gardens along the shores of the Mediterranean.

Plant hunting became more systematic when intrepid private collectors such as the two John Tradescants (father and son) made trips specifically to look for plants on the eastern coasts of North America, particularly Virginia. As the world was mapped and colonized in the eighteenth century, an explosion of botanical interest brought many plants from the New World, notably the western coasts of the American continent, South Africa, Australia and New Zealand. In the twentieth century, the greatest rewards for the determined plant collector were to be found in the diverse flora of eastern Asia. Although not an easy region for Westerners

GENTIANA SINO-ORNATA
George Forrest had a special interest in gentians, collecting hundreds of specimens during his trips to China. He first discovered this plant in 1904, during a hazardous expedition high in the mountain ranges of northwestern Yunnan.

Plant Hunters

A desire to see the world was the original incentive for the earliest botanists but, as interest in new and rare plants developed, private collectors began to bring back plants with them. These exotic novelties proved extremely popular, especially in fashionable gardens, and fuelled the demand for further new plants for garden adornment. To encourage this new market, commercial and scientific organizations began to sponsor the plant hunters. David Douglas was employed in 1824 by the Royal Horticultural Society to travel to America's west coast, where he gathered vast quantities of seed from hitherto unknown species including the Douglas fir. Access to China was restricted until 1842, but in the following year Robert Fortune began an expedition, again sponsored by the Royal Horticultural Society, that was to yield many ornamental garden plants. In his wake went French botanist-missionaries Father Jean Pierre Armand David, who discovered the lovely *Davidia* tree and after whom *Buddleja davidii* is named, and Father Jean Marie Delavay, who found the blue poppy (*Meconopsis betonicifolia*). Japan was also the source of hundreds of garden plants – many being introduced to Europe by the German plant hunter Philipp von Siebold in the nineteenth century.

The golden age of plant hunting was the early twentieth century. E.H. Wilson, one of the most famous plant hunters (see above right), discovered *Magnolia wilsonii* in 1904 and, in the same period, George Forrest introduced many rhododendrons and other plants from China and Tibet. In the 1920s and 1930s, Frank Kingdon Ward collected unusual primulas, rhododendrons, lilies and gentians from the Himalayas.

Today, plant-hunting expeditions are still sponsored and new plants introduced, although in smaller quantities than before. However, the impetus for plant discovery has shifted from garden adornment and novelty to plant conservation and breeding.

Magnolia wilsonii

ERNEST HENRY WILSON
Above: E.H. Wilson, who collected in Asia for the English nursery Messrs Veitch and for the Arnold Arboretum, in Boston, USA, discovered more than 900 new plants species and varieties, including Magnolia Wilsonii.

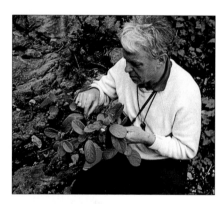

RECENT FINDS
Roy Lancaster (above) is a modern-day plant hunter who has introduced many new species to Britain. Among them are Hypericum lancasteri *and Cotoneaster lancasteri (left), both from China.*

Cotoneaster lancasteri

to explore, thousands of plants, particularly trees and shrubs, were introduced from China, the Himalayan region and Japan.

GENETICS AND HYBRIDIZATION

Natural mutations in plants have been observed for centuries but only in the twentieth century has plant breeding developed into a science used throughout the world. Although Thomas Knight carried out some pioneering plant-breeding experiments in the nineteenth century, and the word 'hybrid' was used by Darwin, it was not until Gregor Mendel's work with sweet peas in 1899 that the process was understood and could therefore be exploited commercially.

Once the mysteries of recessive genes and chromosomes were revealed, it became clear that plants could be bred to be more vigorous and produce more flowers, as well as be altered in other ways. Today, breeders can produce hybrids of a certain shape, colour and .habit. One result of this is that certain successful plant 'cultivars' (**culti**vated **vari**eties) have to be protected (see Coded cultivar names, p.12).

UNDERSTANDING BOTANICAL DIVISIONS

The plant kingdom may be broadly divided into vascular plants and non-vascular plants. Vascular plants are of most interest to the gardener and have specialized conducting tissue that enables them to grow in a wider range of habitats and reach a larger size than the non-vascular plants such as algae,

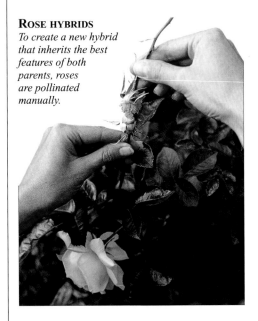

ROSE HYBRIDS
To create a new hybrid that inherits the best features of both parents, roses are pollinated manually.

mosses and liverworts. Vascular plants are classified into many groups, mainly according to the way they bear their seeds. For example conifers, part of the Gymnosperm group, are distinct because they bear their naked seeds in cone-like fruits. The basic division within these groups is the family.

THE FAMILY

Plants are grouped in particular families according to the structure of their flowers, fruits and other organs. This means that families may consist of clearly related and specialized plants such as the orchids (family Orchidaceae) and the bromeliads (family Bromeliaceae), or embrace plants as diverse (in terms of what they offer the gardener) as those in the family Rosaceae: *Alchemilla*, *Cotoneaster*, *Crataegus*, *Geum*, *Malus*, *Prunus*, *Pyracantha*, *Sorbus* and *Spiraea*.

THE GENUS AND ITS SPECIES

A family may contain one genus (for example, *Eucryphia* is the only genus in the family Eucryphiaceae) or many (the daisy family Compositae has over 1,000 genera). Each genus comprises related plants, such as oaks (genus *Quercus*), maples (genus *Acer*) and lilies (genus *Lilium*), with several features in common. A genus may contain one or many species. Thus a reference to a member of the genus *Lilium* could be to any of the lilies, but one to *Lilium candidum* would denote one particular lily (in this case the Madonna lily). Certain genera form separate horticultural groups within families. An example of this would be the heaths or heathers (including *Calluna*, *Daboecia* and *Erica*) within the family Ericaceae, which also includes *Kalmia*, *Rhododendron* and *Vaccinium* (see visual key, opposite).

A species is a group of plants that consistently and naturally reproduces itself, generating a plant population that shares similar characteristics and which is distinguishable from other natural populations.

SUBSPECIES, VARIETIES AND FORMS

In the wild, even plants of the same species can exhibit slight differences, and on the basis of these are often split into three botanically recognized but occasionally overlapping subdivisions. The subspecies (subsp.) is a distinct variant, usually as a result of the plant's particular geographical distribution; the variety (botanical *varietas*, abbreviated to 'var.') differs slightly in its botanical structure; and the form (*forma*, f.) has only minor variations, such as habit or colour of leaf, flower or fruit.

CULTIVARS

Many plants grown in today's gardens may be adequately described by their botanical names, but numerous variants exist in cultivation which differ slightly from the wild form of the species. These forms may be of considerable horticultural interest, for their variegated leaves or other characters. They may be found as individuals in the wild and introduced to cultivation, be selected from a batch of seedlings, or occur as a mutation; all are known as cultivars – a contraction of 'cultivated varieties'. To come true to type, many cultivars need to be propagated vegetatively (by cuttings, grafting or division) or grown annually from specially selected seed.

Cultivars named since 1959 must be given vernacular names, which are printed in Roman type within quotes (e.g. *Phygelius aequalis* 'Yellow Trumpet'); this distinguishes them from wild varieties, which are described by a Latin name in italic type.

HYBRIDS

Sexual crosses between botanically distinct species or genera are known as hybrids and are indicated by a multiplication sign. If the cross is between species in different genera, the result is called an intergeneric hybrid and, when two (occasionally three or more) genera are concerned, the name given is a condensed form of the names of the genera involved: x *Cupressocyparis* covers hybrids between all species of *Chamaecyparis* and *Cupressus*. If more than three genera are involved, then the hybrids are called after a person and given the ending *-ara*. Thus x *Potinara*, covering hybrids of *Brassavola*, *Cattleya*, *Laelia* and *Sophronitis*, commemorates M. Potin of the French orchid society. Most common, however, are hybrids between species in the same genus. These are known as interspecific hybrids and are given a collective name similar to a species name but preceded by a multiplication sign; for example *Epimedium* x *rubrum* covers hybrids between *E. alpinum* and *E. grandiflorum*.

When one plant is grafted onto another, a new plant may occasionally arise at the point of grafting, which contains the tissues of both parents. For naming purposes, these graft chimaeras or graft hybrids are treated in the same way as sexual hybrids, except that they are denoted by a plus sign, as in +*Laburnocytisus adamii*, which is a graft hybrid between species of *Laburnum* and *Chamaecytisus*.

Cultivars of hybrids should be listed under a botanical name if one is available or, if the parentage is complex or obscure, by giving the generic name followed solely by the cultivar name (e.g. *Rosa* 'Buff Beauty').

NAME CHANGES

It is often confusing and frustrating to come across name changes in new publications. Long-established names disappear, only to be replaced by unfamiliar ones. But there are good reasons for such changes: a plant may originally have been incorrectly identified; the same plant may already have been given a different, earlier name; a name may be found to apply to two different plants; or new scientific knowledge may cause a plant's classification to be changed. In this Encyclopedia, numerous synonyms have been given in order to minimize the problems of identifying or purchasing renamed plants.

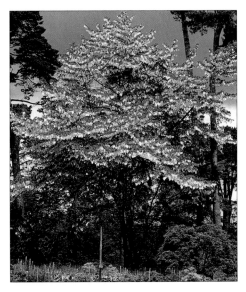

DAVIDIA INVOLUCRATA
This lovely tree from China is named after its discoverer Father Jean Pierre Armand David. It has several common names including Dove tree, Ghost tree and Pocket handkerchief tree.

CODED CULTIVAR NAMES
When plant breeders raise a new cultivar, it is given a code name to ensure its formal identification; this may be different to the name under which the plant is sold. For example, the rose selling under the name Casino also has the code name of 'Macca'; in this Encyclopedia, both names are cited, and styled thus; *Rosa* CASINO ('Macca'). To safeguard their ownership of the cultivar, plant breeders may apply for Plant Breeder's Rights (PBR), which are granted using the code name.

Visual Key to Plant Classification

In horticulture, as in other areas of botany, plants are classified according to a hierarchical system (taxonomy) and named primarily on the basis of Linnaeus's binomial approach (genus followed by species epithet). For a better understanding of this system, part of the family Ericaceae has been set out below, showing all levels from family through genera and species down to cultivars, Groups and hybrids.

FAMILY

A group of several genera that share a set of underlying natural characteristics. Family names usually end in -aceae. Family limits are often controversial.

Ericaceae

GENUS (PL. GENERA)

A group of one or more plants that share a range of distinctive characteristics. Several (rarely one) genera are classified into one family. Each genus contains one or more species and its name is printed in italic type with an initial capital letter.

 Daboecia

 Calluna

 Erica

 Vaccinium

 Kalmia

 Rhododendron

SPECIES

A group of plants that breeds naturally to produce offspring with similar characteristics; these keep it distinct from other populations in nature. Each species has a two-part name printed in italic type.

 Daboecia cantabrica

Daboecia azorica

Erica arborea

 Rhododendron cinnabarinum

 Rhododendron yakushimanum

HYBRID

Sexual crosses between species within a genus give rise to interspecific hybrids (see also box below).

Daboecia x *scotica*

FORMA

A minor variant of a species, often differing in flower colour or habit from others in the species. Indicated by 'f.' in Roman type and an epithet printed in italic type.

 Daboecia cantabrica f. *alba*

VARIETAS

A minor species subdivision, differing slightly in botanical structure. Indicated by 'var.' (short for varietas) *in Roman type and an epithet in italic type.*

 Erica arborea var. *alpina*

SUBSPECIES

A naturally occurring, distinct variant of a species, differing in one or more characteristic. Indicated by 'subsp.' in Roman type and an epithet in italic type.

 Rhododendron cinnabarinum subsp. *xanthocodon*

GROUP (CULTIVAR GROUP)

An assemblage of cultivars with similar characteristics within a genus, species or hybrid. They may be designated with a name in a modern language or in some cases be in Latin form.

Rhododendron cinnabarinum Concatenans Group

Rhododendron cinnabarinum Purpurellum Group

CULTIVAR

Selected or artificially raised, distinct variant of a species, subspecies, varietas, forma or hybrid. Indicated by a vernacular name printed in Roman type within single quotation marks.

 Daboecia cantabrica 'Alba Globosa'

 Daboecia x *scotica* 'William Buchanan'

Daboecia x *scotica* 'Jack Drake'

 Daboecia x *scotica* 'Silverwells'

Rhododendron cinnabarinum 'Copper'

Rhododendron cinnabarinum 'Amber'

Rhododendron yakushimanum 'Koichiro Wada'

 Rhododendron 'Ken Janeck'

HYBRIDS

A graft hybrid is a non-sexual plant created through the merging of plant tissue at the point of graft between a rootstock and its scion. For example, when *Laburnum* and *Chamaecytisus* species are combined they form + *Laburnocytisus adamii*.

A more common type of hybrid is a sexual cross between botanically distinct species or genera. If the resulting hybrids are fertile, several generations of plants may be produced, all sharing characters of both parents. Here two species of viburnum have cross-fertilized to create *Viburnum* x *bodnantense*.

Laburnum anagyroides	+	*Chamaecytisus purpureus*	=	+ *Laburnocytisus adamii*

Viburnum farreri	x	*Viburnum grandiflorum*	=	*Viburnum* x *bodnantense*

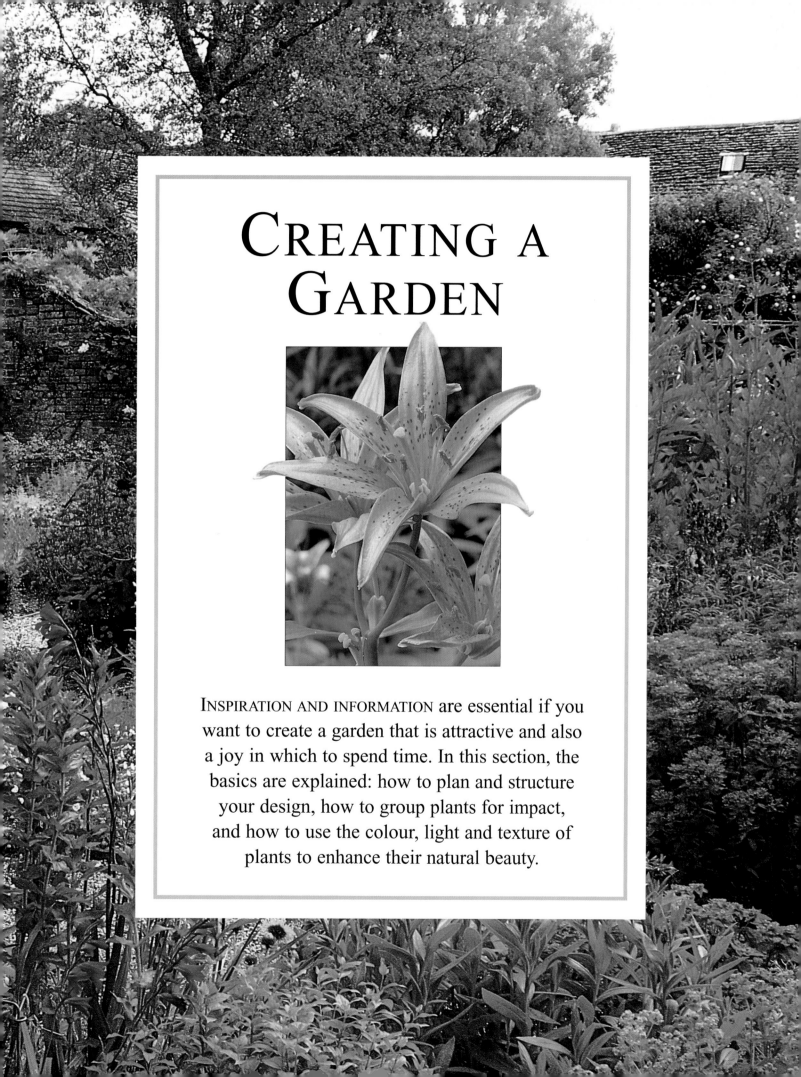

CREATING A
GARDEN

INSPIRATION AND INFORMATION are essential if you
want to create a garden that is attractive and also
a joy in which to spend time. In this section, the
basics are explained: how to plan and structure
your design, how to group plants for impact,
and how to use the colour, light and texture of
plants to enhance their natural beauty.

Style

Gardens, like homes, have many different atmospheres or styles. Some are instantly familiar, such as the haphazard abundance of an English cottage garden or the sparse elegance of a Japanese garden, while others, such as a *jardin sauvage*, are harder to define.

DESIGN INFLUENCES

Styles of garden design may have historical associations and show, for example, the influence of the formal, stepped stone terraces of Renaissance Italy, the elegant grandeur of classical French gardens, such as Versailles, or the showy, colourful and exotic plantings of Edwardian and Victorian England.

Different styles have also developed as a result of regional cultures. This is particularly true of the United States, where East-coast picket gardens, of wooden decks and open white fences, contrast with glamorous West-coast gardens with their patios and pools, or the sleepy gardens of the South with their magnolias and oaks shading the verandah.

These examples may seem too ambitious for the average gardener, but they can provide the source of inspiration and be adapted to a particular site. It may be impossible to reproduce a classical French layout or an elegant Italian hillside landscape in a small city garden, but a sense of classical formality is within the reach of everyone with the use of just a few stone steps, a small fountain and a handsome stone container filled with annuals, or perhaps an architectural, evergreen shrub or clipped tree. When choosing a style, bear in mind the climate, space and soil type.

PROPORTION

To create a style in your own garden, be sensitive to the scale and mood of the surrounding landscape and buildings. A classical-style house, for instance, may well require a garden with a formal layout; the proportions between the windows and doors could suggest the pattern made in the garden by paths, pools, terraces, borders and lawn areas. Take care with the relationships of these elements to each other and the garden as well as to the house. Whereas broad sweeps of colour and grand paths are elegant in a large garden with open views, narrow borders of small flowers and winding paths would be lost in so large a space, although ideally suited to a small, informal cottage garden.

PERSPECTIVE

You can alter the apparent shape of your garden by creating false perspective in your design, using the edges of different areas (paths, beds or terraces) as 'lines'. Horizontal lines will make the site seem wider while vertical lines will increase its length. To accentuate length even more, make vertical lines converge as they approach the bottom of the garden. Skilful placing of upright or prostrate trees and shrubs enhances this effect.

Attention may be drawn to a particular spot, within or beyond the garden, by creating a dynamic, or moving, line such as a curving path that leads to a focal point – a pond, arbour, specimen tree or magnificent view. Formal or enclosed gardens with no dominant point of interest are, however, best served by static patterns, such as those created by box hedges bordering geometric beds.

MATERIALS

Paths, paved areas, fencing and buildings should harmonize with the house and its surroundings in materials as well as in form.

You may have difficulty in deciding what will be appropriate; try determining instead what will not be suitable and continue by a process of elimination. For example, crazy paving will not enhance an eighteenth-century town house.

Try to make the garden a continuation of the interior in terms of colour and style. This concept may be taken further, so that the view from within blends harmoniously with the internal decor and does not jolt the senses, whether you are viewing the interior from the garden, or the garden from the interior. Plants are, of course, the most important 'materials' used to create a garden's style. Your choice will be limited by the location, soil type and climate of the area. Bright Mediterranean flowers such as rock roses will not thrive in a shady woodland, nor will heathers and camellias flourish on open, alkaline land. Take advantage of the assets at your disposal and do not try to fight nature. Not only will

ITALIAN-STYLE TERRACE
Above: This elegant terrace has been created on a modest scale using terracotta pots and a small, wall-mounted fountain. The strong, horizontal lines of the pergola are softened by climbing roses, honeysuckle and the decorative leaves of Vitis coignetiae.

EXOTIC GARDEN
Left: A Japanese mood has been conjured here by combining a clear stream, cascading down stepped rocks, with a distinctive, dwarf Japanese maple (Acer palmatum 'Dissectum Atropurpureum').

SEMI-FORMAL GARDEN
Right: The classical pavilion sets the formal tone of this country garden. Shrubs and hedges are clipped into strong, but related, architectural shapes and lead the eye towards the austere building and to the bonsai tree, on a plinth in front of it, which provides the elegant focal point. The path has been designed with materials that harmonize with the pavilion in texture and colour.

inappropriate plants never thrive, but very often when they are grown away from their natural habitat they also look out of place.

MAKING A STYLE YOUR OWN

Most important of all, do not forget your own relationship with the garden – let it reflect your personality. If you are a relaxed person who likes pottering, you might allow herbaceous perennials to overspill their formal boundaries, or leave a few self-sown seedlings to interrupt a well-groomed gravel path. On the other hand, if you like everything around you to be ordered and tidy, you will probably be happier with a neat, symmetrical layout, perhaps blocks of annuals or Hybrid Tea (modern) roses rather than old-fashioned (old garden) varieties.

Do not overlook any more practical requirements, either. If you have a young family, there is little point in siting an attractive lily pond in the middle of the garden as you will have to cover it with ugly safety mesh. Instead lay large areas to lawn and plant robust trees and shrubs. If a person using a wheelchair will be spending time in the garden, any stepped levels should be removed or replaced with gently sloping ramps or undulating banks. You might also build some raised beds; these make gardening easier for the handicapped or for elderly gardeners.

Consider realistically how much time you are willing to spend on maintenance, as some gardens are much more time-consuming than others. If time is limited, concentrate on trees, shrubs and ground cover; perennials and bulbs provide variety of colour, form and texture, but usually demand rather more gardening time. For maximum commitment grow more specialized plants, for example rock plants that may have demanding cultivation requirements, or plant or sow annuals and biennials.

KEEPING THE PLANTING SIMPLE

A common mistake made by gardeners is to include too many varieties of plants in a small area. There is something to be learnt from a specialist's garden – the rose grower's, for example, or that of the enthusiast who cultivates only conifers and heathers. Their gardens look good because the choice of plants is restricted, giving rise to a comparatively simple design.

COTTAGE-STYLE GARDEN

Below left: A haphazard mixture of mainly perennial plants is here combined with the shrub Piptanthus nepalensis, *which grows against an old stone wall, while beneath it* Corydalis ochroleuca, Hypericum 'Hidcote' *and lady's mantle* (Alchemilla mollis) *intermingle happily. Note the limited colour range of the planting, which makes it appear informal rather than chaotic.*

JAPANESE-STYLE GARDEN

Below right: Bamboo, stepping stones and, in the distance, complementary foliage plants evoke a tranquil atmosphere in this Japanese-style garden. Such a style may be adapted to suit sunny or shaded sites and requires very little maintenance.

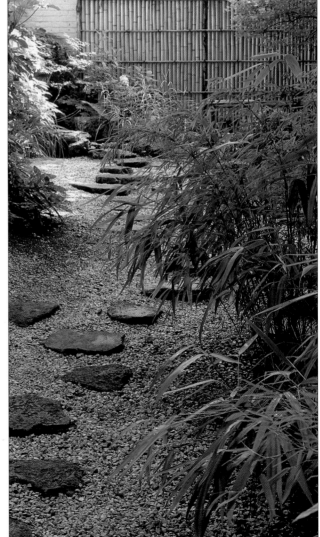

If this is too limiting, you can prevent a mixed planting from becoming over complex and unfocused by designing within a particular colour range and by grouping different varieties of plants together. This also applies to foliage, as is shown so effectively in the famous white garden at Sissinghurst in Kent.

REMEMBERING THE DETAIL

Once the overall style and layout of your garden have been decided upon and the range of plants within it chosen, make sure that the furnishings do not ruin the effect. A wrought-iron bench, for instance, might be too elaborate for many gardens, whereas a simple wooden one would rarely jar. A decorated Italianate urn is probably too grand for an informal, suburban garden, even if planted with humble daisies. A period garden might be difficult to furnish economically, but on the whole plain containers and ornaments are successful, especially in small, confined areas, and also suit a variety of plantings. Once you have decided on the style of garden furniture, keep to your original concept, as slight deviations will create a sense of clutter and all your planning will have been in vain.

ROMANTIC GARDEN
Left: A circular seat is placed in the leafy shade of a country garden made romantic by rough grass and a beautiful, sprawling shrub rose.

INFORMAL GARDEN
Below: Even in this deceptively simple planting of herbaceous perennials, bulbs, annuals and shrubs, each plant has been carefully selected to balance the others in form, colour and texture. The barberry (Berberis) *and elegant, arching sprays of Solomon's seal* (Polygonatum x hybridum) *provide continuity and cohesion to the scheme.*

Structure

'Structuring' a garden does not mean physically shifting earth or laying paving slabs, but developing it from a basic ground plan using elements of the planting together with man-made features, such as paths and gravel areas, to relate a garden to its setting.

INTRODUCING DIFFERENT LEVELS

Once you have decided on the style of garden you wish to create and have sketched a layout, you can start to turn your plan into three-dimensional reality. Consider the differences in height that occur, or could be introduced to the site, and then decide on the plant masses, their relationship to the landscape beyond the garden and to the other elements in the garden, including each other.

Changes in ground level may already exist and can be accentuated by building steps at these points or to a pool, a vantage point or a summerhouse. Fences and walls or structures such as pergolas, dovecotes and arbours all give a vertical emphasis or become useful screens, as can hedges, trees or certain shrubs. Raised beds are invaluable for adding interest to a flat plot, and variety can be introduced by arranging plants of different heights.

USING STRUCTURAL PLANTS
An upright tree such as a juniper may dominate too small a group of plants (A), but may help relate that group to the scale of a wall behind it (B). The same tree may block a view (C) or sited to one side of it act as a counterbalance (D). By incorporating another similar group within the field of vision, a more interesting, repetitive effect may be created. Movement and progression will result from placing one juniper forward of the other (E), but sited equidistant from the viewpoint the two plantings provide an elegant frame (F).

VISUALLY RESHAPING A FLAT SITE
Above: The forms of trees and shrubs may be used to introduce a variety of levels to a site. Prostrate and dwarf conifers contrast with the light, horizontal branches of golden-leaved abies, the open-branched locust tree (Robinia pseudoacacia) and, in the background, the dark, upright form of picea.

CHANGES IN LEVEL
Left: Steps and a low wall serve to emphasize a change in level. The domed forms of the topiary yews (Taxus), flanking a flowering crab apple (Malus), highlight the sobriety of the former and the fresh abandon of the latter.

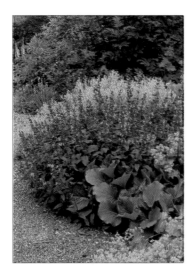

CREATING HARMONY
Purple-leaved elder helps relate the background trees to the foreground perennials, including Salvia officinalis '*Purpurascens*'

PROPORTIONATE PLANTINGS

When planning your design, avoid crowding the basic pattern with a 'liquorice allsorts' sprinkling of plants. Think instead in terms of proportionate masses and build up the structure by adding key plants judiciously. There is much more to the look of a garden than the sum total of the individual plants that are growing within it; no matter how special a plant might be, to create a harmonious whole, it must relate to its neighbour. Moreover, each group of plants must then be in proportion to the bed in which it is situated, which in turn should relate to the whole garden.

The three-dimensional shape of the garden is largely determined by the plant masses and their siting. When you next come across a satisfying group of shrubs or perennials, analyse how the individual shapes of the plant masses are working structurally and how together they combine to form a unified whole.

You will find that it is the proportionate relationship that they create with each other that makes the colour masses work.

USING STRUCTURAL PLANTS

No selection of plants is seen in isolation – there is always the backdrop of a garage, wall, neighbour's house or view. The style and planting of a garden should blend rather than jar with this background. By introducing structural, or architectural plants (those with strong outlines or forms), you can provide the bridge between the garden and what lies beyond, help to relate the garden to the house or bind together scattered plants. Whether spiky and aggressive like a yucca or soft and romantic like a weeping willow, the distinctive outline will add a focal point to the design. Structural plants contribute solidity and scale and, by using key plants of diminishing size, create an illusion of space.

SENSITIVE USE OF PROPORTION
This satisfyingly mixed border is well proportioned. The strong forms of two cupressus, neatly linked to the house by a Chinese wisteria (Wisteria sinensis) *growing along the wall, encourage an easy transition from the starkly outlined mass of the house to the softer groupings of the plants. The cupressus are in turn counterbalanced by a whitebeam* (Sorbus aria '*Lutescens*'). *Shrubs and herbaceous perennials* have been arranged so that the smallest are at the front of the border – yet these are all planted in sufficient quantity to make each group solid and balanced. An alternative planting (below left) has been devised for a hotter climate, using a Ti tree (Cordyline fruticosa) as the dominant feature; considerably fewer plants are used in the underplanting, but the proportions of the schemes are similar.*

Gardening through the Year

The most successful gardens are those that provide interest throughout the year. Since no individual plant is at its peak for all twelve months, its impact in a group will alter as the year progresses. For example, a tree that is spectacular in spring when covered in blossom may fade into the background during the rest of the year. The appearance of the group as a whole will therefore change with the seasons.

When selecting plants, remember to take into account seasonal variations in their appearance and thus ensure that each grouping sustains year-round interest. A planting of summer-flowering perennials alone may look dull in spring, autumn and winter. Consider all the merits of each plant – its size, habit, leaf form, colour, bark and texture – not merely the flower colour. These are the long-term qualities of a plant, which will be on display after its main season of interest has passed.

Ideally, you should provide a succession of 'feature' plants against a relatively unchanging background of shrubs and trees. In this way, when the eye-catching flowers of one plant in the bed are over, another begins to blossom. Alternatively, you might like to plan this succession in the garden as a whole, rather than just one border. In this way, the focal point will move around the garden.

SPRING
In the rock garden, Narcissus cyclamineus *nod cheerfully above* Euphorbia myrsinites.

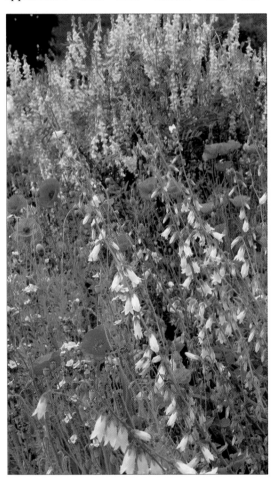

MID-SUMMER
Above: In this cottage garden – suggestive of a wild meadow – red poppies, perhaps garish in a more dense planting, look delightful sprinkled among the cooler tones of white bellflowers and a few pale blue delphiniums.

LATE AUTUMN
Right: Evergreen and berried trees and shrubs may now be fully appreciated. Upright, dark green conifers contrast attractively with the dazzling, silvery-white leaves of Elaeagnus umbellata, *while the red berries of* Cotoneaster horizontalis *provide a colourful foreground.*

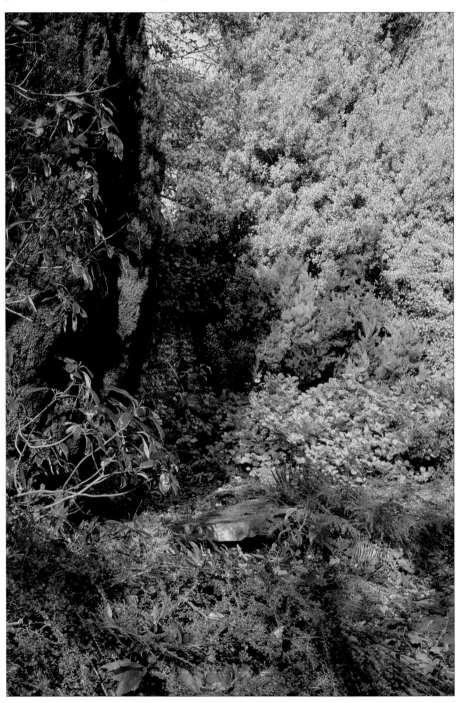

WINTER TO SPRING

During winter, flower interest in the garden is likely to be minimal, and it is then that the bold shapes and foliage colour provided by evergreens, such as conifers, holly and ivy, come into their own. Less obviously, the colours and textures of twigs, branches, bark and berries of deciduous trees and shrubs also have roles to play in providing visual interest during the winter months. The branches of the elegant willow, for instance, can look quite brilliant in winter sunlight; silver birches are especially attractive, graceful, open trees with lovely, white bark that glistens on even the greyest day. The shapes of deciduous as well as evergreen plants play an important part at this time, whether silhouetted against a clear, winter sky or bearing a cloak of snow.

With the arrival of spring, the garden is soon awash with colour. Some is provided by spring-flowering trees and shrubs, such as flowering cherries and magnolias, and by myriad rock plants, but most of the colour comes from an abundance of flowering bulbs and corms. As these die down, they are followed by early flowering shrubs like forsythia, and the fresh green of young leaves, with scented viburnum and lilac flowers appearing in succession through late spring.

SUMMER TO AUTUMN

In early summer, more colour is added by a profusion of perennials and biennials, often lasting until autumn. Shrub interest diminishes as the season progresses, which is when the annuals make their contribution, brightening up the heavy green face of summer. Annual flowers, although often extremely bright, last for only short periods, so it is necessary to sow seeds and transplant seedlings successively to maintain the display. Self-seeding annuals will emerge year after year in a random way, often providing short explosions of colour in unexpected places. The wealth of interesting plants that bloom in late summer, including clematis, remontant (repeat-flowering) roses, as well as annuals and herbaceous perennials, creates a pitfall of its own: you must be selective otherwise the effect as a whole will be overwhelming.

As summer fades, the greenery starts to flare into the fiery colours of autumn, the intensity of the colours and their duration depending on the weather. In your planting include trees or shrubs with spectacular autumn leaves, such as maples; they can make the garden as handsome in this season as in any other. Late-flowering perennials, such as Michaelmas daisies and chrysanthemums, brighten up the garden until the arrival of the first frosts and, when the browned leaves fall, returning us to the winter landscape.

SEASONAL PLANTING
In this small plot of about 9 square metres (97 square feet), the interplay between a group of shrubs, perennials and bulbs can be followed throughout the seasons. Although plants will have changing roles to play at different times of year, each has been chosen to relate successfully within the whole as well as to its neighbour.

WINTER
Evergreen rosemary contrasts with fleshy, purple Bergenia *leaves, variegated* Iris foetidissima *foliage and feathery twigs of* Acer palmatum *'Sango-kaku'. Snowdrops and winter aconites (*Eranthis hyemalis*) will stud the ground by early spring.*

SPRING
Bergenia *now bears its tight, red flower clusters and the scented blooms of* Viburnum opulus *open. Fresh green is provided by young acer leaves and delphinium shoots.*

SUMMER
Blue spikes of delphinium dominate early on. Foreground interest moves from the fern-like, grey leaves of the achillea to its long-lasting, plate-like, yellow flower heads.

AUTUMN
Yellowish acer and bronze-red viburnum foliage command most attention, although later the viburnum berries will also become noteworthy. Iris seed pods open to reveal their orange fruits and late-flowering chrysanthemums brighten the foreground.

23

Planning

A visually satisfying composition of plants comprises several elements. Look at the characteristics of the individual plants, and consider the effects those characteristics have on each other. The shapes and forms of their leaves and flowers, their colour and texture are all important. Think also about the changing size of plants: a small shrub planted now may dominate the garden in five years' time.

Any combination of plants should not be seen in isolation but should be considered in relation to the overall garden plan, the house and its surroundings. For example, a small tree or large shrub backing a small group of iris, daylilies and meadow rue would work well, but replace the single tree or shrub with a bank of trees and more of the smaller plants would be needed to prevent them from being 'swamped'. Similarly, two irises, three daylilies and a meadow rue would probably be too few plants when sited against a two-storey house.

RESTRICTING YOUR CHOICE OF PLANTS

Most people tend to be shy of buying more than one or two of a particular kind of plant,

or, with such a wide range of suitable subjects available, cannot resist the temptation of including yet another species. It is just this magpie instinct that makes overall planting schemes look fractured and detracts from the strong, simple lines of the basic concept. The plant collector and the garden designer are very often a difficult pair to reconcile!

Aim for simple, bold plant masses to begin with; later, if the effect seems too stark, widen the range of plants slightly to add a little light relief. Keep your choice of suitable plants narrow and try to see them growing, by visiting well-established gardens, before you make your final selection.

The magnificent, large-scale plantings within grand borders in the gardens of historic houses that can be admired by the general public are made up of groups of perhaps twelve of this plant and eight of that; to simulate them on a domestic scale calls for an iron discipline. The same applies to planting bulbs – twos and threes tend to look messy; try groups or drifts instead. Remember, your planting is garden furnishing, and you would not cover individual chairs in the same room with contrasting fabrics if you wished to create a calm atmosphere to relax in and enjoy.

SHAPE AND SCALE
Above left: Huge-leaved
Gunnera manicata, *tall giant lily*
(Cardiocrinum giganteum), *bushy
ferns and yellow flag irises* (Iris
pseudacorus), *although very varied
in shape and scale, still form a
cohesive planting for a damp site.*

COLOUR RANGES
*Above: The transition in colour
tone from the golden fronds of*
Juniperus x pfitzeriana *'William
Pfitzer' through the orange-yellow
clump of coneflowers* (Rudbeckia)
to the reddish-orange montbretia
(Crocosmia) *is smooth and
pleasing. More varieties in smaller
quantities might be difficult for the
eye to absorb within this strong
colour range.*

SIMPLE, BOLD PLANT MASSES
*Far left: Erect, silvery-blue Arizona
cypress* (Cupressus arizonica *var.*
glabra) *is balanced by the
horizontal, golden foliage of* Acer
shirasawanum *'Aureum'; both trees
seem stabilized by the solid-looking
plants at their feet.*

STRUCTURED INFORMALITY
*Left: Old stone slabs and exposed
gravel punctuate the planting of
lady's mantle* (Alchemilla mollis),
*variegated cornus, roses and sweet
Williams, which might otherwise
appear unruly.*

25

SITING YOUR PLANTS

A useful discipline when selecting and siting plants is to start with the largest and work towards the smallest. First decide on the background planting, or 'chorus line'. This could be either trees or shrubs, depending on the scale of the location. Forest trees may provide a link with a wood beyond, but they can become too large for the average town garden, whereas medium-sized trees will provide privacy, shelter and a 'backdrop' for your garden. Climbers may be grown around the trees or trained along garden walls or fencing. Against this background, site an occasional decorative small tree or shrub.

Think in the same way about shrubs. Use a backing group to cover a fence, to provide a screen between your garden and your neighbour's or to camouflage unsightly buildings. Evergreens are much more suitable for this than deciduous shrubs. Many conifers are too demanding in both their shape and colour for inclusion in the chorus line and make better specimen plants. Plant a group of shrubs – two or three in a small town garden, perhaps seven or eight in a larger country one.

In front of these shrubs, plant the flowering specimens and among the perennials and biennials introduce the smallest shrubs, including many herbs such as thyme, sage or lavender. At this stage consider carefully the position of any feature plants.

ALLOWING FOR GROWTH

It is essential, when planning where to site your plants, to envisage your scaled blocks of plant masses not only as they appear now but

CREATING A BACKDROP
Above: Climbing plants such as Clematis *'Nelly Moser', here grown through* Rosa *'American Pillar', may be used to soften or screen buildings as well as to act as a foil for other plants.*

VERDANT CHORUS LINE
Left: The large shrubs Chimonanthus praecox *and* Corokia cotoneaster *form a verdant 'chorus line' for smaller, more decorative flowering plants, in this case purple sage, lady's mantle* (Alchemilla mollis) *and* Campanula persicifolia. *The stone wall also makes a handsome, contrasting backdrop.*

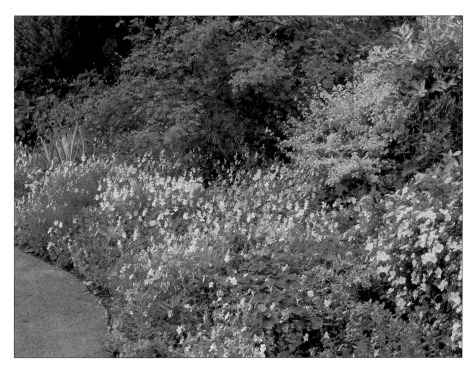

also as they will have developed in five years' time. Site the plants to allow enough room for them to expand and merge together over that time span. Beware of selecting trees that will ultimately become far too large for the scale of your garden as a whole, even if they look delightful at the garden centre.

If the planting seems too far apart initially, fill in the gaps between your groupings with bulbs, annuals or short-lived perennials that may easily be moved later. These will then bulk out the planting scheme, providing a temporary source of interest and colour, until the larger plants have reached maturity.

CLASSIC BORDER PLANTING
The striking foliage of Elaeagnus pungens *'Maculata', the rich red rose and the golden-yellow flowers of* Potentilla fruticosa *provide a classic background for a mass of low-growing perennials and violas.*

PLANTING FOR THE FUTURE
It is easy to forget how quickly trees and shrubs grow, so they should be well spaced. It may help to mark out 1-metre (3-feet) sections with string. This bed has been planted for winter interest. Rosebud cherry (Prunus × subhirtella 'Autumnalis') dominates the bed, while two evergreen Mexican orange blossoms (Choisya ternata) contrast with darker Sarcococca humilis, which bears fragrant flowers in late winter. Against these, the variegated Iris foetidissima stands out well. White-flowered Bergenia 'Silberlicht' is placed under the cherry and beyond the Mexican orange blossoms are grouped three Helleborus argutifolius.

YEAR 1

YEAR 3

CONTINUING CARE AND MAINTENANCE
This bed should reach its peak of glory after about five years. Trimming may be necessary 6–10 years after planting.

YEAR 5

Prunus × subhirtella 'Autumnalis'

Helleborus argutifolius

Bergenia 'Silberlicht'

Sarcococca humilis

Choisya ternata

Iris foetidissima

27

Using Colour

Everyone interprets the moods that colours create in different ways, and many people change their minds according to the weather, the time of day or their emotional state. Individuals with perfectly normal colour vision perceive colours differently, and colour blindness is a surprisingly common phenomenon.

Colour choice is first and foremost about personal preferences. Although there are some fundamental design rules on how to use colour, including the avoidance of such obvious clashes as hot orange with delicate pink, they really constitute only a broad guide for the use of flat planes of basic colour. Often they have little to do with the realities of a garden – the textures of living plants, the changing light, the varying hues of a colour range, the season of the year and the location.

THE INTRICACIES OF COLOUR PERCEPTION

The key to perceiving colour is light. Soft colours look wonderful in the early morning, in the evening and in dull or damp weather. In the Mediterranean sunshine, these colours would look blanched, and strong colours, which may be overpowering in a soft light,

come into their own. Happily nature has ensured that plants with strong-coloured flowers are usually native to sunny regions.

The damp light of a temperate climate is quite unlike humid, tropical light or clear, desert light; sharp, winter light is quite distinct from the hazy light of a summer noon, and both differ from misty, autumnal and dusky, evening lights. All have different effects on colours, altering our perception of them and transforming the mood of the garden. If you are only going to be using your garden at one time of day, for example the evening, bear this in mind when choosing your plants: white flowers can take on a luminous quality in fading light but dark blue ones will be invisible.

Apart from climatic conditions, other factors determine how we notice colour. The sea, for example, can alter colour perception, reflecting light for some distance inland. A background building or fence will also influence colour tones by reflecting or absorbing light: whether shiny or matt, made of glass, stone, brick or timber, it will influence our view of the colours of plants grown in front of it. Colours themselves affect each other too. The many shades of green modify any colours placed in front of them, as

GLOWING PINKS
Right: The pinks and purple-blues of this late summer bed set off each other excellently. The key to this success is the positioning of Artemisia ludoviciana 'Silver Queen' *and agapanthus between the strong pinks of* Aster novae-angliae 'Andenken an Alma Pötschke' *and ice-plant (Sedum spectabile 'Brilliant').*

AUTUMNAL HUES
Far right: Rich bronze-red Japanese maple (Acer palmatum) and golden-yellow Fothergilla major *– in classic colours associated with a temperate autumn – glow even in the rather misty light typical of this season.*

SUBTLE COLOURS
Far left: The pastel colours of catmint (Nepeta x faassenii) *and* Campanula lactiflora *'Loddon Anna' are used here to provide a subtle backdrop for the vivid carmine-red of the phlox.*

COLOUR AND TEXTURE
Left: This planting deliberately juxtaposes extremes of colour and texture, producing an almost layered effect. The sword-shaped leaves and reddish-orange flowers of montbretia (Crocosmia) *contrast strongly with the yellow of feathery dill and erect, spiky verbascum; the yellow creates a link between the foreground and the background.*

STRONG COMPOSITIONS
Below: This interesting contrast of a deep yellow daylily (Hemerocallis) *set against the intense purple-blues of hydrangea and agapanthus makes a striking statement.*

do the mousey-brown colours of a wintry landscape. The individual colour masses in a group influence each other, as well as affecting the whole planting. A largely white planting with a touch of purple will create one mood; but what about the reverse – a largely purple planting with a touch of white? The mood of one will be bright and sharp, the other sombre and tranquil.

CONSIDERING THE CHARACTER OF THE SITE

In the days before the introduction of foreign species and mass hybridization, there was an indigenous range of colours in every area. To help design a harmonious garden you might keep to this spirit of planting by analyzing the location of the garden; the particular flavour of a place is dictated by its climate and the shapes and colours of its natural plant forms.

The background colour may be a dark, coniferous green with the grey of granite or it may be deciduous green with mellower sandstone or limestone. In limestone areas, indigenous vegetation might include a proportion of grey foliage with the darker greens of yew or box. Although there are

some bright-coloured flowers in the temperate zones, the really brilliantly coloured flowers originate in hotter climates, where the intensity of the sun accentuates them. Thus the nearer the equator you go, the brighter the indigenous flowers.

SEASONAL COLOUR ASSOCIATIONS

As well as geographical factors, there is a natural progression of dominant colours through the seasons. Pale spring colours transmute into the blues of early summer; hotter pinks of mid-summer are transformed into yellows and bronzes in autumn, before turning into the browns of winter. When choosing plants for individual plant groups it is wise to avoid certain colours against these seasonal back-drops, lest they introduce a jarring note. For example, refrain from setting soft pink against spring green, using purple in summer or planting bright blue in autumn.

Even within the walls of a town garden with a backdrop of bricks and mortar, the seasons will still influence your colour choices. In temperate zones, for a natural look, try whites and pale lemon in spring; pinks, blues

FOLIAGE AND FLOWERS
Below right: Foliage and flower colours may be combined with equal dominance. In this planting, the huge, variegated leaves of Siberian bugloss (Brunnera macrophylla 'Dawson's White') are well set off by the surrounding, pale pink Potentilla nepalensis 'Miss Willmott', pink astilbe flowers and golden-leaved Lamium maculatum 'Aureum'

SATISFYING CONTRASTS
Below: Not only do the textures of Bowles' golden sedge (Carex elata 'Aurea') and the two hostas combine excellently but also the colour and form of these plants further complement the design.

and greys in mid-summer; in late summer a little red but mainly yellows; and in autumn some bronze and purple.

COLOUR PREFERENCES

There remain, of course, more personal preferences for certain colour combinations. Strong colours are often more appreciated by the young because they are invigorating. It follows that strong colours may be more appropriate when associated with various kinds of activity – near a tennis court, for instance, or around a pool. Softer colours, such as shades of grey and pink, are more restful.

MAKING YOUR PERSONAL MARK

Your individual style and feelings about the moods that different colours create will be the final factors affecting the colours in your garden, just as they are in the decoration of your home. If the garden is small, the result of linking the colours with those in the room adjacent to it will have a dramatic effect on both room and garden. Where room and garden meet, avoid startling clashes such as pink roses against orange-red brick or curtains. Conversely, where the garden is larger, gradually change the colours in it so that, although those of the flowers nearest the house still link with the interior, those at the bottom of the garden work with the backdrop of the fence, hedge or countryside beyond.

Colour may be used to enhance perspective, too: hotter ranges of colour (reds, oranges and pinks) look better closer to the house, while cool colours (blues and whites) introduced at a distance from it will increase the sense of space.

A SENSE OF CALM
Above: Soft colours and forms intermingle harmoniously in this shady site, where the pinkish-mauve of the lacecap hydrangea is echoed in the foreground by the purple ajuga leaves and the tiny, pink flowers of Lamium maculatum. *The delicate tracery of the ferns blends comfortably with the bolder, bluish leaves of* Hosta sieboldiana *var.* elegans.

SYMPATHETIC PLANTING
Right: This damp corner in a cottage garden contains a deliberately limited colour scheme, yet with invigorating results. When set against the ferns and grasses, the yellow heads of giant cowslip (Primula florindae) *and* Ligularia przewalskii *seem natural, because they have an affinity with the character and location of the site.*

Providing Texture

A successful design is one in which the gardener has considered the whole range of an individual plant's ornamental features to create effective combinations of plants and has not relied purely on colour associations. Plant texture, particularly that of foliage, plays an essential role, not only for visual impact but also because its mass and duration far outlive the more transient attractions of flowers, seed heads or fruit, although these can also provide texture. Indeed, some of the most innovative designs depend on the variety and interplay of foliage texture to form a backcloth that is visually pleasing in its own right, while – almost incidentally – providing a foil to enhance the beauty of the flowers.

The overall effect of growing together groups of plants with markedly different textures is far greater since the distinctive texture of each plant is emphasized and enhanced by that very contrast.

CONTRASTING TEXTURE

The textural variety of leaves is derived from their differing sizes, forms and surface finishes. When considering trees, for example, it is worth noting that many of the birches and some of the smaller sorbus with their small leaves and leaflets create airy, fine-textured canopies. These can be brought into sharp

PLAY ON TEXTURES
Above: Spiky branches of Scotch thistle (Onopordum acanthium) *provide a most effective foil for glossy-leaved ivy, soft-leaved nicotiana and fine-leaved lilies and marguerites. The paving slabs, the smooth terracotta pot (planted with marguerites) and the carved stone container (with* Helichrysum petiolare 'Limelight') *add further variety to the scene.*

DISTINCTIVE GRASSES
Far left: The creamy plumes of pampas grass (Cortaderia selloana) *will help to add a textural dimension to any garden, but they must be in proportion to the surrounding trees and shrubs if they are not to look out of place.*

SUCCESSFUL COMBINATIONS
Left: This blend of flowers and leaves skilfully exploits the contrast of textures and colours between the leaves of Bowles' golden sedge (Carex elata 'Aurea'), *the feathery plumes of deep red astilbes and pink candelabra primulas, and the huge leaves of* Gunnera manicata.

relief by a dense coniferous backdrop of the dark-needled *Pinus peuce* or *P. nigra*. Or consider the contrasting effects to be gained from associating the fine-textured surface of small-leaved shrubs, such as box (*Buxus microphylla* or *B. sempervirens*) or possibly *Osmanthus delavayi*, with the larger, glossy textures of *Viburnum tinus* or camellias; then go further and add another dimension with the elegantly cut leaves of tree peonies or *Melianthus major*.

Perennials offer some of the most useful and distinctive plant textures. Contrast the daintily cut filigree of many artemisias, such as *Artemisia pontica* or the jagged *A. ludoviciana*, the soft, finely divided leaves of the dicentras or ferns and the feathery pulsatillas, with bolder, larger foliage such as the huge, wrinkled leaves of the rheums and the deeply veined and architectural leaves of rodgersias. The hostas offer several textures, from the strongly ribbed, glossy leaves of *Hosta plantaginea* to the undulating, puckered leaves of *H. sieboldiana* 'Frances Williams'.

Grasses, sedges and rushes all have more or less linear leaves that create some of the finest textures. They can be introduced in a number of planting situations to provide a range of effects, from the low, spiky, blue-green mounds of *Festuca glauca* 'Blaufuchs', through the corkscrew, hair-like leaves of *Juncus effusus* 'Spiralis' to the tall, flowering plumes of *Cortaderia selloana*. Even short-lived annuals and biennials have numerous textures to offer. When used to fill gaps in a border, the filamentous leaves of *Cosmos bipinnatus* or the spiky forms of *Onopordum acanthium* will provide a visual feast.

SURFACE QUALITIES

Varying foliage surfaces influence the way that light is reflected, absorbed or diffused by the plant so that the massed effect of matt leaves, for example, will be notably different from that of glossy leaves, which can give rise to glittering reflections in bright light. Here too, there is a wide range of surfaces available, from the glossy-leaved hollies (*Ilex*) to matt-leaved *Phlomis russeliana*; from rough symphytums to smooth *Crinum* x *powellii*. Certain plants, among them *Allium karataviense* and *Paeonia mlokosewitschii*, have a greyish bloom to their leaves that can look exquisite when beaded with raindrops.

Leaf hairs add a further dimension when used as a foil for leaves of other textures. Hairy-leaved plants range from the bristly-hairy begonias to the almost shaggy, golden-tinted hairs of *Meconopsis napaulensis*.

The principles of texture apply equally to flowers, seed heads and fruit, and it is also important to mention the contribution made by inanimate objects. Large stones and sea-washed pebbles, and areas of gravel and wooden decking, as well as different plant pots, can all create interesting texture within a design.

DELICATE TOUCHES
Below left: The spiky seed heads of Allium cristophii *contrast with the lobed leaves and satiny flowers of* Geranium x riversleaianum *'Russell Prichard'. Seed heads offer a final flourish of interest that lasts from the allium's early summer flowering until well into the autumn.*

STRONG SHAPES
Below right: The huge, silver-downy leaves and white-woolly, yellow flower spikes of Verbascum olympicum *are a textural treat in their own right, but here their impact is lent additional weight by association with the tiny, dusky, red-purple leaves of* Berberis thunbergii *f.* atropurpurea.

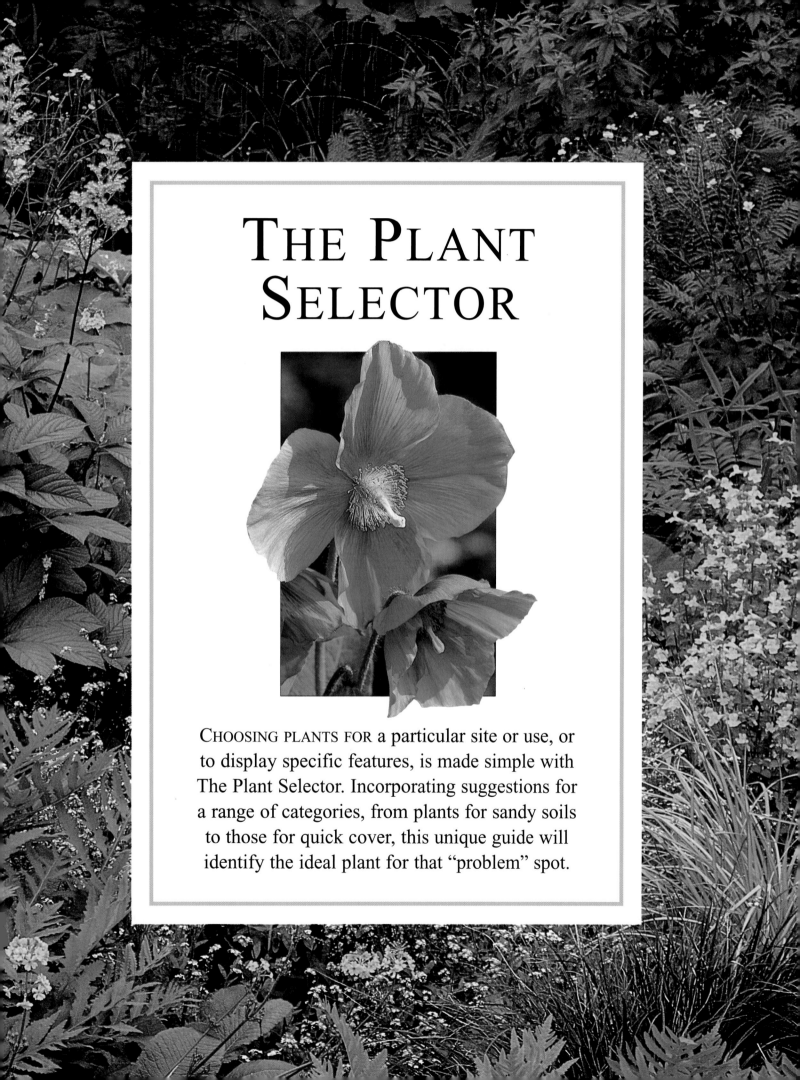

THE PLANT SELECTOR

CHOOSING PLANTS FOR a particular site or use, or
to display specific features, is made simple with
The Plant Selector. Incorporating suggestions for
a range of categories, from plants for sandy soils
to those for quick cover, this unique guide will
identify the ideal plant for that "problem" spot.

How to Use This Section

The following lists suggest plants that are suitable for growing in particular situations, or that have special uses or characteristics. For each category the list is broadly subdivided into plant groups, following the arrangement of The Plant Catalogue, pp.60–480. Plants listed here that are featured in The Plant Catalogue are followed by page numbers. Refer to The Plant Dictionary if a whole genus or a plant not followed by a page number is recommended.

If a plant is listed for a particular purpose (coastal sites, shade, etc.) it should thrive there happily in normal growing conditions, even if the situation is not the plant's naturally preferred location. Bear in mind, however, that plants are not always consistent in their growing habits and much of their success depends on climate, aspect and available nutrients.

The following symbols occur in this section:

○ indicates evergreen or semi-evergreen plants, including those with overwintering rosettes of leaves.

△ (regarding hedges and windbreaks) the plant is moderately to fast growing.

□ (regarding clay soils) the plant tolerates slow-draining soil; all others require reasonable drainage.

▣ the plant is illustrated in this section.

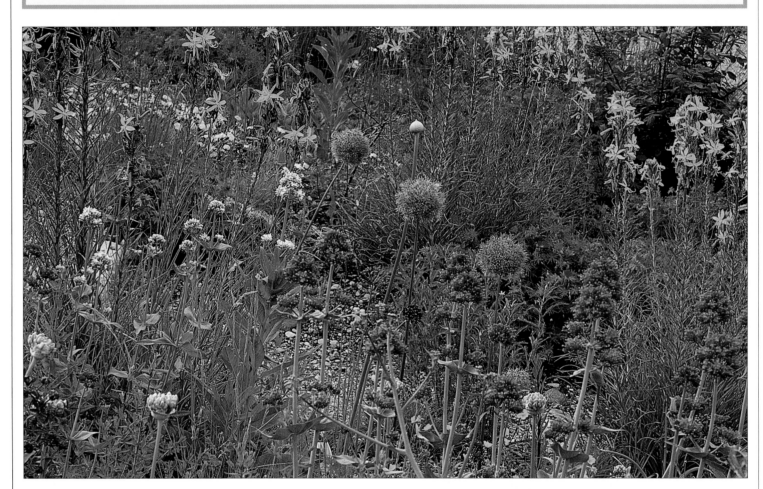

Plants for Sandy Soil

Sandy soils are often termed 'light' or 'hungry' soils. They are usually well-drained, but dry out rapidly during drier summer periods and hold only low reserves of plant foods. Many plants have adapted to such soils by developing deeply penetrating root systems. Their leaves are also modified to reduce moisture loss: small and reflexed, evergreen and glossy, or densely covered with fine grey or silver hairs. Once established, they will usually grow steadily with little attention. To improve moisture retention, incorporate some organic matter when planting in autumn; little watering is then needed and plants can establish well before summer.

Trees
Acacia dealbata, p.83 ○
Agonis flexuosa, p.90 ○
Amelanchier lamarckii, p.116
Betula ermanii, p.72 ▣
Betula pendula 'Dalecarlica', p.73
Castanea sativa
Celtis australis, p.67

Cercis siliquastrum, p.88
Crataegus laevigata 'Paul's Scarlet', p.91
Genista aetnensis, p.93
Nothofagus obliqua, p.68
Phoenix canariensis ○
Quercus ilex ○
Robinia pseudoacacia 'Frisia', p.81

Betula ermanii

A GARDEN ON SANDY GRAVEL
Above: Red centranthus, purple alliums and yellow asphodeline all thrive in sandy soil.

Conifers
Abies grandis, p.104 ○
Cupressocyparis x *leylandii* and cvs ○
Juniperus ○
Larix decidua
Pinus pinaster, p.103 ○
Pinus radiata, p.104 ○
Pseudotsuga menziesii var. *glauca*, p.102 ○
Thuja occidentalis and cvs ○

Shrubs
Artemisia arborescens 'Faith Raven', p.175 ○
Berberis empetrifolia, p.157 ○
Boronia megastigma, p.156 ○
Brachyglottis Dunedin Hybrids 'Sunshine', p.140 ○

Calluna vulgaris and cvs ○
Caragana arborescens 'Lorbergii'
Ceanothus thyrsiflorus and forms ○
Chamelaucium uncinatum, pp.149, 150 ○
Chorizema ilicifolium, p.157 ○
Cistus ○
Convolvulus cneorum, p.158 ○
Cotoneaster lacteus, p.125 ○
Elaeagnus pungens 'Maculata', p.127 ○
Enkianthus cernuus f. *rubens*, p.131
Erica arborea var. *alpina*, p.178 ○
Erica cinerea and cvs ○
Gaultheria mucronata 'Mulberry Wine', p.174 ○
Gaultheria mucronata 'Wintertime', p.173 ○
Genista tinctoria, p.157
x *Halimiocistus sahucii*, p.159 ○
Halimium 'Susan', p.169 ○
Hippophäe rhamnoides, p.124
Hypericum 'Hidcote', p.170 ○
Lavandula ○
Leucospermum reflexum, p.131 ○
Olearia nummulariifolia, p.136 ○
Perovskia 'Blue Spire', p.168
Phlomis fruticosa, p.170 ○
Robinia hispida, p.141
Rosa pimpinellifolia, p.184
Rosmarinus officinalis and cvs ○
Salvia fulgens, p.166 ○
Santolina pinnata subsp. *neapolitana* 'Sulphurea', p.169 ○
Spartium junceum, p.147
Tamarix ramosissima, p.121
Teucrium fruticans 'Azureum' ○
Yucca gloriosa, p.137 ○

Climbers
Clianthus puniceus, p.204 ○
Eccremocarpus scaber, p.217 ○
Kennedia rubicunda, p.204 ○
Lapageria rosea, p.210 ○
Petrea volubilis, p.206 ○
Solanum wendlandii, p.214 ○
Streptosolen jamesonii, p.220 ○
Tropaeolum tricolorum, p.205
Vitis vinifera 'Purpurea', p.218

Perennials
Acanthus spinosus, p.251
Achillea 'Moonshine', p.291
Aphelandra squarrosa 'Louisae', p.256 ○
Artemisia absinthium 'Lambrook Silver' ○
Artemisia ludoviciana var. *albula*, p.266
Asphodeline ▣
Baptisia australis, p.252
Billbergia nutans, p.265 ○

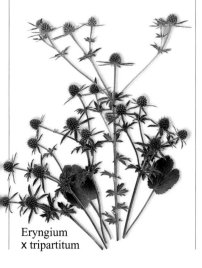

Eryngium
x tripartitum

Centranthus ruber, p.245 ▣
Cryptanthus zonatus ○
Echinops sphaerocephalus, p.226
Eryngium x *tripartitum*, p.253 ▣
Gaillardia x *grandiflora* cvs
Gazania rigens var. *uniflora*, p.292
Limonium latifolium 'Blue Cloud', p.286
Nepeta x *faassenii*, p.286
Oenothera fruticosa 'Fyrverkeri', p.291
Origanum vulgare 'Aureum', p.290
PELARGONIUMS, pp.246–7 ○
Phlomis russeliana, p.255 ○
Platycodon grandiflorus, p.284
Romneya coulteri, p.226
Ruellia devosiana, p.277 ○
Sansevieria trifasciata 'Laurentii', p.267 ○
Solidago 'Goldenmosa', p.255
Strelitzia reginae, p.267 ○
Verbascum dumulosum, p.359 ○

Annuals and biennials
Antirrhinum majus and cvs
Brachyscome iberidifolia, p.334
Bracteantha bracteata Monstrosum Series, p.340
Cleome hassleriana and cvs ▣
Coreopsis tinctoria, p.336

Cleome hassleriana
'Colour Fountain'

Eschscholzia californica, p.339
Impatiens walleriana Novette Series, p.327 ○
Limnanthes douglasii, p.336
Limonium sinuatum, p.332
Linaria maroccana 'Fairy Lights', p.330
Mentzelia lindleyi, p.336
Papaver rhoeas Shirley Series, pp.322, 328
Portulaca grandiflora Series and cvs
Psylliostachys suworowii, p.330
Schizanthus
Senecio cineraria 'Silver Dust', p.334 ○ ▣
Tagetes
Tanacetum parthenium, p.319
Verbena x *hybrida* Series and cvs
Xanthophthalmum segetum, p.337

Rock plants
Acaena caesiiglauca, p.390 ○
Achillea x *kellereri*, p.375 ○
Aethionema 'Warley Rose', p.376 ○
Andromeda polifolia 'Compacta', p.347 ○
Arenaria montana, p.374
Armeria juniperifolia, p.365 ○
Cytisus x *beanii*, p.349

Senecio cineraria '*Silver Dust*'

Dianthus deltoides ○
Gaultheria procumbens, p.387 ○
Gypsophila repens ○
Helianthemum ○
Maianthemum canadense, p.383
Petrorhagia saxifraga, p.375
Phlox bifida, p.381 ○
Saponaria ocymoides, p.378
Sedum ○

Sempervivum ○
Tanacetum argenteum, p.360 ○
Vaccinium vitis-idaea subsp. *minus*, p.366 ○

Bulbs, corms and tubers
Allium ▣
Babiana rubrocyanea, p.431
Crocus
Freesia
Ipheion uniflorum 'Froyle Mill', p.431
IRISES (bulbous species), pp.234–5
Ixia
Muscari
Narcissus tazetta and Div.8 hybrids
Nerine bowdenii, p.424
Ornithogalum
Romulea bulbocodium, p.431
Scilla
Zephyranthes

Cacti and other succulents (all)

CONTRASTING FOLIAGE
Against a backdrop of ivy, a diversity of plants flourishes in a sunny, wall-side border, their leafy growth keeping the sandy soil shaded, cool and moist.

Plants for Clay Soils

Clay soil is usually wet, glutinous and heavy in winter, and during drier summers sometimes shrinks and cracks, damaging plant roots. Whether establishing a new garden on clay or renovating an older one, always choose plants that will tolerate and grow satisfactorily in clay soil. Prepare the soil thoroughly, digging in the autumn, then leaving roughly dug over winter to benefit from the weathering effects of frost and winter rains. Dig in coarse organic matter, and work in grit or sharp sand to ensure the soil is well drained. Plant in early spring, at the beginning of the growing season, to avoid losses over winter.

Trees
Alnus glutinosa □
Castanospermum australe ○
Drimys winteri, p.78 ○
Fraxinus
Juglans nigra, p.67
Melaleuca viridiflora var.
    rubriflora ○ □
Oxydendrum arboreum, p.78 □
Populus □
Pterocarya fraxinifolia □
Quercus palustris, p.69
Quercus robur
Salix x *sepulcralis* var. *chrysocoma*,
    p.74 □
Salix babylonica var. *pekinensis*
    'Tortuosa', p.85 □

Conifers
Cryptomeria ○ □
Metasequoia □
Taxodium distichum, p.104 □

Shrubs
Aronia arbutifolia, p.130 □
Calycanthus floridus □

Viburnum opulus 'Xanthocarpum'

WATERSIDE PLANTING
Above: In the rich, moist clay found at the boggy margins of pools and slow-moving streams, candelabra primulas of many colours grow and flower well in association with butterfly-like irises.

Clethra alnifolia
Cornus alba 'Sibirica', p.150 □
Kalmia latifolia, p.141 ○
Ledum groenlandicum, p.154 ○ □
Magnolia virginiana ○
Salix caprea □
Salix purpurea □
Sambucus racemosa
Tetrapanax papyrifer, p.126 ○
Viburnum lentago
Viburnum opulus and cvs ▣

Climbers
Celastrus scandens
Humulus lupulus 'Aureus', p.206
Rosa filipes 'Kiftsgate', p.196
Vitis coignetiae, p.218

Ferns
Matteuccia struthiopteris, p.312 □
Onoclea sensibilis, p.312 □
Osmunda regalis, p.312 □
Polystichum setiferum Groups, pp.311,
    313 ○
Thelypteris palustris, p.312 □
Woodwardia radicans ○ □

Perennials
Aruncus dioicus, p.226 □
Cyperus papyrus, p.307 ○ □
Darmera peltata, p.238 □

Houttuynia cordata
'Chameleon'

Filipendula ulmaria 'Aurea', p.290 □
Gunnera manicata, p.228 □
Helonias bullata ○ □
Houttuynia cordata 'Chameleon',
    p.447 □ ▣
Iris laevigata, p.235 □
Lythrum □
Mimulus guttatus □
Primula florindae, p.273 □
Primula japonica □
Scrophularia auriculata 'Variegata' □
Trollius □

Water plants
Butomus umbellatus, p.448 □
Caltha palustris, p.451 □
Lysichiton americanus, p.451 □
Pontederia cordata, p.448 □
Ranunculus lingua, p.451 □
Sagittaria latifolia, p.446 □
Thalia dealbata □

Plants requiring Neutral to Acid Soil

Some plants, notably camellias, rhododendrons and most heathers, grow naturally in regions such as open woodland, hillsides or moorland where the soil is neutral to acid, and are intolerant of alkaline soils such as chalk or limestone. These are often termed 'lime-haters' or 'acid-lovers'. Before planting, ensure that the soil is suitable for lime-hating plants, and work in some acidic planting compost or humus. After planting, keep woody plants well mulched. In drier regions, check water needs regularly.

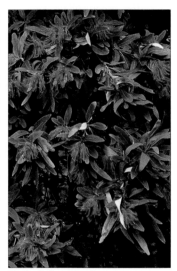

Embothrium coccineum

Trees

Arbutus menziesii ○
Arbutus unedo, p.93 ○
CAMELLIAS, pp.128–9 ○
Embothrium coccineum, p.93 ○ ▣
Eucryphia (most) most ○
Michelia doltsopa, p.83 ○
Nyssa sinensis, p.82
Nyssa sylvatica, p.71
Oxydendrum arboreum, p.78
Pterostyrax hispida
Stewartia
Styrax japonicus, p.77

Conifers

Abies ○
Picea (most) ○
Pinus densiflora ○
Pinus pumila ○
Pseudolarix amabilis, p.107
Pseudotsuga ○
Sciadopitys verticillata, p.106 ○
Tsuga heterophylla ○

Shrubs

Amelanchier lamarckii, p.116
Andromeda polifolia 'Compacta', p.347 ○

Leucothöe fontanesiana *SCARLETTA*

Arctostaphylos (some) ○
Boronia megastigma, p.156 ○
CAMELLIAS, pp.128–9 ○
Chamaedaphne calyculata ○
Crinodendron hookerianum, p.142 ○
Cyrilla racemiflora ○
Desfontainia spinosa, p.143 ○
Enkianthus some ○
Epacris impressa, p.155 ○
Fothergilla major, p.127
Gardenia augusta ○
Gaultheria ○ ▣
Hamamelis
HEATHERS, pp.178–9, most ○ ▣
Kalmia
Ledum groenlandicum, p.154 ○
Leiophyllum buxifolium ○
Leucothöe ○ ▣
Lyonia ligustrinum
Menziesia ciliicalyx var. *purpurea*, p.155
Philesia magellanica ○
Pieris ○
Pimelea ferruginea, p.162 ○

Protea
RHODODENDRONS, pp.132–4, most ○ ▣
Styrax officinalis, p.118
Telopea speciosissima, p.142 ○
Vaccinium, most ○ ▣
Zenobia pulverulenta, p.138

Climbers

Agapetes (several) ○
Allamanda cathartica ○
Asteranthera ovata ○
Berberidopsis corallina, p.211 ○
Mitraria coccinea, p.205 ○

Perennials

Adiantum some ○
Blechnum ○
Cryptogramma crispa, p.313
Cypripedium reginae, p.296
Dianella tasmanica, p.253 ○
Drosera ○
Lilium speciosum var. *rubrum*, p.404
Lilium superbum, p.405
Nepenthes ○
Sarracenia flava, p.290
Smilacina racemosa, p.233
Tolmiea menziesii ○
Trillium
Uvularia

Rock plants

Arctostaphylos ○
Cassiope ○
Cornus canadensis, p.374 ○
Corydalis cashmeriana
Cyananthus
Epigaea ○
Galax urceolata, p.351 ○

Bilberry
(Vaccinium myrtillus)

Gaultheria ○
Gentiana sino-ornata, p.387
Leucothöe keiskei ○
Linnaea borealis, p.375 ○
Lithodora diffusa cvs ○
Mitchella repens ○
Ourisia ○
Phlox adsurgens ○
Phlox stolonifera ○
Phyllodoce ○
Pieris nana ○
Shortia ○

SPRING COLOUR

Acid-loving heathers, flanked by gaultherias and backed by two early-flowering, pink rhododendrons, provide a broad strip of colour to mark the end of winter.

Plants for Limestone

Limestone regions are rich in wildflowers and wildlife, and where there is a reasonable depth of topsoil above limestone a wide range of attractive garden plants can be grown. Often, there are only a few centimetres of soil above bedrock and here there is an increased risk of drought in summer. It may be necessary to excavate planting holes and to incorporate organic matter to increase humus levels. On well-drained soil, plant in autumn or spring; on less than well-drained soils, defer planting until spring. Keep all young woody plants well mulched.

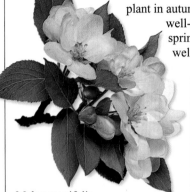

Malus prunifolia

HONESTY WITH TULIPS

Below: A biennial that tolerates dry, chalky soil, honesty (Lunaria annua) flowers in spring, here with Tulipa batalinii and forget-me-nots. The long-lasting, purple flowers give way to coin-like, translucent seed pods.

Trees
Acer negundo 'Variegatum', p.79
Aesculus x *carnea* 'Briotii, p.64
Catalpa bignonioides, p.78
Cercis siliquastrum, p.88
Crataegus
Fagus sylvatica, p.68
Fraxinus ornus, p.76
Gleditsia triacanthos 'Sunburst', p.77
Ilex aquifolium cvs, pp.98–9 ○
Laurus nobilis ○
Malus ▣
Morus nigra ▣
Phillyrea latifolia ○
Prunus avium 'Plena', p.76
Robinia pseudoacacia 'Frisia', p.81
Sorbus aria and cvs
Tilia tomentosa

Morus nigra

Conifers
Calocedrus decurrens, p.106 ○
Cedrus libani, p.103 ○
Chamaecyparis lawsoniana and cvs ○
Cupressocyparis x *leylandii* and cvs ○
Cupressus glabra ○
Ginkgo biloba, p.103 ○
Juniperus ○
Picea omorika, p.103 ○
Pinus nigra ○
Taxus baccata and cvs ○
Thuja orientalis and cvs ○
Thuja plicata and cvs ○

Shrubs
Abutilon 'Kentish Belle', p.171 ○
Aucuba japonica 'Crotonifolia', p.152 ○
Azara microphylla, p.125 ○
Berberis darwinii, p.117 ○
Buddleja davidii and cvs
Carpenteria californica, p.138 ○
Ceanothus impressus, p.145 ○
Choisya ternata, p.127 ○
Cistus ○
Cornus mas 'Variegata', p.119
Cotoneaster, some ○ ▣
Deutzia
Forsythia suspensa, p.131
Fremontodendron 'California Glory', p.123 ○
Fuchsia 'Riccartonii', p.164
Hebe 'Great Orme', p.163 ○
Hypericum 'Hidcote', p.170 ○
LILACS, p.120
Malus sargentii, p.116
Malus sieboldii, p.130
Nerium oleander, p.121 ○

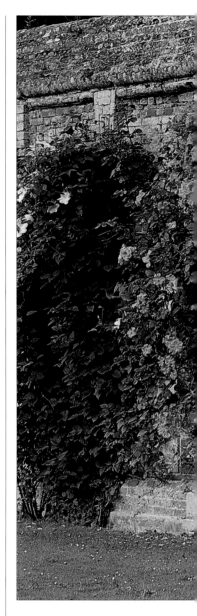

LIME-LOVING CLIMBERS

Above: A weathered brick wall provides support for summer-flowering clematis and climbing roses. Both kinds of plant tolerate limestone soil, but need ample water when in growth.

Paeonia lutea var. *ludlowii*, p.237
Philadelphus
Phlomis fruticosa, p.170 ○
Photinia x *fraseri* 'Red Robin' ○
Potentilla (all shrubby species)
ROSES (most), pp.184–99, some ○ ▣
Rosmarinus officinalis 'Miss Jessopp's Upright' ○
Sambucus nigra 'Guincho Purple'
Spartium junceum, p.147
Spiraea nipponica 'Snowmound', p.139
Viburnum tinus, p.149 ○
Vitex agnus-castus
Weigela florida 'Variegata'
Yucca aloifolia, p.153 ○

Climbers
Actinidia kolomikta, p.209
Campsis radicans
Celastrus orbiculatus
CLEMATIS, pp.212–13, some ○ ▣
Eccremocarpus scaber, p.217 ○

Cotoneaster '*Rothschildianus*'

Matthiola
Salvia viridis, p.331
Tagetes
Ursinia anthemoides, p.338
Xeranthemum annuum
Zinnia

Rock plants
Aethionema ○
Alyssum ○
Androsace lanuginosa, p.377 ○
Aster alpinus, p.381
Campanula (most rock garden species),
  some ○
Dianthus (most rock garden species) ○
Draba ○
Erysimum helveticum, p.373 ○
Gypsophila repens ○
Helianthemum ○ ▣
Lathyrus vernus, p.270
Leontopodium alpinum, p.346
Linum arboreum, p.358 ○
Origanum dictamnus
Papaver burseri
Penstemon pinifolius, p.354 ○
Rhodanthemum hosmariense, p.346 ○
Saponaria ocymoides, p.378
Saxifraga (most) ○
Thymus caespititius, p.375 ○
Veronica (all rock garden species),
  some ○

Bulbs, corms and tubers
Babiana
Chionodoxa
Colchicum
Crinum x *powellii*, p.398
Crocus
Cyclamen hederifolium, p.438
DAFFODILS, pp.416–18
GLADIOLI, p.399
Hermodactylus tuberosus, p.414
Leucocoryne ixioides, p.413
Lilium regale, p.404
Muscari
Pancratium illyricum, p.419
Scilla
TULIPS, pp.410–12 ▣
Zephyranthes

Honeysuckle
(Lonicera)

IVIES, p.221 ○
Jasminum officinale f. *affine*, p.208 ○
Lonicera, some ○ ▣
Parthenocissus henryana
Passiflora caerulea, p.214 ○
Rosa 'Albéric Barbier', p.196 ○
Rosa 'Albertine', p.197 ○
Rosa banksiae 'Lutea', p.198 ○
Solanum crispum 'Glasnevin',
  p.214 ○
Trachelospermum jasminoides,
  p.207 ○
Wisteria sinensis, p.215

Ferns
Asplenium scolopendrium, p.313 ○
Asplenium trichomanes, p.313 ○
Dryopteris filix-mas, p.310
Polypodium vulgare 'Cornubiense',
  p.312 ○

Perennials
Acanthus spinosus, p.251
Achillea filipendulina 'Gold Plate',
  p.256
Aster novae-angliae and cvs
Aster novi-belgii and cvs
Bergenia ○
Doronicum
Eryngium, some ○
Gypsophila paniculata cvs ▣
Helenium
IRISES (most), pp.234–5, some ○
Rudbeckia 'Goldquelle', p.229
Salvia nemorosa
Scabiosa caucasica 'Clive Greaves',
  p.285
Sidalcea
Verbascum ○
Veronica spicata

Annuals and biennials
Ageratum houstonianum and cvs
Calendula officinalis and Series and
  cvs
Callistephus chinensis Series and cvs

Calomeria amaranthoides, p.330
Erysimum cheiri and Series and cvs ○
Gomphrena globosa, p.331
Lavatera trimestris 'Silver Cup', p.324
Limonium sinuatum, p.322
Lobularia maritima
Lunaria annua, p.325 ▣

Gypsophila paniculata
'Bristol Fairy'

Helianthemum
'Rhodanthe Carneum'

41

Plants for Coastal Sites

In coastal regions, and near some highways, salt from sea spray is carried a considerable distance on the wind, causing problems for many plants. Some, however, show tolerance of higher levels of salt; these frequently have hard-surfaced or high-gloss leaves with low absorbency levels, or leaves covered with fine hairs that prevent salt reaching the surface. Coastal gardens are often exposed, so protect plants with hedges or wattle hurdles. Prepare sandy soil by incorporating organic matter and garden loam, to encourage deep root penetration, and use dense ground-cover plants to stabilize the sand and keep root areas cool.

Strawberry tree
(Arbutus unedo)

Trees
Acer pseudoplatanus and cvs
Agonis flexuosa, p.90 ○
Alnus incana, p.66
Arbutus unedo, p.93 ○ ▣
Castanea sativa
Cordyline australis ○
Crataegus laevigata 'Paul's Scarlet', p.91
Crataegus x *lavallei* 'Carrierei'
Eucalyptus coccifera, p.72 ○
Eucalyptus globulus ○
Eucalpytus gunnii, p.72 ○
Ficus macrophylla ○
Fraxinus excelsior
Ilex aquifolium cvs, pp.98–9 ○
Laurus nobilis ○
Melaleuca viridiflora var. *rubriflora* ○
Melia azedarach, p.76
Populus alba, p.64
Quercus ilex ○
Salix alba
Schefflera actinophylla, p.84 ○
Schinus molle ○
Sorbus aria 'Lutescens', p.78
Tabebuia chrysotricha, p.97
Thevetia peruviana, p.93 ○
Tipuana tipu

Conifers
Cupressocyparis x *leylandii* ○
Cupressus macrocarpa ○

Juniperus conferta ○
Pinus contorta var. *latifolia*, p.106 ○
Pinus nigra subsp. *nigra*, p.104 ○
Pinus radiata, p.104 ○

Shrubs
Acacia verticillata ○
Atriplex halimus ○
Baccharis halimifolia
Berberis darwinii, p.117 ○
Brachyglottis Dunedin Hybrids 'Sunshine', p.170 ○
Buddleja globosa, p.123 ○
Bupleurum fruticosum, p.146 ○
Cassinia leptophylla subsp. *fulvida* ○
Chamaerops humilis, p.176 ○
Choisya ternata, p.127 ○
Cistus ladanifer, p.159 ○
Colutea arborescens, p.146
Corokia x *virgata* ○
Cytisus x *spachianus* ○
Duranta erecta, p.150 ○
Elaeagnus x *ebbingei* ○
Elaeagnus pungens 'Maculata', p.127 ○
Erica arborea var. *alpina*, p.178 ○
Erica cinerea 'Eden Valley', p.179 ○
Erica vagans 'Lyonesse', p.178 ○
Escallonia rubra 'Crimson Spire' ○
Euonymus japonicus ○
Euphorbia characias subspp., p.156 ○
Fabiana imbricata 'Prostrata' ○
Felicia amelloides 'Santa Anita', p.168 ○
Fuchsia magellanica, p.164
Fuchsia 'Riccartonii', p.164
Garrya elliptica 'James Roof' ○
Genista hispanica, p.170
Griselinia littoralis ○
Halimium lasianthum subsp. *formosum*, p.169 ○
Hebe x *franciscana* 'Blue Gem' ○
Hebe salicifolia ○
Hebe 'White Gem', p.158 ○
Helichrysum italicum ○
Hibiscus rosa-sinensis ○
Hippophäe rhamnoides, p.124
Hydrangea macrophylla and cvs
Lavandula 'Hidcote', p.167 ○ ▣
Lavatera 'Rosea', p.141 ○
Leptospermum scoparium 'Red Damask', p.131 ○
Leycesteria formosa
Lonicera pileata, p.176 ○
Lycium barbarum
Malvaviscus arboreus, p.121 ○
Nerium oleander, p.121 ○
Olearia x *haastii*, p.139 ○
Olearia macrodonta ○
Ozothamnus ledifolius, p.160 ○
Parahebe perfoliata, p.286 ○
Phillyrea latifolia ○

Phlomis fruticosa, p.170 ○
Pittosporum tobira ○
Pyracantha coccinea 'Lalandei' ○
Rhamnus alaternus 'Argenteovariegata' ○
Rosa pimpinellifolia
Rosa rugosa, p.187
Rosmarinus officinalis, p.167 ○
Sambucus racemosa and cvs
Santolina chamaecyparissus ○
Spartium junceum, p.147
Tamarix ramosissima, p.121 ○
Ulex europaeus 'Flore Pleno' ○
Viburnum tinus, p.149 ○
Yucca gloriosa, p.137 ○

Climbers
Antigonon leptopus, p.209 ○
Bougainvillea glabra, p.214 ○
Eccremocarpus scaber, p.217 ○
Ercilla volubilis ○
Euonymus fortunei 'Coloratus' ○
Fallopia baldschuanica, p.217
Ficus pumila ○
Hedera canariensis var. *algeriensis* ○
Muehlenbeckia complexa
Pandorea jasminoides, p.208 ○
Pyrostegia venusta, p.218 ○
Schisandra rubriflora, p.211 ○
Solandra maxima, p.206 ○
Tripterygium regelii

Lavandula '*Hidcote*'

SEASIDE EXTRAVAGANZA
Left: Plants that are equipped to cope with salty sea air include tall, red kniphofias as well as tender succulents, which can survive winters outdoors because of the mild coastal climate.

Argyranthemum frutescens, p.240 ○
Artemisia absinthium 'Lambrook Silver' ○
Carpobrotus edulis
Centaurea hypoleuca 'John Coutts', p.279
Centranthus ruber, p.245
Crambe maritima, p.276
Echinacea purpurea
Erigeron 'Charity', p.278
Eryngium variifolium, p.286 ○
Euphorbia griffithii 'Fireglow', p.258
Geranium sanguineum, p.354
IRISES, pp.234–5, some ○
Kniphofia, some ○ ▣
Lampranthus aurantiacus, p.468
Myosotidium hortensia, p.287 ○
Osteospermum jucundum, p.279 ○
Peperomia obtusifolia 'Variegata', p.305 ○
Pericallis x *hybrida*
Phormium tenax ○
Pilea cadierei, p.300 ○
Romneya coulteri, p.226
Senecio cineraria 'Silver Dust', p.334 ○
Stachys byzantina, p.304 ○
Tradescantia fluminensis ○

Annuals and biennials
Antirrhinum majus and cvs
Bassia scoparia f. *trichophylla*, p.335
Calendula officinalis Series and cvs
Clarkia amoena and Series
Coreopsis tinctoria, p.336
Cynoglossum amabile 'Firmament', p.334
Dahlia 'Coltness Gem', p.329
Dianthus chinensis Series
Dorotheanthus bellidiformis
Echium ▣
Eschscholzia californica, p.338
Gilia capitata, p.333
Impatiens walleriana Novette Series, p.327 ○
Lavatera trimestris cvs ▣
Limnanthes douglasii, p.336
Matthiola
Portulaca grandiflora Series and cvs

Lavatera trimestris '*Silver Cup*'

Tagetes Antigua Series '*Antigua Gold*'

Rhodanthe chlorocephala subsp. *rosea*, p.321
Tagetes ▣

Rock plants
Achillea clavennae, p.373 ○
Aethionema grandiflorum, p.352 ○
Armeria maritima 'Vindictive', p.380 ○
Aubrieta deltoidea 'Argenteovariegata', p.368 ○
Dianthus deltoides ○
Draba aizoides ○
Epilobium glabellum of gardens, p.351 ○
Iberis sempervirens, p.346 ○
Origanum laevigatum, p.354
Oxalis enneaphylla
Parahebe catarractae, p.356 ○

Tropaeolum tuberosum var. *lineamaculatum* 'Ken Aslet', p.216
Wisteria sinensis, p.215

Grasses (including bamboos)
Cortaderia selloana 'Sunningdale Silver', p.306 ○
Pseudosasa japonica, p.308 ○

Perennials
Anaphalis margaritacea, p.239
Anchusa azurea 'Loddon Royalist', p.254
Anthurium andraeanum, p.264 ○

A COASTAL ROCK GARDEN
Above: This cliff-side rock garden provides sunny, sheltered conditions in beds and rock crevices for many plants, among them centranthus, dorotheanus, echium, erigeron, hebe and phlomis.

Phlox subulata 'Marjorie', p.378 ○
Pulsatilla vulgaris, p.348
Saxifraga paniculata ○
Sedum spathulifolium 'Cape Blanco', p.391 ○
Sempervivum arachnoideum, p.389 ○
Silene schafta, p.379
Thlaspi cepaeifolium subsp. *rotundifolium*, p.365
Viola cornuta, p.349

Bulbs, corms and tubers
Amaryllis belladonna, p.408
Crinum
Crocosmia 'Lucifer', p.401
Crocus
DAFFODILS, pp.416–18
Eucharis x *grandiflora*, p.425 ○
Freesia
Galtonia candicans, p.397
Hippeastrum
HYACINTHS, p.431
Hymenocallis
Nerine
Scilla
Sprekelia formosissima, p.413
TULIPS, pp.410–12
Veltheimia bracteata, p.425
Zantedeschia aethiopica ○

Trees and Shrubs for Exposed Sites

In cold, inland gardens, particularly those exposed to strong winter winds, only the hardiest plants thrive without the protection of a windbreak. Where providing one is not practical, it is essential to establish a basic framework of trees, shrubs and conifers that are fully hardy. Carefully positioned within the garden, in groups, they provide sheltered situations where less hardy plants can be grown, while still retaining a degree of openness if desired.

Sorbus americana

Trees
Acer negundo
Acer rubrum, p.70
Aesculus glabra
Amelanchier laevis, p.85
Betula papyrifera, p.72
Betula pendula
Carpinus carolinianus
Celtis occidentalis
Cornus alternifolia
Crataegus x *mordenensis* 'Toba'
Fraxinus nigra 'Fallgold'
Juglans nigra, p.67

Maackia amurensis, p.90
Ostrya virginiana, p.77
Phellodendron amurensis
Populus alba, p.64
Populus nigra 'Italica', p.66
Prunus maackii, p.84
Prunus padus, p.76
Quercus alba
Salix alba 'Tristis'
Ulmus americana

Conifers
Juniperus chinensis ○
Juniperus sabina ○
Juniperus scopulorum ○
Larix decidua ○
Larix laricina ○
Picea glauca ○
Picea pungens ○

Pinus cembra, p.106 ○
Pinus contorta var. *latifolia*, p.106 ○
Pinus resinosa ○
Pinus strobus, p.102 ○
Pinus sylvestris ○
Thuja occidentalis ○

Shrubs
Acer tataricum ssp. *ginnala*, p.95
Amelanchier alnifolia
Caragana arborescens
Cornus stolonifera and cvs.
Elaeagnus angustifolius, p.122
Euonymus alatus, p.148
Hippophae rhamnoides, p.124
Hydrangea paniculata 'Grandiflora'
Lonicera tatarica
Philadelphus cvs (some), p.136
Physocarpus opulifolius
Potentilla fruticosa cvs.
Prunus cistena, p.154
Ribes alpinum
Rhus typhina
Sambucus racemosa
Shepherdia argentia
Spiraea japonica and cvs, p.163
Spiraea x *vanhouttei*, p.154
Syringa vulgaris cvs
Viburnum lantana
Viburnum trilobum

Ground cover
Arctostaphylos uva-ursi, p.388 ○
Cornus canadensis, p.374

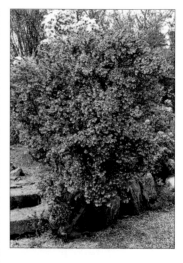

MAXIMUM EXPOSURE
Where it is hardy, evergreen Berberis darwinii *provides shelter for more tender plants with the bonus of masses of spring flowers.*

Cotoneaster nanshen
Genista tinctoria, p.157
Juniperus horizontalis and cvs. ○
Microbiota decussata, p.110 ○
Pachysandra terminalis, p.388 ○
Paxistima canbyi ○

Climbers and Shrubs for Sunless Walls

Against cold, sunless walls, it is essential to choose climbers that grow naturally in shade or semi-shade. These provide reliable and effective foliage cover, and some have attractive flowers. Climbing roses also may flower reasonably well in sunless situations and, together with shade-tolerant shrubs, add colour to shaded walls and wallside borders. Shade-growing plants prefer moist, leafy, woodland-type soils; when planting, enrich the soil well with organic matter, such as leaf mould.

Climbers
Akebia quinata, p.206 ○
Berberidopsis corallina, p.211 ○
Celastrus scandens
Clematis (many), some ○
Clematis alpina 'Frances Rivis', p.213 ○
Ercilla volubilis ○
Euonymus fortunei 'Coloratus' ○
Euonymus fortunei 'Silver Queen', p.151 ○
Hedera colchica 'Dentata Variegata' ○
Hedera colchica 'Sulphur Heart', p.221 ○
Hedera helix cvs ○
Hedera hibernica, p.221 ○
Hydrangea petiolaris, p.208
Lapageria rosea and forms, p.210 ○
Lonicera japonica 'Halliana', p.215 ○
Lonicera periclymenum and cvs
Lonicera tragophylla
Parthenocissus henryana
Parthenocissus quinquefolia (rough surfaces)
Parthenocissus tricuspidata and cvs
Pileostegia viburnoides, p.208
Schisandra rubriflora, p.211
Schizophragma hydrangeoides
Schizophragma integrifolium, p.208

Shrubs
Azara microphylla, p.125 ○
Camellia japonica cvs ○
Camellia x *williamsii* cvs ○
Chaenomeles speciosa 'Moerloosei', p.130
Chaenomeles x *superba* 'Rowallane', p.155
Choisya ternata, p.127 ○
Cotoneaster horizontalis, p.172
Cotoneaster lacteus, p.125 ○
Crinodendron hookerianum, p.142 ○
Drimys winteri, p.78 ○
Eucryphia x *nymansensis* 'Nymansay', p.81 ○

Lapageria rosea *var.* albiflora

x *Fatshedera lizei*, p.152 ○
Fatsia japonica ○
Forsythia suspensa, p.131
Garrya elliptica 'James Roof' ○
Itea ilicifolia, p.146 ○
Jasminum nudiflorum, p.151
Mahonia japonica, p.151 ○
Mahonia x *media* 'Charity', p.125 ○
Muehlenbeckia complexa
Osmanthus decorus ○
Pyracantha 'Orange Glow' ○
Pyracantha x *watereri*, p.136 ○
Ribes laurifolium, p.175 ○
Rosa 'Albéric Barbier', p.196 ○

COOL SECLUSION
Variegated Hedera colchica *'Sulphur Heart' and a decorative stone urn make a feature of a sunless wall.*

Rosa 'Félicité Perpétue', p.196 ○
Rosa 'Gloire de Dijon', p.196
Rosa 'Golden Showers', p.199
Rosa 'Maigold', p.199
Rosa 'Madame Alfred Carrière', p.196
Rosa 'Madame Grégoire Staechelin', p.197 ○

Deer-resistant plants

In many parts of Canada, deer are becoming a major problem in gardens because they can easily gain access and browse on choice plants by jumping fences. Erecting special fences is expensive, and not very practical in smaller urban gardens. Other deterrents do not always work for very long and are difficult to renew in mid-winter when the garden is deep in snow. The plants on the following list are usually avoided by deer, but may be eaten if they are really hungry.

Trees and shrubs
Acer negundo
Acer palmatum
Aralia elata
Arbutus menziesii ○
Berberis
Betula pendula
Buddleja davidii
Buxus ○
Ceanothus
Choisya ternata, p.127
Cotinus coggygria
Cytisus scoparius

Daphne mezereum, p.174
Elaeagnus angustifolius, p.122
Elaeagnus commutata
Erica, most
Euonymes japonicus
Forsythia
Fraxinus
HEATHERS, p.178, most ○
HOLLIES, p.98, except smooth-leaved species ○
Kalmia latifolia, p.141
Kerria japonica
LILACS, p.120
Liquidambar styraciflua, p.70
MAGNOLIA, p.75
Mahonia aquifolium, p.157 ○
Pieris japonica, p.116
Populus nigra 'Italica', p.66
Potentilla fruticosa
RHODODENDRON, pp.132–4, but not azalea ○
Ribes alpinum
Robinia pseudoacacia
ROSES, especially species and many shrub types, pp.184–8
Sambucus racemosa
Spiraea
Symphorecarpos albus
Viburnum
Yucca

Conifers
Abies ○
Juniperus, most ○
Larix decidua
Picea ○

Choisya ternata SUNDANCE

DEER RESISTERS
Above: The golden pampas grass (Cortaderia selloana 'Gold Band') and summer-flowering Agapanthus 'Loch Hope' should escape the attentions of hungry deer.

Syringa vulgaris 'Decaisne'

Pinus ○
Taxus ○

Climbers
Celastris scandens
CLEMATIS, p.212
IVIES, p.221 ○
Ipomoea
Wisteria

Perennials
Achillea
Agapanthus
Alchemilla mollis, p.290
Anemone x hybrida
Aquilegia
Campanula persicifolia
Centranthus ruber, p.245
DAYLILIES, p.257
DELPHINIUMS, p.230

Dicentra spectabilis, p.245
FERNS, most
Filipendual rubra, p.227
Geranium
Heleborus ○
Hesperis matrionalis, p.239
HOSTAS, pp.288–9
IRISES, pp.234–5
Leucanthemum x superbum
Lupinus
Lychnis coronaria, p.282
Monarda
Papaver orientale
PEONIES, pp.236–7
Perovskia atriplicifolia
Rosmarinum officinalis, p.167
Rudbeckia hirta
Salvia
Stachys byzantina, p.304

Grasses (including bamboos)
BAMBOO, most species
Cortaderia selloana
Festuca glauca
Miscanthus sinensis

Ground covers
Ajuga reptans
Arctostaphylos uva-ursi, p.388 ○
Cerastium tomentosum, p.361
Cotoneaster horizontalis, p.172
Dicentra formosa
Epimedium
Galium odoratum, p.275
Gaultheria shallon, p.162 ○
Hypericum calycinum, p.170 ○
Lamium maculatum, p.269
Liriope ○
Vinca minor, p.176 ○

Annuals and perennials
Ageratum houstonianum
Antirrhinum majus
Calendula officinalis
Campanula medium
Catharanthus roseus, p.160
Eschscholzia californica, p.339
Impatiens walleriana
Moluccella laevis, p.335
Myosotis sylvatica
Papaver croceum
Scabiosa atropurpurea
Senecio cineria
Verbena x hybrida
Zinnia

Bulbs, corms and tubers
Allium, most
Begonia x tuberhybrida
Crocosmia
DAFFODILS, pp.416–18
Fritillaria imperialis, p.396
Leucojum aestivum, p.396
Mirabilis jalapa, p.245
TULIPS, pp.410–12
Zantedeschia

Daffodil (Narcissus 'Quince')

Plants for Hedges and Windbreaks

Plants for hedging are often selected for their ornamental qualities, but there are also other aspects to consider. Boundary hedges may provide visual privacy, or screen unsightly buildings; they may also be bushy or thorny to keep out animals or intruders. Make sure that plants for screening will grow to the required height, choosing conifers or evergreen shrubs for year-round effect. In exposed situations, trees and larger conifers may be used as windbreaks; two or three staggered rows are usually much more effective than a single, close-planted one.

HYDRANGEA HEDGES
Above: Parallel hedges of tall lacecap hydrangeas look spectacular in late summer, the flower colours deepening with the evening sun. Between them a gravel walk leads to an archway in a high, carefully trimmed windbreak, passing to a grassy orchard beyond.

Rosa rugosa *var.* rosea

Trees
Alnus cordata, p.66 △
Arbutus unedo, p.93 ○
Carpinus betulus
Carpinus betulus 'Fastigiata', p.100
Crataegus monogyna
Fagus sylvatica, p.68
Ilex aquifolium, p.98 ○
Ilex aquifolium 'Argentea Marginata', p.98 ○
Laurus nobilis ○
Melaleuca viridiflora var. *rubriflora* ○ △
Metrosideros excelsus, p.83 ○ △
Nothofagus dombeyi, p.68 ○ △
Nothofagus obliqua, p.68 △
Olea europaea ○
Populus x *canadensis* 'Robusta', p.65 △
Prunus lusitanica ○
Syzygium paniculatum, p.81 ○
Umbellularia californica, p.74 ○
Zelkova serrata, p.71

Conifers
Abies grandis, p.104 ○ △
Cedrus deodara
Cephalotaxus harringtonii ○
Chamaecyparis lawsoniana ○
Cupressocyparis x *leylandii* ○ △
Cupressus macrocarpa ○ △
Juniperus communis ○
Larix decidua △
Picea omorika, p.103 ○ △

Pinus nigra ○
Pinus radiata, p.104 ○ △
Pseudotsuga menziesii var. *glauca*, p.102 ○ △
Taxus baccata ○
Thuja plicata ○ △
Tsuga canadensis, p.107 ○ △

Shrubs
Berberis darwinii, p.117 ○
Buxus sempervirens 'Suffruticosa', p.177 ○
Choisya ternata, p.127 ○
Codiaeum variegatum var. *pictum*, p.177 ○
Cotoneaster simonsii, p.148 △
Dodonaea viscosa 'Purpurea', p.151 ○ △

Cherry laurel
(Prunus laurocerasus)

Duranta erecta, p.150 ○ △
Elaeagnus x *ebbingei* ○ △
Escallonia 'Langleyensis', p.142 ○
Euonymus japonicus 'Macrophyllus' ○
Griselinia littoralis ○
Hibiscus rosa-sinensis ○
Hippophäe rhamnoides, p.124
Hydrangea macrophylla cvs ▣
Lavandula cvs ○
Leptospermum scoparium cvs ○ △
Ligustrum ovalifolium, p.126 ○ △
Lonicera nitida ○
Photinia x *fraseri* 'Birmingham', p.117 ○ △
Pittosporum tenuifolium, p.127 ○ △
Prunus laurocerasus ○ ▣
Prunus lusitanica ○
Pyracantha x *watereri*, p.136 ○ △
Rosmarinus officinalis and cvs ○
Tamarix ramosissima, p.121 △

Roses
Rosa californica △
Rosa 'Céleste', p.185 △
Rosa 'Felicia', p.185 △
Rosa 'Frühlingsmorgen' △
Rosa gallica var. *officinalis* △
Rosa gallica 'Versicolor', p.187 △
Rosa glauca, p.186 △
Rosa 'Great Maiden's Blush', p.185 △
Rosa 'Marguerite Hilling', p.186 △
Rosa moyesii 'Geranium', p.187 △
Rosa 'Nevada', p.185 △
Rosa 'Penelope', p.184 △
Rosa 'Président de Sèze' △

Rosa rugosa, p.187 △ ▣
Rosa 'Tuscany Superb' △

Grasses (including bamboos)
Arundo donax △
Cortaderia selloana 'Sunningdale Silver', p.306 ○
Fargesia nitida ○
Phyllostachys bambusoides, p.308 ○ △
Pseudosasa japonica, p.308 ○
Semiarundinaria fastuosa, p.308 ○
Stipa gigantea, p.307 ○

Perennials
Echinops bannaticus, p.228 △
Eupatorium purpureum, p.231 △
Filipendula camtschatica △
Helianthus atrorubens 'Monarch'
Macleaya microcarpa 'Kelway's Coral Plume', p.227 △
Phormium tenax ○
Rudbeckia 'Goldquelle', p.229 △

Architectural Plants

In gardens, plants that stand out, immediately drawing the eye with their strong, distinctive appearance, are termed 'architectural' plants. Whether by chance or design, such plants give character and substance, and help form the basic framework of a garden. Most are trees, conifers and shrubs, which provide a permanent effect throughout the year. They impress by shape, as in strongly vertical, conical or fastigiate forms of conifer, or with striking foliage – the immense leaf size of gunneras or the sword-like leaves of phormiums. In established gardens, areas attracting little attention may be improved by introducing plants with good architectural qualities.

Trees
Cordyline ○
Dracaena draco, p.100 ○
Eucalyptus (many) ○
Jacaranda mimosifolia, p.79
Kalopanax septemlobus, p.80
MAGNOLIAS, p.75, some ○
Paulownia tomentosa, p.77
Phoenix canariensis ○
Salix (several)
Trachycarpus fortunei, p.84 ○
Trochodendron aralioides, p.84 ○
Washingtonia ○

Conifers
Abies ○
Araucaria ○
Calocedrus decurrens, p.106 ○
Cedrus ○
Juniperus x *pfitzeriana* 'William Pfitzer', p.111 ○
Metasequoia glyptostroboides, p.102
Picea ○
Pseudolarix amabilis, p.107
Sciadopitys verticillata, p.106 ○
Sequoia sempervirens ○
Sequoiadendron giganteum, p.102 ○
Taxodium distichum, p.104
Tsuga heterophylla ○

Shrubs
Aesculus parviflora, p.119
Brachyglottis repanda, p.127 ○
Cycas revoluta, p.152 ○
Daphniphyllum macropodum, p.117 ○
Eriobotrya japonica ○
Fatsia japonica ○
Fatsia japonica 'Variegata', p.151 ○
Mahonia (most) ○
Parkinsonia aculeata ○
Protea ○
Rhus typhina
Rhus typhina 'Dissecta', p.124
Yucca ○ ▣

Climbers
Epipremnum aureum 'Marble Queen', p.219 ○
Hedera colchica 'Dentata', p.221 ○
Monstera deliciosa, p.220 ○
Schizophragma hydrangeoides
Schizophragma integrifolium, p.208
Vitis coignetiae, p.218

Ferns
Asplenium scolopendrium Marginatum Group, p.313 ○
Blechnum tabulare ○
Cyathea australis, p.100 ○
Dicksonia antarctica, p.310 ○
Matteuccia struthiopteris, p.312 ▣
Platycerium bifurcatum, p.310 ○
Polystichum munitum, p.316 ○
Woodwardia radicans ○

Grasses (including bamboos)
Chusquea culeou, p.308 ○
Cortaderia selloana 'Sunningdale Silver', p.306 ○

Perennials
Acanthus spinosus, p.251
Angelica archangelica, p.228
Berkheya macrocephala, p.258
Crambe cordifolia, p.226
Cynara cardunculus, p.228
Darmera peltata, p.238
Echinops bannaticus, p.228
Echium wildpretii ○
Ensete ventricosum, p.233 ○
Euphorbia characias subsp. *characias*, p.156 ○
Gunnera manicata, p.228
Heliconia ○
Hosta (many)
Kniphofia caulescens, p.263 ○
Ligularia (most)
Macleaya
Meconopsis (most), several ○
Phormium tenax and cvs ○
Puya chilensis, p.265 ○
Rheum palmatum 'Atrosanguineum'
Rodgersia
Strelitzia reginae, p.267 ○
Veratrum nigrum, p.228
Verbascum olympicum, p.229 ○

Annuals and biennials
Alcea rosea, p.321
Amaranthus tricolor cvs

Ostrich fern
(Matteuccia
struthiopteris)

Calomeria amaranthoides, p.330
Helianthus annuus and cvs
Onopordum acanthium, p.322 ▣
Silybum marianum, p.322
Verbascum densiflorum ○

Bulbs, corms and tubers
Arisaema (most)
Arum creticum, p.415
Begonia rex and hybrids ○
Cardiocrinum giganteum, p.398
Dracunculus vulgaris, p.401
GLADIOLI, p.399 most
Sauromatum venosum, p.413
Zantedeschia aethiopica ○

Water plants
Colocasia esculenta and cvs ○
Eichhornia crassipes, p.448 ○
Lysichiton americanus, p.451 ○
Nelumbo nucifera and cvs
Orontium aquaticum, p.451
Pontederia cordata, p.448
Sagittaria
Thalia dealbata

Cacti and other succulents
Most of the larger species, especially:
Aeonium tabuliforme, p.478 ○
Agave americana 'Striata', p.457 ○
Aloe (most) ○
Carnegiea gigantea, p.456 ○
Cereus (most) ○
Cyphostemma juttae, p.459
Euphorbia candelabrum ○
Opuntia (most) ○

SILVER SCULPTURE
Below: In this quiet, shady corner, the eye is immediately caught by the architectural merits of three Scotch thistles (Onopordum acanthium), their silvery-grey stems and foliage effectively displayed against a dark background.

Yucca elephantipes *'Variegata'*

Plants for Quick Cover

In new gardens there are often steep banks or large spaces impractical to turf or plant, and in older gardens areas may become neglected or there may be little time for maintenance. Such problems may be resolved by using plants that have good ground-covering qualities – rapid, dense, low, and leafy or twiggy growth that helps to suppress weeds permanently. Always select plants that are suitable for the soil conditions and, in large areas, use vigorous ones such as ivy (*Hedera*), which may be spaced to give good cover in two or three seasons.

Conifers
Juniperus conferta ○
Juniperus sabina var. *tamariscifolia*, p.110 ○

Shrubs
Ceanothus thyrsiflorus var. *repens*, p.168 ○
Cotoneaster conspicuus ○
Cotoneaster 'Gnom' ○
Cotoneaster 'Skogholm' ○
Gaultheria shallon, p.162 ○
Hypericum calycinum, p.170 ○
Lantana camara ○
Rosa GROUSE ('Korimro'), p.189
Rosa PINK BELLS ('Poulbells'), p.190
Rubus tricolor ○
Stephanandra incisa 'Crispa'

Symphoricarpos x *chenaultii* 'Hancock'

Climbers
Hedera canariensis var. *algeriensis* 'Ravensholst' ○
Hedera colchica 'Dentata', p.221 ○
Hedera helix (small cvs) ○
Hedera hibernica, p.221 ○
Hydrangea petiolaris, p.208 ▣
Lonicera japonica cvs ○
Pueraria lobata
Trachelospermum asiaticum ○
Trachelospermum jasminoides, p.207 ○

Ferns
Dryopteris dilatata

Polystichum aculeatum ○
Polystichum setiferum Groups, pp.311, 313 ○

Perennials
Aegopodium podagraria 'Variegatum', p.276
Alchemilla mollis, p.290
Anthemis punctata subsp. *cupaniana*, p.276 ○
Asarum europaeum, p.390 ○
Campanula portenschlagiana, p.382 ○
Cerastium tomentosum, p.361 ○
Chelidonium majus 'Flore Pleno', p.238
Duchesnea indica ○
Euphorbia amygdaloides var. *robbiae*, p.271 ○
Geranium macrorrhizum, p.279 ○
Geranium x *oxonianum* 'Claridge Druce' ○
Glechoma hederacea 'Variegata', p.300 ○
Heterocentron elegans, p.284 ○
Lamium maculatum and cvs ○
Osteospermum jucundum, p.279 ○
Phalaris arundinacea var. *picta*, p.306 ○

Hydrangea petiolaris

Mother of thousands (Saxifraga stolonifera)

Prunella grandiflora 'Pink Loveliness' ○
Pulmonaria (most), some ○
Stachys byzantina, p.304 ○
Symphytum x *uplandicum* 'Variegatum', p.238

Annuals and biennials
Lathyrus odoratus 'Bijou', p.324
Portulaca grandiflora Series and cvs
Sanvitalia procumbens, p.336
Tropaeolum majus Series and cvs

Rock plants
Acaena anserinifolia of gardens ○
Arabis caucasica and cvs ○
Aubrieta ○
Campanula poscharskyana, p.381 ○
Helianthemum ○
Persicaria affinis and cvs
Persicaria vacciniifolia, p.387 ○
Phlox douglasii cvs ○
Phlox subulata ○
Phuopsis stylosa, p.352 ○
Saxifraga stolonifera ○ ▣
Tiarella cordifolia, p.347 ○
Waldsteinia ○

Sarcococca confusa

Ground-cover Plants for Shade

An area that is shaded for some or most of the day may be regarded by some gardeners as a problem space, when in fact it should be viewed as a fortunate opportunity to experiment with a different, and often equally exciting, range of plants from those more suited to sunny positions. The following ground-cover plants may be planted in any depth of shade, given reasonably fertile soil conditions.

Shrubs
Cotoneaster conspicuus ○
Cotoneaster 'Gnom' ○
Cotoneaster 'Herbstfeuer' ○
Daphne laureola subsp. *philippi*, p.156 ○
Epigaea asiatica ○
Euonymus fortunei 'Kewensis' ○
Gaultheria shallon, p.162 ○
Hypericum calycinum, p.170 ○
Leucothöe fontanesiana ○
Lonicera pileata, p.176 ○

Mahonia aquifolium, p.157 ○
Mahonia repens ○
Pachysandra terminalis, p.388 ○
Paxistima canbyi ○
Prunus laurocerasus 'Otto Luyken', p.154 ○
Rubus tricolor ○
Ruscus hypoglossum, p.176 ○
Sarcococca confusa ○ ▣
Sarcococca humilis, p.174 ○
Vinca difformis ○
Vinca minor, p.176 ○

Climbers
Asteranthera ovata ○
Berberidopsis corallina, p.211 ○
Epipremnum aureum 'Marble Queen', p.219 ○
Ficus pumila ○
Hedera colchica 'Dentata', p.221 ○
Hedera helix 'Green Ripple', p.221 ○
Hedera helix 'Ivalace', p.221 ○
Hedera hibernica, p.221 ○
Hydrangea petiolaris, p.208 ○
Rhoicissus capensis ○
Rhoicissus rhomboidea ○
Schizophragma hydrangeoides

Ferns
Adiantum venustum, p.313 ○
Athyrium filix-femina
Blechnum penna-marina ○ ▣
Blechnum spicant ○
Polypodium vulgare, p.313 ○
Polystichum setiferum Groups, pp.311, 313 ○

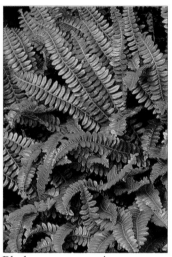

Blechnum penna-marina

Perennials
Acanthus spinosus, p.251
Ajuga pyramidalis ○
Ajuga reptans 'Atropurpurea',
    p.303 ○
Alchemilla mollis, p.290
Anemone apennina
Arisarum proboscideum
Asarum caudatum ○
Asarum europaeum, p.390 ○
Aspidistra elatior ○
Astrantia maxima, p.277
Bergenia cordifolia 'Purpurea',
    p.269 ○
Brunnera macrophylla
Campanula portenschlagiana,
    p.382 ○

Campanula poscharskyana, p.381
Ceratostigma plumbaginoides, p.360
Chelidonium majus 'Flore Pleno',
    p.238
Convallaria majalis, p.268
Dicentra formosa
Dicentra spectabilis, p.245
Duchesnea indica ○
Elatostema repens, p.303 ○
Epimedium perralderianum ○
Euphorbia amygdaloides var. *robbiae*,
    p.271 ○
Fittonia argyroneura, p.300 ○
Galax urceolata, p.351 ○
Galium odoratum, p.275
Geranium macrorrhizum, p.279 ○

Spotted deadnettle
(Lamium maculatum)

Geranium nodosum, p.270
Geranium renardii, p.277
Geranium sanguineum, p.354
Geranium wallichianum 'Buxton's
    Variety', p.287
Glechoma hederacea 'Variegata',
    p.300 ○
HOSTAS (some), pp.288–9 ▣
Hypsela reniformis
Iris foetidissima ○
Lamium maculatum, p.269 ○ ▣
Liriope muscari, p.294 ○
Luzula sylvatica 'Marginata' ○
Maianthemum bifolium
Meehania urticifolia
Omphalodes cappadocica, p.349
Pachyphragma macrophyllum, p.267
Persicaria affinis 'Donald Lowndes',
    p.376 ○
Persicaria campanulata, p.259
Phalaris arundinacea var. *picta*,
    p.306 ○
Plectranthus oertendahlii ○
Pulmonaria saccharata, p.271 ○
Saxifraga x *geum*, p.347 ○
Symphytum grandiflorum of gardens
Tellima grandiflora Rubra Group,
    p.302 ○
Tiarella cordifolia, p.347 ○
Tolmiea menziesii ○

ORNAMENTAL GROUND COVER
*Below: Hostas thrive in cool, shady
surroundings, and offer a variety of
leaf texture, colour and form. Many
plants grow well on the fringes of
woodland, as long as conditions are
not too densely shaded nor too dry.*

Waldsteinia ternata

Tradescantia fluminensis 'Variegata',
    p.300 ○
Vancouveria hexandra, p.347
Viola riviniana 'Purpurea', p.369
Waldsteinia ternata, p.385 ○ ▣

Rock plants
Asarina procumbens, p.384
Cardamine trifolia, p.362
Cornus canadensis, p.374
Homogyne alpina ○
Mitchella repens ○
Prunella grandiflora, p.381 ○
Saxifraga stolonifera ○
Saxifraga x *urbium* ○
Tiarella cordifolia, p.347 ○

Tropaeolum *Alaska Series*

Phlomis russeliana, p.255
Rheum palmatum 'Atrosanguineum',
  p.227
Stachys byzantina, p.304 ○
Veronica prostrata and cvs
Waldsteinia ternata, p.385 ○

Annuals and biennials
Any of spreading habit, such as
  Tropaeolum ▣

Rock plants
Acaena microphylla, p.389 ○
Antennaria dioica var. *rosea*, p.366 ○
Arabis alpina subsp. *caucasica*
  'Variegata', p.362 ○
Armeria maritima 'Vindictive', p.380
  ○
Aubrieta cvs ○
Aurinia saxatilis, p.350 ○
Campanula portenschlagiana,
  p.382 ○
Campanula poscharskyana, p.381
Dianthus gratianopolitanus,
  p.377 ○
Dryas octopetala, p.375 ○
Helianthemum 'Ben More', p.354 ○
Hypericum olympicum
Iberis sempervirens, p.346 ○
Lithodora diffusa 'Heavenly Blue',
  p.357 ○ ▣
Nierembergia repens, p.374 ○
Persicaria affinis and cvs
Phlox douglasii 'Crackerjack',
  p.379 ○
Phuopsis stylosa, p.352
Thymus serpyllum ○
Veronica prostrata 'Kapitan', p.357

Ground-cover Plants for Sun

Many plants grow naturally in dry, sunny conditions. Some have developed foliage characteristics to minimize moisture loss from their leaves; others are densely branched, keeping the soil surface shaded and cool. Most have extensive root systems that penetrate deeply to find moisture. These plants are adapted to well-drained soils; in poorly drained situations, they may not survive prolonged wet conditions. Although adapted to poorer, dry soils, young plants may have been grown in richer composts and well watered, so when planting incorporate organic matter, such as leaf mould or coir, and check water needs until well established.

NATURAL SPREADERS
Several of the mat-forming acaenas provide attractive, summer-flowering ground cover in exposed, sunny sites.

Symphoricarpos x *chenaultii* 'Hancock'
Ulex europaeus 'Flore Pleno'
Vinca minor and cvs ○
Vinca major 'Variegata', p.175 ○

Climbers
Anredera cordifolia ○
Campsis radicans
Clematis armandii, p.212 ○
Clematis rehderiana, p.213
Clematis tangutica, p.213
Decumaria sinensis ○
Hardenbergia comptoniana, p.206 ○
Hedera canariensis var. *algeriensis*
  'Ravensholst' ○
Hedera colchica 'Dentata
  Variegata' ○
Hedera hibernica, p.221 ○
Hibbertia scandens ○
Kennedia rubicunda, p.204 ○
Lathyrus latifolius, p.211 ○
Lonicera japonica 'Halliana',
  p.215 ○
Parthenocissus tricuspidata, p.218
Pueraria lobata
Pyrostegia venusta, p.218 ○
Trachelospermum asiaticum ○
Vitis coignetiae, p.218

Perennials
Alchemilla mollis, p.290
Anthemis punctata subsp. *cupaniana*,
  p.276 ○
Artemisia alba 'Canescens' ○
Centaurea montana, p.284
Darmera peltata, p.238
Euphorbia polychroma, p.275
Geranium sanguineum, p.354
Heterocentron elegans, p.284 ○
Liriope muscari, p.294 ○
Lysimachia punctata, p.255
Nepeta x *faassenii*, p.286
Origanum vulgare 'Aureum', p.290
Osteospermum jucundum, p.279 ○

Juniperus squamata *'Blue Star'*

Conifers
Juniperus communis 'Prostrata' ○
Juniperus horizontalis 'Wiltonii' ○
Juniperus sabina var. *tamariscifolia*,
  p.110 ○
Juniperus squamata 'Blue Carpet' ○
Juniperus squamata 'Blue Star' ○ ▣
Microbiota decussata, p.110 ○
Picea abies 'Inversa' ○

Shrubs
Arctostaphylos nevadensis ○
Arctostaphylos nummularia ○
Arctostaphylos uva-ursi, p.388 ○

Berberis wilsoniae ○
Brachyglottis Dunedin Hybrids
  'Sunshine', p.170 ○
Calluna vulgaris 'White Lawn' ○
Ceanothus thyrsiflorus var. *repens*,
  p.168 ○
Cotoneaster cochleatus of gardens ○
Cotoneaster 'Skogholm' ○
Cytisus x *beanii*, p.349
Cytisus scoparius subsp. *maritimus*
Ephedra gerardiana ○
Erica carnea 'Springwood White',
  p.178 ○
Euonymus fortunei 'Emerald
  Gaiety' ○
Euonymus fortunei 'Kewensis' ○
Gaultheria myrsinoides ○
Genista hispanica, p.170
x *Halimiocistus sahucii*, p.159 ○
Hebe pinguifolia 'Pagei', p.351 ○
Hebe 'Youngii' ○
Hypericum calycinum, p.170 ○
Lantana montevidensis, p.167 ○
Leiophyllum buxifolium ○
Leptospermum rupestre, p.160 ○
Potentilla fruticosa 'Abbotswood',
  p.158
Rosa GROUSE ('Korimro'), p.189
Rosa 'Nozomi', p.189
Rosa PINK BELLS ('Poulbells'), p.190
Rosmarinus officinalis 'Prostratus' ○
Salix repens, p.156
Santolina chamaecyparissus ○
Stephanandra incisa 'Crispa'

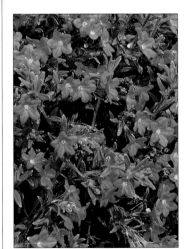

Lithodora diffusa *'Heavenly Blue'*

Plants for Dry Shade

Dry, shady conditions persist under evergreen trees throughout the year. Under the summer leaf canopy of deciduous trees, too, very little moisture penetrates, except during prolonged rainfall. A few early-flowering bulbs, such as bluebells (*Hyacinthoides non-scripta*), and small woodland plants grow naturally in deciduous woodlands, dying down as the trees resume growth in spring. In gardens, dry shade occurs under larger, low-branched trees or where eaves extend over borders. Planting should be done in the autumn so that roots are well established by the following spring. Feed regularly and monitor water needs until the plants are established.

Trees and conifers
Ilex aquifolium, p.98 ○
Taxus baccata 'Adpressa' ○
Taxus cuspidata, p.109 ○
Tsuga canadensis, p.107 ○

Shrubs
Aucuba japonica 'Crotonifolia', p.153 ○
Buxus sempervirens ○
Choisya ternata, p.127 ○
Cotoneaster horizontalis, p.172
Daphne laureola and forms ○ ▣

Daphne laureola *subsp.* philippi

Elaeagnus x *ebbingei* ○
Euonymus japonicus ○
Fatsia japonica ○
Gaultheria shallon, p.162 ○
Hedera colchica var. *algeriensis* 'Ravensholst', p.221 ○
Hedera helix ○
Hedera hibernica, p.221 ○
Hypericum calycinum, p.170 ○
Hypericum x *inodorum* 'Elstead', p.170
Hypericum x *moserianum*
Lonicera pileata, p.176 ○
Mahonia aquifolium, p.157 ○
Osmanthus decorus ○
Osmanthus delavayi, p.116 ○
Pachysandra terminalis, p.388 ○
Prunus laurocerasus 'Otto Luyken', p.154 ○
Prunus laurocerasus 'Zabeliana', p.154 ○
Prunus lusitanica ○
Rubus tricolor ○
Ruscus aculeatus ○
Ruscus hypoglossum, p.176 ○
Sambucus nigra 'Guincho Purple'
Sarcococca humilis, p.174 ○
Symphoricarpos albus var. *laevigatus*

Vaccinium angustifolium var. *laevifolium*, p.172
Viburnum rhytidophyllum, p.118 ○
Viburnum tinus, p.149 ○
Vinca major ○
Vinca minor, p.176 ○

Climbers
Berberidopsis corallina, p.211 ○
Celastrus orbiculatus
Cissus striata ○
Epipremnum aureum 'Marble Queen', p.219 ○
Euonymus fortunei 'Emerald Gaiety' ○
Hedera canariensis var. *algeriensis* ○
Lapageria rosea, p.210 ○
Lonicera japonica 'Halliana', p.215 ○
Lonicera periclymenum and cvs
Philodendron scandens, p.220 ○

Ferns
Asplenium ceterach, p.311 ○
Asplenium scolopendrium, p.313 ○
Cyrtomium falcatum, p.311 ○
Davallia canariensis
Dryopteris affinis ○
Nephrolepis exaltata, p.312 ○
Polypodium vulgare, p.313 ○
Polystichum aculeatum ○
Pteris cretica, p.311 ○

Perennials
Acanthus spinosus, p.251
Achimenes
Ajuga reptans cvs ○
Alchemilla mollis, p.290
Chelidonium majus 'Flore Pleno', p.238
Chirita ○
Corydalis lutea, p.359 ○

Bishop's hat
Epimedium grandiflorum 'Crimson Beauty'

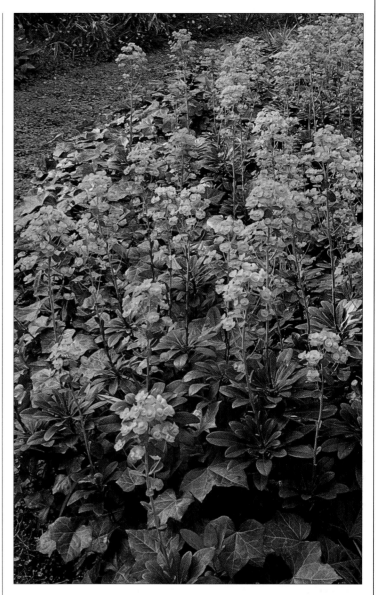

A LIGHT TOUCH
Above: The close-set, dark green leaves of Euphorbia amygdaloides var. robbiae, shown here growing in association with a dark-leaved ivy, provide good ground cover in dry shade, where soil may be poor. Rounded heads of lime-green flowers add light to the clump in spring.

Digitalis purpurea
Doronicum x *excelsum* 'Harpur Crewe'
Epimedium grandiflorum and cvs ▣
Epimedium pinnatum subsp. *colchicum* ○
Euphorbia amygdaloides var. *robbiae*, p.271 ○ ▣
Geranium macrorrhizum, p.279
Geranium phaeum, p.238
Iris foetidissima ○
Kohleria digitaliflora, p.244
Lamium maculatum, p.269 ○
Lunaria rediviva
Luzula sylvatica 'Marginata' ○
Pachysandra terminalis, p.388 ○
Polygonatum x *hybridum*, p.238
Scopolia carniolica, p.271
Sedum spathulifolium, p.389 ○
Streptocarpus saxorum, p.284 ○
Symphytum 'Goldsmith' ▣
Symphytum ibericum

Symphytum '*Goldsmith*'

Tellima grandiflora ○
Tolmiea menziesii ○
Tradescantia zebrina 'Quadricolor' ○
Viola riviniana 'Purpurea', p.369

Bulbs, corms and tubers
Clivia miniata, p.419 ○
Colchicum autumnale, p.437
Haemanthus albiflos ○
Hyacinthoides hispanica, p.414
Hyacinthoides non-scripta, p.414

Helleborus **x** ballardiae
'*December Dawn*'

Plants for Moist Shade

In areas with high rainfall, the soil in parts of the garden that receive little or no sun may be cool and moist throughout the year. Low-lying gardens with a high water table or drainage problems may have shady, permanently moist areas. Similar conditions occur along the margins of natural streams, or when an artificial bog is created beside a garden pond. Take advantage of these situations to grow plants such as broad-leaved hostas, ferns and taller moisture-loving primulas. Plant in spring, enriching lighter soils with organic material. During extended dry periods, keep a check on moisture levels.

A COOL, MOIST CORNER
Above: Ferns and large-leaved hostas grow to perfection in moist shade at the side of a garden pool.

Sword fern
(Polystichum
munitum)

Shrubs
Anopterus glandulosus, p.116 ○
Cassiope lycopodioides, p.363 ○
Clethra arborea ○ ▣
Crataegus laevigata 'Punicea'
Cyathodes colensoi, p.360 ○
Danäe racemosa ○
Gaultheria procumbens, p.387 ○
Kalmia latifolia, p.141 ○
Ledum groenlandicum, p.154 ○
Leucothöe fontanesiana ○
Lindera benzoin, p.131
Lyonia ligustrina
Neillia thibetica, p.140
Paeonia lutea var. *ludlowii*,
    p.237

Paeonia suffruticosa subsp.
    rockii, p.236
Paxistima canbyi ○
Pieris formosa var. *forrestii*
    'Wakehurst', p.142 ○
Pittosporum eugenioides ○
Prunus laurocerasus ○
RHODODENDRONS, pp.132–4,
    most ○
Salix magnifica
Sarcococca ruscifolia ○
Skimmia japonica, p.175 ○
Viburnum 'Pragense', p.139 ○
Xanthorhiza simplicissima

Climbers
Akebia quinata, p.206, some ○
Asteranthera ovata ○
Decumaria sinensis, p.206 ○
Dioscorea discolor, p.219 ○
Humulus lupulus 'Aureus', p.206
Hydrangea petiolaris, p.208
Lonicera tragophylla
Macleania insignis ○
Mikania scandens ○
Passiflora coccinea, p.205 ○
Pileostegia viburnoides, p.208 ○
Schizophragma integrifolium, p.208
Smilax china
Thunbergia mysorensis, p.207 ○
Trachelospermum jasminoides,
    p.207 ○

Ferns
Athyrium nipponicum, p.313
Blechnum tabulare ○
Cyathea australis, p.100 ○

Cyathea medullaris ○
Dicksonia antarctica, p.310 ○
Dryopteris goldieana
Lygodium japonicum ○
Matteuccia struthiopteris, p.312
Onoclea sensibilis, p.312
Osmunda claytoniana
Polystichum munitum, p.310 ○ ▣
Selaginella martensii, p.311 ○
Woodwardia radicans ○

Perennials
Actaea pachypoda, p.259
Ajuga reptans 'Atropurpurea',
    p.303 ○
Anemone **x** *hybrida* cvs
Anemonella thalictroides, p.364
Anthurium scherzerianum, p.302 ○
Aruncus dioicus, p.226
Asarum europaeum, p.390 ○
Begonia rex and hybrids ○
Bergenia ○

Brunnera macrophylla
Calathea zebrina, p.266 ○
Cardamine pentaphyllos, p.270
Cimicifuga racemosa
Convallaria majalis, p.268
Cortusa matthioli, p.354
Cyathodes colensoi, p.360 ○
Darmera peltata, p.238
Deinanthe caerulea
Dichorisandra reginae, p.252 ○
Digitalis **x** *mertonensis* ○
Epigaea gaultherioides, p.364 ○
Galax urceolata, p.351 ○
Geranium nodosum, p.270
Hacquetia epipactis, p.371
Hedyotis michauxii, p.383
Helleborus **x** *ballardiae* 'December
    Dawn' ▣
Helleborus **x** *hybridus*, p.302 ○
HOSTAS, pp.288–9 ▣
Isopyrum thalictroides
Jeffersonia diphylla, p.347
Kirengeshoma palmata, p.263
Lamium galeobdolon subsp. *montanum*
    'Florentinum' ○
Lamium maculatum, p.269 ○
Lathraea clandestina, p.271
Lithophragma parviflorum, p.346
Maianthemum canadense, p.363
Maranta leuconeura 'Erythroneura',
    p.303 ○
Mitella breweri, p.384
Omphalodes cappadocica, p.349
Ourisia caespitosa, p.374 ○
Pachysandra terminalis, p.388 ○
Periscaria campanulata, p.259
Polygonatum **x** *hybridum*, p.238
Pratia pedunculata, p.383 ○
PRIMULAS (many), pp.272–3
Prunella grandiflora, p.381 ○
Pulmonaria, some ○
Ranzania japonica
Ruellia devosiana, p.277 ○
Tiarella cordifolia, p.347 ○
Trillium grandiflorum, p.268
Uvularia grandiflora, p.274
Vancouveria hexandra, p.347
Xanthosoma sagittifolium, p.266

Bulbs, corms and tubers
Arisaema
Arisarum proboscideum
Arum italicum 'Marmoratum', p.434
Camassia leichtlinii, p.397
Galanthus elwesii, p.439
Galanthus nivalis and cvs
Galanthus plicatus subsp. *plicatus*
Leucojum aestivum, p.396
Leucojum vernum, p.426
Narcissus cyclamineus, p.418

Clethra arborea

Shrubs preferring Wall Protection

Walls can provide favourable growing conditions for shrubs, mostly evergreen, that are only moderately frost hardy. Some winter-flowering shrubs also flower more reliably and freely when given wall protection. The best wall-side situations are warm and sunny, and give good shelter from the cold winds of winter and early spring. The warmth from heat loss through house walls, and the well-drained conditions near the base of such walls, also assist the survival of less hardy shrubs.

Fremontodendron
'Pacific Sunset'

Abelia floribunda ○
Abutilon megapotamicum ○
Acacia podalyriifolia, p.135 ○
Acacia pravissima, p.97 ○
Acca sellowiana, p.143 ○
Aloysia triphylla, p.143 ○
Artemisia arborescens, p.175 ○
Azara serrata, p.135 ○
Buddleja asiatica ○
Buddleja crispa, p.143 ○
Callistemon citrinus 'Splendens', p.143 ○
Cantua buxifolia, p.155 ○
Carpenteria californica, p.138 ○
Ceanothus impressus, p.145 ○
Chaenomeles speciosa 'Moerloosei', p.130
Chimonanthus praecox
Coronilla valentina subsp. *glauca*, p.157 ○ ▣
Cytisus x *spachianus* ○
Daphne odora 'Aureomarginata', p.174 ○

Dendromecon rigida, p.147 ○
Drimys winteri, p.78 ○
Elsholtzia stauntonii, p.173
Escallonia 'Iveyi', p.118 ○
Fabiana imbricata f. *violacea*, p.145 ○
Fremontodendron 'California Glory', p.123 ○
Fremontodendron 'Pacific Sunset' ○ ▣
Garrya elliptica, p.125 ○
Itea ilicifolia, p.146 ○
Jasminum mesnyi, p.207 ○
Lagerstroemia indica, p.91
Leptospermum scoparium 'Red Damask', p.131 ○

SHELTERED POSITION
Borderline-hardy Coronilla valentina subsp. glauca may flower early when grown against a warm wall.

Lonicera fragrantissima
Luma apiculata, p.119 ○
Melianthus major ○
Myrtus communis, p.127 ○
Olearia x *scilloniensis* ○

Osteomeles schweriniae, p.138 ○
Piptanthus nepalensis, p.146 ○
Robinia hispida, p.141
Rosa banksiae 'Lutea', p.198 ○
Rosa 'Mermaid', p.198
Rosmarinus officinalis, p.167 ○
Salvia involucrata 'Bethellii', p.231
Solanum crispum 'Glasnevin', p.214 ○
Tibouchina urvilleana, p.122
Vestia foetida ○

Plants for Paving and Wall Crevices

In mountainous regions, many alpine plants grow in deep cracks and crevices in the rock. Some are clump-forming or trailing in habit; others, such as saxifrages and sempervivums, grow as rosettes extending by means of runners. If laying irregularly shaped paving, leave crevices for small plants, but restrict planting to little-used areas where the plants can survive. When building stone retaining walls, tilt rock slabs slightly backwards to create deep pockets, planting as the wall is being constructed. Most wall plants thrive in sunny situations, but ramondas and most small ferns prefer cool, moist shade.

FLORAL COVERING
Fleabane (Erigeron karvinskianus), with its daisy-like flower heads in summer, is excellent in crevices.

Lobelia erinus cvs
Lobularia maritima
Malcolmia maritima, p.323
Nemophila maculata, p.319
Nemophila menziesii, p.333
Portulaca grandiflora Series and cvs

Rock plants
Acaena microphylla, p.389 ○
Acantholimon glumaceum (wall), p.377 ○
Achillea x *kellereri*, p.375 ○
Achillea x *lewisii* 'King Edward' ○
Aethionema 'Warley Rose', p.376 ○
Alyssum montanum ○
Androsace sarmentosa ○
Antennaria dioica ○
Armeria maritima 'Vindictive', p.380 ○
Artemisia pedemontana ○
Artemisia schmidtiana ○
Asplenium ceterach, p.311 ○
Aubrieta ○
Aurinia saxatilis 'Citrina', p.349 ○
Campanula cochleariifolia, p.383
Campanula poscharskyana, p.381
Cassiope 'Edinburgh', p.346 ○
Chamaemelum nobile ○
Chiastophyllum oppositifolium (wall), p.349 ○
Cyananthus microphyllus, p.383
Cymbalaria muralis ○
Dianthus deltoides ○ ▣
Draba aizoides ○
Dryas octopetala, p.375 ○
Erigeron karvinskianus, p.377 ▣
Erinus alpinus, p.366 ○
Gypsophila repens and cvs ○
Haberlea rhodopensis 'Virginalis', p.373 ○

Annuals and biennials (not walls)
Ageratum houstonianum (small cvs)
Ionopsidium acaule
Limnanthes douglasii, p.336

Dianthus deltoides

Helianthemum ○
Hypericum olympicum
Lithodora diffusa 'Heavenly Blue', p.357 ○
Mazus reptans, p.368
Mentha requienii ○
Nierembergia repens, p.374
Parahebe lyallii ○
Phlox douglasii cvs ○
Physoplexis comosa (wall), p.380
Ramonda myconi (wall only), p.382 ○
Saxifraga cotyledon, p.352 ○
Sedum spathulifolium 'Cape Blanco', p.391 ○
Sempervivum montanum, p.390 ○
Thymus serpyllum and cvs ○
Vitaliana primuliflora, p.372 ○

Plants for Containers

Containers full of plants can brighten patios, courtyards and balconies. These situations are often sheltered and sunny, so use large containers which retain more moisture than small ones. Small trees, conifers or shrubs in small groups, together with perennials, will give long-term interest in shape and foliage, with periods of flowering. For colourful displays, plant spring-flowering bulbs, followed by petunias and tagetes, which will flower throughout the summer.

Trees
Acer negundo
Cordyline australis and cvs ○
Crataegus laevigata and cvs
Eucalyptus (when young) ○
Ficus (most) ○
Ilex aquifolium and cvs ○
Jacaranda mimosifolia, p.79
Laurus nobilis ○ ▣
Malus (small species and cvs)
Melia azederach, p.76
Olea europaea ○
Phoenix canariensis ○
Prunus (small species and cvs)
Sorbus (small species and cvs)
Washingtonia ○

Sweet bay
(Laurus nobilis)

Conifers
All the small species and cvs of:
Abies ○
Chamaecyparis ○
Juniperus ○
Picea ○
Pinus ○
Thuja ○
Thujopsis dolabrata ○

Shrubs
Buxus sempervirens and cvs ○
Catharanthus roseus, p.160
Erica ○
FUCHSIAS, pp.164–5
Hebe ○
HYDRANGEAS, p.144
Lavandula ○
Myrtus communis, p.130 ○
Pittosporum ○
RHODODENDRONS (most), pp.132–4, most ○
ROSES (most), pp.184–8, some ○
Santolina ○
Senecio (shrubby species) ○
Spiraea
Viburnum tinus, p.149 ○

Climbers
Cissus antarctica, p.220 ○
CLEMATIS (small cvs), pp.212–13, some ○
Cobaea scandens, p.214 ○
Eccremocarpus scaber, p.217 ○

YEAR-ROUND ATTRACTION
An informal grouping of flowering and foliage plants in separate containers allows a flexible design. Plants can be replaced when their flowering period is over, yet a pleasing air of permanence is retained for the whole arrangement.

Hedera helix and cvs ○
Ipomoea, some ○
Jasminum (climbing species), some ○
Lathyrus (climbing species)
Lonicera (climbing species), some ○
Mandevilla ○
Passiflora ○
Stephanotis floribunda, p.204 ○
Tropaeolum (climbing species)

Ferns
Adiantum (most)
Asplenium scolopendrium Marginatum Group, p.313 ○
Athyrium niponicum, p.312
Polypodium vulgare 'Cornubiense', p.312 ○
Polystichum setiferum Divisilobum Group, p.311 ○

Perennials
Agapanthus
Bergenia ○
DAYLILIES, p.257
Geranium, some ○
Geum
HOSTAS, pp.288–9
Phormium ○
PRIMULAS (tall species and cvs), pp.272–3
Pulmonaria, some ○
Rudbeckia fulgida var. *sullivantii* 'Goldsturm', p.256
Salvia (many)
Stachys, some ○
Verbena, some ○

Annuals and biennials
Ageratum
Bassia scoparia f. *trichophylla*, p.335
Browallia speciosa, p.266
Calendula officinalis Series and cvs
Callistephus chinensis Series and cvs
Lobelia erinus cvs
Nemesia strumosa and Series
Petunia
Salpiglossis sinuata Series and cvs
Solenostemon scutellarioides Series and cvs, pp.324, 329
Tagetes
Viola x *wittrockiana* hybrids

Rock plants
All rock plants are suitable, the following being particularly recommended:
Campanula (many), some ○
Dianthus (many) ○
Geranium (several), some ○
Hebe ○
Helianthemum ○
Iberis sempervirens, p.346 ○
Penstemon (many), some ○
Periscaria affinis
Phlox (several) ○
Primula auricula and hybrids
Saponaria ocymoides, p.378
Saxifraga (many) ○
Silene schafta, p.379

Bulbs, corms and tubers
All bulbous plants are suitable, the following being particularly recommended:
CROCUSES, pp.428–9
DAFFODILS, pp.416–18
HYACINTHS, p.431
IRISES (bulbous species), pp.234–5
LILIES (most), pp.404–5
TULIPS, pp.410–12 ▣
Zantedeschia aethiopica 'Crowborough', p.397 ○

Tulipa '*Keizerskroon*'

Water plants
Watertight containers are ideal for the following:
Acorus calamus 'Argenteostriatus', p.447 ○
Aponogeton distachyos, p.447
Azolla filiculoides, p.448
Eichhornia crassipes, p.448 ○
Menyanthes trifoliata, p.446
Nelumbo nucifera and cvs
Pontederia cordata, p.448
Thalia dealbata
WATER LILIES (small cvs), p.450

Trailing Plants for Walls or Baskets

Many plants grow naturally in crevices, their trailing stems covering large areas of vertical rock. In gardens, trailing alpines may be planted in pockets of earth in dry stone walls. If a garden has retaining walls, climbers or low-growing conifers, trailing from the top, can soften brickwork. Smaller trailing plants, such as tender perennials or annuals, are ideal for hanging baskets. After planting, baskets may be set on large, inverted pots on a patio or old tree stump, the plants forming a conical mound of tumbling stems and flowers.

Conifers
Juniperus conferta ○
Juniperus horizontalis and cvs ○
Juniperus squamata 'Blue Carpet' ○
Microbiota decussata, p.110 ○

Shrubs
Arctostaphylos uva-ursi, p.388 ○
Ceanothus thyrsiflorus var. *repens*,
  p.168 ○
Chorizema ilicifolium, p.157 ○
Cotoneaster microphyllus ○
Euonymus fortunei 'Coloratus' ○
Fuchsia procumbens, p.165 ○
Genista lydia, p.359
Hebe pinguifolia 'Pagei', p.351 ○
Helichrysum petiolare, p.175 ○ ▣
Lantana montevidensis, p.167 ○
Leptospermum rupestre, p.160 ○
Loiseleuria procumbens, p.377 ○
Nematanthus strigillosus ○
Salix lindleyana
Salix repens, p.156

Perennials
Achimenes 'Peach Blossom'
Aeschynanthus speciosus, p.293 ○
Aporocactus flagelliformis, p.463
Campanula isophylla ○
Carpobrotus edulis
Columnea (most) ○
Convolvulus sabatius, p.356
Cyanotis kewensis ○
Elatostema repens, p.303 ○
Episcia cupreata, p.301 ○
Episcia dianthiflora, p.299 ○
Glechoma hederacea 'Variegata',
  p.300 ○ ▣
Hedera colchica 'Dentata
  Variegata' ○
Hedera colchica 'Sulphur Heart' ◑

Lampranthus spectabilis, p.463
Lotus berthelotii, p.283 ○
Pelargonium peltatum ○
Peperomia scandens ○
Plectranthus verticillatus ○
Ruellia devosiana, p.277 ○
Sarmienta repens ○
Tradescantia fluminensis and cvs ○
Tradescantia zebrina, p.301 ○
Tropaeolum polyphyllum, p.293 ○
Verbena peruviana ○
Verbena 'Sissinghurst', p.282

Annuals and biennials
Calceolaria integrifolia ▣
Limnanthes douglasii, p.336
Lobelia erinus cvs ▣
Nemophila maculata, p.319
Nolana paradoxa

Petunia *Surfinia Series*
'*Surfinia Purple*'

Petunia Cascade Series
Petunia Jamboree Series
Petunia Surfinia Series ▣
Portulaca grandiflora Series and cvs
Sanvitalia procumbens, p.336
Tropaeolum majus Series and cvs

Rock plants
Acaena 'Blue Haze' ○ ▣
Androsace lanuginosa, p.377 ○
Arabis caucasica ○
Campanula cochleariifolia, p.383
Cymbalaria muralis ○
Cytisus x *beanii*, p.349
Euphorbia myrsinites, p.371 ○
Gypsophila repens ○
Iberis sempervirens, p.346 ○
Lithodora diffusa cvs ○
Lysimachia nummularia, p.386 ○
Oenothera macrocarpa, p.385
Othonna cheirifolia, p.358 ○
Parahebe catarractae, p.356 ○
Parochetus communis, p.384 ○
Periscaria vacciniifolia, p.387 ○
Phlox subulata ○
Pterocephalus perennis, p.380 ○
Saxifraga stolonifera ○

HIGH-SUMMER DISPLAY
Above: Various kinds of plant container can be fixed to walls to hold colourful seasonal displays. Here fuchsias, lobelias and petunias are planted among yellow calceolarias and trailing red and white pelargoniums.

SOFT HARMONY
Left: This well-filled hanging basket of pastel hues and variegated foliage includes Glechoma hederacea 'Variegata' and Helichrysum petiolare. It will remain attractive and fresh throughout summer.

Acaena '*Blue Haze*'

Plants with Aromatic Foliage

The leaves of many plants contain essential aromatic oils, used in medicine or cooking. For gardeners, their value lies in the pleasant, pungent aromas released naturally or when bruised. Those of culinary value, such as rosemary, are often grown in herb gardens. Low-growing thymes may be planted next to paths or between paving stones to give off scent when trodden underfoot. The fragrance from trees may be best appreciated as it drifts through the garden on the wind.

Trees
Agonis flexuosa, p.90 ○
Atherosperma moschatum ○
Eucalyptus ○
Juglans regia, p.66
Laurus nobilis ○
Phellodendron chinense, p.81
Populus balsamifera
Populus trichocarpa
Sassafras albidum, p.68
Umbellularia californica, p.74 ○

Conifers
Calocedrus decurrens, p.106 ○
Chamaecyparis ○
Cupressus ○
Juniperus ○
Pseudotsuga menziesii ○
Thuja (most) ○

Shrubs
Aloysia triphylla, p.143
Artemisia abrotanum, p.176
Boronia megastigma, p.156 ○
Caryopteris x *clandonensis* 'Arthur Simmonds', p.168
Choisya ternata, p.127 ○
Cistus laurifolius ○
Elsholtzia stauntonii, p.173
Gaultheria procumbens, p.387 ○
Helichrysum italicum ○
Hyssopus officinalis, p.168

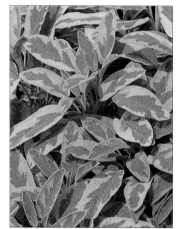

Salvia officinalis 'Icterina'

Lavandula (most) ○
Lindera
Myrtus communis, p.130 ○
PELARGONIUMS (scented-leaved forms), pp.246–7 ○
Perovskia 'Blue Spire', p.168
Phlomis fruticosa, p.170 ○
Prostanthera ○
Rhododendron cinnabarinum subsp. *xanthocodon*, p.133 ○
Rhododendron rubiginosum ○

PATH-SIDE AROMATICS
Above: Shrubby culinary herbs, such as sage and thyme, can be combined with small ornamental shrubs grown for their aromatic foliage.

Ribes sanguineum 'Brocklebankii', p.155
Rosa rubiginosa, p.185
Rosmarinus officinalis, p.167 ○
Salvia officinalis cvs ○ ▣
Santolina chamaecyparissus ○
Zanthoxylum piperitum, p.145

Perennials
Artemisia absinthium 'Lambrook Silver' ○

Chamaemelum nobile ○
Galium odoratum, p.275
Geranium macrorrhizum, p.279 ○
Houttuynia cordata 'Chameleon', p.447
Kaempferia pulchra, p.283
Mentha, some ○
Monarda didyma
Myrrhis odorata, p.240
Origanum vulgare
Perovskia atriplicifolia
Tanacetum parthenium, p.319

Rock plants
Mentha requienii ○
Origanum laevigatum, p.354
Satureja montana
Thymus ○ ▣

Plants with Fragrant Flowers

Fragrance is released from the flowers of numerous plants. It can be strong, pervading the air around the plant, or apparent only when you are close to individual blooms. Some plants release scent continually, but with others it is more noticeable at night. A sunny, sheltered patio is an ideal situation for small fragrant plants. Position large scented shrubs close to paths, and train fragrant climbers around doorways. Hyacinths in pots bring welcome early spring fragrance indoors.

Trees
Acacia dealbata, p.83 ○
Aesculus hippocastanum, p.64
Bauhinia variegata, p.97
Clethra arborea ○
Crataegus monogyna
Drimys winteri, p.78 ○
Eucryphia lucida, p.90 ○
Fraxinus ornus, p.76
Genista aetnensis, p.93
Laburnum x *watereri* 'Vossii', p.92
MAGNOLIAS, p.75
Malus coronaria 'Charlottae'
Malus hupehensis, p.74
Malus 'Profusion', p.77
Pittosporum tenuifolium, p.127 ○
Pittosporum undulatum ○
Plumeria rubra, p.96
Prunus mume 'Beni-chidori', p.130
Prunus padus 'Grandiflora', p.76
Prunus x *yedoensis*, p.87
Pterostyrax hispida

Robinia pseudoacacia
Styrax japonicus, p.77
Styrax obassia
Tilia x *euchlora*
Tilia 'Petiolaris', p.68
Virgilia oroboides ○

Shrubs
Abelia x *grandiflora*, p.121 ○
Abeliophyllum distichum
Azara microphylla, p.125 ○
Berberis x *stenophylla*, p.135 ○
Boronia megastigma, p.156 ○
Brugmansia arborea ○
Buddleja asiatica ○
Buddleja davidii and cvs
Camellia sasanqua 'Narumigata', p.128 ○
Chimonanthus praecox
Choisya ternata, p.127 ○
Clerodendrum bungei, p.148 ○
Clerodendrum trichotomum, p.147

Pittosporum tobira

Clethra delavayi, p.121
Colletia hystrix, p.147
Coronilla valentina subsp. *glauca*, p.157 ○
Corylopsis pauciflora, p.131 ○
Cytisus battandieri, p.123 ○
Daphne (many), most ○
Deutzia x *elegantissima* cvs

Edgeworthia chrysantha
Elaeagnus x *ebbingei* 'Limelight', p.153 ○
Erica arborea ○
Erica lusitanica ○
Fothergilla major, p.127
Gardenia augusta 'Veitchii', p.158 ○
Hamamelis mollis
Heliotropium arborescens, p.167 ○
Itea ilicifolia, p.146 ○
Lavandula 'Hidcote', p.167 ○
Lavandula stoechas, p.167 ○
Ligustrum lucidum 'Excelsum Superbum', p.127 ○
LILACS (most), p.120
Lonicera fragrantissima
Lupinus arboreus, p.169 ○
MAGNOLIAS, p.75
Osmanthus ○
Philadelphus (many)
Pittosporum tobira ○ ▣
ROSES (many), pp.184–8, some ○ ▣
Sarcococca ○
Viburnum (many), some ○

Climbers
Clematis montana 'Elizabeth'
Hoya carnosa, p.208 ○
Jasminum (many), most ○
Lathyrus odoratus and cvs
Lonicera (many), some ○ ▣
Mandevilla laxa
ROSES (many), pp.184–8, some ○
Stephanotis floribunda, p.204 ○

INTERMINGLING FRAGRANCE *A combination of climbing roses (Rosa) and honeysuckles (Lonicera) looks delightful and gives out a delicious fragrance.*

Trachelospermum ○
Wattakaka sinensis
Wisteria

Perennials
Anemone sylvestris, p.268
CARNATIONS and PINKS (most), pp.280–1 ○
Clematis heracleifolia 'Wyevale', p.213
Convallaria majalis, p.268
Cosmos atrosanguineus, p.249
Crambe cordifolia, p.226
Galium odoratum, p.275
Hedychium gardnerianum, p.232
Hemerocallis lilioasphodelus, p.257
Hesperis matronalis, p.239
HOSTAS (some), pp.288–9
Iris graminea
Iris unguicularis ○
Meehania urticifolia
Mirabilis jalapa, p.245
Myrrhis odorata, p.240
Nicotiana sylvestris, p.226
Petasites fragrans ○
Primula elatior, p.273
Primula veris, p.273
Tulbaghia natalensis
Verbena x *hybrida* Series and cvs ○
Viola odorata ○

Annuals and biennials
Amberboa moschata, p.335
Antirrhinum majus Series
Argemone mexicana, p.335
Dianthus barbatus Roundabout Series, p.326
Erysimum cheiri Series and cvs ○
Exacum affine, p.381 ○
Iberis amara, p.318
Lathyrus odoratus and cvs ▣
Limnanthes douglasii, p.336
Matthiola incana
Mentzelia lindleyi, p.336
Nicotiana alata, p.239

Sweet pea
Lathyrus odoratus
'Jayne Amanda'

Primula Primrose Group
Reseda odorata, p.319
Scabiosa atropurpurea
Verbena x *hybrida* (most)

Rock plants
Alyssum montanum ○
Dianthus (most) ○
Erysimum helveticum, p.373 ○
Papaver croceum
Primula auricula
Viola odorata ○

Bulbs, corms and tubers
Amaryllis belladonna, p.408
Arisaema candidissimum, p.435
Chlidanthus fragrans, p.436
Crinum bulbispermum
Crinum x *powellii*, p.398
Crocus angustifolius
Crocus longiflorus
Cyclamen persicum, p.440
Cyclamen repandum
Eucharis x *grandiflora*, p.425 ○
Freesia (most)
Hyacinthus orientalis and cvs
Hymenocallis
LILIES (several), pp.404–5 ▣
Muscari armeniacum, p.433
Narcissus jonquilla and Div.7 hybrids
Narcissus tazetta and Div.8 hybrids
Ornithogalum arabicum, p.420
Polianthes tuberosa

Orchids
Cattleya J.A.Carbone, p.297 ○
Coelogyne flaccida, p.296 ○

Lilium 'Mont Blanc'

Cacti
Epiphyllum laui, p.461

Water plants
Aponogeton distachyos, p.449
Nymphaea 'Blue Beauty', p.450
Nymphaea 'James Brydon', p.450
Nymphaea odorata 'Sulphurea Grandiflora'

57

Iris foetidissima

Iris foetidissima ○ ▣
Ophiopogon ○
Physalis alkekengi ▣
Phytolacca
Podophyllum
Smilacina racemosa, p.233

Annuals and biennials
Briza maxima
Capsicum annuum 'Holiday Cheer'
Coix lacryma-jobi, p.308
Lagurus ovatus, p.306
Lunaria annua, p.325 ▣

Decorative Fruits or Seed Heads

As winter approaches, dull corners of the garden or featureless borders can be brightened with the colourful fruits or berries of berberis, cotoneasters, viburnums and other ornamental free-fruiting shrubs. On pergolas and trellis, *Celastrus orbiculatus* and *Clematis orientalis* provide late-season interest with trailing skeins of yellow fruits and feathery seeds. Wall-trained pyracanthas will colour drab winter walls with yellow, orange or scarlet fruits. Hollies (*Ilex*) also provide berried material for winter decoration. The dried seed heads of many plants are used in flower arrangements, to give a contrast in form and texture.

ROSE HIPS AND LANTERNS
Above: Rose hips and the inflated papery calyces that enclose the fruits of Chinese lantern (Physalis alkekengi) – seen here set against the crowded, deep pink flower heads of a sedum – bring warm, glowing colours to autumn mornings.

Lunaria annua

Trees
Annona reticulata
Arbutus ○
Cornus kousa
Cotoneaster frigidus ▣

Crataegus (most)
HOLLIES (most), pp.98–9, most ○
Koelreuteria paniculata, p.92
MAGNOLIAS, p.75, some ○
Malus (most)
Photinia davidiana, p.94 ○
Schinus molle ○
Sorbus (most)

Conifers
Abies (some) ○
Cedrus (some) ○
Picea (some) ○
Pinus (some) ○

Shrubs
Aucuba japonica, p.152 ○
Berberis (most), some ○
Callicarpa bodinieri var. *giraldii*, p.148
Chaenomeles
x *Citrofortunella microcarpa*, p.151 ○
Cotoneaster (most), some ○ ▣
Cyphomandra betacea, p.125 ○
Decaisnea fargesii, p.122
Euonymus (many), some ○
Gaultheria mucronata and cvs ○

Hippophäe rhamnoides, p.124
Hypericum x *inodorum* 'Elstead', p.170
Leycesteria formosa
Poncirus trifoliata
Pyracantha ○
ROSES (most), pp.184–8, some ○
Sambucus racemosa
Sarcococca hookeriana var. *digyna*, p.174 ○
Shepherdia argentea
Skimmia (some) ○
Symphoricarpos
Symplocos paniculata, p.138
Vaccinium vitis-idaea ○
Viburnum (several), some ○

Climbers
Actinidia deliciosa
Akebia, some ○
Billardiera longiflora, p.218 ○
Cardiospermum halicacabum
Celastrus orbiculatus
Clematis orientalis
Holboellia coriacea ○
ROSES (several), pp.184–8, some ○ ▣
Trichosanthes cucumerina var. *anguina*
Tropaeolum speciosum, p.210

Perennials
Actaea
Clintonia borealis
Disporum hookeri
Duchesnea indica ○

Martynia annua, p.320
Nicandra physalodes
Nigella damascena and cvs
Pulsatilla vulgaris, p.348
Solanum capsicastrum ○
Zea mays

Rock plants
Acaena microphylla, p.389 ○
Cornus canadensis, p.374
Dryas octopetala, p.375 ○
Gaultheria (most) ○
Maianthemum
Margyricarpus pinnatus ○
Mitchella repens ○
Nertera granadensis, p.335 ○
Pulsatilla (most)

Bulbs, corms and tubers
Allium cristophii, p.421
Arisaema triphyllum, p.414
Arum italicum 'Marmoratum', p.434
Cardiocrinum giganteum, p.398

Water plants
Nelumbo
Nuphar lutea, p.451
Thalia dealbata

Cotoneaster frigidus

Flowers for Cutting

With careful selection, flowers can be cut from the garden at most times of the year, from the Christmas rose (*Helleborus niger*) in mid-winter to *Nerine bowdenii* in autumn. In small gardens, integrate plants for cutting into the general scheme, and leave some blooms for display; or plant away from the house so that the cutting is less noticeable. Feed regularly to counteract the weakening effects of cutting plants.

Carnation
(Dianthus '*Doris*')

ROSES (some), pp.184–8, some ○
Salix caprea
Turraea obtusifolia, p.142 ○

Perennials
Alstroemeria Ligtu Hybrids, p.423
Anaphalis
Anchusa azurea
Anemone x *hybrida* cvs
Astrantia major, p.277
CARNATIONS and PINKS,
  pp.280–1 ○ ▣
Cattleya (most)
CHRYSANTHEMUMS, pp.260–1
Cymbidium (most) ○
DELPHINIUMS (most), p.230
Helleborus niger, p.301
Phalaenopsis (most) ○
Phlox paniculata cvs
Rudbeckia (most)
Strelitzia reginae, p.267 ○

Annuals and biennials
Amaranthus caudatus, p.326
Amberboa moschata, p.335
Callistephus chinensis Series and cvs

Shrubs
Calluna vulgaris (tall cvs) ○
Camellia japonica cvs ○
Erica ○
Forsythia
Hamamelis mollis
LILACS, p.120
Lonicera fragrantissima
Philadelphus

CUT FLOWERS
In large gardens, a warm, sunny, sheltered border may be used to grow flowers specially for cutting.

Centaurea cyanus and cvs
Clarkia
Eustoma grandiflorum, p.319
Gaillardia pulchella 'Lollipops', p.338
Gypsophila elegans, p.318
Lathyrus odoratus and cvs
Malope trifida, p.324
Matthiola cvs
Moluccella laevis, p.335
Rhodanthe chlorocephala
  subsp. *rosea*, p.321

Xeranthemum annuum
Zinnia elegans Series and cvs (tall hybrids)

Bulbs, corms and tubers
Allium (tall species)
Alstroemeria (tall species and cvs)
DAFFODILS (tall species and cvs), pp.416–18
DAHLIAS, pp.406–7
GLADIOLI (most), p.399
LILIES (some), pp.404–5
Nerine bowdenii, p.424
Ornithogalum thyrsoides, p.420
Polianthes tuberosa
TULIPS (tall cvs), pp.410–12
Zantedeschia aethiopica ○

Flowers for Drying

Many garden flowers may be dried, and are ideally cut just before reaching perfection. In borders, intersperse plants for drying with others that will not be cut. Groups of annuals for drying are best grown separately, away from the house, in rows to facilitate weeding and gathering; sow in well-drained, fertile soil in a sunny situation to encourage strong balanced growth and good-quality flowers.

Trees
Acacia dealbata, p.83 ○
Acacia longifolia ○
Acacia verticillata ○

Shrubs
Acacia (most) ○
Calluna vulgaris and cvs ○
Cassinia ○
Erica cinerea ○
Fothergilla major, p.127
Garrya elliptica, p.125 ○
Helichrysum (most) ○
Holodiscus discolor, p.119
Lavandula ○
LILACS, p.120
Phlomis fruticosa, p.170 ○
ROSES, pp.184–8
Rosmarinus officinalis and cvs ○

TEASEL HEADS
The prickly, cone-shaped seed heads of teasel (Dipsacus fullonum) persist throughout winter. A soft pinkish-purple when in bloom, teasels are best in a wild garden or at the back of a border. Cut when ripe, the heads are excellent in dried arrangements.

Perennials
Achillea, some ○
Aconitum napellus
Alchemilla mollis, p.290
Allium x *hollandicum*, p.402
Anaphalis margaritacea, p.239
Anigozanthos flavidus, p.254
Artemisia (several), some ○
Astilbe (most)
Astrantia
Catananche caerulea 'Major', p.285
Cirsium rivulare 'Atropurpureum'
Dictamnus albus, p.240
Echinops
Eryngium, some ○
Eupatorium (some)
Gypsophila paniculata 'Bristol Fairy', p.239
Liatris spicata, p.279
Limonium (most)
Lythrum
Ranunculus asiaticus, pp.421, 423
Rodgersia
Scabiosa caucasica and cvs
Solidago (most)
Trachelium caeruleum, p.330
Typha

Annuals and biennials
Amaranthus caudatus, p.326
Bracteantha bracteata Monstrosum Series, p.340
Centaurea cyanus
Consolida ambigua Series
Dipsacus fullonum ▣
Gilia capitata, p.333
Gomphrena globosa, p.331
Gypsophila elegans, p.318
Limonium sinuatum, p.322
Moluccella laevis, p.335
Onopordum acanthium, p.322
Psylliostachys suworowii, p.330
Rhodanthe
Salvia viridis and Series
Scabiosa atropurpurea
Tagetes erecta
Xeranthemum annuum ▣

Xeranthemum annuum

TREES
including Conifers

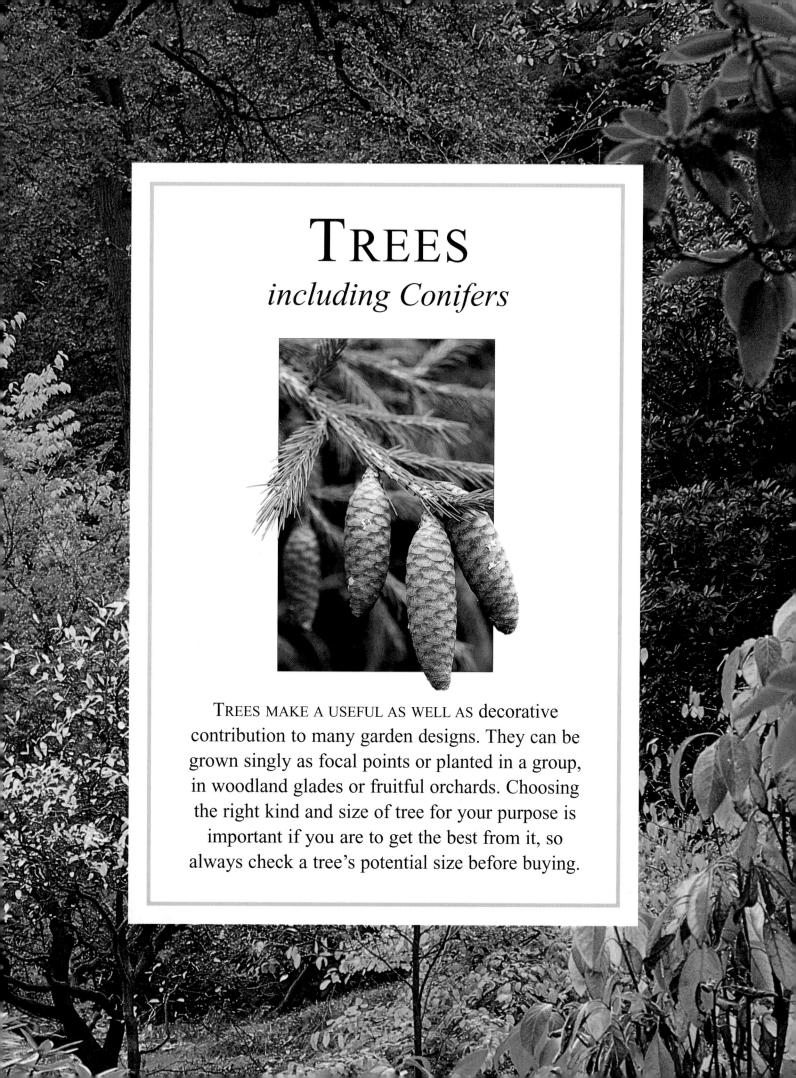

TREES MAKE A USEFUL AS WELL AS decorative
contribution to many garden designs. They can be
grown singly as focal points or planted in a group,
in woodland glades or fruitful orchards. Choosing
the right kind and size of tree for your purpose is
important if you are to get the best from it, so
always check a tree's potential size before buying.

Trees

Trees are the most permanent elements in any planting scheme. Fortunately there is a wealth of ornamental trees in cultivation to suit the individual climate and growing conditions in your garden.

WHAT ARE TREES?

Tree are long-lived, deciduous or evergreen, perennial, woody plants that have a lifespan ranging from decades to several centuries. Most have a single stem, with a crown of branches above a clear trunk, although many species produce multiple stems, either naturally or as a result of pruning and training. Trees are diverse in size, ranging from dwarf conifers at 1m (3ft) tall, to forest giants at 90m (300ft) or more in height. They are equally variable in shape, from narrowly conical, through columnar to rounded and spreading, offering strong design elements within the garden. Most conifers are evergreen and cone-bearing.

CHOOSING TREES

Since a tree is probably the most expensive of garden plants and usually the most prominent, selection and siting are the most important decisions – even more so in a small garden with room for only one or two specimens. If it is to thrive, you must consider whether a tree is suitable for your garden's climate, soil type and degree of exposure. It is then vital to research the tree's final height and spread, and site it where it will have room to mature unimpeded by and not interfering with walls, pipes, drains or cables.

DESIGNING WITH TREES

Trees make a strong visual impact in a planting scheme by virtue of their size alone; they can also contribute to the garden's structure. For example, several trees can be planted to form enclosures or define spaces; they can be used in pairs to frame a view, or in rows to form an avenue or an arch. In exposed or very large gardens, a row of trees can provide wind protection to an area five times its own height. In smaller gardens, trees that tolerate clipping, notably hornbeam (*Carpinus betulus*), beech (*Fagus sylvatica*) and yew (*Taxus baccata*), are ideal for a wind- and noise-filtering hedge that also affords a degree of privacy.

When a tree is grown singly as a specimen plant, it can create an interesting focal point, which is especially effective if it can be viewed from several angles. The tree's shape and ornamental qualities also influence the style of the garden. The neat, crisp outlines of the narrowly columnar *Juniperus chinensis* 'Obelisk', for example, or the flame-shaped *Carpinus betulus* 'Fastigiata' would suit a formal garden design, whereas the rounded, relaxed branch structure of mountain ash (*Sorbus aucuparia*) or the crab apple (*Malus floribunda*) provide a natural informality.

If you have room for several trees, you can develop a woodland-style garden, in the shelter of which shade-loving plants can be established. In an oriental-style garden, Japanese maples (*Acer* species) and Japanese cherries such as *Prunus* 'Shirofugen' are ideal.

FRUIT FOR COLOUR
In autumn, the rowans (Sorbus) offer berries of many colours, among them the creamy yellow fruits of S. 'Joseph Rock' (left), the pearly white fruits of S. cashmiriana and the rich scarlets of S. aucuparia. Many also have splendid autumn foliage.

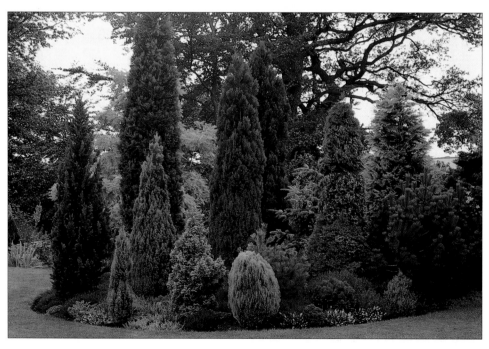

CONIFERS ON DISPLAY
Above: The extraordinary and exciting diversity of size, form, texture and colour to be found in dwarf conifers can be used to create a garden with year-round interest. If grouped in an island bed, as here, conifers can be viewed and enjoyed from many angles.

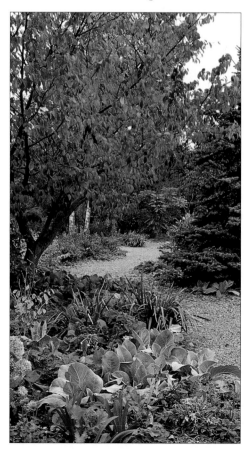

ALL-ROUND INTEREST
Right: Cherries (Prunus) often have more than one season of interest and are among the most valuable of trees for smaller gardens. As well as a glorious display of blossom in spring, many also provide fine autumn colour. Some, such as P. maaekii, also have attractive bark.

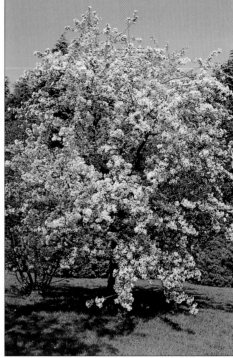

SPRING BENEFITS
Above: With the glorious Malus *'Katherine', a profusion of large double flowers in spring gives rise to tiny, red-flushed, yellow fruits in autumn.*

SUMMER PROMISE
Left: Acer shirasawanum *'Aureum' is noted for its elegant habit, compact size and vibrant leaf colour – the verdant greens of late spring and summer turning into peerless autumn brilliance.*

ATTRACTIVE BARK
Below: Many eucalyptus, such as this Eucalyptus pauciflora *subsp.* niphophila, *are renowned for their beautiful, peeling and flaking bark.*

Many small trees can be grown in containers and then used to decorate patios, courtyards and roof gardens.

MAINTAINING YEAR-ROUND INTEREST
Broadleaved evergreens, such as hollies (*Ilex*) and *Quercus coccifera*, provide an invaluable green backdrop throughout the year, while conifers can provide a useful contrast in shape and texture: many have a strong conical outline; others, such as *Picea breweriana*, weep gracefully. Dwarf conifers range from the neat, rounded domes of *Pinus mugo* 'Gnom' to the spreading *Juniperus* x *pfitzeriana*.

Broadleaved, deciduous trees offer a seasonally changing palette of leaf colour, from the fresh, lemon-yellows and lime-greens of spring to the ruddy brilliance of autumn. The form of their foliage is infinitely variable: why not try interesting textural contrasts such as the delicate leaves of false acacia (*Robinia pseudoacacia*) with the architectural leaves of *Catalpa bignonioides*.

Although most flowering and fruiting trees bloom in spring, some produce a welcome burst of colour at other times. *Maackia amurensis*, many eucryphias and *Arbutus unedo* bear their flowers in late summer and autumn, while *Magnolia campbellii* and *Prunus* x *subhirtella* 'Autumnalis' brighten the dark days of winter.

SIZE CATEGORIES USED WITHIN THIS GROUP		
Large	**Medium**	**Small**
over 15m (50ft)	10–15m (30–50ft)	up to 10m (30ft)

TREES large SPRING INTEREST

◼️◼️◻️ WHITE–YELLOW

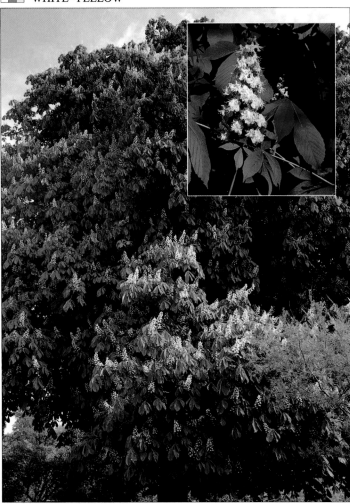

Aesculus hippocastanum
(Horse-chestnut)
Vigorous, deciduous, spreading tree. Has large leaves with 5 or 7 leaflets and spires of white flowers, flushed pink and yellow in centres, in spring. Spiny fruits contain glossy, brown nuts in autumn.

☼ ◊ ❗ Zone 4b   100ft 30m / 75ft 22.5m / 0

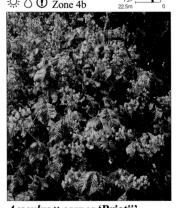

Aesculus × carnea 'Briotii'
Deciduous, round-headed tree. Leaves, consisting of 5 or 7 leaflets, are glossy, dark green. Panicles of red flowers are borne in late spring.

☼ ◊ ❗ Zone 5   100ft 30m / 75ft 22.5m / 0

Acer macrophyllum
(Oregon maple)
Deciduous, round-headed tree with large, deeply lobed, dark green leaves that turn yellow and orange in autumn. Yellowish-green flowers in spring are followed by pale green fruits.

☼ ◊ Zone 6   100ft 30m / 75ft 22.5m / 0

OTHER RECOMMENDED PLANTS: MAGNOLIAS, illus. p.75
Acer cappadocicum 'Aureum'
Calodendrum capense
Fraxinus excelsior 'Jaspidea'

TREES large SUMMER INTEREST

◻️ WHITE

Populus maximowiczii
Fast-growing, deciduous, conical tree. Oval, heart-shaped, bright green leaves have green-veined, white undersides and turn yellow in autumn. Bears long, pendent seed heads surrounded by silky, white hairs in late summer.

☼ ◗ Zone 5   100ft 30m / 75ft 22.5m / 0

Aesculus chinensis
(Chinese horse-chestnut)
Slow-growing, deciduous, spreading tree. Leaves are glossy, dark green with 7 leaflets. Slender spires of white flowers are produced in mid-summer.

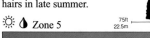

☼ ◊ ❗ Zone 7   100ft 30m / 75ft 22.5m / 0

Populus alba
(White poplar)
Deciduous, spreading tree with wavy-margined or lobed leaves, dark green above, white beneath, turning yellow in autumn.

☼ ◗ Zone 2   100ft 30m / 75ft 22.5m / 0

OTHER RECOMMENDED PLANTS:
Acer platanoides 'Drummondii'   Ceiba pentandra
Aesculus indica   Robinia pseudoacacia
Castanea sativa   Schima wallichii

Castanea sativa 'Albomarginata'
Deciduous, spreading tree. Has glossy, white-edged, dark green leaves that turn yellow in autumn. Spikes of creamy-yellow flowers in summer are followed by edible fruits in autumn.

☼ ◊ Zone 5b

Prunus serotina
(Black cherry, Wild rum cherry)
Deciduous, spreading tree. Spikes of fragrant, white flowers appear in early summer followed by red fruits that turn black in autumn. Glossy, dark green leaves become yellow in autumn.

☼ ◊ ⓘ Zone 5

Acer platanoides 'Crimson King'
Vigorous, deciduous, spreading tree. Leaves are large, lobed and deep reddish-purple, turning orange in autumn. Tiny, red-tinged, deep yellow flowers are carried in mid-spring.

☼ ◊ Zone 4b

Populus × canescens
(Grey poplar)
Vigorous, deciduous, spreading tree with slightly lobed leaves, grey when young, glossy, dark green in summer and yellow in autumn. Usually bears greyish-red catkins in spring.

☼ ◖ Zone 2

Liriodendron tulipifera (Tulip tree)
Vigorous, deciduous, spreading tree. Deep green leaves, with a cut-off or notched tip and lobed sides, turn yellow in autumn. Tulip-shaped, orange-marked, greenish-white flowers appear in mid-summer.

☼ ◊ pH Zone 5b

Brachychiton acerifolius,
syn. *Sterculia acerifolia*
(Illawarra flame tree)
Deciduous tree with clusters of bright scarlet flowers in late winter, spring or summer before 3–7-lobed, lustrous leaves develop.
Min. 7–10°C (45–50°F).

☼ ◊ pH

Fagus sylvatica f. **purpurea**
(Copper beech, Purple beech)
Deciduous, round-headed tree with oval, wavy-margined, purple leaves. In autumn, leaves turn a rich coppery colour.

☼ ◊ Zone 6

Populus × canadensis 'Robusta'
Fast-growing, deciduous, conical tree with upright branches. Broadly oval, bronze, young leaves mature to glossy, dark green. Bears long, red catkins in spring.

☼ ◖ Zone 2

Acer platanoides 'Royal Red'
Fagus sylvatica 'Dawyck Purple'
Fagus sylvatica 'Riversii'
Fagus sylvatica 'Rohanii'

Knightia excelsa
Lagerstroemia speciosa
MAGNOLIAS, illus. p.75
Toona sinensis, illus. p.79

Acer platanoides
Acer platanoides 'Emerald Queen'
Acer saccharinum
Acer velutinum

Ailanthus altissima
MAGNOLIAS, illus. p.75
Salix alba var. caerulea
Sorbus thibetica

TREES large SUMMER INTEREST

■ GREEN

Populus × canadensis 'Serotina de Selys', syn.
P. × c. 'Serotina Erecta'
Fast-growing, deciduous, upright tree.
Has broadly oval, grey-green leaves,
pale green when young, and
red catkins in spring.

☀ ◐ Zone 2

Fagus sylvatica f. **pendula**, syn.
F.s. 'Pendula' (Weeping beech)
Deciduous, weeping tree with oval,
wavy-edged, mid-green leaves that in
autumn take on rich hues of yellow and
orange-brown.

☀ ◌ Zone 6

Alnus cordata (Italian alder)
Fast-growing, deciduous, conical tree.
Yellow, male catkins appear in late
winter and early spring, followed by
heart-shaped, glossy, deep green
leaves. Has persistent, round,
woody fruits in autumn.

☀ ◐ Zone 6

Quercus canariensis
(Algerian oak, Mirbeck's oak)
Deciduous or semi-evergreen tree,
narrow when young, broadening with
age. Large, shallowly lobed, rich green
leaves become yellowish-
brown in autumn, often
persisting into late winter.

☀ ◌ Zone 8

Quercus macranthera
(Caucasian oak)
Deciduous, spreading, stout-branched,
handsome tree with large, deeply
lobed, dark green leaves.

☀ ◌ Zone 7

Quercus robur f. **fastigiata**
Deciduous, upright, columnar tree of
dense habit carrying lobed, dark green
leaves.

☀ ◌ Zone 4b

Populus nigra 'Italica'
(Lombardy poplar)
Very fast-growing, deciduous, narrowly
columnar tree with erect branches,
diamond-shaped, bright green leaves
and red catkins in mid-
spring.

☀ ◐ Zone 4

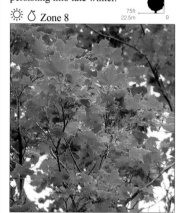

Acer cappadocicum subsp. **lobelii**,
syn. *A. lobelii* (Lobel's maple)
Deciduous tree of narrow, upright
habit, well-suited for growing in
restricted space. Has wavy-edged,
lobed leaves that turn yellow
in autumn.

☀ ◌ Zone 7

Juglans regia (Walnut)
Deciduous tree with a spreading head.
Leaves, usually with 5 or 7 leaflets, are
aromatic, bronze-purple when young,
glossy, mid-green when mature.
Produces edible nuts.

☀ ◌ Zone 6

Alnus incana (Grey alder)
Deciduous, conical tree useful for cold,
wet areas and poor soils. Yellow-brown
catkins are carried in late winter and
early spring, followed by oval, dark
green leaves.

☀ ◐ Zone 4

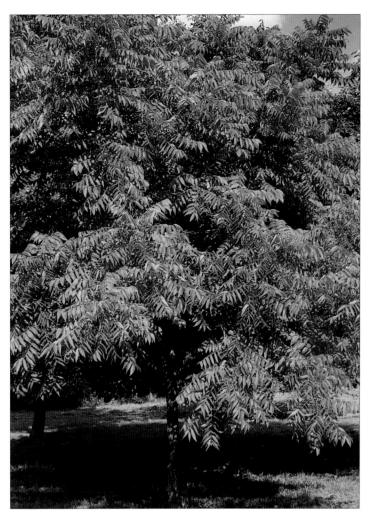

Tilia oliveri
Deciduous, spreading, open tree with pointed, heart-shaped leaves, bright green above and silvery-white beneath. Produces small, fragrant, greenish-yellow flowers in summer, followed by winged fruits.

☼ ◊ Zone 7

Juglans nigra (Black walnut)
Fast-growing, deciduous, handsome, spreading tree with large, aromatic leaves of many pointed, glossy, dark green leaflets. Produces edible nuts in autumn.

☼ ◊ Zone 3

Quercus muehlenbergii
Deciduous, round-headed tree with sharply toothed, bright green leaves.

Celtis australis (Nettle tree)
Deciduous, spreading tree. Has oval, pointed, sharply toothed, dark green leaves and small, purple-black fruits.

Platanus x hispanica, syn.
P. x acerifolia (London plane)
Vigorous, deciduous, spreading tree with ornamental, flaking bark. Has large, sharply lobed, bright green leaves. Spherical fruit clusters hang from shoots in autumn.

Nothofagus procera, syn.
N. x alpina (Rauli, Southern beech)
Fast-growing, deciduous, conical tree. Leaves, with many impressed veins, are dark green, turning orange and red in autumn.

☼ ◊ Zone 4

☼ ◊ Zone 7

☼ ◊ ① Zone 6b

☼ ◖ Zone 9

TREES large SUMMER INTEREST

■ GREEN

Nothofagus obliqua
(Roblé, Southern beech)
Fast-growing, deciduous, elegant tree with slender, arching branches. Has deep green leaves that turn orange and red in autumn.

☼ ◗ Zone 9

Quercus petraea 'Columna'
Deciduous, upright, slender tree with large, wavy-edged, leathery, dark green leaves, tinged bronze when young.

☼ ◗ Zone 4

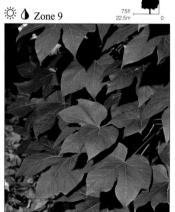

Firmiana simplex, syn.
F. platanifolia, Sterculia platanifolia (Chinese parasol tree)
Robust, deciduous tree with large, lobed leaves, small, showy, lemon-yellow flowers and papery, leaf-like fruits.
Min. 2°C (36°F).

☼ ◗

Quercus castaneifolia
Deciduous, spreading tree with sharply toothed leaves, glossy, dark green above, grey beneath.

☼ ◗ Zone 8

Sassafras albidum
Deciduous, upright, later spreading tree. Aromatic, glossy, dark green leaves vary from oval to deeply lobed and turn yellow or red in autumn. Has insignificant, yellowish-green flowers in spring.

☼ ◗ pH Zone 5b

Juglans ailantifolia var.
cordiformis, syn. *J. cordiformis*
Deciduous, spreading tree with large, aromatic leaves consisting of many glossy, bright green leaflets. Long, yellow-green, male catkins are borne in early summer. In autumn has edible nuts.

☼ ◗ Zone 3b

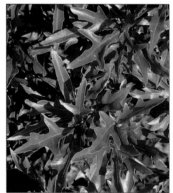

Quercus nigra (Water oak)
Deciduous, spreading tree with glossy, bright green foliage retained until well into winter.

☼ ◗ Zone 8

Tilia 'Petiolaris', syn. *T. petiolaris*
(Weeping silver linden)
Deciduous, spreading tree with pendent branches. Pointed, heart-shaped leaves, dark green above, silver beneath, shimmer in the breeze. Has fragrant, creamy-yellow flowers in late summer.

☼ ◗ ❶ Zone 4b

Fagus sylvatica (European beech)
Deciduous, spreading tree with oval, wavy-edged leaves. These are pale green when young, mid- to dark green when mature, and turn rich yellow and orange-brown in autumn, when nuts are produced.

☼ ◗ Zone 6

☐ GREEN

Quercus frainetto
(Hungarian oak)
Fast-growing, deciduous, spreading
tree with a large, domed head and
handsome, large, deeply lobed, dark
green leaves.

☼ ◊ Zone 7

Quercus palustris (Pin oak)
Fast-growing, deciduous, spreading
tree with slender branches, pendulous
at the tips. Deeply lobed, glossy, bright
green leaves turn scarlet or red-brown
in autumn.

☼ ◊ Zone 4

Carya ovata (Shag-bark hickory)
Deciduous tree with flaking, grey bark.
Has dark green leaves, usually
consisting of 5 slender leaflets, that
turn golden-yellow in autumn.

☼ ◊ Zone 4b

☐☐ GREEN–YELLOW

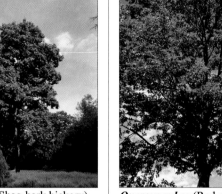

Quercus rubra (Red oak)
Fast-growing, deciduous, spreading
tree. Attractively lobed leaves, often
large, are deep green becoming
reddish- or yellowish-brown in autumn.

☼ ◊ Zone 3

**Liriodendron tulipifera
'Aureomarginatum'**
Vigorous, deciduous tree. Deep green
leaves have yellow margins, cut-off or
notched tips and lobed sides. Bears
cup-shaped, greenish-white
flowers, splashed orange, in
summer on mature trees.

☼ ◊ pH Zone 5b

Populus alba 'Raket',
syn. *P.a.* 'Rocket'
Deciduous, upright, narrow tree.
Leaves, often lobed, are dark green
with white undersides. In autumn,
foliage turns yellow.

☼ ◊ Zone 2

Quercus laurifolia
Deciduous, round-headed tree with
narrow, glossy, bright green leaves,
bronze-tinged when young, that are
retained until late in the year.

☼ ◊ Zone 8

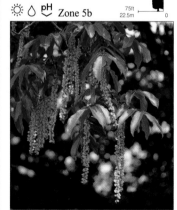

Pterocarya x rehderiana
Very fast-growing, deciduous,
spreading tree. Has glossy, bright green
leaves consisting of narrow, paired
leaflets that turn yellow in autumn and
long catkins of winged fruits
in late summer and autumn.

☼ ◊ Zone 7

Tilia platyphyllos
Tilia tomentosa
Ulmus americana
Ulmus glabra

Ulmus x *hollandica*
Ulmus x *hollandica* 'Vegeta'
Ulmus minor
Ulmus minor 'Sarniensis'

Ulmus procera
Zelkova carpinifolia

Alnus incana 'Aurea'
Fagus sylvatica 'Aurea Pendula'
Populus alba 'Richardii'
Robinia pseudoacacia 'Frisia', illus. p.81

TREES large AUTUMN INTEREST

 PINK–RED

Chorisia speciosa (Floss silk tree)
Fast-growing, deciduous tree, the trunk and branches studded with thick, conical thorns. Pink to burgundy flowers appear as indented, light green leaves fall. Min. 15°C (59°F).

☀ ◊

Liquidambar styraciflua
(Sweet gum)
Deciduous, conical to spreading tree. Shoots develop corky ridges. Lobed, glossy, dark green leaves turn brilliant orange, red and purple in autumn.

☀ ◐ Zone 6

Quercus ellipsoidalis
Deciduous, spreading tree with deeply lobed, glossy, dark green leaves that turn dark purplish-red, then red in autumn.

☀ ◊ Zone 3

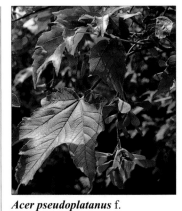

Acer pseudoplatanus f. ***erythrocarpum***
Vigorous, deciduous, spreading tree with lobed, deep green leaves. Wings of young autumn fruits are bright red.

☀ ◊ Zone 6

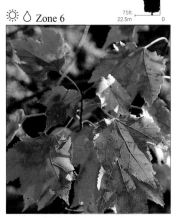

***Acer rubrum* 'Schlesingeri'**
Deciduous, round-headed tree. In early autumn, dark green leaves turn deep red. Tiny, red flowers appear on bare wood in spring.

☀ ◊ Zone 4b

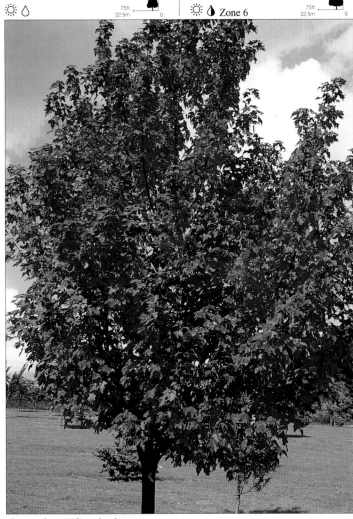

***Acer rubrum* 'Scanlon'**
Deciduous, upright tree. Has lobed, dark green foliage that in autumn becomes bright red, particularly on acid or neutral soil. Clusters of small, red flowers decorate bare branches in spring.

☀ ◊ Zone 4b

Quercus coccinea (Scarlet oak)
Deciduous, round-headed tree. Glossy, dark green leaves have deeply cut lobes ending in slender teeth. In autumn, they turn bright red, usually persisting for several weeks on the tree.

☀ ◊ Zone 4b

Acer rubrum (Red maple)
Deciduous, round-headed tree. Dark green leaves turn bright red in autumn, producing best colour on acid or neutral soil. In spring, bare branches are covered with tiny, red flowers.

☀ ◊ Zone 3

OTHER RECOMMENDED PLANTS:
Acer rubrum 'Columnare', illus. p.81
Acer rubrum 'October Glory'
Acer rubrum 'Red Sunset'

Acer saccharum 'Green Mountain'
Lagerstroemia speciosa
Quercus coccinea 'Splendens'

■■■ RED–YELLOW

Cercidiphyllum japonicum
(Katsura tree)
Fast-growing, deciduous, spreading tree. Leaves, bronze when young, turn rich green, then yellow to purple in autumn, especially on acid soil. Fallen leaves smell of burnt toffee.

☀ ◊ Zone 5

Spathodea campanulata (African tulip tree, Flame-of-the-forest)
Evergreen, showy tree. Leaves have 9–19 deep green leaflets. Clusters of tulip-shaped, scarlet or orange-red flowers appear intermittently. Min. 16–18°C (61–4°F).

☀ ◊

Quercus phellos (Willow oak)
Deciduous, spreading tree of elegant habit. Narrow, willow-like, pale green leaves turn yellow then brown in autumn.

☀ ◊ Zone 8

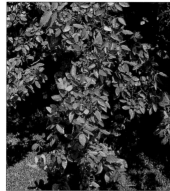

Zelkova serrata
Deciduous, spreading tree with sharply toothed, finely pointed, dark green leaves that turn yellow or orange in autumn.

☀ ◊ Zone 5b

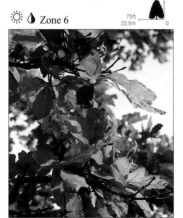

Nyssa sylvatica
(Black gum, Tupelo)
Deciduous, broadly conical tree with oval, glossy, dark to mid-green leaves that turn brilliant yellow, orange and red in autumn.

☀ ◊ Zone 6

Prunus avium
(Gean, Wild cherry)
Deciduous, spreading tree with red-banded bark. Has sprays of white flowers in spring, deep red fruits and dark green leaves that turn red and yellow in autumn.

☀ ◊ ⓘ Zone 4b

***Sophora japonica* 'Violacea'**
Fast-growing, deciduous, round-headed tree. Large sprays of pea-like, white flowers, tinged with lilac-pink, appear in late summer and early autumn.

☀ ◊ Zone 6

Quercus alba
(American white oak)
Deciduous, spreading tree. Deeply lobed, glossy, dark green leaves turn reddish-purple in autumn.

☀ ◊ Zone 2b

***Acer platanoides* 'Palmatifidum'**, syn. *A.p.* 'Lorbergii'
Vigorous, deciduous, spreading tree. Deeply divided, pale green leaves with slender lobes turn yellow or reddish-orange in autumn. Tiny, yellow flowers appear in mid-spring.

☀ ◊ Zone 5

TREES large WINTER/ALL YEAR INTEREST

☐☐ WHITE–GREEN

Betula ermanii

Deciduous, open-branched, elegant tree that has peeling, pinkish-white bark, distinctively marked with large lenticels. Oval, glossy, green leaves give excellent autumn colour.

☼ ◊ Zone 5

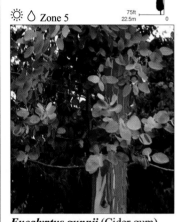

Eucalyptus dalrympleana
(Mountain gum)

Vigorous, evergreen tree. Creamy-white, young bark becomes pinkish-grey, then peels. Leaves are long, narrow and pendent. Clusters of white flowers appear in late summer and autumn.

☼ ◊ Zone 8

Eucalyptus gunnii (Cider gum)

Evergreen, conical tree with peeling, cream, pinkish and brown bark. Leaves are silver-blue when young, blue-green when mature. Clusters of white flowers, with numerous stamens, appear in mid-summer.

☼ ◊ Zone 8

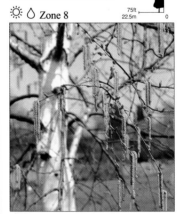

Betula papyrifera
(Canoe birch, Paper birch)

Vigorous, deciduous, open-branched, round-headed tree with peeling, shiny, white bark, yellowish catkins in spring and oval, coarsely serrated leaves that turn clear yellow in autumn.

☼ ◊ Zone 2

Ficus elastica 'Doescheri'
(Rubber plant)

Strong-growing, evergreen, upright then spreading tree with oblong to oval, leathery, lustrous, deep green leaves, patterned with grey-green, yellow and white. Min. 10°C (50°F).

☼ ◊ ①

☐ GREEN

Ficus benghalensis (Banyan)

Evergreen, wide-spreading tree with trunk-like prop roots. Has oval, leathery leaves, rich green with pale veins, to 20cm (8in) long, and small, fig-like, brown fruits. Min. 15–18°C (59–64°F).

☼ ◊ ①

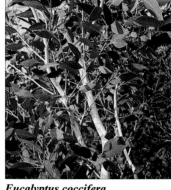

Eucalyptus coccifera
(Tasmanian snow gum)

Evergreen tree with peeling, blue-grey and white bark and aromatic, pointed, grey-green leaves. Bears clusters of white flowers, with numerous stamens, in summer.

☼ ◊ Zone 9?

Archontophoenix alexandrae
(Alexandra palm, Northern bungalow palm)

Evergreen palm with feather-shaped, arching leaves. Mature trees bear sprays of small, white or cream flowers. Min. 15°C (59°F).

☼ ◊

OTHER RECOMMENDED PLANTS:
Betula pendula
Betula utilis
Betula utilis var. *jacquemontii*, illus. p.83

Eucalyptus globulus
Ficus elastica 'Decora'
Metrosideros robustus
Tilia platyphyllos 'Prince's Street'

Archontophoenix cunninghamiana
Castanospermum australe
Ficus benjamina
Ficus lyrata

Ficus macrophylla
Ficus religiosa
Ficus rubiginosa
Nothofagus menziesii

Quercus x _turneri_
Semi-evergreen, rounded, dense tree.
Lobed, leathery, dark green leaves fall
just before new foliage appears in
spring.

☼ ○ Zone 8   100ft 30m / 75ft 22.5m / 0

Nothofagus dombeyi
Evergreen, loosely conical tree of
elegant habit with shoots that droop at
the tips. Leaves are sharply toothed,
glossy and dark green.

☼ ◐ Zone 9   100ft 30m / 75ft 22.5m / 0

Quercus suber (Cork oak)
Evergreen, round-headed tree with
thick, corky bark. Oval, leathery leaves
are glossy, dark green above and
greyish beneath.

☼ ○ Zone 8   100ft 30m / 75ft 22.5m / 0

Betula pendula 'Tristis'
(Weeping birch)
Deciduous, slender, elegant tree with a
strongly weeping habit and white bark.
Oval, bright green leaves, with toothed
margins, provide excellent
golden colour in autumn.

☼ ○ Zone 2   100ft 30m / 75ft 22.5m / 0

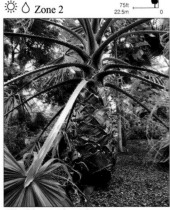

Washingtonia robusta
(Thread palm)
Fast-growing, evergreen palm with
large, fan-shaped leaves and, in summer,
tiny, creamy-white flowers in large,
long-stalked sprays. Black
berries appear in winter-
spring. Min. 10°C (50°F).

☼ ○   100ft 30m / 75ft 22.5m / 0

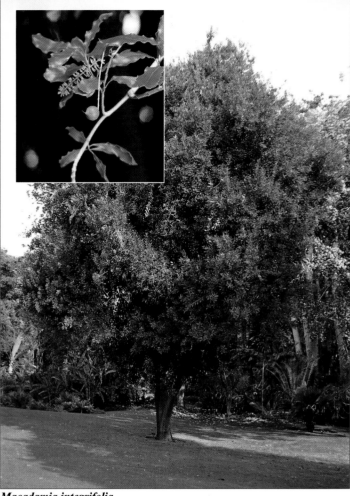

Macadamia integrifolia
(Macadamia nut, Queensland nut)
Evergreen, spreading tree with edible,
brown nuts in autumn. Has whorls of
leathery, semi-glossy leaves and
panicles of small, creamy-
yellow flowers in spring.
Min. 10–13°C (50–55°F).

☼ ◐   100ft 30m / 75ft 22.5m / 0

Syagrus romanzoffiana, syn.
Arecastrum romanzoffianum
(Queen palm)
Majestic, evergreen palm. Has feather-
shaped leaves with lustrous, green
leaflets. Mature trees carry
clusters of yellow flowers in
summer. Min. 18°C (64°F).

☼ ○   100ft 30m / 75ft 22.5m / 0

**_Quercus_ x _hispanica_
'Lucombeana'**, syn.
_Q._ x _lucombeana_ 'William
Lucombe' (Lucombe oak)
Semi-evergreen, spreading tree with
toothed leaves, glossy, dark
green above, grey beneath.

☼ ○ Zone 8   100ft 30m / 75ft 22.5m / 0

TREES large WINTER/ALL YEAR INTEREST

■ GREEN

Betula albosinensis
(Chinese paper birch)
Deciduous, open-branched, elegant tree
with serrated, oval to lance-shaped,
pale green leaves. Peeling bark is
honey-coloured or reddish-
maroon with a grey bloom.

☀ ◊ Zone 4   75ft 22.5m   0   100ft 30m

Nothofagus betuloides
Evergreen, columnar tree with dense
growth of oval, glossy, dark green
leaves on bronze-red shoots.

☀ ◐ Zone 9   75ft 22.5m   0   100ft 30m

□ YELLOW

Umbellularia californica
(Californian laurel)
Evergreen, spreading tree with
aromatic, leathery, glossy, dark green
leaves and creamy-yellow flowers in
late spring. Pungent leaves
may cause nausea and
headache when crushed.

☀ ◐ ❗ Zone 8   75ft 22.5m   0   100ft 30m

Salix alba var. **vitellina**
(Golden willow)
Deciduous, spreading tree, usually cut
back hard to promote growth of strong,
young shoots that are bright orange-
yellow in winter. Lance-
shaped, mid-green leaves
appear in spring.

☀ ◐ Zone 2   75ft 22.5m   0   100ft 30m

Salix × **sepulcralis** var.
chrysocoma (Golden weeping
willow)
Deciduous tree with slender, yellow
shoots falling to the ground as a
curtain. Yellow-green,
young leaves mature to
mid-green.

☀ ◐ Zone 4b   75ft 22.5m   0   100ft 30m

Alnus incana 'Aurea'
Alnus incana 'Ramulis Coccineis'
Betula maximowicziana
Corylus colurna

TREES medium SPRING INTEREST

□ WHITE

Malus hupehensis (Hupeh crab)
Vigorous, deciduous, spreading tree.
Has deep green leaves, large, fragrant,
white flowers, pink in bud, from mid-
to late spring, followed by small, red-
tinged, yellow crab apples
in late summer and autumn.

☀ ◊ Zone 5   50ft 15m   0   50ft 15m

Salix daphnoides (Violet willow)
Fast-growing, deciduous, spreading
tree. Has lance-shaped, glossy, dark
green leaves, silver, male catkins in
spring and purple shoots with bluish-
white bloom in winter.

☀ ◐ Zone 2b   50ft 15m   0   50ft 15m

Malus baccata var. **mandschurica**
Vigorous, deciduous, spreading tree
with dark green leaves and a profusion
of white flowers in clusters in mid-
spring, followed by long-lasting, small,
red or yellow crab apples.

☀ ◊ Zone 3   50ft 15m   0   50ft 15m

OTHER RECOMMENDED PLANTS:
Dillenia indica
MAGNOLIAS, illus. p.75
Malus baccata

Malus prattii

Magnolias

A mature magnolia in full bloom is one of the most spectacular sights in the spring garden. Most magnolias are elegant in habit and though slow-growing, eventually form imposing trees and shrubs that are valuable as focal points or as single specimens in lawns. Some species, such as *Magnolia stellata*, may be successfully grown in the smallest of gardens.

Magnolia flowers are generally saucer- or goblet-shaped and often have a subtle fragrance. The colour range includes pure white or white flushed or stained with pink or purple, pink and rich wine-purple. The genus also includes some evergreen, summer-flowering species. These, and cultivars that are not fully hardy, make excellent subjects for planting against a sunny wall. Some magnolias prefer acid or neutral soil, but most tolerate any soil provided it is humus-rich. Plenty of organic matter should be dug into the soil before planting.

M. wilsonii

M. grandiflora 'Exmouth'

M. campbellii

M. × *soulangeana* 'Rustica Rubra'

M. stellata 'Water Lily'

M. tripetala

M. campbellii subsp. *mollicomata*

M. 'Norman Gould'

M. cylindrica

M. denudata

M. hypoleuca

M. × *s.* 'Etienne Soulange-Bodin'

M. liliiflora 'Nigra'

M. 'Wada's Memory'

M. salicifolia

M. sprengeri

M. 'Charles Coates'

M. × *veitchii* 'Peter Veitch'

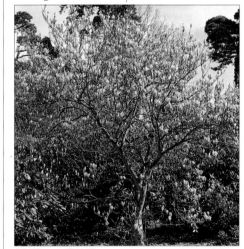

M. 'Heaven Scent'

M. kobus

M. 'Manchu Fan'

M. campbellii 'Charles Raffill'

M. stellata

M. × *wieseneri*

M. fraseri

M. × *loebneri* 'Leonard Messel'

M. sprengeri 'Wakehurst'

M. campbellii 'Darjeeling'

TREES

☐ WHITE

Pyrus calleryana 'Chanticleer'
Deciduous, conical tree with glossy leaves that turn purplish in autumn. Sprays of small, white flowers appear in spring. Resists fireblight.

☀ ◊ Zone 5b

Prunus mahaleb
Deciduous, round-headed, bushy tree that bears a profusion of fragrant, cup-shaped, white flowers from mid- to late spring. Rounded, glossy, dark green leaves turn yellow in autumn.

☀ ◊ ① Zone 7

Halesia monticola
(Silver bell, Snowdrop tree)
Fast-growing, deciduous, conical or spreading tree. Masses of pendent, bell-shaped, white flowers appear in late spring before leaves, followed by 4-winged fruits in autumn.

☀ ◐ Zone 5b

Prunus padus (Bird cherry)
Deciduous, spreading tree, conical when young. Bears fragrant, white flowers in pendent spikes during late spring, followed by small, black fruits in late summer. Dark green leaves turn yellow in autumn.

☀ ◊ ① Zone 2

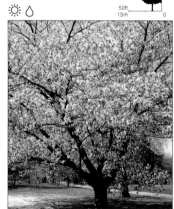

Prunus avium 'Plena'
Deciduous, spreading tree with reddish-brown bark and masses of double, pure white flowers in spring. Dark green foliage turns red in autumn.

☀ ◊ ① Zone 4b

Melia azedarach
(Bead tree, Persian lilac)
Deciduous, spreading tree. Has dark green leaves with many leaflets and fragrant, star-shaped, pinkish-lilac flowers in spring, followed by pale orange-yellow fruits in autumn. Min. 7°C (45°F).

☀ ◊

Cornus nuttallii
(Mountain dogwood, Pacific dogwood)
Deciduous, conical tree. Large, white bracts, surrounding tiny flowers, appear in late spring. Has oval, dark green leaves.

☀ ◊ ① Zone 7

Fraxinus ornus (Manna ash)
Deciduous, round-headed tree. Has deep green leaves with 5–9 leaflets. Panicles of scented, creamy-white flowers appear in late spring and early summer.

☀ ◊ ① Zone 7

Prunus jamasakura,
syn. *P. serrulata* var. *spontanea*
(Hill cherry)
Deciduous, spreading tree bearing cup-shaped, white or pink flowers from mid- to late spring. Oval leaves, bronze when young, mature to deep green.

☀ ◊ ① Zone 6

☐ PINK–YELLOW

☐ WHITE

Prunus 'Kanzan'
Deciduous, vase-shaped tree. Large, double, pink to purple flowers are borne profusely from mid- to late spring amid bronze, young leaves that mature to dark green.

☼ ◐ ① Zone 6   50ft 15m / 15m 0

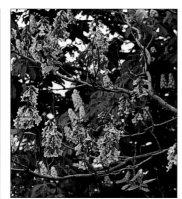

Paulownia tomentosa,
syn. *P. imperialis*
(Foxglove tree, Empress tree)
Deciduous, spreading tree. Has large, lobed, mid-green leaves and terminal sprays of fragrant, foxglove-like, pinkish-lilac flowers in spring.

☼ ◐ Zone 6b   50ft 15m / 15m 0

Styrax japonicus
Deciduous, spreading tree bearing in early summer a profusion of pendent, fragrant, bell-shaped, white flowers amid glossy, dark green foliage.

☼ ◐ pH ᴗ Zone 5b   50ft 15m / 15m 0

Ostrya virginiana (American hop hornbeam, Ironwood)
Deciduous, conical tree with dark brown bark and deep green leaves, yellow in autumn. Has yellowish catkins in spring, followed by greenish-white fruit clusters.

☼ ◐ Zone 3   50ft 15m / 15m 0

Malus 'Profusion'
Deciduous, spreading tree. Dark green foliage is purple when young. Cup-shaped, deep purplish-pink flowers are freely borne in late spring, followed by small, reddish-purple crab apples in late summer and autumn.

☼ ◐ Zone 4   50ft 15m

Gleditsia triacanthos 'Sunburst'
Deciduous, spreading tree with fern-like, glossy foliage that is golden-yellow when young, deep green in summer.

☼ ◐ Zone 4   50ft 15m / 15m 0

Davidia involucrata
(Dove tree, Ghost tree, Pocket handkerchief tree)
Deciduous, conical tree with heart-shaped, vivid green leaves, felted beneath. Large, white bracts appear on mature trees from late spring.

☼ ◐ Zone 7   50ft 15m / 15m 0

Aesculus x *neglecta* 'Erythroblastos', illus. p.89
Catalpa x *erubescens* 'Purpurea'
Cercis siliquastrum, illus. p.88
MAGNOLIAS, illus. p.75

Prunus 'Okame'
Tabebuia rosea

OTHER RECOMMENDED PLANTS:
Acer rufinerve 'Hatsuyuki'
Arbutus menziesii
Catalpa ovata

Cladrastis kentukea, illus. p.82
Cornus controversa
Cunonia capensis
Eucryphia cordifolia

TREES medium SUMMER INTEREST

□ WHITE

Oxydendrum arboreum
(Sorrel tree, Sourwood)
Deciduous, spreading tree with glossy, dark green foliage that turns bright red in autumn. Sprays of white flowers appear in late summer and autumn.

☀ ◊ pH Zone 6

Catalpa speciosa
Deciduous, spreading tree. Heads of large, white flowers marked with yellow and purple are borne in mid-summer among glossy, mid-green leaves.

☀ ◊ Zone 5

Drimys winteri, syn. *Wintera aromatica* (Winter's bark)
Evergreen, conical, sometimes shrubby tree with long, glossy, pale or dark green leaves, usually bluish-white beneath. Bears clusters of fragrant, star-shaped, white flowers in early summer.

☀ ◊ Zone 9

Quercus cerris 'Argenteovariegata', syn. *Q.c.* 'Variegata'
Deciduous, spreading tree. Strongly toothed or lobed, glossy, dark green leaves are edged with creamy-white.

☀ ◊ Zone 8

Sorbus vestita, syn. *S. cuspidata*
Deciduous, broadly conical tree. Has very large, veined, grey-green leaves, white-haired when young. Heads of pink-stamened, white flowers in late spring or early summer are followed by russet or yellowish-red fruits.

☀ ◊ ① Zone 7

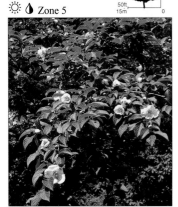

Stewartia pseudocamellia
Deciduous, spreading tree with ornamental, peeling bark. Bears white flowers in mid-summer. Foliage is mid-green, turning orange and red in autumn.

☀ ◊ pH Zone 6

Catalpa bignonioides
(Indian bean tree)
Deciduous, spreading tree. Large, light green leaves are purplish when young. White flowers marked with yellow and purple appear in summer, followed by long, cylindrical, pendent pods.

☀ ◊ Zone 5

Cornus macrophylla
Deciduous, spreading tree. Clusters of small, creamy-white flowers appear in summer. Glossy, bright green leaves are large, pointed and oval.

☀ ◊ ① Zone 8

Sorbus aria 'Lutescens'
Deciduous, spreading tree, upright when young. Young foliage is silvery, maturing to grey-green. White flowers in late spring and early summer are followed by orange-red fruits in autumn.

☀ ◊ ① Zone 4

Gevuina avellana
Hoheria populnea
Lyonothamnus floribundus subsp.
asplenifolius

MAGNOLIAS, illus. p.75
Malus trilobata
Pterostyrax hispida
Stewartia monadelpha, illus. p.82

Stewartia sinensis
Styrax obassia
Weinmannia trichosperma

WHITE–PINK

Acer pseudoplatanus 'Simon Louis Frères'
Deciduous, spreading tree. Young leaves are marked with creamy-white and pink; older foliage is pale green with white markings.

☀ ◊ Zone 6

Acer negundo 'Variegatum'
Fast-growing, deciduous, spreading tree. Has pinkish- then white-margined, bright green leaves with 3 or 5 leaflets. Inconspicuous, greenish-yellow flowers appear in late spring.

☀ ◊ Zone 7

Aesculus indica 'Sydney Pearce'
Deciduous, spreading tree with glossy, dark green leaves, bronze when young and orange or yellow in autumn. Pinkish-white flowers, marked red and yellow, appear from early to mid-summer.

☀ ◊ ⓘ Zone 8

PURPLE–GREEN

Jacaranda mimosifolia, syn. *J. acutifolia* of gardens, *J. ovalifolia*
Fast-growing, deciduous, rounded tree with fern-like leaves of many tiny, bright green leaflets. Has trusses of vivid blue to blue-purple flowers in spring and early summer. Min. 7°C (45°F).

☀ ◊

Sorbus thibetica 'John Mitchell', syn. *S.* 'Mitchellii'
Strong-growing, deciduous, conical tree with dark green leaves, silvery beneath. Has white flowers in spring and brown fruits in late summer.

☀ ◊ ⓘ Zone 6

Toona sinensis, syn. *Cedrela sinensis*
Deciduous, spreading tree with shaggy bark when old. Dark green leaves with many leaflets turn yellow in autumn. Bears fragrant, white flowers in mid-summer. Shoots are onion-scented.

☀ ◊ Zone 7

Broussonetia papyrifera
(Paper mulberry)
Deciduous, round-headed tree. Dull green leaves are large, broadly oval, toothed and sometimes lobed. In early summer, small globes of purple flowers appear on female plants.

☀ ◊ Zone 7

Hovenia dulcis (Raisin-tree)
Deciduous, spreading tree with large, glossy, dark green leaves. In summer it may bear small, greenish-yellow flowers, the stalks of which become red, fleshy and edible.

☀ ◊ Zone 6b

Populus tremula 'Pendula'
(Weeping aspen)
Vigorous, deciduous, weeping tree. Leaves, reddish when young, grey-green in summer and yellow in autumn, tremble in the wind. Has purplish catkins in late winter and spring.

☀ ◊ Zone 2

TREES medium SUMMER INTEREST

◻ GREEN

Quercus marilandica
(Black Jack oak)
Deciduous, spreading tree. Large leaves, 3-lobed at the apex, are glossy, dark green above, paler beneath, and turn yellow, red or brown in autumn.

☼ ◊ Zone 6

Fraxinus velutina (Arizona ash)
Deciduous, spreading tree. Leaves vary but usually consist of 3 or 5 narrow, velvety, grey-green leaflets.

☼ ◊ ⓘ Zone 7

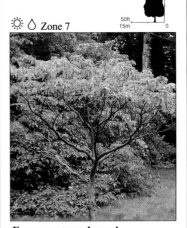

Quercus garryana (Oregon oak)
Slow-growing, deciduous, spreading tree with deeply lobed, glossy, bright green leaves.

☼ ◊ Zone 7

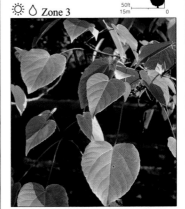

***Tilia cordata* 'Rancho'**
Deciduous, conical, dense tree, spreading when young. Has small, oval, glossy, dark green leaves and clusters of small, fragrant, cup-shaped, yellowish flowers are borne in mid-summer.

☼ ◊ Zone 3

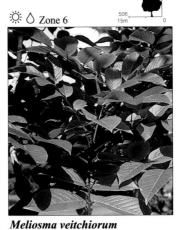

Meliosma veitchiorum
Deciduous, spreading tree with stout, grey shoots and large, dark green, red-stalked leaves with 9 or 11 leaflets. Small, fragrant, white flowers in late spring are followed by violet fruits in autumn.

☼ ◊ Zone 9?

Gleditsia japonica
Deciduous, conical tree with a trunk armed with spines. Shoots are purplish when young. Fern-like leaves consist of many small, mid-green leaflets.

☼ ◊ Zone 9

Emmenopterys henryi
Deciduous, spreading tree. Large, pointed, dark green leaves are bronze-purple when young. Clusters of white flowers (some bearing a large, white bract) are rarely produced except in hot summers.

☼ ◊ Zone 8

Idesia polycarpa
Deciduous, spreading tree with large, heart-shaped, glossy, dark green leaves on long stalks. Small, fragrant, yellow-green flowers in mid-summer are followed in autumn, on female plants, by red fruits hanging in clusters.

☼ �◖ Zone 7

Kalopanax septemlobus,
syn. *Acanthopanax ricinifolius*,
K. pictus, *K. ricinifolius*
Deciduous, spreading tree with spiny stems, large, 5–7-lobed, glossy, dark green leaves and umbels of small, white flowers, then black fruits in autumn.

☼ ◖ Zone 4b

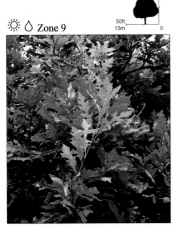

Quercus macrocarpa (Bur oak)
Slow-growing, deciduous, spreading tree. Large, oblong-oval, lobed, glossy, dark green leaves turn yellow or brown in autumn.

☼ ◊ Zone 2

Quercus macrolepis, syn.
Q. aegilops, *Q. ithaburensis* subsp.
macrolepsis
Deciduous or semi-evergreen, spreading tree. Has grey-green leaves with angular lobes.

☼ ◊ Zone 9

***Quercus rubra* 'Aurea'**
Slow-growing, deciduous, spreading tree. Large, lobed leaves are clear yellow when young, becoming green by mid-summer. Produces best colour in an open but sheltered position.

☼ ◊ Zone 4

TREES medium AUTUMN INTEREST

 GREEN–YELLOW

 WHITE–RED

Phellodendron chinense
Deciduous, spreading tree. Aromatic leaves, with 7–13 oblong leaflets, are dark green, turning yellow in autumn. Pendent racemes of greenish flowers in early summer are followed on female trees by berry-like, black fruits.

☼ ◊ Zone 6

Robinia pseudoacacia 'Frisia'
Deciduous, spreading tree with luxuriant leaves divided into oval leaflets, golden-yellow when young, greenish-yellow in summer and orange-yellow in autumn.

☼ ◊ ⓘ Zone 4

Ulmus minor 'Dicksonii' (Cornish golden elm, Dickson's golden elm)
Slow-growing, deciduous, conical tree of dense habit. Carries small, broadly oval, bright golden-yellow leaves.

☼ ◊ Zone 5b

Alnus glutinosa 'Aurea'
Catalpa bignonioides 'Aurea'
Quercus robur 'Concordia'

Eucryphia x nymansensis 'Nymansay'
Evergreen, columnar tree. Some of the leathery, glossy, dark green leaves are simple, others consist of 3 (rarely 5) leaflets. Clusters of large, white flowers open in late summer or early autumn.

☼ ◉ Zone 9

Syzygium paniculatum (Australian brush cherry)
Evergreen tree with glossy leaves, coppery when young. Has creamy-white flowers, with reddish sepals, and fragrant, rose-purple fruits.
Min. 10°C (50°F).

☼ ◊

OTHER RECOMMENDED PLANTS:
Chorisia speciosa, illus. p.70
Cornus capitata
MAGNOLIAS, illus. p.75

Acer davidii 'Madeline Spitta'
Deciduous tree with upright branches that are striped green and white. Glossy, dark green foliage turns orange in autumn after the appearance of winged, green fruits that ripen reddish-brown.

☼ ◊ Zone 6

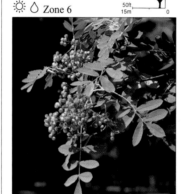

Sorbus hupehensis 'Rosea', syn. *S.h.* var. *obtusa*
Deciduous, spreading tree with leaves of 4–8 pairs of blue-green leaflets turning orange-red in late autumn. White flowers in spring are followed by long-lasting, pink fruits.

☼ ◊ ⓘ Zone 6

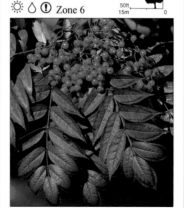

Sorbus commixta, syn. *S. discolor* of gardens
Vigorous, deciduous, spreading tree. Leaves have 6–8 pairs of glossy, deep green leaflets that turn orange and red in autumn. White flowers in spring are followed by bright red fruits.

☼ ◊ ⓘ Zone 6

Rhus potaninii
Rhus verniciflua
Sorbus americana
Sorbus esserteauana

Sorbus aucuparia
(Mountain ash, Rowan)
Deciduous, spreading tree. Leaves have mid-green leaflets that turn red or yellow in autumn. Bears white flowers in spring and red fruits in autumn.

☼ ◊ ⓘ Zone 3

Acer rubrum 'Columnare'
Deciduous, slender, upright tree with lobed, dark green foliage becoming a fiery column of red and yellow in autumn.

☼ ◊ Zone 4b

Sorbus hupehensis
Sorbus scalaris

TREES

Acer rufinerve
(Snake-bark maple)
Deciduous tree with arching branches
striped green and white. In autumn,
lobed, dark green leaves turn brilliant
red and orange.

☀ ◊ Zone 7

Aesculus flava, syn. *A. octandra*
(Sweet buckeye, Yellow buckeye)
Deciduous, spreading tree. Glossy, dark
green leaves, with 5 or 7 oval leaflets,
redden in autumn. Has yellow flowers
in late spring and early
summer followed by round
fruits (chestnuts).

☀ ◊ ① Zone 3b

Nyssa sinensis
Deciduous, spreading tree. Has long,
narrow, pointed leaves that are purplish
when young, dark green when mature
and brilliant scarlet in autumn.

☀ ◐ Zone 7

Quercus × heterophylla
(Bartram's oak)
Deciduous, spreading tree with
toothed, glossy, bright green leaves that
turn orange-red and yellow in autumn.

☀ ◊ Zone 7

Stewartia monadelpha
Deciduous, spreading tree with peeling
bark and glossy, dark green leaves that
turn orange and red in autumn. Small,
violet-anthered, white flowers appear
in mid-summer, followed
by small fruits.

☀ ◐ pH Zone 7

Acer henryi, syn. *A. cissifolium*
subsp. *henryi*
Deciduous, spreading tree. Dark green
leaves with 3 oval, toothed leaflets turn
bright orange and red in autumn.

☀ ◊ Zone 5b

***Sorbus* 'Joseph Rock'**
Deciduous, upright tree. Bright green
leaves composed of many leaflets turn
orange, red and purple in autumn.
White flowers in late spring are
followed by large clusters
of small, yellow berries in
late summer and autumn.

☀ ◊ ① Zone 5

***Acer saccharum* 'Temple's
Upright'**
Deciduous, columnar tree. In autumn,
large, lobed leaves turn brilliant orange
and red.

☀ ◊ Zone 4

Parrotia persica (Persian ironwood)
Deciduous, spreading, short-trunked
tree with flaking, grey and fawn bark.
Rich green leaves turn yellow, orange
and red-purple in autumn. Small, red
flowers are borne on bare
wood in early spring.

☀ ◐ Zone 7

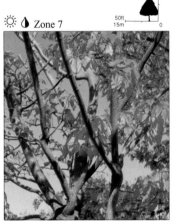

Acer capillipes
(Snake-bark maple)
Deciduous, spreading tree. Has lobed,
bright green leaves that turn brilliant
red and orange in autumn. Older
branches are striped green
and white.

☀ ◊ Zone 6

Cladrastis kentukea (Yellow wood)
Deciduous, round-headed tree. Leaves
of 7 or 9 rounded-oval leaflets are dark
green, turning yellow in autumn.
Clusters of fragrant, pea-like, yellow-
marked, white flowers
appear in early summer.

☀ ◊ Zone 4b

Acer maximowiczianum
Diospyros kaki
Dipteronia sinensis
HOLLIES, illus. pp.98–99

Liquidambar formosana
Maclura pomifera
Malus 'Hopa'
Malus hupehensis, illus. p.74

Malus 'Profusion', illus. p.77
Malus × robusta
Malus × robusta 'Yellow Siberian'
Morus nigra

Oxydendrum arboreum, illus. p.78
Sorbus aucuparia 'Fructu Luteo'
Sorbus decora

TREES medium WINTER INTEREST

☐ WHITE–YELLOW

Betula utilis var. **jacquemontii**
syn. *B. jacquemontii*
(White-barked Himalayan birch)
Deciduous, open-branched, elegant tree
with bright white bark. Oval, serrated,
mid-green leaves turn clear
yellow in autumn.

☼ ◊ Zone 3

Michelia doltsopa
Evergreen, rounded tree with oval,
glossy, dark green leaves, paler
beneath. Strongly scented, magnolia-
like flowers, with white to pale yellow
petals, appear in winter-
spring. Min. 5°C (41°F).

☼ ◊ pH

Acacia dealbata
(Mimosa, Silver wattle)
Fast-growing, evergreen, spreading
tree. Has feathery, blue-green leaves
with many leaflets. Racemes of
globular, fragrant, bright
yellow flower heads are
borne in winter-spring.

☼ ◊ Tender

OTHER RECOMMENDED PLANTS:
Bauhinia variegata
Salix daphnoides, illus. p.74
Tabebuia chrysotricha, illus. p.97

■ RED

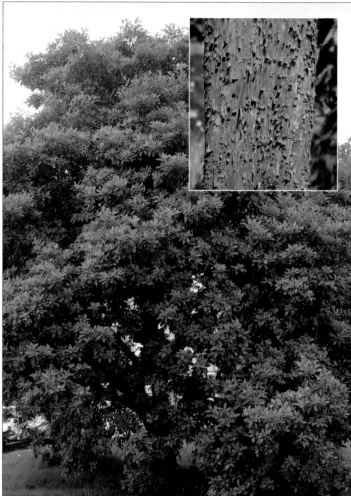

Arbutus × andrachnoides
Evergreen, bushy, spreading tree with
peeling, reddish-brown bark and
glossy, dark green foliage. Clusters of
small, white flowers in autumn to
spring are followed by
small, strawberry-like,
orange or red fruits.

☼ ◊ Zone 9

Metrosideros excelsus
(New Zealand Christmas tree,
Pohutukawa)
Evergreen, wide-spreading tree. Oval,
grey-green leaves are white felted
beneath. Bears showy tufts
of crimson stamens in
winter. Min. 5°C (41°F).

☼ ◊

TREES medium ALL YEAR INTEREST

WHITE–GREEN

***Ficus benjamina* 'Variegata'**
Evergreen, dense, round-headed,
weeping tree, often with aerial roots.
Has slender, pointed, lustrous leaves
that are rich green with white
variegation.
Min. 15–18°C (59–64°F).

☼ ◊ ① 50ft 15m

Trochodendron aralioides
Evergreen, broadly conical tree with
glossy, dark green foliage. In late
spring and early summer bears clusters
of unusual, petal-less, wheel-like, green
flowers.

☼ ◊ Zone 7

Schefflera actinophylla
(Queensland umbrella tree)
Evergreen, upright tree with large,
spreading leaves of 5–16 leaflets. Has
large sprays of small, dull red flowers
in summer or autumn.
Min. 16°C (61°F).

☼ ◊

Acer pensylvanicum
(Snake-bark maple)
Deciduous, upright tree. Shoots are
boldly striped green and white. Large,
lobed, mid-green leaves turn bright
yellow in autumn.

☼ ◊ Zone 2b

Eucalyptus pauciflora
(White Sallee)
Evergreen, spreading tree with peeling,
white, young bark and red, young
shoots. In summer, white flower
clusters appear amid glossy,
bright grey-green foliage.

☼ ◊ Zone 9?

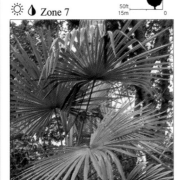

Trachycarpus fortunei
(Chusan palm, Windmill palm)
Evergreen palm with unbranched stem
and a head of large, deeply divided,
fan-like, mid-green leaves. Sprays of
fragrant, creamy-yellow
flowers appear in early
summer.

☼ ◊ Zone 8

***Eucalyptus pauciflora* subsp.
niphophila, syn. *E. niphophila***
(Snow gum)
Evergreen, spreading tree. Has
patchwork-like, flaking bark, red-
rimmed, grey-green leaves
and white flowers in
summer.

☼ ◊ Zone 8

Quercus myrsinifolia
Evergreen, rounded tree with narrow,
pointed, glossy, dark green leaves,
reddish-purple when young.

☼ ◊ Zone 8

Prunus maackii
Deciduous, spreading tree with peeling,
yellowish-brown bark. Produces spikes
of small, white flowers in mid-spring
and pointed, dark green leaves that turn
yellow in autumn.

☼ ◊ ① Zone 2b

OTHER RECOMMENDED PLANTS:
Acer davidii
Betula 'Jermyns'
Cinnamomum camphora

Cordyline australis 'Veitchii'
Cyathea medullaris
Eucalyptus glaucescens
Ficus lyrata

HOLLIES, illus. pp.98–9
Laurelia sempervirens
Laurus nobilis
Lithocarpus densiflorus

MAGNOLIAS, illus. p.75
Salix x *rubens* 'Basfordiana'

GREEN–ORANGE

Jubaea chilensis, syn. *J. spectabilis*
(Chilean wine palm, Coquito)
Slow-growing, evergreen palm with a
massive trunk and large, silvery-green
leaves. Has small, maroon and yellow
flowers in spring and
woody, yellow fruits
in autumn.

☀ ◊ Zone 9

Livistona chinensis (Chinese fan
palm, Chinese fountain palm)
Slow-growing, evergreen palm with a
stout trunk. Has fan-shaped, glossy
leaves, 1–3m (3–10ft) across. Mature
trees bear loose clusters of
berry-like, black fruits in
autumn. Min. 7°C (45°F).

☀ ◊

Quercus agrifolia
(Californian live oak)
Evergreen, spreading tree bearing rigid,
spiny-toothed, glossy, dark green
leaves. Min. 2°C (35°F).

☀ ◊

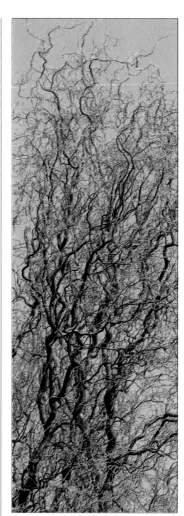

Salix babylonica var. *pekinensis*
'**Tortuosa**' (Dragon's-claw willow,
Corkscrew willow)
Fast-growing, deciduous, spreading
tree with curiously twisted shoots and
contorted, narrow, tapering,
bright green leaves.

☀ ◊ Zone 5

Corynocarpus laevigatus
Evergreen, upright tree, spreading with
age. Has leathery leaves and clusters of
small, greenish flowers in spring-
summer. Plum-like, orange fruits
appear in winter. Min.
7–10°C (45–50°F).

☀ ◊

TREES small SPRING INTEREST

☐ WHITE

Mespilus germanica (Medlar)
Deciduous, spreading tree or shrub.
Has dark green leaves that turn orange-
brown in autumn, white flowers in
spring-summer and brown fruits in
autumn, edible when half
rotten.

☀ ◊ Zone 7

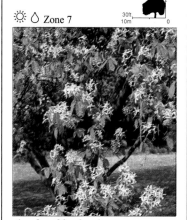

Amelanchier laevis
Deciduous, spreading tree or large
shrub. Oval, bronze, young leaves turn
dark green in summer, red and orange
in autumn. Sprays of white flowers in
spring are followed by
rounded, fleshy, red fruits.

☀ ◊ Zone 3b

Crataegus laciniata,
syn. *C. orientalis*
Deciduous, spreading tree with deeply
lobed, hairy, dark green leaves. A
profusion of white flowers in late
spring or early summer is
followed by red fruits
tinged with yellow.

☀ ◊ ! Zone 7

Cornus florida '**White Cloud**'
Deciduous, spreading tree. Massed
flower heads, comprising large, white
bracts around tiny flowers, appear in
spring. Oval, pointed, dark green
leaves turn red and purple
in autumn.

☀ ◊ ! Zone 6b

Aesculus californica
(California buckeye)
Deciduous, spreading, sometimes
shrubby tree. Dense heads of fragrant,
sometimes pink-tinged, white flowers
appear in spring and early
summer. Small, dark green
leaves have 5–7 leaflets.

☀ ◊ ! Zone 8

Betula alleghaniensis
HOLLIES, illus. pp.98–9
Prunus serrula
Thespesia populnea

OTHER RECOMMENDED PLANTS:
Agonis flexuosa, illus. p.90
Amelanchier arborea
Amelanchier asiatica

Arbutus andrachne
Bauhinia variegata 'Candida', illus. p.97
Cornus 'Eddie's White Wonder', illus. p.96
Crataegus crus-galli

TREES small SPRING INTEREST
□ WHITE

Prunus 'Shogetsu',
syn. *P.* 'Shimidsu'
Deciduous, round-topped tree. In late spring, pink buds open to large, double, white flowers that hang in clusters from long stalks. Mid-green leaves turn orange and red in autumn.

☼ ◊ ❶ Zone 6

Cornus 'Porlock'
Deciduous, spreading tree. Creamy-white bracts around tiny flowers turn to deep pink in summer. These are often followed by heavy crops of strawberry-like fruits in autumn.

☼ ◊ ❶ Zone 6b

Prunus incisa (Fuji cherry)
Deciduous, spreading tree. White or pale pink flowers appear in early spring. Sharply toothed, dark green leaves are reddish when young, orange-red in autumn.

☼ ◊ ❶ Zone 7

Prunus 'Taihaku' (Great white cherry)
Vigorous, deciduous, spreading tree. Very large, single, pure white flowers are borne in mid-spring among bronze-red, young leaves that mature to dark green.

☼ ◊ ❶ Zone 6

Prunus 'Ukon'
Vigorous, deciduous, spreading tree. Semi-double, pale greenish-white flowers open from pink buds in mid-spring amid pale bronze, young foliage that later turns dark green.

☼ ◊ ❶ Zone 6

Prunus 'Shirotae',
syn. *P.* 'Mount Fuji'
Deciduous, spreading tree with slightly arching branches. Large, fragrant, single or semi-double, pure white flowers appear in mid-spring. Foliage turns orange-red in autumn.

☼ ◊ ❶ Zone 6

Crataegus ellwangeriana
Crataegus x *lavallei* 'Carrierei'
Docynia delavayi
Gordonia axillaris

Halesia tetraptera
MAGNOLIAS, illus. p.75
Malus 'Frettingham's Victoria'
Malus 'Golden Hornet', illus. p.97

Malus 'John Downie', illus. p.95
Malus prunifolia, illus. p.95
Malus toringoides
Malus transitoria

Malus 'Veitch's Scarlet', illus. p.94
Parrotiopsis jacquemontiana
Prunus 'Hally Jolivette'

■ PINK

Prunus x *yedoensis*
(Yoshino cherry)
Deciduous, round-headed tree with spreading, arching branches and dark green foliage. Sprays of pink buds open to white or pale pink flowers in early spring.

☼ ◊ ! Zone 7

Prunus 'Spire',
syn. *P.* x *hillieri* 'Spire'
Deciduous, vase-shaped tree, conical when young. Soft pink flowers appear profusely from early to mid-spring. Dark green leaves, bronze when young, turn brilliant orange-red in autumn.

☼ ◊ ! Zone 7

Prunus 'Hokusai',
syn. *P.* 'Uzuzakura'
Deciduous, spreading tree. Oval, bronze, young leaves mature to dark green, then turn orange and red in autumn. Semi-double, pale pink flowers are borne in mid-spring.

☼ ◊ ! Zone 6

Prunus x *subhirtella* 'Stellata'
Deciduous, spreading tree. Pink flowers with narrow, pointed petals, red in bud, open from early to mid-spring. Dark green leaves turn yellow in autumn.

☼ ◊ ! Zone 7

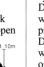

Prunus 'Pandora'
Deciduous tree, upright when young, later spreading. Massed, pale pink flowers appear in early spring. Leaves are bronze when young, dark green in summer and often orange and red in autumn.

☼ ◊ ! Zone 7

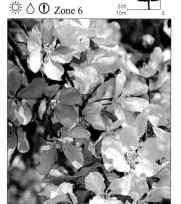

Malus x *arnoldiana*
Deciduous, low, spreading tree with arching branches. In mid- to late spring red buds open to fragrant, pink flowers that fade to white. Bears small, red-flushed, yellow crab apples in autumn. Leaves are oval.

☼ ◊ Zone 5

Prunus sargentii (Sargent cherry)
Deciduous, spreading tree. Oval, dark green leaves are red when young, turning brilliant orange-red in early autumn. Clusters of blush-pink flowers appear in mid-spring.

☼ ◊ ! Zone 5

Prunus 'Shirofugen'
Deciduous, spreading tree with bronze-red leaves turning orange-red in autumn. Pale pink buds open to fragrant, double, white blooms that turn pink before they fade in late spring.

☼ ◊ ! Zone 6

Prunus 'Pink Perfection'
Deciduous, upright tree that bears double, pale pink flowers in late spring. Oval leaves are bronze when young, dark green in summer.

☼ ◊ ! Zone 6

TREES small SPRING INTEREST

☐ PINK

Prunus 'Accolade'
Deciduous, spreading tree with clusters of deep pink buds opening to semi-double, pale pink flowers in early spring. Toothed, mid-green leaves turn orange-red in autumn.

☼ ◊ ① Zone 7

Prunus x *subhirtella* 'Pendula Rubra', syn. *P. pendula* 'Pendula Rubra'
Deciduous, weeping tree that bears deep pink flowers in spring before oval, dark green leaves appear; these turn yellow in autumn.

☼ ◊ ① Zone 7

Malus 'Magdeburgensis'
Deciduous, spreading tree with dark green foliage. Dense clusters of large, semi-double, deep pink flowers appear in late spring, occasionally followed by small, yellow crab apples in autumn.

☼ ◊ Zone 4b

Cercis siliquastrum (Judas tree)
Deciduous, spreading, bushy tree. Clusters of pea-like, bright pink flowers appear in mid-spring, before or with heart-shaped leaves, followed by long, purplish-red pods in late summer.

☼ ◊ Zone 7

Prunus persica 'Prince Charming'
Deciduous, upright, bushy-headed tree with narrow, bright green leaves. Double, deep rose-pink flowers are produced in mid-spring.

☼ ◊ Zone 6

Prunus 'Kiku-shidare-zakura', syn. *P.* 'Cheal's Weeping'
Deciduous, weeping tree. Has double, bright pink flowers that cover pendent branches from mid- to late spring.

☼ ◊ ① Zone 6

Malus floribunda
Deciduous, spreading, dense-headed tree with pale pink flowers, red in bud, appearing from mid- to late spring, followed by tiny, pea-shaped, yellow crab apples in autumn.

☼ ◊ Zone 6b

Dombeya x *cayeuxii* (Pink snowball)
Evergreen, bushy tree with rounded, toothed, hairy leaves to 20cm (8in) long. Pink flowers appear in pendent, ball-like clusters in winter or spring.
Min. 10–13°C (50–55°F).

☼ ◊

Prunus 'Yae-murasaki'
Deciduous, spreading tree with bright green leaves, bronze when young, orange-red in autumn. Semi-double, deep pink flowers are produced in mid-spring.

☼ ◊ ① Zone 7

RED–YELLOW

☐ WHITE

Malus 'Royalty'
Deciduous, spreading tree with glossy, purple foliage. Crimson-purple flowers appear from mid- to late spring, followed by dark red crab apples in autumn. Disease susceptible.

 ☼ ◊ Zone 2b

Acer pseudoplatanus 'Brilliantissimum'
Slow-growing, deciduous, spreading tree. Lobed leaves are salmon-pink when young, then turn yellow and finally dark green in summer.

 ☼ ◊ Zone 5b

Cornus alternifolia 'Argentea'
Deciduous, spreading tree, grown for its attractive, narrowly oval, white-variegated leaves. Has small heads of white flowers in spring.

 ☼ ◊ ! Zone 4

Acer crataegifolium 'Veitchii'
Deciduous, bushy tree with branches streaked with green and white. Small, pointed, dark green leaves, blotched with white and paler green, turn deep pink and reddish-purple in autumn.

☼ ◊ Zone 7

Malus 'Lemoinei'
Deciduous, spreading tree. Oval leaves are deep reddish-purple when young, later becoming tinged with bronze. Wine-red flowers in late spring are followed by dark reddish-purple crab apples in autumn.

 ☼ ◊ Zone 5

Michelia figo
Evergreen tree or rounded shrub. Has oval, glossy, rich green leaves and banana-scented, creamy-yellow flowers, edged maroon, in spring-summer. Min. 5°C (41°F).

☼ ◊

Cornus controversa 'Variegata' (Wedding-cake tree)
Deciduous tree with layered branches. Clusters of small, white flowers appear in summer. Leaves are bright green with broad, creamy-white margins and turn yellow in autumn.

 ☼ ◊ ! Zone 6

Aesculus x *neglecta* 'Erythroblastos'
Deciduous, spreading tree. Leaves with 5 leaflets emerge bright pink, turn yellow, then dark green, and finally orange and yellow in autumn. May bear panicles of flowers in summer.

 ☼ ◊ ! Zone 6b

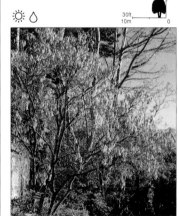

Sophora tetraptera
Semi-evergreen, spreading tree or large shrub with dark green leaves composed of many tiny leaflets. Clusters of golden-yellow flowers appear in late spring. Min. 2°C (35°F).

 ☼ ◊

TREES small SUMMER INTEREST

☐ WHITE

Crataegus flava
(Yellow haw)
Deciduous, spreading tree. Has small, dark green leaves and white flowers in late spring and early summer, followed by greenish-yellow fruits.

☀ ◯ ⓘ Zone 8

Agonis flexuosa
(Peppermint tree, Willow myrtle)
Evergreen, weeping tree. Aromatic, lance-shaped, leathery leaves are bronze-red when young. In spring-summer, mature trees bear masses of small, white flowers. Min. 10°C (50°F).

☀ ◯

Eucryphia glutinosa
Deciduous, upright or spreading tree. Glossy, dark green leaves, consisting of 3–5 leaflets, turn orange-red in autumn. Large, fragrant, white flowers appear from mid- to late summer.

☀ ◐ pH Zone 9

Hoheria angustifolia
Evergreen, columnar tree with narrow, dark green leaves. Shallowly cup-shaped, white flowers are borne from mid- to late summer.

☀ ◯ Zone 9?

Hoheria lyallii
Deciduous, spreading tree with deeply toothed, grey-green leaves. Clusters of white flowers are borne in mid-summer.

☀ ◯ Zone 9

Eucryphia lucida
Evergreen, upright, bushy tree with narrow, glossy, dark green leaves and fragrant, white flowers in early or mid-summer. Min. –1°C (30°F).

☀ ◐ ◯ pH Zone 9

Maackia amurensis
Deciduous, spreading tree with deep green leaves consisting of 7–11 leaflets. Dense, upright spikes of white flowers appear from mid- to late summer.

☀ ◯ Zone 3

Albizia julibrissin (Silk tree)
Deciduous, spreading tree. Large leaves are light to mid-green and divided into many leaflets. Clusters of brush-like, clear pink flowers appear in late summer or autumn.

☀ ◯ Zone 6b

Cornus florida 'Spring Song'
Deciduous, spreading tree. Pink bracts, surrounding tiny flowers, appear in spring-summer. Leaves are oval, pointed and dark green, turning red and purple in autumn.

☀ ◯ ⓘ Zone 6b

Crataegus x prunifolia
Crataegus tanacetifolia
Elaeocarpus cyaneus
Franklinia alatamaha

Fraxinus sieboldiana
Hoheria 'Glory of Amlwch'
Hoheria sexstylosa
MAGNOLIAS, illus. p.75

Plumeria alba
Sophora japonica 'Pendula'
Xanthoceras sorbifolium, illus. p.118

Rothmannia capensis

PINK–PURPLE

PURPLE–GREEN

Lagerstroemia indica
(Crape myrtle)
Deciduous, rounded tree or large shrub. Has trusses of flowers with strongly waved, pink, white or purple petals in summer and early autumn.

☼ ◊ Zone 8

Malus yunnanensis var. **veitchii**
Deciduous, upright tree with lobed, heart-shaped leaves, covered with grey down beneath. Bears white, sometimes pink-tinged, flowers in late spring and a mass of small, red-flushed, brown crab apples in late summer and autumn.

☼ ◊ Zone 7

Aesculus pavia 'Atrosanguinea'
Deciduous, round-headed, sometimes shrubby tree. In summer, panicles of deep red flowers appear among glossy, dark green leaves, which have 5 narrow leaflets.

☼ ◊ ① Zone 6

Prunus cerasifera 'Nigra'
Deciduous, round-headed tree with deep purple leaves, red when young. Pink flowers are borne in profusion from early to mid-spring.

☼ ◊ ① Zone 4

Crataegus laevigata
'Paul's Scarlet'
Deciduous, spreading tree. Has toothed, glossy, dark green leaves and a profusion of double, red flowers in late spring and early summer.

☼ ◊ ① Zone 6

Cercis canadensis 'Forest Pansy'
Deciduous, spreading tree or shrub. In mid-spring has flowers that are magenta in bud, opening to pale pink, before heart-shaped, reddish-purple leaves appear.

☼ ◊ Zone 6

Ehretia dicksonii
Deciduous, spreading tree with stout, ridged branches and large, dark green leaves. Large, flattish heads of small, fragrant, white flowers are borne in mid-summer.

☼ ◊ Zone 8

Pyrus salicifolia 'Pendula'
Deciduous, weeping, mound-shaped tree with white flowers in mid-spring and narrow, grey leaves.

☼ ◊ Zone 5

91

TREES small SUMMER INTEREST

☐ GREEN

Pseudopanax ferox
Evergreen, upright tree with long, narrow, rigid, sharply toothed leaves that are dark bronze-green overlaid white or grey.

☀ ◊ Zone 9

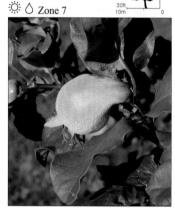

Juglans microcarpa,
syn. *J. rupestris*
(Little walnut, Texan walnut)
Deciduous, bushy-headed tree with large, aromatic leaves of many narrow, pointed leaflets that turn yellow in autumn.

☀ ◊ Zone 7

Acer carpinifolium
(Hornbeam maple)
Deciduous tree of elegant habit, often with several main stems. Prominent-veined, hornbeam-like leaves turn golden-brown in autumn.

☀ ◊ Zone 5b

Koelreuteria paniculata
(Golden-rain tree, Pride of India)
Deciduous, spreading tree with mid-green leaves, turning yellow in autumn. Bears sprays of yellow flowers in summer, followed by inflated, bronze-pink fruits.

☀ ◊ Zone 7

Cydonia oblonga 'Vranja'
Deciduous, spreading tree. Pale green leaves, grey-felted beneath, mature to dark green and set off large, white or pale pink flowers in late spring and, later, very fragrant, golden-yellow fruits.

☀ ◊ Zone 5b

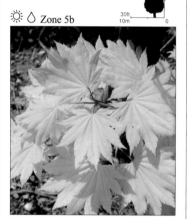

Acer shirasawanum 'Aureum',
syn. *A. japonicum* 'Aureum'
Deciduous, bushy tree or large shrub. Has rounded, many-lobed, pale yellow leaves.

☀ ◊ Zone 6

Ulmus glabra 'Camperdownii',
syn. *U.* 'Camperdownii'
Deciduous, strongly weeping tree with sinuous branches. Leaves are very large, rough and dull green.

☀ ◊ Zone 5

Betula pendula 'Youngii'
(Young's weeping birch)
Deciduous, weeping tree forming a mushroom-shaped dome of thread-like branchlets. Has triangular, serrated leaves and smooth, white bark that is fissured black at maturity.

☀ ◊ Zone 2

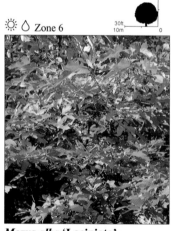

Morus alba 'Laciniata'
Deciduous, spreading tree. Has rounded, deeply lobed, glossy leaves that turn yellow in autumn and bears edible, pink, red or purple fruits in summer.

☀ ◊ Zone 4

Laburnum × watereri 'Vossii'
(Voss's laburnum)
Deciduous, spreading tree. Leaves, consisting of 3 leaflets, are glossy, deep green. Pendent chains of large, yellow flowers are borne in late spring and early summer.

☀ ◊ ⓘ Zone 6

Aralia elata
Celtis sinensis
Cornus alternifolia
Neolitsea sericea

Pseudopanax arboreus
Quercus pontica
Tetracentron sinense
Zelkova abelicea

Aralia elata 'Aureovariegata'
Laburnum anagyroides
Michelia figo, illus. p.89

TREES small AUTUMN INTEREST

Genista aetnensis
(Mount Etna broom)
Almost leafless, rounded tree with
many slender, bright green branches
and a profusion of fragrant, pea-like,
golden-yellow flowers in
mid-summer.

☼ ◊ Zone 9

Sorbus cashmiriana
Deciduous, spreading tree with leaves
consisting of 6–9 pairs of rich green
leaflets. Pink-flushed, white flowers in
early summer are followed by large,
white fruits in autumn.

☼ ◊ ① Zone 5

Cornus florida 'Welchii'
Deciduous, spreading tree. Bears white
bracts, surrounding tiny flowers, in
spring. Dark green leaves, edged with
white and pink, turn red and purple in
autumn.

☼ ◊ ① Zone 6b

Paraserianthes lophantha, syn.
Albizia distachya, A. lophantha
Fast-growing, deciduous, spreading
tree. Has fern-like, dark green leaves
comprising many leaflets. Creamy-
yellow flower spikes appear
in spring-summer.

☼ ◊ Zone 9

Thevetia peruviana,
syn. *T. neriifolia* (Yellow oleander)
Evergreen, erect tree with narrow,
lance-shaped, rich green leaves and
funnel-shaped, yellow or orange-
yellow flowers from winter
to summer.
Min. 16–18°C (61–4°F).

☼ ◊ ①

Arbutus unedo (Strawberry tree)
Evergreen, spreading tree or shrub with
rough, brown bark and glossy, deep
green leaves. Pendent, urn-shaped,
white flowers appear in autumn-winter
as previous season's
strawberry-like, red fruits
ripen.

☼ ◊ Zone 7

Laburnum alpinum
(Scotch laburnum)
Deciduous, spreading tree. Leaves
consist of 3 leaflets and are glossy, dark
green. Long, slender chains of bright
yellow flowers appear in
late spring or early summer.

☼ ◊ ① Zone 5b

Embothrium coccineum
(Chilean firebush)
Evergreen or semi-evergreen, upright,
suckering tree with lance-shaped,
glossy, deep green leaves. Clusters of
brilliant orange-red flowers
are borne in late spring and
early summer.

☼ ◊ pH Zone 9

Caesalpinia gilliesii, illus. p.123
Plumeria rubra, illus. p.96
Tecoma stans, illus. p.96

TREES small AUTUMN INTEREST

■ RED

Sorbus vilmorinii
Deciduous, spreading, arching, elegant tree. Leaves of 9–14 pairs of dark green leaflets become orange- or bronze-red in autumn. Has white blooms in late spring and small, deep pink fruits in autumn.

☼ ◊ ! Zone 3

Crataegus macrosperma var. **acutiloba**
Deciduous, spreading tree with broad, sharply toothed, dark green leaves. White flowers with red anthers in late spring are followed by bright red fruits in autumn.

☼ ◊ ! Zone 4b

Photinia davidiana
Evergreen, spreading tree or large shrub with narrow, glossy, dark green leaves, older ones turning red in autumn. Sprays of white flowers in early summer are followed by clusters of bright red fruits in autumn.

☼ ◊ Zone 8

Malus 'Cowichan'
Deciduous, spreading tree. Has dark green foliage, reddish-purple when young. Pink flowers appear in mid-spring, followed by reddish-purple crab apples.

☼ ◊ Zone 2b

Malus 'Veitch's Scarlet'
Deciduous, spreading tree with dark green foliage. Carries white flowers in late spring and crimson-flushed, scarlet crab apples in autumn.

☼ ◊ Zone 6

Acer palmatum var. **coreanum**
Deciduous, bushy-headed tree or large shrub. Leaves are deeply lobed and mid-green, turning brilliant red in autumn. Small, reddish-purple flowers are borne in spring.

☼ ◊ Zone 6

Cotoneaster frigidus
+ Crataegomespilus dardarii 'Jules d'Asnières'
Crataegus crus-galli

Crataegus ellwangeriana
Crataegus laevigata 'Punicea'
Crataegus monogyna
Crataegus phaenopyrum

HOLLIES, illus. pp.98–9
Malus 'Chilko'
Malus x purpurea
Malus 'Red Jade'

Rhus typhina
Sorbus sargentiana

■ RED

***Acer japonicum* 'Aconitifolium'**
Deciduous, bushy tree or large shrub.
Deeply divided, mid-green leaves turn
red in autumn. Reddish-purple flowers
appear in mid-spring.

☀️◐ ◊ Zone 6

***Acer japonicum* 'Vitifolium'**
Vigorous, deciduous, bushy tree or
large shrub with large, rounded, lobed,
mid-green leaves that turn brilliant red,
orange and purple in autumn.

☀️ ◊ Zone 6

Crataegus pedicellata
Deciduous, spreading tree with sharply
toothed, lobed, dark green leaves that
turn orange and red in autumn. White
flowers with red anthers in late spring
are followed by bright red
fruits in autumn.

☀️ ◊ ① Zone 7

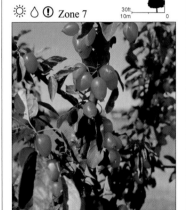

***Malus* 'John Downie'**
Deciduous tree, narrow and upright
when young, conical when mature.
White flowers, borne amid bright green
foliage in late spring, are followed by
large, edible, red-flushed,
orange crab apples in
autumn.

☀️ ◊ Zone 6

Rhus trichocarpa
Deciduous, spreading tree. Large, ash-
like leaves with 13–17 leaflets are
pinkish when young, dark green in
summer and purple-red to orange in
autumn. Bears pendent,
bristly, yellow fruits.

☀️ ◊ Zone 9

Malus prunifolia
Deciduous, spreading tree. Has dark
green leaves and fragrant, white
flowers in mid-spring. In autumn bears
long-lasting, small, red or occasionally
yellowish crab apples.

☀️ ◊ Zone 5

***Acer tataricum* subsp. *ginnala*,**
syn. *A. ginnala* (Amur maple)
Deciduous, spreading tree or large
shrub. Clusters of fragrant, creamy-
white flowers are borne in early
summer amid dainty, bright
green leaves that turn red in
autumn.

☀️ ◊ Zone 2

TREES small AUTUMN INTEREST

■ RED

***Malus* 'Professor Sprenger'**
Deciduous, rounded, dense tree. Dark
green leaves turn yellow in late
autumn. White flowers, pink in bud,
open from mid- to late spring and are
followed by orange-red
crab apples in autumn.

☼ ◊ Zone 5

Acer triflorum
Slow-growing, deciduous, spreading
tree with peeling, grey-brown bark.
Leaves, composed of 3 leaflets, are
dark green, turning brilliant orange-red
in autumn. Clusters of tiny,
yellow-green flowers
appear in late spring.

☼ ◊ Zone 6

***Cornus* 'Eddie's White Wonder'**
Deciduous, spreading tree or shrub.
Large, white bracts, surrounding
insignificant flowers, appear in late
spring. Oval leaves are mid-green,
turning red and purple in
autumn.

☼ ◊ ❶ Zone 7

Plumeria rubra (Frangipani)
Deciduous, spreading tree or large
shrub, sparingly branched. Has fragrant
flowers, in shades of yellow, orange,
pink, red and white, in summer-
autumn. Min. 13°C (55°F).

☼ ◊ ❶

***Malus* x *zumi* 'Calocarpa'**,
syn. *M.* x *z.* var. *calocarpa*
Deciduous, spreading tree. Dark green
leaves are sometimes deeply lobed.
White flowers in late spring are
followed by dense clusters
of long-lasting, cherry-like,
red crab apples in autumn.

☼ ◊ Zone 4

***Malus* 'Marshall Oyama'**
Deciduous, upright tree with dark
green leaves. Pink-flushed, white
flowers borne in late spring are
followed by a profusion of large,
rounded, crimson and
yellow crab apples in
autumn.

☼ ◊ Zone 6

Tecoma stans, syn.
Bignonia stans, *Stenolobium stans*
(Yellow bells, Yellow elder)
Evergreen, rounded, upright tree or
large shrub. Leaves have 5–13 leaflets.
Has funnel-shaped, yellow
flowers from spring to
autumn. Min. 13°C (55°F).

☼ ◊

□ YELLOW

Picrasma quassioides,
syn. *P. ailanthoides* (Quassia)
Deciduous, spreading tree with glossy,
bright green leaves, composed of
9–13 leaflets, that turn brilliant yellow,
orange and red in autumn.

☼ ◊ Zone 6

Malus 'Golden Hornet',
syn. *M.* x *zumi* 'Golden Hornet'
Deciduous, spreading tree with dark
green foliage and open cup-shaped,
white flowers in late spring. In autumn,
branches are weighed down
by a profusion of golden-
yellow crab apples.

☼ ◊ Zone 4b

Crataegus tanacetifolia
Cydonia oblonga 'Lusitanica'
Cydonia oblonga 'Vranja', illus. p.92
HOLLIES, illus. pp.98–9

▭ WHITE–PINK

Bauhinia variegata 'Candida'
Deciduous tree, rounded when young,
spreading with age. Has broadly oval,
deeply notched leaves and fragrant,
pure white flowers, 10cm (4in) across,
in winter-spring or
sometimes later.
Min. 15–18°C (59–64°F).

☼ ◊

Bauhinia variegata
Deciduous, rounded tree with broadly
oval, deeply notched leaves. Fragrant,
magenta to lavender flowers, to 10cm
(4in) across, appear in winter-spring,
sometimes later.
Min. 15–18°C (59–64°F).

☼ ◊

OTHER RECOMMENDED PLANTS:
Dombeya x *cayeuxii*, illus. p.88
Prunus incisa 'February Pink'
Prunus x *subhirtella* 'Autumnalis'

□ YELLOW

Acacia pravissima (Ovens wattle)
Evergreen, spreading, arching tree or
shrub. Has triangular, spine-tipped,
silver-grey phyllodes (flat, leaf-like
stalks) and small heads of bright
yellow flowers in late
winter or early spring.
Min. 5°C (41°F).

☼ ◊

Acacia baileyana
(Cootamundra wattle)
Evergreen, spreading, graceful tree with
arching branches and finely divided,
blue-grey leaves. Clusters of small,
golden-yellow flower heads
appear in winter-spring.
Min. 5°C (41°F).

☼ ◊

Tabebuia chrysotricha
(Golden trumpet tree)
Deciduous, round-headed tree with
dark green leaves, divided into 3–5 oval
leaflets, and rich yellow flowers, 7cm
(3in) long, borne in late
winter or early spring.
Min. 16–18°C (61–4°F).

☼ ◊

Azara microphylla, illus. p.125

Hollies

The common holly, *Ilex aquifolium*, is one of the best-known evergreen trees, but there are many other hollies, including lesser-known *Ilex* cultivars, that make attractive garden plants. In size they range from tall, specimen trees to small shrubs useful in the rock garden or for growing in containers. Hollies respond well to pruning and many may be clipped to form good hedges. Leaves of different species and cultivars may be smooth-edged or spiny and vary considerably in colour, several having gold, yellow, cream, white or grey variegation. Small, often white, male and female flowers, borne on separate plants during summer, are followed by attractive, red, yellow or black berries. In almost all cases hollies are unisexual, that is the berries are borne only on female plants, so to obtain fruits it is usually necessary to grow plants of both sexes. Although some hollies are tender, those described here are hardy in the UK.

I. fargesii var. *brevifolia* ①

I. aquifolium 'Pyramidalis' ①

I. aquifolium 'Argentea Marginata Pendula' ①

I. × *altaclerensis* 'Camelliifolia' ①

I. aquifolium 'Argentea Marginata' ①

I. ciliospinosa ①

I. pernyi ①

I. crenata var. *paludosa* ①

I. fargesii ①

I. aquifolium 'Scotica' ①

I. × *altaclerensis* 'Lawsoniana' ①

I. macrocarpa ①

I. × *koehneana* ①

I. crenata 'Helleri' ①

I. × *altaclerensis* 'Balearica' ①

I. crenata 'Latifolia' ①

I. cornuta 'Burfordii' ①

I. × *altaclerensis* 'N.F. Barnes' ①

I. verticillata ①

I. aquifolium ①

I. opaca ①

I. × *aquipernyi* ①

I. crenata 'Convexa' ①

I. × *altaclerensis* 'Belgica' ①

I. × *meserveae* 'Blue Princess' ①

I. aquifolium 'Silver Milkmaid' ①

TREES small ALL YEAR INTEREST

I. aquifolium 'Silver Queen' ①

I. aquifolium 'Golden Milkboy' ①

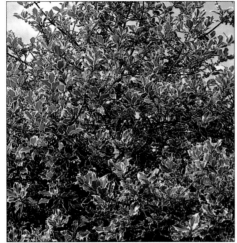

I. aquifolium 'Madame Briot' ①

I. x altaclerensis 'Belgica Aurea' ①

I. aquifolium 'Crispa Aureopicta' ①

I. aquifolium 'Ovata Aurea' ①

I. aquifolium 'Aurifodina' ①

I. aquifolium 'Watereriana' ①

I. serrata f. leucocarpa ①

I. aquifolium 'Pyramidalis Aureomarginata' ①

I. x altaclerensis 'Camelliifolia Variegata' ①

I. purpurea ①

I. crenata 'Variegata' ①

I. pedunculosa ①

Pittosporum crassifolium 'Variegatum'
Evergreen, bushy-headed, dense tree or shrub with grey-green leaves edged with white. Clusters of small, fragrant, deep reddish-purple flowers appear in spring.

☼ ◊ Zone 9?

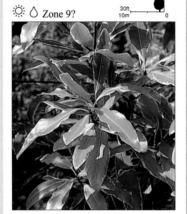

Pittosporum eugenioides 'Variegatum'
Evergreen, columnar tree. Wavy-edged, glossy, dark green leaves have white margins. Honey-scented, pale yellow flowers are borne in spring.

☼ ◊ Zone 9?

Acer laxiflorum, syn.
A. pectinatum subsp. **laxiflorum**
Deciduous, spreading tree with arching branches streaked white and green. In late summer has pale red, winged fruits. Pointed, red-stalked, dark green leaves turn orange in autumn.

☼ ◊ Zone 7

Grevillea banksii
Evergreen, loosely branched tree or tall shrub. Has leaves divided into 5–11 slender leaflets, silky-downy beneath. Spider-like, red flowers appear in dense heads intermittently throughout the year. Min. 10°C (50°F).

☼ ◊ pH ①

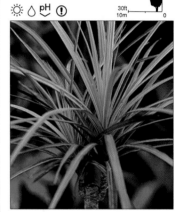

Dracaena marginata 'Tricolor'
Slow-growing, evergreen, upright tree or shrub with narrow, strap-shaped, cream-striped, rich green leaves, prominently edged with red. Min. 13°C (55°F).

☼ ◊

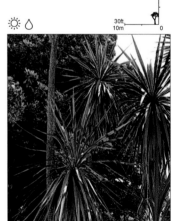

Cordyline australis 'Atropurpurea'
Slow-growing, evergreen tree with purple to purplish-green leaves. Has terminal sprays of white flowers in summer and small, globular, white fruits in autumn. Min. 5°C (41°F).

☼ ◊

OTHER RECOMMENDED PLANTS:
Eriobotrya japonica
Kigelia africana
Pittosporum tenuifolium, illus. p.127

Polyscias guilfoylei 'Victoriae', illus. p.126

TREES small ALL YEAR INTEREST

GREY–GREEN

Leucadendron argenteum
(Silver tree)
Evergreen, conical to columnar tree, spreading with age. Leaves are covered with long, silky, white hairs. Has insignificant flowers set in silvery bracts in autumn-winter. Min. 7°C (45°F).

Butia capitata,
syn. *Cocos capitata* (Jelly palm)
Slow-growing, evergreen palm. Feather-shaped leaves, composed of many leathery leaflets, are strongly arching to recurved, 2m (6ft) or more long. Min. 5°C (41°F).

Carpinus betulus 'Fastigiata',
syn. *C.b.* 'Pyramidalis'
Deciduous, erect tree, with a very distinctive, flame-like outline, that becomes more open with age. Oval, prominently veined, dark green leaves turn yellow and orange in autumn.
Zone 4

Cyathea australis, syn. *Alsophila australis* (Australian tree fern)
Evergreen, upright tree fern with a robust, almost black trunk. Finely divided leaves, 2–4m (6–12ft) long, are light green, bluish beneath. Min. 13°C (55°F).

Eucalyptus perriniana
(Spinning gum)
Fast-growing, evergreen, spreading tree with a wide-branched head. Stems and young leaves are grey-blue; young leaves joined around stems. Leaves on mature trees are long and pendulous. White flowers appear in late summer.
Zone 9?

Meryta sinclairii (Puka, Pukanui)
Evergreen, round-headed tree with large, glossy, deep green leaves. Greenish flowers appear sporadically in spring to autumn, followed by berry-like, black fruits. Min. 5°C (41°F).

Pittosporum dallii
Evergreen, rounded, dense tree or shrub. Has purplish stems and sharply toothed, deep green leaves. Clusters of small, fragrant, shallowly cup-shaped, white flowers are borne in summer.
Zone 9?

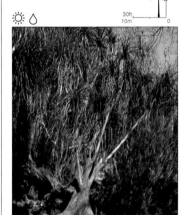

Beaucarnea recurvata, syn. *Nolina recurvata*, *N. tuberculata* (Elephant's foot, Pony-tail)
Slow-growing, evergreen tree or shrub with a sparsely branched stem. Recurving leaves, 1m (3ft) long, persist after turning brown. Min. 7°C (45°F).

Dracaena draco (Dragon tree)
Slow-growing, evergreen tree, eventually with a wide-branched head. Has stiff, lance-shaped, grey- or blue-green leaves. Mature trees bear clusters of orange berries, usually from mid- to late summer. Min. 13°C (55°F).

Lithocarpus henryi
Slow-growing, evergreen, broadly conical tree with glossy, pale green leaves that are long, narrow and pointed.
Zone 9

Dypsis lutescens
(Golden-feather palm, Yellow palm)
Evergreen, suckering palm, forming clumps of robust, cane-like stems. Has long, arching leaves of slender, yellowish-green leaflets. Min. 16°C (61°F).

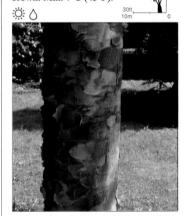

Acer griseum (Paper-bark maple)
Deciduous, spreading tree with striking, peeling, orange-brown bark. Dark green leaves have 3 leaflets and turn red and orange in autumn.
Zone 6

Castanopsis cuspidata
Eucalyptus ficifolia
HOLLIES, illus. pp.98–9
Howea forsteriana

Ligustrum lucidum 'Excelsum Superbum', illus. p.127
Pandanus tectorius
Pisonia umbellifera

Pittosporum crassifolium
Pittosporum tobira
Quercus alnifolia
Quercus coccifera

Ravenala madagascariensis
Sapium sebiferum
Schefflera digitata

CONIFERS large

■ BLUE–GREEN

***Abies concolor* 'Argentea'**, syn.
A.c. 'Candicans'
Conical conifer with silvery foliage
that contrasts well with dark grey bark.
Oblong to ovoid, pale blue
or green cones are 8–12cm
(3–5in) long.

☼ ◊ Zone 4

Pinus* × *holfordiana
(Holford pine)
Broadly conical, open conifer with
large cones, brown when ripe.
Pendent, glaucous blue-green leaves
are held in 5s.

☼ ◊ Zone 7

Cupressus cashmeriana
(Kashmir cypress)
Handsome, broadly conical conifer,
spreading with age, with aromatic
foliage borne in pendent, flat,
glaucous blue sprays. Bears
small, globose, dark brown,
mature cones.

☼ ◊ Zone 7b

**× *Cupressocyparis leylandii*
'Haggerston Grey'**
Vigorous, upright, columnar conifer,
tapering at the apex. Has smooth bark,
becoming stringy with age, flat sprays
of pointed, grey-green leaves,
and dark brown female cones.
A popular screening plant.

☼ ◊ ① Zone 7

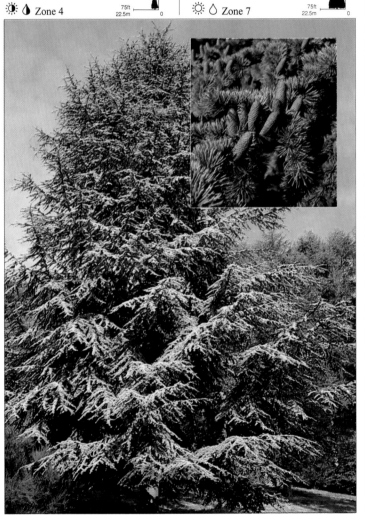

Cedrus atlantica* f. *glauca
(Blue Atlas cedar)
Conical conifer with silvery-blue
foliage that is very bright, especially in
spring. Erect, cylindrical cones are
produced in autumn. Is widely
planted as a specimen tree.

☼ ◊ Zone 6

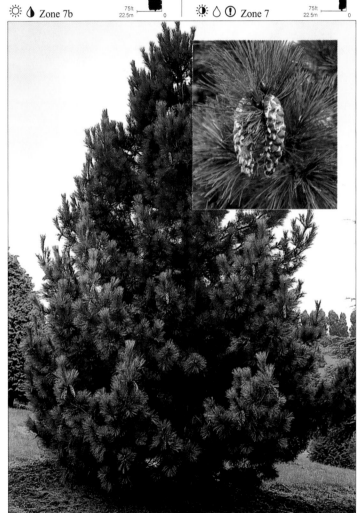

Pinus peuce (Macedonian pine)
Upright conifer, forming a slender
pyramid. Has dense, grey-green foliage
and cylindrical, green cones with white
resin that ripen brown in autumn. Is an
attractive tree that grows
consistently well in all sites.

☼ ◊ Zone 4

OTHER RECOMMENDED PLANTS:
Abies concolor
Abies forrestii, illus. p.105
Abies procera

Cedrus atlantica
Cedrus atlantica f. *fastigiata*
Cedrus deodara
Cedrus libani, illus. p.103

Chamaecyparis lawsoniana 'Triomf van
  Boskoop'
Chamaecyparis lawsoniana 'Wisselii'
Chamaecyparis nootkatensis

Cupressus lusitanica
Juniperus virginiana
Larix kaempferi
Picea pungens

CONIFERS large

■ GREEN

Chamaecyparis lawsoniana 'Intertexta'
Elegant, weeping conifer with aromatic, grey-green foliage carried in lax, pendulous sprays. Old trees become columnar with some splayed branches.

☀ ◐ ⓘ Zone 6

Pseudotsuga menziesii var. glauca (Blue Douglas fir)
Fast-growing, conical conifer with thick, grooved, corky, grey-brown bark, aromatic, glaucous blue-green leaves, and sharply pointed buds. Cones have projecting, 3-pronged bracts.

☀ ◐ Zone 4

Metasequoia glyptostroboides (Dawn redwood)
Fast-growing, deciduous, upright conifer with fibrous, reddish bark. Soft, blue-green leaves turn yellow, pink and red in autumn. Cones are globose to ovoid, 2cm (¾in) long.

☀ ◐ Zone 5b

Pinus strobus (Eastern white pine)
Conifer with an open, sparse, whorled crown. Has grey-green foliage and cylindrical cones. Smooth, grey bark becomes fissured with age. Does not tolerate pollution.

☀ ◐ Zone 2b

Pinus coulteri
(Big-cone pine, Coulter pine)
Fast-growing conifer with large, broadly ovoid, prickly cones, each 1–2kg (2–4½lb). Grey-green leaves in crowded clusters are sparsely set on branches. Grows in all soils, even heavy clays.

☀ ◐ Zone 9

Abies veitchii (Veitch fir)
Upright conifer with dark green leaves, silvery beneath, and cylindrical, violet-blue cones.

☀ ◐ Zone 4

Sequoiadendron giganteum
(Big tree, Giant redwood, Wellingtonia)
Very fast-growing, conical conifer. Has thick, fibrous, red-brown bark and sharp, bluish-green leaves. Is one of the world's largest trees when mature.

☀ ◐ Zone 6

■ GREEN

Cedrus libani (Cedar of Lebanon)
Spreading conifer, usually with several arching stems. Branches carry flat layers of dark grey-green foliage and oblong to ovoid, greyish-pink cones, 8–15cm (3–6in) long.

☼ ◐ Zone 6

Pinus muricata (Bishop pine)
Fast-growing, often flat-topped conifer. Leaves are blue- or grey-green and held in pairs. Ovoid cones, 7–9cm (3–3½in) long, rarely open. Does particularly well in a poor, sandy soil.

☼ ◌ Zone 9

Picea omorika (Serbian spruce)
Narrow, conical conifer, resembling a church spire, with dark green leaves that are white below. Branches are pendulous and arch out at tips. Violet-purple cones age to glossy brown. Grows steadily in all soils.

☼ ◐ Zone 3b

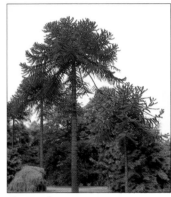

Araucaria araucana
(Chile pine, Monkey puzzle)
Open, spreading conifer with grey bark, wrinkled like elephant hide. Has flattened and sharp, glossy, dark green leaves and 15cm (6in) long cones. Makes a fine specimen tree.

☼ ◐ Zone 7

Pinus ponderosa
(Western yellow pine)
Conical or upright conifer, grown for its distinctive, deeply fissured bark, with smooth, brown plates, and bold greyish-green foliage. Bears ovoid, purplish-brown cones.

☼ ◐ Zone 2b

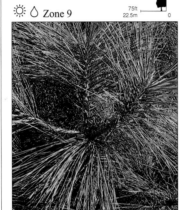

Pinus jeffreyi
(Black pine, Jeffrey pine)
Upright, narrow-crowned conifer with stout, grey-green leaves, 12–26cm (5–10in) long. Bark is black with fine, deep fissures and shoots have an attractive, greyish bloom.

☼ ◌ Zone 5

Pinus wallichiana, syn. *P. chylla*, *P. excelsa*, *P. griffithii*
(Bhutan pine, Himalayan pine)
Conical conifer with long, drooping, blue-green leaves in 5s. Has smooth bark, grey-green on young trees, later fissured and dark, and cylindrical cones.

☼ ◌ Zone 4

Pinus pinaster
(Cluster pine, Maritime pine)
Vigorous, domed conifer with a long, branchless trunk. Has grey-green leaves and whorls of rich brown cones. Purple-brown bark is deeply fissured. Is well-suited to a dry, sandy soil.

☼ ◌ Zone 9

Ginkgo biloba (Maidenhair tree)
Long-lived, deciduous conifer, upright when young, spreading with age. Has fan-shaped, 12cm (5in) long, bright green leaves. Bears ill-smelling fruits, with edible kernels, in late summer and autumn, if male and female plants are grown together. Fruit pulp can cause dermatitis. [Named forms are male and don't produce fruit.]

☼ ◌ ⊕ Zone 3

CONIFERS large

■ GREEN

Pinus nigra subsp. *nigra*
(Austrian pine)
Broadly crowned conifer, with well-spaced branches, often with several stems. Paired, dark green leaves are densely tufted. Tolerates an exposed site.

☼ ◗ Zone 4   100ft 30m / 75ft 22.5m / 0

Pinus radiata, syn. *P. insignis*
(Monterey pine)
Very fast-growing conifer, conical when young, domed when mature. Black bark contrasts well with soft, bright green leaves. Makes an excellent windbreak.

☼ ◗ Zone 9   100ft 30m / 75ft 22.5m / 0

Abies grandis (Giant fir, Grand fir)
Very vigorous, narrow, conical conifer, with a neat habit. Mid-green leaves have an orange aroma when crushed. Cones, 7–8cm (3in) long, ripen red-brown. Makes a useful specimen tree.

☼ ◗ Zone 6   100ft 30m / 75ft 22.5m / 0

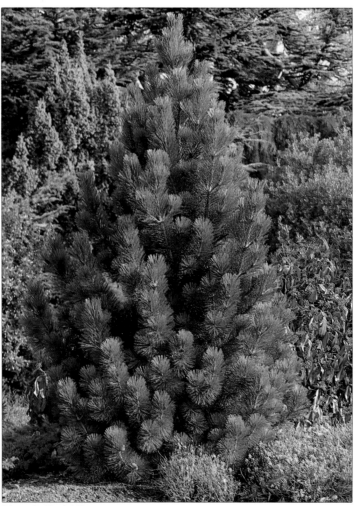

Pinus heldreichii, syn.
P. heldreichii var. *leucodermis*,
P. leucodermis (Bosnian pine)
Dense, conical conifer with dark green leaves held in pairs. Ovoid cones, 5–10cm (2–4in) long, are cobalt-blue in their second summer, brown when ripe.

☼ ◗ Zone 5b   100ft 30m / 75ft 22.5m / 0

Picea abies
(Common spruce, Norway spruce)
Fast-growing, pyramidal conifer with dark green leaves. Narrow, pendulous, glossy, brown cones are 10–20cm (4–8in) long. Much used as a Christmas tree but less useful as an ornamental.

☼ ◗ Zone 2b   100ft 30m / 75ft 22.5m / 0

x *Cupressocyparis leylandii* 'Harlequin'
(Variegated Leyland cypress)
Fast-growing, columnar conifer with a conical tip. Grey-green foliage, with patches of clear ivory-white, is held in plume-like sprays.

☼ ◗ ① Zone 7   100ft 30m / 75ft 22.5m / 0

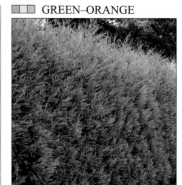

x *Cupressocyparis leylandii* 'Castlewellan'
Upright, vigorous conifer, slightly slower-growing than the species, grown for its bronze-yellow foliage.

☼ ◗ ① Zone 7   100ft 30m / 75ft 22.5m / 0

Picea orientalis 'Skylands'
Dense, upright, graceful conifer that retains the gold coloration of short, glossy leaves throughout the year. Narrowly oblong cones are dark purple, males turning brick-red in spring.

☼ ◗ Zone 5   100ft 30m / 75ft 22.5m / 0

Taxodium distichum
(Bald cypress, Swamp cypress)
Deciduous, broadly conical conifer with small, globose to ovoid cones. Yew-like, fresh green leaves turn rich brown in late autumn. Grows in a very wet site, producing special breathing roots.

☼ ◗ Zone 5   100ft 30m / 75ft 22.5m / 0

x *Cupressocyparis leylandii* 'Robinson's Gold'
Picea orientalis 'Aurea'
Thuja plicata 'Aurea'

CONIFERS medium

■■ BLUE–GREEN

Picea pungens 'Koster'
Upright conifer with whorled branches. Has scaly, grey bark and attractive, needle-like, silvery-blue leaves, which fade to green with age. Tends to suffer from aphid attack.

☼ ◊ Zone 2

Picea glauca 'Coerulea'
Dense, upright, conical conifer with needle-like, blue-green to silver leaves and ovoid, light brown cones.

☼ ◊ Zone 2

Juniperus chinensis 'Keteleeri'
Dense, regular, slender, columnar conifer with scale-like, aromatic, greyish-green leaves and peeling, brown bark. Makes a reliable, free-fruiting form for formal use.

☼ ◊ Zone 5

Picea breweriana
(Brewer's spruce)
Upright conifer with level branches and completely pendulous branchlets, to 2m (6ft) long. Leaves are stout and blue-green. Bears oblong, purplish cones, 6–8cm (2½–3in) long.

☼ ◊ Zone 5b

Picea engelmannii (Engelmann spruce, Mountain spruce)
Broadly conical conifer. Leaves encircle shoots and are prickly or soft, lush, glaucous or bluish-green. Bears small, cylindrical cones. Is good for a very poor site.

☼ ◊ Zone 3

Abies forrestii (Forrest fir)
Conical conifer with an open, whorled habit and smooth, silvery-grey bark. Shoots are red-brown, with spherical, white buds. Has dark green leaves, silvery-white beneath, and ovoid-cylindrical, violet-blue cones.

☼ ◊ Zone 6

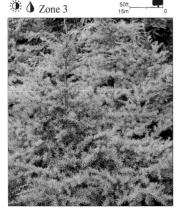

Tsuga mertensiana 'Glauca'
Slow-growing, dwarf or medium-sized, columnar-conical conifer with red-brown shoots bearing spirally arranged, needle-like, flattened, glaucous, silver-grey leaves. Cones are yellow-green to purple, ripening to dark brown.

☼ ◊ Zone 6

Chamaecyparis lawsoniana 'Pembury Blue'
Magnificent, conical conifer with aromatic, bright blue-grey foliage held in pendulous sprays.

☼ ◊ ① Zone 6

Pinus parviflora
(Japanese white pine)
Slow-growing, conical or spreading conifer with fine, bluish foliage and purplish-brown bark. Leaves are held in 5s. Bears ovoid cones, 5–10cm (2–4in) long.

☼ ◊ Zone 5b

OTHER RECOMMENDED PLANTS:
Abies lasiocarpa
Chamaecyparis lawsoniana 'Fletcheri'
Chamaecyparis lawsoniana 'Wisselii'

Chamaecyparis nootkatensis 'Pendula'
Chamaecyparis pisifera 'Squarrosa'
Cupressus arizonica var. *glabra*
Cupressus cashmeriana, illus. p.101

Juniperus recurva
Picea glauca
Picea likiangensis
Picea mariana

Picea pungens 'Hoopsii'
Pinus armandii
Pinus x *holfordiana*, illus. p.101
Tsuga mertensiana

CONIFERS medium

◼ GREEN

Fitzroya cupressoides, syn.
F. patagonica (Patagonian cypress)
Vase-shaped to sprawling conifer with
red-brown bark that peels in long
strips. White-lined, dark green
leaves are held in
open, pendulous,
wiry sprays.

☀ ◌ Zone 7

Pinus rigida (Northern pitch pine)
Conical conifer, often with sucker
shoots from trunk. Twisted, dark green
leaves are borne in 3s. Ovoid to
globose, red-brown cones, 3–8cm
(1¼–3in) long, persist,
open, on the tree.

☀ ◌ Zone 5

Cunninghamia lanceolata
(Chinese fir)
Upright conifer, mop-headed on a dry
site, with distinctive, thick and deeply
furrowed, red-brown bark. Glossy,
green leaves are sharply
pointed and lance-shaped.

◐ ◌ Zone 7

Calocedrus decurrens,
syn. *Libocedrus decurrens*
(Incense cedar)
Upright conifer with short, horizontal
branches and flaky, grey bark, brown
beneath. Has flat sprays of
aromatic, dark green leaves.
Resists honey fungus.

◐ ◌ Zone 6

Podocarpus salignus
Upright conifer. Leaves are willow-
like, 5–11cm (2–4in) long, and glossy
above. Attractive, fibrous, red-brown
bark peels in strips.

☀ ◌ Zone 9

Phyllocladus trichomanoides
Slow-growing conifer, conical when
young, developing a more rounded top
with age. Leaf-like, deep green,
modified shoots, 10–15cm (4–6in)
long, have 5–10 lobed
segments. Min. 2°C (35°F).

☀ ◌

Pinus cembra (Swiss stone pine)
Dense, conical conifer with dark green
or bluish-green leaves grouped in 5s.
Ovoid, bluish or purplish cones, 6–8cm
(2½– 3in) long, ripen brown.

☀ ◌ Zone 2

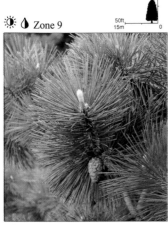

Pinus thunbergii
(Japanese black pine)
Rounded conifer, conical when young,
with dark green leaves and grey-brown
cones, 4–6cm (1½–2½in) long. Buds are
covered with a silky
cobweb of white hairs.
Tolerates sea spray well.

☀ ◌ Zone 4b

Austrocedrus chilensis,
syn. *Libocedrus chilensis*
(Chilean incense cedar)
Conical conifer with flattened, feathery
sprays of 4-ranked, small, dark green
leaves, white beneath.

☀ ◌ Zone 9

Sciadopitys verticillata
(Japanese umbrella pine)
Conical conifer with reddish-brown
bark. Deep green leaves, yellowish
beneath, are whorled at the ends of
shoots, like umbrella
spokes. Ovoid cones ripen
over 2 years.

☀ ◌ Zone 6

Pinus contorta var. *latifolia*
(Lodgepole pine)
Conical conifer with bright green
leaves, 6–9cm (2½–4in) long. Small,
oval cones remain closed on the tree.
Is suitable for a wet or
coastal site.

☀ ◌ Zone 1

Abies amabilis
Abies delavayi
Abies veitchii, illus. p.102
Chamaecyparis lawsoniana 'Kilmacurragh'

Juniperus chinensis
Picea omorika, illus. p.103
Pinus coulteri, illus. p.102
Pinus heldreichii, illus. p.104

Pinus wallichiana, illus. p.103
Saxegothaea conspicua
Taxus baccata
Taxus baccata 'Fastigiata'

Thuja orientalis
Tsuga caroliniana
Tsuga diversifolia

Pseudolarix amabilis,
syn. *P. kaempferi* (Golden larch)
Deciduous, open-crowned conifer,
slow-growing when young. Has
clusters of linear, fresh green leaves,
2.5–6cm (1–2½in) long,
which gradually turn bright
orange-gold in autumn.

☼ ◑ Zone 5b

Pinus banksiana (Jack pine)
Slender, conical, scrubby-looking
conifer with fresh green leaves in
twisted, divergent pairs. Curved cones,
3–6cm (1¼–2½in) long, point forward
along shoots.

☼ ◯ Zone 1

Picea morrisonicola
(Taiwan spruce)
Upright, conical conifer, becoming
columnar with age. Needle-like, deep
green leaves are pressed down on
slender, pale brown shoots.
Cones are cylindrical and
5–7cm (2–3in) long.

☼ ◑ Zone 8

Torreya californica
(California nutmeg)
Upright conifer with very prickly,
glossy, dark green leaves, yellowish-
green beneath, similar to those of yew.
Fruits are olive-like.

☼ ◑ Zone 8

**Chamaecyparis lawsoniana
'Green Pillar'**
Conical conifer with upright branches.
Aromatic foliage is bright green and
becomes tinged with gold in spring. Is
suitable for hedging as
requires little clipping.

☼ ◑ ① Zone 6

Chamaecyparis thyoides
(White false cypress)
Upright conifer with aromatic, green
or blue-grey leaves in rather erratic,
fan-shaped sprays on very fine shoots.
Cones are small, round and
glaucous blue-grey.

☼ ◑ ① Zone 4

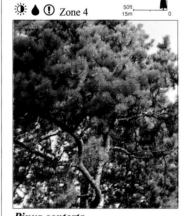

Pinus contorta
(Beach pine, Shore pine)
Dense, conical or domed conifer. Has
paired, bright green leaves and conical
to ovoid cones, 3–8cm (1¼–3in) long.
Is well-suited to a windy,
barren site and tolerates
waterlogged ground.

☼ ◯ Zone 4

Tsuga canadensis (Canada
hemlock, Eastern hemlock)
Broadly conical conifer, often with
several stems. Grey shoots have
2-ranked, dark green leaves, often
inverted to show silver lines
beneath. Cones are ovoid
and light brown.

☼ ◑ Zone 4

Pinus halepensis (Aleppo pine)
Conical, open-crowned conifer with an
open growth of bright green leaves,
6–11cm (2½–4½in) long, and ovoid,
glossy, brown cones. Young trees retain
glaucous, juvenile needles
for several years.

☼ ◯ Zone 9?

**Chamaecyparis lawsoniana
'Lanei'**
Upright conifer that forms a neat
column of aromatic, golden-yellow-
tipped foliage.

☼ ◑ ① Zone 6

Pinus virginiana
(Scrub pine, Virginia pine)
Conifer of untidy habit. Grey- to
yellow-green leaves are 4–7cm (1½–3in)
long. Young shoots have a pinkish-
white bloom. Bears oblong
to conical, red-brown
cones, 6cm (2½in) long.

☼ ◯ Zone 3

Chamaecyparis obtusa 'Crippsii', illus.
p.109
Chamaecyparis pisifera 'Filifera Aurea',
illus. p.111

Chamaecyparis pisifera 'Plumosa'
Cupressus macrocarpa 'Goldcrest', illus.
p.109
Juniperus chinensis 'Aurea'

Juniperus drupacea
Pinus densiflora
Taxus baccata 'Fastigiata Aurea'
Thuja occidentalis

Thuja occidentalis 'Fastigiata'
Thujopsis dolabrata

CONIFERS small

◻ GREEN

Juniperus chinensis 'Robust Green', syn. *J. virginiana* 'Robusta Green'
Slow-growing, column-like, conical conifer, making only 7–8cm (3in) a year, with aromatic, green foliage and small, grey-green juniper berries.

☀ ◑ Zone 4

Pinus bungeana (Lace-bark pine)
Slow-growing, bushy conifer with dark green foliage, planted for its exquisite, grey-green bark that flakes to reveal creamy-yellow patches, darkening to red or purple.

☀ ◑ Zone 5b

Picea mariana 'Doumetii'
Densely branched, globose or broadly conical conifer with short, needle-like, silvered, dark green leaves and pendulous, ovoid, purplish cones.

☀ ◑ Zone 3

Chamaecyparis lawsoniana 'Columnaris'
Narrow, upright conifer that forms a neat column of aromatic, blue-grey foliage. Will tolerate poor soil and some clipping. Is an effective, small, specimen tree.

☀ ◑ ① Zone 6

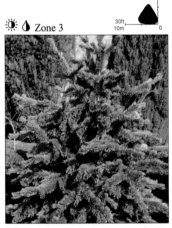

Pinus aristata (Bristle-cone pine)
Slow-growing, bushy conifer. Leaves are in bundles of 5, very dense and blue-white to grey-green, flecked with white resin. Ovoid cones, 4–10cm (1½–4in) long, have bristly prickles. Is the oldest-known living plant, over 4000 years old.

☀ ◊ Zone 3

Juniperus recurva
(Drooping juniper, Himalayan weeping juniper)
Slow-growing, conical conifer with aromatic, incurved, grey- or blue-green leaves and fleshy, black berries. Smooth bark flakes in thin sheets.

☀ ◊ Zone 8

Pinus sylvestris 'Fastigiata', syn. *P.s.* f. *fastigiata*
Upright conifer with erect branches forming a narrow, obelisk shape. Has flaky, red-brown bark, blue-green foliage and conical cones. Suffers wind-damage in an exposed site.

☀ ◊ Zone 3

Juniperus chinensis 'Obelisk'
Slender, irregularly columnar conifer. Has ascending branches and long, prickly, needle-like, aromatic, dark green leaves. Tolerates a wide range of soils and conditions but is particularly suited to a hot, dry site.

☀ ◊ Zone 4

OTHER RECOMMENDED PLANTS:
Cephalotaxus harringtonii
Chamaecyparis lawsoniana 'Ellwoodii'
Chamaecyparis lawsoniana 'Fletcheri'

Juniperus communis
Juniperus rigida
Juniperus scopulorum 'Skyrocket', illus. p.110

Juniperus squamata 'Meyeri'
Juniperus virginiana 'Hetzii'
Picea breweriana, illus. p.105
Pinus pumila

Podocarpus alpinus
Podocarpus macrophyllus
Pseudotsuga menziesii 'Fletcheri'
Taxus baccata 'Adpressa'

Pinus cembroides
(Mexican stone pine, Pinyon)
Slow-growing, bushy conifer, rarely
more than 6–7m (20–22ft) high. Scaly
bark is a striking silver-grey or greyish-
brown. Leaves, in 2s and
3s, are sparse and dark
green to grey-green.

☼ ◊ Zone 8

***Thujopsis dolabrata* 'Variegata'**
Slow-growing, broadly conical, bushy
conifer. Stout, hatchet-shaped leaves
have irregular, creamy patches above
and are silvery beneath.

☼◐ ◊ Zone 6

Taxus cuspidata (Japanese yew)
Evergreen, spreading conifer. Leaves
are dark green above, yellowish-green
beneath, sometimes becoming tinged
red-brown in cold weather. Tolerates
very dry and shady
conditions.

☼ ◊ ⊘ Zone 4

***Chamaecyparis obtusa* 'Crippsii'**
Attractive, small-garden, conical
conifer, grown for its flattened sprays
of aromatic, bright golden foliage. Bark
is stringy and red-brown. Cones are
round, 1cm (½in) across,
and brown.

☼◐ ◊ ⊘ Zone 5b

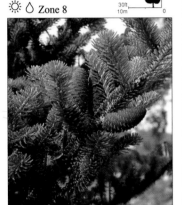

Abies koreana (Korean fir)
Broadly conical conifer. Produces
cylindrical, violet-blue cones when less
than 1m (3ft) tall. Leaves are dark
green above, silver beneath.

☼◐ ◊ Zone 4

***Cryptomeria japonica*
'Pyramidata'**
Narrowly columnar or obelisk-shaped
conifer. Foliage is blue-green when
young, maturing to dark green.

☼ ◊ Zone 6

***Cedrus deodara* 'Aurea'**
Slow-growing, upright conifer with
pendent branch tips and golden-yellow
leaves when young in spring-summer.
Foliage matures to yellowish-green.
Makes a dramatic, small-
garden evergreen.

☼◐ ◊ Zone 6

***Cryptomeria japonica* 'Cristata'**
Conical conifer with twisted, curved
shoots and soft, fibrous bark. Foliage is
bright green, ageing brown.

☼◐ ◊ Zone 6b

Pinus pinea
(Stone pine, Umbrella pine)
Conifer with a rounded crown on a
short trunk. Leaves are dark green, but
blue-green, juvenile foliage is retained
on young trees. Broadly
ovoid cones ripen shiny
brown; seeds are edible.

☼ ◊ Zone 9?

***Cupressus macrocarpa*
'Goldcrest'**
Fast-growing, conical conifer with
aromatic, golden-yellow foliage held in
plume-like sprays that are useful in
flower arrangements.
Dislikes clipping.

☼ ◊ Zone 8

Chamaecyparis obtusa 'Tetragona Aurea'
Taxus baccata Aurea Group, illus. p.111
Taxus baccata 'Semperaurea'
Thuja koraiensis

Thuja occidentalis 'Rheingold'
Tsuga canadensis 'Aurea', illus. p.111

Dwarf conifers

Dwarf conifers are valuable plants, especially for the small garden, requiring very little attention and providing year-round interest. They can be planted as features in their own right, displaying to advantage their varied shapes, habits and often striking colours, or, in the rock garden for example, to provide scale or act as a foil for other plants such as bulbs. Several species and cultivars are spreading and good for ground cover.

Almost all conifers are suitable for a wide range of growing conditions, although *Cedrus* and *Juniperus* do not tolerate shade and *Juniperus* and *Pinus* are best for dry, freely drained, sandy soils. Most *Abies*, *Taxus*, *Thuja* and *Tsuga* are particularly shade tolerant. Some species may be clipped to form a low hedge but new growth will seldom be made if plants are cut back into wood more than 3 or 4 years old.

Picea pungens 'Montgomery'

Abies lasiocarpa var. **arizonica 'Compacta'**

Juniperus squamata 'Holger'

Pinus sylvestris 'Doone Valley'

Picea × mariorika 'Gnom'

Juniperus scopulorum 'Springbank'

Juniperus squamata 'Blue Star'

Juniperus horizontalis 'Douglasii'

Juniperus squamata 'Chinese Silver'

Abies concolor 'Compacta'

Juniperus virginiana 'Grey Owl'

Juniperus × pfitzeriana 'Glauca'

Juniperus sabina 'Mas'

Juniperus chinensis 'Stricta'

Thuja occidentalis 'Caespitosa' ①

Microbiota decussata

Juniperus procumbens

Juniperus scopulorum 'Skyrocket'

Juniperus procumbens 'Nana'

Juniperus horizontalis 'Turquoise Spreader'

Abies balsamea 'Nana'

Abies cephalonica 'Meyer's Dwarf'

Pseudotsuga menziesii 'Fretsii'

Abies lasiocarpa 'Roger Watson'

Picea mariana 'Nana'

Podocarpus nivalis

Juniperus sabina 'Cupressifolia'

Juniperus recurva 'Densa'

Juniperus sabina var. **tamariscifolia**

Picea abies 'Ohlendorffii'

Picea abies 'Reflexa'

Pinus sylvestris 'Watereri'

Pseudotsuga menziesii 'Oudemansii'

Chamaecyparis lawsoniana 'Gnome' ①

Chamaecyparis lawsoniana 'Minima' ①

Picea abies 'Gregoryana'

Chamaecyparis obtusa 'Intermedia' ①

Juniperus × *pfitzeriana* 'William Pfitzer'

Pinus heldreichii 'Smidtii'

Chamaecyparis obtusa 'Nana Pyramidalis' ①

Juniperus communis 'Hibernica'

Picea glauca var. *albertiana* 'Conica'

Cedrus libani 'Sargentii'

Pinus heldreichii 'Compact Gem'

Thuja orientalis 'Aurea Nana' ①

Thuja orientalis 'Semperaurea' ①

Thuja occidentalis 'Filiformis' ①

Thuja plicata 'Hillieri' ①

Juniperus chinensis 'Expansa Variegata'

Juniperus × *pfitzeriana* 'Aurea'

Juniperus chinensis 'Plumosa Aurea'

Cryptomeria japonica 'Spiralis'

Juniperus chinensis 'Blue and Gold'

Cryptomeria japonica 'Sekkan-sugi'

Taxus baccata 'Dovastonii Aurea' ①

Chamaecyparis obtusa 'Nana Aurea' ①

Chamaecyparis pisifera 'Filifera Aurea' ①

Thuja plicata 'Collyer's Gold' ①

Taxus baccata Aurea Group ①

Tsuga canadensis 'Aurea'

Pinus sylvestris 'Aurea'

Pinus sylvestris 'Gold Coin'

Abies nordmanniana 'Golden Spreader'

Thuja plicata 'Stoneham Gold' ①

Cryptomeria japonica 'Elegans Compacta'

111

SHRUBS

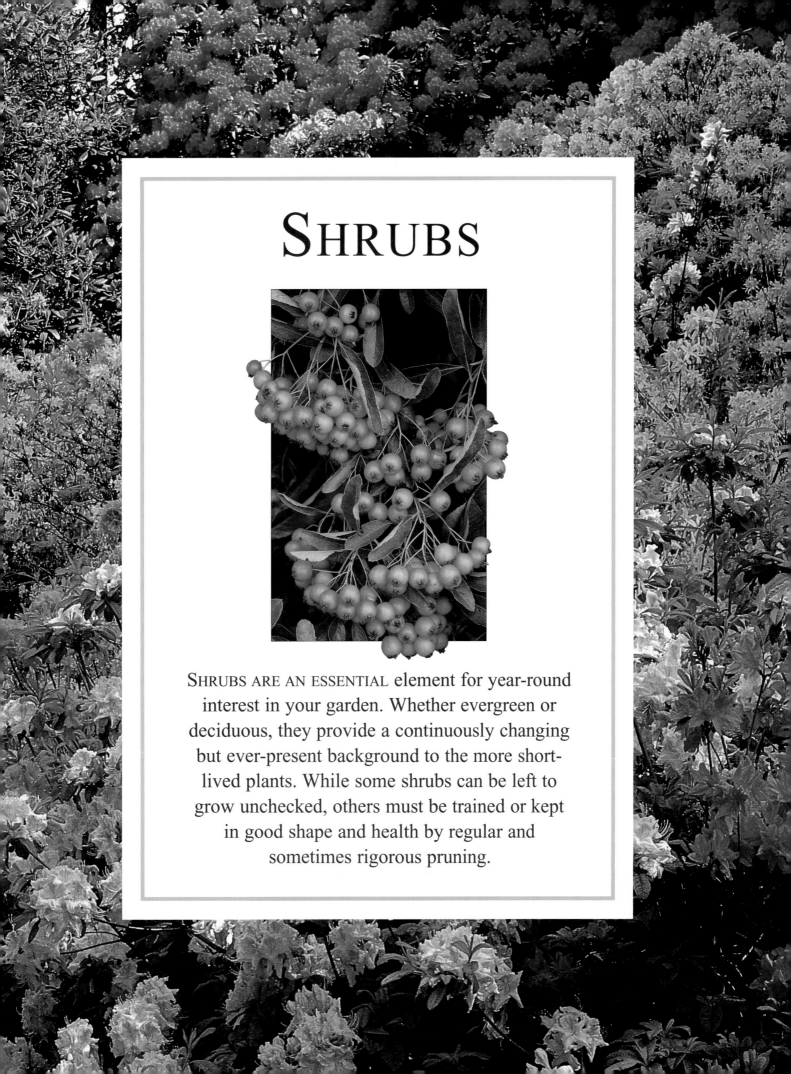

SHRUBS ARE AN ESSENTIAL element for year-round interest in your garden. Whether evergreen or deciduous, they provide a continuously changing but ever-present background to the more short-lived plants. While some shrubs can be left to grow unchecked, others must be trained or kept in good shape and health by regular and sometimes rigorous pruning.

Shrubs

Shrubs can form the backbone of your garden design, and with their variety of foliage, flowers, fruits and stems they also provide interest through the seasons.

WHAT ARE SHRUBS?

Shrub are woody-stemmed, deciduous or evergreen plants that branch freely at or near ground level. Some shrubs grow to more than 6m (20ft) in height, although most species and cultivars attain less than half this size. There is some overlap between shrubs and other plant groups because larger shrubs, such as certain lilacs (*Syringa* species and cultivars), can be grown on a single stem and may equally well be classified as trees, while others, called sub-shrubs, are woody only at the base. In these, as in ceratostigma and fuchsias, softer top growth dies back annually with the onset of winter frosts, and so they are commonly treated as herbaceous

COLOURFUL UNDERPLANTING
Above: The flowering stems of Exochorda x macrantha *'The Bride' arch gracefully above forget-me-nots* (Myosotis sylvatica), *daisies* (Bellis perennis) *and* Tulipa *'Couleur Cardinal'.*

EYE-CATCHING IMPACT
Above right: In a glorious scheme, the golds of senecio, Hypericum *'Hidcote' and violas are set against greys of santolina and* Stachys byzantina.

CONTRASTING FOLIAGE
Right: The golden leaves of Choisya ternata SUNDANCE *('Lich') provide a glowing contrast with those of* Cotinus coggygria *'Royal Purple' and* Berberis thunbergii *'Rose Glow'.*

perennials in cold climates. Some shrubs, such as *Jasminum nudiflorum*, can be wall trained, and many are grown like this because it is the neatest way to manage their sprawling growth. They also benefit from the additional warmth and shelter a wall provides, giving them some frost protection and helping their wood to ripen and so improve flowering.

CHOOSING SHRUBS

When selecting a shrub, as with all garden plants, it is essential to match its hardiness and cultural requirements to the conditions in your garden. It is also vital to consider the shrub's final dimensions and to site it with sufficient room to mature. If you frequently have to prune a shrub to restrict its size, not only does this make unnecessary work but it may also weaken that shrub's resistance to disease.

DESIGNING WITH SHRUBS

Whatever the size or style of your garden, the permanent woody structure of shrubs can form a key element in its framework. Many shrubs can be used formally or informally to create hedges, enclosures or screens. These range in size from small, domed forms, as in *Buxus microphylla* 'Green Pillow', to almost tree-like rhododendrons and amelanchiers.

The low, spreading, prostrate or mat-forming shrubs, such as *Juniperus procumbens* or *Dryas octopetala*, or the tiered branch structure of shrubs such as *Viburnum plicatum* 'Mariesii' and *Cornus alternifolia*, provide strong horizontal lines in a composition. These can be planted so they lead the eye to contrasting rounded forms, found in many hebes or *Spiraea japonica* and its variants, or to the strong verticals of *Eucryphia* x *nymansensis* 'Nymansay' or *Viburnum dentatum*, which may also be used to make a focal point.

Certain shrubs are ideal for topiary, but they must be able to tolerate close regular clipping and preferably have small leaves that permit fine surface texture and detailed shaping. Suitable shrubs include box (*Buxus*), yew (*Taxus*) and *Lonicera nitida*.

The gracefully arching or weeping shrubs, among them *Kerria japonica* 'Pleniflora', *Forsythia suspensa*, *Kolkwitzia amabilis* and *Malus* x *arnoldiana* can be used to link other elements in a border.

Shrubs can be planted alone in a shrub border, or in a mixed border as a backdrop to the more

SHRUBS IN TUBS
Left: In this planting of elegant simplicity, the pink flowers of a standard fuchsia are echoed by an underplanting of pastel busy lizzies (Impatiens). After a prolonged display, the container can be moved under glass for protection during winter.

transient bulbs, annuals and perennials. Compact shrubs such as bay (*Laurus*) are ideal for growing in containers.

MAINTAINING YEAR-ROUND INTEREST

Providing fragrance and colour during the warmer months is relatively simple. For autumn interest, pyracanthas, cotoneasters and *Skimmia japonica* have brilliantly coloured fruits, while most species of euonymus, disanthus and enkianthus offer vibrant foliage. In winter, the spirits can be lifted with the fragrant flowers of witch hazel (*Hamamelis*) and *Lonicera* x *purpusii*, and the coloured stems of *Cornus alba* 'Sibirica' and *Rubus biflorus*, while the swags of *Garrya elliptica* come into their own in the soft, golden winter sun.

SIZE CATEGORIES USED WITHIN THIS GROUP		
Large	**Medium**	**Small**
over 3m (10ft)	1.5–3m (5–10ft)	up to 1.5m (5ft)

AUTUMN COLOUR
Top: Hamamelis x intermedia *'Diane', which bears its spidery, deep red flowers from mid- to late winter, gives added ornamental value with its vibrant autumn colour.*

WINTER INTEREST
Above: The vivid red berries of a female Skimmia japonica, *produced where plants of both sexes are grown together, persist well into winter and are at their most perfect when rimed with frost.*

☐ WHITE

Osmanthus delavayi,
syn. *Siphonosmanthus delavayi*
Evergreen, rounded, bushy shrub with
arching branches. Has small, glossy,
dark green leaves and a profusion of
very fragrant, tubular, white
flowers from mid- to late
spring.

☀ ◊ Zone 8

Pieris japonica
Evergreen, rounded, bushy, dense
shrub with glossy, dark green foliage
that is bronze when young. Produces
drooping racemes of white flowers
during spring.

☀◑ ◊ pH ⚠ Zone 5b

Amelanchier lamarckii
Deciduous, spreading shrub. Young
leaves unfold bronze as abundant
sprays of star-shaped, white flowers
open from mid- to late spring. Foliage
matures to dark green, then
turns brilliant red and
orange in autumn.

☀ ◊ Zone 4

Osmanthus x burkwoodii,
syn. x *Osmarea burkwoodii*
Evergreen, rounded, dense shrub.
Glossy foliage is dark green and sets
off a profusion of small, very fragrant,
white flowers from mid-
to late spring.

☀ ◊ Zone 7

Malus sargentii,
syn. *M. toringo* subsp. *sargentii*
Deciduous, spreading shrub or small
tree. A profusion of white flowers in
late spring is followed by long-lasting,
deep red fruits. Oval, dark
green leaves are sometimes
lobed.

☀ ◊ Zone 5

Anopterus glandulosus
Evergreen, bushy shrub or,
occasionally, small tree. Has narrow,
glossy, dark green leaves, amid which
clusters of cup-shaped, white or pink
flowers appear from mid-
to late spring.
Min. 2°C (36°F).

☀ ◊ pH

Viburnum plicatum 'Mariesii'
Deciduous, bushy, spreading shrub
with tiered branches clothed in dark
green leaves, which turn reddish-purple
in autumn. Large, rounded heads of
flowers with white bracts
appear in late spring and
early summer.

☀ ◊ ⚠ Zone 5b

Dipelta yunnanensis
Deciduous, arching shrub with peeling
bark and glossy leaves. In late spring
produces tubular, creamy-white
flowers, marked orange inside.

☀ ◊ Zone 8

Staphylea pinnata (Bladder nut)
Deciduous, upright shrub that in late
spring carries clusters of white flowers,
tinted pink with age, followed by
bladder-like, green fruits. Foliage
is divided and bright green.

☀ ◊ Zone 7

OTHER RECOMMENDED PLANTS:
Amelanchier canadensis
Amelanchier laevis, illus. p.85
CAMELLIAS, illus. pp.128–9

Exochorda racemosa
Halesia tetraptera
HEATHERS, illus. pp.178–9
LILACS, illus. p.120

Lophomyrtus bullata
MAGNOLIAS, illus. p.75
Parrotiopsis jacquemontiana
Pieris formosa 'Henry Price'

Poncirus trifoliata
Prunus laurocerasus
RHODODENDRONS, illus. pp.132–4
Staphylea colchica

◼◻◻ WHITE–RED

Dipelta floribunda
Vigorous, deciduous, upright, tree-like shrub with peeling, pale brown bark. Fragrant, pale pink flowers, marked yellow inside, open in late spring and early summer. Has pointed, mid-green leaves.

☼ ◐ Zone 7

Enkianthus campanulatus
Deciduous, bushy, spreading shrub with red shoots and tufts of dull green leaves that turn bright red in autumn. Small, bell-shaped, red-veined, creamy-yellow flowers appear in late spring.

☼ ◐ pH Zone 5b

Viburnum × carlcephalum
Deciduous, rounded, bushy shrub. In late spring large, rounded heads of pink buds open to fragrant, white flowers. These are borne amid dark green foliage that often turns red in autumn.

☼ ◐ ⓘ Zone 6

Staphylea holocarpa 'Rosea'
Deciduous, upright shrub or spreading, small tree. From mid- to late spring bears pink flowers, followed by bladder-like, pale green fruits. Bronze, young leaves mature to blue-green.

☼ ◐ Zone 7

Photinia × fraseri 'Birmingham'
Evergreen, upright, bushy, dense shrub with glossy, dark green leaves that are bright purple-red when young. Broad heads of small, white flowers are carried in late spring.

☼ ◐ Zone 7

◼◻◻ PURPLE-ORANGE

Daphniphyllum macropodum, syn. D. himalense subsp. macropodum
Evergreen, bushy, dense shrub with stout shoots and dark green leaves. Small flowers, green on female plants, purplish on male plants, appear in late spring.

☼ ◐ Zone 8

Corylopsis glabrescens
Deciduous, open shrub. Oval leaves, with bristle-like teeth along margins, are dark green above, blue-green beneath. Drooping spikes of fragrant, bell-shaped, pale yellow flowers appear in mid-spring on bare branches.

☼ ◐ pH Zone 7

Berberis darwinii
(Darwin's barberry)
Vigorous, evergreen, arching shrub. Has small, glossy, dark green leaves and a profusion of rounded, deep orange-yellow flowers from mid- to late spring, followed by bluish berries.

☼ ◐ ⓘ Zone 7

SHRUBS large SUMMER INTEREST

☐ WHITE

Escallonia leucantha
Evergreen, upright shrub. Narrow, oval, glossy, dark green leaves set off large racemes of small, shallowly cup-shaped, white flowers in mid-summer.

☀ ◊ Zone 9

Olearia virgata
Evergreen, arching, graceful shrub with very narrow, dark grey-green leaves. Produces an abundance of small, star-shaped, white flower heads in early summer, arranged in small clusters along stems.

☀ ◊ Zone 8

Viburnum rhytidophyllum
Vigorous, evergreen, open shrub with long, narrow, deep green leaves. Dense heads of small, creamy-white flowers in late spring and early summer are succeeded by red fruits that mature to black.

☀ ◊ ❢ Zone 5b

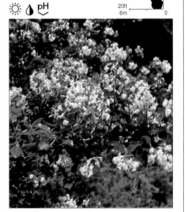

Styrax officinalis
Deciduous, loose to dense shrub or small tree. Fragrant, bell-shaped, white flowers appear in early summer among oval, dark green leaves with greyish-white undersides.
Min. 2°C (35°F).

☀ ◊ pH

Sparrmannia africana
(African hemp)
Evergreen, erect shrub or small tree. Has large, shallowly lobed leaves and clusters of white flowers, with yellow and red-purple stamens, in late spring and summer.
Min. 7°C (45°F).

☀ ◊

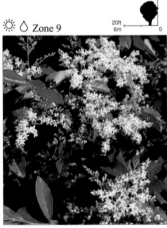

Ligustrum sinense
Deciduous or semi-evergreen, bushy, upright shrub with oval, pale green leaves. Large panicles of fragrant, tubular, white flowers are borne in mid-summer, followed by small, purplish-black fruits.

☀ ◊ ❢ Zone 8

Buddleja davidii 'Peace'
Vigorous, deciduous, arching shrub. Long, pointed, dark green leaves, white-felted beneath, set off long plumes of fragrant, white flowers from mid-summer to autumn.

☀ ◊ Zone 5b

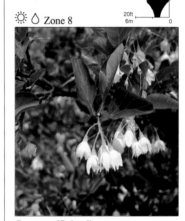

Escallonia 'Iveyi'
Evergreen, upright shrub. Glossy, dark green foliage sets off large racemes of fragrant, tubular, pure white flowers, with short lobes, borne from mid- to late summer.

☀ ◊ Zone 8

Xanthoceras sorbifolium
Deciduous, upright shrub or small tree with bright green leaves divided into many slender leaflets. In late spring and early summer produces spikes of white flowers with red patches inside at the base of the petals.

☀ ◊ Zone 4b

OTHER RECOMMENDED PLANTS:
Clethra arborea
Clethra barbinervis, illus. p.138
Cotoneaster lacteus, illus. p.125

Cotoneaster 'Rothschildianus'
Cotoneaster x *watereri* 'John Waterer'
Deutzia scabra, illus. p.136
Elaeocarpus cyaneus

Eucryphia milliganii, illus. p.137
HEATHERS, illus. pp.178–9
Hibiscus syriacus 'Diana'
HYDRANGEAS, illus. p.144

LILACS, illus. p.120
Lophomyrtus bullata
MAGNOLIAS, illus. p.75
Melaleuca armillaris

☐ WHITE

Brugmansia × candida,
syn. *Datura* × *candida*
Semi-evergreen, rounded shrub or
small tree. Has downy, oval leaves and
strongly scented, pendulous, white
flowers, sometimes cream
or pinkish, in summer-
autumn. Min. 10°C (50°F).

☀ ◌ ❢

Luma apiculata, syn. *Amomyrtus
luma, Myrceugenia apiculata,
Myrtus apiculata, M. luma*
Strong-growing, evergreen shrub with
peeling, golden-brown and grey-white
bark and cup-shaped
flowers amid aromatic
leaves in summer-autumn.

☀ ◌ Zone 9?

Abutilon vitifolium var. **album**
Fast-growing, deciduous, upright
shrub. Large, bowl-shaped, white
blooms, pink-tinged when young,
are freely borne in late spring and
early summer amid deeply
lobed, sharply toothed,
grey-green leaves.

☀ ◌ Zone 9?

Abelia triflora
Vigorous, deciduous, upright shrub
with pointed, deep green leaves. Small,
extremely fragrant, white flowers,
tinged pale pink, appear in
mid-summer.

☀ ◌ Zone 8

Chionanthus virginicus
(Fringe tree)
Deciduous, bushy shrub or small tree.
Has large, glossy, dark green leaves
that turn yellow in autumn. Drooping
sprays of fragrant, white
flowers appear in early
summer.

☀ ◑ Zone 5

Cornus mas 'Variegata'
Deciduous, bushy, dense shrub or small
tree. Small, star-shaped, yellow flowers
appear on bare branches in early spring
before white-edged, dark green
leaves develop.

☀ ◌ ❢ Zone 4

Holodiscus discolor
Fast-growing, deciduous, arching
shrub. Has lobed, toothed, dark green
leaves and large, pendent sprays of
small, creamy-white flowers in
mid-summer.

☀ ◌ Zone 7

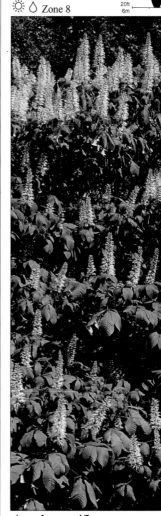

Aesculus parviflora
(Bottlebrush buckeye)
Deciduous, open shrub. Leaves are
bronze when young, dark green in
summer and yellow in autumn.
Panicles of red-centred,
white flowers appear from
mid- to late summer.

☀ ◌ ❢ Zone 4

Lilacs

The heady scent of the lilac (*Syringa*) epitomizes early summer. The flowers are produced in abundance and are excellent for cutting. Apart from the classic lilacs and mauves, colours include white, pink, cream and rich red-purple; double forms are also available. Most lilacs grown in gardens are vigorous shrubs derived from *S. vulgaris*. They may eventually become tree-like and are therefore best planted at the back of a shrub border or in groups in a wild garden; they may also be used as an informal hedge. Where space is restricted choose from the smaller-growing species, some of which may be grown in containers. Spent flower heads are best removed, but care should be taken not to damage the new shoots that form below the flowers. Otherwise little pruning is required, though older, straggly plants may be rejuvenated by hard pruning in winter.

S. vulgaris 'Michel Buchner'

S. vulgaris 'Monge'

S. vulgaris 'Masséna'

S. meyeri 'Palibin'

S. vulgaris 'Madame Florent Stepman'

S. vulgaris 'Maréchal Foch'

S. vulgaris 'Paul Thirion'

S. vulgaris 'Charles Joly'

S. × persica

S. vulgaris 'Madame F. Morel'

S. vulgaris 'Decaisne'

S. vulgaris 'Président Grévy'

S. vulgaris 'Jan van Tol'

S. vulgaris 'Madame Lemoine'

S. vulgaris 'Mrs Edward Harding'

S. × hyacinthiflora 'Clarke's Giant'

S. × hyacinthiflora 'Cora Brandt'

S. × chinensis 'Alba'

S. vulgaris 'Congo'

S. vulgaris 'Madame Antoine Buchner'

S. × hyacinthiflora 'Esther Staley'

S.p. subsp. microphylla 'Superba'

S. yunnanensis

S. × hyacinthiflora 'Blue Hyacinth'

S. vulgaris 'Primrose'

SHRUBS large SUMMER INTEREST

□ WHITE–PINK

■ RED–PURPLE

Clethra delavayi
Deciduous, open shrub with lance-shaped, toothed, rich green leaves. Dense, spreading clusters of pink buds opening to scented, white flowers appear in mid-summer.

☼ ◊ pH Zone 8   20ft/6m

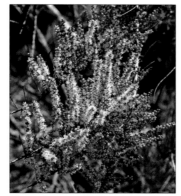

Tamarix ramosissima,
syn. *T. pentandra*
Deciduous, arching, graceful shrub or small tree with tiny, narrow, blue-green leaves. In late summer and early autumn bears large, upright plumes of small, pink flowers.

☼ ◊ Zone 3   20ft/6m

Buddleja davidii 'Royal Red'
Vigorous, deciduous, arching shrub. Has long, pointed, dark green leaves, with white-felted undersides, and plumes of fragrant, rich purple-red flowers from mid-summer to autumn.

☼ ◊ Zone 5b   20ft/6m

Acer palmatum f. atropurpureum
Deciduous, bushy-headed shrub or small tree with lobed, reddish-purple foliage that turns brilliant red in autumn. Small, reddish-purple flowers are borne in mid-spring.

☼ ◊ Zone 6   20ft/6m

Abelia x grandiflora
Vigorous, semi-evergreen, arching shrub. Has glossy, dark green foliage and an abundance of fragrant, pink-tinged, white flowers from mid-summer to mid-autumn.

☼ ◊ Zone 7   20ft/6m

Nerium oleander (Oleander)
Evergreen, upright, bushy shrub with leathery, deep green leaves. Clusters of salver-form, pink, white, red, apricot or yellow flowers appear from spring to autumn, often on dark red stalks. Min. 10°C (50°F).

☼ ◊ ⊙ Zone   20ft/6m

Buddleja davidii 'Harlequin'
Vigorous, deciduous, arching shrub. Leaves are long, pointed and dark green with creamy-white margins. Plumes of fragrant, red-purple flowers appear from mid-summer to autumn.

☼ ◊ Zone 5b   20ft/6m

Buddleja colvilei
Deciduous, arching shrub, often tree-like with age. Large, white-centred, deep pink to purplish-red flowers are borne in drooping racemes amid dark green foliage during early summer.

☼ ◊ Zone 9   20ft/6m

Kolkwitzia amabilis 'Pink Cloud'
Deciduous, arching shrub that bears a mass of bell-shaped, pink flowers amid small, oval, mid-green leaves in late spring and early summer.

☼ ◊ Zone 5   20ft/6m

Malvaviscus arboreus
(Sleepy mallow)
Vigorous, evergreen, rounded shrub. Serrated, bright green leaves are soft-haired. Has bright red flowers with protruding stamens in summer-autumn. Min. 13–16°C (55–61°F).

☼ ◊   20ft/6m

Cotinus coggygria 'Notcutt's Variety'
Deciduous, bushy shrub with deep reddish-purple foliage. Long-lasting, purplish-pink plumes of massed, small flowers are produced in late summer.

☼ ◊ Zone 5   20ft/6m

■ RED–PURPLE

Acer palmatum var. *heptalobum* 'Rubrum'

Deciduous, bushy-headed shrub or small tree. Large leaves are red when young, bronze in summer and brilliant red, orange or yellow in autumn. Has small, reddish-purple flowers in mid-spring.

☼ ◊ Zone 6

Buddleja alternifolia

Deciduous, arching shrub that can be trained as a weeping tree. Has slender, pendent shoots and narrow, grey-green leaves. Neat clusters of fragrant, lilac-purple flowers appear in early summer.

☼ ◊ Zone 4

□ GREEN–YELLOW

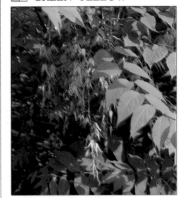

Decaisnea fargesii

Deciduous, semi-arching, open shrub with blue-bloomed shoots and large, deep green leaves of paired leaflets. Racemes of greenish flowers in early summer are followed by pendent, sausage-shaped, bluish fruits.

☼ ◊ Zone 8

Elaeagnus angustifolia (Oleaster)

Deciduous, bushy shrub or spreading, small tree. Has narrow, silvery-grey leaves and small, fragrant, creamy-yellow flowers, with spreading lobes, in early summer, followed by small, oval, yellow fruits.

☼ ◊ Zone 2b

Prunus spinosa 'Purpurea'

Deciduous, dense, spiny shrub or small tree. Bright red, young leaves become deep reddish-purple. Bears saucer-shaped, pale pink flowers from early to mid-spring, followed by blue-bloomed, black fruits.

☼ ◊ Zone 5b

Tibouchina urvilleana (Glory bush)

Evergreen, slender-branched shrub. Velvet-haired leaves are prominently veined. Has satiny, blue-purple flowers in clusters from summer to early winter. Min. 7°C (45°F).

☼ ◊ pH

Corylus maxima 'Purpurea'

Vigorous, deciduous, open shrub or small tree with deep purple leaves and purplish catkins, with yellow anthers, that hang from bare branches in late winter. Edible nuts mature in autumn.

☼ ◊ Zone 5

Acer palmatum var. *heptalobum* 'Lutescens'

Deciduous, bushy-headed shrub or small tree. Large, lobed leaves become clear yellow in autumn. In mid-spring produces small, reddish-purple flowers, followed by winged fruits.

☼ ◊ Zone 6

Paliurus spina-christi (Christ's thorn, Jerusalem thorn)

Deciduous, bushy shrub with slender, thorny shoots. Has oval, glossy, bright green leaves, tiny, yellow flowers in summer and curious, woody, winged fruits in autumn.

☼ ◊ Zone 8

Brugmansia × candida 'Grand Marnier'
Evergreen, robust shrub with large, oval to elliptic leaves. Pendent, flared, trumpet-shaped, apricot flowers open from an inflated calyx in summer.
Min. 7–10°C (45–50°F).

Brugmansia sanguinea
Semi-evergreen, erect to rounded shrub or small tree with lobed, young leaves. Has large, trumpet-shaped, yellow and orange-red flowers from late summer to winter.
Min. 10°C (50°F).

Crotalaria agatiflora
(Canary-bird bush)
Evergreen, loose, somewhat spreading shrub with grey-green leaves. Racemes of greenish-yellow flowers appear in summer and also intermittently during the year. Min. 15°C (59°F).

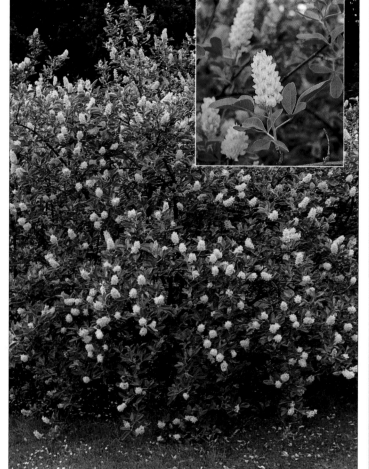

Cytisus battandieri,
syn. *Argyrocytisus battandieri*
(Moroccan broom, Pineapple broom)
Semi-evergreen, open shrub. Leaves have 3 silver-grey leaflets. Pineapple-scented, yellow flowers appear in summer.
☼ ◊ ❶ Zone 7b

Caesalpinia gilliesii,
syn. *Poinciana gilliesii*
Deciduous, open shrub or small tree. Has finely divided, dark green leaves and bears short racemes of yellow flowers with long, red stamens from mid- to late summer. Min. 5°C (41°F).
☼ ◊

Genista cinerea
Deciduous, arching shrub that produces an abundance of fragrant, pea-like, yellow blooms from early to mid-summer. Has silky, young shoots and narrow, grey-green leaves.
☼ ◊ Zone 8

Buddleja globosa
Deciduous or semi-evergreen, open shrub with dark green foliage. Dense, rounded clusters of orange-yellow flowers are carried in early summer.
☼ ◊ Zone 8

Fremontodendron 'California Glory'
Very vigorous, evergreen or semi-evergreen, upright shrub. Has rounded, lobed, dark green leaves and large, bright yellow flowers from late spring to mid-autumn.
☼ ◊ ❶ Zone 8

Ligustrum ovalifolium 'Aureum'
Luma apiculata 'Glanleam Gold'
Osmanthus fragrans f. *aurantiacus*
Sambucus canadensis 'Aurea'

Senna didymobotrya, illus. p.147
Spartium junceum, illus. p.147
Tecoma stans, illus. p.96

SHRUBS

Cotoneaster 'Cornubia'
Vigorous, semi-evergreen, arching shrub. Clusters of white flowers, produced in early summer amid dark green foliage, are followed by large, pendent clusters of decorative, bright red fruits.

☀ ◊ ① Zone 7   20ft 6m / 0

Rhus typhina 'Dissecta'
Deciduous, spreading, open shrub or small tree with velvety shoots. Fern-like, dark green leaves turn brilliant orange-red in autumn, when deep red fruit clusters are also borne.

☀ ◊ Zone 3   20ft 6m / 0

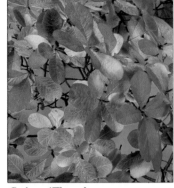

Cotinus 'Flame'
Deciduous, bushy, tree-like shrub with dark green leaves that turn brilliant orange-red in autumn. From late summer, showy, plume-like, purplish-pink flower heads appear above the foliage.

☀ ◊ Zone 5   20ft 6m / 0

Hippophäe rhamnoides
(Sea buckthorn)
Deciduous, bushy, arching shrub or small tree with narrow, silvery leaves. Tiny, yellow flowers borne in mid-spring are followed in autumn by bright orange berries on female plants.

☀ ◊ Zone 2b   20ft 6m / 0

Acer palmatum var. heptalobum
Deciduous, bushy-headed shrub or small tree with large, lobed, mid-green leaves that turn brilliant red, orange or yellow in autumn. Bears small, reddish-purple flowers in mid-spring.

☀ ◊ Zone 6   20ft 6m / 0

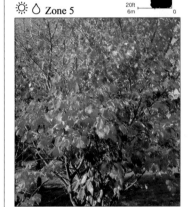

Hamamelis vernalis 'Sandra'
Deciduous, upright, open shrub. Bears small, fragrant, spidery, deep yellow blooms in late winter and early spring. Oval leaves are purple when young, mid-green in summer, purple, red, orange and yellow in autumn.

☀ ◊ pH Zone 5b   20ft 6m / 0

Acer palmatum 'Sango-kaku',
syn. *A.p.* 'Senkaki'
(Coral-bark maple)
Deciduous, bushy-headed shrub or tree. Has coral-pink, young shoots in winter. Palmate, orange-yellow leaves turn green, then in autumn pink, then yellow.

☀ ◊ Zone 6   20ft 6m / 0

Euonymus myrianthus
Evergreen, bushy shrub with pointed, leathery, mid-green leaves. Dense clusters of small, greenish-yellow flowers in summer are followed by yellow fruits that open to show orange-red seeds.

☀ ◑ ① Zone 8   20ft 6m / 0

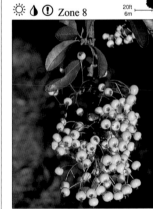

Pyracantha atalantioides 'Aurea'
Vigorous, evergreen, upright, spiny shrub, arching with age. Has narrowly oval, glossy, dark green leaves and white flowers in early summer, followed by large clusters of small, yellow berries in early autumn.

☀ ◊ ① Zone 8   20ft 6m / 0

OTHER RECOMMENDED PLANTS:
Acer japonicum 'Vitifolium', illus. p.95
Acer tataricum subsp. *ginnala*, illus. p.95
Cotinus coggygria 'Royal Purple'

Cotinus obovatus
Cotoneaster x *watereri* 'John Waterer'
Decaisnea fargesii, illus. p.122
Hibiscus mutabilis

Photinia davidiana, illus. p.94
Pyracantha 'Golden Charmer', illus. p.149
Pyracantha 'Mohave'
Sorbus aucuparia 'Fastigiata'

Tibouchina urvilleana, illus. p.122
Viburnum betulifolium, illus. p.148

□ YELLOW

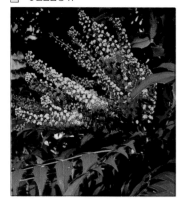

Mahonia × media 'Charity'
Evergreen, upright, dense shrub with large leaves composed of many spiny, dark green leaflets. Slender, upright, later spreading spikes of fragrant, yellow flowers are borne from early autumn to early spring.

☼ ◊ Zone 9?

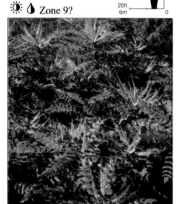

Mahonia × media 'Buckland'
Evergreen, upright, dense shrub. Has large leaves with many spiny, dark green leaflets. Clustered, upright then spreading, long, branched spikes of fragrant, yellow flowers appear from late autumn to early spring.

☼ ◊ Zone 9?

Hamamelis virginiana
(Virginian witch hazel)
Deciduous, open, upright shrub. Small, fragrant, spidery, yellow flowers with 4 narrow petals open in autumn as leaves fall. Broadly oval leaves turn yellow in autumn.

☼ ◊ pH Zone 4b

Brugmansia aurea
Cotoneaster 'Rothschildianus'
HOLLIES, illus. pp.98–9
Tecoma stans, illus. p.96

■ RED

Cotoneaster lacteus
Evergreen, arching shrub suitable for hedging. Oval, dark green leaves set off shallowly cup-shaped, white flowers from early to mid-summer. Long-lasting, red fruits are carried in large clusters in autumn-winter.

☼ ◊ ! Zone 8

Hamamelis × intermedia 'Diane'
Deciduous, open, spreading shrub that produces fragrant, spidery, deep red flowers on bare branches from mid- to late winter. Broadly oval, mid-green leaves turn yellow and red in autumn.

☼ ◊ pH Zone 6b

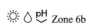

Cyphomandra betacea,
syn. *C. crassicaulis* (Tree tomato)
Evergreen, sparingly branched shrub or small tree, upright when young, with large, heart-shaped, rich green leaves. Has edible, tomato-like, red fruits from summer to winter. Min. 10°C (50°F).

☼ ◊

OTHER RECOMMENDED PLANTS:
Euphorbia pulcherrima, illus. p.150
Euphorbia pulcherrima 'Paul Mikkelson'
HEATHERS, illus. pp.178–9

□□ GREEN–YELLOW

Garrya elliptica (Silk-tassel bush)
Evergreen, bushy, dense shrub with leathery, wavy-edged, dark green leaves. Grey-green catkins, longer on male than female plants, are borne from mid-winter to early spring.

☼ ◊ Zone 8

Azara microphylla
Elegant, evergreen shrub or small tree. Has tiny, glossy, dark green leaves and small clusters of vanilla-scented, deep yellow flowers in late winter and early spring.

☼ ◊ Zone 9

Corylus avellana 'Contorta'
Deciduous, bushy shrub with curiously twisted shoots and broad, sharply toothed, mid-green leaves. In late winter, bare branches are covered with pendent, pale yellow catkins.

☼ ◊ Zone 5

Cornus mas
Hamamelis × intermedia 'Pallida'
Hamamelis japonica
Mahonia napaulensis

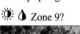

☐ YELLOW

SHRUBS large ALL YEAR INTEREST

☐☐ WHITE–GREEN

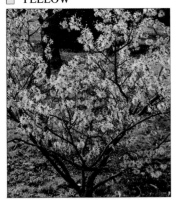

Hamamelis x *intermedia* 'Arnold Promise'
Deciduous, open, spreading shrub. Large, fragrant, spidery, yellow flowers with 4 narrow, crimped petals appear from mid- to late winter. Broadly oval, green leaves turn yellow in autumn.
☼ ◊ pH Zone 6b

Hamamelis japonica 'Sulphurea'
Deciduous, upright, open shrub. In mid-winter, fragrant, spidery, pale yellow flowers with 4 narrow, crimped petals are borne on leafless branches. Broadly oval, dark green leaves turn yellow in autumn.
☼ ◊ pH Zone 6

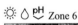

Hamamelis mollis 'Coombe Wood'
Deciduous, open, spreading shrub. From mid- to late winter bears very fragrant, spidery, golden-yellow flowers with 4 narrow petals. Broadly oval, mid-green leaves turn yellow in autumn.
☼ ◊ pH Zone 6

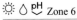

Acacia pravissima, illus. p.97
Buddleja madagascariensis
Jasminum nudiflorum, illus. p.151
Senecio grandifolius

Dracaena fragrans Deremensis Group 'Warneckei'
Slow-growing, evergreen shrub. Erect to arching, lance-shaped leaves are banded grey-green and cream. Min. 15–18°C (59–64°F).
◑ ◊

Ligustrum ovalifolium
Vigorous, evergreen or semi-evergreen, upright, dense shrub with glossy, mid-green leaves. Dense racemes of small, rather unpleasantly scented, tubular, white flowers appear in mid-summer, followed by black fruits.
☼ ◊ ① Zone 7

Prunus lusitanica 'Variegata'
Slow-growing, evergreen, bushy shrub with reddish-purple shoots. Has oval, glossy, dark green, white-edged leaves. Fragrant, shallowly cup-shaped, creamy-white flowers in summer are followed by purple fruits.
☼ ◊ ① Zone 8

Prunus lusitanica subsp. *azorica*
Evergreen, bushy shrub with reddish-purple shoots and bright green leaves, red when young. Bears spikes of small, fragrant, white flowers in summer, followed by purple fruits.
☼ ◊ ① Zone 8

Tetrapanax papyrifer, syn. *Fatsia papyrifera* (Rice-paper plant)
Evergreen, upright, suckering shrub. Long-stalked, circular leaves are deeply lobed. Has bold sprays of small, creamy-white flowers in summer and black berries in autumn-winter.
☼ ◊ Zone 7

Griselinia littoralis 'Variegata'
Evergreen, upright shrub of dense, bushy habit. Leathery leaves are grey-green, marked with bright green and creamy-white. Bears inconspicuous, yellow-green flowers in late spring.
☼ ◊ Zone 9

Pittosporum 'Garnettii'
Evergreen, columnar or conical shrub of dense, bushy habit. Rounded, grey-green leaves, irregularly edged creamy-white, become tinged with deep pink in cold areas. May bear small, greenish-purple flowers in spring-summer.
☼ ◊ Zone 9?

Polyscias guilfoylei 'Victoriae' (Lace aralia)
Slow-growing, evergreen, rounded shrub or small tree with leaves that are divided into several oval to rounded, serrated, white-margined, deep green leaflets. Min. 15–18°C (59–64°F).
◑ ◊

SHRUBS

GREEN–YELLOW

□ WHITE

Schefflera elegantissima, syn.
Aralia elegantissima, Dizygotheca
elegantissima (False aralia)
Evergreen, upright, open shrub. Large
leaves have 7–10 coarsely toothed,
lustrous, grey-green,
sometimes bronze-tinted,
leaflets. Min. 13°C (55°F).

Ligustrum lucidum 'Excelsum
Superbum'
Evergreen, upright shrub or small tree.
Large, glossy, bright green leaves are
marked with pale green and yellow-
edged. Small, tubular, white
flowers open in late
summer and early autumn.

Zone 9

Pieris floribunda
(Fetterbush, Mountain fetterbush)
Evergreen, bushy, dense, leafy shrub
with oval, glossy, dark green leaves.
Greenish-white flower buds appear
in winter, opening to urn-
shaped, white blooms from
early to mid-spring.

Zone 5b

Enkianthus perulatus
Deciduous, bushy, dense shrub. Dark
green leaves turn bright red in autumn.
A profusion of small, pendent,
urn-shaped, white flowers is
borne in mid-spring.

Zone 7

Brachyglottis repanda
(Pukapuka, Rangiora)
Evergreen, bushy shrub or tree, upright
when young, with robust, downy, white
stems. Has veined leaves, white
beneath, and fragrant, white
flower heads in summer.
Min. 3°C (37°F).

Osmanthus heterophyllus
'Aureomarginatus'
Evergreen, upright shrub. Sharply
toothed, holly-like, glossy, bright green
leaves have yellow margins. Small,
fragrant, white flowers are
produced in autumn.

Zone 7

Fothergilla major,
syn. *F. monticola*
Deciduous, upright shrub with glossy,
dark green leaves, slightly bluish-white
beneath, that turn red, orange and
yellow in autumn. Tufts of
fragrant, white flowers
appear in late spring.

Zone 5b

Pieris japonica 'Scarlett O'Hara'
Evergreen, rounded, bushy, dense
shrub. Young foliage and shoots are
bronze-red, leaves becoming glossy,
dark green. Produces sprays of white
flowers in spring.

Zone 5b

Pittosporum tenuifolium
Evergreen, columnar, later rounded
shrub or small tree with purple shoots
and wavy-edged, oval, glossy,
mid-green leaves. Bears honey-
scented, purple flowers
in late spring.

Zone 9?

Elaeagnus pungens 'Maculata',
syn. *E.p.* 'Aureovariegata'
Evergreen, bushy, slightly spiny shrub.
Glossy, dark green leaves are marked
with a central, deep yellow patch. Very
fragrant, urn-shaped,
creamy-white flowers open
from mid- to late autumn.

Zone 8

Choisya ternata
(Mexican orange blossom)
Evergreen, rounded, dense shrub with
aromatic, glossy, bright green leaves
composed of 3 leaflets. Clusters of
fragrant, white blooms
open in late spring and
often again in autumn.

Zone 8

Beaucarnea recurvata, illus. p.100
Castanopsis cuspidata
Cycas revoluta, illus. p.152
Elaeagnus x *ebbingei* 'Gilt Edge'

Euonymus japonicus 'Ovatus Aureus'
Pittosporum tenuifolium 'Margaret Turnbull'
Schefflera arboricola
Schefflera digitata

OTHER RECOMMENDED PLANTS:
Buddleja asiatica
CAMELLIAS, illus. pp.128–9
Gardenia thunbergia

Osmanthus x *burkwoodii*, illus. p.116
Pieris japonica Taiwanensis Group
RHODODENDRONS, illus. pp.132–4
Viburnum x *burkwoodii* 'Anne Russell'

Camellias

These evergreen shrubs have long been valued for their luxuriant, rich green foliage and masses of showy flowers, borne mainly in winter and spring. Once thought suitable only for glasshouses, many camellias are hardy outdoors in milder climates if grown in sheltered positions, although blooms may suffer frost and rain damage. Camellias require lime-free soil. The main flower forms are illustrated below.

Single – shallowly cup-shaped flowers each have not more than 8 petals, arranged in a single row, and a conspicuous, central boss of stamens.

Semi-double – cup-shaped flowers each have 2 or more rows of 9–21 regular or irregular petals and conspicuous stamens.

Anemone – rounded flowers each have one or more rows of large, outer petals lying flat or undulating; the domed centre has a mass of intermingled petaloids and stamens.

Peony-form – rounded, domed flowers have usually irregular petals intermingled with petaloids and stamens.

Rose-form – cup-shaped flowers each have several rows of overlapping petals and open to reveal stamens in the centre.

Formal double – rounded flowers have many rows of regular, neatly overlapping petals that obscure stamens. **Irregular double** forms are similar but often have more loosely arranged, sometimes irregular, petals.

C. × *williamsii* '**Jury's Yellow**' (anemone)

C. '**Shirowabisuke**' (single)

C. × *williamsii* '**Francis Hanger**' (single)

C. '**Cornish Snow**' (single)

C. japonica '**Alba Simplex**' (single)

C. japonica '**Janet Waterhouse**'(semi-dbl.)

C. tsai (single)

C. japonica '**Mrs D.W. Davis**' (semi-double)

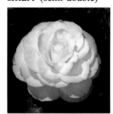

C. japonica '**Lady Van-sittart**' (semi-double)

C.j. '**Tomorrow's Dawn**'(irreg. double)

C. japonica '**Berenice Boddy**' (semi-double)

C. × *williamsii* '**J.C. Williams**' (single)

C. japonica '**Lavinia Maggi**' (formal dbl.)

C. × *williamsii* '**Donation**' (semi-double)

C. japonica '**Margaret Davis**' (irregular double)

C. × *williamsii* '**Dream Boat**' (formal double)

C. × *w.* '**E.G. Water-house**' (formal double)

C. saluenensis (single)

C. × *williamsii* '**Joan Trehane**' (rose)

C. j. '**Betty Sheffield Supreme**' (irreg. double)

C. × *williamsii* '**Bow Bells**' (single)

C. × *w.* '**Brigadoon**' (semi-double)

C. × *williamsii* '**Saint Ewe**' (single)

C. × *williamsii* '**Jury's Yellow**' (anemone)

C. sasanqua '**Narumigata**' (single)

C. 'Inspiration'
(semi-double)

C. 'Francie L'
(semi-double)

C. reticulata 'Arch of
Triumph' (peony)

C. reticulata 'Mandalay
Queen' (semi-double)

C. japonica 'Guilio
Nuccio' (semi-double)

C. reticulata 'Captain
Rawes' (semi-double)

C. 'Satan's Robe'
(semi-double)

C. japonica 'R.L.
Wheeler' (variable)

C. japonica 'Apollo'
(semi-double)

C. japonica 'Elegans'
(anemone)

C. 'Innovation' (peony)

C.j. 'Rubescens Major'
(formal double)

C. japonica 'Julia
Drayton' (variable)

C. x *williamsii* 'Water
Lily' (formal double)

C. 'Leonard Messel'
(semi-double)

C. japonica 'Gloire de
Nantes' (semi-double)

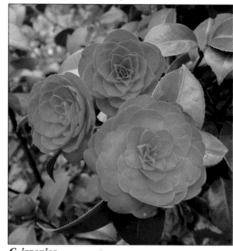

C. reticulata 'Houye
Diechi' (semi-double)

C. japonica
'Mathotiana' (formal double)

C. 'William Hertrich'
(semi-double)

C. 'Dr Clifford Parks'
(variable)

C. japonica 'Adolphe
Audusson'(semi-double)

C. 'Black Lace'
(formal double)

C. x *williamsii* 'Golden
Spangles' (single)

C. japonica 'Alexander
Hunter' (single)

C. japonica 'Bob's
Tinsie' (anemone)

C. x *williamsii* 'George
Blandford' (semi-
double)

C. japonica 'Jupiter'
(single)

C. 'Anticipation'
(peony)

C. japonica
'Althaeiflora' (peony)

C. japonica 'Coquettii'
(variable)

☐☐ WHITE–PINK

Aronia arbutifolia
(Red chokeberry)
Deciduous shrub, upright when young, later arching. Clusters of small, white flowers with red anthers appear in late spring, followed by red berries. Dark green foliage turns red in autumn.

☼ ◊ Zone 4b

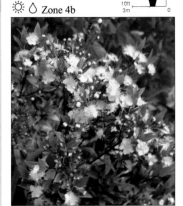

Myrtus communis
(Common myrtle)
Evergreen, bushy shrub with aromatic, glossy, dark green foliage. Fragrant, white flowers are borne from mid-spring to early summer, followed by purple-black berries.

☼ ◊ Zone 9

Malus sieboldii
Deciduous, spreading shrub with arching branches. Bears white or pale to deep pink flowers in mid-spring followed by small, red or yellow fruits. Dark green leaves, often lobed, turn red or yellow in autumn.

☼ ◊ Zone 3

Prunus mume 'Omoi-no-mama', syn. *P.m.* 'Omoi-no-wac'
Deciduous, spreading shrub with fragrant, semi-double, occasionally single, pink-flushed, white flowers wreathing young growths in early spring, before oval, toothed leaves appear.

☼ ◊ ⓘ Zone 5b

Viburnum plicatum 'Pink Beauty'
Deciduous, bushy shrub. Dark green leaves become reddish-purple in autumn. In late spring and early summer bears white, later pink, blooms, followed by red, then black, fruits.

☼ ◊ ⓘ Zone 5b

Chaenomeles speciosa 'Moerloosei'
Vigorous, deciduous, bushy shrub. Has glossy, dark green leaves and pink-flushed, white flowers in early spring, followed by greenish-yellow fruits.

☼ ◊ Zone 5b

☐☐ PINK–RED

Cotoneaster divaricatus
Deciduous, bushy, spreading shrub. Leaves are glossy, dark green, turning red in autumn. Shallowly cup-shaped, pink-flushed, white flowers in late spring and early summer are followed by deep red fruits.

☼ ◊ ⓘ Zone 5

Ribes sanguineum 'Pulborough Scarlet'
Deciduous, upright shrub that in spring bears pendent, tubular, deep red flowers amid aromatic, dark green leaves, with 3–5 lobes, sometimes followed by black fruits with a white bloom.

☼ ◊ Zone 6b

Prunus mume 'Beni-chidori', syn. *P.m.* 'Beni-shidon', *P.m.* 'Beni-shidori'
Deciduous, spreading shrub with fragrant, single, carmine flowers in early spring before pointed, dark green leaves appear.

☼ ◊ ⓘ Zone 5b

Acer palmatum 'Corallinum'
Very slow-growing, deciduous, bushy-headed shrub or small tree. Lobed, bright reddish-pink, young foliage becomes mid-green, then brilliant red, orange or yellow in autumn. Reddish-purple flowers appear in mid-spring.

☼ ◊ Zone 6

Banksia coccinea
Evergreen, dense shrub with toothed, dark green leaves, grey-green beneath. Flower heads comprising clusters of bright red flowers with prominent styles and stigmas are borne in late winter and spring.
Min. 10°C (50°F).

☼ ◊

SHRUBS

Enkianthus cernuus f. **rubens**
Deciduous, bushy shrub with dense clusters of dull green leaves that turn deep reddish-purple in autumn. Small, bell-shaped, deep red flowers appear in late spring.

☼ ◑ pH ♥ Zone 7

Greyia sutherlandii
Deciduous or semi-evergreen, rounded shrub. Coarsely serrated, leathery leaves turn red in autumn. Spikes of small, bright red flowers appear in spring with new foliage.
Min. 7–10°C (45–50°F).

☼ ◑

Corylopsis pauciflora
Deciduous, bushy, dense shrub. Oval, bright green leaves, bronze when young, have bristle-like teeth. Bears fragrant, tubular to bell-shaped, pale yellow flowers from early to mid-spring.

☼ ◑ pH ♥ Zone 7

Leucospermum reflexum
Evergreen, erect shrub with ascending branchlets. Has small, blue-grey or grey-green leaves. Slender, tubular, crimson flowers with long styles are carried in tight, rounded heads in spring-summer.
Min. 10°C (50°F).

☼ ◑

Leptospermum scoparium 'Red Damask'
Evergreen, upright, bushy shrub. Narrow, aromatic, dark green leaves set off sprays of double, dark red flowers in late spring and summer.
Min. 2°C (35°F).

☼ ◑

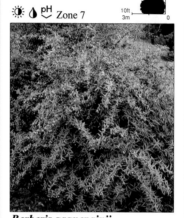

Berberis gagnepainii var. **lanceifolia**
Evergreen, bushy, dense shrub. Massed, globose to cup-shaped, yellow flowers appear among long, narrow, pointed, dark green leaves in late spring. Forms blue-bloomed, black berries.

☼ ◊ ① Zone 7

Kerria japonica 'Pleniflora'
Vigorous, deciduous, graceful shrub. Double, golden-yellow flowers are borne along green shoots from mid- to late-spring. Leaves are narrowly oval, sharply toothed and bright green.

☼ ◊ Zone 5b

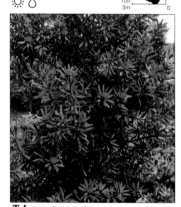

Telopea truncata (Tasmanian waratah)
Evergreen, upright shrub, bushy with age. Has deep green leaves and dense, rounded heads of small, tubular, crimson flowers in late spring and summer.
Min. 2°C (35°F).

☼ ◊ pH

Berberis thunbergii f. **atropurpurea**
Deciduous, arching, dense shrub. Reddish-purple foliage turns bright red in autumn. Globose to cup-shaped, red-tinged, pale yellow flowers in mid-spring are followed by red fruits.

☼ ◊ ① Zone 4b

Lindera benzoin (Benjamin, Spice bush)
Deciduous, bushy shrub with aromatic, bright green leaves that turn yellow in autumn. Tiny, greenish-yellow flowers in mid-spring are followed by red berries on female plants.

☼ ◑ pH ♥ Zone 6

Forsythia suspensa
Deciduous, arching, graceful shrub with slender shoots. Nodding, narrowly trumpet-shaped, bright yellow flowers open from early to mid-spring, before mid-green leaves appear.

☼ ◊ Zone 5b

Rhododendrons and Azaleas

Rhododendrons and azaleas both belong to the huge genus *Rhododendron*, one of the largest in the plant kingdom. 'Azalea' is the common name used for all the deciduous species and hybrids and many of the dwarf, small-leaved evergreens. In stature the genus ranges from alpine shrubs only a few inches high to tall, spreading trees, in the wild reaching 24m (80ft).

Like most of the related heathers (also Ericaceae), rhododendrons should be grown in an acid soil rich in organic matter but with excellent drainage. Most prefer cool, woodland conditions although many dwarf forms will thrive in more open sites. Many will grow well in containers, in which it is often easier to provide suitable growing conditions. Once established, they require very little attention apart from an annual mulch and occasional feeding, and will provide a colourful display for many years.

R. 'Palestrina'
(azalea) ①

R. 'Seven Stars'
(rhododendron) ①

R. 'Mrs G.W. Leak'
(rhododendron) ①

R. occidentale
(azalea) ①

R. souliei
(rhododendron) ①

R. auriculatum
(rhododendron) ①

R. yakushimanum
(rhododendron) ①

R. argyrophyllum
(rhododendron) ①

R. yunnanense
(rhododendron) ①

R. 'Azuma-kagami'
(azalea) ①

R. fulvum
(rhododendron) ①

R. sutchuenense
(rhododendron) ①

R. 'Seta'
(rhododendron) ①

R. 'Strawberry Ice'
(azalea) ①

R. rex subsp. **fictolac-teum** (rhododendron) ①

R. 'Silver Moon'
(azalea) ①

R. calophytum
(rhododendron) ①

R. Nobleanum Group
(rhododendron) ①

R. 'Corneille'
(azalea) ①

R. 'Kirin'
(azalea) ①

R. 'Beauty of Littleworth'
(rhododendron) ①

R. racemosum
(rhododendron) ①

R. williamsianum
(rhododendron) ①

R. schlippenbachii
(azalea) ①

R. orbiculare
(rhododendron) ①

R. 'Percy Wiseman'
(rhododendron) ①

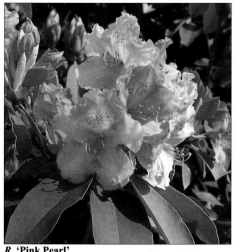

R. 'Pink Pearl'
(rhododendron) ①

R. 'Elizabeth'
(rhododendron) ①

R. davidsonianum
(rhododendron) ①

R. 'Queen Elizabeth II' (rhododendron) ①

R. oreotrephes
(rhododendron) ①

R. wardii
(rhododendron) ①

R. 'Rosalind'
(rhododendron) ①

R. 'Hinode-giri'
(azalea) ①

R. 'May Day'
(rhododendron) ①

R. kaempferi
(azalea) ①

R. 'Blue Peter'
(rhododendron) ①

R. lutescens
(rhododendron) ①

R. calostrotum
(rhododendron) ①

R. thomsonii
(rhododendron) ①

R. cinnabarinum
(rhododendron) ①

R. hippophaeoides
(rhododendron) ①

R. 'Hinomayo'
(azalea) ①

R. 'President Roosevelt'
(rhododendron) ①

R. 'John Cairns'
(azalea) ①

R. 'Irohayama'
(azalea) ①

R. augustinii
(rhododendron) ①

R. cinnabarinum subsp. **xanthocodon** (rho.) ①

R. 'Hatsugiri'
(azalea) ①

R. arboreum
(rhododendron) ①

R. 'Cynthia'
(rhododendron) ①

R. 'Vuyk's Scarlet'
(azalea) ①

R. 'Homebush'
(azalea) ①

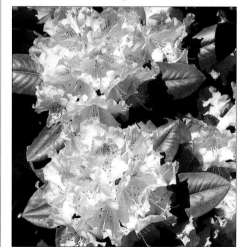

R. 'Susan'
(rhododendron) ①

Rhododendrons and Azaleas continued

R. 'Narcissiflorum'
(azalea) ①

R. 'Freya' (azalea) ①

R. 'Crest'
(rhododendron) ①

R. luteum (azalea) ①

R. 'Medway'
(azalea) ①

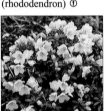

R. 'Curlew'
(rhododendron) ①

R. 'George Reynolds'
(azalea) ①

R. 'Fabia'
(rhododendron) ①

R. 'Yellow Hammer'
(rhododendron) ①

R. 'Glory of Littleworth'
(azalea x rhodo.) ①

R. 'Frome' (azalea) ①

**R. 'Moonshine
Crescent'** (rhodo.) ①

R. macabeanum
(rhododendron) ①

R. 'Gloria Mundi'
(azalea) ①

SHRUBS medium SPRING INTEREST

☐ YELLOW

Berberis verruculosa
Slow-growing, evergreen, bushy shrub.
Has glossy, dark green leaves with
blue-white undersides. Clusters of
small, cup-shaped, bright yellow
flowers in late spring and
early summer are followed
by blue-black fruits.

☀ ◊ ① Zone 4

Berberis julianae
Evergreen, bushy, dense shrub. Has
glossy, dark green leaves, yellow
flowers in late spring and early
summer and egg-shaped, blue-
black fruits in autumn.

☀ ◊ ① Zone 6

**Forsythia x intermedia
'Spectabilis'**
Vigorous, deciduous, spreading shrub
with stout growths. A profusion of
large, deep yellow flowers is borne
from early to mid-spring
before sharply toothed,
dark green leaves appear.

☀ ◊ Zone 6

Hibbertia cuneiformis, illus. p.146
Kerria japonica 'Pleniflora', illus. p.131
Mahonia napaulensis
Mahonia 'Undulata'

Ochna serrulata
Ribes odoratum

YELLOW–ORANGE

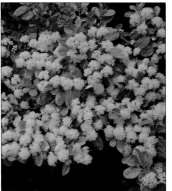

Azara serrata
Evergreen, upright shrub with glossy, bright green foliage and rounded bunches of fragrant, yellow flowers in late spring or early summer.

☼ ◊ Zone 9

Forsythia x *intermedia* 'Beatrix Farrand'
Vigorous, deciduous, bushy, arching shrub with stout shoots. A profusion of large, deep yellow flowers appears from early to mid-spring before oval, coarsely toothed, mid-green leaves emerge.

☼ ◊ Zone 6

Acacia podalyriifolia
(Mount Morgan wattle, Queensland silver wattle)
Evergreen, arching shrub that produces racemes of bright yellow flowers in spring. Has blue-green phyllodes (flattened, leaf-like stalks).

☼ ◊ Tender

Berberis x *stenophylla*
Evergreen, arching shrub with slender shoots and narrow, spine-tipped, deep green leaves, blue-grey beneath. Massed, golden-yellow flowers appear from mid- to late spring followed by small, blue-black fruits.

☼ ◊ ! Zone 6b

Berberis x *lologensis* 'Stapehill'
Vigorous, evergreen, arching shrub. Glossy, dark green foliage sets off profuse racemes of globose to cup-shaped, orange flowers from mid- to late spring.

☼ ◊ ! Zone 7

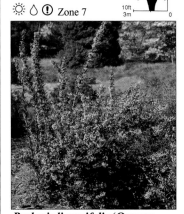

Berberis linearifolia 'Orange King'
Evergreen, upright, stiff-branched shrub with narrow, rigid, dark green leaves. Bears large, globose to cup-shaped, deep orange flowers in late spring.

☼ ◊ ! Zone 7

WHITE

Carissa macrocarpa 'Tuttlei', syn. *C. grandiflora* 'Tuttlei'
Evergreen, compact and spreading shrub with thorny stems and leathery leaves. Has fragrant flowers in spring-summer and edible, plum-like, red fruits in autumn. Min. 13°C (55°F).

☼ ◊ !

Philadelphus 'Beauclerk'
Deciduous, slightly arching shrub. Large, fragrant flowers, white with a small, central, pale purple blotch, are produced from early to mid-summer. Leaves are dark green.

☼ ◊ Zone 5

Exochorda x *macrantha* 'The Bride'
Deciduous, arching, dense shrub that forms a mound of pendent branches. Large, white flowers are produced in abundance amid dark green foliage in late spring and early summer.

☼ ◊ Zone 5b

□ WHITE

Deutzia scabra

Deciduous, upright shrub with narrowly oval, dark green leaves that, from early to mid-summer, set off dense, upright clusters of 5-petalled, white blooms.

☀ ◊ Zone 7

Philadelphus 'Belle Etoile'

Deciduous, arching shrub. Very fragrant, white flowers, each with a pale purple mark at the base, are borne profusely among mid-green foliage in late spring and early summer.

☀ ◊ Zone 5

Pyracantha x watereri, syn. P. 'Waterer's Orange'

Evergreen, upright, dense, spiny shrub with glossy, dark green foliage. Shallowly cup-shaped, white flowers in early summer are succeeded by bright red berries in autumn.

☀ ◊ ⓘ Zone 7

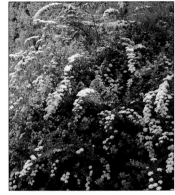

Spiraea canescens

Deciduous shrub with upright shoots arching at the top. Small heads of white flowers are borne in profusion amid narrowly oval, grey-green leaves from early to mid-summer.

☀ ◊ Zone 8

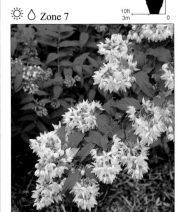

Deutzia x magnifica 'Staphyleoides'

Vigorous, deciduous, upright shrub. Large, 5-petalled, pure white blooms, borne in dense clusters in early summer, have recurved petals. Leaves are bright green.

☀ ◊ Zone 7

Aronia melanocarpa (Black chokeberry)

Deciduous, bushy shrub. White flowers appear in late spring and early summer, followed by black fruits. Has glossy, dark green leaves that turn red in autumn.

☀ ◊ Zone 4

Fallugia paradoxa (Apache plume)

Deciduous, bushy shrub that bears white flowers in mid-summer, followed by silky, pink- and red-tinged, green fruits. Dark green leaves are finely cut and feathery.

☀ ◊ Zone 7

Rubus 'Benenden', syn. R. 'Tridel'

Deciduous, arching, thornless shrub with peeling bark. Large, rose-like, pure white flowers are borne among lobed, deep green leaves in late spring and early summer.

☀ ◊ Zone 6

Olearia nummulariifolia

Evergreen, rounded shrub with stiff, upright shoots densely covered with small, very thick, mid- to dark green leaves. Small, fragrant, white flowers appear in mid-summer.

☀ ◊ Zone 8

SHRUBS

Sorbaria sorbifolia,
syn. *Spiraea sorbifolia*
Deciduous, upright shrub that forms
thickets by suckering. Mid-green
leaves consist of many sharply toothed
leaflets. Large panicles
of small, white flowers
appear in summer.

☼ ◊ Zone 2

Yucca gloriosa (Spanish dagger)
Evergreen shrub with a stout stem
crowned with a tuft of long, pointed,
deep green leaves, blue-green when
young. Bears very long panicles of
bell-shaped, white flowers
in summer-autumn.

☼ ◊ Zone 8

Philadelphus 'Dame Blanche'
Deciduous, bushy, compact shrub with
dark, peeling bark. Dark green foliage
sets off slightly fragrant, semi-double
to loosely double, pure white flowers
borne in profusion from
early to mid-summer.

☼ ◊ Zone 4b

Philadelphus 'Boule d'Argent'
Deciduous, bushy, arching shrub with
dark green foliage that sets off clusters
of slightly fragrant, semi-double to
double, pure white flowers from early
to mid-summer.

☼ ◊ Zone 5

Prinsepia uniflora
Deciduous, arching, spiny shrub. From
late spring to summer bears small,
fragrant, white flowers amid narrow,
glossy, dark green leaves followed by
cherry-like, deep red fruits.
Grows best in hot sun.

☼ ◊ Zone 4

Eucryphia milliganii
Evergreen, upright, narrow shrub. Has
tiny, dark green leaves, bluish-white
beneath, and small, white flowers,
borne in mid-summer.

☼ ◊ pH Zone 9

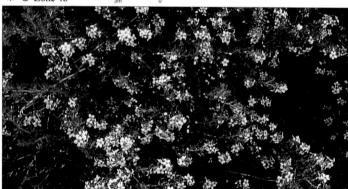

Escallonia virgata
Deciduous, spreading, graceful shrub
with arching shoots and small, glossy,
dark green leaves. Bears racemes of
small, open cup-shaped, white flowers
from early to mid-summer.

☼ ◊ Zone 8

SHRUBS medium SUMMER INTEREST

☐ WHITE

Osteomeles schweriniae
Evergreen, arching shrub with long, slender shoots. Leaves, consisting of many small leaflets, are dark green. Clusters of small, white flowers in early summer are followed by red, later blue-black, fruits.

☼ ◊ Zone 8

Styrax wilsonii
Deciduous, bushy shrub with slender shoots that produce an abundance of yellow-centred, white flowers in early summer. Leaves are small and deep green.

☼ ◑ pH Zone 8

Ceanothus incanus
Evergreen, bushy shrub. Has spreading, spiny shoots, broad, grey-green leaves and large racemes of white flowers in late spring and early summer.

☼ ◊ Zone 9

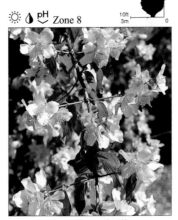

Philadelphus 'Lemoinei', syn. *P.* x *lemoinei*
Deciduous, upright, slightly arching shrub that produces profuse racemes of small, extremely fragrant, white flowers from early to mid-summer.

☼ ◊ Zone 4

Ozothamnus rosmarinifolius, syn. *Helichrysum rosmarinifolium*
Evergreen, upright, dense shrub with woolly, white shoots and narrow, dark green leaves. Clusters of fragrant, white flower heads open in early summer.

☼ ◊ Zone 9

Zenobia pulverulenta
Deciduous or semi-evergreen, slightly arching shrub, often with bluish-white-bloomed shoots. Glossy leaves have a bluish-white reverse when young. Bears fragrant, bell-shaped, white flowers from early to mid-summer.

☼ ◑ ◊ pH Zone 6

Carpenteria californica
Evergreen, bushy shrub. Glossy, dark green foliage sets off fragrant, yellow-centred, white flowers borne during summer.

☼ ◑ Zone 9

Symplocos paniculata
(Sapphire berry)
Deciduous, bushy shrub or small tree. Panicles of small, fragrant, white flowers in late spring and early summer are followed by small, metallic-blue berries. Has dark green leaves.

☼ ◊ Zone 6

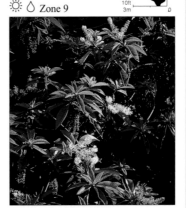

Clethra barbinervis
Deciduous, upright shrub with peeling bark. Has oval, toothed, dark green leaves that turn red and yellow in autumn. Racemes of fragrant, white flowers are borne in late summer and early autumn.

☼ ◑ pH Zone 7

Cornus alba 'Elegantissima'
Vigorous, deciduous shrub. Young shoots are bright red in winter. Has white-edged, grey-green leaves and small, creamy-white flowers in late spring and early summer followed by white fruits.

☼ ◊ ① Zone 2

Viburnum dilatatum 'Catskill'
Deciduous, low, spreading shrub with sharply toothed, dark green leaves that turn yellow, orange and red in autumn. Flat heads of creamy-white flowers in late spring and early summer are followed by bright red fruits.
☼ ◊ ① Zone 5

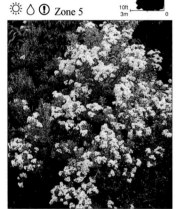

Olearia × _haastii_
Evergreen, bushy, dense shrub, good for hedging. Has small, oval, glossy, dark green leaves and is covered with heads of fragrant, daisy-like, white flowers from mid- to late summer. Min. 2°C (35°F).
☼ ◊

Philadelphus coronarius 'Variegatus'
Deciduous, bushy shrub with racemes of very fragrant, creamy-white flowers in late spring and early summer and mid-green leaves broadly edged with white.
☼ ◊ Zone 3

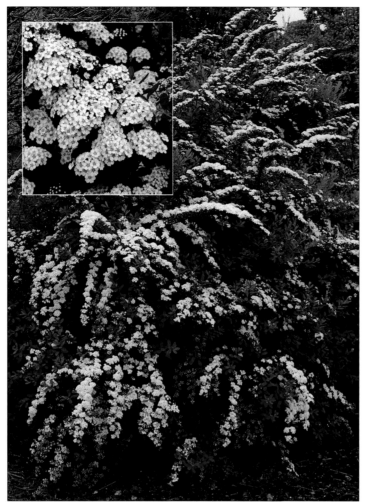

Spiraea nipponica 'Snowmound', syn. _S.n._ var. _tosaensis_ of gardens
Deciduous, spreading shrub with stout, arching, reddish branches. Small, narrow, dark green leaves set off profuse, dense clusters of small, white flowers in early summer.
☼ ◊ Zone 3

Eriogonum giganteum (St Catherine's lace)
Evergreen, rounded shrub with oblong to oval, woolly, white leaves. Small, white flowers are carried in branching clusters to 30cm (12in) or more wide in summer. Min. 5°C (41°F).
☼ ◊

Viburnum 'Pragense', syn. _V._ × _pragense_
Evergreen, rounded, bushy shrub that has dark green foliage and domed heads of white flowers opening from pink buds in late spring and early summer.
☼ ◊ ① Zone 7

Leptospermum polygalifolium, syn. _L. flavescens_
Evergreen, arching, graceful shrub with small, glossy, bright green leaves. Bears an abundance of small, pink-tinged, white flowers in mid-summer. Min. 2°C (35°F).
☼ ◊

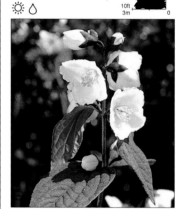

Philadelphus delavayi f. _melanocalyx_
Deciduous, upright shrub, grown for its extremely fragrant flowers, with pure white petals and deep purple sepals, opening from early to mid-summer. Leaves are dark green.
☼ ◊ Zone 7

Hibiscus syriacus 'Red Heart'
Deciduous, upright shrub that bears large, white flowers, with conspicuous red centres, from late summer to mid-autumn. Oval leaves are lobed and deep green.
☼ ◊ Zone 6

WHITE–PINK

 PINK

Lonicera xylosteum
(Fly honeysuckle)
Deciduous, upright, bushy, dense shrub. Creamy-white flowers are produced amid grey-green leaves in late spring and early summer and are followed by red berries.

☼ ◊ ! Zone 2

Acer palmatum 'Butterfly'
Slow-growing, deciduous, mounded shrub or small tree with lobed, grey-green leaves edged with cream and pink. In mid-spring bears small, reddish-purple flowers.

☼ ◊ Zone 6

Deutzia longifolia 'Veitchii'
Deciduous, arching shrub with narrow, pointed leaves and large clusters of 5-petalled, deep pink flowers from early to mid-summer.

☼ ◊ Zone 8

Protea neriifolia
Evergreen, bushy, upright shrub with narrow leaves. Flower heads, about 13cm (5in) long, are red, pink or white, the bracts tipped with tufts of black hair, and appear in spring-summer.
Min. 5–7°C (41–5°F).

☼ ◊ pH

Lonicera tatarica
Deciduous, bushy shrub. Tubular to trumpet-shaped, 5-lobed, white, pink or red flowers cover dark green foliage in late spring and early summer and are succeeded by red berries.

☼ ◊ ! Zone 2

Stephanandra tanakae
Deciduous, arching shrub with orange-brown shoots and sharply toothed, mid-green leaves that turn orange and yellow in autumn. Small, yellow-green buds open to white flowers from early to mid-summer.

☼ ◊ Zone 4b

Escallonia 'Donard Seedling'
Vigorous, evergreen, arching shrub with small, glossy, dark green leaves. Masses of pink flower buds open to white blooms, flushed with pale pink, from early to mid-summer.

☼ ◊ Zone 8

Neillia thibetica,
syn. *N. longiracemosa*
Deciduous, arching shrub. Slender spikes of rose-pink flowers are borne profusely in late spring and early summer. Leaves are sharply toothed.

☼ ◊ Zone 7

Deutzia pulchra
Deutzia scabra 'Plena'
Justicia adhatoda
Melastoma candidum

Neillia sinensis
RHODODENDRONS, illus. pp.132–4

Abelia × grandiflora, illus. p.121
Ceanothus 'Marie Simon'
Deutzia × elegantissima 'Fasciculata'
Grevillea rosmarinifolia

HYDRANGEAS, illus. p.144
Kolkwitzia amabilis
LILACS, illus. p.120
Weigela florida

SHRUBS

Escallonia 'Apple Blossom'
Evergreen, bushy, dense shrub. From early to mid-summer apple-blossom-pink flowers are borne in profusion amid glossy, dark green leaves.

☼ ◊ Zone 8

Robinia hispida (Rose acacia)
Deciduous shrub of loose habit with brittle, bristly stems that carry dark green leaves composed of 7–13 leaflets. Pendent racemes of deep rose-pink blooms open in late spring and early summer.

☼ ◊ ① Zone 3b

Indigofera heterantha, syn. *I. gerardiana*
Deciduous, slightly arching shrub. Has greyish-green leaves consisting of many small leaflets and spikes of small, purplish-pink flowers from early summer to early autumn.

☼ ◊ Zone 7

Lavatera 'Rosea', syn. *L. olbia* 'Rosea'
Semi-evergreen, erect shrub that produces abundant clusters of hollyhock-like, deep pink flowers throughout summer. Has lobed, sage-green leaves.

☼ ◊ Zone 9

Medinilla magnifica
Evergreen, upright shrub, with sparingly produced, 4-angled, robust stems and boldly veined leaves. Pink to coral-red flowers hang in long trusses beneath large, pink bracts in spring-summer. Min. 16–18°C (61–4°F).

☼ ◊

Hibiscus syriacus 'Woodbridge'
Deciduous, upright shrub. From late summer to mid-autumn large, reddish-pink flowers, with deeper-coloured centres, appear amid lobed, dark green leaves.

☼ ◊ Zone 6

Kalmia latifolia (Calico bush)
Evergreen, bushy, dense shrub. In early summer large clusters of pink flowers open from distinctively crimped buds amid glossy, rich green foliage.

☼ ◊ pH ① Zone 5b

Hibiscus rosa-sinensis 'The President'
Evergreen, bushy shrub with toothed, oval, glossy, dark green leaves. In summer bears large, magenta-centred, bright pink flowers with prominent, yellow anthers. Min. 15°C (59°F).

☼ ◊

Lavatera assurgentiflora
Semi-evergreen shrub with twisted, grey stems. Clusters of hollyhock-like, darkly veined, deep cerise blooms open in mid-summer. Palmate, mid-green leaves are white-haired beneath. Min. 2°C (35°F).

☼ ◊

Ceanothus 'Perle Rose', illus. p.163
Escallonia 'Edinensis'
FUCHSIAS, illus. pp.164–5
HEATHERS, illus. pp.178–9

HYDRANGEAS, illus. p.144
Justicia carnea, illus. p.163
Kalmia latifolia 'Ostbo Red'
LILACS, illus. p.120

RHODODENDRONS, illus. pp.132–4
Richea scoparia
Robinia hispida var. *kelseyi*
Rondeletia amoena

Rubus ulmifolius 'Bellidiflorus'
Spiraea x *billiardii*

◼◻ PINK–RED

Melaleuca elliptica
(Granite bottlebrush)
Evergreen, rounded shrub with long,
leathery, usually greyish-green leaves.
Flowers, consisting of a brush of red
stamens, are borne in dense,
terminal spikes in spring-
summer. Min. 5°C (41°F).

Cestrum elegans
Vigorous, evergreen, arching shrub.
Nodding shoots carry downy, deep
green foliage. Dense racemes of
tubular, purplish-red flowers in
late spring and summer are
followed by deep red fruits.
Min. 5°C (41°F).

◼ RED

Pieris formosa var. **forrestii**
'Wakehurst'
Evergreen, bushy, dense shrub. Young
leaves are brilliant red in early summer,
becoming pink, creamy-yellow and
finally dark green. Bears
urn-shaped, white flowers
in spring-summer.

Zone 8

Lonicera ledebourii
Deciduous, bushy shrub. Red-tinged,
orange-yellow flowers are borne amid
dark green foliage in late spring and
early summer and are followed by
black berries. As these
ripen, deep red bracts
enlarge around them.

Zone 6

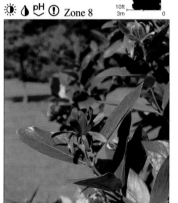

Escallonia 'Langleyensis'
Evergreen or semi-evergreen, arching
shrub with small, glossy, bright green
leaves and an abundance of rose-pink
flowers from early to mid-summer.

Zone 8

Calycanthus occidentalis
(California allspice)
Deciduous, bushy shrub. Leaves are
large, aromatic and dark green.
Fragrant, purplish-red flowers with
many strap-shaped petals
appear during summer.

Zone 7

Crinodendron hookerianum,
syn. **Tricuspidaria lanceolata**
(Lantern tree)
Evergreen, stiff-branched shrub. In late
spring and early summer, lantern-like,
red flowers hang from
shoots clothed with narrow,
dark green leaves.

Zone 9

Bauhinia galpinii,
syn. **B. punctata**
Semi-evergreen or evergreen,
spreading shrub, occasionally semi-
climbing. Has 2-lobed leaves and,
in summer, fragrant,
bright brick-red flowers.
Min. 5°C (41°F).

Telopea speciosissima (Waratah)
Evergreen, erect, fairly bushy shrub
with coarsely serrated leaves. Has
tubular, red flowers in dense, globose
heads, surrounded by bright red bracts,
in spring-summer.
Min. 5°C (41°F).

Escallonia 'Donard Beauty'	Pavonia hastata
Hibiscus schizopetalus	Spiraea x billiardii 'Triumphans'
Leptospermum scoparium 'Nicholsii'	Spiraea japonica cvs, illus. p.163
Lonicera tatarica 'Hack's Red'	Sutherlandia frutescens, illus. p.165

Abelia floribunda	Cestrum 'Newellii'
Abutilon 'Ashford Red'	Correa 'Mannii'
Callistemon speciosus	Escallonia rubra 'Crimson Spire'
Callistemon subulatus	FUCHSIAS, illus. pp.164–5

Erythrina crista-galli
(Cockspur coral-tree)
Deciduous, mainly upright shrub or
small tree. Leaves have 3 oval leaflets.
Has leafy racemes of crimson flowers
in summer-autumn. Dies
back to ground level in
winter. Min. –1°C (30°F).

Erythrina x bidwillii
Deciduous, upright shrub with pale to
mid-green leaves divided into
3 leaflets, up to 10cm (4in) long. Bright
red flowers are carried in racemes in
late summer or autumn.
Min. –1°C (30°F).

Acca sellowiana, syn. *Feijoa
sellowiana* (Pineapple guava)
Evergreen, bushy shrub or tree. Dark
green leaves have white undersides.
In mid-summer bears large, dark red
flowers with white-edged
petals, followed by edible,
red-tinged, green fruits.
Zone 9

Aloysia triphylla, syn. *Lippia
citriodora* (Lemon verbena)
Deciduous, bushy shrub. Leaves
are pale green and lemon-scented.
Racemes of tiny, lilac-tinged,
white flowers appear
in early summer.
Zone 9

Desfontainia spinosa
Evergreen, bushy, dense shrub with
spiny, holly-like, glossy, dark green
leaves. Long, tubular, drooping, red
flowers, tipped with yellow, are
borne from mid-summer
to late autumn.
pH Zone 9

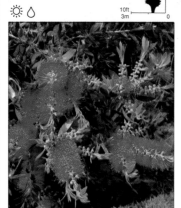

Callistemon citrinus 'Splendens'
Evergreen, arching shrub with broad,
lemon-scented, grey-green leaves that
are bronze-red when young. In early
summer bright red flowers are borne
in bottlebrush-like spikes.
Min. 2°C (35°F).

Acer palmatum 'Bloodgood'
Deciduous, bushy-headed shrub or
small tree with deep reddish-purple
leaves that turn brilliant red in autumn.
Small, reddish-purple flowers in mid-
spring are often followed
by decorative, winged,
red fruits.
Zone 5b

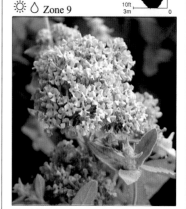

Buddleja crispa
Deciduous, upright, bushy shrub that,
from mid- to late summer, bears
racemes of small, fragrant, lilac flowers
with white eyes. Has woolly, white
shoots and oval, greyish-
green leaves.
Zone 9

Callistemon rigidus
Evergreen, bushy, slightly arching
shrub with long, narrow, sharply
pointed, dark green leaves and dense
spikes of deep red flowers in late
spring and early summer.
Min. 2°C (35°F).

Rhus glabra (Smooth sumach)
Deciduous, bushy shrub with bluish-
white-bloomed, reddish-purple stems.
Deep blue-green leaves turn red in
autumn. Bears panicles of greenish-red
flower heads in summer
followed by red fruits
on female plants.
Zone 2b

Acalypha wilkesiana
(Copperleaf, Jacob's coat)
Evergreen, bushy shrub. Oval, serrated
leaves are 10cm (4in) or more long,
rich copper-green, variably splashed
with shades of red.
Min. 16°C (61°F).

**Hibiscus sinosyriacus 'Lilac
Queen'**
Deciduous, spreading, open shrub.
From late summer to mid-autumn
produces large, pale lilac flowers with
red centres. Broad, lobed
leaves are dark green.
Zone 7

Hydrangeas

Valued for their late summer flowers, hydrangeas are versatile shrubs that thrive in a variety of situations. Larger-growing species, some of which may become tree-like with age, are best suited to light woodland, while there is a wide range of cultivars, mostly of *H. macrophylla*, that make excellent border plants. Some may also be grown in containers. Colours range from white through pink, red and purple to blue, but the truest blue is obtained only on acid soil. Lacecap hydrangeas have a central corymb of small, fertile flowers surrounded by showy, large, coloured bracts; mopheads (or hortensias) have domed heads of sterile bracts only. *H. paniculata* cultivars bear larger though fewer cone-shaped flower heads if pruned hard in spring. Hydrangea flower heads persist on the plants for many months, and may be dried for winter decoration indoors.

H. paniculata
'Floribunda' ①

H. villosa ①

H. paniculata
'Unique' ①

H. macrophylla
'Lanarth White' ①

H. macrophylla
'Lilacina' ①

H. quercifolia ①

H. paniculata
'Praecox' ①

H. heteromalla
'Bretschneideri' ①

H. involucrata
'Hortensis' ①

H. macrophylla
'Veitchii' ①

H. macrophylla **'Blue Wave'** ①

H. arborescens
'Grandiflora' ①

H. paniculata **'Brussels Lace'** ①

H.m. **'Générale Vicomtesse de Vibraye'** ①

H. arborescens
'Annabelle' ①

H. macrophylla
'Hamburg' ①

H. serrata
'Bluebird' ①

H. paniculata Pink
Diamond ①

H. macrophylla
'Altona' ①

H. serrata ①

H. macrophylla **'Blue Bonnet'** ①

SHRUBS medium SUMMER INTEREST

■ PURPLE

Prostanthera ovalifolia
Evergreen, bushy, rounded shrub with tiny, sweetly aromatic, oval, thick-textured leaves. Cup-shaped, 2-lipped, purple flowers appear in short, leafy racemes in spring-summer. Min. 5°C (41°F).

☼ ◊ 10ft 3m / 10ft 3m / 0

Melaleuca nesophila, syn. *M. nesophylla* (Western tea-myrtle)
Evergreen, bushy shrub or small tree with oval, grey-green leaves. Flowers, consisting of a brush of lavender to rose-pink stamens, are borne in rounded, terminal heads in summer. Min. 5°C (41°F).

☼ ◊ 10ft 3m / 10ft 3m / 0

Abutilon x *suntense* 'Violetta'
Fast-growing, deciduous, upright, arching shrub that carries an abundance of large, bowl-shaped, deep violet flowers in late spring and early summer. Vine-like leaves are sharply toothed and dark green. Min. 5°C (41°F).

☼ ◊ 10ft 3m / 10ft 3m / 0

Prostanthera rotundifolia (Round-leaved mint-bush)
Evergreen, bushy, rounded shrub with tiny, sweetly aromatic, deep green leaves and short, leafy racemes of bell-shaped, lavender to purple-blue flowers in late spring or summer. Min. 2°C (35°F).

☼ ◊ 10ft 3m / 10ft 3m / 0

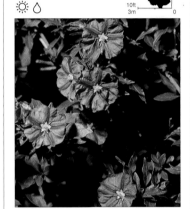

Solanum rantonnetii 'Royal Robe'
Evergreen, loosely rounded shrub with smooth, bright green leaves. In summer has clusters of rich purple-blue flowers that open almost flat. Min. 7°C (45°F).

☼ ◊ ! 10ft 3m / 10ft 3m / 0

Sophora davidii, syn. *S. viciifolia*
Deciduous, bushy shrub with arching shoots. Produces short racemes of small, pea-like, purple and white flowers in late spring and early summer. Grey-green leaves have many leaflets.

☼ ◊ Zone 7 10ft 3m / 10ft 3m / 0

■ PURPLE–BLUE

Fabiana imbricata f. *violacea*, syn. *F.i.* 'Violacea'
Evergreen, upright shrub with shoots that are densely covered with tiny, heath-like, deep green leaves. Tubular, lilac flowers are borne profusely in early summer.

☼ ◊ Zone 9? 10ft 3m / 10ft 3m / 0

Hibiscus syriacus 'Oiseau Bleu', syn. *H.s.* 'Blue Bird'
Deciduous, upright shrub that carries large, red-centred, lilac-blue flowers from late summer to mid-autumn. Has lobed, deep green leaves.

☼ ◊ Zone 6 10ft 3m / 10ft 3m / 0

Ceanothus impressus
Evergreen, bushy shrub. Spreading growth is covered with small, crinkled, dark green leaves. Deep blue flowers appear in small clusters from mid-spring to early summer.

☼ ◊ Zone 9 10ft 3m / 10ft 3m / 0

Ceanothus x *veitchianus*
HYDRANGEAS, illus. p.144
Teucrium fruticans 'Azureum'
Tibouchina urvilleana, illus. p.122

■ GREEN

Eleutherococcus sieboldianus
Deciduous, bushy, elegant shrub. Has glossy, bright green leaves, divided into 5 leaflets, and is armed with spines. Clusters of small, greenish flowers appear in early summer.

☼ ◊ Zone 5 10ft 3m / 10ft 3m / 0

Zanthoxylum piperitum (Japan pepper)
Deciduous, bushy, spiny shrub or small tree with aromatic, glossy, dark green leaves composed of many leaflets. Small, red fruits follow tiny, greenish-yellow, spring flowers.

☼ ◊ Zone 7 10ft 3m / 10ft 3m / 0

Ptelea trifoliata 'Aurea'
Deciduous, bushy, dense shrub or low tree. Leaves, consisting of 3 leaflets, are bright yellow when young, maturing to pale green. Bears racemes of greenish flowers in summer, followed by winged, green fruits.

☼ ◊ Zone 4 10ft 3m / 10ft 3m / 0

Oplopanax horridus
Rhamnus imeretina
Ricinus communis, illus. p.335
Sambucus racemosa 'Plumosa'

SHRUBS medium SUMMER INTEREST

GREEN–YELLOW

Itea ilicifolia
Evergreen, bushy shrub with arching shoots and oval, sharply toothed, glossy, dark green leaves. Long, catkin-like racemes of small, greenish flowers appear in late summer and early autumn.

☀ ◊ Zone 8

Cornus alba 'Spaethii'
Vigorous, deciduous shrub with bright red, young shoots in winter. Bright green leaves are yellow-edged. Bears small, creamy-white flowers in late spring and early summer, followed by rounded, white fruits.

☀ ◊ ① Zone 2

Piptanthus nepalensis,
syn. *P. laburnifolius*
Deciduous or semi-evergreen, open shrub with leaves consisting of 3 large, dark blue-green leaflets. Racemes of pea-like, bright yellow flowers appear in spring-summer. Min. 2°C (35°F).

☀ ◊

Hibbertia cuneiformis,
syn. *Candollea cuneiformis*
Evergreen, upright, bushy shrub with small, oval leaves, serrated at tips. Has small clusters of bright yellow flowers, with spreading petals, in spring-summer.
Min. 5–7°C (41–5°F).

☀ ◊

Callistemon pallidus
Evergreen, arching shrub. Grey-green foliage is pink-tinged when young and in early summer is covered with dense spikes of creamy-yellow flowers that resemble bottlebrushes.
Min. 5°C (41°F).

☀ ◊

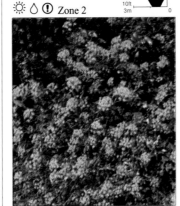

Bupleurum fruticosum
(Shrubby hare's ear)
Evergreen, bushy shrub with slender shoots. From mid-summer to early autumn rounded heads of small, yellow flowers are borne amid glossy, dark bluish-green foliage.

☀ ◊ Zone 8

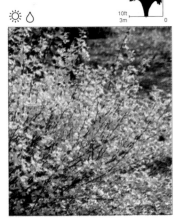

Physocarpus opulifolius 'Dart's Gold'
Deciduous, compact shrub with peeling bark and oval, lobed, golden-yellow leaves. Produces clusters of shallowly cup-shaped, white or pale pink flowers in late spring.

☀ ◊ pH Zone 2b

Colutea arborescens
(Bladder senna)
Fast-growing, deciduous, open shrub. Has pale green leaves with many leaflets, pea-like, yellow flowers throughout summer and bladder-like seed pods in late summer and autumn.

☀ ◊ ① Zone 5

Jasminum humile
(Yellow jasmine)
Evergreen, bushy shrub that bears bright yellow flowers on long, slender, green shoots from early spring to late autumn. Leaves, with 5 or 7 leaflets, are bright green.

☀ ◊ Zone 8

Colutea × media
Vigorous, deciduous, open shrub.
Grey-green leaves have many leaflets.
Racemes of yellow flowers, tinged
with copper-orange, appear in summer,
followed by bladder-like,
papery, red-tinged seed
pods.

 Zone 5

Dendromecon rigida
Vigorous, evergreen, upright shrub,
best grown against a wall. Large,
fragrant, golden-yellow flowers appear
amid grey-green foliage from spring
to autumn.

 Zone 9

Colletia hystrix, syn. *C. armata*
Almost leafless, arching, stoutly
branched shrub armed with rigid, grey-
green spines. Pink flower buds open
in late summer to fragrant, tubular,
white blooms that
last into autumn.

 Zone 8

Calliandra haematocephala
[pink form]
Evergreen, spreading shrub. Leaves
have 16–24 narrowly oval leaflets.
Flower heads consist of many
pink-stamened florets
from late autumn to spring.
Min. 7°C (45°F).

Senna corymbosa,
syn. *Cassia corymbosa*
Vigorous, evergreen or semi-evergreen
shrub. Leaves have 4–6 oval, bright
green leaflets; sprays of bowl-shaped,
rich yellow flowers
appear in late summer.
Min. 7°C (45°F).

Senna didymobotrya, syn. *Cassia
didymobotrya* (Golden wonder)
Evergreen, rounded, sometimes
spreading shrub with leaves of several
leaflets. Spikes of rich yellow flowers
open from glossy, blackish-
brown buds throughout
the year. Min. 13°C (55°F).

Clerodendrum trichotomum
Deciduous, upright, bushy-headed,
tree-like shrub. Clusters of deep pink
and greenish-white buds open to
fragrant, white flowers above large
leaves from late summer to
mid-autumn, followed by
decorative, blue berries.

 Zone 6

Euonymus hamiltonianus subsp.
sieboldianus 'Red Elf'
Deciduous, upright shrub with mid- to
dark green foliage. Decorative, deep
pink fruits, borne in profusion after
tiny, green flowers in early
summer, open in autumn to
reveal red seeds.

 Zone 6

Spartium junceum
(Spanish broom)
Deciduous, almost leafless, upright
shrub that arches with age. Fragrant,
pea-like, golden-yellow flowers appear
from early summer to early
autumn on dark green
shoots.

 Zone 7

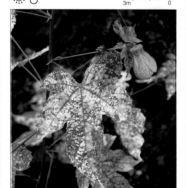

Abutilon pictum 'Thompsonii'
Robust, evergreen, upright shrub with
3–5-lobed, serrated, rich green, heavily
yellow-mottled leaves. Yellow-orange
flowers with crimson veins are borne
from summer to autumn.
Min. 5–7°C (41–5°F).

Viburnum farreri,
syn. *V. fragrans*
Deciduous, upright shrub. In late
autumn and during mild periods in
winter and early spring bears fragrant,
white or pale pink flowers.
Dark green foliage is
bronze when young.

 Zone 5b

**Euonymus europaeus 'Red
Cascade'**
Deciduous, bushy shrub or small tree
with narrowly oval, mid-green leaves
that redden in autumn as red fruits open
to show orange seeds. Has
inconspicuous, greenish
flowers in early summer.

 Zone 4

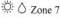
Abutilon 'Golden Fleece'
Banksia baxteri
Cestrum aurantiacum
Colutea orientalis

Juanulloa mexicana, illus. p.171
Justicia spicigera, illus. p.172
Ochna serrulata
Senna × floribunda

OTHER RECOMMENDED PLANTS:
Berberis 'Rubrostilla', illus. p.172
Brugmansia arborea
Euonymus cornutus var. *quinquecornutus*

Eupatorium ligustrinum
Symphoricarpos albus var. *laevigatus*
Turraea obtusifolia, illus. p.172
Viburnum opulus 'Compactum', illus. p.172

SHRUBS medium AUTUMN INTEREST

■ RED

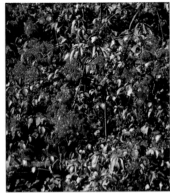

Viburnum betulifolium
Deciduous, upright, arching shrub.
Bright green leaves are slightly glossy
beneath. Heads of small, white flowers
in early summer are succeeded by
profuse nodding clusters of
decorative, bright red fruits
in autumn-winter.

☼ ◊ ① Zone 6

Euonymus latifolius
Deciduous, open shrub. Mid-green
foliage turns brilliant red in late
autumn. At the same time large, deep
red fruits with prominent wings open
to reveal orange seeds.

☼ ◊ ① Zone 7

Euonymus alatus (Winged spindle)
Deciduous, bushy, dense shrub with
shoots that develop corky wings. Dark
green leaves turn brilliant red in
autumn. Inconspicuous, greenish
flowers in summer are
followed by small,
purple-red fruits.

☼ ◊ ① Zone 3

Nymania capensis
Evergreen, more or less rounded,
rigidly branched shrub or small tree.
In spring has flowers with upright, pink
to rose-purple petals. Bears papery,
inflated, red fruits in
autumn.
Min. 7–10°C (45–50°F).

☼ ◊

Cornus alba 'Kesselringii'
Vigorous, deciduous shrub with deep
purplish stems. Dark green leaves
become flushed reddish-purple in
autumn. Creamy-white flowers in
late spring and early
summer are followed
by white fruits.

☼ ◊ ① Zone 2

■■ PURPLE–BLUE

Callicarpa bodinieri var. giraldii
Deciduous, bushy shrub. Leaves are
pale green, often bronze-tinged when
young. Tiny, lilac flowers in mid-
summer are followed by small,
violet berries.

☼ ◊ Zone 6b

Clerodendrum bungei
Evergreen or deciduous, upright,
suckering shrub or sub-shrub with
heart-shaped, coarsely serrated leaves.
Has domed clusters of small, fragrant,
red-purple to deep pink
flowers in late summer
and early autumn.

☼ ◊ Zone 8b

Ceanothus 'Autumnal Blue'
Fast-growing, evergreen, bushy shrub.
Has glossy, bright green foliage and
large panicles of pale to mid-blue
flowers from late spring to autumn.

☼ ◊ Zone 9

□ ORANGE

Berberis x carminea 'Barbarossa'
Semi-evergreen, arching shrub. Has
narrowly oval, dark green leaves and
racemes of rounded, yellow flowers
in late spring and early summer,
followed by globose,
orange-scarlet fruits.

☼ ◊ ① Zone 7

Zanthoxylum simulans
Deciduous, bushy shrub or small tree
with stout spines. Aromatic, glossy,
bright green leaves consist of 5 leaflets.
Tiny, yellowish-green flowers in
late spring and early
summer are followed
by orange-red fruits.

☼ ◊ Zone 7

Cotoneaster simonsii
Deciduous or semi-evergreen, upright
shrub, suitable for hedging. Has oval,
glossy, dark green leaves, shallowly
cup-shaped, white flowers in early
summer and long-lasting,
orange-red fruits
in autumn.

☼ ◊ ① Zone 7

Berberis x carminea 'Pirate King'
Cotoneaster bullatus 'Firebird'
Cotoneaster hupehensis
Cotoneaster 'Hybridus Pendulus'

Disanthus cercidifolius
Grevillea 'Poorinda Constance'
Vaccinium corymbosum 'Pioneer',
     illus. p.173

Callicarpa bodinieri
Elsholtzia stauntonii, illus. p.173
HEATHERS, illus. pp.178–9
Vitex agnus-castus

Corokia x virgata
Cotoneaster franchetii
Pyracantha angustifolia
Pyracantha rogersiana

ORANGE–YELLOW

WHITE

Colquhounia coccinea
Evergreen or semi-evergreen, open
shrub. Has aromatic, sage-green leaves
and whorls of scarlet or orange flowers
in late summer and autumn.

☼ ◊ Zone 9

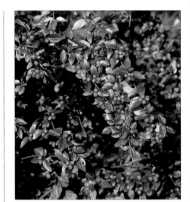

Cotoneaster sternianus,
syn. *C. franchetii* var. *sternianus*
Evergreen or semi-evergreen, arching
shrub. Leaves are grey-green, white
beneath. Pink-tinged, white flowers
in early summer are
followed by orange-red
fruits.

☼ ◊ ① Zone 8

Rubus biflorus
Deciduous, upright shrub with chalky-
white, young shoots in winter. Leaves,
consisting of 5–7 oval leaflets, are dark
green above, white beneath. White
flowers in late spring and
early summer are followed
by edible, yellow fruits.

☼ ◊ Zone 7

Viburnum tinus (Laurustinus)
Evergreen, bushy, dense shrub with
oval, dark green leaves. Freely
produced flat heads of small, white
blooms open from pink buds during
late winter and spring.

☼ ◊ ① Zone 9

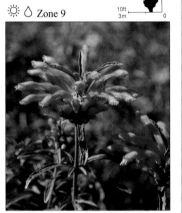

Leonotis leonurus (Lion's ear)
Semi-evergreen, sparingly branched,
erect shrub. Has lance-shaped leaves
and whorls of tubular, bright orange
flowers in late autumn and early winter.
Min. 5°C (41°F).

☼ ◊

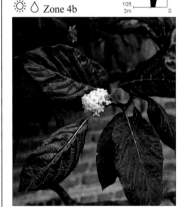

Rubus thibetanus
Deciduous, arching shrub with white-
bloomed, brownish-purple, young
shoots in winter and fern-like, glossy,
dark green foliage, white beneath.
Small, pink flowers from
mid- to late summer are
followed by black fruits.

☼ ◊ Zone 4b

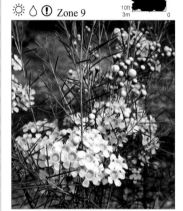

Chamelaucium uncinatum [white
form] (Geraldton waxflower)
Evergreen, wiry-stemmed, bushy shrub.
Each needle-like leaf has a tiny, hooked
tip. Flowers ranging from deep rose-
purple to pink, lavender or
white appear in late winter
or spring. Min. 5°C (41°F).

☼ ◊ pH

Pyracantha 'Golden Charmer'
Evergreen, bushy, arching, spiny shrub
with glossy, bright green leaves.
Flattish clusters of white flowers in
early summer are succeeded by large,
bright orange berries
in early autumn.

☼ ◊ ① Zone 6

Pyracantha 'Golden Dome'
Evergreen, rounded, very dense, spiny
shrub. Dark green foliage sets off white
flowers borne in early summer. These
are followed by orange-yellow berries
in early autumn.

☼ ◊ Zone 7

Viburnum foetens,
syn. *V. grandiflorum* f. *foetens*
Deciduous, bushy shrub that has
aromatic, dark green leaves. Dense
clusters of pink buds open to very
fragrant, white flowers
from mid-winter to
early spring.

☼ ◊ ① Zone 7

Calliandra haematocephala
[white form]
Evergreen, spreading shrub. Leaves
have 16–24 leaflets. Flower heads
comprising many white-stamened
florets appear from late
autumn to spring.
Min. 7°C (45°F).

☼ ◊

Chaenomeles speciosa
HEATHERS, illus. pp.178–9
HOLLIES, illus. pp.98–9
Nicotiana glauca

Stephanandra incisa

OTHER RECOMMENDED PLANTS:
Buddleja asiatica
Gardenia thunbergia
Lonicera fragrantissima

Lonicera x *purpusii*, illus. p.173
Lonicera standishii
Rubus cockburnianus
Salix irrorata

WHITE–PINK

Dombeya burgessiae,
syn. *D. mastersii*
Evergreen shrub with rounded, 3-lobed, downy leaves and dense clusters of fragrant, white flowers, with pink to red veins, in autumn-winter. Min. 5°C (41°F).

Chamelaucium uncinatum [pink form] (Geraldton waxflower)
Evergreen, wiry-stemmed, bushy shrub. Each needle-like leaf has a tiny, hooked tip. Flowers ranging from deep rose-purple to pink, lavender or white appear in late winter or spring. Min. 5°C (41°F).

RED–PURPLE

Cornus alba 'Sibirica'
Deciduous, upright shrub with scarlet, young shoots in winter. Has dark green foliage and heads of creamy-white flowers in late spring and early summer, succeeded by rounded, white fruits.

☼ ◊ ① Zone 2

YELLOW

Stachyurus praecox
Deciduous, spreading, open shrub with purplish-red shoots. Drooping spikes of pale greenish-yellow flowers open in late winter and early spring, before pointed, deep green leaves appear.

☼ ◊ pH Zone 7b

Acokanthera oblongifolia, syn. *A. spectabilis, Carissa spectabilis* (Wintersweet)
Evergreen, rounded shrub. Has fragrant, white or pinkish flowers in late winter and spring and poisonous, black fruits in autumn. Min. 10°C (50°F).

☼ ◊ ①

Viburnum x bodnantense 'Dawn'
Deciduous, upright shrub with oval, bronze, young leaves that mature to dark green. Racemes of deep pink buds open to fragrant, pink flowers during mild periods from late autumn to early spring.

☼ ◊ ① Zone 7

Ardisia crenata, syn. *A. crenulata* (Coralberry, Spiceberry)
Evergreen, upright, open shrub. Has fragrant, star-shaped, white flowers in early summer, followed by long-lasting, bright red fruits. Min. 10°C (50°F).

☽ ◊

Daphne bholua
Evergreen, occasionally deciduous, upright shrub with leathery, dark green foliage. Terminal clusters of richly fragrant, purplish-pink and white flowers are borne in winter.

☼ ◊ ① Zone 9

Euphorbia pulcherrima
(Poinsettia)
Evergreen, sparingly branched shrub. Has small, greenish-red flowers surrounded by bright red, pink, yellow or white bracts from late autumn to spring. Min. 15°C (59°F).

☼ ◊

Iochroma cyanea,
syn. *I. tubulosa*
Evergreen, semi-upright, slender-branched shrub. Tubular, deep purple-blue flowers, with flared mouths, appear in dense clusters from late autumn to early summer. Min. 7–10°C (45–50°F).

☼ ◊

Duranta erecta,
syn. *D. plumieri, D. repens* (Pigeon berry, Skyflower)
Fast-growing, usually evergreen, bushy shrub. Has spikes of lilac-blue flowers, mainly in summer, followed by yellow fruits. Min. 10°C (50°F).

☼ ◊

SHRUBS

☐☐☐ WHITE–PURPLE

Mahonia japonica
Evergreen, upright shrub with deep green leaves consisting of many spiny leaflets. Long, spreading sprays of fragrant, yellow flowers appear from late autumn to spring, succeeded by purple-blue fruits.

☼ ◊ Zone 7

Jasminum nudiflorum
(Winter jasmine)
Deciduous, arching shrub with oval, dark green leaves. Bright yellow flowers appear on slender, leafless, green shoots in winter and early spring.

☼ ◊ Zone 7

Euonymus japonicus 'Latifolius Albomarginatus'
Evergreen, upright, bushy and dense shrub with oval, dark green leaves broadly edged with white. Produces clusters of insignificant, greenish-white flowers in late spring.

☼ ◊ ① Zone 5b

Fatsia japonica 'Variegata'
Evergreen, rounded, bushy and dense shrub with palmate, glossy, dark green leaves, variegated marginally with creamy-white, and large sprays of small, white flowers in autumn.

☼ ◊ Zone 8

Euonymus fortunei 'Silver Queen'
Evergreen, bushy, sometimes scandent shrub with a dense growth of dark green leaves, broadly edged with white. Produces insignificant, greenish-white flowers in spring.

☼ ◊ ① Zone 5

Nandina domestica 'Firepower'
Evergreen or semi-evergreen, elegant, bamboo-like, dwarf shrub. Leaves have dark green leaflets, purplish-red when young and in autumn-winter. Bears small, white flowers in summer followed in warm areas by orange-red fruits.

☼ ◊ Zone 7

x *Citrofortunella microcarpa*,
syn. x *C. mitis*, *Citrus mitis*
(Calamondin)
Evergreen, bushy shrub with leathery, leaves. Intermittently has tiny, fragrant flowers followed by orange-yellow fruits.
Min. 5–10°C (41–50°F).

☼ ◊

Dracaena sanderiana
(Ribbon plant)
Evergreen, upright shrub with seldom branching, cane-like stems. Lance-shaped leaves, 15–25cm (6–10in) long, are pale to grey-green, with bold, creamy-white edges.
Min. 13°C (55°F).

☼ ◊

Dodonaea viscosa 'Purpurea'
Evergreen, bushy shrub or tree. Firm-textured leaves are flushed copper-purple. Has clusters of small, reddish or purplish seed capsules in late summer or autumn. Makes a good hedge in a windy site. Min. 5°C (41°F).

☼ ◊

Acacia podalyriifolia, illus. p.135
Cornus stolonifera 'Flaviramea'
Cytisus x *spachianus*
Edgeworthia chrysantha

HEATHERS, illus. pp.178–9
Stachyurus chinensis

OTHER RECOMMENDED PLANTS:
Acalypha hispida
Cleyera japonica 'Tricolor'
x *Fatshedera lizei* 'Variegata'

Mackaya bella
Pandanus tectorius 'Veitchii', illus. p.175
Polyscias filicifolia 'Marginata'
Rhamnus alaternus 'Argenteovariegata'

SHRUBS

Corokia cotoneaster
(Wire-netting bush)
Evergreen, bushy, open shrub with
interlacing shoots. Has small, spoon-
shaped, dark green leaves, fragrant,
yellow flowers in late
spring and red fruits
in autumn.

☼ ◊ Zone 9

Encephalartos ferox
Slow-growing, evergreen, palm-like
plant, almost trunkless for many years.
Feather-shaped leaves, 60–180cm
(2–6ft) long, have many serrated and
spine-tipped, leathery,
greyish leaflets.
Min. 10–13°C (50–55°F).

☼ ◊

Cycas revoluta
(Japanese sago palm)
Slow-growing, evergreen, palm-like
plant that may produce several trunks.
Leaves have spine-tipped leaflets with
rolled margins. Bears tight
clusters of reddish fruits in
autumn. Min. 13°C (55°F).

☼ ◊

Aucuba japonica
Evergreen, dense, bushy shrub with
stout, green shoots and glossy, dark
green leaves. Small, purplish flowers
in mid-spring are followed on female
plants by rounded to egg-
shaped, bright red berries.

☼ ◊ Zone 7b

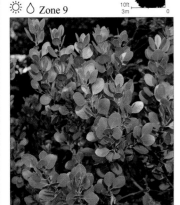

Arctostaphylos patula
Evergreen, rounded shrub with reddish-
brown bark and bright grey-green
foliage. Urn-shaped, white or pale
pink flowers appear from mid-
to late spring, followed
by brown fruits.

☼ ◊ pH Zone 7

Rhapis excelsa
(Bamboo palm, Slender lady palm)
Evergreen fan palm, eventually
forming clumps. Leaves are 20–30cm
(8–12in) long, composed of 20 or more
narrow, glossy, deep green
lobes in fan formation.
Min. 15°C (59°F).

☼ ◊

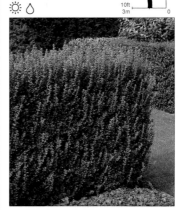

**Buxus sempervirens
'Handsworthensis'**
Vigorous, evergreen, bushy, upright
shrub or small tree. Has broad, very
dark green leaves. A dense habit makes
it ideal for hedging or
screening.

☼ ◊ ① Zone 6

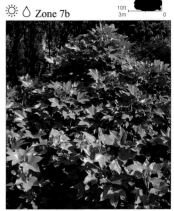

× Fatshedera lizei (Tree ivy)
Evergreen, loose-branched shrub that
forms a mound of deeply lobed, glossy,
deep green leaves. May also be trained
as a climber. Sprays of small, white
flowers appear in autumn.

☼ ◊ Zone 7

Ficus deltoidea (Mistletoe fig)
Slow-growing, evergreen, bushy shrub
with bright green leaves, red-brown-
tinted beneath. Bears small, greenish-
white fruits that mature to dull yellow.
Min. 15–18°C (59–64°F).

☼ ◊ ①

Philodendron bipinnatifidum,
syn. *P. selloum*
Evergreen, unbranched shrub. Glossy
leaves, to 60cm (2ft) or more long, are
divided into many finger-like lobes.
Occasionally produces
greenish-white spathes.
Min. 15–18°C (59–64°F).

☼ ◊ ①

Polyscias filicifolia
(Fern-leaf aralia)
Evergreen, erect, sparingly branched
shrub. Leaves are 30cm (12in) long and
are divided into many small, serrated,
bright green leaflets.
Min. 15–18°C (59–64°F).

☼ ◊

Chamaedorea elegans,
syn. *Neanthe bella* (Dwarf
mountain palm, Parlour palm)
Evergreen, slender palm, suckering
with age. Feather-shaped leaves of
many glossy leaflets are
60–100cm (2–3ft) long.
Min. 18°C (64°F).

☼ ◊

GREEN–YELLOW

Portulacaria afra (Elephant bush)
Semi-evergreen, upright shrub with
horizontal branches and tiny, fleshy,
bright green leaves. Clusters of pale
pink flowers appear in late spring and
summer.
Min. 7–10°C (45–50°F).

:☼: ◊

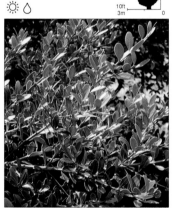

Buxus balearica
(Balearic box)
Evergreen, tree-like shrub suitable for
hedging in mild areas. Has broadly
oval, bright green leaves.

:☼: ◊ ① Zone 9

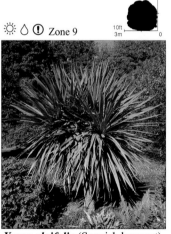

Yucca aloifolia (Spanish bayonet)
Slow-growing, evergreen shrub or
small tree with few branches. Has
sword-shaped, deep green leaves,
50–75cm (20–30in) long, and large
panicles of purple-tinted,
white flowers in summer-
autumn. Min. 7°C (45°F).

:☼: ◊

Elaeagnus × ebbingei 'Limelight'
Evergreen, bushy, dense shrub with
glossy, dark green leaves, silver
beneath, centrally marked yellow and
pale green. Bears small, fragrant, white
flowers in autumn.

:☼: ◊ Zone 7

Ligustrum 'Vicaryi',
syn. *L.* × *vicaryi*
Semi-evergreen, bushy, dense shrub
with broad, oval, golden-yellow leaves.
Dense racemes of small, white flowers
appear in mid-summer.

:☼: ◊ ① Zone 6

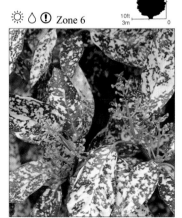

Aucuba japonica 'Crotonifolia'
Evergreen, bushy, dense shrub with
stout, green shoots. Large, glossy, dark
green leaves are heavily mottled
yellow. Small, purplish flowers
in mid-spring are followed
by bright red berries.

:☼: ◊ Zone 7b

SHRUBS small SPRING INTEREST

☐ WHITE

Salix hastata 'Wehrhahnii'
Deciduous, upright-branched shrub
with deep purple stems that contrast
with silver-grey catkins borne in early
spring before foliage appears. Stems
later turn yellow. Has oval,
bright green leaves.

:☼: ◑ Zone 7

Deutzia gracilis
Deciduous, upright or spreading shrub.
Massed, 5-petalled, pure white flowers
are borne in upright clusters amid
bright green foliage in late spring
and early summer.

:☼: ◊ Zone 5b

Prunus glandulosa 'Alba Plena'
Deciduous, open shrub, with narrowly
oval, mid-green leaves, bearing
racemes of double, white flowers
in late spring.

:☼: ◊ ① Zone 5

☐ WHITE | ☐ WHITE–PINK

Ledum groenlandicum
(Labrador tea)
Evergreen, bushy shrub. Foliage is dark green and aromatic. Rounded heads of small, white flowers are carried from mid-spring to early summer.

☀ ◑ pH Zone 2

Azorina vidalii,
syn. *Campanula vidalii*
Evergreen sub-shrub with erect stems. Has coarsely serrated, glossy, dark green leaves and racemes of bell-shaped, white or pink flowers in spring and summer. Min. 5°C (41°F).

☀ ◌

Gaultheria × wisleyensis 'Wisley Pearl', syn. × *Gaulnettya* 'Wisley Pearl'
Evergreen, bushy, dense shrub with oval, deeply veined, dark green leaves. Bears small, white flowers in late spring and early summer, then purplish-red fruits.

☀ ◑ pH ① Zone 6

Viburnum × juddii
Deciduous, rounded, bushy shrub with dark green foliage. Rounded heads of very fragrant, pink-tinged, white flowers open from pink buds from mid- to late spring.

☀ ◌ ① Zone 5

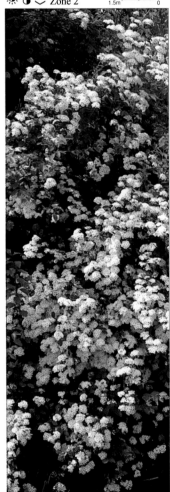

Spiraea × vanhouttei
(Bridal wreath)
Deciduous, compact shrub with slender, arching shoots. In late spring and early summer abundant, small, dense clusters of white flowers appear amid diamond-shaped, dark green leaves.

☀ ◌ Zone 3

Prunus laurocerasus 'Zabeliana'
Evergreen, wide-spreading, open shrub. Leaves are very narrow and glossy, dark green. Spikes of white flowers in late spring are followed by cherry-like, red, then black, fruits.

☀ ◌ ① Zone 8

Deutzia × rosea
Deciduous, bushy, dense shrub. In late spring and early summer produces massed, broad clusters of 5-petalled, pale pink flowers. Leaves are oval and dark green.

☀ ◌ Zone 7

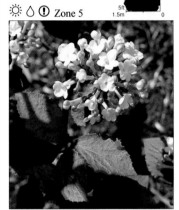

Viburnum carlesii
Deciduous, bushy, dense shrub with dark green leaves that redden in autumn. Rounded heads of very fragrant, white and pink flowers, pink in bud, appear from mid- to late spring, followed by decorative, black fruits.

☀ ◌ ① Zone 5b

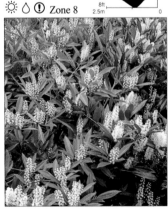

Prunus laurocerasus 'Otto Luyken'
Evergreen, very dense shrub. Has upright, narrow, glossy, dark green leaves, spikes of white flowers in late spring, followed by cherry-like, red, then black, fruits.

☀ ◌ ① Zone 8

Prunus × cistena
Slow-growing, deciduous, upright shrub with deep reddish-purple leaves, red when young. Small, pinkish-white flowers from mid- to late spring may be followed by purple fruits.

☀ ◌ ① Zone 3

Daphne × burkwoodii 'Somerset'
Semi-evergreen, upright shrub that bears dense clusters of very fragrant, white and pink flowers in late spring and sometimes again in autumn. Leaves are lance-shaped and pale to mid-green.

☀ ◌ ① Zone 5

Bauera rubioides
Centradenia floribunda
Diosma ericoides
Gaultheria × wisleyensis 'Pink Pixie'

HEATHERS, illus. pp.178–9
RHODODENDRONS, illus. pp.132–4
Vinca minor 'Bowles' White'

Daphne retusa
Evergreen, densely branched, rounded shrub clothed with leathery, glossy leaves notched at the tips. In late spring and early summer, deep purple buds open to very fragrant, pink-flushed, white flowers borne in terminal clusters.

☀ ◊ ① Zone 8

Menziesia ciliicalyx var. *purpurea*, syn. *M.c.* var. *lasiophylla*
Deciduous, bushy shrub with bright green foliage and racemes of nodding, purplish-pink blooms in late spring and early summer.

☀ ◊ pH Zone 7

Euphorbia milii (Crown of thorns)
Fairly slow-growing, mainly evergreen, spiny, semi-succulent shrub. Clusters of tiny, yellowish flowers, enclosed by 2 bright red bracts, open intermittently during the year.
Min. 8°C (46°F).

☀ ◊ ①

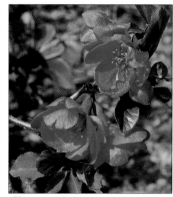

Chaenomeles x *superba* 'Rowallane'
Deciduous, low, spreading shrub. Has glossy, dark green foliage and bears a profusion of large, red flowers during spring.

☀ ◊ Zone 5b

Prunus tenella
Deciduous, bushy shrub with upright shoots and narrowly oval, glossy leaves. Shallowly cup-shaped, bright pink flowers appear from mid- to late spring.

☀ ◊ ① Zone 2

Ribes sanguineum 'Brocklebankii'
Deciduous, spreading shrub. Has aromatic, pale yellow leaves and pendent clusters of small, pale pink flowers in spring, followed by white-bloomed, black fruits.

☀ ◊ Zone 6b

Epacris impressa (Australian heath)
Evergreen, usually erect, fairly open, heath-like shrub with short, red-tipped leaves. Tubular, pink or red flowers appear in late winter and spring. Min. 5°C (41°F).

☀ ◊ pH

Cantua buxifolia, syn. *C. dependens*
Evergreen, arching, bushy shrub. Has grey-green foliage and drooping clusters of bright red and magenta flowers from mid- to late spring.

☀ ◊ Zone 9?

SHRUBS

■■ RED–GREEN

□□ GREEN–YELLOW

Chaenomeles x *superba* 'Nicoline'
Deciduous, bushy, dense shrub. Has glossy, dark green leaves and a profusion of large, scarlet flowers in spring, followed by yellow fruits.

☼ ◊ Zone 5b

Salix lanata (Woolly willow)
Deciduous, bushy, dense shrub with stout, woolly, grey shoots and broad, silver-grey leaves. Large, yellowish-green catkins appear in late spring with foliage.

☼ ◊ Zone 5

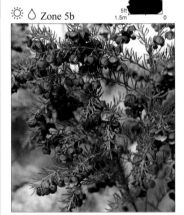

Boronia megastigma
Evergreen, well branched, wiry-stemmed shrub. Small leaves have 3–5 narrow leaflets. Fragrant, bowl-shaped, brownish-purple and yellow flowers hang from leaf axils in late winter and spring. Min. 7–10°C (45–50°F).

☼ ◊ pH

Euphorbia characias subsp. *characias*
Evergreen, upright shrub with clusters of narrow, grey-green leaves. During spring and early summer, bears dense spikes of pale yellowish-green flowers with deep purple centres.

☼ ◊ ① Zone 8

Euphorbia characias subsp. *wulfenii*
Evergreen, upright shrub. Stems are biennial, producing clustered, grey-green leaves one year and spikes of yellow-green blooms the following spring.

☼ ◊ ① Zone 8

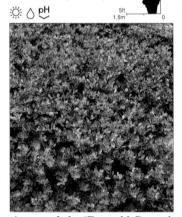

Arctostaphylos 'Emerald Carpet'
Evergreen shrub that, with a low, dense growth of oval, bright green leaves and purple stems, makes excellent ground cover. Bears small, urn-shaped, white flowers in spring.

☼ ◊ pH Zone 8

Daphne laureola subsp. *philippi*
Evergreen, dwarf shrub with oval, dark green leaves. Slightly fragrant, tubular, pale green flowers with short, spreading lobes appear in late winter and early spring, followed by black fruits.

☼ ◊ ① Zone 8

Salix repens (Creeping willow)
Deciduous, prostrate or semi-upright and bushy shrub. Silky, grey catkins become yellow from mid- to late spring, before small, narrowly oval leaves, which are grey-green above, silvery beneath, appear.

☼ ◊ Zone 1

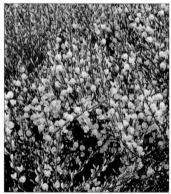

Cytisus x *praecox* 'Warminster' (Warminster broom)
Deciduous, densely branched shrub. From mid- to late spring, pea-like, creamy-yellow flowers appear in profusion amid tiny, silky, grey-green leaves with 3 leaflets.

☼ ◊ ① Zone 6b

Agathosma pulchella
Barleria obtusa
Brunfelsia pauciflora
HEATHERS, illus. pp.178–9

RHODODENDRONS, illus. pp.132–4
Vinca major
Xanthorhiza simplicissima

Mahonia aquifolium
(Oregon grape)
Evergreen, open shrub. Leaves, with
glossy, bright green leaflets, often turn
red or purple in winter. Bunches of
small, yellow flowers in
spring are followed by
blue-black berries.

☀ ◊ Zone 4b

Berberis empetrifolia
Evergreen, arching, prickly shrub with
narrow, grey-green leaves, globose,
golden-yellow flowers in late spring
and black fruits in autumn.

☀ ◊ ① Zone 8

Genista tinctoria
(Dyers' greenweed)
Deciduous, spreading, dwarf shrub that
bears dense spires of pea-like, golden-
yellow flowers in spring and summer.
Leaves are narrow and
dark green.

☀ ◊ Zone 3

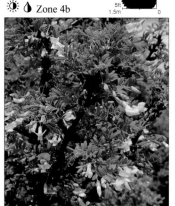

Caragana arborescens 'Nana'
Deciduous, bushy, dwarf shrub with
mid-green leaves consisting of many
oval leaflets. Pea-like, yellow flowers
are borne in late spring.

☀ ◊ Zone 2

Cytisus × praecox 'Allgold'
Deciduous, densely branched shrub
with silky, grey-green leaves, divided
into 3 leaflets, and a profusion of pea-
like, yellow flowers from mid- to late
spring.

☀ ◊ ① Zone 5b

Coronilla valentina subsp. glauca,
syn. C. glauca
Evergreen, bushy, dense shrub. Has
blue-grey leaves with 5 or 7 leaflets.
Fragrant, pea-like, yellow flowers are
borne from mid-spring to
early summer.

☀ ◊ Zone 9

Chorizema ilicifolium
(Holly flame pea)
Evergreen, sprawling or upright shrub,
with spiny-toothed, leathery leaves.
Has spikes of bicoloured, orange
and pinkish-red flowers
in spring-summer.
Min. 7°C (45°F).

☀ ◊ pH

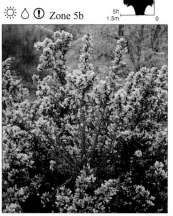

Pachystachys lutea
(Lollipop plant)
Evergreen, loose, more or less rounded
shrub, often grown annually from
cuttings. Has tubular, white flowers
in tight, golden-bracted
spikes in spring-summer.
Min. 13–15°C (55–9°F).

☀ ◊

Ulex europaeus (Gorse)
Leafless or almost leafless, bushy shrub
with year-round, dark green shoots and
spines that make it appear evergreen.
Bears massed, fragrant, pea-like,
yellow flowers in spring.

☀ ◊ pH ① Zone 7

Acacia pulchella
(Western prickly Moses)
Semi-evergreen or deciduous shrub of
diffuse habit, with spiny twigs and rich
green foliage. Tiny, deep yellow
flowers appear in dense,
globular heads in spring.
Min. 5–7°C (41–5°F).

☀ ◊

Nematanthus gregarius, syn.
Hypocyrta radicans, N. radicans
Evergreen, prostrate or slightly
ascending shrub with fleshy, glossy
leaves. Inflated, orange and yellow
flowers appear mainly
from spring to autumn.
Min. 13–15°C (55–9°F).

◑ ◊

Acacia ulicifolia
Berberis calliantha
Caragana frutex 'Globosa'
Genista tinctoria 'Royal Gold'

Hermannia incana
Mahonia 'Heterophylla'
Mahonia repens
RHODODENDRONS, illus. pp.132–4

Daphne giraldii
Halimium lasianthum
Lantana camara
Nematanthus strigillosus

SHRUBS small SUMMER INTEREST

☐ WHITE

Deutzia monbeigii
Deciduous, arching, elegant shrub.
Clusters of small, 5-petalled, white
flowers appear in profusion among
small, dark green leaves from early
to mid-summer.

☀ ◊ Zone 7

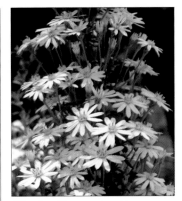

Olearia phlogopappa var.
subrepanda
Evergreen, upright, compact shrub.
Heads of daisy-like, white flowers are
borne profusely from mid-spring to
early summer amid narrow,
toothed, grey-green leaves.
Min. 2°C (35°F).

☀ ◊

Westringia fruticosa
(Australian rosemary)
Evergreen, rounded, compact shrub.
Crowded leaves, in whorls of 4, are
white-felted beneath. White to palest
blue flowers open
in spring-summer.
Min. 5–7°C (41–5°F).

☀ ◊

Potentilla fruticosa 'Abbotswood',
syn. *P*. 'Abbotswood'
Deciduous, bushy shrub. Large, pure
white flowers are borne amid dark
blue-green leaves, divided
into 5 narrowly oval
leaflets, throughout
summer-autumn.

☀ ◊ Zone 1

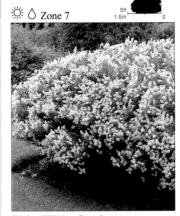

Hebe 'White Gem',
syn. *H. brachysiphon* 'White Gem'
Evergreen, rounded shrub that
produces a dense mound of small,
glossy leaves covered in early summer
with tight racemes of
small, white flowers.

☀ ◊ Zone 9

Cuphea hyssopifolia
(False heather)
Evergreen, rounded, dense shrub with
tiny, narrowly lance-shaped, deep green
leaves. Rose-purple to lilac or white
flowers appear in summer-
autumn. Min. 7°C (45°F).

☀ ◊

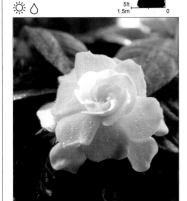

Gardenia augusta
'Veitchii'
Fairly slow-growing, evergreen, leafy
shrub with oval, glossy leaves up to
10cm (4in) long and fragrant, double,
white flowers from
summer to winter.
Min. 15°C (59°F).

☀◐ ◊ pH

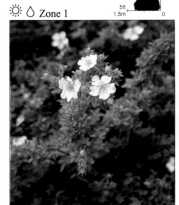

Potentilla fruticosa 'Manchu'
Deciduous, mound-forming shrub with
reddish-pink, prostrate shoots. Pure
white flowers are borne amid divided,
silvery-grey leaves from late spring to
early autumn.

☀ ◊ Zone 3

Rhodotypos scandens,
syn. *R. kerrioides* (White kerria)
Deciduous, upright or slightly arching
shrub. In late spring and early summer,
amid sharply toothed leaves, bears
shallowly cupped, white
flowers, followed by small,
pea-shaped, black fruits.

☀ ◊ Zone 5b

Philadelphus 'Manteau
d'Hermine'
Deciduous, bushy, compact shrub.
Clusters of fragrant, double, creamy-
white flowers appear amid small, pale
to mid-green leaves from
early to mid-summer.

☀ ◊ Zone 5

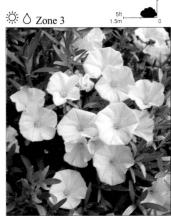

Convolvulus cneorum
Evergreen, rounded, bushy, dense
shrub. Pink-tinged buds opening to
white flowers with yellow centres are
borne from late spring to late summer
among narrow, silky,
silvery-green leaves.

☀ ◊ Zone 8

OTHER RECOMMENDED PLANTS:
Berzelia lanuginosa
Boenninghausenia albiflora
Cyrilla racemiflora

Cytisus albus
FUCHSIAS, illus. pp.164–5
HEATHERS, illus. pp.178–9
Hebe albicans 'Cranleigh Gem'

Hebe macrantha
Hebe ochracea
Hebe rakaiensis
Hebe vernicosa, illus. p.351

Helichrysum splendidum
RHODODENDRONS, illus. pp.132–4
Rubus tricolor

Halimium umbellatum,
syn. *Helianthemum umbellatum*
Evergreen, upright shrub. Narrow,
glossy, dark green leaves are white
beneath. White flowers, centrally
blotched with yellow, are
produced in early summer
from reddish buds.

☀ ◊ Zone 9?

Cistus salviifolius
Evergreen, bushy, dense shrub with
slightly wrinkled, grey-green foliage.
White flowers, with central, yellow
blotches, appear in profusion during
early summer.

☀ ◊ Zone 9

**Potentilla fruticosa 'Farrer's
White'**, syn. *P.* 'Farrer's White'
Deciduous, bushy shrub with divided,
grey-green leaves. Bears an abundance
of white flowers during
summer-autumn.

☀ ◊ Zone 3

Cistus monspeliensis
Evergreen, bushy shrub with narrow,
wrinkled, dark green leaves and small,
white flowers freely borne from early
to mid-summer.

☀ ◊ Zone 9

Cistus × cyprius
Evergreen, bushy shrub with sticky
shoots and narrow, glossy, dark green
leaves. In early summer bears large,
white flowers, with a red blotch at each
petal base, that appear in
succession for some weeks
but last only a day.

☀ ◊ Zone 9

× Halimiocistus sahucii,
syn. *Cistus revolii* of gardens
Evergreen, bushy, dense shrub with
narrow, dark green leaves that set
off an abundance of pure white flowers
in late spring and
early summer.

☀ ◊ Zone 9

Cistus × hybridus,
syn. *C.* × *corbariensis*
Evergreen, bushy, dense shrub. Has
wrinkled, wavy-edged, dark green
leaves and massed white flowers, with
central, yellow blotches,
carried in late spring and
early summer.

☀ ◊ Zone 9

Cistus × aguilarii 'Maculatus'
Evergreen, bushy shrub with narrow,
wavy-edged, slightly sticky, rich green
leaves. Large, white flowers, with a
central, deep red and yellow pattern,
appear from early to mid-
summer.

☀ ◊ Zone 9

Cistus ladanifer,
syn. *C. ladaniferus*
Evergreen, open, upright shrub. Leaves
are narrow, dark green and sticky.
Bears large, white flowers, with red
markings around the
central tuft of stamens, in
profusion in early summer.

☀ ◊ Zone 9

Chamaebatiaria millefolium
× *Halimiocistus wintonensis*
Sibiraea altaiensis

159

Vaccinium corymbosum
(Highbush blueberry)
Deciduous, upright, slightly arching shrub. Small, white or pinkish flowers in late spring and early summer are followed by sweet, edible, blue-black berries. Foliage turns red in autumn.

☀ ◖ pH Zone 3

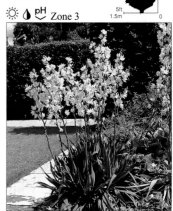

Leptospermum rupestre
Evergreen, semi-prostrate, widely arching shrub with reddish shoots and small, dark green leaves that turn bronze-purple in winter. Small, open cup-shaped, white flowers, red- flushed in bud, appear in early summer.
Min. 2°C (35°F).

☀ ◖

Yucca whipplei,
syn. *Hesperoyucca whipplei*
Evergreen, virtually stemless shrub that forms a dense tuft of slender, pointed, blue-green leaves. Very long panicles of fragrant, greenish-white flowers are produced in late spring and early summer.

☀ ◖ Zone 6

Yucca flaccida 'Ivory',
syn. *Y. filifera* 'Ivory'
Evergreen, very short-stemmed shrub that produces tufts of narrow, dark green leaves and long panicles of bell-shaped, white flowers from mid- to late summer.

☀ ◖ Zone 4

Catharanthus roseus, syn. *Vinca rosea* (Rose periwinkle)
Evergreen, spreading shrub, becoming untidy with age. Has white to rose-pink flowers in spring to autumn, also in winter in warm areas.
Min. 5–7°C (41–5°F).

☀ ◖

Rhaphiolepis umbellata,
syn. *R. japonica, R. ovata*
Evergreen, bushy shrub with rounded, leathery, dark green leaves and clusters of fragrant, white flowers in early summer.

☀ ◖ Zone 9

Weigela florida 'Variegata'
Deciduous, bushy, dense shrub. Carries a profusion of funnel-shaped, pink flowers in late spring and early summer and has mid-green leaves broadly edged with creamy-white.

☀ ◖ Zone 5

Ozothamnus ledifolius,
syn. *Helichrysum ledifolium*
Evergreen, dense shrub. Yellow shoots are covered with small, aromatic leaves, glossy, dark green above, yellow beneath. Small, white flower heads are borne in early summer.

☀ ◖ Zone 9?

Bouvardia longiflora
Cistus x *dansereaui*
FUCHSIAS, illus. pp.164–5
HEATHERS, illus. pp.178–9

Philadelphus 'Sybille'
RHODODENDRONS, illus. pp.132–4
Spiraea trilobata

Lomatia silaifolia
Evergreen, bushy shrub. Spikes of creamy-white flowers, each with 4 narrow, twisted petals, are borne amid deeply divided, dark green leaves from mid- to late summer.
Min. –2°C (28°F).

  ☼ ◊ pH

Cassinia leptophylla subsp.
vauvilliersii, syn. *C. vauvilliersii*
Evergreen, upright shrub. Whitish shoots are covered with tiny, dark green leaves and heads of small, white flowers from mid- to late summer.

☼ ◊ Zone 9

Viburnum acerifolium
Deciduous, upright-branched shrub with bright green leaves that turn orange, red and purple in autumn. Decorative, red fruits, which turn purple-black, follow heads of creamy-white flowers in early summer.

☼ ◊ ① Zone 5

Eriogonum arborescens
Evergreen, sparingly branched shrub. Small leaves have recurved edges and woolly, white undersides. Leafy umbels of small, white or pink flowers appear from spring to autumn.
Min. 5°C (41°F).

 ☼ ◊

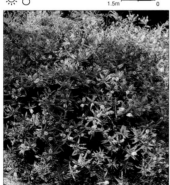

Hebe recurva
Evergreen, open, spreading shrub. Leaves are narrow, curved and blue-grey. Small spikes of white flowers appear from mid- to late summer.

 ☼ ◊ Zone 9?

Hebe albicans
Evergreen shrub that forms a dense mound of blue-grey foliage covered with small, tight clusters of white flowers from early to mid-summer.

 ☼ ◊ Zone 9?

Deutzia 'Mont Rose'
Deciduous, bushy shrub that produces clusters of pink or pinkish-purple flowers, in early summer, with yellow anthers and occasionally white markings. Leaves are sharply toothed and dark green.

 ☼ ◊ Zone 7

Potentilla fruticosa 'Daydawn',
syn. *P.* 'Daydawn'
Deciduous, bushy, rather arching shrub. Creamy-yellow flowers, flushed with orange-pink, appear among divided, mid-green leaves from early summer to mid-autumn.

 ☼ ◊ Zone 3

Protea cynaroides (King protea)
Evergreen, bushy, rounded shrub. Water lily-shaped flower heads, 13–20cm (5–8in) wide, with silky-haired, petal-like, pink to red bracts, appear in spring-summer. Leaves are oval and mid- to dark green.
Min. 5–7°C (41–5°F).

 ☼ ◊ pH

Abelia 'Edward Goucher'
Deciduous or semi-evergreen, arching shrub. Oval, bright green leaves are bronze when young. Bears a profusion of lilac-pink flowers from mid-summer to autumn.

 ☼ ◊ Zone 7

Azorina vidalii, illus. p.154
Cistus parviflorus
Cistus 'Peggy Sammons'
FUCHSIAS, illus. pp.164–5

HEATHERS, illus. pp.178–9
HYDRANGEAS, illus. p.144
Lotus hirsutus
RHODODENDRONS, illus. pp.132–4

■ PINK

Abelia schumannii
Deciduous, arching shrub. Pointed, mid-green leaves are bronze when young. Yellow-blotched, rose-purple and white flowers appear from mid-summer to mid-autumn.

☀ ◊ Zone 8

Myoporum parvifolium
Evergreen, spreading to prostrate shrub with semi-succulent leaves. In summer has clusters of small, honey-scented flowers, white or pink with purple spots, and tiny, purple fruits in autumn. Min. 2–5°C (36–41°F).

☀ ◊

Cistus × skanbergii
Evergreen, bushy shrub. A profusion of pale pink flowers appears amid narrow, grey-green leaves from early to mid-summer.

☀ ◊ Zone 9

Pimelea ferruginea
Evergreen, dense, rounded shrub with tiny, recurved, deep green leaves. Small, tubular, rich pink flowers appear in dense heads in spring or early summer. Min. 7°C (45°F).

☀ ◊ pH

Gaultheria shallon (Shallon)
Evergreen, bushy shrub. Red shoots carry broad, sharply pointed, dark green leaves. Racemes of urn-shaped, pink flowers in late spring and early summer are followed by purple berries.

☀ ◑ pH ① Zone 7

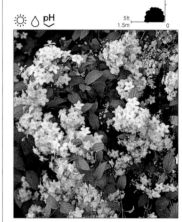

Deutzia × elegantissima 'Rosealind'
Deciduous, rounded, bushy, dense shrub that produces clusters of 5-petalled, deep pink flowers from late spring to early summer.

☀ ◊ Zone 7

Phlomis italica
Evergreen, upright shrub. In mid-summer, whorls of lilac-pink flowers are borne at the ends of shoots amid narrow, woolly, grey-green leaves.

☀ ◊ Zone 9

Indigofera dielsiana
Deciduous, upright, open shrub. Dark green leaves consist of 7–11 oval leaflets. Slender, erect spikes of pale pink flowers are borne from early summer to early autumn.

☀ ◊ Zone 7

Cistus 'Peggy Sammons'
Evergreen, bushy shrub with oval, grey-green leaves. Saucer-shaped, pale purplish-pink flowers are produced freely during early summer.

☀ ◊ Zone 9

☐ PINK

Weigela florida 'Foliis Purpureis'
Deciduous, low, bushy shrub that bears funnel-shaped flowers, deep pink outside, pale pink to white inside, in late spring and early summer. Leaves are dull purple or purplish-green.

☼ ◊ Zone 5

Ceanothus 'Perle Rose'
Deciduous, bushy shrub that from mid-summer to early autumn bears dense racemes of bright carmine-pink flowers amid broad, oval, mid-green leaves.

☼ ◊ Zone 9

Spiraea japonica 'Little Princess'
Slow-growing, deciduous, mound-forming shrub that produces copious small heads of rose-pink blooms from mid- to late summer. Small, dark green leaves are bronze when young.

☼ ◊ Zone 3

Hebe 'Great Orme'
Evergreen, rounded, open shrub. Has deep purplish shoots and glossy, dark green foliage. Slender spikes of deep pink flowers that fade to white are produced from mid-summer to mid-autumn.

☼ ◊ Zone 9

Penstemon isophyllus
Slightly untidy, deciduous shrub or sub-shrub that, from mid- to late summer, carries long sprays of large, white- and red-throated, deep pink flowers above spear-shaped, glossy, mid-green leaves.

☼ ◊ Zone 9

Spiraea japonica 'Goldflame'
Deciduous, upright, slightly arching shrub with orange-red, young leaves turning to bright yellow and finally pale green. Bears heads of deep rose-pink flowers from mid- to late summer.

☼ ◊ Zone 2b

Justicia carnea, syn. *Jacobinia carnea, J. pohliana* (King's crown)
Evergreen, sparingly branched shrub with velvety-haired leaves. Has spikes of pink to rose-purple flowers in summer-autumn.
Min. 10–15°C (50–59°F).

☼ ◊

Pentas lanceolata, syn. *P. carnea* (Egyptian star, Star-cluster)
Mainly evergreen, loosely rounded shrub with hairy, bright green leaves. In summer-autumn produces dense clusters of pink, lilac, red or white flowers.
Min. 10–15°C (50–59°F).

☼ ◊

Spiraea japonica 'Anthony Waterer'
Deciduous, upright, compact shrub. Red, young foliage matures to dark green. Heads of crimson-pink blooms appear from mid- to late summer.

☼ ◊ Zone 2b

Cistus 'Silver Pink'
FUCHSIAS, illus. pp.164–5
HEATHERS, illus. pp.178–9
Hebe 'Eveline'

HYDRANGEAS, illus. p.144
Indigofera decora
RHODODENDRONS, illus. pp.132–4

Fuchsias

With their vividly coloured blooms and long flowering season (usually throughout summer and well into autumn), fuchsias make outstanding shrubs for the greenhouse and for the garden. Single to double flowers often have flared or elegantly recurved sepals. In mild areas fuchsias may be grown outside all year; in cool climates most are best grown in a greenhouse or as summer bedding, although some are slightly hardy.

Fuchsias raised from cuttings are sparingly branched and often become straggly unless pruned from an early stage by pinching out the growing tips. To produce standard plants, the leader shoot is left, supported, but emerging side-shoots are pinched back to one pair of leaves. When the stem has reached the required height and has produced 2 or 3 pairs of leaves above this, it is then pinched out and the plant is left to develop naturally.

F. 'Jack Shahan'

F. arborescens

F. 'Lady Thumb'

F. 'Dollar Princess'

F. 'Gruss aus dem Bodethal'

F. 'Harry Gray'

F. 'Pink Galore'

F. 'Ballet Girl'

F. 'Nellie Nuttall'

F. 'Peppermint Stick'

F. 'Tom Thumb'

F. 'Annabel'

F. 'Bicentennial'

F. 'Golden Dawn'

F. 'Autumnale'

F. magellanica

F. 'Other Fellow'

F. 'Rufus'

F. 'Riccartonii'

F. 'Golden Marinka'

F. 'Leonora'

F. 'Swingtime'

F. 'Heidi Weiss'

F. 'Red Spider'

F. 'Mrs Popple'

F. x *bacillaris*

F. 'Thalia'

F. 'Tom West'

F. 'Celia Smedley'

F. 'Cascade'

F. 'Estelle Marie'

F. boliviana
var. *alba*

F. 'La Campanella'

F. 'Love's Reward'

F. 'Mrs Lovell
Swisher'

F. 'Rose of Castile'

F. procumbens

F. 'Lye's Unique'

F. fulgens

F. 'Coralle'

SHRUBS small SUMMER INTEREST

■■ PINK–RED

Cistus creticus,
syn. *C. incanus* subsp. *creticus*
Evergreen, bushy shrub. Pink or
purplish-pink flowers, each with a
central, yellow blotch, appear amid
grey-green leaves from
early to mid-summer.

☼ ◊ Zone 9

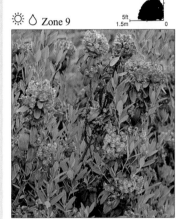

Kalmia angustifolia f. ***rubra***,
syn. *K.a.* 'Rubra' (Sheep laurel)
Evergreen, bushy, mound-forming
shrub with oval, dark green leaves and
clusters of small, deep red flowers in
early summer.

☼ ◊ pH ① Zone 3

Crossandra nilotica
Evergreen, upright to spreading, leafy
shrub with oval, pointed, rich green
leaves. Small, tubular, apricot to pale
brick-red flowers with spreading petals
are carried in short spikes
from spring to autumn.
Min. 15°C (59°F).

☼ ◊

Escallonia rubra 'Woodside'
Evergreen, bushy, dense shrub. Has
small, glossy, dark green leaves and
short racemes of small, tubular,
crimson flowers in summer-autumn.

☼ ◊ Zone 8

Sutherlandia frutescens
Evergreen, upright shrub. Has leaves
of 13–21 grey-haired, deep green
leaflets; bright red flowers in late
spring and summer are followed by
pale green, later red-
flushed, inflated seed pods.
Min. 10°C (50°F).

☼ ◊

Ixora coccinea
Evergreen, rounded shrub with glossy,
dark green leaves to 10cm (4in) long.
Small, tubular, red, pink, orange or
yellow flowers appear in dense heads
in summer.
Min. 13–16°C (55–61°F).

☼ ◊

Anisodontea capensis
Cistus x *purpureus*
Coleonema pulchrum
 HEATHERS, illus. pp.178–9

Philesia magellanica
Potentilla fruticosa 'Royal Flush'
RHODODENDRONS, illus. pp.132–4

SHRUBS

Salvia microphylla var. **neurepia**
Evergreen, well-branched, upright
shrub with pale to mid-green leaves.
Has tubular, bright red flowers from
purple-tinted, green calyces in late
summer and autumn.
Min. 2°C (35°F).

Justicia brandegeeana,
syn. *Beloperone guttata*, *Drejerella
guttata* (Shrimp plant)
Evergreen, rounded shrub intermittently,
but mainly in summer, producing white
flowers surrounded by
shrimp-pink bracts.
Min. 10–15°C (50–59°F).

Potentilla fruticosa 'Red Ace'
Deciduous, spreading, bushy, dense
shrub. Bright vermilion flowers, pale
yellow on the backs of petals, are
produced among mid-green leaves
from late spring to mid-
autumn but fade quickly in
full sun.

 Zone 3

Grevillea 'Robyn Gordon'
Evergreen, sprawling shrub with
leathery, dark green leaves. At intervals
from early spring to late summer,
arching stems bear racemes of crimson
flowers with protruding,
recurved styles.
Min. 5–10°C (41–50°F).

Acer palmatum 'Chitoseyama'
Deciduous, arching, mound-forming
shrub or small tree with lobed, mid-
green foliage that gradually turns
brilliant red from late summer to
autumn. Produces small,
reddish-purple flowers
in mid-spring.

☼ ◊ Zone 6

Phygelius aequalis
Evergreen or semi-evergreen, upright
sub-shrub. Clusters of tubular, pale red
flowers with yellow throats appear
from mid-summer to early autumn.
Leaves are oval and dark
green.

 Zone 7

Salvia fulgens
Evergreen, upright sub-shrub. Oval
leaves are white and woolly beneath,
hairy above. Racemes of tubular,
2-lipped, scarlet flowers appear
in late summer.
Min. 2°C (35°F).

Acer palmatum 'Dissectum
Atropurpureum'
Deciduous shrub that forms a mound
of deeply divided, bronze-red or purple
foliage, which turns brilliant red, orange
or yellow in autumn. Has
small, reddish-purple
flowers in mid-spring.

 Zone 5b

Hebe hulkeana 'Lilac Hint'
Evergreen, upright, open-branched shrub with toothed, glossy, pale green leaves. A profusion of small, pale lilac flowers appears in large racemes in late spring and early summer.

☼ ◊ Zone 9?

Desmodium elegans, syn. *D. tiliifolium*
Deciduous, upright sub-shrub. Mid-green leaves consist of 3 large leaflets. Large racemes of pale lilac to deep pink flowers appear from late summer to mid-autumn.

☼ ◊ Zone 9

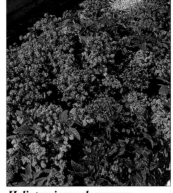

Heliotropium arborescens, syn. *H. peruvianum*
Evergreen, bushy shrub. Semi-glossy, dark green leaves are finely wrinkled. Purple to lavender flowers are borne in dense, flat clusters from late spring to winter.
Min. 7°C (45°F).

☼ ◊

Lavandula stoechas
(French lavender)
Evergreen, bushy, dense shrub. Heads of tiny, fragrant, deep purple flowers, topped by rose-purple bracts, appear in late spring and summer. Mature leaves are silver-grey and aromatic.

☼ ◊ Zone 9

Rosmarinus officinalis (Rosemary)
Evergreen, bushy, dense shrub with aromatic, narrow leaves. Small, purplish-blue to blue flowers appear from mid-spring to early summer and sometimes in autumn.
Used as a culinary herb.

☼ ◊ Zone 7

Hebe 'E.A. Bowles'
Evergreen, rounded, bushy shrub with narrow, glossy, pale green leaves and slender spikes of lilac flowers produced from mid-summer to late autumn.

☼ ◊ Zone 9?

Polygala × dalmaisiana, syn. *P. myrtifolia* var. *grandiflora* of gardens
Evergreen, erect shrub with small, greyish-green leaves. White-veined, rich purple flowers appear from late spring to autumn. Min. 7°C (45°F).

☼ ◊

Hebe 'Autumn Glory'
Evergreen shrub that forms a mound of purplish-red shoots and rounded, deep green leaves, over which dense racemes of deep purple-blue flowers appear from mid-summer to early winter.

☼ ◊ Zone 9?

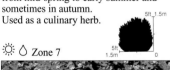

Lantana montevidensis, syn. *L. delicatissima*, *L. sellowiana*
Evergreen, trailing or mat-forming shrub with serrated leaves. Has heads of rose-purple flowers, each with a yellow eye, intermittently all year but mainly in summer.
Min. 10–13°C (50–55°F).

☼ ◊ (!)

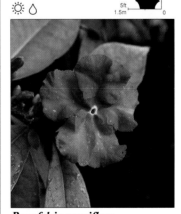

Brunfelsia pauciflora 'Macrantha'
Evergreen, spreading shrub with leathery leaves. Blue-purple flowers, ageing to white in about 3 days, appear from winter to summer.
Min. 10–13°C (50–55°F).

☼ ◊

Lavandula 'Hidcote', syn. *L. angustifolia* 'Hidcote'
Evergreen, bushy shrub with dense spikes of fragrant, deep purple flowers from mid- to late summer and narrow, aromatic, silver-grey leaves.

☼ ◊ Zone 6

SHRUBS small SUMMER INTEREST

■■ PURPLE–BLUE

■■ GREEN–YELLOW

Hebe 'Purple Queen',
syn. *H.* 'Amy'
Evergreen, bushy, compact shrub with glossy, deep green leaves that are purple-tinged when young. Dense racemes of deep purple flowers appear from early summer to mid-autumn.

☼ ◊ Zone 9?

Ceanothus thyrsiflorus var. **repens** (Creeping blue blossom)
Evergreen, dense shrub that forms a mound of broad, glossy, dark green leaves. Racemes of blue flowers are borne in late spring and early summer.

☼ ◊ Zone 8

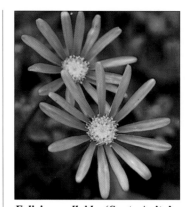

Felicia amelloides 'Santa Anita'
Evergreen, bushy, spreading shrub. Blue flower heads, with bright yellow centres, are borne on long stalks from late spring to autumn among round to oval, bright green leaves.
Min. 2°C (35°F).

☼ ◊

Symphoricarpos orbiculatus 'Foliis Variegatis',
syn. *S.o.* 'Variegatus'
Deciduous, bushy, dense shrub with bright green leaves edged with yellow. Occasionally bears white or pink flowers in summer-autumn.

☼ ◊ ① Zone 3

Hyssopus officinalis (Hyssop)
Semi-evergreen or deciduous, bushy shrub with aromatic, narrowly oval, deep green leaves. Small, blue flowers appear from mid-summer to early autumn. Sometimes used as a culinary herb.

☼ ◊ Zone 7

Caryopteris x clandonensis 'Arthur Simmonds'
Deciduous, bushy sub-shrub. Masses of blue to purplish-blue flowers appear amid narrowly oval, irregularly toothed, grey-green leaves from late summer to autumn.

☼ ◊ Zone 7

Justicia brandegeeana 'Chartreuse'
Evergreen, arching shrub producing white flowers surrounded by pale yellow-green bracts mainly in summer but also intermittently during the year.
Min. 10–15°C (50–59°F).

☼ ◊

Hebe 'Bowles' Variety'
Evergreen, rounded shrub with ovate-oblong, slightly glossy, mid-green leaves. In summer, bears mauve-blue flowers in compact, tapered, terminal racemes.

☼ ◊ Zone 9?

Ceanothus 'Gloire de Versailles',
syn. *C.* x *delileanus* 'Gloire de Versailles'
Vigorous, deciduous, bushy shrub. Has broad, oval, mid-green leaves and large racemes of pale blue flowers from mid-summer to early autumn.

☼ ◊ Zone 8

Perovskia 'Blue Spire'
Deciduous, upright sub-shrub with grey-white stems. Profuse spikes of violet-blue flowers appear from late summer to mid-autumn above aromatic, deeply cut, grey-green leaves.

☼ ◊ Zone 5

Weigela middendorffiana
Deciduous, bushy, arching shrub. From mid-spring to early summer funnel-shaped, sulphur-yellow flowers, spotted with orange inside, are borne amid bright green foliage.

☼ ◊ Zone 4

Brunfelsia pauciflora
Hebe 'Fairfieldii'
Hebe x *franciscana* 'Blue Gem'
Hebe hulkeana

HYDRANGEAS, illus. p.144
Lavandula angustifolia 'Munstead'
Perovskia 'Hybrida'
Phlomis cashmeriana

RHODODENDRONS, illus. pp.132–4

Berberis 'Parkjuweel'
Muehlenbeckia complexa
Myrsine africana

Phygelius aequalis
'Yellow Trumpet'
Evergreen or semi-evergreen, upright sub-shrub. Bears clusters of pendent, tubular, pale creamy-yellow flowers from mid-summer to early autumn.

☼ ◊ Zone 7

Potentilla fruticosa
'Friedrichsenii'
Vigorous, deciduous, upright shrub. From late spring to mid-autumn pale yellow flowers are produced amid grey-green leaves.

☼ ◊ Zone 3

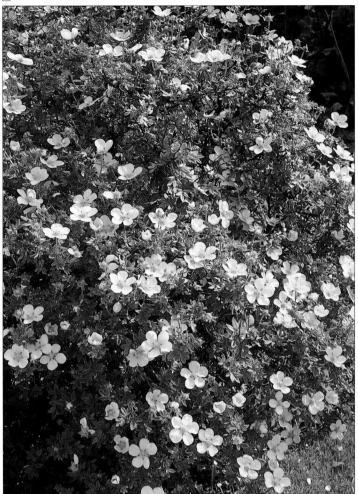

Potentilla fruticosa
'Vilmoriniana'
Deciduous, upright shrub that bears pale yellow or creamy-white flowers from late spring to mid-autumn. Leaves are silver-grey and divided into narrow leaflets.

☼ ◊ Zone 3

Potentilla fruticosa 'Elizabeth',
syn. *P.* 'Elizabeth'
Deciduous, bushy, dense shrub with small, deeply divided leaves and large, bright yellow flowers that appear from late spring to mid-autumn.

☼ ◊ Zone 3

Halimium 'Susan'
Evergreen, spreading shrub with narrow, oval, grey-green leaves. Numerous single or semi-double, bright yellow flowers with central, deep purple-red markings are borne in small clusters along branches in summer.

☼ ◊ Zone 9?

Santolina pinnata subsp.
neapolitana 'Sulphurea'
Evergreen, rounded, bushy shrub with aromatic, deeply cut, feathery, grey-green foliage. Produces heads of pale primrose-yellow flowers in mid-summer.

☼ ◊ Zone 9?

Lupinus arboreus (Tree lupin)
Fast-growing, semi-evergreen, sprawling shrub that in early summer usually bears short spikes of fragrant, clear yellow flowers above hairy, pale green leaves composed of 6–9 leaflets.

☼ ◊ ! Zone 9

Grevillea juniperina f. **sulphurea**,
syn. *G. sulphurea*
Evergreen, rounded, bushy shrub. Has needle-like leaves, recurved, dark green above, silky-haired beneath and groups of small, spidery, pale yellow flowers in spring-summer. Min. –1°C (30°F).

☼ ◊ pH !

Halimium lasianthum subsp.
formosum, syn. *H. formosum*
Evergreen, spreading, bushy shrub. Has grey-green foliage and golden-yellow flowers, with central, deep red blotches, borne in late spring and early summer.

☼ ◊ Zone 9?

□ YELLOW

Phlomis fruticosa
(Jerusalem sage)
Evergreen, spreading shrub with
upright shoots. Whorls of deep golden-
yellow flowers are produced amid
sage-like, grey-green
foliage from early
to mid-summer.

☀ ◊ Zone 9

Hypericum calycinum
(Aaron's beard, Rose of Sharon)
Evergreen or semi-evergreen dwarf
shrub that makes good ground cover.
Has large, bright yellow flowers from
mid-summer to mid-
autumn and dark
green leaves.

☀ ◊ Zone 5b

Hypericum kouytchense
Deciduous or semi-evergreen, arching
shrub. Golden-yellow flowers with
conspicuous stamens are borne among
foliage from mid-summer to early
autumn and followed by
decorative, bronze-red
fruit capsules.

☀ ◊ Zone 6

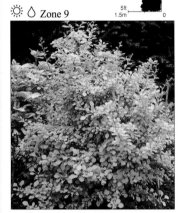

Berberis thunbergii 'Aurea'
Deciduous, bushy, spiny shrub with
small, golden-yellow leaves. Racemes
of small, red-tinged, pale yellow
flowers in mid-spring are followed
by red berries in autumn.

☀ ◊ ① Zone 5

Genista hispanica (Spanish gorse)
Deciduous, bushy, very spiny shrub
with few leaves. Bears dense clusters
of golden-yellow flowers profusely
in late spring and early summer.

☀ ◊ Zone 8

Hypericum 'Hidcote'
Evergreen or semi-evergreen, bushy,
dense shrub. Bears an abundance of
large, golden-yellow flowers from mid-
summer to early autumn amid narrowly
oval, dark green leaves.

☀ ◊ Zone 6

Reinwardtia indica,
syn. *R. trigyna* (Yellow flax)
Evergreen, upright sub-shrub, branching
from the base. Has greyish-green
leaves and small clusters of yellow
flowers mainly in summer
but also during the year.
Min. 10°C (50°F).

☀ ◊

Cytisus nigricans,
syn. *Lembotropis nigricans*
Deciduous, upright shrub with dark
green leaves composed of 3 leaflets.
Has a long-lasting display of tall,
slender spires of yellow
flowers during summer.

☀ ◊ ① Zone 7

**Brachyglottis Dunedin Hybrids
'Sunshine'**, syn. *Senecio* 'Sunshine'
Evergreen, bushy shrub that forms a
mound of silvery-grey, young leaves,
later turning dark green. Bears bright
yellow flower heads on
felted shoots from early
to mid-summer.

☀ ◊ Zone 9

Hypericum × inodorum 'Elstead'
Deciduous or semi-evergreen, upright
shrub. Abundant, small, yellow flowers
borne from mid-summer to early
autumn are followed by ornamental,
orange-red fruits. Dark
green leaves are aromatic
when crushed.

☀ ◊ Zone 7

Euryops pectinatus
Evergreen, upright shrub. Deeply cut,
grey-green leaves set off large heads of
daisy-like, bright yellow flowers, borne
in late spring and early summer and
often again in winter.
Min. 5–7°C (41–5°F).

☀ ◊

Brachyglottis compacta
Hermannia incana
Hypericum × moserianum
Lantana camara

Oxalis hedysaroides
Potentilla fruticosa
Potentilla fruticosa 'Beesii'
Potentilla fruticosa 'Elizabeth'

Potentilla fruticosa 'Gold Drop'
Santolina chamaecyparissus
Santolina rosmarinifolia

SHRUBS

Brachyglottis monroi
Evergreen, bushy, dense shrub that makes an excellent windbreak in mild, coastal areas. Has small, wavy-edged, dark green leaves with white undersides. Bears heads of bright yellow flowers in mid-summer.

☀ ◊ Zone 9

Abutilon 'Kentish Belle'
Semi-evergreen, arching shrub with purple shoots and deeply lobed, purple-veined, dark green leaves. Bears large, pendent, bell-shaped, orange-yellow and red flowers in summer-autumn. Min. 2˚C (37˚F).

☀ ◊

Isoplexis canariensis,
syn. *Digitalis canariensis*
Evergreen, rounded, sparingly branched shrub. Bears foxglove-like, yellow to red- or brownish-orange flowers in dense, upright spikes, to 30cm (12in) tall, in summer. Min. 7˚C (45˚F).

☀ ◊

Potentilla fruticosa 'Sunset',
syn. *P.* 'Sunset'
Deciduous shrub, bushy at first, later arching. Deep orange flowers, fading in hot sun, appear from early summer to mid-autumn. Mid-green leaves are divided into narrowly oval leaflets.

☀◑ ◊ Zone 2b

Grindelia chiloensis,
syn. *G. speciosa*
Mainly evergreen, bushy shrub with sticky stems. Sticky, lance-shaped, serrated leaves are up to 12cm (5in) long. Has large, daisy-like, yellow flower heads in summer. Min. 2˚C (35˚F).

☀ ◌

Mimulus aurantiacus, syn.
Diplacus glutinosus, M. glutinosus
Evergreen, domed to rounded shrub with sticky, lance-shaped, glossy, rich green leaves. Has tubular, orange, yellow or red-purple flowers from late spring to autumn.

☀ ◊ Zone 8

Juanulloa mexicana,
syn. *J. aurantiaca*
Evergreen, upright, sparingly branched shrub. Leaves are felted beneath. Has orange flowers, each with a ribbed calyx, in short, nodding clusters in summer. Min. 13–15˚C (55–9˚F).

☀ ◊

Cytisus scoparius f. **andreanus**
Deciduous, arching shrub with narrow, dark green leaves that are divided into 3 leaflets. Bears a profusion of bright yellow-and-red flowers along elegant, green branchlets in late spring and early summer.

☀ ◊ ⓘ Zone 6b

Lantana 'Spreading Sunset'
Evergreen, rounded to spreading shrub with finely wrinkled, deep green leaves. Has tiny, tubular flowers in a range of colours, carried in dense, rounded heads from spring to autumn. Min. 10–13˚C (50–55˚F).

☀ ◊ ⓘ

Brachyglottis laxifolia
Halimium lasianthum
Halimium ocymoides
Hypericum bellum

Hypericum x *cyathiflorum* 'Gold Cup'
Hypericum patulum
Nematanthus gregarius, illus. p.157
Nematanthus strigillosus

Phlomis chrysophylla
Phlomis longifolia var. *bailanica*
Potentilla fruticosa 'Goldfinger'
Potentilla fruticosa 'Jackman's Variety'

RHODODENDRONS, illus. pp.132–4

■ ORANGE

Cuphea ignea,
syn. *C. platycentra* (Cigar flower)
Evergreen, spreading, bushy sub-shrub
with bright green leaves. From spring
to autumn has tubular, dark orange-red
flowers, each with a dark
band and white ring at the
mouth. Min. 2°C (36°F).

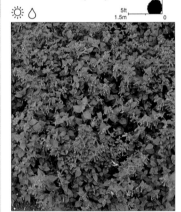

Cuphea cyanea
Evergreen, rounded sub-shrub with
narrowly oval, sticky-haired leaves.
Tubular flowers, orange-red, yellow
and violet-blue, are carried in summer.
Min. 7°C (45°F).

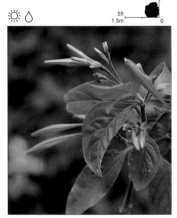

Justicia spicigera,
syn. *J. ghiesbreghtiana* of gardens,
Jacobinia spicigera
Evergreen, well-branched shrub
with spikes of tubular, orange or
red flowers in summer and
occasionally other seasons.
Min. 10–15°C (50–59°F).

Potentilla fruticosa 'Tangerine'

SHRUBS small AUTUMN INTEREST

▢▢■ WHITE–RED

Turraea obtusifolia
Evergreen, rounded, bushy, arching
shrub with oval to lance-shaped leaves.
Bears fragrant, white flowers from
autumn to spring, followed by orange-
yellow fruits like tiny,
peeled tangerines.
Min. 13°C (55°F).

Calliandra eriophylla
(Fairy duster)
Evergreen, stiff, dense shrub. Leaves
have numerous tiny leaflets. From late
spring to autumn has pompons of tiny,
pink-anthered, white florets,
followed by brown seed
pods. Min. 13°C (55°F).

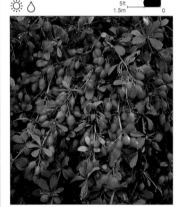

***Berberis* 'Rubrostilla'**
Deciduous, arching shrub. Globose
to cup-shaped, pale yellow flowers,
appearing in early summer, are
followed by a profusion of large,
coral-red fruits. Grey-
green leaves turn brilliant
red in late autumn.
 Zone 8

OTHER RECOMMENDED PLANTS:
Anisodontea capensis
Bouvardia longiflora
Cuphea hyssopifolia, illus. p.158

Cotoneaster horizontalis
(Wall-spray)
Deciduous, stiff-branched, spreading
shrub. Glossy, dark green leaves redden
in late autumn. Bears pinkish-white
flowers from late spring to
early summer, followed by
red fruits.
Zone 5

***Vaccinium angustifolium* var.
*laevifolium*** (Low bush blueberry)
Deciduous, bushy shrub with bright
green leaves that redden in autumn.
Edible, blue fruits follow white,
sometimes pinkish, spring
flowers.
 Zone 2

Cyrilla racemiflora
HEATHERS, illus. pp.178–9
Pentas lanceolata, illus. p.163
Salvia leucantha

***Viburnum opulus* 'Compactum'**
Deciduous, dense shrub. Has deep
green leaves, red in autumn, and
profuse white flowers in spring and
early summer, followed by bunches
of bright red berries.
Zone 2b

SHRUBS

SHRUBS small WINTER INTEREST

◼ RED

◼ PURPLE–YELLOW

☐ WHITE

Bouvardia ternifolia,
syn. *B. triphylla* (Scarlet trompetilla)
Mainly evergreen, bushy, upright shrub
with leaves in whorls of 3. Has tubular,
bright scarlet flowers from summer to
early winter.
Min. 7–10°C (45–50°F).

☼ ◊

Elsholtzia stauntonii (Mint bush)
Deciduous, open sub-shrub. Sharply
toothed, mint-scented, dark green
leaves turn red in autumn. Slender
spires of pale purplish flowers
appear during late summer
and autumn.

☼ ◊ Zone 6

Skimmia japonica 'Fructo Albo'
Evergreen, bushy, dense, dwarf shrub.
Has aromatic, dark green leaves and
dense clusters of small, white flowers
from mid- to late spring, succeeded by
white berries.

☼◐ ◊ ① Zone 7

**Vaccinium corymbosum
'Pioneer'**
Deciduous, upright, slightly arching
shrub. Dark green leaves turn bright
red in autumn. Small, white or pinkish
flowers in late spring are
followed by sweet, edible,
blue-black berries.

☼ ◊ pH Zone 3

Ceratostigma willmottianum
Deciduous, open shrub. Has leaves that
turn red in late autumn and bright, rich
blue flowers from late summer until
well into autumn.

☼ ◊ Zone 7

Vaccinium parvifolium
Deciduous, upright shrub. Has small,
dark green leaves that become bright
red in autumn. Edible, bright red fruits
are produced after small, pinkish-white
flowers borne in late
spring and early summer.

☼ ◊ pH Zone 6

Coriaria terminalis var.
xanthocarpa
Deciduous, arching sub-shrub. Leaves
have oval leaflets and turn red in
autumn. Greenish flowers in late spring
are followed by decorative,
succulent, yellow fruits in
late summer and autumn.

☼ ◊ ① Zone 9

**Gaultheria mucronata
'Wintertime'**
Evergreen, bushy, dense shrub. Has
prickly, glossy, dark green leaves and
white flowers in late spring and early
summer, followed by
large, long-lasting, white
berries.

☼◐ ◊ pH ① Zone 7

Lonicera x purpusii
Semi-evergreen, bushy, dense shrub
with oval, dark green leaves. Small
clusters of fragrant, short-tubed, white
flowers, with spreading petal lobes and
yellow anthers, appear in
winter and early spring.

☼ ◊ ① Zone 8

Cotoneaster adpressus
Cotoneaster microphyllus
Crossandra infundibuliformis
Salvia microphylla var. *microphylla*

Ceratostigma griffithii
HEATHERS, illus. pp.178–9
Heliotropium arborescens, illus. p.167
Rosmarinus officinalis 'Severn Sea'

OTHER RECOMMENDED PLANTS:
Daphne mezereum f. *alba*
HEATHERS, illus. pp.178–9
Sarcococca confusa

Sarcococca hookeriana
Sarcococca ruscifolia
Turraea obtusifolia, illus. p.172

☐ WHITE–PINK

SHRUBS

Sarcococca humilis,
syn. *S. hookeriana* var. *humilis*
Evergreen, low, clump-forming shrub.
Tiny, fragrant, white flowers with pink
anthers appear amid glossy, dark green
foliage in late winter and
are followed by spherical,
black fruits.

☀◐ ◊ Zone 7

Sarcococca hookeriana var.
digyna
Evergreen, clump-forming, suckering,
dense shrub with narrow, bright green
leaves. Tiny, fragrant, white flowers,
with pink anthers, open in
winter and are followed by
spherical, black fruits.

☀ ◊ Zone 7

Gaultheria mucronata 'Mulberry
Wine'
Evergreen, bushy, dense shrub with
large, globose, magenta berries that
mature to deep purple. These follow
white flowers borne in
spring-summer. Leaves
are glossy, dark green.

☀◐ ◊ pH ⊘ Zone 7

☐ RED

Skimmia japonica 'Rubella'
Evergreen, upright, dense shrub with
aromatic, red-rimmed, bright green
foliage. Deep red flower buds in
autumn and winter open to dense
clusters of small, white
flowers in spring.

☀◐ ◊ ⊘ Zone 7

Daphne odora 'Aureomarginata'
Evergreen, bushy shrub with glossy,
dark green leaves narrowly edged with
yellow. Clusters of very fragrant, deep
purplish-pink and white flowers appear
from mid-winter to early
spring.

☀ ◊ ⊘ Zone 6

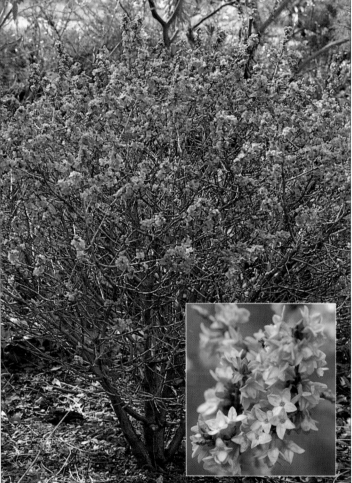

Daphne mezereum (Mezereon)
Deciduous, upright shrub. Very
fragrant, purple or pink blooms clothe
the bare stems in late winter and early
spring, followed by red fruits. Mature
leaves are narrowly oval
and dull grey-green.

☀ ◊ ⊘ Zone 5

Correa pulchella
Evergreen, fairly bushy, slender-
stemmed shrub with oval leaves.
Small, pendent, tubular, rose-red
flowers appear from summer to
winter, sometimes at other
seasons. Min. 3°C (37°F).

☀ ◊ pH

Skimmia japonica subsp.
reevesiana 'Robert Fortune',
syn. *S. reevesiana*
Evergreen, bushy, rather weak-growing
shrub with aromatic leaves. Small,
white flowers in spring are
followed by crimson
berries.

☀◐ ◊ ⊘ Zone 7b

SHRUBS small ALL YEAR INTEREST

■□ RED–GREEN

□□□ WHITE–GREEN

Viburnum davidii

Evergreen shrub that forms a dome of dark green foliage, over which heads of small, white flowers appear in late spring. If plants of both sexes are grown, female plants bear decorative, metallic-blue fruits.

☼ ◊ ① Zone 7

Vinca major 'Variegata'

Evergreen, prostrate, arching, spreading sub-shrub. Has bright green leaves broadly edged with creamy-white and large, bright blue flowers borne from late spring to early autumn.

◐ ◊ ① Zone 6

Helichrysum petiolare,
syn. *H. petiolatum* of gardens

Evergreen shrub with mounds of silver-green shoots and grey-felted leaves. Has yellow flower heads in summer. Usually grown as an annual for ground cover and edging. Min. 5°C (41°F).

☼ ◊

Skimmia japonica

Evergreen, bushy, dense shrub. Has aromatic, mid- to dark green leaves and dense clusters of small, white flowers from mid- to late spring, followed on female plants by bright red fruits if plants of both sexes are grown.

☼ ◊ ① Zone 7

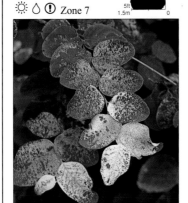

Breynia disticha, syn. *B. nivosa*, *Phyllanthus nivosus* (Snow bush)

Evergreen, well-branched shrub with slender stems. Leaves are green with white marbling. Tiny, greenish flowers, borne intermittently, have no petals. Min. 13°C (55°F).

◐ ◊

Pandanus tectorius 'Veitchii',
syn. *P. veitchii* (Veitch's screw pine)

Evergreen, upright, arching shrub with rosettes of long, light green leaves that have spiny, white to cream margins. Min. 13–16°C (55–61°F).

☼ ◊

Leucophyta brownii

Evergreen, intricately branched shrub with velvety, grey branches and tiny, scale-like leaves. Clusters of flower heads, silver in bud, yellowish when expanded, appear in summer. Min. 7–10°C (45–50°F).

☼ ◊

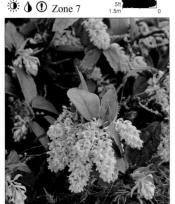

Ribes laurifolium

Evergreen, spreading shrub. Has leathery, deep green leaves and pendent racemes of greenish-yellow flowers in late winter and early spring. Produces edible, black berries on female plants if plants of both sexes are grown.

☼ ◊ Zone 8

Coprosma × kirkii 'Variegata'

Evergreen, densely branched shrub, prostrate when young, later semi-erect. White-margined leaves are borne singly or in small clusters. Tiny, translucent, white fruits appear in autumn on female plants if both sexes are grown.

☼ ◊ Zone 9

Artemisia arborescens

Evergreen, upright shrub, grown for its finely cut, silvery-white foliage. Heads of small, bright yellow flowers are borne in summer and early autumn.

☼ ◊ Zone 6

Brunfelsia pauciflora 'Macrantha', illus. p.167
Eranthemum pulchellum
HEATHERS, illus. pp.178–9
Vinca difformis

OTHER RECOMMENDED PLANTS:
Artemisia arborescens 'Faith Raven'
Breynia disticha 'Roseopicta'
DWARF CONIFERS, illus. pp.110–11

Euonymus fortunei 'Coloratus'
Euonymus fortunei 'Emerald Gaiety'
Pseuderanthemum atropurpureum
Pseudowintera colorata

Ruta graveolens 'Jackman's Blue', illus. p.177
Sideritis candicans
Ursinia sericea

SHRUBS small ALL YEAR INTEREST

☐ GREEN

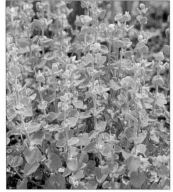

Ballota acetabulosa
Evergreen sub-shrub that forms a mound of rounded, grey-green leaves, felted beneath. Whorls of small, pink flowers open from mid- to late summer.

☼ ◊ Zone 9

Vaccinium glaucoalbum
Evergreen shrub with deep green leaves that, when young, are pale green above, bluish-white beneath. Pink-tinged, white flowers in late spring and early summer are followed by white-bloomed, blue-black fruits.

☼ ◊ pH Zone 9?

Hebe cupressoides
Evergreen, upright, dense shrub with cypress-like, grey-green foliage. On mature plants tiny, pale lilac flowers are borne from early to mid-summer.

☼ ◊ Zone 9

Ruscus hypoglossum
Evergreen, clump-forming shrub with arching shoots. Pointed, glossy, bright green 'leaves' are actually flattened shoots that bear tiny, yellow flowers in spring, followed by large, bright red berries.

☼ ◊ Zone 9

Vinca minor (Lesser periwinkle)
Evergreen, prostrate, spreading sub-shrub that forms extensive mats of small, glossy, dark green leaves. Bears small, purple, blue or white flowers, mainly from mid-spring to early summer.

☼ ◐ ① Zone 3

Mimosa pudica
(Humble plant, Sensitive plant)
Short-lived, evergreen shrub with prickly stems; needs support. Fern-like leaves fold when touched. Has minute, pale mauve-pink flowers in summer-autumn.
Min. 13–16°C (55–61°F).

☼ ◊

Eurya emarginata
Slow-growing, evergreen, densely branched, rounded shrub with small, leathery, deep green leaves. Small, greenish-white flowers in late spring or summer are followed by tiny, purple-black berries.

☼ ◊ Zone 9?

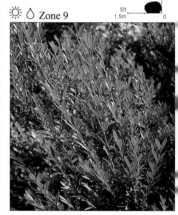

Lonicera pileata
Evergreen, low, spreading, dense shrub with narrow, dark green leaves and tiny, short-tubed, creamy-white flowers in late spring, followed by violet-purple berries. Makes good ground cover.

☼ ◊ ① Zone 6

Chamaerops humilis (Dwarf fan palm, European fan palm)
Slow-growing, evergreen palm, suckering with age. Fan-shaped leaves, 60–90cm (2–3ft) across, have green to grey-green lobes. Has tiny, yellow flowers in summer.
Min. 7°C (45°F).

☼ ◊

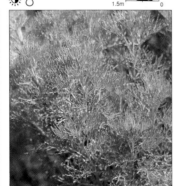

Artemisia abrotanum (Lad's love, Old man, Southernwood)
Deciduous or semi-evergreen, moderately bushy shrub. Aromatic, grey-green leaves have many very slender lobes. Has clusters of small, yellowish flower heads in late summer.

☼ ◊ Zone 6

Buxus microphylla 'Green Pillow'
Evergreen, compact, dwarf shrub, forming a dense, rounded mass of small, oval, dark green leaves. Bears insignificant flowers in late spring or early summer.

☼ ◊ ① Zone 6

Sabal minor (Dwarf palmetto)
Evergreen, suckering fan palm with stems mainly underground. Has leaves of 20–30 green or grey-green lobes. Erect sprays of small, white flowers are followed by shiny, black berries.
Min. 5°C (41°F).

☼ ◊

Brachyglottis rotundifolia
Buxus microphylla
Coprosma x kirkii
Danäe racemosa

DWARF CONIFERS, illus. pp.110–11
Daphne laureola
Ephedra gerardiana
Euonymus fortunei 'Kewensis'

Euonymus fortunei 'Sarcoxie'
Hymenanthera crassifolia
Macrozamia spiralis
Ruscus aculeatus

Salvia officinalis cvs
Serissa foetida

Buxus sempervirens 'Suffruticosa'

Evergreen, dwarf shrub that forms a tight, dense mass of oval, bright green leaves. Bears insignificant flowers in late spring or early summer. Trimmed to about 15cm (6in) is used for edging.

☼ ◊ ⓘ Zone 6

Ruta graveolens 'Jackman's Blue'

Evergreen, bushy, compact sub-shrub. Has aromatic, finely divided, blue foliage. In summer, clusters of small, mustard-yellow flowers are borne.

☼ ◊ ⓘ Zone 5

Leucothöe fontanesiana 'Rainbow'

Evergreen, arching shrub with sharply toothed, leathery, dark green leaves that age from pink- to cream-variegated. Racemes of white flowers open below shoots in spring.

☼ ◊ pH Zone 6

Lonicera nitida 'Baggesen's Gold'

Evergreen, bushy shrub with long, arching shoots covered with tiny, bright yellow leaves. Insignificant, yellowish-green flowers in mid-spring are occasionally followed by mauve fruits.

☼ ◊ ⓘ Zone 7

Salvia officinalis 'Icterina'

Evergreen or semi-evergreen, bushy shrub used as a culinary herb. Has aromatic, grey-green leaves variegated with pale green and yellow. Occasionally bears small spikes of tubular, 2-lipped, purplish flowers.

☼ ◊ Zone 5b

Codiaeum variegatum var. *pictum* (Croton)

Evergreen, erect, sparingly branched shrub. Leathery, glossy leaves vary greatly in size and shape, and are variegated with red, pink, orange or yellow. Min. 10–13°C (50–55°F).

☼◐ ◖ ⓘ

Sanchezia speciosa, syn. *S. nobilis* of gardens

Evergreen, erect, soft-stemmed shrub. Glossy leaves have yellow- or white-banded main veins. Tubular, yellow flowers appear in axils of red bracts, in summer. Min. 15–18°C (59–64°F).

☼ ◖

Euonymus fortunei 'Emerald 'n' Gold'

Evergreen, bushy shrub with bright green leaves, margined with bright yellow and tinged with pink in winter.

☼ ◊ ⓘ Zone 5

Pittosporum tenuifolium 'Tom Thumb'

Evergreen, rounded, dense shrub with pale green, young leaves that contrast with deep reddish-brown, older foliage. Bears cup-shaped, purplish flowers in summer.

☼ ◊ Zone 9?

DWARF CONIFERS, illus. pp.110–11

Euonymus fortunei 'Gold Tip'
Euonymus fortunei 'Sunspot'

Heathers

As a group of plants, heathers (or heaths) are remarkable in that there are species and cultivars available to provide interest at all times of the year. Several are grown for their golden foliage, which often turns a deep burnt orange in winter, while others flower for a long period during summer, autumn or winter. Flowers are in a variety of colours, and are occasionally bicoloured; those with double flowers may be dried for winter decoration. In habit heathers vary from tree-heaths of up to 6m (20ft) to dwarf, prostrate forms, many of which are excellent for providing ground cover.

There are three genera: *Calluna*, *Daboecia* and *Erica*. All *Calluna* and *Daboecia* cultivars and most *Erica* species must be grown in acid soil but otherwise heathers require little attention. Main seasons of interest are given for each plant.

E. tetralix 'Alba Mollis' (sum.-aut.)

E. vagans 'Lyonesse' (sum.-aut.)

E. ciliaris 'White Wings' (sum.)

C. vulgaris 'County Wicklow' (sum.-aut.)

E. × watsonii 'Dawn' (sum.)

C. vulgaris 'Kinlochruel' (sum.-aut.)

E. cinerea 'Hookstone White' (sum.)

E. arborea var. *alpina* (win.-spr.)

E. ciliaris 'David McClintock' (sum.)

C. vulgaris 'Silver Queen' (sum.-aut.)

C. vulgaris 'Elsie Purnell' (sum.-aut.)

E. × darleyensis 'Darley Dale' (win.-spr.)

E. × williamsii 'P.D. Williams' (sum.)

C. vulgaris 'Spring Cream' (spr.-aut.)

E. mackaiana 'Dr Ronald Gray' (sum.)

E. canaliculata (win.-spr.)

C. vulgaris 'My Dream' (sum.-aut.)

E. × darleyensis 'Ghost Hills' (win.-spr.)

D. × scotica 'Silver-wells' (spr.-aut.)

E. carnea 'Golden Starlet' (all year)

E. × darleyensis 'White Perfection' (win.-spr.)

C. vulgaris 'Anthony Davis' (sum.-aut.)

C. vulgaris 'J.H. Hamilton' (sum.-aut.)

E. mackaiana 'Plena' (sum.)

E. × darleyensis 'White Glow' (win.-spr.)

E. × veitchii 'Exeter' (win.-spr.)

E. × veitchii 'Pink Joy' (win.-spr.)

E. carnea 'Springwood White' (win.-spr.)

E. × darleyensis 'Archie Graham' (win.-spr.)

D. cantabrica 'Bicolor' (spr.-aut.)

D. x *scotica* 'William Buchanan' (spr.-aut.)

E. vagans 'Birch Glow' (sum.-aut.)

E. tetralix 'Pink Star' (sum.-aut.)

E. ciliaris 'Corfe Castle' (sum.)

E. cinerea 'C.D. Eason' (sum.)

E. tetralix 'Con Underwood' (sum.-aut.)

C. vulgaris 'Alexandra' (aut.-win.)

E. cinerea 'Eden Valley' (sum.)

E. erigena 'Brightness' (spr.)

E. carnea 'December Red' (win.)

C. vulgaris 'Peter Sparkes' (sum.-aut.)

C. vulgaris 'Tib' (sum.)

C. vulgaris 'Darkness' (sum.-aut.)

E. cinerea 'Purple Beauty' (sum.)

E. carnea 'Vivellii' (win.-spr.)

C. vulgaris 'Silver Knight' (sum.-aut.)

E. carnea 'Rosalie' (all year)

C. vulgaris 'Foxii Nana' (all year)

E. carnea 'Westwood Yellow' (all year)

E. erigena 'Golden Lady' (all year)

E. vagans 'Valerie Proudley' (all year)

E. carnea 'Ann Sparkes' (all year)

C. vulgaris 'Golden Feather' (all year)

C. vulgaris 'Firefly' (all year)

C. vulgaris 'Gold Haze' (all year)

E. cinerea 'Windlebrooke' (all year)

E. cinerea 'Fiddler's Gold' (aut.-win.)

C. vulgaris 'Boskoop' (all year)

C. vulgaris 'Robert Chapman' (all year)

C. vulgaris 'Beoley Gold' (all year)

C. vulgaris 'Multicolor' (all year)

ROSES

THE CULTIVATION OF THE ROSE goes back many
centuries and has a fascinating history, yet roses
are also a valuable element in any modern garden.
Grown in a sunny spot with their roots well fed
and watered, roses will repay your care and
attention with wonderful blooms and scents
throughout the summer months.

Roses

These most romantic of flowers are unsurpassed in beauty and fragrance by any other single group of plants. Roses are cultivated and prized by many, and for some they are an almost indispensable element in the modern garden.

GROWING ROSES

With some 150 species and thousands of cultivars, both ancient and modern, there are members of the genus *Rosa* to suit an enormous number of garden situations. They come from a wide range of habitats throughout the northern hemisphere and, because of this diversity, have a wide range of hardiness. Given attention to their cultivation needs, they will repay the gardener with a profusion of blooms.

All roses do well when grown in open, sunny sites in fertile, humus-rich, moist but well-drained soil. However, avoid planting in soil that has grown roses before as roses may be affected by soil sickness, which is caused by a build-up of harmful soil organisms.

Roses can be grown among bulbs, perennials and other shrubs in a mixed border provided that their fellow plants do not compete directly for moisture and nutrients. Choose companions that are shallow-rooted, such as the many herbaceous geraniums and pinks (*Dianthus* cultivars), or space plants at a sufficient distance to allow for mulching and feeding around the rose's root zone.

MAINTAINING YEAR-ROUND INTEREST

As a group, roses have a long flowering season, from the early summer blooms of 'Frühlingsmorgen' through the main flourish in mid-summer to the first frosts, thanks to the repeat-flowering roses. Some also have attractive fruits (hips) that prolong the season, notably the tomato-like hips of the Rugosas, the flask-shaped, vibrant scarlet fruits of *R. moyesii* and the rounded, black hips of *R. pimpinellifolia*. Regular dead-heading extends the season because it redirects the expenditure of energy from seed formation into flower production.

ORNAMENTAL FEATURES

Roses embrace almost every shade of the spectrum, excluding true blue, and some have a strong fragrance, which can range from the heady, sweet scent of the Damasks to that of musk or spice. A few roses have ornamental thorns, notably *R. sericea* subsp. *omeiensis* f. *pteracantha*, with its large triangular thorns that glow blood-red when backlit.

Foliage can also make an impact: the soft grey-purple leaves of *R. glauca* and the blue-green of the Alba roses are both perfect foils to crimson and purple flowers. Foliage textures range from glossy to matt, from delicately fern-like to robustly wrinkled, as in *R. rugosa*.

DESIGNING WITH ROSES

Roses can be used for a variety of design functions in the garden since they have a diversity of habit that

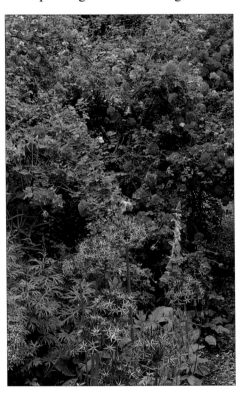

RELAXED INFORMALITY
Above: In this informal planting, the profuse blooms of the gracefully arching shrub Rosa *'Cerise Bouquet' are complemented by the rounded, pink heads of* Allium cristophii *and the vivid spires of foxgloves (*Digitalis purpurea*).*

FORMAL DRESSING
Right: Here, a sturdy arch clothed with clematis and a vigorous, free-flowering rambler lends height to the scheme and forms a perfect frame to draw the eye to an elegant focal point.

10m (30ft) or more in height when scrambling through large trees. Using taller cultivars of dense, thorny shrub roses, such as the Rugosa roses, you can create divisions within the garden. These may take the form of large impenetrable boundary hedges that give privacy and security or, if you use lower-growing roses, they can form garden compartments defined by low hedging or edging.

Climbing and rambling roses are extremely versatile, and can be trained on a wall to act as a colourful backdrop to foreground plantings, or on trellis to form a screen. Like all climbers, they are invaluable for lending height when grown on pillars, pergolas and arches, and can make a focal point if grown on free-standing structures such as tripods and

SUMMER BEDFELLOWS
Above: Alliums and bearded irises are perfect companions to roses in a mid-summer border, while grey-leaved artemisias lend a neutral foil to the intense colours. As a bonus, Crambe cordifolia *adds its subtle topnotes to the fragrance of the roses.*

POTTED ROSES
Right: Small bush roses, notably the miniatures and patio roses, are ideal for container planting. Alternatively, use trailing ground-cover roses in hanging baskets.

includes the mound-forming, sometimes stem-rooting, ground-cover roses, the densely thorny Gallicas and the open, gracefully arching Chinas and Damasks. Many are versatile enough to be used in more than one way.

A rose garden laid out in a formal style is perhaps the most traditional way to use roses, and geometrically ordered beds are particularly suited to the neatly upright growth of many bush roses. Roses can be used equally well as specimens, although the selection of a single favourite is difficult with so many exquisite cultivars to choose from.

Roses range in size from the tiny Miniature bushes such as *R.* 'Rouletii', which at 20cm (8in) high are perfect for containers and window boxes, to the most rampant of ramblers, such as *R.* 'Bobbie James', which can achieve

pyramids. Many of the trailing sorts are also available trained as weeping standards, for elegant focal features.

The ground-cover roses are ideal for clothing sunny and inaccessible banks, since most require little regular pruning.

CONTAINER-GROWING
Smaller roses, especially the Miniature bush roses, are perfect for containers. The smallest – BABY MASQUERADE ('Tanba') and DARLING FLAME ('Meilucca') – are suitable for window boxes, while the trailing or spreading cultivars such as KENT ('Poulcov') are fine for baskets.

ROSES shrub and old garden

☐ WHITE

R. 'Madame Hardy'
Vigorous, upright Damask rose with
plentiful, leathery, matt leaves. Richly
fragrant, quartered-rosette, fully
double flowers, 10cm (4in) across,
white with green eyes, are borne in
summer. H 1.5m (5ft), S 1.2m (4ft).

☼ ◊ Zone 5

R. 'Boule de Neige'
Upright Bourbon rose with arching
stems and very fragrant, cupped to
rosette, fully double flowers. White
flowers, sometimes tinged with pink,
8cm (3in) across, appear in summer-
autumn. Leaves are glossy and dark
green. H 1.5m (5ft), S 1.2m (4ft).

☼ ◊ Zone 6

R. pimpinellifolia 'Plena'
Dense, spreading, prickly species rose
with cupped, double, creamy-white
flowers, 4cm (1½in) across, in early
summer. Has small, fern-like, dark
green leaves and blackish hips.
H 1m (3ft), S 1.2m (4ft).

☼ ◊ Zone 4

R. 'Penelope'
Dense, bushy shrub rose, with plentiful,
dark green foliage, that bears many
scented, cupped, double, pink-cream
flowers, 8cm (3in) across, in clusters
in summer-autumn. H and S 1m (3ft),
more if lightly pruned.

☼ ◊ Zone 6

Categories of Rose

Grown for the extraordinary beauty of their
flowers, roses have been in cultivation for
some hundreds of years. They have been
widely hybridized, producing a vast number
of shrubs suitable for growing as specimen
plants, in the border, as hedges and as climbers
for training on walls, pergolas and pillars.
Roses are classified into three main groups:

Species
Species, or wild, roses and **species hybrids**, which
share most of the characteristics of the parent
species, bear flowers generally in one flush in
summer and hips in autumn.

Old Garden roses
Alba – large, freely branching roses with clusters
of flowers in mid-summer and abundant, greyish-
green foliage.
Bourbon – open, remontant shrub roses that may
be trained to climb. Flowers are borne, often 3 to a
cluster, in summer-autumn.
China – remontant shrubs with flowers borne singly
or in clusters in summer-autumn; provide shelter.
Damask – open shrubs bearing loose clusters of
usually very fragrant flowers mainly in summer.
Gallica – fairly dense shrubs producing richly
coloured flowers, often 3 to a cluster, in the
summer months.
Hybrid Perpetual – vigorous, remontant shrubs with
flowers borne singly or in 3s in summer-autumn.
Moss – often lax shrubs with a furry, moss-like
growth on stems and calyx, and flowers in summer.
Noisette – remontant climbing roses that bear large
clusters of flowers, with a slight spicy fragrance, in
summer-autumn; provide shelter.
Portland – upright, rather dense, remontant shrubs
bearing loose clusters of flowers in summer-autumn.
Provence (Centifolia) – lax, thorny shrubs bearing
scented flowers in summer.
Sempervirens – semi-evergreen climbing roses that
bear numerous flowers in late summer.
Tea – remontant shrubs and climbers with elegant,
pointed buds that open to loose flowers with a spicy
fragrance; provide shelter.

Modern Garden roses
Shrub – a diverse group, illustrated here with
the Old Garden roses because of their similar
characteristics. Most are remontant and are larger
than bush roses, with flowers borne singly or in
sprays in summer and/or autumn.

Flower shapes

With the mass hybridization that has occurred
in recent years, roses have been developed
to produce plants with a wide variety of
characteristics, in particular different forms
of flower, often with a strong fragrance. These
flower types, illustrated below, give a general
indication of the shape of the flower at its perfect
state (which in some cases may be before it has
opened fully). Growing conditions may affect
the form of the flower. Flowers may be single
(4–7 petals), semi-double (8–14 petals), double
(15–30 petals) or fully double (over 30 petals).

Flat – open, usually
single or semi-double
flowers have petals that
are almost flat.

Cupped – open, single
to fully double flowers
have petals curving out-
wards gently from the
centre.

Pointed – elegant,
'Hybrid Tea' shape;
semi-double to fully
double flowers have
high, tight centres.

Urn-shaped – classic,
curved, flat-topped,
semi-double to fully
double flowers are of
'Hybrid Tea' type.

Rounded – usually
double or fully double
flowers have even-sized,
overlapping petals that
form a bowl-shaped or
rounded outline.

Rosette – usually
double or fully double
flowers are rather flat
with many confused,
slightly overlapping
petals of uneven size.

Quartered-rosette –
rather flat, usually
double or fully double
flowers have confused
petals of uneven size
arranged in a quartered
pattern.

Pompon – small,
rounded, double or fully
double flowers, usually
borne in clusters, have
masses of small petals.

Large-flowered bush (Hybrid Tea) – remontant
shrubs with large flowers borne in summer-autumn.
Cluster-flowered bush (Floribunda) – remontant
shrubs with usually large sprays of flowers in
summer-autumn.
Dwarf clustered-flowered bush (Patio) – neat,
remontant shrubs with sprays of flowers borne in
summer-autumn.
Miniature bush – very small, remontant shrubs
with sprays of tiny flowers in summer-autumn.

Polyantha – tough, compact, remontant shrubs with
many small flowers in summer-autumn.
Ground cover – trailing and spreading roses, some
flowering in summer only, others remontant,
flowering in summer-autumn.
Climbing – vigorous climbing roses, diverse in
growth and flower, some flowering in summer only,
others remontant, flowering in summer-autumn.
Rambler – vigorous climbing roses with flexible
stems that bear clusters of flowers mostly in summer.

R. 'Fantin-Latour'
Vigorous, shrubby Provence rose.
Flowers appear in summer and are
fragrant, cupped to flat, fully double,
blush-pink, with neat, green button
eyes, and 10cm (4in) across. Has
broad, dark green leaves.
H 1.5m (5ft), S 1.2m (4ft).

☼ ◊ Zone 3

R. 'Conrad Ferdinand Meyer'
Vigorous, arching shrub rose with
cupped, fully double, pink flowers,
7cm (3in) across, that are richly
fragrant and borne in large numbers
in summer, fewer in autumn. Foliage
is leathery and prone to rust.
H 2.5m (8ft), S 1.2m (4ft).

☼ ◊ Zone 2b

R. 'Dupontii', syn. *R. moschata*
var. *nivea* (Snowbush rose)
Upright, bushy shrub rose with
abundant, greyish foliage. Bears
many clusters of fragrant, flat, single,
white flowers, tinged with blush-pink,
6cm (2½in) across, in mid-summer.
H and S 2.2m (7ft).

☼ ◊ Zone 6

R. 'Great Maiden's Blush',
syn. *R.* 'Cuisse de Nymphe',
R. 'La Séduisante'
Vigorous, upright Alba rose. Very
fragrant, rosette, fully double, pinkish-
white flowers, 8cm (3in) across,
appear in mid-summer.
H 2m (6ft), S 1.3m (4½ft).

☼ ◊ Zone 3

R. 'Céleste', syn. *R.* 'Celestial'
Vigorous, spreading, bushy Alba rose.
Fragrant, cupped, double, light pink
flowers, 8cm (3in) across, appear in
summer. Makes a good hedge.
H 1.5m (5ft), S 1.2m (4ft).

☼ ◊ Zone 3

R. 'Nevada'
Dense, arching shrub rose with
abundant, light green leaves. Scented,
flat, semi-double, creamy-white
flowers, 10cm (4in) across, are borne
freely in summer and more sparsely in
autumn. H and S 2.2m (7ft).

☼ ◊ Zone 2

R. Pearl Drift ('Leggab')
Bushy, spreading shrub rose that
produces clusters of lightly scented,
cupped, double, blush-pink flowers,
10cm (4in) across, in summer-autumn.
Leaves are plentiful and glossy.
H 1m (3ft), S 1.2m (4ft).

☼ ◊ Zone 6

R. 'Felicia'
Vigorous shrub rose with abundant,
healthy, greyish-green foliage. Scented,
cupped, double flowers, 8cm (3in)
across, are light pink, tinged with
apricot, and are borne in summer-
autumn. H 1.5m (5ft), S 2.2m (7ft).

☼ ◊ Zone 6

R. rubiginosa, syn. *R. eglanteria*
(Eglantine, Sweet briar)
Vigorous, arching, thorny species rose
that has distinctive, apple-scented
foliage. Bears cupped, single, pink
flowers, 2.5cm (1in) across, in mid-
summer and red hips in autumn.
H and S 2.4m (8ft).

☼ ◊ Zone 6

R. 'Aimée Vibert'
R. 'Alba Semiplena'
R. 'Blanche Moreau'
R. 'Jacqueline du Pré'

R. 'Mousseline'
R. 'Noisette Carnée'
R. 'Souvenir de la Malmaison'

R. 'Cécile Brünner'
R. 'Félicité Parmentier'
R. 'Kathleen Harrop'
R. 'Omar Khayyám'

ROSES shrub and old garden

☐ PINK

R. ROSY CUSHION ('Interall')
Dense, spreading shrub rose with
plentiful, glossy, dark green leaves.
Bears clusters of scented, cupped, semi-
double flowers, 6cm (2½in) across, that
are pink with ivory centres, in summer-
autumn. H 1m (3ft), S 1.2m (4ft).

☼ ◊ Zone 6

R. glauca, syn. *R. rubrifolia*
Vigorous, arching species rose, grown
for its fine, greyish-purple leaves and
red stems. Flat, single, cerise-pink
flowers, 4cm (1½in) across, with pale
centres and gold stamens, appear in
early summer, followed by red hips in
autumn. H 2m (6ft), S 1.5m (5ft).

☼ ◊ Zone 2b

R. Marguerite Hilling,
syn. *R.* 'Pink Nevada'
Dense, arching shrub rose. Many
scented, flat, semi-double, rose-pink
flowers, 10cm (4in) across, are borne
in summer and a few in autumn. Has
light green foliage. H and S 2.2m (7ft).

☼ ◊ Zone 6

R. 'Reine Victoria'
Lax Bourbon rose with slender stems
and light green leaves. Sweetly
scented, rosette, double flowers, 8cm
(3in) across, in shades of pink, are
borne in summer-autumn. Grows well
on a pillar. H 2m (6ft), S 1.2m (4ft).

☼ ◊ Zone 6

R. 'Complicata'
Very vigorous Gallica rose, with
thorny, arching growth, useful as
a large hedge. Slightly fragrant,
cupped, single flowers, 11cm (4½in)
across, are pink with pale centres and
appear in mid-summer.
H 2.2m (7ft), S 2.5m (8ft).

☼ ◊ Zone 4

R. 'Königin von Dänemark',
syn. *R.* 'Belle Courtisanne'
Vigorous, rather open Alba rose.
Heavily scented, quartered-rosette,
fully double, warm-pink flowers, 8cm
(3in) across and with green button
eyes, appear in mid-summer.
H 1.5m (5ft), S 1.2m (4ft).

☼ ◊ Zone 3

R. BONICA ('Meidonomac'),
syn. *R.* 'Bonica '82'
Vigorous, spreading shrub rose bearing
large sprays of slightly fragrant, cup-
shaped, fully double, rose-pink flowers,
7cm (3in) across, in summer-autumn.
Foliage is glossy and plentiful.
H 1m (3ft), S 1.1m (3½ft).

☼ ◊ Zone 6

R. 'Pink Grootendorst'
Upright, bushy shrub rose with
plentiful, small leaves. Rosette, double
flowers, 5cm (2in) across, have
serrated, clear pink petals. Blooms are
carried in sprays in summer-autumn.
H 2m (6ft), S 1.5m (5ft).

☼ ◊ Zone 2b

R. CONSTANCE SPRY ('Austance')
Shrub rose of arching habit that will
climb if supported. Cupped, fully
double, pink flowers, 12cm (5in)
across, with a spicy scent, are borne
freely in summer. Leaves are large and
plentiful. H 2m (6ft), S 1.5m (5ft).

☼ ◊ Zone 3

R. x *centifolia* 'Cristata'
R. x *centifolia* 'Muscosa'
R. 'Frühlingsmorgen'
R. 'Gloire des Mousseux'

R. 'Ispahan'
R. 'Louise Odier'
R. 'Madame Ernest Calvat'
R. 'Madame Pierre Oger'

R. 'Mary Rose'
R. 'Perle d'Or'
R. 'Saint Nicholas'
R. 'Tricolore de Flandre'

ROSES

R. 'Mrs John Laing'
Bushy Hybrid Perpetual rose with plentiful, light green foliage. Produces many richly fragrant, rounded, fully double, pink flowers, 12cm (5in) across, in summer and a few in autumn. H 1m (3ft), S 80cm (2½ft).

☀ ◊ Zone 5

R. × odorata 'Mutabilis',
syn. *R. chinensis* 'Mutabilis'
Open species rose with coppery young foliage. In summer-autumn bears shallowly cup-shaped, single, buff-yellow flowers, 6cm (2½in) across, that age to coppery-pink or -crimson. H and S 1m (3ft), to 2m (6ft) against a wall.

☀ ◊ Zone 6

R. rugosa
(Hedgehog rose, Japanese rose)
Vigorous, dense species rose with wrinkled leaves and large, red hips. Cupped, single, white or purplish-red flowers, 9cm (3½in) across, appear in good succession in summer-autumn. H and S 1–2m (3–6ft).

☀ ◊ Zone 2b

R. 'Roseraie de l'Haÿ'
Vigorous, dense shrub rose. Bears many strongly scented, cupped to flat, double, reddish-purple flowers, 11cm (4½in) across, in summer-autumn. Leaves are abundant and disease-resistant. H 2.2m (7ft), S 2m (6ft).

☀ ◊ Zone 2

R. × odorata 'Pallida' (Old blush china, Parson's pink china)
Bushy China rose that may be trained as a climber on a sheltered wall. Cupped, double, pink flowers, 6cm (2½in) across, are produced freely from summer to late autumn.
H 1m (3ft), S 80cm (2½ft) or more.

☀ ◊ Zone 6

R. moyesii 'Geranium',
syn. *R.* 'Geranium'
Vigorous, arching species rose. Flat, single flowers, 5cm (2in) across, are dusky scarlet with yellow stamens and are borne on branches in summer. Has small, dark green leaves and in autumn large, red hips. H 3m (10ft), S 2.5m (8ft).

☀ ◊ Zone 6

R. gallica 'Versicolor'
(Rosa mundi)
Neat, bushy Gallica rose. In summer produces striking, slightly scented, flat, semi-double flowers, 5cm (2in) across, very pale blush-pink with crimson stripes. H 75cm (2½ft), S 1m (3ft).

☀ ◊ Zone 4

R. 'Madame Isaac Pereire'
Vigorous, arching Bourbon rose. Fragrant, cupped to quartered-rosette, fully double flowers, 15cm (6in) across, are deep purplish-pink and are produced freely in summer-autumn. H 2.2m (7ft), S 2m (6ft).

☀ ◊ Zone 6

R. 'Henri Martin',
syn. *R.* 'Red Moss'
Vigorous, upright Moss rose. Rosette, double, purplish-crimson flowers, 9cm (3½in) across, appear in summer and have a light scent and some furry, green 'mossing' of the calyces underneath. H 1.5m (5ft), S 1m (3ft).

☀ ◊ Zone 5

R. 'Armada'
R. 'Commandant Beaurepaire'
R. 'Du Maître d'Ecole'
R. 'Fellenberg'

R. gallica var. *officinalis*
R. 'Honorine de Brabant'
R. macrophylla
R. moyesii

R. 'Président de Sèze'
R. 'Variegata di Bologna'

ROSES shrub and old garden

ROSES

■■ RED–PURPLE   □ YELLOW

R. 'Empereur du Maroc'
Compact, shrubby Hybrid Perpetual
rose. Fragrant, quartered-rosette, fully
double flowers, 8cm (3in) across, are
rich purplish-crimson and are borne
freely in summer and more sparsely
in autumn. H 1.2 m (4ft), S 1m (3ft).

☼ ◊ Zone 5

R. 'Belle de Crécy'
Gallica rose of rather lax growth and
few thorns. Rosette, fully double
flowers, 8cm (3in) across, are pink,
tinged greyish-purple with green eyes,
have a rich, spicy fragrance and are
produced in summer.
H 1.2 m (4ft), S 1m (3ft).

☼ ◊ Zone 5

R. primula (Incense rose)
Lax, arching species rose that bears
scented, cupped, single, primrose-
yellow flowers, 4cm (1½in) across,
in late spring. Foliage is plentiful,
aromatic and fern-like. May die back
in hard winters. H and S 2m (6ft).

☼ ◊ Zone 6

R. CARDINAL HUME ('Harregale')
Bushy, spreading shrub rose. Cupped,
fully double, reddish-purple flowers,
7.5cm (3in) across, are borne in dense
clusters in summer-autumn and have a
musky scent. H and S 1m (3ft).

☼ ◊ Zone 6

R. 'William Lobb',
syn. R. 'Duchesse d'Istrie'
Moss rose with strong, arching, prickly
stems that will climb if supported. In
summer bears rosette, double, deep
purplish-crimson flowers, 9cm (3½in)
across, that fade to lilac-grey.
H and S 2m (6ft).

☼ ◊ Zone 3

R. 'Cardinal de Richelieu'
Vigorous, compact Gallica rose that
bears plentiful, dark green foliage and
fragrant, rounded, fully double, deep
burgundy-purple flowers, 8cm (3in)
across, in summer.
H 1.2m (4ft), S 1m (3ft).

☼ ◊ Zone 5

R. 'Tour de Malakoff'
Provence rose of open habit. Scented,
rosette, double flowers, 12cm (5in)
across, are magenta with violet veins,
fading to greyish-purple, and appear in
summer. H 2m (6ft), S 1.5m (5ft).

☼ ◊ Zone 5

R. foetida 'Persiana',
syn. R. 'Persian Yellow'
Upright, arching species rose with
cupped, double, yellow flowers, 2.5cm
(1in) across, in early summer. Glossy
leaves are prone to blackspot. Prune
spent branches only and shelter from
cold winds. H and S 1.5m (5ft).

☼ ◊ Zone 2

R. ecae
Erect, wiry species rose. Cupped,
single, bright yellow flowers, 2cm
(¾in) across, with a musky scent, are
borne close to reddish stems in late
spring. Foliage is fern-like and
graceful. Needs shelter.
H 1.5m (5ft), S 1.2m (4ft).

☼ ◊ Zone 8

R. 'Assemblage des Beautés'
R. 'Capitaine John Ingram'
R. 'Charles de Mills'
R. 'Nuits de Young'

R. 'Robert le Diable'
R. 'Souvenir d'Alphonse Lavallée'
R. 'Tuscany Superb'
R. 'Zigeunerknabe'

R. 'Buff Beauty'
R. 'Golden Wings'

ROSES modern

R. ICEBERG ('Korbin'),
syn. *R.* 'Schneewittchen'
Cluster-flowered bush rose. Produces
many sprays of cupped, fully double,
white flowers, 7cm (3in) across, in
summer-autumn. Has abundant, glossy
leaves. H 75cm (30in), S 65cm (26in),
more if not pruned hard.

☼ ◊ Zone 5b

R. *xanthina* **'Canary Bird'**
Vigorous, dense, arching species
hybrid with small, fern-like leaves.
Cupped, single, yellow flowers, 5cm
(2in) across, with a musky scent,
appear in late spring and sparsely in
autumn. May die back in hard winters.
H and S 2.1m (7ft).

☼ ◊ Zone 4b

R. MARGARET MERRIL
('Harkuly')
Upright, cluster-flowered bush rose.
Very fragrant, double, blush-white or
white flowers, are well-formed, urn-
shaped and 10cm (4in) across, and are
borne singly or in clusters in summer-
autumn. H 1m (3ft), S 60cm (2ft).

☼ ◊ Zone 6

R. 'Elizabeth Harkness'
Neat, upright, large-flowered bush rose
with abundant, dark green foliage.
Fragrant, pointed, fully double flowers,
12cm (5in) across, are pale creamy-
pink, tinted buff, and are borne in
summer-autumn.
H 80cm (30in), S 60cm (24in).

☼ ◊ Zone 6

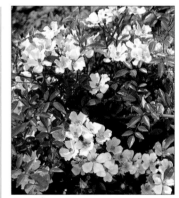

R. GRAHAM THOMAS ('Ausmas')
Vigorous, arching shrub rose, lax in
habit, with glossy, bright green leaves.
In summer-autumn bears cupped, fully
double, yellow flowers, 11cm (4½in)
across, with some scent.
H 1.2m (4ft), S 1.5m (5ft).

☼ ◊ Zone 5

R. GROUSE ('Korimro')
Trailing, ground-cover rose with
very abundant, glossy foliage and
flat, single, blush-pink flowers, 4cm
(1½in) across, borne close to stems
in summer-autumn. Has a pleasant
fragrance. H 45cm (1½ft), S 3m (10ft).

☼ ◊ Zone 6

R. 'The Fairy'
Dense, cushion-forming, dwarf cluster-
flowered bush rose with abundant,
small, glossy leaves. Rosette, double,
pink flowers, 2.5cm (1in) across, are
borne freely in late summer and
autumn. H and S 60cm (2ft).

☼ ◊ Zone 5

R. 'Nozomi', syn.
R. 'Heideröslein'
Creeping, ground-cover rose bearing
flat, single, blush-pink and white
flowers, 2.5cm (1in) across, close to
stems in summer. Has small, dark green
leaves. May be used for a container.
H 45cm (1½ft), S 1.2m (4ft).

☼ ◊ Zone 6

OTHER RECOMMENDED PLANTS:
R. 'City of London'
R. 'Elina'
R. 'English Miss'

R. 'Hannah Gordon'
R. 'Langford Light'
R. 'Len Turner'
R. 'Ophelia'

R. 'Pascali'
R. 'Yvonne Rabier'

☐ PINK

R. PINK BELLS ('Poulbells')
Very dense, spreading, ground-cover rose with abundant, small, dark green leaves and many pompon, fully double, pink flowers, 2.5cm (1in) across, borne in clusters in summer. H 75cm (2½ft), S 1.2m (4ft).

☼ ◊ Zone 6

R. 'Queen Elizabeth'
Upright, cluster-flowered bush rose that bears long-stemmed, rounded, fully double, pink flowers, 10cm (4in) across, singly or in clusters, in summer-autumn. Leaves are large and leathery. H 1.5m (5ft), S 75cm (2½ft), more if not pruned hard.

☼ ◊ Zone 6

R. 'Iced Ginger'
Upright, cluster-flowered bush rose with sparse, reddish foliage. Pointed, fully double, buff to copper-pink flowers, 11cm (4⅓in) across, are borne singly or in clusters in summer-autumn. H 90cm (36in), S 70cm (28in).

☼ ◊ Zone 6

R. 'Alpine Sunset'
Compact, large-flowered bush rose with fragrant, rounded, fully double, peach-yellow flowers, 20cm (8in) across, appearing on short stems in summer-autumn. Has large, semi-glossy leaves. May die back in hard winters. H and S 60cm (2ft).

☼ ◊ Zone 4b

R. PEEK-A-BOO ('DICGROW'),
syn. *R.* 'Brass Ring'
Dense, cushion-forming, dwarf cluster-flowered bush rose with sprays of urn-shaped, double, apricot-pink flowers, 4cm (1½in) across, from summer to early winter. Leaves are narrow and dark green. H and S 45cm (18in).

☼ ◊ Zone 6

R. ROSEMARY HARKNESS ('Harrowbond')
Vigorous, large-flowered bush rose with abundant, glossy leaves. Bears fragrant, pointed, double flowers, 10 cm (4in) across, in shades of salmon-pink and orange, singly or in clusters in summer-autumn. H 1m (3ft), S 75cm (2½ft).

☼ ◊ Zone 6

R. SEXY REXY ('Macrexy')
Compact, bushy, cluster-flowered bush rose. Bears clusters of slightly fragrant, cupped, camellia-like, fully double, pink flowers, 8cm (3in) across, in summer-autumn. Leaves are dark green. H and S 60cm (2ft).

☼ ◊ Zone 6

R. LOVELY LADY ('Dicjubell')
Dense, rounded, large-flowered bush rose. Slightly scented, pointed, fully double, rose-pink flowers, 10cm (4in) across, are produced freely in summer-autumn. H 80cm (30in), S 70cm (28in).

☼ ◊ Zone 6

R. 'Blessings'
Upright, large-flowered bush rose with slightly fragrant, salmon-pink flowers that are urn-shaped and fully double, 10 cm (4in) across, and are borne singly or in clusters in summer-autumn. Has large, dark green leaves. H 1m (3ft), S 75cm (2½ft).

☼ ◊ Zone 6

R. 'Gentle Touch'
R. 'Petit Four'
R. 'Pink Parfait'
R. 'Royal Highness'

■ PINK

R. ANISLEY DICKSON ('Dickimono'), syn. *R.* 'Dicky', *R.* 'Münchner Kindl'
Vigorous, cluster-flowered bush rose. Carries large clusters of slightly fragrant, pointed, double, salmon-pink flowers, 8cm (3in) across, in summer-autumn. H 1m (3ft), S 75cm (2½ft).

☼ ◊ Zone 6

R. PAUL SHIRVILLE ('Harqueterwife')
Spreading, large-flowered bush rose. Bears fragrant, pointed, fully double, rosy salmon-pink flowers, 9cm (3½in) across, in summer-autumn. Leaves are glossy, reddish and abundant. H and S 75cm (30in).

☼ ◊ Zone 6

R. 'Silver Jubilee'
Dense, upright, large-flowered bush rose. Bears slightly scented, pointed, fully double, soft salmon-pink flowers, 12cm (5in) across, very freely in summer-autumn. Foliage is abundant and glossy.
H 1.1m (3½ft), S 75cm (2½ft).

☼ ◊ Zone 6

R. KEEPSAKE ('Kormalda')
Neat, bushy, large-flowered bush rose with plentiful, glossy leaves. Slightly scented, rounded, fully double, pink flowers, 12cm (5in) across, are freely produced in summer-autumn.
H 75cm (30in), S 60cm (24in).

☼ ◊ Zone 6

R. DOUBLE DELIGHT ('Andeli')
Large-flowered bush rose of upright, uneven growth. Fragrant, rounded, fully double flowers, 12cm (5in) across, are creamy-white, edged with red, and are borne in summer-autumn.
H 1m (3ft), S 60cm (2ft).

☼ ◊ Zone 5

■ PINK–RED

R. ESCAPADE ('Harpade')
Dense, cluster-flowered bush rose. Fragrant, cupped, semi-double, rose-violet flowers, 8cm (3in) across, with white eyes, are borne in sprays in summer-autumn. Foliage is light green and glossy.
H 75cm (30in), S 60cm (24in).

☼ ◊ Zone 6

R. ANNA FORD ('Harpiccolo')
Dwarf cluster-flowered bush rose. Has urn-shaped (opening flat), double, orange-red flowers, 4cm (1½in) across, borne in summer-autumn, and many small, dark green leaves.
H 45cm (18in), S 38cm (15in).

☼ ◊ Zone 6

R. TRUMPETER ('Mactru')
Neat, bushy, cluster-flowered bush rose with many cupped, fully double, bright red flowers, 6cm (2½in) across, in summer-autumn. Leaves are deep green and semi-glossy.
H 60cm (24in), S 50cm (20in).

☼ ◊ Zone 6

ROSES modern

■ RED　　　　　　　　　　　　　　　　　　　　　　　　　□ YELLOW

R. ROYAL WILLIAM ('Korzaun'),
syn. *R.* 'Duftzauber '84'
Vigorous, large-flowered bush rose
with large, dark green leaves. Slightly
scented, pointed, fully double, deep
crimson flowers, 12cm (5in) across,
are carried on long stems in summer-
autumn. H 1m (3ft), S 75cm (2½ft).

☼ ◊ Zone 6

R. 'Precious Platinum',
syn. *R.* 'Opa Potschke'
Vigorous, large-flowered bush rose
with abundant, glossy leaves. Bears
slightly scented, rounded, fully double,
deep crimson-scarlet flowers, 10cm
(4in) across, in summer-autumn.
H 1m (3ft), S 60cm (2ft).

☼ ◊ Zone 6

R. WEE JOCK ('Cocabest')
Dense, bushy, dwarf cluster-flowered
bush rose. Bears rosette, fully double,
crimson flowers, 4cm (1½in) across,
in summer-autumn. Plentiful leaves are
small and dark green.
H and S 45cm (18in).

☼ ◊ Zone 5b

**R. CHAMPAGNE COCKTAIL
('Horflash')**
Upright, cluster-flowered bush rose.
Fragrant, cupped, double, yellow-pink
flowers, 9cm (3½in) across, opening
wide, are borne in summer-autumn.
H 1m (3ft), S 60cm (2ft).

☼ ◊ Zone 5b

R. THE TIMES ROSE ('Korpeahn')
Spreading, cluster-flowered bush rose.
Slightly scented, cupped, double, deep
crimson flowers, 8cm (3in) across, are
borne in wide clusters in summer-
autumn. Foliage is dark green and
plentiful. H 60cm (24in), S 75cm (30in).

☼ ◊ Zone 6

R. PEACE ('Madame A. Meilland')
syn. *R.* 'Gioia', *R.* 'Gloria Dei'
Vigorous, shrubby, large-flowered bush
rose with scented, pointed to rounded,
fully double flowers, 15cm (6in) across,
borne freely in clusters in summer-
autumn. Has abundant, large, glossy
foliage. H 1.2m (4ft), S 1m (3ft).

☼ ◊ Zone 6

R. ALEXANDER ('Harlex'),
syn. *R.* 'Alexandra'
Vigorous, upright, large-flowered bush
rose with abundant, dark green foliage.
Slightly scented, pointed, double,
bright red flowers, 12cm (5in) across,
are borne on long stems in summer-
autumn. H 1.5m (5ft), S 75cm (2½ft).

☼ ◊ Zone 6

R. ALEC'S RED ('Cored')
Vigorous, large-flowered bush rose
bearing strongly fragrant, deep cherry-
red flowers that are pointed and fully
double, 15cm (6in) across, in summer-
autumn. H 1m (3ft), S 60cm (2ft).

☼ ◊ Zone 6

R. GOLDEN PENNY ('Rugul'),
syn. *R.* 'Guletta', *R.* 'Tapis Jaune'
Compact, dense, dwarf cluster-
flowered bush rose with cupped to flat,
double, yellow flowers, 5cm (2in)
across, that are borne in summer-
autumn, and rich green leaves.
H 30cm (12in), S 40cm (16in).

☼ ◊ Zone 6

R. 'Blue Moon'　　　　　　　*R.* 'Ingrid Bergman'　　　　　*R.* 'National Trust'　　　　　*R.* 'Julia's Rose'
R. 'Drummer Boy'　　　　　*R.* 'Intrigue'　　　　　　　　*R.* 'Shocking Blue'　　　　　*R.* 'Sheila's Perfume'
R. 'Fragrant Cloud'　　　　*R.* 'Invincible'

R. 'Grandpa Dickson',
syn. *R.* 'Irish Gold'
Neat, upright, large-flowered bush rose
with sparse, pale, glossy foliage. Bears
many slightly scented, pointed, fully
double, light yellow flowers, 18cm
(7in) across, in summer-autumn.
H 80cm (30in), S 60cm (24in).

☼ ◊ Zone 4b

R. SIMBA ('Korbelma'),
syn. *R.* 'Goldsmith'
Upright, large-flowered bush rose with
lightly fragrant, urn-shaped, fully
double, yellow flowers, 9cm (3½in)
across, borne freely in summer-autumn.
Leaves are large and dark green.
H 75cm (30in), S 60cm (24in).

☼ ◊ Zone 6

**R. MOUNTBATTEN
('Harmantelle')**
Shrubby, cluster-flowered bush rose
with disease-resistant foliage. Bears
scented, rounded, fully double, yellow
flowers, 10cm (4in) across, singly or in
clusters, in summer-autumn.
H 1.2m (4ft), S 75cm (2½ft).

☼ ◊ Zone 6

R. 'Korresia', syn. *R.* 'Friesia'
Bushy, upright, cluster-flowered bush
rose. Bears open sprays of strongly
scented, urn-shaped, double flowers,
8cm (3in) across, with waved, yellow
petals, in summer-autumn.
H 75cm (30in), S 60cm (24in).

☼ ◊ Zone 6

R. BRIGHT SMILE ('Dicdance')
Low, bushy, cluster-flowered bush rose
with bright, glossy leaves. Bears
clusters of slightly scented, flat,
semi-double, yellow flowers, 8cm (3in)
across, in summer-autumn.
H and S 45cm (18in).

☼ ◊ Zone 6

R. FREEDOM ('Dicjem')
Neat, large-flowered bush rose, with
many shoots and abundant, glossy
foliage. Bears many lightly scented,
rounded, double, bright yellow
flowers, 9cm (3½in) across, in
summer-autumn.
H 75cm (30in), S 60cm (24in).

☼ ◊ Zone 6

R. 'Glenfiddich'
Upright, cluster-flowered bush rose.
Slightly fragrant, urn-shaped, double,
amber-yellow flowers, 10cm (4in)
across, are borne singly or in clusters
in summer-autumn.
H 75cm (30in), S 60cm (24in).

☼ ◊ Zone 6

R. AMBER QUEEN ('Harroony')
Spreading, cluster-flowered bush rose.
Amber flowers are fragrant, rounded
and fully double, 8cm (3in) across, and
are borne in summer-autumn. Has
abundant, reddish foliage.
H and S 50cm (20in).

☼ ◊ Zone 6

R. 'Arthur Bell'
R. 'Dutch Gold'
R. 'Princess Alice'

R. 'Princess Michael of Kent'

193

ROSES modern

YELLOW–ORANGE

R. POT O' GOLD ('Dicdivine')
Large-flowered bush rose of neat,
even growth. Fragrant, rounded, fully
double, golden-yellow flowers, 9cm
(3½in) across, are carried singly or
in wide sprays in summer-autumn.
H 75cm (30in), S 60cm (24in).

☼ ◊ Zone 6

R. SWEET MAGIC ('Dicmagic')
Bushy, dwarf cluster-flowered bush
rose. Bears sprays of lightly fragrant,
urn-shaped, double, pink-flushed,
golden-orange flowers, 4cm (1½in)
across, in summer-autumn.
H 38cm (15in), S 30cm (12in).

☼ ◊ Zone 6

R. TROIKA ('Poumidor'),
syn. *R.* 'Royal Dane'
Vigorous, dense, large-flowered bush
rose with semi-glossy leaves. Fragrant,
pointed, double flowers, 15cm (6in)
across, are orange-red, tinged with
pink, and are borne in summer-autumn.
H 1m (3ft), S 75cm (2½ft).

☼ ◊ Zone 6

R. PICCADILLY ('Macar')
Vigorous, bushy, large-flowered bush
rose with pointed, double, red and
yellow flowers, 12cm (5in) across,
produced freely singly or in clusters
in summer-autumn. Abundant foliage
is reddish and glossy.
H 1m (3ft), S 60cm (2ft).

☼ ◊ Zone 6

R. 'Southampton',
syn. *R.* 'Susan Ann'
Upright, cluster-flowered bush rose.
Bears fragrant, pointed, double, apricot
flowers, 8cm (3in) across, singly or in
clusters in summer-autumn. Foliage is
glossy and disease-resistant.
H 1m (3ft), S 60cm (2ft).

☼ ◊ Zone 6

R. 'Doris Tysterman'
Vigorous, upright, large-flowered bush
rose with lightly scented, pointed, fully
double, orange-red flowers, 10cm (4in)
across, borne in summer-autumn.
Leaves are large, glossy and dark
green. H 1.2m (4ft), S 75cm (2½ft).

☼ ◊ Zone 6

R. ANNE HARKNESS
('Harkaramel')
Upright, cluster-flowered bush rose.
Urn-shaped, double, amber flowers,
8cm (3in) across, are borne in sprays
of many blooms in late summer and
autumn. H 1.2m (4ft), S 60cm (2ft).

☼ ◊ Zone 6

R. REMEMBER ME ('Cocdestin')
Vigorous, dense, large-flowered
bush rose with pointed, fully double,
copper-orange flowers, 9cm (3½in)
across, freely borne in summer-autumn.
Leaves are abundant and glossy.
H 1m (3ft), S 75cm (2½ft).

☼ ◊ Zone 6

R. 'Just Joey'
Branching, open, large-flowered bush
rose with leathery, dark green foliage.
Bears rounded, fully double flowers,
12cm (5in) across, with waved,
copper-pink petals and some scent,
in summer-autumn.
H 75cm (30in), S 60cm (24in).

☼ ◊ Zone 6

R. 'Clarissa'
R. 'Disco Dancer'
R. 'Matangi'
R. 'Sweet Dream'

R. 'Typhoon'
R. 'Whisky Mac'

ROSES miniature

WHITE–PINK

RED

R. SNOWBALL ('Macangeli'),
syn. *R.* 'Angelita'
Compact, creeping, miniature bush
rose with pompon, fully double, white
flowers, 2.5cm (1in) across, that are
borne in summer-autumn. Leaves are
small, glossy and plentiful.
H 20cm (8in), S 30cm (12in).

☼ ◊ Zone 6

R. BABY MASQUERADE ('Tanba'),
syn. *R.* 'Baby Carnival'
Dense, miniature bush rose with
plentiful, leathery foliage and clusters
of rosette, double, yellow-pink flowers,
2.5cm (1in) across, in summer-autumn.
H and S 40cm (16in), more if not
pruned.

☼ ◊ Zone 5b

R. ANGELA RIPPON ('Ocaru')
syn. *R.* 'Ocarina'
Miniature bush rose with slightly
fragrant, urn-shaped, fully double,
salmon-pink flowers, 4cm (1½in)
across, in summer-autumn, and many
small, dark green leaves.
H 45cm (18in), S 30cm (12in).

☼ ◊ Zone 6

R. SHERI ANNE ('Morsherry')
Upright, miniature bush rose with
glossy, leathery foliage. Slightly
scented, rosette, double, light red
flowers, 2.5cm (1in) across, are borne
in summer-autumn.
H 45cm (18in), S 30 cm (12in).

☼ ◊ Zone 6

R. 'Stacey Sue'
Spreading, miniature bush rose with
plentiful, dark green foliage and
rosette, fully double, pink flowers,
2.5cm (1in) across, that are borne
freely in summer-autumn.
H and S 38cm (15in).

☼ ◊ Zone 6

R. 'Hula Girl'
Wide, bushy, miniature bush rose with
glossy, dark green foliage. Slightly
scented, urn-shaped, fully double,
salmon-orange flowers, 2.5cm (1in)
across, are produced freely in summer-
autumn. H 45cm (18in), S 40cm (16in).

☼ ◊ Zone 6

R. 'Fire Princess'
Upright, miniature bush rose with
small, glossy leaves. Bears sprays of
rosette, fully double, scarlet flowers,
4cm (1½in) across, in summer-autumn.
H 45cm (18in), S 30cm (12in).

☼ ◊ Zone 6

R. RED ACE ('Amruda')
Compact, miniature bush rose with
rosette, double, dark red flowers,
4cm (1½in) across, borne in
summer-autumn.
H 35cm (14in), S 30cm (12in).

☼ ◊ Zone 6

OTHER RECOMMENDED PLANTS:
R. 'Easter Morning'
R. 'Snow Carpet'

ROSES climbing

□ WHITE

R. ORANGE SUNBLAZE
('Meijikitar'), syn. *R.* 'Sunblaze'
Compact, miniature bush rose. Rosette,
fully double, bright orange-red
flowers, 4cm (1½in) across, are freely
produced in summer-autumn. Has
plentiful, dark green leaves.
H and S 30cm (12in).

☼ ◊ Zone 6

R. 'Albéric Barbier'
Vigorous, semi-evergreen rambler rose.
Slightly fragrant, rosette, fully double,
creamy-white flowers, 8cm (3in)
across, appear in clusters in summer.
Leaves are small and bright green.
Tolerates a north-facing wall.
H to 5m (15ft), S 3m (10ft).

☼ ◊ Zone 6

R. 'Rise 'n' Shine',
syn. *R.* 'Golden Sunblaze'
Bushy, upright, miniature bush rose
with dark green leaves that bears
rosette, fully double, yellow flowers,
2.5cm (1in) across, in summer-autumn.
H 40cm (16in), S 25cm (10in).

☼ ◊ Zone 5

R. 'Paul's Lemon Pillar'
Stiff, upright climbing rose with large
leaves and scented, pointed to rounded,
fully double, lemon-white flowers,
15cm (6in) across, that appear in
summer. Prefers a sunny, sheltered
wall. H 5m (15ft), S 3m (10ft).

☼ ◊ Zone 6

R. 'Félicité Perpétue'
Sempervirens climbing rose with long,
slender stems. Clusters of rosette, fully
double, blush-pink to white flowers,
4cm (1½in) across, appear in mid-
summer. Small leaves are semi-
evergreen. Prune spent wood only.
H 5m (15ft), S 4m (12ft).

☼ ◊ Zone 6b

R. COLIBRE '79 ('Meidanover')
Upright, rather open, miniature bush
rose. Urn-shaped, double, red-veined,
orange flowers, 4cm (1½in) across, are
borne in summer-autumn.
H 38cm (15in), S 25cm (10in).

☼ ◊ Zone 6

R. filipes 'Kiftsgate'
Rampant climbing rose with abundant,
glossy, light green foliage. Cupped to
flat, single, creamy-white flowers,
2.5cm (1in) across, appear in late
summer in spectacular clusters. Use to
grow up a tree or in a wild garden.
H and S 10m (30ft) or more.

☼ ◊ Zone 6

R. 'Madame Alfred Carrière'
Noisette climbing rose with slender,
smooth stems. Very fragrant, rounded,
double flowers are creamy-white,
tinged pink, 4cm (1½in) across, and
are borne in summer-autumn.
H to 5.5m (18ft), S 3m (10ft).

☼ ◊ Zone 6

R. 'Gloire de Dijon'
Stiffly branched Noisette or climbing
Tea rose. Fragrant, quartered-rosette,
fully double, creamy-buff flowers,
10cm (4in) across, are borne in
summer-autumn.
H 4m (12ft), S 2.5m (8ft).

☼ ◊ Zone 6

R. 'Magic Carousel'

OTHER RECOMMENDED PLANTS:
R. banksiae
R. 'Niphetos'

R. 'Wedding Day'
R. 'White Cockade'

ROSES

■ PINK

R. 'New Dawn'
Vigorous, very hardy climbing rose.
Fragrant, cupped, double, pale pearl-pink flowers, 8cm (3in) across, are
borne in clusters in summer-autumn.
Tolerates a north-facing wall.
H and S 5m (15ft).

☼ ◊ Zone 6

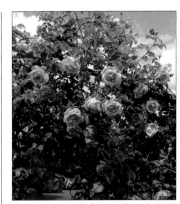

R. HANDEL ('Macha')
Stiff, upright climbing rose. Slightly
scented, urn-shaped, double flowers,
8cm (3in) across, are cream, edged
with pinkish-red, and produced in
clusters in summer-autumn. Has glossy,
dark green foliage.
H 3m (10ft), S 2.2m (7ft).

☼ ◊ Zone 6

R. 'Madame Grégoire Staechelin',
syn. *R.* 'Spanish Beauty'
Vigorous, arching climbing rose with
large clusters of blooms in summer.
Bears rounded to cupped, fully double
flowers, 13cm (5in) across, with
ruffled, clear pink petals, shaded
carmine. H to 6m (20ft), S to 4m (12ft).

☼ ◊ Zone 6

R. 'Pink Perpétué'
Stiffly branched climbing rose that
may be pruned to grow as a shrub.
Bears clusters of cupped to rosette,
double, deep pink flowers, 8cm (3in)
across, in summer-autumn. Leathery
foliage is plentiful.
H 2.8m (9ft), S 2.5m (8ft).

☼ ◊ Zone 6

R. BREATH OF LIFE
('Harquanne')
Stiff, upright climbing rose with large,
lightly scented, rounded, fully double,
pinkish-apricot flowers, 10cm (4in)
across, borne in summer-autumn.
Leaves are semi-glossy.
H 2.8m (9ft), S 2.2m (7ft).

☼ ◊ Zone 6

R. 'Zéphirine Drouhin'
(Thornless rose)
Lax, arching Bourbon rose that will
climb if supported. Bears fragrant,
cupped, double, deep pink flowers,
8cm (3in) across, in summer-autumn.
Is prone to mildew. May be grown as a
hedge. H to 2.5m (8ft), S to 2m (6ft).

☼ ◊ Zone 6

R. 'Albertine'
Vigorous rambler rose with arching,
thorny, reddish stems. Scented, cup-shaped, fully double, salmon-pink
flowers, 8cm (3in) across, are borne in
abundant clusters in summer. Is prone
to mildew in a dry site.
H to 5m (15ft), S 3m (10ft).

☼ ◊ Zone 6

R. 'Chaplin's Pink Companion'
Vigorous climbing rose with glossy,
dark green foliage and slightly scented,
rounded, double, light pink flowers,
5cm (2in) across, borne freely in large
clusters in summer. H and S 3m (10ft).

☼ ◊ Zone 6

R. 'Rosy Mantle'
Stiff, open-branched climbing rose.
Very fragrant, pointed, fully double,
rose-pink flowers, 10cm (4in) across,
are borne in summer-autumn. Dark
green foliage is rather sparse.
H 2.5m (8ft), S 2m (6ft).

☼ ◊ Zone 6

R. 'Aimée Vibert'
R. 'Aloha'
R. 'Belle Portugaise'
R. 'Blush Rambler'

R. 'Compassion'
R. 'François Juranville'
R. 'Kathleen Harrop'
R. 'Lady Waterlow'

R. 'Morning Jewel'
R. 'Noisette Carnée'
R. 'Paul's Himalayan Musk'
R. 'Paul Transon'

ROSES climbing

□□ WHITE-PINK

■ RED

R. CITY GIRL ('Harzorba')
Vigorous, free-branching climbing
rose. Abundant, glossy, dark green
leaves are borne on arching stems.
Scented, semi-double, saucer-shaped,
salmon-pink flowers, 11cm (4½in)
across, appear in summer-autumn.
H and S 2.2m (7ft).

☼ ◊ Zone 6

R. 'Danse du Feu',
syn. *R.* 'Spectacular'
Vigorous, stiffly branched climbing
rose with abundant, glossy foliage.
Bears rounded, double, scarlet flowers,
8cm (3in) across, in summer-autumn.
H and S 2.5m (8ft).

☼ ◊ Zone 6

R. DUBLIN BAY ('Macdub')
Dense, shrubby climbing rose that may
be pruned to grow as a shrub. Bears
clusters of cupped, double, bright
crimson flowers, 10cm (4in) across,
in summer-autumn. Foliage is glossy,
dark green and plentiful.
H and S 2.2m (7ft).

☼ ◊ Zone 6

R. 'Rambling Rector'
Rampant rambler rose. Clusters of
scented, cupped to flat, semi-double,
creamy-white flowers, 4cm (1½in)
across, with golden stamens, appear in
summer, followed by red hips. Arching
stems are covered in greyish-green
foliage. H and S 6m (20ft).

☼ ◊ Zone 6

R. 'Compassion',
syn. *R.* 'Belle de Londres'
Upright, free-branching climbing rose
with glossy, dark leaves on reddish
stems. Fragrant, rounded, double, pink-
tinted, salmon-apricot flowers, 10cm
(4in) across, are borne in summer-
autumn. H 3m (10ft), S 2.5m (8ft).

☼ ◊ Zone 6

R. HIGH HOPES ('Haryup')
Vigorous, upright and arching, long-
stemmed climbing rose. Scented, urn-
shaped to rounded, double, light pink
flowers, 8cm (3in) across, are freely
borne in summer-autumn. Has purplish
green foliage. Good for high walls and
pergolas. H 4m (12ft), S 2.2m (7ft).

☼ ◊ Zone 6

R. 'Aloha'
Strong-growing, bushy climbing rose.
Fragrant, cupped, fully double, rose-
and salmon-pink flowers, 9cm (3½in)
across, appear in summer-autumn.
Leaves are leathery and dark green.
May be grown as a shrub.
H and S 2.5m (8ft).

☼ ◊ Zone 6

R. 'Dortmund'
Upright climbing rose that may be
pruned to make a shrub. Flat, single,
red flowers, 10cm (4in) across, with
white eyes and a slight scent, are borne
freely in clusters in summer-autumn.
Has healthy, dark green foliage.
H 3m (10ft), S 1.8m (6ft).

☼ ◊ Zone 6

R. 'Sympathie'
Vigorous, free-branching climbing
rose. Slightly scented, cupped, fully
double, bright deep red flowers, 8cm
(3in) across, are borne in summer-
autumn, usually in clusters. Has
plentiful, glossy, dark green foliage.
H 3m (10ft), S 2.5m (8ft).

☼ ◊ Zone 6

R. 'Fellenberg'
R. 'John Cabot'
R. 'Ramona'
R. 'John Davis'

R. 'Louis Jolliet'

R. 'Alister Stella Gray'
R. 'Emily Gray'
R. 'Henry Kelsey'
R. 'William Baffin'

R. 'Fortune's Double Yellow'
R. 'Goldfinch'
R. 'Maréchal Niel'

RED-YELLOW

R. 'Guinée'
Vigorous, stiffly branched climbing rose. Fragrant, cupped, fully double, blackish-red to maroon flowers, 11cm (4½in) across, are borne in summer. Leaves are large and leathery. H 5m (15ft), S 2.2m (7ft).

☼ ◊ Zone 6

R. 'Veilchenblau', syn. R. 'Blue Rambler'
Vigorous rambler rose. Rosette, double, violet flowers, streaked white, 2.5cm (1in) across, have a fruity scent and appear in clusters in summer. H 4m (12ft), S 2.2m (7ft).

☼ ◊ Zone 6

R. 'Mermaid'
Slow-growing climbing rose that produces flat, single, primrose-yellow flowers, 12cm (5in) across, in summer-autumn. Has stiff, reddish stems, large, hooked thorns and glossy, dark green leaves. Prefers a sunny, sheltered wall. H and S to 6m (20ft).

☼ ◊ Zone 6

R. 'Emily Gray'
Semi-evergreen rambler rose with long, lax stems. Small trusses of slightly fragrant, cupped, fully double, butter-yellow flowers, 5cm (2in) across, appear in summer. Leaves are lustrous, dark green. Is prone to mildew. H 5m (15ft), S 3m (10ft).

☼ ◊ Zone 6

R. CASINO ('Macca'), syn. R. 'Gerbe d'Or'
Upright, free-branching climbing rose. Sparse, dark green leaves appear on stiffly arching stems. Rounded, double, fragrant, yellow flowers, 9cm (3½in) across, are borne in summer-autumn. H 3m (10ft), S 2.2m (7ft).

☼ ◊ Zone 6

R. 'Golden Showers'
Stiff, upright climbing rose that may be pruned to grow as a shrub. In summer-autumn produces many fragrant, pointed, double, yellow flowers, 10cm (4in) across, that open flat. H 2m (6ft), S 2.2m (7ft) or more.

☼ ◊ Zone 6

YELLOW

R. LAURA FORD ('Chewarvel')
Upright, stiffly branching climbing rose with small, dark, glossy leaves. Sprays of scented, urn-shaped to flat, yellow flowers, 4.5cm (1¾in) across, appear in summer-autumn. Good for pillars. H 2.2m (7ft), S 1.2m (4ft).

☼ ◊ Zone 5

R. banksiae 'Lutea'
(Yellow banksian)
Vigorous climbing rose bearing clusters of many scentless, rosette, fully double, yellow flowers, 2cm (¾in) across, in late spring. Needs a sunny, sheltered wall and pruning of spent wood only. H and S to 10m (30ft).

☼ ◊ Zone 6

R. 'Maigold'
Vigorous climbing rose with prickly, arching stems that may be pruned to grow as shrub. Fragrant, cupped, semi-double, bronze-yellow flowers, 10cm (4in) across, are borne freely in early summer and sparsely in autumn. H and S 2.5m (8ft).

☼ ◊ Zone 3

CLIMBERS

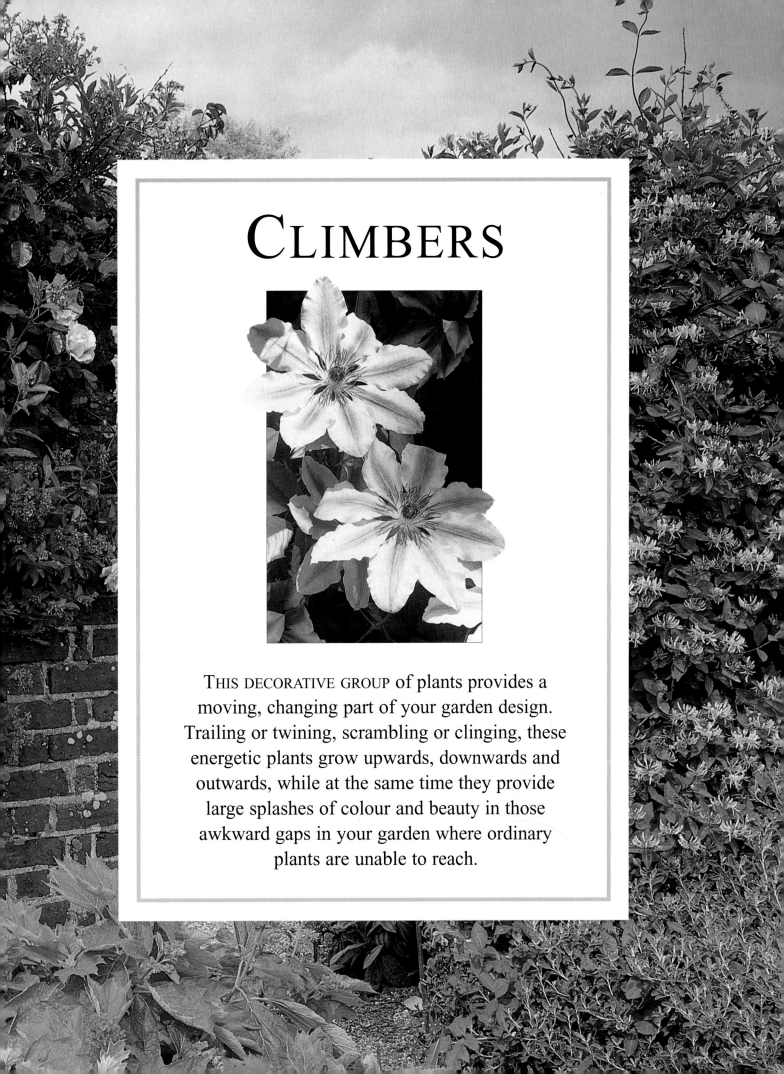

THIS DECORATIVE GROUP of plants provides a moving, changing part of your garden design. Trailing or twining, scrambling or clinging, these energetic plants grow upwards, downwards and outwards, while at the same time they provide large splashes of colour and beauty in those awkward gaps in your garden where ordinary plants are unable to reach.

Climbers

One of the most versatile of plant groups, climbers are able to spread fast and trail decoratively over or through other plants and buildings and across the ground, offering enormous scope for imaginative design.

WHAT ARE CLIMBERS?

Most climbers are woody, evergreen or deciduous plants, while a few are herbaceous perennials or annuals that die back with the onset of winter. They have one of several methods of climbing. They can be self-clinging or twining (with or without tendrils), or scandent, scrambling species that do not cling. It is important to identify the type, since this dictates which method of support is most appropriate.

Self-clingers such as Virginia creeper (*Parthenocissus quinquefolia*) climb by means of adhesive pads or, as in the case of ivies (*Hedera*) and the Swiss cheese plant (*Monstera deliciosa*), by aerial roots which attach themselves to any surface offering purchase such as tree trunks, cliff faces, walls and stout fences. In contrast, twiners such as wisteria draw themselves up by encircling their support, while passion flowers (*Passiflora*) secure their stems with coiling tendrils. Both these types

require the support of tree branches, or a system of wires, mesh or trellis if they are wall-trained. Self-clinging and twining climbers need initial guidance to the support but are self-supporting once established.

Scandent, scrambling plants such as winter jasmine (*Jasminum nudiflorum*) attach themselves loosely, if at all, by threading long, flexible stems through those of a host plant or by mounding their new stems over those made in previous seasons. Their stems must be tied in to their support throughout their life, but in more naturalistic plantings they can be allowed to cascade over walls or tumble down banks as they do in the wild.

ORNAMENTAL FEATURES

Climbing plants provide a range of foliage forms, from the fine-textured, divided leaves of *Tropaeolum speciosum* to the sculptural, heart-shaped ones of *Actinidia deliciosa*. Leaf surfaces alone provide limitless possibilities for interesting textural contrasts, from the softly downy *Vitis vinifera* to the highly glossy ivies (*Hedera* cultivars). The colour range includes the golden-hued *Humulus lupulus* 'Aureus' to the deep green of many jasmines, as well as the intense purple tints of plants such as *Vitis vinifera* 'Purpurea'. Many have such attractive foliage that they make beautiful specimens in their own right – among them *Actinidia kolomikta*, with its green leaves splashed with cream and pink, or the subtle, silver-veined *Parthenocissus henryana*. Some, most notably species of parthenocissus and vitis, reserve their particularly brilliant foliage displays until the autumn. In winter, the architectural forms of twiners such as wisteria and celastrus come into their own.

Climbers bear some of the most beautiful flowers – as shown by the intricate blooms of the passifloras and the elegant chains of wisteria – and many,

especially the honeysuckles (*Lonicera*), sweet peas (*Lathyrus odoratus*) and jasmines, have fragrances that pervade the air over some distance. The flower colours of climbers span the spectrum from the creamy whites of *Schizophragma integrifolium* and *Hydrangea petiolaris* to the vivid magentas of bougainvillea and sombre, chocolate-

WISTERIA ARCH
A sturdy arch forms the ideal support for training climbers, such as Wisteria sinensis, *since it displays the pendent flowers to perfection. When grown around a window, as shown here, the subtle scent of the fragrant flowers can be appreciated both indoors and out.*

FRAGRANT POT
*Graceful climbers such as this honeysuckle (*Lonicera*) lend elegance and fragrance to a patio. For stability, plant in a terracotta or stoneware container in a heavy, loam-based compost.*

SPECTACULAR FLOWERS
*Above: This passion flower (*Passiflora caerulea *'Constance Elliot') produces exquisite blooms. To display them attractively, support these plants against trellis or wires fitted to a wall or fence.*

PRETTY CLIMBER
Left: Here, the self-clinging Hydrangea petiolaris *clothes a wall, forming a superb backdrop for foreground plantings while framing a view to the garden beyond.*

AUTUMN DISPLAY
Below: The tendril-climbing ornamental vine, Vitis coignetiae, *is perfect for wall-training and equally suited to pergolas and arches. Reaching some 15m (50ft) in height, its splendid autumn colour is spectacular en masse.*

maroon of *Rhodochiton atrosanguineus*. With many climbers their season is further prolonged by decorative, silky seed heads, as in clematis, or striking berries, like the shiny blue fruits of *Ampelopsis brevipedunculata* and the orange-yellow fruits of *Celastrus orbiculatus* that split when ripe to reveal bright red seeds within.

DESIGNING WITH CLIMBERS

Growing climbers vertically to create a backdrop to other, lower, foreground plantings is one of the most obvious ways of providing height in a design, although climbers can be used in a variety of other imaginative ways. Grown on free-standing supports, they can form living screens to provide privacy and wind-filtering shelter, or visual and physical barriers between areas in the garden. If grown through trees or on pillars and pyramids, climbers can form a splendid focal point, and on arches they can provide a frame for a vista. On pergolas, climbers

act as a shade-forming element, linking different parts of the garden, and if you use a scented plant to clothe an arbour, it can provide both fragrance and seclusion for quiet contemplation.

When covering walls or buildings, climbers can complement the warmth of brick or stone walls or soften their hard lines, while the most vigorous are indispensable for camouflaging unsightly garden structures. If unsupported, many climbers trail along the ground and, when pegged at the nodes, will root to develop a dense carpet of ground cover. Such a strongly horizontal design element draws the eye into a scheme.

Some climbers look very effective when scrambling through other plants, which must be matched carefully for vigour and pruning requirements. This extends their season of interest if they flower before or after the host plant, but you can also achieve attractive associations of colour and texture when they flower simultaneously.

WHITE–PINK

PINK–RED

Beaumontia grandiflora
(Herald's trumpet)
Vigorous, evergreen, woody-stemmed,
twining climber with rich green leaves
that are hairy beneath. Has large,
fragrant, white flowers from late
spring to summer.
H 8m (25ft). Min. 7–10°C (45–50°F).

☀ ◊

Stephanotis floribunda
(Madagascar jasmine, Wax flower)
Moderately vigorous, evergreen,
woody-stemmed, twining climber with
leathery, glossy leaves. Scented, waxy,
white flowers appear in small clusters
from spring to autumn. H 5m (15ft) or
more. Min. 13–16°C (55–61°F).

☀ ◊

Mandevilla splendens,
syn. *Dipladenia splendens*
Evergreen, woody-stemmed, twining
climber. Has lustrous leaves and
trumpet-shaped, rose-pink flowers,
with yellow centres, appearing in late
spring or early summer.
H 3m (10ft). Min. 7–10°C (45–50°F).

☀ ◊ ①

Clianthus puniceus (Parrot's bill)
Evergreen or semi-evergreen, woody-
stemmed, scrambling climber with
leaves composed of many leaflets.
In spring and early summer bears
drooping clusters of unusual, claw-like,
brilliant red flowers. H 4m (12ft).

☀ ◊ Zone 8

Clianthus puniceus f. **albus**
Evergreen or semi-evergreen, woody-
stemmed, scrambling climber, grown
for its drooping clusters of claw-like,
creamy-white flowers that open in
spring and early summer. Mid-green
leaves consist of many small leaflets.
H 4m (12ft).

☀ ◊ Zone 8

Decumaria sinensis
Evergreen, woody-stemmed, root
climber with oval, often toothed leaves,
2.5–8cm (1–3in) long. Conical clusters
of small, honey-scented, cream flowers
are produced in late spring and early
summer. H to 2m (6ft) or more.

☀ ◊ Zone 8

Ercilla volubilis, syn. *E. spicata*
Evergreen, root climber with oval
to heart-shaped, mid-green leaves,
2.5–5cm (1–2in) long. Spikes of
petalless flowers, each consisting of 5
greenish or purple sepals and 6–8 white
stamens, are borne in spring. H to 10m
(30ft) or more. Min. 0°C (32°F).

☀ ◊

Distictis buccinatoria,
syn. *Phaedranthus buccinatorius*
(Mexican blood flower)
Vigorous, evergreen, woody-stemmed,
tendril climber. Has trumpet-shaped,
rose-crimson flowers, orange-yellow
within, from early spring to summer.
H to 5m (15ft) or more. Min. 5°C (41°F).

☀ ◊

OTHER RECOMMENDED PLANTS:
CLEMATIS, illus. pp.212–13
Decumaria sinensis, illus. p.204

CLEMATIS, illus. pp.212–13
Pandorea jasminoides, illus. p.208
Podranea ricasoliana
Thunbergia coccinea

Kennedia rubicunda
(Dusky coral pea)
Fast-growing, evergreen, woody-stemmed, twining climber with leaves divided into 3 leaflets. Coral-red flowers are borne in small trusses in spring-summer.
H to 3m (10ft). Min. 5–7°C (41–5°F).

Agapetes serpens
Evergreen, arching to pendulous, scandent shrub, best grown with support as a perennial climber. Has small, lance-shaped, lustrous leaves and pendent flowers, rose-red with darker veins, in spring.
H 2–3m (6–10ft). Min. 5°C (41°F).

Akebia quinata (Chocolate vine)
Woody-stemmed, twining climber, semi-evergreen in mild winters or warm areas, with leaves of 5 leaflets. Vanilla-scented, brownish-purple flowers appear in late spring, followed by sausage-shaped, purplish fruits.
H 10m (30ft) or more.

☼ ◊ Zone 5b

Passiflora coccinea
(Red passion flower)
Vigorous, evergreen, woody-stemmed, tendril climber with rounded, oblong leaves. Has bright deep scarlet flowers, with red, pink and white crowns, from spring to autumn.
H 3–4m (10–12ft). Min. 15°C (59°F).

Mitraria coccinea
Evergreen, woody-stemmed, scrambling climber with oval, toothed leaves. Small, tubular, orange-red flowers are borne singly in leaf axils during late spring to summer.
H to 2m (6ft).

☼ ◊ pH Zone 9?

Hoya macgillivrayi
Strong-growing, twining climber with thick stems and lustrous, dark green leaves. From spring to summer, bears large, cup-shaped, red-purple, purple or brownish-red flowers, with dark red, occasionally white-centred coronas.
H 5–8m (15–25ft). Min. 7°C (45°F).

Clytostoma callistegioides
Fast-growing, evergreen, woody-stemmed, tendril climber. Each leaf has 2 oval leaflets and a tendril. Small, nodding clusters of purple-veined, lavender flowers, fading to pale pink, are borne in spring-summer. H to 5m (15ft). Min. 10–13°C (50–55°F).

Tropaeolum tricolorum
Herbaceous climber with delicate stems, small tubers and 5–7-lobed leaves. Small, orange or yellow flowers with black-tipped, reddish-orange calyces are borne from early spring to early summer.
H to 1m (3ft). Min. 5°C (41°F).

Manettia luteorubra, syn.
M. bicolor, M. inflata (Brazilian firecracker)
Fast-growing, evergreen, semi-woody-stemmed, twining climber with glossy leaves. Has small, funnel-shaped, red flowers, with yellow tips, in spring-summer. H 2m (6ft). Min. 5°C (41°F).

Akebia x pentaphylla
Mainly deciduous, woody-stemmed, twining climber. Mid-green leaves, bronze-tinted when young, have 3 or 5 oval leaflets. Pendent racemes of small, 3-petalled, purple flowers (female at base, male at apex) are borne in spring.
H to 10cm (30ft).

☼ ◊ Zone 6

Holboellia coriacea
Evergreen, twining climber with glossy, green leaves. Clusters of tiny, mauve, male flowers and, lower down stems, larger, purple-tinged, green-white female flowers are borne in spring, followed by sausage-shaped, purple fruits. H to 7m (22ft) or more.

☼ ◊ Zone 8

■■ PURPLE–BLUE

Ipomoea indica, syn. *I. acuminata*, *I. learii* (Blue dawn flower)
Vigorous, perennial climber with evergreen, mid-green leaves. From late spring to autumn bears abundant, funnel-shaped, rich purple-blue to blue flowers, often maturing to purplish-red. H 6m (20ft) or more. Min. 7°C (45°F).

☼ ◊ ❗

Hardenbergia comptoniana
Evergreen, woody-stemmed, twining climber with leaves of 3 or 5 lance-shaped leaflets. Has racemes of pea-like, deep purple-blue flowers in spring.
H to 2.5m (8ft). Min. 3°C (37°F).

☼ ◊

Petrea volubilis
Strong-growing, evergreen, woody-stemmed, twining climber with elliptic, rough-textured leaves and deep violet and lilac-blue flowers carried in simple or branched spikes from late winter to late summer. H 6m (20ft) or more. Min. 13–15°C (55–9°F).

☼ ◊

***Hardenbergia violacea* 'Happy Wanderer'**
Evergreen, woody-stemmed, twining climber. In spring, bears pendent panicles of deep mauve-purple flowers, with yellow marks on upper petals.
H to 3m (10ft). Min. 7°C (45°F).

☼ ◊

Solanum seaforthianum
(Italian jasmine, St Vincent lilac)
Evergreen, scrambling climber with nodding clusters of star-shaped, blue, purple, pink, or white flowers, with yellow stamens, from spring to autumn, followed by scarlet berries.
H 2–3m (6–10ft). Min. 7°C (45°F).

☼ ◊ ❗

Sollya heterophylla
Evergreen, woody-based, twining climber with narrowly lance-shaped to oval leaves, 2–6cm (¾-2½in) long. Nodding clusters of 4–9 broadly bell-shaped, sky-blue flowers are carried from spring to autumn.
H to 3m (10ft). Min. 2°C (35°F).

☼ ◊

□□ GREEN–YELLOW

Strongylodon macrobotrys
(Jade vine)
Fast-growing, evergreen, woody-stemmed, twining climber with claw-like, luminous, blue-green flowers in long, pendent spikes in winter-spring. Leaves have 3 oval, glossy leaflets.
H to 20m (70ft). Min. 18°C (64°F).

☼ ◊

***Humulus lupulus* 'Aureus'**
Herbaceous, twining climber with rough, hairy stems and toothed, yellowish leaves divided into 3 or 5 lobes. Greenish, female flower spikes are borne in pendent clusters in autumn. H to 6m (20ft).

☼ ◊

***Tecoma capensis* 'Aurea'**,
syn. *Tecomaria capensis* 'Aurea'
Erect, scrambling, evergreen shrub or climber with lustrous, mid- to dark green leaves. Racemes, to 15cm (6in) long, of slender, tubular, yellow flowers, to 5cm (2in) long, are borne mainly in summer. Min. 5°C (41°F).

☼ ◊

Gelsemium sempervirens
Moderately vigorous, evergreen, twining climber with pointed, lustrous leaves. Clusters of fragrant, funnel-shaped, pale to deep yellow flowers are borne from late spring to late summer. H to 6m (20ft).

☼ ◊ Zone 8

Solandra maxima (Copa de oro, Golden-chalice vine)
Strong-growing, evergreen, woody-stemmed, scrambling climber with glossy leaves. In spring-summer bears fragrant, pale yellow, later golden flowers. H 7–10m (23–30ft) or more. Min. 13–16°C (55–61°F).

☼ ◊

Stigmaphyllon ciliatum, illus. p.216

☐ YELLOW

☐ WHITE

Thunbergia mysorensis
Evergreen, woody-stemmed, twining climber. Has narrow leaves and pendent spikes of flowers with yellow tubes and recurved, reddish-brown lobes from spring to autumn. H 6m (20ft). Min. 15°C (59°F).

Jasminum mesnyi, syn.
J. primulinum (Primrose jasmine)
Evergreen or semi-evergreen, woody-stemmed, scrambling climber. Leaves are divided into 3 leaflets; semi-double, pale yellow flowers appear in spring. H to 3m (10ft).

☼ ◊ Zone 9

Bougainvillea glabra 'Snow White'
Vigorous, evergreen or semi-evergreen, woody-stemmed, scrambling climber with rounded-oval leaves. In summer has clusters of white floral bracts with green veins. H to 5m (15ft). Min. 7–10°C (45–50°F).

☼ ◊

Solanum jasminoides 'Album'
Semi-evergreen, woody-stemmed, scrambling climber. Oval to lance-shaped leaves are sometimes lobed or divided into leaflets. Has star-shaped, white flowers, 2–2.5cm (¾–1in) across, in summer-autumn. H to 6m (20ft).

☼ ◊ ① Zone 9

Trachelospermum jasminoides
(Confederate jasmine, Star jasmine)
Evergreen, woody-stemmed, twining climber with oval leaves up to 10cm (4in) long. Very fragrant, white flowers in summer, followed by pairs of pods, up to 15cm (6in) long, bearing tufted seeds. H to 9m (28ft). Min. 2°C (35°F).

☼ ◊

Wisteria sinensis 'Alba'
Vigorous, deciduous, woody-stemmed, twining climber. Leaves are 25–30cm (10–12in) long with 11 leaflets. Has strongly scented, pea-like, white flowers in racemes, 20–30cm (8–12in) long, in early summer. H to 30m (100ft).

☼ ◊ ① Zone 6

Wisteria floribunda 'Alba',
syn. *W.f.* 'Shiro Noda'
Deciduous, woody-stemmed, twining climber with leaves of 11–19 oval leaflets. Scented, pea-like, white flowers are carried in drooping racemes, up to 60cm (2ft) long, in early summer. H to 9m (28ft).

☼ ◊ ① Zone 6

Araujia sericifera (Cruel plant)
Evergreen, woody-stemmed, twining climber with leaves that are white-downy beneath. Has scented, white flowers, often striped pale maroon inside, from late summer to autumn. H to 7m (23ft). Min. 1°C (34°F).

☼ ◊

☐ WHITE   ▭☐ WHITE–PINK

Hydrangea petiolaris, syn.
H. anomala subsp. *petiolaris*
(Climbing hydrangea)
Deciduous, woody-stemmed, root
climber. Has toothed leaves and lacy
heads of small, white flowers in
summer, only sparingly borne on
young plants. H to 15m (50ft).

☼ ◊ ① Zone 5

Clerodendrum thomsoniae
Vigorous, evergreen, woody-stemmed,
scandent shrub with oval, rich green
leaves. Flowers with crimson petals
and bell-shaped, pure white calyces
appear in clusters in summer.
H 3m (10ft) or more. Min. 16°C (61°F).

☼ ◊

Hoya lanceolata subsp. **bella**,
syn. *H. bella*
Evergreen, woody-stemmed, trailing
shrub with narrowly oval, pointed
leaves. In summer bears tiny, star-
shaped, white flowers, with red centres,
in pendulous, flattened clusters. H 45cm
(18in). Min. 10–12°C (50–54°F).

☼ ◊

Hoya australis
Moderately vigorous, evergreen,
woody-stemmed, twining, root climber
with fleshy, rich green leaves. Has
trusses of 20–50 fragrant, star-shaped
flowers, white with red-purple
markings, in summer.
H to 5m (15ft). Min. 15°C (59°F).

☼ ◊

Pandorea jasminoides, syn.
Bignonia jasminoides (Bower vine)
Evergreen, woody-stemmed, twining
climber with leaves of 5–9 leaflets.
Has clusters of funnel-shaped, white
flowers, with pink-flushed throats,
from late winter to summer.
H 5m (15ft). Min. 5°C (41°F).

☼ ◊

Hoya carnosa (Wax plant)
Fairly vigorous, evergreen, woody-
stemmed, twining, root climber.
Scented, star-shaped flowers, white,
fading to pink, with deep pink centres,
are borne in dense trusses in summer-
autumn. H to 5m (15ft) or more.
Min. 5–7°C (41–5°F).

☼ ◊

Pileostegia viburnoides,
syn. *Schizophragma viburnoides*
Slow-growing, evergreen, woody-
stemmed, root climber. Tiny, white or
cream flowers, with many prominent
stamens, are borne in heads from late
summer to autumn. H to 6m (20ft).

☼ ◊ Zone 8

Schizophragma integrifolium
Deciduous, woody-stemmed, root
climber with oval or heart-shaped
leaves. In summer, white flowers are
borne in flat heads up to 30cm (12in)
across, marginal sterile flowers each
having a large, white bract.
H to 12m (40ft).

☼ ◊ Zone 6

Jasminum officinale f. **affine**,
syn. *J. grandiflorum* of gardens
Semi-evergreen or deciduous, woody-
stemmed, twining climber with leaves
comprising 7 or 9 leaflets. Clusters of
fragrant, 4- or 5-lobed flowers, white
inside and pink outside, are borne in
summer-autumn. H to 12m (40ft).

☼ ◊ Zone 7

Lathyrus odoratus 'Selana'
Vigorous, annual, tendril climber with
oval, mid-green leaves and large,
fragrant, pink-flushed, white flowers
in summer to early autumn. H 2m (6ft).

☼ ◊ ①

Fallopia baldschuanica, illus. p.217
Mandevilla boliviensis
Mandevilla laxa
Schizophragma hydrangeoides

Stephanotis floribunda, illus. p.204
Wisteria brachybotrys 'Shiro Kapitan'

CLEMATIS, illus. pp.212–13
Dregea sinensis
Hoya coronaria
Pandorea pandorana

Passiflora x *allardii*

CLIMBERS

Actinidia kolomikta
Deciduous, woody-stemmed, twining climber with 8–16cm (3–6in) long leaves, the upper sections often creamy-white and pink. Has small, cup-shaped, white flowers in summer, male and female on separate plants. H 4m (12ft).
☼ ◊ Zone 3

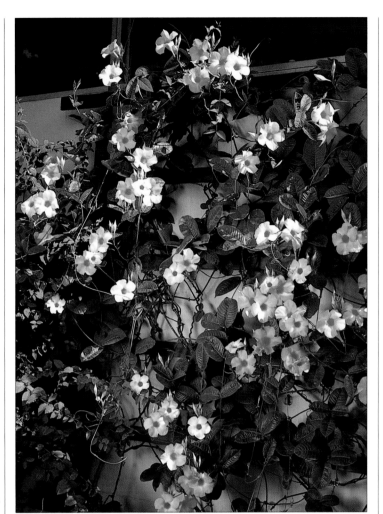

Mandevilla × amoena 'Alice du Pont', syn. *M. × amabilis* 'Alice du Pont'
Vigorous, evergreen, woody-stemmed, twining climber with oval, impressed leaves. Has large clusters of trumpet-shaped, glowing pink flowers in summer. H 3m (10ft). Min. 7–10°C (45–50°F).
☼ ◊ ①

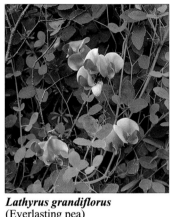

Lathyrus grandiflorus
(Everlasting pea)
Herbaceous, tendril climber with unwinged stems and neat racemes of pink-purple and red flowers in summer. H to 1.5m (5ft).
☼ ◊ ①

Lonicera × heckrottii 'Gold Flame', syn. *L.* 'Gold Flame'
Deciduous, woody-stemmed, twining climber that needs support. Leaves are oblong or oval, bluish beneath, upper ones joined into shallow cups. Scented, orange-throated, pink flowers appear in clusters in summer. H to 5m (15ft).
☼ ◊ ① Zone 5

Lathyrus odoratus 'Xenia Field'
Moderately fast-growing, slender, annual, tendril climber with oval, mid-green leaves. Large, fragrant, pink-and-cream flowers appear from summer to early autumn. H 2m (6ft).
☼ ◊ ①

Antigonon leptopus (Coral vine)
Fast-growing, evergreen, woody-stemmed, tendril climber with crinkly, pale green leaves. Has dense trusses of bright pink, sometimes red or white, flowers mainly in summer but all year in tropical conditions.
H 6m (20ft). Min. 15°C (59°F).
☼ ◊

Lophospermum erubescens
Evergreen, soft-stemmed, scandent, perennial climber, sometimes woody-stemmed, often grown as an annual. Stems and leaves are downy. Rose-pink flowers, 7cm (2¾in) long, are borne in summer-autumn.
H to 3m (10ft) or more. Min. 5°C (41°F).
☼ ◊

Ipomoea horsfalliae
Strong-growing, evergreen, woody-stemmed, twining climber. Leaves have 5–7 radiating lobes or leaflets; stalked clusters of deep rose-pink or rose-purple flowers, 6cm (2½in) long, appear from summer to winter. H 2–3m (6–10ft). Min. 7–10°C (45–50°F).
☼ ◊ ①

CLEMATIS, illus. pp.212–13
Lathyrus sylvestris
Mandevilla splendens, illus. p.204
Mutisia oligodon

Passiflora × *exoniensis*
Passiflora mollissima
× *Philageria veitchii*
Podranea ricasoliana

Sarmienta repens

■■ PINK–RED

Lonicera sempervirens
(Coral honeysuckle)
Evergreen or deciduous, woody-stemmed, twining climber with oval leaves, bluish beneath, upper ones united and saucer-like. Has salmon-red to orange flowers, yellow inside, in whorls on shoot tips in summer. H to 4m (12ft).

☀ ◊ ! Zone 5

Lapageria rosea
(Chilean bellflower, Copihue)
Evergreen, woody-stemmed, twining climber with oblong to oval, leathery leaves. Has pendent, fleshy, pink to red flowers, 7–9cm (2¾–3½in) long, with paler flecks, from summer to late autumn. H to 5m (15ft). Min. 2°C (35°F).

☀ ◊

Lathyrus odoratus 'Red Ensign'
Vigorous, annual, tendril climber with oval, mid-green leaves and large, sweetly scented, rich scarlet flowers from summer to early autumn. H 2m (6ft).

☀ ◊ !

Lonicera x brownii 'Dropmore Scarlet'
Deciduous, woody-stemmed, twining climber with oval, blue-green leaves. Small, fragrant, red flowers with orange throats are borne throughout summer. H to 4m (12ft).

☀ ◊ ! Zone 2b

Bougainvillea 'Miss Manila',
syn. *B.* 'Tango'
Vigorous, mainly evergreen, woody-stemmed, scrambling climber with rounded-oval leaves. Bears clusters of pink floral bracts in summer.
H to 5m (15ft). Min. 7–10°C (45–50°F).

☀ ◊

Ipomoea lobata, syn. *I. versicolor*,
Mina lobata, *Quamoclit lobata*
Deciduous or semi-evergreen, twining climber with 3-lobed leaves, usually grown as an annual. One-sided racemes of small, tubular, dark red flowers fade to orange, then creamy-yellow, in summer. H to 5m (15ft). Min. 10°C (50°F).

☀ ◊ !

Bougainvillea 'Dania'
Vigorous, mainly evergreen, woody-stemmed, scrambling climber.
Has rounded-oval, mid-green leaves and bears clusters of deep pink floral bracts in summer.
H to 5m (15ft). Min. 7–10°C (45–50°F).

☀ ◊

Ipomoea quamoclit, syn.
Quamoclit pennata (Cypress vine)
Annual, twining climber with oval, bright green leaves cut into many thread-like segments. Slender, tubular, orange or scarlet flowers are carried in summer-autumn. H 2–4m (6–12ft).

☀ ◊ !

Tropaeolum speciosum (Flame creeper, Flame nasturtium)
Herbaceous, twining climber with a creeping rhizome and lobed, blue-green leaves. Bears scarlet flowers in summer, followed by bright blue fruits surrounded by deep red calyces. Roots should be in shade. H to 3m (10ft).

☀ ◊

Quisqualis indica
(Rangoon creeper)
Fairly fast-growing, deciduous or semi-evergreen, scandent shrub, often grown as an annual. From late spring to late summer has fragrant flowers, varying from orange to red, sometimes pink.
H 3–5m (10–15ft). Min. 10°C (50°F).

☀ ◊

Rhodochiton atrosanguineus,
syn. *R. volubilis*
Evergreen, leaf-stalk climber, usually grown as an annual, with toothed leaves. Has tubular, blackish-purple flowers, with bell-shaped, red-purple calyces, from late spring to late autumn.
H to 3m (10ft). Min. 5°C (41°F).

☀ ◊

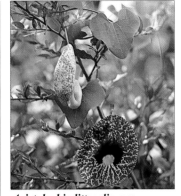

Aristolochia littoralis, syn.
A. elegans (Calico flower)
Fast-growing, evergreen, woody-stemmed, twining climber with heart-to kidney-shaped leaves. Heart-shaped, 12cm (5in) wide flowers, maroon with white marbling, are carried in summer.
H to 7m (23ft). Min. 13°C (55°F).

☀ ◊

Lathyrus latifolius
(Everlasting pea, Perennial pea)
Herbaceous, tendril climber with winged stems. Leaves have broad stipules and a pair of leaflets. Has small racemes of pink-purple flowers in summer and early autumn.
H 2m (6ft) or more.

☀ ◊ ⓘ

Schisandra rubriflora, syn.
S. grandiflora var. *rubriflora*
Deciduous, woody-stemmed, twining climber with leathery, toothed leaves, paler beneath. Has small, crimson flowers in spring or early summer and drooping, red fruits in late summer.
H to 6m (20ft).

☀ ◊ Zone 8

Berberidopsis corallina
(Coral plant)
Evergreen, woody-stemmed, twining climber with oval to heart-shaped, leathery leaves edged with small spines. Pendent clusters of globular, deep red flowers are produced in summer to early autumn. H 4.5m (14ft).

☀ ◊ pH Zone 9

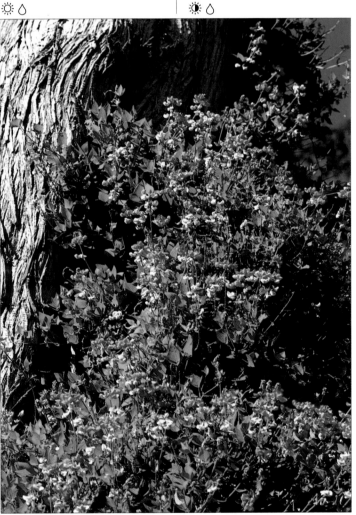

Lablab purpureus, syn. *Dolichos lablab*, *D. purpureus* (Indian bean, Hyacinth bean, Lablab)
Deciduous, woody-stemmed, twining climber, often grown as an annual. Purple, pinkish or white flowers in summer are followed by long pods with edible seeds.
H 10m (30ft). Min. 5°C (41°F).

☀ ◊

Bougainvillea glabra 'Variegata',
syn. *B.g.* 'Sanderiana'
Vigorous, mainly evergreen, woody-stemmed, scrambling climber. Rounded-oval, dark green leaves are edged with creamy-white. Has many bright purple floral bracts in summer.
H to 5m (15ft). Min. 7–10°C (45–50°F).

☀ ◊

Aristolochia griffithii
Bougainvillea x *buttiana* 'Mrs Butt'
Bougainvillea spectabilis
CLEMATIS, illus. pp.212–13

Cryptostegia grandiflora
Hoya imperialis
Ipomoea horsfalliae, illus. p.209
Ipomoea horsfalliae 'Briggsii'

Lathyrus rotundifolius
Lonicera henryi
Lonicera periclymenum 'Serotina'
Mucuna pruriens var. *utilis*

Pueraria lobata

Clematis

Among the climbers, clematis are unsurpassed in their long period of flowering (with species flowering from early spring to late fall), variety of flower shapes and colours and tolerance of almost any aspect and climate. Some spring-flowering species and cultivars are vigorous and excellent for rapidly covering buildings, old trees and pergolas. Other, less rampant cultivars display often large, exquisite blooms from early summer to autumn in almost every colour. Clematis look attractive when trained on walls or trellises and when grown in association with other climbers, trees or shrubs, treating them as hosts. Less vigorous cultivars may also be left unsupported to scramble at ground level, where their flowers will be clearly visible.

The various types of clematis (see the Plant Dictionary) may be divided into 3 groups, each of which has different pruning requirements. Incorrect pruning may result in cutting out the stems that will produce flowers in the current season, so the following guidelines should be followed closely.

Group 1
Early-flowering species, Alpina, Macropetala and Montana types
Flower stems are produced direct from the previous season's ripened stems. Prune after flowering to allow new growth to be produced and ripened for the next season. Remove dead or damaged stems and cut back other shoots that have outgrown their allotted space.

Flower stem direct from the previous season's ripened stems

Group 2
Early, large-flowered cultivars
Flowers are produced on short, current season's stems, so prune before new growth starts, in early spring. Remove dead or damaged stems and cut back all others to where strong, leaf-axil buds are visible. (These buds will produce the first crop of flowers.)

Current season's stems each have one flower and are 15–45cm (6–18in) long

Discarded previous season's old flower stem

Discarded previous season's leaves

Group 3
Late, large-flowered cultivars, Late-flowering species, Small-flowered cultivars and Herbaceous types
Flowers are produced on the current season's growth only, so prune before new growth commences, in early spring. Remove all of the previous season's stems down to a pair of strong, leaf-axil buds, 15–30cm (6–12in) above the soil.

Flowering stems on current season's growth only

C. florida 'Sieboldii' (3, small-fl.)

C. 'Mrs George Jackman' (2, early large-fl.)

C. flammula (3, late-fl.)

C. 'Huldine' (3, late large-fl.)

C.m. 'Mark-ham's Pink' (1, Macrop.)

C. recta (3, herbaceous)

C. montana var. *rubens* (1, Montana)

C. montana 'Tetrarose' (1, Montana)

C. 'Hagley Hybrid' (3, late large-fl.)

C. 'Henryi' (2, early large-fl.)

C. armandii (1, early-fl.)

C. montana (1, Montana)

C. ARCTIC QUEEN (2, early large-fl.)

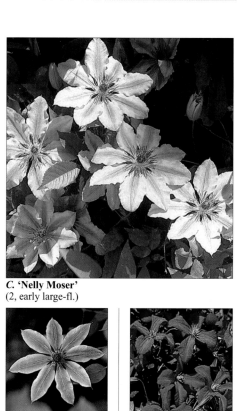

C. 'Nelly Moser'
(2, early large-fl.)

C. 'Lincoln Star'
(2, early large-fl.)

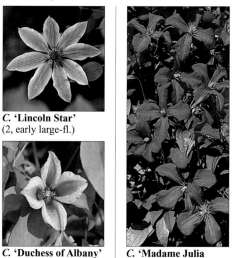

C. 'Duchess of Albany'
(3, small-fl.)

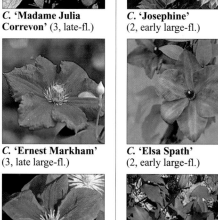

C. 'Madame Julia Correvon' (3, late-fl.)

C.v. **'Purpurea Plena Elegans'** (3, late-fl.)

C. 'Ernest Markham'
(3, late large-fl.)

C. 'Abundance'
(3, late-fl.)

C. ANNA LOUISE
(2, early large-fl.)

C. 'Gravetye Beauty'
(3, small-fl.)

C. 'Star of India'
(3, late large-fl.)

C. ROYAL VELVET
(2, early large-fl.)

C. 'The President'
(2, early large-fl.)

C. BLUE MOON
(2, early large-fl.)

C. 'Josephine'
(2, early large-fl.)

C. 'Elsa Spath'
(2, early large-fl.)

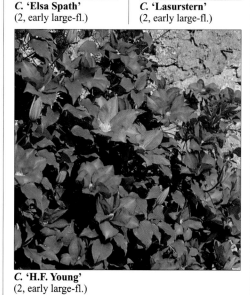

C. 'H.F. Young'
(2, early large-fl.)

C. 'Vyvyan Pennell'
(2, early large-fl.)

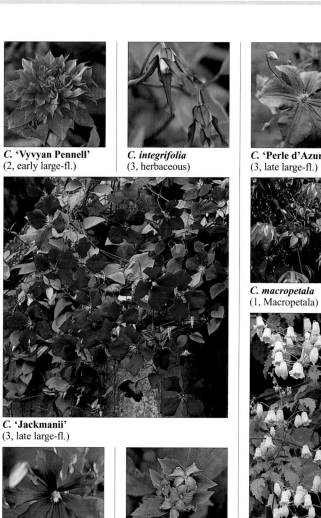

C. 'Jackmanii'
(3, late large-fl.)

C. 'Etoile Violette'
(3, late-fl.)

C. 'Lasurstern'
(2, early large-fl.)

C. integrifolia
(3, herbaceous)

C. heracleifolia **'Wyevale'** (3, herbaceous)

C. PETIT FAUCON
(3, small-fl.)

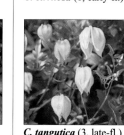

C. 'Ascotiensis'
(3, late large-fl.)

C. alpina **'Frances Rivis'** (1, Alpina)

C. 'Perle d'Azur'
(3, late large-fl.)

C. macropetala
(1, Macropetala)

C. rehderiana
(3, late-fl.)

C. cirrhosa (1, early-fl.)

C. tangutica (3, late-fl.)

C. **'Bill MacKenzie'**
(3, late-fl.)

Bougainvillea glabra
Vigorous, evergreen or semi-evergreen, woody-stemmed, scrambling climber with rounded-oval leaves. Clusters of floral bracts, in shades of cyclamen-purple, appear in summer.
H to 5m (15ft). Min. 7–10°C (45–50°F).

Lathyrus odoratus 'Lady Diana'
Moderately fast-growing, slender, annual, tendril climber with oval, mid-green leaves. Fragrant, pale violet-blue flowers are borne from summer to early autumn. H 2m (6ft).

Solanum crispum 'Glasnevin'
Vigorous, evergreen or semi-evergreen, woody-stemmed, scrambling climber with oval leaves. Has clusters of lilac to purple flowers, 2.5cm (1in) across, in summer. H to 6m (20ft).

 Zone 9?

Passiflora × caponii 'John Innes'
Strong-growing, evergreen, woody-stemmed, tendril climber with 3-lobed leaves. Has bowl-shaped, nodding, white flowers, flushed claret-purple, with purple-banded, white crowns, in summer-autumn.
H 8m (25ft). Min. 7–10°C (45–50°F).

Ipomoea hederacea
(Morning glory)
Annual, twining climber with heart-shaped or 3-lobed, mid- to bright green leaves. Has funnel-shaped, red, purple, pink or blue flowers in summer to early autumn. H 3–4m (10–12ft).

Codonopsis convolvulacea
Herbaceous, twining climber with 5cm (2in) long, oval or lance-shaped leaves. Widely bell- to saucer-shaped, bluish-violet flowers, 2.5–5cm (1–2in) across, are borne in summer. H to 2m (6ft).

Zone 5

Cobaea scandens
(Cup-and-saucer vine)
Evergreen or deciduous, woody-stemmed, tendril climber, grown as an annual. From late summer to first frosts has flowers that open yellow-green and age to purple.
H 4–5m (12–15ft). Min. 4°C (39°F).

Solanum wendlandii
Robust, mainly evergreen, prickly-stemmed, scrambling climber with oblong, variably lobed leaves. Lavender flowers appear in late summer and autumn.
H 3–6m (10–20ft). Min. 10°C (50°F).

Passiflora caerulea (Blue passion flower, Common passion flower)
Fast-growing, evergreen or semi-evergreen, woody-stemmed, tendril climber. Has white flowers, sometimes pink-flushed, with blue- or purple-banded crowns, in summer-autumn.
H 10m (30ft).

Zone 7

CLIMBERS

Passiflora quadrangularis
(Giant granadilla)
Strong-growing, evergreen, woody-
stemmed climber with angled, winged
stems. White, pink, red or pale violet
flowers, the crowns banded white and
deep purple, appear mainly in summer.
H 5–8m (15–25ft). Min. 10°C (50°F).

☀ ◊

**Ipomoea tricolor 'Heavenly
Blue'**, syn. *I. rubrocaerulea*
'Heavenly Blue'
Fast-growing, annual, twining climber
with heart-shaped leaves and large,
funnel-shaped, sky-blue flowers borne
from summer to early autumn.
H to 3m (10ft).

☀ ◊ ⊕

Lonicera × americana, syn.
L. × italica of gardens
Very free-flowering, deciduous,
woody-stemmed, twining climber.
Leaves are oval, upper ones united and
saucer-like. Has clusters of strongly
fragrant, yellow flowers, flushed with
red-purple, in summer. H to 7m (23ft).

☀ ◊ ⊕ Zone 7

Lonicera japonica 'Halliana'
Evergreen or semi-evergreen, woody-
stemmed, twining climber with soft-
haired stems and oval, sometimes
lobed, bright green leaves. Very
fragrant, white flowers, ageing
to pale yellow, are borne in summer
and autumn. H to 10m (30ft).

☀ ◊ ⊕ Zone 6

Wisteria × formosa
Deciduous, woody-stemmed, twining
climber with leaves of 9–15 narrowly
oval leaflets. Scented, pea-like, mauve
and pale lilac flowers are carried in
early summer in drooping racemes,
25cm (10in) long, followed by velvety
pods. H to 25m (80ft) or more.

☀ ◊ ⊕ Zone 7

Plumbago auriculata,
syn. *P. capensis* (Cape leadwort)
Fast-growing, evergreen, woody-
stemmed, scrambling climber. Trusses
of sky-blue flowers are carried from
summer to early winter.
H 3–6m (10–20ft). Min. 7°C (45°F).

☀ ◊

Wisteria sinensis, syn.
W. chinensis (Chinese wisteria)
Vigorous, deciduous, woody-stemmed,
twining climber. Has leaves of 11
leaflets and fragrant, lilac or pale violet
flowers, in racemes 20–30cm (8–12in)
long, in early summer, followed by
velvety pods. H to 30m (100ft).

☀ ◊ ⊕ Zone 6

Tweedia caerulea,
syn. *Oxypetalum caeruleum*
Herbaceous, twining climber with
white-haired stems. Small, fleshy, pale
blue flowers, maturing purple, appear
in summer and early autumn; has green
fruits to 15cm (6in) long.
H to 1m (3ft). Min. 5°C (41°F).

☀ ◊

**Lonicera periclymenum 'Graham
Thomas'**
Deciduous, woody-stemmed, twining
climber. Oval or oblong leaves are
bluish beneath; fragrant, white flowers
ageing to yellow, are borne in summer.
H to 7m (23ft).

☀ ◊ ⊕ Zone 4b

Allamanda cathartica
'Hendersonii'
Fast-growing, evergreen, woody-stemmed, scrambling climber. Has lance-shaped leaves in whorls and trumpet-shaped, rich bright yellow flowers in summer-autumn.
H to 5m (15ft). Min. 13–15°C (55–9°F).

Thunbergia alata
(Black-eyed Susan)
Moderately fast-growing, annual, twining climber. Toothed, oval to heart-shaped leaves. Rounded, rather flat, small flowers, orange-yellow with dark brown centres. Early summer to early autumn. H 3m (10ft). Min. 7°C (45°F).

Thladiantha dubia
Fast-growing, herbaceous or deciduous, tendril climber. Oval to heart-shaped, mid-green leaves, 10cm (4in) long, are hairy beneath; bell-shaped, yellow flowers are carried in summer.
H 3m (10ft).

Zone 8

Stigmaphyllon ciliatum
Fast-growing, evergreen, woody-stemmed, twining climber with heart-shaped, pale green leaves fringed with hairs. Bright yellow flowers with ruffled petals appear in spring-summer.
H 5m (15ft) or more.
Min. 15–18°C (59–64°F).

Macfadyena unguis-cati
(Cat's claw)
Fast-growing, evergreen, woody-stemmed, tendril climber. Leaves have 2 leaflets and a tendril. Has yellow flowers, 10cm (4in) long, in late spring or early summer.
H 8–10m (25–30ft). Min. 5°C (41°F).

Tropaeolum tuberosum var.
lineamaculatum 'Ken Aslet'
Herbaceous climber with yellowish, red-streaked tubers and blue-green leaves. From mid-summer to autumn has flowers with red sepals and orange petals. In cool areas, lift and store tubers in winter. H to 2.5m (8ft).

CLIMBERS AUTUMN INTEREST

Bomarea caldasii, syn. *B. kalbreyeri* of gardens
Herbaceous, twining climber with rounded clusters of 5–40 tubular to funnel-shaped, orange-red flowers, spotted crimson within, in summer.
H 3–4m (10–12ft).
Tender, min. 5°C (41°F).

☀ ◐

Lonicera × tellmanniana
Deciduous, woody-stemmed, twining climber with oval leaves; upper ones are joined and resemble saucers. Bright yellowish-orange flowers are carried in clusters at the ends of shoots in late spring and summer. H to 5m (15ft).

☀ ◐ ① Zone 8

Fallopia baldschuanica (Mile-a-minute plant, Russian vine)
Vigorous, deciduous, woody-stemmed, twining climber with drooping panicles of pink or white flowers in summer-autumn. H 12m (40ft) or more.

☀ ◐ Zone 5b

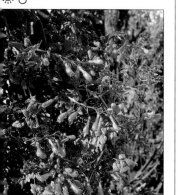

Eccremocarpus scaber
(Chilean glory flower, Glory vine)
Evergreen, sub-shrubby, tendril climber, often grown as an annual. In summer has racemes of small, orange-red flowers, followed by inflated fruit pods containing many winged seeds.
H 2–3m (6–10ft). Min. 2°C (35°F).

☀ ◐

Thunbergia gregorii,
syn. *T. gibsonii*
Evergreen, woody-stemmed, twining climber, usually grown as an annual. Triangular-oval leaves have winged stalks. Glowing orange flowers are carried in summer.
H to 3m (10ft). Min. 10°C (50°F).

☀ ◐

Senecio confusus, syn.
Pseudogynoxys chenopodioides
(Mexican flame vine)
Evergreen, woody-stemmed, twining climber bearing clusters of daisy-like, orange-yellow flower heads, ageing to orange-red, mainly in summer. H to 3m (10ft) or more. Min. 7–10°C (45–50°F).

☀ ◐ ①

Mutisia decurrens
Evergreen, tendril climber with narrowly oblong leaves, 7–13cm (2³/₄–5in) long. Flower heads, 10–13cm (4–5in) across with red or orange ray flowers, are produced in summer. Proves difficult to establish, but is worthwhile. H to 3m (10ft).

☀ ◐ Zone 9

Campsis × tagliabuana 'Madame Galen'
Deciduous, woody-stemmed, root climber with leaves of 7 or more narrowly oval, toothed leaflets. Trumpet-shaped, orange-pink flowers are borne in pendent clusters from late summer to autumn. H to 10m (30ft).

☀ ◐ Zone 6

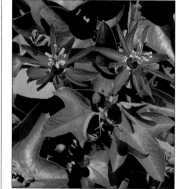

Passiflora manicata
Fast-growing, evergreen, woody-stemmed, tendril climber with slender, angular stems and 3-lobed leaves. Red flowers, with deep purple and white crowns, appear in summer-autumn.
H 3–5m (10–15ft). Min. 7°C (45°F).

☀ ◐

Bignonia capreolata
Campsis radicans
Mitraria coccinea, illus. p.205
Streptosolen jamesonii, illus. p.220

Tecoma capensis

OTHER RECOMMENDED PLANTS:
Cobaea scandens f. *alba*
Lapageria rosea, illus. p.210
Lophospermum erubescens, illus. p.209

Pileostegia viburnoides, illus. p.208
Stephanotis floribunda, illus. p.204
Tecomanthe speciosa

CLIMBERS

■■ RED–PURPLE

Parthenocissus tricuspidata
(Boston ivy, Japanese ivy)
Vigorous, deciduous, woody-stemmed,
tendril climber. Has spectacular,
crimson, autumn leaf colour and dull
blue berries. Will cover large expanses
of wall. H to 20m (70ft).

☀◐ ◊ ① Zone 4b

Parthenocissus tricuspidata
'Lowii'
Vigorous, deciduous, woody-stemmed,
tendril climber with deeply cut and
crinkled, 3–7-lobed leaves that turn
crimson in autumn. Has insignificant
flowers, followed by dull blue berries.
H to 20m (70ft).

☀◐ ◊ ① Zone 4b

Vitis coignetiae
(Crimson glory vine)
Vigorous, deciduous, woody-stemmed,
tendril climber. Large leaves, brown-
haired beneath, are brightly coloured in
autumn. Has tiny, pale green flowers in
summer, followed by purplish-bloomed,
black berries. H to 15m (50ft).

☀◐ ◊ Zone 5

Parthenocissus thomsonii, syn.
Cayratia thomsonii, Vitis thomsonii
Deciduous, woody-stemmed, tendril
climber. Has glossy, green leaves
with 5 leaflets that turn red-purple
in autumn, and black berries. Provide
some shade for best autumn colour.
H to 10m (30ft).

☀◐ ◊ ① Zone 5

Vitis vinifera 'Purpurea'
Deciduous, woody-stemmed, tendril
climber with toothed, 3- or 5-lobed,
purplish leaves, white-haired when
young. Has tiny, pale green flowers
in summer and tiny, green or purple
berries. H to 7m (23ft).

☀ ◊ Zone 6

Parthenocissus tricuspidata
'Veitchii', syn. *Ampelopsis veitchii*
Vigorous, deciduous, woody-stemmed,
tendril climber. Has spectacular, red-
purple, autumn leaf colour and dull
blue berries. Greenish flowers are
insignificant. H to 20m (70ft).

☀◐ ◊ ① Zone 4b

■■ PURPLE–ORANGE

Billardiera longiflora
Evergreen, woody-stemmed, twining
climber with narrow leaves. Small,
bell-shaped, sometimes purple-tinged,
green-yellow flowers are produced
singly in leaf axils in summer, followed
by purple-blue fruits in autumn.
H to 2m (6ft).

☀◐ ◊ Zone 9

Tropaeolum tuberosum
Herbaceous, tuberous-rooted, leaf-stalk
climber. Greyish-green leaves have
3–5 lobes; from mid-summer to late
autumn has cup-shaped flowers with
orange-yellow petals, orange-red sepals
and a long spur. H 2–3m (6–10ft).

☀ ◊

Pyrostegia venusta, syn. *P. ignea*
(Flame flower, Flame vine, Golden
shower)
Fast-growing, evergreen, woody-
stemmed, tendril climber with clusters
of tubular, golden-orange flowers from
autumn to spring. H 10m (30ft) or more.
Min. 13–15°C (55–9°F).

☀ ◊

CLIMBERS

Jasminum polyanthum
Evergreen, woody-stemmed, twining climber. Dark green leaves have 5 or 7 leaflets. Large clusters of fragrant, 5-lobed, white flowers, sometimes reddish on the outside, are carried from late summer to winter.
H 3m (10ft) or more.

☼ ◊ Zone 9

Agapetes variegata var. **macrantha**
Evergreen or semi-evergreen, loose, scandent shrub that may be trained against supports. Has lance-shaped leaves and narrowly urn-shaped, white or pinkish-white flowers, patterned in red, in winter. H 1–2m (3–6ft).
Min. 15–18°C (59–64°F).

☼ ◊ pH

Canarina canariensis,
syn. *C. campanula*
(Canary Island bellflower)
Herbaceous, tuberous, scrambling climber with triangular, serrated leaves. Has waxy, orange flowers with red veins from late autumn to spring.
H 2–3m (6–10ft). Min. 7°C (45°F).

☼ ◊

Asparagus scandens
Evergreen, scrambling climber with lax stems and short, curved, leaf-like shoots in whorls of 3. Tiny, nodding, white flowers appear in clusters of 2–3 in summer, followed by red berries.
H 1m (3ft) or more. Min. 10°C (50°F).

☼ ◊

Senecio macroglossus
'Variegatus'
Evergreen, woody-stemmed, twining climber with triangular, fleshy leaves, bordered in white to cream, and, mainly in winter, daisy-like, cream flower heads. H 3m (10ft).
Min. 7°C (45°F), but best at 10°C (50°F).

☼ ◊ ①

Epipremnum aureum 'Marble Queen', syn. *Scindapsus aureus* 'Marble Queen'
Fairly fast-growing, evergreen, woody-stemmed, root climber. Leaves are streaked and marbled with white. Is less robust than the species. H 3–10m (10–30ft). Min. 15–18°C (59–64°F).

☼ ◊ ①

Epipremnum pictum
'Argyraeum', syn. *Scindapsus pictus* 'Argyraeus' (Silver vine)
Slow-growing, evergreen, woody-stemmed, root climber. Heart-shaped leaves are dark green with silver markings. H 2–3m (6–10ft) or more. Min. 15–18°C (59–64°F).

☼ ◊ ①

Syngonium podophyllum
'Trileaf Wonder'
Evergreen, woody-stemmed, root climber with tufted stems and arrow-head-shaped leaves when young. Mature leaves have 3 glossy leaflets with pale green or silvery-grey veins. H 2m (6ft) or more. Min. 18°C (64°F).

☼ ◊ ①

Dioscorea discolor
(Ornamental yam)
Evergreen, woody-stemmed, twining climber. Heart-shaped, olive-green leaves are 12–15cm (5–6in) long, marbled silver, paler green and brown, and are red beneath.
H to 2m (6ft). Min. 5°C (41°F).

☼ ◊

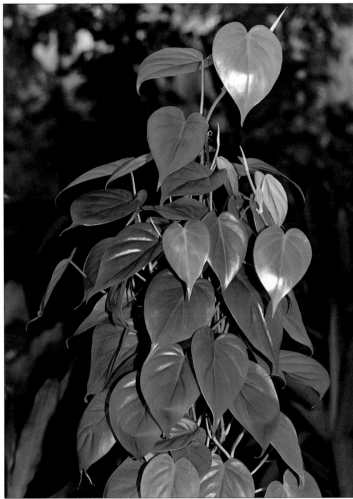

Syngonium podophyllum, syn.
Nephthytis triphylla of gardens
Evergreen, woody-stemmed,
root climber with tufted stems and
arrowhead-shaped leaves when young.
Mature plants have leaves of 7–9
glossy leaflets up to 30cm (12in) long.
H 2m (6ft). Min. 16–18˚C (61–4˚F).

Tetrastigma voinierianum, syn.
Cissus voinieriana (Chestnut vine)
Strong-growing, evergreen, woody-
stemmed, tendril climber. Young
stems and leaves are rust-coloured and
hairy; mature leaves turn lustrous,
deep green above. H 10m (30ft) or more.
Min. 15–18˚C (59–64˚F).

Philodendron melanochrysum
Robust, fairly slow-growing,
evergreen, woody-based, root climber.
Heart-shaped leaves, to 75cm (30in)
long, are lustrous, deep olive green
with a coppery sheen and have pale
veins. H 3m (10ft) or more.
Min. 15–18˚C (59–64˚F).

Cissus antarctica (Kangaroo vine)
Moderately vigorous, evergreen,
woody-stemmed, tendril climber. Oval,
pointed, coarsely serrated leaves are
lustrous, rich green. H to 5m (15ft).
Min. 7˚C (45˚F).

Philodendron scandens
(Heart leaf)
Fairly fast-growing, evergreen, woody-
based, root climber. Rich green leaves
are 10–15cm (4–6in) long when
young, to 30cm (12in) long on mature
plants. H 4m (12ft) or more.
Min. 15–18˚C (59–64˚F).

Gynura aurantiaca (Velvet plant)
Evergreen, woody-based, soft-
stemmed, semi-scrambling climber or
lax shrub with purple-haired stems and
leaves. Clusters of daisy-like, orange-
yellow flower heads are borne in
winter. H 2–3m (6–10ft), less as a
shrub. Min. 16˚C (61˚F).

Monstera deliciosa
(Swiss-cheese plant)
Robust, evergreen, woody-stemmed,
root climber with large-lobed, holed
leaves, 40–90cm (16–36in) long.
Mature plants bear cream spathes,
followed by scented, edible fruits. H to
6m (20ft). Min. 15–18˚C (59–64˚F).

Cissus rhombifolia,
syn. *Rhoicissus rhombifolia,*
R. rhomboidea (Grape ivy)
Moderately vigorous, evergreen,
woody-stemmed, tendril climber with
lustrous leaves divided into 3 coarsely
toothed leaflets.
H 3m (10ft) or more. Min. 7˚C (45˚F).

Streptosolen jamesonii
(Marmalade bush)
Evergreen or semi-evergreen, loosely
scrambling shrub. Has oval, finely
corrugated leaves and, mainly in
spring-summer, many bright orange
flowers. H 2–3m (6–10ft).
Min. 7˚C (45˚F).

CLIMBERS

Ivies

Ivies (*Hedera*) are evergreen, climbing and trailing plants suitable for growing up walls and fences or as ground cover. Plants take a year or so to establish but thereafter growth is rapid. There is a large number of cultivars available, of which the non-variegated forms are shade-tolerant. With height and access to light, the typical, ivy-shaped leaves may become less lobed. Not all ivies are fully hardy.

H. hibernica 'Gracilis' ①

H. hibernica 'Digitata' ①

H. helix 'Adam' ①

H. helix 'Erecta' ①

H. helix 'Merion Beauty' ①

H. helix 'Nigra' ①

H. helix 'Heise' ①

H. helix 'Eva' ①

H. helix 'Ivalace' ①

H. helix 'Woeneri' ①

H. helix 'Glacier' ①

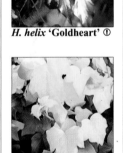

H. helix 'Angularis Aurea' ①

H. colchica 'Dentata' ①

H. helix 'Telecurl' ①

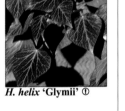

H. helix 'Lobata Major' ①

H. helix 'Glymii' ①

H. helix 'Anne Marie' ①

H. helix 'Goldheart' ①

H. helix 'Pedata' ①

H. hibernica 'Deltoidea' ①

H. hibernica 'Sulphurea' ①

H. helix 'Manda's Crested' ①

H. helix 'Buttercup' ①

H. hibernica ①

H. cana. var. *algeriensis* 'Ravensholst' ①

H. helix 'Green Ripple' ①

H. helix 'Pittsburgh' ①

H. helix 'Parsley Crested' ①

H. helix 'Atropurpurea' ①

H. colchica 'Sulphur Heart' ①

PERENNIALS
including Grasses, Bamboos, Rushes, Sedges and Ferns

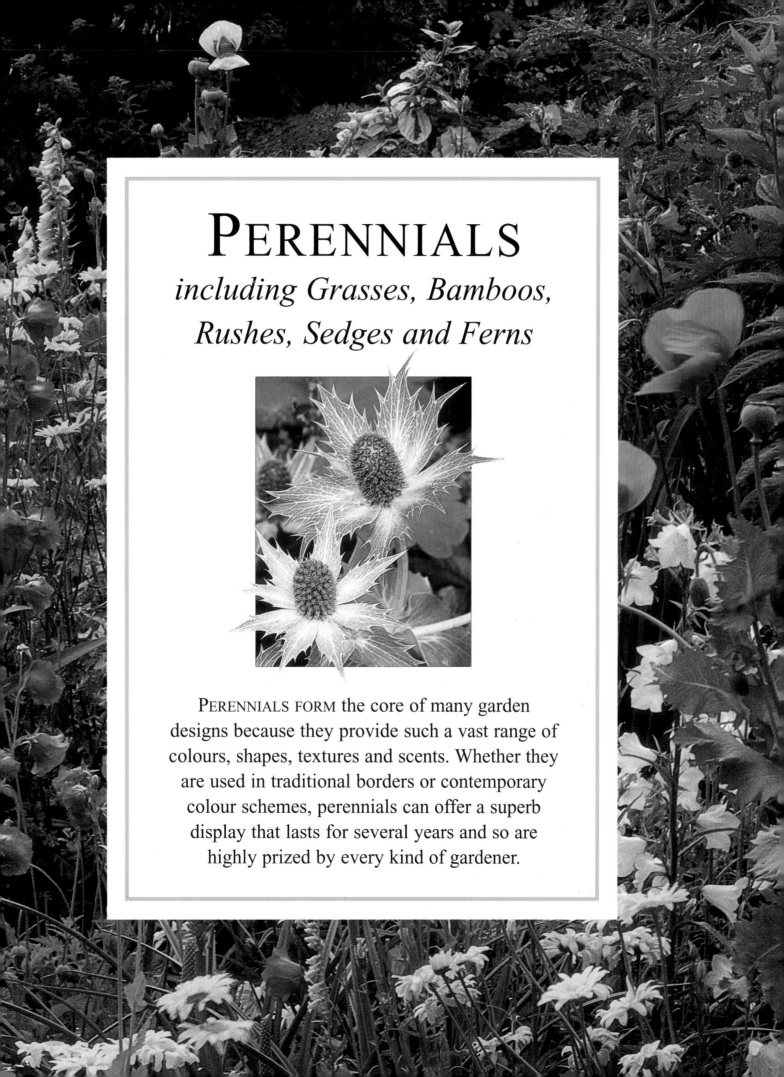

PERENNIALS FORM the core of many garden designs because they provide such a vast range of colours, shapes, textures and scents. Whether they are used in traditional borders or contemporary colour schemes, perennials can offer a superb display that lasts for several years and so are highly prized by every kind of gardener.

Perennials

One of the largest and most versatile of plant groups, perennials offer a large, seasonally changing, diversity of colour, fragrance, form and texture to the designer and a wealth of plants to suit every size and style of garden.

WHAT ARE PERENNIALS?

Perennials are non-woody plants that live for two or more years and, when mature, produce flowers annually. In gardens, the term is also applied to woody-based sub-shrubs, like lavender or artemisia, and often encompasses the grasses and ferns. Although some perennials are evergreen, most are herbaceous and die back each autumn. While this leaves borders bare in winter, many gardeners value this characteristic because it reflects the turning of the seasons: the new growth heralds spring and anticipates the glories of the forthcoming summer.

SEED HEADS
Above: The sculptural forms of biennial teasels (Dipsacus fullonum) *add height and contrast to perennials in high summer, while the seed heads that follow ensure interest well into winter.*

SUMMER BORDER
Right: In this mixed border, drifts of Alstroemeria Ligtu Hybrids *lead the eye to a strong focal point formed by the architectural spikes of verbascum, which are cleverly echoed by the purple spires of* Salvia x superba *in the foreground.*

CHOOSING PERENNIALS

All successful plantings reflect the care taken in selecting plants that suit the climate, soil type and light levels in the garden, and this is especially true when designing with perennials. A plant that is struggling in unsuitable conditions will not fulfil its intended purpose if it fails to flower or grow well enough to fill its allotted space. The best results are usually gained by grouping plants with similar cultivation needs. Most ferns, for example, do well in shady borders in moist, humus-rich soil, as do bamboos such as *Phyllostachys nigra*, which thrive in similar soil conditions.

When perennials are massed together in borders, it is vital to consider their eventual height and spread if the robust and vigorous are not to swamp more delicate specimens.

ORNAMENTAL FEATURES

The form of perennial flowers includes strong contrasts, from the vertical spires of delphiniums or verbascums to the more horizontal shapes provided by the dense, flat flower heads of achillea. Those with arching flowers include *Polygonatum* x *hybridum*.

As foliage is such a large textural mass it has great impact on a border design. Fortunately leaf forms of perennials span a vast range: from the boldly pleated foliage of veratrum to the delicate, pinnate leaves of *Polemonium caeruleum* and *Matteuccia struthiopteris*. Textural contrasts in the foliage also abound: from silky *Stachys byzantina* to the glossy foliage of *Acanthus mollis*.

DESIGNING WITH PERENNIALS

The traditional herbaceous border – a long rectangle flanked by smooth turf and backed by a wall or well-tended hedge – has long been used to display perennials. Its width – often 3m (10ft) or more – allows for banked effects from front to back so that small plants are not obscured by taller neighbours. While only the largest of gardens have space for such grand effects, the principles used can be adapted to more modest plantings.

PATIO PLANTING
Pleasing arrangements of complementary colours and differing textures can be created in containers, as shown here with purple Heuchera micrantha var. diversifolia 'Palace Purple', Houttuynia cordata 'Chameleon' and Tolmiea menziesii.

SIZE CATEGORIES USED WITHIN THIS GROUP		
Large	**Medium**	**Small**
over 1.2m (4ft)	60cm–1.2m (2–4ft)	up to 60cm (2ft)

Low, ground-covering perennials such as *Cerastium tomentosum* and *Tiarella cordifolia* are ideal for the front of a border and, for greatest impact, small and medium-sized plants are best massed in odd-numbered groups. Superb effects can then be created by using single large specimens as focal points, especially those of architectural form such as *Cynara cardunculus*, *Rheum palmatum*, *Rodgersia aesculifolia* or a tall grass such as *Stipa gigantea*. Variety of shape and texture can be introduced by combining, for example, the rounded form of *Sedum spectabile* with the upright spires of *Kniphofia*, or the lacy foliage of dicentras with the bolder outlines of hostas.

The disadvantage of planting herbaceous perennials on their own in a border is that, when they fade in autumn, only bare earth will show until the new growing season. A border mixed with shrubs to provide structure, however, and annuals, biennials and bulbs, will prolong interest.

☐ WHITE

Epilobium angustifolium* f. *album
(White rosebay)
Vigorous, upright perennial bearing
sprays of pure white flowers along
wand-like stems in late summer.Leaves
are small and lance-shaped. May
spread rapidly. H 1.2–1.5m (4–5ft),
S 50cm (20in) or more.

Crambe cordifolia
Robust perennial with clouds of small,
fragrant, white flowers borne in
branching sprays in summer above
mounds of large, crinkled and lobed,
dark green leaves.
H to 2m (6ft), S 1.2m (4ft).

Eremurus himalaicus
Upright perennial with strap-shaped,
basal leaves. In early summer has huge,
dense racemes of open cup-shaped,
pure white blooms with long stamens.
Cover crowns in winter with compost
or bracken. Needs staking.
H 2–2.5m (6–8ft), S 1m (3ft).

Sanguisorba canadensis
(Canadian burnet)
Clump-forming perennial. In late
summer bears slightly pendent spikes
of bottlebrush-like, white flowers on
stems that arise from toothed, divided,
mid-green leaves.
H 1.2–2m (4–6ft), S 60cm (2ft).

Nicotiana sylvestris
(Flowering tobacco)
Branching perennial, often grown
as an annual, carrying panicles of
fragrant, tubular, white flowers at the
ends of stems in late summer. Has long,
rough, mid-green leaves.
H 1.5m (5ft), S 75cm (2½ft).

Eryngium eburneum,
syn. *E. paniculatum*
Evergreen, arching perennial bearing
heads of thistle-like, green flowers
with white stamens on branched stems
in late summer. Has arching, spiny,
grass-like leaves.
H 1.5–2m (5–6ft), S 60cm (2ft).

Romneya coulteri
(Tree poppy)
Vigorous, bushy, sub-shrubby
perennial, grown for its large, fragrant,
white flowers, with prominent centres
of golden stamens, that appear in late
summer. Has deeply divided, grey
leaves. H and S 2m (6ft).

Echinops sphaerocephalus
Massive, bushy perennial with deeply
cut, mid-green leaves, pale grey
beneath, and grey stems bearing round,
greyish-white flower heads in late
summer. H 2m (6ft), S 1m (3ft).

Aruncus dioicus, syn. *A. sylvester*,
Spiraea aruncus (Goat's beard)
Hummock-forming perennial carrying
large leaves with lance-shaped leaflets
on tall stems and above them, in mid-
summer, branching plumes of tiny,
creamy-white flowers.
H 2m (6ft), S 1.2m (4ft).

OTHER RECOMMENDED PLANTS:
Aconitum 'Ivorine'
Aconitum napellus 'Albidum'
Campanula pyramidalis

Cimicifuga racemosa
Filipendula camtschatica
Macleaya cordata

Selinum wallichianum
Veratrum album

PERENNIALS

Artemisia lactiflora
(White mugwort)
Vigorous, erect perennial. Many sprays
of creamy-white buds open to off-white
flower heads in summer. Dark green
leaves are jagged-toothed. Needs staking
and is best as a foil to stronger colours.
H 1.2–1.5m (4–5ft), S 50cm (20in).

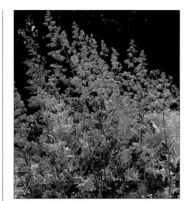

**Macleaya microcarpa 'Kelway's
Coral Plume'**
Clump-forming perennial that in
summer produces branching spikes of
rich pink-buff flowers. Large, rounded,
lobed leaves are grey-green above,
grey-white beneath.
H 2–2.5m (6–8ft), S 1–1.2m (3–4ft).

Lavatera cachemiriana,
syn. *L. cachemirica*
Semi-evergreen, woody-based
perennial or sub-shrub with wiry stems
bearing panicles of trumpet-shaped,
silky, clear pink flowers in summer.
Has ivy-shaped, downy, mid-green
leaves. H 1.5–2m (5–6ft), S 1m (3ft).

☼ ○ Zone 9

Filipendula rubra
Vigorous, upright perennial with large,
jagged leaves and feathery plumes
of tiny, soft pink flowers on tall,
branching stems in mid-summer.
Will rapidly colonize a boggy site.
H 2–2.5m, (6–8ft), S 1.2m (4ft).

Alpinia zerumbet, syn. *A. nutans*
of gardens, *A. speciosa* (Shell
flower, Shell ginger)
Evergreen, clump-forming perennial.
Has racemes of white flowers, with
yellow lips and pink- or red-marked
throats, mainly in summer. H 3m (10ft),
S 1m (3ft). Min. 18°C (64°F).

Campanula lactiflora
'Loddon Anna'
Upright, branching perennial with
narrowly oval leaves. In summer,
slender stems bear racemes of large,
nodding, bell-shaped, soft dusty-pink
flowers. Needs staking on a windy site.
H 1.2m (4ft), S 60cm (2ft).

Eremurus robustus
Upright perennial with strap-like
leaves that die back during summer
as huge racemes of cup-shaped, pink
blooms appear. Cover crowns in winter
with compost or bracken. Needs
staking. H 2.2m (7ft), S 1m (3ft).

**Rheum palmatum
'Atrosanguineum'**
Clump-forming perennial with very
large, lobed, deeply cut leaves that are
deep red-purple when young. Bears
large, fluffy panicles of crimson
flowers in early summer.
H and S 2m (6ft).

PERENNIALS

■ PURPLE–BLUE

Veratrum nigrum
(Black false hellebore)
Erect, stately perennial that from late summer onwards bears long spikes of chocolate-purple flowers at the ends of stout, upright stems. Stems are clothed with ribbed, oval to narrowly oval leaves. H 2m (6ft), S 60cm (2ft).

☀ ◐ ⓘ

Verbena bonariensis,
syn. *V. patagonica*
Perennial often grown as an annual with a basal clump of dark green leaves. Upright, wiry stems carry tufts of tiny, purplish-blue flowers in summer-autumn.
H 1.5m (5ft), S 60cm (2ft).

☀ ◐

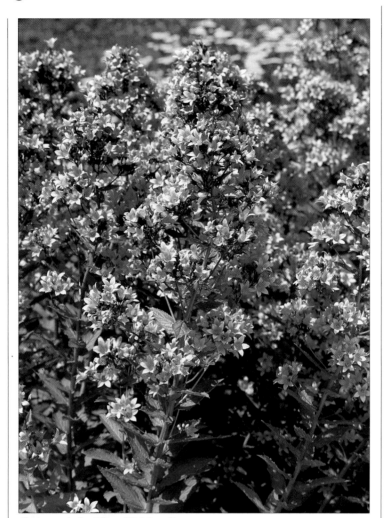

***Campanula lactiflora* 'Prichard's Variety'**
Upright perennial with slender stems carrying branching heads of large, nodding, bell-shaped, violet-blue flowers from early summer to late autumn. May need staking.
H 1.2–1.5m (4–5ft), S 60cm (2ft).

☀ ◐

□ GREEN–YELLOW

Gunnera manicata
Architectural perennial with rounded, prickly-edged leaves, to 1.5m (5ft) across. Has conical, light green flower spikes in early summer, followed by orange-brown seed pods. Needs mulch cover for crowns in winter and a sheltered site. H 2m (6ft), S 2.2m (7ft).

☀ ◐

Angelica archangelica (Angelica)
Upright perennial, usually grown as a biennial, with deeply divided, bright green leaves and white or green flowers in late summer. Stems have culinary usage and when crystallized may be used for confectionery decoration.
H 2m (6ft), S 1m (3ft).

☀ ◐

Cynara cardunculus (Cardoon)
Stately perennial with large clumps of arching, pointed, divided, silver-grey leaves, above which rise large, thistle-like, blue-purple flower heads borne singly on stout, grey stems in summer. Flower heads dry well.
H 2m (6ft), S 1m (3ft).

☀ ◐

Echinops bannaticus
Upright perennial with narrow, deeply cut leaves and globose, pale to mid-blue heads of flowers, borne on branching stems in late summer. Flower heads dry well.
H 1.2–1.5m (4–5ft), S 75cm (2½ft).

☀ ◐

***Galega* 'Lady Wilson'**
Vigorous, upright perennial with spikes of small, pea-like, blue and pinkish-white flowers in summer above bold leaves divided into oval leaflets. Needs staking. H to 1.5m (5ft), S 1m (3ft).

☀ ◐

Ferula communis (Giant fennel)
Upright perennial. Large, cow-parsley-like umbels of yellow flowers are borne from late spring to summer on the tops of stems that arise from a mound of finely cut, mid-green foliage.
H 2–2.3m (6–7ft), S 1–1.2m (3–4ft).

☀ ◐

PERENNIALS

Heliopsis helianthoides subsp. **scabra 'Light of Loddon'**, syn. *H.* 'Light of Loddon'
Upright perennial bearing dahlia-like, double, bright orange flower heads on strong stems in late summer. Dark green leaves are coarse and serrated.
H 1.2–1.5m (4–5ft), S 60cm (2ft).

☼ ◊

Verbascum olympicum
Semi-evergreen, rosette-forming biennial or short-lived perennial. Branching stems, arising from felt-like, grey foliage at the plant base, bear sprays of 5-lobed, bright golden flowers from mid-summer onwards.
H 2m (6ft), S 1m (3ft).

☼ ◊

Ligularia przewalskii , syn. *Senecio przewalskii*
Loosely clump-forming perennial with stems clothed in deeply cut, round, dark green leaves. Narrow spires of small, daisy-like, yellow flower heads appear from mid- to late summer.
H 1.2–2m (4–6ft), S 1m (3ft).

☼ ◖

Hedychium densiflorum
Clump-forming, rhizomatous perennial bearing a profusion of short-lived, fragrant, orange or yellow flowers in dense spikes during late summer. Broadly lance-shaped leaves are glossy, mid-green.
H 1.2–2m (4–6ft), S 60cm (2ft).

☼ ◖

Rudbeckia 'Goldquelle'
Erect perennial. In late summer and autumn, daisy-like, double, bright yellow flower heads with green centres are borne singly on stout stems. Has deeply divided, mid-green foliage.
H 1.5–2m (5–6ft), S 60–75 cm (2–2½ft).

☼ ◊

Inula magnifica
Robust, clump-forming, upright perennial with a mass of lance-shaped to elliptic, rough leaves. Leafy stems bear terminal heads of large, daisy-like, yellow flower heads in late summer. Needs staking.
H 1.8m (6ft), S 1m (3ft).

☼ ◊

Ligularia stenocephala
Loosely clump-forming perennial with jagged-edged, round, mid-green leaves. Large heads of daisy-like, yellow-orange flowers open on purplish stems from mid- to late summer.
H 1.2m (4ft) or more, S 60cm (2ft).

☼ ◖

Heliconia psittacorum (Parrot's flower, Parrot's plantain)
Tufted perennial with long-stalked, lance-shaped leaves. In summer, mature plants carry green-tipped, orange flowers with narrow, glossy, orange-red bracts. H to 2m (6ft), S 1m (3ft). Min. 18°C (64°F).

◐ ◊

Achillea filipendulina 'Gold Plate', illus. p.258
CHRYSANTHEMUMS, illus. pp.260–61
Helianthus atrorubens 'Monarch'

Helianthus x *multiflorus* 'Loddon Gold', illus. p.232
Ligularia 'Gregynog Gold'
Meconopsis paniculata

Rudbeckia 'Herbstsonne', illus. p.232
Silphium laciniatum
Telekia speciosa
Thalictrum flavum

Heliopsis helianthoides 'Incomparabilis'
Heliopsis helianthoides subsp. *scabra*
Kniphofia 'Samuel's Sensation'
Wachendorfia thyrsiflora

Delphiniums

Delphiniums are among the most attractive of the tall perennials, with their showy spires of flowers making a spectacular display in the summer herbaceous border. In addition to the classic blues, hybrids are available in a broad range of colours, from white through the pastel shades of dusky-pink and lilac to the richer mauves and violet-purples. Plants should be securely staked to support the heavy flower spikes.

D. 'Butterball' ①

D. 'Emily Hawkins' ①

D. 'Bruce' ①

D. 'Cliveden Beauty' ①

D. 'Loch Leven' ①

D. 'Fanfare' ①

D. 'Gillian Dallas' ①

D. 'Lord Butler' ①

D. 'Blue Nile' ①

D. 'Sandpiper' ①

D. 'Strawberry Fair' ①

D. 'Mighty Atom' ①

D. 'Spindrift' ①

D. grandiflorum 'Blue Butterfly' ①

D. 'Chelsea Star' ①

D. 'Olive Poppleton' ①

D. 'Langdon's Royal Flush' ①

D. 'Blue Dawn' ①

D. 'Sungleam' ①

PERENNIALS large AUTUMN INTEREST

◻◻ WHITE–PINK

◻◻ PINK–PURPLE

Cimicifuga simplex
Upright perennial with arching spikes
of tiny, slightly fragrant, star-shaped,
white flowers in autumn. Leaves are
glossy and divided. Needs staking.
H 1.2–1.5m (4–5ft), S 60cm (2ft).

☀ ◐

Eupatorium purpureum
(Joe Pye weed)
Stately, upright perennial with terminal
heads of tubular, pinkish-purple flowers
borne in late summer and early autumn.
Coarse, oval leaves are arranged in
whorls along purplish stems.
H to 2.2m (7ft), S to 1m (3ft).

☀ ◊

**Anemone × hybrida 'Honorine
Jobert'**
Vigorous, branching perennial. Slightly
cupped, white flowers with contrasting
yellow stamens are carried on wiry
stems in late summer and early autumn
above deeply divided, dark green
leaves. H 1.5m (5ft), S 60cm (2ft).

☀ ◊ ⓘ

**Anemone hupehensis 'September
Charm'**
Vigorous, branching perennial. In
late summer and early autumn bears
slightly cupped, clear pink flowers on
wiry stems. Leaves are deeply divided
and dark green.
H 75cm (30in), S 50cm (20in).

☀ ◊ ⓘ

Salvia involucrata 'Bethellii'
Sub-shrubby perennial that produces
long racemes of large, cerise-crimson
blooms, with pink bracts, in late
summer and autumn. Leaves are oval
to heart-shaped. H 1.2–1.5m (4–5ft),
S 1m (3ft). Min. 2°C (35°F).

☀ ◊

**Anemone hupehensis var.
japonica 'Bressingham Glow'**
Vigorous, branching perennial with
slightly cupped, rose-purple flowers
borne on wiry stems in late summer
and early autumn over clumps of
deeply divided, dark green leaves.
H 1.2–1.5m (4–5ft), S 60cm (2ft).

☀ ◊ ⓘ

OTHER RECOMMENDED PLANTS:
Anemone hupehensis var. *japonica* 'Prinz
  Heinrich'
Anemone × *hybrida* 'Max Vogel'

CHRYSANTHEMUMS, illus. pp.260–61
Cimicifuga simplex 'Prichard's Giant'
Leucanthemella serotina
MICHAELMAS DAISIES, illus. p.262

Aconitum carmichaelii 'Arendsii'
Campanula lactiflora 'Prichard's Variety',
  illus. p.228
Helenium 'Riverton Gem'

MICHAELMAS DAISIES, illus. p.262
Phytolacca americana
Salvia uliginosa
Verbena bonariensis, illus. p.228

GREEN–YELLOW

PINK–PURPLE

Gomphocarpus physocarpus,
syn. *Asclepias physocarpa*
Deciduous, erect, hairy sub-shrub, leaves
lance-shaped. 10cm (4in) long. Umbels
of 5-horned, creamy-white flowers in
summer. Large, inflated, globose seed
pods with soft bristles. H to 2m (6ft),
S to 60cm (2ft). Min. 2°C (35°F).

☼ ◊ ①

**Helianthus × multiflorus
'Loddon Gold'**
Upright perennial bearing showy,
large, vivid deep yellow flower heads
with rounded, double centres in late
summer and early autumn. Needs
staking and may spread quickly.
H 1.5m (5ft), S 60cm (2ft).

☼ ◊ ①

Strelitzia nicolai
Evergreen, palm-like perennial with
a stout trunk. Has leaves, 1.5m (5ft)
or more long, on very long stalks and
intermittently bears beak-like, white
and pale blue flowers in boat-shaped,
dark purple bracts. H 8m (25ft),
S 5m (15ft). Min. 5–10°C (41–50°F).

☼ ◊

Hedychium gardnerianum
Upright, rhizomatous perennial. In late
summer and early autumn has many
spikes of short-lived, fragrant, lemon-
yellow and red flowers. Lance-shaped
leaves are greyish-green, most markedly
when young. H 1.5–2m (5–6ft),
S 75cm (2½ft). Min. 5°C (41°F).

☼ ◖

Rudbeckia 'Herbstsonne'
Erect perennial bearing daisy-like,
yellow flower heads, with conical,
green centres, that are carried singly on
tall stems in late summer and autumn.
Mid-green leaves are shallowly lobed.
H 1.5–2.3m (5–7ft),
S 60–75cm (2–2½ft).

☼ ◊

Musa ornata (Flowering banana)
Evergreen, palm-like, suckering
perennial with oblong, waxy, bluish-
green leaves to 2m (6ft) long. In
summer has erect, yellow-orange
flowers with pinkish bracts and
greenish-yellow fruits. H to 3m (10ft),
S 2.2m (7ft). Min. 18°C (64°F).

☼ ◊

Calathea sanderiana
Evergreen, clump-forming perennial.
Broadly oval, leathery, glossy leaves,
to 60cm (2ft) long, are dark green with
pink to white lines above, and purple
beneath. Intermittently has short spikes
of white to mauve flowers. H 1.2–1.5m
(4–5ft), S 1m (3ft). Min. 15°C (59°F).

☼ ◊

Helianthus × multiflorus
Upright perennial. Has large, yellow
flower heads, with double centres
surrounded by larger, rayed segments,
that are borne in late summer and early
autumn. Needs staking and may spread
rapidly. H 1.5m (5ft), S 60cm (2ft).

☼ ◊ ①

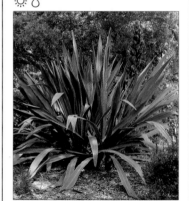

Doryanthes palmeri
Evergreen perennial with a rosette
of arching, ribbed leaves, to 2m (6ft)
long. Intermittently bears panicles of
small, red-bracted, orange-red flowers,
white within. Flowers are often
replaced by bulbils. H 2–2.5m (6–8ft),
S 2.5m (8ft). Min. 10°C (50°F).

☼ ◊

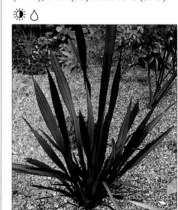

**Phormium tenax Purpureum
Group**
Evergreen, upright perennial with bold,
stiff, pointed leaves that are rich
reddish-purple to dark copper. In
summer, panicles of reddish flowers
appear on purplish-blue stems.
H 2–2.5m (6–8ft), S 1m (3ft).

☼ ◖

CHRYSANTHEMUMS, illus. pp.260–61
Helianthus salicifolius
Kniphofia caulescens, illus. p.263
Rudbeckia laciniata 'Golden Glow'

Solidago 'Golden Wings'

OTHER RECOMMENDED PLANTS:
Calathea majestica 'Roseolineata'
Costus speciosus
Impatiens sodenii

ORCHIDS, illus. pp.296–9

PERENNIALS

□ WHITE

BLUE–GREEN

Pycnostachys dawei
Strong-growing, bushy perennial with toothed, oblong leaves, 12–30cm (5–12in) long, that are reddish below. Has compact spikes of tubular, 2-lipped, bright blue flowers in winter-spring. H 1.2–1.5m (4–5ft), S 30–90cm (1–3ft). Min. 15°C (59°F).

☼ ◊

Musa basjoo, syn. *M. japonica* (Japanese banana)
Evergreen, palm-like, suckering perennial with arching leaves to 1m (3ft) long. Has drooping, pale yellow flowers with brownish bracts in summer followed by green fruits. H 3–5m (10–15ft), S 2–2.5m (6–8ft).

☼ ◊

Ranunculus aconitifolius 'Flore Pleno' (Fair maids of France)
Clump-forming perennial with deeply divided, dark green leaves. Double, pure white flowers are borne on strong, branched stems in spring-summer. H 60–75cm (24–30in), S 50cm (20in).

☼ ◊ ①

Ranunculus aconitifolius
Vigorous, clump-forming perennial with deeply divided, dark green leaves. Single, white flowers, about 3cm (1in) across, are borne in spring and early summer. H and S 1m (3ft).

☼ ◊ ①

Ensete ventricosum, syn. *Musa arnoldiana, M. ensete*
Evergreen, palm-like perennial with small, banana-like fruits. Has 6m (20ft) long leaves with reddish midribs and, intermittently, reddish-green flowers with dark red bracts. H 6m (20ft), S 3m (10ft) or more. Min. 10°C (50°F).

☼ ◊

Smilacina racemosa (False spikenard)
Arching perennial. Has oval, light green leaves terminating in feathery sprays of white flowers that appear from spring to mid-summer and are followed by fleshy, reddish fruits. H 75–90cm (30–36in), S 45cm (18in).

☼ ◊ pH

Aciphylla scott-thomsonii
Artemisia ludoviciana var. *albula*, illus. p.266
Nepenthes rafflesiana
Phormium cookianum

Phormium cookianum subsp. *hookeri* 'Tricolor'
Phormium cookianum 'Variegatum'
Phormium tenax

OTHER RECOMMENDED PLANTS:
Asphodelus aestivus
Asphodelus albus, illus. p.239
Dicentra spectabilis f. *alba*, illus. p.239

IRISES, illus. pp.234–5
PEONIES, illus. pp.236–7
Polygonatum hirtum
Polygonatum multiflorum 'Flore Pleno'

PERENNIALS

233

Irises

These beautiful flowers were originally named after Iris, the Greek goddess of the rainbow, as the shades of their colouring and markings are reminiscent of those of the rainbow. Their distinctive flowers often have 'beards' (short hairs) or crests along the centres of the falls.

The genus is classified into many divisions, some of which are used horticulturally for irises with similar characteristics or cultural requirements. Of these, the easiest to grow are the bearded, crested, Xiphium and dwarf Reticulata groups. Siberian and Japanese types are excellent in a bog garden or by water, but also tolerate drier conditions. Others, such as Juno, Oncocyclus and Regelia irises, may be less easy to cultivate, though their flowers are among the most beautiful. Full details of all groups and guidance on their cultivation are given in the Plant Dictionary.

I. cristata (Evansia) ①

I. 'Rippling Rose' (bearded) ①

I. rosenbachiana (Juno) ①

I. latifolia (Xiphium) ①

I. 'Wisley White' (Siberian) ①

I. iberica (Oncocyclus) ①

I. 'Bold Print' (bearded) ①

I. 'Krasnia' (bearded) ①

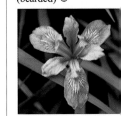

I. 'Mary Frances' (bearded) ①

I. 'Dreaming Yellow' (Siberian) ①

I. 'Geisha Gown' (Japanese) ①

I. pallida 'Variegata' (bearded) ①

I. 'Ruffled Velvet' (Siberian) ①

I. × *fulvala* (beardless) ①

I. douglasiana (Pacific Coast) ①

I. bucharica (Juno) ①

I. 'Joette' (bearded) ①

I. tenax (Pacific Coast) ①

I. 'Magic Man' (bearded) ①

I. magnifica (Juno) ①

I. missouriensis (Pacific Coast) ①

I. 'Annabel Jane' (bearded) ①

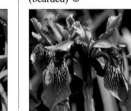

I. versicolor (beardless) ①

I. chrysographes (Siberian) ①

I. 'Paradise Bird' (bearded) ①

I. tectorum (Evansia) ①

I. 'Matinata' (bearded) ①

I. 'Lady of Quality' (Siberian) ①

I. japonica
(Evansia) ①

I. histrioides 'Major'
(Reticulata) ①

I. 'Harmony'
(Reticulata) ①

I. winogradowii
(Reticulata) ①

I. innominata (Pacific Coast) ①

I. danfordiae
(Reticulata) ①

I. 'Peach Frost'
(bearded) ①

I. 'Carnaby'
(bearded) ①

I. 'Sapphire Star'
(Japanese) ①

I. laevigata
(Japanese) ①

I. hoogiana
(Regelia) ①

I. 'Joyce'
(Reticulata) ①

I. pseudacorus
(beardless) ①

I. xiphium 'Wedgwood'
(Xiphium) ①

I. 'Katharine Hodgkin'
(Reticulata) ①

I. setosa
(beardless) ①

I. 'Early Light'
(bearded) ①

I. 'Sun Miracle'
(bearded) ①

I. fulva (beardless) ①

I. reticulata 'Cantab'
(Reticulata) ①

I. ensata 'Galathea'
(Japanese) ①

I. 'Bronze Queen'
(Xiphium) ①

I. variegata
(bearded) ①

I. 'Eyebright'
(bearded) ①

I. 'Blue-eyed Brunette'
(bearded) ①

I. 'Mountain Lake'
(Siberian) ①

I. 'Lavender Royal'
(Pacific Coast) ①

I. 'Butter and Sugar'
(Siberian) ①

I. forrestii
(Siberian) ①

I. 'Shepherd's Delight'
(bearded) ①

I. 'Flamenco'
(bearded) ①

Peonies

Peonies (*Paeonia* species and cultivars) have long been valued for their showy blooms, filling the border with subtle shades of mainly whites, pinks and reds in late spring and early to mid-summer. Peony flowers vary from single to double or anemone form (with broad, outer petals and a mass of petaloids in the centre) and are often heavily scented. The flowers are also good for cutting. Peony foliage is also striking, often tinged bronze when young and assuming rich reddish tints in autumn. Besides the wide variety of border hybrids available, there are many attractive species as well as several tree peonies (cultivars of *P. suffruticosa*), open shrubs often over 2m (6ft) high.

Peonies are long-lived plants that should, if possible, be left undisturbed, as they resent transplanting. If it is necessary to divide the clumps, lift and divide them in late summer or early spring.

P. emodi (single) ①

P. suffruticosa 'Godaishu' (double) ①

P. suffruticosa subsp. *rockii* (semi-dbl.) ①

P. 'Krinkled White' (single) ①

P. obovata var. *alba* (single) ①

P. 'White Wings' (single) ①

P. 'Whitleyi Major' (single) ①

P. 'Baroness Schroeder' (double) ①

P. officinalis 'Alba Plena' (double) ①

P. 'Duchesse de Nemours' (dbl.) ①

P. 'Alice Harding' (double) ①

P. 'Cornelia Shaylor' (double) ①

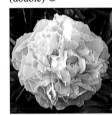

P. 'Shirley Temple' (double) ①

P. 'Mother of Pearl' (single) ①

P. 'Kelway's Supreme' (double) ①

P. suffruticosa 'Hana-kisoi' (double) ①

P. 'Avant Garde' (single) ①

P. suffruticosa 'Reine Elizabeth' (double) ①

P. 'Sarah Bernhardt' (double) ①

P. 'Ballerina' (double) ①

P. 'Bowl of Beauty' (anemone) ①

P. mascula subsp. *mascula* (single) ①

P. 'Globe of Light' (anemone) ①

P. 'Evening World' (anemone) ①

P. cambessedesii (single) ①

P. suffruticosa 'Kamadu-nishiki' (double) ①

P. 'Silver Flare' (single) ①

P. tenuifolia (single) ①

P. wittmanniana (single) ①

P. 'L'Espérance' (single) ①

P. veitchii (single) ①

P. 'Magic Orb' (double) ①

P. 'Instituteur Doriat' (anemone) ①

P. 'Chocolate Soldier' (semi-double) ①

P. 'Laura Dessert' (double) ①

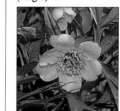

P. potaninii var. *trollioides* (single) ①

P. × *smouthii* (single) ①

P. 'Sir Edward Elgar' (single) ①

P. mlokosewitschii (single) ①

P. suffruticosa 'Cardinal Vaughan' (semi-double) ①

P. 'Defender' (single) ①

P. delavayi (single) ①

P. 'Kelway's Gorgeous' (single) ①

P. officinalis 'China Rose' (single) ①

P. suffruticosa 'Hana-daijin' (double) ①

P. officinalis 'Rubra Plena' (double) ①

P. 'Argosy' (single) ①

P. 'Auguste Dessert' (semi-double) ①

P. peregrina 'Otto Froebel' (single) ①

P. 'Knighthood' (double) ①

P. lutea var. *ludlowii* (single) ①

P. 'Souvenir de Maxime Cornu' (double) ①

P. 'Madame Louis Henri' (semi-double) ①

◻◻◼◼ **WHITE–BLUE**

Polygonatum x hybridum
(Solomon's seal)
Arching, leafy perennial with fleshy rhizomes. In late spring, clusters of small, pendent, tubular, greenish-white flowers are produced in axils of neat, oval leaves. H 1.2m (4ft), S 1m (3ft).

☀ ◊ ①

Geranium phaeum
(Mourning widow)
Clump-forming perennial with lobed, soft green leaves and maroon-purple flowers, with reflexed petals, borne on rather lax stems in late spring. H 75cm (30in), S 45cm (18in).

☀ ◊

Darmera peltata,
syn. *Peltiphyllum peltatum*
(Umbrella plant)
Spreading perennial with large, rounded leaves. Has clusters of white or pale pink flowers in spring on white-haired stems before foliage appears. H 1–1.2m (3–4ft), S 60cm (2ft).

☀ ◊

Symphytum caucasicum
Clump-forming perennial carrying clusters of pendent, azure-blue flowers in spring above rough, hairy, mid-green foliage. Is best suited to a wild garden. H and S 60–90cm (24–36in).

☀ ◊ ①

◼◻ **BLUE–YELLOW**

Symphytum x uplandicum 'Variegatum'
Perennial with large, hairy, grey-green leaves that have broad, cream margins. In late spring and early summer, pink or blue buds open to tubular, blue or purplish-blue flowers. H 1m (3ft), S 60cm (2ft).

☀ ◊ ①

Doronicum columnae 'Miss Mason'
Clump-forming, rhizomatous perennial with heart-shaped leaves. Slender stems bear daisy-like, bright yellow flower heads, 8cm (3in) across, held well above the foliage, in mid- and late spring. H and S 60cm (24in).

☀ ◊

Chelidonium majus 'Flore Pleno'
Upright perennial with divided, bright green leaves and many cup-shaped, double, yellow flowers borne on branching sprays in late spring and early summer. Seeds freely and is best in a wild garden. H 60–90cm (24–30in), S 30cm (12in).

☀ ◊ ①

Tanacetum coccineum 'Brenda',
syn. *Pyrethrum* 'Brenda'
Erect perennial with somewhat aromatic, feathery leaves. Daisy-like, single, magenta-pink flower heads are borne in late spring and early summer. H 60cm (24in), S 45cm (18in) or more.

☀ ◊ ①

Aciphylla aurea
(Golden Spaniard)
Evergreen, rosette-forming perennial with long, bayonet-like, yellow-green leaves. Bears spikes of golden flowers up to 2m (6ft) tall from late spring to early summer. H and S in leaf 60–75cm (24–30in).

☀ ◊

Asphodeline lutea
(Yellow asphodel)
Neat, clump-forming perennial that bears dense spikes of star-shaped, yellow flowers amid narrow, grey-green leaves in late spring. H 1–1.2m (3–4ft), S 60cm–1m (2–3ft).

☀ ◊

Gypsophila paniculata 'Bristol Fairy'
Perennial with small, dark green leaves and wiry, branching stems bearing panicles of tiny, double, white flowers in summer.
H 60–75cm (2–2½ft), S 1m (3ft).

☼ ◊

Libertia grandiflora
(New Zealand satin flower)
Loosely clump-forming, rhizomatous perennial that in early summer produces spikes of white flowers above grass-like, dark green leaves, which turn brown at the tips. Has decorative seed pods in autumn. H 75cm (30in), S 60cm (24in).

☼ ◊

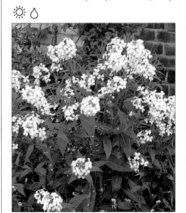

Hesperis matronalis
(Dame's violet, Sweet rocket)
Upright perennial with long spikes of many 4-petalled, white or violet flowers borne in summer. Flowers have a strong fragrance in the evening. Leaves are smooth and narrowly oval.
H 75cm (30in), S 60cm (24in).

☼ ◊

Asphodelus albus
(White asphodel)
Upright perennial with clusters of star-shaped, white flowers borne in late spring and early summer. Has narrow, basal tufts of mid-green leaves.
H 1m (3ft), S 45cm (1½ft).

☼ ◊

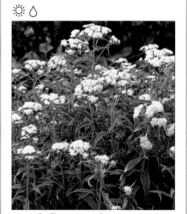

Anaphalis margaritacea
(Pearl everlasting)
Bushy perennial that has lance-shaped, grey-green or silvery-grey leaves with white margins and many heads of small, white flowers borne on erect stems in late summer. Flower heads dry well.
H 60–75cm (24–30in), S 60cm (24in).

☼ ◊

Achillea ptarmica 'The Pearl'
Upright perennial with large heads of small, pompon-like, white flowers in summer and tapering, glossy, dark green leaves. May spread rapidly.
H and S 75cm (30in).

☼ ◊ ①

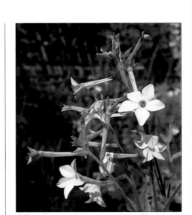

Nicotiana alata, syn. *N. affinis*
Rosette-forming perennial, often grown as an annual, that in late summer bears clusters of tubular, creamy-white flowers, pale brownish-violet externally, which are fragrant at night. Has oval, mid-green leaves.
H 75cm (30in), S 30cm (12in).

☼ ◊ ①

Dicentra spectabilis f. **alba**
Leafy perennial forming a hummock of fern-like, deeply cut, light green foliage with arching sprays of pendent, heart-shaped, pure white flowers in late spring and summer.
H 60–75cm (24–30in), S 60cm (24in).

◐ ◊ ①

PERENNIALS

239

☐ WHITE

Eupatorium rugosum,
syn. *E. ageratoides, E. urticifolium*
(Hardy age, Mist flower, White
snakeroot)
Erect perennial with nettle-like, grey-
green leaves. In late summer bears
dense, flat, white flower heads.
H 1.2m (4ft), S 45cm (1½ft).

Thalictrum aquilegiifolium
'White Cloud'
Perennial with divided, greyish-green
leaves. In summer produces terminal
sprays of delicate, fluffy, white flowers.
H 1–1.2m (3–4ft), S 30cm (1ft).

Leucanthemum × superbum
'Elizabeth', syn. *Chrysanthemum
maximum* of gardens 'Elizabeth',
C. × superbum 'Elizabeth'
Robust perennial with large, daisy-like,
single, pure white flower heads borne
singly in summer. Divide and replant
every 2 years. H 1m (3ft), S 60cm (2ft).

Rodgersia podophylla
Clump-forming, rhizomatous perennial
with large, many-veined leaves that are
bronze when young and later become
mid-green, then copper-tinted. Panicles
of creamy-white flowers are borne
well above foliage in summer.
H 1.2m (4ft), S 1m (3ft).

Dictamnus albus,
syn. *D. fraxinella* (Burning bush)
Upright perennial bearing, in early
summer, spikes of fragrant, star-
shaped, white flowers with long
stamens. Light green leaves are
divided into oval leaflets. Dislikes
disturbance. H 1m (3ft), S 60cm (2ft).

Rodgersia sambucifolia
Clump-forming, rhizomatous perennial
with emerald-green, sometimes
bronze-tinged leaves composed of
large leaflets. Sprays of creamy-white
flowers appear above foliage in
summer. H 1–1.2m (3–4ft), S 1m (3ft).

Myrrhis odorata (Sweet Cicely)
Graceful perennial that resembles cow
parsley. Has aromatic, fern-like, mid-
green foliage and fragrant, bright
creamy-white flowers in early summer.
H 60–90cm (24–36in), S 60cm (24in).

Argyranthemum frutescens,
syn. *Chrysanthemum frutescens*
(Marguerite)
Evergreen, woody-based, bushy
perennial that bears many daisy-like,
white, yellow or pink flower heads
throughout summer. Attractive leaves
are fresh green. H and S 1m (3ft).

***Aruncus dioicus* 'Kneiffii'**
Hummock-forming perennial that has
deeply cut, feathery leaves with lance-
shaped leaflets on elegant stems and
bears branching plumes of tiny, star-
shaped, creamy-white flowers in mid-
summer. H 90cm (3ft), S 50cm (20in).

Lysimachia clethroides
Vigorous, clump-forming, spreading
perennial carrying spikes of small,
white flowers above mid-green foliage
in late summer.
H 1m (3ft), S 60cm–1m (2–3ft).

☼ ◊

Rodgersia aesculifolia
Clump-forming, rhizomatous perennial
that is excellent for a bog garden or
pool side. In mid-summer, plumes
of fragrant, pinkish-white flowers rise
from crinkled, bronze foliage like that
of a horse-chestnut tree.
H and S 1m (3ft).

☼ ◊

Morina longifolia
Evergreen perennial that produces
rosettes of large, spiny, thistle-like,
rich green leaves. Whorls of hooded,
tubular, white flowers, flushed pink
within, are borne well above foliage in
mid-summer.
H 60–75cm (2–2½ft), S 30cm (1ft).

☼ ◊

**Veronicastrum virginicum
f. album**
Upright perennial. In late summer,
spires of small, white flowers, with
pink-flushed bases and pink anthers,
crown stems clothed with whorls of
narrow, dark green leaves.
H 1.2m (4ft), S 45cm (1½ft).

☼ ◊

**Papaver orientale 'Perry's
White'**
Hairy-leaved perennial with deep,
fleshy roots. Satiny, white flowers with
purple centres appear on strong stems
in early summer. May need support.
H 80cm (32in), S 60cm (24in).

☼ ◊

Digitalis ferruginea
Perennial, best treated as a biennial,
with long, slender spikes bearing many
funnel-shaped, pale orange-brown and
white flowers in mid-summer above
basal rosettes of oval, rough leaves.
Propagate from seed.
H 1–1.2m (3–4ft), S 30cm (1ft).

☼ ◊ ①

Gillenia trifoliata
Upright perennial with many wiry,
branching stems carrying clusters of
dainty, white flowers with reddish-
brown calyces in summer. Leaves are
dark green and lance-shaped. Needs
staking. Thrives in most situations.
H 1–1.2m (3–4ft), S 60cm (2ft).

☼ ◊

Valeriana officinalis
(Cat's valerian, Common valerian)
Clump-forming, fleshy perennial that
bears spikes of white to deep pink
flowers in summer. Leaves are deeply
toothed and mid-green. Has
disadvantage of attracting cats.
H 1–1.2m (3–4ft), S 1m (3ft).

☼ ◊

Campanula persicifolia 'Fleur de Neige'
Gaura lindheimeri
Leucanthemum x *superbum* 'Aglaia'
Leucanthemum x *superbum* 'Wirral Supreme'

PHLOX, illus. p.242
Ranunculus aconitifolius 'Flore Pleno',
   illus. p.233
Smilacina racemosa, illus. p.233

Xerophyllum tenax

Phlox

Border phlox (cultivars of *Phlox maculata* and *P. paniculata*) are considered to be some of the most elegant and stately of garden plants and are a mainstay of the herbaceous border in mid- to late summer. Their dome-shaped or conical panicles of flowers, which are often delicately scented, are produced in shades that include white, pink, red and purple. Many of the flowers have attractive, contrasting eyes. Some cultivars have strikingly variegated foliage and make a bold feature before the flowers appear.

Phlox thrive in sun or partial shade and in humus-rich, well-drained soil. Taller varieties may need staking. If larger flowers are required, reduce the number of stems in spring, when the plant is about a quarter to a third of its eventual height, by pinching out or cutting back the weakest shoots. To prolong the flowering season, cutting back the central part of the flower head as the blooms fade will encourage the sideshoots to flower. Once the plants have finished flowering in autumn they should be cut back to the ground.

Border phlox are particularly susceptible to eelworm; to avoid infestation, plant only young, healthy stock propagated from root cuttings taken from clean stock. Any plants that show signs of disease should be dug up and burnt. It is advisable not to replant infested soil with phlox for at least two seasons.

P. paniculata 'Eva Cullum'

P. paniculata 'Brigadier'

P. paniculata 'Eventide'

P. paniculata 'Norah Leigh'

P. paniculata 'Graf Zeppelin'

P. paniculata 'Balmoral'

P. paniculata 'Harlequin'

P. maculata 'Alpha'

P. paniculata 'Windsor'

P. paniculata 'Le Mahdi'

P. paniculata 'Fujiyama'

P. paniculata 'Sandringham'

P. maculata 'Omega'

P. paniculata 'Mia Ruys'

P. paniculata 'White Admiral'

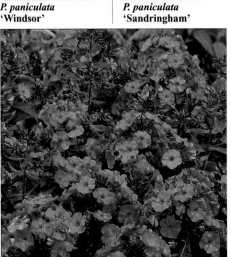

P. paniculata 'Mother of Pearl'

P. paniculata 'Prince of Orange'

P. paniculata 'Amethyst'

P. paniculata 'Hampton Court'

☐ PINK

***Linaria purpurea*
'Canon J. Went'**
Upright perennial bearing spikes of
snapdragon-like, pink blooms with
orange-tinged throats from mid- to
late summer. Has narrow,
grey-green leaves.
H 60cm–1m (2–3ft), S 60cm (2ft).

***Geranium* x *oxonianum*
'Winscombe'**
Semi-evergreen, carpeting perennial
with dense, dainty, lobed leaves and
cup-shaped, deep pink flowers,
which fade to pale pink, borne
throughout summer.
H 60–75cm (24–30in), S 45cm (18in).

Malva moschata
Bushy, branching perennial producing
successive spikes of saucer-shaped,
rose-pink flowers during early summer.
Narrow, lobed, divided leaves are
slightly scented.
H 60cm–1m (2–3ft), S 60cm (2ft).

Dictamnus albus* var. *purpureus
Upright perennial. In early summer
bears stiff spikes of fragrant, star-
shaped, purplish-pink, sometimes paler,
flowers with long stamens. Has light
green leaves divided into oval leaflets.
Dislikes disturbance.
H 1m (3ft), S 60cm (2ft).

***Persicaria bistorta* 'Superba'**, syn.
Polygonum bistorta 'Superbum'
Vigorous, clump-forming perennial
that from early to late summer
produces spikes of soft pink flowers
above oval leaves.
H 60–75cm (24–30in), S 60cm (24in).

***Monarda* 'Croftway Pink'**
Clump-forming perennial carrying
whorls of hooded, soft pink blooms
throughout summer above neat mounds
of aromatic foliage.
H 1m (3ft), S 45cm (1½ft).

***Argyranthemum* 'Mary
Wootton'**, syn. *Chrysanthemum
frutescens* 'Mary Wootton'
Evergreen, woody-based, bushy
perennial bearing daisy-like, pink
flower heads throughout summer.
Has attractive, fern-like, divided, pale
green foliage. H and S to 1m (3ft).

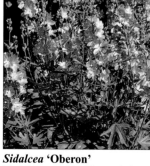

***Sidalcea* 'Oberon'**
Upright perennial with rounded,
deeply cut leaves divided into
narrowly oblong segments. In
summer, produces racemes of
shallowly cup-shaped, clear pink
flowers. H 60cm (24in), S 45cm (18in).

Anemone hupehensis 'Hadspen Abundance',
 illus. p.259
Astrantia major, illus. p.277
Astrantia maxima, illus. p.277

Campanula lactiflora 'Loddon Anna'
Chelone obliqua, illus. p.259
Lythrum virgatum 'Rose Queen'
PELARGONIUMS, illus. pp.246–7

PEONIES, illus. pp.236–7
Sidalcea 'Loveliness'
Sidalcea 'Oberon'
Tanacetum coccineum 'Brenda', illus. p.238

Tanacetum coccineum 'Eileen May
 Robinson'
Tanacetum coccineum 'James Kelway'

PERENNIALS *(side tab)*

Physostegia virginiana 'Variegata'
Erect perennial. In late summer produces spikes of tubular, purplish-pink blooms that can be placed into position. Toothed, mid-green leaves are white-variegated.
H 1–1.2m (3–4ft), S 60cm (2ft).

 ☀ ◐

Rehmannia elata,
syn. *R. angulata* of gardens
Straggling perennial bearing foxglove-like, yellow-throated, rose-purple flowers in leaf axils of notched, stem-clasping, soft leaves from early to mid-summer. H 1m (3ft), S 45cm (1½ft). Min. 1°C (34°F).

 ☀ ◐

Astilbe 'Venus'
Leafy perennial bearing feathery, tapering plumes of tiny, pale pink flowers in summer. Foliage is broad and divided into leaflets; flowers remain on the plant, dried and brown, well into winter. Prefers humus-rich soil. H and S to 1m (3ft).

 ☀ ◐

Lupinus 'The Chatelaine'
Clump-forming perennial carrying spikes of pink-and-white flowers above divided, mid-green foliage in early summer.
H 1.2m (4ft), S 45cm (1½ft).

 ☀ ◐ ①

Astilbe 'Straussenfeder'
Leafy perennial with handsome, divided foliage and arching, feathery, tapering plumes of tiny, coral-pink flowers in summer. Dry, brown flowers remain on the plant well into winter. Prefers humus-rich soil.
H and S to 1m (3ft).

 ☀ ◐

Echinacea purpurea 'Robert Bloom'
Upright perennial. Has lance-shaped, dark green leaves and large, daisy-like, deep crimson-pink flower heads, with conical, brown centres, borne singly on strong stems in summer. Needs humus-rich soil. H 1.2m (4ft), S 50cm (20in).

 ☀ ◐

Centaurea pulcherrima
Upright perennial with deeply cut, silvery leaves. Rose-pink flower heads, with thistle-like centres paler than surrounding star-shaped ray petals, are borne singly on slender stems in summer. H 75cm (2½ft), S 60cm (2ft).

☀ ◐

Kohleria digitaliflora
Erect, bushy, rhizomatous perennial with white-haired stems. Has scalloped, hairy leaves and stalked clusters of tubular, very hairy, pink-and-white flowers, with purple-spotted, green lobes, in summer-autumn. H 60cm (24in) or more, S 45cm (18in). Min. 15°C (59°F).

 ☀ ◐

Caladium x *bicolor* 'Pink Cloud'
Chrysanthemum 'Clara Curtis', illus. p.259
DAYLILIES, illus. p.257

Dierama dracomontanum
Erigeron 'Foerster's Liebling'
Heuchera 'Coral Cloud'
Heuchera 'Scintillation'

Liatris pycnostachya
Lythrum salicaria 'Robert'
Papaver orientale 'Mrs Perry'
PEONIES, illus. pp.236–7

PHLOX, illus. p.242
Rodgersia pinnata 'Superba'
Verbascum 'Pink Domino'

Dicentra spectabilis (Bleeding heart, Dutchman's trousers)
Leafy perennial forming a hummock of fern-like, deeply cut, mid-green foliage, above which rise arching stems carrying pendent, heart-shaped, pinkish-red and white flowers in late spring and summer. H 75cm (30in), S 50cm (20in).

☀ ◊ ⓘ

Lythrum salicaria 'Feuerkerze', syn. *L.s.* 'Firecandle'
Clump-forming perennial for a waterside or bog garden. Bears spikes of intense rose-red blooms from mid- to late summer. Cultivation may be prohibited. H 1m (3ft), S 45cm (1½ft).

☀ ◕

Mirabilis jalapa (Four o'clock flower, Marvel of Peru)
Bushy, tuberous perennial. Fragrant, trumpet-shaped, crimson, pink, white or yellow flowers, opening in evening, cover mid-green foliage in summer. H 60cm–1.2m (2–4ft), S 60–75cm (2–2½ft). Min. 2°C (35°F).

☀ ◊

Lupinus 'Inverewe Red'
Upright perennial with divided, bright green leaves. In early summer bears tall, upright racemes of red flowers. Cut back after flowering. May be short-lived. H 1–1.2m (3–4ft), S 60cm (2ft).

☀ ◊ ⓘ

Filipendula purpurea
Upright perennial with deeply divided leaves. Produces large, terminal heads of masses of tiny, rich reddish-purple flowers in summer. Makes a good waterside plant.
H 1.2m (4ft), S 60cm (2ft).

☀ ◕

Lythrum virgatum 'The Rocket'
Clump-forming perennial that carries slender spikes of rose-red flowers above mid-green foliage during summer. Good for a waterside or bog garden. Cultivation may be prohibited. H 1m (3ft), S 45cm (1½ft).

☀ ◕

Geranium psilostemon, syn. *G. armenum*
Clump-forming perennial that has broad, deeply cut leaves with good autumn colour and many cup-shaped, single, black-centred, magenta flowers in mid-summer. H and S 1.2m (4ft).

☀ ◊

Centranthus ruber (Red valerian)
Perennial forming spreading colonies of fleshy leaves. Branching heads of small, star-shaped, deep reddish-pink or white flowers are borne above foliage from late spring to autumn. Thrives in poor, exposed sites. H 60–90cm (24–36in), S 45–60cm (18–24in) or more.

☀ ◊

Pelargoniums

Pelargoniums are cultivated for their colourful flowers. They grow happily in containers or beds and flower almost continuously in warm climates or in a greenhouse. To flower well, they need warmth, sunshine (without too much humidity) and well-drained soil.

Zonal – the common geranium: plants with rounded leaves, distinctively marked with a darker 'zone' and single to double flowers.
Regal – shrubby plants with deeply serrated leaves and exotic, broadly trumpet-shaped flowers that are prone to weather damage in the open.
Ivy-leaved – trailing plants, ideal for hanging baskets, with lobed, somewhat fleshy leaves and single to double flowers.
Scented-leaved and **species** – plants with small, often irregularly star-shaped flowers; scented-leaved forms are grown for their fragrant leaves.
Unique – tall-growing sub-shrubs with regal-like, brightly coloured flowers that are borne continuously through the season. Leaves, which may be scented, vary in shape.

P. 'Dale Queen'
(zonal) ①

P. 'Purple Emperor'
(regal) ①

P. 'Fragrans'
(scented-leaved) ①

P. 'Butterfly Lorelei'
(zonal) ①

P. 'Apple Blossom Rosebud' (zonal) ①

P. 'Timothy Clifford'
(zonal) ①

P. 'Ivalo' (zonal) ①

P. 'Clorinda'
(scented-leaved) ①

P. 'Mauritania'
(zonal) ①

P. 'Golden Lilac Mist'
(zonal) ①

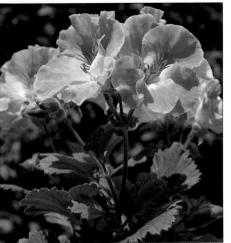

P. 'Autumn Festival'
(regal) ①

P. 'Cherry Blossom'
(zonal) ①

P. 'Rica'
(zonal) ①

P. 'Fraiche Beauté'
(zonal) ①

P. 'Fair Ellen'
(scented-leaved) ①

P. 'Francis Parrett'
(zonal) ①

P. acetosum
(species) ①

P. 'Mr Henry Cox'
(zonal) ①

P. 'Schöne Helena'
(zonal) ①

P. 'Leslie Judd'
(regal) ①

P. 'Mr Everaarts'
(zonal) ①

P. 'Manx Maid'
(regal) ①

P. 'Brookside Primrose' (zonal) ①

P. 'The Boar'
(species) ①

P. 'Lachskönigin'
(ivy-leaved) ①

P. 'Lachsball'
(zonal) ①

P. 'Alberta'
(zonal) ①

P. 'Amethyst'
(ivy-leaved) ①

P. 'Mini Cascade'
(ivy-leaved) ℗

P. 'Madame Fournier'
(zonal) ℗

P. 'Bredon'
(regal) ℗

P. 'Gustav Emich'
(zonal) ℗

P. 'L'Elégante'
(ivy-leaved) ℗

P. 'Caligula' (zonal) ℗

P. 'Paton's Unique'
(unique) ℗

P. 'Rouletta'
(ivy-leaved) ℗

P. 'Dolly Varden'
(zonal) ℗

P. 'Voodoo' (unique) ℗

P. 'Royal Oak'
(scented-leaved) ℗

P. 'Tip Top Duet'
(regal) ℗

P. 'Paul Humphries'
(zonal) ℗

P. 'Flower of Spring'
(zonal) ℗

P. 'Robe' (zonal) ℗

P. capitatum
(scented-leaved) ℗

P. tomentosum
(scented-leaved) ℗

P. 'Friesdorf'
(zonal) ℗

P. 'Irene'
(zonal) ℗

P. 'Mrs Pollock'
(zonal) ℗

P. 'Polka' (unique) ℗

P. 'Purple Unique'
(unique) ℗

P. crispum 'Variegatum'
(scented-leaved) ℗

P. 'Tavira'
(ivy-leaved) ℗

P. 'Purple Wonder'
(zonal) ℗

P. 'Mabel Grey'
(scented-leaved) ℗

P. 'Rollisson's
Unique' (unique) ℗

P. 'Capen' (zonal) ℗

P. 'Orange Ricard'
(zonal) ℗

P. 'Prince of Orange'
(scented-leaved) ℗

P. 'Mrs Quilter'
(zonal) ℗

Penstemons

Increasingly valued by gardeners for their long racemes of foxglove-like flowers, penstemons are among the most elegant and reliable of border perennials. A large number of excellent cultivars is available, in a subtle range of colours that includes white, pastel and deep pink, warm cherry-red, clear blue and dusky purple. Many penstemon flowers have contrasting white throats or are attractively streaked with other colours.

Penstemons flower most prolifically in summer, but the display can be prolonged into autumn provided the plants are regularly dead-headed throughout the season. Some taller cultivars may benefit from being staked.

Penstemons thrive in well-drained soil, preferably with full sun as some are not fully hardy. Where winters are expected to be severe, the plants should be lifted after flowering and before the first frosts and overwintered in a cool basement. Plants are more likely to survive freezing if they are grown in a sheltered spot in free-draining soil.

Penstemons are generally not long-lived plants and tend to become woody at the base after a few seasons; they should be regularly replaced with younger plants propagated from softwood cuttings of non-flowering shoots taken in mid- to late summer.

P. 'Apple Blossom'

P. 'Pennington Gem'

P. 'Schoenholzeri'

P. 'Alice Hindley'

P. 'Rubicundus'

P. cardwellii

P. 'Maurice Gibbs'

P. 'Chester Scarlet'

P. 'Burgundy'

P. 'Stapleford Gem'

P. fruticosus subsp. *scouleri* f. *albus*

P. 'Evelyn'

P. 'Countess of Dalkeith'

P. heterophyllus

P. 'White Bedder'

P. 'Beech Park'

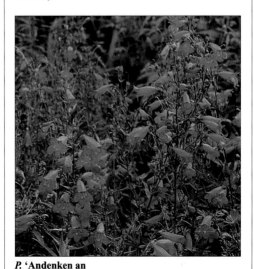

P. 'Andenken an Friedrich Hahn'

P. 'Sour Grapes'

PERENNIALS medium SUMMER INTEREST

■ RED

***Aquilegia vulgaris* 'Nora Barlow'**
Leafy perennial that in summer has several short-spurred, funnel-shaped, double, red flowers, pale green at the tips, on long stems. Leaves are grey-green, rounded and deeply divided.
H 60–75cm (24–30in), S 50cm (20in).

☼ ◊ ①

***Persicaria amplexicaulis*
'Firetail'**, syn. *Polygonum amplexicaule* 'Firetail'
Clump-forming perennial that carries slender spikes of bright red flowers above heart-shaped leaves in summer-autumn. H and S 1–1.2m (3–4ft).

☼ ◗ ①

Lychnis chalcedonica
(Jerusalem cross, Maltese cross)
Neat, clump-forming perennial that bears flat heads of small, vermilion flowers at the tips of stout stems in early summer. Foliage is mid-green.
H 1–1.2m (3–4ft), S 30–45cm (1–1½ft).

☼ ◊

***Lobelia* 'Cherry Ripe'**
Clump-forming perennial bearing spikes of cerise-scarlet flowers from mid- to late summer. Leaves, usually fresh green, are often tinged red-bronze. H 1m (3ft), S 23cm (9in).

☼ ◗

***Astilbe* 'Montgomery'**
Leafy perennial bearing feathery, tapering plumes of tiny, deep salmon-red flowers in summer. Foliage is broad and divided into leaflets; flowers, brown when dried, remain on the plant well into winter. Prefers humus-rich soil. H 75cm (2½ft), S to 1m (3ft).

☼ ◗

***Knautia macedonica*,**
syn. *Scabiosa rumelica*
Upright perennial with deeply divided leaves and many rather lax, branching stems bearing double, almost globular, bright crimson flower heads in summer. Needs staking.
H 75cm (30in), S 60cm (24in).

☼ ◊

***Cosmos atrosanguineus*,**
syn. *Bidens atrosanguinea*
(Chocolate cosmos)
Upright, tuberous perennial with chocolate-scented, maroon-crimson flower heads in late summer. In warm areas tubers may overwinter if protected.
H 60cm (24in) or more, S 45cm (18in).

☼ ◊

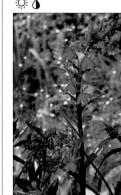

***Lobelia* 'Queen Victoria'**
Clump-forming perennial. From late summer to mid-autumn spikes of blazing red flowers on branching stems arise from basal, deep red-purple foliage. H 1m (3ft), S 30cm (1ft).

☼ ◗

***Ruellia graecizans*,** syn. *R. amoena*
Evergreen, bushy sub-shrub with wide-spreading stems. Oval, pointed leaves are 10cm (4in) long. Intermittently bears clusters of small, tubular, scarlet flowers on stalks to 10cm (4in) long.
H and S 60cm (24in) or more.
Min. 15°C (59°F).

☼ ◗

 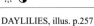
PERENNIALS

249

■ RED

■ RED–PURPLE

Hedysarum coronarium
(French honeysuckle)
Spreading, shrubby perennial or
biennial. Spikes of pea-like, bright red
flowers are produced in summer above
divided, mid-green leaves.
H and S 1m (3ft).

☼ ◊

Russelia equisetiformis,
syn. *R. juncea* (Coral plant)
Evergreen, branching, bushy sub-shrub
with rush-like stems and tiny leaves.
Showy, pendent clusters of tubular,
scarlet flowers appear in summer-
autumn. H to 1m (3ft) or more,
S 60cm (2ft). Min. 15°C (59°F).

☼ ◊

Anigozanthos manglesii
(Red-and-green kangaroo paw)
Vigorous, bushy perennial that bears
racemes of large, tubular, woolly, red-
and-green flowers in spring and early
summer. Has long, narrow, grey-green
leaves. H 1m (3ft), S 45cm (1½ft).
Min. 5°C (41°F).

☼ ◊ pH

Kohleria eriantha
Robust, bushy, rhizomatous perennial
with reddish-haired stems. Oval leaves,
to 13cm (5in) long, are edged with red
hairs. Has tubular, red flowers, with
yellow-spotted lobes, in nodding
clusters in summer. H and S 1m (3ft)
or more. Min. 15°C (59°F).

☼ ◊

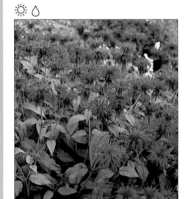

***Monarda* 'Cambridge Scarlet'**
Clump-forming perennial that
throughout summer bears whorls of
hooded, rich red flowers above neat
mounds of aromatic, hairy foliage.
H 1m (3ft), S 45cm (1½ft).

☼ ◊

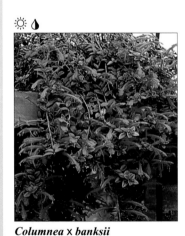

Columnea* x *banksii
Evergreen, trailing perennial with oval,
fleshy leaves, glossy above, purplish-
red below. Tubular, hooded, brilliant
red flowers, to 8cm (3in) long, appear
from spring to winter. Makes a useful
plant for a hanging basket. H 1m (3ft),
S indefinite. Min. 15°C (59°F).

☼ ◊

***Papaver orientale* 'Allegro'**,
syn. *P.o.* 'Allegro Viva'
Hairy-leaved perennial with very
deep, fleshy roots. Papery, bright
scarlet flowers are borne in summer
on strong stems.
H 60–75cm (24–30in), S 45cm (18in).

☼ ◊

***Papaver orientale* 'Beauty of
Livermere'**
Hairy-leaved perennial with deep,
fleshy roots. Large, solitary, cup-
shaped, crimson-scarlet flowers, with
a black mark at the base of each petal,
are borne from late spring to mid-
summer. H 1–1.2m (3–4ft), S 1m (3ft).

☼ ◊

Glycyrrhiza glabra (Liquorice)
Upright perennial that has pea-like,
purple-blue and white flowers, borne
in short spikes on erect stems in late
summer, and large leaves divided into
oval leaflets. Is grown commercially
for production of liquorice.
H 1.2m (4ft), S 1m (3ft).

☼ ◊

Asclepias curassavica
Calceolaria integrifolia
Gaillardia x *grandiflora* 'Dazzler',
  illus. p.283

Geum 'Fire Opal'
Geum 'Mrs J. Bradshaw'
ORCHIDS, illus. pp.296–9
Papaver orientale

Smithiantha zebrina

PELARGONIUMS, illus. pp.246–7

PERENNIALS

Acanthus hungaricus,
syn. *A. balcanicus, A. longifolius*
Perennial with long, deeply cut, basal, dark green leaves. Spikes of white or pink-flushed flowers, set in spiny, red-purple bracts, are carried in summer.
H 60cm–1m (2–3ft), S 1m (3ft).

Linaria triornithophora
(Three birds toadflax)
Upright perennial that from early to late summer produces spikes of snapdragon-like, purple and yellow flowers above narrow, grey-green leaves. H 1m (3ft), S 60cm (2ft).

Monarda fistulosa
Clump-forming perennial that produces small heads of lilac-purple flowers from mid- to late summer.
H 1.2m (4ft), S 45cm (1½ft).

Campanula glomerata 'Superba'
Vigorous, clump-forming perennial with dense, rounded heads of large, bell-shaped, purple flowers borne in summer. Bears oval leaves in basal rosettes and on flower stems. Must be divided and replanted regularly.
H 75cm (2½ft), S 1m (3ft) or more.

Acanthus spinosus
Stately perennial that has very large, arching, deeply cut and spiny-pointed, glossy, dark green leaves. Spires of funnel-shaped, soft mauve and white flowers are borne freely in summer.
H 1.2m (4ft), S 60cm (2ft) or more.

Geranium sylvaticum 'Mayflower'
Upright perennial with a basal clump of deeply lobed leaves, above which rise branching stems of cup-shaped, violet-blue flowers in early summer.
H 1m (3ft), S 60cm (2ft).

Thalictrum aquilegiifolium
Clump-forming perennial with a mass of finely divided, grey-green leaves, resembling those of maidenhair fern. Bunched heads of fluffy, lilac-purple flowers are borne on strong stems in summer.
H 1–1.2m (3–4ft), S 45cm (1½ft).

Veronica spicata 'Romiley Purple'
Clump-forming perennial that in summer freely produces large spikes of purple flowers above whorled, mid-green leaves.
H 1–1.2m (3–4ft), S 30–60cm (1–2ft).

■ PURPLE

Campanula trachelium
(Nettle-leaved bellflower)
Upright perennial with rough, serrated,
oval, pointed, basal leaves. Wide, bell-
shaped, blue or purple-blue flowers are
spaced along erect stems in summer.
H 60cm–1m (2–3ft), S 30cm (1ft).

☼ ◊

Dichorisandra reginae
Evergreen, erect, clump-forming
perennial. Glossy, often silver-banded
and flecked leaves are purple-red
beneath. Has small spikes of densely
set, purple-blue flowers in summer-
autumn. H 60–75cm (24–30in),
S to 30cm (12in). Min. 20°C (68°F).

◑ ◊

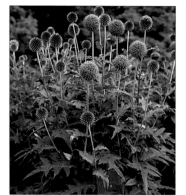

***Echinops ritro* 'Veitch's Blue'**
Upright perennial with round, thistle-
like, purplish-blue heads of flowers
carried in late summer on silvery
stems. Sharply divided leaves have
pale down beneath.
H 1.2m (4ft), S 75cm (2½ft).

☼ ◊

Galega orientalis
Vigorous, upright but compact
perennial that in summer bears spikes
of pea-like, blue-tinged, violet flowers
above delicate leaves divided into oval
leaflets. Needs staking. Spreads freely.
H 1.2m (4ft), S 60cm (2ft).

☼ ◊

***Campanula trachelium* 'Bernice'**
Upright perennial that has wide, bell-
shaped, double, purple-violet flowers
carried along erect stems in summer.
Leaves are mostly basal and are rough,
serrated, oval and pointed.
H 75cm (30in), S 30cm (12in).

☼ ◊

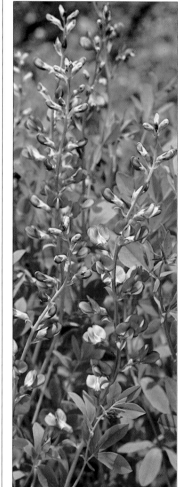

***Salvia* × *superba* 'Mainacht',**
syn. *S.* × *s.* 'May Night'
Neat, clump-forming perennial with
narrow, wrinkled, mid-green leaves.
In late spring and summer bears stiff
racemes of violet-blue flowers.
H 1m (3ft), S 45cm (1½ft).

☼ ◊

***Aconitum* × *cammarum* 'Bicolor',**
syn. *A.* × *bicolor*
Compact, tuberous perennial with
violet-blue and white flowers borne in
summer along upright stems. Has
deeply cut, divided, glossy, dark green
leaves and poisonous roots.
H 1.2m (4ft), S 50cm (20in).

☼ ◊ ⓘ

Baptisia australis (False indigo)
Upright perennial bearing spikes
of pea-like, violet-blue flowers in
summer. Bright green leaves are
divided into oval leaflets. Dark grey
seed pods may be used for winter
decoration.
H 75cm (30in), S 60cm (24in).

☼ ◊

Dianella tasmanica
Upright perennial with nodding, star-shaped, bright blue or purple-blue flowers carried in branching sprays in summer, followed by deep blue berries in autumn. Has untidy, evergreen, strap-shaped leaves. H 1.2m (4ft), S 50cm (20in). Min. 2°C (35°F).

Eryngium alpinum
Upright perennial with basal rosettes of heart-shaped, deeply toothed, glossy foliage, above which rise stout stems bearing, in summer, heads of conical, purplish-blue flower heads, surrounded by blue bracts and soft spines.
H 75cm–1m (2½–3ft), S 60cm (2ft).

Eryngium x tripartitum
Perennial with wiry stems above a basal rosette of coarsely toothed, grey-green leaves. Conical, metallic-blue flower heads on blue stems are borne in summer-autumn and may be dried for winter decoration.
H 1–1.2m (3–4ft), S 50cm (20in).

Meconopsis grandis (Blue poppy)
Erect perennial with oblong, slightly toothed, hairy, mid-green leaves produced in rosettes at the base. Stout stems bear slightly nodding, cup-shaped, deep blue flowers in early summer. Divide every 2–3 years.
H 1–1.5m (3–5ft), S 30cm (1ft).

Campanula persicifolia 'Telham Beauty'
Perennial with basal rosettes of narrow, bright green leaves. In summer, large, nodding, cup-shaped, light blue flowers are borne on slender spikes.
H 1m (3ft), S 30cm (1ft).

Meconopsis betonicifolia (Blue poppy)
Clump-forming perennial that bears blue flowers in late spring and early summer. Oblong, mid-green leaves are produced in basal rosettes and in decreasing size up flowering stems.
H 1–1.2m (3–4ft), S 45cm (1½ft).

Eryngium x oliverianum
Upright perennial that produces large, rounded heads of thistle-like, blue to lavender-blue flowers in late summer. Has heart-shaped, jagged-edged, basal, mid-green leaves. H 60cm–1m (2–3ft), S 45–60cm (1½–2ft).

Cichorium intybus (Chicory)
Clump-forming perennial with basal rosettes of light green leaves and daisy-like, bright blue flower heads borne along upper parts of willowy stems in summer. Flowers are at their best before noon.
H 1.2m (4ft), S 45cm (1½ft).

Agapanthus 'Dorothy Palmer'
Clump-forming perennial bearing rounded heads of rich blue flowers, fading to reddish-mauve, on erect stems in late summer. Leaves are narrow and greyish-green. Protect crowns in winter with mulch or bring inside. H 1m (3ft), S 50cm (20in).

PERENNIALS

■ BLUE

▣▢ GREEN–YELLOW

Agapanthus praecox subsp. orientalis, syn. *A. orientalis*
Perennial with large, dense umbels of sky-blue flowers borne on strong stems in late summer over clumps of broad, almost evergreen, dark green leaves. Makes a good plant for pots. H 1m (3ft), S 60cm (2ft). Min. 2°C (35°F).

☀ ◊

Euphorbia schillingii
Robust, clump-forming perennial that produces long-lasting, yellow cyathia and rounded, greenish-yellow bracts from mid-summer to mid-autumn. Stems are erect and leaves are dark green with pale green or white veins. H 1m (3ft), S 30cm (1ft).

◐ ◊ ⚠

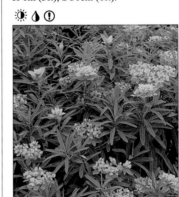

Euphorbia sikkimensis
Spreading, upright perennial bearing yellow cyathia cupped by pale to greenish-yellow involucres in mid- to late summer. Young shoots are bright pink and the leaves deep green. H 1.2m (4ft), S 45cm (1½ft).

◐ ◊ ⚠

Verbascum 'Gainsborough'
Semi-evergreen, rosette-forming, short-lived perennial bearing branched racemes of 5-lobed, pale sulphur-yellow flowers throughout summer above oval, mid-green leaves borne on flower stems. H 60cm–1.2m (2–4ft), S 30–60cm (1–2ft).

☀ ◊

Nepeta sibirica,
syn. *Dracocephalum sibiricum,*
N. macrantha
Erect, leafy perennial that bears long, whorled cymes of blue to lavender-blue flowers in mid- and late summer. Leaves are dark green and aromatic. H 90cm (36in), S 45cm (18in).

☀ ◊

Anchusa azurea 'Loddon Royalist'
Upright perennial that bears flat, single, deep blue flowers on branching spikes in early summer. Most of the lance-shaped, coarse, hairy leaves are at the base of plant. Needs staking. H 1.2m (4ft), S 60cm (2ft).

☀ ◊

Anigozanthos flavidus (Yellow kangaroo paw)
Bushy perennial, large, woolly, tubular racemes, at times red-tinged, yellowish-green flowers with reddish anthers, borne in spring-summer. Narrow leaves, 60cm (2ft) long, mid-green. H 1.2m (4ft), S 45cm (1½ft). Min. 5°C (41°F).

☀ ◊ pH

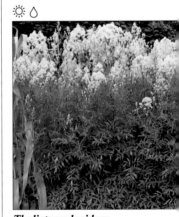

Thalictrum lucidum
Perennial with glossy leaves composed of numerous leaflets. Strong stems bear loose panicles of fluffy, greenish-yellow flowers in summer. H 1–1.2m (3–4ft), S 50cm (20in).

☀ ◊

DELPHINIUMS, illus. p.230
Echinops bannaticus 'Taplow Blue'
Gentiana asclepiadea, illus. p.263
IRISES, illus. pp.234–5

Meconopsis grandis
Salvia nemorosa
Veronica exaltata
Veronica longifolia

Artemisia pontica, illus. p.290
Euphorbia nicaeensis
HOSTAS, illus. pp.288–9
ORCHIDS, illus. pp.296–9

Paris polyphylla
Polygonum virginianum 'Painter's Palette', illus. p.290

PERENNIALS

Argyranthemum 'Jamaica Primrose', syn. *Chrysanthemum frutescens 'Jamaica Primrose'*
Evergreen, woody-based perennial with fern-like, pale green leaves. Daisy-like, single, soft yellow flower heads are borne in summer. Take stem cuttings in early autumn. H and S to 1m (3ft).

☼ ◊

Aconitum lycoctonum subsp. vulparia, syn. *A. orientale of gardens, A. vulparia (Wolf's bane)*
Upright, fibrous perennial that has hooded, straw-yellow flowers in summer. Leaves are dark green and deeply divided. Needs staking. H 1–1.2m (3–4ft), S 30–60cm (1–2ft).

☼◐ ◊ ⓘ

Gentiana lutea *(Great yellow gentian)*
Erect, unbranched perennial with oval, stalkless leaves to 30cm (1ft) long. In summer has dense whorls of tubular, yellow flowers in axils of greenish bracts. H 1–1.2m (3–4ft), S 60cm (2ft).

☼ ◊

Phlomis russeliana
Evergreen perennial, forming excellent ground cover, with large, rough, heart-shaped leaves. Stout flower stems bear whorls of hooded, butter-yellow flowers in summer.
H 1m (3ft), S 60cm (2ft) or more.

☼ ◊

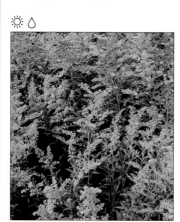

Solidago 'Goldenmosa'
Clump-forming perennial. Sprays of tufted, mimosa-like, yellow flower heads are carried in late summer and autumn above lance-shaped, toothed, hairy, yellowish-green leaves. H 1m (3ft), S 60cm (2ft).

☼ ◊

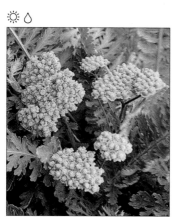

Anthemis tinctoria 'E.C. Buxton'
Clump-forming perennial with a mass of daisy-like, lemon-yellow flower heads borne singly in summer on slim stems. Cut back hard after flowering to promote a good rosette of crinkled leaves for winter. H and S 1m (3ft).

☼ ◊

Lysimachia punctata *(Garden loosestrife)*
Clump-forming perennial that in summer produces spikes of bright yellow flowers above mid-green leaves. H 60–75cm (24–30in), S 60cm (24in).

☼ ◐

Achillea 'Schwellenberg'
Low-growing, spreading perennial with branched stems and grey-green foliage. Silvery buds are followed by lemon-yellow flower heads from early summer to early autumn.
H 45cm (18in), S 60cm (24in).

☼ ◊ ⓘ

PERENNIALS

Thermopsis rhombifolia,
syn. *T. montana*
Upright perennial bearing spikes of
bright yellow flowers above divided,
mid-green leaves in summer.
H 60cm–1m (2–3ft), S 60cm (2ft).

Inula hookeri
Clump-forming perennial with lance-
shaped to elliptic, hairy leaves and
a mass of slightly scented, daisy-like,
greenish-yellow flower heads borne
in summer.
H 75cm (30in), S 45cm (18in).

Aphelandra squarrosa 'Louisae'
Evergreen, erect perennial. Long, oval,
glossy, slightly wrinkled, dark green
leaves have white veins and midribs.
Bears dense spikes of golden-yellow
flowers from axils of yellow bracts in
late summer to autumn. H to 1m (3ft),
S 60cm (2ft). Min. 13°C (55°F).

Solidago 'Laurin'
Compact perennial bearing spikes of
deep yellow flowers in late summer.
Foliage is mid-green.
H 60–75cm (24–30in), S 45cm (18in).

Achillea 'Coronation Gold'
Upright perennial with feathery,
silvery leaves. Bears large, flat heads of
small, golden flower heads in summer
that dry well for winter decoration.
Should be divided and replanted every
third year. H 1m (3ft), S 60cm (2ft).

Rudbeckia fulgida var. **sullivantii**
'Goldsturm'
Erect perennial. In late summer and
autumn, daisy-like, golden flower
heads with conical, black centres
are borne at the ends of strong stems.
Has narrow, rough, mid-green leaves.
H 75cm (30in), S 30cm (12in) or more.

Verbascum nigrum
Semi-evergreen, clump-forming
perennial bearing narrow spikes of
small, 5-lobed, purple-centred, yellow
flowers during summer and autumn.
Oblong, mid-green leaves are
downy beneath.
H 60cm–1m (2–3ft), S 60cm (2ft).

Inula royleana,
syn. *I. macrocephala* of gardens
Upright, clump-forming perennial with
dark green stems and ovate, hairy
leaves. Bears solitary, orange-yellow
flower heads, 10–12cm (4–5in) across,
from mid-summer to early autumn.
H 45–60cm (18–24in), S 45cm (18in).

Daylilies

Although they belong to the lily family (Liliaceae), daylilies (*Hemerocallis*) are not true lilies; their common name comes from the lily-like flowers that generally last only a day. Daylilies range in size from compact plants that grow only to 30–38cm (12–15in) tall, to large plants that may reach 1.5m (5ft). Modern cultivars are available in a wide range of colours, from creamy-white, through shades of yellow, orange, red, pink and purple, to almost black; some flowers have differently coloured bands on the petals. The flower forms are usually classified as single, double or spider. Some species and a few cultivars are strongly fragrant. Most daylilies flower for four to six weeks; they thrive in almost any soil, except poorly drained clay, in sun or shade, but bloom best if they are in sun for at least half the day. The clumps may be divided in early spring.

H. 'Super Purple'

H. 'Solano Bulls Eye'

H. 'Prairie Blue Eyes'

H. 'Lady Fingers'

H. 'Golden Chimes'

H. 'Joan Senior'

H. 'Jolyene Nichole'

H. 'Gentle Shepherd'

H. 'Chorus Line'

H. lilioasphodelus

H. 'Real Wind'

H. 'Betty Woods'

H. 'Cat's Cradle'

H. 'Ruffled Apricot'

H. 'Millie Schlumpf'

H. 'Marion Vaughn'

H. 'Hyperion'

H. 'Mauna Loa'

H. 'Brocaded Gown'

H. 'Eenie Weenie'

H. 'Siloam Virginia Henson'

H. 'Scarlet Orbit'

H. citrina

H. 'Corky'

H. fulva 'Flore Pleno'

☐ YELLOW

Berkheya macrocephala
Upright perennial bearing large,
daisy-like, yellow flower heads on
branched, spiny-leaved stems
throughout summer. Prefers rich soil
and a warm, sheltered position.
H and S 1m (3ft). Min. 2°C (35°F).

☼ ◊

Achillea filipendulina 'Gold Plate'
Upright perennial with stout, leafy
stems carrying broad, flat, terminal
heads of yellow flowers in summer,
above filigree foliage. Flower heads
retain colour if dried.
Divide plants regularly.
H 1.2m (4ft) or more, S 60cm (2ft).

☼ ◊ ⓘ

☐☐ YELLOW–ORANGE

Kniphofia 'Royal Standard'
Upright perennial with grass-like, basal
tufts of leaves and terminal spikes of
scarlet buds, opening to lemon-yellow
flowers, borne on erect stems in late
summer. Protect crowns with winter
mulch. H 1–1.2m (3–4ft), S 60cm (2ft).

☼ ◊

Sphaeralcea ambigua
Branching, shrubby perennial. Broadly
funnel-shaped, orange-coral blooms
are produced singly in leaf axils from
summer until the onset of cold weather.
Leaves are soft, hairy and mid-green.
H and S 75–90cm (30–36in).

☼ ◊

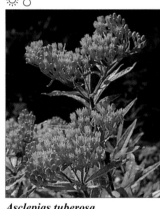

Asclepias tuberosa
(Butterfly weed)
Erect, tuberous perennial with long,
lance-shaped leaves. Small, 5-horned,
bright orange-red flowers are borne
in summer and followed by narrow,
pointed pods, to 15cm (6in) long.
H to 75cm (30in), S 45cm (18in).

☼ ◊ ⓘ

Heliopsis 'Ballet Dancer'
Upright perennial flowering freely
in late summer and bearing double,
yellow flower heads with frilled
petals. Dark green leaves are
coarse and serrated.
H 1–1.2m (3–4ft), S 60cm (2ft).

☼ ◊

Kniphofia thomsonii var.
snowdenii
Upright perennial with grass-like,
basal foliage. In summer bears coral-
pink flowers, with yellowish interiors,
spaced widely along terminal spikes.
Protect crowns with winter mulch.
H 1m (3ft), S 50cm (20in).

☼ ◊

Euphorbia griffithii 'Fireglow'
Bushy perennial that bears orange-red
flowers in terminal umbels in early
summer. Leaves are lance-shaped,
mid-green and have pale red midribs.
H to 1m (3ft), S 50cm (20in).

☼ ◊ ⓘ

PERENNIALS

PERENNIALS medium AUTUMN INTEREST

WHITE–PINK

Actaea pachypoda, syn. *A. alba*
(Doll's eyes, White baneberry)
Compact, clump-forming perennial
with spikes of small, fluffy, white
flowers in summer and clusters of
white berries, borne on stiff, fleshy
scarlet stalks, in autumn.
H 1m (3ft), S 50cm (20in).

☀ ◑ ⊕

Persicaria campanulata,
syn. *Polygonum campanulatum*
Compact, mat-forming perennial
bearing elegant, branching heads of
bell-shaped, pink or white flowers
from mid-summer to early autumn.
Has oval leaves, brown-felted beneath.
H and S 1m (3ft).

☀ ◑ ⊕

Chelone obliqua (Turtle-head)
Upright perennial that bears terminal
spikes of hooded, lilac-pink flowers in
late summer and autumn. Leaves are
dark green and lance-shaped.
H 1m (3ft), S 50cm (20in).

☀ ◑

Tricyrtis formosana,
syn. *T. stolonifera*
Upright, rhizomatous perennial. In
early autumn bears spurred flowers,
heavily spotted with purplish-pink and
with yellow-tinged throats. Glossy,
dark green leaves clasp stems.
H 60cm–1m (2–3ft), S 45cm (1½ft).

☀ ◑

**Anemone hupehensis 'Hadspen
Abundance'**
Erect, branching perennial that bears
pink flowers with rounded, dark
reddish-pink outer tepals from summer
to autumn. Leaves are dark green and
deeply divided, with toothed leaflets.
H 60cm–1.2m (2–4ft), S 45cm (1½ft).

☀ ◑ ⊕

Chrysanthemum 'Clara Curtis',
syn. *C. rubellum* 'Clara Curtis'
Bushy perennial producing many
clusters of flat, daisy-like, clear pink
flower heads throughout summer and
autumn. Divide plants every other
spring. H 75cm (30in), S 45cm (18in).

☀ ◑

OTHER RECOMMENDED PLANTS:
Centranthus ruber, illus. p.245
CHRYSANTHEMUMS, illus. pp.260–61
Cimicifuga simplex 'Elstead'

Kohleria digitaliflora, illus. p.244
MICHAELMAS DAISIES, illus. p.262
PELARGONIUMS, illus. pp.246–7
Schizostylis coccinea 'Sunrise', illus. p.294

Chrysanthemums

PERENNIALS

Florists' chrysanthemum hybrids (botanically now classified under the genus *Dendranthema*) are grouped according to their differing flower forms, approximate flowering season (early, mid- or late autumn) and habit (see also the Plant Dictionary under *Chrysanthemum*). The best groups for garden decoration are the sprays, pompons and early reflexed chrysanthemums. The dwarf charms, forming a dense, dome-shaped mass of flowers, look most attractive displayed in pots. Most groups have only one large flower per stem, although the sprays, charms and pompons have several. The various flower forms are described below.

Incurved – fully double, dense, spherical flowers have incurved petals arising from the base of the flower and closing tightly over the crown.

Fully reflexed – fully double flowers have curved, pointed petals reflexing outwards and downwards from the crown, back to touch the stem.

Reflexed – fully double flowers are similar to those of fully reflexed forms except that the petals are less strongly reflexed and form an umbrella-like or spiky outline.

Intermediate – fully double, roughly spherical flowers have loosely incurving petals, which may close at the crown or may reflex for the bottom half of each flower.

Anemone-centred – single flowers each have a central, dome-shaped disc, up to half the diameter of the bloom, and up to 5 rows of flat, or occasionally spoon-type, ray petals at right angles to the stem.

Single – flowers each have about 5 rows of flat petals, borne at right angles to the stem, that may incurve or reflex at the tips; the prominent, central disc is golden throughout or has a small, green centre.

Pompon – fully double, dense, spherical, or occasionally hemispherical, flowers have tubular petals with flat, rounded tips, growing outwards from the crown.

Spoon-type – flowers are similar to those of single forms except that the ray petals are tubular and open out at their tips to form a spoon shape.

Spider-form – double flower heads with long, thin ray-florets; the outer ray-florets are more or less pendent, the inner ones curling upwards.

Quill-shaped – double flower heads with tubular ray-florets that open out at their tips to form spoon shapes.

C. **'Enbee Wedding'**
(spray, single, early)

C. **'Senkyo Emiaki'**
(spider-form, early)

C. **'Keith Luxford'**
(incurved, late)

C. **'Marian Gosling'**
(reflexed, early)

C. **'Elsie Prosser'**
(reflexed, late)

C. **'Madeleine'** (spray, reflexed, early)

C. **'Brietner'**
(reflexed, early)

C. **'Woking Rose'**
(intermediate, late)

C. **'Pennine Flute'**
(quill-shaped, early)

C. **'Bill Wade'**
(intermediate, early)

C. **'Lundy'**
(reflexed, late)

C. **'Alison Kirk'**
(incurved, early)

C. **'Pennine Oriel'** (spray, anemone, early)

C. **'John Wingfield'**
(reflexed, late)

C. **'Fairweather'**
(incurved, late)

C. **'Ringdove'**
(charm, late)

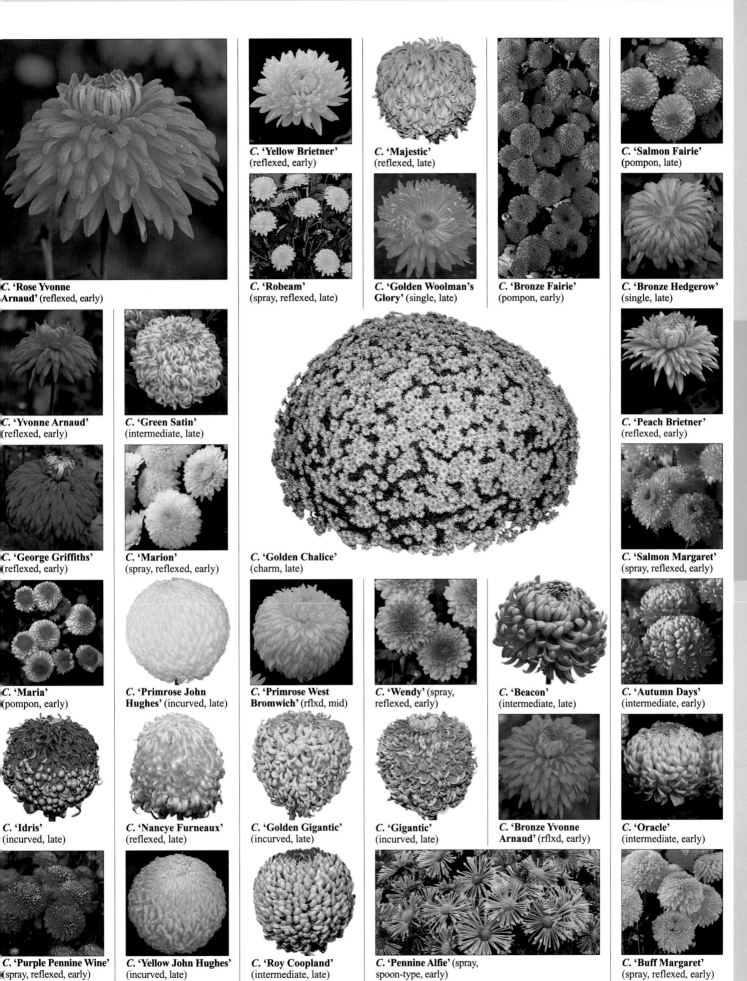

C. 'Rose Yvonne
Arnaud' (reflexed, early)

C. 'Yellow Brietner'
(reflexed, early)

C. 'Majestic'
(reflexed, late)

C. 'Salmon Fairie'
(pompon, late)

C. 'Robeam'
(spray, reflexed, late)

C. 'Golden Woolman's
Glory' (single, late)

C. 'Bronze Fairie'
(pompon, early)

C. 'Bronze Hedgerow'
(single, late)

C. 'Yvonne Arnaud'
(reflexed, early)

C. 'Green Satin'
(intermediate, late)

C. 'Peach Brietner'
(reflexed, early)

C. 'George Griffiths'
(reflexed, early)

C. 'Marion'
(spray, reflexed, early)

C. 'Golden Chalice'
(charm, late)

C. 'Salmon Margaret'
(spray, reflexed, early)

C. 'Maria'
(pompon, early)

C. 'Primrose John
Hughes' (incurved, late)

C. 'Primrose West
Bromwich' (rflxd, mid)

C. 'Wendy' (spray,
reflexed, early)

C. 'Beacon'
(intermediate, late)

C. 'Autumn Days'
(intermediate, early)

C. 'Idris'
(incurved, late)

C. 'Nancye Furneaux'
(reflexed, late)

C. 'Golden Gigantic'
(incurved, late)

C. 'Gigantic'
(incurved, late)

C. 'Bronze Yvonne
Arnaud' (rflxd, early)

C. 'Oracle'
(intermediate, early)

C. 'Purple Pennine Wine'
(spray, reflexed, early)

C. 'Yellow John Hughes'
(incurved, late)

C. 'Roy Coopland'
(intermediate, late)

C. 'Pennine Alfie' (spray,
spoon-type, early)

C. 'Buff Margaret'
(spray, reflexed, early)

Michaelmas daisies

Michaelmas daisies (*Aster* species and cultivars, mostly of *A. novae-angliae* and *A. novi-belgii*) are invaluable border plants as they flower later than most other perennials and continue the display until late autumn. The daisy-like, single or double flowers, usually with yellow centres, range in colour from white, through pink and red, to purple and blue and are excellent for cutting. For larger flowers pinch out or cut back weaker shoots in spring; pinching out the top 2.5–5cm (1–2in) of the remaining shoots produces bushier plants that will bear a greater quantity of smaller flowers. Tall cultivars may need staking. Michaelmas daisies thrive in sun or partial shade in well-drained soil; many are susceptible to mildew, so in areas where this is a problem treat the plants regularly with a fungicide or choose from the resistant varieties available.

A. novae-angliae 'Harrington's Pink'

A. novi-belgii 'Lassie'

A. novi-belgii 'Royal Ruby'

A. novi-belgii 'Freda Ballard'

A. 'Professor Anton Kippenburg'

A. ericoides 'White Heather'

A. ericoides 'Golden Spray'

A. novi-belgii 'Fellowship'

A. n.-a. 'Andenken an Alma Pötschke'

A. frikartii 'Wunder von Stäfa'

A. novae-angliae 'Herbstschnee'

A. lateriflorus 'Horizontalis'

A. novae-angliae 'Barr's Pink'

A. novi-belgii 'Chequers'

A. amellus 'Nocturne'

A. frikartii 'Mönch'

A. novi-belgii 'Sandford White Swan'

A. novi-belgii 'Patricia Ballard'

A. novi-belgii 'Royal Velvet'

A. amellus 'King George'

A. novi-belgii 'Marie Ballard'

A. cordifolius 'Silver Spray'

A. novi-belgii 'Carnival'

A. novi-belgii 'Peace'

A. novi-belgii 'Kristina'

A. novi-belgii 'Apple Blossom'

A. novi-belgii 'Orlando'

A. thomsonii 'Nanus'

A. linosyris

■■▭ PURPLE–YELLOW

Strobilanthes atropurpureus
Upright, branching perennial with oval, toothed leaves. Spikes of numerous, violet-blue to purple flowers appear in summer-autumn. H to 1.2m (4ft), S to 60cm (2ft).

☀ ◊

Gentiana asclepiadea
(Willow gentian)
Arching perennial with narrow, oval leaves to 8cm (3in) long. In late summer to autumn has arching sprays of trumpet-shaped, deep blue flowers, spotted and striped inside.
H to 90cm (36in), S to 60cm (24in).

☀◐ ◊

▭▭ YELLOW–ORANGE

Kirengeshoma palmata
Upright perennial with rounded, lobed, bright green leaves, above which strong stems bearing clusters of narrowly funnel-shaped, creamy yellow flowers appear in late summer to autumn.
H 1m (3ft), S 60cm (2ft).

☀◐ ◊ pH

Kniphofia rooperi,
syn. *K.* 'C.M. Prichard' of gardens
Robust, evergreen perennial with arching, linear, dark green leaves. From early to late autumn, produces broadly ellipsoid racemes of orange-red flowers, becoming orange-yellow. H 1.2m (4ft), S 60cm (2ft).

☀ ◊

Helenium 'Wyndley'
Bushy perennial with branching stems bearing sprays of daisy-like, orange-yellow flower heads for a long period in late summer and autumn. Foliage is dark green. Needs regular division in spring or autumn.
H 80cm (30in), S 50cm (20in).

☀ ◊ ⓘ

Kniphofia 'Percy's Pride'
Upright perennial with large, terminal spikes of creamy flowers, tinged green and yellow, borne on erect stems in autumn. Protect crowns with winter mulch. H 1m (3ft), S 50cm (20in).

☀ ◊

Kniphofia caulescens
Stately, evergreen, upright perennial with basal tufts of narrow, blue-green leaves and smooth, stout stems bearing terminal spikes of reddish-salmon flowers in autumn.
H 1.2m (4ft), S 60cm (2ft).

☀ ◊

Helenium 'Moerheim Beauty'
Upright perennial with strong, branching stems bearing sprays of daisy-like, rich reddish-orange flower heads in early autumn above dark green foliage. Needs regular division in spring or autumn.
H 1m (3ft), S 60cm (2ft).

☀ ◊ ⓘ

◫ WHITE–PINK   ■ RED

Ctenanthe oppenheimiana 'Tricolor'
Robust, evergreen, bushy perennial. Has leathery, lance-shaped leaves, to over 30cm (12in) long, splashed with large, cream blotches, and, intermittently, spikes of 3-petalled, white flowers. H and S 1m (3ft). Min 15°C (59°F).

☼ ◊

Anthurium crystallinum
(Crystal anthurium)
Evergreen, erect, tufted perennial. Long, velvety, dark green leaves are distinctively pale green- to white-veined. Has long-lasting, red-tinged, green spathes. H to 75cm (30in), S to 60cm (24in). Min. 15°C (59°F).

☼ ◊ ⊘

Anthurium andraeanum
(Tail flower)
Evergreen, erect perennial. Long-stalked, oval leaves, with a heart-shaped base, are 20cm (8in) long. Has long-lasting, bright red spathes with yellow spadices. H 60–75cm (24–30in), S 50cm (20in). Min. 15°C (59°F).

☼ ◊ ⊘

Nepenthes × hookeriana
Evergreen, epiphytic, insectivorous perennial with oval, leathery leaves to 30cm (12in) long and pendent, pale green pitchers, with reddish-purple markings and a spurred lid, to 13cm (5in) long. H 60–75cm (24–30in). Min. 18°C (64°F).

☼ ◊

Plectranthus forsteri 'Marginatus'
Evergreen, bushy perennial. Oval leaves, to 6cm (2½in) long, are greyish-green with scalloped, white margins. Irregularly has tubular, white to pale mauve flowers. H and S 60cm (24in) or more. Min. 10°C (50°F).

☼ ◊

Hypoestes phyllostachya,
syn. H. sanguinolenta of gardens (Freckle face, Polka-dot plant)
Evergreen, bush perennial or sub-shrub. Dark green leaves are covered with irregular, pink spots. Bears small, tubular, lavender flowers intermittently. H and S 75cm (30in). Min. 10°C (50°F).

☼ ◊

Dieffenbachia seguine 'Exotica', syn. D. 'Exotica', D. maculata 'Exotica'
Evergreen, tufted perennial, sometimes woody at the base. Broadly lance-shaped leaves, to 45cm (18in) long, are blotched with creamy-white. H and S 1m (3ft) or more. Min. 15°C (59°F).

☼ ◊ ⊘

Caladium bicolor 'Pink Beauty'
Tufted, tuberous perennial. Has long-stalked, triangular, pink-mottled, green leaves, to 45cm (18in) long, with darker pink veins. White spathes appear in summer.
H and S 90cm (3ft). Min. 19°C (66°F).

☼ ◊ ⊘

Phormium 'Dazzler'
Evergreen, upright perennial with tufts of bold, stiff, pointed leaves in tones of yellow, salmon-pink, orange-red and bronze. Bluish-purple stems carry panicles of reddish flowers in summer. H 2–2.5m (6–8ft) in flower, S 1m (3ft).

☼ ◊

PERENNIALS

Bromeliads

Bromeliads, or plants that belong to the family Bromeliaceae, are distinguished by their bold, usually rosetted foliage and showy flowers. Although many are epiphytes, or air plants (absorbing their food through moisture in the atmosphere and not from the host on which they grow), and are suitable for growing outdoors only in tropical regions, they will grow happily indoors in cooler climates.

Aechmea fasciata

Billbergia nutans

Bromelia balansae

Tillandsia lindenii

Cryptanthus zonatus 'Zebrinus'

Ananas bracteatus 'Tricolor'

Puya alpestris

Tillandsia caput-medusae

Neoregelia carolinae 'Tricolor'

Guzmania monostachya

Dyckia remotiflora

Tillandsia argentea

Aechmea distichantha

Aechmea Foster's Favorite Group

Guzmania lingulata var. minor

Cryptanthus bivittatus

Tillandsia usneoides

Cryptanthus 'Pink Starlight'

Aechmea recurvata

Guzmania lingulata

Tillandsia fasciculata

Tillandsia stricta

Vriesea splendens

Neoregelia concentrica

Tillandsia cyanea

Puya chilensis

■■■ PURPLE–GREEN

Browallia speciosa (Bush violet)
Bushy perennial, usually grown as an
annual, propagated by seed each year.
Has oval leaves to 10cm (4in) long and
showy, violet-blue flowers with white
eyes, the season depending when sown.
H 60–75cm (24–30in), S 45cm (18in).
Min. 10–15°C (50–59°F).

☀ ◊

Artemisia ludoviciana var. ***albula***
Bushy perennial, grown for its
aromatic, lance-shaped leaves which
are silvery-white and woolly on both
surfaces and have jagged margins.
Bears slender plumes of tiny, greyish-
white flower heads in summer.
H 1.2m (4ft), S 60cm (2ft).

☀ ◊

Aciphylla squarrosa
(Bayonet plant)
Evergreen, clump-forming perennial
with tufts of pointed, divided leaves.
In summer bears spiky, yellow flowers
in compound umbels with male and
female flowers often mixed.
H and S 1–1.2m (3–4ft).

☀ ◊

Asparagus densiflorus
Evergreen, trailing perennial with
clusters of narrow, bright green, leaf-
like stems. In summer has pink-tinged,
white flowers, followed by red berries.
Suits a hanging basket. H to 1m (3ft),
S 50cm (20in). Min. 10°C (50°F).

☀ ◊

Alocasia cuprea
Evergreen, tufted perennial. Oval
leaves are 30cm (12in) long, with a
metallic sheen and darker, impressed
veins above, purple below; leaf stalks
arise from the lower surface. Purplish
spathes appear intermittently.
H and S to 1m (3ft). Min. 15°C (59°F).

☀ ◊ ⓘ

Xanthosoma sagittifolium
Spreading, tufted perennial with thick
stems. Broadly arrow-shaped leaves,
60cm (2ft) or more long, on long leaf
stalks, are green with a greyish bloom.
Has green spathes intermittently during
the year. H to 2m (6ft) in flower,
S 2m (6ft) or more. Min. 15°C (59°F).

☀ ◊

Columnea microphylla
'Variegata'
Evergreen, trailing perennial. Has
rounded leaves narrowly bordered with
cream and tubular, hooded, scarlet
flowers, with yellow throats, in winter-
spring. H 1m (3ft) or more,
S indefinite. Min. 15°C (59°F).

☀ ◊

Calathea zebrina (Zebra plant)
Robust, evergreen, clump-forming
perennial with long-stalked, velvety,
dark green leaves, to 60cm (2ft) long
(less if pot-grown), with paler veins,
margins and midribs. Bears short spikes
of white to pale purple flowers. H and
S to 90cm (3ft). Min. 15°C (59°F).

☀ ◊

PERENNIALS

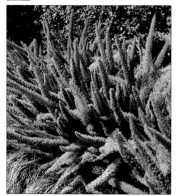

Asparagus densiflorus 'Myersii',
syn. *A. meyeri*, *A.* 'Myers'
(Foxtail fern)
Evergreen, erect perennial with spikes
of tight, feathery clusters of leaf-like
stems and pinkish-white flowers in
summer, then red berries. H to 1m
(3ft), S 50cm (20in). Min. 10°C (50°F).

Globba winitii
Evergreen, clump-forming perennial
with lance-shaped leaves to 20cm (8in)
long. Intermittently has pendent
racemes of tubular, yellow flowers with
large, reddish-purple, reflexed bracts.
H 1m (3ft), S 30cm (1ft).
Min. 18°C (64°F).

Epimedium x youngianum
'Niveum'
Compact, ground-cover perennial with
heart-shaped, serrated, bronze-tinted
leaflets that turn green in late spring,
when small, cup-shaped, snow-white
flowers are borne.
H 15–30cm (6–12in), S 30cm (12in).

Pachyphragma macrophyllum,
syn. *Thlaspi macrophyllum*
Creeping, mat-forming perennial with
rosettes of rounded, long-stalked,
glossy, bright green leaves, each to
10cm (4in) long. Bears many racemes
of tiny, white flowers in spring.
H to 30cm (12in), S indefinite.

**Dieffenbachia seguine 'Rudolph
Roehrs'**, syn. *D. maculata*
'Rudolph Roehrs', *D.s.* 'Roehrsii'
Evergreen, tufted perennial, sometimes
woody at the base. Leaves, to 45cm
(18in) long, are yellowish-green or
white with green midribs and margins.
H and S 1m (3ft). Min. 15°C (59°F).

**Peristrophe hyssopifolia
'Aureovariegata'**
Evergreen, bushy perennial. Small
leaves are broadly lance-shaped with
long, pointed tips and central, creamy-
yellow blotches. Has tubular, rose-pink
flowers in winter. H to 60cm (2ft) or
more, S 1.2m (4ft). Min. 15°C (59°F).

**Lamium maculatum 'White
Nancy'**
Semi-evergreen, mat-forming
perennial with white-variegated, mid-
green foliage and spikes of hooded,
white flowers in late spring and
summer. H 15cm (6in), S 1m (3ft).

Trillium cernuum
Clump-forming perennial with
nodding, maroon-centred, white
flowers borne in spring beneath
luxuriant, 3-parted, mid-green leaves.
H 30–45cm (12–18in), S 30cm (12in).

Sansevieria trifasciata 'Laurentii'
Evergreen, stemless perennial with a
rosette of about 5 stiff, erect, lance-
shaped and pointed leaves with yellow
margins. Occasionally has pale green
flowers. Propagate by division to avoid
reversion. H 45cm–1.2m (1½–4ft),
S 10cm (4in). Min. 10–15°C (50–59°F).

Strelitzia reginae
(Bird-of-paradise flower)
Evergreen, clump-forming perennial
with long-stalked, bluish-green leaves.
Has beak-like, orange-and-blue flowers
in boat-shaped, red-edged bracts
mainly in spring. H over 1m (3ft),
S 75cm (2½ft). Min. 5–10°C (41–50°F).

**Pulmonaria officinalis
'Sissinghurst White'**
Semi-evergreen, clump-forming
perennial that bears funnel-shaped,
white flowers in spring above
long, elliptic, mid-green, paler
spotted leaves.
H 30cm (12in), S 45–60cm (18–24in).

Lamium maculatum 'Album'
Semi-evergreen, mat-forming perennial
that has dark green leaves with central,
white stripes. Bears clusters of hooded,
white flowers in spring-summer.
H 20cm (8in), S 1m (3ft).

Astilbe 'Straussenfeder', illus. p.244
Astilbe 'Venus', illus. p.244
BROMELIADS, illus. p.265
Ctenanthe lubbersiana

Dasylirion texanum
Dieffenbachia seguine
Sansevieria cylindrica
Sansevieria trifasciata

OTHER RECOMMENDED PLANTS:
Convallaria majalis 'Fortin's Giant'
Helleborus x hybridus [white form],
   illus. p.300

Helleborus niger, illus. p.301
PRIMULAS, illus. pp.272–3
Sanguinaria canadensis 'Plena'
Trillium grandiflorum 'Flore Pleno'

PERENNIALS

□ WHITE

Convallaria majalis
(Lily-of-the-valley)
Low-growing, rhizomatous perennial
with narrowly oval, mid- to dark
green leaves and sprays of small, very
fragrant, pendulous, bell-shaped, white
flowers. Likes humus-rich soil.
H 15cm (6in), S indefinite.

Trillium ovatum
Clump-forming perennial with white
flowers, later turning pink, that are
carried singly in spring just above red-
stalked, 3-parted, dark green foliage.
H 25–38cm (10–15in), S 20cm (8in).

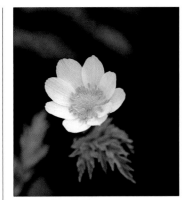

Adonis brevistyla
Clump-forming perennial. Buttercup-
like flowers, borne singly at tips of
stems in early spring, are white, tinged
blue outside. Has finely cut, mid-green
leaves. H and S 15–23cm (6–9in).

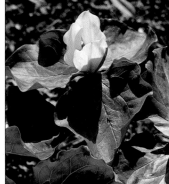

Trillium chloropetalum
Clump-forming perennial with
reddish-green stems carrying 3-parted,
grey-marbled, dark green leaves.
Flowers vary from purplish-pink to
white and appear above foliage in
spring. H and S 30–45cm (12–18in).

Podophyllum hexandrum,
syn. *P. emodi*
(Himalayan May apple)
Perennial with pairs of 3-lobed, brown-
mottled leaves followed by white or
pink flowers in spring and fleshy, red
fruits in summer.
H 30–45cm (12–18in), S 30cm (12in).

Epimedium pubigerum
Evergreen, carpeting perennial, grown
for its dense, smooth, heart-shaped,
divided foliage and clusters of cup-
shaped, creamy-white or pink flowers
in spring. H and S 45cm (18in).

Trillium grandiflorum
(Wake robin)
Clump-forming perennial. Large, pure
white flowers that turn pink with age
are borne singly in spring just above
large, 3-parted, dark green leaves.
H 38cm (15in), S 30cm (12in).

Anemone sylvestris
(Snowdrop windflower)
Carpeting perennial that may be
invasive. Fragrant, semi-pendent, white
flowers with yellow centres are borne
in spring and early summer. Has
divided, mid-green leaves.
H and S 30cm (12in).

***Bergenia* 'Silberlicht'**,
syn. *B.* 'Silver Light'
Evergreen, clump-forming perennial
that has flat, oval, mid-green leaves
with toothed margins. Clusters of
white flowers, sometimes suffused
with pink, are borne on erect stems in
spring. H 30cm (12in), S 50cm (20in).

Bergenia cordifolia 'Purpurea'
Evergreen, clump-forming perennial, useful for ground cover, with large, rounded, purple-tinged, deep green leaves. Clusters of bell-shaped, rose-pink flowers are carried on red stems from late winter to early spring.
H and S 50cm (20in).

☀ ◊

Epimedium × rubrum
Carpeting perennial with dense, heart-shaped, divided leaves that are dark brownish-red in spring, when clusters of cup-shaped, crimson flowers with yellow spurs appear.
H 30cm (12in), S 20cm (8in).

◐ ◊

Epimedium grandiflorum 'Rose Queen'
Carpeting perennial with dense, heart-shaped, divided leaves, tinged with copper, and wiry stems bearing clusters of cup-shaped, spurred, deep pink flowers in spring. H and S 30cm (12in).

◐ ◊

Trillium erectum
(Birthroot, Squawroot)
Clump-forming perennial with 3-lobed, mid-green leaves and bright maroon-purple flowers in spring.
H 30–45cm (12–18in), S 30cm (12in).

☀ ◊

Bergenia ciliata
Evergreen, clump-forming perennial with attractive, large, rounded, hairy leaves. In spring bears clusters of white flowers that age to pink. Leaves are often damaged by frost, although fresh ones will appear in spring.
H 30cm (12in), S 50cm (20in).

☀ ◊

Geranium macrorrhizum 'Ingwersen's Variety'
Compact, carpeting perennial, useful as weed-suppressing ground cover. Small, soft rose-pink flowers appear in late spring and early summer. Aromatic leaves turn bronze- and scarlet-tinted in autumn. H 30cm (12in), S 60cm (24in).

☀ ◊

Heloniopsis orientalis
Clump-forming perennial with basal rosettes of narrowly lance-shaped leaves, above which rise nodding, rose-pink flowers in spring.
H and S 30cm (12in).

◐ ◊

Lamium maculatum
Semi-evergreen, mat-forming perennial with mauve-tinged, often pink-flushed leaves that have central, silvery stripes. Clusters of hooded, mauve-pink flowers are borne in mid-spring. H 15cm (6in), S 90cm (36in).

☀ ◊

Trillium sessile
(Toadshade, Wake robin)
Clump-forming perennial that in spring bears red-brown flowers, nestling in a collar of 3-lobed leaves, marked white, pale green or bronze. H 30–38cm (12–15in), S 30–45cm (12–18in).

◐ ◊

Bergenia 'Abendglut'
Bergenia cordifolia
Bergenia 'Morgenröte'
Bergenia × schmidtii

Bergenia stracheyi
Bergenia 'Sunningdale'
Dicentra 'Adrian Bloom'
Dicentra 'Spring Morning', illus. p.278

Dicentra 'Stuart Boothman', illus. p.278
Helleborus × hybridus [pink form], illus. p.301
PRIMULAS, illus. pp.272–3
Rehmannia glutinosa

Epimedium alpinum
Pulmonaria rubra

■ PURPLE

Anemone nemorosa 'Allenii'
Carpeting perennial with many large,
cup-shaped, single, rich lavender-blue
flowers appearing in spring over deeply
divided, mid-green leaves.
H 15cm (6in), S 30cm (12in) or more.

☀ ◊ ①

Glaucidium palmatum
Leafy perennial that has large, lobed
leaves and, in spring, large, delicate,
cup-shaped, lavender flowers. A
woodland plant, it requires humus-
rich soil and a sheltered position.
H and S 50cm (20in).

◐ ◖

Geranium nodosum
Clump-forming perennial with lobed,
glossy leaves and delicate, cup-shaped,
lilac or lilac-pink flowers borne in
spring-summer. Thrives in deep shade.
H and S 45cm (18in).

☀ ◊

Lathyrus vernus
Clump-forming perennial bearing in
spring small, pea-like, bright purple
and blue flowers veined with red,
several on each slender stem. Leaves
are soft and fern-like. Proves difficult
to transplant successfully.
H and S 30cm (12in).

☀ ◊ ①

**Anemone nemorosa
'Robinsoniana'**
Carpeting perennial with flat, star-
shaped, lavender-blue flowers, pale
creamy-grey beneath, borne singly
on maroon stems. Leaves are deeply
divided into lance-shaped segments.
H 15cm (6in), S 30cm (12in).

 ☀ ◊ ①

Cardamine pentaphyllos,
syn. *Dentaria pentaphyllos*
Upright perennial spreading by fleshy,
horizontal rootstocks. Produces clusters
of large, white or pale purple flowers
in spring. H 30–60cm (12–24in),
S 45–60cm (18–24in).

 ☀ ◊

Cardamine pratensis 'Flore Pleno'
Chirita lavandulacea, illus. p.294
Helleborus x *hybridus* [purple form],
　illus. p.302

Helonias bullata
IRISES, illus. pp.234–5
ORCHIDS, illus. pp.296–9
PEONIES, illus. pp.236–7

PRIMULAS, illus. pp.272–3
Sarracenia purpurea

PERENNIALS

Pulmonaria saccharata
Semi-evergreen, clump-forming
perennial. In spring bears funnel-
shaped flowers, opening pink and
turning to blue. Long, elliptic leaves
are variably spotted with creamy-
white. H 30cm (12in), S 60cm (24in).

☀ ◊

Lathraea clandestina (Toothwort)
Spreading perennial that grows as a
parasite on willow or poplar roots.
Fleshy, underground stems have
colourless scales instead of leaves.
Bears bunches of hooded, purple
flowers from late winter to early
spring. H 10cm (4in), S indefinite.

☀ ◊

**Brunnera macrophylla 'Dawson's
White'**, syn. *B.m.* 'Variegata'
Ground-cover perennial with heart-
shaped leaves, marked creamy-white.
In spring bears delicate sprays of
small, bright blue flowers. Shelter
from wind to prevent leaf damage.
H 45cm (18in), S 60cm (24in).

☀ ◊

Euphorbia seguieriana
Bushy perennial with large, terminal
clusters of yellowish-green flowers in
late spring and narrow, lance-shaped,
glaucous leaves on slender stems.
H and S 45cm (18in).

☀ ◊ ①

Lamium orvala
Clump-forming perennial that forms a
mound of mid-green leaves, sometimes
with central white stripes. Clusters of
pink or purple-pink flowers open in
late spring to early summer.
H and S 30cm (12in).

☀ ◊

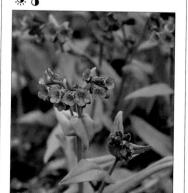

Pulmonaria 'Mawson's Blue'
Clump-forming perennial that in early
spring bears clusters of funnel-shaped,
blue flowers, tinged red with age,
above narrow leaves.
H and S 23cm (9in).

☀ ◊

Meconopsis quintuplinervia
(Harebell poppy)
Mat-forming perennial. Lavender-blue
flowers, deepening to purple at the
bases, are carried singly on hairy stems
in late spring and early summer above
a dense mat of large, mid-green leaves.
H 30–45cm (12–18in), S 30cm (12in).

☀ ◊ pH

Scopolia carniolica
Clump-forming perennial that carries
spikes of nodding, purple-brown
flowers, yellow inside, in early spring.
H and S 60cm (24in).

☀ ◊ ①

Mertensia pulmonarioides,
syn. *M. virginica*
Elegant perennial with rich blue
flowers, hanging in clusters in spring.
Leaves are soft blue-green. Dies down
in summer. Crowns are prone to slug
damage. H 30–60cm (12–24in),
S 30–45cm (12–18in).

☀ ◊

Euphorbia amygdaloides var.
robbiae, syn. *E. robbiae*
Evergreen, spreading perennial with
rosettes of dark green leaves, useful as
ground cover even in poor, dry soil
and semi-shade. Bears open, rounded
heads of lime-green flowers in spring.
H 45–60cm (18–24in), S 60cm (24in).

☀ ◊ ①

Euphorbia cyparissias
Rounded, leafy perennial with a mass
of slender, grey-green leaves and
umbels of small, bright lime-green
flowers in late spring. May be
invasive. H and S 30cm (12in).

☀ ◊ ①

Ajuga pyramidalis
Brunnera macrophylla
Cyanotis somaliensis, illus. p.303
IRISES, illus. pp.234–5

Meehania urticifolia
Pulmonaria angustifolia
Pulmonaria longifolia
Symphytum 'Hidcote Blue'

Chirita sinensis
Helleborus argutifolius, illus. p.304
Helleborus cyclophyllus
Helleborus foetidus, illus. p.305

Helleborus viridis, illus. p.305
IRISES, illus. pp.234–5
Linum narbonense, illus. p.287
Sarracenia flava, illus. p.290

PERENNIALS

271

Primulas

There are primulas to suit almost every kind of garden situation, ranging from the poolside to the scree, but most have particular needs and care should be taken with their cultivation. Among the various botanical groups, Candelabra and Auricula primulas are the most widely known, and have a distinctive arrangement of their flowers. (For fuller details see the Plant Dictionary.)

P. allionii

P. vulgaris 'Gigha White'

P. sinensis

P. sieboldii 'Wine Lady'

P. polyneura

P. sonchifolia

P. 'Craddock White'

P. malacoides [single]

P. warshenewskiana

P. secundiflora

P. frondosa

P. denticulata var. *alba*

P. farinosa

P. malacoides [double]

P. melanops

P. japonica 'Miller's Crimson' (Candelabra)

P. petiolaris

P. japonica 'Postford White' (Candelabra)

P. vulgaris subsp. *sibthorpii*

P. x scapeosa

P. clusiana

P. modesta var. *fauriae*

P. vialii

P. gracilipes

P. pulverulenta 'Bartley' (Candelabra)

P. clarkei

P. rosea

P. hirsuta

P. sieboldii

P. nana

P. 'Mrs J.H. Wilson' (Auricula)

P. 'Janet'

P. 'Mark'
(Auricula)

P. 'Linda Pope'

P. aureata

P. florindae

P. bulleyana
(Candelabra)

P. 'Adrian'
(Auricula)

P. reidii var. williamsii

P. alpicola var. alpicola

P. 'Adrian'
(Auricula)

P. denticulata

P. vulgaris

P. sikkimensis

P. forrestii

P. 'Janie Hill'
(Auricula)

P. 'Moonstone'
(Auricula)

P. elatior

P. veris

P. 'Blossom'
(Auricula)

P. marginata
'Prichard's Variety'

P. bhutanica

P. 'Blairside Yellow'
(Auricula)

P. chungensis
(Candelabra)

P. 'Inverewe'
(Candelabra)

P. flaccida

P. 'Margaret Martin'
(Auricula)

P. prolifera
(Candelabra)

P. x kewensis

P. marginata

P. 'Chloë'
(Auricula)

P. palinuri

P. verticillata

P. Gold Laced Group

PERENNIALS

☐ YELLOW

Valeriana phu 'Aurea'
Perennial with rosettes of lemon- to
butter-yellow young foliage that turns
mid-green by summer, when heads of
insignificant, white flowers appear.
H 38cm (15in), S 30–38cm (12–15in).

☼ ◊

Petasites japonicus
Spreading, invasive perennial that in
early spring produces dense cones of
small, daisy-like, yellowish-white
flowers before large, light green leaves
appear. H 60cm (2ft), S 1.5m (5ft).

☼ ◗

Cardamine enneaphyllos,
syn. *Dentaria enneaphyllos*
Lax perennial spreading by fleshy,
horizontal rootstocks. In spring,
nodding, pale yellow or white flowers
open at the ends of shoots arising from
deeply divided leaves. H 30–60cm
(12–24in), S 45–60cm (18–24in).

☼ ◗

**Epimedium × versicolor
'Neosulphureum'**
Carpeting perennial with dense,
heart-shaped, divided leaves, tinted
reddish-purple in spring when it bears
cup-shaped, pale yellow flowers in
small, pendent clusters on wiry stems.
H and S 30cm (12in).

◐ ◊

Anemone × lipsiensis, syn.
A. × *intermedia, A.* × *seemannii*
Prostrate, carpeting perennial that in
spring has many single, pale yellow
flowers with bright yellow stamens.
Leaves are deeply cut with long
leaflets. H 15cm (6in), S 30cm (12in).

☼ ◊ ①

Uvularia grandiflora
(Bellwort, Merry-bells)
Clump-forming perennial. Clusters of
long, bell-shaped, yellow flowers hang
gracefully from slender stems in
spring.
H 45–60cm (18–24in), S 30cm (12in).

☼ ◊

Trollius × cultorum 'Alabaster'
Clump-forming perennial producing
rounded, yellowish-white flowers in
spring. These emerge from a basal
mass of rounded, deeply divided,
mid-green leaves.
H 60cm (24in), S 45cm (18in).

☼ ◗

Anemone ranunculoides
Spreading perennial for damp woodland, bearing buttercup-like, single,
deep yellow flowers in spring. Divided
leaves have short stalks.
H and S 20cm (8in).

◐ ◗ ①

Trollius europaeus (Globeflower)
Clump-forming perennial that in spring
bears rounded, lemon- to mid-yellow
flowers above deeply divided, mid-
green leaves.
H 60cm (24in), S 45cm (18in).

Adonis amurensis
Clump-forming perennial that in
late winter and early spring bears
buttercup-like, golden blooms singly
at the tips of stems. Mid-green
foliage is finely cut.
H 30cm (12in), S 23–30cm (9–12in).

Campanula alliariifolia
Mound-forming perennial with heart-
shaped leaves, above which rise
nodding, bell-shaped, creamy-white
flowers borne along arching, wiry
stems throughout summer.
H 60cm (24in), S 50cm (20in).

Anemone rivularis
Perennial with stiff, free-branching
stems bearing delicate, cup-shaped,
white flowers in summer above deeply
divided, dark green leaves.
H 60cm (24in), S 30cm (12in).

Euphorbia polychroma,
syn. *E. epithymoides*
Rounded, bushy perennial with mid-
green leaves and heads of bright
yellow flowers carried for several
weeks in spring. H and S 50cm (20in).

Meconopsis cambrica
(Welsh poppy)
Spreading perennial that in late spring
carries lemon-yellow or rich orange
blooms. Double forms are available.
Has deeply divided, fern-like foliage.
H 30–45cm (12–18in), S 30cm (12in).

Anemone narcissiflora
Leafy perennial that in late spring and
early summer produces cup-shaped,
single, white flowers with a blue or
purplish-pink stain on reverse of
petals. Leaves are dark green and
deeply divided.
H to 60cm (24in), S 50cm (20in).

Adonis vernalis
Clump-forming perennial that in
early spring produces buttercup-like,
greenish-yellow blooms singly at the
tips of stems. Mid-green leaves are
delicately dissected.
H and S 23–30cm (9–12in).

Epimedium × warleyense
Carpeting perennial with heart-shaped,
divided, light green leaves, tinged
purple-red, and cup-shaped, rich
orange flowers borne in clusters on
wiry stems in spring.
H and S 30cm (12in).

Galium odoratum, syn. *Asperula
odorata* (Woodruff)
Carpeting perennial that bears whorls
of star-shaped, white flowers above
neat, whorled leaves in summer. All
parts of plant are aromatic.
H 15cm (6in), S 30cm (12in) or more.

Leucanthemum × superbum
'Esther Read',
syn. *Chrysanthemum maximum*
of gardens 'Esther Read'
Robust perennial with large, daisy-like,
double, white flower heads borne
singly on strong stems in summer.
H and S 45cm (18in).

OTHER RECOMMENDED PLANTS:

☐ WHITE

Anthemis punctata subsp. **cupaniana**
Evergreen, carpeting perennial with dense, finely cut, silvery foliage that turns green in winter. Small, daisy-like, white flower heads with yellow centres are borne singly on short stems in early summer. H and S 30cm (12in).

Anaphalis nepalensis var. **monocephala**, syn. *A. nubigena*
Dwarf, leafy perennial that has woolly, silvery stems and lance-shaped leaves. Carries dense, terminal clusters of white flower heads in late summer. H 20–30cm (8–12in), S 15cm (6in).

Aegopodium podagraria '**Variegatum**' (Variegated Bishop's weed, Variegated gout weed)
Vigorous, spreading perennial, excellent for ground cover, with lobed, creamy-white-variegated leaves. Insignificant, white flowers borne in summer are best removed. H 10cm (4in), S indefinite.

Tradescantia Andersoniana Group '**Osprey**', syn. *T.* 'Osprey'
Clump-forming perennial with narrow, lance-shaped leaves, 15–30cm (6–12in) long. Has clusters of white flowers with purple-blue stamens, surrounded by 2 leaf-like bracts, in summer. H to 60cm (24in), S 45cm (18in).

Anthericum liliago
(St Bernard's lily)
Upright perennial that in early summer bears tall racemes of trumpet-shaped, white flowers above clumps of long, narrow, grey-green leaves. H 45–60cm (18–24in), S 30cm (12in).

Mentha suaveolens '**Variegata**', syn. *M. rotundifolia* of gardens 'Variegata' (Variegated apple mint)
Spreading perennial with soft, woolly, mid-green leaves, splashed with white and cream, that smell of apples. Seldom produces flowers. H 30–45cm (12–18in), S 60cm (24in).

Astilbe '**Irrlicht**'
Leafy perennial bearing tapering, feathery plumes of tiny, white flowers in summer. Foliage is dark green and flowers remain on the plant, dried and brown, well into winter. Prefers humus-rich soil.
H 45–60cm (1½–2ft), S to 1m (3ft).

Geranium clarkei '**Kashmir White**', syn. *G. pratense* 'Kashmir White'
Carpeting, rhizomatous perennial with divided leaves and loose clusters of cup-shaped flowers, white with pale lilac-pink veins, borne for a long period in summer. H and S 45–60cm (18–24in).

Crambe maritima (Sea kale)
Robust perennial with a mound of wide, curved, lobed, silvery-green leaves. Bears large heads of small, fragrant, white flowers, opening into branching sprays in summer. H and S 60cm (24in).

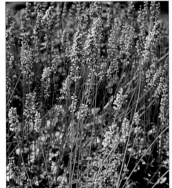

Heuchera cylindrica '**Greenfinch**'
Evergreen, clump-forming perennial with rosettes of lobed, heart-shaped leaves and, in summer, graceful spikes of small, bell-shaped, pale green or greenish-white flowers. H 45–60cm (18–24in), S 50cm (20in).

Streptocarpus caulescens
Erect perennial with small, narrow to oval, fleshy, dark green leaves. Stalked clusters of small, tubular, violet-striped violet or white flowers are carried in leaf axils intermittently. H and S to 45cm (18in) or more. Min. 10–15°C (50–59°F).

PERENNIALS

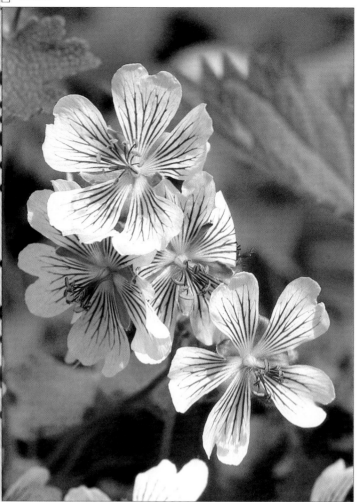

Geranium renardii
Compact, clump-forming perennial
with lobed, circular, sage-green leaves
and purple-veined, white flowers,
borne in early summer.
H and S 30cm (12in).

☼ ◊

Ruellia devosiana
Evergreen, bushy sub-shrub with
spreading, purplish branches. Leaves
are broadly lance-shaped, dark green
with paler veins above and purple
below. Has mauve-tinged, white
flowers in spring-summer. H and S to
45cm (18in) or more. Min. 15°C (59°F).

☼ ◖

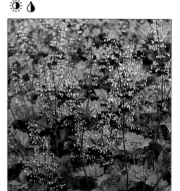

Heuchera micrantha var.
diversifolia 'Palace Purple'
Clump-forming perennial with
persistent, heart-shaped, deep purple
leaves and sprays of small, white
flowers in summer. Cut leaves last
well in water. H and S 45cm (18in).

☼ ◊

Astrantia major subsp. **involucrata**,
syn. *A.m.* subsp. *carinthiaca*
Clump-forming perennial very similar
to *A. major* (below) but with longer
bracts surrounding centres of flower
heads. H 60cm (24in), S 45cm (18in).

☼ ◊

Astrantia major (Masterwort)
Clump-forming perennial producing
greenish-white, sometimes pink-tinged
flower heads throughout summer-
autumn above a dense mass of divided,
mid-green leaves.
H 60cm (24in), S 45cm (18in).

☼ ◊

Diplarrhena moraea
Clump-forming perennial with fans of
long, strap-shaped leaves and clusters
of iris-like, white flowers, with centres
of yellow and purple, borne on wiry
stems in early summer.
H 45cm (18in), S 23cm (9in).

☼ ◊

Osteospermum 'Whirlygig',
syn. *O.* 'Whirligig'
Evergreen, clump-forming, semi-
woody perennial of lax habit that bears
bluish-white flower heads singly, but
in great profusion, during summer.
Leaves are grey-green.
H 60cm (24in), S 30–45cm (12–18in).

☼ ◊

Melittis melissophyllum
(Bastard balm)
Erect perennial that in early summer
bears white flowers with purple lower
lips in axils of rough, oval, mid-green
leaves. H and S 30cm (12in).

☼ ◊

Astrantia maxima
Clump-forming perennial that bears
rose-pink flower heads during
summer-autumn.
H 60cm (24in), S 30cm (12in).

☼ ◊

Arctotis venusta
Osteospermum 'Blue Streak'
Osteospermum ecklonis

Sinningia concinna
Tricyrtis hirta var. alba, illus. p.294

Geranium incanum
Sedum populifolium

☐ PINK

Mimulus 'Andean Nymph'
Spreading perennial, with hairy leaves,
that in summer bears snapdragon-like,
rose-pink flowers tipped with creamy-
yellow and spotted deep pink.
H 23cm (9in), S 25cm (10in).
Min. 2°C (35°F).

☼ ◑

Dicentra 'Spring Morning'
Neat, leafy perennial with small,
heart-shaped, pink flowers hanging
in arching sprays in late spring and
summer. Attractive, fern-like foliage
is grey-green and finely cut.
H and S 30cm (12in).

☼ ◊ ①

Dicentra 'Stuart Boothman'
Tufted perennial with oval, finely cut,
deep grey-green leaves. In spring-
summer, produces arching sprays
of heart-shaped, carmine flowers.
H 30cm (12in), S 40cm (16in).

☼ ◊ ①

Diascia 'Blackthorn Apricot'
Mat-forming perennial with narrowly
heart-shaped, tapering leaves. From
summer to autumn, produces loose
racemes of apricot-pink flowers with
small, narrow 'windows' and almost
straight, downward-pointing spurs.
H 25cm (10in), S to 50cm (20in).

☼ ◊

x Heucherella tiarelloides
Evergreen, ground-cover perennial
that has dense clusters of leaves and
feathery sprays of tiny, bell-shaped,
pink flowers in early summer.
H and S 45cm (18in).

☼ ◊

**x Heucherella alba 'Bridget
Bloom'**
Evergreen, clump-forming perennial
with dense, bright green leaves and,
in early summer, many feathery sprays
of tiny, bell-shaped, rose-pink flowers,
which continue intermittently until
autumn. H 45cm (18in), S 30cm (12in).

☼ ◊

Erigeron 'Charity'
Clump-forming perennial with a mass
of daisy-like, light pink flower heads
with greenish-yellow centres borne for
a long period in summer. May need
some support. H and S to 60cm (24in).

☼ ◊

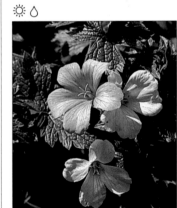

Geranium endressii
Semi-evergreen, compact, carpeting
perennial with small, lobed leaves and
cup-shaped, rose-pink flowers borne
throughout summer.
H 45cm (18in), S 60cm (24in).

☼ ◊

Geranium X oxonianum 'Wargrave Pink'

Semi-evergreen, carpeting perennial with dense, dainty, lobed, basal leaves acting as weed-suppressing ground cover. Cup-shaped, bright salmon-pink flowers are borne throughout summer. H 45cm (18in), S 60cm (24in).

Osteospermum jucundum, syn. O. barberae of gardens, Dimorphotheca barberae of gardens

Evergreen, neat, clump-forming perennial with mid-green leaves. In late summer, soft pink flower heads, mostly dark-eyed, are borne singly but in great abundance. H and S 30cm (12in).

Erodium manescaui, syn. E. manescavii

Mound-forming perennial with divided, ferny, blue-green leaves. Produces loose clusters of single, deep pink, darker blotched flowers throughout summer. H 45cm (18in), S 60cm (24in).

Mimulus lewisii

Upright perennial with downy, sticky, grey leaves that provide an excellent foil for snapdragon-like, deep rose-pink flowers borne singly in summer. Tolerates dry soil. H 60cm (24in), S 45cm (18in).

Lychnis flos-jovis

Clump-forming perennial with rounded clusters of deep rose-pink flowers, opening in mid-summer, that are set off by grey foliage. H and S 45cm (18in).

Centaurea hypoleuca 'John Coutts'

Upright perennial. Deep rose-red flower heads, with thistle-like centres encircled by star-shaped ray petals, are borne singly on slender stems in summer. Deeply divided leaves are white-grey beneath. H 60cm (24in), S 45cm (18in).

Incarvillea mairei

Compact, clump-forming perennial that has short stems bearing several trumpet-shaped, purplish-pink flowers in early summer. Leaves are divided into oval leaflets. Protect crowns with winter mulch. H and S 30cm (12in).

Geranium macrorrhizum

Semi-evergreen, carpeting perennial bearing magenta flowers in early summer. Rounded, divided, aromatic leaves make good, weed-proof ground cover and assume bright tints in autumn. H 30–38cm (12–15in), S 60cm (24in).

Persicaria macrophylla, syn. P. sphaerostachya, Polygonum macrophyllum, P. sphaerostachyum

Compact perennial carrying neat spikes of rich rose-pink blooms above narrow, lance-shaped, glaucous leaves in late summer. H 45–60cm (18–24in), S 30cm (12in).

Liatris spicata, syn. L. callilepis of gardens

Clump-forming perennial. In late summer bears spikes of crowded, rose-purple flower heads on stiff stems that arise from basal tufts of grassy, mid-green foliage. H 60cm (24in), S 30cm (12in).

Physostegia virginiana 'Vivid' (Obedient plant)

Erect, compact perennial that in late summer and early autumn bears spikes of tubular, dark lilac-pink flowers that can be placed in postion. Has toothed, mid-green leaves. H and S 30–60cm (12–24in).

Carnations and Pinks

Although perhaps best known for providing excellent cut flowers, carnations and pinks (*Dianthus* cultivars) are highly ornamental border subjects, valued for their usually fragrant blooms, produced mainly in summer, and their distinctive, silvery- or grey-green foliage. Shorter-growing cultivars – the old-fashioned and modern pinks – are excellent edging plants. Many of the flowers are attractively marked or have fringed petals. Carnations and pinks need an open, sunny position, preferably in alkaline soil. All except the perpetual-flowering carnations are hardy. Carnations and pinks are divided into the following groups:

Border carnations – plants are of upright habit and flower prolifically once in mid-summer; each stem bears 5 or more flowers.

Perpetual-flowering carnations – similar in habit to border carnations, they are usually grown for cut flowers and bloom year-round under glass. Plants are normally disbudded, leaving one flower per stem, but spray forms have up to 5 flowers per stem.

Malmaison carnations – these produce very fragrant flowers sporadically throughout the year under glass.

Old-fashioned pinks – these have a low, spreading habit and form neat cushions of foliage; masses of fragrant flowers are produced in mid-summer.

Modern pinks – usually more vigorous than old-fashioned pinks, they are repeat-flowering with 2 or 3 main flushes of flowers in summer.

Alpine pinks – in early summer, these plants form cushions of small, scented flowers.

D. 'Eva Humphries'
(border carnation)

D. 'London Brocade'
(modern pink)

D. 'Fair Folly'
(modern pink)

D. 'Alice'
(modern pink)

D. 'Prudence'
(old-fashioned pink)

D. 'Emile Paré'
(old-fashioned pink)

D. 'Forest Treasure'
(border carnation)

D. 'Doris'
(modern pink)

D. 'Mrs Sinkins'
(old-fashioned pink)

D. 'Gran's Favourite'
(old-fashioned pink)

D. Pierrot (perpetual-flowering carnation)

D. 'Truly Yours'
(perpetual-fl. carnation)

D. 'Haytor'
(modern pink)

D. 'White Ladies'
(old-fashioned pink)

D. 'Musgrave's Pink'
(old-fashioned pink)

D. 'Nives' (perpetual-flowering carnation)

D. 'Dad's Favourite'
(old-fashioned pink)

D. 'Becky Robinson'
(modern pink)

D. 'Pink Jewel'
(alpine pink)

D. 'Joy'
(modern pink)

D. 'Bovey Belle'
(modern pink)

D. 'Astor' (perpetual-
flowering carnation)

D. 'Lavender Clove'
(border carnation)

D. 'Aldridge Yellow'
(border carnation)

D. 'Monica Wyatt'
(modern pink)

**D. 'Duchess of
Westminster'** (Mal. car.)

D. 'Laced Monarch'
(modern pink)

D. 'Valencia' (perpetual-
flowering carnation)

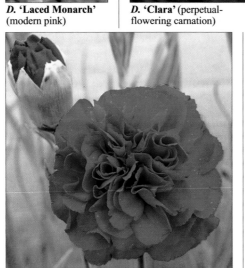

D. 'Clara' (perpetual-
flowering carnation)

D. 'Raggio di Sole'
(perpetual-fl. carnation)

D. 'Houndspool Ruby'
(modern pink)

D. 'Crompton Princess'
(perpetual-fl. carnation)

D. 'Christine Hough'
(border carnation)

D. 'Nina' (perpetual-
flowering carnation)

D. 'Cream Sue'
(perpetual-fl. carnation)

D. 'Albisola' (perpetual-
flowering carnation)

D. 'Christopher'
(modern pink)

D. 'Bookham Perfume'
(border carnation)

D. 'Bookham Fancy'
(border carnation)

D. 'Happiness'
(border carnation)

D. 'Golden Cross'
(border carnation)

PERENNIALS small SUMMER INTEREST

☐ PINK

Achimenes 'Little Beauty'
Bushy perennial with oval, toothed leaves. Large, funnel-shaped, deep pink flowers with yellow eyes are carried in summer. H 25cm (10in), S 30cm (12in).
Min. 10°C (50°F).

☼ ◊

Sinningia 'Red Flicker'
Short-stemmed, tuberous perennial with rosettes of oval, velvety leaves, to 20cm (8in) long. In summer has fleshy, nodding, funnel-shaped, pinkish-red flowers, pouched on lower sides.
H to 30cm (12in), S 45cm (18in).
Min. 15°C (59°F).

◐ ◉

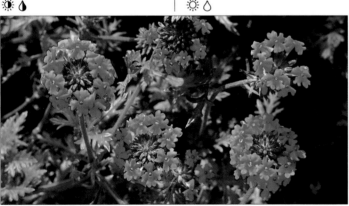

Verbena 'Sissinghurst'
Mat-forming perennial that throughout summer bears heads of brilliant pink flowers above mid-green foliage. Is excellent for edging a path or growing in a tub.
H 15–20cm (6–8in), S 45cm (18in).

☼ ◊

Sedum spectabile 'Brilliant', illus. p.294

Incarvillea delavayi
Clump-forming perennial with deeply divided leaves and erect stems bearing several trumpet-shaped, pinkish-red flowers in early summer. Has attractive seed pods. H 45–60cm (18–24in), S 30cm (12in).

☼ ◊

Potentilla nepalensis 'Miss Willmott'
Clump-forming perennial with palmate, strawberry-like, bright green leaves. Numerous slender, branching stems carry cherry-red-centred, pink flowers throughout summer.
H 50cm (20in), S 60cm (24in).

☼ ◊

☐ RED

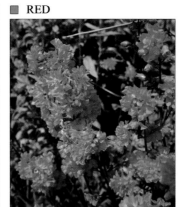

Lychnis viscaria 'Splendens Plena'
Clump-forming perennial bearing spikes of double, magenta flowers in early summer. Stems and large, oval to lance-shaped, basal leaves are covered in sticky hairs. H 30–45cm (12–18in), S 23cm (9in) or more.

☼ ◊

Lychnis coronaria
Clump-forming perennial, often grown as a biennial. From mid- to late summer, brilliant rose-crimson flowers are borne in panicles on branched, grey stems that rise from neat, grey leaves. H 45–60cm (18–24in), S 45cm (18in).

☼ ◊

Sinningia 'Switzerland'
Short-stemmed, tuberous perennial with rosettes of oval, velvety leaves, to 20cm (8in) long. In summer has large, fleshy, trumpet-shaped, bright scarlet flowers with ruffled, white borders.
H to 30cm (12in), S 45cm (18in).
Min. 15°C (59°F).

◐ ◉

Alonsoa warscewiczii, illus. p.329
Geum 'Lionel Cox'
Lychnis viscaria
Potentilla 'Monsieur Rouillard'

Astilbe 'Fanal'
Leafy perennial with strong stems. In summer bears neat, tapering, feathery panicles of tiny, crimson-red flowers that turn brown and keep their shape in winter. Broad leaves are divided into leaflets. Prefers humus-rich soil. H 60cm (24in), S to 90cm (36in).

◐ ◉

Heuchera 'Red Spangles'
Evergreen perennial forming clumps of heart-shaped, purplish-green leaves. Bears spikes of small, bell-shaped, crimson-scarlet flowers in summer. H and S 30cm (12in).

◐ ◊

Salvia blepharophylla
Stachys coccinea
Verbena peruviana

Lotus berthelotii (Coral gem)
Semi-evergreen, straggling perennial
suitable for a hanging basket or large
pan in an alpine house. Has hairy,
silvery branches and leaves, and
clusters of pea-like, scarlet flowers in
summer. H 30cm (12in), S indefinite.
Min. 5°C (41°F).

Columnea crassifolia
Evergreen, shrubby perennial with
fleshy, lance-shaped leaves. Erect,
tubular, hairy, scarlet flowers, about
8cm (3in) long, each with a yellow
throat, are carried from spring to
autumn. H and S to 45cm (18in).
Min. 15°C (59°F).

Potentilla atrosanguinea
Clump-forming perennial with hairy,
palmate, strawberry-like leaves. Loose
clusters of dark red flowers are borne
throughout summer.
H 45cm (18in), S 60cm (24in).

Polemonium carneum
Clump-forming perennial that carries
clusters of cup-shaped, pink or lilac-
pink flowers in early summer. Foliage
is finely divided. H and S 45cm (18in).

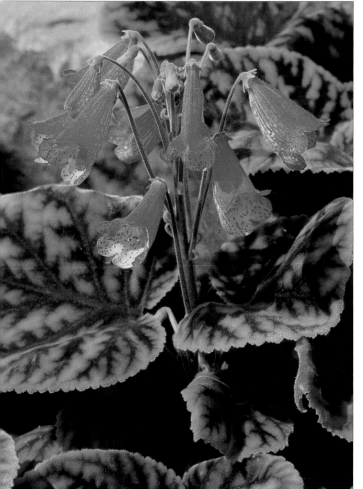

Smithiantha 'Orange King'
Strong-growing, erect, rhizomatous
perennial. Large, scalloped, velvety
leaves are emerald-green with dark red-
marked veins. In summer-autumn has
tubular, orange-red flowers, red-spotted
within and with yellow lips. H and
S to 60cm (24in). Min. 15°C (59°F).

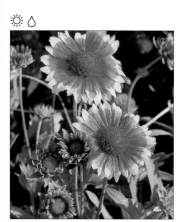

Gaillardia x *grandiflora* 'Dazzler'
Upright, rather open perennial bearing
large, terminal, daisy-like, yellow-
tipped, red flower heads for a long
period in summer. Leaves are soft and
divided. Needs staking and may be
short-lived.
H 60cm (24in), S 50cm (20in).

Kaempferia pulchra
Tufted, rhizomatous perennial with
horizontal, aromatic, dark green
leaves, variegated with paler green
above. Short spikes of lilac-pink
flowers appear from the centre of tufts
in summer. H 15cm (6in),
S 30cm (12in). Min. 18°C (64°F).

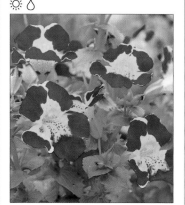

Mimulus 'Royal Velvet'
Compact perennial, often grown as an
annual, producing in summer many
large, snapdragon-like, mahogany-red
flowers with mahogany-speckled, gold
throats. Leaves are mid-green.
H 30cm (12in), S 23cm (9in).

Tulbaghia violacea
Vigorous, semi-evergreen, clump-
forming perennial that in summer-
autumn carries umbels of lilac-purple
or lilac-pink flowers above a mass of
narrow, glaucous, blue-grey leaves.
H 45–60cm (18–24in), S 30cm (12in).

■ PURPLE

Streptocarpus saxorum
(False African violet)
Evergreen, rounded, woody-based
perennial with small, oval, hairy leaves
in whorls. Lilac flowers with white
tubes arise from leaf axils in summer-
autumn. H and S 30cm (12in) or more.
Min. 10–15°C (50–59°F).

☼ ◐

Verbena rigida, syn. *V. venosa*
Neat, compact perennial bearing heads
of pale violet flowers from mid-
summer onwards. Has lance-shaped,
rough, mid-green leaves borne on
flower stems.
H 45–60cm (18–24in), S 30cm (12in).

☼ ◊

Heterocentron elegans, syn. *Heeria
elegans*, *Schizocentron elegans*
Evergreen, mat-forming perennial with
dense, creeping, mid-green foliage.
Massed, bright deep purple flowers
open in summer-autumn and, under
glass, in winter. H 5cm (2in),
S indefinite. Min. 5°C (41°F).

☼ ◊

***Tradescantia* Andersoniana
Group 'Purple Dome'**
Clump-forming perennial with narrow,
lance-shaped leaves, 15–30cm (6–12in)
long. Has clusters of rich purple
flowers, surrounded by 2 leaf-like
bracts, in summer.
H to 60cm (24in), S 45cm (18in).

☼ ◐ ⚠

Centaurea montana
Spreading perennial with many rather
lax stems carrying, in early summer,
one or more large, purple, blue, white
or pink flower heads with thistle-like
centres encircled by star-shaped ray
petals. H 50cm (20in), S 60cm (24in).

☼ ◊

Polemonium pulcherrimum
Vigorous perennial with bright green
leaves divided into leaflets. Tubular,
purple-blue flowers with throats of
yellow or white are borne in summer.
H 50cm (20in), S 30cm (12in).

☼ ◊

***Erigeron* 'Serenity'**
Clump-forming perennial. Many daisy-
like, violet flower heads, with yellow
centres, are borne in early and mid-
summer. Needs some support.
H and S to 60cm (24in).

☼ ◊

Platycodon grandiflorus
(Balloon flower)
Neat, clump-forming perennial that in
summer bears clusters of large, balloon-
like buds opening to bell-shaped, blue
or purplish flowers. Stems are clothed
with bluish-green leaves. H 45–60cm
(18–24in), S 30–45cm (12–18in).

☼ ◊

PERENNIALS

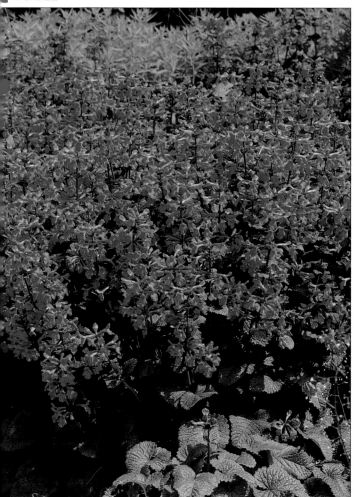

Stachys macrantha 'Superba'
Clump-forming perennial with heart-shaped, soft, wrinkled, mid-green leaves, from which arise stout stems producing whorls of hooded, purple-violet flowers in summer. H 30–45cm (12–18in), S 30–60cm (12–24in).

☼ ◊

Geranium himalayense,
syn. *G. grandiflorum*, *G. meeboldii*
Clump-forming perennial with large, cup-shaped, violet-blue flowers borne on long stalks in summer over dense tufts of neatly cut leaves.
H 30cm (12in), S 60cm (24in).

☼ ◊

Geranium pratense 'Mrs Kendall Clark'
Clump-forming perennial with hairy stems and deeply divided leaves. In early and mid-suumer, bears erect, saucer-shaped, pearl-grey or violet-blue flowers with white or pale pink veins.
H 60–90cm (24–36in), S 60cm (24in).

☼ ◊

Scabiosa caucasica 'Clive Greaves'
Clump-forming perennial that throughout summer has violet-blue flower heads with pincushion-like centres. Basal, mid-green leaves are lance-shaped and slightly lobed on the stems. H and S 45–60cm (18–24in).

☼ ◊

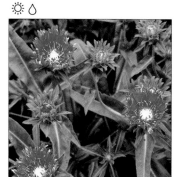

Stokesia laevis
Perennial with overwintering, evergreen rosettes. In summer, cornflower-like, lavender- or purple-blue flower heads are borne freely. Leaves are narrow and mid-green.
H and S 30–45cm (12–18in).

☼ ◊

Geranium × magnificum
Clump-forming perennial with hairy, deeply lobed leaves and cup-shaped, prominently veined, violet-blue flowers borne in small clusters in summer.
H 45cm (18in), S 60cm (24in).

☼ ◊

Geranium 'Johnson's Blue'
Vigorous, clump-forming perennial with many divided leaves and cup-shaped, deep lavender-blue flowers borne throughout summer.
H 30cm (12in), S 60cm (24in).

☼ ◊

Polemonium caeruleum
(Jacob's ladder)
Clump-forming perennial. Clusters of cup-shaped, lavender-blue flowers with orange-yellow stamens open in summer amid finely divided foliage.
H and S 45–60cm (18–24in).

☼ ◊

Catananche caerulea 'Major'
Perennial forming clumps of grassy, grey-green leaves, above which rise wiry, branching stems each carrying a daisy-like, lavender-blue flower head in summer. Propagate regularly by root cuttings.
H 45–60cm (18–24in), S 30cm (24in).

☼ ◊

■ PURPLE

■ BLUE

***Limonium latifolium* 'Blue Cloud'**
Clump-forming perennial. In late summer carries diffuse clusters of bluish-mauve flowers that can be dried for indoor decoration. Has large, leathery, dark green leaves.
H 30cm (12in), S 45cm (18in).

☀ ◊

***Campanula* 'Burghaltii'**
Mound-forming perennial with long, pendent, funnel-shaped, pale lavender flowers displayed on erect, wiry stems in summer. Leaves are oval, soft and leathery. May need staking.
H 60cm (24in), S 30cm (12in).

☀ ◊

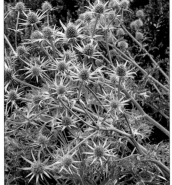

Eryngium bourgatii
Clump-forming perennial that, from mid- to late summer, carries heads of thistle-like, blue-green, then lilac-blue, flowers on branched, wiry stems well above deeply cut, basal, grey-green leaves. H 45–60cm (18–24in), S 30cm (12in).

☀ ◊

***Amsonia orientalis*,**
syn. *Rhazya orientalis*
Neat, clump-forming perennial. In summer, heads of small, star-shaped, grey-blue flowers open on tops of wiry stems clothed with green, sometimes greyish, leaves. H 45–60cm (18–24in), 30–45cm (12–18in).

☀ ◊ ⓘ

***Parahebe perfoliata*, syn. *Veronica perfoliata* (Digger's speedwell)**
Evergreen sub-shrub with willowy stems clasped by leathery, glaucous leaves. Elegant, long, branching sprays of blue flowers are borne in summer.
H 45–60cm (18–24in), S 45cm (18in).

☀ ◊

Anemonopsis macrophylla
(False anemone)
Clump-forming perennial with waxy, nodding, purplish-blue flowers, borne on slender, branching stems in summer above fern-like leaves.
H 45–60cm (18–24in), S 50cm (20in).

◑ ◊

***Nepeta* x *faassenii* (Catmint)**
Bushy, clump-forming perennial, useful for edging. Forms mounds of small, greyish-green leaves, from which loose spikes of tubular, soft lavender-blue flowers appear in early summer. H and S 45cm (18in).

☀ ◊

Eryngium variifolium
Evergreen, rosette-forming perennial with stiff stems that, in late summer, bear heads of thistle-like, grey-blue flowers, each with a collar of white bracts. Jagged-edged leaves are mid-green, marbled with white.
H 45cm (18in), S 25cm (10in).

☀ ◊

Campanula isophylla
Chirita lavandulacea, illus. p.294
IRISES, illus. pp.234–5
Nepeta nervosa

Veronica gentianoides
Mat-forming perennial with spikes of very pale blue flowers opening in early summer on tops of stems that arise from glossy, basal leaves.
H and S 45cm (18in).

☼ ◊

Linum narbonense
Clump-forming, short-lived perennial, best renewed frequently from seed. Has lance-shaped, greyish-green leaves and heads of somewhat cup-shaped, pale to deep blue flowers in spring-summer.
H 30–60cm (12–24in), S 30cm (12in).

☼ ◊

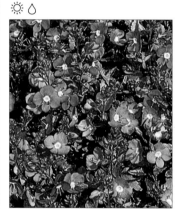

Veronica peduncularis
Mat-forming perennial with ovate to lance-shaped, glossy, purple-tinged, mid-green leaves. Bears abundant, saucer-shaped, deep blue flowers, with small, white eyes, over a long period from early spring to summer.
H to 10cm (4in), S 60cm (24in) or more.

☼ ◊

Veronica spicata subsp. *incana*, syn. *V. incana*
Mat-forming perennial, densely covered with silver hairs, with linear to lance-shaped leaves. In summer, bears spikes of small, star-shaped, clear blue flowers. H and S 30cm (12in).

◑ ◊

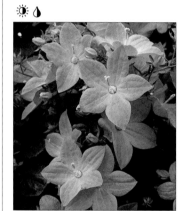

Campanula isophylla Kristal Hybrids 'Stella Blue'
Compact, free-flowering perennial, strong stems and small, heart-shaped, toothed, light green leaves. Large, upright, saucer-shaped, pale blue flowers in mid-summer. H 15–20cm (6–8in), S to 30cm (12in). Min. 5°C (41°F).

◑ ◊

Amsonia tabernaemontana
Clump-forming perennial with willowy stems bearing drooping clusters of small, tubular, pale blue flowers in summer. Leaves are small and narrow.
H 45–60cm (18–24in), S 30cm (12in).

☼ ◊ ①

Myosotidium hortensia
(Chatham Island forget-me-not)
Evergreen, clump-forming perennial bearing large clusters of forget-me-not-like, blue flowers in summer above a basal mound of large, ribbed, glossy leaves. H 45–60cm (18–24in), S 60cm (24in). Min. 0°C (32°F).

☼ ◐

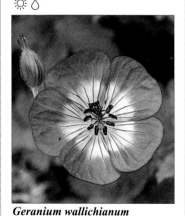

Geranium wallichianum 'Buxton's Variety', syn. *G.w.* 'Buxton's Blue'
Spreading perennial with luxuriant, white-flecked leaves and large, white-centred, blue or blue-purple flowers from mid-summer to autumn.
H 30–45cm (12–18in), S 90cm (36in).

☼ ◊

Salvia patens 'Cambridge Blue'
Erect, branching perennial with ovate, mid-green leaves. From mid-summer to mid-autumn, produces loose terminal racemes of paired, pale blue flowers, 5cm (2in) long, with wide open mouths. H 45–60cm (18–24in), S 45cm (18in).

☼ ◊

Hostas

The luxuriance of their foliage and attractive habit have made hostas, or plantain lilies, increasingly sought after as plants for every garden, large or small. Native to the East, they also add an exotic touch to any waterside or damp, shady corner.

Hosta species vary in size from plants a few centimetres high to vigorous forms that will make a clump of up to 1.5m (5ft) across in a few years. Their elegant leaves are diverse in shape, texture and coloration, with subtle variegations and shadings. Many hostas also produce decorative spikes of flowers, which rise gracefully above the foliage in mid-summer.

Suitable for a range of situations from containers to borders and pool sides, hostas are essentially shade- and moisture-loving plants, preferring rich, well-drained soils. Leaves must be protected from slugs to avoid damage.

H. sieboldii

H. 'Love Pat'

H. undulata var. **univittata**

H. 'Ginko Craig'

H. 'Krossa Regal'

H. sieboldiana var. **elegans**

H. tokudama

H. 'Shade Fanfare'

H. 'Snowden'

H. 'Francee'

H. undulata var. **albomarginata**

H. 'Regal Splendor'

H. tokudama 'Aureonebulosa'

H. 'Hadspen Blue'

H. 'Ground Master'

H. sieboldiana

H. 'Halcyon'

H. tardiflora

H. 'Blue Wedgwood'

H. ventricosa

H. 'Tall Boy'

H. 'Honeybells'

H. 'Yellow River'

H. 'Zounds'

H. plantaginea

H. 'Royal Standard'

H. fortunei 'Albopicta'

H. 'Golden Tiara'

H. 'Kabitan'

H. venusta

H. montana 'Aureomarginata'

H. 'Wide Brim'

H. 'Great Expectations'

H. 'Grand Tiara'

H. ventricosa 'Variegata'

H. 'Gold Standard'

H. sieboldiana 'Frances Williams'

H. fortunei 'Aureomarginata'

H. 'Piedmont Gold'

H. 'Golden Prayers'

H. 'Moonlight'

H. 'Sum and Substance'

PERENNIALS small SUMMER INTEREST

Artemisia pontica
(Roman wormwood)
Vigorous, upright perennial with
aromatic, feathery, silver-green foliage
and tall spikes of small, greyish flower
heads in summer. May spread.
H 60cm (24in), S 20cm (8in).

☼ ◊

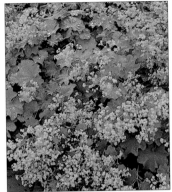

Alchemilla mollis (Lady's mantle)
Clump-forming, ground-cover
perennial that has rounded, pale green
leaves with crinkled edges. Bears small
sprays of tiny, bright greenish-yellow
flowers, with conspicuous outer
calyces, in mid-summer that may
be dried. H and S 50cm (20in).

◑ ◊

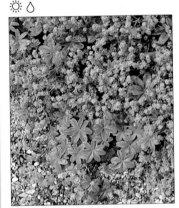

Alchemilla conjuncta
Clump-forming perennial that has neat,
wavy, star-shaped leaves with pale
margins. Loose clusters of tiny,
greenish-yellow flowers, with
conspicuous, outer calyces, appearing
in mid-summer, may be dried for
winter decoration. H and S 30cm (12in).

☼ ◊

Sarracenia flava
(Trumpets, Yellow pitcher plant)
Erect perennial with red-marked,
yellow-green pitchers (modified leaves)
that have hooded tops. From late spring
to early summer bears nodding, yellow
or greenish-yellow flowers.
H and S 45cm (18in).

☼ ●

Sisyrinchium striatum
Semi-evergreen perennial that forms
tufts of long, narrow, grey-green
leaves. Bears slender spikes of purple-
striped, straw-yellow flowers in
summer. Self seeds freely.
H 45–60cm (18–24in), S 30cm (12in).

☼ ◊

Kniphofia 'Little Maid'
Upright perennial with grass-like
leaves and short, erect stems bearing
terminal spikes of pale creamy-yellow
flowers in summer. Protect crowns
with winter mulch.
H 60cm (24in), S 45cm (18in).

☼ ◊

Persicaria virginiana 'Painter's
Palette'
Mounded perennial grown for its
attractive leaves, which are green with
central, brown zones, ivory-yellow
splashes and stripes and an overall
deep pink tinge. Seldom flowers in
cultivation. H and S 60cm (24in).

☼ ◗ ①

Origanum vulgare 'Aureum'
Woody-based perennial forming a
dense mat of aromatic, golden-yellow,
young leaves that turn pale yellow-
green in mid-summer. Occasionally
bears tiny, mauve flowers in summer.
H in leaf 8cm (3in), S indefinite.

☼ ◊

Filipendula ulmaria 'Aurea'
Leafy perennial, grown for its divided
foliage, which is bright golden-yellow
in spring and pale green in summer.
Clusters of creamy-white flowers are
carried in branching heads in mid-
summer. H and S 30cm (12in).

◑ ◗

Osteospermum 'Buttermilk'
Evergreen, upright, semi-woody
perennial. Daisy-like, pale yellow
flower heads, with dark eyes, are borne
singly amid grey-green foliage from
mid-summer to autumn.
H 60cm (24in), S 30cm (12in).
Min. 5°C (41°F).

☼ ◊

Aeschynanthus marmoratus
Clintonia borealis
Elatostema repens var. *pulchra*
Mentha x *gracilis* 'Variegata'

Mentha x *piperita* f. *citrata*
Mentha suaveolens 'Variegata', illus. p.276
Nicotiana 'Lime Green'

Farfugium japonicum 'Aureomaculatum'
IRISES, illus. pp.234–5
Mimulus moschatus

PRIMULAS, illus. pp.272–3
Scrophularia auriculata 'Variegata'

PERENNIALS

Stachys byzantina 'Primrose Heron'
Evergreen, mat-forming perennial with woolly, yellowish-grey leaves, to 10cm (4in) long. Erect stems bear interrupted spikes of pink-purple flowers from early summer to early autumn.
H 45cm (18in), S 60cm (24in).

☼ ◊

Achillea 'Moonshine'
Upright perennial that bears flat heads of bright yellow flowers throughout summer above a mass of small, feathery, grey-green leaves. Divide plants regularly in spring.
H 60cm (24in), S 50cm (20in).

☼ ◊ ⓘ

Barbarea vulgaris 'Variegata'
Perennial with rosettes of long, toothed, glossy leaves, blotched with cream, above which rise branching heads of small, silvery-yellow flowers in early summer.
H 25–45cm (10–18in), S to 23cm (9in).

☼ ◊

Gaillardia aristata (Blanket flower)
Upright, rather open perennial that has large, terminal, daisy-like, single flower heads, rich yellow with red centres, for a long period in summer, and soft, aromatic, divided leaves. Needs staking and may be short-lived.
H 60cm (24in), S 50cm (20in).

☼ ◊

Achillea 'Taygetea',
syn. *A. aegyptica* of gardens
Perennial with erect stems bearing flat heads of lemon-yellow flowers throughout summer above clumps of feathery, grey leaves. Divide and replant every third year.
H 60cm (24in), S 50cm (20in).

☼ ◊ ⓘ

Potentilla recta 'Warrenii',
syn. *P.r.* 'Macrantha'
Clump-forming perennial with lobed, mid-green leaves. Rich golden-yellow flowers are borne on open, branched stems throughout summer.
H 50cm (20in), S 60cm (24in).

☼ ◊

x Solidaster luteus,
syn. x *S. hybridus*
Clump-forming perennial. From mid-summer onwards, slender stems carry dense heads of bright creamy-yellow flowers above narrow, mid-green leaves. H 60cm (24in), S 75cm (30in).

☼ ◊

Helichrysum 'Schwefellicht',
syn. *H.* 'Sulphur Light'
Clump-forming perennial that bears silver-grey leaves and a mass of ever-lasting, fluffy, sulphur-yellow flower heads from mid- to late summer.
H 40–60cm (16–24in), S 30cm (12in). Min. 5°C (41°F).

☼ ◊

Oenothera fruticosa 'Fyrverkeri',
syn. *O.f.* 'Fireworks'
Clump-forming perennial that from mid- to late summer bears spikes of fragrant, cup-shaped flowers. Has reddish stems and glossy, mid-green foliage. H and S 30–38cm (12–15in).

☼ ◊

☐ YELLOW

Ranunculus constantinopolitanus 'Plenus'
Clump-forming perennial with divided, toothed leaves sometimes spotted grey and white. Neat, pompon-like, double, yellow flowers appear in early summer. H 50cm (20in), S 30cm (12in).

Geum 'Lady Stratheden', syn. *G.* 'Goldball'
Clump-forming perennial with lobed leaves and cup-shaped, double, bright yellow flowers with prominent, green stamens borne on slender, branching stems for a long period in summer. H 45–60cm (18–24in), S 45cm (18in).

Gazania rigens var. **uniflora**
Mat-forming perennial, grown as an annual in all except mildest areas. Yellow or orange-yellow flower heads, sometimes with central white spots, are borne singly in early summer above rosettes of narrow, silver-backed leaves. H 23cm (9in), S 20–30cm (8–12in).

Potentilla 'Yellow Queen'
Clump-forming perennial with strawberry-like, dark green leaves and bright yellow flowers in mid-summer. H to 60cm (24in) or more, S 45cm (18in).

Mimulus luteus (Yellow musk)
Spreading perennial. Throughout summer, snapdragon-like, occasionally red-spotted, yellow flowers are freely produced above hairy, mid-green foliage. H and S 30cm (12in).

Potentilla megalantha
Clump-forming perennial with large, palmate, hairy, soft green leaves. Large, rich yellow flowers are produced in summer. H 20cm (8in), S 15cm (6in).

Meconopsis integrifolia
(Lampshade poppy)
Rosette-forming biennial or short-lived perennial carrying spikes of large, pale yellow flowers in late spring and early summer. Has large, pale green leaves. H 45–60cm (18–24in), S 60cm (24in).

Buphthalmum salicifolium
(Yellow ox-eye)
Spreading perennial that carries daisy-like, deep yellow flower heads singly on willowy stems throughout summer. May need staking. Divide regularly; spreads on rich soil. H 60cm (24in), S 90cm (36in).

Ranunculus acris 'Flore Pleno'
(Double meadow buttercup)
Clump-forming perennial. Wiry stems with lobed and cut leaves act as a foil for rosetted, double, golden-yellow flowers in late spring and early summer. H and S 45–60cm (18–24in).

PERENNIALS

Sedum aizoon 'Aurantiacum'
Erect perennial with red stems carrying fleshy, toothed, dark green leaves. In summer produces gently rounded heads of dark yellow flowers followed by red seed capsules. H and S 45cm (18in).

☼ ◊ ⓘ

Hieracium lanatum
Clump-forming perennial that produces mounds of broad, downy, grey leaves, above which dandelion-like, yellow flower heads appear on wiry stems in summer.
H 30–45cm (12–18in), S 30cm (12in).

☼ ◊

Eriophyllum lanatum,
syn. *Bahia lanata*
Perennial forming low cushions of divided, silvery leaves. Daisy-like, yellow flower heads are produced freely in summer, usually singly, on grey stems. H and S 30cm (12in).

☼ ◊

Aeschynanthus speciosus,
syn. *A. splendens*
Evergreen, trailing perennial with waxy, narrowly oval leaves usually carried in whorls. Erect, tubular, bright orange-red flowers are borne in large clusters in summer. H and S 30–60cm (12–24in). Min. 18°C (64°F).

☼◑ ◊

Tropaeolum polyphyllum
Prostrate perennial with spurred, short, trumpet-shaped, rich yellow flowers, borne singly in summer above trailing, grey-green leaves and stems. May spread widely once established but is good on a bank. H 5–8cm (2–3in), S 30cm (12in) or more.

☼ ◊

Coreopsis verticillata
Bushy perennial with finely divided, dark green foliage and many tiny, star-shaped, golden flower heads borne throughout summer. Divide and replant in spring.
H 40–60cm (16–24in), S 30cm (12in).

☼ ◊

Inula ensifolia
Clump-forming perennial with small, lance-shaped to elliptic leaves, bearing many daisy-like, yellow flower heads, singly on wiry stalks, in late summer. H and S 30cm (12in).

☼ ◊

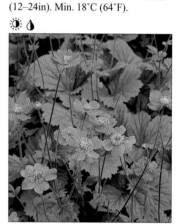

Geum coccineum,
syn. *Geum* x *borisii* of gardens
Clump-forming perennial with irregularly lobed leaves, above which in summer rise slender, branching, hairy stems bearing single, orange flowers with prominent, yellow stamens. H and S 30cm (12in).

☼ ◊

Coreopsis lanceolata
Bushy perennial that in summer freely produces daisy-like, bright yellow flower heads on branching stems. Lance-shaped leaves are borne on lower stems. Propagate by seed or division.
H 45cm (18in), S 30cm (12in).

☼ ◊

Impatiens repens
Evergreen, creeping perennial with rooting stems. Has small, oval to rounded leaves and, in summer, yellow flowers, each with a large, hairy spur.
H to 5cm (2in), S indefinite.
Min. 10°C (50°F).

☼ ◑

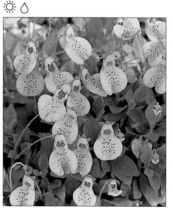

Calceolaria 'John Innes'
Vigorous, evergreen, clump-forming perennial that in spring-summer produces large, pouch-like, reddish-brown-spotted, deep yellow flowers, several to each stem. Has broadly oval, basal, mid-green leaves. H 15–20cm (6–8in), S 25–30cm (10–12in).

☼ ◊

Rhodiola heterodonta,
syn. *Sedum heterodontum, S. rosea* var. *heterodontum*
Clump-forming perennial with heads of yellow or red, sometimes greenish flowers from spring to early summer. Stems bear toothed, blue-green leaves. H 45cm (18in), S 25cm (10in).

☼ ◊

PERENNIALS

☐ WHITE–PINK

▨▨☐ RED–YELLOW

Tricyrtis hirta var. **alba**
Upright, rhizomatous perennial that
bears clusters of large, bell-shaped,
spurred, white flowers, occasionally
purple-spotted, in upper leaf axils of
hairy, stem-clasping, dark green leaves
during late summer and early autumn.
H 45–60cm (18–24in), S 45cm (18in).

☼ ◗

Sedum spectabile 'Brilliant'
(Ice-plant)
Clump-forming perennial that from late
summer to autumn produces flat heads
of bright rose-pink flowers. These are
borne profusely over a mass of fleshy,
grey-green leaves and attract butterflies.
H and S 30–45cm (12–18in).

☼ ◊ ⊙

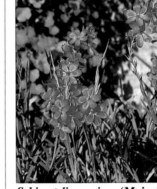

Schizostylis coccinea 'Major',
syn. *S.c.* 'Grandiflora'
Rhizomatous perennial with long,
narrow, grass-like leaves. Gladiolus-
like spikes of cup-shaped, bright
crimson flowers appear in autumn.
H 60cm (24in) or more,
S 30cm (12in) or more.

☼ ◗

Liriope muscari
Evergreen, spreading perennial that
in autumn carries spikes of thickly
clustered, rounded-bell-shaped,
lavender or purple-blue flowers
among narrow, glossy, dark green
leaves. H 30cm (12in), S 45cm (18in).

☼ ◊

Cautleya spicata
Upright perennial that in summer and
early autumn bears spikes of light
orange or soft yellow flowers in
maroon-red bracts. Has handsome,
long, mid-green leaves. Needs a
sheltered site and rich, deep soil.
H 60cm (24in), S 50cm (20in).

☼ ◗

Chirita lavandulacea
Evergreen, erect perennial with downy,
pale green leaves to 20cm (8in) long.
In leaf axils has clusters of lavender-
blue flowers with white tubes. May
be sown in succession to flower from
spring to autumn. H and S 60cm (24in).
Min. 15°C (59°F).

☼ ◊

Schizostylis coccinea 'Sunrise'
Clump-forming, rhizomatous perennial
that in early autumn produces spikes of
large, shallowly cup-shaped, pink
flowers above grassy, mid-green
foliage.
H 60cm (24in), S 23–30cm (9–12in).

☼ ◗

Senecio pulcher
Perennial with leathery, hairy, dark
green leaves. In summer-autumn
produces handsome, daisy-like,
yellow-centred, bright purplish-pink
flower heads. H 45–60cm (18–24in), S
50cm (20in). Min. 0°C (32°F).

☼ ◊ ⊙

Arctotheca calendula
(Cape dandelion)
Carpeting perennial. Leaves are woolly
below, rough-haired above. Heads of
daisy-like, bright yellow flowers, with
darker yellow centres, appear from late
spring to autumn. H 30cm (12in),
S indefinite. Min. 5°C (41°F).

☼ ◊

Begonias

The genus *Begonia* is one of the most versatile, providing interest year-round. Semperflorens begonias are excellent for summer bedding, while the Rex-cultorum group has distinctive and handsome foliage. Others, such as the Tuberhybrida cultivars with their large and showy blooms, are grown mainly for their flowers. Many also make attractive plants for hanging baskets.

B. 'Billie Langdon'

B. scharffii

B. 'Merry Christmas'

B. masoniana

B. prismatocarpa

B. albopicta

B. 'Weltoniensis'

B. 'Orpha C. Fox'

B. 'Flamboyant'

B. bowerae

B. 'Apricot Cascade'

B. foliosa

B. 'Ingramii'

B. 'Roy Hartley'

B. 'Helen Lewis'

B. 'Can-Can'

B. olsoniae

B. metallica

B. 'Lucerna'

B. 'Duartei'

B. manicata 'Crispa'

B. 'Orange Rubra'

B. manicata

B. serratipetala

B. 'Red Ascot'

B. 'Thurstonii'

B. 'Tiger Paws'

B. 'Organdy'

B. pustulata 'Argentea'

B. 'Oliver Twist'

B. sutherlandii

Orchids

Flamboyant, exotic, even seductive, orchids are prized for their unusual flowers. Their aura of mystique and many popular misconceptions may have discouraged gardeners from growing these beautiful plants, but their cultivation is not always difficult and some will thrive happily indoors as house plants.

There are two main groups. Terrestrials grow in a wide range of habitats in the wild; many are at least frost hardy. Epiphytes, the more showy of the two and mostly native to the tropics, cling to tree branches or rocks, obtaining nourishment through their leaves and aerial roots. They need special composts and in cool climates must be grown under glass (see also 'Orchids', p.637).

(Key: x *Brass.* – x *Brassolaeliocattleya*; *Cym.* – *Cymbidium*; x *Oda.* – x *Odontioda*; *Odm.* – *Odontoglossum*; *Paphioped.* – *Paphiopedilum*; x *Soph.* – x *Sophrolaeliocattleya*; e – epiphyte; t – terrestrial)

Coelogyne cristata [e]

Masdevallia infracta [e]

Lemboglossum rossii [e]

Cypripedium acaule [t]

Masdevallia tovarensis [e]

Dendrobium infundibulum [e]

Coelogyne flaccida [e]

Calanthe vestita [t]

Lemboglossum cervantesii [e]

Dendrobium aphyllum [e]

Phalaenopsis Allegria [e]

Odm. Royal Occasion [e]

Paphiopedilum Freckles [t] ①

Paphiopedilum fairrieanum [t] ①

Oncidium ornithorrhynchum [e]

Paphiopedilum niveum [t] ①

Coelogyne nitida [e]

Cymbidium Portelet Bay [e] ①

Angraecum sesquipedale [e]

Paphiopedilum callosum [t] ①

Cypripedium reginae [t]

Spiranthes cernua [t]

Odm. crispum [e]

Cymbidium Strathbraan [e] ①

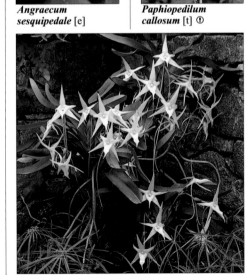

Brassavola nodosa [e]

Paphiopedilum appletonianum [t] ①

Miltoniopsis Robert Strauss 'Ardingly' [e]

Paphiopedilum bellatulum [t] ①

Lemboglossum bictoniense [e]

Dendrobium nobile [e]

Ophrys enthredinifera [t]

x *Brass.* Hetherington Horace 'Coronation' [e]

Laelia anceps [e]

x *Brassocattleya* Mount Adams [e]

Phalaenopsis Lady Jersey x Lippeglut [e]

Calypso bulbosa [t]

Pleione bulbocodioides [t]

Bletilla striata [t]

x *Brass.* St Helier [e]

Cattleya bowringiana [e]

Masdevallia coccinea [e]

Cattleya J.A. Carbone [e]

x *Soph.* Trizac 'Purple Emperor' [e]

Miltoniopsis Anjou 'St Patrick' [e]

Odm. Le Nez Point [e]

x *Oda.* Petit Port [e]

x *Laeliocattleya* Rojo 'Mont Millais' [e]

x *Oda.* Mount Bingham [e]

x *Vuylstekeara* Cambria 'Lensing's Favorite' [e]

Epidendrum ibaguense [e]

Cym. Strathdon 'Cooksbridge Noel' [e] ①

Phaius tankervilleae [t]

Cymbidium Strath Kanaid [e] ①

Cymbidium Pontac 'Mont Millais' [e] ①

Rossioglossum grande [e]

Paphiopedilum Maudiae [t] ①

Paphiopedilum Lyric 'Glendora' [t] ①

Lemboglossum cordatum [e]

x *Wilsonara* Hambuhren Stern 'Cheam' [e]

x *Oda.* Pacific Gold x *Odm. cordatum* [e]

x *Odontocidium* Artur Elle 'Colombian' [e]

x *Odontocidium* Tiger Butter x *Wilsonara* Wigg's 'Kay' [e]

PERENNIALS

297

Orchids continued

Phalaenopsis cornu-cervi [e]

Cymbidium devonianum [e] ①

Paphiopedilum sukhakulii [t] ①

Gomesa planifolia [e]

Paphioped. Buckhurst 'Mont Millais' [t] ①

Miltonia candida [e]

Zygopetalum mackaii [e]

Paphiopedilum haynaldianum [t] ①

Odm. Eric Young [e]

x *Aliceara* Dark Warrior [e]

Zygopetalum Perrenoudii [e]

Coelogyne speciosa [e]

Masdevallia wagneriana [e]

x *Odontocidium* Tigersun 'Orbec' [e]

Gongora quinquenervis [e]

Ophrys fusca [t]

Cymbidium King's Loch 'Cooksbridge' [e] ①

Phalaenopsis Lundy [e]

Oncidium tigrinum [e]

Bulbophyllum careyanum [e]

Orchis morio [t]

Cymbidium hookerianum [e] ①

Cymbidium Caithness Ice 'Trinity' [e] ①

Cymbidium elegans [e] ①

Ophrys lutea [t]

Miltonia clowesii [e]

Vanda Rothschildiana [e]

Cymbidium tracyanum [e] ①

Epidendrum difforme [e]

Cypripedium calceolus [t]

Cypripedium macranthos [t]

PERENNIALS

Maxillaria porphyrostele [e]

× *Potinara* Cherub 'Spring Daffodil' [e]

Laelia cinnabarina [e]

Dendrobium chrysotoxum [e]

Lycaste cruenta [e]

Psychopsis papilio [e]

× *Odontocidium* Tiger Hambuhren [e]

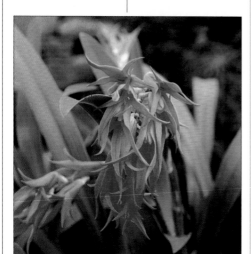

Oncidium flexuosum [e]

Ada aurantiaca [e]

Cypripedium pubescens [t]

× *Soph.* Hazel Boyd 'Apricot Glow' [e]

Cymbidium Christmas Angel 'Cooksbridge Sunburst' [e] ①

Paphiopedilum venustum [t] ①

× *Oda.* (Chantos × Marzorka) × *Odm.* Buttercrisp [e]

□ WHITE

Spathiphyllum 'Mauna Loa'
Robust, evergreen, tufted perennial with rhizomes. Has long, lance-shaped, glossy leaves. Irregularly bears fleshy, white spadices of fragrant flowers enclosed in large, oval, white spathes. H and S 45–60cm (18–24in). Min. 15°C (59°F).

☀ ◊ ①

Episcia dianthiflora, syn. *Alsobia dianthiflora* (Lace flower)
Evergreen perennial with creeping, prostrate stems. Has thick, velvety leaves with brownish midribs and, intermittently, pure white flowers with fringed petals. H 10cm (4in), S indefinite. Min. 15°C (59°F).

☀ ◊

Hemigraphis repanda
Evergreen, prostrate perennial with spreading, rooting stems. Lance-shaped, toothed, purple-tinged leaves, 5cm (2in) long, are darker purple below. Has tiny, tubular, white flowers intermittently. H to 15cm (6in), S indefinite. Min. 15°C (59°F).

☀ ◊

OTHER RECOMMENDED PLANTS:
AFRICAN VIOLETS, illus. p.302
Aglaonema commutatum
Aglaonema 'Malay Beauty'

BROMELIADS, illus. p.265
Peperomia argyreia
Sonerila margaritacea

☐ WHITE

Spathiphyllum wallisii
(Peace lily, White sails)
Evergreen, tufted, rhizomatous
perennial. Has clusters of long, lance-
shaped leaves. Fleshy, white spadices
of fragrant flowers in white spathes are
irregularly produced. H and S 30cm
(12in) or more. Min. 15°C (59°F).

☼ ◊ ①

Pilea cadierei (Aluminium plant)
Evergreen, bushy perennial with
broadly oval leaves, each with a
sharply pointed tip and raised, silvery
patches that appear quilted. Has
insignificant, greenish flowers.
H and S 30cm (12in).
Min. 10°C (50°F).

☼ ◊

Tradescantia fluminensis
'Variegata', syn. *T. albiflora*
'Variegata'
Evergreen, trailing perennial with
rooting stems and leaves, irregularly
striped creamy-white. Intermittently
has clusters of white flowers. H 30cm
(12in), S indefinite. Min. 15°C (59°F).

☼ ◊ ①

Fittonia albivenis Argyroneura
Group (Silver net-leaf)
Evergreen, creeping perennial with
small, oval, white-veined, olive-green
leaves. Remove flowers if they form.
H to 15cm (6in), S indefinite.
Min. 15°C (59°F).

☼ ◊

Tradescantia fluminensis
'Albovittata', syn. *T. albiflora*
'Albovittata'
Strong-growing, evergreen perennial
with trailing, rooting stems. Bluish-
green leaves have broad, white stripes.
Bears small, white flowers. H 30cm
(12in), S indefinite. Min. 15°C (59°F).

☼ ◊ ①

Aglaonema commutatum
'Treubii'
Evergreen, erect, tufted perennial.
Lance-shaped leaves, to 30cm (12in)
long, are marked with pale green or
silver. Occasionally has greenish-white
spathes. H and S to 45cm (18in).
Min. 15°C (59°F).

☼ ◊

***Glechoma hederacea* 'Variegata'**
(Variegated ground ivy)
Evergreen, carpeting perennial that has
small, heart-shaped leaves, with white
marbling, on trailing stems. Bears
insignificant flowers in summer.
Spreads rapidly but is useful for a
container. H 15cm (6in), S indefinite.

☼ ◊

Helleborus* × *hybridus
(Lenten rose) [white form]
Evergreen, clump-forming perennial
with dense, divided foliage, above
which rise nodding, cup-shaped, white,
pink or purple flowers, sometimes
darker spotted, in winter or early
spring. H and S 45cm (18in).

☼ ◊ ①

Peperomia caperata
(Emerald ripple)
Evergreen, bushy perennial with
pinkish leaf stalks. Has oval, fleshy,
wrinkled, dark green leaves, to 5cm
(2in) long, with sunken veins; spikes of
white flowers appear irregularly. H and
S to 15cm (6in). Min. 10°C (50°F).

☼ ◊

Sonerila margaritacea 'Argentea'
Sonerila margaritacea 'Hendersonii'
Spathiphyllum floribundum
Spathiphyllum wallisii 'Clevelandii'

Chlorophytum comosum 'Vittatum'
Evergreen, tufted, rosette-forming perennial. Long, narrow, lance-shaped, creamy-white leaves have green stripes and margins. Irregularly has small, star-shaped, white flowers on thin stems. H and S 30cm (12in). Min. 5°C (41°F).

☀ ◊

Aspidistra elatior 'Variegata'
Evergreen, rhizomatous perennial with upright, narrow, glossy, dark green leaves which are longitudinally cream-striped. Occasionally has inconspicuous, cream to purple flowers near soil level. H 60cm (24in), S 45cm (18in). Min. 5–10°C (41–50°F).

◖ ◊

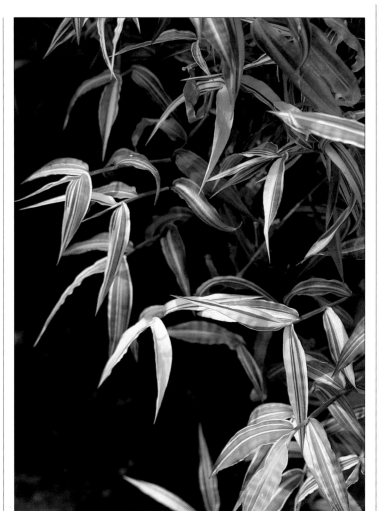

Oplismenus africanus 'Variegatus',
syn. *O. hirtellus* 'Variegatus'
Evergreen, creeping, perennial grass with wiry, rooting stems. White-striped leaves, with wavy margins, are often tinged pink. Bears inconspicuous flowers intermittently. H 20cm (8in) or more, S indefinite. Min. 12°C (54°F).

◐ ◊

Streptocarpus 'Nicola'
Evergreen, stemless perennial with a rosette of strap-shaped, wrinkled leaves. Funnel-shaped, rose-pink flowers are produced intermittently in small clusters. H 25cm (10in), S 50cm (20in). Min. 10–15°C (50–59°F).

☀ ◊

Tradescantia zebrina, syn.
Zebrina pendula (Silver inch plant)
Evergreen, trailing or mat-forming perennial. Bluish-green leaves, purple-tinged beneath, have 2 broad, silver bands. Has pink or violet-blue flowers intermittently during the year. H 15cm (6in), S indefinite. Min. 15°C (59°F).

☀ ◊ ①

Helleborus niger (Christmas rose)
Evergreen, clump-forming perennial with divided, deep green leaves and cup-shaped, nodding, white flowers, with golden stamens, borne in winter or early spring. H and S 30cm (12in).

☀ ◊ ①

Helleborus x sternii
Evergreen, clump-forming perennial with divided leaves and cup-shaped, often pink-tinged, pale green flowers borne in terminal clusters in winter and early spring. H and S 45cm (18in).

☀ ◊ ①

Helleborus x hybridus
(Lenten rose) [pink form]
Evergreen, clump-forming perennial with dense, divided foliage, above which rise nodding, cup-shaped, white, pink or purple flowers, sometimes darker spotted, in winter or early spring. H and S 45cm (18in).

◐ ◊ ①

Episcia cupreata (Flame violet)
Evergreen, creeping perennial. Has small, downy, wrinkled leaves, usually silver-veined or -banded, and, intermittently, scarlet flowers marked yellow within. H 10cm (4in), S indefinite. Min. 15°C (59°F).

☀ ◊

African violets

African violet is the common name for the genus *Saintpaulia*, although it is often used for the many cultivars derived from *S. ionantha*. These small, rosetted perennials may be grown as summer bedding in warm, humid climates but also make attractive indoor pot plants, flowering freely if kept in a draught-free, light, humid position. A wide range of flower colours and forms is available.

S. 'Rococo Anna'

S. 'Garden News'

S. 'Starry Trail'

S. 'Pip Squeek'

S. 'Colorado'

S. 'Porcelain'

S. 'Ice Maiden'

S. 'Zoja'

S. 'Bright Eyes'

S. 'Delft'

Anthurium scherzerianum
(Flamingo flower)
Evergreen, tufted perennial with erect, leathery, dark green leaves to 20cm (8in) long. Has large, long-lasting, bright red spathes and fleshy, orange to yellow spadices. H and S 30–60cm (12–24in). Min. 15°C (59°F).

☀ ⬤ ⓘ

Helleborus* x *hybridus
(Lenten rose) [purple form]
Evergreen, clump-forming perennial with dense, divided foliage, above which rise nodding, cup-shaped, white, pink or purple flowers, sometimes darker spotted, in winter or early spring. H and S 45cm (18in).

☀ ◌ ⓘ

Gerbera jamesonii
(Barberton daisy)
Evergreen, upright perennial with daisy-like, variably coloured flower heads, borne intermittently on long stems, and basal rosettes of large, jagged leaves. Flowers excellent for cutting. H 60cm (24in), S 45cm (18in). Min. 5°C (41°F).

☀ ◌

***Phormium* 'Bronze Baby'**
Evergreen, upright perennial with tufts of bold, stiff, pointed, wine-red leaves. Panicles of reddish flowers are occasionally produced on purplish stems during summer. H and S 45–60cm (18–24in). Min. 2°C (35°F).

☀ ⬤

***Tellima grandiflora* Rubra Group**, syn. *T.g.* 'Purpurea'
Semi-evergreen, clump-forming perennial with a mass of hairy, basal, reddish-purple leaves, underlaid dark green. In late spring, erect stems bear spikes of bell-shaped, pinkish-cream flowers. H and S 60cm (24in).

☀ ◌

***Fittonia albivenis* Verschaffeltii Group**, syn. *F. verschaffeltii*
(Painted net-leaf)
Evergreen, creeping perennial with small, oval, red-veined, olive-green leaves. Flowers are best removed if they form. H to 15cm (6in), S indefinite. Min. 15°C (59°F).

☀ ◌

Alternanthera ficoidea var. *amoena*
Alternanthera ficoidea 'Versicolor'
Bergenia purpurascens
Bertolonia marmorata

ORCHIDS, illus. pp.296–9

PERENNIALS

Ophiopogon planiscapus 'Nigrescens'
Evergreen, spreading, clump-forming perennial, grown for its distinctive, grass-like, black leaves. Racemes of lilac flowers in summer are followed by black fruits. H 23cm (9in), S 30cm (12in).

Elatostema repens
(Watermelon begonia)
Evergreen, creeping perennial with rooting stems. Broadly oval, olive-green leaves have purplish-brown edges and paler green centres. Flowers are insignificant. H 10cm (4in), S indefinite. Min. 15°C (59°F).

Tetranema roseum,
syn. *T. mexicanum* (Mexican foxglove, Mexican violet)
Short-stemmed perennial with crowded, stalkless leaves, bluish-green beneath. Intermittently, has nodding, purple flowers with paler throats. H to 20cm (8in), S 30cm (12in). Min. 13°C (55°F).

Cyanotis somaliensis (Pussy ears)
Evergreen, creeping perennial. Small, narrow, glossy, dark green leaves with white hairs surround stems. Has purplish-blue flowers in leaf axils in winter-spring. H 5cm (2in), S indefinite. Min. 10–15°C (50–59°F).

Tradescantia pallida 'Purpurea'
Evergreen, creeping perennial with dark purple stems and slightly fleshy leaves. Has pink or pink-and-white flowers in summer. H 30–40cm (12–16in), S 30cm (12in) or more. Min. 15°C (59°F).

Ajuga reptans 'Multicolor',
syn. *A.r.* 'Rainbow'
Evergreen, mat-forming perennial. Dark green leaves, marked with cream and pink, make good ground cover. Spikes of small, blue flowers appear in spring. H 12cm (5in), S 45cm (18in).

Maranta leuconeura 'Erythroneura', syn. *M.l.* 'Erythrophylla' (Herringbone plant)
Evergreen perennial. Oblong leaves have veins marked red, with paler yellowish-green midribs, and are upright at night, flat by day. H and S to 30cm (12in). Min. 15°C (59°F).

Ajuga reptans 'Atropurpurea'
Evergreen, ground-cover perennial, spreading freely by runners, with small rosettes of glossy, deep bronze-purple leaves. Short spikes of blue flowers appear in spring. H 15cm (6in), S 90cm (36in).

Tradescantia sillamontana,
syn. *T. pexata, T. velutina*
Evergreen, erect perennial. Oval, stem-clasping leaves are densely covered with white, woolly hairs. Has clusters of small, bright purplish-pink flowers in summer. H and S to 30cm (12in). Min. 10–15°C (50–59°F).

Streptocarpus 'Constant Nymph'
Evergreen, stemless perennial with a rosette of strap-shaped, wrinkled leaves. Funnel-shaped, purplish-blue flowers, darker veined and yellow-throated, are intermittently produced in small clusters. H 25cm (10in), S 50cm (20in). Min. 10–15°C (50–59°F).

Sansevieria trifasciata 'Hahnii'
Evergreen, stemless perennial with a rosette of about 5 stiff, erect, broadly lance-shaped and pointed leaves, banded horizontally with pale green or white. Occasionally has small, pale green flowers. H 15–30cm (6–12in), S 10cm (4in). Min. 15°C (59°F).

PERENNIALS

◻ GREEN

Calathea makoyana
(Peacock plant)
Evergreen, clump-forming perennial.
Horizontal leaves, 30cm (12in) long,
are dark and light green above, reddish-
purple below. Intermittently has short
spikes of white flowers. H to 60cm (2ft),
S to 1.2m (4ft). Min. 15°C (59°F).

Maranta leuconeura var.
kerchoviana (Rabbit tracks)
Evergreen perennial that intermittently
bears white to mauve flowers. Oblong
leaves with dark brown blotches
become greener with age and are
upright at night, flat by day. H and
S to 30cm (12in). Min. 15°C (59°F).

Stachys byzantina,
syn. *S. lanata*, *S. olympica*
(Bunnies' ears, Lamb's tongue)
Evergreen, mat-forming perennial with
woolly, grey foliage that is excellent
for a border front or as ground cover.
Bears mauve-pink flowers in summer.
H 30–38cm (12–15in), S 60cm (24in).

Aglaonema pictum
Evergreen, erect, tufted perennial.
Oval leaves, to 15cm (6in) long, are
irregularly marked with greyish-white
or grey-green. Has creamy-white
spathes in summer. H and S to
60cm (24in). Min. 15°C (59°F).

Welwitschia mirabilis,
syn. *W. bainesii*
Evergreen perennial with a short, woody
trunk. Has 2 strap-shaped leaves, to
2.5m (8ft) long, with tips splitting to
form many tendril-like strips. Bears
small, reddish-brown cones. H to 30cm
(12in), S indefinite. Min. 10°C (50°F).

Ophiopogon japonicus
Evergreen, clump or mat-forming
perennial with grass-like, glossy, dark
green foliage. Spikes of lilac flowers
in late summer are followed by blue-
black berries. H 30cm (12in),
S indefinite.

Soleirolia soleirolii, syn.
Helxine soleirolii (Baby's tears,
Mind-your-own-business)
Usually evergreen, invasive, prostrate
perennial with small, round, vivid
green leaves that form a carpet. May
choke other plants if not controlled.
H 5cm (2in), S indefinite.

***Aglaonema* 'Silver King'**
Evergreen, erect, tufted perennial.
Broadly lance-shaped, mid-green
leaves, to 30cm (12in) long, are
marked with dark and light green. Has
greenish-white spathes in summer.
H and S to 45cm (18in).
Min. 15°C (59°F).

Peperomia marmorata
(Silver heart)
Evergreen, bushy perennial with
insignificant flowers. Has oval, long-
pointed, fleshy, dull green leaves,
marked with greyish-white and quilted
above, reddish below. H and S to
20cm (8in). Min. 10°C (50°F).

Helleborus argutifolius
Clump-forming perennial with
evergreen, divided, spiny, dark green
leaves and cup-shaped, pale green
flowers borne in large clusters in
winter-spring.
H 60cm (24in), S 45cm (18in).

Callisia repens
Evergreen, creeping perennial with
rooting stems and densely packed
leaves, sometimes white-banded and
often purplish beneath. Rarely, has
inconspicuous, white flowers in winter.
H 10cm (4in), S indefinite.
Min. 15°C (59°F).

Ajuga pyramidalis 'Metallica Crispa'
Ajuga reptans 'Jungle Beauty'
Aspidistra elatior
Callisia navicularis

Chamaemelum nobile
Chamaemelum nobile 'Treneague'
Chlorophytum comosum
Peperomia clusiifolia

Peperomia griseoargentea
Peperomia metallica
Peperomia obtusifolia
Peperomia rubella

Plectranthus oertendahlii
Plectranthus verticillatus
Tradescantia fluminensis

PERENNIALS

Drosera spatulata
Evergreen, insectivorous perennial with rosettes of spoon-shaped leaves that have sensitive, red, glandular hairs. Has many small, pink or white flowers on leafless stems in summer. H and S to 8cm (3in). Min. 5–10°C (41–50°F).

Drosera capensis (Cape sundew)
Evergreen, insectivorous perennial. Rosettes of narrow leaves have sensitive, red, glandular hairs. Many small, purple flowers are borne on leafless stems in summer. H and S to 15cm (6in). Min. 5–10°C (41–50°F).

Helleborus foetidus
(Stinking hellebore)
Evergreen, clump-forming perennial with deeply divided, dark green leaves and, in late winter and early spring, panicles of cup-shaped, red-margined, pale green flowers.
H and S 45cm (18in).

Peperomia glabella (Wax privet)
Evergreen perennial with wide-spreading, red stems. Has broadly oval, fleshy, glossy, bright green leaves, to 5cm (2in) long, and insignificant flowers. H to 15cm (6in), S 30cm (12in). Min. 10°C (50°F).

Peperomia obtusifolia 'Variegata'
Evergreen, bushy perennial with spade-shaped, fleshy leaves, to 20cm (8in) long, that have irregular, yellowish-green to creamy-white margins and usually greyish centres. Flowers are insignificant. H and S to 15cm (6in). Min. 10°C (50°F).

Iresine herbstii 'Aureoreticulata'
Evergreen, bushy perennial with red stems and inconspicuous flowers. Rounded, mid-green leaves, 10cm (4in) long, have yellow or red veins and notched tips.
H to 60cm (24in), S 45cm (18in). Min. 10–15°C (50–59°F).

Sansevieria trifasciata 'Golden Hahnii'
Evergreen, stemless perennial with a rosette of about 5 stiff, erect, broadly lance-shaped leaves with wide, yellow borders. Sometimes bears small, pale green flowers. H 15–30cm (6–12in), S 10cm (4in). Min. 15°C (59°F).

Helleborus viridis
(Green hellebore)
Clump-forming perennial with deciduous, divided, dark green leaves. Bears cup-shaped, green fl owers in late winter or early spring. H and S 30cm (12in).

Pilea nummulariifolia
(Creeping Charlie)
Evergreen, mat-forming perennial with creeping, rooting, reddish stems. Rounded, pale green leaves, about 2cm (¾in) wide, have a corrugated surface. Flowers are insignificant. H to 5cm (2in), S 30cm (12in). Min. 10°C (50°F).

Dionaea muscipula (Venus flytrap)
Evergreen, insectivorous perennial with rosettes of 6 or more spreading, hinged leaves, pink-flushed inside, edged with stiff bristles. Clusters of tiny, white flowers are carried in summer. H 10cm (4in), S 30cm (12in). Min. 5°C (41°F).

Nautilocalyx lynchii
Robust, evergreen, erect, bushy perennial. Broadly lance-shaped, slightly wrinkled leaves are glossy, greenish-red above, reddish beneath. In summer has tubular, red-haired, pale yellow flowers with red calyces. H and S to 60cm (24in). Min. 15°C (59°F).

BROMELIADS, illus. p.265
Helleborus lividus
ORCHIDS, illus. pp.296–9
Tolmiea menziesii

Adonis amurensis, illus. p.275
BROMELIADS, illus. p.265
ORCHIDS, illus. pp.296–9
Peperomia obtusifolia 'Greengold'

Pilea involucrata
Tradescantia spathacea 'Vittata'

GRASSES, BAMBOOS, RUSHES *and* SEDGES

WHITE–GREEN

PERENNIALS

Cortaderia selloana 'Silver Comet'
Evergreen, clump-forming, perennial grass with very narrow, sharp-edged, recurved leaves, 1m (3ft) long, that have silver margins. Carries plume-like panicles of spikelets from late summer. H 1.2–1.5m (4–5ft), S 1m (3ft).

Pleioblastus variegatus, syn. *Arundinaria fortunei*, *A. variegata* (Dwarf white-stripe bamboo)
Evergreen, slow-spreading bamboo with narrow, slightly downy, white-striped leaves. Stems are branched near the base. H 80cm (30in), S indefinite.

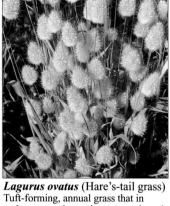

Lagurus ovatus (Hare's-tail grass)
Tuft-forming, annual grass that in early summer bears dense, egg-shaped, soft panicles of white flower spikes, with golden stamens, lasting well into autumn. Leaves are long, narrow and flat. Self seeds readily.
H 45cm (18in), S 15cm (6in).

Glyceria maxima 'Variegata', syn. *G. aquatica* 'Variegata'
Herbaceous, spreading, perennial grass with cream-striped leaves, often tinged pink at the base. Bears open panicles of greenish spikelets in summer.
H 80cm (30in), S indefinite.

Phalaris arundinacea var. **picta**, syn. *P.a.* 'Picta' (Gardener's garters)
Evergreen, spreading, perennial grass with broad, white-striped leaves. Produces narrow panicles of spikelets in summer. Can be invasive.
H 1m (3ft), S indefinite.

Arundo donax var. **versicolor**, syn. *A.d.* 'Variegata'
Herbaceous, rhizomatous, perennial grass with strong stems bearing broad, creamy-white-striped leaves. May bear dense, erect panicles of whitish-yellow spikelets in late summer.
H 2.5–3m (8–10ft), S 60cm (2ft).

Miscanthus sinensis 'Zebrinus'
Herbaceous, clump-forming, perennial grass. Leaves, hairy beneath, have transverse, yellowish-white ring markings. May carry awned, hairy, white spikelets in fan-shaped panicles in autumn. H 1.2m (4ft), S 45cm (1½ft).

Holcus mollis 'Albovariegatus', syn. *H.m.* 'Variegatus' (Variegated creeping soft grass)
Evergreen, spreading, perennial grass with white-striped leaves and hairy nodes. In summer carries purplish-white flower spikes.
H 30–45cm (12–18in), S indefinite.

Sasa veitchii, syn. *S. albomarginata*
Evergreen, slow-spreading bamboo. Leaves, 25cm (10in) long, soon develop white edges. Stems, often purple, produce a single branch at each node. White powder appears beneath nodes. H to 1.5m (5ft), S indefinite.

Cortaderia selloana 'Sunningdale Silver'
Evergreen, clump-forming, perennial grass with narrow, sharp-edged, recurved leaves, 1.5m (5ft) long. Bears long-lasting, feathery panicles of creamy-white spikelets in late summer.
H 2.1m (7ft), S 1.2m (4ft).

Schoenoplectus lacustris subsp. **tabernaemontani 'Zebrinus'**
Evergreen, spreading, perennial sedge with leafless stems, striped horizontally with white, and brown spikelets in summer. Withstands brackish water.
H 1.5m (5ft), S indefinite.

OTHER RECOMMENDED PLANTS:
Arrhenatherum elatius subsp. *bulbosum* 'Variegatum'
Arundo donax

Carex riparia 'Variegata'
Chionochloa conspicua
Cortaderia selloana
Cyperus albostriatus 'Variegatus'

Dactylis glomerata 'Variegata'
Luzula sylvatica 'Marginata'
Scirpoides holoschoenus 'Variegatus'
Stenotaphrum secundatum 'Variegatum'

Luzula nivea (Snowy woodrush)
Evergreen, slow-spreading, perennial rush with fairly dense clusters of shining, white flower spikes in early summer. Leaves are edged with white hairs.
H 60cm (24in), S 45–60cm (18–24in).

☀ ◐ ◊

Hordeum jubatum
(Foxtail barley, Squirrel tail grass)
Tufted, short-lived perennial or annual grass. In summer to early autumn has flat, arching, feathery, plume-like flower spikes with silky awns.
H 30–60cm (12–24in), S 30cm (12in).

☀ ◊

Pennisetum villosum,
syn. *P. longistylum* (Feather-top)
Herbaceous, tuft-forming, perennial grass with long-haired stems. In autumn has panicles of creamy-pink spikelets, fading to pale brown, with very long, bearded bristles.
H to 1m (3ft), S 50cm (20in).

☀ ◊

Stipa gigantea (Golden oats)
Evergreen, tuft-forming, perennial grass with narrow leaves, 45cm (18in) or more long. In summer carries elegant, open panicles of silvery spikelets, with long awns and dangling, golden anthers, which persist well into winter. H 2.5m (8ft), S 1m (3ft).

☀ ◊

Cyperus papyrus
(Paper reed, Papyrus)
Evergreen, clump-forming, perennial sedge with stout, triangular, leafless stems, each carrying huge umbels of spikelets with up to 100 rays in summer. Grows in water. H to 3–5m (10–15ft), S 1m (3ft). Min 7–10˚C (45–50˚F).

☀ ●

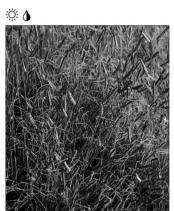

Helictotrichon sempervirens, syn.
Avena candida, A. sempervirens
(Blue oat grass)
Evergreen, tufted, perennial grass with stiff, silvery-blue leaves up to 30cm (12in) or more long. Produces erect panicles of straw-coloured flower spikes in summer. H 1m (3ft), S 60cm (2ft).

☀ ◊

Bambusa multiplex, syn.
B. glaucescens (Hedge bamboo)
Evergreen, clump-forming bamboo with narrow leaves, 10–15cm (4–6in) long. Useful for hedges and windbreaks. H to 15m (50ft), S indefinite.

☀ ◐

Bouteloua gracilis,
syn. *B. oligostachya*
(Blue grama, Mosquito grass)
Semi-evergreen, tuft-forming, narrow-leaved, perennial grass. In summer bears comb-like flower spikes, 4cm (1½in) long, held at right-angles to stems. H 50cm (20in), S 20cm (8in).

☀ ◊

***Melica altissima* 'Atropurpurea'**
Evergreen, tuft-forming, perennial grass with broad leaves, short-haired beneath. Purple spikelets in narrow panicles, 10cm (4in) long, hang from the tops of stems during summer.
H and S 60cm (24in).

☀ ◊

GRASSES, BAMBOOS, RUSHES *and* SEDGES

☐ GREEN

PERENNIALS

Yushania anceps,
syn. *Arundinaria anceps,*
A. jaunsarensis, Sinarundinaria
jaunsarensis (Anceps bamboo)
Evergreen, spreading bamboo with
erect, later arching, stems bearing
several branches at each node.
H 2–3m (6–10ft), S indefinite.

Semiarundinaria fastuosa,
syn. *Arundinaria fastuosa*
(Narihira bamboo)
Evergreen, clump-forming bamboo with
15cm (6in) long leaves and short, tufted
branches at each node. Culm sheaths
open to reveal polished, purplish
interiors. H 6m (20ft), S indefinite.

Shibataea kumasasa
Evergreen, clump-forming bamboo
with stubby, side branches on greenish-
brown stems. Leaves are broad,
5–10cm (2–4in) long.
H 1–1.5m (3–5ft), S 30cm (1ft).

Panicum capillare
(Old-witch grass)
Tuft-forming, annual grass with broad
leaves and hairy stems. Top half of
each stem carries a dense panicle
of numerous, minute, greenish-brown
spikelets on delicate stalks in summer.
H 60cm–1m (2–3ft), S 30cm (1ft).

Phyllostachys nigra var. ***henonis,***
syn. *P.* 'Henonis'
Evergreen, clump-forming bamboo
with bristled auricles on culm sheaths
and a profusion of leaves.
H 10m (30ft), S 2–3m (6–10ft).

Juncus effusus 'Spiralis', syn.
J.e. f. *spiralis, Scirpus lacustris*
'Spiralis' (Corkscrew rush)
Evergreen, tuft-forming, perennial rush
with leafless stems that twist and curl
and are often prostrate. Fairly dense,
greenish-brown flower panicles form
in summer. H 1m (3ft), S 60cm (2ft).

Chusquea culeou
(Chilean bamboo)
Slow-growing, evergreen, clump-
forming bamboo. Bears long-lasting
culm sheaths, shining white when
young, at the swollen nodes of stout,
solid stems.
H to 5m (15ft), S 2.5m (8ft) or more.

Cyperus involucratus,
syn. *C. alternifolius* of gardens,
C. flabelliformis
Evergreen, tuft-forming, perennial
sedge with leaf-like bracts forming
a whorl beneath the clustered flower
spikes in summer. H to 1m (3ft),
S 30cm (1ft). Min. 4–7°C (39–45°F).

Pseudosasa japonica,
syn. *Arundinaria japonica*
(Arrow bamboo, Metake)
Evergreen, clump-forming bamboo that
may run. Has long-persistent, roughly
pubescent, brown sheaths and broad
leaves, 35cm (14in) long.
H 5m (15ft), S indefinite.

Phyllostachys bambusoides
(Timber bamboo)
Evergreen, clump-forming bamboo
with stout, erect, green stems. Bears
leaf sheaths with prominent bristles,
and large, broad leaves.
H 6–8m (20–25ft), S indefinite.

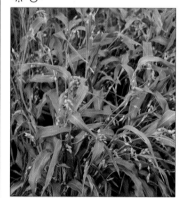

Coix lacryma-jobi (Job's tears)
Tuft-forming, annual grass with broad
leaves and insignificant spikelets
followed by hard, bead-like, green
fruits turning shiny, greyish-mauve
in autumn. H 45cm–90cm (18–36in),
S 10–15cm (4–6in).

Phyllostachys flexuosa
(Zigzag bamboo)
Evergreen, clump-forming bamboo
with slender, markedly zigzag stems
that turn black with age. Leaf sheaths
have no bristles. Leaves stay fresh
green all winter.
H 6–8m (20–25ft), S indefinite.

Miscanthus sinensis 'Gracillimus'
Herbaceous, clump-forming, perennial grass with very narrow leaves, hairy beneath, often turning bronze. May bear fan-shaped panicles of awned, hairy, white spikelets in early autumn. H 1.2m (4ft), S 45cm (1½ft).

☼ ◊

Spartina pectinata 'Aureomarginata',
syn. *S.p.* 'Aureovariegata'
Herbaceous, spreading, rhizomatous grass with long, arching, yellow-striped leaves, which turn orange-brown in late autumn to winter.
H to 2m (6ft), S indefinite.

☼ ◆

Pleioblastus auricomus,
syn. *Arundinaria auricoma*,
A. viridistriata, P. viridistriatus
Evergreen, slow-spreading bamboo with purple stems and broad, softly downy, bright yellow leaves with green stripes. H 1.5m (5ft), S indefinite.

☼ ◊

Alopecurus pratensis 'Aureovariegatus',
syn. *A.p.* 'Aureomarginatus'
(Golden foxtail)
Herbaceous, tuft-forming, perennial grass with yellow or yellowish-green-streaked leaves and dense flower spikes in summer. H and S 23–30cm (9–12in).

☼ ◊

Carex pendula
(Pendulous sedge)
Evergreen, tuft-forming, graceful, perennial sedge with narrow, green leaves, 45cm (18in) long. Solid, triangular stems freely produce pendent, greenish-brown flower spikes in summer. H 1m (3ft), S 30cm (1ft).

◑ ◊

Carex hachijoensis 'Evergold',
syn. *C. oshimensis* 'Evergold'
Evergreen, tuft-forming, perennial sedge with narrow, yellow-striped leaves, 20cm (8in) long. Solid, triangular stems may carry insignificant flower spikes in summer. H 20cm (8in), S 15–20cm (6–8in).

☼ ◊

Phyllostachys viridiglaucescens
Evergreen, clump-forming bamboo with greenish-brown stems that arch at the base. Has white powder beneath nodes. H 6–8m (20–25ft), S indefinite.

☼ ◊

Carex elata 'Aurea',
syn. *C. stricta* 'Aurea'
(Bowles' golden sedge)
Evergreen, tuft-forming, perennial sedge with golden-yellow leaves. Solid, triangular stems bear blackish-brown flower spikes in summer.
H to 40cm (16in), S 15cm (6in).

☼ ◆

Hakonechloa macra 'Aureola'
Slow-growing, herbaceous, shortly rhizomatous grass with purple stems and green-striped, yellow leaves that age to reddish-brown. Open panicles of reddish-brown flower spikes may appear in early autumn and last into winter.
H 40cm (16in), S 45–60cm (18–24in).

☼ ◊

Eleocharis acicularis
Isolepis setaceus
Lamarckia aurea
Melica altissima

Melinis repens
Milium effusum 'Aureum'
Molinia caerulea 'Variegata'
Phyllostachys aurea

Phyllostachys aureosulcata
Sasa palmata
Stipa arundinacea

PERENNIALS

309

FERNS

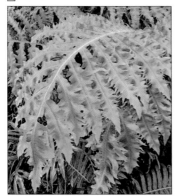

Phlebodium aureum
'Mandaianum'
Evergreen fern with creeping rhizomes.
Has arching, deeply lobed, glaucous
fronds with attractive, orange-yellow
sporangia on reverses; pinnae are
deeply cut and wavy. H 1–1.5m
(3–5ft), S 60cm (2ft). Min. 5°C (41°F).

Dryopteris filix-mas (Male fern)
Deciduous or semi-evergreen fern with
'shuttlecocks' of elegantly arching,
upright, broadly lance-shaped, mid-
green fronds that arise from crowns of
large, upright, brown-scaled rhizomes.
H 1.2m (4ft), S 1m (3ft).

Platycerium bifurcatum
(Common stag's-horn fern)
Evergreen, epiphytic fern with broad,
plate-like sterile fronds and long,
arching or pendent, forked, grey-green
fertile fronds bearing velvety, brownish
spore patches beneath.
H and S 1m (3ft). Min. 5°C (41°F).

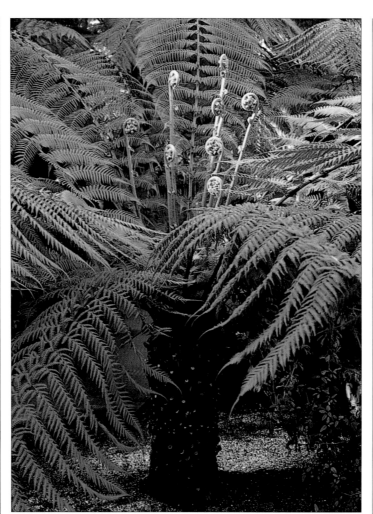

Dicksonia antarctica
(Australian tree fern)
Evergreen, tree-like fern. Stout trunks
are covered with brown fibres and
crowned by spreading, somewhat
arching, broadly lance-shaped, much-
divided, palm-like fronds. H 10m (30ft)
or more, S 4m (12ft). Min. 2°C (35°F).

Polystichum aculeatum
'Pulcherrimum'
Evergreen or semi-evergreen fern with
broadly lance-shaped, daintily cut,
sharp-edged fronds that are yellowish-
green in spring and mature to a glossy,
rich dark green.
H 60cm (24in), S 75cm (30in).

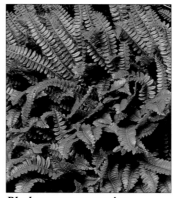

Blechnum penna-marina,
syn. *B. alpinum*
Fast-growing, evergreen, carpeting
fern. Has narrow, ladder-like, dark
green fronds, red-tinged when young.
Outer, sterile fronds are spreading;
inner, fertile ones erect. H 15–30cm
(6–12in), S 30–45cm (12–18in).

Polystichum munitum
(Giant holly fern)
Evergreen fern with erect, leathery,
lance-shaped, dark green fronds that
consist of small, spiny-margined
pinnae. H 1.2m (4ft), S 30cm (1ft).

Polypodium glycyrrhiza
(Liquorice fern)
Deciduous fern. Has oblong-triangular
to narrowly oval, divided, mid-green
fronds, with lance-shaped to oblong
pinnae, that arise from a liquorice-
scented rootstock.
H and S 45cm (18in).

Microlepia speluncae
Large, terrestrial fern with a spreading
rhizome and triangular, divided, softly
hairy fronds, consisting of triangular to
lance-shaped pinnae. H to 1.2m (4ft),
S to 2m (6ft). Min. 5–10°C (41–50°F).

OTHER RECOMMENDED PLANTS:
Asplenium bulbiferum
Blechnum penna-marina
Blechnum spicant

Cyrtomium fortunei
Dicksonia fibrosa
Dicksonia squarrosa
Dryopteris marginalis

Nephrolepis cordifolia
Pellaea atropurpurea
Polystichum acrostichoides
Polystichum aculeatum

Polystichum tsussimense
Pteris ensiformis
Pteris ensiformis 'Arguta'

PERENNIALS

Polypodium scouleri
Evergreen, creeping fern with
triangular to oval, leathery, divided
fronds that arise from a spreading
rootstock. H and S 30–40cm (12–16in).
Min. 2°C (35°F).

☀ ◊

Pteris cretica 'Wimsettii'
Evergreen or semi-evergreen fern with
broadly ovate fronds divided into
narrow pinnae, each with an incised
margin and crested tip. H 45cm (18in),
S 30cm (12in). Min. 5°C (41°F).

☀ ◖

Adiantum aleuticum
Semi-evergreen fern with a short rootstock. Has glossy, dark brown or
blackish stems and dainty, divided,
finger-like fronds, with blue-green
pinnae, that are more crowded than
those of *A. pedatum*. Grows well in
alkaline soils. H and S to 45cm (18in).

☀ ◖

Phlebodium aureum,
syn. *Polypodium aureum*
Evergreen fern with creeping, golden-
scaled rhizomes. Has arching, deeply
lobed, mid-green or glaucous fronds
with attractive, orange-yellow
sporangia on reverses. H 90cm–1.5m
(3–5ft), S 60cm (2ft). Min. 5°C (41°F).

☀ ◊

Selaginella martensii
Evergreen, moss-like perennial with
dense, much-branched, frond-like
sprays of glossy, rich green foliage.
H and S 23cm (9in). Min. 5°C (41°F).

☀ ◊

Asplenium ceterach
(Rusty-back fern)
Semi-evergreen fern with lance-shaped,
leathery, dark green fronds divided into
alternate, bluntly rounded lobes. Backs
of young fronds are covered with
silvery scales that mature to reddish-
brown. H and S 15cm (6in).

☀ ◖

Cyrtomium falcatum
(Fishtail fern, Holly fern)
Evergreen fern. Fronds are lance-
shaped and have holly-like, glossy,
dark green pinnae; young fronds are
often covered with whitish or brown
scales. H 30–60cm (12–24in),
S 30–45cm (12–18in).

☀ ◖

Asplenium trichomanes (Maidenhair spleenwort)
Semi-evergreen fern that has long,
slender, tapering fronds with glossy,
black, later brown, midribs bearing
many rounded-oblong, bright green
pinnae. Is suitable for limestone soils.
H 15cm, S 15–30cm (6–12in).

☀ ◖

**Polystichum setiferum
Divisilobum Group**
Evergreen or semi-evergreen fern.
Broadly lance-shaped or oval,
soft-textured, much-divided, spreading
fronds are clothed with white scales
as they unfurl. H 60cm (24in),
S 45cm (18in).

☀ ◊

Adiantum raddianum 'Fritz-Luthi'
Adiantum tenerum
Blechnum tabulare
Cheilanthes tomentosa

Davallia canariensis
Davallia mariesii
Didymochlaena truncata
Dryopteris carthusiana

Dryopteris cycadina
Dryopteris dilatata
Dryopteris filix-mas 'Grandiceps Wills'
Dryopteris wallichiana

Lygodium japonicum
Matteuccia orientalis
Oreopteris limbosperma
Phegopteris connectilis

FERNS

PERENNIALS

Thelypteris palustris
(Marsh buckler fern, Marsh fern)
Deciduous fern. Has strong, erect,
lance-shaped, pale green fronds, with
widely separated, deeply cut pinnae,
produced from wiry, creeping, blackish
rhizomes. Grows well beside a pool or
stream. H 75cm (30in), S 30cm (12in).

☼ ◑

Nephrolepis exaltata (Sword fern)
Evergreen fern. Has erect, sometimes
spreading, lance-shaped, divided, pale
green fronds borne on wiry stems.
H and S 90cm (36in) or more.
Min. 5°C (41°F).

☼ ◑

Polypodium vulgare
'Cornubiense'
Evergreen fern with narrow, lance-
shaped, divided, fresh green fronds;
segments are further sub-divided to
give an overall lacy effect.
H and S 25–30cm (10–12in).

☼ ◊

Osmunda regalis (Royal fern)
Deciduous fern with elegant, broadly
oval to oblong, divided, bright green
fronds, pinkish when young. Mature
plants bear tassel-like, rust-brown
fertile flower spikes at ends of taller
fronds. H 2m (6ft), S 1m (3ft).

◑ ◑

Onoclea sensibilis (Sensitive fern)
Deciduous, creeping fern with
handsome, arching, almost triangular,
divided, fresh pale green fronds, often
suffused pinkish-brown in spring.
In autumn, fronds turn an attractive
yellowish-brown. H and S 45cm (18in).

◑ ◑

Selaginella kraussiana
Evergreen, trailing, more or less
prostrate, moss-like perennial with
bright green foliage.
H 1cm (½in). S indefinite.
Min. 5°C (41°F).

☼ ◊

Adiantum pedatum
(Northern maidenhair fern)
Semi-evergreen fern with a stout,
creeping rootstock. Dainty, divided,
finger-like, mid-green fronds are
produced on glossy, dark brown or
blackish stems.
H and S to 45cm (18in).

☼ ◑ pH

Matteuccia struthiopteris
(Ostrich-feather fern, Ostrich fern)
Deciduous, rhizomatous fern. Lance-
shaped, erect, divided fronds are
arranged like a shuttlecock; outermost,
fresh green sterile fronds surround
denser, dark brown fertile fronds.
H 1m (3ft), S 45cm (1½ft).

◑ ◑

Polystichum setiferum
Plumosodivisilobum Group
Evergreen fern that produces a
'shuttlecock' of lance-shaped, divided
fronds with segments narrowed
towards the frond tips; lower pinnae
often overlap. H 1.2m (4ft), S 1m (3ft).

☀ ◊

Asplenium nidus (Bird's-nest fern)
Evergreen fern. Produces broadly
lance-shaped, glossy, bright green
fronds in a shuttlecock-like
arrangement. H 60cm–1.2m (2–4ft),
S 30–60cm (1–2ft). Min. 5°C (41°F).

☀ ◖

Athyrium niponicum,
syn. *A. goeringianum, A.*
nipponicum (Japanese painted fern)
Deciduous fern. Broad, triangular,
divided, purple-tinged, greyish-green
fronds arise from a scaly, creeping,
brownish or reddish rootstock.
H and S 30cm (12in).

☀ ◖

Cryptogramma crispa
(Parsley fern)
Deciduous fern with broadly oval to
triangular, finely divided, bright pale
green fronds that resemble parsley. In
autumn, fronds turn bright rusty-brown
and persist during winter. H 15–23cm
(6–9in), S 15–30cm (6–12in).

☀ ◊ pH

Polypodium vulgare
(Common polypody, Polypody)
Evergreen fern with narrow, lance-
shaped, divided, herring-bone-like,
mid-green fronds, arising from
creeping rhizomes covered with
copper-brown scales. Suits a rock
garden. H and S 25–30cm (10–12in).

☀ ◊

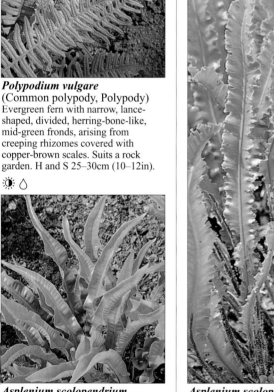

Asplenium scolopendrium,
syn. *Phyllitis scolopendrium,*
Scolopendrium vulgare
(Hart's-tongue fern)
Evergreen fern with stocky rhizomes
and tongue-shaped, leathery, bright
green fronds. Is good in alkaline soils.
H 45–75cm (18–30in), S to 45cm (18in).

☀ ◖

Asplenium scolopendrium
Marginatum Group
Evergreen fern with stocky, upright
rhizomes and lobed, slightly frilled,
tongue-shaped fronds that are leathery
and bright green. Is good in alkaline
soils. H and S 30cm (12in) or more.

☀ ◖

Adiantum venustum
Deciduous fern. Bears delicate, pale
green fronds, tinged brown when
young, consisting of many small,
triangular pinnae, on glossy stems.
H 23cm (9in), S 30cm (12in).

☀ ◖ pH

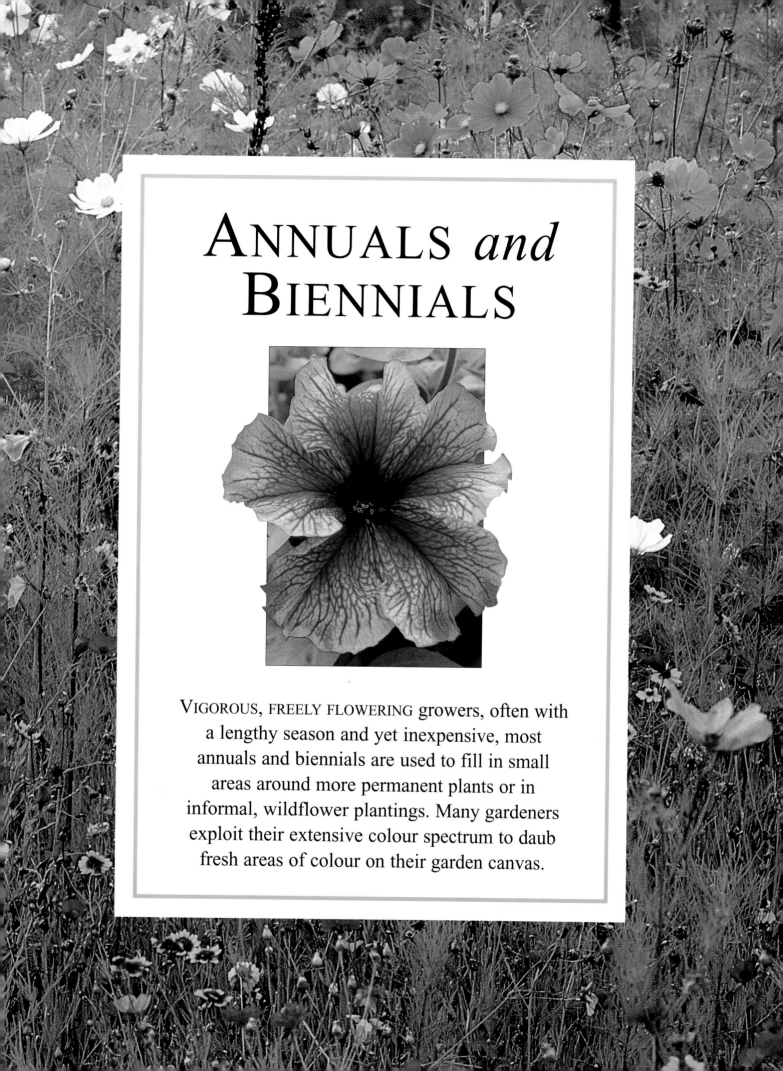

ANNUALS *and* BIENNIALS

VIGOROUS, FREELY FLOWERING growers, often with a lengthy season and yet inexpensive, most annuals and biennials are used to fill in small areas around more permanent plants or in informal, wildflower plantings. Many gardeners exploit their extensive colour spectrum to daub fresh areas of colour on their garden canvas.

Annuals and Biennials

The rapid growth and relatively low cost of annuals and biennials make them ideal for providing immediate colour in new gardens until more permanent plantings of trees, shrubs and perennials are established. They are also invaluable in formal settings as bedding plants to fill gaps or create specific effects, as well as in informal situations, especially natural areas and wildflower meadows.

WHAT ARE ANNUALS AND BIENNIALS?
Annuals are plants that grow, bloom, set seed and die in a single growing season. Biennials complete their life cycle in two seasons: most are sown in summer and make leafy growth in the first year, then flower, set seed and die in the next.

GROWING ANNUALS AND BIENNIALS
Hardy annuals withstand some frost and so can be sown *in situ* in early autumn or spring. Semi-hardy and tender annuals are sown under glass between late winter and early spring and are planted out when all danger of frost has passed. Gardeners often use other types of plants in the same way as annuals, in particular tender perennials, such as pelargoniums or busy lizzies (*Impatiens*), which grow vigorously and flower freely in their first year from seed. Like annuals, such tender perennials are cleared away at the end of the season.

ORNAMENTAL FEATURES
Annuals and biennials are available in an enormous range of sizes and habits, from the lowest hummock-forming cultivars of *Ageratum houstonianum* and trailing nasturtiums (*Tropaeolum majus*) to the tall spires of foxgloves (*Digitalis purpurea*) or the grandeur of the Scotch thistle (*Onopordum acanthium*). They include climbers such as Canary creeper (*Tropaeolum peregrinum)* and fragrant sweet peas (*Lathyrus odoratus*), as well as a number grown primarily for foliage effects, for instance the feathery leaved *Bassia scoparia* f. *trichophylla* or *Senecio cineraria* with its grey foliage. The flower range, in all colours and tones, is also huge, and presents a bewildering choice. Colours extend from the opalescent whites of *Lavatera trimestris* 'Mont Blanc' to the vibrant scarlets of pelargoniums or the intense magentas and purples of petunias, as well as the more subtle pastel shades exhibited by plants such as China aster (*Callistephus chinensis*).

MAINTAINING YEAR-ROUND COLOUR
The long and prolific season of annuals and biennials has traditionally been exploited in formal beds devoted entirely to achieving brilliant, seasonally

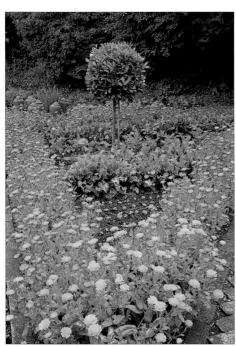

MULTI-PURPOSE MARIGOLDS
Above: Forming a strong edging in a potager, the edible flowers of marigolds (Calendula officinalis) attract beneficial insects such as hoverflies to prey on any aphid pests.

EARLY SEASON SCENTS
Right: Self-sown Dame's violet (Hesperis matronalis) and poached egg plant (Limnanthes douglasii) add scents and a natural informality.

changing displays. Spring displays of primulas and forget-me-nots (*Myosotis*) are sometimes used as a carpet beneath spring bulbs, then lifted to make way for a summer scheme juxtaposing, for example, the exotic foliage of *Ricinus communis* with swathes of hot colour provided by zinnias or pelargoniums. As summer fades, the entire display may be replaced with winter-flowering pansies (*Viola* x *wittrockiana*) or spring wallflowers (*Erysimum cheiri*).

This potential for year-round colour can also be employed in more domestic situations, albeit scaled down to suit modest plots. While the uniformity of habit and colour of many modern annuals are perfect where formality or complex patternwork is needed, they are equally adaptable to more informal plantings. Sinuous drifts of graduated height suggest a cottage-garden style, while yet more naturalistic effects are possible by using cornfield annuals like corncockle (*Agrostemma githago*), cornflower (*Centaurea cyanus*) or field poppy (*Papaver rhoeas*).

If there is room, annuals and biennials can be grown in a border for cutting, especially stocks (*Matthiola incana*), *Cleome hassleriana* and China asters (*Callistephus*) for fresh displays, and everlastings such as *Bracteantha bracteata* and *Limonium sinuatum* for dried arrangements. In a mixed border annuals and biennials are invaluable, whether used to add textural qualities or colour highlights among more permanent plants, or as fillers to mask gaps left by the foliage of perennials that dies back after flowering.

SUMMER HARMONIES
Above: Opium poppies (Papaver somniferum) *and foxgloves* (Digitalis purpurea) *are used here to add subtle colour to a mixed border.*

ANNUALS IN POTS
Right: Use annuals in pots to bring summer-long colour to patio plantings. Here, these vivid nasturtiums (Tropaeolum majus) *will flower continuously, well into early autumn.*

WILDFLOWER GARDENS
Below: Sown en masse, corn marigold (Xanthophthalmum segetum), *field poppies* (Papaver rhoeas) *and cornflowers* (Centaurea cyanus) *look entirely natural.*

PLANTING IN CONTAINERS
Annuals and biennials can create eye-catching features in pots, tubs and hanging baskets. Use them alone in compositions in which trailers, such as the ivy-leaved geraniums or cascading lobelias, surround mound-forming verbenas or busy lizzies, and link them with the airy foliage of brachyscome or felicia. Or add colour to container-grown dwarf conifers, such as *Juniperus communis* 'Compressa', or trailing evergreen ivy (*Hedera* cultivars).

317

☐ WHITE

Digitalis purpurea f. **albiflora**, syn. *D.p.* f. *alba*
Slow-growing, short-lived perennial, grown as a biennial. Has a rosette of large, pointed-oval leaves and erect stems carrying tubular, white flowers in summer.
H 1–1.5m (3–5ft), S 30–45cm (1–1½ft).

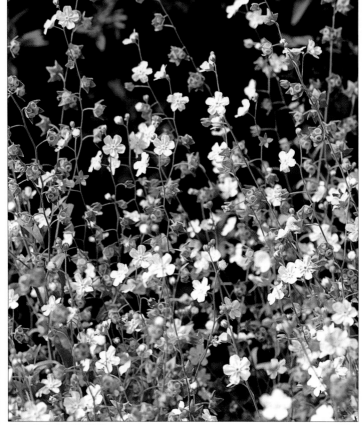

Omphalodes linifolia
(Venus's navelwort)
Fairly fast-growing, slender, erect annual with lance-shaped, grey-green leaves. Tiny, slightly scented, rounded, white flowers, rarely tinged blue, are carried in summer.
H 15–30cm (6–12in), S 15cm (6in).

Gypsophila elegans
Fast-growing, erect, bushy annual. Has lance-shaped, greyish-green leaves and clouds of tiny, white flowers in branching heads from summer to early autumn.
H 60cm (24in), S 30cm (12in) or more.

Lavatera trimestris 'Mont Blanc'
Moderately fast-growing, erect, branching annual with oval, lobed leaves. Shallowly trumpet-shaped, brilliant white flowers appear from summer to early autumn.
H to 60cm (24in), S 45cm (18in).

Iberis amara
Fast-growing, erect, bushy annual with lance-shaped, mid-green leaves. Has flattish heads of small, scented, 4-petalled, white flowers in summer.
H 30cm (12in), S 15cm (6in).

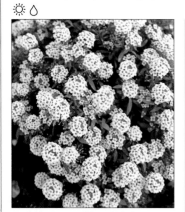

Lobularia maritima 'Little Dorrit', syn. *Alyssum maritimum* 'Little Dorrit'
Fast-growing, compact annual with lance-shaped, greyish-green leaves and heads of scented, 4-petalled, white flowers in summer and early autumn.
H 8–15cm (3–6in), S 20–30cm (8–12in).

Matthiola 'Giant Imperial'
Fast-growing, erect, bushy biennial, grown as an annual. Has lance-shaped, greyish-green leaves and long spikes of highly scented, white to creamy-yellow flowers in summer. Produces excellent flowers for cutting.
H to 60cm (24in), S 30cm (12in).

Petunia Recoverer Series [white]
Moderately fast-growing, branching, bushy perennial, grown as an annual. Has oval, mid- to deep green leaves and large, flared, trumpet-shaped, white flowers in summer-autumn.
H 15–30cm (6–12in), S 30cm (12in).

OTHER RECOMMENDED PLANTS:
Adlumia fungosa
Antirrhinum majus and cvs
Bracteantha bracteata cvs

Callistephus chinensis and cvs
Campanula medium and cvs
Centaurea cyanus

Consolida ajacis Dwarf Hyacinth Series
Dianthus chinensis and cvs
Eustoma grandiflorum Heidi Series
Iberis umbellata

Lobelia erinus 'Colour Cascade'
Lobularia maritima

Dimorphotheca pluvialis,
syn. *D. annua* (Rain daisy)
Branching annual with oval, hairy,
deep green leaves. In summer has
small, daisy-like flower heads, the rays
purple beneath and white above, with
brownish-purple centres.
H 20–30cm (8–12in), S 15cm (6in).

☼ ◊

Nemophila maculata
(Five-spot baby)
Fast-growing, spreading annual with
lobed leaves. Small, bowl-shaped,
white flowers with purple-tipped petals
are carried in summer.
H and S 15cm (6in).

☼ ◊

Tanacetum parthenium, syn.
Chrysanthemum parthenium,
Pyrethrum parthenium (Feverfew)
Moderately fast-growing, short-lived,
bushy perennial, grown as an annual.
Has aromatic leaves and small, white
flower heads in summer and early
autumn. H and S 20–45cm (8–18in).

☼ ◊ ⓘ

Euphorbia marginata (Snow-in-
summer, Snow-on-the-mountain)
Moderately fast-growing, upright,
bushy annual. Has pointed-oval, bright
green leaves; upper leaves are white-
margined. Broad, petal-like, white
bracts surround insignificant flowers in
summer. H 60cm (24in), S 30cm (12in).

☼ ◊ ⓘ

**Viola × wittrockiana Floral Dance
Series** [white]
Bushy perennial, grown as an annual
or biennial. Has oval, mid-green leaves
and rounded, 5-petalled, white
flowers in winter.
H 15–20cm (6–8in), S 20cm (8in).

☼ ◊

ANNUALS *and* BIENNIALS

**Nicotiana × sanderae Domino
Series**
Fairly slow-growing, bushy annual
with pointed-oval leaves. Somewhat
trumpet-shaped flowers, to 8cm (3in)
long, appear in a wide range of colours
in summer and early autumn.
H and S 30cm (12in).

☼ ◊ ⓘ

Reseda odorata (Mignonette)
Moderately fast-growing, erect,
branching annual with oval leaves.
Conical heads of small, very fragrant,
somewhat star-shaped, white flowers
with orange-brown stamens are carried
in summer and early autumn.
H 30–60cm (12–24in), S 30cm (12in).

☼ ◊

Eustoma grandiflorum
Slow-growing, upright annual with
lance-shaped, deep green leaves.
Poppy-like, pink, purple, blue or white
flowers, 5cm (2in) wide, are carried in
summer.
H 60cm (24in), S 30cm (12in).
Min. 4–7°C (39–45°F).

☼ ◊

319

WHITE–PINK

Hibiscus trionum
(Flower-of-the-hour)
Fairly fast-growing, upright annual with oval, serrated leaves. Trumpet-shaped, creamy-white or pale yellow flowers, with purplish-brown centres, are borne from late summer to early autumn. H 60cm (24in), S 30cm (12in).

☼ ◊

Martynia annua
(Unicorn plant)
Fairly fast-growing, upright annual with long-stalked leaves. Has foxglove-like, lobed, creamy-white flowers marked red, pink and yellow in summer, followed by horned, green, then brown, fruits. H 60cm (24in), S 30cm (12in).

☼ ◊

Lathyrus odoratus 'Knee Hi'
Fast-growing annual with oval, divided, mid-green leaves and large, fragrant flowers, in shades of pink, red, blue or white, that are borne in summer or early autumn. H and S 90cm (3ft).

☼ ◊ ⓘ

Crepis rubra
Fairly fast-growing, rosette-forming annual with lance-shaped, serrated leaves. In summer bears dandelion-like, pink, occasionally red or white flower heads. H 30cm (12in), S 15cm (6in).

☼ ◊

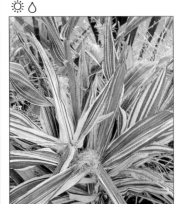

Zea mays 'Gracillima Variegata'
Fairly fast-growing, erect annual with lance-shaped leaves, striped green and creamy-white. Has tassel-like, silvery flower heads, followed by large, bright yellow seed heads (cobs).
H 90cm (3ft), S 30–45cm (1–1½ft).

☼ ◊

Impatiens balsamina (Balsam)
Fairly fast-growing, erect, compact, bushy annual with lance-shaped leaves. Small, cup-shaped, spurred, pink or white flowers are borne in summer and early autumn.
H to 75cm (30in), S 45cm (18in).

☼ ◐

Ismelia carinata 'Monarch Court Jesters'
Fast-growing, erect, branching annual. Has feathery, grey-green leaves and, in summer, daisy-like, zoned flower heads, to 8cm (3in) wide, in various colour combinations.
H 60cm (24in), S 30cm (12in).

☼ ◊

Silene coeli-rosa, syn.
Agrostemma coeli-rosa, Lychnis coeli-rosa, Viscaria elegans
Moderately fast-growing, erect annual with lance-shaped, greyish-green leaves. Has 5-petalled, pinkish-purple flowers with white centres in summer. H 45cm (18in), S 15cm (6in).

☼ ◊

Cleome hassleriana
Impatiens balsamina 'Blackberry Ice'

Rhodanthe chlorocephala
subsp. ***rosea***
Moderately fast-growing, erect annual.
Lance-shaped leaves are greyish-green;
small, daisy-like, papery, semi-double,
pink flower heads appear in summer.
Flowers dry well.
H 30cm (12in), S 15cm (6in).

***Antirrhinum majus* Coronette
Series**
Erect, bushy, compact perennial, grown
as an annual, with lance-shaped leaves.
Spikes of tubular, 2-lipped flowers in
a wide range of colours are produced
from spring to autumn.
H 60cm (24in), S 30cm (12in).

***Papaver somniferum*
'Peony Flowered'**
Fast-growing, erect annual with lobed,
pale greyish-green leaves. Has large,
rounded, often cup-shaped, double
flowers in a mixture of colours – red,
pink, purple or white – in summer.
H 75cm (30in), S 30cm (12in).

Alcea rosea, syn. ***Althaea rosea***
(Hollyhock)
Biennial with tall, erect stems and
lobed, rough-textured leaves. Spikes of
single flowers, in a range of colours
including pink, yellow and cream,
appear in summer and early autumn.
H 1.5–2m (5–6ft), S to 60cm (2ft).

***Primula* 'Dreamer'** (Primrose
Group)
Rosette-forming perennial, normally
grown as a biennial, with oval leaves.
In spring, has flat flowers in cream,
apricot, pink or rose-pink; all bicolours
have darker eyes and yellow centres.
H 8–10cm (3–4in), S 15–20cm (6–8in).

***Matthiola* Brompton Group**
Fast-growing, erect, bushy biennial,
grown as an annual. Lance-shaped
leaves are greyish-green; long spikes
of highly scented flowers in shades of
pink, red, purple, yellow or white are
borne in summer.
H 45cm (18in), S 30cm (12in).

***Salvia splendens* Cleopatra
Series** [salmon]
Slow-growing, bushy perennial, grown
as an annual. Oval, serrated leaves are
fresh green; dense racemes of tubular,
salmon-pink flowers are carried in
summer and early autumn.
H to 30cm (12in), S 20–30cm (8–12in).

***Matthiola* 'Giant Excelsior'**
Fast-growing, erect, bushy biennial,
grown as an annual. Lance-shaped
leaves are greyish-green; long spikes
of highly scented flowers in shades
of pink, red, pale blue or white appear
in summer.
H to 75cm (30in), S 30cm (12in).

Rhodanthe manglesii,
syn. ***Helipterum manglesii***
Moderately fast-growing, erect annual.
Has pointed-oval, greyish-green leaves
and daisy-like, papery, red, pink or
white flower heads, in summer and
early autumn. Flowers dry well.
H 30cm (12in), S 15cm (6in).

***Pelargonium* Orbit Series**
[salmon]
Slow-growing, evergreen, branching,
bushy perennial, grown as an annual,
with lobed leaves, zoned with bronze
or red. Has large, rounded heads of
salmon-pink flowers in summer-
autumn. H and S 30–60cm (12–24in).

***Impatiens walleriana* Swirl Series**
Subshrubby perennial, usually grown
as an annual, with light green to red-
flushed stems and leaves. In summer,
bears flattened, slender-spurred, pink-
and-orange flowers margined in rose-
red. H 15–20cm (6–8in),
S to 60cm (24in). Min. 10°C (50°F).

Ageratum houstonianum 'Swing Pink'
Silene pendula

ANNUALS *and* BIENNIALS

***Petunia* Aladdin Series**
Fairly fast-growing, branching, bushy
perennial, grown as an annual. Has
oval leaves and in summer-autumn
produces flowers in a range of colours,
including strong shades of red and
salmon-pink. H to 30cm (12in),
S 30–90cm (12–36in).

☼ ◊

***Papaver rhoeas* Shirley Series**
[double]
Fast-growing, slender, erect annual
with lobed, light green leaves. Rounded,
often cup-shaped, double flowers, in
shades of red, pink or white, including
bicolours, are borne in summer.
H 60cm (24in), S 30cm (12in).

☼ ◊

***Cleome hassleriana* 'Colour
Fountain'**
Fast-growing, bushy annual with hairy
stems and divided leaves. In summer
has heads of narrow-petalled flowers,
with long, protruding stamens, in shades
of pink, mauve, purple or white.
H 1–1.2m (3–4ft), S 45–60cm (1½–2ft).

☼ ◊

***Lobularia maritima*
'Wonderland'**, syn. *Alyssum
maritimum* 'Wonderland'
Fast-growing, compact annual with
lance-shaped leaves. Bears heads of
tiny, scented, deep purplish-pink
flowers in summer and early autumn.
H to 15cm (6in), S to 30cm (12in).

☼ ◊

***Zinnia elegans* Thumbelina
Series**
Moderately fast-growing, sturdy, erect
annual with oval to lance-shaped
leaves. In summer and early autumn
has large, daisy-like, double and semi-
double flower heads in a range of
colours. H 15cm (6in), S 30cm (12in).

☼ ◊

***Schizanthus* 'Hit Parade'**
Moderately fast-growing, erect, bushy
annual with deeply divided leaves.
Tubular flowers, in a mixture of rich
colours including pink, red, purple or
white, often with contrasting markings
inside, appear in summer-autumn.
H and S 30cm (12in). Min. 5°C (41°F).

☼ ◊

***Centaurea cyanus* [tall, rose]
(Cornflower)**
Fast-growing, erect, branching annual
with lance-shaped, grey-green leaves.
Branching heads of daisy-like, rose-
pink flower heads are carried in
summer and early autumn.
H to 90cm (3ft), S 30cm (1ft).

☼ ◊

Limonium sinuatum
Fairly slow-growing, bushy, upright
perennial, grown as an annual. Has
lance-shaped, lobed, deep green leaves
and, in summer and early autumn, tiny,
blue, pink or white flowers borne in
clusters on winged stems.
H 45cm (18in), S 30cm (12in).

☼ ◊

***Eschscholzia californica*
Ballerina Series**
Fast-growing, slender, erect annual.
Has feathery, bluish-green leaves and
cup-shaped, 4-petalled, frilled, double
flowers, in shades of red, yellow, pink
or orange, in summer-autumn.
H 30cm (12in), S 15cm (6in).

☼ ◊

Onopordum acanthium
(Cotton thistle, Scotch thistle)
Slow-growing, erect, branching
biennial. Large, lobed, spiny leaves are
hairy and bright silvery-grey; winged,
branching flower stems bear deep
purplish-pink flower heads in summer.
H 1.8m (6ft), S 90cm (3ft).

☼ ◊

Silybum marianum
(Blessed Mary's thistle)
Biennial with a basal rosette of deeply
lobed, very spiny, heavily white-
marbled, deep green leaves. Has thistle-
like, dark purplish-pink flower heads on
erect stems in summer and early
autumn. H 1.2m (4ft), S 60cm (2ft).

☼ ◊

***Iberis umbellata* Fairy Series**
Fast-growing, upright, bushy annual
with lance-shaped, mid-green leaves.
Heads of small, 4-petalled flowers, in
shades of pink, red, purple or white, are
carried in summer and early autumn.
H and S 20cm (8in).

☼ ◊

Agrostemma githago
Alcea rosea 'Majorette'
Bellis perennis cvs
Campanula medium and cvs

Clarkia amoena
Consolida ajacis Dwarf Hyacinth Series
Eustoma grandiflorum Heidi Series
Impatiens cvs

Matthiola cvs
Salvia viridis cvs

Petunia Primetime Series
Moderately fast-growing perennial, grown as an annual. In summer-autumn, bears flowers in a very wide range of colours, including white, blue, pink or red, some with dark veins or central stars, or picotee margins.
H to 35cm (14in), S 30–90cm (12–36in).

Agrostemma githago 'Milas'
Fast-growing, slender, upright, thin-stemmed annual. Has lance-shaped leaves and 5-petalled, purplish-pink flowers, 8cm (3in) wide, in summer.
H 60–90cm (2–3ft), S 30cm (1ft).

Malcolmia maritima
(Virginian stock)
Fast-growing, slim, erect annual with oval, greyish-green leaves. Carries tiny, fragrant, 4-petalled, pink, red or white flowers from spring to autumn. Sow seeds in succession for a long flowering season. H 20cm (8in), S 5–8cm (2–3in).

Matthiola Brompton Group
[pink]
Fast-growing, erect, bushy biennial, grown as an annual, with lance-shaped, greyish-green leaves. Long spikes of highly scented, pink flowers are carried in summer.
H 45cm (18in), S 30cm (12in).

Lunaria annua 'Variegata'
Fast-growing, erect biennial with pointed-oval, serrated, white-variegated leaves. Heads of small, scented, 4-petalled, deep purplish-pink flowers are borne in spring and early summer followed by rounded, silvery seed pods. H 75cm (30in), S 30cm (12in).

Silene armeria 'Electra'
Moderately fast-growing, erect annual with oval, greyish-green leaves. Heads of 5-petalled, bright rose-pink flowers are carried in summer and early autumn. H 30cm (12in), S 15cm (6in).

Clarkia amoena 'Sybil Sherwood'
Erect annual with lance-shaped, sometimes toothed leaves. Single, fluted, salmon-pink flowers, fading to white at the margins, are borne at the tips of long, leafy shoots in summer. H to 45cm (18in), S 30cm (12in).

☼ ◊

Brassica oleracea forms (Ornamental cabbage)
Moderately fast-growing, evergreen, rounded biennial, grown as an annual. Has heads of large, often crinkled leaves, in combinations of red/green, white/pink, pink/green. Do not allow to flower. H and S 30–45cm (12–18in).

☼ ◊

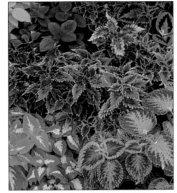

Solenostemon scutellarioides, syn. *Coleus blumei* var. *verschaffeltii*
Fast-growing, bushy perennial, grown as an annual. Leaves are a mixture of colours, including pink, red, green or yellow. Flower spikes should be removed. H to 45cm (18in), S 30cm (12in) or more. Min. 10°C (50°F).

☼ ◊

Malope trifida
Moderately fast-growing, erect, branching annual with rounded, lobed leaves. Flared, trumpet-shaped, reddish-purple flowers, to 8cm (3in) wide and with deep pink veins, are carried in summer and early autumn. H 90cm (3ft), S 30cm (1ft).

☼ ◊

Lavatera trimestris 'Silver Cup'
Moderately fast-growing, erect, branching annual with oval, lobed leaves. Shallowly trumpet-shaped, rose-pink flowers are carried in summer and early autumn. H 60cm (24in), S 45cm (18in).

☼ ◊

Dianthus chinensis Baby Doll Series
Neat, bushy annual or biennial, grown as an annual. Light or mid-green leaves are lance-shaped; small, single, zoned flowers in various colours are carried in summer and early autumn. H 15cm (6in), S 15–30cm (6–12in).

☼ ◊

Lathyrus odoratus 'Bijou'
Fast-growing annual with oval, divided, mid-green leaves and large, fragrant flowers, in shades of pink, red or blue, that are carried in summer or early autumn. H and S 45cm (18in).

☼ ◊

Clarkia 'Brilliant'
Fast-growing, erect, bushy annual with oval leaves. Large, rosette-like, double, bright reddish-pink flowers are carried in long spikes in summer and early autumn. H to 60cm (24in), S 30cm (12in).

☼ ◊

Callistephus chinensis Milady Super Series [rose]
Moderately fast-growing, erect, bushy annual with oval, toothed leaves. Has large, daisy-like, double, rose-pink flower heads in summer and early autumn. H 25–30cm (10–12in), S 30–45cm (12–18in).

☼ ◊

ANNUALS *and* BIENNIALS

***Matthiola* Ten-week Group**[dwarf]
Fast-growing, erect, bushy biennial,
grown as an annual. Lance-shaped
leaves are greyish-green; long spikes of
highly scented, single to double flowers,
in shades of pink, red or white, appear
in summer. H and S 30cm (12in).

Lunaria annua*, syn. *L. biennis
(Honesty)
Fast-growing, erect biennial with
pointed-oval, serrated leaves. Heads of
scented, 4-petalled, white to deep purple
flowers in spring and early summer are
followed by rounded, silvery seed pods.
H 75cm (30in), S 30cm (12in).

***Silene coeli-rosa* 'Rose Angel'**
Moderately fast-growing, slim, erect
annual. Has lance-shaped, greyish-
green leaves and 5-petalled, deep rose-
pink flowers in summer.
H 30cm (12in), S 15cm (6in).

Dorotheanthus bellidiformis
'Magic Carpet'
Carpeting annual with succulent,
lance-shaped, pale green leaves.
Daisy-like flower heads, in bright
shades of red, pink, yellow or white,
open only in summer sunshine.
H 15cm (6in), S 30cm (12in).

***Petunia* Resisto Series**
[rose-pink]
Moderately fast-growing, branching,
bushy perennial, grown as an annual.
Has oval leaves and rain-resistant,
flared, trumpet-shaped, rose-pink
flowers in summer-autumn.
H 15–30cm (6–12in), S 30cm (12in).

***Cosmos bipinnatus* Sensation**
Series
Moderately fast-growing, bushy, erect
annual. Has feathery, mid-green leaves
and daisy-like flower heads, to 10cm
(4in) wide, in shades of red, pink or
white, from early summer to early
autumn. H 90cm (3ft), S 60cm (2ft).

***Antirrhinum majus* Princess**
Series [white, with purple eye]
Erect perennial, grown as an annual,
branching from the base. Has lance-
shaped leaves and spikes of tubular,
2-lipped, white and pinkish-purple
flowers borne from spring to autumn.
H and S 45cm (18in).

***Xeranthemum annuum* [double]**
Erect annual with lance-shaped, silvery
leaves and branching heads of daisy-
like, papery, double flower heads in
shades of pink, mauve, purple or white,
in summer. Produces good dried
flowers. H 60cm (24in), S 45cm (18in).

***Impatiens balsamina* Tom**
Thumb Series
Dwarf, sparsely branched, slightly
hairy annual with toothed leaves. From
summer to early autumn, bears double,
pink, scarlet, violet or white flowers.
H to 30cm (12in), S 45cm (18in).
Min. 5°C (41°F).

◼◻ PINK–RED

Phlox drummondii 'Chanal'
Erect to spreading, but compact, bushy,
hairy annual with very variable, stem-
clasping leaves. In late spring, bears
cymes of double, almost rose-like, pink
flowers. H 10–45cm (4–18in),
S to 25cm (10in) or more.

☼ ◊

Verbena × hybrida 'Showtime'
Fairly slow-growing, bushy perennial,
grown as an annual. Has lance-shaped,
serrated, mid- to deep green leaves and
clusters of small, tubular flowers, in a
range of colours, in summer-autumn.
H 20cm (8in), S 30cm (12in).

☼ ◊

**Dianthus barbatus Roundabout
Series [dwarf]**
Slow-growing, upright, bushy biennial
with lance-shaped leaves. In early
summer has flat heads of zoned and
eyed flowers in shades of pink, red
or white.
H 15cm (6in), S 20–30cm (8–12in).

☼ ◊

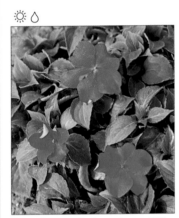

**Impatiens walleriana Super Elfin
Series 'Lipstick'** (Busy lizzie)
Fast-growing, evergreen, bushy
perennial, grown as an annual. Has
pointed-oval, fresh green leaves and
small, flat, spurred, rose-red flowers
from spring to autumn.
H and S 20cm (8in).

◑ ◕

**Portulaca grandiflora Sundance
Hybrids**
Slow-growing, semi-trailing annual
with lance-shaped, succulent, bright
green leaves. Cup-shaped flowers, with
conspicuous stamens, appear in a
mixture of colours in summer and early
autumn. H to 20cm (8in), S 15cm (6in).

☼ ◊

Amaranthus caudatus
(Love-lies-bleeding, Tassel flower)
Bushy annual with oval, pale green
leaves. Pendulous panicles of tassel-
like, red flowers, 45cm (18in) long, are
carried in summer-autumn.
H to 1.2m (4ft), S 45cm (1½ft).

☼ ◊

**Petunia Picotee Series
'Picotee Rose'**
Fairly fast-growing, compact perennial,
grown as an annual, with oval leaves.
In summer-autumn, has large, deep
rose-pink flowers with white margins.
H to 20cm (8in), S 45cm (18in).

☼ ◊

**Nicotiana × sanderae Starship
Series**
Upright, woody-based, sticky annual
or short-lived perennial that bears open
racemes or panicles of tubular, pink,
red, rose-pink, white or lime-green
flowers in summer.
H 30cm (12in), S 30–40cm (12–16in).

◑ ◊

Petunia 'Mirage Velvet'
Branching, bushy perennial, grown as
an annual, with oval, dark green
leaves. Large, flared, trumpet-shaped,
rich red flowers, with almost black
centres, appear in summer-autumn.
H 25cm (10in), S 30cm (12in).

☼ ◊

**Phlox drummondii
'Sternenzauber'**
Moderately fast-growing, slim, erect
annual. Lance-shaped leaves are pale
green; heads of star-shaped flowers in
a bright mixture of colours, some with
contrasting centres, are carried in
summer. H 15cm (6in), S 10cm (4in).

☼ ◊

ANNUALS *and* BIENNIALS

Alcea rosea 'Chater's Double'
Erect biennial with lobed, rough-textured leaves. Spikes of rosette-like, double flowers in several different colours are carried on upright stems in summer and early autumn.
H 1.8–2.4m (6–8ft), S to 60cm (2ft).

☼ ◊

Viola x wittrockiana Imperial Series 'Imperial Frosty Rose'
Erect, bushy perennial, grown as an annual or biennial, with oval leaves. In summer, bears large, unusual, rose-purple flowers fading to pink and white. H 16–23cm (6–9in), S 23–30cm (9–12in).

☼ ◊

Impatiens walleriana Novette Series 'Red Star' (Busy lizzie)
Fast-growing, evergreen, bushy perennial, grown as an annual. Has pointed-oval, fresh green leaves and from spring to autumn small, flat, spurred, red flowers with star-shaped, white markings. H and S 15cm (6in).

☼◑ ◆

Impatiens Confection Series (Busy lizzie)
Fast-growing, evergreen, bushy perennial, grown as an annual. Has fresh green leaves and small, flat, spurred, double or semi-double flowers, in shades of red or pink, from spring to autumn. H and S 20–30cm (8–12in).

☼◑ ◆

Bellis perennis Pomponette Series
Slow-growing, carpeting perennial, grown as a biennial. Has oval leaves and small, daisy-like, double flower heads, in red, pink or white, in spring. H and S 10–15cm (4–6in).

☼ ◊

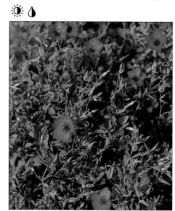

Linum grandiflorum 'Rubrum'
Fairly fast-growing, slim, erect annual. Lance-shaped leaves are grey-green; small, rounded, flattish, deep red flowers are carried in summer.
H 45cm (18in), S 15cm (6in).

☼ ◊

Salvia splendens Sizzler Series
Slow-growing, bushy perennials, grown as annuals, with flowers in bright shades of cerise-red, lavender-blue, salmon-pink, purple, scarlet or white, available as single colours, borne in early summer. H 25–30cm (10–12in), S 23–35cm (9–14in).

☼ ◊

Dianthus chinensis 'Fire Carpet'
Slow-growing, bushy annual or biennial, grown as an annual. Lance-shaped leaves are light or mid-green. Small, rounded, single, bright red flowers are carried in summer and early autumn.
H 20cm (8in), S 15–30cm (6–12in).

☼ ◊

Phlox drummondii 'African Sunset'
Erect to spreading, bushy, hairy annual with very variable, stem-clasping leaves. In late spring, produces tubular, hairy, dusky to deep red flowers.
H 10–45cm (4–18in),
S to 25cm (10in) or more.

☼ ◊

ANNUALS *and* BIENNIALS

■ RED

***Zinnia elegans* Ruffles Series**
[scarlet]
Moderately fast-growing, sturdy,
upright annual with oval to lance-
shaped leaves. Ruffled, daisy-like,
double, scarlet flower heads are carried
in summer and early autumn.
H 60cm (24in), S 30cm (12in).

☀ ◊

***Salvia splendens* 'Scarlet King'**
Slow-growing, compact, bushy
perennial, usually grown as an annual,
with oval, toothed, dark green leaves.
Produces long-tubed, bright scarlet
flowers in dense, terminal spikes in
early summer. H to 25cm (10in),
S 23–35cm (9–14in).

☀ ◊

***Pelargonium* Multibloom Series**
Erect, bushy, evergreen perennials,
grown as annuals. Abundant flowers
in white or shades of pink or red are
borne in clusters over a long period
throughout summer.
H 25–30cm (10–12in), S 30cm (12in).
Min. 2°C (36°F).

☀ ◊ ⚠

***Petunia* Carpet Series**
Moderately fast-growing, compact,
spreading perennial, grown as an
annual, with oval leaves. In summer-
autumn, bears flowers in a colour range
that includes strong reds and oranges.
H 20–25cm (8–10in),
S 30–90cm (12–36in).

☀ ◊

***Papaver rhoeas* Shirley Series**
[single]
Fast-growing, slender, erect annual
with lobed, light green leaves.
Rounded, often cup-shaped, single
flowers, in shades of red, pink, salmon
or white, appear in summer.
H 60cm (24in), S 30cm (12in).

☀ ◊

***Nemesia strumosa* Carnival
Series**
Fairly fast-growing, bushy annual with
serrated, pale green leaves. In summer
has small, somewhat trumpet-shaped
flowers in a range of colours, including
yellow, red, orange, purple and white.
H 20–30cm (8–12in), S 15cm (6in).

☀ ◊

***Verbena* x *hybrida* Sandy Series**
Compact, erect, bushy perennial,
grown as an annual. Has lance-shaped,
serrated, mid- to deep green leaves. In
summer and autumn, produces clusters
of small flowers in rose-pink, rose-pink
with white eyes, magenta, scarlet or
white. H 20cm (8in), S 30cm (12in).

☀ ◊

***Petunia* Picotee Series** [red]
Fairly fast-growing, branching, bushy
perennial, grown as an annual, with
oval leaves. Has flared, somewhat
trumpet-shaped, red flowers, edged
with white, in summer-autumn.
H 15–30cm (6–12in), S 30cm (12in).

☀ ◊

***Primula* Pacific Series** [dwarf]
Rosette-forming perennial, normally
grown as a biennial, with lance-shaped
leaves. Has heads of large, fragrant, flat
flowers in shades of blue, yellow, red,
pink or white in spring.
H 10–15cm (4–6in), S 20cm (8in).

☀ ◊

ANNUALS *and* BIENNIALS

**Zinnia elegans Ruffles Series
[mixed]**
Moderately fast-growing, sturdy,
upright annual with pale or mid-green
leaves. Ruffled, pompon, double flower
heads in a mixture of colours are
carried in summer and early autumn.
H 60cm (24in), S 30cm (12in).

Salpiglossis sinuata Casino Series
Erect, compact annual with slender,
freely branching stems. From summer
to autumn, has broadly funnel-shaped,
5-lobed flowers in blue, purple, red,
yellow or orange, often heavily veined.
H to 60cm (24in), S to 30cm (12in).

**Ismelia carinata 'Monarch Court
Jesters'**
Fast-growing, erect, branching annual.
In summer has feathery, grey-green
leaves and daisy-like, zoned flower
heads, to 8cm (3in) wide, in various
colour combinations.
H 60cm (24in), S 30cm (12in).

**Viola × wittrockiana Floral Dance
Series**
Fairly fast-growing, bushy perennial,
grown as an annual or biennial. Has
oval, mid-green leaves and rounded,
5-petalled flowers in a wide range of
colours in winter.
H 15–20cm (6–8in), S 20cm (8in).

Alonsoa warscewiczii
(Mask flower)
Perennial, grown as an annual, with
slender, branching, red stems carrying
oval, toothed, deep green leaves.
Spurred, bright scarlet flowers are
produced during summer-autumn.
H 30–60cm (12–24in), S 30cm (12in).

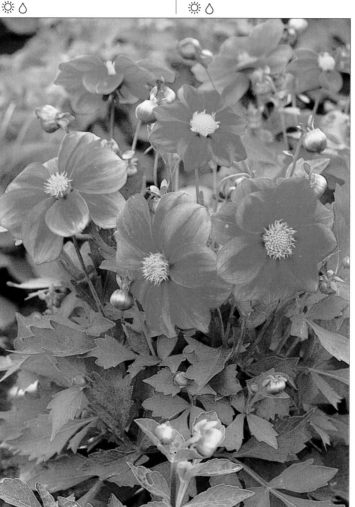

Dahlia 'Coltness Gem'
Well-branched, erect, bushy, tuberous
perennial, grown as an annual. Has
deeply lobed leaves and daisy-like,
single flower heads in many colours
throughout summer until autumn frosts.
H and S 45cm (18in).

Tagetes 'Cinnabar'
Fast-growing, bushy annual with
aromatic, very feathery, deep green
leaves. Heads of rounded, daisy-like,
single, rich rust-red flowers, yellow-
red beneath, are carried in summer and
early autumn. H and S 30cm (12in).

**Solenostemon scutellarioides
'Brightness'**, syn. *Coleus blumei*
var. *verschaffeltii* 'Brightness'
Fast-growing, bushy perennial, grown
as an annual. Has rust-red leaves,
edged with green. Flower spikes should
be removed. H to 45cm (18in), S 30cm
(12in) or more. Min 10°C (50°F).

Petunia cvs
Portulaca grandiflora
Salpiglossis sinuata cvs
Salvia splendens

Solanum capsicastrum
Solanum pseudocapsicum 'Fancy'
Solenostemon scutellarioides, illus. p.324
Tagetes patula

Tropaeolum majus

ANNUALS *and* BIENNIALS

ANNUALS *and* BIENNIALS

■ RED

■ PURPLE

Amaranthus hypochondriacus
(Prince's feather)
Bushy annual with upright, sometimes
flattened panicles, 15cm (6in) or more
long, of dark red flowers in summer-
autumn. Leaves are heavily suffused
purple. H to 1.2m (4ft), S 45cm (1½ft).

☼ ◊

Ricinus communis 'Impala'
Fast-growing, evergreen, erect shrub,
usually grown as an annual. Has
deeply lobed, bronze leaves to 30cm
(12in) wide and clusters of small, red
flowers in summer, followed by
globular, prickly, red seed heads.
H 1.5m (5ft), S 90cm (3ft).

☼ ◊ ①

Calomeria amaranthoides
(Incense plant)
Erect, branching biennial with a strong
fragrance of incense. Has lance-shaped
leaves and heads of tiny, pink,
brownish-red or crimson flowers in
summer-autumn. H to 1.8m (6ft),
S 90cm (3ft). Min. 4°C (39°F).

☼ ◊

Trachelium caeruleum
(Throatwort)
Moderately fast-growing, erect
perennial, grown as an annual. Has
oval, serrated leaves and clustered
heads of small, tubular, lilac-blue or
white flowers in summer.
H 60–90cm (2–3ft), S 30cm (1ft).

☼ ◊

Psylliostachys suworowii, (Statice)
Fairly slow-growing, erect, branching
annual with lance-shaped leaves. Bears
branching spikes of small, tubular, pink
to purple flowers in summer and early
autumn. Flowers are good for drying.
H 45cm (18in), S 30cm (12in).

☼ ◊

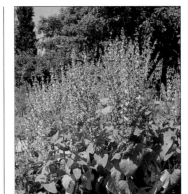

Salvia sclarea var. **turkestanica**
Moderately fast-growing, erect
biennial, grown as an annual. Has
aromatic, oval, hairy leaves and
panicles of tubular, white and lavender-
purple flowers with prominent,
lavender-purple bracts in summer.
H 75cm (30in), S 30cm (12in).

☼ ◊

Schizanthus pinnatus
Moderately fast-growing, upright, bushy
annual with feathery, light green leaves.
In summer-autumn has rounded, lobed,
multicoloured flowers in shades of pink,
purple, white or yellow.
H 30cm–1.2m (1–4ft), S 30cm (1ft).
Min. 5°C (41°F).

☼ ◊

**Linaria maroccana 'Fairy
Lights'**
Fast-growing, erect, bushy annual with
lance-shaped, pale green leaves. Tiny,
snapdragon-like flowers, in shades of
red, pink, purple, yellow or white, are
borne in summer.
H 20cm (8in), S 15cm (6in).

☼ ◊

Amaranthus tricolor 'Joseph's Coat'
Atriplex hortensis var. *rubra*
Nicotiana x *sanderae* 'Crimson Rock'
Scabiosa atropurpurea

Antirrhinum majus
Centaurea cyanus
Consolida ajacis Dwarf Hyacinth Series
Iberis umbellata

Impatiens balsamina Tom Thumb Series
Ionopsidium acaule
Lobelia erinus 'Colour Cascade'
Matthiola cvs

Nemesia strumosa
Proboscidea fragrans
Xeranthemum annuum

Exacum affine (Persian violet)
Evergreen, bushy biennial, usually grown as an annual. Has oval, glossy leaves and masses of tiny, scented, saucer-shaped, purple flowers, with yellow stamens, in summer and early autumn. H and S 20–30cm (8–12in). Min. 7–10°C (45–50°F).

☼ ◊

Echium vulgare [dwarf]
Moderately fast-growing, erect, bushy annual or biennial with lance-shaped, dark green leaves. Spikes of tubular flowers, in shades of white, pink, blue or purple, appear in summer. H 30cm (12in), S 20cm (8in).

☼ ◊ ①

Orychophragmus violaceus
Moderately fast-growing, upright annual or biennial with branching flower stems and pointed-oval, pale green leaves. Heads of 4-petalled, purple-blue flowers are carried in spring. H 30–60cm (12–24in), S 30cm (12in).

☼ ◊

Petunia Daddy Series 'Sugar Daddy'
Fairly fast-growing, branching, bushy, perennial, grown as an annual, with oval leaves. In early summer to autumn, has large, purple flowers with dark veins. H to 35cm (14in), S 30–90cm (12–36in).

☼ ◊

Collinsia grandiflora
Moderately fast-growing, slender-stemmed annual. Upper leaves are lance-shaped; lower are oval. Whorls of pale purple flowers, with purplish-blue lips, are carried in spring-summer. H and S 15–30cm (6–12in).

◑ ◊

Nierembergia caerulea 'Purple Robe'
Moderately fast-growing, rounded, branching perennial, grown as an annual, with narrow, lance-shaped leaves. Has cup-shaped, dark bluish-purple flowers in summer and early autumn. H and S 15–20cm (6–8in).

☼ ◊

Callistephus chinensis Ostrich Plume Series
Fast-growing, bushy annual with long, branching stems. From late summer to late autumn, produces spreading, feathery, reflexed, double flower heads, mainly in pinks and crimsons. H to 60cm (2ft), S 30cm (1ft).

☼ ◊

Salvia splendens Cleopatra Series [violet]
Slow-growing, bushy perennial, grown as an annual. Oval, serrated leaves are dark green; dense racemes of tubular, deep violet-purple flowers are carried in summer and early autumn. H to 30cm (12in), S 20–30cm (8–12in).

☼ ◊

Campanula medium 'Bells of Holland'
Slow-growing, evergreen, clump-forming, erect biennial with lance-shaped, toothed leaves. In spring and early summer has bell-shaped flowers in a mixture of blue, lilac, pink or white. H to 60cm (24in), S 30cm (12in).

☼ ◊

Salvia viridis, syn. *S. horminum*
Moderately fast-growing, upright, branching annual with oval leaves. Tubular, lipped flowers, enclosed by purple, pink or white bracts, are carried in spikes at tops of stems in summer and early autumn. H 45cm (18in), S 20cm (8in).

☼ ◊

Gomphrena globosa (Globe amaranth)
Moderately fast-growing, upright, bushy annual with oval, hairy leaves. Has oval, clover-like flower heads in pink, yellow, orange, purple or white in summer and early autumn. H 30cm (12in), S 20cm (8in).

☼ ◊

Cerinthe major 'Purpurascens'
Annual of lax habit with oval to spoon-shaped leaves, to 6cm (2½in) long. Bears terminal sprays of nodding, tubular, pale to mid-yellow flowers, with violet-tinged tips. Bracts around flowers are strongly suffused purple. H and S 60cm (2ft).

☼ ◊

ANNUALS *and* BIENNIALS

Pericallis x hybrida 'Spring Glory' (Cineraria)
Slow-growing, evergreen, mound- or dome-shaped perennial, grown as a biennial, with large, oval, serrated leaves. Bears heads of large flowers in a mixture of colours in spring. H 20cm (8in), S 30cm (12in). Min. 5°C (41°F).
☼ ◊

Callistephus chinensis Milady Super Series [blue]
Moderately fast-growing, erect, bushy annual with oval, toothed leaves. Has large, daisy-like, double, purplish-blue flower heads in summer and early autumn. H 25–30cm (10–12in), S 30–45cm (12–18in).
☼ ◊

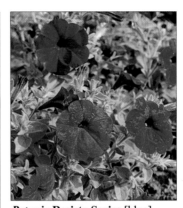

Petunia Resisto Series [blue]
Moderately fast-growing, branching, bushy perennial, grown as an annual. Has oval leaves and rain-resistant, flared, trumpet-shaped, intense blue flowers in summer–autumn. H 15–30cm (6–12in), S 30cm (12in).
☼ ◊

Lobelia erinus 'Sapphire'
Slow-growing, pendulous, spreading annual or occasionally perennial. Oval to lance-shaped leaves are pale green; small, sapphire-blue flowers with white centres are produced continuously in summer and early autumn. H 20cm (8in), S 15cm (6in).
☼ ◊

Convolvulus tricolor 'Blue Flash'
Moderately fast-growing, upright, bushy annual with oval to lance-shaped leaves. Has small, saucer-shaped, intense blue flowers with cream and yellow centres in summer. H 20–30cm (8–12in), S 20cm (8in).
☼ ◊

Viola x wittrockiana Joker Series
Bushy, spreading perennial, usually grown as an annual or biennial. Large, rounded, 5-petalled, purplish-blue flowers, with black and white 'faces' and yellow eyes, appear in summer. H and S 15cm (6in).
☼ ◊

Consolida ajacis Giant Imperial Series (Giant larkspur)
Fast-growing, upright, branching annual with feathery leaves. Long spikes of rounded, spurred, double flowers, pink, blue or white, are carried in summer. H 1.2 m (4ft), S 30cm (1ft).
☼ ◊

Salvia farinacea 'Victoria'
Moderately fast-growing perennial, grown as an annual, with many erect stems. Has oval or lance-shaped leaves and spikes of tubular, violet-blue flowers in summer. H 45cm (18in), S 30cm (12in).
☼ ◊

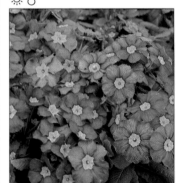

Primula Super Giants Series [blue]
Rosette-forming perennial, usually grown as a biennial, with lance-shaped leaves. Heads of large, fragrant, flat, blue flowers appear in spring. H and S to 30cm (12in).
☼ ◊

Browallia speciosa, illus. p.266
Ipomoea purpurea

Torenia fournieri
(Wishbone flower)
Moderately fast-growing, erect, branching annual with serrated, light green leaves. Dark blue-purple flowers, paler and yellow within, are carried in summer and early autumn. H 30cm (12in), S 20cm (8in). Min. 5°C (41°F).

☀ ◊

Gilia capitata
Erect, branching annual. Has very feathery, mid-green leaves and tiny, dense, rounded heads of soft lavender-blue flowers in summer and early autumn. Is good for cut flowers.
H 45cm (18in), S 20cm (8in).

☀ ◊

Ageratum houstonianum
'Blue Mink'
Moderately fast-growing, hummock-forming annual. Has pointed-oval leaves and clusters of feathery, brush-like, pastel blue flower heads in summer-autumn. Makes a useful edging plant. H and S 20–30cm (8–12in).

☀ ◊

***Nigella damascena* 'Miss Jekyll'**
Fast-growing, slender, erect annual. Feathery leaves are bright green; small, rounded, many-petalled, semi-double, blue flowers are carried in summer, followed by inflated seed pods which can be cut and dried.
H 45cm (18in), S 20cm (8in).

☀ ◊

Ageratum houstonianum
'Blue Danube'
Moderately fast-growing, hummock-forming annual with pointed-oval leaves. Has clusters of feathery, brush-like, lavender-blue flower heads in summer-autumn. Makes a useful edging plant. H and S 15cm (6in).

☀ ◊

Nemophila menziesii,
syn. *N. insignis* (Baby blue-eyes)
Fast-growing, spreading annual with serrated, grey-green leaves. Small, bowl-shaped, blue flowers with white centres are carried in summer.
H 20cm (8in), S 15cm (6in).

☀ ◊

***Nigella damascena* Persian Jewels Series**
Fast-growing, erect annual with feathery leaves. Small, semi-double flowers, in shades of blue, pink or white, appear in summer, followed by inflated seed pods which can be cut and dried.
H 45cm (18in), S 20cm (8in).

☀ ◊

Sedum caeruleum
Moderately fast-growing annual with branching flower stems. Oval, light green leaves become red-tinged when clusters of small, star-shaped, light blue flowers with white centres are borne in summer. H and S 10-15cm (4-6in).

☀ ◊ ⓘ

***Viola* x *wittrockiana* 'True Blue'**
Erect, bushy perennial, grown as an annual or biennial, with spreading stems and oval leaves. In winter or summer, bears large, clear sky-blue flowers each with a small, yellow eye.
H 16–23cm (6–9in),
S 23–30cm (9–12in).

☀ ◊

Callistephus chinensis
Consolida ajacis Dwarf Hyacinth Series
Lobelia erinus 'Blue Cascade'
Nolana paradoxa

Petunia cvs
Phacelia tanacetifolia
Phlox drummondii cvs
Salvia viridis cvs

Trachymene coerulea
Viola x *wittrockiana* cvs

■ BLUE　　　　　　　　　　　　　　　　　　　　　　　　　　□□ BLUE–GREEN

Centaurea cyanus [tall, blue]
(Cornflower)
Fast-growing, erect, branching annual.
Has lance-shaped, grey-green leaves
and branching heads of daisy-like, blue
flowers in summer and early autumn.
H to 90cm (3ft), S 30cm (1ft).

Myosotis sylvatica 'Blue Ball'
Slow-growing, bushy, compact
perennial, often grown as a biennial.
Has lance-shaped leaves and, in spring
and early summer, spikes of tiny,
5-lobed, deep blue flowers.
H to 20cm (8in), S 15cm (6in).

Phacelia campanularia
(California bluebell)
Moderately fast-growing, branching,
bushy annual with oval, serrated, deep
green leaves. Bell-shaped, pure blue
flowers, 2.5cm (1in) wide, are carried
in summer and early autumn.
H 20cm (8in), S 15cm (6in).

Lobelia erinus 'Crystal Palace'
Slow-growing, spreading, compact,
bushy annual or occasionally
perennial. Bronzed leaves are oval to
lance-shaped; small, deep blue flowers
are produced continuously in summer
and early autumn. H 10–20cm (4–8in),
S 10–15cm (4–6in).

Brachyscome iberidifolia
(Swan River daisy)
Moderately fast-growing, thin-stemmed,
bushy annual with deeply cut leaves.
Has small, fragrant, daisy-like flower
heads, usually blue but also pink,
mauve, purple or white, in summer and
early autumn. H and S to 45cm (18in).

Cynoglossum amabile
'Firmament'
Slow-growing, upright, bushy annual
or biennial with lance-shaped, hairy,
grey-green leaves. Pendulous, tubular,
pure sky-blue flowers are carried in
summer. H 45cm (18in), S 30cm
(12in).

Anchusa capensis 'Blue Angel'
Bushy biennial, grown as an annual.
Has lance-shaped, bristly leaves. Heads
of shallowly bowl-shaped, brilliant
blue flowers are borne in summer.
H and S 20cm (8in).

Senecio cineraria 'Silver Dust',
syn. *S. maritimus* 'Silver Dust'
Moderately fast-growing, evergreen,
bushy sub-shrub, usually grown as an
annual, with deeply lobed, silver
leaves. Small, daisy-like, yellow flower
heads appear in summer but are best
removed. H and S 30cm (12in).

Felicia bergeriana
(Kingfisher daisy)
Fairly fast-growing, mat-forming
annual. Has lance-shaped, hairy, grey-
green leaves. Small, daisy-like, blue
flower heads with yellow centres open
only in sunshine in summer and early
autumn. H and S 15cm (6in).

Commelina coelestis (Day flower)
Fairly fast-growing, upright perennial,
usually grown as an annual, with
lance-shaped, mid-green leaves. Small,
3-petalled, bright pure blue flowers
are freely produced from late summer
to mid-autumn.
H to 45cm (18in), S 30cm (12in).

Borago officinalis (Borage)
Spreading, clump-forming, annual
herb. Has oval, crinkled, rough-haired
leaves and sprays of star-shaped, blue
flowers in summer and early autumn.
Young leaves are sometimes used as a
coolant in drinks. Self seeds
prolifically. H 90cm (3ft), S 30cm (1ft).

Nicotiana langsdorffii
Fairly slow-growing, erect, branching
perennial, grown as an annual,
with oval to lance-shaped leaves.
Slightly pendent, bell-shaped, pale
green to yellow-green flowers
appear in summer.
H 1–1.5m (3–5ft), S 30cm (1ft).

Moluccella laevis
(Bells of Ireland, Shell flower)
Fairly fast-growing, erect, branching annual. Rounded leaves are pale green; spikes of small, tubular, white flowers, each surrounded by a conspicuous, pale green calyx, appear in summer.
H 60cm (24in), S 20cm (8in).

Ricinus communis
(Castor-oil plant)
Fast-growing, evergreen, erect shrub, usually grown as an annual. Has large, deeply lobed, mid-green leaves and heads of green and red flowers in summer, followed by globular, prickly seed pods. H 1.5m (5ft), S 90cm (3ft).

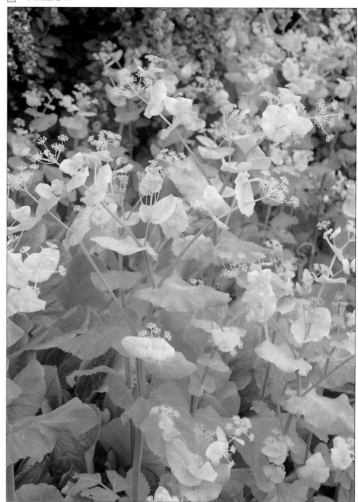

Smyrnium perfoliatum
Slow-growing, upright biennial. Upper leaves, rounded and yellow-green, encircle stems which bear heads of yellowish-green flowers in summer.
H 60cm–1m (2–3ft), S 60cm (2ft).

Zinnia elegans 'Envy'
Moderately fast-growing, sturdy, erect annual. Has oval to lance-shaped, pale or mid-green leaves and large, daisy-like, double, green flower heads in summer and early autumn.
H 60cm (24in), S 30cm (12in).

Amberboa moschata, syn.
Centaurea moschata (Sweet sultan)
Fast-growing, upright, slender-stemmed annual with lance-shaped, greyish-green leaves. Large, fragrant, cornflower-like flower heads, in a range of colours, are carried in summer and early autumn.
H 45cm (18in), S 20cm (8in).

Bassia scoparia f. **trichophylla**,
syn. *Kochia scoparia* f. *trichophylla*
(Burning bush, Summer cypress)
Moderately fast-growing, erect, very bushy annual. Narrow, lance-shaped, light green leaves, 5–8cm (2–3in) long, turn red in autumn. Has insignificant flowers. H 90cm (3ft), S 60cm (2ft).

Platystemon californicus
(Cream cups)
Moderately fast-growing, upright, compact annual with lance-shaped, greyish-green leaves. Saucer-shaped, cream or pale yellow flowers, about 2.5cm (1in) across, appear in summer.
H 30cm (12in), S 10cm (4in).

Argemone mexicana
(Devil's fig, Prickly poppy)
Spreading perennial, grown as an annual, with leaves divided into white-marked, greyish-green leaflets. In summer has fragrant, poppy-like, yellow or orange flowers, 8cm (3in) wide. H to 60cm (24in), S 30cm (12in).

Glaucium flavum (Horned poppy)
Slow-growing, erect biennial with oval, lobed, light greyish-green leaves. Poppy-like, vivid yellow flowers, 8cm (3in) wide, appear in summer and early autumn.
H 30–60cm (12–24in), S 45cm (18in).

Angelica archangelica, illus. p.228
Nicandra physalodes
Nicotiana 'Lime Green'
Solenostemon scutellarioides, illus. p.324

Tanacetum parthenium 'Aureum'

Calendula officinalis 'Fiesta Gitana'
Tagetes Gem Series 'Lemon Gem'
Xanthophthalmum coronarium

☐ YELLOW

Viola x wittrockiana 'Clear Sky Primrose'
Erect, bushy perennial, grown as an annual or biennial, with spreading stems and oval leaves. In winter, produces primrose-yellow flowers brushed in canary yellow. H 16–23cm (6–9in), S 23–30cm (9–12in).

☼ ◊

Limnanthes douglasii (Meadow foam, Poached-egg flower)
Fast-growing, slender, erect annual. Feathery leaves are glossy, light green; slightly fragrant, cup-shaped, white flowers with yellow centres are carried from early to late summer.
H 15cm (6in), S 10cm (4in).

☼ ◊

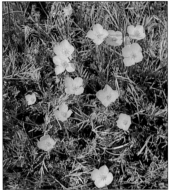

Eschscholzia caespitosa
Fast-growing, slender, erect annual with feathery, bluish-green leaves. Cup-shaped, 4-petalled, yellow flowers, 2.5cm (1in) wide, appear in summer and early autumn. H and S 15cm (6in).

☼ ◊

Antirrhinum majus Tahiti Series
Erect perennial, grown as an annual, branching from the base, with lance-shaped leaves. In summer and autumn, bears 2-lipped flowers in red, orange, rose-pink and bronze, with a pink and white bicolour. Rust resistant.
H 20–30cm (8–12in), S 30cm (12in).

☼ ◊

Helianthus annuus 'Music Box'
Fast-growing, free-flowering, many-branched, hairy-stemmed annual. Bears daisy-like flower heads, 10–12cm (4–5in) across, with ray-florets ranging from creamy-yellow to dark red, and black disc-florets, in summer.
H 70cm (28in), S to 60cm (24in).

☼ ◊ ⓘ

Lindheimera texana (Star daisy)
Moderately fast-growing, erect, branching annual with hairy stems and oval, serrated, hairy leaves. Daisy-like, yellow flower heads appear in late summer and early autumn.
H 30–60cm (12–24in), S 30cm (12in).

☼ ◊

Viola x wittrockiana 'Super Chalon Giants'
Fairly fast-growing, bushy perennial, grown as an annual or biennial. Has oval, serrated leaves and, in summer-autumn, 5-petalled, ruffled and waved, bicoloured flowers.
H 15–20cm (6–8in), S 20cm (8in).

☼ ◊

Calendula officinalis Kablouna Series
Fast-growing, bushy annual with strongly aromatic, lance-shaped leaves. From spring to autumn has crested, daisy-like, orange, gold or yellow flower heads. H 60cm (24in), S 30–60cm (12–24in).

☼ ◊

Mentzelia lindleyi,
syn. *Bartonia aurea*
Fairly fast-growing, bushy annual with fleshy stems and lance-shaped, serrated leaves. Has fragrant, cup-shaped, deep yellow flowers, with conspicuous stamens, in summer.
H 45cm (18in), S 20cm (8in).

☼ ◊

Tagetes 'Gold Coins'
[Erecta Group]
Fast-growing, erect, bushy annual. Has aromatic, feathery, glossy, deep green leaves and large, daisy-like, double flower heads in shades of yellow and orange in summer and early autumn.
H 90cm (3ft), S 30–45cm (1–1½ft).

☼ ◊ ⓘ

Sanvitalia procumbens
(Creeping zinnia)
Moderately fast-growing, prostrate annual with pointed-oval leaves. Daisy-like, yellow flower heads, 2.5cm (1in) wide, with black centres, are borne in summer. H 15cm (6in), S 30cm (12in).

☼ ◊

Amaranthus tricolor 'Joseph's Coat'
Antirrhinum majus
Arctotis Harlequin Hybrids 'Sunshine'
Bracteantha bracteata cvs

Calceolaria Anytime Series
Calceolaria 'Monarch'
Cosmos bipinnatus 'Sea Shells'
Erysimum cheiri

Gaillardia pulchella [double, mixed]
Gazania Daybreak Series
Helianthus annuus 'Russian Giant'
Helianthus annuus 'Teddy Bear', illus. p.337

Hunnemannia fumariifolia 'Sunlite'
Ismelia carinata Tricolor Series
Layia platyglossa
Nemesia strumosa

Coreopsis tinctoria (Tick-seed)
Fast-growing, erect, bushy annual with lance-shaped leaves. Large, daisy-like, bright yellow flower heads with red centres are carried in summer and early autumn.
H 60–90cm (2–3ft), S 20cm (8in).

Xanthophthalmum segetum
Moderately fast-growing, erect annual with lance-shaped, grey-green leaves. Daisy-like, single flower heads, to 8cm (3in) wide, in shades of yellow, are carried in summer and early autumn. Is excellent for cut flowers.
H 45cm (18in), S 30cm (12in).

Coreopsis 'Sunray'
Spreading, clump-forming perennial, grown as an annual by sowing under glass in early spring. Has lance-shaped, serrated leaves and daisy-like, double, bright yellow flower heads in summer.
H 45cm (18in), S 30–45cm (12–18in).

Helianthus annuus
Fast-growing, erect annual with oval, serrated, mid-green leaves. Daisy-like, yellow flower heads to 30cm (12in) or more wide, with brown or purplish centres, appear in summer.
H 1–3m (3–10ft), S 30–45cm (1–1½ft).

Viola x wittrockiana Clear Crystals Series
[yellow]
Bushy perennial, grown as an annual or biennial. Has oval, mid-green leaves and rounded, 5-petalled, yellow flowers in summer.
H 15–20cm (6–8in), S 20cm (8in).

Cladanthus arabicus
Moderately fast-growing, hummock-forming annual with aromatic, feathery, light green leaves. Has fragrant, daisy-like, single, deep yellow flower heads, 5cm (2in) wide, in summer and early autumn. H 60cm (24in), S 30cm (12in).

Viola x wittrockiana Crystal Bowl Series
[yellow]
Bushy, spreading perennial, usually grown as an annual or biennial, with oval, mid-green leaves. Large, rounded, 5-petalled, yellow flowers are carried in summer. H and S 15cm (6in).

Antirrhinum majus Sonnet Series
Erect, bushy, early flowering perennial, grown as an annual, branching from the base, with lance-shaped leaves. From spring to autumn, freely produces 2-lipped flowers in bronze, pink, carmine-red, crimson, burgundy, white and yellow. H and S 45cm (18in).

Helianthus annuus 'Teddy Bear'
Fast-growing, compact, hairy-stemmed annual with toothed, roughly hairy leaves. Produces daisy-like, double, deep yellow flower heads, to 13cm (5in) across, in summer.
H 90cm (36in), S to 60cm (24in).

Portulaca grandiflora
Salpiglossis sinuata Bolero Hybrids
Schizanthus cvs
Solenostemon scutellarioides, illus. p.324

Tolpis barbata
Tropaeolum majus
Tuberaria guttata
Viola x wittrockiana cvs

Zinnia cvs

ANNUALS *and* BIENNIALS

337

☐ YELLOW

***Zinnia elegans* 'Belvedere'**
Moderately fast-growing, sturdy, erect
annual with oval to lance-shaped, pale
or mid-green leaves. Large, daisy-like,
double flower heads in a mixture of
colours appear in summer and early
autumn. H and S 30cm (12in).

☼ ◊

Ursinia anthemoides
Moderately fast-growing, bushy annual
with feathery, pale green leaves. Small,
daisy-like, purple-centred flower heads
with orange-yellow rays, purple
beneath, appear in summer and early
autumn. H 30cm (12in), S 20cm (8in).

☼ ◊

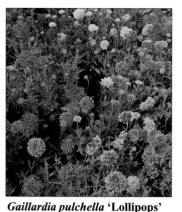

***Gaillardia pulchella* 'Lollipops'**
Moderately fast-growing, upright
annual with lance-shaped, hairy,
greyish-green leaves. Daisy-like,
double, red-and-yellow flower heads,
5cm (2in) wide, are carried in summer.
H and S 30cm (12in).

☼ ◊

***Calceolaria* 'Bright Bikinis'**
Compact, bushy annual or biennial.
Has oval, slightly hairy, mid-green
leaves, and heads of small, rounded,
pouched flowers in shades of yellow,
orange or red in summer.
H and S 20cm (8in). Min. 5°C (41°F).

☼ ◊

***Tagetes* Solar Series**
Bushy annual bearing large, densely
double flower heads, in colours
including orange with red flecking,
sulphur-yellow and golden-yellow,
some with crested centres, from late
spring to early autumn.
H 35cm (14in), S 30–40cm (12–16in).

☼ ◊ ⓘ

***Tagetes* 'Naughty Marietta'**
Fast-growing, bushy annual with
aromatic, deeply cut, deep green
leaves. Heads of daisy-like, bicoloured
flowers, deep yellow and maroon, are
carried in summer and early autumn.
H and S 30cm (12in).

☼ ◊ ⓘ

***Calendula officinalis* Pacific
Beauty Series 'Lemon Queen'**
Fast-growing, erect annual with softly
hairy, aromatic leaves. Daisy-like,
double, lemon-yellow flower heads,
with red-brown disc-florets, are borne
from summer to autumn. H to 45cm
(18in), S 30–45cm (12–18in).

☼ ◊

***Viola* x *wittrockiana* Forerunner
Series**
Erect, bushy perennials, grown as
annuals or biennials, with oval leaves.
In winter and spring, bears medium-
sized flowers in a range of bright, single
colours and bicolours. H 16–23cm
(6–9in), S 23–30cm (9–12in).

☼ ◊

***Eschscholzia californica* [mixed]**
Fast-growing, slender, erect annual.
Feathery leaves are bluish-green; cup-
shaped, 4-petalled, single flowers, in
shades of red, orange, yellow or cream,
are borne in summer-autumn.
H 30cm (12in), S 15cm (6in).

☼ ◊

Rudbeckia hirta
Rudbeckia hirta 'Irish Eyes'
Tagetes patula

Eschscholzia californica
Fast-growing, slender, erect annual
with feathery, bluish-green leaves.
Cup-shaped, 4-petalled, vivid orange-
yellow flowers are borne in summer-
autumn. H 30cm (12in), S 15cm (6in).

☼ ◊

**Eschscholzia californica Thai
Silk Series**
Fast-growing, compact, slender, erect
annual with feathery, bluish-green
leaves. In summer-autumn, produces
single or semi-double, fluted, bronze-
tinged flowers in red, pink or orange.
H 20–25cm (8–10in), S 15cm (6in).

☼ ◊

Tropaeolum Alaska Series
Fast-growing, bushy annual with
rounded, variegated leaves. Spurred,
trumpet-shaped flowers, in shades of
red or yellow, appear in summer and
early autumn. H and S 30cm (12in).

☼ ◊

Primula Pacific Series
(Polyanthus)
Rosette-forming perennial, normally
grown as a biennial, with lance-shaped
leaves. Has heads of large, fragrant,
flat flowers in shades of blue, yellow,
red, pink or white in spring.
H and S 20–22cm (8–9in).

☼ ◊

**Nemesia strumosa Triumph
Series**
Fairly fast-growing, bushy, compact
annual with lance-shaped, serrated,
pale green leaves. Small, somewhat
trumpet-shaped flowers, in a range of
bright colours, are borne in summer.
H 20cm (8in), S 15cm (6in).

☼ ◊

**Viola x wittrockiana Universal
Series** [apricot]
Bushy, spreading perennial, usually
grown as a biennial. Large, rounded,
5-petalled, deep apricot flowers are
borne in winter-spring.
H and S 15–20cm (6–8in).

☼ ◊

Calceolaria 'Sunshine'
Evergreen, compact, bushy perennial,
grown as an annual. Has oval, mid-
green leaves and heads of small,
rounded, pouched, bright golden-
yellow flowers in late spring and
summer. H and S 20cm (8in).

☼ ◊

**Calendula officinalis
'Fiesta Gitana'**
Fast-growing, bushy annual with
strongly aromatic, lance-shaped, pale
green leaves. Daisy-like, double flower
heads, ranging from cream to orange
in colour, are carried from spring
to autumn. H and S 30cm (12in).

☼ ◊

Calceolaria Anytime Series
Calceolaria 'Monarch'

ANNUALS *and* BIENNIALS

☐ ORANGE

Rudbeckia hirta 'Marmalade'
Moderately fast-growing, erect, branching perennial, grown as an annual, with lance-shaped leaves. In summer-autumn bears daisy-like, deep golden-orange flower heads, 8cm (3in) wide, with black centres.
H 45cm (18in), S 30cm (12in).

☼ ◊

Rudbeckia hirta 'Goldilocks'
Moderately fast-growing, erect, branching perennial, grown as an annual. Has lance-shaped leaves and daisy-like, double or semi-double, golden-orange flower heads, 8cm (3in) across, in summer-autumn.
H 60cm (24in), S 30cm (12in).

☼ ◊

Tagetes 'Tangerine Gem'
Fast-growing, bushy annual with aromatic, feathery leaves. Small, single, deep orange flower heads appear in summer and early autumn.
H 20cm (8in), S 30cm (12in).

☼ ◊ ⊘

Rudbeckia hirta 'Rustic Dwarfs'
Moderately fast-growing, erect, branching perennial, grown as an annual, with lance-shaped, mid-green leaves. Bears daisy-like, yellow, mahogany or bronze flower heads, 8cm (3in) wide, in summer-autumn.
H 60cm (24in), S 30cm (12in).

☼ ◊

Tithonia rotundifolia 'Torch'
Slow-growing, erect annual with rounded, lobed leaves. Has daisy-like, bright orange or scarlet flower heads, 5–8 cm (2–3in) wide, in summer and early autumn.
H 90cm (3ft), S 30cm (1ft).

☼ ◊

Tagetes 'Orange Winner'
Fast-growing, bushy annual with aromatic, feathery, deep green leaves. Crested, daisy-like, double, bright orange flower heads are carried in summer and early autumn.
H 15cm (6in), S to 30cm (12in).

☼ ◊ ⊘

Tagetes Boy Series
Compact annual that bears double, crested flower heads in a range of colours, including shades of golden-yellow, yellow, orange or reddish-brown, with deep orange or yellow crests, in late spring and early summer.
H to 15cm (6in), S to 30cm (12in).

☼ ◊ ⊘

Erysimum x allionii 'Orange Bedder'
Slow-growing, short-lived, evergreen, bushy perennial, grown as a biennial. Has lance-shaped, mid-green leaves. Heads of scented, 4-petalled, brilliant orange flowers appear in spring.
H and S 30cm (12in).

☼ ◊

Bracteantha bracteata Monstrosum Series
Moderately fast-growing, erect, branching annual. Has daisy-like, papery, double flower heads, in pink, red, orange, yellow or white, in summer and early autumn. Flowers dry well. H 90cm (3ft), S 30cm (1ft).

☼ ◊

Antirrhinum majus
Arctotis Harlequin Hybrids 'Tangerine'
Arctotis Harlequin Hybrids 'Torch'
Erysimum cheiri

Gazania Daybreak Series
Portulaca grandiflora
Salpiglossis sinuata Bolero Hybrids
Tagetes patula

Tropaeolum majus

Calendula officinalis 'Geisha Girl'
Fast-growing, bushy annual with strongly aromatic, lance-shaped, pale green leaves. Heads of double, orange flowers with incurved petals are borne from late spring to autumn.
H 60cm (24in), S 30–60cm (12–24in).

☼ ◊

Solanum pseudocapsicum 'Balloon'
Evergreen, bushy shrub, grown as an annual. Has lance-shaped leaves and, in summer, small, star-shaped, white flowers. Large, cream fruits turn orange in winter. H 30cm (12in), S 30–45cm (12–18in). Min. 5°C (41°F).

☼ ◊

Sanvitalia procumbens 'Mandarin Orange'
Moderately fast-growing, prostrate annual. Has pointed-oval, mid-green leaves and daisy-like, orange flower heads, 2.5cm (1in) wide, in summer.
H 15cm (6in), S 30cm (12in).

☼ ◊

Zinnia haageana 'Orange Star', syn. *Z. angustifolia* 'Orange Star', *Z. haageana* 'Classic'
Dwarf, bushy annual with daisy-like, broad-petalled, orange flower heads, borne in summer. Is mildew-resistant and good for ground cover.
H to 25cm (10in), S to 30cm (12in).

☼ ◊

Erysimum cheiri 'Fire King', syn. *Cheiranthus cheiri* 'Fire King'
Moderately fast-growing, evergreen, bushy perennial, grown as a biennial. Lance-shaped leaves are mid- to deep green; heads of 4-petalled, reddish-orange flowers are carried in spring.
H 38cm (15in), S 30–38cm (12–15in).

☼ ◊

Solanum pseudocapsicum 'Red Giant'
Fairly slow-growing, evergreen, bushy shrub, usually grown as an annual. Has lance-shaped, deep green leaves, small, white flowers in summer and large, round, orange-red fruits in winter.
H and S 30cm (12in). Min. 5°C (41°F).

☼ ◊

Dahlia 'Dandy'
Well-branched, erect, bushy, tuberous perennial, grown as an annual. Has pointed-oval, serrated leaves and heads of daisy-like flowers, with contrasting central collars of quilled petals, in shades of red, yellow or orange in summer. H and S 60cm (2ft).

☼ ◊

Tropaeolum Jewel Series
Fast-growing, bushy annual with rounded leaves. Spurred, trumpet-shaped flowers, in shades of red, yellow or orange, are held well above leaves from early summer to early autumn. H and S 30cm (12in).

☼ ◊

Emilia coccinea (Tassel flower)
Moderately fast-growing, upright annual with lance-shaped, greyish-green leaves and double, red or yellow flower heads in summer.
H 30–60cm (12–24in),
S 30cm (12in) or more.

☼ ◊

Clarkia amoena Princess Series [salmon]
Fast-growing annual with slender, upright stems and lance-shaped, mid-green leaves. Spikes of frilled, salmon-pink flowers are carried in summer.
H and S 30cm (12in).

☼ ◊

Celosia argentea 'Fairy Fountains'
Moderately fast-growing, erect, bushy perennial, grown as an annual. Has pointed-oval leaves and conical, feathery flower heads, to 15cm (6in) tall, in a wide range of colours in summer-autumn. H and S 30cm (12in).

☼ ◊

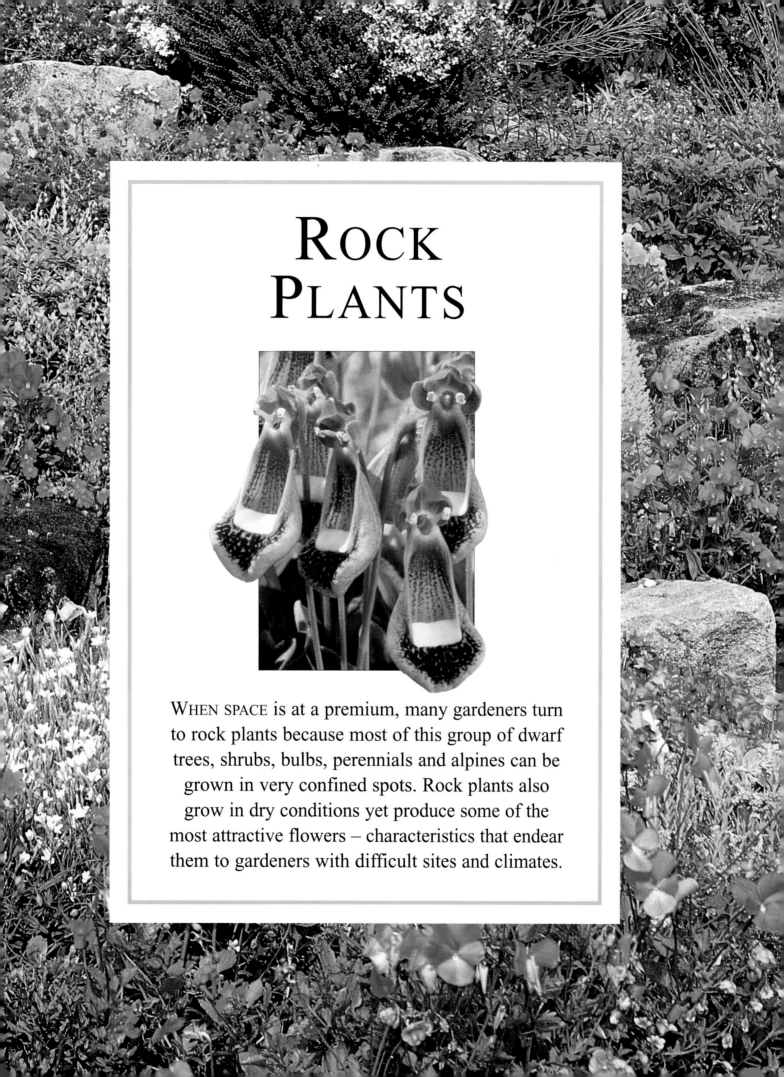

ROCK PLANTS

WHEN SPACE is at a premium, many gardeners turn to rock plants because most of this group of dwarf trees, shrubs, bulbs, perennials and alpines can be grown in very confined spots. Rock plants also grow in dry conditions yet produce some of the most attractive flowers – characteristics that endear them to gardeners with difficult sites and climates.

Rock Plants

Noted for their natural charm and simple, clear-coloured, abundant flowers, in spring and early summer, rock plants are suited to almost every situation, from the tiniest trough to the grandest rock garden.

WHAT ARE ROCK PLANTS?

The term rock plants includes bulbs and mat- and cushion-forming perennials (many of which are evergreen) as well as dwarf, evergreen, coniferous and deciduous trees and shrubs. They may be true alpines or simply plants of small stature that are suitable for rock garden plantings. While many of the alpines have specialized needs, the group includes many species and cultivars, such as aubrieta and *Aurinia saxatilis*, that are undemanding in cultivation and thrive in any well-drained site of suitable aspect.

True alpines grow at high altitudes above the tree-line, on scree slopes, in rock crevices or in short turf, while sub-alpine plants live below the tree-line on rocky slopes or in high pastures or meadow land. Most alpines are compact in habit and frequently deep-rooting, usually with small leaves that are leathery, fleshy or covered in fine hair. These adaptations help them survive the drying, high-velocity winds, brilliant, burning sun and extreme temperature fluctuations of their natural habitat.

Most rock plants grow in areas characterized by stony soils with rapid drainage, and so cannot withstand the combination of constant wetness at the roots and winter cold that is experienced in some regions. Such species also dislike warm, humid summers which may be the main limiting factor. In the wild, plants are insulated from winter cold by a blanket of snow,

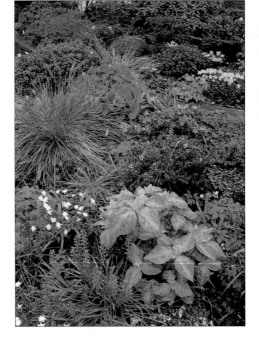

WOODLAND PLANTS
Above: Natives of mountain woodland, such as the trilliums seen here, generally need moist, neutral to acid soil and are perfectly at home in a peat bed in dappled shade.

PLANNING A ROCK GARDEN
Right: Siting a rock garden on a gentle slope assists rapid drainage, while carefully placed rocks form a niche where penetrating roots can be kept cool and moist during the summer.

beneath which they remain dormant till spring, conditions that occur in many parts of Canada. Those environments that mimic conditions in the wild, such as rock gardens, scree beds, troughs, raised beds, open frames and alpine houses, are therefore best for cultivating rock plants, which must have sharp drainage and, usually, protection from excessive winter moisture.

DESIGNING WITH ROCK PLANTS

One of the major attractions of this group is their diminutive size, which can satisfy the gardener's hunger for diversity because many

CONTAINER PLANTING
Troughs are ideal for creating landscapes in miniature but to provide perfect drainage they must be filled with gritty compost. Here, the flowers of alpine poppies, campanulas and lewisias lend colour to the neat, lime-encrusted rosettes of high-alpine saxifrages.

different plants can be grown in a relatively confined space. In a rock garden – as in larger-scale plantings – small shrubs, such as the highly fragrant *Daphne cneorum* and *D. retusa* or berried shrubs like *Cotoneaster horizontalis*, can be used to form the structural framework of a design. Miniature conifers, such as *Juniperus communis* 'Compressa', can create vertical emphasis and year-round colour, in contrast to plants of rounded habit, such as the evergreen *Hebe cupressoides* 'Boughton Dome'.

This structure can then be filled in with mat- and cushion-forming plants, such as sandworts (*Arenaria*) or *Dianthus deltoides*, at the feet of taller, feathery-leaved pulsatillas or the airy *Linum narbonense*. There are also tight, dome-forming saxifrages, rosette-forming sedums and fleshy-leaved sempervivums, whose surfaces contrast perfectly with the white-haired leaves of edelweiss (*Leontopodium*) or the silky, silver leaves of the celmisias.

MAINTAINING YEAR-ROUND INTEREST

Evergreen and structural plantings are more important in rock gardens than in other styles of garden because most alpines bloom in one burst between spring and early summer. The season can be extended, however, by planting early spring bulbs, such as alpine narcissus or crocuses, by using later-flowering rock plants such as helianthemums, phlox or veronicas, and by planting the autumn-flowering *Persicaria vacciniifolia* and cyclamen, or the berry-bearing gaultherias.

MINIATURE LANDSCAPES

In courtyards or tiny gardens, or where the soil in the open garden is too heavy or drainage is inadequate, rock plants can be grown in troughs or raised beds to create landscapes in miniature. The latter also bring small plants closer to eye level and are ideal for gardeners of reduced mobility.

Dry stone walls are also potential planting sites for many crevice-lovers, such as lewisias or ramonda, while the tops of the walls are ideal planting positions for cascading specimens, such as *Saxifraga* 'Tumbling Waters'.

SIZE CATEGORIES USED WITHIN THIS GROUP		
Large	**Medium**	**Small**
over 15cm (6in)	—	up to 15cm (6in)

ROCK PLANTS FOR EDGING
Above: Robust, low-growing mat-formers such as aubrieta and mossy saxifrages make excellent edging plants at the front of a rock garden.

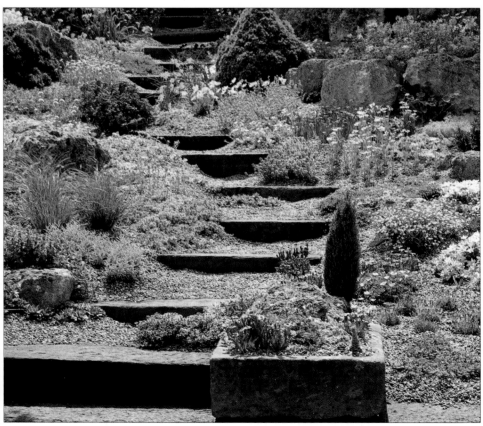

A PERFECT PARTNERSHIP
Left: In an open site in full sun, dwarf shrubs and conifers provide a permanent, structural framework for the profuse spring and early summer flowers that are typical of alpine plants.

345

☐ WHITE

ROCK PLANTS

Leontopodium alpinum (Edelweiss)
Short-lived perennial with tufts of lance-shaped, woolly leaves. Clusters of small, silvery-white flower heads, borne in spring or early summer, are surrounded by petal-like, thick, felted bracts that form a star shape. Dislikes winter and summer wet. H and S 15–20cm (6–8in).

☼ ◊

Lithophragma parviflorum
Clump-forming, tuberous perennial that has small, open clusters of campion-like, white or pink flowers in spring above a basal cluster of deeply toothed, kidney-shaped leaves. Lies dormant in summer.
H 15–20cm (6–8in), S to 20cm (8in).

◑ ◊

Iberis sempervirens, syn. *I. commutata*
Evergreen, spreading sub-shrub, with narrow, oblong, dark green leaves, bearing dense, rounded heads of white flowers in late spring and early summer. Trim after flowering. H 15–30cm (6–12in), S 45–60cm (18–24in).

☼ ◊

Pulsatilla alpina (Alpine anemone)
Tufted perennial with feathery leaves that bears upright, or somewhat nodding, cup-shaped, white, sometimes blue- or pink-flushed flowers singly in spring and early summer, followed by feathery seed heads.
H 15–30cm (6–12in), S to 10cm (4in).

☼ ◊ ⓘ

Saxifraga granulata (Fair maids of France, Meadow saxifrage)
Clump-forming perennial that loses its kidney-shaped, crumpled, glossy leaves in summer. Sticky stems carry loose panicles of rounded, white flowers in late spring. H 23–38cm (9–15in), S to 15cm (6in) or more.

◑ ◊

Rhodanthemum hosmariense
Evergreen, shrubby perennial with finely cut, bright silvery-green leaves that clothe lax, woody stems. From late spring to early autumn, white flower heads are borne singly above foliage.
H 15cm (6in) or more, S 30cm (12in).

☼ ◊

Andromeda polifolia 'Alba'
Evergreen, open, twiggy shrub bearing terminal clusters of pitcher-shaped, white flowers in spring and early summer. Glossy, dark green leaves are leathery and lance-shaped.
H 45cm (18in), S 60cm (24in).

☼ ◊ pH Zone 2

Cassiope 'Muirhead'
Evergreen, loose, bushy shrub with scale-like, dark green leaves on upright branches. In spring, these bear tiny, virtually stemless, bell-shaped, white flowers along their length.
H and S 20cm (8in).

☼ ◊ pH Zone 4

Cassiope 'Edinburgh'
Evergreen, dwarf shrub with tiny, dark green leaves tightly pressed to upright stems. In spring, many small, bell-shaped, white flowers are borne singly in leaf axils. H and S 20cm (8in).

◑ ◊ pH Zone 2

OTHER RECOMMENDED PLANTS:
Achillea clavennae, illus. p.373
Cassiope fastigiata
Cassiope mertensiana, illus. p.364

Cassiope selaginoides
Corydalis ochroleuca, illus. p.351
Cyathodes colensoi, illus. p.360
DAFFODILS, illus. pp.416–18

Daphne alpina
Galax urceolata, illus. p.351
x *Halimiocistus wintonensis*
Hebe carnosula

Hebe pinguifolia 'Pagei', illus. p.351
Houttuynia cordata 'Flore Pleno'
Iberis sempervirens 'Schneeflocke'
IRISES, illus. pp.234–5

Saxifraga hirsuta
Evergreen, mound-forming perennial with rosettes of round, hairy leaves and loose panicles of tiny, star-shaped, white flowers, often yellow-spotted at the base of petals, in late spring and early summer.
H 15–20cm (6–8in), S 20cm (8in).

Tiarella cordifolia (Foamflower)
Vigorous, evergreen, spreading perennial. Lobed, pale green leaves sometimes have darker marks; veins turn bronze-red in winter. Bears many spikes of profuse white flowers in late spring and early summer. H 15–20cm (6–8in), S to 30cm (12in) or more.

Dodecatheon meadia f. **album**
Clump-forming perennial with basal rosettes of oval, pale green leaves. In spring, strong stems bear several white flowers with dark centres and reflexed petals. Lies dormant in summer.
H 20cm (8in), S 15cm (6in).

Andromeda polifolia 'Compacta'
Evergreen, compact, twiggy shrub that bears delicate, terminal clusters of pitcher-shaped, coral-pink flowers, with white undertones, in spring and early summer. Leaves are lance-shaped and glossy, dark green.
H 15–23cm (6–9in), S 30cm (12in).

 Zone 2

Jeffersonia diphylla
Slow-growing, tufted perennial with distinctive, 2-lobed, light to mid-green leaves. Bears solitary cup-shaped, white flowers with prominent, yellow stamens in late spring. Do not disturb roots.
H 15–23cm (6–9in), S to 23cm (9in).

Saxifraga 'Tumbling Waters'
Slow-growing, evergreen, mal-forming perennial with a tight rosette of narrow, lime-encrusted leaves. After several years produces arching sprays of white flowers in conical heads; main rosette then dies but small offsets survive.
H to 60cm (24in), S to 20cm (8in).

Saxifraga × geum
Evergreen, mat-forming perennial with shallow-rooted rosettes of spoon-shaped, hairy leaves. In summer, star-shaped, pink-spotted, white flowers, deep pink in bud, are borne on loose panicles on slender stems.
H 15–20cm (6–8in), S 30cm (12in).

Dodecatheon hendersonii, syn. *D. latifolium*
Clump-forming perennial with a flat rosette of kidney-shaped leaves, above which deep pink flowers with reflexed petals appear in late spring. Needs a dry, dormant summer period.
H 30cm (12in), S 8cm (3in).

Daphne blagayana
Evergreen, prostrate shrub with trailing branches each bearing a terminal cluster of oval, leathery leaves and, in early spring, dense clusters of fragrant, tubular, white flowers. Likes humus-rich soil. H 30–40cm (12–16in), S 60–80cm (24–32in) or more.

 Zone 8

Vancouveria hexandra
Vigorous, spreading perennial with open sprays of many tiny, white flowers in late spring and early summer. Leathery leaves are divided into almost hexagonal leaflets. Makes good woodland ground cover.
H 20cm (8in), S indefinite.

Andromeda polifolia
Evergreen, open, twiggy shrub with narrow, leathery, glossy, mid-green leaves. Bears terminal clusters of pitcher-shaped, pink flowers in spring and early summer.
H 30–45cm (12–18in), S 60cm (24in).

 Zone 2

Phyllodoce × intermedia 'Drummondii'
Evergreen, bushy, dwarf shrub with narrow, heath-like, glossy leaves. From late spring to early summer bears terminal clusters of pitcher-shaped, rich pink flowers on slender, red stalks. H and S 23cm (9in).

☼ ◑ pH Zone 3

ROCK PLANTS

■ PINK–PURPLE

Daphne cneorum
Evergreen, low-growing shrub with trailing branches clothed in small, oval, leathery, dark green leaves. Fragrant, deep rose pink flowers are borne in terminal clusters in late spring. Prefers humus-rich soil.
H 23cm (9in), S to 2m (6ft).

☀ ◌ ① Zone 2b

Phyllodoce empetriformis
Evergreen, mat-forming shrub with fine narrow, heath like leaves and terminal clusters of bell-shaped, purplish-pink flowers in late spring and early summer.
H 15–23cm (6–9in), S 20cm (8in).

☀ ◔ pH Zone 3

Dodecatheon 'Red Wings'
Clump-forming perennial with a basal cluster of oblong, soft, pale green leaves. In late spring and early summer bears small, loose clusters of deep magenta flowers, with reflexed petals, on strong stems. Lies dormant in summer. H 20cm (8in), S 10cm (4in).

☀ ◌

Phyllodoce caerulea,
syn. *P. taxifolia*
Evergreen, dwarf shrub with fine, narrow, heath-like leaves. Bears bell-shaped, purple to purplish-pink flowers, singly or in clusters, in late spring and summer.
H and S to 30cm (12in).

☀ ◔ pH Zone 3

Pulsatilla vulgaris (Pasque flower)
Tufted perennial with feathery, light green leaves. In spring bears nodding, cup-shaped flowers, in shades of purple, red, pink or white, with bright yellow centres. Flower stems rapidly elongate as feathery seeds mature.
H and S 15–23cm (6–9in).

☀ ◌ ①

■ PURPLE–BLUE

Erinacea anthyllis,
syn. *E. pungens* (Hedgehog broom)
Slow growing, evergreen sub-shrub with hard, blue-green spines. Pea-like, soft lavender flowers appear in axils of spines in late spring to early summer.
H and S 15–25cm (6–10in).

☀ ◌ Zone 8

Pulsatilla halleri
Tufted perennial, intensely hairy in all parts, that in spring bears nodding, later erect, cup-shaped flowers in shades of purple. Has feathery leaves and seed heads. H 15–38cm (6–15in), S 15–20cm (6–8in).

☀ ◌ ①

Aquilegia alpina
(Alpine columbine)
Short-lived, upright perennial with spurred, clear blue or violet-blue flowers on slender stems in spring and early summer. Has basal rosettes of rounded, finely divided leaves. Needs rich soil. H 45cm (18in), S 15cm (6in).

☀ ◌ ①

Viola cornuta (Horned violet)
Rhizomatous perennial with oval, toothed leaves and flat-faced, rather angular, spurred, pale to deep purplish-blue, occasionally white flowers in spring and much of summer.
H 12–20cm (8in), S to 20cm (8in) or more.

Omphalodes verna
Semi-evergreen, clump-forming perennial that in spring bears long, loose sprays of flat, bright blue flowers with white eyes. Leaves are oval and mid-green.
H and S 20cm (8in) or more.

Omphalodes cappadocica
Spreading perennial with creeping underground stems and many loose sprays of flat, bright blue flowers in spring-summer above tufts of oval, hairy, basal leaves.
H 15–20cm (6–8in),
S 25cm (10in) or more.

IRISES, illus. pp.234–5
Lithodora zahnii
Pulsatilla halleri subsp. *grandis*

Salix helvetica
Deciduous, spreading, much-branched, dwarf shrub that has small, oval, glossy leaves, white-haired beneath. In spring bears short-stalked, silky, grey, then yellow catkins.
H 60cm (24in), S 30cm (12in).

 Zone 6

Betula nana (Arctic birch)
Deciduous, bushy, dwarf shrub with small, toothed leaves that turn bright yellow in autumn. Has tiny, yellowish-brown catkins in spring.
H 30cm (12in), S 45cm (18in).

 Zone 2

Corydalis cheilanthifolia
Evergreen perennial with fleshy roots. Produces spreading rosettes of fern-like, near-prostrate, sometimes bronze-tinted, mid-green leaves. Dense spikes of short-spurred, yellow flowers are borne in late spring and early summer. H 20–30cm (8–12in), S 15–20cm (6–8in).

DAFFODILS, illus. pp.416–18
IRISES, illus. pp.234–5
Paeonia mlokosewitschii, illus. p.237
PRIMULAS, illus. pp.272–3

Corydalis wilsonii
Evergreen perennial with a fleshy rootstock. Forms rosettes of near-prostrate, divided, bluish-green leaves. Loose racemes of spurred, green-tipped, yellow flowers are produced in spring. H and S 10–25cm (4–10in).

Aurinia saxatilis 'Citrina',
syn. *Alyssum saxatile* 'Citrinum'
Evergreen, clump-forming perennial with oval, hairy, grey-green leaves. Bears racemes of many, small, pale lemon-yellow flowers in late spring and early summer.
H 23cm (9in), S 30cm (12in).

Aurinia saxatilis 'Variegata',
syn. *Alyssum saxatile* 'Variegatum'
Evergreen perennial that bears racemes of many small, yellow flowers in spring above a mat of large, oval, soft grey-green leaves with cream margins.
H 23cm (9in), S 30cm (12in).

Pulsatilla alpina subsp. *apiifolia*
Salix arbuscula

Chiastophyllum oppositifolium,
syn. *Cotyledon simplicifolia*
Evergreen, trailing perennial with large, oblong, serrated, succulent leaves. In late spring and early summer bears many tiny, yellow flowers in arching sprays.
H 15–20cm (6–8in), S 15cm (6in).

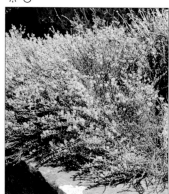

Cytisus × beanii
Deciduous, low-growing shrub with arching sprays of pea-like, golden-yellow flowers that appear in late spring and early summer on previous year's wood. Leaves, divided into 3 leaflets, are small, linear and hairy. H 15–40cm (6–16in), S 30–75cm (12–30in).

Zone 5

☐☐ YELLOW–ORANGE

Hylomecon japonica
Vigorous, spreading perennial with large, cup-shaped, bright yellow flowers that are borne singly on slender stems in spring. Soft, dark green leaves are divided into 4 unequal lobes. H to 30cm (12in), S 20cm (8in).

☀ ◖

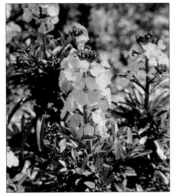

Erysimum 'Bredon',
syn. *Cheiranthus* 'Bredon'
Semi-evergreen, rounded, woody perennial clothed in oval, dark green leaves. In late spring bears dense spikes of flat, bright mustard-yellow flowers. H 30–45cm (12–18in), S 45cm (18in).

☀ ◊

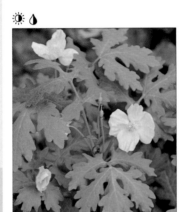

Stylophorum diphyllum
Perennial with basal rosettes of large, lobed, hairy leaves. Bears open cup-shaped, golden-yellow flowers in spring on upright, branched stems. Prefers rich, woodland conditions. H and S to 30cm (12in) or more.

☀ ◖

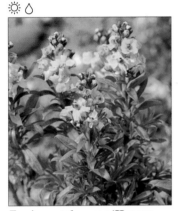

Erysimum × kewense 'Harpur Crewe'
Evergreen, shrubby perennial with stiff stems and narrow leaves. Fragrant, double, deep yellow flowers open in succession from late spring to mid-summer. Grows best in poor soil and a sheltered site. H and S 30cm (12in).

☀ ◊

Aurinia saxatilis,
syn. *Alyssum saxatile* (Gold dust)
Evergreen perennial forming low clumps of oval, hairy, grey-green leaves. Has substantial spikes of small, chrome-yellow flowers in spring. H 23cm (9in), S 30cm (12in).

☀ ◊

Berberis × stenophylla 'Corallina Compacta'
Evergreen, neat, dwarf shrub with spiny stems clothed in small, narrowly oval leaves. In late spring bears many tiny, bright orange flowers. Is slow-growing and difficult to propagate. H and S to 25cm (10in).

☀ ◊ ⓘ Zone 5

☐ WHITE

Parnassia palustris
(Grass of Parnassus)
Perennial with low, basal tufts of heart-shaped, pale to mid-green leaves. Bears saucer-shaped, white flowers, with dark green or purplish-green veins, on erect stems in late spring and early summer. H 20cm (8in), S 6cm (2½in) or more.

☀ ◆

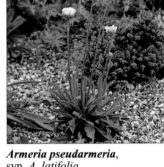

Armeria pseudarmeria,
syn. *A. latifolia*
Evergreen, clump-forming perennial with large, spherical heads of white flowers occasionally suffused pink; these are borne in summer on stiff stems above long, narrow, glaucous leaves. H and S 30cm (12in).

☀ ◊

Celmisia walkeri,
syn. *C. webbiana*
Evergreen, loose, spreading perennial with long, oval or lance-shaped leaves, glossy, green above and hairy, white beneath. Has large, daisy-like, white flower heads in summer. H 23cm (9in), S to 2m (6ft).

☀ ◖ pH

ROCK PLANTS

Helianthemum apenninum
Evergreen, spreading, much-branched shrub that bears saucer-shaped, pure white flowers in mid-summer. Stems and small, linear leaves are covered in white down. H and S 45cm (18in).

☼ ◊ Zone 7

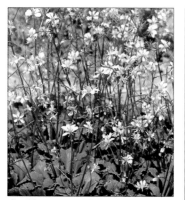

Saxifraga cuneifolia
Evergreen, carpeting perennial with neat rosettes of rounded leaves. In late spring and early summer bears panicles of tiny, white flowers, frequently with yellow, pink or red spots, on slender stems. H 15–20cm (6–8in), S 30cm (12in) or more.

◐ ◖

Chamaecytisus purpureus f. **albus**, syn. **Cytisus purpureus** f. **albus**
Deciduous, low-growing shrub with semi-erect stems clothed in leaves, divided into 3 leaflets. A profusion of pea-like, white flowers appear in early summer on previous year's wood. H 45cm (18in), S 60cm (24in).

☼ ◊ Zone 5

Helianthemum 'Wisley White'
Evergreen, spreading shrub, with oblong, grey-green leaves, bearing saucer-shaped, white flowers for a long period in summer.
H 23cm (9in), S 30cm (12in) or more.

☼ ◊ Zone 7

Galax urceolata, syn. *G. aphylla*
Evergreen, clump-forming perennial. Large, round, leathery, mid-green leaves on slender stems turn bronze in autumn-winter. Has dense spikes of small, white flowers in late spring and early summer.
H 15–20cm (6–8in), S to 30cm (12in).

☼ ◖ pH

Epilobium glabellum of gardens
Semi-evergreen, clump-forming perennial. Bears outward-facing, cup-shaped, white flowers singly on slender stems in summer above oval, mid-green leaves. Makes useful ground cover.
H to 20cm (8in), S 15cm (6in).

◐ ◊

Hebe pinguifolia 'Pagei'
Evergreen, semi-prostrate shrub with small, oblong, slightly cupped, intensely glaucous leaves. Bears short spikes of small, pure white flowers in late spring or early summer. Is excellent for ground or rock cover. H 15–30cm (6–12in), S 60cm–1m (24–36in).

☼ ◊ Zone 6b

Corydalis ochroleuca, syn. *Pseudofumaria ochroleuca*
Evergreen, clump-forming perennial with fleshy, fibrous roots and much divided, basal, grey-green leaves. Bears slender, yellow-tipped, creamy-white flowers in late spring and summer.
H and S 20–30cm (8–12in).

☼ ◊

Hebe vernicosa
Evergreen, bushy, compact shrub with small, oval, glossy, dark green leaves densely packed on stems. In early and mid-summer, spikes of small, 4-lobed, white flowers are freely produced.
H 60cm (2ft), S 1.2m (4ft).

☼ ◊ Zone 9?

Deinanthe bifida
Eomecon chionantha
Fabiana imbricata 'Prostrata'
x *Halimiocistus wintonensis*

Hebe buchananii
HOSTAS, illus. pp.288–9
Iberis sempervirens 'Schneeflocke'
IRISES, illus. pp.234–5

Leontopodium alpinum, illus. p.346
Luetkea pectinata
Papaver burseri
Phyllodoce nipponica

PRIMULAS, illus. pp.272–3
Rhodanthemum hosmariense, illus. p.346
Stephanandra incisa 'Crispa'
Tiarella cordifolia, illus. p.347

ROCK PLANTS

◻◻ WHITE–PINK   ◻ PINK

ROCK PLANTS

Saxifraga cotyledon
Evergreen perennial with large, pale green rosettes of leaves, dying after flowering. In late spring and early summer produces arching, conical panicles of cup-shaped, white flowers sometimes strongly marked red internally. H and S to 30cm (12in).

Onosma alborosea
Semi-evergreen, clump-forming perennial covered in fine hairs, which may irritate skin. Clusters of long, pendent, tubular flowers, borne for a long period in summer, open white and then turn pink.
H 15–30cm (6–12in), S 20cm (8in).

Aethionema grandiflorum, syn.
A. pulchellum (Persian stone cress)
Short-lived, evergreen or semi-evergreen, lax shrub. Bears tiny, pale to deep rose-pink flowers in loose sprays in spring-summer. Blue-green leaves are narrow and lance-shaped.
H 30cm (12in), S 23cm (9in).

***Saxifraga* 'Southside Seedling'**
Evergreen, mat-forming perennial, with large, pale green rosettes of leaves, dying after flowering. In late spring and early summer bears arching panicles of open cup-shaped, white flowers, strongly red-banded within.
H and S to 30cm (12in).

Rhodothamnus chamaecistus
Evergreen, low-growing, dwarf shrub with narrow, oval leaves, edged with bristles. In late spring and early summer bears cup-shaped, rose- to lilac-pink flowers, with dark stamens, in leaf axils.
H 15–20cm (6–8in), S to 25cm (10in).

☼ ◊ pH Zone 8

Anthyllis montana
Rounded, bushy or somewhat spreading perennial with loose branches and finely cut foliage. Heads of clover-like, pale pink flowers with red markings are borne in late spring and early summer.
H and S 30cm (12in).

Phuopsis stylosa,
syn. *Crucianella stylosa*
Low-growing perennial with whorls of pungent, pale green leaves and rounded heads of small, tubular, pink flowers in summer. Is good grown over a bank or large rock.
H 30cm (12in), S 30cm (12in) or more.

***Lewisia* 'George Henley'**
Evergreen, clump-forming perennial with rosettes of narrow, fleshy, dark green leaves. Bears dense sprays of open cup-shaped, deep pink flowers, with magenta veins, from late spring to late summer.
H 15cm (6in) or more, S 10cm (4in).

Astilbe 'Perkeo',
syn. *A.* x *crispa* 'Perkeo'
Erect, compact perennial bearing small plumes of tiny, salmon-pink flowers from mid- to late summer on fine stems. Has stiff, deeply cut, crinkled leaves. H 15–20cm (6–8in), S 10cm (4in).

☼ ◗

Crassula sarcocaulis
Evergreen or semi-evergreen, bushy sub-shrub with tiny, oval, succulent leaves. Bears terminal clusters of tiny, red buds opening to pale pink flowers in summer.
H and S 30cm (12in). Min. 5°C (41°F).

☼ ◊

Origanum 'Kent Beauty'
Prostrate perennial with trailing stems clothed in aromatic, rounded-oval leaves. In summer bears short spikes of tubular, pale pink flowers with darker bracts. Is suitable for a wall or ledge. H 15–20cm (6–8in), S 30cm (12in).

☼ ◊

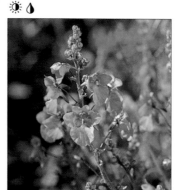

Diascia cordata of gardens
Prostrate perennial with stems clothed in heart-shaped, pale green leaves. Bears terminal clusters of spurred, flat-faced, bright pink flowers in summer and early autumn.
H 15–20cm (6–8in), S 20cm (8in).

☼ ◊

Ononis fruticosa
(Shrubby restharrow)
Deciduous shrub that in summer bears pendent clusters of large, pea-like, purplish-pink blooms with darker streaks. Leaves are divided into 3 serrated leaflets, which are hairy when young. H and S 30–60cm (12–24in).

☼ ◊ Zone 8

Helianthemum 'Rhodanthe Carneum', syn. *H.* 'Wisley Pink'
Evergreen, lax shrub with saucer-shaped, soft, pale pink flowers with orange centres borne for a long period in summer. Has oblong, grey-green leaves. H and S 30cm (12in) or more.

☼ ◊ Zone 7

Oxalis tetraphylla, syn. *O. deppei*
Tuft-forming, tuberous perennial with brown-marked, basal leaves, usually divided into 4 leaflets. Produces loose sprays of widely funnel-shaped, deep pink flowers in late spring and summer. Needs a sheltered site. H 15–30cm (6–10in), S 10–15cm (4–6in).

☼ ◊

Diascia rigescens
Trailing perennial with semi-erect stems covered in heart-shaped, mid-green leaves. Spurred, flat-faced, salmon-pink flowers are borne along stem length in summer and early autumn.
H 23cm (9in), S to 30cm (12in).

☼ ◊

Geranium orientalitibeticum
Perennial spreading by tuberous, underground runners. Has cup-shaped, pink flowers, with white centres, in summer. Leaves are deeply cut and marbled in shades of green. May be invasive. H in flower 15–25cm (6–10in), S indefinite.

☼ ◊

Incarvillea mairei 'Frank Ludlow'
Ononis rotundifolia
Ourisia 'Loch Ewe'
PEONIES, illus. pp.236–7

Potentilla nitida
PRIMULAS, illus. pp.272–3
Teucrium polium, illus. p.379

ROCK PLANTS

353

ROCK PLANTS large SUMMER INTEREST

☐ PINK

Cortusa matthioli
Clump-forming perennial with a basal rosette of rounded, dull green leaves and, in late spring and early summer, one-sided racemes of small, pendent, bell-shaped, reddish- or pinkish-purple flowers.
H 15–20cm (6–10in), S 10cm (4in).

Geranium sanguineum
(Bloody cranesbill)
Hummock-forming, spreading perennial with many cup-shaped, deep magenta-pink flowers borne in summer above round, deeply divided, dark green leaves. Makes good ground cover. H to 25cm (10in), S 30cm (12in) or more.

☐ RED

Penstemon newberryi f. **humilior**
Evergreen, mat-forming shrub with arching branches clothed in small, leathery, dark green leaves. Bears short sprays of tubular, lipped, cherry-red to deep pink flowers in early summer.
H 15–20cm (6–8in), S 30cm (12in).

Helianthemum 'Ben More'
Evergreen, spreading, twiggy shrub that bears a succession of saucer-shaped, reddish-orange flowers in loose, terminal clusters in late spring and summer. Has small, glossy, dark green leaves.
H 23–30cm (9–12in), S 30cm (12in).

Zone 7

Origanum laevigatum
Deciduous, mat-forming sub-shrub with small, aromatic, dark green leaves, branching, red stems and a profusion of tiny, tubular, cerise-pink flowers, surrounded by red-purple bracts, in summer. H 23–30cm (9–12in), S 20cm (8in) or more.

Zone 8

Lewisia Cotyledon Hybrids
Evergreen, clump-forming perennials with rosettes of large, thick, toothed leaves. In early summer bear clusters of flowers, in various shades of pink to purple, on erect stems. Is good for a rock crevice or an alpine house.
H to 30cm (12in), S 15cm (6in) or more.

Helianthemum 'Raspberry Ripple'
Evergreen, spreading shrub with saucer-shaped, red-centred, white flowers that are borne in mid-summer. Has small, linear, grey-green leaves.
H 15–23cm (6–9in),
S 23–30cm (9–12in).

Zone 7

Penstemon pinifolius
Evergreen, bushy shrub with branched stems clothed in fine, dark green leaves. In summer, very narrow, tubular, orange-red flowers are borne in loose, terminal spikes.
H 10–20cm (4–8in), S 15cm (6in).

Zone 5

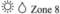

Dianthus carthusianorum
Evergreen perennial carrying rounded, upward-facing, cherry-red or deep pink flowers on slender stems in summer above small tufts of grass-like leaves.
H 20cm (8in), S 6cm (2½in).

Helianthemum 'Fire Dragon'
Evergreen, spreading shrub with saucer-shaped, orange-scarlet flowers in late spring and summer. Leaves are linear and grey-green.
H 23–30cm (9–12in), S 45cm (18in).

Zone 7

Anthyllis montana 'Rubra'
Astilbe chinensis var. pumila
Dianthus armeria
Micromeria juliana

Origanum rotundifolium
Phyllodoce caerulea, illus. p.348
Phyllodoce x intermedia 'Drummondii', illus. p.347

Armeria 'Bees Ruby'
Helianthemum 'Ben Hope'
PEONIES, illus. pp.236–7
Phyllodoce x intermedia 'Fred Stoker'

PRIMULAS, illus. pp.272–3
Zauschneria californica
Zauschneria californica subsp. cana

***Zauschneria californica* subsp.
cana 'Dublin'**, syn. *Z.c.* 'Glasnevin'
Clump-forming, woody-based
perennial with lance-shaped, grey-
green leaves. From late summer to
early autumn bears terminal clusters
of tubular, deep orange-scarlet flowers.
H 30cm (12in), S 45cm (18in).

☼ ◊

Punica granatum* var. *nana
(Dwarf pomegranate)
Slow-growing, deciduous, rounded
shrub that, in summer, bears funnel-
shaped, red flowers with somewhat
crumpled petals, followed by small,
rounded, orange-red fruits.
H and S 30–90cm (12–36in).

☼ ◊ Zone 9

Delphinium nudicaule
Short-lived, upright perennial with
erect stems bearing deeply divided,
basal leaves and, in summer, spikes of
hooded, red or occasionally yellow
flowers, with contrasting stamens.
H 20cm (8in), S 5–10cm (2–4in).

☼ ◊ ①

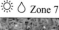

Calceolaria arachnoidea
Evergreen, clump-forming perennial
with a basal rosette of wrinkled leaves,
covered in white down. Upright stems
carry spikes of many pouch-shaped,
dull purple flowers in summer.
Is best treated as a biennial.
H 25cm (10in), S 12cm (5in).

☼ ◖

Erodium cheilanthifolium
Compact, mound-forming perennial
with pink flowers, veined and marked
with purple-red, borne on stiff stems in
late spring and summer. Greyish-green
leaves are crinkled and deeply cut.
H 15–20cm (6–8in),
S 20cm (8in) or more.

☼ ◊

Scabiosa lucida
Clump-forming perennial with tufts of
oval leaves and rounded heads of pale
lilac to deep mauve flowers, borne on
erect stems in summer.
H 20cm (8in), S 15cm (6in).

☼ ◊

Penstemon serrulatus,
syn. *P. diffusus*
Semi-evergreen sub-shrub, deciduous
in severe climates, that has small,
elliptic, dark green leaves and tubular,
blue to purple flowers borne in loose
spikes in summer. Soil should not be
too dry. H 60cm (24in), S 30cm (12in).

☼ ◊ Zone 7

Erigeron alpinus
(Alpine fleabane)
Clump-forming perennial of variable
size that bears daisy-like, lilac-pink
flower heads on erect stems in summer.
Leaves are long, oval and hairy. Suits
a sunny border, bank or large rock
garden. H 25cm (10in), S 20cm (8in).

☼ ◊

Semiaquilegia ecalcarata
Short-lived, upright perennial with
narrow, lobed leaves. In summer each
slender stem bears several pendent,
open bell-shaped, dusky-pink to purple
flowers, with no spurs.
H 20cm (8in), S 6cm (2½in).

☼ ◊

Chamaecytisus purpureus
Geranium procurrens
IRISES, illus. pp.234–5
Oxalis hirta

PEONIES, illus. pp.236–7
Scabiosa graminifolia

ROCK PLANTS

355

PURPLE–BLUE

Parahebe catarractae
Evergreen sub-shrub with oval, toothed, mid-green leaves and, in summer, loose sprays of small, open funnel-shaped, white flowers, heavily zoned and veined pinkish-purple. H and S 30cm (12in). Min. 2°C (35°F).

Wulfenia amherstiana
Evergreen perennial with rosettes of narrowly spoon-shaped, toothed leaves. Erect stems bear loose clusters of small, tubular, purple or pinkish-purple flowers in summer. H 15–30cm (6–12in), S to 30cm (12in).

Phlox divaricata subsp. **laphamii** 'Chatahoochee'
Short-lived, clump-forming perennial that has saucer-shaped, red-eyed, bright lavender flowers throughout summer-autumn. Narrow, pointed leaves are dark reddish-purple when young. H 15–20cm (6–8in), S 30cm (12in).

Campanula barbata
(Bearded bellflower)
Evergreen perennial with a basal rosette of oval, hairy, grey-green leaves. In summer bears one-sided racemes of bell-shaped, white to lavender-blue flowers. Is short lived but sets seed freely. H 20cm (8in), S 12cm (5in).

Phlox divaricata subsp. **laphamii**
Semi-evergreen, creeping perennial with oval leaves and upright stems bearing loose clusters of saucer-shaped, pale to deep violet-blue flowers in summer. H 30cm (12in) or more, S 20cm (8in).

Convolvulus sabatius,
syn. *C. mauritanicus*
Trailing perennial with slender stems clothed in small, oval leaves and open trumpet-shaped, vibrant blue-purple flowers in summer and early autumn. Shelter in a rock crevice in a cold site. H 15–20cm (6–8in), S 30cm (12in).

Sisyrinchium graminoides, syn. *S. angustifolium*, *S. bermudiana*
Semi-evergreen, erect perennial with tufts of grass-like leaves. Small, iris-like, pale to dark purplish-blue flowers with yellow bases are borne in terminal clusters in late spring and early summer. H to 30cm (12in), S 8cm (3in).

Lithodora oleifolia,
syn. *Lithospermum oleifolium*
Evergreen shrub with oval, pointed, silky, mid-green leaves. Curving stems carry loose sprays of several small, funnel-shaped, light blue flowers in early summer. H 15–20cm (6–8in), S to 1m (3ft).
Zone 8

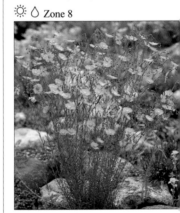

Linum perenne
Upright perennial with slender stems, clothed in grass-like leaves, that bear terminal clusters of open funnel-shaped, clear blue flowers in succession throughout summer. H 30cm (12in), S to 15cm (6in).

Aster alpinus, illus. p.381
Carmichaelia enysii
CARNATIONS and PINKS, illus. pp.280–1
Deinanthe caerulea

Dracocephalum ruyschiana
Erinacea anthyllis, illus. p.348
Erysimum linifolium
Horminum pyrenaicum

IRISES, illus. pp.234–5
Moltkia petraea
Penstemon hirsutus
Penstemon procerus

Phlox divaricata
Satureja montana
Viola cornuta, illus. p.349
Wulfenia carinthiaca

ROCK PLANTS

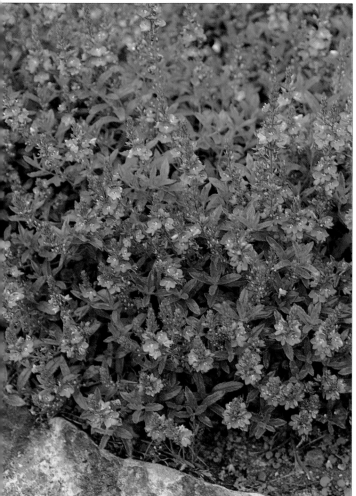

Veronica prostrata, syn.
V. rupestris (Prostrate speedwell)
Dense, mat-forming perennial that has
upright spikes of small, saucer-shaped,
brilliant blue flowers in early summer.
Foliage is narrow, oval and toothed.
H to 30cm (12in), S indefinite.

☼ ◊

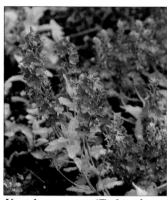

Moltkia suffruticosa
Deciduous, upright sub-shrub. In
summer bears clusters of funnel-
shaped, bright blue flowers, pink in
bud, on hairy stems. Leaves are long,
pointed and hairy.
H 15–40cm (6–16in), S 30cm (12in).

☼ ◊ Zone 8

Veronica prostrata 'Kapitan'
Dense, mat-forming perennial bearing
erect spikes of small, saucer-shaped,
bright deep blue flowers in early
summer. Foliage is narrow, oval and
toothed. H to 30cm (12in), S indefinite.

☼ ◊

Veronica prostrata 'Trehane'
Dense, mat-forming perennial bearing
upright spikes of small, saucer-shaped,
deep violet-blue flowers in early
summer above narrow, toothed, yellow
or yellowish-green leaves.
H in flower 15–20cm (6–8in),
S indefinite.

☼ ◊

Mertensia echioides
Clump-forming perennial with basal
rosettes of long, oval, hairy,
blue-green leaves. Slender stems
carry many open funnel-shaped, dark
blue flowers in summer.
H 15–23cm (6–9in), S 15cm (6in).

☼ ◊

Phyteuma scheuchzeri
Tufted perennial with narrow, dark
green leaves and terminal heads of
spiky, blue flowers that are borne in
summer. Seeds freely; dislikes winter
wet. H 15–20cm (6–8in), S 10cm (4in).

☼ ◊

Symphyandra wanneri
Clump-forming perennial with
branching stems and hairy, oval leaves.
In summer bears pendent, bell-shaped,
blue to violet-blue flowers in loose,
terminal spikes.
H 15–23cm (6–9in), S 25cm (10in).

☼ ◊

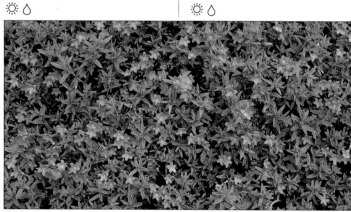

Lithodora diffusa 'Heavenly Blue'
Evergreen, prostrate shrub with trailing
stems bearing pointed, oblong, hairy
leaves and, in summer, a profusion of
open funnel-shaped, deep blue flowers
in leaf axils. Trim stems hard after
flowering. H 15–30cm (6–12in),
S to 45cm (18in).

☼ ◊ pH Zone 7

◫ BLUE–YELLOW   ☐ YELLOW

Veronica austriaca subsp.
teucrium, syn. *V. teucrium*
Spreading perennial with narrow
spikes of small, flat, outward-facing,
bright blue flowers in summer. Leaves
are small, divided, hairy and greyish-
green. H and S 25–60cm (10–24in).

☼ ◊

Verbascum 'Letitia'
Evergreen, stiff-branched shrub with
toothed, grey leaves. Bears outward-
facing, 5-lobed, bright yellow
flowers with reddish-orange centres
continuously from late spring to mid-
autumn. Hates winter wet; is good in an
alpine house. H and S to 25cm (10in).

☼ ◊ Zone 6

**Helianthemum 'Wisley
Primrose'**
Fast-growing, evergreen, compact
shrub with saucer-shaped, soft pale
yellow flowers in summer. Has
oblong, grey-green leaves.
H 23cm (9in), S 30cm (12in) or more.

☼ ◊ Zone 7

Othonna cheirifolia,
syn. *Othonnopsis cheirifolia*
Evergreen shrub with narrow,
somewhat fleshy, grey leaves. In early
summer bears daisy-like, yellow flower
heads singly on upright stems. Needs
a warm, sheltered site. H 20–30cm
(8–12in), S 30cm (12in) or more.

☼ ◊ Zone 9

Erodium chrysanthum
Mound-forming perennial, grown for
its dense, silvery stems and finely cut,
fern-like leaves. Has small sprays of
cup-shaped, sulphur- or creamy-yellow
flowers in late spring and summer.
H and S 23cm (9in).

☼ ◊

Euryops acraeus,
syn. *E. evansii* of gardens
Evergreen, dome-shaped shrub
with stems clothed in toothed, silvery-
blue leaves. Bears solitary daisy-like,
bright yellow flower heads in late
spring and early summer.
H and S 30cm (12in).

☼ ◊ Zone 9?

Hypericum olympicum
f. **uniflorum** 'Citrinum'
Deciduous, dense, rounded sub-shrub
with tufts of upright stems, clothed in
small, oval, grey-green leaves. Bears
terminal clusters of lemon-yellow
flowers throughout summer.
H and S 15–30cm (6–12in).

☼ ◊ Zone 5b

Linum arboreum
Evergreen, compact shrub with blue-
green leaves. In summer has a
succession of funnel-shaped, bright
yellow flowers opening in sunny
weather and borne in terminal clusters.
H to 30cm (12in), S 30cm (12in).

☼ ◊ Zone 7

Eriogonum umbellatum
Evergreen, prostrate to upright
perennial with mats of green leaves,
white and woolly beneath. In summer
carries heads of tiny, yellow flowers
that later turn copper. Dwarf forms
are available. H 8–30cm (3–12in),
S 15–30cm (6–12in).

☼ ◊

ROCK PLANTS

Corydalis lutea,
syn. _Pseudofumaria lutea_
Evergreen, clump-forming perennial
with fleshy, fibrous roots, semi-erect,
basal, grey-green leaves. Bears
racemes of slender, yellow flowers,
with short spurs, in late spring and
summer. H and S 20–30cm (8–12in).

☼ ◊

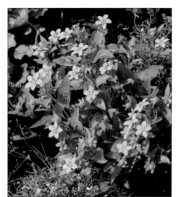

Chrysogonum virginianum
Mat-forming perennial with daisy-like,
yellow flower heads borne on short
stems in summer-autumn and oval,
toothed, mid-green leaves. Although
plant spreads by underground runners,
it is not invasive. H 15–20cm (6–8in),
S 10–15cm (4–6in) or more.

☼ ◐

Ononis natrix
(Large yellow restharrow)
Deciduous, compact, erect shrub with
pea-like, red-streaked, yellow flowers
in pendent clusters in summer. Hairy
leaves are divided into 3 leaflets.
H and S 30cm (12in) or more.

☼ ◊ Zone 8

Verbascum dumulosum
Evergreen, mat-forming, shrubby
perennial with hairy, grey or grey-green
leaves. In late spring and early summer
bears a succession of 5-lobed, bright
yellow flowers in short racemes.
Dislikes winter wet. H 15cm (6in) or
more, S 23–30cm (9–12in) or more.

☼ ◊

Sedum rupestre, syn. _S. reflexum_
(Reflexed stonecrop)
Evergreen perennial with loose mats
of rooting stems bearing narrow, fleshy
leaves. Carries flat, terminal heads of
tiny, bright yellow flowers in summer.
Makes good ground cover.
H 15–20cm (6–8in), S indefinite.

☼ ◊ ①

Ranunculus gramineus
Erect, slender perennial with grass-like,
blue-green leaves. Bears several cup-
shaped, bright yellow flowers in late
spring and early summer. Prefers rich
soil. Seedlings will vary in height and
flower size. H 40–50cm (16–20in),
S 8–10cm (3–4in).

☼ ◊ ①

Genista lydia
Deciduous, domed shrub with slender,
arching branches and blue-green leaves.
Massed terminal clusters of pea-like,
bright yellow flowers appear in late
spring and early summer. Will trail
over a large rock or wall. H 45–60cm
(18–24in), S 60cm (24in) or more.

☼ ◊ Zone 5

Crepis aurea
Clump-forming perennial with a basal
cluster of oblong, light green leaves.
In summer produces dandelion-like,
orange flower heads, singly, on stems
covered with black and white hairs.
H 10–30cm (4–12in), S 15cm (6in).

☼ ◊

ROCK PLANTS

WHITE–BLUE

  WHITE–GREY

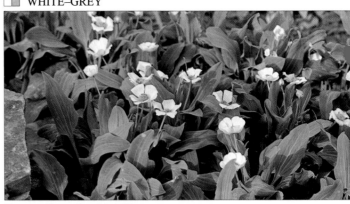

Gaultheria cuneata
Evergreen, compact shrub with stiff
stems clothed in leathery, oval leaves.
In summer bears nodding, urn-shaped,
white flowers, in leaf axils, followed
by white berries in autumn.
H and S 30cm (12in).

☼ ◊ pH ① Zone 7

Ceratostigma plumbaginoides
Bushy perennial that bears small,
terminal clusters of single, brilliant
blue flowers on reddish, branched
stems in late summer and autumn.
Oval leaves turn rich red in autumn.
H 45cm (18in), S 20cm (8in).

☼ ◊

Ranunculus calandrinioides
Clump-forming perennial that loses its
long, oval, blue-green leaves in
summer; in a reasonable winter will
bear a succession of cup-shaped, pink-
flushed, white flowers for many
weeks. Needs very sharp drainage.
H and S to 20cm (8in).

☼ ◊ ①

Sorbus reducta
Deciduous shrub forming a low thicket
of upright branches. Small, grey-green
leaves, divided into leaflets, turn
bronze-red in late autumn. In early
summer bears loose clusters of flat,
white flowers, followed by pink berries.
H and S to 30cm (12in) or more.

☼ ◊ ① Zone 4b

Celmisia semicordata,
syn. *C. coriacea* of gardens
Evergreen perennial with sword-like,
silver leaves in large clumps and, in
summer, daisy-like, white flower
heads borne singly on hairy stems.
H and S 30cm (12in).

☼ ◊ pH

Gentiana septemfida
Evergreen perennial with many upright,
then arching stems clothed with oval
leaves. Bears heads of trumpet-shaped,
mid-blue flowers in summer-autumn.
Likes humus-rich soil but tolerates
reasonably drained, heavy clay.
H 15–20cm (6–8in), S 30cm (12in).

☼ ◊

Cyathodes colensoi
Evergreen, low-growing shrub with
stiff stems clothed in tiny, grey-green
leaves. Bears clusters of small, tubular,
white flowers in spring at the ends
of new growth. Red or white berries
in late summer are rare in cultivation.
H and S 30cm (12in).

 ◐ ◗ Zone 9

Tanacetum argenteum,
syn. *Achillea argentea*
Mat-forming perennial, usually
evergreen, grown for its finely cut,
bright silver leaves. Has a profusion of
small, daisy-like, white flower heads in
summer. H in flower 15–23cm (6–9in),
S 20cm (8in).

☼ ◊ ①

OTHER RECOMMENDED PLANTS:
Chrysogonum virginianum, illus. p.359
Convolvulus sabatius, illus. p.356
Diascia rigescens, illus. p.353

Gaultheria miqueliana
Persicaria affinis 'Darjeeling Red'
Rhodanthemum hosmariense, illus. p.346

OTHER RECOMMENDED PLANTS:
Eriogonum crocatum
Eriogonum ovalifolium
Euonymus fortunei 'Emerald Gaiety'

Persicaria affinis

ROCK PLANTS

■■ GREY–GREEN

☐ WHITE

Tanacetum densum subsp. **amani**, syn. *Chrysanthemum densum*
Clump-forming perennial retaining fern-like, hairy, grey leaves in winter in mild climates. Bears daisy-like, yellow flower heads with woolly bracts in summer. Dislikes winter wet. H and S 20cm (8in).

☼ ◊ ⚠

Hebe cupressoides 'Boughton Dome'
Slow-growing, evergreen, dome-shaped shrub with scale-like, stem-clasping, dark grey-green leaves. Has terminal clusters of small, 4-lobed, blue-tinged, white flowers in summer. H 30cm (12in), S to 60cm (24in).

☼ ◊ Zone 9

Cerastium tomentosum
(Snow-in-summer)
Very vigorous, ground-cover perennial, only suitable for a hot, dry bank, with prostrate stems covered by tiny, grey leaves. In late spring and summer bears star-shaped, white flowers above foliage. H 8cm (3in), S indefinite.

☼ ◊

Ozothamnus coralloides, syn. *Helichrysum coralloides*
Evergreen, upright shrub with grey stems clothed in neat, dark green leaves, marked silver. Occasionally bears fluffy, yellow flower heads. Suits a cold frame or an alpine house. Hates winter wet. H 15–23cm (6–9in), S 15cm (6in).

☼ ◊ Zone 9

Ozothamnus selago, syn. *Helichrysum selago*
Evergreen, upright shrub with stiff stems covered in scale-like leaves. Intermittently bears fluffy, creamy-white flower heads. Makes a good foil for spring bulbs. H and S 15–23cm (6–9in).

☼ ◊ Zone 9?

Salix x boydii
Very slow-growing, deciduous, upright shrub forming a gnarled, branched bush. Has oval, rough-textured leaves; catkins are rarely produced. Will tolerate light shade. H to 15–23cm (6–9in), S to 30cm (12in).

☼ ◊ Zone 7

Ballota pseudodictamnus
Evergreen, mound-forming sub-shrub with rounded, grey-green leaves and stems covered with woolly, white hairs. In summer bears whorls of small, pink flowers with conspicuous, enlarged, pale green calyces. H 60cm (2ft), S 90cm (3ft).

☼ ◊ Zone 8

Androsace pyrenaica
Evergreen perennial with small rosettes of tiny, hairy leaves, tightly packed to form hard cushions. Minute, stemless, single, white flowers appear in spring. H 4cm (1½in), S to 10cm (4in).

☼ ◊

Arenaria tetraquetra
Evergreen perennial that forms a hard, grey-green cushion of small leaves. Stemless, star-shaped, white flowers appear in late spring. Is well-suited for a trough or an alpine house. H 2.5cm (1in), S 15cm (6in) or more.

☼ ◊

Arctostaphylos 'Emerald Carpet', illus. p.156
Buxus microphylla 'Green Pillow', illus. p.176
Euonymus fortunei 'Golden Prince'

Myrsine africana
Pachysandra axillaris
Paxistima canbyi
Rubus tricolor

OTHER RECOMMENDED PLANTS:
Androsace chamaejasme
Androsace cylindrica
Androsace hirtella

Arabis procurrens 'Variegata', illus. p.388
Callianthemum coriandrifolium
Cassiope wardii
Claytonia megarhiza

□ WHITE

ROCK PLANTS

Arabis alpina subsp. **caucasica** 'Variegata'
Evergreen, mat-forming perennial with rosettes of oval, cream-splashed, mid-green leaves. Bears bunches of single, sometimes pink-flushed, white flowers from early spring to summer. H and S 15cm (6in).

Cardamine trifolia
Ground-cover perennial with creeping stems clothed in rounded, toothed, 3-parted leaves. In late spring and early summer bears loose heads of open cup-shaped, white flowers on bare stems. H 10–15cm (4–6in), S 30cm (12in).

Saxifraga scardica
Slow-growing, evergreen perennial with hard cushions composed of blue-green rosettes of leaves. In spring bears small clusters of upward-facing, cup-shaped, white flowers. Does best in an alpine house or sheltered scree. H 2.5cm (1in), S 8cm (3in).

Arenaria balearica
Prostrate perennial that is evergreen in all but the most severe winters. Will form a green film over a wet, porous rock face. Minute, white flowers stud mats of foliage in late spring and early summer.
H less than 1cm (½in), S indefinite.

Androsace vandellii,
syn. *A. imbricata*
Evergreen, dense, cushion-forming perennial with narrow, grey leaves and a profusion of stemless, white flowers in spring. Needs careful cultivation with a deep collar of grit under the cushion. H 2.5cm (1in), S to 10cm (4in).

Weldenia candida
Perennial with rosettes of strap-shaped, wavy-margined leaves, growing from tuberous roots. Bears a succession of upright, cup-shaped, pure white flowers in late spring and early summer. H and S 8–15cm (3–6in).

Dicentra cucullaria
(Dutchman's breeches)
Compact perennial with fern-like foliage and arching stems each bearing a few small, yellow-tipped, white flowers, like tiny, inflated trousers, in spring. Lies dormant in summer. H 15cm (6in), S to 30cm (12in).

Maianthemum canadense
Vigorous, ground-cover, rhizomatous perennial with large, upright, oval, wavy-edged, glossy leaves. Slender stems bear sprays of small, white flowers in late spring and early summer followed by red berries.
H 10cm (4in), S indefinite.
☀ ◑ pH

Sanguinaria canadensis
(Bloodroot)
Rhizomatous perennial with fleshy, underground stems that exude red sap when cut. In spring bears white flowers, sometimes pink-flushed or slate-blue on reverses, as blue-grey leaves unfurl.
H 10–15cm (4–6in), S 30cm (12in).
◐ ◑

Ranunculus alpestris
(Alpine buttercup)
Short-lived, evergreen, clump-forming perennial that bears cup-shaped, white flowers on erect stems from late spring to mid-summer. Glossy, dark green leaves are rounded and serrated.
H 2.5–12cm (1–5in), S 10cm (4in).
☀ ◑ ①

Cassiope lycopodioides
Evergreen, prostrate, mat-forming shrub with slender stems densely set with minute, scale-like, dark green leaves. In spring, short, reddish stems carry tiny, bell-shaped, white flowers, in red calyces, singly in leaf axils.
H 8cm (3in), S 30cm (12in).
◐ ◑ pH Zone 3

Saxifraga burseriana
Slow-growing, evergreen perennial with hard cushions of spiky, grey-green leaves. In spring bears open cup-shaped, white flowers on short stems.
H 2.5–5cm (1–2in), S to 10cm (4in).
◐ ◑

Pulsatilla vernalis
Tufted perennial with rosettes of feathery leaves. Densely hairy, brown flower buds appear in late winter and open in early spring to somewhat nodding, open cup-shaped, pearl-white flowers. Buds dislike winter wet.
H 5–10cm (2–4in), S 10cm (4in).
☀ ◑ ①

Androsace villosa
Evergreen, mat-forming perennial with very hairy rosettes of tiny leaves. Bears umbels of small, white flowers, with yellow centres that turn red, in spring. H 2.5cm (1in), S 20cm (8in).
☀ ◑

Salix apoda
Slow-growing, deciduous, prostrate shrub. In early spring, male forms bear fat, silky, silver catkins with orange to pale yellow stamens and bracts. Oval, leathery leaves are hairy when young, becoming dark green later.
H to 15cm (6in), S 30–60cm (12–24in).
☀ ◑ Zone 7

Ranunculus ficaria 'Albus'
Mat-forming perennial bearing in early spring cup-shaped, single, creamy-white flowers with glossy petals. Leaves are heart-shaped and dark green. Can spread rapidly; is good for a wild garden.
H 5cm (2in), S 20cm (8in).
☀ ◑ ①

Saxifraga burseriana 'Crenata'
Saxifraga burseriana 'Gloria'
Silene alpestris, illus. p.373
Tanakaea radicans

Thlaspi alpinum

WHITE–PINK

Cassiope mertensiana
Evergreen, dwarf shrub with scale-like, dark green leaves tightly pressed to stems. In early spring carries bell-shaped, creamy-white flowers, with green or red calyces, in leaf axils.
H 15cm (6in), S 20cm (8in).

☀ ◊ pH Zone 2

Scoliopus bigelowii, syn.
S. bigelovii
Compact perennial with basal, veined leaves, sometimes marked brown. In early spring bears flowers with purple inner petals and greenish-white outer petals with deep purple lines.
H 8–10cm (3–4in), S 10–15cm (4–6in).

☀ ◊

Gypsophila cerastioides
Prostrate perennial with a profusion of small, saucer-shaped, purple-veined, white flowers borne in late spring and early summer above mats of rounded, velvety, mid-green foliage.
H 2cm (¾in), S to 10cm (4in) or more.

☀ ◊

Paraquilegia anemonoides, syn.
P. grandiflora
Tufted perennial with fern-like, blue-green leaves. In spring, pale lavender-blue buds open to pendent, cup-shaped, almost white flowers borne singly on arching stems. May be difficult to establish. H and S 10–15cm (4–6in).

☀ ◊

Corydalis popovii
Tuberous perennial with leaves divided into 3–6 bluish-green leaflets. In spring bears loose racemes of deep red-purple and white flowers, each with a long spur. Keep dry when dormant.
H and S 10–15cm (4–6in).

☀ ◊

Leptinella atrata subsp. **luteola**
Evergreen, mat-forming perennial that in late spring and early summer bears blackish-red flower heads with creamy-yellow stamens. Leaves are small, finely cut and dark green. Needs adequate moisture; best in an alpine house.
H 2.5cm (1in), S to 25cm (10in).

☀ ◊

Anemonella thalictroides
Perennial with delicate, fern-like leaves growing from a cluster of small tubers. From spring to early summer bears small, cup-shaped, white or pink flowers, singly on finely branched stems. Needs humus-rich soil.
H 10cm (4in), S 4cm (1½in) or more.

☀ ◊

Lewisia tweedyi
Evergreen, rosetted perennial with large, fleshy leaves and stout, branched stems that bear open cup-shaped, many-petalled, white to pink flowers in spring. Best grown in an alpine house.
H 15cm (6in), S 12–15cm (5–6in).

☀ ◊ pH

Shortia galacifolia (Oconee bells)
Evergreen, clump-forming, dwarf perennial with round, toothed, leathery, glossy leaves. In late spring bears cup- to trumpet-shaped, often pink-flushed, white flowers with deeply serrated petals.
H to 15cm (6in), S 15–23cm (6–9in).

☀ ◊ pH

Daphne jasminea
Evergreen, compact shrub. Bears small, white flowers, pink-flushed externally, in late spring and early summer and again in autumn. Brittle stems are clothed in grey-green leaves. Suits an alpine house or a dry wall.
H 8–10cm (3–4in), S to 30cm (12in).

☀ ◊ ① Zone 8

Epigaea gaultherioides,
syn. *Orphanidesia gaultherioides*
Evergreen, prostrate sub-shrub with cup-shaped, shell-pink flowers borne in terminal clusters in spring. Hairy stems carry heart-shaped, dark green leaves. Is difficult to grow and propagate. H to 10cm (4in), S to 25cm (10in) or more.

☀ ◊ pH Zone 9

ROCK PLANTS

Trillium rivale
Perennial with oval leaves, divided into 3 leaflets. In spring bears open cup-shaped, white or pale pink flowers with dark-spotted, heart-shaped petals, singly on upright, later arching stems.
H to 15cm (6in), S 10cm (4in).

☀ ◌

Saxifraga × irvingii 'Jenkinsiae', syn. *S.* 'Jenkinsiae'
Slow-growing perennial with very tight, grey-green cushions of foliage. Carries a profusion of open cup-shaped, lilac-pink flowers on slender stems in early spring.
H 8–10cm (3–4in), S to 15cm (6in).

☀ ◌

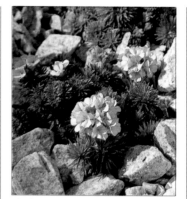

Androsace carnea
Evergreen, cushion-forming perennial that has small rosettes of pointed leaves with hairy margins. In spring, 2 or more stems rise above each rosette, bearing tiny, single, pink flowers. Suits a trough. H and S 5cm (2in).

☀ ◌

Thlaspi cepaeifolium subsp. **rotundifolium**
Clump-forming perennial with dense tufts of round leaves and small, open cup-shaped, pale to deep purplish- or lilac-pink flowers in spring. Needs cool conditions. May be short-lived.
H 5–8cm (2–3in), S 10cm (4in).

☀ ◌

Oxalis acetosella var. **subpurpurascens**
Creeping, rhizomatous perennial forming mats of 3-lobed leaves. Cup-shaped, soft pink flowers, each 1cm (½in) across, with 5 darker-veined petals, are produced in spring.
H 5cm (2in), S indefinite.

☀ ◌

Armeria juniperifolia, syn. *A. caespitosa*
Evergreen, cushion-forming perennial composed of loose rosettes of sharp-pointed, mid- to grey-green leaves. Pale pink flowers are borne in spherical umbels in late spring and early summer.
H 5–8cm (2–3in), S 15cm (6in).

☀ ◌

Arenaria purpurascens
Evergreen, mat-forming perennial with sharp-pointed, glossy leaves, above which rise many small clusters of star-shaped, pale to deep purplish-pink flowers in early spring.
H 1cm (½in), S to 15cm (6in).

☀ ◌

Silene acaulis (Moss campion)
Evergreen, cushion-forming perennial with minute, bright green leaves studded with tiny, stemless, 5-petalled, pink flowers in spring. May be difficult to bring into flower; prefers a cool climate.
H to 2.5cm (1in), S 15cm (6in).

☀ ◌

Arabis × arendsii 'Rosabella', syn. *A. caucasica* 'Rosabella'
Evergreen, mat-forming perennial with a profusion of single, deep pink flowers in spring and early summer and large rosettes of small, oval, soft green leaves. H 15cm (6in), S 30cm (12in).

☀ ◌

ROCK PLANTS

☐ PINK

Oxalis adenophylla
Mat-forming, fibrous-rooted, tuberous
perennial with grey-green leaves
divided into narrow, finger-like, wavy
lobes. In spring bears rounded, purplish-
pink flowers, each 2.5–4cm (1–1½in)
across, with darker purple eyes.
H to 5cm (2in), S 8–10cm (3–4in).

Shortia soldanelloides
Evergreen, mat-forming perennial with
rounded, toothed leaves and small,
pendent, bell-shaped and fringed, deep
pink flowers in late spring.
H 5–10cm (2–4in), S 10–15cm (4–6in).

Saxifraga oppositifolia
(Purple mountain saxifrage)
Evergreen, prostrate perennial with
clusters of tiny, white-flecked leaves.
Has open cup-shaped, dark purple,
purplish-pink or, rarely, white flowers
in early spring. Likes an open position.
H 2.5–5cm (1–2in), S 15cm (6in).

Erinus alpinus
Semi-evergreen, short-lived perennial
with rosettes of soft, mid-green leaves
covered, in late spring and summer,
with small, purple, pink or white
flowers. Self seeds freely.
H and S 5–8cm (2–3in).

***Daphne petraea* 'Grandiflora'**
Slow-growing, evergreen, compact
shrub that bears terminal clusters of
fragrant, rich pink flowers in late spring
and tiny, glossy leaves. Suits an alpine
house, a sheltered, humus-rich rock
garden or a trough.
H to 15cm (6in), S to 25cm (10in).

 Zone 6

Claytonia megarhiza* var. *nivalis
Evergreen perennial with a rosette of
spoon-shaped, succulent leaves. Bears
small heads of tiny, deep pink flowers
in spring. Grows best in a deep pot of
gritty compost in an alpine house.
H 1cm (½in), S 8cm (3in).

Antennaria dioica* var. *rosea
Semi-evergreen perennial forming
a spreading mat of tiny, oval, woolly
leaves. Bears fluffy, rose-pink flower
heads in small, terminal clusters in late
spring and early summer. Is good as
ground cover with small bulbs.
H 2.5cm (1in), S to 40cm (16in).

Daphne arbuscula
Evergreen, prostrate shrub. In late
spring bears many very fragrant,
tubular, deep pink flowers in terminal
clusters. Narrow, leathery, dark green
leaves are crowded at the ends of
the branches. Likes humus-rich soil.
H 10–15cm (4–6in), S 50cm (20in).

Zone 6

***Vaccinium vitis-idaea* subsp.
minus, syn. *V.v.-i.* 'Minus'**
Evergreen, mat-forming sub-shrub
with tiny, oval, leathery leaves. In late
spring produces small, erect racemes
of many tiny, bell-shaped, deep pink
or deep pink-and-white flowers.
H 5–8cm (2–3in), S 10–15cm (4–6in).

 Zone 2

Anagallis tenella 'Studland'
Short-lived perennial that forms
prostrate mats of tiny, bright green
leaves studded in spring with
honey-scented, star-shaped,
bright pink flowers.
H 1cm (½in), S 15cm (6in) or more.

☀ ◐

Saxifraga frederici-augustii subsp.
grisebachii 'Wisley Variety', syn.
S. grisebachii 'Wisley Variety'
Evergreen perennial with rosettes of
lime-encrusted leaves. Crosier-shaped
stems with pale pink to bright red hairs,
bear dense racemes of dark red flowers
in spring. H 10cm (4in), S 15cm (6in).

☀ ◊

Saxifraga sempervivum
Evergreen, hummock-forming
perennial with tight rosettes of tufted,
silvery-green leaves. Crosier-shaped
flower stems, covered in silvery hairs
and emerging from rosettes, bear
racemes of dark red flowers in early
spring. H and S 10–15cm (4–6in).

☀ ◊

Corydalis diphylla
Tuberous perennial with semi-erect,
basal leaves, divided into narrow
leaflets, and loose racemes of purple-
lipped flowers with white spurs in
spring. Protect tubers from excess
moisture in summer.
H 10–15cm (4–6in), S 8–10cm (3–4in).

☀ ◊

Polygonatum hookeri
Slow-growing, dense, rhizomatous
perennial that bears loose spikes of
several small, bell-shaped, lilac-pink
flowers in late spring and early
summer. Leaves are tiny and lance-
shaped. Suits a peat bed.
H to 5cm (2in), S to 30cm (12in).

☀ ◊ ①

Androsace carnea subsp. **laggeri**
Evergreen, cushion-forming perennial
composed of small, tight rosettes of
pointed leaves. Cup-shaped, deep pink
flowers are borne in small clusters
above cushions in spring.
H and S 5cm (2in).

☀ ◊

Corydalis solida 'George Baker',
syn. *C.s.* 'G.P. Baker'
Tuberous perennial with fern-like,
divided leaves and dense racemes of
spurred, rich deep rose-red flowers in
spring. H and S 10–15cm (4–6in).

☀ ◊

Leptinella atrata,
syn. *Cotula atrata*
Evergreen, mat-forming perennial with
small, finely cut, greyish-green leaves
and blackish-red flower heads in late
spring and early summer. Is uncommon
and not easy to grow successfully.
H 2.5cm (1in), S to 25cm (10in).

☀ ◊

Aubrieta 'Joy'
Vigorous, evergreen, trailing perennial
that forms mounds of soft green
leaves. In spring bears double, pale
mauve flowers on short stems.
H 10cm (4in), S 20cm (8in).

☀ ◊

Aethionema 'Warley Ruber'
Androsace sempervivoides
Armeria juniperifolia 'Bevan's Variety'
Dodecatheon pulchellum

Penstemon davidsonii
PRIMULAS, illus. pp.272–3
Rhodohypoxis 'Albrighton', illus. p.380
Rhodohypoxis 'Douglas', illus. p.380

PRIMULAS, illus. pp.272–3
Ramonda nathaliae
Ramonda serbica
Viola 'Nellie Britton', illus. p.381

■ PURPLE

Aubrieta deltoidea 'Argenteovariegata'
Evergreen, compact perennial, grown for its trailing, green leaves which are heavily splashed with creamy-white. Produces pinkish-lavender flowers in spring. H 5cm (2in), S 15cm (6in).

Mazus reptans
Prostrate perennial that has tubular, purple or purplish-pink flowers, with protruding, white lips, spotted red and yellow, borne singly on short stems in spring. Narrow, toothed leaves are in pairs along stem.
H to 5cm (2in), S 30cm (12in) or more.

Soldanella villosa
Evergreen, clump-forming perennial with round, leathery, hairy-stalked leaves and nodding, bell-shaped, fringed, purplish-lavender flowers borne on erect stems in early spring. Dislikes winter wet.
H 10cm (4in), S 10–15cm (4–6in).

Aubrieta 'Hartswood Purple', syn. *A.* 'Carnival'
Vigorous, evergreen, mound-forming perennial that carries many short spikes of large, single, violet-purple flowers in spring above small, soft green leaves.
H 10cm (4in), S 30cm (12in).

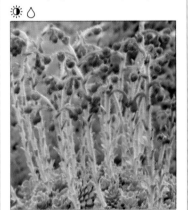

Saxifraga stribrnyi
Evergreen, mound-forming perennial with small, lime-encrusted rosettes of leaves. Crosier-shaped stems, covered in pinkish-buff hairs, bear racemes of deep maroon-red flowers above leaves in late spring and early summer.
H 8cm (3in), S 10–12cm (4–5in).

Polygala chamaebuxus var. *grandiflora*
Evergreen, woody-based perennial that bears terminal clusters of pea-like, reddish-purple and yellow flowers in late spring and early summer. Leaves are small, oval, leathery and dark green.
H to 15cm (6in), S to 30cm (12in).

Zone 7

Soldanella alpina
(Alpine snowbell)
Evergreen, clump-forming perennial with tufts of leaves and short, bell-shaped, fringed, pinkish-lavender or purplish-pink flowers in early spring. Is difficult to flower well.
H to 8cm (3in), S 8–10cm (3–4in).

Aubrieta 'J.S. Baker'
Evergreen perennial with single, purple flowers in spring borne above mounds of small, soft green leaves.
H 10cm (4in), S 20cm (8in).

Viola calcarata
Clump-forming perennial, with oval leaves, that bears flat, outward-facing, single, white, lavender or purple flowers for a long period from late spring to summer. Prefers rich soil.
H 10–15cm (4–6in), S to 20cm (8in).

Aubrieta 'Doctor Mules'
IRISES, illus. pp.234–5
Polygala vayredae
Saxifraga x arco-valleyi 'Arco'

Saxifraga oppositifolia 'Ruth Draper'
Soldanella minima
Soldanella montana
Viola obliqua

Viola odorata
Viola palmata

ROCK PLANTS

Aubrieta 'Cobalt Violet'
Evergreen, mound-forming perennial with single, blue-violet flowers carried in short, terminal spikes in spring above a mat of small, soft green leaves. H 10cm (4in), S 20cm (8in).

☼ ◊

Viola tricolor
(Heartsease, Wild pansy)
Short-lived perennial or annual with neat, flat-faced flowers in combinations of white, yellow and shades of purple from spring to autumn. Self seeds profusely. H 5–15cm (2–6in), S 5–15cm (2–6in) or more.

☼ ◊

Hepatica nobilis var. **japonica**
Slow-growing perennial with leathery, lobed leaves, semi-evergreen in all but very cold or arid climates. Bears slightly cupped, lilac-mauve, pink or white flowers in spring.
H to 8cm (3in), S to 12cm (5in).

◐ ◑

Viola riviniana 'Purpurea',
syn. *V. labradorica* 'Purpurea'
Clump-forming perennial with tiny, flat-faced, purple flowers in spring-summer. Leaves are kidney-shaped and dark purple-green. Is invasive but suits a bank, woodland or wild garden.
H 2.5–5cm (1–2in), S indefinite.

◐ ◊

Jeffersonia dubia,
syn. *Plagiorhegma dubia*
Tufted perennial with 2-lobed, blue-green leaves, sometimes flushed pink when unfolding. Bears cup-shaped, pale lilac to purplish blue flowers singly in spring.
H 10–15cm (4–6in), S to 23cm (9in).

◐ ◑

Jancaea heldreichii
Perennial with rosettes of thick, hairy, silver-green leaves, above which rise slender stems bearing clusters of tiny, lavender-blue flowers in late spring. Is rare and difficult to grow and is best in an alpine house. H and S to 8cm (3in).

◐ ◑

Viola pedata (Bird's-foot violet)
Clump-forming perennial with finely divided foliage and yellow-centred, pale violet, rarely white flowers borne singly on slender stems in late spring and early summer. Needs sharp drainage; grow in an alpine house.
H 5cm (2in) S 8cm (3in).

☼ ◊ pH

Mertensia maritima
Prostrate perennial with oval, fleshy, bright silver-blue or silver-grey leaves. Stout stems carry clusters of pendent, funnel-shaped, sky-blue flowers in spring. Is prone to slug damage. Needs very sharp drainage.
H 10–15cm (4–6in), S 12cm (5in).

☼ ◊

Synthyris stellata
Evergreen, mounded, rhizomatous perennial that bears dense spikes of small, violet-blue flowers in spring above rounded, deeply toothed leaves. Tolerates sun if soil remains moist.
H 10–15cm (4–6in), S 15cm (6in).

◐ ◑

■ BLUE

■■ BLUE–GREEN

Myosotis alpestris, syn.
M. rupicola (Alpine forget-me-not)
Short-lived, clump-forming perennial
producing dense clusters of tiny, bright
blue flowers with creamy-yellow eyes
in late spring and early summer, just
above tufts of hairy leaves. Prefers
gritty soil. H and S 10–15cm (4–6in).

☼ ◊

Anchusa cespitosa
Evergreen, mound-forming perennial
with rosettes of lance-shaped, dark
green leaves. In spring, stemless, white-
centred, blue flowers appear in centres
of rosettes. Old plants do not flower
well; take early summer cuttings.
H 2.5–5cm (1–2in), S to 23cm (9in).

☼ ◊

Gentiana acaulis, syn. *G. excisa*,
G. kochiana (Stemless gentian)
Evergreen, clump-forming perennial
with narrowly oval, glossy leaves. Bears
trumpet-shaped, deep blue flowers, with
green-spotted throats, on short stems in
spring and often in autumn. H in leaf
2cm (¾in), S to 10cm (4in) or more.

☼ ◊

Viola tricolor 'Bowles' Black'
Clump-forming perennial with flat-
faced, very dark violet, almost black,
flowers, borne continuously from
spring to autumn. Oval leaves are
sometimes lobed and toothed.
Is short-lived; treat as biennial.
H 5–15cm (2–6in), S 5–8cm (2–3in).

☼ ◊

Gentiana verna (Spring gentian)
Evergreen perennial, often short-lived,
with small rosettes of oval, dark green
leaves. In early spring, tubular, bright
blue flowers with white throats are
held upright on short stems.
H and S to 5cm (2in).

☼ ◊

Salix reticulata
(Net-veined willow)
Deciduous, spreading, mat-forming
shrub. Carries plump, reddish-brown,
then yellow catkins on male plants in
spring and rounded, slightly crinkled
leaves. Likes cool, peaty soil.
H 5–8cm (2–3in), S 20cm (8in) or more.

☼ ◊ Zone 4

ROCK PLANTS

Mandragora officinarum
Rosetted, fleshy-rooted perennial with coarse, wavy-edged leaves. Bears funnel-shaped, yellowish- or purplish-white flowers in spring, followed by large, tomato-like, shiny yellow fruits.
H 5cm (2in), S 30cm (12in).

Hacquetia epipactis
Clump-forming perennial spreading by short rhizomes. In late winter and early spring bears yellow or yellow-green flower heads, encircled by apple-green bracts, before rounded, 3-parted leaves appear.
H 6cm (2½in), S 15–23cm (6–9in).

Euphorbia myrsinites
Evergreen, prostrate perennial with terminal clusters of bright yellow-green flowers in spring. Woody stems are clothed in small, pointed, fleshy, grey leaves. Is good on a wall or ledge.
H 5–8cm (2–3in),
S to 20cm (8in) or more.

Saxifraga × boydii 'Hindhead Seedling'
Evergreen perennial that forms a hard dome of small, tufted, spiny, blue-green leaves. In spring bears upward-facing, open, cup-shaped, pale yellow flowers, 2 or 3 to each short stem.
H 2.5cm (1in), S 8cm (3in).

Saxifraga × apiculata 'Gregor Mendel'
Evergreen perennial with a tight cushion of bright green foliage. Bears clusters of open, cup-shaped, pale yellow flowers in early spring.
H 10–15cm (4–6in),
S 15cm (6in) or more.

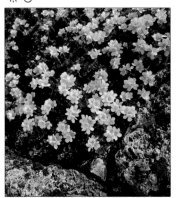

Saxifraga 'Elizabethae',
syn. *S. × elizabethae*
Evergreen, cushion-forming perennial, composed of densely packed, tiny rosettes of spiny leaves. In spring, tight upward-facing, bright yellow flowers are carried on tops of red-based stems.
H 2.5cm (1in), S 10–15cm (4–6in).

Viola aetolica
Clump-forming perennial bearing flat-faced, yellow flowers singly on upright stems in late spring and early summer. Leaves are oval and mid-green.
H 5–8cm (2–3in), S 15cm (6in).

Draba rigida
Evergreen perennial with tight hummocks of minute, dark green leaves. Tiny clusters of bright yellow flowers on fine stems cover hummocks in spring. Suits a rough, scree garden or alpine house. Dislikes winter wet.
H 4cm (1½in), S 6cm (2½in).

Dionysia aretioides
Evergreen perennial forming cushions of soft, hairy, greyish-green leaves that are covered in early spring by scented, stemless, round, bright yellow flowers.
H 5–10cm (2–4in),
S 15–30cm (6–12in).

Draba longisiliqua
Semi-evergreen, cushion-forming perennial composed of firm rosettes of tiny, silver leaves. Bears sprays of small, yellow flowers on long stalks in spring. Needs plenty of water in growth; is best grown in an alpine house. H 5–8cm (2–3in), S 15cm (6in).

Saxifraga sancta
Evergreen, mat-forming perennial with tufts of bright green leaves. Bears short racemes of upward-facing, open cup-shaped, bright yellow flowers in spring. H 5cm (2in), S 15cm (6in).

ROCK PLANTS

Draba mollissima
Semi-evergreen, cushion-forming
perennial covered in spring with clusters
of tiny, yellow flowers on slender stems.
Minute leaves form a soft green dome,
which should be packed beneath with
small stones. Grow in an alpine house.
H 4cm (1½in), S 15cm (6in) or more.

Dionysia tapetodes
Evergreen, prostrate perennial
producing a tight mat of tiny, grey-
green leaves. Bears small, upward-
facing, yellow flowers in early spring.
H 1cm (½in), S to 15cm (6in).

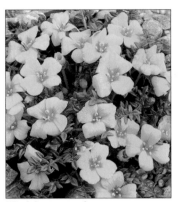

Morisia monanthos,
syn. *M. hypogaea*
Prostrate perennial with flat rosettes
of divided, leathery, dark green leaves.
Bears stemless, flat, bright yellow
flowers in late spring and early
summer. Needs very sharp drainage.
H 2.5cm (1in), S to 8cm (3in).

Ranunculus ficaria 'Flore Pleno'
Mat-forming perennial with heart-
shaped, dark green leaves and, in early
spring, double, bright yellow flowers
with glossy petals. May spread rapidly.
Is good for a wild garden.
H 2.5–5cm (1–2in), S 20cm (8in).

Vitaliana primuliflora,
syn. *Douglasia vitaliana*
Evergreen, prostrate perennial with
a mat of rosetted, mid-green leaves
that are covered in spring with many
small clusters of stemless, tubular,
bright yellow flowers.
H 2.5cm (1in), S 20cm (8in).

Viola 'Jackanapes'
Clump-forming perennial with oval,
toothed leaves. Produces flat-faced
flowers with reddish-brown, upper
petals and yellow, lower ones
throughout late spring and summer.
H 8–12cm (3–5in),
S to 20cm (8in) or more.

Ranunculus ficaria 'Brazen Hussy'
Salix herbacea
Sarcocapnos enneaphylla
Saxifraga aizoides

Saxifraga brunonis
Saxifraga burseriana 'Brookside'
Saxifraga ferdinandi-coburgi
Saxifraga 'Valerie Finnis'

Sedum acre 'Aureum', illus. p.385
Townsendia parryi
Viola glabella
Viola lutea

Waldsteinia ternata, illus. p.385

☐ YELLOW

☐ WHITE

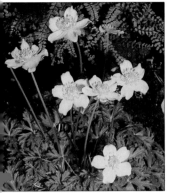

Trollius pumilus
Tufted perennial with leaves divided
into 5 segments, each further lobed.
Carries solitary cup-shaped, bright
yellow flowers in late spring and
early summer.
H 15cm (6in), S 15cm (6in) or more.

☼ ◗

Silene alpestris,
syn. *Heliosperma alpestris*
Perennial with branching stems and
narrow leaves. Bears small, rounded,
fringed, white, occasionally pink-
flushed flowers in late spring and early
summer. Self seeds freely.
H 10–15cm (4–6in), S 20cm (8in).

☼ ◊

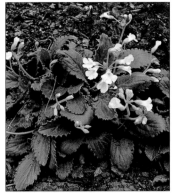

**Haberlea rhodopensis
'Virginalis'**
Evergreen perennial with small,
arching sprays of funnel-shaped, pure
white flowers borne in late spring and
early summer above neat rosettes of
oval, toothed, dark green leaves.
H and S in flower 10–15cm (4–6in).

☼ ◗

Cyananthus lobatus f. **albus**
Prostrate perennial with branched
stems clothed in small, wedge-shaped,
dull green leaves. Bears funnel-shaped,
single, white flowers with spreading
lobes in late summer.
H 8cm (3in), S 30cm (12in).

☼ ◊

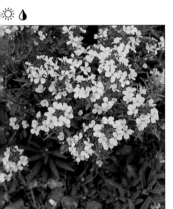

Erysimum helveticum,
syn. *E. pumilum*
Semi-evergreen, clump-forming
perennial with closely-packed tufts of
long, narrow leaves and many fragrant,
bright yellow flowers borne in flat
heads in late spring and early summer.
H 10cm (4in), S 15cm (6in).

☼ ◊

Phlox stolonifera 'Ariane'
Evergreen, low-growing perennial
with flowering side shoots that bear
heads of open, saucer-shaped, white
blooms in early summer. Has oval,
pale green leaves. Cut back flowered
shoots by half after flowering.
H to 15cm (6in), S 30cm (12in).

☼ ◊ pH

Potentilla alba
Vigorous mat-forming perennial
bearing loose sprays of flat, single,
white flowers in summer. Leaves
are divided into oval leaflets and are
silvery beneath.
H 5–8cm (2–3in), S 8cm (3in).

☼ ◊

**Campanula carpatica
'Bressingham White'**
Clump-forming perennial bearing open
cup-shaped, white flowers, singly on
unbranched stems, in summer. Has
abundant, rounded, bright green leaves.
H 10–15cm (4–6in), S 15cm (6in).

☼ ◊

**Ranunculus ficaria
'Aurantiacus'**
Mat-forming perennial bearing in early
spring cup-shaped, single, orange
flowers with glossy petals. Leaves are
heart-shaped and mid-green. May
spread rapidly. Is good for a wild
garden. H 5cm (2in), S 20cm (8in).

☼ ◗ ⚠

Achillea clavennae
Semi-evergreen, carpeting perennial
that bears loose clusters of white flower
heads with gold centres from summer
to mid-autumn. Leaves are narrowly
oval, many-lobed and covered with
fine, white hairs. Dislikes winter wet.
H 15cm (6in), S 23cm (9in) or more.

☼ ◊ ⚠

Lewisia rediviva [white form]
(Bitter root)
Tufted, rosetted perennial with clusters
of fine, narrow leaves that are summer-
deciduous. Bears large, white flowers
that open in bright weather in late
spring and early summer.
H 1–4cm (½–1½in), S to 5cm (2in).

☼ ◊ pH

DAFFODILS, illus. pp.416–18
Hypericum cerastioides
IRISES, illus. pp.234–5
Leucogenes grandiceps, illus. p.389

OTHER RECOMMENDED PLANTS:
Aethionema iberideum
Arabis alpina subsp. *caucasica*
Arabis alpina subsp. *caucasica* 'Flore Pleno'

Arabis alpina subsp. *caucasica* 'Variegata',
  illus. p.362
Arctostaphylos nevadensis
Arenaria balearica, illus. p.362

Artemisia schmidtiana 'Nana', illus. p.389
Cardamine trifolia, illus. p.362
Celmisia bellidioides
Celmisia traversii

373

☐ WHITE

ROCK PLANTS

Arenaria montana
Prostrate perennial that forms loose mats of small, narrowly oval leaves and bears large, round, white flowers in summer. Suits a wall or rock crevice. Must have adequate moisture. H 5cm (2in), S 12cm (5in).

☀ ◊

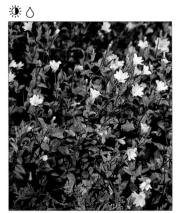

Epilobium chlorifolium var. *kaikourense*
Clump-forming, woody-based perennial with deciduous but persistent, oval, hairy, bronze and dark green leaves. In summer has short spikes of funnel-shaped, white to pink flowers. H 10cm (4in), S 15cm (6in).

☀ ◊

Gentiana saxosa
Evergreen, hummock-forming perennial clothed in small, spoon-shaped, fleshy, dark green leaves. Produces small, upturned, bell-shaped, white flowers in early summer. Is a short-lived scree plant. H 5cm (2in), S 15cm (6in).

☀ ◊

Iberis saxatilis
Evergreen, dwarf sub-shrub that in late spring and early summer produces large heads of numerous small, white flowers, which become tinged violet with age. Glossy, dark leaves are linear and cylindrical. Trim after flowering. H 8–12cm (3–5in), S 30cm (12in).

☀ ◊ Zone 7

Cornus canadensis
(Creeping dogwood)
Ground-cover sub-shrub with whorls of oval leaves. In late spring and early summer bears green, sometimes purple-tinged flowers, within white bracts, followed by red berries. H 10–15cm (4–6in), S 30cm (12in) or more.

☀ ◊ pH ① Zone 2

Celmisia ramulosa
Evergreen, shrubby perennial with small, hairy, grey-green leaves. Daisy-like, white flower heads are borne singly on short stems in late spring and early summer. H and S 10cm (4in).

☀ ◊ pH

Ourisia caespitosa
Evergreen, prostrate perennial with creeping rootstocks and stems bearing tiny, oval leaves and many outward-facing, open cup-shaped, white flowers in late spring and early summer. H 2.5cm (1in), S 10cm (4in).

☀ ◊

Nierembergia repens
Mat-forming perennial with upright, open bell-shaped, yellow-centred, white flowers, occasionally flushed pink with age, borne for a long period in summer. Leaves are small, oval and light green. Is useful for cracks in paving. H 5cm (2in), S 20cm (8in) or more.

☀ ◊

Anacyclus pyrethrum var. *depressus*, syn. *A. depressus*
Short-lived, prostrate perennial that has white flower heads, with red reverses to ray petals, in summer. Flowers close in dull light. Stems are clothed in fine leaves. Dislikes wet. H 2.5–5cm (1–2in) or more, S 10cm (4in).

☀ ◊

Petrocosmea kerrii
Evergreen perennial with compact rosettes of oval, pointed, hairy, rich green leaves. In summer bears clusters of short, outward-facing, tubular, open-mouthed white flowers. Suits an alpine house. H to 8cm (3in), S 12–15cm (5–6in). Min. 2–5°C (36–41°F).

☀ ◊

Dryas octopetala

Evergreen, prostrate perennial forming mats of oval, lobed, leathery, dark green leaves on stout stems. In late spring and early summer, cup-shaped, creamy-white flowers are borne just above foliage, followed by attractive, feathery seeds. H 6cm (2½in), S indefinite.

Linnaea borealis (Twin flower)

Evergreen, mat-forming, sub-shrubby perennial with rooting stems bearing small, oval leaves, above which in summer rise thread-like stems bearing pairs of small, fragrant, tubular, pale pink and white flowers.
H 2cm (¾in), S 30cm (12in) or more.

Achillea x *kellereri*

Semi-evergreen perennial that bears daisy-like, white flower heads in loose clusters in summer. Leaves are feathery and grey-green. Is good for a wall or bank. Dislikes winter wet and must have perfect drainage.
H 15cm (6in), S 23cm (9in) or more.

Dianthus pavonius,
syn. *D. neglectus*
Evergreen, prostrate perennial with comparatively large, rounded, pale to deep pink flowers, buff on reverses, borne on short stems in summer above low mats of spiky leaves.
H 5cm (2in), S 8cm (3in).

Petrorhagia saxifraga, syn.
Tunica saxifraga (Tunic flower)
Mat-forming perennial with tufts of grass-like leaves. In summer bears a profusion of small, pale pink flowers, veined deeper pink, on slender stems. Grows best on poor soil and self-seeds easily. H 10cm (4in), S 15cm (6in).

Carlina acaulis (Alpine thistle)

Clump-forming perennial that in summer-autumn bears large, stemless, thistle-like, single, off-white or pale brown flower heads, with papery bracts, on rosettes of long, spiny-margined, deeply-cut leaves.
H 8–10cm (3–4in), S 15–23cm (6–9in).

Gypsophila repens 'Dorothy Teacher'

Semi-evergreen, prostrate perennial. Sprays of small, rounded, white flowers, which age to deep pink, cover mats of narrow, bluish-green leaves in summer. trim stems after flowering. H 2.5–5cm (1–2in), S 30cm (12in) or more.

Thymus caespititius,
syn. *T. azoricus*, *T. micans*
Evergreen, mat-forming, aromatic sub-shrub with slender, woody stems covered in minute, hairy, mid-green leaves. Bears tiny, pale lilac or lilac-pink flowers in small clusters in summer. H 2.5cm (1in), S 20cm (8in).
Zone 5

Convolvulus althaeoides

Vigorous perennial with long, trailing stems clothed in heart-shaped, cut, mid-green leaves, overlaid silver. Bears large, open trumpet-shaped pink flowers in summer. May be invasive in a mild climate.
H 5cm (2in), S indefinite.

ROCK PLANTS

375

□ PINK

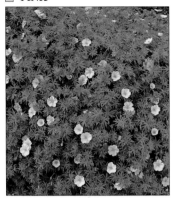

Geranium sanguineum
var. ***striatum***
Hummock-forming, spreading
perennial that has cup-shaped, pink
flowers, with darker veins, borne
singly in summer above round, deeply
divided, dark green leaves. H 10–15cm
(4–6in), S 30cm (12in) or more.

☀ ◊

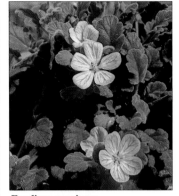

Erodium corsicum
Compact, clump-forming perennial that
has soft, grey-green leaves with wavy
margins. Bears flat-faced, pink flowers,
with darker veins, on stiff, slender stems
in late spring and summer. Grows best
in an alpine house as dislikes winter
wet. H 8cm (3in), S 15cm (6in).

☀ ◊

Saponaria × ***olivana***
Compact perennial with a firm cushion
of narrow leaves. Flowering stems,
produced around edges of the cushion,
bear flat, single, pale pink flowers in
summer. Needs very sharp drainage.
H 8cm (3in), S 10cm (4in).

☀ ◊

Aethionema 'Warley Rose'
Short-lived, evergreen or semi-
evergreen, compact sub-shrub with
tiny, linear, bluish-green leaves. Bears
racemes of small, pink flowers on
short stems in profusion in spring-
summer. H and S 15cm (6in).

☀ ◊ Zone 5b

Ourisia microphylla
Semi-evergreen, mat-forming
perennial, with neat, scale-like, pale
green leaves, bearing a profusion of
small, pink flowers in late spring and
early summer. Is difficult to grow
in an arid climate.
H 5–10cm (2–4in), S 15cm (6in).

☀ ◊ ◊

Rhodohypoxis 'Margaret Rose'
Perennial with a tuber-like rootstock
and an erect, basal tuft of narrowly
lance-shaped, hairy leaves. Bears a
succession of upright, flattish, pale pink
flowers on slender stems in spring and
early summer.
H 5–10cm (2–4in), S 2.5–5cm (1–2in).

☀ ◊

Phlox adsurgens 'Wagon Wheel'
Evergreen, prostrate perennial forming
wide mats of woody stems, clothed in
oval leaves. Bears heads of wheel-
shaped, pink flowers with narrow
petals in summer. Needs humus-rich
soil. H 10cm (4in), S 30cm (12in).

☀ ◊ pH

Asperula suberosa
Clump-forming perennial with a
mound of loose stems bearing tiny,
hairy, grey leaves and, in early summer,
many tubular, pale pink flowers.
Dislikes winter wet but needs moist
soil in summer. Is best in an alpine
house. H 8cm (3in), S to 30cm (12in).

☀ ◊

Persicaria affinis 'Donald
Lowndes'
Evergreen, mat-forming perennial that
has stout, branching, spreading stems
clothed with pointed leaves. In summer
bears dense spikes of small, red
flowers, which become paler with age.
H 8–15cm (3–6in), S to 15cm (6in).

☀ ◊ ①

Geranium traversii var. *elegans*
Lychnis alpina
Origanum amanum
Petrorhagia saxifraga 'Rosette'

PRIMULAS, illus. pp.272–3
Sedum spurium
Silene hookeri
Vaccinium myrtillus

ROCK PLANTS

Geranium dalmaticum
Prostrate, spreading perennial with outward-facing, almost flat, shell-pink flowers borne in summer above divided, dark green leaves. Will grow taller in partial shade and is evergreen in all but severest winters. H 8–10cm (3–4in) or more, S 12–20cm (5–8in).

☀ ◊

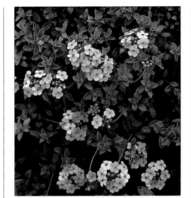

Androsace lanuginosa
Evergreen, trailing perennial with loose stems, covered in silky hairs, carrying deep green leaves and, in summer, clusters of small, flat, lilac-pink or pale pink flowers with dark pink or yellow eyes. H 4cm (1½in), S to 18cm (7in).

☀ ◊

Loiseleuria procumbens
(Alpine azalea, Trailing azalea)
Evergreen, prostrate shrub with small, oval leaves, hairy and beige beneath. Has terminal clusters of open funnel-shaped, rose-pink to white flowers in early summer.
H to 8cm (3in), S 10–15cm (4–6in).

☀ ◊ pH Zone 2

Erigeron karvinskianus,
syn. *E. mucronatus*
Spreading perennial with lax stems bearing narrow, lance-shaped, hairy leaves and, in summer-autumn, daisy-like flower heads that open white, turn pink and fade to purple.
H 10–15cm (4–6in), S indefinite.

☀ ◊

Dianthus 'Little Jock'
Evergreen, compact, clump-forming perennial with spiky, silvery-green foliage. In summer produces strongly fragrant, rounded, semi-double, pink flowers, with darker eyes, above foliage. H and S 10cm (4in).

☀ ◊

Aethionema armenum
Short-lived, evergreen or semi-evergreen, dense sub-shrub with narrow, blue-green leaves. Carries loose sprays of tiny, pale to deep pink flowers in summer.
H and S 15cm (6in).

☀ ◊

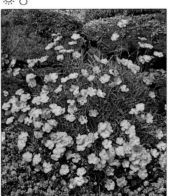

Dianthus gratianopolitanus,
syn. *D. caesius* (Cheddar pink)
Evergreen perennial with loose mats of narrow, grey-green leaves. In summer, produces very fragrant, flat, pale pink flowers on slender stems.
H to 15cm (6in), S to 30cm (12in).

☀ ◊

Acantholimon glumaceum
Evergreen, cushion-forming perennial with hard, spiny, dark green leaves and short spikes of small, star-shaped, pink flowers in summer.
H 10cm (4in), S 20cm (8in).

☀ ◊

377

☐ PINK

Dianthus 'Pike's Pink'
Evergreen, compact, cushion-forming
perennial, with spiky, grey-green
foliage, that bears fragrant, rounded,
double, pink flowers in summer.
H and S 10cm (4in).

☼ ◊

Saponaria caespitosa
Mat-forming perennial with small,
lance-shaped leaves. Tiny, flat, single,
pink to purple flowers are borne in
small heads in summer. Needs very
sharp drainage.
H 8cm (3in), S 10cm (4in).

☼ ◊

Oxalis depressa, syn. *O. inops*
Tuberous perennial with 3-lobed leaves
and short-stemmed, widely funnel-
shaped, bright rose-pink flowers, 2cm
(¾in) across, in summer. Needs a
sheltered site or cool greenhouse.
H 5cm (2in), S 8–10cm (3–4in).

☼ ◊

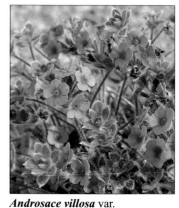

Androsace villosa var.
jacquemontii
Evergreen, mat-forming perennial with
small rosettes of hairy, grey-green
leaves. Bears tiny, pinkish-purple
flowers on red stems in late spring and
early summer. Suits an alpine house.
H 1–4cm (½–1½in), S 20cm (8in).

☼ ◊

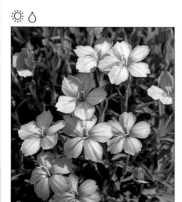

Dianthus microlepis
Evergreen perennial with tiny tufts of
minute, fine, grass-like leaves, above
which rise numerous small, rounded,
pink flowers in early summer.
Is best suited to a trough.
H 5cm (2in), S 20cm (8in).

☼ ◊

Saponaria ocymoides
(Tumbling Ted)
Perennial with compact or loose,
sprawling mats of hairy, oval leaves,
above which a profusion of tiny, flat,
pale pink to crimson flowers is carried
in summer. Is excellent on a dry bank.
H 2.5–8cm (1–3in), S 40cm (16in).

☼ ◊

Dianthus myrtinervius
Evergreen, spreading perennial with
numerous small, rounded, pink flowers
that appear in summer above tiny,
grass-like leaves.
H 5cm (2in), S 20cm (8in).

☼ ◊

Dianthus 'La Bourboule',
syn. *D.* 'La Bourbille'
Evergreen perennial with small clumps
of tufted, spiky foliage. Bears a
profusion of strongly fragrant, small,
single, pink flowers in summer.
H 5cm (2in), S 8cm (3in).

☼ ◊

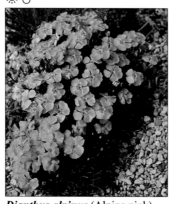

Dianthus alpinus (Alpine pink)
Evergreen, compact perennial that
bears comparatively large, rounded,
rose-pink to crimson flowers, singly in
summer, above mats of narrow, dark
green foliage. Likes humus-rich soil.
H 5cm (2in), S 8cm (3in).

☼ ◊

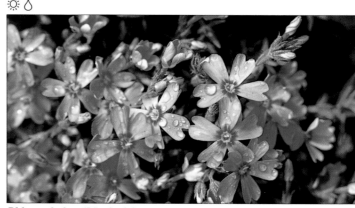

Phlox subulata 'Marjorie'
Evergreen, mound-forming perennial
with fine leaves and a profusion of flat,
star-shaped, bright rose-pink flowers in
early summer. Trim after flowering.
H 10cm (4in), S 20cm (8in).

☼ ◊

PRIMULAS, illus. pp.272–3
Prunella grandiflora 'Pink Loveliness'
Vaccinium nummularia

ROCK PLANTS

Dianthus 'Annabelle'
Evergreen, compact, clump-forming perennial with spiky, grey-green foliage. In summer bears fragrant, rounded, semi-double, cerise-pink flowers, singly on slender stems. H and S 10cm (4in).

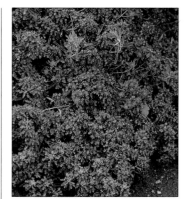

Teucrium polium
Deciduous, dome-shaped sub-shrub that has much-branched, woolly, white or yellowish stems and leaves with scalloped margins. Bears yellowish-white or pinkish-purple flowers in flat heads in summer. Requires very sharp drainage. H and S 15cm (6in).

 Zone 9

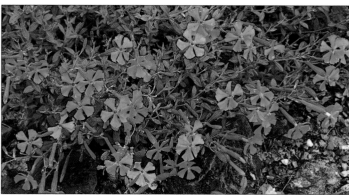

Silene schafta
Spreading perennial with tufts of narrow, oval leaves. Bears sprays of 5-petalled, rose-magenta flowers from late spring to late autumn.
H 10–15cm (4–6in), S 8–10cm (3–4in).

Phlox 'Camla'
Evergreen mound-forming perennial with wiry, arching stems and fine leaves. Has a profusion of open saucer-shaped, rich pink flowers in early summer. Trim after flowering. Needs humus-rich soil.
H 12cm (5in), S 30cm (12in).

Lewisia rediviva [pink form]
(Bitter root)
Tufted, rosetted perennial. Clusters of narrow leaves are summer-deciduous. Large, many-petalled, pink flowers open in bright weather in late spring and early summer. Suits an alpine house.
H 1–4cm (½–1½in), S to 5cm (2in).

Geranium cinereum 'Ballerina'
Spreading, rosetted perennial that bears cup-shaped, purplish-pink flowers, with deep purple veins, on lax stems in late spring and summer. Basal leaves are round, deeply divided and soft. H 10cm (4in), S 30cm (12in).

Phlox douglasii 'Crackerjack'
Evergreen, compact, mound-forming perennial. Has a profusion of saucer-shaped, bright crimson or magenta flowers in early summer. Leaves are lance-shaped and mid-green.
Cut back after flowering.
H to 8cm (3in), S 20cm (8in).

Geranium cinereum
var. **subcaulescens**, syn.
G. subcaulescens
Spreading perennial with round, deeply divided, soft leaves. In summer bears brilliant purple-magenta flowers, with striking, black eyes and stamens, on lax stems. H 10cm (4in), S 30cm (12in).

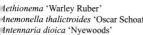

ROCK PLANTS

379

☐ PINK

***Rhodohypoxis* 'Albrighton'**
Perennial with tuber-like rootstock and
an erect, basal tuft of narrowly lance-
shaped, hairy leaves. Bears a
succession of erect, deep pink flowers
singly on slender stems in spring and
early summer.
H 5–10cm (2–4in), S 2.5–5cm (1–2in).

***Armeria maritima* 'Vindictive'**
Evergreen, clump-forming perennial
with grass-like, dark blue-green leaves,
above which rise stiff stems bearing
spherical heads of small, deep rose-
pink flowers for a long period in
summer. H 10cm (4in), S 15cm (6in).

***Dianthus deltoides* 'Leuchtfunk'**,
syn. *D.d.* 'Flashing Light'
Evergreen, mat-forming perennial.
Many small, flat, upward-facing,
brilliant cerise flowers are borne singly
above tiny, oblong, pointed leaves.
H 10–15cm (4–6in), S 20cm (8in).

☐ RED–PURPLE

***Rhodohypoxis* 'Douglas'**
Perennial with a tuber-like rootstock
and an erect, basal tuft of narrowly
lance-shaped, hairy leaves. Bears a
succession of upright, flattish, rich
deep red flowers singly on slender
stems in spring and early summer.
H 5–10cm (2–4in), S 2.5–5cm (1–2in).

Penstemon hirsutus
var. ***pygmaeus***
Short-lived, evergreen, compact sub-
shrub that bears tubular, lipped, hairy,
purple- or blue-flushed, white flowers
in summer. Has tightly packed, dark
green leaves and is suitable for
a trough. H and S 8cm (3in).

☼ ◊ Zone 4

Pterocephalus perennis,
syn. *P. parnassi*
Semi-evergreen, mat-forming perennial
with crinkled, hairy leaves. Bears tight,
rounded heads of tubular, pinkish-
lavender flowers, singly on short stems
in summer, followed by feathery seed
heads. H 5cm (2in), S 10cm (4in).

☼ ◊

☐ PURPLE

***Phlox douglasii* 'Boothman's
Variety'**
Evergreen, mound-forming perennial
with lance-shaped leaves and masses of
pale lavender-blue flowers, with violet-
blue markings around eyes, in early
summer. Cut back after flowering.
H to 5cm (2in), S 20cm (8in).

☼ ◊

Physoplexis comosa, syn.
Phyteuma comosum
Tufted perennial with deeply cut leaves
and round heads of bottle-shaped,
violet-blue, rarely white, flowers in
summer. Suits crevices but dislikes
winter wet. H 8cm (3in), S 10cm (4in).

Globularia meridionalis, syn.
G. bellidifolia, G. cordifolia subsp.
bellidifolia, G. pygmaea
Evergreen, dome-shaped sub-shrub.
In summer, globular, fluffy, lavender
to lavender-purple flower heads are
borne singly just above glossy leaves.
H to 10cm (4in), S to 20cm (8in).

☼ ◊ Zone 6

ROCK PLANTS

Thymus leucotrichus
Evergreen, aromatic, mound-forming
sub-shrub with fine, twiggy stems and
narrow leaves fringed with white hairs.
Bears dense heads of small,
pinkish-purple flowers with purple
bracts in summer.
H 10–12cm (4–5in), S 15cm (6in).

 Zone 6

***Phlox* 'Emerald Cushion'**
Evergreen perennial with emerald-
green mounds of fine leaves, studded
in late spring and early summer with
large, saucer-shaped, bright violet-blue
flowers. Trim after flowering.
H 8cm (3in), S 15cm (6in).

Phlox bifida (Sand phlox)
Evergreen, mound-forming perennial
with lance-shaped leaves. Bears a
profusion of small heads of star-
shaped, lilac or white flowers with
deeply cleft petals in summer. Cut
back stems by half after flowering.
H 10–15cm (4–6in), S 15cm (6in).

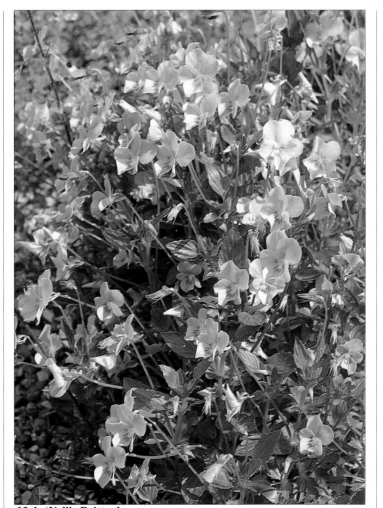

***Viola* 'Nellie Britton',**
syn. *V.* 'Haslemere'
Clump-forming perennial with small,
oval, toothed leaves and flat-faced,
lavender-pink flowers borne from late
spring to late summer. Soil should not
be too dry.
H 8–15cm (3–6in), S to 20cm (8in).

Campanula poscharskyana
Rampant, spreading perennial with
bell-shaped, violet flowers borne on
leafy stems in summer. Leaves are
round with serrated edges. Vigorous
runners make it suitable for a bank
or a wild garden.
H 10–15cm (4–6in), S indefinite.

***Prunella grandiflora* 'Loveliness',**
syn. *P.* x *webbiana* 'Loveliness'
Semi-evergreen, basal-rosetted, ground-
cover perennial. Bears whorls of pale
purple flowers in terminal spikes on
leafy stems in summer. May be invasive;
cut old flower stems before they seed.
H 10–15cm (4–6in), S 30cm (12in).

Aster alpinus
Clump-forming, spreading perennial
with lance-shaped, dark green leaves.
Bears daisy-like, purplish-blue or
pinkish-purple flower heads,
with yellow centres, from mid-
to late summer.
H 15cm (6in), S 30–45cm (12–18in).

Thymus herba-barona
(Caraway thyme)
Evergreen sub-shrub with a loose mat
of tiny, caraway-scented, dark green
leaves. In summer, small, lilac flowers
are borne in terminal clusters.
H in flower 5–10cm (2–4in),
S to 20cm (8in).

Zone 7

Edraianthus serpyllifolius,
syn. *Wahlenbergia serpyllifolia*
Evergreen, prostrate perennial with
tight mats of tiny leaves and small,
bell-shaped, deep violet flowers, borne
on short stems in early summer. Is
uncommon and seldom sets seed in
gardens. H 1cm (½in), S to 5cm (2in).

■ PURPLE

Prunella grandiflora, syn.
P. x *webbiana* (Large self-heal)
Semi-evergreen, spreading, mat-
forming perennial with basal rosettes
of leaves. In mid-summer bears
short spikes of funnel-shaped, purple
flowers in whorls.
H 10–15cm (4–6in), S 30cm (12in).

☼ ◐

Campanula 'Birch Hybrid'
Vigorous, evergreen perennial with
tough, arching, prostrate stems and
ivy-shaped, bright green leaves. Bears
many open bell-shaped, deep violet
flowers in summer.
H 10cm (4in), S 30cm (12in) or more.

☼ ◊

Campanula portenschlagiana
Vigorous, evergreen, prostrate
perennial with dense mats of small,
ivy-shaped leaves and large clusters of
erect, open bell-shaped, violet flowers
in summer. H 15cm (6in), S indefinite.

☼ ◊

Ramonda myconi,
syn. *R. pyrenaica*
Evergreen, rosette-forming perennial
with hairy, crinkled leaves and, in late
spring and early summer, flat, blue-
mauve, pink or white flowers, borne
on branched stems.
H 8cm (3in), S to 10cm (4in).

☀ ◐

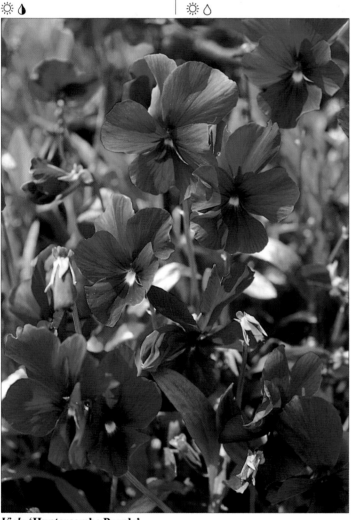

Viola 'Huntercombe Purple'
Perennial forming wide clumps of neat,
oval, toothed leaves. Has a profusion of
flat-faced, rich violet flowers from
spring to late summer. Divide clumps
every 3 years.
H 10–15cm (4–6in),
S 15–30cm (6–12in) or more.

☼ ◊

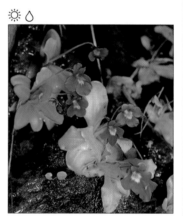

Pinguicula grandiflora
Clump-forming perennial with a basal
rosette of sticky, oval, pale green
leaves. In summer bears spurred,
open funnel-shaped, violet-blue to
purple flowers singly on upright,
slender stems.
H 12–15cm (5–6in), S 5cm (2in).

☼ ●

Campanula 'G.F. Wilson'
Neat, mound-forming perennial with
large, upturned, bell-shaped, violet
flowers in summer. Has rounded, pale
yellow-green leaves.
H 8–10cm (3–4in), S 12–15cm (5–6in).

☼ ◊

Edraianthus pumilio
Short-lived perennial with low tufts of
fine, grass-like leaves. In early
summer, upturned, bell-shaped, pale to
deep lavender flowers, on very short
stems, appear amid foliage.
H 2.5cm (1in), S 8cm (3in).

☼ ◊

Delphinium brunonianum
IRISES, illus. pp.234–5
Polygala chamaebuxus var. *grandiflora*,
   illus. p.368

Scutellaria scordiifolia
Thalictrum kiusianum

ROCK PLANTS

Cyananthus microphyllus
Mat-forming perennial with very fine,
~~red~~ stems clothed in tiny leaves. Bears
~~funnel~~-shaped, violet-blue flowers at
~~the~~ end of each stem in late summer.
~~Likes~~ humus-rich soil.
~~H~~ 2cm (¾in), S 20cm (8in).

Townsendia grandiflora
Short-lived, evergreen perennial with
basal rosettes of small, spoon-shaped
leaves. Upright stems carry solitary
daisy-like, violet or violet-blue flower
heads in late spring and early summer.
H to 15cm (6in), S 10cm (4in).

Sisyrinchium idahoense
Semi-evergreen, upright, clump-
forming perennial that for a long period
in summer and early autumn has many
flowering stems carrying tiny tufts of
iris-like, blue to violet-blue flowers.
Foliage is grass-like. Self seeds readily.
H to 12cm (5in), S 10cm (4in).

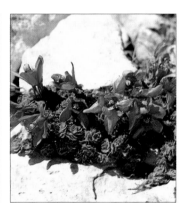

Aquilegia jonesii
Compact perennial that bears short-
spurred, violet-blue flowers in summer,
a few to each slender stem. Has small
rosettes of finely divided, blue-grey or
grey-green leaves. Is uncommon,
suitable for an alpine house only.
H 2.5cm (1in), S to 5cm (2in).

Pratia pedunculata
Vigorous, evergreen, creeping
perennial with small leaves and a
profusion of star-shaped, pale to mid-
blue or occasionally purplish-blue
flowers borne in summer. Makes good
ground cover in a moist site.
H 1cm (½in), S indefinite.

Hedyotis michauxii,
syn. *Houstonia serpyllifolia*
(Creeping bluets)
Vigorous perennial with rooting stems.
Produces mats of mid-green foliage
studded with star-shaped, violet-blue
flowers in late spring and early
summer. H 8cm (3in), S 30cm (12in).

Globularia cordifolia
Evergreen, mat-forming, dwarf shrub
with creeping, woody stems clothed
in tiny, oval leaves. Bears stemless,
round, fluffy, blue to pale lavender-blue
flower heads in summer.
H 2.5–5cm (1–2in), S to 20cm (8in).

☼ ◊ Zone 5

Campanula cochleariifolia,
syn. *C. pusilla* (Fairy thimbles)
Spreading perennial. Runners produce
mats of rosetted, tiny, round leaves.
Bears small clusters of white, lavender
or pale blue flowers in summer on
many thin stems above foliage.
H 8cm (3in), S indefinite.

Trachelium asperuloides,
syn. *Diosphaera asperuloides*
Mat-forming perennial with thread-like
stems clothed in minute, mid-green
leaves, above which rise many tiny,
upright, tubular, pale blue flowers in
summer. Do not remove old stems in
winter. H 8cm (3in), S to 15cm (6in).

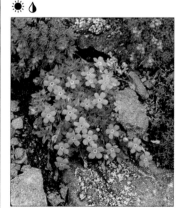

Eritrichium nanum
Clump-forming perennial with tufts of
hairy, grey-green leaves. Bears small,
stemless, flat, pale blue flowers in late
spring and early summer. Requires
sharp drainage. Is only suitable for
an alpine house.
H 2cm (¾in), S 2.5cm (1in).

ROCK PLANTS

ROCK PLANTS (side tab)

■ BLUE

Parochetus communis
(Shamrock pea)
Evergreen, prostrate perennial with
clover-like leaves and pea-like,
brilliant blue flowers that are borne
almost continuously. Grows best in an
alpine house.
H 2.5–5cm (1–2in), S indefinite.

☼◐ ◊

***Polygala calcarea* 'Bulley's
Form'**
Evergreen, prostrate perennial with
rosettes of small, narrowly oval leaves
and loose heads of deep blue flowers
in late spring and early summer. Likes
humus-rich soil. Suits a trough.
H 2.5cm (1in), S 8–10cm (3–4in).

☼ ◊

Polygala calcarea
Evergreen, prostrate, occasionally
upright, perennial. Has small, narrowly
oval leaves and pale to dark blue flowers
in loose heads in late spring and early
summer. Likes humus-rich soil. Suits a
trough. May be difficult to establish.
H 2.5cm (1in), S to 15cm (6in).

☼ ◊

Gentiana clusii
Gentiana gracilipes
Wahlenbergia albomarginata

▣ GREEN–YELLOW

Gunnera magellanica
Mat-forming perennial, grown for its
rounded, toothed leaves, often bronze-
tinged when young, on short, creeping
stems. Small, green, unisexual flowers,
with reddish-bracts, are borne on male
and female plants. Likes peaty soil.
H 2.5cm (1in), S to 30cm (12in).

☼◐ ◊

Mitella breweri
Neat, clump-forming, rhizomatous
perennial with slender, hairy stems
bearing small, pendent, tubular,
greenish-white flowers, with flared
mouths, in summer. Has lobed,
kidney-shaped, basal leaves.
H and S 15cm (6in).

☼ ◊

Sedum acre (Biting stonecrop,
Common stonecrop)
Evergreen, mat-forming perennial with
dense, spreading shoots, clothed in tiny,
fleshy, pale green leaves. Bears flat,
terminal heads of tiny, yellow flowers in
summer. Is invasive but easily controlled.
H 2.5–5cm (1–2in), S indefinite.

☼ ◊ ⓘ

Alchemilla alpina
Arctostaphylos alpina
Salix lindleyana
Satureja montana 'Prostrate White'

☐ YELLOW

***Asarina procumbens*,**
syn. *Antirrhinum asarina*
Semi-evergreen perennial with trailing
stems bearing soft, hairy leaves and
tubular, pale cream flowers, with yellow
palates, throughout summer. Dislikes
winter wet. Self seeds freely. H 1–2.5cm
(½–1in), S 23–30cm (9–12in).

☼ ◊

***Papaver fauriei*,**
syn. *P. miyabeanum* of gardens
Short-lived, clump-forming perennial
with basal rosettes of finely cut, hairy,
soft grey leaves. Bears pendent, open
cup-shaped, pale yellow flowers in
summer. Dislikes winter wet.
H and S 5–10cm (2–4in).

☼ ◊

Alyssum montanum
Alyssum wulfenianum
Calceolaria fothergillii
Calceolaria polyrrhiza

Polygala chamaebuxus
Evergreen, woody-based perennial
with tiny, hard, dark green leaves.
In late spring and early summer bears
many racemes of small, pea-like,
white-and-yellow flowers, sometimes
marked brown. Needs humus-rich soil.
H 5cm (2in), S 20cm (8in).

☀ ◊ Zone 7

Sedum acre 'Aureum'
Evergreen, dense, mat-forming perennial
with spreading shoots, yellow-tipped
in spring and early summer, and clothed
in tiny, fleshy, yellow leaves. Bears flat
heads of tiny, bright yellow flowers in
summer. Is invasive but easy to control.
H 2.5–5cm (1–2in), S indefinite.

☀ ◊ ⓘ

Scutellaria orientalis
Rhizomatous perennial with hairy,
grey, rooting stems. Has terminal
spikes of tubular, yellow flowers, with
brownish-purple lips, in summer.
Leaves are toothed and oval. May be
invasive in a small space.
H 5–10cm (2–4in), S to 23cm (9in).

☀ ◊

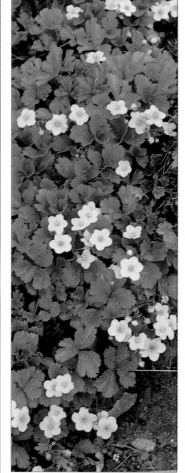

Waldsteinia ternata,
syn. *W. trifolia*
Semi-evergreen perennial with loose,
spreading mats of toothed, 3-parted
leaves. Bears saucer-shaped, yellow
flowers in late spring and early
summer. Is good on a bank.
H 10cm (4in), S 20–30cm (8–12in).

☀ ◊

Oenothera macrocarpa,
syn. *O. missouriensis*
Spreading perennial with stout stems
and oval leaves. Throughout summer
bears a succession of wide, bell-
shaped, yellow flowers, sometimes
spotted red, that open at sundown. H to
10cm (4in), S to 40cm (16in) or more.

☀ ◊

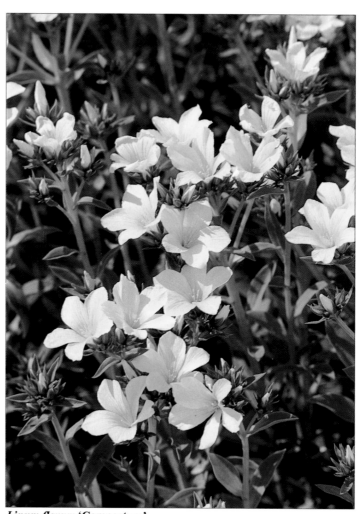

Linum flavum 'Compactum'
Shrubby perennial with narrow leaves
and terminal clusters of many upward-
facing, open funnel-shaped, single,
bright yellow flowers in summer.
Provide a sunny, sheltered position
and protection from winter wet.
H and S 15cm (6in).

☀ ◊

Potentilla eriocarpa
Clump-forming perennial with tufts
of oval, dark green leaves divided
into leaflets. Flat, single, pale yellow
flowers are borne throughout summer
just above leaves.
H 5–8cm (2–3in), S 10–15cm (4–6in).

☀ ◊

Calceolaria tenella
Vigorous, evergreen, prostrate
perennial with creeping, reddish stems
and oval, mid-green leaves, above
which rise small spikes of pouch-
shaped, red-spotted, yellow flowers
in summer. H 10cm (4in), S indefinite.

☀ ◌

ROCK PLANTS small SUMMER INTEREST

☐ YELLOW

☐☐ YELLOW–ORANGE

Genista sagittalis, syn.
Chamaespartium sagittale
Deciduous, semi-prostrate shrub with
winged stems bearing a few oval, dark
green leaves. Pea-like, yellow flowers
appear in dense, terminal clusters in early
summer, followed by hairy seed pods.
H 8cm (3in), S 30cm (12in) or more.

☀ ◌ Zone 5

Lysimachia nummularia 'Aurea'
(Golden creeping Jenny)
Prostrate perennial. Creeping, rooting
stems bear pairs of round, soft yellow
leaves, which later turn greenish-yellow
or green in dense shade. Has bright
yellow flowers in leaf axils in summer.
H 2.5–5cm (1–2in), S indefinite.

☀ ◌

Hypericum empetrifolium
var. *prostratum* of gardens
Evergreen, prostrate shrub with angled
branches and bright green leaves that
have curled margins. Bears flat heads
of small, bright yellow flowers in
summer. Needs winter protection.
H 2cm (¾in), S 30cm (12in).

☀ ◌ Zone 8

Hippocrepis comosa
(Horseshoe vetch)
Vigorous perennial with prostrate,
rooting stems bearing small, open
spikes of pea-like, yellow flowers in
summer and leaves divided into leaflets.
Self seeds freely and may spread
rapidly. H 5–8cm (2–3in), S indefinite.

☀ ◌

Calceolaria 'Walter Shrimpton'
Evergreen, mound-forming perennial
with glossy, dark green leaves. In early
summer bears short spikes of many
pouch-shaped, bronze-yellow flowers,
spotted rich brown, with white bands
across centres.
H 10cm (4in), S 23cm (9in).

☀ ◌

Cytisus ardoinoi, syn. *C. ardoinii*
Deciduous, hummock-forming,
dwarf shrub with arching stems. In late
spring and early summer, pea-like,
bright yellow flowers are produced in
pairs in leaf axils. Leaves are divided
into 3 leaflets.
H 10cm (4in), S 15cm (6in).

☀ ◌ ⚠ Zone 7

Potentilla aurea
Rounded perennial, with a woody
base, that in late summer bears loose
sprays of flat, single, yellow flowers
with slightly darker eyes. Leaves are
divided into oval, slightly silvered
leaflets. H 10cm (4in), S 20cm (8in).

☀ ◌

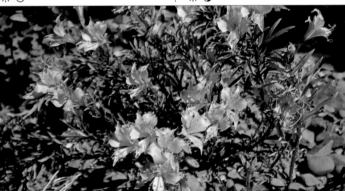

Alstroemeria hookeri
Tuberous perennial with narrow leaves
and loose heads of widely flared,
orange-suffused, pink flowers in
summer; upper petals are spotted and
blotched red and yellow. H 10–15cm
(4–6in), S 45–60cm (18–24in).
Min. –1°C (30°F).

☀ ◌ ⚠

PRIMULAS, illus. pp.272–3
Ranunculus montanus 'Molten Gold'
Saxifraga aizoides
Trollius pumilus, illus. p.373

Viola aetolica, illus. p.371
Viola biflora
Viola 'Jackanapes', illus. p.372
Viola lutea

Achillea x *lewisii* 'King Edward'
Crepis aurea, illus. p.359
Erigeron aurantiacus
Geum montanum

Helianthemum nummularium 'Amy Baring'
Hypericum cerastioides
Inula acaulis
Potentilla x *tonguei*

■■ PINK–BLUE

■■■ BLUE–ORANGE

Persicaria vacciniifolia,
syn. *Polygonum vacciniifolium*
Evergreen, perennial with woody, red
stems. Leaves are tinged red in autumn.
Bears deep pink or rose-red flowers in
late summer and autumn.
H 10–15cm (4–6in), S to 30cm (12in).

☼ ◊ ①

Gentiana sino-ornata
Evergreen, prostrate, spreading
perennial that, in autumn, bears
trumpet-shaped, rich blue flowers
singly at the ends of stems. Leaves are
narrow. Lift and divide every 3 years.
Needs moist soil. H in flower 5cm
(2in), S to 30cm (12in).

☼ ◊ pH

Gaultheria procumbens
Vigorous, evergreen sub-shrub with
prostrate stems carrying clusters of
oval, leathery leaves that turn red in
winter. In summer, solitary bell-shaped,
pink-flushed, white flowers appear in
leaf axils, followed by scarlet berries.
H 5–15cm (2–6in), S indefinite.
☼ ◊ pH ① Zone 5

**Gentiana × macaulayi 'Wells's
Variety'**, syn. *G.* 'Wellsii'
Evergreen, prostrate perennial with
trumpet-shaped, mid-blue flowers in
late summer and autumn. Spreading
stems are clothed in narrow, mid-green
leaves. Soil should be quite moist.
H in flower 5cm (2in), S 20cm (8in).
☼ ◊ pH

Oxalis lobata
Clump-forming perennial with woolly-
coated tubers. Mid-green leaves have
up to 5 rounded lobes. Produces
racemes of widely funnel-shaped,
bright yellow flowers, 1–2cm (½–¾in)
across, in late summer and autumn.
H 5cm (2in), S 8–10cm (3–4in).
☼ ◊

Nertera granadensis,
syn. *N. depressa* (Bead plant)
Prostrate perennial, dense mats of tiny,
bright green leaves. In early summer
bears minute, greenish-white flowers,
then many shiny, orange berries. Needs
ample moisture in summer. H to 1cm
(½in), S 10cm (4in). Min. 5°C (41°F).
☼ ◊

OTHER RECOMMENDED PLANTS:
Arctostaphylos nevadensis
Cornus canadensis
Sedum cauticola

Sedum ewersii

Carlina acaulis, illus. p.375
Gentiana ornata
Gentiana 'Susan Jane'
Sedum kamtschaticum

Sedum kamtschaticum 'Variegatum',
    illus. p.391
Solidago virgaurea subsp. *minuta*
Vaccinium nummularia

▭▭▤ WHITE–RED

Arabis procurrens 'Variegata'
Evergreen, mat-forming perennial with
small, oval, green leaves, splashed with
cream. Bears small, white flowers in
spring and early summer. May revert
to type, with plain green leaves.
H 2cm (¾in), S 30cm (12in).

☼ ◊

**Arctostaphylos uva-ursi
'Point Reyes'**
Evergreen, prostrate shrub with long
shoots and glossy leaves. In late spring
and early summer bears terminal
clusters of urn-shaped, pale pink to
white flowers, followed by red berries.
H 10cm (4in), S 50cm (20in).

☼ ◊ pH Zone 3

Pachysandra terminalis
Evergreen, creeping perennial that has
smooth leaves clustered at the ends of
short stems. Bears spikes of tiny, white
flowers, sometimes flushed purple, in
early summer. Makes excellent ground
cover in a moist or dry site.
H 10cm (4in), S 20cm (8in).

☀ ◊

Sedum lydium
Evergreen, mat-forming perennial
with reddish stems and narrow, fleshy,
often red-flushed leaves. Bears flat-
topped, terminal clusters of tiny, white
flowers in summer.
H 5cm (2in), S to 15cm (6in).

☼ ◊ ①

Jovibarba hirta,
syn. **Sempervivum hirtum**
Evergreen, mat-forming perennial with
rosettes of hairy, mid-green leaves,
often suffused red, and terminal
clusters of star-shaped, pale yellow
flowers in summer. Dislikes winter
wet. H 8–15cm (3–6in), S 10cm (4in).

☼ ◊

Arctostaphylos uva-ursi
Evergreen, low-growing shrub with
arching, intertwining stems clothed in
small, oval, bright green leaves. Bears
urn-shaped, pinkish-white flowers in
summer followed by scarlet berries.
H 10cm (4in), S 50cm (20in).

☼ ◊ pH Zone 1

Sedum obtusatum
Evergreen, prostrate perennial with
small, fat, succulent leaves that turn
bronze-red in summer. Loose, flat
sprays of tiny, bright yellow flowers
are borne in summer. Dislikes summer
wet. H 5cm (2in), S 10–15cm (4–6in).

☼ ◊ ①

Trifolium repens 'Purpurascens'
Vigorous, semi-evergreen, ground-cover
perennial, grown for its divided, bronze-
green foliage, variably edged bright
green. Produces heads of small, pea-
like, white blooms throughout summer.
Suits a wild bank. H in flower 8–12cm
(3–5in), S 20–30cm (8–12in) or more.

☼ ◊

OTHER RECOMMENDED PLANTS:
Ajuga reptans 'Multicolor', illus. p.303
Briggsia muscicola
Pachysandra terminalis 'Variegata'

Paronychia capitata

Acaena microphylla
Compact, mat-forming perennial, usually evergreen, with leaves divided into tiny leaflets, bronze-tinged when young. Heads of small flowers with spiny, dull red bracts are borne in summer and develop into decorative burs. H 5cm (2in), S 15cm (6in).

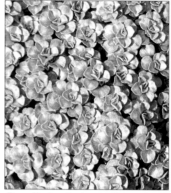

Raoulia hookeri var. **albo-sericea**
Evergreen, prostrate perennial with tiny rosettes of silver leaves. Flower heads appear briefly in summer as fragrant, yellow fluff. Is best in poor, gritty humus in an alpine house. Dislikes winter wet.
H to 1cm (½in), S 25cm (10in).

Artemisia schmidtiana 'Nana'
Prostrate perennial with fern-like, silver foliage. Has insignificant sprays of daisy-like, yellow flowers in summer. Is suitable for a wall or bank.
H 8cm (3in), S 20cm (8in).

Sempervivum tectorum (Common houseleek, Roof houseleek)
Vigorous, evergreen perennial with purple-tipped leaves, sometimes suffused deep red. In summer has clusters of star-shaped, reddish-purple flowers on stems 30cm (12in) tall.
H 10–15cm (4–6in), S to 20cm (8in).

Sempervivum arachnoideum (Cobweb houseleek)
Evergreen, mat-forming perennial. Rosettes of oval, fleshy leaves with red tips are covered in a web of white hairs. Bears loose clusters of star-shaped, rose-red flowers in summer. H 5–12cm (2–5in), S to 10cm (4in) or more.

Sedum spathulifolium
Evergreen, mat-forming perennial with rosettes of fleshy, green or silver leaves, usually strongly suffused bronze-red, and small clusters of tiny, yellow flowers borne just above foliage in summer. Tolerates shade.
H 5cm (2in), S indefinite.

Leucogenes grandiceps
Evergreen, dense, woody-based perennial with neat rosettes of downy, silver leaves. Yellow flower heads, within woolly, white bracts, are borne singly in spring or early summer.
H and S 10–15cm (4–6in).

Sempervivum ciliosum
Evergreen, mat-forming perennial with rosettes of hairy, grey-green leaves and, in summer, heads of small, star-shaped, yellow flowers. Dislikes winter wet; is best grown in an alpine house.
H 8–10cm (3–4in), S 10cm (4in).

Acaena 'Blue Haze'
Acaena buchananii
Acaena novae-zelandiae
Acantholimon venustum

Ajuga reptans 'Atropurpurea', illus. p.303
Raoulia eximia
Saxifraga stolonifera 'Tricolor'
Sempervivum 'Commander Hay'

Sempervivum grandiflorum
Thymus pseudolanuginosus
Tiarella wherryi
Viola odorata

ROCK PLANTS

389

□ GREEN

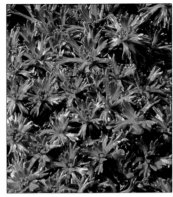

Raoulia australis
Evergreen, carpeting perennial
forming a hard mat of grey-green
leaves. Bears tiny, fluffy, sulphur-
yellow flower heads in summer.
H to 1cm (½in), S 25cm (10in).

☼ ◊

Acaena caesiiglauca
Vigorous, ground-cover perennial,
usually evergreen. Has hairy, glaucous
blue leaves divided into leaflets. Heads
of small flowers with spiny, brownish-
green bracts, borne in summer, develop
into brownish-red burs.
H 5cm (2in), S 75cm (30in) or more.

☼ ◊

Sempervivum montanum
Evergreen, mat-forming perennial with
dark green rosettes of fleshy, hairy
leaves. Star-shaped, wine-red flowers
are borne in terminal clusters in
summer. Is a variable plant that
hybridizes freely.
H 10–15cm (3–6in), S 10cm (4in).

☼ ◊

Azorella trifurcata,
syn. *A. nivalis*
Evergreen perennial forming tight, hard
cushions of tiny, leathery, oval leaves
in rosettes. Bears many small, stalkless
umbels of yellow flowers in summer.
H to 10cm (4in), S 15cm (6in).

☼ ◊

Asarum europaeum (Asarabacca)
Vigorous, evergreen, prostrate,
rhizomatous perennial with large,
kidney-shaped, leathery, glossy
leaves that hide tiny, brown flowers
appearing in spring.
H 15cm (6in), S indefinite.

☀ ◊

Sagina boydii
Evergreen perennial with hard cushions
of minute, stiff, bottle-green leaves
in small rosettes. Bears insignificant
flowers in summer. Is difficult and
slow-growing.
H 1cm (½in), S to 20cm (8in).

☼ ◊

Acantholimon glumaceum, illus. p.377
Arctostaphylos hookeri 'Monterey Carpet'
Asarum caudatum
Asarum hartwegii

Asarum shuttleworthii
Euonymus fortunei 'Kewensis'
Homogyne alpina
Jovibarba sobolifera

Mitchella repens
Thymus 'Porlock'
Thymus serpyllum
Thymus serpyllum 'Annie Hall'

Thymus serpyllum 'Elfin'

Sempervivum giuseppii
Vigorous, evergreen, prostrate perennial. Leaves are hairy, especially in spring, and have dark spots at tips. Produces terminal clusters of star-shaped, deep pink or red flowers in summer. H in flower 8–10cm (3–4in), S 10cm (4in).

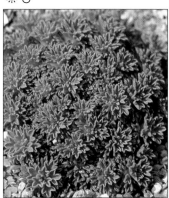

Bolax gummifera
Very slow-growing, evergreen perennial with neat rosettes of small, blue-green leaves forming extremely hard cushions. Insignificant, yellow flowers are rarely produced. Grows well on tufa.
H 2.5cm (1in), S 10cm (4in).

Raoulia haastii
Evergreen perennial forming low, irregular hummocks of minute leaves that are apple-green in spring, dark green in autumn and chocolate-brown in winter. Occasionally has small, fluffy, sulphur-yellow flower heads in summer. H to 1cm (½in), S 25cm (10in).

Sedum kamtschaticum 'Variegatum'
Semi-evergreen, prostrate perennial with fleshy leaves, edged with cream. Has tracery of fleshy stems and leaf buds in winter and loose, terminal clusters of orange-flushed, yellow flowers in early autumn. H 5–8cm (2–3in), S 20cm (8in).

Plantago nivalis
Evergreen perennial with neat rosettes of thick, silver-haired, green leaves. Bears spikes of insignificant, dull grey flowers in summer. Dislikes winter wet. H in leaf 2.5cm (1in), S 5cm (2in).

Paronychia kapela subsp. *serpyllifolia*
Evergreen, very compact, mat-forming perennial with minute, silver leaves. Inconspicuous flowers, borne in summer, are surrounded by papery, silver bracts. Is good for covering tufa. H to 1cm (½in), S 20cm (8in).

Sedum spathulifolium 'Cape Blanco'
Evergreen perennial with rosettes of fleshy leaves, frequently suffused purple. Tiny, yellow flowers appear above foliage in summer. Tolerates shade. H 5cm (2in), S indefinite.

Saxifraga exarata subsp. *moschata* 'Cloth of Gold'
Evergreen hummock-forming perennial, grown for its small, soft rosettes of bright golden foliage; produces best colour in shade. Has star-shaped, white flowers on slender stems in summer. H 10–15cm (4–6in), S 15cm (6in).

Leucogenes leontopodium
Thymus x *citriodorus* 'Aureus'

ROCK PLANTS

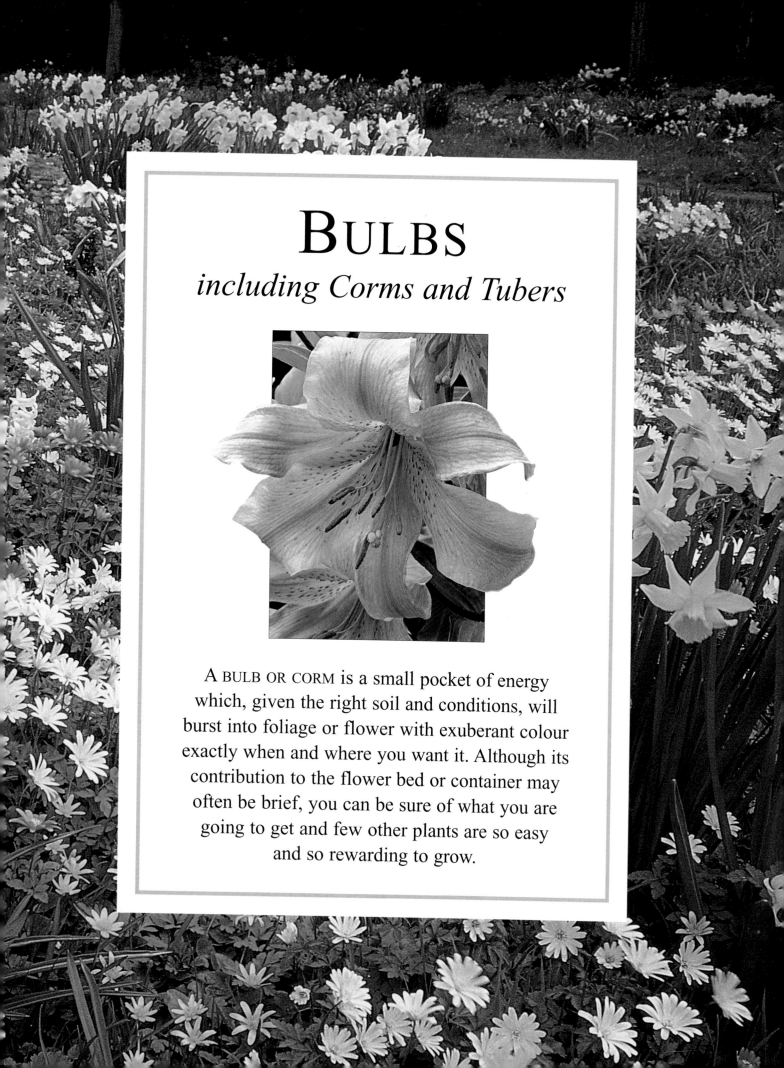

BULBS
including Corms and Tubers

A BULB OR CORM is a small pocket of energy which, given the right soil and conditions, will burst into foliage or flower with exuberant colour exactly when and where you want it. Although its contribution to the flower bed or container may often be brief, you can be sure of what you are going to get and few other plants are so easy and so rewarding to grow.

Bulbs

Bulbous plants are found throughout the world in habitats as varied as woodland and scrub, meadows, the sides of rivers and streams and on rocky hills and mountains. They provide some of the loveliest of flowers in the plant kingdom.

WHAT ARE BULBS?

The term bulb can be used to describe all swollen, underground, food-storage organs, and includes true bulbs as well as corms, rhizomes and tubers. True bulbs have fleshy scales – modified leaves or leaf bases – that are tightly overlapping and can be enclosed in a papery tunic, as in the narcissus, or be naked and loosely arranged, as in the lily. Corms are compressed and enlarged stem bases, usually enclosed in a fibrous or papery tunic, as in the crocus. Each corm lasts one year, and is replaced by a new one after flowering. Tubers, seen in plants such as cyclamen or dahlia, are solid, underground sections of modified stem or root and they seldom possess scales or tunics. Rhizomes are modified stems that creep at or just below soil level; they may be thin and wiry, as in lily-of-the-valley, (*Convallaria*), or swollen and fleshy, as in bearded irises.

Although a few bulbs are evergreen, most grow and bloom during a fairly short season, then die back to below ground level. Although they are then described as dormant, bulbs are far from quiescent, as they are ripening and developing the following year's flowers. This is why the siting of bulbs is often crucial to their continued success. Those bulbs that originated in dry, summer climates usually need warm, dry conditions when dormant to aid ripening and flower formation, while those bulbs from woodland or other damp, shaded habitats require a cool and slightly moist position. Since their leaves produce the food store for the following year, it is vital to leave bulb foliage in place until it has died down naturally.

DESIGNING WITH BULBS

There are bulbs to suit almost every garden site and design, from the tiny *Iris danfordiae* or the autumn daffodil (*Sternbergia lutea*) for the rock garden, to the carpeting erythroniums or the towering *Cardiocrinum giganteum* for the dappled shade of woodland gardens.

Bulbs are extremely versatile when used to define a garden style. The strongly upright habit and sculptural flower forms of many hybrid tulips, the precise formation of the dahlias or the flamboyant spires of gladioli are ideal in formal beds. Amaryllis, lilies and agapanthus, often grown in containers to add formal elegance to patio plantings, are equally at home among perennials and roses. Many bulbs thrive in pots, whether indoors or outside. Bulbs can be planted in informal groups in

CONTAINER COMBINATION
Left: Planting two different tulip bulbs together can highlight the beauty of both. Site the container where it can be appreciated at close quarters.

NATURALIZED BULBS
Above: Short turf sprinkled with naturalized early crocuses (here, cultivars of Crocus chrysanthus*) confirm the onset of spring.*

SUMMER COLOUR
Right: From mid-summer to early autumn, the robust, vibrantly coloured flower spikes of cormous perennial Crocosmia 'Lucifer' lend height and arching grace to the mixed border.

Spring beauty
Left: As spring eases into summer, the crown imperials (Fritillaria imperialis) *raise their majestic heads above a carpet of late-flowering narcissi and grape hyacinths.*

Autumn highlights
Below: Autumn-flowering colchicums here providing a startling finale to the season next to the scarlet-flowered Stachys coccinea.

a border with annuals, shrubs and perennials for year-round interest. In a woodland setting, drifts of white wake-robin (*Trillium grandiflorum*) and erythroniums look natural, while short turf spangled with crocuses or snake's-head fritillaries (*Fritillaria meleagris*) mimics their wild habitat to perfection.

MAINTAINING YEAR-ROUND INTEREST
Most bulbs have a distinct flowering season, which might be considered a disadvantage, yet with careful planning it is possible to extend or enhance this period of interest.

The first snowdrops (*Galanthus*) and early narcissus mark the onset of spring, and begin the gardening year. Most bulbs bloom in spring and early summer, producing splashes of colour before the summer-flowering shrubs and perennials reach their peak. The combination of certain genera, notably narcissus and tulip, can provide constant colour from spring to summer. Summer-flowering species such as *Galtonia candicans* and many alliums offer colourful highlights or allow subtle associations of contrasting form in the border. As summer draws to an end,

the crinums, nerines and crocosmias are at their best, and often continue to bloom into autumn.

The autumn-flowering crocuses, colchicums and cyclamen give their best displays with the onset of autumn rains, when much else in the garden is fading quietly. Some bulbs, for example *Arum italicum* 'Marmoratum' or *Cyclamen hederifolium*, have pretty marbled foliage that persists through winter. These, and early-flowering bulbs such as winter aconites (*Eranthis*), *Anemone blanda* and dwarf narcissus (*Narcissus* 'February Gold', for example) brighten the garden before most shrubs come into leaf. Grape hyacinths, chionodoxas, scillas and dwarf irises can create complementary carpets of blue beneath flowering shrubs such as corylopsis, forsythia and witch hazel (*Hamamelis*).

Many bulbs, notably lilies, also offer an intense fragrance and are ideal for blending with other highly scented plants such as roses or philadelphus.

SIZE CATEGORIES USED WITHIN THIS GROUP		
Large	Medium	Small
over 60cm (2ft)	23cm–60cm (9in–2ft)	up to 23cm (9in)

BULBS large SPRING INTEREST

☐ WHITE

Leucojum aestivum
(Summer snowflake)
Spring-flowering bulb with long, strap-shaped, semi-erect, basal leaves. Bears heads of pendent, long-stalked, bell-shaped, green-tipped, white flowers on leafless stems. H 50cm–1m (1½–3ft), S 10–12cm (4–5in).

☀ ◑

Fritillaria raddeana
Robust, spring-flowering bulb with lance-shaped leaves in whorls on lower half of stem. Has a head of up to 20 widely conical, pale yellow or greenish-yellow flowers, 3–4cm (1¼–1½in) long, topped by a 'crown' of small leaves. H to 1m (3ft), S 15–23cm (6–9in).

☀ ◊

■■ PURPLE–ORANGE

Fritillaria persica
Spring-flowering bulb with narrow, lance-shaped, grey-green leaves along stem. Produces a spike of 10–20 or more narrow, bell-shaped, blackish- or brownish-purple flowers, 1.5–2cm (⅝–¾in) long. H to 1.5m (5ft), S 10cm (4in).

☀ ◊

Fritillaria recurva
(Scarlet fritillary)
Spring-flowering bulb with whorls of narrow, lance-shaped, grey-green leaves. Bears a spike of up to 10 narrow, yellow-chequered, orange or red flowers with flared tips. H to 1m (3ft), S 8–10cm (3–4in).

☀ ◊

Fritillaria verticillata
Spring-flowering bulb with slender leaves in whorls up stem, which bears a loose spike of 1–15 bell-shaped, white flowers, 2–4cm (¾–1½in) long and chequered green or brown. H to 1m (3ft), S 8–10cm (3–4in).

☀ ◊

Fritillaria imperialis
(Crown imperial)
Spring-flowering bulb with glossy, pale green leaves carried in whorls on leafy stems. Has up to 5 widely bell-shaped, orange flowers crowned by small, leaf-like bracts. H to 1.5m (5ft), S 23–30cm (9–12in).

☀ ◊

OTHER RECOMMENDED PLANTS:
Albuca canadensis
Canna iridiflora, illus. p.403
Chasmanthe aethiopica

Fritillaria imperialis 'Lutea'
Fritillaria imperialis 'Rubra Maxima'
Hymenocallis x *festalis*
Phaedranassa carmioli, illus. p.400

BULBS

BULBS large SUMMER INTEREST

⬜ WHITE

Crinum × powellii 'Album'
Late summer- or autumn-flowering
bulb, with a long neck, producing a
group of semi-erect, strap-shaped
leaves. Leafless flower stems carry
heads of fragrant, widely funnel-
shaped, white flowers.
H to 1m (3ft), S 60cm (2ft).

Hymenocallis × macrostephana
Evergreen, spring- or summer-
flowering bulb with strap-shaped,
semi-erect, basal leaves. Bears fragrant,
white or cream- to greenish- yellow
flowers, 15–20cm (6–8in) wide.
H 80cm (32in), S 30–45cm (12–18in).
Min. 15°C (59°F).

Eucomis pallidiflora (Giant pineapple flower, Giant pineapple lily)
Summer-flowering bulb with sword-
shaped, crinkly edged, semi-erect, basal
leaves. Bears a dense spike of star-
shaped, greenish-white flowers, crowned
with a cluster of leaf-like bracts.
H to 75cm (30in), S 30–60cm (12–24in).

**Zantedeschia aethiopica 'Green
Goddess'**
Very robust, summer-flowering tuber
with arrow-shaped, semi-erect, basal,
deep green leaves. Bears a succession of
green spathes each with a large, central,
green-splashed, white area. H 45cm–1m
(1½–3ft), S 45–60cm (1½–2ft).

Galtonia candicans
(Summer hyacinth)
Late summer- or autumn-flowering
bulb with widely strap-shaped, fleshy,
semi-erect, basal, grey-green leaves.
Leafless stem has a spike of up to 30
pendent, short-tubed, white flowers.
H 1–1.2m (3–4ft), S 18–23cm (7–9in).

**Zantedeschia aethiopica
'Crowborough'**
Early to mid-summer-flowering tuber
with arrow-shaped, semi-erect, basal,
deep green leaves. Produces a
succession of arum-like, white spathes,
each with a yellow spadix.
H 45cm–1m (1½–3ft), S 35–45cm.

Camassia leichtlinii
Tuft-forming bulb with long, narrow,
erect, basal leaves. Each leafless stem
bears a dense spike of 6-petalled, star-
shaped, bluish-violet or white flowers,
4–8in (1½–3in) across, in summer.
H 1–1.5m (3–5ft), S 20–30cm (8–12in).

Camassia leichtlinii 'Semiplena'
Tuft-forming bulb with long, narrow,
erect, basal leaves. Each leafless stem
carries a dense spike of narrow-
petalled, double, creamy-white flowers,
4–8cm (1½–3in) across, in summer.
H 1–1.5m (3–5ft), S 20–30cm (8–12in).

OTHER RECOMMENDED PLANTS:
Camassia quamash
Cardiocrinum giganteum, illus. p.398
Chlorogalum pomeridianum

DAHLIAS, illus. pp.406–407
GLADIOLI, illus. p.399
LILIES, illus. pp.404–405
Polianthes tuberosa

Nomocharis saluenensis

Crinum moorei
Summer-flowering bulb, long neck, up
to 1m (3ft) tall, and strap-shaped, semi-
erect, grey-green leaves grouped at neck
top. Leafless flower stems bear heads of
long-tubed, funnel-shaped, white to deep
pink flowers. H 50–70cm (20–28in), S
60cm (24in).   Min. 5°C (41°F).

☼ ◊ ⓘ

Nectaroscordum siculum subsp.
bulgaricum, syn. *N. dioscoridis*
Late spring- to early summer-
flowering bulb with pendent, bell-
shaped, white flowers, flushed purple-
red and green. In seed, stalks bend
upwards, holding dry seed pods erect.
H to 1.2m (4ft), S 30–45cm (1–1½ft).

☼ ◊

Cardiocrinum giganteum
(Giant lily)
Stout, leafy-stemmed bulb. In summer
has long spikes of fragrant, slightly
pendent, cream flowers, 15cm (6in)
long, with purple-red streaks inside,
then brown seed pods. H to 3m (10ft),
S 75cm–1.1m (2½–3½ft).

☼ ◊

Eucomis comosa
Clump-forming bulb with strap-shaped,
wavy-margined leaves, spotted purple
beneath. Purple-spotted stem bears
a spike of white or greenish-white,
sometimes pink-tinted flowers, with
purple ovaries. H to 70cm (28in),
S 30–60cm (12–24in).

☼ ◊

Nomocharis pardanthina,
syn. *N. mairei*
Summer-flowering bulb with stems
bearing whorls of lance-shaped leaves
and up to 15 outward-facing, white or
pale pink flowers, each with purple
blotches and a dark purple eye.
H to 1m (3ft), S 12–15cm (5–6in).

☼ ◊

Crinum × powellii
Late summer- or autumn-flowering
bulb with a long neck producing a
group of strap-shaped, semi-erect
leaves. Leafless flower stems bear
heads of fragrant, widely funnel-
shaped, pink flowers.
H to 1m (3ft), S 60cm (2ft).

☼ ◊ ⓘ

Gladioli

Gladiolus hybrids produce excellent flowers for garden decoration, flower arrangements and exhibition. They are divided into the Grandiflorus Group, with long, densely packed flower spikes, categorized as miniature, small, medium-sized, large or giant according to the width of the lowest flowers, and the Primulinus and Nanus Groups, with loose spikes of small flowers. (See also the Plant Dictionary.)

G. **'Ice Cap'**
(large)

G. **'White Ice'**
(medium)

G. **'The Bride'**
(Nanus Group)

G. **'Halley'**
(Nanus Group)

G. **'Amanda Mahy'**
(Nanus Group)

G. **'Rose Supreme'**
(giant)

G. **'Miss America'**
(medium)

G. **'Inca Queen'**
(large)

G. **'Anna Leorah'**
(large)

G. **'Pulchritude'**
(medium)

G. **'Mi Mi'** (small)

G. **'Pink Lady'**
(large)

G. **'Drama'**
(large)

G. **'Black Lash'**
(small)

G. **'Victor Borge'**
(large)

G. **'Vaucluse'**
(giant)

G. **'Stardust'**
(miniature)

G. **'Green Woodpecker'**
(medium)

G. **'Tesoro'**
(medium)

G. **'Esta Bonita'**
(giant)

G. **'Melodie'**
(small)

G. **'Peter Pears'**
(large)

G. **'Little Darling'**
(Primulinus Group)

■ PINK–RED

Notholirion campanulatum
Early summer-flowering bulb with long, narrow leaves in a basal tuft. Leafy stem bears a spike of 10–40 pendent, funnel-shaped flowers, each 4–5cm (1½–2in) long, with green-tipped, deep rose-purple petals. H to 1m (3ft), S 8–10cm (3–4in).

Watsonia borbonica
Very robust, summer-flowering corm with narrowly sword-shaped leaves both at base and on stem. Produces a loose, branched spike of rich pink flowers, with 6 spreading, pointed, rose-red lobes. H 1–1.5m (3–5ft), S 45–60cm (1½–2ft). Min. 2°C (35°F).

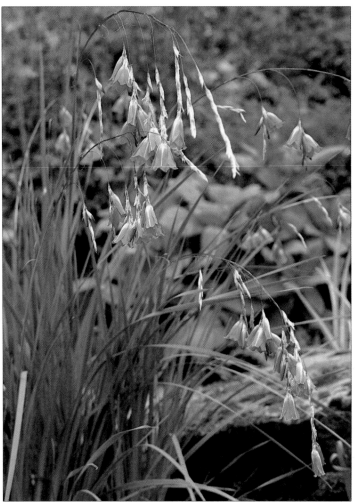

Dierama pulcherrimum
Upright, summer-flowering corm with long, narrow, strap-like, evergreen leaves, above which rise elegant, arching, wiry stems bearing funnel-shaped, deep pink flowers. Prefers deep, rich soil. H 1.5m (5ft), S 30cm (1ft).

Watsonia pillansii, syn. W. beatricis
Summer-flowering corm with long, sword-shaped, erect leaves, some basal and some on stem. Stem carries a dense, branched spike of tubular, orange-red flowers, each 6–8cm (2½–3in) long, with 6 short lobes. H to 1m (3ft), S 30–45cm (1–1½ft). Min. 2°C (35°F).

Gladiolus italicus, syn. G. segetum
Early summer-flowering corm with a fan of erect, sword-shaped leaves from the basal part of stem. Carries a loose spike of up to 20 pinkish-purple flowers, 4–5cm (1½–2in) long. H to 1m (3ft), S 10–15cm (4–6in).

Gladiolus communis subsp. byzantinus, syn. G. byzantinus
Early summer-flowering corm with a dense spike of up to 20 deep purplish-red or purplish-pink flowers, 4–6cm (1½–2½in) long. Produces a fan of sword-shaped, erect, basal leaves. H to 70cm (28in), S 10–15cm (4–6in).

Phaedranassa carmioli
Spring- and summer-flowering bulb with upright, elliptic or lance-shaped, basal leaves. Bears a head of 6–10 pendent, pinkish-red flowers, with green bases and yellow-edged, green lobes at each apex. H 50–70cm (20–28in), S 30–45cm (12–18in). Min. 7°C (45°F).

Alstroemeria Margaret ('Stacova')
Mid- to late summer-flowering tuber with narrow, lance-shaped, twisted, bright green leaves. Stout, leafy stems bear widely flared, funnel-shaped, deep red flowers. H 1m (3ft), S 60cm–1m (2–3ft).

x *Amarcrinum memoria-corsii*, illus. p.408
DAHLIAS, illus. pp.406–407
LILIES, illus. pp.404–405
Watsonia merianiae

BULBS

Dracunculus vulgaris, syn. *Arum dracunculus* (Dragon's arum)
Spring- and summer-flowering tuber with deeply divided leaves at apex of thick, blotched stem. A blackish-maroon spadix protrudes from a deep maroon-purple spathe, 35cm (14in) long.
H to 1m (3ft), S 45–60cm (1½–2ft).

☼ ◊

Gloriosa superba 'Rothschildiana' (Glory lily)
Deciduous, summer-flowering, tuberous, tendril climber. Upper leaf axils each bear a large flower that has 6 reflexed, red petals with scalloped, yellow edges. H to 2m (6ft), S 30–45cm (1–1½ft). Min. 8°C (46°F).

☼ ◊ ①

Crocosmia 'Bressingham Blaze'
Clump-forming, late summer-flowering corm with sword-shaped, pleated, basal, erect leaves. Branched stem bears widely funnel-shaped, fiery-red flowers.
H 75cm (30in), S 15–20cm (6–8in).

☼ ◊

Scadoxus multiflorus subsp. **katherinae**, syn. *Haemanthus katherinae* (Blood flower)
Very robust, clump-forming bulb with lance-shaped, wavy-edged leaves. Bears an umbel of up to 200 red flowers in summer. H to 1.2m (4ft), S 30–45cm (1–1½ft). Min. 10°C (50°F).

◐ ◊

Canna 'Assaut', syn. *C.* 'Assault'
Summer-flowering, rhizomatous perennial with stout, leafy stems bearing wide, purple-green leaves. Has a spike of scarlet flowers surrounded by purple bracts. H to 1.2m (4ft), S 45–60cm (1½–2ft). Min. 2°C (35°F).

☼ ◐

Allium stipitatum
Summer-flowering bulb with stout stems and strap-like, semi-erect, basal leaves. Carries 50 or more star-shaped, purplish-pink flowers in a spherical umbel, 8–12cm (3–5in) across. H to 1–1.5m (3–4ft), S 15–20cm (6–8in).

☼ ◊ ①

Crocosmia 'Lucifer'
Robust, clump-forming corm with sword-shaped, erect, basal, bright green leaves. Bears funnel-shaped, deep rich red flowers in dense, branching spikes in mid-summer.
H to 1m (3ft), S 20–25cm (8–10in).

☼ ◊

Crocosmia masoniorum
Robust, clump-forming corm with erect, basal, deep green leaves, pleated lengthways. Erect, branched stem has a horizontal, upper part which carries upright, reddish-orange flowers in summer-autumn.
H to 1.5m (5ft), S 30–45cm (1–1½ft).

☼ ◊

Dierama pendulum, syn. *D. ensifolium* (Angel's fishing rod)
Clump-forming, late summer-flowering corm with arching, basal leaves. Bears pendulous, loose racemes of bell-shaped, pinkish-purple flowers, 2.5cm (1in) long.
H to 1.5m (5ft), S 15–20cm (6–8in).

☼ ◐

Allium giganteum
Robust, summer-flowering bulb with long, wide, semi-erect, basal leaves. Produces a stout stem with a dense, spherical umbel, 12cm (5in) across, of 50 or more star-shaped, purple flowers. H to 2m (6ft), S 30–35cm (12–14in).

Allium x hollandicum,
syn. *A. aflatunense* of gardens
Summer-flowering bulb with mid-green, basal leaves dying away by flowering time. Carries numerous star-shaped, purplish-pink flowers in a dense, spherical umbel, 10cm (4in) across. H 1m (3ft), S 10cm (4in).

Aristea major, syn. *A. thyrsiflora*
Robust, evergreen, clump-forming rhizome with sword-shaped, erect leaves, to 2.5cm (1in) across, and dense spikes of purple-blue flowers on short stalks in summer. H to 1m (3ft), S 45–60cm (1½–2ft). Min. 2°C (35°F).

Dichelostemma congestum,
syn. *Brodiaea congesta*
Early summer-flowering bulb with semi-erect, basal leaves dying away when a dense head of funnel-shaped, purple flowers, each 1.5–2cm (⅝–¾in) long, appears.
H to 1m (3ft), S 8–10cm (3–4ft).

Neomarica caerulea
Summer-flowering rhizome with sword-shaped, semi-erect leaves in basal fans. Stems each bear a leaf-like bract and a succession of iris-like, blue flowers, with white, yellow and brown central marks. H to 1m (3ft), S 1–1.5m (3–5ft). Min. 10°C (50°F).

Dietes bicolor
Evergreen, tuft-forming, summer-flowering rhizome. Tough, long, narrow, erect, basal leaves. Branching stems each bear a succession of flattish, iris-like, pale to mid-yellow flowers; each large petal has a brown patch. H to 1m (3ft), S 30–60cm (1–2ft). Min. 2°C (35°F).

Galtonia viridiflora
Clump-forming, summer-flowering bulb with widely strap-shaped, fleshy, semi-erect, basal, grey-green leaves. Leafless stem bears a spike of up to 30 pendent, short-tubed, funnel-shaped, pale green flowers.
H 1–1.2m (3–4ft), S 18–23cm (7–9in).

Arisaema consanguineum
Summer-flowering tuber with robust, spotted stems and erect, umbrella-like leaves with narrow leaflets. Produces purplish-white- or white-striped, green spathes, 15–20cm (6–8in) long, and bright red berries.
H to 1m (3ft), S 30–45cm (1–1½ft).

Fritillaria chitralensis
Spring- to early summer-flowering bulb with ovate, mid- to light green leaves and open umbels of 4 or 5 conical, pendent, bright yellow flowers. Similar to *F. imperialis*.
H 50–80cm (20–32in), S 10cm (4in).

Moraea ramosissima
Late spring- to early summer-flowering corm with numerous, semi-erect, narrowly linear, channelled, basal leaves. Yellow flowers, with deeper yellow marks on the inner petals, on many-branched stems. H 50–120cm (20–48in), S 10cm (4in). Min. 2°C (35°F).

Zantedeschia elliottiana
(Golden arum lily)
Summer-flowering tuber with heart-shaped, semi-erect, basal leaves with transparent marks. Bears a 15cm (6in) long, yellow spathe surrounding a yellow spadix. H 60cm–1m (2–3ft), S 45–60cm (1½–2ft). Min. 10°C (50°F).

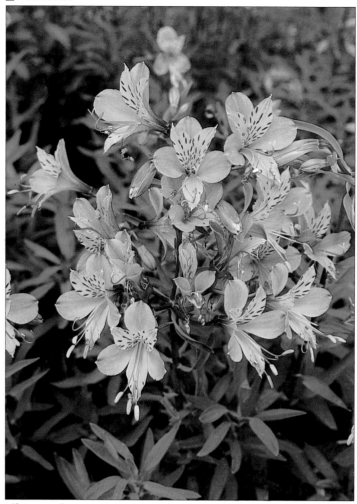

***Crocosmia* 'Golden Fleece',**
syn. *C.* 'Citronella' of gardens
Clump-forming, late summer-
flowering corm with sword-shaped,
erect, basal, grey-green leaves.
Flowers are funnel-shaped and clear
golden-yellow. H 60–75cm (24–30in),
S 15–20cm (6–8in).

☼ ◊

***Alstroemeria aurea*,**
syn. *A. aurantiaca*
Summer-flowering, tuberous perennial
with narrow, lance-shaped, twisted
leaves and loose heads of orange
flowers, tipped with green and
streaked dark red.
H to 1m (3ft), S 60cm–1m (2–3ft).

☼ ◊ ⓘ

BULBS

Moraea huttonii
Summer-flowering corm with long,
narrow, semi-erect, basal leaves.
Tough stem bears a succession of iris-
like, yellow flowers, 5–7cm (2–3in)
across, with brown marks near the
centre. H 75cm–1m (2½–3ft),
S 15–25cm (6–10in).

☼ ◊

***Crocosmia* 'Star of the East'**
Late summer-flowering corm with
sword-shaped, erect, basal, mid-green
leaves. Bears horizontal-facing, funnel-
shaped, clear orange flowers, each with
a paler orange centre, on branched
stems. H 70cm (28in), S 8cm (3in).

☼ ◊

Littonia modesta
Deciduous, summer-flowering,
tuberous, scandent climber. Has slender
stems bearing lance-shaped leaves with
tendrils at apex. Leaf axils bear pendent,
bell-shaped, orange flowers, 4–5cm
(1½–2in) across. H 1–2m (3–6ft),
S 10–15cm (4–6in). Min. 16°C (61°F).

☼ ◊

Canna iridiflora
Very robust, spring- or summer-
flowering, rhizomatous perennial with
broad, oblong leaves and spikes of
pendent, long-tubed, reddish-pink or
orange flowers, each 10–15cm (4–6in)
long, with reflexed petals. H 3m (10ft),
S 45–60cm (1½–2ft). Min. 2°C (35°F).

☼ ◊

Alstroemeria 'Walter Fleming'
DAHLIAS, illus. pp.406–407
GLADIOLI, illus. p.399
Gladiolus papilio, illus. p.408

Gloriosa superba
Moraea spathulata

Belamcanda chinensis
Canna 'Orange Perfection'
Crocosmia aurea
Crocosmia paniculata

DAHLIAS, illus. pp.406–407
GLADIOLI, illus. p.399

403

Lilies

Lilies (*Lilium* species and cultivars) are graceful plants and bring elegance to the summer border. Their attractive, flamboyant flowers are in various shapes, some nodding, others upright or trumpet-shaped, others in the distinctive turkscap form (with recurving petals), and are borne usually several per stem. Many have a distinctive, powerful fragrance, though a few species are unpleasantly scented. Most widely grown are the numerous hybrids, available in a dazzling array of colours – white, pink, red and rich shades of yellow and orange – but among the species are several that have been undeservedly neglected. Lily flowers are often attractively spotted with a darker or contrasting colour, or have conspicuous stamens or pollen. Lilies thrive in sun and well-drained soil. Once established, they are best left undisturbed, as the bulbs are easily damaged.

L. 'Mont Blanc'

L. 'Bronwen North'

L. 'Sterling Star'

L. martagon

L. 'Star Gazer'

L. 'Casa Blanca'

L. martagon var. *album*

L. 'Bright Star'

L. rubellum

L. 'Côte d'Azur'

L. candidum

L. Olympic Hybrids

L. Imperial Gold Group

L. mackliniae

L. 'Black Magic'

L. 'Corsage'

L. 'Montreux'

L. 'Journey's End'

L. longiflorum

L. duchartrei

L. speciosum var. *rubrum*

L. regale

L. auratum var. *platyphyllum*

L. 'Magic Pink'

L. 'Angela North'

L. × *dalhansonii*

BULBS

L. 'Black Beauty'

L. nepalense

L. 'Rosemary North'

L. 'Amber Gold'

L. lancifolium var. *splendens*

L. 'Lady Bowes Lyon'

L. hansonii

L. 'Brushmarks'

L. tsingtauense

L. 'Karen North'

L. Golden Splendor Group

L. canadense

L. pyrenaicum var. *rubrum*

L. 'Roma'

L. monadelphum

L. 'Apollo'

L. bulbiferum var. *croceum*

L. chalcedonicum

L. Golden Clarion Group

L. 'Destiny'

L. pyrenaicum

L. 'Enchantment'

L. 'Harmony'

L. pardalinum

L. 'Connecticut King'

L. superbum

L. medeoloides

L. davidii var. *willmottiae*

Dahlias

The variety of border hybrids offers a dazzling display of colour and form to every gardener, and no special skills are required to cultivate or propagate them. In colour the flowers range from deep reds, crimsons, purples, hues of mauve, and vibrant pinks to whites, apricots, oranges, bronzes, and brilliant scarlets, in size from the tiny pompons of 52mm (2in) to huge exhibition blooms greater than 254mm (10in) across.

Dahlias are excellent for providing cut flowers and will bloom vigorously throughout summer until the first frosts – in the right conditions a single plant may produce up to 100 blooms. Their various flower types (shown below) form the basis of the recognized groups.

Single – each flower usually has 8–10 broad petals surrounding an open, central disc.

Anemone – fully double flowers each have one or more rings of flattened ray petals surrounding a dense group of shorter, tubular petals, usually longer than disc petals found in single dahlias.

Collerette – single flowers each have broad, outer petals, usually 8–10, and an inner 'collar' of smaller petals surrounding an open, central disc.

Water-lily – fully double flowers have large, generally sparse ray petals, which are flat or with slightly incurved or recurved margins, giving the flower a flat appearance.

Decorative – fully double flowers have broad, flat petals that incurve slightly at their margins and usually reflex to the stem.

Ball – flattened to spherical, fully double flowers have densely packed, almost tubular petals.

Pompon – flattened to spherical, fully double flowers are no more than 52mm (2in) across – a miniature form of ball flowers.

Cactus – fully double flowers have narrow, pointed petals that can be straight or curl inwards and have recurved edges for more than two-thirds of their length.

Semi-cactus – fully double flowers are similar to cactus flowers but have broader-based petals, the edges of which are generally recurved towards their tips.

Miscellaneous – flowers are in a wide range of unclassified types, including orchid-like (shown right), single and double forms.

D. 'Rhonda' (pompon)

D. 'Gay Princess' (decorative)

D. 'Vicky Crutchfield' (water-lily)

D. 'Mi Wong' (pompon)

D. 'Pearl of Heemstede' (water-lily)

D. 'Pontiac' (cactus)

D. 'Noreen' (pompon)

D. 'Fascination' (miscellaneous)

D. 'Pink Symbol' (semi-cactus)

D. 'Pink Shirley Alliance' (cactus)

D. 'White Klankstad' (cactus)

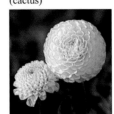

D. 'White Ballet' (water-lily)

D. 'Easter Sunday' (collerette)

D. 'Small World' (pompon)

D. 'Wootton Cupid' (ball)

D. 'White Alva's' (decorative)

D. 'Hayley Jayne'
(semi-cactus)

D. 'Zorro'
(decorative)

D. 'Moor Place'
(pompon)

D. 'Butterball'
(decorative)

D. 'Wootton Impact'
(semi-cactus)

D. 'Grenidor Pastelle'
(semi-cactus)

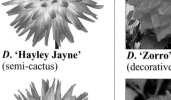

D. 'Pink Jupiter'
(semi-cactus)

D. 'Comet' (anemone)

D. 'Hamari Katrina'
(semi-cactus)

D. 'Mark Hardwick'
(decorative)

D. 'East Anglian'
(decorative)

D. 'Yelno Firelight'
(water-lily)

D. 'Lavender Athalie'
(cactus)

D. 'Bishop of Llandaff'
(miscellaneous)

**D. 'Davenport Sun-
light'** (semi-cactus)

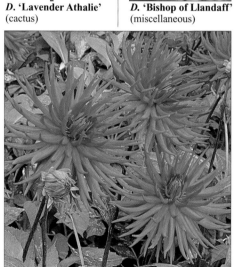

D. 'Hillcrest Royal'
(cactus)

D. 'Yellow Hammer'
(single)

D. 'Wanda's Capella'
(decorative)

D. 'Hamari Gold'
(decorative)

D. 'Clair de Lune'
(collerette)

D. 'Jeanette Carter'
(decorative)

D. 'So Dainty'
(semi-cactus)

D. 'Jescot Julie'
(miscellaneous)

D. 'Jim Branigan'
(semi-cactus)

D. 'Preston Park'
(single)

D. 'Shandy'
(semi-cactus)

D. 'Kathryn's Cupid'
(ball)

D. 'Whale's Rhonda'
(pompon)

D. 'Chimborazo'
(collerette)

D. 'Hamari Accord'
(semi-cactus)

D. 'Shirley Alliance'
(cactus)

**D. 'Biddenham
Sunset'** (decorative)

Amaryllis belladonna 'Hathor'
Autumn-flowering bulb with a stout, purple stem bearing fragrant, pure white flowers, 10cm (4in) long, with yellow throats. Strap-shaped, semi-erect, basal leaves appear in late winter or spring. H 50–80cm (20–32in), S 30–45cm (12–18in).

☼ ◊

× Amarcrinum memoria-corsii,
syn. × *A. howardii*,
× *Crinodonna corsii*
Evergreen, clump-forming bulb with wide, semi-erect, basal leaves. Stout stems carry fragrant, rose-pink flowers in loose heads in late summer and autumn. H and S to 1m (3ft).

☼ ◊

Amaryllis belladonna
(Belladonna lily)
Autumn-flowering bulb with a stout, purple stem bearing fragrant, funnel-shaped, pink flowers, 10cm (4in) long. Forms strap-shaped, semi-erect, basal leaves after flowering. H 50–80cm (20–32in), S 30–45cm (12–18in).

☼ ◊

Erythronium oregonum
Clump-forming, spring-flowering tuber with 2 semi-erect, mottled, basal leaves. Has up to 3 pendent, white flowers, with yellow eyes and often brown rings near centre; petals reflex as flowers open. Increases rapidly by offsets.
H to 35cm (14in), S 12cm (5in).

☼ ◊

× Amarygia parkeri,
syn. × *Brunsdonna parkeri*
Early autumn-flowering bulb. Stout stem carries a large head of funnel-shaped, deep rose flowers with yellow and white throats. Produces strap-shaped, semi-erect, basal leaves after flowering.
H to 1m (3ft), S 60cm–1m (2–3ft).

☼ ◊

Gladiolus papilio,
syn. *G. purpureoauratus*
Clump-forming, summer- or autumn-flowering corm with stolons. Bears up to 10 yellow or white flowers, suffused violet, with hooded, upper petals and darker yellow patches on lower petals.
H to 1m (3ft), S 15cm (6in).

☼ ◊

Allium neapolitanum,
syn. *A. cowanii*
Spring-flowering bulb with narrow, semi-erect leaves on the lower quarter of flower stems. Stems each develop an umbel, 5–10cm (2–4in) across, of up to 40 white flowers. H 20–50cm (8–20in), S 10–12cm (4–5in).

☼ ◊ !

Calochortus venustus
Late spring-flowering bulb with 1 or 2 narrow, erect leaves near the base of the branched stem. Bears 1–4 white, yellow, purple or red flowers, with a dark red, yellow-margined blotch on each large petal. H 20–60cm (8–24in), S 5–10cm (2–4in).

☼ ◊

OTHER RECOMMENDED PLANTS:
Crinum macowanii
Crinum × powellii, illus. p.398
Crinum × powellii 'Album', illus. p.397

Crocosmia masoniorum, illus. p.401
Galtonia candicans, illus. p.397
Urginea maritima
Worsleya rayneri

OTHER RECOMMENDED PLANTS:
Crinum asiaticum, illus. p.419
DAFFODILS, illus. pp.416–18
Freesia 'White Swan'

Hippeastrum 'White Dazzler'
Hymenocallis narcissiflora, illus. p.420
Leucojum aestivum, illus. p.396
Ornithogalum umbellatum

BULBS

Erythronium californicum 'White Beauty'

Vigorous, clump-forming tuber with basal, mottled leaves. In spring has a loose spike of 1–10 reflexed, white flowers, each with a brown ring near the centre. Spreads rapidly. H 20–30cm (8–12in), S 10–12cm (4–5in).

Erythronium hendersonii

Spring-flowering tuber with 2 semi-erect, basal, brown- and green-mottled leaves. Flower stem carries up to 10 lavender or lavender-pink flowers, with reflexed petals and deep purple, central eyes. H 20–30cm (8–12in), S 10–12cm (4–5in).

Calochortus albus
(Fairy lantern, Globe lily)

Spring-flowering bulb with long, narrow, erect, grey-green leaves near the base of the loosely branched stem. Each branch carries a pendent, globose, white or pink flower. H 20–50cm (8–20in), S 5–10cm (2–4in).

Pamianthe peruviana

Evergreen, spring-flowering bulb with a stem-like neck and semi-erect leaves with drooping tips. Stem has a head of 2–4 fragrant, white flowers, each with a bell-shaped cup and 6 spreading petals. H 50cm (20in), S 45–60cm (18–24in). Min. 12°C (54°F).

Allium unifolium

Late spring-flowering bulb with one semi-erect, basal, grey-green leaf. Each flower stem carries a domed umbel, 5cm (2in) across, of up to 30 purplish-pink flowers. H to 30cm (12in), S 8–10cm (3–4in).

Erythronium revolutum
Freesia corymbosa
Hippeastrum 'Apple Blossom', illus. p.425
Hippeastrum 'Bouquet'

Rhodophiala advena, illus. p.421

BULBS

Tulips

Tulips suit a wide range of planting schemes and are excellent in the rock garden, in formal bedding, as elegant cut flowers and for containers. Their bold flowers are generally simple in outline and held upright, with colours that are often bright and strong. Many of the species deserve to be more widely grown, alongside the large variety of hybrids now available. *Tulipa* is classified in 15 divisions, described below.

Div.1 Single early – cup-shaped, single flowers, often opening wide in the sun, are borne from early to mid-spring.

Div.2 Double early – long-lasting, double flowers open wide in early and mid-spring.

Div.3 Triumph – sturdy stems bear rather conical, single flowers, becoming more rounded, in mid- and late spring.

Div.4 Darwin hybrids – large, single flowers are borne on strong stems from mid- to late spring.

Div.5 Single late – single flowers, variable but usually with pointed petals, are borne in late spring and very early summer.

Div.6 Lily-flowered – strong stems bear narrow-waisted, single flowers, with long, pointed, often reflexed petals, in late spring.

Div.7 Fringed – flowers are similar to those in Div.6, but have fringed petals.

Div.8 Viridiflora – variable, single flowers, with partly greenish petals, are borne in late spring.

Div.9 Rembrandt – flowers are similar to those in Div.6, but have striped or feathered patterns caused by virus, and appear in late spring.

Div.10 Parrot – has large, variable, single flowers, with frilled or fringed and usually twisted petals, in late spring.

Div.11 Double late (peony-flowered) – usually bowl-shaped, double flowers appear in late spring.

Div.12 Kaufmanniana hybrids – single flowers are usually bicoloured, open flat in the sun and appear in early spring. Leaves are usually mottled or striped.

Div.13 Fosteriana hybrids – large, single flowers open wide in the sun from early to mid-spring. Leaves are often mottled or striped.

Div.14 Greigii hybrids – large, single flowers appear in mid- and late spring. Mottled or striped leaves are often wavy-edged.

Div.15 Miscellaneous – a diverse category of other species and their cultivars and hybrids. Flowers appear in spring and early summer.

T. turkestanica (Div.15) ⓘ

T. 'Diana' (Div.1) ⓘ

T. 'Angélique' (Div.11) ⓘ

T. 'Don Quichotte' (Div.3) ⓘ

T. 'Purissima' (Div.13) ⓘ

T. 'Groenland' (Div.8) ⓘ

T. saxatilis (Div.15) ⓘ

T. 'Page Polka' (Div.3) ⓘ

T. 'Spring Green' (Div.8) ⓘ

T. 'Ballade' (Div.6) ⓘ

T. 'White Triumphator' (Div.6) ⓘ

T. 'White Parrot' (Div.10) ⓘ

T. 'Carnaval de Nice' (Div.11) ⓘ

T. 'Menton' (Div.5) ⓘ

T. 'White Dream' (Div.3) ⓘ

T. biflora (Div.15) ⓘ

T. 'Fancy Frills' (Div.10) ⓘ

T. 'New Design' (Div.3) ⓘ

T. 'China Pink' (Div.6) ⓘ

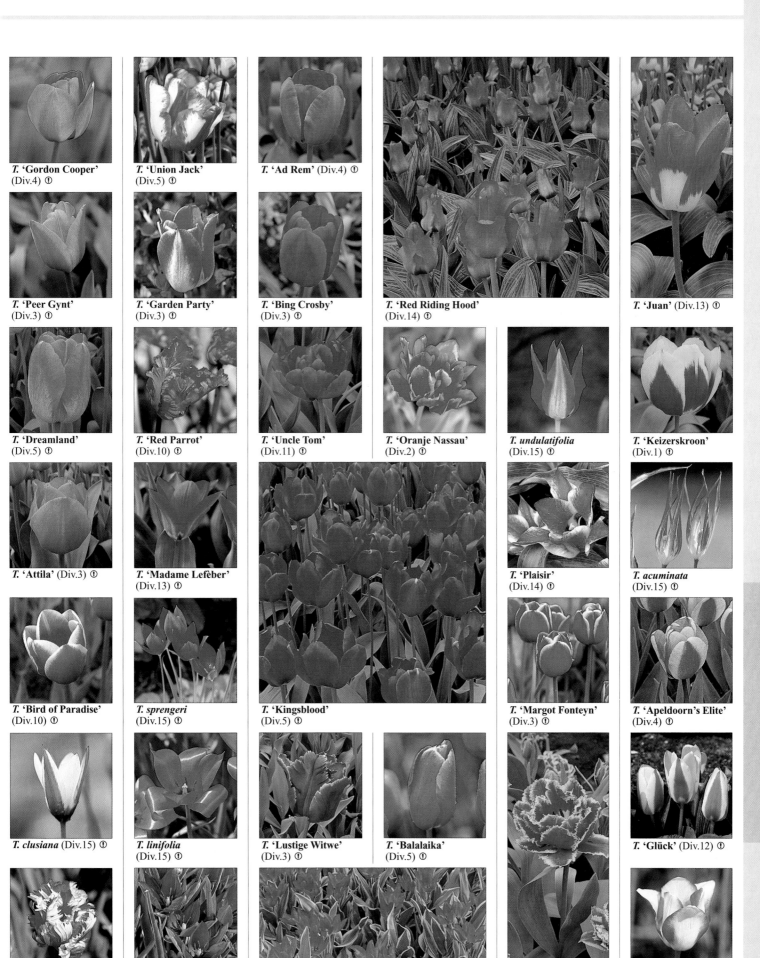

T. 'Gordon Cooper' (Div.4) ①

T. 'Union Jack' (Div.5) ①

T. 'Ad Rem' (Div.4) ①

T. 'Peer Gynt' (Div.3) ①

T. 'Garden Party' (Div.3) ①

T. 'Bing Crosby' (Div.3) ①

T. 'Red Riding Hood' (Div.14) ①

T. 'Juan' (Div.13) ①

T. 'Dreamland' (Div.5) ①

T. 'Red Parrot' (Div.10) ①

T. 'Uncle Tom' (Div.11) ①

T. 'Oranje Nassau' (Div.2) ①

T. undulatifolia (Div.15) ①

T. 'Keizerskroon' (Div.1) ①

T. 'Attila' (Div.3) ①

T. 'Madame Lefèber' (Div.13) ①

T. 'Plaisir' (Div.14) ①

T. acuminata (Div.15) ①

T. 'Bird of Paradise' (Div.10) ①

T. sprengeri (Div.15) ①

T. 'Kingsblood' (Div.5) ①

T. 'Margot Fonteyn' (Div.3) ①

T. 'Apeldoorn's Elite' (Div.4) ①

T. clusiana (Div.15) ①

T. linifolia (Div.15) ①

T. 'Lustige Witwe' (Div.3) ①

T. 'Balalaika' (Div.5) ①

T. 'Glück' (Div.12) ①

T. 'Estella Rijnveld' (Div.10) ①

T. hageri (Div.15) ①

T. praestans 'Unicum' (Div.15) ①

T. 'Fringed Beauty' (Div.7) ①

T. marjollettii (Div.15) ①

Tulips continued

T. 'Dreaming Maid'
(Div.3) ①

T. batalinii
(Div.15) ①

T. 'West Point'
(Div.6) ①

T. sylvestris (Div.15) ①

T. 'Candela'
(Div.13) ①

T. 'Dreamboat'
(Div.14) ①

T. 'Greuze' (Div.5) ①

T. urumiensis
(Div.15) ①

T. clusiana var. **chry-santha** (Div.15) ①

T. 'Artist' (Div.8) ①

T. 'Shakespeare'
(Div.12) ①

T. violacea (Div.15) ①

T. kaufmanniana
(Div.15) ①

T. 'Dillenburg'
(Div.5) ①

T. orphanidea
(Div.15) ①

T. humilis (Div.15) ①

T. tarda (Div.15) ①

T. 'Golden Apeldoorn'
(Div.4) ①

T. 'Prinses Irene'
(Div.1) ①

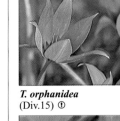
T. praestans 'Van Tuber-gen's Variety' (Div.15)①

T. 'Blue Parrot'
(Div.10) ①

T. 'Maja' (Div.7) ①

T. 'Yokohama'
(Div.1) ①

T. 'Cape Cod'
(Div.14) ①

T. 'Queen of Night'
(Div.5) ①

T. 'Bellona' (Div.1) ①

T. 'Golden Artist'
(Div.8) ①

T. 'Apricot Beauty'
(Div.1) ①

T. whittallii (Div.15) ①

■ RED–PURPLE

■ PURPLE

Anemone pavonina
Leafy tuber with cup-shaped, single, dark-centred, scarlet, purple or blue flowers rising above divided, frilly leaves in early spring. H 40cm (16in), S 20cm (8in). Min. 7°C (45°F).

☀ ◊ ⓘ .

Sprekelia formosissima
(Aztec lily, Jacobean lily)
Clump-forming, spring-flowering bulb with semi-erect, basal leaves. Stem bears a deep red flower, 12cm (5in) wide, that has 6 narrow petals with green-striped bases. H 15–35cm (6–14in), S 12–15cm (5–6in). Min. 7°C (45°F).

☀ ◊

Sauromatum venosum,
syn. *S. guttatum*
(Monarch-of-the-East, Voodoo lily)
Early spring-flowering tuber. Bears a large, acrid, purple-spotted spathe, then a lobed leaf on a long, spotted stalk. H 30–45cm (12–18in), S 30–35cm (12–14in). Min. 5–7°C (41–5°F).

◑ ◊

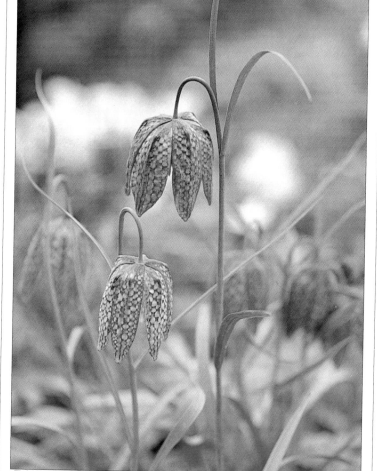

Fritillaria meleagris
(Snake's-head fritillary)
Spring-flowering bulb with slender stems producing scattered, narrow, grey-green leaves. Has solitary bell-shaped, prominently chequered flowers, in shades of pinkish-purple or white. H to 30cm (12in), S 5–8cm (2–3in).

☀ ◊

Fritillaria pyrenaica
Spring-flowering bulb with scattered, lance-shaped leaves, often rather narrow. Develops 1, or rarely 2, broadly bell-shaped flowers with flared-tipped, chequered, deep brownish- or blackish-purple petals. H 15–30cm (6–12in), S 5–8cm (2–3in).

☀ ◊

Muscari latifolium
Spring-flowering bulb with one strap-shaped, semi-erect, basal, grey-green leaf. Has a dense spike of tiny, bell-shaped, blackish-violet to -blue flowers with constricted mouths; upper ones are paler and smaller. H to 25cm (10in), S 5–8cm (2–3in).

☀ ◊

Fritillaria camschatcensis
(Black sarana)
Spring-flowering bulb. Stout stems carry lance-shaped, glossy leaves, mostly in whorls. Bears up to 8 deep blackish-purple or brown flowers. Needs humus-rich soil. H 15–60cm (6–24in), S 8–10cm (3–4in).

◑ ◊

Leucocoryne ixioides
(Glory-of-the-sun)
Spring-flowering bulb with long, narrow, semi-erect, basal leaves that are withered by flowering time. Wiry, slender flower stem has a loose head of up to 10 lilac-blue flowers. H 30–40cm (12–16in), S 8–10cm (3–4in). Min. 5°C (41°F).

☀ ◊

BULBS

BULBS medium SPRING INTEREST

■ BLUE

Hyacinthoides hispanica,
syn. *Endymion hispanicus, Scilla campanulata, S. hispanica*
(Spanish bluebell)
Spring-flowering bulb with strap-shaped, glossy leaves and pendent, bell-shaped, blue, white or pink flowers.
H to 30cm (12in), S 10–15cm (4–6in).
☼ ◐ ◊ ①

Hyacinthoides non-scripta, syn.
Endymion non-scriptus, Scilla non-scripta, S. nutans (English bluebell)
Tuft-forming, spring-flowering bulb with strap-shaped leaves. An erect stem, arching at the apex, bears fragrant, blue, pink or white flowers. H 20–40cm (8–16in), S 8–10cm (3–4in).
☼ ◊ ①

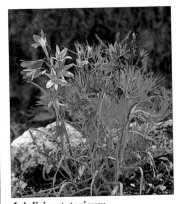

Ixiolirion tataricum,
syn. *I. montanum*
Spring- to early summer-flowering bulb with long, narrow, semi-erect leaves on the lower part of stem. Has a loose cluster of blue flowers with a darker, central line along each petal.
H to 40cm (16in), S 8–10cm (3–4in).
☼ ◊

Aristea ecklonii
IRISES, illus. pp.234–5
Moraea polystachya

■ GREEN

Fritillaria acmopetala
Spring-flowering bulb with slender stems that bear narrowly lance-shaped, scattered leaves, and 1 or 2 broadly bell-shaped, green flowers, with brown-stained petals flaring outwards at the tips. H 15–40cm (6–16in), S 5–8cm (2–3in).
◐ ◊

Arisaema triphyllum, syn.
A. atrorubens (Jack-in-the-pulpit)
Summer-flowering tuber with 3-lobed, erect leaves. Produces green or purple spathes, hooded at tips, followed by bright red berries. H 40–50cm (16–20in), S 30–45cm (12–18in).
☼ ◊

Hermodactylus tuberosus,
syn. *Iris tuberosa* (Widow iris)
Spring-flowering perennial with finger-like tubers. Very long, narrow, grey-green leaves are square in cross-section. Has a fragrant, yellowish-green flower with large, blackish-brown-tipped petals.
H 20–40cm (8–16in), S 5–8cm (2–3in).
☼ ◊

Bellevalia pycnantha

Fritillaria pontica
Spring-flowering bulb with stems carrying lance-shaped, grey-green leaves, the topmost in a whorl of 3. Has solitary broadly bell-shaped, green flowers, 3–4.5cm (1¼–1¾in) long, often suffused brown. H 15–45cm (6–18in), S 5–8cm (2–3in).
☼ ◊

Ixia viridiflora
Spring- to early summer-flowering corm with very narrow, erect leaves mostly at stem base. Carries a spike of flattish, jade-green flowers, 2.5–5cm (1–2in) across, with purple-black eyes.
H 30–60cm (12–24in), S 2.5–5cm (1–2in). Min. 2°C (35°F).
☼ ◊

Fritillaria cirrhosa
Spring-flowering bulb with slender stems and narrow, whorled leaves; upper leaves have tendril-like tips. Produces up to 4 widely bell-shaped flowers, purple or yellowish-green with dark purple chequered patterns.
H to 60cm (24in), S 5–8cm (2–3in).
☼ ◊

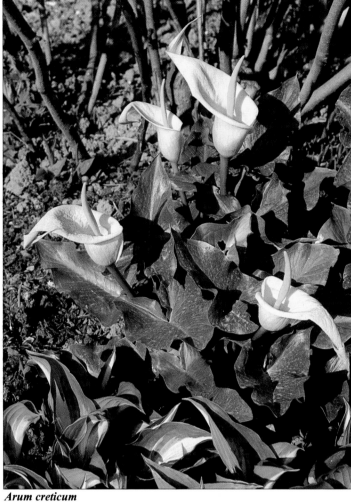

Fritillaria pallidiflora
Robust, spring-flowering bulb with
broadly lance-shaped, grey-green
leaves, scattered or in pairs on stem.
Has 1–5 widely bell-shaped, yellow
to greenish-yellow flowers, usually
faintly chequered brownish-red within.
H 15–70cm (6–28in), S 8–10cm (3–4in).

☼ ◊

Arum creticum
Spring-flowering tuber that bears white
or yellow spathes, each bottle-shaped
at the base, slightly reflexed at the apex
and with a protruding, yellow spadix.
Has arrow-shaped, semi-erect, deep
green leaves in autumn. H 30–50cm
(12–20in), S 20–30cm (8–12in).

☼ ◊

Ferraria crispa, syn. *F. undulata*
Spring-flowering corm, leafy stem with a
succession of upward-facing, brown or
yellowish-brown flowers, 4–5cm
(1½–2in) across, with 6 wavy-edged,
spreading petals that are conspicuously
lined and blotched. H 20–40cm (8–16in),
S 8–10cm (3–4in). Min. 2°C (35°F).

☼ ◊

Gladiolus 'Christabel'
Spring-flowering corm with a wiry
stem producing a loose spike of
fragrant, widely funnel-shaped,
primrose-yellow flowers, 6–8cm
(2½–3in) across, with purple-brown-
veined, upper petals. H to 45cm (18in),
S 8–10cm (3–4in).

☼ ◊

Erythronium 'Pagoda'
Robust, spring-flowering tuber with
2 semi-erect, basal, faintly mottled,
glossy leaves. Flower stem produces
up to 10 pendent, pale yellow flowers
with reflexed petals. H 25–35cm
(10–14in), S 15–20cm (6–8in).

◐ ◊

Calochortus luteus
(Yellow mariposa)
Late spring-flowering bulb with long,
narrow, erect leaves near the base of
the loosely branched stem. Each branch
bears a 3-petalled, yellow flower with
central, brown blotches. H 20–45cm
(8–18in), S 5–10cm (2–4in).

☼ ◊

Bloomeria crocea
Calochortus amabilis, illus. p.434
DAFFODILS, illus. pp.416–18
Erythronium grandiflorum

Erythronium tuolumnense
Fritillaria acmopetala
Homeria ochroleuca
Hymenocallis 'Sulphur Queen'

IRISES, illus. pp.234–5
TULIPS, illus. pp.410–12

415

Daffodils

The charm and beauty of the daffodil (botanically known as *Narcissus*) grace the garden early in the year. The diversity of its flowers provides infinite variation, from the tiny Cyclamineus daffodil, with its swept back petals, to the stately trumpet daffodil. Many may be naturalized, forming a golden carpet in grass or a wild garden, but dwarf forms are best in rock gardens or troughs, brightening the landscape before most other plants emerge.

The genus is classified in 13 divisions. Their flower forms are illlustrated below, with the exception of Div.12, miscellaneous, and Div.13, mostly wild species. Both have varying flowers, including hoop-petticoat forms, produced between autumn and early summer.

Div.1 Trumpet – usually solitary flowers each have a trumpet that is as long as, or longer, than the petals. Early to late spring-flowering.

Div.2 Large-cupped – solitary flowers each have a cup at least one-third the length of, but shorter than, the petals. Spring-flowering.

Div.3 Small-cupped – flowers are often borne singly; each has a cup not more than one-third the length of the petals. Spring- or early summer-flowering.

Div.4 Double – most have solitary large, fully or semi-double flowers with the cup and petals, or just the cup, replaced by petaloid structures. Some have smaller flowers in clusters of 4 or more. Spring- or early summer-flowering.

Div.5 Triandrus – nodding flowers, with short, sometimes straight-sided cups and narrow, reflexed petals, are borne 2–6 per stem. Spring-flowering.

Div.6 Cyclamineus – flowers are borne usually 1 or 2 per stem with cups that are sometimes flanged and often longer than those of Div.5. Petals are narrow, pointed and reflexed. Early to mid-spring flowering.

Div.7 Jonquil – sweetly scented flowers are borne usually 2 or more per stem. Cups are short, sometimes flanged; petals are often flat, fairly broad and rounded. Spring-flowering.

Div.8 Tazetta – flowers are borne in clusters of either 12 or more small, fragrant flowers per stem or 3 or 4 large ones. Cups are small and often straight-sided, petals broad and mostly pointed. Late autumn- to mid-spring-flowering.

Div.9 Poeticus – flowers each have a small, coloured cup and glistening white petals. They are borne usually 1 but sometimes 2 per stem and may be sweetly fragrant. Late spring- or early summer-flowering.

Div.10 Bulbocodium – flowers usually borne singly on very short stems, with insignificant petals and large, widely flaring cups. Winter- to spring-flowering.

Div.11 Split-cupped – usually solitary flowers that have cups split for more than half their length. Spring-flowering.

(a) Collar – wide cup segments lie back on the petals.

(b) Papillon – narrower cup segments have tips arranged at the margin of the petals.

N. cantabricus (Div.13) ①

N. 'Irene Copeland' (Div.4) ①

N. 'Aircastle' (Div.3) ①

N. 'Canisp' (Div.2) ①

N. 'Ice Follies' (Div.2) ①

N. 'Trousseau' (Div.1) ①

N. 'Cheerfulness' (Div.4) ①

N. 'Thalia' (Div.5) ①

N. rupicola subsp. *watieri* (Div.10) ①

N. 'Portrush' (Div.3) ①

N. 'White Lady' (Div.3) ①

N. × *medioluteus* (Div.13) ①

N. 'Silver Chimes'
(Div.8) ①

N. 'Rockall'
(Div.3) ①

N. 'Jack Snipe'
(Div.6) ①

N. triandrus
(Div.13) ①

N. 'Empress of
Ireland' (Div.1) ①

N. 'Merlin'
(Div.3) ①

N. 'Rainbow'
(Div.2) ①

N. 'Dove Wings'
(Div.6) ①

N. 'Canaliculatus'
(Div.8) ①

N. 'Cassata'
(Div.11a) ①

N. 'Passionale'
(Div.2) ①

N. 'Woodland Star'
(Div 3)

N. 'Broadway Star'
(Div.11b) ①

N. 'Bravoure'
(Div.1) ①

N. 'Belcanto'
(Div.11a) ①

N. 'Spellbinder'
(Div.1) ①

N. 'Satin Pink'
(Div.2) ①

N. 'Pride of Cornwall'
(Div.8) ①

N. 'Acropolis'
(Div.4) ①

N. 'February Silver'
(Div.6) ①

N. 'Avalanche'
(Div.8) ①

N. 'Minnow'
(Div.8) ①

N. 'Actaea'
(Div.9) ①

N. 'Kilworth'
(Div.2) ①

N. poeticus var. *recurvus*
(Div.13) ①

N. romieuxii
(Div.13) ①♀

N. 'Cantabile'
(Div.9) ①

N. 'Bridal Crown'
(Div.4) ①

N. 'Honeybird'
(Div.1) ①

N. 'Binkie' (Div.2) ①

Daffodils continued

N. pseudonarcissus
(Div.13) ①

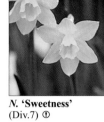

N. 'Rip van Winkle'
(Div.4) ①

N. 'Sweetness'
(Div.7) ①

N. 'Stratosphere'
(Div.7) ①

N. 'Ambergate'
(Div.2) ①

N. rupicola
(Div.13) ①

N. 'February Gold'
(Div.6) ①

N. 'Suzy' (Div.7) ①

N. 'Liberty Bells'
(Div.5) ①

N. jonquilla
(Div.13) ①

N. cyclamineus
(Div.13) ①

N. 'Saint Keverne'
(Div.11b) ①

N. 'Jetfire'
(Div.6) ①

N. 'Home Fires'
(Div.2) ①

N. 'Pipit' (Div.7) ①

N. minor (Div.13) ①

N. 'Pencrebar'
(Div.4) ①

N. 'Golden Ducat'
(Div.4) ①

N. 'Tahiti' (Div.4) ①

N. 'Hawera'
(Div.5) ①

N. 'Fortune' (Div.2) ①

N. 'Tête-à-Tête'
(Div.12) ①

N. 'Bartley' (Div.6) ①

N. 'Shining Light'
(Div.2) ①

N. 'Scarlet Gem'
(Div.8) ①

N. 'Charity May'
(Div.6) ①

N. x *odorus* 'Rugulosus'
(Div.7) ①

N. 'Jumblie'
(Div.12) ①

N. 'Kingscourt'
(Div.1) ①

N. 'Grand Soleil d'Or'
(Div.8) ①

N. 'Altruist' (Div.3) ①

BULBS

418

BULBS medium SPRING INTEREST

☐ ORANGE

Stenomesson variegatum,
syn. *S. incarnatum*
Clump-forming bulb. Bears reddish-yellow, pink or white flowers, with 6 green lobes at the apex, in winter or spring. H 30–60cm (12–24in), S 30cm (12in). Min. 10°C (50°F).

Stenomesson miniatum,
syn. *Urceolina peruviana*
Late spring-flowering bulb with strap-shaped, semi-erect, basal leaves. Bears a head of red or orange flowers, 2–4cm (¾–1½in) long, with yellow anthers. H 20–30cm (8–12in), S 10–15cm (4–6in). Min. 5°C (41°F).

Clivia miniata
Evergreen, tuft-forming rhizome with strap-shaped, semi-erect, basal, dark green leaves, 40–60cm (16–24in) long. Stems each produce a head of 10–20 orange or red flowers in spring or summer. H 40cm (16in), S 30–60cm (12–24in). Min. 10°C (50°F).

BULBS medium SUMMER INTEREST

☐ WHITE

Crinum asiaticum
Clump-forming bulb with strap-shaped, semi-erect, basal, dark green leaves, 1m (3ft) long. Leafless flower stems produce heads of long-tubed, white flowers, with narrow petals, in spring or summer. H 45–60cm (1½–2ft), S 60cm–1m (2–3ft). Min. 16°C (61°F).

Pancratium illyricum
Summer-flowering bulb with strap-shaped, semi-erect, basal, greyish-green leaves. Leafless stem has a head of 5–12 fragrant, 6-petalled, white flowers, 8cm (3in) across. H to 45cm (18in), S 25–30cm (10–12in).

Triteleia hyacinthina, syn.
Brodiaea hyacinthina, *B. lactea*
Late spring- to early summer-flowering corm with long, narrow, semi-erect or spreading, basal leaves. Heads of white, sometimes purple-tinged flowers are borne on wiry stems. H 30–50cm (12–20in), S 8–10cm (3–4in).

Ornithogalum narbonense
Clump-forming, late spring- to summer-flowering bulb with long, narrow, semi-erect, basal, grey-green leaves. Leafless stem produces a spike of star-shaped, white flowers, 2cm (¾in) wide. H 30–40cm (12–16in), S 10–15cm (4–6in).

Arisaema sikokianum
Early summer-flowering tuber with erect leaves divided into 3–5 leaflets. Produces deep brownish-purple and white spathes, 15cm (6in) long, with club-like, white spadices protruding from the mouths. H 30–50cm (12–20in), S 30–45cm (12–18in).

BULBS

□ WHITE

Ornithogalum thyrsoides
(Chincherinchee)
Summer-flowering bulb with strap-shaped, semi-erect, basal leaves. Bears a dense, conical spike of cup-shaped, white flowers, 2–3cm (¾–1¼in) across. H 30–45cm (12–18in), S 10–15cm (4–6in).

Zigadenus fremontii
Clump-forming, early summer-flowering bulb with long, strap-shaped, semi-erect, basal leaves. Stem produces a spike of star-shaped, pale creamy-green flowers with darker green nectaries on petal bases. H 30–50cm (12–20in), S 10–15cm (4–6in).

Ornithogalum arabicum
Early summer-flowering bulb with strap-shaped, semi-erect leaves in a basal cluster. Has a flattish head of up to 15 scented, white or creamy-white flowers, 4–5cm (1½–2in) across, with black ovaries in centres. H 30–45cm (12–18in), S 10–15cm (4–6in).

Alstroemeria pelegrina,
syn. *A. gayana*
Summer-flowering tuber with narrow, lance-shaped leaves. Each leafy stem has 1–3 white flowers, stained pinkish-mauve and spotted yellow and brownish-purple. H 30–60cm (1–2ft), S 60cm–1m (2–3ft).

Allium cernuum
Clump-forming, summer-flowering bulb with narrow, semi-erect, basal leaves. Each stem produces up to 30 cup-shaped, pink or white flowers in a loose, nodding umbel, 2–4cm (¾–1½in) across. H 30–70cm (12–28in), S 8–12cm (3–5in).

Tritonia disticha subsp.
rubrolucens, syn. *T. rosea*,
T. rubrolucens
Late summer-flowering corm with narrowly sword-shaped, erect leaves in a flattish, basal fan. Has pink flowers in a loose, one-sided spike. H 30–50cm (12–20in), S 8–10cm (3–4in).

Hymenocallis narcissiflora,
syn. *H. calathina, Ismene calathina*
(Peruvian daffodil)
Spring- or summer-flowering bulb with semi-erect, basal leaves, dying in winter. Bears a loose head of 2–5 fragrant, white flowers. H to 60cm (24in), S 30–45cm (12–18in). Min. 5°C (41°F).

Allium senescens subsp.
montanum
Vigorous, clump-forming, summer-flowering bulb with strap-shaped, often twisted, grey-green leaves. Has dense umbels, 2cm (¾in) across, of up to 30 long-lasting, cup-shaped, pink flowers. H 45cm (18in), S 60cm (24in).

Lycoris radiata (Red spider lily)
Late summer-flowering bulb with a head of 5 or 6 bright rose-red flowers with narrow, wavy-margined, reflexed petals and conspicuous anthers. Has strap-shaped, semi-erect, basal leaves after flowering time. H 30–40cm (12–16in), S 10–15cm (4–6in).

Allium campanulatum
LILIES, illus. pp.404–405

BEGONIAS, illus. p.295
Bessera elegans
GLADIOLI, illus. p.399
Haemanthus coccineus, illus. p.435

Haemanthus sanguineus
Zantedeschia rehmannii
Zephyranthes grandiflora, illus. p.424

BULBS

Rhodophiala advena,
syn. *Hippeastrum advenum*
Clump-forming, spring- to summer-
flowering bulb with basal, grey-green
leaves. Leafless stem carries a head of
2–8 narrowly funnel-shaped, red
flowers, 5cm (2in) long. H to 40cm
(16in), S 15–20cm (6–8in).

☼ ◊

Allium cristophii,
syn. *A. albopilosum*, *A. christophii*
Summer-flowering bulb with semi-
erect, hairy, grey leaves that droop at
tips. Has a large, spherical umbel of
50 or more star-shaped, purplish-violet
flowers, which dry well. H 15–40cm
(6–16in), S 15–20cm (6–8in).

☼ ◊ ⓘ

BULBS

Ranunculus asiaticus [red form]
(Persian buttercup)
Early summer-flowering perennial with
claw-like tubers and long-stalked
leaves both at base and on stem. Has
single or double flowers in red, white,
pink, yellow or orange. H 45–55cm
(18–22in), S 10cm (4in).

☼ ◊ ⓘ

Allium schubertii
Early summer-flowering bulb with
widely strap-shaped, semi-erect, basal
leaves. Bears large umbels of 40 or
more star-shaped, pink or purple flowers
on very unequal stalks, followed by
brown seed capsules. H 30–60cm
(12–24in), S 15–20cm (6–8in).

☼ ◊ ⓘ

Patersonia umbrosa
Evergreen, clump-forming, spring- and
early summer-flowering rhizome with
erect, basal leaves. Tough flower stems
each carry a succession of iris-like,
purple-blue flowers, 3–4cm (1¼–1½in)
across. H 30–45cm (12–18in),
S 30–60cm (12–24in). Min. 5°C (41°F).

☼ ◊

Gloxinia perennis
Late summer- to autumn-flowering
rhizome with heart-shaped, toothed,
hairy leaves on spotted stems. Has bell-
shaped, lavender-blue flowers, with
rounded lobes and purple-blotched
throats. H to 60cm (24in), S 30–35cm
(12–14in). Min. 10°C (50°F).

◑ ◊

■ BLUE

Allium caeruleum, syn. *A. azureum*
Clump-forming, summer-flowering
bulb with narrow, erect leaves on the
lower third of slender flower stems,
which bear 30–50 star-shaped, blue
flowers in a dense, spherical umbel,
3–4cm (1¼–1½in) across. H 20–80cm
(8–32in), S 10–15cm (4–6in).

☀ ◊ ①

Triteleia laxa, syn. *Brodiaea laxa*
Early summer-flowering corm with
narrow, semi-erect, basal leaves. Stem
carries a large, loose umbel of funnel-
shaped, deep to pale purple-blue
flowers, 2–5cm (¾–2in) long, mostly
held upright. H 10–50cm (4–20in),
S 8–10cm (3–4in).

☀ ◊

Aristea ecklonii
Ixiolirion tataricum, illus. p.414

☐☐ GREEN–YELLOW

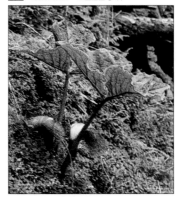

Arisaema griffithii
Summer-flowering tuber with large,
erect leaves above a green or purple
spathe, 20–25cm (8–10in) long,
strongly netted with paler veins and
expanded like a cobra's hood. Protect in
winter or lift for frost-free storage. H to
60cm (24in), S 45–60cm (18–24in).

☀◑ ◊

Arisaema jacquemontii
Summer-flowering tuber with 1 or 2
erect leaves, divided into wavy-edged
leaflets. Produces slender, white-lined,
green spathes that are hooded at tips and
drawn out into long points. H 30–50cm
(12–20in), S 30–38cm (12–15in).

☀◑ ◊

Eucomis bicolor
Summer-flowering bulb with wavy-
margined, semi-erect, basal leaves.
Stem, often spotted purple, bears a spike
of green or greenish-white flowers, with
6 purple-edged petals, topped by a
cluster of leaf-like bracts. H 30–50cm
(12–20in), S 30–60cm (12–24in).

☀ ◊

Cyrtanthus breviflorus
Hymenocallis 'Sulphur Queen'
Ixia viridiflora, p.414
Lycoris aurea

Allium flavum
Clump-forming, summer-flowering
bulb. Leaves are linear and semi-erect
on lower half of slender flower stem.
Produces a loose umbel of up to 60
small, bell-shaped, yellow flowers on
thin, arching stalks. H 10–35cm
(4–14in), S 5–8cm (2–3in).

☀ ◊ ①

Cyrtanthus mackenii var. **cooperi**
Clump-forming, summer-flowering bulb
with long, narrow, semi-erect, basal
leaves. Leafless stems each carry a head
of up to 10 fragrant, tubular, cream or
yellow flowers, 5cm (2in) long and
slightly curved. H 30–40cm (12–16in),
S 8–10cm (3–4in). Min. 2°C (35°F).

☀ ◊

Calochortus barbatus,
syn. *Cyclobothra lutea*
Summer-flowering bulb with narrow,
erect leaves near the base of the loosely
branched stem. Each branch bears a
pendent, yellow or greenish-yellow
flower that is hairy inside. H 30–60cm
(12–24in), S 5–10cm (2–4in).

☀ ◊

Triteleia ixioides

BULBS

Ranunculus asiaticus
[yellow form] (Persian buttercup)
Early summer-flowering perennial
with claw-like tubers and long-stalked,
palmate leaves at base and on stem.
Has single or double flowers in yellow,
white, pink, red or orange. H 45–55cm
(18–22in), S 8–10cm (3–4in).

☼ ◊ ⚠

Cypella herbertii
Summer-flowering bulb with a fan of
narrow, sword-shaped, erect, basal
leaves. Branched flower stem carries a
succession of short-lived, iris-like,
orange-yellow flowers, with spotted
purple centres. H 30–50cm (12–20in),
S 8–10cm (3–4in). Min. 2°C (35°F).

☼ ◊

Alstroemeria Ligtu Hybrids
Summer-flowering tuber with narrow,
twisted leaves and heads of widely
flared flowers in shades of pink, yellow
or orange, often spotted or streaked
with contrasting colours. H 45–60cm
(1½–2ft), S 60cm–1m (2–3ft).

☼ ◊ ⚠

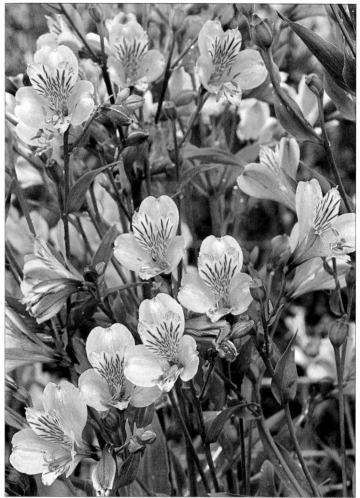

Alstroemeria 'Parigo Charm'
Summer-flowering tuber with narrow,
twisted, mid- to grey-green leaves and
umbels of salmon-pink flowers. The
inner tepals are primrose-yellow,
marked carmine-red.
H 1m (3ft), S 60cm (24in).

☼ ◊ ⚠

Sandersonia aurantiaca
(Chinese-lantern lily)
Deciduous, summer-flowering, tuberous
climber. Slender stem bearing scattered,
lance-shaped leaves, some tendril-tipped.
Orange flowers are produced in axils of
upper leaves. H 60cm (24in), S 25–30cm
(10–12in). Min. 2°C (35°F).

☼ ◊

Crocosmia 'Jackanapes'
Clump-forming, late summer-
flowering corm with sword-shaped,
erect, basal leaves. Produces striking
bicoloured, yellow and orange-red
flowers. H 40–60cm (16–24in),
S 15–20cm (6–8in).

☼ ◊

Polianthes geminiflora,
syn. *Bravoa geminiflora*
Summer-flowering tuber, strap-shaped
narrow, semi-erect leaves in a basal tuft.
Stems carry long spikes of downward-
curving, tubular, red or orange flowers in
pairs. H 20–40cm (8–16in), S 10–15cm
(4–6in). Min. 15°C (59°F).

☼ ◊

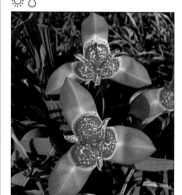

Tigridia pavonia
(Peacock flower, Tiger flower)
Summer-flowering bulb. Sword-shaped,
pleated, erect leaves near stem base.
Succession of short-lived flowers from
white to orange, red or yellow, often
with contrasting spots. H to 45cm (18in),
S 12–15cm (4–6in). Min. 8°C (46°F).

☼ ◊

Clivia miniata, illus. p.419
Crocosmia 'Emily McKenzie'
LILIES, illus. pp.404–405

BULBS

◻️ WHITE–PINK

Nerine bowdenii f. *alba*
Autumn-flowering bulb with a stout stem and strap-shaped, semi-erect, basal leaves. Produces a head of 5–10 white, often pink-flushed flowers; petals widen slightly towards wavy-margined, recurved tips. H 45–60cm (18–24in), S 12–15cm (5–6in).

☀️ ◊ ⚠️

Nerine 'Orion'
Autumn-flowering bulb with strap-shaped, semi-erect, basal leaves. Stout, leafless stem bears a head of pale pink flowers with very wavy-margined petals that have recurved tips. H 30–50cm (12–20in), S 20–25cm (8–10in).

☀️ ◊ ⚠️

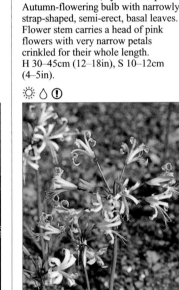

Nerine undulata, syn. *N crispa*
Autumn-flowering bulb with narrowly strap-shaped, semi-erect, basal leaves. Flower stem carries a head of pink flowers with very narrow petals crinkled for their whole length. H 30–45cm (12–18in), S 10–12cm (4–5in).

☀️ ◊ ⚠️

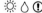

Nerine bowdenii
Autumn-flowering bulb with a stout stem and strap-shaped, semi-erect, basal leaves. Carries a head of 5–10 glistening, pink flowers with petals that widen slightly towards wavy-margined, recurved tips. H 45–60cm (18–24in), S 12–15cm (5–6in).

☀️ ◊ ⚠️

◻️ PINK–ORANGE

Zephyranthes grandiflora
Late summer- to early autumn-flowering bulb with narrowly strap-shaped, semi-erect, basal leaves. Each stem bears a funnel-shaped, pink flower, held almost erect. H 20–30cm (8–12in), S 8–10cm (3–4in). Min. 2°C (35°F).

☀️ ◊

Scilla scilloides, syn. *S. chinensis, S. japonica*
Late summer- and autumn-flowering bulb with 2–4 narrowly strap-shaped, semi-erect, basal leaves. Stem bears a slender, dense spike of up to 30 flattish, pink flowers, 0.5–1cm (¼–½in) across. H to 30cm (12in), S 5cm (2in).

☀️ ◊

Nerine 'Brian Doe'
Autumn-flowering bulb with strap-shaped, semi-erect, basal leaves. Stout, leafless stem bears a head of salmon flowers with 6 reflexed, wavy-margined petals. H 30–50cm (12–20in), S 20–25cm (8–10in).

☀️ ◊ ⚠️

Nerine sarniensis (Guernsey lily)
Autumn-flowering bulb with strap-shaped, semi-erect, basal leaves. Leafless stem carries a spherical head of up to 20 deep orange-pink flowers, 6–8cm (2½–3in) across, with wavy-margined petals. H 45–60cm (18–24in), S 12–15cm (5–6in).

☀️ ◊ ⚠️

OTHER RECOMMENDED PLANTS:
Amaryllis belladonna, illus. p.408
Crinum macowanii
Habranthus robustus, illus. p.437

Nerine 'Blanchefleur'
Nerine filifolia
Nerine flexuosa

Brunsvigia josephinae
Eucomis autumnalis
Gloxinia perennis, illus. p.421
Nerine 'Bagdad'

Nerine 'Corusca Major'
Nerine 'Fothergillii Major'

BULBS

WHITE–RED

Eucharis × grandiflora,
syn. *E. amazonica* of gardens
Evergreen, clump-forming bulb with
strap-shaped, semi-erect, basal leaves.
Bears a head of up to 6 fragrant, slightly
pendent, white flowers at almost any
season. H 40–60cm (16–24in),
S 60cm–1m (2–3ft). Min. 15°C (59°F).

Veltheimia bracteata
Clump-forming, winter-flowering bulb
with semi-erect, strap-shaped, basal,
glossy leaves and dense spikes of
pendent, tubular, pink, red or
yellowish-red flowers. H 30–45cm
(12–18in), S 25–38cm (10–15in).
Min. 10°C (50°F).

Hippeastrum 'Red Lion'
Tuft-forming, winter- and spring-
flowering bulb with a stout stem
bearing a head of 2–6 dark red flowers
with yellow anthers. Strap-shaped
leaves appear with or just after
flowers. H 30–50cm (12–20in),
S 30cm (12in). Min. 13°C (55°F).

RED–YELLOW

Hippeastrum 'Orange Sovereign'
Winter- to spring-flowering bulb with
strap-shaped, semi-erect, basal, grey-
green leaves produced as, or just after,
flowers form. Stout stem carries a
head of 2–6 rich orange-red flowers.
H 30–50cm (12–20in), S 30cm
(12in). Min. 13°C (55°F).

Hippeastrum 'Apple Blossom'
Winter- to spring-flowering bulb with
strap-shaped, semi-erect, basal leaves
produced as, or just after, flowers
form. Stout stem has a head of
2–6 white flowers, becoming pink
at petal tips. H 30–50cm (12–20in),
S 30cm (12in). Min. 13°C (55°F).

Lachenalia orchioides var.
glaucina, syn. *L. glaucina*
Late winter- and early spring-flowering
bulb with 2 strap-shaped, semi-erect,
basal leaves, usually spotted purple.
Has a spike of fragrant, whitish-blue
or pale lilac flowers. H to 30cm (12in),
S 5–8cm (2–3in). Min. 2°C (35°F).

Hippeastrum 'Striped'
Winter- to spring-flowering bulb with
strap-shaped, semi-erect, basal leaves
produced with or just after flowers.
Stout stem has a head of 2–6 widely
funnel-shaped flowers, striped white
and red. H 50cm (20in), S 30cm
(12in). Min. 13°C (55°F).

Hippeastrum aulicum,
syn. *H. morelianum*
Winter- and spring-flowering bulb with
a basal cluster of strap-shaped, semi-
erect leaves. Stout stem bears two red
flowers with green-striped petals and
green throats. H 30–50cm (12–20in),
S 30cm (12in). Min. 13–15°C (55–59°F).

Freesia 'Oberon'
Winter- and spring-flowering corm
with narrow, erect, basal leaves.
Produces yellow flowers, 4–5cm
(1½–2in) long, light blood-red inside;
the throats are lemon-yellow with
small, red veins. H to 40cm (16in),
S 4–6cm (1½–2⅓in). Min. 2°C (35°F).

OTHER RECOMMENDED PLANTS:
Freesia lactea
Freesia corymbosa
Hippeastrum 'Belinda'

Hippeastrum 'Bouquet'
Hippeastrum 'White Dazzler'
Hymenocallis speciosa
Lachenalia rubida

Stenomesson variegatum, illus. p.419
Veltheimia capensis

Freesia 'Romany'
Lachenalia mutabilis
Moraea polystachya

BULBS

☐ WHITE

Anemone blanda 'White Splendour'
Knobbly tuber with semi-erect leaves that have 3 deeply toothed lobes. Bears upright, flattish, white flowers, 4–5cm (1½–2in) across, with 9–14 narrow petals, in early spring. H 5–10cm (2–4in), S 10–15cm (4–6in).

☼ ◊ ⚠

Ornithogalum balansae, syn. *O. oligophyllum* of gardens
Spring-flowering bulb with 2 almost prostrate, inversely lance-shaped, mid-green basal leaves. Has a broad head of 2–5 flowers, glistening white inside, bright green outside, that open wide. H 5–15cm (2–6in), S 5–8cm (2–3in).

☼ ◊ ⚠

Leucojum vernum
(Spring snowflake)
Spring-flowering bulb with strap-shaped, semi-erect, basal leaves. Leafless stem carries 1 or 2 pendent, bell-shaped flowers, 1.5–2cm (⅝–¾in) long, with 6 green-tipped, white petals. H 10–15cm (4–6in), S 8–10cm (3–4in).

☼ ◊

Ornithogalum montanum
Clump-forming, spring-flowering bulb with strap-shaped, semi-erect, basal, grey-green leaves. Leafless stem produces a head of star-shaped, white flowers, 3–4cm (1¼–1½in) across, striped green outside. H and S 10–15cm (4–6in).

☼ ◊ ⚠

Puschkinia scilloides var. **libanotica 'Alba'**
Spring-flowering bulb with usually 2 strap-shaped, semi-erect, basal leaves. Produces a dense spike of star-shaped, white flowers, 1.5–2cm (⅝–¾in) across.
H 15cm (6in), S 2.5–5cm (1–2in).

☼ ◊

Sternbergia candida
Spring-flowering bulb. Strap-shaped, semi-erect, basal, greyish-green leaves appear together with a fragrant, funnel-shaped, white flower, 4–5cm (1½–2in) long, borne on a leafless stem.
H 10–20cm (4–8in), S 8–10cm (3–4in).

☼ ◊

Ornithogalum lanceolatum
Spring-flowering, dwarf bulb with a flattish rosette of prostrate, lance-shaped, basal leaves. Carries a head of flattish, star-shaped, white flowers, 3–4cm (1¼–1½in) across, broadly striped green outside. H 5–10cm (2–4in), S 10–15cm (4–6in).

☼ ◊ ⚠

OTHER RECOMMENDED PLANTS:
CROCUSES, illus. pp.428–9
Cyclamen creticum
DAFFODILS, illus. pp.416–18

Fritillaria bucharica
Gagea graeca
Galanthus 'Atkinsii', illus. p.439
Galanthus elwesii, illus. p.439

Galanthus gracilis, illus. p.439
Galanthus ikariae, illus. p.440
Galanthus nivalis 'Flore Pleno', illus. p.439

Galanthus nivalis 'Pusey Green Tip', illus. p.439
Galanthus nivalis 'Sandersii', illus. p.440
Galanthus nivalis 'Scharlockii', illus. p.440

BULBS

Erythronium californicum
Clump-forming, spring-flowering tuber.
Bears 2 semi-erect, basal, mottled leaves.
Up to 3 white or creamy-white flowers,
sometimes red-brown externally, have
reflexed petals, yellow eyes and often
brown rings near centres. H 15–35cm
(6–14in), S 10–12cm (4–5in).

Chionodoxa forbesii 'Pink Giant'
Early spring-flowering bulb with
2 narrow, semi-erect, basal leaves.
Leafless stem produces a spike of
5–10 flattish, white-eyed, pink flowers,
2–2.5cm (¾–1in) across. H 10–25cm
(4–10in), S 2.5–5cm (1–2in).

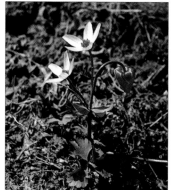

Allium akaka
Spring-flowering bulb with 1–3 broad,
prostrate and basal, grey-green leaves
and an almost stemless, spherical
umbel, 5–7cm (2–3in) across of 30–40
star-shaped, white to pinkish-white
flowers with red centres. H 15–20cm
(6–8in), S 12–15cm (5–6in).

Allium karataviense
Late spring-flowering bulb with
narrowly elliptic to elliptic, prostrate,
basal, greyish-purple leaves. Stem
bears 50 or more star-shaped, pale
purplish-pink flowers in a spherical
umbel, 15cm (6in) or more across.
H to 20cm (8in), S 25–30cm (10–12in).

Cyclamen libanoticum
Spring-flowering tuber with ivy-shaped,
dull green leaves with lighter patterns
and purplish-green undersides. Flowers
are musty-scented, clear pink, each with
deep carmine marks at the mouth. Grows
best in an alpine house. H to 10cm (4in),
S 10–15cm (4–6in). Min. 2°C (35°F).

Anemone tschaernjaewii
Spring-flowering tuber with 3-palmate,
oval, mid-green leaves, the leaflets
shallowly lobed. Bears 5-petalled,
saucer-shaped, purple-centred, white or
pink flowers, 2–4.5cm (¾–1¾in) across.
Needs warm, dry, summer dormancy.
H 5–10cm (2–4in), S 5–8cm (2–3in).

BULBS

427

Crocuses

Crocuses (*Crocus* species and cultivars) are possibly the most versatile and reliable of dwarf bulbous plants, most flowering in late winter or early spring, though some species flower in autumn. A wide colour range is available, from white through pinkish-lilac to rich purples, creams and yellows. Many are also attractively striped or feathered with other colours. Their usually goblet-shaped flowers, sometimes produced before the leaves, open wide in full sun, in some cases to reveal contrasting centres or conspicuous stamens. Most crocuses are also fragrant. To appreciate their scent to the full, plant in bowls or shallow pans for indoor display; start them into growth in a bulb frame outside, then bring them inside a week or two before they would normally bloom in the garden, so that the warmth stimulates them into flower.

Outside, crocuses may be used in rock gardens in association with other early-flowering dwarf bulbs or perennials, or planted *en masse* in drifts or beneath deciduous trees and shrubs, where they will rapidly colonize large areas and provide pleasure for many years. To promote vigour, feed the plants once the flowers have faded and while the leaves are in full growth. If naturalized in grass, delay mowing until the leaves have died down. Congested clumps may be dug up after flowering and divided.

C. 'Eyecatcher'

C. hadriaticus

C. 'Blue Bird'

C. kotschyanus

C. dalmaticus

C. minimus

C. tommasinianus
f. *albus*

C. vernus subsp.
albiflorus

C. sieberi 'Bowles'
White'

C. laevigatus

C. pulchellus

C. sieberi subsp.
sublimis f. *tricolor*

C. etruscus
'Zwanenburg'

C. malyi

C. boryi

C. goulimyi

C. medius

C. 'Snow Bunting'

C. imperati 'De Jager'

C. 'Blue Pearl'

C. nudiflorus

BULBS

C. banaticus

C. etruscus

C. longiflorus

C. baytopiorum

C. speciosus
'Conqueror'

C. vernus 'Queen of
the Blues'

C. biflorus

C. 'Advance'

C. vernus

C. tommasinianus
'Ruby Giant'

C. vernus 'Prinses
Juliana'

C. vernus 'Pickwick'

C. 'Dorothy'

C. 'Ladykiller'

C. cvijicii

C. tommasinianus
'Whitewell Purple'

C. speciosus

C. vernus 'Purpureus
Grandiflorus'

C. cartwrightianus

C. 'Cream Beauty'

C. speciosus 'Oxonian'

C. 'E. A. Bowles'

C. gargaricus

C. vernus
'Remembrance'

BULBS

429

BULBS small SPRING INTEREST

☐ PINK

Erythronium dens-canis
(Dog's-tooth violet)
Spring-flowering tuber with 2 basal, mottled leaves. Stem has a pendent, pink, purple or white flower, with bands of brown, purple and yellow near the centre and reflexed petals. H 15–25cm (6–10in), S 8–10cm (3–4in).

☼ ◊

Allium acuminatum
Spring-flowering bulb with 2–4 long, narrow, semi-erect, basal leaves. Stem bears an umbel, 5cm (2in) across, of up to 30 small, purplish-pink flowers. H 10–30cm (4–12in), S 5–8cm (2–3in).

☼ ◊ ⓘ

Allium oreophilum,
syn. *A. ostrowskianum*
Spring- and summer-flowering, dwarf bulb with 2 narrow, semi-erect, basal leaves. Has loose, domed umbels of up to 10 widely bell-shaped, deep rose-pink flowers, 1.5–2cm (⅝–¾in) across. H 5–10cm (2–4in), S 8–10cm (3–4in).

☼ ◊ ⓘ

Anemone blanda 'Radar'
Knobbly tuber with semi-erect, deep green leaves with 3 deeply toothed lobes. In early spring, stems each bear an upright, flattish, white-centred, deep reddish-carmine flower with 9–14 narrow petals. H 5–10cm (2–4in), S 10–15cm (4–6in).

☼ ◊ ⓘ

■ RED–PURPLE

Anemone × fulgens
Spring- or early summer-flowering tuber with deeply divided, semi-erect, basal leaves. Stout stems each carry an upright, bright red flower, 5–7cm (2–3in) across, with 10–15 petals. H 10–30cm (4–12in), S 8–10cm (3–4in).

☼ ◊ ⓘ

Sparaxis tricolor
Spring-flowering corm, lance-shaped, erect, leaves in a basal fan. Stem has a loose spike of up to 5 flattish, orange, red, purple, pink or white flowers, 5–6cm (2–2½in) across, with black or red centres. H 10–30cm (4–12in), S 8–12cm (3–5in). Min. 5°C (41°F).

☼ ◊

Bulbocodium vernum
Spring-flowering corm with stemless, widely funnel-shaped, reddish-purple flowers. Narrow, semi-erect, basal leaves appear with flowers but do not elongate until later. Dies down in summer. H 3–4cm (1¼–1½in), S 3–5cm (1¼–2in).

☼ ◊

BULBS

Babiana rubrocyanea (Winecups)
Spring-flowering corm with lance-shaped, erect, folded leaves in a basal fan. Carries short spikes of 5–10 flowers, each with 6 petals, purple-blue at the top and red at the base. H 15–20cm (6–8in), S 5–8cm (2–3in). Min. 10°C (50°F).

☼ ◊

Ipheion uniflorum 'Froyle Mill'
Spring-flowering bulb with narrow, semi-erect, basal, pale green leaves that smell of onions if crushed. Each leafless stem carries a star-shaped, violet-blue flower, 3–4cm (1¼–1½in) across. H 10–15cm (4–6in), S 5–8cm (2–3in).

◑ ◊

Romulea bulbocodium
Spring-flowering corm with long, semi-erect, thread-like leaves in a basal tuft. Slender flower stems each carry 1–6 upward-facing flowers, usually pale lilac-purple with yellow or white centres. H 5–10cm (2–4in). S 2.5–5cm (1–2in).

☼ ◊

Hyacinths

Grown for their sweet, penetrating scent, hyacinths (*Hyacinthus*) are deservedly popular spring bulbs. The most widely offered for sale are showy cultivars derived from *H. orientalis* and are available in an increasingly wide colour range: white, many shades of pink, lilac, blue, purple, yellow and warm salmon-orange. In the garden they are most effective if planted *en masse* in blocks of a single colour, or in containers positioned near the house where their fragrance can be appreciated to the full. They are also excellent for growing in bowls indoors; the bulbs may later be planted out in the garden. Specially treated bulbs for indoor culture are available that flower in mid-winter. (For details see the Plant Dictionary.) These forced bulbs may afterwards be planted outdoors in a sheltered spot, where they should flower again in later years. To keep the bulbs healthy and productive, feed them well after the flower spikes have faded.

H. orientalis
'Delft Blue' ①

H. orientalis
'White Pearl' ①

H. orientalis
'Lady Derby' ①

H. orientalis
'Ostara' ①

*H.o.***'Queen of the Pinks'** ①

H. orientalis
'Jan Bos' ①

H. orientalis
'Blue Jacket' ①

H. orientalis
'Distinction' ①

H. orientalis
'Violet Pearl' ①

H. orientalis
'City of Haarlem' ①

H. orientalis
'Princess Maria Christina' ①

Gynandriris sisyrinchium
Spring-flowering corm with 1 or
2 semi-erect, narrow, basal leaves.
Wiry stems each carry a succession of
lavender- to violet-blue flowers, 3–4cm
(1¼–1½in) across, with white or orange
patches on the 3 larger petals.
H 10–20cm (4–8in), S 8–10cm (3–4in).

☼ ◊

Hyacinthella leucophaea
Spring-flowering bulb with 2 narrowly
strap-shaped, semi-erect, basal leaves
and a thin, wiry, leafless flower stem.
Carries a short spike of tiny, bell-
shaped, very pale blue, almost white
flowers. H 10cm (4in),
S 2.5–5cm (1–2in).

☼ ◊

Bellevalia hyacinthoides,
syn. *Strangweja spicata*
Spring-flowering bulb with prostrate,
narrow leaves in a basal cluster. Bears
a dense spike of up to 20 bell-shaped,
pale lavender-blue, almost white
flowers with darker, central veins.
H 5–15cm (2–6in), S 5cm (2in).

☼ ◊

Scilla mischtschenkoana, syn.
S. tubergeniana, S. 'Tubergeniana'
Early spring-flowering bulb with 2 or
3 strap-shaped, semi-erect, basal, mid-
green leaves. Stems elongate as cup-
shaped or flattish, pale blue flowers,
with darker blue veins, open.
H 5–10cm (2–4in), S 5cm (2in).

☼ ◊

Muscari comosum 'Plumosum',
syn. *M.c.* 'Monstrosum'
(Feather grape hyacinth)
Spring-flowering bulb with up to 5 strap-
shaped, semi-erect, basal, grey-green
leaves. Sterile flowers are replaced by
a fluffy mass of purple threads. H to
25cm (10in), S 10–12cm (4–5in).

☼ ◊

Tecophilaea cyanocrocus var.
leichtlinii, syn. *T.c.* 'Leichtlinii'
Spring-flowering corm with 1 or 2
narrowly lance-shaped, semi-erect,
basal leaves and solitary upward-
facing, widely funnel-shaped, pale
blue flowers with large, white centres.
H 8–10cm (3–4in), S 5–8cm (2–3in).

☼ ◊

Puschkinia scilloides var.
libanotica (Striped squill)
Spring-flowering bulb with usually
2 strap-shaped, semi-erect, basal
leaves. Carries a dense spike of star-
shaped, pale blue flowers with a darker
blue stripe down each petal centre.
H 15cm (6in), S 2.5–5cm (1–2in).

☼ ◊

Brimeura amethystina,
syn. *Hyacinthus amethystinus*
Late spring-flowering bulb with very
narrow, semi-erect, basal leaves.
Each leafless stem bears a spike of
up to 15 pendent, tubular, blue flowers.
H 10–25cm (4–10in), S 2.5–5cm
(1–2in).

◑ ◊

Scilla siberica 'Atrocoerulea'
Early spring-flowering bulb with
2–4 strap-shaped, semi-erect, basal,
glossy leaves, widening towards tips.
Bell-shaped, deep rich blue flowers,
1–1.5cm (½–⅝in) long, are borne in
a short spike. H 10–15cm (4–6in),
S 5cm (2in).

☼ ◊

BULBS

Muscari aucheri,
syn. *M. lingulatum*
Spring-flowering bulb with 2 strap-shaped, greyish-green leaves. Bears small, almost spherical, bright blue flowers with white-rimmed mouths; upper flowers are often paler.
H 5–15cm (2–6in), S 5–8cm (2–3in).

Chionodoxa luciliae,
syn. *C. gigantea*
Early spring-flowering bulb with 2 somewhat curved, semi-erect, basal leaves. Leafless stem bears 1–3 upward-facing, blue flowers with white eyes. H 5–10cm (2–4in), S 2.5–5cm (1–2in).

Chionodoxa forbesii, syn.
C. luciliae of gardens, *C. siehei*, *C. tmolusii*
Early spring-flowering bulb with 2 semi-erect, narrow, basal leaves. Bears a spike of 5–10 outward-facing, rich blue-lilac flowers with white eyes. H 10–25cm (4–10in), S 2.5–5cm (1–2in).

Tecophilaea cyanocrocus (Chilean blue crocus)
Spring-flowering corm with 1 or 2 lance-shaped, semi-erect, basal leaves. Carries upward-facing, funnel-shaped, deep gentian-blue flowers, 4–5cm (1½–2in) across, with white throats. H 8–10cm (3–4in), S 5–8cm (2–3in).

Muscari armeniacum
Spring-flowering bulb with 3–6 long, narrow, semi-erect, basal leaves. Carries a dense spike of small, fragrant, bell-shaped, deep blue flowers with constricted mouths that have a rim of small, paler blue or white 'teeth'. H 15–20cm (6–8in), S 8–10cm (3–4in).

Muscari neglectum,
syn. *M. racemosum*
Spring-flowering bulb. Bears 4–6 often prostrate leaves from autumn to early summer. Has small, ovoid, deep blue or blackish-blue flowers with white-rimmed mouths. Increases rapidly. H 10–20cm (4–8in), S 8–10cm (3–4in).

***Anemone blanda* 'Atrocaerulea'**
Knobbly tuber with semi-erect, dark green leaves that have 3 deeply toothed lobes. In early spring, stems each bear an upright, flattish, bright blue flower, 4–5cm (1½–2in) across, with 9–14 narrow petals. H 5–10cm (2–4in), S 10–15cm (4–6in).

x *Chionoscilla allenii*
Early spring-flowering bulb with 2 narrow, semi-erect, basal, dark green leaves and flattish, star-shaped, deep blue flowers, 1–2cm (½–¾in) across, in a loose spike. H 10–15cm (4–6in), S 2.5–5cm (1–2in).

HYACINTHS, illus. p.431

▢ GREEN–YELLOW

***Ledebouria socialis*,**
syn. *Scilla socialis, S. violacea*
Evergreen, spring-flowering bulb with
lance-shaped, semi-erect, basal, dark-
spotted, grey or green leaves. Produces
a short spike of bell-shaped, purplish-
green flowers. H 5–10cm (2–4in),
S 8–10cm (3–4in). Min. 2°C (35°F).

☼ ◊

Muscari macrocarpum
Spring-flowering bulb with 3–5 semi-
erect, basal, greyish-green leaves.
Carries a dense spike of fragrant,
brown-rimmed, bright yellow flowers.
Upper flowers may initially be
brownish-purple. H 10–20cm (4–8in),
S 10–15cm (4–6in).

☼ ◊

▢ YELLOW–ORANGE

Calochortus amabilis (Golden
fairy lantern, Golden globe tulip)
Spring-flowering bulb with one long,
narrow, erect leaf, near the base of the
loosely branched stem. A fringed, deep
yellow, sometimes green-tinged flower
hangs from each branch. H 10–30cm
(4–12in), S 5–10cm (2–4in).

☼ ◊

Colchicum luteum
Spring-flowering corm with wineglass-
shaped, yellow flowers – the only
known yellow *Colchicum*. Semi-erect,
basal leaves are short at flowering time
but later expand. H 5–10cm (2–4in),
S 5–8cm (2–3in).

☼ ◊ ⓘ

Erythronium americanum
Spring-flowering tuber with 2 semi-
erect, basal leaves, mottled green and
brown, and a pendent, yellow flower,
often bronze outside, with petals
reflexing in sunlight. Forms clumps
by stolons. H 5–25cm (2–10in),
S 5–8cm (2–3in).

◑ ◊

Fritillaria pudica
(Yellow fritillary)
Spring-flowering bulb with stems
bearing scattered, narrowly lance-
shaped, grey-green leaves. Has 1 or
2 deep yellow, sometimes red-tinged
flowers, 1–2.5cm (½–1in) long.
H 5–20cm (2–8in), S 5cm (2in).

☼ ◊

***Arum italicum* 'Marmoratum'**
Late spring-flowering tuber. Produces
semi-erect leaves, with cream or white
veins, in autumn, followed by pale
green or creamy-white spathes, then
red berries in autumn. Is good for
flower arrangements. H 15–25cm
(6–10in), S 20–30cm (8–12in).

☼ ◊

Dipcadi serotinum
Spring-flowering bulb with 2–5 very
narrow, semi-erect, basal leaves.
Leafless stem has a loose spike of
nodding, tubular, brown or dull orange
flowers, 1–1.5cm (½–⅝in) long.
H 10–30cm (4–12in), S 5–8cm (2–3in).

☼ ◊

BULBS

BULBS small SUMMER INTEREST

◨ WHITE–PINK

Lloydia serotina
Early summer-flowering bulb with
wiry stems bearing scattered, thread-
like, semi-erect leaves near stem base.
Carries 1 or 2 bell-shaped, white
flowers, 1–1.5cm (½–⅝in) long, with
purple or purple-red veins. H 5–15cm
(2–6in), S 2.5–5cm (1–2in).

☽ ◊

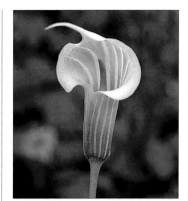

Arisaema candidissimum
Early summer-flowering tuber with
large, cowl-like, pink-striped, white
spathes, enclosing tiny, fragrant flowers
on spadices, followed by broad,
3-palmate, semi-erect leaves, 30cm
(12in) long. H 10–15cm (4–6in),
S 30–45cm (12–18in).

☼ ◊

■ RED

Hippeastrum striatum,
syn. *H. rutilum*
Spring- and summer-flowering bulb
with strap-shaped, semi-erect, basal,
bright green leaves. Funnel-shaped
flowers have pointed, scarlet petals with
central, green stripes. H 30cm (12in),
S 20–25cm (8–10in). Min. 15°C (59°F).

☼ ◊ ⓘ

Cyrtanthus brachyscyphus
Clump-forming, summer-flowering
bulb with strap-shaped, semi-erect,
basal, bright green leaves. Leafless
stem bears a head of 6–12 tubular,
orange- or brilliant red flowers with
6 lobes. H 20–30cm (8–12in),
S 10–15cm (4–6in). Min. 5°C (41°F).

☼ ◊

Albuca humilis
Summer-flowering, dwarf bulb with
very narrow, basal, dark green leaves.
Carries a loose head of 1–3 cup-
shaped, white flowers, 1cm (½in) long,
striped green, later reddish, outside.
H 5–10cm (2–4in), S 5–8cm (2–3in).
Min. 5°C (41°F).

☼ ◊

Allium schoenoprasum (Chives)
Clump-forming, summer-flowering
bulb with narrow, hollow, erect, dark
green leaves at base. Stems each carry
up to 20 tiny, bell-shaped, pale purple
or pink flowers in a dense umbel up to
5cm (2in) across. H 12–25cm
(5–10in), S 5–10cm (2–4in).

☼ ◊ ⓘ

Haemanthus coccineus (Blood lily)
Summer-flowering bulb with 2 elliptic
leaves, hairy beneath, that lie flat on the
ground. Spotted stem, forming before
leaves, bears a cluster of tiny, red flowers
with prominent stamens, within fleshy,
red or pink bracts. H to 30cm (12in),
S 20–30cm (8–12in). Min. 10°C (50°F).

☼ ◊ ⓘ

Cyclamen purpurascens,
syn. *C. europaeum, C. fatrense*
Summer- and autumn-flowering tuber
with rounded, silver-patterned leaves.
Bears very fragrant, lilac-pink to
reddish-purple flowers. H to 10cm
(4in), S 10–15cm (4–6in).

☽ ◊ ⓘ

OTHER RECOMMENDED PLANTS:
Allium campanulatum
Allium oreophilum, illus. p.430
Caloscordum neriniflorum

Habranthus robustus, illus. p.437
Triteleia peduncularis
Zephyranthes atamasco

Anomatheca laxa
BEGONIAS, illus. p.295
Habranthus tubispathus

■ PURPLE

Allium narcissiflorum,
syn. *A. pedemontanum* of gardens
Clump-forming, summer-flowering
bulb with very narrow, erect, grey-
green leaves on the lower part of the
flower stem. Has an umbel of up to 15
bell-shaped, pinkish-purple flowers.
H 15–30cm (6–12in), S 8–10cm (3–4in).

☼ ◊ ⓘ

Allium cyathophorum var. *farreri*
Clump-forming, summer-flowering bulb
with tufts of narrow, erect, basal leaves.
Each stem bears a small, loose umbel,
1.5–4cm (⅝–1½in) wide, of up to 30
bell-shaped, dark reddish-purple flowers
with sharply pointed petals. H 15–30cm
(6–12in), S 10–15cm (4–6in).

☼ ◊ ⓘ

□▭ BLUE–YELLOW

Scilla peruviana
Early summer-flowering bulb with a
basal cluster of up to 10 lance-shaped,
semi-erect leaves. Stem bears a
broadly conical head of up to 50
flattish, violet-blue flowers, 1.5–3cm
(⅝–1¼in) across. H 10–25cm
(4–10in), S 15–20cm (6–8in).

☼ ◊

Chlidanthus fragrans
Summer-flowering bulb with narrow,
semi-erect leaves in a basal tuft.
Leafless stem carries a head of
3–5 fragrant, funnel-shaped, yellow
flowers, 4–7cm (1½–2¾in) long.
H 10–30cm (4–12in), S 8–10cm
(3–4in). Min. 5°C (41°F).

☼ ◊

Roscoea humeana
Summer-flowering tuber. Erect, broadly
lance-shaped, rich green leaves form a
stem-like sheath at base. Carries up to
10 long-tubed, purple flowers, each with
a hooded, upper petal, a wide, pendent
lip and 2 narrower petals. H 15–25cm
(6–10in), S 15–20cm (6–8in).

☼ ◊

Roscoea cautleyoides
Summer-flowering tuber. Erect, lance-
shaped leaves form a stem-like sheath
at base. Has up to 5 long-tubed, yellow
flowers, each with a hooded, upper
petal, a broad, 2-lobed, lower lip and
2 narrower petals. H 15–25cm
(6–10in), S 10–15cm (4–6in).

☼ ◊

Allium moly
Clump-forming, summer-flowering
bulb with 1–3 broad, semi-erect, basal,
grey-green leaves. Stems each bear up
to 40 star-shaped, yellow flowers in a
fairly dense umbel, 4–8cm (1½–3in)
across. H 10–35cm (4–14in),
S 10–12cm (4–5in).

☼ ◊ ⓘ

Calochortus monophyllus
Summer-flowering bulb with an erect,
branched stem with 1–3 slender leaves
and one long, narrow basal leaf. Bears
cup-shaped, deep yellow flowers, often
with a reddish mark on the claws.
Petals are fringed and densely bearded.
H 8–20cm (3–8in), S 5cm (2in).

☼ ◊

Hypoxis angustifolia
Summer-flowering corm with slender,
hairy, semi-erect, basal leaves. Stems
each carry 3–7 star-shaped, yellow
flowers, 1.5–2cm (⅝–¾in) across.
H 10–20cm (4–8in), S 5–8cm (2–3in).
Min. 2°C (35°F).

☼ ◊

BULBS

BULBS small AUTUMN INTEREST

☐ WHITE

Cyclamen hederifolium
f. albiflorum
Autumn-flowering tuber. Pure white
flowers, with reflexed petals, appear
before or with leaves, which vary but
are often ivy-shaped with silvery-
green patterns. H to 10cm (4in),
S 10–15cm (4–6in).
☼ ◊ ⚠

Colchicum speciosum 'Album'
Vigorous, autumn-flowering corm with
large, semi-erect, basal leaves in late
winter or spring. Cup-shaped, white
flowers successfully withstand bad
weather. H and S 15–20cm (6–8in).
☼ ◊ ⚠

Leucojum autumnale
(Autumn snowflake)
Autumn-flowering bulb with thread-
like, erect, basal leaves appearing with,
or just after, flowers. Slender stems
each produce a head of 14 bell-shaped,
white flowers, tinged pink at bases.
H 10–15cm (4–6in), S 2.5–5cm (1–2in).
☼ ◊

☐◼ WHITE–PINK

Zephyranthes candida
Autumn-flowering bulb with narrow,
erect, basal leaves forming rush-like
tufts. Each leafless stem carries crocus-
like, white flowers, to 6cm (2½in)
across. H 15–25cm (6–10in),
S 5–8cm (2–3in).
☼ ◊

Cyclamen africanum
Autumn-flowering tuber with ivy-
shaped, deep green leaves with lighter
patterns. Bears pendent, white or pink
flowers, with reflexed petals and
darker stains around mouths, as or just
before leaves appear. H to 10cm (4in),
S 10–15cm (4–6in).
◑ ◊ ⚠

Cyclamen mirabile
Autumn-flowering tuber with pale
pink flowers with toothed petals and
dark purple-stained mouths. Heart-
shaped, patterned leaves, purplish-
green beneath, are minutely toothed
on margins. H to 10cm (4in),
S 5–8cm (2–3in).
◑ ◊ ⚠

Habranthus robustus
Late summer- to early autumn-
flowering bulb with narrowly strap-
shaped, semi-erect, basal leaves.
Leafless flower stems each bear a
funnel-shaped, pink flower inclined
at an angle. H 20–30cm (8–12in),
S 8–10cm (3–4in). Min. 2°C (35°F).
☼ ◊

Colchicum autumnale
(Autumn crocus, Meadow saffron)
Autumn-flowering corm with up to
8 long-tubed, wineglass-shaped,
purple, pink or white flowers, followed
by 3–5 large, strap-shaped, semi-erect,
basal, glossy leaves in spring. H and
S 10–15cm (4–6in).
☼ ◊ ⚠

Colchicum byzantinum
Robust, autumn-flowering corm with
up to 20 large, funnel-shaped, pale
purplish-pink flowers, 10–15cm
(4–6in) long. In spring produces very
broad, semi-erect, basal leaves, ribbed
lengthways. H and S 15–20cm (6–8in).
☼ ◊ ⚠

BULBS

☐ PINK

Cyclamen graecum
Autumn-flowering tuber with heart-shaped, toothed, velvety, dark green leaves, patterned silver or light green. Flowers are pink or white, with purple stains around mouths. Grows best in an alpine house. H to 10cm (4in), S 10–15cm (4–6in).

Cyclamen rohlfsianum
Autumn-flowering tuber with coarsely toothed leaves, zoned with light and dark green patterns, and pale pink-lilac flowers, stained darker at mouths. H to 10cm (4in), S 10–15cm (4–6in).

Cyclamen cilicium
Autumn-flowering tuber with broadly heart-shaped leaves that have light and dark green zones. Has white or pink flowers, each with a dark purple stain at the mouth, just before or with leaves. H to 10cm (4in), S 5–10cm (2–4in).

Colchicum cilicicum
Autumn-flowering corm with large, cup-shaped, pale pink to deep rose-purple flowers, sometimes slightly chequered. Very broad, semi-erect, basal leaves, ribbed lengthways, appear soon after flowers have faded. H and S 15–20cm (6–8in).

Cyclamen hederifolium,
syn. *C. neapolitanum*
Autumn-flowering tuber. Pale to deep pink flowers, stained darker at mouths, appear before or with foliage. Leaves vary but are often ivy-shaped with silvery-green patterns. H to 10cm (4in), S 10–15cm (4–6in).

Colchicum bivonae,
syn. *C. bowlesianum, C. sibthorpii*
Autumn-flowering corm with large, funnel-shaped, pinkish-purple flowers, strongly chequered darker purple and with purple anthers. Produces 8–10 erect leaves in spring. H 10–15cm (4–6in), S 15–20cm (6–8in).

BULBS

BULBS small WINTER INTEREST

▨ PINK–PURPLE

Colchicum agrippinum
Early autumn-flowering corm. Narrow, slightly waved, semi-erect, basal leaves develop in spring. Bears erect, funnel-shaped, bright purplish-pink flowers with a darker chequered pattern and pointed petals. H 10–15cm (4–6in), S 8–10cm (3–4in).

☀ ◊ ⓘ

Colchicum 'Waterlily'
Autumn-flowering corm with rather broad, semi-erect, basal leaves in winter or spring. Tightly double flowers have 20–40 pinkish-lilac petals. H 10–15cm (4–6in), S 15–20cm (6–8in).

☀ ◊ ⓘ

Merendera montana,
syn. *M. bulbocodium*
Autumn-flowering corm with narrowly strap-shaped, semi-erect, basal leaves, produced just after upright, broad-petalled, funnel-shaped, rose- or purple-lilac flowers appear. H to 5cm (2in), S 5–8cm (2–3in).

☀ ◊

Biarum eximium
Colchicum 'The Giant'
CROCUSES, illus. pp.428–9
Cyclamen purpurascens, illus. p.435

▨ PURPLE–YELLOW

Biarum tenuifolium
Late summer- or autumn-flowering tuber producing clusters of acrid, narrow, erect, basal leaves after stemless, upright and often twisted, blackish-purple spathes appear. H to 20cm (8in), S 8–10cm (3–4in).

☀ ◊

Arum pictum
Autumn-flowering tuber. Arrow-shaped, semi-erect, glossy leaves, with cream veins, appear at the same time as a cowl-like, deep purple-brown spathe and dark purple spadix. H 15–25cm (6–10in), S 15–20cm (6–8in).

☀ ◊

Sternbergia lutea
Autumn-flowering bulb with strap-shaped, semi-erect, basal, deep green leaves appearing together with a funnel-shaped, bright yellow flower, 2.5–6cm (1–2½in) long, on a leafless stem. H 2.5–15cm (1–6in), S 8–10cm (3–4in).

☀ ◊

CROCUSES, illus. pp.428–9
Sternbergia clusiana
Sternbergia sicula
Zephyranthes citrina

☐ WHITE

Galanthus nivalis 'Flore Pleno'
(Double common snowdrop)
Late winter- and early spring-flowering bulb with semi-erect, basal, grey-green leaves. Bears rosetted, many-petalled, double, white flowers, some inner petals having a green mark at the apex. H 10–15cm (4–6in), S 5–8cm (2–3in).

◑ ◊ ⓘ

Galanthus nivalis 'Pusey Green Tip'
Late winter- and early spring-flowering bulb with narrowly strap-shaped, semi-erect, basal, grey-green leaves. Each stem bears a white flower with many mostly green-tipped petals. H 10–15cm (4–6in), S 5–8cm (2–3in).

◑ ◊ ⓘ

Galanthus gracilis
Late winter- and early spring-flowering bulb with slightly twisted, strap-shaped, semi-erect, basal, grey-green leaves. Bears white flowers with 3 inner petals, each marked with a green blotch at the apex and base. H 10–15cm (4–6in), S 5–8cm (2–3in).

◑ ◊ ⓘ

OTHER RECOMMENDED PLANTS:
Galanthus nivalis
Galanthus plicatus subsp. *plicatus*

Galanthus rizehensis
Late winter- and early spring-flowering bulb with very narrow, strap-shaped, semi-erect, basal, dark green leaves. Produces white flowers, 1.5–2cm (⅝–¾in) long, with a green patch at the apex of each inner petal. H 10–20cm (4–8in), S 5cm (2in).

◑ ◊

Galanthus elwesii
Late winter- and early spring-flowering bulb with semi-erect, basal, grey-green leaves that widen gradually towards tips. Each inner petal of the white flowers bears green marks at the apex and base, which may merge. H 10–30cm (4–12in), S 5–8cm (2–3in).

◑ ◊ ⓘ

Galanthus 'Atkinsii'
Vigorous, late winter- and early spring-flowering bulb with strap-shaped, semi-erect, basal, grey-green leaves. Each stem carries a slender, white flower with a green mark at the apex of each inner petal. H 10–25cm (4–10in), S 5–9cm (2–3½in).

◑ ◊ ⓘ

☐ WHITE

Galanthus nivalis 'Sandersii',
syn. *G.n.* 'Lutescens'
Late winter- and early spring-flowering
bulb with narrowly strap-shaped, semi-
erect, basal, grey-green leaves. Flowers,
1.5–2cm (⅝–¾in) long, are white with
yellow patches at the apex of each inner
petal. H 10cm (4in), S 2.5–5cm (1–2in).

Galanthus ikariae
Late winter- and early spring-flowering
bulb with strap-shaped, semi-erect,
basal, glossy, bright green leaves.
Produces one white flower, 1.5–2.5cm
(⅝–1in) long, marked with a green
patch at the apex of each inner petal.
H 10–25cm (4–10in), S 5–8cm (2–3in).

Galanthus nivalis 'Scharlockii'
Vigorous, late winter- and early spring-
flowering bulb with semi-erect, basal,
grey-green leaves. Has white flowers,
with green marks at the apex of inner
petals, overtopped by 2 narrow spathes
that resemble donkeys' ears.
H 10–15cm (4–6in), S 5–8cm (2–3in).

Galanthus plicatus subsp.
byzantinus
Late winter- and early spring-flowering
bulb. Semi-erect, basal, deep green
leaves have a grey bloom and reflexed
margins. White flowers have green
marks at bases and tips of inner petals.
H 10–20cm (4–8in), S 5–8cm (2–3in).

Cyclamen coum f. **albissimum**,
syn. *C.c.* 'Album'
Winter-flowering tuber with rounded,
deep green leaves, sometimes silver-
patterned. Carries white flowers, each
with a maroon mark at the mouth.
H to 10cm (4in), S 5–10cm (2–4in).

☐ PINK

Cyclamen persicum
Winter- or spring-flowering tuber with
heart-shaped leaves, marked light and
dark green and silver. Bears fragrant,
slender, white or pink flowers, 3–4cm
(1¼–1½in) long and stained carmine at
mouths. H 10–20cm (4–8in), S 10–15cm
(4–6in). Min. 5–7°C (41–5°F).

Cyclamen persicum 'Pearl Wave'
Winter- and spring-flowering tuber
with heart-shaped leaves, marked light
and dark green and silver. Produces
fragrant, slender, deep pink flowers,
with 5–6cm (2–2½in) long, frilly-edged
petals. H 10–20cm (4–8in), S 10–15cm
(4–6in). Min. 5–7°C (41–5°F).

Cyclamen coum
Winter-flowering tuber with rounded
leaves, plain deep green or silver-
patterned. Produces bright carmine
flowers with dark stains at mouths.
H to 10cm (4in), S 5–10cm (2–4in).

Cyclamen coum subsp. *caucasicum*
HYACINTHS, illus. p.431

***Cyclamen persicum* 'Esmeralda'**
Winter-flowering tuber with heart-shaped, silver-patterned leaves and broad-petalled, carmine-red flowers. H 10–20cm (4–8in), S 15–20cm (6–8in). Min. 5–7°C (41–5°F).

☼ ◊ ①

***Cyclamen persicum* 'Renown'**
Winter- and spring-flowering tuber with heart-shaped, bright silver-green leaves, each with a central, dark green mark. Carries fragrant, slender, scarlet flowers, 5–6cm (2–2½in) long. H 10–20cm (4–8in), S 10–15cm (4–6in). Min. 5–7°C (41–5°F).

☼ ◊ ①

Lachenalia aloides* var. *quadricolor
Winter- to spring-flowering bulb with 2 strap-shaped, semi-erect, basal leaves. Has a spike of 10–20 purplish-red buds opening to greenish-yellow or -orange flowers. H 15–25cm (6–10in), S 5–8cm (2–3in). Min. 2°C (35°F).

☼ ◊

***Lachenalia aloides* 'Nelsonii'**, syn. *L.* 'Nelsonii'
Winter- to spring-flowering bulb. Has 2 strap-shaped, purple-spotted, semi-erect, basal leaves, a spike of 10–20 pendent, tubular, greenish, bright yellow flowers, 3cm (1¼in) long. H 15–25cm (6–10in), S 5–8cm (2–3in). Min. 2°C (35°F).

☼ ◊

***Cyclamen persicum* Kaori Series**
Winter-flowering tuber with neat, heart-shaped, silver-marbled leaves. Produces fragrant flowers, 4cm (1½in) long, in a wide range of colours. H 10–20cm (4–8in), S 10–15cm (4–6in). Min. 5–7°C (41–5°F).

☼ ◊ ①

Eranthis hyemalis
(Winter aconite)
Clump-forming tuber. Bears stalkless, cup-shaped, yellow flowers, 2–2.5cm (¾–1in) across, from late winter to early spring. A dissected, leaf-like bract forms a ruff beneath each bloom. H 5–10cm (2–4in), S 8–10cm (3–4in).

☼ ◊ ①

HYACINTHS, illus. p.431
Lachenalia aloides
Lachenalia rubida

Eranthis x *tubergenii* 'Guinea Gold'
HYACINTHS, illus. p.431

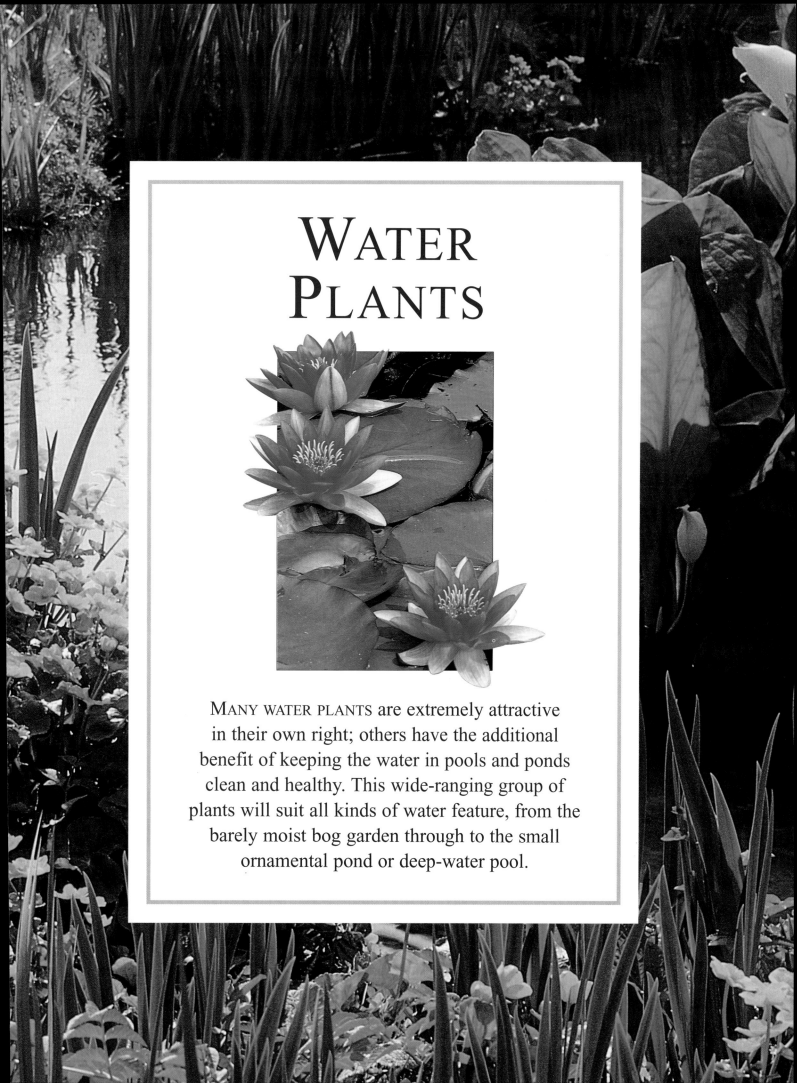

WATER PLANTS

MANY WATER PLANTS are extremely attractive
in their own right; others have the additional
benefit of keeping the water in pools and ponds
clean and healthy. This wide-ranging group of
plants will suit all kinds of water feature, from the
barely moist bog garden through to the small
ornamental pond or deep-water pool.

Water Plants

The sound- and light-reflecting qualities of water have long been used to bring vitality to garden designs. For many, still or moving water is the soul of the garden and it also greatly extends the range of plants that can be grown.

WHAT ARE WATER PLANTS?

The broad definition of water plants includes all plants that grow rooted, submerged or floating in water. They may be further sub-divided into deep-water, surface-floating, marginal, bog, or moisture-loving plants, depending on the depth of water that is required for them to thrive.

WHY CULTIVATE WATER PLANTS?

Water plants differ from other plant groups in that they are seldom grown for ornament alone. Nearly all are important for the creation of the healthy ecosystem that is essential if you wish to maintain a water feature's beauty. To do this you need to introduce a balanced range of water plants to regulate the light, oxygen and nutrient levels, thus producing conditions in which plants and animals alike can thrive.

Submerged plants, such as water milfoil (*Myriophyllum*), act as 'oxygenators', providing the dissolved oxygen that is vital for all pond life. They also remove excess nutrients from the water and help keep it clear by controlling algal growth, which causes cloudy, green water and blocks out the light necessary for healthy, aquatic plant and pond life. Surface-floaters, such as the fairy moss (*Azolla filiculoides*) or water hyacinth (*Eichhornia crassipes*), also reduce dissolved nutrients by absorbing them through their slender roots. Apart from being very attractive in themselves, deep-water plants, such as *Nuphar* and water lilies (*Nymphaea*), with their roots at the pond bottom and flowers and foliage floating at the surface, provide shelter for pond life and also shade out algal growth.

ORNAMENTAL WATER FEATURES

Whether tiny or large, formal or informal, every garden has room for a water feature and its associated plants. In restricted spaces, aquatics such as the dwarf water lily *Nymphaea tetragona* 'Helvola' or slender water irises (*Iris laevigata*) can be grown, while in larger

FORMAL FEATURE
Above: This formal, split-level pool not only makes an elegant focal point within the garden, but also cleverly provides different water depths to accommodate the needs of various types of water plant, from deep-water perennials like water lilies to the shallow-water marginals such as Houttuynia cordata.

MARGINAL PLANTING
Below: The curving edges of an informal pool offer perfect conditions for marginals such as pickerel weed (Pontederia cordata) and arrowhead (Sagittaria latifolia), which root in water up to 15cm (6in) deep. Marginals disguise and soften pool edges and provide invaluable shelter for wildlife.

areas *Typha latifolia* will look effective. In a sunken or raised formal pool, using those plants with an architectural outline, such as *Pontederia cordata* or *Zantedeschia aethiopica*, can provide an elegant focal point and emphasize the formal style. The advantage of an informal pond is that it offers great versatility: its sinuous margins are longer than straight-sided ponds of similar size, and its sloping banks can provide a range of planting depths, greatly increasing your choice of marginal plants. With its sloping and possibly boggy banks, it is also much easier to attract wildlife into the garden.

WATER LILIES
Water lilies (Nymphaea), *which need still water to thrive, perform a dual function: they are incomparably ornamental and their floating leaves shade out algal growth and provide shelter for fish and their fry.*

This lends an extra dimension of interest and also benefits both gardener and plants, because many amphibians, birds and small mammals actively prey on garden pests.

DESIGNING WITH WATER PLANTS

A water feature should be designed following the same principles that apply to other plant groups, using contrasting and complementary colours, textures and forms. Water plants can offer a wide succession of interest if you choose those that provide diversity in foliage, flower colour and shape, and seed heads.

To accommodate a range of water plants, however, it is essential to provide differing depths of water. Deep-water plants, such as Cape pondweed (*Aponogeton distachyos*) with its very fragrant white flowers at the water surface, and the floating water soldier (*Stratiotes aloides*) with its spiky, aloe-like leaves, require a depth of about 1m (3ft). Water lilies (*Nymphaea*), with their pristine flowers in colours ranging from pure white to deepest red, need to root at depths of 15–100cm (½–3ft), depending on the species or cultivar.

Marginal plants, which thrive in conditions ranging from pure mud to water that is 30–45cm (1–1½ft) deep, are the most diverse of aquatics. They are invaluable for disguising edges of artificial and natural ponds, for creating interesting reflections and for providing wildlife cover. Marginals have a range of habits: from bog bean (*Menyanthes trifoliata*), with its dainty clusters of

STREAM-SIDE PLANTING
Above right: The damp soil of a stream bank makes an ideal home for moisture-loving perennials like the candelabra primulas, while water crowfoot (Ranunculus aquatilis), *which thrives in fast-moving water, is a good choice for planting in the stream bed.*

CONTRASTING FOLIAGE
Right: A lush profusion of foliage makes a strong design statement if plants of contrasting form are set side by side. Here, the horizontal, flat shapes of water lilies bring into high relief the vertical heart-shaped foliage of pickerel weed.

white flowers in spring and glossy leaves that spill out across the water surface, to the flowering rush (*Butomus umbellatus*), with its upright stems bearing umbels of small pink flowers, and the substantial skunk cabbages (*Lysichiton*), with their large arum-like blooms and handsome foliage.

In a bog garden, saturated soil provides perfect conditions for many bog natives and moisture-lovers, including the robust candelabra primulas, the globeflower (*Trollius europaeus*), with its deeply divided foliage, and the elegant, ostrich fern *Matteuccia struthiopteris*.

☐ WHITE

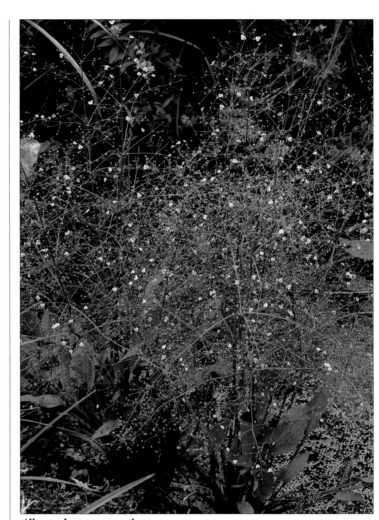

Menyanthes trifoliata
(Bog bean, Buckbean)
Deciduous, perennial, marginal water plant that has 3-parted, mid-green leaves and fringed, white flowers borne in spring. H 23cm (9in), S 30cm (12in).

☼ ●

Alisma plantago-aquatica
(Water plantain)
Deciduous, perennial, marginal water plant with upright, oval, bright green leaves that emerge well above water. Loose, conical panicles of small, pinkish to white flowers appear in summer. H 75cm (30in), S 45cm (18in).

☼ ●

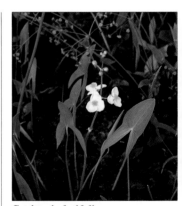

Lysichiton camtschatcensis
(water skunk cabbage)
Vigorous, deciduous, perennial, marginal water or bog plant. Pure white spathes, surrounding spikes of insignificant, small flowers, are borne in spring, before oblong to oval, bright green leaves emerge. H 75cm (30in), S 60cm (24in).

☼ ●

Hydrocharis morsus-ranae
(Frogbit)
Deciduous, perennial, floating water plant with rosettes of kidney-shaped, olive-green leaves and small, white flowers during summer. S 10cm (4in), but young plantlets remain attached to form a mass up to 1m (3ft) across.

☼ ●

Calla palustris (Bog arum)
Deciduous or semi-evergreen, perennial, spreading, marginal water plant with heart-shaped, glossy, mid- to dark green leaves. In spring produces large, white spathes usually followed by red or orange fruits. H 25cm (10in), S 30cm (12in).

☼ ● ⚠

Sagittaria latifolia
(American arrowhead, Duck potato)
Deciduous, perennial, marginal water plant with curved, soft green leaves and sprays of white flowers in summer. H 1.5m (5ft), S 60cm (2ft).

☼ ●

OTHER RECOMMENDED PLANTS:
Luronium natans
Nelumbo nucifera 'Alba Grandiflora'
Sagittaria sagittifolia

Sagittaria sagittifolia 'Flore Pleno'
WATER LILIES, illus. p.450

WATER PLANTS

Saururus cernuus (Lizard's tail, Swamp lily, Water dragon)
Deciduous, perennial, marginal water or bog plant. Has clumps of heart-shaped, mid-green leaves and racemes of creamy flowers in summer. H 23cm (9in), S 30cm (12in).

☼ ◆

Hottonia palustris (Water violet)
Deciduous, perennial, submerged water plant. Dense whorls of much-divided, light green leaves form a spreading mass of foliage. Lilac or whitish flowers appear above water surface in summer. S indefinite.

☼ ◆

Acorus gramineus 'Variegatus'
Semi-evergreen, perennial, marginal or submerged water plant. Narrow, stiff, grass-like leaves are dark green with cream variegation.
H 25cm (10in), S 15cm (6in).

☼ ◆

Stratiotes aloides (Water soldier)
Semi-evergreen, perennial, submerged, free-floating water plant. Spiny, olive-green leaves are arranged in rosettes. Produces cup-shaped, white, sometimes pink-tinged flowers in summer. Increases by producing small water buds. S 30cm (12in).

☼ ◆

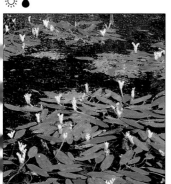

Aponogeton distachyos
(Cape pondweed, Water hawthorn)
Deciduous, perennial, deep-water plant with floating, oblong, mid- to dark green leaves, often splashed with purple. Very fragrant, 'forked', white flowers with black stamens are produced throughout summer. S 1.2m (4ft).

☼ ◆

Acorus calamus 'Argenteostriatus',
syn. *A.c.* 'Variegatus'
Semi-evergreen, perennial, marginal water plant. Sword-like, tangerine-scented, mid-green leaves have cream variegation and are flushed rose-pink in spring. H 75cm (30in), S 60cm (24in).

☼ ◆

Houttuynia cordata 'Chameleon',
syn. *H.c.* 'Variegata'
Vigorous, deciduous, perennial, ground-cover, marginal water plant. Aromatic, leathery leaves are splashed yellow and red. Has small sprays of white flowers in summer. Needs some sun to enhance variegation. H 10cm (4in), S indefinite.

◐ ◆

Caltha leptosepala
(Alpine marsh-marigold)
Deciduous, perennial, marginal water plant with heart-shaped, dark green leaves and buttercup-like, white flowers produced in spring.
H and S 30cm (12in).

☼ ◆

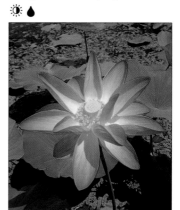

Nelumbo nucifera (Sacred lotus)
Vigorous, deciduous, perennial, marginal water plant. Sturdy stems carry very large, plate-like, blue-green leaves and, in summer, large, vivid rose-pink flowers, maturing to flesh-pink. H 1–1.5m (3–5ft) above water surface, S 1.2m (4ft). Min. 7°C (45°F).

☼ ◆

Nelumbo nucifera 'Alba Striata'
Nelumbo nucifera 'Rosea Plena'
WATER LILIES, illus. p.450

WATER PLANTS

WATER PLANTS

Butomus umbellatus
(Flowering rush)
Deciduous, perennial, rush-like, marginal water plant with narrow, twisted, mid-green leaves and umbels of pink to rose-red flowers in summer. H 1m (3ft), S 45cm (1½ft).
☼ ●

Myosotis scorpioides 'Mermaid'
Deciduous, perennial, marginal water plant for mud or very shallow water. Narrow, mid-green leaves form sprawling mounds. Bears small, blue, forget-me-not flowers throughout summer. H 15cm (6in), S 30cm (12in).
☼ ●

Typha latifolia (cattail)
Deciduous, perennial, marginal water plant with large clumps of mid-green foliage. Produces spikes of beige flowers in late summer, followed by decorative, cylindrical, dark brown seed heads. Is invasive.
H to 2.5m (8ft), S 60cm (2ft).
☼ ●

Eichhornia crassipes, syn. *E. speciosa* (Water hyacinth)
Evergreen or semi-evergreen, perennial water plant, with glossy leaves, floating on air-filled leaf stalks. Bears spikes of blue-and-lilac flowers in summer. May be invasive in warm conditions. S 23cm (9in). Min. 1°C (34°F).
☼ ●

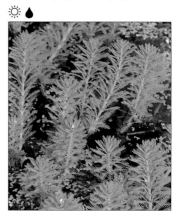

Myriophyllum aquaticum, syn. *M. proserpinacoides* (Parrot feather)
Deciduous, perennial, partially or completely submerged water plant. Spreading, finely divided, blue-green foliage turns reddish in autumn if it surfaces. S indefinite.
☼ ●

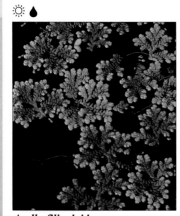

Azolla filiculoides, syn. *A. caroliniana* (Fairy moss, Water fern)
Deciduous, perennial, floating water fern with divided fronds that vary from red to purple in full sun and from pale green to blue-green in shade. Helps reduce algae. S indefinite.
☼ ●

Pontederia cordata
(Pickerel weed)
Deciduous, perennial, marginal water plant. In late summer, dense spikes of blue flowers emerge between lance-shaped, glossy, dark green leaves. H 75cm (30in), S 45cm (18in).
☼ ●

Colocasia esculenta (Taro)
Deciduous, perennial, marginal water plant with large, bold, mid- to dark green leaves, often with prominent, white veins. Bears insignificant spathes in summer. May be grown in wet soil in a pot. H 1.1m (3½ft), S 60cm (2ft). Min. 1°C (34°F).
☼ ● ⊕

Potamogeton crispus
(Curled pondweed)
Deciduous, perennial, submerged water plant that produces spreading colonies of seaweed-like, bronze- or mid-green foliage. Insignificant, reddish flowers are borne in summer. Prefers cool water. S indefinite.
☼ ●

Colocasia esculenta 'Illustris'
Cryptocoryne spiralis
Thalia dealbata
Thalia geniculata

WATER LILIES, illus. p.450

WATER LILIES, illus. p.450

WATER PLANTS

Pistia stratiotes (Water lettuce)
Deciduous, perennial, floating water
plant for a pool or aquarium, evergreen
in tropical conditions. Hairy, soft green
foliage is lettuce-like in arrangement.
Produces tiny, greenish flowers at
varying times. H and S 10cm (4in).
Min. 10–15°C (50–59°F).

Lagarosiphon major,
syn. _Elodea crispa_ of gardens
Semi-evergreen, perennial, spreading,
submerged water plant that forms dense,
underwater swards of foliage. Ascending
stems are covered in narrow, reflexed,
dark green leaves. Bears insignificant
flowers in summer. S indefinite.

Euryale ferox
Annual, deep-water plant. Has
floating, rounded, spiny, olive-green
leaves with rich purple undersides and
bears small, violet-purple flowers in
summer. Is suitable only for a tropical
pool. S 1.5m (5ft). Min. 5°C (41°F).

Sparganium erectum, syn.
S. ramosum (Branched bur reed)
Vigorous, deciduous or semi-
evergreen, perennial, marginal water
plant with narrow, mid-green leaves.
Bears small, greenish-brown burs in
summer.
H 1m (3ft), S 60cm (2ft).

Salvinia auriculata
Deciduous, perennial, floating water
plant, evergreen in tropical conditions,
that forms spreading colonies. Has
rounded, pale to mid-green leaves,
sometimes suffused purplish-brown, in
pairs on branching stems. S indefinite.
Min. 10–15°C (50–59°F).

Myriophyllum verticillatum
(Whorled water milfoil)
Deciduous, perennial, spreading,
submerged water plant, overwintering
by club-shaped winter buds. Slender
stems are covered with whorls of finely
divided, olive-green leaves.
S indefinite.

Trapa natans
(Jesuit's nut, Water chestnut)
Annual, floating water plant with
diamond-shaped, mid-green leaves,
often marked purple, arranged in
neat rosettes. Bears white flowers
in summer. S 23cm (9in).

Typha minima (Dwarf cattail)
Deciduous, perennial, marginal water
plant with grass-like leaves. Spikes of
rust-brown flowers in late summer are
succeeded by decorative, cylindrical
seed heads. H 45–60cm (18–24in),
S 30cm (12in).

Hydrocleys nymphoides
(Water poppy)
Deciduous, perennial, deep-water
plant, evergreen in tropical conditions,
with floating, oval, mid-green leaves.
Poppy-like, yellow flowers are held
above foliage during summer.
S to 60cm (2ft). Min. 1°C (34°F).

WATER PLANTS

449

Water lilies

The serene beauty of a water lily (*Nymphaea*) will add a focal point and colour to any water garden. Neat, small-leaved plants will grow in only 8cm (3in) of water, but more vigorous plants may need up to 1m (3ft). Their large, plate-like leaves provide shelter for fish and also help to reduce the spread of algae. Usually hardy, water lilies make few demands, although they prefer an open, sunny site and still water.

N. 'American Star'

N. 'Lucida'

N. 'Virginia'

N. tetragona 'Alba'

N. 'Gladstoneana'

N. 'Attraction'

N. 'James Brydon'

N. Laydekeri Group 'Fulgens'

N. 'Blue Beauty'

N. Marliacea Group 'Albida'

N. 'Firecrest'

N. 'Froebelii'

N. tetragona 'Helvola'

N. Marliacea Group 'Chromatella'

N. 'General Pershing'

N. 'Rose Arey'

N. 'Escarboucle'

N. 'Sunrise'

WATER PLANTS

☐ YELLOW

Lysichiton americanus,
syn. *L. americanum* (Yellow skunk cabbage)
Vigorous, deciduous, perennial, marginal water or bog plant. In spring, before large, fresh green leaves appear, produces showy, bright yellow spathes. H 1m (3ft), S 75cm (2½ft).
☼ ●

Caltha palustris 'Flore Pleno'
Deciduous, perennial, marginal water plant with rounded, dark green leaves. Bears clusters of double, bright golden-yellow flowers in spring. H and S 25cm (10in).
☼ ●

Nymphoides peltata
(Fringed water lily, Water fringe)
Deciduous, perennial, deep-water plant with floating, small, round, mid-green leaves, often spotted and splashed with brown. Produces small, fringed, yellow flowers throughout summer. S 60cm (24in).
☼ ●

Caltha palustris
(Kingcup, Marsh marigold)
Deciduous, perennial, marginal water plant that has rounded, dark green leaves and bears clusters of cup-shaped, bright golden-yellow flowers in spring. H 60cm (24in), S 45cm (18in).
☼ ●

Ranunculus lingua
(Greater spearwort)
Deciduous, perennial, marginal water plant with stout stems and lance-shaped, glaucous leaves. Clusters of yellow flowers are borne in late spring. H 90cm (3ft), S 45cm (1½ft).
☼ ● ①

Nuphar lutea
(Brandy bottle, Yellow water lily)
Vigorous, deciduous, perennial, deep-water plant for a large pool. Mid-green leaves are leathery. Small, sickly-smelling, bottle-shaped, yellow flowers open in summer and are followed by decorative seed heads. S 1.5m (5ft).
◐ ●

Orontium aquaticum
(Golden club)
Deciduous, perennial, deep-water plant or, less suitably, marginal water plant. In spring, pencil-like, gold-and-white flower spikes emerge from floating, oblong, blue-grey or blue-green leaves. S 60cm (24in).
☼ ●

WATER PLANTS

451

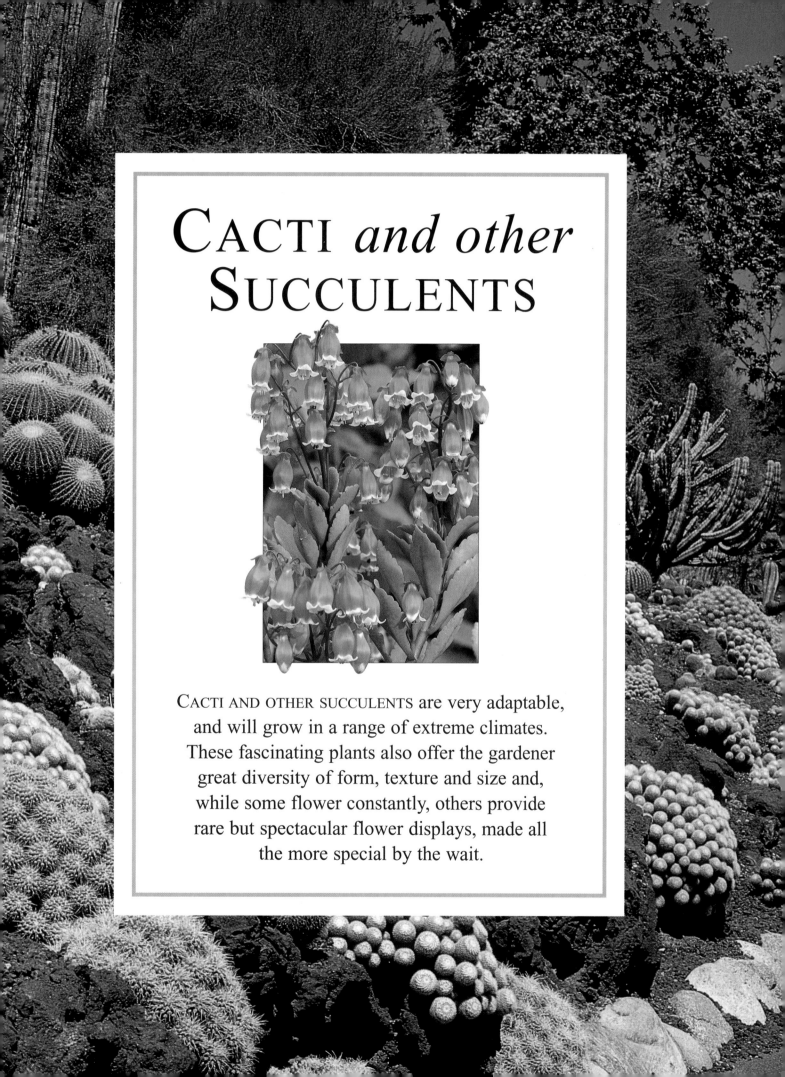

CACTI *and other* SUCCULENTS

CACTI AND OTHER SUCCULENTS are very adaptable,
and will grow in a range of extreme climates.
These fascinating plants also offer the gardener
great diversity of form, texture and size and,
while some flower constantly, others provide
rare but spectacular flower displays, made all
the more special by the wait.

Cacti and other Succulents

The world's harshest climates have imposed evolutionary pressures on the plant life that survives in them, and these have resulted in a group of plants unrivalled in the strangeness and diversity of their forms.

WHAT ARE CACTI AND SUCCULENTS?
Succulents are plants in which the leaves, stems or roots have become adapted for water storage, enabling them to sustain life during seasons of drought. Cacti differ from other succulents in that they have areoles, which are cushion-like growths on their stems.

Since their leaves are primary sites of water loss, many succulents either drop them during periods of drought, or do without them altogether. Their surfaces have also developed to conserve moisture and be protected from harsh light and extreme heat, and range from the waxy, blue-grey-bloomed leaves of pachyphytum and the leathery gasterias to the densely hairy *Oreocereus celsianus* or fiercely spiny echinocactus. Spines, which are prized by gardeners as an ornamental feature, in fact protect plants from predators and also condense droplets of atmospheric moisture which then fall onto the roots.

CHOOSING SUCCULENTS
In order to grow succulents successfully it is important to understand and imitate their natural environments as closely as possible. The most familiar cacti and other succulents are native to arid desert and semi-desert conditions, but some originate from cold, high-alpine

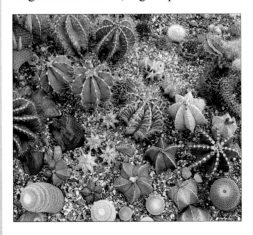

DISPLAYING SMALL SUCCULENTS
Here, neat architectural forms of ribbed parodias and astrophytums provide strong contrasts with the more globose mammillarias.

habitats – the sempervivums for instance – while others, such as the epiphyllums, come from sub-tropical and tropical rainforests.

Gardeners who live in frost-free, dry climates can therefore grow desert cacti and other succulents outside, in large, architectural compositions in a border. In such areas, rainfall is often highly seasonal, but when it does occur it stimulates spectacular floral displays.

In frost-free, humid regions, conditions are perfect for the rainforest cacti and other succulents such as selenicereus, schlumbergera and epiphyllums. These need a little shade, and can be planted where they will cascade from the branches of a host tree. Meanwhile their often nocturnal and sometimes highly fragrant flowers may scent the air over some distance.

In cooler, frost-prone regions, tender species must be grown indoors or in a greenhouse or conservatory. Most need a minimum temperature of 10–15°C (50–59°F) while some tropical species require at least 20°C (68°F). Borders in open ground or raised beds provide a home for such hardy genera as sempervivum, jovibarba, sedum and some of the euphorbias. Most require sharp drainage and grow well with true alpines, which have similar drainage, light and moisture needs.

DESIGNING WITH SUCCULENTS
Succulent textures and shapes range from the tight cushions of fleshy, rosetted leaves of the echeverias, through the spiny, cylindrical, branching desert cacti cereus and cleistocactus to the gracefully pendent, rainforest tree-clingers (epiphytes) rhipsalis and schlumbergera. There are also globose and ribbed forms, as in mammillaria, haageocereus and the very small, pebble-like lithops.

Such a distinctive range has many decorative uses. The majestic, highly sculptural globes, cylinders and branching, candelabra-shaped types, for example, offer scope

HANGING BEAUTY
Left: Rainforest cacti such as aporocactus and epiphyllums and their hybrids often flower along the length of trailing stems. Here, x Aporophyllum *'Sussex Pink' is shown to perfection in a hanging basket.*

for exciting designs when contrasted with the basal-rosetted aloes, agaves and yuccas, with their spiky leaves

GROWING IN CONTAINERS
Most cacti and other succulents adapt successfully to container cultivation, and impressive displays can be created to decorate outdoor patios and terraces during the warmer months. In winter they will need a sunny window-sill or a greenhouse. The most important rule for effective compositions of different species in containers is to group plants of similar growth rates and

GLORIOUS FLOWERS

Above: The brilliant, hot shades of the summer-flowering Echinopsis 'Glorious', which are typical of many cactus flowers, add vibrant colour to a display of sculptural forms.

IN A NATURAL SETTING

Left: In their native hot, dry climates, cacti and other succulents can achieve spectacular dimensions, as here, where the rosettes of agaves are used as a foil to the living, columnar sculptures of the saguaro cactus (Carnegiea gigantea) and pad-forming opuntias.

GREENHOUSE CULTIVATION

Below: Although there are hardy species, in cool temperate climates most cacti and other succulents need protection from frost, cold and damp. The greenhouse and the home provide the ideal conditions for the cultivation and display of their many and varied forms.

cultivation needs together, so that they will thrive without outgrowing their allotted space and overwhelming their companions.

Many cacti and other succulents, such as the jade tree (*Crassula ovata*), *Aeonium arboreum* and many agaves, make splendid specimens when grown alone in attractive containers. These, along with plants such as sansevieria, *Senecio rowleyanus* or *Ceropegia linearis* subsp. *woodii*, are often so long-lived, easily propagated and extraordinarily tolerant of neglect that specimens and their offspring have been passed from generation to generation between families and friends.

Be careful where you site cacti with spines because they are capable of inflicting injury. They must be placed well away from eye-level and out of reach of children and pets.

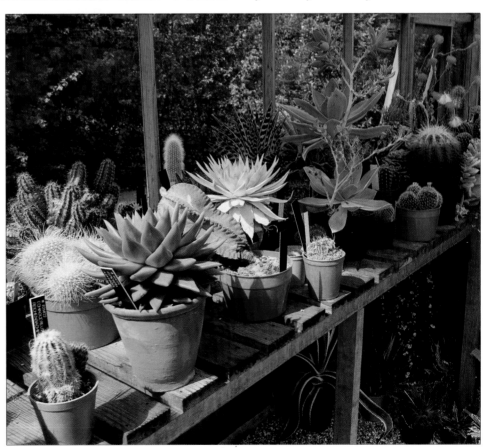

SIZE CATEGORIES USED WITHIN THIS GROUP		
Large	**Medium**	**Small**
over 1m (3ft)	23cm–1m (9in–3ft)	up to 23cm (9in)

CACTI *and other* SUCCULENTS large

☐ WHITE

Selenicereus grandiflorus
(Queen-of-the-night)
Climbing, perennial cactus. Has
7-ribbed, 1–2cm (½–¾in) wide, green
stems with yellow spines. White
flowers, 18–30cm (7–12in) across,
open at night in summer. H 3m (10ft),
S indefinite. Min. 5°C (41°F).

☼ ◊

Echinopsis lageniformis, syn.
E. bridgesii, Trichocerus bridgesii
Columnar, perennial cactus with
4–8-ribbed stems branching at base.
Areoles each produce up to 6 spines.
Scented, funnel-shaped, white flowers
open at night in summer. H to 5m
(15ft), S 1m (3ft). Min. 10°C (50°F).

☼ ◊

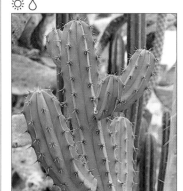

Myrtillocactus geometrizans
(Blue candle)
Columnar, perennial cactus with a
much-branched, 5- or 6-ribbed, blue-
green stem. Bears short, black spines,
on plants over 30cm (1ft) tall, and white
flowers at night in summer. H to 4m
(12ft), S 2m (6ft). Min. 12°C (54°F).

☼ ◊

Cereus validus, syn. *C. forbesii*
Columnar, perennial cactus with a
branching, blue-green stem bearing
dark spines on 4–7 prominent ribs.
Has 25cm (10in) long, cup-shaped, white
flowers at night in summer, followed
by red fruits. H 7m (22ft), S 3m (10ft).
Min. 7°C (45°F).

☼ ◊

Cereus uruguayansus
Columnar, perennial cactus. Has a
branching, silvery-blue stem with golden
spines on 4–8 sharply indented ribs.
Carries cup-shaped, white flowers, 10cm
(4in) across, at night in summer, followed
by pear-shaped, red fruits. H 5m (15ft),
S 4m (12ft). Min. 7°C (45°F).

☼ ◊

Browningia hertlingiana,
syn. *Azureocereus hertlingianus*
Slow-growing, columnar, perennial
cactus with a silvery-blue stem, golden
spines and tufted areoles. Nocturnal,
white flowers appear in summer, only
on plants over 1m (3ft) high. H 8m
(25ft), S 4m (12ft). Min. 7°C (45°F).

☼ ◊

Pachypodium lamerei
Tree-like, perennial succulent with a
spiny, pale green stem crowned by
linear leaves. Has fragrant, trumpet-
shaped, creamy-white flowers in
summer, on plants over 1.5m (5ft) tall.
Stems branch after each flowering. H 6m
(20ft), S 2m (6ft). Min. 11°C (52°F).

☼ ◊

Carnegiea gigantea (Saguaro)
Very slow-growing, perennial cactus
with a thick, 12–24-ribbed, spiny, green
stem. Tends to branch and bears short,
funnel-shaped, fleshy, white flowers at
stem tips in summer, only when over
4m (12ft) high. H to 12m (40ft), S 3m
(10ft). Min. 7°C (45°F).

☼ ◊

OTHER RECOMMENDED PLANTS:
Agave americana
Echinopsis candicans, illus. p.461
Epiphyllum anguliger, illus. p.461

Lepismium warmingianum, illus. p.461
Rhipsalis floccosa, illus. p.461

CACTI *and other* SUCCULENTS

Pachycereus marginatus
(Organ-pipe cactus)
Columnar, perennial cactus with a 5- or
6-ribbed, branching, shiny stem. Areoles
bear minute spines. Produces funnel-
shaped, white flowers in summer. H 7m
(22ft), S 3m (10ft). Min. 11°C (52°F).

☀ ◊

Agave parviflora
Basal-rosetted, perennial succulent.
Has narrow, white-marked, dark green
leaves with white fibres peeling from
edges. Produces white flowers in
summer. H 1.5m (5ft), S 50cm (20in).
Min. 5°C (41°F).

☀ ◊

Stetsonia coryne
Tree-like, perennial cactus with a short,
swollen trunk bearing 8- or 9-ribbed,
blue-green stems. Black spines fade
with age to white with black tips.
Funnel-shaped, white flowers appear at
night in summer. H 8m (25ft), S 4m
(12ft). Min. 10°C (50°F).

☀ ◊

Crassula ovata (Friendship tree,
Jade tree, Money tree)
Perennial succulent with a swollen
stem crowned by glossy, green leaves,
at times red-edged. Bears 5-petalled,
white flowers in autumn-winter. H 4m
(12ft), S 2m (6ft). Min. 5°C (41°F).

☀ ◊

Echinopsis spachiana
(Torch cactus)
Clump-forming, perennial cactus with
glossy, green stems bearing 10–15 ribs
and pale golden spines. Fragrant,
funnel-shaped, white flowers open at
night in summer. H and S 2m (6ft).
Min. 8°C (46°F).

☀ ◊

Espostoa lanata (Cotton ball,
Peruvian old-man cactus)
Very slow-growing, columnar,
perennial cactus with a branching,
woolly, green stem. Foul-smelling,
white flowers appear in summer, only
on plants over 1m (3ft) high. H to 4m
(12ft), S 2m (6ft). Min. 10°C (50°F).

☀ ◊

Pereskia aculeata (Barbados
gooseberry, Lemon vine)
Fast-growing, deciduous, climbing
cactus with broad, glossy leaves.
Orange-centred, creamy-white flowers
appear in autumn, only on plants over
1m (3ft) high. H to 10m (30ft), S 5m
(15ft). Min. 5°C (41°F).

☀ ◊

Agave americana 'Striata'
Basal-rosetted, perennial succulent.
Has sharply pointed, sword-shaped,
blue-green leaves with yellow edges.
Stem carries white flowers, each 9cm
(3½in) long, in spring-summer.
Offsets freely. H and S 2m (6ft).
Min. 6°C (41°F).

☀ ◊

CACTI *and other* SUCCULENTS *(side tab)*

Haageocereus versicolor
Columnar, perennial cactus. Dense, radial spines, golden, red or brown, at times form coloured bands around a longer, central spine up the green stem. Long-tubed, white flowers appear near crown of plant in summer. H to 2m (6ft), S 1m (3ft). Min. 11°C (52°F).

☼ ◊

Crassula arborescens
(Silver jade plant)
Perennial succulent with a thick, robust stem crowned by branches bearing rounded, silvery-blue leaves, often with red edges. Has 5-petalled, pink flowers in autumn-winter. H 4m (12ft), S 2m (6ft). Min. 7°C (45°F).

☼ ◊

Pereskia grandifolia,
syn. *Rhodocactus grandifolius*
(Rose cactus)
Deciduous, bushy, perennial cactus with black spines. Single rose-like, pink flowers form in summer-autumn only on plants over 30cm (1ft) high. H 5m (15ft), S 3m (10ft). Min. 10°C (50°F).

☼ ◊

Adenium obesum
Tree-like, perennial succulent with a fleshy, tapering, green trunk and stems crowned by oval, glossy, green leaves, dull green beneath. Carries funnel-shaped, pink to pinkish-red flowers, white inside, in summer. H 2m (6ft), S 50cm (20in). Min. 15°C (59°F).

☼◐ ◊ ⓘ

Pachycereus schottii,
syn. *Lophocereus schottii*
Columnar, perennial cactus, branching with age. Olive- to dark green stem, covered with small, white spines, bears 4–15 ribs. Funnel-shaped, pink flowers are produced at night in summer. H 7m (22ft), S 2m (6ft). Min. 10°C (50°F).

☼ ◊

Pilosocereus leucocephalus,
syn. *P. palmeri*
Columnar, perennial cactus with a 10–12-ribbed stem and white-haired crown. Bears tubular, pink flowers, with cream anthers, at night in summer, on plants over 1.5m (5ft) tall. H to 6m (20ft), S 1m (3ft). Min. 11°C (52°F).

☼ ◊

Ceropegia linearis subsp. *woodii*, illus. p.462
Haageocereus chosicensis
Oreocereus celsianus, illus. p.462

Pachycereus schottii 'Monstrosus'
Senecio rowleyanus, illus. p.462

Aloe arborescens 'Variegata'
Evergreen, bushy, succulent-leaved
shrub. Each stem is crowned by
rosettes of long, slender, blue-green
leaves with toothed edges and cream
stripes. Produces numerous spikes of
red flowers in late winter and spring.
H and S 2m (6ft). Min. 7°C (45°F).

☼ ◊

Aloe ferox
Evergreen, succulent tree with a woody
stem crowned by a dense rosette of
sword-shaped, blue-green leaves that
have spined margins. Carries an erect
spike of bell-shaped, orange-scarlet
flowers in spring. H to 3m (10ft),
S 1.5–2m (5–6ft). Min. 7°C (45°F).

☼ ◊

Cyphostemma juttae,
syn. *Cissus juttae*
Perennial succulent. Swollen stem has
peeling bark and deciduous, scandent
branches with broad leaves. Bears
inconspicuous, yellow-green flowers in
summer. Green fruits turn yellow or red.
H and S 2m (6ft). Min. 10°C (50°F).

☼ ◊

**Pedilanthus tithymaloides
'Variegata'** (Redbird flower)
Bushy, perennial succulent with stems
angled at each node. Leaves have white
or pink marks. Stem tips carry small,
greenish flowers in red to yellowish-
green bracts in summer. H to 3m (10ft),
S 30cm (1ft). Min. 10°C (50°F).

◑ ◊ ⓘ

Aloe ciliaris
Climbing, perennial succulent with a
slender stem crowned by a rosette of
narrow, green leaves. Has white teeth
where leaf base joins stem. Bears bell-
shaped, scarlet flowers, with yellow
and green mouths, in spring. H 5m
(15ft), S 30cm (1ft). Min. 7°C (45°F).

☼ ◊

Neobuxbaumia euphorbioides
Columnar, perennial cactus. Has grey-
green to dark green stems, 10cm (4in)
across, with 8–10 ribs and 1 or 2 black
spines per areole. Funnel-shaped, wine-
red flowers appear in summer. H to 3m
(10ft), S 1m (3ft). Min. 15°C (59°F).

☼ ◊

Cleistocactus strausii (Silver torch)
Fast-growing, columnar, perennial
cactus with 8cm (3in) wide stems
carrying short, dense, white spines.
Masses of long, tubular, red flowers
appear in spring, only on plants over
60cm (2ft) high. H 3m (10ft), S 1–2m
(3–6ft). Min. 5°C (41°F).

☼ ◊

Aloe arborescens
Cereus uruguayanus 'Monstrosus'
Crassula perfoliata var. *minor*, illus. p.464
Opuntia cylindrica

Pedilanthus tithymaloides
Tylecodon paniculatus

CACTI *and other* SUCCULENTS large

▭▭ GREEN–YELLOW

Cephalocereus senilis
(Old-man cactus)
Very slow-growing, columnar,
perennial cactus with a green stem
covered in long, white hairs, masking
short, white spines. Is unlikely to
flower in cultivation. H 15m (50ft),
S 15cm (6in). Min. 5°C (41°F).

Furcraea foetida 'Mediopicta'
Basal-rosetted, perennial succulent with
broad, sword-shaped, green leaves,
striped with creamy-white, to 2.5m (8ft)
long. Has bell-shaped, green flowers,
with white interiors, in summer. H 3m
(10ft), S 5m (15ft). Min. 6°C (43°F).

Bowiea volubilis
Bulbous succulent with climbing,
much-branched, slender stems and no
proper leaves. Produces small, star-
shaped, green flowers at tips of stems
in summer. Provide support.
H 1–2m (3–6ft), S 45–60cm (1½–2ft).
Min. 10°C (50°F).

Kalanchoe beharensis
Bushy, perennial succulent with
triangular to lance-shaped, olive-green
leaves, covered with fine, brown hairs.
Bell-shaped, yellow flowers appear in
late winter, only on plants over 2m
(6ft) high. H and S to 4m (12ft).
Min. 10°C (50°F).

Ferocactus cylindraceus
Slow-growing, columnar, perennial
cactus, spherical when young. Green,
10–20-ribbed stem is covered with large,
hooked, red or yellow spines. Funnel-
shaped, yellow flowers form in summer
on plants over 25cm (10in) across. H 3m
(10ft), S 80cm (32in). Min. 5°C (41°F).

Pachycereus pringlei
Slow-growing, columnar, perennial
cactus with a branched, bluish-green
stem that has 10–15 ribs. Large areoles
each have 15–25 black-tipped, white
spines. Is unlikely to flower in
cultivation. H 11m (35ft), S 3m (10ft).
Min. 10°C (50°F).

Echinocactus grusonii (Golden
barrel cactus, Mother-in-law's seat)
Slow-growing, hemispherical, perennial
cactus. Spined, green stem has 30 ribs.
Woolly crown bears a ring of straw-
coloured flowers in summer, only on
stems over 38cm (15in) wide.
H and S to 2m (6ft). Min. 11°C (52°F).

Opuntia robusta
Bushy, perennial cactus. Silvery-blue
stem has flattened, oval segments with
either no spines or 8–12 white ones, to
5cm (2in) long, per areole. Saucer-
shaped, yellow flowers, 7cm (3in)
across, appear in spring-summer.
H and S 5m (15ft). Min. 5°C (41°F).

CACTI *and other* SUCCULENTS

☐ WHITE

Gymnocalycium gibbosum
Spherical to columnar, perennial cactus that has a dark green stem with 12–19 rounded ribs, pale yellow spines, darkening with age, and white flowers, to 7cm (3in) long, in summer. H 30cm (12in), S 20cm (8in). Min. 5°C (41°F).

☼ ◊

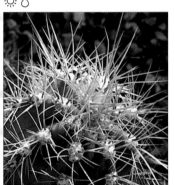

Echinopsis candicans, syn. *Trichocereus candicans*
Clump-forming, branching, perennial cactus with up to 11 ribs. Areoles each have 10–15 radial spines and 4 central ones. Fragrant, funnel-shaped, white flowers open at night in summer. H 1m (3ft), S indefinite. Min. 8°C (46°F).

☼ ◊

Echinopsis oxygona, syn. *E. multiplex*
Spherical to columnar, perennial cactus with a 13–15-ribbed, green stem and long spines. Has 10cm (4in) wide, tubular, white to lavender flowers, to 20cm (8in) long, in spring-summer. H and S 30cm (12in). Min. 5°C (41°F).

◊ ◊

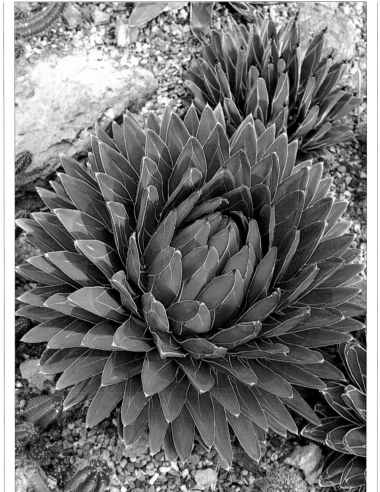

Agave victoriae-reginae
(Royal agave)
Very slow-growing, domed, perennial succulent with a basal rosette of spine-less, white-striped and -edged leaves. Has cream flowers on a 4m (12ft) tall stem in spring-summer after 20–30 years. H and S 60cm (2ft). Min. 5°C (41°F).

☼ ◊

Rhipsalis cereuscula (Coral cactus)
Pendent, perennial cactus with 4- or 5-angled or cylindrical, green stems and branches, to 3cm (1¼in) long in whorls. Stem tips each bear bell-shaped, white flowers in winter-spring. H 60cm (24in), S 50cm (20in). Min. 10°C (50°F).

☼ ◊

Epiphyllum laui
Bushy, perennial cactus, usually with strap-shaped, red-tinged, glossy stems which may also be spiny, cylindrical or 4-angled. Has fragrant, white flowers, with brown sepals, in spring-summer. H 30cm (12in), S 50cm (20in). Min. 10°C (50°F).

☼ ◊

Epiphyllum anguliger
(Fishbone cactus)
Erect, then pendent, perennial cactus. Has strap-shaped, flattened, green stems with indented margins. Produces tubular, 10cm (4in) wide, white flowers in summer. H 1m (3ft), S 40cm (16in). Min. 11°C (52°F).

☼ ◊

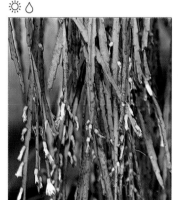

Lepismium warmingianum
Erect, then pendent, perennial cactus with slender, notched, cylindrical, green branches, sometimes tinged red or brown, with 2–4 angles. Has green-white flowers in winter-spring, followed by violet berries. H 1m (3ft), S 50cm (20in). Min. 11°C (52°F).

◐ ◊

Rhipsalis floccosa
Pendent, perennial cactus with cylindrical, green stems, to 1cm (½in) across, branching less than many other *Rhipsalis* species. Has masses of very pale pink flowers in early summer, then pinkish-white berries. H 1m (3ft), S 50cm (20in). Min. 10°C (50°F).

◐ ◊

OTHER RECOMMENDED PLANTS:
Echinopsis eyriesii
Haageocereus decumbens
Hatiora clavata

Hylocereus undatus
Neoporteria chilensis
Rhipsalis capilliformis
Rhipsalis crispata

Rhipsalis paradoxa
Ruschia crassa

CACTI *and other* SUCCULENTS medium

🔲 WHITE–PINK

🔲 PINK

Senecio articulatus 'Variegatus'
Deciduous, spreading, perennial succulent with grey-marked stems. Has cream- and pink-marked, blue-green leaves in summer and yellow flower heads from autumn to spring. H 60cm (2ft), S indefinite. Min. 10°C (50°F).

☀ ◊ ⓘ

Hesperaloe parviflora,
syn. *Yucca parviflora*
Basal-rosetted, perennial succulent, often with peeling, white fibres at leaf edges. Flower stems each bear a raceme of bell-shaped, pink to red flowers in summer-autumn. H 1m (3ft) or more, S 2m (6ft). Min. 3°C (37°F).

☀ ◊

Senecio rowleyanus
(String-of-beads)
Pendent, perennial succulent. Very slender, green stems bear cylindrical, green leaves. Has heads of fragrant, tubular, white flowers from spring to autumn. Suits a hanging pot. H 1m (3ft), S indefinite. Min. 5°C (41°F).

☀ ◊ ⓘ

Ceropegia linearis subsp. **woodii**,
syn. *C. woodii* (Heart vine, Rosary vine, String-of-hearts)
Semi-evergreen, trailing, succulent sub-shrub with tuberous roots. Leaves redden in sun. Has hairy, pinkish-green flowers from spring to autumn. H 1m (3ft), S indefinite. Min. 7°C (45°F).

☀ ◊

Nopalxochia phyllanthoides 'Deutsche Kaiserin'
Pendent, epiphytic, perennial cactus with flattened, toothed, glossy, green stems, each 5cm (2in) across. Stem margins each bear pink flowers, to 10cm (4in) across, in spring. H 60cm (2ft), S 1m (3ft). Min. 10°C (50°F).

☀ ◊

Oreocereus celsianus,
syn. *Borzicactus celsianus,*
Cleistocactus celsianus
(Old man of the Andes)
Slow-growing, perennial cactus. Has heavy and wispy spines. Mature plants bear pink flowers in summer. H 1m (3ft), S 30cm (1ft). Min. 10°C (50°F).

☀ ◊

Kalanchoe fedtschenkoi 'Variegata'
Bushy, perennial succulent. Blue-green and cream leaves also colour red. Bears a new plantlet in each leaf notch. Has brownish-pink flowers in late winter. H and S to 1m (3ft). Min. 10°C (50°F).

☀ ◊

Echinocereus schmollii,
syn. *Wilcoxia schmollii*
(Lamb's-tail cactus)
Erect to prostrate, tuberous cactus with 8–10-ribbed, purplish-green stems and mostly white spines. Has pinkish-purple flowers in spring-summer. H and S 30cm (12in). Min. 8°C (46°F).

☀ ◊

Kalanchoe daigremontiana
(Mexican hat plant)
Erect, perennial succulent with a stem bearing fleshy, boat-shaped, toothed leaves. Produces a plantlet in each leaf notch. Umbels of pink flowers appear at stem tops in winter. H to 1m (3ft), S 30cm (1ft). Min. 7°C (45°F).

☀ ◊

Echinocereus reichenbachii
var. **baileyi**, syn. *E. baileyi*
Columnar, perennial cactus with a slightly branched stem bearing 12–23 ribs and yellowish-white, 3cm (1¼in) long spines. Produces pink flowers with darker bases in spring. H 30cm (12in), S 20cm (8in). Min. 7°C (45°F).

☀ ◊

Echinopsis rhodotricha

Kalanchoe 'Wendy'
Semi-erect, perennial succulent with
narrowly oval, glossy, green leaves,
7cm (3in) long. In late winter bears
bell-shaped, pinkish-red flowers, 2cm
(¾in) long, with yellow tips. Is ideal for
a hanging basket. H and S 30cm (12in).
Min. 10°C (50°F).

Aporocactus flagelliformis
(Rat's-tail cactus)
Pendent, perennial cactus with pencil-
thick, green stems bearing short,
golden spines. Has double, cerise
flowers along stems in spring. Is good
for a hanging basket. H 1m (3ft),
S indefinite. Min. 10°C (50°F).

Nopalxochia 'Gloria'
Erect, then pendent, perennial cactus.
Strap-shaped, flattened, green stems
have toothed edges. Produces pinkish-
red flowers, 10cm (4in) across, in
spring. H 30cm (1ft), S 1m (3ft).
Min. 10°C (50°F).

Nopalxochia 'M.A. Jeans'
Erect, then pendent, perennial cactus.
Strap-shaped, flattened, green stems
have shallowly toothed edges. In spring
has deep pink flowers, 8cm (3in)
across, with white anthers.
H 30cm (12in), S 50cm (20in).
Min. 10°C (50°F).

Echinocereus pentalophus
Clump-forming, perennial cactus with
spined, green stems, 3–4cm (1¼–1½in)
wide, that have 4–8 ribs, later rounded.
Has trumpet-shaped, bright pink
flowers, paler at base, to 12cm (5in)
across, in spring. H 60cm (2ft), S 1m
(3ft). Min. 5°C (41°F).

Lampranthus spectabilis
Spreading, perennial succulent with
erect stems and narrow, cylindrical,
grey-green leaves. In summer produces
daisy-like flowers, cerise with yellow
centres or golden-yellow throughout.
H 30cm (1ft), S indefinite.
Min. 5°C (41°F).

Echinocereus cinerascens
Echinocereus pectinatus
Echinocereus reichenbachii
Kalanchoe fedtschenkoi

Lampranthus haworthii
Neoporteria chilensis
Oreocereus trollii

CACTI *and other* SUCCULENTS

463

CACTI *and other* SUCCULENTS medium

■■ PINK–RED

Kalanchoe blossfeldiana Hybrids
Bushy, perennial succulent with oval to oblong, toothed, glossy, green leaves. Produces clusters of yellow, orange, pink, red or purple flowers, year-round. Makes an excellent house plant.
H and S 30cm (1ft). Min. 10°C (50°F).

☀ ◊

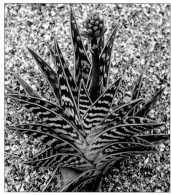

Gymnocalycium mihanovichii 'Red Head'
Perennial cactus with a red stem, 8 angular ribs and curved spines. Must be grafted on to any fast-growing stock as it contains no chlorophyll. Has pink flowers in spring-summer. H and S as per graft stock. Min. 10°C (50°F).

☀ ◊

Aloe variegata, syn. *A. punctata* (Partridge-breasted aloe)
Humped, perennial succulent. Has triangular, white-marked, dark green leaves with pronounced keels beneath. Bears a spike of pinkish-red flowers in spring. Is a good house plant. H 30cm (12in), S 10cm (4in). Min. 7°C (45°F).

☀ ◊

Echeveria pulvinata (Plush plant)
Bushy, perennial succulent with brown-haired stems each crowned by a rosette of thick, rounded, green leaves that become red-edged in autumn. Leaves have short, white hairs. Bears red flowers in spring. H 30cm (12in), S 50cm (20in). Min. 5°C (41°F).

☀ ◊

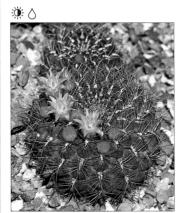

Oroya peruviana,
Spherical, perennial cactus with a much-ribbed stem covered in yellow spines, 1.5cm (⅝in) long, with darker bases. Pink flowers, with yellow bases, open in spring-summer. H 25cm (10in), S 20cm (8in). Min. 10°C (50°F).

☀ ◊

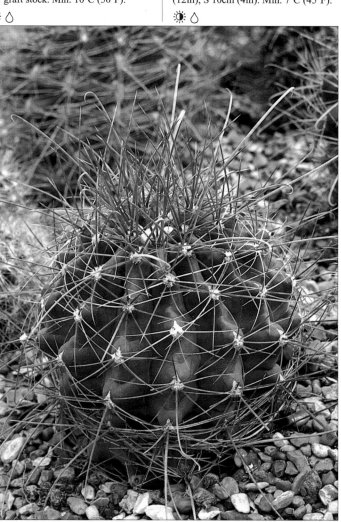

Ferocactus hamatacanthus,
syn. *Hamatocactus hamatacanthus*
Slow-growing, spherical to columnar, perennial cactus with a 13-ribbed stem that bears hooked, red spines, to 12cm (5in) long. Has yellow blooms in summer, then spherical, red fruits.
H and S 60cm (2ft). Min. 5°C (41°F).

☀ ◊

Dudleya pulverulenta
Basal-rosetted, perennial succulent with strap-shaped, pointed, silvery-grey leaves. Bears masses of star-shaped, red flowers in spring-summer. H 60cm (2ft), S 30cm (1ft). Min. 7°C (45°F).

☀ ◊

Kalanchoe 'Tessa'
Prostrate to pendent, perennial succulent with narrowly oval, green leaves, 3cm (1¼in) long. Bears tubular, orange-red flowers, 2cm (¾in) long, in late winter. H 30cm (1ft), S 60cm (2ft). Min. 10°C (50°F).

☀ ◊

Crassula perfoliata var. **minor**, syn. *C. falcata* (Aeroplane propeller)
Bushy, perennial succulent that branches freely. Long leaves each twist like a propeller. Has large clusters of fragrant, red flowers in late summer. H and S 1m (3ft). Min. 7°C (45°F).

☀ ◊

Echeveria gibbiflora
Mammillaria magnimamma
Neoporteria subgibbosa
Oreocereus haynei

Pachypodium succulentum

CACTI *and other* SUCCULENTS

Mammillaria hahniana (Old-lady cactus, Old–woman cactus)
Spherical to columnar, perennial cactus with a green stem bearing long, woolly, white hairs. Carries cerise flowers in spring and spherical, red fruits in autumn. H 40cm (16in), S 15cm (6in). Min. 5°C (41°F).

☼ ◊

Opuntia erinacea
Bushy, perennial cactus with a green stem consisting of 15cm (6in) long, flattened segments. Areoles bear 6–15 flattened, 20cm (8in) long, hair-like spines. Has masses of saucer-shaped, red or yellow flowers in summer. H 50cm (20in), S 2m (6ft). Min. 5°C (41°F).

☼ ◊ ⓘ

Beschorneria yuccoides
Clump-forming, perennial succulent with a basal rosette of up to 20 rough, greyish-green leaves, to 1m (3ft) long and 5cm (2in) across. Produces pendent, tubular, bright red flowers in summer in spikes over 2m (6ft) tall. H 1m (3ft), S 3m (10ft). Min. 7°C (45°F).

☼ ◊

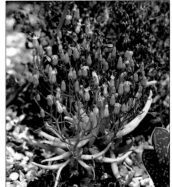

Tylecodon reticulatus,
syn. *Cotyledon reticulata*
(Barbed-wire plant)
Deciduous, bushy, succulent shrub. Swollen branches bear cylindrical leaves in winter. Has tubular, green-yellow flowers on a woody stem in autumn. H and S 30cm (1ft). Min. 7°C (45°F).

☼ ◊

Mammillaria geminispina
Clump-forming, perennial cactus. Has a spherical, green stem densely covered with short, white, radial spines and very long, white, central spines. Has red flowers, 1–2cm (½–¾in) across, in spring. H 25cm (10in), S 50cm (20in). Min. 5°C (41°F).

☼ ◊

Agave filifera (Thread agave)
Basal-rosetted, perennial succulent with narrow, green leaves, each spined at the tip. White leaf margins gradually break away, leaving long, white fibres. Carries yellow-green flowers on a 2.5m (8ft) tall stem in summer. Offsets freely. H 1m (3ft), S 2m (6ft). Min. 10°C (50°F).

☼ ◊

Crassula coccinea
Drosanthemum hispidum
Echeveria gibbiflora
Echinocereus triglochidiatus

Hoodia gordonii
Kalanchoe blossfeldiana
Mammillaria elegans of gardens
Mammillaria rhodantha

Nopalxochia ackermannii
Tylecodon wallichii

CACTI and other SUCCULENTS

465

CACTI *and other* SUCCULENTS medium

Aloe vera, syn. *A. barbadensis*
Clump-forming, perennial succulent
with basal rosettes of tapering, thick
leaves, mottled green, later grey-green.
Flower stems carry bell-shaped, yellow
flowers in summer. Propagate by
offsets as plant is sterile. H 60cm (2ft),
S indefinite. Min. 10°C (50°F).

☼ ◊

Astrophytum myriostigma
(Bishop's cap, Bishop's mitre)
Slow-growing, spherical to slightly
elongated, perennial cactus. A fleshy
stem has 4–6 ribs and is flecked with
tiny tufts of white spines. Bears yellow
flowers in summer. H 30cm (12in),
S 20cm (8in). Min. 5°C (41°F).

☼ ◊

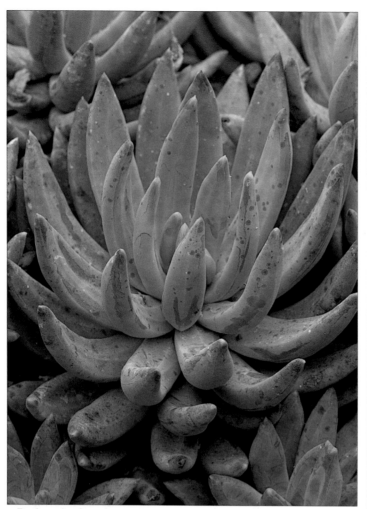

x Pachyveria glauca
Clump-forming, perennial succulent
with a dense, basal rosette of fleshy,
incurved, oval, silvery-blue leaves, to
6cm (2½in) long, with darker marks.
Bears star-shaped, yellow flowers,
each with a red tip, in spring. H and
S 30cm (12in). Min. 7°C (45°F).

☼ ◊

Aeonium haworthii (Pinwheel)
Bushy, perennial succulent. Freely
branching stems bear rosettes, 12cm
(5in) across, of blue-green leaves, often
with red margins. Has a terminal spike
of star-shaped, pink-tinged, pale yellow
flowers in spring. H 60cm (2ft), S 1m
(3ft). Min. 5°C (41°F).

◑ ◊

Agave parryi
Basal-rosetted, perennial succulent with
stiff, broad, grey-green leaves, each to
30cm (12in) long with a solitary dark
spine at its pointed tip. Flower stem, to
4m (12ft) long, bears creamy-yellow
flowers in summer. H 50cm (20in),
S 1m (3ft). Min. 5°C (41°F).

☼ ◊

Leuchtenbergia principis
Basal-rosetted, perennial cactus with
narrow, angular, dull grey-green
tubercles, each 10cm (4in) long and
crowned by papery spines to 10cm (4in)
long. Crown bears yellow flowers, to
7cm (3in) across, in summer. H and
S 30cm (12in). Min. 6°C (43°F).

☼ ◊

Copiapoa cinerea
Very slow-growing, clump-forming,
perennial cactus. Blue-green stem bears
up to 25 ribs and black spines. Has a
woolly, white-grey crown and, on
plants over 10cm (4in) across, yellow
flowers in spring-summer. H 50cm
(20in), S 2m (6ft). Min. 10°C (50°F).

◑ ◊

CACTI *and other* SUCCULENTS

Opuntia microdasys var. **alpispina**
Bushy, perennial cactus with green, flattened, oval segments. Spineless areoles, with slender, barbed, white hairs, are set in diagonal rows. Funnel-shaped, yellow flowers appear in summer. H 60cm (2ft), S 30cm (1ft). Min. 10°C (50°F).

☀ ◊ ❗

Kalanchoe tomentosa
(Panda plant, Pussy ears)
Bushy, perennial succulent with thick, oval, grey leaves, covered with velvety bristles and often edged with brown at tips. Has yellowish-purple flowers in winter. H 50cm (20in), S 30cm (12in). Min. 10°C (50°F).

☀ ◊

Agave attenuata
Perennial succulent with a thick stem crowned by a rosette of sword-shaped, spineless, pale green leaves. Arching flower stem, to 1.5m (5ft) long, is densely covered with yellow flowers in spring-summer. H 1m (3ft), S 2m (6ft). Min. 5°C (41°F).

☀ ◊

Thelocactus setispinus
Slow-growing, perennial cactus with a 13-ribbed stem and yellow or white spines. Fragrant, yellow flowers with red throats appear in summer, only on plants over 5cm (2in) across.
H and S 30cm (12in). Min. 7°C (45°F).

☀ ◊

Dioscorea elephantipes,
syn. **Testudinaria elephantipes**
(Elephant's foot)
Very slow-growing, deciduous, perennial succulent with a domed, woody trunk, annual, climbing stems and yellow flowers in autumn. H 50cm (20in), S 1m (3ft). Min. 10°C (50°F).

☀ ◊

Lobivia haageana
Columnar, perennial cactus with a 20–25-ribbed, bluish- to dark green stem that has yellow, radial spines with longer, darker, central ones. In summer produces yellow flowers, 7cm (3in) across, with red throats. H 30cm (12in), S 15cm (6in). Min. 5°C (41°F).

☀ ◊

Nopalxochia 'Jennifer Ann'
Erect, then pendent, perennial cactus. Has strap-shaped, flattened, green stems with toothed margins. Bears yellow flowers, 15cm (6in) across, in spring. H 30cm (12in), S 50cm (20in). Min. 10°C (50°F).

◑ ◊

Aeonium arboreum
Copiapoa coquimbana
Cyphostemma bainesii
Ferocactus chrysacanthus

Hoodia bainii
Opuntia microdasys
Parodia scopa

Parodia chrysacanthion
Spherical, perennial cactus with a much-ribbed, green stem densely covered with bristle-like, golden spines, each 1–2cm (½–¾in) long. Crown bears yellow flowers in spring and, often, pale yellow wool.
H and S 30cm (1ft). Min. 10°C (50°F).

☀️◐ ◌

Parodia leninghausii,
syn. *Notocactus leninghausii*
(Golden ball cactus)
Clump-forming, perennial cactus. Woolly crown always slopes towards sun. In summer, on plants over 10cm (4in) tall, yellow blooms open flat. H 1m (3ft), S 30cm (1ft). Min. 10°C (50°F).

☀️ ◌

Opuntia tunicata
Mounded, perennial cactus. Has cylindrical, green stem segments densely covered with 5cm (2in) long, golden spines that are enclosed in a silver papery sheath. Bears shallowly saucer-shaped, yellow flowers in spring-summer. H 60cm (2ft), S 1m (3ft). Min. 10°C (50°F).

☀️ ◌ ❗

Aeonium 'Zwartkop', syn.
A. arboreum 'Schwarzkopf'
Bushy, perennial succulent with stems each crowned by a rosette, to 15cm (6in) across, of narrow, purple leaves. Bears golden pyramids of flowers in spring on 2–3-year-old stems, which then die. H to 60cm (2ft), S 1m (3ft). Min. 5°C (41°F).

☀️◐ ◌

Hatiora salicornioides
(Bottle plant, Drunkard's dream)
Bushy, perennial, epiphytic cactus with freely branching, 3cm (1¼in) long stems. Has joints with expanded tips and terminal, bell-shaped, golden-yellow flowers in spring.
H and S 30cm (1ft). Min. 11°C (52°F).

☀️◐ ◌

Kalanchoe delagoensis
Erect, perennial succulent with long, almost cylindrical, grey-green leaves with reddish-brown mottling and flat-tened, notched tips that form plantlets. Bears an umbel of orange-yellow flowers in late winter. H to 1m (3ft), S 30cm (1ft). Min. 8°C (46°F).

☀️ ◌

Aloe striata
Basal-rosetted, perennial succulent. Has broad, blue-green leaves, with white margins and marks, that become suffused red in full sun. Has a panicle of reddish-orange flowers in spring. Makes a good house plant. H and S 1m (3ft). Min. 7°C (45°F).

☀️ ◌

Cotyledon orbiculata var. **oblonga**
Evergreen, upright, succulent sub-shrub with a swollen stem bearing oval, green leaves, densely coated in white wax, with flat, wavy tips. Each 70cm (28in) long flower stem bears a bell-shaped, orange flower in autumn.
H and S 50cm (20in). Min. 7°C (45°F).

☀️ ◌

Lampranthus aurantiacus
Erect, then prostrate, sparse-branching perennial succulent with short, cylindrical, tapering, grey-green leaves. Masses of daisy-like, bright orange flowers, 5cm (2in) wide, open in summer sun. H 50cm (20in), S 70cm (28in). Min. 5°C (41°F).

☀️ ◌

Cleistocactus baumannii
Cotyledon orbiculata
Drosanthemum speciosum

CACTI *and other* SUCCULENTS

CACTI *and other* SUCCULENTS small

☐ WHITE

Mammillaria plumosa
Clump-forming, perennial cactus. Has
a spherical, green stem completely
covered with feathery, white spines.
Carries cream flowers in mid-winter.
Is difficult to grow. Add calcium to
soil. H 12cm (5in), S 40cm (16in).
Min. 10°C (50°F).

☀ ◊

Gibbaeum velutinum
Clump-forming, perennial succulent
with paired, finger-like, velvety, bluish
grey-green leaves, to 6cm (2½in) long.
Produces daisy-like, pink, lilac or
white flowers, 5cm (2in) across, in
spring. H 8cm (3in), S 30cm (12in).
Min. 5°C (41°F).

☀ ◊

Haworthia truncata
Clump-forming, perennial succulent
with a basal fan of broad, erect, rough,
blue-grey leaves with pale grey lines
and flat ends. Produces small, tubular,
white flowers, with spreading petals,
from spring to autumn. H 2cm (¾in),
S 10cm (4in). Min. 10°C (50°F).

☀ ◊

Lithops marmorata
Egg-shaped, perennial succulent,
divided into 2 unequal-sized, swollen,
pale grey leaves with dark grey marks
on convex, upper surfaces. Bears a
white flower in late summer or early
autumn. H 2–3cm (¾–1¼in), S 5cm
(2in). Min. 5°C (41°F).

☀ ◊

Lithops karasmontana
Egg-shaped, perennial succulent,
divided into 2 unequal-sized, grey
leaves, that have pink, upper surfaces
with sunken, darker pink marks. Bears
a white flower in late summer or early
autumn. H to 4cm (1½in), S 5cm (2in).
Min. 5°C (41°F).

☀ ◊

Adromischus maculatus
Clump-forming, perennial succulent
with rounded, glossy, green leaves with
purple marks. Leaf tips are often wavy.
Carries tubular, purplish-white flowers,
on a 30cm (12in) tall stem, in summer.
H 6cm (2½in), S 10–15cm (4–6in).
Min. 7°C (45°F).

☀ ◊

Echinocereus leucanthus,
syn. *Wilcoxia albiflora*
Clump-forming, tuberous cactus with
spined, 6- or 7-ribbed, prostrate stems.
In spring bears often terminal, dark-
throated, white flowers, softly streaked
purple, with green stigmas. H 20cm
(8in), S 30cm (12in). Min. 8°C (46°F).

☀ ◊

Trichodiadema mirabile
Bushy to prostrate, perennial succulent
with cylindrical, dark green leaves
tipped with dark brown bristles and
covered in papillae. Stem tip bears
white flowers, 4cm (1½in) across, from
spring to autumn. H 15cm (6in),
S 30cm (12in). Min. 5°C (41°F).

☀ ◊

Haworthia attenuata f. **clariperla**
Clump-forming, perennial succulent
with a basal rosette of triangular, 3cm
(1¼in) long, dark green leaves, that
have pronounced white dots. Has
tubular, white flowers, with spreading
petals, from spring to autumn. H 7cm
(3in), S 25cm (10in). Min. 5°C (41°F).

☀ ◊

OTHER RECOMMENDED PLANTS:
Cheiridopsis denticulata
Gymnocalycium quehlianum
Lithops fulleri

Lithops julii
Orostachys chanetii

CACTI *and other* SUCCULENTS

CACTI *and other* SUCCULENTS small

☐ WHITE

Crassula socialis
Spreading, perennial succulent with short, dense rosettes, to 1cm (½in) across, of fleshy, triangular, green leaves. Produces clusters of star-shaped, white flowers on 3cm (1¼in) tall stems in spring. H 5cm (2in), S indefinite. Min. 5°C (41°F).

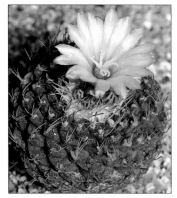

Strombocactus disciformis
Very slow-growing, hemispherical, perennial cactus with a grey-green to brown stem set with a spiral of blunt tubercles. Woolly crown has bristle-like spines, which soon fall off, and cream flowers in summer. H 3cm (1¼in), S 10cm (4in). Min. 5°C (41°F).

Mammillaria schiedeana
Clump-forming, perennial cactus. Green stem is covered with short, feathery, yellow spines that turn white. Produces cream flowers and narrow, red seed pods in late summer. H 10cm (4in), S 30cm (12in). Min. 10°C (50°F).

Neoporteria villosa
Clump-forming, perennial cactus with a branched, green to dark grey-green stem. Has dense, sometimes curved, grey spines, 3cm (1¼in) long. Produces tubular, pink or white flowers in spring or autumn. H 15cm (6in), S 10cm (4in). Min. 8°C (46°F).

Oophytum nanum
Clump-forming, perennial succulent with 2 united, very fleshy, bright green leaves. Has daisy-like, white flowers, 1cm (½in) across, in autumn. Is covered in a dry, paper-like sheath, except in spring. H 2cm (¾in), S 1cm (½in). Min. 5°C (41°F).

Lithops lesliei var. *albinica*
Egg-shaped, perennial succulent, divided into 2 unequal-sized leaves; convex, pale green, upper surfaces have dark green and yellow marks. Bears a white flower in late summer or early autumn. H 2–3cm (¾–1¼in), S 5cm (2in). Min. 5°C (41°F).

Haworthia arachnoidea, syn. *H. setata*
Slow-growing, clump-forming, perennial succulent with a basal rosette of triangular leaves. Bears soft, white teeth along leaf margins. Has white flowers from spring to autumn. H 5cm (2in), S 10cm (4in). Min. 6°C (43°F).

Conophytum truncatum
Slow-growing, clump-forming, perennial succulent with pea-shaped, dark spotted, blue-green leaves, each with a sunken fissure at the tip. Produces cream flowers, 1.5cm (⅝in) across, in autumn. H 1.5cm (⅝in), S 15cm (6in). Min. 4°C (39°F).

Mammillaria elongata
(Lace cactus)
Clump-forming, perennial cactus. Has a columnar, green stem, 3cm (1¼in) across, densely covered with yellow, golden or brown spines. Bears cream flowers in summer. Offsets freely. H 15cm (6in), S 30cm (12in). Min. 5°C (41°F).

Aptenia cordifolia 'Variegata'
Crassula lactea
Haworthia attenuata
Haworthia x cuspidata

Haworthia fasciata
Lithops bella
Mammillaria gracilis
Mammillaria gracilis var. fragilis

Mammillaria prolifera
Ophthalmophyllum maughanii

CACTI *and other* SUCCULENTS

Mammillaria bocasana
(Powder-puff cactus)
Clump-forming, perennial cactus. Long, white hairs cover a hemispherical stem. Has cream or rose-pink flowers in summer and red seed pods the following spring-summer. H 10cm (4in), S 30cm (12in). Min. 5°C (41°F).

☀ ◊

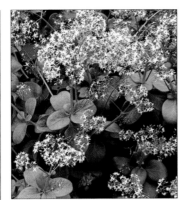

Crassula multicava
Bushy, perennial succulent with oval, grey-green leaves, 8cm (3in) across. Carries numerous clusters of small, star-shaped, pink flowers on elongated stems in spring, followed by small plantlets. H 15cm (6in), S 1m (3ft). Min. 7°C (45°F).

◐ ◊

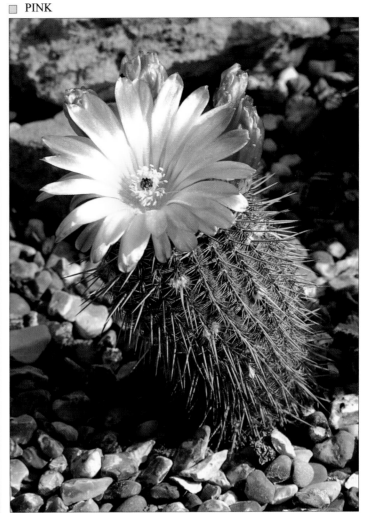

Parodia rutilans, syn.
Notocactus rutilans
Columnar, perennial cactus. Areoles each have about 15 radial spines and 2 upward- or downward-pointing, central spines. Has cream-centred, pink flowers in summer. H 10cm (4in), S 5cm (2in). Min. 10°C (50°F).

◐ ◊

Neoporteria napina
Flattened spherical, perennial cactus with very short, grey spines pressed flat against a greenish-brown stem. Produces white, pink, carmine or brown flowers, 5cm (2in) across, from crown in summer. H 2cm (¾in), S 3.5cm (1½in). Min. 8°C (46°F).

☀ ◊

Lampranthus deltoides
Spreading, perennial succulent. Has chunky, triangular, blue-green leaves, to 1cm (½in) long, with small-toothed, often reddened leaf margins. Fragrant, pink flowers, 1–2cm (½–¾in) wide, appear in early summer. H 15cm (6in), S 1m (3ft). Min. 7°C (45°F).

☀ ◊

Lophophora williamsii
(Dumpling cactus, Mescal button)
Very slow-growing, clump-forming, perennial cactus with an 8-ribbed, blue-green stem. Masses of pink flowers appear in summer on plants over 3cm (1¼in) high. H 5cm (2in), S 8cm (3in). Min. 10°C (50°F).

☀ ◊

Epithelantha micromeris
Slow-growing, spherical, perennial cactus with a green stem completely obscured by close-set areoles bearing tiny, white spines. Bears funnel-shaped, pale pinkish-red flowers, 0.5cm (¼in) across, on a woolly crown in summer. H and S 4cm (1½in). Min. 10°C (50°F).

☀ ◊

Echeveria elegans
Clump-forming, perennial succulent with a basal rosette of broad, fleshy, pale silvery-blue leaves, edged with red, and yellow-tipped, pink flowers in summer. Keep dry in winter. Makes a good bedding plant. H 5cm (2in), S 50cm (20in). Min. 5°C (41°F).

☀ ◊

Escobaria vivipara
Spherical, perennial cactus with a green stem densely covered with grey spines. Bears funnel-shaped, pink flowers, 3.5cm (1½in) across, in summer. Is much more difficult to grow than many other species in this genus. H and S 5cm (2in). Min. 5°C (41°F).

☀ ◊

Crassula exilis subsp. *cooperi*
Gymnocalycium schickendantzii
Mammillaria candida
Ophthalmophyllum longum

Schlumbergera 'Wintermärchen'

Ruschia acuminata
Stenocactus lamellosus

☐ PINK

Schlumbergera 'Gold Charm'
Erect, then pendent, perennial cactus.
Has flattened, oblong, green stem
segments with toothed margins. Yellow
flowers in early autumn turn pinkish-
orange in winter. H 15cm (6in), S 30cm
(12in). Min. 10°C (50°F).

☀ ◊

Mammillaria sempervivi
Slow-growing, spherical, perennial
cactus. Has a dark green stem with
short, white spines. Has white wool
between short, angular tubercles on
plants over 4cm (1½in) high. Bears
cerise flowers in spring.
H and S 7cm (3in). Min. 5°C (41°F).

☀ ◊

Melocactus intortus,
syn. *M. communis* (Melon cactus)
Flattened spherical, perennial cactus.
Has an 18–20-ribbed stem with yellow-
brown spines. Crown matures to a
white column with fine, brown spines.
Bears pink flowers in summer. H 20cm
(8in), S 25cm (10in). Min. 15°C (59°F).

☀ ◊

Ariocarpus fissuratus
Very slow-growing, flattened spherical,
perennial cactus. Grey stem is covered
with rough, triangular tubercles each
producing a tuft of wool. Has 4cm
(1½in) wide, pink-red flowers in
autumn. H 10cm (4in), S 15cm (6in).
Min. 5°C (41°F).

☀ ◊

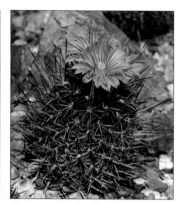

Stenocactus obvallatus, syn.
S. pentacanthus, S. violaciflorus
Spherical, perennial cactus with wavy-
margined ribs. White areoles each bear
5–12 greyish-brown spines. In spring,
has pale yellow to pale pink flowers,
with a purplish-red stripe on each petal.
H and S 8cm (3in). Min. 7°C (45°F).

☀ ◊

Aptenia cordifolia, syn.
Mesembryanthemum cordifolium
Fast-growing, prostrate, perennial
succulent with oval, glossy, green
leaves and, in summer, daisy-like,
bright pink flowers. Is ideal for ground
cover. H 5cm (2in), S indefinite.
Min. 7°C (45°F).

☀ ◊

Hatiora rosea
Bushy, perennial cactus with slender,
3- or 4-angled, bristly, green stem
segments, usually tinged purple, to
5cm (2in) long. Has masses of bell-
shaped, pink flowers, to 4cm (1½in)
across, in spring.
H and S 10cm (4in). Min. 10°C (50°F).

☀ ◊

Ophthalmophyllum villetii
Clump-forming, perennial succulent
with 2 fleshy, grey-green leaves that
are broad, erect and united for most of
their length but have distinctly divided,
upper lobes. Pale pink flowers appear
in late summer. H 2.5cm (1in), S 1cm
(½in). Min. 5°C (41°F).

☀ ◊

Thelocactus bicolor
Spherical to columnar, perennial
cactus with an 8–13-ribbed stem.
Areoles each have 4 usually flattened,
yellow, central spines, or bicoloured
yellow and red, and numerous shorter,
radial spines. Flowers are purple-pink.
H and S 20cm (8in). Min. 7°C (45°F).

☀ ◊

Rebutia minuscula
Clump-forming, perennial cactus with
a tuberculate, dark green stem. Areoles
each produce 15–20 brown spines, to
0.5cm (¼in) long. Has trumpet-shaped,
deep pink to violet flowers, to 2cm
(¾in) across, in spring. H 5cm (2in),
S 15cm (6in). Min. 5°C (41°F).

☀ ◊

Aptenia cordifolia 'Variegata'
Carpobrotus edulis
Kalanchoe pumila
Melocactus bahiensis

Melocactus matanzanus
Rebutia pygmaea
Rebutia senilis
Ruschia macowanii

CACTI *and other* SUCCULENTS

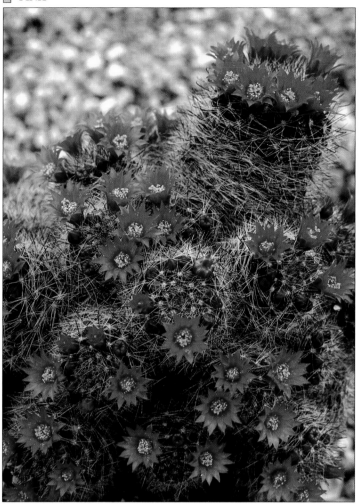

Mammillaria zeilmanniana
(Rose pincushion)
Clump-forming, perennial cactus with
a spherical, green stem that has hooked
spines and bears a ring of deep pink to
purple flowers in spring. H 15cm (6in),
S 30cm (12in). Min. 10°C (50°F).

☼ ◊

Frithia pulchra
Basal-rosetted, perennial succulent
with erect, rough, grey leaves,
cylindrical with flattened tips.
Produces masses of stemless, daisy-
like, bright pink flowers, with paler
centres, in summer. H 3cm (1¼in),
S 6cm (2½in). Min. 10°C (50°F).

☼ ◊

Graptopetalum bellum,
syn. *Tacitus bellus*
Basal-rosetted, perennial succulent
with triangular to oval, grey leaves,
5cm (2in) long. Has clusters of deep
pink to red flowers, 2cm (¾in) across,
in spring-summer. H 3cm (1¼in),
S 15cm (6in). Min. 10°C (50°F).

☼ ◊

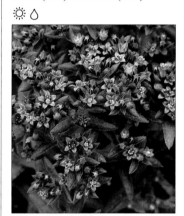

Crassula schmidtii
Carpeting, perennial succulent with
dense rosettes of linear, dark green
leaves, pitted and marked, each 3–4cm
(1¼–1½in) long. Bears masses of star-
shaped, bright pinkish-red flowers in
clusters in winter. H 10cm (4in),
S 30cm (12in). Min. 7°C (45°F).

☼ ◊

Argyroderma pearsonii,
syn. *A. schlechteri*
Prostrate, egg-shaped, perennial
succulent. A united pair of very fleshy,
silvery-grey leaves has a deep fissure
in which a red flower, 3cm (1¼in)
across, appears in summer. H 3cm
(1¼in), S 5cm (2in). Min. 5°C (41°F).

☼ ◊

Echinopsis backebergii,
syn. *Lobivia backebergii*
Clump-forming, almost spherical,
perennial cactus with a 10–15-ribbed,
spined, dark green stem. Has funnel-
shaped, pink, red or purple flowers,
with paler throats, in summer. H 10cm
(4in), S 15cm (6in). Min. 5°C (41°F).

☼ ◊

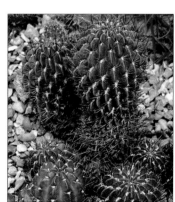

Echinopsis pentlandii,
syn. *Lobivia pentlandii*
Clump-forming or solitary, variable,
perennial cactus with a 10–20-ribbed
stem and 6–20 spined aeroles. Has
white, pink, purple or orange flowers,
with paler throats, in summer. H 8cm
(3in), S 10cm (4in). Min. 5°C (41°F).

☼ ◊

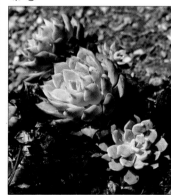

Echeveria secunda
Clump-forming, perennial succulent
with short stems each crowned by a
rosette of broad, fleshy, light green to
grey leaves, reddened towards tips.
Bears cup-shaped, red-and-yellow
flowers in spring-summer. H 4cm
(1½in), S 30cm (12in). Min. 5°C (41°F).

☼ ◊

Schlumbergera truncata,
syn. *Zygocactus truncatus*
(Crab cactus, Lobster cactus)
Erect, then pendent, perennial cactus.
Oblong stem segments have toothed
margins. Bears purple-red flowers in
early autumn and winter. H 15cm (6in),
S 30cm (12in). Min. 10°C (50°F).

☼ ◊

Melocactus oaxacensis

Cheiridopsis purpurea
Echinopsis cinnabarina
Gibbaeum petrense
Huernia pillansii

Lampranthus roseus
Neoporteria nidus
Trichodiadema densum

■ RED

Cephalophyllum alstonii
(Red spike)
Prostrate, perennial succulent with
cylindrical, grey-green leaves, to 7cm
(3in) long. Carries daisy-like,
dark red flowers, 8cm (3in) across, in
summer. H 10cm (4in), S 1m (3ft).
Min. 5°C (41°F).

Parodia microsperma
Clump-forming, perennial cactus. Has
a much-ribbed, green stem densely
covered with brown, radial spines and
red, central spines, some of which are
hooked. Bears blood-red, occasionally
yellow flowers in spring. H 8cm (3in),
S 30cm (12in). Min. 10°C (50°F).

Rebutia krainziana
Clump-forming, perennial cactus with
a tuberculate, dark green stem. Bears
prominent, white areoles with very
short, white spines. Trumpet-shaped,
bright red flowers, to 5cm (2in) across,
appear at stem base in spring. H 5cm
(2in), S 20cm (8in). Min. 5°C (41°C).

Parodia nivosa
Ovoid, perennial cactus that has a
much-ribbed, green stem with stiff,
white spines, each 1–2cm (½–¾in) long.
Has a white, woolly crown and bright
red flowers, to 5cm (2in) across, in
summer. H to 15cm (6in), S 10cm
(4in). Min. 10°C (50°F).

Rebutia tiraquensis,
syn. *Sulcorebutia tiraquensis*
Variable, perennial cactus with a green
stem. Elongated areoles bear spines of
gold or bicoloured red and white. Has
dark pink- or orange-red flowers in
spring. H 15cm (6in), S 10cm (4in).
Min. 10°C (50°F).

Argyroderma fissum,
syn. *A. brevipes*
Clump-forming, perennial succulent
with finger-shaped, fleshy leaves,
5–10cm (2–4in) long and often reddish
at the tip. Has light red flowers
between leaves in summer. H 15cm
(6in), S 10cm (4in). Min. 5°C (41°F).

Cotyledon ladismithensis
Evergreen, freely branching, later
prostrate, succulent sub-shrub with
fleshy, green leaves, swollen and blunt
at tips and covered with short, golden-
brown hairs. Clusters of tubular,
brownish-red flowers appear in autumn.
H and S 20cm (8in). Min. 5°C (41°F).

Opuntia verschaffeltii
Clump-forming, perennial cactus with
cylindrical, usually spineless stems, to
25cm (10in) long. Stem tips each bear
short-lived, cylindrical leaves from
spring to autumn. Has orange-red
flowers in spring. H 15cm (6in),
S 1–2m (3–6ft). Min. 5°C (41°F).

Echeveria agavoides
Basal-rosetted, perennial succulent
with tapering, light green leaves, often
red-margined. Carries cup-shaped, red
flowers, 1cm (½in) long, in summer.
H 15cm (6in), S 30cm (12in).
Min. 5°C (41°F).

Aloe brevifolia
Ferocactus latispinus
Rebutia minuscula
Rebutia senilis

CACTI *and other* SUCCULENTS

Rebutia spegazziniana

Clump-forming, perennial cactus with a spherical, spined, green stem, to 4cm (1½in) across, becoming columnar with age. Bears masses of slender-tubed, orange-red flowers at base in late spring. H 10cm (4in), S 20cm (8in). Min. 5°C (41°F).

Parodia haselbergii,
syn. *Notocactus haselbergii*
(Scarlet ball cactus)

Slow-growing, perennial cactus with a stem covered in white spines. Slightly sunken crown bears red flowers, with yellow stigmas, in spring. H 10cm (4in), S 25cm (10in). Min. 10°C (50°F).

Echinocereus triglochidiatus
var. *paucispinus*

Clump-forming, perennial cactus with a 10cm (4in) wide, dark green stem that has 6 or 7 ribs, and 4–6 spines, 3–4cm (1¼–1½in) long, per areole. Has orange-red flowers in spring. H 20cm (8in), S 50cm (20in). Min. 5°C (41°C).

Schlumbergera 'Bristol Beauty'

Erect, then pendent, perennial cactus with flattened, green stem segments with toothed margins. Bears reddish-purple flowers, with silvery-white tubes, in early autumn and winter. H 15cm (6in), S 30cm (12in). Min. 10°C (50°F).

Echinopsis chamaecereus
(Peanut cactus)

Clump-forming, perennial cactus with spined stems, initially erect, then prostrate. Has funnel-shaped, orange-red flowers in late spring. H 10cm (4in), S indefinite. Min. 3°C (37°F).

Neolloydia conoidea

Clump-forming, perennial cactus. Has a columnar, blue-green stem densely covered with white, radial spines and longer, black, central spines. Bears funnel-shaped, purple-violet flowers in summer. H 10cm (4in), S 15cm (6in). Min. 10°C (50°F).

Hatiora gaertneri
(Easter cactus)

Bushy, perennial cactus with flat, oblong, glossy, green stem segments, each to 5cm (2in) long, often tinged red at edges. Segment ends each bear orange-red flowers in spring. H 15cm (6in), S 20cm (13in). Min. 13°C (55°F).

Pachyphytum oviferum
(Moonstones, Sugared-almond plum)

Clump-forming, perennial succulent with a basal rosette of oval, pinkish-blue leaves. Stem bears 10–15 bell-shaped flowers, with powder-blue calyces and orange-red petals, in spring. H 10cm (4in), S 30cm (12in). Min. 10°C (50°F).

Caralluma joannis

Clump-forming, perennial succulent with blue-grey stems and rudimentary leaves on stem angles. Bears clusters of star-shaped, purple flowers, with short, fine hairs on petal tips, in late summer near stem tips. H 20cm (8in), S 1m (3ft). Min. 11°C (52°F).

Echeveria harmsii
Echeveria setosa
Schlumbergera 'Zara'

Schlumbergera X *buckleyi*
Thelocactus macdowellii

CACTI *and other* SUCCULENTS small

Argyroderma delaetii,
syn. *A. aureum*, *A. blandum*
Prostrate, egg-shaped, perennial
succulent with 2 very fleshy, silvery-
green leaves between which daisy-like,
pink-purple flowers, 5cm (2in) across,
appear in late summer. H 3cm (1½in),
S 5cm (2in). Min. 5°C (41°F).

☼ ◊

Duvalia corderoyi
Clump-forming, perennial succulent.
Has a prostrate, leafless stem with 6
often purple, indistinct ribs. Bears star-
shaped, dull green flowers, 1cm (½in)
across and covered in purple hairs, in
summer-autumn. H 5cm (2in), S 60cm
(24in). Min. 10°C (50°F).

◐ ◊

Crassula deceptor, syn. *C. deceptrix*
Slow-growing, clump-forming,
perennial succulent with branching
stems surrounded by fleshy, grey leaves
set in 4 rows. Each leaf has minute lines
around raised dots. Bears insignificant
flowers in spring.
H and S 10cm (4in). Min. 5°C (41°F).

☼ ◊

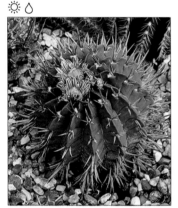

Stenocactus coptonogonus
Spherical, perennial cactus. White
areoles each have 3–5 flat, upward-
curving, pale brownish-red spines.
Bears purple to white flowers, with
pink-purple or violet-purple stripes, in
spring. H 10cm (4in), S 16cm (6in).
Min. 7°C (45°F).

☼ ◊

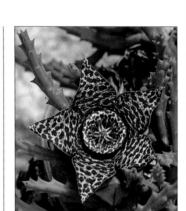

Orbea variegata, syn. *Stapelia*
variegata (Star flower)
Clump-forming, branching, perennial
succulent with 4-angled, indented
stems. Flowers, variable in colour and
blotched yellow, purple- or red-brown,
appear in summer-autumn. H to 10cm
(4in), S indefinite. Min. 11°C (52°F).

◐ ◊

Huernia macrocarpa var. **arabica**
Clump-forming, perennial succulent
with finger-shaped, 4- or 5-sided,
green stems. Produces short-lived,
deciduous leaves and, in autumn, bell-
shaped, white-haired, dark purple flowers with recurved petal tips.
H and S 10cm (4in). Min. 8°C (46°F).

◐ ◊

Stapelia grandiflora
Clump-forming, perennial succulent
with 4-angled, hairy, toothed, green
stems. In summer-autumn carries star-
shaped, purple-brown flowers, to 10cm
(4in) across, ridged with white or
purple hairs. H to 20cm (8in),
S indefinite. Min. 11°C (52°F).

◐ ◊

Stapelia gigantea
Clump-forming, perennial succulent. In
summer-autumn bears star-shaped, red-
marked, yellow-brown flowers, 30cm
(12in) across, with white-haired,
recurved edges. H to 20cm (8in),
S indefinite. Min. 11°C (52°F).

☼ ◊

Rebutia rauschii

Huernia zebrina
Parodia graessneri
Sclerocactus scheeri

Sclerocactus scheeri
Spherical to columnar, perennial
cactus. Stem bears spines and, in
spring, funnel-shaped, straw-coloured
flowers. Lowest and longest spines are
darker and hooked. H 10cm (4in),
S 6cm (2½in). Min. 7–10°C (45–50°F).

☼ ◊

Maihuenia poeppigii
Slow-growing, clump-forming, perennial
cactus. Has a cylindrical, branched, spiny,
green-brown stem. Most branches produce
a spike of cylindrical, green leaves at the
tip, crowned by a funnel-shaped, yellow
flower in summer. H 6cm (2½in), S 30cm
(12in). Min. 2°C (35°F).

☼ ◊

**Aichryson × domesticum
'Variegatum'** (Cloud grass)
Prostrate, perennial succulent with
stems crowned by rosettes of hairy,
cream-marked, green leaves, sometimes
pure cream. Has star-shaped, yellow
flowers in spring. H 15cm (6in), S 40cm
(16in). Min. 5°C (41°F).

☼ ◊

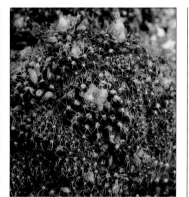

Frailea pygmaea
Columnar, perennial cactus with a
much-ribbed, dark green stem bearing
white to light brown spines. Buds,
which rarely open to flattish, yellow
flowers in summer, become tufts of
spherical, spiny seed pods. H to 5cm
(2in), S 2cm (¾in). Min. 5°C (41°F).

☼◐ ◊

Aloinopsis schooneesii
Dwarf, mounded, perennial succulent
with tuberous roots and fleshy, almost
spherical, blue-green leaves arranged
tightly in tufts. Produces flattish,
yellow flowers in winter-spring.
H 3cm (1½in), S to 7cm (3in).
Min. 7°C (45°F).

☼ ◊

Parodia mammulosa,
syn. *Notocactus mammulosus*
Spherical, perennial cactus. Green stem
has about 20 ribs and straight, stiff,
yellow-brown to white spines, to 1cm
(½in) long. Woolly crown produces
masses of golden flowers in summer.
H and S 10cm (4in). Min. 10°C (50°F).

☼ ◊

Astrophytum ornatum
Elongated, spherical, perennial cactus
with a very fleshy, 8-ribbed stem.
Crown of each rib bears 5–11cm
(2–4½in) long spines on each raised
areole. Has yellow flowers, 8cm (3in)
across, in summer. H 15cm (6in),
S 12cm (5in). Min. 5°C (41°F).

☼ ◊

Gymnocalycium andreae
Clump-forming, spherical, perennial
cactus with a glossy, dark green stem
bearing 8 rounded ribs and up to 8 pale
yellow-white spines per areole. Has
5cm (2in) wide, yellow flowers in
spring-summer. H 6cm (2½in), S 10cm
(4in). Min. 10°C (50°F).

☼ ◊

Euphorbia obesa
(Gingham golf ball)
Spherical, perennial succulent.
Spineless, dark green stem, often
chequered light green, has 8 low ribs.
Crown bears rounded heads of cupped,
yellow flowers in summer. H 12cm
(5in), S 15cm (6in). Min. 10°C (50°F).

☼ ◊ ⓘ

Carpobrotus edulis
Copiapoa echinoides
Dudleya brittonii
Echinopsis aurea

Ferocactus latispinus
Huernia macrocarpa
Huernia thurettii var. *primulina*
Mammillaria densispina

Neoporteria napina
Stomatium agninum
Stomatium patulum
Titanopsis schwantesii

☐ YELLOW

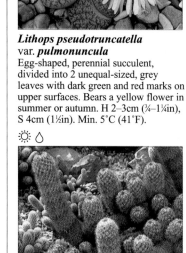

Rhombophyllum rhomboideum
Clump-forming, perennial succulent.
Linear, glossy, grey-green leaves have
expanded middles and white margins.
Stems, 2–5cm (¾–2in) long, bear
3–7 yellow flowers, to 4cm (1½in)
across, in summer. H 5cm (2in),
S 15cm (6in). Min. 5°C (41°F).

☼ ◊

Schwantesia ruedebuschii
Mat-forming, perennial succulent with
cylindrical, bluish-green leaves, 3–5cm
(1–2in) long, with expanded tips. Leaf
edges each produce 3–7 minute, blue
teeth with brown tips. Has yellow
flowers in summer. H 5cm (2in),
S 20cm (8in). Min. 5°C (41°F).

☼ ◊

Pleiospilos compactus
Clump-forming, perennial succulent
with 1 or 2 pairs of thick, grey leaves,
to 8cm (3in) long. Bears coconut-
scented, yellow flowers in early
autumn. H 10cm (4in), S 30cm (12in).
Min. 5°C (41°F).

☼ ◊

Lithops pseudotruncatella
var. **pulmonuncula**
Egg-shaped, perennial succulent,
divided into 2 unequal-sized, grey
leaves with dark green and red marks on
upper surfaces. Bears a yellow flower in
summer or autumn. H 2–3cm (¾–1¼in),
S 4cm (1½in). Min. 5°C (41°F).

☼ ◊

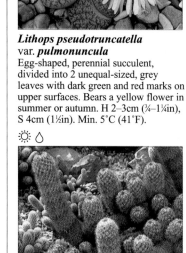

Aeonium tabuliforme
Prostrate, almost stemless, short-lived,
perennial succulent with a basal rosette,
to 30cm (12in) across, like a flat, bright
green plate. Has star-shaped, yellow
flowers in spring, then dies. Propagate
from seed. H 5cm (2in), S 30cm (12in).
Min. 5°C (41°F).

◐ ◊

Lithops schwantesii, syn.
L. schwantesii var. *kuibisensis*
Egg-shaped, perennial succulent,
divided into 2 unequal-sized leaves
with blue or red marks on upper
surface. Has a yellow flower in late
summer or autumn. H 2–3cm (¾–1¼in),
S 3cm (1¼in). Min. 5°C (41°F).

☼ ◊

Lithops dorotheae
Egg-shaped, perennial succulent,
divided into 2 unequal-sized leaves, pale
pink-yellow to green with darker marks
and red dots and lines on upper surfaces.
Produces a daisy-like, yellow flower in
summer or autumn. H 2–3cm (¾–1¼in),
S 5cm (2in). Min. 5°C (41°F).

☼ ◊

Mammillaria microhelia
Columnar, perennial cactus with a 5cm
(2in) wide, green stem bearing cream
or brown spines, discolouring with age.
Has 1.5cm (⅝in) wide, yellow or pink
flowers in spring. Offsets slowly with
age. H 20cm (8in), S 40cm (16in).
Min. 5°C (41°F).

☼ ◊

Opuntia compressa
Prostrate, perennial cactus. Each areole
bears up to 3 spines, 3cm (1¼in) long.
Has flat, rounded to oval, purple-tinged,
dark green stem segments, 7–18cm
(3–7in) long. Bears 8cm (3in) wide,
yellow flowers in spring-summer. Keep
dry in winter. H 15cm (6in), S 1m (3ft).

☼ ◊ ⓘ

Agave utahensis
Basal-rosetted, perennial succulent
with rigid, blue-grey leaves, each with
spines up margins and a long, dark
spine at tip. Flower stem, to 1.5m (5ft)
long, carries yellow flowers in
summer. H 23cm (9in) or more,
S 2m (6ft). Min. 10°C (50°F).

☼ ◊

Graptopetalum paraguayense
(Mother-of-pearl plant)
Clump-forming, perennial succulent
with a basal rosette, 15cm (6in) across,
of grey-green leaves, often tinged pink.
Bears star-shaped, yellow-and-red
flowers in summer. H 10cm (4in),
S 1m (3ft). Min. 5°C (41°F).

☼ ◊

CACTI *and other* SUCCULENTS

Coryphantha cornifera,
syn. *C. radians*
Spherical to columnar, perennial cactus
with angular tubercles, each bearing a
curved, dark, central spine and shorter,
radial spines. Has funnel-shaped,
yellow flowers in summer. H 15cm
(6in), S 10cm (4in). Min. 5°C (41°F).

Conophytum bilobum
Slow-growing, clump-forming,
perennial succulent with 2-lobed,
fleshy, green leaves, each 4cm (1½in)
long and 2cm (¾in) wide. Has a flared,
yellow flower, 3cm (1¼in) across, in
autumn. H 4cm (1½in), S 15cm (6in).
Min. 4°C (39°F).

Faucaria tigrina (Tiger-jaws)
Clump-forming, stemless, perennial
succulent. Fleshy, green leaves, 5cm
(2in) long, have 9 or 10 teeth along
each margin. Bears daisy-like, yellow
flowers, 5cm (2in) across, in autumn.
H 10cm (4in), S 50cm (20in).
Min. 6°C (43°F).

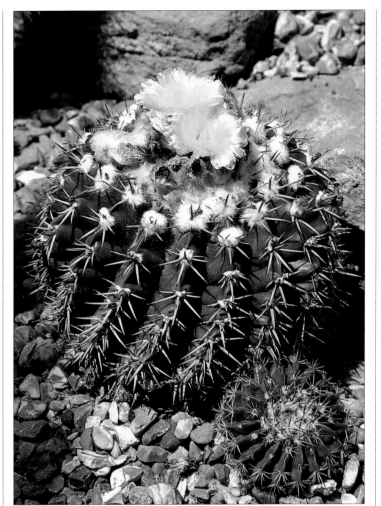

Parodia erinacea
(Colombian ball cactus)
Slow-growing, flattened spherical,
perennial cactus with a glossy stem, up
to 20 wart-like ribs, bearing yellow-
white spines, and yellow blooms in
summer. H 8cm (3in), S 9cm (3½in).
Min. 10°C (50°F).

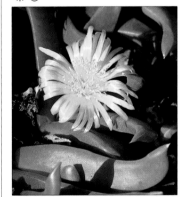

Glottiphyllum nelii
Clump-forming, perennial succulent
with semi-cylindrical, fleshy, green
leaves, to 5cm (2in) long. Carries
daisy-like, golden-yellow flowers, 4cm
(1½in) across, in spring-summer.
H 5cm (2in), S 30cm (12in).
Min. 5°C (41°F).

Lobivia shaferi
Columnar, perennial cactus. Has
narrow, much-ribbed, green stems
covered with pale, radial spines often
surrounded by 1–3 very stout, central
spines, to 2.5cm (1in) long. Produces
yellow flowers in summer.
H and S 10cm (4in). Min. 5°C (41°F).

Fenestraria aurantiaca
(Baby's toes)
Clump-forming, perennial succulent
with a basal rosette of glossy leaves.
Has yellow flowers in late summer and
autumn. H 5cm (2in), S 30cm (12in).
Min. 6°C (43°F).

Titanopsis calcarea
Clump-forming, perennial succulent
with a basal rosette of very fleshy,
triangular, blue-grey leaves covered
in wart-like, grey-white and beige
tubercles. Has yellow flowers from
autumn to spring. H 3cm (1¼in),
S 10cm (4in). Min. 8°C (46°F).

Pleiospilos bolusii
(Living rock, Mimicry plant)
Clump-forming, perennial succulent
with 1 or 2 pairs of grey leaves, often
wider than long and narrowing at
incurved tips. Has golden-yellow
flowers in early autumn. H 10cm (4in),
S 20cm (8in). Min. 5°C (41°F).

Glottiphyllum semicylindricum
Parodia concinna
Parodia ottonis
Thelocactus leucacanthus

CACTI *and other* SUCCULENTS small

Rebutia arenacea,
syn. *Sulcorebutia arenacea*
Spherical, perennial cactus. Has a
brown-green stem with white spines on
spirally arranged tubercles. Has
golden-yellow blooms, to 3cm (1¼in)
across, in spring. H 5cm (2in), S 6cm
(2½in). Min. 10°C (50°F).

Gasteria bicolor var. **liliputana,**
syn. *G. liliputana*
Perennial succulent that forms rosettes
of dark green leaves blotched with
white. Flower stems, to 15cm (6in)
long, bear spikes of bell-shaped, orange-green flowers in spring. H 7cm
(3in), S 10cm (4in). Min. 5°C (41°F).

Pachyphytum compactum
Clump-forming, perennial succulent
with a basal rosette of green leaves,
each narrowing to a blunt point, with
angular, paler edges. Stems each bear
3–10 flowers with green to pink calyces
and orange petals in spring. H 15cm
(6in), S indefinite. Min. 5°C (41°F).

Conophytum notabile
Slow-growing, spherical, perennial
succulent forming clumps of 2-lobed,
very fleshy, grey-green leaves, often
with a red spot on edge of fissure
between the lobes. Carries copper-
orange flowers in autumn. H 3cm
(1¼in). S indefinite. Min. 4°C (39°F).

Malephora crocea
Erect or spreading, perennial succulent
with semi-cylindrical, blue-green
leaves on short shoots. Carries solitary
daisy-like, orange-yellow flowers,
reddened on outsides, in spring-
summer. H 20cm (8in), S 1m (3ft).
Min. 5°C (41°F).

Oreocereus aurantiacus,
syn. *Borzicactus aurantiacus,*
Matucana aurantiaca
Spherical, perennial cactus with a
15–17-ribbed stem. Elongated areoles
each bear up to 30 spines. Has orange-
yellow flowers in summer. H 12cm
(5in), S 40cm (16in). Min. 10°C (50°F).

Aloe aristata
(Lace aloe, Torch plant)
Clump-forming, perennial succulent
that has a basal rosette of pointed, dark
green leaves with white spots and soft-
toothed edges. Has orange flowers in
spring. Offsets freely. H 10cm (4in),
S 30cm (12in). Min. 7°C (45°F).

Rebutia aureiflora
Clump-forming, perennial cactus with
a dark green stem, often tinged violet-
red, that has stiff, radial spines and
longer, soft, central spines. Has masses
of yellow, violet or red flowers in late
spring. H 10cm (4in), S 20cm (8in).
Min. 5°C (41°F).

Gasteria carinata var. **verrucosa,**
syn. *G. verrucosa*
Clump-forming, perennial succulent
with stiff, dark green leaves, with
raised, white dots and incurved edges.
Has spikes of bell-shaped, orange-
green flowers in spring. H 10cm (4in),
S 30cm (12in). Min. 5°C (41°F).

Rebutia fiebrigii, syn. *R. muscula*
Clump-forming, perennial cactus. Has
a dark green stem densely covered
with soft, white spines, to 0.5cm (¼in)
long. Bears bright orange flowers,
2–3cm (¾–1¼in) across, in late spring.
H 10cm (4in), S 15cm (6in).
Min. 5°C (41°F).

Aloe humilis
Echeveria derenbergii
Gasteria caespitosa
Rebutia neocumingii

Rebutia senilis

THE PLANT DICTIONARY

including common names

A complete listing of more than 8,000 plants, suitable for growing in temperate gardens worldwide. Includes full descriptions of the characteristics and cultivation of 4,000 plants not already described in The Plant Catalogue.

Aaron's beard. See *Hypericum calycinum*, illus. p.170.

ABELIA

CAPRIFOLIACEAE

Genus of deciduous, semi-evergreen or evergreen shrubs, grown for their foliage and freely borne flowers. Does best against a south- or west-facing wall at the limits of hardiness. Requires a sheltered, sunny position and fertile, well-drained soil. Remove dead wood in late spring and prune out older branches after flowering to restrict growth, if required. Propagate by softwood cuttings in summer.

A. **'Edward Goucher'** illus. p.161.
A. floribunda. Evergreen, arching shrub. H 3m (10ft), S 4m (12ft). Has oval, glossy, dark green leaves and, in early summer, drooping, tubular, bright red flowers. Zone 9.
A. × *grandiflora* illus. p.121.
'Francis Mason' is a vigorous, semi-evergreen, arching shrub. H 2m (6ft), S 3m (10ft). Has coppery-yellow, young shoots and oval, yellowish-green leaves, darker in centres. Bears a profusion of fragrant, bell-shaped, white flowers, tinged with pink, from mid-summer to mid-autumn. Zone 7.
A. schumannii illus. p.162.
A. triflora illus. p.119.

ABELIOPHYLLUM

OLEACEAE

Genus of one species of deciduous shrub, grown for its winter flowers. In cold areas grow against a south- or west-facing wall. Requires plenty of sun and fertile, well-drained soil. Thin out excess older shoots after flowering each year to encourage vigorous, young growth. Propagate by softwood cuttings in summer.

A. distichum. Deciduous, open shrub. H and S 1.2m (4ft). In late winter produces fragrant, star-shaped, white flowers, tinged with pink, on bare stems; flowers may be damaged by hard frosts. Leaves are oval and dark green. Zone 5b.

ABIES

Silver fir

PINACEAE

Genus of tall conifers with whorled branches. Spirally arranged leaves are needle-like, flattened, usually soft and often have silvery bands beneath. Bears erect cones that ripen in their first autumn to release seeds and scales. See also CONIFERS.

A. alba. Fast-growing, conical conifer. H 15–25m (50–80ft), S 5–8m (15–25ft). Has silvery-grey bark and dull green leaves, silvery beneath. Cylindrical cones, 10–15cm (4–6in) long, ripen to red-brown. Zone 4.

A. amabilis (Pacific fir). Conical conifer. H 15m (50ft), S 4–5m (12–15ft). Dense, notched, square-tipped, glossy, dark green leaves, banded with white beneath, are borne on hairy, grey shoots. Oblong, violet-blue cones are 9–15cm (3½–6in) long. Zone 6.
'Spreading Star', H 50cm (20in), S 4–5m (12–15ft), is a procumbent form suitable for ground cover.
A. balsamea (Balsam fir).
f. *hudsonia* is a dense, dwarf conifer of flattened to globose habit. H and S 60cm–1m (2–3ft). Has smooth, grey bark and grey-green leaves that are semi-spirally arranged. Zone 2.
'Nana' (illus. p.110) is another dwarf form that makes a dense, globose mound with spirally arranged leaves.
A. cephalonica (Greek fir). Upright conifer with a conical crown; old trees have massive, spreading, erect branches. H 20–30m (70–100ft), S 5–10m (15–30ft). Sharp, stiff, glossy, deep green leaves are whitish-green beneath. Cylindrical, tapered cones, 10–15cm (4–6in) long, are brown when ripe. Zone 6. **'Meyer's Dwarf'** (syn. *A.c.* 'Nana'; illus. p.110), H 50cm (20in), S 1.5m (5ft), has short leaves and forms a spreading, flat-topped mound.
A. concolor (White fir). Upright conifer. H 15–30m (50–100ft), S 5–8m (15–25ft). Has widely spreading, blue-green or grey leaves and cylindrical, green or pale blue cones, 8–12cm (3–5in) long. Zone 4. **'Argentea'** (syn. *A.c.* 'Candicans'; illus. p.101).
'Compacta' (syn. *A.c.* 'Glauca Compacta'; illus. p.110), H to 2m (6ft), S 2–3m (6–10ft), is a cultivar with steel-blue foliage. Zone 4.
A. delavayi (Delavay's fir). Upright conifer producing tiered, spreading branches. H 10–15m (30–50ft), S 4–6m (12–20ft). Has maroon shoots and curved, bright deep green leaves, spirally arranged, with vivid silver bands beneath and rolled margins. Cones are narrowly cylindrical, 6–15cm (2½–6in) long, and violet-blue. Zone 8.
A. forrestii illus. p.105.
A. grandis illus. p.104.
A. homolepis (Nikko fir). Conifer that is conical when young, later columnar. H 15m (50ft), S 6m (20ft). Pink-grey bark peels in fine flakes. Has pale green leaves, silver beneath, and cylindrical, violet-blue cones, 8–12cm (3–5in) long. Tolerates urban conditions. Zone 5.
A. koreana illus. p.109.
A. lasiocarpa (Subalpine fir). Narrowly conical conifer. H 10–15m (30–50ft), S 3–4m (10–12ft). Has grey or blue-green leaves and cylindrical, violet-blue cones, 6–10cm (2½–4in) long. Zone 2b. Var. *arizonica* **'Compacta'** (illus. p.110), H 4–5m (12–15ft), S 1.5–2m (5–6ft), is a slow-growing, ovoid to conical tree with corky bark and blue foliage. **'Roger Watson'** (illus. p.110), H and S 75cm (2½ft), is dwarf and conical, with silvery-grey leaves. All zone 3.

A. nordmanniana (Caucasian fir). Columnar, dense conifer. H 15–25m (50–80ft), S 5m (15ft). Luxuriant foliage is rich green. Cylindrical cones, 10–15cm (4–6in) long, are green-brown, ripening to brown. Zone 5.
'Golden Spreader' (illus. p.111), H and S 1m (3ft), is a dwarf form with a spreading habit and bright golden-yellow leaves. Zone 5b.
A. procera (Noble fir). Narrowly conical conifer. H 15m (50ft), S 5m (15ft). Has attractive, smooth, silvery-grey bark and grey-green or bright blue-grey leaves. Produces stoutly cylindrical, green cones, 15–25cm (6–10in) long, that ripen to brown. Zone 5b.
A. veitchii illus. p.102.

ABUTILON

MALVACEAE

Genus of evergreen, semi-evergreen or deciduous shrubs, perennials and annuals, grown for their flowers and foliage. Tender, min. 5–7°C (41–5°F). Needs full sun or partial shade and fertile, well-drained soil. Water containerized specimens freely when in full growth, less at other times. In the growing season, young plants may need tip pruning to promote bushy growth. Mature specimens may have previous season's stems cut back hard annually in early spring. Tie lax-growing species to a support if necessary. Propagate by seed in spring or by softwood, greenwood or semi-ripe cuttings in summer. Whitefly and spider mite may be troublesome.

A. **'Ashford Red'.** Strong-growing, evergreen, erect to spreading shrub. H and S 2–3m (6–10ft). Has maple- to heart-shaped, serrated, pale to mid-green leaves. Pendent, bell-shaped, crimson flowers are carried from spring to autumn.
A. **'Golden Fleece'.** Strong-growing, evergreen, rounded shrub. H and S 2–3m (6–10ft). Has maple- to heart-shaped, serrated, rich green leaves. Pendent, bell-shaped, yellow flowers are carried from spring to autumn.
A. **'Kentish Belle'** illus. p.171.
A. megapotamicum. Evergreen shrub with long, slender branches normally trained against a wall. H and S to 3m (10ft). Pendent, bell-shaped, yellow-and-red flowers appear from late spring to autumn. Leaves are oval, with heart-shaped bases, and dark green.
A. pictum, syn. *A. striatum* of gardens. **'Thompsonii'** illus. p.147.
A. striatum of gardens. See *A. pictum*.
A. × *suntense*. Fast-growing, deciduous, upright, arching shrub. H 5m (15ft), S 3m (10ft). Has oval, lobed, toothed, dark green leaves. Produces an abundance of large, bowl-shaped, pale to deep purple, occasionally white, flowers from late spring to early summer. **'Violetta'** illus. p.145.
A. vitifolium. Fast-growing, deciduous,

upright shrub. H 4m (12ft), S 2.5m (8ft). Masses of large, bowl-shaped, purplish-blue flowers are produced in late spring and early summer. Has oval, lobed, sharply toothed, grey-green leaves. var. *album* illus. p.119.

ACACIA

Mimosa

LEGUMINOSAE/MIMOSACEAE

Genus of evergreen, semi-evergreen or deciduous trees and shrubs, grown for their tiny flowers, composed of massed stamens, and for their foliage. Many species have phyllodes instead of true leaves. Not hardy in most regions, min. 5–7°C (41–5°F). Requires full sun and well-drained soil. Propagate by seed in spring. Spider mite and mealy bug may be problematic.

A. baileyana illus. p.97.
A. dealbata illus. p.83.
A. juniperina. See *A. ulicifolia*.
A. longifolia (Sydney golden wattle). Evergreen, spreading tree. H and S 6m (20ft). Has narrowly oblong, dark green phyllodes. Bears cylindrical clusters of golden-yellow flowers in early spring.
A. podalyriifolia illus. p.135.
A. pravissima illus. p.97.
A. pulchella illus. p.157.
A. ulicifolia, syn. *A. juniperina*. Evergreen, bushy shrub. H 1m (3ft), S 1.5m (5ft). Has very narrow, cylindrical, spine-like, rich green phyllodes and, in mid-spring, globular clusters of pale yellow flowers.
A. verticillata (Prickly Moses). Evergreen, spreading tree or bushy shrub. H and S 9m (28ft). Has needle-like, dark green phyllodes and, in spring, dense, bottlebrush-like spikes of bright yellow flowers.

Acacia
False. See *Robinia pseudoacacia*.
Rose. See *Robinia hispida*, illus. p.141.

ACAENA

ROSACEAE

Genus of mainly summer-flowering sub-shrubs and perennials, evergreen in all but the severest winters, grown for their leaves and coloured burs and as ground cover. Has tight, rounded heads of small flowers. Is good for a rock garden but some species may be invasive. Needs sun or partial shade and well-drained soil. Propagate by division in early spring or by seed in autumn.

A. anserinifolia of gardens. See *A. novae-zelandiae*.
A. **'Blue Haze'**, syn. *A.* 'Pewter'. Vigorous, evergreen, prostrate perennial. H 10cm (4in), S 75cm (30in) or more. Leaves are divided into 9–15 oval, toothed, steel-blue leaflets. Produces spherical, brownish-red flower heads that develop in autumn to dark red burs with pinkish-red spines.

A. buchananii. Vigorous, evergreen, prostrate perennial. H 2cm (¾in), S 75cm (30in) or more. Bears glaucous leaves composed of 11–17 oval, toothed leaflets. Globose, green flower heads are borne in summer and develop into spiny, yellow-green burs.
A. caerulea. See *A. caesiiglauca.*
A. caesiiglauca, syn. *A. caerulea,* illus. p.390.
A. microphylla illus. p.389
A. novae-zelandiae, syn.
A. anserinifolia of gardens. Vigorous, evergreen, prostrate sub-shrub. H 10cm (4in), S 75cm (30in) or more. Has brown-green leaves, divided into 9–13 oval, toothed leaflets. In summer, red-spined, brownish burs develop from spherical heads of greenish-brown flowers.
A. 'Pewter'. See *A.* 'Blue Haze'.

ACALYPHA

EUPHORBIACEAE

Genus of evergreen shrubs and perennials, grown for their flowers and foliage. Tender, min. 10–13°C (50–55°F), but best at min. 16°C (61°F). Needs partial shade and humus-rich, well-drained soil. Water containerized plants freely when in full growth, much less at other times and in low temperatures. Stem tips may be removed in growing season to promote branching of young plants. Propagate by softwood, greenwood or semi-ripe cuttings in summer. Spider mite, whitefly and mealy bug may be troublesome.
A. hispida (Red-hot cat's tail). Evergreen, upright, soft-stemmed shrub. H 2m (6ft) or more, S 1–2m (3–6ft). Has oval, toothed, lustrous, deep green leaves. Tiny, crimson flowers hang in long, dense, catkin-like spikes, intermittently year-round. May be grown as a short-lived cordon.
A. wilkesiana illus. p.143.

ACANTHOLIMON

PLUMBAGINACEAE

Genus of evergreen perennials, grown for their flowers and tight cushions of spiny leaves. Is suitable for rock gardens and walls. Prefers sun and well-drained soil. Dislikes damp winters. Seed is rarely set in cultivation. Propagate by softwood cuttings in late spring.
A. glumaceum illus. p.377.
A. venustum. Evergreen, cushion-forming perennial. H and S 10cm (4in). Small spikes of star-shaped, pink flowers, on 3cm (1¼in) stems, are produced from late spring to early summer amid rosetted, spear-shaped, spiny, blue-green leaves that are edged with silver. Needs a very hot, well-drained site. Makes an excellent alpine house plant.

Acanthopanax. Reclassified as *Eleutherococcus* except for:
A. ricinifolius for which see *Kalopanax septemlobus.*

ACANTHUS
Bear's breeches

ACANTHACEAE

Genus of perennials, some of which are semi-evergreen, grown for their large, deeply cut leaves and their spikes of flowers. Prefers full sun, warm conditions and well-drained soil, but will tolerate shade. Protect crowns in first winter after planting. Long, thong-like roots make plants difficult to eradicate if wrongly placed. Propagate by seed or division in early autumn or spring or by root cuttings in winter.
A. balcanicus. See *A. hungaricus.*
A. dioscoridis. Upright, architectural perennial. H to 1m (3ft), S 45cm (18in). Has oval, deeply cut, rigid, basal leaves and hairy stems. Dense spikes of small, funnel-shaped, purple-and-white flowers are produced in summer.
A. hungaricus, syn. *A. balcanicus,* *A. longifolius,* illus. p.251.
A. longifolius. See *A. hungaricus.*
A. mollis. Semi-evergreen, stately, upright perennial. H 1.2m (4ft), S 45cm (18in). Has long, oval, deeply cut, bright green leaves and, in summer, produces many spikes of funnel-shaped, mauve-and-white flowers.
A. spinosus illus. p.251.

ACCA,
syn. FEIJOA

MYRTACEAE

Genus of evergreen, opposite-leaved shrubs, grown for their shallowly cup-shaped flowers. Needs a sheltered, sunny site and light, well-drained soil. Propagate by seed sown as soon as ripe or by semi-ripe cuttings in summer.
A. sellowiana illus. p.143. Zone 9.

ACER
Maple

ACERACEAE

Genus of deciduous or evergreen trees and shrubs, grown for their foliage, which often colours brilliantly in autumn and, in some cases, for their ornamental bark or stems. Small, but often attractive flowers are followed by 2-winged fruits. Requires sun or semi-shade and fertile, moist but well-drained soil. Many acers produce their best autumn colour on neutral to acid soil. Propagate species by seed as soon as ripe or in autumn; cultivars by various grafting methods in late winter or early spring, or by budding in summer. Leaf-eating caterpillars or aphids sometimes infest plants, and maple tar spot and leaf galls may affect some species.
A. buergerianum (Trident maple). Deciduous, spreading tree. H 10m (30ft) or more, S 8m (25ft). Has 3-lobed, glossy, dark green leaves, usually providing an attractive, long-lasting display of red, orange and purple in autumn. Zone 5b.
A. capillipes illus. p.82.
A. cappadocicum (Cappadocian maple). Deciduous, spreading tree. H 20m (70ft), S 15m (50ft). Has 5-lobed, bright green leaves that turn yellow in autumn. Zone 7.
'Aureum' has bright yellow, young

leaves that turn light green in summer and assume yellow autumn tints. subsp. *lobelii* (syn. *A. lobelii*) illus. p.66.
A. carpinifolium illus. p.92.
A. circinatum (Vine maple). Deciduous, spreading, bushy tree or shrub. H 5m (15ft) or more, S 6m (20ft). Rounded, 7–9-lobed, mid-green leaves turn brilliant orange and red in autumn. Bears clusters of small, purple-and-white flowers in spring. Zone 7.
A. cissifolium. Deciduous, spreading tree. H 8m (25ft), S 12m (40ft). Leaves consist of 3 oval, toothed leaflets, bronze-tinged when young, dark green in summer, turning red and yellow in autumn. Does best in semi-shade and on neutral to acid soil. Zone 5b. subsp. *henryi* see *A. henryi.*
A. crataegifolium (Hawthorn maple). Deciduous, arching tree. H and S 10m (30ft). Branches are streaked green and white. Small, oval, mid-green leaves turn orange in autumn. Zone 7.
'Veitchii' illus. p.89.
A. davidii (Père David's maple, Snake-bark maple). Deciduous tree with upright branches. H and S 15m (50ft). Branches are striped green and white. Oval, glossy, dark green leaves often turn yellow or orange in autumn. Zone 6. Subsp. *grosseri* (syn. *A. grosseri, A.g.* var. *hersii, A. hersii;* Hers's maple, Snake-bark maple) is a deciduous, upright and spreading tree. H and S 10m (30ft). Has white-striped trunk and branches. Broadly oval, deeply lobed, bright green leaves turn red in autumn. Zone 6b. 'Madeline Spitta' illus. p.81.
A. x *freemanii.* A hybrid between *A. rubrum* and *A. saccharinum.* 'Autumn Blaze'. Fast growing, oval-headed, deciduous tree. H 15m (50ft) S 12m (40ft). Has deeply lobed, mid-green leaves that turn orange in fall and keep their colour for several weeks. Zone 3b. 'Celebration'. Upright, deciduous tree. H 14m (45ft) S 8m (25ft). Leaves turn red then gold in autumn. Does not have fruit. Zone 3b.
A. ginnala. See *A. tataricum* subsp. *ginnala.*
A. giraldii. Deciduous, spreading tree. H and S 10m (30ft). Shoots have a blue-grey bloom. Large, sycamore-like, shallowly lobed leaves, with long, pink stalks, are dark green above, blue-white beneath. Zone 8.
A. grandidentatum. See *A. saccharum* subsp. *grandidentatum.*
A. griseum illus. p.100.
A. grosseri. See *A. davidii* subsp. *grosseri.* var. *hersii* see *A. davidii* subsp. *grosseri.*
A. henryi, syn. *A. cissifolium* subsp. *henryi,* illus. p.82.
A. hersii. See *A. davidii* subsp. *grosseri.*
A. japonicum (Full-moon maple, Japanese maple). Deciduous, bushy tree or shrub. H and S 10m (30ft). Rounded, lobed leaves are midgreen, turning red in autumn. Clusters of small, reddish-purple flowers open in mid-spring. Shelter from strong winds. Zone 6. 'Aconitifolium' illus. p.95. 'Aureum' see *A. shirasawanum* 'Aureum'. 'Vitifolium' illus. p.95.
A. laxiflorum, syn. *A. pectinatum* subsp. *laxiflorum,* illus. p.99.

A. lobelii. See *A. cappadocicum* subsp. *lobelii.*
A. macrophyllum illus. p.64.
A. maximowiczianum, syn. *A. nikoense* (Nikko maple). Slow-growing, deciduous, round-headed tree. H and S 12m (40ft). Leaves have 3 oval, bluish-green leaflets that turn brilliant red and yellow in autumn. Zone 7.
A. monspessulanum (Montpelier maple). Deciduous, usually compact, round-headed tree or shrub. H and S 12m (40ft). Small, 3-lobed, glossy, dark green leaves remain on tree until late autumn. Zone 5.
A. negundo (Manitoba maple, Box elder). Fast-growing, deciduous, spreading tree. H 15m (50ft), S 8m (25ft). Bright green leaves have 3–5 oval leaflets. Clusters of inconspicuous, greenish-yellow flowers are borne in late spring. Zone 1b. 'Variegatum' illus. p.79. Var. *violaceum* has purplish branchlets covered in a glaucous bloom and prominent clusters of tassel-like, purplish-pink flowers. Zone 2.
A. nikoense. See *A. maximowiczianum.*
A. opalus (Italian maple). Deciduous, round-headed tree. H and S 15m (50ft). Clusters of small, yellow flowers emerge from early to mid-spring before foliage. Leaves are broad, 5-lobed and dark green, turning yellow in autumn. Zone 6.
A. palmatum (Japanese maple). Deciduous, bushy-headed shrub or tree. H and S 6m (20ft) or more. Palmate, deeply lobed, mid-green leaves turn brilliant orange, red or yellow in autumn. Clusters of small, reddish-purple flowers are borne in mid-spring. Zone 6. f. *atropurpureum* illus. p121. 'Bloodgood' illus. p.143. 'Butterfly' illus. p.140. 'Chitoseyama' illus. p.166. 'Corallinum' illus. p.130. var. *coreanum* illus. p.94. 'Dissectum Atropurpureum' illus. p.166. var. *heptalobum* illus. p.124. var. *heptalobum* 'Lutescens' illus. p.122. var. *heptalobum* 'Rubrum' illus. p.122. 'Osakazuki' has larger leaves, with 7 lobes, that turn brilliant scarlet in autumn. 'Sango-kaku' (syn. *A.p.* 'Senkaki') illus. p.124.
A. pectinatum subsp. *laxiflorum.* See *A. laxiflorum.*
A. pensylvanicum (Snake-bark maple) illus. p.84.
'Erythrocladum' is a deciduous, upright tree. H 10m (30ft), S 6m (20ft). Has brilliant candy-pink, young shoots in winter and large, boldly lobed, mid-green leaves that turn bright yellow in autumn. Zone 4.
A. platanoides (Norway maple). Vigorous, deciduous, spreading tree. H 25m (80ft), S 15m (50ft). Has large, broad, sharply lobed, bright green leaves that turn yellow or orange in autumn and clusters of yellow flowers borne in mid-spring before the leaves appear. Zone 5. 'Columnare', H 12m (40ft), S 8m (25ft), is dense and columnar. 'Crimson King' illus. p.65. 'Drummondii' has leaves broadly edged with creamy-white. 'Emerald Queen' is upright when young. 'Globosum', H 8m (25ft) S 10m (30ft), has a dense, round crown. 'Lorbergii' see *A.p.* 'Palmatifidum'.

'Palmatifidum' (syn. *A.p.* 'Lorbergii') illus. p.71. **'Royal Red'** has deep reddish-purple leaves. Those of **'Schwedleri'** are bright red when young, maturing to purplish-green in summer and turn orange-red in autumn. **'Summershade'** has dark green leaves. All zone 5.

A. pseudoplatanus (Sycamore maple). Fast-growing, deciduous, spreading tree. H 30m (100ft), S 15m (50ft). Has broadly 5-lobed, dark green leaves. Makes a fine specimen tree and is good for an exposed position. Zone 5b. **'Brilliantissimum'** illus. p.89. f. *erythrocarpum* illus. p.70. **'Simon Louis Frères'** illus. p.79.

A. rubrum (Red maple) illus. p.70. **'Columnare'** illus. p.81. **'Morgan.'** See **'Red Sunset'**. **'October Glory'** is a deciduous, spreading tree. H 20m (70ft), S 12m (40ft). Has 3- or 5-lobed, glossy, dark green leaves that become intense red in autumn, particularly on neutral to acid soil. In spring, bare branches are covered with clusters of tiny, red flowers. **'Red Sunset'** (syn. **'Morgan'**) has dense growth that also turns brilliant red in autumn. **'Scanlon'** and **'Schlesingeri'** illus. p.70. All zone 4b.

A. rufinerve (Snake-bark maple) illus. p.82. **'Hatsuyuki'** (syn. *A.r.* f. *albolimbatum*) is a deciduous, arching tree. H 10m (30ft), S 8m (25ft). Branches are striped green and white. Has 3-lobed, mid-green leaves, mottled and edged with white, that turn orange and red in autumn. Zone 7.

A. saccharinum (Silver maple). Fast-growing, deciduous, spreading tree. H 25m (80ft), S 15m (50ft). Deeply lobed, mid-green leaves, with silver undersides, turn yellow in autumn. Zone 2b. f. *laciniatum* **'Wieri'** (syn. *A.s.* 'Laciniatum Wieri') has pendent, lower branches and deeply lobed leaves.

A. saccharum (Sugar maple). subsp. *grandidentatum* (syn. *A. grandidentatum)* is a deciduous, spreading tree. H and S 10m (30ft) or more. Broad 3- or 5-lobed, bright green leaves turn bright orange-red in early autumn. Zone 4. **'Green Mountain'**, H 20m (70ft), S 12m (40ft), is upright. Large, 5-lobed, leaves turn brilliant scarlet in autumn. **'Temple's Upright'** illus. p.82.

A. shirasawanum **'Aureum'**, syn. *A. japonicum* 'Aureum', illus. p.92. *A. tataricum* subsp. *ginnala*, syn. *A. ginnala*, illus. p.95. *A. triflorum* illus. p.96. *A. velutinum*. Deciduous, spreading tree. H 20m (70ft), S 15m (50ft). Produces large, sycamore-like, lobed, dark green leaves, with undersides covered with pale brown down. var. *vanvolxemii* (Van Volxem's maple) has even larger leaves, slightly glaucous and smooth beneath. Zone 8.

ACHILLEA
Yarrow

ASTERACEAE/COMPOSITAE

Genus of mainly upright perennials, some of which are semi-evergreen, suitable for borders and rock gardens. Has fern-like foliage and large, usually plate-like, flower heads mainly in summer. Flower heads may be dried for winter decoration. Tolerates most soils but does best in a sunny, well-drained site. Tall species and cultivars need staking. Propagate by division in early spring or autumn or by softwood cuttings in early summer. Contact with foliage may aggravate skin allergies.

A. aegyptica of gardens. See *A.* 'Taygetea'.
A. argentea. See *Tanacetum argenteum.*
A. argentea of gardens. See *A. clavennae.*
A. clavennae, syn. *A. argentea* of gardens, illus. p.373.
A. clypeolata. Semi-evergreen, upright perennial. H 45cm (18in), S 30cm (12in). Has divided, hairy, silver leaves and dense, flat heads of small, yellow flowers in summer. Divide plants regularly in spring.
A. **'Coronation Gold'** illus. p.256.
A. filipendulina **'Gold Plate'** illus. p.258.
A. x *kellereri* illus. p.375.
A. x *lewisii* **'King Edward'**. Semi-evergreen, rounded, compact, woody-based perennial. H 10cm (4in), S 23cm (9in) or more. Has feathery, soft, grey-green leaves. Bears compact heads of minute, buff-yellow flower heads in summer. Is suitable for a rock garden, wall or bank.
A. millefolium (Yarrow). **'Fire King'** is a vigorous, upright perennial. H and S 60cm (24in). Has a mass of feathery, dark green leaves and flat heads of rich red flowers in summer.
A. **'Moonshine'** illus. p.291.
A. ptarmica **'The Pearl'** illus. p.239.
A. **'Schwellenberg'** illus. p.255.
A. **'Taygetea'**, syn. *A. aegyptica* of gardens, illus. p.291.

ACHIMENES
Hot-water plant

GESNERIACEAE

Genus of erect or trailing perennials with small rhizomes and showy flowers. Tender, min. 10°C (50°F). Prefers bright light, but not direct sunlight, and well-drained soil. Use tepid water for watering pot-grown plants. Allow plants to dry out after flowering and store rhizomes in a frost-free place over winter. Propagate by division of rhizomes or by seed, if available, in spring or by stem cuttings in summer.
A. antirrhina. Erect perennial. H and S 35cm (14in) or more. Has oval, toothed leaves, to 5cm (2in) or more long and of unequal size in each opposite pair. In summer bears funnel-shaped, red-orange flowers, to 4cm (1½in) long, with yellow throats.
A. **'Brilliant'**. Erect, compact perennial. H and S 30cm (12in). Has oval, toothed leaves and, in summer, large, funnel-shaped, scarlet flowers.
A. coccinea. See *A. erecta.*
A. erecta, syn. *A. coccinea, A. pulchella.* Erect, bushy, branching perennial. H and S 45cm (18in). Has narrowly oval, toothed leaves, often arranged in whorls of 3. Tubular, scarlet flowers with yellow eyes are produced in summer.
A. grandiflora. Erect perennial. H and S to 60cm (24in). Oval, toothed leaves are often reddish below. In summer has tubular, dark pink to purple flowers with white eyes.
A. **'Little Beauty'** illus. p.282.
A. **'Paul Arnold'**. Erect, compact, free-flowering perennial. H and S 30cm (12in). Has oval, toothed leaves. Bears large, funnel-shaped, purple flowers in summer.
A. **'Peach Blossom'**. Trailing perennial. H and S to 25cm (10in). Has oval, toothed leaves, and large, funnel-shaped, peach-coloured flowers in summer.
A. pulchella. See *A. erecta.*

Achnatherum calamagrostis. See *Stipa calamagrostis.*
Acidanthera bicolor var. *murieliae.* See *Gladiolus callianthus.*
Acidanthera murieliae. See *Gladiolus callianthus.*

ACIPHYLLA
APIACEAE/UMBELLIFERAE

Genus of evergreen perennials, grown mainly for the architectural value of their spiky foliage but also for their flowers, which are produced more freely on male plants. Requires sun and well-drained soil. Protect neck of plant from winter wet with a deep layer of stone chippings. Propagate by seed when fresh, in late summer, or in early spring.
A. aurea illus. p.238.
A. scott-thomsonii (Giant Spaniard). Evergreen, rosette-forming perennial. H to 4.5m (14ft), S 60cm–1m (2–3ft). Much-dissected, spiny foliage is bronze when young, maturing to silver-grey. Prickly spikes of tiny, creamy-yellow flowers are rarely produced. Prefers a moist but well-drained site.
A. squarrosa illus. p.266.

ACOKANTHERA
APOCYNACEAE

Genus of evergreen shrubs and trees, grown for their flowers and overall appearance. Tender, min. 10°C (50°F). Requires full light and good drainage. Water containerized plants moderately, less when not in full growth. Propagate by seed in spring or autumn or by semi-ripe cuttings in summer. The sap and small, plum-like fruits that follow the flowers are highly toxic if ingested.
A. oblongifolia, syn. *A. spectabilis, Carissa spectabilis*, illus. p.150.
A. spectabilis. See *A. oblongifolia.*

Aconite. See *Aconitum*.
Winter. See *Eranthis hyemalis*, illus. p.441.

ACONITUM
Aconite, Monkshood, Wolf's bane

RANUNCULACEAE

Genus of perennials with poisonous, tuberous or fibrous roots and upright, sometimes scandent, stems, bearing curious, hooded flowers in summer. Leaves are mostly rounded in outline. Is good when grown in rock gardens and borders. Prefers a position in sun, but tolerates some shade and this may enhance flower colour. Requires fertile, well-drained soil. Propagate by division in autumn, every 2–3 years, or by seed in autumn. Contact with the foliage may irritate skin; all parts are highly toxic if ingested.
A. anthora. Compact, tuberous perennial. H 60cm (24in), S 50cm (20in). Has erect, leafy stems that bear several hooded, yellow flowers in summer. Leaves are divided and dark green.
A. x *bicolor.* See *A.* x *cammarum* 'Bicolor'.
A. **'Bressingham Spire'**. Compact, upright, tuberous perennial. H 1m (3ft), S 50cm (20in). Very erect spikes of hooded, violet-blue flowers are produced in summer. Bears deeply divided leaves that are glossy and dark green.
A. x *cammarum* **'Bicolor'**, syn. *A.* x *bicolor*, illus. p.252.
A. carmichaelii **'Arendsii'**, syn. *A.c.* 'Arends'. Erect, tuberous perennial. H 1.5m (5ft), S 30cm (1ft). Has divided, rich green leaves and, in autumn, spikes of hooded, rich deep blue flowers. Upright stems may need staking, particularly if planted in a shady site.
A. hemsleyanum, syn. *A. volubile* of gardens. Wiry, scandent, fibrous perennial. H 2–2.5m (6–8ft), S 1–1.2m (3–4ft). Hooded, lilac flowers are produced in drooping clusters in late summer. Leaves are divided and mid-green. Is best grown where it can scramble through a shrub or be supported.
A. **'Ivorine'**. Upright, tuberous perennial. H 1.5m (5ft), S 50cm (20in). Bears hooded, creamy-white flowers in erect spikes in early summer. Strong stems bear deeply divided, glossy, green leaves.
A. lycoctonum subsp. *vulparia*, syn. *A. orientale* of gardens, *A. vulparia*, illus. p.255.
A. napellus (Helmet flower, Monkshood). Upright, tuberous perennial. H 1.5m (5ft), S 30cm (1ft). Bears tall, slender spires of hooded, light indigo-blue flowers in late summer and deeply cut, mid-green leaves. **'Albidum'** (syn. *A.n.* f. *album*) has white flowers.
A. **'Newry Blue'**. Upright, tuberous perennial. H 1.2m (4ft), S 50cm (20in). Produces hooded, dark blue flowers on erect stems in summer and has deeply divided, glossy, dark green leaves.
A. orientale of gardens. See *A. lycoctonum* subsp. *vulparia*.
A. **'Sparks' Variety'**. Upright, tuberous perennial. H 1.2m (4ft), S 50cm (20in). Bears violet-blue flowers on branching stems in summer and has deeply divided, glossy, dark green leaves.
A. volubile of gardens. See *A. hemsleyanum.*
A. vulparia. See *A. lycoctonum* subsp. *vulparia*.

ACORUS
ARACEAE

Genus of semi-evergreen, perennial, marginal and submerged water plants, grown for their frequently aromatic foliage. Needs an open, sunny position.

A. calamus requires up to 25cm (10in) depth of water. Tidy up fading foliage in autumn and lift and divide plants every 3 or 4 years, in spring, as clumps become congested.
A. calamus 'Argenteostriatus', syn. *A.c.* 'Variegatus', illus. p.447.
A. gramineus 'Pusillus'. Semi-evergreen, perennial, marginal water plant or submerged aquarium plant. H and S 10cm (4in). Has narrow, grass-like, stiff leaves. Rarely, insignificant, greenish flower spikes are produced in summer. 'Variegatus' illus. p.447.

Acroclinium. Reclassified as *Rhodanthe.*

ACTAEA
Baneberry

RANUNCULACEAE

Genus of clump-forming perennials, grown for their colourful, poisonous berries. Likes woodland conditions – moist, peaty soil and shade. Propagate by division in spring or by seed in autumn. The berries are highly toxic if ingested.
A. alba. See *A. pachypoda.*
A. erythrocarpa of gardens. See *A. rubra.*
A. pachypoda, syn. *A. alba*, illus. p.259.
A. rubra, syn. *A. erythrocarpa* of gardens (Red baneberry). Clump-forming perennial. H 50cm (20in), S 30cm (12in). Small, fluffy, white flowers are followed in autumn by clusters of poisonous, rounded, scarlet berries, borne above oval, divided, bright green leaves.

ACTINIDIA

ACTINIDIACEAE

Genus of mainly deciduous, woody-stemmed, twining climbers. Some are tender, min. 10°C (50°F). Grows in partial shade but needs sun for fruit to form and ripen. Grow in any well-drained soil that does not dry out. Prune in winter if necessary. Propagate by seed in spring or autumn, by semi-ripe cuttings in mid-summer or by layering in winter.
A. chinensis of gardens. See *A. deliciosa.*
A. deliciosa, syn. *A. chinensis* of gardens (Chinese gooseberry, Kiwi fruit). Vigorous, mainly deciduous, woody-stemmed, twining climber. H 9–10m (28–30ft). Heart-shaped leaves are 13–20cm (5–8in) long. In summer bears clusters of cup-shaped, white flowers that later turn yellowish, followed by edible, hairy, brown fruits. To obtain fruits, both male and female plants must usually be grown. Zone 7.
A. kolomikta illus. p.209.
A. polygama (Silver vine). Mainly deciduous, woody-stemmed, twining climber. H 4–6m (12–20ft). Heart-shaped leaves, 7–13cm (3–5in) long, are bronze when young and sometimes have creamy upper sections. In summer has scented, cup-shaped, white flowers, usually arranged in groups of 3 male, female or bisexual, followed by edible but not very palatable, egg-shaped, bright yellow fruits. Zone 5.

ADA

See also ORCHIDS.
A. aurantiaca (illus. p.299). Evergreen, epiphytic orchid for a cool greenhouse. H 23cm (9in). Bears sprays of tubular, orange flowers, 2.5cm (1in) long, early spring. Has narrowly oval leaves, 10cm (4in) long. Needs shade in summer.

Adam's needle. See *Yucca filamentosa.*

ADANSONIA
Baobab

BOMBACACEAE

Genus of deciduous or semi-evergreen, mainly spring-flowering trees, grown for their characteristically swollen trunks, their foliage and for shade. Has flowers only on large, mature specimens. Tender, min. 13–16°C (55–61°F). Requires full light and sharply drained soil. Allow soil of containerized specimens almost to dry out between waterings. Propagate by seed sown in spring. Pot specimens kept under glass are susceptible to spider mite.
A. digitata. Slow-growing, semi-evergreen, rounded tree. H and S 15m (50ft) or more. Has palmate leaves of 5–7 lustrous, green leaflets. Produces fragrant, pendent, long-stalked, white flowers, with 5 reflexed petals, in spring, followed by edible, sausage-shaped, brown fruits.

ADENIUM
Desert rose

APOCYNACEAE

Genus of perennial succulents with fleshy, swollen trunks. Tender, min. 15°C (59°F). Needs sun or partial shade and well-drained soil; plants are very prone to rotting. Propagate by seed sown in spring or summer. The milky sap that exudes from broken stems may irritate skin and cause severe discomfort if ingested.
A. obesum illus. p.458.

ADENOPHORA
Gland bellflower

CAMPANULACEAE

Genus of summer-flowering, fleshy-rooted perennials. Requires a site in full sun and rich, well-drained but not over-dry soil. May sometimes become invasive but resents disturbance. Propagate by basal cuttings taken in early spring or by seed sown in autumn.
A. potaninii. Rosette-forming perennial. H 45cm (18in) or more, S 60cm (24in). Arching sprays of bell-shaped, pale bluish-lavender flowers are produced in late summer. Has oval to lance-shaped, basal, mid-green leaves.

Adhatoda duvernoia. See *Justicia adhatoda.*

ADIANTUM

ADIANTACEAE/PTERIDACEAE

Genus of deciduous, semi-evergreen or evergreen ferns. Some are tender, min. 7–13°C (45–55°F). Prefers semi-shade

and moist, neutral to acid soil (*A. aleuticum* prefers alkaline soil). Remove fading fronds regularly. Propagate by spores in summer.
A. aleuticum, syn. *A. pedatum* var. *aleuticum*, illus. p.311.
A. capillus-veneris (Maidenhair fern). Semi-evergreen or evergreen fern. H and S 30cm (12in). Has dainty, triangular to oval, segmented, arching, light green fronds borne on black stems.
A. cuneatum. See *A. raddianum.*
A. pedatum illus. p.312.
var. *aleuticum.* See *A. aleuticum.*
A. raddianum, syn. *A. cuneatum* (Delta maidenhair). Semi-evergreen or evergreen fern. H and S 30cm (12in). Tender, min. 7°C (45°F). Triangular, divided, pale green segments are borne on finely dissected fronds that have purplish-black stems.
'Fritz-Luthi' has bright green fronds.
'Grandiceps' (Tassel maidenhair) has elegant, tasselled fronds.
A. tenerum. Semi-evergreen or evergreen fern. H 30cm–1m (1–3ft), S 60cm–1m (2–3ft). Tender, min. 13°C (55°F). Broadly lance-shaped, much-divided, spreading, mid-green fronds consist of rounded or diamond-shaped pinnae.
A. venustum illus. p.313.

ADLUMIA

FUMARIACEAE/PAPAVERACEAE

Genus of one species of herbaceous, biennial, leaf-stalk climber, grown for its leaves and flowers. Grow in semi-shade in any soil. Propagate by seed in spring.
A. cirrhosa. See *A. fungosa.*
A. fungosa, syn. *A. cirrhosa* (Allegheny vine, Climbing fumitory). Herbaceous, biennial, leaf-stalk climber. H 3–4m (10–12ft). Delicate leaves have numerous leaflets. Tiny, tubular, spurred, white or purplish flowers are carried in drooping panicles in summer.

ADONIS

RANUNCULACEAE

Genus of spring-flowering perennials, grown for their foliage and flowers. Some thrive in semi-shade; others need an open, well-drained site. Propagate by seed when fresh, in late summer, or by division after flowering.
A. amurensis illus. p.275.
A. brevistyla illus. p.268.
A. vernalis illus. p.275.

ADROMISCHUS

CRASSULACEAE

Genus of perennial succulents and evergreen sub-shrubs with rounded, thin or fat leaves. Tender, min. 7°C (45°F). Needs partial shade and very well-drained soil. Propagate by leaf or stem cuttings in spring or summer.
A. clavifolius. See *A. cooperi.*
A. cooperi, syn. *A. clavifolius*, *Cotyledon cooperi*, *Echeveria cooperi.* Freely branching perennial succulent. H 10cm (4in), S to 15cm (6in). Has greyish-brown stems and inversely lance-shaped, glossy, grey-green leaves, to 5cm (2in) long, often purple-marked above. In summer produces

tubular, green-and-red flowers, with white-margined, pink or purple lobes, on a stem 25cm (10in) or more long.
A. maculatus illus. p.469.

AECHMEA

BROMELIACEAE

Genus of evergreen, rosette-forming, epiphytic perennials, cultivated for their foliage, flowers and fruits. Tender, min. 10–15°C (50–59°F). May be grown in full light or a semi-shaded site. Provide a rooting medium of equal parts humus-rich soil and either sphagnum moss or bark or plastic chips used for orchid culture. Using soft water, water moderately in summer, sparingly at all other times, and keep cup-like, rosette centres filled with water from spring through to autumn. Propagate by offsets in late spring.
A. distichantha (illus. p.265). Evergreen, basal-rosetted, epiphytic perennial. H and S to 1m (3ft). Forms dense rosettes of narrowly oblong, round-tipped, arching leaves that are dull green above, grey and scaly beneath. Has panicles of small, tubular, purple or blue flowers among white-felted, pink bracts, usually in summer.
A. fasciata, syn. *Billbergia rhodocyanea* (Silver vase plant, Urn plant; illus. p.265). Evergreen, tubular-rosetted, epiphytic perennial. H 40–60cm (16–24in), S 30–50cm (12–20in). Has loose rosettes of broadly oblong, round-tipped, incurved, arching leaves with dense, grey scales and silver cross-banding. Bears dense, pyramidal panicles of tubular, blue-purple flowers among pink bracts, just above foliage, from spring to autumn.
A. Foster's Favorite Group (Lacquered wine-cup; illus. p.265). Evergreen, basal-rosetted, epiphytic perennial. H and S 30–60cm (12–24in). Has loose rosettes of strap-shaped, arching, lustrous, wine-red leaves. Drooping spikes of small, tubular, deep purple-blue flowers are borne in summer, followed later by pear-shaped, red fruits.
A. fulgens (Coral berry). Evergreen, basal-rosetted, epiphytic perennial. H and S 40–75cm (16–30in). Forms loose rosettes of broadly oblong, arching, glossy, mid-green leaves with grey scales beneath and rounded or pointed tips. In summer produces, above foliage, erect panicles of small, tubular, violet-purple flowers that turn red with age. These are succeeded by small, rounded to ovoid, red fruits on red stalks.
A. nudicaulis. Evergreen, basal-rosetted, epiphytic perennial. H and S 40–75cm (16–30in). Produces loose rosettes of a few broadly strap-shaped, arching, olive-green leaves with spiny edges and usually banded with grey scales beneath. Spikes of small, tubular, yellow flowers open above large, red bracts in summer.
A. recurvata (illus. p.265). Evergreen, basal-rosetted, epiphytic perennial. H and S 15–20cm (6–8in). Narrowly triangular, tapered, spiny-edged, arching, red-flushed, mid-green leaves are produced in dense rosettes. In summer bears a short, dense spike of tubular, red-and-white flowers, with red bracts, just above leaves.

485

AEGOPODIUM
Bishop's weed, Gout weed, Ground elder

APIACEAE/UMBELLIFERAE

Genus of invasive, rhizomatous perennials, most of which are weeds although *A. podagraria* 'Variegatum' provides excellent ground cover. Tolerates sun or shade and any well-drained soil. Propagate by division of rhizomes in spring or autumn.
A. podagraria **'Variegatum'** illus. p.276.

AEONIUM

CRASSULACEAE

Genus of perennial succulents, some of which are short-lived, and evergreen, succulent shrubs, grown for their rosettes of bright green or blue-green, occasionally purple, leaves. Tender, min. 5°C (41°F). Prefers partial shade and very well-drained soil. Most species grow from autumn to spring and are semi-dormant in mid-summer. Propagate by seed in summer or, for branching species, by stem cuttings in spring or summer.
A. arboreum. Bushy, perennial succulent. H to 60cm (2ft), S 1m (3ft). Branched stems are each crowned by a rosette, up to 15cm (6in) across, of broadly lance-shaped, glossy, bright green leaves. In spring produces cones of small, star-shaped, golden flowers on 2–3-year-old stems, which then die back.
'Schwarzkopf' see *A.* 'Zwartkop'.
A. haworthii illus. p.466.
A. tabuliforme illus. p.478.
A. **'Zwartkop'**, syn. *A. arboreum* 'Schwarzkopf', illus. p.468.

Aeroplane propeller. See *Crassula perfoliata* var. *minor*, illus. p.464.

AESCHYNANTHUS

GESNERIACEAE

Genus of evergreen, climbing, trailing or creeping perennials, useful for growing in hanging baskets. Tender, min. 15–18°C (59–64°F). Needs a fairly humid atmosphere and a position out of direct sun. Water sparingly in low temperatures. Propagate by tip cuttings in spring or summer.
A. **'Black Pagoda'.** Semi-trailing perennial. H 60cm (24in), S to 45cm (18in). Has elliptic leaves, to 10cm (4in) long, pale green with dark brown marbling above, and purple beneath. Bears terminal clusters of deep burnt-orange flowers, with green calyces, from summer to winter.
A. marmoratus, syn. *A. zebrinus.* Evergreen, trailing perennial. H and S to 60cm (24in). Oval, waxy leaves are dark green, veined yellowish-green above, purplish below. Produces tubular, greenish flowers, with dark brown markings, borne in terminal clusters in summer.
A. pulcher (Lipstick plant, Royal red bugler). Evergreen, climbing or trailing perennial. H and S indefinite. Produces thick, oval leaves and small, tubular, hooded, bright red flowers, with yellow throats, borne in terminal clusters from summer to winter.

A. speciosus, syn. *A. splendens,* illus. p.293.
A. splendens. See *A. speciosus.*
A. zebrinus. See *A. marmoratus.*

AESCULUS
Buckeye, Horse-chestnut

HIPPOCASTANACEAE

Genus of deciduous trees and shrubs, grown for their bold, divided leaves and conspicuous, upright panicles or clusters of flowers, followed by fruits (horse-chestnuts) sometimes with spiny outer casings. Requires sun or semi-shade and fertile, well-drained soil. Propagate species by sowing seed in autumn, cultivars by budding in late summer or by grafting in late winter. Leaf spot may affect young foliage, and coral spot fungus may attack damaged wood. All parts of these plants may cause mild stomach upset if ingested.
A. californica illus. p.85.
A. × *carnea* (Red horse-chestnut).
'Briotii' illus. p.64.
A. chinensis illus. p.64.
A. flava, syn. *A. octandra,* illus. p.82.
A. glabra (Ohio buckeye). Deciduous, round-headed, sometimes shrubby tree. H and S 10m (30ft). Leaves, usually composed of 5 narrowly oval leaflets, are dark green. Bears 4-petalled, greenish-yellow flowers in upright clusters in late spring and early summer. Zone 3a.
A. hippocastanum (Horse-chestnut) illus. p.64. **'Baumannii'** is a vigorous, deciduous, spreading tree. H 30m (100ft), S 15m (50ft). Large, dark green leaves, consisting of 5 or 7 narrowly oval leaflets, turn yellow in autumn. Has large panicles of long-lasting, double, yellow- or red-marked, white flowers from mid- to late spring. Zone 4b.
A. indica (Indian horse-chestnut). Deciduous, spreading, elegant tree. H 20m (70ft), S 12m (40ft). Glossy, dark green leaves with usually 7 narrowly oval leaflets are bronze when young, orange or yellow in autumn. Upright panicles of 4-petalled, pink-tinged, white flowers, marked with red or yellow, appear in mid-summer. Zone 8.
'Sydney Pearce' illus. p.79.
A. × *neglecta* (Sunrise horse-chestnut). **'Erythroblastos'** illus. p.89.
A. octandra. See *A. flava.*
A. parviflora illus. p.119.
A. pavia (Red buckeye). Deciduous, round-headed, sometimes shrubby tree. H 5m (15ft), S 3m (10ft). Glossy, dark green leaves consist of 5 narrowly oval leaflets. Has panicles of 4-petalled, red flowers in early summer. Zone 5b.
'Atrosanguinea' illus. p.91. Zone 5b.
A. turbinata (Japanese horse-chestnut). Deciduous, spreading, stout-branched tree. H 20m (70ft), S 12m (40ft). Large, dark green leaves consist of 5 or 7 narrowly oval leaflets. Panicles of creamy-white flowers appear in late spring and early summer. Zone 7.

AETHIONEMA

BRASSICACEAE/CRUCIFERAE

Genus of short-lived, evergreen or semi-evergreen shrubs, sub-shrubs and perennials, grown for their prolific flowers. Needs sun and well-drained soil. Propagate by softwood cuttings in spring or by seed in autumn. Most species self seed readily.
A. armenum illus. p.377.
A. grandiflorum, syn. *A. pulchellum,* illus. p.352.
A. iberideum. Evergreen or semi-evergreen, rounded, compact shrub. H and S 15cm (6in). Bears small, lance-shaped, grey-green leaves and, in summer, 2cm (¾in) stems each bear a raceme of small, saucer-shaped, white flowers.
A. pulchellum. See *A. grandiflorum.*
A. **'Warley Rose'** illus. p.376.
A. **'Warley Ruber'.** Evergreen or semi-evergreen, rounded, compact sub-shrub. H and S 15cm (6in). Has tiny, linear, bluish-green leaves. Racemes of small, deep rose-pink flowers appear on 2–3cm (¾–1¼in) stems in spring-summer.

African daisy. See *Arctotis venusta;* *Dimorphotheca.*
African fountain grass. See *Pennisetum setaceum.*
African hemp. See *Sparrmannia africana,* illus.p.118.
African lily. See *Agapanthus africanus.*
African marigold. See *Tagetes erecta.*
African red alder. See *Cunonia capensis.*
African tulip tree. See *Spathodea campanulata,* illus. p.71.
African violet. See *Saintpaulia.*
  False. See *Streptocarpus saxorum,* illus. p.284.

AGAPANTHUS

AGAPANTHACEAE/LILIACEAE

Genus of clump-forming perennials, some of which are evergreen, with erect stems that carry large umbels of bell- to tubular-bell-shaped or trumpet-shaped flowers, usually blue and often fading to purple with age. Leaves are strap-shaped. Narrow-leaved forms may survive from zone 6. Grow in full sun and in moist but well-drained soil. Protect crowns in winter with mulch. Plants increase slowly but may be propagated by division in spring; may also be raised from seed in autumn or spring. Named cultivars will not come true from seed.
A. africanus (African lily). Evergreen, clump-forming perennial. H 1m (3ft), S 50cm (20in). In late summer has rounded umbels of deep blue flowers on upright stems, above broad, dark green leaves.
A. **'Alice Gloucester'.** Clump-forming perennial. H 1m (3ft), S 50cm (20in). Produces large, dense, rounded umbels of white flowers in summer, above narrow, mid-green leaves.
A. **'Ben Hope'.** Clump-forming perennial. H 1–1.2m (3–4ft), S 50cm (20in). Erect stems support dense, rounded umbels of deep blue flowers in late summer and early autumn, borne over narrow, greyish-green leaves.
A. campanulatus. Clump-forming perennial. H 60cm–1.2m (2–4ft), S 50cm (20in). Rounded umbels of blue flowers are borne on strong stems in summer, above narrow, greyish-

green leaves.
A. **'Cherry Holley'.** Clump-forming perennial. H 1m (3ft), S 50cm (20in). Rounded umbels of dark blue flowers, carried in summer above narrow leaves, do not fade to purple with age.
A. **'Dorothy Palmer'** illus. p.253.
A. inapertus. Clump-forming perennial. H 1.5m (5ft), S 60cm (2ft). Pendent, narrowly tubular, blue flowers are borne on very erect stems, above narrow, bluish-green leaves, in late summer and autumn.
A. **'Lilliput'.** Compact, clump-forming perennial. H 80cm (32in), S 50cm (20in). Has small, rounded umbels of dark blue flowers that are produced in summer. Leaves are narrow and mid-green.
A. **'Loch Hope'.** Clump-forming perennial. H 1–1.2m (3–4ft), S 50cm (20in). Bears large, rounded umbels of deep blue flowers in late summer and early autumn, above narrow, greyish-green leaves.
A. orientalis. See *A. praecox* subsp. *orientalis.*
A. praecox subsp. *orientalis,* syn. *A. orientalis,* illus. p.254.

AGAPETES,
syn. PENTAPTERYGIUM

ERICACEAE

Genus of evergreen or deciduous, scandent shrubs and semi-scrambling climbers, grown for their flowers. Tender, min. 5–18°C (41–64°F). Provide full light or partial shade and a humus-rich, well-drained but not dry, neutral to acid soil. Water potted specimens freely when in full growth, but moderately at other times. Overlong stems may be cut back to promote branching, but they are best tied to supports. Propagate by seed sown in spring or by semi-ripe cuttings taken in late summer.
A. **'Ludgvan Cross'.** Evergreen, scandent shrub with arching or pendulous stems. H and S 2–3m (6–10ft). Min. 5°C (41°F). Lance-shaped leaves are dark green. Urn-shaped, red flowers with darker patterns are produced in spring.
A. macrantha. See *A. variegata* var. *macrantha.*
A. rugosa. See *A. variegata* var. *rugosa.*
A. serpens illus. p.205.
A. variegata var. *macrantha,* syn. *A. macrantha,* illus. p.219. var. *rugosa* (syn. *A. rugosa*) is an evergreen, loose shrub with arching or spreading stems. H and S to 3m (10ft). Min. 5°C (41°F). Leaves are lance-shaped, wrinkled and bright green. In spring, clusters of pendent, urn-shaped, white flowers, patterned with purple-red, are borne from leaf axils.

AGASTACHE
Mexican giant hyssop

LABIATAE/LAMIACEAE

Genus of summer-flowering perennials with aromatic leaves. Needs full sun and fertile, well-drained soil. Plants are short-lived and should be propagated each year by softwood or semi-ripe cuttings taken in late summer.

A. mexicana, syn. *Brittonastrum mexicanum*, *Cedronella mexicana*. Upright perennial with aromatic leaves. H to 1m (3ft), S to 30cm (1ft). In summer bears whorls of small, tubular flowers in shades of pink to crimson. Leaves are oval, pointed, toothed and mid-green.

Agathaea. Reclassified as *Felicia*.

AGAVE

AGAVACEAE

Genus of rosetted, perennial succulents with sword-shaped, sharp-toothed leaves. Small species, to 30cm (1ft) high, flower only after 5–10 years; tall species, to 5m (15ft) high, may take 20–40 years to flower. The majority of species that have hard, blue-grey leaves are slighty hardy; grey-green- or green-leaved species are usually tender, requiring min. 5°C (41°F). Agave needs full sun and well-drained soil. Propagate by seed or offsets in spring or summer.
A. americana (Century plant). Basal-rosetted, perennial succulent. H 1–2m (3–6ft), S 2–3m (6–10ft) or more. Has sharply pointed, toothed leaves, to 1.5–2m (5–6ft) long. Branched flower stem, to 8m (25ft) long, bears dense, tapering spikes of bell-shaped, white to pale creamy-yellow flowers, each 9cm (3½in) long, in spring-summer. Offsets freely. 'Mediopicta', H and S 2m (6ft), has central, yellow stripes along leaves. 'Striata' illus. p.457.
A. attenuata illus. p.467.
A. filifera illus. p.465.
A. parryi illus. p.466.
A. parviflora illus. p.457.
A. utahensis illus. p.478.
A. victoriae-reginae illus. p.461.

Agave
> **Royal**. See *Agave victoriae-reginae*, illus. p.461.
> **Thread**. See *Agave filifera*, illus. p.465.
Ageratina ligustrina. See *Eupatorium ligustrinum*.

AGERATUM
Floss flower

ASTERACEAE/COMPOSITAE

Genus of annuals and biennials. Grow in sun and in fertile, well-drained soil, which should not be allowed to dry out otherwise growth and flowering will be poor. Plants must be dead-headed regularly to ensure continuous flowering. Propagate by seed sown outdoors in late spring.
A. houstonianum. Moderately fast-growing, hummock-forming annual. Tall cultivars, H and S 30cm (12in); medium, H and S 20cm (8in); dwarf, H and S 15cm (6in). All have oval, mid-green leaves and clusters of feathery, brush-like flower heads throughout summer and into autumn. Is useful for bedding. 'Blue Danube' (dwarf) and 'Blue Mink' (tall) illus. p.333. **Hawaii Series** includes uniform, compact plants, with deep to pale blue or white flower heads. 'Pacific'

(medium) is neat, with tight clusters of deep violet-blue flower heads. 'Swing Pink' (dwarf) has attractive, pink flower heads.

AGLAONEMA
Chinese evergreen

ARACEAE

Genus of evergreen, erect, tufted perennials, grown mainly for their foliage. Tender, most species requiring min. 15°C (59°F). Tolerates shade, although the variegated forms need more light, and prefers moist but well-drained soil. Water moderately when in full growth, less in winter. Propagate by division or stem cuttings in summer. Mealy bug may be a problem.
A. commutatum. Evergreen, erect, tufted perennial. H and S 45cm (18in) or more. Broadly lance-shaped leaves are 30cm (12in) long and dark green with irregular, greyish-white patches along lateral veins. Has greenish-white spathes produced in summer. 'Malay Beauty' (syn. *A.c.* 'Pewter') bears very dark green leaves mottled greenish-white and cream. 'Pewter' see *A.c.* 'Malay Beauty'. 'Treubii' illus. p.300.
A. pictum illus. p.304.
A. 'Silver King' illus. p.304.

AGONIS
Willow myrtle

MYRTACEAE

Genus of evergreen, mainly spring-flowering shrubs and trees, grown for their foliage, flowers and graceful appearance. Tender, min. 10°C (50°F). Needs full light and well-drained but moisture-retentive soil. Water containerized specimens moderately, scarcely at all in winter. Pruning is tolerated when necessary. Propagate by seed in spring or by semi-ripe cuttings in summer.
A. flexuosa illus. p.90.

AGROSTEMMA
Corn cockle

CARYOPHYLLACEAE

Genus of summer-flowering annuals. Grow in sun; flowers best in very well-drained soil that is not very fertile. Support with sticks and dead-head to prolong flowering. Propagate by seed sown *in situ* in spring or early autumn. Seeds may cause severe discomfort if ingested.
A. coeli-rosa. See *Silene coeli-rosa*.
A. githago. Fast-growing, erect annual with thin stems. H 60cm–1m (2–3ft), S 30cm (1ft). Has lance-shaped, mid-green leaves and, in summer, 5-petalled, open trumpet-shaped, pink flowers, 8cm (3in) wide. Seeds are tiny, rounded, dark brown and poisonous. 'Milas' illus. p.323.

AICHRYSON

CRASSULACEAE

Genus of annual and perennial succulents, often shrub-like, grown for their fleshy, spoon-shaped to rounded, hairy leaves. Most species are short-lived, dying after flowering. Tender,

min. 5°C (41°F). Needs full sun or partial shade and very well-drained soil. Propagate by seed or stem cuttings in spring or summer.
A. × domesticum 'Variegatum' illus. p.477.

Air plant, South American. See *Kalanchoe fedtschenkoi*.

AILANTHUS

SIMAROUBACEAE

Genus of deciduous trees, grown for their foliage and 3–5-winged fruits; they can be particularly useful as they are extremely tolerant of urban pollution. Needs sun or semi-shade and deep, fertile, well-drained soil. To grow as shrubs, cut back hard in spring, after which vigorous shoots bearing very large leaves are produced. Propagate by seed sown in autumn or by suckers or root cuttings taken in winter. Male flowers are unpleasantly scented; the pollen may cause an allergic reaction.
A. altissima (Tree of heaven). Fast-growing, deciduous, spreading tree. H 25m (80ft), S 15m (50ft). Large, dark green leaves consist of 15–30 paired, oval leaflets. Large clusters of small, green flowers in mid-summer are followed by attractive, winged, green, then reddish-brown fruits. Zone 6.

AJUGA

LABIATAE/LAMIACEAE

Genus of annuals and perennials, some of which are semi-evergreen or evergreen and excellent as ground cover. Tolerates sun or shade and any soil, but grows more vigorously in moist conditions. Propagate by division in spring.
A. pyramidalis (Pyramidal bugle). Semi-evergreen perennial. H 15cm (6in), S 45cm (18in). Forms a creeping carpet of oblong to spoon-shaped, deep green leaves, above which appear spikes of whorled, 2-lipped, blue flowers in spring. 'Metallica Crispa' has crisp, curled leaves, with a metallic-bronze lustre, and dark blue flowers.
A. reptans 'Atropurpurea' illus. p.303. 'Jungle Beauty' is a semi-evergreen, mat-forming perennial. H 38cm (15in), S 60cm (24in). Has large, oval, toothed or slightly lobed, dark green leaves, sometimes suffused purple, and, in spring, spikes of whorled, 2-lipped, blue flowers. 'Multicolor' (syn. *A.r.* 'Rainbow') illus. p.303. 'Rainbow' see *A.r.* 'Multicolor'.

AKEBIA

LARDIZABALACEAE

Genus of deciduous or semi-evergreen, woody-stemmed, twining climbers, grown for their leaves and flowers. Individual plants seldom produce fruits; cross-pollination between two individuals is required for fruit formation. Prefers a position in full sun and any good, well-drained soil. Tolerates an east- or north-facing position. Dislikes disturbance. May be propagated in a number of ways:

by seed sown in autumn or spring; by semi-ripe cutings taken in summer; or by layering in winter.
A. lobata. See *A. trifoliata*.
A. × pentaphylla illus. p.205.
A. quinata illus. p.205.
A. trifoliata, syn. *A. lobata*. Deciduous, woody-stemmed, twining climber. H to 10m (30ft) or more. Mid-green leaves, bronze-tinted when young, have 3 oval leaflets; drooping racemes of 3-petalled, purple flowers appear in spring, followed by sausage-shaped, purplish fruits. Zone 6.

Albany bottlebrush. See *Callistemon speciosus*.

ALBIZIA

LEGUMINOSAE/MIMOSACEAE

Genus of deciduous or semi-evergreen trees, grown for their feathery foliage and unusual flower heads, composed of numerous stamens and resembling bottlebrushes. Best grown against a south- or west-facing wall; in cold areas do not risk planting out until late spring. Requires full sun and well-drained soil. *A. julibrissin* may be grown as a summer bedding plant for its foliage. Propagate by seed in autumn.
A. distachya. See *Paraserianthes lophantha*.
A. julibrissin illus. p.90.
A. lophantha. See *Paraserianthes lophantha*.

ALBUCA

HYACINTHACEAE/LILIACEAE

Genus of spring- or summer-flowering bulbs. Tender, min. 10°C (50°F). Needs an open, sunny position and well-drained soil. Dies down in spring or late summer after flowering. Propagate by seed in spring or by offsets when dormant.
A. canadensis, syn. *A. major*, *A. minor*. Spring-flowering bulb. H 15cm (6in), S 8–10cm (3–4in). Has 3–6 narrowly lance-shaped, erect, basal leaves. Produces a loose spike of tubular, yellow flowers, 1.5–2cm (⅝–¾in) long, with a green stripe on each petal.
A. humilis illus. p.435.
A. major. See *A. canadensis*.
A. minor. See *A. canadensis*.

ALCEA
Hollyhock

MALVACEAE

Genus of biennials and short-lived perennials, grown for their tall spikes of flowers. Needs full sun and well-drained soil. Propagate by seed in late summer or spring. Rust may be a problem.
A. rosea, syn. *Althaea rosea* (biennial), illus. p.321. 'Chater's Double' (biennial), illus. p.327. 'Majorette' is an erect biennial, grown as an annual. H 60cm (24in), S to 30cm (12in). Rounded, lobed, pale green leaves have a rough texture. Spikes of rosette-like, double flowers, in several different colours, are produced during summer and early autumn. 'Summer Carnival' (annual or biennial), H 1.8–2.4m (6–8ft), S to 60cm (2ft), has double flowers in mixed colours.

ALCHEMILLA
Lady's mantle

ROSACEAE

Genus of perennials that produce sprays of tiny, greenish-yellow flowers, with conspicuous outer calyces, in summer. Some are good for ground cover. Grow in sun or partial shade, in all but boggy soils. Propagate by seed or division in spring or autumn.

A. alpina (Alpine lady's mantle). Mound-forming perennial. H 15cm (6in), S 60cm (24in) or more. Rounded, lobed, pale green leaves are covered in silky hairs. Bears upright spikes of tiny, greenish-yellow flowers, with conspicuous, green, outer calyces, in summer. Is suitable for ground cover and a dry bank.

A. conjuncta illus. p.290.
A. mollis illus. p.290.

Alder. See *Alnus*.
  African red. See *Cunonia capensis*.
  Black. See *Alnus glutinosa*.
  Common. See *Alnus glutinosa*.
  Grey. See *Alnus incana*, illus. p.66.
  Italian. See *Alnus cordata*, illus. p.66.
  Witch. See *Fothergilla gardenii*.
Alder buckthorn. See *Rhamnus frangula*.
Aleppo pine. See *Pinus halepensis*, illus. p.107.
Alexandra palm. See *Archontophoenix alexandrae*, illus. p.72.
Alexandrian laurel. See *Danäe racemosa*.
Algerian iris. See *Iris unguicularis*.
Algerian ivy. See *Hedera canariensis* var. *algeriensis*.
Algerian oak. See *Quercus canariensis*, illus. p.66.
Algerian winter iris. See *Iris unguicularis*.

x ALICEARA

See also ORCHIDS.
x *A.* Dark Warrior (illus. p.298). Evergreen, epiphytic orchid for a cool greenhouse. H 25cm (10in). Produces sprays of wispy, mauve-brown, cream-yellow or green flowers, 4cm (1½in) across; flowering season varies. Leaves, 10cm (4in) long, are narrowly oval. Grow in semi-shade in summer.

ALISMA

ALISMATACEAE

Genus of deciduous, perennial, marginal water plants, grown for their foliage and flowers. Requires an open, sunny position in mud or up to 25cm (10in) depth of water. Tidy up fading foliage in autumn and remove dying flower spikes before ripening seeds are dispersed. May be propagated by division in spring or by seed in late summer. Contact with sap may irritate skin; all parts may cause mild stomach upset if ingested.

A. natans. See *Luronium natans*.
A. plantago-aquatica illus. p.446.
A. ranunculoides. See *Baldellia ranunculoides*.

ALLAMANDA

APOCYNACEAE

Genus of evergreen, woody-stemmed, scrambling climbers, grown for their trumpet-shaped flowers. Tender, min. 13–15°C (55–9°F). Prefers partial shade in summer and humus-rich, well-drained, neutral to acid soil. Water regularly, less when not in full growth. Stems must be tied to supports. Prune previous season's growth back to 1 or 2 nodes in spring. Propagate by softwood cuttings in spring or summer. Whitefly and spider mite may be troublesome. Contact with sap may irritate skin; all parts may cause mild stomach upset if ingested.

A. cathartica (Golden trumpet).
'Hendersonii' illus. p.216.

Allegheny vine. See *Adlumia fungosa*.

ALLIUM
Onion

ALLIACEAE/LILIACEAE

Genus of perennials, some of which are edible, with bulbs, rhizomes or fibrous rootstocks. Nearly all have narrow, basal leaves smelling of onions when crushed, and most have small flowers packed together in a dense, spherical or shuttlecock-shaped umbel. Dried umbels of tall border species are good for winter decoration. Requires an open, sunny situation and well-drained soil; is best left undisturbed to form clumps. Plant in autumn. Propagate by seed in autumn or by division of clumps – spring-flowering varieties in late summer and summer-flowering ones in spring. Contact with the bulbs may irritate skin or aggravate skin allergies.

A. acuminatum, syn. *A. murrayanum*, illus. p.430.
A. aflatunense of gardens. See *A.* x *hollandicum*.
A. akaka illus. p.427.
A. albopilosum. See *A. cristophii*.
A. azureum. See *A. caeruleum*.
A. beesianum. Clump-forming, late summer-flowering bulb. H 20–30cm (8–12in), S 5–10cm (2–4in). Has linear, grey-green leaves and, in late summer, pendent heads of bell-shaped, blue flowers.
A. caeruleum, syn. *A. azureum*, illus. p.422.
A. campanulatum. Clump-forming, summer-flowering bulb. H 10–30cm (4–12in), S 5–10cm (2–4in). Linear, semi-erect, basal leaves die away before flowering time. Bears a domed umbel, 2.5–7cm (1–3in) wide, of up to 30 small, star-shaped, pale pink or white flowers.
A. carinatum subsp. *pulchellum*, syn. *A. pulchellum*. Clump-forming, summer-flowering bulb. H 30–60cm (12–24in), S 8–10cm (3–4in). Linear, semi-erect leaves sheath lower two-thirds of stem. Has an umbel of pendent, cup-shaped, purple flowers.
A. cernuum illus. p.420.

A. christophii. See *A. cristophii*.
A. cowanii. See *A. neapolitanum*.
A. cristophii, syn. *A. albopilosum*, *A. christophii*, illus. p.421.
A. cyaneum. Tuft-forming, summer-flowering bulb. H 10–30cm (4–12in), S 5–8cm (2–3in). Leaves are thread-like and erect. Stems each bear a small, dense umbel of 5 or more pendent, cup-shaped, blue or violet-blue flowers, 0.5cm (¼in) long.
A. cyathophorum var. *farreri* illus. p.436.
A. flavum illus. p.422.
A. giganteum illus. p.402.
A. x *hollandicum*, syn. *A. aflatunense* of gardens, illus. p.402.
A. kansuense. See *A. sikkimense*.
A. karataviense illus. p.427.
A. macranthum. Tuft-forming, summer-flowering bulb. H 20–30cm (8–12in), S 10–12cm (4–5in). Has linear leaves on lower part of flower stem, which bears a loose umbel of up to 20 bell-shaped, deep purple flowers, each 1cm (½in) long, on slender stalks.
A. mairei. Clump-forming, late summer- to autumn-flowering bulb. H 10–20cm (4–8in), S 10–12cm (4–5in). Leaves are erect, thread-like and basal. Wiry stems, each carry a small, shuttlecock-shaped umbel of up to 20 upright, bell-shaped, pink flowers, each 1cm (½in) long.
A. moly illus. p.436.
A. murrayanum. See *A. acuminatum*.
A. narcissiflorum, syn. *A. pedemontanum* of gardens, illus. p.436.
A. neapolitanum, syn. *A. cowanii*, illus. p.408.
A. oreophilum, syn. *A. ostrowskianum*, illus. p.430.
A. ostrowskianum. See *A. oreophilum*.
A. pedemontanum of gardens. See *A. narcissiflorum*.
A. pulchellum. See *A. carinatum* subsp. *pulchellum*.
A. schoenoprasum illus. p.435.
A. schubertii illus. p.421.
A. senescens var. *calcareum*. See *A.s.* subsp. *montanum*.
subsp. *montanum* (syn. *A.s.* var. *calcareum*) illus. p.420.
A. sikkimense, syn. *A. kansuense*. Tuft-forming, summer-flowering bulb. H 10–25cm (4–10in), S 5–10cm (2–4in). Leaves are linear, erect and basal. Up to 15 bell-shaped, blue flowers, 0.5–1cm (¼–½in) long, are borne in a small, pendent umbel.
A. sphaerocephalon. Clump-forming, summer-flowering bulb. H to 60cm (24in), S 8–10cm (3–4in). Has linear, semi-erect leaves on basal third of slender, wiry stems and a very dense umbel, 2–4cm (¾–1½in) across, of up to 40 small, bell-shaped, pinkish-purple flowers.
A. stipitatum illus. p.401.
A. unifolium illus. p.409.

Allspice
  California. See *Calycanthus occidentalis*, illus. p.142.
  Carolina. See *Calycanthus floridus*.
Almond. See *Prunus dulcis*.
  Indian. See *Terminalia catappa*.
  Tropical. See *Terminalia catappa*.

ALNUS
Alder

BETULACEAE

Genus of deciduous trees and shrubs, grown mainly for their ability to thrive in wet situations. Flowers are borne in catkins in late winter or early spring, the males conspicuous and attractive, the females forming persistent, woody, conelike fruits. Most do best in sun and any moist or even waterlogged soil, but *A. cordata* will also grow well on poor, dry soils. Propagate species by seed sown in autumn, cultivars by budding in late summer or by hardwood cuttings taken in early winter.

A. cordata illus. p.66.
A. glutinosa (Black alder, Common alder). 'Aurea' is a slow-growing, deciduous, conical tree. H to 25m (80ft), S 10m (30ft). Has rounded leaves, bright yellow until mid-summer, later becoming pale green. Produces yellow-brown catkins in early spring. Is useful grown in a boggy area. Zone 4. 'Imperialis', H 10m (30ft), S 4m (12ft), is slow-growing and has deeply cut, lobed leaves.
A. incana (Grey alder) illus. p.66. 'Aurea' is a deciduous, conical tree. H 20m (70ft), S 8m (25ft). Has reddish-yellow or orange shoots in winter and broadly oval, yellow leaves. Reddish-yellow or orange catkins are borne in late winter and early spring. Is useful for cold, wet areas and poor soils. 'Ramulis Coccineis' has red, winter shoots and buds, and orange catkins. Zone 4.

ALOCASIA

ARACEAE

Genus of evergreen perennials with underground rhizomes, grown for their attractive foliage. Produces tiny flowers on a spadix enclosed in a leaf-like spathe. Tender, min. 15°C (59°F). Needs high humidity, partial shade and well-drained soil. Propagate by seed, stem cuttings or division of rhizomes in spring. Contact with sap may irritate skin; all parts may cause mild stomach upset if ingested.

A. cuprea illus. p.266.
A. lowii var. *veitchii*. See *A. veitchii*.
A. macrorrhiza (Giant elephant's ear, Taro). Evergreen, tufted perennial with a thick, trunk-like stem. H to 3m (10ft) or more, S 2m (6ft). Broad, arrow-shaped, glossy, green leaves, to 1m (3ft) long, are carried on stalks 1m (3ft) long. Has yellowish-green spathes to 20cm (8in) high.
A. picta. See *A. veitchii*.
A. veitchii, syn. *A. lowii* var. *veitchii*, *A. picta*. Evergreen, tufted perennial. H 1m (3ft) or more, S 75cm (30in). Narrow leaves, triangular with arrow-shaped bases, are 45cm (18in) long and green with greyish midribs, veins and margins, purple below. Greenish spathes.

ALOE

ALOEACEAE/LILIACEAE

Genus of evergreen, rosetted trees, shrubs, perennials and scandent climbers with succulent foliage and tubular to bell-shaped flowers. Tender, min. 7–10°C (45–50°F). Tree aloes and shrubs with a spread over 30cm (1ft) prefer full sun; most smaller species prefer partial shade. Needs very well-drained soil. Propagate by seed, stem cuttings or offsets in spring or summer.

A. arborescens. Evergreen, bushy, succulent-leaved shrub. H and S 2m (6ft). Stems are crowned by rosettes of widely spreading, long, slender, curved, dull blue-green leaves with toothed margins. Long flower stems produce masses of tubular to bell-shaped, red flowers in late winter and spring. **'Variegata'** illus. p.459.

A. aristata illus. p.480.

A. barbadensis. See *A. vera*.

A. brevifolia. Basal-rosetted, perennial succulent, producing many offsets. H 15cm (6in), S 30cm (12in). Has broadly sword-shaped, fleshy, blue-green leaves with a few teeth along edges. In spring, flower stems, 50cm (20in) long, carry narrowly bell-shaped, bright red flowers.

A. ciliaris illus. p.459.

A. ferox illus. p.459.

A. humilis. Rosetted, perennial succulent. H 10cm (4in), S 30cm (12in). Has a dense, basal rosette of narrowly sword-shaped, spine-edged, fleshy, blue-green leaves, often erect, with incurving tips. Produces flower stems 30cm (12in) long, each bearing a spike of narrowly bell-shaped, orange flowers in spring. Offsets freely.

A. punctata. See *A. variegata*.

A. striata illus. p.468.

A. variegata, syn. *A. punctata*, illus. p.464.

A. vera, syn. *A. barbadensis*, illus. p.466.

Aloe
Lace. See *Aloe aristata*, illus. p.480.
Partridge-breasted. See *Aloe variegata*, illus. p.464.

ALOINOPSIS
AIZOACEAE

Genus of dwarf, tuberous, perennial succulents with daisy-like flowers from late summer to early spring. Tender, min. 7°C (45°F). Requires a sunny site and very well-drained soil. Is very susceptible to overwatering. Propagate by seed in summer.

A. schooneesii illus. p.477.

ALONSOA
SCROPHULARIACEAE

Genus of perennials, grown as annuals. May be used for cut flowers. Grow in sun and in rich, well-drained soil. Flowering may be poor outdoors in a wet summer. Young plants should have growing shoots pinched out to encourage bushy growth. Propagate by seed sown outdoors in late spring. Aphids may be troublesome, particularly under glass.

A. warscewiczii illus. p.329.

ALOPECURUS
GRAMINEAE/POACEAE

See also GRASSES, BAMBOOS, RUSHES and SEDGES.

A. pratensis 'Aureovariegatus', syn. *A.p.* 'Aureomarginatus', illus. p.309.

ALOYSIA
VERBENACEAE

Genus of deciduous or evergreen, summer-flowering shrubs, grown for their aromatic foliage and sprays of tiny flowers. Plant against a south- or west-facing wall or raise afresh each year. Needs full sun and well-drained soil. Cut out any dead wood in early summer. Propagate by softwood cuttings in summer.

A. triphylla, syn. *Lippia citriodora*, illus. p.143.

Alpine anemone. See *Pulsatilla alpina*, illus. p.346.
Alpine avens. See *Geum montanum*.
Alpine azalea. See *Loiseleuria procumbens*, illus. p.377.
Alpine buttercup. See *Ranunculus alpestris*, illus. p.363.
Alpine catchfly. See *Lychnis alpina*.
Alpine cinquefoil. See *Potentilla crantzii*.
Alpine coltsfoot. See *Homogyne alpina*.
Alpine columbine. See *Aquilegia alpina*, illus. p.348.
Alpine currant. See *Ribes alpinum*.
Alpine fleabane. See *Erigeron alpinus*, illus. p.355.
Alpine forget-me-not. See *Myosotis alpestris*, illus. p.370.
Alpine heath. See *Erica carnea*.
Alpine lady's mantle. See *Alchemilla alpina*.
Alpine mouse-ear. See *Cerastium alpinum*.
Alpine penny-cress. See *Thlaspi alpinum*.
Alpine pink. See *Dianthus alpinus*, illus. p.378.
Alpine poppy. See *Papaver burseri*.
Alpine snowbell. See *Soldanella alpina*, illus. p.368.
Alpine thistle. See *Carlina acaulis*, illus. p.375.
Alpine toadflax. See *Linaria alpina*.
Alpine totara. See *Podocarpus nivalis*, illus. p.110.

ALPINIA
ZINGIBERACEAE

Genus of mainly evergreen perennials with fleshy rhizomes, grown for their flowers in well-drained soil with plenty of humus, a moist atmosphere, and partial shade. Tender, min. 18°C (64°F). Not successful in containers. Propagate by division in late spring or early summer. Spider mite may be a problem.

A. calcarata (Indian ginger). Evergreen, upright, clump-forming perennial. H and S to 1m (3ft). Has stalkless, aromatic, lance-shaped leaves, to 30cm (1ft) long. At any time of year may bear horizontal spikes of whitish flowers, with 2.5cm (1in) long, yellow lips marked reddish-purple.

A. nutans of gardens. See *A. zerumbet*.

A. speciosa. See *A. zerumbet*.

A. zerumbet, syn. *A. nutans* of gardens, *A. speciosa*, illus. p.227.

Alsobia dianthiflora. See *Episcia dianthiflora*.
Alsophila. Reclassified as *Cyathea*.

ALSTROEMERIA
ALSTROEMERIACEAE

Genus of mostly summer-flowering, tuberous perennials with showy, multicoloured flowers. Flowers are good for cutting as they last well. Where hardy, protect by covering dormant tubers with dry bracken or loose peat. Needs sun and well-drained soil. Propagate by seed or division in early spring. Contact with foliage may aggravate skin allergies.

A. aurantiaca. See *A. aurea*.

A. aurea, syn. *A. aurantiaca*, illus. p.403.

A. gayana. See *A. pelegrina*.

A. hookeri illus. p.386.

A. Ligtu Hybrids illus. p.423.

A. MARGARET ('Stacova') illus. p.400

A. 'Parigo Charm' illus. p.423

A. pelegrina, syn. *A. gayana*, illus. p.420.

A. 'Stacova'. See *A. MARGARET*.

A. 'Walter Fleming'. Summer-flowering, tuberous perennial. H to 1m (3ft), S 60cm–1m (2–3ft). Each leafy stem produces narrowly lance-shaped, twisted leaves and widely funnel-shaped, deep yellow flowers, 5–6cm (2–2½in) across, flushed purple with reddish-purple spots.

ALTERNANTHERA
AMARANTHACEAE

Genus of bushy perennials, grown for their attractive, coloured foliage. Is useful for carpeting or bedding. Tender, min. 15–18°C (59–64°F). Needs sun or partial shade and moist but well-drained soil. Propagate by tip cuttings or division in spring.

A. amoena. See *A. ficoidea* var. *amoena*.

A. ficoidea (Parrot leaf). var. **amoena** (syn. *A. amoena*) is a mat-forming perennial. H 5cm (2in), S indefinite. Has narrowly oval, green leaves, marked red, yellow and orange, with wavy margins. **'Versicolor'** (syn. *A. versicolor*) is an erect form, H and S to 30cm (12in), with rounded to spoon-shaped leaves shaded brown, red and yellow.

A. versicolor. See *A. ficoidea* 'Versicolor'.

Althaea rosea. See *Alcea rosea*.
Aluminium plant. See *Pilea cadierei*, illus. p.300.

ALYSSUM
BRASSICACEAE/CRUCIFERAE

Genus of perennials, some of which are evergreen, and annuals, grown for their flowers. Requires a sunny site and well-drained soil. Cut back lightly after flowering. Propagate either by softwood cuttings taken in late spring or by seed sown in autumn.

A. maritimum. See *Lobularia maritima*.

A. montanum. Evergreen, prostrate perennial. H and S 15cm (6in). Leaves are small, oval, hairy and grey. Flower stems, 15cm (6in) long, each bear an open, spherical raceme carrying small, highly fragrant, soft yellow flowers in summer. Is a good plant for a rock garden.

A. saxatile. See *Aurinia saxatilis*.

A. spinosum, syn. *Ptilotrichum spinosum*. Semi-evergreen, rounded, compact shrub. H 20cm (8in) or more, S 30cm (12in). Intricate branches bear spines and narrowly oval to linear, silver leaves. Spherical heads of tiny, 4-petalled, white to purple-pink flowers appear in early summer.

A. wulfenianum. Prostrate perennial. H 2cm (¾in), S 20cm (8in). Loose heads of small, bright yellow flowers appear in summer above small, oval, grey leaves.

Alyssum, Sweet. See *Lobularia maritima*.
Amaranth, Globe. See *Gomphrena globosa*, illus. p.331.

AMARANTHUS
AMARANTHACEAE

Genus of annuals, grown for their dense panicles of tiny flowers or their colourful foliage. Tender. Grow in a sunny position in rich or fertile, well-drained soil. Propagate from seed sown outdoors in late spring. Aphids may be a problem.

A. caudatus illus. p.326.

A. hypochondriacus illus. p.330.

A. tricolor 'Joseph's Coat'. Bushy annual. H to 1m (3ft), S 45cm (1½ft) or more. Has oval, scarlet, green and yellow leaves, to 20cm (8in) long, and produces small panicles of tiny, red flowers in summer. Leaves of **'Molten Fire'** are crimson, bronze and purple.

x AMARCRINUM
AMARYLLIDACEAE

Hybrid genus (*Amaryllis* x *Crinum*) of one robust, evergreen bulb, grown for its large, funnel-shaped flowers. Tender. Needs a sunny position and well-drained soil. Plant with neck just covered by soil. Propagate by division in spring.

x A. howardii. See x *A. memoria-corsii*.

x A. memoria-corsii, syn. x *A. howardii*, x *Crinodonna corsii*, illus. p.408.

x AMARYGIA
AMARYLLIDACEAE

Hybrid genus (*Amaryllis* x *Brunsvigia*) of stout, autumn-flowering bulbs, which are cultivated for their large, showy flowers. Tender. Needs full sun and, preferably, the shelter of a wall. Plant bulbs just beneath the surface of well-drained soil. Propagate by division in spring.

x A. parkeri, syn. x *Brunsdonna parkeri*, illus. p.408.

AMARYLLIS
AMARYLLIDACEAE

Genus of autumn-flowering bulbs, grown for their funnel-shaped flowers. Slightly hardy, in cool areas grow against a south-facing wall for protection. Grow in a sheltered, sunny

situation and in well-drained soil. Plant bulbs under at least 8cm (3in) of soil. Propagate by division in late spring, as leaves die down, or in late summer, before growth recommences.
A. belladonna and **'Hathor'** illus. p.408.

Amaryllis, Blue. See *Worsleya.*

AMBERBOA
Sweet sultan

ASTERACEAE/COMPOSITAE

Genus of erect annuals or biennials, grown for their attractive, cornflower-like flower heads, which are borne from spring to autumn. Needs full sun and moderately fertile, well-drained soil. Dead-head to prolong flowering. Propagate by seed in spring or autumn.
A. moschata, syn. *Centaurea moschata,* illus. p.335.

AMELANCHIER
Juneberry, Serviceberry, Shadbush

ROSACEAE

Genus of deciduous, spring-flowering trees and shrubs, grown primarily for their profuse flowers and their foliage, which is frequently brightly coloured in autumn. Requires sun or semi-shade and well-drained but not too dry, preferably neutral to acid soil. Propagate in autumn by seed, in late autumn to early spring by layering or, in the case of suckering species, by division. Fireblight may sometimes be troublesome.
A. alnifolia. Deciduous, upright, suckering shrub. H 4m (12ft) or more, S 3m (10ft) or more. Leaves are oval to rounded and dark green. Erect spikes of star-shaped, creamy-white flowers are borne in late spring, followed by small, edible, juicy, rounded, purple-black fruits. Zone 2b.
A. arborea. Deciduous, spreading, sometimes shrubby, tree. H 10m (30ft), S 12m (40ft). Clusters of star-shaped, white flowers appear in mid-spring as oval, white-haired, young leaves unfold. Foliage matures to dark green, turning to red or yellow in autumn. Rounded fruits are small, dry and reddish-purple. Zone 2b.
A. asiatica. Deciduous, spreading tree or shrub of elegant habit. H 8m (25ft), S 10m (30ft). Leaves are oval and dark green, usually woolly when young and turning yellow or red in autumn. Star-shaped, white flowers are borne profusely in late spring, followed by edible, juicy, rounded, blackcurrant-like fruits. Zone 6.
A. canadensis. Deciduous, upright, dense shrub. H 6m (20ft), S 3m (10ft). Star-shaped, white flowers are borne from mid- to late spring amid unfolding, oval, white-haired leaves that mature to dark green and turn orange-red in autumn. Fruits are edible, rounded, blackish-purple, sweet and juicy. Zone 3b.
A. laevis illus. p.85.
A. lamarckii illus. p.116.
American arbor-vitae. See *Thuja occidentalis.*
American arrowhead. See *Sagittaria latifolia,* illus. p.446.

American aspen. See *Populus tremuloides.*
American beech. See *Fagus grandifolia.*
American bittersweet. See *Celastrus scandens.*
American bladdernut. See *Staphylea trifoliata.*
American chestnut. See *Castanea dentata.*
American cranberry bush. See *Viburnum trilobum.*
American elder. See *Sambucus canadensis.*
American holly. See *Ilex opaca,* illus. p.98.
American hop hornbeam. See *Ostrya virginiana,* illus. p.77.
American hornbeam. See *Carpinus caroliniana.*
American linden. See *Tilia americana.*
American lotus. See *Nelumbo lutea.*
American mountain ash. See *Sorbus americana.*
American spatterdock. See *Nuphar advena.*
American elm. See *Ulmus americana.*
American white oak. See *Quercus alba,* illus. p.71.
Amomyrtus luma. See *Luma apiculata.*
***Amomyrtus luma* 'Glanleam Gold'.** See *Luma apiculata* 'Glanleam Gold'.

AMORPHA
LEGUMINOSAE/PAPILIONACEAE

Genus of deciduous shrubs and sub-shrubs, grown for their flowers and foliage. Is a useful plant for cold, dry, exposed positions. Requires full sun and well-drained soil. May be propagated by softwood cuttings taken in summer or by seed sown in autumn.
A. canescens (Lead plant). Deciduous, open sub-shrub. H 1m (3ft), S 1.5m (5ft). Dense spikes of tiny, pea-like, purple flowers, with orange anthers, are produced in late summer and early autumn, amid oval, grey-haired leaves divided into 21–41 narrowly oval leaflets. Zone 2b.

AMPELOPSIS
VITACEAE

Genus of deciduous, woody-stemmed, tendril climbers, some of which are twining, grown for their leaves. Grow in a sheltered position, in sun or partial shade in any soil. Needs plenty of room as grows quickly and can cover a large area. Propagate by greenwood or semi-ripe cuttings in mid-summer.
A. aconitifolia, syn. *Vitis aconitifolia.* Fast-growing, deciduous, woody-stemmed, twining, tendril climber. H to 12m (40ft). Rounded leaves have 3 or 5 toothed, lobed, dark green leaflets; inconspicuous, greenish flowers appear in late summer, followed later by orange berries. Zone 6.
A. brevipedunculata var. *maximowiczii,* syn. *A. glandulosa* var. *brevipedunculata, A. heterophylla, Vitis heterophylla.* Vigorous, deciduous, woody-stemmed, twining, tendril climber with hairy, young stems. H to 5m (15ft) or more. Has dark green leaves that vary in size and shape and

are almost hairless beneath. Inconspicuous, greenish flowers are produced in summer, followed by bright blue berries. Zone 4.
A. glandulosa var. *brevipedunculata.* See *A. brevipedunculata* var. *maximowiczii.*
A. heterophylla. See *A. brevipedunculata* var. *maximowiczii.*
A. sempervirens. See *Cissus striata.*
A. veitchii. See *Parthenocissus tricuspidata* 'Veitchii'.

AMSONIA
Blue star

APOCYNACEAE

Genus of slow-growing, clump-forming, summer-flowering perennials. Grow in full sun and in well-drained soil. Is best left undisturbed for some years. May be propagated by division in spring, by softwood cuttings in summer or by seed in autumn. Contact with the milky sap may irritate skin.
A. orientalis, syn. *Rhazya orientalis,* illus. p.286.
A. tabernaemontana illus. p.287.

Amur cork tree. See *Phellodendron amurense.*
Amur grape. See *Vitis amurensis.*
Amur maple. See *Acer tataricum* subsp. *ginnala,* illus. p.95.
Amur silver grass. See *Miscanthus sacchariflorus.*
Anacharis densa. See *Egeria densa.*

ANACYCLUS
ASTERACEAE/COMPOSITAE

Genus of summer-flowering, prostrate perennials with stems radiating from a central rootstock. Needs full sun and well-drained soil. Propagate by softwood cuttings in spring or by seed in autumn.
A. depressus. See *A. pyrethrum* var. *depressus.*
A. pyrethrum var. *depressus,* syn. *A. depressus,* illus. p.374.

ANAGALLIS
PRIMULACEAE

Genus of annuals and creeping perennials, grown for their flowers. Plant in an open, sunny site in fertile, moist soil. Propagate by seed or division in spring. Raise *A. tenella* by soft tip cuttings in spring or early summer.
A. tenella (Bog pimpernel). **'Studland'** illus. p.367.

ANANAS
BROMELIACEAE

Genus of evergreen, rosette-forming perennials, grown for their foliage and edible fruits (pineapples). Tender, min. 13–15°C (55–9°F). Prefers full light, but tolerates some shade. Needs fertile, well-drained soil. Water moderately during growing season, sparingly at other times. Propagate by suckers or cuttings of 'leafy' fruit tops in spring or summer.
A. bracteatus (Red pineapple, Wild pineapple). **'Tricolor'** (syn. *A.b.* 'Striatus', *A.b.* var. *tricolor*; illus.

p.265) is an evergreen, basal-rosetted perennial. H and S 1m (3ft). Forms dense rosettes of strap-shaped, spiny-edged, arching, deep green leaves, longitudinally yellow-striped and often with marginal, red spines. Dense spikes of small, tubular, lavender-violet flowers, with prominent, reddish-pink bracts, appear usually in summer. These are followed by brownish-orange-red fruits that are 15cm (6in) or more long.
A. comosus **'Variegatus',** syn. *A.c.* var *variegatus.* Evergreen, basal-rosetted perennial. H and S 60cm (24in) or more. Produces very narrowly strap-shaped, channelled, rigid, grey-green leaves that are suffused pink, have cream margins, are grey-scaled beneath and sometimes have spiny edges. Produces tubular, purple-blue flowers with inconspicuous, green bracts; fruits are the edible pineapples grown commercially, but are much smaller on pot-grown plants.

ANAPHALIS
Pearly everlasting

ASTERACEAE/COMPOSITAE

Genus of perennials with heads of small, papery flowers, used dried for winter decoration. Prefers sun but will grow in semi-shade. Soil should be well-drained but not too dry. Propagate by seed in autumn or by division in winter or spring.
A. margaritacea illus. p.239.
A. nepalensis var. *monocephala,* syn. *A. nubigena,* illus. p.276.
A. nubigena. See *A. nepalensis* var. *monocephala.*

Anceps bamboo. See *Yushania anceps,* illus. p.308.

ANCHUSA
Alkanet

BORAGINACEAE

Genus of annuals, biennials and perennials, some of which are evergreen, with usually blue flowers. Needs sun and well-drained soil; resents too much winter wet. Tall, perennial species may need to be staked and allowed room to spread. Propagate perennials by root cuttings in winter, annuals and biennials by seed in autumn or spring.
A. azurea, syn. *A. italica.* **'Little John'** is a clump-forming perennial. H 50cm (20in), S 60cm (24in). Mainly basal leaves are narrowly oval and hairy. Bears branching racemes of large, open cup-shaped, dark blue flowers in early summer. **'Loddon Royalist'** illus. p.254. **'Opal',** H 1.2m (4ft), has paler blue flowers.
A. caespitosa. See *A. cespitosa.*
A. capensis **'Blue Angel'** illus. p.334. **'Blue Bird'** is a bushy biennial, grown as an annual. H to 45cm (18in), S 20cm (8in). Has lance-shaped, bristly, mid-green leaves and, in summer, heads of shallowly bowl-shaped, sky-blue flowers.
A. cespitosa, syn. *A. caespitosa,* illus. p.370.
A. italica. See *A. azurea.*

Ancistrocactus megarhizus. See *Sclerocactus scheeri.*

Ancistrocactus scheeri. See *Sclerocactus scheeri.*

Ancistrocactus uncinatus. See *Sclerocactus uncinatus.*

ANDROMEDA
Bog rosemary

ERICACEAE

Genus of evergreen shrubs with an open, twiggy habit. Needs full light and humus-rich, moist, acid soil. Propagate by semi-ripe cuttings taken in late summer or by seed sown in spring.
A. polifolia illus. p.347. **'Alba'** illus. p.346. **'Compacta'** illus. p.347.

ANDROSACE
Rock jasmine

PRIMULACEAE

Genus of annuals and evergreen perennials, usually compact cushion-forming and often with soft, hairy leaves. Many species are suitable for cold greenhouses and troughs with winter snow cover. Needs sun and very well-drained soil; some species prefer acid soil. Resents wet foliage in winter. Propagate by tip cuttings in summer or by seed in autumn. Is prone to botrytis and attack by aphids.
A. carnea illus. p.365. subsp *laggeri* illus. p.367.

A. chamaejasme. Evergreen, basal-rosetted, variable perennial with easily rooted stolons. H 3–6cm (1¼–2½in), S to 15cm (6in). Has open, hairy rosettes of oval leaves. In spring bears clusters of 2–8 flattish, white flowers, each with a yellow eye that sometimes turns red with age.

A. cylindrica. Evergreen, basal-rosetted perennial. H 1–2cm (½–¾in), S 10cm (4in). Leaves are linear and glossy. Flower stems each carry up to 10 small, flattish, white flowers, each with a yellow-green eye, in early spring. Is suitable for a cold greenhouse.

A. hedraeantha. Evergreen, tight cushion-forming perennial. H 1–2cm (½–¾in), S to 10cm (4in). Bears loose rosettes of narrowly oval, glossy leaves. Umbels of 5–10 flattish, yellow-throated, pink flowers are produced in spring. Is best in a cold greenhouse.

A. hirtella. Evergreen, tight cushion-forming perennial. H 1cm (½in), S to 10cm (4in). Produces rosettes of small, thick, linear to oblong, hairy leaves. Almond-scented, flattish, white flowers are borne in spring on very short stems, 1 or 2 per rosette.

A. imbricata. See *A. vandellii.*

A. lanuginosa illus. p.377.

A. pyrenaica illus. p.361.

A. sarmentosa. Evergreen, mat-forming perennial, spreading by runners. H 4–10cm (1½–4in), S 30cm (12in). Has open rosettes of small, narrowly elliptic, hairy leaves. Large clusters of flattish, yellow-eyed, bright pink flowers open in spring. Is a good rock plant in all but extremely wet areas.

A. sempervivoides. Evergreen, mat-forming, rosetted perennial with stolons. H 1–7cm (½–3in), S 30cm (12in). Has leathery, oblong or spoon-shaped leaves. In spring produces small heads of 4–10 flattish, pink flowers, with yellow, then red, eyes. Is a good rock plant.

A. vandellii, syn. *A. imbricata,* illus. p.362.

A. villosa illus. p.363. var. *jacquemontii* illus. p.378.

ANEMONE
Windflower

RANUNCULACEAE

Genus of spring-, summer- and autumn-flowering perennials, sometimes tuberous or rhizomatous, with mainly rounded, shallowly cup-shaped flowers. Leaves are rounded to oval, often divided into 3–15 leaflets. Most species thrive in full light or semi-shade in humus-rich, well-drained soil. Propagate by division in spring, by seed sown in late summer, when fresh, or by root cuttings in winter. Contact with the sap may irritate skin.

A. apennina (Apennine anemone). Spreading, spring-flowering, rhizomatous perennial. H and S 15–20cm (6–8in). Fern-like leaves have 3 deeply toothed lobes. Each stem carries a large, up-right, flattish, blue, white or pink flower, with 10–20 narrow petals.

A. blanda. Spreading, early spring-flowering perennial with a knobbly tuber. H 5–10cm (2–4in), S 10–15cm (4–6in). Leaves are broadly oval and semi-erect, with 3 deeply toothed lobes. Each stem bears an upright, flattish, blue, white or pink flower, 4–5cm (1½–2in) across, with 9–14 narrow petals. **'Atrocaerulea'** illus. p.433. **'Ingramii'** bears purple-backed, deep blue flowers. **'Radar'** illus. p.430. **'White Splendour'** illus. p.426.

A. coronaria. Spring-flowering perennial with a misshapen tuber. H 5–25cm (2–10in), S 10–15cm (4–6in). Produces parsley-like, divided, semi-erect leaves. Each stiff stem carries a large, 5–8-petalled, shallowly cup-shaped flower in shades of red, pink, blue or purple. Garden groups include **De Caen Group** and **St Brigid Group,** which have larger flowers varying in colour from white through red to blue.

A. x *fulgens* illus. p.430.

A. hepatica. See *Hepatica nobilis.*

A. hupehensis **'Hadspen Abundance'** illus. p.259. var. *japonica* **'Bressingham Glow'** (syn. *A* x *hybrida* 'Bressingham Glow'; semi-double) illus. p.231. Var. *japonica* **'Prinz Heinrich'** (syn. *A.* x *hybrida* 'Prince Henry') has single, deep pink flowers on slender stems. **'September Charm'** (single) illus. p.231.

A. x *hybrida,* syn. *A. japonica* of gardens (Japanese anemone). Group of vigorous, branching, perennials. H 1.5m (5ft), S 60cm (2ft). Bears shallowly cup-shaped, single, semi-double or double flowers in late summer and early autumn. Leaves are deeply divided and dark green. **'Bressingham Glow'** see *A. hupehensis* var. *japonica* 'Bressingham Glow'. **'Honorine Jobert'** (single) illus. p.231. **'Max Vogel'** has semi-double, pinkish-mauve flowers on wiry stems. **'Prince Henry'**

see *A. hupehensis* var. *japonica* 'Prinz Heinrich'.

A. x *intermedia.* See *A.* x *lipsiensis.*

A. japonica of gardens. See *A.* x *hybrida.*

A. x *lipsiensis,* syn. *A.* x *intermedia, A.* x *seemannii,* illus. p.274.

A. narcissiflora illus. p.275.

A. nemorosa (Wood anemone). Vigorous, carpeting, rhizomatous perennial. H 15cm (6in), S 30cm (12in). Produces masses of star-shaped, single, white flowers, with prominent, yellow stamens, in spring and early summer, above deeply cut, mid-green leaves. Likes woodland conditions. **'Allenii'** and **'Robinsoniana'** illus. p.270. **'Vestal'** has anemone-centred, double, white flowers. **'Wilks' Giant'** (syn. *A.n.* 'Wilk's Giant') has larger, single, white flowers.

A. pavonina illus. p.413.

A. ranunculoides illus. p.274. **'Pleniflora'** (syn *A.r.* 'Flore Pleno') is a spreading, rhizomatous perennial. H and S 20cm (8in). Bears buttercup-like, double, yellow flowers in spring. Leaves are divided. Likes damp, woodland conditions.

A. rivularis illus. p.275.

A. x *seemannii.* See *A.* x *lipsiensis.*

A. sylvestris illus. p.268. **'Macrantha'** is a clump-forming perennial that can be invasive. H and S 30cm (12in). Large, fragrant, semi-pendent, shallowly cup-shaped, white flowers are produced in spring and early summer. Leaves are divided and mid-green.

A. tschaernjaewii illus. p.427.

A. vitifolia. Branching, clump-forming perennial. H 1.2m (4ft), S 50cm (20in). In summer bears open cup-shaped, occasionally pink-flushed, white flowers with yellow stamens. Vine-like leaves are woolly beneath.

Anemone
Alpine. See *Pulsatilla alpina,* illus. p.346.
Apennine. See *Anemone apennina.*
False. See *Anemonopsis.*
Japanese. See *Anemone* x *hybrida,* illus. p.231.
Wood. See *Anemone nemorosa.*

ANEMONELLA

RANUNCULACEAE

Genus of one species of tuberous perennial, grown for its flowers. Needs shade and humus-rich, moist soil. Propagate by seed when fresh or by division every 3–5 years in autumn.
A. thalictroides illus. p.364. **'Oscar Schoaf'** (syn. *A.t.* 'Schoaf's Double') is a slow-growing, tuberous perennial. H 10cm (4in), S 4cm (1½in) or more. Has delicate, fern-like leaves. From spring to early summer bears small, cup-shaped, double, strawberry-pink flowers, singly on finely branched, slender stems.

ANEMONOPSIS
False anemone

RANUNCULACEAE

Genus of one species of perennial, related to *Anemone.* Likes a sheltered, semi-shaded position and humus-rich,

moist but well-drained soil. Propagate by division in spring or by seed sown in late summer, when fresh.
A. macrophylla illus. p.286.

ANGELICA

APIACEAE/UMBELLIFERAE

Genus of summer-flowering, often short-lived perennials, some of which have culinary and medicinal uses. Grows in sun or shade and in any well-drained soil. Remove seed heads when produced, otherwise plants may die. Propagate by seed when ripe.
A. archangelica illus. p.228.

A. gigas. Upright perennial with leaves divided into three parts and 30-40cm (12-16in) long. H 1-2m(3-6ft), S 1.2m (4ft). In summer has very showy inflated reddish leaf bases and flat umbels of purple flowers up to 15cm (6in) across with purple bracts and stems. An attractive border plant.

Angelica. See *Angelica archangelica,* illus. p.228.
Angelica tree, Japanese. See *Aralia elata.*
Angel's fishing rod. See *Dierama.*
Angel's tears. See *Billbergia* x *windii; Narcissus triandrus,* illus. p.417.
Angels' trumpets. See *Brugmansia.*
Angels' wings. See *Caladium bicolor.*
Angelwing begonia. See *Begonia coccinea.*
Angled Solomon's seal. See *Polygonatum odoratum.*

ANGRAECUM

See also ORCHIDS.
A. sesquipedale, syn. *Macroplectrum sesquipedale* (Star-of-Bethlehem orchid; illus. p.296). Evergreen, epiphytic orchid for an intermediate greenhouse. H 30cm (12in) or more. Waxy, apple-white flowers, 8cm (3in) across, each with a 30cm (12in) long spur, are borne, usually 2 to a stem, in winter. Has narrowly oval, semi-rigid, horizontal leaves, 15cm (6in) long. Needs shade in summer.

ANGULOA

See also ORCHIDS.
A. clowesii (Cradle orchid). Deciduous, epiphytic orchid for a cool greenhouse. H 60cm (24in). Fragrant, erect, cup-shaped, lemon-yellow flowers, 10cm (4in) long, each with a loosely hinged, yellow lip, are produced singly in early summer. Broadly oval, ribbed leaves are 45cm (18in) long. Grow in semi-shade in summer.

ANIGOZANTHOS
Kangaroo paw

HAEMODORACEAE

Genus of perennials, with thick root-stocks and fans of sword-shaped leaves, grown for their curious flowers. Needs an open, sunny position and does best in well-drained, peaty or leafy, acid soil. Propagate by division in spring or by seed when fresh, in late summer.
A. flavidus illus. p.254.
A. manglesii illus. p.250.

Anise
Chinese. See *Illicium anisatum*.
Purple. See *Illicium floridanum*.

ANISODONTEA

MALVACEAE

Genus of evergreen shrubs and perennials, grown for their flowers. Tender, min. 3–5°C (37–41°F). Needs full light and well-drained soil. Water containerized plants freely when in full growth, very little at other times. In growing season, young plants may need tip pruning to promote a bushy habit. Propagate by seed in spring or by greenwood or semi-ripe cuttings in late summer.

A. capensis, syn. *Malvastrum capensis*. Evergreen, erect, bushy shrub. H to 1m (3ft), S 60cm (2ft) or more. Each oval leaf has 3–5 deep lobes. Bowl-shaped, 5-petalled, rose-magenta flowers, with darker veins, appear from spring to autumn.

ANNONA

Cherimoya, Custard apple, Sweet sop

ANNONACEAE

Genus of deciduous or evergreen shrubs and trees, grown for their edible fruits and ornamental appearance. Tender, min. 15°C (59°F), preferably higher. Needs full light or partial shade and fertile, moisture-retentive but well-drained soil. Water containerized specimens moderately when in full growth, sparingly in winter. Propagate by seed in spring or by semi-ripe cuttings in late summer. Spider mite may be a nuisance.

A. reticulata (Bullock's heart, Custard apple). Mainly deciduous, rounded tree. H 6m (20ft) or more, S 3–5m (10–15ft). Has oblong to lance-shaped, 13–25cm (5–10in) long leaves. Cup-shaped, olive-green flowers, often flushed purple, appear in summer, followed by edible, heart-shaped, red-flushed, greenish-brown fruits, each 13cm (5in) long.

Annual phlox. See *Phlox drummondii*.
Anoiganthus breviflorus. See *Cyrtanthus breviflorus*.
Anoiganthus luteus. See *Cyrtanthus breviflorus*.

ANOPTERUS

ESCALLONIACEAE

Genus of evergreen shrubs or small trees, grown for their foliage and flowers. Needs shade or semi-shade and moist but well-drained, lime-free soil. Propagate by semi-ripe cuttings in summer.

A. glandulosus illus. p.116.

ANREDERA

Madeira vine, Mignonette vine

BASELLACEAE

Genus of evergreen, tuberous, twining climbers, grown for their luxuriant foliage and small, scented flowers.

Tender, min. 7°C (45°F). If grown in cool areas will die down in winter. Requires a position in full light and well-drained soil. Water moderately in growing season, but sparingly at other times. Provide support. Cut back the previous season's growth by half or to just above ground level in spring. Propagate by tubers, produced at stem bases, in spring or by softwood cuttings in summer.

A. cordifolia, syn. *Boussingaultia basselloides* of gardens. Fast-growing, evergreen, tuberous, twining climber. H to 6m (20ft). Has oval to lance-shaped, fleshy leaves and tiny, fragrant, white flowers borne in clusters from upper leaf axils in summer.

Antarctic beech. See *Nothofagus antarctica*.

ANTENNARIA

Cat's ears, Pussy-toes

ASTERACEAE/COMPOSITAE

Genus of evergreen or semi-evergreen perennials, grown for their almost stemless flower heads and mats of often woolly leaves. Makes good ground cover. Needs sun and well-drained soil. Propagate by seed or division in spring.

A. dioica. Semi-evergreen, mat-forming, dense perennial. H 2.5cm (1in), S 25cm (10in). Leaves are tiny, oval, usually woolly and greenish-white. Short stems carry fluffy, white or pale pink flower heads in late spring and early summer. Is good when grown in a rock garden. Compact **'Nyewoods'** has very deep rose-pink flowers. **'Rosea'** see *A.d.* var. *rosea*.
Var. *rosea* (syn. *A.d.* 'Rosea', *A. rosea*) illus. p.366.
A. rosea. See *A. dioica* var. *rosea*.

ANTHEMIS

Dog's fennel

ASTERACEAE/COMPOSITAE

Genus of carpeting and clump-forming perennials, some of which are evergreen, grown for their daisy-like flower heads and fern-like foliage. Prefers a position in sun and well-drained soil. May need staking for support. Cut to ground level after flowering to produce good leaf rosettes in winter. Propagate by division in spring or, for some species, by basal cuttings in late summer, autumn or spring.

A. nobilis. See *Chamaemelum nobile*.
A. punctata subsp. *cupaniana* illus. p.276.
A. sancti-johannis. Evergreen, spreading, bushy perennial. H and S 60cm (24in). In summer bears many daisy-like, bright orange flower heads among fern-like, shaggy, mid-green leaves.
A. tinctoria. Evergreen, clump-forming perennial. H and S 1m (3ft). Produces a mass of daisy-like, yellow flower heads in mid-summer, borne singly above a basal clump of fern-like, crinkled, mid-green leaves. Propagate by basal cuttings in spring or late summer. **'E.C. Buxton'** illus. p.255.

ANTHERICUM

Spider plant

ANTHERICACEAE/LILIACEAE

Genus of upright perennials with saucer- or trumpet-shaped flowers rising in spike-like racemes from clumps of leaves. Likes a sunny site and fertile, well-drained soil that does not dry out in summer. Propagate by division in spring or by seed in autumn.

A. graminifolium. See *A. ramosum*.
A. liliago illus. p.276.
A. ramosum, syn. *A. graminifolium*. Upright perennial. H 1m (3ft), S 30cm (1ft). Erect racemes of small, saucer-shaped, white flowers are borne in summer above a clump of grass-like, greyish-green leaves.

Antholyza paniculata. See *Crocosmia paniculata*.

ANTHURIUM

Flamingo flower

ARACEAE

Genus of evergreen, erect, climbing or trailing perennials, some grown for their foliage and others for their bright flower spathes. Tender, min. 15°C (59°F). Prefers bright light in winter and indirect sun in summer; needs a fairly moist atmosphere and moist, but not waterlogged, peaty soil. Propagate by division in spring. If ingested, all parts may cause mild stomach disorder; contact with sap may irritate skin.

A. andraeanum illus. p.264.
A. crystallinum illus. p.264.
A. scherzerianum illus. p.302.
'Rothschildianum' is an evergreen, erect, short-stemmed perennial. H and S 30cm (12in). Produces upright, oblong leaves, to 20cm (8in) long. Intermittently bears a long-lasting, red spathe, spotted with white, that surrounds a yellow spadix.
A. veitchii (King anthurium). Evergreen, erect, short-stemmed perennial. H 1m (3ft) or more, S to 1m (3ft). Glossy, corrugated leaves, to 1m (3ft) long, are oval, with heart-shaped bases on 60cm–1m (2–3ft) long leaf stalks. Intermittently bears a long-lasting, leathery, green to white spathe that surrounds a cream spadix.

Anthurium
Crystal. See *Anthurium crystallinum*, illus. p.264.
King. See *Anthurium veitchii*.

ANTHYLLIS

PAPILIONACEAE

Genus of rounded, bushy perennials, grown for their flowers and finely divided leaves. Needs sun and well-drained soil. Propagate by softwood cuttings in summer or by seed in autumn.

A. hermanniae. Rounded, bushy perennial. H and S to 60cm (24in). Spiny, tangled stems bear simple or 3-parted, bright green leaves. Has small, pea-like, yellow flowers in summer. Is good for a rock garden.
A. montana illus. p.352.

'Rubra' is a rounded or spreading, woody-based perennial. H and S 30cm (12in). Divided leaves consist of 17–41 narrowly oval leaflets. Heads of clover-like, bright pink flowers are borne in late spring and early summer. Is good for a rock garden.

ANTIGONON

Coral vine

POLYGONACEAE

Genus of evergreen, woody-stemmed, tendril climbers, grown for their foliage and profuse clusters of small flowers. Tender, min. 15°C (59°F). Grow in full light and any fertile, well-drained soil. Water freely in growing season, sparingly at other times. Needs tropical conditions to flower well. Provide support. Thin out congested growth in early spring. Propagate by seed in spring or by softwood cuttings in summer.

A. leptopus illus. p.209.

ANTIRRHINUM

Snapdragon

SCROPHULARIACEAE

Genus of perennials and semi-evergreen sub-shrubs, usually grown as annuals, flowering from spring to autumn. Needs sun and rich, well-drained soil. Dead-head to prolong flowering season. Propagate by seed sown outdoors in late spring or by stem cuttings in early autumn or spring. Rust disease may be a problem with *A. majus*, but rust-resistant cultivars are available.

A. asarina. See *Asarina procumbens*.
A. majus. Erect perennial that branches from the base. Cultivars are grown as annuals and are grouped according to size and flower type: tall, H 60cm–1m (2–3ft), S 30–45cm (12–18in); intermediate, H and S 45cm (18in); dwarf, H 20–30cm (8–12in), S 30cm (12in); regular tubular-shaped (hyacinth-like) flowers; penstemon, trumpet-shaped flowers; double; and irregular tubular-shaped flowers. All have lance-shaped leaves and, from spring to autumn, carry spikes of usually 2-lipped, sometimes double, flowers in a variety of colours, including white, pink, red, purple, yellow and orange. **Bells Series** (dwarf, regular) is early-flowering, with long-lasting flowers in purple, purple and white, red, rose-pink, pink, bronze, yellow, or white. **Bells Series 'Pink Bells'** has pink flowers. **'Chimes'** (dwarf, regular) is very compact, producing flowers in a wide colour range including several bicolours. **Coronette Series** (tall, regular) illus. p.321. **'Floral Showers** (dwarf, regular) is early-flowering, bearing flowers in up to 10 colours, including some bicolours; tolerates wet weather. **Kim Series** (intermediate, regular) has flowers in scarlet, deep rose, deep orange, primrose-yellow and white as well as orange bicolour. **Madame Butterfly Series** (tall, peloric) is available in a mixture of colours. **Princess Series** (intermediate, peloric) has flowers in a mixture of colours (white with purple eye, illus. p.325).

Rocket Series (tall, regular) is vigorous, with flowers in a broad colour range; they are excellent for cut flowers. **Sonnet Series** (intermediate, regular) illus. p.337. **Tahiti Series** (dwarf, regular) illus. p.336. **'Trumpet Serenade'** (dwarf, penstemon) has bicoloured flowers in a mixture of pastel shades.

Apache plume. See *Fallugia paradoxa*, illus. p.136.

Apennine anemone. See *Anemone apennina*.

APHELANDRA

ACANTHACEAE

Genus of evergreen shrubs and perennials with showy flowers. Tender, min. 13°C (55°F). Grows best in bright light but out of direct sun in summer. Use soft water and keep soil moist but not waterlogged. Benefits from feeding when flower spikes are forming. Propagate by seed or tip cuttings from young stems in spring.
A. squarrosa (Zebra plant). **'Dania'** is an evergreen, compact perennial. H 1m (3ft), S slightly less. Oval, glossy, dark green leaves, with white veins and mid-ribs, are nearly 30cm (1ft) long. Has dense, 4-sided spikes, to 15cm (6in) long, of 2-lipped, bright yellow flowers in axils of yellow bracts in autumn. **'Louisae'** illus. p.256.

APHYLLANTHES

APHYLLANTHACEAE/LILIACEAE

Genus of one species of summer-flowering perennial. Best if given shelter from cold wind. Grow in a sunny, warm, sheltered corner, preferably in an alpine house, and in well-drained, sandy, peaty soil. Resents disturbance. Propagate by seed in autumn or spring.
A. monspeliensis. Tuft-forming perennial. H 15–20cm (6–8in), S 5cm (2in). Star-shaped, pale to deep blue flowers are borne singly or in small groups at tops of wiry, glaucous green stems from early to mid-summer. Leaves are reduced to red-brown sheaths surrounding stems.

APONOGETON

APONOGETONACEAE

Genus of deciduous, perennial, deep-water plants, grown for their floating foliage and often heavily scented flowers. Requires an open, sunny position. Tidy fading foliage in autumn. Propagate by division in spring or by seed while still fresh.
A. distachyos illus. p.447.

APOROCACTUS

CACTACEAE

Genus of perennial cacti, grown for their pendent, slender, fleshy stems and bright flowers. Is suitable for hanging baskets. Tender, min. 5°C (41°F). Needs partial shade and very well-drained soil. Occasional light watering in winter will stop stems dying back

from the tips. Propagate by stem cuttings in spring or summer.
A. flagelliformis illus. p.463.

Apple
  Custard. See *Annona.*
  Elephant. See *Dillenia indica.*
  May. See *Podophyllum peltatum.*
  Pitch. See *Clusia major.*
Apple mint. See *Mentha suaveolens.*
Apple of Peru. See *Nicandra physalodes.*
Apricot, Japanese. See *Prunus mume.*

AQUILEGIA
Columbine

RANUNCULACEAE

Genus of graceful, clump-forming, short-lived perennials, grown for their mainly bell-shaped, spurred flowers in spring and summer. Is suitable for rock gardens. Prefers an open, sunny site and well-drained soil. Propagate species by seed in autumn or spring. Selected forms only occasionally come true from seed (e.g. *A. vulgaris* 'Nora Barlow') as they cross freely; they should be widely segregated. Is prone to aphid and leaf miner attack. Contact with sap may irritate skin.
A. akitensis. See *A. flabellata.*
A. alpina illus. p.348.
A. canadensis (Canadian columbine). Clump-forming, leafy perennial. H 60cm (24in), S 30cm (12in). In early summer bears semi-pendent, bell-shaped flowers, with yellow sepals and red spurs, several per slender stem, above fern-like, dark green foliage.
A. chrysantha. Vigorous, clump-forming perennial. H 1.2m (4ft), S 60cm (2ft). Bears semi-pendent, bell-shaped, soft yellow flowers, with long spurs, several per stem, in early summer. Has fern-like, divided, mid-green leaves.
A. flabellata, syn. *A. akitensis.* Clump-forming perennial. H 25cm (10in), S 10cm (4in). Bell-shaped, soft blue flowers, each with fluted petals and a short spur, are produced in summer. Rounded, finely divided leaves form an open, basal rosette. Needs semi-shade and moist soil. Var. *pumila* f. *alba* (syn. *A.f.* 'Nana Alba'), H 10cm (4in), is compact and has white flowers.
A. jonesii illus. p.383.
A. longissima. Clump-forming, leafy perennial. H 60cm (24in), S 50cm (20in). Bell-shaped, pale yellow flowers, with very long, bright yellow spurs, are borne, several per stem, in early summer, above fern-like, divided, mid-green leaves.
A. **'Mrs Scott Elliott'.** See *A.* Mrs Scott Elliott Hybrids.
A. **Mrs Scott Elliott Hybrids**, syn. *A.* 'Mrs Scott Elliott'. Clump-forming, leafy perennial. H 1m (3ft), S 50cm (20in). Bell-shaped flowers of various colours, often bicoloured, have long spurs and appear in early summer on branching, wiry stems. Has fern-like, divided, bluish-green leaves.
A. scopulorum. Clump-forming perennial. H 6cm (2½in), S 9cm (3½in). In summer produces bell-shaped, fluted, pale blue, or rarely pink, flowers, each with a cream centre and

very long spurs. Leaves are divided into 9 oval, glaucous leaflets.
A. vulgaris (Granny's bonnets). Clump-forming, leafy perennial. H 1m (3ft), S 50cm (20in). Many funnel-shaped, short-spurred flowers, in shades of pink, crimson, purple and white, are borne, several per long stem, in early summer. Leaves are grey-green, rounded and divided into leaflets. **'Nora Barlow'** illus. p.249.

ARABIS
Rock cress

BRASSICACEAE/CRUCIFERAE

Genus of robust, evergreen perennials. Makes excellent ground cover in a rock garden. Needs sun and well-drained soil. Propagate by softwood cuttings in summer or by seed in autumn.
A. albida. See *A. alpina* subsp. *caucasica.*
A. alpina subsp. *caucasica*, syn. *A. albida*, *A. caucasica.* Evergreen, mat-forming perennial. H 15cm (6in), S 50cm (20in). Bears loose rosettes of obovate, toothed, mid-green leaves and, in late spring and summer, fragrant, 4-petalled, white, occasionally pink, flowers. Is excellent on a dry bank. Trim back after flowering. **'Flore Pleno'** (syn. *A. caucasica* 'Plena') has double, white flowers. **'Variegata'** (syn. *A. caucasica* 'Variegata') illus. p.362.
A. × *arendsii* **'Rosabella'**, syn. *A. caucasica* 'Rosabella', illus. p.365.
A. blepharophylla. Short-lived, evergreen, mat-forming perennial. H 12cm (5in), S 20cm (8in). Dislikes winter wet. Has oval, toothed, dark green leaves, with hairy, grey margins, borne in loose rosettes. Fragrant, 4-petalled, bright pink to white flowers are produced in spring.
A. caucasica. See *A. alpina* subsp. *caucasica.* **'Plena'** see *A. alpina* subsp. *caucasica* 'Flore Pleno'. **'Rosabella'** see *A.* × *arendsii* 'Rosabella'. **'Variegata'** see *A. alpina* subsp. *caucasica* 'Variegata'.
A. ferdinandi-coburgi **'Variegata'.** See *A. procurrens* 'Variegata'.
A. procurrens **'Variegata'**, syn. *A. ferdinandi-coburgi* 'Variegata', illus. p.388.

ARALIA

ARALIACEAE

Genus of deciduous trees, shrubs and perennials, grown for their bold leaves and small, but profusely borne flowers. Requires sun or semi-shade, some shelter and fertile, well-drained soil. Propagate those listed below by seed in autumn or by suckers or root cuttings in late winter.
A. elata (Japanese angelica tree). Deciduous tree or suckering shrub with sparse, stout, prickly stems. H and S 10m (30ft). Has large, dark green leaves with numerous oval, paired leaflets. Billowing heads of tiny, white flowers, forming a large panicle, 30–60cm (12–24in) long, are borne in late summer and autumn. Zone 5.
'Albomarginata' see *A.e.* 'Variegata'.
'Aureovariegata' has leaflets broadly edged with yellow. Leaflets of

'Variegata' (syn. *A.e.* 'Albomarginata') have creamy-white margins.
A. elegantissima. See *Schefflera elegantissima.*
A. japonica. See *Fatsia japonica.*
A. sieboldii. See *Fatsia japonica.*

Aralia
  False. See *Schefflera elegantissima*, illus. p.127.
  Fern-leaf. See *Polyscias filicifolia*, illus. p.152.
  Japanese. See *Fatsia japonica.*
  Lace. See *Polyscias guilfoylei* 'Victoriae', illus. p.126.

ARAUCARIA

ARAUCARIACEAE

See also CONIFERS.
A. araucana illus. p.103.
A. excelsa of gardens. See *A. heterophylla.*
A. heterophylla, syn. *A. excelsa* of gardens (Norfolk Island pine). Upright conifer. H 30m (100ft), S 5–8m (15–25ft). Tender. Has spirally set, needle-like, incurved, fresh green leaves. Cones are seldom produced in cultivation. Is often grown as a shade-tolerant house plant.

ARAUJIA

ASCLEPIADACEAE

Genus of evergreen, twining climbers with woody stems that exude milky juice when cut. Needs sun and fertile, well-drained soil. Propagate by seed in spring or by stem cuttings in late summer or early autumn.
A. sericifera illus. p.207.

Arbor-vitae
  American. See *Thuja occidentalis.*
  Chinese. See *Thuja orientalis.*
  Russian. See *Microbiota.*

ARBUTUS

ERICACEAE

Genus of evergreen trees and shrubs, grown for their leaves, clusters of small, urn-shaped flowers, ornamental bark and strawberry-like fruits, which are edible but insipid. Must be protected from strong, cold winds when young. Prefers a position in full sun and needs fertile, well-drained soil; *A. menziesii* requires acid soil. May be propagated by semi-ripe cuttings in late summer or by seed sown in autumn.
A. andrachne (Grecian strawberry tree). Evergreen, spreading tree or shrub. H and S 6m (20ft). Has oval, glossy, dark green leaves and peeling, reddish-brown bark. Panicles of urn-shaped, white flowers in late spring, are followed by orange-red fruits. Prefers a sheltered position. Zone 8.
A. × *andrachnoides* illus. p.83.
A. menziesii (Madroña, Madroñe). Evergreen, spreading tree. H and S 15m (50ft). Has smooth, peeling, reddish bark and oval, dark green leaves. Large, upright, terminal panicles of urn-shaped, white flowers in early summer are followed by orange or red fruits. Zone 7.
A. unedo illus. p.93.

Arbutus, Trailing. See *Epigaea repens*.

ARCHONTOPHOENIX
King palm

ARECACEAE/PALMAE

Genus of evergreen palms, grown for their majestic appearance. Tender, min. 15°C (59°F). Needs full light or partial shade and humus-rich, well-drained soil. Water containerized specimens moderately, much less when temperatures are low. Propagate by seed in spring at not less than 24°C (75°F). Spider mite may be troublesome.
A. alexandrae illus. p.72.
A. cunninghamiana (Illawarra palm, Piccabeen palm). Evergreen palm. H 15–20m (50–70ft), S 2–5m (6–15ft). Has long, arching, feather-shaped leaves. Mature trees produce large clusters of small, lavender or lilac flowers in summer, followed by large, egg-shaped, red fruits.

Arcterica nana. See *Pieris nana*.
Arctic birch. See *Betula nana*, illus. p.349.

ARCTOSTAPHYLOS
Manzanita, Bearberry

ERICACEAE

Genus of evergreen trees and shrubs, grown for their foliage, flowers and fruits. Some species are also grown for their bark, others for ground cover. Some species are tender, min. 7°C (45°F). Provide shelter from strong winds. Does best in full sun and well-drained, acid soil. Propagate by semi-ripe cuttings in summer or by seed in autumn.
A. alpina, syn. *Arctous alpinus*. Deciduous, creeping shrub. H 5cm (2in), S to 12cm (5in). Has drooping, terminal clusters of tiny, urn-shaped, pink-flushed, white flowers in late spring, followed by rounded, purple-black berries. Leaves are oval, toothed, glossy and bright green. Zone 2.
A. diversifolia, syn. *Comarostaphylis diversifolia* (Summer holly). Evergreen, upright shrub or tree. H 5m (15ft), S 3m (10ft). Leaves are oblong, glossy and dark green. Terminal racemes of fragrant, urn-shaped, white flowers appear from early to mid-spring, followed by spherical, red fruits. Zone 8.
A. 'Emerald Carpet' illus. p.156.
A. hookeri 'Monterey Carpet', syn. A. *uva-ursi* subsp. *hookeri* 'Monterey Carpet'. Evergreen, open shrub. H 10–15cm (4–6in), S 40cm (16in) or more. Has hairy branchlets bearing glossy, pale green leaves and, in early summer, urn-shaped, white flowers, sometimes flushed pink, that are followed by globose, red fruits. Zone 9.
A. manzanita. Evergreen, upright shrub. H and S 2m (6ft) or more. Has peeling, reddish-brown bark and oval, leathery, grey-green leaves. From early to mid-spring produces small, urn-shaped, deep pink flowers. Zone 9.

A. nevadensis (Pine-mat manzanita). Evergreen, prostrate shrub. H 10cm (4in), S 1m (3ft). Has small, oval leaves. In summer, pendent, urn-shaped, white flowers are borne in clusters in leaf axils, followed by globose, brownish-red fruits. Is useful as ground cover. Zone 8.
A. nummularia. Evergreen, erect to prostrate shrub. H 30cm (1ft) or more, S 1m (3ft). Leaves are small, rounded, leathery and toothed. Pendent, urn-shaped, white flowers are borne in clusters from leaf axils in summer, followed by globose, green fruits. Makes good ground cover. Zone 7.
A. patula illus. p.152.
A. stanfordiana (Stanford manzanita). Evergreen, erect shrub. H and S 1.5m (5ft). Bark is smooth and reddish-brown. Has narrowly oval, glossy, bright green leaves. Bears drooping clusters of urn-shaped, pink flowers from early to mid-spring. Zone 8.
A. uva-ursi illus. p.388. subsp. *hookeri* 'Monterey Carpet' see *A. hookeri* 'Monterey Carpet'. **'Point Reyes'** illus. p.388. **'Vancouver Jade'** is an evergreen, trailing, sometimes arching shrub. H 10cm (4in), S 50cm (20in). Has small, oval, bright green leaves and bears urn-shaped, white flowers in summer. Zone 4.

ARCTOTHECA

ASTERACEAE/COMPOSITAE

Genus of creeping perennials. Tender, min. 5°C (41°F). Needs bright light and fertile, well-drained soil; dislikes humid conditions. Propagate by seed or division in spring.
A. calendula, syn. *Cryptostemma calendulaceum*, illus. p.294.

ARCTOTIS,
syn. X VENIDIOARCTOTIS

ASTERACEAE/COMPOSITAE

Genus of annuals and perennials, grown for their flower heads and foliage. Tender, min. 1–5°C (34–41°F). Requires full sun and leafy loam with sharp sand added. Propagate by seed in autumn or spring or by stem cuttings year-round.
A. **Harlequin Hybrids**, syn. *A.* x *hybrida*, x *Venidioarctotis*. Fairly slow-growing, upright, branching perennial, usually grown as an annual. H and S 45cm (18in). Lance-shaped, lobed leaves are greyish-green above, white below. In summer has large, daisy-like flower heads in many shades, including yellow, orange, bronze, purple, pink, cream and red. **'Bacchus'** has purple flower heads; **'China Rose'** deep pink; **'Sunshine'** yellow; **'Tangerine'** orange-yellow; and **'Torch'** bronze.
A. x *hybrida*. See *A.* Harlequin Hybrids.
A. stoechadifolia. See *A. venusta*.
A. venusta, syn. *A. stoechadifolia* (African daisy). Compact perennial, often grown as an annual. H 50cm (20in) or more, S 40cm (16in). Daisy-like, creamy-white flower heads with blue centres are borne singly throughout summer and into autumn.

Chrysanthemum-like leaves are dark green above, grey beneath.

Arctous alpinus. See *Arctostaphylos alpina*.

ARDISIA

MYRSINACEAE

Genus of evergreen shrubs and trees, grown for their fruits and foliage. Tender, min. 10°C (50°F). Needs partial shade and humus-rich, well-drained but not dry soil. Water potted plants freely when in full growth, moderately at other times.
Cut back old plants in early spring if required. Propagate by seed in spring or by semi-ripe cuttings in summer.
A. crenata, syn. *A. crenulata*, illus. p.150.
A. crenulata. See *A. crenata*.

Areca lutescens. See *Dypsis lutescens*.
Arecastrum romanozoffianum. See *Syagrus romanozoffiana*.
Aregelia carolinae. See *Neoregelia carolinae*.

ARENARIA
Sandwort

CAROPHYLLACEAE

Genus of spring- and summer-flowering annuals and perennials, some of which are evergreen. Most need sun and well-drained, sandy soil. Propagate by division or softwood cuttings in early summer or by seed in autumn or spring.
A. balearica illus. p.362.
A. montana illus. p.374.
A. purpurascens illus. p.365.
A. tetraquetra illus. p.361.

ARGEMONE

PAPAVERACEAE

Genus of robust perennials, most of which are best treated as annuals. Grow in sun and in very well-drained soil without supports. Dead-head plants to prolong the flowering season. Propagate by seed sown outdoors in late spring.
A. mexicana illus. p.335.

ARGYRANTHEMUM

ASTERACEAE/COMPOSITAE

Genus of evergreen sub-shrubs, grown for their daisy-like flowers. Needs full sun and moderately fertile, well-drained soil. Propagate by semi-ripe cuttings in summer or root greenwood cuttings in spring.
A. frutescens, syn. *Chrysanthemum frutescens* (Marguerite), illus. p.240.
A. 'Jamaica Primrose', syn. *Chrysanthemum frutescens* 'Jamaica Primrose', illus. p255.
A. 'Mary Wootton', syn. *Chrysanthemum frutescens* 'Mary Wootton', illus. p.243.

Argyrocytisus battandieri. See *Cytisus battandieri*.

ARGYRODERMA

AIZOACEAE

Genus of perennial succulents, grown for their very fleshy, grey-green leaves united in a prostrate, egg shape. In summer, daisy-like flowers appear in central split between leaves. Tender, min. 5°C (41°F). Needs full sun and very well-drained soil. Over-watering causes leaves to split or plant to rot. Propagate by seed in summer.
A. aureum. See *A. delaetii*.
A. blandum. See *A. delaetii*.
A. brevipes. See *A. fissum*.
A. delaetii, syn. *A. aureum*, *A. blandum*, illus. p.476.
A. fissum, syn. *A. brevipes*, illus. p.474.
A. pearsonii, syn. *A. schlechteri*, illus. p.473.
A. schlechteri. See *A. pearsonii*.

ARIOCARPUS
Living rock

CACTACEAE

Genus of extremely slow-growing, perennial cacti with large, swollen roots. Produces flattened, spherical, green stems with angular tubercles and tufts of wool. Tender, min. 5°C (41°F). Prefers full sun and extremely well-drained, lime-rich soil. Is very prone to rotting. Propagate by seed in spring or summer.
A. fissuratus illus. p.472.

ARISAEMA

ARACEAE

Genus of tuberous perennials, grown for their large, curious, hooded spathes, each enclosing a pencil-shaped spadix. Forms spikes of fleshy, red fruits in autumn, before dying down. Needs sun or partial shade and moist but well-drained humus-rich soil. Plant tubers 15cm (6in) deep in spring. Propagate by seed in autumn or spring or by offsets in spring.
A. atrorubens. See *A. triphyllum*.
A. candidissimum illus. p.435.
A. consanguineum illus. p.402.
A. griffithii illus. p.422.
A. jacquemontii illus. p.422.
A. ringens. Early spring-flowering, tuberous perennial. H 25–30cm (10–12in), S 30–45cm (12–18in). Bears 2 erect leaves, each with 3 long-pointed lobes, and a widely hooded, green spathe, enclosing the spadix, that has paler green stripes and is edged with dark brown-purple.
A. sikokianum illus. p.419.
A. tortuosum. Summer-flowering, tuberous perennial. H 30cm–1m (1–3ft), S 30–45cm (1–1½ft). Each dark green-mottled, pale green stem bears 2–3 erect leaves, divided into several oval leaflets. A hooded, green or purple spathe, with a protruding, S-shaped spadix, overtops leaves. Produces spikes of attractive, fleshy, red fruits in autumn.
A. triphyllum, syn. *A. atrorubens*, illus. p.414.

ARISARUM

ARACEAE

Genus of tuberous perennials, grown mainly for their curious, hooded spathes enclosing spadices with minute flowers. Needs partial shade and humus-rich, well-drained soil. Propagate in autumn by division of an established clump of tubers, which produce offsets freely.

A. proboscideum (Mouse plant). Clump-forming, spring-flowering, tuberous perennial. H to 10cm (4in), S 20–30cm (8–12in). Leaves are arrow-shaped and prostrate. Produces a spadix of minute flowers concealed in a hooded, dark brown spathe that is drawn out into a tail up to 15cm (6in) long – a mouse-like effect.

ARISTOLOCHIA
Dutchman's pipe

ARISTOLOCHIACEAE

Genus of evergreen or deciduous, woody-stemmed, twining and scrambling climbers, grown for their foliage and flowers. Some are tender, min. 10–13°C (50–55°F). Requires partial shade in summer and well-drained soil. Water regularly, less when not in full growth. Provide support. Cut back previous season's growth to 2 or 3 nodes in spring.Propagate by seed in spring or by semi-ripe cuttings in summer. Spider mite and whitefly may be a nuisance.

A. clurior. See *A. macrophylla.*
A. elegans. See *A. littoralis.*
A. gigas. See *A. grandiflora.*
A. grandiflora, syn. *A. gigas* (Pelican flower, Swan flower). Fast-growing, evergreen, woody-stemmed, twining climber. H 7m (22ft) or more. Tender. Leaves are broadly oval, 15–25cm (6–10in) long. In summer bears large, unpleasant-smelling, tubular, purple-veined, white flowers, each with a long tail and expanding at the mouth into a heart-shaped lip.
A. littoralis, syn. *A. elegans,* illus. p.211.
A. macrophylla, syn. *A. durior, A. sipho.* Vigorous, deciduous twining vine. H 8-10m (25-30ft). Has large, heart-shaped leaves 10-30cm (4-12in) long that are dark green above and lighter beneath. Small greenish flowers mottled with purple and brown produced in mid summer. Zone 5.
A. sipho. See *A. macrophylla.*

Arizona ash. See *Fraxinus velutina,* illus. p.80.
Arizona cypress. See *Cupressus arizonica* var. *glabra.*
Armand pine. See *Pinus armandii.*
Armenian oak. See *Quercus pontica.*

ARMERIA
PLUMBAGINACEAE

Genus of evergreen perennials and, occasionally, sub-shrubs, grown for their tuft-like clumps or rosettes of leaves and their flower heads. Requires sun and well-drained soil. Propagate by semi-ripe cuttings in summer or by seed in autumn.

A. 'Bees Ruby', syn. *A. pseudarmeria* 'Bees Ruby'. Evergreen, clump-forming, dwarf sub-shrub. H and S 30cm (12in). Round heads of many small, ruby-red flowers are produced in summer on stiff stems above narrow,

grass-like, dark green leaves.
A. caespitosa. See *A. juniperifolia.*
A. juniperifolia, syn. *A. caespitosa,* illus. p.365. **'Bevans Variety'** is an evergreen, densely cushioned sub-shrub. H 5–8cm (2–3in), S 15cm (6in). Has narrow, pointed, mid- to grey-green leaves in loose rosettes. Round heads of small, deep pink flowers are borne in late spring and early summer.
A. latifolia. See *A. pseudarmeria.*
A. maritima (Sea pink, Thrift). Evergreen, clump-forming perennial or dwarf sub-shrub. H 10cm (4in), S 15cm (6in). Leaves are narrow, grass-like and dark green. Stiff stems carry round heads of many small, white to pink flowers in summer. Makes a good edging plant.
'Vindictive' illus. p.380.
A. pseudarmeria, syn. *A. latifolia,* illus. p.350. **'Bees Ruby'** see *A.* 'Bees Ruby'.

ARNICA
ASTERACEAE/COMPOSITAE

Genus of rhizomatous perennials, grown for their large, daisy-like flower heads. Is suitable for large rock gardens. Prefers sun and humus-rich, well-drained soil. Propagate by division or seed in spring. All parts may cause severe discomfort if ingested, and contact with sap may aggravate skin allergies.

A. montana. Tufted, rhizomatous perennial. H 30cm (12in), S 15cm (6in). Bears narrowly oval to oval, hairy, grey-green leaves and, in summer, solitary daisy-like, golden flower heads, 5cm (2in) wide. Prefers acid soil.

ARONIA
Chokeberry

ROSACEAE

Genus of deciduous shrubs, cultivated for their flowers, fruits and colourful autumn foliage. Needs sun (for autumn colour at its best) or semi-shade and fertile, well-drained soil. May be propagated in several ways: by softwood or semi-ripe cuttings taken in summer; by seed sown in autumn; or by division from early autumn to spring.

A. arbutifolia illus. p.130.
A. melanocarpa illus. p.136.
A. × prunifolia. Deciduous, upright shrub. H 3m (10ft), S 2.5m (8ft). Oval, glossy, dark green leaves redden in autumn. Produces star-shaped, white flowers in late spring and early summer, followed by spherical, purplish-black fruits. Zone 5.

ARRHENATHERUM
GRAMINAE/POACEAE

See also GRASSES, BAMBOOS, RUSHES and SEDGES.

A. elatius (False oat grass). subsp. **bulbosum 'Variegatum'** is a loosely tuft-forming, herbaceous, perennial grass. H 50cm (20in), S 20cm (8in). Has a basal stem swelling, hairless, grey-green leaves, with white margins, and open panicles of brownish spikelets in summer.

Arrow bamboo. See *Pseudosasa japonica,* illus. p.308.
Arrowhead. See *Sagittaria.*
American. See *Sagittaria latifolia,* illus. p.446.
Common. See *Sagittaria sagittifolia.*
Japanese. See *Sagittaria sagittifolia* 'Flore Pleno'.
Arrowroot
East Indian. See *Tacca leontopetaloides.*
South Sea. See *Tacca leontopetaloides.*
Arrow-wood. See *Viburnum dentalum.*

ARTEMISIA
Wormwood

ASTERACEAE/COMPOSITAE

Genus of perennials and spreading, dwarf sub-shrubs and shrubs, some of which are evergreen or semi-evergreen, grown mainly for their fern-like, silvery foliage that is sometimes aromatic. Prefers an open, sunny, well-drained site; dwarf types benefit from a winter protection of sharp grit or gravel. Trim lightly in spring. Propagate by division in spring or autumn or by softwood or semi-ripe cuttings in summer.

A. abrotanum illus. p.176.
A. absinthium 'Lambrook Silver'. Evergreen, bushy perennial, woody at base. H 80cm (32in), S 50cm (20in). Has a mass of finely divided, aromatic, silvery-grey leaves. Produces tiny, insignificant, grey flower heads, borne in long panicles, in summer. Needs protection in an exposed site.
A. alba 'Canescens', syn. *A. canescens, A. splendens.* Semi-evergreen, bushy perennial. H 50cm (20in), S 30cm (12in). Has delicate, finely cut, curling, silvery-grey leaves. In summer, insignificant, yellow flower heads are borne on erect, silver stems. Makes good ground cover.
A. arborescens illus. p.175. **'Brass Band'** see *A.* 'Powis Castle'. **'Faith Raven'** is an evergreen, upright shrub. H 1.2m (4ft), S 1m (3ft). Differs from the species in that it is hardier. Has finely cut, aromatic, silvery-white foliage and, in summer and early autumn, rounded heads of small, bright yellow flowers.
A. assoana. See *A. caucasica.*
A. canescens. See *A. alba* 'Canescens'.
A. caucasica, syn. *A. assoana, A. lanata, A. pedemontana.* Evergreen or semi-evergreen, prostrate perennial. H and S 30cm (12in). Fern-like foliage is densely covered with silvery-white hairs. Small clusters of small, rounded, yellow flower heads are borne in summer. Suits a rock garden or wall.
A. lactiflora illus. p.227.
A. lanata. See *A. caucasica.*
A. ludoviciana var. *albula* illus. p.266. **'Silver Queen'** is a semi-evergreen, clump-forming perennial. H 75cm (30in), S 60cm (24in) or more. Has large, lance-shaped, downy, silvery-white leaves, which become greener with age. From mid-summer to autumn bears densely white-woolly panicles of brownish-yellow flower heads.
A. pedemontana. See *A. caucasica.*
A. pontica illus. p.290.
A. 'Powis Castle', syn.

A. arborescens 'Brass Band'. Vigorous, evergreen sub-shrub. H 1m (3ft), S 1.2m (4ft). Has abundant, finely cut, aromatic, silvery-grey foliage and sprays of insignificant, yellowish-grey flower heads in summer.
A. schmidtiana. Semi-evergreen, hummock-forming perennial with creeping stems. H 8–30cm (3–12in), S 60cm (24in). Has fern-like, very finely and deeply cut, silver leaves and, in summer, produces short racemes of small, rounded, pale yellow flower heads. Is good for a large rock garden, wall or bank. Needs sandy, peaty soil. **'Nana'** illus. p.389.
A. splendens. See *A. alba* 'Canescens'.
A. stelleriana. Evergreen, rounded, rhizomatous perennial with a woody base. H 30–60cm (1–2ft), S 60cm–1m (2–3ft). White-haired, silver leaves are deeply lobed or toothed. Bears slender sprays of small, yellow flower heads in summer. Needs light soil. **'Boughton Silver'** (syn. *A.s.* 'Mori', *A.s.* 'Silver Brocade'), S 1m (3ft), is vigorous and arching in habit. **'Mori'** see *A.s.* 'Boughton Silver'. **'Silver Brocade'** see *A.s.* 'Boughton Silver'.

ARUM
Cuckoo pint, Lords and ladies

ARACEAE

Genus of tuberous perennials, grown for their leaves and spathes, each enclosing a pencil-shaped spadix of tiny flowers. Requires sun or partial shade and moist but well-drained soil. Propagate by seed in autumn or by division in early autumn.

A. creticum illus. p.415.
A. dioscoridis. Spring-flowering, tuberous perennial. H 20–35cm (8–14in), S 30–45cm (12–18in). Has a sail-like, green or purple spathe, · blotched dark purple, surrounding a blackish-purple spadix. Arrow-shaped, semi-erect leaves appear in autumn. Needs a sheltered, sunny site.
A. dracunculus. See *Dracunculus vulgaris.*
A. italicum 'Marmoratum', syn. *A.i.* 'Pictum', illus. p.434.
A. pictum illus. p.439.

Arum
Bog. See *Calla palustris,* illus. p.446.
Dragon's. See *Dracunculus vulgaris,* illus. p.401.
Pink. See *Zantedeschia rehmannii.*
Arum lily. See *Zantedeschia aethiopica.*

ARUNCUS
ROSACEAE

Genus of perennials, grown for their hummocks of broad, fern-like leaves and their plumes of white flowers in summer. Thrives in full light and any well-drained soil. Propagate by seed in autumn or by division in spring or autumn.

A. dioicus, syn. *A. sylvester, Spiraea aruncus,* illus. p.226. **'Kneiffii'** illus. p.240.

A. sylvester. See *A. dioicus.*
Arundinaria anceps. See *Yushania anceps.*
Arundinaria auricoma. See *Pleioblastus auricomus.*
Arundinaria falconeri. See *Himalayacalamus falconeri.*
Arundinaria fastuosa. See *Semiarundinaria fastuosa.*
Arundinaria fortunei. See *Pleioblastus variegatus.*
Arundinaria japonica. See *Pseudosasa japonica.*
Arundinaria jaunsarensis. See *Yushania anceps.*
Arundinaria murieliae. See *Fargesia murieliae.*
Arundinaria nitida. See *Fargesia nitida.*
Arundinaria variegata. See *Pleioblastus variegatus.*
Arundinaria viridistriata. See *Pleioblastus auricomus.*

ARUNDO

GRAMINAE/POACEAE

See also GRASSES, BAMBOOS, RUSHES and SEDGES.
A. donax (Giant reed). Herbaceous, rhizomatous, perennial grass. H to 6m (20ft), S 1m (3ft). Has thick stems that bear broad, floppy, blue-green leaves. Produces dense, erect panicles of whitish-yellow spikelets in summer. Can be grown in moist soil. Var. **versicolor** (syn. *A.d.* 'Variegata') illus. p.306.
'**Variegata**' see *A.d.* var. **versicolor**.

Asarabacca. See *Asarum europaeum*, illus. p.390.

ASARINA

SCROPHULARIACEAE

Genus of evergreen climbers and perennials, often with scandent stems, grown for their flowers. Is herbaceous in cold climates. Grow in a position with full light and in any well-drained soil. Propagate by seed in spring.
A. barclayana. See *Maurandya barclayana.*
A. erubescens. See *Lophospermum erubescens.*
A. procumbens, syn. *Antirrhinum asarina*, illus. p.384.

ASARUM,
syn. HEXASTYLIS
Wild ginger

ARISTOLOCHIACEAE

Genus of rhizomatous perennials, some of which are evergreen, with pitcher-shaped flowers carried under kidney- or heart-shaped leaves. Makes good ground cover, although leaves may become damaged in severe weather. Prefers shade and humus-rich, moist but well-drained soil. Propagate by division in spring. Self seeds readily.
A. caudatum. Evergreen, prostrate, rhizomatous perennial. H 8cm (3in), S 25cm (10in) or more. Heart-shaped, leathery, glossy, dark green leaves, 5–10cm (2–4in) across, conceal small, pitcher-shaped, reddish-brown or brownish-purple flowers, with tail-like lobes, in early summer.
A. europaeum illus. p.390.
A. hartwegii. Evergreen, prostrate, rhizomatous perennial. H 8cm (3in), S 25cm (10in) or more. Pitcher-shaped, very dark brown, almost black, flowers, with tail-like lobes, appear in early summer beneath heart-shaped, silver-marked, mid-green leaves, 5–10cm (2–4in) wide.
A. shuttleworthii. Evergreen, prostrate, rhizomatous perennial. H 8cm (3in), S 25cm (10in) or more. Has broadly heart-shaped, usually silver-marked, mid-green leaves, 8cm (3in) across. Bears pitcher-shaped, dark brown flowers, mottled violet inside, in early summer.

ASCLEPIAS
Silk weed, Milk weed

ASCLEPIADACEAE

Genus of tuberous perennials or subshrubs, some of which are evergreen, grown for their flowers. Stems exude milky, white latex when cut. Some species are tender, min. 5–10°C (41–50°F). Hardy species prefer a position in sun and a humus-rich, well-drained soil. Propagate by division or seed in spring. Tender species require sun and a moist atmosphere; cut back during periods of growth. Water very sparingly in low temperatures. Propagate by tip cuttings or seed in spring. Contact with the milky sap may irritate skin.
A. hallii. Upright, tuberous perennial. H to 1m (3ft), S 60cm (2ft). Has oblong leaves, to 13cm (5in) long. Umbels of small, 5-horned, dark pink flowers are carried in summer; tightly packed silky seeds are enclosed in narrowly ovoid fruits, to 15cm (6in) long.
A. physocarpa. See *Gomphocarpus physocarpus.*
A. syriaca. Upright, tuberous perennial. H and S 1m (3ft) or more. Bears oval leaves to 20cm (8in) long. Produces umbels of small, 5-horned, purplish-pink flowers carried on drooping flower stalks in summer, followed by narrowly ovoid fruits, to 15cm (6in) long and filled with silky seeds.
A. tuberosa illus. p.258.

Ash. See *Fraxinus.*
 Arizona. See *Fraxinus velutina*, illus. p.80.
 Black. See *Fraxinus nigra.*
 Blueberry. See *Elaeocarpus cynaneus.*
 Claret. See *Fraxinus angustifolia* 'Raywood'.
Ash (continued)
 European. See *Fraxinus excelsior.*
 Green. See *Fraxinus pennsylvanica.*
 Manna. See *Fraxinus ornus*, illus. p.76.
 Mountain. See *Sorbus aucuparia*, illus. p.81.
 Narrow-leaved. See *Fraxinus angustifolia.*
 Red. See *Fraxinus pennsylvanica.*
 White. See *Fraxinus americana.*
Ash-leaved maple. See *Acer negundo.*
Asian chain fern. See *Woodwardia unigemmata.*

ASIMINA

ANNONACEAE

Genus of deciduous or evergreen shrubs and trees, grown for their foliage and flowers. Prefers full sun and fertile, deep, moist but well-drained soil. Propagate by seed in autumn or by layering or root cuttings in winter.
A. triloba (Pawpaw). Deciduous, open shrub. H and S 4m (12ft). Large, oval, mid-green leaves emerge in late spring or early summer, just after, or at the same time as, 6-petalled, purplish-brown flowers. Later it produces small, globular, brownish fruits. Zone 6.

ASPARAGUS

ASPARAGACEAE

Genus of perennials and scrambling climbers and shrubs, some of which are evergreen, grown for their foliage. Hardy to tender, min. 10°C (50°F). Grow in partial shade or bright light, but not direct sun, in any fertile, well-drained soil. Propagate by seed or division in spring.
A. densiflorus illus. p.266.
 '**Myersii**' (syn. *A. meyeri*, *A.* 'Myers') illus. p.267.
A. meyeri. See *A. densiflorus* 'Myersii'.
A. '**Myers**'. See *A. densiflorus* 'Myersii'.
A. scandens illus. p.219.

Aspen. See *Populus tremula.*
 American. See *Populus tremuloides.*
 Quaking. See *Populus tremuloides.*
 Weeping. See *Populus tremula* 'Pendula', illus. p.79.

ASPERULA

RUBIACEAE

Genus of annuals and perennials; some species make good alpine house plants. Most species need sun and well-drained soil with moisture at roots. Dislikes winter wet on crown. Propagate by softwood cuttings or seed in early summer.
A. athoa of gardens. See *A. suberosa.*
A. odorata. See *Galium odoratum.*
A. suberosa, syn. *A. athoa* of gardens, illus. p.376.

Asphodel. See *Asphodelus aestivus.*
 White. See *Asphodelus albus*, illus. p.239.
 Yellow. See *Asphodeline lutea*, illus. p.238.

ASPHODELINE

ASPHODELACEAE/LILIACEAE

Genus of perennials with thick, fleshy roots. Requires sun and not over-rich soil. Propagate by division in early spring, taking care not to damage roots, or by seed in autumn or spring.
A. liburnica. Neat, clump-forming perennial. H 25–60cm (10–24in), S 30cm (12in). In spring produces racemes of shallowly cup-shaped, yellow flowers on slender stems above linear, grey-green leaves.
A. lutea illus. p.238.

ASPHODELUS

ASPHODELACEAE

Genus of spring- or summer-flowering annuals and perennials. Requires sun; most prefer fertile, well-drained soil. *A. albus* prefers light, well-drained soil. Propagate by division in spring or by seed in autumn.
A. acaulis. Prostrate perennial. H 5cm (2in), S 23cm (9in). In spring or early summer, stemless, funnel-shaped, flesh-pink flowers appear in the centre of each cluster of grass-like, mid-green leaves. Is suitable for an alpine house.
A. aestivus, syn. *A. microcarpus* (Asphodel). Upright perennial. H 1m (3ft), S 30cm (1ft). Dense panicles of star-shaped, white flowers are borne in late spring. Has basal rosettes of upright, then spreading, grass-like, channelled, leathery, mid-green leaves.
A. albus illus. p.239.
A. microcarpus. See *A. aestivus.*

ASPIDISTRA

CONVALLARIACEAE/LILIACEAE

Genus of evergreen, rhizomatous perennials that spread slowly, grown mainly for their glossy foliage. Tender, min. 5–10°C (41–50°F). Very tolerant, but is best grown in a cool, shady position away from direct sunlight and in well-drained soil. Water frequently when in full growth, less at other times. Propagate by division of rhizomes in spring.
A. elatior (Cast-iron plant). Evergreen, rhizomatous perennial. H 60cm (24in), S 45cm (18in). Has upright, narrow, pointed-oval leaves, to 60cm (24in) long; inconspicuous, cream to purple flowers are occasionally produced on short stalks near soil level.
'**Variegata**' illus. p.301.

ASPLENIUM

ASPLENIACEAE

Genus of evergreen or semi-evergreen ferns. Hardy to tender, min. 5°C (41°F). Plants described prefer partial shade, but *A. trichomanes* tolerates full sun. Grow in any moist soil, although containerized plants should be grown in a compost including chopped sphagnum moss or coarse peat. Remove fading fronds regularly. Propagate by spores or bulbils, if produced, in late summer.
A. bulbiferum (Hen-and-chicken fern, Mother spleenwort). Semi-evergreen or evergreen fern. H 15–30cm (6–12in), S 30cm (12in). Tender. Lance-shaped, finely divided, dark green fronds produce bulbils from which young plants develop.
A. ceterach, syn. *Ceterach officinarum*, illus. p.311.
A. nidus illus. p.313.
A. scolopendrium, syn. *Phyllitis scolopendrium*, *Scolopendrium vulgare*, illus. p.313. **Marginatum Group** (syn. *Phyllitis scolopendrium* 'Marginatum') illus. p.313.
A. trichomanes illus. p.311.

ASTER
Michaelmas daisy

ASTERACEAE/COMPOSITAE

Genus of perennials and deciduous or evergreen sub-shrubs with daisy-like flower heads borne in summer-autumn. Prefers sun or partial shade and fertile, well-drained soil, with adequate moisture all summer. Tall asters require staking. Propagate by softwood cuttings in spring or by division in spring or autumn. Spray modern forms of *A. novi-belgii* against mildew and insect attack. Other species may suffer too. See also feature panel p.262.

A. acris. See *A. sedifolius*.

A. albescens, syn. *Microglossa albescens*. Deciduous, upright, slender-stemmed sub-shrub. H 1m (3ft), S 1.5m (5ft). Has narrowly lance-shaped, grey-green leaves and flattish sprays of lavender-blue flower heads, with yellow centres, in mid-summer.

A. alpinus illus. p.381. **'Dark Beauty'** see *A.a.* 'Dunkle Schöne'. **'Dunkle Schöne'** (syn. *A.a.* 'Dark Beauty') is a clump-forming perennial. H 25cm (10in), S 45cm (18in). Leaves are lance-shaped and dark green. Deep purple flower heads are borne from mid- to late summer.
Is suitable for a rock garden.

A. amellus **'King George'** (illus. p.262). Bushy perennial. H and S 50cm (20in). In autumn, carries many large, terminal, daisy-like, deep blue-violet flower heads with yellow centres. Leaves are oval and rough. **'Mauve Beauty'** bears clusters of large, violet flower heads, with yellow centres, in autumn. Leaves are lance-shaped, coarse and mid-green. **'Nocturne'** (illus. p.262), H 75cm (30in), has deep lilac flower heads with yellow centres. **'Rudolph Goethe'** with large, violet-blue flower heads, **'Sonia'** with pink flower heads and **'Veilchenkönigin'** (syn. *A.a.* 'Violet Queen') with deep violet flower heads are other good cultivars. **'Violet Queen'** see *A.a.* 'Veilchenkönigin'.

A. capensis. See *Felicia amelloides*.

A. cordifolius **'Silver Spray'** (illus. p.262). Bushy perennial. H 1.2m (4ft), S 1m (3ft). Dense, arching stems carry sprays of small, pink-tinged, white flower heads in autumn. Mid-green leaves are lance-shaped. Needs staking.

A. diffusus. See *A. lateriflorus*.

A. ericoides **'Golden Spray'** (illus. p.262). Bushy perennial. H 1m (3ft), S 30cm (1ft). Produces daisy-like, pink-tinged, white flower heads, with bold, golden-yellow centres, from late summer to late autumn. Has small, lance-shaped, mid-green leaves and slender, freely branched stems. **'White Heather'** (illus. p.262) has long-lasting, neat, white flower heads in late autumn and wiry stems that may need support.

A. frikartii **'Mönch'** (illus. p262). Bushy perennial. H 75cm (30in), S 45cm (18in). Bears daisy-like, single, soft lavender-blue flower heads with yellowish-green centres continuously from mid-summer to late autumn. Leaves are oval and rough. May need staking. **'Wunder von Stäfa'** (illus. p.262) is similar but has

lavender flowers.

A. lateriflorus, syn. *A. diffusus*. Branching perennial. H 60cm (24in), S 50cm (20in). Bears sprays of tiny, mauve flower heads, with pinkish-brown centres, in autumn. Lance-shaped leaves are small and dark green. **'Horizontalis'** (illus. p.262) has flowers heads that are sometimes tinged pink, with darker pink centres.

A. linosyris (Goldilocks; illus. p.262). Upright, unbranched perennial. H 60cm (24in), S 30cm (12in). Bears numerous small, dense, single, golden-yellow flower heads in late summer-autumn. Leaves are narrowly lance-shaped.

A. novae-angliae **'Andenken an Alma Pötschke'**, syn. *A.n.-a.* 'Alma Pötschke' (illus. p.262). Vigorous, upright perennial. H 75cm (30in), S to 60cm (24in). In autumn produces clusters of single, pink flower heads on stiff stems. Has lance-shaped, rough leaves. May need staking. **'Autumn Snow'** see *A.n.-a.* 'Herbstschnee'. **'Barr's Pink'** (illus. p.262) bears semi-double, bright rose-pink flower heads in summer-autumn. **'Harrington's Pink'** (illus. p.262), H 1.2–1.5m (4–5ft), has single, clear pink flower heads with yellow centres. Those of **'Herbstschnee'** (syn. *A.n.-a.* 'Autumn Snow'; illus. p.262), H 75cm–1.1m (2½–3½ft), are white with yellow centres.

A. novi-belgii **'Apple Blossom'** (illus. p.262). Vigorous, spreading perennial. H 90cm (36in), S 60–75cm (24–30in). Panicles of single, pale soft pink flowers are borne in autumn amid lance-shaped, mid-green leaves. **'Carnival'** (illus. p.262), H 75cm (30in), S to 45cm (18in), bears double, cerise-red flower heads with yellow centres. Leaves are dark green. Is prone to mildew. **'Chequers'** (illus. p.262), H 90cm (36in), S 60–75cm (24–30in), has single, purple flowers. **'Climax'**, H 1.5m (5ft), S 60cm (2ft), bears single, light blue flowers. Is mildew-resistant. The flower heads of **'Fellowship'** (illus. p.262), H 1.2m (4ft), S 50cm (20in), are large, double and clear, deep pink; those of **'Freda Ballard'** (illus. p.262) are semi-double and rich rose-red. **'Kristina'** (illus. p.262), H 30cm (12in), S 45cm (18in), has large, semi-double, white flower heads with yellow centres. **'Lassie'** (illus. p.262), H 1.2m (4ft), S 75cm (30in), produces large, single, clear pink flowers. **'Little Pink Beauty'**, H 45cm (18in), S 50cm (20in), is a good dwarf semi-double, pink cultivar. **'Marie Ballard'** (illus. p.262), H to 1m (3ft), S to 45cm (18in), has double, mid-blue flowers. Is prone to mildew. **'Orlando'** (illus. p.262), H 1m (3ft), S to 45cm (18in), has large, single, bright pink flower heads with golden centres. Leaves are dark green. Mildew may be a problem. **'Patricia Ballard'** (illus. p.262), H 1.2m (4ft), S 75cm (30in), produces semi-double, pink flowers. Large, single flowers of **'Peace'** (illus. p.262) are mauve; those of **'Raspberry Ripple'**, H 75cm (30in), S 60cm (24in), are smaller and reddish-violet. **'Royal Ruby'** (illus. p.262), H and S to 45cm (18in), bears semi-double, rich red flower heads with

yellow centres. Is prone to mildew. **'Royal Velvet'** (illus. p.262), H 1.2m (4ft), S 75cm (30in), has single deep violet flowers. **'Sandford White Swan'** (illus. p.262), H 90cm (36in), S 60cm (24in), bears white flower heads.

A. pilosus var. *demotus*, syn. *A. tradescantii* of gardens. Erect perennial. H 1.2m (4ft), S 50cm (20in). Has lance-shaped, mid-green leaves. In autumn, clusters of small, white flower heads appear on wiry, leafy stems and provide a good foil to bright, autumn leaf colours.

A. **'Professor Anton Kippenburg'** (illus. p.262) is a compact, bushy perennial. H 30cm (12in), S to 45cm (18in). Carries large clusters of daisy-like, yellow-centred, clear blue flower heads in autumn.

A. sedifolius, syn. *A. acris*. Bushy perennial. H 1m (3ft), S 60cm (2ft). Produces clusters of almost star-shaped, lavender-blue flower heads, with yellow centres, in autumn. Has small, narrowly oval, bright green leaves. **'Nanus'**, H and S 50cm (20in), makes a compact dome of blooms.

A. thomsonii. Upright perennial. H 1m (3ft), S 50cm (20in). Produces long-petalled, pale lilac flower heads, freely in autumn. Leaves are slightly heart-shaped. **'Nanus'** (illus. p.262) is more compact, H 45cm (18in), S 23cm (9in).

A. tongolensis. Mat-forming perennial. H 50cm (20in), S 30cm (12in). Large, lavender-blue flower heads, with orange centres, are borne singly in early summer. Has lance-shaped, hairy, dark green leaves.

A. tradescantii of gardens. See *A. pilosus* var. *demotus*.

Aster, China. See *Callistephus*.

ASTILBE

SAXIFRAGACEAE

Genus of summer-flowering perennials, grown for their panicles of flowers that remain handsome even when dried brown in winter. Is suitable for borders and rock gardens. Needs partial shade in most species, and a rich, moist soil. Leave undisturbed if possible, and give an annual spring mulch of well-rotted compost. Propagate species by seed sown in autumn, others by division in spring or autumn.

A. **'Bressingham Beauty'**. Leafy, clump-forming perennial. H and S to 1m (3ft). In summer bears feathery, tapering panicles of small, star-shaped, rich pink flowers on strong stems. Broad leaves are divided into oblong to oval, toothed leaflets.

A. chinensis var. *pumila*. Clump-forming perennial. H 30cm (12in), S 20cm (8in). Lower two-thirds of flower stem bears deeply dissected, coarse, toothed, hairy, dark green leaves. Dense, fluffy spikes of tiny, star-shaped, deep raspberry-red flowers appear in autumn. Is good for a shaded, moist rock garden.

A. x *crispa* **'Perkeo'**. See *A.* 'Perkeo'.

A. **'Fanal'** illus. p.282.

A. **'Gnom'**, syn. *A. simplicifolia* 'Gnom'. Arching, clump-forming, slender-stemmed perennial. H 15cm

(6in), S 10cm (4in). Has oval, deeply lobed or cut, crimped, reddish-green leaves in a basal rosette. Produces dense racemes of tiny, star-shaped, pink flowers in summer. Is good for a shaded, moist rock garden or peat bed. Self seeds in damp places but will not come true.

A. **'Granat'**. Clump-forming, leafy perennial. H 60cm (2ft), S to 1m (3ft). Produces pyramidal trusses of tiny, star-shaped, deep red flowers in summer above broad, bronze-flushed, rich green leaves, which are divided into oblong to oval, toothed leaflets.

A. **'Irrlicht'** illus. p.276.

A. **'Montgomery'** illus. p.249.

A. **'Ostrich Plume'**. See *A.* 'Straussenfeder'.

A. **'Perkeo'**, syn. *A.* x *crispa* 'Perkeo', illus. p.353.

A. simplicifolia **'Gnom'**. See *A.* 'Gnom'.

A. **'Sprite'**. Clump-forming, dwarf, leafy perennial. H 50cm (20in), S to 1m (3ft). Has feathery, tapering panicles of tiny, star-shaped, shell-pink flowers in summer, borne above broad leaves divided into narrowly oval, toothed leaflets.

A. **'Straussenfeder'**, syn *A.* 'Ostrich Plume', illus. p.244.

A. **'Venus'** illus. p.244.

ASTRANTIA
Masterwort

APIACEAE/UMBELLIFERAE

Genus of perennials, widely used in flower arrangements. Needs sun or semi-shade and well-drained soil. Propagate by division in spring or by seed when fresh, in late summer.

A. major illus. p.277. subsp. *carinthiaca* see *A.m.* subsp. *involucrata*. **'Hadspen Blood'** has dark red bracts and flowers. subsp. *involucrata* (syn. *A.m.* subsp. *carinthiaca*) illus. p.277.

A. maxima illus. p.277.

ASTROPHYTUM

CACTACEAE

Genus of slow-growing, perennial cacti, grown for their freely produced, flattish, yellow flowers, some with red centres. Tender, min. 5°C (41°F). Prefers sun and very well-drained, lime-rich soil. Allow to dry completely in winter. Is prone to rot if wet. Propagate by seed sown in spring or summer.

A. asterias, syn. *Echinocactus asterias* (Sea urchin, Silver dollar cactus). Slow-growing, slightly domed, perennial cactus. H 8–10cm (3–4in), S 10cm (4in). Spineless stem has about 8 low ribs bearing small, tufted areoles. Produces bright yellow flowers, to 6cm (2½in) across, in summer.

A. myriostigma, syn. *Echinocactus myriostigma*, illus. p.466.

A. ornatum, syn. *Echinocactus ornatus*, illus. p.477.

Asystasia bella. See *Mackaya bella*.
Atamasco lily. See *Zephyranthes atamasco*.

ATHROTAXIS

TAXODIACEAE

Genus of conifers with awl-shaped leaves that clasp stems. See also CONIFERS.

A. selaginoides (King William pine). Irregularly conical conifer. H 15m (50ft) or more, S 5m (15ft). Has tiny, thick-textured, loosely overlapping, dark green leaves and insignificant, globular cones. Zone 9.

ATHYRIUM

ATHYRIACEAE/WOODSIACEAE

Genus of deciduous or, occasionally, semi-evergreen ferns. Hardy to tender, min. 5°C (41°F). Needs shade and humus-rich, moist soil. Remove fading fronds regularly. Propagate by spores in late summer or by division in autumn or winter.

A. filix-femina (Lady fern). Deciduous fern. H 60cm–1.2m (2–4ft), S 30cm–1m (1–3ft). Dainty, lance-shaped, much-divided, arching fronds are pale green. Has very variable frond dissection.

A. goeringianum. See A. niponicum.

A. niponicum, syn. A. goeringianum, A. nipponicum, illus. p.313.

A. nipponicum. See A. niponicum.

A. otophorum. Semi-evergreen fern. H and S to 75cm (30in). Has arching, broadly ovate, mid-green or purple-tinged, divided fronds, 45–75cm (18–30in) long. Stalk and midrib are a contrasting deep wine-purple.

Atlas cedar. See Cedrus atlantica

ATRIPLEX

CHENOPODIACEAE

Genus of annuals, perennials and evergreen or semi-evergreen shrubs, grown for their foliage. Grows well by the coast. Needs full sun and well-drained soil. Propagate by softwood cuttings taken in summer or by seed sown in autumn.

A. halimus (Tree purslane). Semi-evergreen, bushy shrub. H 2m (6ft), S 3m (10ft). Oval leaves are silvery-grey. Produces flowers very rarely. Zone 8.

A. hortensis var. **rubra** (Red mountain spinach, Red orach). Fast-growing, erect annual. H 1.2m (4ft), S 30cm (1ft). Triangular, deep red leaves, to 15cm (6in) long, are edible. Bears insignificant flowers in summer.

AUBRIETA

BRASSICACEAE/CRUCIFERAE

Genus of evergreen, trailing and mound-forming perennials. Is useful on dry banks, walls and in rock gardens. Thrives in sun and in any well-drained soil. To maintain a compact shape, cut back hard after flowering. Propagate by greenwood cuttings in summer or by semi-ripe cuttings in late summer and autumn.

A. 'Carnival'. See A. 'Hartswood Purple'.

A. 'Cobalt Violet' illus. p.369.

A. deltoidea 'Argenteovariegata' illus. p.368.

A. 'Doctor Mules'. Vigorous, evergreen, mound-forming perennial. H 5–8cm (2–3in), S 30cm (12in). Has rounded, toothed, soft green leaves and, in spring, large, single, rich purple flowers on short spikes.

A. 'Gurgedyke'. Evergreen, mound-forming perennial. H 10cm (4in), S 20cm (8in). Bears rounded, toothed, soft green leaves. Produces 4-petalled, deep purple flowers in spring.

A. 'Hartswood Purple', syn. A. 'Carnival', illus. p.368.

A. 'Joy' illus. p.367.

A. 'J.S. Baker' illus. p.368.

AUCUBA

CORNACEAE

Genus of evergreen shrubs, grown for their foliage and fruits. To obtain fruits, grow both male and female plants. Makes good house plants when kept in a cool, shaded position. Tolerates full sun through to dense shade. Grow in any but water-logged soil. To restrict growth, cut old shoots back hard in spring. Propagate by semi-ripe cuttings taken in summer.

A. japonica illus. p.152. **'Crotonifolia'** (male) illus. p.153. **'Gold Dust'** is an evergreen, bushy, dense, female shrub. H and S 2.5m (8ft). Has stout, green shoots and oval, glossy, gold-speckled, dark green leaves. Small, star-shaped, purple flowers in mid-spring are followed by egg-shaped, bright red fruits. Bright green leaves of **'Picturata'** (male) each have a central, golden blotch. Some plants of 'Crotonifolia' and 'Picturata' are known to be female and have produced fruits. Zone 7.

AURINIA

BRASSICACEAE/CRUCIFERAE

Genus of evergreen perennials, grown for their grey-green foliage and showy flower sprays. Is suitable for rock gardens, walls and banks. Needs sun and well-drained soil. Propagate by softwood or greenwood cuttings in early summer or by seed in autumn.

A. saxatilis, syn. Alyssum saxatile, illus. p.350. **'Citrina'** illus. p.349. **'Dudley Nevill'** is an evergreen, clump-forming perennial. H 23cm (9in), S 30cm (12in). Has oval, hairy, grey-green leaves and, in late spring and early summer, produces racemes of many small, 4-petalled, buff-yellow flowers. **'Variegata'** illus. p.349.

Australian banyan. See Ficus macrophylla.
Australian brush cherry. See Syzygium paniculatum, illus. p 81.
Australian cabbage palm. See Livistona australis.
Australian firewheel tree. See Stenocarpus sinuatus.
Australian heath. See Epacris impressa, illus. p.155.
Australian rosemary. See Westringia fruticosa, illus. p.158.
Australian sarsparilla. See Hardenbergia violacea.
Australian sassafras. See Atherosperma moschatum.
Australian tree fern. See Cyathea australis, illus. p.100; Dicksonia antarctica, illus. p.310.
Australian violet. See Viola hederacea.
Austrian pine. See Pinus nigra subsp. nigra, illus. p.104.

AUSTROCEDRUS

CUPRESSACEAE

Genus of conifers with flattish sprays of scale-like leaves. See also CONIFERS.

A. chilensis, syn. Libocedrus chilensis, illus. p.106.

Autograph tree. See Clusia major.
Autumn crocus. See Colchicum autumnale, illus. p.437; Crocus nudiflorus, illus. p.428.
Autumn snowdrop. See Galanthus reginae-olgae.
Autumn snowflake. See Leucojum autumnale, illus. p.437.
Avena candida. See Helictotrichon sempervirens.
Avena sempervirens. See Helicto-trichon sempervirens.
Avens. See Geum.
  Alpine. See Geum montanum.
  Mountain. See Dryas.
Azalea. See Rhododendron.
  Alpine. See Loiseleuria procumbens, illus. p.377.
  Flame. See Rhododendron calendulaceum.
  Trailing. See Loiseleuria procumbens, illus. p.377.

AZARA

FLACOURTIACEAE

Genus of evergreen shrubs and trees, grown for their foliage and also for their yellow flowers that are composed of a mass of stamens. Where hardy, plants are best grown situated against a south- or west-facing wall for added protection. Grows in sun or shade, and in fertile, well-drained soil. Propagate by semi-ripe cuttings in summer.

A. lanceolata. Evergreen, bushy shrub or spreading tree. H and S 6m (20ft). Has narrowly oval, sharply toothed, bright green leaves. Small, rounded clusters of pale yellow flowers are carried in late spring or early summer. Zone 9.

A. microphylla illus. p.125.

A. serrata illus. p.135.

AZOLLA

AZOLLACEAE

Genus of deciduous, perennial, floating water ferns, grown for their decorative foliage and also to control algal growth by reducing light in water beneath. Grows in sun or shade. If not kept in check, may be invasive; reduce spread by removing portions with a net. Propagate by redistributing clusters of plantlets when they appear.

A. caroliniana. See A. filiculoides.

A. filiculoides, syn A. caroliniana, illus. p.448.

AZORELLA

APIACEAE/UMBELLIFERAE

Genus of evergreen, tufted or spreading perennials, grown for their flowers and neat, rosetted foliage. Is useful as alpine house plants. Thrives in full light and well-drained soil. Propagate by division in spring.

A. nivalis. See A. trifurcata.

A. trifurcata, syn. A. nivalis, illus. p.390.

AZORINA

CAMPANULACEAE

Genus of one species of erect evergreen shrub with bell-shaped flowers. Tender, min. 5°C (41°F). Needs full light and fertile, moist but well-drained soil. Propagate by seed in spring or take softwood or semi-ripe cuttings in summer.

Azorina vidalii, syn. Campanula vidalii, illus. p.154.

Azureocereus hertlingianus. See Browningia hertlingiana.
Aztec lily. See Sprekelia formosissima, illus. p.413.
Aztec marigold. See Tagetes erecta.

B

BABIANA
IRIDACEAE

Genus of spring- and early summer-flowering corms, valued for their brightly coloured flowers, which are somewhat like freesias. Tender, min. 10°C (50°F). Requires a position in sun and well-drained soil. Propagate in autumn by seed or natural division of corms.
B. disticha. See *B. plicata*.
B. plicata, syn. *B. disticha*. Spring-flowering corm. H 10–20cm (4–8in), S 5–8cm (2–3in). Has a fan of lance-shaped, erect, basal leaves and short spikes of funnel-shaped, violet-blue flowers, 4–5cm (1½–2in) long, with yellow-patched petals.
B. rubrocyanea illus. p.431.
B. stricta. Spring-flowering corm. H 10–20cm (4–8in), S 5–8cm (2–3in). Produces a fan of narrowly lance-shaped, erect, basal leaves and short spikes of up to 10 funnel-shaped, purple, blue, cream or pale yellow flowers, 2.5–4cm (1–1½in) long and sometimes red-centred.

Baby blue-eyes. See *Nemophila menziesii*, illus. p.333.
Baby rubber plant. See *Peperomia clusiifolia*.
Baby's tears. See *Soleirolia*.
Baby's toes. See *Fenestraria aurantiaca*, illus. p.479.

BACCHARIS
ASTERACEAE/COMPOSITAE

Genus of evergreen or deciduous, mainly autumn-flowering shrubs, grown for their foliage and fruits. Is useful for exposed, coastal gardens and dry soil. Requires a position in full sun and well-drained soil. Propagate by softwood cuttings in summer.
B. halimifolia (Bush groundsel). Vigorous, deciduous, bushy shrub. H and S 4m (12ft). Has grey-green, sharply toothed, oval leaves. Large clusters of tiny, white flower heads in mid-autumn are followed by fluffy, white heads of tiny fruits. Zone 4.

Bacopa. See *Sutera cordata*.
Bahia lanata. See *Eriophyllum lanatum*.
Bald cypress. See *Taxodium distichum*, illus. p.104.

BALDELLIA
ALISMATACEAE

Genus of deciduous or evergreen, perennial, bog plants and submerged water plants, grown for their foliage. Prefers a position in sun, but tolerates shade. Remove fading foliage and excess growth as required. Propagate by division in spring or summer.

B. ranunculoides, syn. *Alisma ranunculoides*, *Echinodorus ranunculoides*. Deciduous, perennial, bog plant or submerged water plant. H 23cm (9in), S 15cm (6in). Has lance-shaped, mid-green leaves and, in summer, umbels of small, 3-parted, pink or white flowers with basal, yellow marks.

Baldmoney. See *Meum athamanticum*.
Balearic box. See *Buxus balearica*, illus. p.153.
Balkan blue grass. See *Sesleria heufleriana*.
Balloon flower. See *Platycodon*.
Balloon vine. See *Cardiospermum halicacabum*.

BALLOTA
LABIATEA/LAMIACEAE

Genus of perennials and evergreen or deciduous sub-shrubs, grown for their foliage and flowers. Requires very well-drained soil and full sun. Cut back in spring before growth starts. Propagate by semi-ripe cuttings in summer.
B. acetabulosa illus. p.176.
B. pseudodictamnus illus. p.361.

Balm
  Bastard. See *Melittis*.
  Bee. See *Monarda didyma*.
Balm of Gilead. See *Populus* x *candicans*.
Balsam. See *Impatiens balsamina*, illus. p.320.
Balsam fir. See *Abies balsamea*.
Balsam poplar. See *Populus balsamifera*.
Bamboo. See Grasses, Bamboos, Rushes and Sedges.
  Anceps. See *Yushania anceps*, illus. p.308.
  Arrow. See *Pseudosasa japonica*, illus. p.308.
  Black. See *Phyllostachys nigra*.
  Chilean. See *Chusquea culeou*, illus. p.308.
  Dwarf white-stripe. See *Pleioblastus variegatus*, illus. p.306.
  Fishpole. See *Phyllostachys aurea*.
  Golden. See *Phyllostachys aurea*.
  Golden-groove. See *Phyllostachys aureosulcata*.
  Heavenly. See *Nandina domestica*.
  Hedge. See *Bambusa multiplex*, illus. p.307.
  Muriel. See *Fargesia murieliae*.
  Narihira. See *Semiarundinaria fastuosa*, illus. p.308.
  Sacred. See *Nandina domestica*.
  Timber. See *Phyllostachys bambusoides*, illus. p.308.
  Zigzag. See *Phyllostachys flexuosa*, illus. p.308.
Bamboo palm. See *Rhapis excelsa*, illus. p.152.

BAMBUSA
GRAMINEAE/POACEAE

See also GRASSES, BAMBOOS, RUSHES and SEDGES.
B. glaucescens. See *B. multiplex*.
B. multiplex, syn. *B. glaucescens*, illus. p.307.

Banana. See *Musa*.
  Flowering. See *Musa ornata*, illus. p.232.
  Japanese. See *Musa basjoo*, illus. p.233.
  Scarlet. See *Musa coccinea*.
Banana passion fruit. See *Passiflora antioquiensis*.
Baneberry. See *Actaea*.
  Red. See *Actaea rubra*.
  White. See *Actaea pachypoda*, illus. p.259.

BANKSIA
PROTEACEAE

Genus of evergreen shrubs and trees, grown for their flowers and foliage. Tender, min. 7–10°C (45–50°F). Requires full light and sharply drained, sandy soil that contains little phosphates or nitrates. Water containerized plants moderately when in full growth, sparingly at other times. Freely ventilate plants grown under glass. Propagate by seed in spring.
B. baxteri. Evergreen, spreading, open shrub. H and S 2–3m (6–10ft). Leathery, mid-green leaves are strap-shaped, cut from the midrib into triangular, sharply pointed lobes. Produces dense, spherical heads of small, tubular, yellow flowers in summer.
B. coccinea illus. p.130.
B. ericifolia (Heath banksia). Evergreen, irregularly rounded, wiry, freely branching shrub. H and S to 3m (10ft). Has small, needle-like leaves and dense, upright, bottlebrush-like spikes, each 10–15cm (4–6in) long, of small, tubular, bronze-red or yellow flowers in late winter and spring.
B. serrata. Evergreen, bushy, upright shrub or tree. H 3–10m (10–30ft), S 1.5–3m (5–10ft). Oblong to lance-shaped, saw-toothed, leathery leaves are mid- to deep green. Small, tubular, reddish-budded, cream flowers appear in dense, upright, bottlebrush-like spikes, each 10–15cm (4–6in) long, from spring to late summer.

Banksia
  Heath. See *Banksia ericifolia*.
  Yellow. See *Rosa banksiae* 'Lutea', illus. p.198.
Banksian rose. See *Rosa banksiae*.
Banyan. See *Ficus benghalensis*, illus. p.72.
  Australian. See *Ficus macrophylla*.
Baobab. See *Adansonia*.

BAPTISIA
LEGUMINOSAE/PAPILIONACEAE

Genus of summer-flowering perennials, grown for their flowers. Requires full sun and deep, well-drained, preferably neutral to acid soil. Is best not disturbed once planted. Propagate by division in early spring or by seed in autumn.
B. australis illus. p.252.

Barbacenia elegans. See *Vellozia elegans*.
Barbados gooseberry. See *Pereskia aculeata*, illus. p.457.
Barbados pride. See *Caesalpinia pulcherrima*.

BARBAREA
BRASSICACEAE/CRUCIFERAE

Genus of summer-flowering perennials, biennials and annuals. Most species are weeds or winter salad plants, but the variegated form of *B. vulgaris* is grown for decorative purposes. Grows in a sunny or shady position and in any well-drained but not very dry soil. Propagate by seed or division in spring.
B. vulgaris (Winter cress, Yellow rocket). 'Variegata' illus. p.291.

Barbed-wire plant. See *Tylecodon reticulatus*, illus. p.465.
Barberry. See *Berberis*.
  Darwin's. See *Berberis darwinii*, illus. p.117.
Barberton daisy. See *Gerbera jamesonii*, illus. p. 302.

BARLERIA
ACANTHACEAE

Genus of evergreen shrubs and perennials, grown for their flowers. Tender, min. 7–18°C (45–64°F). Needs full light or partial shade and fertile soil. Water potted plants well when in full growth, moderately at other times. In the growing season, prune tips of young plants to encourage branching. For a more compact habit, shorten long stems after flowering. May be propagated by seed in spring or by greenwood or semi-ripe cuttings in summer.
B. cristata (Philippine violet). Evergreen, semi-erect shrub. H and S 60cm–1.2m (2–4ft). Min. 15–18°C (59–64°F). Has elliptic, coarsely haired leaves. Tubular, light violet flowers, sometimes pale pink or white, are produced from upper leaf axils in summer.
B. obtusa. Evergreen, erect, spreading shrub. H and S to 1m (3ft). Min. 7–10°C (45–50°F). Leaves are elliptic. Tubular, mauve flowers are produced from upper leaf axils during winter-spring.

Barley, Foxtail. See *Hordeum jubatum*, illus. p.307.

Barosma pulchella. See *Agathosma pulchella*.

Barrel cactus. See *Ferocactus*.

Barrenwort. See *Epimedium*.

Bartonia aurea. See *Mentzelia lindleyi*.

Bartram's oak. See *Quercus* x *heterophylla*, illus. p.82.

Basket grass. See *Oplismenus africanus*.

Basket oak. See *Quercus prinus*.

BASSIA,
syn. KOCHIA

CHENOPODIACEAE

Genus of annuals and perennials, grown for their habit, the feathery effect of their leaves and their autumn tints. Does best in sun and in fertile, well-drained soil. May require support in very windy areas. Propagate by seed sown under glass in early to mid-spring, or outdoors in late spring.

B. scoparia f. ***trichophylla*** illus. p.335.

Basswood. See *Tilia americana*.

Bastard balm. See *Melittis*.

Bat flower. See *Tacca chantrieri*.

BAUERA

CUNONIACEAE

Genus of evergreen shrubs, grown mainly for their flowers. Tender, min. 3–5°C (37–41°F). Needs full sun and humus-rich, well-drained, neutral to acid soil. Water potted plants moderately, less when not in full growth. Remove straggly stems after flowering. May be propagated by seed sown in spring or by semi-ripe cuttings taken in late summer.

B. rubioides. Evergreen, bushy, wiry-stemmed shrub, usually of spreading habit. H and S 30–60cm (1–2ft). Leaves each have 3 oval to lance-shaped, glossy leaflets. Bowl-shaped, pink or white flowers appear in early spring and summer.

BAUHINIA

LEGUMINOSAE/PAPILIONACEAE

Genus of evergreen, semi-evergreen or deciduous trees, shrubs and scandent climbers, grown for their flowers. Tender, min. 5–18°C (41–64°F). Requires full light and fertile, well-drained soil. Water containerized specimens freely when in full growth, less in winter. Thin out congested growth after flowering. Propagate by seed in spring.

B. galpinii, syn. *B. punctata*, illus. p.142.

B. punctata. See *B. galpinii*.

B. variegata and **'Candida'** illus. p.97.

Bay
Bull. See *Magnolia grandiflora*.
Loblolly. See *Gordonia lasianthus*.
Sweet. See *Laurus nobilis*; *Magnolia virginiana*.

Bay laurel. See *Laurus nobilis*.

Bay tree. See *Laurus*.

Bay willow. See *Salix pentandra*.

Bayonet plant. See *Aciphylla squarrosa*, illus. p.266.

Bayonet, Spanish. See *Yucca aloifolia*, illus. p.153.

Beach pine. See *Pinus contorta*, illus. p.107.

Bead plant. See *Nertera granadensis*, illus. p.387.

Bead tree. See *Melia azedarach*, illus. p.76.

Bean
Black. See *Kennedia nigricans*.
Bog. See *Menyanthes trifoliata*, illus. p.446.
Hyacinth. See *Lablab purpureus*, illus. p.211.

Bean tree
Black. See *Castanospermum*.
Indian. See *Catalpa bignonioides*, illus. p.78.

Bearberry. See *Arctostaphylos*.

Bear grass. See *Dasylirion*.

Bear's breeches. See *Acanthus*.

Bearded bellflower. See *Campanula barbata*, illus. p.356.

BEAUCARNEA

AGAVACEAE/DRACAENACEAE

Genus of evergreen shrubs and trees, grown mainly for their intriguing, overall appearance. Tender, min. 7°C (45°F). Needs full light and sharply drained, fertile soil; drought conditions are tolerated. Water potted specimens moderately; allow compost almost to dry out between waterings. Propagate by seed or suckers in spring or by stem-tip cuttings in summer.

B. recurvata, syn. *Nolina recurvata*, *N. tuberculata*, illus. p.100.

BEAUMONTIA

APOCYNACEAE

Genus of evergreen, woody-stemmed, twining climbers, grown for their large, fragrant flowers and handsome leaves. Tender, min. 7–10°C (45–50°F). Requires fertile, well-drained soil and full light. Water freely in growing season, sparingly otherwise. Provide support. Thin out previous season's growth after flowering. Propagate by semi-ripe cuttings in late summer.

B. grandiflora illus. p.204.

Beauty bush. See *Kolkwitzia amabilis*.

Bedstraw. See *Galium*.

Bee balm. See *Monarda didyma*.

Beech. See *Fagus*.
American. See *Fagus grandifolia*.
Antarctic. See *Nothofagus antarctica*.
Blue. See *Carpinus caroliniana*.
Copper. See *Fagus sylvatica* f. *purpurea*, illus. p.65.
European. See *Fagus sylvatica*, illus. p.68.
Oriental. See *Fagus orientalis*.
Purple. See *Fagus sylvatica* f. *purpurea*, illus. p.65.
Silver. See *Nothofagus menziesii*.
Southern. See *Nothofagus*.
Weeping. See *Fagus sylvatica* f. *pendula*, illus. p.66.

Beech fern. See *Phegopteris connectilis*.

Beefsteak plant. See *Iresine herbstii*.

BEGONIA

BEGONIACEAE

Genus of evergreen or deciduous shrubs and small, tree-like plants, perennials and annuals, grown for their colourful flowers and/or ornamental leaves. Prefers slightly acidic soil. Is susceptible to powdery mildew and botrytis from late spring to early autumn. Commonly cultivated begonias are divided into the following groupings, each with varying cultivation requirements. See also feature panel p.295.

Cane-stemmed begonias
Evergreen, woody perennials, many known as 'Angelwings', with usually erect, cane-like stems bearing regularly spaced, swollen nodes and flowers in large, pendulous panicles. Encourage branching by pinching out growing tips. New growth develops from base of plant. Tender, min. 10°C (50°F). Grow under glass in good light but not direct sun (poor light reduces quantity of flowers) and in free-draining, loam-based compost. Stake tall plants. Propagate in spring by seed or tip cuttings.

Rex-cultorum begonias
Mostly evergreen, rhizomatous perennials of variable habit derived from crosses of *B. rex* and related species. They are grown for their brilliantly coloured, oval to lance-shaped leaves, 8–30cm (3–12in) long, that are sometimes spirally twisted. Tender, min. 13–15°C (55–9°F), but preferably 21–4°C (70–75°F), with 40–75% relative humidity. Grow under glass in cool climates, in partial shade and in well-drained soil; water only sparingly. Do not allow water to remain on the leaves, otherwise they become susceptible to botrytis. Propagate in spring by seed, leaf cuttings or division of rhizomes.

Rhizomatous begonias
Variable, mostly evergreen, rhizomatous perennials, grown for their foliage and small, single flowers. Smooth, crested or puckered, green or brown leaves, 8–30cm (3–12in) long, often marked silver, are sometimes spirally twisted. Creeping cultivars are more freely branched than erect ones and are useful for hanging baskets. Tender, min. 13–15°C (55–9°F), but preferably 19°C (66°F), with 40–75% relative humidity. Grow under glass in cool climates, in partial shade and in well-drained soil; water only sparingly. Do not allow water to remain on the leaves, otherwise they become susceptible to botrytis. Propagate in spring by seed, leaf cuttings or division of rhizomes.

Semperflorens begonias
Evergreen, bushy perennials, derived from *B. cucullata* var. *hookeri*, *B. schmidtiana* and other species, often grown as bedding annuals. Stems are soft, succulent and branch freely, bearing generally rounded, green, bronze or variegated leaves, 5cm (2in) long. Flowers are single or double.

Pinch out growing tips to produce bushy plants. Tender, min. 10–15°C (50–59°F). Requires sun or partial shade and well-drained soil. Propagate in spring by seed or stem cuttings.

Shrub-like begonias
Evergreen, multi-stemmed, bushy perennials, usually freely branched with flexible, erect or pendent stems, often hairy. Leaves may be hairy or glabrous and up to 15cm (6in) across, 10–30cm (4–12in) long. Single flowers are pink, cream or white. Tender, min. 7°C (45°F) with 55% relative humidity. Grow under glass in good light and moist but well-drained soil. Propagate in spring by seed or stem cuttings.

Tuberous begonias (including the Tuberhybrida, Multiflora and Pendula begonias)
Mostly upright, bushy, tuberous, winter-dormant perennials grown for their foliage and flowers. Tuberhybrida begonias, H and S 75cm (30in), vary from pendent to erect, with sparsely branched, succulent stems and oval, pointed, glossy, bright to dark green leaves, 20cm (8in) long. Most are summer flowering and mainly double-flowered. Multiflora cultivars, H and S 30cm (12in), are more bushy and have 8cm (3in) long leaves and single, semi-double or double, flowers, each 4–5cm (1½–2in) across, in summer; tolerates full sun. Pendula cultivars, H to 1m (3ft), have long, thin, trailing stems; leaves are 6–8cm (2½–3in) long. Masses of single or double flowers are borne in summer. Tender, min. 5–7°C (41–5°F). Outdoors, grow in dappled shade and moist conditions; under glass, plant in cool shade with 65–70% relative humidity. Tubers are dormant in winter. Start into growth in spring for mid-summer to early autumn flowering. Remove all flower buds until stems show at least 3 pairs of leaves; with large-flowered types allow only central male bud to flower, so remove flanking buds. Plants may require staking. Propagate in spring by seed, stem or basal cuttings or division of tubers.

Winter-flowering begonias
Evergreen, low-growing, very compact perennials, with succulent, thin stems, that are often included in the tuberous group. Two main groups are recognized: the single-flowered, usually pink or white, Lorraine, Cheimantha or Christmas begonias; and the single, semi-double or double, Elatior and Rieger begonias that occur in a wide range of colours. Leaves are green or bronze, 5cm (2in) long. Flowers are borne mainly from late autumn to mid-spring. Tender, min. 18°C (64°F) with 40% relative humidity. Indirect sun and moist soil are preferred. Cut back old stems to 10cm (4in) after flowering. Propagate in spring by seed or stem cuttings.

B. albopicta (illus. p.295). Fast-growing, evergreen, cane-stemmed begonia. H to 1m (3ft), S 30cm (1ft). Freely branched, green stems turn brown-green when mature. Narrowly oval to lance-chaped, wavy-edged, green leaves are silver-spotted. Has clusters of single, green-white flowers in summer-autumn.

B. angularis. See *B. stipulacea*.

B. 'Apricot Cascade' (illus. p.295). Pendent Tuberhybrida begonia. H and S 60cm (2ft). Has emerald-green leaves and, from early summer to mid-autumn, double, orange-apricot flowers. Other cascades are **'Bridal Cascade'** (pink-edged, white petals), **'Crimson Cascade'**, **'Gold Cascade'** and **'Orange Cascade'**.

B. 'Beatrice Haddrell'. Evergreen, creeping, rhizomatous begonia. H 20–30cm (8–12in), S 25–30cm (10–12in). Oval leaves are deeply cleft, 8–15cm (3–6in) long, and dark green with paler veins. Produces single, pink flowers, above foliage, in winter and early spring.

B. 'Bethlehem Star'. Evergreen, creeping, rhizomatous begonia. H 20–30cm (8–12in), S 25–30cm (10–12in). Oval, slightly indented, almost black leaves, less than 8cm (3in) long, each have a central, creamy-green star. Bears masses of single, pale pink flowers, with darker pink spots, from late winter to early spring.

B. 'Billie Langdon' (illus. p.295). Upright Tuberhybrida begonia. H 60cm (2ft), S 45cm (18in). In summer has masses of heavily veined, double, white flowers, each 18cm (7in) across, with a perfect rose-bud centre.

B. 'Bokit'. Evergreen, erect, rhizomatous begonia. H 20–30cm (8–12in), S 25–35cm (10–14in). Has oval, spirally twisted, yellow-green leaves with brown tiger stripes. Bears masses of single, white flowers, flecked with pink, in winter.

B. bowerae (Eyelash begonia; illus. p.295). Evergreen, creeping, rhizomatous begonia. H 25–30cm (10–12in), S 20–25cm (8–10in). Has oval, bright green leaves, 2.5cm (1in) long, with chocolate marks and bristles around edges. Bears single, pink-tinted, white flowers freely in winter.

B. 'Bridal Cascade'. See *B.* 'Apricot Cascade'.

B. 'Can-Can' (illus. p.295). Upright Tuberhybrida begonia. H 1m (3ft), S 45cm (18in). Has double, yellow flowers, each 20cm (8in) wide, with rough-edged, red petals, in summer. Produces few side shoots.

B. 'City of Ballarat'. Vigorous, upright Tuberhybrida begonia. H 60cm (2ft), S 45cm (18in). Leaves are rich dark green. Carries double, glowing orange flowers, each 18cm (7in) across, with broad petals and a formal centre, in summer.

B. coccinea (Angelwing begonia). Evergreen, cane-stemmed begonia. H 1.2m (4ft), S 30cm (1ft). Produces narrowly oval, glossy, green leaves, buff-coloured beneath, and, in spring, profuse, single, pink or coral-red flowers.

B. 'Cocktail'. Semperflorens begonia. H and S 20–30cm (8–12in). Produces rounded, wavy, green-bronze leaves and pink, red or white flowers from summer until autumn frosts.

B. 'Corallina de Lucerna'. See *B.* 'Lucerna'.

B. 'Crimson Cascade'. See *B.* 'Apricot Cascade'.

B. 'Curly Merry Christmas'. Rex-cultorum begonia. H 25cm (10in), S 30cm (12in). Is a sport of *B.* 'Merry Christmas' with spirally twisted leaves.

B. dichroa. Evergreen, cane-stemmed begonia. H 35cm (14in), S 25cm (10in). Oval leaves are mid-green, 12cm (5in) long; occasionally new leaves bear silver spots. Produces small, single, orange flowers, each with a white ovary, in summer.

B. disticha. See *B. stipulacea*.

B. dregei (Mapleleaf begonia). Semi-tuberous begonia. H 75cm (30in), S 35cm (14in). Has small, maple-like, lobed, purple-veined, bronze leaves, with red beneath and occasionally silver-speckled when young. Profuse, pendent, single, white flowers are borne in summer. Needs winter rest.

B. 'Duartei' (illus. p.295). Rex-cultorum begonia. H and S 45–60cm (18–24in). Has spirally twisted, red-haired, very dark green leaves, over 15cm (6in) long, with silver-grey streaks and almost black edges. Is difficult to grow to maturity.

B. x erythrophylla. See *B.* 'Erythrophylla'.

B. 'Erythrophylla', syn. *B. x erythrophylla*, *B.* 'Feastii'. Evergreen, creeping, rhizomatous begonia. H 20cm (8in), S 23–30cm (9–12in). Thick, mid-green leaves, 8–15cm (3–6in) long, are almost rounded, with leaf stalks attached to centre of red undersides; slightly wavy margins have white hairs. Produces single, light pink flowers well above foliage, in early spring.

B. 'Feastii'. See *B.* 'Erythrophylla'.

B. 'Flamboyant' (illus. p.295). Upright Tuberhybrida begonia. H 17cm (7in), S 15cm (6in). Leaves are slender and bright green. Has single, scarlet flowers in profusion in summer.

B. foliosa (illus. p.295). Evergreen, shrub-like begonia. H 30–50cm (12–20in), S 30–35cm (12–14in). Bears erect, then arching stems and oval, toothed, dark green leaves, 1cm (½in) long. Has very small, single, white flowers in spring and autumn. Is susceptible to whitefly. var. *miniata* see *B. fuchsioides*.

B. fuchsioides, syn. *B. foliosa* var. *miniata* (Fuchsia begonia). Evergreen, shrub-like begonia. H to 1.2m (4ft), S 30cm (1ft). Oval, toothed leaves are numerous and dark green, 4cm (1½in) long. Pendent, single, bright red flowers are borne in winter.

B. 'Gloire de Lorraine' (Christmas begonia, Lorraine begonia). Evergreen, winter-flowering, Cheimantha begonia. H 30cm (12in), S 30–35cm (12–14in). Is well-branched with rounded, bright green leaves and single, white to pale pink flowers. Male flowers are sterile, female, highly infertile.

B. 'Gold Cascade'. See *B.* 'Apricot Cascade'.

B. gracilis var. *martiana*, syn. *B. martiana*. Tuberous begonia. H 60–75cm (24–30in), S 40cm (16in). Has small, oval to lance-shaped, lobed, pale green or brown-green leaves with tapering tips and large, fragrant, single, pink flowers, 2.5cm (1in) across, in summer.

B. haageana. See *B. scharffii*.

B. 'Helen Lewis' (illus. p.295). Rex-cultorum begonia. H and S 45–60cm (18–24in). Has an erect rhizome and silky, deep royal purple leaves, 15–20cm (6–8in) long, with silver bands. Slightly hairy, single, cream flowers are produced in early summer.

B. 'Ingramii' (illus. p.295). Evergreen, shrub-like begonia. H 70cm (28in), S 45cm (18in). Produces elliptic, toothed, bright green leaves, 8cm (3in) long, and, intermittently from spring to autumn, masses of single, pink flowers on spreading branches.

B. 'Iron Cross'. See *B. masoniana*.

B. 'Krefeld'. Evergreen, winter-flowering, Rieger begonia. H 25cm (10in), S 30cm (12in). Is semi-tuberous with succulent stems, oval, mid-green leaves and masses of single, vivid orange or bright crimson flowers. Is very susceptible to botrytis and mildew at base of stems, so water by pot immersion.

B. 'Lucerna', syn. *B.* 'Corallina de Lucerna' (illus. p.295). Vigorous, evergreen, cane-stemmed begonia. H 2–2.2m (6–7ft), S 45–60cm (1½–2ft). Has oval, silver-spotted, bronze-green leaves, 25–35cm (10–14in) long, with tapered tips and, year-round, large panicles of single, deep pink flowers; male flowers remain almost closed.

B. 'Mac's Gold'. Evergreen, creeping, rhizomatous begonia. H and S 20–25cm (8–10in). Star-shaped, lobed, yellow leaves, 8–15cm (3–6in) long, have chocolate-brown marks. Has single, pink flowers intermittently in spring-summer but in moderate quantity.

B. 'Madame Richard Galle'. Upright Tuberhybrida begonia. H 25cm (10in), S 20cm (8in). Has masses of small, double, soft apricot flowers in summer.

B. manicata (illus. p.295). Evergreen, erect, rhizomatous begonia. H 60cm (24in), S 30–40cm (12–16in). Bears large, oval, brown-mottled, green leaves and, below each leaf base, a collar of stiff, red hairs around leaf stalk. Produces single, pale pink flowers in very early spring. Propagate by plantlets during growing season. **'Crispa'** (syn *B.m.* 'Cristata'; illus. p.295) has deeper pink flowers and light green leaves with crested margins. **'Cristata'** see *B.m.* 'Crispa'.

B. martiana. See *B. gracilis* var. *martiana*.

B. masoniana, syn. *B.* 'Iron Cross' (Iron cross begonia; illus. p.295). Evergreen, creeping, rhizomatous begonia. H 45–60cm (18–24in), S 30–45cm (12–18in). Bears oval, toothed, rough, bright green leaves, 15cm (6in) long, with tapering tips and cross-shaped, black or dark brown centres. Has single, pink-flushed, white flowers during summer.

B. mazae. Evergreen, trailing, rhizomatous begonia. H to 23cm (9in), S indefinite. Bears rounded, red-veined, bronze-green leaves and in early spring fragrant, single, red-spotted, pink flowers. Is good for a hanging basket.

B. 'Merry Christmas' (syn. *B.* 'Ruhrtal'; illus. p.295). Rex-cultorum begonia. H and S 25–30cm (10–12in). Has satiny, red leaves, 15–20cm (6–8in) long, each with an outer, broad band of emerald-green and a

deep velvet-red centre, sometimes edged with grey.

B. metallica (Metal-leaf begonia; illus. p.295). Evergreen, shrub-like begonia. H 50cm–1.2m (20in–4ft), S 45cm (18in). Bears white-haired stems and oval, toothed, silver-haired, bronze-green leaves, 18cm (7in) long, with dark green veins, red beneath. Has single, pink flowers, with red bristles, in summer-autumn.

B. 'Oliver Twist' (illus. p.295). Evergreen, creeping, rhizomatous begonia. H 45–60cm (18–24in), S 25–45cm (10–18in). Oval leaves are pale to mid-green, to 30cm (12in) long, with heavily crested edges. Has single, pink flowers in early spring.

B. olsoniae (illus. p.295). Evergreen, compact, shrub-like begonia. H 23–30cm (9–12in), S 30cm (12in). Rounded, satiny, bronze-green leaves have cream veins. Bears single, very pale pink flowers, year-round, on arching, 30cm (12in) long stems.

B. 'Orange Cascade'. See *B.* 'Apricot Cascade'.

B. 'Orange Rubra' (illus. p.295). Slow-growing, evergreen, cane-stemmed begonia. H 50cm (20in), S 45cm (18in). Oval leaves are light green. Produces abundant clusters of single, orange flowers all year.

B. 'Organdy' (illus. p.295). Weather-resistant Semperflorens begonia. H and S 15cm (6in). Has rounded, waxy, green-bronze leaves and pink, red or white flowers throughout summer until autumn frosts.

B. 'Orpha C. Fox' (illus. p.295). Evergreen, cane-stemmed begonia. H 1m (3ft), S 30cm (1ft). Oval, silver-spotted, olive-green leaves, 15cm (6in) long, are maroon beneath. Produces large clusters of single, bright pink flowers year-round.

B. paulensis. Evergreen, creeping, rhizomatous begonia. H and S 25–30cm (10–12in). Erect stems bear rounded, mid-green leaves, 15cm (6in) long, with 'seersucker' surfaces criss-crossed with a spider's web of veins. Produces single, cream-white flowers, with wine-coloured hairs, in late spring.

B. 'Président Carnot'. Vigorous, evergreen, cane-stemmed begonia. H to 2.2m (7ft), S 45cm (1½ft). Erect stems bear 28cm (11in) long, 'angelwing', green leaves, with lighter spots. Produces large panicles of single, pink flowers, each 4cm (1½in) across, year-round.

B. 'Princess of Hanover'. Rex-cultorum begonia. H and S 25–30cm (10–12in). Has spirally twisted, deep green leaves, 20cm (8in) long, with bands of silver edged with ruby-red; entire leaf surfaces are covered with fine, pink hairs.

B. prismatocarpa (illus. p.295). Evergreen, creeping, rhizomatous begonia. H 15–20cm (6–8in), S 20–25cm (8–10in). Leaves are oval, lobed, light green and less than 8cm (3in) long. Produces single, bright yellow flowers year-round. Needs 60–65% relative humidity.

B. pustulata. Evergreen, creeping, rhizomatous begonia. H 15–20cm (6–8in), S 20–25cm (8–10in). Bears oval, fine-haired, dark green leaves,

with small blisters or pustules, and single, rose-pink flowers in summer. Prefers min. 22–4°C (72–5°F) and 70–75% relative humidity. **'Argentea'** (syn. *B.* 'Silver'; illus. p.295) has silver-splashed leaves and creamy-white flowers.
B. 'Red Ascot' (illus. p.295). Semperflorens begonia. H and S 15cm (6in). Has rounded, emerald-green leaves and masses of crimson-red flowers in summer.
B. rex. Rhizomatous begonia, the parent of the Rex-cultorum begonias. H 25cm (10in), S 30cm (12in). Has 20–25cm (8–10in) long, heart-shaped, deep green leaves, with a metallic sheen zoned silvery-white above. Produces pink flowers in winter.
B. 'Roy Hartley' (illus. p.295). Upright Tuberhybrida begonia. H 60cm (2ft), S 45cm (18in). In summer, bears double, salmon-coloured flowers, with soft pink tinge. Colour depth depends on light intensity. Has few side shoots.
B. 'Ruhrtal'. See *B.* 'Merry Christmas'.
B. scharffii, syn. *B. haageana* (illus. p.295). Evergreen, shrub-like begonia. H 60cm–1.2m (2–4ft), S 60cm (2ft). Stems are often covered with white hairs. Has oval, fine-haired, dark metallic-green leaves, 28cm (11in) long, with very tapered tips and reddish-green undersides. Produces single, pinkish-white flowers, each with a pink beard, from autumn to summer.
B. 'Scherzo'. Evergreen, creeping, rhizomatous begonia. H 25–30cm (10–12in), S 30–35cm (12–14in). Oval leaves are small, highly serrated and yellow with black marks. Bears single, white flowers in early spring.
B. serratipetala (illus. p.295). Evergreen, trailing, shrub-like begonia. H and S 45cm (18in). Obliquely oval leaves are highly serrated and bronze-green, with raised, deep pink spots. Produces mostly female, single, deep pink flowers intermittently throughout the year. Prefers 60% relative humidity, but with fairly dry roots.
B. 'Silver'. See *B. pustulata* 'Argentea'.
B. 'Silver Helen Teupel'. Rex-cultorum begonia. H and S 30–35cm (12–14in). Has long, deeply cut, silver leaves, each with a glowing pink centre, giving a feathered effect.
B. stipulacea, syn. *B. angularis,* *B. disticha, B. zebrina.* Evergreen, cane-stemmed begonia. H 60cm–1.2m (2–4ft), S 30cm (1ft). Bears well-branched, angular stems and oval, wavy-edged, 20cm (8in) long, grey-green leaves, with silver-grey veins, pale green beneath. Single, white flowers are produced in winter-spring.
B. 'Sugar Candy'. Tuberhybrida begonia. H 60cm (24in), S 45cm (18in). Leaves are mid-green. Produces double, clear pink flowers in summer.
B. sutherlandii (illus. p.295). Trailing, tuberous begonia. H 1m (3ft), S indefinite. Slender stems carry small, lance-shaped, lobed, bright green leaves, with red veins, and, in summer, loose clusters of single, orange flowers in profusion. In late autumn, leaves and stems collapse prior to winter dormancy. Makes an excellent hanging-

502

basket plant. Is particularly susceptible to mildew.
B. 'Thurstonii' (illus. p.295). Evergreen, shrub-like begonia. H to 1.2m (4ft), S 45cm (1½ft). Has rounded to oval, smooth, glossy, bronze-green leaves, with dark red veins, and, in summer, bears single, pink flowers.
B. 'Tiger Paws' (illus. p.295). Evergreen, creeping, rhizomatous begonia. H 15cm (6in), S 25–30cm (10–12in). Small, rounded, striking bright green leaves, with yellow and brown splashes, have bristly, white hairs on the margins. Many clusters of small, white flowers are carried well above the foliage in spring.
B. versicolor. Evergreen, creeping, rhizomatous begonia. H 15cm (6in), S 15–30cm (6–12in). Produces broadly oval or oblong, velvety leaves, 8cm (3in) long, in shades of mahogany, apple-green and maroon, and, in spring-summer, single, salmon-pink flowers. Provide min. 16–19°C (61–6°F) with 65–70% relative humidity.
B. × weltoniensis. See *B.* 'Weltoniensis'.
B. 'Weltoniensis', syn. *B. × weltoniensis.* (Mapleleaf begonia; illus. p.295). Semi-tuberous begonia with a shrub-like habit. H 30–50cm (12–20in), S 30cm (12in). Has small, oval, long-pointed, toothed, dark green leaves. Heads of 5–8 single, pink or white flowers appear from leaf axils in summer.
B. xanthina. Evergreen, bushy, creeping, rhizomatous begonia. H 25–30cm (10–12in), S 30–35cm (12–14in). Bears oval, dark green leaves, 15–23cm (6–9in) long, with yellow veins, purple and hairy beneath. Pendent, single, orange-yellow flowers are borne in summer. Provide min. 21–4°C (70–75°F) with 75% relative humidity.
B. zebrina. See *B. stipulacea.*

Begonia
  Angelwing. See *Begonia coccinea.*
  Christmas. See *Begonia* 'Gloire de Lorraine'.
  Eyelash. See *Begonia bowerae,* illus. p.295.
  Fuchsia. See *Begonia fuchsioides.*
  Iron cross. See *Begonia masoniana,* illus. p.295.
  Lorraine. See *Begonia* 'Gloire de Lorraine'.
  Mapleleaf. See *Begonia dregei;* *Begonia* 'Weltoniensis', illus. p.295.
  Metal-leaf. See *Begonia metallica,* illus. p.295.
  Watermelon. See *Elatostema repens,* illus. p.303.

BELAMCANDA

IRIDACEAE

Genus of summer-flowering bulbs, grown for their iris-like flowers. Protect in cold winters at the limits of their range. Needs sun and well-drained, humus-rich soil. Propagate by seed in spring.
B. chinensis (Blackberry lily).

Summer-flowering bulb. H 45cm–1m (1½–3ft), S 15–25cm (6–10in). Carries a fan of sword-shaped, semi-erect leaves. A loosely branched stem bears a succession of flattish, orange-red flowers, 4–5cm (1½–2in) across, with darker blotches. Seeds are shiny and blackberry-like.

Bell
  Canterbury. See *Campanula medium.*
  Silver. See *Halesia.*
  Spring. See *Olsynium douglasii.*
Bell heather. See *Erica cinerea.*
Belladonna lily. See *Amaryllis belladonna,* illus. p.408.

BELLEVALIA

HYACINTHACEAE/LILIACEAE

Genus of spring-flowering bulbs, similar to *Muscari,* but with longer, more tubular flowers. Some species have ornamental value, but most are uninteresting horticulturally. Needs an open, sunny position and well-drained soil that dries out in summer. Propagate by seed, preferably in autumn.
B. hyacinthoides, syn. *Strangweja spicata,* illus. p.432.
B. paradoxa of gardens. See *B. pycnantha.*
B. pycnantha, syn. *B. paradoxa* of gardens, *Muscari paradoxum* of gardens, *M. pycnantha.* Spring-flowering bulb. H to 40cm (16in), S 5–8cm (2–3in). Has strap-shaped, semi-erect, basal, greyish-green leaves. Tubular, deep dusky-blue flowers, 0.5cm (¼in) long and with yellow tips, appear in a dense, conical spike.

Bellflower. See *Campanula.*
  Bearded. See *Campanula barbata,* illus. p.356.
  Canary Island. See *Canarina canariensis,* illus.p.219.
  Chilean. See *Lapageria rosea,* illus. p.210.
  Chimney. See *Campanula pyramidalis.*
  Gland. See *Adenophora.*
  Nettle-leaved. See *Campanula trachelium,* illus. p.252.
Bell-flowered cherry. See *Prunus campanulata.*

BELLIS

Daisy

ASTERACEAE/COMPOSITAE

Genus of perennials, some grown as biennials for spring bedding. Grow in sun or semi-shade and in fertile, very well-drained soil. Dead-head regularly. Propagate by seed in early summer or by division after flowering.
B. perennis (Common daisy). Stoloniferous, carpeting perennial. Cultivars are grown as biennials. H and S 15–20cm (6–8in). All have inversely lance-shaped to spoon-shaped, mid-green leaves and semi-double to fully double flower heads in spring. Large-flowered (flower heads to 8cm/3in) wide) and miniature-flowered (flower heads to 2½cm/1in) wide) cultivars are available. **Habanera Series**

cultivars bear long-petalled, pink, white or red flower heads, to 6cm (2.5in) across, in early summer. **Pomponette Series** (illus. p.327) cultivars bear double, pink, white or red flower heads, to 4cm (1½in) across, with quilled petals. **Roggli Series** cultivars flower early and prolifically, with semi-double, red, rose-pink, salmon-pink or white flower heads, to 3cm (1¼in) across. **Tasso Series** cultivars have double, pink, white or red flower heads, to 6cm (2½in) across, with quilled petals.

Bells
  Fairy. See *Disporum.*
  Temple. See *Smithiantha cinnabarina.*
  Yellow. See *Tecoma stans,* illus. p.96.
Bells of Ireland. See *Moluccella laevis,* illus. p.335.
Bellwort. See *Uvularia grandiflora,* illus. p.274.
Beloperone guttata. See *Justicia brandegeeana.*
Benjamin. See *Lindera benzoin,* illus. p.131.
Bentham's cornel. See *Cornus capitata.*

BERBERIDOPSIS

FLACOURTIACEAE

Genus of one species of evergreen, woody-stemmed, twining climber. Dislikes strong winds and strong sun and is best grown in a north or west aspect. Soil, preferably lime-free, should be moist but well-drained. Cut out dead growth in spring; train to required shape. Propagate by seed in spring or by stem cuttings or layering in late summer or autumn.
B. corallina illus. p.211.

BERBERIS

Barberry

BERBERIDACEAE

Genus of deciduous, semi-evergreen or evergreen, spiny shrubs, grown mainly for their rounded to cup-shaped flowers, with usually yellow sepals and petals, and for their fruits. The evergreens are also cultivated for their leaves, the deciduous shrubs for their colourful autumn foliage. Requires sun or semi-shade and any but waterlogged soil. Propagate species by seed in autumn, deciduous hybrids and cultivars by softwood or semi-ripe cuttings in summer, evergreen hybrids and cultivars by semi-ripe cuttings in summer. All parts may cause mild stomach upset if ingested; contact with the spines may irritate skin. Many *Berberis* are an alternate host of wheat rust. Their cultivation is prohibited in Canada.
B. aggregata. Deciduous, bushy shrub. H and S 1.5m (5ft). Oblong to oval, mid-green leaves redden in autumn. Dense clusters of pale yellow flowers appear in late spring or early summer and are followed by egg-shaped, white-bloomed, red fruits. Zone 7.
B. buxifolia. Semi-evergreen or deciduous, arching shrub. H 2.5m (8ft), S 3m (10ft). Has oblong to oval, spine-tipped, leathery, dark green leaves. Deep orange-yellow flowers appear

from early to mid-spring and are followed by spherical, black fruits with a white bloom. Zone 5b.

B. calliantha. Evergreen, bushy shrub. H and S 1–1.5m (3–5ft). Has oblong, sharply spiny, glossy, green leaves, white beneath, and large, pale yellow flowers in late spring, followed by egg-shaped, black fruits with a white bloom. Zone 8.

B. candidula. Evergreen, bushy, compact shrub. H and S 1m (3ft). Leaves are narrowly oblong, glossy, dark green, white beneath. Has bright yellow flowers in late spring, then egg-shaped, blue-purple fruits. Zone 7.

B. × carminea 'Barbarossa' illus. p.148. **'Pirate King'** is a deciduous, arching shrub. H 2m (6ft), S 3m (10ft). Bears oblong, dark green leaves. In late spring and early summer produces clusters of yellow flowers, followed by spherical, pale red fruits. Zone 7.

B. 'Chenault'. See B. 'Chenaultii'.
B. 'Chenaultii', syn. B. 'Chenault'. Evergreen, bushy shrub. H 1.5m (5ft), S 2m (6ft). Narrowly oblong, wavy-edged, glossy, dark green leaves set off golden-yellow flowers in late spring and early summer. Bears egg-shaped, blue-black fruits. Zone 7.

B. coxii. Evergreen, bushy, dense shrub. H 2m (6ft), S 3m (10ft). Produces narrowly oval, glossy, dark green leaves with white undersides and, in late spring, yellow flowers. Egg-shaped, blue-black fruits have a grey-blue bloom. Zone 8.

B. darwinii illus. p.117.
B. empetrifolia illus. p.157.
B. gagnepainii var. *lanceifolia* illus. p.131.

B. jamesiana. Vigorous, deciduous, arching shrub. H and S 4m (12ft). Yellow flowers in late spring are followed by pendent racemes of spherical, red berries. Oval, dark green leaves redden in autumn. Zone 8.

B. julianae illus. p.134.
B. linearifolia 'Orange King' illus. p.135.

B. × lologensis. Vigorous, evergreen, arching shrub. H 3m (10ft), S 5m (15ft). Has broadly oblong, glossy, dark green leaves. Profuse clusters of orange flowers are borne from mid- to late spring. Zone 7. **'Stapehill'** illus. p.135.

B. × ottawensis 'Purpurea'. See B. × o. 'Superba'. **'Superba'** (syn. B. × o. 'Purpurea') is a deciduous, arching shrub. H and S 2.5m (8ft). Produces rounded to oval, deep reddish-purple leaves. Bears small, red-tinged, yellow flowers in late spring, then egg-shaped, red fruits in autumn. Zone 5.

B. 'Park Jewel'. See B. 'Parkjuweel'.
B. 'Parkjuweel', syn. B. 'Park Jewel'. Semi-evergreen, bushy, rounded shrub. H and S 1m (3ft). Leaves are oval, glossy and bright green; some turn red in autumn. Flowers are of little value. Zone 7.

B. polyantha of gardens. See B. prattii.
B. prattii, syn. B. polyantha of gardens. Deciduous, bushy shrub. H and S 3m (10ft). Has oblong, glossy, dark green leaves. Large clusters of small, yellow flowers in late summer are followed by a profusion of long-lasting, egg-shaped, coral-pink fruits. Zone 7.

B. × rubrostilla. See B. 'Rubrostilla'.

B. 'Rubrostilla', syn. B. × *rubrostilla*, illus. p.172.
B. sargentiana. Evergreen, bushy shrub. H and S 2m (6ft). Leaves are oblong, glossy, bright green. Yellow flowers produced in late spring and early summer are succeeded by egg-shaped, blue-black fruits. Zone 8.
B. × stenophylla illus. p.135. **'Corallina Compacta'** illus. p.350.
B. thunbergii. Deciduous, arching, dense shrub. H 2m (6ft), S 3m (10ft). Broadly oval, pale to mid-green leaves turn brilliant orange-red in autumn. Small, red-tinged, pale yellow flowers appear in mid-spring, followed by egg-shaped, bright red fruits. Zone 4. f. *atropurpurea* illus. p.131. **'Atropurpurea Nana'** (syn. *B.t.* 'Crimson Pygmy'), H and S 60cm (24in), bears reddish-purple foliage. **'Aurea'** illus. p.170. **'Crimson Pygmy'** see *B.t.* 'Atropurpurea Nana'. Upright branches of **'Erecta'** spread with age. **'Golden Ring'** has purple leaves narrowly margined with golden-yellow, turning red in autumn, and produces red fruit. All zone 4. **'Rose Glow'** has reddish-purple leaves marbled with pink and white.
B. verruculosa illus. p.134.
B. wilsoniae. Deciduous or semi-evergreen, bushy shrub. H 1m (3ft), S 1.5m (5ft). Narrowly oblong, grey-green leaves turn bright orange-red in autumn. In late spring and early summer has yellow flowers, then showy, spherical, coral-red fruits. Zone 7.

BERCHEMIA

RHAMNACEAE

Genus of deciduous, twining climbers, grown for their leaves and fruit. Is useful for covering walls, fences and tree stumps. Grow in sun or shade, in any well-drained soil. Propagate by seed in autumn or spring, by semi-ripe cuttings in summer or by layering or root cuttings in winter.

B. racemosa 'Variegata'. Deciduous, twining climber. H 5m (15ft) or more. Has heart-shaped, green leaves, 3–8cm (1¼–3in) long and paler beneath, that are variegated creamy-white. Small, bell-shaped, greenish-white flowers in summer, are followed by rounded, green fruits that turn red, then black. Zone 7.

Bergamot. See *Monarda*.

BERGENIA,
syn. MEGASEA
Elephant's ears, pigsqueek

SAXIFRAGACEAE

Genus of evergreen perennials with thick, usually large, rounded to oval or spoon-shaped, leathery leaves, with indented veins, that make ideal ground cover. Tolerates sun or shade and any well-drained soil, but leaf colour is best on poor soil and in full sun. Propagate by division in spring after flowering.

B. 'Abendglut', syn. B. 'Evening Glow'. Evergreen, clump-forming perennial. H 23cm (9in), S 30cm (12in). Bears rosettes of oval, crinkled, short-stemmed, maroon leaves, from which arise racemes of open cup-

shaped, semi-double, deep magenta flowers in spring.
B. 'Ballawley'. Evergreen, clump-forming perennial. H and S 60cm (24in). Large, rounded to oval, flat, deep green leaves turn red in winter. Racemes of cup-shaped, bright crimson flowers are borne on red stems in spring. Shelter from cold winds.
B. beesiana. See B. purpurascens.
B. ciliata illus. p.269.
B. cordifolia. Evergreen, clump-forming perennial. H 45cm (18in), S 60cm (24in). Leaves are rounded, puckered and crinkle-edged. Produces racemes of open cup-shaped, light pink flowers in spring.
'Purpurea' illus. p.269.
B. crassifolia. Evergreen, clump-forming perennial. H 30cm (12in), S 45cm (18in). Has oval- or spoon-shaped, fleshy, flat leaves that turn mahogany in winter. Bears spikes of open cup-shaped, lavender-pink flowers in spring.
B. 'Evening Glow'. See B. 'Abendglut'.
B. 'Morgenröte', syn. B. 'Morning Red'. Evergreen, clump-forming perennial. H 45cm (18in), S 30cm (12in). Leaves are rounded, crinkled and deep green. Spikes of open cup-shaped, deep carmine flowers in spring are often followed by a second crop in summer.
B. 'Morning Red'. See B. 'Morgenröte'.
B. purpurascens, syn. B. beesiana. Evergreen, clump-forming perennial. H 45cm (18in), S 30cm (12in). Oval to spoon-shaped, flat, dark green leaves turn beetroot-red in late autumn. In spring bears racemes of open cup-shaped, rich red flowers.
B. × schmidtii. Evergreen, clump-forming perennial. H 30cm (12in), S 60cm (24in). Oval, flat leaves have toothed margins. Sprays of open cup-shaped, soft pink flowers are borne in early spring on short stems.
B. 'Silberlicht', syn. B. 'Silver Light', illus. p.268.
B. 'Silver Light'. See B. 'Silberlicht'.
B. stracheyi. Evergreen, clump-forming perennial. H 23cm (9in), S 30cm (12in). Small, rounded, flat leaves form neat rosettes, among which nestle heads of open cup-shaped, white or pink flowers in spring.
B. 'Sunningdale'. Evergreen, clump-forming perennial. H 60cm (24in), S 30cm (12in). Rounded, slightly crinkled, deep green leaves are mahogany beneath. Bears racemes of open cup-shaped, lilac-carmine flowers on red stalks in spring.

BERKHEYA

ASTERACEAE/COMPOSITAE

Genus of summer-flowering perennials. In mild areas, grow most species against a south- or west-facing wall. Needs full sun and fertile, well-drained soil. Sow seed in autumn or divide in spring.
B. macrocephala illus. p.258.

Berlin poplar. See *Populus* × *berolinensis*.
Berry bladder fern. See *Cystopteris*

bulbifera.

BERTOLONIA

MELASTOMATACEAE

Genus of evergreen perennials, grown for their foliage. Tender, min. 15°C (59°F) but preferably warmer. Requires a fairly shaded position and high humidity, although soil should not be waterlogged. Propagate by tip or leaf cuttings in spring or summer.
B. marmorata. Evergreen, rosette-forming perennial. H 15cm (6in) or more in flower, S 45cm (18in). Broadly oval, slightly fleshy leaves have heart-shaped bases, silvery midribs and puckered surfaces, and are reddish-purple below, velvety green above. Intermittently produces spikes of saucer-shaped, pinkish-purple flowers.

BERZELIA

BRUNIACEAE

Genus of evergreen, heather-like, summer-flowering shrubs, grown for their flowers. Tender, min. 7°C (45°F). Requires full sun and well-drained, neutral to acid soil. Water containerized plants moderately, less when not in full growth. Plants may be cut back lightly after flowering. Propagate by seed in spring or by semi-ripe cuttings in late summer.
B. lanuginosa. Evergreen, erect shrub with soft-haired, young shoots. H and S to 1m (3ft). Has small, heather-like leaves. Compact, spherical heads of tiny, creamy-white flowers are carried in dense, terminal clusters in summer.

BESCHORNERIA

AGAVACEAE

Genus of perennial succulents with narrowly lance-shaped leaves forming erect, almost stemless, basal rosettes. Tender, min. 7°C (45°F). Needs full sun and very well-drained soil. Propagate by seed or division in spring or summer.
B. yuccoides illus. p.465.

Besom heath. See *Erica scoparia*.

BESSERA

ALLIACEAE/LILIACEAE

Genus of summer-flowering bulbs, grown for their striking, brightly coloured flowers. Needs an open, sunny situation and well-drained soil. Propagate by seed in spring. Overwinter indoors.
B. elegans (Coral drops). Summer-flowering bulb. H to 60cm (24in), S 8–10cm (3–4in). Has long, narrow, erect, basal leaves. Each leafless stem bears pendent, bell-shaped, bright red flowers on long, slender stalks.

Betonica officinalis. See *Stachys officinalis*.
Betony. See *Stachys officinalis*.

BETULA
Birch

BETULACEAE

Genus of deciduous trees and shrubs, grown for their bark and autumn colour. Needs sun and moist but well-drained soil; some species prefer acid soil. Transplant young trees in autumn. Propagate by grafting in late winter or by softwood cuttings in early summer. May be subject to leaf-miner, borer, and crown die-back.

B. albosinensis illus. p.74.

B. alleghaniensis, syn. *B. lutea* (Yellow birch). Deciduous, upright, open tree, often multi-stemmed. H 12m (40ft) or more, S 3m (10ft). Smooth, glossy, golden-brown bark peels in thin shreds. Oval, mid- to pale green leaves rapidly turn gold in autumn. Bears yellow-green catkins in spring. Zone 3b.

B. ermanii illus. p.72.

B. jacquemontii. See *B. utilis* var. *jacquemontii*.

B. lutea. See *B. alleghaniensis*.

B. maximowicziana (Monarch birch). Fast-growing, deciduous, broad-headed tree. H 18m (60ft), S 3m (10ft). Has orange-brown or pink bark, and racemes of yellowish catkins in spring. Large, oval, mid-green leaves turn bright butter-yellow in autumn. Zone 7.

B. nana illus. p.349.

B. nigra (river birch). Conical tree that grows well in wetter soils. H 18m (60ft). Cinnamon-brown bark peels in layers, even on young trees. Yellow fall colour. 'Heritage' has white to pale salmon young bark that darkens to a rusty-brown with age. Resistant to leaf miners and bronze birch borer. Zone 3.

B. papyrifera illus. p.72.

B. pendula (European white birch). Deciduous, broadly columnar or conical, graceful tree. H 25m (80ft) or more, S 10m (30ft). Has slender, drooping shoots and silver-white bark that becomes black and rugged at base of trunk with age. Yellow-brown catkins appear in spring. Oval, bright green leaves turn yellow in autumn. Zone 2. 'Dalecarlica' has a more upright habit, with pendant, shorter shoots at the end of the branches, and much more deeply cut leaves. Zone 2. 'Laciniata' has a narrow crown. 'Tristis' illus. p.73. 'Youngii' illus. p.92.

B. platyphylla var. *szechuanica*. See *B. szechuanica*.

B. szechuanica, syn. *B. platyphylla* var. *szechuanica* (Szechuan birch). Vigorous, deciduous, open tree with stiff branches. H 14m (46ft), S 2.5m (8ft). Bark is strikingly chalky-white when mature. Has triangular to oval, serrated, leathery, deep green leaves that turn brilliant gold in autumn. Bears yellow-green catkins in spring. Zone 7b.

B. utilis (Himalayan birch). Deciduous, upright, open tree. H 18m (60ft), S 10m (30ft). Paper-thin, peeling bark varies from creamy-white to dark copper-brown. Yellow-brown catkins are borne in spring. Oval, mid-green leaves, hairy beneath when young, turn golden-yellow in autumn. Zone 3.
var. *jacquemontii* (syn *B. jacquemontii*) illus. p.83.

Bhutan pine. See *Pinus wallichiana*, illus. p.103.

BIARUM

ARACEAE

Genus of mainly autumn-flowering, tuberous perennials with tiny flowers carried on a pencil-shaped spadix, enclosed within a tubular spathe. Upper part of spathe is hooded or flattened out and showy. In winter protect in a cold frame or greenhouse. Needs a sunny position and well-drained soil. Dry out tubers when dormant in summer. Propagate in autumn by seed or offsets.

B. eximium. Early autumn-flowering, tuberous perennial. H and S 8–10cm (3–4in). Lance-shaped, semi-erect, basal leaves follow stemless, tubular, velvety, blackish-maroon spathe, up to 15cm (6in) long and often lying flat on ground. Upper part is flattened out. Spadix is upright and black.

B. tenuifolium illus. p.439.

BIDENS

ASTERACEAE/COMPOSITAEE

Genus of annuals, perennials and shrubs grown for their spreading habit and summer flowers. Tender, min. 5ºC (41ºF). Requires fertile, well drained soil in full sun. Propagate by seed in spring or stem cuttings in fall or early spring from plants over-wintered indoors.

B. atrosanguinea. See Cosmos atrosanguinea

B. ferulifera. Spreading, short-lived perennial usually treated as an annual. H 30cm (12in) S indefinite. Grown for its finely divided bright green foliage and golden yellow, single flowers freely produced. Good for baskets and planters.

Big tree. See *Sequoiadendron giganteum*, illus. p.102.

Big-cone pine. See *Pinus coulteri*, illus. p.102.

BIGNONIA
Cross vine

BIGNONIACEAE

Genus of one species of evergreen, tendril climber. In cool areas may lose its leaves in winter. Needs sun and fertile soil to flower well. If necessary, prune in spring. Propagate by stem cuttings in summer or autumn or by layering in winter.

B. capensis. See *Tecoma capensis*.

B. capreolata, syn. *Doxantha capreolata* (Cross vine, Trumpet flower). Evergreen, tendril climber. H 10m (30ft) or more. Each leaf has 2 narrowly oblong leaflets and a branched tendril. In summer, funnel-shaped, reddish-orange flowers appear in clusters in leaf axils. Pea-pod-shaped fruits, to 15cm (6in) long, are produced in autumn. Zone 7.

B. grandiflora. See *Campsis grandiflora*.

B. jasminoides. See *Pandorea jasminoides*.

B. pandorana. See *Pandorea pandorana*.

B. radicans. See *Campsis radicans*.

B. stans. See *Tecoma stans*.

Bilberry. See *Vaccinium myrtillus*.

Bilderdykia. Reclassified as *Fallopia*.

BILLARDIERA

PITTOSPORACEAE

Genus of evergreen, woody-stemmed, twining climbers, grown mainly for their fruits. Grow in any well-drained soil, in a sheltered position and partial shade. Propagate by seed in spring or stem cuttings in summer or autumn.

B. longiflora illus. p.218.

BILLBERGIA

BROMELIACEAE

Genus of evergreen, rosette-forming perennials, grown for their flowers and foliage. Tender, min. 5–7°C (41–5°F). Requires semi-shade and well-drained soil, ideally adding sphagnum moss or plastic chips used for orchid culture. Water moderately when in full growth, sparingly at other times. Propagate by division or offsets after flowering or in late spring.

B. nutans (Queen's tears; illus. p.265). Evergreen, clump-forming, tubular-rosetted perennial. H and S to 40cm (16in). Strap-shaped leaves are usually dark green. In spring, pendent clusters of tubular, purple-blue-edged, lime-green flowers emerge from pink bracts.

B. rhodocyanea. See *Aechmea fasciata*.

B. × windii (Angel's tears). Evergreen, clump-forming, tubular-rosetted perennial. H and S to 40cm (16in). Is similar to *B. nutans*, but produces broader, spreading, grey-green leaves and larger bracts. Flowers intermittently from spring to autumn.

Biota orientalis. See *Thuja orientalis*.

Birch. See *Betula*.
  Arctic. See *Betula nana*, illus. p.349.
  Canoe. See *Betula papyrifera*, illus. p.72.
  Chinese paper. See *Betula albosinensis*, illus. p.74.
  European white. See *Betula pendula*.
  Himalayan. See *Betula utilis*.
  Monarch. See *Betula maximowicziana*.
  Paper. See *Betula papyrifera*, illus. p.72.
  Szechuan. See *Betula szechuanica*.
  Weeping. See *Betula pendula* 'Tristis', illus. p.73.
  White-barked Himalayan. See *Betula utilis* var. *jacquemontii*, illus. p.83.
  Yellow. See *Betula alleghaniensis*.
  Young's weeping. See *Betula pendula* 'Youngii', illus. p.92.

Bird cherry. See *Prunus padus*, illus. p.76.
  Virginian. See *Prunus virginiana*.

Bird's-eye primrose. See *Primula farinosa*, illus. p.272.

Bird's-foot ivy. See *Hedera helix* 'Pedata', illus. p.221.

Bird's-foot violet. See *Viola pedata*, illus. p.369.

Bird's-nest bromeliad. See *Nidularium innocentii*.

Bird's-nest fern. See *Asplenium nidus*, illus. p.313.

Bird-catcher tree. See *Pisonia umbellifera*.

Bird-of-paradise flower. See *Strelitzia*.

Birthroot. See *Trillium erectum*, illus. p.269.

Bishop pine. See *Pinus muricata*, illus. p.103.

Bishop's cap. See *Astrophytum myriostigma*, illus. p.466.

Bishop's mitre. See *Astrophytum myriostigma*, illus. p.466.

Bishop's weed, Variegated. See *Aegopodium podagraria* 'Variegatum', illus. p.276.

Bistort. See *Persicaria bistorta*.

Biting stonecrop. See *Sedum acre*, illus. p.384.

Bitter cress. See *Cardamine*.

Bitter orange, Japanese. See *Poncirus trifoliata*.

Bitter root. See *Lewisia rediviva*, illus. pp.373 and 379.

Bitternut. See *Carya cordiformis*.

Bitternut hickory. See *Carya cordiformis*.

Bittersweet
  American. See *Celastrus scandens*.
  Oriental. See *Celastrus orbiculatus*.

Black alder. See *Alnus glutinosa*.

Black bamboo. See *Phyllostachys nigra*.

Black bean. See *Kennedia nigricans*.

Black bean tree. See *Castanospermum*.

Black cherry. See *Prunus serotina*, illus. p.65.

Black chokeberry. See *Aronia melanocarpa*, illus. p.136.

Black cottonwood. See *Populus trichocarpa*.

Black false hellebore. See *Veratrum nigrum*, illus. p.228.

Black gum. See *Nyssa sylvatica*, illus. p.71.

Black huckleberry. See *Gaylussacia baccata*.

Black Jack oak. See *Quercus marilandica*, illus. p.80.

Black mulberry. See *Morus nigra*.

Black oak. See *Quercus velutina*.

Black pine. See *Pinus jeffreyi*, illus. p.103; *Pinus nigra*.
  Japanese. See *Pinus thunbergii*, illus. p.106.

Black poplar. See *Populus nigra*.

Black sarana. See *Fritillaria camschatcensis*, illus. p.413.

Black spruce. See *Picea mariana*.

Black tree fern. See *Cyathea medullaris*.

Black walnut. See *Juglans nigra*, illus. p.67.

Black willow. See *Salix gracilistyla* 'Melanostachys'.

Blackberry. See *Rubus*.

Blackboy. See *Xanthorrhoea*.

Black-eyed Susan. See *Rudbeckia fulgida*; *Thunbergia alata*, illus. p.216.

Blackthorn. See *Prunus spinosa*.

Bladder cherry. See *Physalis alkekengi*.

Bladder nut. See *Staphylea*.

Bladder senna. See *Colutea arborescens*, illus. p.146.

Blanket flower. See *Gaillardia*.

Blazing star. See *Liatris*.

BLECHNUM
Hard fern
BLECHNACEAE

Genus of evergreen or semi-evergreen ferns. Hardy to tender, min. 5°C (41°F). Most species prefer semi-shade. Requires moist, neutral to acid soil. Remove fading fronds regularly. Propagate *B. penna-marina* by division in spring, other species by spores in late summer.

B. alpinum. See *B. penna-marina.*
B. chilense of gardens. See *B. tabulare.*
B. magellanicum. See *B. tabulare.*
B. penna-marina, syn. *B. alpinum,* illus. p.310.
B. spicant (Hard fern). Evergreen fern. H 30–75cm (12–30in), S 30–45cm (12–18in). Bears narrowly lance-shaped, indented, leathery, spreading, dark green fronds. Prefers shade and peaty or leafy soil.
B. tabulare, syn. *B. chilense* of gardens, *B. magellanicum.* Evergreen or semi-evergreen fern. H 30cm–1m (1–3ft), S 30–60cm (1–2ft). Outer, mid-green, sterile fronds are broadly lance-shaped, heavily indented and arranged symmetrically. Inner fertile fronds are brown and fringed.

Bleeding heart. See *Dicentra spectabilis,* illus. p.245.
Blessed Mary's thistle. See *Silybum marianum,* illus. p.322.

BLETILLA

See also ORCHIDS.
B. hyacinthina. See *B. striata.*
B. striata, syn. *B. hyacinthina* (illus. p.297). Deciduous, terrestrial orchid. H to 60cm (24in). In late spring or early summer bears magenta or white flowers, 3cm (1¼in) long, and broadly lance-shaped leaves, 50cm (20in) long. Needs shade in summer.

Blood flower. See *Asclepias curassavica; Scadoxus multiflorus* subsp. *katherinae,* illus.p.401.
Mexican. See *Distictis buccinatoria,* illus. p.204.
Blood leaf. See *Iresine lindenii.*
Blood lily. See *Haemanthus coccineus,* illus. p.435.
Bloodroot. See *Sanguinaria canadensis,* illus. p.363.
Bloody cranesbill. See *Geranium sanguineum,* illus. p.354.

BLOOMERIA
ALLIACEAE/LILIACEAE

Genus of onion-like, spring-flowering bulbs, with spherical flower heads on leafless stems, which die down in summer. Needs a sheltered, sunny situation and well-drained soil. Propagate by seed in autumn or by division in late summer or autumn.
B. crocea. Late spring-flowering bulb. H to 30cm (12in), S to 10cm (4in). Long, narrow, semi-erect, basal leaves die at flowering time. Each leafless stem carries a loose, spherical head, 10–15cm (4–6in) across, of star-shaped, dark-striped, yellow flowers.

Blue amaryllis. See *Worsleya.*
Blue Atlas cedar. See *Cedrus atlantica* f. *glauca,* illus. p.101.
Blue candle. See *Myrtillocactus geometrizans,* illus. p.456.
Blue cupidone. See *Catananche.*
Blue dawn flower. See *Ipomoea indica,* illus. p.205.
Blue Douglas fir. See *Pseudotsuga menziesii* var. *glauca,* illus. p.102.
Blue fan flower. See *Scaevola.*
Blue fescue. See *Festuca glauca.*
Blue flag. See *Iris versicolor,* illus. p.234.
Blue grama. See *Bouteloua gracilis,* illus. p.307.
Blue gum. See *Eucalyptus globulus.*
Blue holly. See *Ilex* x *meserveae.*
Blue lace flower. See *Trachymene coerulea.*
Blue marguerite. See *Felicia amelloides.*
Blue oat grass. See *Helictotrichon sempervirens,* illus. p.307.
Blue passion flower. See *Passiflora caerulea,* illus. p.214.
Blue poppy. See *Meconopsis betonicifolia,* illus. p.253; *M. grandis,* illus. p.253.
Blue potato bush. See *Solanum rantonnetii.*
Blue star. See *Amsonia.*
Blue trumpet vine. See *Thunbergia grandiflora.*
Bluebell. See *Hyacinthoides.*
  California. See *Phacelia campanularia,* illus. p.334.
  English. See *Hyacinthoides non-scripta,* illus. p.414.
  New Zealand. See *Wahlenbergia albomarginata.*
  Spanish. See *Hyacinthoides hispanica,* illus. p.414.
Bluebell creeper. See *Sollya.*
Blueberry
  Highbush. See *Vaccinium corymbosum,* illus. p.160.
  Low-bush. See *Vaccinium angustifolium* var. *laevifolium,* illus. p.172.
Blueberry ash. See *Elaeocarpus cyaneus.*
Bluebottle. See *Centaurea cyanus.*
Blue-flowered torch. See *Tillandsia lindenii,* illus. p.265.
Bluets, Creeping. See *Hedyotis michauxii,* illus. p.383.
Blushing bromeliad. See *Neoregelia carolinae; Nidularium fulgens.*
Blushing philodendron. See *Philodendron erubescens.*
Bo. See *Ficus religiosa.*
Boat lily. See *Tradescantia spathacea.*
Bocconia cordata. See *Macleaya cordata.*

BOENNINGHAUSENIA
RUTACEAE

Genus of one species of deciduous sub-shrub, usually with soft, herbaceous stems, grown for its foliage and flowers. Where hardy, cut to ground level in winter. Needs full sun and fertile, well-drained but not too dry soil. Propagate by softwood cuttings in summer or by seed in autumn.
B. albiflora. Deciduous, bushy sub-shrub. H and S 1m (3ft). Has pungent, mid-green leaves, divided into oval leaflets. Loose panicles of small,

cup-shaped, white flowers appear from mid-summer to early autumn. Zone 7.

Bog arum. See *Calla palustris,* illus. p.446.
Bog bean. See *Menyanthes trifoliata,* illus. p.446.
Bog pimpernel. See *Anagallis tenella.*
Bog sage. See *Salvia uliginosa.*

BOLAX
APIACEAE/UMBELLIFERAE

Genus of evergreen, hummock- and cushion-forming perennials, often included in *Azorella.* Is grown for its symmetrical rosettes of small, thick, tough leaves. Flowers only rarely in cultivation. Is suitable for gritty screes, troughs and alpine houses. Needs sun and humus-rich, well-drained soil. Propagate by rooting rosettes in summer.
B. gummifera illus. p.391.

BOMAREA
ALSTROEMERIACEAE/LILIACEAE

Genus of herbaceous or evergreen, tuberous-rooted, scrambling and twining climbers, grown for their tubular or bell-shaped flowers. Tender, min. 5°C (41°F). Grow in any well-drained soil and in full light. Water regularly in growing season, sparingly when dormant. Provide support. Cut out old flowering stems at ground level when leaves turn yellow. Propagate by seed or division in early spring.
B. andimarcana, syn. *B. pubigera* of gardens. Evergreen, scrambling climber with straight, slender stems. H 2–3m (6–10ft). Has lance-shaped leaves, white and hairy beneath. Bears nodding, tubular, green-tipped, pale yellow flowers, suffused pink, from early summer to autumn.
B. caldasii, syn. *B. kalbreyeri* of gardens, illus. p.217.
B. kalbreyeri of gardens. See *B. caldasii.*
B. pubigera of gardens. See *B. andimarcana.*

Bonin Isles juniper. See *Juniperus procumbens,* illus. p.110.
Borage. See *Borago.*

BORAGO
Borage
BORAGINACEAE

Genus of annuals and perennials, grown for culinary use as well as for their flowers. Requires sun and fertile, well-drained soil. For culinary use gather only young leaves. Propagate by seed sown outdoors in spring. Some species will self seed prolifically and may become invasive.
B. officinalis illus. p.334.

BORONIA
RUTACEAE

Genus of evergreen shrubs, grown primarily for their flowers. Tender, min. 7–10°C (45–50°F). Requires full light and sandy, neutral to acid soil. Water potted specimens moderately, less

when not in full growth. For a compact habit, shorten long stems after flowering. Propagate by seed in spring or by semi-ripe cuttings in late summer. Spider mite may be a problem.
B. megastigma illus. p.156.

Borzicactus. Reclassified as *Oreocereus.*
Bosnian pine. See *Pinus heldreichii,* illus. p.104.
Boston ivy. See *Parthenocissus tricuspidata,* illus. p.218.
Bottle, Brandy. See *Nuphar lutea,* illus. p.468.
Bottle plant. See *Hatiora salicornioides,* illus. p.468.
Bottlebrush. See *Callistemon.*
  Albany. See *Callistemon speciosus.*
  Granite. See *Melaleuca elliptica,* illus. p.142.
Bottlebrush buckeye. See *Aesculus parviflora,* illus. p.119.

BOUGAINVILLEA
NYCTAGINACEAE

Genus of deciduous or evergreen, woody-stemmed, scrambling climbers, grown for their showy floral bracts. Tender, min. 7–10°C (45–50°F). Grow in fertile, well-drained soil and in full light. Water moderately in the growing season; keep containerized plants almost dry when dormant. Tie to a support. Cut back previous season's lateral growths in spring, leaving 2–3cm (¾–1¼in) long spurs. Propagate by semi-ripe cuttings in summer or by hardwood cuttings when dormant. Whitefly and mealy bug may attack.
B. x buttiana. Vigorous, evergreen, woody-stemmed, scrambling climber. H 8–12m (25–40ft). Has ovate, mid-green leaves, to 8cm (3in) long, lighter below. Bears large clusters of strongly waved, golden-yellow, purple or red floral bracts from summer to autumn. **'California Gold'** see *B.* x *b.* 'Golden Glow'. **'Crimson Lake'** see *B.* x *b.* 'Mrs Butt'. Floral bracts of **'Golden Glow'** (syn. *B.* x *b.* 'California Gold') are orange-yellow; those of **'Mrs Butt'** (syn. *B.* x *b.* 'Crimson Lake') are crimson-magenta; and those of **'Scarlet Queen'** are scarlet.
B. 'Dania' illus. p.210.
B. glabra illus. p.214. **'Sanderiana'** see *B.g.* 'Variegata'. **'Snow White'** illus. p.207. **'Variegata'** (syn *B.g.* 'Sanderiana') illus. p.211.
B. 'Miss Manila', syn. *B.* 'Tango', illus. p.210.
B. spectabilis. Strong-growing, mainly evergreen, woody-stemmed, scrambling climber; stems usually have a few spines. H to 7m (22ft). Has elliptic to oval leaves and, in summer, large trusses of red-purple floral bracts.
B. 'Tango'. See *B.* 'Miss Manila'.

Boussingaultia basselloides of gardens. See *Anredera cordifolia.*

BOUTELOUA
GRAMINEAE/POACEAE

See also GRASSES, BAMBOOS, RUSHES and SEDGES.
B. gracilis, syn. *B. oligostachya,*

illus. p.307.
B. oligostachya. See *B. gracilis*.

BOUVARDIA

RUBIACEAE

Genus of deciduous, semi-evergreen or evergreen shrubs and perennials, grown for their flowers. Tender, min. 7–10°C (45–50°F), but 13–15°C (55–9°F) for winter-flowering species. Prefers full light and fertile, well-drained soil. Water freely when in full growth, moderately at other times. Cut back stems by half to three-quarters after flowering. Propagate by softwood cuttings in spring or by greenwood or semi-ripe cuttings in summer. Whitefly and mealy bug may be troublesome.
B. humboldtii. See *B. longiflora*.
B. longiflora, syn. *B. humboldtii*. Semi-evergreen, spreading shrub. H and S 1m (3ft) or more. Min. 13–15°C (55–9°F) until flowering ceases, then 7°C (45°F). Has lance-shaped leaves, and terminal clusters of fragrant, white flowers, with slender tubes and 4 petal lobes, from summer to early winter.
B. ternifolia, syn. *B. triphylla*, illus. p.173.
B. triphylla. See *B. ternifolia*.

Bower vine. See *Pandorea jasminoides*, illus. p.208.

BOWIEA

HYACINTHACEAE/LILIACEAE

Genus of summer-flowering, bulbous succulents with scrambling, branched, green stems that produce no proper leaves. Tender, min. 10°C (50°F). Needs sun and well-drained soil; plant with half of bulb above soil level. Support with sticks or canes. Propagate by seed, sown under glass in winter or spring. May produce offsets.
B. volubilis illus. p.460.

Bowles' golden sedge. See *Carex elata* 'Aurea', illus. p.309.

BOYKINIA

SAXIFRAGACEAE

Genus of mound-forming perennials. Most species require shade and humus-rich, moist but well-drained, acid soil. Propagate by division in spring or by seed in autumn.
B. aconitifolia. Mound-forming perennial. H 1m (3ft), S 15cm (6in). Has rounded to kidney-shaped, lobed leaves. In summer, flower stems carry very small, bell-shaped, white flowers.
B. jamesii, syn. *Telesonix jamesii*. Mound-forming, rhizomatous perennial. H and S 15cm (6in). Each woody stem bears a rosette of kidney-shaped leaves with lacerated edges. In early summer bears open bell-shaped, frilled, pink flowers with green centres.

Box. See *Buxus*.
  Balearic. See *Buxus balearica*, illus. p.153.
  Brisbane. See *Lophostemon confertus*.
Box (continued)

  Christmas. See *Sarcococca*.
  Common. See *Buxus sempervirens*.
  Himalayan. See *Buxus wallichiana*.
  Small-leaved. See *Buxus microphylla*.
  Sweet. See *Sarcococca*.
  Victorian. See *Pittosporum undulatum*.
Box elder. See *Acer negundo*.
Box-leaved holly. See *Ilex crenata*.
Bracelet honey myrtle. See *Melaleuca armillaris*.
Brachychilum horsfieldii. See *Hedychium horsfieldii*.

BRACHYCHITON

STERCULIACEAE

Genus of evergreen or deciduous, mainly spring- and summer-flowering trees, grown for their flowers and overall appearance. Tender, min. 7–10°C (45–50°F). Needs full light and humus-rich, well-drained, preferably acid soil. Water containerized plants moderately, much less in winter. Prune if needed. Propagate by seed in spring. Spider mite may be a nuisance.
B. acerifolius, syn. *Sterculia acerifolia*, illus. p.65.
B. populneus, syn. *Sterculia diversifolia* (Kurrajong). Evergreen, conical tree, pyramidal when young. H and S 15–20m (50–70ft). Pointed or 3–5-lobed, glossy, deep green leaves are chartreuse when young. In spring-summer has panicles of saucer-shaped, cream or greenish-white flowers with red, purple or yellow throats.

BRACHYGLOTTIS

ASTERACEAE/COMPOSITAE

Genus of evergreen shrubs and trees, grown for their bold foliage and daisy-like flower heads. Hardy to tender, min. 3°C (37°F). Needs full light or partial shade and well-drained soil. Water plants in containers freely in summer. Take semi-ripe cuttings in late summer.
B. compacta, syn. *Senecio compactus*. Evergreen, bushy, dense shrub. H 1m (3ft), S 2m (6ft). Bears small, oval, white-edged, dark green leaves, white below, and daisy-like, bright yellow flowers in clustered heads from mid- to late summer. Felt-like, white hairs cover the shoots. Zone 9.
B. Dunedin Hybrids, syn. *Senecio* Dunedin Hybrids, *S. greyi* of gardens, *S. laxifolius* of gardens. Spreading, bushy, mound-forming shrubs. H 1.5m (5ft), S 2m (6ft) or more. Leaves are obovate to elliptic, often wavy-margined, white-hairy, later hairless, and mid- to dark green. Loose, terminal panicles of bright yellow flower heads, with conspicuous ray florets, are produced from summer to autumn. Zone 9. **'Sunshine'** (syn. *Senecio* 'Sunshine') illus. p.170.
B. laxifolia, syn. *Senecio laxifolius*. Evergreen, bushy, spreading shrub. H 1m (3ft), S 2m (6ft). Oval, grey-white leaves become dark green. Has large clusters of daisy-like, golden-yellow flower heads in summer. Zone 9.
B. monroi, syn. *Senecio monroi*, illus. p.171.
B. repanda illus. p.127.
B. rotundifolia, syn. *Senecio reinholdii*, *S. rotundifolius*. Evergreen, rounded,

dense shrub. H and S 1m (3ft). Has rounded, leathery, glossy leaves, dark green above, white-felted below, and tiny, yellow flower heads from early to mid-summer. Withstands salt winds in mild coastal areas. Zone 9.

BRACHYSCOME

ASTERACEAE/COMPOSITAE

Genus of annuals and perennials, grown for their daisy-like flower heads and very variable, often finely divided foliage. Requires sun, a sheltered position and rich, well-drained soil. Pinch out growing shoots of young plants to encourage a bushy habit. Propagate by seed sown under glass in spring or outdoors in late spring.
B. iberidifolia illus. p.334.

BRACTEANTHA

ASTERACEAE/COMPOSITAE

Genus of herbaceous perennials and annuals, grown for their daisy-like flower heads with papery bracts. Stalkless, hairy leaves are borne on erect, branching stems. Needs full sun and moderately fertile, moist but well-drained soil. Propagate by seed sown in spring. *B. bracteata* is often grown for cutting and drying.
B. bracteata (Everlasting flower, Immortelle, Strawflower). **'Bright Bikini'** is a moderately fast-growing, upright, branching annual. H and S 30cm (12in). Has lance-shaped, mid-green leaves. From summer to early autumn produces papery, daisy-like flower heads in many colours, including red, pink, orange, yellow and white. **Monstrosum Series** illus. p.340.

Brake
  Cretan. See *Pteris cretica*.
  Purple rock. See *Pellaea atropurpurea*.
  Purple-stemmed cliff. See *Pellaea atropurpurea*.
  Snow. See *Pteris ensiformis*.
Bramble. See *Rubus*.
Branched bur reed. See *Sparganium erectum*, illus. p.449.
Brandy bottle. See *Nuphar lutea*, illus. p.451.
Brass buttons. See *Cotula coronopifolia*.
Brassaia. Reclassified as *Schefflera*.

BRASSAVOLA

See also ORCHIDS.
B. nodosa (Lady-of-the-night; illus. p.296). Evergreen, epiphytic orchid for an intermediate greenhouse. H 23cm (9in). Narrow-petalled, pale green flowers, 5cm (2in) across and each with a white lip, are produced, 1–3 to a stem, in spring; they are fragrant at night. Leaves, 8–10cm (3–4in) long, are thick and cylindrical. Is best grown on a bark slab. Provide good light in summer.

BRASSICA

BRASSICACEAE/CRUCIFERAE

Genus of annuals and evergreen biennials and perennials. Most are edible vegetables, e.g. cabbages and

kales, but forms of *B. oleracea* are grown for their ornamental foliage. Grow in sun and in fertile, well-drained soil. Lime-rich soil is recommended, though not essential. Propagate by seed sown outdoors in spring or under glass in early spring. Is susceptible to club root.
B. oleracea forms illus. p.324.

x BRASSOCATTLEYA

See also ORCHIDS.
x B. Mount Adams (illus. p.297). Evergreen, epiphytic orchid for an intermediate greenhouse. H 45cm (18in). Intermittently produces lavender-pink flowers, to 15cm (6in) across, each with a darker lip marked yellow and red, up to 4 per stem. Has oval, stiff leaves, 10–15cm (4–6in) long. Needs good light in summer.

x BRASSOLAELIO-CATTLEYA

See also ORCHIDS.
x B. Hetherington Horace 'Coronation' (illus. p.297). Evergreen, epiphytic orchid for an intermediate greenhouse. H 45cm (18in). Bears stiff, oval leaves, 10–15cm (4–6in) long, and fragrant, light pink flowers, 10cm (4in) across, each with a deep pink-yellow lip, up to 4 to a stem, mainly in spring.
x B. St Helier (illus. p.297). Evergreen, epiphytic orchid for an intermediate greenhouse. H 45cm (18in). Produces oval, stiff leaves, 10–15cm (4–6in) long. Pinkish-purple flowers, to 10cm (4in) across, each with a white-marked, rich red lip, are borne 1–4 to a stem, mainly in spring. Grow in good light in summer.

Bravoa geminiflora. See *Polianthes geminiflora*.
Brazilian firecracker. See *Manettia luteo-rubra*, illus. p.205.
Breath of heaven. See *Diosma ericoides*.
Brewer's spruce. See *Picea breweriana*, illus. p.105.

BREYNIA

EUPHORBIACEAE

Genus of evergreen shrubs and trees, grown for their foliage. Tender, min. 13°C (55°F). Needs full light or partial shade and fertile, well-drained soil. Water containerized plants freely when in full growth, moderately at other times. Large bushes should be cut back hard after flowering. Propagate by greenwood or semi-ripe cuttings in summer. Whitefly, spider mite and mealy bug may be troublesome.
B. disticha, syn. *B. nivosa*, *Phyllanthus nivosus*, illus. p.175. **'Roseopicta'** is an evergreen, rounded, well-branched shrub with slender stems. H and S to 1m (3ft). Has broadly oval, green leaves variably bordered and splashed with white and flushed pink. Insignificant, petalless flowers are borne in spring-summer.
B. nivosa. See *B. disticha*.

Briar, Sweet. See *Rosa rubiginosa*, illus. p.185.

Bridal bouquet. See *Porana paniculata*.

Bridal wreath. See *Francoa appendiculata*; *Spiraea* 'Arguta'; *Spiraea* x *vanhouttei*, illus. p.154.

Bridgesia. Reclassified as *Ercilla*.

BRIGGSIA

GESNERIACEAE

Genus of evergreen perennials, grown for their rosettes of hairy leaves. Tender, min. 2–5°C (36–41°F). Needs shade and peaty soil with plenty of moisture in summer and good air circulation in winter. Protect against damp in winter. Propagate by seed in spring.

B. muscicola. Evergreen, basal-rosetted perennial. H 8–10cm (3–4in), S 23cm (9in). Leaves are oval, silver-haired and pale green. Arching flower stems bear loose clusters of tubular, pale yellow flowers, with protruding tips, in early summer. Is best grown in an alpine house.

BRIMEURA

HYACINTHACEAE

Genus of spring-flowering bulbs, similar to miniature bluebells, cultivated for their attractive flowers. Is suitable for rock gardens and shrub borders. Requires partial shade and prefers humus-rich, well-drained soil. Propagate by sowing seed in autumn or by division in late summer.

B. amethystina, syn. *Hyacinthus amethystinus*, illus. p.432.

Brisbane box. See *Lophostemon confertus*.

Bristle club-rush. See *Isolepis setaceus*.

Bristle-cone pine. See *Pinus aristata*, illus. p.108.

Bristle-pointed iris. See *Iris setosa*, illus. p.235.

Brittle bladder fern. See *Cystopteris fragilis*.

Brittonastrum mexicanum. See *Agastache mexicana*.

BRIZA

Quaking grass

GRAMINEAE/POACEAE

See also GRASSES, BAMBOOS, RUSHES and SEDGES.

B. maxima (Greater quaking grass). Robust, tuft-forming, annual grass. H to 50cm (20in), S 8–10cm (3–4in). Mid-green leaves are mainly basal. Produces loose panicles of up to 10 pendent, purplish-green spikelets, in early summer, that dry particularly well for winter decoration. Self seeds readily.

B. media (Common quaking grass). Evergreen, tuft-forming, rhizomatous, perennial grass. H 30–60cm (12–24in), S 8–10cm (3–4in). Mid-green leaves are mainly basal. In summer produces open panicles of up to 30 pendent, purplish-brown spikelets that dry well for winter decoration.

Broad buckler fern. See *Dryopteris dilatata*.

Broadleaf. See *Griselinia littoralis*.

BRODIAEA

ALLIACEAE/LILIACEAE

Genus of mainly spring-flowering bulbs with colourful flowers produced in loose heads on leafless stems. Needs a sheltered, sunny situation and light, well-drained soil. Dies down in summer. Propagate in autumn by seed or in late summer and autumn by freely produced offsets.

B. capitata. See *Dichelostemma pulchellum*.

B. congesta. See *Dichelostemma congestum*.

B. coronaria, syn. *B. grandiflora*. Late spring- to early summer-flowering bulb. H 10–25cm (4–10in), S 8–10cm (3–4in). Long, narrow, semi-erect, basal leaves die down by flowering time. Leafless stems each carry a loose head of erect, funnel-shaped, violet-blue flowers on long, slender stalks.

B. grandiflora. See *B. coronaria*.

B. hyacinthina. See *Triteleia hyacinthina*.

B. ida-maia. See *Dichelostemma ida-maia*.

B. ixioides. See *Triteleia ixioides*.

B. lactea. See *Triteleia hyacinthina*.

B. laxa. See *Triteleia laxa*.

B. lutea. See *Triteleia ixioides*.

B. peduncularis. See *Triteleia peduncularis*.

B. pulchella. See *Dichelostemma pulchellum*.

BROMELIA

BROMELIACEAE

Genus of evergreen, rosette-forming perennials, grown for their overall appearance. Tender, min. 5–7°C (41–5°F). Needs full light and well-drained soil. Water moderately in summer, sparingly at other times. Propagate by suckers in spring.

B. balansae (Heart of flame; illus. p.265). Evergreen, clump-forming, basal-rosetted perennial. H 1m (3ft), S 1.5m (5ft). Produces narrowly strap-shaped, arching, mid- to grey-green leaves with large, hooked spines. Club-shaped panicles of tubular, red- or violet-purple flowers, with long, bright red bracts, are borne in spring-summer or sometimes later.

Bromeliad. See feature panel p.265.

Bird's-nest. See *Nidularium innocentii*.

Blushing. See *Neoregelia carolinae*; *Nidularium fulgens*.

Bromeliads, King of the. See *Vriesea hieroglyphica*.

Brompton stock. See *Matthiola incana*.

BROMUS

GRAMINEAE/POACEAE

See also GRASSES, BAMBOOS, RUSHES and SEDGES.

B. ramosus (Hairy brome grass). Evergreen, tuft-forming, perennial grass. H to 2m (6ft), S 30cm (1ft). Mid-green

leaves are lax and hairy. Produces long, arching panicles of nodding, grey-green spikelets in summer. Prefers shade.

Bronvaux medlar. See + *Crataegomespilus dardarii*.

Broom. See *Cytisus*; *Genista*.

Butcher's. See *Ruscus aculeatus*.

Climbing butcher's. See *Semele androgyna*.

Common. See *Cytisus scoparius*.

Hedgehog. See *Erinacea anthyllis*, illus. p.348.

Moroccan. See *Cytisus battandieri*, illus. p.123.

Mount Etna. See *Genista aetnensis*, illus. p.93.

Pineapple. See *Cytisus battandieri*, illus. p.123.

Pink. See *Notospartium carmichaeliae*.

Purple. See *Chamaecytisus purpureus*.

Spanish. See *Spartium junceum*, illus. p.147.

Warminster. See *Cytisus* x *praecox* 'Warminster', illus. p.156.

BROUSSONETIA

MORACEAE

Genus of deciduous trees and shrubs, grown for their foliage and unusual flowers. Male and female flowers are produced on different plants. Requires a position in full sun and well-drained soil. Propagate by softwood cuttings in summer or by seed in autumn.

B. papyrifera illus. p.79.

BROWALLIA

SOLANACEAE

Genus of shrubby perennials, usually grown as annuals, with showy, open trumpet-shaped flowers. Tender, min. 4–15°C (39–59°F). Grows best in sun or partial shade and in fertile, well-drained soil that should not dry out completely. Feed when flowering if pot-grown and pinch out young shoots to encourage bushiness. Propagate by seed in spring; for winter flowers, sow in late summer.

B. americana, syn. *B. elata*. Moderately fast-growing, bushy perennial, usually grown as an annual. H 30cm (12in), S 15cm (6in). Min. 4°C (39°F). Has oval, mid-green leaves and, in summer, trumpet-shaped, blue flowers, 4cm (1½in) wide.

B. elata. See *B. americana*.

B. speciosa illus. p.266.

BROWNINGIA

CACTACEAE

Genus of slow-growing, eventually tree-like, perennial cacti. Spiny, silvery- or green-blue stems, with up to 20 or more ribs, are crowned by stiff, erect, green-blue branches. Tender, min. 7°C (45°F). Requires a position in full sun and very well-drained soil. Propagate by seed in spring or summer.

B. hertlingiana, syn. *Azureocereus hertlingianus*, illus. p.456.

Bruckenthalia spiculifolia. See *Erica spiculifolia*.

BRUGMANSIA,

syn. DATURA

Angels' trumpets

SOLANACEAE

Genus of evergreen or semi-evergreen shrubs, trees and annuals, cultivated for their flowers borne mainly in summer-autumn. Tender, min. 7–10°C (45–50°F). Prefers full light and fertile, well-drained soil. Water containerized specimens freely in full growth, moderately at other times. May be pruned hard in early spring. Propagate by seed sown in spring or by greenwood or semi-ripe cuttings in early summer or later. Whitefly and spider mite may be troublesome. All parts are highly toxic if ingested.

B. arborea, syn. *B. versicolor* of gardens. Evergreen or semi-evergreen, rounded, robust shrub. H and S to 3m (10ft). Bears narrowly oval leaves, each 20cm (8in) or more long. Bears strongly fragrant, pendent, trumpet-shaped, white flowers, each 16–20cm (6–8in) long with a spathe-like calyx, in summer-autumn.

B. aurea. Evergreen, rounded shrub or tree. H and S 6–11m (20–35ft). Has oval leaves, 15cm (6in) long, and, in summer-autumn, pendent, trumpet-shaped, white or yellow flowers, 15–25cm (6–10in) long.

B. x candida illus. p.119. **'Grand Marnier'** (syn. *B.* 'Grand Marnier') illus. p.123.

B. 'Grand Marnier'. See *B.* x *candida* 'Grand Marnier'.

B. rosei of gardens. See *B. sanguinea*.

B. sanguinea, syn. *B. rosei* of gardens, illus. p.123.

B. versicolor of gardens. See *B. arborea*.

BRUNFELSIA

SOLANACEAE

Genus of evergreen shrubs, grown for their flowers. Tender, min. 10–13°C (50–55°F), but 15–18°C (59–64°F) for good winter flowering. Needs semi-shade and humus-rich, well-drained soil. Water containerized plants moderately, much less in low temperatures. Remove stem tips to promote branching in growing season. Propagate by semi-ripe cuttings in summer. Mealy bug and whitefly may be a problem.

B. calycina. See *B. pauciflora*.

B. eximia. See *B. pauciflora*.

B. pauciflora, syn. *B. calycina*, *B. eximia* (Yesterday-today-and-tomorrow). Evergreen, spreading shrub. H and S 60cm (2ft) or more. Bears oblong to lance-shaped, leathery, glossy leaves. Blue-purple flowers, each with a tubular base and 5 overlapping, wavy-edged petals, are carried from winter to summer. **'Macrantha'** illus. p.167.

BRUNNERA

BORAGINACEAE

Genus of spring-flowering perennials. Prefers light shade and moist soil. Propagate by division in spring or autumn or by seed in autumn.

B. macrophylla (Siberian bugloss).

507

Clump-forming perennial. H 45cm (18in), S 60cm (24in). Delicate sprays of small, star-shaped, forget-me-not-like, bright blue flowers in early spring are followed by heart-shaped, rough, long-stalked leaves. Makes good ground cover. **'Dawson's White'** (syn. *B.m.* 'Variegata') illus. p.271.

x **Brunsdonna parkeri.** See x *Amarygia parkeri*.

BRUNSVIGIA

AMARYLLIDACEAE

Genus of autumn-flowering bulbs with heads of showy flowers. Requires sun and well-drained soil. Water in autumn to encourage bulbs into growth and continue watering until summer, when the leaves will die away and dormant bulbs should be kept fairly dry and warm. Propagate by seed sown in autumn or by offsets in late summer.
B. josephinae (Josephine's lily). Autumn-flowering bulb. H to 45cm (18in), S 45–60cm (18–24in). Bears a stout, leafless stem with a spherical head of 20–30 funnel-shaped, red flowers, 7–9cm (3–3½in) long, with recurved petal tips. Semi-erect, oblong leaves appear after flowering.

Brush-box tree. See *Lophostemon confertus*.
Bryophyllum. Reclassified as *Kalanchoe*.
Buckbean. See *Menyanthes trifoliata*, illus. p.446.
Buckeye. See *Aesculus*.
  Bottlebrush. See *Aesculus parviflora*, illus. p.119.
  California. See *Aesculus californica*, illus. p.85.
  Ohio. See *Aesculus glabra*.
  Red. See *Aesculus pavia*.
  Sweet. See *Aesculus flava*, illus. p.82.
  Yellow. See *Aesculus flava*, illus. p.82.
Buckthorn. See *Rhamnus*.
  Alder. See *Rhamnus frangula*.
  Italian. See *Rhamnus alaternus*.
  Sea. See *Hippophäe rhamnoides*, illus. p.124.
Buckwheat, Wild. See *Eriogonum*.

BUDDLEJA

BUDDLEJACEAE

Genus of deciduous, semi-evergreen or evergreen shrubs and trees, grown for their clusters of small, often fragrant flowers. Requires full sun and fertile, well-drained soil. *B. crispa*, *B. davidii*, *B. fallowiana*, *B.* 'Lochinch' and *B.* x *weyeriana* should be cut back hard in spring. Prune *B. alternifolia* by removing shoots that have flowered. Other species may be cut back lightly after flowering. Propagate by semi-ripe cuttings in summer.
B. alternifolia illus. p.122.
B. asiatica. Evergreen, arching shrub. H and S 3m (10ft). Long plumes of very fragrant, tubular, white flowers appear amid long, narrow, dark green leaves in late winter and early spring.

Grow against a south- or west-facing wall. Zone 9.
B. colvilei illus. p.121. **'Kewensis'** is a deciduous, arching shrub, often tree-like with age. H and S 5m (15ft). Has lance-shaped, dark green leaves. Large, tubular, white-throated, deep red flowers hang in drooping clusters in early summer. Zone 9.
B. crispa illus. p.143.
B. davidii (Butterfly bush). **'Black Knight'** is a vigorous, deciduous, arching shrub. H and S 5m (15ft). Leaves are long, lance-shaped and dark green with white-felted undersides. Dense clusters of fragrant, tubular, dark violet-purple flowers are borne from mid-summer to autumn. Zone 5b. Flowers of **'Empire Blue'** are rich violet-blue. **'Harlequin'** illus. p.121. **'Peace'** illus. p.118. **'Pink Pearl'** produces pale lilac-pink flowers. **'Royal Red'** illus. p.121.
B. fallowiana. Deciduous, arching shrub. H 2m (6ft), S 3m (10ft). Shoots and lance-shaped leaves, when young, are covered with white hairs; foliage then becomes dark grey-green. Has fragrant, tubular, lavender-purple flowers in late summer and early autumn. Is often damaged in very severe winters; grow against a wall in cold areas. var. **alba** has white flowers. Zone 8.
B. globosa illus. p.123.
B. 'Lochinch'. Deciduous, arching shrub. H and S 3m (10ft). Long plumes of fragrant, tubular, lilac-blue flowers are borne above lance-shaped, grey-green leaves in late summer and autumn. Zone 7.
B. madagascariensis, syn. *Nicodemia madagascariensis*. Evergreen, arching shrub. H and S 4m (12ft) or more. Has narrowly lance-shaped, dark green leaves, white beneath, and, in late winter and spring, long clusters of tubular, orange-yellow flowers. Grow against a south- or west-facing wall. Tender, min. 5°C (41°F).
B. x weyeriana. Deciduous, arching shrub. H and S 4m (12ft). Bears lance-shaped, dark green leaves, and loose, rounded clusters of tubular, orange-yellow flowers, often tinged purple, from mid-summer to autumn. Zone 7.

Buffalo berry. See *Shepherdia argentea*.
Buffalo currant. See *Ribes odoratum*.
Bugbane. See *Cimicifuga*.
Bugle, Pyramidal. See *Ajuga pyramidalis*.
Bugler, Royal red. See *Aeschynanthus pulcher*.
Bugloss, Siberian. See *Brunnera macrophylla*.

BULBOCODIUM

COLCHICACEAE/LILIACEAE

Genus of spring-flowering corms, related to *Colchicum* and with funnel-shaped flowers. Is particularly suitable for rock gardens and cool greenhouses. Requires an open, sunny site and well-drained soil. Propagate by seed sown in

autumn or by division in late summer and early autumn.
B. vernum illus. p.430.

BULBOPHYLLUM

See also ORCHIDS.
B. careyanum (illus. p.298). Evergreen, epiphytic orchid for an intermediate greenhouse. H 8cm (3in). Oval leaves are 8–10cm (3–4in) long. In spring produces tight sprays of many slightly fragrant, brown flowers, 0.5cm (¼in) across. Grows best in a hanging basket. Needs semi-shade in summer.

Bull bay. See *Magnolia grandiflora*.
Bullock's heart. See *Annona reticulata*.
Bunch-flowered daffodil. See *Narcissus tazetta*.
Bunnies' ears. See *Stachys byzantina*, illus. p.304.
Bunny ears. See *Opuntia microdasys*.

BUPHTHALMUM

ASTERACEAE/COMPOSITAE

Genus of summer-flowering perennials. Requires full sun; grows well in any but rich soil. Propagate by seed in spring or autumn or by division in autumn. Needs frequent division to curb invasiveness.
B. salicifolium illus. p.292.
B. speciosum. See *Telekia speciosa*.

BUPLEURUM

APIACEAE/UMBELLIFERAE

Genus of perennials and evergreen shrubs, grown for their foliage and flowers. Grows well in coastal gardens. Needs full sun and well-drained soil. Propagate by semi-ripe cuttings in summer.
B. fruticosum illus. p.146.

Bur oak. See *Quercus macrocarpa*, illus. p.80.
Bur reed. See *Sparganium*.
Burnet. See *Sanguisorba*.
  Canadian. See *Sanguisorba canadensis*, illus. p.226.
  Great. See *Sanguisorba officinalis*.
Burnet rose. See *Rosa pimpinellifolia*.
Burning bush. See *Dictamnus albus*, illus. p.240; *Bassia scoparia* f. *trichophylla*, illus. p.335.
Burro's tail. See *Sedum morganianum*.
Bush-cranberry
  High. See *Viburnum tribulum*.
Bush groundsel. See *Baccharis halimifolia*.
Bush violet. See *Browallia speciosa*, illus. p.266.
Busy lizzie. See *Impatiens walleriana* cvs.
Butcher's broom. See *Ruscus aculeatus*.

BUTIA

Yatay palm

ARECACEAE/PALMAE

Genus of evergreen palms, grown for their overall appearance. Tender, min. 5°C (41°F). Grow in any fertile, well-

drained soil and in full light or partial shade. Water regularly, less in winter. Propagate by seed in spring at not less than 24°C (75°F). Spider mite may be a problem.
B. capitata, syn. *Cocos capitata*, illus. p.100.

BUTOMUS

BUTOMACEAE

Genus of one species of deciduous, perennial, rush-like, marginal water plant, grown for its fragrant, cup-shaped flowers. Requires an open, sunny situation in up to 25cm (10in) depth of water. Propagate by division in spring or by seed in spring or late summer.
B. umbellatus illus. p.448.

Butter tree. See *Tylecodon paniculatus*.
Buttercup. See *Ranunculus*.
  Alpine. See *Ranunculus alpestris*, illus. p.363.
  Double meadow. See *Ranunculus acris* 'Flore Pleno', illus. p.292.
  Giant. See *Ranunculus lyallii*.
  Meadow. See *Ranunculus acris*.
  Persian. See *Ranunculus asiaticus*, illus. pp.421 and 423.
Butterfly bush. See *Buddleja davidii*.
Butterfly flower. See *Schizanthus*.
Butterfly orchid. See *Psychopsis papilio*, illus. p.299.
Butterfly weed. See *Asclepias tuberosa*, illus. p.258.
Butternut. See *Juglans cinerea*.
Button-fern. See *Pellaea rotundifolia*.
Buttons, Brass. See *Cotula coronopifolia*.
Buttonwood. See *Platanus occidentalis*.

BUXUS

Box

BUXACEAE

Genus of evergreen shrubs and trees, grown for their foliage and habit. Is excellent for edging, hedging and topiary work. Flowers are insignificant. Requires sun or semi-shade and any but waterlogged soil. Trim hedges in summer. Promote new growth by cutting back stems to 30cm (12in) or less in late spring. Propagate by semi-ripe cuttings in summer. Contact with box sap may irritate skin.
B. balearica illus. p.153.
B. microphylla (Small-leaved box). Evergreen, bushy shrub. H 1m (3ft), S 1.5m (5ft). Forms a dense, rounded mass of small, oblong, dark green leaves. Zone 6. **'Green Pillow'** illus. p.176.
var. **koreana** is hardier and hybrids between this and *B. sempervirens*, such as **'Green Gem'** and **'Green Velvet'** are hardy to zone 5.
B. sempervirens (Common box). Evergreen, bushy shrub or tree. H and S 5m (15ft). Produces leaves that are oblong, glossy and dark green. Is useful for hedging and screening. Zone 6. **'Handsworthensis'** illus. p.152. **'Suffruticosa'** illus. p.177.

C

Cabbage
  Ornamental. See *Brassica oleracea* forms, illus. p.324.
  Yellow skunk. See *Lysichiton americanus*, illus. p.451.
Cabbage palm
  Australian. See *Livistona australis*.
  New Zealand. See *Cordyline australis*.

CABOMBA

CABOMBACEAE

Genus of deciduous or semi-evergreen, perennial, submerged water plants with finely divided foliage. Is suitable for aquariums. Tender, min. 5°C (41°F). Prefers partial shade. Propagate by stem cuttings in spring or summer.
C. caroliniana (Fanwort, Carolina water shield). Deciduous or semi-evergreen, perennial, submerged water plant. S indefinite. Forms dense, spreading hummocks of fan-shaped, coarsely cut, bright green leaves. Is used as an oxygenating plant.

Cactus
  Barrel. See *Ferocactus*.
  Chain. See *Rhipsalis paradoxa*.
  Christmas. See *Schlumbergera* x *buckleyi*.
  Colombian ball. See *Parodia erinacea*, illus. p.479.
  Coral. See *Rhipsalis cereuscula*, illus. p.461.
  Crab. See *Schlumbergera truncata*, illus. p.473.
  Dumpling. See *Lophophora williamsii*, illus. p.471.
  Easter. See *Hatiora gaertneri*, illus. p.475.
  Fishbone. See *Epiphyllum anguliger*, illus. p.461.
  Golden ball. See *Parodia leninghausii*, illus. p.468.
  Golden barrel. See *Echinocactus grusonii*, illus. p.460.
  Lace. See *Mammillaria elongata*, illus. p.470.
  Lamb's-tail. See *Echinocereus schmollii*, illus. p.462.
  Lobster. See *Schlumbergera truncata*, illus. p.473.
  Melon. See *Melocactus intortus*, illus. p.472.
  Mistletoe. See *Rhipsalis*.
  Old-lady. See *Mammillaria hahniana*, illus. p.465.
  Old-man. See *Cephalocereus senilis*, illus. p.460.
  Old-woman. See *Mammillaria hahniana*, illus. p.465.
  Orchid. See *Epiphyllum*.
  Organ-pipe. See *Pachycereus marginatus*, illus. p.457.
  Peanut. See *Echinopsis chamaecereus*, illus. p.475.
  Peruvian old-man. See *Espostoa lanata*, illus. p.457.
  Pincushion. See *Mammillaria*.
  Powder-puff. See *Mammillaria bocasana*, illus. p.471.

Cactus (continued)
  Rat's-tail. See *Aporocactus flagelliformis*, illus. p.463.
  Red orchid. See *Nopalxochia ackermannii*.
  Rose. See *Pereskia grandifolia*, illus. p.458
  Scarlet ball. See *Parodia haselbergii*.
  Silver ball. See *Parodia scopa*.
  Silver dollar. See *Astrophytum asterias*.
  Strap. See *Epiphyllum*.
  Strawberry. See *Mammillaria prolifera*.
  Torch. See *Echinopsis spachiana*, illus. p.457.

CAESALPINIA

CAESALPINIACEAE/LEGUMINOSAE

Genus of deciduous or evergreen shrubs, trees and scrambling climbers, grown for their foliage and flowers. Tender, min. 5–10°C (41–50°F). Needs full sun and fertile, well-drained soil. Propagate by softwood cuttings in summer or by seed in autumn or spring.
C. gilliesii, syn. *Poinciana gilliesii*, illus. p.123.
C. pulcherrima, syn. *Poinciana pulcherrima* (Barbados pride). Evergreen shrub or tree of erect to spreading habit. H and S 3–6m (10–20ft). Has fern-like leaves composed of many small, mid-green leaflets. In summer bears cup-shaped, yellow flowers, 3cm (1¼in) wide, with very long, red anthers, in short, dense, erect racemes.

CALADIUM

ARACEAE

Genus of perennials with tubers from which arise long-stalked, ornamental leaves. Tender, min. 18–19°C (64–6°F). Requires partial shade and moist, humus-rich soil. After leaves die down, store tubers in a frost-free, dark place. Propagate by separating small tubers when planting in spring. Contact with all parts may irritate skin, and may cause mild stomach upset if ingested.
C. bicolor (Angels' wings).
'**Candidum**' is a tufted perennial. H and S to 90cm (36in). Triangular, green-veined, white leaves, to 45cm (18in) long, have arrow-shaped bases and long leaf stalks. Intermittently bears white spathes; small flowers clustered on spadix sometimes produce whitish berries. '**John Peed**' has purple stems and waxy, green leaves with metallic orange-red centres and scarlet veins. '**Pink Beauty**' illus. p.264. '**Pink Cloud**' has large, dark green leaves with mottled pink centres, and pink to white areas along the veins.

Calamondin. See x *Citrofortunella microcarpa*, illus. p.151.

Calandrinia megarhiza. See *Claytonia megarhiza*.

CALANTHE

See also ORCHIDS.
C. vestita (illus. p.296). Deciduous, terrestrial orchid. H 60cm (24in). Tender, min. 18°C (64°F). In winter bears sprays of many white flowers, 4cm (1½in) across, each with a large, red-marked lip. Has broadly oval, ribbed, soft leaves, 30cm (12in) long. In summer requires semi-shade and regular feeding.

CALATHEA

MARANTACEAE

Genus of evergreen perennials with brightly coloured and patterned leaves. Tender, min. 15°C (59°F). Prefers a shaded, humid position, without fluctuations of temperature, in humus-rich, well-drained soil. Water with soft water, sparingly in low temperatures, but do not allow to dry out completely. Propagate by division in spring.
C. lindeniana. Evergreen, clump-forming perennial. H 1m (3ft), S 60cm (2ft). Lance-shaped, long-stalked, more or less upright leaves, over 30cm (1ft) long, are dark green, with paler green, feathered midribs above and marked with reddish-purple below. Intermittently bears short, erect spikes of 3-petalled, pale yellow flowers.
C. majestica '**Roseolineata**', syn. *C. ornata* '**Roseolineata**'. Evergreen, clump-forming, stemless perennial. H to 2m (6ft), S to 1.5m (5ft). Narrowly oval, leathery leaves, to 60cm (2ft) long, are dark green, with close-set, fine, pink stripes along the lateral veins and reddish-purple below. Intermittently bears short, erect spikes of 3-petalled, white to mauve flowers.
'**Sanderiana**' see *C. sanderiana*.
C. makoyana illus. p.304.
C. oppenheimiana. See *Ctenanthe oppenheimiana*.
C. ornata '**Roseolineata**'. See *C. majestica* '**Roseolineata**'.
C. sanderiana, syn. *C. majestica* '**Sanderiana**', illus. p.232.
C. zebrina illus. p.266.

CALCEOLARIA

Pouch flower, Slipper flower

SCROPHULARIACEAE

Genus of annuals, biennials and evergreen perennials, sub-shrubs and scandent climbers, some of which are grown as annuals. Hardy to tender, min. 5–7°C (41–5°F). Most prefer sun but some like a shady, cool site and moist but well-drained soil, incorporating sharp sand and compost, and dislike wet conditions in winter. Propagate by softwood cuttings in late spring or summer or by seed in autumn.
C. acutifolia. See *C. polyrrhiza*.
C. Anytime Series. Compact, bushy annuals or biennials. H 20cm (8in), S 15cm (6in). Has oval, slightly hairy, mid-green leaves and, in spring-summer, heads of 5cm (2in) long, rounded, pouched flowers in red and yellow shades, including bicolours.
C. arachnoidea illus. p.355.
C. '**Bright Bikinis**' illus. p.338.
C. darwinii. See *C. uniflora* var. *darwinii*.
C. fothergillii. Evergreen, clump-forming, short-lived perennial. H and S 12cm (5in). Has a rosette of rounded, light green leaves with hairy edges and, in summer, solitary pouch-shaped, sulphur-yellow flowers with crimson spots. Is good for a sheltered rock ledge or trough or in an alpine house. Needs gritty, peaty soil. Is prone to aphid attack.
C. integrifolia. Evergreen, upright sub-shrub, sometimes grown as an annual. H to 1.2m (4ft), S 60cm (2ft). In summer bears crowded clusters of pouch-shaped, yellow to red-brown flowers above oblong to elliptic, mid-green leaves, sometimes rust-coloured beneath.
C. '**John Innes**' illus. p.293.
C. '**Monarch**'. Group of bushy annuals or biennials. H and S 30cm (12in). Has oval, lightly hairy, mid-green leaves and, in spring-summer, bears heads of large, rounded, pouched flowers, 5cm (2in) long, in a wide range of colours.
C. pavonii. Robust, evergreen, scandent climber. H 2m (6ft) or more. Tender, min. 7°C (45°F). Has oval, serrated, soft-haired leaves with winged stalks. Pouched, yellow flowers with brown marks appear in large trusses from late summer to winter.
C. polyrrhiza, syn. *C. acutifolia*. Evergreen, prostrate perennial. H 2.5cm (1in), S 15cm (6in). Has rounded, hairy, mid-green leaves along flower stem, which bears pouch-shaped, purple-spotted, yellow flowers in summer. Is good for a shady rock garden. May also be propagated by division in autumn or spring.
C. '**Sunshine**' illus. p.339.
C. tenella illus. p.385.
C. uniflora var. *darwinii*, syn. *C. darwinii*. Evergreen, clump-forming, short-lived perennial. H 8cm (3in), S 10cm (4in). Bears rounded, wrinkled, glossy, dark green leaves. In late spring, flower stems carry pendent, pouch-shaped, yellow flowers with dark brown spots on lower lips and central, white bands. Is difficult to grow. Needs a sheltered, sunny site in moist, gritty, peaty soil. Is prone to attack by aphids.
C. '**Walter Shrimpton**' illus. p.386.

CALENDULA

Marigold

ASTERACEAE/COMPOSITAE

Genus of annuals and evergreen shrubs. Annuals may be hardy; shrubs are tender, min. 4°C (39°F). Grow in sun or partial shade and in any well-drained soil. Dead-head regularly to prolong flowering. Propagate annuals by seed sown outdoors in spring or autumn, shrubs by stem cuttings in summer. Annuals may self-seed. Cucumber mosaic virus and powdery mildew may cause problems.

C. officinalis (Pot marigold). Fast-growing, bushy annual. Tall cultivars, H and S 60cm (24in); dwarf forms, H and S 30cm (12in). All have lance-shaped, strongly aromatic, pale green leaves. Daisy-like, single or double flower heads in a wide range of yellow and orange shades are produced from spring to autumn. **'Fiesta Gitana'** illus. p.339. **'Geisha Girl'** (tall) illus. p.341. **Kablouna Series** (tall) illus. p.336. **Pacific Beauty Series 'Lemon Queen'** illus. p.338.

Calico bush. See *Kalmia latifolia*, illus. p.141.
Calico flower. See *Aristolochia littoralis*, illus. p.211.
California allspice. See *Calycanthus occidentalis*, illus. p.142.
California bluebell. See *Phacelia campanularia*, illus. p.334.
California buckeye. See *Aesculus californica*, illus. p.85.
California nutmeg. See *Torreya californica*, illus. p.107.
California poppy. See *Eschscholzia*.
Californian laurel. See *Umbellularia californica*, illus. p.74.
Californian live oak. See *Quercus agrifolia*, illus. p.85.
Californian pepper-tree. See *Schinus molle*.

CALLA
ARACEAE
Genus of one species of deciduous or semi-evergreen, perennial, spreading, marginal water plant, grown for its foliage and showy spathes that surround insignificant flower clusters. Requires a sunny position, in mud or in water to 25cm (10in) deep. Propagate by division in spring or by seed in late summer. Contact with the foliage may aggravate skin allergies.
C. palustris illus. p.446.

Callery pear. See *Pyrus calleryana*.

CALLIANDRA
LEGUMINOSAE/MIMOSACEAE
Genus of evergreen trees, shrubs and scandent semi-climbers, grown for their flowers and overall appearance. Tender, min. 7–18°C (45–64°F). Requires full light or partial shade and well-drained soil. Water containerized plants freely when in full growth, much less when temperatures are low. To restrict growth, cut back stems by one-half to two-thirds after flowering. Propagate by seed sown indoors in spring. Whitefly and mealy bug may be troublesome.
C. eriophylla illus. p.172.
C. haematocephala [pink form] illus. p.147, [white form] illus. p.149.

CALLIANTHEMUM
RANUNCULACEAE
Genus of perennials, grown for their daisy-like flowers and thick, dissected leaves. Is excellent for rock gardens and alpine houses. Needs sun and moist but well-drained soil. Propagate by seed when fresh.
C. coriandrifolium, syn. *C. rutifolium*. Prostrate perennial with upright flower stems. H 8cm (3in), S 20cm (8in). Leaves, forming open rosettes, are long-stalked, very dissected and blue-green. In spring has short-stemmed, many-petalled, white flowers with yellow centres. Is susceptible to slugs.
C. rutifolium. See *C. coriandrifolium*.

CALLICARPA
VERBENACEAE
Genus of deciduous, summer-flowering shrubs, grown for their small but striking, clustered fruits. Does best in full sun and fertile, well-drained soil. Propagate by softwood cuttings in summer.
C. bodinieri. Deciduous, bushy shrub. H 3m (10ft), S 2.5m (8ft). Has oval, dark green leaves. Tiny, star-shaped, lilac flowers in mid-summer are followed by dense clusters of spherical, violet fruits. Zone 6. var. **giraldii** illus. p.148.

CALLISIA
COMMELINACEAE
Genus of evergreen, prostrate perennials, grown for their ornamental foliage and trailing habit. Tender, min. 10–15°C (50–59°F). Grow in full light, but out of direct sunlight, in fertile, well-drained soil. Propagate by tip cuttings in spring, either annually or when plants become straggly.
C. navicularis, syn. *Tradescantia navicularis*. Evergreen, low-growing perennial with creeping, rooting shoots, 50cm (20in) or more long. H 5–8cm (2–3in), S indefinite. Has 2 rows of oval, keeled leaves, 2.5cm (1in) long, sheathing the stem, and stalkless clusters of small, 3-petalled, pinkish-purple flowers in leaf axils in summer-autumn.
C. repens illus. p.304.

CALLISTEMON
Bottlebrush
MYRTACEAE
Genus of evergreen shrubs, usually with narrow, pointed leaves, grown for their clustered flowers, which, with their profusion of long stamens, resemble bottlebrushes. Tender, min. 5°C (41°F); in cool areas, grow against a south- or west-facing wall or in a cool greenhouse. Requires full sun and fertile, well-drained soil. Propagate by semi-ripe cuttings in summer or by seed in autumn or spring.
C. citrinus 'Splendens' illus. p.143.
C. pallidus illus. p.146.
C. paludosus. See *C. sieberi*.
C. pityoides. Evergreen, compact, upright shrub. H 1.5m (5ft), S 1m (3ft). Is densely covered with sharply

pointed, dark green leaves, and has short spikes of yellow flowers in mid- and late summer.
C. rigidus illus. p.143.
C. sieberi, syn. *C. paludosus*. Evergreen, bushy, dense shrub. H 1.5m (5ft), S 1m (3ft). Has short, narrowly lance-shaped, rigid, mid-green leaves and, from mid- to late summer, small clusters of pale yellow flowers.
C. speciosus (Albany bottlebrush). Evergreen, bushy shrub. H and S 3m (10ft). Produces long, narrow, grey-green leaves. Cylindrical clusters of bright red flowers appear in late spring and early summer.
C. subulatus. Evergreen, arching shrub. H and S 1.5m (5ft). Leaves are narrowly oblong and bright green. Dense spikes of crimson flowers are produced in summer.
C. viminalis. Evergreen, arching shrub. H and S 5m (15ft). Narrowly oblong, bronze, young leaves mature to dark green. Bears clusters of bright red flowers in summer.

CALLISTEPHUS
China aster
ASTERACEAE/COMPOSITAE
Genus of one species of annual. Requires sun, a sheltered position and fertile, well-drained soil. Tall cultivars need support; all should be dead-headed. Propagate by seed sown under glass in spring; seed may also be sown outdoors in mid-spring. Wilt disease, virus diseases, foot rot, root rot and aphids may be a problem.
C. chinensis. Moderately fast-growing, erect, bushy annual. Tall cultivars, H 60cm (24in), S 45cm (18in); intermediate, H 45cm (18in), S 30cm (12in); dwarf, H 25–30cm (10–12in), S 30–45cm (12–18in); very dwarf, H 20cm (8in), S 30cm (12in). All have oval, toothed, mid-green leaves and flower in summer and early autumn. Different forms are available in a wide colour range, including pink, red, blue and white. **Duchesse Series** (tall) has incurved, chrysanthemum-like flower heads. **Milady Super Series** (dwarf) has incurved, fully double flower heads available either in mixed or single colours (blue, illus. p.332; rose, illus. p.324). **Ostrich Plume Series** (tall) illus. p.331. **Pompon Series** (tall) has small, double flower heads. **Princess Series** (tall) has double flower heads with quilled petals.

CALLUNA
ERICACEAE
See also HEATHERS.
C. vulgaris (Ling, Scotch heather). Evergreen, bushy shrub. H to 60cm (24in), S 45cm (18in). Slightly fleshy, linear leaves, in opposite and overlapping pairs, may range in colour from bright green to many shades of grey, yellow, orange and red. Spikes of bell- to urn-shaped, single or double flowers are produced from mid-summer to late autumn.
Unlike *Erica*, most of the flower colour derives from the sepals. The following cultivars are H 45cm (18in),

have mid-green leaves and bear single flowers in late summer and early autumn, unless otherwise stated. Zone 3.
'Alba Plena', H 30–45cm (12–18in), bears double, white flowers.
'Alexandra' (illus. p.179), H 30cm (12in), S 40cm (16in), has an upright habit, dark green foliage, and deep crimson buds until early winter.
'Alicia', H 30cm (12in), S 40cm (16in), has white buds until early winter, and a neat, compact habit.
'Allegro', H 60cm (24in), is compact in habit and produces purple-red flowers. **'Alportii'**, H 60–90cm (24–36in), has purple-red flowers.
'Anette', H 35cm (14in), S 40cm (16in), has clear pink buds until early winter. **'Annemarie'**, H 50cm (20in), S 60cm (24in), has outstanding, double, rose-pink flowers, ideal for cutting.
'Anthony Davis' (illus. p.178) has grey leaves and white flowers. **'Beoley Gold'** (illus. p.179), S 50cm (20in), has golden foliage and white flowers.
'Beoley Silver', H 40cm (16in), has silver foliage and white flowers.
'Blazeaway', H 35cm (14in), S 60cm (24in), has gold foliage in summer that turns orange, then fiery red in winter.
'Bonfire Brilliance', H 30cm (12in), has bright, flame-coloured foliage and mauve-pink flowers. **'Boskoop'** (illus. p.179), H 30cm (12in), is compact with golden foliage that turns deep orange in winter and lilac-pink flowers.
'County Wicklow' (illus. p.178), H 30cm (12in), S 35cm (14in), is compact with double, shell-pink flowers. **'Dark Beauty'**, H 20cm (8in), S 35cm (14in), is neat and compact, and bears bright, semi-double, crimson flowers. **'Darkness'** (illus. p.179), H 40cm (16in), S 35cm (14in), is compact with crimson flowers. **'Elsie Purnell'** (illus. p.178) is a spreading cultivar with greyish-green leaves and double, pale pink flowers. **'Finale'** bears dark pink flowers from late autumn to early winter. **'Firefly'** (illus. p.179), S 50cm (20in), with deep mauve flowers, has foliage that is terracotta in summer, brick-red in winter. **'Foxii Nana'** (illus. p.179), H 15cm (6in), forms low mounds of bright green foliage and produces a few mauve-pink flowers. **'Fred J. Chapple'** has bright pink- and coral-tipped foliage in spring; mauve-pink flowers are borne on long stems. **'Gold Haze'** (illus. p.179) has bright golden foliage and white flowers. **'Golden Feather'** (illus. p.179) has bright yellow foliage, turning orange in winter, and mauve-pink flowers.
'Hammondii Aureifolia', H 30cm (12in), S 40cm (16in), has white flowers. Foliage is light green, tipped yellow in spring and early summer.
'H.E. Beale', H 50cm (20in), is one of the best double-flowered heathers, with pale pink flowers on long stems.
'J.H. Hamilton' (illus. p.178), H 20cm (8in), S 40cm (16in), is compact with double, salmon-pink flowers. **'Joy Vanstone'** has golden foliage, turning to orange and bronze, and mauve-pink flowers. **'Kerstin'**, H 30cm (12in), produces mauve flowers and has downy, deep lilac-grey

foliage in winter, tipped pale yellow and red in spring. **'Kinlochruel'** (illus. p.178), H 30cm (12in), S 35cm (14in), bears an abundance of large, double, white flowers. **'Loch Turret'**, H 30cm (12in), has emerald-green foliage and produces white flowers in early summer. **'Mair's Variety'**, an old cultivar, has white flowers on long spikes. **'Marleen'** is unusual in that its long-lasting, dark mauve flower buds, borne from early to late autumn, do not open fully. **'Mullion'** H 25cm (10in), S 50cm (20in), is a spreading cultivar with rich mauve-pink flowers. **'Multicolor'** (illus. p.179), H 20cm (8in), is compact with foliage in shades of yellow, orange, red and green year-round; flowers are mauve-pink. **'My Dream'** (syn. *C.v.* 'Snowball'; illus. p.178), H 50cm (20in), produces double, white flowers that are borne on long, tapering stems. **'Peter Sparkes'** (illus. p.179), H 50cm (20in), S 55cm (22in), bears double, deep pink flowers. **'Robert Chapman'** (illus. p.179) is a spreading cultivar and grown mainly for its foliage, which is golden-yellow in summer, turning orange and brilliant red in winter; flowers are mauve-pink. **'Ruth Sparkes'**, H 25cm (10in), has golden foliage and white flowers. **'Silver Knight'** (illus. p.179), H 30cm (12in), is of upright habit with grey leaves and mauve-pink flowers. **'Silver Queen'** (illus. p.178), H 40cm (16in), S 55cm (22in), is a spreading cultivar with dark mauve-pink flowers. **'Sir John Charrington'** has bright-coloured foliage, varying from golden-yellow in summer to orange and red in winter, and dark mauve-pink flowers. **'Sister Anne'**, H 15cm (6in), has grey leaves and pale mauve-pink flowers. **'Snowball'** see *C.v.* 'My Dream'. **'Spring Cream'** (illus. p.178) has bright green leaves, which have cream tips in spring, and white flowers. **'Spring Torch'**, H 40cm (16in), S 60cm (24in), has mauve flowers with cream, orange and red tips in spring. **'Sunset'**, H 25cm (10in), has brightly coloured foliage, changing from golden-yellow in spring to orange in summer and fiery red in winter; flowers are mauve-pink. **'Tib'** (illus. p.179), H 30cm (12in), S 40cm (16in), is the earliest-flowering double cultivar, producing small, double, deep pink flowers in early summer. **'White Lawn'**, H 10cm (4in), is a creeping cultivar with bright green foliage and white flowers on long stems; is suitable for a rock garden. **'Wickwar Flame'** is primarily a foliage plant with leaves in shades of yellow, orange and flame that are particularly effective in winter; flowers are mauve-pink. All zone 3.

CALOCEDRUS

CUPRESSACEAE

See also CONIFERS.
C. decurrens, syn. *Libocedrus decurrens*, illus. p.106.

Calocephalus brownii. See *Leucophyta brownii.*

CALOCHONE

RUBIACEAE

Genus of evergreen, scrambling climbers, grown for their showy flowers. Tender, min. 18°C (64°F). Requires full light and humus-rich, well-drained soil. Water regularly, less in cold weather. Needs tying to a support. Thin out crowded stems after flowering. Propagate by semi-ripe cuttings in summer.
C. redingii. Moderately vigorous, evergreen, scrambling climber. H 3–5m (10–15ft). Has oval, pointed, hairy leaves, 7–12cm (3–5in) long. Trusses of primrose-shaped, red to orange-pink flowers appear in winter.

CALOCHORTUS

Cat's ears, Fairy lantern, Mariposa tulip

LILIACEAE

Genus of bulbs, grown for their spring and summer flowers. Needs a sheltered, sunny position and well-drained soil. In cold, damp climates, cover or lift spring-flowering species when dormant (in summer), or grow in cold frames or cold houses. After flowering, remove bulbils formed in leaf axils for propagation. Propagate by seed or bulbils – spring-flowering species in autumn, summer-flowering species in spring.
C. albus illus. p.409.
C. amabilis illus. p.434.
C. barbatus, syn. *Cyclobothra lutea*, illus. p.422.
C. luteus illus. p.415.
C. monophyllus illus. p.436.
C. splendens. Late spring-flowering bulb. H 20–60cm (8–24in), S 5–10cm (2–4in). Bears 1 or 2 linear, erect leaves near base of branched stem and 1–4 upward-facing, saucer-shaped, pale purple flowers, 5–7cm (2–3in) across, with a darker blotch at the base of each of the 3 large petals.
C. superbus. Late spring-flowering bulb. H 20–60cm (8–24in), S 5–10cm (2–4in). Is similar to *C. splendens*, but flowers are white, cream or pale lilac, with a brown mark near the base of each of the 3 large petals.
C. venustus illus. p.408.
C. vestae. Late spring-flowering bulb. H 20–60cm (8–24in), S 5–10cm (2–4in). Is similar to *C. splendens*, but flowers are white or purple, with a rust-brown mark near the base of each of the 3 large petals.
C. weedii. Summer-flowering bulb. H 30–60cm (12–24in), S 5–10cm (2–4in). Has a linear, erect leaf near base of stem. Carries usually 2 upright, saucer-shaped flowers, 4–5cm (1½–2in) across, that are orange-yellow with brown lines and flecks and hairy inside.

CALODENDRUM

RUTACEAE

Genus of evergreen trees, grown for their flowers that are produced mainly in spring-summer. Tender, min. 7–10°C (45–50°F). Needs full light and fertile, well-drained but moisture-retentive soil. Water containerized specimens freely when in full growth, less at other times. Tolerates some pruning. Propagate by seed in spring or by semi-ripe cuttings in summer.
C. capense (Cape chestnut). Fairly fast-growing, evergreen, rounded tree. H and S to 15m (50ft) or more. Has oval leaves patterned with translucent dots. Terminal panicles of 5-petalled, light pink to deep mauve flowers appear from spring to early summer.

CALOMERIA,
syn. HUMEA

ASTERACEAE/COMPOSITAE

Genus of perennials and evergreen shrubs. Only *C. amaranthoides* is cultivated, usually as a biennial. Tender, min. 4°C (39°F). Needs sun and fertile, well-drained soil. Propagate by seed sown under glass in mid-summer.
C. amaranthoides, syn. *C. elegans*, illus. p.330.
C. elegans. See *C. amaranthoides.*

Calonyction aculeatum. See *Ipomoea alba.*

CALOSCORDUM

ALLIACEAE/LILIACEAE

Genus of one species of summer-flowering bulb, related and similar to *Allium*. Is suitable for a rock garden. Needs an open, sunny situation and well-drained soil. Lies dormant in winter. Propagate in early spring by seed or division before growth starts.
C. neriniflorum, syn. *Nothoscordum neriniflorum*. Clump-forming bulb. H 10–25cm (4–10in), S 8–10cm (3–4in). Thread-like, semi-erect, basal leaves die down at flowering time. Each leafless stem produces a loose head of 10–20 small, funnel-shaped, pinkish-red flowers in late summer.

CALOTHAMNUS

MYRTACEAE

Genus of evergreen, summer-flowering shrubs, grown for their flowers and overall appearance. Thrives in a dryish, airy environment. Tender, min. 5°C (41°F). Requires full sun and well-drained, sandy soil. Water containerized plants moderately when in full growth, less at other times. Propagate by seed or semi-ripe cuttings in summer.
C. quadrifidus (common net bush). Erect to spreading, evergreen shrub. H 2–4m (6–12ft), S 2–5m (6–15ft). Has linear, greyish to dark green or grey leaves. Irregular, axillary, one-sided spikes of rich red, feathery flowers, 2.5cm (1in) long, are produced from late spring to autumn, often forming clusters, 20cm (8in) or more across, around the stems.

CALTHA

RANUNCULACEAE

Genus of deciduous, perennial, marginal water plants, bog plants and rock garden plants, grown for their attractive flowers. Most prefer an open, sunny position. Smaller growing species are suitable for rock gardens, troughs and alpine houses and require moist but well-drained soil; larger species are best in marginal conditions. Propagate species by seed in autumn or by division in autumn or early spring, selected forms by division in autumn or early spring.
C. leptosepala illus. p.447.
C. palustris illus. p.451. var. *alba* (syn. *C.p.* 'Alba') is a compact, deciduous, perennial, marginal water plant. H 22cm (9in), S 30cm (12in). Has rounded, glossy, dark green leaves, and bears solitary, white flowers with yellow stamens in early spring, often before the foliage develops. **'Flore Pleno'** illus. p.451.

CALYCANTHUS

CALYCANTHACEAE

Genus of deciduous, summer-flowering shrubs, grown for their purplish- or brownish-red flowers with strap-shaped petals. Requires sun or light shade and fertile, deep, moist but well-drained soil. Propagate by softwood cuttings in summer or by seed in autumn.
C. floridus (Carolina allspice). Deciduous, bushy shrub. H and S 2m (6ft). Has oval, aromatic, dark green leaves and, from early to mid-summer, fragrant, brownish-red flowers with masses of spreading petals. Zone 5.
C. occidentalis illus. p.142.

CALYPSO

See also ORCHIDS.
C. bulbosa (illus. p.297). Deciduous, terrestrial orchid. H 5–20cm (2–8in). Corm-like stem produces a single, oval, pleated leaf, 3–10cm (1¼–4in) long. Purplish-pink flowers, 1.5–2cm (⅝–¾in) long, with hairy, purple-blotched, white or pale pink lips, are produced singly in late spring or early summer. Requires a damp, semi-shaded position with a mulch of leaf mould.

CAMASSIA

HYACINTHACEAE/LILIACEAE

Genus of summer-flowering bulbs, suitable for borders and pond margins. Requires sun or partial shade and deep, moist soil. Plant bulbs in autumn, 10cm (4in) deep. Lies dormant in autumn-winter. Propagate by seed in autumn or by division in late summer. If seed is not required, cut off stems after flowering.
C. esculenta. See *C. quamash*.
C. leichtlinii illus. p.397. **'Semiplena'** illus. p.397.
C. quamash, syn. *C. esculenta* (Common camassia, Quamash). Clump-forming, summer-flowering bulb. H 20–80cm (8–32in), S 20–30cm (8–12in). Produces long, narrow, erect, basal leaves. Leafless stems each bear a dense spike of star-shaped, blue, violet or white flowers, to 7cm (3in) across.

Camassia, Common. See *Camassia quamash.*

CAMELLIA

THEACEAE

Genus of evergreen shrubs and trees, grown for their flowers and foliage. Flowers are classified according to the following types: single, semi-double, anemone-form, peony-form, rose-form, formal double and irregular double. See feature panel pp.128–9 for illustrations and descriptions. Grows well against walls and in containers. Hardy to tender, min. 7–10°C (45–50°F). Most forms prefer a sheltered position and semi-shade. Well-drained, neutral to acid soil is essential. Prune to shape after flowering. Propagate by semi-ripe or hardwood cuttings from mid-summer to early winter or by grafting in late winter or early spring. Aphids, thrips and scale insects may cause problems under glass.

C. 'Anticipation' (illus. p.129). Robust, evergreen, upright shrub. H 3m (10ft), S 1.5m (5ft). Has lance-shaped, dark green leaves. Large, peony-form, deep rose-pink blooms are freely produced in spring. Zone 8.

C. 'Black Lace' (illus. p.129). Slow-growing, dense, upright shrub. H 1.5–2.5m (5–8ft), S 1–2.5m (3–8ft). Has ovate, dark green leaves, 8cm (3in) long, and large, formal double, deep velvet-red flowers from early to late spring. Zone 9.

C. chrysantha. See *C. nitidissima.*

C. 'Cornish Snow' (illus. p.128). Fast-growing, evergreen, upright, bushy shrub. H 3m (10ft), S 1.5m (5ft). Has lance-shaped leaves, bronze when young, maturing to dark green. In early spring bears a profusion of small, cup-shaped, single, white flowers. Zone 8.

C. cuspidata. Evergreen, upright shrub becoming bushy with age. H 3m (10ft), S 1.5m (5ft). Has small, lance-shaped leaves, bronze when young, maturing to purplish-green. Small, cup-shaped, single, pure white flowers are freely produced from leaf axils in early spring. Zone 8.

C. 'Dr Clifford Parks' (illus. p.129). Evergreen, spreading shrub. H 4m (12ft), S 2.5m (8ft). In mid-spring has large, flame-red flowers, often semi-double, peony- and anemone-form on the same plant. Leaves are large, oval and dark green. Zone 8.

C. 'Francie L.' (illus. p.129). Vigorous shrub with long, fan-shaped branches. H 5m (15ft), S 6m (20ft). Leaves are lance-shaped and dark green, 6–10cm (2½–4in) long. Has large, semi-double, salmon-red to deep rose-red flowers from late winter to late spring. Zone 8.

C. granthamiana. Evergreen, open shrub. H to 3m (10ft), S 2m (6ft). Oval, leathery leaves are crinkly and glossy, deep green. In late autumn bears large, saucer-shaped, single, white flowers, to 18cm (7in) across, with up to 8 broad petals. Zone 8.

C. hiemalis. Evergreen, upright, bushy shrub. H 2–3m (6–10ft), S 1.5m (5ft). Has small, lance-shaped leaves and fragrant, single, cup-shaped, semi- or irregular double, white, pink or red flowers borne in late autumn and winter. Is good for hedging. Zone 8.

C. hongkongensis. Evergreen, bushy shrub or tree. H to 3m (10ft), S 2m

(6ft). Lance-shaped leaves, 10cm (4in) long, are dark red when young, maturing to dark green. Bears cup-shaped, single, deep crimson flowers, velvety beneath, in late spring. Zone 8.

C. 'Innovation' (illus. p.129). Evergreen, open, spreading shrub. H 5m (15ft), S 3m (10ft). Has large, oval, leathery leaves and, in spring, produces large, peony-form, lavender-shaded, claret-red flowers with twisted petals. Zone 8.

C. 'Inspiration' (illus. p.129). Evergreen, upright shrub. H 4m (12ft), S 2m (6ft). Leaves are oval and leathery. Saucer-shaped, semi-double, phlox-pink flowers are freely produced in spring. Zone 8.

C. japonica (Common camellia). Evergreen shrub that is very variable in habit, foliage and floral form. H 10m (30ft), S 8m (25ft). Numerous cultivars are available; they are spring-flowering unless otherwise stated. All zone 8 unless noted.

'Adolphe Audusson' (illus. p.129) is a very reliable, old cultivar that is suitable for all areas and will withstand lower temperatures than most other variants. Produces large, saucer-shaped, semi-double, dark red flowers with prominent, yellow stamens. Leaves are broadly lance-shaped and dark green. Zone 7.

'Alba Simplex' (illus. p.128) is bushy in habit with broadly lance-shaped, mid- to yellow-green leaves and cup-shaped, single, white flowers in early spring. Zone 8.

'Alexander Hunter' (illus. p.129), an upright, compact shrub, has flattish, single, deep crimson flowers, with some petaloids, and lance-shaped, dark green leaves. Zone 8.

'Althaeiflora' (illus. p.129) has a vigorous, bushy habit, large, peony-form, dark red flowers and broadly oval, very dark green leaves. Zone 8.

'Apollo' (syn. *C.j.* 'Paul's Apollo'; illus. p.129) is a vigorous, branching shrub that produces semi-double, red flowers sometimes blotched with white. Leaves are glossy, dark green. Zone 8.

'Berenice Boddy' (illus. p.128) is a vigorous shrub that bears semi-double, light pink flowers amid lance-shaped, dark green leaves. Zone 8.

'Betty Sheffield Supreme' (illus. p.128) is upright in habit with lance-shaped, mid-green leaves. Irregular double flowers have white petals bordered with shades of rose-pink. Zone 8.

'Bob's Tinsie' (illus. p.129) has a dense, upright habit, and bears miniature, anemone-form, brilliant red flowers from early to late spring.

'Coquettii' (syn. *C.j.* 'Glen 40'; illus. p.129) is a slow-growing, erect shrub. In early and mid-spring, bears profuse, medium to large, deep red flowers, sometimes formal double, sometimes peony-form.

'Donckelaeri' see *C.j.* 'Masayoshi'.

'Elegans' (illus. p.129) has a spreading habit and anemone-form, deep rose-pink flowers with central petaloids often variegated white. Leaves are broadly lance-shaped and dark green.

'Glen 40' see *C.j.* 'Coquettii'.

'Gloire de Nantes' (illus. p.129) is an upright shrub, becoming bushy with age, that bears flattish to cup-shaped, semi-double, bright rose-pink flowers over a long period. Has oval to lance-shaped, glossy, dark green leaves.

'Guilio Nuccio' (illus. p.129) is an upright, free-flowering cultivar that spreads with age. Produces large, cup-shaped, semi-double, rose-red flowers with wavy petals and often a confused centre of petaloids and golden stamens. Dark green leaves are lance-shaped and occasionally have 'fish-tail' tips.

'Hagoromo' (syn. *C.j.* 'Magnoliiflora') has a bushy habit and flattish to cup-shaped, semi-double, blush-pink flowers. Twisted, light green leaves point downwards.

'Janet Waterhouse' (illus. p.128) is strong-growing and has semi-double, white flowers with golden anthers borne amid dark green foliage.

'Julia Drayton' (illus. p.129) has an upright habit and large, crimson flowers varying from formal double to rose-form. Dark green leaves are oval to lance-shaped and slightly twisted.

'Jupiter' (illus. p.129) is an upright shrub that bears lance-shaped, dark green leaves and large, saucer-shaped, single, pinkish-red flowers with golden stamens.

'Kumasaka' (syn. *C.j.* 'Lady Marion') has an upright habit with narrowly lance-shaped, mid-green leaves. Produces formal double, or occasionally peony-form, deep rose-pink flowers. Zone 7.

'Lady Marion' see *C.j.* 'Kumasaka'.

'Lady Vansittart' (illus. p.128) is upright, with unusual, holly-like, twisted, mid-green foliage. Saucer-shaped, semi-double, white flowers are flushed rose-pink; flower colour is variable and often self-coloured mutations appear.

'Lavinia Maggi' (illus. p.128) has an upright habit and formal double, white flowers striped with pink and carmine. Sometimes sports red flowers.

'Magnoliiflora' see *C.j.* 'Hagoromo'.

'Margaret Davis' (illus. p.128) is a spreading cultivar, with oval to lance-shaped, dark green leaves. Has irregular double blooms with ruffled, creamy-white petals, often lined with pink. Edges of each petal are bright rose-red.

'Masayoshi' (syn. *C.j.* 'Donckelaeri') is slow-growing, bushy and pendulous with saucer-shaped, semi-double, red flowers, often white-marbled. Has lance-shaped, dark green leaves. Zone 8.

'Mathotiana' (illus. p.129) is of spreading habit. Very large, formal double, velvety, dark crimson flowers become purplish with age and in warm climates often have rose-form centres. Leaves are lance-shaped to oval, slightly twisted and dark green. Zone 8.

'Mrs D.W. Davis' (illus. p.128) is a dense, spreading cultivar that bears very large, pendulous, cup-shaped, semi-double, delicate pink flowers that are backed by oval to lance-shaped, dark green leaves. Zone 8.

'Paul's Apollo' see *C.j.* 'Apollo'.

'R.L. Wheeler' (illus. p.129) has a

robust, upright growth, large, broadly oval, leathery, very dark green leaves and very large, flattish, anemone-form to semi-double, rose-pink flowers, with distinctive rings of golden stamens, often including some petaloids.

'Rubescens Major' (illus. p.129) is an upright cultivar, becoming bushy with age, with oval to lance-shaped, dark green leaves. Bears formal double, crimson-veined, rose-red flowers.

'Sieboldii' see *C.j.* 'Tricolor'.

'Tomorrow Park Hill', one of the best of many mutations of 'Tomorrow', is of vigorous, upright habit. Has lance-shaped, mid-green leaves and bears irregular double flowers with deep pink, outer petals gradually fading to soft pink centres that are often variegated with white.

'Tomorrow's Dawn' (illus. p.128) is similar to 'Tomorrow Park Hill', but produces pale pink flowers, each with a white border and frequently red-streaked.

'Tricolor' (syn. *C.j.* 'Sieboldii') has bright green, crinkled, holly-like leaves, and bears medium, single or semi-double, red flowers, striped pink and white, in early spring.

C. 'Leonard Messel' (illus. p.129). Evergreen, open shrub. H 4m (12ft), S 2.5m (8ft). Has large, oval, leathery, dark green leaves. In spring bears a profusion of large, flattish to cup-shaped, semi-double, rose-pink flowers. Zone 8.

C. x *maliflora.* Evergreen, upright, bushy shrub. H 2m (6ft), S 1m (3ft). Has small, lance-shaped, thin-textured, light green leaves and, in spring, produces flattish to cup-shaped, semi-double, pale pink- or white-centred flowers with rose-pink margins. Zone 8.

C. nitidissima, syn. *C. chrysantha.* Fast-growing, evergreen, open shrub or tree. H 6m (20ft) or more, S 3m (10ft). Has large, oval, leathery, veined leaves. Small, stalked, cup-shaped, single, clear yellow flowers are produced from leaf axils in spring. Zone 7.

C. oleifera. Evergreen, bushy shrub. H 2m (6ft), S 1.5m (5ft). Leaves are oval and dull green. Has cup-shaped, single, sometimes pinkish, white flowers in early spring. Zone 7.

C. reticulata. Evergreen, open, tree-like shrub. H 10m (30ft) or more, S 5m (15ft). Has large, oval, leathery leaves; large, saucer-shaped, single, rose-pink and salmon-red flowers are borne in spring. Needs shelter. Zone 8b.

'Arch of Triumph' (illus. p.129) bears very large, loose peony-form, orange-tinted, crimson-pink flowers. 'Butterfly Wings' see *C.r.* 'Houye Diechi'.

'Captain Rawes' (illus. p.129) has a profusion of large, semi-double, carmine-rose blooms. 'Houye Diechi' (syn. *C.r.* 'Butterfly Wings'; illus. p.129) produces very large, flattish to cup-shaped, semi-double, rose-pink flowers with wavy, central petals.

'Mandalay Queen' (illus. p.129) has large, semi-double, deep rose-pink flowers. 'Robert Fortune' see *C.r.* 'Songzilin'. 'Songzilin' (syn. *C.r.* 'Robert Fortune') is upright and has large, formal double, deep red flowers. All zone 8b.

C. rosiflora. Evergreen, spreading

shrub. H and S 1m (3ft). Leaves are oval and dark green. In spring bears small, saucer-shaped, single, rose-pink flowers. Zone 8.

C. saluenensis (illus. p.128). Fast-growing, evergreen, bushy shrub. H to 4m (12ft), S to 2.5m (8ft). Has lance-shaped, stiff, dull green leaves. Cup-shaped, single, white to rose-red flowers are freely produced in early spring. Some forms may withstand lower temperatures. Zone 8.

C. sasanqua. Fast-growing, evergreen, dense, upright shrub. H 3m (10ft), S 1.5m (5ft). Has lance-shaped, glossy, bright green leaves. In autumn bears a profusion of fragrant, flattish to cup-shaped, single, rarely semi-double, white flowers; they may occasionally be pink or red. Does best in a hot, sunny site. Zone 8. **'Narumigata'** (illus. p.128) has large, cup-shaped, single, white flowers, sometimes pink-flushed. **'Shishigashira'** has small, semi-double to rose-form double, pinkish-red flowers.

C. **'Satan's Robe'** (illus. p.129). Vigorous, erect shrub. H 3–5m (10–15ft), S 2–3m (6–10ft). Leaves are broadly elliptic, glossy and dark green, 12–16cm (5–6in) long. From early to late spring, produces large, semi-double, bright carmine-red flowers, with yellow stamens. Zone 8.

C. **'Shirowabisuke'** (illus. p.128). Slow-growing, compact shrub. H 2.5m (8ft), S 1.5m (5ft). Has narrow, mid-green leaves. From mid-winter to early spring produces small, single, bell-shaped, white flowers. Zone 8.

C. tsai (illus. p.128). Evergreen, bushy shrub. H 4m (12ft), S 3m (10ft). Small, lance-shaped, light green leaves turn bronze with age. Small, cup-shaped, single, white flowers are freely produced in spring. Zone 9.

C. x *vernalis.* Fast-growing, evergreen, upright shrub. H to 3m (10ft), S 1.5m (5ft). Has lance-shaped, bright green leaves and, in late winter, fragrant, flattish to cup-shaped, single, white, pink or red flowers. Some forms produce irregular double flowers. Zone 8.

C. **'William Hertrich'** (illus. p.129). Strong-growing, evergreen, open shrub. H 5m (15ft), S 3m (10ft). Is free-flowering with large, flattish to cup-shaped, semi-double blooms of a bright cherry-red in spring. Petal formation is very irregular, and petals often form a confused centre with only a few golden stamens. Leaves are large, oval and deep green. Zone 8.

C. x *williamsii* **'Bow Bells'** (illus. p.128). Evergreen, upright, spreading shrub. H 4m (12ft), S 2.5m (8ft). Has small, lance-shaped, mid-green leaves and, in early spring, masses of cup-shaped, single, rose-pink flowers with deeper pink centres and veins. Zone 8b. **'Brigadoon'** (illus. p.128) is a bushy shrub, bearing semi-double, rose-pink flowers with broad, down-curving petals. **'Donation'** (illus. p.128) is a compact, upright plant that is very floriferous, with large, cup-shaped, semi-double, pink flowers. **'Dream Boat'** (illus. p.128) has a spreading habit, and bears medium, formal double, pale purplish-pink flowers, with incurved petals, in mid-spring.

'E.G. Waterhouse' (illus. p.128) is an upright, free-flowering cultivar bearing formal double, pink flowers among pale green foliage. **'Elizabeth de Rothschild'** is vigorous and upright; cup-shaped, semi-double, rose-pink flowers appear among glossy foliage. **'Francis Hanger'** (illus. p.128) has an upright habit and carries single, white flowers with gold stamens. **'George Blandford'** (illus. p.129) is spreading and bears semi-double, bright crimson-pink flowers in early spring. **'Golden Spangles'** (illus. p.129) is a cup-shaped, single, deep pink cultivar with unusual, variegated foliage, yellowish in centres of leaves with dark green margins. **'J.C. Willams'** (illus. p.128) is of pendulous habit when mature and bears cup-shaped, single, pink flowers from early winter to late spring. **'Joan Trehane'** (illus. p.128) has strong, upright growth and large, rose-form double, rose-pink flowers. **'Jury's Yellow'** (illus. p.128) is narrow and erect, bearing medium, anemone-form, white flowers, with centres of yellow petaloids. **'Saint Ewe'** (syn. *C.* x *w.* 'St Ewe'; illus. p.128) has glossy, light green foliage and funnel-shaped, single, deep pink flowers. **'Water Lily'** (illus. p.129) is an upright, compact cultivar with dark green leaves that bears formal double, mid-pink flowers with incurving petals in mid- to late spring. All zone 8b.

Camellia, Common. See *Camellia japonica.*

CAMPANULA
Bellflower

CAMPANULACEAE

Genus of spring- and summer-flowering annuals, biennials and perennials, some of which are evergreen. Grows in sun or shade, but delicate flower colours are preserved best in shade. Most forms prefer moist but well-drained soil. Propagate by softwood or basal cuttings in summer or by seed or division in autumn or spring. Is prone to slug attack, and rust may be a problem in autumn.

C. alliariifolia illus. p.275.
C. barbata illus. p.356.
C. betulifolia. Prostrate, slender-stemmed perennial. H 2cm (¾in), S 30cm (12in). In summer, long, branching flower stems each carry a cluster of open bell-shaped, single, white to pink flowers, deep pink outside. Leaves are wedge-shaped.
C. **'Birch Hybrid'** illus. p.382.
C. x *burghaltii.* See *C.* 'Burghaltii'.
C. **'Burghaltii'**, syn. *C.* x *burghaltii*, illus. p.286.
C. carpatica. Clump-forming perennial. H 8–10cm (3–4in), S to 30cm (12in). Leafy, branching stems bear rounded to oval, toothed leaves and, in summer, broadly bell-shaped, blue or white flowers. **'Bressingham White'** illus. p.373. **'Jewel'** has deep violet flowers. Flowers of **'Turbinata'** (syn. *C.c.* var. *turbinata*) are pale lavender.
C. cochleariifolia, syn. *C. pusilla*, illus. p.383.
C. garganica. Spreading perennial. H 5cm (2in), S 30cm (12in). Has small,

ivy-shaped leaves along stems. Clusters of star-shaped, single, pale lavender flowers are produced from leaf axils in summer. Makes an excellent wall or bank plant. **'W.H. Paine'** has bright lavender-blue flowers, each with a white eye.
C. **'G.F. Wilson'** illus. p.382.
C. glomerata **'Superba'** illus. p.251.
C. x *haylodgensis.* See *C.* x *haylodgensis* 'Plena'.
C. x *haylodgensis* **'Plena'**, syn. *C.* x *haylodgensis.* Spreading perennial. H 5cm (2in), S 20cm (8in). Has small, heart-shaped leaves and, in summer, bears pompon-like, double, deep lavender-blue flowers. Is suitable for a rock garden or wall.
C. isophylla. Evergreen, dwarf, trailing perennial often grown as an annual. H 10cm (4in), S 30cm (12in). In summer, star-shaped, blue or white flowers are borne above small, heart-shaped, toothed leaves. Is ideal for a hanging basket. **Kristal Hybrids 'Stella Blue'** illus. p.287.
C. **'Joe Elliott'.** Mound-forming perennial. H 8cm (3in), S 12cm (5in). In summer, large, funnel-shaped, mid-lavender-blue flowers almost obscure small, heart-shaped, downy, grey-green leaves. Is good for an alpine house, trough or rock garden. Needs well-drained, alkaline soil. Protect from winter wet. Is prone to slug attack.
C. lactiflora. Upright, branching perennial. H 1.2m (4ft), S 60cm (2ft). In summer, slender stems bear racemes of large, nodding, bell-shaped, blue, occasionally pink or white flowers. Leaves are narrowly oval. Needs staking on a windy site. **'Loddon Anna'** illus. p.227. **'Prichard's Variety'** illus. p.228.
C. latifolia **'Brantwood'.** Clump-forming, spreading perennial. H 1.2m (4ft), S 60cm (2ft). Strong stems are clothed with bell-shaped, rich violet-purple flowers in summer. Oval leaves are rough-textured.
C. latiloba. Rosette-forming perennial. H 1m (3ft), S 45cm (1½ft). Leaves are oval. Widely cup-shaped flowers, in shades of blue, occasionally white, are borne in summer. **'Percy Piper'** has lavender flowers.
C. medium (Canterbury bell). Slow-growing, evergreen, erect, clump-forming biennial. Tall cultivars, H 1m (3ft), S 30cm (1ft); dwarf, H 60cm (2ft), S 30cm (1ft). All have lance-shaped, toothed, fresh green leaves. Bell-shaped, single or double flowers, white or in shades of blue and pink, are produced in spring and early summer. **'Bells of Holland'** illus. p.331.
C. morettiana. Tuft-forming perennial. H 2.5cm (1in), S 7cm (3in). Leaves are ivy-shaped with fine hairs. Arching flower stems each carry a solitary erect, bell-shaped, violet-blue flower in late spring and early summer. Needs gritty, alkaline soil and a dry but not arid winter climate. Spider mite may be troublesome.
C. persicifolia. Rosette-forming, spreading perennial. H 1m (3ft), S 30cm (1ft). In summer, nodding, bell-shaped, papery, white or blue flowers are borne above narrowly lance-shaped, bright green leaves.

'Fleur de Neige' has double, white flowers. **'Pride of Exmouth'** bears double, powder-blue flowers. **'Telham Beauty'** illus. p.253.
C. portenschlagiana illus. p.382.
C. poscharskyana illus. p.381.
C. pulla. Often short-lived perennial that spreads by underground runners. H 2.5cm (1in), S 10cm (4in). Tiny, rounded leaves form 1cm (½in) wide rosettes, each bearing a flower stem with a solitary pendent, bell-shaped, deep violet flower from late spring to early summer. Is good for a scree or rock garden. Needs gritty, alkaline soil that is not too dry. Slugs may prove troublesome.
C. pusilla. See *C. cochleariifolia.*
C. pyramidalis (Chimney bellflower). Erect, branching biennial. H 2m (6ft), S 60cm (2ft). Produces long racemes of star-shaped, blue or white flowers in summer. Leaves are heart-shaped. Needs staking.
C. raineri. Perennial that spreads by underground runners. H 4cm (1½in), S 8cm (3in). Leaves are oval, toothed and grey-green. Flower stems each carry a large, upturned, bell-shaped, pale lavender flower in summer. Is suitable for an alpine house or trough that is protected from winter wet. Requires semi-shade.
C. trachelium and **'Bernice'** illus. p.252.
C. vidalii. See *Azorina vidalii.*
C. zoysii. Tuft-forming perennial. H 5cm (2in), S 10cm (4in). Has tiny, rounded, glossy green leaves. In summer, flower stems each bear a bottle-shaped, lavender flower held horizontally. Needs gritty, alkaline soil. Is difficult to grow and flower well, dislikes winter wet and is prone to slug attack.

Campernelle jonquil. See *Narcissus* x *odorus.*
Campion. See *Silene.*
   Double sea. See *Silene uniflora* 'Robin Whitebreast'.
   Moss. See *Silene acaulis*, illus. p.365.

CAMPSIS

BIGNONIACEAE

Genus of deciduous, woody-stemmed, root climbers, grown for their flowers. At limits of hardiness, needs protection of a sunny wall. Grow in sun in fertile, well-drained soil, and water regularly in summer. Prune in spring. Propagate by semi-ripe cuttings in summer or by layering in winter.
C. chinensis. See *C. grandiflora.*
C. grandiflora, syn. *Bignonia grandiflora, Campsis chinensis, Tecoma grandiflora* (Chinese trumpet creeper, Chinese trumpet vine). Deciduous, woody-stemmed, root climber. H 7–10m (22–30ft). Leaves have 7 or 9 oval, toothed leaflets, hairless beneath. Drooping clusters of trumpet-shaped, deep orange or red flowers, 5–8cm (2–3in) long, are produced in late summer and autumn, abundantly in warm areas. Zone 8.
C. radicans, syn. *Bignonia radicans, Tecoma radicans* (Trumpet creeper,

Trumpet vine). Deciduous, woody-stemmed, root climber. H to 12m (40ft). Leaves of 7–11 oval, toothed leaflets are downy beneath. Small clusters of trumpet-shaped, orange, scarlet or yellow flowers, 6–8cm (2½–3in) long, open in late summer and early autumn. Zone 5b.
C. x tagliabuana 'Madame Galen' illus. p.217.

Canada hemlock. See *Tsuga canadensis*, illus. p.107.
Canada lily. See *Lilium canadense*.
Canada moonseed. See *Menispermum canadense*.
Canada wild rice. See *Zizania aquatica*.
Canadian burnet. See *Sanguisorba canadensis*, illus. p.226.
Canadian columbine. See *Aquilegia canadensis*.
Canadian poplar. See *Populus x canadensis*.

CANARINA

CAMPANULACEAE

Genus of herbaceous, tuberous, scrambling climbers, grown for their flowers. Tender, min. 7°C (45°F). Grow in full light and in any fertile, well-drained soil. Water moderately from early autumn to late spring, then keep dry. Needs tying to a support. Remove dead stems when dormant. Propagate by basal cuttings or seed sown in spring or autumn.
C. campanula. See *C. canariensis*.
C. canariensis, syn. *C. campanula*, illus. p.219.

Canary creeper. See *Tropaeolum peregrinum*.
Canary Island bellflower. See *Canarina canariensis*, illus. p.219.
Canary Island date palm. See *Phoenix canariensis*.
Canary Island ivy. See *Hedera canariensis*.
Canary-bird bush. See *Crotalaria agatiflora*, illus. p.123.
Candle plant. See *Senecio articulatus*.
Candle, Blue. See *Myrtillocactus geometrizans*, illus. p.456.
Candollea cuneiformis. See *Hibbertia cuneiformis*.
Candytuft. See *Iberis*.
Cane, Dumb. See *Dieffenbachia*.

CANNA

CANNACEAE

Genus of robust, showy, rhizomatous perennials, grown for their striking flowers and ornamental foliage. Is generally used for summer-bedding displays and container growing. Tender, min. 5–15°C (41–59°F). Requires a warm, sunny position and humus-rich, moist soil. If grown under glass or for summer bedding, encourage into growth in spring at 16°C (61°F) and store rhizomes in slightly damp soil or peat in winter. Propagate in spring by division or in winter by seed sown at 20°C (68°F) or more.
C. 'Assault'. See *C. 'Assaut'*.

C. 'Assaut', syn. *C. 'Assault'*, illus. p.401.
C. 'Black Knight'. Rhizomatous perennial. H 1.8m (6ft), S 45–60cm (1½–2ft). Stout stems bear broadly lance-shaped, bronze-green leaves. From mid-summer to early autumn has large racemes of gladiolus-like, very dark red flowers, 7cm (3in) across, with wavy petals.
C. iridiflora illus. p.403.
C. 'Lucifer'. Rhizomatous perennial. H 1m (3ft), S 45–60cm (1½–2ft). Has broadly lance-shaped, mid-green leaves, and profuse racemes of iris-like, yellow-edged, red flowers from mid-summer to early autumn.

Canoe birch. See *Betula papyrifera*, illus. p.72.
Canterbury bell. See *Campanula medium*.

CANTUA

POLEMONIACEAE

Genus of evergreen shrubs, grown for their showy flowers in spring. Only one species is in general cultivation, and is best grown against a south- or west-facing wall. Requires full sun and fertile, well-drained soil. Propagate by semi-ripe cuttings in summer.
C. buxifolia, syn. *C. dependens*, illus. p.155.
C. dependens. See *C. buxifolia*.

Cape blue water lily. See *Nymphaea capensis*.
Cape chestnut. See *Calodendrum capense*.
Cape dandelion. See *Arctotheca calendula*, illus. p.294.
Cape grape. See *Rhoicissus capensis*.
Cape honeysuckle. See *Tecoma capensis*.
Cape jasmine. See *Gardenia augusta*.
Cape leadwort. See *Plumbago auriculata*, illus. p.215.
Cape marigold. See *Dimorphotheca*.
Cape myrtle. See *Myrsine africana*.
Cape pondweed. See *Aponogeton distachyos*, illus. p.447.
Cape primrose. See *Streptocarpus rexii*.
Cape sundew. See *Drosera capensis*, illus. p.305.
Cappadocian maple. See *Acer cappadocicum*.

CAPSICUM

SOLANACEAE

Genus of evergreen shrubs, sub-shrubs and short-lived perennials, usually grown as annuals. Some species produce edible fruits (e.g. sweet peppers), others small, ornamental ones. Tender, min. 4°C (39°F). Grow in sun and in fertile, well-drained soil. Spray flowers with water to encourage fruit to set. Propagate by seed sown under glass in spring. Spider mite may cause problems.
C. annuum (Ornamental pepper). **'Holiday Cheer'** is a moderately fast-growing, evergreen, bushy perennial, grown as an annual. H and S 20–30cm (8–12in). Has oval, mid-green leaves.

Bears small, star-shaped, white flowers in summer and, in autumn-winter, spherical, green fruits maturing to red.

CARAGANA

LEGUMINOSAE/PAPILIONACEAE

Genus of deciduous shrubs, grown for their foliage and flowers. Needs full sun and fertile but not over-rich, well-drained soil. Propagate species by softwood cuttings in summer or by seed in autumn, cultivars by softwood or semi-ripe cuttings or budding in summer or by grafting in winter.
C. arborescens. Fast-growing, deciduous, upright shrub. H 6m (20ft), S 4m (12ft). Has spine-tipped, dark green leaves, each composed of 8–12 oblong leaflets. Produces clusters of pea-like, yellow flowers in late spring. Zone 2. Arching **'Lorbergii'**, H 3m (10ft), S 2.5m (8ft), has very narrow leaflets and smaller flowers and is often grown as a tree by top-grafting. **'Nana'** illus. p.157. **'Walker'**, H 30cm (1ft), S 2–3m (6–10ft), is prostrate but is usually top-grafted to form a weeping tree, H 2m (6ft), S 75cm (2½ft).
C. frutex 'Globosa'. Slow-growing, deciduous, upright shrub. H and S 30cm (1ft). Mid-green leaves each have 4 oblong leaflets. Pea-like, bright yellow flowers are borne only rarely in late spring. Zone 2.

CARALLUMA

ASCLEPIADACEAE

Genus of perennial succulents with 4–6-ribbed, finger-like, blue-grey or blue-green to purple stems. Tender, min. 11°C (52°F). Needs sun and extremely well-drained soil. Water sparingly, only in the growing season. May be difficult to grow. Propagate by seed or stem cuttings in summer.
C. europaea, syn. *Stapelia europaea*. Clump-forming, perennial succulent. H 20cm (8in), S 1m (3ft). Rough, 4-angled, erect to procumbent, grey stems often arch over and root. Has clusters of small, star-shaped, yellow and brownish-purple flowers near stem crown from mid- to late summer, then twin-horned, grey seed pods. Flowers smell faintly of rotten meat. Is one of the easier species to grow.
C. joannis illus. p.475.

Caraway thyme. See *Thymus herba-barona*, illus. p.381.

CARDAMINE

Bitter cress

BRASSICACEAE/CRUCIFERAE

Genus of spring-flowering annuals and perennials. Some are weeds, but others are suitable for informal and woodland gardens. Requires sun or semi-shade and moist soil. Propagate by seed or division in autumn.
C. enneaphyllos, syn. *Dentaria enneaphyllos*, illus. p.274.
C. pentaphyllos, syn. *Dentaria pentaphyllos*, illus. p.270.

C. pratensis (Cuckoo flower, Lady's smock). **'Flore Pleno'** is a neat, clump-forming perennial. H 45cm (18in), S 30cm (12in). Bears dense sheaves of double, lilac flowers in spring. Mid-green leaves are divided into rounded leaflets. May also be propagated by leaf-tip cuttings in mid-summer. Prefers moist or wet conditions.
C. trifolia illus. p.362.

Cardinal climber. See *Ipomoea x multifida*.
Cardinal flower. See *Lobelia cardinalis*.
Cardinal's guard. See *Pachystachys coccinea*.

CARDIOCRINUM

LILIACEAE

Genus of summer-flowering, lily-like bulbs, grown for their spectacular flowers in mild climates. Needs partial shade and deep, humus-rich, moist soil. Where hardy, plant bulbs just below soil surface, in autumn. Water well in summer and mulch with humus. Provide a deep mulch in winter. After flowering, main bulb dies, but produces offsets. To produce flowers in up to 5 years, propagate by offsets in autumn; may also be propagated by seed in autumn or winter and will then flower in 7 years.
C. giganteum (Giant lily) illus. p.398. var. **yunnanense** is a stout, leafy-stemmed bulb. H 1.5–2m (5–6ft), S 75cm–1m (2½–3ft). Has bold, heart-shaped, bronze-green leaves. Fragrant, pendent, trumpet-shaped, cream flowers, 15cm (6in) long, with purpled-red streaks inside, are borne in long spikes in summer and are followed by decorative seed heads.

CARDIOSPERMUM

SAPINDACEAE

Genus of herbaceous or deciduous, shrubby climbers, grown mainly for their attractive fruits. Is useful for covering bushes or trellises. Tender, min. 5°C (41°F). Grow in full light and any soil. Propagate by seed in spring.
C. halicacabum (Balloon vine, Heart pea, Heart seed, Winter cherry). Deciduous, shrubby, scandent, perennial climber, usually grown as an annual or biennial. H to 3m (10ft). Has toothed leaves of 2 oblong leaflets. Inconspicuous, whitish flowers are produced in summer, followed by downy, spherical, inflated, 3-angled, straw-coloured fruits containing black seeds, each with a heart-shaped, white spot.

Cardoon. See *Cynara cardunculus*, illus. p.228.

CAREX

CYPERACEAE

See also GRASSES, BAMBOOS, RUSHES and SEDGES.
C. buchananii (Leatherleaf sedge). Evergreen, tuft-forming, perennial sedge. H to 60cm (24in), S 20cm (8in).

Very narrow, copper-coloured leaves turn red towards base. Solid, triangular stems bear insignificant, brown spikelets in summer.
C. elata, syn. *C. stricta* (Tufted sedge). Evergreen, tuft-forming, perennial sedge. H to 1m (3ft), S 15cm (6in). Leaves are somewhat glaucous. Solid, triangular stems bear blackish-brown spikelets in summer. **'Aurea'** illus. p.309.
C. grayi (Mace sedge). Evergreen, tuft-forming, perennial sedge. H to 60cm (24in), S 20cm (8in). Has bright green leaves. Large, female spikelets, borne in summer, mature to pointed, knobbly, greenish-brown fruits.
C. hachijoensis 'Evergold', syn. *C. oshimensis* 'Evergold', illus. p.309.
C. morrowii of gardens. See *C. oshimensis*.
C. oshimensis, syn. *C. morrowii* of gardens. Evergreen, tuft-forming, perennial sedge. H 20–50cm (8–20in), S 20–25cm (8–10in). Has narrow, mid-green leaves. Solid, triangular stems bear insignificant spikelets in summer. **'Evergold'** see *C. hachijoensis* 'Evergold'.
C. pendula illus. p.309.
C. riparia (Greater pond sedge). **'Variegata'** is a vigorous, evergreen, perennial sedge. H 60cm–1m (2–3ft), S indefinite. Has broad, white-striped, mid-green leaves and solid, triangular stems that bear narrow, bristle-tipped, dark brown spikelets in summer.
C. stricta. See *C. elata*.

Caricature plant. See *Graptophyllum pictum*.

CARISSA
APOCYNACEAE

Genus of evergreen, spring- to summer-flowering shrubs, grown for their flowers and overall appearance. Tender, min. 10–13°C (50–55°F). Needs partial shade and well-drained soil. Water containerized specimens moderately, less when temperatures are low. Propagate by seed when ripe or in spring or by semi-ripe cuttings in summer. The seeds are poisonous.
C. grandiflora. See *C. macrocarpa*.
C. macrocarpa, syn. *C. grandiflora* (Natal plum). **'Tuttlei'** illus. p.135.
C. spectabilis. See *Acokanthera oblongifolia*.

CARLINA
Thistle
ASTERACEAE/COMPOSITAE

Genus of annuals, biennials and perennials, grown for their ornamental flower heads. Requires a sunny position and well-drained soil. Propagate by seed: annuals in spring, perennials in autumn.
C. acaulis illus. p.375.

CARMICHAELIA
LEGUMINOSAE/PAPILIONACEAE

Genus of deciduous, usually leafless shrubs, grown for their profusion of tiny flowers in summer. Flattened, green shoots assume function of leaves.

Needs full sun and well-drained soil. Cut out dead wood in spring. Propagate by semi-ripe cuttings in summer or by seed in autumn or spring.
C. arborea, syn. *C. australis*. Deciduous, upright shrub. H 2m (6ft), S 1.5m (5ft). Small clusters of pea-like, pale lilac flowers appear from early to mid-summer. May need staking when mature. Zone 9.
C. australis. See *C. arborea*.
C. enysii. Deciduous, mound-forming, dense shrub. H and S 30cm (1ft). Shoots are rigid. Pea-like, violet flowers are borne in mid-summer. Is best grown in a rock garden. Zone 9.

Carnation. See *Dianthus*.

CARNEGIEA
CACTACEAE

Genus of one species of very slow-growing, perennial cactus with thick, 12–24-ribbed, spiny stems. Is unlikely to flower or branch at less than 4m (12ft) high. Tender, min. 7°C (45°F). Requires full sun and very well-drained soil. Propagate by seed in spring or summer.
C. gigantea illus. p.456.

Carolina allspice. See *Calycanthus floridus*.
Carolina hemlock. See *Tsuga caroliniana*.
Carolina jasmine. See *Gelsemium sempervirens*, illus. p.206.
Carolina poplar. See *Populus* x *canadensis* 'Eugenes'.
Carolina water shield. See *Cabomba*.

CARPENTERIA
HYDRANGEACEAE/PHILADELPHACEAE

Genus of one species of evergreen, summer-flowering shrub, cultivated for its flowers and foliage. Grows well against a south- or west-facing wall. Prefers full sun and fairly moist but well-drained soil. Propagate by greenwood cuttings in summer or by seed in autumn.
C. californica illus. p.138.

CARPINUS
Hornbeam
CORYLACEAE

Genus of deciduous trees, grown for their foliage, autumn colour and clusters of small, winged nuts. Needs sun or semi-shade and fertile, well-drained soil. Propagate species by seed in autumn, cultivars by budding in late summer.
C. betulus (European hornbeam). Deciduous, round-headed tree. H 25m (80ft), S 20m (70ft). Has a fluted trunk and oval, prominently veined, dark green leaves that turn yellow and orange in autumn. Bears green catkins from late spring to autumn, when clusters of winged nuts appear. Zone 4.
'Fastigiata' (syn. *C.b.* 'Pyramidalis'; illus. p.100). **'Pyramidalis'** see *C.b.* 'Fastigiata'.
C. caroliniana (American hornbeam, Blue beech). Deciduous, spreading tree

with branches that droop at tips. H and S 10m (30ft). Has a fluted, grey trunk, green catkins in spring and oval, bright green leaves that turn orange and red in autumn, when clusters of winged nuts appear. Zone 3b.
C. tschonoskii. Deciduous, rounded tree of elegant habit, with branches drooping at tips. H and S 12m (40ft). Has oval, sharply toothed, glossy, dark green leaves. Green catkins are carried in spring and clusters of small, winged nuts appear in autumn. Zone 7.
C. turczaninowii. Deciduous, spreading tree of graceful habit. H 12m (40ft), S 10m (30ft). Green catkins are borne in spring. Produces clusters of small, winged nuts in autumn, when small, oval, glossy, deep green leaves turn orange. Zone 7.

CARPOBROTUS
AIZOACEAE

Genus of mat-forming, perennial succulents with triangular, fleshy, dark green leaves and daisy-like flowers. Is excellent for binding sandy soils. Tender, min. 5°C (41°F). Needs full sun and well-drained soil. Propagate by seed or stem cuttings in spring or summer.
C. edulis (Hottentot fig, Kaffir fig). Carpeting, perennial succulent. H 15cm (6in), S indefinite. Prostrate, rooting branches bear leaves 1.5cm (⅝in) thick and 12cm (5in) long. Yellow, purple or pink flowers, 12cm (5in) across, open in spring-summer from about noon in sun. Bears edible, fig-like, brownish fruits in late summer and autumn.

CARRIEREA
FLACOURTIACEAE

Genus of deciduous trees. Only *C. calycina*, grown for its flowers, is in general cultivation. Requires full sun and fertile, well-drained soil. Propagate by softwood cuttings in summer.
C. calycina. Deciduous, spreading tree. H 8m (25ft), S 10m (30ft). Oval, glossy, mid-green leaves set off upright clusters of cup-shaped, creamy-white or greenish-white flowers borne in early summer. Zone 9.

CARYA
Hickory
JUGLANDACEAE

Genus of deciduous trees, grown for their stately habit, divided leaves, autumn colour and, in some cases, edible nuts. Has insignificant flowers in spring. Requires sun or semi-shade and deep, fertile soil. Plant young seedlings in a permanent position during their first year since older plants resent transplanting. Propagate by seed in autumn.
C. cordiformis (Bitternut, Bitternut hickory). Vigorous, deciduous, spreading tree. H 25m (80ft), S 15m (50ft). Bark is smooth at first, later fissured. Bright green, winter leaf buds develop into large, dark green leaves, with usually 7 oval to oblong leaflets; these turn yellow in autumn. Nuts are pear-shaped or rounded,

2–4cm (¾–1½in) long, each with a bitter kernel. Zone 4.
C. glabra (Pignut, Pignut hickory). Deciduous, spreading tree. H 25m (80ft), S 20m (70ft). Dark green leaves, with usually 5 narrowly oval leaflets, turn bright yellow and orange in autumn. Pear-shaped or rounded nuts, 2–4cm (¾–1½in) long, each have a bitter kernel. Zone 6.
C. ovata illus. p.69.

CARYOPTERIS
VERBENACEAE

Genus of deciduous sub-shrubs, grown for their foliage and small, but freely produced, blue flowers. Prefers full sun and light, well-drained soil. Cut back hard in spring. Propagate species by greenwood or semi-ripe cuttings in summer or by seed in autumn; propagate cultivars by cuttings only, in summer.
C. x clandonensis 'Arthur Simmonds' illus. p.168. **'Heavenly Blue'** is a deciduous, bushy sub-shrub. H and S 1m (3ft). Forms an upright, compact mass of lance-shaped, grey-green leaves. Dense clusters of tubular, blue to purplish-blue flowers, with prominent stamens, are borne from late summer to autumn. Zone 7.
C. incana, syn. *C. mastacanthus*. Deciduous, bushy sub-shrub. H and S 1.2m (4ft). Bears tubular, violet-blue flowers, with prominent stamens, amid lance-shaped, grey-green leaves from late summer to early autumn. Zone 8.
C. mastacanthus. See *C. incana*.

Caspian locust. See *Gleditsia caspica*.

CASSIA
CAESALPINIACEAE/LEGUMINOSAE

Genus of annuals, perennials and evergreen or deciduous trees and shrubs, grown for their flowers mainly produced from winter to summer. Tender, min. 7–18°C (45–64°F). Needs full light and fertile, well-drained soil. Water containerized specimens freely when in full growth, moderately to sparingly in winter. Pruning is tolerated, severe if need be, but trees are best left to grow naturally. Propagate by seed in spring.
C. artemisioides. See *Senna artemisioides*.
C. corymbosa. See *Senna corymbosa*. var. **plurijuga** of gardens. See *Senna* x *floribunda*.
C. didymobotrya. See *Senna didymobotrya*.
C. fistula (Golden shower, Indian laburnum, Pudding pipe-tree). Fast-growing, almost deciduous, ovoid tree. H 8–10m (25–30ft), S 4–6m (12–20ft). Tender, min. 16°C (61°F). Has 30–45cm (12–18in) long leaves, each with 4–8 pairs of oval leaflets, coppery when young. In spring produces racemes of small, fragrant, 5-petalled, cup-shaped, bright yellow flowers. Cylindrical, dark brown pods, to 60cm (24in) long, yield cassia pulp.
C. x floribunda. See *Senna* x *floribunda*.
C. siamea. See *Senna siamea*.

Cassia
Silver. See *Senna artemisioides*.
Wormwood. See *Senna artemisioides*.

CASSINIA

ASTERACEAE/COMPOSITAE

Genus of evergreen shrubs, grown for their foliage and flowers. Where hardy, avoid cold, exposed positions. Needs full sun and fertile, well-drained soil. Propagate by softwood cuttings in summer.
C. fulvida. See *C. leptophylla* subsp. *fulvida*.
C. leptophylla subsp. *fulvida*, syn. *C. fulvida*. Evergreen, bushy shrub. H and S 2m (6ft). Has yellow shoots, small, oblong, dark green leaves and, in mid-summer, clustered heads of minute, white flowers. Is useful as a coastal hedging plant. Zone 9.
subsp. *vauvilliersii* (syn. *C. vauvilliersii*) illus. p.161.
C. vauvilliersii. See *C. leptophylla* subsp. *vauvilliersii*.

CASSIOPE

ERICACEAE

Genus of evergreen, spring-flowering shrubs, suitable for peat beds and walls and for rock gardens. Needs a sheltered, shaded or semi-shaded site and moist, peaty, acid soil. Propagate by semi-ripe or greenwood cuttings in summer or by seed in autumn or spring.
C. 'Edinburgh' illus. p.346.
C. fastigiata. Evergreen, upright, loose shrub. H 30cm (12in), S 15–20cm (6–8in). In spring, bell-shaped, creamy-white flowers, resting in green or red calyces, are borne on short stalks in leaf axils. Leaves are tiny and scale-like. Needs semi-shade. Zone 2.
C. lycopodioides illus. p.363.
C. mertensiana illus. p.364.
C. 'Muirhead' illus. p.346.
C. selaginoides. Evergreen, spreading shrub. H 25cm (10in), S 15cm (6in). Stem is hidden by dense, scale-like, mid-green leaves. Bears solitary relatively large, pendent, bell-shaped, white flowers in spring. Needs a shaded site. Zone 8.
C. tetragona. Evergreen, upright shrub. H 10–25cm (4–10in), S 10–15cm (4–6in). Dense, scale-like, dark green leaves conceal branched stems. In spring, leaf axils bear solitary pendent, bell-shaped, white flowers in red calyces. Needs a semi-shaded site. Zone 2.
C. wardii. Evergreen, upright to spreading, loose shrub. H 15cm (6in), S 20cm (8in). Semi-upright stems are densely clothed with scale-like, dark green leaves that give them a squared appearance. Bell-shaped, white flowers, set close to stems, open in spring. Needs shade in all but cool areas. May also be propagated by division of runners in spring. Zone 5.

CASTANEA

Chestnut

FAGACEAE

Genus of deciduous, summer-flowering trees and shrubs, grown for their foliage, stately habit, flowers and edible fruits (chestnuts). Requires sun or semi-shade; does particularly well in hot, dry areas. Needs fertile, well-drained soil; grows poorly on shallow, chalky soil. Propagate species by seed in autumn, cultivars by budding in summer or by grafting in late winter.
C. mollissima (Chinese chestnut). Deciduous, spreading tree with attractive bark. H & S 20m (70ft). Leaves are oblong to oval, mid-green and up to 20cm (8in) long. Pale yellow, unpleasantly scented flowers in early summer. Edible fruit in very prickly husks produced in fall. Resistant to chestnut blight. Zone 5b.
C. sativa (Spanish chestnut, Sweet chestnut). Deciduous, spreading tree. H 30m (100ft), S 15m (50ft). Bark becomes spirally ridged with age. Oblong, glossy, dark green leaves turn yellow in autumn. Spikes of small, creamy-yellow flowers in summer are followed by edible fruits in rounded, spiny husks. Zone 5b. 'Albomarginata' illus. p.65.

CASTANOPSIS

FAGACEAE

Genus of evergreen shrubs and trees, grown for their habit and foliage. Flowers are insignificant. Needs a sheltered position in sun or semi-shade and fertile, well-drained but not too dry, acid soil. Propagate by seed when ripe, in autumn.
C. cuspidata. Evergreen, bushy, spreading shrub or tree with drooping shoots. H and S 8m (25ft) or more. Bears long, oval, slender-tipped, leathery leaves, glossy, dark green above, bronze beneath. Zone 9.

CASTANOSPERMUM

Black bean tree, Moreton Bay chestnut

LEGUMINOSAE/PAPILIONACEAE

Genus of one species of evergreen tree, grown for its overall ornamental appearance and for shade. Tender, min. 10–15°C (50–59°F). Requires full light and fertile, moisture-retentive but well-drained soil. Water containerized specimens freely when in full growth, moderately at other times. Propagate by seed in spring.
C. australe. Strong-growing, evergreen, rounded tree. H 15m (50ft) or more, S 8m (25ft) or more. Has 45cm (18in) long leaves of 8–17 oval leaflets. Racemes of large, pea-like, yellow flowers, that age to orange and red, are produced in autumn, but only on mature trees, and are succeeded by cylindrical, reddish-brown pods, each 25cm (10in) long, containing large, chestnut-like seeds.

Cast-iron plant. See *Aspidistra elatior*.
Castor-oil plant. See *Ricinus communis*, illus. p.335.
Catalina ironwood. See *Lyonothamnus floribundus*.

CATALPA

BIGNONIACEAE

Genus of deciduous, summer-flowering trees and shrubs, extremely resistant to urban pollution, grown for their foliage and bell- or trumpet-shaped flowers with frilly lobes. Trees are best grown as isolated specimens. Prefers full sun and does best in hot summers. Needs deep, fertile, well-drained but not too dry soil. Propagate species by seed in autumn, cultivars by softwood cuttings in summer or by budding in late summer.
C. bignonioides (Indian bean tree) illus. p.78. 'Aurea' is a deciduous, spreading tree. H and S 10m (30ft). Has broadly oval, bright yellow leaves, bronze when young. Bell-shaped, white flowers, marked with yellow and purple, appear in summer, followed by long, pendent, cylindrical pods, often persisting after leaf fall. Zone 5.
C. × *erubescens* 'Purpurea'. Deciduous, spreading tree. H and S 15m (50ft). Broadly oval or 3-lobed, very dark purple, young leaves mature to dark green. Fragrant, bell-shaped, white flowers, marked with yellow and purple, appear from mid- to late summer. Zone 5.
C. ovata. Deciduous, spreading tree. H and S 10m (30ft). Bears 3-lobed, purplish leaves when young, maturing to pale green. Has large clusters of bell-shaped, white flowers, spotted with red and yellow, from mid- to late summer.
C. speciosa illus. p.78. Zone 5.

CATANANCHE

Blue cupidone, Cupid's dart

ASTERACEAE/COMPOSITAE

Genus of perennials with daisy-like flower heads that may be successfully dried for winter flower arrangements. Needs sun and light, well-drained soil. Propagate by seed in spring or by root cuttings in winter.
C. caerulea 'Major' illus. p.285.

CATHARANTHUS

APOCYNACEAE

Genus of evergreen shrubs, grown for their flowers. *C. roseus* is often grown annually from seed or cuttings and used as a summer bedding plant. Tender, min. 5–7°C (41–5°F). Needs full light and well-drained soil. Water potted specimens moderately, less when temperatures are low. Prune long or straggly stems in early spring to promote a more bushy habit. Propagate by seed in spring or by greenwood or semi-ripe cuttings in summer.
C. roseus, syn. *Vinca rosea*, illus. p.160.

Cat's claw. See *Macfadyena unguis-cati*, illus. p.216.
Cat's ears. See *Antennaria*; *Calochortus*.
Cat's tail, Red-hot. See *Acalypha hispida*.
Cat's valerian. See *Valeriana officinalis*, illus. p.241.
Cat's whiskers. See *Tacca chantrieri*.

Catalina ironwood. See *Lyonothamnus floribundus*.
Catchfly. See *Silene*.
Alpine. See *Lychnis alpina*.
Nodding. See *Silene pendula*.
Catmint. See *Nepeta*.
Cattail. See *Typha latifolia*, 516illus. p.448.
Dwarf. See *Typha minima*, illus. p.449.

CATTLEYA

See also ORCHIDS.
C. bowringiana (illus. p.297). Evergreen, epiphytic orchid for a cool greenhouse. H 45cm (18in). In autumn bears large heads of rose-purple-lipped, magenta flowers, 8cm (3in) across. Has oval, stiff leaves, 8–10cm (3–4in) long. Grow in semi-shade during summer and do not spray overhead.
C. J.A. Carbone (illus. p.297). Evergreen, epiphytic orchid for an intermediate greenhouse. H 45cm (18in). Large heads of fragrant, pinkish-mauve flowers, 10cm (4in) across and each with a yellow-marked, deep pink lip, open in early summer. Has oval, stiff leaves, 10–15cm (4–6in) long. Avoid spraying from above.

Caucasian elm. See *Zelkova carpinifolia*.
Caucasian fir. See *Abies nordmanniana*, illus. p.111.
Caucasian oak. See *Quercus macranthera*, illus. p.66.
Caucasian spruce. See *Picea orientalis*.
Caucasian whortleberry. See *Vaccinium arctostaphylos*.
Caucasian wing nut. See *Pterocarya fraxinifolia*.

CAUTLEYA

ZINGIBERACEAE

Genus of summer- and autumn-flowering perennials. Grow in a sunny, wind-free position and in deep, rich, moist but well-drained soil. Propagate by seed or division in spring.
C. spicata illus. p.294.

Cayratia thomsonii. See *Parthenocissus thomsonii*.

CEANOTHUS

RHAMNACEAE

Genus of evergreen or deciduous shrubs and small trees, grown for their small but densely clustered, mainly blue flowers. At the edge of their hardiness plant against a south- or west-facing wall. Needs a sheltered site in full sun and light, well-drained soil. Cut dead wood from evergreens in spring and trim their side-shoots after flowering. Cut back shoots of deciduous species to basal framework in early spring. Propagate by semi-ripe cuttings in summer.
C. 'Autumnal Blue' illus. p148.
C. 'Blue Mound'. Evergreen, bushy, dense shrub. H 1.5m (5ft), S 2m (6ft). Forms a mound of oblong, glossy, dark green leaves,

covered, in late spring, with rounded clusters of deep blue flowers. Zone 9.

C. 'Burkwoodii'. Evergreen, bushy, dense shrub. H 1.5m (5ft), S 2m (6ft). Has oval, glossy, dark green leaves, downy and grey beneath. Produces dense panicles of bright blue flowers from mid-summer to mid-autumn. Zone 9.

C. 'Burtonensis'. Evergreen, bushy, spreading shrub. H 2m (6ft) or more, S 4m (12ft). Has small, rounded, almost spherical, crinkled leaves that are lustrous and dark green. Small, deep blue flowers appear in clusters, 2cm (¾in) wide, from mid-spring to early summer. Zone 9.

C. 'Cascade'. Vigorous, evergreen, arching shrub. H and S 4m (12ft). Leaves are narrowly oblong, glossy and dark green. Large panicles of powder-blue flowers open in late spring and early summer. Zone 9.

C. 'Delight'. Fast-growing, evergreen, bushy shrub. H 3m (10ft), S 5m (15ft). Bears oblong, glossy, deep green leaves. Long clusters of rich blue flowers appear in late spring. Zone 9.

C. x delileanus 'Gloire de Versailles'. See *C.* 'Gloire de Versailles'.

C. dentatus. Evergreen, bushy, dense shrub. H 1.5m (5ft), S 2m (6ft). Produces small, oblong, glossy, dark green leaves and is covered, in late spring, with rounded clusters of bright blue flowers. Zone 9.

C. dentatus of gardens. See *C.* x *lobbianus*.

C. 'Gloire de Versailles', syn. *C.* x *delileanus* 'Gloire de Versailles', illus. p.168.

C. gloriosus. Evergreen, prostrate shrub. H 30cm (1ft), S 2m (6ft). Leaves are oval and dark green. Rounded clusters of deep blue or purplish-blue flowers appear from mid- to late spring. May suffer from chlorosis on chalky soils. Zone 7.

C. impressus illus. p.145.

C. incanus illus. p.138.

C. 'Italian Skies'. Evergreen, bushy, spreading shrub. H 1.5m (5ft), S 3m (10ft). Has small, oval, glossy, dark green leaves. Produces dense, conical clusters of bright blue flowers during late spring. Zone 9.

C. x lobbianus, syn. *C. dentatus* of gardens. Evergreen, bushy, dense shrub. H and S 2m (6ft). Rounded clusters of bright deep blue flowers are borne in late spring and early summer amid oval, dark green leaves. Zone 9.

C. 'Marie Simon'. Deciduous, bushy shrub. H and S 1.5m (5ft). Has broadly oval, mid-green leaves. Conical clusters of soft pink flowers are carried in profusion from mid-summer to early autumn. Zone 9.

C. papillosus. Evergreen, arching shrub. H 3m (10ft), S 5m (15ft). Leaves are narrowly oblong, glossy, dark green and sticky. Produces dense racemes of blue or purplish-blue flowers during late spring. Zone 9.

C. 'Perle Rose' illus. p.163.

C. rigidus (Monterey ceanothus). Evergreen, bushy shrub of dense, spreading habit. H 1.2m (4ft), S 2.5m

(8ft). Bears oblong to rounded, glossy, dark green leaves and, from mid-spring to early summer, produces rounded clusters of deep purplish-blue flowers. Zone 9.

C. 'Southmead'. Evergreen, bushy, dense shrub. H and S 1.5m (5ft). Has small, oblong, glossy, dark green leaves. Deep blue flowers are produced in rounded clusters in late spring and early summer. Zone 9.

C. thyrsiflorus. Evergreen, bushy shrub or spreading tree. H and S 6m (20ft). Has broadly oval, glossy, mid-green leaves and, in late spring and early summer, bears rounded clusters of pale blue flowers. Zone 8. var. *repens* illus. p.168.

C. 'Trewithen Blue'. Vigorous, evergreen, bushy, spreading shrub. H 6m (20ft), S 8m (25ft) or more. In spring and early summer, large, pyramidal clusters of rich blue flowers are borne amid broadly oval to rounded, dark green leaves. Zone 9.

C. x veitchianus. Vigorous, evergreen, bushy shrub. H and S 3m (10ft). Dense, oblong clusters of deep blue flowers are borne in late spring and early summer amid oblong, glossy, dark green leaves. Zone 9.

Ceanothus, Monterey. See *Ceanothus rigidus*.
Cedar. See *Cedrus*.
  Atlas. See *Cedrus atlantica*.
  Blue Atlas. See *Cedrus atlantica* f. *glauca*, illus. p.101.
  Chilean incense. See *Austrocedrus chilensis*, illus. p.106.
  Eastern white. See *Thuja occidentalis*.
  Incense. See *Calocedrus decurrens*, illus. p.106.
  Japanese. See *Cryptomeria japonica*.
  Pencil. See *Juniperus virginiana*.
  Western red. See *Thuja plicata*.
  White. See *Thuja occidentalis*.
Cedar of Goa. See *Cupressus lusitanica*.
Cedar of Lebanon. See *Cedrus libani*, illus. p.103.
Cedrela sinensis. See *Toona sinensis*.
Cedronella mexicana. See *Agastache mexicana*.

CEDRUS
Cedar

PINACEAE

See also CONIFERS.

C. atlantica, syn. *C. libani* subsp. *atlantica* (Atlas cedar). Conifer that is conical when young, broadening with age. H 15–25m (50–80ft), S 5–10m (15–30ft). Leaves are spirally arranged, needle-like, dull green or bright blue-grey. Has ovoid cones, males pale brown, females pale green, ripening to brown. Zone 6. f. *fastigiata* (syn. *C.a.* Fastigiata Group), S 4–5m (12–15ft), has a narrower, more upright habit. f. *glauca* (syn. *C.a.* Glauca Group) illus. p.101.

C. deodara (Deodar). Fast-growing conifer, densely conical with weeping tips when young, broader when mature. H 15–25m (50–80ft), S 5–10m (15–30ft). Has spirally arranged,

needle-like, grey-green leaves and barrel-shaped, glaucous cones, 8–12cm (3–5in) long, ripening to brown. Zone 6.
'Aurea' illus. p.109.

C. libani (Cedar of Lebanon; illus. p.103). Open conifer with tiered, arching branches. H 25m (80ft), S 15m (50ft). Spirally arranged, needle-like, grey-green foliage is produced in dense, flat layers. Has greyish-pink cones. Zone 6. subsp. *atlantica* see *C. atlantica*. **'Comte de Dijon'**, H 1–2m (3–6ft), S 60cm–1.2m (2–4ft), is a dwarf form that grows only 5cm (2in) a year. **'Sargentii'** (illus. p.111), H and S 1–1.5m (3–5ft), has horizontal, then weeping branches and makes a bush that is rounded in shape.

CEIBA
BOMBACACEAE

Genus of evergreen, semi-evergreen or deciduous trees, grown for their overall appearance and for shade. Tender, min. 15°C (59°F). Requires full light or light shade and fertile, moisture-retentive but well-drained soil. Water potted specimens freely while in full growth, less at other times. Pruning is tolerated if necessary. Propagate by seed in spring or by semi-ripe cuttings in summer.

C. pentandra (Kapok, Silk cotton tree). Fast-growing, semi-evergreen tree with a spine-covered trunk. H and S 25m (80ft) or more. Hand-shaped leaves have 5–9 elliptic leaflets, red when young, becoming mid-green. Bears clusters of 5-petalled, white, yellow or pink flowers in summer, followed by woody, brownish seed pods containing silky kapok fibre.

Celandine. See *Chelidonium*.
  Greater. See *Chelidonium*.
  Lesser. See *Ranunculus ficaria*.
Celandine crocus. See *Crocus korolkowii*.

CELASTRUS
CELASTRACEAE

Genus of deciduous shrubs and twining climbers, grown for their attractive fruits. Most species bear male and female flowers on separate plants, so both sexes must be grown to obtain fruits; hermaphrodite forms of *C. orbiculatus* are available. Grow in any soil and in full or partial shade. Likes regular feeding. Prune in spring to cut out old wood and maintain shape. Propagate by seed in autumn or spring or by semi-ripe cuttings in summer.

C. articulatus. See *C. orbiculatus*.
C. orbiculatus, syn. *C. articulatus* (Oriental bittersweet, Staff vine). Vigorous, deciduous, twining climber. H to 14m (46ft). Has small, rounded, toothed leaves. Clusters of 2–4 small, green flowers are produced in summer; tiny, long-lasting, spherical fruits begin green, turn black in autumn, then split and show yellow insides and red seeds. Zone 4.

C. scandens (American bittersweet, Staff tree). Deciduous, twining climber. H to 10m (30ft). Oval leaves are

5–10cm (2–4in) long. Tiny, greenish flowers are borne in small clusters in leaf axils in summer. Long-lasting, spherical fruits are produced in bunches, 5–8cm (2–3in) long; each fruit splits to show an orange interior and scarlet seeds. Zone 3.

CELMISIA
ASTERACEAE/COMPOSITAE

Genus of evergreen, late spring- and summer-flowering perennials, grown for their foliage and daisy-like flower heads. Is suitable for rock gardens and peat beds, but may be difficult to grow in hot, dry climates. Needs a sheltered, sunny site and humus-rich, moist but well-drained, sandy, acid soil. Propagate by division in early summer or by seed when fresh.

C. bellidioides. Evergreen, mat-forming perennial. H 2cm (¾in), S to 15cm (6in). Dark green leaves are rounded and leathery. Bears almost stemless, 1cm (½in) wide, daisy-like, white flower heads in early summer.

C. coriacea of gardens. See *C. semicordata*.

C. ramulosa illus. p.374.

C. semicordata, syn. *C. coriacea* of gardens, illus. p.360.

C. traversii. Slow-growing, evergreen, clump-forming perennial. H 15cm (6in), S 20cm (8in). Sword-shaped, dark green leaves have reddish-brown margins and cream undersides. In summer carries 6–7cm (2½–3in) wide, daisy-like, white flower heads. Is difficult to establish.

C. walkeri, syn. *C. webbiana*, illus. p.350.

C. webbiana. See *C. walkeri*.

CELOSIA
AMARANTHACEAE

Genus of erect perennials, grown as annuals. Grows best in a sunny, sheltered position and in fertile, well-drained soil. Propagate by seed sown under glass in spring.

C. argentea. Moderately fast-growing, erect, bushy perennial, grown as an annual. H 30–60cm (12–24in), S to 45cm (18in). Has oval to lance-shaped, pale to mid-green leaves and, in summer, silvery-white, pyramid-shaped, feathery flower heads, to 10cm (4in) long. Cultivars are available in red, orange, yellow and cream. Dwarf cultivars, H 30cm (12in), include **'Fairy Fountains'**, illus. p.341, and **Olympia Series**, which has crested, coral-like heads of tightly clustered flowers, 8–12cm (3–5in) across, in colours such as golden yellow, scarlet, light red, deep cerise and purple.

CELTIS
Hackberry, Nettle tree

ULMACEAE

Genus of deciduous trees, with inconspicuous flowers in spring, grown for their foliage and small fruits. Needs full sun (doing best in hot summers) and fertile, well-drained soil. Propagate by seed in autumn.

C. australis illus. p.67.

C. occidentalis (Common hackberry). Deciduous, spreading tree. H and S 20m (70ft). Oval, sharply toothed, glossy, bright green leaves turn yellow in autumn, when they are accompanied by globose, yellowish-red, then red-purple fruits. Zone 2b.

C. sinensis. Deciduous, rounded tree. H and S 10m (30ft). Has oval, glossy, dark green leaves, with fine teeth, and small, globose, orange fruits. Zone 6b.

CENTAUREA
Knapweed

ASTERACEAE/COMPOSITAE

Genus of annuals and perennials, grown for their flower heads that each have a thistle-like centre surrounded by a ring of slender ray petals. Requires sun; grows in any well-drained soil, even poor soil. Propagate by seed or division in autumn or spring.

C. cyanus (Bluebottle, Cornflower). Fast-growing, upright, branching annual. H 30cm–1m (1–3ft), S 30cm (1ft). Has lance-shaped, grey-green leaves and, in summer and early autumn, branching stems with usually double, daisy-like flower heads in shades of blue, pink, red, purple or white. Flowers are excellent for cutting. Tall (blue, illus. p.334; rose, illus. p.322) and dwarf cultivars are available.

Baby Series (dwarf), H to 30cm (1ft), has blue, white or pink flower heads.

C. dealbata. Erect perennial. H 1m (3ft), S 60cm (2ft). Lilac-purple flower heads are borne freely in summer, one or more to each stem. Has narrowly oval, finely cut, light green leaves.

'Steenbergii', H 60cm (2ft), has carmine-lilac flowers.

C. hypoleuca **'John Coutts'** illus. p.279.

C. macrocephala. Robust, clump-forming perennial. H 1m (3ft), S 60cm (2ft). In summer, stout stems bear large, yellow flower heads, enclosed in papery, silvery-brown bracts. Mid-green leaves are narrowly oval and deeply cut.

C. montana illus. p.284.

C. moschata. See *Amberboa moschata.*

C. pulcherrima illus. p.244.

CENTRADENIA

MELASTOMATACEAE

Genus of evergreen perennials and shrubs, grown for their flowers and foliage. Tender, min. 13°C (55°F). Needs light shade and fertile, well-drained soil. Water containerized plants freely when in full growth, moderately at other times. Tip prune young plants to promote a bushy habit; old plants become straggly unless trimmed each spring. Propagate from early spring to early summer by seed or by softwood or greenwood cuttings. If grown as pot plants, propagate annually.

C. floribunda. Evergreen, loosely rounded, soft-stemmed shrub. H and S to 60cm (24in). Lance-shaped leaves are prominently veined, glossy, green above, bluish-green beneath. Large, terminal clusters of 4-petalled, pink or white flowers develop from pink buds in late winter and spring.

CENTRANTHUS

VALERIANACEAE

Genus of late spring- to autumn-flowering perennials. Requires sun. Thrives in an exposed position and in poor, alkaline soil. Propagate by seed in autumn or spring.

C. ruber illus. p.245.

Century plant. See *Agave americana.*

CEPHALARIA

DIPSACACEAE

Genus of coarse, summer-flowering perennials, best suited to large borders and wild gardens. Prefers sun and well-drained soil. Propagate by division in spring or by seed in autumn.

C. gigantea, syn. *C. tatarica* (Giant scabious, Yellow scabious). Robust, branching perennial. H 2m (6ft), S 1.2m (4ft). In early summer, wiry stems bear pincushion-like heads of primrose-yellow flowers well above lance-shaped, deeply cut, dark green leaves.

C. tatarica. See *C. gigantea.*

CEPHALOCEREUS

CACTACEAE

Genus of slow-growing, columnar, perennial cacti with 20–30-ribbed, green stems. Tender, min. 5°C (41°F). Prefers full sun and extremely well-drained, lime-rich soil. Is prone to rot if overwatered. Propagate by seed in spring or summer.

C. senilis illus. p.460.

CEPHALOPHYLLUM

AIZOACEAE

Genus of clump-forming, bushy, perennial succulents with semi-cylindrical to cylindrical, green leaves. Flowers are borne after 1 or 2 years. Tender, min. 5°C (41°F). Requires sun and well-drained soil. Propagate by seed in spring or summer.

C. alstonii illus. p.474.

C. pillansii. Clump-forming, perennial succulent. H 8cm (3in), S 60cm (24in). Leaves are cylindrical, 6cm (2½in) long, dark green and covered in darker dots. Short flower stems produce daisy-like, red-centred, yellow flowers, 6cm (2½in) across, from spring to autumn.

CEPHALOTAXUS

CEPHALOTAXACEAE

See also CONIFERS.

C. harringtonii (Cow's-tail pine, Plum yew). Bushy, spreading conifer. H 5m (15ft), S 3m (10ft). Needle-like, flattened leaves are glossy, dark green, greyish beneath, radiating around erect shoots. Bears ovoid, fleshy, green fruits that ripen to brown. Zone 7.

CERASTIUM

CAROPHYLLACEAE

Genus of annuals and perennials with star-shaped flowers. Some species are useful as ground cover. Needs sun and well-drained soil. Propagate by division in spring.

C. alpinum (Alpine mouse-ear). Prostrate perennial. H 8cm (3in), S 40cm (16in). Tiny, oval, grey leaves cover stems. Flower stems carry solitary 1cm (½in) wide, star-shaped, white flowers throughout summer.

C. tomentosum illus. p.361.

CERATOPHYLLUM

CERATOPHYLLACEAE

Genus of deciduous, perennial, submerged water plants, grown for their foliage. Is suitable for pools and cold-water aquariums. Prefers an open, sunny position, but tolerates shade better than most submerged plants. Propagation occurs naturally when scaly, young shoots or winter buds separate from main plants. Alternatively, take stem cuttings in the growing season.

C. demersum (Hornwort). Deciduous, perennial, spreading, submerged water plant that occasionally floats. S indefinite. Has small, dark green leaves with 3 linear lobes. Is best suited to a cool-water pool.

CERATOPTERIS

PARKERIACEAE

Genus of deciduous or semi-evergreen, perennial, floating water ferns, grown for their attractive foliage. Is suitable for aquariums. Tender, min. 10°C (50°F). Prefers a sunny position. Remove fading fronds regularly. Propagate in summer by division or by buds that develop on the leaves.

C. thalictroides (Water fern). Semi-evergreen, perennial, spreading, floating water fern that sometimes roots and becomes submerged. S indefinite. Lance- or heart-shaped, soft green fronds are wavy-edged.

CERATOSTIGMA

PLUMBAGINACEAE

Genus of deciduous, semi-evergreen or evergreen shrubs and perennials, grown for their blue flowers and autumn colour. Some species are tender, min. 10°C (50°F). Requires a sunny position, with well-drained soil. Cut out old, dead wood from shrubs in spring. Propagate shrubs by softwood cuttings in summer, perennials by division in spring.

C. griffithii. Evergreen or semi-evergreen, bushy, dense shrub. H 1m (3ft), S 1.5m (5ft). Spoon-shaped, bristly, purple-edged, dull green leaves redden in autumn. Clusters of tubular, bright blue flowers, with spreading petal lobes, appear in late summer and autumn. Zone 9.

C. plumbaginoides illus. p.360.

C. willmottianum illus. p.173.

CERCIDIPHYLLUM

CERCIDIPHYLLACEAE

Genus of deciduous trees, grown for their foliage and often spectacular autumn colour. Late frosts may damage young foliage, but do not usually cause lasting harm. Requires sun or semi-shade and fertile, moist

but well-drained soil. Propagate by seed in autumn.

C. japonicum illus. p.71.

CERCIS
Judas tree, Redbud

LEGUMINOSAE/PAPILIONACEAE

Genus of deciduous shrubs and trees with sometimes shrubby growth, cultivated for their foliage and small, pea-like flowers, borne profusely in spring. Requires a position in full sun with deep, fertile, well-drained soil. Plant out as young specimens. Resents transplanting. Propagate species by seed sown in autumn, cultivars by budding in summer.

C. canadensis (Eastern redbud). Deciduous, spreading tree or shrub. H and S 10m (30ft). Heart-shaped, dark green leaves turn yellow in autumn. Pea-like flowers are magenta in bud, opening to pale pink in mid-spring before leaves emerge. Zone 6.

'Forest Pansy' illus. p.91.

C. siliquastrum illus. p.88.

CEREUS

CACTACEAE

Genus of columnar, perennial cacti with spiny stems, most having 4–10 pronounced ribs. Cup-shaped flowers usually open at night. Tender, min. 7°C (45°F). Needs full sun and very well-drained soil. Propagate in spring by seed or, for branching species, by stem cuttings.

C. forbesii. See *C. validus.*

C. peruvianus of gardens. See *C. uruguayanus.*

C. spachianus. See *Echinopsis spachiana.*

C. uruguayanus, syn. *C. peruvianus* of gardens, illus. p.456. **'Monstrosus'** is a columnar, perennial cactus. H 5m (15ft), S 4m (12ft). Swollen, occasionally fan-shaped, silvery-blue stems bear golden spines on 4–8 (or more) uneven ribs. Is unlikely to flower in cultivation.

C. validus, syn. *C. forbesii,* illus. p.456.

Cereus, Night-blooming. See *Hylocereus undatus.*

CERINTHE

BORAGINACEAE

Genus of annuals, biennials, and perennials with somewhat fleshy stems and leaves. Requires a site in full sun, with dry to moist, but well-drained soil. Propagate by seed sown in autumn or spring.

C. major **'Purpurascens'** illus. p.331.

CEROPEGIA

ASCLEPIADACEAE

Genus of semi-evergreen, succulent shrubs and sub-shrubs, most with slender, climbing or pendent stems, grown for their unusual flowers. Tender, min. 7–11°C (45–52°F). Needs partial shade and very well-drained soil. Propagate by seed or stem cuttings in spring or summer. *C. woodii* is often used as grafting stock for difficult asclepiads.

C. distincta subsp. **haygarthii.** See *C. haygarthii.*

C. haygarthii, syn. *C. distincta* subsp. *haygarthii.* Semi-evergreen, climbing, succulent sub-shrub. H 2m (6ft) or more, S indefinite. Min. 11°C (52°F). Bears oval or rounded, dark green leaves, 1–2cm (½–¾in) long. In summer, produces masses of small, white or pinkish-white flowers, each with a pitcher-shaped tube, widening towards the top and then united at the tip by purplish-spotted petals that form a short stem ending in 5 'knobs' edged with fine hairs. The whole resembles an insect hovering over a flower.

C. linearis subsp. **woodii,** syn. *C. woodii,* illus. p.462.

C. sandersoniae. See *C. sandersonii.*

C. sandersonii, syn. *C. sandersoniae* (Fountain flower, Parachute plant). Semi-evergreen, scrambling, succulent sub-shrub. H 2m (6ft), S indefinite. Min. 11°C (52°F). Leaves are triangular to oval, fleshy and 2cm (¾in) long. In summer-autumn has tubular, green flowers, 5cm (2in) long, with paler green to white marks; the petals are flared widely at tips to form 'parachutes'.

C. woodii. See *C. linearis* subsp. *woodii.*

CESTRUM

SOLANACEAE

Genus of deciduous or evergreen shrubs and semi-scrambling climbers, grown for their showy flowers. Foliage has an unpleasant scent. Hardy to tender, min. 7–10°C (45–50°F). Grow hardiest species against a south- or west-facing wall or in a greenhouse. Requires a sheltered, sunny position and fertile, well-drained soil. Water containerized specimens freely when in full growth, moderately at other times. Support is needed for scrambling species. Propagate hardy species by softwood cuttings in summer, tender species by seed in spring or by semi-ripe cuttings in summer.

C. aurantiacum. Mainly evergreen semi-scrambler that remains a rounded shrub if cut back annually. H and S to 2m (6ft). Tender, min. 7–10°C (45–50°F); is deciduous at low temperatures. Bears oval, bright green leaves. Tubular, bright orange flowers are carried in large, terminal trusses in summer and may be followed by spherical, white fruits. Prune annually, cutting out old stems to near base after flowering.

C. elegans, syn. *C. purpureum,* illus. p.142.

C. 'Newellii'. Evergreen, arching shrub. H and S 3m (10ft). Slightly hardy. Bears clusters of tubular, crimson flowers in late spring and summer. Leaves are large, broadly lance-shaped and dark green. Zone 9?.

C. parqui. Deciduous, open shrub. H and S 2m (6ft). Large clusters of tubular, yellowish-green flowers, fragrant at night, are borne in profusion in summer amid narrowly lance-shaped, mid-green leaves. Zone 9.

C. purpureum. See *C. elegans.*

Ceterach officinarum. See *Asplenium ceterach.*

CHAENOMELES

Flowering quince, Japonica

ROSACEAE

Genus of deciduous, usually thorny, spring-flowering shrubs, grown for their showy flowers and fragrant fruits, produced in autumn and used for preserves. Prefers sun and well-drained soil. On wall-trained shrubs cut back side-shoots after flowering to 2 or 3 buds and shorten shoots growing away from wall during growing season. Propagate species by softwood or greenwood cuttings in summer or by seed in autumn, cultivars by cuttings only in summer. Fireblight and, on alkaline soils, chlorosis are common problems.

C. cathayensis. Deciduous, spreading, open shrub with thorns. H and S 3m (10ft) or more. Produces long, narrow, pointed, mid-green leaves. Small, 5-petalled, pink-flushed, white flowers appear from early to mid-spring, followed by large, egg-shaped, yellow-green fruits. Zone 8.

C. japonica (Japanese quince, Japonica). Deciduous, bushy, spreading shrub with thorns. H 1m (3ft), S 2m (6ft). Has oval, mid-green leaves and, in spring, a profusion of 5-petalled, red or orange-red flowers, then spherical, yellow fruits. Zone 5.

C. speciosa. Vigorous, deciduous, bushy shrub with thorns. H 2.5m (8ft), S 5m (15ft). Leaves are oval, glossy and dark green. Clustered, 5-petalled, red flowers are borne from early to mid-spring, and are followed by spherical, greenish-yellow fruits. Zone 5b.

'Moerloosei' illus. p.130. Flowers of **'Nivalis'** are pure white. **'Simonii',** H 1m (3ft), S 2m (6ft), bears masses of semi-double, deep red flowers.

C. x superba 'Crimson and Gold'. Deciduous, bushy, dense shrub with thorns. H 1m (3ft), S 2m (6ft). Has oval, glossy, dark green leaves. Bears masses of 5-petalled, deep red flowers, with conspicuous, golden-yellow anthers, in spring, followed by round, yellow fruits. Flowers of **'Etna',** H 1.5m (5ft), S 3m (10ft), are scarlet. **'Knap Hill Scarlet',** H 1.5m (5ft), S 3m (10ft), produces large, brilliant red flowers. **'Nicoline'** illus. p.156. **'Rowallane'** illus. p.155. Zone 5b.

Chain cactus. See *Rhipsalis paradoxa.*
Chain fern. See *Woodwardia radicans.*
 Asian. See *Woodwardia unigemmata.*

Chamaecereus silvestrii. See *Echinopsis chamaecereus.*

CHAMAEBATIARIA

ROSACEAE

Genus of one species of deciduous shrub, grown for its foliage and summer flowers. Needs a sheltered,

sunny position and well-drained soil. Propagate by semi-ripe cuttings in summer.

C. millefolium. Deciduous, upright, open shrub. H and S 1m (3t). Has finely divided, aromatic, grey-green leaves. Shallowly cup-shaped, white flowers, with yellow stamens, are borne in terminal, branching panicles from mid-to late summer. Zone 6b.

CHAMAECYPARIS

False cypress

CUPRESSACEAE

Contact with the foliage may aggravate skin allergies. See also CONIFERS.

C. lawsoniana (Lawson False cypress). Upright, columnar conifer with branches drooping at tips. H 15–25m (50–80ft), S 3–4m (10–12ft). Bears flattened sprays of scale-like, aromatic, dark green leaves and globular cones, the males brick-red, the females insignificant and green. Zone 5b. **'Columnaris'** illus. p.108. **'Ellwoodii',** H 3m (10ft), S 1.5m (5ft), is erect with incurved, blue-grey leaves. **'Fletcheri',** H 5–12m (15–40ft), S 2–3m (6–10ft), has grey leaves that are incurved. **'Gnome'** (illus. p.111), H and S 50cm (20in), is a dwarf, bun-shaped form with blue foliage. **'Green Pillar'** illus. p.107. **'Intertexta'** illus. p.102. c **'Kilmacurragh',** H 10–15m (30–50ft), S 1m (3ft), has very bright green foliage. **'Lanei'** illus. p.107. **'Minima'** (illus. p.111), H and S 1m (3ft), is dwarf and globular, and has light green foliage. **'Pembury Blue'** illus. p.105. **'Tamariscifolia'** (syn. *C.l.* Tamariscifolia Group), H 3m (10ft), S 4m (12ft), is a dwarf, spreading form. **'Triomf van Boskoop',** H 20m (70ft), is broadly columnar, with grey-blue foliage. **'Wisselii',** H 15m (50ft), S 2–3m (6–10ft), is fast-growing, with erect branches and blue-green leaves.

C. nootkatensis (Nootka False cypress). Almost geometrically conical conifer. H 15m (50ft), S 6m (20ft). Bears long, pendent sprays of scale-like, aromatic, grey-green leaves and globular, hooked, dark blue and green cones that ripen to brown. Zone 5b. **'Pendula'** has a gaunt crown of arching, weeping foliage. Zone 5.

C. obtusa (Hinoki False cypress). Conical conifer. H 15–20m (50–70ft), S 5m (15ft). Has stringy, red-brown bark and scale-like, aromatic, dark green leaves with bright silver lines at sides and incurving tips. Small, rounded cones ripen to yellow-brown. Zone 5. **'Coralliformis',** H to 50cm (20in), S 1m (3ft), is dwarf, with thread-like shoots. **'Crippsii'** illus. p.109. **'Intermedia'** (illus. p.111), H to 30cm (12in), S 40cm (16in), is a globular, open, dwarf shrub with downward-spreading, light green foliage. **'Kosteri',** H 1–2m (3–6ft), S 2–3m (6–10ft), forms a sprawling bush with twisted, lustrous foliage. Extremely slow-growing **'Nana',** eventual H 1m (3ft), S 1.5–2m (5–6ft), makes a flat-topped bush. **'Nana Aurea'** (illus. p.111), H and S 2m (6ft), is a form with golden-yellow leaves. **'Nana Gracilis',** H 2m (6ft), S 1.5–2m

(5–6ft), is a form with glossy foliage. **'Nana Pyramidalis'** (illus. p.111), H and S to 60cm (2ft), is a slow-growing, dense, conical, dwarf cultivar with horizontal, cup-shaped leaves. **'Tetragona Aurea',** H 10m (30ft), S 2–3m (6–10ft), produces golden- or bronze-yellow leaves. Zones 5–5b.

C. pisifera (Sawara False cypress). Conical conifer with horizontal branches. H 15m (50ft), S 5m (15ft). Has ridged, peeling, red-brown bark, scale-like, aromatic, fresh green leaves, white at sides and beneath, and angular, yellow-brown cones. Zone 4. **'Boulevard'** has silver-blue foliage. **'Filifera'** has whip-like, hanging shoots and dark green foliage. **'Filifera Aurea'** (illus. p.111), H 12m (40ft), S 3–5m (10–15ft), also has whip-like shoots, but with golden-yellow leaves. **'Filifera Nana',** H 60cm (2ft), S 1m (3ft), is a dwarf form with whip-like branches. **'Nana',** H and S 50cm (20in), is also dwarf, with dark bluish-green foliage. **'Plumosa'** is broadly conical to columnar, with yellowish-grey-green leaves. **'Plumosa Rogersii',** H 2m (6ft), S 1m (3ft), has yellow foliage. Slow-growing **'Squarrosa',** H to 20m (70ft), has a broad crown and soft, blue-grey foliage. Zones 4–4b.

C. thyoides illus. p.107. **'Andelyensis'** is a slow-growing, conical, dwarf conifer. H 3m (10ft), S 1m (3ft). Has wedge-shaped tufts of scale-like, aromatic, blue-green leaves. Globular cones are glaucous blue-grey. Zone 4.

CHAMAECYTISUS

LEGUMINOSAE/PAPILIONACEAE

Genus of evergreen and deciduous trees, shrubs and sub-shrubs, grown for their pea-like flowers. Best in full sun and moderately fertile, well-drained soil. Propagate by seed in autumn or spring or by semi-ripe cuttings in summer.

C. albus. See *Cytisus albus.*

C. demissus, syn. *C. hirsutus* var. *demissus, Cytisus demissus.* Slow-growing, deciduous, prostrate shrub. H 8cm (3in), S 20–30cm (8–12in). Densely hairy stems bear tiny, bright green leaves with 3-palmate, obovate leaflets. Produces axillary clusters of 2–4 bright yellow flowers, each with a brown keel, in early summer. Is good for a rock garden or trough. Zone 7.

C. hirsutus var. **demissus.** See *C. demissus.*

C. purpureus, syn. *Cytisus purpureus* (Purple broom). Deciduous, arching shrub. H 45cm (18in), S 60cm (24in). Semi-erect stems are clothed with leaves of 3-palmate, obovate leaflets. Clusters of 2–3 pale lilac to purple flowers open in early summer on previous year's growth. Is good for a bank or sunny border. Zone 5. f. **albus** illus. p.351.

C. supinus, syn. *Cytisus supinus.* Deciduous, bushy, rounded shrub. H and S 1m (3ft). Dense, terminal heads of large, yellow flowers are borne from mid-summer to autumn amid grey-green leaves with 3-palmate, oblong-elliptic leaflets. Zone 6.

CHAMAEDAPHNE

ERICACEAE

Genus of one species of evergreen shrub, grown for its white flowers. Needs sun or semi-shade and moist, peaty, acid soil. Propagate by semi-ripe cuttings in summer.

C. calyculata (Leatherleaf). Evergreen, arching, open shrub. H 75cm (2½ft), S 1m (3ft). Leaves are small, oblong, leathery and dark green. Leafy racemes of small, urn-shaped flowers appear on slender branches in mid- to late spring. Zone 3.

CHAMAEDOREA

ARECACEAE/PALMAE

Genus of evergreen palms, grown for their overall appearance. Tender, min. 18°C (64°F). Needs shade or semi-shade and humus-rich, well-drained soil. Water containerized plants moderately, less when temperatures are low. Propagate by seed in spring at not less than 25°C (77°F). Spider mite may be troublesome.

C. elegans, syn. *Neanthe bella*, illus. p.152.

CHAMAEMELUM

ASTERACEAE/COMPOSITAE

Genus of evergreen perennials, suitable as ground cover or for a lawn. Flowers may be used to make tea. Needs sun and well-drained soil. Propagate by division in spring or by seed in autumn.

C. nobile, syn. *Anthemis nobilis* (Chamomile). Evergreen, mat-forming, invasive perennial. H 10cm (4in), S 45cm (18in). Has finely divided, aromatic leaves and daisy-like heads of white flowers, with yellow centres, borne in late spring or summer. **'Treneague'** is a non-flowering, less invasive cultivar that, requiring less mowing, is better for a lawn.

Chamaenerion. Reclassified as *Epilobium.*
Chamaepericlymenum canadense. See *Cornus canadensis.*

CHAMAEROPS

ARECACEAE/PALMAE

Genus of evergreen palms, cultivated for their overall appearance. Tender, min. 7°C (45°F). Needs full light and fertile, well-drained soil. Water containerized plants moderately, less when not in full growth. Propagate by seed in spring at not less than 22°C (72°F) or by suckers in late spring. Spider mite may be a nuisance.
C. humilis illus. p.176.

Chamaespartium sagittale. See *Genista sagittalis.*
Chamaespartium sagittale subsp. **delphinense.** See *Genista delphinensis.*

CHAMELAUCIUM

MYRTACEAE

Genus of evergreen shrubs, grown for their flowers and overall appearance.

Tender, min. 5°C (41°F), but best at 7–10°C (45–50°F). Requires full sun and well-drained, sandy, neutral to acid soil. Water containerized specimens moderately, sparingly when not in full growth. To maintain a more compact habit, cut back flowered stems by half when the last bloom falls. Propagate by seed in spring or by semi-ripe cuttings in summer.

C. uncinatum [pink form] illus. p.150, [white form] illus. p.149.

Chamomile. See *Chamaemelum nobile.*
Channelled heath. See *Erica canaliculata*, illus. p.178.
Chaste tree. See *Vitex agnus-castus.*
Chatham Island forget-me-not. See *Myosotidium.*
Cheddar pink. See *Dianthus gratianopolitanus*, illus. p.377.

CHASMANTHE

IRIDACEAE

Genus of corms, grown for their showy flowers. Requires a site in full sun or partial shade and well-drained soil, with plenty of water in growing season (late winter and early spring). Reduce watering in summer-autumn. Propagate by division in autumn.

C. aethiopica. Spring- and early summer-flowering corm. H to 80cm (32in), S 12–18cm (5–7in). Has narrowly sword-shaped, erect, basal leaves in a flat fan. Produces a spike of scarlet flowers, all facing one way, with yellow tubes, 5–6cm (2–2½in) long, and hooded, upper lips.
C. floribunda. Summer-flowering corm. H to 80cm (32in), S 12–18cm (5–7in). Is similar to *C. aethiopica*, but the leaves are much wider, and the longer, orange or scarlet flowers do not all face in the same direction.

CHEILANTHES

ADIANTACEAE

Genus of evergreen ferns. Needs full light and humus-rich, well-drained soil. Do not overwater containerized plants or splash water on fronds. Remove fading foliage regularly. Propagate by spores in summer.

C. lanosa of gardens. See *C. tomentosa.*
C. tomentosa, syn. *C. lanosa* of gardens. Evergreen fern. H and S 15–23cm (6–9in). Leaves are triangular or lance-shaped and have much divided, soft green fronds on hairy, black stems.

Cheiranthus. Reclassified as *Erysimum.*

CHEIRIDOPSIS

AIZOACEAE

Genus of clump-forming, perennial succulents with pairs of semi-cylindrical leaves. Tender, min. 5°C (41°F). Needs sun and well-drained soil. Water in autumn to encourage flowers. Propagate by seed or stem cuttings in spring or summer.

C. candidissima. See *C. denticulata.*
C. denticulata, syn. *C. candidissima*. Clump-forming, perennial succulent. H 10cm (4in), S 20cm (8in). Has semi-cylindrical, slender, fleshy, blue-grey leaves, each 10cm (4in) long with a flat top, joined in pairs for almost half their length. Bears daisy-like, shiny, white flowers, to 6cm (2½in) across, in spring.
C. purpurata. See *C. purpurea.*
C. purpurea, syn. *C. purpurata*. Carpeting, perennial succulent. H 10cm (4in), S 30cm (12in). Has semi-cylindrical, thick, short, glaucous green leaves, each with a flat top. In early spring produces daisy-like, purple-pink flowers, 4cm (1½in) across.

CHELIDONIUM

Celandine, Greater celandine

PAPAVERACEAE

Genus of one species of perennial that rapidly forms ground cover. Grows in sun or shade and in any but very wet soil. Propagate by seed or division in autumn. Contact with the sap may cause skin blisters.

C. majus 'Flore Pleno' illus. p.238.

CHELONE

Turtle-head

SCROPHULARIACEAE

Genus of summer- and autumn-flowering perennials. Needs semi-shade and moist soil. Propagate by soft-tip cuttings in summer or by division or seed in autumn or spring.

C. barbata. See *Penstemon barbatus.*
C. obliqua illus. p.259.

Cherimoya. See *Annona.*
Cherry. See *Prunus.*
  Australian brush. See *Syzygium paniculatum*, illus. p.81.
  Bell-flowered. See *Prunus campanulata.*
  Bird. See *Prunus padus*, illus. p.76.
  Black. See *Prunus serotina*, illus. p.65.
  Bladder. See *Physalis alkekengi.*
  Cornelian. See *Cornus mas.*
  Downy. See *Prunus tomentosa.*
  Fuji. See *Prunus incisa*, illus. p.86.
  Great white. See *Prunus* 'Taihaku', illus. p.86.
  Higan. See *Prunus* x *subhirtella.*
  Hill. See *Prunus jamasakura*, illus. p.76.
  Jerusalem. See *Solanum pseudocapsicum.*
  Pin. See *Prunus pensylvanica.*
  Rosebud. See *Prunus* x *subhirtella.*
  Sargent. See *Prunus sargentii*, illus. p.87.
  Taiwan. See *Prunus campanulata.*
  Virginian bird. See *Prunus virginiana.*
  Wild. See *Prunus avium*, illus. p.71.
  Wild rum. See *Prunus serotina*, illus. p.65.
  Winter. See *Cardiospermum halicacabum*; *Physalis alkekengi*; *Solanum capsicastrum.*
  Yoshino. See *Prunus* x *yedoensis*, illus. p.87.
Cherry laurel. See *Prunus laurocerasus.*
Cherry plum. See *Prunus cerasifera.*

Cherry prinsepia. See *Prinsepia sinensis.*
Chestnut. See *Castanea.*
  Cape. See *Calodendrum capense.*
  Chinese. See *Castanea mollissima.*
  Moreton Bay. See *Castanospermum.*
  Spanish. See *Castanea sativa.*
  Sweet. See *Castanea sativa.*
  Water. See *Trapa natans*, illus. p.449.
Chestnut oak. See *Quercus prinus.*
Chestnut vine. See *Tetrastigma voinierianum*, illus. p.220.

CHIASTOPHYLLUM

CRASSULACEAE

Genus of one species of evergreen perennial, grown for its succulent leaves and attractive sprays of small, yellow flowers. Thrives in rock crevices. Needs shade and well-drained soil that is not too dry. Propagate by side-shoot cuttings in early summer or by seed in autumn.

C. oppositifolium, syn. *Cotyledon simplicifolia*, illus. p.349.

Chicory. See *Cichorium.*
Chile pine. See *Araucaria araucana*, illus. p.103.
Chilean bamboo. See *Chusquea culeou*, illus. p.308.
Chilean bellflower. See *Lapageria rosea*, illus. p.210.
Chilean blue crocus. See *Tecophilaea cyanocrocus*, illus. p.433.
Chilean firebush. See *Embothrium coccineum*, illus. p.93.
Chilean glory flower. See *Eccremocarpus scaber*, illus. p.217.
Chilean hazel. See *Gevuina avellana.*
Chilean incense cedar. See *Austrocedrus chilensis*, illus. p.106.
Chilean jasmine. See *Mandevilla laxa.*
Chilean laurel. See *Laurelia sempervirens.*
Chilean wine palm. See *Jubaea chilensis*, illus. p.85.
Chimney bellflower. See *Campanula pyramidalis.*

CHIMONANTHUS

CALYCANTHACEAE

Genus of deciduous or evergreen, winter-flowering shrubs, grown for their flowers. At limits of hardiness reduce susceptibility of flowers to frost by training plants against a south- or west-facing wall. Needs full sun and fertile, well-drained soil. Propagate species by seed when ripe, in late spring and early summer, cultivars by softwood cuttings in summer.

C. fragrans. See *C. praecox.*
C. praecox, syn. *C. fragrans* (Wintersweet). Deciduous, bushy shrub. H 2.5m (8ft) or more, S 3m (10ft). Has oval, rough, glossy, dark green leaves. Bears very fragrant, many-petalled, cup-shaped, yellow flowers, with purple centres, on bare branches in mild periods during winter. Zone 7.
'Concolor' (syn. *C.p.* var. *concolor*, *C.p.* 'Luteus', *C.p.* var. *luteus*) has pure yellow flowers.

China aster. See *Callistephus*.
Chincherinchee. See *Ornithogalum thyrsoides*, illus. p.420.
Chinese anise. See *Illicium anisatum*.
Chinese arbor-vitae. See *Thuja orientalis*.
Chinese box thorn. See *Lycium barbarum*.
Chinese elm. See *Ulmus parvifolia*.
Chinese evergreen. See *Aglaonema*.
Chinese fan palm. See *Livistona chinensis*, illus. p.85.
Chinese fir. See *Cunninghamia lanceolata*, illus. p.106.
Chinese fountain grass. See *Pennisetum alopecuroides*.
Chinese fountain palm. See *Livistona chinensis*, illus. p.85.
Chinese fringe tree. See *Chionanthus retusus*.
Chinese gooseberry. See *Actinidia deliciosa*.
Chinese hat plant. See *Holmskioldia sanguinea*.
Chinese horse-chestnut. See *Aesculus chinensis*, illus. p.64.
Chinese juniper. See *Juniperus chinensis*.
Chinese lantern. See *Physalis*.
Chinese necklace poplar. See *Populus lasiocarpa*.
Chinese parasol tree. See *Firmiana simplex*, illus. p.68.
Chinese pear. See *Pyrus ussuriensis*.
Chinese persimmon. See *Diospyros kaki*.
Chinese privet. See *Ligustrum lucidum*.
Chinese tallow tree. See *Sapium sebiferum*.
Chinese thuja. See *Thuja orientalis*.
Chinese trumpet creeper. See *Campsis grandiflora*.
Chinese trumpet vine. See *Campsis grandiflora*.
Chinese tulip tree. See *Liriodendron chinense*.
Chinese walnut. See *Juglans cathayensis*.
Chinese wing nut. See *Pterocarya stenoptera*.
Chinese wisteria. See *Wisteria sinensis*, illus. p.215.
Chinese witch hazel. See *Hamamelis mollis*.
Chinese-lantern lily. See *Sandersonia aurantiaca*, illus. p.423.

CHIONANTHUS

OLEACEAE

Genus of deciduous shrubs, grown for their profuse, white flowers. Flowers more freely in areas with hot summers. Prefers full sun and fertile, well-drained but not too dry soil. Propagate by seed in autumn.
C. retusus (Chinese fringe tree). Deciduous, often tree-like, arching shrub. H and S 3m (10ft). From early to mid-summer, star-shaped, pure white flowers appear in large clusters amid oval, bright green leaves. Zone 7.
C. virginicus illus. p.119.

CHIONOCHLOA

GRAMINEAE/POACEAE

See also GRASSES, BAMBOOS, RUSHES and SEDGES.
C. conspicua (Hunangemoho grass).

Evergreen, tussock-forming, perennial grass. H 1.2–1.5m (4–5ft), S 1m (3ft). Very long, mid-green leaves are tinged reddish-brown. Has stout, arching stems with long, loose, open panicles of cream spikelets in summer.

CHIONODOXA
Glory-of-the-snow

HYACINTHACEAE/LILIACEAE

Genus of spring-flowering bulbs, related to *Scilla*. Is suitable for rock gardens and for naturalizing under shrubs, in sun or partial shade. Requires well-drained soil, top dressed with leaf mould or mature garden compost in autumn. Propagate by seed in autumn or by division in late summer or autumn.
C. forbesii, syn. *C. luciliae* of gardens, *C. siehei*, *C. tmolusii*, illus. p.433.
'Pink Giant' illus. p.427.
C. gigantea. See *C. luciliae*.
C. luciliae, syn. *C. gigantea*, illus. p.433.
C. luciliae of gardens. See *C. forbesii*.
C. sardensis. Early spring-flowering bulb. H 10–20cm (4–8in), S 2.5–5cm (1–2in). Has 2 narrowly lance-shaped, semi-erect, basal leaves. Leafless stem produces 5–10 flattish, slightly pendent or outward-facing, deep rich blue flowers, 1.5–2cm (⅝–¾in) across and without white eyes.
C. siehei. See *C. forbesii*.
C. tmolusii. See *C. forbesii*.

x CHIONOSCILLA

HYACINTHACEAE/LILIACEAE

Hybrid genus (*Chionodoxa* x *Scilla*) of spring-flowering bulbs, suitable for rock gardens. Needs full sun or partial shade and humus-rich, well-drained soil. Propagate by division in late summer or autumn.
x *C. allenii* illus. p.433.

CHIRITA

GESNERIACEAE

Genus of evergreen perennials or sub-shrubs, grown for their flowers. Tender, min. 15°C (59°F). Requires well-drained soil, a fairly humid atmosphere and a light position out of direct sunlight. Propagate by tip cuttings in summer or, if available, seed in late winter or spring.
C. lavandulacea illus. p.294.
C. sinensis. Evergreen, stemless, rosetted perennial. H to 15cm (6in), S 25cm (10in) or more. Has oval, almost fleshy leaves, the corrugated, hairy surfaces usually patterned with silver marks. In spring-summer, clusters of tubular, lavender flowers are held above leaves.

Chives. See *Allium schoenoprasum*, illus. p.436.

CHLIDANTHUS

AMARYLLIDACEAE

Genus of one species of summer-flowering bulb, grown for its showy, funnel-shaped flowers. Needs a sunny site and well-drained soil. Plant in the

open in spring and after flowering, if necessary, lift and dry off for winter. Propagate by offsets in spring.
C. fragrans illus. p.436.

CHLOROGALUM

HYACINTHACEAE/LILIACEAE

Genus of summer-flowering bulbs, grown more for botanical interest than for floral display. Marginally hardy, so plant in a sheltered site. Requires sun and well-drained soil. Propagate by seed in autumn or spring.
C. pomeridianum. Summer-flowering bulb. H to 2.5m (8ft). S 15–20cm (6–8in). Semi-erect, basal leaves are long, narrow and grey-green, with wavy margins. Carries a large, loosely branched head of small, saucer-shaped, white flowers, with a central, green or purple stripe on each petal, that open after midday.

CHLOROPHYTUM

ANTHERICACEAE/LILIACEAE

Genus of evergreen, stemless perennials with short rhizomes, grown for their foliage. Tender, min. 5°C (41°F). Grow in a light position, away from direct sun, in fertile, well-drained soil. Water freely in growing season but sparingly at other times if pot-grown. Propagate by seed, division or plantlets (produced on flower stems of some species) at any time except winter.
C. capense. Evergreen, tufted perennial. H 30cm (12in), S indefinite. Forms rosettes of lance- or strap-shaped, bright green leaves, to 60cm (24in) long. Tiny, white flowers in racemes, to 60cm (24in) long, are borne in summer. Does not produce plantlets.
C. capense of gardens. See *C. comosum*.
C. comosum, syn. *C. capense* of gardens (Spider plant). Evergreen, tufted perennial. H 30cm (12in), S indefinite. Very narrow leaves, to 45cm (18in) long, spread from a rosette. Racemes of many small, star-shaped, white flowers are carried on thin stems, 60cm (24in) or more long, at any time. Small rosettes of leaves may appear on flower stems, forming plantlets.
'Vittatum' illus. p.301.

Chocolate cosmos. See *Cosmos atrosanguineus*, illus. p.249.
Chocolate vine. See *Akebia quinata*, illus. p.205.

CHOISYA

RUTACEAE

Genus of evergreen shrubs, grown for their foliage and flowers. Where hardy may need some shelter. Requires full sun and fertile, well-drained soil. Propagate by semi-ripe cuttings in late summer.
C. ternata (Mexican orange blossom) illus. p.127. SUNDANCE ('Lich') is an evergreen, rounded, dense shrub. H and S 2.5m (8ft). Aromatic, glossy, bright yellow leaves each consist of 3 oblong leaflets. Fragrant, star-shaped, white flowers are produced in clusters in late spring and often again in autumn. Zone 8.

Chokeberry. See *Aronia*.
Black. See *Aronia melanocarpa*, illus. p.136.
Red. See *Aronia arbutifolia*, illus. p.130.

CHORDOSPARTIUM

LEGUMINOSAE/PAPILIONACEAE

Genus of one species of deciduous, almost leafless shrub, grown for its habit and flowers. Slender, green shoots assume function of leaves. Requires a sheltered, sunny position and fertile, well-drained soil. Propagate by seed in autumn.
C. stevensonii. Deciduous, almost leafless, arching shrub. H 3m (10ft), S 2m (6ft). Produces small, pea-like, purplish-pink flowers in cylindrical racemes in mid-summer. Zone 9.

CHORISIA

BOMBACACEAE

Genus of deciduous trees, usually with spine-covered trunks, grown mainly for their flowers in autumn and winter and their overall appearance. Tender, min. 15°C (59°F). Needs full light and well-drained soil. Water containerized specimens freely when in full growth, very little when leafless. Pruning is tolerated if necessary. Propagate by seed in spring. Spider mite may be troublesome.
C. speciosa illus. p.70.

CHORIZEMA

LEGUMINOSAE/PAPILIONACEAE

Genus of evergreen sub-shrubs, shrubs and scandent climbers, grown mainly for their flowers. Tender, min. 7°C (45°F). Requires full light and humus-rich, well-drained, sandy soil, preferably neutral to acid. Water potted plants moderately, less when not in full growth. Tie climbers to supports, or grow in hanging baskets. Propagate by seed in spring or by semi-ripe cuttings in summer.
C. ilicifolium illus. p.157.

Christ's thorn. See *Paliurus spina-christi*, illus. p.122.
Christmas begonia. See *Begonia* 'Gloire de Lorraine'.
Christmas berry. See *Photinia arbutifolia*.
Christmas box. See *Sarcococca*.
Christmas cactus. See *Schlumbergera* x *buckleyi*.
Christmas fern. See *Polystichum acrostichoides*.
Christmas rose. See *Helleborus*.
Christmas tree, New Zealand. See *Metrosideros excelsus*, illus. p.83.
Chrysalidocarpus lutescens. See *Dypsis lutescens*.

CHRYSANTHEMUM

ASTERACEAE/COMPOSITAE

Genus of annuals, perennials, some of which are evergreen, and evergreen sub-shrubs, grown for their flowers. Each flower head is referred to horticulturally as a flower, even though it does in fact comprise a large number of individual flowers or florets; this horticultural usage has been followed in the descriptions below. Leaves are usually deeply lobed or cut, often feathery, oval to lance-shaped. Florists' chrysanthemums (nowadays considered to belong to the genus *Dendranthema*) comprise the vast majority of chrysanthemums now cultivated and are perennials grown for garden decoration, cutting and exhibition. Annuals are slightly hardy. Florists' chrysanthemums are fully hardy to tender, min. 10°C (50°F); those that are tender should be lifted and stored in a frost-free place over winter. The hardiness of other perennial chrysanthemums depends on minimum temperature. Provide a sunny site and reasonably fertile, well-drained soil. If grown for exhibition will require regular feeding. Pinch out growing tips to encourage lateral growths on which flowers will be borne, and stake tall plants with canes. Propagate annuals by seed sown in position in spring; thin out, but do not transplant. Propagate hardy perennials by division in autumn, after flowering, or in early spring. Florists' chrysanthemums should be propagated from basal softwood cuttings in spring. Spray regularly to control aphids, capsids, froghoppers, earwigs, mildew and white rust.

Florists' chrysanthemums
Florists' chrysanthemums are grouped according to their widely varying flower forms, approximate flowering season (early, mid- or late autumn) and habit. They are divided into disbudded and non-disbudded types. For descriptions and illustrations of flower forms see feature panel pp.260–61.

Disbudded types – single, anemone-centred, incurved, intermediate and reflexed – are so called because all buds, except the one that is to flower, are removed from each stem. To produce exhibition flowers, incurved, intermediate and reflexed chrysanthemums may be restricted to only 2 blooms per plant by removing all except the 2 most vigorous lateral growths. In gardens, allow 4 or 5 blooms per plant to develop. Single and anemone-centred flowers should be reduced to 4–8 blooms per plant for exhibition, according to their vigour, and 10 or more for garden decoration or cutting.

Non-disbudded types – charm, pompon and spray chrysanthemums – have several flowers per stem.
Charm chrysanthemums are dwarf plants that produce hundreds of star-shaped, single flowers, 2.5cm (1in) across, densely covering each plant to form a hemispherical to almost spherical head. For exhibition, finish growing in at least 30cm (12in) pots. Plants for indoor decoration are grown in smaller pots and have correspondingly smaller, though equally dense, heads of blooms.
Pompon chrysanthemums are also dwarf. Each plant has 50 or more dense, spherical or occasionally

hemispherical, fully double flowers that have tubular petals (for illustrations see p.261). They are excellent for growing in borders.
Spray chrysanthemums have a variety of flower forms: single, anemone-centred, intermediate, reflexed, pompon, spoon-type (in which each straight, tubular floret opens out like a spoon at its tip), quill-shaped and spider-form. Each plant should be allowed to develop 4 or 5 stems with at least 5 flowers per stem. Grow late-flowering sprays on up to 3 stems per plant. With controlled day length, to regulate flowering dates for exhibition purposes, late sprays should be allowed to develop at least 12 flowers per stem; without day length control, 6 or 7 flowers per stem.

Those most suitable for garden decoration are sprays, pompons and early reflexed chrysanthemums. All are suitable for cutting, except for charms. Late-flowering chrysanthemums are only suitable for growing under glass as flowers need protection from poor weather; they should be grown in pots and placed in a greenhouse in early autumn, when the flower buds have developed. Intermediate cultivars are also less suitable for garden decoration as florets may collect and retain rain and thus become damaged. Those cultivars suitable for exhibition are noted below. Measurements of flowers given are the greatest normally achieved and may vary considerably depending on growing conditions.

C. 'Alison Kirk' (illus. p.260). Incurved florists' chrysanthemum. H 1.2m (4ft), S 30–60cm (1–2ft). Produces white flowers, to 12–15cm (5–6in) across, in early autumn. Is more suitable for exhibition than for garden use.
C. alpinum. See *Leucanthemopsis alpina.*
C. 'Amber Yvonne Arnaud'. Reflexed florists' chrysanthemum. H 1.2m (4ft), S 60–75cm (2–2½ft). Is a sport of *C.* 'Yvonne Arnaud' with fully reflexed, amber flowers in early autumn.
C. 'Autumn Days' (illus. p.261). Intermediate florists' chrysanthemum. H 1.1–1.2m (3½–4ft), S to 75cm (2½ft). Bears loosely incurving, bronze flowers, 12cm (5in) across, in early autumn.
C. 'Beacon' (illus. p.261). Intermediate florists' chrysanthemum. H 1.2m (4ft), S 60cm (2ft). Tender. Bears red, sometimes bronze, flowers, to 18cm (7in) wide, in late autumn. Is good for exhibition.
C. 'Bill Wade' (illus. p.260). Intermediate florists' chrysanthemum. H 1.35m (4½ft), S 60cm (2ft). Loosely incurving, white flowers, 18–20cm (7–8in) across, are produced in early autumn. Is more suitable for exhibition than for garden use.
C. 'Brietner' (illus. p.260). Reflexed florists' chrysanthemum. H 1.1–1.2m (3½–4ft), S 75cm (2½ft). Fully reflexed, pink flowers, to 12cm (5in) wide, appear in early autumn.
C. 'Bronze Fairie' (illus. p.261). Pompon florists' chrysanthemum.

H 30–60cm (1–2ft), S 60cm (2ft). Has bronze flowers, 4cm (1½in) across, in early autumn.
C. 'Bronze Hedgerow' (illus. p.261). Single florists' chrysanthemum. H 1.5m (5ft), S 75cm–1m (2½–3ft). Tender. Produces bronze flowers, 12cm (5in) across, in late autumn.
C. 'Bronze Yvonne Arnaud' (illus. p.261). Reflexed florists' chrysanthemum. H 1.2m (4ft), S 60–75cm (2–2½ft). Is a sport of *C.* 'Yvonne Arnaud' with fully reflexed, bronze flowers in early autumn.
C. 'Buff Margaret' (illus. p.261). Spray florists' chrysanthemum. H 1.2m (4ft), S to 75cm (2½ft). Has reflexed, pale bronze flowers, to 9cm (3½in) wide, in early autumn.
C. carinatum. See *Ismelia carinata.*
C. 'Chessington'. Intermediate florists' chrysanthemum. H 2–2.2m (6–7ft), S 75cm (2½ft). Produces fairly tightly incurving, white flowers, 18–20cm (7–8in) across, in early autumn. Is more suitable for exhibition than for garden use.
C. 'Christina'. Intermediate florists' chrysanthemum. H 1.35–1.5m (4½–5ft), S 60–75cm (2–2½ft). Bears loosely incurving, white flowers, to 14cm (5½in) wide, in early autumn. Is suitable for exhibition.
C. 'Claire Louise'. Reflexed florists' chrysanthemum. H 1.2–1.35m (4–4½ft), S 75cm (2½ft). Produces fully reflexed, bronze flowers, to 15cm (6in) across, in early autumn. Is ideal for exhibition.
C. 'Clara Curtis', syn. *C. rubellum* 'Clara Curtis', illus. p.259.
C. coccineum. See *Tanacetum coccineum.*
C. coronarium. See *Xanthophthalmum coronarium.*
C. densum. See *Tanacetum densum* subsp. *amani.*
C. 'Elsie Prosser' (illus. p.260). Fully reflexed florists' chrysanthemum. H 1.3–1.5m (4½–5ft), S 30cm (1ft). Tender. Bears pink flowers, 25cm (10in) wide, in late autumn. Is good for exhibition.
C. 'Enbee Wedding' (illus. p.260). Spray florists' chrysanthemum. H 1.2m (4ft), S 75cm (2½ft). Has single, light pink flowers, to 8cm (3in) wide, in early autumn. Is good for exhibition.
C. 'Fairweather' (illus. p.260). Incurved florists' chrysanthemum. H 1.1m (3½ft), S 60cm (2ft). Tender. Bears pale purplish-pink flowers, 14cm (5½in) wide, in late autumn. Is good for exhibition.
C. 'Fiona Lynn'. Reflexed florists' chrysanthemum. H 1.5m (5ft), S 75cm (2½ft). Fully reflexed, pink flowers, to 18–20cm (7–8in) across, appear in early autumn. Is ideal for exhibition.
C. frutescens. See *Argyranthemum frutescens.* 'Jamaica Primrose' see *A.* 'Jamaica Primrose'. 'Mary Wootton' see *A.* 'Mary Wootton'.
C. 'George Griffiths' (illus. p.261). Reflexed florists' chrysanthemum. H 1.2–1.35m (4–4½ft), S 75cm (2½ft). Produces fully reflexed, deep red flowers, to 14cm (5½in) wide, in early autumn. Is excellent for exhibition.
C. 'Gigantic' (illus. p.261). Tightly

incurved or loosely reflexed florists' chrysanthemum, its form depending on the amount of warmth provided. H 1.3m (4½ft), S 30cm (1ft). Tender. Has salmon-pink flowers, 25–27cm (10–11in) wide, in late autumn. Is good for exhibition.
C. 'Ginger Nut'. Intermediate florists' chrysanthemum. H 1.2m (4ft), S 60–75cm (2–2½ft). Bears tightly incurving, light bronze flowers, to 14cm (5½in) across, occasionally closing at top to form a true incurved flower, in early autumn. Is good for exhibition.
C. 'Golden Chalice' (illus. p.261). Charm florists' chrysanthemum. H and S 1m (3ft). Tender. Bears single, yellow flowers, 2.5cm (1in) wide, in late autumn. Is good for exhibition.
C. 'Golden Gigantic' (illus. p.261). Tightly incurved or loosely reflexed florists' chrysanthemum. H 1.3m (4½ft), S 30cm (1ft). Tender. Produces large, gold flowers, 25–27cm (10–11in) wide, in late autumn. Is good for exhibition.
C. 'Golden Woolman's Glory' (illus. p.261). Single florists' chrysanthemum. H 1.5m (5ft), S 1m (3ft). Tender. Golden flowers, to 18cm (7in) across, appear in late autumn. Is excellent for exhibition.
C. 'Green Satin' (illus. p.261). Intermediate florists' chrysanthemum. H 1.2m (4ft), S 60cm (2ft). Tender. Produces loosely incurving, green flowers, to 12cm (5in) wide, in late autumn.
C. haradjanii. See *Tanacetum haradjanii.*
C. hosmariense. See *Rhodanthemum hosmariense.*
C. 'Idris' (illus. p.261). Incurved florists' chrysanthemum. H 1.3m (4½ft), S 45cm (1½ft). Tender. Has salmon-pink flowers, 21–25cm (8–10in) wide, in late autumn.
C. 'John Wingfield' (illus. p.260). Reflexed florists' chrysanthemum. H 1.5m (5ft), S 45–60cm (1½–2ft). Tender. Produces white, often pink-flushed, flowers, 12cm (5in) wide, in late autumn. Is good for exhibition.
C. 'Keith Luxford' (illus. p.260). Incurved florists' chrysanthemum. H 1.5m (5ft), S 45cm (1½ft). Tender. Bears pink flowers, 21–25cm (8–10in) wide, in late autumn. Is good for exhibition.
C. 'Lundy' (illus. p.260). Fully reflexed florists' chrysanthemum. H 1.5m (5ft), S 45cm (1½ft). Tender. Bears white flowers, 21–25cm (8–10in) wide, often broader than they are deep, in late autumn. Is good for exhibition.
C. 'Madeleine' (illus. p.260). Spray florists' chrysanthemum. H 1.2m (4ft), S 75cm (2½ft). Has reflexed, pink flowers, to 8cm (3in) across, in early autumn. Is good for exhibition.
C. 'Majestic' (illus. p.261). Fully reflexed florists' chrysanthemum. H 1.3m (4½ft), S 45cm (1½ft). Tender. Has light bronze flowers, 21–25cm (8–10in) wide, in late autumn. Is good for exhibition.
C. 'Maria' (illus. p.261). Pompon florists' chrysanthemum. H 45cm (1½ft), S 30–60cm (1–2ft). Bears

masses of pink flowers, to 4cm (1½in) across, in early autumn.

C. **'Marian Gosling'** (illus. p.260). Reflexed florists' chrysanthemum. H 1.2–1.35m (4–4½ft), S 60cm (2ft). Fully reflexed, pale pink flowers, to 14cm (5½in) wide, appear in early autumn. Is good for exhibition.

C. **'Marion'** (illus. p.261). Spray florists' chrysanthemum. H 1.2m (4ft), S 75cm (2½ft). Produces reflexed, pale yellow flowers, to 8cm (3in) wide, from late summer.

C. **'Mason's Bronze'**. Single florists' chrysanthemum. H 1.35–1.5m (4½–5ft), S to 1m (3ft). Tender. Has bronze flowers, to 12cm (5in) wide, in late autumn. Is excellent for exhibition.

C. maximum of gardens. See *Leucanthemum* × *superbum*.

C. **'Nancye Furneaux'** (illus. p.261). Reflexed florists' chrysanthemum. H 1.5m (5ft), S 45cm (1½ft). Tender. Has yellow flowers, 21–25cm (8–10in) wide, in late autumn. Is good for exhibition.

C. **'Oracle'** (illus. p.261). Intermediate florists' chrysanthemum. H 1.2m (4ft), S 60–75cm (2–2½ft). Produces loosely incurving, pale bronze flowers, to 12cm (5in) wide, in early autumn. Is useful for exhibition.

C. parthenium. See *Tanacetum parthenium.*

C. **'Peach Brietner'** (illus. p.261). Reflexed florists' chrysanthemum. H 1.1–1.2m (3½–4ft), S 75cm (2½ft). Is a sport of *C.* 'Brietner' with fully reflexed, peach-coloured flowers.

C. **'Pennine Alfie'** (illus. p.261). Spray florists' chrysanthemum. H 1.2m (4ft), S 60–75cm (2–2½ft). Spoon-type, pale bronze flowers, to 6–8cm (2½–3in) wide, appear in early autumn. Is suitable for exhibition.

C. **'Pennine Flute'** (illus. p.260). Quill-shaped florists' chrysanthemum. H 1.2m (4ft), S 60–75cm (2–2½ft). Is similar to *C.* 'Pennine Alfie', but has pink flowers.

C. **'Pennine Oriel'** (illus. p.260). Spray florists' chrysanthemum. H 1.2m (4ft), S 60–75cm (2–2½ft). Anemone-centred, white flowers, to 9cm (3½in) across, are produced in early autumn. Is very good for exhibition.

C. **'Peter Rowe'**. Incurved florists' chrysanthemum. H 1.35m (4½ft), S 60–75cm (2–2½ft). Produces yellow flowers, to 14cm (5½in) across, in early autumn. Is ideal for exhibition.

C. **'Primrose Fairweather'**. Incurved florists' chrysanthemum. H 1–1.1m (3–3½ft), S to 75cm (2½ft). Produces pale yellow flowers, to 14–15cm (5½–6in) wide, in late autumn. Is good for exhibition.

C. **'Primrose John Hughes'** (illus. p.261). Perfectly incurved florists' chrysanthemum. H 1.2m (4ft), S 60–75cm (2–2½ft). Tender. Bears primrose-yellow flowers, 12–14cm (5–5½in) wide, in late autumn. Is good for exhibition.

C. **'Primrose West Bromwich'** (illus. p.261). Reflexed florists' chrysanthemum. H 2.2m (7ft), S 45–60cm (1½–2ft). Fully reflexed, pale yellow flowers, to 18cm (7in) or more wide, appear in mid-autumn. Use only for exhibition.

C. **'Purple Pennine Wine'** (illus. p.261). Spray florists' chrysanthemum. H 1.2m (4ft), S 60–75cm (2–2½ft). Bears reflexed, purplish-red flowers, to 8cm (3in) wide, in early autumn. Is very good for exhibition.

C. **'Ringdove'** (illus. p.260). Charm florists' chrysanthemum. H and S 1m (3ft). Tender. Has masses of pink flowers, 2.5cm (1in) across, in late autumn. Is excellent for exhibition.

C. **'Robeam'** (illus. p.261). Spray florists' chrysanthemum. H 1.5m (5ft), S 75–100cm (2½–3ft). Tender. Produces reflexed, yellow flowers, to 8cm (3in) wide, in late autumn. Is good for exhibition.

C. **'Rose Yvonne Arnaud'** (illus. p.261). Reflexed florists' chrysanthemum. H 1.2m (4ft), S 60–75cm (2–2½ft). Is a sport of *C.* 'Yvonne Arnaud', producing fully reflexed, red flowers in early autumn.

C. **'Roy Coopland'** (illus. p.261). Intermediate to loosely incurved florists' chrysanthemum. H 1.3m (4½ft), S 60cm (2ft). Tender. Produces bronze flowers, 15cm (6in) wide, in late autumn. Is good for exhibition.

C. rubellum **'Clara Curtis'**. See *C.* 'Clara Curtis'.

C. **'Salmon Fairie'** (illus. p.261). Pompon florists' chrysanthemum. H 30–60cm (1–2ft), S 60cm (2ft). Is similar to *C.* 'Bronze Fairie', but has salmon flowers.

C. **'Salmon Margaret'** (illus. p.261). Spray florists' chrysanthemum. H 1.2m (4ft), S to 75cm (2½ft). Is similar to *C.* 'Buff Margaret', but has salmon flowers.

C. segetum. See *Xanthophthalmum segetum.*

C. **'Senkyo Emiaki'** (illus. p.260). Spider-form florists' chrysanthemum. H 30–60cm (1–2ft), S to 60cm (2ft). Tender. Bears light pink flowers, 15cm (6in) wide, in early autumn. Is good for exhibition.

C. serotinum. See *Leucanthemella serotina.*

C. × *superbum.* See *Leucanthemum* × *superbum.*

C. tricolor. See *Ismelia carinata.*

C. uliginosum. See *Leucanthemella serotina.*

C. **'Venice'**. Reflexed florists' chrysanthemum. H 1.2m (4ft), S 60–75cm (2–2½ft). Reflexed, pink flowers, to 15cm (6in) wide, are produced in early autumn. Is good for exhibition.

C. **'Wendy'** (illus. p.261). Spray florists' chrysanthemum. H 1.2m (4ft), S 60–75cm (2–2½ft). Produces reflexed, pale bronze flowers, to 8cm (3in) wide, in early autumn. Is excellent for exhibition.

C. **'Woking Rose'** (illus. p.260). Intermediate florists' chrysanthemum. H 1.5m (5ft), S 45cm (1½ft). Tender. Has rose-pink flowers, to 21cm (8in) wide, in late autumn. Is good for exhibition.

C. **'Yellow Brietner'** (illus. p.261). Reflexed florists' chrysanthemum. H 1.1–1.2m (3½–4ft), S 75cm (2½ft). Is a sport of *C.* 'Brietner' with fully reflexed, yellow flowers in early autumn.

C. **'Yellow John Hughes'** (illus. p.261). Incurved florists'

chrysanthemum. H 1.2m (4ft), S 60–75cm (2–2½ft). Tender. Yellow flowers, to 12–14cm (5–5½in) wide, appear in late autumn. Is excellent for exhibition.

C. **'Yvonne Arnaud'** (illus. p.261). Reflexed florists' chrysanthemum. H 1.2m (4ft), S 60–75cm (2–2½ft). Fully reflexed, purple flowers, to 12cm (5in) wide, are produced in early autumn.

CHRYSOGONUM

ASTERACEAE/COMPOSITAE

Genus of one species of summer- to autumn-flowering perennial. Suits a rock garden. Needs partial shade and moist but well-drained, peaty, sandy soil. Propagate by division in spring or by seed when fresh.

C. virginianum illus. p.359.

Chusan palm. See *Trachycarpus fortunei*, illus. p.84.

CHUSQUEA

GRAMINEAE/POACEAE

See also GRASSES, BAMBOOS, RUSHES and SEDGES.

C. culeou illus. p.308.

CICERBITA,

syn. MULGEDIUM

ASTERACEAE/COMPOSITAE

Genus of perennials, grown for their attractive flower heads. Requires shade and damp but well-drained soil. Propagate by division in spring or by seed in autumn. Some species may be invasive.

C. alpina, syn. *Lactuca alpina* (Mountain sow thistle). Branching, upright perennial. H to 2m (6ft), S 60cm (2ft). Mid-green leaves are lobed, with a large, terminal lobe. Elongated panicles of thistle-like, pale blue flower heads are produced in summer.

C. bourgaei, syn. *Lactuca bourgaei.* Rampant, erect perennial. H to 2m (6ft), S 60cm (2ft). Leaves are oblong to lance-shaped, toothed and light green. Many-branched panicles of thistle-like, mauve-blue or purplish-blue flower heads appear in summer.

CICHORIUM

Chicory

ASTERACEAE/COMPOSITAE

Genus of annuals, biennials and perennials, grown mainly as ornamental plants (*C. intybus* has edible leaves). Needs full sun and well-drained soil. Propagate by seed in autumn or spring. Contact with all parts of the plants may irritate skin or aggravate skin allergies.

C. intybus illus. p.253.

Cider gum. See *Eucalyptus gunnii*, illus. p.72.
Cigar flower. See *Cuphea ignea*, illus. p.172.

CIMICIFUGA

Bugbane

RANUNCULACEAE

Genus of perennials, grown for their flowers, which have an unusual, slightly unpleasant smell. Grow in light shade and moist soil. Needs staking. Propagate by seed when fresh or by division in spring.

C. racemosa. Clump-forming perennial. H 30–150cm (1–5ft), S 60cm (2ft). Spikes of bottlebrush-like, pure white flowers are borne in mid-summer above broadly oval, divided, fresh green leaves.
var. *cordifolia* see *C. rubifolia.*
C. rubifolia, syn. *C. racemosa* var. *cordifolia.*
Clump-forming perennial. H 1.5m (5ft), S 60cm (2ft). Feathery plumes of star-shaped, creamy-white flowers are produced in mid-summer above broadly oval to lance-shaped, dissected, light green leaves.
C. simplex illus. p.231.
'Elstead' is an upright perennial. H 1.2m (4ft), S 60cm (2ft). Purple stems bear arching racemes of fragrant, bottlebrush-like, white flowers in autumn. Has broadly oval to lance-shaped, divided, glossy leaves.
'Prichard's Giant', H 2.2m (7ft), has large, much-divided leaves and produces white flowers on arching panicles.

Cineraria cruentus of gardens. See *Pericallis* × *hybrida.*
Cineraria × *hybridus.* See *Pericallis* × *hybrida.*
Cineraria. See *Pericallis* × *hybrida.*

CINNAMOMUM

LAURACEAE

Genus of evergreen trees, grown for their foliage and to provide shade. Tender, min. 10°C (50°F). Requires full light or partial shade and fertile, moisture-retentive but well-drained soil. Water containerized specimens freely when in full growth but less at other times. May be pruned if necessary. Propagate by seed in spring or by semi-ripe cuttings in summer.

C. camphora. Moderately fast-growing, evergreen, rounded tree. H and S 12m (40ft) or more. Oval, lustrous, rich green leaves, tinted blue-grey beneath, reddish or coppery when young, are camphor-scented when bruised. Has insignificant flowers in spring.

Cinnamon fern. See *Osmunda cinnamomea.*
Cinquefoil, Alpine. See *Potentilla crantzii.*

CIONURA

ASCLEPIADACEAE

Genus of one species of deciduous, twining climber, grown for its flowers. Grow in any soil and in full sun. Prune after flowering. Propagate by seed in spring or by stem cuttings in late summer or early autumn. Contact with the latex exuded by cut leaves and stems may irritate skin or cause blisters, and may cause severe discomfort if ingested.

C. erecta, syn. *Marsdenia erecta*. Deciduous, twining climber. H 3m (10ft) or more. Heart-shaped, greyish-green leaves are 3–6cm (1¼–2½in) long. In summer, clusters of fragrant, white flowers, with 5 spreading petals, are borne in leaf axils, followed by 7cm (3in) long fruits, containing many silky seeds, in autumn. Zone 9?.

CIRSIUM

ASTERACEAE/COMPOSITAE

Genus of annuals, biennials and perennials. Most species are not cultivated – indeed some are pernicious weeds – but *C. rivulare* has decorative flower heads. Tolerates sun or shade and any but wet soil. Propagate by division in spring or by seed in autumn.

C. rivulare 'Atropurpureum'. Erect perennial. H 1.2m (4ft), S 60cm (2ft). Heads of pincushion-like, deep crimson flowers are borne on erect stems in summer. Leaves are narrowly oval to oblong or lance-shaped and deeply cut, with weakly spiny margins.

CISSUS

VITACEAE

Genus of evergreen, woody-stemmed, mainly tendril climbers, grown for their attractive foliage. Bears insignificant, greenish flowers, mainly in summer. Tender, min. 7–18°C (45–64°F). Provide fertile, well-drained soil, with semi-shade in summer. Water regularly, less in cold weather. Needs tying to supports. Thin out crowded stems in spring. Propagate by semi-ripe cuttings in summer.

C. antarctica illus. p.220.
C. bainesii. See *Cyphostemma bainesii*.
C. discolor (Rex begonia vine). Moderately vigorous, evergreen, tendril climber with slender, woody stems. H to 3m (10ft). Tender, min. 18°C (64°F). Has oval, pointed leaves, 10–15cm (4–6in) long, that are deep green with silver bands above, maroon beneath.
C. hypoglauca. Evergreen, woody-stemmed, scrambling climber. H 2–3m (6–10ft). Tender, min. 7°C (45°F). Leaves are divided into 4 or 5 oval leaflets that are pale green above and blue-grey beneath.
C. juttae. See *Cyphostemma juttae*.
C. rhombifolia, syn. *Rhoicissus rhombifolia, R. rhomboidea*, illus. p.220.
C. striata, syn. *Ampelopsis sempervirens, Parthenocissus striata, Vitis striata* (Ivy of Uruguay, Miniature grape ivy). Fast-growing, evergreen, woody-stemmed, tendril climber. H 10m (30ft) or more. Tender, min. 7°C (45°F). Has leaves of 3–5 oval, serrated, lustrous, green leaflets. Mature plants may produce pea-shaped, glossy, black berries in autumn.
C. voinieriana. See *Tetrastigma voinierianum*.

CISTUS
Rock rose

CISTACEAE

Genus of evergreen shrubs, grown for a succession of freely borne, short-lived, showy flowers. Is good in coastal areas, withstanding sea winds well. Needs shelter at the limit of hardiness. Does best in full sun and light, well-drained soil. Resents being transplanted. Cut out any dead wood in spring, but do not prune hard. Propagate species by softwood or greenwood cuttings in summer or by seed in autumn, hybrids and cultivars by cuttings only in summer.

C. × aguilarii 'Maculatus' illus. p.159.
C. albidus. Evergreen, bushy shrub. H and S 1m (3ft). Leaves are oblong and white-felted. Saucer-shaped, pale rose-pink flowers, each with a central, yellow blotch, open in early summer. Zone 9.
C. algarvensis. See *Halimium ocymoides*.
C. × corbariensis. See *C. × hybridus*.
C. creticus, syn. *C. incanus* subsp. *creticus*, illus. p.165.
C. × cyprius illus. p.159.
C. × dansereaui, syn. *C. × lusitanicus* of gardens. Evergreen, bushy, compact shrub. H and S 1m (3ft). Leaves are narrowly oblong and dark green. Saucer-shaped, white flowers, each with a central, deep red blotch, appear from early to mid-summer. Zone 9.
C. × hybridus, syn. *C. × corbariensis*, illus. p.159.
C. incanus subsp. **creticus**. See *C. creticus*.
C. ladanifer, syn. *C. ladaniferus*, illus. p.159.
C. ladaniferus. See *C. ladanifer*.
C. laurifolius. Evergreen, bushy, dense shrub. H and S 2m (6ft). Has oval, aromatic, dark green leaves and, in summer, saucer-shaped, white flowers, each with a central, yellow blotch. Zone 9.
C. × lusitanicus of gardens. See *C. × dansereaui*.
C. monspeliensis illus. p.159.
C. parviflorus. Evergreen, bushy, dense shrub. H and S 1m (3ft). Small, saucer-shaped, pale pink flowers appear among oval, grey-green leaves in early summer. Zone 9.
C. 'Peggy Sammons' illus. p.162.
C. × purpureus. Evergreen, bushy, rounded shrub. H and S 1m (3ft). Produces saucer-shaped, deep purplish-pink flowers, each blotched with deep red, from early to mid-summer. Leaves are narrowly lance-shaped and grey-green. Zone 9.
C. revolii of gardens. See × *Halimiocistus sahucii*.
C. salviifolius illus. p.159.
C. 'Silver Pink'. Evergreen, bushy shrub. H 60cm (2ft), S 1m (3ft). Oval, dark green leaves set off large, saucer-shaped, clear pink flowers, each with conspicuous, yellow stamens, from early to mid-summer.
C. × skanbergii illus. p.162. Zone 9.

× CITROFORTUNELLA

RUTACEAE

Hybrid genus (*Citrus* × *Fortunella*) of evergreen shrubs and trees, grown for

their flowers, fruits and overall appearance. Tender, min. 5–10°C (41–50°F). Requires full light and fertile, well-drained but not dry soil. Water containerized specimens freely when in full growth, moderately at other times. Propagate by seed when ripe or by greenwood or semi-ripe cuttings in summer. Whitefly, spider mite, mealy bug, lime-induced and magnesium-deficiency chlorosis may be troublesome.

× C. microcarpa, syn. × *C. mitis, Citrus mitis*, illus. p.151.
× C. mitis. See × *C. microcarpa*.

Citrus mitis. See × *Citrofortunella microcarpa*.

CLADANTHUS

ASTERACEAE/COMPOSITAE

Genus of one species of annual, grown for its fragrant foliage and daisy-like flower heads. Grow in sun and in reasonably fertile, very well-drained soil. Dead-head to prolong flowering. Propagate by seed sown outdoors in mid-spring.

C. arabicus illus. p.337.

CLADRASTIS

LEGUMINOSAE/PAPILIONACEAE

Genus of deciduous, summer-flowering trees, grown for their pendent, wisteria-like flower clusters and autumn foliage. Requires full sun and fertile, well-drained soil. Propagate by seed in autumn or by root cuttings in late winter. The wood is brittle: old trees are prone to damage by strong winds.

C. kentukea, syn. *C. lutea*, illus. p.82.
C. lutea. See *C. kentukea*.

Claret ash. See *Fraxinus angustifolia* 'Raywood'.

CLARKIA,
syn. GODETIA

ONAGRACEAE

Genus of annuals, grown for their flowers, which are good for cutting. Grow in sun and in reasonably fertile, well-drained soil. Avoid rich soil as this encourages vegetative growth at the expense of flowers. Propagate by seed sown outdoors in spring, or in early autumn in mild areas. Botrytis may be troublesome.

C. amoena. Fast-growing annual with upright, thin stems. H to 60cm (24in), S 30cm (12in). Has lance-shaped, mid-green leaves. Spikes of 5-petalled, single or double flowers, in shades of lilac to pink, are produced in summer. Tall forms, H 60cm (24in), have double flowers in shades of pink or red. **Grace Series**, intermediate, H to 50cm (20in), has single, lavender-pink, red, salmon-pink or pink flowers with contrasting centres. **Princess Series**, dwarf, H 30cm (12in), has frilled flowers in shades of pink, including salmon (illus. p.341). **Satin Series**, dwarf, H to 20cm (8in), has single flowers in various colours, many with white margins or contrasting centres.

'Sybil Sherwood' illus. p.324.
C. 'Brilliant' illus. p.324.

CLAYTONIA

PORTULACACEAE

Genus of mainly evergreen perennials with succulent leaves; is related to *Lewisia*. Grows best in alpine houses. Tolerates sun or shade and prefers well-drained soil. Propagate by seed or division in autumn. May be difficult to grow.

C. megarhiza, syn. *Calandrinia megarhiza*. Evergreen, basal-rosetted perennial with a long tap root. H 1cm (½in), S 8cm (3in). Leaves are spoon-shaped and fleshy. Bears small heads of tiny, bowl-shaped, white flowers in spring. Prefers sun and gritty soil. Is prone to aphid attack. var. **nivalis** illus. p.366.
C. virginica (Spring beauty). Clump-forming perennial with flat, black tubers. H 10cm (4in), S 20cm (8in) or more. Narrowly spoon-shaped leaves, reddish when young, later turn green and glossy. Branched stems bear cup-shaped, white or pink flowers, striped deep pink, in early spring. Needs shade.

CLEISTOCACTUS,
syn. BORZICACTUS

CACTACEAE

Genus of columnar, perennial cacti with branched, cylindrical, much-ribbed stems with spines. Is one of the faster-growing cacti, some reaching 2m (6ft) in 5 years or less. Tubular flowers contain plenty of nectar and are pollinated by hummingbirds. Tender, min. 5°C (41°F). Needs full sun and very well-drained soil. Propagate by seed or stem cuttings in spring or summer.

C. baumannii. Erect, then prostrate, perennial cactus. H 1m (3ft) or more, S 5m (15ft). Thick stems produce long, uneven, variable-coloured spines. Has S-shaped, tubular, bright orange-red flowers in spring-summer.
C. celsianus. See *Oreocereus celsianus*.
C. smaragdiflorus. Erect, then prostrate, perennial cactus. H 1.5m (5ft), S 6m (20ft). Is similar to *C. baumannii*, but has straight, tubular flowers with green-tipped petals.
C. straussii illus. p.459.
C. trollii. See *Oreocereus trollii*.

CLEMATIS
Old man's beard, Travellers' joy

RANUNCULACEAE

Genus of evergreen or deciduous, mainly twining climbers and herbaceous perennials, cultivated for their mass of flowers, often followed by decorative seed heads, and grown on walls and trellises and together with trees, shrubs and other host plants. Only early-flowering species are evergreen, although some later-flowering species are semi-evergreen. Most species have nodding, bell-shaped flowers, with 4 petals (botanically known as perianth segments), or flattish flowers, each usually with 4–6 generally pointed petals. Large-flowered cultivars also bear flattish flowers, but with 4–10 petals. Flower colour may vary according to climatic conditions: in general, the warmer the climate, the darker the flower colour. May be grown in partial shade or full sun, but prefers rich, well-drained soil with roots shaded. Propagate cultivars in early summer by softwood or semi-ripe cuttings or layering, species from seed sown in autumn. Aphids, mildew and clematis wilt may cause problems.

Clematis may be divided into groups according to their approximate flowering seasons, habit and pruning needs. See also feature panel pp.212–13.

Group 1

Early-flowering species preferring a sheltered, sunny site with well-drained soil. Small, single flowers, either bell-shaped or open-bell-shaped, 2–5cm (¾–2in) long, or saucer-shaped, 4–5cm (1½–2in) across, are borne on the previous season's ripened shoots in spring or, occasionally, in late winter. Leaves are evergreen and glossy, or deciduous, and usually divided into 3 lance-shaped, 12cm (5in) long leaflets or into 3 fern-like, 5cm (2in) long leaflets.

C. alpina, *C. macropetala* **and their cultivars** tolerate cold, exposed positions. Small, bell-shaped to open bell-shaped, single, semi-double, or double flowers, 3–7cm (1¼–3in) across, are borne on the previous season's ripened shoots in spring, occasionally also on the current season's shoots in summer. Deciduous, pale to mid-green leaves are divided into 3–5 lance-shaped to broadly oblong, toothed leaflets, 3cm (1¼in) long.

C. montana **and its cultivars** are vigorous, deciduous climbers, suitable for growing over large buildings and trees. Small, flat to saucer-shaped, usually single flowers, 5–7cm (2–3in) across, are borne on the previous season's ripened shoots in late spring. Leaves are mid- to purplish-green and divided into 3 lance-shaped to broadly oval, serrated leaflets, 8cm (3in) long with pointed tips.

Prune all group 1 clematis after flowering to allow new growth to be produced and ripened for the following season. Remove dead or damaged stems and cut back other shoots that have outgrown their allotted space. This will encourage production of new growth to bear flowers in the following season.

Group 2

Early- to mid-season, large-flowered cultivars bearing mostly saucer-shaped, single, semi-double, or fully double flowers, 10–20cm (4–8in) across, that are borne on the previous season's ripened shoots, in late spring and early summer, and on new shoots in mid- and late summer. Generally the second flush of flowers on semi-double and double forms produces single flowers. Deciduous, pale to mid-green leaves are usually 10–15cm (4–6in) long and divided into 3 ovate or lance-shaped leaflets, or are simple and ovate, and to 10cm (4in) long.

Prune before new growth starts, in early spring. Remove any dead or damaged stems and cut back all remaining shoots to where strong buds are visible. These buds provide a framework of second-year shoots which, in turn, produce sideshoots that flower in late spring and early summer. The flowers may then be removed. Young shoots bear more flowers later in the summer.

Group 3

Late, large-flowered cultivars producing outward-facing, usually saucer-shaped, single flowers, 7–15cm (3–6in) across, borne on new shoots in summer or early autumn. Leaves are deciduous and similar to those of early cultivars (group 2), described above.

Late-flowering species and **small-flowered cultivars** that bear small, single or double flowers on the current season's shoots in summer-autumn. Flowers vary in shape and may be star-shaped, tubular, bell-shaped, flattish or resembling nodding lanterns; they vary in size from 1cm (½in) to 10cm (4in) across. Have generally deciduous, pale to dark green or grey-green leaves divided into 3 lance-shaped to broadly oval leaflets, each 1cm (½in) long, or hairy and/or toothed leaves divided into 5 or more lance-shaped to broadly oval leaflets, each 1–10cm (½–4in) long.

Herbaceous species and cultivars producing single flowers that are either saucer-shaped, 1–2cm (½–¾in) wide, or bell-shaped or tubular, 1–4cm (½–1½in) long, and are produced on the current season's shoots in summer. Mid- to dark green or grey-green leaves are simple and lance-shaped to elliptic, 2.5–15cm (1–6in) long, or are divided into 3–5 lance-shaped to ovate, serrated leaflets, each 10–15cm (4–6in) long with a pointed tip.

Prune all group 3 clematis before new growth begins, in early spring. Cut back all the previous season's stems to a pair of strong buds, 15–20cm (6–8in) above soil level.

C. **'Abundance'**, syn. *C. viticella* 'Abundance' (illus. p.213). Late-flowering clematis (group 3). H 2–3m (6–10ft), S 1m (3ft). Produces flattish, deep purplish-red flowers, 5cm (2in) across, with cream anthers, in summer. Zone 3.

C. **'Aljonushka'**. Semi-herbaceous, non-clinging clematis (group 3). H 1–1.2m (3–4ft), S 1m (3ft). In mid-summer to early autumn, produces single, rich mauvish-pink flowers, 6–8cm (2½–3in) wide, with a satin sheen when young, with deep ridges on the reverse and crumpled edges; the petal tips recurve and twist as they age. Zone 6.

C. alpina. Alpina clematis (group 1). H 2–3m (6–10ft), S 1.5m (5ft). Has lantern-shaped, single, blue flowers, 4–7cm (1½–3in) long, in spring and, occasionally, summer. Forms attractive, fluffy, silvery seed heads in summer. Is ideal for a north-facing or very exposed site. **'Columbine'** has 5cm (2in) long, pale blue petals. **'Constance'** has semi-double, deep purplish-pink flowers. **'Frances Rivis'** (illus. p.213) is free-flowering, with slightly twisted, 7cm (3in) long, mid-blue petals. **'Frankie'** has light to mid-blue flowers with cream petaloid stamens tipped pale blue. Zones 1–3.

C. **ANNA LOUISE** ('Evithree') (illus. p.213). Compact, early, large-flowered clematis (group 2). H 1–1.2m (3–4ft), S 1m (3ft). Freely produces single flowers with violet petals with a contrasting red-purple central bar, and striking brown anthers, in late spring to early summer, and again in late summer to early autumn. Zone 4.

C. **ARCTIC QUEEN** ('Evitwo') (illus. p.212). Early, large-flowered clematis (group 2). H 3m (10ft), S 1m (3ft). From early summer to early autumn, freely produces double, clear creamy-white flowers, 10–18cm (4–7in) across, with yellow anthers. Zone 4.

C. armandii (illus. p.212). Strong-growing, evergreen, early-flowering clematis (group 1). H 3–5m (10–15ft), S 2–3m (6–10ft). Bears scented, flattish, single, white flowers, 4cm (1½in) across, in early spring. Needs a sheltered, south- or south-west-facing site. Zone 6.

C. **'Ascotiensis'** (illus. p.213). Vigorous, late, large-flowered clematis (group 3). H 3–4m (10–12ft), S 1m (3ft). Single, bright violet-blue flowers, 9–12cm (3½–5in) across, with pointed petals and brownish-green anthers, are produced in summer. Zone 4.

C. **'Bees Jubilee'**. Compact, early, large-flowered clematis (group 2). H 2.5m (8ft), S 1m (3ft). In early summer bears a profusion of single, deep pink flowers, 10–12cm (4–5in) across with brown anthers and a central, rose-madder stripe on each petal. Prefers partial shade. Zone 3b.

C. **'Bill MacKenzie'** (illus. p.213). Vigorous, late-flowering clematis (group 3). H 7m (22ft), S 3–4m (10–12ft). Has dark green leaves. Flowers are yellow and 6–7cm (2½–3in) wide. Is best pruned with shears. Zone 4.

C. **BLUE MOON** ('Evirin') (illus. p.213). Compact, free-flowering, early, large-flowered clematis (group 2). H 2.5–3m (8–10ft), S 1m (3ft). Bears single, white flowers, 15–18cm (6–7in) wide, suffused with pale lilac becoming darker at the wavy petal edges, in late spring to early summer. In late summer to early autumn, flowers are slightly smaller and darker. Zone 4.

C. calycina. See *C. cirrhosa*.

C. **'Carnaby'**. Compact, early, large-flowered clematis (group 2). H 2.5m (8ft), S 1m (3ft). In early summer has a profusion of single, deep pink flowers, 8–10cm (3–4in) across, with a darker stripe on each petal and red anthers. Prefers partial shade. Zone 4.

C. **'Charissima'**. Free-flowering, early, large-flowered clematis (group 2). H 2.5–3m (8–10ft), S 1m (3ft). In late spring to early summer, produces single flowers, 15–18cm (6–7in) across, with pointed, cerise-pink petals, a deeper pink bar and veins throughout the flower, and dark maroon anthers. Zone 4.

C. cirrhosa, syn. *C. calycina* (illus. p.213). Evergreen, early-flowering clematis (group 1). H 2–3m (6–10ft), S 1–2m (3–6ft). Produces bell-shaped, cream flowers, 3cm (1¼in) across and spotted red inside, in late winter and early spring during frost-free weather. Zone 5.

C. **'Comtesse de Bouchaud'**. Strong-growing, late, large-flowered clematis (group 3). H 2–3m (6–10ft), S 1m (3ft). In summer has masses of single, bright mauve-pink flowers, 8–10cm (3–4in) across, with yellow anthers. Zone 3.

C. **'Daniel Deronda'**. Vigorous, early, large-flowered clematis (group 2). H 3m (10ft), S 1m (3ft). Has double and semi-double, deep purple-blue flowers, 10–14cm (4–5½in) across, with cream anthers, then single flowers in late summer. Zone 4.

C. **'Doctor Ruppel'**. Early, large-flowered clematis (group 2). H 2.5m (8ft), S 1m (3ft). Single flowers, 10–15cm (4–6in) across, with deep rose-pink petals with darker central bands and light chocolate anthers, are freely produced throughout summer. Zone 4.

C. **'Duchess of Albany'** (illus. p.213). Vigorous, small-flowered clematis (group 3). H 2.5m (8ft), S 1m (3ft). In summer and early autumn has masses of small, tulip-like, single, soft pink flowers, 6cm (2½in) long, with brown anthers and a deeper pink stripe inside each petal. Zone 2.

C. **'Duchess of Edinburgh'**. Early, large-flowered clematis (group 2). H 2–3m (6–10ft), S 1m (3ft). In summer produces double, white flowers, 8–10cm (3–4in) across, with yellow anthers and green, outer petals. May be weak-growing. Zone 3b.

C. x *durandii*. Semi-herbaceous, late-flowering clematis (group 3). H 1–2m (3–6ft), S 45cm–1.5m (1½–5ft). In summer has flattish, single, deep blue flowers, 6–8cm (2½–3in) across, with 4 petals and yellow anthers. Leaves are elliptic. Zone 5.

C. **'Elsa Spath'** (illus. p.213). Early, large-flowered clematis (group 2). H 2–3m (6–10ft), S 1m (3ft). Bears masses of single, 12cm (5in) wide flowers, with overlapping, rich mauve-blue petals and red anthers, throughout summer. Zone 4b.

C. **'Ernest Markham'** (illus. p.213). Vigorous, late, large-flowered clematis (group 3). H 3–4m (10–12ft), S 1m (3ft). In summer bears 10cm (4in) wide, single flowers with blunt-tipped, vivid magenta petals and chocolate anthers. Thrives in full sun. Zone 3b.

C. **'Etoile Violette'**, syn. *C. viticella* 'Etoile Violette' (illus. p.213). Vigorous, late-flowering clematis (group 3). H 3–5m (10–15ft), S 1.5m (5ft). Produces masses of flattish, single, violet-purple flowers, 4–6cm (1½–2½in) wide, with yellow anthers, in summer. Zone 3.

C. **'Evifour'**. See *C.* ROYAL VELVET.
C. **'Evirin'**. See *C.* BLUE MOON.
C. **'Evisix'**. See *C.* PETIT FAUCON.
C. **'Evithree'**. See *C.* ANNA LOUISE.
C. **'Evitwo'**. See *C.* ARCTIC QUEEN.
C. flammula (illus. p.212). Vigorous, late-flowering clematis; may be semi-evergreen (group 3). H 3–5m (10–15ft), S 2m (6ft). Produces masses of almond-scented, flattish, single, white flowers, 2cm (¾in) across, in summer and early autumn. Zone 8.

C. florida 'Sieboldii', syn. *C. florida* 'Bicolor' (illus. p.212). Weak-growing, small-flowered clematis (group 3). H 2–3m (6–10ft), S 1m (3ft). In summer has passion-flower-like, single blooms, each 8cm (3in) wide with creamy-white petals and a domed boss of petal-like, rich purple stamens. Needs a sheltered aspect. Zone 5b.

C. 'Général Sikorski'. Early, large-flowered clematis (group 2). H 3m (10ft), S 1m (3ft). Has numerous 10cm (4in) wide, single flowers with large, overlapping, blue petals and cream anthers, in summer. Zone 4.

C. 'Gipsy Queen'. Vigorous, late, large-flowered clematis (group 3). H 3m (10ft), S 1m (3ft). Bears single, 10cm (4in) wide flowers, with velvety, violet-purple petals and red anthers, in summer. Zone 3.

C. 'Gravetye Beauty' (illus. p.213). Vigorous, small-flowered clematis (group 3). H 2.5m (8ft), S 1m (3ft). In summer and early autumn has masses of small, tulip-like, single, bright red flowers, 6cm (2½in) long, with brown anthers. Is similar to *C.* 'Duchess of Albany', but flowers are more open. Zone 2.

C. 'Guernsey Cream'. Early, large-flowered clematis (group 2). H 2.5m (8ft), S 1m (3ft). Bears single flowers, 12cm (5in) across, with creamy yellow petals and anthers, in early summer. Flowers are smaller and creamy white in late summer. Fades in full sun. Zone 4.

C. 'Hagley Hybrid' (illus. p.212). Vigorous, late, large-flowered clematis (group 3). H 2.5m (8ft), S 1m (3ft). Produces 8–10cm (3–4in) wide, single flowers with boat-shaped, rose-mauve petals and red anthers, in summer. Prefers partial shade. Zone 3.

C. 'Henryi' (illus. p.212). Vigorous, early, large-flowered clematis (group 2). H 3m (10ft), S 1m (3ft). Has 12cm (5in) wide, single flowers, with white petals and dark chocolate anthers, in summer. Zone 4.

C. heracleifolia var. *davidiana*. Herbaceous clematis (group 3). H 1m (3ft), S 75cm (2½ft). In summer, thick stems bear axillary clusters of scented, tubular, single, pale blue flowers, 2–3cm (¾–1¼in) long, with reflexed petal tips. 'Wyevale' (illus. p.213) has strongly scented, dark blue flowers. Zone 5.

C. 'H.F. Young' (illus. p.213). Compact, early, large-flowered clematis (group 2). H 2.5m (8ft), S 1m (3ft). Bears 10cm (4in) wide, single flowers, with violet-tinged, blue petals and cream anthers, in summer. Is ideal for a container or patio garden. Zone 4.

C. 'Huldine' (illus. p.212). Very vigorous, late, large-flowered clematis (group 3). H 3–4m (10–12ft), S 2m (6ft). In summer has 6cm (2½in) wide, single, white flowers, mauve beneath and with cream anthers. Is ideal for an archway or pergola. Zone 3.

C. integrifolia (illus. p.213). Herbaceous clematis (group 3). H and S 75cm (30in). Leaves are narrowly lance-shaped. In summer bears bell-shaped, single, deep blue flowers, 3cm (1¼in) long with cream anthers, followed by attractive, grey-brown seed heads. Zone 3.

C. 'Jackmanii' (illus. p.213). Vigorous, late, large-flowered clematis (group 3). H 3m (10ft), S 1m (3ft). Bears masses of velvety, single, dark purple flowers, fading to violet, 8–10cm (3–4in) across, with light brown anthers, in mid-summer. Zone 2.

C. 'Jackmanii Superba'. Vigorous, late, large-flowered clematis (group 3). Is similar to *C.* 'Jackmanii', but has more rounded, darker flowers. Zone 4.

C. 'John Huxtable'. Late, large-flowered clematis (group 3). H 2–3m (6–10ft), S 1m (3ft). Bears masses of 8cm (3in) wide, single, white flowers, with cream anthers, in mid-summer. Zone 4.

C. 'Josephine' (illus. p.213). Early, large-flowered clematis (group 2). H 2.5m (8ft), S 1m (3ft). From early summer to early autumn, bears double flowers, 12cm (5in) across, with almost bronze, green-tinged petals with a darker central bar; the petals become lilac in mid-summer, with a pink bar. Best colour in sun. Zone 4.

C. x *jouiniana*. Sprawling, sub-shrubby, late-flowering clematis (group 3). H 1m (3ft), S 3m (10ft). Has coarse foliage and, in summer, masses of tubular, single, soft lavender or off-white flowers, 2cm (¾in) wide, with reflexed petal tips. Is non-clinging. 'Praecox' has slightly darker flowers, 2 weeks earlier. Zone 2b.

C. 'Kathleen Wheeler'. Early, large-flowered clematis (group 2). H 2.5–3m (8–10ft), S 1m (3ft). Has single, plum-mauve flowers, 12–14cm (5–5½in) across with yellow anthers, in early summer. Zone 4.

C. 'Lasurstern' (illus. p.213). Vigorous, early, large-flowered clematis (group 2). H 2–3m (6–10ft), S 1m (3ft). In summer bears single, blue flowers, 10–12cm (4–5in) across, with overlapping, wavy-edged petals and cream anthers. Zone 4.

C. 'Lincoln Star' (illus. p.213). Early, large-flowered clematis (group 2). H 2–3m (6–10ft), S 1m (3ft). Has 10–12cm (4–5in) wide, single, raspberry-pink flowers, with red anthers, in early summer. Early flowers are darker than late ones, which have very pale pink petal edges. Prefers partial shade. Zone 4.

C. macropetala (illus. p.213). Macropetala clematis (group 1). H 3m (10ft), S 1.5m (5ft). During late spring and summer has masses of semi-double, mauve-blue flowers, 5cm (2in) long and lightening in colour towards the centre, followed by fluffy, silvery seed heads. Zone 1. 'Markham's Pink' (illus. p.212) has pink flowers.

C. 'Madame Edouard André'. Late, large-flowered clematis (group 3). H 2.5m (8ft), S 1m (3ft). Freely produces single, deep red flowers, 8–10cm (3–4in) across, with silver undersides, pointed petals, and yellow anthers, in mid-summer. Zone 4.

C. 'Madame Julia Correvon', syn. *C. viticella* 'Madame Julia Correvon' (illus. p.213). Late-flowering clematis (group 3). H 2.5–3.5m (8–11ft), S 1m (3ft). Has flattish, single, wine-red flowers, 5–7cm (2–3in) wide, with twisted petals, in summer. Zone 3.

C. 'Madame Le Coultre'. See *C.* 'Marie Boisselot'.

C. 'Marie Boisselot', syn. *C.* 'Madame Le Coultre'. Vigorous, early, large-flowered clematis (group 2). H 3m (10ft), S 1m (3ft). Bears single flowers, 12cm (5in) across, with overlapping, white petals and cream anthers, in summer. Zone 4.

C. 'Miss Bateman'. Compact, early, large-flowered clematis (group 2). H 2.5m (8ft), S 1m (3ft). Masses of single, white flowers, 8–10cm (3–4in) across with red anthers, are produced in summer. Is good for a container or patio garden. Zone 4.

C. montana (illus. p.212). Vigorous, Montana clematis (group 1). H 7–12m (22–40ft), S 2–3m (6–10ft). In late spring bears masses of single, white flowers, 4–5cm (1½–2in) across, with yellow anthers. Zone 6. 'Broughton Star', H 4–5m (12–15ft), bears semi-double to fully double, cup-shaped, dusty pink flowers, with slightly darker veins. 'Elizabeth', H 10–12m (30–40ft), has scented, soft pink flowers with widely spaced petals. Flowers of var. *rubens* (illus. p.212) are pale pink. 'Tetrarose' (illus. p.212), H 7–8m (22–25ft), has coarse, 8cm (3in) long leaflets and 6–7cm (2½–3in) wide, deep satin-pink flowers.

C. 'Mrs Cholmondeley'. Early, large-flowered clematis (group 2). H 2–3m (6–10ft), S 1m (3ft). In summer has single, light bluish-lavender flowers, 10–12cm (4–5in) across with widely spaced petals and light chocolate anthers. Zone 3b.

C. 'Mrs George Jackman' (illus. p.212). Early, large-flowered clematis (group 2). H 2–3m (6–10ft), S 1m (3ft). Bears 10cm (4in) wide, semi-double flowers, with creamy-white petals and light brown anthers, in early summer. Zone 4.

C. 'Mrs N. Thompson'. Compact, early, large-flowered clematis (group 2). H 2.5m (8ft), S 1m (3ft). Produces masses of 8–10cm (3–4in) wide, single, magenta flowers, with a central, slightly darker stripe on each bluish-purple-edged petal and red anthers, in summer. Is good for a container or patio garden. Zone 3b.

C. 'Nelly Moser' (illus. p.213). Early, large-flowered clematis (group 2). H 3.5m (11ft), S 1m (3ft). In early summer has 12–16cm (5–6½in) wide, single, rose-mauve flowers, with reddish-purple anthers and, on each petal, a carmine stripe that fades in strong sun. Prefers a shaded, east-, west- or north-facing situation. Zone 3b.

C. 'Niobe'. Early, large-flowered clematis (group 2). H 2–3m (6–10ft), S 1m (3ft). Throughout summer produces masses of single, rich deep red flowers, 10–14cm (4–5½in) across with yellow anthers. Zone 4.

C. orientalis. Late-flowering clematis (group 3). H 3–4m (10–12ft), S 1.5m (5ft). Leaves are grey- to dark green. In summer lantern-shaped, single, greenish-yellow flowers, 3cm (1¼in) wide with recurved petal tips, are followed by feathery seed heads. Zone 3.

C. 'Perle d'Azur' (illus. p.213). Late, large-flowered clematis (group 3). H 3m (10ft), S 1m (3ft). Single, azure-blue flowers, 8cm (3in) across, with recurved petal tips and creamy-green anthers, open in summer. Zone 3.

C. PETIT FAUCON ('Evisix') (illus. p.213). Non-clinging, mid-season, small-flowered clematis (group 3). H 1.5m (5ft), S 1m (3ft). From mid-summer to mid-autumn, freely produces nodding, single, deep blue flowers, 7–9cm (3–3½in) across, with orange-yellow stamens that become creamy-white with age. Zone 5.

C. 'Purpurea Plena Elegans'. See *C. viticella* 'Purpurea Plena Elegans'.

C. 'Ramona'. Early, large-flowered clematis (group 2). H 3m (10ft), S 1m (3ft). Has coarse, dark green leaves offset, in summer, by single, pale blue flowers, 10–12cm (4–5in) across with red anthers. Prefers a south- or south-west-facing position. Zone 3b.

C. recta (illus. p.212). Clump-forming, herbaceous clematis (group 3). H 1–2m (3–6ft), S 50cm (20in). Leaves are dark or grey-green. Bears masses of sweetly scented, flattish, single, white flowers, 2cm (¾in) across, in mid-summer. Zone 5.

C. rehderiana (illus. p.213). Vigorous, late-flowering clematis (group 3). H 6–7m (20–22ft), S 2–3m (6–10ft). Bears loose clusters of fragrant, tubular, single, yellow flowers, 1–2cm (½–¾in) long, in late summer and early autumn. Leaves are coarse-textured. Zone 6.

C. 'Rhapsody'. Compact, early, large-flowered clematis (group 2). H 2.5m (8ft), S 1m (3ft). From early summer to early autumn, bears single, sapphire-blue flowers, 10–13cm (4–5in) across, with splayed, creamy-yellow anthers. Colour deepens with age. Zone 4.

C. 'Richard Pennell'. Early, large-flowered clematis (group 2). H 2–3m (6–10ft), S 1m (3ft). Produces 10–12cm (4–5in) wide, single flowers, with rich purple-blue petals and golden-yellow anthers, in summer. Zone 4.

C. 'Rouge Cardinal'. Early, large-flowered clematis (group 3). H 2–3m (6–10ft), S 1m (3ft). In summer has single, velvety, crimson flowers, 8–10cm (3–4in) across, with red anthers. Zone 4.

C. ROYAL VELVET ('Evifour') (illus. p.213). Early, large-flowered clematis (group 2). H 2–2.5m (6–8ft), S 1m (3ft). In early and mid-summer, bears single flowers, 10–15cm (4–6in) wide, with bluish, rich velvet-purple petals, with darker central bands, and red anthers. Zone 4.

C. 'Souvenir du Capitaine Thuilleaux'. Compact, early, large-flowered clematis (group 2). H 2.5m (8ft), S 1m (3ft). In early summer bears 8–10cm (3–4in) wide, single flowers, with red anthers and deep pink-striped, cream-pink petals. Is ideal for a container or patio garden. Zone 4.

C. 'Star of India' (illus. p.213). Vigorous, late, large-flowered clematis (group 3). H 3m (10ft), S 1m (3ft). Bears masses of 8–10cm (3–4in) wide, single, deep purple-blue flowers, with light brown anthers, in mid-summer; each petal has a deep carmine-red stripe. Zone 3b.

C. tangutica (illus. p.213). Vigorous, late-flowering clematis (group 3). H 5–6m (15–20ft), S 2–3m (6–10ft). Has lantern-shaped, single, yellow flowers, 4cm (1½in) long, throughout summer and early autumn, followed by fluffy, silvery seed heads. Zone 1b.
C. 'The President' (illus. p.213). Early, large-flowered clematis (group 2). H 2–3m (6–10ft), S 1m (3ft). In early summer bears masses of single, rich purple flowers, silver beneath, 10cm (4in) wide, with red anthers. Zone 3b.
C. 'Ville de Lyon'. Late, large-flowered clematis (group 3). H 2–3m (6–10ft), S 1m (3ft). In mid-summer has single, bright carmine-red flowers, 8–10cm (3–4in) across, with darker petal edges and yellow anthers. Lower foliage tends to become scorched by late summer. Zone 3b.
C. viticella. Late-flowering clematis (group 3). H 2–3m (6–10ft), S 1m (3ft). Produces nodding, open bell-shaped, single, purple-mauve flowers, 3.5cm (1½in) long, in summer. Zone 3.
'Abundance' see *C.* 'Abundance'. **'Etoile Violette'** see *C.* 'Etoile Violette'. **'Madame Julia Correvon'** see *C.* 'Madame Julia Correvon'. **'Purpurea Plena Elegans'** (syn *C.* 'Purpurea Plena Elegans'; illus. p.213) bears abundant, double flowers, with many purplish-mauve sepals, occasionally green outer sepals, and no anthers, from mid-summer to late autumn. Zone 3.
C. 'Vyvyan Pennell' (illus. p.213). Early, large-flowered clematis (group 2). H 2–3m (6–10ft), S 1m (3ft). Has double, lilac flowers, 10–12cm (4–5in) wide with a central, lavender-blue rosette of petals and golden-yellow anthers, in early summer, then single, blue-mauve flowers. Zone 3b.
C. 'W.E. Gladstone'. Vigorous, early, large-flowered clematis (group 2). H 3–4m (10–12ft), S 1m (3ft). Produces single, lavender flowers, 15cm (6in) wide with red anthers, in summer. Zone 4.
C. 'William Kennett'. Early, large-flowered clematis (group 2). H 2–3m (6–10ft), S 1m (3ft). In summer has masses of single flowers, 10–12cm (4–5in) across, with red anthers and tough, lavender-blue petals each bearing a central, darker stripe that fades as the flower matures. Zone 3b.

CLEOME
Spider flower
CAPPARACEAE

Genus of annuals and a few evergreen shrubs, grown for their unusual, spidery flowers. Tender, min. 4°C (39°F). Grow in sun and in fertile, well-drained soil. Remove dead flowers. Propagate by seed sown outdoors in late spring. Aphids may be a problem.
C. hassleriana, syn. *C. spinosa.* Fast-growing, bushy annual. H to 1.2m (4ft), S 45cm (1½ft). Has hairy, spiny stems and mid-green leaves divided into lance-shaped leaflets. Large, rounded heads of narrow-petalled, pink-flushed, white flowers, with long, protruding stamens, appear in summer. **'Colour**

Fountain' illus. p.322. **'Rose Queen'** has rose-pink flowers.
C. spinosa. See *C. hassleriana.*

CLERODENDRUM
VERBENACEAE

Genus of evergreen or deciduous, small trees, shrubs, sub-shrubs and woody-stemmed, twining climbers, grown for their showy flowers. Hardy to tender, min. 10–16°C (50–61°F). Needs humus-rich, well-drained soil and full sun, with partial shade in summer. Water freely in growing season, less at other times. Stems require support. Thin out crowded growth in spring. Propagate by seed in spring, by softwood cuttings in late spring or by semi-ripe cuttings in summer. Whitefly, spider mite and mealy bug may be a problem.
C. bungei illus. p.148.
C. chinense **'Pleniflorum'**, syn. *C. fragrans* 'Pleniflorum', *C. philippinum.* Evergreen or deciduous, bushy shrub. H and S to 2.5m (8ft). Tender, min. 10°C (50°F). Leaves are broadly oval, coarsely and shallowly toothed and downy. Fragrant, double, pink or white flowers are borne in domed, terminal clusters in summer.
C. fallax. See *C. speciosissimum.*
C. fragrans **'Pleniflorum'**. See *C. chinense* 'Pleniflorum'.
C. philippinum. See *C. chinense* 'Pleniflorum'.
C. speciosissimum, syn. *C. fallax.* Evergreen, erect to spreading, sparingly branched shrub. H and S to 3m (10ft). Tender, min. 15°C (59°F). Bears broadly heart-shaped, wavy-edged leaves, each to 30cm (1ft) across, on long stalks and, from late spring to autumn, tubular, scarlet flowers, with spreading petal lobes, in 30cm (1ft) long, terminal clusters. Makes a good pot plant.
C. splendens. Vigorous, evergreen, woody-stemmed, twining climber. H 3m (10ft) or more. Tender, min. 15°C (59°F). Has oval to elliptic, rich green leaves. Clusters of 5-petalled, tubular, scarlet flowers, 2.5cm (1in) wide, are produced in summer.
C. thomsoniae illus. p.208.
C. trichotomum illus. p.147.

CLETHRA
CLETHRACEAE

Genus of deciduous or evergreen shrubs and trees, grown for their fragrant, white flowers. Needs semi-shade and moist, peaty, acid soil. Propagate by softwood cuttings in summer or by seed in autumn.
C. alnifolia (Sweet pepper-bush). Deciduous, bushy shrub. H and S 2.5m (8ft). Has oval, toothed, mid-green leaves and, in late summer and early autumn, slender spires of small, bell-shaped flowers. Zone 5.
C. arborea (Lily-of-the-valley tree). Evergreen, bushy, dense shrub or tree. H 8m (25ft), S 6m (20ft). Bears long, nodding clusters of small, strongly fragrant, bell-shaped flowers among oval, toothed, rich green leaves from late summer to mid-autumn. Zone 9.
C. barbinervis illus. p.138.
C. delavayi illus. p.121.

CLEYERA
THEACEAE

Genus of evergreen, summer-flowering shrubs and trees, grown for their foliage and flowers. Requires a sheltered position in sun or semi-shade and moist, acid soil. Propagate by semi-ripe cuttings in summer.
C. fortunei **'Variegata'**. See *C. japonica* 'Tricolor'.
C. japonica. Evergreen, bushy shrub. H and S 3m (10ft). Small, fragrant, bowl-shaped, creamy-white flowers are borne in summer and narrowly oblong to oval-oblong, glossy, dark green leaves. Occasionally has small, spherical, red fruits, ripening to black. **'Tricolor'** (syn. *C. fortunei* 'Variegata', *Eurya japonica* 'Variegata' of gardens), H and S 2m (6ft), produces pink-flushed, young leaves, later green edged with creamy-white. Both zone 9.

CLIANTHUS
LEGUMINOSAE/PAPILIONACEAE

Genus of evergreen or semi-evergreen, woody-stemmed, scrambling climbers, grown for their attractive flowers. Tender, min. 7°C (45°F). Grow outdoors in warm areas in well-drained soil and full sun. In cooler areas needs to be under glass. In spring prune out growing tips to give a bushier habit and cut out any dead wood. Propagate by seed in spring or stem cuttings in late summer.
C. puniceus and f. *albus* illus. p.204.

Climbing butcher's broom. See *Semele androgyna.*
Climbing dahlia. See *Hidalgoa.*
Climbing fumitory. See *Adlumia fungosa.*
Climbing hydrangea. See *Hydrangea petiolaris*, illus. p.208.

CLINTONIA
CONVALLARIACEAE/LILIACEAE

Genus of late spring- or summer-flowering, rhizomatous perennials. Prefers shade and moist but well-drained, peaty, neutral to acid soil. Propagate by division in spring or by seed in autumn.
C. andrewsiana. Clump-forming, rhizomatous perennial. H 60cm (24in), S 30cm (12in). In early summer produces clusters of small, bell-shaped, pinkish-purple flowers at tops of stems, above sparse, broadly oval, glossy, rich green leaves. Bears globose, blue fruits in autumn.
C. borealis. (Corn lily). Clump-forming, rhizomatous perennial. H and S 30cm (12in). Is similar to *C. andrewsiana*, but has nodding, yellowish-green flowers and small, globose, blackish fruits.
C. uniflora (Queencup). Spreading, rhizomatous perennial. H 15cm (6in), S 30cm (12in). Has oval, glossy, green leaves. Slender stems bear solitary star-shaped, white flowers in late spring, then large, globose, blue-black fruits.

CLITORIA
LEGUMINOSAE/PAPILIONACEAE

Genus of perennials and evergreen shrubs and twining climbers, grown for their large, pea-like flowers. Tender, min. 15°C (59°F). Grow in full light and in any fertile, well-drained soil. Water moderately, less when not in full growth. Provide support for stems. Thin out crowded stems in spring. Propagate by seed in spring or by softwood cuttings in summer. Whitefly and spider mite may be a problem.
C. ternatea. Evergreen, twining climber with slender stems. H 3–5m (10–15ft). Leaves are divided into 3 or 5 oval leaflets. Clear bright blue flowers, 7–12cm (3–5in) wide, are carried in summer.

CLIVIA
AMARYLLIDACEAE

Genus of robust, evergreen, rhizomatous perennials, cultivated for their funnel-shaped flowers. Suits borders and large containers. Tender, min. 10°C (50°F). Needs partial shade and well-drained soil. Water well in summer, less in winter. Propagate by seed in winter or spring or by division in spring or summer after flowering. Mealy bugs may cause problems. All parts of *C. miniata* may cause mild stomach upset if ingested, and the sap may irritate skin.
C. miniata illus. p.419.
C. nobilis. Evergreen, spring- or summer-flowering, rhizomatous perennial. H 30–40cm (12–16in), S 30–60cm (12–24in). Has strap-shaped, semi-erect, basal leaves, 40–60cm (16–24in) long. Each leafless stem bears a dense, semi-pendent head of over 20 narrowly funnel-shaped, red flowers, with green tips and yellow margins to petals.

Cloth-of-gold crocus. See *Crocus angustifolius.*
Cloud grass. See *Aichryson* x *domesticum* 'Variegatum', illus. p.477.
Clover. See *Trifolium.*
Club, Devil's. See *Oplopanax horridus.*
Club-rush.
  Bristle. See *Isolepis setaceus.*
  Round-headed. See *Scirpoides holoschoenus.*

CLUSIA
CLUSIACEAE

Genus of evergreen, mainly summer-flowering climbers, shrubs and trees, grown for their foliage and flowers. Tender, min. 16–18°C (61–4°F). Needs partial shade and well-drained soil. Water potted specimens moderately, very little when temperatures are low. Pruning is tolerated if necessary. Propagate by layering in spring or by semi-ripe cuttings in summer. Whitefly and spider mite may be a problem.
C. major, syn. *C. rosea* (Autograph tree, Copey, Fat pork tree, Pitch apple). Slow-growing, evergreen, rounded tree or shrub. H and S to 15m (50ft). Bears

oval, lustrous, deep green leaves. Cup-shaped, pink flowers, 5cm (2in) wide, are produced in summer, followed by globose, greenish fruits that yield a sticky resin.

Cluster pine. See *Pinus pinaster*, illus. p.103.
Clustered ivy. See *Hedera helix* 'Conglomerata'.

CLYTOSTOMA
BIGNONIACEAE

Genus of evergreen, woody-stemmed, tendril climbers, grown for their flowers. Tender, min. 10–13°C (50–55°F). Grow in well-drained soil, with partial shade in summer. Water freely in summer, less at other times. Provide support for stems. Thin out congested growth after flowering or in spring. Propagate by semi-ripe cuttings in summer.
C. callistegioides, syn. *Pandorea lindleyana*, illus. p.205.

Coast redwood. See *Sequoia sempervirens*.

COBAEA
COBAEACEAE/POLEMONIACEAE

Genus of evergreen or deciduous, woody-stemmed, tendril climbers. Only one species, *C. scandens*, is generally cultivated. Tender, min. 4°C (39°F). Grow outdoors in warm areas in full light and in any well-drained soil. In cool regions may be grown under glass or treated as an annual. Propagate by seed in spring.
C. scandens illus. p.214.
f. *alba* is an evergreen, woody-stemmed, tendril climber. H 4–5m (12–15ft). Has long-stalked, bell-shaped, green, then white flowers from late summer until first frosts. Leaves have 4 or 6 oval leaflets.

Cobnut. See *Corylus avellana*.
Cobweb houseleek. See *Sempervivum arachnoideum*, illus. p.389.
Cock's foot. See *Dactylis glomerata*.
Cockle, Corn. See *Agrostemma*.
Cockspur coral-tree. See *Erythrina crista-galli*, illus. p.143.
Cockspur thorn. See *Crataegus crus-galli*.
Cocos capitata. See *Butia capitata*.

CODIAEUM
EUPHORBIACEAE

Genus of evergreen shrubs, grown for their foliage. Tender, min. 10–13°C (50–55°F). Prefers partial shade and fertile, moist but well-drained soil. Remove tips from young plants to promote a branched habit. Propagate by greenwood cuttings from firm stem tips in spring or summer. Mealy bug and soft scale may be a nuisance. Contact with the foliage may aggravate skin allergies.
C. variegatum var. *pictum* illus. p.177.

CODONOPSIS
CAMPANULACEAE

Genus of perennials and mostly herbaceous, twining climbers, grown for their bell- or saucer-shaped flowers. Requires a position in semi-shade, with light, well-drained soil. Train over supports or leave to scramble through other, larger plants. Propagate by seed sown in autumn or spring.
C. clematidea. Herbaceous, twining climber. H to 1.5m (5ft). Has small, oval, mid-green leaves. In summer produces nodding, bell-shaped flowers, 2.5cm (1in) long; they are white, tinged with blue, and marked inside with darker veining and 2 purple rings.
C. convolvulacea illus. p.214.
C. ovata. Upright perennial with scarcely twining stems. H to 30cm (12in). Has small, oval leaves and, in summer, small, bell-shaped, pale blue flowers, often with darker veins.

COELOGYNE
See also ORCHIDS.
C. cristata (illus. p.296). Evergreen, epiphytic orchid for a cool greenhouse. H 15cm (6in). In winter produces sprays of crisp, white flowers, 5cm (2in) across, and marked orange on each lip. Narrowly oval leaves are 8–10cm (3–4in) long. Needs a position in good light in summer.
C. flaccida (illus. p.296). Evergreen, epiphytic orchid for a cool greenhouse. H 15cm (6in). During spring bears drooping spikes of fragrant, star-shaped, light buff flowers, 4cm (1½in) across, with yellow and brown marks on each lip. Has narrowly oval, semi-rigid leaves, 8–10cm (3–4in) long. Grow in semi-shade in summer.
C. nitida, syn. *C. ochracea* (illus. p.296). Evergreen, epiphytic orchid for a cool greenhouse. H 12cm (5in). In spring produces sprays of very fragrant, white flowers, 2.5cm (1in) across and with a yellow mark on each lip. Narrowly oval, semi-rigid leaves are 8–10cm (3–4in) long. Requires semi-shade in summer.
C. ochracea. See *C. nitida*.
C. speciosa (illus. p.298). Vigorous, evergreen, epiphytic orchid for an intermediate greenhouse. H 25cm (10in). In summer, produces pendent, light green flowers, 6cm (2½in) across, with brown- and white-marked lips, that open in succession along stems. Has broadly oval leaves, 23–5cm (9–10in) long. Grow in good light in summer.

Coffee, Wild. See *Polyscias guilfoylei*.
Coffee tree, Kentucky. See *Gymnocladus dioica*.

COIX
GRAMINEAE/POACEAE
See also GRASSES, BAMBOOS, RUSHES and SEDGES.
C. lacryma-jobi illus. p.308.

COLCHICUM
COLCHICACEAE/LILIACEAE

Genus of spring- and autumn-flowering corms, grown for their mainly goblet-shaped blooms, up to 20cm (8in) long, most of which emerge before leaves. Each corm bears 2–7 narrowly strap-shaped to broadly elliptic, basal leaves. Needs an open, sunny situation and well-drained soil. Propagate by seed or division in autumn. All parts are highly toxic if ingested and, if in contact with skin, may cause irritation.
C. agrippinum illus. p.439.
C. autumnale illus. p.437.
'Alboplenum' is an autumn-flowering corm. H and S 10–15cm (4–6in). In spring has 3–5 large, semi-erect, basal, glossy, green leaves. Produces a bunch of up to 8 long-tubed, rounded, double, white flowers with 15–30 narrow petals.
C. 'Beaconsfield'. Robust, autumn-flowering corm. H and S 15–20cm (6–8in). Bears large, goblet-shaped, rich pinkish-purple flowers, faintly chequered and white in centres. Large, semi-erect, basal leaves appear in spring.
C. bivonae, syn. *C. bowlesianum*, *C. sibthorpii*, illus. p.438.
C. bowlesianum. See *C. bivonae*.
C. byzantinum illus. p.437.
C. cilicicum illus. p.438.
C. 'Lilac Wonder'. Vigorous, autumn-flowering corm. H and S 15–20cm (6–8in). Produces goblet-shaped, deep lilac-pink flowers, 15–20cm (6–8in) long. Broad, semi-erect, basal leaves appear in spring.
C. luteum illus. p.434
C. sibthorpii. See *C. bivonae*.
C. speciosum. Vigorous, autumn-flowering corm. H and S 15–20cm (6–8in). Bears goblet-shaped, pale to deep pinkish-purple flowers, 15–20cm (6–8in) long, often with white throats. Large, semi-erect, basal leaves develop in winter or spring.
'Album' illus. p.437.
C. 'The Giant'. Robust, autumn-flowering corm. H and S 15–20cm (6–8in). Produces up to 5 funnel-shaped, deep mauve-pink flowers, each 15–20cm (6–8in) long and fading to white in the centre. Broad, semi-erect, basal leaves form in winter or spring.
C. variegatum. Autumn-flowering corm. H 10–15cm (4–6in), S 8–10cm (3–4in). Bears widely funnel-shaped, reddish-purple flowers with strong chequered patterns. More or less horizontal, basal leaves with wavy margins appear in spring. Needs a hot, sunny site.
C. 'Waterlily' illus. p.439.

COLEONEMA
RUTACEAE

Genus of evergreen, heath-like shrubs, grown for their flowers and overall appearance. Tender, min. 3–5°C (37–41°F). Requires a position in full sun and well-drained, neutral to acid soil. Water potted plants moderately when in full growth, sparingly at other times. For a more compact habit, clip after flowering. Propagate by seed

sown in spring or by semi-ripe cuttings in late summer.
C. pulchrum. Evergreen, spreading to domed shrub with wiry stems. H 60cm–1.2m (2–4ft), S 1–1.5m (3–5ft). Has soft, needle-like, bright green leaves. Carries 5-petalled, pale pink to red flowers in spring-summer.

Coleus. Reclassified as *Solenostemon* except for:
C. thyrsoideus for which see *Plectranthus thyrsoideus*.
Coleus, Prostrate. See *Plectranthus oertendahlii*.

COLLETIA
RHAMNACEAE

Genus of deciduous, usually leafless shrubs, grown for their curious, spiny shoots and profuse, small flowers. Shoots assume function of leaves. Requires a sheltered, sunny site and well-drained soil. Propagate by semi-ripe cuttings in late summer.
C. armata. See *C. hystrix*.
C. cruciata. See *C. paradoxa*.
C. hystrix, syn. *C. armata*, illus. p.147.
'Rosea' is a deciduous, stoutly branched shrub. H 2.5m (8ft), S 5m (15ft). Shoots have rigid, grey-green spines. Bears fragrant, tubular, pink flowers in late summer and early autumn. Zone 8.
C. paradoxa, syn. *C. cruciata*. Deciduous, arching shrub with stiff branches. H 3m (10ft), S 5m (15ft). Has stout, flattened, blue-green spines. Fragrant, tubular, white flowers are borne in late summer and early autumn. Zone 8.

COLLINSIA
SCROPHULARIACEAE

Genus of spring- to summer-flowering annuals. Grow in partial shade and in fertile, well-drained soil. Support with thin sticks. Propagate by seed sown outdoors in spring or early autumn.
C. grandiflora illus. p.331.

COLOCASIA
ARACEAE

Genus of deciduous or evergreen, perennial, marginal water plants, grown for their foliage. Has edible tubers, known as 'taros', for which it is widely cultivated. Is suitable for the edges of frost-free pools; may also be grown in wet soil in pots. Tender, min. 1°C (34°F); with min. 25°C (77°F) is evergreen. Grows in sun or light shade and in mud or shallow water. Propagate by division in spring. All parts may cause mild stomach upset if ingested without cooking, and contact with the sap may irritate the skin.
C. antiquorum. See *C. esculenta*.
C. esculenta, syn. *C. antiquorum*, illus. p.448. 'Fontanesii' is a deciduous, perennial, marginal water plant. H 1.1m (3½ft), S 60cm (2ft). Has large, bold, oval, mid-green leaves with dark green veins and margins and blackish-violet leaf stalks and spathe tubes. 'Illustris' has brownish-purple leaf stalks and dark green leaf blades with purple spots.

Colombian ball cactus. See *Parodia erinacea*, illus. p.479.

Colorado spruce. See *Picea pungens*.

COLQUHOUNIA

LABIATAE/LAMIACEAE

Genus of evergreen or semi-evergreen shrubs, grown for their flowers in late summer and autumn. Just hardy, but is cut to ground level in cold winters. Needs a sheltered, sunny position and well-drained soil. Propagate by softwood cuttings in summer.

C. coccinea illus. p.149.

Coltsfoot, Alpine. See *Homogyne alpina*.

Columbine. See *Aquilegia*.

Alpine. See *Aquilegia alpina*, illus. p.348.

Canadian. See *Aquilegia canadensis*.

COLUMNEA

GESNERIACEAE

Genus of evergreen, creeping or trailing perennials or sub-shrubs, grown for their showy flowers. Trailing species are useful for hanging baskets. Tender, min. 15°C (59°F). Needs bright but indirect light, a fairly humid atmosphere and moist soil, except in winter. Propagate by tip cuttings after flowering.

C. x *banksii* illus. p.250.

C. crassifolia illus. p.283.

C. gloriosa (Goldfish plant). Evergreen, trailing perennial with more or less unbranched stems. H or S to 90cm (3ft). Oval leaves have reddish hairs. Has tubular, hooded, scarlet flowers, to 8cm (3in) long with yellow throats, in winter-spring.

C. microphylla. Evergreen perennial, sparsely branched on each trailing stem. H or S 1m (3ft) or more. Has small, rounded leaves with brown hairs. Hooded, tubular, scarlet flowers, to 8cm (3in) long with yellow throats, in winter-spring. **'Variegata'** illus. p.266.

COLUTEA

LEGUMINOSAE/PAPILIONACEAE

Genus of deciduous, summer-flowering shrubs, grown for their foliage, pea-like flowers and bladder-shaped seed pods. Grow in full sun and any but water-logged soil. Propagate by softwood cuttings in summer or by seed in autumn. Seeds may cause mild stomach upset if ingested.

C. arborescens illus. p.146.

C. x *media* illus. p.147.

C. orientalis. Deciduous, bushy shrub. H and S 2m (6ft). Has blue-grey leaves consisting of 7 or 9 oval leaflets. Clusters of yellow-marked, coppery-red flowers produced in summer are followed by inflated, green, then pale brown seed pods. Zone 5.

Comarostaphylis diversifolia. See *Arctostaphylos diversifolia*.

Comfrey. See *Symphytum*.

Russian. See *Symphytum* x *uplandicum*.

COMBRETUM

COMBRETACEAE

Genus of evergreen trees, shrubs and scandent to twining climbers, grown for their small, showy flowers. Tender, min. 16°C (61°F). Provide humus-rich, well-drained soil, with partial shade in summer. Water freely in summer, less at other times. Support for stems is necessary. Thin out and spur back congested growth after flowering. Propagate by semi-ripe cutting in summer. Spider mite may be a problem.

C. grandiflorum. Moderately vigorous, evergreen, scandent to twining climber. H to 6m (20ft). Has oblong to elliptic, pointed leaves, 10–20cm (4–8in) long. Tubular, bright red flowers with long stamens are borne in summer in one-sided spikes, 10–13cm (4–5in) long.

COMMELINA

COMMELINACEAE

Genus of perennials, usually grown as annuals. Grow in a sunny, sheltered position and in fertile, well-drained soil. Crowns should be lifted before the frosts and overwintered in slightly moist, frost-free conditions. Propagate by seed sown under glass or by division of the crown in spring.

C. coelestis, syn. *C. tuberosa* Coelestis Group, illus. p.334.

C. tuberosa Coelestis Group. See *C. coelestis*.

Common alder. See *Alnus glutinosa*.

Common arrowhead. See *Sagittaria sagittifolia*.

Common ash. See *Fraxinus excelsior*.

Common beech. See *Fagus sylvatica*, illus. p.68.

Common box. See *Buxus sempervirens*.

Common broom. See *Cytisus scoparius*.

Common camassia. See *Camassia quamash*.

Common camellia. See *Camellia japonica*.

Common devil's claw. See *Proboscidea louisianica*.

Common English ivy. See *Hedera helix*.

Common gardenia. See *Gardenia augusta*.

Common German flag. See *Iris germanica*.

Common hackberry. See *Celtis occidentalis*.

Common hawthorn. See *Crataegus monogyna*.

Common holly. See *Ilex aquifolium*, illus. p.98.

Common honeysuckle. See *Lonicera periclymenum*.

Common hop. See *Humulus lupulus*.

Common hornbeam. See *Carpinus betulus*.

Common houseleek. See *Sempervivum tectorum*, illus. p.389.

Common jasmine. See *Jasminum officinale*.

Common juniper. See *Juniperus communis*.

Common laburnum. See *Laburnum anagyroides*.

Common morning glory. See *Ipomoea purpurea*.

Common moss rose. See *Rosa* x *centifolia* 'Muscosa'.

Common myrtle. See *Myrtus communis*, illus. p.130.

Common net bush. See *Calothamnus quadrifidus*.

Common oak. See *Quercus robur*.

Common passion flower. See *Passiflora caerulea*, illus. p.214.

Common pear. See *Pyrus communis*.

Common pitcher plant. See *Sarracenia purpurea*.

Common polypody. See *Polypodium vulgare*, illus. p.313.

Common quaking grass. See *Briza media*.

Common rue. See *Ruta graveolens*.

Common snowdrop. See *Galanthus nivalis*.

Common spruce. See *Picea abies*, illus. p.104.

Common stag's-horn fern. See *Platycerium bifurcatum*, illus. p.310.

Common stonecrop. See *Sedum acre*, illus. p.384.

Common unicorn plant. See *Proboscidea louisianica*.

Common valerian. See *Valeriana officinalis*, illus. p.241.

Compass plant. See *Silphium laciniatum*.

CONANDRON

GESNERIACEAE

Genus of one species of tuberous perennial, grown for its fleshy leaves and drooping flower clusters. Grow in alpine houses. Needs shade and humus-rich, well-drained soil. Keep containerized plants moist in summer, dry when dormant in winter. Propagate by division or seed in spring.

C. ramondioides. Hummock-forming, tuberous perennial. H 30cm (12in), S 20cm (8in). Bears broadly oval, fleshy, wrinkled, mid-green leaves with toothed edges. In mid-summer, each flower stem carries 5–25 tubular flowers, usually lilac, but white, purple or pink forms also occur.

Coneflower. See *Echinacea*; *Rudbeckia*.

Confederate jasmine. See *Trachelospermum jasminoides*, illus. p.207.

Confederate rose. See *Hibiscus mutabilis*.

CONIFERS

Group of trees and shrubs distinguished botanically from others by producing seeds exposed or uncovered on the scales of fruits. Most conifers are evergreen, have needle-like leaves and bear woody fruits (cones). All genera in the Cupressaceae family, however, have needle-like juvenile leaves and, excepting many junipers and some other selected forms, scale-like adult leaves. Conifers described in this book are evergreen unless otherwise stated.

Conifers are excellent garden plants. Most provide year-round foliage, which may be green, blue, grey, bronze, gold or silver. They range in height from trees 30m (100ft) or more tall to dwarf shrubs that grow less than 5cm (2in) every 10 years. Tall conifers may be planted as specimen trees or to provide shelter, screening or hedging. Dwarf conifers make good features in their own right as well as in groups; they also associate well with heathers, add variety to rock gardens and provide excellent ground cover. They may also be grown in containers.

Hardiness

Nearly all conifers described in this book are hardy. Some, such as *Picea sitchensis*, *P. pungens* and *Pinus contorta* var *latifolia*, thrive in the coldest, most windswept sites. *Araucaria*, *Cupressus* and *Pinus* are good for coastal conditions. *Athrotaxis*, *Austrocedrus*, *Cephalotaxus*, *Podocarpus* and certain species noted in other genera flourish only in mild localities. Elsewhere they will not survive unless grown indoors as dwarf plants.

Frost may damage new growth of several genera, especially *Abies*, *Larix*, *Picea* and *Pseudotsuga*, and severe cold, dry spells in winter may temporarily harm mature foliage.

Position and soil

x *Cupressocyparis*, *Cupressus*, *Larix* and *Pinus* need full sun. *Cedrus*, *Juniperus* and *Pseudolarix* do not tolerate shade. All other conifers will thrive in sun or shade, and most *Abies* and all *Cephalotaxus*, *Podocarpus*, *Taxus*, *Thuja*, *Torreya* and *Tsuga* will grow in deep shade once established.

Conifers grow well on most soils, but certain genera and species will not do well on soils over limestone. In this book such conifers are: *Abies*, *Pseudolarix*, *Pseudotsuga* and *Tsuga*; also *Picea*, except *P. likiangesis*, *P. omorika* and *P. pungens*; and *Pinus*, except *P. aristata*, *P. armandii*, *P. cembroides*, *P. halepensis*, *P. heldreichii*, *P. nigra*, *P. peuce* and *P. wallichiana*.

Certain conifers tolerate extreme conditions. *Abies alba*, *A. homolepis*, *A. nordmanniana*, *Cryptomeria*, *Cunninghamia*, *Metasequoia*, *Pinus coulteri*, *P. peuce*, *P. ponderosa*, *Sciadopitys*, *Sequoia*, *Sequoiadendron* and *Taxodium* will grow on heavy clay soils. *Picea omorika*, *P. sitchensis*, *Pinus contorta*, *Sciadopitys verticillata* and *Thuja plicata* are all happy on wet soil, and *Metasequoia* and *Taxodium* thrive in waterlogged conditions. *Cupressus*, *Juniperus* and *Pinus* grow well on dry, sandy soil.

Pruning

If a conifer produces more than one leader, remove all but one. Bear in mind when trimming hedges that most conifers will not make new growth when cut back into old wood or from branches that have turned brown. This does not, however, apply to *Cephalotaxus*, *Cryptomeria*, *Cunninghamia*, *Sequoia*, *Taxus* and *Torreya*, and these conifers may be kept to a reasonable size in the garden by cutting back the main stem, which will later coppice (make new growth).

Young specimens of *Araucaria*, *Ginkgo*, *Metasequoia* and *Taxodium* will sometimes do the same.

Propagation

Seed is the easiest method of propagation, but forms selected for leaf colour (other than blue in some species) do not come true. Sow in autumn or spring. All genera apart from *Abies*, *Cedrus*, *Picea* (except young plants or dwarf forms), *Pinus*, *Pseudolarix*, *Pseudotsuga* and *Tsuga* (except young plants or dwarf forms) may be raised fairly easily from cuttings: current growth from autumn to spring for evergreens, softwood cuttings in summer for deciduous conifers. Tall-growing forms of Pinaceae (*Abies*, *Cedrus*, *Picea*, *Pinus*, *Pseudolarix*, *Pseudotsuga* and *Tsuga*) are usually propagated by grafting in late summer, winter or early spring. Layering may be possible for some dwarf conifers.

Pests and diseases

Honey fungus attacks many conifers, especially young plants. Most resistant to the disease are *Abies*, *Calocedrus*, *Larix*, *Pseudotsuga* and *Taxus*. Green spruce aphid and spruce budworm may be a problem on *Picea*, and conifer mites may defoliate *Abies*, *Picea* and some *Pinus*.

Conifers are illustrated on pp.101–109, dwarf forms on pp.110–111. See also *Abies*, *Araucaria*, *Athrotaxis*, *Austrocedrus*, *Calocedrus*, *Cedrus*, *Cephalotaxus*, *Chamaecyparis*, *Cryptomeria*, *Cunninghamia*, x *Cupressocyparis*, *Cupressus*, *Fitzroya*, *Ginkgo*, *Juniperus*, *Larix*, *Metasequoia*, *Microbiota*, *Phyllocladus*, *Picea*, *Pinus*, *Podocarpus*, *Pseudolarix*, *Pseudotsuga*, *Saxegothaea*, *Sciadopitys*, *Sequoia*, *Sequoiadendron*, *Taxodium*, *Taxus*, *Thuja*, *Thujopsis*, *Torreya* and *Tsuga*.

CONOPHYTUM

AIZOACEAE

Genus of slow-growing, clump-forming, perennial succulents with spherical or 2-eared leaves that grow for only 2 months each year, after flowering. In early summer, old leaves gradually shrivel to papery sheaths from which new leaves and flowers emerge in late summer. Tender, min. 4°C (39°F) if dry. Needs full sun and well-drained soil. Keep dry in winter. Propagate by seed from spring to autumn or by division in late summer.
C. bilobum illus. p.479.
C. longum. See *Ophthalmophyllum longum.*
C. notabile illus. p.480.
C. truncatum illus. p.470.

CONSOLIDA

Larkspur

RANUNCULACEAE

Genus of annuals, providing excellent cut flowers. Needs sun and fertile, well-drained soil. Support stems of tall-growing plants with sticks. Propagate by seed sown outdoors in spring, or in early autumn in mild areas. Protect young plants from slugs and snails. The seeds are poisonous.
C. ajacis, syn. *C. ambigua*, *Delphinium consolida.* Fast-growing, upright, branching annual. Giant forms, H to 1.2m (4ft), S 30cm (1ft); dwarf, H and S 30cm (1ft). All have feathery, mid-green leaves and, throughout summer, spikes of rounded, spurred flowers. **Dwarf Hyacinth Series** has spikes of tubular flowers in shades of pink, mauve, blue or white. **Giant Imperial Series** illus. p.332.
C. ambigua. See *C. ajacis.*

CONVALLARIA

Lily-of-the-valley

CONVALLARIACEAE/LILIACEAE

Genus of spring-flowering, rhizomatous perennials. Prefers partial shade and does best in humus-rich, moist soil. Propagate by division after flowering or in autumn. The seeds of *C. majalis* may cause mild stomach upset if ingested.
C. majalis illus. p.268. **'Flore Pleno'** is a low-growing, rhizomatous perennial. H 23–30cm (9–12in), S indefinite. Sprays of small, very fragrant, pendent, bell-shaped flowers that are double and white open in spring. Narrowly oval leaves are mid- to dark green. **'Fortin's Giant'**, H 45cm (18in), has larger flowers and leaves that appear a little earlier.

CONVOLVULUS

CONVOLVULACEAE

Genus of dwarf, bushy and climbing annuals, perennials and evergreen shrubs and sub-shrubs. Hardy to tender, min 2°C (36°F). Grow in sun and in poor to fertile, well-drained soil. Dead-head to prolong flowering. Propagate by seed sown outdoors in mid-spring for hardy plants or under glass in spring for tender plants, perennials and sub-shrubs by softwood cuttings in late spring or summer.
C. althaeoides illus. p.375.
C. cneorum illus. p.158.
C. mauritanicus. See *C. sabatius.*
C. minor. See *C. tricolor.*
C. purpureus. See *Ipomoea purpurea.*
C. sabatius, syn. *C. mauritanicus*, illus. p.356.
C. tricolor, syn. *C. minor.* Moderately fast-growing, upright, bushy or climbing annual. H 20–30cm (8–12in), S 20cm (8in). Has oval to lance-shaped, mid-green leaves. In summer bears saucer-shaped, blue or white flowers, 2.5cm (1in) wide, with yellowish-white throats. Tall, climbing forms, H to 3m (10ft), are half hardy and have flowers to 10cm (4in) wide. **'Blue Flash'** (bushy) illus. p.332. **'Flying Saucers'** (climber) has blue-and-white-striped flowers.

COPIAPOA

CACTACEAE

Genus of slow-growing, perennial cacti with funnel-shaped, yellow flowers. Many species have large tap roots.

Tender, min. 8–10°C (46–50°F). Needs partial shade and very well-drained soil. Propagate by seed or grafting in spring or summer.
C. cinerea illus. p.466.
C. coquimbana. Clump-forming, spherical, then columnar, perennial cactus. H to 30cm (1ft), S 1m (3ft). Min. 8°C (46°F). Dark grey-green stem has 10–17 ribs. Areoles each bear 8–10 dark brown radial spines and 1 or 2 stouter central spines. Yellow flowers, 3cm (1¼in) across, appear in summer. Is slow to form clumps.
C. echinoides. Flattened spherical, perennial cactus, ribbed like a sea-urchin. H 15cm (6in), S 10cm (4in). Min. 10°C (50°F). Solitary grey-green stem bears dark brown spines, 3cm (1¼in) long, which soon fade to grey. In summer produces pale yellow flowers, 4cm (1½in) across.
C. marginata. Clump-forming, perennial cactus. H 60cm (2ft), S 30cm (1ft). Min. 10°C (50°F). Grey-green stem bears very close-set areoles with dark-tipped, pale brown spines, to 3cm (1¼in) long. Has yellow flowers, 2–5cm (¾–2in) across, in spring-summer.

Cootamundra wattle. See *Acacia baileyana*, illus. p.97.
Copa de oro. See *Solandra maxima*, illus. p.206.
Copey. See *Clusia major.*
Copihue. See *Lapageria rosea*, illus. p.210.
Copper beech. See *Fagus sylvatica* f. *purpurea*, illus. p.65.
Copperleaf. See *Acalypha wilkesiana*, illus. p.143.

COPROSMA

RUBIACEAE

Genus of evergreen shrubs and trees, grown for their foliage and fruits. Separate male and female plants are needed to obtain fruits. Hardy to tender, min. 2–5°C (36–41°F). Prefers full light and well-drained soil. Water containerized specimens freely in summer, moderately at other times. Propagate by seed in spring or by semi-ripe cuttings in late summer.
C. baueri. See *C. repens.*
C. baueriana. See *C. repens.*
C. x *kirkii.* Evergreen, prostrate, then semi-erect, densely branched shrub. H to 1m (3ft), S 1.2–2m (4–6ft). Narrowly oblong to lance-shaped, leathery, glossy leaves are borne singly or in small clusters. In late spring has insignificant flowers, followed on female plants by tiny, egg-shaped, translucent, white fruits with red speckles. Zone 9.
'Variegata' illus. p.175.
C. repens, syn. *C. baueri*, *C. baueriana.* Evergreen, spreading, then erect shrub. H and S to 2m (6ft). Tender, min. 2°C (36°F). Has broadly oval, leathery, lustrous, rich green leaves. Carries insignificant flowers in late spring, followed on female plants by egg-shaped, orange-red fruits from late summer to autumn. Leaves of **'Picturata'** each have a central, cream blotch.

Coquito. See *Jubaea chilensis*, illus. p.85.
Coral bells. See *Heuchera.*
Coral berry. See *Aechmea fulgens.*
Coral bush. See *Templetonia retusa.*
Coral cactus. See *Rhipsalis cereuscula*, illus. p.461.
Coral drops. See *Bessera elegans.*
Coral gem. See *Lotus berthelotii*, illus. p.283.
Coral honeysuckle. See *Lonicera sempervirens*, illus. p.210.
Coral pea. See *Hardenbergia violacea.*
Coral plant. See *Berberidopsis corallina*, illus. p.211; *Russelia equisetiformis*, illus. p.250.
Coral tree
　Flame. See *Erythrina coralloides.*
　Naked. See *Erythrina coralloides.*
Coral vine. See *Antigonon.*
Coral-bark maple. See *Acer palmatum* 'Sango-kaku', illus. p.124
Coralberry. See *Ardisia crenata*, illus. p.150; *Symphoricarpos orbiculatus.*
Coral-tree, Cockspur. See *Erythrina crista-galli*, illus. p.143.

CORDYLINE

AGAVACEAE

Genus of evergreen shrubs and trees, grown primarily for their foliage, although some also have decorative flowers. Hardy to tender, min. 5–16°C (41–61°F). Provide fertile, well-drained soil and full light or partial shade. Water potted plants moderately, less in winter. Propagate by seed or suckers in spring or by stem cuttings in summer. Spider mite may be a nuisance.
C. australis, syn. *Dracaena australis* (New Zealand cabbage palm). Slow-growing, evergreen, sparsely branched tree. H 15m (50ft) or more, S 5m (15ft) or more. Each stem is crowned by a rosette of strap-shaped, 30cm–1m (1–3ft) long leaves. Has small, scented, white flowers in large, open panicles in summer and, in autumn, globose, white fruits. Zone 9. **'Atropurpurea'** illus. p.99. Long, sword-shaped leaves of **'Veitchii'** have red bases and midribs.
C. fruticosa, syn. *C. terminalis* (Good-luck plant, Ti tree). Slow-growing, evergreen, upright shrub, sparingly branched and suckering. H 2–4m (6–12ft), S 1–2m (3–6ft). Tender, min. 13°C (55°F). Broadly lance-shaped, glossy, deep green leaves are 30–60cm (1–2ft) long. Produces branched panicles of small, white, purplish or reddish flowers in summer. Foliage of **'Baptisii'** is deep green with pink and yellow stripes and spots. **'Imperialis'** has red- or pink-marked, deep green leaves.
C. indivisa, syn. *Dracaena indivisa.* Slow-growing, evergreen, erect tree or shrub. H 3m (10ft) or more, S 2m (6ft). Tender, min 5°C (41°F). Bears lance-shaped, 60cm–2m (2–6ft) long, green leaves, orange-brown veined above, blue-grey tinted beneath. In summer tiny, star-shaped, white flowers in dense clusters, 60cm (2ft) or more long, are followed by tiny, spherical, blue-purple fruits.
C. terminalis. See *C. fruticosa.*

COREOPSIS
Tickseed
ASTERACEAE/COMPOSITAE

Genus of annuals and perennials, grown for their daisy-like flower heads. Needs full sun and fertile, well-drained soil. Propagate annuals by seed in spring; *C. lanceolata* by seed or division in spring; *C. auriculata* 'Superba', *C.* 'Goldfink' and *C. grandiflora* 'Badengold' by softwood cuttings or division in spring or summer; and *C. verticillata* by division in spring.

C. auriculata 'Superba'. Bushy perennial. H and S 45cm (18in). Daisy-like, rich yellow flower heads, with central, purple blotches, are borne in summer. Oval to lance-shaped leaves are lobed and light green. Some plants grown as *C. auriculata* are the closely related annual *C. basalis*.

C. 'Goldfink'. Short-lived, dwarf, bushy perennial. H and S 30cm (12in). Sprays of daisy-like, deep yellow flower heads appear in summer above narrowly oval, deep green leaves.

C. grandiflora 'Badengold'. Short-lived, erect perennial with lax stems. H 75cm (30in), S 60cm (24in). Bears large, daisy-like, rich buttercup-yellow flower heads in summer and broadly lance-shaped, divided, bright green leaves.

C. lanceolata illus. p.293.
C. 'Sunray' illus. p.337.
C. tinctoria illus. p.337. **'Golden Crown'** is a fast-growing, upright, bushy annual. H 60cm (24in), S 20cm (8in). Has lance-shaped, deep green leaves and, in summer and early autumn, large, daisy-like, deep yellow flower heads with brown centres.
C. verticillata illus. p.293.

CORIARIA
CORIARIACEAE

Genus of deciduous, spring- or summer-flowering shrubs and sub-shrubs, grown for their habit, foliage and fruits. Needs full sun and fertile, well-drained soil. Propagate by softwood cuttings in summer or by seed in autumn. The leaves and fruits of some species may cause severe stomach upset if ingested; in other species, the fruits are edible, although the seeds are thought to be poisonous.
C. terminalis. Deciduous, arching sub-shrub. H 1m (3ft), S 2m (6ft). Broadly lance-shaped, fern-like, mid-green leaves turn red in autumn. Minute, green flowers in late spring are succeeded by small, spherical, black fruits. Zone 9. var. *xanthocarpa* illus. p.173.

Cork oak. See *Quercus suber*, illus. p.73.
Cork tree, Amur. See *Phellodendron amurense*.
Corkscrew rush. See *Juncus effusus* 'Spiralis', illus. p.308.
Corkscrew willow. See *Salix babylonica* var *pekinensis* 'Tortuosa'.
Corn
 Indian. See *Zea*.
 Sweet. See *Zea mays*.

Corn cockle. See *Agrostemma*.
Corn plant. See *Dracaena fragrans*.
Corn poppy. See *Papaver rhoeas*.
Cornel, Bentham's. See *Cornus capitata*.
Cornelian cherry. See *Cornus mas*.
Cornflower. See *Centaurea cyanus*.
Cornish elm. See *Ulmus minor* 'Cornubiensis'.
Cornish golden elm. See *Ulmus minor* 'Dicksonii', illus. p.81.
Cornish heath. See *Erica vagans*.

CORNUS
Dogwood
CORNACEAE

Genus of deciduous shrubs and deciduous or evergreen trees, grown for their flowers, foliage or brightly coloured winter stems. Needs sun or semi-shade and fertile, well-drained soil. Those grown for winter stem colour do best in full sun. *C. florida*, *C. kousa* and *C. nuttallii* dislike shallow, alkaline soil. *C. canadensis* prefers acid soil. Plants grown for their stems should be cut back almost to ground level each year in early spring. Propagate *C. alba* and *C. stolonifera* 'Flaviramea' by softwood cuttings in summer or by hardwood cuttings in autumn or winter; variegated forms of *C. alternifolia* and *C. controversa* by grafting in winter; *C. canadensis* by division in spring or autumn; *C. capitata*, *C. florida* and *C. kousa* by seed in autumn or by softwood cuttings in summer; *C. nuttallii* by seed in autumn; all others described here by softwood cuttings in summer. The fruits of some species may cause mild stomach upset if ingested; contact with the leaf hairs may irritate skin.
C. alba (Red twig dogwood). Vigorous, deciduous, upright, then spreading shrub. H and S 3m (10ft). Young shoots are bright red in winter. Has oval, dark green leaves, often red or orange in autumn. Bears flattened heads of star-shaped, creamy-white flowers in late spring and early summer, followed by spherical, sometimes blue-tinted, white fruits. Zone 2.
'Elegantissima' illus. p.138.
'Gouchaultii' has pink-flushed leaves broadly edged with yellow.
'Kesselringii' illus. p.148. **'Sibirica'** illus. p.150. **'Spaethii'** illus. p.146.
C. alternifolia. Deciduous, spreading tree or bushy shrub, with tiered branches. H and S 6m (20ft). Oval, bright green leaves, which each taper to a point, often turn red in autumn. Clusters of tiny, star-shaped, creamy-white flowers in early summer are followed by small, rounded, blue-black fruits. Zone 3b. **'Argentea'** illus. p.89.
C. canadensis, syn. *Chamaepericlymenum canadense*, illus. p.374.
C. capitata, syn. *Dendrobenthamia capitata* (Bentham's cornel). Evergreen or semi-evergreen, spreading tree. H and S up to 12m (40ft). Pale yellow bracts, surrounding insignificant flowers, appear in early summer, followed by large, strawberry-like, red fruits. Has oval, grey-green leaves. Is good for mild coastal areas. Zone 9.
C. controversa. Deciduous tree with

layered branches. H and S 15m (50ft). Clusters of small, star-shaped, white flowers appear in summer. Leaves are oval, pointed and bright green, turning purple in autumn. Zone 7. **'Variegata'** illus. p.89.
C. 'Eddie's White Wonder' illus. p.96.
C. florida (Flowering dogwood). Deciduous, spreading tree. H 6m (20ft), S 8m (25ft). In late spring bears white or pinkish-white bracts surrounding tiny, insignificant flowers. Oval, pointed, dark green leaves turn red and purple in autumn. Zone 6. **'Apple Blossom'** has pale pink bracts. f. *rubra* bears pink or red bracts. **'Spring Song'** illus. p.90. **'Welchii'** illus. p.93. **'White Cloud'** illus. p.85.
C. kousa. Deciduous, vase-shaped tree or shrub. H 7m (22ft), S 5m (15ft). Flower heads of large, white bracts, surrounding insignificant flowers, appear in early summer, followed, after a hot summer, by strawberry-like fruits. Oval, glossy, dark green leaves turn bright red-purple in autumn. Zone 6b. var. *chinensis* has larger flower heads and more narrowly pointed bracts. Zone 6.
C. macrophylla illus. p.78.
C. mas (Cornelian cherry). Deciduous, spreading, open shrub or tree. H and S 5m (15ft). Oval, dark green leaves change to reddish-purple in autumn. Produces small, star-shaped, yellow flowers on bare shoots in late winter and early spring, then edible, oblong, bright red fruits. Zone 4.
'Aureoelegantissima' (syn. *C.m.* 'Elegantissima'), H 2m (6ft), S 3m (10ft), has pink-tinged leaves edged with yellow.
'Elegantissima' see *C.m.* 'Aureoelegantissima'.
'Variegata' illus. p.119.
C. 'Norman Hadden'. Deciduous, spreading tree. H and S 8m (25ft). Creamy-white bracts around tiny flowers turn to deep pink in summer. These are often followed by strawberry-like fruits in autumn. Zone 8.
C. nuttallii illus. p.76.
C. 'Porlock' illus. p.86.
C. stolonifera 'Flaviramea'. Vigorous, deciduous, spreading shrub with creeping, underground stems. H 2m (6ft), S 4m (12ft). Has bright greenish-yellow, young shoots in winter and oval, dark green leaves. Small, star-shaped, white flowers appear in late spring and early summer, and are followed by spherical, white fruits. Zone 1b.

COROKIA
ESCALLONIACEAE

Genus of evergreen shrubs, grown for their habit, foliage, flowers and fruits. Is good in mild, coastal areas, where it is very wind-tolerant. Protect from strong winds at limits of hardiness. Needs full sun and fertile, well-drained soil. Propagate by softwood cuttings in summer.
C. buddlejoides. Evergreen, upright shrub. H 3m (10ft), S 2m (6ft). Has slender, grey shoots and narrowly oblong, glossy, dark green leaves.

Produces panicles of star-shaped, yellow flowers in late spring, followed by spherical, blackish-red fruits. Zone 9.
C. cotoneaster illus. p.152.
C. x virgata. Evergreen, upright, dense shrub. H and S 3m (10ft). Leaves are oblong and glossy, dark green above, white beneath. Produces star-shaped, yellow flowers in mid-spring, then egg-shaped, bright orange fruits. Makes a good hedge, especially in coastal areas. Zone 9.

CORONILLA
LEGUMINOSAE/PAPILIONACEAE

Genus of deciduous or evergreen shrubs and perennials, grown for their foliage and flowers. Grow against a south- or west-facing wall. Requires full sun and light, well-drained soil. Propagate by softwood cuttings in summer.
C. glauca. See *C. valentina* subsp. *glauca*.
C. valentina subsp. *glauca*, syn. *C. glauca*, illus. p.157.

CORREA
RUTACEAE

Genus of evergreen shrubs, grown for their flowers. Tender, min. 3–5°C (37–41°F). Prefers full light or partial shade and fertile, well-drained, neutral to acid soil. Water potted specimens moderately, less when not in flower. Propagate by seed in spring or by semi-ripe cuttings in late summer.
C. backhouseana. Evergreen, rounded, well-branched shrub. H and S 2m (6ft). Leaves are oval to elliptic and dark green, with dense, pale buff down beneath. Tubular, pale yellow-green to white flowers appear in spring and intermittently until autumn.
C. x harrisii. See *C.* 'Mannii'.
C. 'Harrisii'. See *C.* 'Mannii'.
C. 'Mannii', syn. *C. x harrisii*, *C.* 'Harrisii'. Evergreen, bushy, slender-stemmed shrub. H and S 2m (6ft). Has narrowly oval leaves with short hairs beneath. Tubular, scarlet flowers are carried in summer-autumn, sometimes in other seasons.
C. pulchella illus. p.174.
C. reflexa, syn. *C. speciosa*. Evergreen, bushy, slender-stemmed shrub. H and S to 2m (6ft). Oval leaves have thick down beneath. Bears tubular, greenish-yellow to crimson or rose flowers, with greenish-white petal tips, in summer-autumn, sometimes in other seasons.
C. speciosa. See *C. reflexa*.

Corsican heath. See *Erica terminalis*.
Corsican mint. See *Mentha requienii*.
Corsican pine. See *Pinus nigra* subsp. *laricio*.

CORTADERIA
GRAMINEAE/POACEAE

See also GRASSES, BAMBOOS, RUSHES and SEDGES.
C. selloana (Pampas grass). Evergreen, clump-forming, stately, perennial grass. H to 2.5m (8ft), S 1.2m (4ft). Has narrow, very sharp-edged, outward-

curving leaves, 1.5m (5ft) long. In late summer, erect, plume-like, silvery panicles, up to 60cm (2ft) long, are borne above mid-green leaves. Male and female flowers are produced on separate plants; females, with long, silky hairs, are more decorative. **'Aureolineata'** (syn. *C.s.* 'Gold Band'), H to 2.2m (7ft), is compact, and has leaves with rich yellow margins ageing to dark golden-yellow. **'Gold Band'** see *C.s.* 'Aureolineata'. **'Silver Comet'** and **'Sunningdale Silver'** illus. p.306.

CORTUSA

PRIMULACEAE

Genus of clump-forming, spring- and summer-flowering perennials, related to *Primula*, with one-sided racemes of bell-shaped flowers. Is not suited to hot, dry climates as needs shade and humus-rich, moist soil. Propagate by seed when fresh or by division in autumn.
C. matthioli illus. p.354.

CORYDALIS

PAPAVERACEAE

Genus of spring- and summer-flowering annuals and tuberous or fibrous-rooted perennials, some of which are evergreen, grown for their tubular, spurred, 2-lipped flowers or for their fern-like leaves. Needs full sun or partial shade and well-drained soil; some require humus-rich soil and cool growing conditions. Propagate by seed in autumn or by division when dormant: autumn for spring-flowering species, spring for summer-flowering species.
C. ambigua of gardens. See *C. fumariifolia*.
C. bulbosa of gardens. See *C. cava*.
C. cashmeriana. Tuft-forming, fibrous-rooted perennial. H 10–25cm (4–10in), S 8–10cm (3–4in). Has divided, semi-erect, basal leaves and, in summer, dense spikes of 2-lipped, brilliant blue flowers. Needs cool, partially shaded, humus-rich, neutral to acid soil. Is good for a rock garden. Dies down in winter.
C. cava, syn. *C. bulbosa* of gardens. Spring-flowering, tuberous perennial. H 10–20cm (4–8in), S 8–10cm (3–4in). Leaves are semi-erect, basal and much divided. Carries dense spikes of tubular, dull purple flowers. Dies down in summer.
C. cheilanthifolia illus. p.349.
C. diphylla illus. p.367.
C. fumariifolia, syn. *C. ambigua* of gardens. Tuberous perennial, flowering from spring to early summer. H to 15cm (6in), S to 10cm (4in). Stem bears much-divided leaves and a short spike of 2-lipped, azure blue or purplish-blue flowers, with flattened, triangular spurs. Dies down in summer.
C. halleri. See *C. solida*.
C. lutea, syn. *Pseudofumaria lutea*, illus. p.359.
C. nobilis. Perennial with long, fleshy, fibrous roots. H and S 20–35cm (8–14in). Bears much-divided leaves on lower part of flower

stems, each of which carries a dense spike of long-spurred, pale yellow flowers, with lips tipped green or brown, in spring.
C. ochroleuca, syn. *Pseudofumaria ochroleuca*, illus. p.351.
C. popovii illus. p.364.
C. solida, syn. *C. halleri*. Tuft-forming, tuberous perennial. H 10–20cm (4–8in), S 8–12cm (3–5in). Leaves alternate on flower stems, each of which carries a dense spike of dull purplish-red flowers in spring. Dies down in summer.
'George Baker' (syn. *C.s.* 'G.P. Baker') illus. p.367.
C. wilsonii illus. p.349.

CORYLOPSIS

HAMAMELIDACEAE

Genus of deciduous shrubs and trees, grown for their fragrant, yellow flowers, which are produced before hazel-like leaves emerge. Late frosts may damage flowers. Prefers semi-shade and fertile, moist but well-drained, acid soil. Propagate by softwood cuttings in summer or by seed in autumn.
C. glabrescens illus. p.117.
C. pauciflora illus. p.131.
C. sinensis, syn. *C. willmottiae*. Vigorous, deciduous, spreading, open shrub. H and S 4m (12ft). Leaves are bright green above, blue-green beneath. Clusters of bell-shaped, pale yellow flowers open from early to mid-spring. **'Spring Purple'** has deep plum-purple, young leaves. Zone 7.
C. spicata. Deciduous, spreading, open shrub. H 2m (6ft), S 3m (10ft). Bristle-toothed leaves are dull, pale green above, blue-green beneath. Drooping clusters of bell-shaped, pale yellow flowers are borne in mid-spring. Zone 6.
C. willmottiae. See *C. sinensis*.

CORYLUS

Hazel

CORYLACEAE

Genus of deciduous trees and shrubs, grown for their habit, catkins and often edible fruits (nuts). Prefers sun or semi-shade and fertile, well-drained soil. Cut out suckers as they arise. Propagate species by seed in autumn, cultivars by grafting in late summer or by suckers or layering in late autumn to early spring. Mildew may cause defoliation; other fungi and insects may spoil nuts.
C. avellana (Cobnut). **'Contorta'** illus. p.125.
C. colurna (Turkish hazel). Deciduous, conical tree. H 20m (70ft), S 7m (22ft). Has broadly oval, strongly toothed, almost lobed, dark green leaves. Long, yellow catkins are borne in late winter. Clusters of nuts are set in fringed husks. Zone 5.
C. maxima (Filbert). Vigorous, deciduous, bushy, open shrub or tree. H 6m (20ft), S 5m (15ft). Bears oval, toothed, mid-green leaves, long, yellow catkins in late winter and edible, egg-shaped, brown nuts. Zone 5b.
'Purpurea' illus. p.122.

CORYNOCARPUS

CORYNOCARPACEAE

Genus of evergreen trees, grown for their foliage and overall appearance. Tender, min. 7–10°C (45–50°F). Needs full light or partial shade and fertile, moisture-retentive but well-drained soil. Water containerized specimens moderately, less when temperatures are low. Pruning is tolerated if necessary. Propagate by seed when ripe or by semi-ripe cuttings in summer.
C. laevigatus illus. p.85.

CORYPHANTHA

CACTACEAE

Genus of perennial cacti with roughly spherical, spiny, green stems. Stems have elongated areoles in grooves running along upper sides of tubercles; many species only show this groove on very old plants. Funnel-shaped flowers are produced in summer, followed by cylindrical, green seed pods. Tender, min. 5°C (41°F). Needs a site in full sun with very well-drained soil. Propagate by seed in spring or summer.
C. cornifera, syn. *C. radians*, illus. p.479.
C. radians. See *C. cornifera*.
C. vivipara. See *Escobaria vivipara*.

COSMOS

ASTERACEAE/COMPOSITAE

Genus of summer- and early autumn-flowering annuals and tuberous perennials. Hardy to tender, min. 5°C (41°F). Needs sun and does best in moist but well-drained soil. In mild areas, tubers of *C. atrosanguineus* may be overwintered in ground if protected with a deep mulch. Propagate perennial species by basal cuttings in spring, annuals by seed in autumn or spring.
C. atrosanguineus, syn. *Bidens atrosanguinea*, illus. p.249.
C. bipinnatus. Upright, bushy annual. H to 1.5m (5ft), S 45cm (1½ft). Has feathery, mid-green leaves, and, throughout summer, produces solitary, bowl- or saucer-shaped flower heads in white, pink, or crimson, with yellow centres. **'Candy Stripe'**, H to 90cm (3ft), has white flower heads, edged and flecked with crimson. **'Sea Shells'**, H to 90cm (3ft), produces carmine-red, pink, or white flower heads with tubular florets. **Sensation Series** illus. p.325.
C. sulphureus **Ladybird Series**. Group of upright, bushy annuals. H 30–40cm (12–16in), S 20cm (8in). Has feathery, mid-green leaves, and in summer produces clusters of semi-double, bowl-shaped flower heads in yellow, orange, or scarlet, with black centres.

Cosmos, Chocolate. See *Cosmos atrosanguineus*, illus. p.249.

COSTUS

ZINGIBERACEAE

Genus of mostly clump-forming, rhizomatous perennials, grown for their showy, solitary or paired, tubular

flowers with basal bracts. Tender, min. 18°C (64°F). Grow in a humid atmosphere, out of direct sunlight, in humus-rich soil. Propagate by division in spring. Pot-grown plants may be attacked by spider mite.
C. speciosus (Malay ginger). Clump-forming, rhizomatous perennial. H 2m (6ft) or more, S 1m (3ft). Has narrowly oval, downy leaves, to 25cm (10in) long. Reddish bracts are spine-tipped, each surrounding one white or pink-flushed flower, to 10cm (4in) wide with a broad, yellow-centred lip; flowers are produced intermittently throughout the year.

COTINUS

ANACARDIACEAE

Genus of deciduous shrubs and trees, grown for their foliage, flower heads and autumn colour. Individual flowers are inconspicuous. Requires a position in full sun or semi-shade, with fertile but not over-rich soil. Purple-leaved forms need full sun to bring out their best colours. Propagate species by softwood or greenwood cuttings in summer or by seed in autumn, cultivars by cuttings only in summer.
C. americanus. See *C. obovatus*.
C. coggygria, syn. *Rhus cotinus* (Smoke tree, Venetian sumach). Deciduous, bushy shrub. H and S 5m (15ft). Leaves are rounded or oval and light green, becoming yellow or red in autumn. From late summer, as insignificant fruits develop, masses of tiny flower stalks form showy, pale fawn, later grey, plume-like clusters. Zone 4b.
'Flame' see *C.* 'Flame'. **'Notcutt's Variety'** illus. p.121. **'Royal Purple'** has deep pink plumes and deep purplish-red leaves.
C. **'Flame'**, syn. *C. coggygria* 'Flame', illus. p.124.
C. obovatus, syn. *C. americanus*, *Rhus cotinoides*. Vigorous, deciduous, bushy shrub or tree. H 10m (30ft), S 8m (25ft). Has large, oval leaves that are bronze-pink when young, maturing to mid-green and turning orange, red and purple in autumn. Zone 5.

COTONEASTER

ROSACEAE

Genus of deciduous, semi-evergreen or evergreen shrubs and trees, grown for their foliage, flowers and fruits. Some species make fine specimen plants; others may be used for hedging or ground cover. Deciduous species and cultivars prefer full sun, but evergreens do well in either sun or semi-shade. All resent waterlogged soil and are particularly useful for dry sites. Propagate species by cuttings in summer or by seed in autumn, hybrids and cultivars by cuttings only, in summer. Take semi-ripe cuttings for evergreens and semi-evergreens, softwood cuttings for deciduous plants. Fireblight is a common problem. The seeds may cause mild stomach upset if ingested.
C. adpressus. Deciduous, arching shrub. H 30cm (1ft), S 2m (6ft). Rounded, wavy-edged, dark green

leaves redden in autumn. Produces small, 5-petalled, pink flowers in early summer, then spherical, red fruits. Zone 4 var. *praecox* see *C. nanshen*.
C. 'Autumn Fire'. See
C. 'Herbstfeuer'.
C. bullatus 'Firebird', syn.
C. 'Firebird'. Deciduous, bushy, open shrub. H and S 3m (10ft). Large, oval, deeply veined, dark green leaves redden in autumn. Small, 5-petalled, white flowers in early summer are followed by masses of spherical, bright red fruits. Zone 5b. var. **macrophyllus** see *C. rehderi*.
C. cashmiriensis, syn. *C. cochleatus* of gardens, *C. microphyllus* var. *cochleatus* of gardens. Evergreen, prostrate shrub. H to 45cm (1½ft), S 2m (6ft). Has small, oval, notched, dark green leaves. Small, white flowers are produced in late spring, followed by spherical, red fruits. Zone 5.
C. cochleatus of gardens. See *C. cashmiriensis*.
C. congestus. Evergreen, prostrate shrub. H 20cm (8in), S 2m (6ft). Forms dense mounds of oval, dull green leaves. Produces small, 5-petalled, pinkish-white flowers in early summer, followed by spherical, bright red fruits. Is excellent for a rock garden. Zone 5b.
C. conspicuus, syn. *C.c.* var. *decorus*. Evergreen, prostrate, arching shrub. H 30cm (1ft), S 2–3m (6–10ft). Leaves are oblong, glossy, very dark green. Small, 5-petalled, white flowers in late spring are succeeded by large, spherical, scarlet or orange-red fruits. Zone 7.
C. 'Coral Beauty'. Evergreen, arching, dense shrub. H 1m (3ft), S 2m (6ft). Has small, oval, glossy, dark green leaves and, in early summer, produces small, 5-petalled, white flowers. Fruits are spherical and bright orange-red. Zone 4.
C. 'Cornubia' illus. p.124.
C. dielsianus. Deciduous, arching shrub. H and S 2.5m (8ft). Slender shoots are clothed in oval, dark green leaves. Produces small, 5-petalled, pink flowers in early summer, followed by spherical, glossy, red fruits. Zone 7.
C. divaricatus illus. p.130.
C. 'Firebird'. See *C. bullatus* 'Firebird'.
C. franchetii. Evergreen or semi-evergreen, arching shrub. H and S 3m (10ft). Oval, grey-green leaves are white beneath. Bears small, 5-petalled, pink-tinged, white flowers in early summer, then a profusion of oblong, bright orange-red fruits. Zone 6b. var. **sternianus** see *C. sternianus*.
C. frigidus (Tree cotoneaster). Vigorous, deciduous tree, upright when young, arching when mature. H and S 10m (30ft). Has large, broadly oval, wavy-edged, dull green leaves and broad heads of small, 5-petalled, white flowers borne in early summer, followed by large clusters of long-lasting, small, spherical, bright red fruits.
C. glaucophyllus. Evergreen, arching, open shrub. H and S 3m (10ft). Leaves are oval, dark green, bluish-white beneath. Produces small, 5-petalled, white flowers in mid-summer, followed by small, spherical, deep red fruits in autumn. var. **serotinus** see *C. serotinus*. Zone 8.

C. 'Gnom', syn. *C.* 'Gnome', *C. salicifolius* 'Gnom'. Evergreen, prostrate shrub. H 20cm (8in), S 2m (6ft). Bears narrowly lance-shaped, dark green leaves, small, 5-petalled, white flowers, in early summer, and clusters of small, spherical, red fruits. Makes good ground cover. Zone 6.
C. 'Gnome'. See *C. 'Gnom'*.
C. 'Herbstfeuer', syn. *C.* 'Autumn Fire'. Evergreen, prostrate or arching shrub. H 30cm (1ft), S 2m (6ft). Has lance-shaped, bright green leaves. Small, 5-petalled, white flowers in early summer are followed by spherical, bright red fruits. May be grown as ground cover or as a weeping standard. Zone 6.
C. horizontalis illus. p.172.
C. hupehensis. Deciduous, arching shrub. H 2m (6ft), S 3m (10ft). Oval, bright green leaves become yellow in autumn. Masses of small, 5-petalled, white flowers in late spring are succeeded by large, spherical, bright red fruits. Zone 5b.
C. 'Hybridus Pendulus'. Evergreen, prostrate shrub, almost always grown as a weeping standard. H 2m (6ft), S 1.5m (5ft). Has oblong, dark green leaves. Small, 5-petalled, white flowers in early summer are followed by spherical, deep red fruits. Zone 7.
C. lacteus illus. p.125.
C. linearifolius, syn. *C. microphyllus* var. *thymifolius* of gardens. Evergreen, prostrate shrub. H 60cm (2ft), S 2m (6ft). Rigid branches bear tiny, narrow, blunt-ended, glossy leaves. Produces small, white flowers in late spring, followed by spherical red fruits. Zone 7.
C. lucidus (Hedge cotoneaster). Upright growth produces a rounded shrub. H & S 2-3m (6-10ft). Shiny, dark green leaves are hairy beneath. Small clusters of pale pink flowers in late spring and shiny black fruit in fall. Often used for hedging, especially in the Montreal area. Zone 2.
C. microphyllus. Evergreen, spreading, dense shrub. H 1m (3ft), S 2m (6ft). Rigid shoots are clothed in small, oval, dark green leaves. Small, 5-petalled, white flowers in late spring are followed by spherical, red fruits. Zone 5. var. **cochleatus** of gardens see *C. cashmiriensis*. var. **thymifolius** of gardens see *C. linearifolius*.
C. nanshen syn. *C. adpressus* var. *praecox*. A low, creeping, deciduous plant that is a good ground cover for stabilizing banks and slopes. H 45cm (18in) S 1.2m (4ft). Rounded foliage is mid-green turning red in fall. Pink flowers in late spring give persistant bright red fruits. Zone 3. 'Boer' has larger, earlier fruits.
C. prostratus of gardens. See *C. rotundifolius*.
C. rehderi, syn. *C. bullatus* var. *macrophyllus*. Deciduous, bushy, open shrub. H 5m (15ft), S 3m (10ft). Very large, oval, deeply veined, dark green leaves change to red in autumn. Clusters of small, 5-petalled, pink flowers appear in late spring and early summer, succeeded by spherical, bright red fruits. Zone 7.
C. 'Rothschildianus'. Evergreen or semi-evergreen, arching shrub. H and S 5m (15ft). Has narrowly oval, bright

green leaves, small, 5-petalled, white flowers, in early summer, and large clusters of spherical, golden-yellow fruits. Zone 7.
C. rotundifolius, syn. *C. prostratus* of gardens. Evergreen, arching shrub. H 1.5m (5ft), S 2.5m (8ft). Has small, oval, glossy, dark green leaves. Produces small, 5-petalled, white flowers in early summer, followed by spherical, deep red fruits. Zone 8.
C. salicifolius. Vigorous, evergreen, arching shrub. H and S 5m (15ft). Has narrowly lance-shaped, dark green leaves. Small, 5-petalled, white flowers, in early summer, are followed by clusters of small, spherical, red fruits. Zone 5b. **'Gnom'** see *C. 'Gnom'*.
C. serotinus, syn. *C. glaucophyllus* var. *serotinus*. Evergreen, arching, open shrub. H and S 6m (20ft). Has oval, dark green leaves. Small white flowers are borne from mid- to late summer and the fruits last until spring. Zone 8.
C. simonsii illus. p.148.
C. 'Skogholm', syn. *C.* 'Skogsholmen'. Evergreen, arching, wide-spreading shrub. H 60cm (2ft), S 3m (10ft). Leaves are small, oval and glossy, dark green. Bears small, 5-petalled, white flowers during early summer, then rather sparse, spherical, red fruits. Makes good ground cover. Zone 4.
C. 'Skogsholmen'. See *C. 'Skogholm'*.
C. sternianus, syn. *C. franchetii* var. *sternianus*, illus. p.149.
C. x watereri 'John Waterer'. Vigorous, evergreen or semi-evergreen, arching shrub. H and S 5m (15ft). Has lance-shaped, dark green leaves. Bears small, 5-petalled, white flowers, in early summer, and produces a profusion of spherical, red fruits in large clusters. Zone 7.

Cotoneaster, Tree. See *Cotoneaster frigidus*.
Cotton ball. See *Espostoa lanata*, illus. p.457.
Cotton lavender. See *Santolina chamaecyparissus*.
Cotton rose. See *Hibiscus mutabilis*.
Cotton thistle. See *Onopordum acanthium*, illus. p.322.
Cotton tree, Silk. See *Ceiba pentandra*.
Cottonwood. See *Populus deltoides*.
   Black. See *Populus trichocarpa*.
   Eastern. See *Populus deltoides*.

COTULA
ASTERACEAE/COMPOSITAE
Genus of perennials and a few marginal water plants, most of which are evergreen, grown for their neat foliage and button-like flower heads. Many species are useful in cracks in paving stones, but may be invasive. Most need a position in full sun, with well-drained soil that is not too dry. Propagate by division in spring.
C. atrata. See *Leptinella atrata*.
C. coronopifolia (Brass buttons). Short-lived, deciduous, perennial, marginal water plant. H 15cm (6in), S 30cm (12in). Has fleshy stems, small, lance-shaped, mid-green leaves and, in summer, button-like, yellow flower heads.

COTYLEDON
CRASSULACEAE
Genus of evergreen, succulent shrubs and sub-shrubs, grown for their diverse foliage that ranges from large, oval, grey leaves to small, cylindrical, mid-green leaves. Tender, min. 5–7°C (41–5°F). Likes a sunny or partially shaded site and very well-drained soil. Propagate by seed or stem cuttings in spring or summer.
C. cooperi. See *Adromischus cooperi*.
C. ladismithensis illus. p.474.
C. orbiculata. Evergreen, upright, succulent shrub. H and S 50cm (20in) or more. Min. 7°C (45°F). Swollen stem bears thin, oval, mid-green leaves, densely coated in white wax and sometimes red-edged. Flower stems, to 70cm (28in) long, have pendent, tubular, orange flowers in autumn. var. **oblonga** (syn. *C. undulata*) illus. p.468.
C. paniculata. See *Tylecodon paniculatus*.
C. reticulata. See *Tylecodon reticulatus*.
C. simplicifolia. See *Chiastophyllum oppositifolium*.
C. undulata. See *C. orbiculata* var. *oblonga*.
C. wallichii. See *Tylecodon papillaris* subsp. *wallichii*.

Coulter pine. See *Pinus coulteri*, illus. p.102.
Cowberry. See *Vaccinium vitrs-ideae*.
Cow-parsley. See *Heracleum*.
Cow's-tail pine. See *Cephalotaxus harringtonii*.
Cowslip. See *Primula veris*, illus. p.273.
   Giant. See *Primula florindae*, illus. p.273.
Crab
   Purple. See *Malus x purpurea*.
   Siberian. See *Malus baccata*.
Crab apple. See *Malus*.
Crab cactus. See *Schlumbergera truncata*, illus. p.473.
Crack willow. See *Salix fragilis*.
Cradle orchid. See *Anguloa clowesii*.

CRAMBE
BRASSICACEAE/CRUCIFERAE
Genus of annuals and perennials, grown for their bold leaves and large sprays of white flowers in summer. Leaf shoots of *C. maritima* (Sea kale) are eaten as a spring vegetable. Will grow in any well-drained soil; prefers an open position in full sun but tolerates some shade. Propagate by division in spring or by seed in autumn or spring.
C. cordifolia illus. p.226.
C. maritima illus. p.276.

Cranberry bush American. See *Viburnum trilobum*.
Cranesbill. See *Geranium*.
   Bloody. See *Geranium sanguineum*, illus. p.354.
   Meadow. See *Geranium pratense*.
Crape myrtle. See *Lagerstroemia indica*, illus. p.91.

CRASPEDIA

ASTERACEAE/COMPOSITAE

Genus of basal-rosetted, summer-flowering perennials, some of which are bet treated as annuals. Tender, min. 5°C (41°F). Needs a site in sun and well-drained soil. Propagate by seed sown when very fresh in summer.

C. incana. Basal-rosetted perennials. H 20–30cm (8–12in), S 10cm (4in). Has narrowly oval, basal leaves, with dense, woolly, white hairs beneath, and smaller leaves on flower stem. In summer, many domed heads of 3–10 tiny, tubular, yellow flowers are produced in large, terminal clusters.

CRASSULA

CRASSULACEAE

Genus of perennial succulents and evergreen, succulent shrubs and sub-shrubs, ranging from 2cm (¾in) high, very succulent-leaved species to 5m (15ft) shrubby ones. Most are easy to grow. Tender, min. 5–7°C (41–5°F). Most prefer full sun; others like partial shade. Needs very well-drained soil and a little water in winter. Propagate by seed or stem cuttings in spring or autumn.

C. arborescens illus. p.458.
C. argentea of gardens. See *C. ovata.*
C. coccinea, syn. *Rochea coccinea.* Evergreen, erect, succulent shrub. H to 60cm (24in), S 30cm (12in) or more. Tender, min. 5°C (41°F). Alternate pairs of fleshy, oval to oblong-oval, hairy-margined, dull green leaves, each united at the base, are arranged at right angles in 4 rows up the woody, green stems. Produces umbels of tubular, bright red flowers in summer or autumn.
C. cooperi. See *C. exilis* subsp. *cooperi.*
C. deceptor, syn. *C. deceptrix,* illus. p.476.
C. deceptrix. See *C. deceptor.*
C. exilis subsp. *cooperi,* syn. *C. cooperi.* Carpeting, perennial succulent. H 2cm (¾in), S 30cm (12in). Tender, min. 7°C (45°F). Has small, spoon- to lance-shaped, light green leaves, pitted with darker green or blackish-green marks. Produces clusters of minute, 5-petalled, white to pale pink flowers in winter.
C. falcata. See *C. perfoliata* var. *minor.*
C. lactea. Prostrate to semi-erect, perennial succulent. H 20cm (8in), S 1m (3ft). Tender, min. 5°C (41°F). Leaves are triangular-oval, glossy and dark green. In winter produces masses of small, 5-petalled, white flowers in terminal clusters. Likes partial shade.
C. lycopodioides. See *C. muscosa.*
C. muscosa, syn. *C. lycopodioides.* Dense, bushy, woody-based, perennial succulent. H 15cm (6in), S 30cm (12in). Tender, min. 5°C (41°F). Bears small, scale-like, neatly overlapping, mid-green leaves arranged in 4 rows around erect stems. In spring, produces tiny, 5-petalled, greenish-yellow flowers. Likes partial shade.
C. multicava illus. p.471.
C. ovata, syn. *C. argentea* of gardens, *C. portulacea,* illus. p.457.
C. perfoliata var. *minor,*
syn. *C. falcata,* illus. p.464.
C. portulacea. See *C. ovata.*
C. sarcocaulis illus. p.353.
C. schmidtii illus. p.473.
C. socialis illus. p.470.

+ CRATAEGOMESPILUS

ROSACEAE

Group of grafted, hybrid, deciduous trees (*Crataegus* and *Mespilus*), grown for their flowers, foliage and fruits. Requires sun or semi-shade and fertile, well-drained soil. Propagate by grafting in late summer.
+ **C. dardarii** (Bronvaux medlar). **'Jules d'Asnières'** is a deciduous, spreading tree. H and S 6m (20ft). Has drooping branches and spiny shoots. Variable, oval or deeply lobed, dark green leaves, grey when young, turn orange and yellow in autumn. Clusters of saucer-shaped, white, sometimes rose-tinted, flowers in late spring or early summer are followed by small, rounded, red-brown fruits. Zone 7.

CRATAEGUS

Hawthorn

ROSACEAE

Genus of deciduous, or more rarely semi-evergreen, spiny, often spreading trees and shrubs, grown for their clustered, 5-petalled, occasionally double flowers in spring-summer, ornamental fruits and, in some cases, autumn colour. Prefers full sun but is suitable for most sites and may be grown in any but very wet soil. Is useful for growing in polluted urban areas, exposed sites and coastal gardens. Propagate species by seed in autumn, cultivars by budding in late summer. Fireblight is sometimes a problem. The seeds may cause mild stomach upset if ingested.
C. cordata. See *C. phaenopyrum.*
C. crus-galli (Cockspur thorn). Deciduous, flat-topped tree. H 8m (25ft), S 10m (30ft). Has shoots armed with long, curved thorns and oval, glossy, dark green leaves that turn bright crimson in autumn. Clusters of white flowers, with pink anthers, in late spring are followed by long-lasting, rounded, bright red fruits. Zone 2b.
C. crus-galli of gardens. See *C. flava* illus. p.90.
C. laciniata, syn. *C. orientalis,* illus. p.85.
C. laevigata, syn. *C. oxyacantha* of gardens (Hawthorn, May). **'Paul's Scarlet'** illus. p.91. **'Punicea'** is a deciduous, spreading tree. H and S 6m (20ft). In late spring and early summer, oval, lobed, toothed, glossy, dark green leaves set off clusters of crimson flowers, which are followed by rounded, red fruits. Zone 6.
C. x lavallei 'Carrierei'. Vigorous, deciduous, spreading tree. H 7m (22ft), S 10m (30ft). Oval, glossy, dark green leaves turn red in late autumn. Has clusters of white flowers in late spring, followed by long-lasting, rounded, orange-red fruits. Zone 5.
C. macrosperma var. *acutiloba* illus. p.94.
C. mollis. Deciduous, spreading tree. H 10m (30ft), S 12m (40ft). Large, broadly oval, lobed, dark green leaves have white-haired undersides when young. Bears heads of large, white flowers in late spring, followed by short-lived, rounded, red fruits. Zone 3.
C. monogyna (Common hawthorn). Deciduous, round-headed tree. H 10m (30ft), S 8m (25ft). Has broadly oval, deeply lobed, glossy, dark green leaves. Clusters of fragrant, white flowers are borne from late spring to early summer, followed by rounded, red fruits. Makes a dense hedge. Zone 4b. **'Biflora'** (Glastonbury thorn) has flowers and leaves in mild winters as well as in spring.
C. x mordenensis. A rounded, deciduous tree with very few thorns. H & S 6m (20ft). Foliage is dark green and turns bronze in fall. Double flowers are freely produced in late spring and followed by sparse, spherical, red fruit that persist into winter. Zone 3. 'Toba' has pale pink flowers that darken with age, 'Snowbird' is white.
C. orientalis. See *C. laciniata.*
C. oxyacantha of gardens. See *C. laevigata.*
C. pedicellata illus. p.95.
C. persimilis 'Prunifolia', syn. *C. crus-galli* of gardens, *C. x prunifolia.* Deciduous, spreading, thorny tree. H 8m (25ft), S 10m (30ft). Oval, glossy, dark green leaves turn red or orange in autumn. Has clusters of white flowers, with pink anthers, in early summer, then rounded, dark red fruits. Zone 2b.
C. phaenopyrum, syn. *C. cordata* (Washington thorn). Deciduous, round-headed tree. H and S 10m (30ft). Broadly oval leaves are sharply lobed, glossy and dark green. Clusters of white flowers, with pink anthers, are produced from early to mid-summer, followed by rounded, glossy, red fruits that last through winter. Zone 5.
C. x prunifolia. See *C. persimilis* 'Prunifolia'.
C. viridis 'Winter King'. A round-headed tree with slender thorns and attractive green new bark. H 6m (20ft) S 4.5m (15ft). Foliage is glossy, mid-green turning red in fall. White flowers (with yellow anthers) give masses of showy bright red fruit that last well into winter. Older bark flakes off in plates giving winter interest. Zone 5.

Cream cups. See *Platystemon californicus,* illus. p.335.
Creeper
  Canary. See *Tropaeolum peregrinum.*
  Flame. See *Tropaeolum speciosum,* illus. p.210.
  Rangoon. See *Quisqualis indica,* illus. p.211.
  Snow. See *Porana paniculata.*
  Trumpet. See *Campsis radicans.*
  Virginia. See *Parthenocissus quinquefolia.*
Creeping blue blossom. See *Ceanothus thyrsiflorus* var. *repens,* illus. p.168.
Creeping bluets. See *Hedyotis michauxii,* illus. p.383.
Creeping Charlie. See *Pilea nummulariifolia,* illus. p.305. and *Glechoma hederacea.*
Creeping dogwood. See *Cornus canadensis,* illus. p.374.

Creeping fig. See *Ficus pumila.*
Creeping juniper. See *Juniperus horizontalis.*
Creeping phlox. See *Phlox stolonifera.*
Creeping soft grass. See *Holcus mollis.*
Creeping willow. See *Salix repens,* illus. p.156.
Creeping zinnia. See *Sanvitalia procumbens,* illus. p.336.

CREMANTHODIUM

ASTERACEAE/COMPOSITAE

Genus of basal-rosetted perennials, grown for their pendent, half-closed, daisy-like flower heads. Is often very difficult to grow in all but very cool areas with snow cover. Dislikes winter wet. Needs shade and humus-rich, moist but well-drained soil. Propagate by seed when fresh.
C. reniforme. Basal-rosetted perennial. H and S 20cm (8in). Leaves are large and kidney-shaped. Stout stems each carry a large, daisy-like, yellow flower head in summer.

CREPIS

Hawk's beard

ASTERACEAE/COMPOSITAE

Genus of summer-flowering annuals, biennials and perennials, some of which are evergreen, with long tap roots and leaves in flat rosettes. Many species are persistent weeds, but some are grown for their many-petalled, dandelion-like flower heads. Tolerates sun or shade and prefers well-drained soil. Propagate annuals and biennials by seed in autumn, perennials by root cuttings (not from tap root) in late winter, although most species self-seed freely.
C. aurea illus. p.359.
C. incana (Pink dandelion). Basal-rosetted perennial. H 20cm (8in), S 10cm (4in). Bears oblong, divided, hairy, greyish-green leaves. Uneven discs of ragged, pink flower heads are produced on stiff stems in summer. Is good for a sunny rock garden or border.
C. rubra illus. p.320.

Cress
  Bitter. See *Cardamine.*
  Persian stone. See *Aethionema grandiflorum,* illus. p.352.
  Violet. See *Ionopsidium acaule.*
  Winter. See *Barbarea vulgaris.*
Crested moss rose. See *Rosa* x *centifolia* 'Cristata'.
Cretan brake. See *Pteris cretica.*
Cretan dittany. See *Origanum dictamnus.*
Cricket-bat willow. See *Salix alba* var. *caerulea.*
Crimean linden. See *Tilia* x *euchlora.*
Crimson glory vine. See *Vitis coignetiae,* illus. p.218.

CRINODENDRON

ELAEOCARPACEAE

Genus of evergreen shrubs and trees, grown for their flowers and foliage. Requires shade or semi-shade, with plant base in cool shade. Soil should be fertile, moist but well-drained, and

acid. Propagate by softwood cuttings in summer or by seed in autumn.
C. hookerianum, syn. *Tricuspidaria lanceolata*, illus. p.142.

× Crinodonna corsii. See
× *Amarcrinum memoria-corsii*.

CRINUM

AMARYLLIDACEAE

Genus of robust bulbs, grown for their often fragrant, funnel-shaped flowers. Tender, min. 5–16°C (41–61°F). Needs full sun, shelter and rich, well-drained soil. Propagate by offsets in spring or by seed when fresh or in spring. All parts may cause severe discomfort if ingested; contact with the sap may irritate skin.
C. americanum. Tuft-forming, spring- and summer-flowering bulb. H 40–75cm (16–30in), S 60cm (24in). Min. 10°C (50°F). Has 6–10 strap-shaped, semi-erect, basal leaves. Leafless stem bears a head of up to 6 fragrant, long-tubed, white flowers with narrow petals.
C. asiaticum illus. p.419.
C. bulbispermum, syn. *C. longifolium*. Summer-flowering bulb. H to 1m (3ft), S 60cm (2ft). Min. 5°C (41°F). Leafless flower stem has a head of fragrant, long-tubed, white or pinkish-red flowers with darker red stripes. Bears long, strap-shaped, semi-erect leaves grouped in a tuft on a short stalk.
C. longifolium. See *C. bulbispermum*.
C. macowanii. Autumn-flowering bulb. H and S 60cm (2ft) or more. Min. 5°C (41°F). Is similar to *C. bulbispermum*, but leaves are wavy-edged.
C. moorei illus. p.398.
C. × powellii illus. p.398. **'Album'** illus. p.397.

CROCOSMIA

Montbretia

IRIDACEAE

Genus of corms, grown for their brightly coloured flowers produced mainly in summer. Forms dense clumps of sword-shaped, erect leaves. Requires well-drained soil and an open, sunny site. In cold areas, plant in a sheltered position or lift and store corms over winter. Propagate by division as growth commences in spring.
C. aurea. Tuft-forming, summer-flowering corm. H 50–75cm (20–30in), S 15–20cm (6–8in). Erect, basal leaves are long, narrow and sword-shaped. Carries a loosely branched spike of tubular, orange or yellow flowers, each 3–5cm (1–2in) long and with 6 spreading petals.
C. 'Bressingham Blaze' illus. p.401.
C. 'Citronella' of gardens. See *C.* 'Golden Fleece'.
C. 'Emily McKenzie'. Compact, late summer-flowering corm. H to 60cm (24in), S 15–20cm (6–8in). Leaves are erect, basal and sword-shaped. Bears a dense spike of widely funnel-shaped, deep orange flowers, each with a dark mahogany throat.
C. 'Golden Fleece', syn. *C.* 'Citronella' of gardens, illus. p.403.
C. 'Jackanapes' illus. p.423.

C. 'Lucifer' illus. p.401
C. masoniorum, syn. *C. masonorum*, illus. p.401.
C. masonorum. See *C. masoniorum*.
C. paniculata, syn. *Antholyza paniculata, Curtonus paniculatus*. Summer-flowering corm. H to 1.5m (5ft), S 30–45cm (1–1½ft). Has sword-shaped, erect, basal leaves, pleated lengthways. Carries long-tubed, orange flowers on branched stems, which are strongly zig-zag in shape.
C. 'Star of the East' illus. p.403.

CROCUS

IRIDACEAE

Genus of mainly spring- or autumn-flowering corms with funnel-shaped to rounded, long-tubed flowers. Has long, very narrow, semi-erect, basal leaves, each with a white line along centre, usually 1–5 per corm. Some autumn-flowering species have no leaves at flowering time, these appearing in winter or spring. Most species are less than 10cm (4in) tall when in flower and have a spread of 2.5–8cm (1–3in). Is ideal for rock gardens and for slight forcing in bowls for an early indoor display. Most require well-drained soil and a sunny situation; *C. banaticus* prefers moist soil and semi-shade. Plant 5–6cm (2–2½in) deep, in late summer or early autumn. Propagate in early autumn by seed or division if clumps of corms have formed. See also feature panel pp.428–9.
C. 'Advance' (illus. p.429). Late winter- to mid-spring flowering corm. Funnel-shaped flowers are buttercup yellow inside and paler yellow outside, suffused violet-bronze.
C. aerius of gardens. See *C. biflorus* subsp. *pulchricolor*.
C. ancyrensis. Spring-flowering corm. Produces up to 7 fragrant, bright orange-yellow flowers, 5–6cm (2–2½in) long.
C. angustifolius, syn. *C. susianus* (Cloth-of-gold crocus). Spring-flowering corm. Fragrant flowers are bright golden-yellow, striped or stained bronze outside.
C. aureus. See *C. flavus*.
C. balansae. See *C. olivieri* subsp. *balansae*.
C. banaticus, syn. *C. iridiflorus* (illus. p.429). Autumn-flowering corm. Usually has one long-tubed, pale violet flower; outer 3 petals are much larger than inner 3. Very narrow, semi-erect, basal leaves, each with a paler line along the centre, appear in spring.
C. baytopiorum (illus. p.429). Spring-flowering corm. Each corm bears 1 or 2 rounded, clear torquoise-blue, slightly darker-veined flowers.
C. biflorus (illus. p.429). Early spring-flowering corm. Has narrow, semi-erect, basal leaves, each with a white line along the centre. Bears fragrant, white or purplish-white flowers, with yellow throats, vertically striped purple outside. subsp. *alexandri* has fragrant, deep violet flowers, with white insides. subsp. *pulchricolor* (syn. *C. aerius* of gardens) has rich deep blue flowers with golden-yellow centres.
C. 'Blue Bird' (illus. p.428). Late winter- to mid-spring-flowering corm.

Funnel-shaped flowers are white inside with deep yellow throats and violet margined with white outside.
C. 'Blue Pearl' (illus. p.428). Early spring-flowering corm. Produces narrow, semi-erect, basal leaves, with white lines along the centres. Fragrant, long-tubed, funnel-shaped, soft lavender-blue flowers, bluish-white within, have golden-yellow throats.
C. boryi (illus. p.428). Autumn-flowering corm. Flowers are ivory-white, sometimes veined or flushed with mauve outside.
C. cancellatus. Autumn-flowering corm. Slender flowers are pale blue, slightly striped outside. Leaves form after flowering, in spring.
C. cartwrightianus (illus. p.429). Autumn-flowering corm. Produces leaves at same time as strongly veined, violet or white flowers, each 4–6cm (1½–2½in) across and with 3 long, bright red stigmas, similar to those of *C. sativus*.
C. chrysanthus. Spring-flowering corm. Scented flowers are orange-yellow throughout with deeper orange-red stigmas.
C. 'Cream Beauty' (illus. p.429). Spring-flowering corm. Scented rich cream flowers, with deep yellow throats, are stained purplish-brown outside at base. Bears very narrow, semi-erect, basal, dark green leaves, each with a white, central line.
C. cvijicii (illus. p.429). Spring-flowering corm. Usually has one funnel-shaped, yellow flower. Produces very narrow, semi-erect, basal leaves, each with a white line along the centre, which scarcely show at flowering time.
C. dalmaticus (illus. p.428). Spring-flowering corm. Very narrow, semi-erect leaves have central, white lines. Bears 1-3 purple-veined, pale violet flowers, with yellow centres, overlaid with silver or yellow outside.
C. 'Dorothy' (illus. p.429). Spring-flowering corm. Scented flowers are pale lemon-yellow.
C. 'Dutch Yellow'. See *C.* 'Golden Yellow'.
C. 'E.A. Bowles' (illus. p.429). Early spring-flowering corm. Has scented, funnel-shaped, deep yellow flowers, stained bronze near base on outside. Has narrow, semi-erect leaves, each with a central white line. Increases well by offsets.
C. etruscus (illus. p.429). Spring-flowering corm. Has very narrow, semi-erect, basal, dark green leaves with central, white lines. Bears long-tubed, funnel-shaped, pale purple-blue flowers, washed silver outside, with violet veining. **'Zwanenburg'** (illus. p.428) has pale purple-blue flowers, washed with biscuit-brown and flecked violet outside.
C. 'Eyecatcher' (illus. p.428). Late winter- to mid-spring-flowering corm. Produces funnel-shaped, grey-white, yellow-throated flowers with white-edged, deep purple outer segments.
C. flavus, syn. *C. aureus*. Spring-flowering corm. Fragrant flowers are bright yellow or orange-yellow throughout; often several flowers are produced together or in quick succession.

C. gargaricus (illus. p.429). Spring-flowering corm. Bears yellow flowers, 4–5cm (1½–2in) long. Increases by stolons. Tolerates slightly damper conditions than most crocuses.
C. 'Golden Yellow', syn. *C.* 'Dutch Yellow', *C. × luteus* 'Golden Yellow'. Very vigorous, clump-forming, spring-flowering corm. Bears yellow flowers, 8–10cm (3–4in) long and faintly striped outside at bases. Naturalizes well in grass.
C. goulimyi (illus. p.428). Autumn-flowering corm. Usually has one long-tubed, pale lilac to pinkish-lilac flower, with a white throat and 3 inner petals usually paler than the 3 outer ones. Leaves and flowers appear together. Needs a warm site.
C. hadriaticus (illus. p.428). Autumn-flowering corm. Leaves appear with the white flowers, which usually have yellow throats and may be lilac-feathered at the base.
C. imperati. Strikingly bicoloured, spring-flowering corm. Develops 1 or 2 scented, purple flowers, 6–8cm (2½–3in) long, fawn with purple striping outside and with yellow throats. In **'De Jager'** (illus. p.428) flowers are rich violet-purple inside and biscuit-coloured with violet feathering outside.
C. iridiflorus. See *C. banaticus*.
C. korolkowii (Celandine crocus). Spring-flowering corm. Produces up to 20 narrow leaves. Carries fragrant, yellow flowers that are speckled or stained brown or purple outside. When open in sun, petals have glossy surfaces.
C. kotschyanus, syn. *C. zonatus* (illus. p.428). Autumn-flowering corm. Pinkish-lilac or purplish-blue flowers have yellow centres and white anthers. Narrow, semi-erect, basal leaves, with white lines along centres, appear in winter-spring. var. *leucopharynx* has pale lilac-blue flowers with white centres and white anthers. Leaves appear in winter-spring.
C. 'Ladykiller' (illus. p.429). Late winter- to mid-spring-flowering corm. Has funnel-shaped flowers, white or pale lilac within and deep violet-purple with white margins outside.
C. laevigatus (illus. p.428). Very variable corm, flowering intermittently for a month or more in autumn or winter depending on the form. Fragrant flowers appear with leaves and are usually lilac-purple with bold stripes on outside; inside each has a yellow eye and cream-white anthers.
C. longiflorus. (illus. p.429). Autumn-flowering corm. Produces fragrant, slender, purple flowers, which are striped darker purple outside, at the same time as leaves. Flowers have yellow centres and anthers and red stigmas.
C. × luteus 'Golden Yellow'. See *C.* 'Golden Yellow'.
C. malyi (illus. p.428). Spring-flowering corm. Has 1 or 2 funnel-shaped, white flowers with yellow throats, brown or purple tubes and showy, bright orange stigmas. Leaves are very narrow, semi-erect and basal with central, white lines.
C. medius (illus. p.428). Autumn-

flowering corm. Has 1 or 2 funnel-shaped, uniform rich purple flowers, with yellow anthers and red stigmas cut into many thread-like branches. Linear, basal leaves appear in winter-spring, after flowering.

C. minimus (illus. p.428). Late spring-flowering corm. Has very narrow, semi-erect, basal, dark green leaves that have central, white lines. Bears 1 or 2 flowers, purple inside and stained darker violet or sometimes darker striped on outside.

C. niveus. Autumn-flowering corm. Produces 1 or 2 white or pale lavender flowers, 10–15cm (4–6in) long, with conspicuous, yellow throats. Leaves appear with flowers or just afterwards. Needs a warm, sunny site.

C. nudiflorus (Autumn crocus; illus. p.428). Autumn-flowering corm. Has linear, basal leaves in winter-spring. Usually bears one slender, long-tubed, rich purple flower, with a frilly, bright orange or yellow stigma. Naturalizes in grass.

C. olivieri. Spring-flowering corm. Bears rounded, bright orange flowers. Flowers of subsp. **balansae** (syn. *C. balansae*) are stained or striped bronze-brown outside.

C. pulchellus (illus. p.428). Autumn-flowering corm. Bears long-tubed, pale lilac-blue flowers with darker veins, conspicuous, yellow throats and white anthers. Leaves are very narrow, semi-erect and basal, with white lines along centres.

C. salzmannii. See *C. serotinus* subsp. *salzmannii*.

C. sativus, syn. *C.s.* var. *cashmirianus* (Saffron crocus). Autumn-flowering corm. Leaves appear with saucer-shaped, dark-veined, purple flowers, 5–7cm (2–3in) across, each with 3 long, bright red stigmas that yield saffron.

C. serotinus subsp. **salzmannii,** syn. *C. salzmannii.* Autumn-flowering corm. Lilac-blue flowers, to 10cm (4in) long, sometimes with yellow throats, appear with leaves.

C. sieberi. Spring-flowering corm. Has white flowers with yellow throats and purple staining outside, either in horizontal bands or vertical stripes. **'Albus'** see *C.s.* 'Bowles' White'. subsp. *atticus* has pale lilac to violet-blue flowers with frilly, orange stigmas. **'Bowles' White'** (syn. *C.s.* 'Albus'; illus. p.428) produces pure white flowers with large, deep yellow areas in throats. **'Hubert Edelsten'** has yellow-throated, pale lilac flowers, the outer segments of which are white, tipped, centrally marked and feathered with rich purple. subsp. **sublimis** f. **tricolor** (illus. p.428) has unusual flowers, divided into 3 distinct bands of lilac, white and golden yellow. **C. 'Snow Bunting'** (illus. p.428). Spring-flowering corm. Fragrant long-tubed, funnel-shaped, white flowers have mustard-yellow centres and orange stigmas. Very narrow, semi-erect, basal leaves are dark green with white, central lines.

C. speciosus (illus. p.429). Autumn-flowering corm. Produces lilac-blue to

deep purple-blue flowers, usually with a network of darker veins and a much-divided, orange stigma. Leaves appear in winter-spring.

'Conqueror' (illus. p.429) has large, deep sky-blue flowers.

'Oxonian' (illus. p.429) produces dark violet-blue flowers with prominent darker veining externally.

C. susianus. See *C. angustifolius*.

C. tommasinianus. Spring-flowering corm. H to 10cm (4in), S 2.5–8cm (1–3in). Bears slender, long-tubed, funnel-shaped flowers, varying in colour from lilac or purple to violet, sometimes with darker tips to petals and occasionally silver outside. Naturalizes well. f. **albus** (illus. p.428) has white flowers. **'Ruby Giant'** (illus. p.429) bears clusters of large rich reddish-purple flowers. **'Whitewell Purple'** (illus. p.429) has slender, reddish-purple flowers.

C. tournefortii. Autumn-flowering corm. Leaves appear at same time as 1 or 2 pale lilac-blue flowers that open flattish to reveal a much-divided, orange stigma and white anthers. Requires a warm, sunny site.

C. vernus (Dutch crocus; Spring crocus; illus. p.429). Spring-flowering corm. H to 10cm (4in), S 2.5–8cm (1–3in). Variable in colour from white to purple or violet and often striped and feathered. Stigmas are large, frilly and orange or yellow. Is suitable for naturalizing. subsp. **albiflorus** (illus. p.428) has small, white flowers sometimes slightly marked or striped purple.

'Jeanne d'Arc' has white flowers with a deep purple base. **'Pickwick'** (illus. p.429) has pale, greyish-white flowers, with dark violet stripes and purplish bases. **'Prinses Juliana'** (illus. p.429) has mid-purple flowers with darker veins. **'Purpureus Grandiflorus'** (illus. p.429) has shiny, violet-purple flowers. **'Queen of the Blues'** (illus. p.429) has rich blue flowers that have higher margins and a darker base. **'Remembrance'** (illus. p.429) has shiny, violet flowers. **'Vanguard'**, a very early cultivar, has bluish-lilac flowers, paler and silvered outside.

C. 'Zephyr'. Autumn-flowering corm. Bears very pale silver-blue flowers, veined darker, each with a conspicuous, yellow throat and white anthers.

C. zonatus. See *C. kotschyanus*.

C. 'Zwanenburg Bronze'. Spring-flowering corm. H to 10cm (4in), S 2.5–8cm (1–3in). Has bicoloured flowers, rich yellow inside, stained bronze outside.

Crocus
   Autumn. See *Colchicum autumnale*, illus. p.437; *Crocus nudiflorus*, illus. p.428.
   Celandine. See *Crocus korolkowii*.
   Chilean blue. See *Tecophilaea cyanocrocus*, illus. p.433.
   Cloth-of-gold. See *Crocus angustifolius*.
   Dutch. See *Crocus vernus*, illus. p.429.
   Saffron. See *Crocus sativus*.

Crocus (continued)
   Spring. See *Crocus vernus*, illus. p.429.
Cross vine. See *Bignonia capreolata*.

CROSSANDRA
ACANTHACEAE

Genus of evergreen perennials, sub-shrubs and shrubs, grown mainly for their flowers. Tender, min. 15°C (59°F). Needs partial shade or full light and humus-rich, well-drained soil. Water potted plants freely when in full growth, moderately at other times. For a strong branch system, cut back flowered growth by at least half in late winter. Propagate by seed in spring or by greenwood cuttings in late spring or summer. Whitefly may be troublesome.

C. infundibuliformis, syn. *C. undulifolia.* Evergreen, erect to spreading, soft-stemmed shrub or sub-shrub. H to 1m (3ft), S 60cm (2ft). Has oval to lance-shaped, glossy, deep green leaves and, in summer-autumn or earlier, fan-shaped, salmon-red flowers in conical spikes, each 10cm (4in) long.

C. nilotica illus. p.165.

C. undulifolia. See *C. infundibuliformis*.

Cross-leaved heath. See *Erica tetralix*.

CROTALARIA
LEGUMINOSAE/PAPILIONACEAE

Genus of evergreen shrubs, perennials and annuals, grown mainly for their flowers. Tender, min. 10–15°C (50–59°F). Requires full light and well-drained soil. Water containerized specimens freely when in full growth, less at other times. For a more compact habit, cut back old stems by half after flowering. Propagate by seed in spring or by semi-ripe cuttings in summer. Spider mite may be troublesome.

C. agatiflora illus. p.123.

Croton. See *Codiaeum variegatum* var. *pictum*, illus. p.177.
Crowfoot, Water. See *Ranunculus aquatilis*.
Crown imperial. See *Fritillaria imperialis*, illus. p.396.
Crown of thorns. See *Euphorbia milii*, illus. p.155.
Crucianella stylosa. See *Phuopsis stylosa*.
Cruel plant. See *Araujia sericifera*, illus. p.207.
Crusaders' spears. See *Urginea maritima*.

CRYPTANTHUS
BROMELIACEAE

Genus of evergreen, rosette-forming perennials, grown for their attractive foliage. Tender, min. 10–13°C (50–55°F). Needs semi-shade and well-drained soil, preferably mixed with sphagnum moss. Water moderately during the growing season, sparingly at other times. Propagate by offsets or suckers in late spring.

C. acaulis (Green earth star). Evergreen, clump-forming, basal-rosetted perennial.

H to 10cm (4in), S 15–30cm (6–12in). Loose, flat rosettes of lance-shaped to narrowly triangular, wavy, mid-green leaves have serrated edges. A cluster of fragrant, tubular, white flowers appears in each rosette centre, usually in summer.

'Ruber' has red-flushed foliage.

C. bivittatus (illus. p.265). Evergreen, clump-forming, basal-rosetted perennial. H to 15cm (6in), S 25–38cm (10–15in). Loose, flat rosettes of broadly lance-shaped, wavy, mid- to yellowish-green leaves have finely toothed margins and are striped length-ways with 2 coppery-fawn to buff bands. Small clusters of tubular, white flowers appear from centre of each rosette, usually in summer.

C. bromelioides (Rainbow star). Evergreen, spreading, basal-rosetted perennial. H 20cm (8in) or more, S 35cm (14in) or more. Strap-shaped, wavy, finely toothed, arching, mid- to bright green leaves are produced in dense rosettes. Occasionally bears clusters of tubular, white flowers in centre of each rosette, usually in summer. **'Tricolor'** has carmine-suffused, white-striped foliage.

C. 'Pink Starlight' (illus. p.265). Vigorous, evergreen, spreading, basal-rosetted perennial. H 20cm (8in) or more, S 35cm (14in) or more. Strap-shaped, wavy, finely toothed, arching, green leaves are striped yellowish-green, and heavily suffused deep pink. Clusters of tubular, white flowers occasionally appear from each rosette centre in summer.

C. zonatus. Evergreen, basal-rosetted perennial. H 10–15cm (4–6in), S 30–40cm (12–16in). Forms loose, flat rosettes of strap-shaped, wavy, finely toothed, sepia-green leaves, cross-banded with grey-buff and with greyish-white scales beneath. A cluster of tubular, white flowers opens in each rosette, usually in summer. **'Zebrinus'** (illus. p.265) has silver-banded foliage.

---

x CRYPTBERGIA
BROMELIACEAE

Hybrid genus (*Cryptanthus* x *Billbergia*) of evergreen, rosette-forming perennials, grown for their foliage. Tender, min. 8–10°C (46–50°F). Needs semi-shade and fertile, well-drained soil. Water moderately during growing season, sparingly in winter. Propagate by suckers or offsets in spring.

x C. 'Rubra'. Evergreen, clump-forming, basal-rosetted perennials. H and S 15–30cm (6–12in). Loose rosettes comprise strap-shaped, pointed, bronze-red leaves. Rarely, small, tubular, white flowers are produced in rosette centres in summer.

CRYPTOCORYNE
ARACEAE

Genus of semi-evergreen, perennial, submerged water plants and marsh plants, grown for their foliage. Is suitable for tropical aquariums. Tender, min. 10°C (50°F). Needs sun and rich soil. Remove fading foliage, and divide plants periodically. Propagate by division in spring or summer.

C. beckettii var. *ciliata.* See *C. ciliata.*
C. ciliata, syn. *C. beckettii* var. *ciliata.* Semi-evergreen, perennial, submerged water plant. S 15cm (6in). Lance-shaped, deep green leaves have paler midribs. Small, hooded, fringed, purplish spathes appear intermittently at base of plant.
C. spiralis. Semi-evergreen, perennial, submerged water plant. S 15cm (6in). Small, hooded, purplish spathes are borne intermittently among lance-shaped, purplish-green leaves.

CRYPTOGRAMMA

CRYPTOGRAMMACEAE

Genus of deciduous or semi-evergreen ferns. Needs partial shade and moist but well-drained, neutral or acid soil. Remove fading fronds. Propagate by spores in late summer.
C. crispa illus. p.313.

CRYPTOMERIA

TAXODIACEAE

See also CONIFERS.
C. japonica (Japanese cedar). Fast-growing, columnar to conical, open conifer. H 15–20m (50–70ft), S 5–8m (15–25ft). Has soft, fibrous, red-brown bark, needle-like, incurved, mid- to dark green leaves, spirally arranged, and globular, brown cones.
'Bandai-sugi', H and S 2m (6ft), makes an irregularly rounded shrub with foliage that turns bronze in winter. Zone 6. 'Cristata' illus. p.109.
'Elegans Compacta' (illus. p.111), H 2–5m (6–15ft), S 2m (6ft), is a dwarf form. 'Pyramidata' illus. p.109.
'Sekkan-sugi' (illus. p.111), H 10m (30ft), S 3–4m (10–12ft), has semi-pendulous branches and light golden-cream foliage. Zone 6. 'Spiralis' (illus. p.111), H and S 2–3m (6–10ft), forms a tree or dense shrub with spirallytwisted foliage and is very slow-growing. Zone 6b.
'Vilmoriniana', H and S 1m (3ft), forms a globular mound of yellow-green foliage that turns bronze in winter. Zone 5b.

CRYPTOSTEGIA

ASCLEPIADACEAE

Genus of evergreen, twining climbers, grown for their flowers. Tender, min. 15°C (59°F). Provide fertile, well-drained soil and full light. Water regularly, less when not in full growth. Stems require support. Spur back previous season's old flowering stems in spring. Propagate by seed in spring or by softwood cuttings in summer.
C. grandiflora (Rubber vine). Strong-growing, evergreen, twining climber. H 10m (30ft) or more. Has thick-textured, oval, glossy leaves. Funnel-shaped, reddish to lilac-purple flowers appear in summer. Stems yield a poisonous latex that may cause severe discomfort if ingested.

Cryptostemma calendulaceum. See *Arctotheca calendula.*
Crystal anthurium. See *Anthurium crystallinum,* illus. p.264.

CTENANTHE

MARANTACEAE

Genus of evergreen, bushy perennials, grown for their ornamental foliage. Tender, min. 15°C (59°F). Requires a humid atmosphere, even temperature and partial shade. Prefers moist but well-drained soil and soft water; do not allow to dry completely. Propagate by division in spring.
C. lubbersiana. Evergreen, clump-forming, bushy perennial. H and S to 75cm (30in) or more. Long-stalked, lance-shaped, sharply pointed leaves are 25cm (10in) long, green above, irregularly marked and striped with pale yellowish-green, and pale greenish-yellow below. Intermittently bears dense, one-sided spikes of many small, 3-petalled, white flowers.
C. oppenheimiana, syn. *Calathea oppenheimiana.* Robust, evergreen, bushy perennial. H and S 1m (3ft) or more. Lance-shaped, leathery leaves are over 30cm (1ft) long, red below, dark green above with pale green or white bands along veins on either side of midribs. Dense, one-sided spikes of many small, 3-petalled, white flowers are produced intermittently.
'Tricolor' illus. p.264.

Cuban royal palm. See *Roystonea regia.*
Cuckoo flower. See *Cardamine pratensis.*
Cuckoo pint. See *Arum.*
Cucumber tree. See *Magnolia acuminata.*
Cudrania tricuspidata. See *Maclura tricuspidata.*

CUNNINGHAMIA

TAXODIACEAE

See also CONIFERS.
C. lanceolata illus. p.106.

CUNONIA

CUNONIACEAE

Genus of evergreen, summer-flowering trees, grown for their foliage, flowers and overall appearance. Tender, min. 10°C (50°F). Requires full light and well-drained soil. Water potted plants moderately, less in winter. Pruning is tolerated. Propagate by seed in spring or by semi-ripe cuttings in summer.
C. capensis (African red alder). Moderately fast-growing, evergreen, rounded tree. H and S 10–15m (30–50ft), more in rich soil. Has lustrous, dark green leaves, divided into pairs of lance-shaped, serrated leaflets. Tiny, long-stamened, white flowers appear in dense, bottlebrush-like spikes, each 10–13cm (4–5in) long, in late summer.

Cup-and-saucer vine. See *Cobaea scandens,* illus. p.214.

CUPHEA

LYTHRACEAE

Genus of annuals, perennials and evergreen shrubs and sub-shrubs, grown for their flowers. Tender, min. 2–7°C (36–45°F). Prefers full sun and fertile, well-drained soil. Water freely when in full growth, moderately at other times. Remove flowered shoots after flowering to maintain a bushy habit. Propagate by seed in spring or by greenwood cuttings in spring or summer. Spider mite may be troublesome.
C. cyanea illus. p.172.
C. hyssopifolia illus. p.158.
C. ignea, syn. *C. platycentra,* illus. p.172.
C. platycentra. See *C. ignea.*

Cupid peperomia. See *Peperomia scandens.*
Cupidone, Blue. See *Catananche.*

x CUPRESSOCYPARIS

CUPRESSACEAE

Contact with the foliage may aggravate skin allergies. See also CONIFERS.
x *C. leylandii* 'Castlewellan' illus. p.104. 'Haggerston Grey' illus. p.101. 'Harlequin' illus. p.104. 'Leighton Green' is a very fast-growing, columnar conifer with a conical tip. H 25–35m (80–120ft), S 4–5m (12–15ft). Bears flattened sprays of paired, scale-like, rich green leaves and globular, glossy, dark brown cones.
'Robinson's Gold', H 15–20m (50–70ft), has bright golden leaves. All zone 7.

CUPRESSUS

Cypress

CUPRESSACEAE

See also CONIFERS.
C. arizonica var. *glabra,* syn. *C. glabra* (Arizona cypress, Smooth cypress). Conical conifer. H 10–15m (30–50ft), S 3–5m (10–15ft). Has smooth, flaking, reddish-purple bark and upright, spirally arranged sprays of scale-like, aromatic, glaucous blue-grey leaves that are flecked with white resin. Globular cones are chocolate-brown.
C. cashmeriana, syn. *C. torulosa* 'Cashmeriana', illus. p.101.
C. glabra. See *C. arizonica* var. *glabra.*
C. lusitanica (Cedar of Goa, Mexican cypress). Conical conifer. H 20m (70ft), S 5–8m (15–25ft). Has fissured bark and spreading, spirally arranged sprays of scale-like, aromatic, grey-green leaves. Bears small, globular cones that are glaucous blue when young, ripening to glossy brown. Zone 9.
C. macrocarpa (Monterey cypress). Fast-growing, evergreen conifer, columnar when young, often wide-spreading with age. H 20m (70ft), S 6–25m (20–80ft). Bark is shallowly fissured. Scale-like, aromatic, bright to dark green leaves are borne in plume-like sprays. Globular cones are glossy and brown. Zone 8.
'Goldcrest' illus. p.109.
C. torulosa 'Cashmeriana'. See *C. cashmeriana.*

Curled pondweed. See *Potamogeton crispus,* illus. p.448.
Currant. See *Ribes.*
Alpine. See *Ribes alpinum.*

Currant (continued)
Buffalo. See *Ribes odoratum.*
Flowering. See *Ribes sanguineum.*
Fuchsia-flowered. See *Ribes speciosum.*
Indian. See *Symphoricarpos orbiculatus.*
Curry plant. See *Helichrysum italicum.*
Curtonus paniculatus. See *Crocosmia paniculata.*
Cushion bush. See *Leucophyta.*
Custard apple. See *Annona.*

CYANANTHUS

CAMPANULACEAE

Genus of late summer-flowering perennials, suitable for rock gardens, walls and troughs. Needs partial shade and humus-rich, moist but well-drained soil. Propagate by softwood cuttings in spring or by seed in autumn.
C. lobatus. Prostrate perennial. H 2cm (¾in), S 20cm (8in). Branched stems are clothed in small, wedge-shaped, dull green leaves. In late summer, each stem carries a funnel-shaped, blue flower. f. *albus* illus. p.373.
C. microphyllus illus. p.383.

CYANOTIS

COMMELINACEAE

Genus of evergreen, creeping perennials, grown for their foliage. Tender, min. 10–15°C (50–59°F). Prefers a position in sun or partial shade, with humus-rich, well-drained soil. Propagate by tip cuttings from spring to autumn.
C. kewensis (Teddy-bear vine). Evergreen perennial forming rosettes with trailing stems. H 5cm (2in), S 30cm (12in). Clasping the stem are 2 rows of overlapping, oval leaves, to 5cm (2in) long, dark green above, purple with velvety, brown hairs below. Stalkless clusters of 3-petalled, purplish-pink flowers are produced in axils of leaf-like bracts almost all year round.
C. somaliensis illus. p.303.

CYATHEA,
syn. ALSOPHILA, SPHAEROPTERIS

CYATHEACEAE

Genus of evergreen tree ferns, grown for their foliage and overall appearance. Tender, min. 10–13°C (50–55°F). Needs a humid atmosphere, sun or partial shade and humus-rich, moisture-retentive but well-drained soil. Water potted plants freely in summer, moderately at other times. Propagate by spores in spring.
C. australis illus. p.100.
C. medullaris (Black tree fern, Mamaku). Evergreen, upright tree fern with a slender, black trunk. H 7–16m (22–52ft), S 6–12m (20–40ft). Has arching fronds, each to 7m (22ft) long, divided into small, oblong, glossy, dark green leaflets, paler beneath.

CYATHODES

EPACRIDACEAE

Genus of evergreen, heath-like shrubs, suitable for rock gardens and peat beds. Hardy to tender, min. 7°C (45°F).

Needs a sheltered, shaded site and gritty, moist, peaty soil. Propagate in summer by seed or semi-ripe cuttings. *C. colensoi*, syn. *Leucopogon colensoi*, illus. p.360.

CYBISTAX

BIGNONIACEAE

Genus of deciduous trees, grown for their spring flowers and for shade. Tender, min. 16–18°C (61–4°F). Needs full light and fertile, moisture-retentive but well-drained soil. Will not bloom when confined to a container. Young plants may be pruned to shape when leafless; otherwise pruning is not required. Propagate by seed or air-layering in spring or by semi-ripe cuttings in summer.

C. donnell-smithii, syn. *Tabebuia donnell-smithii*. Fairly fast-growing, deciduous, rounded tree. H and S 10m (30ft) or more. Leaves have 5–7 oval, 5–20cm (2–8in) long leaflets. Bell-shaped, 5-lobed, bright yellow flowers appear in spring before the leaves, often in great profusion.

CYCAS

CYCADACEAE

Genus of slow-growing, evergreen, woody-stemmed perennials, grown for their palm-like appearance. Tender, min. 10–13°C (50–55°F). Prefers a position in full light and humus-rich, well-drained soil. Water potted specimens moderately, less when not in full growth. Propagate in spring by seed or suckers taken from mature plants.

C. revoluta illus. p.152.

CYCLAMEN

PRIMULACEAE

Genus of tuberous perennials, some of which are occasionally evergreen, grown for their pendent flowers, each with 5 reflexed petals and a mouth often stained with a darker colour. Hardy to tender, min. 5–7°C (41–5°F). Grow in sun or partial shade, and in humus-rich, well-drained soil. If grown in containers, in summer dry off tubers of all except *C. purpurascens* (which is evergreen and flowers in summer); repot in autumn and water to restart growth. Propagate by seed in late summer or autumn. *C. persicum* and its cultivars are susceptible to black root rot. All parts may cause severe discomfort if ingested.

C. africanum illus. p.437.
C. alpinum. See *C. trochopteranthum*.
C. caucasicum. See *C. coum* subsp. *caucasicum*.
C. cilicium illus. p.438.
C. coum and f. *albissimum* (syn. *C.c.* 'Album') illus. p.440. subsp. *caucasicum* (syn. *C. caucasicum*) is a winter-flowering, tuberous perennial. H to 10cm (4in), S 5–10cm (2–4in). Has heart-shaped, silver-patterned leaves and produces a succession of bright carmine flowers, each with a dark stain at the mouth.
C. creticum. Spring-flowering, tuberous perennial. H to 10cm (4in), S 5–10cm (2–4in). Produces

heart-shaped, dark green leaves, sometimes silver-patterned, and fragrant, white flowers.
C. cyprium. Autumn-flowering, tuberous perennial. H to 10cm (4in), S 5–10cm (2–4in). Heart-shaped, toothed, dark green leaves, patterned with lighter green, appear with or just after fragrant, white flowers, each with carmine marks around the mouth.
C. europaeum. See *C. purpurascens*.
C. fatrense. See *C. purpurascens*.
C. graecum illus. p.438.
C. hederifolium, syn. *C. neapolitanum*, illus. p.438. f. *albiflorum* illus. p.437.
C. libanoticum illus. p.427.
C. mirabile illus. p.437.
C. neapolitanum. See *C. hederifolium*.
C. persicum illus. p.440. 'Esmeralda' illus. p.441. Halios Series is a late summer- or autumn-flowering, tuberous perennial. H 30cm (12in), S 18cm (7in). Tender. Blunt-toothed, heart-shaped, dark green leaves have silver marbling. Produces a succession of white, pink, scarlet, lilac or purple flowers. Kaori Series illus. p.441. 'Pearl Wave' illus. p.440. 'Renown' illus. p.441. 'Scentsation', H 15cm (6in), bears strongly scented flowers in pink, carmine-red or crimson from early winter to early spring.
C. pseudibericum. Spring-flowering, tuberous perennial. H to 10cm (4in), S 10–15cm (4–6in). Has heart-shaped, toothed leaves patterned with silvery- and dark green zones. Flowers are deep carmine-purple with darker, basal stains and white-rimmed mouths.
C. purpurascens, syn. *C. europaeum*, *C. fatrense*, illus. p.435.
C. repandum. Spring-flowering, tuberous perennial. H to 10cm (4in), S 10–15cm (4–6in). Has heart-shaped, jagged-toothed, dark green leaves with lighter patterns. Bears fragrant, slender, reddish-purple flowers.
C. rohlfsianum illus. p.438.
C. trochopteranthum, syn. *C. alpinum*. Spring-flowering, tuberous perennial. H 10cm (4in), S 5–10cm (2–4in). Bears rounded or heart-shaped leaves, zoned with silver. Produces musty-scented, pale carmine or white flowers, stained dark carmine at mouths; petals are twisted and propeller-shaped.

Cyclobothra lutea. See *Calochortus barbatus*.

CYDONIA

ROSACEAE

Genus of one species of deciduous, spring-flowering tree, grown for its flowers and fruits, which are used as a flavouring and for preserves. Grow against a south- or west-facing wall at the limits of hardiness. Requires sun and fertile, well-drained soil. Propagate species by seed in autumn, cultivars by softwood cuttings in summer. Mildew, brown rot and fireblight are sometimes a problem.
C. oblonga (Quince). Portugal ('Lusitanica') is a deciduous, spreading tree. H and S 5m (15ft). Broadly oval, dark green leaves are grey-felted beneath. Has a profusion of large, 5-petalled, pale pink flowers in

late spring, followed by fragrant, pear-shaped, deep yellow fruits. Zone 5b. 'Vranja' illus. p.92.
C. sinensis. See *Pseudocydonia sinensis*.

CYMBALARIA

SCROPHULARIACEAE

Genus of annuals, biennials and short-lived perennials, related to *Linaria*, grown for their tiny flowers on slender stems. Is good for rock gardens, walls and banks, but may be invasive. Needs shade and moist soil. Propagate by seed in autumn. Self-seeds readily.
C. muralis (Ivy-leaved toadflax, Kenilworth ivy). Spreading perennial. H 5cm (2in), S 12cm (5in). Bears small, ivy-shaped, pale green leaves and, in summer, masses of tiny, tubular, spurred, sometimes purple-tinted, white flowers.

CYMBIDIUM

Contact with the foliage may aggravate skin allergies. See also ORCHIDS.
C. Caithness Ice 'Trinity' (illus. p.298). Evergreen, epiphytic orchid for a cool greenhouse. H 75cm (30in). Sprays of green flowers, 10cm (4in) across, each with a red-marked, white lip, are borne in early spring. Has narrowly oval leaves, to 60cm (24in) long. Needs a position in semi-shade in summer.
C. Christmas Angel 'Cooksbridge Sunburst' (illus. p.299). Evergreen, epiphytic orchid for a cool greenhouse. H 75cm (30in). In winter produces sprays of yellow flowers, 10cm (4in) across and with red-spotted lips. Narrowly oval leaves are up to 60cm (24in) long. Grow in semi-shade in summer.
C. devonianum (illus. p.298). Evergreen, epiphytic orchid for a cool greenhouse. H 60cm (24in). In early summer bears pendent spikes of 2.5cm (1in) wide, olive-green flowers overlaid with purple and with purple lips. Has broadly oval, semi-rigid leaves, to 30cm (12in) long. Needs semi-shade in summer.
C. elegans, syn. *Cyperorchis elegans* (illus. p.298). Evergreen, epiphytic orchid for a cool greenhouse. H 75cm (30in). Dense, pendent sprays of fragrant, tubular, yellow flowers, 4cm (1½in) across, appear in early summer. Has narrowly oval leaves, to 60cm (24in) long. Requires semi-shade in summer.
C. grandiflorum. See *C. hookerianum*.
C. hookerianum, syn. *C. grandiflorum* (illus. p.298). Evergreen, epiphytic orchid for a cool greenhouse. H 75cm (30in). In winter produces sprays of deep green flowers, 8cm (3in) across, each with a hairy, brown-spotted, creamy-white lip. Narrowly oval leaves are up to 60cm (24in) long. Grow in semi-shade in summer.
C. King's Loch 'Cooksbridge' (illus. p.298). Evergreen, epiphytic orchid for a cool greenhouse. H 60cm (24in). Sprays of green flowers, 5cm (2in) across and each

with a purple-marked, white lip, open in spring. Leaves are narrowly oval and up to 60cm (24in) long. Provide semi-shade in summer.
C. Pontac 'Mont Millais' (illus. p.297). Evergreen, epiphytic orchid for a cool greenhouse. H 75cm (30in). Bears sprays of 8cm (3in) wide, rich deep red flowers, edged and marked with white, in spring. Has narrowly oval leaves, to 60cm (24in) long. Grow in semi-shade in summer.
C. Portelet Bay (illus. p.296). Evergreen, epiphytic orchid for a cool greenhouse. H 75cm (30in). Red-lipped, white flowers, 10cm (4in) across, are borne in sprays in spring. Has narrowly oval leaves, to 60cm (24in) long. Provide semi-shade in summer.
C. Strath Kanaid (illus. p.297). Evergreen, epiphytic orchid for a cool greenhouse. H 60cm (24in). In spring bears arching spikes of deep red flowers, 5cm (2in) across. Lips are white, marked deep red. Narrowly oval leaves are up to 60cm (24in) long. Requires semi-shade in summer.
C. Strathbraan (illus. p.296). Evergreen, epiphytic orchid for a cool greenhouse. H 60cm (24in). In spring produces slightly arching spikes of off-white flowers, 5cm (2in) across, with red marks on each lip. Leaves are narrowly oval, to 60cm (24in) long. Requires semi-shade in summer.
C. Strathdon 'Cooksbridge Noel' (illus. p.297). Evergreen, epiphytic orchid for a cool greenhouse. H 1m (3ft). Sprays of rich pink flowers, 5cm (2in) across, with red-spotted, yellow-tinged lips, appear in winter. Has narrowly oval leaves, up to 60cm (24in) long. Needs semi-shade in summer.
C. tracyanum (illus. p.298). Evergreen, epiphytic orchid for a cool greenhouse. H 75cm (30in). In autumn produces long spikes of fragrant, olive-green flowers, 8cm (3in) across, overlaid with reddish dots and dashes. Has narrowly oval leaves, to 60cm (24in) long. Grow in semi-shade in summer.

CYNARA

ASTERACEAE/COMPOSITAE

Genus of architectural perennials, grown for their large heads of flowers. The plant described is grown both as a vegetable and as a decorative border plant. Requires sun and fertile, well-drained soil. Propagate by seed or division in spring.
C. cardunculus illus. p.228.

CYNOGLOSSUM

Hound's tongue

BORAGINACEAE

Genus of annuals, biennials and perennials, grown for their long flowering period from late spring to early autumn. Needs sun and fertile but not over-rich soil. Propagate by division in spring or by seed in autumn or spring.
C. amabile 'Firmament' illus. p.334.

CYPELLA
IRIDACEAE

Genus of summer-flowering bulbs, grown for their short-lived, iris-like flowers that have 3 large, spreading outer petals and 3 small, incurved inner ones. May survive outdoors in warm areas if planted near a sunny wall. Needs full sun and well-drained soil. Lift bulbs when dormant; partially dry off in winter. Propagate by seed in spring.
C. herbertii illus. p.423.

Cyperorchis elegans. See *Cymbidium elegans.*

CYPERUS
CYPERACEAE

See also GRASSES, BAMBOOS, RUSHES and SEDGES.
C. albostriatus, syn. *C. diffusus* of gardens, *C. elegans* of gardens. Evergreen, perennial sedge. H 60cm (24in), S indefinite. Tender, min. 7°C (45°F). Stem has prominently veined, mid-green leaves and up to 8 leaf-like, green bracts surrounding a well-branched umbel of brown spikelets, produced in summer. 'Variegatus' has white-striped leaves and bracts.
C. alternifolius of gardens. See *C. involucratus.*
C. diffusus of gardens. See *C. albostriatus.*
C. elegans of gardens. See *C. albostriatus.*
C. flabelliformis. See *C. involucratus.*
C. involucratus, syn. *C. alternifolius* of gardens, *C. flabelliformis*, illus. p.308.
C. isocladus of gardens. See *C. papyrus* 'Nanus'.
C. longus (Galingale). Deciduous, spreading, perennial sedge. H 1.5m (5ft), S indefinite. Bears rough-edged, glossy, dark green leaves and, in summer, attractive umbels of narrow, flattened, milk-chocolate-coloured spikelets that keep their colour well. Tolerates its roots in water.
C. papyrus illus. p.307. 'Nanus' (syn. *C. isocladus* of gardens) is an evergreen, spreading, perennial sedge with a red rhizome; it is a dwarf variant of the species, sometimes considered distinct, and is often grown under misapplied names. H 80cm (32in), S indefinite. Tender, min. 7–10°C (45–50°F). Triangular, leafless stems bear umbels of brown spikelets on 8–10cm (3–4in) stalks in summer.

CYPHOMANDRA
SOLANACEAE

Genus of evergreen shrubs and trees, grown for their fruits and foliage. Tender, min. 10°C (50°F). Grow in full light or partial shade and in well-drained soil. Water containerized specimens freely when in growth, sparingly at other times, when some leaves may fall. Tip prune at intervals while young to promote branching. Propagate by seed in spring. Whitefly and spider mite may cause problems.

C. betacea, syn. *C. crassicaulis*, illus. p.125.
C. crassicaulis. See *C. betacea.*

CYPHOSTEMMA
VITACEAE

Genus of deciduous, perennial succulents with very thick, fleshy, almost woody caudices and branches. Leaf undersides often exude droplets of resin. Tender, min. 10°C (50°F). Needs full sun and very well-drained soil. Keep dry in winter. Is difficult to grow. Propagate by seed in spring.
C. bainesii, syn. *Cissus bainesii.* Deciduous, perennial succulent. H and S 60cm (24in). Has a thick, swollen, bottle-shaped trunk, often unbranched, covered in peeling, papery, yellow bark. Fleshy, silvery-green leaves, with deeply serrated edges, are divided into 3 oval leaflets, silver-haired when young. Bears tiny, cup-shaped, yellow-green flowers in summer, then grape-like, red fruits.
C. juttae, syn. *Cissus juttae*, illus. p.459.

Cypress. See *Cupressus.*
  Arizona. See *Cupressus arizonica* var. *glabra.*
  Bald. See *Taxodium distichum*, illus. p.104.
  False. See *Chamaecyparis.*
  Hinoki. See *Chamaecyparis obtusa.*
  Kashmir. See *Cupressus cashmeriana*, illus. p.101.
  Lawson. See *Chamaecyparis lawsoniana.*
  Mexican. See *Cupressus lusitanica.*
  Monterey. See *Cupressus macrocarpa.*
  Nootka. See *Chamaecyparis nootkatensis.*
  Patagonian. See *Fitzroya cupressoides*, illus. p.106.
  Sawara. See *Chamaecyparis pisifera.*
  Smooth. See *Cupressus arizonica* var. *glabra.*
  Summer. See *Bassia scoparia* f. *trichophylla*, illus. p.335.
  Swamp. See *Taxodium distichum*, illus. p.104.
  Variegated Leyland. See x *Cupressocyparis leylandii* 'Harlequin', illus. p.104.
  White. See *Chamaecyparis thyoides*, illus. p.107.
Cypress vine. See *Ipomoea quamoclit*, illus. p.210.

CYPRIPEDIUM
Slipper orchid

See also ORCHIDS.
C. acaule (Moccasin flower; illus. p.296). Deciduous, terrestrial orchid. H to 40cm (16in). Yellowish-green or purple flowers, 4–6cm (1½–2½in) long, each with a pouched, pink or white lip, are borne singly in spring-summer. Leaves are broadly lance-shaped, pleated and 10–30cm (4–12in) long. Does best in partial shade.
C. calceolus (Lady's slipper orchid, Yellow lady's slipper orchid; illus. p.298). Deciduous, terrestrial orchid. H 75cm (30in). In spring-summer bears paired or solitary yellow-pouched,

purple flowers, 3–7cm (1¼–3in) long. Broadly lance-shaped leaves, 5–20cm (2–8in) long, are arranged in a spiral up stem. Stems and leaves are slightly hairy. Prefers partial shade. var. *pubescens* see *C. pubescens.*
C. macranthon. See *C. macranthos.*
C. macranthos, syn. *C. macranthon* (illus. p.298). Deciduous, terrestrial orchid. H 50cm (20in). Pouched, violet or purplish-red flowers, 4–6cm (1½–2½in) long, usually borne singly, open in spring-summer. Stems and oval leaves, 4–7cm (1½–3in) long, are slightly hairy. Prefers partial shade.
C. pubescens, syn. *C. calceolus* var. *pubescens* (illus. p.299). Deciduous, terrestrial orchid. H 75cm (30in). Has large, purple-marked, greenish-yellow flowers, 8–10cm (3–4in) long, in spring-summer. Large, broadly lance-shaped leaves, 15–20cm (6–8in) long, are arranged in a spiral up stem. Stems and leaves are hairy. Prefers partial shade.
C. reginae (Showy lady's slipper orchid; illus. p.296). Deciduous, terrestrial orchid. H to 1m (3ft). In spring-summer, white flowers, 2–5cm (¾–2in) long, each with a pouched, white-streaked, pink lip, are borne singly or in groups of 2 or 3. Stem and oval leaves, 10–25cm (4–10in) long, are hairy. Does best in partial shade.

Cyprus turpentine. See *Pistacia terebinthus.*

CYRILLA
CYRILLACEAE

Genus of one very variable species of deciduous or evergreen shrub, grown for its flowers in late summer and autumn. Prefers full sun and needs peaty, acid soil. Propagate by semi-ripe cuttings in summer.
C. racemiflora (Leatherwood). Deciduous or evergreen, bushy shrub. H and S 1.2m (4ft). Oblong, glossy, dark green leaves redden in autumn. Slender spires of small, 5-petalled, white flowers are borne in late summer and autumn. Zone 7.

CYRTANTHUS
AMARYLLIDACEAE

Genus of bulbs with brightly coloured flowers, usually in summer. Hardy to tender, min. 15°C (59°F). Requires full sun and free-draining, light soil. In frost-free areas may flower for much of the year. Plant in spring. Water freely in the growing season. Propagate by seed or offsets in spring.
C. brachyscyphus, syn. *C. parviflorus*, illus. p.435.
C. breviflorus, syn. *Anoiganthus breviflorus, A. luteus.* Clump-forming summer-flowering bulb. H 20–30cm (8–12in), S 8–10cm (3–4in). Has narrowly strap-shaped, semi-erect, basal leaves. Leafless flower stem bears up to 6 funnel-shaped, yellow flowers, 2–3cm (¾–1¼in) long. Prefers a warm, sheltered situation.
C. elatus, syn. *C. purpureus, Vallota speciosa.* Clump-forming, summer-flowering bulb. H 30–50cm (12–20in),

S 12–15cm (5–6in). Bears widely strap-shaped, semi-erect, basal, bright green leaves. Stout stem produces a head of up to 5 widely funnel-shaped, scarlet flowers, 8–10cm (3–4in) long. Makes an excellent house plant.
C. mackenii. Clump-forming, summer-flowering bulb. H 30–40cm (12–16in), S 8–10cm (3–4in). Bears strap-shaped, semi-erect, basal leaves. Leafless stems each carry an umbel of up to 10 fragrant, tubular, white flowers, 5cm (2in) long and slightly curved. var. *cooperi* illus. p.422.
C. obliquus. Clump-forming, summer-flowering bulb. H 20–60cm (8–24in), S 12–15cm (5–6in). Bears widely strap-shaped, semi-erect, basal, greyish-green leaves, twisted lengthways. Carries a head of up to 12 pendent, tubular, red-and-yellow flowers, each 7cm (3in) long.
C. parviflorus. See *C. brachyscyphus.*
C. purpureus. See *C. elatus.*
C. sanguineus. Clump-forming, summer-flowering bulb. H 30–50cm (12–20in), S 12–15cm (5–6in). Has strap-shaped, semi-erect, basal, bright green leaves. Stout stem bears 1 or 2 long-tubed, scarlet flowers, 8–10cm (3–4in) long.

CYRTOMIUM
AMARYLLIDACEAE

Genus of evergreen ferns. Does best in semi-shade and humus-rich, moist soil. Remove fading fronds. Propagate by division in spring or summer or by spores in summer.
C. falcatum illus. p.311.
C. fortunei, syn. *Phanerophlebia fortunei.* Evergreen fern. H 60cm (24in). S 40cm (16in). Has erect, dull, pale green fronds, 30–60cm (12–24in) long, with broadly sickle-shaped pinnae, 2.5–5cm (1–2in) long.

CYSTOPTERIS
WOODSIACEAE

Genus of deciduous ferns, suitable for rock gardens. Does best in semi-shade and in soil that is never allowed to dry out. Remove fronds as they fade. Propagate by division in spring, by spores in summer or by bulbils when available.
C. bulbifera (Berry bladder fern). Deciduous fern. H 15cm (6in), S 23cm (9in). Broadly lance-shaped, much-divided, dainty, pale green fronds produce tiny bulbils along their length. Propagate by bulbils as soon as mature.
C. dickieana. Deciduous fern. H 15cm (6in), S 23cm (9in). Has broadly lance-shaped, divided, delicate, pale green fronds, with oblong, blunt, indented pinnae, that arch downwards.
C. fragilis (Brittle bladder fern). Deciduous fern. H 15cm (6in), S 23cm (9in). Broadly lance-shaped, pale green fronds are delicate and much divided into oblong, pointed, indented pinnae.

CYTISUS
Broom
LEGUMINOSAE/PAPILIONACEAE

Genus of deciduous or evergreen shrubs, grown for their abundant, pea-like flowers. Prefers full sun and fertile, but not over-rich, well-drained soil. Resents being transplanted. Propagate species by semi-ripe cuttings in summer or by seed in autumn, hybrids and cultivars by semi-ripe cuttings in late summer. All parts, especially the seeds, may cause mild stomach upset if ingested.

C. albus, syn. *Chamaecytisus albus*, *Cytisus leucanthus*. Deciduous, spreading shrub. H 30cm (1ft), S 1m (3ft). Has oval leaves, each with 3 tiny leaflets and, from early to mid-summer, creamy-white flowers borne in dense clusters. Zone 7.

C. ardoinii. See *C. ardoinoi.*

C. ardoinoi, syn. *C. ardoinii*, illus. p.386.

C. battandieri, syn. *Argyrocytisus battandieri*, illus. p.123.

C. x *beanii* illus. p.349.

C. canariensis of gardens. See *C.* x *spachianus*.

C. demissus. See *Chamaecytisus demissus.*

C. 'Firefly'. Deciduous, bushy shrub with slender, arching shoots. H and S 1.5–2m (5–6ft). Small, mid-green leaves are oblong and have 3 tiny leaflets. Produces masses of yellow flowers, marked with red, from late spring to early summer. Zone 7.

C. x *kewensis.* Deciduous, arching shrub. H 30cm (1ft), S to 2m (6ft). Has leaves, each composed of 3 tiny leaflets, along downy stems. In late spring bears creamy-white flowers. Is good for a bank or large rock garden. Zone 7.

C. leucanthus. See *C. albus.*

C. nigricans, syn. *Lembotropis nigricans*, illus. p.170.

C. x *praecox* '**Allgold**' illus. p.157. '**Warminster**' illus. p.156.

C. purpureus. See *Chamaecytisus purpureus.*

C. racemosus of gardens. See *C.* x *spachianus*.

C. scoparius (Common broom). f. *andreanus* illus. p.171. subsp. *maritimus* (syn. *C.s.* var. *prostratus*) is a deciduous, prostrate shrub forming dense mounds of interlocking shoots. H 20cm (8in), S 1.2–2m (4–6ft). Small, grey-green leaves usually have 3 oblong leaflets, but may be reduced to a single leaflet. Has masses of golden-yellow flowers in late spring and early summer. Zone 7. var. *prostratus* see *C.s.* subsp. *maritimus.*

C. x *spachianus*, syn. *C. canariensis* of gardens, *C. racemosus* of gardens, *Genista fragrans* of gardens, *G.* x *spachiana*. Vigorous, evergreen,

arching shrub. H and S 3m (10ft). Has dark green leaves with 3 oval leaflets. Produces long, slender clusters of fragrant, golden-yellow flowers in winter and early spring. Is often grown as a houseplant. Zone 9.

C. supinus. See *Chamaecytisus supinus.*

C. 'Windlesham Ruby'. Deciduous, bushy shrub with slender, arching shoots. H and S 1.5–2m (5–6ft). Small, mid-green leaves have 3 oblong leaflets. Large, rich red flowers are borne in profusion in late spring and early summer. Zone 7.

C. 'Zeelandia'. Deciduous, bushy shrub with slender, arching shoots. H and S 1.5–2m (5–6ft). Small, mid-green leaves have 3 oblong leaflets. Has masses of bicoloured, creamy-white and lilac-pink flowers from late spring to early summer. Zone 6.

D

DABOECIA

ERICACEAE

See also HEATHERS.

D. azorica. Evergreen, compact shrub. H to 15cm (6in), S to 60cm (24in). Lance-shaped leaves are dark green above, silver-grey beneath. Urn-to bell-shaped flowers are vivid red and open in late spring or early summer. Zone 9.

D. cantabrica (St Dabeoc's heath). Evergreen, straggling shrub. H to 45cm (18in), S 60cm (24in). Top growth may be damaged by frost and cold winds, but plants respond well to hard pruning and produce new growth from base. Leaves are lance-shaped to oval, dark green above, silver-grey beneath. Bears bell- to urn-shaped, single or double, white, purple or mauve flowers from late spring to mid-autumn. Zone 6. **'Bicolor'** (illus. p.178) bears white, purple and striped flowers on the same plant. **'Praegerae'**, H 35cm (14in), has glowing deep pink flowers. **'Snowdrift'** has bright green foliage and long racemes of large, white flowers.

D. x scotica. Evergreen, compact shrub. H to 15cm (6in), S to 60cm (2ft). Lance-shaped to oval leaves are dark green above, silver-grey beneath. Bears bell- to urn-shaped, white, purple or mauve flowers from late spring to mid-autumn. Zone 6. **'Jack Drake'**, H 20cm (8in), has small, dark green leaves and ruby-coloured flowers. **'Silverwells'** (illus. p.178) has small, bright green leaves and large, white flowers. **'William Buchanan'** (illus. p.179), H 45cm (18in), is a vigorous cultivar with dark green leaves and deep purple flowers.

DACTYLIS

GRAMINAE/POACEAE

See also GRASSES, BAMBOOS, RUSHES and SEDGES.

D. glomerata (Cock's-foot, Orchard grass). **'Variegata'** is an evergreen, tuft-forming, perennial grass. H 1m (3ft), S 20–25cm (8–10in). Silver-striped, grey-green leaves arise from tufted rootstock. In summer bears panicles of densely clustered, awned, purplish-green spikelets.

DACTYLORHIZA

See also ORCHIDS.

D. elata, syn. *Orchis elata.* Deciduous, terrestrial orchid. H 1.1m (3½ft). Spikes of pink or purple flowers, 1–2cm (½–¾in) long, open in spring-summer. Lance-shaped leaves, 15–25cm (6–10in) long, are spotted with brownish-purple and arranged spirally on stem. Requires shade outdoors; keep pot plants semi-shaded in summer.

D. foliosa, syn. *D. maderensis, Orchis maderensis.* Deciduous, terrestrial orchid. H 70cm (28in). Spikes of bright purple or pink flowers, 1–2cm (½–¾in) long, are borne in spring-summer. Has lance-shaped or triangular leaves, 10–20cm (4–8in) long, arranged spirally on stem. Cultivate as for *D. elata.*

D. maderensis. See *D. foliosa.*

Daffodil. See *Narcissus.*
  Bunch-flowered. See *Narcissus tazetta.*
  Hoop-petticoat. See *Narcissus bulbocodium* subsp. *bulbocodium.*
  Peruvian. See *Hymenocallis narcissiflora,* illus. p.420.
  Poet's. See *Narcissus poeticus.*
  Polyanthus. See *Narcissus tazetta.*
  Queen Anne's double. See *Narcissus* 'Eystettensis'.
  Sea. See *Pancratium maritimum.*
  Tenby. See *Narcissus obvallaris.*
  Wild. See *Narcissus pseudonarcissus,* illus. p.417.

DAHLIA

ASTERACEAE/COMPOSITAE

Genus of bushy, summer- and autumn-flowering, tuberous perennials, grown as bedding plants or for their flower heads, which are good for cutting or exhibition. Dwarf forms are used for mass-planting and are also suitable for containers. Needs a sunny position and well-drained soil. All apart from dwarf forms require staking. After flowering, lift tubers and store in a frost-free place; replant once all frost danger has passed. In frost-free areas, plants may be left in ground as normal herbaceous perennials, but they benefit from regular propagation to maintain vigour. Propagate dwarf forms by seed sown under glass in late winter, others in spring by seed, basal shoot cuttings or division of tubers. Dahlias may be subject to attack by aphids, spider mite and thrips. In recent years, powdery mildew has become a problem in certain areas, and spraying is essential. Dahlias also succumb quickly to virus infection. See also feature panel, pp.406–407.

Border dahlias

Prolific and long-flowering, various species of *Dahlia* have been hybridized and, with constant breeding and selection, have developed into many forms and have a wide colour range (although there is no blue). Shoots may be stopped, or pinched out, to promote vigorous growth and a bushy shape. Spread measurements depend on the amount of stopping carried out and the time at which it is done: early stopping encourages a broader shape, stopping later in the growing season results in a taller plant with much less spread, even in the same cultivar. Leaves are generally mid-green and divided into oval leaflets, some with rounded tips and some with toothed margins. Each flower head is referred to horticulturally as a flower, even though it does in fact comprise a large number of individual flowers. This horticultural usage has been followed in the descriptions below. All forms with flower heads to 152mm (6in) across are suitable for cutting; those suitable for exhibition are so noted.

Groups and flower sizes

Dahlias are divided into groups, according to the size and type of their flower heads, although the latter may vary in colour and shape depending on soil and weather conditions. The groups are: (1) single; (2) anemone; (3) collerette; (4) water-lily; (5) decorative; (6) ball; (7) pompon; (8) cactus; (9) semi-cactus; (10) miscellaneous. For illustrations and descriptions, see p.406. Certain groups have been subdivided; flower sizes are as follows:

Group 4
C – medium-flowered; usually 152–203mm (6–8in) in diameter.
D – small-flowered; usually 102–152mm (4–6in) in diameter.
E – miniature-flowered; usually not exceeding 102mm (4in) in diameter.

Groups 5, 8 and 9
A – giant-flowered; usually over 254mm (10in) in diameter.
B – large-flowered; usually 203–254mm (8–10in) in diameter.
C – medium-flowered; usually 152–203mm (6–8in) in diameter.
D – small-flowered; usually 102–152mm (4–6in) in diameter.
E – miniature-flowered; usually not exceeding 102mm (4in) in diameter.

Group 6
A – small ball dahlias; usually 102–152mm (4–6in) in diameter.
B – miniature ball dahlias; usually 52–102mm (2–4in) in diameter.

Group 7
Pompon dahlias; not exceeding 52mm (2in) in diameter.

D. 'Alloway Cottage'. Medium-flowered decorative dahlia. H 1.2m (4ft), S 60cm (2ft). Bears very full, formal, soft yellow flowers, with a touch of lavender-blue on the tip of each petal, in summer-autumn. Is good for exhibition.

D. 'Alva's Doris'. Small-flowered cactus dahlia. H 1.2m (4ft), S 60cm (2ft). Freely produces blood-red flowers, on strong stems, in summer-autumn. Is good for exhibition.

D. 'Alva's Supreme'. Giant-flowered decorative dahlia. H 1.1m (3½ft), S 60cm (2ft). In summer-autumn bears pale yellow flowers. Is good for exhibition.

D. 'Apricot Honeymoon Dress'. Small-flowered decorative dahlia. H 1.2m (4ft), S 60cm (2ft). In summer-autumn bears apricot flowers. Is good for exhibition.

D. 'Banker'. Small-flowered cactus dahlia. H 1.2m (4ft), S 60cm (2ft). In summer-autumn produces red flowers that are good for exhibition.

D. 'Biddenham Sunset' (illus. p.407).

Small-flowered decorative dahlia. H 1.1m (3½ft), S 60cm (2ft). Orange-red flowers are borne in mid-summer to autumn.

D. 'Bishop of Llandaff' (illus. p.407). Miscellaneous dahlia. H 1m (3ft), S 45cm (18in). Has bronze-green leaves and single, open-centred, dark red flowers, 78mm (3in) across, in summer-autumn. It is excellent as a bedding plant.

D. 'Black Monarch'. Giant-flowered decorative dahlia. H 1.2m (4ft), S 60cm (2ft). Produces oxblood-red flowers, shading to crimson, in summer-autumn.

D. 'Butterball' (illus. p.407). Miniature-flowered decorative dahlia. H 60cm (2ft), S 30cm (1ft). Produces bright yellow flowers in early summer.

D. 'Candy Cupid'. Miniature ball dahlia. H 1.1m (3½ft), S 60cm (2ft). In summer-autumn bears lavender-pink flowers that are good for exhibition.

D. 'Chimborazo' (illus. p.407). Collerette dahlia. H 1.1m (3½ft), S 60cm (2ft). Leaves are glossy, dark green. Has 102mm (4in) wide flowers, with red, outer petals and yellow, inner petals, in summer-autumn. Flowers are good for exhibition.

D. 'Clair de Lune' (illus. p.407). Collerette dahlia. H 1.1m (3½ft), S 60cm (2ft). Has 102mm (4in) wide flowers, with lemon-yellow, outer petals and paler yellow, inner petals, in summer-autumn, good for exhibition.

D. 'Coltness Gem' illus. p.329.

D. 'Comet' (illus. p.407). Anemone dahlia. H 1.1m (3½ft), S 60cm (2ft). Leaves are glossy, dark green. Dark red flowers, 102–152mm (4–6in) across, are produced in summer-autumn.

D. 'Cryfield Bryn'. Small-flowered semi-cactus dahlia. H 1.1m (3½ft), S 60cm (2ft). In summer-autumn has butter-yellow flowers, excellent for exhibition.

D. 'Daddy's Choice'. Small-flowered semi-cactus dahlia. H 1.3m (4½ft), S 60cm (2ft). In summer-autumn, bears pale lemon-yellow flowers, with a pale lilac tinge.

D. 'Dana Iris'. Small-flowered cactus dahlia. H 1.3m (4½ft), S 60cm (2ft). Bears outstanding red flowers in summer-autumn. Is good for exhibition.

D. 'Dandy' illus. p.341.

D. 'Davenport Honey'. Miniature-flowered decorative dahlia. H 1.2m (4ft), S 60cm (2ft). In summer-autumn, has amber flowers that are good for exhibition.

D. 'Davenport Sunlight' (illus. p.407). Medium-flowered semi-cactus dahlia. H 1.2m (4ft), S 60cm (2ft). Has bright yellow flowers in summer-autumn that are good for exhibition.

D. 'David Howard'. Miniature-flowered decorative dahlia. H 1m (3ft), S 60cm (2ft). Dark, bronze-coloured foliage offsets orange-bronze flowers, produced in summer-autumn.

D. 'Debra Ann Craven'. Giant-flowered semi-cactus dahlia. H 1.3m (4½ft), S 60cm (2ft). Deep red flowers are held well above the foliage on strong stems in summer-autumn. Is good for exhibition.

D. Disco Series. Group of well-branched, erect, perennial dahlias, grown as annuals. H and S 45cm (18in). Leaves are divided into oval leaflets. Daisy-like, semi-double and double flower heads, with quilled florets, in a wide colour range, appear throughout summer and until autumn frosts.

D. 'East Anglian' (illus. p.407). Small-flowered decorative dahlia. H 1m (3ft), S 60cm (2ft). Has orange-yellow flowers in summer-autumn.

D. 'Easter Sunday' (illus. p.406). Collerette dahlia. H 1m (3ft), S 60cm (2ft). Leaves are glossy, dark green. Produces 102mm (4in) wide flowers, with white, inner and outer petals and dark yellow centres, in summer-autumn. Is good for exhibition.

D. 'Eastwood Moonlight'. Medium-flowered semi-cactus dahlia. H 1.1m (3½ft), S 60cm (2ft). Bears bright yellow flowers in summer-autumn. Is a very good exhibition cultivar.

D. 'Fascination' (illus. p.406). Dwarf miscellaneous dahlia. H 45cm (18in), S 30cm (12in). Has single, light purple flowers, 78mm (3in) across, in summer-autumn. Is useful for bedding.

D. 'Gateshead Festival'. Small-flowered decorative dahlia. H 1.2m (4ft), S 60cm (2ft). In summer-autumn, bears peach to orange flowers with lemon-yellow petal bases. Is good for exhibition.

D. 'Gay Princess' (illus. p.406). Small-flowered decorative dahlia. H 1.2m (4ft), S 60cm (2ft). Produces lilac-lavender flowers in summer-autumn.

D. 'Geerling's Indian Summer', syn. *D.* 'Indian Summer'. Small-flowered cactus dahlia. H 1.2m (4ft), S 60cm (2ft). Has red flowers in summer-autumn. Very free-flowering.

D. 'Gerrie Hoek'. Small-flowered water-lily dahlia. H 1.1m (3½ft), S 60cm (2ft). Flowers have pale pink outer petals and dark pink inner petals, borne in summer-autumn.

D. 'Grenidor Pastelle' (illus. p.407). Medium-flowered semi-cactus dahlia. H 1.3m (4½ft), S 60cm (2ft). Bears salmon-pink flowers, with cream petal bases, in summer-autumn. Is good for exhibition.

D. 'Hallmark'. Pompon dahlia. H 1.1m (3½ft), S 60cm (2ft). Has spherical, pink flowers in summer-autumn. Is good for exhibition.

D. 'Hamari Accord' (illus. p.407). Large-flowered semi-cactus dahlia. H 1.2m (4ft), S 60cm (2ft). Has pale, clear yellow flowers held well above the foliage on strong stems in summer-autumn, that are good for exhibition.

D. 'Hamari Bride'. Medium-flowered semi-cactus dahlia. H 1.2m (4ft), S 60cm (2ft). Bears clear white flowers in summer-autumn. Is a good exhibition cultivar.

D. 'Hamari Gold' (illus. p.407). Giant-flowered decorative dahlia. H 1.1m (3½ft), S 60cm (2ft). Has golden orange-bronze flowers in summer-autumn. Is suitable for exhibition.

D. 'Hamari Katrina' (illus. p.407). Large-flowered semi-cactus dahlia. H 1.2m (4ft), S 60cm (2ft). Bears deep butter-yellow flowers in summer-autumn that are good for exhibition.

D. 'Hayley Jane' (illus. p.407). Small-flowered semi-cactus dahlia. H 1.1m (3½ft), S 60cm (2ft). Produces white flowers, evenly tipped purple-red, in summer-autumn. Is good for exhibition.

D. 'Hillcrest Hillton'. Large-flowered semi-cactus dahlia. H 1.2m (4ft), S 60cm (2ft). In summer-autumn, produces weather-resistant, deep rich yellow flowers. Is good for exhibition.

D. 'Hillcrest Royal' (illus. p.407). Medium-flowered cactus dahlia. H 1.1m (3½ft), S 60cm (2ft). In summer-autumn, has rich purple flowers with incurving petals, held on strong stems.

D. 'Indian Summer'.
See *D.* 'Geerling's Indian Summer'.

D. 'Jeanette Carter' (illus. p.407). Miniature-flowered decorative dahlia. H 1.1m (3½ft), S 60cm (2ft). Bears pale yellow flowers, sometimes flushed pink in the centres, in summer-autumn.

D. 'Jescot Julie' (illus. p.407). Miscellaneous dahlia. H 60cm (24in), S 45cm (18in). Has sparse, mid-green foliage and orchid-like, double, orange-purple flowers, 78mm (3in) across, with purple-backed petals, in summer-autumn.

D. 'Jim Branigan' (illus. p.407). Large-flowered semi-cactus dahlia. H 1.3m (4½ft), S 60cm (2ft). Bright red flowers are held well above the foliage in summer-autumn. Is good for exhibition.

D. 'Kathryn's Cupid' (illus. p.407). Miniature ball dahlia. H 1.2m (4ft), S 60cm (2ft). In summer-autumn, produces peach flowers that are good for exhibition.

D. 'Klankstad Kerkrade'. Small-flowered cactus dahlia. H 1.2m (4ft), S 60cm (2ft). Has glossy, dark green leaves and bears soft sulphur-yellow flowers in summer-autumn that are good for exhibition.

D. 'Lady Linda'. Small-flowered decorative dahlia. H 1.2m (4ft), S 60cm (2ft). Well-formed, primrose-yellow flowers are held well above the foliage in summer-autumn. Very vigorous and free-flowering. Is good for exhibition.

D. 'Lavender Athalie' (illus. p.407). Small-flowered cactus dahlia. H 1.2m (4ft), S 60cm (2ft). Is a sport of *D.* 'Athalie'. Bears soft lilac-lavender flowers in summer-autumn.

D. 'Linda's Chester'. Small-flowered cactus dahlia. H 1.2m (4ft), S 60cm (2ft). In summer-autumn, produces yellow flowers, overlaid with bronze at the petal tips. Is good for exhibition.

D. 'Mariposa'. Collerette dahlia. H 1m (3ft), S 60cm (2ft). In summer-autumn has white flowers; outer petals are tinged with lilac. Is good for exhibition.

D. 'Mark Damp'. Large-flowered semi-cactus dahlia. H 1–1.2m (3–4ft), S 60cm (2ft). Bears bronze-orange flowers, tinged with peach, in summer-autumn. Is suitable for exhibition.

D. 'Mark Hardwick' (illus. p.407). Giant-flowered decorative dahlia.

H 1.1m (3½ft), S 60cm (2ft). Compact plant bearing bright, deep yellow flowers, on strong stems, in summer-autumn. Is good for exhibition.

D. 'Mi Wong' (illus. p.406). Pompon dahlia. H 1.1m (3½ft), S 60cm (2ft). Bears white flowers, suffused pink, in summer-autumn. Is good for exhibition.

D. 'Moor Place' (illus. p.407). Pompon dahlia. H 1m (3ft), S 60cm (2ft). Leaves are glossy, dark green. Has royal purple flowers in summer-autumn. Is a good exhibition cultivar.

D. 'Nationwide'. Small-flowered decorative dahlia. H 1–1.2m (3–4ft), S 60cm (2ft). Bears yellowish-orange flowers in summer-autumn.

D. 'Noreen' (illus. p.406). Pompon dahlia. H 1m (3ft) S 60cm (2ft). In summer-autumn produces dark pinkish-purple flowers that are good for exhibition.

D. 'Pearl of Heemstede' (illus. p.406). Small-flowered water-lily dahlia. H 1m (3ft), S 45cm (18in). Low-growing, very free-flowering dahlia that produce pale silvery-pink flowers on long, thin stems in summer-autumn.

D. 'Pink Jupiter' (illus. p.407). Giant-flowered semi-cactus dahlia. H 1.3m (4½ft), S 60cm (2ft). In summer-autumn, produces deep pinkish-mauve flowers. Is good for exhibition.

D. 'Pink Shirley Alliance' (illus. p.406). Small-flowered cactus dahlia. H 1.2m (4ft), S 60cm (2ft). Has soft lilac-pink flowers in summer-autumn.

D. 'Pink Symbol' (illus. p.406). Medium-flowered semi-cactus dahlia. H 1–1.2m (3–4ft), S 60cm (2ft). Bears pink flowers in summer-autumn. Is good for exhibition.

D. 'Pontiac' (illus. p.406). Small-flowered cactus dahlia. H 1m (3ft), S 60cm (2ft). Leaves are glossy, dark green. Bears dark pinkish-purple flowers in summer-autumn.

D. 'Porcelain'. Small-flowered water-lily dahlia. H 1m (3ft), S 60cm (2ft). Produces whitish-lilac flowers in summer-autumn. Is useful for exhibition.

D. 'Preston Park' (illus. p.407). Dwarf single dahlia. H 45cm (18in), S 30cm (12in). Bedding plant with nearly black foliage. In summer-autumn, bears bright scarlet flowers, to 78mm (3in) across, with prominent yellow anthers in the centre, on short stems.

D. 'Redskin'. Well-branched, perennial dahlia, grown as an annual. H and S 30cm (12in). Has bronze-green to maroon leaves, divided into oval leaflets. Throughout summer and until autumn frosts, bears daisy-like, double flower heads, in many colours.

D. 'Reginald Keene'. Large-flowered semi-cactus dahlia. H 1.1–1.2m (3½–4ft), S 60cm (2ft). In summer-autumn has orange-flame flowers. Is good for exhibition.

D. 'Rhonda' (illus. p.406). Pompon dahlia. H 1m (3ft), S 60cm (2ft). In summer-autumn produces whitish-lilac flowers that are suitable for exhibition.

D. 'Ruby Wedding'. Miniature-flowered decorative dahlia. H 1m (3ft), S 60cm (2ft). Bears deep purple flowers in summer-autumn. Is suitable for exhibition.

D. 'Scottish Relation'. Small-flowered semi-cactus dahlia. H 1.1m (3½ft), S 60cm (2ft). Bears vivid purple flowers, with cream petal bases, in summer-autumn. Is good for exhibition.

D. 'Shandy' (illus. p.407). Small-flowered semi-cactus dahlia. H 1m (3ft), S 60cm (2ft). Produces pale brown flowers in summer-autumn.

D. 'Sherwood Standard'. Medium-flowered decorative dahlia. H 1.2m (4ft), S 60cm (2ft). Has orange flowers in summer-autumn. Is suitable for exhibition.

D. 'Shirley Alliance' (illus. p.407). Small-flowered cactus dahlia. H 1.3m (4½ft), S 60cm (2ft). In summer-autumn, bears soft orange flowers, with a gold base to each petal. Is good for exhibition.

D. 'Small World' (illus. p.406). Pompon dahlia. H 1m (3ft), S 60cm (2ft). Leaves are glossy, dark green. Has white flowers in summer-autumn. Is suitable for exhibition.

D. 'So Dainty' (illus. p.407). Miniature-flowered semi-cactus dahlia. H 1.1m (3½ft), S 60cm (2ft). Produces bronze-coloured flowers in summer-autumn that are suitable for exhibition.

D. 'Trengrove Jill'. Medium-flowered decorative dahlia. H 1.3m (4½ft), S 60cm (2ft). Deep bronze flowers are held well above the foliage on strong stems in summer-autumn.

D. 'Vicky Crutchfield' (illus. p.406). Small-flowered water-lily dahlia. H 1m (3ft), S 60cm (2ft). Bears pink flowers in summer-autumn. Is suitable for exhibition.

D. 'Wanda's Capella' (illus. p.407). Giant-flowered decorative dahlia. H 1.2m (4ft), S 60cm (2ft). Has bright yellow flowers in summer-autumn. Is good for exhibition.

D. 'Whale's Rhonda' (illus. p.407). Pompon dahlia. H 1m (3ft), S 60cm (2ft). Leaves are glossy, very dark green. In summer-autumn has purple flowers that are good for exhibition.

D. 'White Alva's' (illus. p.406). Giant-flowered decorative dahlia. H 1.2m (4ft), S 60cm (2ft). Produces pure white flowers, held well above the foliage on strong stems, in summer-autumn. Is good for exhibition.

D. 'White Ballet' (illus. p.406). Small-flowered water-lily dahlia. H 1m (3ft), S 60cm (2ft). Produces pure white flowers in summer-autumn.

D. 'White Klankstad' (illus. p.406). Small-flowered cactus dahlia. H 1.1–1.2m (3½–4ft), S 60cm (2ft). Is a sport of *D.* 'Klankstad Kerkrade' with white flowers in summer-autumn.

D. 'White Moonlight'. Medium-flowered semi-cactus dahlia. H 1.2m (4ft), S 60cm (2ft). Produces white flowers in summer-autumn. Is good for exhibition.

D. 'Willo's Violet'. Pompon dahlia. H 1m (3ft), S 60cm (2ft). Has glossy, dark green leaves and bears violet-purple flowers in summer-autumn. Is suitable for exhibition.

D. 'Wootton Cupid' (illus. p.406). Miniature ball dahlia. H 1.1–1.2m (3½–4ft), S 60cm (2ft). Produces pink flowers in summer-autumn. Is good for exhibition.

D. 'Wootton Impact' (illus. p.407). Medium-flowered semi-cactus dahlia. H 1.2m (4ft), S 60cm (2ft). Has flowers in shades of bronze, held well above the foliage on strong stems, in summer-autumn. Is good for exhibition.
D. 'Yellow Hammer' (illus. p.407). Dwarf, single dahlia. H 45cm (18in), S 30cm (12in). Has rich yellow flowers, 78mm (3in) across, in summer-autumn.
D. 'Yelno Firelight' (illus. p.407). Small-flowered water-lily dahlia. H 1.2m (4ft), S 60cm (2ft). In summer-autumn, has red and yellow flowers, with a neat petal formation, held on strong stems.
D. 'Yelno Velvena'. Small-flowered water-lily dahlia. H 1.2m (4ft), S 60cm (2ft). Deep maroon flowers are held on strong stems in summer-autumn.
D. 'Zorro' (illus. p.407). Giant-flowered decorative dahlia. H 1.2m (4ft), S 60cm (2ft). Produces bright blood-red flowers in summer-autumn, that are good for exhibition.

Dahlia, Climbing. See *Hidalgoa*.
Daimio oak. See *Quercus dentata*.
Daiswa polyphylla. See *Paris polyphylla*.
Daisy. See *Bellis*.
　African. See *Arctotis stoechadifolia*; *Dimorphotheca*.
　Barberton. See *Gerbera jamesonii*, illus. p.302.
　Common. See *Bellis perennis*.
　Kingfisher. See *Felicia bergeriana*, illus. p.334.
　Livingstone. See *Dorotheanthus bellidiformis*.
　Michaelmas. See *Aster*.
　Rain. See *Dimorphotheca pluvialis*, illus. p.319.
　Shasta. See *Leucanthemum* x *superbum*.
　Star. See *Lindheimera texana*, illus. p.336.
　Swan River. See *Brachyscome iberidifolia*, illus. p.334.
Daisy bush. See *Olearia*.
Dalmatian iris. See *Iris pallida*.
Dalmatian laburnum. See *Petteria ramentacea*.
Dalmatian toadflax. See *Linaria genistifolia* var. *dalmatica*.
Dame's violet. See *Hesperis matronalis*, illus. p.239.

DANÄE
LILIACEAE/RUSCACEAE

Genus of one species of evergreen shrub, with inconspicuous flowers, grown for its attractive, flattened, leaf-like shoots. Grows in sun or shade and in moist soil. Propagate by seed in autumn or by division from autumn to spring.
D. racemosa (Alexandrian laurel). Evergreen, arching, dense shrub. H and S 1m (3ft). Has slender stems, lance-leaf-like, glossy, bright green shoots and pointed, glossy, bright green 'leaves'. Occasionally bears spherical, red berries.

Dancing-doll orchid. See *Oncidium flexuosum*, illus. p.299.

Dandelion.
　Cape. See *Arctotheca calendula*, illus. p.294.
　Pink. See *Crepis incana*.

DAPHNE
THYMELAEACEAE

Genus of evergreen, semi-evergreen or deciduous shrubs, grown for their usually fragrant, tubular flowers, each with 4 spreading lobes, and, in some species, for their foliage or fruits (seeds are poisonous). Dwarf species and cultivars are good for rock gardens. Most need full sun (although *D. alpina*, *D. arbuscula*, and *D. blagayana* may be grown in semi-shade and *D. laureola* tolerates deep shade) and fertile, well-drained but not over-dry soil. Resents being transplanted. Propagate species by seed when fresh or by semi-ripe cuttings in summer, cultivars by cuttings only. Is susceptible to viruses that cause leaf mottling. All parts, including the seed, are highly toxic if ingested, and contact with the sap may irritate skin.
D. alpina. Deciduous, erect shrub. H 50cm (20in), S 40cm (16in). Leaves are oval, downy, and grey-green. Carries terminal clusters of fragrant, white flowers in late spring. Is suitable for a rock garden. Zone 5.
D. arbuscula illus. p.366.
D. bholua illus. p.150.
D. blagayana illus. p.347.
D. x burkwoodii 'Somerset' illus. p.154. **'Somerset Variegated'** is a semi-evergreen, upright shrub. H 1.5m (5ft), S 1m (3ft). Bears dense clusters of very fragrant, white-throated, pink flowers in late spring, sometimes again in autumn. Narrowly oblong, grey-green leaves are edged with creamy-white or pale yellow. Zone 5.
D. cneorum illus. p.348. **'Eximia'** is an evergreen, prostrate shrub. H 10cm (4in), S to 50cm (20in) or more. Has small, oval, leathery, dark green leaves and, in late spring, terminal clusters of fragrant, white flowers, crimson outside and often pink-flushed within. Zone 2b.
D. collina. Evergreen, domed, compact shrub. H and S 50cm (20in). Oval, dark green leaves densely cover upright branches. Has terminal clusters of small, fragrant, purple-rose flowers in late spring. Is good for a rock garden or shrubbery. Zone 8.
D. genkwa. Deciduous, upright, open shrub. H and S 1.5m (5ft). Oval, dark green leaves are bronze when young. Large, faintly scented, lilac flowers are borne from mid- to late spring. Zone 7.
D. giraldii. Deciduous, upright shrub. H and S 60cm (2ft). Clusters of fragrant, golden-yellow flowers are produced amid oblong, pale blue-green leaves in late spring and early summer and are followed by egg-shaped, red fruits. Zone 5b.
D. jasminea illus. p.364.
D. laureola (Spurge laurel). Evergreen, bushy shrub. H 1m (3ft), S 1.5m (5ft). Has oblong, dark green leaves. Slightly fragrant, pale green flowers are borne from late winter to early spring, followed by spherical, black fruits. Zone 8. subsp. *philippi* illus. p.156.
D. mezereum illus. p.174. f. *alba* is a

deciduous, upright to spreading shrub. H and S 1.2m (4ft). Bears very fragrant, white or creamy-white flowers that clothe bare stems in late winter and early spring. Has spherical, yellow fruits. Leaves are oblong and dull grey-green. Zone 5.
D. odora. Evergreen, bushy shrub. H and S 1.5m (5ft). Has oval, glossy, dark green leaves and, from mid-winter to early spring, very fragrant, deep purplish-pink-and-white flowers. Zone 6. **'Aureomarginata'** illus. p.174.
D. petraea 'Grandiflora' illus. p.366.
D. retusa illus. p.155.
D. tangutica. Evergreen, bushy shrub with stout shoots. H and S 1m (3ft). Narrowly oval, leathery leaves are dark green. Bears clusters of fragrant, white-flushed, purple-pink flowers in mid- to late spring. Zone 5.

DAPHNIPHYLLUM
DAPHNIPHYLLACEAE

Genus of evergreen trees and shrubs, grown for their habit and foliage. Male and female flowers are borne on separate plants. Needs a sheltered position in sun or semi-shade and deep, fertile, well-drained but not too dry soil. Propagate by semi-ripe cuttings in summer.
D. himalense subsp. *macropodum*. See *D. macropodum*.
D. macropodum, syn. *D. himalense* subsp. *macropodum*, illus. p.117.

Darling pea. See *Swainsona galegifolia*.

DARMERA,
syn. PELTIPHYLLUM
Umbrella plant
SAXIFRAGACEAE

Genus of one species of perennial, grown for its unusual foliage. Makes fine marginal water plants. Grows in sun or shade and requires moist soil. Propagate by division in spring or by seed in autumn or spring.
D. peltata illus. p.238.

Darwin's barberry. See *Berberis darwinii*, p.117.

DASYLIRION
Bear grass
DRACAENACEAE

Genus of evergreen, palm-like perennials, grown for their foliage and flowers. Male and female flowers are produced on separate plants. Tender, min. 10°C (50°F). Requires well-drained soil and a sunny position. Water freely when in full growth, sparingly at other times. Propagate by seed in spring.
D. texanum. Evergreen, palm-like perennial with a 75cm (30in) high trunk. H over 1m (3ft), S 3m (10ft). Has a rosette of narrow, drooping, green leaves, each 60–90cm (2–3ft) long, with yellowish prickles along margins. Stems, 5m (15ft) long, emerge from centre of plant carrying dense, narrow panicles of small,

bell-shaped, whitish flowers in summer. Dry, 3-winged fruits appear in autumn.

Date plum. See *Diospyros lotus*.
Datura. Reclassified as *Brugmansia*.

DAVALLIA
DAVALLIACEAE

Genus of evergreen or semi-evergreen, often epiphytic ferns, best suited to growing in pots and hanging baskets. Tender, min. 5°C (41°F). Requires semi-shade and very fibrous, moist, peaty soil. Remove fading fronds regularly. Propagate by division in spring or summer or by spores in summer.
D. canariensis (Hare's-foot fern). Semi-evergreen fern. H and S 30cm (12in). Broadly lance-shaped, leathery, mid-green fronds, with numerous triangular pinnae, arise from a scaly, brown rootstock.
D. mariesii (Squirrel's-foot fern). Evergreen fern. H 15cm (6in), S 23cm (9in). Broadly triangular, delicately divided, leathery, mid-green fronds arise from a creeping, scaly, brown rootstock.

DAVIDIA
CORNACEAE/DAVIDIACEAE

Genus of one species of deciduous, spring- and summer-flowering tree, grown for its habit and showy, white bracts surrounding insignificant flower heads. Needs shelter from strong winds. Requires sun or semi-shade and fertile, well-drained but preferably moist soil. Propagate by semi-ripe cuttings in spring or by seed when ripe in autumn.
D. involucrata illus. p.77.

David's peach. See *Prunus davidiana*.
David's pine. See *Pinus armandii*.
Dawn flower, Blue. See *Ipomoea indica*.
Dawn redwood. See *Metasequoia glyptostroboides*, illus. p.102.
Day flower. See *Commelina coelestis*, illus. p.334.
Daylily. See *Hemerocallis*.
　Fulvous. See *Hemerocallis fulva*.
　Grass-leaved. See *Hemerocallis minor*.
　Tawny. See *Hemerocallis fulva*.
Deadnettle. See *Lamium*.

DECAISNEA
LARDIZABALACEAE

Genus of deciduous, summer-flowering shrubs, grown for their foliage, flowers and sausage-shaped fruits. Requires a sheltered, sunny situation and fertile soil that is not too dry. Propagate by seed in autumn.
D. fargesii illus. p.122.

DECUMARIA
HYDRANGEACEAE

Genus of evergreen or deciduous, woody-stemmed, root climbers. Prefers sun and loamy, well-drained soil that does not dry out. Prune, if necessary, after flowering. Propagate by stem cuttings in late summer or early autumn.

D. sinensis illus. illus. p.204.

DEINANTHE

HYDRANGEACEAE

Genus of slow-growing perennials with creeping, underground rootstocks. Is useful for rock gardens and peat beds. Needs shaded, moist soil. Propagate by division in spring or by seed when fresh.

D. bifida. Slow-growing, mound-forming perennial. H 20cm (8in), S 10–20cm (4–8in). Nodding, star-shaped, white flowers are produced in summer amid rounded, crinkled leaves with 2-lobed, lacerated tips.

D. caerulea. Slow-growing, mound-forming perennial. H 20cm (8in), S to 15cm (6in). Stems, each carrying a cluster of nodding, bowl-shaped, pale violet-blue flowers, rise above 3–4 oval, toothed leaves in summer.

Delairea odorata. See *Senecio mikanioides*.
Delavay's fir. See *Abies delavayi*.

DELOSPERMA

AIZOACEAE

Genus of densely branched, trailing, perennial, sometimes shrubby succulents, some with tuberous roots. Tender, min. 5°C (41°F). Requires full sun and very well-drained soil. Propagate by seed or stem cuttings in spring or summer.

D. cooperi. Spreading, mat-forming, perennial succulent. H 5cm (2in), S indefinite. Has cylindrical, fleshy, light green leaves, 5cm (2in) long, and, in mid- to late summer, solitary, daisy-like, magenta flowers.

DELPHINIUM

RANUNCULACEAE

Genus of perennials, biennials, and annuals, grown for their spikes of irregularly cup-shaped, sometimes hooded, spurred flowers. Needs an open, sunny position and fertile or rich, well-drained soil. Tall cultivars need staking and ample feeding and watering in spring and early summer. In spring remove thin growths from well-established plants, leaving 5–7 strong shoots. If flower spikes are removed after they fade, a second flush may be produced in late summer, provided plants are fed and watered well. Propagate species by seed in autumn or spring; Belladonna Group cultivars by division or basal cuttings of young shoots in spring; Elatum Group cultivars by cuttings only. All parts may cause severe discomfort if ingested, and contact with foliage may irritate skin. See also feature panel, p.230.

For ease of reference, delphinium cultivars have been grouped as follows:

Belladonna Group. Upright, branched perennials with palmately lobed leaves. H 1–1.2m (3–4ft), S to 45cm (18in).

Wiry stems bear loose, branched spikes, 30cm (12in) long, of elf cap-shaped, single flowers, 2cm (¾in) or more across, with spurs up to 3cm (1¼in) long, in early and late summer.
Elatum Group. Erect perennials with large, palmate leaves. H 1.5–2m (5–6ft), S 60–90cm (24–36in). In summer, produce closely packed spikes, 40cm–1.2m (16in–4ft) long, of regularly spaced, semi-double, rarely fully double flowers, 8–10cm (3–4in) wide, in a range of colours from white to blue and purple, sometimes red-pink, usually with contrasting eyes.
Pacific Hybrids. Similar to Elatum Group cultivars, but grown as annuals or biennials. They produce short-lived, large, semi-double flowers on spikes in early and mid-summer.

D. 'Balkleid'. Belladonna Group perennial. H 1–1.2m (3–4ft). Bears spikes of widely spaced, mid-blue flowers on spikes 30cm (12in) long.
D. 'Blue Dawn' (illus. p.230). Elatum Group perennial. H 2–2.2m (6–7ft). Bears pinkish-purple-flushed, pale blue flowers, with dark brown eyes, on spikes to 1.2m (4ft) long.
D. 'Blue Nile' (illus. p.230). Elatum Group perennial. H 1.5–1.7m (5–5½ft). Has rich blue flowers, with lightly blue-streaked, white eyes, on spikes to 68cm (27in) long.
D. 'Bruce' (illus. p.230). Elatum Group perennial. H 1.7–2.2m (5½–7ft). Bears deep violet-purple flowers, silver-flushed towards centres and with grey-brown eyes, on spikes to 1.2m (4ft) long.
D. brunonianum. Upright perennial. H and S to 20cm (8in). Hairy stems bear rounded, 3- or 5-lobed leaves. In early summer, flower stems each produce a spike, to 15cm (6in) long, of hooded, single, pale blue to purple flowers, 4cm (1½in) wide, with short, black spurs. Is good for a rock garden.
D. 'Butterball' (illus. p.230). Elatum Group perennial. H 1.5–1.7m (5–5½ft). Produces cream-eyed, white flowers, overlaid with very pale greenish-yellow, on spikes to 50cm (20in) long.
D. cardinale. Short-lived, upright perennial. H 1–2m (3–6ft), S 60cm (2ft). In summer has single, scarlet flowers, 4cm (1½in) wide, with yellow eyes, on spikes, 30–45cm (12–18in) long, above palmate, finely divided leaves.
D. 'Chelsea Star' (illus. p.230). Elatum Group perennial. H 2m (6ft). Has rich deep violet flowers, with white eyes, on spikes to 1.1m (3½ft) long.
D. chinense. See *D. grandiflorum*.
D. 'Cliveden Beauty' (illus. p.230). Belladonna Group perennial. H 1–1.2m (3–4ft). Produces sky-blue flowers on spikes 30cm (12in) long.
D. consolida. See *Consolida ajacis*.
D. 'Emily Hawkins' (illus. p.230). Elatum Group perennial. H 2–2.2m (6–7ft). Has lilac-flushed, pale blue flowers, with fawn eyes, on spikes to 80cm (32in) long.
D. 'Fanfare' (illus. p.230). Elatum Group perennial. H 2–2.2m (6–7ft). Bears pale blue to silvery-mauve flowers, with white-and-violet eyes, on spikes 60–75cm (2–2½ft) long.

D. 'Fenella'. Elatum Group perennial. H 1.1–1.5m (3½–5ft). Bears purple-flushed, gentian-blue flowers, with black eyes, on spikes to 1m (3ft) long.
D. 'Gillian Dallas' (illus. p.230). Elatum Group perennial. H 2m (6ft). Has spikes, to 80cm (32in) long, of white-eyed, pale lilac flowers, shading to even paler lilac on outer edges.
D. grandiflorum, syn. *D. chinense*. **'Blue Butterfly'** (illus. p.230) is a short-lived, erect perennial, usually grown as an annual. H 45cm (1½ft), S 30cm (1ft). Has palmate, divided leaves. In summer produces loose, branching spikes, to 15cm (6in) long, of single, deep blue flowers, 3.5cm (1½in) wide. Is useful as a bedding plant.
D. 'Langdon's Royal Flush' (illus. p.230). Elatum Group perennial. H 2m (6ft). Has cream-eyed, pinkish-purple flowers on spikes to 85cm (34in) long; upper petals are a darker shade than lower ones.
D. 'Loch Leven' (illus. p.230). Elatum Group perennial. H 1.7m (5½ft). Bears mid-blue flowers, with white eyes, on spikes to 1m (3ft) long.
D. 'Loch Nevis'. Elatum Group perennial. H 2m (6ft). Has mid-blue flowers, with white eyes, on spikes to 1.1m (3½ft) long.
D. 'Lord Butler' (illus. p.230). Elatum Group perennial. H 1.5–1.7m (5–5½ft). Produces mid-blue flowers, lightly flushed with pale lilac and with blue-marked, white eyes, on spikes to 75cm (30in) long.
D. 'Mighty Atom' (illus. p.230). Elatum Group perennial. H 1.5–2m (5–6ft). Has mid-violet flowers, with violet-marked, yellowish-brown eyes, on spikes to 75cm (2½ft) long.
D. nudicaule illus. p.355.
D. 'Olive Poppleton' (illus. p.230). Elatum Group perennial. H 2–2.5m (6–8ft). Produces white flowers, with fawn eyes, on spikes to 1m (3ft) long.
D. Pacific Hybrids. Perennials, often grown as annuals and available in single colours and as a mixture. Seedlings may not come true. Flowers are produced in spikes, 45cm–1m (1½–3ft) long.
D. 'Sandpiper' (illus. p.230). Elatum Group perennial. H 1–1.35m (3–4½ft). Has white flowers, with creamy-brown eyes, on spikes to 75cm (2½ft) long.
D. 'Spindrift' (illus. p.230). Elatum Group perennial. H 1.7–2m (5½–6ft). Produces spikes, to 1m (3ft) long, of pinkish-purple flowers, overlaid with pale blue and with creamy-white eyes; towards centres, the pinkish-purple becomes paler and the blue darker. Flower colour varies with different types of soil; on acid soil, flowers are greenish.
D. 'Strawberry Fair' (illus. p.230). Elatum Group perennial. H 1.7m (5½ft). Has white-eyed, mulberry-pink flowers on spikes to 78cm (31in) long.
D. 'Sungleam' (illus. p.230). Elatum Group perennial. H 1.7–2m (5½–6ft). Produces spikes, 40–75cm (16–30in) long, of white flowers, overlaid with pale yellow and with ½ yellow eyes.
D. tatsienense. Short-lived, upright perennial. H 30cm (12in),

S 5–10cm (2–4in). Loose spikes, to 15cm (6in) long, of small-spurred, single, bright blue flowers, 2.5cm (1in) long, are borne in summer. Leaves are rounded to oval and deeply cut. Suits a rock garden. Needs gritty soil.
D. 'Völkerfrieden'. Belladonna Group perennial. H 1–1.2m (3–4ft). Produces deep blue flowers on spikes 30cm (12in) long.

Delta maidenhair. See *Adiantum raddianum*.
Dendrobenthamia capitata. See *Cornus capitata*.

DENDROBIUM

See also ORCHIDS.
D. aphyllum, syn. *D. pierardii* (illus. p.296). Deciduous, epiphytic orchid for an intermediate greenhouse. H to 60cm (24in). In early spring produces pairs of soft pink flowers, 4cm (1½in) across and each with a large, cream lip. Has oval leaves, 5–8cm (2–3in) long. Requires semi-shade in summer. Is best grown hanging from a bark slab.
D. chrysotoxum (illus. p.299). Deciduous, epiphytic orchid for an intermediate greenhouse. H 60cm (24in). Trusses of cup-shaped, deep yellow flowers, 2cm (¾in) across and with hairy, red-marked lips, are borne in spring. Oval leaves are 5–8cm (2–3in) long. Provide good light in summer.
D. infundibulum (illus. p.296). Evergreen, epiphytic orchid for a cool greenhouse. H 30cm (12in). In spring, stems each produce up to 6 pure white flowers, 8cm (3in) wide and each with a yellow-marked lip. Has oval leaves, 5–8cm (2–3in) long. Grow in semi-shade in summer.
D. nobile (illus. p.297). Deciduous, epiphytic orchid (often evergreen in cultivation) for a cool greenhouse. H 30cm (12in). Trusses of delicate, rose-pink flowers, 5cm (2in) across and each with a prominent, maroon lip, are borne along stems in spring. Oval leaves are 5–8cm (2–3in) long. Requires semi-shade in summer.
D. pierardii. See *D. aphyllum*.

DENDROCHILUM

See also ORCHIDS.
D. glumaceum (Silver chain). Evergreen, epiphytic orchid for a cool greenhouse. H 10cm (4in). Pendent sprays of fragrant, pointed, orange-lipped, creamy-white flowers, 1cm (½in) long, are produced in autumn. Narrowly oval leaves are 15cm (6in) long. Requires semi-shade in summer.

DENDROMECON

PAPAVERACEAE

Genus of evergreen shrubs, grown for their foliage and showy flowers. Plant against a south- or west-facing wall where hardy. Requires full sun and very well-drained soil. Propagate by softwood cuttings in summer, by seed in autumn or spring or by root cuttings in winter.

D. rigida illus. p.147.

Dentaria enneaphyllos. See
Cardamine enneaphyllos.
Dentaria pentaphyllos. See *Cardamine
pentaphyllos.*
Deodar. See *Cedrus deodara.*
Deptford pink. See *Dianthus armeria.*

DESCHAMPSIA

GRAMINEAE/POACEAE

See also GRASSES, BAMBOOS,
RUSHES and SEDGES.
D. cespitosa (Tufted hair grass).
Evergreen, tuft-forming, perennial grass.
H to 1m (3ft), S 25–30cm (10–12in).
Has dense, narrow, rough-edged, dark
green leaves. In summer produces
dainty, open panicles of minute, pale
brown spikelets that last well into
winter. Tolerates sun or shade.

Desert fan palm. See *Washingtonia
filifera.*
Desert rose. See *Adenium.*

DESFONTAINIA

DESFONTAINIACEAE/LOGANIACEAE

Genus of evergreen shrubs, grown for
their foliage and showy, tubular
flowers. Provide shelter in cold areas.
Needs some shade, particularly in dry
regions, and moist, peaty, preferably
acid soil. Propagate by semi-ripe
cuttings in summer.
D. spinosa illus. p.143.

DESMODIUM

LEGUMINOSAE/PAPILIONACEAE

Genus of perennials and deciduous
shrubs and sub-shrubs, grown for their
flowers. Needs full sun and well-
drained soil. Propagate by softwood
cuttings in late spring or by seed in
autumn. May also be divided in spring.
D. elegans, syn. *D. tiliifolium,* illus.
p.167.
D. tiliifolium. See *D. elegans.*

DEUTZIA

HYDRANGEACEAE

Genus of deciduous shrubs, grown for
their profuse, 5-petalled flowers. Needs
full sun and fertile, well-drained soil.
Plants benefit from regular thinning out
of old shoots after flowering. Propagate
by softwood cuttings in summer.
D. × elegantissima 'Fasciculata'.
Deciduous, upright shrub. H 2m (6ft),
S 1.5m (5ft). From late spring to early
summer produces large clusters of
5-petalled, pale pink flowers. Leaves
are oval, toothed and mid-green.
Zone 7. 'Rosealind' illus. p.162.
D. gracilis illus. p.153.
D. 'Joconde'. Deciduous, upright
shrub. H and S 1.5m (5ft). Bears
5-petalled, white flowers, striped purple
outside, in early summer. Oval, mid-
green leaves are long-pointed. Zone 7.
D. longifolia. Deciduous, arching
shrub. H 2m (6ft), S 3m (10ft). Large
clusters of 5-petalled, deep pink
flowers are produced from early to
mid-summer. Narrowly lance-shaped
leaves are grey-green. Zone 8.
'Veitchii' illus. p.140.

D. × magnifica. Vigorous, deciduous,
upright shrub. H 2.5m (8ft), S 2m (6ft).
Produces dense clusters of 5-petalled,
pure white flowers in early summer.
Leaves are narrowly oval and bright
green. Zone 7. 'Staphyleoides'
illus. p.136.
D. monbeigii illus. p.158.
D. 'Mont Rose' illus. p.161.
D. pulchra. Vigorous, deciduous,
upright shrub. H 2.5m (8ft), S 2m (6ft).
Has peeling, orange-brown bark and
lance-shaped, dark green leaves.
Slender, pendulous panicles of
5-petalled, pink-tinged, white
lowers appear in late spring and early
summer. Zone 8.
D. × rosea illus. p.154.
D. scabra illus. p.136. 'Plena' (syn.
D.s. 'Flore Pleno') is a deciduous,
upright shrub. H 3m (10ft), S 2m (6ft).
Narrowly oval, dark green leaves set
off dense, upright clusters of double,
white flowers, purplish-pink outside,
from early to mid-summer. Zone 7.
D. setchuenensis var. *corymbiflora.*
Deciduous, upright shrub with peeling,
pale brown bark when mature. H 2m
(6ft), S 1.5m (5ft). Small, 5-petalled,
white flowers are borne in broad
clusters in early and mid-summer.
Produces lance-shaped, long-pointed,
grey-green leaves. Zone 7.

Devil's club. See *Oplopanax horridus.*
Devil's fig. See *Argemone mexicana,*
illus. p.335.

DIANELLA

Flax lily

LILIACEAE/PHORMIACEAE

Genus of evergreen, summer-flowering
perennials. Is suitable outdoors only in
mild areas and elsewhere requires a
cold greenhouse or frame. Needs sun
and well-drained, neutral to acid
soil. Propagate by division or seed
in spring.
D. caerulea. Evergreen, tuft-forming
perennial. H 75cm (30in), S 30cm
(12in). In summer has panicles of
small, star-shaped, blue flowers,
above grass-like leaves, followed by
blue berries.
D. tasmanica illus. p.253.

DIANTHUS

Carnation, Pink

CARYOPHYLLACEAE

Genus of evergreen or semi-evergreen,
mainly summer-flowering perennials,
annuals and biennials, grown for their
mass of flowers, often scented, some
of which are excellent for cutting.
Carnations and pinks (see below)
are excellent for cut flowers and
border decoration, the biennial
D. barbatus (Sweet William) is suitable
for bedding and smaller, tuft-forming
species and cultivars are good for rock
gardens. Needs an open, sunny position
and well-drained, slightly alkaline soil,
except for *D. pavonius,* which prefers
acid soil. Dead-heading of repeat-
flowering types is beneficial. Tall forms
of carnations and pinks have a loose
habit and need staking. Propagate
border carnations by layering in late

summer, other named forms by
softwood cuttings in early to
mid-summer and species by seed at any
time. Is susceptible to rust, spider mite
and virus infection through aphids, but
many cultivars are available from
virus-free stock.
Carnations and pinks have narrowly
lance-shaped, silvery- or grey-green
leaves, scattered up flower stems,
which may coil outwards on carnations.
They are divided into the following
groups, all with self-coloured and
bicoloured cultivars. See also feature
panel, pp.280–81.

Carnations
Border carnations are annuals or
evergreen perennials that flower
prolifically once in mid-summer and
are good for border decoration and
cutting. Each stem bears 5 or more
often scented, semi-double or double
flowers, to 8cm (3in) across; picotee
forms (with petals outlined in a darker
colour) are available. H 75cm–1.1m
(2½–3½ft), S to 30cm (1ft).
Perpetual-flowering carnations are
evergreen perennials that flower year-
round if grown in a greenhouse, but
more prolifically in summer. They are
normally grown for cut flowers: flower
stems should be disbudded, leaving
one terminal bud per stem. Fully
double flowers, to 10cm (4in) across,
are usually unscented and are often
flecked or streaked. H 1–1.5m (3–5ft),
S 30cm (1ft) or more.
    Spray forms are not disbudded so
have 5 or more flowers per stem, each
5–6cm (2–2½in) across. H 60cm–1m
(2–3ft), S to 30cm (1ft).
Malmaison carnations are evergreen
perennials, derived from *D.* 'Souvenir
de la Malmaison'. Grown under glass,
they bear large, double, scented flowers
sporadically during the year. The flowers
can reach up to 13cm (5in) across.
They are mostly self-coloured, and
tend to split their calyces. H 50–70cm
(20–28in), S 40cm (16in).

Pinks
Evergreen, clump-forming perennials,
grown for border decoration and cutting,
that in summer produce a succession of
basal shoots, each bearing 4–6 fragrant,
single to fully double flowers, 3.5–6cm
(1½–2½in) across. H 30–45cm
(12–18in), S 23–30cm (9–12in)
or more.
Old-fashioned pinks have a low,
spreading habit and produce masses of
flowers in one flowering period in mid-
summer. Mule types (a border carnation
crossed with a Sweet William) and
laced types (in which the central colour
extends as a loop around each petal)
are available.
Modern pinks, obtained by crossing
an old-fashioned pink with a perpetual-
flowering carnation, are more vigorous
than old-fashioned pinks, and are
repeat-flowering with two or three
main flushes of flowers in summer.
Alpine pinks are evergreen species and
cultivars forming neat mat or cushion
plants. They will grow at the edge of a
border or in a rock garden, trough or
alpine house. In early summer, they
bear single, semi-double or double,

often scented flowers. Foliage is
grey-green. H 8–10cm (3–4in),
S 20cm (8in).

D. 'A.J. MacSelf'. See *D.* 'Dad's
Favourite'.
D. 'Albisola' (illus. p.281). Perpetual-
flowering carnation. Fully double
flowers are clear tangerine-orange.
D. 'Aldridge Yellow' (illus. p.281).
Border carnation. Semi-double flowers
are clear yellow.
D. 'Alice' (illus. p.280). Modern
pink. Has clove-scented, semi-double,
ivory-white flowers, each with a bold,
crimson eye.
D. alpinus illus. p.378.
D. 'Annabelle' illus. p.379.
D. 'Arctic'. Perpetual-flowering, spray
carnation. Fully double flowers are
white with pink flecks.
D. armeria (Deptford pink). Evergreen,
tuft-forming perennial, sometimes
grown as an annual. H 30cm (12in),
S 45cm (18in). Has narrowly lance-
shaped, dark green leaves. In summer,
tall stems each carry small, 5-petalled,
cerise-pink flowers in small bunches.
Is good for a rock garden or bank.
D. 'Astor' (illus. p.281).
Perpetual-flowering carnation.
Produces fully double, scarlet flowers;
is one of the few scented,
perpetual-flowering cultivars.
D. barbatus (Sweet William).
Roundabout Series (dwarf) illus. p.326.
D. 'Becky Robinson' (illus. p.280).
Modern pink. Bears clove-scented,
fully double, rose-pink flowers with
ruby-red lacing. Is good for exhibition.
D. 'Bombardier'. Evergreen, tuft-
forming perennial. H and S 10cm (4in).
Has a basal tuft of linear, grey-green
leaves and, in summer, small,
double, scarlet flowers. Is good for
a rock garden.
D. 'Bookham Fancy' (illus. p.281).
Border carnation. Produces bright
yellow flowers, edged and flecked
carmine-purple, on short, stiff stems.
D. 'Bookham Perfume' (illus. p.281).
Perennial border carnation. Has
scented, semi-double, crimson flowers.
D. 'Bovey Belle' (illus. p.281). Modern
pink. Has clove-scented,
fully double, bright purple flowers
that are excellent for cutting.
D. 'Brympton Red'. Old-fashioned
pink. Flowers are single, bright crimson
with deeper shading.
D. caesius. See *D. gratianopolitanus.*
D. carthusianorum illus. p.354.
D. 'Charles Musgrave'. See
D. 'Musgrave's Pink'.
D. chinensis (Indian pink). Slow-
growing, bushy annual. H and
S 15–30cm (6–12in). Lance-shaped
leaves are pale or mid-green.
Tubular, single or double flowers,
2.5cm (1in) or more wide and with
open, spreading petals, in shades
of pink, red or white, are produced
in summer and early autumn. **Baby
Doll Series** illus. p.324; **'Fire Carpet'**
illus. p.327; **Heddewigii Group**,
H 30cm (12in), has flowers in
mixed colours.
D. 'Christine Hough' (illus. p.281).
Perennial border carnation. Semi-
double flowers are apricot, overlaid
and streaked with rose-pink.

D. 'Christopher' (illus. p.281). Modern pink. Produces lightly scented, fully double, bright salmon-red flowers.

D. 'Clara' (illus. p.281). Perpetual-flowering carnation. Fully double flowers are yellow with salmon flecks.

D. 'Constance Finnis'. See D. 'Fair Folly'.

D. 'Cream Sue' (illus. p.281). Perpetual-flowering carnation. Flowers are cream. Is a sport of D. 'Apricot Sue'.

D. 'Crompton Princess' (illus. p.281). Perpetual-flowering carnation. Flowers are pure white.

D. 'Dad's Favourite', syn. D. 'A.J. MacSelf' (illus. p.280). Old-fashioned pink. Bears scented, semi-double, white flowers with chocolate-brown lacing.

D. deltoides (Maiden pink). Evergreen, mat-forming, basal-tufted perennial. H 15cm (6in), S 30cm (12in). In summer, small, 5-petalled, white, pink or cerise flowers are borne singly above tiny, lance-shaped leaves. Is good for a rock garden or bank. Trim back after flowering. 'Leuchtfunk' (syn. D.d. 'Flashing Light') illus. p.380.

D. 'Denis'. Modern pink. Strongly clove-scented, fully double, magenta flowers are freely produced.

D. 'Doris' (illus. p.280). Modern pink. Has compact growth and an abundance of fragrant, semi-double, pale pink flowers, each with a salmon-red ring towards base of flower. Is one of the most widely grown cultivars and provides excellent flowers for cutting.

D. 'Duchess of Westminster' (illus. p.281). Vigorous Malmaison carnation. Produces salmon-pink flowers with stronger calyces than most Malmaison carnations.

D. 'Edenside'. Perennial border carnation. Semi-double flowers are clear white.

D. 'Emile Paré' (illus. p.280). Old-fashioned, mule pink. Has clusters of semi-double, salmon-pink flowers and, unusually for a pink, mid-green foliage.

D. 'Eva Humphries' (illus. p.280). Perennial border carnation. Has fragrant, semi-double flowers with white petals outlined in purple.

D. 'Fair Folly', syn. D. 'Constance Finnis' (illus. p.280). Modern pink. Flowers are single and of variable colour, usually dusky-pink to dusky-purple with 2 white splashes on each petal.

D. 'Forest Treasure' (illus. p.280). Perennial border carnation. Has double, white flowers with reddish-purple splashes on each petal.

D. 'Freckles'. Modern pink. A compact cultivar, it has fully double flowers that are red-speckled and dusky-pink.

D. 'Golden Cross' (illus. p.281). Border carnation. Produces bright yellow flowers on short, stiff stems.

D. 'Gran's Favourite' (illus. p.280). Old-fashioned pink. Bears fragrant, semi-double, white flowers with deep raspberry lacing.

D. gratianopolitanus, syn. D. caesius, illus. p.377.

D. 'Green Eyes'. See D. 'Musgrave's Pink'.

D. haematocalyx. Evergreen, tuft-forming perennial. H 12cm (5in),

S 10cm (4in). Leaves are lance-shaped and usually glaucous. Bears 5-petalled, toothed, beige-backed, deep pink flowers on slender stems in summer. Suits a rock garden or scree.

D. 'Happiness' (illus. p.281). Perennial border carnation. Semi-double flowers are yellow, striped scarlet-orange.

D. 'Haytor', syn. D. 'Haytor White' (illus. p.280). Modern pink. Fully double, white flowers, borne on strong stems, have a good scent. Is widely grown, especially to provide cut flowers.

D. 'Haytor White'. See D. 'Haytor'.

D. 'Hidcote'. Evergreen, tufted, compact perennial. H and S 10cm (4in). Bears a basal tuft of linear, spiky, grey-green leaves and, in summer, double, red flowers. Suits a rock garden.

D. 'Houndspool Ruby', syn. D. 'Ruby', D. 'Ruby Doris' (illus. p.281). Modern pink. Is a sport of D. 'Doris' with strongly scented, ruby-pink flowers that each have a deeper eye.

D. 'Ibiza'. Perpetual-flowering, spray carnation. Fully double flowers are shell-pink.

D. 'Iceberg'. Modern pink. Fragrant flowers are semi-double and pure white. Has a somewhat looser habit than D. 'Haytor'.

D. 'Joy' (illus. p.281). Modern pink. Bears semi-double, pink flowers that are strongly scented and good for cutting.

D. 'Kobusa'. See D. PIERROT.

D. 'La Bourbille'. See D. 'La Bourboule'.

D. 'La Bourboule', syn. D. 'La Bourbille', illus. p.378.

D. 'Laced Monarch' (illus. p.281). Modern pink. Double flowers are pink, laced with maroon-red.

D. 'Laced Prudence'. See D. 'Prudence'.

D. 'Lavender Clove' (illus. p.281). Vigorous border carnation. Bears lavender-grey flowers on long stems.

D. 'Little Jock' illus. p.377.

D. 'London Brocade' (illus. p.280). Modern pink. Has clove-scented, crimson-laced, pink flowers.

D. 'London Delight'. Old-fashioned pink. Fragrant flowers are semi-double and lavender, laced with purple.

D. 'Manon'. Perpetual-flowering carnation. Is one of the best deep pink cultivars with fully double flowers.

D. 'Mars'. Evergreen, tuft-forming perennial. H and S 10cm (4in). Has small, double, cherry-red flowers in summer. Bears a basal tuft of linear, grey-green leaves. Is good in a rock garden.

D. 'Master Stuart'. Perennial border carnation. Has striking, semi-double flowers that are white with scarlet stripes.

D. microlepis illus. p.378.

D. 'Monica Wyatt' illus. p.281. Modern pink. Very fragrant, fully double flowers are cyclamen-pink, each with a magenta eye. Is very free-flowering and provides excellent cut flowers.

D. monspessulanus. Evergreen, mat-forming perennial. H 30cm (12in), S 10–15cm (4–6in). In summer, masses

of strongly fragrant, 5-petalled, deeply fringed, pale lavender flowers rise on slender stems above short tufts of fine, grass-like leaves. Is good for a rock garden. Needs gritty soil.

D. 'Mrs Sinkins' (illus. p.280). Old-fashioned pink. Flowers are heavily scented, fringed, fully double and white.

D. 'Murcia'. Perpetual-flowering carnation. Has fully double, deep golden-yellow flowers.

D. 'Musgrave's Pink', syn. D. 'Charles Musgrave', D. 'Green Eyes' (illus. p.280). Old-fashioned pink. An old cultivar, it bears single, white flowers with green eyes.

D. myrtinervius illus. p.378.

D. neglectus. See D. pavonius.

D. 'Nina' (illus. p.281). Perpetual-flowering carnation. Is one of the best crimson cultivars. Fully double flowers have smooth-edged petals.

D. 'Nives' (illus. p.280). Perpetual-flowering carnation. Fully double flowers are clear white and are borne on short stems.

D. pavonius, syn. D. neglectus, illus. p.375.

D. PIERROT ('Kobusa') (illus. p.280). Perpetual-flowering carnation. Bears fully double, light rose-lavender flowers with purple-edged petals.

D. 'Pike's Pink' illus. p.378.

D. 'Pink Calypso'. See D. 'Truly Yours'.

D. 'Pink Jewel' (illus. p.281). Alpine pink. Has strongly scented, semi-double, pink flowers.

D. 'Prudence', syn. D. 'Laced Prudence' (illus. p.280). Old-fashioned pink. Fragrant flowers are semi-double and pinkish-white with purple lacing. Has a spreading habit.

D. 'Raggio di Sole' (illus. p.281). Perpetual-flowering carnation. Fully double flowers are bright orange.

D. 'Red Barrow'. Perpetual-flowering, spray carnation. Fully double, bright scarlet flowers are borne in abundance.

D. 'Ruby'. See D. 'Houndspool Ruby'.

D. 'Ruby Doris'. See D. 'Houndspool Ruby'.

D. 'Sam Barlow'. Old-fashioned pink. Bears very fragrant, frilly, fully double, white flowers with chocolate-brown centres.

D. 'Show Ideal'. Modern pink. Flat-petalled, semi-double flowers are white with red eyes and are strongly scented. Is excellent for exhibition.

D. 'Sops-in-wine'. Old-fashioned pink. Bears fragrant, single, maroon flowers with white markings.

D. superbus. Evergreen, mat-forming perennial. H to 20cm (8in), S 15cm (6in). Has narrowly lance-shaped, pale green leaves. In summer, slender stems bear very fragrant, 5-petalled, deeply fringed, pink flowers with darker centres. Suits a rock garden.

D. 'Tigré'. Perpetual-flowering carnation. Has fully double, yellow flowers with a uniform, pinkish-purple stripe and edging to each petal.

D. 'Tony'. Perpetual-flowering, spray carnation. Fully double flowers are yellow with red stripes.

D. 'Truly Yours', syn. D. 'Pink Calypso' (illus. p.280). Perpetual-flowering carnation. Fully double flowers are a good pink.

D. 'Valda Wyatt'. Modern pink. Flowers are very fragrant, fully double and rose-lavender.

D. 'Valencia' (illus. p.281). Perpetual-flowering carnation. Has fully double, golden-orange flowers.

D. 'White Ladies' (illus. p.280). Old-fashioned pink. Bears very fragrant, fully double, white flowers with greenish centres.

D. 'Widecombe Fair'. Modern pink. Semi-double flowers, borne on strong stems, are of unusual colouring – peach-apricot, opening to blush-pink.

DIAPENSIA

DIAPENSIACEAE

Genus of evergreen, spreading sub-shrubs, suitable for rock gardens and troughs. Needs partial shade and peaty, sandy, acid soil. Is very difficult to grow in hot, dry climates at low altitudes. Propagate by seed in spring or by semi-ripe cuttings in summer.

D. lapponica. Evergreen, spreading sub-shrub. H and S 7cm (3in). Has tufts of small, rounded, leathery leaves. Carries solitary tiny, bowl-shaped, white flowers in early summer. Zone 1.

DIASCIA

SCROPHULARIACEAE

Genus of summer- and autumn-flowering annuals and perennials, some of which are semi-evergreen, grown for their tubular, pink flowers. Is suitable for banks and borders. Needs sun and humus-rich, well-drained soil that is not too dry. Cut back old stems in spring. Propagate by softwood cuttings in late spring, by semi-ripe cuttings in summer or by seed in autumn.

D. barberae 'Ruby Field'. Mat-forming perennial. H 8cm (3in), S 15cm (6in). Heart-shaped, pale green leaves clothe short, wiry stems. Produces tubular, wide-lipped, salmon-pink flowers throughout summer.

D. 'Blackthorn Apricot' illus. p.278.

D. cordata of gardens illus. p.353.

D. rigescens illus. p.353.

D. vigilis. Prostrate perennial. H 30–40cm (12–16in), S 60cm (24in). Leaves are small, rounded, toothed and pale green. Upright branchlets carry loose spikes of flattish, outward-facing, pale pink flowers in summer.

DICENTRA

PAPAVERACEAE

Genus of perennials, grown for their elegant sprays of pendent flowers. Most do best in semi-shade and humus-rich, moist but well-drained soil. Propagate by division when dormant in late winter, species also by seed in autumn. Contact with the foliage may aggravate skin allergies.

D. 'Adrian Bloom'. Spreading, tuft-forming perennial. H 45cm (18in), S 30cm (12in). Produces sprays of pendent, heart-shaped, rich carmine-pink flowers above oval, grey-green leaves.

D. cucullaria illus. p.362.

D. eximia of gardens. See D. formosa.

D. formosa, syn. D. eximia of gardens. Spreading, tufted perennial. H 45cm (18in), S 30cm (12in). In spring-summer

bears slender, arching sprays of pendent, heart-shaped, pink or dull red flowers above oval, finely cut, grey-green leaves.
D. peregrina. Tuft-forming perennial. H 8cm (3in), S to 5cm (2in). Locket-shaped, pink flowers appear in spring-summer above fern-like, blue-green leaves. Needs gritty soil. Is suitable for an alpine house.
D. spectabilis illus. p.245.
f. **alba** illus. p.239.
D. 'Spring Morning' illus. p.278.
D. 'Stuart Boothman' illus. p.278.

DICHELOSTEMMA

ALLIACEAE/LILIACEAE

Genus of summer-flowering bulbs, grown for their dense flower heads on leafless stems. Is related to *Brodiaea* and is similar to *Allium* in appearance. Where hardy, grow in a sheltered position. Needs a sunny site and well-drained soil. Water freely in spring, but dry out after flowering. Propagate by seed in autumn or spring or by offsets in autumn before growth commences.
D. congestum, syn. *Brodiaea congesta*, illus. p.402.
D. ida-maia, syn. *Brodiaea ida-maia*. Early summer-flowering bulb. H to 1m (3ft), S 8–10cm (3–4in). Long, narrow leaves are semi-erect and basal. Leafless stem carries a dense head of 2–2.5cm (¾–1in) long flowers, each with a red tube and 6 green petals.
D. pulchellum, syn. *Brodiaea capitata, B. pulchella*. Early summer-flowering bulb. H 30–60cm (12–24in), S 8–10cm (3–4in). Long, narrow leaves are semi-erect and basal. Leafless stem produces a dense head of narrowly funnel-shaped, pale to deep violet flowers, 1–2cm (½–¾in) long, with violet bracts.

DICHORISANDRA

COMMELINACEAE

Genus of erect, clump-forming, evergreen perennials, grown for their ornamental foliage. Tender, min. 15–20°C (59–68°F). Prefers fertile, moist but well-drained soil, humid conditions and partial shade. Propagate by division in spring or by stem cuttings in summer.
D. reginae illus. p.252.

DICKSONIA

DICKSONIACEAE

Genus of evergreen or semi-evergreen, tree-like ferns that resemble palms and that are sometimes used to provide height in fern plantings. Tender, min. 5°C (41°F). Needs semi-shade and humus-rich, moist soil. Remove faded fronds regularly. Propagate by spores in summer.
D. antarctica illus. p.310.
D. fibrosa. Evergreen, tree-like fern (deciduous in cold climates). H to 6m (20ft), S to 4m (12ft). Stout trunks are crowned by a rosette of spreading, divided, lance-shaped, dark green fronds, to 2m (6ft) long.
D. squarrosa. Evergreen, tree-like fern (deciduous in cold climates). H to 6m (20ft), S to 4m (12ft). Slender trunks are crowned by a rosette of spreading, divided, lance-shaped, mid-green

fronds, to 2m (6ft) long, with blackish stalks and midribs.

Dickson's golden elm. See *Ulmus minor* 'Dicksonii', illus. p.81.

DICTAMNUS

RUTACEAE

Genus of summer-flowering perennials. Requires full sun and fertile, well-drained soil. Resents disturbance. Propagate by seed sown in late summer when fresh. The foliage, roots and seeds of *D. albus* may cause mild stomach upset if ingested, and contact with the foliage may cause photodermatitis.
D. albus, syn. *D. fraxinella*, illus. p.240. var. **purpureus** illus. p.243.
D. fraxinella. See *D. albus*.

Didiscus coeruleus. See *Trachymene coerulea*.

DIEFFENBACHIA

Dumb cane, Leopard lily

ARACEAE

Genus of evergreen, tufted perennials, grown for their foliage. Tender, min. 15°C (59°F). Grow in fertile, well-drained soil and in partial shade. Propagate in spring or summer by stem cuttings or pieces of leafless stem placed horizontally in compost. Scale insect or spider mite may be troublesome. All parts may cause severe discomfort if ingested, and contact with sap may irritate skin.
D. amoena of gardens. See *D. seguine* 'Amoena'.
D. 'Exotica'. See *D. seguine* 'Exotica'.
D. maculata 'Exotica'. See *D. seguine* 'Exotica'. **'Rudolph Roehrs'** see *D. seguine* 'Rudolph Roehrs'.
D. 'Memoria'. See *D. seguine* 'Memoria Corsii'.
D. seguine. Evergreen, tufted perennial. H and S 1m (3ft) or more. Broadly lance-shaped leaves, to 45cm (18in) long, are glossy and dark green. Insignificant, tiny, greenish-white flowers, clustered on the spadix, are surrounded by a narrow, leaf-like spathe that appears intermittently. **'Amoena'** (syn *D. amoena* of gardens) is robust, H to 2m (6ft), with creamy-white bars along lateral veins on the leaves. **'Exotica'** (syn. *D. 'Exotica', D. maculata* 'Exotica') illus. p.264. **'Memoria Corsii'** (syn. *D. 'Memoria'*) has grey-green leaves, marked dark green and spotted white. **'Rudolph Roehrs'** (syn. *D. maculata* 'Rudolph Roehrs', *D.s.* 'Roehrs') illus. p.267.

DIERAMA

Angel's fishing rod, Wandflower

IRIDACEAE

Genus of evergreen, clump-forming, summer-flowering corms with pendent, funnel- or bell-shaped flowers on long, arching, wiry stems. Flourishes near pools. Prefers a warm, sheltered, sunny site and well-drained soil that should be kept moist in summer when in growth. Dies down

partially in winter. Propagate by division of corms in spring or by seed in autumn or spring. Resents disturbance, and divisions take a year or more to settle and start flowering again.
D. 'Blackbird'. Evergreen, upright perennial. H 1.5m (5ft), S 30cm (1ft). Produces cascades of nodding, funnel-shaped, violet-mauve flowers on wiry, pendulous stems in summer above grass-like leaves.
D. dracomontanum, syn. *D. pumilum* of gardens. Vigorous, evergreen, upright perennial. H 75cm (30in), S 30cm (12in). In summer freely produces nodding, funnel-shaped flowers, in shades of pink and violet, on wiry stems. Leaves are grass-like.
D. ensifolium. See *D. pendulum.*
D. pendulum, syn. *D. ensifolium*, illus. p.401.
D. pulcherrimum illus. p.400.
D. pumilum of gardens. See *D. dracomontanum.*

DIERVILLA

CAPRIFOLIACEAE

Genus of deciduous, summer-flowering shrubs, grown for their overall appearance. Is similar to *Weigela*. Tolerates partial shade or full light and moderately fertile, well-drained soil. For a more shapely shrub remove 2- and 3-year-old stems in winter or after flowering. Propagate by semi-ripe cuttings in late summer or by hardwood cuttings in autumn.
D. sessilifolia. Deciduous, spreading shrub. H and S 1–1.5m (3–5ft). Narrowly oval, pointed, serrated, green leaves are often copper-tinted when young. Has terminal and lateral clusters of tubular, pale yellow flowers in summer. To treat as an herbaceous perennial, cut back to ground level each spring and apply a mulch and a fertilizer. Zone 6.

DIETES

IRIDACEAE

Genus of evergreen, iris-like, rhizomatous perennials, grown for their attractive flowers in spring or summer. Needs sun or partial shade and humus-rich, well-drained soil that does not dry out excessively. Propagate by seed in autumn or spring or by division in spring (although divisions do not become re-established very readily).
D. bicolor illus. p.402.
D. iridioides, syn. *D. vegeta* of gardens. Evergreen, spring- and summer-flowering, rhizomatous perennial. H to 60cm (2ft), S 30–60cm (1–2ft). Bears sword-shaped, semi-erect, basal leaves in a spreading fan. Branching, wiry stems bear iris-like, white flowers, 6–8cm (2½–3in) across. Each of the 3 large petals has a central, yellow mark.
D. vegeta of gardens. See *D. iridioides.*

Digger's speedwell. See *Parahebe perfoliata*, illus. p.286.

DIGITALIS

Foxglove

SCROPHULARIACEAE

Genus of biennials and perennials, some of which are evergreen, grown for their flower spikes in summer. Species mentioned grow in most conditions, even dry, exposed sites, but do best in semi-shade and moist but well-drained soil. Propagate by seed in autumn. All parts may cause severe discomfort if ingested. Contact with foliage may irritate skin.
D. ambigua. See *D. grandiflora.*
D. canariensis. See *Isoplexis canariensis.*
D. eriostachya. See *D. lutea.*
D. ferruginea illus. p.241.
D. grandiflora, syn. *D. ambigua* (Yellow foxglove). Evergreen, clump-forming perennial. H 75cm (30in), S 30cm (12in). Racemes of downward-pointing, tubular, creamy-yellow flowers appear in summer above a rosette of oval to oblong, smooth, strongly veined leaves.
D. lutea, syn. *D. eriostachya*. Upright perennial. H 75cm (30in), S 30cm (12in). In summer, delicate spires of downward-pointing, narrowly tubular, creamy-yellow flowers are borne above a rosette of oval, smooth, mid-green leaves.
D. × mertonensis. Clump-forming perennial. H 75cm (30in), S 30cm (12in). Produces spikes of downward-pointing, tubular, rose-mauve to coppery flowers in summer, above a rosette of oval, hairy, soft leaves. Divide after flowering.
D. purpurea. Upright, short-lived perennial, grown as a biennial. H 1–1.5m (3–5ft), S 60cm (2ft). Has a rosette of oval, rough, deep green leaves and, in summer, tall spikes of tubular flowers in shades of pink, red, purple or white. f. **albiflora** (syn. *D.p.* f. *alba*) illus. p.318.

DILLENIA

DILLENIACEAE

Genus of evergreen or briefly deciduous, spring-flowering trees, grown for their flowers and foliage and for shade. Tender, min. 16°C (61°F). Needs moisture-retentive, fertile soil and full light. Water potted plants freely while in full growth, less in winter. Propagate by seed in spring.
D. indica (Elephant apple). Briefly deciduous, spreading tree. H and S 8–12m (25–40ft). Has oval, serrated, boldly parallel-veined, glossy leaves, each 30cm (1ft) long. Nodding, cup-shaped, white flowers, each 15–20cm (6–8in) wide, are produced in spring, followed by edible, globular, greenish fruits.

DIMORPHOTHECA

African daisy, Cape marigold

ASTERACEAE/COMPOSITAE

Genus of annuals, perennials and evergreen sub-shrubs. Grow in sun and in fertile, very well-drained soil. Dead-head to prolong flowering. Propagate annuals by seed sown under glass in mid-spring, perennials by semi-

ripe cuttings in summer. Is susceptible
to botrytis in wet summers.
D. annua. See *D. pluvialis.*
D. barberae of gardens. See
Osteospermum jucundum.
D. pluvialis, syn. *D. annua,* illus. p.319.

DIONAEA

DROSERACEAE

Genus of evergreen, insectivorous,
rosette-forming perennials. Tender,
min. 5°C (41°F). Needs partial shade
and a humid atmosphere; grow in a
mixture of peat and moss, kept
constantly moist. Propagate by seed or
division in spring.
D. muscipula illus. p.305.

DIONYSIA

PRIMULACEAE

Genus of evergreen, cushion-forming
perennials. Grow in an alpine house in
sun and very gritty, well-drained soil.
Position deep collar of grit under cushion
and ensure good ventilation at all
times. Dislikes winter wet. Propagate
by softwood cuttings in summer. Plants
are susceptible to botrytis.
D. aretioides illus. p.371.
D. microphylla. Evergreen perennial.
H 5cm (2in), S 15cm (6in). Rosettes of
oval to rounded, often sharply pointed,
grey-green leaves, with a mealy, yellow
coating beneath, form tight cushions.
Small, short-stemmed, 5-petalled,
white-eyed, pale to deep violet-yellow
flowers, with darker petal bases, appear
in early spring.
D. tapetodes illus. p.372.

DIOSCOREA

DIOSCOREACEAE

Genus of tuberous perennials, some
of which are succulent, and herbaceous
or evergreen, twining climbers, grown
mainly for their decorative leaves.
Insignificant flowers are generally
yellow. Tender, min. 5–13°C
(41–55°F). Prefers full sun or partial
shade and fertile, well-drained soil.
Propagate by division, or by cutting off
sections of tuber in spring or autumn or
by seed in spring.
D. discolor illus. p.219.
D. elephantipes, syn. *Testudinaria
elephantipes,* illus. p.467.

DIOSMA

RUTACEAE

Genus of evergreen, wiry-stemmed
shrubs, grown for their flowers and
overall appearance. Tender, min. 7°C
(45°F). Needs full light and well-drained,
neutral to acid soil. Water potted
specimens moderately, less when not in
full growth. To create a compact habit
shorten flowered stems after flowering.
Propagate by seed in spring or by semi-
ripe cuttings in late summer.
D. ericoides (Breath of heaven). Fast-
growing, evergreen, loosely rounded
shrub. H and S 30–60cm (1–2ft).
Aromatic, needle-like leaves are
crowded on stems. In winter-spring
carries a profusion of small, fragrant,
5-petalled, white flowers, sometimes
tinted red.

Diosphaera. Reclassified as
Trachelium.

DIOSPYROS

EBENACEAE

Genus of deciduous or evergreen trees
and shrubs, grown for their foliage and
fruits. Needs full sun and does best in
hot summers. Requires fertile, well-
drained soil. To obtain fruits, plants of
both sexes should be grown. Propagate
by seed in autumn.
D. kaki (Chinese persimmon, Kaki,
Persimmon). Deciduous, spreading tree.
H 10m (30ft), S 7m (22ft). Oval, glossy,
dark green leaves turn orange, red and
purple in autumn. Tiny, yellowish-white
flowers in summer are followed on
female trees by large, edible, rounded,
yellow or orange fruits. Zone 8.
D. lotus (Date plum). Deciduous,
spreading tree. H 10m (30ft), S 6m
(20ft). Has oval, glossy, dark green
leaves, tiny, red-tinged, green flowers
from mid- to late summer and, on
female trees, unpalatable, rounded,
purple or yellow fruits. Zone 7.

DIPCADI

HYACINTHACEAE/LILIACEAE

Genus of spring-flowering bulbs, grown
mainly for botanical interest. Will not
tolerate cold, wet winters, so is best
grown in a cold frame or alpine house.
Needs a warm, sunny situation and
light, well-drained soil. Is dormant in
summer. Propagate by seed in autumn.
D. serotinum illus. p.434.

DIPELTA

CAPRIFOLIACEAE

Genus of deciduous shrubs, with bold,
long-pointed leaves, grown for their
showy, tubular flowers and peeling bark.
After flowering, bracts beneath flowers
enlarge and become papery and brown,
surrounding the fruits. Requires sun or
semi-shade and fertile, well-drained soil.
Benefits from the occasional removal of
old shoots after flowering. Propagate by
softwood cuttings in summer.
D. floribunda illus. p.117.
D. yunnanensis illus. p.116.

DIPHYLLEIA

BERBERIDACEAE

Genus of perennials with creeping
rootstocks and umbrella-like leaves.
Is best suited to woodland gardens.
Needs semi-shade and moist soil.
Propagate by division in spring or
by seed in autumn.
D. cymosa (Umbrella leaf). Rounded
perennial. H 60cm (24in), S 30cm
(12in). Has large, rounded, 2-lobed
leaves. In spring bears loose heads of
inconspicuous, white flowers followed
by indigo-blue berries on red stalks.

Dipidax. Reclassified as *Onixotis.*
Diplacus glutinosus. See *Mimulus
aurantiacus.*
Dipladenia. Reclassified as
Mandevilla.

DIPLARRHENA

IRIDACEAE

Genus of one species of summer-
flowering perennial. Needs sun and
well-drained soil. Propagate by seed
or division in spring.
D. moraea illus. p.277.

DIPSACUS

Teasel

DIPSACACEAE

Genus of biennials or short-lived
perennials grown for their flower heads,
which are good for drying. Requires
sun or partial shade and any fertile soil,
including heavy clay. Propagate by
seed in autumn or spring.
D. fullonum. Prickly biennial.
H 1.5–2m (5–6ft), S 30–80cm
(12–32in). In the first year produces a
basal rosette of toothed, dark green
leaves covered in spiny pustules.
Thistle-like, pinkish-purple or white
flower heads, with stiff, prickly bracts,
are borne terminally on upright stems
with paired leaves in mid- and late
summer of the second year.

DIPTERONIA

ACERACEAE

Genus of deciduous trees, grown for
their foliage and fruits. Needs full sun
and fertile, well-drained soil. Propagate
by softwood cuttings in summer or by
seed in autumn.
D. sinensis. Deciduous, spreading,
sometimes shrubby tree. H 10m (30ft),
S 6m (20ft). Large, mid-green leaves
have 7–11 oval to lance-shaped leaflets.
Inconspicuous, greenish-white flowers
in summer are followed by large
clusters of winged, red fruits. Zone 9.

DISA

See also ORCHIDS.
D. uniflora. Deciduous, terrestrial
orchid. H 45–60cm (1½–2ft). Tender,
min. 7–10°C (45–50°F). Has narrowly
lance-shaped, glossy, dark green leaves,
to 22cm (9in) long, that clasp stems. In
early summer each stem bears up to 7
hooded, scarlet flowers, 8–10 cm
(3–4in) long, that have darker veins and
are suffused yellow. Is the parent of
many hybrids cultivated commercially
for cut flowers. Needs partial shade and
continually moist soil. Raise from seed
or propagate by division of offsets
when dormant.

DISANTHUS

HAMAMELIDACEAE

Genus of one species of deciduous,
autumn-flowering shrub, grown for its
overall appearance and autumn colour.
Needs partial shade and humus-rich,
moist but not wet, neutral to acid soil.
Propagate by layering in spring or by
seed when ripe or in spring.
D. cercidifolius. Deciduous, rounded
shrub. H and S to 3m (10ft). Bears
broadly oval to almost circular, bluish-
green leaves that turn yellow, orange,
red or purple in autumn. Has small,
dark red flowers in autumn as the
leaves fall, or later. Zone 6b.

DISCARIA

RHAMNACEAE

Genus of deciduous or almost leafless
shrubs and trees, grown for their habit
and flowers. Spiny, green shoots assume
function of leaves. Needs a sheltered,
sunny site and fertile, well-drained
soil. Propagate by softwood cuttings
in summer.
D. toumatou (Wild Irishman).
Deciduous or almost leafless,
bushy shrub. H and S 2m (6ft).
Shoots have sharp, rigid spines. Tiny,
star-shaped, greenish-white flowers are
borne in dense clusters in late spring.
Zone 9.

Disk-leaved hebe. See *Hebe
pinguifolia.*

DISPORUM

Fairy bells

CONVALLARIACEAE/LILIACEAE

Genus of spring- or early summer-
flowering perennials. Is best suited to
woodland gardens. Requires a cool,
semi-shaded position and humus-rich
soil. Propagate by division in spring or
by seed in autumn.
D. hookeri. Clump-forming perennial.
H 75cm (30in), S 30cm (12in).
Leaves are narrowly oval and mid-
green. Orange-red berries in autumn
follow clusters of drooping, open
bell-shaped, greenish-white flowers
in spring.
D. sessile 'Variegatum'. Rapidly
spreading, clump-forming perennial.
H 45cm (18in), S 30cm (12in).
Solitary tubular-bell-shaped to bell-
shaped, creamy-white flowers are
produced in spring. Narrowly
oval, pleated leaves are irregularly
striped with white.

DISTICTIS

BIGNONIACEAE

Genus of evergreen, woody-stemmed,
tendril climbers, grown for their
colourful, trumpet-shaped flowers.
Tender, min. 5–7°C (41–5°F). Well-
drained soil is suitable with full light.
Water freely in summer, less at other
times. Support for stems is necessary.
Thin out congested growth in spring.
Propagate by softwood cuttings in early
summer or by semi-ripe cuttings in
late summer.
D. buccinatoria, syn. *Phaedranthus
buccinatorius,* illus. p.204.

DISTYLIUM

HAMAMELIDACEAE

Genus of evergreen shrubs and trees,
grown for their foliage and flowers.
Prefers a sheltered, partially shaded
position and moist, peaty soil.
Propagate by semi-ripe cuttings
in summer.
D. racemosum. Evergreen, arching
shrub. H 2m (6ft), S 3m (10ft).
Leaves are oblong, leathery, glossy
and dark green. Small flowers, with
red calyces and purple anthers, are
borne in late spring and early summer.
Zone 8.

Dittany. See *Origanum*.
　Cretan. See *Origanum dictamnus*.
Dizygotheca elegantissima. See
　Schefflera elegantissima.

DOCYNIA

ROSACEAE

Genus of evergreen or semi-evergreen,
spring-flowering trees, grown for
their flowers and foliage; is related to
Cydonia. Requires full light and
well-drained soil. Other than
shaping while young, pruning is
not necessary. Propagate by seed in
spring or autumn, by budding in
summer or by grafting in winter.
Is usually trouble-free, though
caterpillars may be troublesome.
D. delavayi. Evergreen or semi-
evergreen, spreading tree. H and S 8m
(25ft) or more. Oval to lance-shaped
leaves are white-felted beneath. In
spring has fragrant, 5-petalled, white
flowers, pink in bud, followed by
ovoid, downy, yellow fruits in autumn.
Zone 9.

DODECATHEON

Shooting stars

PRIMULACEAE

Genus of spring- and summer-flowering
perennials, grown for their distinctive
flowers, with reflexed petals and
prominent stamens. Once fertilized,
flowers turn skywards – hence their
common name. Is dormant after
flowering. Prefers sun or partial shade
and moist but well-drained soil.
Propagate by seed in autumn or by
division in winter.
D. dentatum. Clump-forming
perennial. H 7cm (3in), S 25cm (10in).
Leaves are long, oval and toothed. In
late spring, frail stems bear white
flowers with prominent, dark stamens
and reflexed petals. Prefers a partially
shaded position.
D. hendersonii, syn. *D. latifolium*,
illus. p.347.
D. latifolium. See *D. hendersonii*.
D. meadia. Clump-forming perennial.
H 20cm (8in), S 15cm (6in). Leaves are
oval and pale green. In spring, strong
stems carry pale pink flowers, with
reflexed petals, above foliage. Prefers a
partially shaded position. f. ***album***
illus. p.347.
D. pauciflorum of gardens. See
D. pulchellum.
D. pulchellum, syn. *D. pauciflorum* of
gardens. Clump-forming perennial. H
15cm (6in), S 10cm (4in). Is similar to
D. meadia, but flowers are usually
deep cerise.
D. 'Red Wings' illus. p.348.

DODONAEA

SAPINDACEAE

Genus of evergreen trees and shrubs,
grown mainly for their foliage
and overall appearance. Tender,
min. 3–5°C (37–41°F). Prefers full
sun and well-drained soil. Water
potted plants freely when in full
growth, less at other times. Cut back
in late summer and in spring if
needed, to maintain a balanced shape.

Propagate by seed in spring or by
semi-ripe cuttings in late summer.
***D. viscosa* 'Purpurea'** illus. p.151.

Dog's fennel. See *Anthemis*.
Dog's-tooth violet. See *Erythronium
　dens-canis*, illus. p.430.
Dogwood. See *Cornus*.
　Creeping. See *Cornus canadensis*,
　　illus. p.374.
　Flowering. See *Cornus florida*.
　Mountain. See *Cornus nuttallii*,
　　illus. p.76.
　Pacific. See *Cornus nuttallii*,
　　illus. p.76.
　Red-barked. See *Cornus alba*.
Dolichos lablab. See *Lablab purpureus*.
Dolichos purpureus. See *Lablab
　purpureus*.
Doll's eyes. See *Actaea pachypoda*,
　illus. p.259.

DOMBEYA

STERCULIACEAE

Genus of evergreen shrubs and trees,
grown for their flowers. Tender, min.
5–13°C (41–55°F). Needs full light or
partial shade and fertile, well-drained
soil. Water potted specimens freely when
in full growth, less at low temperatures.
May be cut back after flowering.
Propagate by seed in spring or by
semi-ripe cuttings in summer. Whitefly
and spider mite may be a nuisance.
D. burgessiae, syn. *D. mastersii*,
illus. p.150.
D. × cayeuxii illus. p.88.
D. mastersii. See *D. burgessiae*.

Dondia. Reclassified as *Hacquetia*.
Donkey-tail. See *Sedum morganianum*.

DORONICUM

Leopard's bane

ASTERACEAE/COMPOSITAE

Genus of perennials, grown for their
daisy-like flower heads, which are good
for cutting. Most prefer full light or
shade and moist, well-drained soil.
Propagate by division in autumn.
D. austriacum. Clump-forming
perennial. H 45cm (18in), S 30cm
(12in). Daisy-like, pure yellow flower
heads are produced singly on slender
stems in spring. Heart-shaped, bright
green leaves are hairy and wavy-edged.
D. columnae, syn. *D. cordatum*. **'Miss
Mason'** illus. p.238.
D. cordatum. See *D. columnae*.
***D. × excelsum* 'Harpur Crewe',** syn.
D. plantagineum 'Excelsum'. Elegant,
clump-forming perennial. H 1m (3ft),
S 60cm (2ft). Large, daisy-like,
buttercup-yellow flower heads are
borne, 3 or 4 to a stem, in spring.
Leaves are heart-shaped and bright
green. Is good for a dry, shaded site.
D. 'Frühlingspracht', syn *D.* 'Spring
Beauty'. Clump-forming perennial.
H 45cm (18in), S 30cm (12in).
Produces daisy-like, double, bright
yellow flower heads in spring. Bears
heart-shaped, bright green leaves.
***D. plantagineum* 'Excelsum'.** See
D. × excelsum 'Harpur Crewe'.
D. 'Spring Beauty'. See
D. 'Frühlingspracht'.

DOROTHEANTHUS

AIZOACEAE

Genus of succulent annuals, suitable for
hot, dry places such as rock gardens,
banks and gaps in paving. Needs sun
and grows well in poor, very well-
drained soil. Dead-head to prolong
flowering. Propagate by seed sown under
glass in early spring, or outdoors in mid-
spring. Protect from slugs and snails.
D. bellidiformis, syn.
Mesembryanthemum criniflorum
(Ice-plant, Livingstone daisy).
'Magic Carpet' illus. p.325.

Dorset heath. See *Erica ciliaris*.

DORYANTHES

DORYANTHACEAE/LILIACEAE

Genus of evergreen, rosette-forming
perennials, grown for their flowers.
Tender, min. 10°C (50°F). Needs a
sunny position and humus-rich,
well-drained soil. Propagate by mature
bulbils, by seed in spring or by suckers
after flowering.
D. palmeri illus. p.232.

Dorycnium hirsutum. See *Lotus
　hirsutus*.
Double common snowdrop. See
　Galanthus nivalis 'Flore Pleno',
　illus. p.439.
Double meadow buttercup. See
　Ranunculus acris 'Flore Pleno',
　illus. p.292.
Double sea campion. See *Silene
　uniflora* 'Robin Whitebreast'.
Double soapwort. See *Saponaria
　officinalis* 'Rubra Plena'.
Douglas fir. See *Pseudotsuga menziesii*.
Douglasia vitaliana. See *Vitaliana
　primuliflora*.
Dove tree. See *Davidia involucrata*,
　illus. p.77.
Doxantha. Reclassified as *Macfadyena*
　except for:
D. capreolata for which see *Bignonia
　capreolata*.

DRABA

BRASSICACEAE/CRUCIFERAE

Genus of spring-flowering annuals
and evergreen or semi-evergreen,
cushion- or mat-forming perennials
with extensive root systems. Some
species form soft, green cushions that
in winter turn brown except at the tips,
appearing almost dead. Is suitable for
alpine houses. Needs sun and gritty,
well-drained soil. Dislikes winter wet.
Propagate by softwood cuttings of
the rosettes in late spring or by seed
in autumn.
D. aizoides (Yellow whitlow grass).
Semi-evergreen, mat-forming perennial.
H 2.5cm (1in), S 15cm (6in). Has
lance-shaped, stiff-bristled
leaves in rosettes and, in spring,
4-petalled, bright yellow flowers.
Suits a scree.
D. bryoides. See *D. rigida* var. *bryoides*.
D. hispanica. Semi-evergreen, cushion-
forming perennial. H 5cm (2in),
S 10cm (4in). Leaves are oval, soft,

fragile and pale green. Clusters of flat,
4-petalled, pale yellow flowers are
borne in spring.
D. longisiliqua illus. p.371.
D. mollissima illus. p.372.
D. polytricha. Semi-evergreen,
cushion-forming perennial. H 6cm
(2½in), S 15cm (6in). Has minute,
rounded leaves in neat, symmetrical
rosettes. Frail stems carry flat,
4-petalled, golden-yellow flowers in
spring. Is difficult to grow. Keep stones
under cushion at all times. Remove
dead rosettes at once.
D. rigida illus. p.371. var. ***bryoides***
(syn. *D. bryoides*) is an evergreen, tight
hummock-forming perennial. H 4cm
(1½in), S 6cm (2½in). Leaves are tiny,
rounded, hard and dark green. Produces
small clusters of almost stemless,
4-petalled, bright yellow flowers that
cover hummocks in spring. Also suited
to a trough or scree.

DRACAENA

AGAVACEAE/DRACAENACEAE

Genus of evergreen trees and
shrubs, grown for their foliage and
overall appearance. Tender, min.
13–18°C (55–64°F). Needs full
light or partial shade and well-drained
soil. Water containerized plants
moderately, much less in low
temperatures. Rejuvenate leggy
plants by cutting back to near soil
level in spring. Propagate by seed or
air-layering in spring or by tip or stem
cuttings in summer. Mealy bug may be
a nuisance.
D. australis. See *Cordyline australis*.
D. deremensis. See *D. fragrans*
Deremensis Group. **'Souvenir de
Schrijver'** see *D. fragrans* Deremensis
Group 'Warneckei'. **'Warneckei'** see
D. fragrans Deremensis Group
'Warneckei'.
D. draco illus. p.100.
D. fragrans (Corn plant). **Deremensis
Group,** syn. *D. deremensis*, is a slow-
growing, evergreen, erect, sparsely
branched shrub. H 2m (6ft) or more,
S 1m (3ft) or more. Has lance-shaped,
erect to arching, glossy, deep green
leaves, to 45cm (18in) long. Mature
plants may occasionally bear large
panicles of small, red-and-white
flowers in summer. **Deremensis Group
'Warneckei'** (syn. *D. deremensis*
'Souvenir de Schrijver', *D.d.*
'Warneckei') illus. p.126.
'Massangeana'. Evergreen, erect,
sparsely branched shrub. H 3–6m
(10–20ft), S 1–3m (3–10ft). Has
strap-shaped, arching leaves, to 60cm
(2ft) long, with longitudinal bands
of yellow and pale green. In early
summer, fragrant, star-shaped,
yellow flowers, rarely produced, are
followed by rounded-oblong,
orange-red fruits.
D. indivisa. See *Cordyline indivisa*.
D. marginata (Madagascar dragon
tree). Slow-growing, evergreen,
erect shrub or tree. H 3m (10ft) or
more, S 1–2m (3–6ft) or more.
Leaves are narrowly strap-shaped
and rich green with red margins.
Flowers are rarely produced. **'Tricolor'**
illus. p.99.
D. sanderiana illus. p.151.

DRACOCEPHALUM
Dragon's head
LABIATAE/LAMIACEAE

Genus of summer-flowering annuals and perennials, suitable for rock gardens and borders. Prefers sun and fertile, well-drained soil. Propagate by seed or division in spring or autumn or by basal cuttings of young growth in spring.

D. ruyschiana. Erect perennial. H 45–60cm (18–24in), S 30cm (12in). Freely bears whorled spikes of 2-lipped, violet-blue flowers from early to mid-summer. Mid-green leaves are linear to lance-shaped.

D. sibiricum. See *Nepeta sibirica*.

DRACUNCULUS
ARACEAE

Genus of robust, tuberous perennials that produce roughly triangular, foul-smelling spathes. Where hardy, protect dormant tubers with a heavy mulch. Needs sun and well-drained soil that dries out in summer. Propagate by freely borne offsets in late summer or by seed in autumn.

D. vulgaris, syn. *Arum dracunculus*, illus. p.401.

Dragon tree. See *Dracaena draco*, illus. p.100.
  Madagascar. See *Dracaena marginata*.
Dragon's arum. See *Dracunculus vulgaris*, illus. p.401.
Dragon's head. See *Dracocephalum*.
Dragon's mouth. See *Horminum pyrenaicum*.
Dragon's-claw willow. See *Salix babylonica* var. *pekinensis* 'Tortuosa', illus. p.85.

DREGEA
ASCLEPIADACEAE

Genus of evergreen, woody-stemmed, twining climbers, grown for botanical interest. Grow in sun and in any well-drained soil. Propagate by seed in spring or by stem cuttings in summer or autumn.

D. corrugata. See *D. sinensis*.
D. sinensis, syn. *D. corrugata*, *Wattakaka sinensis*. Evergreen, woody-stemmed, twining climber. H to 3m (10ft). Oval, mid-green leaves, heart-shaped at base, 3–10cm (1¼–4in) long, are greyish beneath. In summer has clusters of 10–25 small, fragrant, star-shaped flowers, white or cream with red dots and streaks, followed by pairs of slender pods, 5–7cm (2–3in) long. Zone 9?.

Drejerella guttata. See *Justicia brandegeeana*.
Drepanostachyum falconeri. See *Himalayacalamus falconeri*.

DRIMYS
WINTERACEAE

Genus of evergreen trees and shrubs, grown for their foliage and star-shaped flowers. Where hardy, grow against a south- or west-facing wall. Needs sun or semi-shade and fertile, moist but well-drained soil. Propagate by semi-ripe cuttings in summer or by seed in autumn.

D. aromatica. See *D. lanceolata*.
D. axillaris. See *Pseudowintera axillaris*.
D. colorata. See *Pseudowintera colorata*.
D. lanceolata, syn. *D. aromatica* (Mountain pepper). Evergreen, upright, dense shrub or tree. H 4m (12ft), S 2.5m (8ft). Has deep red shoots and oblong, dark green leaves. Produces clusters of star-shaped, white flowers in spring. Zone 9.
D. winteri, syn. *Wintera aromatica*, illus. p.78.

Drooping juniper. See *Juniperus recurva*, illus. p.108.
Drooping star-of-Bethlehem. See *Ornithogalum nutans*.
Dropwort. See *Filipendula vulgaris*.

DROSANTHEMUM
AIZOACEAE

Genus of erect or prostrate, succulent shrubs with slender stems and masses of flowers in summer. Leaves are finely covered in papillae. Tender, min. 5°C (41°F). Needs full sun and very well-drained soil. Propagate by seed or stem cuttings in spring or summer.

D. hispidum. Succulent shrub, with arching or spreading branches that root down. H 60cm (2ft), S 1m (3ft). Has cylindrical, light green leaves, 1.5–2.5cm (⅝–1in) long. In summer, masses of shiny, daisy-like, purple flowers, to 3cm (1¼in) across, are borne.
D. speciosum. Erect, shrubby succulent. H 60cm (2ft), S 1m (3ft). Has semi-cylindrical leaves, 1–2cm (½–¾in) long. Masses of daisy-like, green-centred, orange-red flowers, to 5cm (2in) across, appear in summer.

DROSERA
Sundew
DROSERACEAE

Genus of evergreen, insectivorous perennials. Hardy to tender, min. 5–10°C (41–50°F). Grow in sun, in a mixture of peat and moss that is not allowed to dry out. Propagate by seed or division in spring.

D. capensis illus. p.305.
D. spatulata illus. p.305.

Drumstick primula. See *Primula denticulata*, illus. p.273.
Drunkard's dream. See *Hatiora salicornioides*, illus. p.468.

DRYANDRA
PROTEACEAE

Genus of evergreen, spring- to summer-flowering shrubs and trees, grown for their flowers, foliage and overall appearance. Tender, min. 7°C (45°F). Needs full light and well-drained, sandy soil that contains few nitrates or phosphates. Is difficult to grow. Water containerized specimens moderately, less in low temperatures. Plants under glass must be freely ventilated. Propagate by seed in spring.

D. formosa. Evergreen, bushy shrub. H 2–5m (6–15ft), S 1.5–3m (5–10ft). Strap-shaped leaves are divided into triangular, closely set lobes, creating a saw-blade effect. In spring carries small, scented, tubular, orange-yellow flowers in domed, terminal heads.

DRYAS
Mountain avens
ROSACEAE

Genus of evergreen, prostrate, woody-based perennials with oak-like leaves and cup-shaped flowers. Is useful on banks and walls, in rock gardens and as ground cover. Prefers sun and gritty, well-drained, peaty soil. Propagate by seed when fresh or by semi-ripe cuttings in summer.

D. drummondii. Evergreen, prostrate, woody-based perennial. H 5cm (2in), S indefinite. Stout stems are clothed in small, oval, lobed, leathery, dark green leaves. Nodding, creamy-white flowers are borne in early summer but never fully open.
D. octopetala illus. p.375.
D. × suendermannii. Evergreen, prostrate, woody-based perennial. H 5cm (2in), S indefinite. Is similar to *D. drummondii*, but has slightly nodding, pale cream flowers that open horizontally.

DRYOPTERIS
ASPIDIACEAE/DRYOPTERIDACEAE

Genus of deciduous or semi-evergreen ferns, many of which form regular, shuttlecock-like crowns. Requires shade and moist soil. Regularly remove fading fronds. Propagate by spores in summer or by division in autumn or winter.

D. affinis, syn. *D. borreri*, *D. pseudomas* (Golden male fern). Virtually evergreen fern. H and S to 1m (3ft). Produces a 'shuttlecock' of lance-shaped, divided fronds, 20–80cm (8–32in) tall, from an erect rhizome. Fronds are pale green as they unfurl in spring, in contrast to the scaly, golden brown midribs; they mature to dark green and often remain green through winter. Distinguished from *D. filix-mas* by a dark spot where each pinna joins the midrib.
D. atrata of gardens. See *D. cycadina*.
D. austriaca. See *D. dilatata*.
D. borreri. See *D. affinis*.
D. carthusiana (Narrow buckler fern). Deciduous or semi-evergreen, creeping, rhizomatous fern. H 1m (3ft), S 45cm (18in). Produces lance-shaped, much-divided, mid-green fronds with triangular to oval pinnae.
D. cycadina, syn. *D. atrata* of gardens, *D. hirtipes*. Deciduous fern. H 60cm (24in), S 45cm (18in). Has an erect rhizome producing a 'shuttlecock' of lance-shaped, divided, bright green fronds, 45cm (18in) tall, with green midribs.
D. dilatata, syn. *D. austriaca* (Broad buckler fern). Deciduous or semi-evergreen fern. H 1m (3ft), S 45cm (18in). Has much-divided,

arching, mid-green fronds, with triangular to oval pinnae, on stout, dark brown stems.

D. erythrosora (Japanese shield fern). Deciduous fern. H 45cm (18in), S 30cm (12in). Broadly triangular, coppery-pink fronds, divided into triangular to oval pinnae, persist until mid-winter.
D. filix-mas illus. p.310. **'Grandiceps Wills'** is a deciduous fern. H and S 90m (3ft). Has 'shuttlecocks' of broadly lance-shaped, tasselled, elegantly arching, mid-green fronds, arising from crowns of large, upright, brown-scaled rhizomes. The tip of each frond has a heavy crest, and the pinnae are also finely crested.
D. goldieana (Giant wood fern). Deciduous fern. H 1m (3ft), S 60cm (2ft). Has broadly oval, light green fronds divided into numerous oblong, indented pinnae.
D. hirtipes. See *D. cycadina*.
D. marginalis. Deciduous fern. H 60cm (24in), S 30cm (12in). Fronds are lance-shaped, dark green and divided into numerous oblong, slightly indented pinnae.
D. pseudomas. See *D. affinis*.
D. sieboldii. Semi-evergreen, tufted fern. H and S 30–60cm (1–2ft). Produces long-stalked, erect or arching, yellowish-green fronds, 20–50cm (8–20in) long, with up to 6 pairs of narrowly lance-shaped pinnae, 15–30cm (6–12in) long.
D. wallichiana (Wallich's wood fern). Deciduous fern. H 1–1.8m (3–6ft), S 75cm (30in). Produces an erect rhizome and a 'shuttlecock' of lance-shaped, divided, dark green fronds, yellow-green when young, 1m (3ft) or more long. Midribs are covered with dark brown or black scales, providing attractive colour contrasts in spring.

DUCHESNEA
ROSACEAE

Genus of perennials, some of which are semi-evergreen, grown as ground cover as well as for their flowers. May be used in hanging baskets. Grow in well-drained soil and in sun or partial shade. Propagate by division in spring, by rooting plantlets formed at ends of runners in summer or by seed in autumn.

D. indica, syn. *Fragaria indica*. Semi-evergreen, trailing perennial. H to 10cm (4in), S indefinite. Dark green leaves have 3 toothed leaflets like those of strawberries. Solitary, 5-petalled, bright yellow flowers, to 2.5cm (1in) wide and with leafy, green frills of sepals, appear from spring to early summer. Strawberry-like, tasteless, red fruits appear in late summer.

Duck potato. See *Sagittaria latifolia*, illus. p.446.
Duckweed. See *Wolffia*.
  Least. See *Wolffia arrhiza*.

DUDLEYA
CRASSULACEAE

Genus of basal-rosetted, perennial succulents, closely related to *Echeveria*. Tender, min. 7°C (45°F). Requires full sun and very well-drained soil. Water sparingly when plants are semi-dormant in mid-summer. Propagate by seed or division in spring or summer.

D. brittonii. Basal-rosetted, perennial succulent. H 20cm (8in)–60cm (24in) or more when in flower, S 50cm (20in). Has narrowly lance-shaped, tapering, fleshy, silvery-white leaves. Masses of star-shaped, pale yellow flowers are produced in spring-summer.

D. pulverulenta illus. p.464.

Duke of Argyll's tea-tree. See *Lycium barbarum.*

Dumb cane. See *Dieffenbachia.*

Dumpling cactus. See *Lophophora williamsii,* illus. p.471.

DURANTA

VERBENACEAE

Genus of fast-growing, evergreen or partially deciduous trees and shrubs, grown for their flowers and overall appearance. Tender, min. 10–13°C (50–55°F). Needs full light and fertile, well-drained soil. Water potted plants freely when in full growth, moderately at other times. Prune as necessary to curb vigour. Propagate by seed in spring or by semi-ripe cuttings in summer. Whitefly may be troublesome.

D. erecta, syn. *D. plumieri, D. repens,* illus. p.150.

D. plumieri. See *D. erecta.*

D. repens. See *D. erecta.*

Durmast oak. See *Quercus petraea.*

Dusky coral pea. See *Kennedia rubicunda,* illus. p.205.

Dutch crocus. See *Crocus vernus,* illus. p.429.

Dutch elm. See *Ulmus* x *hollandica.*

Dutchman's breeches. See *Dicentra cucullaria,* illus. p.362.

Dutchman's pipe. See *Aristolochia.*

Dutchman's trousers. See *Dicentra spectabilis,* illus. p.245.

DUVALIA

ASCLEPIADACEAE

Genus of clump-forming or carpeting, perennial succulents with short, thick, leafless stems; is closely related to *Stapelia.* Star-shaped flowers have thick, fleshy petals recurved at tips. Tender, min. 10°C (50°F), but best at 20°C (68°F). Requires partial shade and very well-drained soil. Propagate by seed or stem cuttings in spring or summer.

D. corderoyi illus. p.476.

Duvernoia adhatodoides. See *Justicia adhatoda.*

Dwarf bearded iris. See *Iris pumila.*

Dwarf cattail. See *Typha minima,* illus. p.449.

Dwarf fan palm. See *Chamaerops humilis,* illus. p.176.

Dwarf mountain palm. See *Chamaedorea elegans,* illus. p.152.

Dwarf palmetto. See *Sabal minor,* illus. p.176.

Dwarf pine. See *Pinus mugo.*

Dwarf pomegranate. See *Punica granatum* var. *nana,* illus. p.355.

Dwarf Siberian pine. See *Pinus pumila.*

Dwarf sumach. See *Rhus copallina.*

Dwarf white wood lily. See *Trillium nivale.*

Dwarf white-stripe bamboo. See *Pleioblastus variegatus,* illus. p.306.

Dwarf willow. See *Salix herbacea.*

DYCKIA

BROMELIACEAE

Genus of evergreen, rosette-forming perennials, grown for their overall appearance. Tender, min. 7–10°C (45–50°F). Requires full light and well-drained soil containing sharp sand or grit. Water moderately in summer, scarcely or not at all in winter, sparingly at other times. Propagate by offsets or division in spring.

D. remotiflora (illus. p.265). Evergreen, basal-rosetted perennial. H and S 30–50cm (12–20in). Has dense rosettes of very narrowly triangular, pointed, thick-textured, arching, dull green leaves with hooked spines and grey scales beneath. Woolly spikes of tubular, orange-yellow flowers appear above foliage in summer-autumn.

Dyers' greenweed. See *Genista tinctoria,* illus. p.157.

DYPSIS

ARECACEAE/PALMAE

Genus of evergreen palms, grown for their elegant appearance. Tender, min. 16°C (61°F). Needs full light or partial shade and fertile, well-drained soil. Water potted specimens moderately, much less when temperatures are low. Propagate by seed in spring at not less than 26°C (79°F). Spider mite may sometimes be a nuisance.

D. lutescens, syn. *Areca lutescens, Chrysalidocarpus lutescens,* illus. p.100.

East Indian arrowroot. See *Tacca leontopetaloides.*
Easter cactus. See *Hatiora gaertneri,* illus. p.475.
Easter lily. See *Lilium longiflorum,* illus. p.404.
Eastern cottonwood. See *Populus deltoides.*
Eastern hemlock. See *Tsuga canadensis,* illus. p.107.
Eastern redbud. See *Cercis canadensis.*
Eastern white cedar. See *Thuja occidentalis.*
Eastern white pine. See *Pinus strobus,* illus. p.102.
Eau-de-Cologne mint. See *Mentha* x *piperita* f. *citrata.*

ECCREMOCARPUS
BIGNONIACEAE

Genus of evergreen, sub-shrubby, tendril climbers grown for their attractive flowers, produced over a long season. One species only is commonly grown. Usually treated as an annual. Grow in full light and in any well-drained soil. Propagate by seed in early spring.
E. scaber illus. p.217.

ECHEVERIA
CRASSULACEAE

Genus of rosetted, perennial succulents with long-lasting flowers. Leaves take on their brightest colours from autumn to spring. Tender, min. 5–7°C (41–5°F). Needs sun, good ventilation and very well-drained soil. Propagate by seed, stem or leaf cuttings, division or offsets in spring or summer.
E. agavoides illus. p.474.
E. cooperi. See *Adromischus cooperi.*
E. derenbergii. Clump-forming, perennial succulent. H 4cm (1½in), S 30cm (12in). Min. 5°C (41°F). Produces a short-stemmed rosette of rounded, grey-green leaves. Flower stem, 8cm (3in) long, produces cup-shaped, yellow-and-red or orange flowers in spring. Offsets freely. Is often used as a parent in breeding.
E. elegans illus. p.471.
E. gibbiflora. Rosetted, perennial succulent. H 10–25cm (4–10in), S 30cm (12in). Min. 7°C (45°F). Rosettes of spoon-shaped, pointed, grey-green leaves, often tinged red-brown, are stemless or borne on short stems. Cup-shaped, red flowers, yellow within, are borne on stems, 90cm (3ft) long, in autumn-winter. **'Metallica'** (syn. *E.g.* var. *metallica*) has white- or red-margined, purple-green leaves that mature to green-bronze.
E. harmsii, syn. *Oliveranthus elegans.* Bushy, perennial succulent. H 20cm (8in), S 30cm (12in). Min. 7°C (45°F). Erect stems are each crowned by a 6cm (2½in) wide rosette of short, narrowly lance-shaped, pale green leaves,

covered in short hairs. In spring bears cup-shaped, orange-tipped, red flowers, yellow within.
E. pulvinata illus. p.464.
E. secunda illus. p.473.
E. setosa (Mexican firecracker). Basal-rosetted, perennial succulent. H 4cm (1½in), S 30cm (12in). Min. 7°C (45°F). Has long, narrow, mid-green leaves covered in short, thick, white hairs. Bears cup-shaped, red-and-yellow flowers in spring. Is prone to rotting: do not water foliage.

ECHINACEA
Coneflower
ASTERACEAE/COMPOSITAE

Genus of summer-flowering perennials. Prefers sun and humus-rich, moist but well-drained soil. Propagate by division or root cuttings in spring. May seed freely.
E. purpurea, syn. *Rudbeckia purpurea.* **'Robert Bloom'** illus. p.244. **'White Lustre'** is a vigorous, upright perennial. H 1.2m (4ft), S 45cm (1½ft). Large, daisy-like, white flower heads, each with a prominent, central, orange-brown cone, are borne singly on strong stems in summer. Has lance-shaped, dark green leaves.

ECHINOCACTUS
CACTACEAE

Genus of slow-growing, hemispherical, perennial cacti. Tender, min. 11°C (52°F); lower temperatures cause yellow patches on *E. grusonii.* Requires full sun and very well-drained soil. Yellow-flowered species are easy to grow. Propagate by seed in spring.
E. asterias. See *Astrophytum asterias.*
E. chilensis. See *Neoporteria chilensis.*
E. eyriesii. See *Echinopsis eyriesii.*
E. grusonii illus. p.460.
E. ingens. See *E. platyacanthus.*
E. myriostigma. See *Astrophytum myriostigma.*
E. ornatus. See *Astrophytum ornatum.*
E. platyacanthus, syn. *E. ingens.* Slow-growing, hemispherical, perennial cactus. H 3m (10ft), S 2m (6ft). Grey-blue stem has a woolly crown and up to 50 ribs. Funnel-shaped, yellow flowers, 3cm (1¼in) across, appear in summer only on plants over 40cm (16in) in diameter.
E. scheeri. See *Sclerocactus scheeri.*
E. uncinatus. See *Sclerocactus uncinatus.*

ECHINOCEREUS
CACTACEAE

Genus of spherical to columnar, perennial cacti, freely branching with age, some with tuberous rootstocks. Buds, formed inside spiny stem, burst through skin, producing long-lasting flowers, with reflexed petal tips and prominent, green stigmas, followed by pear-shaped, spiny seed pods. Tender,

min. 5–8°C (41–6°F); some species tolerate light frost if dry. Needs full sun and very well-drained soil. Propagate by seed or stem cuttings in spring or summer.
E. baileyi. See *E. reichenbachii* var. *baileyi.*
E. cinerascens. Clump-forming, perennial cactus. H 30cm (1ft), S 1m (3ft). Min. 5°C (41°F). Has 7cm (3in) wide stems, each with 5–12 ribs. Areoles each bear 8–15 yellowish-white spines. Mature plants produce masses of trumpet-shaped, bright pink or purple flowers, 12cm (5in) across and with paler petal bases, in spring.
E. leucanthus, syn. *Wilcoxia albiflora,* illus. p.469.
E. pectinatus. Columnar, perennial cactus. H 35cm (14in), S 20cm (8in). Min. 7°C (45°F). Has sparsely branched, green stems with 12–23 ribs and short, comb-like spines, often variably coloured. In spring produces trumpet-shaped, purple, pink or yellow flowers, 12cm (5in) across, with paler petal bases.
E. pentalophus, syn. *E. procumbens,* illus. p.463.
E. procumbens. See *E. pentalophus.*
E. reichenbachii. Columnar, perennial cactus. H 35cm (14in), S 20cm (8in). Min. 7°C (45°F). Has a slightly branched, multicoloured stem with 12–23 ribs and comb-like spines, 1.5cm (⅝in) long. Carries trumpet-shaped, pink or purple flowers, 12cm (5in) across, with darker petal bases, in spring. var. *baileyi* (syn. *E. baileyi*) illus. p.462.
E. schmollii, syn. *Wilcoxia schmollii,* illus. p.462.
E. triglochidiatus. Clump-forming, perennial cactus. H 30cm (12in), S 15cm (6in). Min. 5°C (41°F). Has a short, thick, dark green stem with 3–5 spines, each to 2.5cm (1in) long, per areole. In spring bears funnel-shaped, bright red flowers, 7cm (3in) across, with prominent, red stamens and green stigmas. var. *paucispinus* illus. p.475.

Echinodorus ranunculoides. See *Baldellia ranunculoides.*
Echinofossulocactus. Reclassified as *Stenocactus.*
Echinomastus macdowellii. See *Thelocactus macdowellii.*

ECHINOPS
Globe thistle
ASTERACEAE/COMPOSITAE

Genus of summer-flowering perennials, grown for their globe-like, spiky flower heads. Does best in full sun and in poor soil. Propagate by division or seed in autumn or by root cuttings in winter.
E. bannaticus illus. p.228. **'Taplow Blue'** is an erect perennial, H 1.2m (4ft), S 1m (3ft). Wiry stems produce thistle-like, rounded heads of powder-

blue flowers in summer. Narrowly oval leaves are divided and greyish-green.
E. ritro **'Veitch's Blue'** illus. p.252.
E. sphaerocephalus illus. p.226.

ECHINOPSIS
CACTACEAE

Genus of spherical to columnar, perennial cacti, mostly freely branching; it is sometimes held to include *Trichocereus.* Tender, min. 5–10°C (41–50°F). Requires full sun and well-drained soil. Tolerates long periods of neglect. Propagate by seed or offsets in spring or summer.
E. aurea, syn. *Lobivia aurea, L. cylindrica, Pseudolobivia aurea.* Clump-forming, perennial cactus. H 12cm (5in), S 20cm (8in). Green stem, with 14 or 15 ribs, is densely covered with white, radial spines and a longer, darker, central spine. Produces funnel-shaped to flattish, yellow flowers, 8cm (3in) across, in summer.
E. backebergii, syn. *Lobivia backebergii,* illus. p.473.
E. bridgesii. See *E. lageniformis.*
E. candicans, syn. *Trichocereus candicans,* illus. p.461.
E. chamaecereus, syn. *Chamaecereus silvestrii, Lobivia silvestrii,* illus. p.475.
E. cinnabarina, syn. *Lobivia cinnabarina.* Spherical, perennial cactus. H and S 15cm (6in). Glossy, dark green stem has about 20 warty ribs and mostly curved, dark spines. In summer bears funnel-shaped to flattish, carmine-red flowers, 8cm (3in) across. *E. eyriesii,* syn. *Echinocactus eyriesii.* Flattened spherical, perennial cactus. H 30cm (12in), S 50cm (20in). Has slowly branching, mid-green stems with 11–18 ribs and very short spines. Tubular, white flowers appear in spring-summer.
E. lageniformis, syn. *E. bridgesii, Trichocereus bridgesii,* illus. p.456.
E. multiplex. See *E. oxygona.*
E. oxygona, syn. *E. multiplex,* illus. p.461.
E. pentlandii, syn. *Lobivia pentlandii,* illus. p.473.
E. rhodotricha. Spherical to columnar, perennial cactus. H 60cm (2ft), S 20cm (8in). Produces branching, dark green stems, 9cm (3½in) across, with 8–13 ribs. Curved, dark spines, 2cm (¾in) long, later turn pale. Has tubular, white to pink flowers in spring-summer.
E. spachiana, syn. *Cereus spachianus, Trichocereus spachianus,* illus. p.457.

Echioides longiflorum. See *Arnebia pulchra.*

ECHIUM
BORAGINACEAE

Genus of annuals and evergreen shrubs, biennials and perennials, grown for their flowers. Hardy to tender, min. 3°C (37°F). Needs full sun and fertile, well-drained soil. Water containerized specimens freely in summer, moderately at other times. Propagate by seed in spring or by greenwood or semi-ripe cuttings in summer. Whitefly may sometimes be troublesome. All parts may cause mild stomach upset if ingested; contact with the foliage may irritate skin.

E. bourgaeanum. See *E. wildpretii.*
E. vulgare [dwarf] illus. p.331.
E. wildpretii, syn. *E. bourgaeanum.* Evergreen, erect, unbranched biennial that dies after fruiting. H 2.5m (8ft) or more, S 60cm (2ft). Narrowly lance-shaped, silver-haired leaves, 30cm (1ft) long, form a dense rosette. Has compact spires, 1–1.5m (3–5ft) long, of small, funnel-shaped, red flowers in late spring and early summer.

Edelweiss. See *Leontopodium.*
  New Zealand. See *Leucogenes.*
  North Island. See *Leucogenes leontopodium.*

EDGEWORTHIA
THYMELAEACEAE

Genus of deciduous shrubs, grown for their flowers in late winter and early spring. Just hardy, but flowers are susceptible to frost damage. Is best grown against a south- or west-facing wall in most areas. Requires full sun and well-drained soil. Dislikes being transplanted. Propagate by semi-ripe cuttings in summer or by seed in autumn.

E. chrysantha, syn. *E. papyrifera.* Deciduous, rounded, open shrub. H and S 1.5m (5ft). Very supple shoots produce terminal, rounded heads of fragrant, tubular, yellow flowers in late winter and early spring. Has oval, dark green leaves. Zone 9.
E. papyrifera. See *E. chrysantha.*

Edible prickly pear. See *Opuntia ficus-indica.*

EDRAIANTHUS
CAMPANULACEAE

Genus of short-lived perennials, some of which are evergreen, usually growing from central rootstocks. In winter, a small, resting bud is just visible from each rootstock. In spring, prostrate stems radiate to carry leaves and flowers. Is suitable for rock gardens, screes and troughs. Needs sun and well-drained soil. Propagate by softwood cuttings from side shoots in early summer or by seed in autumn.

E. dalmaticus. Upright, then arching perennial. H 10cm (4in), S 15cm (6in). Bears narrowly lance-shaped, pale green leaves and, in early summer, terminal clusters of bell-shaped, violet-blue flowers, 2.5cm (1in) across.
E. pumilio illus. p.382.
E. serpyllifolius, syn. *Wahlenbergia serpyllifolia,* illus. p.381. **'Major'** is an evergreen, prostrate perennial. H 1cm (½in), S to 5cm (2in). Has tight mats of tiny, oval, dark green leaves. In early summer, bell-shaped, deep violet flowers, 1.5cm (⅝in) wide, are borne

on very short stems. Needs a sheltered site. Seldom sets seed.

Edwardsia microphylla. See *Sophora microphylla.*
Eel grass. See *Vallisneria spiralis.*

EGERIA
HYDROCHARITACEAE

Genus of semi-evergreen or evergreen, perennial, floating or submerged water plants, grown for their foliage. Is similar to *Elodea,* but has more conspicuous flowers, held above water surface. Tender, min. 1˚C (34˚F). Needs a sunny position. Propagate by stem cuttings in spring or summer.

E. densa, syn. *Anacharis densa, Elodea densa.* Semi-evergreen, perennial, spreading, submerged water plant. S indefinite. Forms a dense mass of whorled, small, lance-shaped, dark green leaves borne on long, wiry stems. Small, 3-parted, white flowers appear in summer.

Eglantine. See *Rosa rubiginosa,* illus. p.185.
Egyptian star. See *Pentas lanceolata,* illus. p.163.

EHRETIA
BORAGINACEAE

Genus of deciduous, summer-flowering trees, grown for their foliage and star-shaped flowers. Is susceptible to frost damage when young. Requires sun or semi-shade and fertile, well-drained soil. Propagate by softwood cuttings in summer.

E. dicksonii illus. p.91.

EICHHORNIA
PONTEDERIACEAE

Genus of evergreen or semi-evergreen, perennial, floating and marginal water plants. Tender, min. 1˚C (34˚F). Needs an open, sunny position in warm water. Grows prolifically and requires regular thinning year-round. Propagate by detaching young plants as required.

E. crassipes, syn. *E. speciosa,* illus. p.448.
E. speciosa. See *E. crassipes.*

ELAEAGNUS
ELAEAGNACEAE

Genus of deciduous or evergreen shrubs and trees, grown for their foliage and small, usually very fragrant flowers, often followed by ornamental fruits. Evergreen species are good for providing shelter or for hedging, particularly in coastal areas. Most evergreen species thrive in sun or shade, but those with silver leaves and deciduous species prefer full sun. Needs fertile, well-drained soil. Trim hedges in late summer. Propagate species by seed in autumn, evergreen forms also by semi-ripe cuttings in summer, deciduous forms by softwood or semi-ripe cuttings in summer.

E. angustifolia illus. p.122.
E. commutata (Silverberry). Dense,

deciduous shrub that spreads by suckers and is good for stabilizing slopes and on poor soils. H 4m (12ft) S 2m (6ft). Both shoots and leaves are covered with silvery scales. Fragrant pale yellow flowers in spring give silvery-red, mealy fruits in late fall. Zone 2.

E. × ebbingei. Evergreen, bushy, dense shrub. H and S 5m (15ft). Has oblong to oval, glossy, dark green leaves, silvery beneath. Fragrant, bell-shaped, silvery-white flowers are borne from mid- to late autumn. Zone 7. Leaves of **'Gilt Edge'** have golden-yellow margins. **'Limelight'** illus. p.153.
E. macrophylla. Evergreen, bushy, dense shrub. H and S 3m (10ft). Broadly oval leaves are silvery-grey when young, becoming glossy, dark green above, but remaining silvery-grey beneath, when mature. Fragrant, bell-shaped, creamy-yellow flowers, silvery outside, appear from mid- to late autumn, followed by egg-shaped, red fruits. Zone 8.
E. pungens 'Maculata', syn. *E. pungens* 'Aureovariegata', illus. p.127.
E. umbellata. Vigorous, deciduous, bushy shrub. H and S 5m (15ft). Oblong, wavy-edged, bright green leaves are silvery when young. Has fragrant, bell-shaped, creamy-yellow flowers in late spring and early summer, then egg-shaped, red fruits. Zone 5.

ELATOSTEMA,
syn. PELLIONIA
URTICACEAE

Genus of evergreen, creeping perennials and sub-shrubs with attractive foliage that often tends to lie flat, making useful ground cover. Tender, min. 15˚C (59˚F). Requires a humid atmosphere away from draughts, indirect light and moist soil. Propagate from stem cuttings in spring or summer.

E. pulchra, syn. *E. repens* var. *pulchra.* Evergreen, slightly fleshy perennial with rooting, creeping stems. H 8–10cm (3–4in), S 60cm (2ft) or more. Broadly oval leaves, 5cm (2in) long, are blackish-green with dark green veins above, purple below. Flowers are insignificant.
E. repens, syn. *Pellionia daveauana, P. repens,* illus. p.303. var. **pulchra** see *E. pulchra.*

Elder. See *Sambucus.*
  American. See *Sambucus canadensis.*
  Box. See *Acer negundo.*
  European. See *Sambucus nigra.*
  European Golden. See *Sambucus nigra* 'Aurea'.
  Red-berried. See *Sambucus racemosa.*
  Yellow. See *Tecoma stans,* illus. p.96.

ELEOCHARIS
CYPERACEAE

See also GRASSES, BAMBOOS, RUSHES and SEDGES.
E. acicularis (Needle spike-rush). Evergreen, spreading, rhizomatous, perennial sedge. H to 10cm (4in),

S indefinite. Basal, mid-green leaves are very narrow. Hairless, unbranched, square stems bear solitary minute, brown spikelets in summer.

Elephant apple. See *Dillenia indica.*
Elephant bush. See *Portulacaria afra,* illus. p.153.
Elephant's ear. See *Philodendron domesticum.*
Elephant's ear, Giant. See *Alocasia macrorrhiza.*
Elephant's ears. See *Hedera colchica* 'Dentata', illus. p.221.
Elephant's foot. See *Beaucarnea recurvata,* illus. p.100; *Dioscorea elephantipes,* illus. p.467.

ELEUTHEROCOCCUS,
syn. ACANTHOPANAX
ARALIACEAE

Genus of deciduous shrubs and trees, grown for their foliage and fruits. Produces tiny, usually greenish-white flowers. Prefers full sun and needs well-drained soil. Propagate by seed in spring or by root cuttings in late winter.
E. sieboldianus illus. p.145.

Elliottia paniculata. See *Tripetaleia paniculata.*
Elm. See *Ulmus.*
  American. See *Ulmus americana.*
  Caucasian. See *Zelkova carpinifolia.*
  Chinese. See *Ulmus parvifolia.*
  Cornish. See *Ulmus minor* 'Cornubiensis'.
  Cornish golden. See *Ulmus minor* 'Dicksonii', illus. p.81.
  Dickson's golden. See *Ulmus minor* 'Dicksonii', illus. p.81.
  Dutch. See *Ulmus × hollandica.*
  English. See *Ulmus procera.*
  Exeter. See *Ulmus glabra* 'Exoniensis'.
  Goodyer's. See *Ulmus minor* subsp. *angustifolia.*
  Huntingdon. See *Ulmus ×* *hollandica* 'Vegeta'.
  Jersey. See *Ulmus minor* 'Sarniensis'.
Elm
  Siberian. See *Ulmus pumila.*
  Smooth-leaved. See *Ulmus minor.*
  Wheatley. See *Ulmus minor* 'Sarniensis'.
  White. See *Ulmus americana.*
  Wych. See *Ulmus glabra.*
Elodea crispa of gardens. See *Lagarosiphon major.*
Elodea densa. See *Egeria densa.*

ELSHOLTZIA
LABIATAE/LAMIACEAE

Genus of perennials and deciduous shrubs and sub-shrubs, grown for their flowers, generally in autumn. Needs full sun and fertile, well-drained soil. Cut back old shoots hard in early spring. Propagate by softwood cuttings in summer.
E. stauntonii illus. p.173.

Elymus arenarius. See *Leymus arenarius.*

EMBOTHRIUM
PROTEACEAE

Genus of evergreen or semi-evergreen trees, grown for their flowers. Just hardy, but shelter from cold winds. Needs semi-shade and moist but well-drained, lime-free soil. Propagate by suckers in spring or autumn or by seed in autumn.
E. coccineum illus. p.93.

Emerald ripple. See *Peperomia caperata*, illus. p.300.

EMILIA,
syn. CACALIA
ASTERACEAE/COMPOSITAE

Genus of annuals and perennials with flower heads that are good for cutting. Is ideal for hot, dry areas and coastal soils. Requires sun and very well-drained soil. Propagate by seed sown under glass in spring, or outdoors in late spring.
E. coccinea, syn. *E. flammea*, *E. javanica* of gardens, illus. p.341.
E. flammea. See *E. coccinea*.
E. javanica of gardens. See *E. coccinea*.

EMMENOPTERYS
RUBIACEAE

Genus of deciduous trees, grown mainly for their foliage; flowers appear only rarely, during hot summers. Even where hardy, young growths may be damaged by late frosts. Needs full sun and deep, fertile, well-drained soil. Propagate by softwood cuttings in summer.
E. henryi illus. p.80.
Empress tree. See *Paulownia tomentosa*, illus. p.77.

ENCEPHALARTOS
ZAMIACEAE

Genus of evergreen shrubs and trees, grown for their palm-like appearance. Tender, min. 10–13°C (50–55°F). Needs full light and well-drained soil. Water plotted plants moderately when in full growth, less at other times. Propagate by seed in spring.
E. ferox illus. p.152.
E. longifolius. Slow-growing, evergreen, palm-like tree, sometimes branched with age. H 3m (10ft) or more, S 1.5–2.5m (5–8ft). Has feather-shaped leaves, each 60cm–1.5m (2–5ft) long, divided into narrowly lance-shaped to oval, blue-green leaflets, usually with hook-tipped teeth. Cone-like, brownish flower heads appear intermittently.

ENCYCLIA

See also ORCHIDS.
E. cochleata. Evergreen, epiphytic orchid for a cool greenhouse. H 30cm (12in). Upright spikes of green flowers, 5cm (2in) long, with dark purple lips at the top and ribbon-like sepals and petals, are produced in summer and, on mature plants, intermittently throughout the year. Leaves are narrowly oval and 15cm (6in) long. Requires semi-shade in summer.
E. radiata. Evergreen, epiphytic orchid

for a cool greenhouse. H 25cm (10in). Bears upright spikes of very fragrant, well-rounded, creamy-white flowers, 1cm (½in) across, with red-lined white lips, in summer. Narrowly oval leaves are 10–15cm (4–6in) long. Needs semi-shade in summer.

Endymion. Reclassified as *Hyacinthoides*.
Engelmann spruce. See *Picea engelmannii*, illus. p.105.
English bluebell. See *Hyacinthoides non-scripta*, illus. p.414.
English elm. See *Ulmus procera*.
English iris. See *Iris latifolia*, illus. p.234.
English lavender. See *Lavandula* x *intermedia*.

ENKIANTHUS
ERICACEAE

Genus of deciduous or semi-evergreen, spring-flowering shrubs and trees, grown for their mass of small, bell- or urn-shaped flowers and their autumn colour. Needs sun or semi-shade and moist, peaty, acid soil. Propagate by semi-ripe cuttings in summer or by seed in autumn.
E. campanulatus illus. p.117.
E. cernuus f. *rubens* illus. p.131.
E. perulatus illus. p.127.

ENSETE
MUSACEAE

Genus of evergreen perennials, grown for their foliage, which resembles that of bananas, and fruits. Has false stems made of overlapping leaf sheaths that die after flowering. Tender, min. 10°C (50°F). Grow in sun or partial shade and humus-rich soil. Propagate by seed in spring or by division year-round.
E. ventricosum, syn. *Musa arnoldiana*, *M. ensete*, illus. p.233.

EOMECON
PAPAVERACEAE

Genus of one species of perennial that spreads rapidly and deeply underground. Is suitable for large rock gardens. Needs sun and well-drained soil. Propagate by seed or runners in spring.
E. chionantha (Snow poppy). Vigorous, spreading perennial. H to 40cm (16in), S indefinite. Leaves are large, palmate and grey. Erect stems each carry a long panicle of small, poppy-like, white flowers in summer.

EPACRIS
EPACRIDACEAE

Genus of evergreen, heath-like shrubs, grown for their flowers. Tender, min. 5°C (41°F). Needs full sun and humus-rich, well-drained, neutral to acid soil. Water potted plants moderately when in full growth, less at other times. Flowered stems may be shortened after flowering to maintain a neat habit. Propagate by seed in spring or semi-ripe cuttings in late summer.
E. impressa illus. p.155.

Epaulette tree. See *Pterostyrax hispida*.

EPHEDRA
EPHEDRACEAE

Genus of evergreen shrubs, grown for their habit and green shoots. Makes good ground cover in dry soil. Grow male and female plants together in order to obtain fruits. Requires full sun and well-drained soil. Propagate by seed in autumn or by division in autumn or spring.
E. gerardiana. Evergreen, spreading shrub with slender, erect, rush-like, green shoots. H 60cm (2ft), S 2m (6ft). Leaves and flowers are inconspicuous. Bears small, spherical, red fruits. Zone 6.

EPIDENDRUM

See also ORCHIDS.
E. difforme (illus. p.298). Evergreen, epiphytic orchid for an intermediate greenhouse. H 23cm (9in). Large heads of semi-translucent, green flowers, 0.5cm (¼in) across, open in autumn. Has oval, rigid leaves, 2.5–5cm (1–2in) long. Requires shade in summer. Avoid spraying, which can cause spotting of leaves. Propagate by division in spring.
E. ibaguense, syn. *E. radicans* (illus. p.297). Evergreen, epiphytic orchid for a cool greenhouse. H 2m (6ft) or more. Flowers more or less constantly, bearing a succession of feathery-lipped, deep red blooms, 0.5cm (¼in) across. Leaves, 2.5–5cm (1–2in) long, are oval and rigid. Grow in semi-shade during summer. Propagate by tip cuttings in spring.
E. radicans. See *E. ibaguense*.

EPIGAEA
ERICACEAE

Genus of evergreen, prostrate, spring-flowering sub-shrubs. Needs shade and humus-rich, moist, acid soil. Most are difficult to cultivate. Propagate by seed in spring or by softwood cuttings in early summer.
E. asiatica. Evergreen, creeping sub-shrub. H to 10cm (4in), S to 20cm (8in). Stems and heart-shaped, deep green leaves are covered with brown hairs. Bears terminal clusters of 3–6 tiny, slightly fragrant, urn-shaped, white or pink flowers in spring. Zone 6.
E. gaultherioides, syn. *Orphanidesia gaultherioides*, illus. p.364.
E. repens (Mayflower, Trailing arbutus). Evergreen, creeping sub-shrub. H 10cm (4in), S 30cm (12in). Hairy stems, bearing heart-shaped, leathery leaves, root at intervals. In spring produces terminal clusters of 4–6 cup-shaped, white flowers, sometimes flushed pink. Is relatively easy to grow. Zone 2.

EPILOBIUM,
syn. CHAMAENERION
Willow herb
ONAGRACEAE

Genus of annuals, biennials, perennials and deciduous sub-shrubs, grown for

their deep pink to white flowers in summer. Is useful on dry banks; many species are invasive. Tolerates sun or shade and prefers moist but well-drained soil. Propagate species by seed in autumn, selected forms by softwood cuttings from side-shoots in spring.
E. angustifolium f. *album* illus. p.226.
E. californicum. See *Zauschneria californica*.
E. canum. See *Zauschneria californica* subsp. *cana*.
E. chlorifolium var. *kaikourense* illus. p.374.
E. glabellum of gardens illus. p.351.
E. obcordatum. Clump-forming perennial. H 15cm (6in), S 10cm (4in). Oval leaves are glossy green. Spikes of open cup-shaped, deep rose-pink flowers are borne in summer. Is good for a rock garden or alpine house. Needs a sheltered site and full sun. In cultivation may not retain character, especially in mild climates.
E. septentrionale. See *Zauschneria septentrionalis*.

EPIMEDIUM
Barrenwort
BERBERIDACEAE

Genus of spring-flowering perennials, some of which are evergreen. Flowers are cup-shaped with long or short spurs. Makes good ground cover. Does best in partial shade and humus-rich, moist but well-drained soil. Cut back just before new growth appears in spring. Propagate by division in spring or autumn.
E. alpinum. Evergreen, clump-forming perennial. H 23cm (9in), S 30cm (12in). Racemes of pendent, short-spurred flowers, with crimson sepals and yellow petals, appear in spring. Has finely toothed, glossy leaves divided into oval, angled, mid-green leaflets, bronze when young.
E. grandiflorum 'Crimson Beauty' (illus. p.51). Clump-forming perennial. H and S 30cm (12in). Racemes of pendent, long-spurred, copper-crimson flowers are produced in spring at the same time as heart-shaped, copper-marked, light green leaves, divided into oval leaflets, which mature to mid-green. 'Rose Queen' illus. p.269. f. *violaceum* has young leaves that are flushed bronze and produces purple-and-white flowers.
E. x perralchicum. Evergreen, carpeting perennial. H 45cm (18in), S 30cm (12in). Short spires of pendent, yellow flowers, with short spurs, are borne on slender stems in spring. Leaves, divided into rounded to oval leaflets, are dark green.
E. perralderianum. Semi-evergreen, carpeting perennial. H 30cm (12in), S 45cm (18in). Clusters of small, pendent, short-spurred, bright yellow flowers are borne in spring. Has large, toothed, glossy, deep green leaves, divided into rounded to oval leaflets.
E. pinnatum subsp. *colchicum*. Evergreen, carpeting perennial. H and S 30cm (12in). In spring, clusters of small, pendent, bright yellow flowers, with short spurs, are produced above dark green leaves, divided into rounded to oval leaflets, that are hairy when young.

E. pubigerum illus. p.268.
E. × *rubrum* illus. p.269.
E. × *versicolor*. Clump-forming perennial. H and S 30cm (12in). Small, pendent clusters of yellow flowers, with long, red-tinged spurs, appear in spring. Heart-shaped, fresh green leaves are divided into oval leaflets that are tinted reddish-purple.
'**Neosulphureum**' illus. p.274.
E. × *warleyense* illus. p.275.
E. × *youngianum* '**Niveum**' illus. p.267.

EPIPHYLLUM
Orchid cactus, Strap cactus

CACTACEAE

Genus of perennial cacti with strap-shaped, flattened, green stems that have notched edges. Flowers are produced at notches. Tender, min. 5–11°C (41–52°F). Grow in sun or partial shade and in rich, well-drained soil. Propagate by stem cuttings in spring or summer.
E. ackermannii. See *Nopalxochia ackermannii*.
E. anguliger illus. p.461.
E. crenatum. Erect, then pendent, perennial cactus. H and S 3m (10ft). Min. 11°C (52°F). Has a flattened stem. Bears lightly perfumed, funnel-shaped, broad-petalled, white flowers, 20cm (8in) across, in spring-summer. Is often used as a parent for breeding.
E. laui illus. p.461.
E. oxypetalum. Erect, then pendent, perennial cactus. H 3m (10ft), S 1m (3ft). Min. 11°C (52°F). Produces freely branching, flattened stems, 12cm (5in) across. In spring-summer bears nocturnal, tubular, white flowers, 25cm (10in) long. Makes a good house plant.

EPIPREMNUM,
syn. POTHOS

ARACEAE

Genus of evergreen, woody-stemmed, root climbers, including *Pothos*, grown for their handsome leaves. Tender, min. 15–18°C (59–64°F). Grow in light shade away from direct sun; any well-drained, moisture-retentive soil is suitable. Water regularly, less in cold weather. Stems need good supports. Remove shoot tips to induce branching at any time. Propagate by leaf-bud or stem-tip cuttings in late spring or by layering in summer. All parts may cause severe discomfort if ingested, and contact with the sap of *E. aureum* may irritate skin.
E. aureum '**Marble Queen**', syn. *Scindapsus aureus* 'Marble Queen', illus. p.219.
E. pictum '**Argyraeum**', syn. *Scindapsus pictus* 'Argyraeus', illus. p.219.

EPISCIA

GESNERIACEAE

Genus of evergreen, low-growing and creeping perennials, grown for their ornamental leaves and colourful flowers. Is useful as ground cover or in hanging baskets. Tender, min. 15°C (59°F). Requires high humidity and a

fairly shaded position in humus-rich, well-drained soil. Keep well watered, but avoid waterlogging. Propagate in summer by stem cuttings, division or removing rooted runners.
E. cupreata (Flame violet) illus. p.301.
'**Metallica**' is an evergreen, creeping perennial. H 10cm (4in), S indefinite. Has oval, downy, wrinkled leaves, tinged pink to copper and with broad, silvery bands along midribs. Funnel-shaped, orange-red flowers, marked yellow within, are borne intermittently. '**Tropical Topaz**' has yellow flowers.
E. dianthiflora, syn. *Alsobia dianthiflora*, illus. p.299.
E. lilacina. Evergreen, low-growing perennial, with runners bearing plantlets. H 10cm (4in), S indefinite. Has oval, hairy, pale green leaves, to 8cm (3in) long. Funnel-shaped, white flowers, tinged mauve and with yellow eyes, are produced in small clusters from autumn to spring. Leaves of '**Cuprea**' are bronze-tinged.

EPITHELANTHA

CACTACEAE

Genus of very slow-growing, spherical, perennial cacti densely covered with very short spines. Tender, min. 10°C (50°F). Needs full sun and well-drained soil, and is prone to rot if overwatered. Is easier to cultivate if grafted. Propagate by seed or stem cuttings in spring or summer.
E. micromeris illus. p.471

ERANTHEMUM

ACANTHACEAE

Genus of perennials and evergreen shrubs, grown for their flowers. Tender, min. 15–18°C (59–64°F). Requires full light or partial shade and fertile, well-drained soil. Water containerized plants freely when in full growth, moderately at other times. In spring or after flowering remove at least half of each spent flowering stem to encourage a bushier habit. Propagate by softwood cuttings in late spring. Whitefly may be a nuisance.
E. atropurpureum. See *Pseuderanthemum atropurpureum*.
E. nervosum. See *E. pulchellum*.
E. pulchellum, syn. *E. nervosum*. Evergreen, erect shrub. H 1–1.2m (3–4ft), S 60cm (2ft) or more. Produces elliptic to oval, prominently veined, deep green leaves. Blue flowers, each with a 3cm (1¼in) long tube and rounded petal lobes, are produced in winter-spring.

ERANTHIS

RANUNCULACEAE

Genus of clump-forming perennials, with knobbly tubers, grown for their cup-shaped flowers surrounded by leaf-like ruffs of bracts. Prefers partial shade and humus-rich soil, well-drained but not drying out excessively. Dies down in summer. Propagate by seed in autumn or by division of clumps immediately after flowering while still in leaf. All parts may cause mild stomach upset if ingested, and contact with the sap may irritate skin.

E. hyemalis illus. p.441.
E. × *tubergenii* '**Guinea Gold**'. Late winter- or early spring-flowering, tuberous perennial. H 8–10cm (3–4in), S 4–6cm (1½–2⅜in). Stems each bear a stalkless, deep golden-yellow flower, 3–4cm (1¼–1½in) across, surrounded by a bronze-green bract, cut into narrow lobes. Rounded leaves are divided into finger-shaped lobes.

ERCILLA,
syn. BRIDGESIA

PHYTOLACCACEAE

Genus of evergreen, root climbers, grown for their neat, green leaves and green and purple flower spikes. Grow in sun or partial shade and in any well-drained soil. Prune after flowering, if required. Propagate by stem cuttings in late summer or autumn.
E. spicata. See *E. volubilis*.
E. volubilis, syn. *E. spicata*, illus. p.204.

EREMURUS
Foxtail lily, King's spear

ASPHODELACEAE/LILIACEAE

Genus of perennials, with fleshy, finger-like roots, grown for their stately spires of shallowly cup-shaped flowers in summer. Requires a sunny, warm position and well-drained soil. Tends to come into growth very early, and young shoots may be frosted. Provide a covering of dry bracken in late winter to protect the crowns when shoots are first developing. Stake tall species and hybrids. Propagate by division in spring or early autumn or by seed in autumn.
E. himalaicus illus. p.226.
E. robustus illus. p.227.
E. **Shelford Hybrids**. Group of perennials of varying habit and flower colour. H 1.5m (5ft), S 60cm (2ft). Long racemes of orange, buff, pink or white flowers are borne freely in mid-summer. Leaves are strap-shaped, in basal rosettes.
E. spectabilis. Erect perennial. H 1.2m (4ft), S 60cm (2ft). Bears long racemes of pale yellow flowers, with brick-red anthers, in early summer. Leaves are strap-shaped, in basal rosettes.

ERIA

See also ORCHIDS.

E. coronaria, syn. *Trichosma suavis*. Evergreen, epiphytic orchid for a cool greenhouse. H 23cm (9in). Sprays of fragrant, rounded, creamy-white flowers, 1cm (½in) across, each with a red- and yellow-marked lip, open in autumn. Has broadly oval, glossy leaves, 10cm (4in) long. Needs semi-shade in summer and moist compost year-round.

ERICA

ERICACEAE

See also HEATHERS.
E. arborea (Tree heath). Evergreen, upright, shrub-like tree heath. H 6m (20ft), S 1.5m (5ft). Hardy to tender. Liable to damage from frost and cold winds. Has needle-like, bright green

leaves in whorls of 3 or 4 and bears scented, bell-shaped, white flowers from late winter to late spring. May tolerate slightly alkaline soil. Zone 8. '**Albert's Gold**', H 2m (6ft), retains its golden foliage year-round. var. *alpina* (illus. p.178) has vivid green foliage that contrasts well with compact racemes of white flowers. May be pruned hard to keep its shape and to encourage new growth. Zone 9.
E. australis (Spanish heath, Spanish tree heath). Evergreen, shrub-like tree heath. H to 2.2m (7ft), S 1m (3ft). Stems may be damaged by snow and frost. Has needle-like leaves in whorls of 4 and tubular to bell-shaped, white or purplish-pink flowers in spring. May tolerate slightly alkaline soil. Zone 8. '**Mr Robert**' has white flowers. '**Riverslea**' has bright purple-pink flowers, mostly in clusters of 4.
E. canaliculata (Channelled heath; illus. p.178). Evergreen, erect shrub. H to 3m (10ft), S 1m (3ft). Dark green leaves are narrow and needle-like in whorls of 3. Cup-shaped, pearl-white flowers, sometimes rose-tinted, with dark brown, almost black anthers, are borne in winter (under glass) or early spring (in the open). Requires acid soil. Zone 9.
E. carnea, syn. *E. herbacea* (Alpine heath, Winter heath). Evergreen, spreading shrub. H to 30cm (12in), S to 45cm (18in) or more. Produces whorls of needle-like, mid- to dark green leaves and bears tubular to bell-shaped flowers that are in shades of pink and red, occasionally white, from early winter to late spring. Tolerates limestone and some shade. Makes good ground cover. Zone 4. '**Altadena**' has golden foliage and pale pink flowers. '**Ann Sparkes**' (illus. p.179), H 15cm (6in), has golden foliage, turning to bronze in winter, and rose-pink flowers. '**Bell's Extra Special**', H 15cm (6in), S 40cm (16in), has a neat habit, with crimson flowers borne on distinctive, whisky-coloured foliage, flecked with tints of orange and gold. '**Cecilia M. Beale**', H 15cm (6in), bears an abundance of white flowers from mid-winter to early spring. '**December Red**' (illus. p.178) has a spreading habit and vigorous growth. Deep rose-pink flowers are borne in winter. '**Foxhollow**', a vigorous, spreading cultivar, has foliage that is golden-yellow in summer, with orange tips in spring, and a few pale pink flowers. '**Golden Starlet**' (illus. p.178), H 15cm (6in), S 40cm (16in), bears white flowers set on lime-green foliage that turns a glowing yellow in summer. '**Ice Princess**', H 15cm (6in), S 35cm (14in), has white flowers held erect on bright green foliage. '**Isabell**', H 15cm (6in), S 35cm (14in), has large, white flowers on bright green foliage, and an erect but spreading habit. '**King George**', H 20cm (8in), has dark green foliage and deep rose-pink flowers from early winter to mid-spring. '**Loughrigg**', H 15cm (6in), produces dark purplish-red flowers from late winter to spring. '**March Seedling**' has a spreading habit, dark green foliage and rich, rose-purple flowers. '**Myretoun Ruby**', H 20cm (8in), is

vigorous but compact with brilliant deep purple-red flowers in late winter and early spring. **'Nathalie'**, H 15cm (6in), S 40cm (16in), the deepest and brightest of the *E. carnea* cultivars, has purple flowers, neat, dark green foliage and a compact, upright habit. **'Pink Spangles'**, H 15cm (6in), is vigorous with flowers that have shell-pink sepals and deeper pink corollas. **'Pirbright Rose'** is very floriferous with bright pink flowers from early winter to early spring. **'R.B. Cooke'**, H 20cm (8in), bears clear pink flowers from early winter to early spring. **'Rosalie'** (illus. p.179), H 15cm (6in), S 35cm (14in), has bright pink flowers, bronze-green foliage and a low, upright but spreading habit. **'Springwood White'** (illus. p.178), H 15cm (6in), the most vigorous white cultivar, is excellent as ground cover and bears large, white flowers, with brown anthers, from late winter to spring. **'Vivellii'** (illus. p.179), H 15cm (6in), has dark bronze-green foliage and bears deep purple-pink flowers from late winter to spring. **'Westwood Yellow'** (illus. p.179) is compact with golden-yellow foliage and deep pink flowers. **'Winter Sun'** see *E.c.* 'Wintersonne'. **'Wintersonne'** (syn. *E.c.* 'Winter Sun'), H 15cm (6in), S 35cm (14in), has magenta flowers and red-brown foliage. All Zone 4.
E. ciliaris (Dorset heath). Evergreen, loose shrub. H to 30cm (12in), S 40cm (16in). May be damaged in severe weather. Has needle-like, dark green leaves in whorls of 3. Bears long racemes of bell-shaped, bright pink flowers in tiers of 3 or 4 in summer. Requires acid soil and prefers warm, moist conditions. Zone 6. **'Aurea'** has somewhat straggly growth with golden foliage and clear pink flowers. **'Corfe Castle'** (illus. p.179) produces salmon-pink flowers from summer to early autumn. **'David McClintock'** (illus. p.178) has light grey-green foliage and bears white flowers, with deep pink tips, from summer to early autumn. **'Mrs C.H. Gill'** has dark grey-green foliage and clear red flowers. **'White Wings'** (illus. p.178), a sport of 'Mrs C.H. Gill', has dark grey-green foliage and white flowers.
E. cinerea (Bell heather). Evergreen, compact shrub. H 30cm (12in), S 45–60cm (18–24in). Has needle-like, mid- to deep green leaves and bears bell-shaped flowers that are in shades of pink and dark red, occasionally white, from early summer to autumn. Prefers a warm, dry position. Requires acid soil. Zone 6. **'Atropurpurea'** has deep purple flowers in long racemes. **'C.D. Eason'** (illus. p.179) has distinctive, dark green foliage and bright red flowers. **'Cevennes'** is upright in habit and bears a profusion of mauve flowers. **'C.G. Best'** has mid-green foliage and rose-pink flowers. **'Domino'** produces white flowers that contrast with dark brown stems and sepals and almost black stigmas. **'Eden Valley'** (illus. p.179), H 20cm (8in), bears white flowers with lavender-mauve tips. **'Fiddler's Gold'** (illus. p.179), H 25cm (10in), has golden-yellow foliage, deepening to red in winter, and

lilac-pink flowers. **'Golden Hue'**, H 35cm (14in), has amethyst flowers set on pale yellow foliage, tipped orange in winter. **'Hookstone White'** (illus. p.178), H 35cm (14in), has bright green foliage and bears long racemes of large, white flowers. **'Lime Soda'**, H 35cm (14in), produces soft lavender flowers in profusion on attractive, lime-green foliage. **'Pentreath'** has rich purple flowers. **'Pink Ice'**, H 20cm (8in), is compact with soft pink flowers. **'P.S. Patrick'** is a vigorous cultivar with purple flowers and dark green foliage. **'Purple Beauty'** (illus. p.179) has purple flowers and dark foliage. **'Stephen Davis'**, H 25cm (10in), has brilliant, almost fluorescent, red flowers. **'Velvet Night'**, H 25cm (10in), produces very dark purple, almost black flowers. **'Windlebrooke'** (illus. p.179), H 25cm (10in), is vigorous, with golden foliage, turning bright orange-red in winter, and mauve flowers. All Zone 6.
E. × darleyensis. Evergreen, bushy shrub. H 45cm (18in), S 1m (3ft) or more. Has needle-like, mid-green foliage, with cream, pink or red, young growth in late spring. Bell-shaped, white, pink or purple flowers are borne in racemes from early winter to late spring. Tolerates limestone. Zone 5. **'Archie Graham'** (illus. p.178), H 50cm (20in), is vigorous with mauve-pink flowers. **'Arthur Johnson'**, H 1m (3ft), has young foliage with cream and pink tips in spring and long racemes of mauve-pink flowers from mid-winter to spring. **'Darley Dale'** (illus. p.178) bears pale mauve flowers from mid-winter to spring. **'George Rendall'** carries deep pink flowers from early winter to early spring. **'Ghost Hills'** (illus. p.178) has cream-tipped foliage in spring and a profusion of pink flowers from mid-winter to spring. **'Jack H. Brummage'**, H 30cm (12in), has golden foliage, with yellow and orange tints, and mauve flowers. **'J.W. Porter'**, H 30cm (12in), has reddish, young shoots in spring and mauve-pink flowers from mid-winter to late spring. **'Kramer's Rote'** (syn. *E. × d.* 'Kramer's Red') has dark bronze-green foliage with deep purple-red flowers from late autumn to late spring. Spring foliage does not have cream or red tips. **'Molten Silver'** see *E. × d.* 'Silberschmelze'. **'Silberschmelze'** (syn. *E. × d.* 'Molten Silver') is vigorous and produces young shoots with creamy-pink tips in spring and white flowers. **'White Glow'** (illus. p.178), H 30cm (12in), bears white flowers. **'White Perfection'** (illus. p.178) has bright green foliage and white flowers. All Zone 5.
E. erigena, syn. *E. hibernica*, *E. mediterranea*. Evergreen, upright shrub. H to 2.5m (8ft), S to 1m (3ft). Top growth may be damaged in severe weather, but plant recovers well from the base. Has needle-like, mid-green leaves and, usually, bell-shaped, mauve-pink flowers from early winter to late spring. Tolerates limestone. Flowers of some cultivars have a pronounced scent of honey. Zone 7.

'Brightness' (illus. p.179), H 45cm (18in), has bronze-green foliage and mauve-pink flowers in spring. **'Golden Lady'** (illus. p.179), H 30cm (12in), has a neat, compact habit with year-round, golden foliage and white flowers in late spring. **'Irish Dusk'**, H 45cm (18in), has dark green foliage and salmon-pink flowers from mid-winter to early spring. **'Superba'**, H 2m (6ft), bears strongly scented, rose-pink flowers during spring. **'W.T. Rackliff'**, H 60cm (2ft), has dark green foliage and produces thick clusters of white flowers from late winter to late spring.
E. gracilis. Evergreen, compact shrub. H and S to 30cm (12in). Tender, min. 5°C (41°F). Has needle-like, mid-green leaves and clusters of small, bell-shaped, cerise flowers from early autumn to early spring. Is usually grown as a pot plant; may be planted outdoors in summer in a sheltered site.
E. herbacea. See *E. carnea*.
E. hibernica. See *E. erigena*.
E. × hiemalis. Evergreen, bushy shrub. H and S 30cm (12in). Tender. Has needle-like, mid-green foliage and racemes of tubular to bell-shaped, pink-tinged, white flowers from late autumn to mid-winter.
E. lusitanica (Portuguese heath). Evergreen, upright, bushy, tree heath. H to 3m (10ft), S 1m (3ft). Has feathery, bright green leaves and, from late autumn to late spring, bears tubular to bell-shaped flowers that are pink in bud but pure white when fully open. Zone 9. **'George Hunt'** has golden foliage; needs a sheltered position.
E. mackaiana, syn. *E. mackayana* (Mackay's heath). Evergreen, spreading shrub. H to 25cm (10in), S 40cm (16in). Fully hardy. Has needle-like, mid-green leaves and bears umbels of rounded, pink, mauve-pink or white flowers from mid-summer to early autumn. Likes damp, acid soil. Zone 5. **'Dr Ronald Gray'** (illus. p.178), H 15cm (6in), has dark green foliage and pure white flowers. **'Plena'** (illus. p.178), H 15cm (6in), has double, deep-pink flowers, shading to white in centres.
E. mackayana. See *E. mackaiana*.
E. mediterranea. See *E. erigena*.
E. pageana. Evergreen, bushy shrub. H to 60cm (2ft), S 30cm (1ft). Has needle-like, mid-green leaves and, from late spring to early summer, bell-shaped, rich yellow flowers. Tender.
E. × praegeri. See *E. × stuartii*.
E. scoparia (Besom heath). Evergreen, bushy shrub. H to 3m (10ft), S 1m (3ft). Has needle-like, dark green leaves. Clusters of rounded, bell-shaped, greenish-brown flowers appear in late spring and early summer. Requires acid soil. Zone 9. **'Minima'**, H 30cm (12in), has bright green foliage.
E. spiculifolia, syn. *Bruckenthalia spiculifolia* (Spike heath). Evergreen, heath-like shrub. H and S 15cm (6in). Tiny, needle-like, glossy, dark green leaves clothe stiff stems. Terminal clusters of tiny, pink flowers appear in summer. Zone 6.
E. stricta. See *E. terminalis*.
E. × stuartii, syn. *E. × praegeri*. Evergreen, compact shrub. H 15cm (6in), S 30cm (12in). Has needle-like,

dark green leaves. Numerous umbels of bell-shaped, pink flowers are produced in late spring and summer. Prefers moist, acid soil. Zone 5.
'Irish Lemon' produces young foliage with lemon-yellow tips in spring and bright pink flowers. **'Irish Orange'** has orange-tipped young foliage and dark pink flowers.
E. terminalis, syn. *E. stricta* (Corsican heath). Evergreen, shrub-like tree heath with stiff, upright growth. H and S to 2.5m (8ft). Has needle-like, mid-green foliage. Bell-shaped, mauve-pink flowers, borne from early summer to early autumn, turn russet as they fade in winter. Tolerates limestone. Zone 8.
E. tetralix (Cross-leaved heath). Evergreen, spreading shrub. H to 30cm (12in), S 45cm (18in). Has needle-like, grey-green leaves in whorls of 4. Large umbels of bell-shaped, pink flowers appear from summer to early autumn. Requires acid, preferably moist soil. Zone 5. **'Alba Mollis'** (illus. p.178) has silver-grey foliage and bears white flowers from early summer to late autumn. **'Con Underwood'** (illus. p.179) has dark red flowers. **'Hookstone Pink'** has silver-grey foliage and bears rose-pink flowers from late spring to early autumn. **'Pink Star'** (illus. p.179) produces pink flowers held upright in a star-like pattern.
E. umbellata. Evergreen, bushy shrub. H and S 60cm (2ft). Has needle-like, mid-green foliage and bell-shaped, mauve flowers, with chocolate-brown anthers, in late spring. Zone 8.
E. vagans (Cornish heath). Vigorous, evergreen, bushy shrub. H and S 75cm (30in). Leaves are needle-like and mid-green. Rounded, bell-shaped, pink, mauve or white flowers appear from mid-summer to late autumn. Tolerates some limestone. Responds well to hard pruning. Zone 5. **'Birch Glow'** (illus. p.179), H 45cm (18in), has bright green foliage and glowing rose-pink flowers. **'Lyonesse'** (illus. p.178), H 45cm (18in), has dark green foliage and long, tapering spikes of white flowers with brown anthers. **'Mrs D.F. Maxwell'**, H 45cm (18in), has dark green foliage and glowing deep pink flowers. **'St Keverne'**, H 45cm (18in), is a neat, bushy shrub with rose-pink flowers; may be used for a low hedge. **'Valerie Proudley'** (illus. p.179), H 45cm (18in), has golden foliage year-round when grown in full light, and bears sparse, white flowers in late summer and autumn.
E. × veitchii. Evergreen, bushy, shrub-like tree heath. H to 2m (6ft), S 1m (3ft). Has needle-like, mid-green leaves. Scented, tubular to bell-shaped, white flowers are produced in dense clusters from mid-winter to spring. Zone 8. **'Exeter'** (illus. p.178) has a profusion of white flowers, almost obscuring the foliage. **'Gold Tips'** is similar to 'Exeter', but young foliage has golden tips in spring. **'Pink Joy'** (illus. p.178) has pink flower buds that open to clear white.
E. verticillata. Evergreen, erect shrub. H to 60cm (2ft), S 30cm (1ft). Tender, min. 5–7°C (41–5°F). Has a very unusual and attractive arrangement of

flowers tightly packed in whorls at intervals along an otherwise almost bare stem. Bears tubular, pale mauve-pink flowers, 1.5cm (½in) long, intermittently throughout the year.
E. × watsonii. Evergreen, compact shrub. H 30cm (12in), S 38cm (15in). Needle-like, mid-green leaves often have bright-coloured tips in spring. Bears rounded, bell-shaped, pink flowers from mid- to late summer. Zone 5. **'Cherry Turpin'** has long racemes of pale pink flowers from mid-summer to mid-autumn. **'Dawn'** (illus. p.178) produces young foliage with orange-yellow tips and bears deep mauve-pink flowers in compact clusters all summer.
E. × williamsii. Evergreen, spreading shrub. H 30cm (12in), S 60cm (24in). Has needle-like, dark green leaves, with bright yellow tips when young in spring. Bears bell-shaped, mauve or pink flowers in mid-summer. Prefers acid soil. Zone 5. **'Gwavas'** has pale pink flowers on a neat, compact plant from mid-summer to autumn. **'P.D. Williams'** (illus. p.178), H 45cm (18in), has dark mauve-pink flowers; sometimes keeps its golden foliage tips all summer.

ERIGERON
Fleabane

ASTERACEAE/COMPOSITAE

Genus of mainly spring- and summer-flowering annuals, biennials and perennials, grown for their daisy-like flower heads. Is good for rock gardens or herbaceous borders. Prefers sun and well-drained soil but should not be allowed to dry out during growing season. Resents winter damp. Propagate by division in spring or early autumn or by seed in autumn, selected forms by softwood cuttings in early summer.
E. alpinus illus. p.355.
E. aurantiacus. Clump-forming perennial. H 15cm (6in), S 30cm (12in). Has long, oval, grey-green leaves and produces daisy-like, brilliant orange flower heads in summer. Propagate by seed or division in spring.
E. aureus. Short-lived, clump-forming perennial. H 5–10cm (2–4in), S 15cm (6in). Bears small, spoon-shaped to oval, hairy leaves. Slender stems each bear a relatively large, daisy-like, golden-yellow flower head in summer. Dislikes winter wet with no snow cover. Is excellent for a scree, trough or alpine house; is prone to aphid attack. **'Canary Bird'**, H to 10cm (4in), is longer lived, and bears bright canary-yellow flower heads.
E. 'Charity' illus. p.278.
E. 'Darkest of All'. See *E.* 'Dunkelste Aller'.
E. 'Dunkelste Aller', syn. *E.* 'Darkest of All'. Clump-forming perennial. H 80cm (32in), S 60cm (24in) or more. Produces a mass of daisy-like, deep purple flower heads, with yellow centres, in summer. Has narrowly oval, greyish-green leaves.
E. 'Foerster's Liebling'. Clump-forming perennial. H 80cm (32in), S 60cm (24in). In summer daisy-like, semi-double, pink flower heads, with

yellow centres, are borne above narrowly oval, greyish-green leaves.
E. glaucus 'Elstead Pink'. Tufted perennial. H 30cm (12in), S 15cm (6in). Daisy-like, dark lilac-pink flower heads appear throughout summer above oval, grey-green leaves.
E. karvinskianus, syn. *E. mucronatus*, illus. p.377.
E. mucronatus. See *E. karvinskianus*.
E. 'Quakeress'. Clump-forming perennial. H 80cm (32in), S 60cm (24in). Produces a mass of daisy-like, delicate lilac-pink flower heads, with yellow centres, in summer. Narrowly oval leaves are greyish-green.
E. 'Serenity' illus. p.284.

ERINACEA
LEGUMINOSAE/PAPILIONACEAE

Genus of one species of slow-growing, evergreen sub-shrub with hard, sharp, blue-green spines and pea-like flowers. In spring produces short-lived, soft leaves. Needs a sheltered position with full sun and deep, gritty, well-drained soil. Propagate by seed when available or by softwood cuttings in late spring or summer. Zone 8.
E. anthyllis, syn. *E. pungens*, illus. p.348.
E. pungens. See *E. anthyllis*.

ERINUS
Fairy foxglove

SCROPHULARIACEAE

Genus of short-lived, semi-evergreen perennials, suitable for rock gardens, walls and troughs. Needs sun and well-drained soil. Propagate species by seed in autumn (but seedlings will vary considerably), selected forms by softwood cuttings in early summer. Self-seeds freely.
E. alpinus illus. p.366. **'Dr Hähnle'** (syn. *E.a.* 'Dr Haenele') is a semi-evergreen, basal-rosetted perennial. H and S 5–8cm (2–3in). Small, flat, 2-lipped, deep pink flowers open in late spring and summer. Leaves are small, oval and mid-green.

ERIOBOTRYA
ROSACEAE

Genus of evergreen, autumn-flowering trees and shrubs, grown for their foliage, flowers and edible fruits. Where hardy, best against a south- or west-facing wall. Fruits, which ripen in spring, may be damaged by hard frosts. Requires sunny, fertile, well-drained soil. Propagate by seed in autumn or spring.
E. japonica (Loquat). Evergreen, bushy shrub or spreading tree. H and S 8m (25ft). Has stout shoots and large, oblong, prominently veined, glossy, dark green leaves. Fragrant, 5-petalled, white flowers are borne in large clusters in early autumn, followed by pear-shaped, orange-yellow fruits. Zone 9.

ERIOGONUM
Wild buckwheat

POLYGONACEAE

Genus of annuals, biennials and evergreen perennials, sub-shrubs and shrubs, grown for their rosetted, hairy,

often silver or white leaves. Hardy to tender, min. 5°C (41°F). Needs full sun and well-drained, even poor soil. In cool, wet-winter areas protect shrubby species and hairy-leaved perennials. Water potted plants moderately in summer, less in spring and autumn, very little in winter. Remove flower heads after flowering unless seed is required. Propagate by seed in spring or autumn or by semi-ripe cuttings in summer. Divide perennial root clumps in spring.
E. arborescens illus. p.161.
E. crocatum. Evergreen, sub-shrubby perennial. H to 20cm (8in), S 15cm (6in). Oval, hairy leaves have woolly, white undersides. Heads of minute, sulphur-yellow flowers are borne in summer. Is a good alpine house plant. Zone 9?.
E. giganteum illus. p.139.
E. ovalifolium. Evergreen, domed perennial. H 30cm (12in), S 10cm (4in). In summer carries tiny, bright yellow flowers in umbels above branched stems bearing tiny, spoon-shaped, hairy, grey leaves. Is excellent for an alpine house.
E. umbellatum illus. p.358.

ERIOPHYLLUM
ASTERACEAE/COMPOSITAE

Genus of summer-flowering perennials and evergreen sub-shrubs, with, usually, silvery foliage and attractive, daisy-like flower heads, suitable for rock gardens and front of borders. Needs sun and well-drained soil. Propagate by division in spring or by seed in autumn.
E. lanatum, syn. *Bahia lanata*, illus. p.293.

ERITRICHIUM
BORAGINACEAE

Genus of short-lived perennials with soft, grey-green leaves and forget-me-not-like flowers. Is suitable for rock gardens and alpine houses. Needs sun and well-drained, peaty, sandy soil with a deep collar of grit; dislikes damp conditions. Is extremely difficult to grow. Propagate by seed when available or by softwood cuttings in summer.
E. elongatum. Tuft-forming perennial. H 2cm (¾in), S 3cm (1¼in). Leaves are oval, hairy and grey-green. Short flower stems each carry small, rounded, flat, blue flowers in early summer.
E. nanum illus. p.383.

ERODIUM
GERANIACEAE

Genus of mound-forming perennials, suitable for rock gardens. Needs sun and well-drained soil. Propagate by semi-ripe cuttings in summer or by seed when available.
E. chamaedryoides. See *E. reichardii*.
E. cheilanthifolium, syn. *E. petraeum* subsp. *crispum*, illus. p.355.
E. chrysanthum illus. p.358.
E. corsicum illus. p.376.
E. foetidum, syn. *E. petraeum*. Compact, mound-forming perennial. H 15–20cm (6–8in), S 20cm (8in).

Produces saucer-shaped, single, red-veined, pink flowers in summer. Oval, grey leaves have deeply cut edges.
E. manescaui, syn. *E. manescavii*, illus. p.279.
E. manescavii. See *E. manescaui*.
E. petraeum. See *E. foetidum*. subsp. *crispum* see *E. cheilanthifolium*.
E. reichardii, syn. *E. chamaedryoides*. Mound-forming perennial. H 2.5cm (1in), S 6–8cm (2½–3in). In summer saucer-shaped, single flowers, either white or pink with darker veins, are borne above tiny, oak-like leaves. Is good for a rock garden or trough.
E. × variabile 'Flore Pleno'. Variable, cushion-forming or spreading perennial. H 10cm (4in), S 30cm (12in). Has oval to narrowly oval, dark to grey-green leaves with scalloped edges and long stalks. From spring to autumn flower stems each bear 1 or 2 rounded, double, pink flowers with darker veins; outer petals are rounded, inner petals narrower. **'Ken Aslet'** has prostrate stems, mid-green leaves and single, deep pink flowers.

Erpetion reniforme. See *Viola hederacea*.

ERYNGIUM
Sea holly

APIACEAE/UMBELLIFERAE

Genus of biennals and perennials, some of which are evergreen, grown for their flowers, foliage and habit. Thrives in sun and fertile, well-drained soil. Propagate species by seed in autumn, selected forms by division in spring or by root cuttings in winter.
E. agavifolium, syn. *E. bromeliifolium* of gardens. Evergreen, clump-forming perennial. H 1.5m (5ft), S 60cm (2ft). Forms rosettes of sword-shaped, sharply toothed, rich green leaves. Thistle-like, greenish-white flower heads are produced on branched stems in summer.
E. alpinum illus. p.253.
E. amethystinum. Rosette-forming perennial. H and S 60cm (24in). Oval leaves are divided, spiny and mid-green. Produces much-branched stems that, in summer, bear heads of small, thistle-like, blue flowers surrounded by spiky, darker blue bracts.
E. bourgatii illus. p.286.
E. bromeliifolium of gardens. See *E. agavifolium*.
E. eburneum, syn. *E. paniculatum*, illus. p.226.
E. giganteum. Clump-forming biennial or short-lived perennial that dies after flowering. H 1–1.2m (3–4ft), S 75cm (2½ft). Heart-shaped, basal leaves are mid-green. Large, rounded heads of thistle-like, blue flowers, surrounded by broad, spiny, silvery bracts, are produced in late summer.
E. × oliverianum illus. p.253.
E. paniculatum. See *E. eburneum*.
E. × tripartitum illus. p.253.
E. variifolium illus. p.286.
E. × zabelii 'Violetta'. Upright perennial. H 75cm (30in), S 60cm (24in). Has rounded, mid-green leaves divided into 3–5 segments. Loose heads of thistle-like, deep violet

flowers, surrounded by narrow, spiny, silvery-blue bracts, appear in late summer.

ERYSIMUM

BRASSICACEAE/CRUCIFERAE

Genus of annuals, biennials, evergreen or semi-evergreen, short-lived perennials and sub-shrubs, grown for their flowers. Is closely related to *Cheiranthus* and is suitable for borders, banks and rock gardens. Needs sun and well-drained soil. Propagate by seed in spring or autumn or by softwood cuttings in summer.

E. x allionii, syn. *Cheiranthus x allionii* (Siberian wallflower). **'Orange Bedder'** illus. p.340.

E. **'Bowles Mauve'**, syn. *Cheiranthus* 'Bowles Mauve', *E.* 'E.A. Bowles'. Bushy perennial. H to 75cm (30in), S 45cm (18in). Narrowly lance-shaped, dark green leaves are 5cm (2in) long. Many clusters of small, rich mauve flowers, each with 4 spreading petals, are borne in spring and early summer.

E. **'Bredon'**, syn. *Cheiranthus* 'Bredon', illus. p.350.

E. cheiri, syn. *Cheiranthus cheiri*. Moderately fast-growing, evergreen, bushy perennial, grown as a biennial. H 25–80cm (10–32in), S 30–40cm (12–16in). Has lance-shaped, mid- to deep green leaves. Heads of fragrant, 4-petalled flowers in many colours, including red, yellow, bronze, white and orange, are produced in spring. **Bedder Series** is dwarf and has golden-yellow, primrose-yellow, orange or scarlet-red flowers. **Fair Lady Series** bears flowers in pale pink, yellow and creamy white, with some reds. **'Fire King'** illus. p.341. Flowers of **'Ivory White'** are creamy white.

E. **'E.A. Bowles'**. See *E.* 'Bowles' Mauve'.

E. helveticum, syn. *E. pumilum*, illus. p.373.

E. x kewense **'Harpur Crewe'**, syn. *Cheiranthus cheiri* 'Harpur Crewe', illus. p.350.

E. linifolium. Short-lived, semi-evergreen, open, dome-shaped sub-shrub. H to 30cm (12in), S 20cm (8in) or more. Leaves are narrowly lance-shaped and blue-grey. Tight heads of small, 4-petalled, pale violet flowers appear in early summer.

E. **'Moonlight'**, syn. *Cheiranthus* 'Moonlight'. Evergreen, mat-forming perennial. H 5cm (2in), S 20cm (8in) or more. Leaves are small and narrowly oval. Leafy stems each carry clusters of 4-petalled, pale yellow flowers, opening in succession during summer. Makes a good rock garden plant. Needs a sheltered, sunny site and poor, gritty soil.

E. pumilum. See *E. helveticum*.

ERYTHRINA

LEGUMINOSAE/PAPILIONACEAE

Genus of deciduous or semi-evergreen trees, shrubs and perennials, grown for their flowers from spring to autumn. Tender, min. 5°C (41°F). Requires full light and well-drained soil. Water containerized plants moderately, very

little in winter or when leafless. Propagate by seed in spring or by semi-ripe cuttings in summer. Spider mite may be troublesome.

E. americana. See *E. coralloides*.

E. x bidwillii illus. p.143.

E. coralloides, syn. *E. americana* (Flame coral tree, Naked coral tree). Deciduous, untidily rounded shrub or tree with somewhat prickly stems. H and S 3–6m (10–20ft). Tender, min. 5°C (41°F). Has leaves of 3 triangular leaflets, the largest central one 11cm (4½in) long. Racemes of pea-like, red flowers are borne on leafless stems in early spring and summer.

E. crista-galli illus. p.143.

ERYTHRONIUM

LILIACEAE

Genus of spring-flowering, tuberous perennials, grown for their pendent flowers and in some cases attractively mottled leaves. Requires partial shade and humus-rich, well-drained soil, where tubers will not become too hot and dry in summer while dormant. Prefers cool climates. Propagate by seed in autumn. Some species increase by offsets, which should be divided in late summer. Do not allow tubers to dry out before replanting, 15cm (6in) deep.

E. americanum illus. p.434.

E. californicum illus. p.427.

'White Beauty' illus. p.409.

E. dens-canis illus. p.430.

E. grandiflorum. Spring-flowering, tuberous perennial. H 10–30cm (4–12in), S 5–8cm (2–3in). Has 2 lance-shaped, semi-erect, basal, plain bright green leaves. Stem carries 1–3 pendent, bright yellow flowers with reflexed petals.

E. hendersonii illus. p.409.

E. oregonum illus. p.408.

E. **'Pagoda'** illus. p.415.

E. revolutum. Spring-flowering, tuberous perennial. H 20–30cm (8–12in), S 15cm (6in). Produces 2 lance-shaped, semi-erect, basal, brown-mottled, green leaves and a loose spike of 1–4 pendent, pale to deep pink flowers with reflexed petals.

E. tuolumnense. Spring-flowering, tuberous perennial. H to 30cm (12in), S 12–15cm (5–6in). Has 2 lance-shaped, semi-erect, basal, glossy, plain green leaves. Carries a spike of up to 10 pendent, bright yellow flowers with reflexed petals. Increases rapidly by offsets.

ESCALLONIA

ESCALLONIACEAE/GROSSULARIACEAE

Genus of evergreen, semi-evergreen or deciduous shrubs and trees, grown for their profuse, 5-petalled flowers and glossy foliage. Thrives in mild areas, where *Escallonia* is wind-resistant and ideal for hedging in coastal gardens. At the limits of hardiness, protect from strong winds and grow against a south- or west-facing wall. Requires full sun and fertile, well-drained soil. Trim hedges and wall-trained plants after flowering. Propagate by softwood cuttings in summer.

E. **'Apple Blossom'** illus. p.141.

E. **'Donard Beauty'**. Evergreen,

arching shrub with slender shoots. H and S 1.5m (5ft). Bears deep pink flowers from early to mid-summer among small, oval, dark green leaves. Zone 8.

E. **'Donard Seedling'** illus. p.140.

E. **'Edinensis'**. Vigorous, evergreen, arching shrub. H 2m (6ft), S 3m (10ft). Bears small, oblong, bright green leaves. Small, pink flowers are produced from early to mid-summer. Is one of the more hardy escallonias. Zone 7.

E. **'Iveyi'** illus. p.118.

E. **'Langleyensis'** illus. p.142.

E. leucantha illus. p.118.

E. rubra **'Crimson Spire'**. Very vigorous, evergreen, upright shrub. H and S 3m (10ft). Has oval, rich green leaves and, throughout summer, tubular, deep red flowers. Zone 8.

'Woodside' illus. p.165.

E. virgata illus. p.137.

ESCHSCHOLZIA

Califorinia poppy

PAPAVERACEAE

Genus of annuals, grown for their bright, poppy-like flowers. Is suitable for rock gardens and gaps in paving. Requires sun and grows well in poor, very well-drained soil. Dead-head regularly to ensure a long flowering period. Propagate by seed sown outdoors in spring or early autumn.

E. caespitosa illus. p.336.

E. californica illus. p.339, [mixed] illus. p.338. **Ballerina Series** illus. p.322. **Thai Silk Series** illus. p.339.

ESCOBARIA

CACTACEAE

Genus of mainly spherical to columnar perennial cacti. The stems are studded with tubercles (each with a furrow immediately above it) and very spiny, generally white areoles. Tender, min. 5°C (41°F). Needs full sun and poor to moderately fertile, well-drained soil. Propagate by seed in spring or by offsets in summer.

E. vivipara, syn. *Coryphantha vivipara*, illus. p.471.

ESPOSTOA

CACTACEAE

Genus of columnar, perennial cacti, each with a 10–30-ribbed stem, eventually becoming bushy or tree-like with age. Most species are densely covered in woolly, white hairs masking short, sharp spines. Bears cup-shaped flowers, as well as extra wool down the side of stems facing the sun, only after about 30 years. Tender, min. 10°C (50°F). Needs full sun and very well-drained soil. Propagate by seed in spring or summer.

E. lanata illus. p.457.

Etruscan honeysuckle. See *Lonicera etrusca*.

EUCALYPTUS

Gum tree

MYRTACEAE

Genus of evergreen trees and shrubs, grown for their bark, flowers and aromatic foliage. Hardy to tender, min.

1–10°C (34–50°F). Needs full sun, shelter from strong, cold winds and fertile, well-drained soil. Plant smallest obtainable trees. Water potted plants moderately, less in winter. Attractive, young foliage of some species, normally lost with age, may be retained by cutting growth back hard in spring. Propagate by seed in spring or autumn.

E. camaldulensis (Murray red gum, River red gum). Fast-growing, evergreen, irregularly rounded tree. H 30m (100ft) or more, S 20m (70ft) or more. Tender, min. 3–5°C (37–41°F). Young bark is grey, brown and cream; leaves are lance-shaped, slender, green or blue-green. Has umbels of small, cream flowers in summer. Is a drought-resistant tree.

E. coccifera illus. p.72.

E. dalrympleana illus. p.72.

E. ficifolia (Flowering gum). Moderately fast-growing, evergreen, rounded tree. H and S to 8m (25ft). Tender, min. 1–3°C (34–7°F). Has broadly lance-shaped, glossy, deep green leaves and, in spring-summer, large panicles of many-stamened, pale to deep red flowers. Is best in acid soil.

E. glaucescens (Tingiringi gum). Evergreen, spreading tree. H 12m (40ft), S 8m (25ft). Tender, min. –1°C (30°F). Young bark is white. Leaves are silvery-blue and rounded when young, long, narrow and blue-grey when mature. In autumn bears clusters of many-stamened, white flowers.

E. globulus (Blue gum, Tasmanian blue gum). Very fast-growing, evergreen, spreading tree. H 30m (100ft), S 12m (40ft). Bark peels in ribbons. Large, oval to oblong, silvery-blue leaves are long, narrow and glossy, mid-green when mature. White flowers, consisting of tufts of stamens, appear in summer-autumn, often year-round. Zone 9.

E. gunnii illus. p.72.

E. niphophila. See *E. pauciflora* subsp. *niphophila*.

E. pauciflora illus. p.84.

subsp. *niphophila* (syn. *E. niphophila*) illus. p.84.

E. perriniana illus. p.100.

E. viminalis (Manna gum, Ribbon gum). Vigorous, evergreen, spreading tree. H 30m (100ft), S 15m (50ft). Tender, min. 5°C (41°F). Bark peels on upper trunk. Lance-shaped, dark green leaves become very long, narrow and pale green when mature. Bears clusters of stamened, white flowers in summer.

EUCHARIS

AMARYLLIDACEAE

Genus of evergreen bulbs, grown for their fragrant, white flowers that resemble large, white daffodils, with a cup and 6 spreading petals. Tender, min. 15°C (59°F). Prefers at least 50% relative humidity. Needs partial shade and humus-rich soil. Water freely in summer. Propagate by seed when ripe or by offsets in spring.

E. amazonica of gardens. See *E. x grandiflora*.

E. x grandiflora, syn. *E. amazonica* of gardens, illus. p.425.

EUCOMIS
Pineapple flower
EUCOMIS

HYACINTHACEAE/LILIACEAE

Genus of summer- and autumn-flowering bulbs, grown for their dense spikes of flowers, which are overtopped by a tuft of small, leaf-like bracts, as in a pineapple. Where not hardy, lift in fall and over-winter indoors. Needs full sun and well-drained soil. Plant in spring and water freely in summer. Propagate by seed or division of clumps in spring.

E. autumnalis, syn. *E. undulata*. Late summer- to autumn-flowering bulb. H 20–30cm (8–12in), S 60–75cm (24–30in). Has strap-shaped, wavy-edged leaves in a semi-erect, basal tuft. Leafless stem bears small, star-shaped, pale green or white flowers in a dense spike, with cluster of leaf-like bracts at apex.

E. bicolor illus. p.422.
E. comosa illus. p.398.
E. pallidiflora illus. p.397.
E. undulata. See *E. autumnalis*.

EUCOMMIA
EUCOMMIACEAE

Genus of one species of deciduous tree, grown for its unusual foliage. Needs full sun and fertile, well-drained soil. Propagate by softwood cuttings in summer.

E. ulmoides (Hardy rubber tree). Deciduous, spreading tree. H 12m (40ft), S 8m (25ft). Drooping, oval leaves are pointed and glossy, dark green; when pulled apart, leaf pieces stay joined by rubbery threads. Inconspicuous flowers appear in late spring before leaves. Zone 5b.

EUCRYPHIA
EUCRYPHIACEAE

Genus of evergreen, semi-evergreen or deciduous trees and shrubs, grown for their foliage and often fragrant, white flowers. Needs a sheltered, semi-shaded position in all but mild, wet areas, where it will withstand more exposure. Does best with roots in a cool, moist, shaded position and crown in sun. Requires fertile, well-drained, lime-free soil, except in the case of *E. cordifolia* and *E.* x *nymansensis*. Propagate by semi-ripe cuttings in late summer.

E. cordifolia (Ulmo). Evergreen, columnar tree. H 15m (50ft), S 8m (25ft). Has oblong, wavy-edged, dull green leaves, with grey down beneath. Large, rose-like, white flowers are borne in late summer and autumn. Zone 9.

E. glutinosa illus. p.90.
E. lucida illus. p.90.
E. milliganii illus. p.137.
E. x *nymansensis* **'Nymansay'** illus. p.81.

Eugenia australis of gardens. See *Syzygium paniculatum*.
Eugenia paniculata. See *Syzygium paniculatum*.
Eugenia ugni. See *Ugni molinae*.
Euodia. Reclassified as *Tetradium*.

EUONYMUS
CELASTRACEAE

Genus of evergreen or deciduous shrubs and trees, sometimes climbing, grown for their foliage, autumn colour and fruits. Needs sun or semi-shade and any well-drained soil, although, for evergreen species in full sun, soil should not be very dry. Propagate by semi-ripe cuttings in summer or by seed in autumn. *E. europaeus* and *E. japonicus* may be attacked by caterpillars; *E. japonicus* is susceptible to mildew. All parts may cause mild stomach upset if ingested.

E. alatus illus. p.148.
'Compactus' is a deciduous, bushy, dense shrub. H 1m (3ft), S 3m (10ft). Shoots have corky wings. Oval, dark green leaves turn brilliant red in autumn. Bears inconspicuous, greenish-white flowers in summer, followed by small, 4-lobed, purple or red fruits. Zone 3.
E. europaeus (Spindle tree). **'Red Cascade'** illus. p.147.
E. fortunei. Evergreen shrub, grown only as var. *radicans* and its cultivars, which are climbing or creeping and prostrate. H 5m (15ft) if supported, S indefinite. Bears oval, dark green leaves and inconspicuous, greenish-white flowers from early to mid-summer. Makes good ground cover. Foliage of **'Coloratus'** turns reddish-purple in autumn-winter. Zone 5. **'Emerald Gaiety'**, H 1m (3ft), S 1.5m (5ft), is bushy, with rounded, white-edged, deep green leaves. **'Emerald 'n' Gold'** illus. p.177. **'Gold Tip'** see *E.f.* 'Golden Prince'. Young, rounded leaves of **'Golden Prince'** (syn. *E.f.* 'Gold Tip') are edged bright yellow, ageing to creamy-white. **'Kewensis'**, H 10cm (4in) or more, has slender stems and tiny leaves, and forms dense mats of growth. **'Sarcoxie'**, H and S 1.2m (4ft), is vigorous, upright and bushy, with glossy, dark green leaves. **'Silver Queen'** illus. p.151. **'Sunspot'** bears deep green leaves, each marked in centre with golden-yellow.
E. hamiltonianus subsp. *sieboldianus*, syn. *E. yedoensis*. Deciduous, tree-like shrub. H and S 6m (20ft) or more. Oval, mid-green leaves often turn pink and red in autumn. Tiny, green flowers in late spring and early summer are followed by 4-lobed, pink fruits. Zone 6. subsp. *sieboldianus* **'Red Elf'** illus. p.147.
E. japonicus (Japanese spindle). **'Latifolius Albomarginatus'** (syn. *E.j.* 'Macrophyllus Albus') illus. p.151. **'Macrophyllus'** is an evergreen, upright, dense shrub. H 4m (12ft), S 2m (6ft). Has very large, oval, glossy, dark green leaves and, in summer, small, star-shaped, green flowers, sometimes succeeded by spherical, pink fruits with orange seeds. Is good for hedging, particularly in coastal areas. Zone 5b. **'Macrophyllus Albus'** see *E.j.* 'Latifolius Albomarginatus'. Leaves of **'Ovatus Aureus'** are broadly edged with golden-yellow.
E. latifolius illus. p.148.
E. myrianthus illus. p.124.
E. nanus (Dwarf burning bush). Dwarf, slightly spreading, deciduous shrub H 1m (3ft) S 1.2m (4ft). Leaves

are dark green, toothed and turn brilliant red in fall; they may be alternate or in whorls. Fruits are pink with red to orange seeds. Zone 2. var. *turkestanicus* is more upright and most readily available. Zone 3.
E. oxyphyllus. Deciduous, upright shrub or tree. H and S 2.5m (8ft). Oval, dull green leaves become purplish-red in autumn. Produces tiny, greenish-white flowers in late spring, followed by globose, 4- or 5-lobed, deep red. Zone 7.
E. planipes, syn. *E. sachalinensis* of gardens. Deciduous, upright, open shrub. H and S 3m (10ft). Bears oval, mid-green leaves that turn to brilliant red in autumn, as large, 4- or 5-lobed, red fruits open to reveal bright orange seeds. Star-shaped, green flowers open in late spring. Zone 5.
E. sachalinensis of gardens. See *E. planipes*.
E. yedoensis. See *E. hamiltonianus* var. *sieboldianus*.

EUPATORIUM
ASTERACEAE/COMPOSITAE

Genus of perennials, sub-shrubs and shrubs, many of which are evergreen, grown mainly for their flowers, some also for their architectural foliage. Hardy to tender, min. 5–13°C (41–55°F). Requires full light or partial shade. Will grow in any conditions, although most species prefer moist but well-drained soil. Water containerized plants freely when in full growth, moderately at other times. Prune shrubs lightly after flowering or in spring. Propagate by seed in spring; shrubs and sub-shrubs may also be propagated by softwood or greenwood cuttings in summer, perennials by division in early spring or autumn. Spider mite and whitefly may be troublesome.

E. ageratoides. See *E. rugosum*.
E. ligustrinum, syn. *E. Ageratina ligustrina*, *E. micranthum*, *E. weinmannianum*. Evergreen, rounded shrub. H and S 2–4m (6–12ft). Tender, min. 5°C (41°F). Has elliptic to lance-shaped, bright green leaves and, in autumn, fragrant, groundsel-like, white or pink flowers are produced in flattened clusters, 10–20cm (4–8in) wide.
E. maculatum (Joe Pye weed). Upright perennial with lance-shaped foliage in whorls. H 2.2m (7ft) S 1m (3ft). Flat-topped corymbs of purple flowers in late summer. Grows best on moist, alkaline soils. **'Atropurpureum'** has purple tinged leaves and dark purple flower heads.
E. micranthum. See *E. ligustrinum*.
E. purpureum illus. p.231.
E. rugosum, syn. *E. ageratoides*, *E. urticifolium*, illus. p.240.
E. urticifolium. See *E. rugosum*.
E. weinmannianum. See *E. ligustrinum*.

EUPHORBIA
Milkweed, Spurge
EUPHORBIACEAE

Genus of shrubs, succulents and perennials, some of which are semi-evergreen or evergreen, and annuals.

Flower heads consist of cup-shaped bracts, in various colours and usually each containing several flowers lacking typical sepals and petals. Hardy to tender, min. 5–15°C (41–59°F). Does best in sun or partial shade and in moist but well-drained soil. Propagate by basal cuttings in spring or summer, by division in spring or early autumn or by seed in autumn or spring. All parts may cause severe discomfort if ingested; contact with their milky sap may irritate skin.

E. amygdaloides (Wood spurge). **'Purpurea'** is a semi-evergreen, erect perennial. H and S 30cm (1ft). Stems and narrowly oval leaves are green, heavily suffused purple-red. Has flower heads of cup-shaped, yellow bracts in spring. Is susceptible to mildew. var. *robbiae* (syn. *E. robbiae*) illus. p.271.
E. biglandulosa. See *E. rigida*.
E. candelabrum. Deciduous, tree-like, perennial succulent. H 10m (30ft), S 5m (15ft). Tender, min. 10°C (50°F). Erect, 3–5-angled, deeply indented, glossy, dark green stems, often marbled white, branch and rebranch candelabra-like. Has short-lived, spear-shaped leaves. Rounded heads of small flowers, with cup-shaped, yellow bracts, are produced in spring.
E. characias subsp. *characias* and subsp. *wulfenii* illus. p.156.
E. cyparissias illus. p.271.
E. epithymoides. See *E. polychroma*.
E. fulgens (Scarlet plume). Evergreen shrub of erect and arching habit. H 1–1.5m (3–5ft), S 60cm–1m (2–3ft). Tender, min. 5–7°C (41–5°F). Has elliptic to lance-shaped, mid- to deep green leaves, to 10cm (4in) long. From winter to spring, bears leafy, wand-like sprays of small flowers, each cluster surrounded by 5 petal-like, bright scarlet bracts, 2–3cm (¾–1¼in) across.
E. gorgonis (Gorgon's head). Deciduous, hemispherical, perennial succulent. H 8cm (3in), S 10cm (4in). Tender, min. 10°C (50°F). Has a much-ribbed, green main stem crowned by 3–5 rows of prostrate, 1cm (½in) wide stems that are gradually shed. In spring, crown also bears rounded heads of small, fragrant flowers with cup-shaped, yellow bracts.
E. griffithii **'Fireglow'** illus. p.258.
E. marginata illus. p.319.
E. milii illus. p.155. var. *splendens* (syn. *E. splendens*) is a slow-growing, mainly evergreen, spreading, spiny, semi-succulent shrub. H to 2m (6ft), S to 1m (3ft). Tender, min. 5–7°C (41–5°F). Has oblong to oval leaves and, intermittently year-round but especially in spring, clusters of tiny flowers enclosed in large, petal-like, red bracts.
E. myrsinites illus. p.371.
E. nicaeensis. Clump-forming perennial with a woody base. H 75cm (30in), S 45cm (18in). Has narrowly oval, fleshy, grey-green leaves. Umbels of greenish-yellow flower heads with cup-shaped bracts are borne throughout summer.
E. obesa illus. p.477.
E. palustris. Bushy perennial. H and S 1m (3ft). Clusters of yellow-green flower heads with cup-shaped bracts

appear in spring above oblong to lance-shaped, yellowish-green leaves.

E. polychroma, syn. *E. epithymoides*, illus. p.275.

E. pulcherrima illus. p.150. **'Paul Mikkelson'** is a mainly evergreen, erect, freely branching shrub. H and S 3–4m (10–12ft). Tender, min. 5–7°C (41–5°F). Bears oval to lance-shaped, shallowly lobed leaves. From late autumn to spring, has flattened heads of small, greenish-white flowers with large, leaf-like, bright red bracts.

E. rigida, syn. *E. biglandulosa*. Evergreen, erect perennial. H and S 45cm (18in). In early spring produces terminal heads of yellow flowers with cup-shaped bracts above oblong to oval, pointed, grey-green leaves. Zone 8.

E. robbiae. See *E. amygdaloides* var. *robbiae*.

E. schillingii illus. p.254.

E. seguieriana illus. p.271.

E. sikkimensis illus. p.254.

E. splendens. See *E. milii* var. *splendens*.

European elder. See *Sambucus nigra*.
European fan palm. See *Chamaerops humilis*, illus. p.176.
European larch. See *Larix decidua*.
European linden. See *Tilia* x *europea*.
European white linden. See *Tilia tomentosa*.

EURYA

THEACEAE

Genus of evergreen shrubs and trees, grown for their foliage. Insignificant flowers are produced from spring

to summer. Tolerates partial shade or full light and needs fertile, well-drained soil. Water containerized specimens freely when in full growth, less at other times. Propagate by seed when ripe or in spring or by semi-ripe cuttings in late summer.

E. emarginata illus. p.176.

E. japonica. Evergreen, bushy shrub or small tree. H and S 10m (30ft). Has elliptic to lance-shaped, bluntly toothed, leathery, dark green leaves. Inconspicuous, green flowers, borne from spring to summer, are followed on female plants by tiny, spherical, purple-black fruits. Zone 7.

'Variegata' of gardens see *Cleyera japonica* 'Tricolor'.

EURYALE

NYMPHAEACEAE

Genus of one species of annual, deep-water plant, grown for its floating foliage; is suitable only for a tropical pool. Tender, min. 5°C (41°F). Needs full light, constant warmth and heavy feeding. Propagate by seed in spring.

E. ferox illus. p.449.

EURYOPS

ASTERACEAE/COMPOSITAE

Genus of evergreen shrubs and sub-shrubs, grown for their attractive leaves and showy, daisy-like flower heads. Is suitable for borders and rock gardens. Marginally hardy to tender, min. 5–7°C (41–5°F). Needs sun and moist but well-drained soil. May not tolerate root disturbance. Propagate by

softwood cuttings in summer.

E. acraeus, syn. *E. evansii* of gardens, illus. p.358.

E. evansii of gardens. See *E. acraeus*.

E. pectinatus illus. p.170.

EUSTOMA

GENTIANACEAE

Genus of annuals and perennials with poppy-like flowers that are good for cutting. Makes good pot plants. Tender, min. 4–7°C (39–45°F). Needs sun and well-drained soil. Propagate by seed sown under glass in late winter.

E. grandiflorum, syn. *E. russellianum*, *Lisianthus russellianus*, illus. p.319.

Heidi Series has flowers in shades of rose-pink, blue, white and bicolours.

E. russellianum. See *E. grandiflorum*.

Evening primrose. See *Oenothera*.
  White. See *Oenothera speciosa*.
Everlasting flower. See *Bracteantha bracteata*.
Everlasting pea. See *Lathyrus grandiflorus*, illus. p.209; *Lathyrus latifolius*, illus. p.211; *Lathyrus sylvestris*.
Evodia. Reclassified as *Tetradium*.

EXACUM

GENTIANACEAE

Genus of annuals, biennials and perennials, grown for their profusion of flowers, that are excellent as pot plants. Tender, min. 7–10°C (45–50°F). Grow in sun and in well-drained soil. Propagate by seed

sown in early spring for flowering the same year or in late summer for the following year.

E. affine illus. p.331.

Exeter elm. See *Ulmus glabra* 'Exoniensis'.

EXOCHORDA

ROSACEAE

Genus of deciduous shrubs, grown for their abundant, showy, white flowers. Does best in full sun and fertile, well-drained soil. Improve vigour and flowering by thinning out old shoots after flowering. Propagate by softwood cuttings in summer or by seed in autumn. Chlorosis may be a problem on shallow, alkaline soil.

E. giraldii. Deciduous, widely arching shrub. H and S 3m (10ft). Has pinkish-green, young growths and oblong leaves. Bears upright racemes of large, 5-petalled, white flowers in late spring. Zone 4.

***E.* x *macrantha* 'The Bride'** illus. p.135.

E. racemosa. Deciduous, arching shrub. H and S 4m (12ft). Has upright clusters of 5-petalled, white flowers in late spring. Leaves are oblong and deep blue-green. Prefers acid soil.

Eyelash begonia. See *Begonia bowerae*, illus. p.295.

FABIANA

SOLANACEAE

Genus of evergreen shrubs, grown for their foliage and flowers. Even where hardy needs a sheltered position. Requires full sun and fertile, well-drained soil. Propagate by softwood cuttings in summer.

F. imbricata 'Prostrata'. Evergreen, mound-forming, very dense shrub. H 1m (3ft), S 2m (6ft). Shoots are densely covered with tiny, heath-like, deep green leaves. Bears a profusion of tubular, white flowers in early summer. Zone 9. f. **violacea**, syn. *F.i.* 'Violacea', illus. p.145.

FAGUS

Beech

FAGACEAE

Genus of deciduous trees, grown for their habit, foliage and autumn colour. Insignificant flowers appear in late spring and hairy fruits ripen in autumn to release edible, triangular nuts. Requires sun or semi-shade; purple-leaved forms prefer full sun, yellow-leaved forms a little shade. Grows well in any but waterlogged soil. *F. sylvatica*, when used as hedging, should be trimmed in summer. Propagate species by seed sown in autumn, and selected forms by budding in late summer. Problems may be caused by bracket fungi, canker-causing fungi, and aphids.

F. americana. See *F. grandifolia*.
F. grandifolia, syn. *F. americana* (American beech). Deciduous, spreading tree. H and S 10m (30ft). Oval, silky, pale green young leaves mature to dark green in summer, then turn golden-brown in autumn. Zone 4.
F. orientalis (Oriental beech). Deciduous, spreading tree. H 20m (70ft), S 15m (50ft). Has large, oval, wavy-edged, dark green leaves that turn yellow in autumn. Zone 7.
F. sylvatica (European beech) illus. p.68. f. **atropunicea** see *F.s.* f. *purpurea*. 'Aurea Pendula' is a deciduous, slender tree with pendulous branches. H 30m (100ft), S 25m (80ft). Oval, wavy-edged leaves are bright yellow and become rich yellow and orange-brown in autumn. 'Dawyck', S 7m (22ft), is columnar, with erect branches; pale green leaves mature to mid- to dark green, and turn rich yellow and orange-brown in autumn. 'Dawyck Purple' is similar, but has deep purple foliage. Leaves of f. **laciniata** are deeply cut. f. **pendula** (syn. *F.s.* 'Pendula') illus. p.66. f. **purpurea** (syn. *F.s.* f. *atropunicea*) illus. p.65. 'Purpurea Pendula', H and S 3m (10ft), has stiff, weeping branches and blackish-purple foliage. Leaves of 'Riversii' are very dark purple. Those of 'Rohanii' are deeply cut and reddish-purple. 'Zlatia' produces yellow, young foliage that later becomes mid- to dark green. All zone 6.

Fair maids of France. See *Saxifraga granulata*, illus. p.346, *Ranunculus aconitifolius* 'Flora Pleno', illus. p.233.
Fairy bells. See *Disporum*.
Fairy duster. See *Calliandra eriophylla*, illus. p.172.
Fairy foxglove. See *Erinus*.
Fairy lantern. See *Calochortus*.
  Golden. See *Calochortus amabilis*, illus. p.434.
Fairy moss. See *Azolla filiculoides*, illus. p.448.
Fairy thimbles. See *Campanula cochleariifolia*, illus. p.383.

FALLOPIA,

syn. BILDERDYKIA, REYNOUTRIA

POLYGONACEAE

Genus of rhizomatous, climbing or scrambling, woody-based perennials that are good for training on pergolas and deciduous trees or for covering unsightly structures. Grow in full sun or partial shade and moist but well-drained soil. Propagate by seed sown as soon as ripe or in spring or by semi-ripe cuttings in summer or hardwood cuttings in autumn.

F. aubertii, syn. *Polygonum aubertii* (Mile-a-minute plant, Russian vine). Vigorous, deciduous, woody-stemmed, twining climber. H to 12m (40ft) or more. Leaves are broadly heart-shaped. Panicles of small, white or greenish flowers, ageing to pink, are carried in summer-autumn; they are followed by angled, pinkish-white fruits. Is often confused with *F. baldschuanica*. Zone 6.
F. aubertii of gardens. See *Fallopia baldschuanica*.
F. baldschuanica, syn. *F. aubertii* of gardens, *Polygonum baldschuanicum*, illus. p.217.

FALLUGIA

ROSACEAE

Genus of one species of deciduous shrub, grown for its flowers and showy fruit clusters. But in cold areas protect in winter. Needs a hot, sunny position and well-drained soil. Propagate by softwood cuttings taken in summer or by seed sown in autumn.
F. paradoxa illus. p.136.

False acacia. See *Robinia pseudoacacia*.
False African violet. See *Streptocarpus saxorum*, illus. p.284.
False anemone. See *Anemonopsis*.
False aralia. See *Schefflera elegantissima*, illus. p.127.
False cypress. See *Chamaecyparis*.
False heather. See *Cuphea hyssopifolia*, illus. p.158.
False indigo. See *Baptisia australis*, illus. p.252.
False jasmine. See *Gelsemium sempervirens*, illus. p. 206.

False oat grass. See *Arrhenatherum elatius*.
False spikenard. See *Smilacina racemosa*, illus. p.233.
Fanwort. See *Cabomba caroliniana*.

FARFUGIUM

ASTERACEAE/COMPOSITAE

Genus of perennials, grown for their foliage and daisy-like flower heads. Grow in sun or semi-shade and in moist but well-drained soil. Propagate by division in spring or by seed in autumn or spring.
F. japonicum, syn. *Ligularia tussilaginea*. Loosely clump-forming perennial. H and S 60cm (24in). Has large, rounded, toothed, basal, mid-green leaves, above which rise woolly, branched stems bearing clusters of daisy-like, pale yellow flower heads in late summer. 'Aureomaculatum' (Leopard plant) has variegated, gold-and-white leaves and is less hardy.

FARGESIA

GRAMINEAE/POACEAE

See also GRASSES, BAMBOOS, RUSHES and SEDGES.
F. murieliae, syn. *Arundinaria murieliae*, *Fargesia spathacea* of gardens, *Sinarundinaria murieliae*, *Thamnocalamus murieliae*, *T. spathaceus* of gardens (Muriel bamboo). Evergreen, clump-forming bamboo. H 4m (12ft), S indefinite. Has attractive, grey young culms with loose, light brown leaf sheaths and broad, apple-green leaves, each very long, drawn-out at its tip. Flower spikes are unimportant.
F. nitida, syn. *Arundinaria nitida*, *Sinarundinaria nitida*. Evergreen, clump-forming bamboo. H 5m (15ft), S indefinite. Has small, pointed, mid-green leaves on dark purple stalks and several branches at each node. Stems are often purple with close sheaths.
F. spathacea of gardens. See *F. murieliae*.

Fat pork tree. See *Clusia major*.

x FATSHEDERA

ARALIACEAE

Hybrid genus (*Fatsia japonica* 'Moseri' x *Hedera helix* 'Hibernica') of one evergreen, autumn-flowering shrub, grown for its foliage. Is good trained against a wall or pillar or, if supported by canes, grown as a house plant. Thrives in sun or shade and in fertile, well-drained soil. Propagate by semi-ripe cuttings in summer.
x F. lizei illus. p.152. 'Variegata' is an evergreen, mound-forming, loose-branched shrub. H 1.5m (5ft), or more if trained as a climber, S 3m (10ft). Has rounded, deeply lobed, glossy, deep green leaves, narrowly edged with

creamy-white. From mid- to late autumn bears sprays of small, white flowers. Zone 7.

FATSIA

ARALIACEAE

Genus of one species of evergreen, autumn-flowering shrub, grown for its foliage, flowers and fruits. Is excellent for conservatories. At limits of hardiness, shelter from strong winds. Tolerates sun or shade and requires fertile, well-drained soil. May be propagated by semi-ripe cuttings taken in summer or by seed sown in autumn or spring.
F. japonica, syn. *Aralia japonica*, *A. sieboldii* (Japanese aralia). Evergreen, rounded, dense shrub. H and S 3m (10ft). Has stout shoots and very large, rounded, deeply lobed, glossy, dark green leaves. In mid-autumn, produces dense clusters of tiny, white flowers, followed by rounded, black fruits. Zone 7. 'Variegata' illus. p.151.
F. papyrifera. See *Tetrapanax papyrifer*.

FAUCARIA

AIZOACEAE

Genus of clump-forming, stemless, perennial succulents with semi-cylindrical or 3-angled, fleshy, bright green leaves and yellow flowers that open in late afternoons in autumn. Buds and dead flowers may appear orange or red. Tender, min. 6°C (43°F). Needs full sun and well-drained soil. Keep dry in winter and water sparingly in spring. Propagate by seed or stem cuttings in spring or summer.
F. tigrina illus. p.479.

Feather grape hyacinth. See *Muscari comosum* 'Plumosum', illus. p.432.
Feather-top. See *Pennisetum villosum*, illus. p.307.
Feijoa. Reclassified as *Acca*.

FELICIA,

syn. AGATHAEA

ASTERACEAE/COMPOSITAE

Genus of annuals, evergreen sub-shrubs and (rarely) shrubs, grown for their daisy-like, mainly blue flower heads. Hardy to tender, min. 5–7°C (41–5°F). Requires a position in full sun and well-drained soil. Water potted plants moderately, less when not in full growth; dislikes wet conditions, particularly in low temperatures. Cut off dead flowering stems and cut back straggly shoots regularly. Propagate by seed in spring or by greenwood cuttings in summer or early autumn.
F. amelloides, syn. *Aster capensis* (Blue marguerite). Bushy sub-shrub, grown as an annual. Bears deep green leaves, to 3cm (1¼in) long, and light

to deep blue flowers from summer to autumn. **'Santa Anita'** illus. p.168. *F. bergeriana* illus. p.334.

FENESTRARIA

AIZOACEAE

Genus of clump-forming, perennial succulents with basal rosettes of fleshy leaves that have grey 'windows' in their flattened tips. Tender, min. 6°C (43°F). Needs sun and very well-drained soil. Keep bone dry in winter. Propagate by seed in spring or summer.
F. aurantiaca illus. p.479.
f. *rhopalophylla* is a clump-forming, perennial succulent. H 5cm (2in), S 20cm (8in). Forms open cushions of erect, club-shaped, glossy, glaucous to mid-green leaves, each with a flattened tip. Bears daisy-like, white flowers on long stems in late summer and autumn.

Fennel. See *Foeniculum vulgare*.
  Dog's. See *Anthemis*.
  Giant. See *Ferula*.
Fennel-leaved pondweed. See *Potamogeton pectinatus*.
Fern
  Asian chain. See *Woodwardia unigemmata*.
  Beech. See *Phegopteris connectilis*.
  Berry bladder. See *Cystopteris bulbifera*.
  Bird's-nest. See *Asplenium nidus*, illus. p.313.
  Brittle bladder. See *Cystopteris fragilis*.
  Broad buckler. See *Dryopteris dilatata*.
  Button. See *Pellaea rotundifolia*.
  Chain. See *Woodwardia radicans*.
  Christmas. See *Polystichum acrostichoides*.
  Cinnamon. See *Osmunda cinnamomea*.
  Common stag's-horn. See *Platycerium bifurcatum*, illus. p.310.
  Fishtail. See *Cyrtomium falcatum*, illus. p.311.
Fern
  Foxtail. See *Asparagus densiflorus* 'Myersii', illus. p.267.
  Giant holly. See *Polystichum munitum*, illus. p.310.
  Giant wood. See *Dryopteris goldieana*.
  Golden male. See *Dryopteris affinis*.
  Hard. See *Blechnum spicant*.
  Hard shield. See *Polystichum aculeatum*.
  Hare's-foot. See *Davallia canariensis*.
  Hart's-tongue. See *Asplenium scolopendrium*, illus. p.313.
  Hen-and-chicken. See *Asplenium bulbiferum*.
  Holly. See *Cyrtomium falcatum*, illus. p.311.
  Interrupted. See *Osmunda claytoniana*.
  Japanese climbing. See *Lygodium japonicum*.
  Japanese painted. See *Athyrium nipponicum*, illus. p.313.
  Japanese shield. See *Dryopteris erythrosora*.
  Ladder. See *Nephrolepis cordifolia*.
  Lady. See *Athyrium filix-femina*.

Fern (continued)
  Liquorice. See *Polypodium glycyrrhiza*, illus. p.310.
  Maidenhair. See *Adiantum capillus-veneris*.
  Male. See *Dryopteris filix-mas*, illus. p.310.
  Marsh. See *Thelypteris palustris*, illus. p.312.
  Marsh buckler. See *Thelypteris palustris*, illus. p.312.
  Mountain. See *Oreopteris limbosperma*.
  Mountain buckler. See *Oreopteris limbosperma*.
  Mountain wood. See *Oreopteris limbosperma*.
  Narrow buckler. See *Dryopteris carthusiana*.
  Northern maidenhair. See *Adiantum pedatum*, illus. p.312.
  Oak. See *Gymnocarpium dryopteris*.
  Ostrich. See *Matteuccia struthiopteris*, illus. p.312.
  Ostrich-feather. See *Matteuccia struthiopteris*, illus. p.312.
  Parsley. See *Cryptogramma crispa*, illus. p.313.
  Prickly shield. See *Polystichum aculeatum*.
  Royal. See *Osmunda regalis*, illus. p.312.
  Rusty-back. See *Asplenium ceterach*, illus. p.311.
  Sensitive. See *Onoclea sensibilis*, illus. p.312.
  Soft shield. See *Polystichum setiferum*.
  Squirrel's-foot. See *Davallia mariesii*.
  Stag's-horn. See *Platycerium*.
  Sword. See *Nephrolepis cordifolia*; *Nephrolepis exaltata*, illus. p.312.
  Wallich's wood. See *Dryopteris wallichiana*.
  Water. See *Azolla filiculoides*, illus. p.448; *Ceratopteris thalictroides*.
  Wintergreen. See *Polypodium cambricum*.
Fern-leaf aralia. See *Polyscias filicifolia*, illus. p.152.

FEROCACTUS
Barrel cactus

CACTACEAE

Genus of slow-growing, spherical, perennial cacti, becoming columnar after many years. Tender, min. 5°C (41°F). Needs full sun and very well-drained soil. Propagate by seed in spring or summer. Treat blackened areoles with systemic fungicide and ensure plants have good ventilation.
F. acanthodes of gardens. See *F. cylindraceus*.
F. chrysacanthus. Slow-growing, spherical, perennial cactus. H 1m (3ft), S 60cm (2ft). Green stem, with 15–20 ribs, is fairly densely covered with curved, yellow-white spines. In summer bears funnel-shaped, yellow, rarely red, flowers, 5cm (2in) across, only on plants 25cm (10in) or more in diameter.
F. cylindraceus, syn. *F. acanthodes* of gardens, illus. p.460.
F. hamatacanthus, syn. *Hamatocactus hamatacanthus*, illus. p.464.
F. latispinus. Slow-growing, flattened spherical, perennial cactus. H 20cm

(8in), S 40cm (16in). Green stem, with 15–20 ribs, bears broad, hooked, red or yellow spines. Funnel-shaped, pale yellow or red flowers appear in summer on plants over 10cm (4in) wide.
F. setispinus. See *Thelocactus setispinus*.
F. wislizenii. Slow-growing, spherical, perennial cactus. H 2m (6ft), S 1m (3ft). Green stem, with up to 25 ribs, is covered in flattened, fish-hook, usually reddish-brown spines, to 5cm (2in) long. Funnel-shaped, orange or yellow flowers, 6cm (2½in) across, appear in late summer, on plants over 25cm (10in) widem which should attain this size 10–15 years after raising from seed.

FERRARIA

IRIDACEAE

Genus of spring-flowering corms, grown for their curious flowers with 3 large, outer petals and 3 small, inner ones, with very wavy edges. Is unpleasant-smelling to attract flies, which pollinate them. Requires full sun and well-drained soil. Plant in autumn, water during winter and dry off after flowering. Dies down in summer. Propagate by division in late summer or by seed in autumn.
F. crispa, syn. *F. undulata*, illus. p.415.
F. undulata. See *F. crispa*.

FERULA
Giant fennel

APIACEAE/UMBELLIFERAE

Genus of mainly summer-flowering perennials, grown for their bold, architectural form. Should not be confused with culinary fennel, *Foeniculum*. Requires sun and well-drained soil. Propagate by seed when fresh, in late summer.
F. communis illus. p.228.

Fescue, Blue. See *Festuca glauca*.

FESTUCA

GRAMINEAE/POACEAE

See also GRASSES, BAMBOOS, RUSHES and SEDGES.
F. glauca, syn. *F. ovina* var. *glauca* (Blue fescue). Group of evergreen, tuft-forming, perennial grasses. H and S 10cm (4in). Bears narrow leaves in various shades of blue-green to silvery-white. Produces unimportant panicles of spikelets in summer. Is good for bed edging. Divide every 2–3 years in spring.
F. ovina var. *glauca*. See *F. glauca*.

Fetterbush. See *Pieris floribunda*, illus. p.127.
  Mountain. See *Pieris floribunda*, illus. p.127.
Feverfew. See *Tanacetum parthenium*, illus. p.319.

FICUS

MORACEAE

Genus of evergreen or deciduous trees, shrubs and scrambling or root climbers, grown for their foliage and for shade;

a few species also for fruit. All bear insignificant clusters of flowers in spring or summer. Tender, min. 5–18°C (41–64°F). Prefers full light or partial shade and fertile, well-drained soil. Water potted specimens moderately, very little when temperatures are low. Propagate by seed in spring or by leaf-bud or stem-tip cuttings or air-layering in summer. Spider mite may be a nuisance. The foliage may cause mild stomach upset if ingested; the sap may irritate skin or aggravate allergies.
F. benghalensis illus. p.72.
F. benjamina (Weeping fig). Evergreen, weeping tree, often with aerial roots. H and S 18–20m (60–70ft). Tender, min. 10°C (50°F). Has slender, oval leaves, 7–13cm (3–5in) long, in lustrous, rich green. **'Variegata'** illus. p.84.
F. deltoidea illus. p.152.
F. elastica (India rubber tree, Rubber plant). **'Decora'** is a strong-growing, evergreen, irregularly ovoid tree. H to 30m (100ft), S 15–20m (50–70ft). Tender, min. 10°C (50°F). Has broadly oval, leathery, lustrous, deep green leaves, pinkish-bronze when young. **'Doescheri'** illus. p.72. Leaves of **'Variegata'** are cream-edged, mottled with grey-green.
F. lyrata (Fiddle-leaf fig). Evergreen, ovoid, robust-stemmed tree. H 15m (50ft) or more, S to 10m (30ft). Tender, min. 15–18°C (59–64°F). Fiddle-shaped leaves, 30cm (1ft) or more long, are lustrous, deep green.
F. macrophylla (Australian banyan, Moreton Bay fig). Evergreen, wide-spreading, dense tree with a buttressed trunk when mature. H 20–30m (70–100ft), S 30–40m (100–130ft). Tender, min. 15–18°C (59–64°F). Oval leaves, to 20cm (8in) long, are leathery, glossy, deep green.
F. pumila, syn. *F. repens* (Creeping fig). Evergreen, root climber. H 8m (25ft); 1.5m (5ft) as a pot-grown plant. Tender, min. 5°C (41°F). Bright green leaves are heart-shaped and 2–3cm (¾–1¼in) long when young, 3–8cm (1¼–3in) long, leathery and oval when mature. Unpalatable fruits are 6cm (2½in) long, orange at first, then flushed red-purple. Only reaches adult stage in very warm regions or under glass. Pinch out branch tips to encourage branching. The young leaves of **'Minima'** are shorter and narrower.
F. religiosa (Bo, Peepul, Sacred fig tree). Mainly evergreen, rounded to wide-spreading tree with prop roots from branches. H and S 20–30m (70–100ft). Tender, min. 15–18°C (59–64°F). Leaves, 10–15cm (4–6in) long, are broadly oval to almost triangular with long, thread-like tips, pink-flushed when expanding.
F. repens. See *F. pumila*.
F. rubiginosa (Port Jackson fig, Rusty-leaved fig). Evergreen, dense-headed tree with a buttressed trunk. H and S 20–30m (70–100ft) or more. Tender, min. 15–18°C (59–64°F). Elliptic, blunt-pointed leaves, to 10cm (4in) long, are glossy, dark green above, usually with rust-coloured down beneath.

Fiddle-leaf fig. See *Ficus lyrata*.
Field poppy. See *Papaver rhoeas*.
Fig
　Creeping. See *Ficus pumila*.
　Devil's. See *Argemone mexicana*,
　　illus. p.335.
　Fiddle-leaf. See *Ficus lyrata*.
　Hottentot. See *Carpobrotus edulis*.
　Indian. See *Opuntia ficus-indica*.
　Kaffir. See *Carpobrotus edulis*.
　Mistletoe. See *Ficus deltoidea*,
　　illus. p.152.
　Moreton Bay. See *Ficus
　　macrophylla*.
　Port Jackson. See *Ficus rubiginosa*.
　Rusty-leaved. See *Ficus rubiginosa*.
　Weeping. See *Ficus benjamina*.
Fig tree, Sacred. See *Ficus religiosa*.
Figwort. See *Scrophularia*.
　Water. See *Scrophularia auriculata*.
Filbert. See *Corylus maxima*.

FILIPENDULA
Meadowsweet

ROSACEAE

Genus of spring- and summer-
flowering perennials. Most grow in full
sun or partial shade, in moist but well-
drained, leafy soil; some species, e.g.
F. rubra, will thrive in boggy sites.
F. vulgaris needs a drier site, in full
sun. Propagate by seed in autumn or by
division in autumn or winter.
F. camtschatica, syn. *F. kamtschatica*.
Clump-forming perennial. H to 1.5m
(5ft), S 1m (3ft). In mid-summer,
produces frothy, flat heads of scented,
star-shaped, white or pale pink flowers
above large, lance-shaped, divided and
cut leaves.
F. hexapetala. See *F. vulgaris*. **'Flore
Pleno'** see *F. vulgaris* 'Multiplex'.
F. kamtschatica. See *F. camtschatica*.
F. purpurea illus. p.245.
F. rubra illus. p.227.
F. ulmaria, syn. *Spiraea ulmaria*.
'Aurea' illus. p.290.
F. vulgaris, syn. *F. hexapetala*
(Dropwort). **'Multiplex'** (syn.
F. hexapetala 'Flore Pleno') is an
upright, rosette-forming perennial with
fleshy, swollen roots. H 1m (3ft),
S 45cm (1½ft). In summer produces flat
panicles of rounded, double, white
flowers, sometimes flushed pink, above
fern-like, finely divided, toothed,
hairless, dark green leaves.

Finger-leaved ivy. See *Hedera
hibernica* 'Digitata', illus. p.221.
Fir
　Balsam. See *Abies balsamea*.
　Blue Douglas. See *Pseudotsuga
　　menziesii* var. *glauca*, illus. p.102.
　Caucasian. See *Abies
　　nordmanniana*, illus. p.111.
　Chinese. See *Cunninghamia
　　lanceolata*, illus. p.106.
　Delavay's. See *Abies delavayi*.
　Douglas. See *Pseudotsuga menziesii*.
　Forrest. See *Abies forrestii*,
　　illus. p.105.
　Giant. See *Abies grandis*, illus. p.104.
　Grand. See *Abies grandis*,
　　illus. p.104.
　Greek. See *Abies cephalonica*.
　Korean. See *Abies koreana*,
　　illus. p.109.

Fir (continued)
　Nikko. See *Abies homolepis*.
　Noble. See *Abies procera*.
　Pacific. See *Abies amabilis*.
　Silver. See *Abies*.
　Subalpine. See *Abies lasiocarpa*.
　Veitch. See *Abies veitchii*,
　　illus. p.102.
　White. See *Abies concolor*.
Fire lily. See *Lilium bulbiferum*.
Firebush, Chilean. See *Embothrium
　coccineum*, illus. p.93.
Firecracker
　Brazilian. See *Manettia luteorubra*,
　　illus. p.205.
　Mexican. See *Echeveria setosa*.
Firecracker vine. See *Manettia
　cordifolia*.
Firethorn. See *Pyracantha*.
Firewheel tree, Australian. See
　Stenocarpus sinuatus.

FIRMIANA

STERCULIACEAE

Genus of mainly deciduous trees and
shrubs, grown for their foliage and to
provide shade. To reach tree
proportions needs min. 2–5°C
(36–41°F). Requires well-drained but
moisture-retentive, fertile soil and full
light or partial shade. Water
containerized specimens freely when in
full growth, less in winter. Pruning is
tolerated if necessary. Propagate by
seed when ripe or in spring.
F. platanifolia. See *F. simplex*.
F. simplex, syn. *F. platanifolia*,
Sterculia platanifolia, illus. p.68.

Fishbone cactus. See *Epiphyllum
　anguliger*, illus. p.461.
Fishpole bamboo. See *Phyllostachys
　aurea*.
Fishtail fern. See *Cyrtomium falcatum*,
　illus. p.311.

FITTONIA

ACANTHACEAE

Genus of evergreen, creeping
perennials, grown mainly for their
foliage. Is useful as ground cover.
Tender, min. 15°C (59°F). Needs a
fairly humid atmosphere. Grow in a
shaded position and in well-drained
soil; keep well watered but avoid
waterlogging, especially in winter.
If it becomes too straggly, cut back in
spring. Propagate in spring or
summer, with extra heat, by division
or stem cuttings.
F. albivenis **Argyroneura Group**, syn.
F. argyroneura, *F. verschaffeltii* var.
argyroneura, illus. p.300.
Verschaffeltii Group (syn.
F. verschaffeltii) illus. p.302.
F. argyroneura. See *F. albivenis*
Argyroneura Group.
F. verschaffeltii. See *F. albivenis*
Verschaffeltii Group. var. *argyroneura*
see *F. albivenis* Argyroneura Group.

FITZROYA

CUPRESSACEAE

See also CONIFERS.
F. cupressoides, syn. *F. patagonica*,
illus. p.106.
F. patagonica. See *F. cupressoides*.

Five fingers. See *Pseudopanax
　arboreus*; *Syngonium auritum*.
Five-leaved ivy. See *Parthenocissus
　quinquefolia*.
Five-spot baby. See *Nemophila
　maculata*, illus. p.319.
Flag
　Blue. See *Iris versicolor*, illus. p.234.
　Common German. See *Iris
　　germanica*.
　Japanese. See *Iris ensata*.
　Missouri. See *Iris missouriensis*,
　　illus. p.234.
　Myrtle. See *Acorus calamus*.
　Siberian. See *Iris sibirica*.
　Sweet. See *Acorus calamus*.
　Wall. See *Iris tectorum*, illus. p.234.
　Yellow. See *Iris pseudacorus*,
　　illus. p.235.
Flaky juniper. See *Juniperus
　squamata*.
Flame azalea. See *Rhododendron
　calendulaceum*.
Flame coral tree. See *Erythrina
　coralloides*.
Flame creeper. See *Tropaeolum
　speciosum*, illus. p.210.
Flame flower. See *Pyrostegia venusta*,
　illus. p.218.
Flame nasturtium. See *Tropaeolum
　speciosum*, illus. p.210.
Flame tree, Illawarra. See
　Brachychiton acerifolius,
　illus. p.65.
Flame vine. See *Pyrostegia venusta*,
　illus. p.218.
Flame violet. See *Episcia cupreata*,
　illus. p.301.
Flame-of-the-forest. See *Spathodea
　campanulata*, illus. p.71.
Flaming Katy. See *Kalanchoe
　blossfeldiana*.
Flaming sword. See *Vriesea
　splendens*, illus. p.265.
Flamingo flower. See *Anthurium
　scherzerianum*, illus. p.302.
Flannel flower. See *Fremontodendron*.
Flax
　Golden. See *Linum flavum*.
　Holy. See *Santolina rosmarinifolia*.
　Lily. See *Daniella*.
　Mountain. See *Phormium
　　cookianum*.
　New Zealand. See *Phormium*.
　Yellow. See *Linum flavum*;
　　Reinwardtia indica, illus. p.170.
Floating water plantain. See
　Luronium natans.
Floss flower. See *Ageratum*.
Floss silk tree. See *Chorisia speciosa*,
　illus. p.70.
Flowering banana. See *Musa ornata*,
　illus. p.232.
Flowering currant. See *Ribes
　sanguineum*.
Flowering dogwood. See *Cornus
　florida*.
Flowering gum. See *Eucalyptus
　ficifolia*.
Flowering quince. See *Chaenomeles*.
Flowering raspberry. See *Rubus
　odoratus*.
Flowering rush. See *Butomus
　umbellatus*, illus. p.448.
Flowering tobacco. See *Nicotiana
　sylvestris*, illus. p.226.
Flower-of-the-hour. See *Hibiscus
　trionum*, illus. p.320.
Fly honeysuckle. See *Lonicera
　xylosteum*, illus. p.140.

Flytrap, Venus. See *Dionaea
　muscipula*, illus. p.305.
Foam of May. See *Spiraea* 'Arguta'.
Foam, Meadow. See *Limnanthes
　douglasii*, illus. p.336.
Foamflower. See *Tiarella*.

FOENICULUM

APIACEAE/UMBELLIFERAE

Genus of summer-flowering biennials
and perennials, some of which are
grown for their umbels of yellow
flowers. Is also grown for its leaves,
which are both decorative in borders
and used for culinary flavouring. Grow
in an open, sunny position and in
fertile, well-drained soil. Remove
flower heads after fading to prevent self
seeding. Propagate by seed in autumn.
F. vulgare (Fennel). **'Purpureum'** is
an erect, branching perennial. H 2m
(6ft), S 45cm (1½ft). Has very finely
divided, hair-like, bronze leaves and, in
summer, large, flat umbels of small,
yellow flowers.

FONTINALIS
Moss

FONTINALACEAE

Genus of evergreen, perennial,
submerged water plants, grown for
their foliage, which provides dense
cover for fish and a good site for the
deposit of spawn. Grows in sun or
semi-shade in streams and other
running water; tolerates still water if
cool, but then does not grow to full
size. Propagate by division in spring.
F. antipyretica (Water moss, Willow
moss). Evergreen, perennial,
submerged water plant. H 2.5cm (1in),
S indefinite. Forms spreading colonies
of moss-like, dark olive-green leaves.

Foothill penstemon. See *Penstemon
　heterophyllus*.
Forget-me-not. See *Myosotis*.
　Alpine. See *Myosotis alpestris*,
　　illus. p.370.
　Chatham Island. See *Myosotidium*.
　Water. See *Myosotis scorpioides*.
Forrest fir. See *Abies forrestii*,
　illus. p.105.

FORSYTHIA

OLEACEAE

Genus of deciduous, spring-flowering
shrubs, grown for their usually profuse,
yellow flowers, which are produced
before the leaves emerge. *F.* x
intermedia 'Beatrix Farrand' and *F.* x *i.*
'Lynwood' make attractive, flowering
hedges. Prefers a position in full sun
and in fertile, well-drained soil. Many
older varieties fail to flower well
because the flower buds are not as
hardy as the rest of the plant and are
killed above the snow line. Thin out old
shoots and trim hedges immediately
after flowering. Propagate by softwood
cuttings in summer or by hardwood
cuttings in autumn or winter.
F. x *intermedia* **'Beatrix Farrand'**
illus. p.135. **'Lynwood'**, H 3m (10ft),
is very free-flowering, vigorous and
upright. **'Minigold'**, H and S 2m (6ft),
has oblong, mid-green leaves, and

produces masses of small, 4-lobed, yellow flowers from early to mid-spring. **'Spectabilis'** illus. p.134. **'Spring Glory'**, H 2m (6ft), S 1.5m (5ft), has clusters of large, 4-lobed, pale yellow flowers borne in mid-spring and oblong, toothed, bright green leaves. *F.* **'Northern Gold'**, 'Northern Sun', 'Vermont Sun'. New hybrids with improved flower bud hardiness that will still bloom fully in zone 4. *F. ovata.* Deciduous, bushy shrub. H and S 1.5m (5ft). Bears broadly oval, toothed, dark green leaves. Produces small, 4-lobed, bright yellow flowers in early spring. **'Ottawa'** was selected for its bud hardiness and will flower well in zone 3b. It is slightly darker than the species. **'Tetragold'** has larger flowers. *F. suspensa* illus. p.131.

FOTHERGILLA
HAMAMELIDACEAE
Genus of deciduous, spring-flowering shrubs, grown for their autumn colour and fragrant flowers, each with a dense, bottlebrush-like cluster of stamens, which open before or as leaves emerge. Grows in sun or semi-shade, but colours best in full sun. Requires moist, peaty, acid soil. Propagate by softwood cuttings taken in summer.
F. gardenii (Witch alder). Deciduous, bushy, dense shrub. H and S 1m (3ft). Produces dense clusters of tiny, fragrant, white flowers that appear from mid- to late spring, usually before broadly oval, dark blue-green leaves emerge. Leaves turn brilliant red in autumn.
F. major, syn. *F. monticola,* illus. p.127.
F. monticola. See *F. major.*

Fountain flower. See *Ceropegia sandersonii.*
Four o'clock flower. See *Mirabilis.*
Foxglove. See *Digitalis.*
  Fairy. See *Erinus.*
  Mexican. See *Tetranema roseum,* illus. p.303.
  Yellow. See *Digitalis grandiflora.*
Foxglove tree. See *Paulownia tomentosa,* illus. p.77.
Foxtail, Golden. See *Alopecurus pratensis* 'Aureovariegatus', illus. p.309.
Foxtail barley. See *Hordeum jubatum,* illus. p.307.
Foxtail fern. See *Asparagus densiflorus* 'Myersii', illus. p.267.
Foxtail lily. See *Eremurus.*
Foxtail millet. See *Setaria italica.*
Fragaria indica. See *Duchesnea indica.*
Fragrant olive. See *Osmanthus fragrans.*
Fragrant snowbell. See *Styrax obassia.*
Fragrant sumach. See *Rhus aromatica.*

FRAILEA
CACTACEAE
Genus of spherical to columnar, perennial cacti with tuberculate ribs. Bears short spines, mostly bristle-like.

In summer produces masses of buds, most of which develop into small, spherical, shiny pods without opening. Tender, min. 5°C (41°F). Needs partial shade and very well-drained soil. Is not well-adapted to long periods of drought. Propagate by seed in spring or summer.
F. pulcherrima. See *F. pygmaea.*
F. pygmaea, syn. *F. pulcherrima,* illus. p.477.

FRANCOA
SAXIFRAGACEAE
Genus of summer- and early autumn-flowering perennials. Needs full sun and fertile, well-drained soil. Propagate by seed or division in spring.
F. appendiculata (Bridal wreath). Clump-forming perennial. H 60cm (24in), S 45cm (18in). Racemes of small, bell-shaped, pale pink flowers, spotted with deep pink at base, appear on graceful, erect stems from summer to early autumn, above oblong to oval, lobed, hairy, crinkled, dark green leaves.
F. sonchifolia. Clump-forming perennial. H 75cm (30in), S 45cm (18in). Bears racemes of cup-shaped, red-marked, pink flowers from summer to early autumn. Lobed leaves each have a large, terminal lobe.

Frangipani. See *Plumeria.*
Native Australian. See *Hymenosporum flavum.*

FRANKLINIA
THEACEAE
Genus of one species of deciduous tree or shrub, grown for its flowers and autumn colour. Thrives only during hot summers. Needs full sun and moist but well-drained, neutral to acid soil. Propagate by softwood cuttings in summer, by seed in autumn or by hardwood cuttings in early winter.
F. alatamaha. Deciduous, upright tree or shrub. H and S 5m (15ft) or more. Large, shallowly cup-shaped, white flowers with yellow stamens open in late summer and early autumn. Oblong, glossy, bright green leaves turn red in autumn. Zone 6b.

FRAXINUS
Ash
OLEACEAE
Genus of deciduous trees and shrubs, grown mainly for their foliage of paired leaflets; flowers are usually insignificant. Requires a position in sun and fertile, well-drained but not too dry soil. Propagate species by seed in autumn, selected forms by budding in summer. Contact with lichens on the bark may aggravate skin allergies.
F. americana (White ash). Fast-growing, deciduous, spreading tree. H 25m (80ft), S 15m (50ft). Leaves are dark green, with 5–9 oval to lance-shaped leaflets, turning yellow or purple in autumn. Zone 3b. **'Autumn Blaze'** and **'Autumn Purple'** were selected for their reddish-purple fall colour. **'Skyline'** has a more upright form and turns orange-red in fall. All

zone 4.
F. angustifolia, syn. *F. oxycarpa* (Narrow-leaved ash). Deciduous, spreading, elegant tree. H 25m (80ft), S 12m (40ft). Leaves usually consist of 9–11 slender, lance-shaped, glossy, dark green leaflets that are golden-yellow in autumn. **'Raywood'** (Claret ash) is vigorous, H 20m (70ft), S 15m (50ft). Leaves have 5–7 narrowly oval leaflets that turn bright reddish-purple in autumn. Zone 7.
F. excelsior (European ash). Vigorous, deciduous, spreading tree. H 30m (100ft), S 20m (70ft). Dark green leaves, with usually 9–11 oval leaflets, sometimes become yellow in autumn. Black leaf buds are conspicuous in winter. f. *diversifolia* has leaves that are simple or with only 3 leaflets. Leaves of **'Jaspidea'** are yellow in spring and turn golden in autumn; shoots are yellow in winter. **'Pendula'**, H 15m (50ft), S 8–10m (25–30ft), has branches weeping to the ground. Zone 4b.
F. nigra (Black ash). Fast-growing, upright, deciduous tree. H 15m (50ft) S 8m (25ft). Leaves have 11 tapering, dark green leaflets and turn yellow in fall. **'Fallgold'** is a sterile selection with long-lasting golden fall colour. Zone 2b.
F. ornus illus. p.76.
F. oxycarpa. See *F. angustifolia.*
F. pennsylvanica (Green ash, Red ash). Fast-growing, deciduous, spreading tree. H and S 20m (70ft). Leaves of usually 7 or 9 narrowly oval, dull green leaflets are often velvety beneath, like the shoots, and turn yellow in autumn. **'Patmore'** is disease-resistant, with long-lasting, glossy leaves, but does not bear fruit. Zone 3.
F. velutina illus. p.80.

Freckle face. See *Hypoestes phyllostachya,* illus. p.264.

FREESIA
IRIDACEAE
Genus of winter- and spring-flowering corms, grown for their usually fragrant, funnel-shaped flowers, which are popular for cutting. Tender, min. 2°C (35°F).Requires full sun and well-drained soil. Plant in autumn and water throughout winter. Support with twigs or small canes. Dry off corms after flowering. Plant specially prepared corms outdoors in spring for flowering in summer. Propagate by offsets in autumn or by seed in spring.
F. alba of gardens. See *F. lactea.*
F. armstrongii. See *F. corymbosa.*
F. corymbosa, syn. *F. armstrongii.* Late winter- and spring-flowering corm. H to 30cm (12in), S 4–6cm (1½–2½in). Has narrowly sword-shaped, erect, basal leaves. Flower stem bends horizontally near the top and bears a spike of un-scented, upright, pink flowers, 3–3.5cm (1¼–1½in) long, with yellow bases. *F.* **'Golden Melody'**. Winter- and spring-flowering corm. H to 30cm (12in), S 4–6cm (1½–2½in). Is similar to *F. corymbosa,* but has larger, fragrant flowers, yellow throughout.
F. lactea, syn. *F. alba* of gardens,

F. refracta var. *alba.* Late winter- and spring-flowering corm. H 20–30cm (8–12in), S 4–6cm (1½–2½in). Has narrowly sword-shaped, erect leaves in a basal fan. Leafless stems bear loose spikes of very fragrant, white flowers, each 5–8cm (2–3in) long.
F. **'Oberon'** illus. p. 425.
F. refracta var. *alba.* See *F. lactea.*
F. **'Romany'**. Winter- and spring-flowering corm. H to 30cm (12in), S 4–6cm (1½–2½in). Is similar to *F. corymbosa,* but has fragrant, double, pale mauve flowers.
F. **'White Swan'**. Winter- and spring-flowering corm. H to 30cm (12in), S 4–6cm (1½–2½in). Is similar to *F. corymbosa,* but has very fragrant, white flowers with cream throats.

Fremontia. Reclassified as *Fremontodendron.*

FREMONTODENDRON,
syn. FREMONTIA
Flannel flower
STERCULIACEAE
Genus of vigorous, evergreen or semi-evergreen shrubs, grown for their large, very showy flowers. At the limits of hardiness, plant against a south- or west-facing wall. Needs full sun and light, not too rich, well-drained soil. In mild areas may be grown as a spreading shrub, but needs firm staking when young. Resents being transplanted. Propagate by semi-ripe cuttings in summer or by seed in autumn or spring. Contact with the foliage and shoots may irritate the skin.
F. **'California Glory'** illus. p.123.
F. californicum. Vigorous, evergreen or semi-evergreen, upright shrub. H 6m (20ft), S 4m (12ft), when grown against a wall. Large, saucer-shaped, bright yellow flowers are borne amid dark green leaves, each with 3 rounded lobes, from late spring to mid-autumn. Zone 9.
F. mexicanum. Vigorous, evergreen or semi-evergreen, upright shrub. H 6m (20ft), S 4m (12ft) when grown against a wall. Dark green leaves have 5 deep, rounded lobes. Bears a profusion of large, saucer-shaped, deep golden-yellow flowers from late spring to mid-autumn. Zone 9?.
F. **'Pacific Sunset'** (illus. p.53). Upright, evergreen shrub. H 5m (15ft), S 3–4m (10–12ft). Rounded, strongly lobed leaves are dark green. In summer produces saucer-shaped, bright yellow flowers, to 6cm (2½in) across, with long, slender-pointed lobes. Zone 9.

French honeysuckle. See *Hedysarum coronarium,* illus. p.250.
French lavender. See *Lavandula dentata; Lavandula stoechas,* illus. p.167.
French marigold. See *Tagetes patula.*
Friendship plant. See *Pilea involucrata.*
Friendship tree. See *Crassula ovata,* illus. p.457.
Fringe tree. See *Chionanthus virginicus,* illus. p.119.
  Chinese. See *Chionanthus retusus.*
Fringecups. See *Tellima grandiflora.*
Fringed water lily. See *Nymphoides peltata,* illus. p.451.

FRITHIA

AIZOACEAE

Genus of one species of rosette-forming, perennial succulent. Tender, min. 10°C (50°F). Needs sun and well-drained soil. Propagate by seed in spring or summer.
F. pulchra illus. p.473.

FRITILLARIA

LILIACEAE

Genus of spring-flowering bulbs, grown for their pendent, mainly bell-shaped flowers on leafy stems. Protect smaller, 5–15cm (2–6in) high species in cold frames or cold greenhouses. Needs full sun or partial shade and well-drained soil that dries out slightly in summer when bulbs are dormant but that does not become sunbaked. Grow *F. meleagris*, which is good for naturalizing in grass, in moisture-retentive soil. Propagate by offsets in summer or by seed in autumn or winter.
F. acmopetala illus. p.414.
F. bucharica. Spring-flowering bulb. H 10–35cm (4–14in), S 5cm (2in). Stems each bear scattered, lance-shaped, grey-green leaves and a raceme of up to 10 cup-shaped, green-tinged, white flowers, 1.5–2cm (⅝–¾in) long.
F. camschatcensis illus. p.413.
F. chitralensis illus. p.402.
F. cirrhosa illus. p.414.
F. crassifolia. Spring-flowering bulb. H 10–20cm (4–8in), S 5cm (2in). Has scattered, lance-shaped, grey leaves. Stems each produce 1–3 bell-shaped, green flowers, 2–2.5cm (¾–1in) long and chequered with brown.
F. delphinensis. See *F. tubiformis*.
F. imperialis illus. p.396. **'Lutea'** is a spring-flowering bulb. H to 1.5m (5ft), S 23–30cm (9–12in). Leafy stems each bear lance-shaped, glossy, pale green leaves in whorls and a head of up to 5 widely bell-shaped, yellow flowers, 5cm (2in) long, crowned by small, leaf-like bracts. **'Rubra Maxima'** is very robust with red flowers.
F. meleagris illus. p.413.
F. michailovskyi. Spring-flowering bulb. H 10–20cm (4–8in), S 5cm (2in). Has lance-shaped, grey leaves scattered on stem. Bears 1–4 bell-shaped, 2–3cm (¾–1¼in) long flowers, coloured purplish-brown with upper third of petals bright yellow.
F. pallidiflora illus. p.415.
F. persica illus. p.396. **'Adiyaman'** is a spring-flowering bulb. H to 1.5m (5ft), S 10cm (4in). Has narrowly lance-shaped, grey leaves along stem. Produces a spike of 10–20 or more narrowly bell-shaped, deep blackish-purple flowers, 1.5–2cm (⅝–¾in) long.
F. pontica illus. p.414.
F. pudica illus. p.434.
F. pyrenaica illus. p.413.
F. raddeana illus. p.396.
F. recurva illus. p.396.
F. sewerzowii, syn. *Korolkowia sewerzowii.* Spring-flowering bulb. H 15–25cm (6–10in), S 8–10cm (3–4in). Stems bear scattered, broadly lance-shaped leaves. Produces a spike of up to 10 narrowly bell-shaped,

green or metallic purplish-blue flowers, 2.5–3.5cm (1–1½in) long, with flared mouths.
F. tubiformis, syn. *F. delphinensis.* Spring-flowering bulb. H 15–35cm (6–14in), S 5–8cm (2–3in). Stems carry scattered, narrowly lance-shaped, grey leaves and a solitary, broadly bell-shaped, purplish-pink flower, 3.5–5cm (1½–2in) long, conspicuously chequered and suffused grey outside.
F. verticillata illus. p.396.

Fritillary
   Scarlet. See *Fritillaria recurva,* illus. p.396.
   Snake's-head. See *Fritillaria meleagris,* illus. p.413.
   Yellow. See *Fritillaria pudica,* illus. p.434.
Frogbit. See *Hydrocharis morsus-ranae,* illus. p.446.

FUCHSIA

ONAGRACEAE

Genus of deciduous or evergreen shrubs and trees, grown for their flowers, usually borne from early summer to early autumn. Slightly hardy (Zone 8) to tender, min. 5°C (41°F). If temperature remains above 4°C (39°F), deciduous plants are evergreen, but temperatures above 32°C (90°F) should be avoided. Prolonged low temperatures cause loss of top growth. If top growth dies in winter, cut back to ground level in spring. Needs a sheltered, partially shaded position, except where stated otherwise, and fertile, moist but well-drained soil. When grown as pot plants in a greenhouse, fuchsias also need high-nitrogen feeds and, when flowering, plenty of potash. Propagate by softwood cuttings in any season.

Tubular flowers are almost always pendulous and often bicoloured, with petals of one hue, and a tube and 4 sepals of another. Leaves are oval and mid-green unless otherwise stated. Spherical to cylindrical, usually blackish-purple fruits are edible, but mostly poor-flavoured. Upright types may be trained as compact bushes or standards or, with more difficulty, as pyramids. Lax or trailing plants are good for hanging baskets, but may be trained on trellises; if they are used for summer bedding they require staking.

Heights given in descriptions below are of plants grown in frost-free conditions. See also feature panel pp.164–5.

F. **'Alice Hoffman'.** Deciduous, compact shrub. H and S 75cm (2½ft). Has bronze foliage and small, semi-double flowers with rose-red tubes and sepals and rose-veined, white petals.
F. **'Annabel'** (illus. p.164). Deciduous, upright shrub. H 1m (3ft), S 75cm (2½ft). Produces large, double, pink-tinged, creamy-white flowers amid pale green leaves. Makes an excellent standard.
F. **'Applause'.** Deciduous, lax, upright shrub. H 30–40cm (12–18in), S 45–60cm (18–24in). Bears very large, double flowers with short, thick,

pale carmine tubes, very broad, carmine sepals with a pale central streak, and many, spreading, deep orange-red petals. Produces best colour in shade. Needs staking as a bush, but will trail with weights.
F. arborea. See *F. arborescens.*
F. arborescens, syn. *F. arborea* (Tree fuchsia; illus. p.164). Evergreen, upright tree. H 8m (25ft), S 2.5m (8ft). Tender. Foliage is mid- to dark green. Erect heads of tiny, pale mauve to pink flowers, borne year-round, are followed by black fruits with grey-blue bloom. May also be grown as a pot plant.
F. **'Auntie Jinks'.** Deciduous, trailing shrub. H 15–20cm (6–8in), S 20–40cm (8–16in). Bears small, single flowers with pink-red tubes, cerise-margined white sepals, and white-shaded purple petals.
F. **'Autumnale',** syn. *F.* 'Burning Bush' (illus. p.164). Deciduous, lax shrub, grown mainly for its foliage. H 2m (6ft), S 50cm (20in). Bears variegated red, gold and bronze leaves. Flowers have red tubes and sepals with reddish-purple petals. Is suitable for a hanging basket or for training as a weeping standard.
F. × *bacillaris,* syn. *F. parviflora* of gardens (illus. p.165). Group of deciduous, lax shrubs. H and S 75cm (2½ft). Small leaves are mid- to dark green. Bears minute, white, pink or crimson flowers (colour varying according to sun), sometimes followed by glossy, black fruits. Is suitable for a rock garden or hanging basket.
F. **'Ballet Girl'** (illus. p.164). Deciduous, upright shrub. H 30–45cm (12–18in), S 45–75cm (18–30in). Produces large, double flowers with bright cerise tubes and sepals, and white petals with cerise veins at the base.
F. **'Bicentennial'** (illus. p.164). Deciduous, lax shrub. H 30–45cm (12–18in), S 45–60cm (18–24in). Bears medium, double flowers with thin white tubes, orange sepals, and double corollas with magenta centres surrounded by orange petals.
F. boliviana. Fast-growing, deciduous, upright shrub. H 3m (10ft), S 1m (3ft). Tender. Has large, soft, grey-green leaves with reddish midribs. Long-tubed, scarlet flowers, bunched at ends of branches, are followed by pleasantly flavoured, black fruits. Needs a large pot and plenty of space to grow well. Resents being pinched back. Is very susceptible to whitefly. var. *alba* (syn. *F.b.* var. *luxurians* 'Alba', *F. corymbiflora* 'Alba'; illus. p.165) has flowers with white tubes and sepals and scarlet petals, followed by green fruits.
F. **'Bon Accorde'.** Vigorous, deciduous, upright shrub. H 1.5m (5ft), S 50cm (20in). Small, erect flowers have white tubes and sepals and pale purple petals.
F. **'Brookwood Belle'.** Deciduous, lax, bushy shrub with strong, short-jointed stems. H and S 45–60cm (18–24in). Medium, double flowers have deep cerise tubes and sepals, and white petals flushed pink and veined deep rose-pink.
F. **'Brutus'.** Vigorous, deciduous, upright shrub. H 1.5m (5ft), S 1m (3ft).

Single or semi-double flowers have crimson-red tubes and sepals and deep purple petals.
F. **'Burning Bush'.** See *F.* 'Autumnale'.
F. **'Cascade'** (illus. p.165). Deciduous, trailing shrub. H 2m (6ft), S indefinite. Bears red-tinged, white tubes and sepals and deep carmine petals. Is excellent grown in a hanging basket.
F. **'Celia Smedley'** (illus. p.165). Vigorous, deciduous, upright shrub. H 1.5m (5ft), S 1m (3ft). Large, single or semi-double flowers have greenish-white tubes, pale pinkish-white sepals and currant-red petals. Is best when trained as a standard.
F. **'Checkerboard'.** Vigorous, deciduous, upright shrub with strong stems. H 75–90cm (30–36in), S 45–75cm (18–30in). Produces medium, single flowers with slightly recurved, long red tubes, red sepals turning white and white-based, dark red petals.
F. **'Cloverdale Pearl'.** Deciduous, upright shrub. H 1m (3ft), S 75cm (2½ft). Foliage is mid-green with crimson midribs. Flowers have pinkish-white tubes, pink-veined, white petals and green-tipped, pink sepals. Is readily trained as a standard.
F. **'Coquet Bell'.** Vigorous, deciduous, upright shrub. H 1.5m (5ft), S 1m (3ft). Has a profusion of single or semi-double flowers with pinkish-red tubes and sepals and red-veined, pale mauve petals.
F. **'Coralle',** syn. *F.* 'Koralle' (illus. p.165). Deciduous, upright shrub. H and S 1m (3ft). Tender. Foliage is velvety and deep green. Salmon-orange flowers, with long, narrow tubes and small sepals and petals, are bunched at branch ends. Is useful for summer bedding and as a specimen plant. Prefers sun.
F. corymbiflora **'Alba'.** See *F. boliviana* var. *alba.*
F. **'Dark Eyes'.** Deciduous, bushy, upright shrub. H 45–60cm (18–24in), S 60–75cm (24–30in). Bears medium, double flowers that hold their shape for a long period. The tubes and upturned sepals are deep red, and the petals deep violet-blue.
F. denticulata. Deciduous, straggling shrub. H 4m (12ft), S indefinite. Tender. Leaves are glossy, dark green above and reddish-green beneath. Flowers have long, crimson tubes, green-tipped, pale pink sepals and vermilion petals. With good cultivation under glass, flowers appear throughout autumn and winter.
F. **'Display'.** Deciduous, upright shrub. H 1m (3ft), S 75cm (2½ft). Bears saucer-shaped flowers in shades of pink.
F. **'Dollar Princess'** (illus. p.164). Deciduous, upright shrub. H 1m (3ft), S 75cm (2½ft). Small, double flowers have cerise-red tubes and sepals and purple petals.
F. **'Estelle Marie'** (illus. p.165). Deciduous, upright shrub. H 1m (3ft), S 50cm (20in). Flowers with white tubes, green-tipped, white sepals and mauve petals are borne above foliage. Is excellent for summer bedding.
F. **'Flash'.** Fast-growing, deciduous, stiffly erect shrub. H 2.5m (8ft),

S 50cm (20in). Produces small, red flowers amid small leaves.

F. 'Flirtation Waltz'. Vigorous, deciduous, upright shrub. H 1m (3ft), S 75cm (2½ft). Has large, double flowers with petals in shades of pink, and white tubes and sepals.

F. fulgens (illus. p.165). Deciduous, upright shrub with tubers. H 2m (6ft), S 1m (3ft). Tender. Long-tubed, orange flowers hang in short clusters amid large, pale green leaves and are followed by edible but acidic, green fruits. Tubers may be stored dry for winter. May also be propagated by division of tubers in spring. Is highly susceptible to whitefly.

F. 'Garden News'. Deciduous, upright shrub with strong stems. H and S 45–60cm (18–24in). Medium, double flowers have short, thick, pink tubes, frost-pink sepals and magenta-rose petals becoming rose-pink at the base.

F. 'Genii'. Deciduous, erect shrub. H 1.5m (5ft), S 75cm (2½ft). Has golden-green foliage. Produces small flowers with cerise-red tubes and sepals and reddish-purple petals. Makes a good standard.

F. 'Golden Dawn' (illus. p.164). Deciduous, upright shrub. H 1.5m (5ft), S 75cm (2½ft). Flowers are salmon-pink. Is good for training as a standard.

F. 'Golden Marinka' (illus. p.164). Deciduous, trailing shrub. H 2m (6ft), S indefinite. Has red flowers and variegated golden-yellow leaves with red veins. Is excellent for a hanging basket.

F. 'Gruss aus dem Bodethal' (illus. p.164). Deciduous, upright shrub. H 1m (3ft), S 75cm (2½ft). Small, single or semi-double, crimson flowers open almost black, becoming larger and paler with age.

F. 'Harry Gray' (illus. p.164). Deciduous, lax shrub. H 2m (6ft), S indefinite. Bears a profusion of double flowers with pale pink tubes, green-tipped, white sepals and white to pale pink petals. Is excellent in a hanging basket.

F. 'Heidi Weiss', syn. F. 'White Ann' of gardens, F. 'White Heidi Ann' of gardens (illus. p.164). Deciduous, upright shrub. H 1m (3ft), S 75cm (2½ft). Has double flowers with red tubes and sepals and cerise-veined, white petals. Is good for training as a standard.

F. 'Hula Girl'. Deciduous, trailing shrub. H 2m (6ft), S indefinite. Bears large, double flowers with deep rose-pink tubes and sepals and pink-flushed, white petals. Does best in a large hanging basket or when trained against a trellis.

F. 'Jack Shahan' (illus. p.164). Vigorous, deciduous, trailing shrub. H 2m (6ft), S indefinite. Has large, pale to deep pink flowers. Is excellent for a hanging basket or for training into a weeping standard or upright against a trellis.

F. 'Joy Patmore'. Vigorous, deciduous, upright shrub. H 1.5m (5ft), S 1m (3ft). Flowers have white tubes, green-tipped, white sepals and cerise petals with white bases. Makes a good standard.

F. 'Koralle'. See F. 'Coralle'.

F. 'La Campanella' (illus. p.165). Deciduous, trailing shrub. H 1.5m (5ft), S indefinite. Has small, semi-double flowers with white tubes, pink-flushed, white sepals and cerise-purple petals. Does best in a hanging basket or trained against a trellis.

F. 'Lady Thumb' (illus. p.164). Deciduous, upright, dwarf shrub. H and S 50cm (20in). Has small, semi-double flowers with reddish-pink tubes and sepals and pink-veined, white petals. May be trained as a miniature standard.

F. 'Lena'. Deciduous, lax shrub. H and S 1m (3ft). Bears double flowers with pale pink sepals and tubes and pink-flushed, purple petals. Makes a good standard.

F. 'Leonora' (illus. p.164). Vigorous, deciduous, upright shrub. H 1.5m (5ft), S 1m (3ft). Flowers are pink with green-tipped sepals. Is good for training as a standard.

F. 'Love's Reward' (illus. p.165). Deciduous, upright, short-jointed shrub. H and S 30–45cm (12–18in). Small to medium, single flowers have white to pale pink tubes and sepals and violet-blue petals.

F. 'Lye's Unique' (illus. p.165). Vigorous, deciduous, upright shrub. H 1.5m (5ft), S 1m (3ft). Has small flowers with long, white tubes and sepals and orange-red petals. Is excellent for training as a large pyramid.

F. magellanica (Lady's eardrops; illus. p.164). Deciduous, upright shrub. H 3m (10ft), S 2m (6ft). Small flowers with red tubes, long, red sepals and purple petals are followed by black fruits.
'Alba' see F.m. var. molinae. var. molinae (syn. F.m. 'Alba') has very pale pink flowers. Zone 8.
var. molinae 'Enstone' has gold and green, variegated foliage. var. molinae 'Sharpitor' produces cream and pale green, variegated leaves.

F. 'Margaret Brown' (illus. p.45). Deciduous, free-flowering, upright shrub. H and S 60–90cm (2–3ft). Has strong stems and light green foliage, and bears small, single, 2-tone pink flowers in summer.

F. 'Marinka'. Deciduous, trailing shrub. H 2m (6ft), S indefinite. Red flowers with darker petals that are folded at outer edges are produced amid dark green leaves with crimson midribs. Foliage becomes discoloured in full sun or cold winds. Is excellent in a hanging basket.

F. 'Micky Goult'. Vigorous, deciduous, upright shrub. H 1m (3ft), S 75cm (2½ft). Small flowers, with white tubes, pink-tinged, white sepals and pale purple petals, are produced amid pale green foliage.

F. 'Mieke Meursing'. Deciduous, upright shrub. H 1m (3ft), S 75cm (2½ft). Single to semi-double flowers have red tubes and sepals and pale pink petals with cerise veins.

F. 'Mrs Lovell Swisher' (illus. p.165). Deciduous, upright shrub. H 45–60cm (18–24in), S 30–60cm (12–24in). Produces masses of small, single flowers with flesh-pink tubes, pinkish-white sepals and deep rose-pink petals.

F. 'Mrs Popple' (illus. p.164).

Vigorous, deciduous, upright shrub. H 1.5m (5ft), S 75cm (2½ft). Has flowers with red tubes, overhanging, red sepals and purple petals. In a sheltered area may be grown as a hedge.

F. 'Mrs Rundle'. Vigorous, deciduous, lax shrub. H and S 75cm (2½ft). Tender. Produces large flowers with long, pink tubes, green-tipped, pink sepals and vermilion petals. Is good for training as a standard or growing in a large hanging basket.

F. 'Nancy Lou'. Vigorous, deciduous, upright shrub. H and S 1m (3ft). Large, double flowers have pink tubes, upright, green-tipped, pink sepals and bright white petals.

F. 'Nellie Nuttall' (illus. p.164). Vigorous, deciduous, upright shrub. H 1m (3ft), S 75cm (2½ft). Flowers, with rose-red tubes and sepals and white petals, are borne well above foliage. Is especially suitable for summer bedding; is also good as a standard.

F. 'Other Fellow' (illus. p.164). Deciduous, upright shrub. H 1.5m (5ft), S 75cm (2½ft). Has small flowers with white tubes and sepals and pink petals.

F. 'Pacquesa'. Vigorous, deciduous, upright shrub. H 1m (3ft), S 75cm (2½ft). Has flowers with deep red tubes and sepals and red-veined, white petals. Is good for training as a standard.

F. parviflora of gardens. See F. x bacillaris.

F. 'Peppermint Stick' (illus. p.164). Deciduous, upright shrub. H 1.5m (5ft), S 1m (3ft). Large, double flowers have carmine-red tubes and sepals and pink-splashed, purple petals. Makes a good standard.

F. 'Phyllis'. Deciduous, upright shrub. H 2m (6ft), S 1m (3ft). Single to semi-double flowers, with rose-red tubes and sepals and crimson petals, are followed by masses of black fruits. In a sheltered area may be grown as a hedge.

F. 'Pink Fantasia'. Deciduous, stiff, upright shrub. H 30–40cm (12–18in), S 45–60cm (18–24in). Bears single, upward-looking flowers, in profusion, with white tubes and sepals blushed dark pink, and dark purple petals, veined pink, with white bases. Excellent for borders or pots.

F. 'Pink Galore' (illus. p.164). Deciduous, trailing shrub. H 1.5m (5ft), S indefinite. Has large, double, pale pink flowers. Grows best in a large hanging basket or when trained against a trellis.

F. procumbens (illus. p.165). Deciduous, prostrate shrub. H 10cm (4in), S indefinite. Produces tiny, erect, petalless, yellow-tubed flowers with purple sepals and bright blue pollen. Has small, dark green leaves and large, red fruits. Suits a rock garden as well as a hanging basket. Encourage flowering by root restriction or growing in poor, sandy soil.

F. 'Red Spider' (illus. p.164). Deciduous, trailing shrub. H 1.5m (5ft), S indefinite. Has long, red flowers with long, narrow, spreading sepals and darker petals. Is best in a large hanging basket or when trained against a trellis.

F. 'Riccartonii' (illus. p.164). Deciduous, stiff, upright shrub. H 2m

(6ft), S 1.5m (5ft). With good drainage and wind protection is sometimes fully hardy. Has small flowers with red tubes, broad, overhanging, red sepals and purple petals. In a sheltered area may be grown as a hedge. Many plants sold under name of F. 'Riccartonii' are lax hybrids of F. magellanica. Zone 8.

F. 'Rose Fantasia'. Deciduous, stiff, upright shrub. H 30–40cm (12–18in), S 45–60cm (18–24in). Produces single, upward-looking flowers, in profusion, with rose-pink tubes, dark rose-pink sepals with green tips and red-purple petals, veined rose-pink. Excellent plant for either borders or pots.

F. 'Rose of Castile' (illus. p.165). Vigorous, deciduous, upright shrub. H 1.5m (5ft), S 1m (3ft). Produces small flowers with white tubes, green-tipped, white sepals and purple-flushed, pink petals. Makes a good standard.

F. 'Rough Silk'. Vigorous, deciduous, trailing shrub. H 2m (6ft), S indefinite. Bears large flowers with pink tubes, long, spreading, pink sepals and wine-red petals. Grows best in a large hanging basket or when trained against a trellis.

F. 'Royal Velvet'. Vigorous, deciduous, upright shrub. H 1.5m (5ft), S 75cm (2½ft). Has large, double flowers with red tubes and sepals and deep purple petals, splashed deep pink. Is an excellent standard.

F. 'Rufus' (illus. p.164). Vigorous, deciduous, upright shrub. H 1.5m (5ft), S 75cm (2½ft). Has a profusion of small, bright red flowers. Is easily trained as a standard.

F. 'Shellford'. Deciduous, upright, short-jointed shrub. H 35–50cm (14–20in), S 45–60cm (18–24in). Bears masses of medium-sized, single flowers with slightly fluted, baby-pink tubes, long, narrow, baby-pink sepals and white petals with slight pink veining at the base. Suitable for all forms of training.

F. splendens. Deciduous, upright shrub. H 2m (6ft), S 1m (3ft). Small flowers, with broad, orange tubes, pinched in their middles, and short, green sepals and petals, appear in spring amid pale green foliage. Is very susceptible to whitefly.

F. 'Strawberry Delight'. Deciduous, lax shrub. H and S 1m (3ft). Leaves are yellowish-green and slightly bronzed. Large, double flowers have red tubes and sepals and pink-flushed, white petals. Is excellent as a standard or hanging basket plant.

F. 'Swingtime' (illus. p.164). Vigorous, deciduous, lax shrub. H and S 1m (3ft). Has large, double flowers with red tubes and sepals and red-veined, creamy-white petals. Makes a good standard or hanging basket plant.

F. 'Texas Longhorn'. Deciduous, lax shrub. H and S 75cm (2½ft). Very large, double flowers have red tubes, long, spreading, red sepals and cerise-veined, white petals. Grow as a standard or in a hanging basket.

F. 'Thalia' (illus. p.165). Deciduous, upright shrub. H and S 1m (3ft). Tender. Foliage is dark maroon and velvety. Long, slender flowers, with long, red tubes, small, red sepals and small, orange-red petals, are bunched at ends of branches. Makes an excellent specimen plant in summer bedding schemes. Prefers full sun.

F. thymifolia. Deciduous, lax shrub. H and S 1m (3ft). Has pale green foliage and a few minute, greenish-white flowers that age to purplish-pink. Bears black fruits on female plants if pollen-bearing plants of this species or of *F.* x *bacillaris* are also grown.

F. 'Tom Thumb' (illus. p.164). Deciduous, upright shrub. H and S 50cm (20in). Bears small flowers with red tubes and sepals and mauve-purple petals. May be trained as a miniature standard.

F. 'Tom West' (illus. p.165). Deciduous, upright, lax shrub. H and S 30–60cm (12–24in). Has green and cream variegated foliage and small, single flowers with red tubes and sepals, and purple petals.

F. triphylla. Deciduous, upright shrub, sometimes confused with *F.* 'Thalia'. H and S 50cm (20in). Tender. Spikes of narrow, long-tubed, bright reddish-orange flowers, with small petals and sepals, are borne above dark bronze-green leaves that are purple beneath. Is very difficult to grow.

F. 'White Ann' of gardens. See *F.* 'Heidi Weiss'.

F. 'White Heidi Ann' of gardens. See *F.* 'Heidi Weiss'.

Fuchsia, Tree. See *Fuchsia arborescens*, illus. p.164.

Full moon maple. See *Acer japonicum*.

FURCRAEA

AGAVACEAE

Genus of perennial succulents with basal rosettes of sword-shaped, fleshy, toothed leaves; rosettes die after flowering. Resembles *Agave*, but has short-tubed flowers. Tender, min. 6°C (43°F). Requires a sunny position and well-drained soil. Propagate by bulbils, borne on lower stems, when developed.

F. foetida, syn. *F. gigantea*. Basal-rosetted, perennial succulent. H 3m (10ft), S 5m (15ft). Has broadly sword-shaped, fleshy, mid-green leaves, to 2.5m (8ft) long, with edges toothed only at the base. Flower stems, to 8m (25ft), bear scented, bell-shaped, green flowers, white within, in summer.
'Mediopicta' (syn. *F.f.* var. *mediopicta*, *F.f.* 'Variegata') illus. p.460.
F. gigantea. See *F. foetida*.

G

GAGEA
LILIACEAE

Genus of spring-flowering bulbs, grown for their clusters of funnel- or star-shaped, white or yellow flowers. Is suitable for rock gardens. Prefers full light and well-drained soil that does not become too hot and dry. Dies down in summer. Propagate by division in spring or autumn or by seed in autumn.
G. graeca, syn. *Lloydia graeca*. Spring-flowering bulb. H 5–10cm (2–4in), S 3–5cm (1¼–2in). Thread-like, semi-erect leaves form at ground level and on wiry stems. Bears up to 5 widely funnel-shaped, purple-veined, white flowers, 1–1.5cm (½–⅝in) long.
G. peduncularis. Spring-flowering bulb. H 5–15cm (2–6in), S 2.5–5cm (1–2in). Has thread-like, semi-erect leaves at base and on stem. Produces a loose head of flat, star-shaped, yellow flowers, each 1.5–3cm (⅝–1¼in) across, with green stripes outside.

GAILLARDIA
Blanket flower

ASTERACEAE/COMPOSITAE

Genus of summer-flowering annuals and perennials that tend to be short-lived. Requires sun and prefers well-drained soil. May need staking. Propagate species by seed in autumn or spring, selected forms by root cuttings in winter.
G. aristata illus. p.291.
G. × grandiflora 'Dazzler' illus. p.283.
'Wirral Flame' is a clump-forming, short-lived perennial. H 60cm (24in), S 50cm (20in). Produces large, terminal, daisy-like, deep cardinal-red flower heads during summer. Leaves are lance-shaped, lobed and soft green.
G. pulchella. Moderately fast-growing, upright annual or short-lived perennial. H 45cm (18in), S 30cm (12in). Has lance-shaped, hairy, greyish-green leaves and, in summer, daisy-like, double, crimson-zoned, yellow, pink or red flower heads. **'Lollipops'** illus. p.338.

GALANTHUS
Snowdrop

AMARYLLIDACEAE

Genus of bulbs, grown for their pendent, white flowers, one on each slender stem between 2 basal leaves. Is easily recognized by its 3 large, outer petals and 3 small, inner ones forming a cup, which is green-marked. Needs a cool, partially shaded position and humus-rich, moist soil. Do not allow bulbs to dry out excessively. Propagate by division in spring after flowering or in late summer or autumn when bulbs are dormant. All parts may cause mild stomach upset if ingested; contact with the bulbs may irritate skin.
G. 'Atkinsii' illus. p.439.
G. elwesii illus. p.4309.

G. gracilis, syn. *G. graecus* of gardens, illus. p.439.
G. graecus of gardens. See *G. gracilis*.
G. ikariae, syn. *G. latifolius* of gardens, illus. p.440.
G. latifolius of gardens. See *G. ikariae*.
G. nivalis (Common snowdrop). Late winter- and early spring-flowering bulb. H 10–15cm (4–6in), S 5–8cm (2–3in). Produces narrowly strap-shaped, semi-erect, basal, grey-green leaves. Flowers are 2–2.5cm (¾–1in) long with a green mark at the tip of each inner petal.
'Flore Pleno' illus. p.439.
'Lutescens' see *G.n. 'Sandersii'*.
'Pusey Green Tip' illus. p.439.
'Sandersii' (syn. *G.n.* 'Lutescens') and **'Scharlockii'** illus. p.440.
G. plicatus subsp. **plicatus**. Late winter- and early spring-flowering bulb. H 10–20cm (4–8in), S 5–8cm (2–3in). Bears broadly strap-shaped, semi-erect, basal, deep green leaves that have grey bands along the centres and reflexed margins. White flowers, 2–3cm (¾–1¼in) long, have a green patch at the tip of each inner petal. subsp. **byzantinus** illus. p.440.
G. reginae-olgae (Autumn snowdrop). Autumn-flowering bulb. H 10–20cm (4–8in), S 5cm (2in). Has 1.5–2.5cm (⅝–1in) long flowers, with a green patch at the apex of each inner petal, before or just as narrowly strap-shaped, deep green leaves, each with a central, grey stripe, appear.
G. rizehensis illus. p.439.

GALAX
DIAPENSIACEAE

Genus of one species of evergreen perennial, grown for its foliage and for its flowers borne in late spring and summer. Is useful for underplanting shrubs. Needs shade and moist, peaty, acid soil. Propagate by division of rooted runners in spring.
G. aphylla. See *G. urceolata*.
G. urceolata, syn. *G. aphylla*, illus. p.351.

GALEGA
Goat's rue

LEGUMINOSAE/PAPILIONACEAE

Genus of summer-flowering perennials. Grow in an open, sunny position and in any well-drained soil. Requires staking. Propagate by seed in autumn or by division in winter.
G. 'Her Majesty'. See *G. 'His Majesty'*.
G. 'His Majesty', syn. *G. 'Her Majesty'*. Vigorous, upright perennial. H to 1.5m (5ft), S 1m (3ft). In summer produces spikes of small, pea-like, clear lilac-mauve and white flowers. Bold, oblong to lance-shaped leaves consist of oval leaflets.
G. 'Lady Wilson' illus. p.228.
G. orientalis illus. p.252.

Galingale. See *Cyperus longus*.

GALIUM
Bedstraw

RUBIACEAE

Genus of spring- and summer-flowering perennials, many of which are weeds; *G. odoratum* is cultivated as ground cover. Grows well in partial shade, but tolerates sun and thrives in any well-drained soil. Propagate by division in early spring or autumn.
G. odoratum, syn. *Asperula odorata*, illus. p.275.

GALTONIA
HYACINTHACEAE/LILIACEAE

Genus of summer- and autumn-flowering bulbs, grown for their elegant spikes of pendent, funnel-shaped, white or green flowers. Needs a sheltered, sunny site and fertile, well-drained soil that does not dry out in summer. Dies down in winter. May be lifted for replanting in spring. Propagate by seed in spring or by offsets in autumn or spring.
G. candicans illus. p.397.
G. viridiflora illus. p.402.

Gandergoose. See *Orchis morio*, illus. p.298.
Garden loosestrife. See *Lysimachia punctata*, illus. p.255.
Gardener's garters. See *Phalaris arundinacea* var. *picta*, illus. p.306.

GARDENIA
RUBIACEAE

Genus of evergreen shrubs and trees, grown for their flowers and foliage. Tender, min. 15°C (59°F). Prefers partial shade and humus-rich, well-drained, neutral to acid soil. Water containerized specimens freely when in full growth, moderately at other times. After flowering, shorten strong shoots to maintain a shapely habit. Propagate by greenwood cuttings in spring or by semi-ripe cuttings in summer. Whitefly and mealy bug may cause problems.
G. augusta, syn. *G. florida*, *G. grandiflora*, *G. jasminoides* (Cape jasmine, Common gardenia). **'Veitchii'** illus. p.158.
G. capensis. See *Rothmannia capensis*.
G. florida. See *G. augusta*.
G. grandiflora. See *G. augusta*.
G. jasminoides. See *G. augusta*.
G. rothmannia. See *Rothmannia capensis*.
G. thunbergia. Evergreen, bushy shrub with white stems. H and S to 2m (6ft) or more. Has elliptic, glossy, deep green leaves. Fragrant, 7–9-petalled, white flowers, 6–10cm (2½–4in) wide, are borne in winter-spring.

Gardenia, Common. See *Gardenia augusta*.
Garland flower. See *Hedychium*.

GARRYA
GARRYACEAE

Genus of evergreen shrubs and trees, grown for their catkins in winter and spring, which are longer and more attractive on male plants. Hard frosts may damage catkins. Requires a sheltered, sunny site and tolerates any poor soil. Is suitable for a south- or west-facing wall. Dislikes being transplanted. Propagate by semi-ripe cuttings in summer.
G. elliptica illus. p.125. **'James Roof'** is an evergreen, bushy, dense shrub. H and S 4m (12ft). Has oval, wavy-edged, leathery, dark green leaves. Very long, grey-green catkins, with yellow anthers, are borne from mid- or late winter to early spring. Zone 8.

GASTERIA
ALOEACEAE/LILIACEAE

Genus of perennial succulents with thick, fleshy leaves, usually arranged in a fan, later becoming a tight rosette. Tender, min. 5°C (41°F). Is easy to grow, needing sun or partial shade and very well-drained soil. Propagate by seed, leaf cuttings or division in spring or summer.
G. bicolor var. **liliputana**, syn. *G. liliputana*, illus. p.480.
G. caespitosa. Fan-shaped, perennial succulent. H 15cm (6in), S 30cm (12in). Produces triangular, thick, dark green leaves, 15cm (6in) long, with horny borders. Upper leaf surfaces have numerous white or pale green dots, usually in diagonal rows. Bears spikes of bell-shaped, orange-green flowers in summer.
G. carinata var. **verrucosa**, syn. *G. verrucosa*, illus. p.480.
G. liliputana. See *G. bicolor* var. *liliputana*.
G. verrucosa. See *G. carinata* var. *verrucosa*.

× **Gaulnettya 'Pink Pixie'.** See *Gaultheria* × *wisleyensis* 'Pink Pixie'.
× **Gaulnettya 'Wisley Pearl'.** See *Gaultheria* × *wisleyensis* 'Wisley Pearl'.

GAULTHERIA
ERICACEAE

Genus of evergreen shrubs and sub-shrubs, grown for their foliage, flowers and fruits. Grows best in shade or semi-shade and requires moist, peaty, acid soil. Will tolerate sun provided soil is permanently moist. Propagate by semi-ripe cuttings in summer or by seed in autumn; for *G. shallon* and

G. trichophylla propagate by division in autumn or spring. All parts may cause mild stomach upset if ingested, except the fruits, which are edible.
G. cuneata illus. p.360.
G. forrestii. Evergreen, rounded shrub. H and S 1.5m (5ft). Has oblong, glossy, dark green leaves and racemes of small, fragrant, rounded, white flowers, in spring, followed by rounded, blue fruits. Zone 8.
G. miqueliana. Evergreen, compact shrub. H and S 25cm (10in). Has oval, leathery leaves clothing stiff stems. In late spring produces bell-shaped, pink-tinged, white flowers, up to 6 per stem, followed by rounded, white or pink fruits. Zone 7.
G. mucronata, syn. *Pernettya mucronata*. Evergreen, bushy, dense shrub, spreading by underground stems. H and S 1.2m (4ft). Oval, prickly, glossy, dark green leaves set off tiny, urn-shaped, white flowers in late spring and early summer. Has spherical, fleshy fruit varying in colour between cultivars. Sprays of fruit are good for indoor display. Zone 7. Fruits of **'Cherry Ripe'** (female) are large and bright cherry-red. **'Edward Balls'** (male) bears stout, upright, red shoots and sharply spined, bright green leaves. **'Mulberry Wine'** (female) illus. p.174. **'Wintertime'** (female) illus. p.173.
G. myrsinoides, syn. *G. prostrata, Pernettya prostrata*. Evergreen, spreading shrub. H 15–30cm (6–12in), S 30cm (12in) or more. Bears oval, leathery, dark green leaves. Urn-shaped, white flowers are produced in early summer and are followed by large, rounded, blue-purple fruits. Is suitable for a rock garden or peat bed. Zone 8.
G. nummularioides. Evergreen, compact shrub. H 10–15cm (4–6in), S 20cm (8in). Leaves are oval to heart-shaped and leathery. Egg-shaped, pink-flushed, white flowers are produced from the upper leaf axils in late spring or summer. Produces rounded, blue-black fruits, but only rarely. Zone 8.
G. procumbens illus. p.387.
G. prostrata. See *G. myrsinoides*.
G. pumila, syn. *Pernettya pumila*. Evergreen, mat-forming, creeping shrub. H 5cm (2in), S 30–60cm (12–24in). Prostrate branches bear tiny, bell-shaped, white flowers in early summer among tiny, rounded, leathery leaves. Rounded fruits are pink or white. Is good for a rock garden or peat bed. Zone 8.
G. shallon illus. p.162.
G. tasmanica, syn. *Pernettya tasmanica*. Evergreen, mat-forming shrub. H 5–8cm (2–3in), S 20cm (8in). Has oval, toothed, leathery leaves with wavy edges. Bell-shaped, white flowers in early summer are followed by rounded, red fruits. Is good for a rock garden or peat bed. Zone 9.
G. trichophylla. Evergreen, compact shrub with creeping, underground stems. H 7–15cm (3–6in), S 20cm (8in). Bell-shaped, pink flowers in early summer are followed by egg-shaped, blue fruits produced from leaf axils. Leaves are small and oval. Zone 7.
G. × wisleyensis 'Pink Pixie', syn. × *Gaulnettya* 'Pink Pixie'. Evergreen,

dense, bushy shrub. H and S 1m (3ft). Bears broadly oval, deeply veined, dark green leaves. Small, urn-shaped, pale pink flowers, produced in late spring and early summer, are followed by spherical, purplish-red fruits. Zone 6. **'Wisley Pearl'**, syn. × *Gaulnettya* 'Wisley Pearl', illus. p.154.

GAURA
ONAGRACEAE
Genus of summer-flowering annuals and perennials that are sometimes short-lived. Prefers full sun and light, well-drained soil. Propagate by softwood or semi-ripe cuttings in summer or by seed in autumn or spring.
G. lindheimeri. Bushy perennial. H 1.2m (4ft), S 1m (3ft). In summer produces racemes of tubular, pink-suffused, white flowers. Leaves are lance-shaped and mid-green.

Gay feather, Kansas. See *Liatris pycnostachya*.
Gay feathers. See *Liatris*.
Gean. See *Prunus avium*, illus. p.71.

GAYLUSSACIA
Huckleberry
ERICACEAE
Genus of deciduous, occasionally evergreen shrubs, grown for their flowers, fruits, and autumn colour. Needs sun or semi-shade and moist, peaty, acid soil. Propagate by softwood cuttings in summer or by seed in autumn.
G. baccata (Black huckleberry). Deciduous, bushy shrub. H and S 1m (3ft). Oval, sticky, dark green leaves redden in autumn. Produces clusters of small, urn-shaped, dull red flowers in late spring, then edible, spherical, black fruits. Zone 4.

GAZANIA
ASTERACEAE/COMPOSITAE
Genus of evergreen perennials, often grown as annuals and useful for summer bedding, pots and tubs. Requires sun and sandy soil. Propagate by seed in spring or by heel cuttings in spring or summer.
G. Daybreak Series. Carpeting perennial, grown as an annual. H and S 20cm (8in). Has lance-shaped leaves and, in summer, large, daisy-like flower heads in a mixture of orange, yellow, pink, bronze and white. Flowers remain open in dull weather.
G. pinnata. Mat-forming perennial. H 15cm (6in), S 30cm (12in). Daisy-like, orange-red flower heads, with central, black rings, appear singly in early summer above oval, finely cut, hairy, bluish-grey leaves.
G. rigens var. **uniflora**, syn. *G. uniflora*, illus. p.292.
G. Talent Series. Vigorous perennials. H and S to 25cm (3ft). Produce solitary, yellow, orange, pink or brown flower heads on short stems just above the leaves in summer.
G. uniflora. See *G. rigens* var. *uniflora*.

GELSEMIUM
LOGANIACEAE
Genus of evergreen, twining climbers, grown for their fragrant, jasmine-like flowers. In cool climates best grown under glass. Provide full light and fertile, well-drained soil. Water regularly, less in cold weather. Stems require support and should be thinned out after flowering or in spring. Propagate by seed in spring or by semi-ripe cuttings in summer.
G. sempervirens illus. p.206.

GENISTA
Broom
LEGUMINOSAE/PAPILIONACEAE
Genus of deciduous, sometimes almost leafless, shrubs and trees, grown for their mass of small, pea-like flowers. Does best in full sun and not over-rich, well-drained soil. Resents being transplanted. Propagate species by softwood or semi-ripe cuttings in summer or by seed in autumn, selected forms by softwood cuttings only in summer.
G. aetnensis illus. p.93.
G. cinerea illus. p.123.
G. delphinensis, syn. *Chamaespartium sagittale* subsp. *delphinense*, *G. sagittalis* subsp. *delphinensis*. Deciduous, prostrate shrub. H 1cm (½in), S 20cm (8in). Has tangled, winged branches, covered with minute, oval, dark green leaves. Masses of golden-yellow flowers are produced along stems in early summer. Suitable for a rock garden or wall. Zone 7.
G. fragrans of gardens. See *Cytisus* × *spachianus*.
G. hispanica illus. p.170.
G. lydia illus. p.359.
G. monosperma, syn. *Retama monosperma*. Deciduous, almost leafless, graceful, arching shrub. H 1m (3ft), S 1.5m (5ft). Slender, silky-grey shoots bear clusters of very fragrant, white flowers in early spring. Has a few inconspicuous leaves. Grow against a south- or west-facing wall. Zone 7.
G. pilosa. Deciduous, domed shrub. H and S 30cm (12in). Narrowly oval leaves are silky-haired beneath. Bright yellow flowers on short stalks are borne in leaf axils in summer. Is useful on a bank or as ground cover. Propagate by semi-ripe cuttings in summer. Zone 5. 'Vancouver Gold' is more mounded, H 45cm (18in), with golden-yellow flowers. Zone 5.
G. sagittalis, syn. *Chamaespartium sagittale*, illus. p.386. subsp. **delphinensis.** See *G. delphinensis*.
G. × spachiana. See *Cytisus* × *spachianus*.
G. tenera 'Golden Shower'. Vigorous, deciduous, arching shrub. H 3m (10ft), S 5m (15ft). Narrowly oblong leaves are grey-green. Bears racemes of fragrant, golden-yellow flowers in early to mid-summer. Zone 9?.
G. tinctoria illus. p.157. **'Royal Gold'** is a deciduous, upright shrub. H and S 1m (3ft). Produces long, conical panicles of golden-yellow flowers in spring-summer and leaves that are narrowly lance-shaped and dark green. Zone 3.

Gentian. See *Gentiana*.
Great yellow. See *Gentiana lutea*, illus. p.355.
Spring. See *Gentiana verna*, illus. p.370.
Stemless. See *Gentiana acaulis*, illus. p.370.
Trumpet. See *Gentiana clusii*.
Willow. See *Gentiana asclepiadea*, illus. p.263.

GENTIANA
Gentian
GENTIANACEAE
Genus of annuals, biennials and perennials, some of which are semi-evergreen or evergreen, grown for their usually blue flowers. Is excellent for rock gardens and peat beds. Prefers sun or semi-shade and humus-rich, well-drained, moist, neutral to acid soil. Some species grow naturally on limestone soils. Propagate by division or offshoots in spring or by seed in autumn. Divide autumn-flowering species and *G. clusii* every 3 years in early spring and replant in fresh soil.
G. acaulis, syn. *G. excisa, G. kochiana*, illus. p.370.
G. angustifolia. Evergreen, clump-forming perennial. H 10cm (4in), S 20cm (8in). Has rosettes of oblong, dull green leaves and, in summer, solitary, tubular, sky-blue flowers on 7cm (3in) stems. Tolerates alkaline soils.
G. asclepiadea illus. p.263.
G. clusii (Trumpet gentian). Evergreen, clump-forming perennial. H 5cm (2in), S 15–23cm (6–9in). Has rosettes of oval, glossy, dark green leaves. Trumpet-shaped, azure-blue flowers, with green-spotted, paler throats, are borne on 2.5–10cm (1–4in) stems in early summer. Tolerates alkaline soils.
G. excisa. See *G. acaulis*.
G. gracilipes. Semi-evergreen, tufted perennial with arching stems. H 15cm (6in), S 20cm (8in). Forms a central rosette of long, strap-shaped, dark green leaves from which lax flower stems bearing tubular, dark purplish-blue flowers, greenish within, are produced in summer. Tolerates some shade.
G. kochiana. See *G. acaulis*.
G. lutea illus. p.255.
G. × macaulayi 'Wells's Variety', syn. *G.* 'Wellsii', illus. p.387.
G. ornata. Semi-evergreen, clump-forming perennial with small, over-wintering rosettes. H 5cm (2in), S 10cm (4in). Forms a central rosette of grass-like leaves. In autumn, each stem tip carries an upright, bell-shaped, mid-blue flower, with a white throat and deep blue stripes shading to creamy-white outside. Requires acid soil and a moist atmosphere.
G. saxosa illus. p.374.
G. septemfida illus. p.360.
G. sino-ornata illus. p.387.
G. 'Susan Jane'. Vigorous, semi-evergreen, spreading perennial with small, overwintering rosettes. H 5cm (2in), S 30cm (12in). Prostrate stems bear grass-like leaves. Large, trumpet-shaped, white-throated, deep blue flowers, greenish within, appear in autumn. Requires acid soil.
G. verna illus. p.370.

569

G. 'Wellsii'. See *G.* x *macaulayi* 'Wells's Variety'.

Geraldton waxflower. See *Chamelaucium uncinatum*, illus. pp.149 and 150.

GERANIUM
Cranesbill

GERANIACEAE

Genus of perennials, some of which are semi-evergreen, grown for their flowers and often as ground cover. Compact species are suitable for rock gardens. Most species prefer sun, but some do better in shade. Will grow in all but waterlogged soils. Propagate by semi-ripe cuttings in summer or by seed or division in autumn or spring. Cultivars should be propagated by division or cuttings only.

G. anemonifolium. See *G. palmatum*.
G. 'Ann Folkard'. Spreading perennial. H 50cm (20in), S 1m (36in). Has rounded, deeply cut, yellowish-green leaves and, in summer-autumn, masses of shallowly cup-shaped, rich magenta flowers with black veins.
G. armenum. See *G. psilostemon*.
G. cinereum. Semi-evergreen, rosetted perennial with spreading flowering stems. H 15cm (6in), S 30cm (12in). Has cup-shaped flowers, either white to pale pink, strongly veined with purple, or pure white, on lax stems in late spring and summer. Basal leaves are rounded, deeply divided, soft and grey-green. Is good for a large rock garden. **'Ballerina'** and var. **subcaulescens** (syn. *G. subcaulescens*) illus. p.379.
G. clarkei 'Kashmir Purple', syn. *G. pratense* 'Kashmir Purple'. Carpeting, rhizomatous perennial. H and S 45–60cm (18–24in). Bears loose clusters of cup-shaped, deep purple flowers in summer. Rounded leaves are deeply divided and finely veined. **'Kashmir White'** (syn. *G. pratense* 'Kashmir White') illus. p.276.
G. dalmaticum illus. p.377.
G. endressii illus. p.278.
'Wargrave Pink' see *G.* x *oxonianum* 'Wargrave Pink'.
G. farreri. Rosetted perennial with a tap root. H 10cm (4in), S 10–15cm (4–6in) or more. Outward-facing, flattish, very pale mauve-pink flowers set off blue-black anthers in early summer. Has kidney-shaped, matt green leaves. Both flower and leaf stems are red.
G. grandiflorum. See *G. himalayense*.
G. himalayense, syn. *G. grandiflorum*, *G. meeboldii*, illus. p.285.
G. ibericum. Clump-forming perennial. H and S 60cm (24in). In summer produces sprays of 5-petalled, saucer-shaped, violet-blue flowers. Has heart-shaped, lobed or cut, hairy leaves.
G. incanum. Semi-evergreen, spreading, mounded perennial. H 30–38cm (12–15in), S 60–90cm (24–36in). Shallowly cup-shaped flowers are variable, but usually deep pink, and borne singly in summer above aromatic, deeply divided, grey-green leaves with linear segments.
G. 'Johnson's Blue' illus. p.285.

G. macrorrhizum illus. p.279. **'Ingwersen's Variety'** illus. p.269.
G. maculatum. Clump-forming perennial. H 75cm (30in), S 45cm (18in). In spring bears heads of flattish, pinkish-lilac flowers above rounded, lobed or scalloped, mid-green leaves that turn fawn and red in autumn.
G. maderense. Vigorous, semi-evergreen, bushy perennial with a woody base. H and S 1m (3ft). Produces large sprays of shallowly cup-shaped, deep magenta flowers in summer above palmate, finely cut, dark green leaves.
G. x **magnificum** illus. p.285.
G. meeboldii. See *G. himalayense*.
G. nodosum illus. p.270.
G. orientalitibeticum, syn. *G. stapfianum* var. *roseum* of gardens, illus. p.353.
G. x **oxonianum 'Claridge Druce'.** Vigorous, semi-evergreen, carpeting perennial. H and S 60–75cm (24–30in). Bears clusters of cup-shaped, darker-veined, mauve-pink flowers throughout summer. Has dainty, rounded, lobed leaves. **'Wargrave Pink'** (syn. *G. endressii* 'Wargrave Pink') illus. p.279. **'Winscombe'** illus. p.243.
G. palmatum, syn. *G. anemonifolium*. Vigorous, semi-evergreen, bushy perennial with a woody base. H 45cm (18in), S 60cm (24in). Has palmate, deeply lobed, dark green leaves and, in late summer, large sprays of shallowly cup-shaped, purplish-red flowers.
G. phaeum illus. p.238.
G. pratense (Meadow cranesbill). Clump-forming perennial. H 75cm (30in), S 60cm (24in). Bears 5-petalled, saucer-shaped, violet-blue flowers on branching stems in summer. Rounded, lobed to deeply divided, mid-green leaves become bronze in autumn. **'Kashmir Purple'** see *G. clarkei* 'Kashmir Purple'. **'Kashmir White'** see *G. clarkei* 'Kashmir White'. **'Mrs Kendall Clark'** illus. p.285. **'Plenum Violaceum'** is more compact than the species with double, deep violet flowers.
G. procurrens. Carpeting perennial. H 30cm (12in), S 60cm (24in). Has rounded, lobed, glossy leaves and, in summer, clusters of saucer-shaped, deep rose-purple flowers.
G. psilostemon, syn. *G. armenum*, illus. p.245.
G. pylzowianum. Spreading perennial with underground runners and tiny tubers. H 12–25cm (5–10in), S 25cm (10in) or more. Bears semi-circular, deeply cut, dark green leaves and, in late spring and summer, trumpet-shaped, green-centred, deep rose-pink flowers. May be invasive.
G. renardii illus. p.277.
G. x **riversleaianum 'Russell Prichard'.** Semi-evergreen, clump-forming perennial. H 30cm (1ft), S 1m (3ft). Saucer-shaped, clear pink flowers are borne singly or in small clusters from early summer to autumn. Rounded leaves are lobed and grey-green.
G. sanguineum illus. p.354. var. **striatum** (syn. *G.s.* var. *lancastriense*) illus. p.354.
G. stapfianum var. **roseum** of gardens. See *G. orientalitibeticum*.
G. subcaulescens. See *G. cinereum* var. *subcaulescens*.

G. sylvaticum 'Mayflower' illus. p.251.
G. traversii var. **elegans.** Semi-evergreen, rosetted perennial with spreading stems. H 10cm (4in), S 25cm (10in). Large, upward-facing, saucer-shaped, pale pink flowers, with darker veins, rise above rounded, lobed, grey-green leaves in summer. Is suitable for a sheltered ledge or rock garden. Protect from winter wet. Needs gritty soil.
G. wallichianum 'Buxton's Variety', syn. *G.w.* 'Buxton's Blue', illus. p.287.
G. wlassovianum. Clump-forming perennial. H and S 60cm (24in). Has velvety stems and rounded, lobed, dark green leaves. Saucer-shaped, deep purple flowers are borne singly or in small clusters in summer.

Geranium. See *Pelargonium*.
Peppermint. See *Pelargonium tomentosum*, illus. p.247.
Silver-leaved. See *Pelargonium* 'Flower of Spring', illus. p.247.
Strawberry. See *Saxifraga stolonifera* 'Tricolor'.

GERBERA

ASTERACEAE/COMPOSITAE

Genus of perennials, flowering from summer to winter depending on growing conditions. Grow in full sun and in light, sandy soil. Propagate by heel cuttings from side shoots in summer or by seed in autumn or early spring.
G. jamesonii illus. p.302.

German ivy. See *Senecio mikanioides*.
Germander
Shrubby. See *Teucrium fruticans*.
Tree. See *Teucrium fruticans*.

GEUM
Avens

ROSACEAE

Genus of summer-flowering perennials. Does best in sun and prefers moist but well-drained soil. Propagate by division or by seed in autumn.
G. x **borisii** of gardens. See *G. coccineum*.
G. chiloense, syn. *G. coccineum* of gardens. Clump-forming perennial. H 40–60cm (16–24in), S 60cm (24in). Saucer-shaped, scarlet flowers are produced from early to late summer. Pinnate leaves are deeply lobed and toothed.
G. coccineum, syn. *G.* x *borisii* of gardens, illus. p.293.
G. coccineum of gardens. See *G. chiloense*.
G. 'Feuerball'. See *G.* 'Mrs J. Bradshaw'.
G. 'Fire Opal'. Clump-forming perennial. H 80cm (32in), S 45cm (18in). Rounded, double, bronze-scarlet flowers are borne in small clusters in summer above oblong to lance-shaped, lobed, fresh green leaves.
G. 'Goldball'. See *G.* 'Lady Stratheden'.
G. 'Lady Stratheden', syn. *G.* 'Goldball', illus. p.292.
G. 'Lionel Cox'. Clump-forming

perennial. H and S 30cm (12in). In early summer produces small clusters of 5-petalled, cup-shaped, shrimp-red flowers above oblong to lance-shaped, lobed, fresh green leaves.
G. montanum (Alpine avens). Dense, clump-forming, rhizomatous perennial that spreads slowly. H 10cm (4in), S 23cm (9in). Shallowly cup-shaped, golden-yellow flowers in early summer are followed by fluffy, buff-coloured seed heads. Leaves are pinnate, each with a large, rounded, terminal lobe. Suitable for a rock garden.
'Mrs J. Bradshaw', syn. *G.* 'Feuerball'. Clump-forming perennial. H 80cm (32in), S 45cm (18in). Rounded, double, crimson flowers are borne in small sprays in summer. Fresh green leaves are oblong to lance-shaped and lobed.

GEVUINA

PROTEACEAE

Genus of evergreen trees, grown for their foliage and flowers in summer. Needs semi-shade and fertile, moist but well-drained soil. Propagate by semi-ripe cuttings in late summer or by seed in autumn.
G. avellana (Chilean hazel). Evergreen, conical tree. H and S 10m (30ft). Has large, glossy, dark green leaves divided into numerous oval, toothed leaflets. Slender spires of spidery, white flowers in late summer are followed by cherry-like, red, then black fruits. Zone 9.

Ghost tree. See *Davidia involucrata*, illus. p.77.
Giant Burmese honeysuckle. See *Lonicera hildebrandiana*.
Giant buttercup. See *Ranunculus lyallii*.
Giant cowslip. See *Primula florindae*, illus. p.273.
Giant elephant's ear. See *Alocasia macrorrhiza*.
Giant fennel. See *Ferula*.
Giant fir. See *Abies grandis*, illus. p.104.
Giant granadilla. See *Passiflora quadrangularis*, illus. p.215.
Giant hog-weed. See *Heracleum mantegazzianum*.
Giant holly fern. See *Polystichum munitum*, illus. p.310.
Giant larkspur. See *Consolida ajacis* Giant Imperial Series, illus. p.332.
Giant lily. See *Cardiocrinum giganteum*, illus. p.398.
Giant pineapple flower. See *Eucomis pallidiflora*, illus. p.397.
Giant pineapple lily. See *Eucomis pallidiflora*, illus. p.397.
Giant redwood. See *Sequoiadendron giganteum*, illus. p.102.
Giant reed. See *Arundo donax*.
Giant scabious. See *Cephalaria gigantea*.
Giant Spaniard. See *Aciphylla scott-thomsonii*.
Giant wood fern. See *Dryopteris goldieana*.

GIBBAEUM

AIZOACEAE

Genus of clump-forming, perennial succulents with pairs of small, swollen leaves, often of unequal size. Tender, min. 5˚C (41˚F). Needs full sun and very well-drained soil. Water very lightly in early winter. Propagate by seed or stem cuttings in spring or summer.

G. petrense. Carpeting, perennial succulent. H 3cm (1¼in), S 30cm (12in) or more. Each branch carries 1 or 2 pairs of thick, triangular, pale grey-green leaves, 1cm (½in) long. Bears daisy-like, pink-red flowers, 1.5cm (⅝in) across, in spring.

G. velutinum illus. p.469.

GILIA

POLEMONIACEAE

Genus of summer- and autumn-flowering annuals. Grows best in sun and in fertile, very well-drained soil. Stems may need support, especially on windy sites. Propagate by seed sown outdoors in spring, or in early autumn for early flowering the following year.

G. achilleifolia. Fast-growing, upright, bushy annual. H 60cm (24in), S 20cm (8in). Finely divided, mid-green leaves are hairy and sticky. Heads of funnel-shaped, blue flowers, 2.5cm (1in) wide, are produced in summer.

G. capitata illus. p.333.

GILLENIA

ROSACEAE

Genus of summer-flowering perennials. Grow in sun or shade and any well-drained soil. Needs staking. Propagate by seed in autumn or spring.

G. trifoliata illus. p.241.

Ginger
Indian. See *Alpinia calcarata.*
Malay. See *Costus speciosus.*
Shell. See *Alpinia zerumbet*, illus. p.227.
Spiral. See *Costus.*
Wild. See *Asarum.*
Ginger lily. See *Hedychium.*
Gingham golf ball. See *Euphorbia obesa*, illus. p.477.

GINKGO

GINKGOACEAE

See also CONIFERS.
G. biloba illus. p.103.

Gippsland fountain palm. See *Livistona australis.*

GLADIOLUS

IRIDACEAE

Genus of corms, each producing a spike of funnel-shaped flowers and a fan of erect, sword-shaped leaves on basal part of flower stem. Is suitable for cutting or for planting in mixed borders; most hybrids are also good for exhibition. Needs a sunny and fertile, well-drained site. Plant 10–15cm (4–6in) deep and the same distance apart in spring. Water well in summer and support tall cultivars with canes. Lift tender types in autumn, cut off stems and dry corms in a frost-free but cool place. Pot up spring-flowering species and cultivars in autumn and place in a cool greenhouse; after flowering, dry off corms during summer months and repot in autumn.

Propagate by seed or by removal of young cormlets from parent. Seed sown in early spring in a cool greenhouse will take 2–3 years to flower and may not breed true to type. Cormlets, removed after lifting, should be stored in frost-free conditions and then be planted out 5cm (2in) deep in spring; lift in winter as for mature corms. They will flower in 1–2 years.

While in store, corms may be attacked by various rots and pests. Protect sound, healthy corms by treating with a combination fungicide/insecticide dust or dip; store in an airy, cool, frost-free place. Gladiolus scab causes blotches on leaves; gladiolus yellows shows as yellowing stripes on leaves, which then die; in both cases destroy affected corms. Thrips feed on buds causing streaked blooms and overwinter and feed on corms, destroying or weakening them. As a preventative measure, always plant healthy corms in a new site each year. See also feature panel p.399.

Gladiolus hybrids
Most hybrids are derived from *G. x hortulanus*. All have stiff leaves, 20–50cm (8–20in) long, ranging from pale willow-green or steely blue-green to almost bottle-green. All are good for flower arranging. They are divided into Grandiflorus, Primulinus, and Nanus Groups.

Grandiflorus Group produces long, densely packed spikes of funnel-shaped flowers, with ruffled, thick-textured petals or plain-edged, thin-textured ones. Giant-flowered hybrids have a bottom flower of over 14cm (5½in) across (flower head is 65–80cm (26–32in) long); large-flowered 11–14cm (4½–5½in) across (flower head 60cm–1m (24–36in) long); medium-flowered 9–11cm (3½–4½in) across (flower head 60–80cm (24–32in) long); small-flowered 6–9cm (2½–3½in) across (flower head 50–70cm (20–28in) long); and miniature-flowered 3.5–6cm (1½–2½in) across (flower head 40–60cm (16–24in) long).
Primulinus Group has fairly loose spikes of plain-edged, funnel-shaped flowers, 6–8cm (2½–3in) across, each with a strongly hooded, upper petal over the stigma and anthers. Flower heads are 30cm (12in) long.
Nanus Group produces 2 or 3 slender spikes, with loosely arranged flowers, 4–5cm (1½–2in) across. Flower heads are 22–35cm (9–14in) long.

G. 'Amanda Mahy' (illus. p.399). Nanus Group gladiolus. H 80cm (32in), S 8–10cm (3–4in). Produces spikes of up to 7 salmon-pink flowers, with lip tepals flecked violet and white, in early summer.
G. 'Amsterdam'. Grandiflorus Group, giant-flowered gladiolus. H 1.7m (5½ft), S 30cm (1ft). Spikes of up to 27 slightly upward-facing, finely ruffled, white flowers are produced in late summer. Is good for exhibition.
G. 'Amy Beth'. Grandiflorus Group, small-flowered gladiolus. H 1.2m (4ft), S 20–25cm (8–10in). Produces spikes of up to 22 heavily ruffled, lavender flowers, with thick, waxy, cream-lipped petals, in late summer.
G. 'Anna Leorah' (illus. p.399). Grandiflorus Group, large-flowered gladiolus. H 1.6m (5½ft), S 15cm (6in). In mid-summer, bears spikes of up to 25 strongly ruffled, mid-pink flowers with large, white throats. Is good for exhibition.
G. 'Atlantis'. Grandiflorus Group, medium-flowered gladiolus. H 1.5m (5ft), S 20–25cm (8–10in). Produces spikes of up to 20 lightly ruffled, deep violet-blue flowers with small, white throats, in late summer.
G. 'Beau Rivage'. Grandiflorus Group, large-flowered gladiolus. H to 1.2m (4ft), S 30cm (1ft). Spikes of up to 15 ruffled, deep coral-pink flowers are produced in summer. Is good for exhibition.
G. 'Beauty of Holland'. Grandiflorus Group, large-flowered gladiolus. H 1.7m (5½ft), S 15cm (6in). Produces spikes of up to 27 ruffled, pink-margined, white flowers in mid-summer. Is good for exhibition.
G. 'Black Lash' (illus. p.399). Grandiflorus Group, small-flowered gladiolus. H 1.35m (4½ft), S 15–20cm (6–8in). Bears spikes of up to 25 lightly ruffled, deep black-rose flowers, with pointed, slightly reflexed petals, from late summer to early autumn.
G. blandus. See *G. carneus.*
G. byzantinus. See *G. communis* subsp. *byzantinus.*
G. callianthus, syn. *Acidanthera bicolor* var. *murieliae, A. murieliae.* Late summer-flowering corm. H to 1m (3ft), S 10–15cm (4–6in). Has a loose spike of up to 10 fragrant flowers, each with a curved, 10cm (4in) long tube and 6 white petals, each with a deep purple blotch at the base.
G. cardinalis. Summer-flowering corm. H to 1.2m (4ft), S 10–15cm (4–6in). Arching stem bears a spike of up to 12 widely funnel-shaped flowers, each 8cm (3in) long and bright red with spear-shaped, white marks on lower 3 petals.
G. carneus, syn. *G. blandus.* Spring-flowering corm. H 20–40cm (8–16in), S 8–10cm (3–4in). Stem bears a loose spike of 3–12 widely funnel-shaped, white or pink flowers, 4–6cm (1½–2½in) long, marked on lower petals with darker red or yellow blotches.
G. 'Charmer'. Grandiflorus Group, large-flowered gladiolus. H 1.7m (5½ft), S 15cm (6in). In early and mid-summer, produces spikes of up to 27 strongly ruffled, almost translucent, light pink flowers. Is good for exhibition.
G. 'Christabel' illus. p.415.
G. communis subsp. *byzantinus,* syn. *G. byzantinus,* illus. p.400.
G. 'Côte d'Azur'. Grandiflorus Group, giant-flowered gladiolus. H 1.7m (5½ft), S 15cm (6in). Bears spikes of up to 23 ruffled, mid-blue flowers, with pale blue throats, in early summer. Is good for exhibition.

G. dalenii, syn. *G. natalensis, G. primulinus, G. psittacinus.* Vigorous, summer-flowering corm. H to 1.5m (5ft), S 10–15cm (4–6in). Produces up to 14 red, yellow-orange, yellow, or greenish-yellow flowers, 8–12cm (3–5in) long, each with a hooded, upper petal and often flecked or streaked red.
G. 'Drama' (illus. p.399). Grandiflorus Group, large-flowered gladiolus. H 1.7m (5 ft), S 25–30cm (10–12in). In late summer produces spikes of up to 26 lightly ruffled, deep watermelon-pink flowers with red-marked, yellow throats. Is superb for exhibition.
G. 'Dutch Mountain'. Grandiflorus Group, large-flowered gladiolus. H 1.7m (5½ft), S 15cm (6in). In mid-summer, produces spikes of up to 25 slightly ruffled, white flowers with small green marks in the throats. Is good for exhibition.
G. 'Esta Bonita' (illus. p.399). Grandiflorus Group, giant-flowered gladiolus. H 1.7m (5½ft), S 30cm (1ft). Produces spikes of up to 24 apricot-orange flowers, slightly darker towards petal edges, in late summer. Is good for exhibition.
G. 'Firestorm'. Grandiflorus Group, miniature-flowered gladiolus. H 1.1m (3½ft), S 8–10cm (3–4in). Spikes of up to 22 loosely spaced, ruffled, vivid scarlet flowers, with yellowish-white flecks on the outer tepals, are produced in early summer. Is good for exhibition.
G. 'Georgette'. Grandiflorus Group, small-flowered gladiolus. H 1.2m (4ft), S 8–10cm (3–4in). Produces spikes of up to 22 slightly ruffled, yellow-suffused, orange flowers, with large lemon-yellow throats, in mid-summer. Is good for exhibition.
G. 'Green Isle'. Grandiflorus Group, medium-flowered gladiolus. H 1.35m (4½ft), S 20–25cm (8–10in). Spikes carrying up to 22 slightly informal flowers, lime-green throughout with chiselled ruffling, are produced in late summer.
G. 'Green Woodpecker' (illus. p.399). Grandiflorus Group, medium-flowered gladiolus. H 1.5m (5ft), S 30cm (1ft). Has spikes of up to 25 uranium-green flowers, with wine-red throats, in late summer. Is very good for exhibition.
G. 'Halley' (illus. p.399). Nanus Group gladiolus. H 1m (3ft), S 8–10cm (3–4in). In early summer, produces spikes carrying up to 7 white-flushed, pale yellow flowers, each with bright red marks in the throats.
G. 'Ice Cap' (illus. p.399). Grandiflorus Group, large-flowered gladiolus. H 1.7m (5½ft), S 25–30cm (10–12in). Produces spikes of up to 27 heavily ruffled, ice-white flowers from late summer to early autumn.
G. 'Inca Queen' (illus. p.399). Grandiflorus Group, large-flowered gladiolus. H 1.5m (5ft), S 20–25cm (8–10in). Bears spikes of up to 25 heavily ruffled, waxy, deep salmon-pink flowers, with lemon-yellow lip petals and throats, in late summer.
G. italicus, syn. *G. segetum,* illus. p.400.
G. 'Little Darling' (illus. p.399). Primulinus Group gladiolus. H 1.1m (3½ft), S 8–10cm (3–4in). Bears spikes

of up to 16 loosely spaced, salmon- to rose-pink flowers, with lemon lip tepals, in mid-summer. Is good for exhibition.

G. 'Magistral'. Grandiflorus Group, large-flowered gladiolus. H 1.8m (6ft), S 15cm (6in). Produces spikes of up to 24 ruffled, oyster-white flowers, with magenta lines, in mid-summer. Is good for exhibition.

G. 'Melodie' (illus. p.399). Grandiflorus Group, small-flowered gladiolus. H 1.2m (4ft), S 15–20cm (6–8in). Produces spikes of up to 17 salmon-rose flowers, with longitudinal, spear-like, red-orange marks in throats, in late summer.

G. 'Mi Mi' (illus. p.399). Grandiflorus Group, small-flowered gladiolus. H 1.3m (4½ft), S 8–10cm (3–4in). In mid-summer bears spikes of up to 24 strongly ruffled, deep lavender-pink flowers with white throats. Is good for exhibition.

G. 'Miss America' (illus. p.399). Grandiflorus Group, medium-flowered gladiolus. H 1.5m (5ft), S 30cm (1ft). In late summer produces spikes of up to 24 deep pink flowers that are heavily ruffled. Is excellent for exhibition.

G. natalensis. See *G. dalenii*.
G. papilio, syn. *G. purpureoauratus*, illus. p.408.
G. 'Parade'. Grandiflorus Group, giant-flowered gladiolus. H 1.7m (5½ft), S 25–35cm (10–14in). Produces spikes of up to 27 finely ruffled, salmon-pink flowers, with small, cream throats, in early autumn. Is superb for exhibition.

G. 'Peace'. Grandiflorus Group, giant-flowered gladiolus. H 1.7m (5½ft), S 15cm (6in). Bears spikes of up to 26 strongly ruffled, cream flowers, with pale lemon throats and pale pink margins, in mid-summer. Is good for exhibition.

G. 'Peter Pears' (illus. p.399). Grandiflorus Group, large-flowered gladiolus. H 1.7m (5½ft), S 35cm (14in). In late summer bears spikes of up to 26 apricot-salmon flowers with red throat marks. Is excellent for exhibition.

G. 'Pink Flare'. Grandiflorus Group, small-flowered gladiolus. H 1.3m (4½ft), S 8–10cm (3–4in). Spikes of up to 25 ruffled, mid-pink flowers, each with a small, white throat, are produced in mid-summer. Is good for exhibition.

G. 'Pink Lady' (illus. p.399). Grandiflorus Group, large-flowered gladiolus. H 1.5m (5ft), S 25–30cm (10–12in). Has spikes of up to 25 lightly ruffled, deep rose-pink flowers, with large, white throats, in late summer and early autumn.

G. primulinus. See *G. dalenii*.
G. psittacinus. See *G. dalenii*.
G. 'Pulchritude' (illus. p.399). Grandiflorus Group, medium-flowered gladiolus. H 1.3m (4½ft), S 12cm (5in). Produces spikes of up to 27 ruffled, light lavender-pink flowers, deepening at the tepal margins, and with a magenta-red mark on each lip tepal, in mid-summer. Is good for exhibition.

G. purpureoauratus. See *G. papilio*.
G. 'Rose Supreme' (illus. p.399).

Grandiflorus Group, giant-flowered gladiolus. H 1.7m (5½ft), S 25–30cm (10–12in). Spikes of up to 24 rose-pink flowers, flecked and streaked darker pink towards petal tips, and with cream throats, are produced in late summer.

G. 'Royal Dutch'. Grandiflorus Group, large-flowered gladiolus. H 1.7m (5½ft), S 25–30cm (10–12in). Produces spikes of up to 27 flowers, each pale lavender blending into a white throat, from late summer to early autumn. Is very good for exhibition.

G. segetum. See *G. italicus*.
G. 'Stardust' (illus. p.399). Grandiflorus Group, miniature-flowered gladiolus. H 1.2m (4ft), S 8–10cm (3–4in). Has spikes of up to 21 ruffled, pale yellow flowers, with lighter yellow throats, in mid-summer. Is good for exhibition.

G. 'Tendresse'. Grandiflorus Group, medium-flowered gladiolus. H 1.5m (5ft), S 20–25cm (8–10in). In late summer has spikes of up to 28 slightly ruffled, dark pink flowers, with small, cream throats marked with longitudinal, faint rose-pink 'spears'.

G. 'Tesoro' (illus. p.399). Grandiflorus Group, medium-flowered gladiolus. H 1.5m (5ft), S 20–25cm (8–10in). Bears spikes of up to 26 silky flowers, slightly ruffled and glistening yellow, in early autumn. Is among the top exhibition gladioli.

G. 'The Bride' (illus. p.399). Nanus Group gladiolus. H 80cm (32in), S 8–10cm (3–4in). Produces spikes of up to 7 white flowers, with green-marked throats, in early summer.

G. 'Vaucluse' (illus. p.399). Grandiflorus Group, giant-flowered gladiolus. H 1.9m (6ft), S 15cm (6in). In late summer, bears spikes of up to 27 slightly ruffled, vermilion-red flowers with small, creamy-white throats. Is good for exhibition.

G. 'Victor Borge' (illus. p.399). Grandiflorus Group, large-flowered gladiolus. H 1.7m (5½ft), S 35cm (14in). Spikes of up to 22 vermilion-orange flowers, with pale cream throat marks, are produced in late summer.

G. 'White Ice' (illus. p.399). Grandiflorus Group, medium-flowered gladiolus. H 1.5m (5ft), S 12cm (5in). Produces spikes of up to 25 ruffled, white flowers in late summer. Is good for exhibition.

G. 'Zephyr'. Grandiflorus Group, large-flowered gladiolus. H 1.7m (5½ft), S 15cm (6in). In mid-summer has spikes of up to 26 light lavender-pink flowers with small, ivory throats. Is good for exhibition.

Gladwin. See *Iris foetidissima*.
Gland bellflower. See *Adenophora*.
Glandulicactus uncinatus. See *Sclerocactus uncinatus*.
Glastonbury thorn. See *Crataegus monogyna* 'Biflora'.

GLAUCIDIUM

GLAUCIDIACEAE/PAEONIACEAE

Genus of one species of spring-flowering perennial. Is excellent in

woodland gardens. Needs a partially shaded, sheltered position and moist, peaty soil. Propagate by seed in autumn.

G. palmatum illus. p.270.

GLAUCIUM
Horned poppy

PAPAVERACEAE

Genus of annuals, biennials and perennials, grown for their bright, poppy-like flowers. Grow in sun and in fertile, well-drained soil. Propagate annuals by seed sown outdoors in spring; perennials by seed sown outdoors in spring or autumn; biennials by seed sown under glass in late spring or early summer. Roots are toxic if ingested.

G. flavum illus. p.335.

GLECHOMA

LABIATAE/LAMIACEAE

Genus of evergreen, summer-flowering perennials. Makes good ground cover, but may be invasive. Tolerates sun or shade. Prefers moist but well-drained soil. Propagate by division in spring or autumn or by softwood cuttings in spring.

G. hederacea (Ground ivy, Creeping Charlie). **'Variegata'** illus. p.300.

GLEDITSIA

CAESALPINIACEAE/LEGUMINOSAE

Genus of deciduous, usually spiny trees, grown for their foliage. Has inconspicuous flowers, often followed by large seed pods after hot summers. Young plants may suffer frost damage. Requires plenty of sun and fertile, well-drained soil. Propagate species by seed in autumn, selected forms by budding in late summer.

G. caspica (Caspian locust). Deciduous, spreading tree. H 12m (40ft), S 10m (30ft). Trunk is armed with long, branched spines. Has fern-like, glossy, mid-green leaves. Zone 8.
G. japonica illus. p.80.
G. triacanthos (Honey locust). Deciduous, spreading tree. H 20m (70ft), S 15m (50ft). Trunk is very thorny. Fern-like, glossy, dark green leaves turn yellow in autumn. Zone 4. f. *inermis* is thornless. **'Shademaster'** is vigorous, with long-lasting leaves. **'Skyline'** is thornless, broadly conical and has golden-yellow foliage in autumn. Both zone 4. **'Sunburst'** illus. p.77.

GLOBBA

ZINGIBERACEAE

Genus of evergreen, aromatic, clump-forming perennials, grown for their flowers. Tender, min. 18°C (64°F). Needs partial shade, high humidity, and humus-rich, well-drained soil. Keep plants dry when dormant in winter. Propagate by division or seed in spring or by mature bulbils that fall off plants.

G. winitii illus. p.267.

Globe amaranth. See *Gomphrena globosa*, illus. p.331.
Globe lily. See *Calochortus albus*, illus. p.409.
Globe thistle. See *Echinops*.
Globeflower. See *Trollius*.

GLOBULARIA
Globe daisy

GLOBULARIACEAE

Genus of mainly evergreen, summer-flowering shrubs and sub-shrubs, grown for their dome-shaped hummocks and usually blue or purple flower heads. Needs full sun and well-drained soil. Propagate by division in spring, by softwood or semi-ripe cuttings in summer or by seed in autumn.

G. bellidifolia. See *G. meridionalis*.
G. cordifolia illus. p.383. subsp. *bellidifolia* see *G. meridionalis*.
G. meridionalis, syn. *G. bellidifolia*, *G. cordifolia* subsp. *bellidifolia*, *G. pygmaea*, illus. p.380.
G. pygmaea. See *G. meridionalis*.

GLORIOSA

COLCHICACEAE/LILIACEAE

Genus of deciduous, summer-flowering, tendril climbers with finger-like tubers. Tender, min. 8–10°C (46–50°F). Needs full sun and rich, well-drained soil. Water freely in summer and liquid feed every 2 weeks. Provide support. Dry off tubers in winter and keep cool but frost-free. Propagate by seed or division in spring. Highly toxic if ingested; handling tubers may irritate the skin.

G. rothschildiana. See *G. superba* 'Rothschildiana'.
G. superba (Glory lily). Deciduous, tendril climber with tubers. H to 2m (6ft), S 30–45cm (1–1½ft). Min. 8°C (46°F). Slender stems bear scattered, broadly lance-shaped leaves. In summer, upper leaf axils carry large, yellow or red flowers, with 6 sharply reflexed, wavy-edged petals, changing to dark orange or deep red. Stamens are prominent. **'Rothschildiana'** (syn. *G. rothschildiana*) illus. p.401.

Glory bush. See *Tibouchina urvilleana*, illus. p.122.
Glory flower, Chilean. See *Eccremocarpus scaber*, illus. p.217.
Glory lily. See *Gloriosa superba*.
Glory vine. See *Eccremocarpus scaber*, illus. p.217.
Glory-of-the-snow. See *Chionodoxa*.
Glory-of-the-sun. See *Leucocoryne ixioides*, illus. p.413.

GLOTTIPHYLLUM

AIZOACEAE

Genus of clump-forming, perennial succulents with semi-cylindrical leaves often broader at tips. Tender, min. 5°C (41°F). Grow in full sun and poor, well-drained soil. Propagate by seed or stem cuttings in spring or summer.

G. nelii illus. p.479.
G. semicylindricum. Clump-forming, perennial succulent. H 8cm (3in), S 30cm (12in) or more. Has semi-

cylindrical, bright green leaves, 6cm (2½in) long, with a tooth half-way along each margin. Short-stemmed, daisy-like, golden-yellow flowers, 4cm (1½in) across, appear in spring-summer.

GLOXINIA
GESNERIACEAE

Genus of late summer- to autumn-flowering, rhizomatous perennials. Tender, min. 10°C (50°F). Needs partial shade and humus-rich, well-drained soil. Dies down in late autumn or winter; then keep rhizomes nearly dry. Propagate by division or seed in spring or by stem or leaf cuttings in summer.
G. perennis illus. p.421.
G. speciosa. See *Sinningia speciosa.*

Gloxinia. See *Sinningia speciosa.*

GLYCERIA
Manna grass
POACEAE

See also GRASSES, BAMBOOS, RUSHES and SEDGES.
G. aquatica 'Variegata'. See *G. maxima* 'Variegata'.
G. maxima 'Variegata', syn. *G. aquatica* 'Variegata', illus. p.306.

GLYCYRRHIZA
Liquorice
LEGUMINOSAE/PAPILIONACEAE

Genus of summer-flowering perennials. Needs sun and deep, rich, well-drained soil. Propagate by division in spring or seed in autumn or spring.
G. glabra illus. p.250.

Goat willow. See *Salix caprea.*
Goat's beard. See *Aruncus dioicus,* illus. p.226.
Goat's rue. See *Galega.*
Godetia. Reclassified as *Clarkia.*
Gold dust. See *Aurinia saxatilis,* illus. p.350.
Golden arum lily. See *Zantedeschia elliottiana,* illus. p.402.
Golden ball cactus. See *Parodia leninghausii,* illus. p.468.
Golden bamboo. See *Phyllostachys aurea.*
Golden barrel cactus. See *Echinocactus grusonii,* illus. p.460.
Golden chain. See *Laburnum anagyroides.*
Golden creeping Jenny. See *Lysimachia nummularia,* illus. p.386.
Golden club. See *Orontium aquaticum,* illus. p.451.
Golden European elder. See *Sambucus nigra* 'Aurea'.
Golden fairy lantern. See *Calochortus amabilis,* illus. p.434.
Golden flax. See *Linum flavum.*
Golden foxtail. See *Alopecurus pratensis* 'Aureovariegatus', illus. p.309.
Golden globe tulip. See *Calochortus amabilis,* illus. p.434.
Golden larch. See *Pseudolarix amabilis,* illus. p.107.
Golden male fern. See *Dryopteris affinis.*

Golden oak of Cyprus. See *Quercus alnifolia.*
Golden oats. See *Stipa gigantea,* illus. p.307.
Golden rod. See *Solidago.*
Golden shower. See *Cassia fistula; Pyrostegia venusta,* illus. p.218.
Golden Spaniard. See *Aciphylla aurea,* illus. p.238.
Golden spider lily. See *Lycoris aurea.*
Golden top. See *Lamarckia aurea.*
Golden trumpet. See *Allamanda cathartica.*
Golden trumpet tree. See *Tabebuia chrysotricha,* illus. p.97.
Golden weeping willow. See *Salix* x *sepulcralis,* 'Chrysocoma' illus. p.74.
Golden willow. See *Salix alba* var. *vitellina,* illus. p.74.
Golden wonder. See *Senna didymobotrya,* illus. p.147.
Golden-chalice vine. See *Solandra maxima,* illus. p.206.
Golden-eyed grass. See *Sisyrinchium californicum.*
Golden-feather palm. See *Dypsis lutescens,* illus. p.100.
Golden-groove bamboo. See *Phyllostachys aureosulcata.*
Golden-rain tree. See *Koelreuteria paniculata,* illus. p.92.
Golden-rayed lily of Japan. See *Lilium auratum.*
Goldfish plant. See *Columnea gloriosa.*
Goldilocks. See *Aster linosyris,* illus. p.262.
Golf ball, Gingham. See *Euphorbia obesa,* illus. p.477.

GOMESA
See also ORCHIDS.
G. planifolia (illus. p.298). Evergreen, epiphytic orchid for a cool greenhouse. H 23cm (9in). Sprays of star-shaped, pea-green flowers, 0.5cm (¼in) across, are produced in autumn. Narrowly oval leaves are 15cm (6in) long. Grow in semi-shade during summer.

GOMPHOCARPUS
ASCLEPIADACEAE

Genus of evergreen and deciduous sub-shrubs and perennials. Hooded, cup-shaped flowers are followed by seed pods that are usually inflated. Tender, min. 5°C (41°F). Grows in sun or partial shade and in any well-drained soil. Propagate by seed or softwood cuttings in spring. Some species exude a milky sap, which may aggravate skin allergies.
G. physocarpus, syn. *Asclepias physocarpa,* illus. p.232.

GOMPHRENA
AMARANTHACEAE

Genus of annuals, biennials and perennials. Only one species, *G. globosa,* is usually cultivated; its flower heads are good for cutting and drying. Grows best in sun and in fertile, well-drained soil. Propagate by seed sown under glass in spring.
G. globosa illus. p.331.

GONGORA
See also ORCHIDS.
G. quinquenervis (illus. p.298). Evergreen, epiphytic orchid for an intermediate greenhouse. H 25cm (10in). In summer, fragrant, brown, orange and yellow flowers, 1cm (⅖in) across, which resemble birds in flight, are produced in long, pendent spikes. Has oval, ribbed leaves, 12–15cm (5–6in) long. Is best grown in a hanging basket. Requires semi-shade in summer.

Good-luck plant. See *Cordyline fruticosa.*
Goodyer's elm. See *Ulmus minor* subsp. *angustifolia.*
Gooseberry
 Barbados. See *Pereskia aculeata,* illus. p.457.
 Chinese. See *Actinidia deliciosa.*

GORDONIA
THEACEAE

Genus of evergreen shrubs and trees, grown for their flowers and overall appearance. Best at min. 3°C (37°F). Prefers sun or partial shade and humus-rich, acid soil. Water potted plants moderately, less in winter. Propagate by semi-ripe cuttings in late summer or by seed when ripe, in autumn, or in spring.
G. axillaris. Evergreen, bushy shrub or tree. H and S 3–5m (10–15ft), sometimes much more. Has lance-shaped, leathery, glossy leaves, each with a blunt tip, and bears, from autumn to spring, saucer-shaped, white flowers.
G. lasianthus (Loblolly bay). Evergreen, upright tree. H to 20m (70ft), S to 10m (30ft). Lance-shaped to elliptic leaves are shallowly serrated. Has fragrant, saucer- to bowl-shaped, white flowers in summer. Needs sub-tropical summer warmth to grow and flower well.

Gorgon's head. See *Euphorbia gorgonis.*
Gorse. See *Ulex europaeus,* illus. p.157.
Gorse, Spanish. See *Genista hispanica,* illus. p.170.
Gourd, Snake. See *Trichosanthes cucumerina* var. *anguina.*
Gout weed. See *Aegopodium.*
 Variegated. See *Aegopodium podagraria* 'Variegatum', illus. p.276.
Grama, Blue. See *Bouteloua gracilis,* illus. p.307.
Granadilla, Giant. See *Passiflora quadrangularis,* illus. p.215.
Grand fir. See *Abies grandis,* illus. p.104.
Granite bottlebrush. See *Melaleuca elliptica,* illus. p.142.
Granny's bonnets. See *Aquilegia vulgaris.*
Grape
 Amur. See *Vitis amurensis.*
 Cape. See *Rhoicissus capensis.*
 Oregon. See *Mahonia aquifolium,* illus. p.157.
Grape hyacinth. See *Muscari.*
Grape ivy. See *Cissus rhombifolia,* illus. p.220.
Grape vine. See *Vitis vinifera.*

GRAPTOPETALUM
CRASSULACEAE

Genus of rosetted, perennial succulents very similar to *Echeveria,* with which it hybridizes. Tender, min. 5–10°C (41–50°F). Is easy to grow, needing sun or partial shade and very well-drained soil. Propagate by seed or by stem or leaf cuttings in spring or summer.
G. amethystinum. Clump-forming, prostrate, perennial succulent. H 40cm (16in), S 90cm (36in). Min. 10°C (50°F). Produces thick, rounded, blue-grey to red leaves, 7cm (3in) long, in terminal rosettes and star-shaped, yellow-and-red flowers, 1–2cm (½–¾in) across, in spring-summer.
G. bellum, syn. *Tacitus bellus,* illus. p.473.
G. paraguayense illus. p.478.

GRAPTOPHYLLUM
ACANTHACEAE

Genus of evergreen shrubs, grown mainly for their foliage. Tender, min. 16–18°C (61–4°F). Needs partial shade and fertile, well-drained soil. Water potted plants freely when in full growth, much less when temperatures are low. Young plants need tip pruning after flowering to promote branching; leggy specimens may be cut back hard after flowering or in spring. Propagate by greenwood or semi-ripe cuttings in spring or summer.
G. pictum (Caricature plant). Evergreen, erect, loose shrub. H to 2m (6ft), S 60cm (2ft) or more. Has oval, pointed, glossy, green leaves with central, yellow blotches. Bears short, terminal spikes of tubular, red to purple flowers in spring and early summer.

Grass
 African fountain. See *Pennisetum setaceum.*
 Amur silver. See *Miscanthus sacchariflorus.*
 Balkan blue. See *Sesleria heufleriana.*
 Basket. See *Oplismenus africanus.*
 Bear. See *Dasylirion.*
 Blue oat. See *Helictotrichon sempervirens,* illus. p.307.
 Chinese fountain. See *Pennisetum alopecuroides.*
 Cloud. See *Aichryson* x *domesticum* 'Variegata', illus. p.477.
 Common quaking. See *Briza media.*
 Creeping soft. See *Holcus mollis.*
 Eel. See *Vallisneria spiralis.*
 False oat. See *Arrhenatherum elatius.*
 Golden-eyed. See *Sisyrinchium californicum.*
 Greater quaking. See *Briza maxima.*
 Hairy brome. See *Bromus ramosus.*
 Hare's-tail. See *Lagurus ovatus,* illus. p.306.
 Hunangemoho. See *Chionochloa conspicua.*
 Japanese blood. See *Imperata cylindrica.*
 Lyme. See *Leymus arenarius.*
 Mosquito. See *Bouteloua gracilis,* illus. p.307.
 Natal. See *Melinis repens.*

Grass (continued)

Old-witch. See *Panicum capillare*, illus. p.308.
Orchard. See *Dactylis glomerata*.
Pampas. See *Cortaderia selloana*.
Pheasant. See *Stipa arundinacea*.
Quaking. See *Briza*.
Ruby. See *Melinis repens*.
Scurvy. See *Oxalis enneaphylla*.
Squirrel tail. See *Hordeum jubatum*, illus. p.307.
St Augustine. See *Stenotaphrum secundatum*.
Tape. See *Vallisneria spiralis*.
Tufted hair. See *Deschampsia cespitosa*.
Variegated creeping soft. See *Holcus mollis* 'Albovariegatus', illus. p.306.
Variegated purple moor. See *Molinia caerulea* 'Variegata'.
Yellow whitlow. See *Draba aizoides*.
Grass of Parnassus. See *Parnassia palustris*, illus. p.350.
Grass tree. See *Xanthorrhoea*.
Grass widow. See *Olsynium douglasii*.

GRASSES, BAMBOOS, RUSHES AND SEDGES

Group of evergreen or herbaceous, perennial and annual grasses or grass-like plants belonging to the Gramineae (including Bambusoideae), Juncaceae and Cyperaceae families. They are grown mainly as foliage plants, adding grace and contrast to borders and rock gardens, although several grasses have attractive flower heads in summer that may be dried for winter decoration. Dead foliage may be cut back on herbaceous perennials when dormant. Propagate species by seed in spring or autumn or by division in spring; selected forms by division only. Pests and diseases usually give little trouble. Grasses, bamboos, rushes and sedges are illustrated on pp.306–309.

Grasses (Gramineae)
Family of evergreen, semi-evergreen or herbaceous, sometimes creeping perennials, annuals and marginal water plants, usually with rhizomes or stolons, that form tufts, clumps or carpets. All have basal leaves and rounded flower stems that bear alternate, long, narrow leaves. Flowers are bisexual (males and females in same spikelet) and are arranged in panicles, racemes or spikes. Each flower head comprises spikelets, with one or more florets, that are covered with glumes (scales) from which awns (long, slender bristles) may grow. Unless otherwise stated, grasses will tolerate a range of light conditions and flourish in any well-drained soil. Many genera, such as *Briza*, self seed readily.
See also *Alopecurus, Arrhenatherum, Arundo, Bouteloua, Briza, Bromus, Chionochloa, Coix, Cortaderia, Dactylis, Deschampsia, Festuca, Glyceria, Hakonechloa, Helictotrichon, Holcus, Hordeum, Lagurus, Lamarckia, Leymus, Melica, Melinis, Milium, Miscanthus, Molinia, Oplismenus, Panicum, Pennisetum, Phalaris, Sesleria, Setaria, Spartina, Stenotaphrum, Stipa, Zea* and *Zizania*.

Bamboos (Bambusoideae)
Sub-family of Gramineae, comprising evergreen, rhizomatous perennials, sometimes grown as hedging as well as for ornamentation. Most bamboos differ from other perennial grasses in that they have woody stems (culms). These are hollow (except in *Chusquea*), mostly greenish-brown and, due to their silica content, very strong, with a circumference of up to 15cm (6in) in some tropical species. Leaves are lance-shaped with cross veins that give a tessellated appearance, which may be obscured in the more tender species. Flowers are produced at varying intervals but are not decorative. After flowering, stems die down but few plants die completely. Bamboos thrive in a sheltered, not too dry situation in sun or shade, unless otherwise stated.
See also *Bambusa, Chusquea, Fargesia, Himalayacalamus, Phyllostachys, Pleioblastus, Pseudosasa, Sasa, Semiarundinaria, Shibataea* and *Yushania*.

Rushes (Juncaceae)
Family of evergreen, tuft-forming or creeping, mostly rhizomatous annuals and perennials. All have either rounded, leafless stems or stems bearing long, narrow, basal leaves that are flat and hairless except *Luzula* (woodrushes) which has flat leaves, edged with white hairs. Rounded flower heads are generally unimportant. Most rushes prefer sun or partial shade and a moist or wet situation, but *Luzula* prefers drier conditions.
See also *Isolepis, Juncus* and *Luzula*.

Sedges (Cyperaceae)
Family of evergreen, rhizomatous perennials that form dense tufts. Stems are triangular and bear long, narrow leaves, sometimes reduced to scales. Spikes or panicles of florets covered with glumes are produced and contain both male and female flowers, although some species of *Carex* have separate male and female flower heads on the same stem. Grow in sun or partial shade. Some sedges grow naturally in water, but many may be grown in any well-drained soil.
See also *Carex, Cyperus, Eleocharis, Schoenoplectus* and *Scirpoides*.

Grass-leaved daylily. See *Hemerocallis minor*.
Great burnet. See *Sanguisorba officinalis*.
Great Solomon's seal. See *Polygonatum biflorum*.
Great white cherry. See *Prunus* 'Taihaku', illus. p.86.
Great yellow gentian. See *Gentiana lutea*, illus. p.255.
Greater celandine. See *Chelidonium*.
Greater periwinkle. See *Vinca major*.
Greater pond sedge. See *Carex riparia*.
Greater quaking grass. See *Briza maxima*.
Greater spearwort. See *Ranunculus lingua*, illus. p.451.
Greater woodrush. See *Luzula sylvatica*.
Grecian strawberry tree. See *Arbutus andrachne*.

Greek fir. See *Abies cephalonica*.
Green ash. See *Fraxinus pennsylvanica*.
Green earth star. See *Cryptanthus acaulis*.
Green hellebore. See *Helleborus viridis*, illus. p.305.
Green-veined orchid. See *Orchis morio*, illus. p.298.
Greenweed, Dyers'. See *Genista tinctoria*, illus. p.157.

GREVILLEA

PROTEACEAE

Genus of evergreen shrubs and trees, grown for their flowers and foliage. Tender, min. 5–10°C (41–50°F). Grow in full sun and well-drained, preferably acid soil. Water potted specimens moderately, very little in winter. Pruning is tolerated if necessary. Propagate by seed in spring or by semi-ripe cuttings in summer. All parts may aggravate skin allergies.
G. alpestris. See *G. alpina*.
G. alpina, syn. *G. alpestris*. Evergreen, rounded, wiry-stemmed shrub. H and S 30–60cm (1–2ft). Tender, min. 0°C (32°F). Has narrowly oblong or oval leaves, dark green above, silky-haired beneath. Bears tubular, red flowers in small clusters in spring-summer.
G. banksii illus. p.99.
G. juniperina f. *sulphurea*, syn. *G. sulphurea*, illus. p.169.
G. 'Poorinda Constance'. Evergreen, bushy, rounded shrub. H and S to 2m (6ft). Tender, min. 2°C (35°F). Has small, lance-shaped, mid- to deep green leaves with prickly toothed margins. Tubular, bright red flowers in conspicuous clusters are borne from spring to autumn, sometimes longer.
G. robusta (Silky oak). Fast-growing, evergreen, upright to conical tree. H 30m (100ft), S to 15m (50ft). Tender, min. 5°C (41°F). Fern-like leaves are 15–25cm (6–10in) long. Mature specimens bear upturned bell-shaped, bright yellow or orange flowers in dense, one-sided spikes, 10cm (4in) or more long, in spring-summer.
G. 'Robyn Gordon' illus. p.166.
G. rosmarinifolia. Evergreen, rounded, well-branched shrub. H and S to 2m (6ft). Tender, min. 0°C (32°F). Dark green leaves are needle-shaped with reflexed margins, silky-haired beneath. Has short, dense clusters of tubular, red, occasionally pink or white flowers in summer.
G. sulphurea. See *G. juniperina* f. *sulphurea*.

Grey alder. See *Alnus incana*, illus. p.66.
Grey poplar. See *Populus* x *canescens*, illus. p.65.

GREYIA

GREYIACEAE

Genus of evergreen, semi-evergreen or deciduous, spring-flowering shrubs and trees, grown for their flowers and overall appearance. Tender, min. 7–10°C (45–50°F). Needs full light and well-drained soil. Water containerized specimens moderately, less when not in full growth. Remove or shorten flowered

stems after flowering. Propagate by seed in spring or by semi-ripe cuttings in summer. Plants grown under glass need plenty of ventilation.
G. sutherlandii illus. p.131.

GRINDELIA

ASTERACEAE/COMPOSITAE

Genus of annuals, biennials, evergreen perennials and sub-shrubs, grown for their flower heads. Need a warm, sheltered site. Requires sun and well-drained soil. Water potted specimens moderately, less when not in full growth. Remove spent flowering stems either as they die or in following spring. Propagate by seed in spring or by semi-ripe cuttings in late summer.
G. chiloensis, syn. *G. speciosa*, illus. p.171.
G. speciosa. See *G. chiloensis*.

GRISELINIA

CORNACEAE/GRISELINIACEAE

Genus of evergreen shrubs and trees, with inconspicuous flowers, grown for their foliage. Thrives in mild, coastal areas where it is effective as a hedge or windbreak as it is very wind- and salt-resistant. In colder areas provide shelter. Requires sun and fertile, well-drained soil. Restrict growth and trim hedges in early summer. Propagate by semi-ripe cuttings in summer.
G. littoralis (Broadleaf). Fast-growing, evergreen, upright shrub of dense habit. H 6m (20ft), S 5m (15ft). Bears oval, leathery leaves that are bright apple-green. Tiny, inconspicuous, yellow-green flowers are borne in late spring. 'Dixon's Cream', H 3m (10ft), S 2m (6ft), is slower-growing and has central, creamy-white leaf variegation. Zone 9. 'Variegata' illus. p.126.
G. lucida. Fast-growing, evergreen, upright shrub. H 6m (20ft), S 5m (15ft). Is similar to *G. littoralis*, but has larger, glossy, dark green leaves.

Ground elder. See *Aegopodium*.
Ground ivy. See *Glechoma hederacea*.
Groundsel, Bush. See *Baccharis halimifolia*.
Guava, Pineapple. See *Acca sellowiana*, illus. p.143.
Guelder rose. See *Viburnum opulus*.
Guernsey lily. See *Nerine sarniensis*, illus. p.424.
Gum
  Black. See *Nyssa sylvatica*, illus. p.71.
  Blue. See *Eucalyptus globulus*.
  Cider. See *Eucalyptus gunnii*, illus. p.72.
  Flowering. See *Eucalyptus ficifolia*.
  Manna. See *Eucalyptus viminalis*.
  Mountain. See *Eucalyptus dalrympleana*, illus. p.72.
  Murray red. See *Eucalyptus camaldulensis*.
  Oriental sweet. See *Liquidambar orientalis*.
  Ribbon. See *Eucalyptus viminalis*.
  River red. See *Eucalyptus camaldulensis*.
  Snow. See *Eucalyptus pauciflora* subsp. *niphophila*, illus. p.84.
  Spinning. See *Eucalyptus perriniana*, illus. p.100.

Gum (continued)
  Sweet. See *Liquidambar styraciflua*,
    illus. p.70.
  Tasmanian blue. See *Eucalyptus
    globulus*.
  Tasmanian snow. See *Eucalyptus
    coccifera*, illus. p.72.
  Tingiringi. See *Eucalyptus
    glaucescens*.
  Gum tree. See *Eucalyptus*.

GUNNERA

GUNNERACEAE/HALORAGIDACEAE

Genus of summer-flowering perennials, grown mainly for their foliage. Some are clump-forming with very large leaves; others are mat-forming with smaller leaves. Shelter from wind in summer and cover with hay or compost in winter. Some require sun while others do best in partial shade; all need moist soil. Propagate by seed in autumn or spring; small species by division in spring.
G. brasiliensis. See *G. manicata*.
G. chilensis. See *G. tinctoria*.
G. magellanica illus. p.384.
G. manicata, syn. *G. brasiliensis*, illus. p.228.
G. scabra. See *G. tinctoria*.
G. tinctoria, syn. *G. chilensis*, *G. scabra*. Robust, rounded, clump-forming perennial. H and S 1.5m (5ft) or more. Has very large, rounded, puckered and lobed leaves, 45–60cm (1½–2ft) across. In early summer produces dense, conical clusters of tiny, dull reddish-green flowers.

GUZMANIA

BROMELIACEAE

Genus of evergreen, rosette-forming, epiphytic perennials, grown for their overall appearance. Tender, min. 10–15°C (50–59°F). Needs semi-shade and a rooting medium of equal parts humus-rich soil and either sphagnum moss, or bark or plastic chips used for orchid culture. Using soft water, water moderately during growing season, sparingly at other times, and keep rosette centres filled with water from spring to autumn. Propagate by offsets in spring or summer.
G. lingulata (illus. p.265). Evergreen, basal-rosetted, epiphytic perennial. H and S 30–45cm (12–18in). Loose rosettes of broadly strap-shaped, arching, mid-green leaves. Cluster of tubular, white to yellow flowers, surrounded by a rosette of bright red bracts, usually in

summer. var. *minor* (illus. p.265), H and S 15cm (6in), has yellow-green leaves and red or yellow bracts.
G. monostachia. See *G. monostachya*.
G. monostachya, syn. *G. monostachia*, *G. tricolor* (Striped torch; illus. p.265). Evergreen, basal-rosetted, epiphytic perennial. H and S 30–40cm (12–16in). Has dense rosettes of strap-shaped, erect to arching, pale to yellowish-green leaves. In summer, elongated spikes of tubular, white flowers emerge from axils of oval bracts, the upper ones red, the lower ones green with purple-brown stripes.
G. sanguinea. Evergreen, basal-rosetted, epiphytic perennial. H 20cm (8in), S 30–35cm (12–14in). Has dense, slightly flat rosettes of broadly strap-shaped, arching, mid- to deep green leaves. In summer, a compact cluster of tubular, yellow flowers, surrounded by red bracts, appears at the heart of each mature rosette.
G. tricolor. See *G. monostachya*.
G. vittata. Evergreen, basal-rosetted, epiphytic perennial. H and S 35–60cm (14–24in). Produces fairly loose rosettes of strap-shaped, erect, dark green leaves with pale green cross-bands and recurved tips. Stem bears a compact, egg-shaped head of small, tubular, white flowers in summer.

GYMNOCALYCIUM

CACTACEAE

Genus of perennial cacti with masses of funnel-shaped flowers in spring-summer. Crowns generally bear smooth, scaly buds. Tender, min. 5–10°C (41–50°F). Needs full sun or partial shade and very well-drained soil. Propagate by seed or offsets in spring or summer.
G. andreae illus. p.477.
G. gibbosum illus. p.461.
G. mihanovichii **'Red Head'**, syn. *G.m* 'Hibotan', *G.m.* 'Red Cap', illus. p.464.
G. quehlianum. Flattened spherical, perennial cactus. H 5cm (2in), S 7cm (3in). Min. 5°C (41°F). Grey-blue to brown stem has 11 or so rounded ribs. Areoles each produce 5 curved spines. Has white flowers, 5cm (2in) across, with red throats, in spring-summer. Easy to flower.
G. schickendantzii. Spherical, perennial cactus. H and S 10cm (4in). Min. 5°C (41°F). Dark green stem has 7–14 deeply indented ribs and long, red-tipped, grey-brown spines. Bears

greenish-white to pale pink flowers, 5cm (2in) across, in summer.

GYMNOCARPIUM

DRYOPTERIDACEAE/WOODSIACEAE

Genus of about 5 species of deciduous, rhizomatous, terrestrial ferns with triangular fronds, ideal for ground cover. Grow in deep shade and preferably neutral to acid, leafy, moist soil. Propagate from spores when ripe, or divide in spring.
G. dryopteris (Oak fern). Deciduous fern. H 20cm (8in), S indefinite. Bears distinctive, divided fronds, each with a leaf-blade 10–18cm (4–7in) long and across, on a stem 10cm (4in) long. Pinnae are triangular, with oblong to ovate, toothed and scalloped segments. Pale yellowish green when young, the fronds darken to vivid rich green as they mature.

GYMNOCLADUS

CAESALPINIACEAE/LEGUMINOSAE

Genus of deciduous trees, grown for their foliage. Needs full sun and deep, fertile, well-drained soil. Propagate by seed in autumn.
G. dioica (Kentucky coffee tree). Slow-growing, deciduous, spreading tree. H 20m (70ft), S 15m (50ft). Very large leaves, with 4–7 pairs of oval leaflets, are pinkish when young, dark green in summer, then yellow in autumn. Small, star-shaped, white flowers are borne in early summer, followed by long bean-like pods on female plants. [Seeds are toxic.] Zone 5.

GYNANDRIRIS

IRIDACEAE

Genus of iris-like, spring-flowering corms, grown mainly for botanical interest, with very short-lived blooms. Dormant corms require warmth and dryness, so plant in a sunny site that dries out in summer. Needs well-drained soil, but with plenty of moisture in winter-spring. Propagate by seed or by removing cormlets from parent in autumn.
G. sisyrinchium illus. p.432.

GYNURA

ASTERACEAE/COMPOSITAE

Genus of evergreen perennials, shrubs and semi-scrambling climbers, grown

for their ornamental foliage or flower heads. Tender, min. 16°C (61°F). Needs light shade in summer and any fertile, well-drained soil. Water moderately throughout the year, less in cool conditions; do not overwater. Provide support for stems. Remove stem tips to encourage branching. Propagate by softwood or semi-ripe cuttings in spring or summer.
G. aurantiaca illus. p.220. **'Purple Passion'** (syn. *G. sarmentosa* of gardens) is an evergreen, erect, woody-based, soft-stemmed shrub or semi-scrambling climber. H 60cm (2ft) or more. Stems and lance-shaped, lobed, serrated leaves are covered with velvety, purple hairs. Leaves are purple-green above, deep red-purple beneath. In winter produces clusters of daisy-like, orange-yellow flower heads that become purplish as they mature.
G. sarmentosa of gardens. See *G. aurantiaca* 'Purple Passion'.

GYPSOPHILA

CARYOPHYLLACEAE

Genus of spring- to autumn-flowering annuals and perennials, some of which are semi-evergreen. Needs sun. Will grow in dry, sandy and stony soils, but does best in deep, well-drained soil. Resents being disturbed. Cut back after flowering for a second flush of flowers. Propagate *G. paniculata* cultivars by grafting in winter; others by softwood cuttings in summer or by seed in autumn or spring.
G. cerastioides illus. p.364.
G. elegans illus. p.318.
G. paniculata **'Bristol Fairy'** illus. p.239. **'Flamingo'** is a spreading, short-lived perennial. H 60–75cm (2–2½ft), S 1m (3ft). In summer bears panicles of numerous, small, rounded, double, pale pink flowers on wiry, branching stems. Has small, linear, mid-green leaves.
G. repens. Semi-evergreen, prostrate perennial with much-branched rhizomes. H 2.5–5cm (1–2in) or more, S 30cm (12in) or more. In summer produces sprays of small, rounded, white, lilac or pink flowers on slender stems that bear narrowly oval, bluish-green leaves. Is excellent for a rock garden, wall or dry bank. May also be propagated by division in spring.
'Dorothy Teacher' illus. p.375.

H

HAAGEOCEREUS

CACTACEAE

Genus of perennial cacti with ribbed, densely spiny, columnar, green stems branching from the base. Tender, min. 11°C (52°F). Requires full sun and very well-drained soil. Propagate by seed or stem cuttings in spring or summer.
H. ambiguus. See *H. decumbens*.
H. australis. See *H. decumbens*.
H. chosicensis. See *H. multangularis*.
H. decumbens, syn. *H. ambiguus*, *H. australis*, *H. litoralis*. Prostrate, perennial cactus. H 30cm (1ft), S 1m (3ft). Stems, 6cm (2½in) across, with 20 or so ribs, have dark brown, central spines, 5cm (2in) long, and shorter, dense, golden, radial spines. Tubular, white flowers, 8cm (3in) across, produced in summer near crowns, only on mature plants.
H. litoralis. See *H. decumbens*.
H. multangularis, syn. *H. chosicensis*. Upright, perennial cactus. H 1.5m (5ft), S 1m (3ft). Green stem, 10cm (4in) across, with 19 or so ribs, bears white, golden or red, central spines and shorter, dense, bristle-like, white, radial ones. Has tubular, white, lilac-white or pinkish-red flowers, 7cm (3in) long, near crown in summer.
H. versicolor illus. p.458.

HABERLEA

GESNERIACEAE

Genus of evergreen, rosetted perennials, grown for their elegant sprays of flowers. Is useful on walls. Needs partially shaded, moist soil. Resents disturbance to roots. Propagate by seed in spring or by leaf cuttings or offsets in early summer.
H. ferdinandi-coburgii. Evergreen, dense, basal-rosetted perennial. H 10–15cm (4–6in), S 30cm (12in). Has oblong, toothed, dark green leaves, hairy below, almost glabrous above. Sprays of funnel-shaped, blue-violet flowers, each with a white throat, appear on long stems in late spring and early summer.
H. rhodopensis. Evergreen, dense, basal-rosetted perennial. H 10cm (4in), S 15cm (6in) or more. Is similar to *H. ferdinandi-coburgii*, but leaves are soft-haired on both surfaces.
'Virginalis' illus. p.373.

HABRANTHUS

AMARYLLIDACEAE

Genus of summer- and autumn-flowering bulbs with funnel-shaped flowers. Needs a sheltered, sunny site and fertile soil, which is well supplied with moisture in growing season. Propagate by seed or offsets in spring.
H. andersonii. See *H. tubispathus*.
H. brachyandrus. Summer-flowering bulb. H to 30cm (12in), S 5–8cm

(2–3in). Long, linear, semi-erect, narrow leaves form a basal cluster. Each flower stem bears a semi-erect, widely funnel-shaped, pinkish-red flower, 7–10cm (3–4in) long.
H. robustus, syn. *Zephyranthes robusta*, illus. p.437.
H. tubispathus, syn. *H. andersonii*. Summer-flowering bulb. H to 15cm (6in), S 5cm (2in). Has linear, semi-erect, basal leaves and a succession of flower stems each bearing solitary 2.5–3.5cm (1–1½in) long, funnel-shaped flowers, yellow inside, copper-red outside.

Hackberry. See *Celtis*.
Common. See *Celtis occidentalis*.

HACQUETIA,
syn. DONDIA

APIACEAE/UMBELLIFERAE

Genus of one species of clump-forming, rhizomatous perennial that creeps slowly, grown for its yellow or yellow-green flower heads borne on leafless plants in late winter and early spring. Is good in rock gardens. Prefers shade and humus-rich, moist soil. Resents disturbance to roots. Propagate by division in spring, by seed when fresh in autumn or by root cuttings in winter.
H. epipactis illus. p.371.

HAEMANTHUS

AMARYLLIDACEAE

Genus of summer-flowering bulbs with dense heads of small, star-shaped flowers, often brightly coloured. Tender, min. 10°C (50°F). Prefers full sun or partial shade and well-drained soil or sandy compost. Liquid feed in the growing season. Leave undisturbed as long as possible before replanting. Propagate by offsets or seed before growth commences in early spring. All parts may cause mild stomach upset if ingested; contact with the sap may irritate skin.
H. albiflos (Paintbrush). Summer-flowering bulb. H 5–30cm (2–12in), S 20–30cm (8–12in). Has 2–6 almost prostrate, broadly elliptic leaves with hairy edges. Flower stem, appearing between leaves, bears a brush-like head of up to 50 white flowers with very narrow petals and protruding stamens.
H. coccineus illus. p.435.
H. katherinae. See *Scadoxus multiflorus* subsp. *katherinae*.
H. magnificus. See *Scadoxus puniceus*.
H. multiflorus. See *Scadoxus multiflorus*.
H. natalensis. See *Scadoxus puniceus*.
H. puniceus. See *Scadoxus puniceus*.
H. sanguineus. Summer-flowering bulb. H to 30cm (12in), S 20–30cm (8–12in). Bears 2 prostrate, elliptic, rough, dark green leaves, hairy beneath. Brownish-purple-spotted,

green flower stem, forming before leaves, produces a dense head of small, narrow-petalled, red flowers, surrounded by whorls of narrow, leaf-like, red or pink bracts.

Hairy brome grass. See *Bromus ramosus*.

HAKEA

PROTEACEAE

Genus of evergreen shrubs and trees, grown for their often needle-like leaves and their flowers. Is very wind-resistant, except in cold areas. Hardy to tender, min. 5–7°C (41–5°F). Requires a position in full sun and fertile, well-drained soil. Water containerized specimens moderately in growing season, but only sparingly in winter. Propagate by semi-ripe cuttings in summer or by seed in autumn.
H. lissosperma, syn. *H. sericea* of gardens. Evergreen, upright, densely branched shrub of pine-like appearance. H 5m (15ft), S 3m (10ft). Marginally hardy. Bears long, slender, sharply pointed, grey-green leaves and produces, in late spring and early summer, clusters of small, spidery, white flowers. Zone 9?.
H. sericea of gardens. See *H. lissosperma*.
H. suaveolens. Evergreen, rounded shrub. H and S 2m (6ft) or more. Tender. Leaves are divided into cylindrical, needle-like leaflets or occasionally are undivided and lance-shaped. Small, fragrant, tubular, white flowers, carried in short, dense clusters, are produced from summer to winter.

HAKONECHLOA

GRAMINEAE/POACEAE

See also GRASSES, BAMBOOS, RUSHES and SEDGES.
H. macra 'Aureola' illus. p.309.

HALESIA
Silver bell, Snowdrop tree

STYRACACEAE

Genus of deciduous, spring-flowering trees and shrubs, grown for their showy, pendent, bell-shaped flowers and their curious, winged fruits. Needs a sunny, sheltered position. Prefers moist but well-drained, neutral to acid soil. Propagate by softwood cuttings in summer or by seed in autumn.
H. carolina, syn. *H. tetraptera*. Deciduous, spreading tree or shrub. H 8m (25ft), S 10m (30ft). Oval leaves are mid-green. Masses of bell-shaped, white flowers, hanging from bare shoots, are produced in late spring, and are followed by 4-winged, green fruits. Zone 4.
H. monticola illus. p.76.
H. tetraptera. See *H. carolina*.

x HALIMIOCISTUS

CISTACEAE

Hybrid genus (*Cistus* x *Halimium*) of evergreen shrubs, grown for their flowers, but needs shelter at limits of hardiness. Requires full sun and well-drained soil. Propagate by semi-ripe cuttings in summer.
x H. sahucii, syn. *Cistus revolii* of gardens, illus. p.159.
x H. wintonensis, syn. *Halimium wintonense*. Evergreen, bushy shrub. H 60cm (2ft), S 1m (3ft). Saucer-shaped, white flowers, each with deep red bands and a yellow centre, open amid lance-shaped, grey-green leaves in late spring and early summer. Zone 8.

HALIMIUM

CISTACEAE

Genus of evergreen shrubs, grown for their showy flowers. Is good for coastal gardens. Marginally hardy, but needs a sheltered site. Does best in full sun and light, well-drained soil. Propagate by semi-ripe cuttings in summer.
H. formosum. See *H. lasianthum* subsp. *formosum*.
H. lasianthum. Evergreen, bushy, spreading shrub. H 1m (3ft), S 1.5m (5ft). Leaves are oval and grey-green. In late spring and early summer bears saucer-shaped, golden-yellow flowers, sometimes with small, central, red blotches. Zone 9?. subsp. *formosum* (syn. *H. formosum*) illus. p.169.
H. ocymoides, syn. *Cistus algarvensis*. Evergreen, bushy shrub. H 60cm (2ft), S 1m (3ft). Narrowly oval leaves, covered in white hairs when young, mature to dark green. In early summer produces upright clusters of saucer-shaped, golden-yellow flowers, conspicuously blotched with black or purple. Zone 9?. **'Susan'** see *H.* 'Susan'.
H. 'Susan', syn. *H. ocymoides* 'Susan', illus. p.169.
H. umbellatum, syn. *Helianthemum umbellatum*, illus. p.159.
H. wintonense. See x *Halimiocistus wintonensis*.

HAMAMELIS
Witch hazel

HAMAMELIDACEAE

Genus of deciduous, autumn- to early spring-flowering shrubs, grown for their autumn colour and fragrant, frost-resistant flowers, each with 4 narrowly strap-shaped petals. Flourishes in sun or semi-shade and fertile, well-drained, peaty, acid soil, although tolerates good, deep soil over chalk. Propagate species by seed in autumn, selected forms by softwood cuttings in summer, by budding in late summer or by grafting in winter.
H. x intermedia 'Arnold Promise' illus. p.126. **'Diane'** illus. p.125. **'Jelena'** is a deciduous, upright shrub. H and S 4m (12ft) or more. Broadly

oval, glossy, bright green leaves turn bright orange or red in autumn. Bears masses of large, fragrant, orange flowers, along bare branches, from early to mid-winter. Zone 6b. **'Pallida'** (syn. *H. mollis* 'Pallida'), S 3m (10ft), bears dense clusters of large, sulphur-yellow flowers. Zone 6.

H. japonica (Japanese witch hazel). Deciduous, upright, open shrub. H and S 4m (12ft). Broadly oval, glossy, mid-green leaves turn yellow in autumn. Fragrant, yellow flowers, with crinkled petals, are produced on bare branches from mid- to late winter. Zone 6. **'Sulphurea'** illus. p.126. **'Zuccariniana'** bears paler, lemon-yellow flowers in early spring and produces orange-yellow leaves in autumn. Zone 5b.

H. mollis (Chinese witch hazel). Deciduous, upright, open shrub. H and S 4m (12ft) or more. Broadly oval, mid-green leaves turn yellow in autumn. Produces extremely fragrant, yellow flowers, along bare branches, in mid- and late winter. Zone 5b. **'Coombe Wood'** illus. p.126. **'Pallida'** see *H.* x *intermedia* 'Pallida'.

H. vernalis **'Sandra'** illus. p.124.
H. virginiana illus. p.125.

Hamatocactus hamatacanthus. See *Ferocactus hamatacanthus.*
Hamatocactus setispinus. See *Thelocactus setispinus.*
Hamatocactus uncinatus. See *Sclerocactus uncinatus.*
Hard fern. See *Blechnum spicant.*
Hard shield fern. See *Polystichum aculeatum.*

HARDENBERGIA
LEGUMINOSAE/PAPILIONACEAE

Genus of evergreen, woody-stemmed, twining climbers or sub-shrubs, grown for their curtains of leaves and racemes of pea-like flowers. Tender, min. 7°C (45°F). Grows best in sun and in well-drained soil that does not dry out. Propagate by stem cuttings in late summer or autumn or by seed (soaked before sowing) in spring.

H. comptoniana illus. p.206.
H. monophylla. See *H. violacea.*
H. violacea, syn. *H. monophylla* (Australian sarsparilla, Coral pea, Vine lilac). Evergreen, woody-stemmed, twining climber. H to 3m (10ft). Narrowly oval leaves are 2.5–12cm (1–5in) long. Violet, occasionally pink or white, flowers, with yellow blotches on upper petals, are borne in spring. Brownish pods, 3–4cm (1¼–1½in) long, are produced in autumn. **'Happy Wanderer'** illus. p.206.

Hardy age. See *Eupatorium rugosum,* illus. p.240.
Hardy orange. See *Poncirus trifoliata.*
Hare's ear, Shrubby. See *Bupleurum fruticosum,* illus. p.146.
Hare's-foot fern. See *Davallia canariensis.*
Hare's-tail grass. See *Lagurus ovatus,* iilus. p.306.
Harebell poppy. See *Meconopsis quintuplinervia,* illus. p.271.

Harlequin flower. See *Sparaxis.*
Hart's-tongue fern. See *Asplenium scolopendrium,* illus. p.313.
Hat plant
  Chinese. See *Holmskioldia sanguinea.*
  Mandarin's. See *Holmskioldia sanguinea.*
  Mexican. See *Kalanchoe daigremontiana.*

HATIORA
CACTACEAE

Genus of perennial, epiphytic cacti with short, jointed, cylindrical stems, each swollen at one end like a bottle. Tender, min. 10–13°C (50–55°F). Requires partial shade and very well-drained soil. Keep damp in summer; water a little in winter. Propagate by stem cuttings in spring or summer.

H. clavata, syn. *Rhipsalis clavata.* Pendent, perennial, epiphytic cactus. H 60cm (2ft), S 1m (3ft). Min. 11°C (52°F). Multi-branched, cylindrical, dark green stems each widen towards tips. Masses of terminal, bell-shaped, white flowers, 1.5cm (⅝in) wide, appear in late winter and early spring on plants over 30cm (1ft) high.

H. gaertneri, syn. *Rhipsalidopsis gaertneri,* illus. p.475.
H. rosea, syn. *Rhipsalidopsis rosea,* illus. p.472.
H. salicornioides, syn. *Rhipsalis salicornioides,* illus. p.468.

Haw, Yellow. See *Crataegus flava,* illus. p.90.
Hawk's beard. See *Crepis.*
Hawkweed. See *Hieracium.*

HAWORTHIA
ALOEACEA/LILIACEAE

Genus of basal-rosetted, clump-forming, perennial succulents with triangular to rounded, green leaves. Roots tend to wither in winter or during long periods of drought. Tender, min. 5–10°C (41–50°F). Needs partial shade to stay green and grow quickly; if planted in full sun turns red or orange and grows slowly. Requires very well-drained soil. Keep dry in winter. Propagate by seed or division from spring to autumn.

H. arachnoidea, syn. *H. setata,* illus. p.470.
H. attenuata. Clump-forming, perennial succulent. H 7cm (3in), S 25cm (10in). Min. 5°C (41°F). Bears a basal rosette of triangular, dark green leaves, 3cm (1¼in) long, covered in raised, white dots. Has tubular to bell-shaped, white flowers, on long, slender stems, from spring to autumn. f. *clariperla* illus. p.469.
H. x *cuspidata.* Clump-forming, perennial succulent. H 5cm (2in), S 25cm (10in). Min. 5°C (41°F). Produces a basal rosette of smooth, rounded, fleshy, light green leaves covered with translucent marks. Tubular to bell-shaped, white flowers appear from spring to autumn on long, slender stems.
H. fasciata. Slow-growing, clump-forming, perennial succulent. H 15cm

(6in), S 30cm (12in). Min. 5°C (41°F). Has raised, white dots, mostly in bands, on undersides of triangular, slightly incurved leaves, to 8cm (3in) long, which are arranged in a basal rosette. Bears tubular to bell-shaped, white flowers, on long, slender stems, from spring to autumn.
H. setata. See *H. arachnoidea.*
H. truncata illus. p.469.

Hawthorn. See *Crataegus.*
  Common. See *Crataegus monogyna.*
  Indian. See *Rhaphiolepis indica.*
  Water. See *Aponogeton distachyos,* illus. p.447.
Hawthorn maple. See *Acer crataegifolium.*
Hazel. See *Corylus.*
  Chilean. See *Gevuina avellana.*
  Chinese witch. See *Hamamelis mollis.*
  Turkish. See *Corylus colurna.*
  Virginian. See *Hamamelis virginiana.*
  Witch. See *Hamamelis.*
Headache tree. See *Umbellularia.*
Heart leaf. See *Philodendron cordatum; Philodendron scandens,* illus. p.220.
Heart of flame. See *Bromelia balansae,* illus. p.265.
Heart pea. See *Cardiospermum halicacabum.*
Heart seed. See *Cardiospermum halicacabum.*
Heart vine. See *Ceropegia linearis* subsp. *woodii,* illus. p.462.
Hearts-and-honey vine. See *Ipomoea* x *multifida.*
Heartsease. See *Viola tricolor,* illus. p.369.
Heath
  Alpine. See *Erica carnea.*
  Australian. See *Epacris impressa,* illus. p.155.
  Besom. See *Erica scoparia.*
  Channelled. See *Erica canaliculata,* illus. p.178.
  Cornish. See *Erica vagans.*
  Corsican. See *Erica terminalis.*
  Cross-leaved. See *Erica tetralix.*
  Dorset. See *Erica ciliaris.*
  Mackay's. See *Erica mackaiana.*
  Portuguese. See *Erica lusitanica.*
  St Dabeoc's. See *Daboecia cantabrica.*
  Spanish. See *Erica australis.*
  Spanish tree. See *Erica australis.*
  Spike. See *Erica spiculifolia.*
  Tree. See *Erica arborea.*
  Winter. See *Erica carnea.*
Heath banksia. See *Banksia ericifolia.*
Heather
  Bell. See *Erica cinerea.*
  False. See *Cuphea hyssopifolia,* illus. p.158.
  Scotch. See *Calluna vulgaris.*

HEATHERS
ERICACEAE

Heathers (otherwise known as heaths) are evergreen, woody-stemmed shrubs, grown for their flowers and foliage, both of which may provide colour in the garden all year round. There are 3 genera: *Calluna, Daboecia* and *Erica. Calluna* has only one species, *C. vulgaris,* but it contains a large

number of cultivars that flower mainly from mid-summer to late autumn. *Daboecia* has 2 species, both of which are summer-flowering. The largest genus is *Erica,* which, although broadly divided into 2 groups – winter- and summer-flowering species – has some species also flowering in spring and autumn. They vary in height from tree heaths, which may grow to 6m (20ft), to dwarf, prostrate plants that, if planted 30–45cm (12–18in) apart, soon spread to form a thick mat of ground cover.

Heathers are hardy to tender, min. 5–7°C (41–5°F). They prefer an open, sunny position and require humus-rich, well-drained soil. *Calluna* and *Daboecia* dislike limestone and must be grown in acid soil; some species of *Erica* tolerate slightly alkaline soil but all are better grown in acid soils. Prune lightly after flowering each year to keep plants bushy and compact. Propagate species by seed in spring or by softwood cuttings, division or layering in summer. Seed cannot be relied on to come true. All cultivars should be vegetatively propagated. Heathers are illustrated on pp.178–9.

Heavenly bamboo. See *Nandina domestica.*

HEBE
SCROPHULARIACEAE

Genus of evergreen shrubs, grown for their often dense spikes, panicles or racemes of flowers and their foliage. Grows well in coastal areas. Smaller species and cultivars are suitable for rock gardens. Many are marginally hardy and may not survive outside, even in zone 9. Requires position in full sun and well-drained soil. Growth may be restricted, or leggy plants tidied, by cutting back in spring. Propagate by semi-ripe cuttings in summer.

H. albicans illus. p.161. **'Cranleigh Gem'** is an evergreen, rounded shrub. H 60cm (2ft), S 1m (3ft). Has dense spikes of small, 4-lobed, white flowers, with conspicuous, black anthers, amid narrowly oval, grey-green leaves in early summer. Zone 7.
H. **'Alicia Amherst'.** Fast-growing, evergreen, upright shrub. H and S 1.2m (4ft). Has large, oblong, glossy, dark green leaves and, in late summer-autumn, large spikes of small, 4-lobed, deep violet-purple flowers. Zone 9?.
H. **'Amy'.** See *H.* 'Purple Queen'.
H. **'Andersonii Variegata'.** See *H.* x *andersonii* 'Variegata'.
H. x *andersonii* **'Variegata',** syn. *H.* 'Andersonii Variegata'. Evergreen, bushy shrub. H and S 2m (6ft). Probably tender. Leaves are oblong and dark green, each with a grey-green centre and creamy-white margins. Has dense spikes of small, 4-lobed, lilac flowers from mid-summer to autumn.
H. **'Autumn Glory'** illus. p.167.
H. **'Bowles' Variety'** illus. p.168.
H. brachysiphon. Evergreen, bushy, dense shrub. H and S 2m (6ft). Has oblong, dark green leaves. Produces

dense spikes of small, 4-lobed, white flowers in mid-summer. Zone 9.
'White Gem' see *H.* 'White Gem'.
H. buchananii. Evergreen, dome-shaped shrub. H and S 15cm (6in) or more. Very dark stems bear oval, bluish-green leaves. In summer produces clusters of small, 4-lobed white flowers at stem tips. **'Minor'**, H 5–10cm (2–4in), has smaller leaves. Zone 9.
H. canterburiensis, syn. *H.* 'Tom Marshall'. Evergreen, low growing, spreading shrub. H and S 30–90cm (1–3ft). Small, oval, glossy, dark green leaves are densely packed on stems. In early summer, short racemes of small, white flowers are freely produced in leaf axils. Zone 9?.
***H.* 'Carl Teschner'.** See *H.* 'Youngii'.
H. carnosula. Evergreen, prostrate shrub. H 15–30cm (6–12in), S 30cm (12in) or more. Has small, oblong to oval, slightly convex, fleshy, glaucous leaves. Terminal clusters of many small, white flowers, with 4 pointed lobes, are borne in late spring or early summer. Zone 9?.
H. cupressoides illus. p.176.
'Boughton Dome' illus. p.361.
***H.* 'E.A. Bowles'** illus. p.167.
***H.* 'Eveline'**, syn. *H.* 'Gauntlettii'. Evergreen, upright shrub. H and S 1m (3ft). Has long spikes of small, 4-lobed, pink flowers, each with a purplish tube, amid rich green, oblong leaves from late summer to late autumn. Zone 8.
***H.* 'Fairfieldii'.** Evergreen, upright shrub. H and S 60cm (2ft). Oval, toothed, glossy, bright green leaves are red-margined. Large, open panicles of small, 4-lobed, pale lilac flowers are produced in late spring and early summer. Zone 9?.
***H.* × *franciscana* 'Blue Gem'.** Evergreen, spreading shrub. H 60cm (2ft), S 1.2m (4ft). Has oblong, densely arranged, mid-green leaves. Bears dense spikes of small, 4-lobed, violet-blue flowers from mid-summer until early winter. Zone 9.
***H.* 'Gauntlettii'.** See *H.* 'Eveline'.
***H.* 'Great Orme'** illus. p.163.
H. hulkeana. Evergreen, upright, open shrub. H and S 1m (3ft). Oval, toothed, glossy, dark green leaves have red margins. Has masses of small, 4-lobed, pale lilac flowers in large, open panicles in late spring and early summer. Zone 9. **'Lilac Hint'** illus. p.167.
***H.* 'La Séduisante'**, syn. *H.* 'Ruddigore', *H. speciosa* 'Ruddigore'. Evergreen, upright shrub. H and S 1m (3ft). Oval, glossy, deep green leaves are purple beneath. Produces small, 4-lobed, deep purplish-red flowers in large spikes from late summer to late autumn. Zone 9.
H. macrantha. Evergreen, bushy shrub. H 60cm (2ft), S 1m (3ft). Has oval, toothed, fleshy, bright green leaves and produces racemes of large, 4-lobed, pure white flowers in early summer. May become bare at base. Zone 9.
***H.* 'Midsummer Beauty'.** Evergreen, rounded, open shrub. H 2m (6ft), S 1.5m (5ft). Long, narrow, glossy, bright green leaves are reddish-purple beneath. Long spikes of small, 4-lobed, lilac flowers that fade to white are

borne from mid-summer to late autumn. Zone 9.
H. ochracea. Evergreen, bushy, dense shrub. H and S 1m (3ft). Slender shoots are densely covered with tiny, scale-like, ochre-tinged, olive-green leaves. Clusters of small, 4-lobed, white flowers appear in late spring and early summer. Zone 6b.
H. pinguifolia (Disk-leaved hebe). **'Pagei'** illus. p.351.
***H.* 'Purple Queen'**, syn. *H.* 'Amy', illus. p.168.
H. rakaiensis. Evergreen, rounded, compact shrub. H 1m (3ft), S 1.2m (4ft). Produces small, dense spikes of small, 4-lobed, white flowers amid small, oblong, mid-green leaves from early to mid-summer. Zone 8.
H. recurva illus. p.161.
***H.* 'Ruddigore'.** See *H.* 'La Séduisante'.
H. salicifolia. Evergreen, upright shrub. H and S 2.5m (8ft). Has long, narrow, pointed, pale green leaves and, in summer, produces slender spikes of small, 4-lobed, white or pale lilac flowers. Zone 9?.
***H. speciosa* 'Ruddigore'.** See *H.* 'La Séduisante'.
***H.* 'Tom Marshall'.** See *H. canterburiensis*.
H. vernicosa illus. p.351.
***H.* 'White Gem'**, syn. *H. brachysiphon* 'White Gem', illus. p.158.
***H.* 'Youngii'**, syn. *H.* 'Carl Teschner'. Evergreen, prostrate, becoming dome-shaped, shrub. H 15cm (6in), S 30cm (12in) or more. Blackish-brown stems are covered in small, oval, glossy, dark green leaves. Bears short racemes of tiny, 4-lobed, white-throated, purple flowers in summer. Is excellent as a border plant. Zone 6b.

Hebe, Disk-leaved. See *Hebe pinguifolia*.

HEDERA
Ivy

ARALIACEAE

Genus of evergreen, woody-stemmed, trailing perennials and self-clinging climbers with adventitious rootlets, used for covering walls and fences and as ground cover. Takes a year or so to become established, but thereafter growth is rapid. On the ground and while climbing, mostly bears roughly triangular, usually lobed leaves. Given extra height and access to light, leaves become less lobed and, in autumn, umbels of small, yellowish-green flowers are produced, followed by globose, black, occasionally yellow, fruits. Ivies with green leaves are very shade tolerant and do well against a north-facing wall. Those with variegated or yellow leaves prefer more light, are usually less hardy and may sustain frost and wind damage in severe winters. All prefer well-drained, alkaline soil. Prune in spring to control height and spread, and to remove any damaged growth. Propagate in late summer by softwood cuttings or rooted layers. Spider mite may be a problem when plants are grown against a south-facing wall or in dry conditions. All parts of ivy may cause severe

discomfort if ingested; contact with the sap may aggravate skin allergies or irritate skin. See also feature panel p.221.
H. algeriensis. See *H. canariensis* var. *algeriensis*.
H. canariensis (Canary Island ivy). var. ***algeriensis*** (syn. *H. algeriensis*; Algerian ivy) is a fast-growing, evergreen, self-clinging climber. H to 6m (20ft), S 5m (15ft). May be damaged in severe winters but soon recovers. Has oval to triangular, unlobed, glossy, mid-green leaves and reddish-purple stems. Is suitable for growing against a wall in a sheltered area. Zone 7. **'Gloire de Marengo'** has silver-variegated leaves. **'Ravensholst'** (illus. p.221) is vigorous with large leaves; makes good ground cover.
H. colchica (Persian ivy). Evergreen, self-clinging climber or trailing perennial. H 10m (30ft), S 5m (15ft). Has large, oval, unlobed, dark green leaves. Is suitable for growing against a wall. Zone 7.
'Dentata' (Elephant's ears; illus. p.221) is more vigorous and has large, light green leaves that droop, hence its common name. Is good when grown against a wall or for ground cover.
'Dentata Variegata', H 5m (15ft), has variegated, cream-yellow leaves; is useful to brighten a shady corner.
'Paddy's Pride' see 'Sulphur Heart'.
'Sulphur Heart' (syn. *H.c.* 'Paddy's Pride'; illus. p.221), H 5m (15ft), S 3m (10ft), has leaves variegated yellow and light green.
H. helix (Common English ivy). Vigorous, evergreen, self-clinging climber or trailing perennial. H 10m (30ft), S 5m (15ft). Has 5-lobed, dark green leaves. Makes good ground and wall cover, but may be invasive; for a small garden, the more decorative cultivars are preferable. Zone 5b.
'Adam' (illus. p.221), H 1.2m (4ft), S 1m (3ft), has small, light green leaves variegated cream-yellow; may suffer leaf damage in winter, but will recover.
'Angularis Aurea' (illus. p.221), H 4m (12ft), S 2.5m (8ft), has glossy, light green leaves, with bright yellow variegation; is not suitable as ground cover. **'Anne Marie'** (illus. p.221), H 1.2m (4ft), S 1m (3ft), has light green leaves with cream variegation, mostly at margins; may suffer leaf damage in winter. **'Atropurpurea'** (syn. *H.h.* 'Purpurea'; Purple-leaved ivy; illus. p.221), H 4m (12ft), S 2.5m (8ft), has dark green leaves that turn deep purple in winter. var. *baltica* (syn. *H.h.* 'Baltica'), an exceptionally hardy cultivar, has small leaves and makes good ground cover in an exposed area. Zone 4. **'Buttercup'** (illus. p.221), H 2m (6ft), S 2.5m (8ft), has light green leaves that turn rich butter-yellow in full sun. **'Caenwoodiana'** see *H.h.* 'Pedata'. **'Congesta'**, H 45cm (1½ft), S 60cm (2ft), is a non-climbing, erect cultivar with spire-like shoots and small leaves; is suitable for a rock garden. **'Conglomerata'** (Clustered ivy), H and S 1m (3ft), will clamber over a low wall or grow in a rock garden; has small, curly, unlobed leaves. **'Cristata'** see *H.h.* 'Parsley Crested'. **'Curlylocks'** see *H.h.*

'Manda's Crested'. 'Deltoidea' see *H. hibernica* 'Deltoidea'. **'Digitata'** see *H. hibernica* 'Digitata'. **'Erecta'** (illus. p.221), H 1m (3ft), S 1.2m (4ft), is a non-climbing, erect cultivar similar to *H.h.* 'Congesta'. **'Eva'** (illus. p.221), H 1.2m (4ft), S 1m (3ft), has small, grey-green leaves with cream variegation; may suffer leaf damage in winter. **'Glacier'** (illus. p.221), H 3m (10ft), S 2m (6ft), has silvery-grey-green leaves. Zone 5. **'Glymii'** (illus. p.221), H 2.5m (8ft), S 2m (6ft), has glossy, dark green leaves that turn deep purple in winter; is not suitable for ground cover. **'Goldheart'** (syn. *H.h.* 'Jubiläum Goldherz', *H.h.* 'Jubilee Goldheart', *H.h.* 'Oro di Bogliasco'; illus. p.221), H 6m (20ft), has dark green leaves with bright yellow centres; is slow to establish, then grows rapidly; is not suitable for ground cover. Zone 6. **'Gracilis'** see *H. hibernica* 'Gracilis'. **'Green Feather'** see *H.h.* Triton'. **'Green Ripple'** (illus. p.221), H and S 1.2m (4ft), has mid-green leaves with prominent, light green veins; is good for ground cover or for growing against a low wall. **'Hahn's Self-branching'** see *H.h.* 'Pittsburgh'. **'Heise'** (illus. p.221), H 30cm (1ft), S 60cm (2ft), has small, grey-green leaves with cream variegation; is suitable as ground cover for a small, sheltered area. var. *hibernica* see *H. hibernica*. **'Ivalace'** (illus. p.221), H 1m (3ft), S 1.2m (4ft), has curled and crimped, glossy leaves; is good for ground cover and for growing against a low wall. **'Jubiläum Goldherz'** see *H.h.* 'Goldheart'. **'Jubilee Goldheart'** see *H.h.* 'Goldheart'. **'Königers Auslese'** (syn. *H.h.* 'Sagittifolia'), H 1.2m (4ft), S 1m (3ft), has finger-like, deeply cut leaves; is not suitable for ground cover. **'Lobata Major'** (syn. *H. hibernica* 'Lobata Major'; illus. p.221), H 5m (15ft), is vigorous with large, 3-lobed leaves. **'Manda's Crested'** (syn. *H.h.* 'Curlylocks'; illus. p.221), H and S 2m (6ft), has elegant, wavy-edged, mid-green leaves that turn a coppery shade in winter. **'Merion Beauty'** (illus. p.221), H 1.2m (4ft), S 1m (3ft), with delicately lobed leaves; is not suitable for ground cover. **'Nigra'** (illus. p.221), H and S 1.2m (4ft), has small, very dark green leaves that turn purple-black in winter. **'Oro di Bogliasco'** see *H.h.* 'Goldheart'. **'Parsley Crested'** (syn. *H.h.* 'Cristata'; illus. p.221), H 2m (6ft), S 1.2m (4ft), has light green leaves, crested at margins; is not suitable for ground cover. **'Pedata'** (syn. *H.h.* 'Caenwoodiana'; Bird's-foot ivy; illus. p.221), H 4m (12ft), S 3m (10ft), has grey-green leaves shaped like a bird's foot; is not suitable for ground cover. **'Pittsburgh'** (syn. *H.h.* 'Hahn's Self-branching'; illus. p.221), H 1m (3ft), S 1.2m (4ft), has mid-green leaves; is suitable for growing against a low wall and for ground cover. **'Purpurea'** see *H.h.* 'Atropurpurea'. **'Sagittifolia'** see *H.h.* 'Königers Auslese'. **'Telecurl'** (illus. p.221), H and S 1m (3ft), has elegantly twisted, light green leaves. **'Triton'** (syn. *H.h.* 'Green Feather'), H 45cm (1½ft),

S 1m (3ft), is a non-climbing cultivar that has leaves with deeply incised lobes that resemble whips; makes good ground cover. **'Woeneri'** (illus. p.221), H 4m (12ft), S 3m (10ft), is a vigorous cultivar that has bluntly lobed, grey-green leaves, with lighter coloured veins, that turn purple in winter. Most of these cultivars are hardy to zone 5b; known exceptions are noted.

H. hibernica, syn. *H. helix* var. *hibernica* (Irish ivy; illus. p.221). Vigorous, evergreen climber. H 5m (15ft), S 6m (20ft). Has large, mid-green leaves. Is good for covering a large area, either on the ground or against a wall. Zone 7. **'Deltoidea'** (syn. *H. helix* 'Deltoidea'; Shield ivy, Sweetheart ivy; illus. p.221), H 5m (15ft), S 3m (10ft), has heart-shaped leaves; is suitable only for growing against a wall. **'Digitata'** (syn. *H. helix* 'Digitata'; Finger-leaved ivy; illus. p.221), H 6m (20ft), has large leaves; is not suitable for ground cover. **'Gracilis'** (syn. *H. helix* 'Gracilis'; illus. p.221), H 5m (15ft), has sharply lobed, dark green leaves that turn bronze-purple in winter; is not suitable for ground cover. **'Lobata Major'** see *H. helix* 'Lobata Major'. **'Sulphurea'** (illus. p.221), H and S 3m (10ft), has medium-sized leaves with sulphur-yellow variegation; is suitable for growing against a wall or for ground cover, and as a foil for brightly coloured plants.

H. nepalensis (Nepalese ivy). Evergreen, self-clinging climber. H 4m (12ft), S 2.5m (8ft). Young growth may suffer damage from late frosts. Has oval to triangular, toothed, olive-green leaves and is suitable only for growing against a sheltered wall. Zone 5b.

H. pastuchovii. Moderately vigorous, evergreen, self-clinging climber. H 2.5m (8ft), S 2m (6ft). Has shield-shaped, glossy, dark green leaves and should only be grown against a wall. Zone 7.

H. rhombea (Japanese ivy). Evergreen, self-clinging climber. H and S 1.2m (4ft). Has small, fairly thick, diamond-shaped, unlobed, mid-green leaves. Is suitable only for growing against a low wall. Zone 7. **'Variegata'** has leaves with narrow, white margins.

Hedge bamboo. See *Bambusa multiplex,* illus. p.307.
Hedgehog broom. See *Erinacea anthyllis,* illus. p.348.
Hedgehog holly. See *Ilex aquifolium* 'Ferox'.
Hedgehog rose. See *Rosa rugosa,* illus. p.187.

HEDYCHIUM
Garland flower, Ginger lily

ZINGIBERACEAE

Genus of perennials with stout, fleshy rhizomes. Fragrant, showy flowers are short-lived, but borne profusely. Grow in sheltered borders and conservatories. Tender, min. 5°C (41°F). Needs sun and rich, moist soil. Propagate by division in spring; should not be divided when dormant.

H. coronarium (White ginger lily). Upright, rhizomatous perennial.

H 1.5m (5ft), S 60cm–1m (2–3ft). Produces dense spikes of very fragrant, butterfly-like, white flowers with basal, yellow blotches in mid-summer. Lance-shaped, mid-green leaves are downy beneath.

H. densiflorum illus. p.229.
H. gardnerianum illus. p.232.
H. horsfieldii, syn. *Brachychilum horsfieldii.* Clump-forming, tufted perennial. H and S to 1m (3ft). Has short-stalked, lance-shaped, leathery leaves, to 30cm (1ft) long. Produces showy, tubular, yellow-and-white flowers, to 8cm (3in) across, in summer, followed by orange fruits that open to reveal red seeds.

HEDYOTIS,
syn. HOUSTONIA

RUBIACEAE

Genus of mat-forming, summer-flowering perennials. Thrives in shady sites on moist, sandy leaf mould. Propagate by division in spring or by seed in autumn.

H. michauxii illus. p.383.

HEDYSARUM

LEGUMINOSAE/PAPILIONACEAE

Genus of perennials, biennials and deciduous sub-shrubs. Prefers sun and well-drained soil. Resents being disturbed. Propagate by seed in autumn or spring.

H. coronarium illus. p.250.

Heeria. Reclassified as *Heterocentron.*
Heimerliodendron brunonianum. See *Pisonia umbellifera.*

HELENIUM
Sneezeweed

ASTERACEAE/COMPOSITAE

Genus of late summer- and autumn-flowering perennials, grown for their daisy-like flower heads, each with a prominent, central disc. Needs a site in full sun and any well-drained soil. Propagate by division in spring or autumn. All parts may cause severe discomfort if ingested; contact with foliage may aggravate skin allergies.

H. 'Bressingham Gold'. Erect, bushy perennial with stout stems clothed in lance-shaped, mid-green leaves. H 1m (3ft), S 60cm (2ft). Sprays of bright yellow flower heads are produced in late summer and autumn.

H. 'Bruno'. Erect, bushy perennial. H 1.2m (4ft), S 75cm (2½ft). Sprays of deep bronze-red flower heads are produced in late summer-autumn. Stout stems are clothed in lance-shaped leaves.

H. 'Butterpat'. Compact perennial. H 1m (3ft), S 60cm (2ft). Has stout stems clothed in lance-shaped leaves. Bears sprays of rich deep yellow flower heads in late summer and autumn.

H. 'Moerheim Beauty' illus. p.263.
H. 'Riverton Gem'. Erect, bushy perennial. H 1.4m (4½ft), S 1m (3ft). Has sprays of red-and-gold flower heads in late summer-autumn. Stems are clothed in lance-shaped leaves.

H. 'Wyndley' illus. p.263.

HELIANTHEMUM
Rock rose

CISTACEAE

Genus of evergreen, spring- to autumn-flowering shrubs and sub-shrubs, grown for their flowers. Is useful for rock gardens and dry banks. Needs full sun and well-drained soil. Cut back lightly after flowering. Propagate by semi-ripe cuttings in early summer.

H. apenninum illus. p.351.
H. 'Ben Hope'. Evergreen, domed shrub. H 23–30cm (9–12in), S 45cm (18in). Bears small, linear grey-green, leaves and saucer-shaped, carmine-red flowers in mid-summer. Zone 7.
H. 'Ben More' illus. p.354.
H. 'Ben Nevis'. Evergreen, hummock-forming, compact shrub. H and S 15–23cm (6–9in). Has small, linear, dark green leaves and, in mid-summer, saucer-shaped, orange flowers with bronze centres. Zone 7.
H. 'Fire Dragon' illus. p.354.
H. 'Golden Queen'. Evergreen, domed, compact shrub. H 23cm (9in), S 30cm (12in). Saucer-shaped, golden-yellow flowers appear amid small, linear, dark green leaves in mid-summer. Zone 7.
H. guttatum. See *Tuberaria guttata.*
H. 'Jubilee'. Evergreen, domed, compact shrub. H 15–23cm (6–9in), S 23–30cm (9–12in). Has small, linear, dark green leaves. Bears saucer-shaped, double, pale yellow flowers from spring to late summer. Zone 7.
H. nummularium 'Amy Baring'. Evergreen, spreading shrub. H 10–15cm (4–6in), S 60cm (24in). Small, oblong, light grey leaves are hairy beneath. In summer bears a succession of saucer-shaped, orange-centred, deep yellow flowers in loose, terminal clusters. Zone 7.
H. oelandicum subsp. *alpestre.* Evergreen, open, twiggy shrub. H 7–12cm (3–5in), S 15cm (6in) or more. Produces terminal clusters of 3–6 saucer-shaped, bright yellow flowers from early to mid-summer. Leaves are tiny, oblong and mid-green. Is suitable for growing in a trough. Zone 7.
H. 'Raspberry Ripple' illus. p.354.
H. 'Rhodanthe Carneum', syn. *H. 'Wisley Pink', illus. p.353.
H. umbellatum. See *Halimium umbellatum.*
H. 'Wisley Pink'. See *H. 'Rhodanthe Carneum'.*
H. 'Wisley Primrose' illus. p.358.
H. 'Wisley White' illus. p.351.

HELIANTHUS
Sunflower

ASTERACEAE/COMPOSITAE

Genus of summer- and autumn-flowering annuals and perennials, grown for their large, daisy-like, usually yellow flower heads. May be invasive. All need sun and well-drained soil; some prefer moist conditions. Needs staking. Propagate by seed or division in autumn or spring. Contact with the foliage may aggravate skin allergies.

H. annuus (illus. p.337). Fast-growing, upright annual. H 1–3m (3–10ft) or more; S 30–45cm (12–18in). Has large,

oval, serrated, mid-green leaves. Very large, daisy-like, brown- or purplish-centred, yellow flower heads, 30cm (12in) or more wide, are produced in summer. Tall, intermediate and dwarf cultivars are available. **'Music Box'** (dwarf) illus p.336. **'Russian Giant'** (tall), H 3m (10ft) or more, has yellow flower heads with green-brown centres. **'Teddy Bear'** (dwarf) illus. p.337.

H. atrorubens **'Monarch'.** Erect perennial. H 2.2m (7ft), S 1m (3ft). Bears terminal, daisy-like, semi-double, golden-yellow flower heads on branching stems in late summer. Has lance-shaped, coarse, mid-green leaves. Replant each spring to keep in check.

H. debilis subsp. *cucumerifolius* **'Italian White'.** Erect perennial. H 1.2m (4ft), S 45–60cm (1½–2ft). In summer has large, black-centred, creamy-white flower heads. Purple-mottled stems bear coarsely hairy, sharply toothed, glossy, mid-green leaves.

H. × multiflorus illus. p.232.
'Capenoch Star' is an erect perennial. H 1.2m (4ft), S 60cm (2ft). In summer, daisy-like, lemon-yellow flower heads are borne terminally on branching stems. Leaves are lance-shaped, coarse and mid-green.
'Loddon Gold' illus. p.232.
H. orgyalis. See *H. salicifolius.*
H. salicifolius, syn. *H. orgyalis* (Willow-leaved sunflower). Upright perennial. H 2.2m (7ft), S 60cm (2ft). Bears small, daisy-like, yellow flower heads at ends of stout, branching stems in autumn. Has narrow, willow-like, drooping, deep green leaves.

HELICHRYSUM

ASTERACEAE/COMPOSITAE

Genus of summer- and autumn-flowering perennials, annuals and evergreen sub-shrubs and shrubs. When dried, flower heads are 'everlasting'. Hardy to tender, min. 5°C (41°F). Needs sun and well-drained soil. Propagate shrubs and sub-shrubs by heel or semi-ripe cuttings in summer; perennials by division or seed in spring; annuals by seed in spring.

H. angustifolium. See *H. italicum.*
H. bellidioides. Evergreen, prostrate shrub. H 5cm (2in), S 23cm (9in). Has small, rounded, fleshy, dark green leaves and, in early summer, terminal clusters of daisy-like, white flower heads. Zone 8.
H. coralloides. See *Ozothamnus coralloides.*
H. italicum, syn. *H. angustifolium* (Curry plant). Evergreen, bushy sub-shrub. H 60cm (2ft), S 1m (3ft). Has linear, aromatic, silvery-grey leaves. Broad clusters of small, oblong, bright yellow flower heads are produced on long, upright, white shoots during summer. Zone 8. subsp. *serotinum* (syn. *H. serotinum*), H and S 15cm (6in), is dome-shaped; stems and oval leaves are densely felted with white hairs. Dislikes winter wet and cold climates.
H. ledifolium. See *Ozothamnus ledifolius.*
H. marginatum of gardens. See *H. milfordiae.*

H. milfordiae, syn. *H. marginatum* of gardens. Evergreen, mat-forming, dense sub-shrub. H 5cm (2in), S 23cm (9in). On sunny days in early summer, large, conical, red buds open into daisy-like, white flower heads with red-backed petals; they close in dull or wet weather. Has basal rosettes of oval, hairy, silver leaves. Prefers very gritty soil. Dislikes winter wet. Propagate in spring by rooting single rosettes. Zone 9.

H. petiolare, syn. *H. petiolatum* of gardens, illus. p.175. **'Limelight'** is an evergreen, mound-forming shrub. H to 50cm (20in), S 2m (6ft). Tender, min. 2°C (35°F). Trailing, silver-green shoots bear oval to heart-shaped, bright lime-green leaves. In late summer and autumn has daisy-like, off-white flower heads.

H. petiolatum of gardens. See *H. petiolare*.

H. rosmarinifolium. See *Ozothamnus rosmarinifolius*.

H. **'Schwefellicht'**, syn. *H.* 'Sulphur Light', illus. p.291.

H. selago. See. *Ozothamnus selago*.

H. serotinum. See *H. italicum* subsp. *serotinum*.

H. splendidum. Evergreen, bushy, dense shrub. H and S 1.2m (4ft). Woolly, white shoots are clothed in small, oblong, silvery-grey leaves. Small, oblong, bright yellow flower heads produced in clusters from mid-summer to autumn or sometimes into winter. Zone 9?.

H. **'Sulphur Light'**. See *H.* 'Schwefellicht'.

HELICONIA
Lobster claws

HELICONIACEAE/MUSACEAE

Genus of tufted perennials, evergreen in warm climates, grown for their spikes of colourful flowers and for the attractive foliage on younger plants. Tender, min. 18°C (64°F). Needs partial shade and humus-rich, well-drained soil. Water generously in growing season, very sparingly when plants die down in winter. Propagate by seed or division of rootstock in spring.

H. metallica. Tufted perennial. H to 3m (10ft), S 1m (3ft). Oblong, long-stalked leaves, to 60cm (2ft) long, are velvety-green above with paler veins, sometimes purple below. In summer, mature plants bear erect stems with tubular, glossy, greenish-white-tipped, red flowers enclosed in narrow, boat-shaped, green bracts.

H. psittacorum illus. p.229.

HELICTOTRICHON

GRAMINEAE/POACEAE

See also GRASSES, BAMBOOS, RUSHES and SEDGES.

H. sempervirens, syn. *Avena candida*, *A. sempervirens*, illus. p.307.

HELIOPSIS

ASTERACEAE/COMPOSITAE

Genus of summer-flowering perennials. Requires sun and any well-drained soil. Propagate by seed or division in autumn or spring.

H. **'Ballet Dancer'** illus. p.258.

H. helianthoides **'Incomparabilis'**. Upright perennial. H to 1.5m (5ft), S 60cm (2ft). Bears daisy-like, single, orange flower heads in late summer. Leaves are narrowly oval, coarsely toothed and mid-green. **'Patula'** bears flattish, semi-double, orange-yellow flower heads. subsp. *scabra* (syn. *H. scabra*) has very rough stems and leaves and double, orange-yellow flower heads. subsp. *scabra* **'Light of Loddon'** (syn. *H.* 'Light of Loddon') illus. p.229.

H. **'Light of Loddon'**. See *H. helianthoides* subsp. *scabra* 'Light of Loddon'.

H. scabra. See *H. helianthoides* subsp. *scabra*.

Heliosperma alpestris. See *Silene alpestris*.

Heliotrope, Winter. See *Petasites fragrans*.

HELIOTROPIUM
Heliotrope

BORAGINACEAE

Genus of annuals, evergreen sub-shrubs and shrubs, grown for their fragrant flowers. Tender, min. 5–7°C (41–5°F). Needs full sun and fertile, well-drained soil. Water potted plants freely when in full growth, moderately at other times. In spring, tip prune young plants to promote a bushy habit and cut leggy, older plants back hard. Propagate by seed in spring, by greenwood cuttings in summer or by semi-ripe cuttings in early autumn.

H. arborescens, syn. *H. peruvianum*, illus. p.167.

H. peruvianum. See *H. arborescens*.

Helipterum manglesii. See *Rhodanthe manglesii*.

Helipterum roseum. See *Rhodanthe chlorocephala* subsp. *rosea*.

Hellebore

Black false. See *Veratrum nigrum*, illus. p.228.

Green. See *Helleborus viridis*, illus. p.305.

Stinking. See *Helleborus foetidus*, illus. p.305.

White false. See *Veratrum album*.

HELLEBORUS
Christmas rose

RANUNCULACEAE

Genus of perennials, some of which are evergreen, grown for their winter and spring flowers. Most deciduous species retain their old leaves over winter. These should be cut off in early spring as flower buds develop. Is excellent in woodlands. Prefers semi-shade and moisture-retentive, well-drained soil. Propagate by fresh seed or division in autumn or very early spring. Is prone to aphid attack in early summer. All parts may cause severe discomfort if ingested, and the sap may irritate skin on contact.

H. argutifolius, syn. *H. corsicus*, *H. lividus* subsp. *corsicus*, illus p.304.

H. atrorubens. Clump-forming perennial. H and S 30cm (1ft).

Shallowly cup-shaped, deep purple flowers are borne in late winter. Has palmate, deeply divided, toothed, glossy, dark green leaves.

H. × *ballardiae* **'December Dawn'** (illus. p.52). Clump-forming perennial with deep bluish-green leaves. H to 35cm (14in), S 30cm (12in). From mid-winter to early spring bears saucer-shaped, white flowers, 6–8cm (2½–3in) across, flushed pinkish-purple, maturing to a dull metallic purple.

H. corsicus. See *H. argutifolius*.

H. cyclophyllus. Clump-forming perennial. H to 60cm (24in), S 45cm (18in). In early spring produces shallowly cup-shaped, yellow-green flowers with prominent, yellowish-white stamens. Leaves are palmate, deeply divided, and bright green.

H. foetidus illus. p.305.

H. × *hybridus* [white form] illus. p.300, [pink form] illus. p.301, [purple form] illus. p.302.

H. lividus. Evergreen, clump-forming perennial. H and S 45cm (18in). Has 3-parted, mid-green leaves, marbled pale green, purplish-green below, with obliquely oval, slightly toothed or entire leaflets. Produces large clusters of cup-shaped, purple-suffused, yellow-green flowers in late winter. subsp. *corsicus* see *H. argutifolius*.

H. niger illus. p.301.

H. purpurascens. Neat, clump-forming perennial. H and S 30cm (1ft). Small, nodding, cup-shaped, pure deep purple or green flowers, splashed with deep purple on outside, are produced in early spring. Dark green leaves are palmate and deeply divided into narrowly lance-shaped, toothed segments.

H. × *sternii* illus. p.301.

H. viridis illus. p.305.

Helmet flower. See *Aconitum napellus*.

HELONIOPSIS

LILIACEAE/MELANTHIACEAE

Genus of spring-flowering, rosette-forming perennials. Grow in semi-shade and in moist soil. Propagate by division in autumn or by seed in autumn or spring.

H. orientalis illus. p.269.

HELWINGIA

HELWINGIACEAE

Genus of deciduous shrubs, bearing flowers and showy fruits directly on leaf surfaces, grown mainly for botanical interest. Requires separate male and female plants in order to produce fruits. Needs sun or semi-shade and moist soil. Propagate by softwood cuttings in summer.

H. japonica. Deciduous, bushy, open shrub. H and S 1.5m (5ft). Oval, bright green leaves have bristle-like teeth. In early summer, tiny, star-shaped, green flowers appear at centre of each leaf and are followed by spherical, black fruits. Zone 9.

Helxine soleirolii. See *Soleirolia soleirolii*.

HEMEROCALLIDACEAE/LILIACEAE

Genus of perennials, some of which are semi-evergreen or evergreen. Flowers, borne in succession, each last for only a day. Does best in full sun and fertile, moist soil. Propagate by division in autumn or spring. Cultivars raised from seed will not come true to type; species may come true if grown in isolation from other daylilies. Slug and snail control is essential in early spring when young foliage first appears. See also feature panel p.257.

H. **'Betty Woods'** (illus. p.257). Robust, spreading evergreen, clump-forming perennial. H 65cm (26in), S 60cm (2ft). Large, peony-like, yellow flowers are borne in mid- and late summer. Leaves are arching, strap-shaped and mid-green.

H. **'Brocaded Gown'** (illus. p.257). Semi-evergreen, clump-forming perennial. H and S to 60cm (2ft). In summer has rounded, ruffled creamy-yellow flowers amid broad, strap-shaped, mid-green leaves.

H. **'Catherine Woodbery'**. Robust, clump-forming perennial. H 70cm (28in), S 75cm (30in). Fragrant, trumpet-shaped, delicate, pale lavender flowers, with soft lime-green throats, are produced above strap-shaped, mid-green leaves in late summer.

H. **'Cat's Cradle'** (illus. p.257). Semi-evergreen, clump-forming perennial. H 1m (3ft), S 75cm (2½ft). In summer has large, spider-like, bright yellow flowers amid slender grassy leaves.

H. **'Chorus Line'** (illus. p.257). Extended-blooming, semi-evergreen, clump-forming perennial. H 50cm (20in), S 60cm (24in). Produces remontant, triangular, slightly fragrant, bright pink flowers, with pink- and yellow-marked tepals and dark green throats, from early to mid-summer.

H. citrina (illus. p.257). Vigorous, coarse-growing, clump-forming perennial. H and S 75cm (2½ft). Many large, very fragrant, trumpet-shaped, rich lemon-yellow flowers open at night in mid-summer, each lasting only one day. Strap-shaped leaves are dark green.

H. **'Corky'** (illus. p.257). Clump-forming perennial. H and S 45cm (18in). Bears trumpet-shaped, lemon-yellow flowers, brown on outsides, in late spring and early summer above slender, strap-shaped, mid-green leaves. Flowers, borne prolifically, last only a day.

H. dumortieri. Compact, clump-forming perennial. H 45cm (1½ft), S 60cm (2ft). In early summer produces fragrant, trumpet-shaped, brown-backed, golden-yellow flowers. Mid-green leaves are strap-shaped, stiff and coarse.

H. **'Eenie Weenie'** (illus. p.257). Clump-forming perennial. H and S 30cm (1ft). Bears an abundance of clear yellow flowers in early summer. Leaves are narrow and arching.

H. flava. See *H. lilioasphodelus*.

H. **'Frank Gladney'**. Robust, semi-evergreen, clump-forming perennial. In summer produces very large, rounded, vivid coral-pink flowers with golden throats; anthers are black. Broad, strap-shaped leaves are mid-green.

H. fulva (Fulvous daylily, Tawny daylily). Vigorous, clump-forming perennial. H 1m (3ft), S 75cm (2½ft). Trumpet-shaped, tawny-orange flowers appear from mid- to late summer above a mound of strap-shaped, light green leaves. **'Flore Pleno'** (illus. p.257) has double flowers. **'Kwanzo Variegata'** has leaves variably marked with white.

***H.* 'Gentle Shepherd'** (illus. p.257). Semi-evergreen, clump-forming perennial. H 70cm (28in), S 60cm (24in). From early to mid-summer carries ruffled, white flowers with green throats above light green leaves.

***H.* 'Golden Chimes'** (illus. p.257). Clump-forming perennial of graceful habit. H 75cm (2½ft), S 60cm (2ft). Bears small, delicate, trumpet-shaped, golden-yellow flowers with a brown reverse, lasting only a day, from early to mid-summer. Has narrow strap-shaped mid-green leaves.

***H.* 'Hyperion'** (illus. p.257). Clump-forming perennial. H and S 90cm (3ft). In mid-summer, very fragrant, lily-like, pale lemon-yellow flowers are borne above strap-shaped leaves.

***H.* 'Joan Senior'** (illus. p.257). Vigorous, semi-evergreen, clump-forming perennial. H 63cm (25in), S 1m (3ft). Open trumpet-shaped, almost pure white flowers are produced on well-branched stems from mid- to late summer. Leaves are strap-shaped and mid-green.

***H.* 'Jolyene Nichole'** (illus. p.257). Semi-evergreen, clump-forming perennial. H and S 50cm (20in). Bears rounded, ruffled, rose-pink flowers amid lush, blue-green leaves.

***H.* 'Lady Fingers'** (illus. p.257). Semi-evergreen, clump-forming perennial with narrow leaves. H 80cm (32in), S 75cm (30in). In mid-summer, bears spider-shaped, pale yellow-green flowers with green throats and spoon-shaped tepals.

H. lilioasphodelus (syn. *H. flava*; illus. p.257). Robust, clump-forming, spreading perennial. H and S 60cm (2ft) or more. Very fragrant, delicate, lemon- to chrome-yellow flowers, lasting only 1 or 2 days, are borne in late spring and early summer. Strap-shaped leaves are mid-green.

***H.* 'Lullaby Baby'.** Vigorous, semi-evergreen, clump-forming perennial. H and S 50cm (20in). Produces very pale pink flowers with green throats in mid-summer amid strap-shaped, mid-green leaves.

***H.* 'Luxury Lace'.** Compact, clump-forming perennial. H 75cm (2½ft), S 60cm (2ft). In late summer produces small, trumpet-shaped, creamy-lavender-pink flowers with lime-green throats and prominent anthers. Each petal is curled and ruffled and has a near-white midrib. Leaves are strap-shaped and mid-green.

***H.* 'Marion Vaughn'** (illus. p.257). Clump-forming perennial. H 1m (3ft), S 60cm (2ft). Produces fragrant, trumpet-shaped, green-throated, pale lemon-yellow flowers, in late summer, each lasting only a day. Each petal has a raised, near-white midrib. Strap-

shaped leaves are mid-green.

***H.* 'Mauna Loa'** (illus. p.257). Vigorous, free-flowering, evergreen, clump-forming perennial. H 55cm (22in), S 1m (3ft). Produces rounded, bright tangerine-orange flowers, with chartreuse throats and contrasting black anthers, in mid- to late summer.

***H.* 'Millie Schlumpf'** (illus. p.257). Vigorous, free-flowering, evergreen, clump-forming perennial. H 50cm (20in), S 60cm (24in). Triangular to rounded, pale pink flowers, with deeper pink halos and green throats, are borne in early to mid-summer.

H. minor (Grass-leaved daylily). Compact, clump-forming perennial. H 40cm (16in), S 45cm (18in). In early summer, fragrant, trumpet-shaped, lemon-yellow flowers, with tawny-backed, outer petals, overtop narrowly strap-shaped, mid-green leaves that die back in early autumn.

***H.* 'Prairie Blue Eyes'** (illus. p.257). Semi-evergreen, clump-forming perennial. H 80cm (32in), S 90cm (36in). In mid-summer produces lavender flowers, banded with blue-purple, that have green throats. Slender, strap-shaped leaves are mid-green.

***H.* 'Real Wind'** (illus. p.257). Vigorous, free-flowering, evergreen, clump-forming perennial with dense foliage. H 65cm (26in), S 1m (3ft). Produces triangular to round, pale buff to salmon-pink flowers, with bold rose-pink eyes, in mid- to late summer.

***H.* 'Ruffled Apricot'** (illus. p.257). Slow-growing, clump-forming perennial. Large, deep apricot flowers, with lavender-pink midribs, are ruffled at edges. Leaves are stiff, strap-shaped and mid-green.

***H.* 'Scarlet Orbit'** (illus. p.257). Low-growing, semi-evergreen, clump-forming perennial. H 50cm (20in), S 65cm (26in). Scarlet flowers with green throats, open flat amid lush, strap-shaped, mid-green leaves in mid-summer.

***H.* 'Siloam Virginia Henson'** (illus. p.257). Clump-forming perennial. H 45cm (18in), S 65cm (26in). In early summer bears rounded, ruffled, creamy-pink flowers banded with rose-pink and with green throats. Broad, strap-shaped leaves are mid-green.

***H.* 'Solano Bulls Eye'** (illus. p.257). Vigorous, free-flowering, evergreen, clump-forming perennial. H 50cm (20in), S 75cm (30in). Produces round, bright yellow flowers, with deep brownish-purple eyes, over a long period from early to late summer.

***H.* 'Super Purple'** (illus. p.257). Clump-forming perennial. H 68cm (27in), S 65cm (26in). Bears rounded, ruffled, velvety, red-purple flowers, with lime-green throats, in mid-summer amid strap-shaped, light-green leaves.

HEMIGRAPHIS

ACANTHACEAE

Genus of annuals and evergreen perennials, usually grown for their foliage. Tender, min. 15°C (59°F). Grows well in bright but not direct sunlight and in moist but well-drained soil. Water frequently during growing

season, less in winter. Regularly cut back straggly stems to tidy. Propagate by stem cuttings in spring or summer.
H. repanda illus. p.299.

Hemlock
  Canada. See *Tsuga canadensis*, illus. p.107.
  Carolina. See *Tsuga caroliniana*.
  Eastern. See *Tsuga canadensis*, illus. p.107.
  Japanese. See *Tsuga diversifolia*; *Tsuga sieboldii*.
  Mountain. See *Tsuga mertensiana*.
  Northern Japanese. See *Tsuga diversifolia*.
  Southern Japanese. See *Tsuga sieboldii*.
  Western. See *Tsuga heterophylla*.
Hemp, African. See *Sparrmannia africana*, illus. p.118.
Hen-and-chicken fern. See *Asplenium bulbiferum*.

HEPATICA

RANUNCULACEAE

Genus of very variable perennials, some of which are semi-evergreen, flowers are produced in early spring before new leaves are properly formed. Needs partial shade and deep, humus-rich, moist soil. Stout, much-branched rootstock resents disturbance. Propagate by seed when fresh or by division or removing side shoots in spring.
H. angulosa. See *H. transsilvanica*.
***H.* × *media* 'Ballardii'.** Slow-growing, dome-shaped perennial. H 10cm (4in), S 30cm (12in). Has rounded, 3-lobed, stalked, soft green leaves and, in early spring, shallowly cup-shaped, many-petalled, intense blue flowers. Fully double, coloured forms are also known. Propagate by division only.
H. nobilis, syn. *Anemone hepatica*, *H. triloba*. Slow-growing, semi-evergreen, dome-shaped perennial. H 8cm (3in), S 10–12cm (4–5in). Bears rounded, 3-lobed, fleshy, mid-green leaves. Shallowly cup-shaped, many-petalled flowers – white through pink to carmine, pale to deep blue or purple – are produced in early spring. Fully double, coloured forms are also known. Is excellent when grown in woodland or a rock garden. var. *japonica* illus. p.369.
H. transsilvanica, syn. *H. angulosa*. Semi-evergreen, spreading perennial. H 8cm (3in), S 20cm (8in). Shallowly cup-shaped, many-petalled flowers, varying from blue to white or pink, are produced in early spring amid rounded, 3-lobed, hairy, green leaves. Fully double, coloured forms are also known.
H. triloba. See *H. nobilis*.

HEPTACODIUM

Seven-son flower

CAPRIFOLIACEAE

Genus of deciduous shrubs or small trees flowering in late summer. Needs full sun to dappled shade and a well drained soil. Propagate by seed when fresh or stem cuttings in spring.
H. miconioides. Deciduous bushy shrub or small tree. H 6m (20ft) S 2.5-

3m (8-10ft). Foliage is light green in spring, darkening with age, and turning purple in fall. Bark is tan and peeling. Clusters of fragrant, cream flowers appear from late summer to fall and are followed by purple fruits. Zone 5.

Heptapleurum. Reclassified as *Schefflera*.

HERACLEUM

Cow-parsnip

APIACEAE

Genus of tall perennials with alternate, simple, lobed leaves, and compound umbels of flowers. Grow in moist, well drained soil, in full sun to light shade. Propagate by seed sown in place in spring.
H. mantegazzianum (Giant hog-weed). Short-lived, large perennial with hollow, purple-blotched stems. H 3m (10ft) S 1m (3ft). Has very large umbels of white flowers. Can cause severe discomfort if ingested. Foliage can cause skin rash and photodermatitis.

Herald's trumpet. See *Beaumontia grandiflora*, illus. p.204.
Herb Paris. See *Paris*.
Herb, Willow. See *Epilobium*.

HERMANNIA

STERCULIACEAE

Genus of evergreen sub-shrubs and shrubs, grown mainly for their flowers. Tender, min. 7°C (45°F). Prefers full light and fertile, well-drained soil. Water containerized plants freely when in full growth, moderately at other times. Tip prune young plants to produce well-branched specimens. Propagate by softwood or greenwood cuttings in late spring or summer.
H. candicans. See *H. incana*.
H. incana, syn. *H. candicans*. Evergreen, bushy sub-shrub. H and S 60cm (24in) or more. Oval to oblong leaves are covered with white down beneath. Produces small, nodding, bell-shaped, bright yellow flowers, carried in terminal clusters, to 15cm (6in) long, in spring-summer.

HERMODACTYLUS

IRIDACEAE

Genus of one species of spring-flowering tuber, with an elongated, finger-like rootstock, grown mainly for its attractive iris-like flowers. Requires a hot, sunny site, where tubers will ripen well in summer, and well-drained soil. Grows particularly successfully on hot, alkaline soils. Propagate by division in late summer.
H. tuberosus, syn. *Iris tuberosa*, illus. p.414.

Heropito. See *Pseudowintera axillaris*.
Herringbone plant. See *Maranta leuconeura* 'Erythroneura', illus. p.303.
Hers's maple. See *Acer davidii* subsp. *grosseri*.

HESPERALOE

AGAVACEAE

Genus of basal-rosetted, perennial succulents with very narrow, strap-shaped, grooved, dark green leaves, that often have peeling, white fibres at their margins. Is closly related to *Agave* and *Yucca*. Produces offsets freely at base. Tender, min. 3°C (37°F). Grows well in a sunny situation and in very well-drained soil. Propagate by seed or division in spring or summer.
H. parviflora, syn. *Yucca parviflora*, illus. p.462.

HESPERANTHA

IRIDACEAE

Genus of spring-flowering corms with spikes of small, funnel- or cup-shaped flowers. Needs full sun and well-drained soil. Plant in autumn, water through winter and dry off corms after flowering. Propagate by seed in autumn or spring.
H. buhrii. See *H. cucullata*.
H. cucullata, syn. *H. buhrii*. Spring-flowering corm. H 20–30cm (8–12in), S 3–5cm (1¼–2in). Has linear, erect leaves on lower part of branched stems, each of which produces a spike of up to 7 cup-shaped, white flowers, flushed pink or purple outside, that open only at evening.

HESPERIS

BRASSICACEAE/CRUCIFERAE

Genus of late spring- or summer-flowering annuals and perennials. Requires a sunny site and well-drained soil. *H. matronalis* tolerates poor soil. Tends to become woody at base, so raise new stock from seed every few years. Propagate by basal cuttings in spring or by seed in autumn or spring.
H. matronalis illus. p.239.

HESPEROCALLIS

LILIACEAE

Genus of spring- to summer-flowering bulbs. Needs a sunny, well-drained site. Is difficult to cultivate in all but warm, dry areas; in cool, damp climates, protect in a cool greenhouse. Requires ample water in spring, followed by a hot, dry period during its summer dormancy. Propagate by seed in autumn.
H. undulata. Spring- to summer-flowering bulb. H 20–50cm (8–20in), S 10–15cm (4–6in). Has a cluster of long, narrow, wavy-margined leaves, semi-erect or prostrate, at base. Stout stems each bear a spike of upward-facing, funnel-shaped, white flowers, with a central, green stripe along each of the 6 petals.

Hesperoyucca. Reclassified as *Yucca*.

HETEROCENTRON,
syn. HEERIA

MELASTOMATACEAE

Genus of evergreen, summer- and autumn-flowering perennials and shrubs. Tender, min. 5°C (41°F). Requires sun and well-drained soil. Propagate by softwood or stem-tip cuttings in late winter or early spring.
H. elegans, syn. *Schizocentron elegans*, illus. p.284.

Heteromeles arbutifolia. See *Photinia arbutifolia*.

HEUCHERA
Coral bells

SAXIFRAGACEAE

Genus of evergreen, summer-flowering perennials forming large clumps of leaves, that are often tinted bronze or purple. Makes good ground cover. Prefers semi-shaded position and moisture-retentive but well-drained soil. Propagate species by seed in autumn or by division in autumn or spring, and cultivars by division only, using young, outer portions of crown.
H. americana. Evergreen, mound forming perennial. H 45cm (18in) S 30cm (12in). New foliage has brown to copper marbling and veins. Flowers are greenish and not showy. There are many named selections such as **'Chocolate Veil'** with leaves of chocolate brown and silver; **'Pewter Veil'** with silver leaves and charcoal veins; **'Velvet Night'** with almost black leaves.
H. cylindrica **'Greenfinch'** illus. p.276.
H. **'Firebird'**. Evergreen, compact perennial. H 60cm (2ft), S 30cm (1ft). In early summer bears long, feathery sprays of small, pendent, bell-shaped, crimson-scarlet flowers. Leaves are rounded, lobed, toothed and dark green.
H. micrantha var. *diversifolia* **'Palace Purple'** illus. p.277.
H. **'Pearl Drops'**. Evergreen, clump-forming perennial. H 60cm (2ft), S 30cm (1ft). In early summer bears small, pendent, bell-shaped, white flowers tinged pink. Leaves are rounded, lobed, toothed and dark green.
H. **'Red Spangles'** illus. p.282.
H. **'Scintillation'**. Evergreen, clump-forming perennial. H 45–75cm (18–30in), S 30–45cm (12–18in). In early summer produces long, feathery sprays of small, pendent, bell-shaped, deep pink flowers, each rimmed with coral-pink. Bears rounded, lobed, toothed and dark green leaves.

x HEUCHERELLA

SAXIFRAGACEAE

Hybrid genus (*Heuchera* x *Tiarella*) of evergreen, mainly late spring- and summer-flowering perennials. Prefers semi-shade and needs fertile, well-drained soil. Propagate by basal cuttings in spring or by division in spring or autumn.
x *H. alba* **'Bridget Bloom'** illus. p.278.
x *H. tiarelloides* illus. p.278.

Hexastylis. Reclassified as *Asarum*.
Hiba. See *Thujopsis dolabrata*.

HIBBERTIA,
syn. CANDOLLEA

DILLENIACEAE

Genus of evergreen shrubs and twining climbers, grown for their flowers. Tender, min. 5–10°C (41–50°F). Grow in well-drained soil, in full light or semi-shade. Water freely in summer, less at other times. Provide stems with support. Thin out congested growth in spring. Propagate by semi-ripe cuttings in summer.
H. cuneiformis illus. p.146.
H. scandens, syn. *H. volubilis*. Vigorous, evergreen, twining climber. H 6m (20ft). Has 4–9cm (1½–3½in) long, oblong to lance-shaped, glossy, deep green leaves. Saucer-shaped, bright yellow flowers, 4cm (1½in) across, are produced mainly in summer.
H. volubilis. See *H. scandens*.

HIBISCUS

MALVACEAE

Genus of evergreen or deciduous shrubs, trees, perennials and annuals, grown for their flowers. Hardy to tender, min. 5–15°C (41–59°F). Needs full sun and humus-rich, well-drained soil. Water containerized specimens freely when in full growth, moderately at other times. Tip prune young plants to promote bushiness; cut old plants back hard in spring. Propagate by seed in spring; shrubs and trees by greenwood cuttings in late spring or by semi-ripe cuttings in summer; and perennials by division in autumn or spring. Whitefly may cause problems.
H. mutabilis (Confederate rose, Cotton rose). Evergreen, erect to spreading shrub or tree. H and S 3–5m (10–15ft). Tender, min 5°C (41°F). Rounded leaves have 5–7 shallow lobes. In summer-autumn bears funnel-shaped, sometimes double, white or pink flowers, 7–10cm (3–4in) wide, that age from pink to deep red. In light frost dies back to ground level.
H. rosa-sinensis. Evergreen, rounded, leafy shrub. H and S 1.5–3m (5–10ft) or more. Tender, min. 10–13°C (50–55°F). Oval, glossy leaves are coarsely serrated. Produces funnel-shaped, bright crimson flowers, 10cm (4in) wide, mainly in summer but also in spring and autumn. Many colour selections are grown including **'The President'** illus. p.141.
H. schizopetalus. Evergreen, upright, spreading, loose shrub. H to 3m (10ft), S 2m (6ft) or more. Tender, min. 10–13°C (50–55°F). Has oval, serrated leaves and, in summer, pendent, long-stalked flowers, 6cm (2½in) wide, with deeply fringed, reflexed, pink or red petals. May be trained as a climber.
H. sinosyriacus **'Lilac Queen'** illus. p.143.
H. syriacus **'Blue Bird'**. See *H.s.* 'Oiseau Bleu'. **'Diana'** is a deciduous, upright shrub. H 3m (10ft), S 2m (6ft). Has oval, lobed, deep green leaves and very large, trumpet-shaped, pure white flowers, with wavy-edged petals, from late summer to mid-autumn. Zone 6. **'Oiseau Bleu'** (syn. *H.s.* 'Blue Bird') illus. p.145.
'Red Heart' illus. p.139. **'Wood-**

bridge' illus. p.141.
H. trionum illus. p.320.

Hibiscus, Norfolk Island. See *Lagunaria patersonii*.
Hickory. See *Carya*.
   Bitternut. See *Carya cordiformis*.
   Pignut. See *Carya glabra*.
   Shag-bark. See *Carya ovata*, illus. p.69.

HIDALGOA
Climbing dahlia

ASTERACEAE/COMPOSITAE

Genus of evergreen, leaf-stalk climbers, grown for their single, dahlia-like flower heads. Tender, min. 10°C (50°F). Requires full light and humus-rich, well-drained soil. Water freely when in full growth, less at other times. Needs support. In spring thin out crowded stems or cut back all growth to ground level. Propagate by softwood cuttings in spring. Aphids, spider mite and whitefly may be troublesome.
H. wercklei. Moderately vigorous, evergreen, leaf-stalk climber. H 5m (15ft) or more. Oval leaves are divided into 3, 5 or more coarsely serrated leaflets. In summer bears dahlia-like, scarlet flower heads, yellowish in bud.

HIERACIUM
Hawkweed

ASTERACEAE/COMPOSITAE

Genus of perennials; most are weeds, but the species described is grown for its foliage. Needs sun and poor, well-drained soil. Propagate by seed or division in autumn or spring.
H. lanatum illus. p.293.

Higan cherry. See *Prunus* x *subhirtella*.
High bush-cranberry. See *Viburnum trilobum*.
Highbush blueberry. See *Vaccinium corymbosum*, illus. p.160.
Hill cherry. See *Prunus jamasakura*, illus. p.76.

HIMALAYACALAMUS

GRAMINEAE/POACEAE

See also GRASSES, BAMBOOS, RUSHES and SEDGES.
H. falconeri, syn. *Arundinaria falconeri*, *Drepanostachyum falconeri*, *Thamnocalamus falconeri*. Evergreen, clump-forming bamboo. H 5–10m (15–30ft), S 1m (3ft). Greenish-brown stems have a dark purple ring beneath each node. Has 10–15cm (4–6in) long, yellowish-green leaves, without visible tessellation, and unimportant flower spikes.

Himalayan birch. See *Betula utilis*.
Himalayan box. See *Buxus wallichiana*.
Himalayan holly. See *Ilex dipyrena*.
Himalayan honeysuckle. See *Leycesteria formosa*.
Himalayan lilac. See *Syringa emodi*.
Himalayan May apple. See *Podophyllum hexandrum*, illus. p.268.

Himalayan pine. See *Pinus
wallichiana*, illus. p.103.
Himalayan weeping juniper. See
Juniperus recurva, illus. p.108.
Hinoki cypress. See *Chamaecyparis
obtusa*.

HIPPEASTRUM
AMARYLLIDACEAE

Genus of bulbs, grown for their huge,
funnel-shaped flowers. Is often
incorrectly cultivated as *Amaryllis*.
Tender, min. 13–15°C (55–9°F).
Requires a position in full sun or partial
shade and well-drained soil. Plant
large-flowered hybrids in autumn, half
burying bulb; after the leaves die away,
dry off bulb until following autumn.
Smaller, summer-flowering species
should be kept dry while dormant in
winter. Propagate by seed in spring or
by offsets in spring (summer-flowering
species) or autumn (large-flowered
hybrids). All parts may cause mild
stomach upset if ingested.
H. advenum. See *Rhodophiala advena.*
H. 'Apple Blossom' illus. p.425.
H. aulicum, syn. *H. morelianum*, illus.
p.425.
H. 'Belinda'. Winter- and spring-
flowering bulb with a basal leaf cluster.
H 30–50cm (12–20in), S 30cm (12in).
Tender, min. 13°C (55°F). Is similar
to *H. aulicum*, but flowers are deep
velvety-red throughout, stained darker
towards centres.
H. 'Bouquet'. Winter- and spring-
flowering bulb with a basal leaf cluster.
H 30–50cm (12–20in), S 30cm (12in).
Tender, min. 13°C (55°F). Is similar to
H. aulicum, but has very wide, salmon-
pink flowers with deep red veins and
red centres.
H. morelianum. See *H. aulicum.*
H. 'Orange Sovereign' illus. p.425.
H. procerum. See *Worsleya rayneri.*
H. 'Red Lion' illus. p.425.
H. reginae. Summer-flowering bulb.
H to 50cm (20in), S 20–25cm (8–10in).
Tender, min. 13°C (55°F). Flower
stem produces a head of 2–4 scarlet
flowers, each 10–15cm (4–6in) across
and with a star-shaped, green mark
in the throat. Long, strap-shaped,
semi-erect leaves develop at base
after flowering has finished.
H. rutilum. See *H. striatum.*
H. striatum, syn. *H. rutilum*, illus. p.435.
H. 'Striped' illus. p.425.
H. vittatum. Vigorous, spring-flowering
bulb. H 1m (3ft), S 30cm (1ft). Tender,
min. 13°C (55°F). Leaves are broadly
strap-shaped, semi-erect and basal.
Stout, leafless stem precedes leaves
and terminates in a head of 2–6 red-
striped, white flowers, each 12–20cm
(5–8in) across.
H. 'White Dazzler'. Winter- and
spring-flowering bulb with a basal leaf
cluster. H 30–50cm (12–20in), S 30cm
(12in). Tender, min. 13°C (55°F). Is
similar to *H. aulicum*, but has pure
white flowers.

HIPPOCREPIS
Vetch
LEGUMINOSAE/PAPILIONACEAE

Genus of annuals and perennials,

grown for their pea-like flowers.
Requires full sun and well-drained soil.
Propagate by seed in spring or autumn.
Self-seeds readily. May be invasive.
H. comosa (Horseshoe vetch) illus.
p.386. 'E.R. Janes' is a vigorous,
prostrate, woody-based perennial.
H 5–8cm (2–3in), S 15cm (6in) or
more. Rooting stems bear small, loose
spikes of pea-like, yellow flowers from
late spring to late summer. Leaves are
divided, with 3–8 pairs of narrowly
oval leaflets.

HIPPOPHAE
ELAEAGNACEAE

Genus of deciduous shrubs and trees,
with inconspicuous flowers, grown for
their foliage and showy fruits. Separate
male and female plants are required in
order to obtain fruits. Is suitable for
coastal areas, where it is wind-resistant
and excellent when grown as hedging.
Needs a sunny position and is
particularly useful for poor, dry or very
sandy soil. Propagate by softwood
cuttings in summer or by seed
in autumn.
H. rhamnoides illus. p.124.

Hoary willow. See *Salix elaeagnos.*
Hog-weed Giant. See *Heracleum
mantegazzianum.*

HOHERIA
MALVACEAE

Genus of deciduous, semi-evergreen
or evergreen trees and shrubs, grown
for their flowers produced mainly in
summer. Where hardy, grow against a
south- or west-facing wall. Requires sun
or semi-shade and fertile, well-drained
soil. Propagate by semi-ripe cuttings in
summer or by seed in autumn.
H. angustifolia illus. p.90.
H. 'Glory of Amlwch'. Semi-
evergreen, spreading tree. H 7m (22ft),
S 6m (20ft). Has long, narrowly oval,
glossy, bright green leaves and a
profusion of large, 5-petalled, white
flowers from mid- to late summer.
Zone 9.
H. lyallii illus. p.90.
H. populnea (Lace-bark). Evergreen,
spreading tree. H 12m (40ft), S 10m
(30ft). Bears narrowly oval, glossy,
dark green leaves and produces dense
clusters of 5-petalled, white flowers
in late summer and early autumn.
Bark on mature trees is pale brown and
white and often flaky. Zone 9?.
H. sexstylosa (Ribbonwood). Fast-
growing, evergreen, upright tree or
shrub. H 8m (25ft), S 6m (20ft). Glossy,
pale green leaves are narrowly oval and
sharply toothed. Star-shaped, 5-petalled,
white flowers are borne in clusters from
mid- to late summer. Zone 9?.

HOLBOELLIA
LARDIZABALACEAE

Genus of evergreen, twining climbers,
grown mainly for their fine foliage.
Both male and female flowers are
borne on the same plant. Grow in any
well-drained soil, in a position in shade
or full light. Propagate by stem cuttings

in late summer or autumn.
H. coriacea illus. p.205.

HOLCUS
GRAMINEAE/POACEAE

See also GRASSES, BAMBOOS,
RUSHES and SEDGES.
H. mollis (Creeping soft grass).
'Albovariegatus' (syn.
H.m. 'Variegatus') illus. p.306.

Holford pine. See *Pinus* x *holfordiana*,
illus. p.101.
Holly. See *Ilex.*
American. See *Ilex opaca*, illus.
p.98.
Blue. See *Ilex* x *meserveae.*
Box-leaved. See *Ilex crenata.*
Common. See *Ilex aquifolium*, illus.
p.98.
Hedgehog. See *Ilex aquifolium*
'Ferox'.
Himalayan. See *Ilex dipyrena.*
Horned. See *Ilex cornuta.*
Japanese. See *Ilex crenata.*
Moonlight. See *Ilex aquifolium*
'Flavescens'.
Perry's weeping silver. See *Ilex
aquifolium* 'Argentea Marginata
Pendula', illus. p.98.
Sea. See *Eryngium.*
Silver hedgehog. See *Ilex aquifolium*
'Ferox Argentea'.
Silver-margined. See *Ilex aquifolium*
'Argentea Marginata', illus. p.98.
Summer. See *Arctostaphylos
diversifolia.*
Tarajo. See *Ilex latifolia.*
Waterer's gold. See *Ilex aquifolium*
'Watereriana', illus. p.99.
Holly fern. See *Cyrtomium falcatum*,
illus. p.311.
Holly-fern woodsia. See *Woodsia
polystichoides.*
Holly flame pea. See *Chorizema
ilicifolium*, illus. p.157.
Hollyhock. See *Alcea.*
Holm oak. See *Quercus ilex.*

HOLMSKIOLDIA
VERBENACEAE

Genus of evergreen shrubs or
scrambling climbers. Tender, min. 16°C
(61°F). Any fertile, well-drained soil is
suitable in a position in full light. Water
freely in growing season, less at other
times. Requires tying to supports.
Crowded growth should be thinned
out in spring or after flowering has
finished. Propagate by seed in spring
or by softwood or semi-ripe cuttings in
summer. Whitefly and spider mite may
be troublesome.
H. sanguinea (Chinese hat plant,
Mandarin's hat plant). Evergreen,
straggly shrub. H to 5m (15ft), S 2m
(6ft). Leaves are 5–10cm (2–4in) long,
oval and serrated. Produces showy, red
or orange flowers, with saucer-shaped
calyces and central, 5-lobed tubes, in
autumn through to winter.

HOLODISCUS
ROSACEAE

Genus of deciduous shrubs, grown for
their flowers in summer. Needs sun or
semi-shade and any but very dry soil.

Propagate by softwood cuttings
in summer.
H. discolor illus. p.119.

Holy flax. See *Santolina
rosmarinifolia.*

HOMERIA
IRIDACEAE

Genus of spring- or summer-flowering
corms with widely funnel-shaped,
cup-shaped or flattish flowers. Needs a
sunny site and well-drained soil. To
produce flowers in spring, pot in
autumn in a cool greenhouse, water
until after flowering, then dry off for
summer. To produce flowers in summer,
plant in the open in spring. Propagate
by seed, division or offsets in autumn.
H. collina is toxic to livestock.
H. ochroleuca. Spring- or summer-
flowering corm. H to 55cm (22in),
S 5–8cm (2–3in). Slender, wiry stems
each bear 1 or 2 long, narrow, semi-
erect leaves on lower part of stem.
Bears a succession of upright, cup-
shaped to flattish, yellow flowers, each
sometimes with a central, orange stain.

HOMOGYNE
ASTERACEAE/COMPOSITAE

Genus of evergreen perennials, useful
for ground cover in rock gardens and
woodland. Needs shade and moist soil.
Propagate by division in spring or by
seed when fresh.
H. alpina (Alpine coltsfoot).
Evergreen, mat-forming, rhizomatous
perennial. H 8–15cm (3–6in), S 15cm
(6in) or more. Has kidney-shaped,
toothed, glossy leaves and, in summer,
stems, 8–15cm (3–6in) or more long,
each carry a daisy-like, rose-purple
flower head.

Honesty. See *Lunaria.*
Honey locust. See *Gleditsia
triacanthos.*
Honeybush. See *Melianthus major.*
Honeysuckle. See *Lonicera.*
Cape. See *Tecoma capensis.*
Common. See *Lonicera
periclymenum.*
Coral. See *Lonicera sempervirens*,
illus. p.210.
Etruscan. See *Lonicera etrusca.*
Fly. See *Lonicera xylosteum*, illus.
p.140.
Honeysuckle (continued)
French. See *Hedysarum coronarium*,
illus. p.250.
Giant Burmese. See *Lonicera
hildebrandiana.*
Himalayan. See *Leycesteria formosa.*
Japanese. See *Lonicera japonica.*
Late Dutch. See *Lonicera
periclymenum* 'Serotina'.
New Zealand. See *Knightia excelsa.*
Scarlet trumpet. See *Lonicera*
x *brownii.*

HOODIA
ASCLEPIADACEAE

Genus of branching, perennial
succulents with firm, erect, green
stems, generally branching from the

583

base. Tender, min. 10–15°C (50–59°F). Needs full sun and very well-drained soil. Is difficult to cultivate. Water sparingly at all times. Propagate by seed or grafting in spring or summer.

H. bainii. Clump-forming, perennial succulent. H 30cm (12in), S 15cm (6in). Min. 15°C (59°F). Dull green stem has spiral rows of tubercles, each terminating in a sharp thorn. Produces 5-lobed, dull yellow flowers, 7cm (3in) across, from summer to autumn. Keep dry in winter.

H. gordonii. Variable, erect, clump-forming, perennial succulent. H 80cm (32in), S 30cm (12in). Min. 10°C (50°F). Green stem is covered with short, spine-tipped tubercles in distorted rows. Often branches into clumps. Produces 5-lobed, flesh-coloured to brownish flowers in late summer.

Hoop-petticoat daffodil. See *Narcissus bulbocodium* subsp. *bulbocodium.*
Hop. See *Humulus.*
  Common. See *Humulus lupulus.*
Hop hornbeam. See *Ostrya carpinifolia.*
Hop tree. See *Ptelea trifoliata.*

HORDEUM

GRAMINEAE/POACEAE

See also GRASSES, BAMBOOS, RUSHES and SEDGES.
H. jubatum illus. p.307.

HORMINUM

LABIATAE/LAMIACEAE

Genus of one species of basal-rosetted perennial, suitable for rock gardens. Needs sun and well-drained soil. Propagate by division in spring or by seed in autumn.

H. pyrenaicum (Dragon's mouth). Basal-rosetted perennial. H and S 20cm (8in). In summer carries whorls of nodding, short-stalked, funnel-shaped, blue-purple or white flowers above oval, leathery, dark green leaves, 8–10cm (3–4in) long.

Hornbeam. See *Carpinus.*
  American. See *Carpinus caroliniana.*
  American hop. See *Ostrya virginiana,* illus. p.77.
Hornbeam (continued)
  European. See *Carpinus betulus.*
  Hop. See *Ostrya carpinifolia.*
Hornbeam maple. See *Acer carpinifolium,* illus. p.92.
Horned holly. See *Ilex cornuta.*
Horned poppy. See *Glaucium.*
Horned tulip. See *Tulipa acuminata,* illus. p.411.
Horned violet. See *Viola cornuta,* illus. p.349.
Hornwort. See *Ceratophyllum demersum.*
Horse-chestnut. See *Aesculus.*
  Chinese. See *Aesculus chinensis,* illus. p.64.
  Indian. See *Aesculus indica.*
  Japanese. See *Aesculus turbinata.*
  Red. See *Aesculus* x *carnea.*

  Sunrise. See *Aesculus* x *neglecta.*
Horseshoe vetch. See *Hippocrepis comosa,* illus. p.386.

HOSTA
Plantain lily

HOSTACEAE/LILIACEAE

Genus of perennials, grown mainly for their decorative foliage. Forms large clumps that are excellent for ground cover (heights given are those of foliage). Most species prefer shade and rich, moist but well-drained, neutral soil. Propagate by division in early spring. Seed-raised plants (except of *H. ventricosa*) very rarely come true to type. Slug and snail control is essential. See also feature panel pp.288-9.

H. albomarginata. See *H. sieboldii.*

H. **'Blue Moon'.** Slow-growing, compact, clump-forming perennial. H 12cm (5in), S 30cm (12in). Oval to rounded, greyish-blue leaves taper to a point. In mid-summer, dense clusters of trumpet-shaped, mauve flowers are borne just above leaves. Is suitable for a rock garden. Prefers partial shade.

H. **'Blue Wedgwood'** (illus. p.288). Slow-growing, clump-forming perennial. H 30cm (1ft), S 45cm (1½ft). Has wedge-shaped, deeply quilted, blue leaves and, in summer, produces lavender flowers.

H. **'Brim Cup'.** Slow-growing, clump-forming perennial. H 30cm (12in), S 35–40cm (14–16in). Erect, heart-shaped, slightly cupped and puckered, thick, dark green leaves are irregularly margined with cream fading to white. Bears racemes of pale lavender-blue flowers in summer.

H. decorata. Stoloniferous perennial. H 30cm (12in), S 45cm (18in). Oval to rounded, dark green leaves have white margins. Dense racemes of trumpet-shaped, deep violet or sometimes white flowers are borne in mid-summer. f. *normalis* has plain green leaves.

H. fluctuans **'Sagae',** syn. *H.f.* 'Variegated', *H.* 'Sagae'. Vigorous, clump-forming perennial. H and S 1m (3ft). Has undulate, heart-shaped, olive-green leaves, boldly margined creamy-white. Racemes of bell-shaped, near-white flowers are produced in mid- to late summer on leafy, glaucous grey scapes. **'Variegated'** see *H.f.* 'Sagae'.

H. fortunei. Group of vigorous, clump-forming, hybrid perennials. H 75cm–1m (2½–3ft), S 1m (3ft) or more. Leaves are oval to heart-shaped.
'Albopicta' (syn. *H.f.* var. *albopicta;* illus. p.289) has pale green leaves, with creamy-yellow centres, fading to dull green from mid-summer. Racemes of trumpet-shaped, pale violet flowers open above foliage in early summer.
'Aureomarginata' (syn. *H.f.* 'Yellow Edge'; illus. p.289) has mid-green leaves with irregular, creamy-yellow edges. In mid-summer, trumpet-shaped, violet flowers are carried in racemes above foliage. Mass planting produces effective results. Tolerates full sun.
'Yellow Edge' see *H.f.* 'Aureomarginata'.

H. **'Fragrant Bouquet'.** Clump-forming perennial. H 45cm (18in), S 65cm (26in). Has oval to heart-shaped, slightly undulate, glossy, light green leaves with irregular, creamy-yellow margins. Racemes of funnel-shaped, fragrant, mauvish-white flowers are produced in late summer. Tolerates some sun.

H. **'Francee'** (illus. p.288). Vigorous, clump-forming perennial. H 55cm (22in), S 1m (3ft). Has oval to heart-shaped, slightly cupped and puckered, olive-green leaves with irregular, white margins. In summer, produces arching, leafy scapes bearing funnel-shaped, lavender-blue flowers. Is late to emerge.

H. **'Ginko Craig'** (illus. p.288). Low-growing, clump-forming perennial. H and S 30cm (1ft). Has small, narrow, dark green leaves irregularly edged with white. In summer produces spikes of bell-shaped, deep mauve flowers. Is a good edging plant.

H. **'Gold Standard'** (illus. p.289). Vigorous, clump-forming perennial. H 75cm (2½ft), S 1m (3ft). Oval to heart-shaped leaves are pale green, turning to gold from mid-summer, with narrow, regular, dark green margins. Racemes of trumpet-shaped, violet flowers are produced above leaves in mid-summer. Prefers partial shade.

H. **'Golden Prayers'** (illus. p.289). Upright, clump-forming perennial. H 15cm (6in), S 30cm (12in). Cupped leaves are puckered and bright golden green. Flowers are white suffused with pale lavender. Suits a rock garden.

H. **'Golden Tiara'** (illus. p.289). Clump-forming perennial. H 15cm (6in), S 30cm (12in). Neat, broadly heart-shaped, dark green leaves have well-defined, chartreuse-yellow edges. In summer produces tall spikes of lavender-purple flowers.

H. **'Grand Tiara'** (illus. p.289). Vigorous perennial forming a compact mound. H 30cm (12in), S 50cm (20in). Has ovate to heart-shaped, mid-green leaves with irregular, wide, yellow margins. In summer, has scapes of bell-shaped, sometimes remontant, deep purple flowers, each striped lavender-blue within.

H. **'Great Expectations'** (illus. p.289). Clump-forming perennial. H 55cm (22in), S 85cm (34in). Has green-margined, white leaf stalks bearing heart-shaped, stiff, puckered, thick leaves; they are glaucous, blue-green, and irregularly but widely splashed with yellow, fading to white in the centres. In early summer, bell-shaped, greyish-white flowers are borne on leafy scapes.

H. **'Ground Master'** (illus. p.288). Vigorous, stoloniferous, prostrate perennial. H 25cm (10in), S 55cm (22in). Has ovate to lance-shaped, matt, olive-green leaves with wavy, irregular, creamy margins, fading to white. Straight, leafy scapes of funnel-shaped, purple flowers are borne in summer.

H. **'Hadspen Blue'** (illus. p.288). Slow-growing, clump-forming perennial. H and S 30cm (12in). Smooth leaves are heart-shaped and deep glaucous blue. Produces short spikes of lavender flowers in summer.

H. **'Halcyon'** (illus. p.288). Robust, clump-forming perennial. H 30cm

(1ft), S 1m (3ft). Has heart-shaped, tapering, greyish-blue leaves that fade to muddy-green in full sun; texture may be spoiled by heavy rain. Heavy clusters of trumpet-shaped, violet-mauve flowers open just above foliage in mid-summer.

H. **'Honeybells'** (illus. p.289). Clump-forming perennial. H 1m (3ft), S 60cm (2ft). Light green leaves are blunt at the tips and have wavy edges. In late summer bears fragrant, pale lilac flowers.

H. hypoleuca (White-backed hosta). Clump-forming perennial. H 45cm (1½ft), S 1m (3ft). Broadly oval leaves have widely spaced veins and are pale green above, striking white beneath. In late summer bears drooping racemes of trumpet-shaped, milky-violet flowers with mauve-flecked, pale green bracts. Tolerates full sun.

H. **'Kabitan'**, syn. *H. sieboldii* 'Kabitan' (illus. p.289). Clump-forming perennial, spreading by stolons. H to 30cm (1ft), S 60cm (2ft). Lance-shaped, thin-textured, glossy leaves are yellow-centred and have narrow, undulating, dark green margins. In early summer produces a short raceme of small, trumpet-shaped, pale violet flowers. Is suitable for a shaded rock garden. Needs establishing in a pot for first few years.

H. kikutii. Clump-forming perennial. H 40cm (16in), S 60cm (2ft). Has oval to lance-shaped, deeply veined, dark green leaves. Racemes of bell-shaped, near-white flowers are borne in a tight bunch at the top of the raceme on conspicuously leaning scapes, in mid-summer. var. *caput-avis* is smaller, and the flower bud resembles a bird's head. **'Kifukurin'** has larger leaves, attractively margined with cream.

H. **'Krossa Regal'** (illus. p.288). Vase-shaped, clump-forming perennial. H and S 1m (3ft). Arching, deeply ribbed leaves are greyish blue. Produces tall spikes of pale lilac flowers in summer. Tolerates sun.

H. lancifolia. Arching, clump-forming perennial. H 45cm (1½ft), S 75cm (2½ft). Has narrowly lance-shaped, thin-textured, glossy, mid-green leaves. Produces racemes of trumpet-shaped, deep violet flowers above foliage in late summer through to autumn.

H. **'Love Pat'** (illus p.288). Vigorous, clump-forming perennial. H and S to 60cm (2ft). Produces rounded, deeply puckered, deep glaucous blue leaves. Bears racemes of pale lilac flowers during summer.

H. montana. Vigorous, clump-forming perennial. H 1.1m (3½ft), S 1m (3ft). Has oval, prominently veined, glossy, dark green leaves. Racemes of trumpet-shaped, pale violet flowers open well above foliage in mid-summer. Slower-growing **'Aureomarginata'** (illus. p.289) has leaves irregularly edged with golden-yellow. Is always the first hosta to appear in spring.

H. **'Moonlight'** (illus. p.289). Clump-forming perennial. H 50cm (20in), S 70cm (28in). Has pale yellow leaves that emerge olive-green, narrowly margined white. Requires full shade.

H. nigrescens. Vigorous, clump-forming perennial. H 70cm (28in),

S 65cm (26in). Has oval to heart-shaped, concave, puckered, glaucous grey-green leaves, and racemes of funnel-shaped, pearl-grey to white flowers on 1.4m (4½ft) undulating scapes in late summer.
H. 'Paxton's Original'. See *H. sieboldii.*
H. 'Pearl Lake'. Vigorous, clump-forming perennial. H 35–40cm (14–16in), S 1m (3ft). Has heart-shaped, flat, glaucous grey-green leaves, and racemes of bell-shaped, opalescent, lavender-blue flowers on scapes towering above the leaf mound in summer.
H. 'Piedmont Gold' (illus. p.289). Slow-growing, clump-forming perennial. H 60cm (2ft), S 75cm (2½ft). Smooth leaves are bright yellowish-green with fluted margins. Racemes of white flowers are produced in summer. Is best in light shade.
H. plantaginea (illus. p.289). Lax, clump-forming perennial. H 60cm (2ft), S 1.2m (4ft). Leaves are oval and glossy, pale green. Rising well above these are flower stems crowned in late summer and early autumn with fragrant, trumpet-shaped, white flowers that open in the evening. Prefers sunny conditions. **'Grandiflora'** (syn. *H.p.* var. *japonica*) has larger, longer-tubed flowers, to 13cm (5in) long. Prefers sun. var. *japonica* see *H.p.* 'Grandiflora'.
H. rectifolia. Upright, clump-forming perennial. H 1m (3ft), S 75cm (2½ft). Produces oval to lance-shaped, dark green leaves and racemes of large, trumpet-shaped, violet flowers from mid- to late summer.
H. 'Regal Splendor' (illus. p.288). Clump-forming perennial. H and S 1m (3ft). Arching, greyish-blue leaves are suffused white or yellow at the margins. Talls spikes of lilac flowers are produced in summer.
H. 'Royal Standard' (illus. p.289). Upright, clump-forming perennial. H 60cm (2ft), S 1.2m (4ft). Broadly oval leaves are glossy, pale green. Pure white, slightly fragrant, trumpet-shaped flowers are carried well above foliage and open in the evening. Prefers sun.
H. 'Sagae'. See *H. fluctuans* 'Sagae'.
H. 'Shade Fanfare' (illus. p.288). Vigorous, clump-forming perennial. H 45cm (1½ft), S 75cm (2½ft). Heart-shaped leaves are pale green with cream margins. In summer has an abundance of lavender flowers.
H. sieboldiana (illus. p.288). Robust, clump-forming perennial. H 1m (3ft) or more, S 1.5m (5ft). Large, heart-shaped, deeply ribbed, puckered leaves are bluish-grey. Racemes of trumpet-shaped, very pale lilac flowers open in early summer, just above foliage. Makes good ground cover. Tolerates sun, but leaves may then turn dull green. var. *elegans* (illus. p.288) has larger, bluer leaves. **'Frances Williams'** (illus. p.289) has yellow-edged leaves, is slower-growing and should not be grown in full sun.
H. sieboldii, syn. *H. albomarginata, H.* 'Paxton's Original' (illus. p.288). Vigorous, clump-forming perennial. H 45cm (1½ft), S 60cm (2ft). Lance-shaped, round-tipped leaves are mid- to

dark green with narrow, irregular, white edges. Racemes of trumpet-shaped, violet flowers appear at tops of stems in late summer and are followed by ovoid, glossy, dark green, then brown seed heads that are useful for flower arrangements. **'Kabitan'** see *H.* 'Kabitan'.
H. 'Snowden' (illus. p.288). Clump-forming perennial. H and S 1m (3ft) or more. Produces large, pointed glaucous blue leaves that age to sage green. Tall stems bear white tinged with green flowers in summer.
H. 'Sum and Substance' (illus. p.289). Vigorous, clump-forming perennial. H and S to 1m (3ft). Produces large, greenish-gold leaves that are thick in texture and, in mid-summer, tall spikes of pale lavender flowers appear. Tolerates full sun.
H. 'Summer Music'. Clump-forming perennial. H 30cm (12in), S 40cm (16in). Twisted, oval to heart-shaped, white leaves, of thin substance, are widely and irregularly margined light green. Racemes of bell-shaped, pale lavender flowers are produced in summer.
H. 'Tall Boy' (illus. p.289). Clump-forming perennial. H and S 60cm (2ft). Has large, bright green leaves ending in long points. In summer an abundance of rich lilac flowers is produced on stems 1.2m (4ft) tall or more.
H. tardiflora (illus. p.288). Slow-growing, clump-forming perennial. H 30cm (1ft), S 75cm (2½ft). Has narrowly lance-shaped, thick-textured, dark green leaves. Dense racemes of trumpet-shaped, lilac-purple flowers open just above foliage from late summer to early autumn.
H. 'Thomas Hogg'. See *H. undulata* var. *albomarginata.*
H. tokudama (illus. p.288). Very slow-growing, clump-forming perennial. H 45cm (1½ft), S 75cm (2½ft). Produces cup-shaped, puckered, blue leaves. Racemes of trumpet-shaped, pale lilac-grey flowers appear just above foliage in mid-summer.
'Aureonebulosa' (syn. *H.t.* 'Variegata'; illus. p.288) has irregular, cloudy-yellow centres to leaves.
'Flavocircinalis', often mistaken for a juvenile *H.* 'Frances Williams', has heart-shaped leaves with wide, irregular, creamy-yellow margins.
'Variegata' see *H.t.* 'Aureonebulosa'.
H. undulata var. **albomarginata,** syn. *H.* 'Thomas Hogg' (illus. p.288). Clump-forming perennial. H 55cm (22in), S 60cm (24in). Has oval to lance-shaped, round-tipped, mid-green leaves, irregularly margined cream to near-white. Racemes of trumpet-shaped, pale mauve flowers rise well above the foliage in early and mid-summer. var. *erromena* is robust, H 45cm (1½ft), S 60cm (2ft), and bears trumpet-shaped, pale mauve flowers high above oblong, wavy, mid-green leaves. Leaves of var. *undulata* have irregular, white centres on first crop, white streaks on second. Leaf stalks and flower bracts are white with narrow, green margins. var. *univittata* (illus. p.288) is vigorous with oval, mid-green leaves that have narrow, white centres.

H. ventricosa (illus. p.289). Clump-forming perennial. H 70cm (28in), S 1m (3ft) or more. Has heart-shaped to oval, slightly wavy-edged, glossy, dark green leaves. Racemes of bell-shaped, deep purple flowers appear above foliage in late summer. Usually comes true from seed. **'Variegata'** (syn. *H.v.* 'Aureomarginata'; illus. p.289) has leaves with irregular, cream margins.
H. venusta (illus. p.289). Vigorous, mat-forming perennial. H 2.5cm (1in), S to 30cm (12in). Has oval to lance-shaped, mid- to dark green leaves and abundant racemes of trumpet-shaped, purple flowers, borne well above foliage in mid-summer. Is suitable for a rock garden.
H. 'Veronica Lake'. Vigorous, clump-forming perennial. H 35–40cm (14–16in), S 1m (3ft). Has striking, cream-margined, heart-shaped, flat, glaucous grey-green leaves, and racemes of bell-shaped, opalescent, lavender-blue flowers in summer.
H. 'Wide Brim' (illus. p.289). Vigorous, clump-forming perennial. H and S to 75cm (2½ft). Leaves are heavily puckered and dark blue-green with wide irregular, creamy-white margins. Produces white or very pale lavender flowers in summer.
H. 'Yellow River' (illus. p.289). Clump-forming perennial. H 55cm (22in), S 1m (3ft). Has ovate to heart-shaped, pointed, thick, dark green leaves with irregular, yellow margins. Leafy scapes of funnel-shaped, very pale lavender-blue flowers are produced in early summer.
H. 'Zounds' (illus. p.289). Slow-growing, clump-forming perennial. H and S to 1m (3ft). Large, bright gold leaves are heavily puckered and have metallic sheen. White or pale lavender flowers are produced in early summer.

Hosta, White-backed. See *Hosta hypoleuca.*
Hottentot fig. See *Carpobrotus edulis.*

HOTTONIA

PRIMULACEAE

Genus of deciduous, perennial, submerged water plants, grown for their handsome foliage and delicate, primula-like flowers. Needs sun and clear, cool water, still or running. Periodically thin overcrowded growth. Propagate by stem cuttings in spring or summer.
H. palustris illus. p.447.

Hot-water plant. See *Achimenes.*
Hound's tongue. See *Cynoglossum.*
Houseleek. See *Sempervivum.*
  Cobweb. See *Sempervivum arachnoideum*, illus. p.389.
  Common. See *Sempervivum tectorum*, illus. p.389.
  Roof. See *Sempervivum tectorum*, illus. p.389.
Houstonia. Reclassified as *Hedyotis.*

HOUTTUYNIA

SAURURACEAE

Genus of one species of perennial or deciduous marginal water plant, with far-spreading rhizomes. Is suitable for ground cover, although invasive. Prefers position in semi-shade and moist soil or shallow water, beside streams and ponds. Propagate by runners in spring.
H. cordata 'Chameleon', syn. *H.c.* 'Variegata', illus. p.447.
'Flore Pleno' (syn. *H.c.* 'Plena') is a spreading perennial. H 15–60cm (6–24in), S indefinite. Spikes of insignificant flowers, surrounded by 8 or more oval, white bracts, are produced above aromatic, fleshy, leathery, heart-shaped, pointed leaves, in spring. **'Plena'** see *H.c.* 'Flore Pleno'. **'Variegata'** see *H.c.* 'Chamaeleon'.

HOVENIA

RHAMNACEAE

Genus of one species of deciduous, summer-flowering tree, grown for its foliage. Young, unripened growth is susceptible to frost damage. Does best in a position in full sun and requires fertile, well-drained soil. Propagate by softwood cuttings in summer or by seed in autumn.
H. dulcis illus. p.79.

HOWEA,

syn. HOWEIA, KENTIA

ARECACEAE/PALMAE

Genus of evergreen palms, grown for their ornamental appearance. Tender, min. 16–18°C (61–4°F). Needs partial shade and humus-rich, well-drained soil. Water containerized specimens freely in summer, minimally in winter and moderately at other times. Propagate by seed in spring at not less than 26°C (79°F). Is prone to spider mite.
H. forsteriana (Paradise palm, Sentry palm, Thatch-leaf palm). Evergreen, upright palm with a slender stem. H 10m (30ft), S 3–4m (10–12ft). Has spreading, feather-shaped leaves, 1.5–2.5m (5–8ft) long, made up of strap-shaped leaflets. Branching clusters of several spikes of small, greenish-brown flowers are produced in winter.

Howeia. Reclassified as *Howea.*

HOYA

ASCLEPIADACEAE

Genus of evergreen, woody-stemmed, twining and/or root climbers and loose shrubs, grown for their flowers and foliage. Tender, min. 5–18°C (41–64°F). Grow in humus-rich, well-drained soil with semi-shade in summer. Water moderately when in full growth, sparingly at other times. Stems require support. Cut back and thin out crowded stems after flowering or in spring. Propagate by semi-ripe cuttings in summer.
H. australis, syn. *H. darwinii* of

gardens, illus. p.208.
H. bella. See *H. lanceolata* subsp.
bella.
H. carnosa illus. p.208.
H. coronaria. Slow-growing, evergreen,
woody-stemmed, twining and root
climber. H 2–3m (6–10ft). Min. 16–18°C
(61–4°F). Bears thick, leathery, oblong to
oval leaves. In summer, bell-shaped,
yellow to white flowers are produced,
each spotted with red.
  H. darwinii of gardens. See
H. australis.
H. imperialis. Vigorous, evergreen,
woody-stemmed, twining and root
climber. H to 6m (20ft). Min. 16–18°C
(61–4°F). Oval, leathery, leaves are
covered with down and 10–23cm
(4–9in) long. In summer, produces
large, star-shaped, brown-purple to
deep magenta flowers, each with a
cream centre.
H. lanceolata subsp. **bella,** syn.
H. bella, illus. p.208.
H. macgillivrayi illus. p.205.

Huckleberry. See *Gaylussacia.*
  Black. See *Gaylussacia baccata.*

HUERNIA
ASCLEPIADACEAE

Genus of clump-forming, perennial
succulents with finger-like, usually
4-angled stems. Produces minute,
short-lived, deciduous leaves on
new growth. Tender, min. 8–11°C
(46–52°F). Requires a position in sun
or partial shade and extremely well-
drained soil. Is one of easiest stapeliads
to grow. Propagate by seed or stem
cuttings in spring or summer.
H. macrocarpa. Deciduous, clump-
forming, perennial succulent. H and
S 10cm (4in). Min. 8°C (46°F). Has
finger-like, 4- or 5-sided, grey-green
stems. In summer through to autumn
bell-shaped, yellow flowers, with
narrow, purple bands and recurved tips,
are produced at base of new growth.
var. **arabica** illus. p.476.
H. pillansii. Deciduous, clump-
forming, perennial succulent. H 5cm
(2in), S 10cm (4in). Min. 11°C (52°F).
Has a finger-like, light green stem that
is densely covered with short tubercles
with hair-like tips. Produces bell-
shaped, creamy-red flowers, with red
spots, at base of new growth, in
summer through to autumn.
H. primulina. See *H. thuretii* var.
primulina.
H. thuretii var. **primulina,** syn.
H. primulina. Deciduous, clump-
forming, perennial succulent. H 10cm
(4in), S 15cm (6in). Min. 11°C (52°F).
Stems are short, thick and grey-green.
In summer through to autumn bell-
shaped, dull yellow flowers, 2cm (¾in)
across, with reflexed, blackish tips, are
produced at base of new growth.
H. zebrina (Owl-eyes). Deciduous,
clump-forming, perennial succulent.
H 10cm (4in), S 15cm (6in). Min. 11°C
(52°F). Is similar to *H. thuretii* var.
primulina, but produces pale yellow-
green flowers with conspicuous bands
of red-brown.

Humble plant. See *Mimosa pudica,*
illus. p.176.
Humea. Reclassified as *Calomeria.*

HUMULUS
Hop
CANNABACEAE

Genus of herbaceous, twining climbers.
Is useful for concealing unsightly
garden sheds or tree-stumps. Male
and female flowers are produced on
separate plants; female flower spikes
become drooping clusters known as
'hops'. Grow in a position in sun or
semi-shade and in any well-drained
soil. Propagate by tip cuttings in spring.
H. lupulus (Common hop).
'Aureus' illus. p.206.

Hunangemoho grass. See
Chionochloa conspicua.
Hungarian oak. See *Quercus
frainetto,* illus. p.69.

HUNNEMANNIA
PAPAVERACEAE

Genus of poppy-like perennials, usually
grown as annuals. Grow in sun and in
poor to fertile, very well-drained soil.
Dead-head plants regularly. Provide
support, especially in windy areas.
Propagate by seed sown under glass in
early spring, or outdoors in mid-spring.
H. fumariifolia (Mexican tulip poppy).
'Sunlite' is a fast-growing, upright
perennial, grown as an annual. H 60cm
(24in), S 20cm (8in). Has oblong, very
divided, bluish-green leaves and, in
summer and early autumn, poppy-like,
semi-double, bright yellow flowers, to
8cm (3in) wide.

Huntingdon elm. See *Ulmus* x
hollandica 'Vegeta'.
Huntsman's cup. See *Sarracenia
purpurea.*
Hupeh crab. See *Malus hupehensis,*
illus. p.74.
Hupeh rowan. See *Sorbus hupehensis.*
Hyacinth. See *Hyacinthus.*
  Feather grape. See *Muscari
comosum* 'Plumosum', illus. p.432.
  Grape. See *Muscari.*
  Summer. See *Galtonia candicans,*
illus. p.397.
  Tassel grape. See *Muscari comosum.*
  Water. See *Eichhornia crassipes,*
illus. p.448.
Hyacinth bean. See *Lablab purpureus,*
illus. p.211.

HYACINTHELLA
HYACINTHACEAE/LILIACEAE

Genus of spring-flowering bulbs with
short spikes of small, bell-shaped
flowers, suitable for rock gardens and
cold greenhouses. Requires an open,
sunny situation and well-drained soil,
which partially dries out while bulbs
are dormant in summer. Propagate by
seed in autumn.
H. leucophaea illus. p.432.

HYACINTHOIDES,
syn. ENDYMION
Bluebell
HYACINTHACEAE/LILIACEAE

Genus of spring-flowering bulbs,
grown for their bluebell flowers. Is
suitable for growing in borders and for
naturalizing in grass beneath trees and
shrubs. Requires partial shade and
plenty of moisture. Prefers heavy soil.
Plant bulbs in autumn 10–15cm (4–6in)
deep. Propagate by division in late
summer or by seed in autumn. All parts
may irritate skin on contact, and may
cause severe discomfort if ingested.
H. hispanica, syn. *Scilla campanulata,
S. hispanica,* illus. p.414.
H. italica, syn. *Scilla italica.* Spring-
flowering bulb. H 15–20cm (6–8in),
S 5–8cm (2–3in). Produces a basal
cluster of narrowly strap-shaped, semi-
erect leaves. Leafless stem produces
a conical spike of many flattish, star-
shaped, blue flowers, 1cm (½in) across.
H. non-scripta, syn. *Scilla non-scripta,
S. nutans,* illus. p.414.

HYACINTHUS
Hyacinth
HYACINTHACEAE/LILIACEAE

Genus of bulbs, grown for their dense
spikes of fragrant, tubular flowers; is
ideal for spring bedding displays and
for pot cultivation indoors. Needs an
open, sunny situation or partial shade
and well-drained soil. Plant in autumn.
For winter flowers, force large-size,
specially 'treated' bulbs of *H. orientalis*
cultivars by potting in early autumn,
then keep cool and damp for several
weeks to ensure adequate root systems
develop. When shoot tips are visible,
move into max. 10°C (50°F) at first,
raising temperature as more shoot
appears and giving as much light as
possible. After forcing, keep in a cool
place to finish growth, then plant out
to recover. Propagate by offsets in late
summer or early autumn. All parts
may cause stomach upset if ingested;
contact with the bulbs may aggravate
skin allergies. See also feature
panel p.431.
H. amethystinus. See *Brimeura
amethystina.*
H. azureus. See *Muscari azureum.*
H. orientalis 'Amsterdam'. Winter-
or spring-flowering bulb. H 10–20cm
(4–8in), S 6–10cm (2½–4in). Has strap-
shaped, channelled, semi-erect, glossy,
basal leaves that develop fully only
after flowering. Flower stem carries
a dense, cylindrical spike of fragrant,
tubular, bright rose-red flowers, each
with 6 recurving petals. **'Blue Jacket'**
(illus. p.431) has very large spikes of
navy-blue flowers with purple veining.
'City of Haarlem' (illus. p.431) bears
pale yellow flowers in a dense spike.
'Delft Blue' (illus. p.431) has violet-
flushed, soft blue flowers. **'Distinction'**
(illus. p.431) produces slender, open
spikes of reddish-purple flowers; those
of **'Jan Bos'** (illus. p.431) are crimson.
'Lady Derby' (illus. p.431) bears rose-
pink flowers. **'L'Innocence'** has ivory-
white flowers. **'Ostara'** (illus. p.431)
has a large spike of blue flowers, with

a dark stripe along each petal centre.
'Pink Pearl' has a dense spike of
carmine-pink flowers. Flowers of
'Princess Maria Christina' (illus.
p.431) are salmon-pink; those of
'Queen of the Pinks' (illus. p.431) are
soft pink. **'Violet Pearl'** (illus. p.431)
produces spikes of violet flowers.
'White Pearl' (illus. p.431) has pure
white flowers.

HYDRANGEA
HYDRANGEACEAE

Genus of deciduous shrubs and
deciduous or evergreen, root climbers,
grown for their mainly domed or
flattened flower heads. Each head
usually consists of masses of small,
inconspicuous, fertile flowers,
surrounded by or mixed with much
larger, sterile flowers bearing showy,
petal-like sepals. However, in some
forms, all or most of the flowers are
sterile. Prefers a position in full sun or
semi-shade and fertile, moist but well-
drained soil. Requires more shade in
dry areas. Propagate by softwood
cuttings in summer. All parts of
hydrangeas may cause mild stomach
upset if ingested; contact with the
foliage may aggravate skin allergies.
See also feature panel p.144.
H. anomala subsp. **petiolaris.** See
H. petiolaris.
H. arborescens 'Annabelle' (illus.
p.144). Deciduous, open shrub. H and
S 2.5m (8ft). Long-stalked, broadly
oval leaves are glossy, dark green
above, paler beneath. Very large,
rounded heads of mainly sterile, white
flowers are borne in summer. Zone 2b.
'Grandiflora' (illus. p.144) has smaller
flower heads but larger sterile flowers.
Zone 3b.
H. aspera Villosa Group. See
H. villosa. subsp. *sargentiana* see
H. sargentiana.
H. bretschneideri. See *H. heteromalla*
'Bretschneideri'.
H. heteromalla. Deciduous, arching
shrub. H 5m (15ft), S 3m (10ft).
Narrowly oval, dark green leaves turn
yellow in autumn. Broad, flat, open
heads of white flowers are borne in
mid- and late summer, the outer ones
ageing to deep pink. Zone 3b.
'Bretschneideri' (syn.
H. bretschneideri) illus. p.144. Zone 4.
H. involucrata. Deciduous, spreading,
open shrub. H 1m (3ft), S 2m (6ft).
Has broadly heart-shaped, bristly,
mid-green leaves. During late summer
and autumn bears heads of small, blue,
inner flowers surrounded by large, pale
blue to white, outer ones. Zone 8.
'Hortensis' (illus. p.144) is smaller
and has clusters of cream, pink and
green flowers. Zone 8.
H. macrophylla. Deciduous, bushy
shrub. H 1.5–2m (5–6ft), S 2–2.5m
(6–8ft). Has oval, toothed, glossy, light
green leaves. In mid- to late summer,
blue or purple flowers are produced in
acid soils with a pH of up to about 5.5.
In neutral or alkaline soils above this
level, flowers are pink or red. White
flowers are not affected by pH. Prune
older shoots back to base in spring.
Trim back winter-damaged shoots to
new growth and remove spent flower

heads in spring. Is divided into 2 groups: Hortensias, which have domed, dense heads of mainly sterile flowers; and Lacecaps, which have flat, open heads, each with fertile flowers in the centre and larger, sterile flowers on the outside that are green in bud. Zone 6.

'Altona' (Hortensia; illus. p.144), H 1m (3ft), S 1.5m (5ft), has large heads of rich pink to deep purple-blue flowers. **'Ami Pasquier'** (Hortensia), H 60cm (2ft), S 1m (3ft), is compact, with deep crimson or blue-purple flowers. **'Blue Bonnet'** (Hortensia; illus. p.144), H 2m (6ft), S to 2.5m (8ft), produces heads of rich blue or lilac to pink flowers.

'Blue Wave' (syn. *H.m.* 'Mariesii Perfecta', Lacecap; illus. p.144), H 2m (6ft), S to 2.5m (8ft), produces heads of rich blue or lilac to pink flowers. Flower heads of **'Générale Vicomtesse de Vibraye'** (Hortensia; illus. p.144), H and S 1.5m (5ft), are rounded and pale blue or pink. Foliage is light green. **'Hamburg'** (Hortensia; illus. p.144), H 1m (3ft), S 1.5m (5ft), is vigorous and has large, deep pink to deep blue flowers with serrated sepals. **'Lanarth White'** (Lacecap; illus. p.144), H and S 1.5m (5ft), has pink or blue fertile flowers edged with pure white sterile flowers. **'Lilacina'** (Lacecap; illus. p.144), H and S 2m (6ft), has deep, lilac, central flowers and pinkish-purple outer flowers. **'Madame E. Mouillère'** (Hortensia) has white flowers, becoming pale pink, and prefers partial shade. **'Mariesii Perfecta'** see *H.m.* 'Blue Wave'. subsp. *serrata* see *H. serrata*. subsp. *serrata* **'Preziosa'** see *H.* 'Preziosa'. **'Veitchii'** (Lacecap; illus. p.144) has lilac-blue flowers. All zone 6.

H. paniculata **'Brussels Lace'** (illus. p.144). Deciduous, upright, open shrub. H and S to 3m (10ft). Has large, pointed, dark green leaves. Bears delicate, open panicles of white flowers in late summer and early autumn. **'Floribunda'** (illus. p.144) has dense conical heads of small, fertile, central flowers surrounded by large, white ray flowers. **'Grandiflora'** has large, oval and dark green leaves. Large, conical panicles of mostly sterile, white flowers turn pink or red from late summer. Prune back hard in spring to obtain largest panicles. **'Interhydia'** see *H.p.* 'PINK DIAMOND'. Flower heads of **'PINK DIAMOND'** ('Interhydia') (illus. p.144) turn pink with age. **'Praecox'** (illus. p.144) flowers from mid-summer. **'Tardiva'** has both fertile and sterile flowers from early to mid-autumn. **'Unique'** (illus. p.144) is similar to 'Grandiflora' but more vigorous and has larger flowers. All zone 3b.

H. petiolaris, syn. *H. anomala* subsp. *petiolaris*, illus. p.208.

H. **'Preziosa'**, syn. *H. macrophylla* subsp. *serrata* 'Preziosa', *H. serrata* 'Preziosa'. Deciduous, bushy shrub. H 1.5–2m (5–6ft), S 2–2.5m (6–8ft). Has oval, toothed, light green leaves. Bears pink flowers, becoming deep crimson. Zone 5b.

H. quercifolia (Oak-leaved hydrangea; illus. p.144). Deciduous, bushy, mound-forming shrub. H and S 2m

(6ft). Deeply lobed, dark green leaves turn red and purple in autumn. Has white flower heads from mid-summer to mid-autumn. Zone 5b.

H. sargentiana, syn. *H. aspera* subsp. *sargentiana*. Deciduous, upright, gaunt shrub. H 2.5m (8ft), S 2m (6ft). Has peeling bark, stout shoots and very large, narrowly oval, bristly, dull green leaves with grey down beneath. In late summer to mid-autumn bears broad heads of flowers, the inner ones small and blue or deep purple, the outer ones larger and white, sometimes flushed purplish-pink. Zone 6.

H. serrata, syn. *H. macrophylla* subsp. *serrata* (illus p.144). Deciduous, bushy, dense shrub. H and S 1.2m (4ft). Has slender stems and light green leaves. From mid- to late summer bears flat heads of pink, lilac or white inner and pink or blue outer flowers. Zone 6. **'Bluebird'** (illus. p.144) has pale pink, pale purple or blue flowers. Zone 5b. **'Preziosa'** see *H.* 'Preziosa'.

H. villosa (syn. *H. aspera* Villosa Group; illus. p.144). Deciduous, upright shrub. H and S 3m (10ft). Has peeling bark and, from late summer to mid-autumn, heads of small, blue or purple, central flowers and larger, white, sometimes flushed purplish-pink, outer ones. Zone 6.

Hydrangea
　Climbing. See *Hydrangea petiolaris*, illus. p.208.
　Oak-leaved. See *Hydrangea quercifolia*, illus. p.144.

HYDROCHARIS
HYDROCHARITACEAE

Genus of one species of deciduous, perennial, floating water plant, grown for its foliage and flowers. Requires an open, sunny position in still water. Propagate by detaching young plantlets as required.
H. morsus-ranae illus. p.446.

Hydrocleis. Reclassified as *Hydrocleys*.

HYDROCLEYS,
syn. HYDROCLEIS
LIMNOCHARITACEAE

Genus of deciduous or evergreen, annual or perennial, water plants, grown for their floating foliage and attractive flowers. Tender, min. 1°C (34°F). Is best grown in large aquariums and tropical pools with plenty of light. Propagate by seed when ripe or by tip cuttings year-round.
H. nymphoides illus. p.449.

HYGROPHILA
ACANTHACEAE

Genus of deciduous or evergreen, perennial, submerged water plants and marsh plants, grown for their foliage. Tender, min. 13°C (55°F). Remove fading leaves regularly. Propagate by stem cuttings in spring or summer.
H. polysperma. Deciduous, perennial, submerged water plant. S indefinite. Lance-shaped, pale green leaves are

borne on woody stems. Given water above 16°C (61°F), is evergreen. Is suitable for a tropical aquarium.

HYLOCEREUS
CACTACEAE

Genus of fast-growing, perennial cacti with erect, slender, climbing stems that are jointed into sections, and many aerial roots. Makes successful grafting stock except in northern Europe. Tender, min. 11°C (52°F). Requires a position in sun or partial shade and very well-drained soil. Propagate by stem cuttings in spring or summer.
H. undatus (Night-blooming cereus, Queen-of-the-night). Fast-growing, climbing, perennial cactus. H 1m (3ft), S indefinite. Bears freely branching, 3-angled, weakly spined, dark green stems, 7cm (3in) wide and jointed into sections. In summer produces flattish, white flowers, 30cm (12in) across, that last only one night.

HYLOMECON
PAPAVERACEAE

Genus of one species of vigorous perennial, grown for its large, cup-shaped flowers. Is good for rock gardens, borders and woodlands but may be invasive. Prefers partial shade and humus-rich, moist soil. Propagate by division in spring or by seed in autumn.
H. japonica illus. p.350.

Hylotelephium anacampseros. See *Sedum anacampseros.*
Hylotelephium cauticola. See *Sedum cauticola.*
Hylotelephium ewersii. See *Sedum ewersii.*
Hylotelephium populifolium. See *Sedum populifolium.*
Hylotelephium spectabile. See *Sedum spectabile.*
Hylotelephium tatarinowii. See *Sedum tatarinowii.*
Hymenanthera. Reclassified as *Melicytus.*

HYMENOCALLIS
AMARYLLIDACEAE

Genus of bulbs, some of which are evergreen, grown for their fragrant flowers, somewhat like those of large daffodils. Tender, min. 15°C (59°F). Needs a sheltered site, full sun or partial shade and well-drained soil. Plant in early summer, lifting for winter in cold districts. Alternatively, grow in a heated greenhouse; reduce water in winter, without drying out completely, then repot in spring. Propagate by offsets in spring or early summer.
H. calathina. See *H. narcissiflora.*
H. × *festalis.* Spring- or summer-flowering bulb with a basal leaf cluster. H to 80cm (32in), S 30–45cm (12–18in). Bears strap-shaped, semi-erect leaves. Produces a head of 2–5 scented, white flowers, each 20cm (8in) across with a deep, central cup and 6 narrow, reflexed petals.
H. × *macrostephana* illus. p.397.
H. narcissiflora, syn. *H. calathina*, *Ismene calathina*, illus. p.420.

H. speciosa. Evergreen, winter-flowering bulb. H and S 30–45cm (12–18in). Has broadly elliptic, semi-erect, basal leaves. Produces a head of 5–10 fragrant, white or green-white flowers, each 20–30cm (8–12in) wide with a funnel-shaped cup and 6 long, narrow petals.
H. **'Sulphur Queen'.** Spring- or summer-flowering bulb. H 60cm (24in), S 30–45cm (12–18in). Produces widely strap- or lance-shaped, semi-erect, basal leaves. Has a loose head of 2–5 fragrant, yellow-green flowers, each 16–20cm (6–8in) wide with a frilly-edged cup and 6 spreading petals.

HYMENOSPORUM
PITTOSPORACEAE

Genus of one species of evergreen shrub or tree, grown for its flowers and overall appearance. Tender, min. 5–7°C (41–5°F). Prefers full sun, though some shade is tolerated. Requires humus-rich, well-drained soil, ideally neutral to acid. Water containerized specimens freely when in full growth, less at other times. Propagate by seed when ripe, in autumn, or in spring or by semi-ripe cuttings in late summer.
H. flavum (Native Australian frangipani). Evergreen, erect shrub or tree, gradually spreading with age. H 10m (30ft) or more, S 5m (15ft) or more. Has oval to oblong, lustrous, rich green leaves. In spring-summer bears terminal panicles of very fragrant, tubular, 5-petalled, cream flowers that age to deep sulphur-yellow.

HYPERICUM
CLUSIACEAE/GUTTIFERAE

Genus of perennials and deciduous, semi-evergreen or evergreen sub-shrubs and shrubs, grown for their conspicuous, yellow flowers with prominent stamens. Large species and cultivars need sun or semi-shade and fertile, not too dry soil. Smaller types, which are good in rock gardens, do best in full sun and well-drained soil. Propagate species sub-shrubs and shrubs by softwood cuttings in summer or by seed in autumn, cultivars by softwood cuttings only in summer; perennials by seed or division in autumn or spring. Is generally trouble-free but *H.* × *inodorum* 'Elstead' is susceptible to rust, which produces orange spots on leaves, *H.* 'Hidcote' to a virus that makes leaves narrow and variegated.
H. balearicum. Evergreen, compact shrub. H and S to 60cm (2ft). Small, oval, green leaves have wavy edges and rounded tips. Solitary, large, fragrant, shallowly cup-shaped, yellow flowers are produced at stem tips above foliage from early summer to autumn. Zone 9?.
H. beanii **'Gold Cup'.** See *H.* × *cyathiflorum* 'Gold Cup'.
H. bellum. Semi-evergreen, arching, graceful shrub. H 1m (3ft), S 1.5m (5ft). Cup-shaped, golden-yellow flowers are borne from mid-summer to early autumn. Shoots are red. Oval, wavy-edged, mid-green leaves redden in autumn. Zone 6.
H. calycinum illus. p.170.

587

H. cerastioides, syn. *H. rhodoppeum*. Vigorous, evergreen sub-shrub with upright and arching branches. H 15cm (6in) or more, S 40–50cm (16–20in). Leaves are oval, hairy and soft greyish-green. In late spring and early summer produces masses of saucer-shaped, bright yellow flowers in terminal clusters. Cut back hard after flowering. Is suitable for a large rock garden. Zone 7.

H. coris. Evergreen, open, dome-shaped, occasionally prostrate, sub-shrub. H 15–30cm (6–12in), S 20cm (8in) or more. Bears long-stemmed whorls of 3 or 4 pointed-oval leaves. Produces panicles of shallowly cup-shaped, bright yellow flowers, streaked red, in summer. Suits a sheltered rock garden. Zone 8.

H. x *cyathiflorum* **'Gold Cup'**, syn. *H. beanii* 'Gold Cup'. Semi-evergreen, arching shrub. H and S 1m (3ft). Produces pinkish-brown shoots, oval, dark green leaves and, from mid-summer to early autumn, large, cup-shaped, golden-yellow flowers. Zone 5.

H. empetrifolium subsp. *oliganthum.* See *H.e.* var. *prostratum* of gardens. var. *prostratum* of gardens (syn. *H.e.* subsp. *oliganthum*) illus. p.386.

H. **'Hidcote'** illus. p.170.

H. x *inodorum* **'Elstead'** illus. p.170.

H. kouytchense, syn. *H. patulum* var. *grandiflorum*, illus. p.170.

H. x *moserianum.* Deciduous, arching shrub. H 30cm (12in), S 60cm (24in). Small, bowl-shaped, yellow flowers are produced above oval, dark green leaves from mid-summer to mid-autumn. Zone 5b. **'Tricolor'** has leaves that are edged with white and pink. Prefers a sheltered position. Zone 5b.

H. olympicum. Deciduous, upright, slightly spreading, dense sub-shrub.

H 15–30cm (6–12in), S to 15cm (6in). Tufts of upright stems are covered in small, oval, grey-green leaves. Produces terminal clusters of up to 5 cup-shaped, bright yellow flowers in summer. Zone 5b. f. *uniflorum* **'Citrinum'** (syn. *H.o.* 'Sulphureum') illus. p.358.

H. patulum. Evergreen or semi-evergreen, upright shrub. H and S 1m (3ft). Large, cup-shaped, golden-yellow flowers open above oval, dark green leaves from mid-summer to mid-autumn. Zone 8. var. *grandiflorum* see *H. kouytchense.*

H. reptans. Deciduous, mat-forming shrub. H 5cm (2in), S 20cm (8in). Oval, green leaves turn yellow or bright red in autumn. In summer produces flattish, golden-yellow flowers, crimson-flushed outside. Suits a rock garden. Zone 5.

H. rhodoppeum. See *H. cerastioides.*

H. **'Rowallane'.** Semi-evergreen, arching shrub. H and S 1.5m (5ft). Even where hardy, may be cut to ground level in severe winters. Bears large, bowl-shaped, deep golden-yellow flowers from mid-summer to mid- or late autumn. Oval leaves are rich green. Zone 7.

Hypocyrta radicans. See *Nematanthus gregarius.*

Hypocyrta strigillosa. See *Nematanthus strigillosus.*

HYPOESTES

ACANTHACEAE

Genus of mainly evergreen perennials, shrubs and sub-shrubs, grown for their flowers and foliage. Tender, min. 10°C (50°F). Grow in bright light and in well-drained soil. Water frequently in growing season, less in winter. Straggly stems

should be cut back. Propagate by stem cuttings in spring or summer.

H. phyllostachya may be treated as an annual and propagated by seed in spring.

H. aristata. Evergreen, bushy perennial or sub-shrub. H to 1m (3ft), S 60cm (2ft). Has oval, mid-green leaves to 8cm (3in) long. Small, tubular, deep pink to purple flowers are produced in terminal spikes in late winter.

H. phyllostachya, syn. *H. sanguinolenta* of gardens, illus. p.264.

H. sanguinolenta of gardens. See *H. phyllostachya.*

HYPOXIS

HYPOXIDACEAE

Genus of spring- or summer-flowering corms, grown for their flat, star-shaped flowers. Suits rock gardens. Requires full sun and light, well-drained soil. Propagate by seed in autumn or spring.

H. angustifolia illus. p.436.

H. capensis, syn. *H. stellata*, *Spiloxene capensis.* Spring-flowering corm with a basal leaf cluster. H 10–20cm (4–8in), S 5–8cm (2–3in). Has very slender, narrowly lance-shaped, erect leaves. Stems each produce an upward-facing flower with pointed, white or yellow petals and a purple eye.

H. stellata. See *H. capensis.*

HYPSELA

CAMPANULACEAE

Genus of vigorous, creeping perennials, grown for their flowers and heart-shaped leaves. Good as ground cover, especially in rock gardens. Needs shade and moist soil. Propagate by division in spring.

H. longiflora. See *H. reniformis.*

H. reniformis, syn. *H. longiflora.*

Vigorous, creeping, stemless perennial. H 2cm (¾in), S indefinite. Has tiny, heart-shaped, fleshy leaves and, in spring-summer, small, star-shaped, pink-and-white flowers.

Hyssop. See *Hyssopus officinalis*, illus. p.168.

Mexican giant. See *Agastache.*

HYSSOPUS

LABIATAE/LAMIACEAE

Genus of perennials and semi-evergreen or deciduous shrubs, grown for their flowers, which attract bees and butterflies, and for their aromatic foliage, which has culinary and medicinal uses. May be grown as a low hedge. Requires full sun and fertile, well-drained soil. Cut back hard or, if grown as a hedge, trim lightly, in spring. Propagate by softwood cuttings in summer or by seed in autumn.

H. officinalis (Hyssop) illus. p.168. subsp. *aristatus* is a semi-evergreen or deciduous, upright, dense shrub. H 60cm (2ft), S 1m (3ft). Bears aromatic, narrowly lance-shaped leaves that are bright green. Produces densely clustered, small, 2-lipped, dark blue flowers from mid-summer through to early autumn. Zone 7.

I

IBERIS

BRASSICACEAE/CRUCIFERAE

Genus of annuals, perennials, evergreen sub-shrubs and shrubs, grown for their flowers and excellent for rock gardens. Some species are short-lived, flowering themselves to death. Requires sun and well-drained soil. Propagate by seed in spring, sub-shrubs and shrubs by semi-ripe cuttings in summer.

I. amara illus. p.318. **'Giant Hyacinth-flowered'** is a group of fast-growing, upright, bushy annuals. H 30cm (12in), S 15cm (6in). Has lance-shaped, mid-green leaves and, in summer, flattish heads of large, scented, 4-petalled flowers in a variety of colours.

I. commutata. See *I. sempervirens.*
I. saxatilis illus. p.374.
I. sempervirens, syn. *I. commutata,* illus. p.346. **'Schneeflocke'** (syn. *I.s.* 'Snowflake') is an evergreen, spreading sub-shrub. H 15–30cm (6–12in), S 45–60cm (18–24in). Leaves are narrowly oblong, glossy and dark green. Dense, semi-spherical heads of 4-petalled, white flowers are produced in late spring and early summer. Trim after flowering. Zone 5.
I. umbellata. Fast-growing, upright, bushy annual. H 15–30cm (6–12in), S 20cm (8in). Has lance-shaped, mid-green leaves. Heads of small, 4-petalled, white or pale purple flowers, sometimes bicoloured, are carried in summer and early autumn.
Fairy Series illus. p.322.

Iceland poppy. See *Papaver croceum.*
Ice-plant. See *Dorotheanthus bellidiformis; Sedum spectabile.*

IDESIA

FLACOURTIACEAE

Genus of one species of deciduous, summer-flowering tree, grown for its foliage and fruits. Both male and female plants are required to obtain fruits. Needs sun or semi-shade and fertile, moist but well-drained soil, preferably neutral to acid. Propagate by softwood cuttings in summer or by seed in autumn.
I. polycarpa illus. p.80.

ILEX

Holly

AQUIFOLIACEAE

Genus of evergreen or deciduous trees and shrubs, grown for their foliage and fruits (berries). Mainly spherical berries, ranging in colour from red through yellow to black, are produced in autumn, following insignificant, usually white, flowers borne in spring. Almost all plants are unisexual, and to obtain fruits on a female plant a male also needs to be grown. All prefer well-drained soil. Grow in sun or shade, but deciduous plants and those with variegated foliage do best in sun or semi-shade. Hollies resent being transplanted, but respond well to hard pruning and pollarding, which should be carried out in late spring. Propagate by seed in spring or by semi-ripe cuttings from late summer to early winter. Holly leaf miner and holly aphid may cause problems. The berries may cause mild stomach upset if ingested. See also feature panel pp.98–9.

I. x *altaclerensis.* Group of vigorous, evergreen shrubs and trees. Is resistant to pollution and coastal exposure. Zone 8 (unless noted).
'Balearica' (illus. p.98) is an erect, female tree. H 12m (40ft), S 5m (15ft). Has green to olive-green young branches. Large, broadly oval leaves are spiny- or smooth-edged and glossy, dark green. Freely produces large, bright red berries.
'Belgica' (illus. p.98) is an erect, dense, female tree. H 12m (40ft), S 5m (15ft). Young branches are green to yellowish-green. Has large, lance-shaped to oblong, spiny- or smooth-edged, glossy, mid-green leaves. Large, orange-red fruits are freely produced.
'Belgica Aurea' (syn. *I.* x *a.* 'Silver Sentinel', *I. perado* 'Aurea'; illus. p.99) is an upright, female tree. H 8m (25ft), S 3m (10ft). Young branches are green with yellow streaks. Has large, lance-shaped, mainly spineless, dark green leaves, mottled with grey-green and irregularly edged with yellow. Red berries are produced only rarely.
'Camelliifolia' (illus. p.98) is a narrow, pyramidal, female tree. H 14m (46ft), S 3m (10ft). Has purple young branches and large, oblong, mainly smooth-edged, glossy, dark green leaves. Reliably produces large, scarlet fruits; is an excellent specimen tree.
'Camelliifolia Variegata' (illus. p.99). H 8m (25ft), S 3m (10ft). Is similar to *I.* x *a.* 'Camelliifolia', but leaves have broad, yellow margins.
'Golden King' is a bushy, female shrub. H 6m (20ft), S 5m (15ft). Young branches are green with a purplish flush. Has large, oblong to oval, sometimes slightly spiny, dark green leaves, each splashed with grey-green in the centre and with a bright yellow margin that turns to cream on older leaves. Is not a good fruiter, bearing only a few reddish-brown berries, but is excellent as a hedge or a specimen plant. Zone 7.
'Hodginsii' is a vigorous, dense, male tree. H 14m (46ft), S 10m (30ft). Shoots are purple; leaves are broadly oval, sparsely spiny and glossy, blackish-green.
'Lawsoniana' (illus. p.98) is a bushy, female shrub. H 6m (20ft), S 5m (15ft). Is similar to *I.* x *a.* 'Golden King', but has leaves splashed irregularly in the centre with gold and lighter green. Foliage tends to revert to plain green.
'N.F. Barnes' (illus. p.98) is a dense, female shrub. H 5.5m (18ft), S 4m (12ft). Has purple shoots and oval, mainly entire but spine-tipped, glossy, dark green leaves and red berries.
'Silver Sentinel' see *I.* x *a.* 'Belgica Aurea'.
'Wilsonii' is a vigorous, female tree. H 8m (25ft), S 5m (15ft). Has purplish-green young branches and large, oblong to oval, glossy, mid-green leaves with prominent veins and large spines. Freely produces large, scarlet fruits and makes a good hedging or specimen plant.
I. aquifolium (Common holly; illus. p.98). Evergreen, much-branched, erect shrub or tree. H 20m (70ft), S 6m (20ft). Has variably shaped, wavy, sharply spined, glossy, dark green leaves and bright red berries. Zone 7 (unless noted).
'Argentea Marginata' (Silver-margined holly; illus. p.98) is a columnar, female tree. H 14m (46ft), S 5m (15ft). Young branches are green, streaked with cream. Broadly oval, spiny, dark green leaves, with wide, cream margins, are shrimp-pink when young. Bears an abundance of bright red berries. Is good for hedging.
'Argentea Marginata Pendula' (Perry's weeping silver holly; illus. p.98) is a slow-growing, weeping, female tree. H 6m (20ft), S 5m (15ft). Has purple young branches and broadly oval, spiny, dark green leaves, mottled with grey-green and broadly edged with cream. Bears red fruits. Is good as a specimen plant in a small garden.
'Atlas' is an erect, male shrub. H 5m (15ft), S 3m (10ft). Has green young branches and oval, spiny, glossy, dark green leaves. Is useful for landscaping and hedging.
'Aurea Regina' see *I.a.* 'Golden Queen'.
'Aurifodina' (illus. p.99) is an erect, dense, female shrub. H 6m (20ft), S 3m (10ft). Young branches are purplish. Oval, spiny leaves are olive-green with golden-yellow margins that turn tawny-yellow in winter. Produces a good crop of deep scarlet berries.
f. *bacciflava* (syn. *I.a.* 'Bacciflava') is a much-branched, usually erect shrub or tree. H 20m (70ft), S 6m (20ft). Has variably shaped, wavy, sharply spined, glossy, dark green leaves and yellow fruits. Zone 6.
'Crispa Aureopicta' (illus. p.99) is a male tree of open habit. H 10m (30ft), S 6m (20ft). Narrowly oval, twisted, sparsely spiny, blackish-green leaves are centrally blotched with golden-yellow. Foliage tends to revert to plain green.
'Ferox' (Hedgehog holly) is an open, male shrub. H 6m (20ft), S 4m (12ft). Has purple young branches and oval, dark green leaves with spines over entire leaf surface.
'Ferox Argentea' (Silver hedgehog holly) is similar to *I.a.* 'Ferox', but has leaves with cream margins.
'Flavescens' (Moonlight holly) is a columnar, female shrub. H 6m (20ft), S 5m (15ft). Young branches are purplish-red. Variably shaped leaves are dark green, with a yellowish flush when young that will last year-round when grown in good light. Produces plentiful, red berries.
'Golden Milkboy' (illus. p.99) is a dense, male shrub. H 6m (20ft), S 4m (12ft). Has purplish-green young branches and oval, very spiny, bright green leaves with heavily blotched, bright yellow centres. Leaves tend to revert to plain green.
'Golden Queen' (syn. *I.a.* 'Aurea Regina') is a dense tree that, despite its name, is male. H 10m (30ft), S 6m (20ft). Broadly oval, very spiny, mid-green leaves are edged with golden-yellow.
'Golden van Tol', a sport of *I.a.* 'J.C. van Tol', is an upright, female shrub. H 4m (12ft), S 3m (10ft). Young branches are purple. Oval, puckered, slightly spiny, dark green leaves have irregular, clear yellow margins. Produces a sparse crop of red fruits. Is good for hedging or as a specimen plant. Zone 6.
'Handsworth New Silver' is a dense, columnar, female shrub. H 8m (25ft), S 5m (15ft). Branches are purple. Oblong to oval, spiny, dark green leaves have broad, cream margins. Bears a profusion of bright red fruits. Is excellent as a hedge or specimen plant and is good for a small garden.
'Hascombensis' is a slow-growing, dense shrub of unknown sex. H 1.5m (5ft), S 1–1.2m (3–4ft). Has purplish-green young branches and small, oval, spiny, dark green leaves. Does not produce berries. Suits a rock garden.
'J.C. van Tol' is an open, female shrub that does not require cross-fertilization to produce fruits. H 6m (20ft), S 4m (12ft). Branches are dark purple when young. Oval, puckered, slightly spiny leaves are dark green. Produces a good crop of red berries. Is useful as a hedge or for a tub. Zone 6.
'Madame Briot' (illus. p.99) is a vigorous, bushy, female tree. H 10m (30ft), S 5m (15ft). Young branches are purplish-green. Leaves are large, broadly oval, spiny and dark green with bright golden borders. Bears scarlet berries.
'Ovata Aurea' (illus. p.99) is a dense, male shrub. H 5m (15ft), S 4m (12ft). Has reddish-brown young branches and oval, regularly spiny, dark green leaves with bright golden margins.
'Pyramidalis' (illus. p.98) is a dense, female tree that does not require cross-fertilization to produce fruits. H 6m (20ft), S 5m (15ft). Has green young branches and narrowly elliptic,

slightly spiny, mid-green leaves. Produces masses of scarlet fruits. Is suitable for a small garden.

'Pyramidalis Aureomarginata' (illus. p.99) is an upright, female shrub. H 6m (20ft), S 5m (15ft). Young branches are green. Has narrowly elliptic, mid-green leaves with prominent, golden margins and spines on upper half. Bears a large crop of red berries.

'Pyramidalis Fructu Luteo' is a conical, female shrub that broadens with age. H 6m (20ft), S 4m (12ft). Branches are green when young. Has oval, often spineless, dark green leaves and bears yellow berries. Is excellent for a small garden.

'Scotica' (illus. p.98) is a large, stiff, compact, female shrub. H 6m (20ft), S 4m (12ft). Oval, usually spineless, glossy, very dark green leaves are slightly twisted. Bears red fruits.

'Silver King' see *I.a.* 'Silver Queen'.

'Silver Milkboy' see *I.a.* 'Silver Milkmaid'.

'Silver Milkmaid' (syn. *I.a.* 'Silver Milkboy'; illus. p.98) is a dense, female shrub. H 5.5m (18ft), S 4m (12ft). Oval, wavy-edged, very spiny leaves are bronze when young, maturing to bright green, each with a central, creamy-white blotch, but tend to revert to plain green. Produces an abundance of scarlet berries. Makes a very attractive specimen plant.

'Silver Queen' (syn. *I.a.* 'Silver King'; illus. p.99) is a dense shrub that, despite its name, is male. H 5m (15ft), S 4m (12ft). Has purple young branches. Oval, spiny leaves, pink when young, mature to very dark green, almost black, with broad, cream edging.

'Watereriana' (syn. *I.a.* 'Waterer's Gold'; Waterer's gold holly; illus. p.99) is a dense, male bush. H and S 5m (15ft). Young branches are green, streaked with yellow. Oval, spiny- or smooth-edged leaves are greyish-green, with broad, golden margins. Is best grown as a specimen plant.

'Waterer's Gold' see *I.a.* 'Watereriana'.

I. × *aquipernyi* (illus. p.98). Evergreen, upright shrub. H 5m (15ft), S 3m (10ft). Has small, oval, spiny, glossy, dark green leaves with long tips. Berries are large and red. Zone 7.

I. chinensis of gardens. See *I. purpurea*.

I. ciliospinosa (illus. p.98). Evergreen, upright shrub or tree. H 6m (20ft), S 4m (12ft). Has small, oval, weak-spined, dull green leaves and red berries. Zone 6.

I. cornuta (Horned holly). Evergreen, dense, rounded shrub. H 4m (12ft), S 5m (15ft). Rectangular, dull green leaves are spiny except on older bushes. Produces large, red berries. All zone 8. **'Burfordii'** (illus. p.98) is female, S 2.5m (8ft), has glossy leaves with only a terminal spine and bears a profusion of fruits. **'Rotunda'**, H 2m (6ft), S 1.2m (4ft), is also female and produces a small crop of fruits; is useful for a tub or small garden.

I. crenata (Box-leaved holly, Japanese holly). Evergreen, spreading shrub or tree. H 5m (15ft), S 3m (10ft). Has

very small, oval, dark green leaves with rounded teeth. Bears glossy, black fruits. Is useful for landscaping or as hedging. All zone 7.

'Bullata' see *I.c.* 'Convexa'.

'Convexa' (syn. *I.c.* 'Bullata'; illus. p.98) is a dense, female shrub. H 2.5m (8ft), S 1.2–1.5m (4–5ft). Has purplish-green young branches and oval, puckered, glossy leaves. Bears glossy, black fruits.

'Helleri' (illus. p.98) is a spreading, female shrub. H 1.2m (4ft), S 1–1.2m (3–4ft). Has green young branches and oval leaves with few spines. Has glossy, black fruits. Is much used for landscaping.

'Latifolia' (syn. *I.c.* f. *latifolia*; illus. p.98) is a spreading to erect, female shrub or tree. H 6m (20ft), S 3m (10ft). Young branches are green and broadly oval leaves have tiny teeth. Produces glossy, black berries.

var. *paludosa* (illus. p.98) is a prostrate shrub or tree. H 15–30cm (6–12in), S indefinite. Has very small, oval, dark green leaves with rounded teeth. Bears glossy, black fruits.

'Variegata' (illus. p.98) is an open, male shrub. H 4m (12ft), S 2.5m (8ft). Oval leaves are spotted or blotched with yellow, but tend to revert to plain green.

I. dipyrena (Himalayan holly). Evergreen, dense, upright tree. H 12m (40ft), S 8m (25ft). Elliptic, dull green leaves are spiny when young, later smooth-edged. Bears large, red fruits. Zone 8.

I. fargesii (illus. p.98). Evergreen, broadly conical tree or shrub. H 6m (20ft), S 5m (15ft). Has green or purple shoots and oval, small-toothed, mid- to dark green leaves. Produces red berries. Zone 7. Var. *brevifolia* (illus. p.98), H 4m (12ft), is dense and rounded.

I. georgei. Evergreen, compact shrub. H 5m (15ft), S 4m (12ft). Tender, min 1ºC (34ºF). Has small, lance-shaped or oval, weak-spined, glossy, dark green leaves with long tips. Berries are red.

I. glabra (Inkberry). Evergreen, dense, upright shrub. H 2.5m (8ft), S 2m (6ft). Small, oblong to oval, dark green leaves are smooth-edged or may have slight teeth near tips. Produces black fruits. Zone 6.

I. insignis. See *I. kingiana*.

I. integra. Evergreen, dense, bushy shrub or tree. H 6m (20ft), S 5m (15ft). Has oval, blunt-tipped, bright green leaves with smooth edges. Bears large, deep red berries. Zone 9?.

I. **'Jermyns Dwarf'**. See *I. pernyi* 'Jermyns Dwarf'.

I. kingiana, syn. *I. insignis*. Evergreen, upright tree. H 6m (20ft), S 4m (12ft). Very large, oblong, leathery, dark green leaves have small spines. Berries are bright red. Zone 8.

I. × *koehneana* (illus. p.98). Evergreen, conical shrub. H 6m (20ft), S 5m (15ft). Young branches are green. Has very large, oblong, spiny, mid-green leaves and red fruits. Zone 8.

I. latifolia (Tarajo holly). Evergreen, upright shrub. H 6m (20ft), S 5m (15ft). Has stout, olive-green young branches, very large, oblong, dark green leaves with short spines and plentiful, red fruits. Zone 8.

I. macrocarpa (illus. p.98). Deciduous, upright tree. H 10m (30ft), S 6m (20ft). Has large, oval, saw-toothed, mid-green leaves and very large, black berries. Zone 8.

I. × *meserveae* (Blue holly). Group of vigorous, evergreen, dense shrubs. Does not thrive in a maritime climate. Has oval, glossy, greenish-blue leaves. Zone 5. **'Blue Princess'** (illus. p.98), H 3m (10ft), S 1.2m (4ft), is female and has purplish-green young branches, small, oval, wavy, spiny leaves and an abundance of red fruits. Zone 5.

I. opaca (American holly). Evergreen, erect tree. H 14m (46ft), S 1.2m (4ft). Does not thrive in a maritime climate. Oval leaves are dull green above, yellow-green beneath and spiny- or smooth-edged. Has red fruits. Zone 6.

I. pedunculosa (illus. p.99). Evergreen, upright shrub or tree. H 10m (30ft), S 6m (20ft). Oval, dark green leaves are smooth-edged. Bright red berries are borne on very long stalks. Zone 7.

I. perado **'Aurea'**. See *I.* × *altaclerensis* 'Belgica Aurea'.

I. pernyi (illus. p.98). Slow-growing, evergreen, stiff shrub. H 8m (25ft), S 4m (12ft). Has pale green young branches and small, oblong, spiny, dark green leaves. Produces red berries. Zone 7. **'Jermyns Dwarf'** (syn. *I.* 'Jermyns Dwarf'), H 60cm (2ft), S 1.2m (4ft), is low-growing and female, with glossy, very spiny leaves. Zone 7.

I. purpurea, syn. *I. chinensis* of gardens (illus. p.99). Evergreen, upright tree. H 12m (40ft), S 6m (20ft). Oval, thin-textured, glossy, dark green leaves have rounded teeth. Lavender flowers are followed by egg-shaped, glossy, scarlet fruits. Zone 8.

I. serrata. Deciduous, bushy shrub. H 4m (12ft), S 2.5m (8ft). Small, oval, finely toothed, bright green leaves are downy when young. Pink flowers are followed by small, red fruits. Zone 6. f. *leucocarpa* (illus. p.99) bears white berries.

I. verticillata (Winterberry; illus. p.98). Deciduous, dense, suckering shrub. H 2m (6ft), S 1.2–1.5m (4–5ft). Young branches are purplish-green. Produces oval or lance-shaped, saw-toothed, bright green leaves. Bears masses of long-lasting, red berries that remain on bare branches during winter. Zone 5.

I. yunnanensis. Evergreen, spreading to erect shrub. H 4m (12ft), S 2.5m (8ft). Branches are downy. Small, oval leaves, with rounded teeth, are brownish-green when young, glossy, dark green in maturity. Produces red berries. Zone 6.

Illawarra flame tree. See *Brachychiton acerifolius*, illus. p.65.
Illawarra palm. See *Archontophoenix cunninghamiana*.

ILLICIUM

ILLICIACEAE

Genus of evergreen, spring- to early summer-flowering trees and shrubs, grown for their foliage and unusual flowers. Does best in semi-shade or shade and moist, neutral to acid soil.

Propagate by semi-ripe cuttings in summer.

I. anisatum (Chinese anise). Slow-growing, evergreen, conical tree or shrub. H and S 6m (20ft). Produces oval, aromatic, glossy, dark green leaves. Star-shaped, greenish-yellow flowers, with numerous narrow petals, are carried in mid-spring. Zone 9.

I. floridanum (Purple anise). Evergreen, bushy shrub. H and S 2m (6ft). Lance-shaped, leathery, deep green leaves are very aromatic. Star-shaped, red or purplish-red flowers, with numerous, narrow petals, are produced in late spring and early summer. Zone 8.

Immortelle. See *Bracteantha bracteata*; *Xeranthemum*.

IMPATIENS

BALSAMINACEAE

Genus of annuals and mainly tender evergreen perennials and sub-shrubs, often with succulent but brittle stems. Prefers sun or semi-shade and moist but not waterlogged soil. Propagate by seed or by stem cuttings in spring or summer. Spider mite, aphids and whitefly may cause problems under glass.

I. balsamina illus. p.320. **'Blackberry Ice'** is a fast-growing, upright, bushy annual. H 70cm (28in), S 45cm (18in). Has lance-shaped, pale green leaves and, in summer and early autumn, large, double, purple flowers, splashed with white. **Tom Thumb Series** illus. p.325.

I. **Confection Series** illus. p.327.

I. **New Guinea Group.** Hybrid subshrubby perennials, usually grown as annuals from cuttings. H and S 30-60cm (1-2ft). Grown for their attractive, often multi-coloured foliage and large, bright flowers. They grow best in sun or light shade. 'Tango' has dark green leaves, orange flowers and can be raised from seed.

I. niamniamensis. Evergreen, bushy perennial. H to 90cm (3ft), S 30cm (1ft). Has reddish-green stems and oval, toothed leaves to 20cm (8in) long. Showy, 5-petalled, hooded, yellowish-green flowers, 2.5cm (1in) long and each with a long, orange, red, crimson or purple spur, appear in summer-autumn. **'Congo Cockatoo'** has red, green and yellow flowers.

I. oliveri. See *I. sodenii*.

I. repens illus. p.293.

I. sodenii, syn. *I. oliveri*. Evergreen, strong-growing, bushy perennial. H 1.2m (4ft) or more, S 60cm (2ft). Narrowly oval, toothed leaves, in whorls of 4–10, are 15cm (6in) or more long. Almost flat, white or pale pink to mauve flowers, 5cm (2in) or more wide, are produced mainly in summer.

I. walleriana (Busy lizzie). Fast-growing, evergreen, bushy perennial, usually grown as an annual. H and S to 60cm (2ft). Has oval, fresh green leaves. Flattish, 5-petalled, spurred, bright red, pink, purple, violet or white flowers appear from spring to autumn. **Novette Series 'Red Star'** illus. p.327. **Super Elfin Series**, H and S 20cm (8in), has flattish flowers in mixed colours. **Super Elfin Series 'Lipstick'** illus. p.326. **Swirl Series** illus. p.321. Flowers of **Tempo Series**, H to 23cm (9in), include shades of violet, orange, pink and red, as well as bicolours and picotees.

IMPERATA

GRAMINEA/POACEAE

See also GRASSES, BAMBOOS, RUSHES and SEDGES

I. cylindrica **'Rubra'**, syn. *I.c.* 'Red baron'. (Japanese blood grass) A slow-spreading perennial grass forming clumps of green leaves that turn bright red from the tip downwards. H 50cm (20in) S infinite. Fluffy white spikes of flowers are produced in late summer.

INCARVILLEA

BIGNONIACEAE

Genus of late spring- or summer-flowering perennials, suitable for rock gardens and borders. Protect crowns with straw or compost in winter. Requires sun and fertile, well-drained soil. Propagate by seed in autumn or spring.

I. delavayi illus. p.282.
I. mairei illus. p.279. **'Frank Ludlow'** is a compact, clump-forming perennial. H and S 30cm (12in). Short stems bear trumpet-shaped, rich deep pink flowers in early summer. Divided leaves consist of up to 4 pairs of narrowly oval, dark green leaflets.

Incense cedar. See *Calocedrus decurrens*, illus. p.106.
Incense plant. See *Calomeria amaranthoides*, illus. p.330.
Incense rose. See *Rosa primula*, illus. p.188.
India rubber tree. See *Ficus elastica*.
Indian almond. See *Terminalia catappa*.
Indian bean. See *Lablab purpureus*, illus. p.271.
Indian bean tree. See *Catalpa bignonioides*, illus. p.78.
Indian corn. See *Zea*.
Indian currant. See *Symphoricarpos orbiculatus*.
Indian fig. See *Opuntia ficus-indica*.
Indian ginger. See *Alpinia calcarata*.
Indian hawthorn. See *Rhaphiolepis indica*.
Indian horse-chestnut. See *Aesculus indica*.
Indian laburnum. See *Cassia fistula*.
Indian pink. See *Dianthus chinensis*.
Indian plum. See *Oemleria cerasiformis*.
Indigo, False. See *Baptisia australis*, illus. p.252.

INDIGOFERA

LEGUMINOSAE/PAPILIONACEAE

Genus of perennials and deciduous shrubs, grown for their foliage and small, pea-like flowers. Hard frosts may cut plants to ground, but they usually regrow from base in spring. Needs full sun and fertile, well-drained soil. Cut out dead wood in spring. Propagate by softwood cuttings in summer or by seed in autumn.

I. decora. Deciduous, bushy shrub. H 45cm (1½ft), S 1m (3ft). Glossy, dark green leaves each have 7–13 oval leaflets. Long spikes of pink or white flowers appear from mid- to late summer. Zone 8.
I. dielsiana illus. p.162.
I. gerardiana. See *I. heterantha*.
I. heterantha, syn. *I. gerardiana*, illus. p.141.
I. pseudotinctoria. Deciduous, arching shrub. H 1m (3ft) or more, S 2m (6ft). Each dark green leaf has usually 7–9 oval leaflets. Long, dense racemes of small, pale pink flowers are borne in mid-summer to early autumn. Zone 7.

Inkberry. See *Ilex glabra*.
Interrupted fern. See *Osmunda claytoniana*.

INULA

ASTERACEAE/COMPOSITAE

Genus of summer-flowering, clump-forming, sometimes rhizomatous perennials. Most need sun and moist but well-drained soil. Propagate by seed or division in spring or autumn.

I. acaulis. Tuft-forming, rhizomatous perennial. H 5–10cm (2–4in), S 15cm (6in). Has lance-shaped to elliptic, hairy leaves. Solitary, almost stemless, daisy-like, golden-yellow flower heads are produced in summer. Is good for a rock garden.
I. ensifolia illus. p.293.
I. hookeri illus. p.256.
I. macrocephala of gardens. See *I. royleana*.
I. magnifica illus. p.229.
I. oculis-christi. Spreading, rhizomatous perennial. H 45cm (18in), S 60cm (24in). Stems each bear 2 or 3 daisy-like, yellow flower heads, which appear in summer. Has lance-shaped to elliptic, hairy, mid-green leaves.
I. royleana, syn. *I. macrocephala* of gardens, illus. p.256.

IOCHROMA

SOLANACEAE

Genus of evergreen shrubs, grown for their flowers. Tender, min. 7–10°C (45–50°F). Needs full light or partial shade and fertile, well-drained soil. Water potted plants freely when in full growth, moderately at other times. Tip prune young plants to stimulate a bushy habit. Cut back flowered stems by half in late winter. Propagate by greenwood or semi-ripe cuttings in summer. Whitefly and spider mite are sometimes troublesome.

I. cyanea, syn. *I. tubulosa*, illus. p.150.
I. tubulosa. See *I. cyanea*.

IONOPSIDIUM

BRASSICACEAE/CRUCIFERAE

Genus of annuals. Only one species is usually cultivated, for rock gardens and as edging. Grow in semi-shade and in fertile, well-drained soil. Propagate by seed sown outdoors in spring, early summer or early autumn.

I. acaule (Violet cress). Fast-growing, upright annual. H 5–8cm (2–3in), S 2.5cm (1in). Rounded leaves are

mid-green. Tiny, 4-petalled, lilac or white flowers, flushed with deep blue, are produced in summer and early autumn.

IPHEION

ALLIACEAE/LILIACEAE

Genus of bulbs that freely produce many star-shaped, blue, white or yellow flowers in spring and make excellent pot plants in cold greenhouses. Prefers a sheltered situation in dappled sunlight and well-drained soil. Plant in autumn; after flowering, dies down for summer. Propagate by offsets in late summer or early autumn.

I. uniflorum **'Froyle Mill'** illus. p.431. **'Wisley Blue'** is a spring-flowering bulb. H 10–15cm (4–6in), S 5–8cm (2–3in). Bears linear, semi-erect, basal, pale green leaves, which smell of onions if damaged. Leafless stems each produce an upward-facing, pale blue flower, 3–4cm (1¼–1½in) across.

IPOMOEA,

syn. MINA, PHARBITIS

CONVOLVULACEAE

Genus of mainly evergreen shrubs, perennials, annuals and soft- or woody-stemmed, twining climbers. Hardy to tender, min. 7–10°C (45–50°F). Provide full light and humus-rich, well-drained soil. Water freely when in full growth, less at other times. Support is needed. Thin out or cut back congested growth in spring. Propagate by seed in spring or by softwood or semi-ripe cuttings in summer. Whitefly and spider mite may cause problems. Seeds are highly toxic if ingested.

I. acuminata. See *I. indica*.
I. alba, syn. *Calonyction aculeatum*, *I. bona-nox* (Moon flower). Evergreen, soft-stemmed, twining climber with prickly stems that exude milky juice when cut. H 7m (22ft) or more. Tender, min. 10°C (50°F). Oval or sometimes 3-lobed leaves are 20cm (8in) long. Fragrant, tubular, white flowers, to 15cm (6in) long and expanded at the mouths to 15cm (6in) across, open at night in summer.
I. bona-nox. See *I. alba*.
I. coccinea, syn. *Quamoclit coccinea* (Red morning glory, Star ipomoea). Annual, twining climber. H to 3m (10ft). Tender, min. 10°C (50°F). Arrow- or heart-shaped leaves are long-pointed and often toothed. Fragrant, tubular, scarlet flowers, with yellow throats and expanded mouths, are produced in late summer and autumn.
I. hederacea illus. p.214.
I. horsfalliae illus. p.209. **'Briggsii'** is a strong-growing, evergreen, woody-stemmed, twining climber. H 2–3m (6–10ft). Tender, min. 7–10°C (45–50°F). Has leaves with 5–7 radiating lobes or leaflets. Stalked clusters of funnel-shaped, deep rose-pink or rose-purple flowers are produced from summer to winter; flowers are larger and more richly coloured than those of the species.
I. imperialis. See *I. nil*.

I. indica, syn. *I. acuminata*, *I. learii*, illus. p.206.
I. learii. See *I. indica*.
I. lobata, syn. *I. versicolor*, *Quamoclit lobata*, illus. p.210.
I. × *multifida*, syn. *I.* × *sloteri* (Cardinal climber, Hearts-and-honey vine). Annual, twining climber. H 3m (10ft). Tender, min. 10°C (50°F). Triangular-oval leaves are divided into 7–15 segments. Tubular, wide-mouthed, crimson flowers with white eyes appear in summer.
I. nil, syn. *I. imperialis*. **'Early Call'** is a short-lived, soft-stemmed, perennial, twining climber with hairy stems, best grown as an annual. H to 4m (12ft). Leaves are heart-shaped or 3-lobed. From summer to early autumn bears large, funnel-shaped flowers in a range of colours, with white tubes. **'Scarlett O'Hara'** has deep red flowers.
I. purpurea, syn. *Convolvulus purpureus* (Common morning glory). Short-lived, soft-stemmed, perennial, twining climber, best grown as an annual, with hairy stems. H to 5m (15ft). Leaves are heart-shaped or 3-lobed. From summer to early autumn has funnel-shaped, deep purple to bluish-purple or reddish flowers with white throats and bristly sepals.
I. quamoclit, syn. *Quamoclit pennata*, illus. p.210.
I. rubrocaerulea **'Heavenly Blue'.** See *I. tricolor* 'Heavenly Blue'.
I. × *sloteri.* See *I.* × *multifida*.
I. tricolor **'Heavenly Blue'**, syn. *I. rubrocaerulea* 'Heavenly Blue', illus. p.215.
I. tuberosa. See *Merremia tuberosa*.
I. versicolor. See *I. lobata*.

Ipomoea, Star. See *Ipomoea coccinea*.

IPOMOPSIS

POLEMONIACEAE

Genus of perennials and biennials, often grown as pot plants for greenhouses and conservatories. Grow in cool, airy conditions with bright light and in fertile, well-drained soil. Propagate by seed sown under glass in early spring or early summer.

I. aggregata. Slow-growing biennial with upright, slender, hairy stems. H to 1m (3ft), S 30cm (1ft). Mid-green leaves are divided into linear leaflets. Fragrant, trumpet-shaped flowers, borne in summer, are usually brilliant red, sometimes spotted yellow, but may be rose, yellow or white.

IRESINE

AMARANTHACEAE

Genus of perennials, grown for their colourful leaves. Tender, min. 10–15°C (50–59°F). Requires bright light to retain leaf colour and a good, loamy, well-drained soil. Pinch out tips in growing season to obtain bushy plants. Propagate by stem cuttings in spring.

I. herbstii (Beefsteak plant). Bushy perennial. H to 60cm (24in), S 45cm (18in). Has red stems and rounded, purplish-red leaves, notched at their tips and 10cm (4in) long, with paler or yellowish-red veins. Flowers are insignificant. **'Aureoreticulata'** illus. p.305.

I. lindenii (Blood leaf). Bushy perennial. H 60cm (24in), S 45cm (18in). Has lance-shaped, dark red leaves, 5–10cm (2–4in) long. Flowers are insignificant.

IRIS

IRIDACEAE

Genus of upright, rhizomatous or bulbous (occasionally fleshy-rooted) perennials, some of which are evergreen, grown for their distinctive and colourful flowers. Each flower has 3 usually large 'falls' (pendent or semi-pendent petals), which in a number of species have conspicuous beards or crests; 3 generally smaller 'standards' (erect, horizontal or, occasionally, pendent petals); and a 3-branched style. In many irises the style branches are petal-like. Unless otherwise stated below, flower stems are unbranched. Green, then brown seed pods are ellipsoid to cylindrical and often ribbed. Irises are suitable for borders, rock gardens, woodlands, watersides, bog gardens, alpine houses, cold frames and containers. Species and cultivars described are hardy unless otherwise stated, but some groups may thrive only in the specific growing conditions mentioned below. Propagate species by division of rhizomes or offsets in late summer or by seed in autumn, named cultivars by division only. Botanically, irises are divided into a number of sub-genera and sections, and it is convenient, for horticultural purposes, to use some of these botanical names for groups of irises with similar characteristics and requiring comparable cultural treatment. All parts may cause severe discomfort if ingested; contact with the sap may irritate skin. See also feature panel pp.234–5.

Rhizomatous
These irises have rhizomes as rootstocks; leaves are sword-shaped and usually in a basal fan.

Bearded irises are rhizomatous and have 'beards', consisting of numerous often coloured hairs, along the centre of each fall. In some irises, the end of the beard is enlarged into the shape of a horn. The group covers the vast majority of irises, including many named cultivars, grown in gardens; all are derived from *I. pallida* and related species. Bearded irises thrive in full sun in fairly rich, well-drained, preferably slightly alkaline soil. Some are very tolerant and will grow and flower reasonably in partial shade in poorer soil. For horticultural purposes, various groupings of hybrid bearded irises are recognized, based mainly on the height of the plants in flower. These include **Miniature Dwarf**, H to 20cm (8in); **Standard Dwarf**, H 20–40cm (8–16in); **Intermediate**, H 40–70cm (16–28in); and **Standard Tall**, H 70cm (28in) or more (this last category may be further subdivided). In general, the shorter the iris, the earlier the flowering

season (from early spring to early summer).
Oncocyclus irises are rhizomatous, with very large and often bizarrely coloured flowers, one to each stem, which have bearded falls. They require full sun, sharply drained but fairly rich soil and, after flowering, a dry period of dormancy in summer and early autumn. Difficult to cultivate successfully, they are best grown in an alpine house or covered frame in climates subject to summer rains.
Regelia irises are closely related to Oncocyclus irises, differing in having bearded standards as well as falls and in having 2 flowers to each stem. They require similar conditions of cultivation, although a few species, such as *I. hoogiana*, have proved easier to grow than Oncocyclus irises. Hybrids between the 2 groups have been raised and are known as **Regeliocyclus** irises.

Beardless irises, also rhizomatous, lack hairs on the falls; most have very similar cultural requirements to bearded irises but some prefer heavier soil. Various groupings are recognized, of which the following are the most widely known. **Pacific Coast** irises, a group of Californian species and their hybrids, prefer acid to neutral soil and grow well in sun or partial shade, appreciating some humus in the soil; they are best grown from seed as they resent being moved. **Spuria** irises (*I. spuria* and its relatives) grow in sun or semi-shade and well-drained but moist soil. A number of species and hybrids prefers moist, waterside conditions; these include the well-known **Siberian** irises (*I. sibirica* and its relatives) and the **Japanese** water irises, such as *I. ensata* and *I. laevigata*, which may also be grown as border plants, but succeed best in open, sunny, humus-rich, moist sites.

Crested irises, also rhizomatous, have ridges, or cockscomb-like crests, instead of beards. They include the **Evansia** irises, with often widely spreading, creeping stolons. Most have very similar cultivation requirements to bearded irises but some prefer damp, humus-rich conditions; a few are tender, min. 5°C (41°F).

Bulbous
These irises are distinguished by having bulbs as storage organs, sometimes with thickened, fleshy roots, and leaves that are lance-shaped and channelled; 4-sided (more or less square in cross section); or almost cylindrical – unlike the flat and usually sword-shaped leaves of the rhizomatous irises.
Xiphium irises include the commonly grown Spanish, English and Dutch irises, which are excellent both for garden decoration and as cut flowers. All are easy to cultivate in sunny, well-drained sites, preferring slightly alkaline conditions, but also growing well on acid soil. **Spanish** irises are derived from *I. xiphium*, which is variable in flower colour, from blue and violet to yellow and white, and

produces its channelled leaves in autumn. **English** irises have been produced from *I. latifolia*, which varies from blue to violet (occasionally white) and produces its channelled leaves in spring. **Dutch** irises are hybrids of *I. xiphium* and the related pale to deep blue *I. latifolia*. They are extremely variable in flower colour.
Juno irises have bulbs with thickened, fleshy roots, channelled leaves and very small standards that are sometimes only bristle-like and usually horizontally placed. Although very beautiful in flower, they are mostly difficult to grow successfully, requiring the same cultivation conditions as Oncocyclus irises to thrive. Care must be taken not to damage the fleshy roots when transplanting or dividing clumps.

Reticulata irises include the dwarf, bulbous irises valuable for flowering early in the year. Unlike other bulbous irises, they have net-like bulb tunics and leaves that are 4-sided, or occasionally cylindrical. With few exceptions (not described here), Reticulata irises grow well in open, sunny, well-drained sites.

I. acutiloba. Rhizomatous Oncocyclus iris. H 8–25cm (3–10in), S 30–38cm (12–15in). Has narrowly sickle-shaped, mid-green leaves. In late spring produces solitary, strongly purple-violet- or brownish-purple-veined, white flowers, 5–7cm (2–3in) across, with a dark brown blaze around the beard of each fall.
I. 'Annabel Jane' (illus. p.234). Vigorous, rhizomatous, bearded iris (Standard Tall). H 1.2m (4ft), S indefinite. Well-branched stem bears 8–12 flowers, 15–25cm (6–10in) across, with pale lilac falls and paler standards. Flowers in early summer.
I. 'Anniversary'. Rhizomatous, beardless Siberian iris. H 60cm (2ft), S indefinite. From late spring to early summer, branched stem bears 1–4 white flowers, 5–10cm (2–4in) across, with a creamy-white stripe in the throat of each fall. Grows well in moist soil or a bog garden.
I. aphylla. Rhizomatous, bearded iris. H 15–30cm (6–12in), S indefinite. Branched stem produces up to 5 pale to dark purple or blue-violet flowers, 6–7cm (2½–3in) across, in late spring and sometimes again in autumn if conditions suit.
I. aucheri. Bulbous Juno iris. H 15–25cm (6–10in), S 15cm (6in). Has channelled, mid-green leaves packed closely together on stem, looking somewhat leek-like. In late spring bears up to 6 blue to white flowers, 6–7cm (2½–3in) across with yellow-ridged falls, in leaf axils.
I. aurea. See *I. crocea.*
I. bakeriana. Bulbous Reticulata iris. H 10cm (4in), S 5–6cm (2–2½in). In early spring bears a solitary, long-tubed, pale blue flower, 5–6cm (2–2½in) across, with each fall having a dark blue blotch at the tip and a spotted, deep blue centre. Has narrow, almost cylindrical leaves that are very short at flowering time but elongate later.

I. 'Banbury Beauty'. Rhizomatous, beardless Pacific Coast iris. H 45cm (18in), S indefinite. In late spring and early summer, branched stem produces 2–10 light lavender flowers, 10–15cm (4–6in) across, with a purple zone on each fall.
I. 'Bibury'. Rhizomatous, bearded iris (Standard Dwarf). H 30cm (12in), S indefinite. Has 2–4 cream flowers, 10cm (4in) wide, on a branched stem in late spring.
I. 'Blue-eyed Brunette' (illus. p.235). Rhizomatous, bearded iris (Standard Tall). H 1m (3ft), S indefinite. Well-branched stem produces 7–10 brown flowers, 10–15cm (4–6in) wide, with a blue blaze and a golden beard on each fall, in early summer.
I. 'Bold Print' (illus. p.234). Rhizomatous, bearded iris (Intermediate). H 55cm (22in), S indefinite. In late spring or early summer, branched stem bears up to 6 flowers, 13cm (5in) wide, with purple-edged, white standards and white falls that are each purple-stitched at the edge and have a bronze-tipped, white beard.
I. 'Bronze Queen' (illus. p.235). Bulbous Xiphium iris (Dutch). H to 80cm (32in), S 15cm (6in). In spring and early summer produces 1 or 2 golden-brown flowers, 8–10cm (3–4in) wide, flushed bronze and purple. Lance-shaped, channelled, mid-green leaves are scattered up flower stem.
I. 'Brown Lasso'. Rhizomatous, bearded iris (Intermediate). H 55cm (22in), S indefinite. In early summer, sturdy, well-branched stem bears 6–10 flowers, 10–13cm (4–5in) across, with deep butterscotch standards and brown-edged, light violet falls.
I. bucharica (illus. p.234). Vigorous, bulbous Juno iris. H 20–40cm (8–16in), S 12cm (5in). In late spring produces 2–6 flowers, 6cm (2½in) across, golden-yellow to white with yellow falls, from leaf axils. Has narrowly lance-shaped, channelled, glossy, mid-green leaves scattered up flower stem. Is easier to grow than most Juno irises.
I. 'Butter and Sugar' (illus. p.235). Rhizomatous, beardless Siberian iris. H to 1m (3ft), S indefinite. From late spring to early summer produces large, yellow and white flowers.
I. 'Carnaby' (illus. p.235). Rhizomatous, bearded iris (Standard Tall). H to 1m (3ft), S indefinite. Well-branched stem bears 6–8 flowers, 15–18cm (6–7in) wide, with pale pink standards and deep rose-pink falls with orange beards, in early summer.
I. chamaeiris. See *I. lutescens.*
I. chrysographes (illus. p.234). Rhizomatous, beardless Siberian iris. H 40cm (16in), S indefinite. From late spring to early summer, branched stem bears 1–4 deep red-purple or purple-black flowers, 5–10cm (2–4in) wide, with gold etching down falls. Prefers moist conditions.
I. 'Clairette', syn. *I. reticulata* 'Clairette'. Bulbous Reticulata iris. H 10–15cm (4–6in), S 4–6cm (1½–2½in). In early spring bears a solitary, fragrant, long-tubed, pale

blue flower, 4–6cm (1½–2½in) wide, with white-flecked, deep violet falls. Narrow, squared leaves elongate after flowering time.

I. clarkei. Rhizomatous, beardless Siberian iris. H 60cm (2ft), S indefinite. From late spring to early summer, solid stem produces 2–3 branches each with 2 blue to red-purple flowers, 5–10cm (2–4in) across, with a violet-veined, white blaze on each fall. Prefers moist conditions.

I. colchica. See *I. graminea*.

I. confusa. Evergreen or semi-evergreen, rhizomatous Evansia iris with short stolons. H 30cm–1m (1–3ft), S indefinite. Bamboo-like, erect stem is crowned by a fan of lax leaves. In mid-spring, widely branched flower stem produces a long succession of up to 30 white flowers, 4–5cm (1½–2in) across, with yellow and purple spots around a yellow crest on each fall. Prefers well-drained soil and the protection of a south-facing wall.

I. 'Conjuration'. Rhizomatous, bearded iris (Standard Tall). H 90cm (3ft), S indefinite. In early summer, bears 6–11 flowers with standards that are white at the edges, suffusing inwards to pale violet-blue, and white falls suffusing to deep amethyst-violet at the edges. The horned beard is white, tipped with yellow.

I. cristata (illus. p.234). Evansia iris with much-branched rhizomes. H 10cm (4in), S indefinite. Has neat fans of lance-shaped leaves. In early summer produces 1 or 2 virtually stemless, long-tubed, lilac, blue, lavender or white flowers, 3–4cm (1¼–1½in) across, with a white patch and orange crest on each fall. Prefers semi-shade and moist soil; is ideal for peat banks.

I. crocea, syn. *I. aurea*. Rhizomatous, beardless Spuria iris. H 1–1.2m (3–4ft), S indefinite. Has long leaves. Strong, erect, sparsely branched stem produces terminal clusters of 2–10 golden-yellow flowers, 12–18cm (5–7in) across, with wavy-edged falls, in early summer. Resents being disturbed.

I. cuprea. See *I. fulva*.

I. 'Custom Design'. Rhizomatous, beardless Spuria iris. H 1m (3ft), S indefinite. Strong, erect-branched stem produces 2–10 deep maroon-brown flowers, each 5–12cm (2–5in) wide, with a heavily veined, bright yellow blaze on each fall, from early to mid-summer.

I. danfordiae (illus. p.235). Bulbous Reticulata iris. H 5–10cm (2–4in), S 5cm (2in). In early spring bears usually one yellow flower, 3–5cm (1¼–2in) across, with green spots on each fall. Standards are reduced to short bristles. Narrow, squared leaves are very short at flowering time but elongate later. Tends to produce masses of small bulblets and requires deeper planting than other Reticulata irises to maintain bulbs at flowering size.

I. douglasiana (illus. p.234). Evergreen, rhizomatous, beardless Pacific Coast iris. H 25–70cm (10–28in), S indefinite. Leathery, dark green leaves are stained red-purple at base. Branched stem produces 1–3 lavender to purple, occasionally white, flowers, 7–12cm (3–5in) wide, with variable,

central, yellowish zones on the falls, in late spring and early summer.

I. 'Dreaming Spires'. Rhizomatous, beardless Siberian iris. H 1m (3ft), S indefinite. From late spring to early summer, branched stem produces 1–4 flowers, 5–10cm (2–4in) wide, with lavender standards and royal-blue falls. Prefers moist soil.

I. 'Dreaming Yellow' (illus. p.234). Rhizomatous, beardless Siberian iris. H 1m (3ft), S indefinite. From late spring to early summer, branched stem produces 1–4 flowers, 5–10cm (2–4in) across. Standards are white, falls creamy-yellow fading to white with age. Prefers moist soil.

I. 'Early Light' (illus. p.235). Rhizomatous, bearded iris (Standard Tall). H 1m (3ft), S indefinite. In early summer, well-branched stem bears 8–10 flowers, 15–18cm (6–7in) wide, with lemon-flushed, cream standards and slightly darker falls with a yellow beard.

I. 'Elmohr'. Rhizomatous, bearded iris. H 1m (3ft), S indefinite. In early summer, well-branched stem produces 2–5 strongly veined, red-purple flowers, 15–20cm (6–8in) across.

I. ensata, syn. *I. kaempferi* (Japanese flag). Rhizomatous, beardless Japanese iris. H 60cm–1m (2–3ft), S indefinite. Branched stem produces 3–15 purple or red-purple flowers, 8–15cm (3–6in) across, with a yellow blaze on each fall, from early to mid-summer. May be distinguished from the related, smooth-leaved *I. laevigata* by the prominent midrib on the leaves. Has produced many hundreds of garden forms, some with double flowers, in shades of purple, pink, lavender and white, sometimes bicoloured. Prefers partial shade and thrives in a water or bog garden. **'Galathea'** (syn. *I. 'Galathea'*; illus. p.235), H 80cm (32in), has blue-purple flowers with a yellow blaze on each fall.

I. extremorientalis. See *I. sanguinea*.

I. 'Eyebright' (illus. p.235). Rhizomatous, bearded iris (Standard Dwarf). H 30cm (12in), S indefinite. In late spring produces 2–4 bright yellow flowers, 7–10cm (3–4in) wide, each with a brown zone on the falls surrounding the beard, on usually an unbranched stem.

I. 'Flamenco' (illus. p.235). Rhizomatous, bearded iris (Standard Tall). H 1m (3ft), S indefinite. In early summer, well-branched stem produces 6–9 flowers, 15cm (6in) wide, with gold standards, infused red, and white to yellow falls with red borders.

I. foetidissima (Gladwin, Roast-beef plant, Stinking iris). Evergreen, rhizomatous, beardless iris. H 30cm–1m (1–3ft), S indefinite. Branched stem bears up to 9 yellow-tinged, dull purple or occasionally pure yellow flowers, 5–10cm (2–4in) wide, from early to mid-summer. Cylindrical seed pods open to reveal rounded, bright scarlet fruits throughout winter. Thrives in a bog or water garden, although tolerates drier conditions.

I. forrestii (illus. p.235). Rhizomatous, beardless Siberian iris. H 15–40cm (6–16in), S indefinite. From late spring

to early summer, unbranched stem produces 1 or 2 fragrant, yellow flowers, 5–6cm (2–2½in) across, with black lines on each fall and occasionally brownish-flushing on standards. Has linear, glossy, mid-green leaves, grey-green below. Prefers moist, lime-free soil.

I. fosteriana. Bulbous Juno iris. H 10–15cm (4–6in), S 6cm (2½in). In spring produces 1 or 2 long-tubed flowers, 4–5cm (1½–2in) wide, with downward-turned, rich purple standards, which are larger than those of most Juno irises, and creamy-yellow falls. Has narrowly lance-shaped, channelled, silver-edged, mid-green leaves scattered on flower stem. Is difficult to grow and is best in an alpine house or cold frame.

I. 'Frank Elder'. Bulbous Reticulata iris. H 6–10cm (2½–4in), S 5–7cm (2–3in). Has a solitary, very pale blue flower, 6–7cm (2½–3in) wide, suffused pale yellow and veined and spotted darker blue, in early spring. Narrow, squared leaves are very short at flowering time but elongate later.

I. fulva, syn. *I. cuprea* (illus. p.235). Rhizomatous, beardless iris. H 45–80cm (18–32in), S indefinite. In late spring or summer produces a slender, slightly branched stem with 4–6 (occasionally more) copper- or orange-red flowers, 5–7cm (2–3in) across, with 2 flowers per leaf axil. Thrives in a bog or water garden.

I. × fulvala, syn. *I. 'Fulvala'* (illus. p.234). Rhizomatous, beardless iris. H 45cm (18in), S indefinite. In summer, zigzag stem produces 4–6 (occasionally more) velvety, deep red-purple flowers, 5–12cm (2–5in) across, with 2 flowers per leaf axil. Has a yellow blaze on each fall. Thrives in a bog or water garden.

I. 'Galathea'. See *I. ensata* 'Galathea'.

I. 'Geisha Gown' (illus. p.234). Rhizomatous, beardless Japanese iris. H 80cm (32in), S indefinite. In summer, branched stem produces 3–5 double, rose-purple-veined, white flowers, 15–30cm (6–12in) across, with purple styles and a gold blaze on each fall. Leaves are ridged. Prefers sun or semi-shade. Thrives in a bog or water garden.

I. germanica (Common German flag). Rhizomatous, bearded iris. H to 60cm–1.2m (2–4ft), S indefinite. Sparsely branched stem produces up to 6 yellow-bearded, blue-purple or blue-violet flowers, 10–15cm (4–6in) wide, in late spring and early summer.

I. 'Golden Harvest'. Bulbous Xiphium iris (Dutch). H to 80cm (32in), S 15cm (6in). Bears 1 or 2 deep rich yellow flowers, 6–8cm (2½–3in) wide, in spring and early summer. Has scattered, narrowly lance-shaped, channelled, mid-green leaves.

I. gracilipes. Clump-forming, rhizomatous Evansia iris with short stolons. H 15–20cm (6–8in), S indefinite. In late spring and early summer, slender, branched stem produces a succession of 4 or 5 lilac-blue flowers, each 3–4cm (1¼–1½in) across, with a violet-veined, white zone surrounding a yellow-and-white crest.

Has narrow, grass-like leaves. Prefers semi-shade and peaty soil.

I. graeberiana. Bulbous Juno iris. H 15–35cm (6–14in), S 6–8cm (2½–3in). In late spring produces 4–6 bluish-lavender flowers, 6–8cm (2½–3in) across, with a white crest on each fall, from leaf axils. Lance-shaped, channelled leaves are white-margined, glossy, mid-green above, greyish-green below, and scattered up flower stem. Is easier to grow than most Juno irises.

I. graminea, syn. *I. colchica*. Rhizomatous, beardless Spuria iris. H 20–40cm (8–16in), S indefinite. In late spring, narrowly lance-shaped leaves partially hide up to 10 plum-scented flowers, 5–12cm (2–5in) wide, with wine-purple standards and heavily veined, violet-blue falls, borne on flattened, angled stem. Resents being disturbed.

I. 'Harmony' (illus. p.235). Bulbous Reticulata iris. H 6–10cm (2½–4in), S 6–7cm (2½–3in). In early spring bears a solitary, fragrant, long-tubed, clear pale blue flower, 5–6cm (2–2½in) across, with white marks and a yellow ridge down each fall centre. Narrow, squared leaves are very short at flowering time but elongate later.

I. histrioides. Bulbous Reticulata iris. H 6–10cm (2½–4in), S 6–7cm (2½–3in). In early spring produces solitary flowers, 6–7cm (2½–3in) across, which vary from light to deep violet-blue. Each fall is lightly to strongly spotted with dark blue and has white marks and a yellow ridge down centre. Narrow, squared leaves are very short at flowering time but elongate later. **'Lady Beatrix Stanley'** has light blue flowers and heavily spotted falls. **'Major'** (illus. p.235) has darker blue-violet flowers.

I. 'Holden Clough'. Rhizomatous, beardless iris. H 50–70cm (20–28in), S indefinite. In early summer, branched stem bears 6–12 yellow flowers, each 5cm (2in) wide, with very heavy, burnt-sienna veining. Is excellent in a bog or water garden, but also grows well in any rich, well-drained soil.

I. hoogiana (illus. p.235). Regelia iris with stout rhizomes. H 40–60cm (16–24in), S indefinite. Produces 2 or 3 scented, delicately veined, lilac-blue flowers, 7–10cm (3–4in) across, in late spring and early summer. Is relatively easy to cultivate.

I. iberica (illus. p.234). Rhizomatous Oncocyclus iris. H 15–20cm (6–8in), S indefinite. Has narrow, strongly curved, grey-green leaves. Bears solitary, bicoloured flowers, 10–12cm (4–5in) across, in late spring. Standards are white, pale yellow, or pale blue with slight brownish-purple veining; spoon-shaped falls are white or pale lilac, spotted and strongly veined brownish-purple. Grows best in a frame or alpine house.

I. innominata (illus. p.235). Evergreen or semi-evergreen, rhizomatous, beardless Pacific Coast iris. H 16–25cm (6–10in), S indefinite. Stem bears 1 or 2 flowers, 6.5–7.5cm (2½–3in) across, from late spring to early summer. Varies greatly in colour from cream to yellow or orange and from lilac-pink to blue or purple; falls are often veined with maroon or brown.

I. japonica (illus. p.235). Vigorous, rhizomatous Evansia iris with slender stolons. H 45–80cm (18–32in), S indefinite. Has fans of broadly lance-shaped, glossy leaves. In late spring produces branched flower stem with a long succession of flattish, frilled or ruffled, pale lavender or white flowers, 1–8cm (½–3in) across, marked violet around an orange crest on each fall. Prefers the protection of a sheltered, sunny wall.

I. 'Joette' (illus. p.234). Rhizomatous, bearded iris (Intermediate). H 45cm (18in), S indefinite. In late spring or early summer, branched stems carry uniformly lavender-blue flowers with yellow beards. Is excellent in flower arrangements.

I. 'Joyce' (illus. p.235). Bulbous Reticulata iris. H 6–10cm (2½–4in), S 6–7cm (2½–3in). In early spring bears a solitary, fragrant, long-tubed, clear blue flower, 5–6cm (2–2½in) across, with white marks and a yellow ridge down each fall centre. Narrow, squared leaves are very short at flowering time but elongate later.

I. 'June Prom'. Vigorous, rhizomatous, bearded iris (Intermediate). H 50cm (20in), S indefinite. In late spring or early summer, branched stem bears up to 6 pale blue flowers, 8–10cm (3–4in) wide, with a green tinge on each fall.

I. kaempferi. See *I. ensata*.

I. 'Katharine Hodgkin' (illus. p.235). Bulbous Reticulata iris. H 6–10cm (2½–4in), S 5–7cm (2–3in). Is similar to *I.* 'Frank Elder', but has yellower flowers, 6–7cm (2½–3in) wide, suffused pale blue, lined and dotted dark blue. Flowers in early spring.

I. kerneriana. Rhizomatous, beardless Spuria iris. H 25cm (10in), S indefinite. Has very narrow, grass-like leaves. Strong, erect-branched stem bears 2–4 soft lemon- or creamy-yellow flowers, 5–12cm (2–5in) across, from each pair of bracts, in early summer. Resents being disturbed.

I. korolkowii. Regelia iris with stout rhizomes. H 40–60cm (16–24in), S indefinite. From late spring to early summer, each spathe encloses 2 or 3 delicately blackish-maroon- or olive-green-veined, creamy-white or light purple flowers, 6–8cm (2½–3in) across. Is best grown in a bulb frame.

I. 'Krasnia' (illus. p.234). Rhizomatous, bearded iris (Standard Tall). H 1m (3ft), S indefinite. In early summer, well-branched stem produces 8–12 flowers, 13–18cm (5–7in) wide, with purple standards and purple-edged, white falls.

I. 'Lady of Quality' (illus. p.234). Rhizomatous, beardless Siberian iris. H to 1m (3ft), S indefinite. Flowers, produced in mid- or late spring, have light blue-violet standards and lighter blue falls.

I. laevigata (illus. p.235). Rhizomatous, beardless Japanese iris. H 60–90cm (2–3ft) or more, S indefinite. Sparsely branched stem produces 2–4 blue, blue-purple or white flowers, 5–12cm (2–5in) across, from early to mid-summer. Is related to *I. ensata* but has smooth, not

ridged leaves. Grows well in sun or semi-shade in moist conditions or in shallow water. **'Regal'** bears single, cyclamen-red flowers. Flowers of **'Snowdrift'** are double and white. **'Variegata'**, H 25cm (10in), has white-and-green-striped leaves and often flowers a second time in early autumn.

I. latifolia, syn. *I. xiphioides* (English iris; illus. p.234). Bulbous Xiphium iris (English). H 80cm (32in), S 15cm (6in). In late spring and summer, 1 or 2 blue to deep violet flowers, 8–10cm (3–4in) wide, with a yellow stripe down centre of each very broad fall, are produced from the bracts. Lance-shaped, channelled, mid-green leaves are scattered up flower stem. **'Duchess of York'** bears purple flowers. Flowers of **'Mont Blanc'** are pure white. **'Queen of the Blues'** has blue standards and purple-blue falls.

I. 'Lavender Royal' (illus. p.235). Rhizomatous, beardless Pacific Coast iris. H 45cm (18in), S indefinite. In late spring to early summer, branched stems carry lavender flowers with darker flushes.

I. lutescens, syn. *I. chamaeiris*. Fast-growing, very variable, rhizomatous, bearded iris. H 5–30cm (2–12in), S indefinite. Branched stem produces 1 or 2 yellow-bearded, violet, purple, yellow, white or bicoloured flowers, 6–8cm (2½–3in) across, in early summer. **'Nancy Lindsay'** has scented, yellow flowers.

I. 'Magic Man' (illus. p.234). Rhizomatous, bearded iris (Standard Tall). H 1m (3ft), S indefinite. In early summer, branched stems carry flowers that have light blue standards and velvety purple falls with light blue edges; beards are orange.

I. magnifica (illus. p.234). Bulbous Juno iris. H 30–60cm (12–24in), S 15cm (6in). In late spring produces 3–7 very pale lilac flowers, 6–8cm (2½–3in) across, with a central, yellow area on each fall, from leaf axils. Bears scattered, lance-shaped, channelled, glossy, mid-green leaves.

I. 'Margot Holmes'. Rhizomatous, beardless Siberian iris. H 25cm (10in), S indefinite. In early summer produces 2 or 3 purple-red flowers, 10–15cm (4–6in) across, with yellow veining on each fall.

I. 'Marhaba'. Rhizomatous, bearded iris (Miniature Dwarf). H 15cm (6in), S indefinite. Bears 1, rarely 2 deep blue flowers, 5–8cm (2–3in) wide, in mid-spring.

I. 'Mary Frances' (illus. p.234). Rhizomatous, bearded iris (Standard Tall). H 1m (3ft), S indefinite. In early summer, well-branched stem bears 6–9, occasionally to 12 pink-lavender flowers, 15cm (6in) wide.

I. 'Matinata' (illus. p.234). Rhizomatous, bearded iris (Standard Tall). H 1m (3ft), S indefinite. In early summer, well-branched stem produces 6–9, occasionally to 12 flowers, 15cm (6in) wide, that are dark purple-blue throughout.

I. missouriensis, syn. *I. tolmeiana* (Missouri flag; illus. p.234). Very variable, rhizomatous, beardless Pacific Coast iris. H to 75cm (2½ft), S indefinite. Branched stem produces

2 or 3 pale blue, lavender, lilac, blue or white flowers, 5–8cm (2–3in) wide, in each spathe, in late spring or early summer. Falls are veined and usually have a yellow blaze.

I. 'Mountain Lake' (illus. p.235). Rhizomatous, beardless Siberian iris. H 1m (3ft), S indefinite. From late spring to early summer, branched stem produces 1–4 mid-blue flowers, 5–10cm (2–4in) across, with darker veining on falls. Prefers moist soil.

I. ochroleuca. See *I. orientalis*.

I. orientalis, syn. *I. ochroleuca*. Rhizomatous, beardless Spuria iris. H to 90cm (3ft), S indefinite. In late spring each stem, usually with one branch, bears 3–5 white flowers, 8–10cm (3–4in) wide. Falls are white with yellow centres. Leaves are often present over winter.

I. orientalis of gardens. See *I. sanguinea*.

I. pallida (Dalmatian iris). Rhizomatous, bearded iris. H 70–90cm (28–36in) or more, S indefinite. In late spring and early summer produces 2–6 scented, lilac-blue flowers, 8–12cm (3–5in) across and with yellow beards, from silvery spathes on strong, branched stems. Leaves of **'Variegata'** (syn. *I.p.* 'Aurea Variegata'; illus. p.234) are striped green and yellow.

I. 'Paradise Bird' (illus. p.234). Rhizomatous, bearded iris (Standard Tall). H 85cm (34in), S indefinite. In early summer, well-branched stem produces 8–10 flowers, 14–15cm (5½–6in) wide, with magenta falls and paler standards.

I. 'Peach Frost' (illus. p.235). Rhizomatous, bearded iris (Standard Tall). H 1m (3ft), S indefinite. Well-branched stem bears 6–10 flowers, 15cm (6in) wide, in early summer. Standards are peach-pink, falls white with peach-pink borders and tangerine beards.

I. 'Piona'. Rhizomatous, bearded iris (Intermediate). H 45cm (18in), S indefinite. In late spring and early summer, branched stem bears up to 6 deep violet flowers, 8–10cm (3–4in) wide, with golden beards. Mid-green leaves have purple bases.

I. 'Professor Blaauw'. Bulbous Xiphium iris (Dutch). H 80cm (32in), S 15cm (6in). From spring to early summer produces 1 or 2 rich violet-blue flowers, 6–8cm (2½–3in) across. Narrowly lance-shaped, channelled, mid-green leaves are scattered up flower stem.

I. pseudacorus (Yellow flag; illus. p.235). Robust, rhizomatous, beardless iris. H to 2m (6ft), S indefinite. Branched stem produces 4–12 golden-yellow flowers, 5–12cm (2–5in) wide, usually with brown or violet veining and a darker yellow patch on the falls, from early to mid-summer. Leaves are broad, ridged and greyish-green. Prefers semi-shade and thrives in a water garden. **'Variegata'** has yellow-and-green-striped foliage in spring, often turning green before flowering.

I. pumila (Dwarf bearded iris). Rhizomatous, bearded iris. H 10–15cm (4–6in), S indefinite. In mid-spring has a 1cm (½in) long flower stem bearing 2 or 3 long-tubed flowers, 2.5–5cm

(1–2in) wide, varying from violet-purple to white, yellow or blue, with yellow or blue beards on the falls. Prefers very well-drained, slightly alkaline soil.

I. reticulata. Bulbous Reticulata iris. H 10–15cm (4–6in), S 4–6cm (1½–2½in). In early spring bears a solitary, fragrant, long-tubed, deep violet-purple flower, 4–6cm (1½–2½in) wide, with a yellow ridge down each fall centre. Narrow, squared leaves elongate after flowering time. **'Cantab'** (illus. p.235) has clear pale blue flowers with a deep yellow ridge on each fall. **'Clairette'** see *I.* 'Clairette'. Flowers of **'J.S. Dijt'** are reddish-purple with an orange ridge on each fall. **'Violet Beauty'** see *I.* 'Violet Beauty'.

I. 'Rippling Rose' (illus. p.234). Rhizomatous, bearded iris (Standard Tall). H 1m (3ft), S indefinite. In early summer, well-branched stem has 6–10 white flowers, 15cm (6in) wide, with purple marks and lemon-yellow beards.

I. rosenbachiana (illus. p.234). Bulbous Juno iris. H 10–15cm (4–6in), S 6cm (2½in). In spring produces 1 or 2 long-tubed flowers, 4–5cm (1½–2in) wide, with small, downward-turned, rich purple standards and reddish-purple falls, each with a yellow ridge in the centre. Has lance-shaped, channelled, mid-green leaves in a basal tuft. Is difficult to grow and is best in an alpine house or cold frame.

I. 'Ruffled Velvet' (illus. p.234). Rhizomatous, beardless Siberian iris. H to 1m (3ft), S indefinite. In early summer produces 2 or 3 red-purple flowers marked with yellow.

I. 'Saffron Jewel'. Rhizomatous, bearded iris (Intermediate). H 75cm (30in), S indefinite. In early summer, branched stem produces 2–5 flowers, 5–10cm (2–4in) across, with oyster falls, veined chartreuse, and paler standards. Falls each have a blue blaze and beard.

I. sanguinea, syn. *I. extremorientalis*, *I. orientalis* of gardens. Rhizomatous, beardless Siberian iris. H to 1m (3ft), S indefinite. From late spring to early summer, branched stem produces 2 or 3 deep purple or red-purple flowers, 5–10cm (2–4in) wide, from each set of bracts. Falls are red-purple with white throats finely veined purple.

I. 'Sapphire Star' (illus. p.235). Rhizomatous, beardless Japanese iris. H 1.2m (4ft), S indefinite. In summer, branched stem bears 3–5 white-veined, lavender flowers, 15–30cm (6–12in) wide, pencilled with a white halo around a yellow blaze on each fall. Prefers moist soil.

I. setosa (Bristle-pointed iris; illus. p.235). Rhizomatous, beardless iris, very variable in stature. H 10–90cm (4–36in), S indefinite. Bears 2–13 deep blue or purple-blue flowers, 5–8cm (2–3in) across, from each spathe in late spring and early summer. Falls have paler blue or white marks; each standard is reduced to a bristle.

I. 'Shepherd's Delight' (illus. p.235). Rhizomatous, bearded iris (Standard Tall). H 1m (3ft), S indefinite. In early summer, well-branched stem produces

6–10 clear pink flowers, 15–18cm (6–7in) wide, with a yellow cast.

I. sibirica (Siberian flag). Rhizomatous, beardless Siberian iris. H 50–120cm (20–48in), S indefinite. From late spring to early summer, branched stem bears 2 or 3 dark-veined, blue or blue-purple flowers, 5–10cm (2–4in) across, from each spathe. Prefers moist or boggy conditions.

I. 'Splash Down'. Rhizomatous, beardless Siberian iris. H 1m (3ft), S indefinite. From late spring to early summer, branched stem produces 1–4 flowers, 5–10cm (2–4in) across. Standards are pale blue and falls speckled blue on a pale ground. Prefers moist soil.

I. spuria. Very variable, rhizomatous, beardless Spuria iris. H 50–90cm (20–36in), S indefinite. Strong, erect-branched stem produces 2–5 pale blue-purple, sky-blue, violet-blue, white or yellow flowers, 5–12cm (2–5in) across, in early summer. Prefers moist soil.

I. 'Stepping Out'. Rhizomatous, bearded iris (Standard Tall). H 1m (3ft), S indefinite. Well-branched stem produces 8–11 white flowers, 14–15cm (5½–6in) wide, with deep blue-purple marks in early summer.

I. stylosa. See *I. unguicularis*.

I. 'Sun Miracle' (illus. p.235). Rhizomatous, bearded iris (Standard Tall). H 1m (3ft), S indefinite. Well-branched stem produces 7–10 pure yellow flowers, 15–18cm (6–7in) wide, in early summer.

I. susiana (Mourning iris). Rhizomatous Oncocyclus iris. H 35–40cm (14–16in), S indefinite. In late spring produces a solitary, greyish-white flower, 8–15cm (3–6in) wide, heavily veined deep purple. Standards appear larger than incurved falls, which each carry a black blaze and a deep purple beard. Grows best in a frame or alpine house.

I. tectorum (Japanese roof iris, Wall flag; illus. p.234). Evansia iris with stout rhizomes. H 25–35cm (10–14in), S indefinite. Has fans of broadly lance-shaped, ribbed leaves. In early summer, sparsely branched stem produces 2–3 darker-veined, bright lilac flowers, 1–8cm (½–3in) across with a white crest on each fall, from each spathe. Prefers a sheltered, sunny site near a south- or west-facing wall.

I. tenax (illus. p.234). Rhizomatous, beardless Pacific Coast iris. H 15–30cm (6–12in), S indefinite. From late spring to early summer produces 1 or 2 deep purple to lavender-blue flowers, 8–12cm (3–5in) across, often with yellow-and-white marking on falls. White, cream and yellow variants also occur. Narrow, dark green leaves are stained pink at base.

I. 'Theseus'. Rhizomatous Regeliocyclus iris. H 45cm (18in), S indefinite. From late spring to early summer produces usually 2 flowers, 10–15cm (4–6in) across, with violet standards and violet-veined, cream falls. Is best in a frame or alpine house.

I. 'Thornbird'. Rhizomatous, bearded iris (Standard Tall). H 90cm (3ft), S indefinite. In early summer, produces up to 7 flowers, with standards that are pale greenish-white and falls that are

greenish-brown overlaid with deep violet lines. The long, horned beard is violet, tipped with mustard-yellow.

I. tolmeiana. See *I. missouriensis*.

I. tuberosa. See *Hermodactylus tuberosus*.

I. unguicularis, syn. *I. stylosa* (Algerian iris, Algerian winter iris, Winter iris). Evergreen, rhizomatous, beardless iris. H to 20cm (8in), S indefinite. Has narrow, tough leaves. Almost stemless, primrose-scented, lilac flowers, 5–8cm (2–3in) across with yellow centres to the falls and with very long tubes, appear from late autumn to early spring. Buds are prone to slug attack. Is excellent for cutting. Prefers a sheltered site against a south- or west-facing wall. **'Mary Barnard'** has deep violet-blue flowers. Flowers of **'Walter Butt'** are pale silvery-lavender.

I. variegata (Variegated iris; illus. p.235). Rhizomatous, bearded iris. H 30–50cm (12–20in), S indefinite. In early summer, branched stem produces 3–6 flowers, 5–8cm (2–3in) across, with bright yellow standards and white or pale yellow falls, heavily veined red-brown and appearing striped.

I. verna. Rhizomatous, beardless iris. H 5cm (2in), S indefinite. In mid-spring bears 1, occasionally 2, lilac-blue flowers, 2.5–5cm (1–2in) across, with a narrow, orange stripe in the centre of each fall. Prefers semi-shade and moist but well-drained soil.

I. versicolor (Blue flag, Wild iris; illus. p.234). Robust, rhizomatous, beardless iris. H 60cm (2ft), S indefinite. Branched stem produces 3–5 or more purple-blue, reddish-purple, lavender or slate-purple flowers, 5–10cm (2–4in) across, from early to mid-summer. Falls usually have a central white area veined purple. Prefers partial shade and thrives in moist soil or in shallow water. **'Kermesina'** has red-purple flowers.

I. 'Violet Beauty', syn. *I. reticulata* 'Violet Beauty'. Bulbous Reticulata iris. H 10–15cm (4–6in), S 4–6cm (1½–2½in). In early spring bears a solitary, fragrant, long-tubed, deep violet-purple flower, 4–6cm (1½–2½in) wide, with an orange ridge down the centre of each fall. Narrow, squared leaves elongate after flowering time.

I. warleyensis. Bulbous Juno iris. H 20–45cm (8–18in), S 7–8cm (3in). In spring produces up to 5 pale lilac or violet-blue flowers, 5–7cm (2–3in) across, in leaf axils. Each fall has a darker blue apex and a yellow stain in the centre. Bears scattered, lance-shaped, channelled, mid-green leaves. Is best in an unheated greenhouse.

I. 'White Excelsior'. Bulbous Xiphium iris (Dutch). H to 80cm (32in), S 15cm (6in). From spring to early summer bears 1 or 2 white flowers, 6–8cm (2½–3in) wide, with a yellow stripe down each fall centre. Narrowly lance-shaped, channelled, mid-green leaves are scattered on flower stem.

I. winogradowii (illus. p.235). Bulbous Reticulata iris. H 6–10cm (2½–4in), S 6–7cm (2½–3in). Solitary pale primrose-yellow flower, 6–7cm (2½–3in) wide, spotted green on falls, appears in early spring. Narrow,

squared leaves are very short at flowering time but elongate later.

I. 'Wisley White' (illus. p.234). Rhizomatous, beardless Siberian iris. H to 1m (3ft), S indefinite. Each stem carries 2 or 3 white flowers, held well above the foliage, in early summer.

I. xiphioides. See *I. latifolia*.

I. xiphium. Bulbous Xiphium iris (Spanish). H to 80cm (32in), S 15cm (6in). Has 1 or 2 blue or violet, occasionally yellow or white, flowers, 6–8cm (2½–3in) across, with central orange or yellow marks on the falls, in spring and early summer. Narrowly lance-shaped, channelled, mid-green leaves are scattered on flower stem. **'Blue Angel'** produces bright mid-blue flowers with a yellow mark in the centre of each fall. Flowers of **'Lusitanica'** are pure yellow. **'Queen Wilhelmina'** produces white flowers in spring. **'Wedgwood'** (illus. p.235) has bright blue flowers.

Iris

Algerian. See *Iris unguicularis*.
Algerian winter. See *Iris unguicularis*.
Bristle-pointed. See *Iris setosa*, illus. p.235.
Dalmatian. See *Iris pallida*.
Dwarf bearded. See *Iris pumila*.
English. See *Iris latifolia*, illus. p.234.
Japanese roof. See *Iris tectorum*, illus. p.234.
Mourning. See *Iris susiana*.
Stinking. See *Iris foetidissima*.
Variegated. See *Iris variegata*, illus. p.235.
Widow. See *Hermodactylus tuberosus*, illus. p.414.
Wild. See *Iris versicolor*, illus. p.234.
Winter. See *Iris unguicularis*.
Irish ivy. See *Hedera hibernica*, illus. p.221.
Iron cross begonia. See *Begonia masoniana*, illus. p.295.
Ironwood. See *Ostrya virginiana*, illus. p.77.
Catalina. See *Lyonothamnus floribundus*.
Persian. See *Parrotia persica*, illus. p.82.

ISATIS

BRASSICACEAE/CRUCIFERAE

Genus of summer-flowering annuals, biennials and perennials. Needs sun and fertile, well-drained soil. Propagate by seed in autumn or spring.

I. tinctoria (Woad). Vigorous, upright biennial. H to 1.2m (4ft), S 45cm (1½ft). Has oblong to lance-shaped, glaucous leaves and, in summer, large, terminal panicles of 4-petalled, yellow flowers.

ISMELIA

ASTERACEAE/COMPOSITAE

Genus of one species of annuals, grown for its daisy-like flower heads. Needs full sun and well-drained soil. Propagate by seed in spring.

I. carinata, syn. *Chrysanthemum carinatum*, *C. tricolor*. **'Monarch Court Jesters'** (red with yellow

centres) illus. p.329, (white with red centres) illus. p.320. **Tricolor Series** is a group of fast-growing, upright, branching annuals. H 30–60cm (12–24in), S 30cm (12in). Has feathery, light green leaves and, in summer, daisy-like, single or double flower heads, to 8cm (3in) wide, in many colour combinations. Tall cultivars, H 60cm (24in), S 30cm (12in), and dwarf, H and S 30cm (12in), are available.

Ismene calathina. See *Hymenocallis narcissiflora*.

ISOLEPIS

CYPERACEAE

See also GRASSES, BAMBOOS, RUSHES and SEDGES.

I. setaceus, syn. *Scirpus setaceus* (Bristle club-rush). Tuft-forming, annual or short-lived, perennial rush. H 10–15cm (4–6in), S 8cm (3in). Has very slender, lax, basal leaves. Very slender, unbranched stems each bear 1–3 minute, egg-shaped, green spikelets in summer.

ISOPLEXIS

SCROPHULARIACEAE

Genus of evergreen, mainly summer-flowering shrubs, grown for their flowers. Is closely related to *Digitalis*. Tender, min. 7°C (45°F). Tolerates full light or partial shade and prefers well-drained soil. Water potted specimens freely when in full growth, moderately at other times. Remove spent flower spikes. Propagate by seed in spring or by semi-ripe cuttings in late summer.

I. canariensis, syn. *Digitalis canariensis*, illus. p.171.

ISOPYRUM

RANUNCULACEAE

Genus of spring-flowering perennials, grown for their small flowers and delicate foliage. Is suitable for peat beds, woodlands and rock gardens. Requires shade and humus-rich, moist soil. Propagate by seed when fresh or by division in autumn. Self-seeds readily.

I. thalictroides. Dainty, clump-forming perennial. H and S 25cm (10in). Central stalk bears fern-like, 3-parted leaves, each leaflet being cut into 3. Has small, nodding, cup-shaped, white flowers in spring.

Italian alder. See *Alnus cordata*, illus. p.66.
Italian buckthorn. See *Rhamnus alaternus*.
Italian jasmine. See *Solanum seaforthianum*, illus. p.206.
Italian maple. See *Acer opalus*.
Italian millet. See *Setaria italica*.

ITEA

ESCALLONIACEAE

Genus of deciduous or evergreen trees and shrubs, grown for their foliage and flowers. In most areas protect by

growing against a south- or west-facing wall. Needs sun or semi-shade and fertile, well-drained but not too dry soil. Propagate by softwood cuttings in summer.
I. ilicifolia illus. p.146.

Ivy. See *Hedera*.
  Algerian. See *Hedera canariensis* var. *algeriensis*.
  Bird's-foot. See *Hedera helix* 'Pedata', illus. p.221.
  Boston. See *Parthenocissus tricuspidata*, illus. p.218.
  Canary Island. See *Hedera canariensis*.
  Clustered. See *Hedera helix* 'Conglomerata'.
  Common English. See *Hedera helix*.
  Finger-leaved. See *Hedera hibernica* 'Digitata', illus. p.221.
  Five-leaved. See *Parthenocissus quinquefolia*.
  German. See *Senecio mikanioides*.
  Grape. See *Cissus rhombifolia*, illus. p.220.
  Ground. See *Glechoma hederacea*.
  Irish. See *Hedera hibernica*, illus. p.221.

Ivy (continued)
  Japanese. See *Hedera rhombea*; *Parthenocissus tricuspidata*, illus. p.218.
  Kenilworth. See *Cymbalaria muralis*.
  Miniature grape. See *Cissus striata*.
  Natal. See *Senecio macroglossus*.
  Nepalese. See *Hedera nepalensis*.
  Persian. See *Hedera colchica*.
  Purple-leaved. See *Hedera helix* 'Atropurpurea', illus. p.221.
  Shield. See *Hedera hibernica* 'Deltoidea', illus. p.221.
  Swedish. See *Plectranthus oertendahlii*; *Plectranthus verticillatus*.
  Sweetheart. See *Hedera hibernica* 'Deltoidea', illus. p.221.
  Tree. See x *Fatshedera lizei*, illus. p.152.
  Variegated ground. See *Glechoma hederacea* 'Variegata', illus. p.300.
  Ivy of Uruguay. See *Cissus striata*.
  Ivy peperomia. See *Peperomia griseoargentea*.
  Ivy-leaved toadflax. See *Cymbalaria muralis*.
  Ivy-leaved violet. See *Viola hederacea*.

IXIA
IRIDACEAE

Genus of spring- and summer-flowering corms with wiry stems and spikes of flattish flowers. Grow in an open, sunny situation and in well-drained soil. Plant in autumn for spring and early summer flowers; plant in spring for later summer display. Dry off after flowering. Propagate in autumn by seed or by offsets at replanting time.

I. 'Mabel'. Spring- to early summer-flowering corm. H 40cm (16in), S 2.5–5cm (1–2in). Has linear, basal, mid-green leaves and spikes of deep pink flowers.

I. maculata. Spring- to early summer-flowering corm. H 40cm (16in), S 2.5–5cm (1–2in). Leaves are linear, erect and mostly basal. Wiry stem bears a spike of flattish, orange or yellow flowers, 2.5–5cm (1–2in) across, with brown or black centres.

I. monadelpha. Spring- to early summer-flowering corm. H 30cm (12in), S 2.5–5cm (1–2in). Linear, erect leaves are mostly basal. Stem produces a dense spike of 5–10 flattish, white, pink, purple or blue flowers, 3–4cm (1¼–1½in) across,

often with differently coloured eyes.
I. viridiflora illus. p.414.

IXIOLIRION
AMARYLLIDACEAE

Genus of bulbs, grown for their funnel-shaped flowers mainly in spring. Needs a sheltered, sunny site and well-drained soil that becomes hot and dry in summer to ripen the bulb. Propagate, by seed or offsets, in autumn.

I. montanum. See *I. tataricum*.
I. tataricum, syn. *I. montanum*, illus. p.414.

IXORA
RUBIACEAE

Genus of evergreen, summer-flowering shrubs, grown primarily for their flowers, some also for their foliage. Tender, min. 13–16°C (55–61°F). Prefers full sun and humus-rich, well-drained soil. Water containerized specimens freely when in full growth, moderately at other times. Propagate by seed in spring or by semi-ripe cuttings in summer.

I. coccinea illus. p.165.

J

JACARANDA
BIGNONIACEAE

Genus of deciduous or evergreen trees, grown for their flowers and foliage in spring-summer. Tender, min. 7–10°C (45–50°F). Grows in any fertile, well-drained soil and in full light. Water potted specimens freely in full growth, sparingly at other times. Potted plants grown for foliage may be cut back hard in late winter. Propagate by seed in spring or semi-ripe cuttings in summer.
J. acutifolia of gardens. See *J. mimosifolia*.
J. mimosifolia, syn. *J. acutifolia* of gardens, *J. ovalifolia*, illus. p.79.
J. ovalifolia. See *J. mimosifolia*.

Jack pine. See *Pinus banksiana*, illus. p.107.
Jack-in-the-pulpit. See *Arisaema triphyllum*, illus. p.414.
Jacobean lily. See *Sprekelia formosissima*, illus. p.413.
Jacobinia carnea. See *Justicia carnea*.
Jacobinia coccinea. See *Pachystachys coccinea*.
Jacobinia pohliana. See *Justicia carnea*.
Jacobinia spicigera. See *Justicia spicigera*.
Jacob's coat. See *Acalypha wilkesiana*, illus. p.143.
Jacob's ladder. See *Polemonium*.

JACQUEMONTIA
CONVOLVULACEAE

Genus of evergreen, twining climbers, grown for their flowers. Tender, min. 16–18°C (61–4°F). Any well-drained soil is suitable with full light. Water freely except in cold weather. Provide support and thin out by cutting old stems to ground level in spring. Propagate by seed in spring or by semi-ripe cuttings in summer. Spider mite and whitefly may cause problems.
J. pentantha, syn. *J. violacea*. Fast-growing, evergreen, twining climber. H 2–3m (6–10ft). Has heart-shaped, pointed leaves and 2.5cm (1in) wide, funnel-shaped, rich violet-blue or pure blue flowers in long-stalked clusters in summer-autumn.
J. violacea. See *J. pentantha*.

Jade plant, Silver. See *Crassula arborescens*, illus. p.458.
Jade tree. See *Crassula ovata*, illus. p.457.
Jade vine. See *Strongylodon macrobotrys*, illus. p.206.

JAMESIA
HYDRANGEACEAE

Genus of one species of deciduous shrub, grown for its flowers. Needs full sun and fertile, well-drained soil. Propagate by softwood cuttings in summer. Zone 6.
J. americana. Deciduous, bushy shrub. H 1.5m (5ft), S 2.5m (8ft). Rounded, grey-green leaves are grey-white beneath. Clusters of small, slightly fragrant, star-shaped, white flowers are produced during late spring.

JANCAEA,
syn. JANKAEA
GESNERIACEAE

Genus of one species of evergreen, rosetted perennial, grown for its flowers and silver-green leaves. Makes a good alpine house plant. Is difficult to grow, as needs shade from mid-day sun in high summer, a humus-rich, gritty, moist, alkaline soil and a gritty collar. Dislikes winter wet. Propagate by seed in spring or by leaf cuttings in mid-summer.
J. heldreichii illus. p.369.

Jankaea. Reclassified as *Jancaea*.
Japan pepper. See *Zanthoxylum piperitum*, illus. p.145.
Japanese anemone. See *Anemone* x *hybrida*.
Japanese angelica tree. See *Aralia elata*.
Japanese apricot. See *Prunus mume*.
Japanese aralia. See *Fatsia japonica*.
Japanese arrowhead. See *Sagittaria sagittifolia* 'Flore Pleno'.
Japanese banana. See *Musa basjoo*, illus. p.233.
Japanese big-leaf magnolia. See *Magnolia hypoleuca*, illus. p.75.
Japanese black pine. See *Pinus thunbergii*, illus. p.106.
Japanese blood grass. See *Imperata cylindrica*.
Japanese cedar. See *Cryptomeria japonica*.
Japanese climbing fern. See *Lygodium japonicum*.
Japanese flag. See *Iris ensata*.
Japanese hemlock. See *Tsuga diversifolia*; *Tsuga sieboldii*.
Japanese holly. See *Ilex crenata*.
Japanese honeysuckle. See *Lonicera japonica*.
Japanese horse-chestnut. See *Aesculus turbinata*.
Japanese hydrangea vine. See *Schizophragma hydrangeoides*.
Japanese ivy. See *Hedera rhombea*; *Parthenocissus tricuspidata*, illus. p.218.
Japanese larch. See *Larix kaempferi*.
Japanese maple. See *Acer japonicum*; *Acer palmatum*.
Japanese painted fern. See *Athyrium niponicum*, illus. p.313.
Japanese pittosporum. See *Pittosporum tobira*.
Japanese privet. See *Ligustrum japonicum*.
Japanese quince. See *Chaenomeles japonica*.
Japanese red pine. See *Pinus densiflora*.
Japanese roof iris. See *Iris tectorum*, illus. p.234.
Japanese rose. See *Rosa rugosa*, illus. p.187.
Japanese sago palm. See *Cycas revoluta*, illus. p.152.
Japanese shield fern. See *Dryopteris erythrosora*.
Japanese snowball tree. See *Viburnum plicatum*.
Japanese spindle. See *Euonymus japonicus*.
Japanese umbrella pine. See *Sciadopitys verticillata*, illus. p.106.
Japanese walnut. See *Juglans ailantifolia*.
Japanese white pine. See *Pinus parviflora*, illus. p.105.
Japanese wisteria. See *Wisteria floribunda*.
Japanese witch hazel. See *Hamamelis japonica*.
Japanese yew. See *Taxus cuspidata*, illus. p.109.
Japonica. See *Chaenomeles*; *C. japonica*.

JASIONE
CAMPANULACEAE

Genus of summer-flowering annuals, biennials and perennials, grown for their attractive flower heads. Needs sun and sandy soil. Remove old stems in autumn. Propagate by seed in autumn or by division in spring.
J. laevis, syn. *J. perennis* (Sheep's bit). Tufted perennial. H 5–30cm (2–12in), S 10–20cm (4–8in). Has narrowly oblong, very hairy or glabrous, grey-green leaves and, in summer, spiky, spherical, blue flower heads borne on erect stems. Is good for a rock garden.
J. perennis. See *J. laevis*.

Jasmine. See *Jasminum*.
  Cape. See *Gardenia augusta*.
  Carolina. See *Gelsemium sempervirens*, illus. p.206.
  Chilean. See *Mandevilla laxa*.
  Common. See *Jasminum officinale*.
  Confederate. See *Trachelospermum jasminoides*, illus. p.207.
  False. See *Gelsemium sempervirens*, illus. p.206.
  Italian. See *Solanum seaforthianum*, illus. p.206.
  Madagascar. See *Stephanotis floribunda*, illus. p.204.
  Orange. See *Murraya paniculata*.
  Primrose. See *Jasminum mesnyi*, illus. p.207.
  Star. See *Trachelospermum jasminoides*, illus. p.207.
  West Indian. See *Plumeria alba*.
  Winter. See *Jasminum nudiflorum*, illus. p.151.
  Yellow. See *Jasminum humile*, illus. p.146.

JASMINUM
Jasmine
OLEACEAE

Genus of deciduous or evergreen shrubs and woody-stemmed, scrambling or twining climbers, grown for their often fragrant flowers and their foliage. Hardy to tender, min. 7–18°C (45–64°F). Needs full sun and fertile, well-drained soil. *J. nudiflorum*, which needs supporting, benefits from having old shoots thinned out after flowering, when others may be pruned. Propagate by semi-ripe cuttings in summer.
J. angulare, syn. *J. capense*. Evergreen, woody-stemmed, scrambling climber. H 2m (6ft) or more. Tender, min. 7–10°C (45–50°F). Dark green leaves have 3 oval leaflets. Small clusters of fragrant, tubular, 5-lobed, white flowers are carried in late summer.
J. beesianum. Evergreen, woody-stemmed, scrambling climber, deciduous in cool areas. H to 5m (15ft). Tender, min. –1°C (30°F).Has lance-shaped leaves. Fragrant, tubular, usually 6-lobed, pinkish-red flowers, 1–3 together, borne in early summer; then shiny, black berries.
J. capense. See *J. angulare*.
J. grandiflorum of gardens. See *J. officinale* f. *affine*.
J. humile (Yellow jasmine) illus. p.146. 'Revolutum' is an evergreen, bushy shrub. H 2.5m (8ft), S 3m (10ft). Bears large, fragrant, tubular, upright, bright yellow flowers, with 5 spreading lobes, on long, slender, green shoots from early spring to late autumn. Glossy, bright green leaves each consist of 3–7 oval leaflets. Zone 8. f. *wallichianum* has semi-pendent flowers and 7–13 leaflets.
J. mesnyi, syn. *J. primulinum*, illus. p.207.
J. nobile subsp. *rex*, syn. *J. rex*. Evergreen, woody-stemmed, twining climber. H 3m (10ft). Tender, min. 18°C (64°F). Has broadly oval, leathery, deep green leaves, 10–20cm (4–8in) long. Scentless, tubular, 5-lobed, pure white flowers are pink-tinged in bud and appear intermittently all year if warm enough.
J. nudiflorum illus. p.151.
J. officinale (Common jasmine, Jessamine). Semi-evergreen or deciduous, woody-stemmed, twining climber. H to 12m (40ft). Leaves comprise 7 or 9 leaflets. Has clusters of fragrant, 4- or 5-lobed, white flowers in summer-autumn. Zone 7. f. *affine* (syn. *J. grandiflorum* of gardens) illus. p.208.
J. parkeri. Evergreen, domed shrub. H 15cm (6in), S 38cm (18in) or more. Produces a tangled mass of fine stems and twigs bearing minute, oval leaves. Masses of tiny, tubular, 5-lobed, yellow flowers appear from leaf axils in early summer. Zone 8.
J. polyanthum illus. p.219.
J. primulinum. See *J. mesnyi*.
J. rex. See *J. nobile* subsp. *rex*.

JEFFERSONIA
BERBERIDACEAE

Genus of spring-flowering perennials. Needs shade or partial shade and

597

humus-rich, moist soil. Extensive root systems resent disturbance. Top-dress crown in late autumn. Propagate by seed as soon as ripe.
J. diphylla illus. p.347.
J. dubia, syn. *Plagiorhegma dubia*, illus. p.369.

Jeffrey pine. See *Pinus jeffreyi*, illus. p.103.
Jelly palm. See *Butia capitata*, illus. p.100.
Jersey elm. See *Ulmus minor* 'Sarniensis'.
Jerusalem cherry. See *Solanum pseudocapsicum*.
Jerusalem cross. See *Lychnis chalcedonica*, illus. p.249.
Jerusalem sage. See *Phlomis fruticosa*, illus. p.170.
Jerusalem thorn. See *Paliurus spina-christi*, illus. p.122; *Parkinsonia aculeata*.
Jessamine. See *Jasminum officinale*.
Jesuit's nut. See *Trapa natans*, illus. p.449.
Job's tears. See *Coix lacryma-jobi*, illus. p.308.
Joe Pye weed. See *Eupatorium purpureum*, illus. p.231.
Jonquil. See *Narcissus jonquilla*, illus. p.418.
Campernelle. See *Narcissus* x *odorus*.
Queen Anne's. See *Narcissus jonquilla* 'Flore Pleno'.
Wild. See *Narcissus jonquilla*, illus. p.418.
Josephine's lily. See *Brunsvigia josephinae*.

JOVIBARBA
CRASSULACEAE

Genus of evergreen perennials that spread by short stolons and are grown for their symmetrical rosettes of oval to strap-shaped, pointed, fleshy leaves. Makes ground-hugging mats, suitable for rock gardens, screes, walls, banks and alpine houses. Needs sun and gritty soil. Takes several years to reach flowering size. Rosettes die after plants have flowered, but leave numerous offsets. Propagate by offsets in summer.
J. hirta, syn. *Sempervivum hirtum*, illus. p.388.
J. sobolifera, syn. *Sempervivum soboliferum*. Vigorous, evergreen, mat-forming perennial. H 10cm (4in), S 20cm (8in). Rounded, greyish-green or olive-green rosettes are often red-tinged. Flower stems bear terminal clusters of small, cup-shaped, 6-petalled (rarely 5 or 7), pale yellow flowers in summer.

JUANULLOA
SOLANACEAE

Genus of evergreen, summer-flowering shrubs, grown for their flowers. Tender, min. 13–15°C (55–9°F). Low temperatures cause leaf drop. Prefers full light and fertile, freely draining soil. Water potted specimens moderately, less when not in full growth. To encourage a branching habit, tip prune young plants. Propagate by semi-ripe

cuttings in summer. Whitefly, spider mite and mealy bug may be troublesome.
J. aurantiaca. See J. mexicana.
J. mexicana, syn. J. aurantiaca, illus. p.171

JUBAEA
ARECACEAE

Genus of one species of evergreen palm, grown for its overall appearance. Needs full light and fertile, well-drained soil. Water potted specimens moderately, less frequently in winter. Propagate by seed in spring at not less than 25°C (77°F). Spider mite may be a nuisance. Zone 9.
J. chilensis, syn. *J. spectabilis*, illus. p.85.
J. spectabilis. See *J. chilensis*.

Judas tree. See *Cercis*.

JUGLANS
Walnut
JUGLANDACEAE

Genus of deciduous trees, with aromatic leaves, grown for their foliage, stately habit and, in some species, edible nuts (walnuts). Produces greenish-yellow catkins in spring and early summer. Young plants are prone to frost damage. Requires full sun and deep, fertile, well-drained soil. Propagate by seed, when ripe, in autumn.
J. ailantifolia, syn. *J. sieboldiana* (Japanese walnut). Deciduous, spreading tree with stout shoots. H and S 15m (50ft). Very large leaves consist of 11–17 oblong, glossy, bright green leaflets. Bears edible walnuts in autumn. Zone 4b. var. **cordiformis** (syn. *J. cordiformis*) illus. p.68.
J. cathayensis (Chinese walnut). Deciduous, spreading tree. H and S 20m (70ft). Has very large leaves, consisting of 11–17 oval to oblong, dark green leaflets. Bears edible walnuts in autumn. Zone 6.
J. cinerea (Butternut). Fast-growing, deciduous, spreading tree. H 25m (80ft), S 20m (70ft). Leaves are large and very aromatic, with 7–19 oval to oblong, pointed, bright green leaflets. Bears dense clusters of large, rounded nuts in autumn. Zone 3.
J. cordiformis. See *J. ailantifolia* var. *cordiformis*.
J. microcarpa, syn. *J. rupestris*, illus. p.92.
J. nigra illus. p.67.
J. regia illus. p.66. 'Carpathian', zone 4.
J. rupestris. See *J. microcarpa*.
J. sieboldiana. See *J. ailantifolia*.

JUNCUS
JUNCACEAE

See also GRASSES, BAMBOOS, RUSHES AND SEDGES.
J. effusus 'Spiralis', syn. *J. effusus* f. *spiralis*, *Scirpus lacustris* 'Spiralis', illus. p.308.

Juneberry. See *Amelanchier*.
Juniper. See *Juniperus*.

Bonin Isles. See *Juniperus procumbens*, illus. p.110.
Juniper (continued)
Chinese. See *Juniperus chinensis*.
Coffin. See *Juniperus recurva* var. *coxii*.
Common. See *Juniperus communis*.
Creeping. See *Juniperus horizontalis*.
Drooping. See *Juniperus recurva*, illus. p.108.
Flaky. See *Juniperus squamata*.
Himalayan weeping. See *Juniperus recurva*, illus. p.108.
Rocky Mountain. See *Juniperus scopulorum*.
Shore. See *Juniperus conferta*.
Syrian. See *Juniperus drupacea*.
Temple. See *Juniperus rigida*.

JUNIPERUS
Juniper
CUPRESSACEAE

See also CONIFERS.
J. chinensis (Chinese juniper). Conical conifer, making a tree. H 15m (50ft), S 2–3m (6–10ft), or a spreading shrub, H 1–5m (3–15ft), S 3–5m (10–15ft). Has peeling bark. Both scale- and needle-like, aromatic, dark green leaves, paired or in 3s, are borne on same shoot. Globose, fleshy, berry-like fruits are glaucous white. Many cultivars commonly listed under *J. chinensis* are forms of *J.* x *pfitzeriana*. 'Aurea', H 10–15m (30–50ft), S 3–4m (10–12ft), is a slow-growing, oval or conical form with gold foliage and abundant yellow, male cones. 'Blaauw' (syn. *J.* x *media* 'Blaauw'), H and S 2m (6ft), is a spreading shrub with blue-green foliage. 'Blue and Gold' (syn. *J.* x *media* 'Blue and Gold'; illus. p.111), H to 1m (3ft), S 1m (3ft), is a spreading form with leaves variegated sky-blue and gold. 'Expansa Variegata' (syn. *J. davurica* 'Expansa Variegata'; illus. p.111) is a conifer with trailing or ascending branchlets. H 75cm (30in), S 1.5–2m (5–6ft). Bears scale- and needle-like, aromatic, yellow-variegated, bluish-green leaves. 'Kaizuka', H 5m (15ft), S 3–5m (10–15ft), forms a sprawling, irregular bush and has a profusion of cones. 'Keteleeri' illus. p.105. 'Obelisk' illus. p.108. 'Plumosa Aurea' (syn. *J.* x *media* 'Plumosa Aurea'; illus. p.111) is more erect, with green-gold foliage, turning bronze in winter. 'Pyramidalis', H 10m (30ft), S 1–2m (3–6ft), is a columnar, dense form with ascending branches bearing needle-like, blue-green leaves. 'Robust Green' syn. *J. virginiana* 'Robusta Green' (illus. p.108). 'Stricta' (illus. p.110), H to 5m (15ft), S to 1m (3ft), is conical, with soft, blue-green, young foliage. All zone 4.
J. communis (Common juniper). Conifer, ranging from a spreading shrub to a narrow, upright tree. H 30cm–8m (1–25ft), S 1–4m (3–12ft). Has needle-like, aromatic, glossy, mid- or yellow-green leaves in 3s and bears globular to ovoid, fleshy, greenish berries that become glaucous blue, then ripen to black in their third year. 'Compressa', H 75cm (30in), S 15cm (6in), is a dwarf, erect form.

'Hibernica' (illus. p.111), H 3–5m (10–15ft), S 30cm (12in), is columnar. 'Hornibrookii', H 50cm (20in), S 2m (6ft), and 'Prostrata', H 20–30cm (8–12in), S 1–2m (3–6ft), are carpeting plants. Zone 4.
J. conferta, syn. *J. rigida* subsp. *conferta* (Shore juniper). Prostrate, shrubby conifer. H 15cm (6in), S 1–2m (3–6ft). Spreading branches bear dense, needle-like, aromatic, glossy, bright green leaves, glaucous beneath. Produces glaucous black berries. Tolerates salty, coastal air. Zone 5.
J. davurica 'Expansa Variegata'. See *J. chinensis* 'Expansa Variegata'.
J. drupacea (Syrian juniper). Columnar conifer. H 10–15m (30–50ft), S 1–2m (3–6ft). Has needle-like, aromatic, light green leaves, in 3s, and ovoid or almost globose, fleshy, brown berries. Zone 8.
J. horizontalis (Creeping juniper). Prostrate, wide-spreading, shrubby conifer, eventually forming mats up to 50cm (20in) thick. Has scale- or needle-like, aromatic, blue-green or -grey leaves and pale blue-grey berries. Leaves of 'Andorra Compact' (syn. *J.h.* 'Plumosa Compacta') turn bronze-purple in winter. 'Douglasii' (illus. p.110) has glaucous blue foliage that turns plum-purple in winter. 'Plumosa' is less dense than 'Andorra Compact' and has grey-green leaves, becoming purple during winter. 'Plumosa Compacta' see *J.h.* 'Andorra Compact'. 'Prince of Wales' has bright green foliage, tinged blue when young and turning purple-brown in winter. 'Turquoise Spreader' (illus. p.110) has turquoise-green foliage. 'Wiltonii' has bluish-grey leaves that retain their colour over winter. All zone 2.
J. x **media.** See *J.* x *pfitzeriana*.
'Blaauw' see *J. chinensis* 'Blaauw'.
'Blue and Gold' see *J. chinensis* 'Blue and Gold'. 'Hetzii' see *J. virginiana* 'Hetzii'. 'Pfitzeriana' see *J.* x *pfitzeriana* 'William Pfitzer'. 'Pfitzeriana Aurea' see *J.* x *pfitzeriana* 'Aurea'. 'Pfitzeriana Glauca' see *J.* x *pfitzeriana* 'Glauca'. 'Plumosa', H 1m (3ft), S 2–3m (6–10ft), is a spreading shrub with drooping sprays of mid-green foliage. 'Plumosa Aurea' see *J. chinensis* 'Plumosa Aurea'.
J. x **pfitzeriana**, syn. *J.* x *media*. Group of spreading to conical conifers. H 15m (50ft), S 2–3m (6–10ft). Has peeling bark. Mainly scale-like, dark green leaves exude a fetid smell when crushed. Fruits are globose to rounded, white or blue-black. Cultivars are suitable as ground cover or as specimen plants in a small garden. All zone 3. Some forms are commonly listed under *J. chinensis*. 'Aurea' (syn. *J.* x *media* 'Pfitzeriana Aurea'; illus. p.111) has golden foliage. 'Glauca' (syn. *J.* x *media* 'Pfitzeriana Glauca'; illus. p.110) has grey-blue leaves. 'William Pfitzer' (syn. *J.* x *media* 'Pfitzeriana'; illus. p.111), H 3m (10ft), S 3–5m (10–15ft), is a spreading, flat-topped shrub with grey-green leaves.
J. procumbens (Bonin Isles juniper; illus. p.110). Spreading, prostrate, shrubby conifer. H 75cm (30in), S 2m (6ft). Has red-brown bark. Thick branches carry needle-like, aromatic,

light green or yellow-green leaves and globose, fleshy, brown or black berries. Zone 4. **'Nana'** (illus. p.110), H 15–20cm (6–8in), S 75cm (30in),is less vigorous and is mat-forming.

J. recurva (Drooping juniper, Himalayan weeping juniper) illus. p.108. var. *coxii* (Coffin juniper) is a slow-growing, conical conifer. H to 15m (50ft), S to 7m (22ft). Smooth bark flakes in thin sheets. Weeping sprays of long, needle-like, aromatic, incurved leaves are bright green. Globose or ovoid, fleshy berries are black. Zone 7. **'Densa'** (syn. *J. recurva* 'Nana'; illus. p.110), H 30cm (1ft), S 1m (3ft), is a spreading shrub with sprays of green leaves that are erect at tips. **'Nana'** see *J.r.* 'Densa'.

J. rigida (Temple juniper). Sprawling, shrubby conifer. H and S 8m (25ft). Grey or brown bark peels in strips. Very sharp, needle-like, aromatic, bright green leaves, in 3s, are borne in nodding sprays. Globose, fleshy fruits are purplish-black. Zone 4b. subsp. *conferta* see *J. conferta*.

J. sabina (Savin). Spreading, shrubby conifer. H to 4m (12ft), S 3–5m (10–15ft). Has flaking, red-brown bark. Slender shoots bear mainly scale-like, aromatic, dark green leaves that give off a fetid smell when crushed. Bears rounded, blue-black berries. Zone 2. **'Blaue Donau'** (syn. *J.s.* 'Blue Danube'), H 2m (6ft), S 2–4m (6–12ft), is a spreading form with branch tips curved upwards and grey-blue foliage. Zone 2b. **'Blue Danube'** see *J.s.* 'Blaue Donau'. **'Cupressifolia'** (syn. *J.s.* Cupressifolia Group; illus. p.110), H 2m (6ft), S 4m (12ft), is a free-fruiting, female form with horizontal or ascending branches and blue-green leaves. Zone 2b. **'Mas'** (illus. p.110), has ascending branches. Leaves are blue above, green below, purplish in winter. Zone 3. var. *tamariscifolia* (syn. *J.s.* Tamariscifolia Group; illus. p.110), H 1m (3ft), S 2m (6ft), has tiered layers of mainly needle-like, bright green or blue-green leaves. Zone 2.

J. scopulorum (Rocky Mountain juniper). Slow-growing, round-crowned conifer. H 10m (30ft), S 4m (12ft). Reddish-brown bark is furrowed into strips or squares and peels on branches. Scale-like, aromatic leaves are grey-green to dark green. Bears globose, fleshy, blue berries. **'Skyrocket'** (syn. *J. virginiana* 'Skyrocket'; illus. p.110), H 8m (25ft), S 75cm (2½ft), is very narrow in habit with glaucous blue foliage. **'Springbank'** (illus. p.110) is narrowly conical with drooping branch tips and intense silvery-blue foliage. **'Tabletop'**, H 2m (6ft), S 5m (15ft), has a flat-topped habit and silvery-blue leaves. All zone 3.

J. squamata (Flaky juniper). Prostrate to sprawling, shrubby conifer. H 30cm–4m (1–12ft), S 1–5m (3–15ft). Bark is red-brown and flaking. Needle-like, aromatic, fresh green or bluish-green leaves spread at tips of shoots.

Produces ovoid, fleshy, black berries. **'Blue Carpet'**, H 30cm (1ft), S 2–3m (6–10ft), is vigorous and prostrate, with glaucous blue foliage. **'Blue Star'** (illus. p.110), H 50cm (20in), S 60cm (24in), forms a dense, rounded bush and has blue foliage. Zone 3. **'Chinese Silver'** (illus. p.110), H and S 3–4m (10–12ft), has branches with nodding tips and bluish leaves with bright silver undersides. **'Holger'** (illus. p.110), H and S 2m (6ft), has sulphur-yellow young leaves that contrast with steel-blue old foliage. **'Meyeri'**, H and S 5m (15ft), sprawls and has steel-blue foliage. All zone 5 unless marked.

J. virginiana (Pencil cedar). Slow-growing, conical or broadly columnar conifer. H 15–20m (50–70ft), S 6–8m (20–25ft). Both scale- and needle-like, aromatic, grey-green leaves are borne on same shoot. Ovoid, fleshy berries are brownish-violet and very glaucous. **'Grey Owl'** (illus. p.110), H 3m (10ft), S 3–5m (10–15ft), is a low, spreading cultivar with ascending branches and silvery-grey foliage. **'Hetzii'** (syn. *J.* x *media* 'Hetzii'), H 3–4m (10–12ft), S 4m (12ft), has tiers of grey-green foliage. **'Robusta Green'** see *J. chinensis* 'Robust Green'. **'Skyrocket'** see *J. scopulorum* 'Skyrocket'. All zone 3.

JUSTICIA
ACANTHACEAE

Genus of evergreen perennials, sub-shrubs and shrubs, grown mainly for their flowers. Tender, min. 10–15°C (50–59°F). Requires full light or partial shade and fertile, well-drained soil. Water containerized specimens freely when in full growth, moderately at other times. Some species need regular pruning. Propagate by softwood or greenwood cuttings in spring or early summer. Whitefly may cause problems.

J. adhatoda, syn. *Adhatoda duvernoia*, *Duvernoia adhatodoides* (Snake bush). Evergreen, erect shrub. H 2–3m (6–10ft), S 1–2m (3–6ft). Has elliptic, dark green leaves. Fragrant, tubular, white or mauve flowers, with pink, red or purple marks, appear in summer-autumn.

J. brandegeeana, syn. *Beloperone guttata*, *Drejerella guttata*, illus. p.166. **'Chartreuse'** illus. p.168.

J. carnea, syn. *Jacobinia carnea*, *J. pohliana*, illus. p.163.

J. coccinea. See *Pachystachys coccinea*.

J. floribunda. See *J. rizzinii*.

J. ghiesbreghtiana of gardens. See *J. spicigera*.

J. pauciflora. See *J. rizzinii*.

J. rizzinii, syn. *J. floribunda*, *J. pauciflora*, *Libonia floribunda*. Evergreen, rounded, freely branching shrub. H and S 30–60cm (1–2ft). Min. 15°C (59°F) to flower well in winter. Leaves are oval, mid-green. Bears nodding clusters of tubular, yellow-tipped, scarlet flowers mainly autumn-spring; best repropagated every few years.

J. spicigera, syn. *J. ghiesbreghtiana* of gardens, *Jacobinia spicigera*, illus. p.172.

K

KAEMPFERIA

ZINGIBERACEAE

Genus of tufted, rhizomatous perennials, grown for their aromatic leaves and their flowers. Tender, min. 18°C (64°F). Needs a moist atmosphere, partial shade and moist, humus-rich soil. Allow to dry out when plants become dormant. Propagate by division in late spring.
K. pulchra illus. p.283.
K. roscoeana. Rhizomatous perennial without an obvious stem. H 5–10cm (2–4in), S 20–25cm (8–10in). Usually has only 2 almost rounded, aromatic leaves, to 10cm (4in) long, dark green with pale green marks above, reddish-green below, that are held horizontally. A short spike of pure white flowers, each with a deeply lobed lip, appears from the centre of leaf tuft in autumn.

Kaffir fig. See *Carpobrotus edulis.*
Kaffir lily. See *Schizostylis.*
Kaki. See *Diospyros kaki.*

KALANCHOE,
syn. BRYOPHYLLUM

CRASSULACEAE

Genus of perennial succulents or shrubs with very fleshy, mainly cylindrical, oval or linear leaves and bell-shaped to tubular flowers. Many species produce new plantlets from indented leaf margins. Tender, min. 7–15°C (45–59°F). Needs full sun or partial shade and well-drained soil. Keep moist from spring to autumn. Water lightly and only occasionally in winter. Propagate by seed, offsets or stem cuttings in spring or summer.
K. beharensis illus. p.460.
K. blossfeldiana (Flaming Katy). Bushy, perennial succulent. H and S 30cm (12in). Min. 10°C (50°F). Has oval to oblong, glossy, dark green leaves with toothed edges and clusters of tubular, scarlet flowers, 0.5cm (¼in) across, in spring. Prefers partial shade. Many hybrids are available in a range of colours (salmon pink, illus. p.464).
K. daigremontiana illus. p.462.
K. delagoensis, syn. *K. tubiflora,* illus. p.468.
K. fedtschenkoi (South American air plant). Bushy, perennial succulent. H and S 1m (3ft). Min. 10°C (50°F). Produces oval, indented, blue-grey leaves with new plantlets in each notch. Bell-shaped, brownish-pink flowers, 2cm (¾in) long, appear in late winter. Prefers a sunny position. **'Variegata'** illus. p.462.
K. pumila. Creeping, perennial succulent. H 10cm (4in), S indefinite. Min. 10°C (50°F). Has oval, powdery grey-white leaves with indented margins. Tubular, pink flowers, 1cm (½in) long, appear in spring. Suits a hanging basket in a sunny position.
K. 'Tessa' illus. p.464.

K. tomentosa illus. p.467.
K. tubiflora. See *K. delagoensis.*
K. uniflora, syn. *Kitchingia uniflora.* Creeping, perennial succulent. H 6cm (2½in), S indefinite. Min. 15°C (59°F). Produces rounded, mid-green leaves, 0.5–3cm (¼–1¼in) long, and bell-shaped, yellow-flushed, reddish-purple flowers, 1cm (½in) long, in late winter. Prefers partial shade.
K. 'Wendy' illus. p.463.

Kale, Sea. See *Crambe maritima,* illus. p.276.

KALMIA

ERICACEAE

Genus of evergreen, summer-flowering shrubs, grown for their clusters of distinctive, usually cup-shaped flowers. Needs sun or semi-shade and moist, peaty, acid soil. Propagate species by softwood cuttings in summer or by seed in autumn, selected forms by softwood cuttings in summer. All parts may cause severe discomfort if ingested.
K. angustifolia (Sheep laurel). f. *rubra* (syn. *K. angustifolia* 'Rubra') illus. p.165.
K. latifolia (Calico bush) illus. p.141. **'Ostbo Red'** is an evergreen, bushy, dense shrub. H and S 3m (10ft). Has oval, glossy, rich green leaves. Large, showy clusters of deep pink flowers open in early summer from distinctively crimped, deep red buds. Prefers full sun. Zone 5b.

KALMIOPSIS

ERICACEAE

Genus of one species of evergreen, spring-flowering shrub, grown for its flowers. Requires semi-shade and moist, peaty, acid soil. Propagate by softwood or semi-ripe cuttings in summer.
K. leachiana 'La Piniec', syn. *K.l.* 'M. le Piniec'. Evergreen, bushy shrub. H and S 30cm (12in). Terminal clusters of small, widely bell-shaped, purplish-pink flowers are produced from early to late spring. Has small, oval, glossy, dark green leaves. Zone 8.

KALOPANAX

ARALIACEAE

Genus of one species of deciduous, autumn-flowering tree, grown for its foliage and fruits. Unripened wood on young plants is susceptible to frost damage. Does best in sun or semi-shade and in fertile, moist but well-drained soil. Propagate by softwood cuttings in summer.
K. pictus. See *K. septemlobus.*
K. ricinifolius. See *K. septemlobus.*
K. septemlobus, syn. *Acanthopanax ricinifolius, K. pictus, K. ricinifolius,* illus. p.80.

Kangaroo paw. See *Anigozanthos.*
 Red-and-green. See *Anigozanthos manglesii,* illus. p.250.
 Yellow. See *Anigozanthos flavidus,* illus. p.254.
Kangaroo vine. See *Cissus antarctica,* illus. p.220.
Kansas gay feather. See *Liatris pycnostachya.*
Kapok. See *Ceiba pentandra.*
Karo. See *Pittosporum crassifolium.*
Kashmir cypress. See *Cupressus cashmeriana,* illus. p.101.
Katsura. See *Cercidiphyllum japonicum,* illus. p.71.

KELSEYA

ROSACEAE

Genus of one species of extremely small, evergreen sub-shrub. Is difficult to grow and is best in an alpine house as foliage deeply resents both summer and winter wet. Needs full sun and moist, alkaline soil. Propagate by soft-tip cuttings in late spring or by seed in autumn. Is susceptible to moulds, so remove any dead rosettes at once.
K. uniflora. Slow-growing, evergreen, rosetted sub-shrub. H 1cm (½in), S to 20cm (8in). Forms a hard mat of closely packed, small rosettes of tiny, oval, dark green leaves. In early spring carries stemless, star-shaped, occasionally pink-flushed, white flowers. Zone 6.

Kenilworth Ivy. See *Cymbalaria muralis.*

KENNEDIA,
syn. KENNEDYA

LEGUMINOSAE/PAPILIONACEAE

Genus of evergreen, woody-stemmed, trailing and twining climbers, grown for their pea-like flowers. Tender, min. 5–7°C (41–5°F). Provide full light and moderately fertile, sandy soil. Water regularly when in full growth, sparingly in cold weather. Requires support. Thin out congested growth after flowering or in spring. Propagate by seed in spring or by semi-ripe cuttings in summer.
K. nigricans (Black bean). Vigorous, evergreen, woody-stemmed, twining climber. H to 2m (6ft). Leaves are divided into 3 leaflets with notched tips. Has small trusses of pea-like, velvety, black-purple flowers, with yellow blazes, in spring-summer.
K. rubicunda illus. p.205.

Kennedya. Reclassified as *Kennedia.*
Kentia. Reclassified as *Howea.*
Kentucky coffee tree. See *Gymnocladus dioica.*
Kermes oak. See *Quercus coccifera.*

KERRIA

ROSACEAE

Genus of one species of deciduous shrub, grown for its showy, yellow flowers. Needs sun or semi-shade and fertile, well-drained soil. Thin out old shoots after flowering. Propagate by softwood cuttings in summer or by division in autumn.
K. japonica 'Pleniflora' illus. p.131. var. *simplex* is a deciduous, arching, graceful shrub. H and S 2m (6ft). Has bright green foliage. Single, buttercup-like, golden yellow flowers are borne from mid- to late spring. Zone 5.
Kerria white. See *Rhodotypos scandens,* illus. p.158.

KIGELIA

BIGNONIACEAE

Genus of one species of evergreen tree, grown for its flowers, curious, sausage-like fruits and for shade. Tender, min. 16°C (61°F). Requires full light and humus-rich, well-drained soil. Water potted specimens moderately, very little when temperatures low. Propagate by seed in spring at not less than 23°C (73°F).
K. africana, syn. *K. pinnata* (Sausage tree). Evergreen, spreading, fairly bushy tree. H and S 8m (25ft) or more. Leaves have 7–11 oblong to oval leaflets. Scented, bell-shaped, purplish-red flowers open at night from autumn to spring. Bears inedible, cylindrical, hard-shelled, brown fruits, 30–45cm (12–18in) long.
K. pinnata. See *K. africana.*

Kilmarnock willow. See *Salix caprea* 'Kilmarnock'.
King anthurium. See *Anthurium veitchii.*
King of the bromeliads. See *Vriesea hieroglyphica.*
King palm. See *Archontophoenix.*
King protea. See *Protea cynaroides,* illus. p.161.
King William pine. See *Athrotaxis selaginoides.*
King's crown. See *Justicia carnea,* illus. p.163.
King's spear. See *Eremurus.*
Kingcup. See *Caltha palustris,* illus. p.451.
Kingfisher daisy. See *Felicia bergeriana,* illus. p.334.

KIRENGESHOMA

HYDRANGEACEAE

Genus of late summer- and autumn-flowering perennials. Grow in light shade and in deep, moist, lime-free soil. Propagate by seed or division in autumn or spring.
K. palmata illus. p.263.

KITAIBELA,
syn. KITAIBELIA

MALVACEAE

Genus of one species of summer-flowering perennial. Needs full sun and fertile, preferably dry soil. Propagate by seed in autumn or spring.

K. vitifolia. Bushy, upright perennial. H to 1.5m (5ft), S 60cm (2ft). In summer bears small clusters of open cup-shaped, white or rose-pink flowers. Has palmately lobed, coarsely toothed leaves.

Kitaibelia. Reclassified as *Kitaibela*
Kitchingia uniflora. See *Kalanchoe uniflora.*
Kiwi fruit. See *Actinidia deliciosa.*
Kleinia articulata. See *Senecio articulatus.*
Knapweed. See *Centaurea.*

KNAUTIA

DIPSACACEAE

Genus of summer-flowering annuals and perennials. Needs sun and well-drained soil. Requires staking. Propagate by basal cuttings in spring or by seed in autumn.

K. arvensis, syn. *Scabiosa arvensis* (Scabious). Erect perennial. H 1.2m (4ft), S 45cm (1½ft). Produces heads of pincushion-like, bluish-lilac flowers in summer. Stems are clothed in narrowly oval to lyre-shaped, deeply divided leaves.
K. macedonica, syn. *Scabiosa rumelica,* illus. p.249.

KNIGHTIA

PROTEACEAE

Genus of evergreen, summer-flowering trees, grown for their flowers, foliage and overall appearance. Is best at min. 3–5°C (37–41°F). Grows in any reasonably fertile, well-drained soil and in sun or partial shade. Water potted

specimens moderately, less in winter. Propagate by seed in spring.
K. excelsa (New Zealand honeysuckle, Rewa rewa). Evergreen, upright tree. H 20m (70ft) or more, S 2–4m (6–12ft). Has oblong to lance-shaped, coarsely serrated, leathery leaves, glossy and deep green. Dense racemes of slender, tubular, deep red flowers are produced in summer.

KNIPHOFIA
Red-hot poker, Torch lily

ASPHODELACEAE/LILIACEAE

Genus of perennials, some of which are evergreen. Needs full sun and well-drained conditions, with constantly moist soil in summer. Propagate species by seed or division in spring, cultivars by division only in spring.
K. 'Atlanta'. Evergreen, upright perennial. H to 1m (3ft), S 45cm (1½ft). In summer, stout stems bear dense, terminal racemes of tubular, bright orange-yellow flowers. Has thick, grass-like, channelled leaves. Does well in a coastal area.
K. 'Bee's Lemon'. Upright perennial. H 1m (3ft), S 45cm (1½ft). Has dense, terminal racemes of tubular, green-tinged, citron-yellow flowers on stout stems in late summer and autumn. Grass-like, deep green leaves have serrated edges.
K. caulescens illus. p.263.
K. 'C.M. Prichard' of gardens. See *K. rooperi.*
K. 'Little Maid' illus. p.290.
K. 'Maid of Orleans'. Upright perennial. H 1.2m (4ft), S 45cm (1½ft). In summer, slender stems are each crowned with a dense raceme of yellow buds that open to tubular, creamy-white flowers. Leaves are fresh green, basal and strap-shaped.
K. 'Percy's Pride' illus. p.263.
K. rooperi, syn. *K.* 'C.M. Prichard' of gardens, illus. p.263.
K. 'Royal Standard' illus. p.258.
K. 'Samuel's Sensation'. Upright perennial. H 1.5m (5ft), S 60cm (2ft).

In late summer, dense, terminal racemes of tubular, deep orange flowers are produced on stout stems. Has strap-shaped, basal, dark green leaves.
K. snowdenii of gardens. See *K. thomsonii* var. *snowdenii.*
K. thomsonii var. *snowdenii,* syn. *K. snowdenii* of gardens, illus. p.258.
K. uvaria (Red-hot poker). **'Nobilis'** is an upright perennial with erect, then spreading leaves. H 2m (6ft), S 1m (3ft). In late summer and autumn, stout stems each bear a dense, terminal raceme of tubular, bright red flowers. Has strap-shaped, channelled, dark green leaves.

Knotweed. See *Persicaria.*
Kochia. Reclassified as *Bassia.*

KOELREUTERIA

SAPINDACEAE

Genus of deciduous, summer-flowering trees, grown for their foliage, flowers and fruits. Hardy to tender, min. 10°C (50°F). Requires full sun, doing best in hot summers, and fertile, well-drained soil. Propagate by seed in autumn or by root cuttings in late winter.
K. paniculata illus. p.92.

KOHLERIA

GESNERIACEAE

Genus of erect perennials with scaly rhizomes, grown for their showy, tubular flowers borne mainly in summer. Tender, min. 15°C (59°F). Grow in moist but well-drained soil and in full sun or semi-shade. Water sparingly in winter; over-watering will cause rhizomes to rot. Propagate in spring by division of rhizomes or by seed if available.
K. amabilis. Rhizomatous perennial. H 8–16cm (3–6in), S 60cm (2ft). Oval, hairy leaves, to 8cm (3in) long, are often marked with silver and brown above. Small, nodding, tubular, deep pink flowers, with red-marked lobes,

appear in summer. Is useful for a hanging basket.
K. bogotensis. Erect, rhizomatous perennial. H and S 45cm (18in) or more. Oval, velvety, green leaves, to 8cm (3in) long, are sometimes marked with paler green above. In summer has small, tubular flowers, red with a yellow base outside, red-dotted, yellow within.
K. digitaliflora illus. p.244.
K. eriantha illus. p.250.
K. warscewiczii. Erect, rhizomatous perennial. H 1m (3ft), S 60cm (2ft). Oval, dark green leaves have scalloped margins. In summer and autumn has tubular, hairy, yellow-based, scarlet flowers with red- or brown spotted, greenish-yellow or bright yellow lobes.

KOLKWITZIA

CAPRIFOLIACEAE

Genus of one species of deciduous shrub, grown for its abundant flowers. Prefers full sun and fertile, well-drained soil. Cut out old shoots after flowering. Propagate by softwood cuttings in summer.
K. amabilis (Beauty bush). Deciduous, arching shrub. H and S 3m (10ft). Has peeling bark and oval, dark green leaves. Bell-shaped, yellow-throated, white or pink flowers are borne in late spring and early summer. Zone 5.
'Pink Cloud' illus. p.121.

Korean fir. See *Abies koreana,* illus. p.109.
Korean mountain ash. See *Sorbus alnifolia.*
Korean thuja. See *Thuja koraiensis.*
Korolkowia sewerzowii. See *Fritillaria sewerzowii.*
Kowhai. See *Sophora.*
Kudzu vine. See *Pueraria lobata.*
Kurrajong. See *Brachychiton populneus.*
Kusamaki. See *Podocarpus macrophyllus.*

L

LABLAB
PAPILIONACEAE/LEGUMINOSAE

Genus of one species of deciduous, woody-stemmed, twining climber, grown for its attractive, pea-like flowers (in tropics is grown for green manure and animal feed, and for its edible pods and seeds). Is often raised as an annual. Tender, min. 5–10°C (41–50°F). Grow in sun and in any well-drained soil. Propagate by seed in spring.
L. purpureus, syn. *Dolichos lablab*, *D. purpureus*, illus. p.211.

Lablab. See *Lablab purpureus*, illus. p.211.
Labrador tea. See *Ledum groenlandicum*, illus. p.154.

LABURNUM
PAPILIONACEAE/LEGUMINOSAE

Genus of deciduous trees, grown for their profuse, pendent flower clusters in spring and summer. Does best in full sun; grows in any but waterlogged soil. Seeds are very poisonous. Propagate species by seed in autumn, hybrids by budding in summer. All parts are highly toxic if ingested.
L. alpinum illus. p.93.
L. anagyroides, syn. *L. vulgare* (Common laburnum, Golden chain). Deciduous, spreading tree. H and S 7m (22ft). Leaves have 3 oval leaflets and are grey-green. Short, pendent, dense clusters of large, pea-like, yellow flowers appear in late spring and early summer. Zone 6.
L. vulgare. See *L. anagyroides*.
L. × watereri '**Vossii**' illus. p.92.

Laburnum
Common. See *Laburnum anagyroides*.
Dalmatian. See *Petteria ramentacea*.
Indian. See *Cassia fistula*.
Scotch. See *Laburnum alpinum*, illus. p.93.
Voss's. See *Laburnum × watereri* 'Vossii', illus. p.92.
Lace aloe. See *Aloe aristata*, illus. p.480.
Lace aralia. See *Polyscias guilfoylei* 'Victoriae', illus. p.126.
Lace cactus. See *Mammillaria elongata*, illus. p.470.
Lace flower. See *Episcia dianthiflora*, illus. p.299.
Blue. See *Trachymene coerulea*.
Lace-bark. See *Hoheria populnea*.
Lace-bark pine. See *Pinus bungeana*, illus. p.108.

LACHENALIA
HYACINTHACEAE/LILIACEAE

Genus of winter- and spring-flowering bulbs with tubular or bell-shaped flowers; some have attractively mottled leaves. Is useful as pot plants and in open borders. Tender, min. 2°C (35°F). Requires light, well-drained soil and a sunny site. Plant in early autumn; dry off in summer when foliage has died down. Propagate in autumn by seed or freely produced offsets.
L. aloides, syn. *L. tricolor*, *L.* 'Tricolor'. Winter- and spring-flowering bulb. H 15–25cm (6–10in), S 5–8cm (2–3in). Produces 2 strap-shaped, semi-erect, basal, purple-spotted, green leaves. Has a spike of 10–20 pendent flowers, each 3cm (1¼in) long with a yellow tube shading to red at the apex and with flared, green tips. '**Nelsonii**' (syn. *L.* 'Nelsonii') illus. p.441. var. **quadricolor** illus. p.441.
L. angustifolia. See *L. contaminata*.
L. contaminata, syn. *L. angustifolia*. Winter- and spring-flowering bulb. H to 20cm (8in), S 5–8cm (2–3in). Has narrowly strap-shaped, semi-erect leaves in a basal cluster. Bears a spike of bell-shaped, white flowers, 0.5cm (¼in) long, suffused and tipped with red and green.
L. glaucina. See *L. orchioides* var. *glaucina*.
L. mutabilis. Winter- and spring-flowering bulb. H to 30cm (12in), S 5–8cm (2–3in). Has 2 strap-shaped, semi-erect, basal leaves. Stem bears a loose spike of up to 25 tubular, 1cm (½in) long flowers that are purple or lilac in bud and open to reddish-brown-tipped petals with a green tube base.
L. 'Nelsonii'. See *L. aloides* 'Nelsonii'.
L. orchioides. Winter- and spring-flowering bulb. H 15–30cm (6–12in), S 5–8cm (2–3in). Has 2 strap-shaped, semi-erect, basal, green leaves, sometimes spotted blackish- or purple-brown. Stem produces a dense spike of fragrant, semi-erect, tubular, white flowers, 1cm (½in) long, blue-tinged and tipped with green. var. **glaucina** (syn. *L. glaucina*) illus. p.425.
L. rubida. Winter-flowering bulb. H to 25cm (10in), S 5–8cm (2–3in). Bears 2 strap-shaped, purple-spotted, green leaves, semi-erect and basal, and a loose spike of pendent, tubular, red flowers, 2–3cm (¾–1¼in) long, shading to yellow at tips.
L. tricolor. See *L. aloides*.
L. 'Tricolor'. See *L. aloides*.

Lacquered wine-cup. See *Aechmea* Foster's Favorite Group, illus. p.265.
Lactuca alpina. See *Cicerbita alpina*.
Lactuca bourgaei. See *Cicerbita bourgaei*.
Lad's love. See *Artemisia abrotanum*, illus. p.176.
Ladder fern. See *Nephrolepis cordifolia*.

Lady fern. See *Athyrium filix-femina*.
Lady tulip. See *Tulipa clusiana*, illus. p.411.
Lady's eardrops. See *Fuchsia magellanica*, illus. p.164.
Lady's mantle. See *Alchemilla*.
Alpine. See *Alchemilla alpina*.
Lady's slipper orchid. See *Cypripedium calceolus*, illus. p.298.
Showy. See *Cypripedium reginae*, illus. p.296.
Lady's smock. See *Cardamine pratensis*.
Lady-of-the-night. See *Brassavola nodosa*, illus. p.296.

LAELIA
See also ORCHIDS.
L. anceps (illus. p.297). Evergreen, epiphytic orchid for a cool greenhouse. H 25cm (10in). Lilac-pink flowers, 6cm (2½in) wide, each with a deep mauve lip, are carried in tall spikes in autumn. Has oval, rigid leaves, 10–15cm (4–6in) long. Needs semi-shade in summer.
L. cinnabarina (illus. p.299). Evergreen, epiphytic orchid for an intermediate greenhouse. H 15cm (6in). Produces sprays of slender, orange flowers, 5cm (2in) or more across, usually in winter. Has narrowly oval, rigid leaves, 8–10cm (3–4in) long. Needs good light in summer.

× LAELIOCATTLEYA
See also ORCHIDS.
× **L. Rojo 'Mont Millais'** (illus. p.297). Evergreen, epiphytic orchid for an intermediate greenhouse. H 30cm (12in). In winter-spring bears arching heads of slender, reddish-orange flowers, 2cm (¾in) across. Oval leaves are up to 15cm (6in) long. Provide good light in summer.

LAGAROSIPHON
HYDROCHARITACEAE

Genus of semi-evergreen, perennial, spreading, submerged water plants grown for their decorative foliage. Oxygenates water. Needs full sun. Thin regularly to keep under control. Propagate by stem cuttings in spring or summer.
L. major, syn. *Elodea crispa* of gardens, illus. p.449.

LAGERSTROEMIA
LYTHRACEAE

Genus of deciduous or evergreen, summer-flowering shrubs and trees, grown for their flowers. Hardy to tender, min. 3–5°C (37–41°F). Prefers fertile, well-drained soil and full light. Water potted specimens freely when in full growth, less at other times. To maintain as shrubs, cut back hard the previous season's stems each spring. Propagate by seed in spring or by semi-ripe cuttings in summer.
L. indica illus. p.91.
L. speciosa (Pride of India, Queen's crape myrtle). Deciduous, rounded tree. H 15–20m (50–70ft), S 10–15m (30–50ft). Tender. Mid- to deep green leaves are narrowly oval, 8–18cm (3–7in) long. Has panicles of funnel-shaped, rose-pink to rose-purple flowers in summer-autumn, often when leafless.

LAGUNARIA
MALVACEAE

Genus of one species of evergreen tree, grown for its flowers in summer-autumn and its overall appearance. Tender, min. 3–5°C (37–41°F). Prefers fertile, well-drained soil and full light. Water potted plants freely when in full summer growth, moderately at other times. Pruning is tolerated if required. Propagate by seed in spring or by semi-ripe cuttings in summer. Under cover, spider mite may be troublesome. Contact with the seeds may irritate skin.
L. patersonii (Norfolk Island hibiscus, Queensland pyramidal tree). Fast-growing, evergreen, upright tree, pyramidal when young. H 10–14m (30–46ft), S 5–7m (15–22ft). Oval, rough-textured leaves are matt-green above, whitish-green beneath. Bears hibiscus-like, rose-pink flowers, 5cm (2in) wide, in summer.

LAGURUS
Hare's tail
POACEAE/GRAMINEAE

See also GRASSES, BAMBOOS, RUSHES and SEDGES.
L. ovatus illus. p.306.

LAMARCKIA
POACEAE/GRAMINEAE

See also GRASSES, BAMBOOS, RUSHES and SEDGES.
L. aurea (Golden top). Tuft-forming, annual grass. H and S 20cm (8in). Wiry stems bear scattered, pale green leaves and, in summer, erect, dense, one-sided, golden panicles. Needs sun.

Lamb's tongue. See *Stachys byzantina*, illus. p.304.
Lamb's-tail cactus. See *Echinocereus schmollii*, illus. p.462.

LAMIUM
Deadnettle
LAMIACEAE/LABIATAE

Genus of spring- or summer-flowering perennials, most of which are semi-

evergreen, including a number of weeds; some species make useful ground cover. Prefers full or partial shade and moist but well-drained soil. Resents excessive winter wet. Propagate by stem-tip cuttings of non-flowering shoots in mid-summer or by division in autumn or early spring.
L. galeobdolon subsp. **montanum** **'Florentinum'**, syn. *L.g.* 'Variegatum'. Semi-evergreen, carpeting perennial. H to 30cm (12in), S indefinite. Oval, mid-green leaves are marked with silver. Racemes of tubular, 2-lipped, lemon-yellow flowers appear in summer. 'Hermann's Pride' has leaves marked with silver.
L. maculatum illus. p.269. **'Album'** illus. p.267. **'Aureum'** (syn. *L.m.* 'Gold Leaf') is a semi-evergreen, mat-forming perennial. H 20cm (8in), S 60cm (24in). Produces oval, yellow leaves with paler white centres. Whorls of hooded, pink flowers appear on short stems in summer. **'Beacon Silver'** bears mauve-tinged, silver leaves, sometimes with narrow, green margins, and clear pale pink flowers. **'Gold Leaf'** see *L.m.* 'Aureum'. **'White Nancy'** illus. p.267.
L. orvala illus. p.271.

LAMPRANTHUS

AIZOACEAE

Genus of creeping, bushy, perennial succulents and sub-shrubs with daisy-like flowers. Becomes woody after several years, when is best replenished. Plants are good for summer bedding, particularly in arid conditions. Leaves redden in strong sun. Tender, min. 7°C (45°F) if dry. Requires full sun and very well-drained soil. Propagate by seed or stem cuttings in spring or autumn.
L. aurantiacus illus. p.468.
L. deltoides, syn. *Oscularia deltoides*, illus. p.471.
L. haworthii. Erect to creeping, perennial succulent. H 50cm (20in), S indefinite. Blue-grey leaves are cylindrical and 5cm (2in) long. In spring bears masses of daisy-like, cerise flowers, 7cm (3in) across, that only open in sun.
L. multiradiatus. See. *L. roseus*.
L. roseus, syn. *L. multiradiatus*, *Mesembryanthemum multiradiatum*. Creeping, perennial succulent. H 15cm (6in), S indefinite. Produces solid, 3-angled, mid- to glaucous green leaves, 5cm (2in) long. Daisy-like, dark rose-red flowers, 4cm (1½in) across, open only in sun from spring to autumn.
L. spectabilis illus. p.463.

Lampshade poppy. See *Meconopsis integrifolia*, illus. p.292.
Lancewood. See *Pseudopanax crassifolius*.

LANTANA

Shrub verbena

VERBENACEAE

Genus of evergreen perennials and shrubs, grown for their flowers. Tender,

min. 10–13°C (50–55°F). Needs full light and fertile, well-drained soil. Water containerized specimens freely when in full growth, moderately at other times. Tip prune young plants to promote a bushy habit. Propagate by seed in spring or by semi-ripe cuttings in summer. Spider mite and whitefly may be troublesome. All parts may cause severe discomfort if ingested, and contact with foliage may irritate skin.
L. camara. Evergreen, rounded to spreading shrub. H and S 1–2m (3–6ft). Bears oval, finely wrinkled, deep green leaves. From spring to autumn, tiny, tubular, 5-lobed flowers, in dense, domed heads, open yellow, then turn red. Many colour forms have been selected.
L. delicatissima. See *L. montevidensis*.
L. montevidensis, syn. *L. delicatissima*, *L. sellowiana*, illus. p.167.
L. sellowiana. See *L. montevidensis*.
L. 'Spreading Sunset' illus. p.171.

Lantern tree. See *Crinodendron hookerianum*, illus. p.142.
Lantern, Chinese. See *Physalis*.

LAPAGERIA

PHILESIACEAE/LILIACEAE

Genus of one species of evergreen, woody-stemmed, twining climber, grown for its large, waxy blooms. Tender, min. 2°C (35°F). Requires humus-rich, well-drained soil and partial shade. Water moderately, scarcely at all when not in full growth. Provide support. Thin out congested growth in spring. Propagate in spring by seed, soaked for 2 days before sowing, or in spring or autumn by layering.
L. rosea illus. p.210. var. **albiflora** (illus. p.44) is an evergreen, woody-stemmed, twining climber. H to 5m (15ft). Has oblong to oval, leathery, dark green leaves. From summer to late autumn bears pendent, fleshy, narrowly bell-shaped, white flowers.

Lapeirousia cruenta. See *Anomatheca laxa*.
Lapeirousia laxa. See *Anomatheca laxa*.
Larch
   European. See *Larix decidua*.
   Golden. See *Pseudolarix amabilis*, illus. p.107.
   Japanese. See *Larix kaempferi*.

LARDIZABALA

LARDIZABALACEAE

Genus of evergreen, woody-stemmed, twining climbers, grown for their foliage. Male and female flowers are produced on the same plant in late autumn to winter. Is useful for growing on trellises or pergolas. Grow in any well-drained soil and sun or partial shade. Propagate by seed in spring or by stem cuttings in late summer or autumn.
L. biternata. Evergreen, woody-stemmed, twining climber. H 3–4m (10–12ft). Tender, min. 2°C (35°F). Rounded leaves have broadly oval,

leathery, dark green leaflets. In winter produces brown flowers with tiny, whitish petals, the males in drooping spikes, the females solitary. In winter-spring bears many-seeded, berry-like, purple fruits, 5–8cm (2–3in) long.

Large self-heal. See *Prunella grandiflora*, illus. p.382.
Large yellow restharrow. See *Ononis natrix*, illus. p.359.
Large-leaved linden. See *Tilia platyphyllos*.

LARIX

PINACEAE

See also CONIFERS.
L. decidua, syn. *L. europaea* (European larch). Fast-growing, deciduous conifer with a conical crown when young, broadening on maturity, and spaced branches. H 25–30m (80–100ft), S 5–15m (16–50ft). Shoots are yellow-brown in winter. Has light green leaves and small, erect, conical cones. Zone 2b.
L. europaea. See *L. decidua*.
L. kaempferi, syn. *L. leptolepis* (Japanese larch). Fast-growing, deciduous, columnar conifer with a conical tip. H 25–30m (80–100ft), S 5–8m (15–25ft). Shoots are purplish-red and leaves are needle-like, flattened, greyish-green or bluish. Small cones have reflexed scales. Zone 2b.
L. leptolepis. See *L. kaempferi*.

Larkspur. See *Consolida*.
   Giant. See *Consolida ajacis* Giant Imperial Series, illus. p.332.
Late Dutch honeysuckle. See *Lonicera periclymenum* 'Serotina'.

LATHRAEA

SCROPHULARIACEAE

Genus of spreading perennials that grow as parasites on the roots of trees, in the case of *L. clandestina* on willow or poplar. True leaves are not produced. Grows in dappled shade cast by host tree and prefers moist conditions. Roots resent being disturbed. Propagate by seed when fresh, in late summer.
L. clandestina illus. p.271.

LATHYRUS

PAPILIONACEAE/LEGUMINOSAE

Genus of annuals and perennials, many of them tendril climbers, grown for their racemes of attractive flowers. Flowers are followed by long, thin seed pods. Grow in humus-rich, fertile, well-drained soil and in full light. Provide support and remove dead flowers regularly. Cut down perennials in late autumn. Propagate annuals by seed (soaked before sowing) in early spring or early autumn, perennials by seed in autumn or by division in spring. Botrytis and mildew may cause problems. Seeds may cause mild stomach upset if ingested.
L. grandiflorus illus. p.209.
L. latifolius illus. p.211.
L. magellanicus of gardens. See *L. nervosus*.

L. nervosus, syn. *L. magellanicus* of gardens (Lord Anson's blue pea). Herbaceous, tendril climber. H to 5m (15ft). Grey-green leaves each have a pair of leaflets, a 3-branched tendril and large stipules. Fragrant, purplish-blue flowers are borne in long-stalked racemes in summer.
L. odoratus (Sweet pea). Moderately fast-growing, annual, tendril climber. H to 3m (10ft). Has oval, mid-green leaves with tendrils. Scented flowers are produced in shades of pink, blue, purple or white, from summer to early autumn. Dwarf, non-climbing cultivars are available. **'Bijou'** illus. p.324. **'Jayne Amanda'** (illus. p.57) bears racemes of usually 4, rarely 5, rose-pink flowers, and may be grown as a cordon or bush. **'Knee Hi'** illus. p.320. **'Lady Diana'** illus. p.214. **'Red Ensign'** illus. p.210. **'Selana'** illus. p.208. **'Xenia Field'** illus. p.209.
L. rotundifolius (Persian everlasting pea). Herbaceous, tendril climber with winged stems. H to 1m (3ft). Leaves each have narrow stipules, a pair of leaflets and a 3-branched tendril. Has small racemes of 3–8 pink to purplish flowers in summer.
L. sylvestris (Everlasting pea, Perennial pea). Herbaceous, tendril climber with winged stems. H to 2m (6ft). Leaves each have narrow stipules, a pair of leaflets and a terminal, branched tendril. In summer and early autumn bears racemes of 4–10 rose-pink flowers, marked with green and purple.
L. vernus, syn. *Orobus vernus*, illus. p.270. **'Alboroseus'** is a clump-forming perennial. H and S 30cm (12in). In spring, slender stems each bear 3–5 white-and-deep-pink flowers. Has fern-like, much-divided, soft leaves.

Laurel. See *Laurelia*; *Laurus*; *Prunus laurocerasus*; *Prunus lusitanica*.
   Alexandrian. See *Danaë racemosa*.
   Bay. See *Laurus nobilis*.
   Californian. See *Umbellularia californica*, illus. p.74.
   Cherry. See *Prunus laurocerasus*.
   Chilean. See *Laurelia sempervirens*.
   Portugal. See *Prunus lusitanica*.
   Sheep. See *Kalmia angustifolia*.
   Spurge. See *Daphne laureola*.
Laurel willow. See *Salix pentandra*.

LAURELIA

Laurel

ATHEROSPERMATACEAE/MONIMIACEAE

Genus of evergreen trees and shrubs, grown for their aromatic foliage. Tender, min. 2°C (35°F). Requires sun or semi-shade; grows in any but very dry soil. Propagate by semi-ripe cuttings in summer.
L. sempervirens, syn. *L. serrata* of gardens (Chilean laurel). Evergreen, broadly conical tree or shrub. H and S to 15m (50ft). Oval, leathery leaves are glossy, dark green and very aromatic. In summer bears inconspicuous flowers.
L. serrata of gardens. See *L. sempervirens*.

LAURUS
Bay tree, Laurel

LAURACEAE

Genus of evergreen trees, grown for their foliage. Foliage may be scorched by strong, cold winds. Needs a sheltered position in sun or semi-shade and fertile, well-drained soil. In tubs may be grown well as standards, which should be trimmed during summer. Propagate by semi-ripe cuttings in summer or by seed in autumn.

L. nobilis (Bay laurel, Sweet bay). Evergreen, broadly conical tree. H 12m (40ft), S 10m (30ft). Narrowly oval, leathery, glossy, dark green leaves are very aromatic and used in cooking. Has small, star-shaped, pale yellow flowers in spring, followed by globose to ovoid, green, then black fruits. Zone 9.

Laurustinus. See *Viburnum tinus*, illus. p.149.

LAVANDULA
Lavender

LAMIACEAE/LABIATAE

Genus of evergreen, mainly summer-flowering shrubs, with entire or divided, often grey-green leaves, rown for their aromatic foliage and flowers. Makes an effective, low hedge. Needs full sun and fertile, well-drained soil. Trim hedges lightly in spring to maintain a compact habit. Propagate by semi-ripe cuttings in summer.

L. angustifolia 'Hidcote' see *L.* 'Hidcote'. **'Munstead'** is an evergreen, bushy, compact shrub. H and S 60cm (2ft.). Narrowly oblong, narrow, aromatic leaves are grey-green. Produces dense spikes of tiny, fragrant, tubular, blue flowers from mid- to late summer. Zone 5.

L. dentata (French lavender). Evergreen, bushy shrub. H and S 1m (3ft). Aromatic leaves are fern-like, toothed and grey-green. Dense spikes of small, slightly fragrant, tubular, lavender-blue flowers and purple bracts are borne from mid- to late summer. Zone 9.

L. 'Grappenhall'. See *L.* x *intermedia* 'Grappenhall'.

L. 'Hidcote', syn. *L. angustifolia* 'Hidcote', illus. p.167.

L. x *intermedia* (English lavender). **'Grappenhall'**, syn. *L.* 'Grappenhall', is an evergreen, bushy shrub. H 1m (3ft), S 1.5m (5ft). Produces narrowly oblong, aromatic, grey-green leaves. Produces long-stalked spikes of tiny, slightly fragrant, tubular, blue-purple flowers in mid- and late summer. Zone 6.

L. stoechas illus. p.167.

LAVATERA
Tree mallow

MALVACEAE

Genus of mainly summer-flowering annuals, biennials, perennials and semi-evergreen sub-shrubs and shrubs. Needs sun and well-drained soil. Propagate perennials, sub-shrubs and shrubs by softwood cuttings in early spring or summer, annuals and biennials by seed in spring or early autumn.

L. assurgentiflora illus. p.141.
L. 'Barnsley'. Vigorous, semi-evergreen sub-shrub. H and S 2m (6ft). Mid-green, palmate leaves have 3–5 lobes. Throughout summer bears profuse clusters of open funnel-shaped, red-eyed, white flowers, ageing to soft pink, with deeply notched petals.
L. cachemiriana, syn. *L. cachemirica*, illus. p.227.
L. cachemirica. See *L. cachemiriana*.
L. olbia 'Rosea'. See *L.* 'Rosea'.
L. 'Rosea', syn. *L. olbia* 'Rosea', illus. p.141.
L. trimestris 'Mont Blanc' illus. p.318.
'Silver Cup' illus. p.324.

Lavender. See *Lavandula*.
　Cotton. See *Santolina chamaecyparissus*.
　English. See *Lavandula* x *intermedia*.
　French. See *Lavandula dentata*; *Lavandula stoechas*, illus. p.167.
　Sea. See *Limonium*.
Lavender cotton. See *Santolina chamaecyparissus*.
Lawson cypress. See *Chamaecyparis lawsoniana*.

LAYIA

ASTERACEAE/COMPOSITAE

Genus of annuals, useful for hot, dry places. Grow in sun and in poor to fertile, very well-drained soil. Propagate by seed sown outdoors in spring or early autumn.

L. elegans. See *L. platyglossa*.
L. platyglossa, syn. *L. elegans* (Tidy tips). Fast-growing, upright, bushy annual. H 45cm (18in), S 30cm (12in). Has lance-shaped, greyish-green leaves. Daisy-like flower heads, 5cm (2in) wide, with white-tipped, yellow ray petals and yellow centres, are produced from early summer to early autumn. Is suitable for cutting.

Lead plant. See *Amorpha canescens*.
Leadwort, Cape. See *Plumbago auriculata*, illus. p.215.
Least bur reed. See *Sparganium natans*.
Least duckweed. See *Wolffia arrhiza*.
Least snowbell. See *Soldanella minima*.
Least willow. See *Salix herbacea*.
Leatherleaf. See *Chamaedaphne calyculata*.
Leatherleaf sedge. See *Carex buchananii*.
Leatherwood. See *Cyrilla racemiflora*.
Lechenaultia. Reclassified as *Leschenaultia*.

LEDEBOURIA

HYACINTHACEAE/LILIACEAE

Genus of bulbs, some of which are evergreen, with ornamental, narrowly lance-shaped leaves. Produces very small flowers with reflexed tips. Makes good pot plants in cool greenhouses. Needs full light, to allow leaf marks to develop well, and loose, open soil. Propagate by offsets in spring.

L. cooperi, syn. *Scilla adlamii*, *S. cooperi*. Summer-flowering bulb. H 5–10cm (2–4in), S 2.5–5cm (1–2in). Semi-erect, basal, green leaves, with brownish-purple stripes, die away in winter. Stem carries a short spike of small, bell-shaped, greenish-purple flowers.
L. socialis, syn. *Scilla socialis*, *S. violacea*, illus. p.434.

LEDUM

ERICACEAE

Genus of evergreen shrubs, grown for their aromatic foliage and small, white flowers. Needs shade or semi-shade and moist, peaty, acid soil. Benefits from dead-heading. Propagate by semi-ripe cuttings in summer or by seed in autumn.

L. groenlandicum illus. p.154.

LEIOPHYLLUM

ERICACEAE

Genus of one species of evergreen shrub with an extensive, spreading root system. Prefers semi-shade and well-drained, peaty, acid soil. Top-dress regularly with peaty soil. Propagate by seed in spring or by semi-ripe cuttings in summer.

L. buxifolium. Evergreen, dome-shaped shrub. H 25cm (10in), S 45cm (18in). Stems are covered with tiny, oval, leathery, dark green leaves. In late spring, terminal clusters of deep pink buds develop into small, star-shaped, white flowers, with prominent stamens. Zone 7.

Lemaireocereus euphorbioides. See *Neobuxbaumia euphorbioides*.
Lemaireocereus marginatus. See *Pachycereus marginatus*.
Lemaireocereus thurberi. See *Stenocereus thurberi*.

LEMBOGLOSSUM

See also ORCHIDS.

L. bictoniense, syn. *Odontoglossum bictoniense* (illus. p.296). Evergreen, epiphytic orchid for a cool greenhouse. H 23cm (9in). Olive-green flowers, 4cm (1½in) across, barred with dark brown and each with a sometimes pink-flushed, white lip, are produced in spikes in late summer. Leaves are narrowly oval and 10–15cm (4–6in) long. Requires shade in summer.
L. cervantesii, syn. *Odontoglossum cervantesii* (illus. p.296). Evergreen, epiphytic orchid for a cool greenhouse. H 8cm (3in). In winter produces sprays of papery, white flowers, 2.5cm (1in) across, with cobweb-like, light brown marks. Has narrowly oval leaves, 10–15cm (4–6in) long. Grow in shade in summer.
L. cordatum, syn. *Odontoglossum cordatum* (illus. p.297). Evergreen, epiphytic orchid for a cool greenhouse. H 12cm (5in). Sprays of brown-marked, corn-yellow flowers, 2.5cm (1in) across, open in spring. Leaves are narrowly oval and 10–15cm (4–6in)

long. Provide shade in summer and keep very dry in winter.
L. rossii, syn. *Odontoglossum rossii* (illus. p.296). Evergreen, epiphytic orchid for a cool greenhouse. H 8cm (3in). In autumn-winter, white to mushroom-pink flowers, 2.5cm (1in) across and speckled with beige-brown, are borne in spikes. Narrowly oval leaves are 10–15cm (4–6in) long. Needs shade in summer.

Lembotropis nigricans. See *Cytisus nigricans*.
Lemon verbena. See *Aloysia triphylla*, illus. p.143.
Lemon vine. See *Pereskia aculeata*, illus. p.457.
Lent lily. See *Narcissus pseudonarcissus*, illus. p.417.
Lenten rose. See *Helleborus* x *hybridus*.

LEONOTIS

LAMIACEAE/LABIATAE

Genus of annuals, evergreen and semi-evergreen perennials, sub-shrubs and shrubs, grown for their flowers and overall appearance. Tender, min. 5–7°C (41–5°F). Needs full sun and rich, well-drained soil. Water containerized specimens freely when in full growth, much less at other times. Cut back perennials, sub-shrubs and shrubs to within 15cm (6in) of ground in early spring. Propagate by seed in spring or by greenwood cuttings in early summer.
L. leonurus illus. p.149.

LEONTOPODIUM
Edelweiss

COMPOSITAE/ASTERACEAE

Genus of short-lived, spring-flowering, woolly perennials, grown for their flower heads. Is suitable for rock gardens. Needs sun, gritty, well-drained soil and a deep collar of grit. Shelter from prevailing, rain-bearing winds, as crowns are very intolerant of winter wet. Propagate by division in spring or by seed when fresh. Many seeds are not viable.
L. alpinum illus. p.346.
L. stracheyi. Mound-forming, spreading, woolly perennial. H and S 10cm (4in). Star-shaped, glistening, white flower heads are produced among thick, oval, silver leaves in spring. Makes a good alpine house plant.

Leopard lily. See *Dieffenbachia*; *Lilium pardalinum*, illus. p.405.
Leopard plant. See *Farfugium japonicum* 'Aureomaculatum'.
Leopard's bane. See *Doronicum*.
Leopoldia comosa. See *Muscari comosum*.

LEPISMIUM

CACTACEAE

Genus of epiphytic and lithophytic (growing on rocks) perennial cacti often pendulous in habit with cylindrical, ribbed, angled or flat, usually segmented stems. Small,

funnel- to disc-shaped flowers are followed by spherical, often purple or red berries. Tender, min. 6–10°C (43–50°F). Needs partial shade and rich, well-drained soil. Prefers 80% relative humidity – higher than for most cacti. Give only occasional, very light watering in winter. Propagate by seed or stem cuttings in spring or summer.
L. warmingianum, syn. *Rhipsalis warmingiana*, illus. p.461.

LEPTINELLA

ASTERACEAE/COMPOSITAE

Genus of annuals and creeping perennials that are effective as low ground cover. Grow in full sun and moderately fertile, sharply drained soil. Propagate by seed as soon as ripe or by division in spring.
L. atrata, syn. *Cotula atrata*, illus. p.367. subsp. *luteola* illus. p.364.

LEPTOSPERMUM

MYRTACEAE

Genus of evergreen trees and shrubs, grown for their foliage and small, often profuse flowers. Grows well in coastal areas if not too exposed. Tender, min. 2°C (35°F). Needs full sun and fertile, well-drained soil. Propagate by semi-ripe cuttings in summer.
L. flavescens. See *L. polygalifolium*.
L. humifusum. See *L. rupestre*.
L. polygalifolium, syn. *L. flavescens*, illus. p.139.
L. rupestre, syn. *L. humifusum*, illus. p.160.
L. scoparium (Manuka, New Zealand tea-tree). 'Keatleyi' is an evergreen, rounded shrub. H and S 3m (10ft). Narrowly lance-shaped, aromatic, grey-green leaves set off a profusion of large, star-shaped, pale pink flowers during late spring and summer. 'Nicholsii' produces bronze-purple leaves and smaller, crimson flowers. 'Red Damask' illus. p.131.

LESCHENAULTIA,
syn. LECHENAULTIA

GOODENIACEAE

Genus of evergreen shrubs, grown for their flowers. Tender, min. 7–10°C (45–50°F). Needs full light and peaty, well-drained soil with few phosphates and nitrates. Water containerized plants moderately during growing season, sparingly at other times. Shorten over-long stems after flowering. Propagate by seed in spring or by semi-ripe cuttings in summer. Most species are not easy to grow under glass; good ventilation is essential.
L. floribunda. Evergreen, domed, wiry-stemmed shrub. H and S 30–60cm (12–24in). Has narrow, cylindrical, pointed leaves and, in spring-summer, short, tubular, pale blue flowers, each with 5 angular petals, in terminal clusters.

Lesser celandine. See *Ranunculus ficaria*.
Lesser periwinkle. See *Vinca minor*, illus. p.176.

Lettuce, Water. See *Pistia stratiotes*, illus. p.449.

LEUCADENDRON

PROTEACEAE

Genus of evergreen shrubs and trees, grown for their flower heads from autumn to spring and for their foliage. Tender, min. 5–7°C (41–5°F). Needs full light and sharply drained soil, mainly of sand and peat, ideally with very little nitrogen and phosphates. Water potted specimens moderately while in growth, sparingly at other times. Propagate by seed in spring.
L. argenteum illus. p.100.

LEUCANTHEMELLA

ASTERACEAE/COMPOSITAE

Genus of hairy perennials, grown for their daisy-like flower heads in autumn. Grow in full sun or partial shade and reliably moist soil. Propagate by division or basal cuttings in spring.
L. serotina, syn. *Chrysanthemum serotinum*, *C. uliginosum*. Erect perennial. H 1.5m (5ft), S 90cm (3ft). Lance-shaped leaves are toothed and dark green. Leafy stems carry sprays of large, green-centred, white flower heads in late autumn.

LEUCANTHEMOPSIS

ASTERACEAE/COMPOSITAE

Genus of dwarf, tufted, clump- or mat-forming perennials, grown for their solitary, daisy-like flower heads in summer. Grow in full sun and sharply drained soil. Propagate by seed as soon as ripe or by division or basal cuttings in spring.
L. alpina, syn. *Chrysanthemum alpinum*. Tuft-forming, short-lived perennial. H 10cm (4in), S 20cm (8in). Small tufts of deeply cut leaves are produced from short, rhizomatous stems. Has large, white flower heads, with yellow centres, in summer. Is good for a rock garden or scree.

LEUCANTHEMUM

ASTERACEAE/COMPOSITAE

Genus of annuals and perennials, grown for their attractive flowers. Cultivars of *L. x superbum* are valued for their profusion of large daisy-like summer flowers. Some species are suitable for rock gardens. Needs full sun and well-drained soil. Propagate species by seed or division, cultivars by division only.
L. x superbum, syn. *Chrysanthemum maximum* of gardens, *C. x superbum* (Shasta daisy). 'Aglaia' is a robust perennial. H 1m (3ft), S 60cm (2ft). Large, daisy-like, semi-double, white flower heads are borne singly in summer. Has spoon-shaped, coarse, lobed, toothed leaves. Divide every 2 years. 'Elizabeth' illus. p.240. 'Esther Read' illus. p.275 'Wirral Supreme' is double with short, central florets.

LEUCHTENBERGIA

CACTACEAE

Genus of one species of perennial cactus. Looks like *Agave* in foliage,

but its flowers, seed pods and seeds are similar to *Ferocactus*. Tubercles eventually form on short, rough, woody stems. Tender, min. 6°C (43°F). Needs full sun and very well-drained soil. Keep completely dry in winter; water sparingly from spring to autumn. Propagate by seed in spring or summer.
L. principis illus. p.466.

LEUCOCORYNE

ALLIACEAE/LILIACEAE

Genus of spring-flowering bulbs with loose heads of flattish flowers. Needs sun and well-drained soil. Plant in autumn, water when in growth, and keep almost dry when dormant in summer. Propagate by seed or offsets in autumn.
L. ixioides illus. p.413.

LEUCOGENES
New Zealand edelweiss

ASTERACEAE/COMPOSITAE

Genus of evergreen, woody-based perennials, grown mainly for their foliage. Is excellent for alpine houses in areas where summers are cool. Needs sun and gritty, well-drained, peaty soil. Resents winter wet and may be difficult to grow. Propagate by seed when fresh or by softwood cuttings in late spring or early summer.
L. grandiceps illus. p.389.
L. leontopodium, syn. *Raoulia leontopodium* (North Island edelweiss). Evergreen, rosetted perennial. H and S 12cm (5in). Has oblong to oval, overlapping, silvery-white to yellowish leaves. In early summer has up to 15 small, star-shaped, woolly, silvery-white flower heads surrounded by thick, felted, white bracts.

LEUCOJUM
Snowflake

AMARYLLIDACEAE

Genus of bulbs, grown for their pendent, bell-shaped, white or pink flowers in autumn or spring. Some species prefer a moist, partially shaded site, others do best in sun and well-drained soil. Propagate by division in spring or early autumn or by seed in autumn.
L. aestivum illus. p.396.
L. autumnale illus. p.437.
L. roseum. Early autumn-flowering bulb. H to 10cm (4in), S 2.5–5cm (1–2in). Slender stems bear usually solitary, pale pink flowers, 1cm (½in) long. Thread-like, erect, basal leaves appear with, or just after, flowers. Prefers sun and well-drained soil.
L. vernum illus. p.426.

LEUCOPHYTA
Cushion bush

ASTERACEAE/COMPOSITAE

Genus of annuals, evergreen perennials and small shrubs, often grown annually from cuttings and used as summer bedding. Tender, min. 7–10°C (45–50°F). Requires well-drained soil and full light. Water containerized plants moderately when in full growth, sparingly at other times. Remove stem

tips of young plants to promote a bushy habit. Propagate by semi-ripe cuttings in late summer. Botrytis may be troublesome if plants are kept too cool and damp in winter.
L. brownii, syn. *Calocephalus brownii*, illus. p.175.

Leucopogon colensoi. See *Cyathodes colensoi*.

LEUCOSPERMUM

PROTEACEAE

Genus of evergreen shrubs, grown for their flower heads. Tender, min. 7–10°C (45–50°F). Requires full light and sandy, well-drained soil with few phosphates and nitrates. Water containerized specimens moderately when in growth, sparingly at other times. Propagate by seed in spring. Is not easy to cultivate long term under glass; good ventilation is essential.
L. cordifolium, syn. *L. nutans*. Evergreen, rounded to spreading, well-branched shrub. H and S 1.2m (4ft). Elongated, heart-shaped, blue-grey leaves each have a 3-toothed tip. In summer, very slender, tubular, brick-red to orange flowers, each with a long style, are borne in tight heads that resemble single blooms.
L. nutans. See *L. cordifolium*.
L. reflexum illus. p.131.

LEUCOTHÖE

ERICACEAE

Genus of evergreen, semi-evergreen or deciduous shrubs, grown for their white flowers and their foliage. Needs shade or semi-shade and moist, peaty, acid soil. Propagate by semi-ripe cuttings in summer.
L. catesbaei of gardens. See *L. fontanesiana*.
L. fontanesiana, syn. *L. catesbaei* of gardens, *L. walteri*. Evergreen, arching shrub. H 1.5m (5ft), S 3m (10ft). Lance-shaped, leathery, glossy, dark green leaves have long points and sharp teeth. Short racemes of small, urn-shaped, white flowers are borne beneath shoots from mid- to late spring. Zone 6. 'Rainbow' illus. p.177. SCARLETTA ('Zeblid') (illus. p.39) has dark red-purple young foliage, which turns dark green, then bronze in winter. 'Zeblid' see *L.f.* SCARLETTA. Zone 6.
L. keiskei. Evergreen shrub with erect or semi-procumbent stems. H 15–60cm (6–24in), S 30–60cm (12–24in). Oval, thin-textured, glossy, dark green leaves have a red flush when young and a leathery appearance. Bears pendent, urn-shaped, white flowers from leaf axils in summer. Is good for a rock garden, peat bed or alpine house. Prefers mild, damp climates. Zone 7.
L. walteri. See *L. fontanesiana*.

LEWISIA

PORTULACACEAE

Genus of perennials, some of which are evergreen, with rosettes of succulent leaves and deep tap roots. Most species are good in alpine houses, troughs and rock gardens. Evergreen species need semi-shaded, humus-rich, moist or well-drained, neutral to acid soil and resent water in their rosettes at all times. Herbaceous species shed their leaves in summer and require sun and well-drained, neutral to acid soil; dry off after flowering. Propagate herbaceous species by seed in spring or autumn, evergreen species by seed in spring or by offsets in summer. Seed of *L.* Cotyledon Hybrids may not come true.

L. columbiana. Evergreen, basal-rosetted perennial. H 15cm (6in) or more, S 10–15cm (4–6in). Bears thick, narrowly oblong, flat, glossy, green leaves and, in early summer, terminal sprays of small, cup-shaped, deeply veined, white to deep pink flowers. Prefers moist soil.
L. **Cotyledon Hybrids** illus. p.354.
L. **'George Henley'** illus. p.352.
L. nevadensis. Loose, basal-rosetted perennial. H 4–6cm (1½–2½in), S 8cm (3in). In summer, large, almost stemless, cup-shaped, white flowers appear above small clusters of strap-shaped, dark green leaves.
L. rediviva [pink form] illus. p.379; [white form] illus. p.373.
L. tweedyi illus. p.364.

LEYCESTERIA

CAPRIFOLIACEAE

Genus of deciduous shrubs, grown for their showy flower clusters. Suitable for a cool greenhouse. Needs full sun and fertile, well-drained soil. Propagate by softwood cuttings in summer or by seed or division in autumn.
L. formosa (Himalayan honeysuckle). Deciduous, upright shrub. H and S 2m (6ft). Has blue-green shoots and slender, oval, dark green leaves. In summer and early autumn, small, funnel-shaped, white flowers are produced at tip of each pendent cluster of purplish-red bracts and are followed by spherical, reddish-purple fruits. Cut weak shoots to ground level in early spring.

LEYMUS

POACEAE/GRAMINEAE

See also GRASSES, BAMBOOS, RUSHES and SEDGES.
L. arenarius, syn. *Elymus arenarius* (Lyme grass). Vigorous, spreading, herbaceous, rhizomatous, perennial grass. H to 1.5m (5ft), S indefinite. Has broad, glaucous leaves. Has stout, terminal spikes of greyish-green flowers on erect stems in late summer. Is useful for binding coastal dunes.

LIATRIS

Gay feathers, blazing star

ASTERACEAE/COMPOSITAE

Genus of summer-flowering perennials with thickened, corm-like rootstocks. Prefers sun and well-drained soil. Propagate by division in spring.
L. callilepis of gardens. See *L. spicata*.
L. pycnostachya (Kansas gay feather). Clump-forming perennial. H 1.2m (4ft), S 30cm (1ft). In summer bears tall spikes of clustered, feathery,

mauve-pink flower heads. Grass-like, dark green leaves form basal tufts.
L. spicata, syn. *L. callilepis* of gardens, illus. p.279.

LIBERTIA

IRIDACEAE

Genus of rhizomatous perennials, grown for their foliage, decorative seed pods and flowers. Needs a sheltered, sunny or partially shaded site and well-drained soil. Propagate by division in spring or by seed in autumn or spring.
L. grandiflora illus. p.239.
L. ixioides. Clump-forming, rhizomatous perennial. H and S 60cm (24in). Produces panicles of saucer-shaped, white flowers in summer. Grass-like, dark green leaves turn orange-brown during winter.

Libocedrus chilensis. See *Austrocedrus chilensis*.
Libocedrus decurrens. See *Calocedrus decurrens*.
Libonia floribunda. See *Justicia rizzinii*.

LIGULARIA

ASTERACEAE/COMPOSITAE

Genus of perennials, grown for their foliage and large, daisy-like flower heads. Grow in sun or semi-shade and in moist but well-drained soil. Propagate by division in spring or by seed in autumn or spring. Is prone to damage by slugs and snails.
L. clivorum 'Desdemona'. See *L. dentata* 'Desdemona'.
L. dentata 'Desdemona', syn. *L. clivorum* 'Desdemona'. Compact, clump-forming perennial. H 1.2m (4ft), S 60cm (2ft). Has heart-shaped, long-stalked, leathery, basal, dark brownish-green leaves, almost mahogany beneath, and bears terminal clusters of large, daisy-like, vivid orange flower heads on branching stems from mid- to late summer.
L. 'Gregynog Gold'. Clump-forming perennial. H 2m (6ft), S 60cm (2ft). Leaves are large, heart-shaped and deep green. Conical panicles of daisy-like, orange-yellow flower heads are borne from mid- to late summer.
L. przewalskii, syn. *Senecio przewalskii*, illus. p.229.
L. stenocephala illus. p.229.
L. tussilaginea. See *Farfugium japonicum*.

LIGUSTRUM

Privet

OLEACEAE

Genus of deciduous, semi-evergreen or evergreen shrubs and trees, grown for their foliage and, in some species, flowers. Requires sun or semi-shade, the variegated forms doing best in full sun. Thrives on any well-drained soil, including alkaline soil. All except *L. lucidum* occasionally need cutting back in mid-spring to restrict growth. Propagate by semi-ripe cuttings in summer. All parts may cause severe discomfort if ingested.
L. japonicum (Japanese privet).

Evergreen, bushy, dense shrub. H 3m (10ft), S 2.5m (8ft). Has oval, glossy, very dark green leaves and, from mid-summer to early autumn, large, conical panicles of small, tubular, white flowers with 4 lobes. Zone 9. 'Coriaceum' see *L.j.* 'Rotundifolium' **'Rotundifolium'**, syn. *L.j.* 'Coriaceum', is slow-growing, with a dense mass of rounded, leathery leaves. Zone 9.
L. lucidum (Chinese privet). Evergreen, upright shrub or tree. H 10m (30ft), S 8m (25ft). Bears large, oval, glossy, dark green leaves. Produces large panicles of small, tubular, white flowers, with 4 lobes, in late summer and early autumn. Zone 9. 'Excelsum Superbum' illus. p.127.
L. ovalifolium illus. p.126. 'Aureum' is a vigorous, evergreen or semi-evergreen, upright, dense shrub. H 4m (12ft), S 3m (10ft). Leaves are oval, glossy and mid-green, broadly edged with bright yellow. Dense panicles of small, rather unpleasantly scented, tubular, white flowers, with 4 lobes, appear in mid-summer and are succeeded by spherical, black fruits. Cut back hedges to 30cm (1ft) after planting and prune hard for first 2 years; then trim as necessary during the growing season. Zone 7.
L. sinense illus. p.118.
L. 'Vicaryi', syn. *L.* x *vicaryi*, illus. p.153.
L. x *vicaryi*. See *L.* 'Vicaryi'.
L. vulgare. Deciduous or semi-evergreen, bushy shrub. H and S 3m (10ft). Leaves are narrowly lance-shaped and dark green. Produces panicles of small, strongly scented, tubular, white flowers, with 4 lobes, from early to mid-summer, then spherical, black fruits. Cut back hedges to 30cm (1ft) after planting and prune hard for first 2 years; then trim as necessary during the growing season. Zone 5b. 'Lodense', a more compact form. Zone 4. H and S 1.2m (4ft).

Lijiang spruce. See *Picea likiangensis*.
Lilac. See *Syringa*.
  Himalayan. See *Syringa emodi*.
  Japanese tree. See *Syringa reticulata*.
  Persian. See *Melia azedarach*, illus. p.76; *Syringa* x *persica*, illus. p.120.
  Rouen. See *Syringa* x *chinensis*.
  St Vincent. See *Solanum seaforthianum*, illus. p.206.
  Vine. See *Hardenbergia violacea*.

LILIUM

Lily

LILIACEAE

Genus of mainly summer-flowering bulbs, grown for their often fragrant, brightly coloured flowers. Each fleshy-scaled bulb produces one unbranched, leafy stem, in some cases with annual roots in lower part. Mostly lance-shaped or linear leaves, to 22cm (9in) long, are scattered or in whorls, sometimes with bulbils in axils. Flowers, usually several per stem, are mainly trumpet- to bowl-shaped or with the 6 petals strongly reflexed to form a turkscap

shape. (Petals of *Lilium* are known botanically as perianth segments.) Each plant has a spread of up to 30cm (12in). Needs sun and any well-drained soil, unless otherwise stated. Propagate by seed in autumn or spring, by bulb scales in summer or by stem bulbils (where present) in autumn. Virus and fungal diseases (such as botrytis) and lily beetle may cause problems. See also feature panel pp.404–405.
L. amabile. Summer-flowering bulb with stem roots. H 30cm–1m (1–3ft). Scattered leaves are lance-shaped. Has up to 10 unpleasant-smelling, nodding, turkscap, black-spotted, red flowers; each petal is 5–5.5cm (2–2¼in) long.
L. 'Amber Gold' (illus. p.405). Summer-flowering bulb. H 1.2–1.5m (4–5ft). Has nodding, turkscap, deep yellow flowers, each with maroon spots in throat.
L. 'Angela North' (illus. p.404). Mid-summer flowering bulb. H to 1m (3ft). Has slightly fragrant, dark red flowers, spotted darker red, that have strongly recurved petals.
L. 'Apollo' (illus. p.405). Summer-flowering bulb. H 1.2m (4ft). Has downward-facing, turkscap, pale orange flowers with strongly reflexed petals.
L. auratum (Golden-rayed lily of Japan). Summer- and autumn-flowering bulb with stem roots. H 60cm–1.5m (2–5ft). Has long, scattered, lance-shaped leaves. Produces up to 10, sometimes more, fragrant, outward-facing, widely bowl-shaped, white flowers; each petal is 12–18cm (5–7in) long with a central, red or yellow band and often red or yellow spots. Requires semi-shade and neutral to acid soil. var. *platyphyllum* (illus. p.404) has broader leaves; petals have a central, yellow band and fewer spots.
L. 'Black Beauty' (illus. p.405). Summer-flowering bulb. H 1.5–2m (5–6ft). Has outward-facing, flattish, green-centred, very deep red flowers with recurved, white-margined petals.
L. 'Black Dragon'. Summer-flowering bulb. H 1.5m (5ft). Has outward-facing, trumpet-shaped flowers with dark purplish-red outsides and white insides.
L. 'Black Magic' (illus. p.404). Summer-flowering bulb. H 1.2–2m (4–6ft). Scented, outward-facing, trumpet-shaped flowers are purplish-brown outside and white inside.
L. 'Bonfire'. Late summer-flowering bulb. H 1.2–1.5m (4–5ft). Produces outward-facing, bowl-shaped flowers with broad petals, white outside flushed with pink, and dark crimson inside spotted paler crimson.
L. 'Bright Star' (illus. p.404). Summer-flowering bulb. H 1–1.5m (3–5ft). Has flattish, white flowers; petals have recurved tips and a central, orange streak inside.
L. 'Bronwen North' (illus. p.404). Mid-summer-flowering bulb. H to 1m (3ft). In mid-summer, each stem carries 7 or more slightly fragrant flowers with strongly recurving, pale mauve-pink petals, paler at the tips, and pale pink throats with dark spots and lines; nectaries are reddish-black.
L. 'Brushmarks' (illus. p.405). Early summer-flowering bulb. H 1.35m

(4½ft). Upward-facing, cup-shaped, orange flowers are green-throated. Petals each have deep red blotches and sometimes spots.

L. bulbiferum (Fire lily, Orange lily). Summer-flowering bulb with stem roots. H 40cm–1.5m (16in–5ft). Stem bears scattered, lance-shaped leaves and, usually, bulbils in leaf axils. Bears 1–5 or more upward-facing, shallowly cup-shaped, orange-red flowers. Each petal is 6–8.5cm (2½–3¼in) long and spotted black or deep red. var. **croceum** (illus. p.405) has orange flowers and does not normally bear bulbils.

L. canadense (Canada lily, Meadow lily, Wild yellow lily; illus. p.405). Summer-flowering bulb with stem roots. H to 1.5m (5ft). Narrowly to broadly lance-shaped leaves are mainly in whorls. Bears about 10 nodding, bell-shaped, yellow or red flowers; each petal is 5–8cm (2–3in) long, with dark red or purple spots in lower part.

L. candidum (Madonna lily; illus. p.404). Summer-flowering bulb. H 1–2m (3–6ft). Flower stem bears scattered, lance-shaped leaves and 5–20 fragrant, outward-facing, broadly funnel-shaped, white flowers. Each petal is 5–8cm (2–3in) long with a yellow base and a slightly recurved tip. In autumn bears basal leaves, which remain throughout winter but die off as flowering stems mature. Prefers lime-rich soil.

L. carniolicum. See **L. pyrenaicum** subsp. **carniolicum.**

L. 'Casa Blanca' (illus. p.404). Late summer-flowering bulb. H 90cm (3ft). Waxy, white flowers, have yellowish-white midribs and violet-red nectaries.

L. cernuum. Summer-flowering bulb with stem roots. H to 60cm (2ft). Long, linear leaves are scattered. Produces 7–15 fragrant, nodding, turkscap flowers, usually pinkish-purple with purple spots. Each petal is 3.5–5cm (1½–2in) long.

L. chalcedonicum, syn. **L. heldreichii** (Scarlet turkscap lily; illus. p.405). Summer-flowering bulb with stem roots. H 50cm–1.5m (20in–5ft). Leaves are scattered and mostly lance-shaped, lower ones spreading, upper ones smaller and closer to stem. Bears up to 12 slightly scented, nodding, turkscap flowers with red or reddish-orange petals, each 5–7cm (2–3in) long.

L. 'Connecticut King' (illus. p.405). Early to mid-summer-flowering bulb. H 1m (3ft). Flowers are upward-facing, cup-shaped and bright yellow.

L. 'Corsage' (illus. p.404). Summer-flowering bulb. H 1.2m (4ft). Bears outward-facing, bowl-shaped flowers with recurved petals, pink-flushed outside and pink inside with white centres and maroon spots.

L. 'Côte d'Azur' (illus. p.404). Summer-flowering bulb. H 40cm (16in). Strong stems bear deep rose-pink flowers with darker-spotted throats.

L. × dalhansonii (illus. p.404). Variable, summer-flowering bulb. H 1.5–2m (5–6ft). Has unpleasant-smelling, turkscap flowers that are chestnut brown or dark maroon with gold spots. **'Marhan'** see **L. 'Marhan'.**

L. davidii. Summer-flowering bulb with stem roots. H 1–1.4m (3–4½ft). Linear leaves are scattered. Produces 5–20 nodding, turkscap, red or reddish-orange flowers; each petal is 5–8cm (2–3in) long with dark purple spots. var. **willmottiae** (illus. p.405) differs in its slender, arching stems to 2m (6ft) and pendent flower stalks.

L. 'Destiny' (illus. p.405). Early summer-flowering bulb. H 1–1.2m (3–4ft). Flowers are upward-facing, cup-shaped and yellow with brown spots.

L. duchartrei (illus. p.404). Summer-flowering bulb. H 60cm–1m (2–3ft). Lance-shaped leaves are scattered up stems. Has up to 12 fragrant, nodding, turkscap, white flowers that are flushed purple outside and spotted deep purple inside.

L. 'Enchantment' (illus. p.405). Early summer-flowering bulb. H 1m (3ft). Produces upward-facing, cup-shaped, orange-red flowers with black-spotted throats.

L. Golden Clarion Group (illus. p.405). Late spring to early summer-flowering bulb. H 1–2m (3–6ft). Has outward-facing, trumpet-shaped, pale to deep yellow flowers that may be flushed with reddish-purple outside.

L. Golden Splendor Group (illus. p.405). Vigorous, mid- to late summer-flowering bulb with stem roots. H 1.5–2m (5–6ft). Large, funnel-shaped flowers are deep golden yellow with maroon stripes on the back of each petal.

L. hansonii (illus. p.405). Summer-flowering bulb with stem roots. H 1–1.5m (3–5ft). Long leaves in whorls are lance-shaped to oval. Has 3–12 scented, nodding, turkscap, orange-yellow flowers. Each thick petal is 3–4cm (1¼–1½in) long with brown-purple spots towards base.

L. 'Harmony' (illus. p.405). Summer-flowering bulb. H 50cm–1m (1½–3ft). Orange flowers are upward-facing, cup-shaped and spotted with maroon.

L. heldreichii. See **L. chalcedonicum.**

L. henryi. Late summer-flowering bulb with stem roots. H 1–3m (3–10ft). Has scattered, lance-shaped leaves. Produces 5–20, sometimes up to 70, nodding, turkscap, orange flowers; petals are 6–8cm (2½–3in) long with dark spots and prominent warts towards bases. Prefers lime-rich soil.

L. Imperial Crimson Group. Late summer-flowering bulb. H 1.5m (5ft). Fragrant, flattish, deep crimson flowers have white throats and white-edged petals.

L. Imperial Gold Group (illus. p.404). Summer-flowering bulb. H 2m (6ft). Bears fragrant, flattish, white flowers, spotted maroon, and with a yellow stripe up each petal centre.

L. 'Journey's End' (illus. p.404). Late summer-flowering bulb. H 2m (6ft). Outward-facing, bowl-shaped, maroon-spotted, deep pink flowers have recurved petals, white at tips and edges.

L. 'Karen North' (illus. p.405). Summer-flowering bulb. H to 1.4m (4½ft). Turkscap flowers are downward-facing, with orange-pink petals sparsely spotted with deep pink.

L. 'Lady Bowes Lyon' (illus. p.405). Summer-flowering bulb. H 1–1.2m

(3–4ft). Downward-facing, black-spotted, rich red flowers have reflexed petals.

L. lancifolium, syn. **L. tigrinum** (Tiger lily). Summer- to early autumn-flowering bulb with stem roots. H 60cm–1.5m (2–5ft). Produces long, scattered, narrowly lance-shaped leaves. Produces 5–10, sometimes up to 40, nodding, turkscap, pink- to red-orange flowers; each petal is 7–10cm (3–4in) long and spotted with purple. var. **flaviflorum** has yellow-orange flowers. Vigorous var. **splendens** (illus. p.405) bears larger, brighter red-orange flowers.

L. lankongense. Summer-flowering bulb with stem roots. H to 1.2m (4ft). Leaves are scattered and lance-shaped. Has up to 15 scented, nodding, turkscap, pink flowers. Petals, each 4–6.5cm (1½–2½in) long with a central, green stripe and red-purple spots mainly on edges, are often mauve-flushed. Needs partial shade in warm areas.

L. leichtlinii. Summer-flowering bulb with stem roots. H to 1.2m (4ft). Scattered leaves are linear to narrowly lance-shaped. Produces 1–6 nodding, turkscap, yellow flowers; each petal is 6–8.5cm (2½–3¼in) long with dark reddish-purple spots. Needs semi-shade.

L. 'Limelight'. Summer-flowering bulb. H 1–1.5m (3–5ft). Flowers are outward-facing or slightly nodding, trumpet-shaped and yellow-green.

L. longiflorum (Easter lily, White trumpet lily; illus. p.404). Summer-flowering bulb with stem roots. H 30cm–1m (1–3ft). Leaves are scattered and lance-shaped. Produces 1–6 fragrant, outward-facing, funnel-shaped, white flowers. Each petal is 13–20cm (5–8in) long with slightly recurved tips.

L. mackliniae (Manipur lily; illus. p.404). Late spring- to summer-flowering bulb with stem roots. H to 40cm (16in). Small, narrowly lance-shaped to narrowly oval leaves are scattered or whorled near top of stem. Has 1–6 usually nodding, broadly bell-shaped, purplish-pink flowers; each petal is 4.5–5cm (1¾–2in) long. Needs semi-shade.

L. maculatum, syn. **L. thunbergianum.** Summer-flowering bulb with stem roots. H to 60cm (2ft). Scattered leaves are lance-shaped or oval. Has 1–6 upward-facing, cup-shaped, yellow, orange or red flowers with darker spots; each petal is 8–10cm (3–4in) long.

L. 'Magic Pink' (illus. p.404). Early summer-flowering bulb. H 1–1.2m (3–4ft). Flowers are satin pink with darker pink spots.

L. 'Marhan', syn. **L. × dalhansonii** 'Marhan'. Early summer-flowering bulb. H 1.2–2m (4–6ft). Nodding, turkscap, deep orange flowers are spotted red-brown.

L. martagon (Martagon lily; illus. p.404). Summer-flowering bulb with stem roots. H 1–2m (3–6ft). Has lance-shaped to oval leaves in whorls and up to 50 scented, nodding, turkscap flowers. Petals are 3–4.5cm (1¼–1¾in) long and pink or purple, often with darker spots. var. **album** (illus. p.404) has pure white flowers.

L. medeoloides (illus. p.405). Summer-flowering bulb. H to 75cm (2½ft). produces lance-shaped leaves and up to 10 turkscap, apricot to orange-red flowers, usually with darker spots.

L. monadelphum, syn. **L. szovitsianum** (illus. p.405). Summer-flowering bulb with stem roots. H 50cm–2m (1½–6ft). Has scattered, lance-shaped to oval leaves. Produces usually 1–5, sometimes up to 30, scented, nodding, turkscap, yellow flowers, usually with deep red or purple spots inside. Each petal is 6–10cm (2½–4in) long.

L. 'Mont Blanc' (illus. p.404). Summer-flowering bulb. H 90cm (3ft). Has upward-facing, creamy-white flowers, spotted with brown.

L. 'Montreux' (illus. p.404). Mid-summer-flowering bulb. H 1m (3ft). Bears about 8 pink flowers with darker pink midribs; orange-pink throats are spotted with brown.

L. nanum, syn. **Nomocharis nana.** Late spring- or summer-flowering bulb. H 6–45cm (2½–18in). Scattered leaves are linear. Bears a usually nodding, broadly bell-shaped, purplish-pink flower with 4.5–5cm (1¾–2in) long petals. Needs partial shade. var. **flavidum** has pale yellow flowers.

L. nepalense (illus. p.405). Summer-flowering bulb with stem roots. H 70cm–1m (28–36in). Has scattered, lance-shaped leaves. Produces often unpleasant-smelling, nodding, funnel-shaped, greenish-white or greenish-yellow flowers, each with a dark reddish-purple base inside and petals to 15cm (6in) long.

L. Olympic Hybrids (illus. p.404). Summer-flowering bulb. H 1.2–2m (4–6ft). Scented, outward-facing, trumpet-shaped flowers are usually pink or purple outside with yellow throats; white, cream, yellow or pink variants also occur.

L. pardalinum (Leopard lily, Panther lily; illus. p.405). Summer-flowering bulb. H 2–3m (6–10ft). Long, narrowly elliptic leaves are mainly in whorls. Has up to 10 often scented, nodding, turkscap flowers. Each petal is 5–9cm (2–3½in) long with red, upper parts. Orange, lower parts have maroon spots, some of which are encircled with yellow.

L. ponticum. See **L. pyrenaicum** subsp. **ponticum.**

L. pumilum, syn. **L. tenuifolium.** Summer-flowering bulb with stem roots. H 15cm–1m (6–36in). Small, scattered leaves are linear. Produces usually up to 7 but occasionally up to 30 slightly scented, nodding, turkscap flowers; each petal is 3–3.5cm (1¼–1½in) long and scarlet with or without basal, black spots.

L. pyrenaicum (Yellow turkscap lily; illus. p.405). Late spring to early summer-flowering bulb often with stem roots. H 30cm–1.35m (1–4½ft). Has scattered, linear to narrowly elliptic, hairless leaves. Produces up to 12 unpleasant-smelling, nodding, turkscap flowers. Each petal is 4–6.5cm (1½–2½in) long and yellow or green-yellow with deep purple spots and lines. subsp. **carniolicum** (syn. **L. carniolicum**) has red- or orange-spotted flowers. Leaves may be hairless or downy. subsp. **ponticum** (syn.

L. ponticum) bears deep yellow flowers, densely lined and spotted with red-brown or purple; leaves are downy beneath. var. **rubrum** (illus. p.405) has orange-red or dark red flowers.

L. **regale** (Regal lily; illus. p.404). Summer-flowering bulb with stem roots. H 50cm–2m (20in–6ft). Linear leaves are scattered. Produces up to 25 fragrant, outward-facing, funnel-shaped flowers. Petals are each 12–15cm (5–6in) long, white inside with a yellow base and pinkish-purple outside.

L. **'Roma'** (illus. p.405). Early summer-flowering bulb. H 1.5m (5ft). Green buds open to cream flowers that sometimes age to pale greenish-yellow.

L. **'Rosemary North'** (illus. p.405). Mid- to late summer-flowering bulb. H to 1m (3ft). Produces 12 or more slightly fragrant, rich orange flowers that sometimes have darker spots.

L. **rubellum** (illus. p.404). Early summer-flowering bulb with stem roots. H 30–80cm (12–32in). Has scattered, narrowly oval leaves and up to 9 scented, outward-facing, broadly funnel-shaped, pink flowers with dark red spots at bases; each petal is 6–8cm (2½–3in) long.

L. **'Shuksan'**. Summer-flowering bulb. H 1.2–2m (4–6ft). Nodding, turkscap, yellowish-orange flowers are flushed red at petal tips and sparsely spotted with black.

L. **speciosum**. Late summer-flowering bulb with stem roots. H 1–1.7m (3–5½ft). Has long, scattered, broadly lance-shaped leaves. Produces up to 12 scented, nodding, turkscap, white or pink flowers; each petal is up to 10cm (4in) long, with pink or crimson spots. Requires neutral to acid soil. var. **album** has white flowers and purple stems. Flowers of var. **rubrum** (illus. p.404) are carmine, stems are purple.

L. **'Star Gazer'** (illus. p.404). Late summer-flowering bulb. H 90cm (3ft). Fragrant, rich crimson flowers are spotted maroon.

L. **'Sterling Star'** (illus. p.404). Summer-flowering bulb. H 1–1.2m (3–4ft). Has upward-facing, cup-shaped, white flowers with tiny, brown spots.

L. **superbum** (Swamp lily, Turkscap lily; illus. p.405). Late summer- to early autumn-flowering bulb with stem roots. H 1.5–3m (5–10ft). Lance-shaped to elliptic leaves are mainly in whorls. Bears up to 40 nodding, turkscap, orange flowers. Each petal is 6–10cm (2½–4in) long, with a green base inside and usually flushed red and spotted maroon. Requires neutral to acid soil.

L. **szovitsianum**. See L. monadelphum.
L. **tenuifolium**. See L. pumilum.
L. × **testaceum** (Nankeen lily). Summer-flowering bulb. H 1–1.5m (3–5ft). Has scattered, linear, often twisted leaves. Produces 6–12 fragrant, nodding, turkscap, light orange to brownish-yellow flowers; each petal is 8cm (3in) long, usually with reddish spots inside.

L. **thunbergianum**. See L. maculatum.
L. **tigrinum**. See L. lancifolium.
L. **tsingtauense** (illus. p.405). Summer-flowering bulb with stem roots. H 1m (3ft). Lance-shaped leaves are mainly in whorls. Produces 1–5 upward-facing, cup-shaped, orange to orange-

red flowers; petals are up to 5cm (2in) long and spotted with maroon.

L. **wallichianum**. Late summer- to autumn-flowering bulb with stem roots. H to 2m (6ft). Long, scattered leaves are linear or lance-shaped. Bears 1–4 fragrant, outward-facing, funnel-shaped, white or cream flowers that are green or yellow towards bases. Each petal is 15–30cm (6–12in) long.

Lily. See Lilium.
   African. See Agapanthus africanus.
   Arum. See Zantedeschia aethiopica.
   Atamasco. See Zephyranthes atamasco.
   August. See Hosta plantaginea, illus. p.289.
   Aztec. See Sprekelia formosissima, illus. p.413.
   Belladonna. See Amaryllis belladonna, illus. p.408.
   Blackberry. See Belamcanda.
   Blood. See Haemanthus coccineus, illus. p.435.
   Boat. See Tradescantia spathacea.
   Canada. See Lilium canadense.
   Chinese-lantern. See Sandersonia aurantiaca, illus. p.423.
   Dwarf white wood. See Trillium nivale.
   Easter. See Lilium longiflorum, illus. p.404.
   Fire. See Lilium bulbiferum.
   Flax. See Dianella.
   Foxtail. See Eremurus.
   Giant. See Cardiocrinum giganteum, illus. p.398.
   Giant pineapple. See Eucomis pallidiflora, illus. p.397.
   Ginger. See Hedychium.
   Globe. See Calochortus albus, illus. p.409.
   Glory. See Gloriosa superba.
   Golden arum. See Zantedeschia elliottiana, illus. p.402.
   Golden spider. See Lycoris aurea.
   Guernsey. See Nerine sarniensis, illus. p.424.
   Jacobean. See Sprekelia formosissima, illus. p.413.
   Josephine's. See Brunsvigia josephinae.
   Kaffir. See Schizostylis.
   Lent. See Narcissus pseudonarcissus, illus. p.417.
   Leopard. See Dieffenbachia; Lilium pardalinum, illus. p.405.
   Madonna. See Lilium candidum, illus. p.404.
   Manipur. See Lilium mackliniae, illus. p.404.
   Martagon. See Lilium martagon, illus. p.404.
   May. See Maianthemum.
   Meadow. See Lilium canadense.
   Nankeen. See Lilium × testaceum.
   Orange. See Lilium bulbiferum.
   Painted wood. See Trillium undulatum.
   Panther. See Lilium pardalinum, illus. p.405.
   Peace. See Spathiphyllum wallisii, illus. p.300.
   Plantain. See Hosta.
   Rain. See Zephyranthes.
   Red spider. See Lycoris radiata, illus. p.420.
   Regal. See Lilium regale, illus. p.404.

Lily (continued)
   Resurrection. See Lycoris sqwamigera.
   Rienga. See Arthropodium cirratum.
   Rock. See Arthropodium cirratum.
   Scarlet turkscap. See Lilium chalcedonicum, illus. p.405.
   Sea. See Pancratium maritimum.
   St Bernard's. See Anthericum liliago, illus. p.276.
   St Bruno's. See Paradisea liliastrum.
   Swamp. See Lilium superbum; Saururus cernuus, illus. p.447.
   Tiger. See Lilium lancifolium.
   Toad. See Tricyrtis.
   Torch. See Kniphofia.
   Turkscap. See Lilium superbum.
   Voodoo. See Sauromatum venosum, illus. p.413.
   Water. See Nymphaea.
   White ginger. See Hedychium coronarium.
   White trumpet. See Lilium longiflorum, illus. p.404.
   Wild yellow. See Lilium canadense.
   Wood. See Trillium.
   Yellow pond. See Nuphar advena.
   Yellow turkscap. See Lilium pyrenaicum.
Lily of Japan, Golden-rayed. See Lilium auratum.
Lily tree. See Magnolia denudata, illus. p.75.
Lily-of-the-valley. See Convallaria.
   Wild. See Pyrola rotundifolia.
Lily-of-the-valley tree. See Clethra arborea.
Lilyturf. See Liriope.
Limnanthemum nymphoides. See Nymphoides peltata.

LIMNANTHES

LIMNANTHACEAE

Genus of annuals, useful for rock gardens and for edging. Prefers a sunny situation and fertile, well-drained soil. Propagate by seed sown outdoors in spring or early autumn. Self seeds freely.
L. **douglasii** illus. p.336.

LIMONIUM
Sea lavender

PLUMBAGINACEAE

Genus of summer- and autumn-flowering perennials, sometimes grown as annuals, and sub-shrubs, some of which are evergreen. Tender, min. 7–10°C (45–50°F). Grows in full sun and in well-drained soil. Propagate by division in spring, by seed in autumn or early spring or by root cuttings in winter.
L. **bellidifolium**, syn. L. reticulatum. Evergreen, dome-shaped perennial with a woody base. H 15–20cm (6–8in), S 10cm (4in). Has basal rosettes of rounded, dark green leaves. Much-branched flower stems produce masses of small, 'everlasting', trumpet-shaped blue flowers in summer-autumn. Is excellent for a rock garden.
L. **latifolium** **'Blue Cloud'** illus. p.286.
L. **perezii**. Evergreen, rounded sub-shrub. H and S 1m (3ft) or more. Tender, min. 7–10°C (45–50°F). Has long-stalked, oval to diamond-shaped, deep green leaves. Dense clusters, 20cm (8in) wide, of tiny, tubular, deep mauve-blue flowers are carried well

above the leaves in autumn. Needs good ventilation if grown under glass.
L. **reticulatum**. See L. bellidifolium.
L. **sinuatum** illus. p.322. **Fortress Series** is a slow-growing, upright, bushy perennial, grown as an annual. H 45cm (18in), S 30cm (12in). Has lance-shaped, lobed and often wavy-margined, deep green leaves and, in summer and early autumn, clusters of small, tubular flowers in a mixture of shades such as pink, yellow or blue.
L. **suworowii**. See Psylliostachys suworowii.

LINARIA
Toadflax

SCROPHULARIACEAE

Genus of spring-, summer- or autumn-flowering annuals, biennials and perennials, useful for rock gardens and borders. Prefers sun or light shade; thrives in any well-drained soil. Propagate by seed in autumn or spring. Self seeds freely.
L. **alpina** (Alpine toadflax). Tuft-forming, compact, annual, biennial or short-lived perennial with a sparse root system. H 15cm (6in), S 10–15cm (4–6in). Has whorls of linear to lance-shaped, fleshy, grey-green leaves. A succession of snapdragon-like, yellow-centred, purple-violet flowers is borne in loose racemes in summer.
L. **dalmatica**. See L. genistifolia var. dalmatica.
L. **genistifolia**. Upright perennial. H 60cm–1.2m (2–4ft), S 23cm (9in). From mid-summer to autumn produces racemes of small, snapdragon-like, orange-marked, yellow flowers. Lance-shaped, glossy, mid-green leaves clasp the stems.
var. **dalmatica** (syn. L. dalmatica; Dalmatian toadflax), H 1–1.2m (3–4ft), S 60cm (2ft), bears much larger, golden-yellow flowers, from mid- to late summer, and has broader, more glaucous leaves.
L. **maroccana** **'Fairy Lights'** illus. p.330.
L. **purpurea** (Purple toadflax). Upright perennial. H 60cm–1m (2–3ft), S 60cm (2ft). From mid- to late summer, racemes of snapdragon-like, purplish-blue flowers, touched with white at throats, are produced above narrowly oval, grey-green leaves.
'Canon J. Went' illus. p.243.
L. **triornithophora** illus. p.251.

Linden. See Tilia.
Linden. See Tilia.
   American. See Tilia americana.
   Crimean. See Tilia × euchlora.
   European. See Tilia × europaea.
   European white. See Tilia tomentosa.
   Large-leaved. See Tilia platyphyllos.
   Mongolian. See Tilia mongolica.
   Weeping silver. See Tilia 'Petiolaris', illus. p.68.
   Silver. See Tilia tomentosa.
   Small-leaved. See Tilia cordata.

LINDERA

LAURACEAE

Genus of deciduous or evergreen shrubs and trees, grown for their foliage, which

is often aromatic, and their autumn colour. Fruits are produced on female plants if male plants are also grown. Needs semi-shade and moist, acid soil. Propagate by softwood cuttings in summer or by seed in autumn.
L. benzoin illus. p.131.
L. obtusiloba. Deciduous, bushy shrub. H and S 6m (20ft). Bears 3-lobed, aromatic, glossy, dark green leaves, becoming butter-yellow in autumn. Clusters of small, star-shaped, deep yellow flowers, borne on bare shoots from early to mid-spring, are followed by small, spherical, black fruits. Zone 7.

LINDHEIMERA

ASTERACEAE/COMPOSITAE

Genus of late summer- and early autumn-flowering annuals. Grow in sun and in fertile, well-drained soil. Propagate by seed sown under glass in early spring or outdoors in late spring.
L. texana illus. p.336.

Ling. See *Calluna vulgaris*.

LINNAEA
Twin flower

CAPRIFOLIACEAE

Genus of one species of evergreen, creeping, summer-flowering, sub-shrubby perennial that makes an extensive, twiggy mat. Is useful as ground cover on peat beds and rock gardens. Requires partial shade and moist, peaty, acid soil. Propagate by rooted runners in spring, by softwood cuttings in summer or by seed in autumn.
L. borealis illus. p.375.

LINUM

LINACEAE

Genus of annuals, biennials, perennials, sub-shrubs and shrubs, some of which are evergreen or semi-evergreen, grown for their flowers. Is suitable for rock gardens. Even where hardy some species need a sheltered position. Prefers sun and humus-rich, well-drained, peaty soil. Propagate sub-shrubs and shrubs by semi-ripe cuttings in summer or by seed in autumn, annuals, biennials and perennials by seed in autumn.
L. arboreum illus. p.358.
L. flavum (Golden flax, Yellow flax). Bushy perennial with a woody rootstock. H 30cm (12in), S 15cm (6in). Has narrowly oval, green leaves and, in summer, upward-facing, funnel-shaped, yellow flowers in terminal clusters. **'Compactum'** illus. p.385.
L. 'Gemmell's Hybrid'. Semi-evergreen, domed perennial with a woody rootstock. H 15cm (6in), S 20cm (8in). Leaves are oval and grey-green. In summer, short-stalked, broadly funnel-shaped, bright chrome-yellow flowers are produced in terminal clusters. Prefers alkaline soil.
L. grandiflorum 'Rubrum' illus. p.327.
L. narbonense illus. p.287.
L. perenne illus. p.356.

L. salsoloides. See *L. suffruticosum* subsp. *salsoloides*.
L. suffruticosum subsp. **salsoloides**, syn. *L. salsoloides*. Perennial with spreading, sometimes woody-based, stems. H 5–20cm (2–8in), S 8cm (3in). Slender stems produce fine, heath-like, grey-green leaves and, in summer, a succession of short-lived, saucer-shaped, pearl-white flowers, flushed blue or pink, in terminal clusters.

Lion's ear. See *Leonotis leonurus*, illus. p.149.
Lippia citriodora. See *Aloysia triphylla*.
Lipstick plant. See *Aeschynanthus pulcher*.

LIQUIDAMBAR

HAMAMELIDACEAE

Genus of deciduous trees, with inconspicuous flowers, grown for their maple-like foliage and autumn colour. Requires sun or semi-shade and fertile, moist but well-drained soil; grows poorly on shallow, chalky soil. Propagate by softwood cuttings in summer or by seed in autumn.
L. formosana, syn. *L. monticola*. Deciduous, broadly conical tree. H 12m (40ft), S 10m (30ft). Has large, 3-lobed, toothed leaves, purple when young, dark green in summer and turning orange, red and purple in autumn. Zone 8.
L. monticola. See *L. formosana*.
L. orientalis (Oriental sweet gum). Slow-growing, deciduous, bushy tree. H 6m (20ft), S 4m (12ft). Small, 5-lobed, mid-green leaves turn orange in autumn. Zone 8.
L. styraciflua (Sweet gum) illus. p.70.
'Lane Roberts' is a deciduous, broadly conical to spreading tree. H 25m (80ft), S 12m (40ft). Shoots usually have corky ridges. Glossy, green leaves, each with 5 lobes, turn deep reddish-purple in autumn. Zone 6b.

Liquorice fern. See *Polypodium glycyrrhiza*, illus. p.310.
Liquorice. See *Glycyrrhiza*.

LIRIODENDRON

MAGNOLIACEAE

Genus of deciduous trees, grown for their foliage and flowers in summer. Flowers are almost hidden by unusual leaves and are not produced on young trees. Requires sun or semi-shade and deep, fertile, well-drained, preferably slightly acid, soil. Propagate species by seed in autumn, selected forms by budding in late summer.
L. chinense (Chinese tulip tree). Fast-growing, deciduous, spreading tree. H 25m (80ft), S 12m (40ft). Bears large, deep green leaves, cut off at the tips and with a deep lobe on each side; leaves become yellow in autumn. Cup-shaped, orange-based, greenish-white flowers appear in mid-summer. Zone 8.
L. tulipifera illus. p.65.
'Aureomarginatum' illus. p.69.

LIRIOPE
Lilyturf

CONVALLARIACEAE/LILIACEAE

Genus of evergreen perennials with swollen, fleshy rhizomes. Some are grown as ground cover. Requires sun and well-drained soil. Propagate by division in spring or by seed in autumn.
L. graminifolia var. **densiflora**. See *L. muscari*.
L. muscari, syn. *L. graminifolia* var. *densiflora*, *L. platyphylla* (illus. p.294). **'Majestic'** is an evergreen, spreading, rhizomatous perennial. H 30cm (12in), S 45cm (18in). In late autumn produces spikes of thickly clustered, rounded-bell-shaped, violet flowers among linear, glossy, bright green leaves.
L. platyphylla. See *L. muscari*.
L. spicata. Evergreen, spreading, rhizomatous perennial. H 30cm (12in), S 30–40cm (12–16in). Grass-like, glossy, dark green leaves make good ground cover. Produces spikes of rounded-bell-shaped, pale lavender flowers in late summer.

Lisianthus russellianus. See *Eustoma grandiflorum*.

LITHOCARPUS

FAGACEAE

Genus of evergreen trees, grown for their foliage. Needs sun or semi-shade. Prefers well-drained, neutral to acid soil. Shelter from strong winds. Propagate by seed, when ripe, in autumn.
L. densiflorus (Tanbark oak). Evergreen, spreading tree. H and S 10m (30ft). Has sweet chestnut-like, leathery, glossy, dark green leaves and upright, pale yellow flower spikes borne in spring and often again in autumn. Zone 9.
L. henryi illus. p.100.

LITHODORA

BORAGINACEAE

Genus of evergreen sub-shrubs and shrubs, grown for their flowers. Is excellent in rock gardens. Needs full sun and moist, well-drained soil; some species are limestone haters and need acid conditions. Resents root disturbance. Propagate by semi-ripe cuttings in mid-summer or by seed in autumn.
L. diffusa, syn. *Lithospermum diffusum*. **'Grace Ward'** is an evergreen, compact, semi-prostrate shrub. H 15–30cm (6–12in), S to 30cm (12in). Trailing stems bear lance-shaped, hairy, dull green leaves. In early summer bears masses of funnel-shaped, deep blue flowers in terminal clusters. Needs acid soil. Plants should be trimmed back after flowering. Zone 7. **'Heavenly Blue'** illus. p.357.
L. oleifolia, syn. *Lithospermum oleifolium*, illus. p.356.
L. zahnii, syn. *Lithospermum zahnii*. Evergreen, much-branched, upright shrub. H and S 30cm (12in) or more. Stems are covered in oval, hairy, dark green or greyish-green leaves. Funnel-shaped, azure-blue flowers, with spreading lobes, open in succession from

early spring to mid-summer. Sets buds and flowers intermittently until mid-autumn. Prefers alkaline soil. Zone 9.

LITHOPHRAGMA

SAXIFRAGACEAE

Genus of tuberous perennials, grown for their campion-like flowers. Is dormant in summer. Tolerates all but deepest shade and prefers humus-rich, moist soil. Propagate by seed or division in spring or autumn.
L. parviflorum illus. p.346.

LITHOPS
Living stones, Stone plant

AIZOACEAE

Genus of prostrate, egg-shaped, perennial succulents, with almost united pairs of swollen, erect leaves that are separated on upper surface by a fissure from which a daisy-like flower emerges. Each pair of old leaves splits and dries away to papery skin in spring to reveal a pair of new leaves growing at right angles to old ones. Slowly forms clumps after 3–5 years. Tender, min. 5°C (41°F). Needs full sun and extremely well-drained soil or gritty compost. Water regularly in growing season (mid-summer to early autumn), not at all in winter. Propagate by seed in spring or summer.
L. aucampiae. Egg-shaped, perennial succulent. H 1cm (½in), S 3cm (1¼in). Pairs of brown leaves have flat, upper surfaces bearing darker marks. Produces a yellow flower in late summer or early autumn.
L. bella, syn. *L. karasmontana* subsp. *bella*. Egg-shaped, perennial succulent. H 2–3cm (¾–1¼in), S 1.5cm (⅝in). Has pairs of brown to brown-yellow leaves with darker marks on convex, upper surfaces. Produces a white flower in late summer or early autumn.
L. bromfieldii var. **insularis**. See *L. insularis*.
L. dorotheae illus. p.478.
L. fulleri. Egg-shaped, perennial succulent. H and S 2cm (¾in). Pairs of leaves are dove-grey to brown-yellow. Convex, upper surfaces have sunken, darker marks. In late summer or early autumn bears a white flower.
L. hookeri. See *L. turbiniformis*.
L. insularis, syn. *L. bromfieldii* var. *insularis*. Egg-shaped, perennial succulent. H 2–3cm (¾–1¼in), S 2cm (¾in). Slightly convex, upper surfaces of paired, brown leaves have dark green windows and red dots and lines. Produces a yellow flower in late summer or early autumn.
L. julii. Egg-shaped, perennial succulent. H 2–3cm (¾–1¼in), S 5cm (2in). Has paired, pearl- to pink-grey leaves, each with a slightly convex, darker-marked, upper surface. In late summer or autumn produces a white flower.
L. karasmontana illus. p.469. subsp. *bella* see *L. bella*.
L. lesliei. Egg-shaped, perennial succulent. H 1cm (½in), S 2cm (¾in). Is similar to *L. aucampiae*, but upper leaf surfaces are convex. var. **albinica** illus. p.470.
L. marmorata illus. p.469.
L. olivacea. Egg-shaped, perennial

succulent. H and S 2cm (¾in). Paired, dark olive-green leaves have darker windows on convex, upper surfaces. Yellow flower appears in late summer or early autumn.

L. otzeniana. Egg-shaped, perennial succulent. H 3cm (1¼in), S 2cm (¾in). Paired, grey-violet leaves each have a convex, upper surface with a distinctive, light border and large, semi-translucent windows. In late summer or early autumn bears a yellow flower.

L. pseudotruncatella. Egg-shaped, perennial succulent. H 3cm (1¼in), S 4cm (1½in). Bears pairs of pale grey or blue to lilac leaves with darker marks on convex, upper surfaces. Fissure reaches from side to side only on mature plants. Has a yellow flower in late summer or early autumn. var. *pulmonuncula* illus. p.478.

L. schwantesii, syn. *L.s.* var. *kuibisensis,* illus. p.478.

L. turbiniformis, syn. *L. hookeri.* Egg-shaped, perennial succulent. H 4cm (1½in), S 2cm (¾in). Has a flattish, upper surface with, usually, sunken, dark brown marks on paired, brown leaves. Yellow flower appears in late summer or early autumn.

Lithospermum diffusum. See *Lithodora diffusa.*
Lithospermum oleifolium. See *Lithodora oleifolia.*
Lithospermum zahnii. See *Lithodora zahnii.*
Litsia glauca. See *Neolitsia sericea.*
Little walnut. See *Juglans microcarpa,* illus. p.92.

LITTONIA

COLCHICACEAE/LILIACEAE

Genus of deciduous, perennial, scandent, tuberous climbers, grown for their pendent, bell-shaped flowers in summer. Tender, min. 8–16°C (46–61°F). Requires full sun and rich, well-drained soil. Provide support. Dies down in winter; lift and dry off tubers and store in a frost-free place. Propagate by seed in spring; tubers sometimes will divide naturally.

L. modesta illus. p.403.

Living rock. See *Ariocarpus; Pleiospilos bolusii,* illus. p.479.
Living stones. See *Lithops.*
Livingstone daisy. See *Dorotheanthus bellidiformis.*

LIVISTONA

ARECACEAE/PALMAE

Genus of evergreen palms, grown for their overall appearance. Has clusters of insignificant flowers in summer. Tender, min. 7°C (45°F). Needs full light or partial shade and fertile, well-drained soil, ideally neutral to acid. Water potted specimens moderately, less in winter. Propagate by seed in spring at not less than 23°C (73°F). Spider mite may be a nuisance on containerized plants.

L. australis (Australian cabbage palm, Gippsland fountain palm). Slow-growing, evergreen palm with a fairly

slender trunk. H 15–20m (50–70ft), S 3–6m (10–20ft). Has fan-shaped leaves, 1.2–2.5m (4–8ft) wide, divided into narrow, slender-pointed, glossy, green leaflets. Leaf stalks are spiny. *L. chinensis* illus. p.85.

Lizard's tail. See *Saururus cernuus,* illus. p.447.

LLOYDIA

LILIACEAE

Genus of summer-flowering bulbs, grown for their small, graceful, bell-shaped flowers. Is not easy to grow. Requires partial shade and well-drained, peaty soil; provide plenty of moisture in summer but, preferably, keep fairly dry in winter. Propagate by seed in spring.

L. graeca. See *Gagea graeca.*
L. serotina illus. p.435.

LOBELIA

CAMPANULACEAE

Genus of annuals, perennials and deciduous or evergreen shrubs, grown for their flowers. Some are suitable for wild gardens or by the waterside. Hardy to tender, min. 5°C (41°F). Prefers sun and moist but well-drained soil. Resents wet conditions in winter; in cold areas some perennials and shrubs are therefore best lifted in autumn and placed in well-drained compost in frames. Propagate annuals by seed in spring, perennial species by seed or division in spring, perennial cultivars by division only and shrubs by semi-ripe cuttings in summer. Contact with the milky sap of some species may irritate skin.

L. cardinalis (Cardinal flower). Clump-forming perennial. H 1m (3ft), S 23cm (9in). Bears racemes of 2-lipped, brilliant scarlet flowers from mid- to late summer. Lance-shaped leaves may be fresh green or red-bronze. *L.* 'Cherry Ripe' illus. p.249.

L. 'Dark Crusader'. Clump-forming perennial. H 1m (3ft), S 23cm (9in). From mid- to late summer bears racemes of 2-lipped, dark red flowers above lance-shaped, fresh green or red-bronze leaves.

L. erinus 'Blue Cascade'. Slow-growing, pendulous, spreading annual, occasionally perennial. H 10–20cm (4–8in), S 10–15cm (4–6in). Oval to lance-shaped leaves are pale green. Small, 2-lipped, pale blue flowers are produced continuously in summer and early autumn. 'Cambridge Blue' is compact and has blue flowers. 'Colour Cascade' has flowers in a mixture of colours, such as blue, red, pink, mauve or white. 'Crystal Palace' illus. p.334. 'Red Cascade' produces white-eyed, purple-red flowers. 'Sapphire' illus. p.332.

L. fulgens. See *L. splendens.*
L. x *gerardii* 'Vedrariensis', syn *L.* 'Vedrariensis'. Clump-forming perennial. H 1m (3ft), S 30cm (1ft). In late summer produces racemes of 2-lipped, purple flowers. Has lance-shaped, dark green leaves. *L.* 'Queen Victoria' illus. p.249.

L. siphilitica. Clump-forming perennial. H 1m (3ft), S 23cm (9in). Racemes of 2-lipped, blue flowers appear in late summer and autumn above narrowly oval, green leaves. Thrives in damp, heavy soil.

L. splendens, syn. *L. fulgens.* Clump-forming perennial. H 1m (3ft), S 23cm (9in). Racemes of 2-lipped, brilliant scarlet flowers are produced from mid- to late summer. Lance-shaped leaves are reddish-green.

L. tupa. Clump-forming perennial. H 1.5–2m (5–6ft), S 1m (3ft). Bears large spikes of 2-lipped, brick-red flowers in late summer, above narrowly oval, hairy, light green leaves. Does best in a sheltered, sunny site.

L. 'Vedrariensis'. See *L.* x *gerardii* 'Vedrariensis'.

L. 'Will Scarlet'. Clump-forming perennial. H 1m (3ft), S 30cm (1ft). Racemes of 2-lipped, bright red flowers are borne in summer. Lance-shaped leaves are coppery-green.

Lobel's maple. See *Acer cappadocicum* subsp. *lobelii,* illus. p.66.

LOBIVIA

CACTACEAE

Genus of spherical to columnar, perennial cacti, forming clumps with age, with flowers that each last only 1–2 days. Tender, min. 5°C (41°F). Is easy to grow, requiring full sun and well-drained soil. Propagate by seed or stem cuttings from spring to autumn.

L. aurea. See *Echinopsis aurea.*
L. backebergii. See *Echinopsis bachebergii.*
L. cinnabarina. See *Echinopsis cinnabarina.*
L. cylindrica. See *Echinopsis aurea.*
L. haageana illus. p.467.
L. pentlandii. See *Echinopsis pentlandii.*
L. pygmaea. See *Rebutia pygmaea.*
L. shaferi illus. p.479.
L. silvestrii. See *Echinopsis chamaecereus.*

Loblolly bay. See *Gordonia lasianthus.*
Lobster cactus. See *Schlumbergera truncata,* illus. p.473.
Lobster claws. See *Heliconia.*

LOBULARIA

BRASSICACEAE/CRUCIFERAE

Genus of summer- and early autumn-flowering annuals. Grow in sun and in fertile, well-drained soil. Dead-head to encourage continuous flowering. Propagate by seed sown under glass in spring, or outdoors in late spring.

L. maritima, syn. *Alyssum maritimum* (Sweet alyssum). Fast-growing, spreading annual. H 8–15cm (3–6in), S 20–30cm (8–12in). Has lance-shaped, greyish-green leaves. Rounded heads of tiny, scented, 4-petalled, white flowers are produced in summer and early autumn. 'Little Dorrit' illus. p.318. 'Wonderland' illus. p.322.

Locust. See *Robinia pseudoacacia.*
Caspian. See *Gleditsia caspica.*
Honey. See *Gleditsia triacanthos.*
Lodgepole pine. See *Pinus contorta* var. *latifolia,* illus. p.106.

LOISELEURIA

ERICACEAE

Genus of one species of evergreen, creeping, prostrate shrub, grown for its flowers. Requires full light and humus-rich, well-drained, acid soil. Is difficult to grow. Propagate by seed in spring or by softwood or semi-ripe cuttings in summer.

L. procumbens illus. p.377.

Lollipop plant. See *Pachystachys lutea,* illus. p.157.

LOMATIA

PROTEACEAE

Genus of evergreen shrubs and trees, grown for their foliage and flowers, which have 4 narrow, twisted petals. Slightly hardy, but best in cool greenhouse. Requires sun or semi-shade and moist but well-drained, acid soil. Propagate by softwood or semi-ripe cuttings in summer.

L. ferruginea. Evergreen, upright shrub or tree. H 10m (30ft), S 5m (15ft). Stout, brown-felted shoots bear oblong to oval, dark green leaves, deeply cut into 6–15 oblong lobes. Racemes of yellow-and-red flowers are borne in mid-summer. Thrives outside only in mild, moist areas.

L. silaifolia illus. p.161.

Lombardy poplar. See *Populus nigra* 'Italica', illus. p.66.
London plane. See *Platanus* x *hispanica,* illus. p.67.
London pride. See *Saxifraga* x *urbium.*

LONICERA

Honeysuckle

CAPRIFOLIACEAE

Genus of deciduous, semi-evergreen or evergreen shrubs and woody-stemmed, twining climbers, grown mainly for their flowers, which are often fragrant. Flowers are tubular, with spreading, 2-lipped petal lobes. Climbers may be trained into large shrubs. Hardy to tender, min. 5°C (41°F). Grows in any fertile, well-drained soil in sun or semi-shade. Prune out flowered wood of climbers after flowering. Prune shrubs only to remove dead shoots or restrain growth. Propagate by seed in autumn or spring, by semi-ripe cuttings in summer or by hardwood cuttings in late autumn. Aphids may be a problem especially on *L. tatarica.* The berries may cause mild stomach upset if ingested.

L. x *americana,* syn. *L.* x *italica* of gardens, illus. p.215.

L. x *brownii* (Scarlet trumpet honeysuckle). 'Dropmore Scarlet' illus. p.210.

L. etrusca (Etruscan honeysuckle).

Deciduous or semi-evergreen, woody-stemmed, twining climber. H to 4m (12ft). Oval, mid-green leaves are blue-green beneath, the upper ones united into cups. Fragrant, long-tubed, pale yellow flowers, borne in summer-autumn, turn deeper yellow and become red-flushed with age. Grow in sun. Zone 8.

L. fragrantissima. Deciduous or semi-evergreen, bushy, spreading shrub. H 2m (6ft), S 4m (12ft). Bears oval, dark green leaves. Fragrant, short-tubed, creamy-white flowers open in winter and early spring. Zone 6.

L. 'Gold Flame'. See *L.* x *heckrottii* 'Gold Flame'.

L. x *heckrottii.* Deciduous or semi-evergreen, twining climber. H 5m (15ft). Oval, dark green leaves are blue-green beneath, the upper pairs united. Bears terminal whorls of fragrant, pink flowers, orange-yellow inside, in summer, sometimes followed by red berries. Zone 7. **'Gold Flame'** (syn. *L.* 'Gold Flame') illus. p.209.

L. henryi. Evergreen or semi-evergreen, woody-stemmed, twining climber. H to 10m (30ft). Narrowly oval, dark green leaves are paler beneath. Terminal clusters of long-tubed, red-purple flowers appear in summer-autumn, followed by black berries. Zone 6.

L. hildebrandiana (Giant Burmese honeysuckle). Evergreen or semi-evergreen, woody-stemmed, twining climber. H to 20m (70ft). Oval or rounded, mid-green leaves are paler beneath. Long-tubed, white or cream flowers, ageing to creamy-orange or brownish-yellow, appear in pairs in leaf axils or at shoot tips in summer. Grow in sun. Zone 8.

L. x *italica* of gardens. See *L.* x *americana.*

L. japonica (Japanese honeysuckle). **'Aureoreticulata'** is an evergreen or semi-evergreen, twining climber with soft-haired, woody stems. H to 10m (30ft). Oval, sometimes lobed, leaves are bright green with bright yellow veins. Fragrant, long-tubed, white flowers, becoming yellowish, are produced in summer-autumn. Is useful for hiding a tree stump or an unsightly wall or fence. Zone 6. **'Halliana'** illus. p.215.

L. ledebourii illus. p.142.

L. maackii. Vigorous, deciduous, bushy shrub. H and S 5m (15ft). Leaves are oval and dark green. Fragrant, short-tubed, white, later yellow flowers, in early summer, are followed by spherical, bright red fruits. Zone 6.

L. morrowii. Deciduous, spreading shrub with arching branches. H 2m (6ft), S 3m (10ft). Has oval, dark green leaves and, in late spring and early summer, small, short-tubed, creamy-white flowers that age to yellow. Zone 5.

L. nitida. Evergreen, bushy, dense shrub. H 2m (6ft), S 3m (10ft). Leaves are small, oval, glossy and dark green. Tiny, fragrant, short-tubed, creamy-white flowers appear in late spring and are followed by small, spherical, purple fruits. Is good for hedging. Zone 7. **'Baggesen's Gold'** illus. p.177. Zone 7. **'Yunnan'** is more upright, has stouter

shoots and larger leaves and flowers more freely. Zone 7.

L. periclymenum (Common honeysuckle, Woodbine). **'Graham Thomas'** illus. p.215. **'Serotina'** (Late Dutch honeysuckle) is a deciduous H to 7m (22ft). Oval or oblong, mid-green leaves are grey-green beneath. Very fragrant, long-tubed, dark purple flowers, pinkish within, are borne in mid- and late summer. Grow in sun or shade. Zone 6.

L. pileata illus. p.176.

L. x *purpusii* illus. p.173. **'Winter Beauty'** has red-purple shoots and freely bears very fragrant, white flowers. Zone 8.

L. sempervirens illus. p.210.

L. standishii. Evergreen, bushy shrub. H and S 2m (6ft). Has peeling bark, oblong, bristly, dark green leaves and, in winter, fragrant, short-tubed, creamy-white flowers. Zone 6.

L. tatarica illus. p.140. **'Hack's Red'** is a deciduous, bushy shrub. H and S 2.5m (8ft). Produces short-tubed, deep pink flowers in late spring and early summer, followed by spherical, red fruits. Leaves are oval and dark green. Zone 2.

L. x *tellmanniana* illus. p.217.

L. tragophylla. Deciduous, woody-stemmed, twining climber. H 5–6m (15–20ft). Oval leaves are bluish-green, the uppermost pair united into a cup. Produces clusters of up to 20 long-tubed, bright yellow flowers in early summer. Zone 7.

L. x *xylosteoides* **'Clavey's Dwarf'.** Deciduous, upright, dense shrub. H 2m (6ft), S 1m (3ft). Leaves are oval and grey-green. Bears short-tubed, pink flowers in late spring, then spherical, red fruits. Zone 2.

L. xylosteum illus. p.140.

Loosestrife. See *Lysimachia.*
  Garden. See *Lysimachia punctata,* illus. p.255.
  Purple. See *Lythrum.*
Lophocereus schottii. See *Pachycereus schottii.*

LOPHOPHORA
Peyote

CACTACEAE

Genus of very slow-growing, perennial cacti that resemble small, blue dumplings, with up to 10 ribs, each separated by an indented line. Has long tap roots. Flowering areoles each produce tufts of short, white hairs. Tender, min. 5–10°C (41–50°F). Needs sun and well-drained soil. Is very prone to rotting, so water lightly from spring to autumn. Propagate by seed in spring or summer.

L. echinata. See *L. williamsii.*

L. lutea. See *L. williamsii.*

L. williamsii, syn. *L. echinata, L. lutea,* illus. p.471.

LOPHOSPERMUM

SCROPHULARIACEAE

Genus of deciduous and evergreen, perennial climbers and shrubs. Has triangular to rounded leaves and tubular to funnel-shaped flowers. Tender, min.

5°C (41°F). Needs sun and moist but well-drained soil. Propagate by seed in spring or semi-ripe cuttings in late summer.

L. erubescens, syn. *Asarina erubescens, Maurandya erubescens,* illus. p.209.

Loquat. See *Eriobotrya japonica.*
Lord Anson's blue pea. See *Lathyrus nervosus.*
Lords and ladies. See *Arum.*

LOROPETALUM

HAMAMELIDACEAE

Genus of evergreen shrubs, grown for their flowers. Needs min. 5°C (41°F) to flower well. Requires full light or semi-shade and rich, well-drained, neutral to acid soil. Water containerized plants freely when in full growth, moderately at other times. Propagate by layering or seed in spring or by semi-ripe cuttings in late summer.

L. chinense. Evergreen, rounded, well-branched shrub. H and S 1.2m (4ft). Asymmetrically oval leaves are deep green. White flowers, each with 4 strap-shaped petals, are borne in tufted, terminal clusters, mainly in winter-spring.

Lorraine begonia. See *Begonia* 'Gloire de Lorraine'.

LOTUS

PAPILIONACEAE/LEGUMINOSAE

Genus of summer-flowering perennials, some of which are semi-evergreen, and evergreen sub-shrubs, grown for their foliage and flowers. Hardy to tender, min. 5°C (41°F). Prefers sun and well-drained soil. Propagate by softwood cuttings from early to mid-summer or by seed in autumn or spring.

L. berthelotii illus. p.283.

L. hirsutus, syn. *Dorycnium hirsutum.* Deciduous, upright sub-shrub. H and S 60cm (24in). Bears silver-grey leaves with 3 oval leaflets. Dense clusters of pea-like, pink-tinged, white flowers in summer and early autumn are followed by oblong to ovoid, reddish-brown seed pods. Zone 7.

Lotus
  American. See *Nelumbo lutea.*
  Sacred. See *Nelumbo nucifera,* illus. p.447.
Love-in-a-mist. See *Nigella damascena.*
Love-lies-bleeding. See *Amaranthus caudatus,* illus. p.326.
Low-bush blueberry. See *Vaccinium angustifolium* var. *laevifolium,* illus. p.172.
Lucombe oak. See *Quercus* x *hispanica* 'Lucombeana', illus. p.73.

LUCULIA

RUBIACEAE

Genus of evergreen shrubs, grown for their flowers and foliage. Tender, min.

5–10°C (41–50°F). Needs full light or partial shade and fertile, well-drained soil. Water potted specimens freely when in full growth, moderately at other times. Cut back flowered stems hard in spring, if container-grown. Propagate by seed in spring or by semi-ripe cuttings in summer.

L. grandifolia. Evergreen, rounded to upright, robust shrub. H and S 3–6m (10–20ft). Min. 5°C (41°F). Oval, green leaves have red veins and stalks. Fragrant, tubular, white flowers, each 6cm (2½in) long, with 5 rounded, petal lobes, appear in terminal clusters in summer.

LUETKEA

ROSACEAE

Genus of one species of deciduous sub-shrub, grown for its fluffy flower heads. Is suitable for banks and rock gardens. Requires shade and well-drained but not too dry soil. Propagate by division or seed in spring.

L. pectinata. Deciduous, spreading, decumbent sub-shrub. H to 30cm (12in), S 20cm (8in). Stems are clothed in finely dissected, very dark green leaves. In summer has terminal racemes of small, fluffy, off-white flower heads. Zone 7.

LUMA

MYRTACEAE

Genus of evergreen shrubs and small trees, grown for their aromatic leaves and cup-shaped, white flowers. Marginally hardy. Grow in full sun or partial shade and fertile, ideally humus-rich, well-drained soil. Propagate by seed in spring or by semi-ripe cuttings in late summer.

L. apiculata, syn. *Amomyrtus luma, Myrceugenia apiculata, Myrtus apiculata, M. luma,* illus. p.119. **'Glanleam Gold'** is a strong-growing, evergreen, upright shrub. H and S 10m (30ft). Has stout stems, peeling, brown-and-white bark and oval, bright green leaves edged with creamy-yellow. Slightly fragrant flowers are borne from mid-summer to mid-autumn. Zone 9?.

L. chequen, syn. *Myrtus chequen.* Strong growing upright-shrub or small tree. H 6m (20ft) S 5m (15ft). Has broadly ovate, wavy-margined, aromatic, dark green leaves. In late summer and early-autumn bears cup-shaped white flowers singly or in small clusters followed by black berries. Zone 9?.

LUNARIA
Honesty

CRUCIFERAE/BRASSIACEAE

Genus of biennials and perennials, grown for their flowers and silvery seed pods. Will grow in sun or shade, but prefers partial shade and well-drained soil. Propagate perennials by seed in autumn or spring or by division in spring, biennials by seed only. Self seeds prolifically.

L. annua, syn. *L. biennis,* illus. p.325. **'Variegata'** illus. p.323.

L. biennis. See *L. annua.*

L. rediviva. Rosette-forming perennial.

H 60–75cm (24–30in), S 30cm (12in). Produces racemes of 4-petalled, lilac or white flowers in spring, followed by elliptical, silvery seed pods that are useful for indoor decoration. Has oval, coarse, sometimes maroon-tinted, mid-green leaves.

Lungwort. See *Pulmonaria*.
Lupin. See *Lupinus*.
 Tree. See *Lupinus arboreus*,
  illus. p.169.

LUPINUS
Lupin

PAPILIONACEAE/LEGUMINOSAE

Genus of annuals, perennials and semi-evergreen shrubs, grown for their large, imposing racemes of pea-like flowers. Prefers sun and well-drained soil. Remove seed heads of most varieties to prevent self seeding. Propagate species by seed when fresh, in autumn, selected forms by cuttings from non-flowering side-shoots in spring or early summer. The seeds may cause severe discomfort if ingested.
L. arboreus illus. p.169.
L. **'Band of Nobles'.** Clump-forming perennial. H to 1.5m (5ft), S 75cm (2½ft). In early and mid-summer, racemes of flowers in white, yellow, pink, red, blue or bicolours (usually white or yellow in combination with another colour) arise above palmate, deeply divided, mid-green leaves.
L. **'Inverewe Red'** illus. p.245.
L. **'My Castle'.** Clump-forming perennial. H 90cm (3ft), S 75cm (2½ft). Bears racemes of deep rose-pink flowers above palmate, deeply divided, mid-green leaves in early and mid-summer.
L. **'Noble Maiden'.** Clump-forming perennial. H 90m (3ft), S 75cm (2½ft). In early and mid-summer, racemes of creamy-white flowers arise above palmate, deeply divided, mid-green leaves.
L. **'The Chatelaine'** illus. p.244.

LURONIUM

ALISMATACEAE

Genus of deciduous, perennial, marginal water plants and marsh plants, grown for their foliage and flowers. Requires shallow water and full sun. Thin plants when overcrowded. Propagate in spring by seed or division.
L. natans, syn. *Alisma natans* (Floating water plantain). Deciduous, perennial, marginal water plant. H 2.5–5cm (1–2in), S 30cm (12in). Produces small, elliptic to lance-shaped, mid-green leaves and, in summer, small, 3-lobed, yellow-spotted, white flowers.

LUZULA
Woodrush

JUNCACEAE

See also GRASSES, BAMBOOS, RUSHES and SEDGES.
L. maxima. See *L. sylvatica*.
L. nivea illus. p.307.
L. sylvatica, syn. *L. maxima* (Greater

woodrush). **'Marginata'** (syn. *L.s.* 'Aureomarginata') is a slow-growing, evergreen, spreading, rhizomatous, perennial grass. H to 30cm (12in), S indefinite. Produces thick tufts of broad, hairy-edged, mid-green leaves, with white margins. Leafy stems bear terminal, open, brown flower spikes in summer. Tolerates shade.

LYCASTE

See also ORCHIDS.
L. cruenta (illus. p.299). Vigorous, deciduous, epiphytic orchid for a cool greenhouse. H 30cm (12in). Fragrant, triangular, green-and-yellow flowers, 5cm (2in) across, are produced singly in spring. Has broadly oval, ribbed, soft leaves, to 30cm (12in) long. Grow in semi-shade during summer and avoid spraying, which can mark leaves.

LYCHNIS

CARYOPHYLLACEAE

Genus of summer-flowering annuals, biennials and perennials. Requires sun and well-drained soil. Propagate by division or seed in autumn or spring.
L. **'Abbotswood Rose'.** See *L.* x *walkeri* 'Abbotswood Rose'.
L. alpina, syn. *Viscaria alpina* (Alpine catchfly). Tuft-forming perennial. H 5–15cm (2–6in), S 10–15cm (4–6in). Has dense tufts of thick, linear, deep green leaves. In summer, sticky stems each bear a rounded head of pale to deep pink or, rarely, white flowers with spreading, frilled petals. Suits a rock garden.
L. chalcedonica illus. p.249.
L. coeli-rosa. See *Silene coeli-rosa*.
L. coronaria illus. p.282.
L. flos-jovis illus. p.279.
L. x *haageana*, syn. *L.* x *haagena*. Short-lived, clump-forming perennial. H 45cm (18in), S 30cm (12in). Produces clusters of large, 5-petalled, white, orange or red flowers in summer. Oval leaves are mid-green. Is best raised regularly from seed.
L. x *haagena.* See *L.* x *haageana*.
L. x *walkeri* **'Abbotswood Rose'**, syn. *L.* 'Abbotswood Rose'. Neat, clump-forming perennial. H 30–38cm (12–15in), S 23cm (9in). Has oval, grey leaves and grey, branching stems that, from mid- to late summer, bear sprays of rounded, 5-petalled, bright rose-pink flowers.
L. viscaria. Clump-forming perennial. H 30cm (12in), S 30–45cm (12–18in). From early to mid-summer, rather sticky, star-shaped, reddish-purple flowers are borne in dense clusters above narrowly oval to oblong, dark green leaves. Is suitable for the front of a border or a rock garden.
'Splendens Plena' illus. p.282.

Lycianthes rantonnetii. See *Solanum rantonnetii*.

LYCIUM

SOLANACEAE

Genus of deciduous shrubs, sometimes with long, scandent branches, grown

for their habit, flowers and fruits. Is useful for poor, dry soil and coastal gardens. May be grown as a hedge. Prefers full sun and not too rich, well-drained soil. Remove dead wood in winter and cut back to restrict growth if necessary. Cut back hedges hard in spring. Propagate by softwood cuttings in summer, by seed in autumn or by hardwood cuttings in winter.
L. barbarum, syn. *L. halimifolium* (Chinese box thorn, Duke of Argyll's tea-tree). Deciduous, arching, often spiny shrub. H 2.5m (8ft), S 5m (15ft). Funnel-shaped, purple or pink flowers in late spring and summer are followed by spherical, orange-red berries. Leaves are lance-shaped, bright green or grey-green. Zone 6.
L. halimifolium. See *L. barbarum*.

LYCORIS

AMARYLLIDACEAE

Genus of late summer- and early autumn-flowering bulbs with showy flower heads on leafless stems. In cool areas is best grown in pots or planted in greenhouse borders. Needs sun, well-drained soil and a warm period in summer to ripen bulbs so they flower. Provide regular liquid feed while in growth. After summer dormancy, water from early autumn until following summer, when foliage dies away. Propagate by seed when ripe or in spring or summer or by offsets in late summer.
L. aurea (Golden spider lily). Late summer- and early autumn-flowering bulb. H 30–40cm (12–16in), S 10–15cm (4–6in). Produces a head of 5 or 6 bright yellow flowers that have narrow, reflexed petals, with very wavy margins, and conspicuous stamens. Strap-shaped, semi-erect, basal leaves appear after flowering.
L. radiata illus. p.420.
L. squamigera (Resurrection lily). Late summer- or early autumn-flowering bulb. H 45–60cm (18–24in), S 10–15cm (4–6in). Carries a head of 6–8 fragrant, funnel-shaped, rose-pink flowers, 10cm (4in) l ong, with reflexed petal tips. Strap-shaped, semi-erect, basal leaves form after flowers.

LYGODIUM

SCHIZAEACEAE

Genus of deciduous or semi-evergreen, climbing ferns, usually with 2 kinds of fronds: vegetative and fertile. Tender, min. 5°C (41°F). Needs shade or semi-shade and humus-rich, moist, peaty soil. Is best grown among shrubby plants that can provide support. Plants grown under glass in pots need strong, twiggy supports. Remove faded fronds regularly. Propagate by division in spring or by spores in summer.
L. japonicum (Japanese climbing fern). Deciduous, climbing fern. H 2m (6ft), S indefinite. Tender. Mid-green, vegetative fronds consist of delicate,

finger-shaped pinnae; fertile fronds are broader and 3–5 lobed, with a longer, terminal lobe.

Lyme grass. See *Leymus arenarius*.

LYONIA

ERICACEAE

Genus of deciduous, semi-evergreen or evergreen shrubs and trees, grown for their racemes of small, urn-shaped flowers. Needs shade or semi-shade and moist, peaty, acid soil. Propagate by semi-ripe cuttings in summer.
L. ligustrina. (Maleberry) Deciduous, bushy shrub. H and S 2m (6ft). Oval, dark green leaves set off dense racemes of globular urn-shaped, white flowers from mid- to late summer. Zone 5.
L. ovalifolia. Deciduous or semi-evergreen, bushy shrub. H and S 2m (6ft). Produces red shoots and oval, dark green leaves. Racemes of urn-shaped, white flowers appear in late spring and early summer. Zone 7.

LYONOTHAMNUS

ROSACEAE

Genus of one species of evergreen tree, grown for its foliage and flowers. Marginally hardy. Needs sun or semi-shade, a warm, sheltered position and fertile, well-drained soil. Propagate by softwood cuttings in summer or by seed in autumn.
L. floribundus (Catalina ironwood). Evergreen tree grown only in the form subsp. **aspleniifolius**. This slender tree, H 12m (40ft), S 6m (20ft), has rather stringy, reddish-brown bark and much divided, fern-like, dark green leaves. Large, flattened heads of 5-petalled, star-shaped white flowers are produced in early summer. Zone 9?.

LYSICHITON

ARACEAE

Genus of deciduous, perennial, marginal water plants and bog plants, grown for their handsome spathes and very large, glossy foliage. Prefers full sun, but tolerates semi-shade. Tolerates both still and running water. Propagate by seed when fresh, in late summer.
L. americanum. See *L. americanus*.
L. americanus, syn. *L. americanum*, illus. p.451.
L. camtschatcensis illus. p.446.

LYSIMACHIA
Loosestrife

PRIMULACEAE

Genus of summer-flowering annuals and perennials, suitable for the border or rock garden. Prefers sun or semi-shade and moist but well-drained soil. Propagate by division in spring or by seed in autumn.
L. clethroides illus. p.241.
L. ephemerum. Neat, clump-

forming perennial. H 1m (3ft),
S 30cm (1ft). Erect, terminal
racemes of star-shaped, greyish-white
flowers are borne on slender stems in
summer, followed by light green seed
heads. Lance-shaped leaves are
leathery and glaucous.
L. nummularia (Moneywort). **'Aurea'**
illus. p.386.
L. punctata illus. p.255.

LYTHRUM
Purple loosestrife

LYTHRACEAE

Genus of summer-flowering perennials
that thrive by the waterside and in bog
gardens. Grows in full sun or semi-
shade and in moist or wet soil.
Propagate cultivars by division in spring,
species by seed or division in spring or
autumn. Some species have become
noxious weeds in North America.
L. salicaria **'Feuerkerze'**, syn.
L.s. 'Firecandle', illus. p.245.
'Firecandle' see *L.s.* 'Feuerkerze'.
'Robert' is a clump-forming
perennial. H 75cm (30in), S 45cm
(18in). Produces racemes of 4-petalled,
clear pink flowers from mid- to late
summer. Leaves are mid-green and
lance-shaped.
L. virgatum **'Rose Queen'**. Clump-
forming perennial. H 1m (3ft),
S 60cm (2ft). Racemes of 4-petalled,
star-shaped, light pink flowers are
produced from mid- to late summer
above lance-shaped, hairless, mid-green
leaves. **'The Rocket'** illus. p.245.

M

MAACKIA

LEGUMINOSAE/PAPILIONACEAE

Genus of deciduous, summer-flowering trees, grown for their foliage and flowers. Requires full sun and fertile, well-drained soil. Propagate by seed in autumn.
M. amurensis illus. p.90.

MACADAMIA

PROTEACEAE

Genus of evergreen trees, grown for their foliage and fruits. Tender, min. 10–13°C (50–55°F). Prefers full light, though some shade is tolerated. Provide humus-rich, moisture-retentive but well-drained soil. Water freely while in full growth, moderately at other times. Pruning is not usually necessary, but is tolerated in autumn. Propagate by seed when ripe, in autumn, or in spring.
M. integrifolia illus. p.73.

Macadamia nut. See *Macadamia integrifolia*, illus. p.73.
Mace sedge. See *Carex grayi*.
Macedonian pine. See *Pinus peuce*, illus. p.101.

MACFADYENA,
syn. DOXANTHA

BIGNONIACEAE

Genus of evergreen, woody-stemmed, tendril climbers, grown for their foxglove-like flowers. Tender, min. 5°C (41°F). Any fertile, well-drained soil is suitable with full light. Water regularly, less when not in full growth. Stems need support. Thin out crowded shoots after flowering or in spring. Propagate by semi-ripe cuttings in summer.
M. unguis-cati, syn. *Bignonia unguis-cati*, *Doxantha unguis-cati*, illus. p.216.

MACKAYA

ACANTHACEAE

Genus of one species of evergreen shrub, grown for its flowers and overall appearance. Tender, min. 7–10°C (45–50°F). Requires full light or partial shade and fertile, well-drained soil. Water potted plants freely when in full growth, moderately at other times. Pruning is tolerated in winter if necessary. Propagate by greenwood cuttings in spring or by semi-ripe cuttings in summer.
M. bella, syn. *Asystasia bella*. Evergreen, erect, then spreading, well-branched shrub. H to 1.5m (5ft), S 1.2–1.5m (4–5ft). Leaves are oval, pointed, glossy and mid- to deep green. Has spikes of tubular, dark-veined, lavender flowers, each with 5 large, flared petal lobes, from spring to autumn. In warm conditions, above 13°C (55°F), will flower into winter.

Mackay's heath. See *Erica mackaiana*.

MACLEAYA
Plume poppy

PAPAVERACEAE

Genus of summer-flowering perennials, grown for their overall appearance. Grows in sun and in well-drained soil. May spread rapidly. Propagate by division in early spring or by root cuttings in winter.
M. cordata, syn. *Bocconia cordata*. Spreading, clump-forming perennial. H 1.5m (5ft) or more, S 60cm (2ft) or more. Large, rounded, lobed, grey-green leaves, grey-white beneath, are produced at base of plant and up lower parts of stems. Large, feathery panicles of dainty, creamy-white flowers are produced in summer.
M. microcarpa 'Coral Plume'. See *M.m.* 'Kelway's Coral Plume'.
'Kelway's Coral Plume' (syn. *M.m.* 'Coral Plume) illus. p.227.

MACLURA

MORACEAE

Genus of deciduous trees, grown for their foliage and unusual fruits. Both male and female trees need to be planted to obtain fruits. Young plants are susceptible to frost damage. Requires full sun and needs hot summers to thrive in cold areas. Grows in any but waterlogged soil. Propagate by softwood cuttings in summer, by seed in autumn or by root cuttings in late winter.
M. aurantiaca. See *M. pomifera*.
M. pomifera, syn. *M. aurantiaca* (Osage orange). Deciduous, rounded, spreading tree. H 15m (50ft), S 12m (40ft). Has spiny shoots and oval, dark green leaves that turn yellow in autumn. Tiny, cup-shaped, yellow flowers in summer are followed on female trees by large, rounded, wrinkled, pale green fruits. Zone 6.
M. tricuspidata, syn. *Cudrania tricuspidata*. Deciduous, spreading tree. H 7m (22ft), S 6m (20ft). Bears oval, dark green leaves that are sometimes 3-lobed. Produces small, rounded clusters of tiny, green flowers in mid-summer. Zone 6.

Macroplectrum sesquipedale. See *Angraecum sesquipedale*.
Macrotomia echioides. See *Arnebia pulchra*.
Madagascar dragon tree. See *Dracaena marginata*.
Madagascar jasmine. *See Stephanotis floribunda*, illus. p.204.
Madeira vine. See *Anredera*.
Madonna lily. See *Lilium candidum*, illus. p.404.
Madroña. See *Arbutus menziesii*.
Madroñe. See *Arbutus menziesii*.

MAGNOLIA

MAGNOLIACEAE

Genus of deciduous, semi-evergreen or evergreen trees and shrubs, grown for their showy, usually fragrant flowers. Leaves are mainly oval. Flowers and buds of early-flowering magnolias may be damaged by late frosts. Needs sun or semi-shade and shelter from strong winds. Does best in fertile, well-drained soil. *M. delavayi*, *M. kobus*, *M. sieboldii* and *M. wilsonii* grow on alkaline soil. Other species prefer neutral to acid soil, but will grow in alkaline soil if deep and humus-rich. Dry, sandy soils should be generously enriched with manure and leaf mould before planting. Propagate species by semi-ripe cuttings in summer or by seed, when ripe, in autumn, selected forms by semi-ripe cuttings in summer or by grafting in winter. See also feature panel p.75.
M. acuminata (Cucumber tree). Vigorous, deciduous tree, conical when young, later spreading. H 20m (70ft), S 10m (30ft). Fragrant, cup-shaped, bluish-green flowers appear from early to mid-summer amid large, oval, pale green leaves, followed by small, egg-shaped, green, later red fruits. Zone 5.
M. 'Ann'. Deciduous spreading shrub with dark green leaves that are slightly hairy above. H 2.5–3m (8–10ft) S 3m (10ft). Deep purple, goblet-shaped flowers with 7–9 petals, 13cm (5in) across open in spring. Zone 5.
M. 'Betty'. Deciduous shrub with a rounded habit. H and S 4m (12ft). Ovate, mid-green leaves about 15cm (6in) long. Produces 20cm (8in) cup-shaped flowers, with up to 19 petals, that are purple outside and red inside, in mid-spring. Zone 5b.
M. campbellii illus. p.75. Deciduous tree, upright when young, later spreading. H 15m (50ft), S 10m (30ft). Large, slightly fragrant, pale to deep pink flowers are borne on leafless branches from late winter to mid-spring on trees 15–20 years old or more.
'Charles Raffill' (illus. p.75) bears large, fragrant, cup-shaped, purplish-pink flowers from late winter to mid-spring on trees at least 15 years old. Leaves are large, oval and mid-green.
'Darjeeling' (illus. p.75) is similar to the species but has large, very deep pink flowers. **'Kew's Surprise'** bears deep purplish-pink flowers. *mollicomata* (illus. p.75) has lilac-pink flowers slightly earlier in the year. All slightly tender, Zone 9?.
M. 'Charles Coates' (illus. p.75). Deciduous, rounded, open, spreading tree. H 19m (70ft), S 8m (25ft). Extremely fragrant, creamy-white flowers with conspicuous, red stamens are produced in late spring and early summer amid large, light green leaves. Zone 6.
M. cylindrica (illus. p.75). Deciduous, spreading tree or large shrub. H and S

5m (15ft). Fully hardy. Fragrant, upright, creamy-white flowers are produced in mid-spring, after which the young leaves turn dark green. Zone 7.
M. dawsoniana. Deciduous tree or shrub, with a broadly oval head. H 15m (50ft), S 10m (30ft). In early spring, large, fragrant, pendent, open cup-shaped, pale lilac-pink flowers are carried profusely on older plants (20 years from seed, 10 years from grafting). Leaves are oval, leathery and deep green. Zone 7.
M. denudata, syn. *M. heptapeta* (Lily tree, Yulan; illus. p.75). Deciduous, rounded, bushy shrub or spreading tree. H and S 10m (30ft). Produces masses of fragrant, cup-shaped, white flowers from mid- to late spring before oval, mid-green leaves appear. Zone 5b.
M. fraseri (illus. p.75). Deciduous, spreading, open tree. H 10m (30ft), S 8m (25). Fragrant white or pale yellow flowers open in late spring and early summer amid large, pale green leaves. Zone 5.
M. 'Galaxy'. Deciduous, fast growing, conical tree H 12m (40ft) S 8m (25ft). It has 13cm (5in) purple-pink flowers in early spring before the leaves. Flowers at a young age. Zone 6.
M. grandiflora (Bull bay). Evergreen, broadly conical or rounded, dense tree. H and S 10m (30ft). Bears large, very fragrant, bowl-shaped, white flowers intermittently from mid-summer to early autumn. Has oblong, glossy, mid- to dark green leaves. Zone 7.
'Exmouth' (illus. p.75) has creamy-white flowers and narrow, leathery leaves. **'Ferruginea'** has dark green leaves, rust-brown beneath. Both Zone 8.
M. 'Heaven Scent' (illus. p.75). Vigorous, deciduous shrub or tree. H and S 10m (30ft). Fragrant, vase-shaped flowers, each with usually 9 petals that are pink outside, white within, are borne from mid-spring to early summer. Leaves are broadly elliptic and glossy green. Zone 4b.
M. heptapeta. See *M. denudata*.
M. hypoleuca, syn. *M. obovata* (Japanese big-leaf magnolia; illus. p.75). Vigorous, deciduous, upright tree. H 15m (50ft), S 10m (30ft). Large, fragrant, pink-flushed, white or pale cream flowers with crimson stamens appear in early summer. Zone 6.
M. insignis. See *Manglietia insignis*.
M. 'Jane'. Upright deciduous shrub or small tree H 4m (12ft) S 3m (10 ft). Produces fragrant flowers with 10 petals in late spring. Flowers are red-purple outside, white inside. Zone 5.
M. × kewensis 'Wada's Memory'. See *M.* 'Wada's Memory'.
M. kobus (illus. p.75). Deciduous, broadly conical tree. H 10m (30ft), S 8m (25ft). Bears a profusion of fragrant, pure white flowers in mid-spring before small, slightly aromatic, dark green leaves appear. Zone 5b.

M. liliiflora, syn. *M. quinquepeta*.
Deciduous, bushy shrub. H 3m (10ft),
S 4m (12ft). Has fragrant, upright,
vase-shaped, purplish-pink flowers
that are borne amid oval, very dark
green leaves from mid-spring to
mid-summer. **'Nigra'** (illus. p.75)
has large, deep purple flowers.
Both Zone 6.

M. × loebneri **'Leonard Messel'** (illus.
p.75). Deciduous, upright shrub or
small tree. H 8m (25ft), S 6m (20ft). In
mid-spring, fragrant flowers with many
pale lilac-pink petals appear before and
after oval, deep green leaves emerge.
'Merrill' has funnel-shaped, white
flowers. Both Zone 5.

M. **'Manchu Fan'** (illus. p.75).
Vigorous, deciduous shrub or tree.
H 6m (20ft), S 5m (15ft). In late
spring has large, goblet-shaped,
creamy-white flowers with usually
9 petals, the inner ones flushed
purple-pink at the base. Leaves
are ovate. Zone 6b.

M. **'Norman Gould'** (illus. p.75).
Deciduous, spreading tree or bushy
shrub. H and S 5m (15ft). Silky buds
open into fragrant, star-shaped, white
flowers in mid-spring. Leaves are
oblong and dark green. Zone 7.

M. obovata. See *M. hypoleuca*.

M. quinquepeta. See *M. liliiflora*.

M. **'Ricki'**. Spreading deciduous shrub.
H and S 4m (12ft). Flowers open in
mid-spring and are pink outside, paler
within and have 15 twisted petals.
Zone 5b.

M. salicifolia (Willow-leaved
magnolia; illus. p.75). Deciduous,
conical tree. H 10m (30ft), S 5m (15ft).
Fully hardy. Has aromatic, oval leaves,
mid-green above, grey-white beneath.
Fragrant, pure white flowers open
in mid-spring before foliage appears.
Zone 6.

M. sieboldii. Deciduous, arching shrub
or wide-spreading tree. H 8m (25ft),
S 12m (40ft). Fragrant, cup-shaped,
white flowers, with crimson anthers,
are carried above oval, dark green
leaves from late spring to late summer.
subsp. *sinensis* (syn. *M. sinensis*) has
slightly larger, fully pendent flowers
and more rounded, oval leaves.
Both Zone 6b.

M. sinensis. See. *M. sieboldii* subsp.
sinensis.

M. × soulangeana **'Alba'** see *M. × s.*
'Alba Superba'. **'Alba Superba'**
(syn. *M. × s.* 'Alba') is a deciduous,
rounded, spreading shrub or small
tree. H and S 6m (20ft). Bears large,
fragrant, tulip-like, white flowers,
faintly flushed with pink at the bases,
from mid- to early spring, the first
before mid- to dark green leaves
emerge. Zone 5b. **'Brozzonii'**, H 8m
(25ft), S 6m (20ft), is tree-like, with
large, purple-flushed, white flowers.
'Etienne Soulange-Bodin' (illus. p.75)
bears purple-flushed, white blooms.
Flowers of **'Lennei'** are large, goblet-
shaped and deep rose-purple. **'Picture'**,
H 8m (25ft), S 6m (20ft), is vigorous,
compact and upright, with large, erect,
deep reddish-purple flowers. **'Rubra'**
of gardens see *M. × s.* 'Rustica Rubra'.
'Rustica Rubra' (syn. *M. × s.* 'Rubra'
of gardens; illus. p.75) has purplish-red
blooms suffused pink. All Zone 5b.

M. sprengeri (illus. p.75). Deciduous,
spreading tree. H 15m (50ft), S 10m
(30ft). In mid-spring has fragrant,
bowl-shaped, white flowers
sometimes fringed with red or pale
pink, before oval, dark green leaves
appear. **'Wakehurst'** (illus. p.75)
has deep purplish-pink flowers.
Both Zone 8.

M. stellata (Star magnolia; illus. p.75).
Deciduous, bushy, dense shrub.
H 3m (10ft), S 4m (12ft). Fragrant,
star-shaped flowers with many narrow
petals open from silky buds during
early to mid-spring. Leaves are narrow
and deep green. **'Water Lily'** (illus.
p.75) has large, white flowers with
many petals. Both Zone 5.

M. tripetala (illus. p.75). Deciduous,
spreading, open tree, conical when
young. H 10m (30ft), S 8m (25ft).
Has large, dark green leaves, clustered
about shoot tips, and rather
unpleasantly scented, creamy-white
flowers with narrow petals in late
spring and early summer. Zone 5.

M. × veitchii **'Peter Veitch'** (illus.
p.75). Fast-growing, deciduous,
spreading tree. H 20m (60ft), S 15m
(52ft). Bears large, fragrant, pale pink
and white flowers in mid-spring, before
dark green leaves emerge. Usually
flowers within 10 years of planting.
Zone 8.

M. virginiana (Sweet bay). Deciduous
or semi-evergreen, conical shrub or
tree. H 9m (28ft), S 6m (20ft).
Has very fragrant, cup-shaped,
creamy-white flowers from early
summer to early autumn. Oblong,
glossy, mid- to dark green leaves are
bluish-white beneath. Zone 6.

M. **'Wada's Memory'**, syn.
M. × kewensis 'Wada's Memory' (illus.
p.75). Deciduous, conical tree. H 10m
(30ft), S 5m (15ft). Has aromatic, dark
green foliage and a profusion of large,
fragrant, white flowers borne from
mid- to late spring before oval leaves
appear. Zone 6.

M. × watsonii. See *M. × wieseneri*.

M. × wieseneri, syn. *M. × watsonii*
(illus. p.75). Deciduous, spreading,
open tree or shrub. H 8m (25ft), S 5m
(15ft). Rounded, white buds open in
late spring to early summer to fragrant,
creamy-white flowers, flushed pink
outside and with crimson stamens.
Zone 7.

M. wilsonii (illus. p.75). Deciduous,
spreading tree or shrub. H 8m (25ft),
S 7m (22ft). In late spring and early
summer, fragrant, cup-shaped, white
flowers with crimson stamens hang
from arching branches amid narrow,
dark green leaves. Zone 8.

Magnolia
   Japanese big-leaf. See *Magnolia*
     hypoleuca, illus. p.75.
   Star. See *Magnolia stellata*,
     illus. p.75.
   Willow-leaved. See *Magnolia*
     salicifolia, illus. p.75.

---

x MAHOBERBERIS

BERBERIDACEAE

Hybrid genus (*Berberis* × *Mahonia*)
of evergreen shrubs, grown for their

foliage, flowers and botanical interest.
Needs sun or semi-shade and fertile,
well-drained soil. Propagate by semi-
ripe cuttings in summer.

x *M. aquisargentii*. Evergreen, upright,
densely leaved shrub. H and S 2m (6ft).
Leaves are bright green, often with
3 leaflets, some oblong and finely
toothed, others holly-shaped. Terminal
clusters of berberis-like, yellow flowers
are sparsely produced in late spring.
Zone 7.

Mahoe. See *Melicytus ramiflorus*;
   Thespesia populnea.

MAHONIA

BERBERIDACEAE

Genus of evergreen shrubs, grown for
their foliage, their usually short
racemes of often fragrant, rounded,
bell-shaped, yellow flowers and, with
tall species and cultivars, for their
deeply fissured bark. Large mahonias
make good specimen plants; low-
growing ones are excellent for ground
cover. Prefers shade or semi-shade and
fertile, well-drained but not too dry
soil. Propagate species by leaf-bud or
semi-ripe cuttings in summer or by
seed in autumn, selected forms by leaf-
bud or semi-ripe cuttings only.

M. acanthifolia. See *M. napaulensis*.

M. aquifolium illus. p.157.

M. bealei. See *M. japonica* 'Bealei'.

M. **'Heterophylla'**. Evergreen, upright
shrub. H 1m (3ft), S 1.5m (5ft). Has
reddish-purple shoots and glossy,
bright green leaves, each composed of
5 or 7 narrowly lance-shaped, wavy-
edged or curled leaflets, that turn
reddish-purple in winter. Small clusters
of yellow flowers appear in spring.
Sheltered zone 9.

M. japonica illus. p.151. **'Bealei'** (syn.
M. bealei). Bears blue-green leaves
divided into broad leaflets and pale
yellow flowers in shorter,
upright racemes. Zone 7.

M. lomariifolia. Evergreen, very
upright shrub. H 3m (10ft), S 2m (6ft).
Large, dark green leaves each have
19–37 narrow, holly-like, spiny leaflets.
Fragrant, bright yellow flowers are
produced in dense, upright racemes
during late autumn and winter. Zone 9.

M. × media. **'Buckland'** and **'Charity'**
illus. p.125.

M. napaulensis, syn. *M. acanthifolia*.
Evergreen, upright, open shrub. H 2.5m
(8ft), S 3m (10ft). Leaves are
composed of up to 15 holly-like, spiny,
dark green leaflets. Produces long,
slender racemes of yellow flowers in
early and mid-spring. Zone 9.

M. repens. Evergreen, upright shrub
that spreads by underground stems.
H 30cm (1ft), S 2m (6ft). Blue-green
leaves each consist of 3–7 oval leaflets,
with bristle-like teeth. Dense clusters of
deep yellow flowers are borne from
mid- to late spring. Zone 3.

M. **'Undulata'**. Evergreen, upright
shrub. H and S 2m (6ft). Glossy, dark
green leaves each have 5–9 holly-like,
wavy-edged leaflets that become
bronzed in winter. Bears dense
clusters of deep yellow flowers in
mid- and late spring. Zone 9.

MAIANTHEMUM
May lily

CONVALLARIACEAE/LILIACEAE

Genus of perennials with extensive,
spreading rhizomes. Is useful as ground
cover in woodlands and wild areas.
Prefers shade and humus-rich, moist,
sandy, neutral to acid soil. Propagate
by seed in autumn or by division
in any season.

M. bifolium. Spreading, rhizomatous
perennial. H 10cm (4in), S indefinite.
Pairs of large, oval, glossy, dark green
leaves, with wavy edges, arise direct
from rhizomes. Slender stems each
produce a raceme of 4-petalled, white
flowers in early summer, followed
by small, spherical, red berries.
May be invasive.

M. canadense illus. p.363.

Maiden pink. See *Dianthus deltoides*.
Maidenhair
   Delta. See *Adiantum raddianum*.
   Tassel. See *Adiantum raddianum*
     'Grandiceps'.
Maidenhair fern. See *Adiantum*
   capillus-veneris.
Maidenhair spleenwort. See
   Asplenium trichomanes,
   illus. p.311.
Maidenhair tree. See *Ginkgo biloba*,
   illus. p.103.

MAIHUENIA

CACTACEAE

Genus of slow-growing, summer-
flowering, alpine cacti, clump-forming
with age, with cylindrical stems.
Tender, min 2°C (35°F). Requires sun
and well-drained soil. Protect from
winter rain. Propagate by seed or stem
cuttings in spring or summer.

M. poeppigii illus. p.477.

Maiten. See *Maytenus boaria*.
Maize. See *Zea*.
   Ornamental. See *Zea mays*.
Majorcan peony. See *Paeonia*
   cambessedesii, illus. p.237.
Malay ginger. See *Costus speciosus*.

MALCOLMIA

BRASSICACEAE/CRUCIFERAE

Genus of spring- to autumn-flowering
annuals. Grow in sun and in fertile,
well-drained soil. Propagate by seed
sown outdoors in spring, summer or
early autumn. Self-seeds freely.

M. maritima illus. p.323.

Male berry. See *Lyonia ligustrina*.
Male fern. See *Dryopteris filix-mas*,
   illus. p.310.

MALEPHORA

AIZOACEAE

Genus of erect or spreading, perennial
succulents with semi-cylindrical leaves.
Tender, min. 5°C (41°F). Needs sun and
very well-drained soil. Propagate by
seed or stem cuttings in spring
or summer.

M. crocea illus. p.480.

Mallow. See *Malva*.
  Sleepy. See *Malvaviscus arboreus*, illus. p.121.
  Tree. See *Lavatera*.

MALOPE

MALVACEAE

Genus of annuals, grown for their showy flowers that are ideal for cutting. Grow in sun and in fertile, well-drained soil. Propagate by seed sown outdoors in spring. Self-seeds freely.
M. trifida illus. p.324.

Maltese cross. See *Lychnis chalcedonica*, illus. p.249.

MALUS
Crab apple

ROSACEAE

Genus of deciduous, mainly spring-flowering trees and shrubs, grown for their shallowly cup-shaped flowers, fruits, foliage or autumn colour. Crab apples may be used to make preserves. Prefers full sun, but tolerates semi-shade; grows in any but waterlogged soil. In winter, cut out dead or diseased wood and prune to maintain a balanced branch system. Propagate by budding in late summer or by grafting in mid-winter. Trees are sometimes attacked by aphids, caterpillars and spider mite, and are susceptible to fireblight, mildew, and apple scab. Zone 2b.
M. **'Almey'.** Deciduous, rounded tree. H and S 8m (25ft). Oval leaves are reddish-purple when young, maturing to dark green. Single, deep pink flowers, with paler pink, almost white centres, in late spring are followed by long-lasting, rounded, orange-red crab apples, which are subject to apple scab. Zone 2b.
M. **'American Beauty'.** Vigorous, medium-sized, spreading tree with bronze foliage. H 6–8m (20–25ft) S 8–10m (25–30ft). Flowers are double, deep red, but few fruits are produced. Susceptible to scab. Zone 5.
M. × *arnoldiana* illus. p.87.
M. × *atrosanguinea*. Deciduous, spreading tree. H and S 6m (20ft). Produces oval, glossy, dark green leaves. Red flower buds open to single, rich pink blooms in late spring. Bears small, rounded, red-flushed, yellow crab apples. Zone 4.
M. baccata (Siberian crab). Deciduous, spreading tree. H and S 15m (50ft). Has oval, dark green leaves, a profusion of single, white flowers from mid- to late spring and tiny, rounded, red or yellow crab apples. Zone 3. var. *mandschurica* illus. p.74.
M. **'Candied Apple'**, syn. *M.* 'Weeping Candied Apple'. Small weeping tree H and S 5m (15ft). Oval, textured leaves have a reddish tint. Buds are dark red and open to single pink flowers. Fruit is dark red and persistent. Zone 5.
M. **'Chilko'.** Deciduous, spreading tree. H and S 8m (25ft). Oval, dark green leaves are reddish-purple when young. Has single, rose-pink flowers in mid-spring, followed by large, rounded, bright crimson crab apples. Zone 3.

M. coronaria **'Charlottae'.** Deciduous, spreading tree. H and S 9m (28ft). Broadly oval, lobed or deeply toothed leaves are dark green, turning red in autumn. Semi-double, pale pink flowers are borne in late spring and early summer. Zone 4.
M. **'Cowichan'** illus. p.94.
M. **'Dolgo'.** Wide, spreading tree with an open habit. H and S 10m (30ft). Pink buds open to large, fragrant, white flowers. Fruit are glossy red, about 1cm (⅜in) in diameter. They fall early but are tasty and good for jelly. Good disease resistance but only blooms well every other year. Zone 2b.
M. **'Eleyi'**, syn. *M.* × *purpurea* 'Eleyi'. Deciduous, spreading tree. H and S 8m (25ft). Oval leaves are dark reddish-purple when young, dark green when mature. Bears single, deep purplish-red flowers from mid- to late spring and rounded, purplish-red crab apples. Zone 3.
M. floribunda illus. p.88.
M. **'Golden Hornet'**, syn. *M.* × *zumi* 'Golden Hornet', illus. p.97.
M. × *hartwigii* **'Katherine'.** See *M.* 'Katherine'.
M. **'Hopa'.** Deciduous, spreading tree. H and S 10m (30ft). Oval, dark green leaves are reddish-purple when young. Single, deep pink flowers in mid-spring are succeeded by rounded, orange-and-red crab apples. Disease susceptible. Zone 2b.
M. hupehensis illus. p.74.
M. **'Indian Magic'.** Small tree with a rounded habit. H and S 6m (20ft). Buds are red and open to single, deep pink flowers. Fruit is glossy red becoming orange with age, and persisting. Susceptible to scab. Zone 5.
M. **'Inglis'** see *M.* 'White Angel'.
M. **'John Downie'** illus. p.95.
M. **'Lemoinei'**, syn. *M.* × *purpurea* 'Lemoinei', illus. p.89.
M. **'Magdeburgensis'** illus. p.88.
M. **'Marshall Oyama'** illus. p.96.
M. × *moerlandsii* **'Profusion'.** See *M.* 'Profusion'.
M. niedzwetskyana, syn. *M. pumila* var. *niedzwetskyana*. Deciduous, spreading tree. H 6m (20ft), S 8m (25ft). Oval leaves are red when young, later purple. Produces clusters of single, deep reddish-purple flowers in late spring, then very large, conical, reddish-purple crab apples. Zone 5.
M. **'Pink Spires'.** An upright tree with foliage that is tinged red in spring, turning green later. H 8m (25ft) S 5m (15ft). Dark mauve buds open the same colour but fade to pale mauve as the flowers age. Fruit are dark red and last well. Moderately susceptible to scab. Zone 5.
M. prattii. Deciduous tree, upright when young, later spreading. H and S 10m (30ft). Oval, red-stalked, glossy, mid-green leaves become orange and red in autumn. Single, white flowers in late spring are followed by small, rounded or egg-shaped, white-flecked, red crab apples. Zone 7.
M. **'Professor Sprenger'** illus. p.96.
M. **'Profusion'**, syn. *M.* × *moerlandsii* 'Profusion', illus. p.77.
M. prunifolia illus. p.95.
M. pumila var. *niedzwetskyana*. See *M. niedzwetskyana*.

M. × *purpurea* (Purple crab). Deciduous, spreading tree. H 8m (25ft), S 10m (30ft). Oval, young leaves are reddish, maturing to green. Single, deep ruby-red flowers, which become paler with age, are produced in late spring and are followed by rounded, reddish-purple crab apples. Zone 3. **'Eleyi'** see *M.* 'Eleyi'. **'Lemoinei'** see *M.* 'Lemoinei'. **'Neville Copeman'** see *M.* 'Neville Copeman'.
M. **'Red Jade'**, syn. *M.* × *schiedeckeri* 'Red Jade'. Deciduous, weeping tree. H 4m (12ft), S 6m (20ft). In late spring has single, white flowers, sometimes pale pink-flushed, then long-lasting, rounded to egg-shaped, red crab apples. Leaves are dark green and oval. Zone 5.
M. **'Red Splendor'.** Upright open tree. H 10m (30ft) S 6m (20ft). Foliage is dark green but turns purple in fall. Flowers are rose pink, single and the fruit is red. Moderately susceptible to fireblight. Zone 2b.
M. × *robusta*. Vigorous, deciduous, spreading tree. H 12m (40ft), S 10m (30ft). Bears masses of single, white or pink flowers above oval, dark green leaves in late spring. These are followed by long-lasting, rounded, yellow or red crab apples. Both zone 2b. **'Yellow Siberian'** produces white flowers, which are sometimes pink-tinged, and yellow crab apples.
M. **'Royal Beauty'.** A small weeping tree with reddish purple leaves that turn green. H 2m (6ft) S 2.5m (8ft). Flowers are dark red-purple and the fruit is dark red. Zone 5.
M. **'Royalty'** illus. p.89.
M. sargentii, syn. *M. toringo* subsp. *sargentii*, illus. p.116.
M. × *schiedeckeri* **'Red Jade'.** See *M.* 'Jade'.
M. sieboldii, syn. *M. toringo*, illus. p.130.
M. **'Snowdrift'.** Dense, rounded, vigorous tree with glossy, dark green foliage. H and S 6m (20ft). Abundant white flowers and persistent, orange-red fruits. Somewhat susceptible to fireblight. Zone 4.
M. **'Thunderchild'.** A small, upright tree H 4.5m (15ft) S 3m (10ft) with single rose-pink flowers and dark red fruits. Very good disease resistance. Zone 2b.
M. toringo. See *M. sieboldii*. subsp. *sargentii* see *M. sargentii*.
M. toringoides. Deciduous, spreading tree. H 8m (25ft), S 10m (30ft). Oval, deeply lobed, glossy, bright green leaves turn yellow in autumn. Bears single, white flowers in late spring and rounded or egg-shaped, red-flushed, yellow crab apples in autumn. Zone 7.
M. transitoria. Deciduous, spreading, elegant tree. H 8m (25ft), S 10m (30ft). Oval, deeply lobed, mid-green leaves turn yellow in autumn. Has masses of single, white flowers in late spring, followed by small, rounded, pale yellow crab apples. Zone 6.
M. trilobata. Deciduous, conical tree. H 15m (50ft), S 7m (22ft). Has maple-like, lobed, glossy, bright green leaves that often become brightly coloured in autumn. Bears single, white flowers in early summer, followed by small, rounded or pear-shaped, red or yellow crab apples. Zone 6.

M. tschonoskii. Deciduous, conical tree. H 12m (40ft), S 7m (22ft). Broadly oval, glossy, mid-green leaves turn brilliant shades of orange, red and purple in autumn. Single, pink-tinged, white flowers, borne in late spring, are succeeded by rounded, red-flushed, yellowish-green crab apples. Zone 6.
M. **'Van Eseltine'.** Deciduous, upright tree. H 6m (20ft), S 4m (12ft). Bears double, pink flowers in late spring and rounded, yellow crab apples in autumn. Has oval, dark green leaves. Zone 2b.
M. **'Veitch's Scarlet'** illus. p.94.
'Weeping Candied Apple'. See **'Candied Apple'**
M. **'White Angel'**, syn. *M.* 'Inglis'. Rounded tree that tends to lose its shape because of its heavy fruiting. H and S 6m (20ft). Abundant white flowers open from pale pink buds. Fruit is a glossy red and persists well. Quite good disease resistance. Zone 5.
M. yunnanensis var. *veitchii* illus. p.91.
M. × *zumi* **'Calocarpa'**, syn. *M.* × *z.* var. *calocarpa*, illus. p.96. var. *calocarpa* see *M.* × *z.* 'Calocarpa'. **'Golden Hornet'** see *M.* 'Golden Hornet'.

MALVA
Mallow

MALVACEAE

Genus of annuals, biennials and free-flowering, short-lived perennials. Requires sun and fertile, well-drained soil. Propagate species by seed in autumn, selected forms by cuttings from firm, basal shoots in late spring or summer. These shoots may be encouraged by cutting plant back after first flowers have faded.
M. moschata illus. p.243.

Malvastrum capensis. See *Anisodontea capensis.*

MALVAVISCUS

MALVACEAE

Genus of evergreen shrubs and trees, grown for their flowers. Tender, min. 13–16°C (55–61°F). Requires a position in full light and in fertile, well-drained soil. Water containerized plants freely during growing season, moderately at other times. To maintain shape, flowered stems may be cut back hard in late winter. Propagate by seed in spring or by semi-ripe cuttings in summer. Whitefly and spider mite may be troublesome.
M. arboreus illus. p.121.

Mamaku. See *Cyathea medullaris.*

MAMMILLARIA
Pincushion cactus

CACTACEAE

Genus of hemispherical, spherical or columnar cacti, grown for their rings of funnel-shaped flowers that develop near crowns. Flowers, offsets and long, slender to spherical seed pods grow between tubercles on a spiny, green stem with extended areoles. Tender,

min. 5–10°C (41–50°F). Requires full
sun and very well-drained soil. Keep
completely dry in winter, otherwise
plants rot easily. Propagate by seed in
spring or summer.
M. bocasana illus. p.471.
M. candida (Snowball pincushion).
Slow-growing, clump-forming,
perennial cactus. H and S 15cm (6in).
Min. 5°C (41°F). Columnar, green stem
is densely covered with short, stiff,
white spines. Produces cream to rose
flowers, 1–2cm (½–¾in) across, in
spring. Water sparingly in summer.
M. centricirrha. See *M. magnimamma.*
M. conoidea. See *Neolloydia conoidea.*
M. densispina. Slow-growing,
spherical, perennial cactus. H 10cm
(4in), S 20cm (8in). Min. 5°C (41°F).
Has a green stem densely covered with
stout, golden spines and, in spring,
yellow flowers, 1–2cm (½–¾in) wide.
M. elegans of gardens. See
M. haageana.
M. elongata illus. p.470.
M. geminispina illus. p.465.
M. gracilis. Clump-forming, perennial
cactus. H 5cm (2in), S 20cm (8in).
Min. 5°C (41°F). Produces a columnar,
green stem densely covered with pure
white spines. In early summer carries
pale cream flowers, 1–2cm (½–¾in)
across. Stem is shallow-rooted and
reroots readily. var. *fragilis*, H 4cm
(1½in), is more fragile and has off-
white spines.
M. haageana, syn. *M. elegans* of
gardens. Spherical to columnar,
perennial cactus. H 30cm (12in),
S 20cm (8in). Min. 5°C (41°F). Bears
a green stem densely covered with
short, bristly spines and bright red
flowers, 1cm (½in) across, in spring.
Offsets occasionally.
M. hahniana illus. p.465.
M. magnimamma, syn. *M.
centricirrha.* Clump-forming, perennial
cactus. H 30cm (1ft), S 60cm (2ft).
Min. 5°C (41°F). Green stem has
very pronounced, angular, dark green
tubercles with white spines of variable
length. Bears cream, pink or red
flowers, 1–2cm (½–¾in) wide, in spring
and possibly again in late summer.
M. microhelia illus. p.478.
M. plumosa illus. p.469.
M. prolifera (Strawberry cactus).
Clump-forming, perennial cactus.
H 10cm (4in), S 30cm (12in).
Min 5°C (41°F). Green stem bears
dense, golden to white spines.
Produces masses of cream or yellow
flowers, 1–2cm (½–¾in) wide, in
summer, followed by red berries that
taste like strawberries.
M. rhodantha. Spherical to columnar,
perennial cactus. H and S 60cm (2ft).
Min. 5°C (41°F). Green stem,
branching from crown with age, is
densely covered with brown to yellow
spines, often curved. In late summer
produces bright red flowers, 1–2cm
(½–¾in) across.
M. schiedeana illus. p.470.
M. sempervivi illus. p.472.
M. zeilmanniana illus. p.473.

Mandarin's hat plant. See
Holmskioldia sanguinea.

MANDEVILLA,
syn. DIPLADENIA
APOCYNACEAE

Genus of evergreen, semi-evergreen
or deciduous, woody-stemmed, twining
climbers, grown for their large,
trumpet-shaped flowers. Tender, min.
7–10°C (45–50°F). Grow in any well-
drained soil, with light shade in
summer. Water freely when in full
growth, sparingly at other times.
Provide support and thin out and spur
back congested growth in early spring.
Propagate by seed in spring or by
semi-ripe cuttings in summer. Whitefly
and spider mite may cause problems.
Contact with the sap may cause skin
irritation, and all parts may cause mild
stomach upset if ingested.
M. x *amabilis* 'Alice du Pont'. See
M. x *amoena* 'Alice du Pont'.
M. x *amoena* **'Alice du Pont'**,
syn. *M.* x *amabilis* 'Alice du Pont',
illus. p.209.
M. boliviensis, syn. *Dipladenia
boliviensis.* Vigorous, evergreen,
woody-stemmed, twining climber.
Tender. H to 4m (12ft). Oblong,
pointed leaves are lustrous green.
Large, trumpet-shaped, white flowers
with gold eyes are produced in small
clusters in summer.
M. laxa, syn. *M. suaveolens,
M. tweediana* (Chilean jasmine). Fast-
growing, deciduous or semi-evergreen,
woody-stemmed, twining climber.
H 5m (15ft) or more. Tender. Oval
leaves have heart-shaped bases.
Clusters of fragrant, white flowers are
borne in summer.
M. splendens, syn. *Dipladenia
splendens*, illus. p.204.
M. suaveolens. See *M. laxa.*
M. tweediana. See *M. laxa.*

MANDRAGORA
Mandrake
SOLANACEAE

Genus of rosetted perennials with large,
deep, fleshy roots. Needs sun or partial
shade and deep, humus-rich, well-
drained soil. Resents being
transplanted. Propagate by seed in
autumn. Alkaloids in the plant may be
harmful if ingested.
M. officinarum illus. p.371.

Mandrake. See *Mandragora.*

MANETTIA
RUBIACEAE

Genus of evergreen, soft- or semi-
woody-stemmed, twining climbers,
grown for their small but showy
flowers. Tender, min. 5°C (41°F), but
7–10°C (45–50°F) is preferred. Grow in
any humus-rich, well-drained soil, with
partial shade in summer. Water
regularly, sparingly when temperatures
are low. Stems need support. Cut back
if required in spring. Propagate by
softwood or semi-ripe cuttings in
summer. Whitefly is sometimes
a problem.
M. bicolor. See *M. luteorubra.*
M. cordifolia (Firecracker vine). Fast-
growing, evergreen, soft-stemmed,

twining climber. H 2m (6ft) or more.
Has narrowly heart-shaped, glossy
leaves. Funnel-shaped, red flowers,
sometimes yellow flushed on the lobes,
appear in small clusters in summer.
M. inflata. See *M. luteorubra.*
M. luteorubra, syn. *M. bicolor,
M. inflata*, illus. p.205.

MANGLIETIA
MAGNOLIACEAE

Genus of evergreen trees, grown for
their foliage and flowers. Best at min.
3–5°C (37–41°F). Provide humus-rich,
moisture-retentive but well-drained,
acid soil and full light or partial shade.
Water potted plants freely when in full
growth, less at other times. Pruning is
tolerated if necessary. Propagate by
seed in spring.
M. insignis, syn. *Magnolia insignis.*
Evergreen, broadly conical tree.
H 8–12m (25–40ft) or more, S 3–5m
(10–15ft) or more. Leaves are
narrowly oval, lustrous, dark green
above, bluish-green beneath. In early
summer produces solitary, magnolia-
like, pink to carmine flowers that
are cream-flushed.

Manipur lily. See *Lilium mackliniae*,
   illus. p.404.
Manna ash. See *Fraxinus ornus*,
   illus. p.76.
Manna gum. See *Eucalyptus
   viminalis.*
Manuka. See *Leptospermum
   scoparium.*
Manzanita. See *Arctostaphylos.*
   Pine-mat. See *Arctostaphylos
      nevadensis.*
   Stanford. See *Arctostaphylos
      stanfordiana.*
Maple. See *Acer.*
   Amur. See *Acer tataricum* subsp.
      ginnala, illus. p.95.
   Cappadocian. See *Acer
      cappadocicum.*
   Coral-bark. See *Acer palmatum*
      'Sango-kaku', illus. p.124.
   Full-moon. See *Acer japonicum.*
   Hawthorn. See *Acer crataegifolium.*
   Hers's. See *Acer davidii* subsp.
      grosseri.
   Hornbeam. See *Acer carpinifolium*,
      illus. p.92.
   Italian. See *Acer opalus.*
   Japanese. See *Acer japonicum;
      Acer palmatum.*
   Lobel's. See *Acer cappadocicum*
      subsp. *lobelii*, illus. p.66.
   Manitoba. See *Acer negundo.*
   Montpelier. See *Acer
      monspessulanum.*
   Nikko. See *Acer maximowiczianum.*
   Norway. See *Acer platanoides.*
   Oregon. See *Acer macrophyllum*,
      illus. p.64.
   Paper-bark. See *Acer griseum*,
      illus. p.100.
   Père David's. See *Acer davidii.*
   Red. See *Acer rubrum*, illus. p.70.
   Silver. See *Acer saccharinum.*
   Snake-bark. See *Acer capillipes*,
      illus. p.82; *Acer davidii;
      Acer davidii* subsp. *grosseri;
      Acer pensylvanicum*, illus. p.84;
      Acer rufinerve, illus. p.82.
   Sugar. See *Acer saccharum.*

Maple (continued)
   Trident. See *Acer buergerianum.*
   Van Volxem's. See *Acer velutinum*
      var. *van-volxemii.*
   Vine. See *Acer circinatum.*
Mapleleaf begonia. See *Begonia dregei;
   Begonia* 'Weltoniensis', illus. p.295.

MARANTA
MARANTACEAE

Genus of evergreen perennials,
grown for their distinctively patterned,
coloured foliage. Tender, min. 10–15°C
(50–59°F). Needs constant, high
humidity and a shaded position away
from draughts or wind. Grow in
humus-rich, well-drained soil.
Propagate by division in spring or
summer or by stem cuttings in summer.
M. leuconeura (Prayer plant).
'Erythroneura' (syn.
M.l. 'Erythrophylla') illus. p.303.
'Erythrophylla'. See
M.l. 'Erythroneura'. var. *kerchoviana*
illus. p.304. var. *massangeana* is an
evergreen, short-stemmed perennial,
branching at the base. H and S 30cm
(1ft). Each oblong, velvety, dark green
leaf, 15cm (6in) long, has a wide,
irregular, pale midrib, white, lateral
veins and often purplish-green below,
stand upright at night but lie flat during
the day. Bears small, 3-petalled, white
to mauve flowers in slender, upright
spikes year-round.

Marguerite. See *Argyranthemum
   frutescens*, illus. p.240.
   Blue. See *Felicia amelloides.*
Marginatocereus marginatus. See
   Pachycereus marginatus.

MARGYRICARPUS
ROSACEAE

Genus of evergreen shrubs, grown for
their fruits. Is good for rock gardens.
Needs a sheltered, sunny position and
well-drained soil. Propagate by
softwood cuttings in early summer or
by seed in autumn.
M. pinnatus, syn. *M. setosus* (Pearl
berry). Evergreen, prostrate shrub.
H 23–30cm (9–12in), S 1m (3ft). Has
dark green leaves divided into linear,
silky leaflets. Has tiny, inconspicuous,
green flowers in early summer, then
small, globose, glossy, white fruits.
Zone 9.
M. setosus. See *M. pinnatus.*

Marigold. See *Calendula.*
   African. See *Tagetes erecta.*
   Aztec. See *Tagetes erecta.*
   Cape. See *Dimorphotheca.*
   French. See *Tagetes patula.*
   Marsh. See *Caltha palustris*,
      illus. p.451.
   Pot. See *Calendula officinalis.*
Mariposa tulip. See *Calochortus.*
Mariposa, Yellow. See *Calochortus
   luteus*, illus. p.415.
Maritime pine. See *Pinus pinaster*,
   illus. p.103.
Marjoram, Wild. See *Origanum
   vulgare.*
Marmalade bush. See *Streptosolen
   jamesonii*, illus. p.220.

Marsdenia erecta. See *Cionura erecta.*
Marsh buckler fern. See *Thelypteris palustris,* illus. p.312.
Marsh fern. See *Thelypteris palustris,* illus. p.312.
Marsh marigold. See *Caltha palustris,* illus. p.451.
Martagon lily. See *Lilium martagon,* illus. p.404.

MARTYNIA

PEDALIACEAE

Genus of annuals, grown for their flowers and horned fruits. Needs a sunny, sheltered site and fertile, well-drained soil. Propagate by seed sown under glass in early spring.
M. annua illus. p.320.
M. louisianica. See *Proboscidea louisianica.*

Marvel of Peru. See *Mirabilis.*

MASDEVALLIA

See also ORCHIDS.
M. coccinea (illus. p.297). Evergreen, epiphytic orchid for a cool greenhouse. H 15cm (6in). Narrowly oval leaves are 10cm (4in) long. Bears rich cerise flowers, 8cm (3in) long, in summer. Needs shade in summer.
M. infracta (illus. p.296). Evergreen, epiphytic orchid for a cool greenhouse. H 15cm (6in). Narrowly oval leaves are 10cm (4in) long. Bears rounded, red-and-white flowers, 5cm (2in) long, with tail-like, greenish sepals, in summer. Needs shade in summer.
M. tovarensis (illus. p.296). Evergreen, epiphytic orchid for a cool greenhouse. H 15cm (6in). Has oval leaves, 10cm (4in) long, and in autumn milky-white flowers, 4cm (1½in) long, with short-tailed sepals, singly or up to 3 to a stem. Grow in shade in summer.
M. wageneriana (illus. p.298). Evergreen, epiphytic orchid for a cool greenhouse. H 8cm (3in). Narrowly oval leaves are 10cm (4in) long. Bears pale yellow flowers, 4cm (1½in) long, with long, tail-like sepals, singly or in pairs in summer. Needs summer shade.

Mask flower. See *Alonsoa warscewiczii,* illus. p.329.
Masterwort. See *Astrantia.*
Mastic tree. See *Pistacia lentiscus.*
  Peruvian. See *Schinus molle.*

MATTEUCCIA

DRYOPTERIDACEAE/WOODSIACEAE

Genus of deciduous, rhizomatous ferns. Prefers semi-shade and wet soil. Remove faded fronds regularly and divide plants when crowded. Propagate by division in autumn or winter.
M. orientalis. Deciduous, rhizomatous fern. H and S to 1m (3ft). Produces a 'shuttlecock' of sterile, arching, broadly ovate, divided fronds, to 80cm (32in) long, light green when young, becoming darker. Fertile, erect, blackish-green fronds appear from the centre of the plant in summer.
M. struthiopteris illus. p.312.

MATTHIOLA
Stock

BRASSICACEAE/CRUCIFERAE

Genus of annuals, biennials, perennials and evergreen sub-shrubs. Flowers of most annual or biennial stocks are highly scented and excellent for cutting. Hardy to tender, min. 4°C (39°F). Grow in sun or semi-shade and in fertile, well-drained, ideally lime-rich soil. Tall cultivars may need support. If grown as biennials outdoors, provide cloche protection during winter. To produce flowers outdoors the same summer, sow seed of annuals under glass in early spring, or outdoors in mid-spring. Sow seed of perennials under glass in spring. Propagate sub-shrubs by semi-ripe cuttings in summer. Is prone to aphids, flea beetle, club root, downy mildew and botrytis.
M. **Brompton Group** (mixed) illus. p.321, (pink) illus. p.323.
M. **East Lothian Group.** Group of fast-growing, upright, bushy biennials and short-lived perennials, grown as annuals. H and S 30cm (1ft). Has lance-shaped, greyish-green leaves and, in summer, spikes, 15cm (6in) or more long, of scented, 4-petalled, single or double flowers, in shades of pink, red, purple, yellow or white.
M. **'Giant Excelsior'** illus. p.321.
M. **'Giant Imperial'** illus. p.318.
M. incana (Brompton stock). Fast-growing, upright, bushy biennial or short-lived perennial, grown as an annual. H 30–60cm (1–2ft), S 30cm (1ft). Has lance-shaped, greyish-green leaves and, in summer, scented, 4-petalled, light purple flowers borne in spikes, 7–15cm (3–6in) long.
M. **'Mammoth Column'.** Fast-growing, upright, bushy biennial or short-lived perennial, grown as an annual. H to 75cm (2½ft), S 30cm (1ft). Has lance-shaped, greyish-green leaves and, in summer, 30–38cm (12–15in) long spikes, of scented, 4-petalled flowers, available in mixed or single colours. Flowers are excellent for cutting.
M. **Park Series.** Group of fast-growing, upright, bushy biennials and short-lived perennials, grown as annuals. H and S to 30cm (1ft). Lance-shaped leaves are greyish-green. In summer, spikes, at least 15cm (6in) long, of scented, 4-petalled flowers are borne in a wide range of colours.
M. **Ten-week Group.** Group of fast-growing, upright, bushy biennials and short-lived perennials, grown as annuals. H and S to 30cm (1ft). Has lance-shaped, greyish-green leaves. Has scented, 4-petalled flowers, in spikes at least 15cm (6in) long, in a wide range of colours in summer. Dwarf (illus. p.325) and 'selectable' cultivars have double flowers.
M. **'Trysomic'.** Fast-growing, upright, bushy biennial or short-lived perennial, grown as an annual. H and S to 30cm (1ft). Lance-shaped leaves are greyish-green. Spikes, at least 15cm (6in) long, of scented, mostly double flowers are produced in a wide range of colours in summer.

Matucana aurantiaca. See *Oreocereus aurantiacus.*
Matucana haynei. See *Oreocereus haynei.*

MAURANDYA

SCROPHULARIACEAE

Genus of twining, woody-based, perennial climbers, grown against a wall or to clothe a trellis. Marginally hardy. Needs full sun and moderately fertile, moist but well-drained soil. Propagate by seed in spring or softwood cuttings in late spring.
M. barclayana, syn. *Asarina barclayana.* Evergreen, soft-stemmed, scandent climber, herbaceous in cold climates. H to 2m (6ft). Has angular, heart-shaped, hairless leaves. Trumpet-shaped, white, pink or purple flowers, each with a green or whitish throat, 6–7cm (2½–3in) long, are produced in summer-autumn. Zone 9?.
M. erubescens. See *Lophospermum erubescens.*

MAXILLARIA

See also ORCHIDS.
M. picta. Evergreen, epiphytic orchid for a cool greenhouse. H 23cm (9in). Fragrant, deep yellow to white flowers, 2.5cm (1in) across, marked purple to dark reddish-brown outside, are produced singly beneath foliage in winter. Has narrowly oval leaves, 15–23cm (6–9in) long. Requires semi-shade in summer.
M. porphyrostele (illus. p.299). Evergreen, epiphytic orchid for a cool greenhouse. H 8cm (3in). White- and red-lipped, yellow flowers, 1cm (½in) across, are borne singly in summer-autumn. Narrowly oval leaves are 8cm (3in) long. Grow in good light during summer.
M. tenuifolia. Evergreen, epiphytic orchid for a cool greenhouse. H 15cm (6in). Fragrant, yellow flowers, 2.5cm (1in) across, heavily overlaid with red and with white lips, are borne singly throughout summer. Has narrowly oval leaves, 15cm (6in) long. Needs good light in summer.

May. See *Crataegus laevigata.*
May, Foam of. See *Spiraea* 'Arguta'.
May apple. See *Podophyllum peltatum.*
  Himalayan. See *Podophyllum hexandrum,* illus. p.268.
May lily. See *Maianthemum.*
Mayflower. See *Epigaea repens.*

MAZUS

SCROPHULARIACEAE

Genus of creeping, spring-flowering perennials. Is useful for rock gardens and in paving. Needs a sheltered, sunny site and moist soil. Propagate by division in spring or by seed in autumn.
M. reptans illus. p.368.

Meadow buttercup. See *Ranunculus acris.*

Meadow cranesbill. See *Geranium pratense.*
Meadow foam. See *Limnanthes douglasii,* illus. p.336.
Meadow lily. See *Lilium canadense.*
Meadow rue. See *Thalictrum.*
Meadow saffron. See *Colchicum autumnale,* illus. p.437.
Meadow saxifrage. See *Saxifraga granulata,* illus. p.346.
Meadowsweet. See *Filipendula.*

MECONOPSIS

PAPAVERACEAE

Genus of perennials, some short-lived, others monocarpic (die after flowering), grown for their flowers. Needs shade and, in warm areas, a cool position. Most prefer humus-rich, moist, neutral to acid soil. All but *M.* x *sheldonii* may be propagated by seed when fresh, in late summer; *M. cambrica, M. grandis, M. quintuplinervia, M.* x *sheldonii* and their cultivars may also be propagated by division after flowering.
M. betonicifolia illus. p.253.
M. cambrica illus. p.275.
M. grandis illus. p.253.
M. integrifolia illus. p.292.
M. paniculata. Short-lived, clump-forming perennial that dies after flowering. H 1.5m (5ft), S 60cm (2ft). Produces racemes of nodding, shallowly cup-shaped, yellow flowers in late spring or early summer. Bears large rosettes of oblong to lance-shaped, deeply lobed and cut, hairy, yellowish-green leaves.
M. quintuplinervia illus. p.271.
M. x *sheldonii.* Clump-forming perennial. H 1.2–1.5m (4–5ft), S 45–60cm (1½–2ft). In early summer bears clusters of cup-shaped, clear deep blue flowers. Has rosettes of oblong to oval, toothed, hairy, mid-green leaves. Divide every three years to maintain vigour. **'Branklyn'** bears vivid blue flowers and coarsely toothed leaves. **'Slieve Donard'** has slightly smaller flowers and leaves with fewer teeth.

MEDICAGO

LEGUMINOSAE/PAPILIONACEAE

Genus of annuals, perennials and evergreen shrubs, grown for their flowers. Is good in mild, coastal areas as is very wind-resistant. Where hardy, is best planted against a south- or west-facing wall. Requires sun and well-drained soil. Cut out dead wood in spring. Propagate shrubs by semi-ripe or softwood cuttings in summer or by seed in autumn or spring, annuals and perennials by seed in autumn or spring.
M. arborea (Moon trefoil, Tree medick). Evergreen, bushy, dense shrub. H and S 2m (6ft). Bears clusters of small, pea-like, yellow flowers from mid-spring to late autumn or winter, followed by curious, flattened, snail-like, green, then brown seed pods. Has dark green leaves, each composed of 3 narrowly triangular leaflets, which are silky-haired when young. Zone 8.

Medick, Tree. See *Medicago arborea.*

MEDINILLA
MELASTOMATACEAE

Genus of evergreen shrubs and scrambling climbers, grown for their flowers and foliage. Tender, min. 16–18°C (61–4°F). Needs partial shade and humus-rich, well-drained soil. Water potted plants freely when in full growth, moderately at other times. Propagate by greenwood cuttings in spring or summer.
M. magnifica illus. p.141.

Medlar. See *Mespilus*.
   Bronvaux. See + *Crataegomespilus dardarii*.

MEEHANIA
LABIATAE/LAMIACEAE

Genus of perennials often with creeping stems, grown mainly as ground cover. Prefers shade and well-drained but not dry, humus-rich soil. May be propagated by seed, division or stem cuttings in spring.
M. urticifolia. Trailing, hairy perennial with long, creeping, leafy stems and erect flowering stems. H to 30cm (1ft), S indefinite. Oval to triangular, toothed leaves are 10cm (4in) or more long on the creeping stems – smaller on flowering stems. Whorls of fragrant, 2-lipped, purplish-blue flowers, to 5cm (2in) long, are carried in erect spikes in late spring.

Megasea. Reclassified as *Bergenia*.

MELALEUCA
MYRTACEAE

Genus of evergreen, spring- and summer-flowering trees and shrubs, grown for their flowers and overall appearance. Tender, min. 4–7°C (39–45°F). Needs full light and well-drained soil, preferably without much nitrogen. Some species tolerate waterlogged soils. Water containerized specimens moderately, less in low temperatures. Propagate by seed in spring or by semi-ripe cuttings in summer.
M. armillaris (Bracelet honey myrtle). Evergreen, rounded, wiry-stemmed shrub or tree. H 3–6m (10–20ft), S 1.2–3m (4–10ft). Has needle-like, deep green leaves and, in summer, dense, bottlebrush-like clusters, 3–6cm (1¼–2½in) long, each flower consisting of a small brush of white stamens.
M. elliptica illus. p.142.
M. hypericifolia. Evergreen, rounded shrub. H and S 2–5m (6–15ft). Leaves are oblong to elliptic and mid- to deep green above, paler beneath. Crimson flowers, each composed of a 2–2.5cm (¾–1in) long brush of stamens of the same colour, are borne in summer, mainly in bottlebrush-like spikes, 4–8cm (1½–3in) long.
M. nesophila, syn. *M. nesophylla,* illus. p.145.
M. nesophylla. See *M. nesophila.*
M. quinquenervia. See *M. viridiflora* var. *rubriflora.*

M. squarrosa (Scented paper-bark). Evergreen, erect, wiry-stemmed shrub or tree. H 3–6m (10–20ft), S 2–4m (6–12ft). Has tiny, oval, deep green leaves. Bears 4cm (1½in) long spikes of scented flowers, each comprising a tiny brush of cream stamens, in late spring and summer.
M. viridiflora var. *rubriflora,* syn. *M. quinquenervia* (Paper-bark tree). Strong-growing, evergreen, rounded tree. H 6–12m (20–40ft), S 3–6m (10–20ft). Leaves are elliptic and lustrous. Has peeling, papery, tan-coloured bark and, in spring, small, white or creamy-pink flowers in bottlebrush-like clusters. Tolerates waterlogged soil.

MELASPHAERULA
IRIDACEAE

Genus of one species of spring-flowering corm, grown mainly for botanical interest. Needs sun and well-drained soil. Plant in autumn and keep watered until after flowering, then dry off. Propagate by seed or offsets in autumn.
M. graminea. See *M. ramosa.*
M. ramosa, syn. *M. graminea.* Spring-flowering corm. H to 60cm (24in), S 10–15cm (4–6in). Has narrowly sword-shaped, semi-erect leaves in a basal fan. Wiry, branched stem bears loose sprays of small, pendent, funnel-shaped, yellowish-green flowers with pointed petals.

MELASTOMA
MELASTOMATACEAE

Genus of evergreen, mainly summer-flowering shrubs and trees, grown for their flowers and foliage. Tender, min. 10–13°C (50–55°F). Requires full light or partial shade and fertile, well-drained soil. Water containerized specimens freely when in full growth, moderately at other times. Pruning is tolerated in late winter if necessary. Propagate by softwood or greenwood cuttings in spring or summer. Spider mite and whitefly may cause problems.
M. candidum. Evergreen, rounded, bristly-stemmed shrub. H and S 1–2m (3–6ft). Bears oval, leathery, bristly leaves. Small, terminal clusters of fragrant, 5–7-petalled, white or pink flowers are produced profusely in summer.

MELIA
MELIACEAE

Genus of deciduous, spring-flowering trees, grown for their foliage, flowers and fruits. Is useful for very dry soil and does well in coastal gardens in mild areas. Tender. Requires a position in full sun; grows in any well-drained soil. Propagate by seed in autumn.
M. azedarach illus. p.76.

MELIANTHUS
MELIANTHACEAE

Genus of evergreen perennials and shrubs, grown primarily for their foliage. Tender, min. 5°C (41°F). Requires sun and fertile, well-drained soil. Water

potted specimens freely in summer, moderately at other times. Long stems may be shortened in early spring. May be propagated by seed in spring or by greenwood cuttings in summer. Spider mite may be troublesome.
M. major (Honeybush). Evergreen, sprawling, sparingly branched shrub. H and S 2–3m (6–10ft). Marginally hardy, but best at min. 5°C (41°F). Leaves are 25–45cm (10–18in) long, with 7–13 oval, toothed, blue-grey leaflets. Has tubular, rich brownish-red flowers in terminal spikes, 30cm (12in) long, in spring-summer.

Melic
   Siberian. See *Melica altissima*.
   Tall. See *Melica altissima*.

MELICA
GRAMINEAE/POACEAE

See also GRASSES, BAMBOOS, RUSHES and SEDGES.
M. altissima (Siberian melic, Tall melic). Evergreen, tuft-forming, perennial grass. H 60cm (24in), S 20cm (8in). Bears slender stems and broad, mid-green leaves, rough beneath. In summer produces pendent, tawny spikelets in narrow panicles.
'**Atropurpurea**' illus. p.307.

MELICYTUS,
syn. HYMENANTHERA
VIOLACEAE

Genus of evergreen shrubs and trees, grown for their overall appearance and ornamental fruits. Slightly hardy to tender, min. 3–5°C (37–41°F). Requires a position in full light or partial shade and in well-drained soil. Water pot plants moderately, less in winter. Pruning is tolerated if required. Propagate by seed when ripe, in autumn, or in spring.
M. crassifolius, syn. *Hymenanthera crassifolia.* Evergreen, densely twiggy shrub of irregular outline. H and S to 1.2m (4ft). Bears narrowly oval to oblong, leathery, mid-green leaves. Carries tiny, bell-shaped, 5-petalled, yellow flowers in spring-summer, followed by egg-shaped, purple fruits. Zone 9?.
M. ramiflorus (Mahoe, Whiteywood). Evergreen, spreading shrub or tree. H and S 6–10m (20–30ft). Tender. Bark is grey-white. Bears lance-shaped, bluntly serrated, bright green leaves. Small, rounded, greenish flowers are produced in axillary clusters in summer, followed by tiny, violet to purple-blue berries.

MELINIS
GRAMINEAE/POACEAE

See also GRASSES, BAMBOOS, RUSHES and SEDGES.
M. repens, syn. *Rhynchelytrum repens, R. roseum* (Natal grass, Ruby grass). Tuft-forming, annual or short-lived, perennial grass. H 1.2–2m (4–6ft), S 60cm–1m (2–3ft). Tender, min. 5°C (41°F). Leaves are mid-green, flat and finely pointed. Produces loose panicles of awned, pink spikelets in summer.

MELIOSMA
MELIOSMACEAE

Genus of deciduous trees and shrubs, grown for their habit, foliage and flowers, which, however, do not appear reliably. Marginally hardy. Prefers full sun and deep, fertile, well-drained soil. Propagate by seed in autumn.
M. oldhamii. See *M. pinnata* var. *oldhamii.*
M. pinnata var. *oldhamii,* syn. *M. oldhamii.* Deciduous, stout-branched tree, upright when young, spreading when mature. H 10m (30ft), S 6m (20ft). Has very large, dark green leaves divided into 5–13 oval leaflets. Bears large clusters of small, fragrant, star-shaped, white flowers in early summer. Zone 9?.
M. veitchiorum illus. p.80.

MELITTIS
Bastard balm

LABIATAE/LAMIACEAE

Genus of one species of summer-flowering perennial. Does best in light shade and requires fertile, well-drained soil. Propagate by seed in autumn or by division in spring or autumn.
M. melissophyllum illus. p.277.

MELOCACTUS
Turk's cap

CACTACEAE

Genus of spherical, ribbed, perennial cacti. On reaching flowering size, usually 15cm (6in) high, stems produce woolly crowns; then stems appear to stop growing while woolly crowns develop into columns. Has funnel-shaped flowers in summer, followed by elongated or rounded, red, pink or white seed pods. Tender, min. 11–15°C (52–9°F). Requires a position in full sun and extremely well-drained soil. Propagate by seed in spring or summer.
M. actinacanthus. See *M. matanzanus.*
M. bahiensis. Spherical, perennial cactus. H and S 15cm (6in). Min. 15°C (59°F). Dull green stem bears 10–15 ribs. Produces stout, slightly curved, dark brown spines that become paler with age. Crown bears brown bristles and pink flowers, 1–2cm (½–¾in) across, in summer.
M. communis. See *M. intortus.*
M. curvispinus, syn. *M. oaxacensis.* Spherical to columnar, perennial cactus. H 20cm (8in), S 15cm (6in). Min. 15°C (59°F). Green stem has 15 rounded ribs. Areoles each bear a straight central spine and curved radial spines. Flat, woolly crown bears deep pink flowers, 1cm (½in) across, in summer.
M. intortus, syn. *M. communis,* illus. p.472.
M. matanzanus, syn. *M. actinacanthus.* Spherical, perennial cactus. H and S 10cm (4in). Min. 15°C (59°F). Dark green stem has neat, short spines and develops a woolly crown about 5 years from seed. In summer produces pink flowers, 1cm (½in) across.
M. oaxacensis. See *M. curvispinus.*

Melon cactus. See *Melocactus intortus*, illus. p.472.

MENISPERMUM
Moonseed

MENISPERMACEAE

Genus of deciduous, woody or semi-woody, twining climbers, grown for their attractive fruits that each contain a crescent-shaped seed – hence the common name. Male and female flowers are carried on separate plants; to produce fruits, plants of both sexes must be grown. Grow in sun and in any well-drained soil. Propagate by seed or suckers in spring. The fruits may cause severe discomfort if ingested.
M. canadense (Canada moonseed, Yellow parilla). Vigorous, deciduous, woody-stemmed, twining climber, producing a dense tangle of stems and spreading by underground suckers. H to 5m (15ft). Produces oval to heart-shaped, rounded leaves that are usually 3–7-lobed. Small, cup-shaped, greenish-yellow flowers are carried in summer, followed by clusters of poisonous, spherical, glossy, blackish fruits. Zone 4.

MENTHA
Mint

LABIATAE/LAMIACEAE

Genus of perennials, some of which are semi-evergreen, grown for their aromatic foliage, which is both decorative and used as a culinary herb. Plants are invasive, however, and should be used with caution. Grow in a sunny or shady position and in well-drained soil. Propagate by division in spring or autumn.
M. corsica. See *M. requienii*.
M. × gentilis 'Variegata'. See *M. × gracilis* 'Variegata'.
M. × gracilis 'Variegata', syn. *M. × gentilis* 'Variegata'. Spreading perennial. H 45cm (18in), S 60cm (24in). Forms a mat of oval, dark green leaves that are speckled and striped with yellow, most conspicuously in full sun. Produces stems that carry whorls of small, 2-lipped, pale mauve flowers in summer.
M. × piperita f. *citrata* (Eau-de-Cologne mint) is a vigorous, spreading perennial. H 30–60cm (12–24in), S 60cm (24in). Reddish-green stems, bearing terminal spikes of small, 2-lipped, purple flowers in summer, arise from a carpet of oval, slightly toothed, mid-green leaves that have a scent which is similar to eau de Cologne.
M. requienii, syn. *M. corsica* (Corsican mint). Semi-evergreen, mat-forming, creeping perennial. H to 1cm (½in), S indefinite. When they are crushed, the rounded, bright apple-green leaves exude a strong peppermint fragrance. Carries tiny, stemless, lavender-purple flowers in summer. Is suitable for a rock garden or paved path. Needs shade and moist soil.
M. rotundifolia of gardens. See *M. suaveolens*.
M. suaveolens, syn. *M. rotundifolia* of gardens (Apple mint). 'Variegata' illus. p.276.

MENTZELIA

LOASACEAE

Genus of annuals, perennials and evergreen shrubs. Hardy to tender, min. 4°C (39°F). Requires a position in sun and in fertile, very well-drained soil; tender species are best grown in pots under glass. Propagate by seed in spring; shrubs may also be propagated by semi-ripe cuttings in summer.
M. lindleyi, syn. *Bartonia aurea*, illus. p.336.

MENYANTHES

MENYANTHACEAE

Genus of deciduous, perennial, marginal water plants, grown for their foliage and flowers. Prefers an open, sunny position. Remove fading flower heads and foliage, and divide overcrowded clumps in spring. Propagate by stem cuttings in spring.
M. trifoliata illus. p.446.

MENZIESIA

ERICACEAE

Genus of deciduous shrubs, grown for their small, urn-shaped flowers. Needs semi-shade and fertile, moist, peaty, acid soil. Propagate by softwood cuttings in summer or by seed in autumn.
M. ciliicalyx var. *lasiophylla*. See *M.c.* var. *purpurea*. var. **purpurea** (syn. *M.c.* var. *lasiophylla*) illus. p.155.

MERENDERA

COLCHICACEAE/LILIACEAE

Genus of corms similar to *Colchicum* but with less showy flowers. Needs a sunny position and well-drained soil. In cool, damp areas grow in an unheated greenhouse or frame where corms can dry out in summer. Plant in autumn and keep watered through winter and spring. Propagate by seed or offsets in autumn.
M. bulbocodium. See *M. montana*.
M. montana, syn. *M. bulbocodium*, illus. p.439.
M. robusta. Spring-flowering corm. H 8cm (3in), S 5–8cm (2–3in). Narrowly lance-shaped, semi-erect, basal leaves appear at the same time as upright, funnel-shaped flowers, 5–6cm (2–2½in) wide, with narrow, pale purplish-pink or white petals.

MERREMIA

CONVOLVULACEAE

Genus of evergreen, twining climbers, grown for their flowers and fruits. Tender, min. 7–10°C (45–50°F). Prefers fertile, well-drained soil and full light. Water moderately, much less when not in full growth. Provide support. Thin out congested stems during spring. Propagate by seed in spring. Spider mite may be a problem.
M. tuberosa, syn. *Ipomoea tuberosa*, *Operculina tuberosa* (Wood rose, Yellow morning glory). Fast-growing, evergreen, twining climber. H 6m (20ft) or more. Leaves have 7 radiating lobes. In summer bears funnel-shaped, yellow flowers, followed by semi-woody, globose, ivory-brown fruits.

Merry-bells. See *Uvularia grandiflora*, illus. p.274.

MERTENSIA

BORAGINACEAE

Genus of perennials, grown for their funnel-shaped flowers. Requires sun or shade and deep, well-drained soil. Propagate by division in spring or by seed in autumn.
M. echioides illus. p.357.
M. maritima illus. p.369.
M. pulmonarioides, syn. *M. virginica*, illus. p.271.
M. virginica. See *M. pulmonarioides*.

MERYTA

ARALIACEAE

Genus of evergreen trees, grown for their handsome foliage. Tender, min. 5°C (41°F). Requires full light or partial shade and humus-rich, moisture-retentive but moderately drained soil. Water freely containerized plants in full growth, less at other times. Propagate by semi-ripe cuttings in summer or by seed when ripe in late summer.
M. sinclairii illus. p.100.

Mescal button. See *Lophophora williamsii*, illus. p.471.
Mesembryanthemum cordifolium. See *Aptenia cordifolia*.
Mesembryanthemum criniflorum. See *Dorotheanthus bellidiformis*.
Mesembryanthemum multiradiatum. See *Lampranthus roseus*.

MESPILUS
Medlar

ROSACEAE

Genus of one species of deciduous tree or shrub, grown for its habit, flowers, foliage and edible fruits. Needs sun or semi-shade and fertile, well-drained soil. Propagate species by seed in autumn and named forms (for fruit) by budding in late summer.
M. germanica illus. p.85.

Metake. See *Pseudosasa japonica*, illus. p.308.
Metal-leaf begonia. See *Begonia metallica*, illus. p.295.

METASEQUOIA

TAXODIACEAE

See also CONIFERS.
M. glyptostroboides illus. p.102.

METROSIDEROS

MYRTACEAE

Genus of evergreen, winter-flowering shrubs, trees and scrambling climbers, grown for their flowers, the trees also for their overall appearance and for shade. Tender, min. 5°C (41°F). Grows in fertile, well-drained soil and in full light. Water freely containerized specimens in full growth, moderately at other times. Pruning is tolerated if necessary. Propagate by seed in spring or by semi-ripe cuttings in summer.

M. excelsus, syn. *M. tomentosus*, illus. p.83.
M. robustus (Rata). Robust, evergreen, rounded tree. H 20–25m (70–80ft) or more, S 10–15m (30–50ft). Oblong to elliptic, leathery leaves are dark green and lustrous. Produces large clusters of flowers, which are mostly composed of long, dark red stamens, during winter.
M. tomentosus. See *M. excelsus*.

MEUM

APIACEAE/UMBELLIFERAE

Genus of summer-flowering perennials, grown for their aromatic leaves. Is useful on banks and in wild gardens. Needs sun and well-drained soil. Propagate by seed when fresh, in autumn.
M. athamanticum (Baldmoney, Spignel). Upright, clump-forming perennial. H 15–45cm (6–18in), S 10–15cm (4–6in). Mainly basal and deeply dissected leaves have narrowly linear leaflets. In summer produces flattish flower heads consisting of clusters of tiny, white or purplish-white flowers.

Mexican blood flower. See *Distictis buccinatoria*, illus. p.204.
Mexican bush sage. See *Salvia leucantha*.
Mexican cypress. See *Cupressus lusitanica*.
Mexican firecracker. See *Echeveria setosa*.
Mexican flame vine. See *Senecio confusus*, illus. p.217.
Mexican foxglove. See *Tetranema roseum*, illus. p.303.
Mexican giant hyssop. See *Agastache*.
Mexican hat plant. See *Kalanchoe daigremontiana*, illus. p.462.
Mexican orange blossom. See *Choisya ternata*, illus. p.127.
Mexican palo verde. See *Parkinsonia aculeata*.
Mexican stone pine. See *Pinus cembroides*, illus. p.109.
Mexican sunflower. See *Tithonia rotundifolia*.
Mexican tulip poppy. See *Hunnemannia fumariifolia*.
Mexican violet. See *Tetranema roseum*, illus. p.303.
Mezereon. See *Daphne mezereum*, illus. p.174.
Michaelmas daisy. See *Aster*.

MICHELIA

MAGNOLIACEAE

Genus of evergreen, winter- to summer-flowering shrubs and trees, grown for their flowers and foliage. Tender, min. 5°C (41°F). Provide humus-rich, well-drained, neutral to acid soil and full light or partial shade. Water potted specimens freely when in full growth, less in winter. Pruning is seldom necessary. Propagate by semi-ripe cuttings in summer or by seed when ripe, in autumn, or in spring.
M. doltsopa illus. p.83.
M. figo illus. p.89.

Mickey-mouse plant. See *Ochna serrulata*.

MICROBIOTA
Russian arbovitae

CUPRESSACEAE

See also CONIFERS.
M. decussata (illus. p.110). Spreading, shrubby conifer. H 50cm (20in), S 2–3m (6–10ft). Flat sprays of scale-like, yellow-green leave turn bronze in winter. Globose, yellow-brown cones had only one seed. Zone 3.

Microglossa albescens. See *Aster albescens.*

MICROLEPIA

DENNSTAEDTIACEAE

Genus of deciduous, semi-evergreen or evergreen ferns, best grown in pans and hanging baskets. Tender, min. 5°C (41°F). Requires shade or semi-shade and moist soil. Remove faded fronds regularly. Propagate by division in spring or by spores in summer.
M. speluncae illus. p.310.

MICROMERIA

LABIATAE/LAMIACEAE

Genus of evergreen or semi-evergreen shrubs, sub-shrubs and perennials, suitable for rock gardens and banks. Needs sun and well-drained soil. Propagate by seed in spring or by softwood cuttings in early summer.
M. juliana. Evergreen or semi-evergreen, bushy shrub or sub-shrub. H and S 30cm (12in). Has small, oval, aromatic, green leaves pressed close to stems. In summer, minute, tubular, bright deep pink flowers are carried in whorls on upper parts of stems. Zone 8.

Mignonette. See *Reseda.*
Mignonette vine. See *Anredera.*

MIKANIA

ASTERACEAE/COMPOSITAE

Genus of evergreen or herbaceous, scrambling or twining climbers, shrubs and erect perennials, grown for their foliage and flower heads. Tender, min. 7°C (45°F). Any fertile, well-drained soil is suitable, with partial shade in summer. Water regularly, less when not in full growth. Support for stems is needed and ties may be necessary. Thin out congested growth in spring. Propagate by semi-ripe or softwood cuttings in summer. Aphids may be a problem.
M. scandens. Herbaceous, twining climber. H 3–5m (10–15ft). Oval to triangular, mid-green leaves have 2 basal lobes. Tiny, groundsel-like, pink to purple flower heads appear in compact clusters in summer-autumn.

Mile-a-minute plant. See *Fallopia aubertii*; *Fallopia baldschuanica,* illus. p.217.
Milfoil, Whorled water. See *Myriophyllum verticillatum,* illus. p.449.

MILIUM

GRAMINEAE/POACEAE

See also GRASSES, BAMBOOS, RUSHES and SEDGES.
M. effusum (Wood millet). **'Aureum'** is an evergreen, tuft-forming, perennial grass. H 1m (3ft), S 30cm (1ft). Has flat, golden-yellow leaves. Produces open, tiered panicles of greenish-yellow spikelets in summer. Self seeds readily in shade.

Milkweed. See *Asclepias* and *Euphorbia.*

MILLA

ALLIACEAE/LILIACEAE

Genus of summer-flowering bulbs, grown for their fragrant flowers, each comprising a slender tube with 6 spreading, star-shaped petals at the tip. Needs a sheltered, sunny position and well-drained soil. Plant in spring. After flowering lift bulbs and partially dry off for winter. Propagate by seed or offsets in spring.
M. biflora. Summer-flowering bulb. H 30–45cm (12–18in), S 8–10cm (3–4in). Has long, narrow, semi-erect, basal leaves. Stem bears a loose head of 2–6 erect, white flowers, 3–6cm (1¼–2½in) across, each on a slender stalk to 20cm (8in) long.

Millet
Foxtail. See *Setaria italica.*
Italian. See *Setaria italica.*
Wood. See *Milium effusum.*

MILTONIA

See also ORCHIDS.
M. candida (illus. p.298). Evergreen, epiphytic orchid for a cool or intermediate greenhouse. H 20cm (8in). Cream-lipped, green-patterned, brown flowers, 5cm (2in) across, are borne in spikes in autumn. Has narrowly oval leaves, 10–12cm (4–5in) long. Grow in semi-shade in summer.
M. clowesii (illus. p.298). Evergreen, epiphytic orchid for an intermediate greenhouse. H 20cm (8in). In early summer produces large spikes of 4cm (1½in) wide, yellow flowers, barred with reddish-brown and each with a white-and-mauve lip. Has broadly oval leaves, 30cm (12in) long. Grow in semi-shade in summer.

MILTONIOPSIS
Pansy orchid

See also ORCHIDS.
M. Anjou 'St Patrick' (illus. p.297). Evergreen, epiphytic orchid for a cool greenhouse. H 15cm (6in). Has sprays of deep crimson flowers, 10cm (4in) across, with red and yellow patterns on each lip, mainly in summer. Narrowly oval, soft leaves are 10–12cm (4–5in) long. Needs shade in summer.
M. Robert Strauss 'Ardingly' (illus. p.296). Evergreen, epiphytic orchid for a cool greenhouse. H 15cm (6in). Bears sprays of white flowers, 10cm (4in) across, marked reddish-brown and

purple; flowering season varies. Narrowly oval, soft leaves are 10–12cm (4–5in) long. Requires shade in summer.

Mimicry plant. See *Pleiospilos bolusii,* illus. p.479.

MIMOSA

LEGUMINOSAE/MIMOSACEAE

Genus of annuals, evergreen perennials, shrubs, trees and scrambling climbers, cultivated for their flowers and foliage. *M. pudica* is usually grown as an annual. Tender, min. 13–16°C (55–61°F). Needs partial shade and fertile, well-drained soil. Water potted specimens freely when in full growth, moderately at other times. Propagate by seed in spring, shrubs also by semi-ripe cuttings in summer. Spider mite may be a nuisance.
M. pudica illus. p.176.

Mimosa. See *Acacia.*

MIMULUS
Monkey musk

SCROPHULARIACEAE

Genus of annuals, perennials and evergreen shrubs. Small species suit damp pockets in rock gardens. Most prefer full sun and wet or moist soil; some, such as *M. aurantiacus* need a dry site. Propagate perennials by division in spring, sub-shrubs by softwood cuttings in late summer; annuals and all species by seed in autumn or early spring.
M. 'Andean Nymph' illus. p.278.
M. aurantiacus, syn. *Diplacus glutinosus, M. glutinosus,* illus. p.171.
M. glutinosus. See *M. aurantiacus.*
M. guttatus, syn. *M. langsdorffii.* Spreading, mat-forming perennial. H and S 60cm (24in). Snapdragon-like, bright yellow flowers, spotted with reddish-brown on lower lobes, are borne in succession in summer and early autumn. Oval leaves are coarsely or sometimes deeply toothed and mid-green.
M. langsdorffii. See *M. guttatus.*
M. lewisii illus. p.279.
M. luteus illus. p.292.
M. Magic Series. Early-flowering perennial. H 15–20cm (6–8in). Produces small flowers, ranging from bright orange, yellow, and red to more usual pastel shades and bicolours.
M. moschatus (Musk). Spreading, mat-forming perennial. H and S 15–30cm (6–12in). Bears snapdragon-like, pale yellow flowers, lightly speckled with brown, in summer-autumn. Leaves are oval, hairy and pale green.
M. 'Royal Velvet' illus. p.283.
M. 'Whitecroft Scarlet'. Short-lived, spreading perennial. H 20–30cm (8–12in), S 30cm (12in). Bears snapdragon-like, scarlet flowers freely from early to late summer. Has oval, toothed, mid-green leaves.

Mina. Reclassified as *Ipomoea.*
Mind-your-own-business. See *Soleirolia.*

Miniature date palm. See *Phoenix roebelenii.*
Miniature grape ivy. See *Cissus striata.*
Mint. See *Mentha.*
Apple. See *Mentha suaveolens.*
Corsican. See *Mentha requienii.*
Eau-de-Cologne. See *Mentha* x *piperita* f. *citrata.*
Variegated apple. See *Mentha suaveolens* 'Variegata', illus. p.276.
Mint bush. See *Elsholtzia stauntonii,* illus. p.173; *Prostanthera.*
Mint-bush, Round-leaved. See *Prostanthera rotundifolia,* illus. p.145.
Mintleaf. See *Plectranthus madagascariensis.*

MIRABILIS
Four o'clock flower, Marvel of Peru

NYCTAGINACEAE

Genus of summer-flowering annuals and tuberous perennials. Is best grown in a sheltered position in fertile, well-drained soil and in full sun. Lift tubers and store over winter in frost-free conditions. Propagate by seed or division of tubers in early spring.
M. jalapa illus. p.245.

Mirbeck's oak. See *Quercus canariensis,* illus. p.661.

MISCANTHUS

GRAMINEAE/POACEAE

See also GRASSES, BAMBOOS, RUSHES and SEDGES.
M. sacchariflorus (Amur silver grass). Vigorous, herbaceous, slow-spreading, rhizomatous, perennial grass. H 3m (10ft), S indefinite. Hairless, mid-green leaves last into winter, often turning bronze. Has rare, open, branched panicles of hairy, purplish-brown spikelets in summer.
M. sinensis 'Gracillimus' illus. p.309.
'Zebrinus' illus. p.306.

Missouri flag. See *Iris missouriensis,* illus. p.234.
Mist flower. See *Eupatorium rugosum,* illus. p.240.
Mistletoe cactus. See *Rhipsalis.*
Mistletoe fig. See *Ficus deltoidea,* illus. p.152.

MITCHELLA

RUBIACEAE

Genus of evergreen, trailing sub-shrubs, grown for their foliage and fruits. Makes excellent ground cover, especially in woodlands, although is sometimes difficult to establish. Prefers shade and humus-rich, neutral to acid soil. Propagate by division of rooted runners in spring or by seed in autumn.
M. repens (Partridge berry). Evergreen, trailing, mat-forming sub-shrub. H 5cm (2in), S indefinite. Bears small, oval, white-striped, green leaves with heart-shaped bases. In early summer has pairs of tiny, fragrant, tubular, white flowers, sometimes purple-tinged, followed by spherical, bright red fruits. Suits a rock garden or peat bed. Zone 4.

MITELLA

SAXIFRAGACEAE

Genus of clump-forming, summer-flowering, slender-stemmed, rhizomatous perennials. Requires shade and humus-rich, moist soil. Propagate by division in spring or by seed in autumn.

M. breweri illus. p.384.

MITRARIA

GESNERIACEAE

Genus of one species of evergreen, woody-stemmed, scrambling climber. Marginally hardy. Requires a position in semi-shade and in peaty, acid soil. Propagate by seed in spring or by stem cuttings in summer.

M. coccinea illus. p.205.

Moccasin flower. See *Cypripedium acaule*, illus. p.296.
Mock orange. See *Philadelphus coronarius*; *Pittosporum tobira*.

MOLINIA

GRAMINEAE/POACEAE

See also GRASSES, BAMBOOS, RUSHES and SEDGES.
M. altissima. See *M. caerulea* subsp. *arundinacea*.
M. caerulea subsp. **arundinacea**, syn. *M. altissima*. Tuft-forming, herbaceous, perennial grass. H 2.5m (8ft), S 60cm (2ft). Has broad, flat, grey-green leaves and spreading panicles of purple spikelets on stiff, erect stems in summer. Needs a dry, sunny position and acid soil.
'Variegata' (Variegated purple moor grass), H 60cm (2ft), has yellow-striped, mid-green leaves and, in late summer, panicles of purplish spikelets.

MOLTKIA

BORAGINACEAE

Genus of deciduous, semi-evergreen or evergreen sub-shrubs and perennials, grown for their funnel-shaped flowers in summer. Prefers sun and well-drained, neutral to acid soil. Propagate by semi-ripe cuttings in summer or by seed in autumn.
M. x intermedia. Evergreen, open, dome-shaped sub-shrub. H 30cm (12in), S 50cm (20in). Stems are clothed in narrowly linear, dark green leaves. Masses of loose spikes of small, open funnel-shaped, bright blue flowers appear in summer. Zone 8.
M. petraea. Semi-evergreen, bushy shrub. H 30cm (12in), S 60cm (24in). Has long, narrow, hairy leaves and clusters of pinkish-purple buds open into funnel-shaped, violet-blue flowers in summer. Zone 8.
M. suffruticosa illus. p.357.

MOLUCCELLA

LABIATAE/LAMIACEAE

Genus of annuals and perennials, grown for their flowers that may be dried successfully. Grow in sun and in rich, very well-drained soil. May be propagated by seed sown under glass in spring, or outdoors in late spring.
M. laevis illus. p.335.

Monarch birch. See *Betula maximowicziana*.
Monarch-of-the-East. See *Sauromatum venosum*, illus. p.413.

MONARDA

Bergamot

LABIATAE/LAMIACEAE

Genus of annuals and perennials, grown for their aromatic foliage as well as their flowers. Requires sun and moist soil. Propagate species and cultivars by division in spring, species only by seed in spring.
M. 'Adam'. Clump-forming perennial. H 75cm (30in), S 45cm (18in). Bears dense whorls of 2-lipped, cerise flowers throughout summer. Oval, usually toothed, mid-green leaves are aromatic and hairy.
M. didyma (Bee balm, Bergamot).
'Cambridge Scarlet' illus. p.250.
'Croftway Pink' illus. p.243.
M. fistulosa illus. p.251.
M. 'Prairie Night'. See *M.* 'Prärienacht'.
M. 'Prärienacht', syn. *M.* 'Prairie Night'. Clump-forming perennial. H 1.2m (4ft), S 45cm (1½ft). Produces dense whorls of 2-lipped, rich violet-purple flowers from mid- to late summer. Oval, toothed leaves are mid-green.

Money tree. See *Crassula ovata*, illus. p.457.
Moneywort. See *Lysimachia nummularia*.
Mongolian linden. See *Tilia mongolica*.
Monkey musk. See *Mimulus*.
Monkey puzzle. See *Araucaria araucana*, illus. p.103.
Monkshood. See *Aconitum*.

MONSTERA

ARACEAE

Genus of evergreen, woody-stemmed, root climbers, grown for their large, handsome leaves. Bears insignificant, creamy-white flowers with hooded spathes intermittently. Tender, min. 15–18°C (59–64°F). Provide humus-rich, well-drained soil and light shade in summer. Water moderately, less when temperatures are low. Provide support. If necessary, shorten long stems in spring. Propagate by leaf-bud or stem-tip cuttings in summer. All parts except the fruit may cause mild stomach upset when ingested, and contact with the fruit may irritate skin.
M. acuminata (Shingle plant). Evergreen, woody-stemmed, root climber with robust stems. H 3m (10ft) or more. Has lopsided, oval, pointed, rich green leaves with a heart-shaped base, sometimes cleft into a few large lobes, up to 25cm (10in) long.
M. deliciosa illus. p.220.

Montbretia. See *Crocosmia*.
Monterey ceanothus. See *Ceanothus rigidus*.
Monterey cypress. See *Cupressus macrocarpa*.
Monterey pine. See *Pinus radiata*, illus. p.104.
Montpelier maple. See *Acer monspessulanum*.
Moon flower. See *Ipomoea alba*.
Moon trefoil. See *Medicago arborea*.
Moonlight holly. See *Ilex aquifolium* 'Flavescens'.
Moonseed. See *Menispermum*.
Canada. See *Menispermum canadense*.
Moonstones. See *Pachyphytum oviferum*, illus. p.475.

MORAEA

IRIDACEAE

Genus of corms with short-lived, iris-like flowers. Divides into 2 groups: winter- and summer-growing species. Winter-growing species need full sun and well-drained soil; keep dry in summer during dormancy and start into growth by watering in autumn. Summer-growers are dormant in winter; grow in a sheltered, sunny site and well-drained soil. Propagate winter growers by seed in autumn, spring for summer growers.
M. huttonii illus. p.403.
M. polystachya. Winter-growing corm. H to 30cm (12in), S 5–8cm (2–3in). Bears long, narrow, semi-erect, basal leaves. Stem has a succession of erect, flattish, blue or lilac flowers, 8cm (3in) wide, in winter-spring. Outer petals each have a central, yellow mark.
M. ramosissima illus. p.402.
M. spathacea. See *M. spathulata*.
M. spathulata, syn. *M. spathacea*. Summer-growing corm. H to 1m (3ft), S 10–15cm (4–6in). Has one long, narrow, semi-erect, basal leaf. Tough flower stem carries a succession of up to 5 upward-facing, yellow flowers, 5–7cm (2–3in) wide, with reflexed, outer petals, in summer.

Moreton Bay chestnut. See *Castanospermum*.
Moreton Bay fig. See *Ficus macrophylla*.

MORINA

Whorl flower

MORINACEAE

Genus of evergreen perennials, only one species of which is in general cultivation: this is grown for its thistle-like foliage and its flowers. Needs protection from drying spring winds. Needs full sun and well-drained, preferably sandy soil. Propagate by division directly after flowering or by seed when fresh, in late summer.
M. longifolia illus. p.241.

Morinda spruce. See *Picea smithiana*.

MORISIA

BRASSICACEAE/CRUCIFERAE

Genus of one species of rosetted perennial with a long tap root. Is good for rock gardens and alpine houses. Needs sun and gritty, well-drained soil.

Propagate by seed in autumn or by root cuttings in winter.
M. hypogaea. See *M. monanthos*.
M. monanthos, syn. *M. hypogaea*, illus. p.372.

Morning glory. See *Ipomoea hederacea*, illus. p.214.
Common. See *Ipomoea purpurea*.
Red. See *Ipomoea coccinea*.
Woolly. See *Argyreia nervosa*.
Yellow. See *Merremia tuberosa*.
Moroccan broom. See *Cytisus battandieri*, illus. p.123.

MORUS

Mulberry

MORACEAE

Genus of deciduous trees, grown for foliage and edible fruits. Tiny flowers appear in spring. Requires full sun and fertile, well-drained soil. Propagate by softwood cuttings in summer or by seed in autumn.
M. alba (White mulberry). **'Laciniata'** illus. p.92. **'Pendula'** is a deciduous, weeping tree. H 3m (10ft), S 5m (15ft). Rounded, sometimes lobed, glossy, deep green leaves turn yellow in autumn. Edible, oval, fleshy, pink, red or purple fruits ripen in summer. Zone 4.
M. nigra (Black mulberry). Deciduous, round-headed tree. H 12m (40ft), S 15m (50ft). Heart-shaped, dark green leaves turn yellow in autumn. Bears edible, oval, succulent, dark purplish-red fruits in late summer or early autumn. Zone 6.

Moses-in-the-cradle. See *Tradescantia spathacea*.
Mosquito grass. See *Bouteloua gracilis*, illus. p.307.
Moss
Fairy. See *Azolla filiculoides*, illus. p.448.
Spanish. See *Tillandsia usneoides*, illus. p.265.
Water. See *Fontinalis antipyretica*.
Willow. See *Fontinalis antipyretica*.
Moss campion. See *Silene acaulis*, illus. p.365.
Mother of thousands. See *Saxifraga stolonifera*; *Soleirolia*.
Mother spleenwort. See *Asplenium bulbiferum*.
Mother-in-law's seat. See *Echinocactus grusonii*, illus. p.460.
Mother-in-law's tongue. See *Sansevieria trifasciata*.
Mother-of-pearl plant. See *Graptopetalum paraguayense*, illus. p.478.
Mount Etna broom. See *Genista aetnensis*, illus. p.93.
Mount Morgan wattle. See *Acacia podalyriifolia*, illus. p.135.
Mountain ash. See *Sorbus aucuparia*, illus. p.81.
American. See *Sorbus americana*.
Korean. See *Sorbus alnifolia*.
Mountain avens. See *Dryas*.
Mountain buckler fern. See *Oreopteris limbosperma*.
Mountain dogwood. See *Cornus nuttallii*, illus. p.76.
Mountain fern. See *Oreopteris limbosperma*.

Mountain fetterbush. See *Pieris floribunda*, illus. p.127.
Mountain flax. See *Phormium cookianum*.
Mountain gum. See *Eucalyptus dalrympleana*, illus. p.72.
Mountain hemlock. See *Tsuga mertensiana*.
Mountain pansy. See *Viola lutea*.
Mountain pepper. See *Drimys lanceolata*.
Mountain pine. See *Pinus mugo*.
Mountain pride. See *Penstemon newberryi*.
Mountain sow thistle. See *Cicerbita alpina*.
Mountain spruce. See *Picea engelmannii*, illus. p.105.
Mountain tassel. See *Soldanella montana*.
Mountain willow. See *Salix arbuscula*.
Mountain wood fern. See *Oreopteris limbosperma*.
Mourning iris. See *Iris susiana*.
Mourning widow. See *Geranium phaeum*, illus. p.238.
Mouse plant. See *Arisarum proboscideum*.
Mouse-ear, Alpine. See *Cerastium alpinum*.
Moutan. See *Paeonia suffruticosa*.

MUCUNA

LEGUMINOSAE/PAPILIONACEAE

Genus of vigorous, evergreen, twining climbers, grown for their large, pea-like flowers. Tender, min. 18°C (64°F). Humus-rich, moist but well-drained soil is essential, with partial shade in summer. Water freely when in full growth, less at other times. Needs plenty of space to climb; provide support. Thin out crowded stems in spring. Propagate by seed in spring or by layering in late summer. Whitefly and spider mite may cause problems.
M. bennettii. Strong- and fast-growing, evergreen, twining climber. H 15–25m (50–80ft). Leaves are divided into 3 oval leaflets. In summer has pendent clusters of pea-like, orange-scarlet flowers.
M. deeringiana. See *M. pruriens* var. *utilis*.
M. pruriens var. **utilis**, syn. *M. deeringiana*. Vigorous, evergreen, twining climber. H 15m (50ft) or more. Has pea-like, both green- and red-purple flowers in long, pendent clusters in summer-autumn. Leaves, of 3 oval leaflets, are used for fodder and green manure. May be short-lived.

MUEHLENBECKIA

POLYGONACEAE

Genus of deciduous or evergreen, slender-stemmed, summer-flowering shrubs and woody-stemmed, scrambling climbers, grown for their foliage. Grow in sun or shade and in well-drained soil. Propagate by semi-ripe cuttings in summer.
M. axillaris of gardens. See *M. complexa*.
M. complexa, syn. *M. axillaris* of gardens. Deciduous, mound-forming shrub or twining climber. H 60cm–1m (2–3ft), S 1m (3ft). Slender, wiry stems bear variably shaped (oval to fiddle-

shaped), dark green leaves. Produces tiny, star-shaped, greenish-white flowers in mid-summer that are followed by small, spherical, waxy, white fruits. Zone 9.

Mugwort, White. See *Artemisia lactiflora*, illus. p.227.
Mulberry. See *Morus*.
 Black. See *Morus nigra*.
 Paper. See *Broussonetia papyrifera*, illus. p.79.
 White. See *Morus alba*.
Mulgedium. Reclassified as *Cicerbita*.
Mullein. See *Verbascum*.
 White. See *Verbascum lychnitis*.
Muriel bamboo. See *Fargesia murieliae*.
Murray red gum. See *Eucalyptus camaldulensis*.

MURRAYA

RUTACEAE

Genus of evergreen trees and shrubs, grown for their overall appearance. Tender, min. 13–15°C (55–9°F). Requires a position in full light or partial shade and in humus-rich, well-drained soil. Water containerized plants freely when in full growth, moderately at other times. Pruning is tolerated in late winter if necessary. Propagate by seed in spring or by semi-ripe cuttings in summer. Whitefly may be troublesome.
M. exotica. See *M. paniculata*.
M. paniculata, syn. *M. exotica* (Orange jasmine). Evergreen, rounded shrub or tree. H and S 2–4m (6–12ft). Pungently aromatic, edible, glossy, rich green leaves each have 9 or more oval leaflets. Carries fragrant, 5-petalled, white flowers in terminal clusters year-round, followed by tiny, egg-shaped, red fruits.

MUSA
Banana

MUSACEAE

Genus of evergreen, palm-like, suckering perennials, with false stems formed from overlapping leaf sheaths, grown for their foliage, flowers and fruits (bananas), not all of which are edible. Tender, min. 18°C (64°F). Grow in sun or partial shade and in humus-rich, well-drained soil. Propagate by division year-round, by offsets in summer or by suckers after flowering.
M. arnoldiana. See *Ensete ventricosum*.
M. basjoo, syn. *M. japonica*, illus. p.233.
M. coccinea, syn. *M. uranoscopus* (Scarlet banana). Evergreen, palm-like perennial. H to 1m (3ft), S 1.5m (5ft). Bears oblong to oval, dark green leaves, to 1m (3ft) long, that are paler below. In summer produces erect spirals of tubular, yellow flowers, enclosed in red bracts, followed by banana-like, orange-yellow fruits, 5cm (2in) long.
M. ensete. See *Ensete ventricosum*.
M. japonica. See *M. basjoo*.
M. ornata illus. p.232.
M. uranoscopus. See *M. coccinea*.

MUSCARI
Grape hyacinth

HYACINTHACEAE/LILIACEAE

Genus of spring-flowering bulbs, each with a cluster of narrowly strap-shaped, basal leaves, usually appearing in spring just before flowers. Leafless flower stems bear dense spikes of small flowers, most of which have constricted mouths. Needs sun and fairly well-drained soil. Plant in autumn. Propagate by division in late summer or by seed in autumn.
M. armeniacum illus. p.433. **'Blue Spike'** is a spring-flowering bulb. H 15–20cm (6–8in), S 8–10cm (3–4in). Produces 3–6 long, narrow, semi-erect, basal leaves. Bears dense spikes of fragrant, bell-shaped, deep blue flowers; constricted mouths have rims of paler blue or white 'teeth'.
M. aucheri, syn. *M. lingulatum*, illus. p.433.
M. azureum, syn. *Hyacinthus azureus*, *Pseudomuscari azureum*. Spring-flowering bulb. H 10–15cm (4–6in), S 5–8cm (2–3in). Bears 2 or 3 narrow, semi-erect, basal, greyish-green leaves, slightly wider towards the tips. Produces a very dense spike of bell-shaped, pale clear blue flowers; mouths have small 'teeth' with central, dark blue stripes. May self-seed freely.
M. botryoides. Spring-flowering bulb. H 15–20cm (6–8in), S 5–8cm (2–3in). Bears 2–4 narrow, semi-erect, basal leaves that widen slightly at the tips. Each minute, nearly spherical, bright blue flower has a constricted mouth and white-toothed rim.
M. comosum, syn. *Leopoldia comosa* (Tassel grape hyacinth). Late spring-flowering bulb. H 20–30cm (8–12in), S 10–12cm (4–5in). Has up to 5 strap-shaped, semi-erect, basal, grey-green leaves. Bears a loose spike of bell-shaped, fertile, brownish-yellow flowers with a tuft of thread-like, sterile, purplish-blue flowers at the tip.
'Monstrosum' see *M.c.* 'Plumosum'.
'Plumosum' (syn. *M.c.* 'Monstrosum') illus. p.432.
M. latifolium illus. p.413.
M. lingulatum. See *M. aucheri*.
M. macrocarpum illus. p.434.
M. neglectum, syn. *M. racemosum*, illus. p.433.
M. paradoxum of gardens. See *Bellevalia pycnantha*.
M. pycnantha. See *Bellevalia pycnantha*.
M. racemosum. See *M. neglectum*.

Musk. See *Mimulus moschatus*.
 Monkey. See *Mimulus*.
 Yellow. See *Mimulus luteus*, illus. p.292.
Musk willow. See *Salix aegyptiaca*.

MUSSAENDA

RUBIACEAE

Genus of evergreen shrubs and scrambling climbers, grown for their flowers. Tender, min. 16–18°C (61–4°F). Requires a position in full light and fertile, well-drained soil. Water freely when in full growth, less at other times. Provide support and thin out crowded stems in spring. Propagate

by seed in spring or by air-layering in summer. Whitefly and spider mite may cause problems.
M. erythrophylla. Moderately vigorous, evergreen, scrambling climber. H 6–10m (20–30ft). Has broadly oval, bright green leaves and flowers in summer-autumn. Each flower has one greatly enlarged, oval, bract-like, red sepal, a red tube and yellow petal lobes.

MUTISIA

ASTERACEAE/COMPOSITAE

Genus of evergreen, tendril climbers, grown for their long-lasting flower heads. Plant with roots in shade and leafy parts in sun, in well-drained soil. Propagate by seed in spring, by stem cuttings in summer or by layering in autumn.
M. decurrens illus. p.217.
M. oligodon. Evergreen, tendril climber. H to 1.5m (5ft). Oblong, glossy, green leaves with sharply toothed margins are 2.5–3.5cm (1–1½in) long. In summer-autumn produces long-stalked, daisy-like, pink flower heads with yellow centres. Grow against a low wall or through a shrub. Zone 9?.

MYOPORUM

MYOPORACEAE

Genus of evergreen shrubs and trees, grown for their overall appearance and as hedges and windbreaks. Tender, min. 2–5°C (36–41°F). Prefers full light and well-drained soil; will tolerate poor soil. Water potted specimens moderately. Propagate by seed when ripe or in spring or by semi-ripe cuttings in late summer.
M. laetum. Evergreen, rounded to upright shrub or tree. H 3–10m (10–30ft), S 2–5m (6–15ft). Has fleshy, oval, lustrous, bright green leaves and axillary clusters of small, bell-shaped, white flowers, dotted with purple, in spring-summer, then tiny, narrowly oblong, pale to deep red-purple fruits.
M. parvifolium illus. p.162.

MYOSOTIDIUM
Chatham Island forget-me-not

BORAGINACEAE

Genus of one species of evergreen perennial that is suitable for mild, coastal areas. Prefers semi-shade and moist soil. Seaweed is often recommended as a mulch. Is not easy to cultivate, and once established should not be disturbed. Propagate by division in spring or by seed when ripe, in summer or autumn.
M. hortensia, syn. *M. nobile*, illus. p.287. Bears oval to heart-shaped, glossy leaves. H and S 60cm (24in). In early summer produces bell-shaped, pale to dark blue flowers, sometimes with white-margined lobes.
M. nobile. See *M. hortensia*.

MYOSOTIS
Forget-me-not

BORAGINACEAE

Genus of annuals, biennials and perennials, grown for their flowers.

Most species are good for rock gardens and screes; *M. scorpioides* is best grown as a marginal water plant. Most prefer sun or semi-shade and fertile, well-drained soil. Propagate by seed in autumn.

M. alpestris, syn. *M. rupicola*, illus. p.370.

M. australis. Short-lived, tuft-forming perennial. H 12cm (5in), S 8cm (3in). Has oval, rough-textured leaves and, in summer, tight sprays of open funnel-shaped, yellow or white flowers. Is good for a scree.

M. caespitosa. See *M. laxa* subsp. *caespitosa.*

M. laxa subsp. *caespitosa*, syn. *M. caespitosa.* Clump-forming annual or short-lived perennial. H 12cm (5in), S 15cm (6in). Lance-shaped, leathery leaves are dark green. Bears rounded, bright blue flowers in summer.

M. palustris. See *M. scorpioides.*

M. rupicola. See *M. alpestris.*

M. scorpioides, syn. *M. palustris* (Water forget-me-not). 'Mermaid' illus. p.448.

M. sylvatica 'Blue Ball' illus. p.334. 'White Ball' is a slow-growing, short-lived, bushy, compact perennial, grown as a biennial. H to 20cm (8in), S 15cm (6in). Leaves are lance-shaped. Sprays of tiny, 5-lobed, pure white flowers are produced in early summer.

Myrceugenia apiculata. See *Luma apiculata.*

MYRIOPHYLLUM

HALORAGIDACEAE

Genus of deciduous, perennial, submerged water plants, grown for their foliage. Most species are ideal as depositories for fish spawn. Hardy to tender, min. 5°C (41°F). Requires full sun. Spreads widely: keep in check by removing excess growth as required. Propagate by stem cuttings in spring or summer.

M. aquaticum, syn. *M. proserpinacoides*, illus. p.448.

M. hippuroides. Deciduous, perennial, spreading, submerged water plant with thin stems. S indefinite. Produces a dense mass of small, feathery, pale green leaves. Inconspicuous, greenish-cream flowers are borne from the axils of the emergent leaves in summer. Is suitable for a cold-water aquarium.

M. proserpinacoides. See *M. aquaticum.*

M. verticillatum illus. p.449.

Myrobalan. See *Prunus cerasifera.*

MYRRHIS

Sweet Cicely

APIACEAE/UMBELLIFERAE

Genus of one species of summer-flowering perennial. Requires a position in sun or shade and in well-drained soil. Propagate by seed in autumn or spring.

M. odorata illus. p.240.

MYRSINE

MYRSINACEAE

Genus of evergreen shrubs and trees, with inconspicuous flowers, grown mainly for their foliage. Also bears decorative fruits, to obtain which plants of both sexes must be grown. Is suitable for rock and peat gardens. Marginally hardy and needs a very protected location. Requires a position in sun or shade and in any fertile, well-drained soil other than a shallow, alkaline one. Propagate by semi-ripe cuttings in summer.

M. africana (Cape myrtle). Very slow-growing, evergreen, bushy, dense shrub. H and S 75cm (30in). Small, glossy, dark green leaves are aromatic and rounded. Tiny, yellowish-brown flowers in late spring are succeeded by spherical, pale blue fruits. Zone 9?.

MYRTILLOCACTUS

CACTACEAE

Genus of branching, perennial cacti with ribbed, spiny, blue-green stems. Bears star-shaped flowers that open at night. Tender, min. 11–12°C (52–4°F). Needs a sunny, well-drained site. Propagate by seed or stem cuttings in spring or summer.

M. geometrizans illus. p.456.

Myrtle. See *Myrtus.*
   Bracelet honey. See *Melaleuca armillaris.*
   Cape. See *Myrsine africana.*

Myrtle (continued)
   Common. See *Myrtus communis*, illus. p.130.
   Crape. See *Lagerstroemia indica*, illus. p.91.
   Flag. See *Acorus calamus.*
   Queen's crape. See *Lagerstroemia speciosa.*
   Willow. See *Agonis.*

MYRTUS

Myrtle

MYRTACEAE

Genus of evergreen shrubs, sometimes tree-like, grown for their flowers, fruits and aromatic foliage. At limits of hardiness, plant against a south- or west-facing wall. Requires full sun and fertile, well-drained soil. May be pruned in spring. Propagate by semi-ripe cuttings in late summer.

M. apiculata. See *Luma apiculata.*

M. bullata. See *Lophomyrtus bullata.*

M. chequen. See *Luma chequen.*

M. communis (Common myrtle) illus. p.130. subsp. *tarentina* is an evergreen, bushy shrub. H and S 2m (6ft). Bears small leaves that are narrowly oval, glossy and dark green. Produces fragrant, saucer-shaped, white flowers, each with a dense cluster of stamens, from mid-spring to early summer, followed by spherical, white fruits. Is very wind-resistant and good for hedging in mild areas. Zone 9.

M. luma. See *Luma apiculata.*

'Glanleam Gold' see *Luma apiculata* 'Glanleam Gold'.

M. ugni. See *Ugni molinae.*

N

Naked coral tree. See *Erythrina americana*.

NANDINA

BERBERIDACEAE

Genus of one species of evergreen or semi-evergreen, summer-flowering shrub, grown for its foliage and flowers. Prefers a sheltered, sunny site and fertile, well-drained but not too dry soil. On established plants prune untidy, old stems to base in spring. Propagate by semi-ripe cuttings in summer.

N. domestica (Heavenly bamboo, Sacred bamboo). Evergreen or semi-evergreen, upright, elegant shrub. H and S 2m (6ft). Leaves have narrowly lance-shaped, dark green leaflets, purplish-red when young and in autumn-winter. Large panicles of small, star-shaped, white flowers, with large yellow anthers, in mid-summer are followed in warm climates by spherical, red fruits. Zone 7.
'**Firepower**' illus. p.151.

Nankeen lily. See *Lilium* x *testaceum*.
Nannyberry. See *Viburnum lentago*.

NARCISSUS
Daffodil

AMARYLLIDACEAE

Genus of bulbs, grown for their ornamental flowers. Daffodils have usually linear, basal leaves and a spread of up to 20cm (8in). Each flower has a trumpet or cup (the corona) and petals (botanically known as perianth segments). Hardy, except where otherwise stated. Prefer sun or light shade and well-drained soil, but Div.8 cultivars (see below) prefer a sunny site and tolerate lighter soils. Dead-head flowers and remove faded foliage during mid-summer. Most cultivars increase naturally by offsets; dense clumps should be divided no sooner than 6 weeks after flowering every 3–5 years. Species may be propagated by fresh seed in late summer or autumn. Narcissus yellow stripe virus, basal rot, slugs, large narcissus fly and bulb and stem eelworm may cause problems. Contact with the sap of daffodils may irritate skin or aggravate skin allergies.

Horticulturally, *Narcissus* is split into the following divisions. See also feature panel pp.416–18:

Div.1 Trumpet – usually solitary flowers each have a trumpet that is as long as, or longer than, the petals. Early to late spring-flowering.
Div.2 Large-cupped – solitary flowers each have a cup at least one-third the length of, but shorter than, the petals. Spring-flowering.
Div.3 Small-cupped – flowers are often borne singly; each has a cup not

more than one-third the length of the petals. Spring- or early summer-flowering.
Div.4 Double – most have solitary, large, fully or semi-double flowers, sometimes scented, with both cup and petals or cup alone replaced by petaloid structures. Some have smaller flowers, produced in clusters of 4 or more, which are often sweetly fragrant. Spring- or early summer-flowering.
Div.5 Triandrus – nodding flowers, with short, sometimes straight-sided cups and narrow, reflexed petals, are borne 2–6 per stem. Spring-flowering.
Div.6 Cyclamineus – flowers are borne usually 1 or 2 per stem, each with a cup sometimes flanged and often longer than those of Div.5. Petals are narrow, pointed and reflexed. Early to mid-spring-flowering.
Div.7 Jonquil – sweetly scented flowers are borne usually 2 or more per stem. Cup is short, sometimes flanged; petals are often flat, fairly broad and rounded. Spring-flowering.
Div.8 Tazetta – sweetly fragrant flowers of small-flowered cultivars are borne in clusters of 12 or more per stem; large-flowered cultivars have 3 or 4 flowers per stem. All have a small, often straight-sided cup and broad, mostly pointed petals. Late autumn- to mid-spring-flowering. Most are hardy. Autumn-flowering hybrids provide valuable cut flowers; 'prepared' bulbs may be grown in pots for mid-winter flowering.
Div.9 Poeticus – flowers, sometimes borne 2 per stem, may be sweetly fragrant. Each has a small, coloured cup and glistening white petals. Some *N. poeticus* hybrids are categorized as Div.3 or 8. Late spring- or early summer-flowering.
Div.10 Bulbocodium – flowers usually borne singly on very short stems, showing all the hallmarks of hoop-petticoat daffodils (*N. bulbocodium* subsp. *bulbocodium*), with insignificant petals and a disproportionately large, widely flaring cup. Winter- to spring-flowering.
Div.11 Split-cupped – usually solitary flowers that have cups split for more than half their length. In (a), Collar daffodils, the overlapping segments of the cup lie against the petals, but in (b), Papillon daffodils, the segments of the cup tend to be narrower, with their tips arranged at the margin of the petals. Most flowers fall into category (a). Spring-flowering.
Div.12 Miscellaneous – a miscellaneous category containing hybrids with varying, intermediate flower shapes that cannot be satisfactorily classified elsewhere. Autumn- to spring-flowering.
Div.13 Daffodils distinguished solely by botanical name – a wide variety of flowers showing the huge range of floral characteristics of wild daffodils: from the tiny *N. cyclamineus* and the

sweetly scented, many-flowered *N. tazetta* to the stately trumpet species. Flower in early autumn to early summer.

N. '**Acropolis**' (illus. p.417), Div.4. Mid- to late spring-flowering bulb. H 42cm (17in). Large, double flowers have white, outer petals and petaloids; white, inner petals are interspersed with shorter, orange-red petaloids. Is suitable for exhibition.
N. '**Actaea**' (illus. p.417), Div.9. Late spring-flowering bulb. H 40cm (16in). Fragrant flowers have glistening white petals and shallow, flanged, rich lemon cups with narrow, orange-red rims.
N. '**Aircastle**' (illus. p.416), Div.3. Mid-spring-flowering bulb. H 40cm (16in). Flowers have white petals that age greenish; shallow, flat, lemon-yellow cups deepen in colour at the rim.
N. '**Albus Plenus Odoratus**'. See *N. poeticus* 'Plenus'.
N. '**Altruist**' (illus. p.418), Div.3. Mid-spring-flowering bulb. H 45cm (18in). Flowers have smooth, pale orange petals and a neat, ribbed, shallow, orange-red cup.
N. '**Ambergate**' (illus. p.418), Div.2. Mid-spring-flowering bulb. H 45cm (18in). Flowers each have a shallow, widely expanded, fiery scarlet cup and soft tangerine petals.
N. '**Arctic Gold**', Div.1. Mid-spring-flowering bulb. H 40cm (16in). Rich golden-yellow flowers have broad petals and well-proportioned, flanged trumpets with neatly serrated rims. Is suitable for exhibition.
N. assoanus, syn. *N. juncifolius*, *N. requienii*, Div.13. Mid-spring-flowering bulb. H 15cm (6in). Is similar to *N. jonquilla*, but has thin, cylindrical leaves and rounded, bright clear yellow flowers with a sweet, slightly lemony fragrance. Thrives in sunny, gritty soil.
N. asturiensis, syn. *N. minimus*, Div.13. Late winter- or early spring-flowering bulb. H 8cm (3in). Small, pale yellow flowers have waisted trumpets and slender petals. Prefers full sun.
N. '**Avalanche**' (illus. p.417), Div.8. Early spring-flowering bulb. H 35cm (14in). Not as hardy. Produces 8 or more sweetly fragrant flowers, each with white petals and a primrose-yellow cup that scarcely fades. May be forced for mid-winter flowering.
N. '**Bartley**' (illus. p.418), Div.6. Early spring-flowering bulb. H 35cm (14in). Long, slender, golden flowers have reflexed petals and narrow, angled trumpets. Flowers are long-lasting.
N. '**Belcanto**' (illus. p.417), Div.11a. Late spring-flowering bulb. H 45cm (18in). Flowers, 8–12cm (3–5in) across, have rounded perianth segments, almost obscured by the flattened, pale yellow cups.
N. x *biflorus*. See *N.* x *medioluteus*.
N. '**Binkie**' (illus. p.417), Div.2. Early spring-flowering bulb. H 30cm (12in). Flowers open clear pale lemon and

cups turn sulphur-white with ruffled, lemon rims.
N. '**Birma**', Div.3. Mid-spring-flowering bulb. H 45cm (18in). Flowers have soft yellow petals and fiery orange cups with heavily ruffled rims.
N. '**Bravoure**' (illus. p.417), Div.1. Early to mid-spring-flowering bulb. H 38cm (15in). Large flowers have overlapping, white petals and unusually slender, only slightly flared, lemon-yellow trumpets, with entire rims.
N. '**Bridal Crown**' (illus. p.417), Div.4. Late spring-flowering bulb. H 40cm (16in). Long-lasting, small, sweetly scented flowers are semi-double, with rounded, milk-white petals and white petaloids interspersed with shorter, saffron-orange ones towards centre.
N. '**Broadway Star**' (illus. p.417), Div.11b. Mid-spring-flowering bulb. H 40cm (16in). Has white flowers, 8cm (3in) across. The expanded segments of the split cups are flattened against the perianth segments; each has a narrow, orange mid-stripe running lengthways.
N. '**Brunswick**', Div.2. Early spring-flowering bulb. H 40cm (16in). Long-lasting flowers have white petals and long, flared, primrose cups, which fade to lemon, with darker rims. Foliage is a striking bluish-green. Is suitable for cutting.
N. bulbocodium subsp. *bulbocodium* (Hoop-petticoat daffodil), Div.13. Vigorous, spring-flowering bulb. H 8–15cm (3–6in). Flowers are golden-yellow with conical cups and narrow, pointed petals. Thrives in moist turf in full sun. var. *citrinus*, H 15cm (6in), has slender, dark green leaves and clear pale lemon flowers. Hybrids of this species are placed in Div.10.
N. campernelli. See *N.* x *odorus*.
N. '**Canaliculatus**' (illus. p.417), Div.8. Mid-spring-flowering bulb. H 23cm (9in). Produces a cluster of 4 or more small, fragrant flowers per stem, each with reflexed, white petals and a shallow, straight-sided, dark yellow cup.
N. '**Canisp**' (illus. p.416), Div.2. Mid-spring-flowering bulb. H 40cm (16in). A robust garden and exhibition daffodil with large, milk-white flowers, with broad, overlapping petals, lightly reflexed at the apex, and a slightly darker, flanged, trumpet-like cup, with a rolled, crenate mouth.
N. '**Cantabile**' (illus. p.417), Div.9. Late spring-flowering bulb. H 25cm (10in). Stiff stems bear neat, well-rounded, glistening white flowers, with tiny, red-rimmed, yellow cups with a prominent green eye.
N. cantabricus (illus. p.416), Div.13. Spring- and sometimes winter-flowering bulb. H 10cm (4in). Is similar in form to *N. bulbocodium* subsp. *bulbocodium*, but is less robust. Flowers are milk- or ice-white. Thrives in an alpine house or greenhouse.

N. **'Cantatrice'**, Div.1. Mid-spring-flowering bulb. H 40cm (16in). Flowers have pure white petals and slender, milk-white trumpets.

N. **'Capax Plenus'.** See *N.* 'Eystettensis'.

N. **'Cassata'** (illus. p.417), Div.11a. Mid-spring-flowering bulb. H 40cm (16in). Cups are soft primrose and distinctly split into segments with ruffled margins, while petals are broad and milk-white.

N. **'Charity May'** (illus. p.418), Div.6. Early to mid-spring-flowering bulb. H 30cm (12in). Small, pale lemon flowers each have broad, reflexed petals and slightly darker cups.

N. **'Cheerfulness'** (illus. p.416), Div.4. Mid-spring-flowering bulb. H 40cm (16in). Long-lasting, small, sweetly scented, fully double flowers, 5.5cm (2¼in) across, are borne several to a stem, with milk-white petals and petaloids interspersed with shorter, orange-yellow ones at the centre. Is excellent for cutting.

N. cyclamineus (illus. p.418), Div.13. Late winter- to early spring-flowering bulb. H 15cm (6in). Slender, nodding, clear gold flowers have narrow, reflexed petals and long, slender, flanged, waisted trumpets.

N. **'Dove Wings'** (illus. p.417), Div.6. Mid-spring-flowering bulb. H 30cm (12in). Has small flowers with milk-white petals and fairly long, soft primrose cups.

N. **'Empress of Ireland'** (illus. p.417), Div.1. Mid-spring-flowering bulb. H 40cm (16in). Large, robust, milk-white flowers have broad, overlapping petals, reflexed at the apex, and a slightly darker, flanged trumpet with a rolled, crenate mouth.

N. **'Eystettensis'**, syn. *N.* 'Capax Plenus' (Queen Anne's double daffodil), Div.4. Mid-spring-flowering bulb. H 20cm (8in). Dainty, double flowers are composed of pointed, soft pale primrose petaloids neatly arranged in whorls.

N. **'February Gold'** (illus. p.418), Div.6. Early spring-flowering bulb. H 32cm (13in). Solitary, long-lasting flowers have clear golden petals and long, flanged, slightly darker trumpets. Is useful for borders and naturalizing.

N. **'February Silver'** (illus. p.417), Div.6. Robust, early spring-flowering bulb. H 32cm (13in). Has long-lasting flowers with milk-white petals and long, sturdy, nodding trumpets that open rich lemon and age to creamy-yellow.

N. **'Fortune'** (illus. p.418), Div.2. Early to mid-spring-flowering bulb. H 40cm (16in). Flowers have ribbed, dark lemon petals and bold, flared, copper-orange cups; they are good for cutting.

N. **'Foxfire'**, Div.2. Mid-spring-flowering bulb. H 35cm (14in). Has very rounded flowers with conspicuously white petals. Small, greenish-cream cups each have a small, green eye zone and a coral-orange rim.

N. **'Golden Ducat'** (illus. p.418), Div.4. Mid-spring-flowering bulb. H 38cm (15in). Produces variable, sometimes poorly formed, double, rich golden flowers. Is suitable for cutting.

N. **'Grand Primo Citronière'**, Div.8. Late autumn- to early spring-flowering bulb. H 32cm (13in). Tender. Bears 8 or more fragrant flowers, each with milk-white petals and a clear lemon cup, which fades to cream. 'Treated' bulbs may be forced for mid-winter flowering. Is good for cutting.

N. **'Grand Soleil d'Or'** (illus. p.418), Div.8. Late autumn- to early spring-flowering bulb. H 35cm (14in). Tender. Flowers are sweetly scented with a dash of lemon. Each has rich golden petals and a clear tangerine cup. May be forced for mid-winter flowering, but staking is needed. Is excellent for cutting.

N. **'Hawera'** (illus. p.418), Div.5. Mid-spring-flowering bulb. H 20cm (8in). Nodding flowers are a delicate lemon-yellow. Requires a sunny position. Makes a good pot plant.

N. **'Home Fires'** (illus. p.418), Div.2. Early spring-flowering bulb. H 45cm (18in). Flowers each have pointed, rich lemon petals and an orange-scarlet cup with a lobed and frilled rim.

N. **'Honeybird'** (illus. p.417), Div.1. Mid-spring-flowering bulb. H 50cm (20in). Well-proportioned flowers, 10.5cm (4⅛in) across, open greenish-yellow. The trumpets gradually fade almost to pure white.

N. **'Ice Follies'** (illus. p.416), Div.2. Early spring-flowering bulb. H 40cm (16in). Flowers have milk-white petals and very wide, almost flat, primrose-yellow cups, fading to cream.

N. **'Irene Copeland'** (illus. p.416), Div.4. Mid-spring-flowering bulb. H 35cm (14in). Bears large, fully double flowers of neatly arranged, milk-white petaloids interspersed with shorter, pale creamy-yellow ones. Is excellent for cutting.

N. **'Jack Snipe'** (illus. p.417), Div.6. Sturdy, early to mid-spring-flowering bulb. H 23cm (9in). Long-lasting, milk-white flowers are similar to those of *N.* 'Dove Wings', but have narrower petals with incurved margins and medium-length cups of rich dark lemon-yellow.

N. **'Jenny'**, Div.6. Early to mid-spring-flowering bulb. H 30cm (12in). Bears long-lasting flowers, each with milk-white petals and a medium-length, flanged, soft lemon trumpet that turns creamy-white.

N. **'Jetfire'** (illus. p.418), Div.6. Floriferous, early spring-flowering bulb. H 23cm (9in). Flowers have overlapping, reflexed, clear golden-yellow petals and a cylindrical, ribbed, vibrant orange cup, slightly waisted before the crenate rim.

N. jonquilla (Wild jonquil; illus. p.418), Div.13. Mid-spring-flowering bulb. H 30cm (12in). Richly fragrant flowers are borne in a cluster of 6 or more; each has tapering, yellow petals and a shallow, dark gold cup. Distinctive foliage is semi-cylindrical, dark, shining and grooved. **'Flore Pleno'** (Queen Anne's jonquil) has loosely double flowers; broad, incurved, yellow petals are interspersed with short, darker ones.

N. **'Jumblie'** (illus. p.418), Div.12. Early spring-flowering bulb. H 20cm (8in). Bears 2 or 3 long-lasting flowers,

each with broad, golden petals and a sturdy, flanged, orange-yellow cup. Is ideal as a pot plant.

N. juncifolius. See *N. assoanus.*

N. **'Kilworth'** (illus. p.417), Div.2. Vigorous, late spring-flowering bulb. H 38cm (15in). Flowers have pointed, milk-white petals and dark reddish-orange cups with green eyes. Is effective in large groups.

N. **'Kingscourt'** (illus. p.418), Div.1. Sturdy, mid-spring-flowering bulb. H 42cm (17in). Flowers have flanged, flared, rich gold trumpets with broad, rounded, paler gold petals.

N. **'Liberty Bells'** (illus. p.418), Div.5. Sturdy, mid-spring-flowering bulb. H 32cm (13in). Flowers are slightly fragrant and clear lemon.

N. × *medioluteus*, syn. *N.* × *biflorus* (Primrose peerless) (illus. p.416), Div.13. Mid- to late-spring-flowering bulb. H 40cm (16in). Produces neat, medium-sized, sweetly scented flowers of rounded outline, with overlapping, almost pure white petals and a small, shallow, solid primrose-yellow, bowl-shaped cup. Is usually twin-headed.

N. **'Merlin'** (illus. p.417), Div.3. Mid-spring-flowering bulb. H 35cm (14in). Flowers have broad, rounded, glistening white petals and relatively large, almost flat, rich gold cups, each with a small, green eye and a broad, lightly ruffled, orange-red rim. Is excellent for exhibition.

N. minimus. See *N. asturiensis.*

N. **'Minnow'** (illus. p.417), Div.8. Robust, early to mid-spring-flowering bulb. H 18cm (7in). Has a cluster of 4 or more fragrant flowers per stem, each with rounded, creamy-yellow petals and a lemon cup. Increases freely. Is suitable for a container or rock garden.

N. minor, syn. *N. nanus* of gardens (illus. p.418), Div.13. Early spring-flowering bulb. H 20cm (8in). Flowers have slightly overlapping, soft yellow petals and almost straight, darker yellow trumpets with frilled rims. subsp. *pumilus* see *N. pumilus.*

N. minor of gardens. See *N. pumilus.*

N. nanus, Div.13. Early spring-flowering bulb. H 12cm (5in). Flowers each have twisted, cream petals and a stout, straight, dull yellow trumpet with a frilled rim. Leaves are broad. Is suitable for naturalizing.

N. nanus of gardens. See *N. minor.*

N. obvallaris, syn. *N. pseudonarcissus* subsp. *obvallaris* (Tenby daffodil), Div.13. Sturdy, early spring-flowering bulb. H 30cm (12in). Gold flowers have short petals and broad trumpets, borne on stiff stems.

N. × *odorus*, syn. *N. campernelli* (Campernelle jonquil), Div.13. Robust, mid-spring-flowering bulb. H 20–30cm (8–12in). Has usually 2 richly fragrant, dark gold flowers. **'Rugulosus'** (illus. p.418), Div.7, H 28cm (11in), is more vigorous and produces up to 4 small-cupped, rich gold flowers.

N. **'Paper White Grandiflorus'**, syn. *N. papyraceus* 'Grandiflorus', *N.* 'Paper White Snowflake', Div.8. Winter- to mid-spring-flowering bulb. H 35cm (14in). Tender. Produces 10 or more long-lived, heavily fragrant, star-shaped, glistening white flowers, each with long, spreading petals and a small,

flanged cup containing conspicuous, saffron-yellow stamens. Produces flowers continuously through winter indoors.

N. **'Paper White Snowflake'.** See *N.* 'Paper White Grandiflorus'.

N. papyraceus **'Grandiflorus'.** See *N.* 'Paper White Grandiflorus'.

N. **'Passionale'** (illus. p.417), Div.2. Mid-spring-flowering bulb. H 40cm (16in). Each flower has milk-white petals and a long, flanged, apricot-tinged, pink cup.

N. **'Pencrebar'** (illus. p.418), Div.4. Mid-spring-flowering bulb. H 18cm (7in). Fragrant flowers are small, rounded and fully double, often in pairs. Outer petaloids and large, inner ones are pale gold and are evenly interspersed with darker ones.

N. **'Pipit'** (illus. p.418), Div.7. Mid-spring-flowering bulb. H 25cm (10in). Bears up to 3 scented flowers per stem, slightly greenish sulphur-yellow on opening. The ruffled, flared cup and the base of the overlapping petals become almost white at maturity.

N. poeticus (Poet's daffodil, Poet's narcissus), Div.13. Variable, late spring-flowering bulb. H 22–42cm (9–17in). Each fragrant flower comprises glistening white petals and a small, shallow, yellow or orange cup with a red rim. Is ideal for naturalizing in moist turf although slow to establish.
'Flore Pleno' see *N.p.* 'Plenus'.
'Plenus' (syn. *N.* 'Albus Plenus Odoratus', *N.p.* 'Flore Pleno'), H 40cm (16in), has loosely double, pure white flowers, with inconspicuous, greenish-yellow or orange centres, in late spring or early summer. Is good for cutting.
var. *recurvus* (Pheasant's eye; illus. p.417), H 42cm (17in), bears larger, long-lasting flowers with strongly swept-back petals and very shallow, greenish-yellow cups, with crimson rims, in early summer.

N. **'Portrush'** (illus. p.416), Div.3. Late spring- to early summer-flowering bulb. H 35cm (14in). Produces small flowers, each with green-tinged, glistening milk-white petals and a small, shallow, flanged, creamy-white cup with a bright green eye.

N. **'Pride of Cornwall'** (illus. p.417), Div.8. Mid-spring-flowering bulb. H 38cm (15in). Bears several large, fragrant flowers, each with milk-white petals and a rich yellow cup shading to an orange-red rim outside. Is excellent for cutting. *N.* 'Martha Washington' and *N.* 'Geranium' are similar.

N. pseudonarcissus (Lent lily, Wild daffodil; illus. p.418), Div.13. Extremely variable, early spring-flowering bulb. H 15–30cm (6–12in). Nodding flowers have overlapping, straw-yellow petals and large, darker yellow trumpets. Is ideal for naturalizing. subsp. *obvallaris* see *N. obvallaris.*

N. pumilus, syn. *N. minor* of gardens, *N. minor* subsp. *pumilus*, Div.13. Early spring-flowering bulb. H 15–22cm (6–9in). Bears bright gold flowers with separated, slightly paler petals and large trumpets with lobed and frilled rims. **'Plenus'** see *N.* 'Rip van Winkle'.

N. **'Rainbow'** (illus. p.417), Div.2. Vigorous, mid-spring-flowering bulb.

H 45cm (18in). White flowers have cups that are broadly banded with coppery-pink at the rim.

N. requienii. See *N. assoanus.*

N. **'Rip van Winkle'**, syn. *N. pumilus* 'Plenus' (illus. p.418), Div.4. Early spring-flowering bulb. H 15cm (6in). Shaggy, double flowers have densely arranged, flat, tapering, greenish-lemon petals with incurving tips.

N. **'Rockall'** (illus. p.417), Div.3. Mid-spring-flowering bulb. H 50cm (20in). Produces neat flowers with overlapping, white petals and a shallow, ribbed, intense orange-red, bowl-shaped cup.

N. romieuxii (illus. p.417), Div.13. Early spring-flowering bulb. H 10cm (4in). Marginally hardy, but is best grown in a frame or an alpine house. Is similar to *N. bulbocodium* subsp. *bulbocodium*, but each fragrant flower has a large, almost flat, flanged cup of glistening pale primrose.

N. rupicola (illus. p.418), Div.13. Mid-spring-flowering bulb. H 8cm (3in). Is similar to *N. assoanus*, but has more angled, bluish-green foliage and solitary, less scented, lemon flowers, each with a 6-lobed cup. subsp. **watieri** (illus. p.416), H 10cm (4in), produces relatively large, fragrant, crystalline-textured, white flowers with shallow, lobed cups.

N. **'Saint Keverne'** (illus. p.418), Div.11b. Sturdy, early to mid-spring-flowering bulb. H 42cm (17in). Solitary flowers have clear rich golden petals and slightly darker cups of almost trumpet proportions.

N. **'Satin Pink'** (illus. p.417), Div.2. Mid-spring-flowering bulb. H 42cm (17in). Each flower has broad, ribbed, milk-white petals and a long, barely flared, flanged, soft buff-pink cup of almost trumpet proportions.

N. **'Scarlet Gem'** (illus. p.418), Div.8. Mid-spring-flowering bulb. H 35cm (14in). Produces 7–8 scented flowers with golden petals and scarlet or deep orange-red cups.

N. **'Shining Light'** (illus. p.418), Div.2. Mid-spring-flowering bulb. H 42cm (17in). Refined, well-balanced flowers have smooth, overlapping, clear, pale golden-yellow petals, and the slightly ribbed, cup-shaped cup is rich orange-red. The lightly dentate rim is slightly darker. Is good for exhibition.

N. **'Silver Chimes'** (illus. p.417), Div.8. Sturdy, mid- to late spring-flowering bulb. H 32cm (13in). Has up to 10 fragrant flowers, each with broad, milk-white petals and a straight, shallow, creamy-primrose cup. Foliage is dark green. Thrives in a warm site.

N. **'Spellbinder'** (illus. p.417), Div.1. Early spring-flowering bulb. H 42cm (17in). Long-lasting, bright sulphur-yellow flowers each have a slender, flanged trumpet, reversing to palest sulphur-white inside, except for the lobed, rolled-back rim, which is tinged with lemon.

N. **'Stratosphere'** (illus. p.418), Div.7. Mid-spring-flowering bulb. H 40cm (16in). Bears usually 3 fragrant flowers, each with rich golden petals and a darker gold cup. Is excellent for exhibition.

N. **'Suzy'** (illus. p.418), Div.7. Robust, mid-spring-flowering bulb. H 38cm (15in). Produces 3 or 4 long-lasting, large, fragrant flowers, each with clear golden petals and a large, flanged, rich tangerine cup.

N. **'Sweetness'** (illus. p.418), Div.7. Early spring-flowering bulb. H 38cm (15in). Sweetly fragrant flowers, occasionally borne in pairs, have intense, golden-yellow petals and a darker, waved cup of strong substance.

N. **'Tahiti'** (illus. p.418), Div.4. Robust, mid-spring-flowering bulb. H 38cm (15in). Solitary, loosely double flowers have golden petals and petaloids, interspersed with short, fiery orange, inner petaloids.

N. tazetta (Bunch-flowered daffodil, Polyanthus daffodil), Div.13. Extremely variable, late autumn- to mid-spring-flowering bulb. H 30–40cm (12–16in). Bears usually 12 or more fragrant flowers, generally with slender, white or yellow petals and shallow, white or yellow cups.

N. **'Tête-à-Tête'** (illus. p.418), Div.12. Early spring-flowering bulb. H 15–30cm (6–12in). Produces long-lasting flowers, each with reflexed, rich golden petals and a square, flanged, warm yellowish-orange cup. Should be twin-flowered. Is very susceptible to viruses.

N. **'Thalia'** (illus. p.416), Div.5. Vigorous, mid-spring-flowering bulb. H 38cm (15in). Has 3 or more long-lived, charming, milk-white flowers per stem, each with irregularly formed, often propeller-shaped petals and a flanged, bold cup.

N. **'Tresamble'**, Div.5. Sturdy, early spring-flowering bulb. H 40cm (16in). Bears up to 6 flowers per stem, each with milk-white petals and a flanged, creamy-white cup that is paler at the rim.

N. **'Trevithian'**, Div.7. Vigorous, early to mid-spring-flowering bulb. H 45cm (18in). Produces 2 or 3 large, fragrant flowers, rounded and soft primrose, each with broad petals and a short cup.

N. triandrus (Angel's tears; illus. p.417), Div.13. Early spring-flowering bulb. H 12cm (5in). Bears nodding, milk-white flowers, each with narrow, reflexed petals and a fairly long, straight-sided cup. Makes a good container plant.

N. **'Trousseau'** (illus. p.416), Div.1. Early spring-flowering bulb. H 42cm (17in). Flowers each have milk-white petals and a straight, flanged, soft lemon trumpet, with a flared, lobed rim turning rich creamy-buff tinged with pale pink.

N. **'Tudor Minstrel'**, Div.2. Mid-spring-flowering bulb. H 42cm (17in). Produces flowers with white, pointed petals. Chrome-yellow cups are slender and flanged.

N. **'Waterperry'**, Div.7. Mid-spring-flowering bulb. H 25cm (10in). Flowers have dull creamy-white petals; lightly flanged, spreading, primrose cups turn rich buff-yellow, shading to pinkish-apricot rims.

N. **'White Lady'** (illus. p.416), Div.3. Vigorous, mid- to late-spring-flowering bulb. H 45cm (18in). Large, scented flowers have spreading, slightly overlapping, pure white petals. The small, shallow, heavily frilled cup is strong primrose-yellow on opening, becoming more creamy-yellow with maturity.

N. **'Woodland Star'** (illus. p.417), Div.3. Mid-spring-flowering bulb. H 50cm (20in). Large flowers have white petals and small, bowl-shaped, deep red cups.

N. **'W.P. Milner'**, Div.1. Early spring-flowering bulb. H 23cm (9in). Nodding flowers each have slender, twisted, light creamy-yellow petals and a flared, pale lemon trumpet, which fades to palest sulphur.

Narcissus, Poet's. See *Narcissus poeticus.*

Narihira bamboo. See *Semiarundinaria fastuosa*, illus. p.308.

Narrow buckler fern. See *Dryopteris carthusiana.*

Narrow-leaved ash. See *Fraxinus angustifolia.*

Nasturtium. See *Tropaeolum.*
   Flame. See *Tropaeolum speciosum*, illus. p.210.

Natal grass. See *Melinis repens.*

Natal ivy. See *Senecio macroglossus.*

Natal plum. See *Carissa macrocarpa.*

Native Australian frangipani. See *Hymenosporum flavum.*

NAUTILOCALYX

GESNERIACEAE

Genus of evergreen, erect, bushy perennials, grown for their flowers and foliage. Tender, min. 15°C (59°F). Requires high humidity, partial shade and well-drained soil; avoid waterlogging, especially in winter. Propagate by stem cuttings in summer or by seed, if available, in spring.

N. bullatus, syn. *N. tessellatus.* Evergreen, erect, bushy perennial. H and S 60cm (2ft). Narrowly oval, wrinkled leaves, to 23cm (9in) long, are dark green with a bronze sheen above, reddish-green beneath. Clusters of small, tubular, white-haired, pale yellow flowers are produced in the leaf axils mainly in summer.

N. lynchii illus. p.305.

N. tessellatus. See *N. bullatus.*

Navelwort, Venus's. See *Omphalodes linifolia*, illus. p.318

Neanthe bella. See *Chamaedorea elegans.*

NECTAROSCORDUM

ALLIACEAE/LILIACEAE

Genus of flowering bulbs, related to *Allium*, with long, linear, erect leaves. Exudes a very strong onion smell when bruised. Stems with erect, shuttlecock-like seed heads may be dried for winter decoration. Needs partial shade. Grow in rough grass or borders in any soil that is neither too dry nor waterlogged. Propagate by freely produced offsets in late summer or by seed in autumn.

N. dioscoridis. See *N. siculum* subsp. *bulgaricum.*

N. siculum subsp. *bulgaricum*, syn. *N. dioscoridis*, illus. p.398.

Needle spike-rush. See *Eleocharis acicularis.*

NEILLIA

ROSACEAE

Genus of deciduous shrubs, grown for their graceful habit and profuse clusters of small flowers. Requires sun or semi-shade and fertile, well-drained soil. Established plants benefit from having some older shoots cut to base after flowering. Propagate by softwood cuttings in summer or by suckers in autumn.

N. longiracemosa. See *N. thibetica.*

N. sinensis. Deciduous, arching shrub. H and S 2m (6ft). Has peeling brown bark and oval, sharply toothed, mid-green leaves. Bears nodding racemes of small, tubular, pinkish-white flowers in late spring and early summer. Zone 7.

N. thibetica, syn. *N. longiracemosa*, illus. p.140.

NELUMBO

NYMPHAEACEAE

Genus of deciduous, perennial, marginal water plants, grown for their foliage and flowers. Hardy to tender, min. 1–7°C (34–45°F). Needs an open, sunny position and 60cm (24in) depth of water. Remove fading foliage; flowers may be left to develop into decorative seed pods. Divide overgrown plants in spring. Propagate species by seed in spring, selected forms by division in spring.

N. lutea (American lotus). Vigorous, deciduous, perennial, marginal water plant. H and S 1m (3ft). Rounded, blue-green leaves, prominently veined beneath, develop on stout, 30–60cm (1–2ft) long stems. Large, chalice-shaped, yellow flowers open in summer.

N. nucifera illus. p.447. **'Alba Grandiflora'** is a vigorous, deciduous, perennial, marginal water plant. H 1.2–1.8m (4–6ft), S 1.2m (4ft). Min. 1°C (34°F). Has very large, rounded, wavy-margined, dark green leaves, on sturdy stems, with large, fragrant, chalice-shaped, white flowers, 22–25cm (9–10in) across, in summer. **'Alba Striata'** bears white flowers, 15cm (6in) across, with jagged red margins. **'Rosea Plena'** has double, soft pink flowers to 30cm (12in) across.

NEMATANTHUS

GESNERIACEAE

Genus of perennials and soft-stemmed, evergreen shrubs, grown for their flowers and foliage. Tender, min. 13–15°C (55–9°F). Requires partial shade and humus-rich, moist but well-drained soil. Water potted specimens moderately, allowing soil almost to dry out between applications. Tip prune young plants to stimulate branching. Propagate by softwood or greenwood cuttings in summer.

N. gregarius, syn. *Hypocyrta radicans*, *N. radicans*, illus. p.157.

N. radicans. See *N. gregarius.*

N. strigillosus, syn. *Hypocyrta strigillosa.* Evergreen, prostrate shrub.

H 15–30cm (6–12in), S 60cm–1m (2–3ft). Elliptic, slightly cupped leaves are clothed in dense down. Small, tubular, orange or orange-red flowers appear in leaf axils mainly from spring to autumn.

NEMESIA

SCROPHULARIACEAE

Genus of annuals, perennials and evergreen sub-shrubs, grown for summer bedding and as greenhouse plants. Prefers sun and fertile, well-drained soil. Cut back stems after flowering. Pinch out growing shoots of young plants to ensure a bushy habit. Propagate by seed sown under glass in early spring, or outdoors in late spring.
N. strumosa. Fast-growing, bushy annual. H 20–45cm (8–18in), S 15cm (6in). Has lance-shaped, serrated, pale green leaves and, in summer, trumpet-shaped, yellow, white or purple flowers, 2.5cm (1in) across, that are suitable for cutting. **Carnival Series** illus. p.328. **Triumph Series** illus. p.339.

NEMOPHILA

HYDROPHYLLACEAE

Genus of annuals, useful for rock gardens and for edging. Grow in sun or semi-shade and in fertile, well-drained soil. Propagate by seed sown outdoors in spring or early autumn. Is prone to aphids.
N. insignis. See *N. menziesii.*
N. maculata illus. p.319.
N. menziesii, syn. *N. insignis,* illus. p.333.

NEOBUXBAUMIA

CACTACEAE

Genus of columnar or tree-like perennial cacti with cylindrical stems and usually low-set ribs. Nocturnal flowers, produced in summer, are followed by angular fruits, which open like stars when ripe. Tender, min. 15°C (59°F). Requires sun and poor to moderately fertile, sharply drained, gritty soil. Propagate by seed in spring.
N. euphorbioides, syn. *Lemaireocereus euphorbioides, Rooksbya euphorbioides,* illus. p.459.

Neochilenia mitis of gardens. See *Neoporteria napina.*

NEOLITSEA

LAURACEAE

Genus of evergreen trees and shrubs, grown for their foliage. Marginally hardy, it needs shelter from strong winds; does best against a south- or west-facing wall. Requires sun or semi-shade and fertile, well-drained soil. Propagate by semi-ripe cuttings in late summer.
N. glauca. See *N. sericea.*
N. sericea, syn. *Litsea glauca, N. glauca.* Evergreen, broadly conical, dense tree or shrub. H and S 6m (20ft). Frost hardy. Narrowly oval, pointed leaves are glossy, mid-green above, white beneath and, when young, are densely covered with silky, brown

hairs. Small, star-shaped, yellow flowers are borne in autumn. Zone 9?.

NEOLLOYDIA

CACTACEAE

Genus of spherical to columnar, perennial cacti with dense spines and short tubercles in spirals. Most species are exceptionally difficult to cultivate unless grafted. Tender, min. 10°C (50°F). Needs full sun and well-drained soil. Water sparingly from spring to autumn; keep dry in winter. Propagate by seed in spring or summer.
N. conoidea, syn. *Mammillaria conoidea,* illus. p.475.
N. macdowellii. See *Thelocactus macdowellii.*

NEOMARICA

IRIDACEAE

Genus of evergreen, summer-flowering, iris-like, rhizomatous perennials with clusters of short-lived flowers. Tender, min. 10°C (50°F). Needs partial shade and fertile, moist, preferably humus-rich soil. Water freely in summer; reduce water in winter but do not allow plants to dry out. Propagate by seed in spring or by division in spring or summer.
N. caerulea illus. p.402.

Neopanax. Reclassified as *Pseudopanax.*

NEOPORTERIA

CACTACEAE

Genus of spherical to columnar, perennial cacti. Egg-shaped, red, brown or green seed pods are similar to those of *Wigginsia.* Tender, min. 8°C (46°F). Requires full sun and very well-drained soil. Propagate by seed in spring or summer.
N. chilensis, syn. *Echinocactus chilensis.* Spherical, then columnar, perennial cactus. H 30cm (12in), S 10cm (4in). Pale green stem has a dense covering of stout, golden spines of varying lengths. Crown bears flattish, pink-orange or white flowers, to 5cm (2in) across, in summer.
N. litoralis. See *N. subgibbosa.*
N. mitis. See *N. napina.*
N. napina, syn. *Neochilenia mitis* of gardens, *Neoporteria mitis,* illus. p.471. Flattened spherical, perennial cactus. H 3cm (1¼in), S 5cm (2in). Has very short, black spines pressed flat against a chocolate-brown stem. In summer the crown produces flattish, yellow flowers, 5cm (2in) across.
N. nidus. Spherical to columnar, perennial cactus. H 10cm (4in), S 8cm (3in). Long, soft, grey spines completely encircle a dark greenish-brown stem. During spring or autumn the crown produces tubular, pink to cerise flowers that are 3–5cm (1¼–2in) long, with paler bases, and open only at the tips.
N. subgibbosa, syn. *N. litoralis.* Spherical to columnar, perennial cactus. H 30cm (12in), S 10cm (4in). Light green to dark grey-green stem bears large, woolly areoles and stout,

amber spines. In late summer, crown bears flattish, carmine-pink flowers, 4cm (1½in) across.
N. villosa illus. p.470.

NEOREGELIA

BROMELIACEAE

Genus of evergreen, rosette-forming, epiphytic perennials, grown for their overall appearance. Tender, min. 10°C (50°F). Requires semi-shade and a rooting medium of equal parts humus-rich soil and sphagnum moss or bark or plastic chips used for orchid culture. Using soft water, water moderately during growing season, sparingly at other times, and keep rosette centres filled with water from spring to autumn. Propagate by offsets in spring or summer.
N. carolinae, syn. *Aregelia carolinae, Nidularium carolinae* (Blushing bromeliad). Evergreen, spreading, basal-rosetted, epiphytic perennial. H 20–30cm (8–12in), S 40–60cm (16–24in). Strap-shaped, finely spine-toothed, lustrous, bright green leaves are produced in dense rosettes. A compact cluster of tubular, blue-purple flowers, surrounded by red bracts, is borne at the heart of each mature rosette, usually in summer. f. *tricolor* see *N.c.* 'Tricolor'. **'Tricolor'** (syn. *N.c.* f. *tricolor;* illus. p.265) has leaves, striped with ivory-white, that flush pink with age.
N. concentrica (illus. p.265). Evergreen, spreading, basal-rosetted, epiphytic perennial. H 20–30cm (8–12in), S to 70cm (28in). Very broadly strap-shaped to oval, glossy, dark green leaves, with spiny, black teeth and usually with dark blotches, are borne in dense rosettes. In summer, a compact cluster of tubular, pale blue flowers, surrounded by pinkish-lilac bracts, is produced at the heart of each mature rosette. var. *plutonis* (syn. *N.c.* 'Plutonis') has bracts flushed with red. **'Plutonis'** see *N.c.* var. *plutonis.*

Nepalese ivy. See *Hedera nepalensis.*

NEPENTHES
Pitcher plant

NEPENTHACEAE

Genus of evergreen, insectivorous, mostly epiphytic perennials, with leaves adapted to form pendulous, lidded, coloured pitchers that trap and digest insects. Is suitable for hanging baskets. Tender, min. 18°C (64°F). Requires a humid atmosphere, partial shade and moist, fertile soil with added peat and moss. Propagate by seed in spring or by stem cuttings in spring or summer.
N. × hookeriana illus. p.264.
N. rafflesiana. Evergreen, epiphytic, insectivorous perennial. H 3m (10ft), S 1–1.2m (3–4ft). Has lance-shaped, dark green leaves. Greenish-yellow pitchers, to 25cm (10in) long, are mottled purple and brown and have spurred lids. Inconspicuous, green flowers are borne in racemes and produced intermittently.

NEPETA
Catmint

LABIATAE/LAMIACEAE

Genus of summer-flowering perennials, useful for edging, particularly where they can tumble over paving. Grows in sun or partial shade and any well-drained soil. Propagate by division in spring or by stem-tip or softwood cuttings in spring or summer, species only by seed in autumn.
N. 'Blue Beauty'. See *N.* 'Souvenir d'André Chaudon'.
N. × faassenii illus. p.286.
N. grandiflora. Neat, erect perennial. H 40–80cm (16–32in), S 45–60cm (18–24in). Has slightly hairy stems, oval, round-toothed, light green leaves, with heart-shaped bases, and, in summer, racemes of small, hooded, blue flowers.
N. macrantha. See *N. sibirica.*
N. nervosa. Clump-forming perennial. H 35cm (14in), S 30cm (12in). Forms a mound of narrowly oblong to lance-shaped, pointed, prominently veined, mid-green leaves. Produces dense racemes of small, tubular, pale blue flowers from early to mid-summer.
N. sibirica, syn. *Dracocephalum sibiricum, N. macrantha,* illus. p.254.
'Souvenir d'André Chaudron' see *N.* 'Souvenir d'André Chaudron'.
N. 'Souvenir d'André Chaudron', syn. *N.* 'Blue Beauty', *N. sibirica* 'Souvenir d'André Chaudron'. Spreading, clump-forming perennial. H and S 45cm (18in). Tubular, blue flowers are borne throughout summer above oval to lance-shaped, toothed, grey leaves.

NEPHROLEPIS

NEPHROLEPIDACEAE/OLEANDRACEAE

Genus of evergreen or semi-evergreen ferns. Tender, min. 5°C (41°F). Needs a shady position. Prefers moist soil, but is extremely tolerant of both drought and waterlogging. Remove fading fronds and divide regularly. Propagate by division in summer or early autumn.
N. cordifolia (Ladder fern, Sword fern). Semi-evergreen fern. H 45cm (18in), S 30cm (12in). Has narrowly lance-shaped, arching, dark green fronds with rounded, finely serrated pinnae.
N. exaltata illus. p.312.

NEPHTHYTIS

ARACEAE

Genus of evergreen, tufted perennials, with horizontal, creeping rhizomes, grown for their foliage. Tender, min. 18°C (64°F). Requires a humid atmosphere, moist, humus-rich soil and partial shade. Propagate by division in spring or summer.
N. afzelii. Evergreen, creeping, rhizomatous perennial. H to 75cm (30in), S indefinite. Has tufts of arrow-shaped, lobed, dark green leaves, to 25cm (10in) long. Intermittently bears a hooded, greenish spathe, enclosing a green spadix, followed by spherical, orange fruits.
N. triphylla of gardens. See *Syngonium podophyllum.*

NERINE

AMARYLLIDACEAE

Genus of bulbs, some of which are semi-evergreen, grown for their spherical heads of wavy-petalled, pink to red, occasionally white, flowers. Most flower in autumn before leaves appear. Needs full sun and light, sandy soil. Plant in early autumn. Dislikes being disturbed. Water until leaves die down, then dry off. Propagate by seed when fresh or divide offsets in autumn or when leaves have died down. If ingested, all parts may cause mild stomach upset.

N. **'Baghdad'.** Autumn-flowering bulb. H 60cm (24in), S 15–20cm (6–8in). Leaves are strap-shaped, semi-erect and basal. Has crimson flowers, paler towards centres; long, narrow petals have recurved tips and crisped margins.

N. **'Blanchefleur'.** Autumn-flowering bulb. H 30–50cm (12–20in), S 15–20cm (6–8in). Produces strap-shaped, semi-erect, basal leaves and a tight head of 5–10 pure white flowers. Upper parts of petals are twisted.

N. bowdenii illus. p.424. f. *alba* illus. p.424.

N. **'Brian Doe'** illus. p.424.

N. **'Corusca Major'**, syn. *N. sarniensis* var. *corusca* 'Major'. Autumn-flowering bulb. H 60cm (24in), S 12–15cm (5–6in). Forms strap-shaped, semi-erect, basal leaves. Stout stem bears 10–15 scarlet-red flowers with narrow petals. Is useful for cutting.

N. crispa. See *N. undulata.*

N. filifolia. Autumn-flowering bulb. H to 25cm (10in), S 8–10cm (3–4in). Has thread-like, semi-erect leaves in a basal tuft. Slender stem has pale pink flowers with narrow petals.

N. flexuosa. Semi-evergreen, autumn-flowering bulb. H 40–50cm (16–20in), S 12–15cm (5–6in). Bears strap-shaped, semi-erect, basal leaves and 10–15 pink flowers; each petal has a deeper pink mid-vein and a recurved, wavy upper half.

N. **'Fothergillii Major'.** Late summer- to early autumn-flowering bulb. H 45–60cm (18–24in), S 12–15cm (5–6in). Leaves are strap-shaped, semi-erect and basal. Very strong stem has about 10 bright scarlet-salmon flowers with recurved petals.

N. masoniorum. Autumn-flowering bulb. H 15–20cm (6–8in), S 8–10cm (3–4in). Produces thread-like, semi-erect leaves in a basal tuft. Stem bears pink flowers with very crisped petal margins.

N. **'Orion'** illus. p.424.

N. sarniensis illus. p.424. var. *corusca* **'Major'** see *N.* 'Corusca Major'.

N. undulata, syn. *N. crispa,* illus. p.424.

NERIUM

APOCYNACEAE

Genus of evergreen shrubs, grown for their flowers. Tender, min. 10°C (50°F). Requires full sun and well-drained soil. Water containerized plants freely when in full growth, sparingly at other times. Tip prune young plants to promote branching. Propagate by seed in spring

or by semi-ripe cuttings in summer. All parts are highly toxic if ingested; contact with foliage may irritate skin.

N. oleander illus. p.121.

NERTERA

RUBIACEAE

Genus of creeping perennials, grown for their mass of spherical, bead-like fruits in autumn. Makes excellent alpine house plants. Requires a sheltered, semi-shaded position in gritty, moist but well-drained, sandy soil. Resents winter wet. Propagate in spring by seed, division or tip cuttings.

N. depressa. See *N. granadensis.*

N. granadensis, syn. *N. depressa,* illus. p.387.

Net bush, Common. See *Calothamnus quadrifidus.*

Net-leaf
  Painted. See *Fittonia albivenis* Verschaffeltii Group, illus. p.302.
  Silver. See *Fittonia albivenis* Argyroneura Group, illus. p.300.

Nettle tree. See *Celtis.*

Nettle-leaved bellflower. See *Campanula trachelium,* illus. p.252.

Net-veined willow. See *Salix reticulata,* illus. p.370.

New Zealand bluebell. See *Wahlenbergia albomarginata.*

New Zealand cabbage palm. See *Cordyline australis.*

New Zealand Christmas tree. See *Metrosideros excelsus,* illus. p.83.

New Zealand edelweiss. See *Leucogenes.*

New Zealand flax. See *Phormium.*

New Zealand honeysuckle. See *Knightia excelsa.*

New Zealand satin flower. See *Libertia grandiflora,* illus. p.239.

New Zealand tea-tree. See *Leptospermum scoparium.*

NICANDRA

SOLANACEAE

Genus of one species of annual with short-lived flowers. Grow in sun and in rich, well-drained soil. Propagate by seed sown in spring.

N. physalodes (Apple of Peru, Shoo-fly). Fast-growing, upright, branching annual. H 1m (3ft), S 30cm (1ft) or more. Has oval, serrated, mid-green leaves. In summer to early autumn has bell-shaped, white-throated, light violet-blue flowers, over 2.5cm (1in) wide that last one day. Spherical, green fruits, 5cm (2in) wide, are surrounded by purple and green calyces. Is thought to repel flies, hence its name.

Nicodemia madagascariensis. See *Buddleja madagascariensis.*

NICOTIANA

SOLANACEAE

Genus of annuals, perennials, that are usually grown as annuals, and semi-evergreen shrubs. Tender, min. 1°C (34°F). Needs sun or partial shade and fertile, well-drained soil. Propagate

annuals and perennials by seed in early spring, shrubs by seed in spring or by semi-ripe cuttings in summer. Contact with the foliage may irritate skin.

N. affinis. See *N. alata.*

N. alata, syn. *N. affinis,* illus. p.239.

N. glauca. Semi-evergreen, upright shrub. H and S 2.5–3m (8–10ft). Stout, blue-grey shoots bear narrowly oval, fleshy, blue-grey leaves. Showy, tubular, bright yellow flowers are produced in summer and early autumn.

N. langsdorffii illus. p.334.

N. **'Lime Green'.** Upright annual. H 60cm (24in), S 25cm (10in). Mid-green leaves are spoon-shaped. In late summer and autumn produces racemes of open trumpet-shaped, greenish-yellow flowers that are fragrant at night.

N. × *sanderae* **'Crimson Rock'.** Fairly slow-growing, bushy annual. H 60cm (2ft), S 30cm (1ft). Oval leaves are mid-green. Evening-scented, trumpet-shaped, bright crimson flowers, to 8cm (3in) long, are produced throughout summer and early autumn. **Domino Series** illus. p.319. **Nicki Series**, H 38cm (15in), produces fragrant flowers in an extensive colour range that includes white, pink, red and purple. **Starship Series** illus. p.326.

N. sylvestris illus. p.226.

NIDULARIUM

BROMELIACEAE

Genus of evergreen, rosette-forming, epiphytic perennials, grown for their overall appearance. Tender, min. 10–15°C (50–59°F). Requires a position in semi-shade and a rooting medium of equal parts humus-rich soil and sphagnum moss or bark or plastic chips generally used for orchid culture. Using soft water, water moderately during the growing season, sparingly at other times, and keep centres of rosettes filled with water from spring to autumn. Propagate by offsets in spring or summer.

N. carolinae. See *Neoregelia carolinae.*

N. fulgens (Blushing bromeliad). Evergreen, spreading, basal-rosetted, epiphytic perennial. H 20cm (8in) or more, S 40–50cm (16–20in). Has dense rosettes of strap-shaped, spiny-toothed, arching, glossy, rich green leaves. Tubular, white-and-purple flowers, almost hidden in a rosette of bright scarlet bracts, are mainly produced in summer.

N. innocentii (Bird's-nest bromeliad). Evergreen, spreading, basal-rosetted, epiphytic perennial. H 20–30cm (8–12in), S 60cm (24in). Has dense rosettes of strap-shaped, prickle-toothed, arching, dark green, sometimes reddish-green leaves with reddish-purple undersides. Tubular, white flowers, partially hidden in a rosette of bright red bracts, appear mainly in summer.

N. procerum. Evergreen, spreading, basal-rosetted, epiphytic perennial. H 20–30cm (8–12in), S 50–75cm (20–30in). Strap-shaped, spiny-toothed, bright green leaves are produced in dense rosettes. Clusters of small, tubular, blue flowers are produced in summer.

NIEREMBERGIA

SOLANACEAE

Genus of summer-flowering perennials, sometimes grown as annuals, and deciduous or semi-evergreen sub-shrubs. Prefers sun and moist but well-drained soil. Propagate by division in spring, by semi-ripe cuttings in summer or by seed in autumn.

N. caerulea, syn. *N. hippomanica.* **'Purple Robe'** illus. p.331.

N. hippomanica. See *N. caerulea.*

N. repens, syn. *N. rivularis,* illus. p.374.

N. rivularis. See *N. repens.*

NIGELLA

RANUNCULACEAE

Genus of annuals, grown for their attractive flowers, which are suitable for cutting, and their ornamental seed pods. Grows best in sun and in fertile, well-drained soil. Dead-head plants to prolong flowering if seed heads are not required. Propagate by seed sown outdoors in spring or early autumn.

N. damascena (Love-in-a-mist). Fast-growing, upright annual. H 60cm (24in), S 20cm (8in). Has feathery, bright green leaves. Spurred, many-petalled, blue or white flowers appear in summer, followed by inflated, rounded, green, then brown seed pods that may be cut and dried. **'Miss Jekyll'** and **Persian Jewels Series** illus. p.333.

Night-blooming cereus. See *Hylocereus undatus.*

Nikko fir. See *Abies homolepis.*

Nikko maple. See *Acer maximowiczianum.*

Ninebark. See *Physocarpus opulifolius.*

Nirre. See *Nothofagus antarctica.*

Noble fir. See *Abies procera.*

Nodding catchfly. See *Silene pendula.*

NOLANA

SOLANACEAE

Genus of annuals, useful for growing in hot, dry sites and rock gardens and as edging. Grow in sun and in fertile, well-drained soil. Propagate by seed sown outdoors in spring.

N. atriplicifolia. See *N. paradoxa.*

N. grandiflora. See *N. paradoxa.*

N. paradoxa, syn. *N. atriplicifolia, N. grandiflora.* Moderately fast-growing, prostrate annual. H 8cm (3in), S 15cm (6in). Has oval, mid-green leaves and, in summer, funnel-shaped, purplish-blue flowers, to 5cm (2in) wide, that have white-zoned, yellow throats.

Nolina recurvata. See *Beaucarnea recurvata.*

Nolina tuberculata. See *Beaucarnea recurvata.*

NOMOCHARIS

LILIACEAE

Genus of bulbs with a lily-like habit and, in summer, loose spikes of flattish

flowers, often conspicuously spotted.
Requires partial shade and rich, well-
drained soil with a high humus content.
In summer needs moist but not
waterlogged soil. Is dormant
throughout winter. Propagate by seed
in winter or spring.
N. mairei. See *N. pardanthina.*
N. nana. See *Lilium nanum.*
N. pardanthina, syn. *N. mairei*, illus.
p.398.
N. saluenensis. Summer-flowering
bulb. H 85cm (34in), S 12–15cm
(5–6in). Leafy stems bear lance-
shaped, scattered leaves. Has a loose
spike of 2–6 saucer-shaped, white
or pink flowers, with dark purple eyes
and purple spots.

Nootka cypress. See *Chamaecyparis
nootkatensis.*

NOPALXOCHIA

CACTACEAE

Genus of epiphytic, perennial cacti
with flattened, strap-shaped stems.
Is closely related to *Epiphyllum*, with
which it hybridizes. Spines are
insignificant. Stems may die back after
flowering. Tender, min. 10°C (50°F).
Needs partial shade and rich, well-
drained soil. Is easy to grow. Propagate
by stem cuttings in spring or summer.
N. ackermannii, syn. *Epiphyllum
ackermannii* (Red orchid cactus). Erect,
then pendent, epiphytic, perennial
cactus. H 30cm (1ft), S 60cm (2ft).
Has fleshy, toothed, green stems,
to 7cm (3in) across and 40cm (16in)
long; 15cm (6in) wide, funnel-shaped,
red flowers in spring-summer along
indented edges of stems.
N. 'Gloria' illus. p.463.
N. 'Jennifer Ann' illus. p.467.
N. 'M.A. Jeans' illus. p.463.
N. phyllanthoides 'Deutsche
Kaiserin', illus. p.462.

Norfolk Island hibiscus. See
Lagunaria patersonii.
Norfolk Island pine. See *Araucaria
heterophylla.*
North Island edelweiss. See
Leucogenes leontopodium.
Northern bungalow palm. See
Archontophoenix alexandrae, illus.
p.72.
Northern Japanese hemlock. See
Tsuga diversifolia.
Northern maidenhair fern. See
Adiantum pedatum, illus. p.312.
Northern pitch pine. See *Pinus rigida*,
illus. p.106.
Norway maple. See *Acer platanoides.*
Norway spruce. See *Picea abies*,
illus. p.104.

NOTHOFAGUS

Southern beech

FAGACEAE

Genus of deciduous or evergreen trees,
grown for their habit, foliage and, in
the case of deciduous species, autumn
colour. Has inconspicuous flowers in
late spring. Needs sun or semi-shade
and, as it is not very resistant to strong
winds, should have the shelter of other

trees. Prefers deep, fertile, moist but
well-drained soil; is not suitable for
shallow, alkaline soil. Propagate by
seed in autumn.
N. × *alpina.* See *N. procera.*
N. antarctica (Antarctic beech, Nirre).
Deciduous, broadly conical tree,
sometimes with several main stems.
H 15m (50ft), S 10m (30ft). Small,
oval, crinkly-edged, glossy, dark
green leaves turn yellow in autumn.
Zone 7.
N. betuloides illus. p.74.
N. dombeyi illus. p.73.
N. menziesii (Silver beech).
Evergreen, conical tree. H 20m (70ft),
S 12m (40ft). Has tiny, rounded,
sharply toothed, glossy, dark green
leaves. Zone 9.
N. obliqua illus. p.68.
N. procera, syn. *N.* × *alpina*, illus. p.67.

NOTHOLIRION

LILIACEAE

Genus of summer-flowering bulbs,
related to *Lilium*, grown for their
funnel-shaped flowers. Often produces
early leaves, which may be damaged by
spring frosts, so grow in a cool
greenhouse in areas subject to
alternating mild and cold periods in
spring. Prefers partial shade or full
sun and humus-rich, well-drained soil.
Bulb dies after flowering. Propagate in
spring or autumn by offsets, which take
2–3 years to reach flowering size.
Alternatively propagate by seed in
winter or spring.
N. campanulatum illus. p.400.

Nothopanax. Reclassified as
Pseudopanax.
Nothoscordum neriniflorum. See
Caloscordum neriniflorum.
Notocactus apricus. See *Parodia
concinna.*
Notocactus graessneri. See *Parodia
graessneri.*
Notocactus haselbergii. See *Parodia
haselbergii.*
Notocactus leninghausii. See *Parodia
leninghausii.*
Notocactus mammulosus. See *Parodia
mammulosa.*
Notocactus ottonis. See *Parodia
ottonis.*
Notocactus rutilans. See *Parodia
rutilans.*
Notocactus scopa. See *Parodia
scopa.*

NOTOSPARTIUM

LEGUMINOSAE/PAPILIONACEAE

Genus of leafless, summer-flowering
shrubs, grown for their habit, green
shoots and flowers. Where hardy, does
best against a south- or west-facing
wall. Requires a sheltered, sunny
position and well-drained soil. Older
plants may need staking. Propagate by
semi-ripe cuttings in summer or by
seed in autumn.
N. carmichaeliae (Pink broom).
Leafless, arching shrub. H 2m (6ft),
S 1.5m (5ft). Short, dense spikes of pea-
like, purple-blotched, pink flowers are
produced in mid-summer on slender,
drooping, green shoots. Zone 9.

NUPHAR

NYMPHAEACEAE

Genus of deciduous, perennial, deep-
water plants, grown for their floating
foliage and spherical flowers. Grows
in shade or sun and in running or still
water; is often grown for a water-lily
effect in conditions where true water
lilies would not thrive. Remove fading
foliage and flowers, and periodically
divide crowded plants. Propagate by
division in spring.
N. advena (American spatterdock,
Yellow pond lily). Deciduous,
perennial, deep-water plant. S 1.2m
(4ft). Has broadly oval, floating,
mid-green leaves; central ones are
occasionally erect. Small, purple-
tinged, yellow flowers in summer are
followed by decorative seed heads.
N. lutea illus. p.451.

Nutallia. Reclassified as *Oemleria.*
Nutmeg, California. See *Torreya
californica*, illus. p.107.

NYMANIA

ALTONIACEAE/MELIACEAE

Genus of one species of evergreen,
spring-flowering shrub, grown for
its flowers and fruits. Tender, min.
7–10°C (45–50°F). Needs full light
and fertile, well-drained soil. Water
potted specimens moderately, less
when not in full growth. Propagate
by seed in spring or by semi-ripe
cuttings in summer.
N. capensis illus. p.148.

NYMPHAEA

Water lily

NYMPHAEACEAE

Genus of deciduous, summer-
flowering, perennial water plants,
grown for their floating, usually
rounded leaves and brightly coloured
flowers. Hardy or tender, min. 10°C
(50°F). Needs an open, sunny position
and still water. Remove fading foliage
to prevent it polluting water. Plants
have tuber-like rhizomes and require
dividing and replanting in spring or
early summer every 3 or 4 years.
Most or tender plants may be treated as
annuals. May also be propagated
by seed or by separating plantlets in
spring or early summer. See also
feature panel p.450.
N. 'Amabilis'. Deciduous, perennial
water plant with floating leaves.
S 1.5–2.2m (5–7ft). Rounded leaves,
reddish-purple when young, mature
to dark green with red-margined, light
green undersides. In summer, has star-
shaped, pink flowers, 15–19cm (6–7in)
across, with light pink tips and dark
yellow stamens.
N. 'American Star' (illus. p.450).
Deciduous, perennial water plant with
floating leaves. S to 1.2m (4ft). Young
leaves are purplish-green or bronze,
maturing to bright green. Star-shaped
flowers, 10cm (4in) across, are deep
pink and are held above water
throughout summer.
N. 'Attraction' (illus. p.450).
Deciduous, perennial water plant with

floating leaves. S to 2m (6ft). Has dark
green leaves. In summer bears cup-
shaped, garnet-red flowers, 15cm (6in)
across and flecked with white.
N. 'Aurora'. Deciduous, perennial
water plant with floating leaves. S to
75cm (30in). Olive-green leaves are
mottled with purple. In summer has
star-shaped flowers, 5cm (2in) across,
cream in bud, opening to yellow, then
passing through orange to blood-red.
Suits a small- to medium-sized pool.
N. 'Blue Beauty' (illus. p.450).
Deciduous, perennial water plant with
floating leaves. S to 2.5m (8ft). Tender.
Leaves are brown-freckled, dark green
above, purplish-green beneath.
Fragrant, rounded, deep blue flowers,
to 30cm (12in) across, are produced
in summer.
N. capensis (Cape blue water lily).
Deciduous, perennial water plant with
floating leaves. S to 2m (6ft). Tender.
Large, mid-green leaves are often
splashed with purple beneath. Star-
shaped, bright blue flowers, 15–20cm
(6–8in) across, appear in summer.
N. 'Emily Grant Hutchings'.
Deciduous, perennial water plant with
floating leaves. S to 1.2m (4ft). Tender.
Has small, green leaves overlaid with
bronze-crimson. Cup-shaped, pinkish-
red flowers, 15–20cm (6–8in) across,
open at night in summer.
N. 'Escarboucle' (illus. p.450).
Deciduous, perennial water plant
with floating leaves. S to 3m (10ft).
Leaves are dark green. In summer has
cup-shaped, deep crimson flowers,
10–15cm (4–6in) across, with
golden centres.
N. 'Fabiola'. Deciduous, perennial
water plant with floating leaves.
S to 1.5m (5ft). In summer, produces
fragrant, peony-shaped flowers,
15–18cm (6–7in) across, with strongly
flecked pink petals, above mid-green
leaves.
N. 'Firecrest' (illus. p.450). Deciduous,
perennial water plant with floating
leaves. S to 1.2m (4ft). Dark green
leaves are suffused with purple. In
summer bears star-shaped, deep pink
flowers, 15–20cm (6–8in) across, with
red-tipped stamens.
N. 'Froebelii' (illus. p.450).
Deciduous, perennial water plant with
floating leaves. S 90cm (3ft). Has
rounded, pale green leaves, bronzed
when young. In summer, produces cup-
shaped, later star-shaped, burgundy-red
flowers, 10–12cm (4–5in) across, with
orange-red stamens.
N. 'General Pershing' (illus. p.450).
Deciduous, perennial water plant with
floating leaves. S 1.5–1.8m (5–6ft).
Tender. Leaves are rounded, wavy-
margined, olive-green and marked
with purple. In summer, bears day-
blooming, cup-shaped, later flat,
highly fragrant, lavender-pink flowers,
20–27cm (8–11in) across, with
yellow stamens.
N. 'Gladstoneana' (illus. p.450).
Deciduous, perennial water plant with
floating leaves. S to 3m (10ft). Leaves
are mid-green. Star-shaped, white
flowers, 15–30cm (6–12in) across,
appear in summer.
N. 'Gonnère'. Deciduous, perennial
water plant with floating leaves.

S to 1.5m (5ft). Has bright pea-green leaves and, in summer, rounded, white flowers, 15–20cm (6–8in) across.

N. **'Green Smoke'.** Deciduous, perennial water plant with floating leaves. S to 2m (6ft). Tender. Bronze-green leaves have bronze speckling. Star-shaped flowers, 10–20cm (4–8in) across, are chartreuse, shading to blue.

N. **'James Brydon'** (illus. p.450). Deciduous, perennial water plant with floating leaves. S to 2.5m (8ft). Fragrant, peony-shaped, orange-suffused, crimson flowers, 15–20cm (6–8in) across, are borne in summer above dark green leaves.

N. **'Laydekeri Fulgens'.** See *N.* Laydekeri Group 'Fulgens'.

N. **Laydekeri Group 'Fulgens',** syn. *N.* 'Laydekeri Fulgens' (illus. p.450). Deciduous, perennial water plant with floating leaves. S to 1m (3ft). Dark green leaves have purplish-green undersides. Star-shaped, bright crimson flowers, 5–10cm (2–4in) across, appear in summer.

N. **'Lucida'** (illus. p.450). Deciduous, perennial water plant with floating leaves. S 1.5–1.8m (5–6ft). Has broadly ovate, mid-green leaves, and star-shaped flowers, 12–15cm (5–6in) across, with red inner petals, pink-veined, whitish-pink outer petals, and yellow stamens, in summer.

N. **'Madame Wilfon Gonnère'.** Deciduous, perennial water plant with floating leaves. S to 1.5m (5ft). Has mid-green leaves and, in summer, cup-shaped, white flowers, 15cm (6in) across, spotted with deep rose-pink.

N. **Marliacea Group 'Albida'** (illus. p.450). Deciduous, perennial water plant with floating leaves. S to 2m (6ft). Deep green leaves have red or purplish-green undersides. Bears fragrant, cup-shaped, pure white flowers, 15–20cm (6–8in) across, in summer.

'Chromatella' (illus. p.450) has olive-green leaves, heavily mottled with maroon and bronze, and cup-shaped, canary-yellow flowers, 15–20cm (6–8in) across.

N. odorata **'Sulphurea Grandiflora',** syn *N.* 'Odorata Sulphurea Grandiflora'. Deciduous, perennial water plant with floating leaves. S to 1m (3ft). Dark green leaves are heavily mottled with maroon. Bears fragrant, star-shaped, yellow flowers, 10–15cm (4–6in) across, throughout summer.

N. **'Odorata Sulphurea Grandiflora'.** See *N. odorata* 'Sulphurea Grandiflora'.

N. **'Pink Sensation'.** Deciduous, perennial water plant with floating leaves. S 1.2m (4ft). In summer, bears cup-shaped, later star-shaped, pink flowers, 12–15cm (5–6in) across, with yellow inner stamens and pink outer stamens, above rounded, mid-green leaves, purple-green when young.

N. **pygmaea.** See *N. tetragona*.

N. **'Ray Davies'.** Deciduous, perennial water plant with floating leaves. S to 1.5m (5ft). In summer, produces peony-shaped, light pink flowers, 15–18cm (6–7in) across, slightly yellow in the centre, above rounded, deep green leaves.

N. **'Red Flare'.** Deciduous, perennial water plant with floating leaves.

S 1.5–1.8m (5–6ft). Tender. Leaves are rounded, strongly toothed and reddish-green. In summer, bears night-blooming, flat, dark red flowers, 17–25cm (7–10in) across, with light pink or yellowish stamens.

N. **'Rose Arey'** (illus. p.450). Deciduous, perennial water plant with floating leaves. S to 1.5m (5ft). Leaves are reddish-green, purple when young. In summer produces star-shaped, deep rose-pink flowers, 10–15cm (4–6in) across, that pale with age and have a strong aniseed fragrance.

N. **'Saint Louis'.** Deciduous, perennial water plant with floating leaves. S to 2m (6ft). Tender. Bright green leaves are spotted with brown when young. Produces star-shaped, bright yellow flowers, 15–25cm (6–10in) across, in summer.

N. **'Sunrise'** (illus. p.450). Deciduous, perennial water plant with floating leaves. S to 2m (6ft). Mid-green leaves have downy stalks and undersides. Bears star-shaped, yellow flowers, 10–15cm (4–6in) across, in summer.

N. **tetragona,** syn. *N. pygmaea*. **'Alba'** (illus. p.450). Deciduous, perennial water plant with floating leaves. S to 30cm (12in). Has small, dark green leaves, purplish-green beneath, and, in summer, star-shaped, white flowers, 2–3cm (¾–1¼in) across. **'Helvola'** (illus. p.450), S to 45cm (18in), has small, olive-green leaves with heavy purple or brown mottling. Produces star-shaped, yellow flowers, 2–4cm (¾–1½in) across, in summer.

N. **'Virginia'** (illus. p.450). Deciduous,

perennial water plant with floating leaves. S to 1.5m (5ft). Has purplish-green leaves and, in summer, star-shaped, white flowers, 10–15cm (4–6in) across.

N. **'Wood's White Knight'.** Deciduous, perennial water plant with floating leaves. S to 2m (6ft). Tender. Leaves are mid-green, dappled with darker green beneath. In summer, produces star-shaped, creamy-white flowers, 10–20cm (4–8in) across and with prominent, gold stamens, that open at night.

NYMPHOIDES

MENYANTHACEAE

Genus of deciduous, perennial, deep-water plants, with floating foliage, grown for their flowers. Requires an open, sunny position. Propagate by division in spring or summer.

N. **peltata,** syn. *Limnanthemum nymphoides, Villarsia nymphoides,* illus. p.451.

NYSSA

Tupelo

NYSSACEAE

Genus of deciduous trees grown for their foliage and brilliant autumn colour. Needs sun or semi-shade; does best in hot summers. Requires moist, neutral to acid soil. Resents being transplanted. Propagate by softwood cuttings in summer or by seed in autumn.

N. **sinensis** illus. p.82.

N. **sylvatica** illus. p.71.

O

Oak. See *Quercus*.
  Algerian. See *Quercus canariensis*, illus. p.66.
  American white. See *Quercus alba*, illus. p.71.
  Armenian. See *Quercus pontica*.
  Bartram's. See *Quercus* x *heterophylla*, illus. p.82.
  Basket. See *Quercus prinus*.
  Black. See *Quercus velutina*.
  Black Jack. See *Quercus marilandica*, illus. p.80.
  Bur. See *Quercus macrocarpa*, illus. p.80.
  Californian live. See *Quercus agrifolia*, illus. p.85.
  Caucasian. See *Quercus macranthera*, illus. p.66.
  Chestnut. See *Quercus prinus*.
  Common. See *Quercus robur*.
  Cork. See *Quercus suber*, illus. p.73.
  Daimio. See *Quercus dentata*.
  Durmast. See *Quercus petraea*.
  Holm. See *Quercus ilex*.
  Hungarian. See *Quercus frainetto*, illus. p.69.
  Kermes. See *Quercus coccifera*.
  Lucombe. See *Quercus* x *hispanica* 'Lucombeana', illus. p.73.
  Mirbeck's. See *Quercus canariensis*, illus. p.66.
  Oregon. See *Quercus garryana*, illus. p.80.
  Oriental white. See *Quercus aliena*.
  Pedunculate. See *Quercus robur*.
  Pin. See *Quercus palustris*, illus. p.69.
  Pontine. See *Quercus pontica*.
  Red. See *Quercus rubra*, illus. p.69.
  Sawtooth. See *Quercus acutissima*.
  Scarlet. See *Quercus coccinea*, illus. p.70.
  Sessile. See *Quercus petraea*.
  Shingle. See *Quercus imbricaria*.
  Silky. See *Grevillea robusta*.
  Swamp white. See *Quercus bicolor*.
  Tanbark. See *Lithocarpus densiflorus*.
  Turkey. See *Quercus cerris*.
  Water. See *Quercus nigra*, illus. p.68.
  Willow. See *Quercus phellos*, illus. p.71.
Oak fern. See *Gymnocarpium dryopteris*.
Oak of Cyprus, Golden. See *Quercus alnifolia*.
Oak-leaved hydrangea. See *Hydrangea quercifolia*, illus. p.144.
Oats, Golden. See *Stipa gigantea*, illus. p.307.
Obedient plant. See *Physostegia*.

OCHNA

OCHNACEAE

Genus of mainly evergreen trees and shrubs, grown mostly for their flowers and fruits. Tender, min. 10°C (50°F). Prefers full light and well-drained soil. Water containerized specimens moderately, less when not in full growth. Prune, if necessary, in early spring. Propagate by seed in spring or by semi-ripe cuttings in summer.
O. multiflora. See *O. serrulata*.
O. serratifolia of gardens. See *O. serrulata*.
O. serrulata, syn. *O. multiflora*, *O. serratifolia* of gardens (Mickey-mouse plant). Evergreen, irregularly rounded, twiggy shrub that is semi-evergreen in low temperatures. H to 2m (6ft), S 1–2m (3–6ft) or more. Leaves are narrowly elliptic, toothed and glossy. Has 5-petalled, bright yellow flowers in spring-summer, then shuttlecock-shaped, red fruits, each with 1–5 berry-like seeds clustered on top.

Oconee bells. See *Shortia galacifolia*, illus. p.364.

x ODONTIODA

See also ORCHIDS.
x *O.* (*O.* Chantos x *O.* Marzorka) x *Odontoglossum* Buttercrisp (illus. p.299). Evergreen, epiphytic orchid for a cool greenhouse. H 23cm (9in). Produces arching spikes of intricately patterned, red, tan, orange and yellow flowers, 8cm (3in) across; flowering season varies. Has narrowly oval leaves, 10–15cm (4–6in) long. Needs shade in summer.
x *O.* **Mount Bingham** (illus. p.297). Evergreen, epiphytic orchid for a cool greenhouse. H 23cm (9in). Bears pink-edged, red flowers, 9cm (3½in) across, in spikes; flowering season varies. Has narrowly oval leaves, 10–15cm (4–6in) long. Needs shade in summer.
x *O.* **Pacific Gold** x *Odontoglossum cordatum* (illus. p.297). Evergreen, epiphytic orchid for a cool greenhouse. H 23cm (9in). Bears long spikes of yellow-striped and -marked, rich chocolate-brown flowers, 7cm (3in) across; flowering season varies. Leaves are narrowly oval and 10–15cm (4–6in) long. Grow in shade in summer.
x *O.* **Petit Port** (illus. p.297). Evergreen, epiphytic orchid for a cool greenhouse. H 23cm (9in). Bears spikes of rich red flowers, 8cm (3in) across, each with a pink-and-yellow-marked lip; flowering season varies. Narrowly oval leaves are 10–15cm (4–6in) long. Needs shade in summer.

x ODONTOCIDIUM

See also ORCHIDS.
x *O.* **Artur Elle 'Colombian'** (illus. p.297). Evergreen, epiphytic orchid for a cool greenhouse. H 23cm (9in). Produces tall spikes of pale yellow flowers, 6cm (2½in) across and intricately patterned with brown; flowering season varies. Has narrowly oval leaves, 10–15cm (4–6in) long. Requires shade in summer.
x *O.* **Tiger Butter** x *Wilsonara* **Wigg's 'Kay'** (illus. p.297). Evergreen,

epiphytic orchid for a cool greenhouse. H 23cm (9in). Bears spikes of mottled, deep reddish-brown flowers, 5cm (2in) across, each with a rich golden-yellow lip; flowering season varies. Narrowly oval leaves are 10–15cm (4–6in) long. Grow in shade in summer.
x *O.* **Tiger Hambuhren** (illus. p.299). Evergreen, epiphytic orchid for a cool greenhouse. H 23cm (9in). Deep yellow flowers, 8cm (3in) across and heavily patterned with chestnut-brown, are borne in tall spikes; flowering season varies. Has narrowly oval leaves, 10–15cm (4–6in) long. Needs shade in summer.
x *O.* **Tigersun 'Orbec'** (illus. p.298). Evergreen, epiphytic orchid for a cool greenhouse. Is very similar to x *O.* Tiger Hambuhren, but flowers are slightly smaller and have lighter patterning.

ODONTOGLOSSUM

See also ORCHIDS.
O. bictoniense. See *Lemboglossum bictoniense*.
O. cervantesii. See *Lemboglossum cervantesii*.
O. cordatum. See *Lemboglossum cordatum*.
O. crispum (illus. p.296). Evergreen, epiphytic orchid for a cool greenhouse. H 15cm (6in). Bears long sprays of rounded flowers, 8cm (3in) across, white or spotted or flushed with pink, each with a red-and-yellow-marked lip; flowering season varies. Has narrowly oval leaves, 10–15cm (4–6in) long. Requires shade in summer.
O. **Eric Young** (illus. p.298). Evergreen, epiphytic orchid for a cool greenhouse. H 15cm (6in). Has spikes of white-lipped, pale yellow flowers, 8cm (3in) across, spotted with rich yellow; flowering season varies. Bears narrowly oval leaves, 10–15cm (4–6in) long. Grow in shade in summer.
O. grande. See *Rossioglossum grande*.
O. **Le Nez Point** (illus. p.297). Evergreen, epiphytic orchid for a cool greenhouse. H 15cm (6in). Crimson flowers, 6cm (2½in) across, are borne in spikes; flowering season varies. Has narrowly oval leaves, 10–15cm (4–6in) long. Needs shade in summer.
O. rossii. See *Lemboglossum rossii*.
O. **Royal Occasion** (illus. p.296). Evergreen, epiphytic orchid for a cool greenhouse. H 15cm (6in). Has spikes of white flowers, 8cm (3in) across, with deep yellow markings in the centres of the lips, in autumn-winter. Leaves are narrowly oval and 10–15cm (4–6in) long. Shade in summer.

x ODONTONIA

See also ORCHIDS.
x *O.* **Olga.** Evergreen, epiphytic orchid for a cool greenhouse. H 15cm (6in). Pure white flowers, 10cm (4in) across, with large, reddish-brown-blotched lips, are borne in tall, arching racemes,

mainly in autumn. Produces ovoid pseudobulbs and narrowly oval leaves, 12cm (5in) long. Is best grown in shade during the summer.

OEMLERIA,
syn. NUTTALLIA, OSMARONIA

ROSACEAE

Genus of one species of deciduous, early spring-flowering shrub, grown for its fragrant flowers and decorative fruits. Separate male and female plants are needed in order to obtain fruits. Prefers sun or semi-shade and moist soil. To restrict growth remove suckers and cut old shoots back or down to base in late winter. Propagate by suckers in autumn.
O. cerasiformis. (Indian plum, Oso berry). Deciduous, upright, then arching shrub that forms dense thickets. H 2.5m (8ft), S 4m (12ft). Leaves are narrowly oval and dark blue-green. Has nodding clusters of small, fragrant, bell-shaped, white flowers in early spring, then small, plum-shaped, purple fruits. Zone 7.

OENOTHERA
Evening primrose

ONAGRACEAE

Genus of annuals, biennials and perennials, grown for their profuse but short-lived flowers in summer. Needs full sun and well-drained, sandy soil. Propagate by seed or division in autumn or spring or by softwood cuttings in late spring.
O. acaulis. Tuft-forming perennial. H 15cm (6in), S 20cm (8in). Has oblong to oval, deeply toothed or lobed leaves. Cup-shaped, white flowers, turning pink, open at sunset in summer. Suits a rock garden.
O. caespitosa. Clump-forming, stemless perennial. H 12cm (5in), S 20cm (8in). Has narrowly oval, entire or toothed, mid-green leaves. Flowers, opening at sunset in summer, are fragrant, cup-shaped and white, becoming pink with age. Suits a rock garden.
O. fraseri. See *O. fruticosa* subsp. *glauca*.
O. fruticosa 'Fireworks'. See *O.f.* 'Fyrverkeri'. 'Fyrverkeri' (syn. *O.f.* 'Fireworks') illus. p.291. subsp. *glauca* (syn. *O. fraseri, O. glauca, O. tetragona*) is a clump-forming perennial. H 45–60cm (18–24in), S 45cm (18in). Dense spikes of fragrant, cup-shaped, bright yellow flowers appear from mid- to late summer. Leaves, borne on reddish-green stems, are narrowly oval to lance-shaped and glossy, mid-green.
O. glauca. See *O. fruticosa* subsp. *glauca*.
O. macrocarpa, syn. *O. missouriensis*, illus. p.385.
O. missouriensis. See *O. macrocarpa*.
O. perennis, syn. *O. pumila*. Clump-forming perennial. H 15–60cm

(6–24in), S 30cm (12in). In summer, loose spikes of nodding buds open to fragrant, funnel-shaped, yellow flowers above narrowly spoon-shaped, mid-green leaves.

O. pumila. See *O. perennis.*
O. speciosa (White evening primrose). Often short-lived, clump-forming perennial with running rhizomes. H 45cm (18in), S 30cm (12in) or more. In summer bears spikes of fragrant, saucer-shaped, green-centred, pure white flowers that age to pink and open flat. Leaves are narrowly spoon-shaped, deeply cut and mid-green.
O. tetragona. See *O. fruticosa* subsp. *glauca.*

Ohio buckeye. See *Aesculus glabra.*
Old blush china. See *Rosa* x *odorata* 'Pallida'.
Old man. See *Artemisia abrotanum,* illus. p.176.
Old man of the Andes. See *Oreocereus celsianus,* illus. p.462.
Old man's beard. See *Clematis.*
Old pink moss rose. See *Rosa* x *centifolia* 'Muscosa'.
Old-lady cactus. See *Mammillaria hahniana,* illus. p.465.
Old-man cactus. See *Cephalocereus senilis,* illus. p.460.
  Peruvian. See *Espostoa lanata,* illus. p.457.
Old-witch grass. See *Panicum capillare,* illus. p.308.
Old-woman cactus. See *Mammillaria hahniana,* illus. p.465.

OLEA
OLEACEAE

Genus of evergreen trees, grown for their foliage and edible fruits. Marginally hardy and requires the protection of a sheltered, south- or west-facing wall. Needs full sun and deep, fertile, very well-drained soil. Propagate by semi-ripe cuttings in summer or by seed in autumn.
O. europaea (Olive). Slow-growing, evergreen, spreading tree. H and S 10m (30ft). Is very long-lived. Narrowly oblong leaves are grey-green above, silvery beneath. Tiny, fragrant, white flowers, borne in short racemes in late summer, are followed by edible, oval, green, later purple fruits. Zone 9?.

Oleander. See *Nerium oleander,* illus. p.121.
  Yellow. See *Thevetia peruviana,* illus. p.93.

OLEARIA
Daisy bush
ASTERACEAE/COMPOSITAE

Genus of evergreen shrubs and trees, grown for their foliage and daisy-like flower heads. In mild, coastal areas provides good, very wind-resistant shelter. Slightly hardy to tender, (min. 2°C (35°F). Needs full sun and well-drained soil. Cut out dead wood in spring. Propagate by semi-ripe cuttings in summer.
O. albida of gardens. See *O.* 'Talbot de Malahide'.

O. avicenniifolia. Evergreen, rounded, dense shrub. H 3m (10ft), S 5m (15ft). Oval to lance-shaped, dark grey-green leaves are white beneath. Bears wide heads of fragrant, white flowers in late summer and early autumn.
O.* x *haastii illus. p.139.
***O.* 'Henry Travers'**, syn. *O. semidentata* of gardens. Evergreen, rounded, compact shrub. H and S 3m (10ft). Tender. Has white shoots and narrowly lance-shaped, leathery, grey-green leaves. Large heads of purple-centred, lilac flowers appear from early to mid-summer.
O. ilicifolia. Evergreen, bushy, dense shrub. H and S 3m (10ft). Narrowly oblong, rigid leaves are sharply toothed, grey-green and musk-scented. Fragrant, white flower heads are borne in clusters in early summer. Zone 8.
O. lacunosa. Evergreen, upright, dense shrub. H and S 3m (10ft). Narrowly oblong, pointed, rigid leaves have rust-brown hairs when young and mature to glossy, dark green with central, white veins. Produces white flowerheads only rarely. Zone 9.
O. macrodonta. Vigorous, evergreen, upright shrub, often tree-like. H 6m (20ft), S 5m (15ft). Tender. Has holly-shaped, sharply toothed, grey-green leaves, silvery-white beneath. Large heads of fragrant, white flowers appear in early summer.
O.* x *mollis. Evergreen, rounded, dense shrub. H 1m (3ft), S 1.5m (5ft). Has oval, wavy-edged, silvery-grey leaves. Large heads of small, white flowers are borne profusely in late spring. Zone 8.
'Zennorensis', H and S 2m (6ft), has narrowly oblong leaves.
O. nummulariifolia illus. p.136.
O. phlogopappa. Evergreen, upright, compact shrub. H and S 2m (6ft). Tender. Leaves are grey-green and oblong, with wavy edges. Massed, white flower heads are carried in late spring. var. **subrepanda** illus. p.158.
O.* x *scilloniensis. Evergreen, upright, then rounded, dense shrub. H and S 2m (6ft). Narrowly oblong, wavy-edged, dark grey-green leaves set off masses of white flower heads in late spring. Zone 9.
O. semidentata of gardens. See *O.* 'Henry Travers'.
***O.* 'Talbot de Malahide'**, syn. *O. albida* of gardens. Evergreen, bushy, dense shrub. H 3m (10ft), S 5m (15ft). Tender. Oval, dark green leaves are silvery beneath. Bears broad heads of fragrant, white flowers in late summer. Excellent for exposed, coastal gardens.
O. virgata illus. p.118.

Oleaster. See *Elaeagnus angustifolia,* illus. p.122.
Olive. See *Olea europaea.*
  Fragrant. See *Osmanthus fragrans.*
Oliveranthus elegans. See *Echeveria harmsii.*

OLSYNIUM
IRIDACEAE

Genus of fibrous-rooted, clump-forming perennials, grown for their nodding, trumpet- to bell-shaped

flowers in spring. Requires partial shade and moist, humus-rich, moderately fertile soil. Propagate by seed in autumn. Young plants take 2 or 3 years to flower.
***O. biflorum*,** syn. *Phaiophleps biflora, Sisyrinchium odoratissimum.* Clump-forming, spring- to summer-flowering, rhizomatous perennial. H 25–35cm (10–14in), S 5–8cm (2–3in). Has cylindrical, rush-like, erect, basal leaves. Bears a small head of pendent, white flowers that are striped and veined red.
***O. douglasii*,** syn. *Sisyrinchium douglasii, S. grandiflorum* (Grass widow, Spring bell). Stiff, upright, summer-deciduous perennial. H 25cm (10in), S 15cm (6in). Has grass-like leaves sheathing very short, thread-like flowering stems and, in early spring, a succession of pendent, bell-shaped, violet to red-purple, or sometimes white, flowers. Suits a rock garden or alpine house.

OMPHALODES
BORAGINACEAE

Genus of annuals and perennials, some of which are evergreen or semi-evergreen. Makes good ground cover, especially in rock gardens. Needs shade or semi-shade and moist but well-drained soil, except for *O. linifolia* and *O. luciliae,* which prefer sun. Propagate by seed or division in spring.
O. cappadocica illus. p.349.
O. linifolia illus. p.318.
O. luciliae. Semi-evergreen, mound-forming perennial. H 7cm (3in), S 15cm (6in). Has oval, blue-grey leaves. In spring-summer, loose sprays of pink buds develop into flattish, sky-blue flowers. Resents winter wet, so plant in a sheltered site or alpine house. Prefers sun and very gritty soil.
O. verna illus. p.349.

OMPHALOGRAMMA
PRIMULACEAE

Genus of perennials, closely related to *Primula,* grown for their flowers. Makes good rock garden plants, but is difficult to grow, especially in hot, dry areas. Needs shade and gritty, moist but well-drained, peaty soil. Propagate by seed in spring.
O. vinciflorum. Basal-rosetted perennial. H 15cm (6in), S 10cm (4in). Has oval, hairy leaves that are mid-green in colour. In spring produces nodding, funnel-shaped, violet flowers, each with a deeper violet throat and a flat, flared mouth.

ONCIDIUM

See also ORCHIDS.
O. flexuosum (Dancing-doll orchid; illus. p.299). Evergreen, epiphytic orchid for a cool or intermediate greenhouse. H 23cm (9in). In autumn produces terminal sprays of many small, large-lipped, bright yellow flowers, 0.5cm (¼in) across, with red-brown markings on the sepals and petals. Bears narrowly oval leaves, 10cm (4in) long. Is best grown on a bark slab. Keep in semi-shade in summer.

O. ornithorrhynchum (illus. p.296). Evergreen, epiphytic orchid for a cool greenhouse. H 15cm (6in). Dense, arching sprays of very fragrant, rose-lilac flowers, 0.5cm (¼in) across, with a yellow highlight, are borne freely in autumn. Has narrowly oval leaves, 10cm (4in) long. Requires semi-shade in summer.
O. papilio. See *Psychopsis papilio.*
O. tigrinum (illus. p.298). Evergreen, epiphytic orchid for a cool or intermediate greenhouse. H 23cm (9in). Branching spikes of fragrant, yellow-marked, brown flowers, 5cm (2in) across, each with a large, yellow lip, open in autumn. Has oval leaves, 15cm (6in) long. Requires semi-shade in summer.

Onion. See *Allium.*
  Sea. See *Urginea maritima.*

ONIXOTIS,
syn. DIPIDAX
COLCHICACEAE/LILIACEAE

Genus of spring-flowering corms, cultivated mainly for botanical interest. Requires sun and well-drained soil. Plant corms in early autumn and keep them watered until after flowering. Dry off in summer. Propagate by seed in autumn.
***O. triquetra*,** syn. *Dipidax triquetrum.* Spring-flowering corm. H 20–30cm (8–12in), S 5–8cm (2–3in). Long, narrow leaves are semi-erect and basal. Carries a spike of flattish, star-shaped, white flowers, each narrow petal having a basal, red mark.

ONOCLEA
ATHYRIACEAE/DRYOPTERIDACEAE

Genus of one species of deciduous fern that rapidly colonizes wet areas. Grows in sun or shade and in wet soil. Remove fronds as they fade. Propagate by division in autumn or winter.
O. sensibilis illus. p.312.

ONONIS
LEGUMINOSAE/PAPILIONACEAE

Genus of summer-flowering annuals, perennials and deciduous or semi-evergreen shrubs and sub-shrubs, grown for their pea-like flowers. Is good for rock gardens, walls and banks. Needs a sunny position in well-drained soil. Propagate by seed in autumn or spring, shrubs also by softwood cuttings in summer.
O. fruticosa illus. p.353.
O. natrix illus. p.359.
O. rotundifolia. Deciduous or semi-evergreen, glandular, upright sub-shrub. H 20–60cm (8–24in), S 20–30cm (8–12in) or more. Bears small, rounded, 3-parted, toothed, hairy, green leaves, with the terminal leaflet long-stalked. Flowers that are relatively large, red-streaked, and rose-pink appear in small clusters in summer. Zone 8.

Onopordon. Reclassified as *Onopordum.*

ONOPORDUM,
syn. ONOPORDON

ASTERACEAE/COMPOSITAE

Genus of annuals, biennials and perennials, ranging from stemless to tall, branching plants. Grow in sun or semi-shade and in rich, well-drained soil. To prevent self seeding remove dead flower heads. Propagate by seed sown outdoors in autumn or spring. Leaves are prone to slug and snail damage.
O. acanthium illus. p.322.

ONOSMA

BORAGINACEAE

Genus of summer-flowering annuals, semi-evergreen biennials, perennials and sub-shrubs, grown for their long, pendent, tubular flowers. Is suitable for rock gardens and banks. Requires full sun and well-drained soil. Dislikes wet summers. Propagate by softwood cuttings in summer or by seed in autumn.
O. alborosea illus. p.352.
O. stellulata. Semi-evergreen, upright sub-shrub. H and S 15cm (6in). Leaves are oblong and covered in hairs which may irritate the skin. Clusters of yellow flowers open in late spring and summer.

Ontario poplar. See *Populus* x *candicans*.

OOPHYTUM

AIZOACEAE

Genus of clump-forming, egg-shaped, perennial succulents with 2 united, very fleshy leaves. These are covered in dry, papery sheaths, except in spring when sheaths split open, revealing a new pair of leaves. Flowers are produced from a slight central fissure on upper surface. Is difficult to grow. Tender, min. 5°C (41°F). Requires sun and well-drained soil. Propagate by seed or stem cuttings in spring or summer.
O. nanum illus. p.470.

Operculina tuberosa. See *Merremia tuberosa*.

OPHIOPOGON

CONVALLARIACEAE/LILIACEAE

Genus of evergreen perennials, grown mainly for their grass-like foliage. Grows in sun or partial shade and in fertile, well-drained soil. Propagate by division in spring or by seed in autumn.
O. jaburan. Evergreen, clump-forming perennial. H 15cm (6in), S 30cm (12in). Has dark green foliage. In early summer produces racemes of bell-shaped, white flowers, followed by deep blue berries. **'Variegatus'** see *O.j.* **'Vittatus'**. **'Vittatus'** (syn. *O.j.* 'Variegatus') has white- or yellow-striped foliage and is much less robust.
O. japonicus illus. p.304.
O. planiscapus 'Nigrescens' illus. p.303.

OPHRYS

See also ORCHIDS.
O. aranifera. See *O. sphegodes*.
O. fuciflora. See *O. holoserica*.
O. fusca (illus. p.298). Deciduous, terrestrial orchid. H 10–40cm (4–16in). Spikes of greenish, yellow or brown flowers, 0.5cm (¼in) long, each with a yellow-edged, bluish, brown or purple lip, are produced in spring. Has oval or lance-shaped leaves, 8–12cm (3–5in) long. Grow in shade outdoors. Containerized plants require semi-shade in summer.
O. holoserica, syn. *O. fuciflora*. Deciduous, terrestrial orchid. H 15–55cm (6–22in). Spikes of flowers, 1cm (½in) long, from white through pink to blue and green, appear in spring-summer. Leaves are oval to oblong, 5–10cm (2–4in) long. Cultivate as for *O. fusca*.
O. lutea (illus. p.298). Deciduous, terrestrial orchid. H 8–30cm (3–12in). In spring bears short spikes of flowers, 1cm (½in) long, with greenish sepals, yellow petals and brown-centred, bright yellow lips. Has oval, basal leaves, 5–10cm (2–4in) long. Cultivate as for *O. fusca*.
O. speculum. See *O. vernixia*.
O. sphegodes, syn. *O. aranifera* (Spider orchid). Deciduous, terrestrial orchid. H 10–45cm (4–18in). In spring-summer carries spikes of flowers, 1cm (½in) long, that vary from green to yellow and have spider-like, blackish-brown marks on lips. Leaves are oval to lance-shaped and 4–8cm (1½–3in) long. Cultivate as for *O. fusca*.
O. tenthredinifera (Sawfly orchid; illus. p.297). Deciduous, terrestrial orchid. H 15–55cm (6–22in). In spring has spikes of flowers, 1cm (½in) long, in colours of white to pink, or blue and green, each with a violet or bluish lip edged with pale green. Has a basal rosette of oval to oblong leaves, 5–9cm (2–3½in) long. Cultivate as for *O. fusca*.
O. vernixia, syn. *O. speculum*. Deciduous, terrestrial orchid. H 8–30cm (3–12in). In spring produces dense spikes of flowers, 1cm (½in) long, with greenish or yellow sepals, purple petals and 3-centred, brown lips. Has oblong to lance-shaped leaves, 4–7cm (1½–3in) long. Cultivate as for *O. fusca*.

OPHTHALMOPHYLLUM

AIZOACEAE

Genus of clump-forming, perennial succulents related to *Lithops*. Each plant has 2 cylindrical, very fleshy leaves, erect and united for most of their length, but with a fissure between them at the top. Leaves each have a rounded upper surface with a translucent window. Tender, min. 5°C (41°F). Requires sun and well-drained soil. Water in late summer and early autumn; thereafter keep almost dry. Propagate by seed or stem cuttings in spring or summer.
O. herrei. See *O. longum*.
O. longum, syn. *Conophytum longum*, *O. herrei*. Clump-forming, perennial succulent. H 3cm (1¼in), S 1.5cm

(⅜in). Has 2 almost united, cylindrical, very fleshy, erect, grey-green to brown leaves. In late summer bears daisy-like, white to pink flowers, 2cm (¾in) across.
O. maughanii. Clump-forming, perennial succulent. H 4cm (1½in), S 10cm (4in). Produces 2 almost united, cylindrical, very fleshy, erect, yellowish-green leaves with upper surface bearing 0.5–1cm (¼–½in) deep fissure. In late summer bears daisy-like, white flowers, 1.5cm (⅝in) across.
O. villetii illus. p.472.

Opium poppy. See *Papaver somniferum*.

OPLISMENUS

GRAMINEAE/POACEAE

See also GRASSES, BAMBOOS, RUSHES and SEDGES.
O. africanus, syn. *O. hirtellus* (Basket grass). **'Variegatus'** illus. p.301.
O. hirtellus. See *O. africanus*.

OPLOPANAX

ARALIACEAE

Genus of deciduous, summer-flowering shrubs, grown for their habit, fruits and spiny foliage. Young growths may be damaged by late frosts. Does best in a cool, partially shaded position and in moist soil. Propagate by seed in autumn or by root cuttings in late winter.
O. horridus (Devil's club). Deciduous, spreading, open, sparsely branched shrub. H and S 2m (6ft). Prickly stems bear large, oval, 7–9-lobed, toothed, mid-green leaves. Bears dense umbels of small, star-shaped, greenish-white flowers from mid- to late summer, then spherical, red fruits. Zone 7.

OPUNTIA
Prickly pear

CACTACEAE

Genus of perennial cacti, ranging from small, alpine, ground-cover plants to large, evergreen, tropical trees, with at times insignificant glochids – short, soft, barbed spines produced on areoles. Mature plants carry masses of short-spined, pear-shaped, green, yellow, red or purple fruits (prickly pears), edible in some species. Hardy to tender, min. 5–10°C (41–50°F). Needs sun and well-drained soil. Water containerized specimens when in full growth. Propagate by seed or stem cuttings in spring or summer. Contact with the bristles causes intense irritation to skin, and they are difficult to remove.
O. brasiliensis. Tree-like, perennial cactus. H 5.5m (18ft), S 3m (10ft). Tender, min. 10°C (50°F). Has a cylindrical, green stem bearing bright green branches of flattened, oval, spiny segments. Sheds 2–3-year-old side branches. Masses of shallowly saucer-shaped, yellow flowers, 4cm (1½in) across, appear in spring-summer, only on plants over 60cm (2ft) tall, and are followed by small, yellow fruits.
O. compressa, syn. *O. humifusa*, illus. p.478.
O. cylindrica. Bushy, perennial cactus. H 4–6m (12–20ft). S 1m (3ft). Tender,

min. 10°C (50°F). On cylindrical stems, 4–5cm (1½–2in) across, are borne short-lived, cylindrical, dark green leaves, to 2cm (¾in) long, on new growth. Areoles may lack spines or each produce 2 or 3 barbed ones. Shallowly saucer-shaped, pink-red flowers appear in spring-summer, only on plants over 2m (6ft) tall, and are followed by greenish-yellow fruits.
O. engelmannii. See *O. ficus-indica*.
O. erinacea illus. p.465.
O. ficus-indica, syn. *O. engelmannii*, *O. megacantha* (Edible prickly pear, Indian fig). Bushy to tree-like, perennial cactus. H and S 5m (15ft). Tender, min. 10°C (50°F). Bears flattened, oblong, blue-green stem segments, 50cm (20in) long and spineless. In spring-summer has masses of shallowly saucer-shaped, yellow flowers, 10cm (4in) across, followed by edible, purple fruits.
O. humifusa. See *O. compressa*.
O. megacantha. See *O. ficus-indica*.
O. microdasys (Bunny ears). Bushy, perennial cactus. H and S 60cm (2ft). Tender, min. 10°C (50°F). Has flattened, oval, green stem segments, 8–18cm (3–7in) long, that develop brown marks in low temperatures. Bears spineless areoles, with white, yellow, brown or red glochids, closely set in diagonal rows. Masses of funnel-shaped, yellow flowers, 5cm (2in) across, appear in summer on plants over 15cm (6in) tall, and are followed by small, dark red fruits. var. **albispina** illus. p.467.
O. robusta illus. p.460.
O. tunicata illus. p.468.
O. verschaffeltii illus. p.474.

Orach, Red. See *Atriplex hortensis* var. *rubra*.
Orange
  Hardy. See *Poncirus trifoliata*.
  Mock. See *Philadelphus coronarius*; *Pittosporum tobira*.
  Osage. See *Maclura pomifera*.
  Trifoliate. See *Poncirus trifoliata*.
Orange blossom, Mexican. See *Choisya ternata*, illus. p.127.
Orange jasmine. See *Murraya paniculata*.
Orange lily. See *Lilium bulbiferum*.

ORBEA

ASCLEPIADACEAE

Genus of clump-forming, perennial succulents with erect, 4-angled stems. Stem edges are often indented and may produce small leaves that drop after only a few weeks. Tender, min. 11°C (52°F). Needs sun or partial shade and well-drained soil. Propagate by seed or stem cuttings in spring or summer.
O. variegata, syn. *Stapelia variegata*, illus. p.476.

Orchard grass. See *Dactylis glomerata*.
Orchid
  Butterfly. See *Psychopsis papilio*, illus. p.299.
  Cradle. See *Anguloa clowesii*.
  Dancing-doll. See *Oncidium flexuosum*, illus. p.299.

Orchid (continued)

Green-veined. See *Orchis morio*, illus. p.298.

Lady's slipper. See *Cypripedium calceolus*, illus. p.298.

Pansy. See *Miltoniopsis*.

Poor man's. See *Schizanthus*.

Sawfly. See *Ophrys tenthredinifera*, illus. p.297.

Showy lady's slipper. See *Cypripedium reginae*, illus. p.296.

Slipper. See *Cypripedium*; *Paphiopedilum*.

Spider. See *Ophrys sphegodes*.

Star-of-Bethlehem. See *Angraecum sesquipedale*, illus. p.296.

Yellow lady's slipper. See *Cypripedium calceolus*, illus. p.298.

Orchid cactus. See *Epiphyllum*.

ORCHIDS

ORCHIDACEAE

Family of perennials, some of which are evergreen or semi-evergreen, grown for their beautiful, unusual flowers. These consist of 3 outer sepals and 3 inner petals, the lowest of which, known as the lip, is usually enlarged and different from the others in shape, markings and colour. There are about 750 genera and 17,500 species, together with an even greater number of hybrids, bred partly for their vigour and ease of care. They are divided into epiphytic and terrestrial plants. (The spread of an orchid is indefinite.)

Epiphytic orchids

Epiphytes have more flamboyant flowers than terrestrial orchids and are more commonly grown. In the wild, they grow on tree branches or rocks (lithophytes), obtaining nourishment through clinging roots and moisture through aerial roots. Most consist of a horizontal rhizome, from which arise vertical, water-storing, often swollen stems known as pseudobulbs. Flowers and foliage are produced from the newest pseudobulbs. Other epiphytes consist of a continuously growing upright rhizome; on these, flower spikes appear in the axils of leaves growing from the rhizome. In temperate climates, epiphytes need to be grown under glass.

Cultivation of epiphytes

For cultivation purposes, epiphytes, which are all tender, may be divided into 3 groups: cool-greenhouse types, which require min. 10°C (50°F) and max. 24°C (75°F); intermediate-greenhouse types, needing a range of 13–27°C (55–80°F); and warm-greenhouse types, requiring 18–27°C (65–80°F). In summer, temperatures need to be controlled by shading the glass and by ventilation. Cool-greenhouse orchids may be placed outdoors in summer; this improves flowering. Other types may also be grown outdoors if the air temperature remains within these ranges.

The amount of light required in summer is given in individual plant entries. All epiphytic orchids, however, need to be kept out of direct sun in summer to avoid scorching, and require full light in winter.

Epiphytic orchids, whether grown indoors or outside, require a special soil-free compost obtained from an orchid nursery or made by mixing 2 parts fibrous material (such as bark chippings and/or peat) with 1 part porous material (such as sphagnum moss and/or expanded clay pellets). Most epiphytes may be grown in pots, although some may be successfully cultivated in a hanging basket or on a slab of bark (with moss around their roots) suspended in the greenhouse.

In summer, water plants freely and spray regularly. Those suspended on bark slabs need a constantly moist atmosphere. In winter, water moderately and, if plants are in growth, spray occasionally. Some orchids rest in winter and require scarcely any water or none at all. Orchids benefit from weak foliar feeds; apply as for watering. Repot plants every other year, in spring; if they are about to flower, repot after flowering.

Terrestrial orchids

Terrestrial orchids, some of which also produce pseudobulbs, grow in soil or leaf mould, sustaining themselves in the normal way through roots or tubers. Some may be grown in borders, but many in temperate climates need to be cultivated in pots and protected under glass during winter.

Cultivation of terrestrial orchids

Terrestrial orchids are fully hardy to tender, min. 18°C (65°F). *Cypripedium* species may be grown outdoors, preferably in neutral to acid soil, but cannot withstand severe frost, if frozen solid in pots or without snow cover, or tolerate very wet soil in winter. Other terrestrial orchids, except in very mild areas, are best grown in pots; use the same compost as for epiphytes but add 1 part grit to 2 parts compost. Place pots outdoors in a peat bed or in a glasshouse in the growing season. Keep dry when dormant. Under glass, light requirements, watering, feeding and repotting are as for epiphytes.

Orchid propagation

Orchids with pseudobulbs may be increased by removing and replanting old, leafless pseudobulbs when repotting in spring. Take care to retain at least 4 pseudobulbs on the parent plant. Some genera that may be propagated in this way are: *Ada*, x *Aliceara*, *Anguloa*, *Bletilla*, *Brassavola* (large plants only and retaining at least 6 pseudobulbs on the parent), x *Brassocattleya*, x *Brassolaeliocattleya*, *Bulbophyllum*, *Calanthe*, *Cattleya*, *Coelogyne*, *Cymbidium*, *Dendrobium*, *Dendrochilum*, *Encyclia*, *Gomesa*, *Gongora*, *Laelia*, x *Laeliocattleya*, *Lycaste*, *Maxillaria*, *Miltonia*, *Miltoniopsis*, x *Odontioda*, x *Odontocidium*, *Odontoglossum*, x *Odontonia*, *Oncidium*, *Phaius*, *Pleione*, x *Potinara*, x *Sophrolaeliocattleya*, *Stanhopea*, x *Vuylstekeara*, x *Wilsonara* and *Zygopetalum*.

Some orchids without pseudobulbs produce new growth from the base. When a plant has 6 new growths, divide it in spring into 2 and repot both portions. Propagate *Disa*, *Paphiopedilum* and *Phragmipedium* in this way. Large specimens of *Eria*, *Masdevallia* and *Pleurothallis* may be divided in spring, leaving 4–6 stems on each portion.

Propagation of *Phalaenopsis* is by stem cuttings taken soon after flowering. *Vanda* may be increased by removing the top half of the stem once it has produced aerial roots and leaves; new growths will develop from the leafless base. With both these methods achieving success is difficult and not recommended for the beginner.

Propagate terrestrial orchids with tubers by division of the tubers. Genera that may be increased in this way are: *Cypripedium* (in spring), *Dactylorhiza* (spring), *Ophrys* (autumn), *Orchis* (spring), *Serapias* (autumn) and *Spiranthes* (spring). *Calypso* is rarely propagated successfully in cultivation. *Angraecum* should not be propagated in cultivation, because the parent plant is easily endangered.

The most easily increased orchids are *Cymbidium*. Propagation of *Epidendrum* may be extremely difficult; see genus for specific details.

Orchids are illustrated on pp.296–9. See also *Ada*, x *Aliceara*, *Angraecum*, *Anguloa*, *Bletilla*, *Brassavola*, x *Brassocattleya*, x *Brassolaeliocattleya*, *Bulbophyllum*, *Calanthe*, *Calypso*, *Cattleya*, *Coelogyne*, *Cymbidium*, *Cypripedium*, *Dactylorhiza*, *Dendrobium*, *Dendrochilum*, *Encyclia*, *Epidendrum*, *Eria*, *Gomesa*, *Gongora*, *Laelia*, x *Laeliocattleya*, *Lemboglossum*, *Lycaste*, *Masdevallia*, *Maxillaria*, *Miltonia*, *Miltoniopsis*, x *Odontioda*, x *Odontocidium*, *Odontoglossum*, x *Odontonia*, *Oncidium*, *Ophrys*, *Orchis*, *Paphiopedilum*, *Phaius*, *Phalaenopsis*, *Phragmipedium*, *Pleione*, *Pleurothallis*, x *Potinara*, *Psychopsis*, *Rossioglossum*, *Serapias*, x *Sophrolaeliocattleya*, *Spiranthes*, *Stanhopea*, *Vanda*, x *Vuylstekeara*, x *Wilsonara* and *Zygopetalum*.

ORCHIS

See also ORCHIDS.

O. elata. See *Dactylorhiza elata*.

O. morio (Gandergoose, Green-veined orchid; illus. p.298). Deciduous, terrestrial orchid. H 40cm (16in). Reddish-purple, mauve or rarely white flowers, 1cm (½in) long, with green veins on the cupped sepals, open along stems in spring. Has a basal cluster of lance-shaped or broadly oblong, pale to mid-green leaves, 10–16cm (4–6in) long. Requires sun or semi-shade.

Oregon grape. See *Mahonia aquifolium*, illus. p.157.

Oregon maple. See *Acer macrophyllum*, illus. p.64.

Oregon oak. See *Quercus garryana*, illus. p.80.

OREOCEREUS,
syn. BORZICACTUS

CACTACEAE

Genus of mainly columnar, perennial cacti with thick, cylindrical, much-ribbed stems with spines, usually branching from the base, and, in some species, are covered in long hairs. Solitary, tubular-funnel-shaped flowers are produced near stem tips during the day in summer. Tender, min. 10°C (50°F). Requires a position in full sun and very well-drained, slightly alkaline soil. Propagate by seed in spring or summer.

O. aurantiacus, syn. *Matucana aurantiaca*, illus. p.480.

O. celsianus, syn. *Cleistocactus celsianus*, illus. p.462.

O. haynei, syn. *Matucana haynei*. Slow-growing, spherical to columnar, perennial cactus. H 60cm (24in), S 10cm (4in). Has a cylindrical, much-ribbed, grass-green stem densely covered with short, white or yellow spines. Red, orange-brown or purple-crimson flowers appear in summer on plants over 15cm (6in) high.

O. peruviana. See *Oroya peruviana*.

O. trollii, syn. *Cleistocactus trollii* (Old man of the Andes). Slow-growing, columnar, perennial cactus. H 70cm (28in), S 10cm (4in). Cylindrical, green stem, 7–10cm (3–4in), with thick, golden spines is almost hidden by long, wispy, hair-like, white spines. Pink flowers, recurved at tips and 10cm (4in) long, appear in summer on fully mature plants.

OREOPTERIS

THELYPTERIDACEAE

Genus of deciduous ferns. Tolerates sun or semi-shade. Grow in moist or very moist soil. Remove fading fronds regularly. Propagate by division in spring.

O. limbosperma, syn. *Thelypteris oreopteris* (Mountain buckler fern, Mountain fern, Mountain wood fern). Deciduous fern. H 60cm–1m (2–3ft), S 30cm (1ft). Has mainly lance-shaped, much-divided fronds, with oblong to lance-shaped, mid-green pinnae.

Organ-pipe cactus. See *Pachycereus marginatus*, illus. p.457.

Oriental beech. See *Fagus orientalis*.

Oriental bittersweet. See *Celastrus orbiculatus*.

Oriental plane. See *Platanus orientalis*.

Oriental poppy. See *Papaver orientale*.

Oriental spruce. See *Picea orientalis*.

Oriental sweet gum. See *Liquidambar orientalis*.

Oriental white oak. See *Quercus aliena*.

ORIGANUM

Dittany

LABIATAE/LAMIACEAE

Genus of deciduous sub-shrubs and perennials, sometimes with overwintering leaf rosettes. Some species are grown as culinary herbs, others for their clusters of tubular, usually pink flowers. Most species have arching, prostrate stems and are useful for trailing over rocks, banks and walls. Prefers sun and well-drained, alkaline soil. Propagate by division in spring, by cuttings of non-flowering shoots in early summer or by seed in autumn or spring.

O. amanum. Deciduous, rounded, compact sub-shrub. H and S 15–20cm (6–8in). Open funnel-shaped, pale pink or white flowers are borne all summer above small, heart-shaped, pale green leaves. Makes a good alpine house plant; dislikes a damp atmosphere. Zone 6.

O. dictamnus (Cretan dittany). Prostrate perennial. H 12–15cm (5–6in), S 40cm (16in). Arching stems are clothed in rounded, aromatic, hairy, grey-white leaves. Has pendent heads of open funnel-shaped, purplish-pink flowers in summer.

O. 'Kent Beauty' illus. p.353.

O. laevigatum illus. p.354.

O. rotundifolium. Deciduous, prostrate sub-shrub. H 23–30cm (9–12in), S 30cm (12in). Throughout summer bears whorls of pendent, funnel-shaped, pale pink flowers, surrounded by yellow-green bracts. Has small, rounded, mid-green leaves. Zone 8.

O. vulgare (Wild marjoram). Mat-forming, woody-based perennial. H and S 45cm (18in). Has oval, aromatic, dark green leaves, above which branched, wiry stems bear clusters of tiny, tubular, 2-lipped, mauve flowers in summer.

'Aureum' illus. p.290.

Ornamental cabbage. See *Brassica oleracea* forms, illus. p.324.
Ornamental maize. See *Zea mays*.
Ornamental pepper. See *Capsicum annuum*.
Ornamental yam. See *Dioscorea discolor*, illus. p.219.

ORNITHOGALUM
Star-of-Bethlehem

HYACINTHACEAE/LILIACEAE

Genus of bulbs, grown for their mostly star-shaped, white flowers, usually backed with green. Hardy to tender, min. 7°C (45°F). Needs sun or partial shade and well-drained soil. Lift and dry tender species for winter, if grown outside in summer, and replant in spring. Propagate by seed or offsets, in autumn for spring-flowering bulbs, in spring for summer-flowering bulbs. All parts may cause severe discomfort if ingested; the sap may irritate skin.

O. arabicum illus. p.420.

O. balansae, syn. *O. oligophyllum* of gardens, illus. p.426.

O. lanceolatum illus. p.426.

O. montanum illus. p.426.

O. narbonense illus. p.419.

O. nutans (Drooping star-of-Bethlehem). Spring-flowering bulb. H 15–35cm (6–14in), S 8–10cm (3–4in). Has a cluster of linear, channelled, semi-erect, basal leaves. Stem bears a spike of pendent, bell-shaped, translucent, white flowers, 2–3cm (¾–1¼in) long with pale green outsides. Prefers partial shade.

O. oligophyllum of gardens. See *O. balansae*.

O. saundersiae. Summer-flowering bulb. H to 1m (3ft), S 15–20cm (6–8in). Produces a basal cluster of strap- or lance-shaped, semi-erect leaves. Stem bears a flat-topped head of erect, flattish, white or cream flowers, each with a blackish-green ovary forming a dark eye.

O. thyrsoides illus. p.420.

O. umbellatum. Spring-flowering bulb. H 10–30cm (4–12in), S 10–15cm (4–6in). Linear, channelled, semi-erect, green leaves each have a white line on upper surface. Bears a loose, flat-topped head of star-shaped, white flowers, backed with green.

Orobus vernus. See *Lathyrus vernus*.

ORONTIUM

ARACEAE

Genus of one species of deciduous, perennial, deep-water plant, grown for its floating foliage and flower spikes. Needs full sun. Remove faded flower spikes. Propagate by seed when fresh, in mid-summer.

O. aquaticum illus. p.451.

OROSTACHYS

CRASSULACEAE

Genus of short-lived, basal-rosetted, perennial succulents with very fleshy, sword-shaped leaves. Produces flowers 3 years from sowing seed, then dies. Tender, min. 8°C (46°F). Requires sun and well-drained soil. Propagate by seed or division in spring or summer.

O. chanetii. Basal-rosetted, perennial succulent. H 4cm (1½in), S 8cm (3in). Bears grey-green leaves that are shorter in rosette centre. Flower stem produces a dense, tapering spike of star-shaped, white or pink flowers, 1–2cm (½–¾in) across, in spring-summer.

OROYA

CACTACEAE

Genus of spherical, perennial cacti. Inner flower petals form a tube and outer ones open fully. Tender, min. 10°C (50°F). Needs a sunny, well-drained site. Propagate by seed in spring or summer.

O. neoperuviana. See *O. peruviana*.

O. peruviana, syn. *Oreocereus neoperuviana, O. peruviana,* illus. p.464.

Orphanidesia gaultherioides. See *Epigaea gaultherioides*.

ORTHROSANTHUS

IRIDACEAE

Genus of perennials with short, woody rhizomes, grown for their flowers. Tender, min. 5°C (41°F). Prefers sun and well-drained soil. Propagate by division or seed in spring.

O. chimboracensis. Tufted, rhizomatous perennial. H 60cm (2ft) in flower, S 15cm (6in). Has very narrow, grass-like, ribbed, stiff leaves, to 45cm

(18in) long, with finely toothed margins. In summer, produces clusters of short-lived, long-stalked, shallowly bowl-shaped, lavender-blue flowers, each enclosed in 2 leaf-like bracts.

ORYCHOPHRAGMUS

BRASSICACEAE/CRUCIFERAE

Genus of late spring- to summer-flowering annuals. Grow in sun and in fertile, well-drained soil. Propagate by seed in spring.

O. violaceus illus. p.331.

Osage orange. See *Maclura pomifera*.

OSBECKIA

MELASTOMATACEAE

Genus of evergreen, summer-flowering perennials, sub-shrubs and shrubs, grown for their flowers and foliage. Tender, min. 16°C (61°F). Needs full light or partial shade and humus-rich, well-drained soil. Water potted specimens freely when in full growth, moderately at other times. Cut back flowered stems by at least half in early spring to maintain vigour and to produce large flower trusses. Propagate by seed in spring or by greenwood cuttings in summer.

O. stellata. Evergreen, rounded, stiff-stemmed shrub. H and S 1–2m (3–6ft). Has narrowly oval, hairy, prominently veined leaves. Bears terminal clusters of 4-petalled, rose-purple flowers in late summer.

Oscularia deltoides. See *Lampranthus deltoides*.
Osier, Purple. See *Salix purpurea*.

OSMANTHUS

OLEACEAE

Genus of evergreen shrubs and trees, grown for their foliage and small, fragrant flowers. O. x *burkwoodii* and O. *heterophyllus* may be used for hedging. Tolerates sun or shade and fertile, well-drained soil. Restrict growth by cutting back after flowering; trim hedges in mid-summer. Propagate by semi-ripe cuttings in summer.

O. armatus. Evergreen, bushy, dense shrub. H and S 4m (12ft). Large, oblong, dark green leaves are rigid and sharply toothed. Has tubular, 4-lobed, white flowers in autumn, followed by egg-shaped, dark violet fruits. Zone 9.

O. x burkwoodii, syn. x *Osmarea burkwoodii,* illus. p.116.

O. decorus, syn. *Phillyrea decora.* Evergreen, upright, rounded, dense shrub. H 3m (10ft), S 5m (15ft). Has large, oblong, glossy, dark green leaves. Bears tubular, 4-lobed, white flowers in mid-spring, then egg-shaped, blackish-purple fruits. Zone 7.

O. delavayi, syn. *Siphonosmanthus delavayi,* illus. p.116.

O. forrestii. See *O. yunnanensis.*

O. fragrans (Fragrant olive). Evergreen, upright shrub or tree. H and S 6m (20ft). Marginally hardy. Very fragrant, tubular, 4-lobed, white flowers are borne amid oblong, glossy,

dark green leaves from early to late summer, followed by ovoid, blue-black fruits. Is suitable only for very mild areas. f. *aurantiacus* has orange flowers. Zone 9?.

O. heterophyllus 'Aureomarginatus' illus. p.127. **'Gulftide'** is an evergreen, bushy, dense shrub. H 2.5m (8ft), S 3m (10ft). Holly-shaped, sharply toothed, glossy, dark green leaves set off tubular, 4-lobed, white flowers in autumn. Zone 7.

O. yunnanensis, syn. *O. forrestii.* Evergreen, tree-like, upright, then spreading shrub. H and S 10m (30ft). Has large, oblong, glossy, bright green leaves, bronze when young. Produces tubular, 4-lobed, creamy-white flowers in clusters in late winter or early spring. Zone 9.

x **Osmarea burkwoodii.** See *Osmanthus* x *burkwoodii.*
Osmaronia. Reclassified as *Oemleria.*

OSMUNDA

OSMUNDACEAE

Genus of deciduous ferns. Requires shade, except for O. *regalis*, which also tolerates sun. O. *cinnamomea* and O. *claytoniana* need moist soil; O. *regalis* does best in very wet conditions. Remove fading fronds regularly. Propagate by division in autumn or winter or by spores as soon as ripe.

O. cinnamomea (Cinnamon fern). Deciduous fern. H 1m (3ft), S 45cm (18in). Outer, lance-shaped, divided, pale green sterile fronds, with deeply cut pinnae, surround brown fertile fronds, all arising from a fibrous rootstock.

O. claytoniana (Interrupted fern). Deciduous fern. H 60cm (2ft), S 30cm (1ft). Has lance-shaped, pale green fronds, divided into oblong, blunt pinnae; outer sterile fronds are larger than fertile ones at centre of plant.

O. regalis illus. p.312.

Oso berry. See *Oemleria cerasiformis.*

OSTEOMELES

ROSACEAE

Genus of evergreen, summer-flowering shrubs, grown for their habit, foliage and flowers. In most areas plant against a south- or west-facing wall. Requires a position in sun and fertile, well-drained soil. Propagate by semi-ripe cuttings in summer.

O. schwerinae illus. p.138.

OSTEOSPERMUM

ASTERACEAE/COMPOSITAE

Genus of evergreen, semi-woody perennials. Does best in warm areas. Requires sun and well-drained soil. Propagate by cuttings of non-flowering shoots in mid-summer.

O. barberae of gardens. See *O. jucundum.*

O. 'Blue Streak', syn. *O. ecklonis* 'Blue Streak'. Evergreen, upright perennial. H and S 45cm (18in). In summer-autumn, daisy-like flower heads, with dark slate-blue centres and white ray florets, blue on the reverse, are borne above lance-shaped, grey-green leaves.

O. **'Buttermilk'** illus. p.290.

O. **'Cannington Roy'.** Evergreen, clump-forming, prostrate perennial. H 30cm (12in), S 45cm (18in). Large, daisy-like, pink flower heads, with darker eyes, are borne profusely in summer-autumn. Leaves are linear and grey.

O. ecklonis. Evergreen, upright or somewhat straggling perennial. H and S 45cm (18in). In summer-autumn, daisy-like, white flower heads, with dark blue centres, are borne singly above lance-shaped, grey-green leaves.

'Blue Streak' see *O.* 'Blue Streak'.

O. jucundum, syn. *Dimorphotheca barberae* of gardens, *O. barberae* of gardens, illus. p.279.

O. **'Nairobi Purple'.** Evergreen, semi-prostrate perennial. H 30cm (12in), S 30–45cm (12–18in). Bears daisy-like, velvety, deep purple-red flower heads, with darker streaks on outside of ray petals, in summer. Has fresh green, lance-shaped leaves. Will not flower freely in rich soils.

O. **'Whirligig'.** See *O.* 'Whirlygig'.

O. **'Whirlygig',** syn. *O.* 'Whirligig', illus. p.277.

Ostrich fern. See *Matteuccia struthiopteris,* illus. p.312.

Ostrich-feather fern. See *Matteuccia struthiopteris,* illus. p.312.

OSTROWSKIA

CAMPANULACEAE

Genus of one species of summer-flowering perennial. Prefers a warm, sunny situation and rich, moist but well-drained soil. May be difficult to grow as needs a resting period after flowering, so cover with a frame until late autumn to keep dry. Propagate by seed in autumn or spring.

O. magnifica. Erect perennial. H 1.5m (5ft), S 45cm (1½ft). From early to mid-summer produces very large, bell-shaped blooms of delicate light blue-purple, veined with darker purple. Produces whorls of oval, blue-grey leaves.

OSTRYA

BETULACEAE/CORYLACEAE

Genus of deciduous trees, grown for their foliage, catkins and fruits. Needs

sun or semi-shade and fertile, well-drained soil. Propagate by seed in autumn.

O. carpinifolia (Hop hornbeam). Deciduous, rounded tree. H and S 15m (50ft). Has grey bark and oval, glossy, dark green leaves that turn yellow in autumn. Yellow catkins in mid-spring are followed by hop-like, greenish-white fruit clusters that become brown in autumn. Zone 6.

O. virginiana illus. p.77.

OTHONNA,
syn. OTHONNOPSIS

ASTERACEAE/COMPOSITAE

Genus of evergreen shrubs, grown for their daisy-like flower heads in summer. Needs sun and well-drained soil. Propagate by softwood cuttings in early summer.

O. cheirifolia illus. p.358.

Othonnopsis. Reclassified as *Othonna.*

OURISIA

SCROPHULARIACEAE

Genus of evergreen perennials with creeping rootstocks. Excellent for peat beds and walls. Needs shade and moist, peaty soil. Propagate by division or seed in spring.

O. caespitosa illus. p.374.

O. **'Loch Ewe'.** Vigorous, evergreen, rosetted perennial. H and S 30cm (12in). Prostrate stems have heart-shaped, leathery, green leaves. Produces dense spikes of outward-facing, tubular, salmon-pink flowers in late spring and early summer.

O. macrocarpa. Vigorous, evergreen, prostrate perennial. H 60cm (24in), S 20cm (8in). Has rosettes of heart-shaped, leathery, dark green leaves. Produces spikes of open cup-shaped, yellow-centred, white flowers in late spring.

O. magellanica. See *O. ruellioides.*

O. microphylla illus. p.376.

O. ruellioides, syn. *O. magellanica.* Evergreen, straggling perennial. H 4cm (1½in), S to 15cm (6in). In summer produces tubular, scarlet flowers above broadly heart-shaped leaves.

Ovens wattle. See *Acacia pravissima,* illus. p.97.

Owl-eyes. See *Huernia zebrina.*

OXALIS

OXALIDACEAE

Genus of tuberous, rhizomatous or fibrous-rooted perennials and semi-evergreen sub-shrubs, grown for their colourful flowers, which in bud are rolled like an umbrella, and attractive leaves. Leaves are mostly less than 2cm (¾in) across and are divided into 3 or more leaflets. Some species may be invasive; smaller species and cultivars suit a rock garden. Hardy to tender, min. 5°C (41°F). Needs full sun or semi-shade and well-drained soil. Propagate by division in autumn or early spring.

O. acetosella (Wood sorrel). Creeping, spring-flowering, rhizomatous perennial. H 5cm (2in), S 30–45cm (12–18in). Forms mats of clover-like, 3-lobed leaves. Delicate stems bear cup-shaped, white flowers, each 1cm (½in) across with 5 purple-veined petals. Prefers semi-shade.

var. *purpurascens* see *O.a.* var. *subpurpurascens.* var. *subpurpurascens* (syn. *O.a.* var. *purpurascens*) illus. p.365.

O. adenophylla illus. p.366.

O. bowiei, syn. *O. purpurata* var. *bowiei.* Spring- to summer-flowering, tuberous perennial. H to 30cm (12in), S 15cm (6in). Has long-stalked, clover-like, 3-lobed leaves. Stems each produce a loose head of 3–10 widely funnel-shaped, pinkish-purple flowers, 3–4cm (1¼–1½in) across. Needs a sheltered, sunny site.

O. chrysantha. Creeping, fibrous-rooted perennial. H 4–5cm (1½–2in), S 15–30cm (6–12in). Forms mats of clover-like, 3-lobed leaves. Stems each produce a funnel-shaped, bright yellow flower, 2–3cm (¾–1¼in) across, in summer. Needs a sheltered site.

O. deppei. See *O. tetraphylla.*

O. depressa, syn. *O. inops,* illus. p.378.

O. enneaphylla (Scurvy grass). Tuft-forming, rhizomatous perennial. H 5–7cm (2–3in), S 8–10cm (3–4in). Grey-green leaves are divided into narrowly oblong to oval leaflets. In summer, stems bear widely funnel-shaped, 3–4cm (1¼–1½in) wide, lilac-pink or white flowers.

O. hedysaroides. Semi-evergreen, bushy sub-shrub. H 1m (3ft), S 30–45cm (1–1½ft). Stems have clover-like, 3-lobed, green leaves. Leaf axils bear clusters of widely funnel-shaped, yellow flowers, 2–3cm (¾–1¼in) across, in spring-summer.

O. hirta. Late summer-flowering, tuberous perennial. H 30cm (12in),

S 10–15cm (4–6in). Stem produces scattered leaves, with 3 narrowly lance-shaped leaflets. Leaf axils each produce a widely funnel-shaped, rose-purple flower, 2–3cm (¾–1¼in) wide, with a yellow centre.

O. inops. See *O. depressa.*

O. **'Ione Hecker'.** Tuft-forming, rhizomatous perennial. H 5cm (2in), S 5–8cm (2–3in). Grey leaves are composed of narrowly oblong, wavy leaflets. In summer bears funnel-shaped, pale purple-blue flowers, 4cm (1½in) across, with darker veins.

O. laciniata. Tuft-forming, rhizomatous perennial. H 5cm (2in), S 5–8cm (2–3in). Has blue-grey leaves with narrowly oblong, crinkly-edged leaflets. In summer bears wide funnel-shaped, steel-blue flowers, 4cm (1½in) across, with darker veins.

O. lobata illus. p.387.

O. purpurata var. *bowiei.* See *O. bowiei.*

O. tetraphylla, syn. *O. deppei,* illus. p.353.

Ox-eye, Yellow. See *Buphthalmum salicifolium,* illus. p.292.

Oxlip. See *Primula elatior,* illus. p.273.

OXYDENDRUM

ERICACEAE

Genus of one species of deciduous tree, grown for its flowers and spectacular autumn colour. For good colouring plant in an open position in sun or semi-shade. Needs moist, acid soil. Propagate by softwood cuttings in summer or by seed in autumn.

O. arboreum illus. p.78.

Oxypetalum caeruleum. See *Tweedia caerulea.*

OZOTHAMNUS

ASTERACEAE/COMPOSITAE

Genus of evergreen, summer-flowering shrubs, grown for their foliage and small, densely clustered flower heads. Requires full sun and well-drained soil. Propagate by semi-ripe cuttings in summer.

O. coralloides, syn. *Helichrysum coralloides,* illus. p.361.

O. ledifolius, syn. *Helichrysum ledifolium,* illus. p.160.

O. rosmarinifolius, syn. *Helichrysum rosmarinifolium,* illus. p.138.

O. selago, syn. *Helichrysum selago,* illus. p.361.

P

PACHYCEREUS

CACTACEAE

Genus of slow-growing, columnar, perennial cacti, branching with age. The funnel-shaped flowers are unlikely to appear in cultivation as they are produced only on plants over 3m (10ft) high. Tender, min. 10°C (50°F). Requires sun and well-drained soil. Propagate by seed in spring or summer.

P. marginatus, syn. *Lemaireocereus marginatus*, *Marginatocereus marginatus*, *Stenocereus marginatus*, illus. p.457.

P. pecten-aboriginum. Columnar, perennial cactus. H 11m (35ft), S 3m (10ft). Dark green stems bear 9–11 deep ribs. Each areole has 8 radial spines, 1cm (½in) long, and longer central spines. All spines are dark brown with red bases and fade to grey.

P. pringlei illus. p.460.

P. schottii, syn. *Lophocereus schottii*, illus. p.458. **'Monstrosus'** is a columnar, perennial cactus. H 7m (22ft), S 2m (6ft). Irregular, olive- to dark green stems have 4–15 ribs and no spines. Has funnel-shaped, pink flowers, 3cm (1¼in) wide, at night in summer.

PACHYPHRAGMA

BRASSICACEAE/CRUCIFERAE

Genus of perennials with rosettes of basal leaves, often grown as ground cover under shrubs. Needs sun or partial shade and moist soil. Propagate by division or stem cuttings in late spring or by seed in autumn.

P. macrophyllum, syn. *Thlaspi macrophyllum*, illus. p.267.

PACHYPHYTUM

CRASSULACEAE

Genus of rosetted, perennial succulents, closely related to *Echeveria*, with which it hybridizes. Tender, min. 5–10°C (41–50°F). Needs sun and well-drained soil. Propagate by seed, or leaf or stem cuttings in spring or summer.

P. compactum illus. p.480.

P. oviferum illus. p.475.

PACHYPODIUM

APOCYNACEAE

Genus of bushy or tree-like, perennial succulents, mostly with swollen stems, closely related to *Adenium*, except that most species have spines. Tender, min. 10–15°C (50–59°F). Requires full sun and very well-drained soil. May be very difficult to grow. Propagate by seed in spring or summer.

P. lamerei illus. p.456.

P. succulentum. Tree-like, perennial succulent. H 60cm (2ft), S 30cm (1ft). Min. 10°C (50°F). Swollen trunk, 15cm (6in) across, has narrow, vertical, green to grey-brown stems. Has trumpet-shaped, pink-crimson flowers, 2cm (¾in) across, near stem tips in summer.

PACHYSANDRA

BUXACEAE

Genus of evergreen, creeping perennials and sub-shrubs, grown for their tufted foliage. Is useful for ground cover. Tolerates dense shade and will grow well in any but very dry soil. Propagate by division in spring.

P. procumbens (Alleghany spurge). A clump-forming semi-evergreen perennial. H 30cm (12in) S indefinite. Toothed leaves are in whorls and are a dark green, often mottled with brown. Spikes of fragrant white flowers appear with the new foliage in spring.

P. terminalis illus. p.388.

'Variegata' is an evergreen, creeping perennial. H 10cm (4in), S 20cm (8in). Diamond-shaped, cream-variegated leaves are clustered at stem tips. In early summer bears spikes of tiny, white flowers, sometimes flushed purple.

PACHYSTACHYS

ACANTHACEAE

Genus of evergreen perennials and shrubs, grown for their flowers. Tender, min. 13–18°C (55–64°F). Needs partial shade and fertile, well-drained soil. Water potted plants freely when in full growth, moderately at other times. Cut back flowered stems in late winter to maintain a bushy habit. Propagate by greenwood cuttings in early summer. Whitefly and spider mite may cause problems.

P. cardinalis. See *P. coccinea*.

P. coccinea, syn. *Jacobinia coccinea*, *Justicia coccinea*, *P. cardinalis* (Cardinal's guard). Evergreen, erect, robust shrub. H 1.2–2m (4–6ft), S 60cm–1m (2–3ft). Min. 15–18°C (59–64°F) to flower well. Leaves are oval and deep green. Has tubular, bright red flowers in tight, green-bracted spikes, 15cm (6in) long, in winter.

P. lutea illus. p.157.

Pachystima. Reclassified as *Paxistima*.

x PACHYVERIA

CRASSULACEAE

Hybrid genus (*Echeveria* x *Pachyphytum*) of clump-forming, rosetted, perennial succulents, sometimes almost stemless. Tender, min. 5–7°C (41–5°F). Requires a position in full sun or partial shade and very well-drained soil. Propagate by leaf or stem cuttings in spring or summer.

x *P. glauca* illus. p.466.

Pacific dogwood. See *Cornus nuttallii*, illus. p.76.
Pacific fir. See *Abies amabilis*.

PAEONIA

Peony

PAEONIACEAE

Genus of late spring-flowering perennials and deciduous shrubs ('tree peonies'), valued for their bold foliage, showy blooms and, in some species, colourful seed pods. Hardy, unless otherwise stated, although young growth (especially on tree peonies) may be damaged by late spring frosts. Prefers sun (but tolerates light shade) and rich, well-drained soil. Tall and very large-flowered cultivars need support. Propagate all species by seed in autumn (may take up to 3 years to germinate), tuberous species by root cuttings in winter, tree peonies by semi-ripe cuttings in late summer or by grafting in winter. Perennials may also be propagated by division in late summer. Is prone to peony wilt. All parts can cause mild stomach upset if ingested. See also feature panel pp.236–7.

Flower forms

Unless stated otherwise, peonies described below flower between late spring and early to mid-summer and have large, alternate leaves divided into oval to lance-shaped or linear leaflets. Flowers are single, semi-double, double or anemone-form.

Single – flowers are mostly cup-shaped, with 1 or 2 rows of large, often lightly ruffled, incurving petals and a conspicuous central boss of stamens.

Semi-double – flowers are similar to single ones, but have 2 or 3 rows of petals.

Double – flowers are rounded, usually composed of 1 or 2 outer rows of large, often lightly ruffled, incurving petals, the remaining petals being smaller, usually becoming more densely arranged and diminishing in size towards the centre. Stamens are few, inconspicuous, or absent.

Anemone-form (Imperial or Japanese) – flowers usually have 1 or 2 rows of broad, incurving, outer petals; the centre of the flower is often filled entirely with numerous densely arranged, sometimes deeply cut, narrow petaloids derived from stamens.

P. **'Alice Harding'** (illus. p.236). Clump-forming perennial. H and S to 1m (3ft). Bears very large, fragrant, double, creamy-white flowers.

P. **'America'**. Clump-forming perennial. H and S to 1m (3ft). Has large, single flowers with very broad, crimson petals, lightly ruffled at edges.

P. **'Argosy'** (illus. p.237). Deciduous, upright shrub (tree peony). H and S to 1.5m (5ft). Magnificent, large, single flowers are lemon-yellow, each with a crimson-purple blotch at base. Is hard to propagate. Zone 5.

P. arietina. See *P. mascula* subsp. *arietina*.

P. **'Auguste Dessert'** (illus. p.237). Clump-forming perennial. H and S to 75cm (30in). Foliage provides rich autumn colour. Has masses of fragrant, semi-double flowers; carmine petals are tinged salmon-pink and have slightly ruffled, striking silvery-white margins.

P. **'Avant Garde'** (illus. p.236). Clump-forming perennial. H and S to 1m (3ft). Has luxuriant foliage. Medium-sized to large, fragrant, single flowers are pale rose-pink with darker veins and bright golden anthers that have yellow-red filaments. Flowers are borne on stiff, straight stems in mid-spring and are ideal for cutting.

P. **'Ballerina'** (illus. p.236). Clump-forming perennial. H and S 1m (3ft). Foliage provides autumn colour. Fragrant, double flowers are soft blush-pink, tinged lilac at first, later fading to white. Outer rows of petals are loosely arranged, very broad and incurving; inner petals are also incurving, but more densely arranged, narrower, more uneven in size and often have slightly ruffled margins.

P. **'Baroness Schroeder'** (illus. p.236). Vigorous, clump-forming perennial. H and S to 1m (3ft). Is very free-flowering with large, fragrant, globe-shaped, double flowers, tinged with pale flesh-pink on opening but fading to almost pure white. Has several rows of nearly flat, outer petals; inner petals are incurving, ruffled and very tightly arranged. Is one of the best peonies for cutting.

P. **'Barrymore'**. Clump-forming perennial. H and S to 85cm (34in). Has very large, anemone-form flowers with broad, outer petals that are palest blush-pink on opening, later white. Clear pale golden-yellow petaloids are very narrow, relatively short and are neatly and densely arranged.

P. **'Bowl of Beauty'** (illus. p.236). Clump-forming perennial. H and S to 1m (3ft). Has very large, striking, anemone-form flowers with pale carmine-pink, outer petals and numerous narrow, densely arranged, ivory-white petaloids.

P. cambessedesii (Majorcan peony; illus. p.236). Clump-forming perennial. H and S 45cm (18in). Marginally hardy. Has especially attractive foliage, dark green above with veins, stalks and under-surfaces suffused purple-red. Single, deep rose-pink flowers are borne in mid-spring.

P. **'Cheddar Cheese'**. Clump-forming perennial. H and S to 1m (3ft). Produces well-formed, large, double flowers in mid-summer. Neatly and densely arranged, slightly ruffled, ivory-white petals, the inner ones incurving, are interspersed with shorter, yellow petals.

P. **'Chocolate Soldier'** (illus. p.237). Clump-forming perennial. H and S to 1m (3ft). Has mid- to dark green leaves that are often tinged bronze-red when young. Semi-double, purple-red flowers, borne in early summer, have yellow-mottled centres.

P. **'Colonel Heneage'**. Clump-forming perennial of upright habit. H and S to 85cm (34in). Has masses of anemone-form flowers with both outer petals and inner petaloids of dark rose-crimson.

P. **corallina**. See *P. mascula* subsp. *mascula*.

P. **'Cornelia Shaylor'** (illus. p.236). Erect, clump-forming perennial. H and S to 85cm (34in). Fragrant, double flowers, flushed rose-pink on opening and gradually fading to blush-white, are borne freely from early to mid-summer. Ruffled petals are neatly and densely arranged.

P. **'Dayspring'**. Clump-forming perennial. H and S to 70cm (28in). Has an abundance of fragrant, single, clear pink flowers borne in trusses.

P. **decora**. See *P. peregrina*.

P. **'Defender'** (illus. p.237). Clump-forming, vigorous perennial. H and S to 1m (3ft). Single, satiny crimson flowers, to 15cm (6in) across, with a central boss of golden anthers, are carried on strong stems.

P. **delavayi** (illus. p.237). Deciduous, upright, open shrub (tree peony). H to 2m (6ft), S to 1.2m (4ft). Leaves are divided into pointed-oval leaflets, often with reddish stalks. Single flowers are small, bowl-shaped and rich dark red, with conspicuous, leafy bracts below flowers. Zone 5b. var. *ludlowii* see *P. lutea* var. *ludlowii*. var. *lutea* see *P. lutea*.

P. **'Dresden'**. Robust, clump-forming perennial. H and S to 85cm (34in). Foliage provides autumn colour. Single flowers are ivory-white, tinged with soft blush-rose-pink.

P. **'Duchesse de Nemours'**, syn. *P.* 'Mrs Gwyn Lewis' (illus. p.236). Vigorous, clump-forming perennial. H and S to 70cm (28in). Produces masses of richly fragrant, double flowers with very large, incurving, outer petals, tinged palest green at first, soon fading to pure white; inner petals with irregular margins are densely arranged towards the centre and are creamy-yellow at their base.

P. **emodi** (illus. p.236). Clump-forming perennial. H to 1.2m (4ft), S to 1m (3ft). Glossy, green foliage is topped by tall stems bearing several large, fragrant, single, pure white flowers with golden-yellow anthers.

P. **'Evening World'** (illus. p.236). Clump-forming perennial. H and S to 1m (3ft). Has abundant, large, anemone-form flowers with soft blush-pink, outer petals and very tightly arranged, pale flesh-pink petaloids.

P. **'Félix Crousse'**, syn. *P.* 'Victor Hugo'. Vigorous, clump-forming perennial. H and S to 75cm (30in). Bears a profusion of fragrant, double, rich carmine-pink flowers with darker red centres. Petals are ruffled, very numerous and tightly arranged, with edges sometimes tipped silvery-white.

P. **'Festiva Maxima'**. Clump-forming perennial. H and S to 1m (3ft). Has dense, spreading foliage and huge, fragrant, double flowers borne on strong stems. Rather loosely arranged petals are large with irregular margins;

outer petals are pure white, inner ones each have a basal, crimson blotch.

P. **'Flamingo'**. Clump-forming perennial. H and S to 85cm (34in). Foliage provides autumn colour. Double flowers are large and clear pale salmon-pink.

P. **'Globe of Light'** (illus. p.236). Clump-forming perennial. H and S to 1m (3ft). Has large, fragrant, anemone-form flowers. Outer petals are pure rose-pink, petaloids clear golden-yellow.

P. **'Heirloom'**. Compact, clump-forming perennial. H and S to 70cm (28in). Bears masses of large, fragrant, double, pale lilac-pink flowers.

P. **'Instituteur Doriat'** (illus. p.237). Clump-forming perennial. H and S to 1m (3ft). Foliage provides autumn colour. Has abundant, large, anemone-form flowers with reddish-carmine, outer petals and densely arranged, relatively broad petaloids, paler and more pink than outer petals, with ruffled, silvery-white margins.

P. **'Kelway's Gorgeous'** (illus. p.237). Clump-forming perennial. H and S to 85cm (34in). Single, intense clear carmine flowers, with a hint of salmon-pink, are borne very freely.

P. **'Kelway's Majestic'**. Clump-forming perennial. H and S to 1m (3ft). Freely borne, large, fragrant, anemone-form flowers have bright cherry rose-pink, outer petals and lilac-pink petaloids flecked with silver or pale gold.

P. **'Kelway's Supreme'** (illus. p.236). Clump-forming perennial. H and S to 1m (3ft). Foliage provides autumn colour. Has large, strongly fragrant, double flowers, produced over a long period, sometimes borne in clusters on well-established plants. Petals are broad, incurving, soft blush-pink, fading to milk-white. Single or semi-double axillary flowers are often produced.

P. **'Knighthood'** (illus. p.237). Clump-forming perennial. H and S to 75cm (30in). Double flowers have densely arranged, rather narrow, ruffled petals of unusually rich burgundy-red.

P. **'Krinkled White'** (illus. p.236). Robust, clump-forming perennial. H and S to 80cm (32in). Large, bowl-shaped, single, milk-white flowers are sometimes flushed palest pink. Petals are large with ruffled margins.

P. **'Laura Dessert'** (illus. p.237). Clump-forming perennial. H and S to 75cm (30in). Produces fragrant, double flowers with creamy blush-white, outer petals. Densely arranged, incurving, inner petals are flushed rich lemon-yellow, and their margins are sometimes deeply cut.

P. **'L'Espérance'**, syn. *P.* x *lemoinei* 'L'Espérance' (illus. p.237). Has very large, single, primrose-yellow flowers with a carmine blotch at the base of each petal.

P. x *lemoinei* **'L'Espérance'**. See *P.* 'L'Espérance'.

P. **lobata**. See *P. peregrina*.

P. **lutea**, syn. *P. delavayi* var. *lutea*. Deciduous, upright shrub (tree peony). H and S to 1.5m (5ft). Single flowers are usually vivid yellow; brownish- or purplish-yellow forms also occur.

Zone 6. var. *ludlowii* (syn. *P. delavayi* var. *ludlowii*; illus. p.237), H and S to 2.5m (8ft), is grown as much for its large, bright green leaves, divided into deeply cut, pointed leaflets, as for its bowl-shaped, golden-yellow flowers. Zone 6.

P. **'Madame Louis Henri'** (illus. p.237). Deciduous, upright shrub (tree peony). H and S to 1.5m (5ft). Has loosely semi-double, whitish-yellow flowers with large, incurving, outer petals very heavily suffused with rusty-red. Smaller, often darker, inner petals each have a basal, dull red blotch. Zone 5.

P. **'Magic Orb'** (illus. p.237). Clump-forming perennial. H and S to 1m (3ft). Foliage provides autumn colour. Bears masses of large, strongly fragrant, double flowers, each with several outer whorls of fairly broad, ruffled, intense cherry-pink petals and a centre of densely arranged, smaller, incurving petals. Outermost rows of central petals are blush-white, heavily shaded with mid-rose-carmine; the innermost petals are mostly creamy-white.

P. **mascula** subsp. **arietina**, syn. *P. arietina*. Tuberous perennial. H and S to 75cm (30in). Foliage is hairy underneath and dark green; stems are dark red. Has single, reddish-pink flowers. Seed capsules with 2–5 boat-shaped sections split to reveal purplish-black seeds. subsp. **mascula** (syn. *P. corallina*; illus. p.236) is clump-forming, H and S to 1m (3ft), with hairless leaflets. Produces purple- or carmine-red, occasionally pink or white, flowers with bosses of golden-yellow anthers borne on purple filaments.

P. **mlokosewitschii** (illus. p.237). Clump-forming perennial. H and S to 75cm (30in). Soft bluish-green foliage, sometimes edged reddish-purple, is topped by large, single, lemon-yellow flowers.

P. **'Mother of Pearl'** (illus p.236). Clump-forming perennial. H to 75cm (30in) and S to 60cm (24in). Greyish-green leaves provide an attractive foil for the single, dog rose-pink flowers.

P. **'Mrs Gwyn Lewis'**. See *P.* 'Duchesse de Nemours'.

P. **obovata** var. **alba** (illus. p.236). Clump-forming perennial. H and S 70–90cm (28–36in). Has erect stems and large, deep green leaves, each with 9 uneven, broadly elliptic leaflets, pale grey-green and slightly hairy beneath. Bears single, cup-shaped, white flowers with purple filaments.

P. **officinalis**. Clump-forming, tuberous perennial. H and S to 60cm (24in). This single, red apothecaries' peony has long been in cultivation, but is seldom seen today, having been superseded by larger, often double-flowered hybrids, such as the following. **'Alba Plena'** (illus. p.236), H and S to 75cm (30in), has double, white flowers that are sometimes tinged with pink. **'China Rose'** (illus. p.237), H and S to 45cm (18in), has handsome, dark green foliage and single flowers with incurving, clear dark salmon-rose petals contrasting with central bosses of orange-yellow anthers. **'Rubra Plena'** (illus. p.237), H and S to 75cm

(30in), is long-lived and has distinctive foliage, divided into broadly oval leaflets, and double, vivid pinkish-crimson flowers with ruffled petals.

P. **peregrina**, syn. *P. decora*, *P. lobata*. Clump-forming, tuberous perennial. H and S to 1m (3ft). Produces bowl-shaped, single, ruby-red flowers. **'Otto Froebel'** (syn. *P.p.* 'Sunshine'; illus. p.237) has glossy, bright green leaves and bears large, single, vermilion flowers, tinged with salmon-rose.

P. **potaninii**. Deciduous, rhizomatous shrub (tree peony). H to 60cm (24in), S indefinite. Has deeply divided leaves with narrowly oval, irregularly cut or lobed leaflets and small, single, deep maroon-red, or occasionally white flowers. Is similar to *P. delavayi*, but is more invasive and has less conspicuous, leafy bracts below the flowers. Zone 6. var. *trollioides* (illus. p.237) has finely divided leaves and yellow flowers.

P. **'Président Poincaré'**. Clump-forming perennial. H and S to 1m (3ft). Foliage provides autumn colour. Fragrant, double, clear rich ruby-crimson flowers are borne very freely.

P. **rockii**. See *P. suffruticosa* subsp. *rockii*.

P. **'Sarah Bernhardt'** (illus. p.236). Vigorous, erect, clump-forming perennial. H and S to 1m (3ft). Produces an abundance of huge, fragrant, fully double flowers with large, ruffled, slightly dull rose-pink petals, fading to silvery blush-white at margins.

P. **'Shirley Temple'** (illus. p.236). Clump-forming perennial. H and S to 85cm (34in). Profuse, soft rose-pink flowers, fading to palest buff-white, are fully double, with broad petals arranged in whorls; innermost petals are smaller and more loosely packed.

P. **'Silver Flare'** (illus. p.237). Clump-forming perennial. H and S to 1m (3ft). Foliage gives autumn colour. Stems are flushed dull reddish-brown. Produces masses of fragrant, single flowers with rather long, slender, rich carmine-pink petals, each feathering to a striking silvery-white margin.

P. **'Sir Edward Elgar'** (illus. p.237). Clump-forming perennial. H and S to 75cm (30in). Foliage provides autumn colour. Has an abundance of single, chocolate-brown-tinged, rich crimson flowers with bosses of loosely arranged, clear lemon-yellow anthers.

P. x *smouthii* (illus. p.237). Clump-forming perennial. H and S to 60cm (24in). Produces an abundance of fragrant, single, glistening, dark crimson flowers, to 10cm (4in) across, with conspicuous, yellow stamens, although both flowers and foliage may vary in colour.

P. **'Souvenir de Maxime Cornu'** (illus. p.237). Deciduous, upright shrub (tree peony). H and S to 1.5m (5ft). Large, richly fragrant flowers are fully double with warm golden-yellow petals densely arranged towards centres; ruffled margins are dull reddish-orange. Zone 5.

P. **suffruticosa** (Moutan). Deciduous, upright shrub (tree peony). H and S to 2.2m (7ft). Bears variable, large, cup-shaped flowers, single or semi-

double, with incurving, rose-pink or white petals, each sometimes with a basal, usually chocolate-maroon blotch. Has given rise to many cultivars with semi-double and double flowers. **'Cardinal Vaughan'** (illus. p.237) has semi-double, ruby-purple flowers. **'Godaishu'** ('large globe'; illus. p.236) bears semi- or fully double, white flowers with yellow centres amid light green leaves that are fringed and twisted. **'Hana-daijin'** ('magnificent flower'; illus. p.237), H and S 2m (6ft) or more, is a vigorous cultivar that bears masses of double, purple flowers. **'Hana-kisoi'** ('floral rivalry'; illus. p.236) has double, pale cerise-pink flowers. JEWEL IN THE LOTUS (**'Tama-fuyo'**) is vigorous and freely produces double, pink flowers earlier than most other cultivars. **'Joseph Rock'** see *P.s.* subsp. *rockii*. **'Kamadu-nishiki'** ('kamada brocade'; illus. p.237), H and S to 1.2m (4ft), produces large, double flowers, to 20cm (8in) across, that are lilac-pink striped white at the edge of each petal. **'Reine Elizabeth'** (illus. p.236), H and S to 2m (6ft), has large, fully double flowers with broad, salmon-pink petals, flushed with bright copper-red and lightly ruffled at margins. **'Renkaku'** ('flight of cranes'), H and S to 1m (3ft), bears double flowers, each with broad, incurving, slightly ruffled, ivory-white petals, loosely arranged in 3 or more whorls, that surround a large boss of long, golden-yellow anthers. subsp. *rockii* (syn. *P. rockii*, *P.s.* 'Joseph Rock', *P.s.* 'Rock's Variety'; illus. p.236) has large, spreading, semi-double, white flowers; inner petals each have a basal, dark maroon blotch. Is difficult to propagate. **'Rock's Variety'** see *P.s.* subsp. *rockii*. **'Tama-fuyo'** see *P.s.* JEWEL IN THE LOTUS. All Zone 5 with winter mulch.
P. tenuifolia (illus. p.237). Clump-forming perennial. H and S to 45cm (18in). Elegant leaves are finely divided into many linear segments. Has single, dark crimson flowers, with golden-yellow anthers.
P. veitchii (illus. p.237). Clump-forming perennial. H and S to 75cm (30in). Shiny, bright green leaves are divided into oblong to elliptic leaflets. In early summer produces nodding, cup-shaped, single, purple-pink flowers.
P. **'Victor Hugo'.** See *P.* 'Félix Crousse'.
P. **'White Wings'** (illus. p.236). Clump-forming perennial. H and S to 85cm (34in). Glossy, dark green foliage also provides autumn colour. In mid-summer produces masses of large, fragrant, single flowers with broad, white petals, sometimes tinged sulphur-yellow, that are each slightly ruffled at the apex.
P. **'Whitleyi Major'** (illus. p.236). Clump-forming perennial. H to 1m (3ft), S to 60cm (2ft). Foliage and stems are flushed rich reddish-brown. Large, single, ivory-white flowers have a satin sheen and central bosses of clear yellow anthers.
P. wittmanniana (illus. p.237). Clump-forming perennial. H and S to 1m (3ft). Has large, single, pale primrose-yellow

flowers, each with a large, central boss of yellow anthers on purple-red filaments. Leaves are divided into broadly oval leaflets, shiny dark green above, paler beneath.

Pagoda tree. See *Sophora japonica*.
Paintbrush. See *Haemanthus albiflos*.
  Royal. See *Scadoxus puniceus*.
Painted net-leaf. See *Fittonia albivenis* Verschaffeltii Group, illus. p.302.
Painted nettle. See *Solenostemon*.
Painted trillium. See *Trillium undulatum*.
Painted wood lily. See *Trillium undulatum*.

PALIURUS

RHAMNACEAE

Genus of deciduous, spiny, summer-flowering shrubs and trees, grown for their foliage and flowers. *P. spina-christi* is also grown for its religious association, reputedly being the plant from which Christ's crown of thorns was made. Requires full sun and well-drained soil. Propagate by softwood cuttings in summer or by seed in autumn.
P. spina-christi illus. p.122.

Palm
  Alexandra. See *Archontophoenix alexandrae*, illus. p.72.
  Australian cabbage. See *Livistona australis*.
  Bamboo. See *Rhapis excelsa*, illus. p.152.
  Canary Island date. See *Phoenix canariensis*.
  Chilean wine. See *Jubaea chilensis*, illus. p.85.
  Chinese fan. See *Livistona chinensis*, illus. p.85.
  Chinese fountain. See *Livistona chinensis*, illus. p.85.
  Chusan. See *Trachycarpus fortunei*, illus. p.84.
  Cuban royal. See *Roystonea regia*.
  Desert fan. See *Washingtonia filifera*.
  Dwarf fan. See *Chamaerops humilis*, illus. p.176.
  Dwarf mountain. See *Chamaedorea elegans*, illus. p.152.
  European fan. See *Chamaerops humilis*, illus. p.176.
  Gippsland fountain. See *Livistona australis*.
  Golden-feather. See *Dypsis lutescens*, illus. p.100.
  Illawarra. See *Archontophoenix cunninghamiana*.
  Japanese sago. See *Cycas revoluta*, illus. p.152.
  Jelly. See *Butia capitata*, illus. p.100.
  King. See *Archontophoenix*.
  Miniature date. See *Phoenix roebelenii*.
  Northern bungalow. See *Archontophoenix alexandrae*, illus. p.72.
  Paradise. See *Howea forsteriana*.
  Parlour. See *Chamaedorea elegans*, illus. p.152.
  Piccabeen. See *Archontophoenix cunninghamiana*.
  Pygmy date. See *Phoenix roebelenii*.

Palm (continued)
  Queen. See *Syagrus*.
  Royal. See *Roystonea*.
  Sentry. See *Howea forsteriana*.
  Slender lady. See *Rhapis excelsa*, illus. p.152.
  Thatch-leaf. See *Howea forsteriana*.
  Thread. See *Washingtonia robusta*, illus. p.73.
  Virgin's. See *Dioon edule*.
  Windmill. See *Trachycarpus fortunei*, illus. p.84.
  Yatay. See *Butia*.
  Yellow. See *Dypsis lutescens*, illus. p.100.
Palmetto
  Dwarf. See *Sabal minor*, illus. p.176.
  Saw. See *Serenoa repens*.
  Scrub. See *Serenoa repens*.
Palo verde, Mexican. See *Parkinsonia aculeata*.

PAMIANTHE

AMARYLLIDACEAE

Genus of one species of evergreen, spring-flowering bulb, grown for its large, strongly fragrant, showy flowers. Tender, min. 12°C (54°F). Needs partial shade and rich, well-drained soil. Feed with high-potash liquid fertilizer in summer. Reduce watering in winter but do not allow to dry out. Propagate by seed in spring or by offsets in late winter.
P. peruviana illus. p.409.

Pampas grass. See *Cortaderia selloana*.

PANCRATIUM

AMARYLLIDACEAE

Genus of bulbs with large, fragrant, daffodil-like flowers in summer. Needs sun and well-drained soil that is warm and dry in summer when bulbs are dormant. Plant at least 15cm (6in) deep. Feed with a high-potash liquid fertilizer every 2 weeks from autumn to spring. Propagate by seed in autumn or by offsets detached in early autumn.
P. illyricum illus. p.419.
P. maritimum (Sea daffodil, Sea lily). Late summer-flowering bulb. H 45cm (18in), S 25–30cm (10–12in). Has strap-shaped, erect, basal, greyish-green leaves. Produces a head of 5–12 white flowers, each with a large, deep cup in the centre and 6 spreading petals. Is shy-flowering in cultivation.

Panda plant. See *Kalanchoe tomentosa*, illus. p.467.

PANDANUS
Screw pine

PANDANACEAE

Genus of evergreen trees, shrubs and scramblers, grown for their foliage and overall appearance. Flowers and fruits only appear on large, mature specimens. Tender, min. 13–16°C (55–61°F). Requires full light or partial shade and fertile, well-drained soil. Water containerized plants freely when in full growth, moderately at other times. Propagate by seed or suckers

in spring or by cuttings of lateral shoots in summer. Spider mite may be troublesome.
P. odoratissimus. See *P. tectorius.*
P. tectorius, syn. *P. odoratissimus.* Evergreen, rounded tree. H to 6m (20ft), S 3m (10ft) or more. Has rosettes of strap-shaped, deep green leaves, each 1–1.5m (3–5ft) long, with spiny margins and a spiny midrib beneath. Small flowers, the males in clusters, each with a lance-shaped, white bract, appear mainly in summer. Fruits are like round pineapples.
'Veitchii' (syn. *P. veitchii*) illus. p.175.
P. veitchii. See *P. tectorius* 'Veitchii'.

PANDOREA

BIGNONIACEAE

Genus of evergreen, woody-stemmed, twining climbers, grown for their handsome flowers and attractive leaves. Tender, min. 5°C (41°F). Grow in sun and in any well-drained soil. Prune after flowering to restrain growth. Propagate by seed sown in spring or by stem cuttings or layering in summer.
P. jasminoides, syn. *Bignonia jasminoides*, illus. p.208.
P. lindleyana. See *Clytostoma callistegioides*.
P. pandorana, syn. *Bignonia pandorana*, *Tecoma australis* (Wonga-wonga vine). Fast-growing, evergreen, woody-stemmed, twining climber. H 6m (20ft) or more. Leaves have 3–9 scalloped leaflets. Small, funnel-shaped, cream flowers, which are streaked and often spotted with red, brown or purple, are borne in clusters in summer.
P. ricasoliana. See *Podranea ricasoliana*.

PANICUM

GRAMINEAE/POACEAE

See also GRASSES, BAMBOOS, RUSHES and SEDGES.
P. capillare illus. p.308.

Pansy. See *Viola* x *wittrockiana*.
  Mountain. See *Viola lutea*.
  Wild. See *Viola tricolor*, illus. p.369.
Pansy orchid. See *Miltoniopsis*.
Panther lily. See *Lilium pardalinum*, illus. p.405.

PAPAVER
Poppy

PAPAVERACEAE

Genus of annuals, biennials and perennials, some of which are semi-evergreen, grown for their cup-shaped flowers. Needs sun or semi-shade and prefers moist but well-drained soil. Propagate by seed in autumn or spring. *P. orientale* and its cultivars are best propagated by root cuttings in winter. Self-seeds readily.
P. alpinum subsp. *burseri.* See *P. burseri.*
P. atlanticum. Clump-forming, short-lived perennial. H and S 10cm (4in). Has oval, toothed, hairy leaves and, in summer, single, dull orange flowers. Is good for a rock garden.
P. burseri, syn. *P. alpinum* subsp. *burseri*

(Alpine poppy). Semi-evergreen, tuft-forming, short-lived perennial, best treated as an annual or biennial. H 15–20cm (6–8in), S 10cm (4in). Has finely cut, grey leaves. Carries single, white flowers throughout summer. Suits a rock garden, wall, or bank.

P. commutatum, syn. *P.c.* 'Ladybird'. Fast-growing, erect, branching annual. H and S 45cm (18in). Has elliptic, deeply lobed, mid-green leaves and, in summer, single, red flowers, each with a black blotch in centre.

'Ladybird' see *P. commutatum*.

P. croceum, syn. *P. nudicaule* of gardens (Iceland poppy). Tuft-forming perennial. H to 30cm (12in), S 10cm (4in). Hairy stems each produce a fragrant, single, white-and-yellow flower, sometimes marked green outside, in summer. Many colour forms have been selected. Leaves are oval, toothed and soft green. Needs partial shade. Is good for a rock garden.

P. fauriei, syn. *P. miyabeanum* of gardens, illus. p.384.

P. miyabeanum of gardens. See *P. fauriei*.

P. nudicaule of gardens. See *P. croceum*.

P. orientale (Oriental poppy). Rosetted perennial. H 1m (3ft), S 30cm–1m (1–3ft). Single, brilliant vermilion flowers, with dark blotches at bases of petals, are borne in early summer. Has broadly lance-shaped, toothed or cut, rough, mid-green leaves. Flowering stems need support. **'Allegro'** (syn. *P.o.* 'Allegro Viva') illus. p.250. **'Allegro Viva'** see *P.o.* 'Allegro'. **'Beauty of Livermere'** illus. p.250. **'Indian Chief'** has deep mahogany-red flowers. **'May Queen'** bears double, orange flowers. **'Mrs Perry'** has large, salmon-pink flowers. **'Perry's White'** illus. p.241.

P. rhoeas (Corn poppy, Field poppy). **Shirley Series** (double) illus. p.322; (single) illus. p.328.

P. somniferum (Opium poppy). Fast-growing, upright annual. H 75cm (30in), S 30cm (12in). Has oblong, lobed, light greyish-green leaves. Large, single flowers, to 10cm (4in) wide, in shades of red, pink, purple, or white, are produced in summer. Several double-flowered forms are available, including **Carnation-flowered Series**, with fringed flowers in mixed colours; **'Peony Flowered'** illus. p.321; **'Pink Beauty'**, which has salmon-pink flowers; and **'White Cloud'**, which produces large, white flowers.

Paper mulberry. See *Broussonetia papyrifera*, illus. p.79.

Paper reed. See *Cyperus papyrus*, illus. p.307.

Paper-bark maple. See *Acer griseum*, illus. p.100.

Paper-bark tree. See *Melaleuca viridiflora* var. *rubriflora*.

Paper-bark, Scented. See *Melaleuca squarrosa*.

PAPHIOPEDILUM
Slipper orchid

Contact with foliage may aggravate skin allergies. See also ORCHIDS.

P. appletonianum (illus. p.296). Evergreen, terrestrial orchid. H 8cm (3in). Tender, min. 13°C (55°F). In spring, green flowers, 6cm (2½in) across and each with a pouched, brownish lip and pink-flushed petals, are borne singly on tall, slender stems. Has oval, mottled leaves, 10cm (4in) long. Needs shade in summer.

P. bellatulum (illus. p.296). Evergreen, terrestrial orchid. H 5cm (2in). Tender, min. 18°C (64°F). Bears almost stemless, rounded, pouch-lipped, white flowers, 8cm (3in) across, spotted with dark maroon, singly in spring. Oval, marbled leaves are 8cm (3in) long. Grow in shade in summer.

P. Buckhurst 'Mont Millais' (illus. p.298). Evergreen, terrestrial orchid. H 10cm (4in). Tender, min. 13°C (55°F). Rounded, yellow-and-white flowers, to 12cm (5in) across and lined and spotted with red, are produced singly in winter. Has oval leaves, 10cm (4in) long. Requires shade in summer.

P. callosum (illus. p.296). Evergreen, terrestrial orchid. H 8cm (3in). Tender, min. 13°C (55°F). Purple- and green-veined, white flowers, 8cm (3in) across, are borne on tall stems in spring-summer. Has oval, mottled leaves, 10cm (4in) long. Needs shade in summer.

P. fairrieanum (illus. p.296). Evergreen, terrestrial orchid. H 8cm (3in). Tender, min. 10°C (50°F). Rich purple- and green-veined flowers, 5cm (2in) across, with curved petals and orange-brown pouches, are borne singly in autumn. Oval leaves are 8cm (3in) long. Grow in shade in summer.

P. Freckles (illus. p.296). Evergreen, terrestrial orchid. H 10cm (4in). Tender, min. 13°C (55°F). Rounded, reddish-brown-spotted and pouched, white flowers, 10cm (4in) across, are produced singly in winter. Has oval leaves, 10cm (4in) long. Grow in shade in summer.

P. haynaldianum (illus. p.296). Evergreen, terrestrial orchid. H 12cm (5in). Tender, min. 13°C (55°F). In summer, long-petalled, brown-marked, green-, pink-and-white flowers, to 15cm (6in) across, are produced singly. Has oval leaves, 20–23cm (8–9in) long. Requires shade in summer.

P. Lyric 'Glendora' (illus. p.297). Evergreen, terrestrial orchid. H 10cm (4in). Tender, min. 13°C (55°F). Rounded, glossy, white-, red-and-green flowers, 10cm (4in) across, appear singly in winter. Has oval leaves, 15cm (6in) long. Needs shade in summer.

P. Maudiae (illus. p.297). Evergreen, terrestrial orchid. H 10cm (4in). Tender, min. 13°C (55°F). Clear apple-green or deep reddish-purple flowers, 10cm (4in) across, appear singly on long stems in spring or early summer. Has oval, mottled leaves, 10cm (4in) long. Requires shade in summer.

P. niveum (illus. p.296). Evergreen, terrestrial orchid. H 5cm (2in). Tender, min. 13–18°C (55–64°F). White flowers, 4cm (1½in) across, are produced singly, mainly in spring. Oval, marbled leaves are 8cm (3in) long. Needs shade in summer.

P. sukhakulii (illus. p.298). Evergreen, terrestrial orchid. H 8cm (3in). Tender,

min. 13°C (55°F). In spring-summer, purple-pouched, black-spotted, green flowers, 8cm (3in) across, appear singly on tall stems. Has oval, mottled leaves, 10cm (4in) long. Grow in shade in summer.

P. venustum (illus. p.299). Evergreen, terrestrial orchid. H 10cm (4in). Tender, min. 13°C (55°F). Variably coloured flowers, ranging from pink to orange with green veins and darker spots, are 6cm (2½in) across and borne singly in autumn. Has oval, mottled leaves, 10cm (4in) long. Needs shade in summer.

Papyrus. See *Cyperus papyrus*, illus. p.307.

Para para. See *Pisonia umbellifera*.

Parachute plant. See *Ceropegia sandersonii*.

Paradise palm. See *Howea forsteriana*.

PARAHEBE
SCROPHULARIACEAE

Genus of evergreen or semi-evergreen, summer-flowering perennials, sub-shrubs and shrubs, similar to *Hebe* and *Veronica*. Is suitable for rock gardens. Needs sun and well-drained, peaty, sandy soil. Propagate by semi-ripe cuttings in early summer.

P. catarractae illus. p.356.

P. lyallii. Semi-evergreen, prostrate shrub. H 15cm (6in), S 20–25cm (8–10in). Has oval, toothed, leathery leaves and, in early summer, erect stems bearing loose sprays of flattish, pink-veined, white flowers.

P. perfoliata, syn. *Veronica perfoliata*, illus. p.286.

PARAQUILEGIA
RANUNCULACEAE

Genus of tufted perennials, grown for their cup-shaped flowers and fern-like foliage. Is difficult to cultivate and flower successfully. Prefers dry winters and cool climates. Is good in alpine houses and troughs. Needs sun and gritty, well-drained, alkaline soil. Propagate by seed in autumn.

P. anemonoides, syn. *P. grandiflora*, illus. p.364.

P. grandiflora. See *P. anemonoides*.

PARASERIANTHES
LEGUMINOSAE/MIMOSACEAE

Genus of deciduous or semi-evergreen trees, grown for their feathery foliage and unusual flower heads, composed of numerous stamens and resembling bottlebrushes. Tender, min. 4–5°C (39–41°F). In frost-prone areas grow half-hardy species against a south- or west-facing wall and tender species under glass; in cold areas do not plant out until late spring. Requires full sun and well-drained soil. Propagate by seed in spring.

P. lophantha, syn. *Albizia distachya*, *A. lophantha*, illus. p.93.

Parasol tree, Chinese. See *Firmiana simplex*, illus. p.68.

Parilla, Yellow. See *Menispermum canadense*.

Parlour palm. See *Chamaedorea elegans*, illus. p.152.

PARNASSIA
PARNASSIACEAE

Genus of rosetted, mainly summer-flowering perennials, grown for their saucer-shaped flowers. Is good for rock gardens. Needs sun and wet soil. Propagate by seed in autumn.

P. palustris illus. p.350.

PAROCHETUS
LEGUMINOSAE/PAPILIONACEAE

Genus of one species of evergreen perennial. Grows best in alpine houses. Needs semi-shade and gritty, moist soil. Propagate by division of rooted runners in any season.

P. communis illus. p.384.

PARODIA
CACTACEAE

Genus of rounded, perennial cacti with tubercles arranged in ribs that often spiral around green stems. Crown forms woolly buds, then funnel-shaped flowers. Tender, min. 5–10°C (41–50°F). Requires full sun or partial shade and very well-drained soil. Water very lightly in winter; tends to lose roots during a long period of drought. Propagate by seed in spring or summer.

P. aprica. See *P. concinna*.

P. chrysacanthion illus. p.468.

P. concinna, syn. *Notocactus apricus*, *P. aprica*. Flattened spherical, perennial cactus. H 7cm (3in), S 10cm (4in). Min. 10°C (50°F). Much-ribbed, pale green stem is densely covered with short, soft, golden-brown spines. In summer, crown produces flattish, glossy, bright yellow flowers, 8cm (3in) across, with purple stigmas. Prefers partial shade.

P. erinacea, syn. *Wigginsia vorwerkiana*, illus. p.479.

P. graessneri, syn. *Notocactus graessneri*. Slow-growing, flattened spherical, perennial cactus. H 10cm (4in), S 25cm (10in). Min. 10°C (50°F). Bristle-like, golden spines completely cover much-ribbed, green stem. Slightly sunken crown bears funnel-shaped, glossy, greenish-yellow flowers, with yellow stigmas, in early spring. Prefers partial shade.

P. haselbergii, syn. *Notocactus haselbergii*, illus. p.475.

P. leninghausii, syn. *Notocactus leninghausii*, illus. p.468.

P. mammulosa, syn. *Notocactus mammulosus*, illus. p.477.

P. microsperma, syn. *P. sanguiniflora*, illus. p.474.

P. nivosa illus. p.474.

P. ottonis, syn. *Notocactus ottonis*. Variable, spherical, perennial cactus. H and S 10cm (4in). Min. 5°C (41°F). Has pale to dark green stem with 8–12 rounded ribs bearing stiff, golden radial spines and longer, soft, red central spines. In summer, crown bears flattish, glossy, golden flowers, 8cm (3in) across, with purple stigmas. Offsets freely from stolons. Prefers sun.

P. rutilans, syn. *Notocactus rutilans*, illus. p.471.

P. sanguiniflora. See *P. microsperma*.

P. scopa, syn. *Notocactus scopa* (Silver ball cactus). Spherical to columnar, perennial cactus. H 25cm (10in), S 15cm (6in). Min. 10°C (50°F). Stem, with 30–35 ribs, is densely covered with white radial spines and longer, red central spines, 3 or 4 per areole. Crown bears funnel-shaped, glossy, yellow flowers, 4cm (1½in) across, with purple stigmas, in summer. Prefers a sunny position.

PARONYCHIA
CARYOPHYLLACEAE/ILLECEBRACEAE

Genus of evergreen perennials making loose mats of prostrate stems. Is useful for rock gardens and walls. Needs sun and well-drained soil. Propagate by division in spring.

P. capitata. Vigorous, evergreen, mat-forming perennial. H 1cm (½in), S 40cm (16in). Fully hardy. Silvery leaves are small and oval. In summer produces inconspicuous flowers surrounded by papery bracts. Makes good ground cover.

P. kapela subsp. *serpyllifolia* illus. p.391.

Parrot feather. See *Myriophyllum aquaticum*, illus. p.448.

Parrot leaf. See *Alternanthera ficoidea*.

Parrot's bill. See *Clianthus puniceus*, illus. p.204.

Parrot's flower. See *Heliconia psittacorum*, illus. p.229.

Parrot's plantain. See *Heliconia psittacorum*, illus. p.229.

PARROTIA
HAMAMELIDACEAE

Genus of one species of deciduous tree, grown for its flowers and autumn colour. Flower buds may be killed by hard frosts. Requires full sun and grows best in fertile, moist but well-drained soil. Is lime-tolerant, but usually colours best in acid soil. Propagate by softwood cuttings in summer or by seed in autumn.

P. persica illus. p.82.

Parsley fern. See *Cryptogramma crispa*, illus. p.313.

Parson's pink china. See *Rosa* x *odorata* 'Pallida', illus. p.187.

PARTHENOCISSUS
VITACEAE

Genus of deciduous, woody-stemmed, tendril climbers, grown for their leaves, which often turn beautiful colours in autumn. Broad tips of tendrils have sucker-like pads that cling to supports. Has insignificant, greenish flowers in summer. Will quickly cover north- or east-facing walls or fences and may be grown up large trees. Grow in semi-shade or shade and in well-drained soil. Propagate by softwood or greenwood cuttings in summer or by hardwood cuttings in early spring. The berries may cause mild stomach upset if ingested.

P. henryana, syn. *Vitis henryana*. Deciduous, tendril climber with 4-angled, woody stems. H to 10m (30ft) or more. Leaves have 3–5 toothed, oval leaflets, each 4–13cm (1½–5in) long, and are velvety, deep green or bronze with white or pinkish veins. Small, dark blue berries are produced in autumn. Leaf colour is best with a north or east aspect. Zone 6b.

P. quinquefolia, syn. *Vitis quinquefolia* (Five-leaved ivy, Virginia creeper). Deciduous, woody-stemmed, tendril climber. H 15m (50ft) or more. Frost hardy. Leaves have 5 oval, toothed, dull green leaflets, paler beneath, that turn a beautiful crimson in autumn. Blue-black berries are produced in autumn. Is ideal for covering a high wall or building. Zone 2b.

P. striata. See *Cissus striata*.

P. thomsonii, syn. *Cayratia thomsonii*, *Vitis thomsonii*, illus. p.218.

P. tricuspidata, illus. p.218. 'Lowii' and 'Veitchii' (syn. *Ampelopsis veitchii*) illus. p.218.

Partridge berry. See *Mitchella repens*.

Partridge-breasted aloe. See *Aloe variegata*, illus. p.464.

Pasque flower. See *Pulsatilla vulgaris*, illus. p.348.

PASSIFLORA
Passion flower

PASSIFLORACEAE

Genus of evergreen or semi-evergreen, woody-stemmed, tendril climbers, grown for their unique flowers, each one with a central corona of filaments. Produces egg-shaped to rounded, fleshy, edible fruits that mature to orange or yellow in autumn. Hardy to tender, min. 5–16°C (41–61°F). Grow in full sun or partial shade and in any fertile, well-drained soil. Water freely in full growth, less at other times. Stems need support. Thin out and spur back crowded growth in spring. Propagate by seed in spring or by semi-ripe cuttings in summer.

P. x *allardii*, syn. *P.* 'Allardii'. Strong-growing, evergreen, woody-stemmed, tendril climber. H 7–10m (22–30ft). Tender, min. 7°C (45°F). Has 3-lobed leaves. Flowers, 7–10cm (3–4in) wide, are white, tinted pink, with purple-banded crowns, and are carried in summer-autumn.

P. 'Allardii'. See *P.* x *allardii*.

P. antioquiensis, syn. *Tacsonia van-volxemii* (Banana passion fruit). Fast-growing, evergreen, woody-stemmed, tendril climber. H 5m (15ft) or more. Tender, min. 7°C (45°F). Has downy leaves, with 3 deep lobes. Produces long-tubed, rose-red flowers, 10–12cm (4–5in) across, with purplish-blue centres, in summer-autumn.

P. caerulea illus. p.214. 'Constance Elliot' is a fast-growing, evergreen or semi-evergreen, woody-stemmed, tendril climber. H 10m (30ft) or more. Has rich green leaves and, in summer-autumn, produces bowl-shaped, fragrant, white flowers with pale blue or white filaments. Zone 7.

P. x *caeruleoracemosa*. See *P.* x *violacea*.

P. x *caponii* 'John Innes' illus. p.214.

P. coccinea illus. p.205.

P. x *exoniensis*. Fast-growing, evergreen, woody-stemmed, tendril climber. H 8m (25ft) or more. Tender, min. 7°C (45°F). Leaves have 3 deep lobes and are softly downy. Rose-pink flowers, 8cm (3in) across, with purplish-blue crowns, are produced in summer-autumn.

P. manicata illus. p.217.

P. mollissima, syn. *Tacsonia mollissima*. Fast-growing, evergreen, woody-stemmed, tendril climber. H 5m (15ft) or more. Tender, min. 7°C (45°F). Softly downy leaves have 3 deep lobes. Long-tubed, pink flowers, to 8cm (3in) wide, each with a purplish-blue crown, appear in summer-autumn.

P. quadrangularis illus. p.215.

P. racemosa (Red passion flower). Fast-growing, evergreen, tendril climber with slender, woody stems. H 5m (15ft). Tender, min. 15°C (59°F). Has wavy, leathery leaves with 3 deep lobes. In summer-autumn bears terminal racemes of pendent, crimson flowers, 8–10cm (3–4in) across, with white- and purple-banded crowns.

P. sanguinea. See *P. vitifolia*.

P. x *violacea*, syn. *P.* x *caeruleoracemosa*. Vigorous, evergreen, woody-stemmed, tendril climber. H 10m (30ft). Tender, min. 7–10°C (45–50°F). Has 3-lobed leaves. Purple flowers, 8cm (3in) across, appear in summer-autumn.

P. vitifolia, syn. *P. sanguinea*. Evergreen, woody-stemmed, tendril climber; slender stems have fine, brown hairs. H to 5m (15ft). Tender, min. 16°C (61°F). Has 3-lobed, lustrous leaves. In summer-autumn bears bright scarlet flowers, 13cm (5in) wide, each with a short crown, banded red, yellow and white.

Passion flower. See *Passiflora*.
  Blue. See *Passiflora caerulea*, illus. p.214.
  Common. See *Passiflora caerulea*, illus. p.214.
  Red. See *Passiflora coccinea*, illus. p.205; *Passiflora racemosa*.

Passion fruit, Banana. See *Passiflora antioquiensis*.

Patagonian cypress. See *Fitzroya cupressoides*, illus. p.106.

PATERSONIA
IRIDACEAE

Genus of evergreen, clump-forming, spring- and early summer-flowering, rhizomatous perennials. Needs full sun and light, well-drained soil. Leave undisturbed once planted. Propagate by seed in autumn.

P. umbrosa illus. p.421.

PATRINIA
VALERIANACEAE

Genus of perennials, with neat clumps, grown for their flowers. Is suitable for rock gardens and peat beds. Needs a site in partial shade with moist soil. Propagate by division in spring or by seed in autumn. Self-seeds freely.

P. triloba. Clump-forming perennial. H 20–50cm (8–20in), S 15–30cm (6–12in). Neat heads of small, golden-yellow flowers are borne throughout summer. Rounded, 3- to 5-lobed, green leaves turn gold in autumn.

PAULOWNIA
SCROPHULARIACEAE

Genus of deciduous trees, grown for their large leaves and foxglove-like flowers, borne before the foliage emerges. Flower buds and young growth of small plants may be damaged by very hard frosts. Requires full sun and fertile, moist but well-drained soil. In cold areas may be grown for foliage only by cutting back young shoots hard in spring and cutting out all but one of the subsequent shoots; this results in very large leaves. Propagate by seed in autumn or spring or by root cuttings in winter.

P. fortunei. Deciduous, spreading tree. H and S 8m (25ft). Has large, oval, mid-green leaves. In late spring bears large, fragrant flowers, purple-spotted and white inside, pale purple outside. Zone 7.

P. imperialis. See *P. tomentosa*.

P. tomentosa, syn. *P. imperialis*, illus. p.77.

Pawpaw. See *Asimina triloba*.

PAXISTIMA,
syn. PACHYSTIMA

CELASTRACEAE

Genus of evergreen, spreading shrubs and sub-shrubs, grown for their foliage. Is suitable for ground cover. Fully hardy. Prefers shade and humus-rich, moist soil. Propagate by division in spring or by semi-ripe cuttings in summer.

P. canbyi. (Cliff green, ratstripper). Evergreen, spreading sub-shrub. H 15–30cm (6–12in), S 20cm (8in). Leaves are linear or oblong, and short, pendent spikes of tiny, greenish-white flowers are produced in summer. Zone 2b.

Pea
  Australian. See *Lablab purpureus*, illus. p.211.
  Coral. See *Hardenbergia violacea*.
  Darling. See *Swainsona galegifolia*.
  Dusky coral. See *Kennedia rubicunda*, illus. p.205.
  Everlasting. See *Lathyrus grandiflorus*, illus. p.209; *Lathyrus latifolius*, illus. p.211; *Lathyrus sylvestris*.
  Holly flame. See *Chorizema ilicifolium*, illus. p.157.
  Lord Anson's blue. See *Lathyrus nervosus*.
  Perennial. See *Lathyrus latifolius*, illus. p.211; *Lathyrus sylvestris*.
  Persian everlasting. See *Lathyrus rotundifolius*.
  Shamrock. See *Parochetus communis*, illus. p.384.
  Sweet. See *Lathyrus odoratus*.

Peace lily. See *Spathiphyllum wallisii*, illus. p.300.

Peach. See *Prunus persica*.
  David's. See *Prunus davidiana*.

Peacock flower. See *Tigridia pavonia*, illus. p.423.

Peacock plant. See *Calathea makoyana*, illus. p.304.

Peanut cactus. See *Echinopsis chamaecereus*, illus. p.475.

Pear. See *Pyrus*.
  Callery. See *Pyrus calleryana*.
  Chinese. See *Pyrus ussuriensis*.
  Common. See *Pyrus communis*.
  Prickly. See *Opuntia*.

Pearl berry. See *Margyricarpus pinnatus*.

Pearly everlasting. See *Anaphalis*.

PEDILANTHUS

EUPHORBIACEAE

Genus of bushy, summer-flowering, perennial succulents. Produces small, yellowish-green, pink, red or brown bracts that are each shaped like a bird's head. Tender, min. 10–11°C (50–52°F). Needs sun or partial shade and well-drained soil. Propagate by seed or stem cuttings in spring or summer. The stems and leaves contain a milky sap that may cause stomach upset if ingested.

P. tithymaloides. (Devil's backbone). Bushy, perennial succulent. H 3m (10ft), S 30cm (1ft). Min. 10°C (50°F). Has thin, erect stems zigzagging at each node. Leaves are mid-green and boat-shaped, with prominent ribs beneath. Red to yellowish-green bracts are produced at each of the stem tips in summer. Prefers partial shade.
'Variegata' illus. p.459.

Pedunculate oak. See *Quercus robur*.
Peepul. See *Ficus religiosa*.

PELARGONIUM
Geranium

GERANIACEAE

Genus of mainly summer-flowering perennials, most of which are evergreen, often cultivated as annuals. Is grown for its colourful flowers and is useful in pots or as bedding plants; in warm conditions flowers are borne almost continuously. Tender, min. 2°C (36°F), unless otherwise stated. A sunny site with 12 hours of daylight is required for good flowering. Prefers well-drained, neutral to alkaline soil. Dislikes very hot, humid conditions. Dead-head frequently and fertilize regularly if grown in pots; do not overwater. Plants may be kept through winter in the greenhouse by cutting back in autumn-winter to 12cm (5in) and repotting. Propagate by softwood cuttings from spring to autumn. Contact with the foliage may occasionally aggravate skin allergies.

Pelargoniums may be divided into 5 groups; all flower in summer-autumn unless stated otherwise. See also feature panel pp.246–7.

Zonal – plants with rounded leaves, distinctively marked with a darker 'zone', and single (5-petalled), semi-double or fully double flowers.

Regal (Martha Washington)– shrubby plants with rounded to oval, deeply serrated leaves and broadly trumpet-shaped, exotic-coloured flowers that are prone to weather-damage in the open.

Ivy-leaved – trailing plants, ideal for hanging baskets, with rounded, lobed leaves and flowers similar to those of zonal pelargoniums.

Scented-leaved and **species** – plants with small, often irregularly star-shaped flowers; scented-leaved forms are grown for their fragrance.

Unique – Tall-growing sub-shrubs with regal-like, single, brightly coloured flowers that are borne continuously through the season. Leaves, which may be scented, vary in shape.

P. acetosum (illus. p.246). Species pelargonium. H 50–60cm (20–24in), S 20–25cm (8–10in). Stems are succulent with fleshy, grey-green leaves that are often margined red. Bears single, salmon-pink flowers. Is good as a pot plant in a greenhouse.

P. **'Alberta'** (illus. p.246). Evergreen zonal pelargonium. H 45cm (18in), S 30cm (12in). Bears clusters of small, single, crimson-and-white flowers. Is best grown as a bedding plant.

P. **'Amethyst'** (illus. p.246). Evergreen, trailing ivy-leaved pelargonium. H and S to 1.5m (5ft). Leaves are fleshy with pointed lobes. Bears fully double, light mauve-purple flowers.

P. **'Apple Blossom Rosebud'** (illus. p.246). Evergreen zonal pelargonium. H 30cm (12in), S 23cm (9in). Fully double, pinkish-white flowers, edged with red, look like miniature rosebuds.

P. **'Autumn Festival'** (illus. p.246). Evergreen, bushy regal pelargonium. H and S 30cm (12in). Salmon-pink flowers have a pronounced, white throat.

P. **'Bredon'** (illus. p.247). Strong-growing, evergreen regal pelargonium. H 45cm (18in), S to 30cm (12in). Has large, maroon flowers.

P. **'Brookside Primrose'** (illus. p.246). Dwarf zonal pelargonium. H 10–12cm (4–5in), S 7–10cm (3–4in). Bears double, pale pink flowers. Leaves have a butterfly mark in the centre of each leaf. Is good as a pot plant or for bedding.

P. **'Butterfly Lorelei'** (illus. p.246). Fancy-leaved, zonal pelargonium. H 25–30cm (10–12in), S 15–20cm (6–8in). Has butterfly-shaped leaves and double, pale salmon-pink flowers. Is suitable as a pot plant in a greenhouse.

P. **'Caligula'** (illus. p.247). Evergreen, miniature zonal pelargonium. H 15–20cm (6–8in), S 10cm (4in). Has small, double, crimson flowers and tiny, dark green leaves. Suits a windowsill.

P. **'Capen'** (illus. p.247). Bushy zonal pelargonium. H 38–45cm (15–18in), S 15–20cm (6–8in). Bears coral-pink, semi-double flowers. Is good as a pot plant.

P. capitatum (illus. p.247). Evergreen scented-leaved pelargonium. H 30–60cm (12–24in), S 30cm (12in). Has mauve flowers and irregularly 3-lobed leaves that smell faintly of roses. Is mainly used to produce geranium oil for the perfume industry, but may be grown as a pot plant.

P. carnosum. Deciduous, shrubby pelargonium (unclassified), with thick, succulent stems and a woody, swollen, tuber-like rootstock. H and S 30cm (12in). Min. 10°C (50°F). Has long, grey-green leaves with triangular, deeply lobed leaflets. Produces branched, umbel-like flower heads with white or greenish-yellow flowers, the upper petals streaked red and shorter than the green sepals.

P. **'Cherry Blossom'** (illus. p.246). Vigorous, evergreen zonal pelargonium. H and S to 45cm (18in). Semi-double flowers are mauve-pink with white centres.

P. **'Chew Magna'**. Evergreen regal pelargonium. H 30–45cm (12–18in), S to 30cm (12in). Each petal of the pale pink flowers has a wine-red blaze.

P. **'Clorinda'** (illus. p.246). Vigorous, scented-leaved pelargonium. H 45–50cm (18–20in), S 20–25cm (8–10in). Leaves smell of cedar and are 3-lobed. Bears large, single, rose-pink flowers and is excellent in a large pot. Is suitable for a greenhouse or patio.

P. crispum **'Variegatum'** (illus. p.247). Evergreen, upright scented-leaved pelargonium. H to 1m (3ft), S 30–45cm (1–1½ft). Has gold-variegated leaves and small, pale lilac flowers. Foliage tends to become creamy-white in winter.

P. **'Dale Queen'** (illus. p.246). Evergreen, bushy zonal pelargonium. H 23–30cm (9–12in), S 23cm (9in). Single flowers are delicate salmon-pink. Is particularly suitable for a pot.

P. **'Dolly Varden'** (illus. p.247). Evergreen zonal pelargonium. H 30cm (12in), S 23cm (9in). Green leaves have handsome, purple-brown, white and crimson markings. Single, scarlet flowers are insignificant.

P. **'Emma Hössle'.** See *P.* 'Frau Emma Hössle'.

P. **'Fair Ellen'** (illus. p.246). Compact scented-leaved pelargonium. H and S 30cm (12in). Has dark green leaves and pale pink flowers marked with red.

P. **'Flower of Spring'** (Silver-leaved geranium; illus. p.247). Vigorous, evergreen zonal pelargonium. H 60cm (24in), S 30cm (12in). Has green-and-white leaves and single, red flowers.

P. x *fragrans*. See *P.* 'Fragrans'.

P. **'Fragrans'**, syn. *P.* x *fragrans*, *P.* Fragrans Group (illus. p.246). Evergreen, very bushy scented-leaved pelargonium. H and S 30cm (12in). Rounded, shallowly lobed, grey-green leaves smell strongly of pine. Bears small, white flowers.

P. Fragrans Group. See *P.* 'Fragrans'.

P. **'Fraiche Beauté'**, syn. *P.* 'Fraicher Beauty' (illus. p.246). Evergreen zonal pelargonium. H 30cm (12in), S 23cm (9in). Flowers are fully double and perfectly formed with delicate colouring: white with a thin, red edge to each petal. Is excellent as a pot plant.

P. **'Fraicher Beauty'.** See *P.* 'Fraiche Beauté'.

P. **'Francis Parrett'** (illus. p.246). Evergreen, short-jointed zonal pelargonium. H 15–20cm (6–8in), S 10cm (4in). Bears fully double, purplish-mauve flowers and small, green leaves. Is good for a windowsill.

P. **'Frau Emma Hössle'**, syn. *P.* 'Emma Hössle'. Evergreen, dwarf zonal pelargonium. H 20–25cm (8–10in), S 15cm (6in). Bears large, fully double, mauve-pink flowers. Is useful for a window box.

P. **'Friesdorf'** (illus. p.247). Evergreen zonal pelargonium. H 25cm (10in), S 15cm (6in). Has dark green foliage and narrow-petalled, single, orange-scarlet flowers. Is good for a window box or planted in a large group.

P. **'Golden Lilac Mist'** (illus. p.246). Bushy zonal pelargonium. H 25–30cm (10–12in), S 15–20cm (6–8in). Leaves are gold marked with bronze. Bears double, lavender-pink flowers. Is a good window-box plant.

P. **'Gustav Emich'** (illus. p.247). Vigorous, evergreen, zonal pelargonium. H and S to 60cm (24in). Semi-double flowers are vivid scarlet.

P. **'Irene'** (illus. p.247). Evergreen zonal pelargonium. H 45cm (18in), S 23–30cm (9–12in). Bears large, semi-double, light crimson blooms.

P. **'Ivalo'** (illus. p.246). Evergreen, bushy, short-jointed zonal pelargonium. H 23–30cm (9–12in), S 23cm (9in). Large, semi-double flowers are pale pink with crimson-dotted, white centres.

P. **'Lachsball'** (illus. p.246). Vigorous zonal pelargonium. H 45–50cm (18–20in), S 15–20cm (6–8in). Bears semi-double, salmon-pink flowers each with a scarlet eye. Is good for summer bedding.

P. **'Lachskönigin'** (illus. p.246). Evergreen, trailing, brittle-jointed pelargonium. H and S to 60cm (24in). Has fleshy leaves, with pointed lobes, and semi-double, deep rosy-pink flowers. Suits a hanging basket or window box.

P. **'L'Elégante'** (illus. p.247). Evergreen, trailing ivy-leaved pelargonium. H and S to 60cm (24in). Foliage is variegated with creamy-white margins, sometimes turning pink at the edges; semi-double flowers are pale mauve. Is best grown in a hanging basket.

P. **'Leslie Judd'** (illus. p.246). Vigorous, evergreen, bushy regal pelargonium. H 30–45cm (12–18in), S to 30cm (12in). Flowers are soft salmon-pink with a central, red blotch. Pinch out growing tips before flowering to control shape.

P. **'Mabel Grey'** (illus. p.247). Evergreen scented-leaved pelargonium. H 45–60cm (18–24in), S 30–45cm (12–18in). Has diamond-shaped, rough-textured, toothed, strongly lemon-scented leaves, with 5–7 pointed lobes, and mauve flowers.

P. **'Madame Fournier'** (illus. p.247). Evergreen, short-jointed zonal pelargonium. H 15–20cm (6–8in), S 10cm (4in). Small, single, scarlet flowers contrast well with almost black leaves. Is useful for a pot or as a summer bedding plant.

P. **'Manx Maid'** (illus. p.246). Evergreen regal pelargonium. H 30–38cm (12–15in), S 25cm (10in). Flowers and leaves are small for regal type. Pink flowers are veined and blotched with burgundy.

P. **'Mauritania'** (illus. p.246). Evergreen zonal pelargonium. H 30cm (12in), S 23cm (9in). Single, white flowers are ringed towards centres with pale salmon-pink.

P. **'Mini Cascade'** (illus. p.247). Evergreen, trailing, short-jointed ivy-leaved pelargonium. H and S 30–45cm (12–18in). Bears many single, red flowers. Regular dead-heading is essential for continuous display.

P. **'Mr Everaarts'** (illus. p.246). Bushy dwarf zonal pelargonium. H 15–20cm (6–8in), S 10–12cm (4–5in). Bears double, bright pink flowers. Is good in a window box.

P. **'Mr Henry Cox'**, syn. *P.* 'Mrs Henry Cox' (illus. p.246). Evergreen zonal pelargonium. H 30cm (12in), S 15cm (6in). Mid-green leaves are marked with red, yellow and purple-brown. Flowers are single and pink.

P. **'Mrs Henry Cox'**. See *P.* 'Mr Henry Cox'.

P. **'Mrs Pollock'** (illus. p.247). Evergreen zonal pelargonium. H 30cm (12in), S 15cm (6in). Each golden leaf has a grey-green butterfly mark in centre, with a bronze zone running through it. Bears small, single, orange-red flowers.

P. **'Mrs Quilter'** (illus. p.247). Evergreen zonal pelargonium. H 30cm (12in), S 23cm (9in). Has yellow leaves with wide, chestnut-brown zones and single, pink flowers.

P. **Multibloom Series** (illus. p.328). Seed-raised, single-flowered zonal pelargonium. H 25–30cm (10–12in) and S 30cm (12in). Abundant flowers in shades of white, pink and red, some with white eyes, are borne in clusters. Early flowering over a long period. Is tolerant of wet conditions.

P. **'Orange Ricard'** (illus. p.247). Vigorous, robust, evergreen zonal pelargonium. H 45–60cm (18–24in), S 30cm (12in). Produces masses of large, semi-double, orange blooms.

P. **Orbit Series.** Group of slow-growing, evergreen, bushy zonal pelargoniums, grown as annuals. H and S 30–60cm (12–24in). Has rounded, lobed, bronze- or red-zoned, mid-green leaves and large, domed, single flower heads in mixed or separate colours, including shades of white, pink, red and orange (salmon, illus. p.321).

P. **'Paton's Unique'** (illus. p.247). Vigorous unique pelargonium with pungent-smelling leaves. H 38–45cm (15–18in), S 15–20cm (6–8in). Flowers are single, red or pale pink, each with a small, white eye.

P. **'Paul Humphries'** (illus. p.247). Evergreen, bushy, compact zonal pelargonium. H 30cm (12in), S 23cm (9in). Has fully double, deep wine-red flowers. Is good as a pot plant.

P. peltatum. Evergreen, trailing, brittle-jointed pelargonium from which ivy-leaved cultivars have been derived. H and S to 1.5m (5ft). Has fleshy leaves, with pointed lobes, and produces single, mauve or white flowers. Cultivars suit hanging baskets and window boxes.

P. **'Polka'** (illus. p.247). Vigorous unique pelargonium. H 45–50cm (18–20in), S 20–25cm (8–10in). Flowers are semi-double. Upper petals are orange-red, blotched and feathered deep purple; lower ones are salmon-orange.

P. **'Prince of Orange'** (illus. p.247). Scented-leaved pelargonium.

H 25–30cm (10–12in), S 15–20cm (6–8in). Small, rounded leaves smell of orange. Bears single, mauve flowers. Is good as a pot plant indoors.

P. **'Purple Emperor'** (illus. p.246). Evergreen regal pelargonium. H 45cm (18in), S 30cm (12in). Pink-mauve flowers have a deeper, central coloration. Flowers well into autumn.

P. **'Purple Unique'** (illus. p.247). Vigorous, evergreen, upright, shrubby unique pelargonium. H and S 1m (3ft) or more. Rounded, large-lobed leaves are very aromatic. Has single, open trumpet-shaped, light purple flowers. Does well when trained against a sunny wall.

P. **'Purple Wonder'** (illus. p.247). Vigorous zonal pelargonium. H 38–45cm (15–18in), S 20–25cm (8–10in). Bears semi-double, cerise-purple flowers. Is good as a pot plant in the greenhouse or in the garden.

P. **'Rica'** (illus. p.246). Bushy zonal pelargonium. H 30–38cm (12–15in), S 15–20cm (6–8in). Flowers are semi-double and deep rose-pink, each with a large, white eye. Is good in a window box or as a greenhouse pot plant.

P. **'Robe'** (illus. p.247). Vigorous zonal pelargonium. H 38–45cm (15–18in), S 15–20cm (6–8in). Bears semi-double, cerise-crimson flowers. Is suitable as a pot plant in a greenhouse, or as a bedding plant, and is good for exhibition.

P. **'Rollisson's Unique'** (illus. p.247). Evergreen, shrubby pelargonium (unique). H 60cm (24in) or more, S 30cm (12in). Has oval, notched, pungent leaves and small, single, open trumpet-shaped, wine-red flowers with purple veins.

P. **'Rouletta'** (illus. p.247). Vigorous, evergreen, trailing ivy-leaved pelargonium. H and S 60cm–1m (2–3ft). Bears semi-double, red-and-white flowers. To control shape, growing tips should be pinched out regularly.

P. **'Royal Oak'** (illus. p.247). Evergreen, bushy, compact scented-leaved pelargonium. H 38cm (15in), S 30cm (12in). Oak-like, slightly sticky leaves have a spicy fragrance and are dark green with central, brown markings. Flowers are small and mauve-pink.

P. **'Schöne Helena'** (illus. p.246). Evergreen zonal pelargonium. H 30–45cm (12–18in), S 23cm (9in). Produces masses of large, semi-double, salmon-pink blooms.

P. **Sprinter Series.** Group of slow-growing, evergreen, branching, bushy zonal pelargoniums, grown as annuals. H and S 30–60cm (12–24in). Has rounded, lobed, light to mid-green leaves. Bears large, domed, single flower heads in shades of red. Is very free-flowering.

'Tavira' (illus. p.247). Evergreen, trailing, brittle-jointed pelargonium. H and S 30–40cm (12–16in). Has fleshy leaves, with pointed lobes, and single, soft cerise-red flowers. Suits a hanging basket or window box.

P. **'The Boar'** (illus. p.246). Evergreen, trailing pelargonium (species). H and S to 60cm (24in). Has unusual, 5-lobed, notched leaves, each with a central, dark brown blotch, and long-stemmed, single, salmon-pink flowers. Is useful for a hanging basket.

P. **'Timothy Clifford'** (illus. p.246). Evergreen, short-jointed zonal pelargonium. H 15–20cm (6–8in), S 10cm (4in). Has dark green leaves and fully double, salmon-pink flowers. Suits a windowsill.

P. **'Tip Top Duet'** (illus. p.247). Evergreen, bushy, free-branching regal pelargonium. H 30–38cm (12–15in), S 25cm (10in). Leaves and blooms are small for regal type. Bears pink-veined, white flowers; uppermost petals have dark burgundy blotches.

P. tomentosum (Peppermint geranium; illus. p.247). Evergreen, bushy scented-leaved pelargonium. H 30–60cm (12–24in), S 1m (36in). Large, rounded, shallowly lobed, velvety, grey-green leaves have a strong peppermint aroma. Bears clusters of small, white flowers. Growing tips should be pinched out to control spread. Dislikes full sun.

P. **Video Series.** Group of slow-growing, evergreen, branching, bushy zonal pelargoniums, grown as annuals. H and S 30–60cm (12–24in). Has rounded, lobed, bronze-zoned, deep green leaves and large, domed, single flower heads in white and shades of pink or red.

P. **'Voodoo'** (illus. p.247). Unique pelargonium. H 50–60cm (20–24in), S 20–25cm (8–10in). Flowers are single and pale burgundy with a purple-black blaze on each petal. Is suitable as a greenhouse pot plant.

Pelican flower. See *Aristolochia grandiflora.*

PELLAEA

ADIANTACEAE

Genus of deciduous, semi-evergreen or evergreen ferns. Tender, min. 5°C (41°F). Grow in semi-shade and gritty, moist but well-drained soil. Remove fading fronds regularly. Propagate by spores in summer.

P. atropurpurea (Purple rock brake, Purple-stemmed cliff brake). Semi-evergreen or evergreen fern. H and S 30cm (12in). Small, narrowly lance-shaped, divided fronds have oblong, blunt pinnae and are dark green with a purplish tinge.

P. rotundifolia (Button fern). Evergreen fern. H and S 15cm (6in). Small, narrowly lance-shaped, divided fronds are dark green and have rounded pinnae.

Pellionia. Reclassified as *Elatostema.*
Peltiphyllum. Reclassified as *Darmera.*
Pencil cedar. See *Juniperus virginiana.*
Pendulous sedge. See *Carex pendula,* illus. p.309.

PENNISETUM

GRAMINEAE/POACEAE

See also GRASSES, BAMBOOS, RUSHES and SEDGES.
P. alopecuroides, syn. *P. compressum* (Chinese fountain grass). Tuft-forming, herbaceous, perennial grass. H 1m

(3ft), S 45cm (1½ft). Has narrow, mid-green leaves; leaf sheaths each have a hairy tip. In late summer bears arching, cylindrical panicles with decorative, purple bristles that last well into winter.
P. compressum. See *P. alopecuroides.*
P. longistylum. See *P. villosum.*
P. rueppellii. See *P. setaceum.*
P. setaceum, syn. *P. rueppellii* (African fountain grass). Tuft-forming, herbaceous, perennial grass. H 1m (3ft), S 45cm (1½ft). Has very rough, mid-green leaves and stems. In summer bears dense, cylindrical panicles of copper-red spikelets, with decorative, bearded bristles, that last well into winter.
P. villosum, syn. *P. longistylum,* illus. p.307.

Penny-cress, Alpine. See *Thlaspi alpinum.*

PENSTEMON

SCROPHULARIACEAE

Genus of annuals, perennials, sub-shrubs and shrubs, most of which are semi-evergreen or evergreen. Prefers full sun and fertile, well-drained soil. Propagate species by seed in autumn or spring or by softwood or semi-ripe cuttings of non-flowering shoots in mid-summer, cultivars by cuttings only. See also feature panel p.248.
P. **'Alice Hindley'** (illus. p.248). Large-leaved, semi-evergreen perennial. H 90cm (36in), S 45cm (18in). Bears tubular to bell-shaped, pale lilac-blue flowers, white inside, tinged mauve-pink outside, from mid-summer to early or mid-autumn. Leaves are linear to lance-shaped and mid-green.
P. **'Andenken an Friedrich Hahn'**, syn. *P.* 'Garnet' (illus. p.248). H 60–75cm (2–2½ft), S 60cm (2ft). Vigorous, semi-evergreeen, bushy perennial. Bears sprays of tubular, deep wine-red flowers from mid-summer to autumn. Has narrow, fresh green leaves.
P. **'Apple Blossom'** (illus. p.248). Semi-evergreen, bushy perennial. H and S 60cm (24in). Carries sprays of small, tubular, pale pink flowers from mid-summer onwards above narrow, fresh green foliage.
P. barbatus, syn. *Chelone barbata.* Semi-evergreen, rosette-forming perennial. H 1m (3ft), S 30cm (1ft). From mid-summer to early autumn bears racemes of slightly nodding, tubular, 2-lipped, rose-red flowers. Flower stems rise from rosettes of oblong to oval, mid-green leaves.
P. **'Barbara Barker'**. See *P.* 'Beech Park'.
P. **'Beech Park'**, syn. *P.* 'Barbara Barker' (illus. p.248). Semi-evergreen perennial. H and S 60cm (24in). Bears bright pink and white flowers. Leaves are linear and light green.
P. **'Burford Seedling'**. See *P.* 'Burgundy'.
P. **'Burford White'**. See *P.* 'White Bedder'.
P. **'Burgundy'**, syn. *P.* 'Burford Seedling' (illus. p.248). Robust, semi-evergreen perennial. H 1.2m (4ft), S 60cm (2ft). Produces purplish-red

flowers with white throats streaked dark red. Leaves are linear and light green.

P. campanulatus, syn. *P. pulchellus.* Semi-evergreen, upright perennial. H 30–60cm (12–24in), S 30cm (12in). Long racemes of bell-shaped, dark purple, violet, or, occasionally, white flowers appear in early summer above lance-shaped, toothed, mid-green leaves.

P. cardwellii (illus. p.248). Spreading, sometimes stem-rooting, evergreen sub-shrub. H and S 30–50cm (12–20in). In early summer, produces raceme-like panicles of slender, tubular to funnel-shaped, deep purple flowers. Leaves are elliptic, finely toothed, and mid-green. Zone 6.

P. 'Chester Scarlet' (illus. p.248). Semi-evergreen perennial. H and S 90cm (36in). Large, bright red flowers are borne above narrowly lance-shaped, light green leaves.

P. confertus. Semi-evergreen, neat, clump-forming perennial. H 45cm (18in), S 30cm (12in). Bears spikes of tubular, creamy-yellow flowers above long, lance-shaped, mid-green leaves in early summer.

P. 'Countess of Dalkeith' (illus. p.248). Erect, semi-evergreen perennial. H 1m (3ft), S 60cm (2ft). Produces large, deep purple flowers each with a pure white throat. Leaves are linear and light green.

P. davidsonii. Evergreen, prostrate shrub. H 8cm (3in), occasionally more, S 15cm (6in) or more. In late spring and early summer, funnel-shaped, violet to ruby-red flowers, with protruding lips, develop from leaf axils. Leaves are small, oval to rounded and leathery. Trim after flowering. Zone 6. subsp. *menziesii* see *P. menziesii.*

P. diffusus. See *P. serrulatus.*

P. 'Evelyn' (illus. p.248). Semi-evergreen, bushy perennial. H and S 45cm (18in). Racemes of small, tubular, light pink flowers open from mid-summer onwards. Has broadly lance-shaped, mid-green leaves.

P. 'Firebird'. See *P.* 'Schoenholzeri'.

P. fruticosus. Evergreen, upright, woody-based sub-shrub. H and S 15–30cm (6–12in). Has lance-shaped to oval, toothed leaves and, in early summer, funnel-shaped, lipped, lavender-blue flowers. Is suitable for a rock garden. Trim back after flowering. subsp. *scouleri* (syn. *P. scouleri*) has pale to deep purple flowers. subsp. *scouleri* f. *albus* (syn. *P. scouleri* f. *albus*; illus. p.248) has white flowers. All Zone 5.

P. 'Garnet'. See *P.* 'Andenken an Friedrich Hahn'.

P. hartwegii. Semi-evergreen, erect perennial. H 60cm (24in) or more, S 30cm (12in). Bears sprays of slightly pendent, tubular to bell-shaped, scarlet flowers from mid- to late summer. Lance-shaped leaves are mid-green.

P. heterophyllus (Foothill penstemon) (illus. p.248). Evergreen sub-shrub. H and S 30–50cm (12–20in). In summer, produces racemes of tubular to funnel-shaped, pinkish-blue flowers, with blue or lilac lobes. Leaves are linear to lance-shaped, entire, and mid-green or bluish-green. **'True Blue'** has pale green leaves and pure blue

flowers, borne on short side-shoots. Trim back after flowering. Suits a rock garden. Zone 8.

P. hirsutus. Short-lived, evergreen, open sub-shrub. H 60cm–1m (2–3ft), S 30–60cm (1–2ft). In summer produces hairy, tubular, lipped, purple- or blue-flushed, white flowers. Leaves are oval and dark green. Is suitable for a rock garden. Zone 4. var. *pygmaeus* illus. p.380.

P. isophyllus illus. p.163.

P. 'Maurice Gibbs' (illus. p.248). Semi-evergreen perennial. H 90cm (3ft), S 60cm (2ft). Bears claret-red flowers with white throats. Has lance-shaped, light green leaves.

P. menziesii, syn. *P. davidsonii* subsp. *menziesii.* Evergreen, prostrate shrub. H 5cm (2in), S 20cm (8in). In late spring and early summer bears funnel-shaped, lavender-blue flowers. Has small, rounded, toothed leaves. Zone 5.

P. newberryi (Mountain pride). Evergreen, mat-forming shrub. H 15–20cm (6–8in), S 30cm (12in). Branches are covered in small, oval, leathery, dark green leaves. Bears short sprays of tubular, lipped, deep rose-pink flowers in early summer. Trim back after flowering. Is good for a rock garden. Zone 8. f. *humilior* illus. p.354.

P. 'Pennington Gem' (illus. p.248). Vigorous, semi-evergreen perennial. H 1m (3ft), S 45cm (18in). Bears sprays of tubular, pink flowers from mid-summer to autumn. Leaves are narrow and fresh green.

P. pinifolius illus. p.354. **'Mersea Yellow'** is an evergreen, bushy sub-shrub, H 10–20cm (4–8in), S 25cm (10in), with branched stems clothed in fine, dark green leaves. In summer, very narrow, tubular, bright deep yellow flowers are borne in loose, terminal spikes. Zone 5b.

P. procerus. Upright, semi-evergreen perennial. H 50cm (20in), S 20cm (8in). Leaves are oblong to lance-shaped. Produces slim spikes of funnel-shaped, blue-purple flowers in summer. Is suitable for a rock garden.

P. pulchellus. See *P. campanulatus.*

P. 'Royal White'. See *P.* 'White Bedder'.

P. 'Rubicundus' (illus. p.248). Erect, semi-evergreen perennial. H 1.2m (4ft), S 60cm (2ft). Bears very large, bright red flowers each with a white throat. Leaves are linear and light green.

P. rupicola. Evergreen, prostrate shrub. H 5cm (2in), S 15cm (6in). Has rounded to oval, fleshy, blue-grey leaves and, in summer, variable, funnel-shaped, pale to deep pink flowers. Is best grown in a rock garden. Seed may not come true. Zone 5.

P. 'Schoenholzeri', syn. *P.* 'Firebird' (illus. p.248). Vigorous, semi-evergreen, upright perennial. H 1m (3ft), S 30–45cm (1–1½ft). Produces racemes of trumpet-shaped, brilliant scarlet flowers from mid-summer to autumn. Lance-shaped to narrowly oval leaves are mid-green.

P. scouleri. See *P. fruticosus* subsp. *scouleri.* f. *albus* see *P. fruticosus* subsp. *scouleri* f. *albus.*

P. serrulatus, syn. *P. diffusus*, illus. p.355.

P. 'Six Hills'. Evergreen, prostrate shrub. H 5cm (2in), S 15cm (6in). Has rounded, fleshy, grey-green leaves. In summer carries funnel-shaped, cool lilac flowers at stem tips. Is suitable for a rock garden. Zone 6.

P. 'Snow Storm'. See *P.* 'White Bedder'.

P. 'Sour Grapes' (illus. p.248). Semi-evergreen perennial. H 90cm (36in), S 60cm (24in). Light green leaves are narrowly lance-shaped. Bears deep purple-blue flowers suffused violet.

P. 'Stapleford Gem' (illus. p.248). Large-leaved, semi-evergreen perennial. H to 60cm (24in), S 45cm (18in). Bears large, tubular to bell-shaped, lilac-purple flowers from mid-summer to early or mid-autumn; upper lips are pale pink-lilac; lower lips and throats are white with purple lines. Leaves are linear to lance-shaped and mid-green.

P. 'White Bedder', syn. *P.* 'Burford White', *P.* 'Royal White', *P.* 'Snow Storm' (illus p.248). Semi-evergreen, free-flowering perennial. H 70cm (28in), S 60cm (24in). Has white flowers with dark anthers, and linear, fresh green leaves.

PENTACHONDRA

EPACRIDACEAE

Genus of evergreen, spreading shrubs with heath-like leaves. Needs full light and gritty, moist, peaty soil. Is difficult to grow, especially in hot, dry areas. Propagate by rooted offsets in spring, by semi-ripe cuttings in summer or by seed in autumn.

P. pumila. Evergreen, mat-forming, dense shrub. H 3–10cm (1¼–4in), S 20cm (8in) or more. Has oblong to narrowly oval, purplish-green leaves. Small, tubular, white flowers, with reflexed lobes, open in early summer, followed, though rarely in cultivation, by small, spherical, orange fruits. Zone 8.

Pentapterygium. Reclassified as *Agapetes.*

PENTAS

RUBIACEAE

Genus of mainly evergreen perennials and shrubs, grown for their flowers. Tender, min. 10–15°C (50–59°F). Needs full light or partial shade and fertile, well-drained soil. Water freely when in full growth, moderately at other times. May be hard pruned in winter. Propagate by softwood cuttings in summer or by seed in spring. Is prone to whitefly.

P. carnea. See *P. lanceolata.*

P. lanceolata, syn. *P. carnea*, illus. p.163.

Peony. See *Paeonia.*
 Majorcan. See *Paeonia cambessedesii*, illus. p.237.
 Tree. See *Paeonia potaninii.*

PEPEROMIA

PIPERACEAE

Genus of annuals and evergreen perennials, grown for their foliage.

Tender, min. 10°C (50°F). Grow in full light or partial shade, ideally in a peat-based compost. Do not overwater. Propagate by division, by seed or by leaf or stem cuttings in spring or summer.

P. argyreia, syn. *P. sandersii* (Watermelon plant). Evergreen, bushy, compact perennial. H and S 20cm (8in). Has red-stalked, oval, fleshy, dark green leaves, to 10cm (4in) or more long, striped with broad bands of silver. Flowers are insignificant.

P. caperata illus. p.300.

P. clusiifolia (Baby rubber plant). Evergreen perennial with branching, sometimes prostrate, reddish-green stems. H to 20cm (8in), S 25cm (10in). Narrowly oval, fleshy leaves, 8–15cm (3–6in) long, are dark green, edged with red. Flowers are insignificant. Leaves of **'Variegata'** have cream-and-red margins.

P. glabella illus. p.305.

P. griseoargentea, syn. *P. hederifolia* (Ivy peperomia, Silver-leaf peperomia). Evergreen, bushy perennial. H to 15cm (6in), S 20cm (8in). Oval, fleshy leaves, 5cm (2in) or more long, each have a heart-shaped base, a quilted green surface and a silvery sheen. Flowers are insignificant.

P. hederifolia. See *P. griseoargentea.*

P. magnoliifolia. See *P. obtusifolia.*

P. marmorata illus. p.304.

P. metallica. Evergreen perennial with erect, branching, reddish-green stems. H and S to 15cm (6in). Narrowly oval, dark green leaves, to 2.5cm (1in) long, have a metallic sheen, and wide, pale midribs above, reddish-green veins below. Flowers are insignificant.

P. nummariifolia. See *P. rotundifolia.*

P. obtusifolia, syn. *P. magnoliifolia* (Pepper face) Evergreen perennial with leathery, dull green leaves. H and S 25cm (10in). Bears spikes of white flowers. **'Green and Gold'** has green leaves with golden-yellow margins. **'Variegata'** illus. p.305.

P. rotundifolia, syn. *P. nummulariifolia.* Evergreen, creeping perennial. H 5–8cm (2–3in), S 30cm (12in) or more. Very slender stems produce tiny, rounded, fleshy, bright green leaves, 1cm (½in) wide. Flowers are insignificant. Is useful for a hanging basket.

P. rubella. Evergreen perennial with erect, branching, red stems. H and S 15cm (6in). Leaves, in whorls of 4, are 1cm (½in) long, narrowly oval, fleshy and dark green above, crimson below. Flowers are insignificant.

P. sandersii. See *P. argyreia.*

P. scandens (Cupid peperomia). Evergreen, climbing or trailing perennial with pinkish-green stems. H and S to 1m (3ft). Oval, pointed, fleshy leaves, to 5cm (2in) or more long, are waxy and bright green. Flowers are insignificant.

Peperomia
 Cupid. See *Peperomia scandens.*
 Ivy. See *Peperomia griseoargentea.*
 Silver-leaf. See *Peperomia griseoargentea.*
Pepper
 Japan. See *Zanthoxylum piperitum*, illus. p.145.
 Mountain. See *Drimys lanceolata.*

Pepper (continued)
Ornamental. See *Capsicum annuum.*
Pepper-bush, Sweet. See *Clethra alnifolia.*
Pepper face. See *Peperomia obtusifolia.*
Peppermint geranium. See *Pelargonium tomentosum,* illus. p.247.
Peppermint tree. See *Agonis flexuosa,* illus. p.90.
Pepper-tree. See *Pseudowintera axillaris.*
Californian. See *Schinus molle.*
Peruvian. See *Schinus molle.*
Père David's maple. See *Acer davidii.*
Perennial pea. See *Lathyrus latifolius,* illus. p.211; *Lathyrus sylvestris.*

PERESKIA

CACTACEAE

Genus of deciduous cacti, some of which are climbing, with fleshy leaves and woody, green, then brown stems. Is considered the most primitive genus of the *Cactaceae,* producing true leaves unlike most members of the family. Tender, min. 5–10°C (41–50°F). Needs sun and well-drained soil. Water moderately in summer. Propagate by stem cuttings in spring or summer.
P. aculeata illus. p.457. **'Godseffiana'** (syn. *P.a.* var. *godseffiana*) is a fast-growing, deciduous, erect, then climbing cactus. H to 10m (30ft), S 5m (15ft). Min. 5°C (41°F). Broadly oval, slightly fleshy, orange-brown leaves, usually purplish beneath and 9cm (3½in) long, mature to glossy, green. Short flower stems, carrying rose-like, single, orange-centred, cream flowers, 5cm (2in) across, appear in autumn only on plants over 1m (3ft) high. Cut back hard to main stems in autumn.
P. grandifolia, syn. *Rhodocactus grandifolius,* illus. p.458.

PERICALLIS

ASTERACEAE/COMPOSITAE

Genus of perennials and sub-shrubs, sometimes grown as annuals, especially for their daisy-like flower heads. Tender, min. 5°C (41°F). Requires sun or partial shade and fertile, well-drained soil. Propagate by seed sown from spring to mid-summer.
P. x *hybrida,* syn. *Cineraria cruentus* of gardens, *C.* x *hybridus, Senecio* x *hybridus* (Cineraria). H 45–60cm (18–24in), S 25–60cm (10–24in). Slow-growing, evergreen, mound- or dome-shaped perennial. Cultivars are grown as biennials. All have oval, serrated, mid- to deep green leaves. Large, daisy-like, single, semi-double or double flower heads, in shades of blue, red, pink or white, sometimes bicoloured, are produced in winter or spring. **'Brilliant'** has large flower heads in a mixture of white, blue, deep red, copper and rose-pink, and bicolours. **'Royalty'** is late-flowering, with flower heads in sky-blue, cherry-red, lilac with a white eye, and bicolours. **'Spring Glory'** illus. p.332. **'Star Wars',** H 15cm (6in), S 20cm (8in), is compact, with flower heads in a mixture of white, blue, rose-pink, carmine-red and purple; ideal for small containers.

PERILLA

LABIATAE/LAMIACEAE

Genus of annuals, grown for their foliage. Grow in sun and in fertile, well-drained soil. Pinch out growing tips of young plants to encourage a bushy habit. Propagate by seed sown under glass in early spring.
P. frutescens. Moderately fast-growing, upright, bushy annual. H 60cm (24in), S 30cm (12in). Has oval, serrated, aromatic, reddish-purple leaves. In summer produces spikes of very small, tubular, white flowers.

PERISTROPHE

ACANTHACEAE

Genus of mainly evergreen perennials and sub-shrubs, grown usually for their flowers. Tender, min. 15°C (59°F). Grow in sun or partial shade and in well-drained soil; do not overwater in winter. Propagate by stem cuttings in spring or summer.
P. angustifolia. See *P. hyssopifolia.*
P. hyssopifolia, syn. *P. angustifolia.* Evergreen, bushy perennial. H to 60cm (2ft), S 1–1.2m (3–4ft). Broadly lance-shaped leaves, with long-pointed tips, are 8cm (3in) long. Small clusters of tubular, deep rose-pink flowers are borne in winter. **'Aureovariegata'** illus. p.267.

Periwinkle. See *Vinca.*
Greater. See *Vinca major.*
Lesser. See *Vinca minor,* illus. p.176.
Rose. See *Catharanthus roseus,* illus. p.160.
Pernettya mucronata. See *Gaultheria mucronata.*
Pernettya prostrata. See *Gaultheria myrsinoides.*
Pernettya pumila. See *Gaultheria pumila.*
Pernettya tasmanica. See *Gaultheria tasmanica.*

PEROVSKIA

LABIATAE/LAMIACEAE

Genus of deciduous sub-shrubs, grown for their aromatic, grey-green foliage and blue flowers. Needs full sun and very well-drained soil. Cut plants back hard, almost to base, in spring, as new growth starts. Propagate by softwood cuttings in late spring.
P. atriplicifolia. Deciduous, upright sub-shrub. H 1.2m (4ft), S 1m (3ft). Grey-white stems bear narrowly oval, coarsely toothed leaves. Bears 2-lipped, violet-blue flowers in long, slender spikes from late summer to mid-autumn. Zone 5.
P. **'Blue Spire'** illus. p.168.
P. **'Hybrida'.** Deciduous, upright sub-shrub. H 1m (3ft), S 75cm (2½ft). Has oval, deeply lobed and toothed leaves and, from late summer to mid-autumn, tall spires of 2-lipped, deep lavender-blue flowers. Zone 5b.

Perry's weeping silver holly. See *Ilex aquifolium* 'Argentea Marginata Pendula', illus. p.98.

Persian buttercup. See *Ranunculus asiaticus,* illus. pp.421 and 423.
Persian everlasting pea. See *Lathyrus rotundifolius.*
Persian ironwood. See *Parrotia persica,* illus. p.82.
Persian ivy. See *Hedera colchica.*
Persian lilac. See *Melia azedarach,* illus. p.76; *Syringa* x *persica,* illus. p.120.
Persian stone cress. See *Aethionema grandiflorum,* illus. p.352.
Persian violet. See *Exacum affine,* illus. p.331.

PERSICARIA
Knotweed

POLYGONACEAE

Genus of annuals, sometimes invasive perennials and rarely evergreen, semi-evergreen or deciduous sub-shrubs, grown for their autumn leaf colour. Has spikes or panicles of small, usually long-lasting, white, pink or red flowers. Needs sun or partial shade and moist soil. Propagate by seed in spring. Divide perennials in spring or autumn. Contact with all parts may irritate skin; the sap may cause mild stomach upset if ingested.
P. affinis, syn. *Polygonum affine.* Mat-forming, evergreen perennial. H 15–30cm (6–12in), S 30cm (12in) or more. Stout stems bear small, lance-shaped, glossy, green leaves that turn red-bronze in winter. From midsummer to mid-autumn carries dense spikes of small, funnel-shaped, rose-red flowers, fading to pale pink. Is good on a bank or in a rock garden. **'Darjeeling Red',** H 20–25cm (8–10in), has long spikes of deep red flowers. **'Donald Lowndes'** illus. p.376.
P. amplexicaulis, syn. *Polygonum amplexicaule.* Clump-forming, leafy perennial. H and S 1.2m (4ft). Fully hardy. Bears profuse spikes of small, rich red flowers in summer-autumn. Has oval to heart-shaped, mid-green leaves. **'Firetail'** illus. p.249.
P. bistorta, syn. *Polygonum bistorta* (Bistort). **'Superba'** illus. p.243.
P. campanulata, syn. *Polygonum campanulatum,* illus. p.259.
P. capitata, syn. *Polygonum capitatum.* Compact, spreading perennial. H 5cm (2in), S 15–20cm (6–8in). Small, oval leaves are green with darker marks. Small, spherical heads of pink flowers are borne in summer. Is suitable for a rock garden or bank.
P. macrophylla, syn. *P. sphaerostachya, Polygonum macrophyllum, P. sphaerostachyum,* illus. p.279.
P. milletii, syn. *Polygonum milletii.* Compact perennial. H and S 60cm (24in). Fully hardy. Produces slender spikes of rich crimson flowers from mid-summer to early autumn. Narrow, lance-shaped leaves are mid-green.
P. sphaerostachya. See *P. macrophylla.*
P. vacciniifolia, syn. *Polygonum vacciniifolium,* illus. p.387.
P. virginiana **'Painter's Palette',** syn. *Polygonum virginianum* 'Painter's Palette', *Tovara virginiana* 'Painter's Palette', illus. p.290.

Persimmon. See *Diospyros kaki.*
Chinese. See *Diospyros kaki.*
Peruvian daffodil. See *Hymenocallis narcissiflora,* illus. p.420.
Peruvian mastic tree. See *Schinus molle.*
Peruvian old-man cactus. See *Espostoa lanata,* illus. p.457.
Peruvian pepper-tree. See *Schinus molle.*

PETASITES

ASTERACEAE/COMPOSITAE

Genus of invasive perennials, grown for their usually large leaves and value as ground cover. Tolerates sun or shade and prefers moist but well-drained soil. Propagate by division in spring or autumn.
P. fragrans (Winter heliotrope). Spreading, invasive perennial. H 23–30cm (9–12in), S 1.2m (4ft). Has rounded to heart-shaped, dark green leaves. Small, vanilla-scented, daisy-like, pinkish-white flower heads are produced in late winter before foliage.
P. japonicus illus. p.274.

PETREA

VERBENACEAE

Genus of evergreen shrubs and woody-stemmed, twining climbers, grown for their flowers. Tender, min. 13–15°C (55–9°F). Needs full light and fertile, well-drained soil. Water regularly, less when not in full growth. Provide support. Thin out and spur back crowded growth in spring. Propagate by semi-ripe cuttings in summer. Mealy bug and whitefly may cause problems.
P. volubilis illus. p.206.

PETROCOSMEA

GESNERIACEAE

Genus of evergreen, rhizomatous perennials. Tender, min. 2–5°C (36–41°F). Requires shade and well-drained, peaty soil. Propagate by seed in early spring or by leaf cuttings in early summer.
P. kerrii illus. p.374.

PETRORHAGIA

CARYOPHYLLACEAE

Genus of annuals and perennials, grown for their flowers. Is suitable for rock gardens and banks. Prefers sun and well-drained, sandy soil. Propagate by seed in autumn. Self-seeds readily.
P. saxifraga, syn. *Tunica saxifraga* (Tunic flower), illus. p.375. **'Rosette'** is a mat-forming perennial. H 10cm (4in), S 15cm (6in). Has tufts of grass-like leaves. In summer, slender stems carry a profusion of cup-shaped, double, white to pale pink flowers, sometimes veined deeper pink.

PETUNIA

SOLANACEAE

Genus of annuals and perennials, wholly grown as annuals, with showy, colourful flowers. Grow in a sunny position that is sheltered from wind and in fertile, well-drained soil. Dead-head regularly. Propagate by seed sown under glass in autumn or mid-spring. May suffer from viruses, including cucumber mosaic and tomato spotted wilt.

The many cultivars that have been produced are moderately fast-growing, branching, bushy plants, H 15–30cm (6–12in), S 30cm (12in), with oval, mid- to deep green leaves, usually 5–12cm (2–5in) long. In summer-autumn, they produce flared, trumpet-shaped, single or double flowers in a wide range of colours (available in mixtures or singly), including blue, violet, purple, red, pink and white. Some have dark veining, central white stars, halos (throats in contrasting colours), or picotee margins. The cultivars are divided into 2 groups, Grandiflora and Multiflora petunias. **Grandiflora** petunias have very large flowers, 8–10cm (3–4in) wide, but they are easily damaged by rain and, where summer rains are frequent, are best grown in sheltered hanging baskets and containers. **Multiflora** petunias are bushier than the Grandiflora petunias, and produce smaller flowers, 5cm (2in) wide, in greater quantity. They tend to be more resistant to rain damage, and are excellent for summer bedding or for a mixed border.

P. **Aladdin Series.** Grandiflora petunias, illus. p.322.
P. **Carpet Series.** Multiflora petunias, illus. p.328.
P. **Cascade Series.** Grandiflora petunias. H 20–30cm (8–12in), S 30–90cm (12–36in). Trailing stems produce flowers in a wide range of colours.
P. **'Cherry Tart'.** Multiflora petunia. H 15–30cm (6–12in), S 30–60cm (12–24in). Bears double, deep pink-and-white flowers.
P. **'Colour Parade'.** Grandiflora petunia. H 20–30cm (8–12in), S 30–90cm (12–36in). Has a wide colour range of flowers with ruffled petals.
P. **Daddy Series.** Grandiflora petunias. H to 35cm (14in), S 30–90cm (12–36in). Bear large, heavily veined flowers in pastel to deep pink, salmon-pink, purple or lavender-blue. **'Sugar Daddy'** illus p.331.
P. **Flash Series.** Compact, Grandiflora petunias. H 23–40cm (9–16in), S 30–90cm (12–36in). Produce flowers in a range of bright colours, including bicolours.
P. **'Gypsy'.** Multiflora petunia. H 15–30cm (6–12in), S 30–60cm (12–24in). Has salmon-red flowers.
P. **Jamboree Series.** Multiflora petunias. H 15–30cm (6–12in), S 30–90cm (12–36in). Produce pendulous stems bearing flowers in a range of colours.
P. **'Magic Cherry'.** Compact, Grandiflora petunia. H 20–30cm (8–12in), S 30–60cm (12–24in). Has cherry-red flowers.
P. **'Mirage Velvet'.** Multiflora petunia, illus. p.326.
P. **Pearl Series.** Dwarf, Multiflora petunias. H 15–20cm (6–8in), S 20–50cm (8–20in). Bear small flowers in a wide range of colours.
P. **Picotee Ruffled Series.** Multiflora petunias. H 15–30cm (6–12in),

S 30–90cm (12–36in). Bear ruffled flowers, edged with white, in a range of colours.
P. **Picotee Series.** Grandiflora petunias, illus. p.328. **'Picotee Rose'** illus. p.326.
P. **Plum Crazy Series.** Multiflora petunias. H 15–20cm (6–8in), S 30–90cm (12–36in). Produce flowers that have contrasting veins and throats. Colours available include white, with yellow throat and veins, and shades of violet, pink, and magenta, all with darker throats and veins.
P. **Primetime Series.** Multiflora petunias, illus. p.323.
P. **'Razzle Dazzle'.** Grandiflora petunia. H 20–30cm (8–12in), S 30–90cm (12–36in). Has flowers in various colours, striped with white.
P. **Recoverer Series.** Grandiflora petunias, illus. p.318.
P. **'Red Satin'.** Multiflora petunia. H 15–30cm (6–12in), S 30–60cm (12–24in). Has brilliant scarlet flowers.
P. **Resisto Series.** Multiflora petunias, [blue] illus. p.332; [rose-pink] illus. p.325.
P. **Surfinia Series 'Surfinia Purple'** (illus. p.55). Vigorous Grandiflora petunia. H 23–40cm (9–16in), S 30–90cm (12–36in). Bears masses of magenta flowers with purple veining. Has good wet-weather tolerance.

Peyote. See *Lophophora.*

PHACELIA

HYDROPHYLLACEAE

Genus of annuals, biennials, and perennials. Grow in sun and in fertile, well-drained soil. Tall species may need support. Propagate by seed sown outdoors in spring or early autumn. Contact with foliage may aggravate skin allergies.
P. **campanularia** illus. p.334.
P. **tanacetifolia.** Moderately fast-growing, upright annual. H 60cm (24in) or more, S 30cm (12in). Has feathery, deep green leaves. In summer, bears spikes of bell-shaped, lavender-blue flowers.

PHAEDRANASSA

AMARYLLIDACEAE

Genus of bulbs with tubular, often pendent flowers. Needs full sun or partial shade and fairly rich, well-drained soil. Feed with high-potash fertilizer in summer. Reduce watering in winter. Propagate by seed or offsets in spring.
P. **carmioli** illus. p.400.

Phaedranthus buccinatorius. See *Distictis buccinatoria.*
Phaiophleps biflora. See *Olsynium biflorum.*

PHAIUS

See also ORCHIDS.
P. **tankervilleae** (illus. p.297). Semi-evergreen, terrestrial orchid. H 75cm (30in). Tender, min. 10°C (55°F). Tall spikes of flowers, 9cm (3½in) across, brown within, silvery-grey outside and

each with a long, red-marked, pink lip, open in early summer. Leaves are broadly oval, ribbed and 60cm (24in) long. Provide semi-shade in summer.

PHALAENOPSIS

See also ORCHIDS.
P. **Allegria** (illus. p.296). Evergreen, epiphytic orchid for a warm greenhouse. H 15cm (6in). Carries sprays of white flowers, to 12cm (5in) across; flowering season varies. Broadly oval, fleshy leaves are 15cm (6in) long. Needs shade in summer.
P. **cornu-cervi** (illus. p.298). Evergreen, epiphytic orchid for a warm greenhouse. H 15cm (6in). Yellowish-green flowers, 5cm (2in) across, with brown marks, are borne successively, either singly or in pairs, in summer. Has broadly oval leaves, 10cm (4in) long. Needs shade in summer.
P. **Lady Jersey x Lippeglut** (illus. p.297). Evergreen, epiphytic orchid for a warm greenhouse. H 15cm (6in). Tall, pendent spikes of pink flowers, 9cm (3½in) across, appear at varying times of year. Broadly oval leaves are 10cm (4in) long. Requires shade in summer.
P. **Lundy** (illus. p.298). Evergreen, epiphytic orchid for a warm greenhouse. H 15cm (6in). Has sprays of yellow flowers, 8cm (3in) across, with red-stripes; flowering season varies. Broadly oval leaves are 23cm (9in) long. Grow in shade in summer.

PHALARIS

GRAMINEAE/POACEAE

See also GRASSES, BAMBOOS, RUSHES and SEDGES.
P. **arundinacea** var. *picta*, syn. *P.a.* 'Picta', illus. p.306. **'Picta'** see *P.a.* var. *picta*.

Phanerophlebia fortunei. See *Cyrtomium fortunei.*
Pharbitis. Reclassified as *Ipomoea.*
Phaseolus caracalla. See *Vigna caracalla.*
Pheasant grass. See *Stipa arundinacea.*
Pheasant's eye. See *Narcissus poeticus* var. *recurvus*, illus. p.417.

PHEGOPTERIS

THELYPTERIDACEAE

Genus of deciduous ferns. Grow in semi-shade and in humus-rich, moist but well-drained soil. Propagate by division in spring or by spores in summer.
P. **connectilis**, syn. *Thelypteris phegopteris* (Beech fern). Deciduous fern. H 23cm (9in), S 30cm (12in). Broadly lance-shaped, mid-green fronds, each consisting of tiny, triangular pinnae on wiry stalks, arise from a creeping rootstock. Is useful for ground cover.

PHELLODENDRON

RUTACEAE

Genus of deciduous trees, grown for their foliage, which colours well in autumn. Male and female flowers are

produced on different plants. Young growth is susceptible to damage by late frosts. Needs full sun and fertile, well-drained soil. Does best in hot summers. Propagate by softwood cuttings in summer, by seed in autumn or by root cuttings in late winter.
P. **amurense** (Amur cork tree). Deciduous, spreading tree. H 12m (40ft), S 15m (50ft). Has corky, dark bark when old. Aromatic leaves, each with 5 to 11 oblong leaflets, are glossy, dark green, becoming yellow in autumn. Tiny, green flowers in early summer are followed by small, persistent, rounded, black fruits that smell of resin. Zone 3.
P. **chinense** illus. p.81.

PHILADELPHUS

HYDRANGEACEAE/PHILADELPHACEAE

Genus of deciduous, mainly summer-flowering shrubs, grown for their usually fragrant flowers. Needs sun and fertile, well-drained soil. After flowering, cut some older shoots back to young growths, leaving young shoots to flower the following year. Propagate by softwood cuttings in summer. May become infested with aphids.
P. **'Beauclerk'** illus. p.135.
P. **'Belle Etoile'** illus. p.136.
P. **'Boule d'Argent'** illus. p.137.
P. **coronarius** (Mock orange). **'Aureus'** is a deciduous, upright shrub. H 2.5m (8ft), S 1.5m (5ft). Clusters of very fragrant, 4-petalled, creamy-white flowers are produced in late spring and early summer. Oval, golden-yellow, young leaves turn yellow-green in summer. Protect from full sun. Zone 3. **'Variegatus'** illus. p.139.
P. **'Buckley's Quill'.** Upright deciduous shrub. H 2m (6ft) S 1.2m (4ft). Semi-double to double fragrant white flowers with about 30 narrow quill-like petals, divided at their tips, appear in early summer. Leaves are mid-green and slightly toothed. Zone 4.
P. **'Dame Blanche'** illus. p.137.
P. **delavayi.** Deciduous, upright shrub. H 3m (10ft), S 2.5m (8ft). Dense clusters of very fragrant, 4-petalled, white flowers, with sometimes purple-flushed, green sepals, open from early to mid-summer. Leaves are dark green, oval and toothed. f. *melanocalyx* (syn. *P. purpurascens*) illus. p.139.
P. x *lemoinei*. See *P.* 'Lemoinei'.
P. **'Lemoinei'**, syn. *P.* x *lemoinei*, illus. p.138.
P. **'Manteau d'Hermine'** illus. p.158.
P. **purpurascens.** See *P. delavayi* f. *melanocalyx.*
P. **'Snowbelle'.** Semi-dwarf, deciduous shrub with dark green, narrow foliage. H and S 1.2m (4ft). The fragrant white flowers have 8–15 rounded petals in a compact inflorescence. Zone 4.
P. **'Virginal'.** Vigorous, deciduous, upright shrub. H 3m (10ft), S 2.5m (8ft). Has oval, dark green leaves. Produces masses of large, very fragrant, double or semi-double, pure white flowers in loose racemes from early to mid-summer. Zone 4b.

PHILESIA

LILIACEAE/PHILESIACEAE

Genus of one species of evergreen shrub, grown for its showy flowers. Thrives only in mild, moist areas. Needs semi-shade and humus-rich, moist, acid soil. Benefits from an annual dressing of leaf mould. Propagate by semi-ripe cuttings in summer or by suckers in autumn.

P. magellanica. Evergreen, erect shrub. H 1m (3ft), S 2m (6ft). Bears trumpet-shaped, waxy, crimson-pink flowers, in leaf axils, from mid-summer to late autumn. Narrowly oblong, dark green leaves are bluish-white beneath. Zone 8.

Philippine violet. See *Barleria cristata.*

PHILLYREA

OLEACEAE

Genus of evergreen shrubs and trees, with inconspicuous flowers, grown for their foliage. Requires shelter at the limits of hardiness. Does best in full sun and in fertile, well-drained soil. To restrict growth, cut back in spring. Propagate by semi-ripe cuttings in summer.

P. angustifolia. Evergreen, bushy, dense shrub. H and S 3m (10ft). Leaves are narrowly oblong and dark green. Small, fragrant, 4-lobed, greenish-white flowers in late spring and early summer are followed by spherical, blue-black fruits. Zone 8.

P. decora. See *Osmanthus decorus.*

P. latifolia. Evergreen, rounded shrub or tree. H and S 8m (25ft). Has oval, glossy, dark green leaves. Bears tiny, fragrant, 4-lobed, greenish-white flowers from late spring to early summer, then spherical, blue-black fruits. Zone 8.

PHILODENDRON

ARACEAE

Genus of evergreen shrubs and woody-based, root climbers, grown for their handsome leaves. Intermittently bears insignificant flowers. Tender, min. 15–18°C (59–64°F). Needs partial shade and humus-rich, well-drained soil. Water moderately, sparingly in cold weather. Provide support. Young stem tips may be removed to promote branching. Propagate by leaf-bud or stem-tip cuttings in summer. All parts may cause severe discomfort if ingested; contact with sap may irritate skin.

P. auritum of gardens. See *Syngonium auritum.*

P. bipinnatifidum, syn. *P. selloum* (Tree philodendron; illus. p.152). Tree-like shrub with a single, erect stem and very long-stalked leaves.

P. **'Burgundy'.** Slow-growing, evergreen, woody-based, root climber. H 2m (6ft) or more. Leaves are narrowly oblong, red-flushed, deep green above, wine-red beneath, and up to 30cm (12in) long.

P. cordatum (Heart leaf). Moderately vigorous, evergreen, woody-based, root climber. H 3m (10ft) or more. Has heart-shaped, lustrous, rich green leaves, to 45cm (18in) long.

P. domesticum, syn. *P. hastatum* of gardens (Elephant's ear, Spade leaf). Fairly slow-growing, evergreen, woody-based, root climber. H 2–3m (6–10ft). Lustrous, bright green leaves, 30–40cm (12–16in) long, are arrow-shaped on young plants and later have prominent, basal lobes.

P. erubescens (Blushing philodendron). Evergreen, erect, woody-based, root climber. H to 3m (10ft). Oval to triangular leaves, 15–25cm (6–10in) long, have long, red stalks and are dark green with a lustrous, coppery flush.

P. hastatum of gardens. See *P. domesticum.*

P. laciniatum. See *P. pedatum.*

P. melanochrysum illus. p.220.

P. pedatum, syn. *P. laciniatum.* Slow-growing, evergreen, woody-based, root climber. H 2–3m (6–10ft). Has oval, lustrous, deep green leaves, 30–80cm (12–32in) long, cut into 5 or 7 prominent lobes.

P. pinnatifidum. Evergreen, erect, robust, unbranched shrub. H to 3m (10ft), S 1–2m (3–6ft). Glossy, deep green leaves are broadly oval in outline, 40–60cm (16–24in) long and divided into 15 or more finger-like lobes.

P. sagittatum. See *P. sagittifolium.*

P. sagittifolium, syn. *P. sagittatum.* Slow-growing, evergreen, woody-based, root climber. H 2–3m (6–10ft). Oval leaves with basal lobes are up to 40–60cm (16–24in) long and glossy, bright green.

P. scandens illus. p.220.

P. selloum. See *P. bipinnatifidum.*

P. trifoliatum. See *Syngonium auritum.*

Philodendron, Blushing. See *Philodendron erubescens.*

PHLEBODIUM

POLYPODIACEAE

Genus of evergreen or semi-evergreen ferns. Tender, min. 5°C (41°F). Needs full light or semi-shade and humus-rich, moist but well-drained soil. Remove fading fronds regularly. Propagate by division in spring or by spores in summer.

P. aureum, syn. *Polypodium aureum,* illus. p.311. **'Mandaianum'** illus. p.310.

PHLOMIS

LABIATAE/LAMIACEAE

Genus of evergreen, summer-flowering shrubs and perennials, grown for their conspicuous, hooded flowers, which are borne in dense whorls, and for their foliage. Prefers full sun and well-drained soil. Propagate by seed in autumn; increase shrubs from softwood cuttings in summer, perennials by division in spring.

P. cashmeriana. Evergreen, upright shrub. H 60cm (24in), S 45cm (18in). Produces masses of 2-lipped, pale lilac flowers in summer. Narrowly oval, mid-green leaves have woolly, white undersides. Zone 9.

P. chrysophylla. Evergreen, rounded, stiffly branched shrub. H and S 1m (3ft). Bears 2-lipped, golden-yellow flowers in early summer. Oval leaves are grey-green when young, becoming golden-green. Zone 9?.

P. fruticosa illus. p.170.

P. italica illus. p.162.

P. longifolia var. *bailanica.* Evergreen, bushy shrub. H 1.2m (4ft), S 1m (3ft). Leaves are oblong to heart-shaped, deeply veined and bright green. Has 2-lipped, deep yellow flowers from early to mid-summer. Zone 9.

P. russeliana illus. p.255.

PHLOX

POLEMONIACEAE

Genus of mainly late spring- or summer-flowering annuals and perennials, some of which are semi-evergreen or evergreen, grown for their terminal panicles or profusion of brightly coloured flowers. Does best in sun or semi-shade and in fertile, moist but well-drained soil; some species prefer acid soil; in light, dry soils is better grown in partial shade. Trim back rock garden species after flowering. Propagate rock garden species and hybrids by cuttings from non-flowering shoots in spring or summer; species by seed in autumn or spring; *P. maculata, P. paniculata* and their cultivars also by division in early spring or by root cuttings in winter; and annuals by seed in spring. *P. maculata, P. paniculata* and their cultivars are susceptible to eelworm and mildew. See also feature panel p.242.

P. adsurgens. Evergreen, mat-forming, prostrate perennial. H 10cm (4in), S 30cm (12in). Woody-based stems are clothed in oval, light to mid-green leaves. In summer produces terminal clusters of short-stemmed, saucer-shaped, purple, pink or white flowers with overlapping petals. Is good for a rock garden or peat bed. Prefers partial shade and gritty, peaty, acid soil. **'Wagon Wheel'** illus. p.376.

P. amoena **'Variegata'.** See *P.* x *procumbens* 'Variegata'.

P. bifida illus. p.381.

P. caespitosa. Evergreen, mound-forming, compact perennial. H 8cm (3in), S 12cm (5in). Leaves are narrow and needle-like. Solitary almost stemless, saucer-shaped, lilac or white flowers are borne in summer. Suits a rock garden or trough. Needs sun and very well-drained soil.

P. **'Camla'** illus. p.379.

P. **'Chatahoochee'.** See *P. divaricata* subsp. *laphamii* 'Chatahoochee'.

P. divaricata. Semi-evergreen, creeping perennial. H 30cm (12in) or more, S 20cm (8in). In early summer, upright stems carry saucer-shaped, lavender-blue flowers in loose clusters. Leaves are oval. Suits a rock garden or peat bed. Prefers semi-shade and moist but well-drained, peaty soil. subsp. *laphamii* illus. p.356. subsp. *laphamii* **'Chatahoochee'** (syn. *P.* 'Chatahoochee') illus. p.356.

P. douglasii **'Boothman's Variety'** illus. p.380. **'Crackerjack'** illus. p.379. **'May Snow'** is an evergreen, mound-forming perennial. H 8cm (3in), S 20cm (8in). Masses of saucer-shaped, white flowers are carried in early

summer. Leaves are lance-shaped and mid-green. Is suitable for a rock garden, wall, or bank. Vigorous, compact **'Red Admiral'**, H 15cm (6in), has crimson flowers.

P. drummondii (Annual phlox). **'African Sunset'** illus. p.327. **Beauty Series** is a group of moderately fast-growing, compact, upright annuals. H 15cm (6in), S 10cm (4in). Has lance-shaped, pale green leaves and, from summer to early autumn, heads of star-shaped flowers in many colours, including red, pink, blue, purple, and white. **'Carnival'** has larger flowers with contrasting centres. **'Chanal'** illus. p.326. **'Petticoat'** has bicoloured flowers. **'Sternenzauber'** (syn. *P.d.* 'Twinkle') illus. p.326. **'Twinkle'** see *P.d.* 'Sternenzauber'.

P. **'Emerald Cushion'** illus. p.381.

P. hoodii. Evergreen, compact, prostrate perennial. H 5cm (2in), S 10cm (4in). Solitary, flat, white flowers open in early summer above fine, needle-like, hairy leaves. Suits a rock garden. Needs sun and very well-drained soil.

P. maculata. Erect perennial. H 1m (3ft), S 45cm (1½ft). In summer produces cylindrical panicles of tubular, 5-lobed, mauve-pink flowers above oval, mid-green leaves. **'Alpha'** (illus. p.242) has rose-pink flowers. **'Omega'** (illus. p.242) has white flowers, each with a lilac eye.

P. paniculata. Upright perennial, seldom grown, as is replaced in gardens by its more colourful cultivars. H 1.2m (4ft), S 60cm (2ft). Tubular, 5-lobed flowers are borne in conical heads above oval, mid-green leaves in late summer. **'Aida'** is purple-red, each flower with a purple eye. Flowers of **'Amethyst'** (illus. p.242) are pale lilac with paler-edged petals. **'Balmoral'** (illus. p.242) has large, rosy-mauve flowers. **'Brigadier'** (illus. p.242) has deep orange-red flowers. **'Bright Eyes'** has pale pink flowers, each with a red eye. **'Eva Cullum'** (illus. p.242) has clear pink flowers with magenta eyes. **'Eventide'** (illus. p.242) produces lavender-blue flowers. **'Fujiyama'** (illus. p.242) has star-shaped, white flowers. Flowers of **'Graf Zeppelin'** (illus. p.242) are white with red centres. **'Hampton Court'** (illus. p.242) is a mauve-blue cultivar, with dark green foliage. **'Harlequin'** (illus. p.242) has reddish-purple flowers. Leaves are variegated ivory-white. **'Le Mahdi'** (illus. p.242) has deep purple flowers. **'Mia Ruys'** (illus. p.242), H 45cm (18in), has large, white flowers, and is shorter than most other cultivars. **'Mother of Pearl'** (illus. p.242) has white flowers tinted pink. **'Norah Leigh'** (illus. p.242) has pale lilac flowers and ivory-variegated leaves. **'Prince of Orange'** (illus. p.242) is orange-red. **'Russian Violet'** is of open habit and has pale lilac-blue flowers. Flowers of **'Sandringham'** (illus. p.242) have widely spaced petals and are pink with darker centres. **'Sir John Falstaff'** has large, deep salmon flowers, each with a cherry-red eye. **'White Admiral'** (illus. p.242) bears pure white flowers. Those of **'Windsor'** (illus. p.242) are carmine-rose with red eyes.

P. × procumbens 'Millstream'. Evergreen, prostrate perennial. H to 15cm (6in), S 30cm (12in). Has narrowly oval, glossy, green leaves. In early summer produces small, saucer-shaped, deep lavender-pink flowers with white eyes. Is suitable for a rock garden. **'Variegata'** (syn. *P. amoena* 'Variegata'), H 2.5cm (1in), S 25cm (10in), has white-margined leaves and bright cerise-pink flowers.

P. stolonifera (Creeping phlox). Evergreen, prostrate, spreading perennial. H 10–15cm (4–6in), S 30cm (12in) or more. Has small, saucer-shaped, pale blue flowers in early summer. Leaves are oblong to oval. Prefers moist, peaty, acid soil; is good for a peat bed or rock garden. **'Ariane'** illus. p.373. **'Blue Ridge'** has masses of lavender-blue flowers.

P. subulata. Evergreen, mound-forming perennial. H 10cm (4in), S 20cm (8in). Bears fine, needle-like leaves. Masses of star-shaped, white, pink or mauve flowers appear in early summer. Is good for a sunny rock garden. **'Marjorie'** illus. p.378.

Phlox
  Annual. See *Phlox drummondii.*
  Creeping. See *Phlox stolonifera.*
  Sand. See *Phlox bifida,* illus. p.381.

PHOENIX

ARECACEAE/PALMAE

Genus of evergreen palms, grown for their overall appearance and their edible fruits. Tender, min. 10–15°C (50–59°F). Grow in full light, though tolerates partial shade, in any fertile, well-drained soil. Water potted specimens moderately, less during winter. Propagate by seed in spring at not less than 24°C (75°F). Spider mite may be a problem.

P. canariensis (Canary Island date palm). Evergreen, upright palm with a robust trunk. H 18m (60ft) or more, S 10m (30ft) or more. Min. 10°C (50°F). Feather-shaped, arching leaves, each to 5m (15ft) long, are divided into narrowly lance-shaped, leathery, bright green leaflets. Bears large, pendent clusters of tiny, yellowish-brown flowers that on mature specimens are followed by shortly oblong, yellow to red fruits in autumn-winter.

P. roebelenii (Miniature date palm, Pygmy date palm). Evergreen palm with a slender trunk. H 2–4m (6–12ft), S 1–2m (3–6ft). Min. 15°C (59°F). Has feather-shaped, arching, glossy, dark green leaves, 1–1.2m (3–4ft) long, and, in summer, large panicles of tiny, yellow flowers. Egg-shaped, black fruits are borne in pendent clusters, 45cm (18in) long, in autumn.

PHORMIUM
New Zealand flax

AGAVACEAE/PHORMIACEAE

Genus of evergreen perennials, grown for their bold, sword-shaped leaves. Requires sun and moist but well-drained soil. Propagate by division or seed in spring.

P. 'Bronze Baby' illus. p.302.
P. colensoi. See *P. cookianum.*
P. cookianum, syn. *P. colensoi* (Mountain flax). Evergreen, upright perennial. H 1–2m (3–6ft), S 30cm (1ft). Has tufts of sword-shaped, dark green leaves. Panicles of tubular, pale yellowish-green flowers are borne in summer. subsp. *hookeri* **'Tricolor'** has leaves striped vertically with red, yellow and green. **'Variegatum'** has cream-striped leaves.
P. 'Dazzler' illus. p.264.
P. tenax. Evergreen, upright perennial. H 3m (10ft), S 1–2m (3–6ft). Has tufts of sword-shaped, stiff, dark green leaves. Panicles of tubular, dull red flowers are produced on short, slightly glaucous green stems in summer. Thrives by the sea. **'Aurora'** has leaves vertically striped with red, bronze, salmon-pink, and yellow. **Purpureum Group** illus. p.232. **'Veitchianum'** (syn. *P.t.* 'Veitchii') bears broad, creamy-white-striped leaves. **'Veitchii'** see *P.t.* 'Veitchianum'.

PHOTINIA,
syn. STRANVAESIA

ROSACEAE

Genus of evergreen or deciduous shrubs and trees, with small, white flowers, grown for their foliage and, in the case of deciduous species, for their autumn colour and fruits. Protect evergreen species from strong, cold winds. Requires sun or semi-shade and fertile, well-drained soil; some species prefer acid soil. Propagate evergreen and deciduous species by semi-ripe cuttings in summer, deciduous species also by seed in autumn.

P. arbutifolia, syn. *Heteromeles arbutifolia* (Christmas berry, Toyon). Evergreen, bushy, spreading shrub or tree. H 6m (20ft), S 8m (25ft). Frost hardy. Has oblong, sharply toothed, leathery, glossy, dark green leaves. Broad, flat heads of small, 5-petalled, white flowers, produced in late summer, are succeeded by large clusters of rounded, red fruits. Zone 9?.
P. davidiana illus. p.94.
P. × fraseri. Group of evergreen, hybrid shrubs. Has good resistance to damage by late frosts. Leaves are bold and oblong. Young growths are attractive over a long period. Zone 7. **'Birmingham'** illus. p.117. **'Red Robin'** is upright and dense. H 6m (20ft), S 4m (12ft). Glossy, dark green leaves are brilliant red when young. Bears 5-petalled flowers in late spring. Zone 7.
P. nussia. Evergreen, spreading tree. H and S 6m (20ft). Produces oblong, leathery, glossy, dark green leaves and saucer-shaped, 5-petalled, white flowers in mid-summer, followed by rounded, orange-red fruits. Zone 9?.
P. serratifolia, syn. *P. serrulata.* Evergreen, upright shrub or bushy-headed tree. H 10m (30ft), S 8m (25ft). Oblong, often sharply toothed leaves are red when young, maturing to glossy, dark green. Small, 5-petalled flowers from mid- to late spring are sometimes followed by spherical, red fruits. Young growth may be damaged by late frosts. Zone 8.

P. serrulata. See *P. serratifolia.*
P. villosa. Deciduous, upright shrub or spreading tree. H and S 5m (15ft). Oval, dark green leaves, bronze-margined when young, become brilliant orange-red in autumn. Clusters of 5-petalled flowers, produced in late spring, are followed by spherical, red fruits. Prefers acid soil. Zone 6.

PHRAGMIPEDIUM

See also ORCHIDS.
P. caudatum. Evergreen, epiphytic orchid for an intermediate greenhouse. H 23cm (9in). In summer produces sprays of flowers with light green and tan sepals and pouches and drooping, ribbon-like, yellow and brownish-crimson petals, to 30cm (12in) long. Has narrowly oval leaves, 30cm (12in) long. Needs shade in summer.

PHUOPSIS

RUBIACEAE

Genus of one species of mat-forming, summer-flowering perennial, grown for its small, pungent, tubular flowers. Is good for ground cover, especially on banks and in rock gardens. Needs sun and well-drained soil. Propagate by division in spring, by semi-ripe cuttings in summer or by seed in autumn.
P. stylosa, syn. *Crucianella stylosa,* illus. p.352.

PHYGELIUS

SCROPHULARIACEAE

Genus of evergreen or semi-evergreen shrubs and sub-shrubs, grown for their showy, tubular flowers. Grows best if planted in a sheltered position; will attain a considerably greater height when grown against a south- or west-facing wall. Needs sun and fertile, well-drained but not too dry soil. Usually loses leaves or has shoots cut to ground by frosts. Cut back to just above ground level in spring, or, if plants have woody bases, prune to live wood. Propagate by softwood cuttings in summer.

P. aequalis illus. p.166. **'Yellow Trumpet'** illus. p.169.
P. capensis 'Coccineus'. Evergreen or semi-evergreen, upright sub-shrub. H 1.5m (5ft), S 2m (6ft). Tubular, curved, bright orange-red flowers, each with a red mouth and a yellow throat, are produced from mid-summer to early autumn in tall, slender spires amid triangular, dark green leaves. Zone 7.
P. × rectus 'Winchester Fanfare'. Evergreen or semi-evergreen, upright sub-shrub. H 1.5m (5ft), S 2m (6ft). Has pendulous, tubular, dusky, reddish-pink flowers, each with scarlet lobes and a yellow throat, from mid-summer to early autumn, and triangular, dark green leaves. Zone 7.

Phyllanthus nivosus. See *Breynia disticha.*
Phyllitis scolopendrium. See *Asplenium scolopendrium.*
Phyllitis scolopendrium **'Marginatum'.** See *Asplenium scolopendrium* Marginatum Group.

PHYLLOCLADUS

PHYLLOCLADACEAE/PODOCARPACEAE

See also CONIFERS.
P. aspleniifolius (Tasman celery pine). Slow-growing, upright conifer. H 5–10m (15–30ft), S 3–5m (10–15ft). Tender, min. 2°C (35°F). Instead of true leaves has flattened, leaf-like shoots known as phylloclades; these are dull dark green and resemble celery leaves in outline. Produces inedible, white-coated nuts with fleshy, red bases.
P. trichomanoides illus. p.106.

PHYLLODOCE

ERICACEAE

Genus of evergreen shrubs, grown for their heath-like leaves and attractive flowers. Needs semi-shade and moist, peaty, acid soil. Propagate by semi-ripe cuttings in late summer or by seed in spring.
P. caerulea, syn. *P. taxifolia,* illus. p.348.
P. empetriformis illus. p.348.
P. × intermedia 'Drummondii' illus. p.347. **'Fred Stoker'** is an evergreen, upright shrub. H and S 23cm (9in). Has narrow, glossy, green leaves. From late spring to early summer carries terminal clusters of pitcher-shaped, bright reddish-purple flowers on slender, red stalks. Zone 3.
P. nipponica. Evergreen, upright shrub. H 10–20cm (4–8in), S 10–15cm (4–6in). Freely branched stems bear fine, linear leaves and, in late spring and summer, stalked, bell-shaped, white flowers from their tips. Zone 3.
P. taxifolia. See *P. caerulea.*

PHYLLOSTACHYS

GRAMINEAE/POACEAE

See also GRASSES, BAMBOOS, RUSHES and SEDGES.
P. aurea (Fishpole bamboo, Golden bamboo). Evergreen, clump-forming bamboo. H 6–8m (20–25ft), S indefinite. Erect, grooved stems have cup-shaped swellings beneath most nodes, which, towards the base, are often close together and distorted. Bears mid-green leaves. Flowers are unimportant as they are so rarely produced.
P. aureosulcata (Golden-groove bamboo). Evergreen, clump-forming bamboo. H 6–8m (20–25ft), S indefinite. Bears striped sheaths and yellow grooves on rough, brownish-green stems. Mid-green leaves are up to 15cm (6in) long; flowers are unimportant as they are so rarely produced.
P. bambusoides illus. p.308.
P. flexuosa illus. p.308.
P. 'Henonis'. See *P. nigra* var. *henonis.*
P. nigra (Black bamboo). Evergreen, clump-forming bamboo. H 6–8m (20–25ft), S indefinite. Grooved, greenish-brown stems turn black in second season. Almost unmarked culm sheaths bear bristled auricles and mid-green leaves. Flowers are unimportant as they are so rarely produced. var. *henonis* (syn. *P.* 'Henonis') illus. p.308.
P. viridiglaucescens illus. p.309.

PHYSALIS
Chinese lantern

SOLANACEAE

Genus of summer-flowering perennials and annuals, grown mainly for their decorative, lantern-like calyces and fruits, produced in autumn. Grows in sun or shade and in well-drained soil. Propagate by division or softwood cuttings in spring, annuals by seed in spring or autumn. All parts of *P. alkekengi*, except the fully ripe fruit, may cause mild stomach upset if ingested; contact with foliage may irritate skin.

P. alkekengi (Bladder cherry, Winter cherry). Spreading invasive, perennial. H 45cm (18in), S 60cm (24in). Inconspicuous, nodding, star-shaped, white flowers in summer are followed, in autumn, by rounded, bright orange-red fruits, surrounded by inflated, orange calyces. Leaves are mid-green and oval.

PHYSOCARPUS

ROSACEAE

Genus of deciduous, mainly summer-flowering shrubs, grown for their foliage and flowers. Requires sun and fertile, not too dry soil. Prefers acid soil and does not grow well on shallow, alkaline soil. Thin established plants occasionally by cutting some older shoots back to ground level after flowering. Propagate by softwood cuttings in summer.

P. opulifolius (Ninebark). Deciduous, arching, dense shrub. H 3m (10ft), S 5m (15ft). Has peeling bark and broadly oval, toothed and lobed, mid-green leaves. Clusters of tiny, sometimes pink-tinged, white flowers are borne in early summer. Zone 2b.
'Dart's Gold' illus. p.146.

PHYSOPLEXIS

CAMPANULACEAE

Genus of one species of tufted perennial, grown for its flowers. Is good grown on tufa, in rock gardens, troughs and alpine houses. Needs sun and very well-drained, alkaline soil, but should face away from midday sun. Keep fairly dry in winter. Propagate by seed in autumn or by softwood cuttings in early summer. Is susceptible to slug damage.

P. comosa, syn. *Phyteuma comosum*, illus. p.380.

PHYSOSTEGIA
Obedient plant

LABIATAE/LAMIACEAE

Genus of summer- to early autumn-flowering perennials. Needs sun and fertile, moist but well-drained soil. Propagate by division in spring.

P. virginiana. Erect perennial. H 1m (3ft), S 60cm (2ft). In late summer produces spikes of hooded, 2-lipped, rose-purple flowers with hinged stalks that allow flowers to remain in position once moved. Has lance-shaped, toothed, mid-green leaves. subsp. *speciosa* **'Variegata'** see *P.v.* 'Variegata'.
'Summer Snow' has pure white

flowers. **'Variegata'** (syn. *P.v.* subsp. *speciosa* 'Variegata') illus. p.244.
'Vivid' illus. p.279.

PHYTEUMA
Horned rampion

CAMPANULACEAE

Genus of early- to mid-summer-flowering perennials that are useful for rock gardens. Needs sun and well-drained soil. Propagate by seed in autumn.

P. comosum. See *Physoplexis comosa.*
P. scheuchzeri illus. p.357.

PHYTOLACCA

PHYTOLACCACEAE

Genus of perennials and evergreen shrubs and trees, grown for their overall appearance and decorative but poisonous fruits. Tolerates sun or shade and requires fertile, moist soil. Propagate by seed in autumn or spring. All parts may cause severe discomfort if ingested; the fruit of *P. americana* may be lethal if eaten. Contact with the sap may irritate skin.

P. americana, syn. *P. decandra* (Red-ink plant, Virginian pokeweed). Upright, spreading perennial. H and S 1.2–1.5m (4–5ft). Oval to lance-shaped, mid-green leaves are tinged purple in autumn. Shallowly cup-shaped, sometimes pink-flushed, white-and-green flowers, borne in terminal racemes in summer, are followed by poisonous, rounded, fleshy, blackish-purple berries.
P. clavigera. See *P. polyandra.*
P. decandra. See *P. americana.*
P. polyandra, syn. *P. clavigera*. Stout, upright perennial. H and S 1.2m (4ft). Has brilliant crimson stems, oval to lance-shaped, mid-green leaves that turn yellow in autumn. In summer bears clusters of shallowly cup-shaped, pink flowers, followed by poisonous, blackish-purple berries.

Piccabeen palm. See *Archontophoenix cunninghamiana.*

PICEA
Spruce

PINACEAE

Genus of conifers with needle-like leaves set on a pronounced peg on the shoots and arranged spirally. Cones are pendulous and ripen in their first autumn; scales are woody and flexible. See also CONIFERS.

P. abies (Common spruce, Norway spruce; illus. p.104). Fast-growing conifer, narrowly conical when young, broader with age. H 20–30m (70–100ft), S 5–7m (15–22ft). Has needle-like, dark green leaves and bears pendulous cones. Zone 2b.
'Clanbrassiliana', H 5m (15ft), S 3–5m (10–15ft), is slow-growing, rounded and spreading. **'Gregoryana'** (illus. p.111), H and S 60cm (2ft), is slow-growing, with a dense, globose form. **'Inversa'**, H 5–10m (15–30ft), S 2m (6ft), has an erect leader, but pendent side branches. **'Little Gem'**, H and S 30–50cm (12–20in), has a nest-shaped, central depression caused by spreading branches. **'Nidiformis'**,

H 1m (3ft), S 1–2m (3–6ft), is larger and faster-growing. **'Ohlendorffii'** (illus. p.110), H and S 1m (3ft), is slow-growing, initially rounded, becoming conical with age. **'Reflexa'** (illus. p.110), H 30cm (1ft), S 5m (15ft), is prostrate and ground-hugging, but may be trained up a stake, to form a mound of weeping foliage. All Zone 3.
P. breweriana illus. p.105.
P. engelmannii illus. p.105.
P. glauca (White spruce). Narrowly conical conifer. H 10–15m (30–50ft), S 4–5m (12–15ft). Glaucous shoots produce blue-green leaves. Ovoid, light brown cones fall after ripening. Zone 1. var. *albertiana* **'Conica'** (syn. *P.g.* 'Albertiana Conica'; illus. p.111), H 2–5m (6–15ft), S 1–2m (3–6ft), is of neat, pyramidal habit and slow-growing, with longer leaves and smaller cones. Zone 4. **'Albertiana Conica'** see *P.g.* var. *albertiana* 'Conica'. **'Coerulea'** illus. p.105. **'Echiniformis'**, H 50cm (20in), S 90cm (36in), is a dwarf, flat-topped, rounded form. Zone 2.
P. likiangensis (Lijiang spruce). Upright conifer. H 15m (50ft), S 5–10m (15–30ft). Bluish-white leaves are well-spaced. Cones, 8–15cm (3–6in) long, are cylindrical, females bright red when young, ripening to purple, males pink. Zone 7.
P. mariana (Black spruce). Conical conifer, whose lowest branches often layer naturally, forming a ring of stems around the parent plant. H 10–15m (30–50ft), S 3m (10ft). Leaves are bluish-green or bluish-white. Oval cones are dark grey-brown. Zone 3. **'Doumetii'** illus. p.108. **'Nana'** (illus. p.110), H 50cm (20in), S 50–80cm (20–32in), is a neat shrub with blue-grey foliage.
P. x *mariorika* **'Gnom'**, syn. *P. omorika* 'Gnom' is a shrub-like conifer with pendent branches arching at tips. H to 1.5m (5ft), S 1–2m (3–6ft). Fully hardy. Dark green leaves are white beneath. Zone 4.
P. morrisonicola illus. p.107.
P. omorika illus. p.103. **'Gnom'** see *P.* x *mariorika* 'Gnom'. **'Nana'**, H and S 1m (3ft), is a slow-growing, rounded or oval cultivar. Zone 3.
P. orientalis (Caucasian spruce, Oriental spruce). Columnar, dense conifer. H 20m (70ft), S 5m (15ft). Has glossy, deep green leaves and ovoid to conical cones, 6–10cm (2½–4in) long, dark purple, ripening to brown, the males brick-red in spring. Zone 5. **'Aurea'** has golden, young foliage in spring, later turning green. Zone 5. **'Skylands'** illus. p.104.
P. pungens (Colorado spruce). Columnar conifer. H 15m (50ft), S 5m (15ft). Has scaly, grey bark and very sharp, stout, greyish-green or bright blue leaves. Cylindrical, light brown cones have papery scales. Zone 2. **'Hoopsii'**, H 10–15m (30–50ft), has silvery-blue foliage. **'Koster'** illus. p.105. **'Montgomery'** (illus. p.110), H and S 1m (3ft), is dwarf, compact, spreading or conical, with grey-blue leaves. All Zone 2.
P. sitchensis (Sitka spruce). Very vigorous, broadly conical conifer. H 30–50m (100–160ft) in damp

locations, 15–20m (50–70ft) in dry situations, S 6–10m (20–30ft). Bark scales on old trees. Has prickly, bright deep green leaves and cylindrical, papery, pale brown or whitish cones, 5–10cm (2–4in) long. Is good on an exposed or poor site. Zone 2.
P. smithiana (Morinda spruce, West Himalayan spruce). Slow-growing conifer, conical when young, columnar with horizontal branches and weeping shoots when mature. H 25–30m (80–100ft), S 6m (20ft). Has dark green leaves and produces cylindrical, bright brown cones, 10–20cm (4–8in) long. Zone 9.

Pick-a-back plant. See *Tolmiea menziesii.*
Pickerel weed. See *Pontederia cordata*, illus. p.448.

PICRASMA

SIMAROUBACEAE

Genus of deciduous trees, grown for their brilliant autumn colour. Produces insignificant flowers in late spring. Requires sun or semi-shade and fertile, well-drained soil. Propagate by seed in autumn.

P. ailanthoides. See *P. quassioides.*
P. quassioides, syn. *P. ailanthoides*, illus. p.97.

PIERIS

ERICACEAE

Genus of evergreen shrubs, grown for their foliage and small, profuse, urn-shaped flowers. Needs a sheltered site in semi-shade or shade and in moist, peaty, acid soil. *P. floribunda*, however, grows well in any acid soil. Young shoots are sometimes frost-killed in spring and should be cut back as soon as possible. Dead-heading after flowering improves growth. Propagate by soft tip or semi-ripe cuttings in summer. Leaves may cause severe discomfort if ingested.

P. **'Bert Chandler'**. Evergreen, bushy shrub. H 2m (6ft), S 1.5m (5ft). Lance-shaped leaves are bright pink when young, becoming creamy-yellow, then white and finally dark green. Produces white flowers only very rarely. Likes an open position. Zone 5b.
P. floribunda illus. p.127.
P. **'Forest Flame'**. Evergreen, upright shrub. H 4m (12ft), S 2m (6ft). Narrowly oval, glossy leaves are brilliant red when young, then turn pink, cream and finally dark green. White flowers are borne with the young leaves from mid- to late spring. Zone 5b.
P. formosa. Evergreen, bushy, dense shrub. H and S 4m (12ft). Large, oblong, glossy, dark green leaves are bronze when young. Bears large clusters of white flowers from mid- to late spring. Zone 8. var. *forrestii* **'Wakehurst'** illus. p.142. **'Henry Price'** has deep-veined leaves, which are bronze-red when young. Zone 8.
P. japonica illus. p.116. **'Daisen'** is an evergreen, rounded, dense shrub. H and S 3m (10ft). Oval, bronze leaves mature to glossy, dark green. Bears drooping clusters of red-budded, deep

pink flowers in spring. **'Dorothy Wyckoff'** has deep crimson buds, opening to pink blooms; foliage is bronze in winter. Young foliage of **'Mountain Fire'** is brilliant red. All Zone 5b. **'Scarlett O'Hara'** illus. p.127. **Taiwanensis Group** (syn. *P. taiwanensis*), S 5m (15ft), has narrow leaves that are bronze-red when young. Bears clusters of white flowers in early and mid-spring. **'Variegata'** is slow-growing, with small leaves, edged with white. Zone 7.

P. nana, syn. *Arcterica nana*. Evergreen, prostrate, dwarf shrub. H 2.5–5cm (1–2in), S 10–15cm (4–6in). Has tiny, oval, leathery, dark green leaves, usually in whorls of 3, on fine stems that root readily. In early spring bears small, terminal clusters of white flowers with green or red calyces. Is excellent for binding a peat wall or in a rock garden. Zone 3b.

P. taiwanensis. See *P. japonica* Taiwanensis Group.

PILEA

URTICACEAE

Genus of bushy or trailing annuals and evergreen perennials, grown for their ornamental foliage. Tender, min. 10°C (50°F). Grow in any well-drained soil out of direct sunlight and draughts; do not overwater in winter. Pinch out tips in growing season to avoid straggly plants. Propagate perennials by stem cuttings in spring or summer, annuals by seed in spring or autumn. Spider mite may be a problem.

P. cadierei illus. p.300.
P. involucrata, syn. *P. mollis* (Friendship plant). Evergreen, bushy perennial. H 15cm (6in), S 30cm (12in). Oval to rounded leaves, to 5cm (2in) long, have corrugated surfaces and are bronze above, reddish-green below; leaves are green when grown in shade.
P. mollis. See *P. involucrata.*
P. nummulariifolia illus. p.305.

PILEOSTEGIA

HYDRANGEACEAE

Genus of evergreen, woody-stemmed, root climbers. Grows in sun or shade and in any well-drained soil; is therefore useful for planting against a north wall. Prune in spring, if required. Propagate by semi-ripe cuttings in summer.

P. viburnoides, syn. *Schizophragma viburnoides*, illus. p.208.

PILOSOCEREUS

CACTACEAE

Genus of columnar, summer-flowering, perennial cacti with wool-like spines in flowering zones at crowns. Some species are included in *Cephalocereus*. Tender, min. 11°C (52°F). Needs full sun and very well-drained soil. Propagate by seed or stem cuttings in spring or summer.

P. leucocephalus. See *P. palmeri.*
P. palmeri, syn. *P. leucocephalus*, illus. p.458.

PIMELEA

THYMELAEACEAE

Genus of evergreen shrubs, grown for their flowers and overall appearance. Tender, min. 7°C (45°F). Needs full sun and well-drained, neutral to acid soil. Water potted plants moderately, less when temperatures are low. Needs good winter light and ventilation in northern temperate greenhouses. Propagate by seed in spring or by semi-ripe cuttings in late summer.

P. ferruginea illus. p.162.

PINGUICULA

LENTIBULARIACEAE

Genus of summer-flowering perennials with sticky leaves that trap insects and digest them for food. Is useful in pots under glass among plants at risk from aphids. Hardy to tender, min. 7°C (45°F). Needs sun and wet soil. Propagate by division in early spring or by seed in autumn.

P. caudata. See *P. moranensis* var. *caudata.*
P. grandiflora illus. p.382.
P. moranensis var. *caudata*, syn. *P. caudata.* Basal-rosetted perennial. H 12–15cm (5–6in), S 5cm (2in). Tender. Leaves are narrowly oval and dull green with inrolled, purplish margins. In summer, 5-petalled, deep carmine flowers are produced on long stems.

PINUS

Pine

PINACEAE

Genus of small to large conifers with spirally arranged leaves in bundles, usually of 2, 3 or 5 needles. Cones ripen over 2 years and are small in the first year. See also CONIFERS.

P. aristata illus. p.108.
P. armandii (Armand pine, David's pine). Conical, open conifer. H 10–15m (30–50ft), S 5–8m (15–25ft). Has pendent, glaucous blue leaves and conical, green cones, 8–25cm (3–10in) long, ripening to brown. Zone 8.
P. banksiana illus. p.107.
P. bungeana illus. p.108.
P. cembra illus. p.106.
P. cembroides illus. p.109.
P. chylla. See *P. wallichiana.*
P. contorta illus. p.107.
var. *latifolia* illus. p.106. **'Spaan's Dwarf'** is a conical, open, dwarf conifer with short, stiffly erect shoots. H and S 75cm (30in). Has bright green leaves in 2s. Zone 5.
P. coulteri illus. p.102.
P. densiflora (Japanese red pine). Flat-topped conifer. H 15m (50ft), S 5–7m (15–22ft). Has scaling, reddish-brown bark, bright green leaves and conical, yellow or pale brown cones. Zone 4b. **'Alice Verkade'**, H and S 75cm (30in), is a diminutive, rounded form with fresh green leaves. **'Tagyosho'** see *P.d.* 'Umbraculifera'. **'Umbraculifera'** (syn. *P.d.* 'Tagyosho'), H 4m (12ft), S 6m (20ft), is a slow-growing, rounded or umbrella-shaped form. All Zone 4b.
P. excelsa. See *P. wallichiana.*
P. griffithii. See *P. wallichiana.*
P. halepensis illus. p.107.
P. heldreichii, syn. *P.h.* var. *leucodermis*, *P. leucodermis*, illus. p.104. **'Compact Gem'** (syn. *P.h.* var. *leucodermis* 'Compact Gem') is a broadly conical, dense, dwarf conifer. H and S 25–30cm (10–12in). Has very dark green leaves in 2s. Grows only 2.5cm (1in) a year. Zone 7. var. *leucodermis* see *P. heldreichii.* **'Smidtii'** (syn *P.h.* var. *leucodermis* 'Schmidtii'; illus. p.111) is a dwarf form with an ovoid habit and sharp, dark green leaves. Zone 7.
P. x *holfordiana* illus. p.101.
P. insignis. See *P. radiata.*
P. jeffreyi illus. p.103.
P. leucodermis. See *P. heldreichii.*
P. mugo (Dwarf pine, Mountain pine, Swiss mountain pine). Spreading, shrubby conifer. H 3–5m (10–15ft),

S 5–8m (15–25ft). Has bright to dark green leaves in 2s and ovoid, brown cones. **'Gnom'**, H and S to 2m (6ft), and **'Mops'**, H 1m (3ft), S 2m (6ft), are rounded cultivars. All Zone 3.
P. muricata illus. p.103.
P. nigra (Black pine). Upright, later spreading conifer, generally grown in one of the following forms.
'Hornibrookiana', H 1.5–2m (5–6ft), S 2m (6ft), is shrubby with stout, spreading or erect branches and dark green leaves in 2s. subsp. *laricio* (syn. *P.n.* var. *maritima*; Corsican pine), H 25–30m (80–100ft), S 8m (25ft), is fast-growing and narrowly conical with an open crown; bears grey-green leaves, in 2s, and ovoid to conical, yellow- or pale grey-brown cones. var. *maritima* see *P.n.* subsp. *laricio*. subsp. *nigra* illus. p.104. All Zone 4.
P. parviflora illus. p.105.
'Adcock's Dwarf' is a slow-growing, rounded, dense, dwarf conifer. H 2–3m (6–10ft), S 1.5–2m (5–6ft). Bears grey-green leaves in 5s. Zone 7.
P. peuce illus. p.101.
P. pinaster illus. p.103.
P. pinea illus. p.109.
P. ponderosa illus. p.103.
P. pumila (Dwarf Siberian pine). Spreading, shrubby conifer. H 2–3m (6–10ft), S 3–5m (10–15ft). Has bright blue-green leaves in 5s. Ovoid cones are violet-purple, ripening to red-brown or yellow-brown, the males bright red-purple in spring. Zone 2. **'Globe'**, H and S 50cm–1m (1½–3ft), is a rounded cultivar with blue foliage.
P. radiata, syn. *P. insignis*, illus. p.104.
P. resinosa (Red pine). Conical tree with ascendant branches. H 15–25m (50–80ft) S 6-8m (20–25ft). Young shoots are orange-brown and have pairs of long needles. The older branches have flaking red bark. Good on poor, sandy or gravely soils. Zone 2b.
P. rigida illus. p.106.
P. strobus illus. p.102. **'Radiata'** (syn. *P.s.* f. *nana*, *P.s.* 'Nana') is a rounded, dwarf conifer with an open, sparse, whorled crown. H 1–2m (3–6ft), S 2–3m (6–10ft). Grey bark is smooth at first, later fissured. Bears grey-green leaves in 5s. Zone 3.
P. sylvestris (Scots pine). Conifer, upright and with whorled branches when young, that develops a spreading, rounded crown with age. H 15–25m (50–80ft), S 8–10m (25–30ft). Bark is flaking and red-brown on upper trunk, fissured and purple-grey at base. Has blue-green leaves in 2s and conical, green cones that ripen to pale grey- or red-brown. Zone 2. **'Aurea'** (illus. p.111), H 10m (30ft), S 4m (12ft), has golden-yellow leaves in winter-spring, otherwise blue-green.
'Beuvronensis', H and S 1m (3ft), is a rounded shrub. **'Doone Valley'** (illus. p.110), H and S 1m (3ft), is an upright, irregularly shaped shrub. f. *fastigiata* see *P.s.* 'Fastigiata'. **'Fastigiata'** (syn. *P.s.* f. *fastigiata*) illus. p.108. **'Gold Coin'** (illus. p.111), H and S 2m (6ft), is a dwarf version of *P.s.* 'Aurea'.
'Nana' see *P.s.* 'Watereri'. **'Watereri'** (syn. *P.s.* 'Nana'; illus. p.110), H and S 50cm (20in), is a very dense cultivar with widely spaced leaves. All Zone 3.
P. thunbergii illus. p.106.

P. virginiana illus. p.107.
P. wallichiana, syn. *P. chylla*, *P. excelsa*, *P. griffithii*, illus. p.103.

Pinwheel. See *Aeonium haworthii*, illus. p.466.
Pinyon. See *Pinus cembroides*, illus. p.109.

PIPTANTHUS
LEGUMINOSAE/PAPILIONACEAE

Genus of deciduous or semi-evergreen shrubs, grown for their foliage and flowers. Marginally hardy and will need the protection of a south- or west-facing wall. Requires sun and fertile, well-drained soil. In spring cut some older shoots back to ground level and prune any frost-damaged growths back to healthy wood. Propagate by seed in autumn.
P. laburnifolius. See *P. nepalensis.*
P. nepalensis, syn. *P. laburnifolius*, illus. p.146.

PISONIA
NYCTAGINACEAE

Genus of evergreen shrubs and trees, grown for their foliage and overall appearance. Tender, min. 10–15°C (50–59°F). Needs full light or partial shade and humus-rich, well-drained soil. Water containerized specimens freely when in full growth, moderately at other times. Pruning is tolerated if required. Propagate by seed in spring or by semi-ripe cuttings in summer.
P. brunoniana. See *P. umbellifera.*
P. umbellifera, syn. *Heimerliodendron brunonianum*, *P. brunoniana* (Bird-catcher tree, Para para). Evergreen, rounded large shrub or small tree. H and S 3–6m (10–20ft). Bears oval, leathery, lustrous leaves. In spring, produces clusters of tiny, green or pink flowers, followed by 5-winged, sticky, brownish fruits.

PISTACIA
ANACARDIACEAE

Genus of evergreen or deciduous trees, grown for their foliage and overall appearance. Tender, min. 10°C (50°F). Requires full light and free-draining, even dry soil. Water containerized plants moderately when in full growth, sparingly at other times. Pruning is tolerated if necessary. Propagate by seed in spring or by semi-ripe cuttings in summer.
P. lentiscus (Mastic tree). Evergreen, irregularly rounded shrub or tree. H 5m (15ft), S to 3m (10ft). Bears leaves that are divided into 2–5 pairs of oval, leathery, glossy leaflets. Produces auxillary clusters of insignificant flowers from spring to early summer that develop into globose, red, then black fruits in autumn.
P. terebinthus (Cyprus turpentine, Terebinth tree). Deciduous, rounded to ovoid tree. H 6–9m (20–28ft), S 3–6m (10–20ft). Leaves have 5–9 oval, usually lustrous, rich green leaflets. Axillary clusters of small flowers borne in spring and early summer develop into tiny, globular to ovoid, red, then purple-brown fruits in autumn.

PISTIA
ARACEAE

Genus of one species of deciduous, perennial, floating water plant, grown for its foliage. In water above 19–21°C (66–70°F) is evergreen. Is suitable for tropical aquariums and frost-free pools. Tender, min 10–15°C (50–59°F). Grows in sun or semi-shade. Remove fading foliage and thin plants out as necessary. Propagate by separating plantlets in summer.
P. stratiotes illus. p.449.

Pitch apple. See *Clusia major*.
Pitcher plant. See *Nepenthes*; *Sarracenia*.
  Common. See *Sarracenia purpurea*.
  Yellow. See *Sarracenia flava*, illus. p.290.

PITTOSPORUM
PITTOSPORACEAE

Genus of evergreen trees and shrubs, grown for their ornamental foliage and fragrant flowers. Almost tender, may just survive in the milder parts of Zone 9. Grow against a south- or west-facing wall. *P. crassifolium* and *P. ralphii* make wind-resistant hedges in mild, coastal areas; like forms with variegated or purple leaves, prefer sun. Others will grow in sun or semi-shade. All need well-drained soil. Propagate *P. dallii* by budding in summer, other species by seed in autumn or spring or by semi-ripe cuttings in summer; selected forms by semi-ripe cuttings only in summer.
P. crassifolium (Karo). Evergreen, bushy-headed, dense tree or shrub. H 5m (15ft), S 3m (10ft). Has oblong, dark green leaves, grey- felted beneath. Clusters of small, fragrant, star-shaped, dark reddish-purple flowers are borne in spring. Zone 9?.
'Variegatum' illus. p.99.
P. dallii illus. p.100.
P. eugenioides. Evergreen, columnar tree. H 10m (30ft), S 5m (15ft). Narrowly oval, wavy-edged leaves are glossy, dark green. Honey-scented, star-shaped, pale yellow flowers are produced in spring. Zone 9?.
'Variegatum' illus. p.99.
P. **'Garnettii'** illus. p.126.
P. ralphii. Evergreen, bushy-headed tree or shrub. H 4m (12ft), S 3m (10ft). Large leaves are oblong, leathery and grey-green, very hairy beneath. Produces small, fragrant, star-shaped, dark red flowers in spring. Zone 9?.
P. tenuifolium illus. p.127. **'Margaret Turnbull'** is an evergreen, compact shrub. H 1.8m (6ft), S 1m (3ft). Has dark green leaves, centrally splashed golden yellow. Zone 9?. **'Tom Thumb'** illus. p.177.
P. tobira (Japanese pittosporum, Mock orange). Evergreen, bushy-headed, dense tree or shrub. H 6m (20ft), S 4m (12ft). Has oblong to oval, glossy, dark green leaves. Very fragrant, star-shaped, white flowers, opening in late spring, later become creamy-yellow. Zone 9?.
P. undulatum (Victorian box). Evergreen, broadly conical tree. H 12m (40ft), S 8m (25ft). Half hardy. Has

long, narrowly oval, pointed, wavy-edged, dark green leaves. Fragrant, star-shaped, white flowers are borne in late spring and early summer, followed by rounded, orange fruits. Zone 9?.

Pittosporum, Japanese. See *Pittosporum tobira*.

PITYROGRAMMA
ADIANTACEAE/PTERIDACEAE

Genus of semi-evergreen or evergreen ferns, suitable for hanging baskets. Tender, min. 10°C (50°F). Needs semi-shade and humus-rich, moist but well-drained soil. Remove fading fronds regularly. Water carefully to avoid spoiling farina on fronds. Propagate by spores in late summer.
P. triangularis. Semi-evergreen or evergreen fern. H and S 45cm (18in). Has broadly triangular, delicately divided, mid-green fronds with orange or creamy-white farina.

Plagiorhegma dubia. See *Jeffersonia dubia*.
Plane. See *Platanus*.
  London. See *Platanus* x *hispanica*, illus. p.67.

PLANTAGO
PLANTAGINACEAE

Genus of summer-flowering annuals, biennials and evergreen perennials and shrubs. Many species are weeds, but a few are grown for their foliage and architectural value. Hardy to tender, min. 7–10°C (45–50°F). Needs full sun and well-drained soil. Water potted plants moderately, sparingly in winter. Propagate by seed or division in spring.
P. nivalis (illus. p.391) has lance-shaped, silky-hairy, silver-green leaves and tiny, grey-brown flowers.

Plantain
  Floating water. See *Luronium natans*.
  Parrot's. See *Heliconia psittacorum*, illus. p.229.
  Water. See *Alisma plantago-aquatica*, illus. p.446.
Plantain lily. See *Hosta*.

PLATANUS
Plane
PLATANACEAE

Genus of deciduous trees, grown for their habit, foliage and flaking bark. Flowers are inconspicuous. Spherical fruit clusters hang from shoots in autumn. Needs full sun and deep, fertile, well-drained soil. Propagate species by seed in autumn, *P.* x *hispanica* by hardwood cuttings in early winter. All the following are susceptible to the fungal disease plane anthracnose. Contact with the basal tufts of hair on the fruits may irritate the skin and respiratory system.
P. x *acerifolia.* See *P.* x *hispanica*.
P. x *hispanica*, syn. *P.* x *acerifolia*, illus. p.67. **'Suttneri'** is a vigorous, deciduous, spreading tree. H 20m

(70ft), S 15m (50ft). Has flaking bark and large, palmate, 5-lobed, sharply toothed, bright green leaves that are blotched with creamy-white.
P. occidentalis (Buttonwood, Sycamore). Open crowned, vigorous deciduous tree. H 25m (80ft) S 20m (70ft). Has three-lobed leaves up to 20cm (8in) long and attractive, flaking cream and brown bark. Brown globular fruits persist through winter. Zone 5b.

PLATYCARYA
JUGLANDACEAE

Genus of one species of deciduous tree, grown for its foliage and catkins. Requires full sun and fertile, well-drained soil. Propagate by seed in autumn.
P. strobilacea. Deciduous, spreading tree. H and S 10m (30ft). Has ash-like, bright green leaves with 5–15 leaflets. Upright, green catkins are borne from mid- to late summer; males are slender and cylindrical, often drooping at tips, females are cone-like, become brown and persist through winter. Zone 7.

PLATYCERIUM
Stag's-horn fern
POLYPODIACEAE

Genus of evergreen, epiphytic ferns, best grown in hanging baskets or fastened to and suspended from pieces of wood. Produces 2 kinds of fronds: permanent, broad, sterile 'nest leaves' forming the main part of the plant; and strap-shaped, usually partly bifurcated, arching fertile fronds. Tender, min. 5°C (41°F). Thrives in warm, humid conditions in semi-shade, and needs fibrous, peaty compost with hardly any soil. Propagate by detaching buds in spring or summer and planting in compost, or by spores in summer or early autumn.
P. alcicorne of gardens. See *P. bifurcatum.*
P. bifurcatum, syn. *P. alcicorne* of gardens, illus. p.310.

Platycladus. Reclassified as *Thuja.*

PLATYCODON
Balloon flower
CAMPANULACEAE

Genus of one species of perennial, grown for its flowers in summer. Needs sun and light, sandy soil. Propagate by basal cuttings of non-flowering shoots in summer, preferably with a piece of root attached, or by seed in autumn.
P. grandiflorus illus. p.284. var. *mariesii* (syn. *P.g.* 'Mariesii') is a neat, clump-forming perennial. H and S 30–45cm (12–18in). In mid-summer produces solitary terminal, large, balloon-like flower buds opening to bell-shaped, blue or purplish-blue flowers. Has oval, sharply toothed, bluish-green leaves. '**Mariesii**' see *P.g.* var. *mariesii.*

PLATYSTEMON
PAPAVERACEAE

Genus of one species of summer-flowering annual. Grow in sun and

in fertile, well-drained soil. Propagate by seed sown outdoors in spring or early autumn.
P. californicus illus. p.335.

PLECTRANTHUS
LABIATAE/LAMIACEAE

Genus of evergreen, trailing, or bushy perennials, grown for their foliage. Tender, min. 4–10°C (39–50°F). Is easy to grow if kept moist in partial shade or bright light. Cut back stem tips in growing season if plants become too straggly. Propagate by stem cuttings or division in spring or summer.
P. australis of gardens. See *P. verticillatus.*
P. coleoides '**Variegatus**' of gardens. See *P. madagascariensis* 'Variegated Mintleaf'.
P. forsteri '**Marginatus**', illus. p.264.
P. madagascarienis (Mintleaf) Creeping perennial. H 30cm (12in), S indefinite. Min. 10°C (50°F). Has rounded, scalloped, fleshy leaves. Bears 2-lipped, lavender-blue or white flowers, often dotted with red.
'**Variegated Mintleaf**' (syn. *P. coleoides* 'Variegatus' of gardens) has variegated white leaves.
P. oertendahlii (Prostrate coleus, Swedish ivy). Evergreen, prostrate perennial. H to 15cm (6in), S indefinite. Min. 10°C (50°F). Rounded, scalloped, dark green leaves are reddish-green below, with white veins above. Racemes of tubular, white or pale mauve flowers are produced at irregular intervals throughout the year.
P. thyrsoideus, syn. *Coleus thyrsoideus.* Fast-growing, bushy perennial, often grown as an annual. H to 1m (3ft), S 60cm (2ft). Min. 4°C (39°F). Has heart-shaped, serrated, mid-green leaves. Bears spikes of tubular, bright blue flowers at various times of year.
P. verticillatus, syn. *P. australis* of gardens (Swedish ivy). Evergreen, trailing perennial with square stems. H to 15cm (6in), S indefinite. Min. 10°C (50°F). Has rounded, waxy, glossy, green leaves with scalloped edges. Racemes of tubular, white, or pale mauve flowers are produced intermittently through the year.

PLEIOBLASTUS
GRAMINEAE/POACEAE

See also GRASSES, BAMBOOS, RUSHES and SEDGES.
P. auricomus, syn. *Arundinaria auricoma, A. viridistriata, P. viridistriatus,* illus. p.309.
P. variegatus, syn. *Arundinaria fortunei, A. variegata,* illus. p.306.
P. viridistriatus. See *P. auricomus.*

PLEIONE
See also ORCHIDS.
P. bulbocodioides (illus. p.297). Deciduous, terrestrial orchid. H 20cm (8in). In spring, usually before solitary leaf appears, bears pink, rose or magenta flowers, 5–12cm (2–5in) across, with darker purple marks on lips. Leaf is narrowly lance-shaped, 14cm (5½in) long. Is often difficult to flower: regular feeding helps to

increase pseudobulbs to flowering size.
P. x *confusa.* Deciduous, terrestrial orchid. H 15cm (6in). Canary-yellow flowers, 5–8cm (2–3in) across, with brown or purple blotches on lips, appear singly in spring, before foliage. Has lance-shaped leaves, 10–18cm (4–7in) long. Does best in an alpine house. Needs semi-shade.
P. hookeriana. Deciduous, terrestrial orchid. H 8–15cm (3–6in). Lilac-pink, rose or white flowers, 5–7cm (2–3in) across, each with a brown- or purplish-spotted lip, are borne singly in spring with lance-shaped leaves, 5–20cm (2–8in) long. Cultivate as for *P.* x *confusa.*
P. humilis. Deciduous, terrestrial orchid. H 5–8cm (2–3in). In winter, before foliage appears, white flowers, 7–9cm (3–3½in) across, each with a crimson-spotted lip, are borne singly or in pairs. Lance-shaped leaves are 18–25cm (7–10in) long. Cultivate as for *P.* x *confusa.*
P. praecox. Deciduous, terrestrial orchid. H 8–13cm (3–5in). Flowers, to 8cm (3in) across, appear in pairs in autumn, after foliage. They are white to pinkish-purple or lilac-purple, with violet marks. Leaves are oblong to lance-shaped and 15–25cm (6–10in) long. Cultivate as for *P.* x *confusa.*

PLEIOSPILOS
AIZOACEAE

Genus of clump-forming, perennial succulents with almost stemless rosettes bearing up to 4 pairs of fleshy, erect leaves, like pieces of granite, each with a flat upper surface and each pair united at the base. Flowers are daisy-like. Individual species are very similar, and many are difficult to identify. Tender, min. 5°C (41°F). Needs sun and well-drained soil. Propagate by seed or division in spring or summer.
P. bolusii illus. p.479.
P. compactus illus. p.478.

PLEUROTHALLIS
See also ORCHIDS.
P. grobyi. Evergreen, epiphytic orchid for a cool greenhouse. H 2.5cm (1in). In summer produces sprays of minute, white flowers, 0.25cm (⅛in) long. Leaves are oval, fleshy and 0.5cm (¼in) long. Provide shade in summer.

Plum
 Cherry. See *Prunus cerasifera.*
 Date. See *Diospyros lotus.*
 Indian. See *Oemleria cerasiformis.*
 Natal. See *Carissa macrocarpa.*
 Sugared-almond. See *Pachyphytum oviferum,* illus. p.475.
Plum yew. See *Cephalotaxus harringtonii; Prumnopitys andina.*

PLUMBAGO
PLUMBAGINACEAE

Genus of annuals, evergreen or semi-evergreen shrubs, perennials and woody-stemmed, scrambling climbers, grown for their primrose-shaped flowers. Tender, min. 7°C (45°F). Grow in full light or semi-shade and in fertile,

well-drained soil. Water regularly, less when not in full growth. Tie stems to supports. Thin out or spur back all previous year's growth in early spring. Propagate by semi-ripe cuttings in summer. Whitefly may be a problem.
P. auriculata, syn. *P. capensis,* illus. p.215.
P. capensis. See *P. auriculata.*
P. indica, syn. *P. rosea.* Evergreen or semi-evergreen, spreading shrub or semi-climber. H 2m (6ft), S 1–2m (3–6ft). Leaves are oval to elliptic and mid-green. Has terminal racemes of primrose-shaped, red or pink flowers, 2.5cm (1in) long. These are produced in summer, if hard pruned annually in spring, or from late winter onwards, if left unpruned and trained as a climber.
P. rosea. See *P. indica.*

Plume poppy. See *Macleaya.*

PLUMERIA
Frangipani
APOCYNACEAE

Genus of mainly deciduous, fleshy-branched shrubs and trees, grown for their flowers in summer-autumn. Tender, min. 13°C (55°F). Requires full sun and freely draining soil. Water potted specimens moderately while in growth, keep dry in winter when leafless. Stem tips may be cut out to induce branching. Propagate by seed or leafless stem-tip cuttings in late spring. Spider mite may be a nuisance. The milky sap may cause mild stomach upset if ingested.
P. acuminata. See *P. rubra* var. *acutifolia.*
P. acutifolia. See *P. rubra* var. *acutifolia.*
P. alba (West Indian jasmine). Deciduous, rounded, sparingly branched tree. H to 6m (20ft), S to 4m (12ft). Leaves are lance-shaped and slender-pointed, to 30cm (12in) long. Terminal clusters of fragrant, yellow-eyed, white flowers, each with 5 spreading petals and a tubular base, appear in summer.
P. rubra illus. p.96. var. *acutifolia* (syn. *P. acuminata, P. acutifolia*) is a deciduous, spreading, sparsely branched tree or shrub. H and S 4m (12ft) or more. Produces fragrant, yellow-centred, white flowers, with 5 spreading petals, in summer-autumn. Leaves are lance-shaped to oval and 20–30cm (8–12in) long.

Plum-fruited yew. See *Prumnopitys andina.*
Plush plant. See *Echeveria pulvinata,* illus. p.464.
Poached-egg flower. See *Limnanthes douglasii,* illus. p.336.
Pocket handkerchief tree. See *Davidia involucrata,* illus. p.77.
Podocarp, Tasmanian. See *Podocarpus alpinus.*

PODOCARPUS
PODOCARPACEAE

See also CONIFERS.
P. alpinus (Tasmanian podocarp).

Rounded, spreading, shrubby conifer. H 2m (6ft), S 3–5m (10–15ft). Has linear, dull green leaves and rounded, egg-shaped, fleshy, bright red fruits. Zone 8.

P. andinus. See *Prumnopitys andina*.
P. macrophyllus (Kusamaki). Erect conifer. H 10m (30ft), S 3–5m (10–15ft). Long, linear leaves are bright green above, glaucous beneath. May be grown as a shrub, H and S 1–2m (3–6ft), and planted in a tub in hot climates. Zone 8.
P. nivalis (Alpine totara; illus. p.110). Rounded, spreading, shrubby conifer. H 2m (6ft), S 3–5m (10–15ft). Is very similar to *P. alpinus*, but bears longer, broader, more rigid leaves. Zone 8.
P. salignus illus. p.106.

PODOPHYLLUM

BERBERIDACEAE

Genus of spring-flowering, rhizomatous perennials. Young leaves may be damaged by frost. Does best in semi-shade and moist, peaty soil. Propagate by division in spring or by seed in autumn. All parts of the plants are highly toxic if ingested.
P. emodi. See *P. hexandrum*.
P. hexandrum, syn. *P. emodi*, illus. p.268.
P. peltatum (May apple). Vigorous, spreading, rhizomatous perennial. H 30–45cm (12–18in), S 30cm (12in). Palmate, sometimes brown-mottled, light green leaves, with 3–5 deep lobes, push up through soil, looking like closed umbrellas, and are followed, in spring, by nodding, cup-shaped, white flowers. Produces large, fleshy, plum-like, glossy, deep rose-pink fruits in autumn.

Poet's daffodil. See *Narcissus poeticus*.
Poet's narcissus. See *Narcissus poeticus*.
Poinciana gilliesii. See *Caesalpinia gilliesii*.
Poinciana pulcherrima. See *Caesalpinia pulcherrima*.
Poinsettia. See *Euphorbia pulcherrima*, illus. p.150.
Pokeweed, Virginian. See *Phytolacca americana*.

POLEMONIUM

Jacob's ladder

POLEMONIACEAE

Genus of late spring- or summer-flowering annuals and perennials, some perennials tending to be short-lived. Prefers sun and fertile, well-drained soil. Propagate by division in spring or by seed in autumn.
P. caeruleum illus. p.285.
P. carneum illus. p.283.
P. foliosissimum. Vigorous, clump-forming perennial. H 75cm (30in), S 60cm (24in). Terminal clusters of cup-shaped, lilac flowers, with yellow stamens, are borne in summer above oblong to lance-shaped, mid-green leaves, each composed of numerous, small leaflets.
P. pulcherrimum illus. p.284.

POLIANTHES

AGAVACEAE

Genus of tuberous perennials, grown for their fragrant flowers in summer. Tender, min. 15–20°C (59–68°F). Needs a sheltered site in full sun and well-drained soil. Water well in spring-summer; feed liquid fertilizer every 2 weeks when in growth. Dry off after leaves die down in winter. Propagate by seed or offsets in spring.
P. geminiflora, syn. *Bravoa geminiflora*, illus. p.423.
P. tuberosa (Tuberose). Summer-flowering, tuberous perennial. H 60–90cm (24–36in), S 10–15cm (4–6in). Has a basal cluster of strap-shaped, erect leaves; flower stem also bears leaves on lower part. Produces a spike of funnel-shaped, single, white flowers with 6 spreading petals. A double form is also available.

Polka-dot plant. See *Hypoestes phyllostachya*, illus. p.264.
Polyanthus. See *Primula* Pacific Series, illus. p.339 and (dwarf) illus. p. 328.
Polyanthus daffodil. See *Narcissus tazetta*.

POLYGALA

POLYGALACEAE

Genus of annuals, evergreen perennials, shrubs and trees, grown mainly for their pea-like flowers. Hardy to tender, min. 7°C (45°F). Needs full light or partial shade and moist but sharply drained soil. Water potted specimens freely when in full growth, moderately at other times. Lanky stems may be cut back hard in late winter. Propagate by seed in spring or by semi-ripe cuttings in late summer. Is susceptible to whitefly.
P. calcarea illus. p.384. **'Bulley's Form'** illus. p.384.
P. chamaebuxus illus. p.385. var. *grandiflora* (syn. *P.c.* var. *purpurea*, *P.c.* var. *rhodoptera*) illus. p.368. var. *purpurea* see *P.c.* var. *grandiflora*. var. *rhodoptera* see *P.c.* var. *grandiflora*.
P. x *dalmaisiana*, syn. *P. myrtifolia* var. *grandiflora* of gardens, illus. p.167.
P. myrtifolia var. *grandiflora* of gardens. See *P.* x *dalmaisiana*.
P. vayredae. Evergreen, mat-forming shrub. H 5–10cm (2–4in), S 20–30cm (8–12in). Slender, prostrate stems bear small, linear leaves. Pea-like, reddish-purple flowers, each with a yellow lip, are produced in late spring and early summer. Suits a rock garden or alpine house.

POLYGONATUM

Solomon's seal

CONVALLARIACEAE/LILIACEAE

Genus of spring- or early summer-flowering, rhizomatous perennials. Requires a cool, shady situation and fertile, well-drained soil. Propagate by division in early spring or by seed in autumn. Sawfly caterpillar is a common pest. All parts may cause mild stomach upset if ingested.

P. biflorum, syn. *P. canaliculatum*, *P. commutatum*, *P. giganteum* (Great Solomon's seal). Arching, rhizomatous perennial. H 1.5m (5ft) or more, S 60cm (2ft). Bears oval to oblong, mid-green leaves. Pendent clusters of bell-shaped, white flowers are borne in leaf axils during late spring.
P. canaliculatum. See *P. biflorum*.
P. commutatum. See *P. biflorum*.
P. giganteum. See *P. biflorum*.
P. hirtum, syn. *P. latifolium*. Upright, then arching, rhizomatous perennial. H 1m (3ft), S 30cm (1ft). Clusters of 2–5 drooping, tubular, green-tipped, white flowers open in late spring. Undersides of stems, leaf stalks and oval to lance-shaped, mid-green leaves are hairy.
P. hookeri illus. p.367.
P. x *hybridum* illus. p.238.
P. latifolium. See *P. hirtum*.
P. multiflorum. Arching, leafy perennial with fleshy rhizomes. H 1m (3ft), S 30cm (1ft). Bears clusters of 2–6 pendent, tubular, green-tipped, white flowers in late spring, then spherical, black fruit. Has oval to lance-shaped, mid-green leaves. **'Flore Pleno'** has double flowers that look like ballet dancers' skirts. **'Striatum'** (syn. *P.m.* 'Variegatum'), H 60cm (2ft), has leaves with creamy-white stripes. **'Variegatum'** see *P.m.* 'Striatum'.
P. odoratum (Angled Solomon's seal). Arching, rhizomatous perennial. H 60cm (24in), S 30cm (12in). Produces pairs of fragrant, tubular to bell-shaped, green-tipped, white flowers in late spring. Oval to lance-shaped leaves are mid-green.
P. verticillatum (Whorled Solomon's seal). Upright, rhizomatous perennial. H 1.2m (4ft), S 45cm (1½ft). Bears whorls of stalkless, lance-shaped, mid-green leaves. In early summer produces narrowly bell-shaped, greenish-white flowers.

Polygonum affine. See *Persicaria affinis*.
Polygonum amplexicaule. See *Persicaria amplexicaulis*.
Polygonum aubertii. See *Fallopia aubertii*.
Polygonum baldschuanicum. See *Fallopia baldschuanica*.
Polygonum bistorta. See *Persicaria bistorta*.
Polygonum campanulatum. See *Persicaria campanulata*.
Polygonum capitatum. See *Persicaria capitata*.
Polygonum macrophyllum. See *Persicaria macrophylla*.
Polygonum milletii. See *Persicaria milletii*.
Polygonum sphaerostachyum. See *Persicaria macrophylla*.
Polygonum vacciniifolium. See *Persicaria vacciniifolia*.
Polygonum virginianum **'Painter's Palette'**. See *Persicaria virginiana* 'Painter's Palette'.

POLYPODIUM

POLYPODIACEAE

Genus of deciduous, semi-evergreen or evergreen ferns, grown for their sculptural fronds. Hardy to tender, min.

10°C (50°F). Grow in semi-shade and fibrous, moist but well-drained soil. Propagate by division in spring or by spores in late summer.
P. aureum. See *Phlebodium aureum*.
P. australe. See *P. cambricum*.
P. cambricum, syn. *P. australe*, *P. vulgare* subsp. *serratum* (Southern polypody, Wintergreen fern). Deciduous, creeping fern. H 15–60cm (6–24in), S indefinite. Has broadly lance-shaped to broadly triangular-ovate, divided, mid-green fronds, to 60cm (24in) long, with linear or oblong pinnae that often have toothed margins. New fronds appear in late summer and die back by early summer. Sori are conspicuously yellow in winter.
P. glycyrrhiza illus. p.310.
P. scouleri illus. p.311.
P. vulgare illus. p.313. **'Cornubiense'** illus. p.312. **'Cristatum'** is an evergreen, creeping fern. H and S 25–30cm (10–12in). Narrowly lance-shaped, divided, mid-green fronds, with semi-pendulous, terminal crests, grow from creeping rhizomes covered with copper-brown scales. subsp. *serratum* see *P. cambricum*.

Polypody. See *Polypodium vulgare*, illus. p.313.
   Common. See *Polypodium vulgare*, illus. p.313.
   Southern. See *Polypodium cambricum*.

POLYSCIAS

ARALIACEAE

Genus of evergreen trees and shrubs, grown for their foliage. Sometimes has insignificant flowers in summer, but only on large, mature specimens. Tender, 15–18°C (59–64°F). Needs partial shade and humus-rich, well-drained soil. Water containerized plants freely when in full growth, moderately at other times. Straggly stems may be cut out in spring. Propagate by seed in spring or by stem-tip or leafless stem-section cuttings in summer. Spider mite may be troublesome.
P. filicifolia illus. p.152. **'Marginata'** is an evergreen, erect, sparsely branched shrub. H 2m (6ft) or more, S 1m (3ft) or more. Has 30cm (1ft) long leaves with many small, oval to lance-shaped, serrated, bright green leaflets with white edges.
P. guilfoylei (Wild coffee). Slow-growing, evergreen, rounded tree. H 3–8m (10–25ft), S to 2m (6ft) or more. Leaves are 25–40cm (10–16in) long and divided into oval to rounded, serrated, deep green leaflets. **'Victoriae'** illus. p.126.

POLYSTICHUM

DRYOPTERIDACEAE

Genus of evergreen, semi-evergreen or deciduous ferns. Does best in semi-shade and moist but well-drained soil enriched with fibrous organic matter. Remove faded fronds regularly. Propagate species by division in spring or by spores in summer, selected forms by division in spring.

P. acrostichoides (Christmas fern). Evergreen fern. H 60cm (24in), S 45cm (18in). Slender, lance-shaped, deep green fronds have small, holly-like pinnae. Is excellent for cutting.

P. aculeatum (Hard shield fern, Prickly shield fern). Semi-evergreen fern. H 60cm (24in), S 75cm (30in). Broadly lance-shaped, yellowish-green, then deep green fronds, with oblong to oval, spiny-edged, glossy pinnae, are produced on stems often covered in brown scales. **'Pulcherrimum'** illus. p.310.

P. braunii. Evergreen or semi-evergreen fern. H and S 45–75cm (18–30in). Produces a rosette of spreading to arching, lance-shaped, divided, dark green fronds, to 60cm (2ft) long. Young fronds are densely covered with orange-brown scales when unfurling in spring.

P. munitum illus. p.310.

P. polyblepharum. Evergreen fern. H 60–80cm (24–32in), S 90cm (36in). Produces 'shuttlecocks' of spreading, lance-shaped, divided, shiny, dark green fronds, 30–80cm (12–32in) long, covered with golden hairs when they unfurl. Pinnae lobes are oblong-ovate and have spiny-toothed margins.

P. rigens. Evergreen fern. H 40cm (16in), S 60cm (24in). Has 'shuttlecocks' of narrowly ovate-oblong, divided, leathery, harsh-textured, dull green fronds, 30–45cm (12–18in) long. Broad, lance-shaped pinnae are divided into ovate, spiny-toothed lobes. Fronds are yellowish-green in spring.

P. setiferum (Soft shield fern). **'Divisilobum'** see *P.s.* Divisilobum Group. **Divisilobum Group** (syn. *P.s.* 'Divisilobum') illus. p.311. **Plumosodivisilobum Group** illus. p.313.

P. tsussimense. Semi-evergreen fern. H 30cm (12in), S 23cm (9in). Has broadly lance-shaped, dull green fronds divided into oblong, finely spiny-edged pinnae. Is suitable for a peat garden or alpine house.

Pomegranate. See *Punica*.
  Dwarf. See *Punica granatum* var. *nana*, illus. p.355.

PONCIRUS

RUTACEAE

Genus of one species of very spiny, deciduous shrub or small tree, grown for its foliage, showy flowers and orange-like fruits. Is very effective as a protective hedge. Needs sun and fertile, well-drained soil. Cut out dead wood in spring, and trim hedges in early summer. Propagate by semi-ripe cuttings in summer or by seed when ripe, in autumn.

P. trifoliata (Hardy orange, trifoliate orange). Deciduous, bushy shrub or tree. H and S 5m (15ft). Stout, spiny, green shoots bear dark green leaves each composed of 3 oval leaflets. Fragrant, white flowers, with 4 or 5 large petals, borne in late spring and often again in autumn, are followed by rounded, 2–3cm (¾–1¼in) wide fruits. Zone 8.

Pond lily, Yellow. See *Nuphar advena*.
Pondweed
  Cape. See *Aponogeton distachyos*, illus. p.447.
  Curled. See *Potamogeton crispus*, illus. p.448.
  Fennel-leaved. See *Potamogeton pectinatus*.

PONTEDERIA

PONTEDERIACEAE

Genus of deciduous, perennial, marginal water plants, grown for their foliage and flower spikes. Needs full sun and up to 23cm (9in) depth of water. Remove fading flowers regularly. Propagate in spring by division or seed.

P. cordata illus. p.448.

Pontine oak. See *Quercus pontica*.
Pony-tail. See *Beaucarnea recurvata*, illus. p.100.
Poor man's orchid. See *Schizanthus*.
Poplar. See *Populus*.
  Balsam. See *Populus balsamifera*.
  Berlin. See *Populus* x *berolinensis*.
  Black. See *Populus nigra*.
  Canadian. See *Populus* x *canadensis*.
  Carolina. See *Populus* x *canadensis* 'Eugenei'.
  Chinese necklace. See *Populus lasiocarpa*.
  Grey. See *Populus* x *canescens*, illus. p.65.
  Lombardy. See *Populus nigra* 'Italica', illus. p.66.
  Necklace. See *Populus deltoides*.
  Ontario. See *Populus* x *candicans*.
  Theues. See *Populus nigra* 'Theuestina'.
  Western balsam. See *Populus trichocarpa*.
  White. See *Populus alba*, illus. p.64.
Poppy. See *Papaver*.
  Alpine. See *Papaver burseri*.
  Blue. See *Meconopsis betonicifolia*, illus. p.253.
Poppy (continued)
  California. See *Eschscholzia*.
  Corn. See *Papaver rhoeas*.
  Field. See *Papaver rhoeas*.
  Harebell. See *Meconopsis quintuplinervia*, illus. p.271.
  Horned. See *Glaucium*.
  Iceland. See *Papaver croceum*.
  Lampshade. See *Meconopsis integrifolia*, illus. p.292.
  Mexican tulip. See *Hunnemannia fumariifolia*.
  Opium. See *Papaver somniferum*.
  Oriental. See *Papaver orientale*.
  Plume. See *Macleaya*.
  Prickly. See *Argemone mexicana*, illus. p.335.
  Snow. See *Eomecon chionantha*.
  Tree. See *Romneya*.
  Water. See *Hydrocleys nymphoides*, illus. p.449.
  Welsh. See *Meconopsis cambrica*, illus. p.275.

POPULUS

Poplar

SALICACEAE

Genus of deciduous trees, grown for their habit, foliage and very quick growth. Has catkins in late winter or spring. Female trees produce copious amounts of fluffy, white seeds. Prefers full sun and needs deep, fertile, moist but well-drained soil; resents dry soil, apart from *P. alba*, which thrives in coastal gardens. Extensive root systems can undermine foundations and so make poplars unsuitable for planting close to buildings, particularly on clay soil. Propagate by hardwood cuttings in winter. Is susceptible to bacterial canker and fungal diseases.

P. alba illus. p.64. Is much confused with the commoner *P. canescens*. f. *pyramidalis* (syn. *P.a.* 'Pyramidalis') is a vigorous, deciduous, upright tree. H 20m (70ft), S 5m (15ft). Broadly oval, wavy-margined or lobed, dark green leaves, white beneath, turn yellow in autumn. Zone 4. **'Pyramidalis'** see *P.a.* f. *pyramidalis*. **'Raket'** (syn. *P.a.* 'Rocket') illus. p.69. **'Richardii'**, H 15m (50ft), S 12m (40ft), has leaves golden-yellow above. Zone 4. **'Rocket'** see *P.a.* 'Raket'.

P. balsamifera (Balsam poplar, Tacamahac). Fast-growing, deciduous, upright tree. H 30m (100ft), S 8m (25ft). Oval, glossy, dark green leaves, whitish beneath, have a strong fragrance of balsam when young. Zone 1.

P. x **berolinensis** (Berlin poplar). Deciduous, columnar tree. H 25m (80ft), S 8m (25ft). Has broadly oval, bright green leaves with white undersides. Zone 2.

P. x **canadensis** (Canadian poplar). **'Eugenei'** (Carolina poplar) is a deciduous, columnar tree. H 30m (100ft), S 12m (40ft). Has broadly oval, bronze, young leaves, maturing to dark green, and red catkins in spring. Zone 2. **'Robusta'** illus. p.65. **'Serotina de Selys'** (syn. *P.* x *c.* 'Serotina Erecta') illus. p.66.

P. x **candicans**, syn. *P. gileadensis*, *P.* x *jackii* 'Gileadensis' (Balm of Gilead, Ontario poplar). Very fast-growing, deciduous, conical tree. H 25m (80ft), S 10m (30ft). Oval leaves are dark green and, when young, balsam-scented. Is very susceptible to canker. Zone 4. **'Aurora'**, H 15m (50ft) or more, S 6m (20ft), has leaves that are heavily but irregularly blotched with creamy-white. Zone 4.

P. x **canescens** illus. p.65. **'Tower'**. A very narrow selection. H 20m (65ft) S 4m (12ft). It is canker resistant, does not sucker, and sets very little seed. Zone 2.

P. deltoides (Cottonwood, Eastern cottonwood, Necklace poplar). Very fast-growing, deciduous, spreading tree. H 30m (100ft), S 20m (70ft). Has lush growth of broadly oval, glossy, bright green leaves. Zone 3.

P. gileadensis. See *P. candicans*.

P. x **jackii** 'Gileadensis'. See *P.* x *candicans*.

P. lasiocarpa (Chinese necklace poplar). Very fast-growing, deciduous,

spreading tree. H 15m (50ft), S 12m (40ft). Has stout shoots and very large, heart-shaped, mid-green leaves with red veins, on long, red stalks. Bears stout, drooping, yellow catkins in spring. Zone 7.

P. maximowiczii illus. p.64.

P. nigra (Black poplar). Fast-growing, deciduous, spreading tree. H 25m (80ft), S 20m (70ft). Has dark bark. Diamond-shaped, bronze young leaves turn bright green, then yellow in autumn. Male trees bear red catkins in mid-spring. Zone 4. **'Italica'** illus. p.66. **'Thevestina'** (Theves' poplar). Similar to *P. n.* 'Italica' but with a whitish bark and less prone to disease. Zone 2b.

P. 'Northwest'. A fast growing hybrid that forms a large tree at maturity. H 30m (100ft) S 20m (70ft). It is resistant to many of the diseases that attack poplars. Zone 2.

P. szechuanica. Very fast-growing, deciduous, conical tree. H 25m (80ft), S 10m (30ft). Has flaking, pinkish-grey bark and large, heart-shaped, dark green leaves. Zone 5.

P. tremula (Aspen). Vigorous, deciduous, spreading tree. H 15m (50ft), S 10m (30ft). Rounded leaves are bronze-red when young, grey-green when mature and yellow in autumn. Flattened stalks make foliage tremble and rattle in wind. Zone 2. **'Erecta'**, S 5m (15ft), has an upright habit. **'Pendula'** illus. p.79.

P. tremuloides (American aspen, Quaking aspen). Very fast-growing, deciduous, spreading tree. H 15m (50ft) or more, S 10m (30ft). Has rounded, finely toothed, glossy, dark green leaves that flutter in the wind and turn yellow in autumn. Zone 1.

P. trichocarpa (Black cottonwood, Western balsam poplar). Very fast-growing, deciduous, conical tree. H 30m (100ft) or more, S 10m (30ft). Bears dense growth of oval, glossy, dark green leaves with green-veined, white undersides, strongly balsam-scented when young. Foliage turns yellow in autumn. Zone 6.

Port Jackson fig. See *Ficus rubiginosa*.
Portia oil nut. See *Thespesia populnea*.
Portugal laurel. See *Prunus lusitanica*.
Portuguese heath. See *Erica lusitanica*.

PORTULACA

PORTULACACEAE

Genus of fleshy annuals and perennials with flowers that open in sun and close in shade. Needs full light and any well-drained soil. Propagate by seed sown under glass in early spring, or outdoors in late spring. Is prone to attack by aphids.

P. grandiflora (Sun plant). Slow-growing, partially prostrate annual. H 15–20cm (6–8in), S 15cm (6in). Has lance-shaped, succulent, bright green leaves. In summer and early autumn bears shallowly bowl-shaped flowers, 2.5cm (1in) wide and with conspicuous stamens, in shades of yellow, red, orange, pink, or white. **Minilaca**

Hybrids have a double-flowered cultivar. **Sundance Hybrids** illus. p.326. **Sundial Series** has double flowers in a broad colour range. Bred for longer flowering in poor conditions and cooler climates.

PORTULACARIA
PORTULACACEAE

Genus of one species of evergreen or semi-evergreen, succulent-leaved shrub, grown for its foliage and overall appearance. Tender, min. 7–10°C (45–50°F). Needs full sun and well-drained soil. Water potted plants moderately when in full growth, sparingly at other times. Propagate by semi-ripe cuttings in summer.
P. afra illus. p.153. **'Foliisvariegatus'** (syn. *P.a.* 'Variegatus') is an evergreen or semi-evergreen, erect shrub with more or less horizontal branches. H and S 2–3m (6–10ft). Has oval to rounded, fleshy, cream-edged, bright green leaves. From late spring to summer, bears tiny, star-shaped, pale pink flowers in small clusters. **'Variegatus'** see *P.a.* 'Foliisvariegatus'.

Pot marigold. See *Calendula officinalis.*

POTAMOGETON
POTAMOGETONACEAE

Genus of deciduous, perennial, submerged water plants, grown for their foliage. Is suitable for cold-water pools and aquariums. Prefers sun. Remove fading foliage and thin plants as necessary. Propagate by stem cuttings in spring or summer.
P. crispus illus. p.448.
P. pectinatus (Fennel-leaved pondweed). Deciduous, perennial, submerged water plant. S 3m (10ft). Has very narrow, linear, green to brownish-green leaves, and produces inconspicuous flowers in summer. Is suitable for a medium to large pool.

Potato, Duck. See *Sagittaria latifolia,* illus. p.446.
Potato bush, Blue. See *Solanum rantonnetii.*
Potato creeper. See *Solanum seaforthianum,* illus. p.206.
Potato vine. See *Solanum jasminoides.*

POTENTILLA
ROSACEAE

Genus of perennials and deciduous shrubs, grown for their clusters of small, flattish to saucer-shaped flowers and for their foliage. Tall species – particularly the shrubs – are useful in borders. Dwarf potentillas are good for rock gardens. Does best in full sun, but flower colour is better on orange-, red- and pink-flowered cultivars if they are shaded from hottest sun. Needs well-drained soil. Propagate perennial species by seed in autumn or by division in spring or autumn; selected forms by division only in spring or autumn. Shrubby species may be raised by seed in autumn or by softwood or

greenwood cuttings in summer, selected forms by softwood or greenwood cuttings during summer.
P. **'Abbotswood'.** See *P. fruticosa* 'Abbotswood'.
P. alba illus. p.373.
P. **arbuscula.** See *P. fruticosa* var. *arbuscula.*
P. **argyrophylla.** See *P. atrosanguinea* var. *argyrophylla.*
P. atrosanguinea illus. p.283. var. *argyrophylla* (syn. *P. argyrophylla*) is a clump-forming perennial. H 45cm (18in), S 60cm (24in). Saucer-shaped, yellow or yellow-orange flowers are produced in profusion from early to late summer above strawberry-like, silvery leaves.
P. aurea illus. p.386.
P. **'Beesii'.** See *P. fruticosa* 'Beesii'.
P. crantzii (Alpine cinquefoil). Upright perennial with a thick, woody rootstock. H and S 10–20cm (4–8in). Produces wedge-shaped, 5-lobed leaves and, in spring, flattish, yellow flowers with orange centres. Is good in a rock garden.
P. davurica var. *mandschurica* of gardens. See *P. fruticosa* 'Manchu'.
P. **'Daydawn'.** See *P. fruticosa* 'Daydawn'.
P. **'Elizabeth'.** See *P. fruticosa* 'Elizabeth'.
P. eriocarpa illus. p.385.
P. **'Etna'.** Clump-forming perennial. H 75cm (30in), S 45cm (18in). In mid-summer produces saucer-shaped, maroon flowers above strawberry-like, dark green leaves.
P. fruticosa. Deciduous, bushy, dense shrub. H 1m (3ft), S 1.5m (5ft). From late spring to late summer produces saucer-shaped, bright yellow flowers. Dark green leaves have 5 narrowly oblong leaflets. **'Abbotswood'** (syn. *P.* 'Abbotswood') illus. p.158. var. *arbuscula* (syn. *P. arbuscula*), S 1.2m (4ft), bears golden-yellow flowers amid grey-green to silver-grey leaves. **'Beesii'** (syn. *P.* 'Beesii', *P.* 'Nana Argentea'), H 75cm (30in), S 1m (3ft), is slow-growing and compact. Has golden-yellow flowers and silver leaves. Zone 2b. **'Daydawn'** (syn. *P.* 'Daydawn') illus. p.161. **'Elizabeth'** (syn. *P.* 'Elizabeth') illus. p.169. **'Farrer's White'** illus. p.159. **'Friedrichsenii'** illus. p.169. **'Gold Drop'** (syn. *P. parvifolia* 'Gold Drop'), H and S 1.2m (4ft), bears a mass of golden-yellow flowers amid bright green leaves. Zone 2. **'Goldfinger'** (syn. *P.* 'Goldfinger') bears large, rich yellow flowers in profusion. Zone 2b. **'Jackman's Variety'** (syn. *P.* 'Jackman's Variety'), H 1.2m (4ft), has large, bright yellow flowers. Zone 3. **'Maanelys'** (syn. *P.* 'Maanelys', *P.* 'Manelys', *P.* 'Moonlight'), H 1.2m (4ft), S 2m (6ft), has soft yellow flowers and grey-green foliage. Zone 3. **'Manchu'** (syn. *P. davurica* var. *mandschurica* of gardens, *P.* 'Manchu') illus. p.158. **'Red Ace'** (syn. *P.* 'Red Ace') illus. p.166. **'Royal Flush'** (syn. *P.* 'Royal Flush'), H 45cm (18in), S 75cm (30in), produces mid-green leaves and sometimes semi-double, yellow-stamened, rich pink flowers, fading to white in full sun. Zone 3. **'Sunset'** (syn. *P.* 'Sunset') illus. p.171. **'Tangerine'** (syn. *P.* 'Tangerine'),

H 1.2m (4ft), bears yellow flowers, flushed with pale orange-red, amid mid-green leaves. Zone 3. **'Vilmoriniana'** (syn. *P.* 'Vilmoriniana') illus. p.169.
P. **'Gibson's Scarlet'.** Clump-forming perennial. H and S 45cm (18in). Bears saucer-shaped, brilliant scarlet flowers from mid- to late summer. Dark green leaves are strawberry-like.
P. **'Gloire de Nancy'**, syn. *P.* 'Glory of Nancy'. Clump-forming perennial. H and S 45cm (18in). Very large, saucer-shaped, semi-double, orange and coppery-red flowers appear throughout summer. Has strawberry-like, dark green leaves.
P. **'Glory of Nancy'.** See *P.* 'Gloire de Nancy'.
P. **'Goldfinger'.** See *P. fruticosa* 'Goldfinger'.
P. **'Jackman's Variety'.** See *P. fruticosa* 'Jackman's Variety'.
P. **'Maanelys'.** See *P. fruticosa* 'Maanelys'.
P. **'Manchu'.** See *P. fruticosa* 'Manchu'.
P. **'Manelys'.** See *P. fruticosa* 'Maanelys'.
P. megalantha illus. p.292.
P. **'Monsieur Rouillard'.** Clump-forming perennial. H and S 45cm (18in). Bears saucer-shaped, double, blood-red flowers in summer above strawberry-like, dark green leaves.
P. **'Moonlight'.** See *P. fruticosa* 'Maanelys'.
P. **'Nana Argentea'.** See *P. fruticosa* 'Beesii'.
P. nepalensis **'Miss Willmott'** illus. p.282.
P. nitida. Dense, mat-forming perennial. H 2.5–5cm (1–2in), S 20cm (8in). Has rounded, 3-lobed, silver leaves. Flower stems each carry 1–2 rose-pink flowers with dark centres in early summer. Is often shy-flowering. Suits a rock garden or trough.
P. parvifolia **'Gold Drop'.** See *P. fruticosa* 'Gold Drop'.
P. recta. Clump-forming, hairy perennial. H 60cm (24in), S 45cm (18in). From early to late summer bears pale yellow flowers. **'Macrantha'** see *P.r.* 'Warrenii'. **'Warrenii'** (syn. *P.r.* 'Macrantha') illus. p.291.
P. **'Red Ace'.** See *P. fruticosa* 'Red Ace'.
P. **'Royal Flush'.** See *P. fruticosa* 'Royal Flush'.
P. **'Sunset'.** See *P. fruticosa* 'Sunset'.
P. **'Tangerine'.** See *P. fruticosa* 'Tangerine'.
P. x *tonguei.* Mat-forming perennial. H 5cm (2in), S 25cm (10in). Has rounded, 3–5 lobed, green leaves. Prostrate branches bear flattish, orange-yellow flowers with red centres during summer. Is good for a rock garden.
P. **'Vilmoriniana'.** See *P. fruticosa* 'Vilmoriniana'.
P. **'William Rollison'.** Clump-forming perennial. H and S 45cm (18in). From mid- to late summer bears saucer-shaped, semi-double, scarlet-suffused, deep orange flowers with yellow centres. Has dark green leaves.
P. **'Yellow Queen'** illus. p.292

Pothos. Reclassified as *Epipremnum.*

x POTINARA

See also ORCHIDS.
x *P.* Cherub 'Spring Daffodil' (illus. p.299). Evergreen, epiphytic orchid for an intermediate greenhouse. H 15cm (6in). Sprays of yellow flowers, 5cm (2in) across, open in spring. Broadly oval, rigid leaves are 10cm (4in) long. Provide good light in summer.

Powder-puff cactus. See *Mammillaria bocasana,* illus. p.471.

PRATIA
CAMPANULACEAE

Genus of evergreen, mat-forming perennials with small leaves, grown for their mass of star-shaped flowers; is suitable for rock gardens. Is sometimes included in *Lobelia.* Some species may be invasive. Prefers shade and moist soil. Propagate by division or seed in autumn.
P. angulata. Evergreen, creeping perennial. H 1cm (½in), S indefinite. Bears small, broadly oval, dark green leaves. Star-shaped, white flowers, with 5 unevenly spaced petals, are carried in leaf axils in late spring and are followed by globose, purplish-red fruits in autumn.
P. pedunculata illus. p.383. **'County Park'** is a vigorous, evergreen, creeping perennial. H 1cm (½in), S indefinite. Has small, rounded to oval leaves and, in summer, a profusion of star-shaped, rich violet-blue flowers. Makes good ground cover.

Prayer plant. See *Maranta leuconeura.*
Prickly Moses. See *Acacia verticillata.*
Western. See *Acacia pulchella,* illus. p.157.
Prickly pear. See *Opuntia.*
Edible. See *Opuntia ficus-indica.*
Prickly poppy. See *Argemone mexicana,* illus. p.335.
Prickly shield fern. See *Polystichum aculeatum.*
Pride of Bolivia. See *Tipuana tipu.*
Pride of India. See *Koelreuteria paniculata,* illus. p.92; *Lagerstroemia speciosa.*
Primrose. See *Primula; P. vulgaris,* illus. p.273.
Primrose (continued)
Bird's-eye. See *Primula farinosa,* illus. p.272.
Cape. See *Streptocarpus rexii.*
Evening. See *Oenothera.*
Primrose jasmine. See *Jasminum mesnyi,* illus. p.207.
Primrose peerless. See *Narcissus* x *medioluteus.*

PRIMULA
Primrose
PRIMULACEAE

Genus of mainly herbaceous perennials, some woody-based and evergreen. All have leaves in basal rosettes and tubular, bell- or primrose-shaped (flat) flowers. In some primulas, the flower stems, leaves, sepals and, occasionally, sections of the petals are covered with a waxy powder known as farina. There are primulas suitable for almost every type of site: the border, scree garden, rock garden, peat garden, bog garden, pool margin, greenhouse and alpine house. Some may be difficult to grow as they dislike winter damp or summer heat. Hardy to tender, min. 7–10°C (45–50°F). Repot pot-grown plants annually. Tidy up fading foliage and dead-head as flowering ceases. Propagate species by seed when fresh or in spring; increase selected forms when dormant, either by division in autumn-spring, or by root cuttings in winter. Auricula primulas should be propagated by offsets in early spring or early autumn. Border cultivars may be prone to slug damage in damp situations and to attack by root aphids when grown in very dry conditions or in pots.

Primulas are divided into many different horticultural groups, of which the following are in common use. See also feature panel pp.272–3.

Auricula primulas
These are evergreen primulas, derived from hybrids between *P. auricula* and *P. hirsuta*, producing flat, smooth flowers carried in an umbel on a stem above the foliage. There are 3 main sub-groups: alpine, border and show.
Alpine Auricula Group. In these, the colour of the flower centre is strikingly different from that of the petals. They may be either light-centred (white or pale in the centre) or gold-centred (yellow or gold in the centre). There is no meal or 'farina' on either leaves or flowers. Grow in an alpine house or rock garden.
Show Auricula Group has flowers with a distinct circle of white meal or 'paste' in the centre. Some are self-coloured, with one colour, which may be red, yellow, blue or violet, from the central paste to the petal margins; edged cultivars have a black ring surrounding the central paste, feathering out to an often green, grey or white margin; in fancy cultivars the paste is surrounded by a colour other than black, with a green, grey or white margin. Show Auriculas have white farina on their foliage (except those with green-edged flowers), on their flower eyes and, sometimes, on their petal margins. Grow under glass to protect the flowers from rain.
Border Auricula Group has generally robust, garden Auricula primulas, which are often very fragrant. Some have farina on flower stems and leaves. Grow in a mixed or herbaceous border.

Candelabra primulas
These are robust, herbaceous perennials with tubular, flat-faced flowers borne in tiered whorls up tall, sturdy stems. Some are deciduous, dying back to basal buds; others are semi-evergreen, dying back to reduced rosettes. Grow in moist shade or woodland, especially by streams.

Primrose-Polyanthus primulas
A diverse group of evergreen, semi-evergreen, or deciduous, perennial hybrids, derived from *P. vulgaris,*

crossed with *P. veris, P. juliae* and other species. They are divided into two main groups.
Primrose Group Most produce solitary flowers among the leaves. Are mainly grown as herbaceous perennials, flowering in spring, or as biennial, greenhouse container plants flowering in winter-spring.
Polyanthus Group Produce flowers in long-stalked umbels. Usually grown as biennials for bedding, sown in summer to flower in winter and the following spring, or under glass as winter- and spring-flowering container plants.

Cultivation
Primulas have varying cultivation requirements. For ease of reference, these have been grouped as follows:
1 – Full sun or partial shade, in moist, but well-drained, humus-rich soil.
2 – Partial shade, in deep, humus-rich, moist, neutral to acid soil.
3 – Deep or partial shade, in peaty, gritty, moist but sharply drained, acid soil. Protect from excessive winter wet.
4 – Under glass in an alpine house or frame. Avoid wetting foliage of mealy species and hybrids.
5 – Full sun with some midday shade, or partial shade, in moist but sharply drained, gritty, humus-rich, slightly alkaline soil.
6 – In a cool or temperate greenhouse, or as a houseplant, in bright, filtered light.

P. **'Adrian'** (illus. p.273). Alpine Auricula primula. H and S 10cm (4in). Produces flat, light to dark blue flowers, with light centres and paler margins, in mid- to late spring. Leaves are oval to rounded and mid-green. Is useful for exhibition. Cultivation group 1 or 4.
P. allionii (illus. p.272). Rosette-forming, evergreen perennial. H 7–10cm (3–4in), S 20cm (8in). Better grown in an alpine house. Tubular, rose, mauve or white flowers cover a tight cushion of oval, mid-green leaves in spring. Cultivation group 4.
P. alpicola. Compact, rosette-forming perennial. H 50cm (20in), S 30cm (12in). Produces terminal clusters of pendent, bell-shaped, yellow to white or purple flowers on slender stems in early summer. Mid-green leaves are oval to lance-shaped. Cultivation group 2. var. *alpicola* (syn. *P.a.* var. *luna*; illus. p.273) has soft sulphur-yellow flowers. var. *luna* see *P.a.* var. *alpicola.*
P. aurantiaca. Small, rosette-forming Candelabra primula. H 30cm (12in), S 40cm (16in). Tubular, reddish-orange flowers are borne in early summer. Has long, broadly oval to lance-shaped, coarse, mid-green leaves. Cultivation group 2.
P. aureata (illus. p.273). Rosette-forming, evergreen perennial. H 15cm (6in), S 20cm (8in). Produces small umbels of flat, cream to yellow flowers in spring. In summer, oval, toothed, mid-green leaves have striking purple-red midribs; in winter, leaves form tight buds covered with whitish farina. Cultivation group 3 or 4.
P. auricula. Rosette-forming,

evergreen, sometimes white-mealy perennial. H 20cm (8in), S 25cm (10in). Bears fragrant, flat, yellow flowers in large umbels in spring. Oval, soft, pale green to grey-green leaves are densely covered with white farina. Cultivation group 1, 4 or 5.
P. bhutanica (illus. p.273). Rosette-forming perennial. H 15cm (6in), S 20cm (8in). Often short-lived. In spring produces neat umbels of tubular, pale purplish-blue flowers, each with a white or creamy-white eye, close to oval to lance-shaped, crinkled, mid-green leaves. Cultivation group 3.
P. **'Blairside Yellow'** (illus. p.273). Compact, border Auricula primula. H 10cm (4in), S 20cm (8in). In early spring, bell-shaped, golden-yellow flowers nestle in a rosette of tiny, rounded to oval, pale green leaves. Cultivation group 2 or 5.
P. **'Blossom'** (illus. p.273). Vigorous, alpine Auricula primula. H and S 10cm (4in). Flat, deep crimson to bright red flowers with golden centres are borne profusely in spring. Has oval, dark green leaves. Is suitable for exhibition. Cultivation group 1 or 4.
P. bulleyana (illus. p.273). Rosette-forming, semi-evergreen, Candelabra primula. H and S 60cm (24in). Tubular, deep orange flowers appear in early summer. Leaves are oval to lance-shaped, toothed and dark green. Cultivation group 2.
P. chionantha subsp. *melanops.* See *P. melanops.*
P. **'Chloë'** (illus. p.273). Green-edged, show Auricula primula. H and S 10cm (4in). In late spring produces flat, dark-green-edged flowers with a black body colour and brilliant white paste centres. Oval leaves are dark green and have no farina. Is good for exhibition. Cultivation group 4.
P. chungensis (illus. p.273). Vigorous, rosette-forming Candelabra primula. H 80cm (32in), S 60cm (24in). In summer bears tiered whorls of tubular, orange flowers among oval to lance-shaped, mid-green leaves. Cultivation group 2.
P. clarkei (illus. p.272). Small, rosette-forming perennial. H 7cm (3in), S 15cm (6in). In spring has flat, rose-pink flowers, with yellow eyes, just above a clump of rounded to oval, pale green leaves. Cultivation group 2 or 4. Divide in late winter.
P. clusiana (illus. p.272). Small, rosette-forming, evergreen perennial. H 8cm (3in), S 15cm (6in). In spring bears umbels of tubular, rose-pink flowers with white eyes. Leaves are oval, glossy and mid-green. Cultivation group 4 or 5.
P. **'Craddock White'** (illus. p.272). Rosette-forming, deciduous or semi-evergreen, Primrose Group primula. H to 12cm (5in), S 25cm (10in). Fragrant, upward-facing, flat, white flowers, with yellow eyes, are borne in spring just above long, oval, red-veined, dark green leaves. Cultivation group 1 or 2.
P. **'David Green'.** Rosette-forming, Primrose Group primula. H 10cm (4in), S 15–20cm (6–8in). In spring produces flat, bright crimson-purple flowers amid oval, coarse, mid-green leaves.

Cultivation group 1 or 2.
P. denticulata (Drumstick primula; illus. p.273). Robust, rosette-forming perennial. H and S 45cm (18in). From early to mid-spring, dense, rounded heads of flat, lilac, purple or pink flowers are borne on tops of stout stems. Mid-green leaves are broadly lance-shaped and toothed. Cultivation group 1 or 2. var. *alba* (illus. p.272) has white flowers.
P. **'Dreamer'** illus. p. 328; cultivation group 6.
P. edgeworthii. See *P. nana.*
P. elatior (Oxlip; illus. p.273). Variable, rosette-forming, evergreen or semi-evergreen perennial. H 30cm (12in), S 25cm (10in). Umbels of small, fragrant, tubular, yellow flowers appear in spring, above neat, oval to lance-shaped, toothed, mid-green leaves. Cultivation group 1 or 2.
P. **'E.R. Janes'.** Vigorous, rosette-forming, semi-evergreen, Primrose Group primula. H 10–15cm (4–6in), S 30–40cm (12–16in). Flat, pale rose-pink flowers, flushed with orange, are borne in spring amid broadly oval, toothed, mid-green leaves. Cultivation group 1 or 2.
P. farinosa (Bird's-eye primrose; illus. p.272). Rosette-forming perennial. H and S 25cm (10in). In spring, umbels of tubular, lilac-pink, occasionally white, flowers are borne on short, stout stems. Oval, toothed, mid-green leaves are densely covered with white farina. Cultivation group 2 or 4. *P. flaccida,* syn. *P. nutans* of gardens (illus. p.273). Lax, rosette-forming, short-lived perennial. H 50cm (20in), S 30cm (12in). In early summer, each stout stem produces a conical head of pendent, bell-shaped, lavender or violet flowers above narrowly oval, pale to mid-green leaves. Cultivation group 3 or 4.
P. florindae (Giant cowslip; illus. p.273). Bold, rosette-forming perennial. H 1.2m (4ft), S 1m (3ft). In summer, large heads of pendent, bell-shaped, sulphur-yellow flowers appear above broadly lance-shaped, toothed, mid-green leaves. Cultivation group 1 or 2.
P. forrestii (illus. p.273). Rosette-forming, evergreen perennial. H 60cm (24in), S 45cm (18in). Dense umbels of flat, yellow flowers with orange eyes are borne in late spring or early summer. Has oval, toothed, dark green leaves. Cultivation group 4 or 5.
P. frondosa (illus. p.272). Compact, rosette-forming perennial. H 15cm (6in), S 25cm (10in). In spring bears umbels of flat, yellow-eyed, lilac-rose to reddish-purple flowers on short stems above neat, oval, mid-green leaves, densely covered with white farina. Cultivation group 2 or 4.
P. **'Garryarde Guinevere'.** Vigorous, rosette-forming, evergreen Polyanthus Group primula. H 12cm (5in), S 25cm (10in). Flat, purplish-pink flowers with yellow eyes are produced in spring among oval, toothed, bronze-green leaves. Cultivation group 2.
P. **Gold Laced Group** (illus. p.273). Erect, semi-evergreen or evergreen, Polyanthus Group primulas. H 25cm (10in), S 30cm (12in). Produces flat flowers, in a variety of colours, with

gold-laced margins, from mid- to late spring. Leaves are oval and mid-green, sometimes tinged red. Raise annually by seed. Cultivation group 2 or 4.

P. gracilipes (illus. p.272). Rosette-forming, evergreen or semi-evergreen perennial. H 1cm (4in), S 20cm (8in). Tubular, purplish-pink flowers with greenish-yellow eyes are borne singly in spring or early summer among oval, wavy, toothed, mid-green leaves. Cultivation group 3 or 4.

P. 'Harlow Car'. Rosette-forming, Alpine Auricula primula. H 10–15cm (4–6in), S 15–20cm (6–8in). In spring produces flat, white flowers on short stems above oval, soft, mid-green leaves. Cultivation group 1 or 4.

P. helodoxa. See *P. prolifera*.

P. hirsuta, syn. *P. rubra* (illus. p.272). Rosette-forming, evergreen perennial. H 10cm (4in), S 25cm (10in). Produces small umbels of flat, rose or lilac flowers in spring. Has small, rounded to oval, sticky, mid-green leaves. Cultivation group 1, 2, or 4.

P. 'Inverewe' (illus. p.273). Vigorous, rosette-forming, semi-evergreen, Candelabra primula. H 75cm (30in), S 60cm (24in). Tubular, bright orange-red flowers are produced in summer on stems coated with white farina. Has oval to lance-shaped, toothed, coarse, mid-green leaves. Cultivation group 2.

P. ioessa. Rosette-forming perennial. H and S 30cm (12in). Clustered heads of funnel-shaped, pink or pinkish-mauve, or sometimes white, flowers are borne in spring or early summer above oval to lance-shaped, toothed, mid-green leaves. Cultivation group 2, 3, or 4.

P. 'Janet' (illus. p.272). Vigorous, rosette-forming evergreen perennial. H 15–20cm (6–8in), S 15cm (6in). In spring, clusters of outward-facing, flat, purplish-pink flowers are produced above a rosette of oval to rounded, soft, mid-green leaves. Cultivation group 1 or 4. Propagate by offsets after flowering.

P. 'Janie Hill' (illus. p.273). Rosette-forming, alpine Auricula. H 10cm (4in), S 15cm (6in). Flat, dark to golden-brown flowers, with golden centres, open in mid- to late spring. Has oval, mid-green leaves. Is useful for exhibition. Cultivation group 4 or 5.

P. japonica. Robust, rosette-forming, Candelabra primula. H and S 45cm (18in). In early summer produces tubular, deep red flowers on stout stems above oval to lance-shaped, toothed, coarse, pale green leaves. Cultivation group 2. **'Miller's Crimson'** (illus. p.272) has intense crimson flowers. **'Postford White'** (illus. p.272) bears white flowers.

P. × kewensis (illus. p.273). Rosette-forming, evergreen perennial. H 45cm (18in), S 20cm (8in). Tender, min. 2°C (35°F). Produces whorls of fragrant, tubular, bright yellow flowers in winter and early spring. Oval to lance-shaped, toothed, pale green leaves are covered with white farina. Cultivation group 6.

P. 'Linda Pope' (illus. p.273). Vigorous, rosette-forming, evergreen or semi-evergreen perennial. H 15cm (6in), S 30cm (12in). In spring bears flat, mauve-blue flowers on short stems

above oval, toothed, mid-green leaves covered with white farina. Cultivation group 4 or 5.

P. malacoides (single, double, illus. p.272). Erect, rosette-forming, evergreen perennial, usually grown as an annual. H 30–45cm (12–18in), S 20cm (8in). Tender, min. 2°C (35°F). Dense whorls of small, flat, single or double, pink, purplish-pink or white flowers open in winter-spring. Leaves are oval, hairy, soft and pale green. Cultivation group 6.

P. 'Margaret Martin' (illus. p.273). Rosette-forming, show Auricula primula. H 10cm (4in), S 15cm (6in). Bears flat, grey-edged flowers, with a black body colour and white centres, in mid- to late spring. Has spoon-shaped, grey-green leaves covered with white farina. Is excellent for exhibition. Cultivation group 4.

P. marginata (illus. p.273). Rosette-forming, evergreen or semi-evergreen perennial. H 15cm (6in), S 30cm (12in). In spring, clusters of funnel-shaped, blue-lilac flowers appear above oval, toothed, mid-green leaves densely covered with white farina. Cultivation group 4 or 5. **'Prichard's Variety'** (illus. p.273) has lilac-purple flowers with white eyes.

P. 'Mark' (illus. p.273). Vigorous, alpine Auricula primula. H and S 10cm (4in). Produces flat, pink flowers, with light yellow centres, in spring. Leaves are oval and vibrant green. Is a leading exhibition cultivar. Cultivation group 4.

P. melanops, syn. *P. chionantha* subsp. *melanops* (illus. p.272). Rosette-forming perennial. H 35cm (14in), S 50cm (20in). In summer has umbels of pendent, narrowly funnel-shaped, deep violet-purple flowers, with black eyes, above long, strap-shaped, mid-green leaves. Cultivation group 2 or 4.

P. modesta. Rosette-forming perennial. H and S 20cm (8in). Dense heads of small, tubular, pinkish-purple flowers appear on short stems in spring. Rounded to oval, mid-green leaves are covered with yellow farina. Cultivation group 1 or 4. var. *fauriae* (illus. p.272), H and S 5cm (2in), produces yellow-eyed, pinkish-purple flowers and leaves covered with white farina.

P. 'Moonstone' (illus. p.273). Rosette-forming, border Auricula primula. H 12cm (5in), S 15cm (6in). Rounded, double, whitish- or greenish-yellow flowers are produced in profusion in spring. Leaves are oval and mid-green. Preferably, grow under glass. Cultivation group 4 or 5.

P. 'Mrs J.H. Wilson' (illus. p.272). Rosette-forming, alpine Auricula primula. H and S 10–15cm (4–6in). Bears small umbels of flat, white-centred, purple flowers in spring. Oval leaves are greyish-green. Cultivation group 1 or 4.

P. nana, syn. *P. edgeworthii* (illus. p.272). Rosette-forming perennial. H 10cm (4in), S 15cm (6in). Flat, pale mauve flowers with white eyes appear singly among oval, toothed, pale green leaves in spring. Cultivation group 3 or 4.

P. nutans of gardens. See *P. flaccida*.

P. obconica. Erect, rosette-forming, evergreen perennial, usually grown

as an annual. H 23–40cm (9–16in), S 25cm (10in). Tender, min. 2°C (35°F). Flat, purple, lilac or white flowers, with yellow eyes, are borne in dense umbels during winter-spring. Leaves are oval, toothed, hairy and pale green. Cultivation group 6.

P. 'Orb'. Neat, show Auricula primula. H and S 10cm (4in). Flat, dark-green-edged flowers, each with a black body colour and a central zone of white paste, are produced from mid- to late spring. Has spoon-shaped, dark green leaves without farina. Is good for exhibition. Cultivation group 4.

P. Pacific Series (Polyanthus). Polyanthus Group primula illus. p.339, (dwarf) illus. p 328; cultivation group 1, 2, 4, or 6.

P. palinuri (illus. p.273). Rosette-forming, evergreen perennial. H and S 30cm (12in). One-sided clusters of semi-pendent, narrowly funnel-shaped, yellow flowers appear on thick stems in early summer. Has rounded to oval, lightly toothed, thick-textured, powdered, green leaves. Cultivation group 1 or 4; requires full sun.

P. petiolaris (illus. p.272). Rosette-forming, evergreen perennial. H 10cm (4in), S 20cm (8in). Tubular, purplish-pink flowers, with toothed petals, are borne singly in spring. Has small, oval, toothed, mid-green leaves. Cultivation group 3 or 4.

P. polyneura (illus. p.272). Rosette-forming perennial. H and S 45cm (18in). Dense heads of tubular, pale rose, rich rose, or purple-rose flowers are produced in late spring or early summer. Rounded to oval, shallowly lobed, downy, soft leaves are mid-green. Cultivation group 2.

P. prolifera, syn *P. helodoxa* (illus. p.273). Rosette-forming, evergreen, Candelabra primula. H and S 60cm (24in). Bell-shaped, yellow flowers are borne in summer. Leaves are oval, toothed and pale green. Cultivation group 2.

P. pulverulenta (illus. p.272). Rosette-forming, Candelabra primula. H 90cm (36in), S 60cm (24in). In early summer bears tubular, deep red flowers with purple-red eyes on stems covered with white farina. Has broadly lance-shaped, toothed, coarse, mid-green leaves. Cultivation group 2. **'Bartley'** (illus. p.272) has pink flowers.

P. reidii. Robust, rosette-forming perennial. H 5–15cm (2–6in), S 10–15cm (4–6in). Produces dense clusters of bell-shaped, pure white flowers on slender stems in early summer. Has oval, hairy, pale green leaves. Cultivation group 3 or 4. var. *williamsii* (illus. p.273) is more robust and has purplish-blue to pale blue flowers.

P. rosea (illus. p.272). Rosette-forming perennial. H and S 20cm (8in). In early spring bears small clusters of flat, glowing rose-pink flowers on short stems, among oval to lance-shaped, mid-green leaves, often bronze-flushed when young. Cultivation group 2.

P. 'Royal Velvet'. Vigorous, rosette-forming, border Auricula primula. H and S 15–20cm (6–8in). Flat, velvety, blue-tinged, maroon flowers, with frilled petals and large, creamy-

yellow centres, are produced in spring. Has large, spoon-shaped, pale green leaves. Cultivation group 2 or 5.

P. rubra. See *P. hirsuta*.

P. × scapeosa (illus. p.272). Vigorous, rosette-forming perennial. H 10cm (4in), S 25cm (10in). Clusters of outward-facing, flat, mauve-pink flowers, in early spring, are initially hidden by broadly oval, sharply toothed, mid-green leaves covered at first with slight farina; later, flower stem elongates above leaves. Cultivation group 3 or 4.

P. secundiflora (illus. p.272). Rosette-forming, evergreen or semi-evergreen perennial. H 60–90cm (24–36in), S 60cm (24in). Has clusters of pendent, funnel-shaped, reddish-purple flowers in summer above lance-shaped, toothed leaves. Cultivation group 2.

P. sieboldii (illus. p.272). Rosette-forming perennial. H 30cm (12in), S 45cm (18in). Umbels of flat, white, pink or purple flowers, with white eyes, open above oval, round-toothed, downy, soft, pale green leaves in early summer. Cultivation group 2. **'Sumina'** bears large, wisteria-blue flowers. **'Wine Lady'** (illus. p.272) has white flowers, strongly suffused with purplish-red.

P. sikkimensis (illus. p.273). Rosette-forming perennial. H 60–90cm (24–36in), S 60cm (24in). Pendent clusters of funnel-shaped, yellow flowers are borne in summer. Has rounded to oval, toothed, pale green leaves. Cultivation group 2.

P. sinensis (illus. p.272). Erect, rosette-forming, evergreen perennial. H and S 15–20cm (6–8in). Tender, min. 5°C (41°F). Flat, purple, purple-rose, pink or white flowers, with yellow eyes, are produced in neat whorls in winter-spring. Leaves are oval, toothed, hairy and mid-green. Cultivation group 6.

P. sonchifolia (illus. p.272). Rosette-forming, deciduous perennial. H 5cm (2in), S 30cm (12in). Produces dense umbels of tubular, blue-purple flowers with white eyes and yellow margins in spring. Leaves are oval to lance-shaped, toothed and mid-green. Cultivation group 3 or 4.

P. Super Giants Series. Rosette-forming Polyanthus Group primulas, usually grown as biennials. H and S 15–20cm (6–8in). Produce large, fragrant, flat flowers in a wide range of colours in spring (blue, illus. p.332). Cultivation group 1 or 2.

P. 'Tawny Port'. Very dwarf, rosette-forming, evergreen or semi-evergreen, Polyanthus Group primula. H 10–15cm (4–6in), S 15–20cm (6–8in). Bears flat, port-wine-coloured flowers on short stems in spring. Rounded to oval, toothed leaves are reddish-green. Cultivation group 1, 2 or 4.

P. veris (Cowslip; illus. p.273). Very variable, rosette-forming, evergreen or semi-evergreen perennial. H and S 25cm (10in). Tight clusters of fragrant, tubular, yellow flowers are produced on stout stems in spring. Leaves are oval to lance-shaped, toothed and mid-green. Cultivation group 1 or 2.

P. verticillata (illus. p.273). Rosette-forming perennial. H 20–25cm (8–10in), S 15–20cm (6–8in). Tender,

min. 2°C (35°F). Fragrant, bell-shaped, yellow flowers are borne in whorls in spring. Has oval, toothed, mid-green leaves. Cultivation group 4 or 6.
P. vialii (illus. p.272). Rosette-forming, often short-lived perennial. H 30–60cm (12–24in), S 30cm (12in). Dense, conical spikes of tubular, bluish-purple-and-red flowers are produced in late spring. Has lance-shaped, toothed, soft, mid-green leaves. Cultivation group 1 or 2.
P. vulgaris (Primrose; illus. p.273). Rosette-forming, evergreen or semi-evergreen perennial. H 20cm (8in), S 35cm (14in). Flat, soft yellow flowers, with darker eyes, are borne singly among oval to lance-shaped, toothed, bright green leaves in spring. Cultivation group 2. **'Alba Plena'** has double, white flowers. **'Gigha White'** (illus. p.272) is very floriferous and has yellow-eyed, white flowers. subsp. *sibthorpii* (illus. p.272) has pink or purplish-pink flowers.
P. **'Wanda'**. Very vigorous, long-flowering, rosette-forming, evergreen or semi-evergreen perennial. H 10–15cm (4–6in), S 30–40cm (12–16in). In spring, produces clusters of flat, crimson-purple flowers singly amid oval, toothed, purplish-green foliage. Cultivation group 1 or 2. Thrives well in both sun and shade.
P. warshenewskiana (illus. p.272). Rosette-forming perennial. H 7cm (3in), S 15cm (6in). Tiny, flat, white-eyed, bright pink flowers sit just above spoon-shaped, dark green leaves in early spring. Cultivation group 2 or 4. Divide clumps regularly in late winter before flowering.

Primula, Drumstick. See *Primula denticulata*, illus. p.273.
Prince Albert's yew. See *Saxegothaea conspicua*.
Prince's feather. See *Amaranthus hypochondriacus*, illus. p.330.

PRINSEPIA

ROSACEAE

Genus of deciduous, usually spiny, spring- and early summer-flowering shrubs, grown for their habit, flowers and fruits. Needs sun and any not too dry soil. Does well against a south- or west-facing wall. Propagate by softwood cuttings in summer or by seed in autumn.
P. sinensis (Cherry prinsepia). Spreading deciduous shrub with spiny, light gray branches. H 2m (6ft) S 3m (10ft). Clusters of up to 8 bright yellow flowers open in spring and become red to purple edible fruit. Makes a good hedge. Zone 2b.
P. uniflora illus. p.137.

Privet. See *Ligustrum*.
  Chinese. See *Ligustrum lucidum*.
  Japanese. See *Ligustrum japonicum*.
  Wax. See *Peperomia glabella*, illus. p.305.

PROBOSCIDEA

MARTYNIACEAE/PEDALIACEAE

Genus of annuals and perennials. Grow in a sunny, sheltered position and in fertile, well-drained soil. Propagate by seed sown under glass in early spring.
P. fragrans. Moderately fast-growing, upright annual. H 60cm (24in), S 30cm (12in). Has rounded, serrated, or lobed leaves. Fragrant, bell-shaped, crimson-purple flowers, to 5cm (2in) long, appear in summer-autumn, followed by rounded, horned, brown fruits, 8–10cm (3–4in) long, which, if gathered young, may be pickled and eaten.
P. jussieui. See *P. louisianica*.
P. louisianica, syn. *Martynia louisianica*, *P. jussieui*, *P. proboscidea* (Common devil's claw, Common unicorn plant, Ram's horn). Erect to spreading annual. Has rounded to ovate, unlobed leaves. In summer, bears funnel-shaped, fragrant, reddish-purple to purple flowers, followed by narrow, crested fruit, to 6cm (2½in) long, with beak-like projections.
P. proboscidea. See *P. louisianica*.

Prophet flower. See *Arnebia pulchra*.

PROSTANTHERA
Mint bush

LABIATAE/LAMIACEAE

Genus of evergreen shrubs, grown for their flowers and mint-scented foliage. Tender, min. 2°C (35°F). Requires full light or partial shade and fertile, well-drained soil. Water containerized specimens freely when in full growth, moderately at other times. Leggy stems may be cut back after flowering. Propagate by seed in spring or by semi-ripe cuttings in late summer.
P. ovalifolia illus. p.145.
P. rotundifolia illus. p.145.

Prostrate coleus. See *Plectranthus oertendahlii*.
Prostrate speedwell. See *Veronica prostrata*, illus. p.357.

PROTEA

PROTEACEAE

Genus of evergreen shrubs and trees, grown mainly for their colourfully bracted flower heads. Is difficult to grow. Tender, min. 5–7°C (41–5°F). Requires full light and well-drained, neutral to acid soil, low in phosphates and nitrates. Water containerized specimens moderately, less when not in full growth. Plants under glass must have plenty of ventilation throughout the year. Prune, if necessary, in early spring. Propagate by seed in spring or by semi-ripe cuttings in summer.
P. barbigera. See *P. magnifica*.
P. cynaroides illus. p.161.
P. magnifica, syn. *P. barbigera*. Evergreen, rounded to spreading shrub. H and S 1m (3ft). Has oblong to elliptic, leathery, mid- to greyish-green leaves. Spherical flower heads, 15–20cm (6–8in) wide, with petal-like, pink, red, yellow or white bracts,

appear in spring-summer.
P. mellifera. See *P. repens*.
P. neriifolia illus. p.140.
P. repens, syn. *P. mellifera* (Sugar bush). Evergreen, ovoid to rounded shrub. H and S 2–3m (6–10ft). Mid-green leaves are narrowly oblong to elliptic and tinted blue-grey. In spring-summer produces cup-shaped, 13cm (5in) long flower heads, with petal-like, pink, red or white bracts.

Protea, King. See *Protea cynaroides*, illus. p.161.

PRUMNOPITYS

PODOCARPACEAE

See also CONIFERS.
P. andina, syn. *Podocarpus andinus* (Plum yew, Plum-fruited yew). Conifer with a domed crown on several stems. H 15m (50ft), S 8m (25ft). Has smooth, grey-brown bark, needle-like, flattened, bluish-green leaves and edible, yellowish-white fruits like small plums. Zone 9.

PRUNELLA
Self-heal

LABIATAE/LAMIACEAE

Genus of semi-evergreen perennials with spreading mats of leaves from which arise short, stubby flower spikes in mid-summer. Suits rock gardens. Grows well in sun or shade and in moist but well-drained soil. Propagate by division in spring.
P. grandiflora, syn. *P.* x *webbiana* (Large self-heal) illus. p.382. **'Loveliness'** illus. p.381. **'Pink Loveliness'** bears soft pink flowers in terminal spikes in summer. Makes good ground cover, but may be invasive. Cut off old flower stems before they produce seed. **'White Loveliness'** has white flowers.
P. x *webbiana*. See *P. grandiflora*.

PRUNUS
Cherry

ROSACEAE

Genus of deciduous or evergreen shrubs and trees. The trees are grown mainly for their single (5-petalled) to double flowers and autumn colour; the shrubs for their autumn colour, bark, flowers or fruits. All have oval to oblong leaves. Evergreen species tolerate sun or shade; deciduous species prefer full sun. All may be grown in any but waterlogged soil. Trim deciduous hedges after flowering, evergreen ones in early or mid-spring. Propagate deciduous species by seed in autumn, deciduous hybrids and selected forms by softwood cuttings in summer. Increase evergreens by semi-ripe cuttings in summer. Bullfinches may eat flower buds and foliage may be attacked by aphids, caterpillars and the fungal disease silver leaf. Flowering cherries are prone to a fungus that causes 'witches' brooms' (abnormal, crowded shoots). Certain *Prunus* species and cultivars, notably cultivars of the almond (*P. dulcis*) and the peach (*P. persica*), are grown for their edible

fruits. Leaves and fruits of most other species may cause severe discomfort if ingested.
P. **'Accolade'** illus. p.88.
P. **'Amanogawa'**. Deciduous, upright tree. H 10m (30ft), S 4m (12ft). Bears fragrant, semi-double, pale pink flowers in late spring. Oblong to oval, taper-pointed, dark green leaves turn orange and red in autumn. Zone 6.
P. x *amygdalopersica* **'Pollardii'**. Deciduous, spreading tree. H and S 7m (22ft). Large, 5-petalled, bright pink flowers open from early to mid-spring, before oval, glossy, mid-green leaves emerge. Green, then brown fruits are like almonds in shape and taste. Zone 7.
P. avium illus. p.71. **'Plena'** illus. p.76.
P. x *blireana*. Deciduous, spreading shrub or small tree. H and S 4m (12ft). Bears double, pink flowers in mid-spring and has oval, purple leaves. Zone 6.
P. campanulata (Bell-flowered cherry, Taiwan cherry). Deciduous, spreading tree. H and S 8m (25ft). Shallowly bell-shaped, deep rose-red flowers are produced from early to mid-spring, before or with oval, taper-pointed, dark green leaves. Fruits are small, rounded and reddish. Zone 8.
P. cerasifera (Cherry plum, Myrobalan). **'Nigra'** illus. p.91. **'Pissardii'** is a deciduous, round-headed tree. H and S 10m (30ft). Small, 5-petalled, pale pink flowers open from early to mid-spring and are often followed by edible, plum-like, red fruits. Has oval, red, young leaves turning deeper red, then purple. May be used for hedging. Zone 4b.
P. **'Cheal's Weeping'**. See *P.* 'Kiku-shidare-zakura'.
P. x *cistena* illus. p.154.
P. davidiana (David's peach). Deciduous, spreading tree. H and S 8m (25ft). Saucer-shaped, 5-petalled, white or pale pink flowers are carried on slender shoots in late winter and early spring, but are susceptible to late frosts. Leaves are narrowly oval and dark green. Fruits are rounded and reddish. Zone 5.
P. dulcis (Almond). **'Roseoplena'** is a deciduous, spreading tree. H and S 8m (25ft). Bears double, pink flowers in late winter and early spring, before oblong, pointed, toothed, dark green leaves. Zone 6.
P. glandulosa **'Alba Plena'** illus. p.153. **'Rosea Plena'** see *P.g.* 'Sinensis'. **'Sinensis'** (syn. *P.g.* 'Rosea Plena') is a deciduous, rounded, open shrub. H and S 1.5m (5ft). Produces double, bright rose-pink flowers in late spring and oval, mid-green leaves. Flowers best when grown against a south- or west-facing wall. Cut back young shoots to within a few buds of old wood after flowering. Zone 5.
P. **'Hally Jolivette'**. Deciduous, rounded, compact tree. H and S 5m (15ft). Double, white flowers open from pink buds in late spring. Leaves are oval and dark green. Zone 6.
P. x *hillieri* **'Spire'**. See *P.* 'Spire'.
P. **'Hokusai'**, syn. *P.* 'Uzuzakura', illus. p.87.

P. incisa (Fuji cherry) illus. p.86. **'February Pink'** is a deciduous, spreading tree. H and S 8m (25ft). Oval, sharply toothed, dark green leaves are reddish when young, orange-red in autumn. During mild, winter periods bears 5-petalled, pale pink flowers. Has tiny, rounded, reddish fruits. Zone 7.

P. jamasakura, syn. *P. serrulata* var. *spontanea*, illus. p.76.

P. **'Kanzan'** illus. p.77.

P. **'Kiku-shidare-zakura'**, syn. *P.* 'Cheal's Weeping', illus. p.88.

P. **'Kursar'**. Deciduous, spreading tree. H and S 8m (25ft). Bears masses of small, 5-petalled, deep pink flowers in early spring. Oval, dark green leaves turn brilliant orange in autumn. Zone 7.

P. laurocerasus (Cherry laurel, Laurel). Evergreen, dense, bushy shrub becoming spreading and open. H 6m (20ft), S 10m (30ft). Has long spikes of small, single, white flowers from mid- to late spring, large, oblong, glossy, bright green leaves and cherry-shaped, red, then black fruits. Restrict growth by cutting back hard in spring. Zone 7. **'Otto Luyken'** illus. p.154. **'Schipkaensis'**, H 2m (6ft), S 3m (10ft), is fully hardy and of elegant, spreading habit, with narrow leaves and freely borne flowers in upright spikes. Zone 8. **'Zabeliana'** illus. p.154.

P. lusitanica (Laurel, Portugal laurel). Evergreen, bushy, dense shrub or spreading tree. H and S 6–10m (20–30ft). Reddish-purple shoots bear oval, glossy, dark green leaves. Slender spikes of small, fragrant, 5-petalled, white flowers appear in early summer, followed by egg-shaped, fleshy, deep purple fruits. Restrict growth by pruning hard in spring. Zone 8. subsp. *azorica* illus. p.126. **'Variegata'** illus. p.126.

P. maackii illus. p.84.

P. mahaleb illus. p.76.

P. **'Mount Fuji'**. See *P.* 'Shirotae'.

P. mume (Japanese apricot). **'Beni-chidori'** (syn. *P.m.* 'Beni-shidon', *P.m.* 'Beni-shidori') illus. p.130. **'Omoi-no-mama'** (syn. *P.m.* 'Omoi-no-wac') illus. p.130. **'Pendula'** is a deciduous, weeping tree with slender, arching branches. H and S 6m (20ft). Fragrant, 5-petalled, pink flowers appear in late winter or early spring, before broadly oval, bright green leaves, and are sometimes succeeded by edible, apricot-like, yellow fruits. Zone 5b.

P. **'Okame'**. Deciduous, bushy-headed tree. H 10m (30ft), S 8m (25ft). Bears masses of 5-petalled, carmine-pink flowers in early spring. Oval, sharply toothed, dark green leaves turn orange-red in autumn. Zone 8.

P. padus (Bird cherry) illus. p.76. **'Colorata'** is a deciduous, spreading tree, conical when young. H 15m (50ft), S 10m (30ft). Produces pendent racemes of fragrant, cup-shaped, 5-petalled, pink flowers in late spring, followed by small, pea-shaped, black fruits. Oval, reddish-purple young leaves mature to dark green and then turn red or yellow in autumn. **'Grandiflora'** see *P.p.* 'Watereri'. **'Plena'** has long-lasting, double flowers and no fruits. **'Watereri'** (syn.

P.p. 'Grandiflora') bears long racemes of flowers from mid- to late spring. All Zone 2.

P. **'Pandora'** illus. p.87.

P. pendula **'Pendula Rubra'**. See *P.* x *subhirtella* 'Pendula Rubra'.

'Stellata' see *P.* x *subhirtella* 'Stellata'.

P. pensylvanica (Pin cherry). Deciduous, spreading tree. H 15m (50ft), S 10m (30ft). Has peeling, red-banded bark and oval, taper-pointed, bright green leaves. Produces clusters of small, star-shaped, 5-petalled, white flowers from mid- to late spring, followed by small, pea-shaped, red fruits. Zone 1.

P. persica (Peach). **'Klara Meyer'** is a deciduous, spreading tree. H 5m (15ft), S 6m (20ft). Bears double, bright pink flowers in mid-spring. Has slender, lance-shaped, bright green leaves. Is susceptible to the fungal disease peach leaf curl. Zone 6. **'Prince Charming'** illus. p.88.

P. **'Pink Perfection'** illus. p.87.

P **'Pink Star'**. See *P. subhirtella* 'Stellata'.

P. sargentii illus. p.87.

P. serotina illus. p.65.

P. serrula. Deciduous, round-headed tree. H and S 10m (30ft). Has gleaming, coppery-red bark that peels. In late spring bears small, 5-petalled, white flowers amid oval, tapering, toothed, dark green leaves that turn yellow in autumn. Fruits are tiny, rounded and reddish-brown. Zone 7.

P. serrulata var. *spontanea*. See *P. jamasakura*.

P. **'Shirofugen'** illus. p.87.

P. **'Shirotae'**, syn. *P.* 'Mount Fuji', illus. p.86.

P. **'Shogetsu'**, syn. *P.* 'Shimidsu', illus. p.86.

P. spinosa (Blackthorn, Sloe). **'Purpurea'** illus. p.122.

P. **'Spire'**, syn. *P.* x *hillieri* 'Spire', illus. p.87.

P. x *subhirtella* (Higan cherry, Rosebud cherry). Deciduous, spreading tree. H and S 8m (25ft). From early to mid-spring, a profusion of small, 5-petalled, pale pink flowers appear before oval, taper-pointed, dark green leaves, which turn yellow in autumn. Has small, rounded, reddish-brown fruits. Zone 6. **'Autumnalis'** has semi-double, white flowers, pink in bud, in mild periods in winter. **'Pendula Rubra'** (syn. *P. pendula* 'Pendula Rubra') illus. p.88. **'Stellata'** (syn. *P. pendula* 'Stellata', *P.* 'Pink Star') illus. p.87.

P. **'Taihaku'** illus. p.86. All Zone 7.

P. tenella illus. p.155. **'Fire Hill'** is a deciduous, bushy shrub with upright, then spreading branches. H and S 2m (6ft). Narrowly oval, glossy, dark green leaves are a foil for small, almond-like, single, very deep pink flowers borne profusely from mid- to late spring, followed by small, almond-like fruits. Zone 2.

P. tomentosa (Downy cherry). Deciduous, bushy, dense shrub. H 1.5m (5ft), S 2m (6ft). Has small, 5-petalled, pale pink flowers from early to mid-spring before oval, downy, dark green leaves appear. Fruits are spherical and bright red. Thrives in hot summers. Zone 2.

P. **'Trailblazer'**. Deciduous, spreading tree. H and S 5m (15ft). Bears

5-petalled, white flowers from early to mid-spring, sometimes followed by edible, plum-like, red fruits. Oval, light green, young leaves mature to deep red-purple. Zone 7.

P. triloba **'Multiplex'**. Deciduous, bushy, spreading tree or shrub. H and S 4m (12ft). Double, pink flowers are borne in mid-spring. Has oval, dark green leaves, often 3-lobed, that turn yellow in autumn. Does best against a sunny wall. Cut back young shoots to within a few buds of old wood after flowering. Zone 2b.

P. **'Ukon'** illus. p.86.

P. **'Uzuzakura'**. See *P.* 'Hokusai'.

P. virginiana (Virginian bird cherry). **'Shubert'** is a deciduous, conical tree. H 10m (30ft), S 8m (25ft). Produces dense spikes of small, star-shaped, white flowers from mid- to late spring, followed by dark purple-red fruits. Has oval, pale green, young leaves, turning deep reddish-purple in summer. Zone 2.

P. **'Yae-murasaki'** illus. p.88.

P. x *yedoensis* illus. p.87.

PSEUDERANTHEMUM

ACANTHACEAE

Genus of evergreen perennials and shrubs, grown mainly for their foliage. Tender, min. 16°C (61°F). Requires partial shade and fertile, well-drained soil. Water potted plants freely when in full growth, moderately at other times. Tip prune young plants to promote a bushy habit. Cut leggy plants back hard in spring. Propagate annually or biennially as a pot plant by greenwood cuttings in spring or summer. Whitefly may sometimes be troublesome.

P. atropurpureum, syn. *Eranthemum atropurpureum*. Evergreen, erect shrub. H 1–1.2m (3–4ft), S 30–60cm (1–2ft). Has oval, strongly purple-flushed leaves and, mainly in summer, short spikes of tubular, purple-marked, white flowers.

PSEUDOCYDONIA

ROSACEAE

Genus of one species of deciduous or semi-evergreen, spring-flowering tree, grown for its bark, flowers and fruits. Where hardy, best grown against a south- or west-facing wall. Requires full sun and does well only in hot summers. Needs well-drained soil. Propagate by seed in autumn.

P. sinensis, syn. *Cydonia sinensis*. Deciduous or semi-evergreen, spreading tree. H and S 6m (20ft). Has decorative, flaking bark. Shallowly cup-shaped, pink flowers, borne from mid- to late spring, are followed after hot summers by large, egg-shaped, yellow fruits. Oval, finely toothed leaves are dark green. Zone 7.

Pseudofumaria lutea. See *Corydalis lutea.*

Pseudofumaria ochroleuca. See *Corydalis ochroleuca.*

Pseudogynoxys chenopodioides. See *Senecio confusus.*

PSEUDOLARIX

PINACEAE

See also CONIFERS.

P. amabilis, syn. *P. kaempferi*, illus. p.107.

P. kaempferi. See *P. amabilis.*

Pseudolobivia aurea. See *Echinopsis aurea.*

Pseudomuscari azureum. See *Muscari azureum.*

PSEUDOPANAX,
syn. NEOPANAX, NOTHOPANAX

ARALIACEAE

Genus of evergreen trees and shrubs, grown for their unusual foliage and fruits. Is excellent for landscaping and may also be grown in large containers. Insignificant flowers are produced in summer. Grows in sun or semi-shade and in fertile, well-drained soil. Propagate by semi-ripe cuttings in summer or by seed in autumn or spring.

P. arboreus (Five fingers). Evergreen, round-headed, stout-branched tree. H 6m (20ft), S 4m (12ft). Tender, min. 2°C (35°F). Large, glossy, dark green leaves are divided into 5 or 7 oblong leaflets. Produces tiny, honey-scented, green flowers in summer, followed by rounded, purplish-black fruits on female plants.

P. crassifolius (Lancewood). Evergreen tree, unbranched for many years, then becoming round-headed. H 6m (20ft), S 2m (6ft). Marginally hardy. Dark green leaves are extremely variable in shape on young trees, but eventually become long, narrow, rigid and downward-pointing on older specimens. Female plants produce small, rounded, black fruits. Zone 9?.

P. ferox illus. p.92.

P. laetus. Evergreen, round-headed, stout-branched tree or shrub. H and S 3m (10ft). Has large, long-stalked, leathery leaves composed of 5 or 7 oblong, dark green leaflets, to 30cm (12in) long. Bears tiny, greenish-purple flowers, to 20cm (8in) across, in summer, followed by rounded, purplish-black fruits on female plants in autumn. Zone 9.

PSEUDOSASA

GRAMINEAE/POACEAE

See also GRASSES, BAMBOOS, RUSHES and SEDGES.

P. japonica, syn. *Arundinaria japonica*, illus. p.308.

PSEUDOTSUGA

PINACEAE

See also CONIFERS.

P. douglasii. See *P. menziesii.*

P. menziesii, syn. *P. douglasii*, *P. taxifolia* (Douglas fir). Fast-growing, conical conifer. H 25m (80ft), S 8–12m (25–40ft). Has thick, corky, fissured, grey-brown bark. Spirally arranged, aromatic, needle-like, slightly flattened leaves, which develop from sharply pointed buds, are dark green with white bands beneath. Elliptic cones, 8–10cm

(3–4in) long, with projecting bracts, are dull brown. **'Fletcheri'**, H 3m (10ft), S 2–3m (6–10ft), makes a flat-topped shrub. **'Fretsii'** (illus. p.110), H 6m (20ft) or more, S 3–4m (10–12ft), is slow-growing, with very short, dull green leaves. var. *glauca* illus. p.102. **'Oudemansii'** (illus. p.111) is very slow-growing, with ascending branches and short, glossy leaves, dark green all over. All Zone 4.
P. taxifolia. See *P. menziesii*.

PSEUDOWINTERA

WINTERACEAE

Genus of evergreen shrubs and trees, grown for their foliage. Tender, min. 5°C (41°F). Needs full light or partial shade and humus-rich, well-drained but moisture-retentive soil, ideally neutral to acid. Water containerized plants freely when in full growth, only moderately at other times. Pruning is tolerated if needed. Propagate by semi-ripe cuttings taken in summer or by seed when ripe, in autumn, or in spring.
P. axillaris, syn. *Drimys axillaris* (Heropito, Pepper-tree). Evergreen, rounded shrub or tree. H and S 3–8m (10–25ft). Half hardy. Has oval, lustrous, mid-green leaves, blue-grey beneath. Tiny, star-shaped, greenish-yellow flowers appear in spring-summer, followed by bright red fruits.
P. colorata, syn. *Drimys colorata.* Evergreen, bushy, spreading shrub. H 1m (3ft), S 1.5m (5ft). Has oval, leathery, pale yellow-green leaves, to 8cm (3in) long, blotched with pink and narrowly edged with deep red-purple; undersides are bluish-white. Clusters of 2–5 small, star-shaped, greenish-yellow flowers appear in mid-spring. Provide shelter in all but the mildest areas.

PSYCHOPSIS

See also ORCHIDS.
P. papilio, syn. *Oncidium papilio* (Butterfly orchid; illus. p.299). Evergreen, epiphytic orchid for a warm greenhouse. H 15cm (6in). In summer, rich yellow-marked, orange-brown flowers, 8cm (3in) long, are borne singly and in succession on tops of stems. Has oval, semi-rigid, mottled leaves, 10–15cm (4–6in) long. Grow in good light in summer.

PSYLLIOSTACHYS

Statice

PLUMBAGINACEAE

Genus of annuals, perennials and evergreen sub-shrubs, grown for cut flowers and for drying. Is suitable for coastal areas. Grow in sun and fertile, well-drained soil. If required for drying, cut flowers before they are fully open. Cut down dead stems of perennials in autumn. Propagate by seed sown under glass in early spring; perennials and sub-shrubs may also be increased by softwood cuttings in spring. Botrytis and powdery mildew may be troublesome.
P. suworowii, syn. *Limonium suworowii, Statice suworowii,* illus. p.330.

PTELEA

RUTACEAE

Genus of deciduous trees and shrubs, grown for their foliage and fruits. Requires sun and fertile soil. Propagate species by softwood cuttings in summer or by seed in autumn, selected forms by softwood cuttings only in summer.
P. trifoliata (Hop tree). Deciduous, bushy, spreading tree or shrub. H and S 7m (22ft). Produces aromatic, dark green leaves with 3 narrowly oval leaflets. Clusters of small, star-shaped, green flowers from early to mid-summer are succeeded by clusters of winged, pale green fruits. Zone 4.
'Aurea' illus. p.145.

PTERIS

ADIANTACEAE/PTERIDACEAE

Genus of deciduous, semi-evergreen or evergreen ferns. Tender, min. 5°C (41°F). Tolerates sun or shade. Grow in moist, peaty soil. Remove faded fronds regularly. Propagate by division in spring or by spores in summer.
P. cretica (Cretan brake). Evergreen or semi-evergreen fern. H 45cm (18in), S 30cm (12in). Tender, min. 5°C (41°F). Produces triangular to broadly oval, divided, pale green fronds that have finger-like pinnae. var. *albolineata* see *P.c.* 'Albolineata'. **'Albolineata'** (syn. *P.c.* var. *albolineata*) has pale green fronds centrally variegated with creamy-white. Variegated **'Mayi'**, H 30cm (12in), has crested frond tips. **'Wimsettii'** (illus p.311) is compact, with the margins of the pinnae deeply and irregularly lobed.
P. ensiformis (Snow brake). Deciduous or semi-evergreen fern. H 30cm (12in), S 23cm (9in). Dark green fronds, often greyish-white around the midribs, are coarsely divided into finger-shaped pinnae. **'Arguta'**, H 45cm (18in), has deeper green fronds with central, silver-white marks.

PTEROCARYA

Wing nut

JUGLANDACEAE

Genus of deciduous trees, grown for their foliage and catkins. Needs full sun and any deep, moist but well-drained soil. Suckers should be removed regularly. Propagate by softwood cuttings in summer or by suckers or seed, when ripe, in autumn.
P. fraxinifolia (Caucasian wing nut). Deciduous, spreading tree. H 25m (80ft), S 20m (70ft). Large, ash-like glossy, dark green leaves turn yellow in autumn. Long, green catkins are borne in summer, the females developing winged, green, then brown fruits. Zone 6.
P. x rehderiana illus. p.69.
P. stenoptera (Chinese wing nut). Deciduous, spreading tree. H 20m (70ft), S 15m (50ft). Ash-like, bright green leaves, each with a winged stalk, turn yellow in autumn. Produces long, green catkins in summer, the females developing winged, pink-tinged, green fruits. Zone 7.

PTEROCEPHALUS

DIPSACACEAE

Genus of compact, summer-flowering annuals, perennials and semi-evergreen sub-shrubs, grown for their scabious-like flower heads and feathery seed heads. Is useful for rock gardens. Requires sun and well-drained soil. Propagate by softwood or semi-ripe cuttings in summer or by seed in autumn. Self-seeds moderately.
P. parnassi. See *P. perennis.*
P. perennis, syn. *P. parnassi,* illus. p.380.

PTEROSTYRAX

STYRACACEAE

Genus of deciduous trees and shrubs, grown for their foliage and fragrant flowers. Requires sun or semi-shade and deep, well-drained, neutral to acid soil. Propagate by softwood or semi-ripe cuttings in summer or by seed in autumn.
P. hispida (Epaulette tree). Deciduous, spreading tree or shrub with aromatic grey bark. H 15m (50ft), S 12m (40ft). Has oblong to oval, mid-green leaves, 20cm (8in) long. Bears large, drooping panicles of small, bell-shaped, white flowers from early to mid-summer. Zone 6.

Ptilotrichum spinosum. See *Alyssum spinosum.*
Pudding pipe-tree. See *Cassia fistula.*

PUERARIA

LEGUMINOSAE/PAPILIONACEAE

Genus of deciduous, woody-stemmed or herbaceous, twining climbers. Grow in full sun and in any well-drained soil. Propagate by seed in spring.
P. hirsuta. See *P. lobata.*
P. lobata, syn. *P. hirsuta, P. montana* var. *lobata, P. thunbergiana* (Kudzu vine). Deciduous, invasive, woody-stemmed, twining climber with hairy stems. H to 5m (15ft) or to 30m (100ft) in the wild. Leaves have 3 broadly oval leaflets. In summer produces racemes, to 30cm (12in) long, of small, scented, sweet pea-like, reddish-purple flowers, followed by long, slender, hairy pods, 6–8cm (2½–3in) long. In cold areas is best grown as an annual. Zone 8.
P. montana var. *lobata.* See *P. lobata.*
P. thunbergiana. See *P. lobata.*

Puka. See *Meryta sinclairii,* illus. p.100.
Pukanui. See *Meryta sinclairii,* illus. p.100.
Pukapuka. See *Brachyglottis repanda,* illus. p.127.

PULMONARIA

Lungwort

BORAGINACEAE

Genus of mainly spring-flowering perennials, some of which are semi-evergreen with small, overwintering rosettes of leaves. Prefers shade; grows in any moist but well-drained soil. Propagate by division in spring

or autumn.
P. angustifolia. Clump-forming, usually deciduous perennial. H 23cm (9in), S 20–30cm (8–12in) or more. Has lance-shaped, unspotted, mid-green leaves, 40cm (16in) long. In early spring produces heads of tubular, 5-lobed, borage-like, sometimes pink-tinged, deep blue flowers.
P. longifolia. Clump-forming, deciduous perennial. H 30cm (12in), S 45cm (18in). Bears very narrowly lance-shaped, dark green leaves, to 45cm (18in), spotted with silvery white. Heads of tubular, 5-lobed, borage-like, vivid blue flowers appear in late spring.
P. **'Mawson's Blue'** illus. p.271.
P. officinalis **'Sissinghurst White'**, syn. *P. saccharata* 'Sissinghurst White', illus. p.267.
P. rubra. Semi-evergreen, clump-forming perennial. H 30cm (12in), S 60cm (24in). Has oval, velvety, mid-green leaves. Heads of tubular, 5-lobed, borage-like, brick-red flowers open from late winter to early spring.
P. saccharata illus. p.271.
'Sissinghurst White' see *P. officinalis* 'Sissinghurst White'.

PULSATILLA

RANUNCULACEAE

Genus of perennials, some of which are evergreen, grown for their large, feathery leaves, upright or pendent, bell- or cup-shaped flowers, covered in fine hairs, and feathery seed heads. Has fibrous, woody rootstocks. Leaves increase in size after flowering time. Is suitable for large rock gardens. Needs full sun and humus-rich, well-drained soil. Resents disturbance to roots. Propagate by root cuttings in winter or by seed when fresh. All parts of the plant may cause mild stomach upset if ingested, and, in rare instances, contact with the sap may irritate skin.
P. alpina illus. p.346. subsp. *apiifolia* (syn. *P.a.* subsp. *sulphurea*) is a clump-forming perennial. H 15–30cm (6–12in), S to 10cm (4in). Has feathery, soft green leaves. Bears upright, bell-shaped, soft pale yellow flowers in spring, followed by feathery, silvery seed heads. subsp. *sulphurea* see *P.a.* subsp. *apiifolia*.
P. halleri illus. p.348. subsp. *grandis* (syn. *P. vulgaris* subsp. *grandis*) is a clump-forming perennial. H and S 15–23cm (6–9in). In spring, before feathery, light green leaves appear, bears large, upright, shallowly bell-shaped, lavender-blue flowers, 5cm (2in) wide, with bright yellow centres. Flower stems rapidly elongate as feathery, silvery seed heads mature.
P. occidentalis. Clump-forming perennial. H 20cm (8in), S 15cm (6in). In late spring to early summer, solitary nodding buds develop into erect, goblet-shaped, white flowers, stained blue-violet at base outside and sometimes flushed pink, followed by feathery, silvery seed heads. Bears feathery leaves. Is extremely difficult to grow and flower well at low altitudes.
P. vernalis illus. p.363. *P. vulgaris* illus. p.348. subsp. *grandis* see *P. halleri* subsp. *grandis.*

PUNICA
Pomegranate

LYTHRACEAE/PUNICACEAE

Genus of deciduous, summer-flowering shrubs and trees, grown for their bright red flowers and yellow to orange-red fruits, which ripen and become edible only in warm climates. Needs a sheltered, sunny position and well-drained soil. Propagate by seed in spring or by semi-ripe cuttings in summer.

P. granatum. Deciduous, rounded shrub or tree. H and S 2–8m (6–25ft). Has narrowly oblong leaves and, in summer, funnel-shaped, bright red flowers, with crumpled petals. Fruits are spherical and deep yellow to orange. May be grown in a southern or eastern aspect, either free-standing or, in frost-prone climates, against a wall. Zone 9. var. *nana* illus. p.355.

Purple anise. See *Illicium floridanum*.
Purple beech. See *Fagus sylvatica* f. *purpurea*, illus. p.65.
Purple broom. See *Chamaecytisus purpureus*.
Purple crab. See *Malus* x *purpurea*.
Purple loosestrife. See *Lythrum*.
Purple mountain saxifrage. See *Saxifraga oppositifolia*, illus. p.366.
Purple osier. See *Salix purpurea*.
Purple rock brake. See *Pellaea atropurpurea*.
Purple toadflax. See *Linaria purpurea*.
Purple-leaved ivy. See *Hedera helix* 'Atropurpurea', illus. p.221.
Purple-stemmed cliff brake. See *Pellaea atropurpurea*.
Purslane, Tree. See *Atriplex halimus*.

PUSCHKINIA

LILIACEAE

Genus of dwarf, *Scilla*-like bulbs, grown for their early spring flowers. Needs sun or partial shade and humus-rich soil that has grit or sand added to ensure good drainage. Plant in autumn. Dies down in summer. Propagate by offsets in late summer or by seed in autumn.

P. libanotica. See *P. scilloides* var. *libanotica*.
P. scilloides var. **libanotica**, syn. *P. libanotica*, illus. p.432. 'Alba' illus. p.426.

Pussy ears. See *Cyanotis somaliensis*, illus. p.303; *Kalanchoe tomentosa*, illus. p.467.
Pussy toes. See *Antennaria*.
Pussy willow. See *Salix caprea*.

PUYA

BROMELIACEAE

Genus of evergreen, rosette-forming perennials and shrubs, grown for their overall appearance. Tender, min. 5–7°C (41–5°F). Requires full light and well-drained soil. Water moderately during the growing season, sparingly at other times. Propagate by seed or offsets

in spring.

P. alpestris (illus. p.265). Evergreen perennial with stout, branched, prostrate stems. H to 2m (6ft), S 3m (10ft). Linear, tapering, arching, bright green leaves are fleshy, with hooked, spiny teeth along the edges and dense, white scales beneath. Tubular, deep metallic-blue flowers, ageing to purple-red, are borne in stiff, erect panicles and are produced in early summer.
P. chilensis (illus. p.265). Evergreen, upright perennial with a short, woody stem. H and S to 2m (6ft). Stem is crowned by a dense rosette of linear, tapering, arching, fleshy, grey-green leaves with margins of hooked, spiny teeth. Bears tubular, metallic- or greenish-yellow flowers in erect, branched panicles in summer.

PYCNOSTACHYS

LABIATAE/LAMIACEAE

Genus of bushy perennials, grown for their whorled clusters of flowers. Tender, min. 15°C (59°F). Grow in bright light and in fertile, well-drained soil. Propagate by stem cuttings in early summer.

P. dawei illus. p.233.
P. urticifolia. Strong-growing, erect perennial with square stems. H 1–2m (3–6ft), S 20–60cm (8–24in). Has oval, toothed, hairy, mid-green leaves. Bears whorls of small, tubular, bright blue flowers in racemes in winter.

Pygmy date palm. See *Phoenix roebelenii*.

PYRACANTHA
Firethorn

ROSACEAE

Genus of evergreen, spiny, summer-flowering shrubs, grown for their foliage, flowers and fruits. Requires a sheltered site in sun or semi-shade and fertile soil. To produce a compact habit on a plant grown against a wall, train and cut back long shoots after flowering. Propagate by semi-ripe cuttings in summer. Is susceptible to scab and fireblight. The seeds may cause mild stomach upset if ingested.

P. angustifolia. Evergreen, bushy, dense shrub. H and S 3m (10ft). Has narrowly oblong leaves, dark green above, grey beneath. Bears clusters of small, 5-petalled, white flowers in early summer, followed by spherical, orange-yellow fruits, 8mm (⅜in) across, in autumn. Zone 5b.
P. atalantioides. Vigorous, evergreen shrub, part upright, part arching. H 5m (15ft), S 4m (12ft). Oblong leaves are glossy and dark green. Large clusters of small, 5-petalled, white flowers in early summer are followed by spherical, red fruits in early autumn. 'Aurea' illus. p.124.
P. coccinea. Evergreen, dense, bushy shrub. H and S 4m (12ft). Dense clusters of small, 5-petalled, white flowers open amid oval, dark green leaves in early summer and are succeeded by spherical, bright red fruits. 'Lalandei' has larger leaves and larger, orange-red fruits. All Zone 6.

P. 'Golden Charmer' illus. p.149.
P. 'Golden Dome' illus. p.149.
P. 'Mohave'. Vigorous, evergreen, bushy shrub. H 4m (12ft), S 5m (15ft). Produces clusters of small, 5-petalled, white flowers in early summer, then spherical, orange-red fruits. Leaves are broadly oval and dark green. Is disease-resistant. Zone 6.
P. 'Orange Glow'. Evergreen, upright, dense shrub. H 5m (15ft), S 3m (10ft). Has oblong, glossy, dark green leaves. Clusters of small, 5-petalled, white flowers, in early summer, are followed by spherical, orange fruits. Zone 6.
P. rogersiana. Evergreen, upright, then arching shrub. H and S 3m (10ft). Leaves are narrowly oblong, glossy and bright green. Produces clusters of small, 5-petalled, white flowers in early summer, followed by round, orange-red or yellow fruits. Zone 9.
P. x watereri, syn. *P.* 'Waterer's Orange', illus. p.136.
P. 'Waterer's Orange'. See *P.* x *watereri*.

Pyramidal bugle. See *Ajuga pyramidalis*.
Pyrethropsis hosmariense. See *Rhodanthemum hosmariense*.
Pyrethrum. See *Tanacetum coccineum*.
Pyrethrum 'Brenda'. See *Tanacetum coccineum* 'Brenda'.
Pyrethrum coccineum. See *Tanacetum coccineum*.
Pyrethrum parthenium. See *Tanacetum parthenium*.
Pyrethrum roseum. See *Tanacetum coccineum*.

PYROLA
Wintergreen

PYROLACEAE

Genus of evergreen, spreading, spring- and summer-flowering perennials. Needs partial shade, cool conditions and well-drained, peaty, acid soil; is best suited to light woodlands. Resents disturbance. Propagate by seed in autumn or spring or by division in spring.

P. asarifolia. Evergreen, rosette-forming perennial. H 15–25cm (6–10in), S 15cm (6in) or more. Has kidney-shaped, leathery, glossy, light green leaves. Bears open tubular, pale to deep pink flowers in spring.
P. rotundifolia (Round-leaved wintergreen, Wild lily-of-the-valley). Creeping, evergreen, rosette-forming perennial. H 23cm (9in), S 30cm (12in). Produces rounded, leathery, glossy, mid-green leaves and, in late spring and early summer, sprays of fragrant, white flowers that resemble lily-of-the-valley.

PYROSTEGIA

BIGNONIACEAE

Genus of evergreen, woody-stemmed, tendril climbers, grown for their flowers. Tender, min. 13–15°C (55–9°F). Needs full light and fertile, well-drained soil. Water regularly, less in winter. Provide support. Thin stems

after flowering. Propagate by semi-ripe cuttings or layering in summer.
P. ignea. See *P. venusta*.
P. venusta, syn. *P. ignea*, illus. p.218.

PYRUS
Pear

ROSACEAE

Genus of deciduous, spring-flowering trees, grown for their habit, foliage, flowers and edible fruits (pears). Does best in full sun and needs well-drained soil. Propagate species by seed in autumn, cultivars by budding in summer or by grafting in winter. Many species are susceptible to fireblight and scab and, in North America, pear decline.

P. amygdaliformis. Deciduous, spreading tree. H 10m (30ft), S 8m (25ft). Lance-shaped leaves are grey when young, maturing to glossy, dark green. Clusters of 5-petalled, white flowers are produced in mid-spring, and are followed by small, brownish fruits. Zone 7.
P. calleryana (Callery pear). Deciduous, broadly conical tree. H and S to 15m (50ft). Oval, glossy, dark green leaves often turn red in autumn. Bears 5-petalled, white flowers from mid- to late spring and small, brownish fruits. Zone 6. 'Bradford', S 10m (30ft), is resistant to fireblight. Zone 5b. 'Chanticleer' illus. p.76.
P. communis (Common pear). 'Beech Hill' is a deciduous, narrowly conical tree. H 10m (30ft), S 7m (22ft). Oval, glossy, dark green leaves often turn orange and red in autumn. From mid- to late spring produces 5-petalled, white flowers as the leaves emerge, followed by small, brownish fruits. Zone 6.
P. elaeagrifolia. Deciduous, spreading, thorny tree. H and S 8m (25ft). Has lance-shaped, grey-green leaves. Produces loose clusters of 5-petalled, creamy white flowers in mid-spring, followed by small, pear-shaped, brownish fruits. Zone 6.
P. salicifolia. Deciduous, mound-shaped tree with slightly drooping branches. H 5–8m (15–25ft), S 4m (12ft). White flowers, with 5 petals, open as lance-shaped, grey leaves emerge in mid-spring. Fruits are small and brownish. Zone 5. 'Pendula' illus. p.91.
P. ussuriensis (Chinese pear). A broadly conical, deciduous tree with dark green leaves that turn yellow to orange in autumn. H 12m (40ft) S 8m (25ft). White flowers in small upright racemes open in spring and become small almost spherical green fruits. Zone 2b.

Q, R

Quaking aspen. See *Populus tremuloides*.
Quaking grass. See *Briza*. **Common.** See *Briza media*.
Quamash. See *Camassia quamash*.
Quamoclit coccinea. See *Ipomoea coccinea*.
Quamoclit lobata. See *Ipomoea lobata*.
Quamoclit pennata. See *Ipomoea quamoclit*.
Quassia. See *Picrasma quassoides*, illus. p.97.
Quater. See *Vinca major*.
Queen Anne's double daffodil. See *Narcissus* 'Eystettensis'.
Queen Anne's jonquil. See *Narcissus jonquilla* 'Flore Pleno'.
Queen palm. See *Syagrus romanzoffiana*.
Queen's crape myrtle. See *Lagerstroemia speciosa*.
Queen's tears. See *Billbergia nutans*, illus. p.265.
Queencup. See *Clintonia uniflora*.
Queen-of-the-night. See *Hylocereus undatus*; *Selenicereus grandiflorus*, illus. p.456.
Queensland nut. See *Macadamia integrifolia*, illus. p.73.
Queensland pyramidal tree. See *Lagunaria patersonii*.
Queensland silver wattle. See *Acacia podalyriifolia*, illus. p.135.
Queensland umbrella tree. See *Schefflera actinophylla*, illus. p.84.

QUERCUS
Oak

FAGACEAE

Genus of deciduous or evergreen trees and shrubs, grown for their habit, foliage and, in some deciduous species, autumn colour. Produces insignificant flowers from late spring to early summer, followed by egg-shaped to rounded, brownish fruits (acorns). Does best in sun or semi-shade and in deep, well-drained soil. Except where stated otherwise, will tolerate limestone. Propagate species by seed in autumn, selected forms and hybrids by grafting in late winter. May be affected, though not usually seriously, by mildew, various galls, and oak wilt.
Q. acutissima (Sawtooth oak). Deciduous, round-headed tree. H and S 15m (50ft). Has sweet-chestnut-like, glossy, dark green leaves, edged with bristle-tipped teeth, that last until late in the year. Zone 6.
Q. aegilops. See *Q. macrolepis*.
Q. agrifolia illus. p.85.
Q. alba illus. p.71.
Q. aliena (Oriental white oak). Deciduous, spreading tree. H 15m (50ft), S 12m (40ft). Has large, oblong, prominently toothed, glossy, dark green leaves. Zone 7.
Q. bicolor (Swamp white oak). Deciduous spreading tree H 20m (70ft), S 15m (50ft). Has glossy, dark green, shallowly lobed leaves that turn orange

to red in fall. Bark is gray-brown and peels in flakes. Zone 4b.
Q. canariensis illus. p.66.
Q. castaneifolia illus. p.68.
Q. cerris (Turkey oak). Fast-growing, deciduous, spreading tree of stately habit. H 30m (100ft), S 25m (80ft). Oblong, glossy, dark green leaves are deeply lobed. Thrives on shallow, alkaline soil. Zone 6.
'Argenteovariegata' (syn. *Q.c.* 'Variegata') illus. p.78.
Q. coccifera (Kermes oak). Evergreen, bushy, compact tree or shrub. H and S 5m (15ft). Holly-like leaves are glossy, dark green and rigid with spiny margins. Zone 8.
Q. coccinea illus. p.70. **'Splendens'** is a deciduous, round-headed tree. H 20m (70ft), S 15m (50ft). Has oblong, glossy, mid-green leaves, with deep, tooth-like lobes, that turn deep scarlet in autumn. Prefers acid soil. Zone 4b.
Q. dentata (Daimio oak). Deciduous, spreading, stout-branched tree of rugged habit. H 15m (50ft), S 10m (30ft). Has oval, lobed, dark green leaves, 30cm (12in) or more long. Prefers acid soil. Zone 7.
Q. ellipsoidalis illus. p.70.
Q. frainetto illus. p.69.
Q. garryana illus. p.80.
Q. x *heterophylla* illus. p.82.
Q. x *hispanica* 'Lucombeana', syn. *Q.* x *lucombeana* 'William Lucombe', illus. p.73.
Q. ilex (Holm oak). Evergreen, round-headed tree. H 25m (80ft), S 20m (70ft). Glossy, dark green leaves are silvery-grey when young and very variably shaped, but are most often oval. Thrives on shallow chalk and is excellent for an exposed, coastal position. Zone 8.
Q. imbricaria (Shingle oak). Deciduous, spreading tree. H 20m (70ft), S 15m (50ft). Bears long, narrow leaves that are yellowish when young, dark green in summer and yellowish-brown in autumn. Zone 4b.
Q. ithaburensis subsp. *macrolepis.* See *Q. macrolepis*.
Q. laurifolia illus. p.69.
Q. x *lucombeana* **'William Lucombe'.** See *Q.* x *hispanica* 'Lucombeana'.
Q. macranthera illus. p.66.
Q. macrocarpa illus. p.80.
Q. macrolepis, syn. *Q. aegilops*, *Q. ithaburensis* subsp. *macrolepis*, illus. p.80.
Q. marilandica illus. p.80.
Q. mongolica var. *grosseserrata.* Deciduous, spreading tree. H 20m (70ft), S 15m (50ft). Has large, oblong, lobed, dark green leaves with prominent, triangular teeth. Zone 6.
Q. muehlenbergii illus. p.67.
Q. myrsinifolia illus. p.84.
Q. nigra illus. p.68.
Q. palustris illus. p.69.
Q. petraea (Durmast oak, Sessile oak). Deciduous, spreading tree. H 30m (100ft), S 25m (80ft). Has oblong, lobed, leathery, dark green leaves with

yellow stalks. Zone 4b. **'Columna'** illus. p.68.
Q. phellos illus. p.71.
Q. prinus (Chestnut oak, basket oak). Deciduous, rounded tree. H and S 18m (60ft). The shiny, dark green leaves are gray-woolly beneath and turn yellow in fall. Zone 5.
Q. robur (English oak, Pedunculate oak). Deciduous, spreading, rugged tree. H and S 25m (80ft). Bears oblong, wavy, lobed, dark green leaves. Zone 5.
'Concordia', H 10m (30ft), is slow-growing and has golden-yellow, young foliage that becomes yellowish-green in mid-summer. Zone 4. f. *fastigiata* illus. p.66.
Q. rubra illus. p.69. **'Aurea'** illus. p.80.
Q. suber illus. p.73.
Q. x *turneri* illus. p.73.
Q. velutina (Black oak). Fast-growing, deciduous, spreading tree. H 30m (100ft), S 25m (80ft). Large, oblong, lobed, glossy, dark green leaves turn reddish-brown in autumn. Zone 5.

Quince. See *Cydonia oblonga*. **Flowering.** See *Chaenomeles*. **Japanese.** See *Chaenomeles japonica*.

QUISQUALIS

COMBRETACEAE

Genus of evergreen or deciduous, scandent shrubs and twining climbers, grown for their flowers. Tender, min. 10–18˚C (50–64˚F). Provide humus-rich, moist but well-drained soil and full light or semi-shade. Water freely when in full growth, less in cold weather. Stems need support. Thin out crowded growth in spring. Propagate by seed in spring or by semi-ripe cuttings in summer.
Q. indica illus. p.211.

Rabbit tracks. See *Maranta leuconeura* var. *kerchoviana*, illus. p.304.
Rain daisy. See *Dimorphotheca pluvialis*, illus. p.319.
Rain lily. See *Zephyranthes*.
Rainbow star. See *Cryptanthus bromelioides*.
Raisin-tree. See *Hovenia dulcis*, illus. p.79.

RAMONDA

GESNERIACEAE

Genus of evergreen perennials, grown for their rosettes of rounded, crinkled, hairy leaves and for their flowers. Is useful for rock gardens and peat walls. Prefers shade and moist soil. Water plants well if they curl in a dry spell. Propagate by rooting offsets in early summer or by leaf cuttings or seed in early autumn.

R. myconi, syn. *R. pyrenaica*, illus. p.382.
R. nathaliae. Evergreen, basal-rosetted perennial. H and S 10cm (4in). Has small, pale green leaves and, in late spring and early summer, bears umbels of small, outward-facing, flattish, white or lavender flowers, with yellow anthers.
R. pyrenaica. See *R. myconi*.
R. serbica. Evergreen, basal-rosetted perennial. H and S0 10cm (4in). Is similar to *R. nathaliae*, but has cup-shaped, lilac-blue flowers and dark violet-blue anthers. May be difficult to grow.

Ram's horn. See *Proboscidea louisianica*.
Rangiora. See *Brachyglottis repanda*, illus. p.127.
Rangoon creeper. See *Quisqualis indica*, illus. p.211.

RANUNCULUS
Buttercup

RANUNCULACEAE

Genus of annuals, aquatics and perennials, some of which are evergreen or semi-evergreen, grown mainly for their flowers. Many species grow from a thickened rootstock or a cluster of tubers. Some are invasive. Aquatic species are seldom cultivated. Grows in sun or shade and in moist but well-drained soil. Propagate by seed when fresh or by division in spring or autumn. Contact with the sap may irritate skin.
R. aconitifolius and **'Flore Pleno'** illus. p.233.
R. acris (Meadow buttercup). **'Flore Pleno'** illus. p.292.
R. alpestris illus. p.363.
R. amplexicaulis. Upright perennial. H 25cm (10in), S 10cm (4in). Has narrowly oval, blue-grey leaves. In early summer produces clusters of shallowly cup-shaped, white flowers with yellow anthers. Needs humus-rich soil.
R. aquatilis (Water crowfoot). Aquatic annual or usually evergreen perennial. H 1cm (½in), S indefinite. Submerged, branched, slender stems bear dark green leaves, these having many thread-like segments; the floating leaves are kidney-shaped to rounded, deeply divided into 3–7 lobes. In mid-summer, produces solitary, bowl- or saucer-shaped, white-based yellow flowers, 1cm (½in) across, on the surface.
R. asiaticus [red form] illus. p.421, [yellow form] illus. p.423.
R. bulbosus **'Speciosus Plenus'** of gardens. See *R. constantinopolitanus* 'Plenus'.
R. bullatus. Clump-forming perennial with thick, fibrous roots. H 5–8cm (2–3in), S 8–10cm (3–4in). Produces fragrant, shallowly cup-shaped, bright yellow flowers in autumn above neat mounds of foliage. Oblong to oval,

green leaves have sharply toothed tips and are puckered. Suits an alpine house or rock garden.

R. calandrinioides illus. p.360.

***R. constantinopolitanus* 'Plenus'**, syn. *R. bulbosus* 'Speciosus Plenus' of gardens, *R. gouanii* 'Plenus', *R. speciosus* 'Plenus', illus. p.292.

R. crenatus. Semi-evergreen, rosetted perennial with thick, fibrous roots. H and S 10cm (4in). Produces rounded, toothed, green leaves and, in summer, short stems bearing 1 or 2 shallowly cup-shaped, white flowers just above foliage. May also be propagated by removing a flower stem at its first joint in summer; rosettes will form and may then be rooted. Rarely sets seed in cultivation. Suits an alpine house or rock garden.

R. ficaria (Lesser celandine). **'Albus'** illus. p.363. **'Aurantiacus'** illus. p.373. **'Brazen Hussy'** is a mat-forming, tuberous perennial. H 5cm (2in), S to 20cm (8in). Is grown for its heart-shaped, purple-bronze leaves produced in spring. Shallowly cup-shaped, glossy, sulphur-yellow flowers, with bronze reverses, appear in early spring. All *R. ficaria* forms die down in late spring. May spread rapidly; is good for a wild garden. **'Flore Pleno'** illus. p.372.

R. glacialis. Hummock-forming perennial with fibrous roots. H 5–25cm (2–10in), S 5cm (2in) or more. Bears rounded, deeply lobed, glossy, dark green leaves and, in late spring and early summer, clusters of shallowly cup-shaped, white or pink flowers. Is very difficult to grow at low altitudes. Suits a scree or alpine house. Prefers humus-rich, moist, acid soil that is drier in winter. Slugs may be troublesome.

***R. gouanii* 'Plenus'.** See *R. constantinopolitanus* 'Plenus'.

R. gramineus illus. p.359.

R. lingua illus. p.451. **'Grandiflorus'** is a deciduous, perennial, marginal water plant. H 1m (3ft), S 30cm (1ft). Has stout, pinkish-green stems, lance-shaped, glaucous leaves and, in late spring, racemes of large, saucer-shaped, yellow flowers.

R. lyallii (Giant buttercup). Evergreen, stout, upright, tufted perennial. H and S 30cm (12in) or more. Has rounded, leathery, dark green leaves, each 15cm (6in) or more across, and, in summer, bears panicles of large, shallowly cup-shaped, white flowers. Is very difficult to flower in hot, dry climates. Is suitable for an alpine house. Rarely sets seed in cultivation.

***R. montanus* 'Molten Gold'.** Clump-forming, compact perennial. H 15cm (6in), S 10cm (4in). Leaves are rounded and 3-lobed. Flower stems each produce a shallowly cup-shaped, shiny, bright golden-yellow flower in early summer. Is useful for a sunny rock garden.

***R. speciosus* 'Plenus'.** See *R. constantinopolitanus* 'Plenus'.

RANZANIA

BERBERIDACEAE

Genus of one species of perennial, grown for its unusual appearance as well as its flowers. Is ideal for

woodland gardens. Prefers shade or semi-shade and humus-rich, moist soil. Propagate by division in spring or by seed in autumn.

R. japonica. Upright perennial. H 45cm (18in), S 30cm (12in). Produces 3-parted, fresh green leaves and, in early summer, small clusters of nodding, shallowly cup-shaped, pale mauve flowers.

RAOULIA

ASTERACEAE/COMPOSITAE

Genus of evergreen, mat-forming perennials, grown for their foliage. Some species are suitable for alpine houses, others for rock gardens. Needs sun or semi-shade and gritty, moist but well-drained, peaty soil. Propagate by seed when fresh or by division in spring.

R. australis illus. p.390.

R. eximia. Evergreen, cushion-forming perennial. H 2.5cm (1in), S 5cm (2in). Has oblong to oval, overlapping, woolly, grey leaves and, in late spring-summer, small, rounded heads of yellowish-white flowers. Suits an alpine house. Prefers some shade.

R. haastii illus. p.391.

R. hookeri var. ***albo-sericea*** illus. p.389.

R. leontopodium. See *Leucogenes leontopodium*.

Raspberry, Flowering. See *Rubus odoratus*.

Rat's-tail cactus. See *Aporocactus flagelliformis*, illus. p.463.

Rata. See *Metrosideros robustus*.

Rauli. See *Nothofagus procera*, illus. p.67.

RAVENALA

STRELITZIACEAE

Genus of one species of evergreen, palm-like tree, grown for its foliage and overall appearance. Is related to *Strelitzia*. Tender, min. 16°C (61°F). Requires full light and humus-rich, well-drained soil. Water potted specimens freely in summer, less in winter or when temperatures are low. Propagate by seed in spring. Spider mite may be troublesome.

R. madagascariensis (Traveller's tree). Evergreen, upright, fan-shaped tree. H and S to 10m (30ft). Has banana-like, long-stalked leaves, each 3–6m (10–20ft) long, with expanded stalk bases. Groups of boat-shaped spathes with 6-parted, white flowers emerge from leaf axils in summer.

REBUTIA

CACTACEAE

Genus of mostly clump-forming, spherical to columnar, perennial cacti. Produces flowers in profusion from plant bases, usually 2–3 years after raising from seed. Much-ribbed, tuberculate, green stems have short spines. A few species are sometimes included in *Aylostera*. Tender, min. 5–10°C (41–50°F). Requires a position in sun or partial shade and well-drained soil. Is easy to grow. Propagate by seed in spring or summer.

R. arenacea, syn. *Sulcorebutia arenacea*, illus. p.480.

R. aureiflora illus. p.480.

R. fiebrigii, syn. *R. muscula*, illus. p.480.

R. krainziana illus. p.474.

R. minuscula, syn. *R. violaciflora*, illus. p.472

R. muscula. See *R. fiebrigii*.

R. neocumingii, syn. *Weingartia neocumingii*. Spherical, perennial cactus. H and S 10cm (4in). Stem is tuberculate and green. Areoles bear dense clusters of yellow spines, 1.5cm (⅝in) long, some thicker than others, and several cup-shaped, dark yellow flowers, 3cm (¼in) long, in spring.

R. pygmaea, syn. *Lobivia pygmaea*. Clump-forming, columnar, perennial cactus. H 5cm (2in), S 10cm (4in). Very short, comb-like spines are pressed against grey- to purple-green stem. Trumpet-shaped, pink to salmon or rose-purple flowers, to 2cm (¾in) across, appear in spring. Prefers a sunny position.

R. rauschii, syn. *Sulcorebutia rauschii*. Flattened spherical, perennial cactus. H 5cm (2in), S 10cm (4in). Grey-green stem bears very short, comb-like, golden or black spines. Bears flattish, 3cm (1¼) wide, deep purple flowers in spring. Grows better when grafted.

R. senilis. Clump-forming, perennial cactus. H 5cm (2in), S 15cm (6in). Has soft, white spines, 3cm (1¼in) long, matted around a 5cm (2in) wide stem. In spring bears trumpet-shaped, red, yellow, pink, or orange flowers, 5cm (2in) across. Prefers a sunny site.

R. spegazziniana illus. p.475.

R. tiraquensis, syn. *Sulcorebutia tiraquensis*, illus. p.474.

R. violaciflora. See *R. minuscula*.

Red ash. See *Fraxinus pennsylvanica*.

Red baneberry. See *Actaea rubra*.

Red chokeberry. See *Aronia arbutifolia*, illus. p.130.

Red horse-chestnut. See *Aesculus* x *carnea*.

Red maple. See *Acer rubrum*, illus. p.70.

Red morning glory. See *Ipomoea coccinea*.

Red mountain spinach. See *Atriplex hortensis* var. *rubra*.

Red oak. See *Quercus rubra*, illus. p.69.

Red orach. See *Atriplex hortensis* var. *rubra*.

Red orchid cactus. See *Nopalxochia ackermannii*.

Red passion flower. See *Passiflora coccinea*, illus. p.205; *Passiflora racemosa*.

Red pineapple. See *Ananas bracteatus*.

Red rose of Lancaster. See *R. gallica* var. *officinalis*.

Spider lily. See *Lycoris radiata*, illus. p.420.

Red spike. See *Cephalophyllum alstonii*, illus. p.474.

Red valerian. See *Centranthus ruber*, illus. p.245.

Red-and-green kangaroo paw. See *Anigozanthos manglesii*, illus. p.250.

Red-barked dogwood. See *Cornus alba*.

Red-berried elder. See *Sambucus racemosa*.

Redbird flower. See *Pedilanthus tithymaloides* 'Variegata', illus. p.459.

Redbud. See *Cercis*.
  Eastern. See *Cercis canadensis*.

Red-hot cat's tail. See *Acalypha hispida*.

Red-hot poker. See *Kniphofia*; *K. uvaria*.

Red-ink plant. See *Phytolacca americana*.

Redwood. See *Sequoia sempervirens*.
  Coast. See *Sequoia sempervirens*.
  Dawn. See *Metasequoia glyptostroboides*, illus. p.102.
  Giant. See *Sequoiadendron giganteum*, illus. p.102.

Reed
  Branched bur. See *Sparganium erectum*, illus. p.449.
  Bur. See *Sparganium*.
  Giant. See *Arundo donax*.
  Least bur. See *Sparganium natans*.
  Paper. See *Cyperus papyrus*, illus. p.307.

Reflexed stonecrop. See *Sedum rupestre*, illus. p.359.

Regal lily. See *Lilium regale*, illus. p.404.

REHDERODENDRON

STYRACACEAE

Genus of deciduous, spring-flowering trees, grown for their flowers and fruits. Needs sun or semi-shade, some shelter and fertile, moist, but well-drained, acid soil. Propagate by semi-ripe cuttings in summer or by seed in autumn.

R. macrocarpum. Deciduous, spreading tree. H 10m (30ft), S 7m (22ft). Young shoots are red. Pendent clusters of lemon-scented, cup-shaped, pink-tinged, white flowers are borne amid oblong, taper-pointed, red-stalked, glossy, dark green leaves in late spring. Bears cylindrical, woody, red, then brown fruits in autumn. Zone 9.

REHMANNIA

SCROPHULARIACEAE

Genus of spring- and summer-flowering perennials. Tender, min. 1–5°C (34–41°F). Needs a warm, sunny position and light soil. Propagate by seed in autumn or spring or by root cuttings in winter.

R. angulata of gardens. See *R. elata*.

R. elata, syn. *R. angulata* of gardens, illus. p.244.

R. glutinosa. Rosette-forming perennial. H 30cm (12in), S 25cm (10in). Tubular, pink, red-brown or yellow flowers, with purple veins, are borne on leafy shoots in late spring and early summer. Leaves are oval to lance-shaped, toothed, hairy, and light green.

REINWARDTIA

LINACEAE

Genus of evergreen sub-shrubs, grown for their flowers. Tender, min. 7–10°C

(45–50˚F). Needs full light or partial shade and fertile, well-drained soil. Water freely when growing, moderately at other times. Tip prune young plants to promote branching; cut back hard after flowering. Raise softwood cuttings annually in late spring. Spider mite may cause problems.
R. indica, syn. *R. trigyna*, illus. p.170.
R. trigyna. See *R. indica*.

RESEDA
Mignonette

RESEDACEAE

Genus of annuals and biennials with flowers that attract bees and that are also suitable for cutting. Grow in a sunny position and in any fertile, well-drained soil. Dead-heading regularly ensures a prolonged flowering period. Propagate by sowing seed outdoors in spring or early autumn.
R. odorata illus. p.319.

Restharrow
  Large yellow. See *Ononis natrix*, illus. p.359.
  Shrubby. See *Ononis fruticosa*, illus. p.353.
Resurrection lily. See *Lycoris squamigera*.
Resurrection plant. See *Selaginella lepidophylla*.
Retama monosperma. See *Genista monosperma*.
Rewa rewa. See *Knightia excelsa*.
Rex begonia vine. See *Cissus discolor*.
Reynoutria. Reclassified as *Fallopia*.

RHAMNUS
Buckthorn

RHAMNACEAE

Genus of deciduous or evergreen shrubs and trees, with inconspicuous flowers, grown mainly for their foliage and fruits. Requires sun or semi-shade and fertile soil. Propagate deciduous species by seed in autumn, evergreen species by semi-ripe cuttings in summer. All parts may cause severe discomfort if ingested.
R. alaternus (Italian buckthorn). '**Argenteovariegata**' is an evergreen, bushy shrub. H and S 3m (10ft). Has oval, leathery, glossy, grey-green leaves edged with creamy-white. Tiny, yellowish-green flowers are produced from early to mid-summer and followed by spherical, red, then black fruits. Zone 8.
R. frangula (Alder buckthorn). Deciduous, spreading, open shrub. H and S 5m (15ft). Has oval, glossy, dark green leaves that turn red in fall. Small green flowers in summer are followed by spherical red fruit that turn black. Zone 3b. '**Asplenifolia**' has leaves that are much dissected and irregularly scalloped. Zone 3b.

RHAPHIOLEPIS

ROSACEAE

Genus of evergreen shrubs, grown for their flowers and foliage. In most areas does best against a sheltered wall; *R. umbellata* is the most hardy. Needs

sun and fertile, well-drained soil. Propagate by semi-ripe cuttings in late summer.
R. × *delacourii* '**Coates' Crimson**'. Evergreen, rounded shrub. H 2m (6ft), S 2.5m (8ft). Clusters of fragrant, star-shaped, deep pink flowers, produced in spring or summer, are set off by the oval, leathery, dark green leaves. Zone 9.
R. indica (Indian hawthorn). Evergreen, bushy shrub. H 1.5m (5ft), S 2m (6ft). Clusters of fragrant, star-shaped, white flowers, flushed with pink, are borne in spring or early summer amid narrowly lance-shaped, glossy, dark green leaves. Zone 9.
R. japonica. See *R. umbellata*.
R. ovata. See *R. umbellata*.
R. umbellata, syn. *R. japonica*, *R. ovata*, illus. p.160.

RHAPIS

ARECACEAE/PALMAE

Genus of evergreen fan palms, grown for their foliage and overall appearance. May have tiny, yellow flowers in summer. Tender, min. 15˚C (59˚F). Needs partial shade and humus-rich, well-drained soil. Water containerized specimens freely when growing, moderately at other times. Propagate by seed, suckers or division in spring. Is susceptible to spider mite.
R. excelsa, syn. *R. flabelliformis*, illus. p.152.
R. flabelliformis. See *R. excelsa*.

Rhazya orientalis. See *Amsonia orientalis*.

RHEUM
Rhubarb

POLYGONACEAE

Genus of perennials, grown for their foliage and striking overall appearance. Includes the edible rhubarb and various ornamental plants. Some species are extremely large and require plenty of space. Prefers sun or semi-shade and deep, rich, well-drained soil. Propagate by division in spring or by seed in autumn. Leaves may cause severe discomfort if ingested.
R. nobile. Clump-forming perennial. H 1.5m (5ft), S 1m (3ft). Leaves are oblong to oval, leathery, basal, mid-green, 60cm (2ft) long. In late summer produces long stems and conical spikes of large, overlapping, pale cream bracts that hide insignificant flowers.
R. palmatum. Clump-forming perennial. H and S 2m (6ft). Has 60–75cm (2–2½ft) long, rounded, 5-lobed, mid-green leaves. In early summer produces broad panicles of small, creamy-white flowers.
'**Atrosanguineum**' illus. p.227.

Rhipsalidopsis gaertneri. See *Hatiora gaertneri*.
Rhipsalidopsis rosea. See *Hatiora rosea*.

RHIPSALIS
Mistletoe cactus

CACTACEAE

Genus of epiphytic, perennial cacti with usually pendent, variously formed stems. Flowers are followed by spherical, translucent berries. Tender, min. 10–11˚C (50–52˚F). Needs partial shade and rich, well-drained soil. Prefers 80% relative humidity – higher than for most cacti. Give only occasional, very light watering in winter. Propagate by seed or stem cuttings in spring or summer.
R. capilliformis. Pendent, perennial cactus. H 1m (3ft), S 50cm (20in). Min. 10˚C (50˚F). Has freely branching, cylindrical, green stems and, in winter-spring, short, funnel-shaped, white flowers, to 1cm (½in) wide, with recurved tips, then white berries.
R. cereuscula illus. p.461.
R. clavata. See *Hatiora clavata*.
R. crispata. Bushy, then pendent, perennial cactus. H 1m (3ft), S indefinite. Min. 11˚C (52˚F). Has leaf-like, elliptic to oblong, pale green stem segments, to 12cm (5in) long, with undulating edges that produce short, funnel-shaped, cream or pale yellow flowers, to 1cm (½in) across, with recurved tips, in winter-spring, then white berries.
R. floccosa, syn. *R. tucumanensis*, illus. p.461.
R. paradoxa (Chain cactus). Bushy, then pendent, perennial cactus. H 1m (3ft), S indefinite. Min. 11˚C (52˚F). Triangular, green stems have segments alternately set at different angles. Short, funnel-shaped, white flowers, 2cm (¾in) across, with recurved tips, appear from stem edges in winter-spring and are followed by red berries.
R. salicornioides. See *Hatiora salicornioides*.
R. tucumanensis. See *R. floccosa*.
R. warmingiana. See *Lepismium warmingianum*.

RHODANTHE,
syn. ACROCLINIUM
Strawflower

ASTERACEAE/COMPOSITAE

Genus of drought-tolerant annuals, perennials and sub-shrubs, grown for their daisy-like, papery flower heads, which are excellent for cutting and drying. Grow in sun and in poor, very well-drained soil. Propagate by seed sown outdoors in mid-spring. Aphids may cause problems.
R. chlorocephala subsp. *rosea*, syn. *Acroclinium roseum*, *Helipterum roseum*, illus. p.321.
R. manglesii, syn. *Helipterum manglesii*, illus. p.321.

RHODANTHEMUM

ASTERACEAE/COMPOSITAE

Genus of mat-forming, often rhizomatous perennials and sub-shrubs, grown for their solitary, large, daisy-like, white flower heads, surrounded by prominent, usually green bracts. Needs full sun and moderately fertile, very well-drained soil. Propagate by

seed in spring or by softwood cuttings in summer.
R. hosmariense, syn. *Chrysanthemum hosmariense*, *Pyrethropsis hosmariense*, illus. p.346.

RHODIOLA

CRASSULACEAE

Genus of perennials, some dioecious, with thick, fleshy rhizomes producing scaly, brown basal leaves and stiffly erect stems that bear triangular-oval to lance-shaped, fleshy, grey-green leaves. Star-shaped flowers have prominent stamens, and may be unisexual or bisexual. Grow in full sun and moderately fertile soil. Propagate by seed in spring or autumn, divide rhizomes in spring or early summer or take leaf cuttings in summer.
R. heterodonta, syn. *Sedum heterodontum*, *S. rosea* var. *heterodontum*, illus. p.293.
R. rosea, syn. *Sedum rosea* (Roseroot). Clump-forming perennial. H and S 30cm (12in). Stems are clothed with oval to inversely lance-shaped, toothed, fleshy, glaucous leaves and, in late spring or early summer, bear dense, terminal heads of pink buds that open to small, star-shaped, greenish-, yellowish- or purplish-white flowers.

Rhodocactus grandifolius. See *Pereskia grandifolia*.

RHODOCHITON

SCROPHULARIACEAE

Genus of one species of evergreen, leaf-stalk climber, grown for its unusual flowers. Does best when grown as an annual. May be planted against fences and trellises or used as ground cover. Tender, min. 5˚C (41˚F). Grow in sun and in any well-drained soil. Propagate by seed in early spring.
R. atrosanguineus, syn. *R. volubilis*, illus. p.211.
R. volubilis. See *R. atrosanguineus*.

RHODODENDRON
Azalea, Rhododendron

ERICACEAE

Genus of evergreen, semi-evergreen or deciduous shrubs, ranging from a dwarf habit to a tree-like stature, grown mainly for beauty of flower. Hardy unless noted otherwise. Most prefer dappled shade, but a considerable number tolerates full sun, especially in cool climates. Needs neutral to acid soil – ideally, humus-rich and well-drained. Shallow planting is essential, as plants are surface-rooting. Dead-head spent flowers, wherever practical, to encourage energy into growth rather than seed production. Propagate by layering or semi-ripe cuttings in late summer. Yellowing leaves are usually caused by poor drainage, excessively deep planting or lime in soil. Weevils and powdery mildew may also cause problems. The nectar of some rhododendron flowers may cause severe discomfort if ingested. See also feature panel pp.132-4.

Rhododendrons and azaleas
The genus *Rhododendron* includes not only evergreen, large-leaved and frequently large-flowered species and hybrids, but also dwarf, smaller-leaved shrubs, both evergreen and deciduous, with few-flowered clusters of usually small blooms. 'Azalea' is the common name given to the deciduous species and hybrids as well as to a group of compact, evergreen shrubs derived mainly from Japanese species. They are valued for their mass of small colourful blooms produced in late spring. Many of the evergreen azaleas (sometimes known as Belgian azaleas) may also be grown as house plants. Botanically, however, all are classified as *Rhododendron*. The flowers are usually single, but may be semi-double or double, including hose-in-hose (one flower tube inside the other). Unless otherwise stated below, flowers are single and leaves are mid- to dark green and oval.

R. albrechtii. Deciduous, upright, bushy azalea. H to 3m (10ft), S 2m (6ft). Has spoon-shaped leaves, clustered at branch tips, and, in spring, loose clusters of 3–5 bell-shaped, green-spotted, purple or pink flowers. Zone 6.

R. 'America'. Sprawling, evergreen rhododendron. H 1.5m (5ft), S 2m (6ft). Leaves are broadly oval. Produces compact trusses of bell-shaped, dark red flowers in spring. Zone 5.

R. 'Angelo'. Evergreen, bushy rhododendron. H and S to 4m (12ft). Has bold foliage and large, fragrant, bell-shaped, white flowers in mid-summer, good in light woodland. Zone 7.

R. 'Anna H. Hall'. Small, bushy, evergreen rhododendron. H 1m (3ft), S 1.2m (4ft). Narrow leaves with a brown indumentum on the new foliage. Flowers are in trusses of about 15 blooms with bright pink buds that open white in mid spring. Zone 5b.

R. 'Apricot Surprise'. Deciduous bushy azalea. H and S 1.2–1.5m (4–5ft). Apricot flowers with a yellow throat are produced in early summer. Foliage turns a coppery shade in fall. Zone 4.

R. arboreum (illus. p.133). Evergreen, tree-like rhododendron. H to 12m (40ft), S 3m (10ft). Undersides of broadly lance-shaped leaves are silver, fawn or cinnamon. In spring has dense clusters of bell-shaped flowers in colours ranging from red (most tender form) through pink to white. Zone 9.

R. argyrophyllum (illus. p.132). Evergreen, spreading rhododendron. H and S to 5m (15ft). Oblong leaves are silvery-white on undersides. Loose bunches of bell-shaped, rich pink flowers, sometimes with deeper coloured spots, are borne in spring. Is ideal for a light woodland. Zone 7.

R. augustinii (illus. p.133). Evergreen, bushy rhododendron. H and S to 4m (12ft). Has lance-shaped to oblong, light green leaves and, in spring, bears an abundance of multi-stemmed, widely funnel-shaped, pale to deep blue or lavender flowers. Zone 8.

R. auriculatum (illus. p.132). Evergreen, bushy, widely branching rhododendron. H and S to 6m (20ft).

Has large, oblong, hairy leaves with distinct, ear-like lobes at their base. In late summer bears loose bunches of 7–15 large, heavily scented, tubular to funnel-shaped, white flowers. Is best in light woodland. Zone 7.

R. 'Azuma-kagami' (illus. p.132). Evergreen, compact azalea. H and S 1.2m (4ft). Bears many small, hose-in-hose, deep pink flowers in mid-spring. Is best in semi-shade. Zone 7.

R. 'Beauty of Littleworth' (illus. p.132). Evergreen, open, shrubby rhododendron. H and S 4m (12ft). . Bears huge, conical bunches of scented, funnel-shaped, crimson-spotted, white flowers in late spring. Zone 7.

R. 'Belle Heller'. A vigorous, evergreen rhododendron. H and S 1.5m (5ft). Has dense, conical trusses of white flowers with a gold flair. Does well in sun and may rebloom in fall in mild regions. Zone 6.

R. 'Besse Howells'. Compact, evergreen rhododendron. H and S 1.2m (4ft). Has ruffled burgundy red flowers with a darker blotch in globe-shaped trusses in early summer. Zone 5.

R. 'Blue Diamond'. Evergreen, upright rhododendron. H and S to 1.5m (5ft). Small, neat leaves contrast with funnel-shaped, bright blue flowers borne in mid- to late spring. Likes full sun. Zone 6.

R. 'Blue Ensign'. Medium-sized, evergreen rhododendron. H 1.2m (4ft), S 1.5m (5ft). Has pale lavender flowers with a prominent darker blotch in rounded trusses of 15 blooms in early summer. Zone 6.

R. 'Blue Peter' (illus. p.133). Evergreen, bushy rhododendron. H and S to 4m (12ft). In early summer produces bold, open funnel-shaped, 2-tone lavender-purple flowers with frilled petal edges. Zone 5.

R. calendulaceum (Flame azalea). Deciduous, bushy azalea. H and S 2–3m (6–10ft). In early summer bears funnel-shaped, scarlet or orange flowers in bunches of 5–7.

R. calophytum (illus. p.132). Evergreen, widely-branched rhododendron. H and S to 6m (20ft). Produces large, lance-shaped leaves and, in early spring, huge bunches of bell-shaped, white or pale pink flowers with crimson spots. Zone 6.

R. calostrotum (illus. p.133). Evergreen, compact rhododendron. H and S to 1m (3ft). Has attractive, blue-green leaves and, in late spring, saucer-shaped, purple or scarlet flowers in clusters of 2–5. Zone 7.

R. 'Catawbiense Album'. Evergreen, rounded rhododendron. H and S to 3m (10ft). Bears glossy leaves and, in early summer, dense, rounded bunches of bell-shaped, white flowers. Zone 4b.

R. 'Catawbiense Boursault'. Evergreen, rounded rhododendron. H and S to 3m (10ft). Has glossy leaves. Dense, rounded bunches of bell-shaped, lilac-purple blooms are borne in early summer. Zone 4b.

R. 'Chionoides'. Dense, evergreen rhododendron with narrow foliage. H 1.2m (4ft), S 1.5m (5ft). Flowers are in dome-shaped trusses, white with a yellow eye. Zone 6.

R. 'Cilpinense', syn. *R.* x *cilpinense*. Semi-evergreen, compact rhododendron. H and S to 1.5m (5ft). Leaves are dark green and glossy. Bears masses of large, bell-shaped, blush-pink flowers, flushed deeper in bud, in early spring that are vulnerable to frost damage. Zone 8.

R. cinnabarinum (illus. p.133). Evergreen, upright rhododendron. H and S 1.5–4m (5–12ft). Has blue-green leaves with small scales. Narrowly tubular, waxy, orange to red flowers are borne in loose, drooping bunches in late spring. Zone 6.
subsp. *xanthocodon* (syn. *R. xanthocodon*; illus. p.133) is of open, upright habit. H and S 1.5–4m (5–12ft). Aromatic leaves are blue-green when young, maturing to mid-green. Produces loose clusters of bell-shaped, waxy, yellow flowers during late spring. Zone 6b.

R. 'Coccineum Speciosum'. Deciduous, bushy azalea. H and S 1.5–2.5m (5–8ft). Produces open funnel-shaped, brilliant rich orange-red blooms in early summer. Broadly lance-shaped leaves provide good autumn colour. Zone 5.

R. 'Corneille' (illus. p.132). Deciduous, bushy azalea. H and S 1.5–2.5m (5–8ft). In early summer produces fragrant, honeysuckle-like, cream flowers, flushed pink outside. Has attractive autumn foliage. Zone 5b.

R. 'Crest', syn. *R.* 'Hawk Crest' (illus. p.134). Evergreen rhododendron of open habit. H and S 1.5–4m (5–12ft). Has broadly lance-shaped leaves. Bell-shaped flowers are borne in loose, flat-topped bunches, and are apricot in bud, opening to clear sulphur-yellow in late spring. Zone 7.

R. 'Curlew' (illus. p.134). Evergreen rhododendron of compact, spreading habit. H and S 30cm (1ft). Produces dull green leaves and, in late spring, relatively large, open funnel-shaped, yellow flowers. Zone 8.

R. 'Cynthia' (illus. p.133). Vigorous, evergreen, dome-shaped rhododendron. H and S to 6m (20ft). Bears conical bunches of bell-shaped, magenta-purple flowers, marked blackish-red within, in late spring. Is excellent for sun or shade. Zone 8.

R. dauricum. Evergreen, upright rhododendron. H and S to 1.5m (5ft). Produces funnel-shaped, vivid purple flowers in loose clusters throughout winter. Green leaves turn purple-brown in frosty conditions. Zone 4b.

R. davidsonianum (illus. p.133). Deciduous, upright rhododendron. H 1.5–4m (5–12ft). Aromatic leaves are lance-shaped to oblong. In late spring has clusters of funnel-shaped flowers, ranging from pale pink to mid-lilac-mauve. Zone 6.

R. decorum. Evergreen, bushy rhododendron. H and S 4m (12ft). Oblong to lance-shaped leaves are mid-green above, paler beneath. Large, fragrant, funnel-shaped, white or shell-pink flowers, green- or pink-spotted within, are produced in early summer. Zone 8.

R. discolor. See *R. fortunei* subsp. *discolor*.

R. 'Dora Amateis'. Evergreen, compact rhododendron. H and S 60cm (2ft). Leaves are slender, glossy and pointed. Masses of broadly funnel-shaped, white flowers, tinged with pink and marked with green, appear in late spring. Is sun tolerant. Zone 5.

R. 'Elizabeth' (illus. p.133). Evergreen, dome-shaped rhododendron. H and S to 1.5m (5ft). Leaves are oblong. Has large, trumpet-shaped, brilliant red flowers in late spring. Is good in sun or partial shade. Zone 6.

R. 'Elizabeth Lockhart'. Evergreen, dome-shaped rhododendron. H and S 60cm (2ft). Produces shiny, purple-green leaves that become darker in winter. Bell-shaped, deep pink flowers are carried in spring. Zone 7.

R. 'English Roseum'. Evergreen, vigorous, bushy rhododendron. H and S to 2.5m (8ft). Handsome leaves are dark green, paler beneath. Bears compact bunches of funnel-shaped, lilac-rose flowers in late spring. Zone 4.

R. 'Fabia' (illus. p134). Evergreen, dome-shaped rhododendron. H and S 2m (6ft). Leaves are lance-shaped. Loose, flat trusses of funnel-shaped, orange-tinted, scarlet flowers are produced in early summer. Zone 8.

R. 'Fastuosum Flore Pleno'. Evergreen, dome-shaped rhododendron. H and S 1.5–4m (5–12ft). In early summer produces loose bunches of funnel-shaped, double, rich mauve flowers with red-brown marks and wavy edges. Zone 5b.

R. fictolacteum. See *R. rex* subsp. *fictolacteum*.

R. 'Fireball'. Mounded deciduous azalea with coppery-red young foliage. H and S 1m (3ft). Blooms in early summer with deep orange-red flowers. Zone 6.

R. 'Firefly'. See *R.* 'Hexe'.

R. fortunei subsp. *discolor*, syn. *R. discolor*. Evergreen, tree-like rhododendron. H and S to 8m (25ft). Leaves are oblong to oval. Bears fragrant, funnel-shaped, pink flowers that give a magnificent display in mid-summer. Is ideal in a light woodland. Zone 6.

R. 'Freya' (illus. p.134). Deciduous azalea of compact, shrubby habit. H and S 1.5m (5ft). Fragrant, funnel-shaped, pink-flushed, orange-salmon flowers appear from late spring to early summer. Zone 6.

R. 'Frome' (illus. p.134). Deciduous azalea of shrubby habit. H and S to 1.5m (5ft). In spring bears trumpet-shaped, saffron-yellow flowers, overlaid red in throats; petals are frilled and wavy-margined. Zone 5b.

R. fulvum (illus. p.132). Evergreen, bushy rhododendron. H and S 1.5–4m (5–12ft). Oblong to oval, polished, deep green leaves are brown-felted beneath. In early spring has loose bunches of bell-shaped, red-blotched, pink flowers, which fade to white. Zone 8.

R. 'George Reynolds' (illus. p.134). Deciduous, bushy azalea. H and S to 2m (6ft). Large, funnel-shaped, yellow flowers, flushed pink in bud, are borne with or before the leaves in spring. Zone 5.

R. 'Gibraltar'. Vigorous, deciduous azalea that grows well in full sun. H and S 1.5m (5ft). Dark orange buds open to give flame-orange flowers with a yellow flair and frilled petals. Zone 6.

R. 'Gloria Mundi' (illus. p.134). Deciduous, twiggy azalea. H and S to 2m (6ft). Produces fragrant, honeysuckle-like, yellow-flared, orange flowers, with frilled margins, in early summer. Zone 6.

R. 'Glory of Littleworth' (illus. p.134). Evergreen or semi-evergreen, bushy hybrid between a rhododendron and an azalea. H and S 1.5m (5ft). Compact bunches of fragrant, bell-shaped, orange-marked, creamy-white flowers are borne abundantly in late spring and early summer. Is not easy to cultivate. Zone 7.

R. 'Golden Lights'. Upright, deciduous azalea. H and S 2m (6ft). Has fragrant, gold to bright yellow flowers in mid-spring. Zone 4.

R. 'Gomer Waterer'. Evergreen, compact rhododendron. H and S 1.5–4m (5–12ft). Leaves are curved back at margins. Bell-shaped flowers, borne in dense bunches in early summer, are white, flushed mauve, each with a basal, mustard blotch. Likes sun or partial shade. Zone 8.

R. 'Hatsugiri' (illus. p.133). Evergreen, compact azalea. H and S 60cm (2ft). Has small, but very numerous, funnel-shaped, bright crimson-purple flowers in spring. Flowers very reliably. Zone 7.

R. 'Hawk Crest'. See R. 'Crest'.

R. 'Hinode-giri' (illus. p.133). Evergreen, compact azalea. H and S 1.5m (5ft). Funnel-shaped, bright crimson flowers are small, but produced in abundance in late spring. Likes sun or light shade. Zone 7.

R. 'Hinomayo' (illus. p.133). Evergreen, compact azalea. H and S 1.5m (5ft). Small, funnel-shaped, clear pink flowers are produced in great abundance in spring. Likes sun or light shade. Zone 7.

R. hippophaeoides (illus. p.133). Evergreen, erect rhododendron. H and S 1.5m (5ft). Narrowly lance-shaped, aromatic leaves are grey-green. Has small, funnel-shaped, lavender or lilac flowers in spring. Tolerates wet, but not stagnant, soil. Zone 6.

R. 'Homebush' (illus. p.133). Deciduous, compact azalea. H and S 1.5m (5ft). In late spring bears tight, rounded heads of trumpet-shaped, semi-double, rose-purple flowers with paler shading. Zone 6.

R. 'Hotei'. Evergreen, rhododendron of neat, compact habit. H and S 1.5–2.5m (5–8ft). Has excellent foliage. Large, funnel-shaped, deep yellow flowers are freely produced in late spring. Zone 8.

R. impeditum. Slow-growing, evergreen rhododendron. H and S to 60cm (2ft). Aromatic leaves are grey-green.Funnel-shaped, purplish-blue flowers appear in spring. Is ideal for a rock garden. Zone 5.

R. 'Irohayama' (illus. p.133). Evergreen, compact azalea. H and S to 1.5m (5ft). Has abundant, small, funnel-shaped, white flowers, with pale lavender margins and faint brown eyes,

in spring. Does well in light shade. Zone 7.

R. 'John Cairns' (illus. p.133). Evergreen, upright, compact azalea. H and S 1.5–2m (5–6ft). Bears abundant funnel-shaped, orange-red flowers in spring. Grows reliably and consistently in sun or semi-shade. Zone 8.

R. kaempferi (illus. p.133). Semi-evergreen, erect, loosely branched azalea. H and S 1.5–2.5m (5–8ft). Leaves are lance-shaped. Has an abundance of funnel-shaped flowers in various shades of orange or red in late spring and early summer. Zone 6.

R. 'Kilimanjaro'. Evergreen, bushy rhododendron. H and S 1.5–4m (5–12ft). Bears broadly lance-shaped leaves. Produces large, rounded bunches of funnel- to bell-shaped, wavy-edged, maroon-red flowers, spotted chocolate within, in late spring and early summer. Zone 8.

R. 'Kirin' (illus. p.132). Evergreen, compact azalea. H and S to 1.5m (5ft). In spring has numerous hose-in-hose flowers that are deep rose, shaded a delicate silvery-rose. Looks best in light shade. Zone 7.

R. kiusianum. Semi-evergreen azalea of compact habit. H and S to 60cm (2ft). Leaves are narrowly oval. Produces clusters of 2–5 funnel-shaped flowers, usually lilac-rose or mauve-purple, in late spring. Prefers full sun. Zone 6.

R. 'Klondyke'. Mounded, deciduous azalea that grows best in full sun. H and S 2m (6ft). Young foliage has a copper tint and buds are flushed red. Flowers are orange-gold with a red reverse and in large trusses. Zone 6.

R. 'Lady Clementine Mitford'. Evergreen, rounded, dense rhododendron. H and S 4m (12ft). Has broadly oval, glossy, dark green leaves that are silvery when young and, in late spring and early summer, bold bunches of tubular- to bell-shaped flowers, peach-pink fading to white in the centre, with V-shaped, pink, green and brown marks within. Zone 7.

R. 'Lees Dark Purple'. An open, rounded, evergreen rhododendron with slightly wavy foliage. H 2m (6ft), S 1.5m (5ft). Flowers are royal purple with brownish markings inside, in dense rounded trusses. May rebloom in fall in warm climates. Zone 5.

R. 'Loderi King George'. Large, evergreen rhododendron of open habit. H and S 4m (12ft). Has large leaves. In late spring and early summer, pale pink buds open to huge trusses of funnel-shaped, fragrant, pure white flowers, 9–11cm (3½–4½in) long, with subtle green marks in the throats. Zone 7.

R. lutescens (illus. p.133). Semi-evergreen, upright rhododendron. H and S 1.5–3m (5–10ft). Has oval to lance-shaped leaves that are bronze-red when young. In early spring bears funnel-shaped, primrose-yellow flowers. Elegant and delicate, it is effective in a light woodland. Zone 8.

R. luteum (illus. p.134). Open deciduous azalea. H and S 1.5–2.5m (5–8ft). Leaves are oblong to lance-shaped. Has very fragrant, bold yellow, funnel-shaped blooms in spring.

Autumn foliage is rich and colourful. Zone 4.

R. macabeanum (illus. p.134). Evergreen, tree-like rhododendron. H and S up to 13.5m (45ft). Has bold, broadly oval leaves, dark green above, grey-felted beneath, and, in early spring, large bunches of bell-shaped, yellow flowers, blotched purple within. Zone 9?.

R. 'May Day' (illus. p.133). Evergreen, spreading rhododendron. H and S to 1.5m (5ft). Leaves are fresh green above, whitish-felted beneath. Has masses of loose bunches of long-lasting, funnel-shaped, scarlet flowers in late spring; petal-like calyces match the flower colour. Zone 8.

R. 'Medway' (illus. p.134). Deciduous, bushy, open azalea. H and S 1.5–2.5m (5–8ft). In late spring has large, trumpet-shaped, pale pink flowers with darker edges and orange-flashed throats; petal edges are frilled. Zone 6.

R. 'Moonshine Crescent' (illus. p.134). Evergreen, rounded to upright rhododendron. H 2–2.5m (6–8ft), S 2m (6ft). In late spring produces compact trusses of bell-shaped, yellow flowers. Leaves are oblong to oval and dark green. Zone 7.

R. moupinense. Evergreen, rounded, compact rhododendron. H and S to 1.5m (5ft). Produces funnel-shaped, pink blooms in loose bunches in late winter and early spring. Leaves are glossy, dark green above, paler beneath. Is best grown in a sheltered situation to reduce risk of frosted flowers. Zone 7.

R. 'Mrs G.W. Leak' (illus. p.132). Evergreen, upright, compact rhododendron. H and S 4m (12ft). In late spring bears compact, conical bunches of funnel-shaped, pink flowers, with black-brown and crimson marks within. Zone 7.

R. nakaharae. Evergreen, mound-forming azalea. H and S 60cm (2ft). Shoots and oblong to oval leaves are densely hairy. Funnel-shaped, dark brick-red flowers are borne in small clusters. Is valuable for mid-summer flowering and is ideal for a rock garden. Zone 5.

R. 'Nancy Waterer'. Deciduous, twiggy azalea. H and S 1.5–2.5m (5–8ft). Has large, long-tubed and honeysuckle-like, brilliant golden-yellow flowers in early summer. Is ideal in a light woodland or full sun. Zone 5.

R. 'Narcissiflorum' (illus. p.134). Vigorous, deciduous, compact azalea. H and S 1.5–2.5m (5–8ft). Sweetly scented, hose-in-hose, pale yellow flowers, darker outside and in centre, are borne in late spring or early summer. Autumn foliage is bronze. Zone 5.

R. Nobleanum Group (illus. p.132). Evergreen, upright shrub or tree-like rhododendron. H and S to 5m (15ft). Bears large, compact bunches of broadly funnel-shaped, rose-red, pink or white flowers in winter or early spring. Will flower for long periods in mild weather; is best in a sheltered position. Zone 7.

R. 'Norma'. Vigorous, deciduous, compact azalea. H and S to 1.5m (5ft).

Bears masses of hose-in-hose, rose-red flowers with a salmon glow in spring. Grows well in sun or light shade. Zone 6.

R. Northern Lights Group. A strain of deciduous azaleas that form upright, rounded shrubs. H 1.5m (5ft), S 1.2m (4ft). Have dense trusses of funnel-shaped flowers in pastel colours. Zone 3b.

R. 'Nova Zembla'. Vigorous, evergreen, upright rhododendron. H and S 1.5–4m (5–12ft). Has funnel-shaped, dark red flowers in closely set bunches from late spring to early summer. Zone 4.

R. occidentale (illus. p.132). Bushy, deciduous, azalea. H and S 1.5–2.5m (5–8ft). Glossy leaves turn yellow or orange in autumn. Bears fragrant, funnel-shaped, white or pale pink flowers, each with a basal, yellow-orange blotch, in early to mid-summer. Zone 6.

R. 'Olga Mezzit'. Spreading, evergreen, small-leaved rhododendron. H 1.2m (4ft), S 1.5–2m (5–6ft). Has small trusses of pinkish-purple flowers in early summer. Foliage turns light red in cold weather. Zone 5.

R. orbiculare (illus. p.132). Evergreen rhododendron of compact habit. H and S to 3m (10ft). Produces rounded, bright green leaves. Bell-shaped, rose-pink flowers are borne in loose bunches in late spring. Zone 7.

R. 'Orchid Lights'. Upright, deciduous azalea. H 2m (6ft) S 1.5m (5ft). Has tubular orchid-pink flowers in dense trusses in early summer. Zone 4.

R. oreotrephes (illus. p.133). Deciduous, upright shrub or tree-like rhododendron. H and S to 5m (15ft). Has attractive, scaly, grey-green foliage. In spring bears loose bunches of 3–10 broadly funnel-shaped flowers, usually mauve or purple, but variable, often with crimson spots. Zone 7.

R. 'Palestrina' (illus. p.132). Evergreen or semi-evergreen, compact, free-flowering azalea. H and S to 1.2m (4ft). Has large, open funnel-shaped, white flowers, with faint, green marks, in late spring. Grows well in light shade. Zone 8.

R. 'Percy Wiseman' (illus. p.132). Evergreen rhododendron with a domed, compact habit. H and S to 2m (6ft). In late spring produces open funnel-shaped, peach-yellow flowers that fade to white. Zone 6.

R. 'Peter John Mezitt', syn. R. 'P.J.M.' Evergreen, compact rhododendron. H and S up to 1.5m (5ft). Aromatic leaves are small, dark green in summer, bronze-purple in winter. Bears frost-resistant, funnel-shaped, lavender-pink flowers in early spring. Is good in full sun. Zone 4.

R. 'Pink Pearl' (illus. p.133). Vigorous, evergreen, upright, open rhododendron. H and S 4m (12ft) or more. Tall bunches of open funnel-shaped, pink flowers give a spectacular display in late spring. Zone 6.

R. 'P.J.M.' See R. 'Peter John Mezitt'.

R. 'President Roosevelt' (illus. p133). Slow-growing, evergreen, open, weakly branched rhododendron. H and S to 2m (6ft). Leaves are yellow-variegated but have a tendency to revert to plain green. Open bell-shaped, pale pink flowers, lighter towards centres and frilled at margins, appear from mid- to late spring. Zone 8.

R. 'Purple Gem'. Rounded, dwarf, evergreen rhododendron with new foliage tinged blue. H 60cm (2ft), S 1.2m (4ft). Has small trusses of open funnel-shaped, light purple flowers. Good on a rock garden. Zone 6.

R. 'Purple Splendour'. Evergreen, bushy rhododendron. H and S to 3m (10ft). Has well-formed bunches of open funnel-shaped, rich royal-purple flowers, with prominent, black marks in throats, in late spring or early summer. Zone 7.

R. 'Queen Elizabeth II' (illus. p.133). Evergreen, bushy rhododendron. H and S 1.5–4m (5–12ft). Bears funnel-shaped, greenish-yellow flowers in loose bunches in late spring. Leaves are narrowly oval or lance-shaped, glossy and mid-green above, paler beneath. Zone 7.

R. racemosum (illus. p.132). Evergreen, upright, stiffly branched rhododendron. H and S to 2.5m (8ft). Has clusters of widely funnel-shaped, bright pink flowers carried along the stems in spring. Small, broadly oval, aromatic leaves are dull green above, grey-green below. Zone 8.

R. 'Ramapo'. Similar to 'Purple Gem' but slightly smaller. H 45cm (18in), S 1.2m (4ft). New foliage is a blue-gray turning a metallic blue in winter. Flowers are violet-purple. It does best in sun. Zone 4.

R. rex. Vigorous, evergreen, upright shrub or tree-like rhododendron. H and S 4m (12ft) or more. Leaves are pale buff-felted beneath. Pink or white flowers each have a crimson blotch and a spotted throat. Zone 6b.

subsp. *fictolacteum* (syn. *R. fictolacteum*; illus. p.132), H to 13.5m (45ft), has large leaves, green above, brown-felted beneath. Bears bunches of bell-shaped, white flowers in spring, each with a maroon blotch and often a spotted throat. Zone 8.

R. 'Rosalind' (illus. p.133). Vigorous, evergreen rhododendron of open-branched habit. H and S 4m (12ft). Leaves are dull green. Bears broadly funnel-shaped, pink flowers in loose bunches in spring. Zone 7.

R. 'Roseum Elegans'. Vigorous, evergreen, rounded rhododendron. H and S 2.5m (8ft) or more. Foliage is bold and glossy, deep green. In early summer, bears rounded bunches of broadly funnel-shaped, reddish-purple flowers, each marked with yellow-brown. Zone 4.

R. 'Scarlet Wonder'. Small, compact evergreen rhododendron. H 60cm (2ft), S 1.2m (4ft). Has loose trusses of ruby-red, trumpet-shaped flowers with frilly margins. Zone 6.

R. schlippenbachii (illus. p.132). Deciduous, rounded, open azalea. H and S 2.5m (8ft). Spoon-shaped leaves are in whorls at branch ends. Bears loose bunches of 3–6 saucer-shaped, pink flowers in mid-spring. Suits a light woodland. Zone 5.

R. 'Scintillation'. Vigorous, evergreen rhododendron, with long, shiny, waxy foliage. H 1.5m (5ft), S 2m (6ft). Has

large trusses of scented, pastel pink flowers with golden-bronze marking in the throat. Zone 4.

R. 'Seta' (illus. p.132). Evergreen, erect rhododendron. H 1.5m (5ft), S 1–1.5m (3–5ft). In early spring bears loose bunches of tubular, shiny, vivid pink-and-white-striped flowers, fading to white at bases. Zone 8.

R. 'Seven Stars' (illus. p.132). Vigorous, evergreen, upright, dense rhododendron. H and S 2–3m (6–10ft). Has yellowish-green foliage and, in spring, masses of bunches of large, bell-shaped, wavy-margined, white flowers, flushed with apple-blossom pink, pink in bud. Zone 7.

R. 'Silver Moon' (illus. p.132). Evergreen azalea of broad, spreading habit. H and S 1.5–2.5m (5–8ft). Funnel-shaped, white flowers, with pale green-blotched throats and frilled petal edges, appear in spring. Grows best in partial shade. Zone 8.

R. souliei (illus. p.132). Evergreen, open rhododendron. H and S 1.5–4m (5–12ft). Has rounded leaves and, in late spring, saucer-shaped, soft pink flowers. Grows best in areas of low rainfall. Zone 9?.

R. 'Spek's Orange'. Deciduous, bushy azalea. H and S to 2.5m (8ft). In late spring carries bold bunches of large, slender-tubed blooms that are bright reddish-orange with greenish marks within. Zone 5.

R. 'Spicy Lights'. Upright, deciduous azalea. H 1.5m (5ft), S 1.2m (4ft). Has loose trusses of orange-red flowers in early summer. Zone 4.

R. 'Strawberry Ice' (illus. p.132). Deciduous, bushy azalea. H and S 1.5–2.5m (5–8ft). Bears trumpet-shaped flowers, deep pink in bud, opening flesh-pink, and mottled deeper pink at petal edges with deep yellow-marked throats, in late spring. Zone 5.

R. 'Surprise'. Evergreen, dense azalea. H and S to 1.5m (5ft). Has abundant, small, funnel-shaped, light orange-red flowers in mid-spring. Looks effective when mass planted and is ideal in light shade or full sun. Zone 7.

R. 'Susan' (illus. p.133). Close-growing, evergreen rhododendron. H and S 1.5–4m (5–12ft). Handsome foliage is glossy, dark green. In spring bears large bunches of open funnel-shaped flowers in 2 shades of blue-mauve, spotted purple within. Zone 6b.

R. sutchuenense (illus. p.132). Evergreen, spreading shrub or tree-like rhododendron. H and S to 5m (16ft). Has large leaves and, in early spring, large bunches of broadly funnel-shaped, pink flowers, spotted deeper within. Suits a light woodland. Zone 5b.

R. 'Temple Belle'. Evergreen rhododendron of neat, compact habit. H and S 1.5–2.5m (5–8ft). Loose bunches of bell-shaped, clear pink flowers are produced in spring. Rounded leaves are dark green above, grey-green beneath. Zone 8.

R. thomsonii (illus. p.133). Evergreen, rounded rhododendron of open habit. H and S to 5.5m (18ft). Leaves are waxy, dark green above, whiter beneath. Peeling, fawn-coloured bark

contrasts well with bell-shaped, waxy, red flowers in spring. Zone 9?.

R. 'Vulcan'. An evergreen rhododendron with pointed leaves that makes a rounded plant. H and S 1.5m (5ft). Bright red flowers with wavy margins are in dome-shaped trusses in early summer. Zone 5b.

R. 'Vuyk's Scarlet' (illus. p.133). Evergreen, compact azalea. H and S to 60cm (2ft). In spring bears an abundance of relatively large, open funnel-shaped, brilliant red flowers, with wavy petals, that completely cover the glossy foliage. Zone 7.

R. wardii (illus. p.133). Evergreen, compact rhododendron. H and S 1.5–4m (5–12ft). Leaves are rounded. In late spring, bears loose bunches of saucer-shaped, clear yellow flowers, with basal, crimson blotches. Zone 8.

R. 'White Lights'. Hardy, deciduous azalea forming a mounded bush. H 1.5m (5ft), S 1.2m (4ft). Fragrant flowers are very pale pink to white with a yellow centre. Zone 4.

R. williamsianum (illus. p.132). Evergreen rhododendron of compact, spreading habit. H and S 1.5m (5ft). Young leaves are bronze, maturing to mid-green. Has loosely clustered, bell-shaped, pink flowers in spring. Is ideal for a small garden. Zone 8.

R. 'Woodcock'. Evergreen, compact, spreading rhododendron. H and S 1.5–2.5m (5–8ft). Has semi-glossy, dark green leaves and, in spring, masses of loose bunches of funnel-shaped, rose-red flowers. Zone 7.

R. xanthocodon. See *R. cinnabarinum* subsp. *xanthocodon*.

R. yakushimanum (illus. p.132). Evergreen, dome-shaped rhododendron of neat, compact habit. H 1m (3ft), S 1.5m (5ft). Leaves are broadly oval, silvery at first, maturing to deepest green, and brown-felted beneath. In late spring has open funnel-shaped, pink flowers that fade to near white and are flecked green within. Zone 5.

R. 'Yellow Hammer' (illus. p.134). Evergreen, erect, bushy rhododendron. H and S to 2m (6ft). Bears abundant clusters of tubular, bright yellow flowers in spring; frequently flowers again in autumn. Zone 8.

R. yunnanense (illus. p.132). Semi-evergreen, open rhododendron. H and S 1.5–4m (5–12ft). Has aromatic, grey-green leaves and masses of butterfly-like, pale pink or white flowers with blotched throats, in spring. Zone 8.

RHODOHYPOXIS

HYPOXIDACEAE

Genus of dwarf, spring- to summer-flowering, tuberous perennials, grown for their pink, red or white flowers, each comprising 6 petals that meet at the centre, so the flower has no eye. Needs full sun, sandy, peaty soil, plenty of moisture in summer, and to be kept fairly dry while dormant. Propagate in spring by seed or offsets.

R. 'Albrighton' illus. p.380.

R. baurii. Spring- and early summer-flowering, tuberous perennial. H 5–10cm (2–4in), S 2.5–5cm (1–2in). Has an erect, basal tuft of narrowly lance-shaped, hairy leaves. Bears a succession

of erect, flattish, white, pale pink or red flowers, 2cm (¾in) across, on slender stems. var. *platypetala* has 2.5cm (1in) wide, white or very pale pink flowers.

R. 'Douglas' illus. p.380.

R. 'Margaret Rose' illus. p.376.

RHODOLEIA

HAMAMELIDACEAE

Genus of evergreen, mainly spring-flowering trees, grown for their foliage and flowers. Tender, min. 7–10°C (45–50°F). Needs full light or partial shade and humus-rich, well-drained, neutral to acid soil. Water potted specimens freely; sparingly when not in full growth. Tolerates pruning if necessary. Propagate by semi-ripe cuttings in summer or by seed when ripe, in autumn or in spring.

R. championii. Evergreen, bushy tree. H and S 4–8m (12–25ft). Elliptic to oval, bright green leaves, each to 9cm (3½in) long, are borne near the shoot tips. Clusters of tiny flowers, surrounded by petal-like, pink bracts, appear in spring.

RHODOPHIALA

AMARYLLIDACEAE

Genus of bulbs, grown for their large, funnel-shaped flowers. Hardy to tender, min. 13–15°C (55–9°F). Needs full sun or partial shade and well-drained soil. Keep dormant bulbs dry in winter. Propagate by seed in spring or by offsets in spring (summer-flowering species).

R. advena, syn. *Hippeastrum advenum*, illus. p.421.

RHODOTHAMNUS

ERICACEAE

Genus of one species of evergreen, semi-prostrate, open shrub, grown for its flowers. Is suitable for rock gardens and peat beds. Needs sun and humus-rich, well-drained, acid soil. Propagate by seed in spring or by semi-ripe cuttings in summer.

R. chamaecistus illus. p.352.

RHODOTYPOS

ROSACEAE

Genus of one species of deciduous shrub, grown for its flowers. Needs sun or semi-shade and moist but well-drained, fertile soil. After flowering, on established plants, cut some older shoots back or to ground level. Propagate by softwood cuttings in summer or by seed in autumn.

R. kerrioides. See *R. scandens*.

R. scandens, syn. *R. kerrioides*, illus. p.158.

Rhoeo discolor. See *Tradescantia spathacea.*

Rhoeo spathacea. See *Tradescantia spathacea.*

RHOICISSUS

VITACEAE

Genus of evergreen, tendril climbers, grown for their handsome foliage. Bears inconspicuous flowers intermittently during the year. Tender, min. 7–10°C (45–50°F). Grow in any fertile, well-drained soil with light shade in summer. Water regularly, less in cold weather. Provide support. Remove crowded stems when necessary or in early spring. Propagate by seed in spring or by semi-ripe cuttings in summer.

R. capensis (Cape grape). Vigorous, evergreen, tendril climber. H and S to 5m (15ft). Rounded, toothed, lustrous, mid- to deep green leaves, to 20cm (8in) wide, have deeply rounded, heart-shaped bases.
R. rhombifolia. See *Cissus rhombifolia.*
R. rhomboidea. See *Cissus rhombifolia.*

RHOMBOPHYLLUM

AIZOACEAE

Genus of mat-forming, perennial succulents with dense, basal rosettes of linear or semi-cylindrical leaves, each expanded towards middle or tip; leaf tip is reflexed or incurved. Tender, min. 5°C (41°F). Needs sun and very well-drained soil. Propagate by seed or stem cuttings in spring or summer.
R. rhomboideum illus. p.478.

Rhubarb. See *Rheum.*

RHUS
Sumach

ANACARDIACEAE

Genus of deciduous trees, shrubs and scrambling climbers, grown for their divided, ash-like foliage, autumn colour and, in some species, showy fruit clusters. Requires sun and well-drained soil. Propagate by semi-ripe cuttings in summer, by seed in autumn or by root cuttings in winter. May be attacked by coral spot fungus. All parts of *R. verniciflua* are highly toxic if ingested; contact with its foliage, and that of a number of related species, including *R. succedanea*, may aggravate skin allergies.
R. aromatica (Fragrant sumach). Deciduous, bushy shrub. H 1m (3ft), S 1.5m (5ft). Deep green leaves, each composed of 3 oval leaflets, turn orange or reddish-purple in autumn. Tiny, yellow flowers are borne in mid-spring, before leaves, followed by spherical, red fruits. Zone 3.
R. copallina (Dwarf sumach). Deciduous, upright shrub. H and S 1–1.5m (3–5ft), or more. Has glossy, dark green leaves, with numerous lance-shaped leaflets, that turn red-purple in autumn. Minute, greenish-yellow flowers, borne in dense clusters from mid- to late summer, develop into narrowly egg-shaped, bright red fruits. Zone 2b.
R. cotinoides. See *Cotinus obovatus.*
R. cotinus. See *Cotinus coggygria.*
R. glabra illus. p.143.
R. hirta. See *R. typhina* 'Laciniata' see *R. typhina* 'Dissecta'.
R. potaninii. Deciduous, round-headed tree. H 12m (40ft), S 8m (25ft). Has large, dark green leaves, with usually

7–11 oval leaflets that turn red in autumn. In summer produces dense clusters of tiny, yellow-green flowers. Female flower clusters develop into tiny, spherical, black or brownish fruits. Zone 6.
R. succedanea, syn. *Toxicodendron succedaneum* (Wax tree). Deciduous, spreading tree. H and S 10m (30ft). Large, glossy, dark green leaves, each made up of 9–15 oval leaflets, turn red in autumn. Has dense clusters of tiny, yellow-green flowers in summer. Female flowers develop into tiny, spherical, black or brownish fruits. Zone 6.
R. trichocarpa illus. p.95.
R. typhina, syn. *R. hirta* (Stag's horn sumach). Deciduous, spreading, suckering, open shrub or tree. H 5m (15ft), S 6m (20ft). Velvety shoots are clothed in dark green leaves with oblong leaflets. Produces minute, greenish-white flowers from mid- to late summer. Leaves become brilliant orange-red in autumn, accompanying clusters of spherical, deep red fruits on female plants. 'Dissecta' (syn. *R. hirta* 'Laciniata', *R.t.* 'Laciniata' of gardens), illus. p.124. 'Laciniata' of gardens see *R.t.* 'Dissecta'. All zone 3.
R. verniciflua, syn. *Toxicodendron vernicifluum* (Varnish tree). Deciduous, spreading tree. H 15m (50ft), S 10m (30ft). Large, glossy, bright green leaves, with 7–13 oval leaflets, redden in autumn. Bears dense clusters of tiny, yellow-green flowers in summer, followed by berry-like, brownish-yellow fruits. Contact with the sap may severely irritate the skin. Zone 7.

Rhynchelytrum repens. See *Melinis repens.*
Rhynchelytrum roseum. See *Melinis repens.*
Ribbon gum. See *Eucalyptus viminalis.*
Ribbon plant. See *Dracaena sanderiana*, illus. p.151.
Ribbonwood. See *Hoheria sexstylosa.*

RIBES
Currant

GROSSULARIACEAE/SAXIFRAGACEAE

Genus of deciduous or evergreen, mainly spring-flowering shrubs, grown for their edible fruits (currants and gooseberries) or their flowers. Needs full sun and well-drained, fertile soil, but *R. laurifolium* tolerates shade. After flowering cut out some older shoots and, in winter or early spring, prune straggly, old plants hard. Propagate deciduous species by hardwood cuttings in winter, evergreens by semi-ripe cuttings in summer. Aphids attack young foliage.
R. alpinum (Alpine currant). Deciduous, mounded shrub often used for hedges. H 60cm (2ft), S 1m (3ft). Erect racemes of bell-shaped, yellow flowers in spring, with male and female flowers on separate plants. Female plants have dark red spherical fruit in late summer. Zone 2.
R. aureum of gardens. See *R. odoratum.*
R. laurifolium illus. p.175.

R. odoratum, syn. *R. aureum* of gardens (Buffalo currant). Deciduous, upright shrub. H and S 2m (6ft). Clusters of fragrant, tubular, golden-yellow flowers are borne from mid- to late spring, followed by rounded, purple fruits. Rounded, 3-lobed, bright green leaves turn red and purple in autumn. Zone 2.
R. sanguineum (Flowering currant). 'Brocklebankii' illus. p.155. 'King Edward VII' is a deciduous, upright, compact shrub. H and S 2m (6ft). Small, tubular, deep reddish-pink flowers are freely borne amid rounded, 3–5-lobed, aromatic, dark green leaves, from mid- to late spring, and are sometimes succeeded by spherical, black fruits with a white bloom. Is useful for hedging. Zone 6b.
'Pulborough Scarlet' illus. p.130.
'Tydeman's White', H and S 2.5m (8ft), is less compact, with white flowers.
R. speciosum (Fuchsia-flowered currant). Deciduous, bushy, spiny shrub. H and S 2m (6ft). Slender, drooping, tubular, red flowers, with long, red stamens, open mid-late spring. Fruits are spherical and red. Has red, young shoots and oval, 3–5-lobed, glossy, bright green leaves. Train against a south- or west-facing wall. Zone 8.

Rice, Canada wild. See *Zizania aquatica.*
Rice-paper plant. See *Tetrapanax papyrifer*, illus. p.126.

RICHEA

EPACRIDACEAE

Genus of evergreen, summer-flowering shrubs, grown for their foliage and densely clustered flowers. Needs sun or semi-shade and moist, peaty, neutral to acid soil. Propagate by semi-ripe cuttings in summer or by seed in autumn.
R. scoparia. Evergreen, upright shrub. H and S 2m (6ft). Shoots are covered with narrowly lance-shaped, sharp-pointed, dark green leaves. Bears dense, upright spikes of small, egg-shaped, pink, white, orange or maroon flowers in early summer. Zone 9.

RICINUS

EUPHORBIACEAE

Genus of one species of fast-growing, evergreen, tree-like shrub, grown for its foliage. In cool climates is grown as an annual. Needs sun and fertile to rich, well-drained soil. May require support in exposed areas. Propagate by seed sown under glass in early spring. All parts of *R. communis*, particularly the seeds, are highly toxic if ingested; contact with the foliage may aggravate skin allergies.
R. communis illus. p.335. 'Impala' illus. p.330.

Rienga lily. See *Arthropodium cirratum.*
River red gum. See *Eucalyptus camaldulensis.*
Roast-beef plant. See *Iris foetidissima.*

ROBINIA

LEGUMINOSAE/PAPILIONACEAE

Genus of deciduous, mainly summer-flowering trees and shrubs, grown for their foliage and clusters of pea-like flowers. Is useful for poor, dry soil. Needs a sunny position. Grows in any but waterlogged soil. Branches are brittle and may be damaged by strong winds. Propagate by seed or suckers in autumn or by root cuttings in winter. All parts may cause severe discomfort if ingested. Borers may be a problem.
R. × ambigua 'Decaisneana'. Deciduous, spreading tree. H 15m (50ft), S 10m (30ft). Dark green leaves have numerous oval leaflets. Long, hanging clusters of pea-like, pink flowers are borne in early summer. Zone 4.
R. hispida illus. p.141. var. **kelseyi** (syn. *R. kelseyi*) is a deciduous, spreading, open shrub. H 2.5m (8ft), S 4m (12ft). Clusters of pea-like, rose-pink flowers open in late spring or early summer, followed by pendent, red seed pods. Dark green leaves consist of 9 or 11 oval leaflets. Zone 6.
R. kelseyi. See *R. hispida* var. *kelseyi.*
R. pseudoacacia (False acacia, Locust). Fast-growing, deciduous, spreading tree. H 25m (80ft), S 15m (50ft). Dark green leaves consist of 11–23 oval leaflets. Dense, drooping clusters of fragrant, pea-like, white flowers are borne in late spring and early summer. Zone 4. 'Frisia' illus. p.81. 'Umbraculifera' (Mop-head acacia), H and S 6m (20ft), rarely produces a rounded, dense flower head. Zone 4b.

Roblé. See *Nothofagus obliqua*, illus. p.68.
Rochea coccinea. See *Crassula coccinea.*
Rock lily. See *Arthropodium cirratum.*
Rock rose. See *Cistus*; *Helianthemum.*
Rock speedwell. See *Veronica fruticans.*
Rocket
  Sweet. See *Hesperis matronalis*, illus. p.239.
  Yellow. See *Barbarea vulgaris.*
Rocky Mountain juniper. See *Juniperus scopulorum.*

RODGERSIA

SAXIFRAGACEAE

Genus of summer-flowering, rhizomatous perennials. Is ideal for pond sides. Grows in sun or semi-shade and in soil that is moist; requires shelter from strong winds, which may damage foliage. Propagate by division in spring or by seed in autumn.
R. aesculifolia illus. p.241.
R. pinnata 'Superba'. Clump-forming, rhizomatous perennial. H 1–1.2m (3–4ft), S 75cm (2½ft). Leaves are bronze-tinged, emerald-green, with 5–9 narrowly oval leaflets. Long, much-branched, dense panicles of star-shaped, bright pink flowers appear in mid-summer.
R. podophylla illus. p.240.
R. sambucifolia illus. p.240.

Roman wormwood. See *Artemisia pontica*, illus. p.290.

ROMNEYA
Tree poppy

PAPAVERACEAE

Genus of summer-flowering, woody-based perennials and deciduous sub-shrubs. Requires a warm, sunny position and deep, well-drained soil. Is difficult to establish, resents being moved and, in very cold areas, roots may need protection in winter. Once established, may spread rapidly. Propagate by softwood cuttings of basal shoots in early spring, by seed in autumn (transplanting seedlings without disturbing rootballs) or by root cuttings in winter.
R. coulteri illus. p.226.
R. 'White Cloud'. Vigorous, bushy, woody-based perennial. H and S 1m (3ft). Throughout summer produces large, slightly fragrant, shallowly cup-shaped, white flowers with prominent golden stamens. Leaves are oval, deeply lobed and grey.

ROMULEA

IRIDACEAE

Genus of crocus-like corms, grown for their funnel-shaped flowers. Needs full light and well-drained, sandy soil. Water freely during the growing period. Most species die down in summer and then need warmth and dryness. *R. macowanii*, however, is dormant in winter. Propagate by seed in autumn, or in spring for *R. macowanii*.
R. bulbocodioides of gardens. See *R. flava*.
R. bulbocodium illus. p.431.
R. flava, syn. *R. bulbocodioides* of gardens. Early spring-flowering corm. H to 10cm (4in), S 2.5–5cm (1–2in). Has a thread-like, erect, basal leaf and 1–5 upright, widely funnel-shaped, usually yellow flowers, 2–4cm (¾–1½in) across, with deeper yellow centres.
R. longituba. See *R. macowanii* var. *alticola*.
R. macowanii var. *alticola*, syn. *R. longituba*. Summer-flowering corm. H and S 1–2cm (½–¾in). Leaves are thread-like, erect and basal. Produces 1–3 upright, yellow flowers, each 3cm (1¼in) across with a long tube expanding to become a wide funnel shape.
R. sabulosa. Early spring-flowering corm. H 5–15cm (2–6in), S 2.5–5cm (1–2in). Forms thread-like, erect, basal leaves. Stems bear 1–4 upward-facing, funnel-shaped, black-centred, bright red flowers that open flattish, to 4–5cm (1½–2in) across, in the sun.

RONDELETIA

RUBIACEAE

Genus of evergreen, mainly summer-flowering trees and shrubs, grown primarily for their flowers. Tender, min. 13–16°C (55–61°F). Requires full light or partial shade and fertile, well-drained soil. Water containerized specimens freely when in full growth, moderately at other times. Stems may

be shortened in early spring if necessary. Propagate by seed in spring or by semi-ripe cuttings in summer.
R. amoena. Evergreen, rounded shrub. H and S 2–4m (6–12ft). Oval, dark green leaves have dense, brown down on undersides. Produces dense clusters of tubular, 4- or 5-lobed, pink flowers in summer.

Roof houseleek. See *Sempervivum tectorum*, illus. p.389.
Rooksbya euphorbioides. See *Neobuxbaumia euphorbioides*.

ROSA
Rose

ROSACEAE

Genus of deciduous or semi-evergreen, open shrubs and scrambling climbers, grown for their profusion of flowers, often fragrant, and sometimes for their fruits (rose hips). Leaves are divided into usually 5 or 7 oval leaflets, with rounded or pointed tips, that are sometimes toothed. Stems usually bear thorns, or prickles. Most of the bush and climbing roses are hardy to zone 6 (unless otherwise stated) but are often grown in colder zones and protected for the winter by mounding, deep planting, or burying. Prefers an open, sunny site and requires fertile, moist but well-drained soil. Avoid planting in an area where roses have been grown in recent years, as problems due to harmful organisms may occur: either exchange the soil, which may be used satisfactorily elsewhere, or choose another site for the new rose. To obtain blooms of high quality, feed in late winter or early spring with a balanced fertilizer and apply a mulch. In spring and summer feed regularly at 3-weekly intervals. Remove spent flower heads from plants that are 'remontant' ('rising up again'; other terms used are repeat- or perpetual-flowering). May be trimmed for tidiness in early winter. To improve health, flower quality and shape of bush, prune in the dormant season or, preferably, in spring, before young shoots develop from dormant growth buds: remove dead, damaged and dying wood; lightly trim Old Garden and Ground cover roses (see below); remove two-thirds of previous summer's growth of Modern bush, including miniature, roses. Correct treatment of Modern shrub and climbing roses, ramblers and species roses depends on the individual variety but in general they should be pruned only lightly. Propagate by budding in summer or by hardwood cuttings in autumn. All roses are prone to attack by various pests and diseases, including aphids, blackspot, powdery mildew, rust, sawfly, and rose chafer.
Roses are officially classified in three groups, each comprising different types, based, it is claimed, on the functional qualities of each plant, such as whether it is remontant, rather than on any historical, botanical or genetical relationships. Flowers occur in a variety of forms (illustrated and described on p.184) and are single (4–7 petals), semi-double (8–14 petals),

double (15–30 petals) or fully double (over 30 petals). Roses are illustrated on pp.180–99.

Species roses
Species, or wild, roses and **species hybrids** that share most of the characteristics of the parent species. Includes shrubs and climbing roses. Produces usually single flowers mainly in summer, borne generally in one flush, followed by red or black hips in autumn.
Old Garden roses
Alba – large, freely branching shrubs with clusters of, usually, 5–7 semi-double to double flowers in mid-summer. Has abundant, greyish-green leaves. Is very hardy and is good for borders and as specimen plants.
Bourbon – open, remontant shrubs that may be trained to climb. Produces usually fully double flowers, borne commonly in 3s, in summer-autumn. Is suitable for borders and for training over fences, walls and pillars.
China – spindly, remontant shrubs that produce single to double flowers, borne singly or in clusters of 2–13, in summer-autumn. Has pointed, shiny leaflets. Needs a sheltered position. Is suitable for borders and walls.
Damask – open shrubs with usually very fragrant, semi- to fully double flowers, borne singly or in loose clusters of 5–7 mainly in summer. Is suitable for borders.
Gallica – shrubs of fairly dense, free-branching growth. Leaves are dull green. Produces single to fully double, richly coloured flowers, often in clusters of 3, in summer. Is suitable for borders and as hedging.
Hybrid Perpetual – vigorous, free-branching, remontant shrubs that bear fully double flowers, held singly or in 3s, in summer-autumn. Leaves are usually olive-green. Is suitable for beds and borders.
Moss – often lax shrubs with a furry, moss-like growth on stems and calyces. Leaves are usually dark green. Has double to fully double flowers in summer.
Noisette – remontant climbing roses that bear clusters of up to 9 usually double flowers, with a slight spicy fragrance, in summer-autumn. Has generally smooth stems and glossy leaves. Needs a sheltered site. Suitable for a south- or west-facing wall.
Portland – upright, remontant shrubs with semi-double to double flowers, held singly or in 3s, in summer-autumn. Suits beds and borders.
Provence (Centifolia) – lax, thorny shrubs that produce scented, usually double to fully double flowers, borne singly or in 3s, in summer. Leaves are often dark green. Suitable for borders.
Sempervirens – semi-evergreen climbing roses with shiny, light green leaves and, in late summer, numerous semi- to fully double flowers. Is ideal for naturalizing or for growing on fences and pergolas.
Tea – remontant shrubs and climbing roses that produce spicy-scented, slender-stemmed, pointed, semi- to fully double flowers, borne singly or in 3s, in summer-autumn. Leaves are

shiny and pale green. Needs a sheltered position. Is suitable for beds and borders.

Modern roses
Shrub – a diverse group of modern roses, most of which are remontant, that grow larger (mostly H 1–2m (3–6ft)) than most bush roses. Has single to fully double flowers, singly or in sprays, in summer and/or autumn. Is suitable for beds and borders and for growing as specimen plants.
Large-flowered bush (Hybrid Tea) – remontant shrubs with mostly pointed, double flowers, 8cm (3in) or more across, borne singly or in 3s, in summer-autumn. Is excellent for beds, borders, hedges and cutting.
Cluster-flowered bush (Floribunda) – remontant shrubs that produce sprays of usually 3–25 single to fully double flowers in summer-autumn. Is excellent for beds, borders and hedges.
Dwarf cluster-flowered bush (Patio) – neat, remontant shrubs, H 38–60cm (15–24in), S 30–60cm (12–24in), that bear sprays of generally 3–11 single to double flowers in summer-autumn. Is ideal for beds, borders and hedges and for growing in containers.
Miniature bush – remontant shrubs, H to 45cm (18in), S to 40cm (16in), with sprays of usually 3–11 tiny, single to fully double flowers in summer-autumn. Has tiny leaves. Is suitable for rock gardens, small spaces and for growing in containers.
Polyantha – tough, compact, remontant shrubs with sprays of usually 7–15 small, 5-petalled, single to double flowers in summer-autumn. Is suitable for beds.
Ground cover – trailing and spreading roses, many of which are remontant, with single to fully double flowers, borne mostly in clusters of 3–11, in summer and/or autumn. Is suitable for beds, banks and walls.
Climbing – vigorous climbing roses, some of which are remontant, with stiff stems and single to fully double flowers, borne singly or in clusters, from late spring to autumn. Suitable to train over walls, fences and pergolas.
Rambler – vigorous climbing roses with lax stems. Has clusters of 3–21 single to fully double flowers, mainly in summer. Suitable for training over walls, fences, pergolas and trees.

R. 'Adelaide Hoodless'. Vigorous, arching shrub rose. H 1m (3ft), S 60cm (2ft). Has large clusters of up to 35 semi-double red flowers in July and September. Prune off first crop of fruit to encourage second blooming. Zone 2b.
R. 'Agnes'. An upright, *R. rugosa* hybrid shrub rose. H 2m (6ft), S 1.2m (4ft). Has dark green leaves on very thorny canes. Cupped, scented, double, butter yellow flowers open in late spring. It occasionally reblooms. Zone 3.
R. 'Aimée Vibert', syn. *R. 'Bouquet de la Mariée'.* Noisette climbing rose with long, smooth stems. H 5m (15ft), S 3m (10ft). Bears clusters of lightly scented, cupped, fully double, blush-pink to white flowers, 8cm (3in) across, in

summer-autumn. Leaves are glossy, dark green. May be grown as a shrub. Zone 6.

R. 'Alba Semiplena', syn. *R.* x *alba* 'Semiplena'.Vigorous, bushy Alba rose. H 2m (6ft), S 1.5m (5ft). Bears sweetly scented, flat, semi-double, white flowers, 8cm (3in) across, in mid-summer. Has greyish-green leaves. Suitable for a hedge. Zone 3.

R. 'Albéric Barbier' illus. p.196.

R. 'Albertine' illus. p.197.

R. ALEC'S RED ('Cored') illus. p.192.

R. ALEXANDER ('Harlex'), syn. *R.* 'Alexandra', illus. p.192.

R. 'Alexander Mackenzie'. Upright, vigorous shrub rose with excellent mildew and blackspot resistance. H 2m (6ft), S 1.5m (4.5ft). Has deep red, cup-shaped flowers with 40–50 petals in clusters of 10–12. Recurrent blooming. Zone 3.

R. 'Alfred de Dalmas'. See *R.* 'Mousseline'.

R. 'Alister Stella Gray', syn. *R.* 'Golden Rambler'. Noisette climbing rose with long, vigorous, upright stems. H 5m (15ft), S 3m (10ft). Bears clusters of musk-scented, quartered, fully double, yolk-yellow flowers, 6cm (2½in) across, in summer-autumn. Has glossy, mid-green leaves. Zone 6.

R. 'Aloha' illus. p.198.

R. 'Alpine Sunset' illus. p.190.

R. AMBER QUEEN ('Harroony') illus. p.193.

R. 'American Pillar'. Vigorous rambler rose of lax growth. H to 5m (15ft), S 4m (12ft). Large clusters of cupped, single, carmine-red flowers, with white eyes, are borne freely in mid-summer. Leathery foliage is glossy, mid-green. Zone 6.

R. 'Amruda'. See *R.* RED ACE.

R. 'Andeli'. See *R.* DOUBLE DELIGHT.

R. ANGELA RIPPON ('Ocarina'), syn. *R.* 'Ocaru', illus. p.195.

R. 'Angelita'. See *R.* 'Snowball'.

R. ANISLEY DICKSON ('Dickimono'), syn. *R.* 'Dicky', *R.* 'Münchner Kindl', illus. p.191.

R. ANNA FORD ('Harpiccolo') illus. p.191.

R. 'ANNE HARKNESS' ('Harkaramel') illus. p.194.

R. 'Apothecary's Rose'. See *R. gallica* var. *officinalis*.

R. 'Arthur Bell'. Upright, cluster-flowered bush rose. H 1m (3ft), S 60cm (2ft). Clusters of fragrant, cupped, double, yellow flowers, 8cm (3in) across, are borne in summer-autumn. Foliage is bright green.

R. 'Assemblage des Beautés', syn. *R.* 'Rouge Eblouissante'. Upright, dense Gallica rose. H 1.2m (4ft), S 1m (3ft). In summer bears faintly scented, rounded, fully double, green-eyed, cerise to crimson-purple flowers, 8cm (3in) across. Has rich green leaves. Zone 6.

R. 'Ausmary'. See *R.* MARY ROSE.

R. 'Ausmas'. See *R.* GRAHAM THOMAS.

R. 'Austance'. See *R.* CONSTANCE SPRY.

R. 'Baby Carnival'. See *R.* BABY MASQUERADE.

R. BABY MASQUERADE ('Tanba'), syn. 'Baby Carnival', illus. p.195.

R. banksiae, syn. *R.b.* var. *normalis* (Banksian rose). Climbing species rose. H and S 10m (30ft). Dense clusters of fragrant, flat, single, white flowers, 2.5cm (1in) across, are borne on slender, thornless, light green stems in late spring. Leaves are small and pale green. Is uncommon in cultivation. Zone 6. **'Lutea'** (syn. *R.b.* var. *lutea*) illus. p.199.

R. 'Beauty of Glazenwood'. See *R.* x *odorata* 'Pseudindica'.

R. 'Belle Courtisanne'. See *R.* 'Königin von Dänemark'.

R. 'Belle de Crécy' illus. p.188.

R. 'Belle de Londres'. See *R.* 'Compassion'.

R. 'Bizarre Triomphant'. See *R.* 'Charles de Mills'.

R. 'Blanc Double de Coubert'. Dense spreading shrub rose, a *R. rugosa* hybrid. H 1.5m (5ft), S 1.2m (4ft). Has semi-double, fragrant white flowers with prominent yellow stamens from spring to fall. Zone 2b.

R. 'Blanche Moreau'. Moss rose of rather lax growth. H 1.5m (5ft), S 1.2m (4ft). Fragrant, cupped, fully double, white flowers, 10cm (4in) across, with brownish 'mossing', appear in summer. Has dull green leaves. Zone 5.

R. 'Blaze'. Vigorous climbing rose. H and S 2.5m (8ft). Large semi-double bright red flowers are borne from late spring to early autumn.

R. 'Blessings' illus. p.190.

R. BLUE MOON ('Tannacht'), syn. *R.* 'Mainzer Fastnacht', *R.* 'Sissi'. Large-flowered bush rose of open habit. H 1m (3ft), S 60cm (2ft). Sweetly scented, pointed, fully double, lilac flowers, 10cm (4in) across, are borne in summer-autumn. Leaves are large and dark green.

R. 'Blue Rambler'. See *R.* 'Veilchenblau'.

R. 'Blush Noisette'. See *R.* 'Noisette Carnée'.

R. BONICA ('Meidomonac'), syn. *R.* 'Bonica '82', illus. p186.

R. 'Boule de Neige' illus. p.184.

R. 'Bouquet de la Mariée'. See *R.* 'Aimée Vibert'.

R. 'Brass Ring'. See *R.* PEEK-A-BOO.

R. BREATH OF LIFE ('Harquanne') illus. p.197.

R. BRIGHT SMILE ('Dicdance') illus. p.193.

R. 'Buff Beauty'. Rounded shrub rose. H and S 1.2m (4ft). Slightly fragrant, cupped, fully double, apricot-buff flowers, 9cm (3½in) across, are borne freely in summer, sparsely in autumn. Has plentiful, glossy, dark green leaves. Zone 6.

R. 'Canary Bird'. See *R. xanthina* 'Canary Bird'.

R. 'Capitaine John Ingram'. Vigorous, bushy Moss rose. H and S 1.2m (4ft). In summer bears fragrant, cupped, fully double, rich maroon-crimson flowers, 8cm (3in) across; petals are paler on reverses. Foliage is dark green. Zone 6.

R. 'Cardinal de Richelieu' illus. p.188.

R. CARDINAL HUME ('Harregale') illus. p.188.

R. CASINO ('Macca'), syn. *R.* 'Gerbe d'Or', illus. p.199.

R. 'Cécile Brünner', syn. *R.* 'Mignon'.

Upright, spindly China rose with fairly smooth stems. H 75cm (30in), S 60cm (24in). Produces slightly scented, urn-shaped, fully double, light pink flowers, 4cm (1½in) across, in summer-autumn. Small, dark green leaves are sparse. Zone 6.

R. 'Céleste', syn. *R.* 'Celestial', illus. p.185.

R. 'Celestial'. See *R.* 'Céleste'.

R. x centifolia 'Cristata', syn. *R.* 'Chapeau de Napoléon', *R.* 'Cristata' (Crested moss). Bushy, lanky Provence rose. H 1.5m (5ft), S 1.2m (4ft). In summer, very fragrant, cupped, fully double, pink flowers, 9cm (3½in) across and with tufted sepals, are borne on nodding stems amid dull green foliage. May be grown on a support. **'Muscosa'** (Common moss, Old pink moss) is a vigorous, lax Moss rose. H 1.5m (5ft), S 1.2m (4ft). Bears fragrant, rounded to cupped, fully double, mossed, pink flowers, 8cm (3in) across, in summer. Leaves are matt, dull green. Best with support. Both zone 4.

R. CHAMPAGNE COCKTAIL ('Horflash') illus. p.192.

R. 'Champlain'. Free-flowering shrub rose that makes a good informal hedge. H and S 1m (3ft). Has velvety red, slightly fragrant, double flowers. Good resistance to mildew. Zone 3.

R. 'Chapeau de Napoléon'. See *R.* x *centifolia* 'Cristata'.

R. 'Chaplin's Pink Companion' illus. p.197.

R. 'Charles Albanel'. A low, spreading shrub rose that makes a good ground cover. H 0.5m (18in), S 1m (3ft). Medium red, fragrant flowers freely produced in spring and then sporadically through the summer. Excellent black spot and mildew resistance. Zone 2b.

R. 'Charles de Mills', syn. *R.* 'Bizarre Triomphant'. Upright, arching Gallica rose with fairly smooth stems. H 1.2m (4ft), S 1m (3ft). Very fragrant, quartered-rosette, fully double, crimson-purple flowers, 10cm (4in) across, appear in summer. Leaves are plentiful and mid-green. May be grown on a support. Zone 5.

R. 'Chewarvel'. See *R.* LAURA FORD.

R. chinensis var. **minima.** See *R.* 'Rouletii'. **'Mutabilis'** see *R.* x *odorata* 'Mutabilis'.

R. CITY GIRL ('Harzorba') illus. p.198.

R. CITY OF LONDON ('Harukfore'). Rounded, cluster-flowered bush rose. H 1m (3ft), S 75cm (2½ft). In summer-autumn, bears dainty sprays of sweet-smelling, urn-shaped, double, blush-pink flowers, 8cm (3in) across, amid bright green foliage.

R. CLARISSA ('Harprocrustes'). Upright, cluster-flowered bush rose. H 75cm (30in), S 45cm (18in). Dense sprays of slightly scented, urn-shaped, fully double, apricot flowers, 5cm (2in) across, appear in summer-autumn. Has many small, glossy leaves. Makes a good, narrow hedge.

R. 'Cocabest'. See *R.* WEE JOCK.

R. 'Cocdestin'. See *R.* REMEMBER ME.

R. COLIBRE '79 ('Meidanover') illus. p.196.

R. 'Commandant Beaurepaire', syn. *R.* 'Panachée d'Angers'. Vigorous,

spreading Bourbon rose. H and S 1.2m (4ft). Fragrant, cupped, double flowers, 10cm (4in) across, are borne in summer-autumn. They are blush-pink, splashed with mauve, purple, crimson and scarlet. Light green leaflets have wavy margins. Zone 6.

R. 'Compassion', syn. *R.* 'Belle de Londres', illus. p198.

R. 'Complicata' illus. p.186.

R. 'Comte de Chambord'. See *R.* 'Madame Knorr'.

R. CONGRATULATIONS ('Korlift'), syn. *R.* 'Sylvia'. Upright, vigorous, large-flowered bush rose. H 1.2m (4ft), S 1m (3ft). Produces neat, urn-shaped, fully double, deep rose-pink flowers, 11cm (4½in) across, on long stems in summer-autumn. Leaves are large and dark green. Makes a tall hedge.

R. 'Conrad Ferdinand Meyer' illus. p185.

R. CONSTANCE SPRY ('Austance') illus. p.186.

R. 'Cored'. See *R.* ALEC'S RED.

R. 'Cristata'. See *R.* x *centifolia* 'Cristata'.

R. 'Cuisse de Nymphe'. See *R.* 'Great Maiden's Blush'.

R. 'Cuthbert Grant'. A vigorous semi-upright shrub rose. H 1m (3ft), S 60cm (2ft). Strongly fragrant, crimson red, semi-double flowers about 10cm (4in) across are produced in June and September. Plants have excellent resistance to mildew and black spot. Zone 3.

R. 'Danse du Feu', syn. *R.* 'Spectacular', illus. p.198.

R. 'David Thompson'. A *R. rugosa* hybrid shrub rose. H 1.2m (4ft). Free flowering, with 7cm (3in) medium red blooms. It does not set fruit. Highly resistant to black spot and mildew. Zone 2b.

R. 'Dicdance'. See *R.* BRIGHT SMILE.

R. 'Dicdivine'. See *R.* POT O' GOLD.

R. 'Dicgrow'. See *R.* PEEK-A-BOO.

R. 'Dicinfra'. See *R.* DISCO DANCER.

R. 'Dicjana'. See *R.* ELINA.

R. 'Dicjem'. See *R.* FREEDOM.

R. 'Dicjubell'. See *R.* LOVELY LADY.

R. 'Dickimono'. See *R.* ANISLEY DICKSON.

R. 'Dicky'. See *R.* ANISLEY DICKSON.

R. 'Diclittle'. See *R.* LITTLE WOMAN.

R. 'Diclulu'. See *R.* GENTLE TOUCH.

R. 'Dicmagic'. See *R.* SWEET MAGIC.

R. DISCO DANCER ('Dicinfra'). Dense, rounded, cluster-flowered bush rose. H 75cm (30in), S 60cm (24in). Bears dense sprays of slightly fragrant, cupped, double, bright orange-red flowers, 6cm (2½in) across, in summer-autumn, amid a mass of glossy foliage.

R. 'Don Juan', syn. 'Malandrone'. Branching, upright climbing rose. H 3m (10ft), S 2m (6ft). Very fragrant, fully double, dark red cupped flowers in clusters repeated throughout the summer.

R. 'Doris Tysterman' illus. p.194.

R. 'Dortmund' illus. p.198.

R. DOUBLE DELIGHT ('Andeli') illus. p.191.

R. 'Double Velvet'. See *R.* 'Tuscany Superb'.

R. 'Doux Parfum'. See *R.* L'AIMANT.

R. DRUMMER BOY ('Harvacity'). Dwarf cluster-flowered bush rose of bushy, spreading habit. H and

S 50cm (20in). Faintly scented, cupped, double, bright crimson flowers, 5cm (2in) across, appear in dense sprays amid a mass of small, dark green leaves in summer-autumn. Makes a good, low hedge.

R. DUBLIN BAY ('Macdub') illus. p.198.

R. 'Duchesse d'Istrie'. See *R.* 'William Lobb'.

R. 'Duftzauber '84'. See *R.* ROYAL WILLIAM.

R. 'Du Maître d'Ecole'. Bushy, spreading Gallica rose. H 1.2m (4ft), S 1m (3ft). Bears fragrant, quartered-rosette, fully double, carmine to light pink flowers, 10cm (4in) across, in summer. Foliage is dull green. Zone 6.

R. 'Dupontii', syn. *R. moschata* var. *nivea*, illus. p.185.

R. ecae illus. p.188.

R. eglanteria. See *R. rubiginosa*.

R. ELINA ('Dicjana'), syn. *R.* 'Peaudouce'. Vigorous, shrubby, large-flowered bush rose. H 1.1m (3½ft), S 75cm (2½ft). Lightly scented, rounded, fully double, ivory-white flowers, 15cm (6in) across, with lemon-yellow centres, are borne freely in summer-autumn. Has abundant, reddish foliage.

R. 'Elizabeth Harkness' illus. p.189.

R. 'Emily Gray' illus. p199.

R. 'Empereur du Maroc' illus. p.188.

R. ESCAPADE ('Harpade') illus. p.191.

R. 'Fantin-Latour' illus. p.185.

R. FASCINATION ('Poulmax'), syn. *R.* 'Fredensborg'. Vigorous, cluster-flowered bush rose. H 1m (3ft), S 60cm (2ft). In summer-autumn, bears clusters of fragrant, rounded, double, shrimp-pink blooms amid dark green, glossy foliage. Is good for beds and hedges.

R. 'Felicia' illus. p.185.

R. 'Félicité Parmentier'. Vigorous, compact, upright Alba rose. H 1.2m (4ft), S 1m (3ft). Fragrant, cupped to flat, fully double, pale flesh-pink flowers, 6cm (2½in) across, are borne in mid-summer. Has abundant, greyish-green leaves. Makes a good hedge. Zone 3.

R. 'Félicité Perpétue' illus. p.196.

R. filipes 'Kiftsgate' illus. p.196.

R. 'Fire Princess' illus. p.195.

R. 'F.J.Grootendorst'. Very vigorous and spiny shrub rose. H 1.2m (4ft), S 1m (3ft). Has small, crimson, double, very fragrant flowers all summer. Good orange fruit persist into winter. Zone 2b.

R. foetida 'Persiana', syn. *R.* 'Persian Yellow', illus. p.188.

R. 'Fortune's Double Yellow'. See *R.* x *odorata* 'Pseudindica'.

R. FRAGRANT CLOUD ('Tanellis'). Bushy, dense, large-flowered bush rose. H 75cm (30in), S 60cm (24in). Very fragrant, rounded, double, dusky-scarlet flowers, 12cm (5in) across, are borne freely in summer-autumn. Has plentiful, dark green foliage.

R. 'Fragrant Delight'. Bushy, cluster-flowered bush rose of uneven habit. H 1m (3ft), S 75cm (2½ft). Produces an abundance of reddish-green foliage, amid which clusters of fragrant, urn-shaped, double, salmon-pink flowers, 8cm (3in) across, are borne freely in summer-autumn.

R. 'Frau Dagmar Hartopp'. See *R.* 'Fru Dagmar Hastrup'.

R. 'Fredensborg'. See *R.* FASCINATION.

R. FREEDOM ('Dicjem') illus. p.193.

R. 'Friesia'. See *R.* 'Korresia'.

R. 'Fru Dagmar Hastrup', syn. 'Frau Dagmar Hartopp'. A spreading *R. rugosa* hybrid. H 1m (3ft), S 1.2m (4ft). Single, clove-scented, light pink flowers, with cream stamens in spring and occasionally until autumn. Produces large crops of crimson hips that persist well. Zone 2b.

R. 'Frühlingsmorgen', syn. *R.* 'Spring Morning'. Open, free-branching shrub rose. H 2m (6ft), S 1.5m (5ft). Foliage is greyish-green. In late spring produces hay-scented, cupped, single, pink flowers, 12cm (5in) across, with a primrose centre and reddish stamens. Zone 6.

R. gallica var. *officinalis*, syn. *R.* 'Apothecary's Rose', *R. officinalis* (Red rose of Lancaster). Bushy species rose of neat habit. H to 80cm (32in), S 1m (36in). In summer bears flat, semi-double, pinkish-red flowers, 8cm (3in) across, with a moderate scent. Zone 4. 'Versicolor' illus. p.187.

R. 'Gaumo'. See *R.* ROSE GAUJARD.

R. GENTLE TOUCH ('Diclulu'). Upright, dwarf cluster-flowered bush rose. H 50cm (20in), S 30cm (12in). Bears sprays of faintly scented, urn-shaped, semi-double, pale salmon-pink flowers, 5cm (2in) across, in summer-autumn. Leaves are small and dark green. Is good as a low hedge.

R. 'Geranium'. See *R. moyesii* 'Geranium'.

R. 'Gerbe d'Or'. See *R.* 'Casino'.

R. 'Gioia'. See *R.* 'Peace'.

R. 'Gipsy Boy'. See *R.* 'Zigeunerknabe'.

R. glauca, syn. *R. rubrifolia*, illus. p.186.

R. 'Glenfiddich' illus. p.193.

R. 'Gloire de Dijon' illus. p.196.

R. 'Gloire des Mousseux'. Vigorous, bushy Moss rose. H 1.2m (4ft), S 1m (3ft). Has plentiful, light green foliage. In summer bears fragrant, cupped, fully double flowers, 15cm (6in) across. These are bright pink, paling to blush-pink, with light green 'mossing'. Zone 5.

R. 'Gloria Dei'. See *R.* 'Peace'.

R. 'Gold of Ophir'. See *R.* x *odorata* 'Pseudindica'.

R. GOLDEN PENNY ('Rugul'), syn. *R.* 'Guletta', *R.* 'Tapis Jaune', illus. p.192.

R. 'Golden Rambler'. See *R.* 'Alister Stella Gray'.

R. 'Golden Showers' illus. p.199.

R. 'Golden Sunblaze'. See *R.* 'Rise 'n' Shine'.

R. 'Golden Wings'. Bushy, spreading shrub rose. H 1.1m (3½ft), S 1.35m (4½ft). Bears fragrant, cupped, single, pale yellow flowers, 12cm (5in) across, amid light green foliage, in summer-autumn. Is good for a hedge. Zone 3.

R. 'Goldfinch'. Vigorous, arching rambler rose. H 2.7m (9ft), S 2m (6ft). In summer produces lightly scented, rosette, double, yolk-yellow flowers, 4cm (1½in) across, that fade to white. Has plentiful, bright light green leaves. Zone 6.

R. 'Goldsmith'. See *R.* SIMBA.

R. GRAHAM THOMAS ('Ausmas') illus. p.189.

R. 'Grandpa Dickson', syn. *R.* 'Irish Gold', illus. p.193.

R. 'Great Maiden's Blush', syn. *R.* 'Cuisse de Nymphe', *R.* 'La Séduisante', illus. p.185.

R. GROUSE ('Korimro') illus. p.189.

R. 'Guinée' illus. p.199.

R. 'Guletta'. See *R.* GOLDEN PENNY.

R. HANDEL ('Macha') illus. p.197.

R. HANNAH GORDON ('Korweiso'). Bushy, open, cluster-flowered bush rose. H 75cm (30in), S 60cm (2ft). Sprays of slightly fragrant, cupped, double, blush-pink flowers, 8cm (3in) across, margined with reddish-pink, appear in summer-autumn. Leaves are dark green.

R. 'Hansa'. A very free-flowering *R. rugosa* hybrid. H 1.2m (4ft), S 1m (3ft). Highly fragrant, double reddish-purple flowers with fringed petals produced all summer long. One of the best and most floriferous *rugosa* hybrids. Zone 2b.

R. x *harisonii* 'Harison's Yellow'. (Yellow rose of Texas). Upright, spiny rose that makes a good hedge. H 2m (6ft), S 1.2m (4ft). Has cupped, semi-double, bright yellow flowers in spring and blackish-red hips. Zone 2.

R. 'Harkaramel'. See *R.* ANNE HARKNESS.

R. 'Harkuly'. See *R.* MARGARET MERRIL.

R. 'Harlex'. See *R.* ALEXANDER.

R. 'Harmantelle'. See *R.* MOUNTBATTEN.

R. 'Harpade'. See *R.* ESCAPADE.

R. 'Harpiccolo'. See *R.* ANNA FORD.

R. 'Harprocrustes'. See *R.* CLARISSA.

R. 'Harquanne'. See *R.* BREATH OF LIFE.

R. 'Harqueterwife'. See *R.* PAUL SHIRVILLE.

R. 'Harregale'. See *R.* CARDINAL HUME.

R. 'Harroony'. See *R.* AMBER QUEEN.

R. 'Harrowbond'. See *R.* ROSEMARY HARKNESS.

R. 'Harsherry'. See *R.* SHEILA'S PERFUME.

R. 'Harukfore'. See *R.* CITY OF LONDON.

R. 'Harwanna'. See *R.* JACQUELINE DU PRÉ.

R. 'Harwanted'. See *R.* MANY HAPPY RETURNS.

R. 'Haryup'. See *R.* HIGH HOPES.

R. 'Harzorba'. See *R.* CITY GIRL.

R. 'Heartthrob'. See *R.* 'Paul Shirville'.

R. 'Heideröslein'. See *R.* 'Nozomi'.

R. 'Henri Martin', syn. *R.* 'Red Moss', illus. p.187.

R. 'Henry Hudson'. A hardy, semi-dwarf, disease resistant shrub rose. H 60cm (2ft), S 1m (3ft). Fragrant flowers are white with a tinge of pink and produced all summer. Zone 2b.

R. 'Henry Kelsey'. A repeat-flowering climbing rose. H 2.5m (8ft), S 1.5m (4ft). Flowers are medium red with a spicy fragrance and produced in clusters of 5–18 blooms. Good mildew resistance. Zone 3.

R. HIGH HOPES ('Haryup') illus. p.198.

R. 'Honorine de Brabant'. Vigorous, bushy, sprawling Bourbon rose. H and S 2m (6ft). Fragrant, quartered, double flowers, 10cm (4in) across, lilac-pink,

marked with light purple and crimson, are produced in summer-autumn. Has plentiful, light green foliage. Zone 5.

R. 'Horflash'. See *R.* CHAMPAGNE COCKTAIL.

R. 'Hula Girl' illus. p.195.

R. ICEBERG ('Korbin'), syn. *R.* 'Schneewittchen', illus. p.189.

R. 'Iced Ginger' illus. p.190.

R. INGRID BERGMAN ('Poulman'). Upright, branching, large-flowered bush rose. H 75cm (30in), S 60cm (24in). Bears slightly scented, urn-shaped, double, dark red flowers, 11cm (4½in) across, in summer-autumn. Has leathery, semi-glossy, dark green foliage.

R. 'Interall'. See *R.* ROSY CUSHION.

R. INVINCIBLE ('Runatru'). Upright, cluster-flowered bush rose. H 1m (3ft), S 60cm (2ft). Faintly scented, cupped, fully double, bright crimson flowers, 9cm (3½in) across, appear in open clusters in summer-autumn. Leaves are semi-glossy.

R. 'Irish Gold'. See *R.* 'Grandpa Dickson'.

R. 'Ispahan', syn. *R.* 'Pompon des Princes', *R.* 'Rose d'Isfahan'. Vigorous, bushy, dense Damask rose. H 1.5m (5ft), S 1.2m (4ft). Produces fragrant, cupped, double, clear pink flowers, 8cm (3in) across, amid greyish-green foliage throughout summer and autumn. Zone 4.

R. JACQUELINE DU PRÉ ('Harwanna'). Vigorous, arching shrub rose. H 2m (6ft), S 1.5m (5ft). In summer-autumn bears musk-scented, cupped, double, ivory-white flowers, 10cm (4in) across, with scalloped petals and red stamens. Has abundant glossy leaves. Makes a large hedge.

R. 'Jens Munk'. A vigorous, spiny shrub rose with good disease resistance. H 2m (6ft), S 1.5m (4.5m). Semi-double, fragrant, pink flowers during the summer, and showy orange hips that last well into winter. Zone 2b.

R. 'John Cabot'. Vigorous shrub rose. H 1.5m (5ft), S 1.2m (4ft). Has yellow-green leaves and, in summer-autumn, clusters of fragrant, cupped, double, magenta flowers, 6cm (2½in) across. May be grown as a climber or hedge. Zone 2b.

R. 'John Davies'. A free-flowering climbing rose. H 2.5m (8ft), S 1.2m (4ft). Has clusters of up to 18 medium pink flower with a spicy perfume that open from buds like a miniature hybrid tea rose. Excellent disease resistance. Foliage turns a yellow to orange in fall. Zone 3.

R. 'John Franklin'. A bushy, upright shrub rose. H and S 1.2m (4ft). Medium red flowers with fringed petals are borne from spring to fall in large clusters. Zone 4.

R. 'J.P.Connell'. A vigorous, upright shrub rose with good resistance to mildew and blackspot. H 1.5m (4.5ft), S 1.2m (4ft). Semi-double flowers open yellow and fade to a cream but with prominent yellow stamens. Flowers best on established plants. Zone 3.

R. 'Julia's Rose'. Spindly, branching, large-flowered bush rose. H 75cm (30in), S 45cm (18in). In summer-autumn produces faintly scented, urn-shaped, double, brownish-pink to buff

flowers, 10cm (4in) across. Foliage is reddish-green. Is good for flower arrangements.
R. '**Just Joey**' illus. p.194.
R. '**Karl Forster**'. Bushy shrub rose with light green foliage. H 1.5m (5ft), S 1.2m (4ft). Very showy large double white flowers with golden stamens when fully open. Blooms well later in summer. Zone 4b.
R. '**Kathleen Harrop**'. Arching, lax Bourbon rose. H 2.5m (8ft), S 2m (6ft). Fragrant, double, cupped, pale pink flowers, 8cm (3in) across, are borne in summer-autumn. Plentiful, dark green foliage is susceptible to mildew. May be grown as a climber or hedge. Zone 6.
R. KEEPSAKE ('Kormalda') illus. p.191.
R. '**Königin von Dänemark**', syn. *R.* 'Belle Courtisanne', illus. p.186.
R. '**Königliche Hoheit**'. See *R.* 'Royal Highness'.
R. '**Korbelma**'. See *R.* SIMBA.
R. '**Korbin**'. See *R.* ICEBERG.
R. '**Korblue**'. See *R.* SHOCKING BLUE.
R. '**Korimro**'. See *R.* GROUSE.
R. '**Korlift**'. See *R.* CONGRATULATIONS.
R. '**Kormalda**'. See *R.* KEEPSAKE.
R. '**Korpeahn**'. See *R.* THE TIMES ROSE.
R. '**Korresia**', syn. *R.* 'Friesia', illus. p.193.
R. '**Korweiso**'. See *R.* HANNAH GORDON.
R. '**Korzaun**'. See *R.* ROYAL WILLIAM.
R. '**La Séduisante**'. See *R.* 'Great Maiden's Blush'.
R. '**Lanken**'. See *R.* FELICITY KENDAL.
R. LAURA FORD ('Chewarvel') illus. p.199.
R. '**Leggab**'. See *R.* PEARL DRIFT.
R. '**Legnews**'. See *R.* NEWS.
R. '**Lenip**'. See *R.* PASCALI.
R. LITTLE WOMAN ('Diclittle'). Upright, dwarf cluster-flowered bush rose. H 50cm (20in), S 40cm (16in). In summer-autumn bears sprays of faintly fragrant, urn-shaped, double, salmon-pink flowers, 5cm (2in) across. Has small, dark green leaves. Is suitable for a narrow hedge.
R. '**Louise Odier**', syn. *R.* 'Madame de Stella'. Elegant, upright Bourbon rose. H 2m (6ft), S 1.2m (4ft). Has light greyish-green foliage and fragrant, cupped, fully double, warm rose-pink flowers, 12cm (5in) across, borne in summer-autumn. Zone 5.
R. '**Louis Jolliet**'. Disease resistant climbing rose with a trailing habit. H 2m (6ft), S 1.2m (4ft). Pink flowers in small clusters are produced continuously from June to September. Zone 3.
R. LOVELY LADY ('Dicjubell') illus. p.190.
R. '**Macangeli**'. See *R.* SNOWBALL.
R. '**Macar**'. See *R.* PICCADILLY.
R. '**Macca**'. See *R.* CASINO.
R. '**Maccarpe**'. See *R.* SNOW CARPET.
R. '**Macdub**'. See *R.* DUBLIN BAY.
R. '**Macha**'. See *R.* HANDEL.
R. '**Macrexy**'. See *R.* SEXY REXY.
R. macrophylla. Vigorous species rose. H 4m (12ft), S 3m (10ft). Bears moderately fragrant, flat, single, red flowers, 5cm (2in) across, in summer, followed by flask-shaped, red hips. Has

red stems and large, mid-green leaves. Zone 5.
R. '**Mactru**'. See *R.* TRUMPETER.
R. '**Madame Alfred Carrière**' illus. p.196.
R. '**Madame A. Meilland**'. See *R.* PEACE.
R. '**Madame de Stella**'. See *R.* 'Louise Odier'.
R. '**Madame Ernest Calvat**'. Vigorous, arching Bourbon rose. H 2–3m (6–10ft), S 2m (6ft). Fragrant, cupped to quartered-rosette, fully double, rose-pink flowers, 15cm (6in) across, are borne freely in summer-autumn. Has plentiful, large leaves. Zone 6.
R. '**Madame Grégoire Staechelin**', syn. *R.* 'Spanish Beauty', illus. p.197.
R. '**Madame Hardy**' illus. p.184.
R. '**Madame Hébert**'. See *R.* 'Président de Sèze'.
R. '**Madame Isaac Pereire**' illus. p.187.
R. '**Madame Pierre Oger**'. Lax Bourbon rose. H 2m (6ft), S 1.2m (4ft). In summer-autumn, slender stems carry sweetly scented, cupped or bowl-shaped, double, pink flowers, 8cm (3in) across, with rose-lilac tints. Has light green leaves. Grows well on a pillar. Zone 6.
R. MAGIC CAROUSEL ('Moorcar'). Bushy, miniature bush rose. H 40cm (16in), S 30cm (12in). Slightly scented, rosette, fully double, yellow-and-red flowers, 4cm (1½in) across, with petals arranged in diminishing circles, appear in summer-autumn. Has small, glossy leaves.
R. '**Maigold**' illus. p.199.
R. '**Mainzer Fastnacht**'. See *R.* BLUE MOON.
R. '**Malandrone**'. See *R.* 'Don Juan'.
R. MANY HAPPY RETURNS ('Harwanted'), syn. *R.* 'Prima'. Bushy, spreading shrub rose. H 1m (3ft), S 1.2m (4ft). In summer-autumn bears lightly fragrant, cupped, double, blush-pink flowers, 10cm (4in) across, freely amid glossy, dark green leaves. Zone 6.
R. '**Maréchal Davoust**'. Vigorous, bushy Moss rose. H 1.5m (5ft), S 1.2m (4ft). In summer bears moderately fragrant, cupped, fully double, deep reddish-pink to purple flowers, 10cm (4in) across, with a green eye and brownish 'mossing'. Leaves are dull green and lance-shaped. Zone 5.
R. '**Maréchal Niel**'. Vigorous, spreading Noisette or Tea climbing rose. H 3m (10ft), S 2m (6ft). Drooping stems carry rich green foliage and moderately scented, pointed, fully double, clear yellow flowers, 10cm (4in) across, in summer-autumn. Zone 6.
R. MARGARET MERRIL ('Harkuly') illus. p.189.
R. '**Marguerite Hilling**', syn. *R.* 'Pink Nevada', illus. p.186.
R. MARY ROSE ('Ausmary'). Bushy, spreading shrub rose. H and S 1.2m (4ft). Produces moderately fragrant, cupped, fully double, rose-pink flowers, 9cm (3½in) across, in summer-autumn. Has plentiful leaves. Zone 6.
R. '**Meidanover**'. See *R.* COLIBRE '79.
R. '**Meidomonac**'. See *R.* BONICA.
R. '**Meijikitar**'. See *R.* ORANGE SUNBLAZE.

R. '**Mermaid**' illus. p.199.
R. '**Mignon**'. See *R.* 'Cécile Brünner'.
R. '**Moorcar**'. See *R.* MAGIC CAROUSEL.
R. '**Morden Amorette**'. Compact, repeat blooming shrub rose. H 0.5m (18in), S 1m (3ft). Fully double rose carmine flowers have up to 30 rolled petals. Deadheading promotes continuous blooms. Good disease resistance. Zone 3.
R. '**Morden Blush**'. Variable, dwarf, shrub rose. H 0.5–1m (18–36in), S 0.5m (18in). Flowers from June until hard frost with double flat blooms that are pink in cool weather and white in hot. Good disease resistance. Zone 2b.
R. '**Morden Centennial**'. Repeat-blooming dwarf shrub rose. H 1m (3ft), S 60cm (2ft). Fragrant, double, light pink flowers with about 40 petals are borne in small clusters. Main blooming times are June and August-September with some flowers between these flushes. Zone 3b.
R. '**Morning Jewel**'. Free-branching climbing rose. H 2.5m (8ft), S 2.2m (7ft). Has plentiful, glossy foliage and cupped, double, bright pink flowers, 9cm (3½in) across, freely borne, usually in clusters, in summer-autumn. May be pruned to a shrub. Zone 6.
R. '**Morsherry**. See *R.* SHERI ANNE.
R. moschata var. *nivea.* See *R.* 'Dupontii'.
R. MOUNTBATTEN ('Harmantelle') illus. p.193.
R. '**Mousseline**', syn. *R.* 'Alfred de Dalmas'. Bushy Moss rose with twiggy growth. H and S 1m (3ft). Mainly in summer bears pleasantly scented, cupped, fully double, blush-pink flowers, 8cm (3in) across, with little 'mossing'. Has matt green leaves. Zone 6.
R. moyesii. Vigorous, arching species rose. H 4m (12ft), S 3m (10ft). In summer, faintly scented, flat, single, dusky-scarlet flowers, 5cm (2in) across, with yellow stamens, are borne close to branches. Produces long, red hips in autumn. Sparse, small, dark green leaves are composed of 7–13 leaflets. Zone 4.
'**Geranium**' (syn. *R.* 'Geranium') illus. p.187.
R. '**Mrs John Laing**' illus. p.187.
R. '**Münchner Kindl**'. See *R.* ANISLEY DICKSON.
R. '**National Trust**'. Compact, large-flowered bush rose. H 75cm (30in), S 60cm (24in). Slightly scented, urn-shaped, fully double, scarlet-crimson flowers, 10cm (4in) across, are borne freely in summer-autumn. Produces plentiful, dark green foliage. Makes a good, low hedge.
R. '**Nevada**' illus. p.185.
R. '**New Dawn**' illus. p.197.
R. '**Noisette Carnée**', syn. *R.* 'Blush Noisette'. Noisette climbing rose of branching habit and lax growth. H 2–4m (6–12ft), S 2–2.5m (6–8ft). In summer-autumn, smooth stems bear clusters of spice-scented, cupped, double, blush-pink flowers, 4cm (1½in) across. Has matt foliage. May be grown as a shrub. Zone 6.
R. '**Nozomi**', syn. *R.* 'Heideröslein', illus. p.189.
R. '**Nuits de Young**', syn. *R.* 'Old

Black'. Erect Moss rose with wiry stems. H 1.2m (4ft), S 1m (3ft). Bears, in summer, slightly scented, double, flat, dark maroon-purple flowers, 5cm (2in) across, with brownish 'mossing'. Leaves are small and dark green. Zone 6.
R. '**Ocarina**'. See *R.* ANGELA RIPPON.
R. '**Ocaru**'. See *R.* ANGELA RIPPON.
R. x *odorata* '**Mutabilis**', syn. *R. chinensis* 'Mutabilis', illus. p.187. 'Pallida' illus. p.187. '**Pseudindica**' (syn. *R.* 'Beauty of Glazenwood', *R.* 'Fortune's Double Yellow', *R.* 'Gold of Ophir', *R.* 'San Rafael Rose') is a lax climbing rose of restrained growth. H 2.5m (8ft), S 1.5m (5ft). In summer bears small clusters of scented, pointed to cupped, semi-double, copper-suffused, yellow flowers, 5cm (2in) across. Leaves are glossy, light green. Prune very lightly. Zone 6.
R. officinalis. See *R. gallica* var. *officinalis.*
R. '**Old Black**'. See *R.* 'Nuits de Young'.
R. '**Omar Khayyám**'. Dense, prickly Damask rose. H and S 1m (3ft). Fragrant, quartered-rosette, fully double, light pink flowers, 8cm (3in) across, are borne amid downy, greyish foliage in summer. Zone 5.
R. omeiensis f. *pteracantha.* See *R. sericea* subsp. *omeiensis* f. *pteracantha.*
R. '**Opa Potschke**'. See *R.* 'Precious Platinum'.
R. '**Ophelia**'. Upright, open, large-flowered bush rose. H 1m (3ft), S 60cm (2ft). In summer-autumn produces sweetly fragrant, urn-shaped, double, creamy-blush-pink flowers, 10cm (4in) across, singly or in clusters. Dark green foliage is sparse.
R. ORANGE SUNBLAZE ('Meijikitar'), syn. *R.* 'Sunblaze', illus. p.196.
R. '**Panachée d'Angers**'. See *R.* 'Commandant Beaurepaire'.
R. PASCALI ('Lenip'). Upright, large-flowered bush rose. H 1m (3ft), S 60cm (2ft). Bears faintly scented, neat, urn-shaped, fully double, white flowers, 9cm (3½in) across, in summer-autumn. Has deep green leaves.
R. PAUL SHIRVILLE ('Harqueterwife'), syn. *R.* 'Heartthrob', illus. p.191.
R. '**Paul Transon**'. Vigorous, rather lax rambler rose. H 4m (12ft), S 1.5m (5ft). In summer bears slightly fragrant, flat, double, faintly coppery, salmon-pink flowers, 8cm (3in) across, with pleated petals. Plentiful foliage is glossy, dark green. Zone 5.
R. '**Paul's Himalayan Musk**', syn. *R.* 'Paul's Himalayan Musk Rambler'. Very vigorous climbing rose. H and S 10m (30ft). Large clusters of slightly fragrant, rosette, double, blush-pink flowers, 4cm (1½in) across, are freely borne in late summer. Has thorny, trailing shoots and drooping leaves. Is suitable for growing up a tree or in a wild garden. Zone 6.
R. '**Paul's Himalayan Musk Rambler**'. See *R.* 'Paul's Himalayan Musk'.
R. '**Paul's Lemon Pillar**' illus. p.196.
R. PEACE ('Madame A. Meilland'), syn. *R.* 'Gioia', *R.* 'Gloria Dei', illus. p.192.
R. PEARL DRIFT ('Leggab') illus. p.185.

R. 'Peaudouce'. See *R*. ELINA.

R. PEEK-A-BOO ('Dicgrow'), syn.
R. 'Brass Ring', illus. p.190.

R. 'Penelope' illus. p.184.

R. 'Perle d'Or'. China rose that forms
a twiggy, leafy, small shrub. H 75cm
(2½ft), S 60cm (2ft). Small, slightly
scented, urn-shaped, fully double,
honey-pink flowers, 4cm (1½in) across,
are borne in summer-autumn. Leaves
have pointed, glossy leaflets. Zone 6.

R. 'Persian Yellow'. See *R. foetida*
'Persiana'.

R. PETIT FOUR ('Interfour').
Compact, dwarf cluster-flowered bush
rose. H and S 40cm (16in). In summer-
autumn, bears dense clusters of
slightly fragrant, flat, wide-opening,
semi-double, pink-and-white flowers,
4cm (1½in) across, amid plentiful
mid-green foliage.

R. PICCADILLY ('Macar') illus. p.194.

R. pimpinellifolia, syn. *R. spinosissima*
(Burnet rose, Scotch rose). 'Plena'
illus. p.184.

R. PINK BELLS ('Poulbells')
illus. p.190.

R. 'Pink Grootendorst' illus. p.186.

R. 'Pink Nevada'. See *R*. 'Marguerite
Hilling'.

R. 'Pink Parfait'. Bushy, cluster-
flowered bush rose. H 75cm (2½ft),
S 60cm (2ft). In summer-autumn,
slightly fragrant, urn-shaped, double
flowers, 9cm (3½in) across, in shades
of light pink, are produced freely. Has
plentiful foliage.

R. 'Pink Perpétué' illus. p.197.

R. 'Pompon de Paris'. See
R. 'Rouletii'.

R. 'Pompon des Princes'. See
R. 'Ispahan'.

R. POT O' GOLD ('Dicdivine')
illus. p.194.

R. 'Poulbells'. See *R*. PINK BELLS.

R. 'Poulcov'. See *R*. KENT.

R. 'Poulman'. See *R*. INGRID BERGMAN.

R. 'Poulmax'. See *R*. FASCINATION.

R. 'Poumidor'. See *R*. TROIKA.

R. 'Prairie Dawn'. An upright shrub
rose with spiny canes that is good for
hedging. H 1.5m (5ft), S 1m (3ft). Has
fully double, medium pink blooms,
with a good fragrance and disease
resistance. Zone 3b.

R. 'Precious Platinum', syn.
R. 'Opa Potschke', illus. p.192.

R. 'Président de Sèze', syn.
R. 'Madame Hébert'. Vigorous, rather
open Gallica rose. H and S 1.2m (4ft).
Bears fragrant, quartered-rosette, fully
double, magenta-pink to pale lilac-pink
flowers, 10cm (4in) across, in summer.
Zone 6.

R. 'Prima'. See *R*. 'Many Happy
Returns'.

R. primula illus. p.188.

R. PRINCESS MICHAEL OF KENT
('Harlightly'). Neat, compact, cluster-
flowered bush rose. H 60cm (24in),
S 50cm (20in). In summer-autumn
produces pleasantly scented, rounded,
fully double, yellow flowers, 9cm
(3½in) across, singly or in clusters.
Leaves are glossy, bright green and
very healthy. Makes a good, low hedge.

R. 'Queen Elizabeth', syn.
R. 'The Queen Elizabeth',
illus. p.190.

R. 'Queen of the Violets'. See
R. 'Reine des Violettes'.

R. 'Rambling Rector' illus. p.198.

R. 'Ramona', syn. *R*. 'Red Cherokee'.
Rather stiff, open climbing rose.
H 2.7m (9ft), S 3m (10ft). Fragrant,
flat, single, carmine-red flowers, 10cm
(4in) across, with a greyish-red reverse
and gold stamens, appear mainly in
summer, a few later. Has sparse foliage.
Does best against a warm wall. Zone 6.

R. RED ACE ('Amruda') illus. p.195.

R. 'Red Cherokee'. See *R*. 'Ramona'.

R. 'Red Moss'. See *R*. 'Henri Martin'.

R. 'Reine des Violettes', syn.
R. 'Queen of the Violets'. Spreading,
vigorous Hybrid Perpetual rose. H and
S 2m (6ft). Has greyish-toned leaves
and fragrant, quartered-rosette, fully
double, violet to purple flowers, 8cm
(3in) across, in summer-autumn. May
be grown on a support. Zone 6.

R. 'Reine Victoria' illus. p.186.

R. REMEMBER ME ('Cocdestin')
illus. p.194.

R. 'Rise 'n' Shine', syn. *R*. 'Golden
Sunblaze', illus. p.196.

R. 'Robert le Diable'. Lax, bushy
Provence rose. H and S 1m (3ft).
In summer bears slightly scented,
pompon, double flowers, 8cm (3in)
across, in mixed bright and dull purple.
Has narrowly oval, dark green leaves.
Is best trailing over a low support.
Zone 5.

R. 'Rose d'Isfahan'. See *R*. 'Ispahan'.

R. ROSE GAUJARD ('Gaumo').
Upright, strong, large-flowered bush
rose. H 1.1m (3½ft), S 75cm (2½ft). Has
plentiful glossy foliage. Bears slightly
scented, urn-shaped, double, cherry-red
and blush-pink flowers, 10cm (4in)
across, freely in summer-autumn.

R. ROSEMARY HARKNESS
('Harrowbond') illus. p190.

R. 'Roseraie de l'Haÿ' illus. p.187.

R. ROSY CUSHION ('Interall')
illus. p.186.

R. 'Rosy Mantle' illus. p.197.

R. 'Rouge Eblouissante'. See
R. 'Assemblage des Beautés'.

R. 'Rouletii', syn. *R. chinensis* var.
minima, *R*. 'Pompon de Paris'.
Compact miniature China rose with
thin stems. H and S 20cm (8in). Has
mid-green leaves comprising many
lance-shaped leaflets, and freely
produces cupped, double, deep pink
flowers, 2cm (¾in) across, from
summer to autumn. Zone 6.

R. 'Royal Dane'. See *R*. TROIKA.

R. 'Royal Highness', syn.
R. 'Königliche Hoheit'. Upright, large-
flowered bush rose. H 1.1m (3½ft),
S 60cm (2ft). In summer-autumn, firm
stems bear leathery, dark green foliage
and large, fragrant, pointed, fully double,
pearl-pink flowers, 12cm (5in) across.

R. ROYAL WILLIAM ('Korzaun'), syn.
R. 'Duftzauber '84', illus. p.192.

R. rubiginosa, syn. *R. eglanteria*,
illus. p.185.

R. rubrifolia. See *R. glauca*.

R. rugosa illus. p.187. var. *alba* is a
dense, vigorous, species hybrid rose.
H and S 1–2m (3–6ft). Bears a
succession of fragrant, cupped, single,
white flowers, 9cm (3½in) across, in
summer-autumn. They are followed by
large, tomato-shaped hips. Abundant
foliage is leathery, wrinkled and glossy.
Zone 2b.

R. 'Rugul'. See *R*. GOLDEN PENNY.

R. 'Runatru'. See *R*. INVINCIBLE.

R. 'Saint Nicholas'. Vigorous, erect
Damask rose. H and S 1.2m (4ft). In
summer bears lightly scented, cupped,
semi-double, rose-pink flowers, 12cm
(5in) across, with golden stamens,
followed by red hips in autumn. Has
plentiful, dark green foliage. Zone 6.

R. 'San Rafael Rose'. See
R. x *odorata* 'Pseudindica'.

R. 'Schneewittchen'. See
R. ICEBERG.

R. sericea subsp. *omeiensis*
f. *pteracantha*, syn. *R. omeiensis*
f. *pteracantha* (Winged thorn rose).
Stiff, upright, vigorous species rose.
H 2.5m (8ft), S 2.2m (7ft). Has small,
fern-like, light green leaves and large,
red prickles on young stems. In
summer, solitary, flat, white flowers,
2.5–6cm (1–2½in) across, are borne
briefly along the stems. Zone 6.

R. SEXY REXY ('Macrexy')
illus. p.190.

R. SHEILA MACQUEEN
('Harwotnext'). Narrow, upright,
cluster-flowered bush rose. H 75cm
(30in), S 45cm (18in). In summer-
autumn produces dense clusters of
peppery-scented, cupped, double, green
flowers, 6cm (2½in) across, tinged
apricot-pink. Has leathery leaves.

R. SHEILA'S PERFUME ('Harsherry').
Upright, cluster-flowered bush rose.
H 75cm (2½ft), S 60cm (2ft). Has
glossy, reddish foliage. Fragrant,
urn-shaped, double, red-and-yellow
flowers, 9cm (3½in) across, are
produced singly or in clusters in
summer-autumn.

R. SHERI ANNE ('Morsherry')
illus. p.195.

R. SHOCKING BLUE ('Korblue').
Bushy, cluster-flowered bush rose.
H 75cm (2½ft), S 60cm (2ft). Bears, in
summer-autumn, fragrant, pointed,
well-formed, fully double, purple
flowers, 10cm (4in) across, singly or in
clusters. Foliage is dark green.

R. 'Silver Jubilee' illus. p.191.

R. SIMBA ('Korbelma'), syn.
R. 'Goldsmith', illus. p.193.

R. 'Sissi'. See *R*. BLUE MOON.

R. SNOW CARPET ('Maccarpe').
Prostrate, creeping, miniature bush rose.
H 15cm (6in), S 50cm (20in). Has many
small glossy leaves and pompon, fully
double, white flowers, 3cm (1¼in)
across, in summer, a few in autumn.
Makes good, compact ground cover.

R. SNOWBALL ('Macangeli'), syn.
R. 'Angelita', illus. p.195.

R. 'Southampton', syn. *R*. 'Susan
Ann', illus. p.194.

R. 'Souvenir d'Alphonse Lavallée'.
Vigorous, sprawling Hybrid Perpetual
rose. H 2.2m (7ft), S 2m (6ft). Fragrant,
cupped, double, burgundy-red to
maroon-purple flowers, 10cm (4in)
across, are borne in summer-autumn.
Leaves are small and mid-green. Is best
grown on a light support. Zone 6.

R. 'Souvenir de la Malmaison'.
Dense, spreading Bourbon rose. H and
S 1.5m (5ft). Bears spice-scented,
quartered-rosette, fully double, blush-
pink to white flowers, 12cm (5in) across,
in summer-autumn. Rain spoils flowers.
Has large, dark green leaves. Zone 6.

R. 'Spanish Beauty'. See *R*. 'Madame
Grégoire Staechelin'.

R. 'Spectacular'. See *R*. 'Danse du
Feu'.

R. spinosissima. See *R. pimpinellifolia*.

R. 'Spring Morning'. See
R. 'Frühlingsmorgen'.

R. 'Stacey Sue' illus. p.195.

R. 'Sunblaze'. See *R*. ORANGE
SUNBLAZE.

R. SUNSET BOULEVARD
('Harbabble'). Upright cluster-flowered
bush rose. H 1m (3ft), S 60cm (2ft).
Bears open sprays of lightly scented,
pointed to cupped, double, salmon-pink
flowers, 9cm (3½in) across, in summer-
autumn on glossy-foliaged plants. Is
excellent for beds and cutting.

R. 'Susan Ann'. See *R*. 'Southampton'.

R. 'Swan Lake'. A vigorous climbing
rose with an upright habit. H 2.5m (8ft),
S 2m (6ft). Pointed buds open to give
fully double white flowers with a pale
pink flush in the centre. Free flowering.

R. SWEET DREAM ('Fryminicot').
Compact, dwarf cluster-flowered bush
rose. H 40cm (16in), S 35cm (14in).
Clusters of slightly scented, pompon,
fully double, peach-apricot flowers,
6cm (2½in) across, appear in summer-
autumn. Leaves are small.

R. SWEET MAGIC ('Dicmagic')
illus. p.194.

R. 'Sylvia'. See *R*. CONGRATULATIONS.

R. 'Sympathie' illus. p.198.

R. 'Tanba'. See *R*. BABY
MASQUERADE.

R. 'Tanellis'. See *R*. FRAGRANT
CLOUD.

R. 'Tanky'. See *R*. WHISKY MAC.

R. 'Tannacht'. See *R*. BLUE MOON.

R. 'Tapis d'Orient'. See
R. 'Yesterday'.

R. 'Tapis Jaune'. See *R*. GOLDEN
PENNY.

R. 'The Fairy' illus. p.189.

R. 'The Queen Elizabeth'. See
R. 'Queen Elizabeth'.

R. 'Thérèse Bugnet'. A hybrid *rugosa*
rose that does not have the typical
rough foliage. H and S 2m (6ft).
Double fragrant flowers open a ark
pink and fade with age. Blooms from
June to frost and the red canes are
attractive in winter. Zone 2b.

R. THE TIMES ROSE ('Korpeahn')
illus. p.192.

R. 'Tour de Malakoff' illus. p.188.

R. 'Tricolore de Flandre'. Vigorous,
upright Gallica rose. H and S 1m (3ft).
Fragrant, pompon, fully double, blush-
pink flowers, 6cm (2½in) across, striped
with pink and purple, open in summer.
Has dull green leaves.

R. TROIKA ('Poumidor'), syn.
R. 'Royal Dane', illus. p.194.

R. TRUMPETER ('Mactru')
illus. p.191.

R. 'Tuscany Superb', syn. *R*. 'Double
Velvet'. Vigorous, upright Gallica rose.
H 1.1m (3½ft), S 1m (3ft). In summer,
produces, slightly scented, cupped to
flat, double flowers, 5cm (2in) across,
deep crimson-maroon, ageing to
purple, with gold stamens. Leaves are
dark green. Zone 5.

R. 'Variegata di Bologna'. Upright,
arching Bourbon rose. H 2m (6ft),
S 1.4m (4½ft). Has small leaves and, in
summer-autumn, fragrant, quartered-
rosette, fully double flowers, 8cm (3in)
across, blush-pink, striped with rose-
purple. Needs fertile soil and is prone

to blackspot. Zone 6.

R. 'Veilchenblau', syn. *R.* 'Blue Rambler', illus. p.199

R. 'Wedding Day'. Rampant climbing rose. H 8m (25ft), S 4m (12ft). Produces large clusters of fruity-scented, flat, single, creamy-white flowers, 2.5cm (1in) across, that mature to blush-pink, in late summer. Is suitable for growing up a tree or in a wild garden. Zone 7.

R. WEE JOCK ('Cocabest') illus. p.192.

R. WHISKY MAC ('Tanky'). Neat, upright, large-flowered bush rose. H 75cm (2½ft), S 60cm (2ft). Fragrant, rounded, fully double, amber flowers, 9cm (3½in) across, appear freely in summer-autumn. Reddish foliage is prone to mildew. May die back during a hard winter.

R. 'White Cockade'. Slow-growing, bushy, upright, large-flowered climber. H 2–3m (6–10ft), S 1.5m (5ft). Bears slightly fragrant, rounded, well-formed, fully double, white flowers, 9cm (3½in) across, in summer-autumn. May be pruned and grown as a shrub. Zone 6.

R. 'William Baffin'. A tall, upright climbing rose. H 3m (10ft), S 1.2m (4ft). Clusters of up to 30 slightly fragrant, medium red flowers appear from June to September. Highly resistant to black spot and mildew. Zone 2b.

R. 'William Lobb', syn. *R.* 'Duchesse d'Istrie', illus. p.188.

R. 'Winnipeg Parks'. A recurrent-blooming dwarf shrub rose that makes a good container plant. H and S 40–70cm (15–40in). Plants form dense bushes with slightly fragrant medium red blooms in small clusters. Foliage is shiny, dark green and turns red in fall. Zone 2b.

R. xanthina 'Canary Bird', syn. *R.* 'Canary Bird', illus. p.189.

R. 'Yesterday', syn. *R.* 'Tapis d'Orient'. Bushy, arching Polyantha bush rose. H and S 75cm (30in), or more if lightly pruned. Fragrant, rosette, semi-double, lilac-pink flowers, 2.5cm (1in) across, are borne, mainly in clusters, from summer through to early winter. Produces small, dark green leaves. Makes a hedge.

R. 'Yvonne Rabier'. Dense, bushy Polyantha bush rose. H 45cm (18in), S 40cm (16in). Plentiful leaves are bright green. Bears moderately scented, rounded, double, creamy-white flowers, 5cm (2in) across, in summer-autumn.

R. 'Zéphirine Drouhin' illus. p.197.

R. 'Zigeunerknabe', syn. *R.* 'Gipsy Boy'. Vigorous, thorny Bourbon rose of lanky habit. H and S 2m (6ft). Faintly scented, cupped to flat, double, purplish-crimson flowers, 8cm (3in) across, are borne in summer. Leaves are dark green. Zone 6.

R. 'Zonta Rose'. See *R.* PRINCESS ALICE.

Rosa mundi. See *Rosa gallica* 'Versicolor', illus. p.187.

Rosary vine. See *Ceropegia linearis* subsp. *woodii*, illus. p.462.

ROSCOEA

ZINGIBERACEAE

Genus of late summer- and early autumn-flowering, tuberous perennials, related to ginger, grown for their orchid-like flowers. Suits open borders, rock gardens and woodland gardens. Grows in sun or partial shade and in cool, well-drained humus-rich soil that must be kept moist in summer. Dies down in winter, when a top dressing of leaf mould or well-rotted compost is beneficial. Propagate by division in spring or by seed, exposed to frost for best germination, in autumn or winter.

R. cautleyoides illus. p.436.

R. humeana illus. p.436.

R. procera. See *R. purpurea*.

R. purpurea, syn. *R. procera*. Summer-flowering, tuberous perennial. H 20–30cm (8–12in), S 15–20cm (6–8in). Lance-shaped, erect leaves are long-pointed and wrap around each other at base to form a false stem. Has long-tubed, purple flowers, each with a hooded, upper petal, wide-lobed, lower lip and 2 narrower petals.

Rose. See *Rosa*.

Banksian. See *Rosa banksiae*.

Burnet. See *Rosa pimpinellifolia*.

Christmas. See *Helleborus*.

Common moss. *Rosa centifolia* 'Muscosa'.

Confederate. See *Hibiscus mutabilis*.

Cotton. See *Hibiscus mutabilis*.

Crested moss. See *Rosa centifolia* 'Cristata'.

Desert. See *Adenium*.

Guelder. See *Viburnum opulus*.

Hedgehog. See *Rosa rugosa*, illus. p.187.

Incense. See *Rosa primula*, illus. p.188.

Japanese. See *Rosa rugosa*, illus. p.187.

Lenten. See *Helleborus* x *hybridus*.

Old pink moss. See *Rosa centifolia* 'Muscosa'.

Rock. See *Cistus*; *Helianthemum*.

Scotch. See *Rosa pimpinellifolia*.

Snowbush. See *Rosa* 'Dupontii', illus. p.185.

Thornless. See *Rosa* 'Zéphirine Drouhin', illus. p.197.

Winged thorn. See *R. sericea* subsp. *omeiensis* f. *pteracantha*.

Wood. See *Merremia tuberosa*.

Rose acacia. See *Robinia hispida*, illus. p.141.

Rose cactus. See *Pereskia grandifolia*, illus. p.458.

Rose of Jericho. See *Selaginella lepidophylla*.

Rose of Lancaster, Red. See *Rosa gallica* var. *officinalis*.

Rose of Sharon. See *Hypericum calycinum*, illus. p.170.

Rose periwinkle. See *Catharanthus roseus*, illus. p.160.

Rose pincushion. See *Mammillaria zeilmanniana*, illus. p.473.

Rosebay, White. See *Epilobium angustifolium* f. *album*, illus. p.226.

Rosebud cherry. See *Prunus* x *subhirtella*.

Rosemary. See *Rosmarinus officinalis*, illus. p.167.

Australian. See *Westringia fruticosa*, illus. p.158.

Roseroot. See *Rhodiola rosea*.

ROSMARINUS

LABIATAE/LAMIACEAE

Genus of evergreen shrubs, grown for their flowers and aromatic foliage, or as a culinary herb. At limits of hardiness grow against a south- or west-facing wall. Requires sun and well-drained soil. Cut back frost-damaged plants to healthy wood in spring; straggly, old plants may be cut back hard at same time. After flowering, trim hedges. Propagate by semi-ripe cuttings in summer.

R. lavandulaceus of gardens. See *R. officinalis* 'Prostratus'.

R. officinalis (Rosemary) illus. p.167. **'Miss Jessopp's Upright'** is an evergreen, compact, upright shrub. H and S 2m (6ft). From mid- to late spring and sometimes again in autumn bears small, 2-lipped, blue flowers amid narrowly oblong, aromatic, dark green leaves. Is good when grown for hedging. **'Prostratus'** (syn. *R. lavandulaceus* of gardens), H 15cm (6in), is prostrate and the least hardy form. **'Severn Sea'**, H 1m (3ft), is arching, with bright blue flowers. All zone 7.

ROSSIOGLOSSUM

See also ORCHIDS.

R. grande, syn. *Odontoglossum grande* (illus. p.297). Evergreen, epiphytic orchid for a cool greenhouse. H 15cm (6in). Spikes of rich yellow flowers, to 15cm (6in) across and heavily marked chestnut-brown, are produced in autumn. Has broadly oval, stiff leaves, 15cm (6in) long. Provide shade in summer and keep very dry in winter.

ROTHMANNIA

RUBIACEAE

Genus of evergreen, summer-flowering shrubs and trees, grown for their flowers. Is related to *Gardenia*. Tender, min. 16°C (61°F). Needs a position in full light or partial shade and humus-rich, well-drained, neutral to acid soil. Water potted plants freely when in full growth, moderately at other times. Propagate by seed in spring or by semi-ripe cuttings in summer.

R. capensis, syn. *Gardenia capensis*, *G. rothmannia*. Evergreen, ovoid shrub or tree. H 6m (20ft) or more, S 3m (10ft) or more. Leaves are oval, lustrous and rich green. Has fragrant, tubular flowers, each with 5 arching, white to creamy-yellow petal lobes and a purple-dotted throat, in summer.

Rouen lilac. See *Syringa* x *chinensis*.

Round-headed club-rush. See *Scirpoides holoschoenus*.

Round-leaved mint-bush. See *Prostanthera rotundifolia*, illus. p.145.

Round-leaved wintergreen. See *Pyrola rotundifolia*.

Rowan. See *Sorbus aucuparia*, illus. p.81.

Hupeh. See *Sorbus hupehensis*.

Sargent's. See *Sorbus sargentiana*.

Royal agave. See *Agave victoriae-reginae*, illus. p.461.

Royal fern. See *Osmunda regalis*, illus. p.312.

Royal paintbrush. See *Scadoxus puniceus*.

Royal palm. See *Roystonea*.

Cuban. See *Roystonea regia*.

Royal red bugler. See *Aeschynanthus pulcher*.

ROYSTONEA
Royal palm

ARECACEAE/PALMAE

Genus of evergreen palms, grown for their majestic appearance. Produces racemes of insignificant flowers in summer. Tender, min. 16–18°C (61–64°F). Needs full light or partial shade and fertile, well-drained but moisture-retentive soil. Water potted plants freely when in full growth, less at other times, especially when temperatures are low. Propagate by seed in spring at not less than 27°C (81°F). Spider mite may be a problem.

R. regia (Cuban royal palm). Evergreen palm with upright stem, sometimes thickened about the middle. H 20m (70ft) or more, S to 6m (20ft). Leaves are feather-shaped, 3m (10ft) long, upright at first, later arching and pendent, and are divided into narrowly oblong, leathery, bright green leaflets.

Rubber plant. See *Ficus elastica*.

Baby. See *Peperomia clusiifolia*.

Rubber tree

Hardy. See *Eucommia ulmoides*.

Rubber vine. See *Cryptostegia grandiflora*.

RUBUS
Blackberry, Bramble

ROSACEAE

Genus of deciduous, semi-evergreen or evergreen shrubs and woody-stemmed, scrambling climbers. Some species are cultivated solely for their edible fruits, including raspberries and blackberries. Those described here are grown mainly for their foliage, flowers or ornamental, often prickly stems, though some may also bear edible fruits. Deciduous species grown for their winter stems prefer full sun; other deciduous species need sun or semi-shade; evergreens and semi-evergreens tolerate sun or shade. All *Rubus* require fertile, well-drained soil. Cut old stems of *R. biflorus*, *R. cockburnianus* and *R. thibetanus* to ground after fruiting. Propagate by seed or cuttings (semi-ripe for evergreens, softwood or hardwood for deciduous species) in summer or winter.

R. odoratus may be increased by division, and *R.* 'Benenden' and *R. ulmifolius* 'Bellidiflorus' by layering in spring.

R. 'Benenden', syn. *R.* 'Tridel', illus. p.136.

R. biflorus illus. p.149.

R. cockburnianus. Deciduous, arching shrub. H and S 2.5m (8ft). Prickly shoots are brilliant blue-white in winter. Dark green leaves, white beneath, each have usually 9 oval leaflets. Bears panicles of 5-petalled, purple flowers in early summer, followed by unpalatable, spherical, black fruits. Zone 6.

R. henryi var. **bambusarum.** Fast-growing, vigorous, evergreen, woody-stemmed, scrambling climber, grown mainly for its attractive foliage. H to 6m (20ft). Leaves have 3 broadly oval leaflets, white-felted beneath. Tiny, pink flowers are borne in small clusters in summer. Zone 7.

R. odoratus (Flowering raspberry, Thimbleberry). Vigorous, deciduous, upright, thicket-forming shrub. H and S 2.5m (8ft). Thornless, peeling shoots bear large, velvety, dark green leaves, each with 5 broadly triangular lobes. Large, fragrant, 5-petalled, rose-pink flowers appear from early summer to early autumn, and are sometimes followed by unpalatable, flattened, red fruits. Zone 3.

R. thibetanus illus. p.149.

R. tricolor. Evergreen shrub with both prostrate and arching shoots covered in red bristles. H 60cm (2ft), S 2m (6ft). Oval, toothed, glossy, dark green leaves set off cup-shaped, 5-petalled, white flowers borne in mid-summer. Has edible, raspberry-like, red fruits. Makes good ground cover. Zone 8.

R. **'Tridel'**. See *R.* 'Benenden'.

R. ulmifolius **'Bellidiflorus'**. Vigorous, deciduous or semi-evergreen, arching shrub. H 2.5m (8ft), S 4m (12ft). Prickly stems bear dark green leaves, with 3 or 5 oval leaflets, and, in mid- to late summer, large panicles of daisy-like, double, pink flowers. Zone 7.

Ruby grass. See *Melinis repens*.

RUDBECKIA
Coneflower

ASTERACEAE/COMPOSITAE

Genus of annuals, biennials and perennials grown for their flowers. Thrives in sun or shade and well-drained or moist soil. Propagate by division in spring or by seed in autumn or spring.

R. fulgida (Black-eyed Susan). var. *deamii* is an erect perennial. H 1m (3ft), S 60cm (2ft) or more. In late summer and autumn produces daisy-like, yellow flower heads with central, black cones. Has narrowly lance-shaped, mid-green leaves. Prefers

moist soil. var. *sullivantii* **'Goldsturm'** illus. p.256.

R. **'Goldquelle'** illus. p.229.

R. **'Herbstsonne'** illus. p.232.

R. hirta. Moderately fast-growing, upright, branching, short-lived perennial, grown as an annual. H 30cm–1m (1–3ft), S 30–45cm (1–1½ft). Has lance-shaped, mid-green leaves and, in summer-autumn, large, daisy-like, deep yellow flower heads, with conical, purple centres. Needs sun and well-drained soil. **'Goldilocks'** illus. p.340. **'Irish Eyes'**, H to 75cm (2½ft), has yellow flower heads with olive-green centres. **'Marmalade'** and **'Rustic Dwarfs'** illus. p.340.

R. laciniata **'Golden Glow'**. Erect perennial. H 2–2.2m (6–7ft), S 60cm–1m (2–3ft). Bears daisy-like, double, golden-yellow flower heads, with green centres, in late summer and autumn. Mid-green leaves are divided into lance-shaped leaflets, themselves further cut. Prefers well-drained soil.

R. purpurea. See *Echinacea purpurea*.

Rue. See *Ruta*.
    Common. See *Ruta graveolens*.
    Meadow. See *Thalictrum*.

RUELLIA

ACANTHACEAE

Genus of perennials and evergreen sub-shrubs and shrubs with showy flowers. Tender, min. 15°C (59°F). Grow in a humid atmosphere, partial shade and in moist but well-drained soil. Propagate by stem cuttings or seed, if available, in spring.

R. amoena. See *R. graecizans*.

R. devosiana illus. p.277.

R. graecizans, syn. *R. amoena*, illus. p.249.

RUSCHIA

AIZOACEAE

Genus of mostly small, tufted, perennial succulents and evergreen shrubs with leaves united up to one-third of their lengths around stems or with very short sheaths. Tender, min.

5°C (41°F). Needs sun and well-drained soil. Propagate by seed or stem cuttings in spring or summer.

R. acuminata. Evergreen, erect, succulent shrub. H 20cm (8in), S 50cm (20in). Has woody stems as well as non-woody, bluish-green stems with darker dots. Produces solid, 3-angled, 3cm (1¼in) long leaves, each with a blunt keel and a short sheath. Daisy-like, white to pale pink flowers, 3cm (1¼in) across, appear in summer.

R. crassa. Evergreen, erect, succulent shrub. H and S 50cm (20in). Bears solid, 3-angled, bluish-green leaves, 2cm (¾in) long, with short, white hairs; the undersides are keeled, each with a single tooth. Has 2.5cm (1in) wide, daisy-like, white flowers in summer.

R. macowanii. Erect, then spreading, perennial succulent. H 15cm (6in), S 1m (3ft). Has solid, slightly keeled, 3-angled, bluish-green leaves, to 3cm (1¼in) long. In summer carries masses of daisy-like, bright pink flowers, 3cm (1¼in) across, with darker stripes.

RUSCUS

RUSCACEAE/LILIACEAE

Genus of evergreen, clump-forming, spring-flowering shrubs, grown for their foliage and fruits. The apparent leaves are actually flattened shoots, on which flowers and fruits are borne. Usually, separate male and female plants are required for fruiting. Is particularly useful for dry, shady sites. Tolerates sun or shade and any soil other than waterlogged. Cut back dead shoots to base in spring. Propagate by division in spring. The berries of *R. aculeatus* may cause mild stomach upset if ingested.

R. aculeatus (Butcher's broom). Evergreen, erect, thicket-forming shrub. H 75cm (2½ft), S 1m (3ft). Spine-tipped 'leaves' are glossy and dark green. Tiny, star-shaped, green flowers in spring are succeeded by large, spherical, bright red fruits. Zone 8.

R. hypoglossum illus. p.176.

Rush
    Corkscrew. See *Juncus effusus*

f. *spiralis*, illus. p.308.
    Flowering. See *Butomus umbellatus*, illus. p.448.

Rushes. See Grasses, Bamboos, Rushes and Sedges.

RUSSELIA

SCROPHULARIACEAE

Genus of evergreen shrubs and sub-shrubs with showy flowers. Tender, min. 10–15°C (50–59°F). Needs sun or partial shade. Requires humus-rich, light, well-drained soil. Propagate by stem cuttings or division in spring.

R. equisetiformis, syn. *R. juncea*, illus. p.250.

R. juncea. See *R. equisetiformis*.

Russian arborvitae. See *Microbiota*.

Russian comfrey. See *Symphytum* x *uplandicum*.

Russian vine. See *Fallopia aubertii* of gardens; *Fallopia baldschuanica*, illus. p.217.

Rusty-back fern. See *Asplenium ceterach*, illus. p.311.

Rusty-leaved fig. See *Ficus rubiginosa*.

RUTA
Rue

RUTACEAE

Genus of evergreen, summer-flowering sub-shrubs, with deeply divided, aromatic leaves, grown for their foliage and flowers and used as a medicinal herb. Requires a sunny position and well-drained soil. Cut back to old wood in spring to keep compact. Propagate by semi-ripe cuttings in summer. All parts may cause severe discomfort if eaten; the foliage may cause photodermatitis on contact.

R. graveolens (Common rue).

'Jackman's Blue' illus. p.177.

S

SABAL

ARECACEAE/PALMAE

Genus of evergreen fan palms, grown for their foliage and overall appearance. Just tender, min. 5–7°C (41–5°F). Prefers full sun and fertile, well-drained soil. Water moderately, less when not in full growth. Propagate by seed in spring. Spider mite may be troublesome.

S. minor illus. p.176.

Sacred bamboo. See *Nandina domestica.*
Sacred fig tree. See *Ficus religiosa.*
Sacred lotus. See *Nelumbo nucifera,* illus. p.447.
Saffron crocus. See *Crocus sativus.*
Saffron, Meadow. See *Colchicum autumnale,* illus. p.437.
Sage. See *Salvia.*
  Bog. See *Salvia uliginosa.*
  Mexican bush. See *Salvia leucantha.*

SAGINA

CARYOPHYLLACEAE

Genus of mat-forming annuals and evergreen perennials, grown for their foliage. Is suitable for banks and in paving. Some species may be very invasive. Prefers sun and gritty, moist soil; dislikes hot, dry conditions. Propagate by division in spring, by seed in autumn or, for *S. boydii*, by tip cuttings in summer. Aphids and spider mite may cause problems.

S. boydii illus. p.390.

SAGITTARIA

Arrowhead

ALISMATACEAE

Genus of deciduous, perennial, submerged and marginal water plants, grown for their foliage and flowers. Hardy to tender, min. 5°C (41°F). Some species are suitable for pools, others for aquariums. All require full sun. Remove fading foliage as necessary. Propagate by division in spring or summer or by breaking off turions (scaly, young shoots) in spring.

S. japonica. See *S. sagittifolia* 'Flore Pleno'.
S. latifolia illus. p.446.
S. sagittifolia (Common arrowhead). Deciduous, perennial, marginal water plant. H 45cm (18in), S 30cm (12in). Upright, mid-green leaves are acutely arrow-shaped. In summer produces 3-petalled, white flowers with dark purple centres. May be grown in up to 23cm (9in) depth of water. **'Flore Pleno'** (syn. *S. japonica*; Japanese arrowhead) has double flowers.

Saguaro. See *Carnegiea gigantea,* illus. p.456.
St Augustine grass. See *Stenotaphrum secundatum.*

St Bernard's lily. See *Anthericum liliago,* illus. p.276.
St Bruno's lily. See *Paradisea liliastrum.*
St Catherine's lace. See *Eriogonum giganteum,* illus. p.139.
St Dabeoc's heath. See *Daboecia cantabrica.*
St Vincent lilac. See *Solanum seaforthianum.*

SAINTPAULIA

African violet

GESNERIACEAE

Genus of evergreen, rosette-forming perennials, grown for their showy flowers. Tender, min. 15°C (59°F). Needs a constant temperature, a humid atmosphere, partial shade and fertile soil. Propagate by leaf cuttings in summer. Whitefly and mealy bug may cause problems with indoor plants.

African violet cultivars
There are over 2,000 cultivars, mainly derived from *S. ionantha*, with star- or bell-shaped, white, pink, red, blue, violet, bi- or multi-coloured flowers, borne throughout the year. They may be single, semi-double or fully double. Petal edges may be ruffled, rounded, frilled or fringed. The broadly ovate to oval leaves are usually mid- or dark green, and may be feathered, flecked or variegated white, pink or cream. See also feature panel p.302.
  Cultivars are divided into 5 groups, according to rosette size. The measurement given below is the diameter of the rosette; the spread of each cultivar is the same as this:
Micro-miniature – less than 8cm (3in);
Miniature – 8–16cm (3–6in);
Semi-miniature – 16–21cm (6–8in);
Standard – 21–40cm (8–16in);
Large – over 40cm (16in).

S. 'Bright Eyes' (illus. p.302). Standard Group. H to 15cm (6in). Has dark green leaves and single, deep violet-blue flowers with yellow centres.
S. 'Chantabent'. Semi-miniature Group. H 10–15cm (4–6in). Has dark green leaves with deep red undersides, and bears large, single, violet-blue flowers.
S. 'Colorado' (illus. p.302). Standard Group. H 15–20cm (6–8in). Bears dark green leaves and frilled, single, magenta flowers.
S. 'Delft' (illus. p.302). Standard Group. H to 15cm (6in). Leaves are dark green, and flowers are semi-double and violet-blue.
S. 'Dorothy'. Standard Group. H to 15cm (6in). Has long-stalked, light green leaves, and bears large, single, rich pink flowers with frilled, white margins.
S. 'Garden News' (illus. p.302). Standard Group. H to 15cm (6in). Has bright green leaves and double, pure white flowers.

S. 'Ice Maiden' (illus. p.302). Standard Group. H to 15cm (6in). Bears single, white flowers with purple-blue markings.
S. ionantha. Evergreen, stemless, rosette-forming perennial, often forming clumps. H to 10cm (4in), S 25cm (10in). Almost rounded, scalloped, long-stalked, fleshy, usually hairy leaves, to 8cm (3in) long, are mid-green above and often reddish-green below. Loose clusters of 2–8 tubular, 5-lobed, violet-blue flowers, to 2.5cm (1in) across, are produced on stems held above leaves and appear year-round.
S. 'Pip Squeek' (illus. p.302). Micro-miniature Group. H to 8cm (3in). Has oval, unscalloped, deep green leaves, 1–2cm (½–¾in) long, and bell-shaped, pale pink flowers, 1cm (½in) wide.
S. 'Porcelain' (illus. p.302). Standard Group. H to 15cm (6in). Bears semi-double, white flowers with purple-blue edges.
S. 'Rococo Anna', syn. *S.* 'Rococo Pink' (illus. p.302). Standard Group. H to 15cm (6in). Bears double, iridescent pink flowers.
S. 'Starry Trail' (illus. p.302). Standard Group. H to 15cm (6in). Has dark green leaves and narrow-petalled, semi-double to double, white flowers, sometimes flushed pale pink.
S. 'Zoja' (illus. p.302). Standard Group. H to 15cm (6in). Produces large, single to semi-double, purple-blue flowers with a bold white line at the margin of each petal.

SALIX

Willow

SALICACEAE

Genus of deciduous trees and shrubs, grown for their habit, foliage, catkins and, in some cases, colourful winter shoots. Male catkins are more striking than female; each plant usually bears catkins of only one sex. Most prefer full sun. Most species grow well in any but very dry soil; *S. caprea, S. purpurea* and their variants also thrive in dry soil. Plants grown for their colourful winter shoots should be cut back hard in early spring, every 1–3 years. Propagate by semi-ripe cuttings in summer or by hardwood cuttings in winter. Fungal diseases may cause canker, particularly in *S. babylonica* and *S.* x *sepulcralis* var. *chrysocoma.* Willows may become infested with such pests as caterpillars, aphids and gall mites.

S. aegyptiaca (Musk willow). Vigorous, deciduous, bushy shrub or tree. H 4m (12ft), S 5m (15ft). Grey catkins that turn to yellow appear on bare, stout shoots in late winter or early spring, before large, narrowly oval, deep green leaves. Zone 7.
S. alba (White willow). f. **argentea** see *S.a.* var. *sericea.* **'Britzensis'** see *S.a.* var. *vitellina* 'Britzensis'. var. **caerulea** (Cricket-bat willow) is a very

fast-growing, deciduous, conical tree with upright branches. H 25m (80ft), S 10m (30ft). Has long, narrowly lance-shaped, deep bluish-green leaves and, in early spring, small, pendent, yellowish-green catkins. Zone 2. **'Chermesina'** see *S.a.* var. *vitellina* 'Chermesina'. **'Sericea'** see *S.a.* var. *sericea.* var. **sericea** (syn. *S.a.* f. *argentea, S.a.* 'Sericea'; Silver willow), H 15m (50ft), S 8m (25ft), is a spreading tree that is conical when young and has bright silver-grey leaves. Zone 2. **'Tristis'** (syn. *S. vitellina* 'Pendula') has a more weeping habit and only produces female catkins. Zone 2. **'Tristis'** of gardens see *S.* x *sepulcralis* var. *chrysocoma.* var. **vitellina** illus. p.74. var. **vitellina 'Britzensis'** (syn. *S.a.* 'Britzensis'), which has green leaves and bright orange-red, young shoots, is usually cut back to near ground level to provide winter colour. Zone 2. var. **vitellina 'Chermesina'** (syn. *S.a.* 'Chermesina') has carmine-red, young winter shoots. Zone 3.
S. apoda illus. p.363.
S. arbuscula (Mountain willow). Deciduous, spreading shrub. H and S 60cm (2ft) or more. In spring, dark brown stems produce narrowly oval, toothed leaves and white-haired, sometimes red-tinged, yellow catkins. Suits a rock garden. Zone 3.
S. babylonica (Weeping willow). Deciduous, weeping tree with slender, pendent shoots that reach almost to the ground. H and S 12m (40ft). Bears narrowly lance-shaped, long-pointed leaves. Has yellowish-green catkins in early spring. Is susceptible to canker and has been largely replaced in cultivation by *S.* x *sepulcralis* var. *chrysocoma.* Zone 6. var. **pekinensis 'Tortuosa'** (syn. *S. matsudana* 'Tortuosa') illus. p.85.
S. bockii. Deciduous, bushy shrub. H and S 2.5m (8ft). Has slender, upright, grey-hairy shoots and oblong, glossy, bright green leaves, with silky-hairy undersides. Usually female in cultivation; bears green catkins in early and mid-autumn. Zone 5.
S. x **boydii** illus. p.361.
S. caprea (Goat willow, Pussy willow). Deciduous, bushy shrub or tree. H 10m (30ft), S 8m (25ft). Oval leaves are dark green above, grey beneath. Catkins are borne in spring before foliage emerges: females are silky and grey, males are grey with yellow anthers. Zone 4b. **'Kilmarnock'** (Kilmarnock willow), H 1.5–2m (5–6ft), S 2m (6ft), is dense-headed and weeping. From early to mid-spring produces grey catkins that later become yellow. Zone 5.
S. 'Chrysocoma'. See *S.* x *sepulcralis* var. *chrysocoma.*
S. daphnoides illus. p.74.
S. elaeagnos (Hoary willow). Deciduous, upright, dense shrub. H 3m (10ft), S 5m (15ft). In spring, long

shoots bear slender, yellow catkins as leaves appear. These are narrowly oblong and dark green, with white undersides, and turn yellow in autumn. Zone 5.

S. fargesii, syn. *S. moupinensis* of gardens. Deciduous, upright, open shrub. H and S 3m (10ft). Has purplish-red winter shoots and buds. Slender, erect, green catkins are carried in spring, at same time as bold, oblong, glossy, dark green leaves. Zone 6.

S. fragilis (Crack willow). Deciduous tree with a broad, bushy head. H 15m (50ft), S 12–15m (40–45ft). Has long, narrow, pointed, glossy, bright green leaves. Catkins, borne in early spring, are yellow on male plants, green on females. Zone 3b.

S. gracilistyla. Deciduous, bushy shrub. H 3m (10ft), S 4m (12ft). Large, silky, grey catkins with red, then bright yellow anthers are produced from early to mid-spring, and are followed by lance-shaped, silky, grey, young leaves that mature to bright, glossy green. Zone 4b.

'Melanostachys' (syn. *S.* 'Melanostachys'; Black willow) bears almost black catkins, with red anthers, in early spring, before bright green leaves emerge. Zone 4b.

S. hastata 'Wehrhahnii' illus. p.153.

S. helvetica illus. p.349.

S. herbacea (Dwarf willow, Least willow). Deciduous, creeping shrub. H 2.5cm (1in), S 20cm (8in) or more. Has small, rounded to oval leaves and, in spring, small, yellow or yellowish-green catkins are produced. Is good for a rock garden. Needs moist soil. Zone 7.

S. irrorata. Deciduous, upright shrub. H 3m (10ft), S 5m (15ft). Purple, young shoots are white-bloomed in winter. Catkins with red, then yellow anthers appear from early to mid-spring before narrowly oblong, glossy, bright green leaves emerge. Zone 6.

S. lanata illus. p.156. **'Stuartii'** see *S.* 'Stuartii'.

S. lindleyana. Deciduous, creeping, mat-forming shrub with long, creeping stems. H 2–3cm (¾–1¼in), S 40cm (16in) or more. Small, narrowly oval to linear, pale green leaves are densely set on short branchlets that produce brownish-pink catkins, 1cm (½in) long, in spring. Suits a rock garden or bank. Needs partial shade and damp soil. Zone 8. Is often confused with the very similar *S. furcata* (syn. *S. fruticulosa*, *S. hylematica*), which is more lax, with spreading, sometimes erect stems.

S. magnifica. Deciduous, upright shrub. H 5m (15ft), S 3m (10ft). Produces very long, slender, green catkins on stout, red shoots in spring, as large, magnolia-like, blue-green leaves emerge. Zone 6.

S. matsudana 'Tortuosa'. See *S. babylonica* var. *pekinensis* 'Tortuosa'.

S. 'Melanostachys'. See *S. gracilistyla* 'Melanostachys'.

S. moupinensis of gardens. See *S. fargesii*.

S. pentandra (Bay willow, Laurel willow). Deciduous, large shrub, then small tree with broad, bushy head. H and S 10m (30ft). Oval, glossy, green leaves are blue-white beneath. Catkins – males bright yellow, females

grey-green – open in early summer when the tree is in full leaf. Zone 1b.

S. purpurea (Purple osier). Deciduous, bushy, spreading shrub. H and S 5m (15ft). Grey, male catkins, with yellow anthers, and insignificant, female catkins are both borne on slender, often purple shoots in spring, before narrowly oblong, deep green leaves emerge. **'Nana'** (syn. *S.p.* f. *gracilis*, *S.p.* 'Gracilis'), H and S 1.5m (5ft), is dense, with silver-grey leaves; is good as a hedge. Zone 4b.

S. repens illus. p.156.

S. reticulata illus. p.370.

S. × rubens 'Basfordiana'. Deciduous, spreading tree. H 15m (50ft), S 10m (30ft). Has bright orange-yellow, young shoots in winter and long, narrow leaves, grey-green when young, becoming glossy, bright green in summer. Yellowish-green catkins appear in early spring. Zone 7.

S. sachalinensis 'Sekka'. See *S. udensis* 'Sekka'.

S. × sepulcralis var. *chrysocoma*, syn. *S. alba* 'Tristis' of gardens, *S.* 'Chrysocoma', illus. p.74.

S. 'Stuartii', syn. *S. lanata* 'Stuartii'. Slow-growing, deciduous, spreading shrub. H 1m (3ft), S 2m (6ft). Has yellow winter shoots. Stout, grey-green catkins open from orange buds in spring, as oval, woolly, grey leaves emerge. Zone 5.

S. udensis 'Sekka', syn. *S. sachalinensis* 'Sekka'. Deciduous, spreading shrub. H 5m (15ft), S 10m (30ft). Has flattened shoots that are red in winter and lance-shaped, glossy, bright green leaves. Silver catkins are produced in early spring. Zone 4b.

S. vitellina 'Pendula'. See *S. alba* 'Tristis'.

SALPIGLOSSIS

SOLANACEAE

Genus of annuals and biennials. Usually only annuals are cultivated, either for colour in borders or as greenhouse plants. Grow in sun and in rich, well-drained soil. Stems need support. Dead-head regularly. Propagate by seed sown under glass in early spring, or in early autumn for winter flowering indoors. Aphids may be troublesome.

S. sinuata Bolero Hybrids. Group of moderately fast-growing, branching, upright annuals. H 60cm (2ft), S 30cm (1ft). Has lance-shaped, pale green leaves. Outward-facing, widely flared, trumpet-shaped, conspicuously veined flowers, 5cm (2in) across, appear in summer and early autumn. Is available in a mixture of rich colours. **Casino Series** illus. p.329. **'Friendship'** has upward-facing flowers in a range of colours.

SALVIA

Sage

LABIATAE/LAMIACEAE

Genus of annuals, biennials, perennials and evergreen or semi-evergreen shrubs and sub-shrubs, grown for their tubular, 2-lipped, often brightly coloured flowers and aromatic foliage. Leaves of some species may be used for

flavouring foods. Hardy to tender, min. 5°C (41°F). Needs sun and fertile, well-drained soil. Propagate perennials by division in spring, perennials, shrubs and sub-shrubs by softwood cuttings in mid-summer. Sow seed of annuals under glass in early spring and of species outdoors in mid-spring.

S. blepharophylla. Spreading, rhizomatous perennial. H and S 45cm (18in). Tender. Has oval, glossy, dark green leaves and slender racemes of bright red flowers, with maroon calyces, in summer-autumn.

S. bulleyana. Rosette-forming perennial. H and S 60cm (24in). Racemes of nettle-like, yellow flowers, with maroon lips, are borne in summer above a basal mass of broadly oval, coarse, prominently veined, dark green leaves.

S. farinacea f. alba. Moderately fast-growing, upright perennial, grown as an annual. H 1m (3ft), S 30cm (1ft). Has lance-shaped, mid-green leaves. Spikes of white flowers are produced in summer. **'Strata'** has blue and white flowers. **'Victoria'** illus. p.332. Dwarf forms are also available.

S. fulgens illus. p.166.

S. grahamii. See *S. microphylla* var. *microphylla*.

S. greggii. Evergreen, erect sub-shrub. H to 1m (3ft), S to 60cm (2ft). Tender. Leaves are narrowly oblong and matt, deep green. Has terminal racemes of bright red-purple flowers in autumn.

S. haematodes. See *S. pratensis* Haematodes Group.

S. horminum. See *S. viridis*.

S. involucrata. Bushy, woody-based perennial. H 60–75cm (2–2½ft) or more, S 1m (3ft). Has oval, mid-green leaves and, in late summer and autumn, racemes of large, rose-crimson flowers. **'Bethellii'** illus. p.231.

S. jurisicii. Rosette-forming perennial. H 45cm (18in), S 30cm (12in). Stems are clothed with mid-green leaves, divided into 4–6 pairs of linear leaflets. In early summer produces racemes of inverted, violet-blue flowers.

S. leucantha (Mexican bush sage). Evergreen, erect, well-branched shrub. H and S to 60cm (2ft) or more. Tender. Narrowly lance-shaped, finely wrinkled leaves are deep green above, white-downy beneath. In summer-autumn produces terminal spikes of hairy, white flowers, each from a woolly, violet calyx.

S. microphylla var. *microphylla*, syn. *S. grahamii*. Evergreen, erect, well-branched shrub. H and S 1–1.2m (3–4ft). Marginally hardy, but best at 5°C (41°F). Has oval to elliptic, mid- to deep green leaves. Racemes of dark crimson flowers, ageing to purple and with purple-tinted calyces, appear in late summer and autumn. var. *neurepia* illus. p.166.

S. nemorosa, syn. *S. virgata* var. *nemorosa*. Neat, clump-forming perennial. H 1m (3ft), S 45cm (1½ft). Has narrowly oval, rough, mid-green leaves and, in summer, branching racemes densely set with violet-blue flowers. **'East Friesland'** see *S.n.* 'Ostfriesland'. **'Lubecca'**, H 45cm (1½ft), is a dwarf form. **'Ostfriesland'** (syn. *S.n.* 'East Friesland'), H 75cm (2½ft), is smaller.

S. officinalis (Sage). **'Icterina'** illus. p.177. **'Purpurascens'** is an evergreen or semi-evergreen, bushy shrub. H 60cm (2ft), S 1m (3ft). Oblong, grey-green leaves are used as a culinary herb and are purple-flushed when young. Racemes of blue-purple flowers are produced in summer.

S. patens 'Cambridge Blue' illus. p.287.

S. pratensis Haematodes Group, syn. *S. haematodes*. Short-lived, rosette-forming perennial. H 1m (3ft), S 45cm (1½ft). In early summer produces panicles massed with lavender-blue flowers above large, broadly oval, wavy-edged, toothed, rough, dark green leaves.

S. sclarea var. *turkestanica* illus. p.330.

S. splendens. Slow-growing, bushy perennial or evergreen sub-shrub, grown as an annual. H to 30cm (12in), S 20–30cm (8–12in). Has oval, serrated, fresh green leaves, and dense racemes of scarlet flowers in summer and early autumn. **'Blaze of Fire'** has brilliant scarlet flowers. **Cleopatra Series** (salmon, illus. p.321; violet, illus. p.331) are available in mixed or single colours. **'Rambo'**, H to 60cm (24in), is very tall, vigorous, and bushy, with dark green leaves and scarlet flowers. **'Red Riches'** (syn. *S.s.* 'Ryco'), S 30–40cm (12–16in) has dark green leaves and scarlet flowers. **'Ryco'** see *S.s.* 'Red Riches'. **'Scarlet King'** illus. p.328. **Sizzler Series** illus p.327.

S. × superba. Clump-forming, erect, branched perennial. H 60–90cm (24–36in), S 45–60cm (18–24in). Leaves are lance-shaped to oblong, scalloped and mid-green, slightly hairy beneath. Slender, terminal racemes of bright violet or purple flowers, to 1.5cm (½in) long, are produced from mid-summer to early autumn. **'Mainacht'** (syn. *S. × s.* 'May Night') illus. p.252.

S. uliginosa (Bog sage). Graceful, upright, branching perennial. H 2m (6ft), S 45cm (1½ft). Has oblong to lance-shaped, saw-edged, mid-green leaves and, in autumn, long racemes with whorls of bright blue flowers. Prefers moist soil.

S. virgata var. *nemorosa*. See *S. nemorosa*.

S. viridis, syn. *S. horminum*, illus. p.331. **'Bouquet'** (syn. *S.v.* 'Monarch Bouquet') is a moderately fast-growing, upright, branching annual with oval to oblong leaves. H 45–50cm (18–20in), S 23cm (9in). Tubular, lipped flowers, with oval, rose-pink, white, deep carmine-pink, or purple bracts, are carried in spikes at tops of stems in summer and early autumn; also available as single colours. Bracts of **Claryssa Series** are in a wide range of brilliant colours, including white, pink, purple and blue. **'Monarch Bouquet'** see *S.v.* 'Bouquet'. **'Oxford Blue'**, H 30cm (12in), has violet-blue bracts.

SALVINIA

SALVINIACEAE

Genus of deciduous, perennial, floating water ferns, evergreen in tropical conditions and aquariums. Tender, min.

10–15°C (50–59°F). Does best in warm water, with plenty of light. Remove fading foliage, and thin plants when crowded. Propagate by dividing young plants in summer.
S. auriculata illus. p.449.
S. natans. Deciduous, perennial, floating water plant. S indefinite. Oval, elongated, mid-green leaves are borne on branching stems. Tolerates colder conditions than other species and is often used in a cold-water aquarium.

SAMBUCUS
Elder

CAPRIFOLIACEAE

Genus of perennials, deciduous shrubs and trees, grown for their foliage, flowers and fruits. Needs sun and fertile, moist soil. For best foliage effect, either cut all shoots to ground in winter or prune out old shoots and reduce length of young shoots by half. Propagate species by softwood cuttings in summer, by seed in autumn or by hardwood cuttings in winter, some forms by cuttings only. All parts may cause severe discomfort if ingested, although fruits are safe when cooked; contact with the leaves may irritate skin.
S. canadensis (American elder). **'Aurea'** is a deciduous, upright shrub. H and S 4m (12ft). Has large, golden-yellow leaves, each with usually 7 oblong leaflets. In mid-summer bears large, domed heads of small, star-shaped, creamy-white flowers, then spherical, red fruits. Zone 2b.
S. nigra (European elder). **'Aurea'** (Golden European elder) is a deciduous, bushy shrub. H and S 6m (20ft). Has stout, corky shoots and golden-yellow leaves of usually 5 oval leaflets. Flattened heads of fragrant, star-shaped, creamy-white flowers in early summer are followed by spherical, black fruits. Dark green foliage of **'Guincho Purple'** matures to deep blackish-purple. Bears purple-stalked flowers, pink in bud and opening to white within, pink outside. Both zone 4.
S. racemosa (Red-berried elder). Deciduous, bushy shrub. H and S 3m (10ft). Mid-green leaves each have usually 5 oval leaflets. Star-shaped, creamy-yellow flowers, borne in dense, conical clusters in mid-spring, are succeeded by spherical, red fruits. **'Plumosa'** has leaves with finely cut leaflets, as does **'Plumosa Aurea'**, but those of the latter are bronze when young, maturing to golden-yellow. **'Sutherland Gold'** retains its golden-yellow colour throughout the summer. All zone 3.

SANCHEZIA

ACANTHACEAE

Genus of evergreen, mainly summer-flowering perennials, shrubs and scrambling climbers, grown for their flowers and foliage. Tender, min. 15–18°C (59–64°F). Requires full light or partial shade and fertile, well-drained soil. Water potted plants freely when in full growth, less at other times. Tip prune young plants to promote a branching habit. Propagate by greenwood cuttings

in spring or summer. Is prone to whitefly and soft scale.
S. nobilis of gardens. See *S. speciosa.*
S. speciosa, syn. *S. nobilis* of gardens, illus. p.177.

Sand phlox. See *Phlox bifida,* illus. p.381.

SANDERSONIA

COLCHICACEAE/LILIACEAE

Genus of one species of deciduous, tuberous climber with urn-shaped flowers in summer. Needs a sheltered, sunny site and well-drained soil. Support with sticks or canes. Lift tubers for winter. Propagate in spring by seed or by naturally divided tubers.
S. aurantiaca illus. p.423.

Sandwort. See *Arenaria.*

SANGUINARIA
Bloodroot

PAPAVERACEAE

Genus of one species of spring-flowering, rhizomatous perennial. Grow in sun or semi-shade and in humus-rich, moist but well-drained soil. Propagate by division of rhizomes in summer or by seed in autumn.
S. canadensis illus. p.363. **'Plena'** (syn. *S.c.* 'Flore Pleno') is a clump-forming, rhizomatous perennial with fleshy, underground stems that exude red sap when cut. H 15cm (6in), S 30–45cm (12–18in). Short-lived, rounded, fully double, white flowers emerge in spring followed by large, rounded to heart-shaped, scalloped, grey-green leaves with glaucous undersides.

SANGUISORBA
Burnet

ROSACEAE

Genus of perennials, grown for their bottlebrush-like flower spikes. Requires sun and moist soil. Propagate by division in spring or by seed in autumn.
S. canadensis illus. p.226.
S. obtusa. Clump-forming perennial. H 1–1.2m (3–4ft), S 60cm (2ft). Arching stems bear spikes of rose-crimson flowers in mid-summer. Pairs of oval leaflets are pale green above, blue-green beneath.
S. officinalis (Great burnet). **'Rubra'** is a clump-forming perennial. H 1.2m (4ft), S 60cm (2ft). Produces small spikes of red-brown flowers in late summer above a mass of mid-green leaves, divided into oval leaflets.

SANSEVIERIA

AGAVACEAE/DRACAENACEAE

Genus of evergreen, rhizomatous perennials, grown for their rosettes of stiff, fleshy leaves. Tender, min. 10–15°C (50–59°F). Tolerates sun and shade and is easy to grow in most soil conditions if not overwatered. Propagate by leaf cuttings or division in summer.
S. cylindrica. Evergreen, stemless, rhizomatous perennial. H 45cm–1.2m

(1½–4ft), S 10cm (4in). Has a rosette of 3–4 cylindrical, stiff, fleshy, erect leaves, to 1.2m (4ft) long, in dark green with paler horizontal bands. Racemes of small, tubular, 6-lobed, pink or white flowers are occasionally produced.
S. trifasciata (Mother-in-law's tongue). Evergreen, stemless, rhizomatous perennial. H 45cm–1.2m (1½–4ft), S 10cm (4in). Has a rosette of about 5 lance-shaped, pointed, stiff, fleshy, erect leaves, to 1.2m (4ft) long, banded horizontally with pale green and yellow. Occasionally carries racemes of tubular, 6-lobed, green flowers.
'Golden Hahnii' illus. p.305.
'Hahnii' illus. p.303.
'Laurentii' illus. p.267.

SANTOLINA

ASTERACEAE/COMPOSITAE

Genus of evergreen, summer-flowering shrubs, grown for their aromatic foliage and their button-like flower heads, each on a long stem. Needs sun and not too rich, well-drained soil. Cut off old flower heads and reduce long shoots in autumn. Cut straggly, old plants back hard each spring. Propagate by semi-ripe cuttings in summer.
S. chamaecyparissus, syn. *S. incana* (Cotton lavender, Lavender cotton). Evergreen, rounded, dense shrub. H 75cm (2½ft), S 1m (3ft). Shoots are covered with woolly, white growth, and narrowly oblong, finely toothed leaves are also white. Bright yellow flower heads are borne in mid- and late summer. Zone 7.
S. incana. See *S. chamaecyparissus.*
S. neapolitana. See *S. pinnata* subsp. *neapolitana.*
S. pinnata. Evergreen shrub, mainly grown as subsp. *neapolitana* (syn. *S. neapolitana*), which is of rounded and bushy habit. H 75cm (2½ft), S 1m (3ft). Slender flower stems bear a head of lemon-yellow flowers in mid-summer, among feathery, deeply cut, grey-green foliage. Zone 9?. subsp. *neapolitana* **'Sulphurea'** illus. p.169.
S. rosmarinifolia, syn. *S. virens* (Holy flax). Evergreen, bushy, dense shrub. H 60cm (2ft), S 1m (3ft). Has finely cut, bright green leaves. Each slender stem produces a head of bright yellow flowers in mid-summer. **'Primrose Gem'** has pale yellow flower heads.
S. virens. See *S. rosmarinifolia.* Zone 7.

SANVITALIA

ASTERACEAE/COMPOSITAE

Genus of perennials and annuals. Grow in sun and in fertile, well-drained soil. Propagate by seed sown outdoors in spring or early autumn.
S. procumbens illus. p.336.
'Mandarin Orange' illus. p.341.

SAPONARIA
Soapwort

CARYOPHYLLACEAE

Genus of summer-flowering annuals and perennials, grown for their flowers. Is good for rock gardens, screes and banks. Needs sun and well-drained soil. Propagate by seed in spring or

autumn or by softwood cuttings in early summer.
S. **'Bressingham'**, syn. *S.* 'Bressingham Hybrid'. Loose, mat-forming perennial. H 8cm (3in), S 10cm (4in). Has small, narrowly oval leaves. Flattish, deep vibrant pink flowers are produced in clustered heads in summer. Is good for a trough.
S. caespitosa illus. p.378.
S. ocymoides illus. p.378.
S. officinalis **'Rubra Plena'** (Double soapwort). Upright perennial. H to 1m (3ft), S 30cm (1ft). Has oval, rough, mid-green leaves on erect stems. Clusters of ragged, double, red flowers are produced from leaf axils on upper part of flower stems in summer.
S. × *olivana* illus. p.376.

Sapphire berry. See *Symplocos paniculata,* illus. p.138.
Sarana, Black. See *Fritillaria camschatcensis,* illus. p.413.

SARCOCOCCA
Christmas box, Sweet box

BUXACEAE

Genus of evergreen shrubs, grown for their foliage, fragrant, winter flowers and spherical fruits. Flowers are tiny – the only conspicuous part being the anthers. Is useful for cutting in winter. Grows in sun or shade and in fertile, not too dry soil. Propagate by semi-ripe cuttings in summer or by seed in autumn.
S. confusa. Evergreen, bushy, dense shrub. H and S 1m (3ft). Leaves are small, oval, taper-pointed, glossy and dark green. Has tiny, white flowers in winter, then black fruits. Zone 7.
S. hookeriana. Evergreen, upright, dense, suckering shrub. H 1.5m (5ft), S 2m (6ft). Forms clumps of narrowly oblong, pointed, dark green leaves and has tiny, white flowers in the leaf axils during winter. Fruits are black. Zone 7. var. *digyna* illus. p.174. var. *humilis* see *S. humilis.*
S. humilis, syn. *S. hookeriana* var. *humilis,* illus. p.174.
S. ruscifolia. Evergreen, upright, arching shrub. H and S 1m (3ft). Has oval, glossy, dark green leaves and, in winter, creamy-white flowers, then red fruits. Zone 8. var. *chinensis* has narrower leaves.

Sargent cherry. See *Prunus sargentii,* illus. p.87.
Sargent's rowan. See *Sorbus sargentiana.*

SARRACENIA
Pitcher plant

SARRACENIACEAE

Genus of insectivorous perennials, some of which are evergreen, with pitchers formed from modified leaves with hooded tops. Grow in sun or partial shade and in peat and moss. Keep very wet, except in winter, when drier conditions are needed. Propagate by seed in spring.
S. flava illus. p.290.
S. purpurea (Common pitcher plant, Huntsman's cup). Evergreen, erect

to semi-prostrate, rosette-forming perennial. H 30cm (12in), S 30–38cm (12–15in). Inflated, green pitchers, to 15cm (6in) long, are tinged and veined purplish-red. In spring, 5-petalled, purple flowers, 5cm (2in) or more wide, are carried well above pitchers.

Sarsparilla, Australian. See *Hardenbergia violacea.*

SASA

GRAMINEAE/POACEAE

See also GRASSES, BAMBOOS, RUSHES and SEDGES.
S. albomarginata. See *S. veitchii.*
S. palmata. Evergreen, spreading bamboo. H 2m (6ft), S indefinite. A fine foliage plant, it produces very broad, rich green leaves, to 40cm (16in) long. Hollow, purple-streaked stems have one branch at each node. Flower spikes are unimportant.
S. veitchii, syn. *S. albomarginata,* illus. p.306.

SASSAFRAS

LAURACEAE

Genus of deciduous trees, with inconspicuous flowers, grown for their aromatic foliage. Needs sun or light shade and deep, fertile, well-drained, preferably acid soil. Propagate by seed or suckers in autumn or by root cuttings in winter.
S. albidum illus. p.68.

Sassafras
  Australian. See *Atherosperma moschatum.*
  Tasmanian. See *Atherosperma moschatum.*
Satin flower, New Zealand. See *Libertia grandiflora,* illus. p.239.

SATUREJA

LABIATAE/LAMIACEAE

Genus of summer-flowering annuals, semi-evergreen perennials and sub-shrubs, grown for their highly aromatic leaves and attractive flowers. Is useful for rock gardens and dry banks. Needs sun and well-drained soil. Propagate by seed in winter or spring or by softwood cuttings in summer.
S. montana (Winter savory). Semi-evergreen, upright perennial or sub-shrub. H 30cm (12in), S 20cm (8in) or more. Leaves are linear to oval, aromatic and green or greyish-green. Carries loose whorls of tubular, 2-lipped, lavender flowers in summer. **'Prostrate White',** H 7–15cm (3–6in), has a prostrate habit and produces white flowers.

SAUROMATUM

ARACEAE

Genus of spring-flowering, tuberous perennials with tubular spathes that expand into waved, twisted blades. Tubers will flower without soil or moisture, and before leaves appear. Tender, min. 5–7°C (41–5°F). Needs a

sheltered, semi-shaded position and humus-rich, well-drained soil. Water well in summer. Dry off or lift when dormant in winter. Propagate by offsets in spring.
S. guttatum. See *S. venosum.*
S. venosum, syn. *S. guttatum,* illus. p.413.

SAURURUS

SAURURACEAE

Genus of deciduous, perennial, bog and marginal water plants, grown for their foliage. Prefers full sun, but tolerates some shade. Remove faded leaves and divide plants as required to maintain vigour. Propagate by division in spring.
S. cernuus illus. p.447.

Sausage tree. See *Kigelia africana.*
Savin. See *Juniperus sabina.*
Savory, Winter. See *Satureja montana.*
Saw palmetto. See *Serenoa repens.*
Sawara cypress. See *Chamaecyparis pisifera.*
Sawfly orchid. S*ee Ophrys tenthredinifera,* illus. p.297.
Sawtooth oak. See *Quercus acutissima.*

SAXEGOTHAEA

PODOCARPACEAE

See also CONIFERS.
S. conspicua (Prince Albert's yew). Conifer that is conical in mild areas, more bushy in cold districts. H 5–15m (15–50ft), S 4–5m (12–15ft). Needle-like, flattened, dark green leaves are produced in whorls at ends of shoots. Bears globose, fleshy, glaucous green cones.

SAXIFRAGA
Saxifrage

SAXIFRAGACEAE

Genus of often rosetted perennials, most of which are evergreen or semi-evergreen, grown for their flowers and attractive foliage. Is excellent in rock gardens, raised beds and alpine houses. Propagate by seed in autumn or by rooted offsets in winter. For cultivation, saxifrages may be grouped as follows:

1 – Needs protection from midday sun and moist soil.
2 – Needs semi-shaded, well-drained soil. Is good among rocks and screes.
3 – Thrives in well-drained rock pockets, troughs, alpine-house pans etc, shaded from midday sun. Must never be dry at roots. Most form tight cushions and flower in early spring, flower stems being barely visible above leaves.
4 – Needs full sun and well-drained, alkaline soil. Suits rock pockets. Most have hard leaves encrusted in lime.

S. aizoides. Evergreen perennial forming a loose mat. H 15cm (6in), S 30cm (12in) or more. Has small, narrowly oval, fleshy, shiny, green leaves and, in spring-summer, terminal racemes of star-shaped, bright yellow or orange flowers, often spotted red, on

8cm (3in) stems. Cultivation group 1.
S. aizoon. See *S. paniculata.*
S. x anglica 'Cranbourne', syn. *S.* 'Cranbourne'. Evergreen, cushion-forming perennial. H and S 12cm (5in). In early spring produces solitary, cup-shaped, bright purplish-lilac flowers on short stems just above tight rosettes of linear, green leaves. Flower stems are longer if plant is grown in an alpine house. Cultivation group 3.
S. x apiculata 'Gregor Mendel', syn. *S.* 'Gregor Mendel', illus. p.371; Cultivation group 2.
S. 'Arco'. See. *S.* x *arco-valleyi* 'Arco'.
S. x arco-valleyi 'Arco', syn. *S.* 'Arco'. Evergreen perennial forming a tight cushion. H and S 10cm (4in). In early spring produces upturned, cup-shaped to flattish, pale lilac flowers almost resting on tight rosettes of oblong to linear leaves. Cultivation group 3.
S. 'Aretiastrum'. See *S.* 'Valerie Finnis'.
S. 'Bob Hawkins'. Evergreen perennial with a loose rosette of leaves. H 2.5–5cm (1–2in), S 15cm (6in). Carries small, upturned, rounded, greenish-white flowers in summer on 5cm (2in) stems. Oval, green leaves are white-splashed. Cultivation group 1.
S. x boydii 'Hindhead Seedling' illus. p.371; cultivation group 2.
S. 'Brookside'. See *S. burseriana* 'Brookside'.
S. brunoniana. See *S. brunonis.*
S. brunonis, syn. *S. brunoniana.* Semi-evergreen, rosetted perennial. H 10cm (4in), S 20cm (8in). Small, soft green rosettes of lance-shaped, rigid leaves produce masses of long, thread-like, red runners. Many of the rosettes die down to large terminal buds in winter. Short racemes of 5-petalled, spreading, pale yellow flowers are produced in late spring and summer on 5–8cm (2–3in) stems. Is difficult to grow; cultivation group 1.
S. burseriana illus. p.363. **'Brookside'** (syn. *S.* 'Brookside') is a slow-growing, evergreen perennial forming a hard cushion. H 2.5–5cm (1–2in), S to 10cm (4in). Has broadly linear, spiky, grey-green leaves. In early spring bears upturned, rounded, shallowly cup-shaped, bright yellow flowers on short, red stems. Flowers of **'Crenata'** (syn. *S.* 'Crenata') have fringed, white petals and red sepals. **'Gloria'** (syn. *S.* 'Gloria') has dark reddish-brown stems, each bearing 1 or 2 flowers, with red sepals and white petals, in late spring. Cultivation group 3.
S. callosa, syn. *S. lingulata.* Evergreen, tightly rosetted perennial. H 25cm (10in), S to 20cm (8in). Bears long, linear, stiff, lime-encrusted leaves and, in early summer, upright, then arching panicles of star-shaped, white flowers with red-spotted petals. Rosettes die after flowering; new ones are produced annually from short stolons. Cultivation group 4.
S. cochlearis. Evergreen, rosetted perennial. H 20cm (8in), S 25cm (10in). Has spoon-shaped, green leaves with white-encrusted edges. Produces loose panicles of rounded, white flowers, often with red-spotted petals, in early summer. **'Minor',** H and S 12cm (5in), has

smaller leaf rosettes and loose panicles of red-spotted, white flowers on red stems. Is ideal for a trough. Cultivation group 4.
S. cortusifolia var. **fortunei.** See *S. fortunei.*
S. cotyledon illus. p.352; cultivation group 2.
S. 'Cranbourne'. See *S.* x *anglica* 'Cranbourne'.
S. 'Crenata'. See *S. burseriana* 'Crenata'.
S. cuneifolia illus. p.351; cultivation group 1.
S. 'Elizabethae', syn. *S.* x *elizabethae,* illus. p.371; cultivation group 2.
S. exarata subsp. **moschata,** syn. *S. moschata.* Evergreen perennial forming a loose to tight hummock. H and S 10cm (4in). Rosettes comprise small, lance-shaped, sometimes 3-toothed, green leaves. Bears 2–5 star-shaped, creamy-white or dull yellow flowers on slender stems in summer. **'Cloth of Gold'** illus. p.391. Cultivation group 1.
S. ferdinandi-coburgi. Evergreen, cushion-forming perennial. H and S 15cm (6in). Forms rosettes of linear, spiny, glaucous green leaves and, in early spring, bears racemes of open cup-shaped, rich yellow flowers on stems 3–10cm (1–4in) long. Cultivation group 3.
S. fortunei, syn. *S. cortusifolia* var. *fortunei.* Semi-evergreen or herbaceous, clump-forming perennial. H and S 30cm (12in). Has rounded, 5- or 7-lobed, fleshy, green or brownish-green leaves, red beneath. In autumn produces panicles of tiny, moth-like, white flowers, with 4 equal-sized petals and one elongated petal, on upright stems. Propagate by division in spring. **'Rubrifolia'** has dark red flower stems and dark reddish-green leaves with beetroot-red undersides. Cultivation group 1.
S. frederici-augustii subsp. **grisebachii 'Wisley Variety',** syn. *S. grisebachii* 'Wisley Variety', illus. p.367; cultivation group 4.
S. x geum illus. p.347; cultivation group 1.
S. 'Gloria'. See *S. burseriana* 'Gloria'.
S. granulata (Fair maids of France, Meadow saxifrage) illus. p.346. **'Plena'** is a clump-forming perennial. H 23–38cm (9–15in), S to 15cm (6in) or more. Loses its kidney-shaped, glossy, pale to mid-green leaves soon after flowering. Has a loose panicle of large, rounded, double, white flowers in late spring or early summer. Bulbils or resting buds form at base of foliage. Cultivation group 1.
S. 'Gregor Mendel'. See *S.* x *apiculata* 'Gregor Mendel'.
S. grisebachii 'Wisley Variety'. See *S. frederici-augustii* subsp. *grisebachii* 'Wisley Variety'.
S. hirsuta illus. p.347; cultivation group 1.
S. 'Irvingii'. See *S.* x *irvingii* 'Walter Irving'.
S. x irvingii 'Jenkinsiae', syn. *S.* 'Jenkinsiae', illus. p.365; cultivation group 2. **'Walter Irving'** (syn. *S.* 'Irvingii') is a very slow-growing, evergreen, hard-domed perennial. H 2cm (¾in), S 8cm (3in). Bears

minute leaves in rosettes. Stemless, cup-shaped, lilac-pink flowers open in early spring. Cultivation group 3.

S. 'Jenkinsiae'. See *S.* × *irvingii* 'Jenkinsiae'.

S. lingulata. See *S. callosa*.

S. longifolia. Rosetted perennial. H 60cm (24in), S 20–25cm (8–10in). Has long, narrow, lime-encrusted leaves forming attractive rosettes that, after 3–4 years, develop long, arching, conical to cylindrical panicles bearing numerous rounded, 5-petalled, white flowers in late spring and summer. Rosettes die after flowering, and no daughter rosettes are formed, so propagate by seed in spring or autumn. In cultivation, hybridizes readily with other related species. Cultivation group 4.

S. moschata. See *S. exarata* subsp. *moschata*.

S. oppositifolia illus. p.366. **'Ruth Draper'** is an evergreen, loose matforming perennial. H 2.5–5cm (1–2in), S 15cm (6in). Has small, opposite, oblong to oval, white-flecked, dark green leaves closely set along prostrate stems. Large, cup-shaped, deep purple-pink flowers appear in early spring just above foliage. Prefers peaty soil. Cultivation group 1.

S. paniculata, syn. *S. aizoon*. Evergreen, tightly rosetted perennial. H 15–30cm (6–12in), S 20cm (8in). In summer produces loose panicles of rounded, usually white flowers, with or without purplish-red spots, on upright stems above rosettes of oblong to oval, lime-encrusted leaves. Is very variable in size. Pale yellow or pale pink forms also occur. Cultivation group 4.

S. × **primulaize,** syn. *S.* 'Primulaize'. Evergreen, loosely rosetted perennial. H and S 15cm (6in). In summer, branched flower stems, 5–8cm (2–3in) long, produce star-shaped, salmon-pink flowers. Leaves are tiny, narrowly oval, slightly indented and fleshy. Cultivation group 1.

S. sancta illus. p.371; cultivation group 2.

S. sarmentosa. See *S. stolonifera*.

S. scardica illus. p.362; cultivation group 3.

S. sempervivum illus. p.367; cultivation group 3.

S. 'Southside Seedling' illus. p.352; cultivation group 4.

S. stolonifera, syn. *S. sarmentosa* (Mother of thousands). Evergreen, prostrate perennial with runners. H 15cm (6in) or more, S 30cm (12in) or more. Has large, rounded, shallowly lobed, hairy, silver-veined, olive-green leaves that are reddish-purple beneath. Loose panicles of tiny, moth-like, white flowers, each with 4 equal-sized petals and one elongated petal, appear in summer on slender, upright stems. Makes good ground cover. **'Tricolor'** (syn. *S.* 'Tricolor'; Strawberry geranium) has green-and-red leaves with silver marks and is half hardy. Cultivation group 1.

S. stribrnyi illus. p.368; cultivation group 3.

S. 'Tricolor'. See *S. stolonifera* 'Tricolor'.

S. 'Tumbling Waters' illus. p.347; cultivation group 4.

S. × **urbium** (London pride). Evergreen, rosetted, spreading perennial. H 30cm (12in), S indefinite. Has spoon-shaped, toothed, leathery, green leaves. Flower stems bear tiny, star-shaped, at times pink-flushed, white flowers, with red spots, in summer. Is useful as ground cover. Cultivation group 1.

S. 'Valerie Finnis', syn. *S.* 'Aretiastrum'. Evergreen, hard cushion-forming perennial. H and S 10cm (4in). Short, red stems carry upturned, cup-shaped, sulphur-yellow flowers above tight rosettes of oval, green leaves in spring. Cultivation group 3.

Saxifrage. See *Saxifraga*.
   Meadow. See *Saxifraga granulata*, illus. p.346.
   Purple mountain. See *Saxifraga oppositifolia*, illus. p.366.

SCABIOSA
Scabious

DIPSACACEAE

Genus of annuals and perennials, some of which are evergreen, with flower heads that are good for cutting. Prefers sun and fertile, well-drained, alkaline soil. Propagate annuals by seed in spring and perennials by cuttings of young, basal growths in summer, by seed in autumn or by division in early spring.

S. arvensis. See *Knautia arvensis*.

S. atropurpurea (Sweet scabious). Moderately fast-growing, upright, bushy annual. H to 1m (3ft), S 20–30cm (8–12in). Has lance-shaped, lobed, mid-green leaves. Domed heads of scented, pincushion-like, deep crimson flower heads, 5cm (2in) wide, are produced on wiry stems in summer and early autumn. Tall forms, H 1m (3ft), and dwarf, H 45cm (18in), are available with flower heads in shades of blue, purple, red, pink or white.

S. caucasica. 'Clive Greaves' illus. p.285. **'Floral Queen'** is a clump-forming perennial. H and S 60cm (24in). Large, frilled, violet-blue flower heads, with pincushion-like centres, are produced throughout summer. Light green leaves are lance-shaped at base of plant and segmented on stems. **'Miss Willmott'** has creamy-white flowers.

S. columbaria var. **ochroleuca.** See *S. ochroleuca*.

S. graminifolia. Evergreen, clump-forming perennial, often with a woody base. H and S 15–25cm (6–10in). Has tufts of narrow, grass-like, pointed, silver-haired leaves. In summer produces stiff stems with spherical, bluish-violet to lilac flower heads like pincushions. Resents disturbance. Suits a rock garden.

S. lucida illus. p.355.

S. ochroleuca, syn. *S. columbaria* var. *ochroleuca*. Clump-forming perennial. H and S 1m (3ft). In late summer, branching stems carry many heads of frilled, sulphur-yellow flower heads with pincushion-like centres. Has narrowly oval, toothed, grey-green leaves.

S. rumelica. See *Knautia macedonica*.

Scabious. See *Knautia arvensis*; *Scabiosa*.
   Giant. See *Cephalaria gigantea*.
   Sweet. See *Scabiosa atropurpurea*.
   Yellow. See *Cephalaria gigantea*.

SCADOXUS

AMARYLLIDACEAE

Genus of bulbs with dense, mainly spherical, umbels of red flowers. Tender, min. 10–15°C (50–59°F). Requires partial shade and humus-rich, well-drained soil. Reduce watering in winter, when not in active growth. Propagate by seed or offsets in spring.

S. multiflorus, syn. *Haemanthus multiflorus*. Summer-flowering bulb. H to 70cm (28in), S 30–45cm (12–18in). Has broadly lance-shaped, semi-erect, basal leaves. Produces a spherical umbel, 10–15cm (4–6in) wide, of up to 200 narrow-petalled flowers. subsp. **katherinae** (syn. *Haemanthus katherinae*) illus. p.401.

S. puniceus, syn. *Haemanthus magnificus*, *H. natalensis*, *H. puniceus* (Royal paintbrush). Spring- and summer-flowering bulb. H 30–40cm (12–16in), S 30–45cm (12–18in). Has elliptic, semi-erect leaves in a basal cluster. Leaf bases are joined, forming a false stem. Flower stem bears up to 100 tubular, orange-red flowers in a conical umbel surrounded by a whorl of red bracts.

SCAEVOLA
Blue fan flower

GOODENIACEAE

Genus of summer flowering perennials, grown for their arching stems, with spoon-shaped toothed leaves. Tender, min. 5°C (41°F). Grow in full sun or very light shade and well-drained soil, rich in organic matter. Will tolerate sandy soils as long as they are kept moist. Propagate by cuttings in early spring.

S. aemula. Tender perennial, usually grown as an annual from cuttings. H and S 45cm (18in). Pale blue flowers have all the petals on one side giving a fan-like effect. **'Blue Wonder'** is more trailing with lilac-blue flowers from early summer to fall. H 15cm (6in), S 1.2m (4ft). Good for baskets, window boxes and planters.

Scarlet ball cactus. See *Parodia haselbergii*, illus. p.475.
Scarlet banana. See *Musa coccinea*.
Scarlet fritillary. See *Fritillaria recurva*, illus. p.396.
Scarlet oak. See *Quercus coccinea*, illus. p.70.
Scarlet plume. See *Euphorbia fulgens*.
Scarlet trompetilla. See *Bouvardia ternifolia*, illus. p.173.
Scarlet trumpet honeysuckle. See *Lonicera* × *brownii*.
Scarlet turkscap lily. See *Lilium chalcedonicum*, illus. p.405.
Scented paper-bark. See *Melaleuca squarrosa*.

SCHEFFLERA,
syn. BRASSAIA, HEPTAPLEURUM

ARALIACEAE

Genus of evergreen shrubs and trees, grown for their handsome foliage. Tender, min. 3–16°C (37–61°F). Grows in any fertile, well-drained but moisture-retentive soil and in full light or partial shade. Water potted specimens freely when in full growth, moderately at other times. Pruning is tolerated if needed. Propagate by air-layering in spring, by semi-ripe cuttings in summer or by seed as soon as ripe, in late summer.

S. actinophylla illus. p.84.

S. arboricola. Evergreen, erect, well-branched shrub or tree. H 2–5m (6–15ft), S 1–3m (3–10ft). Tender, min. 15°C (59°F). Leaves each have 7–16 oval, stalked, glossy, deep green leaflets. Mature plants carry small, spherical heads of tiny, green flowers in spring-summer.

S. digitata. Evergreen, rounded to ovoid shrub or bushy tree. H and S 3–8m (10–25ft). Tender, min. 5°C (41°F). Leaves are hand-shaped, with 5–10 oval, glossy, rich green leaflets. Has tiny, greenish flowers in large, terminal panicles in spring and tiny, globular, dark violet fruits in autumn.

S. elegantissima, syn. *Aralia elegantissima, Dizygotheca elegantissima*, illus. p.127.

SCHIMA

THEACEAE

Genus of one species of very variable, evergreen tree or shrub, grown for its foliage and flowers. Is related to *Camellia*. Tender, min. 3–5°C (37–41°F). Prefers humus-rich, well-drained, neutral to acid soil and sun or partial shade. Water potted plants freely in full growth, moderately at other times. Pruning is tolerated if necessary. Propagate by seed as soon as ripe or by semi-ripe cuttings in summer.

S. wallichii. Robust, evergreen, ovoid tree or shrub. H 25–30m (80–100ft), S 12m (40ft) or more. Elliptic to oblong, red-veined, dark green leaves are 10–18cm (4–7in) long, red-flushed beneath. In late summer has solitary fragrant, cup-shaped, white flowers, 4cm (1½in) wide, red-flushed in bud.

SCHINUS

ANACARDIACEAE

Genus of evergreen shrubs and trees, grown mainly for their foliage and for shade. Tender, min. 5°C (41°F). Grows in any freely draining soil and in full light. Water potted specimens moderately, hardly at all in winter. Propagate by seed in spring or by semi-ripe cuttings in summer.

S. molle (Californian pepper-tree, Peruvian mastic tree, Peruvian pepper-tree). Fast-growing, evergreen, weeping tree. H and S to 8m (25ft). Fern-like leaves are divided into many narrowly lance-shaped, glossy, rich green leaflets. Has open clusters of tiny, yellow flowers from late winter to summer, followed by pea-sized, pink-red fruits.

S. terebinthifolius. Evergreen shrub or tree, usually of bushy, spreading habit. H 3m (10ft) or more, S 2–3m (6–10ft) or more. Leaves have 3–13 oval, mid- to deep green leaflets. Tiny, white flowers are borne in clusters in summer-autumn, followed by pea-sized, red fruits, but only if plants of both sexes are grown close together.

SCHISANDRA

SCHISANDRACEAE

Genus of deciduous, woody-stemmed, twining climbers. Male and female flowers are borne on separate plants, so grow plants of both sexes if fruits are required. Is useful for growing against shady walls and training up pillars and fences. Grow in sun or partial shade and rich, well-drained soil. Propagate by greenwood or semi-ripe cuttings in summer.

S. grandiflora var. **rubriflora.** See *S. rubriflora.*
S. henryi. Deciduous, woody-stemmed, twining climber, with stems that are angled and winged when young. H 3–4m (10–12ft). Glossy, green leaves are oval or heart-shaped. Small, cup-shaped, white flowers appear in spring. Pendent spikes, 5–7cm (2–3in) long, of spherical, fleshy, red fruits are borne in late summer on female plants.
S. rubriflora, syn. *S. grandiflora* var. *rubriflora,* illus. p.211.

SCHIZANTHUS

Butterfly flower, Poor man's orchid

SOLANACEAE

Genus of annuals, grown for their showy flowers. Makes excellent pot plants. Tender, min. 5°C (41°F). Grow in a sunny, sheltered position and in fertile, well-drained soil. Pinch out growing tips of young plants to ensure a bushy habit. Propagate by seed sown under glass in early spring for summer-autumn flowers and in late summer for plants to flower in pots in late winter or spring. Is prone to damage by aphids.
S. 'Hit Parade' illus. p.322.
S. pinnatus illus. p.330.
S. 'Star Parade'. Compact annual with a distinctive pyramidal habit. H 20–25cm (8–10in), S 23–30cm (9–12in). Has almost fern-like, light green leaves. From spring to autumn, bears tubular, then flared, 2-lipped, white, yellow, pink, purple, or red flowers.

Schizocentron elegans. See *Heterocentron elegans.*

SCHIZOPETALON

BRASSICACEAE/CRUCIFERAE

Genus of annuals. Grow in sun and in well-drained, fertile soil. Propagate by seed sown under glass in early spring.
S. walkeri. Moderately fast-growing, upright, slightly branching annual. H 45cm (18in), S 20cm (8in). Has deeply divided, mid-green leaves and, in summer, almond-scented, white flowers with deeply cut and fringed petals.

SCHIZOPHRAGMA

HYDRANGEACEAE

Genus of deciduous, woody-stemmed, root climbers, useful for training up large trees. Flowers best in sun, but will grow against a north-facing wall. Needs well-drained soil. Tie young plants to supports. Propagate by seed in spring or by greenwood or semi-ripe cuttings in summer.
S. hydrangeoides (Japanese hydrangea vine). Deciduous, woody-stemmed, root climber. H to 12m (40ft). Broadly oval leaves are 10–15cm (4–6in) long. Small, white or creamy-white flowers, in flat heads 20–25cm (8–10in) across, are produced on pendent side-branches in summer; these are surrounded by marginal, sterile flowers, which each have an oval or heart-shaped, pale yellow sepal, 2–4cm (¾–1½in) long. Zone 6.
S. integrifolium illus. p.208.
S. viburnoides. See *Pileostegia viburnoides.*

SCHIZOSTYLIS

Kaffir lily

IRIDACEAE

Genus of rhizomatous perennials with flowers that are excellent for cutting. Requires sun and fertile, moist soil. Divide in spring every few years to avoid congestion.
S. coccinea 'Major', syn. *S.c.* 'Grandiflora', illus. p.294.
'Mrs Hegarty' is a vigorous, clump-forming, rhizomatous perennial. H 60cm (24in), S 23–30cm (9–12in). In mid-autumn produces spikes of shallowly cup-shaped, pale pink flowers above tufts of grass-like, mid-green leaves. **'Sunrise'** illus. p.294. **'Viscountess Byng'** has pink flowers that last until late autumn.

SCHLUMBERGERA

Holiday cactus

CACTACEAE

Genus of bushy, perennial cacti with erect, then pendent stems and flattened, oblong stem segments with indented notches at margins – like teeth in some species. Stem tips produce flowers with prominent stigmas and stamens and with petals of different lengths set in 2 rows. In the wild, often grows over mossy rocks, rooting at ends of stem segments. Tender, min. 10°C (50°F). Needs partial shade and rich, well-drained soil. Propagate by stem cuttings in spring or early summer.
S. bridgesii. See *S.* x *buckleyi.*
S. 'Bristol Beauty' illus. p.475.
S. x **buckleyi,** syn. *S. bridgesii* (Christmas cactus). Erect, then pendent, perennial cactus. H 15cm (6in), S 1m (3ft). Has glossy, green stem segments and produces red-violet flowers in mid-winter.
S. 'Gold Charm' illus. p.472.
S. truncata, syn. *Zygocactus truncatus,* illus. p.473.
S. 'Wintermärchen'. Erect, then pendent, perennial cactus. H 15cm (6in), S 30cm (12in). Has glossy, green stem segments. In early autumn bears

white flowers that become pink-and-white in winter.
S. 'Zara'. Erect, then pendent, perennial cactus. H 15cm (6in), S 30cm (12in). Has glossy, green stem segments. Bears deep orange-red flowers in early autumn and winter.

SCHOENOPLECTUS

CYPERACEAE

See also GRASSES, BAMBOOS, RUSHES and SEDGES.
S. lacustris subsp. **tabernaemontani 'Zebrinus',** syn. *Scirpus lacustris* var. *tabernaemontani* 'Zebrinus', *Scirpus tabernaemontani* 'Zebrinus', illus. p.306.

SCHWANTESIA

AIZOACEAE

Genus of cushion-forming, perennial succulents with stemless rosettes of unequal-sized pairs of keeled leaves and daisy-like, yellow flowers. Tender, min. 5°C (41°F). Needs full sun and well-drained soil. Propagate by seed or stem cuttings in spring or summer.
S. ruedebuschii illus. p.478.

SCIADOPITYS

SCIADOPITYACEAE

See also CONIFERS.
S. verticillata illus. p.106.

SCILLA

HYACINTHACEAE/LILIACEAE

Genus of mainly spring- and summer-flowering bulbs with leaves in basal clusters and spikes of small, often blue flowers. Needs an open site, sun or partial shade and well-drained soil. Propagate by division in late summer or by seed in autumn.
S. adlamii. See *Ledebouria cooperi.*
S. bifolia. Early spring-flowering bulb. H 5–15cm (2–6in), S 2.5–5cm (1–2in). Has 2 narrowly strap-shaped, semi-erect, basal leaves that widen towards tips. Stem produces one-sided spike of up to 20 star-shaped, purple-blue, pink or white flowers.
S. campanulata. See *Hyacinthoides hispanica.*
S. chinensis. See *S. scilloides.*
S. cooperi. See *Ledebouria cooperi.*
S. hispanica. See *Hyacinthoides hispanica.*
S. italica. See *Hyacinthoides italica.*
S. japonica. See *S. scilloides.*
S. litardierei, syn. *S. pratensis.* Clump-forming, early summer-flowering bulb. H 10–25cm (4–10in), S 5–8cm (2–3in). Bears up to 5 narrowly strap-shaped, semi-erect, basal leaves. Stem has a dense spike of flat, star-shaped, violet flowers, 1–1.5cm (½–⅝in) across.
S. mischtschenkoana, syn. *S. tubergeniana, S.* 'Tubergeniana', illus. p.432.
S. natalensis. Clump-forming, summer-flowering bulb. H 30–45cm (12–18in), S 15–20cm (6–8in). Lance-shaped, semi-erect, basal leaves lengthen after flowering. Has a long spike of up to 100 flattish, blue flowers, each 1.5–2cm (⅝–¾in) across.
S. non-scripta. See *Hyacinthoides non-scripta.*

S. nutans. See *Hyacinthoides non-scripta.*
S. peruviana illus. p.436.
S. pratensis. See *S. litardierei.*
S. scilloides, syn. *S. chinensis, S. japonica,* illus. p.424.
S. siberica (Siberian squill). **'Atrocoerulea'** illus. p.432.
S. socialis. See *Ledebouria socialis.*
S. tubergeniana. See *S. mischtschenkoana.*
S. 'Tubergeniana'. See *S. mischtschenkoana.*
S. violacea. See *Ledebouria socialis.*

Scindapsus aureus **'Marble Queen'.** See *Epipremnum aureum* 'Marble Queen'.
Scindapsus pictus **'Argyraeus'.** See *Epipremnum pictum* 'Argyraeum'.

SCIRPOIDES

CYPERACEAE

See also GRASSES, BAMBOOS, RUSHES and SEDGES.
S. holoschoenus, syn. *Scirpus holoschoenus* (Round-headed club-rush). **'Variegatus'** is an evergreen, tuft-forming, perennial rush. H 1m (3ft), S 45cm (1½ft). Rounded, leafless, green stems are striped horizontally with cream and bear long-stalked, dense, spherical heads of egg-shaped, awned, brown spikelets, produced from mid-summer to early autumn.

Scirpus holoschoenus. See *Scirpoides holoschoenus.*
Scirpus lacustris **'Spiralis'.** See *Juncus effusus* 'Spiralis'.
Scirpus lacustris subsp. **tabernaemontani 'Zebrinus'.** See *Schoenoplectus lacustris* subsp. *tabernaemontani* 'Zebrinus'.
Scirpus setaceus. See *Isolepsis setaceus.*
Scirpus tabernaemontani **'Zebrinus'.** See *Schoenoplectus lacustris* subsp. *tabernaemontani* 'Zebrinus'.

SCLEROCACTUS

CACTACEAE

Genus of perennial cacti, grown for their depressed-spherical to club-shaped or columnar stems, each with a long, fleshy tap root and deeply notched or warty ribs. Tender, min. 7–10°C (45–50°F) if completely dry. Needs full sun with some midday shade and very well-drained soil. May rot if overwatered. Propagate by seed in spring.
S. scheeri, syn. *Ancistrocactus megarhizus, A. scheeri, Echinocactus scheeri,* illus. p.477.
S. uncinatus, syn. *Ancistrocactus uncinatus, Echinocactus uncinatus, Glandulicactus uncinatus, Hamatocactus uncinatus.* Globose to columnar, perennial cactus. H 20cm (8in), S 10cm (4in). Stem is blue-green. Areoles each produce 1–4 very long, hooked, reddish spines and 15–18 straight ones. Has cup-shaped, brown-green or reddish flowers, 2cm (¾in) across, in spring.

SCOLIOPUS

LILIACEAE/TRILLIACEAE

Genus of one species of spring-flowering perennial. Is usually grown in alpine houses, where its neat habit and curious flowers, which arise directly from buds on the rootstock early in the season, may be better appreciated. Is also suitable for rock gardens and peat beds. Requires sun or partial shade and moist but well-drained soil. Propagate by seed when fresh, in summer or autumn.

S. bigelowii, syn. *S. bigelovii*, illus. p.364.

Scolopendrium vulgare. See *Asplenium scolopendrium.*

SCOPOLIA

SOLANACEAE

Genus of spring-flowering perennials. Prefers shade and fertile, very well-drained soil. Propagate by division in spring or by seed in autumn. All parts are highly toxic if ingested.

S. carniolica illus. p.271.

Scotch heather. See *Calluna vulgaris.*
Scotch laburnum. See *Laburnum alpinum,* illus. p.93.
Scotch rose. See *Rosa pimpinellifolia.*
Scotch thistle. See *Onopordum acanthium,* illus. p.322.
Scots pine. See *Pinus sylvestris.*
Screw pine. See *Pandanus.*

SCROPHULARIA

Figwort

SCROPHULARIACEAE

Genus of perennials and sub-shrubs, some of which are semi-evergreen or evergreen. Most species are weeds, but some are grown for their variegated foliage. Does best in semi-shade and moist soil. Propagate by division in spring or by softwood cuttings in summer.

S. aquatica 'Variegata'. See *S. auriculata* 'Variegata'.
S. auriculata 'Variegata', syn. *S. aquatica* 'Variegata' (Water figwort). Evergreen, clump-forming perennial. H 60cm (24in), S 30cm (12in) or more. Has attractive, oval, toothed, dark green leaves with cream marks. Remove spikes of insignificant, maroon flowers, borne in summer.

Scrub palmetto. See *Serenoa repens.*
Scrub pine. See *Pinus virginiana,* illus. p.107.
Scurvy grass. See *Oxalis enneaphylla.*

SCUTELLARIA

Skullcap

LABIATAE/LAMIACEAE

Genus of rhizomatous perennials, grown for their summer flowers. Needs sun and well-drained soil. Propagate by softwood cuttings in summer or by seed in autumn.

S. indica. Upright, rhizomatous perennial. H 15–30cm (6–12in), S 10cm (4in) or more. Leaves are oval,

toothed and hairy. Has dense racemes of long-tubed, 2-lipped, slate-blue, occasionally white flowers in summer. Suits a rock garden.

S. orientalis illus. p.385.
S. scordiifolia. Mat-forming, rhizomatous perennial. H and S 15cm (6in) or more. Bears narrowly oval, wrinkled leaves. In summer-autumn has racemes of tubular, hooded, purple flowers, each with a white-streaked lip. Propagate by division in spring.

Sea buckthorn. See *Hippophäe rhamnoides,* illus. p.124.
Sea campion, Double. See *Silene uniflora* 'Robin Whitebreast'.
Sea daffodil. See *Pancratium maritimum.*
Sea holly. See *Eryngium.*
Sea kale. See *Crambe maritima,* illus. p.276.
Sea lavender. See *Limonium.*
Sea lily. See *Pancratium maritimum.*
Sea onion. See *Urginea maritima.*
Sea pink. See *Armeria maritima.*
Sea squill. See *Urginea maritima.*
Sea urchin. See *Astrophytum asterias.*
Sedge
  Bowles' golden. See *Carex elata* 'Aurea', illus. p.309.
  Greater pond. See *Carex riparia.*
  Leatherleaf. See *Carex buchananii.*
  Mace. See *Carex grayi.*
  Pendulous. See *Carex pendula,* illus. p.309.
  Tufted. See *Carex elata.*
Sedges. See Grasses, Bamboos, Rushes and Sedges.

SEDUM

Stonecrop

CRASSULACEAE

Genus of often fleshy or succulent annuals, evergreen biennials, mostly evergreen or semi-evergreen perennials and evergreen shrubs and sub-shrubs, suitable for rock gardens and borders. Hardy to tender, min. 5°C (41°F). Needs sun. Does best in fertile, well-drained soil. Propagate perennials, sub-shrubs and shrubs by division or by softwood cuttings of non-flowering shoots from spring to mid-summer or by seed in autumn or spring. Propagate annuals and biennials by seed, sown under glass in early spring or outdoors in mid-spring. All parts may cause mild stomach upset if ingested; contact with the sap may irritate skin.

S. acre illus. p.384. 'Aureum' illus. p.385.
S. aizoon. Evergreen, erect perennial. H and S 45cm (18in). Mid-green leaves are oblong to lance-shaped, fleshy and toothed. In summer bears flat heads of star-shaped, yellow flowers. 'Aurantiacum' illus. p.293.
S. anacampseros, syn. *Hylotelephium anacampseros.* Semi-evergreen, trailing perennial with overwintering foliage rosettes. H 10cm (4in), S 25cm (10in) or more. Prostrate, loosely rosetted, brown stems bear oblong to oval, fleshy, glaucous green leaves. Dense, sub-globose, terminal heads of small, cup-shaped, purplish-pink flowers appear in summer.
S. caeruleum illus. p.333.

S. cauticola, syn. *Hylotelephium cauticola.* Trailing, shallow-rooted perennial with stolons. H 5cm (2in), S 20cm (8in). Has oval to oblong, stalked, fleshy, blue-green leaves on procumbent, purplish-red stems. Bears leafy, branched, flattish heads of star-shaped, pale purplish-pink flowers in early autumn. Cut back old stems in winter.
S. ewersii, syn. *Hylotelephium ewersii.* Trailing perennial. H 5cm (2in), S 15cm (6in). Is similar to *S. cauticola,* but has more rounded, stem-clasping leaves, often tinted red, and dense, rounded flower heads.
S. heterodontum. See *Rhodiola heterodonta.*
S. kamtschaticum. Semi-evergreen, prostrate perennial with overwintering foliage rosettes. H 5–8cm (2–3in), S 20cm (8in). Bears narrowly oval, toothed, fleshy, mid-green leaves. Spreading, terminal clusters of star-shaped, orange-flushed, yellow flowers appear in summer-autumn. 'Variegatum' illus. p.391.
S. lydium illus. p.388.
S. morganianum (Burro's tail, Donkey-tail). Evergreen, prostrate, succulent perennial. H 30cm (12in) or more, S indefinite. Tender. Stems are clothed in oblong to lance-shaped, almost cylindrical, fleshy, waxy, white leaves. Has terminal clusters of star-shaped, rose-pink flowers in summer.
S. obtusatum illus. p.388.
S. palmeri. Evergreen, clump-forming perennial. H 20cm (8in), S 30cm (12in). Bears sprays of star-shaped, yellow or orange flowers in early summer above oblong-oval to spoon-shaped, fleshy, grey-green leaves.
S. populifolium, syn. *Hylotelephium populifolium.* Semi-evergreen, bushy perennial. H 30–45cm (12–18in), S 30cm (12in). Terminal clusters of hawthorn-scented, star-shaped, pale pink or white flowers are borne in late summer. Has broadly oval, irregularly toothed, fleshy, mid-green leaves.
S. reflexum. See *S. rupestre.*
S. rosea. See *Rhodiola rosea.* var. *heterodontum* see *R. heterodonta.*
S. rupestre, syn. *S. reflexum,* illus. p.359.
S. sempervivoides. Evergreen, basal-rosetted biennial. H 8–10cm (3–4in), S 5cm (2in). Has rosettes that are similar to those of *Sempervivum;* oval to strap-shaped, leathery, glaucous green leaves are strongly marked red-purple. Produces domed heads of star-shaped, scarlet flowers in summer. Dislikes winter wet. Is good for an alpine house.
S. sieboldii 'Mediovariegatum', *S.s.* 'Variegatum'. Evergreen, spreading, tuberous perennial with long, tapering tap roots. H 10cm (4in), S 20cm (8in) or more. Tender. Rounded, fleshy, blue-green leaves, splashed cream and occasionally red-edged, appear in whorls of 3. Bears open, terminal heads of star-shaped, pink flowers in late summer. Is good for an alpine house.
S. spathulifolium illus. p.389. 'Cape Blanco' (syn. *S.s.* 'Cappa Blanca') illus. p.391.
S. spectabile, syn. *Hylotelephium spectabile* (Ice-plant). Clump-forming perennial. H and S 45cm (18in). Has

oval, indented, fleshy, grey-green leaves, above which flat heads of small, star-shaped, pink flowers that attract butterflies are borne in late summer. 'Brilliant' illus. p.294.
S. spurium. Semi-evergreen, mat-forming, creeping perennial. H 10cm (4in) or more, S indefinite. Oblong to oval, toothed leaves are borne along hairy stems. Large, slightly rounded heads of small, star-shaped flowers are borne in summer. Flower colour varies from deep purple to white.
S. tatarinowii, syn. *Hylotelephium tatarinowii.* Arching, spreading, tuberous perennial. H 10cm (4in), S 20cm (8in). Rounded, terminal heads of star-shaped, pink-flushed, white flowers appear in late summer above small, oval, toothed, green leaves borne along purplish stems. Suits an alpine house.

SELAGINELLA

SELAGINELLACEAE

Genus of evergreen, moss-like perennials, grown for their foliage. Tender, min. 5°C (41°F). Prefers semi-shade and needs moist but well-drained, peaty soil. Remove faded foliage regularly. Propagate from pieces with roots attached that have been broken off plant in any season.

S. kraussiana illus. p.312.
'Aurea' is an evergreen, moss-like perennial. H 1cm (½in), S indefinite. Spreading, filigreed, bright yellowish-green fronds are much-branched, denser towards the growing tips and easily root on soil surface.
'Variegata' has foliage splashed with creamy-yellow.
S. lepidophylla (Resurrection plant, Rose of Jericho). Evergreen, moss-like perennial. H and S 10cm (4in). Bluntly rounded, emerald-green fronds, ageing red-brown or grey-green, are produced in dense tufts. On drying, fronds curl inwards into a tight ball; they unfold when placed in water.
S. martensii illus. p.311.

SELENICEREUS

CACTACEAE

Genus of summer-flowering, perennial cacti with climbing, 4–10-ribbed, green stems, to 2cm (¾in) across. Nocturnal, funnel-shaped flowers eventually open flat. Tender, min. 5°C (41°F). Needs sun or partial shade and rich, well-drained soil. Propagate by seed or stem cuttings in spring or summer.

S. grandiflorus illus. p.456.

Self-heal. See *Prunella.*
  Large. See *Prunella grandiflora,* illus. p.382.

SELINUM

APIACEAE/UMBELLIFERAE

Genus of summer-flowering perennials, ideal for informal gardens and backs of borders. Prefers sun, but will grow in semi-shade, and any well-drained soil. Once established, roots resent disturbance. Propagate by seed when fresh, in summer or autumn.

683

S. tenuifolium. See *S. wallichianum*.
S. wallichianum, syn *S. tenuifolium*.
Upright, architectural perennial.
H 1.5m (5ft), S 60cm (2ft). In summer
produces small, star-shaped, white
flowers, borne in large, flat heads, one
above another. Has very finely divided,
mid-green leaves.

SEMELE

LILIACEAE/RUSCACEAE

Genus of one species of evergreen,
twining climber. Male and female
flowers are produced on the same plant.
Tender, min. 5°C (41°F). Needs partial
shade and prefers rich, well-drained
soil. Propagate by division or seed
in spring.
S. androgyna (Climbing butcher's
broom). Evergreen climber, twining in
upper part, branched and bearing oval
cladodes, 5–10cm (2–4in) long. H to
7m (22ft). Star-shaped, cream flowers
appear in early summer, in notches on
cladode margins, followed by orange-
red berries.

SEMIAQUILEGIA

RANUNCULACEAE

Genus of perennials, grown for their
flowers. These differ from those of
Aquilegia, with which it is sometimes
included, by having no spurs. Is good
for rock gardens. Requires sun and
moist but well-drained soil. Propagate
by seed in autumn.
S. ecalcarata illus. p.355.

SEMIARUNDINARIA

GRAMINEAE/POACEAE

See also GRASSES, BAMBOOS,
RUSHES and SEDGES.
S. fastuosa, syn *Arundinaria fastuosa*,
illus. p.308.

SEMPERVIVUM

Houseleek

CRASSULACEAE

Genus of evergreen perennials that
spread by short stolons and are grown
for their symmetrical rosettes of oval
to strap-shaped, pointed, fleshy leaves.
Makes ground-hugging mats, suitable
for rock gardens, screes, walls, banks
and alpine houses. Flowers are star-
shaped with 8–16 spreading petals.
Needs sun and gritty soil. Takes several
years to reach flowering size. Rosettes
die after flowering but leave numerous
offsets. Propagate by offsets in
summer.
S. arachnoideum illus. p.389.
S. ciliosum illus. p.389.
S. 'Commander Hay'. Evergreen,
basal-rosetted perennial. H 15cm (6in),
S to 30cm (12in). Is mainly grown for
its very large, dark red rosettes to 10cm
(4in) across. Bears terminal clusters of
dull greenish-red flowers in summer.
S. giuseppii illus. p.391.
S. grandiflorum. Evergreen, basal-
rosetted perennial. H 10cm (4in), S to
20cm (8in). Variable, densely haired,
red-tinted, dark green rosettes exude a
goat-like smell when crushed. Produces
loose, terminal clusters of yellow-green
flowers, stained purple in centres, on

long flower stems in summer. Prefers
humus-rich, acid soil.
S. hirtum. See *Jovibarba hirta*.
S. montanum illus. p.390.
S. soboliferum. See *Jovibarba
sobolifera*.
S. tectorum illus. p.389.

SENECIO

ASTERACEAE/COMPOSITAE

Genus of annuals, succulent and non-
succulent perennials and evergreen
shrubs, sub-shrubs and twining
climbers, grown for their foliage
and usually daisy-like flower heads.
Some shrubby species are now referred
to the genus *Brachyglottis*. Shrubs are
excellent for coastal gardens. Hardy to
tender, min. 5–10°C (41–50°F). Most
prefer full sun and well-drained soil
(although *S. articulatus* and
S. rowleyanus tolerate partial shade and
need very well-drained soil). Propagate
shrubs and climbers by semi-ripe
cuttings in summer, annuals by seed in
spring, perennials by division in spring
(*S. articulatus* and *S. rowleyanus*
by seed or stem cuttings in spring or
summer). All parts may cause severe
discomfort if ingested.
S. articulatus, syn *Kleinia articulata*
(Candle plant). Deciduous, spreading,
perennial succulent. H 60cm (2ft),
S indefinite. Tender, min. 10°C (50°F).
Branching, grey-marked, blue stems
have weak joints. Bears rounded to
oval, 3–5-lobed, grey leaves and flattish
heads of small, cup-shaped, yellow
flowers from spring to autumn.
Offsets freely from stolons.
'Variegatus' illus. p.462.
S. cineraria, syn *S. maritimus*.
Moderately fast-growing, evergreen,
bushy sub-shrub, often grown as an
annual. H and S 30cm (1ft). Has
long, oval, very deeply lobed,
hairy, silver-grey leaves. Rounded,
yellow flower heads appear in
summer, but are best removed.
'Cirrus' (illus. p.37) has elliptic,
finely toothed or lobed, silvery-green
to white leaves. Zone 9.
'Silver Dust' illus. p.334.
S. clivorum 'Desdemona'. See
Ligularia dentata 'Desdemona'.
S. compactus. See *Brachyglottis
compacta*.
S. confusus, syn *Pseudogynoxys
chenopodioides*, illus. p.217.
S. Dunedin Hybrids. See
Brachyglottis Dunedin Hybrids.
S. elegans. Moderately fast-growing,
upright annual. H 45cm (18in),
S 15cm (6in). Has oval, deeply lobed,
deep green leaves. Daisy-like, purple
flower heads appear on branching
stems in summer.
S. grandifolius, syn *Telanthophora
grandiflora*. Evergreen, erect, robust-
stemmed shrub. H 3–5m (10–15ft),
S 2–3m (6–10ft). Tender, min. 10°C
(50°F) to flower well. Has oval,
toothed, boldly veined leaves, 20–45cm
(8–18in) long, glossy, rich green above,
red-brown-haired beneath. Carries
terminal clusters, 30cm (12in) wide, of
small, daisy-like, yellow flower heads
in winter-spring.
S. greyi of gardens. See *Brachyglottis*
Dunedin Hybrids.

S. × hybridus. See *Pericallis × hybrida*.
S. laxifolius. See *Brachyglottis
laxifolia*.
S. laxifolius of gardens. See
Brachyglottis Dunedin Hybrids.
S. macroglossus (Natal ivy, Wax vine).
Evergreen, woody-stemmed, twining
climber. H 3m (10ft). Tender,
min. 7°C (45°F), best at 10°C (50°F).
Leaves are sharply triangular, fleshy-
textured and glossy. Loose clusters
of daisy-like flower heads, each with
a few white ray petals and a central,
yellow disc, are borne mainly in winter.
'Variegatus' illus. p.219.
S. maritimus. See *S. cineraria*.
S. mikanioides, syn *Delairea odorata*
(German ivy). Evergreen, semi-woody,
twining climber. H 2–3m (6–10ft).
Tender, min. 5°C (41°F), best at 7–10°C
(45–50°F). Has fleshy leaves with 5–7
broad, pointed, radiating lobes. Mature
plants carry large clusters of small,
yellow flower heads in autumn-winter.
S. monroi. See *Brachyglottis monroi*.
S. przewalskii. See *Ligularia
przewalskii*.
S. pulcher illus. p.294.
S. reinholdii. See *Brachyglottis
rotundifolia*.
S. rotundifolius. See *Brachyglottis
rotundifolia*.
S. rowleyanus illus. p.462.
S. smithii. Bushy perennial. H 1–1.2m
(3–4ft), S 75cm–1m (2½–3ft). Woolly
stems are clothed with long, oval,
toothed, leathery, dark green leaves.
Daisy-like, white flower heads, with
yellow centres, are borne in terminal
clusters, up to 15cm (6in) across, in
early summer. Likes boggy conditions.
S. 'Spring Glory'. See *Pericallis ×
hybrida* 'Spring Glory'.
S. 'Sunshine'. See *Brachyglottis*
Dunedin Hybrids 'Sunshine'.
S. tamoides. Evergreen, woody-
stemmed, twining climber. H 5m (15ft)
or more. Tender, min. 5–10°C
(41–50°F). Has ivy-shaped, light green
leaves. In autumn-winter bears yellow
flower heads that are daisy-like, but
with only a few ray petals.

SENNA

CAESALPINIACEAE/LEGUMINOSAE

Genus of evergreen trees, shrubs and
perennials, grown for their pea-like
flowers. Tender, min. 7–18°C
(45–64°F). Requires full sun and moist
but well-drained soil. Propagate by
seed sown in spring, or by semi-ripe
cuttings in summer. Divide perennials
in spring.
S. artemisioides, syn *Cassia
artemisioides* (Silver cassia,
Wormwood cassia). Evergreen, erect to
spreading, wiry shrub. H and S 1–2m
(3–6ft). Tender, min. 10–13°C
(50–55°F). Leaves each have 6–8 linear
leaflets covered with silky, white down.
Axillary spikes of cup-shaped, yellow
flowers appear from winter to
early summer.
S. corymbosa, syn *Cassia corymbosa*,
illus. p.147.
S. didymobotrya, syn *Cassia
didymobotrya*, illus. p.147.
S. × floribunda, syn *Cassia
corymbosa* var. *plurijuga* of gardens,
C. × floribunda. Vigorous, evergreen

or deciduous, rounded shrub with
robust stems. H and S 1.5–2m (5–6ft).
Tender, min. 7°C (45°F). Bright green
leaves consist of 4–6 oval leaflets.
Carries very large clusters of
bowl-shaped, rich yellow flowers
in late summer.
S. siamea, syn *Cassia siamea*. Fast-
growing, evergreen, rounded tree.
H and S 8–10m (25–30ft) or more.
Tender, min. 16–18°C (61–4°F).
Leaves, 15–30cm (6–12in) long, have
7–12 pairs of elliptic leaflets. Large
terminal panicles of small, cup-shaped,
bright yellow flowers are borne in
spring, followed by flat, dark brown
pods, to 23cm (9in) long.

Senna, Bladder. See *Colutea
arborescens*, illus. p.146.
Sensitive fern. See *Onoclea sensibilis*,
illus. p.312.
Sensitive plant. See *Mimosa pudica*,
illus. p.176.
Sentry palm. See *Howea forsteriana*.

SEQUOIA

TAXODIACEAE

See also CONIFERS.
S. sempervirens (Coast redwood,
Redwood). Very vigorous, columnar to
conical conifer with horizontal branches.
H 20–30m (70–100ft), S 5–8m
(15–25ft), although one specimen –
which is believed to be the tallest tree
in the world – has reached 112m
(375ft). Has thick, soft, fibrous, red-
brown bark and needle-like, flattened,
pale green leaves, spirally arranged on
shoots. Produces rounded to cylindrical
cones, initially green, ripening to dark
brown. Will regrow if cut back. Where
hardy, cold winters kill foliage, but
without affecting tree. Zone 7.

SEQUOIADENDRON

TAXODIACEAE

See also CONIFERS.
S. giganteum illus. p.102. **'Pendulum'**
is a weeping conifer. H 10m (30ft),
S 2m (6ft) or more. Bark is thick, soft,
fibrous and red-brown. Has spiralled,
needle-like, incurved, grey-green
leaves that darken and become glossy.
Zone 6b.

SERAPIAS

See also ORCHIDS.
S. cordigera. Deciduous, terrestrial
orchid. H 40cm (16in). Spikes of
reddish or dark purple flowers, 4cm
(1½in) long, are borne in spring. Has
lance-shaped, red-spotted leaves, 15cm
(6in) long. Grow in semi-shade.

Serbian spruce. See *Picea omorika*,
illus. p.103.

SERENOA

ARECACEAE/PALMAE

Genus of one species of evergreen fan
palm, grown for its foliage. Tender,
min. 10–13°C (50–55°F). Requires full
light or partial shade and well-drained
soil. Water potted plants moderately

during growing season, less at other times. Propagate by seed or suckers in spring. Spider mite may be troublesome.
S. repens (Saw palmetto, Scrub palmetto). Evergreen, rhizomatous fan palm, usually stemless. H 60cm–1m (2–3ft), S 2m (6ft) or more. Palmate leaves, 45–75cm (18–30in) wide, are grey to blue-green, and each divided into 6–20 strap-shaped lobes. Clusters of tiny, fragrant, cream flowers are hidden among leaves in summer, followed by egg-shaped, purple-black fruits.

SERISSA

RUBIACEAE

Genus of one species of evergreen shrub, grown for its overall appearance. Tender, min. 7–10°C (45–50°F). Needs sun or partial shade and fertile, well-drained soil. Water containerized specimens moderately, less when not in growth. May be trimmed after flowering. Propagate by semi-ripe cuttings in summer.
S. foetida, syn. *S. japonica*. Evergreen, spreading to rounded, freely branching shrub. H to 60cm (2ft), S 60cm–1m (2–3ft). Tiny, oval leaves are lustrous and deep green. Small, funnel-shaped, 4- or 5-lobed, white flowers are produced from spring to autumn.
S. japonica. See *S. foetida*.

SERRATULA

ASTERACEAE/COMPOSITAE

Genus of perennials, grown for their thistle-like flower heads. Requires sun and well-drained soil. Propagate by seed or by division in spring.
S. seoanei, syn. *S. shawii*. Upright, compact perennial. H 23cm (9in), S 12–15cm (5–6in). Stems bear feathery, finely cut leaves and, in autumn, terminal panicles of small, thistle-like, purple flower heads. Is useful for a rock garden.
S. shawii. See *S. seoanei*.

Service tree of Fontainebleau. See *Sorbus latifolia*.
Serviceberry. See *Amelanchier*.

SESLERIA

GRAMINEAE/POACEAE

See also GRASSES, BAMBOOS, RUSHES and SEDGES.
S. heufleriana (Balkan blue grass). Evergreen, tuft-forming, perennial grass. H 50cm (20in), S 30–45cm (12–18in). Bears rich green leaves, glaucous beneath, and, in spring, compact panicles of purple spikelets.

Sessile oak. See *Quercus petraea*.

SETARIA

GRAMINEAE/POACEAE

See also GRASSES, BAMBOOS, RUSHES and SEDGES.
S. italica (Foxtail millet, Italian millet). Moderately fast-growing, annual grass with stout stems. H 1.5m (5ft), S to 1m (3ft). Has lance-shaped, mid-green leaves, to 45cm (1½ft) long, and loose

panicles of white, cream, yellow, red, brown or black flowers in summer-autumn.

Setcreasea purpurea. See *Tradescantia pallida* 'Purpurea'.
Shadbush. See *Amelanchier*.
Shag-bark hickory. See *Carya ovata*, illus. p.69.
Shallon. See *Gaultheria shallon*, illus. p.162.
Shamrock pea. See *Parochetus communis*, illus. p.384.
Shasta daisy. See *Leucanthemum* x *superbum*.
Sheep laurel. See *Kalmia angustifolia*.
Sheep's bit. See *Jasione laevis*.
Shell flower. See *Alpinia zerumbet*, illus. p.227; *Moluccella laevis*, illus. p.335.
Shell ginger. See *Alpinia zerumbet*, illus. p.227.

SHEPHERDIA

ELAEAGNACEAE

Genus of deciduous or evergreen shrubs, grown for their foliage and fruits. Separate male and female plants are needed in order to obtain fruits. Requires sun and well-drained soil. Propagate by softwood cuttings in summer or by seed in autumn.
S. argentea (Buffalo berry). Deciduous, bushy, often tree-like shrub. H and S 4m (12ft). Bears tiny, inconspicuous, yellow flowers amid oblong, silvery leaves in spring, followed by small, egg-shaped, bright red fruits. Zone 1.

SHIBATAEA

GRAMINEAE/POACEAE

See also GRASSES, BAMBOOS, RUSHES and SEDGES.
S. kumasasa illus. p.308.

Shield fern, Soft. See *Polystichum setiferum*.
Shield ivy. See *Hedera hibernica* 'Deltoidea', illus. p.221.
Shingle oak. See *Quercus imbricaria*.
Shingle plant. See *Monstera acuminata*.
Shoo-fly. See *Nicandra physalodes*.
Shooting stars. See *Dodecatheon*.
Shore juniper. See *Juniperus conferta*.
Shore pine. See *Pinus contorta*, illus. p.107.

SHORTIA

DIAPENSIACEAE

Genus of evergreen, spring-flowering perennials with leaves that often turn red in autumn-winter. Buds may be frosted in areas without snow cover. Is difficult to grow in hot, dry climates. Needs shade or semi-shade and well-drained, peaty, sandy, acid soil. Propagate by runners in summer or by seed when available.
S. galacifolia illus. p.364.
S. soldanelloides illus. p.366. var. *ilicifolia* is an evergreen, mat-forming perennial. H 5–10cm (2–4in), S 10–15cm (4–6in). Has rounded, toothed leaves. In late spring each flower stem carries 4–6 small, pendent, bell-shaped flowers with fringed

edges and rose-pink centres shading to white. Flowers of var. *magna* are rose-pink throughout.
S. uniflora 'Grandiflora'. Vigorous, evergreen, mat-forming perennial with a few rooted runners. H 8cm (3in), S 20cm (8in). Leaves are rounded, toothed, leathery and glossy. Flower stems bear cup-shaped, 5cm (2in) wide, white-pink flowers, with serrated petals, in spring.

Showy lady's slipper orchid. See *Cypripedium reginae*, illus. p.296.
Shrimp plant. See *Justicia brandegeeana*, illus. p.166.
Shrubby germander. See *Teucrium fruticans*.
Shrubby hare's ear. See *Bupleurum fruticosum*, illus. p.146.
Shrubby restharrow. See *Ononis fruticosa*, illus. p.353.
Siberian bugloss. See *Brunnera macrophylla*.
Siberian crab. See *Malus baccata*.
Siberian elm. See *Ulmus pumila*.
Siberian flag. See *Iris sibirica*.
Siberian melic. See *Melica altissima*.
Siberian squill. See *Scilla siberica*.
Siberian wallflower. See *Erysimum* x *allionii*.

SIBIRAEA

ROSACEAE

Genus of deciduous shrubs, grown for their foliage and flowers. Needs sunny, well-drained soil. Established plants benefit from having old or weak shoots cut to base after flowering. Propagate by softwood cuttings in summer.
S. altaiensis, syn. *S. laevigata*. Deciduous, spreading, open shrub. H 1m (3ft), S 1.5m (5ft). Has narrowly oblong, blue-green leaves and, in late spring and early summer, dense, terminal clusters of tiny, star-shaped, white flowers.
S. laevigata. See *S. altaiensis*.

SIDALCEA

MALVACEAE

Genus of summer-flowering perennials, grown for their hollyhock-like flowers. Needs sun and well-drained soil. Propagate by division in spring.
S. 'Loveliness'. Upright perennial. H 1m (3ft), S 45cm (1½ft). Has buttercup-like, divided leaves with narrowly oblong segments. In summer bears racemes of shallowly cup-shaped, shell-pink flowers.
S. 'Oberon' illus. p.243.
S. 'Puck'. Upright perennial. H 60cm (2ft), S 45cm (1½ft). Has buttercup-like, divided leaves with narrowly oblong segments. In summer bears racemes of shallowly cup-shaped, deep pink flowers.
S. 'Sussex Beauty'. Upright perennial. H 1.2m (4ft), S 45cm (1½ft). Has buttercup-like, divided leaves, with narrowly oblong segments, and, in summer, shallowly cup-shaped, deep rose-pink flowers.

SIDERITIS

LABIATAE/LAMIACEAE

Genus of evergreen perennials, sub-shrubs and shrubs, grown mainly for their foliage. Hardy to tender, min.

7–10°C (45–50°F). Needs full light and well-drained soil. Water containerized plants moderately, less when temperatures are low. Remove spent flower spikes after flowering. Propagate by seed in spring or by semi-ripe cuttings in summer.
S. candicans. Evergreen, erect, well-branched shrub. H to 75cm (2½ft), S to 60cm (2ft). Tender. Lance-shaped to narrowly oval or triangular leaves bear dense, white wool. Produces leafy, terminal spikes of tubular, pale yellow-and-light-brown or orange-red flowers in summer.

SILENE

Campion, Catchfly

CARYOPHYLLACEAE

Genus of annuals and perennials, some of which are evergreen, grown for their mass of 5-petalled flowers. Needs sun and fertile, well-drained soil. Propagate by softwood cuttings in spring or by seed in spring or early autumn.
S. acaulis illus. p.365.
S. alpestris, syn. *Heliosperma alpestris*, illus. p.373.
S. armeria 'Electra' illus. p.323.
S. coeli-rosa, syn. *Agrostemma coelirosa*, *Lychnis coeli-rosa*, *Viscaria elegans*, illus. p.320. 'Rose Angel' illus. p.325.
S. elisabethae. Basal-rosetted perennial. H 10cm (4in), S 20cm (8in). Has rosettes of strap-shaped, mid-green leaves. In summer, stems bear large, often solitary, deep rose-red flowers with green centres and long-clawed petals. Is suitable for a rock garden.
S. hookeri. Short-lived, trailing, prostrate, late summer-deciduous perennial with a long, slender tap root. H 5cm (2in), S 20cm (8in). Slender stems bear oval, grey leaves and, in late summer, soft pink, salmon or orange flowers, deeply cleft to base.
S. maritima 'Flore Pleno'. See *S. uniflora* 'Robin Whitebreast'.
S. pendula (Nodding catchfly). Moderately fast-growing, bushy annual. H and S 15–20cm (6–8in). Has oval, hairy, mid-green leaves and, in summer and early autumn, clusters of light pink flowers.
S. schafta illus. p.379.
S. uniflora 'Robin Whitebreast', syn. *S. maritima* 'Flore Pleno', *S.u.* 'Flore Pleno', *S. vulgaris* subsp. *maritima* 'Flore Pleno' (Double sea campion). Lax perennial with deep, wandering roots. H and S 20cm (8in). Leaves are lance-shaped and grey-green. Has pompon-like, double, white flowers on branched stems in summer.
S. vulgaris subsp. *maritima* 'Flore Pleno'. See *S. uniflora* 'Robin Whitebreast'.

Silk cotton tree. See *Ceiba pentandra*.
Silk tree. See *Albizia julibrissin*, illus. p.90.
  Floss. See *Chorisia speciosa*, illus. p.70.
Silk vine. See *Periploca graeca*.
Silk weed. See *Asclepias*.
Silk-tassel bush. See *Garrya elliptica*, illus. p.125.
Silky oak. See *Grevillea robusta*.

Silky wisteria. See *Wisteria brachybotrys* 'Shiro Kapitan'.

SILPHIUM

ASTERACEAE/COMPOSITAE

Genus of fairly coarse, summer-flowering perennials. Does best in sun or semi-shade and in moist but well-drained soil. Propagate by division in spring or by seed when fresh, in autumn.
S. laciniatum (Compass plant). Clump-forming perennial. H 2m (6ft), S 60cm (2ft). Mid-green leaves, composed of opposite pairs of oblong to lance-shaped leaflets, face north and south wherever the plant is grown, hence the common name. Large clusters of slightly pendent, daisy-like, yellow flower heads are borne in late summer.

Silver ball cactus. See *Parodia scopa*.
Silver beech. See *Nothofagus menziesii*.
Silver bell. See *Halesia*.
Silver birch. See *Betula pendula*.
Silver cassia. See *Senna artemisioides*.
Silver chain. See *Dendrochilum glumaceum*.
Silver dollar cactus. See *Astrophytum asterias*.
Silver fir. See *Abies*.
Silver heart. See *Peperomia marmorata*, illus. p.304.
Silver hedgehog holly. See *Ilex aquifolium* 'Ferox Argentea'.
Silver inch plant. See *Tradescantia zebrina*, illus. p.301.
Silver jade plant. See *Crassula arborescens*, illus. p.458.
Silver linden. See *Tilia tomentosa*.
  Pendent. See *Tilia* 'Petiolaris', illus. p.68.
Silver maple. See *Acer saccharinum*.
Silver net-leaf. See *Fittonia albivenis* Argyroneura Group, illus. p.300.
Silver torch. See *Cleistocactus straussii*, illus. p.459.
Silver tree. See *Leucadendron argenteum*, illus. p.100.
Silver vase plant. See *Aechmea fasciata*, illus. p.265.
Silver vine. See *Actinidia polygama*; *Epipremnum pictum* 'Argyraeum', illus. p.219.
Silver wattle. See *Acacia dealbata*, illus. p.83.
Silver willow. See *Salix alba* var. *sericea*.
Silver-leaf peperomia. See *Peperomia griseoargentea*.
Silver-leaved geranium. See *Pelargonium* 'Flower of Spring', illus. p.247.
Silver-margined holly. See *Ilex aquifolium* 'Argentea Marginata', illus. p.98.

SILYBUM

ASTERACEAE/COMPOSITAE

Genus of thistle-like biennials, grown for their spectacular foliage. Grow in sun and in any well-drained soil. Propagate by seed in late spring or early summer. Is prone to slug and snail damage.
S. marianum illus. p.322.

Sinarundinaria jaunsarensis. See *Yushania anceps*.
Sinarundinaria murieliae. See *Fargesia murieliae*.
Sinarundinaria nitida. See *Fargesia nitida*.

SINNINGIA

GESNERIACEAE

Genus of usually summer-flowering, tuberous perennials and deciduous sub-shrubs with showy flowers. Tender, min. 15°C (59°F). Grow in bright light but not direct sun. Prefers a humid atmosphere and moist but not waterlogged, peaty soil. When leaves die down after flowering, allow tubers to dry out; then store in a frost-free area. Propagate in spring by seed or in late spring or summer by stem cuttings or by dividing tubers into sections, each with a young shoot.
S. barbata. Bushy, tuberous perennial with square, red stems. H and S 60cm (2ft) or more. Broadly lance-shaped leaves, to 15cm (6in) long, are glossy, mid-green above, reddish-green beneath. In summer has 5-lobed, pouched, white flowers, 4cm (1½in) long.
S. concinna. Rosetted perennial with very small tubers. H and S to 15cm (6in). Oval to almost round, scalloped, velvety, red-veined, mid-green leaves, 2cm (¾in) long, are red below. Trumpet-shaped, bicoloured, purple and white or yellowish-white flowers, to 2cm (¾in) long, are produced in summer.
S. 'Etoile du Feu'. Short-stemmed, rosetted, tuberous perennial. H 30cm (12in), S 40cm (16in) or more. Has oval, velvety leaves, 20–24cm (8–9½in) long. Upright, trumpet-shaped, carmine-red flowers appear in summer.
S. 'Mont Blanc'. Short-stemmed, rosetted, tuberous perennial. H 30cm (12in), S 40cm (16in) or more. Oval, velvety, mid-green leaves are 20–24cm (8–9½in) long. In summer bears upright, trumpet-shaped, pure white flowers.
S. 'Red Flicker' illus. p.282.
S. speciosa, syn. *Gloxinia speciosa* (Gloxinia). Short-stemmed, rosetted, tuberous perennial. H and S to 30cm (1ft). Oval, velvety, green leaves are 20cm (8in) long. Nodding, funnel-shaped, fleshy, violet, red or white flowers, to 5cm (2in) long and pouched on lower sides, are produced in summer. Is a parent of many named hybrids, of which a selection is included above and below.
S. 'Switzerland' illus. p.282.
S. 'Waterloo'. Short-stemmed, rosetted, tuberous perennial. H 30cm (12in), S 40cm (16in) or more. Has oval, velvety leaves, 20–24cm (8–9½in) long. Upright, trumpet-shaped, bright scarlet flowers open in summer.

SINOFRANCHETIA

LARDIZABALACEAE

Genus of one species of deciduous, twining climber, grown mainly for its handsome leaves. Is suitable for

covering buildings and growing up large trees. Male and female flowers are produced on separate plants. Grow in semi-shade and in any well-drained soil. Propagate by semi-ripe cuttings in summer.
S. chinensis. Deciduous, twining climber. H to 15m (50ft). Mid- to dark green leaves have 3 oblong to oval leaflets, each 5–15cm (2–6in) long. In late spring has small, dull white flowers in pendent racemes, to 10cm (4in) long. Pale purple berries, containing many seeds, follow in summer. Zone 8.

SINOJACKIA

STYRACACEAE

Genus of deciduous shrubs and trees, grown for their flowers. Requires a sheltered position in sun or partial shade and fertile, humus-rich, moist, acid soil. Propagate by softwood cuttings in summer.
S. rehderiana. Deciduous, bushy shrub or spreading tree. H and S 6m (20ft). Nodding, saucer-shaped, white flowers, each with a central cluster of yellow anthers, appear in late spring and early summer. Oval leaves are dark green. Zone 7.

SINOWILSONIA

HAMAMELIDACEAE

Genus of one species of deciduous tree, grown for its foliage and catkins. Requires sun or semi-shade and fertile, moist but well-drained soil. Propagate by seed in autumn.
S. henryi. Deciduous, spreading, sometimes shrubby tree. H and S 8m (25ft). Has oval, toothed, glossy, bright green leaves, and long, pendent, green catkins in late spring. Zone 7.

Siphonosmanthus delavayi. See *Osmanthus delavayi*.

SISYRINCHIUM

IRIDACEAE

Genus of annuals and perennials, some of which are semi-evergreen. Prefers sun, but tolerates partial shade, and well-drained or moist soil. Propagate by division in early spring or by seed in spring or autumn.
S. angustifolium. See *S. graminoides*.
S. bellum of gardens. See *S. idahoense*.
S. bermudiana. See *S. graminoides*.
S. brachypus. See *S. californicum*.
S. californicum (Golden-eyed grass). Semi-evergreen, upright perennial. H 30–60cm (12–24in), S 30cm (12in). Has grass-like tufts of basal, light green leaves. For a long period in spring-summer produces flattish, bright yellow flowers, with slightly darker veins, on winged stems. Outer leaves may die off and turn black in autumn. Dwarf forms are known as *S. brachypus*. Prefers moist soil.
S. douglasii. See *Olsynium douglasii*.
S. graminoides, syn. *S. angustifolium*, *S. bermudiana*, illus. p.356.
S. grandiflorum. See *Olsynium douglasii*.
S. idahoense, syn. *S. bellum* of gardens, illus. p.383.

S. odoratissimum. See *Olsynium biflorum*.
S. striatum illus. p.290. **'Aunt May'** (syn. *S.s.* 'Variegatum') is a semi-evergreen, upright perennial. H 45–60cm (18–24in), S 30cm (12in). Produces tufts of long, narrow, cream-striped, greyish-green leaves. Slender spikes of trumpet-shaped, purple-striped, straw-yellow flowers are borne in summer.

Sitka spruce. See *Picea sitchensis*.

SKIMMIA

RUTACEAE

Genus of evergreen shrubs and trees, grown for their spring flowers, aromatic foliage and their fruits. Except with *S. japonica* subsp. *reevesiana*, separate male and female plants are needed in order to obtain fruits. Needs shade or semi-shade and fertile, moist soil. Poor soil or too much sun may cause chlorosis. Propagate by semi-ripe cuttings in late summer or by seed in autumn. The fruits may cause mild stomach upset if ingested.
S. anquetilia. Evergreen, bushy, open shrub. H 1.2m (4ft), S 2m (6ft). Produces small clusters of tiny, yellow flowers from mid- to late spring, then spherical, scarlet fruits. Leaves are oblong to oval, pointed, strongly aromatic and dark green. Zone 8.
S. × foremanii of gardens. See *S. japonica* 'Veitchii'.
S. japonica illus. p.175. **'Fructo Albo'** (female) illus. p.173. subsp. *reevesiana* **'Robert Fortune'** (syn. *S. reevesiana*; hermaphrodite) and **'Rubella'** (male) illus. p.174. **'Veitchii'** (syn. *S. × foremanii* of gardens) is a vigorous, evergreen, upright, dense, female shrub. H and S 1.5m (5ft). Broadly oval leaves are rich green. In mid- and late spring bears dense clusters of small, star-shaped, white flowers, followed by large, spherical, bright red fruits. Zone 7.
S. reevesiana. See *S. japonica* subsp. *reevesiana* 'Robert Fortune'.

Skullcap. See *Scutellaria*.
Sky plant. See *Tillandsia ionantha*.
Skyflower. See *Duranta erecta*, illus. p.150.
Sleepy mallow. See *Malvaviscus arboreus*, illus. p.121.
Slender lady palm. See *Rhapis excelsa*, illus. p.152.
Slipper orchid. See *Cypripedium*; *Paphiopedilum*.
Sloe. See *Prunus spinosa*.
Small-leaved box. See *Buxus microphylla*.
Small-leaved linden. See *Tilia cordata*.

SMILACINA

CONVALLARIACEAE/LILIACEAE

Genus of perennials, grown for their graceful appearance. Prefers semi-shade and humus-rich, moist, neutral to acid soil. Propagate by division in spring or by seed in autumn.
S. racemosa illus. p.233.

SMILAX

LILIACEAE/SMILACACEAE

Genus of deciduous or evergreen, woody-stemmed or herbaceous, scrambling climbers with tubers or rhizomes. Male and female flowers are borne on separate plants. Hardy to tender, min. 5°C (41°F). Grow in any well-drained soil, in sun or semi-shade. Propagate by division or seed in spring or by semi-ripe cuttings in summer.
S. china. Deciduous, woody-based, scrambling climber with straggling, sometimes spiny stems. H to 5m (15ft). Leaves are broadly oval to rounded. Umbels of yellow-green flowers are produced in spring; tiny, red berries appear in autumn. Zone 8.

SMITHIANTHA

GESNERIACEAE

Genus of bushy, erect perennials with tuber-like rhizomes, grown for their flowers and foliage. Tender, min. 15°C (59°F). Grow in humus-rich, well-drained soil and in bright light but out of direct sun. Reduce watering after flowering and water sparingly in winter. Propagate by division of rhizomes in early spring.
S. cinnabarina (Temple bells). Robust, erect, rhizomatous perennial. H and S to 60cm (2ft). Broadly oval to almost rounded, toothed leaves, to 15cm (6in) long, are dark green with dark red hairs. Bell-shaped, orange-red flowers, lined with pale yellow, are produced in summer-autumn.
S. 'Orange King' illus. p.283.
S. zebrina. Bushy, rhizomatous perennial with velvety-haired stems. H and S to 1m (3ft). Oval, toothed, hairy leaves, to 18cm (7in) long, are deep green marked with reddish-brown. In summer produces tubular flowers, scarlet above, yellow below, spotted red inside and with orange-yellow lobes.

Smoke tree. See *Cotinus coggygria.*
Smooth cypress. See *Cupressus arizonica* var. *glabra.*
Smooth sumach. See *Rhus glabra*, illus. p.143.
Smooth-leaved elm. See *Ulmus minor.*

SMYRNIUM

APIACEAE/UMBELLIFERAE

Genus of biennials, grown for their flowers. Grow in sun and in fertile, well-drained soil. Propagate by seed sown outdoors in autumn or spring.
S. perfoliatum illus. p.335.

Snail flower. See *Vigna caracalla.*
Snake bush. See *Justicia adhatoda.*
Snake gourd. See *Trichosanthes cucumerina* var. *anguina.*
Snake-bark maple. See *Acer capillipes*, illus. p.82; *Acer davidii*; *Acer davidii* subsp. *grosseri*; *Acer pensylvanicum*, illus. p.84; *Acer rufinerve*, illus. p.82.
Snake's-head fritillary. See *Fritillaria meleagris*, illus. p.413.
Snakeroot, White. See *Eupatorium rugosum*, illus. p.240.

Snapdragon. See *Antirrhinum.*
Sneezeweed. See *Helenium.*
Snow brake. See *Pteris ensiformis.*
Snow bush. See *Breynia disticha*, illus. p.175.
Snow creeper. See *Porana paniculata.*
Snow gum. See *Eucalyptus pauciflora* subsp. *niphophila*, illus. p.84.
Snow poppy. See *Eomecon chionantha.*
Snow trillium. See *Trillium nivale.*
Snowball pincushion. See *Mammillaria candida.*
Snowball, Pink. See *Dombeya* x *cayeuxii*, illus. p.88.
Snowball tree, Japanese. See *Viburnum plicatum.*
Snowbell. See *Soldanella.*
  Alpine. See *Soldanella alpina*, illus. p.368.
  Fragrant. See *Styrax obassia.*
  Least. See *Soldanella minima.*
Snowberry. See *Symphoricarpos albus.*
Snowbush rose. See *Rosa* 'Dupontii', illus. p.185.
Snowdrop. See *Galanthus.*
  Autumn. See *Galanthus reginae-olgae.*
  Common. See *Galanthus nivalis.*
  Double common. See *Galanthus nivalis* 'Flore Pleno', illus. p.439.
Snowdrop tree. See *Halesia.*
Snowdrop windflower. See *Anemone sylvestris*, illus. p.268.
Snowflake. See *Leucojum.*
  Autumn. See *Leucojum autumnale*, illus. p.437.
  Spring. See *Leucojum vernum*, illus. p.426.
  Summer. See *Leucojum aestivum*, illus. p.396.
Snow-in-summer. See *Cerastium tomentosum*, illus. p.361; *Euphorbia marginata*, illus. p.319.
Snow-on-the-mountain. See *Euphorbia marginata*, illus. p.319.
Snowy woodrush. See *Luzula nivea*, illus. p.307.
Soapwort. See *Saponaria.*
  Double. See *Saponaria officinalis* 'Rubra Plena'.
Soft shield fern. See *Polystichum setiferum.*

SOLANDRA

SOLANACEAE

Genus of evergreen, woody-stemmed, scrambling climbers, grown for their large, trumpet-shaped flowers. Tender, min. 10°C (50°F), but prefers 13–16°C (55–61°F). Needs full light and fertile, well-drained soil. Water freely when in full growth, sparingly in cold weather. Tie to supports. Thin out crowded stems after flowering. Propagate by semi-ripe cuttings in summer.
S. maxima illus. p.206.

SOLANUM

SOLANACEAE

Genus of annuals, perennials (some of which are evergreen) and evergreen, semi-evergreen or deciduous sub-shrubs, shrubs (occasionally scandent) and woody-stemmed, scrambling or leaf-stalk climbers, grown for their flowers and ornamental fruits. Hardy to tender, min. 5–10°C (41–50°F).

Requires full sun and fertile, well-drained soil. Water regularly but sparingly in winter. Support scrambling climbers. Thin out and spur back crowded growth of climbers in spring. Propagate by seed in spring or by semi-ripe cuttings in summer. Spider mite, whitefly and aphids may cause problems. All parts of most species, especially the fruits of *S. capsicastrum* and *S. pseudocapsicum*, can cause severe discomfort if ingested.
S. capsicastrum (Winter cherry). Fairly slow-growing, evergreen, bushy subshrub, grown as an annual. H and S 30–45cm (1–1½ft). Min. 5°C (41°F). Has lance-shaped, deep green leaves. In summer bears small, star-shaped, white flowers, followed by egg-shaped, pointed, orange-red or scarlet fruits, at least 1cm (⅜in) in diameter, which are at their best in winter.
S. crispum 'Glasnevin' illus. p.214.
S. jasminoides (Potato vine). Semi-evergreen, woody-stemmed, scrambling climber. H to 6m (20ft). Oval to lance-shaped leaves may be lobed or have leaflets at base. Small, 5-petalled, pale grey-blue flowers are produced in summer-autumn; tiny, purple berries appear in autumn. Zone 9.
'Album' illus. p.207.
S. pseudocapsicum (Jerusalem cherry). Fairly slow-growing, evergreen, bushy shrub, usually grown as an annual. H and S to 1.2m (4ft). Min. 5°C (41°F). Has oval or lance-shaped, bright green leaves. Small, star-shaped, white flowers appear in summer and are followed by spherical, scarlet fruits. Has several smaller selections: **'Balloon'** illus. p.341; **'Fancy'**, H 30cm (1ft), with scarlet fruits; **'Red Giant'** illus. p.341; and **'Snowfire'**, H 30cm (1ft), with white fruits that later turn red.
S. rantonnetii, syn. *Lycianthes rantonnetii* (Blue potato bush). **'Royal Robe'** illus. p.145.
S. seaforthianum illus. p.206.
S. wendlandii illus. p.214.

SOLDANELLA

Snowbell

PRIMULACEAE

Genus of evergreen perennials, grown for their early spring flowers. Is good for rock gardens, troughs and alpine houses. Flower buds are set in autumn and may be destroyed by cold if there is no snow cover. Requires partial shade and humus-rich, well-drained, peaty soil. Propagate by seed in spring or by division in late summer. Slugs may attack flower buds.
S. alpina illus. p.368.
S. minima (Least snowbell). Evergreen, prostrate perennial. H 2.5cm (1in), S 10cm (4in). Forms a mat of minute, rounded leaves on soil surface. In early spring produces solitary almost stemless, bell-shaped, pale lavender-blue or white flowers with fringed mouths.
S. montana (Mountain tassel). Evergreen, mound-forming perennial. H 10cm (4in), S 15cm (6in). In early spring produces tall flower stems carrying long, pendent, bell-shaped, lavender-blue flowers with

fringed mouths. Leaves are rounded and leathery.
S. villosa illus. p.368.

SOLEIROLIA

Baby's tears, Mind-your-own-business, Mother of thousands

URTICACEAE

Genus of one species of, usually evergreen, prostrate perennial that forms a dense carpet of foliage. Marginally hardy, although leaves are killed by frost. Recovers to grow vigorously again in spring. Tolerates sun or shade, and prefers moist soil. Propagate by division from spring to mid-summer.
S. soleirolii, syn. *Helxine soleirolii*, illus. p.304.

SOLENOSTEMON

Painted nettle

LABIATAE/LAMIACEAE

Genus of evergreen, bushy, sub-shrubby perennials, grown for their colourful leaves amd flowers. Makes excellent pot plants. Tender, min. 4–10°C (39–50°F). Grow in sun or partial shade and in fertile, well-drained soil, choosing a sheltered position. Water freely in summer, much less at other times. Pinch out growing shoots of young plants to encourage a bushy habit. Propagate by seed sown under glass in spring or by softwood cuttings in spring or summer. Mealy bugs and whitefly may cause problems.
S. scutellarioides, syn. *Coleus blumei* var. *verschaffeltii*, illus. p.324.
'Brightness' illus. p.329. **'Fashion Parade'** is a fast-growing, bushy perennial, grown as an annual. H to 45cm (18in), S 30cm (12in) or more. Min. 10°C (50°F). Has multicoloured, serrated leaves of various shapes, from oval and unlobed to deeply lobed. Spikes of tiny, blue flowers are produced in summer and are best removed. **'Scarlet Poncho'**, with a pendulous habit and oval, serrated, bright red leaves, and **Wizard Series**, also with oval, serrated leaves, but in a very wide range of leaf colours, are both dwarf forms, H 30cm (12in).

SOLIDAGO

Golden rod

ASTERACEAE/COMPOSITAE

Genus of summer- and autumn-flowering perennials, some species of which are vigorous, coarse plants that tend to crowd out others in borders. Most tolerate sun or shade and any well-drained soil. Propagate by division in spring. Occasionally self-seeds.
S. 'Golden Wings'. Upright perennial. H 1.5m (5ft), S 1m (3ft). Bears large, feathery panicles of small, bright yellow flower heads in early autumn. Has lance-shaped, toothed, slightly hairy, mid-green leaves.
S. 'Goldenmosa' illus. p.255.
S. 'Laurin' illus. p.256.
S. virgaurea subsp. **minuta**, syn. *S.v.* subsp. *alpestris*. Mound-forming perennial. H and S 10cm (4in). Has

small, lance-shaped, green leaves and, in autumn, neat spikes of small, yellow flower heads. Is suitable for a rock garden, trough or alpine house. Needs shade and moist soil.

x SOLIDASTER

ASTERACEAE/COMPOSITAE

Hybrid genus (*Solidago* x *Aster*) of one summer-flowering perennial. Grows in sun or shade, and in any fertile soil. Propagate by division in spring.

x **S. hybridus.** See x **S. luteus.**
x **S. luteus,** syn. x **S. hybridus,** illus. p.291.

SOLLYA
Bluebell creeper

PITTOSPORACEAE

Genus of evergreen, woody-based, twining climbers, grown for their attractive flowers. Tender, min. 2°C (35°F). Grow in sun and well-drained soil. Propagate by seed in spring or by softwood or greenwood cuttings in summer.

S. heterophylla illus. p.206.

Solomon's seal. See *Polygonatum.*
 Angled. See *Polygonatum odoratum.*
 Great. See *Polygonatum biflorum.*
 Whorled. See *Polygonatum verticillatum.*

SONERILA

MELASTOMATACEAE

Genus of evergreen, bushy perennials and shrubs, grown for their foliage and flowers. Tender, min. 15°C (59°F). Prefers a humid atmosphere in semi-shade and peaty soil. Propagate by tip cuttings in spring.

S. margaritacea. Evergreen, bushy, semi-prostrate perennial. H and S 20–25cm (8–10in). Red stems produce oval, dark green leaves, 5–8cm (2–3in) long, reddish below, silver-patterned above. Has racemes of 3-petalled, rose-pink flowers in summer. **'Argentea'** has more silvery leaves with green veins; **'Hendersonii'** is more compact with white-spotted leaves.

Sop, Sweet. See *Annona.*

SOPHORA
Kowhai

LEGUMINOSAE/PAPILIONACEAE

Genus of deciduous or semi-evergreen trees and shrubs, grown for their habit, foliage and flowers. Requires full sun (*S. microphylla* and *S. tetraptera* usually need to be grown against a south- or west-facing wall) and fertile, well-drained soil. Propagate by seed in autumn; semi-evergreens may also be raised from softwood cuttings in summer.

S. davidii, syn. *S. viciifolia,* illus. p.145.
S. japonica (Pagoda tree). Deciduous, spreading tree. H and S 20m (70ft).

Dark green leaves consist of 9–15 oval leaflets. On mature trees, long clusters of pea-like, creamy-white flowers appear in late summer and early autumn. Does best in hot summers. Zone 6. **'Pendula',** H and S 3m (10ft), has long, hanging shoots clothed with dark green foliage. Zone 6.
'Violacea' illus. p.71.
S. microphylla, syn. *Edwardsia microphylla.* Semi-evergreen, spreading tree. H and S 8m (25ft). Dark green leaves are composed of numerous tiny, oblong leaflets. Produces clusters of pea-like, deep yellow flowers in late spring. Zone 9?.
S. tetraptera illus. p.89.
S. viciifolia. See *S. davidii.*

x SOPHROLAELIO-CATTLEYA

See also ORCHIDS.
x **S. Hazel Boyd 'Apricot Glow'** (illus. p.299). Evergreen, epiphytic orchid for an intermediate greenhouse. H 10cm (4in). In spring and early summer produces small heads of apricot-orange flowers, 9cm (3½in) across, with crimson marks on lips. Has oval, rigid leaves, 10cm (4in) long. Grow in good light in summer.
x **S. Trizac 'Purple Emperor'** (illus. p.297). Evergreen, epiphytic orchid for an intermediate greenhouse. H 10cm (4in). In spring, has crimson-lipped, pinkish-purple flowers, 6cm (2½in) across, in small heads. Has oval, rigid leaves, 10cm (4in) long. Provide good light in summer.

SORBARIA

ROSACEAE

Genus of deciduous, summer-flowering shrubs, grown for their foliage and large panicles of small, white flowers. Prefers sun and deep, fertile, moist soil. In winter cut out some older stems on mature plants and prune back remaining shoots to growing points. Remove suckers at base to prevent *Sorbaria* spreading too widely. Propagate by softwood cuttings in summer, by division in autumn or by root cuttings in late winter.

S. aitchisonii. See *S. tomentosa* var. *angustifolia.*
S. arborea. See *S. kirilowii.*
S. kirilowii, syn. *S. arborea, Spiraea arborea.* Vigorous, deciduous, arching shrub. H and S 6m (20ft). Leaves are composed of 13–17 lance-shaped, taper-pointed, deep green leaflets. Nodding panicles of star-shaped, white flowers are produced in mid- and late summer. Zone 6.
S. sorbifolia, syn. *Spiraea sorbifolia,* illus. p.137.
S. tomentosa var. **angustifolia,** syn. *S. aitchisonii, Spiraea aitchisonii.* Deciduous, arching shrub. H and S 3m (10ft). Shoots are red when young. Leaves have 11–23 narrowly lance-shaped, taper-pointed, dark green leaflets. Upright panicles of star-shaped, white flowers are produced from mid- to late summer. Zone 6.

SORBUS

ROSACEAE

Genus of deciduous trees and shrubs, grown for their foliage, small, 5-petalled flowers, attractive fruits and, in some species, autumn colour. Leaves may be whole or divided into leaflets. Needs sun or semi-shade and fertile, well-drained but moist soil. Species with leaves composed of leaflets do not grow well in very dry soil. Propagate by softwood cuttings or budding in summer, by seed in autumn or by grafting in winter. Is susceptible to fireblight. Raw fruit may cause mild stomach upset if ingested.

S. alnifolia (Korean mountain ash). Deciduous, conical, then spreading tree. H 15m (50ft), S 8m (25ft). Oval, toothed, bright green leaves turn orange and red in autumn. Has small, white flowers in late spring, then egg-shaped, orange-red fruits. Zone 4.
S. americana (American mountain ash). Deciduous, round-headed tree. H 10m (30ft), S 7m (22ft). Light green leaves, divided into 11–17 narrowly oval leaflets, usually colour well in autumn. Bears small, white flowers in early summer, then rounded, bright red fruits, ripening in early autumn. Zone 3.
S. aria (Whitebeam). Deciduous, spreading tree. H 15m (50ft), S 10m (30ft). Oval, toothed leaves are silver-grey when young, maturing to dark green above, white-felted beneath. Clusters of small, white flowers in late spring are followed by rounded, brown-speckled, deep red fruits. **'Chrysophylla',** H 10m (30ft), S 7m (22ft), bears golden-yellow, young leaves. **'Decaisneana'** see *S.a.* **'Majestica'. 'Lutescens'** illus. p.78. **'Majestica'** (syn. *S.a.* 'Decaisneana') has larger leaves, white-haired when young, and larger fruits. All zone 4.
S. aucuparia (Mountain ash, Rowan) illus. p.81. **'Fastigiata'** (syn. *S. scopulina* of gardens) is a deciduous, dense, conical tree with upright branches. H 8m (25ft), S 5m (15ft). Bears divided, dark green leaves, and clusters of small, white flowers in late spring or early summer followed by large, dark red fruits, 1cm (½in) across. Zone 4. **'Fructu Luteo'** is a spreading tree, H 15m (50ft), S 8m (25ft). Leaves consist of 13–15 narrowly oval, mid-green leaflets that turn yellow or red in autumn. Bears orange-yellow fruits. Zone 3b. Fruits of **'Rossica Major'** (syn. *S.a.* 'Rossica') are large and deep red. Zone 4. **'Sheerwater Seedling',** S 4m (12ft), has a narrow, upright habit. Zone 4.
S. cashmiriana illus. p.93.
S. commixta, syn. *S. discolor* of gardens, illus. p.81. **'Embley'** is a vigorous, deciduous, elegant tree with steeply ascending branches. H 12m (40ft), S 9m (28ft). Glossy, deep green leaves, each with 13–17 slender, lance-shaped leaflets, turn orange and red in late autumn. Bears small, white flowers in late spring, and rounded, bright red fruits in autumn. Zone 6.
S. cuspidata. See *S. vestita.*
S. decora. Deciduous, spreading, sometimes shrubby tree. H 10m (30ft),

S 8m (25ft). Leaves are composed of oblong, blue-green leaflets. Small, white flowers in late spring are succeeded by rounded, orange-red fruits. Zone 2.
S. discolor of gardens. See *S. commixta.*
S. esserteauana. Deciduous, spreading tree. H and S 10m (30ft). Dark green leaves, with broadly oblong leaflets, redden in autumn. Has small, white flowers in late spring, followed by large clusters of rounded, bright red, sometimes orange-yellow fruits. Zone 7.
S. hupehensis (Hupeh rowan). Deciduous, spreading tree. H 12m (40ft), S 8m (25ft). Leaves have 9–17 oblong, blue-green leaflets that turn orange-red in late autumn. Small, white flowers in late spring are followed by clusters of rounded, pink-tinged, white fruits. Zone 6. **'Rosea'** (syn. *S.h.* var. *obtusa*) illus. p.81.
S. insignis. Deciduous, spreading tree. H 8m (25ft), S 6m (20ft). Leaves consist of usually 9–21 large, oblong, glossy, dark green leaflets. Large clusters of small, creamy-white flowers in late spring are followed by rounded, pink fruits that become white in winter. Zone 9?.
S. intermedia (Swedish whitebeam). Deciduous, broad-headed, dense tree. H and S 12m (40ft). Has broadly oval, deeply lobed, dark green leaves. Carries clusters of small, white flowers in late spring, succeeded by rounded, red fruits. Zone 4.
S. 'Joseph Rock' illus. p.82.
S. x kewensis, syn. *S. pohuashanensis* of gardens. Deciduous, spreading tree. H 10m (30ft), S 8m (25ft). Dark green leaves are divided into 11–15 oblong leaflets. Has small, white flowers in late spring, followed by dense clusters of rounded, red fruits. Zone 6.
S. latifolia (Service tree of Fontainebleau). Deciduous, spreading tree. H 12m (40ft), S 10m (30ft). Has peeling bark and broadly oval, sharply lobed, glossy, dark green leaves. Small, white flowers in late spring are succeeded by rounded, brownish-red fruits. Zone 6.
S. 'Mitchellii'. See *S. thibetica* 'John Mitchell'.
S. pohuashanensis of gardens. See *S.* x *kewensis.*
S. prattii. Deciduous, spreading tree. H and S 6m (20ft). Dark green leaves are divided into 21–9 oblong, sharply toothed leaflets. Produces small, white flowers in late spring, followed by rounded, white fruits. Zone 7.
S. reducta illus. p.360.
S. sargentiana (Sargent's rowan). Deciduous, sparsely branched, spreading tree. H and S 6m (20ft). Has stout shoots and large, mid-green leaves, consisting of 7–11 oblong leaflets, that turn brilliant red in autumn. Small, white flowers in late spring are succeeded by rounded, red fruits. Zone 7.
S. scalaris. Deciduous, spreading, graceful tree. H and S 10m (30ft). Produces leaves with 21–33 narrowly oblong, glossy, deep green leaflets that become deep red and purple in autumn. Produces small, white flowers in late spring, followed by rounded, red fruits in large, dense clusters. Zone 4b.

S. scopulina of gardens. See
S. aucuparia 'Fastigiata'.
S. thibetica. Deciduous, conical tree.
H 20m (70ft), S 15m (50ft). Large,
broadly oval, dark green leaves are
silvery-white when young and remain
so on undersides. Heads of small, white
flowers in late spring are followed by
rounded, brown fruits. Zone 6.
'John Mitchell' (syn. *S.* 'Mitchellii')
illus. p.79.
S. × thuringiaca. Deciduous, broadly
conical, compact tree. H 12m (40ft),
S 8m (25ft). Oval, dark green leaves are
deeply lobed and have basal leaflets.
Small, white flowers appear in late
spring, followed by rounded, bright red
fruits. **'Fastigiata'** has upright branches
and a broad, oval, dense crown. Both
zone 5.
S. vestita. syn. *S. cuspidata,* illus. p.78.
S. vilmorinii illus. p.94.
S. **'Wilfred Fox'.** Deciduous tree,
upright when young, later with a dense,
oval head. H 15m (50ft), S 10m (30ft).
Has broadly oval, glossy, dark green
leaves and small, white flowers in late
spring, followed by rounded, orange-
brown fruits. Zone 7.

Sorrel tree. See *Oxydendrum
arboreum,* illus. p.78.
Sorrel, Wood. See *Oxalis
acetosella.*
Sourwood. See *Oxydendrum arboreum.*
South American air plant. See
Kalanchoe fedtschenkoi.
South Sea arrowroot. See *Tacca
leontopetaloides.*
Southern beech. See *Nothofagus.*
Southern Japanese hemlock. See
Tsuga sieboldii.
Southern polypody. See *Polypodium
cambricum.*
Southernwood. See *Artemisia
abrotanum,* illus. p.176.
Spade leaf. See *Philodendron
domesticum.*
Spanish bayonet. See *Yucca aloifolia,*
illus. p.153.
Spanish bluebell. See *Hyacinthoides
hispanica,* illus. p.414.
Spanish broom. See *Spartium
junceum,* illus. p.147.
Spanish chestnut. See *Castanea
sativa.*
Spanish dagger. See *Yucca gloriosa,*
illus. p.137.
Spanish gorse. See *Genista hispanica,*
illus. p.170.
Spanish heath. See *Erica australis.*
Spanish moss. See *Tillandsia
usneoides,* illus. p.265.
Spanish tree heath. See *Erica
australis.*

SPARAXIS
Harlequin flower

IRIDACEAE

Genus of spring- and early summer-
flowering corms, grown for their
very gaudy flowers. Needs a sunny,
well-drained site. Plant in autumn.
Dry off corms after flowering.
Propagate by offsets in late summer
or by seed in autumn.
S. elegans, syn. *Streptanthera cuprea,*
S. elegans. Spring-flowering corm.
H 10–25cm (4–10in), S 8–12cm

(3–5in). Has lance-shaped leaves in an
erect, basal fan. Stem produces a loose
spike of 1–5 flattish, orange or white
blooms, each 3–4cm (1¼–1½in) wide
and with a yellow centre surrounded
by a purple-black band.
S. fragrans subsp. **grandiflora**, syn.
S. grandiflora. Spring-flowering corm.
H 15–40cm (6–16in), S 8–12cm
(3–5in). Has sword-shaped leaves in
an erect, basal fan. Stem bears a loose
spike of up to 5 flattish, yellow-tubed,
deep purple flowers, each 4–5cm
(1½–2in) across.
S. grandiflora. See *S. fragrans* subsp.
grandiflora.
S. tricolor illus. p.430.

SPARGANIUM
Bur reed

SPARGANIACEAE/TYPHACEAE

Genus of deciduous or semi-evergreen,
perennial, marginal water plants, grown
for their foliage. Tolerates deep shade
and cold water. Remove faded foliage
and cut plants back regularly to control
growth. Propagate by seed or division
in spring.
S. erectum, syn. *S. ramosum,*
illus. p.449.
S. minimum. See *S. natans.*
S. natans, syn. *S. minimum* (Least bur
reed). Vigorous, deciduous or semi-
evergreen, perennial, marginal water
plant. H 30cm–1m (1–3ft), S 30cm
(1ft). Mid-green leaves are grass-like,
some erect, some floating. In summer
has insignificant, brownish-green
flowers, in the form of burs.
S. ramosum. See *S. erectum.*

Sparmannia. Reclassified as
Sparrmannia.

SPARRMANNIA,
syn. SPARMANNIA

TILIACEAE

Genus of evergreen trees and shrubs,
grown for their flowers and foliage.
Tender, min. 7°C (45°F). Prefers full
light and fertile, well-drained soil.
Water freely when in full growth,
moderately at other times. Flowered
stems may be cut back after flowering
to promote a more compact habit.
Propagate by greenwood cuttings in
late spring. Is prone to whitefly.
S. africana illus. p.118.

SPARTINA

GRAMINEAE/POACEAE

See also GRASSES, BAMBOOS,
RUSHES and SEDGES.
S. pectinata **'Aureomarginata'**, syn.
S.p. 'Aureovariegata', illus. p.309.

SPARTIUM

LEGUMINOSAE/PAPILIONACEAE

Genus of one species of deciduous,
almost leafless shrub, grown for its
green shoots and showy flowers.
Needs sun and not too rich, well-
drained soil. To maintain a compact
habit, trim in early spring. Propagate
by seed in autumn.
S. junceum illus. p.147.

SPATHIPHYLLUM

ARACEAE

Genus of evergreen perennials, with
rhizomes, grown for their foliage and
flowers. Tender, min. 15°C (59°F).
Prefers a humid atmosphere, humus-rich,
moist soil and partial shade. Propagate
by division in spring or summer. All
parts of the plants may cause mild
stomach upset if ingested, and contact
with the sap may irritate skin.
S. **'Clevelandii'.** See *S. wallisii*
'Clevelandii'.
S. floribundum. Evergreen, tufted, short-
stemmed perennial. H and S to 30cm
(1ft). Has clusters of lance-shaped,
long-pointed, long-stalked, glossy, dark
green leaves, to 15cm (6in) long.
Intermittently, bears narrowly oval,
white spathes, to 8cm (3in) long, each
enclosing a green-and-white spadix.
S. **'Mauna Loa'** illus. p.299.
S. wallisii illus. p.300. **'Clevelandii'**
(syn. *S.* 'Clevelandii') is an evergreen,
tufted perennial. H and S to 60cm (2ft).
Has broadly lance-shaped, semi-erect,
glossy, mid-green leaves, 30cm (1ft) or
more long. Intermittently bears oval,
white spathes, each 15cm (6in) long
with a central, green line, that surround
fragrant, white spadices.

SPATHODEA

BIGNONIACEAE

Genus of evergreen trees, grown for
their flowers, mainly from autumn to
spring, and for their overall appearance.
Tender, min. 16–18°C (61–4°F). Needs
full light and fertile, well-drained but
moisture-retentive soil. Container-
grown and immature plants seldom bear
flowers. Propagate by seed in spring or
by semi-ripe cuttings in summer.
S. campanulata illus. p.71.

Spatterdock, American. See *Nuphar
advena.*
Spearwort, Greater. See *Ranunculus
lingua,* illus. p.451.
Speedwell
  Digger's. See *Parahebe perfoliata,*
    illus. p.286.
  Prostrate. See *Veronica prostrata,*
    illus. p.357.
  Rock. See *Veronica fruticans.*
  Spiked. See *Veronica spicata.*

SPHAERALCEA

MALVACEAE

Genus of perennials and deciduous sub-
shrubs that are evergreen in warm
climates. Requires a warm, sunny
situation and fertile, well-drained soil.
Propagate by seed or division in spring
or by softwood cuttings in mid-summer.
S. ambigua illus. p.258.
S. munroana. Branching, woody-based
perennial. H and S 45cm (18in). Broadly
funnel-shaped, brilliant coral-pink
flowers are borne singly in leaf axils
from summer until first frosts. Has oval,
round-toothed, hairy, mid-green leaves.

Sphaeropteris. Reclassified as *Cyathea.*
Spice bush. See *Lindera benzoin,*
  illus. p.131.

Spiceberry. See *Ardisia crenata,*
  illus. p.150.
Spider flower. See *Cleome.*
Spider orchid. See *Ophrys sphegodes.*
Spider plant. See *Anthericum;*
  Chlorophytum comosum.
Spiderwort. See *Tradescantia.*
Spignel. See *Meum athamanticum.*
Spike heath. See *Erica spiculifolia.*
Spiked speedwell. See *Veronica
spicata.*
Spikenard, False. See *Smilacina
racemosa,* illus. p.233.
Spike-rush, Needle. See *Eleocharis
acicularis.*
Spiloxene capensis. See *Hypoxis
capensis.*
Spinach, Red mountain. See *Atriplex
hortensis* 'Rubra'.
Spindle
  Japanese. See *Euonymus
japonicus.*
  Winged. See *Euonymus alatus,* illus.
    p.148.
Spindle tree. See *Euonymus
europaeus.*
Spinning gum. See *Eucalyptus
perriniana,* illus. p.100.

SPIRAEA

ROSACEAE

Genus of deciduous or semi-evergreen
shrubs, grown for their mass of small
flowers and, in some species, their
foliage. Requires sun and fertile, well-
drained but not over-dry soil. On
species and cultivars that flower on the
current year's growth – *S. × billiardii,*
S. douglasii and *S. japonica* and its
cultivars – cut back young stems and
remove very old ones in early spring.
On species that flower on old wood, cut
out older shoots in early spring, leaving
young shoots to flower that year.
Propagate *S. douglasii* by division
between late autumn and early spring,
other species and cultivars by softwood
cuttings in summer.
S. aitchisonii. See *Sorbaria tomentosa*
var. *angustifolia.*
S. arborea. See *Sorbaria kirilowii.*
S. **'Arguta'** (Bridal wreath, Foam of
May). Deciduous, arching, dense shrub.
H and S 2.5m (8ft). Produces clusters
of 5-petalled, white flowers from mid-
to late spring. Leaves are narrowly
oblong and bright green. Zone 2b.
S. aruncus. See *Aruncus dioicus.*
S. × billiardii. Deciduous, upright,
dense shrub. H and S 2.5m (8ft). Has
oval, finely toothed, dark green leaves
and dense panicles of 5-petalled, pink
flowers in summer. **'Triumphans'** has
large, broadly conical panicles of bright
purplish-pink flowers. Zone 3.
S. canescens illus. p.136.
S. douglasii. Vigorous, deciduous,
upright shrub. H and S 2m (6ft). Dense,
narrow panicles of 5-petalled, purplish-
pink flowers are borne from early to
mid-summer among oblong, mid-green
leaves with grey-white undersides.
Leaves of subsp. *menziesii,* H 1m (3ft),
are green on both sides. Zone 6.
S. japonica **'Anthony Waterer'**,
'Goldflame' and **'Little Princess'**
illus. p.163.
S. nipponica. Deciduous, arching
shrub. H and S 2.5m (8ft). Bears dense
clusters of 5-petalled, white flowers in

early summer. Stout, red shoots carry small, rounded, dark green leaves. **'Halward's Silver'**, H and S 1m (3ft), is slow-growing, very dense and flowers profusely. **'Snowmound'** (syn. *S.n.* var. *tosaensis* of gardens) illus. p.139. All zone 3.
S. prunifolia. Deciduous, arching, graceful shrub. H and S 2m (6ft). In mid- and late spring has clusters of rosette-like, double, white flowers amid rounded to oblong, bright green leaves, colouring to bronze-yellow in autumn. Zone 4.
S. 'Snow White', syn. *S. trichocarpa* 'Snow White'. Deciduous, arching shrub. H and S 2m (6ft). Leaves are oblong and mid-green. Dense clusters of 5-petalled, white flowers are borne in late spring and early summer. Zone 3.
S. sorbifolia. See *Sorbaria sorbifolia*.
S. thunbergii. Deciduous or semi-evergreen, arching, dense shrub. H 1.5m (5ft), S 2m (6ft). Small clusters of 5-petalled, white flowers are borne from early to mid-spring. Has narrowly oblong, pale green leaves. Zone 3.
S. trichocarpa 'Snow White'. See *S.* 'Snow White'.
S. trilobata. Deciduous, arching, graceful shrub. H 1m (3ft), S 1.5m (5ft). In early summer bears 5-petalled, white flowers in clusters along slender shoots. Has rounded, shallowly lobed, toothed, blue-green leaves. Zone 2b.
S. ulmaria. See *Filipendula ulmaria*.
S. × vanhouttei illus. p.154.
S. veitchii. Vigorous, deciduous, upright shrub. H and S 3m (10ft). Has arching, red branches and oblong, dark green leaves. Produces heads of 5-petalled, white flowers from early to mid-summer. Zone 5.

SPIRANTHES

See also ORCHIDS.
S. cernua (illus. p.296). Deciduous, terrestrial orchid. H 50cm (20in). Spikes of delicate, white flowers, 1cm (½in) long, with pale yellow centres, appear in autumn. Has narrowly lance-shaped leaves, 5–12cm (2–5in) long. Requires semi-shade in summer.

Spleenwort
  Maidenhair. See *Asplenium trichomanes*, illus. p.311.
  Mother. See *Asplenium bulbiferum*.

SPREKELIA

AMARYLLIDACEAE

Genus of one species of bulb, grown for its showy, red flowers in spring. Needs an open, sunny site and well-drained soil. Keep dry in winter; start into growth by watering in spring. Propagate by offsets in early autumn.
S. formosissima illus. p.413.

Spring beauty. See *Claytonia virginica*.
Spring bell. See *Olsynium douglasii*.
Spring crocus. See *Crocus vernus*, illus. p.429.
Spring gentian. See *Gentiana verna*, illus. p.370.

Spring snowflake. See *Leucojum vernum*, illus. p.426.
Spruce. See *Picea*.
  Black. See *Picea mariana*.
  Brewer's. See *Picea breweriana*, illus. p.105.
  Caucasian. See *Picea orientalis*.
  Colorado. See *Picea pungens*.
  Common. See *Picea abies*, illus. p.104.
  Engelmann. See *Picea engelmannii*, illus. p.105.
  Lijiang. See *Picea likiangensis*.
  Morinda. See *Picea smithiana*.
  Mountain. See *Picea engelmannii*, illus. p.105.
  Norway. See *Picea abies*, illus. p.104.
  Oriental. See *Picea orientalis*.
  Serbian. See *Picea omorika*, illus. p.103.
  Sitka. See *Picea sitchensis*.
  Taiwan. See *Picea morrisonicola*, illus. p.107.
  West Himalayan. See *Picea smithiana*.
  White. See *Picea glauca*.
Spurge. See *Euphorbia*.
  Wood. See *Euphorbia amygdaloides*.
Spurge laurel. See *Daphne laureola*.
Squawroot. See *Trillium erectum*, illus. p.269.
Squill
  Sea. See *Urginea maritima*.
  Siberian. See *Scilla siberica*.
  Striped. See *Puschkinia scilloides* var. *libanotica*, illus. p.432.
Squirrel tail grass. See *Hordeum jubatum*, illus. p.307.
Squirrel's-foot fern. See *Davallia mariesii*.

STACHYS

LABIATAE/LAMIACEAE

Genus of late spring- or summer-flowering perennials, shrubs and sub-shrubs, some of which are evergreen. Hardy to tender, min. 5°C (41°F). Grows in any well-drained soil, tolerating even poor soil. Species mentioned below prefer an open, sunny position; others are woodland plants and grow better in semi-shade. Propagate by division in spring.
S. byzantina, syn. *S. lanata*, *S. olympica*, illus. p.304. **'Primrose Heron'** illus. p.291. **'Silver Carpet'** is an evergreen, mat-forming perennial. H 15cm (6in), S 60cm (24in). Has oval, woolly, grey leaves. Rarely produces flowers. Makes an excellent front-of-border or ground-cover plant.
S. coccinea. Clump-forming perennial. H 60cm (24in), S 45cm (18in). Tender. Has oval, mid-green leaves with a pronounced network of veins. From early to late summer, spikes of small, hooded, bright scarlet flowers, protruding from purple calyces, arise from leaf axils.
S. lanata. See *S. byzantina*.
S. macrantha. Clump-forming perennial. H and S 30cm (12in). Has heart-shaped, crinkled, round-toothed, soft green leaves. Whorls of large, hooded, rose-purple flowers are produced in summer. **'Superba'** illus. p.285.
S. officinalis, syn. *Betonica officinalis* (Betony). Mat-forming perennial. H 45–60cm (18–24in), S 30–45cm

(12–18in). Bears whorls of hooded, tubular, purple, pink or white flowers on sturdy stems, arising, in summer, from mats of oval to oblong, round-toothed, mid-green leaves. **'Rosea'** has flowers of clearer pink.
S. olympica. See *S. byzantina*.

STACHYURUS

STACHYURACEAE

Genus of deciduous shrubs, grown for their flowers, which are borne before the leaves. Flower spikes, formed in autumn, are usually unharmed by hard frosts. Requires a position in sun or semi-shade, and fertile, moist but well-drained, not too heavy soil, preferably peaty and acid. Does well when trained against a south- or west-facing wall. Propagate by softwood cuttings in summer.
S. chinensis. Deciduous, spreading, open shrub. H 2m (6ft), S 4m (12ft). Pendent spikes of small, bell-shaped, pale yellow flowers open in late winter and early spring. Leaves are oval and deep green. Zone 8.
S. praecox illus. p.150. **'Magpie'** is a deciduous, spreading, open shrub, less vigorous than the species. H 1.5m (5ft), S 2m (6ft). Has arching, red-purple shoots and oval, tapered, grey-green leaves, edged with creamy-white. Bell-shaped, pale yellow flowers are borne in late winter and early spring. Zone 8.

Staff tree. See *Celastrus scandens*.
Staff vine. See *Celastrus orbiculatus*.
Stag's-horn fern. See *Platycerium*.
Stag's-horn sumach. See *Rhus typhina*.
Stanford manzanita. See *Arctostaphylos stanfordiana*.

STANHOPEA

See also ORCHIDS.
S. tigrina. Evergreen, epiphytic orchid for a cool greenhouse. H 23cm (9in). Pendent spikes of fragrant, waxy, rich yellow and maroon flowers, 15cm (6in) across, with red-spotted, white lips, are produced in summer. Has broadly oval, ribbed leaves, 30cm (12in) long. Is best grown in a hanging, slatted basket. Provide semi-shade in summer.

STAPELIA

ASCLEPIADACEAE

Genus of clump-forming, perennial succulents with erect, 4-angled stems. Stem edges are often indented and may bear small leaves that drop after only a few weeks. Flowers are often foul-smelling. Tender, min. 11°C (52°F). Needs a site in sun or partial shade, with well-drained soil. Propagate by seed or stem cuttings in spring or summer.
S. europaea. See *Caralluma europaea*.
S. flavirostris. See *S. grandiflora*.
S. gigantea illus. p.476.
S. grandiflora, syn. *S. flavirostris*, illus. p.476.
S. variegata. See *Orbea variegata*.

STAPHYLEA
Bladder nut

STAPHYLEACEAE

Genus of deciduous, spring-flowering shrubs and trees, grown for their flowers and bladder-like fruits. Requires sun or semi-shade and fertile, moist soil. Propagate species by softwood or greenwood cuttings in summer or by seed in autumn, selected forms by softwood or greenwood cuttings in summer.
S. colchica. Deciduous, upright shrub. H and S 3.5m (11ft). Erect panicles of bell-shaped, white flowers are borne in late spring and are followed by inflated, greenish-white fruits. Bright green leaves each consist of 3–5 oval leaflets. Zone 7.
S. holocarpa 'Rosea' illus. p.117.
S. pinnata illus. p.116.
S. trifoliata (American bladdernut). Upright, deciduous, suckering shrub. H 5m (15ft), S 2.5m (8ft). Leaves have three, sharply pointed leaflets and are softly hairy beneath. Greenish-white flowers in spring give inflated fruit with loose seeds that rattle in the winter winds. Does well in part shade. Zone 3.

Star, Blue. See *Amsonia*.
Star daisy. See *Lindheimera texana*, illus. p.336.
Star flower. See *Orbea variegata*, illus. p.476.
Star ipomoea. See *Ipomoea coccinea*.
Star jasmine. See *Trachelospermum jasminoides*, illus. p.207.
Star magnolia. See *Magnolia stellata*, illus. p.75.
Star-cluster. See *Pentas lanceolata*, illus. p.163.
Star-of-Bethlehem. See *Ornithogalum*.
  Drooping. See *Ornithogalum nutans*.
Star-of-Bethlehem orchid. See *Angraecum sesquipedale*.
Statice. Reclassified as *Limonium* except for:
  S. suworowii for which see *Psylliostachys suworowii*.
Statice. See *Psylliostachys*.

STAUNTONIA

LARDIZABALACEAE

Genus of evergreen, woody-stemmed, twining climbers. Male and female flowers are produced on separate plants. Marginally hardy. Grow in any well-drained soil and in sun or semi-shade. To keep under control, prune in early spring. Propagate by seed in spring or by stem cuttings in summer or autumn.
S. hexaphylla. Evergreen, woody-stemmed, twining climber. H to 10m (30ft) or more. Leaves have 3–7 oval leaflets, each 5–13cm (2–5in) long. In spring has racemes of small, fragrant, cup-shaped, pale violet flowers, followed by egg-shaped, edible, fleshy, purple fruits, 2.5–5cm (1–2in) long, if plants of both sexes are grown together. Zone 9?.

Stemless gentian. See *Gentiana acaulis*, illus. p.370.

STENANTHIUM

LILIACEAE/MELANTHIACEAE

Genus of summer-flowering bulbs, attractive but seldom cultivated. Needs an open, sunny position in any well-drained soil. In cool areas, plant in a warm, sheltered site in light soil that does not dry out excessively. Propagate by seed in autumn or by division in spring.

S. gramineum. Summer-flowering bulb. H to 1.5m (5ft), S 45–60cm (1½–2ft). Has long, narrowly strap-shaped, semi-erect, basal leaves. Stem produces a dense, branched, often arching spike of fragrant, star-shaped, white or green flowers, each 1–1.5cm (½–⅝in) across.

STENOCACTUS,
syn. ECHINOFOSSULOCACTUS

CACTACEAE

Genus of spherical, perennial cacti with spiny, green stems that have very narrow, wavy ribs. Tender, min. 7°C (45°F). Needs a sunny position and well-drained soil. Propagate by seed in spring or summer.

S. coptonogonus illus. p.476.
S. lamellosus. Spherical, perennial cactus. H and S 8cm (3in). Green stem has 30–35 ribs. Funnel-shaped, flesh-coloured or red flowers, 1–3cm (½–1¼in) across, are produced from crown in spring. Has flattened upper radial spines, shorter, more rounded lower ones and longer, rounded central spines with darker tips.
S. obvallatus, syn. *Echinofossulatus pentacanthus*, *E. violaciflorus*, illus. p.472.

STENOCARPUS

PROTEACEAE

Genus of evergreen, summer- and autumn-flowering trees, grown for their flowers and foliage. Tender, min. 5–7°C (41–5°F). Needs full light and fertile, well-drained soil. Water containerized plants moderately, less in winter. Pruning is rarely necessary. Propagate by seed in spring or by semi-ripe cuttings in summer.

S. sinuatus (Australian firewheel tree). Slow-growing, evergreen, upright tree. H 12m (40ft) or more, S 5m (15ft). Has lustrous, deep green leaves, each 12–25cm (5–10in) long, lance-shaped and entire or with pairs of oblong lobes. Bottle-shaped, bright scarlet flowers, clustered like the spokes of a wheel, are produced from late summer to autumn.

STENOCEREUS

CACTACEAE

Genus of tree-like or shrubby, perennial cacti with prominently ribbed stems often densely spined. Tender, min. 13°C (55°F), otherwise plants may become badly marked. Needs full sun and very well-drained soil. Propagate by seed in spring or stem cuttings in summer.

S. marginatus. See *Pachycereus marginatus*.
S. thurberi, syn. *Lemaireocereus thurberi*. Columnar, perennial cactus,

branching from low down. H to 7m (22ft), S 1m (3ft). Has 5- or 6-ribbed, glossy, dark green stems with very short-spined areoles set in close rows down each rib. Produces funnel-shaped, purple or pink flowers with red sepals in summer.

Stenolobium stans. See *Tecoma stans.*

STENOMESSON

AMARYLLIDACEAE

Genus of bulbs, grown for their long, often pendent, tubular flowers. Tender, min. 5–10°C (41–50°F). Needs an open, sunny situation and well-drained soil. Propagate by offsets in autumn.

S. incarnatum. See *S. variegatum*.
S. miniatum, syn. *Urceolina peruviana*, illus. p.419.
S. variegatum, syn. *S. incarnatum*, illus. p.419.

STENOTAPHRUM

GRAMINEAE/POACEAE

See also GRASSES, BAMBOOS, RUSHES and SEDGES.
S. secundatum (St Augustine grass) **'Variegatum'** is an evergreen, spreading, rhizomatous, perennial grass. H 15cm (6in), S indefinite. Tender, min. 5°C (41°F). Leaves are mid-green with cream stripes and last well into winter. Has erect racemes of brownish-green spikelets in summer. In warm climates is used for lawns.

STEPHANANDRA

ROSACEAE

Genus of deciduous, summer-flowering shrubs, grown for their habit, foliage, autumn colour and winter shoots. Needs sun or semi-shade and fertile, not too dry soil. On established plants cut out some older shoots after flowering. Propagate by softwood cuttings in summer or by division in autumn.

S. incisa. Deciduous, arching shrub. H 1.5m (5ft), S 3m (10ft). Oval, deeply lobed and toothed, bright green leaves turn orange-yellow in autumn and stems become rich brown in winter. Produces crowded panicles of tiny, star-shaped, greenish-white flowers in early summer. **'Crispa'**, H 60cm (2ft), has wavy-edged and more deeply lobed leaves.
S. tanakae illus. p.140. Both zone 5.

STEPHANOTIS

ASCLEPIADACEAE

Genus of evergreen, woody-stemmed, twining climbers, grown for their scented, waxy flowers. Tender, min. 13–16°C (55–61°F). Provide a humus-rich, well-drained soil and partial shade in summer. Water moderately, less in cold weather. Provide stems with support. Shorten over-long or crowded stems in spring. Propagate by seed in spring or by semi-ripe cuttings in summer.

S. floribunda illus. p.204.

Sterculia acerifolia. See *Brachychiton acerifolius.*
Sterculia diversifolia. See *Brachychiton populneus.*
Sterculia platanifolia. See *Firmiana simplex.*

STERNBERGIA

AMARYLLIDACEAE

Genus of spring- or autumn-flowering bulbs, grown for their large, crocus-like flowers. Marginally hardy and best grown against a sunny wall. Needs a hot, sunny site and any well-drained, heavy or light soil that dries out in summer, when bulbs die down and need warmth and dryness. Leave undisturbed to form clumps. Propagate by division in spring or autumn.

S. candida illus. p.426.
S. clusiana. Autumn-flowering bulb. H to 2cm (¾in), S 8–10cm (3–4in). Strap-shaped, semi-erect, basal, greyish-green leaves, often twisted lengthways, appear after flowering. Stems carry erect, goblet-shaped, yellow or greenish-yellow flowers, 4–8cm (1½–3in) long.
S. lutea illus. p.439.
S. sicula. Autumn-flowering bulb. H 2.5–7cm (1–3in), S 5–8cm (2–3in). Narrowly strap-shaped, semi-erect, basal, deep green leaves, each with a central, paler green stripe, appear with flowers. Each stem bears a funnel-shaped, bright yellow flower, 2–4cm (¾–1½in) long.

STETSONIA

CACTACEAE

Genus of one species of tree-like, perennial cactus with a stout trunk. Nocturnal, funnel-shaped flowers are 15cm (6in) long. Tender, min. 10°C (50°F). Needs a sunny, well-drained position. Propagate by seed in spring or summer.

S. coryne illus. p.457.

STEWARTIA,
syn. STUARTIA

THEACEAE

Genus of deciduous trees and shrubs, grown for their flowers, autumn colour and usually peeling bark. Needs a sunny position, but preferably with roots in shade, and shelter from strong winds. Requires fertile, moist but well-drained, neutral to acid soil. Resents being transplanted. Propagate by softwood cuttings in summer or by seed in autumn.

S. malacodendron. Deciduous, spreading tree or shrub. H 4m (12ft), S 3m (10ft). Rose-like, purple-stamened, white flowers, some-times purple-streaked, are borne in mid-summer amid oval, dark green leaves. Zone 8.
S. monadelpha illus. p.82.
S. pseudocamellia illus. p.78.
S. sinensis. Deciduous, spreading tree. H 12m (40ft), S 7m (22ft). Has peeling bark and oval, bright green leaves that turn brilliant red in autumn. Fragrant, rose-like, white flowers are produced in mid-summer. Zone 6.

STIGMAPHYLLON

MALPIGHIACEAE

Genus of evergreen, woody-stemmed, twining climbers, grown for their flowers. Tender, min. 15–18°C (59–64°F). Fertile, well-drained soil is needed with partial shade in summer. Water freely when in full growth, less in low temperatures. Provide stems with support. Thin out crowded stems in spring. Propagate by semi-ripe cuttings in summer.

S. ciliatum illus. p.216.

Stinking hellebore. See *Helleborus foetidus*, illus. p.305.
Stinking iris. See *Iris foetidissima*.

STIPA

GRAMINEAE/POACEAE

See also GRASSES, BAMBOOS, RUSHES and SEDGES.
S. arundinacea (Pheasant grass). Evergreen, tuft-forming, perennial grass. H 1.5m (5ft), S 1.2m (4ft). Brownish-green leaves, 30cm (12in) long, turn soft orange in late summer. Has pendent, open panicles of purplish-green flower spikes in autumn.
S. calamagrostis, syn. *Achnatherum calamagrostis*. Evergreen, tuft-forming, perennial grass. H 1m (3ft), S 45cm (1½ft). Leaves are bluish-green and inrolled. In summer bears decorative, large, loose panicles of sand-brown spikelets that dry and last well into winter.
S. gigantea illus. p.307.

Stock. See *Matthiola*.
 Brompton. See *Matthiola incana*.
 Virginian. See *Malcolmia maritima*, illus. p.323.

STOKESIA

ASTERACEAE/COMPOSITAE

Genus of one species of evergreen, summer-flowering perennial. Requires sun or semi-shade and fertile, well-drained soil. Propagate by division in spring or by seed in autumn.

S. laevis illus. p.285. **'Blue Star'** is an evergreen, basal-rosetted perennial. H and S 30–45cm (12–18in). Bears cornflower-like, deep blue flower heads singly at stem tips in summer. Has rosettes of narrowly lance-shaped, dark green leaves.

STOMATIUM

AIZOACEAE

Genus of mat-forming, perennial succulents with short stems, each bearing 4–6 pairs of solid, 3-angled or semi-cylindrical leaves, often with toothed edges and incurved tips. Tender, min. 5°C (41°F). Needs sun and well-drained soil. Propagate by seed or stem cuttings in spring or summer.

S. agninum. Mat-forming, perennial succulent. H 5cm (2in), S 1m (3ft) or more. Has solid, 3-angled or semi-cylindrical, soft grey-green leaves, 4–5cm (1½–2in) long, often without teeth. In summer, fragrant, daisy-like, yellow flowers, 2–5cm (¾–2in) across, open in evening.

S. patulum. Mat-forming, perennial succulent. H 3cm (1¼in), S 1m (3ft). Has semi-cylindrical, grey-green leaves, each 2cm (¾in) long, with rough dots and 2–9 teeth-like tubercles on upper surface. Bears 2cm (¾in) wide, fragrant, daisy-like, pale yellow flowers in evening in summer.

Stone pine. See *Pinus pinea*, illus. p.109.
   Mexican. See *Pinus cembroides*, illus. p.109.
Stone plant. See *Lithops*.
Stonecrop. See *Sedum*.
   Biting. See *Sedum acre*, illus. p.384.
   Common. See *Sedum acre*, illus. p.384.
   Reflexed. See *Sedum rupestre*, illus. p.359.
Strangweja spicata. See *Bellevalia hyacinthoides*.
Stranvaesia. Reclassified as *Photinia*.
Strap cactus. See *Epiphyllum*.

STRATIOTES

HYDROCHARITACEAE

Genus of semi-evergreen, perennial, submerged, free-floating water plants, grown for their foliage. Requires sun. Grows in any depth of cool water. Thin plants as required. Propagate by separating young plants from runners in summer.
S. aloides illus. p.447.

Strawberry cactus. See *Mammillaria prolifera*.
Strawberry geranium. See *Saxifraga stolonifera* 'Tricolor'.
Strawberry tree. See *Arbutus unedo*, illus. p.93.
   Grecian. See *Arbutus andrachne*.
Strawflower. See *Bracteantha bracteata*; *Rhodanthe*.

STRELITZIA

Bird-of-paradise flower

MUSACEAE/STRELITZIACEAE

Genus of large, evergreen, tufted, clump-forming, palm-like perennials, grown for their showy flowers. Tender, min. 5–10°C (41–50°F). Grow in fertile, well-drained soil and in bright light shaded from direct sun in summer. Reduce watering in low temperatures. Propagate by seed or division of suckers in spring.
S. nicolai illus. p.232.
S. reginae illus. p.267.

Streptanthera cuprea. See *Sparaxis elegans*.
Streptanthera elegans. See *Sparaxis elegans*.

STREPTOCARPUS

GESNERIACEAE

Genus of perennials, some of which are evergreen, with showy flowers. Tender, min. 10–15°C (50–59°F). Grow in a humid atmosphere in humus-rich, moist soil and in bright light away from

direct sunlight. Avoid wetting leaves when watering; water less during cold periods. Propagate by seed, if available, in spring, by division after flowering or by tip cuttings from bushy species or leaf cuttings from stemless species in spring or summer.
S. caulescens illus. p.276.
S. 'Constant Nymph' illus. p.303.
S. 'Nicola' illus. p.301.
S. rexii (Cape primrose). Stemless perennial. H to 25cm (10in), S to 50cm (20in). Has a rosette of strap-shaped, wrinkled, green leaves. Stems, 15cm (6in) or more long, bear loose clusters of funnel-shaped, pale blue or mauve flowers, 5cm (2in) long and with darker lines, intermittently at any time of year.
S. saxorum illus. p.284.

STREPTOSOLEN

SOLANACEAE

Genus of one species of evergreen or semi-evergreen, loosely scrambling shrub, grown for its flowers. Tender, min. 7–10°C (45–50°F). Requires full sun and humus-rich, well-drained soil. Water freely when in full growth, less at other times. After flowering or in spring, remove flowered shoots and tie in new growths. Propagate by softwood or semi-ripe cuttings in summer.
S. jamesonii illus. p.220.

String-of-beads. See *Senecio rowleyanus*, illus. p.462.
String-of-hearts. See *Ceropegia linearis* subsp. *woodii*, illus. p.462.
Striped squill. See *Puschkinia scilloides* var. *libanotica*, illus. p.432.
Striped torch. See *Guzmania monostachya*, illus. p.265.

STROBILANTHES

ACANTHACEAE

Genus of perennials and evergreen sub-shrubs, grown for their flowers. Hardy to tender, min. 15°C (59°F). Grow in semi-shade in fertile, well-drained soil. Propagate by seed, basal stem cuttings or division in spring.
S. atropurpureus illus. p.263.

STROMANTHE

MARANTACEAE

Genus of evergreen, creeping perennials, grown mainly for their foliage. Tender, min. 15°C (59°F). Prefers high humidity and partial shade. Grow on open soil or compost, use soft water if possible and do not allow to dry out completely. Propagate by division in spring.
S. sanguinea. Strong-growing, evergreen, creeping perennial. H and S to 1.5m (5ft). Lance-shaped leaves, to 45cm (18in) long, are glossy, green above with paler midribs, reddish below. Bears panicles of small, 3 petalled, white flowers in axils of showy, bright red bracts, usually in spring but also in summer-autumn.

STROMBOCACTUS

CACTACEAE

Genus of extremely slow-growing, hemispherical to cylindrical, perennial cacti. Takes 5 years from seed to reach 1cm (½in) high. Funnel-shaped flowers are 4cm (1½in) across. Tender, min. 5°C (41°F). Needs sun and very well-drained soil. Is difficult to grow and very susceptible to overwatering. Propagate by seed or grafting in spring or summer.
S. disciformis illus. p.470.

STRONGYLODON

LEGUMINOSAE/PAPILIONACEAE

Genus of evergreen, woody-stemmed, twining climbers, grown for their large, claw-like flowers. Tender, min. 18°C (64°F). Needs humus-rich, moist but well-drained soil and partial shade in summer. Water freely when in full growth, less at other times. Provide support. If necessary, thin crowded stems in spring. Propagate by seed or stem cuttings in summer or by layering in spring.
S. macrobotrys illus. p.206.

Stuartia. Reclassified as *Stewartia*.

STYLIDIUM

STYLIDIACEAE

Genus of perennials with grass-like leaves, grown for their unusual flowers that have fused, 'triggered' stamens adapted for pollination by insects. Tender, min. 10°C (50°F). Grow in fertile soil and in bright light. Propagate by division or seed in spring.
S. graminifolium (Trigger plant). Rosetted perennial. H and S to 15cm (6in) or more. Grass-like, stiff, dark green leaves, with toothed margins, rise from ground level. Bears tiny, pale pinkish-mauve flowers in narrow spikes, 30cm (12in) or more long, in summer.

STYLOPHORUM

PAPAVERACEAE

Genus of spring-flowering perennials with large, deeply lobed leaves, nearly all as basal rosettes. Needs semi-shade and humus-rich, moist, peaty soil. Propagate by division in spring or by seed in autumn.
S. diphyllum illus. p.350.

STYRAX

STYRACACEAE

Genus of deciduous, summer-flowering trees and shrubs, grown for their foliage and flowers. Hardy to tender, min. 7–10°C (45–50°F). Prefers a sheltered position in sun or semi-shade and moist, neutral to acid soil. Propagate by softwood cuttings in summer or by seed in autumn.
S. japonicus illus. p.77.
S. obassia (Fragrant snowbell). Deciduous, spreading tree. H 12m (40ft), S 7m (22ft). Bears long, spreading clusters of fragrant, bell- to

funnel-shaped, white flowers in early summer. Has broad, rounded, deep green leaves. Zone 6.
S. officinalis illus. p.118.
S. wilsonii illus. p.138.

Subalpine fir. See *Abies lasiocarpa*.
Sugar bush. See *Protea repens*.
Sugar maple. See *Acer saccharum*.
Sugared-almond plum. See *Pachyphytum oviferum*, illus. p.475.
Sulcorebutia arenacea. See *Rebutia arenacea*.
Sulcorebutia rauschii. See *Rebutia rauschii*.
Sulcorebutia tiraquensis. See *Rebutia tiraquensis*.
Sultan, Sweet. See *Amberboa*.
Sumach. See *Rhus*.
   Dwarf. See *Rhus copallina*.
   Fragrant. See *Rhus aromatica*.
   Smooth. See *Rhus glabra*, illus. p.143.
   Stag's-horn. See *Rhus typhina*.
   Venetian. See *Cotinus coggygria*.
Summer cypress. See *Bassia scoparia* f. *trichophylla*, illus. p.335.
Summer holly. See *Arctostaphylos diversifolia*.
Summer hyacinth. See *Galtonia candicans*, illus. p.397.
Summer snowflake. See *Leucojum aestivum*, illus. p.396.
Sun plant. See *Portulaca grandiflora*.
Sundew. See *Drosera*.
   Cape. See *Drosera capensis*, illus. p.305.
Sunflower. See *Helianthus*.
   Mexican. See *Tithonia rotundifolia*.
   Willow-leaved. See *Helianthus salicifolius*.
Sunrise horse-chestnut. See *Aesculus* x *neglecta*.

SUTERA

SCROPHULARIACEAE

Genus of annuals, perennials and evergreen shrubs, used for summer bedding. Tender, min. 5°C (41°F). Needs a position in sun and in well-drained soil. Propagate by seed or division in spring or by softwood cuttings in summer.
S. cordata (*Bacopa* of gardens). Spreading perennial usually treated as an annual. H 15cm (6in), S 45cm (18in). Has toothed, dark green leaves and small white or pink flowers freely produced. Grows best if shaded during the heat of the day. Do not allow to dry out.
S. grandiflora. (Purple glory plant). Much-branched, sub-shrubby perennial. H 1m (3ft), S 30–45cm (12–18in). Has oval to oblong, round-toothed leaves. Tubular, 5-lobed, frilled, deep purple flowers are produced from mid-summer to autumn.

SUTHERLANDIA

LEGUMINOSAE/PAPILIONACEAE

Genus of evergreen shrubs, grown for their flowers and fruits. Tender, min. 7–10°C (45–50°F). Requires full light and fertile, well-drained soil. Water containerized specimens freely when in full growth, moderately at other times. Remove old, twiggy stems at ground

level in late winter. Propagate by seed in spring. Spider mite may be troublesome.
S. frutescens illus. p.165.

SWAINSONA

LEGUMINOSAE/PAPILIONACEAE

Genus of annuals, evergreen perennials, sub-shrubs and shrubs, grown for their flowers. Tender, min. 5–7°C (41–5°F). Needs full light or partial shade and humus-rich, well-drained soil. Water freely when in active growth, moderately at other times. Propagate by seed in spring or by semi-ripe cuttings in summer.
S. galegifolia (Darling pea). Evergreen, sprawling sub-shrub. H 60cm–1.2m (2–4ft), S 30–60cm (1–2ft). Leaves have 11–25 narrowly oval, mid- to deep green leaflets. Bears pea-like, red, pink, purple, blue or yellow flowers in late spring and summer. Remove old, flowered shoots in late winter.

Swamp cypress. See *Taxodium distichum*, illus. p.104.
Swamp lily. See *Lilium superbum*; *Saururus cernuus*, illus. p.447.
Swamp pink. See *Helonias bullata*.
Swamp white oak. See *Quercus bicolor*.
Swan flower. See *Aristolochia grandiflora*.
Swan River daisy. See *Brachycome iberidifolia*, illus. p.334.
Swedish ivy. See *Plectranthus oertendahlii*; *Plectranthus verticillatus*.
Swedish whitebeam. See *Sorbus intermedia*.
Sweet alyssum. See *Lobularia maritima*.
Sweet bay. See *Laurus nobilis*; *Magnolia virginiana*.
Sweet box. See *Sarcococca*.
Sweet briar. See *Rosa rubiginosa*, illus. p.185.
Sweet buckeye. See *Aesculus flava*, illus. p.82.
Sweet chestnut. See *Castanea sativa*.
Sweet Cicely. See *Myrrhis*.
Sweet corn. See *Zea mays*.
Sweet flag. See *Acorus calamus*.
Sweet gum. See *Liquidambar styraciflua*, illus. p.70.
Sweet pea. See *Lathyrus odoratus*.
Sweet pepper-bush. See *Clethra alnifolia*.
Sweet rocket. See *Hesperis matronalis*, illus. p.239.
Sweet scabious. See *Scabiosa atropurpurea*.
Sweet sop. See *Annona*.
Sweet sultan. See *Amberboa*.
Sweet viburnum. See *Viburnum odoratissimum*.
Sweet violet. See *Viola odorata*.
Sweet William. See *Dianthus barbatus*.
Sweetheart ivy. See *Hedera hibernica* 'Deltoidea', illus. p.221.
Swiss mountain pine. See *Pinus mugo*.
Swiss-cheese plant. See *Monstera deliciosa*, illus. p.220.
Sword fern. See *Nephrolepis cordifolia*; *Nephrolepis exaltata*, illus. p.312.

SYAGRUS
Queen palm

ARECACEAE/PALMAE

Genus of one species of evergreen palm, grown for its majestic appearance. Tender, min. 18°C (64°F). Requires full light or partial shade and humus-rich, well-drained soil. Water containerized specimens moderately, less when temperatures are low. Propagate by seed in spring at not less than 24°C (75°F). Spider mite may be a nuisance.
S. romanzoffiana illus. p.73.

Sycamore. See *Platanus occidentalis*.
Sycamore maple. See *Acer pseudoplatanus*.

SYCOPSIS

HAMAMELIDACEAE

Genus of evergreen trees and shrubs, grown for their foliage and flowers. Needs a sheltered position in sun or semi-shade and fertile, not too dry, peaty soil. Propagate by semi-ripe cuttings in summer.
S. sinensis. Evergreen, upright shrub. H 5m (15ft), S 4m (12ft). Leaves are oval, glossy and dark green. Flowers lack petals but have showy, dense clusters of red-tinged, yellow anthers in late winter or early spring. Zone 9.

Sydney golden wattle. See *Acacia longifolia*.

SYMPHORICARPOS

CAPRIFOLIACEAE

Genus of deciduous shrubs, with inconspicuous, bell-shaped flowers, grown mainly for their clusters of showy, long-persistent fruits. Requires sun or semi-shade and fertile soil. Propagate by softwood cuttings in summer or by division in autumn. Fruits may cause mild stomach upset if ingested; contact with them may irritate skin.
S. albus (Snowberry). var. *laevigatus* is a vigorous, deciduous, dense shrub, part upright, part arching. H and S 2m (6ft). Large, marble-like, white fruits follow pink flowers borne in summer. Rounded leaves are dark green. Zone 3.
S. × chenaultii 'Hancock'. Deciduous, procumbent, dense shrub. H 1m (3ft), S 3m (10ft). Has oval, bronze leaves maturing to bright green. White flowers appear from early to mid-summer. Small, spherical, deep lilac-pink fruits are sparsely borne. Makes excellent ground cover. Zone 5.
S. orbiculatus (Coralberry, Indian currant). Deciduous, bushy, dense shrub. H and S 2m (6ft). White or pink flowers in late summer and early autumn, then spherical, deep purplish-red fruits. Oval leaves are dark green. Does best after a hot summer. Zone 2b. **'Foliis Variegatis'** (syn. *S.o.* 'Variegatus') illus. p.168.

SYMPHYANDRA

CAMPANULACEAE

Genus of short-lived, summer-flowering perennials, best grown as biennials. Suits large rock gardens and

bases of banks. Needs sun and well-drained soil. Propagate by seed in autumn. Self-seeds readily.
S. armena. Upright or spreading perennial. H 30–60cm (1–2ft), S 30cm (1ft). Produces panicles of upright, bell-shaped, blue or white flowers in summer. Leaves are oval, irregularly toothed, hairy and mid-green.
S. pendula. Arching perennial. H 30–60cm (1–2ft), S 30cm (1ft). Produces panicles of pendent, bell-shaped, cream flowers in summer. Has oval, hairy, pale green leaves. Becomes woody at base with age.
S. wanneri illus. p.357.

SYMPHYTUM
Comfrey

BORAGINACEAE

Genus of vigorous, coarse perennials, best suited to wild gardens. Prefers sun or semi-shade and moist soil. Propagate by division in spring or by seed in autumn; usually self-seeds. Propagate named cultivars by division only. Roots and leaves may cause severe discomfort if ingested; contact with foliage may irritate skin.
S. caucasicum illus. p.238.
S. 'Goldsmith', syn. *S. ibericum* 'Jubilee', *S. ibericum* 'Variegatum', *S.* 'Jubilee'. Clump-forming perennial. H and S 30cm (12in). Has ovate, hairy, dark green leaves with gold and cream markings. Bears pale blue flowers, tinged cream or pink, in spring.
S. grandiflorum of gardens. See *S. ibericum*.
S. 'Hidcote Blue'. Clump-forming perennial. H 50cm (20in), S 60cm (24in). Is similar to *S. ibericum*, but has pale blue flowers.
S. ibericum, syn. *S. grandiflorum* of gardens. Clump-forming perennial. H 25cm (10in), S 60cm (24in). Has lance-shaped, hairy, rich green leaves. Bears one-sided racemes of tubular, creamy flowers in spring. Makes good ground cover. **'Jubilee'** see *S.* 'Goldsmith'. **'Variegatum'** see *S.* 'Goldsmith'.
S. 'Jubilee'. See *S.* 'Goldsmith'.
S. × uplandicum (Russian comfrey). **'Variegatum'** illus. p.238.

SYMPLOCOS

SYMPLOCACEAE

Genus of evergreen or deciduous trees and shrubs, of which only the species described is in general cultivation. This is grown for its flowers and fruits. Fruits are most prolific when several plants are grown together. Needs full sun and fertile, moist but well-drained soil. Propagate by seed in autumn.
S. paniculata illus. p.138.

SYNADENIUM

EUPHORBIACEAE

Genus of evergreen, semi-succulent shrubs, grown for their foliage. Tender, min. 7–10°C (45–50°F). Requires full light and fertile, freely draining soil. Water containerized plants moderately, less in winter. Prune in late winter if necessary. Propagate by seed in spring

or by softwood cuttings in summer. All parts are highly toxic if ingested; sap may irritate skin.
S. compactum var. *rubrum*, syn. *S. grantii* 'Rubrum'. Evergreen, erect, robust-stemmed shrub. H 3–4m (10–12ft), S 2m (6ft) or more. Has very small, red flowers in autumn, largely concealed by lance-shaped to oval, glossy, purplish-green leaves, red-purple beneath.
S. grantii 'Rubrum'. See *S. compactum* var. *rubrum*.

SYNGONIUM

ARACEAE

Genus of evergreen, woody-stemmed, root climbers, grown for their ornamental foliage. Flowers are seldom produced in cultivation. Tender, min. 16–18°C (61–4°F). Needs partial shade and humus-rich, well-drained soil. Water moderately, less in low temperatures. Provide support, ideally with moss poles. Remove young stem tips to promote branching. Propagate by leaf-bud or stem-tip cuttings in summer. All parts may cause mild stomach upset if ingested; contact with the sap may irritate skin.
S. auritum, syn. *Philodendron auritum* of gardens, *P. trifoliatum* (Five fingers). Fairly slow-growing, evergreen, woody-stemmed, root climber. H 1–2m (3–6ft). Has glossy, rich green leaves divided into 3, sometimes 5, oval leaflets, the central one the largest.
S. erythrophyllum. Slow-growing, evergreen, root climber with slender, woody stems. H 1m (3ft) or more. Young plants have arrowhead-shaped leaves, flushed purple beneath. Leaves on mature plants have 3 lobes or leaflets and thicker, longer stems.
S. hoffmannii. Moderately vigorous, evergreen, woody-stemmed, root climber. H 2–3m (6–10ft). Young plants have arrowhead-shaped leaves; mature ones have leaves divided into 3 grey-green leaflets with silvery-white veins.
S. podophyllum, syn. *Nephthytis triphylla* of gardens, illus. p.220. **'Trileaf Wonder'** illus. p.219.

SYNTHYRIS

SCROPHULARIACEAE

Genus of evergreen or deciduous, spring-flowering perennials with gently spreading, rhizomatous rootstocks. Is useful for rock gardens and peat beds. Prefers partial shade and moist soil. Propagate in late spring by seed or division.
S. reniformis. Evergreen, clump-forming perennial. H 8–10cm (3–4in), S 15cm (6in). Has kidney-shaped to rounded, toothed, dark green leaves and, in spring, short, dense racemes of small, bell-shaped, blue flowers.
S. stellata illus. p.369.

Syrian juniper. See *Juniperus drupacea*.

SYRINGA

Lilac

OLEACEAE

Genus of deciduous shrubs and trees, grown for their dense panicles of small, tubular flowers, usually extremely fragrant. Needs sun and deep, fertile, well-drained, preferably alkaline soil. Obtain plants on their own roots, since grafted plants usually sucker freely. Remove flower heads from newly planted lilacs, and dead-head for first few years. Cut out weak shoots in winter and, to maintain shape, prune after flowering. Straggly, old plants may be cut back hard in winter, but the next season's flowers will then be lost. Propagate by softwood cuttings in summer. Leaf miners, leaf spot, mildew, and blight may be troublesome.
See also feature panel p.120

S. 'Belle de Nancy'. See *S. vulgaris* 'Belle de Nancy'.
S. 'Blue Hyacinth'. See *S.* x *hyacinthiflora* 'Blue Hyacinth'.
S. 'Charles Joly'. See *S. vulgaris* 'Charles Joly'.
S. x *chinensis* (Rouen lilac). Deciduous, arching shrub. H and S 4m (12ft). Bears large, arching panicles of fragrant, tubular, single, lilac-purple flowers in late spring. Oval leaves are dark green. Zone 2b.
'Alba' (illus. p.120) has white flowers.
S. 'Clarke's Giant'. See *S.* x *hyacinthiflora* 'Clarke's Giant'.
S. 'Congo'. See *S. vulgaris* 'Congo'.
S. 'Cora Brandt'. See *S.* x *hyacinthiflora* 'Cora Brandt'.
S. 'Decaisne'. See *S. vulgaris* 'Decaisne'.
S. emodi (Himalayan lilac). Vigorous, deciduous, upright shrub. H 5m (15ft), S 4m (12ft). Bears unpleasantly scented, tubular, single, very pale lilac flowers in large, upright panicles in early summer. Has large, oval, dark green leaves. Zone 7.
S. 'Esther Staley'. See *S.* x *hyacinthiflora* 'Esther Staley'.
S. 'Fountain'. Vigorous, deciduous, arching, open shrub. H 4m (12ft), S 5m (15ft). Large, nodding panicles of fragrant, tubular, single, deep pink flowers open above large, oval, dark green leaves in early summer. Zone 2.
S. x *hyacinthiflora* **'Blue Hyacinth'**, syn. *S.* 'Blue Hyacinth' (illus. p.120). Deciduous, bushy shrub, upright when young, later spreading. H and S 3m (10ft). Bears large, loose panicles of fragrant, single, pale lilac-blue flowers from mid-spring to early summer and has broadly heart-shaped, mid-green leaves. Vigorous **'Clarke's Giant'** (syn. *S.* 'Clarke's Giant'; illus p.120), H and S 5m (15ft), has lavender flowers, mauve-pink within, opening from mauve-pink buds from mid- to late spring. Has dark green leaves. **'Cora Brandt'** (syn. *S.* 'Cora Brandt'; illus. p.120) produces double, white flowers in large open panicles. **'Esther Staley'** (syn. *S.* 'Esther Staley'; illus. p.120) is vigorous, with broadly conical panicles of red buds opening to

lilac-pink flowers. All zone 2b.
S. 'James Macfarlane'. See *S. prestoniae* 'James Macfarlane'.
S. 'Jan van Tol'. See *S. vulgaris* 'Jan van Tol'.
S. x *josiflexa* **'Royalty'**, syn. *S.* 'Royalty'. Deciduous, upright, then arching shrub. H 4m (12ft), S 5m (15ft). Large panicles of fragrant, tubular, single, bright purple flowers are borne above oval, dark green leaves in late spring and early summer. Zone 2.
S. 'Katherine Havemeyer'. See *S. vulgaris* 'Katherine Havemeyer'.
S. 'Madame Antoine Buchner'. See *S. vulgaris* 'Madame Antoine Buchner'.
S. 'Madame F. Morel'. See *S. vulgaris* 'Madame F. Morel'.
S. 'Madame Florent Stepman'. See *S. vulgaris* 'Madame Florent Stepman'.
S. 'Madame Lemoine'. See *S. vulgaris* 'Madame Lemoine'.
S. 'Maréchal Foch'. See *S. vulgaris* 'Maréchal Foch'.
S. 'Masséna'. See *S. vulgaris* 'Masséna'.
S. 'Maud Notcutt'. See *S. vulgaris* 'Maud Notcutt'.
S. meyeri 'Palibin', syn. *S. palibianina* of gardens, *S. velutina* of gardens (illus. p.120). Slow-growing, deciduous, bushy, dense shrub. H and S 1.5m (5ft). Produces dense panicles of fragrant, tubular, single, lilac-pink flowers in late spring and early summer. Has small, oval deep green leaves. Zone 2b.
S. 'Michel Buchner'. See *S. vulgaris* 'Michel Buchner'.
S. microphylla. See *S. pubescens* subsp. *microphylla*.
S. 'Minuet'. Deciduous, upright, bushy shrub. H 2.5m (8ft), S 2m (6ft). Dense panicles of small, very fragrant, pale pink flowers open from magenta-pink buds in early summer. Very free flowering, even when young, on a rounded bush. Zone 2.
S. 'Monge'. See *S. vulgaris* 'Monge'.
S. 'Mrs Edward Harding'. See *S. vulgaris* 'Mrs Edward Harding'.
S. palibiniana of gardens. See *S. meyeri* 'Palibin'.
S. patula 'Miss Kim'. See *S.pubescens.* ssp. *patula* 'Miss Kim'.
S. 'Paul Thirion'. See *S. vulgaris* 'Paul Thirion'.
S. x *persica* (Persian lilac; illus. p.120). Deciduous, bushy, dense shrub. H and S 2m (6ft). Produces small, dense panicles of fragrant, purple flowers in late spring. Leaves are narrow, pointed and dark green. Zone 2b.
S. 'Président Grévy'. See *S. vulgaris* 'Président Grévy'.
S. x *prestoniae* **'James Macfarlane'**, syn. *S.* 'J. Macfarlane'. Vigorous, deciduous, upright shrub. H and S 4m (12ft). Has large, nodding panicles of fragrant, tubular, single, salmon-pink flowers, paler within, in early summer, and large, oval, dark green leaves. Zone 2.
S. 'Primrose'. See *S. vulgaris* 'Primrose'.
S. pubescens subsp. **microphylla**, syn. *S. microphylla.* Deciduous, bushy shrub. H and S 2m (6ft). Small panicles of

very fragrant, tubular, single, pink flowers appear in early summer, and often again in autumn, amid oval, mid-green leaves. Zone 3. **'Superba'** illus. p.120. ssp. **patula** 'Miss Kim' (syn. *S. patula* 'Miss Kim'). Deciduous, mounded shrub with purple new shoots and foliage that often turns purple in fall. H 2.5m (8ft), S 3m (10ft). Pale lilac-blue flowers are in erect panicles in early summer. Zone 2.
S. reticulata. (Japanese tree lilac) Deciduous, broadly conical tree or shrub. H 10m (30ft), S 6m (20ft). Large panicles of fragrant, tubular, single, creamy-white flowers open above oval, taper-pointed, bright green leaves from early to mid-summer. Zone 2. 'Ivory Silk' is smaller. H 4m (12ft), S 2m (6ft). It is usually grown as a tree and flowers freely when young. Zone 2.
S. 'Royalty'. See *S.* x *josiflexa* 'Royalty'.
S. 'Souvenir de Louis Spaeth'. See *S. vulgaris* 'Andenken an Ludwig Spaeth'.
S. velutina of gardens. See *S. meyeri* 'Palibin'.
S. vulgaris 'Agincourt Beauty' bears short panicles of large, dark purple, single flowers with cupped petals. **'Andenken an Ludwig Spaeth'** (syn. *S.* 'Souvenir de Louis Spaeth'). Deciduous, upright, then spreading shrub. H and S 5m (15ft). Long, slender panicles of fragrant, tubular, single, deep purplish-red flowers are borne profusely above heart-shaped, dark green leaves in late spring. 'Beauty of Moscow'. See 'Krasavitsa Moskvy'. **'Belle de Nancy'** (syn. *S.* 'Belle de Nancy') has large, dense panicles of double, mauve-pink flowers opening from purple-red buds. **'Charles Joly'** (syn. *S.* 'Charles Joly'; illus. p.120), H and S 3m (10ft), carries deep purple-red flowers from mid-spring to early summer. **'Congo'** (syn. *S.* 'Congo'; illus. p.120) bears large panicles of single, deep lilac-purple flowers, purplish-red in bud, in spring. **'Decaisne'** (syn. *S.* 'Decaisne'; illus. p.120) is compact, with masses of single, dark blue flowers that are shaded purple, and mid-green leaves. **'Jan van Tol'** (syn. *S.* 'Jan van Tol'; illus. p.120) bears long, semi-pendent panicles of single, narrow-petalled, pure white flowers. **'Katherine Havemeyer'** (syn. *S.* 'Katherine Havemeyer') has double, lavender-purple, then lavender-pink flowers in dense, conical panicles. **'Krasavitsa Moskvy'** (syn. 'Beauty of Moscow') has dense panicles of double creamy-white flowers that open from lavender-tinted buds. **'Madame Antoine Buchner'** (syn. *S.* 'Madame Antoine Buchner'; illus. p.120) carries long, narrow panicles of deep purple-red buds, which open to double, pinkish-mauve flowers, fading with age. **'Madame F. Morel'** (syn. *S.* 'Madame F. Morel'; illus. p.120) produces large panicles of single, light violet-purple flowers that are purple in bud. **'Madame Florent Stepman'** (syn. *S.* 'Madame Florent Stepman'; illus. p.120) bears large panicles of single,

white flowers. **'Madame Lemoine'** (syn. *S.* 'Madame Lemoine'; illus. p.120) bears compact panicles of large, double, white flowers. **'Maréchal Foch'** (syn. *S.* 'Maréchal Foch'; illus. p.120) has broad, open panicles of very large, single, carmine-pink flowers. **'Masséna'** (syn. *S.* 'Masséna'; illus. p.120). bears loose panicles of large, deep red-purple flowers. **'Maud Notcutt'** (syn. *S.* 'Maud Notcutt') produces large panicles of single, pure white flowers. **'Michel Buchner'** (syn. *S.* 'Michel Buchner'; illus. p.120) has large panicles of double, pink-lilac flowers, each with a white eye. **'Monge'** (syn. *S.* 'Monge'; illus. p.120) produces masses of very large, single, deep purple-red flowers. **'Mrs Edward Harding'** (syn. *S.* 'Mrs Edward Harding'; illus. p.120) has large panicles of double or semi-double, purple-red flowers that fade to pink. **'Paul Thirion'** (syn. *S.* 'Paul Thirion'; illus. p.120) carries double lilac-pink flowers that open from deep purple-red buds. **'Président Grévy'** (syn. *S.* 'Président Grévy'; illus. p.120) bears very large panicles of double, lilac-blue flowers that open from red-violet buds. **'Primrose'** (syn. *S.* 'Primrose'; illus. p.120) produces small, dense panicles of pale yellow flowers. All zone 2. **'Sensation'** has slightly open trusses of single, deep purple flowers, with each petal edged in white.
S. yunnanensis (illus. p.120). Deciduous, upright shrub. H 3m (10ft), S to 3m (10ft). In early summer, large, oval, pointed, dark green leaves set off slender panicles of 4-petalled, pale pink or white flowers. Zone 3.

SYZYGIUM

MYRTACEAE

Genus of evergreen shrubs and trees, grown for their overall appearance. Tender, min. 10–13°C (50–56°F). Prefers full light (but tolerates some shade) and fertile, well-drained soil. Water containerized plants freely when in full growth, moderately at other times. Is very tolerant of pruning, but is best grown naturally. Propagate by seed in spring or semi-ripe cuttings in summer.
S. paniculatum, syn. *Eugenia australis* of gardens, *E. paniculata*, illus. p.81.

Szechuan birch. See *Betula szechuanica*.

T

TABEBUIA

BIGNONIACEAE

Genus of deciduous or evergreen, mainly spring-flowering trees, grown for their flowers and for shade. Tender, min. 16–18°C (61–4°F). Requires full light and fertile, well-drained but not dry soil. Pot-grown plants are unlikely to flower. Pruning, other than shaping while young in autumn, is not needed. Propagate by seed or air-layering in spring or by semi-ripe cuttings in summer.

T. chrysotricha illus. 97.
T. donnell-smithii. See *Cybistax donnell-smithii.*
T. pentaphylla of gardens. See *T. rosea.*
T. rosea, syn. *T. pentaphylla* of gardens (Pink trumpet tree). Fast-growing, evergreen, rounded tree, deciduous in cool climates. H and S 15m (50ft) or more. Leaves have 5 oval leaflets. Produces trumpet-shaped rose- to lavender-pink or white flowers, with yellow throats, in terminal clusters in spring.

Tacamahac. See *Populus balsamifera.*

TACCA

TACCACEAE

Genus of perennials with rhizomes, grown for their curious flowers. Tender, min. 18°C (64°F). Needs a fairly humid atmosphere, partial shade and peaty soil. Water sparingly during resting period in winter. Propagate by division or seed, if available, in spring.

T. chantrierei (Bat flower, Cat's whiskers). Clump-forming, rhizomatous perennial. H and S 30cm (1ft). Narrowly oblong, stalked, arching leaves are 45cm (1½ft) or more long. In summer produces flower umbels with green or purplish bracts on stems up to 60cm (2ft) long. Individual flowers are nodding, bell-shaped, 6-petalled and green, turning purple with long, pendent, maroon to purple threads.

T. leontopetaloides (East Indian arrowroot, South Sea arrowroot). Clump-forming, rhizomatous perennial. H and S 45cm (1½ft). Green leaves, to 1m (3ft) long, are deeply 3-lobed, each lobe also divided, on stalks to over 1m (3ft). In summer, on stems up to 1m (3ft) long, flower umbels are produced with 4–12 purple or brown bracts and 20–40 small, 6-petalled, yellow or purplish-green flowers, with long, purple to brown threads. Rhizomes yield edible starch.

Tacitus bellus. See *Graptopetalum bellum.*
Tacsonia mollissima. See *Passiflora mollissima.*
Tacsonia van-volxemii. See *Passiflora antioquiensis.*

TAGETES

ASTERACEAE/COMPOSITAE

Genus of annuals that flower continuously throughout summer and until the autumn frosts. Is useful as bedding plants and for edging. Grow in sun and in fertile, well-drained soil. Dead-head to ensure a long flowering period. Propagate by seed sown under glass in mid-spring. Is prone to slugs, snails and botrytis. The African marigolds are excellent for formal bedding, whereas the French, Afro-French, and Signet marigolds are more suitable for the edge of a mixed border. All are good in containers and provide long-lasting cut flowers. Contact with the foliage may aggravate skin allergies. Four main hybrid groups are in cultivation.

African marigolds (African Group) Compact annuals, derived from *T. erecta,* with angular, hairless stems and pinnate, sparsely glandular leaves, 5–10cm (2–4in) long, each with 11–17 narrowly lance-shaped, pointed, sharply toothed leaflets, to 5cm (2in) long. Large, densely double, pompon-like, terminal flower heads, usually to 12cm (5in) across, each with 5–8 or more ray-florets and numerous orange to yellow disc-florets, are produced from late spring to autumn. S to 45cm (18in).

French marigolds (French Group) Compact annuals, derived from *T. patula,* with hairless, purple-tinged stems and pinnate leaves, to 10cm (4in) long, with lance-shaped to narrowly lance-shaped, toothed leaflets, to 3cm (1¼in) long. Solitary, usually double flower heads, typically to 5cm (2in) across, with few to many red-brown, yellow, orange, or parti-coloured ray-florets and usually several disc-florets, are borne singly or in cyme-like inflorescences from late spring to autumn. S to 30cm (12in).

Afro-French marigolds (Afro-French Group) Bushy annuals, derived from crosses of *T. erecta* and *T. patula,* with angular to rounded stems, branched and sometimes stained purple, and pinnate leaves, 5–13cm (2–5in) long, with lance-shaped leaflets, to 5cm (2in) long. Numerous small, single or double, yellow or orange flower heads, usually 2.5–6cm (1–2½in) across, often marked red-brown, are borne singly or in cyme-like inflorescences from late spring to autumn. S 30–40cm (12–16in).

Signet marigolds (Signet Group) Upright annuals, derived from *T. tenuifolia,* with cylindrical, simple or many-branched stems and pinnate leaves, 5–13cm (2–5in) long, with narrowly lance-shaped, toothed leaflets, to 2cm (¾in) long. Many single flower heads, usually to 2.5cm (1in) across, with yellow or orange florets (few ray-florets and several disc-florets), are

borne in cyme-like inflorescences from late spring to autumn. S to 40cm (16in).

T. **Antigua Series.** African marigolds. H to 30cm (12in). Bear orange, lemon-yellow, golden-yellow, or primrose-yellow flower heads from late spring to early autumn.

T. **Beaux Series.** Afro-French marigolds. H 35cm (14in). Bear double flower heads of rich golden-yellow, orange with a red splash, or copper-red, from late spring to early autumn.

T. **Bonanza Series.** French marigolds. H 30cm (12in). In summer, they have double flower heads in deep orange-mahogany with gold margins, golden orange-mahogany, or orange-yellow-mahogany.

T. **Boy Series** illus. p.340.
T. **'Cinnabar'** illus. p.329.
T. **Disco Series.** French marigolds. H 20–25cm (8–10in). Single, weather-resistant flower heads in a range of colours, including yellow, golden-yellow with mahogany markings, golden-red and red-orange, are borne from late spring to early autumn.

T. erecta (African marigold, Aztec marigold). Fast-growing, upright, bushy annual. H 30cm–1m (1–3ft), S 30–45cm (1–1½ft). Has very deeply divided, aromatic, glossy, deep green leaves. Daisy-like, double flower heads, 5cm (2in) wide, are carried in summer and early autumn.

T. **Gem Series.** Signet marigolds. H to 23cm (9in). Produce flower heads in lemon-yellow, deep orange, or bright orange with darker markings. **'Lemon Gem'** has lemon-yellow flower heads. **'Tangerine Gem'** illus. p.340.

T. **'Gold Coins'** illus. p.336.
T. **'Honeycomb'.** French marigold. H 25cm (10in). Produces crested, double, yellow- and reddish-orange flower heads.

T. **Lady Series.** African marigolds. H 40–45cm (16–18in). Produce orange, primrose-yellow, yellow, or golden-yellow flower heads from late spring to early autumn.

T. **Marvel Series.** Compact African marigolds. H 45cm (18in). Produce densely double flower heads in gold, orange, yellow, lemon-yellow, or in a formula mixture of colours, from late spring to early autumn.

T. **Mischief Series.** French marigolds. H to 30cm (12in) or more. Have single flower heads in mahogany-red, yellow, or golden-yellow, with some bicolours, from late spring to early autumn.

T. **'Naughty Marietta'** illus. p.338.
T. **'Orange Winner'** illus. p.340.
T. patula (French marigold). Fast-growing, bushy annual. H and S to 30cm (1ft). Has deeply divided, aromatic, deep green leaves. Single or carnation-like, double flower heads, in shades of yellow, orange, red or mahogany, are borne in summer and early autumn.

T. **Safari Series 'Safari Tangerine'** (illus. p.43). French marigolds.

H 20–25cm (8–10in). Has double, broad-petalled, rich tangerine-orange flower heads from late spring to early autumn.

T. **Solar Series** illus. p.338.
T. **'Vanilla'.** African marigold. H to 35cm (14in). Has creamy-white flower heads from late spring to early autumn.

T. **Voyager Series.** Compact African marigolds. H 30–35cm (12–14in). Large, yellow or orange flower heads, to 10cm (4in) across, are borne from late spring to early autumn.

T. **Zenith Series.** Afro-French marigolds. H 30cm (12in). Have flower heads in yellow, golden-yellow, lemon-yellow, red, or orange, from late spring to early autumn.

Tail flower. See *Anthurium andraeanum,* illus. p.264.
Taiwan cherry. See *Prunus campanulata.*
Taiwan spruce. See *Picea morrisonicola,* illus. p.107.
Talbotia elegans. See *Vellozia elegans.*

TALINUM

PORTULACACEAE

Genus of summer-flowering perennials, some of which are evergreen, grown for their flowers and succulent foliage. Is useful for rock gardens, troughs and alpine houses and as pot plants. Needs sun and gritty, not too dry, well-drained soil. Propagate by seed in autumn.

T. okanoganense. Cushion- or mat-forming, prostrate perennial. H to 4cm (1½in), S to 10cm (4in). Succulent stems produce tufts of cylindrical, succulent, greyish-green leaves and, in summer, bear tiny, cup-shaped, white flowers. Is excellent for cultivating in a trough or alpine house.

Tall melic. See *Melica altissima.*
Tallow tree, Chinese. See *Sapium sebiferum.*
Tamarind. See *Tamarindus indica.*

TAMARINDUS

CAESALPINIACEAE/LEGUMINOSAE

Genus of one species of evergreen tree, grown for its edible fruits and overall appearance as well as for shade. Tender, min. 15–18°C (59–64°F). Needs full light and well-drained soil. Propagate by seed or air-layering in spring.

T. indica (Tamarind). Slow-growing, evergreen, rounded tree. H and S to 25m (80ft). Leaves have 10–15 pairs of oblong to elliptic, bright green leaflets. Produces profuse racemes of asymmetric, 5-petalled, pale yellow flowers, veined red, in summer, then long, brownish pods containing edible but acidic pulp.

Tamarisk. See *Tamarix.*

TAMARIX
Tamarisk

TAMARICACEAE

Genus of deciduous or evergreen shrubs and trees, grown for their foliage, habit and abundant racemes of small flowers. In mild areas is very wind-resistant and thrives in exposed, coastal positions, making excellent hedges. Requires sun and fertile, well-drained soil. Restrict growth by cutting back in spring; trim hedges at the same time. Propagate by semi-ripe cuttings in summer or by hardwood cuttings in winter.
T. parviflora. Deciduous spreading shrub. H 5m (15ft), S 6m (20ft). Has arching purple shoots with small pointed leaves. 4-petalled pale pink flowers are borne on arching racemes in late spring. Zone 4.
T. pentandra. See *T. ramosissima.*
T. ramosissima, syn. *T. pentandra,* illus. p.121.

TANACETUM

ASTERACEAE/COMPOSITAE

Genus of perennials, some of which are evergreen, often with aromatic foliage, grown for their daisy-like flower heads. Grow in sun and in fertile, well-drained soil. Propagate by division in spring. Contact with the foliage may aggravate skin allergies.
T. argenteum, syn. *Achillea argentea,* illus. p.360.
T. coccineum, syn. *Chrysanthemum coccineum, Pyrethrum coccineum, Pyrethrum roseum* (Pyrethrum).
'Brenda' (syn. *Pyrethrum* 'Brenda') illus. p.238. **'Eileen May Robinson'** is an upright perennial. H to 75cm (30in), S 45cm (18in). Has slightly aromatic, feathery, recurved leaves, 5cm (2in) long. In summer bears strong-stemmed, pink flower heads, 5cm (2in) wide, with yellow centres. Is useful for cut flowers. **'James Kelway'** has deep crimson flower heads ageing to pink.
T. densum subsp. **amani,** syn. *Chrysanthemum densum,* illus. p.361.
T. haradjanii, syn. *Chrysanthemum haradjanii.* Evergreen, mat-forming, woody-based perennial with a tap root. H and S 23–38cm (9–15in). Has broadly lance-shaped, much-divided, silvery-grey leaves and, in summer terminal clusters of bright yellow flower heads. Is useful for a rock garden or alpine house.
T. parthenium, syn. *Chrysanthemum parthenium, Pyrethrum parthenium,* illus. p.319. **'Aureum'** is a short-lived, bushy perennial, grown as an annual. H and S 20–45cm (8–18in). Has oval, lobed, aromatic, green-gold leaves and, in summer and early autumn, daisy-like, white flower heads.

TANAKAEA

SAXIFRAGACEAE

Genus of one species of evergreen, spreading perennial, grown for its foliage and flowers. Is suitable for rock gardens and peat beds. Needs partial shade and well-drained, peaty, sandy soil. Propagate by runners in spring.
T. radicans. Evergreen, dense, basal-rosetted perennial. H 6–8cm (2½–3in), S 20cm (8in). Leaves are narrowly oval to heart-shaped, leathery and mid- to dark green. Bears small panicles of tiny, outward-facing, star-shaped, white flowers in late spring.

Tanbark oak. See *Lithocarpus densiflorus.*
Tansy-leaved thorn. See *Crataegus tanacetifolia.*
Tape grass. See *Vallisneria spiralis.*

TAPEINOCHILOS

COSTACEAE/ZINGIBERACEAE

Genus of mostly evergreen perennials, grown for their colourful, leaf-like bracts. Tender, min. 18°C (64°F). Needs high humidity, partial shade and humus-rich soil. Is not easy to grow successfully in pots. Propagate by division in spring. Spider mite may be a problem with pot-grown plants.
T. ananassae. Evergreen, tufted perennial. H to 2m (6ft), S 75cm (2½ft). Non-flowering stems are erect and unbranched, with narrowly oval, long-pointed leaves, to 15cm (6in) long. Flowering stems are leafless, to over 1m (3ft) long, and, in summer, bear ovoid, dense spikes, 15cm (6in) or more long, of small, tubular, yellow flowers. Showy, recurved, hard, scarlet bracts enclose and almost hide flowers.

Tarajo holly. See *Ilex latifolia.*
Taro. See *Alocasia macrorrhiza; Colocasia esculenta,* illus. p.448.
Tasman celery pine. See *Phyllocladus aspleniifolius.*
Tasmanian blue gum. See *Eucalyptus globulus.*
Tasmanian podocarp. See *Podocarpus alpinus.*
Tasmanian sassafras. See *Atherosperma moschatum.*
Tasmanian snow gum. See *Eucalyptus coccifera,* illus. p.72.
Tasmanian waratah. See *Telopea truncata,* illus. p.131.
Tassel flower. See *Amaranthus caudatus,* illus. p.326; *Emilia coccinea,* illus. p.341.
Tassel grape hyacinth. See *Muscari comosum.*
Tassel maidenhair. See *Adiantum raddianum* 'Grandiceps'.
Tassel, Mountain. See *Soldanella montana.*
Tawny daylily. See *Hemerocallis fulva.*

TAXODIUM

TAXODIACEAE

See also CONIFERS.
T. distichum illus. p.104.

TAXUS

TAXACEAE

All parts (but not the seed coating) are highly toxic if ingested. See also CONIFERS.
T. baccata (Yew). Slow-growing conifer with a broadly conical, later domed crown. H 10–15m (30–50ft), S 5–10m (15–30ft). Needle-like, flattened leaves are dark green. Female plants bear cup-shaped, fleshy, bright red fruits; only the red part, not the seed, is edible. Will regrow if cut back. The following forms are H 6–10m (20–30ft), S 5–8m (15–25ft) unless otherwise stated. **'Adpressa'** is a shrubby, female form with short, broad leaves. **Aurea Group** (syn. *T.b.* 'Aurea'; illus. p.111) has golden-yellow foliage. **'Dovastoniana'** is spreading, with weeping branchlets. **'Dovastonii Aurea'** (illus. p.111) is similar to *T.b.* 'Dovastoniana', but has golden shoots and yellow-margined leaves. **'Fastigiata',** H 10–15m (30–50ft), S 4–5m (12–15ft), has erect branches and dark green foliage that stands out all around shoots. **'Fastigiata Aurea'** is similar to *T.b.* 'Fastigiata', but has gold-variegated leaves. **'Repandens',** H 60cm (2ft), S 5m (15ft), is a spreading form. **'Semperaurea',** H 3m (10ft), S 5m (15ft), has ascending branches with dense, golden foliage. All zone 6.
T. cuspidata illus. p.109. **'Aurescens'** is a spreading, bushy, dwarf conifer. H 30cm (1ft), S 1m (3ft). Is hardier than *T. baccata* forms. Needle-like, flattened leaves are deep golden-yellow in their first year and mature to dark green. **'Capitata',** H 10m (30ft), S 2m (6ft), is upright in habit. **'Densa',** H 1.2m (4ft), S 6m (20ft), is a female form with short, erect shoots. All zone 4.
T. × media. Dense conifer that is very variably shaped. H and S 3–6m (10–20ft). Has needle-like, flattened leaves, spreading either side of olive-green shoots. Leaves are stiff, broad and widen abruptly at the base. Fruits are similar to those of *T. baccata.* **'Brownii',** H 2.5m (8ft), S 3.5m (11ft), is a dense, globose form with dark green foliage. **'Densiformis',** H 2–3m (6–10ft), is dense and rounded, with masses of shoots that have bright green leaves. **'Hicksii',** H to 6m (20ft), is columnar and has ascending branches. Male and female forms exist. Zone 5b. **'Hillii',** H and S 3m (10ft), is a broadly conical to rounded, dense bush with glossy, green leaves. **'Wardii',** H 2m (6ft), S 6m (20ft), is a flat, globose, female form. Zone 5 except as noted.

Tea, Labrador. See *Ledum groenlandicum,* illus. p.154.
Tea-myrtle, Western. See *Melaleuca nesophila,* illus. p.145.
Tea-tree
    Duke of Argyll's. See *Lycium barbarum.*
    New Zealand. See *Leptospermum scoparium.*
Teasel. See *Dipsacus.*

TECOMA,
syn. TECOMARIA

BIGNONIACEAE

Genus of mainly evergreen shrubs and trees, grown for their flowers from spring to autumn. Tender, min. 5–13°C (41–55°F). Prefers moist but well-drained soil and full light. Water potted specimens moderately, hardly at all in winter. May be pruned annually after flowering to maintain as a shrub. Propagate by seed in spring or by semi-ripe cuttings in summer. Spider mite may be troublesome.
T. australis. See *Pandorea pandorana.*
T. capensis, syn. *Bignonia capensis* (Cape honeysuckle). Evergreen, scrambling climber, shrub-like when young. H 2–3m (6–10ft). Leaves have 5–9 rounded, serrated, glossy, dark green leaflets. Tubular, orange-red flowers are carried in short spikes mainly in spring-summer. **'Aurea'** (syn. *Tecomaria capensis* 'Aurea') illus. p.206.
T. grandiflora. See *Campsis grandiflora.*
T. radicans. See *Campsis radicans.*
T. ricasoliana. See *Podranea ricasoliana.*
T. stans, syn. *Bignonia stans, Stenolobium stans,* illus. p.96.

TECOMANTHE

BIGNONIACEAE

Genus of evergreen, twining climbers, grown for their flowers. Tender, min. 16–18°C (61–4°F). Provide humus-rich, well-drained soil and light shade in summer. Water freely when in full growth, less at other times. Provide stems with support. If necessary, thin out crowded stems in spring. Propagate by seed in spring or by semi-ripe cuttings in summer.
T. speciosa. Strong-growing, evergreen, twining climber. H to 10m (30ft) or more. Has leaves of 3 or 5 oval leaflets. Bears dense clusters of foxglove-like, fleshy-textured, cream flowers, tinged with green, in autumn.

Tecomaria. Reclassified as *Tecoma.*

TECOPHILAEA

LILIACEAE/TECOPHILAEACEAE

Genus of spring-flowering corms, rare in cultivation and extinct in the wild, grown for their beautiful flowers. Hardy, but because of rarity usually grown in a cold greenhouse or cold frame. Requires sun and well-drained soil. Water in winter and spring. Keep corms dry, but not sunbaked, from early summer to autumn, then replant. Propagate in autumn by seed or offsets.
T. cyanocrocus illus. p.433. var. **leichtlinii** (syn. *T.c.* 'Leichtlinii') illus. p.432.

Teddy-bear vine. See *Cyanotis kewensis.*

TELEKIA

ASTERACEAE/COMPOSITAE

Genus of summer-flowering perennials, grown for their bold foliage and large flower heads. Grows in sun or shade and in moist soil. Propagate by division in spring or by seed in autumn.
T. speciosa, syn. *Buphthalmum speciosum.* Upright, spreading perennial. H 1.2–1.5m (4–5ft), S 1–1.2m (3–4ft). Mid-green leaves are heart-shaped at

base of plant, oval on stems. In late summer, branched stems bear large, daisy-like, rich gold flower heads. Is ideal for a pool side or woodland.

Telesonix jamesii. See *Boykinia jamesii.*

TELLIMA

SAXIFRAGACEAE

Genus of one species of semi-evergreen, late spring-flowering perennial. Makes good ground cover and is ideal for cool, semi-shaded woodland gardens and beneath shrubs in sunny borders. Grows in any well-drained soil. Propagate by division in spring or by seed in autumn.

T. grandiflora (Fringecups). Semi-evergreen, clump-forming perennial. H and S 60cm (24in). Has heart-shaped, toothed, hairy, purple-tinted, bright green leaves. Bears racemes of small, bell-shaped, fringed, cream flowers, well above foliage, in late spring. **Rubra Group** (syn. *T.g.* 'Purpurea') illus. p.302.

TELOPEA

PROTEACEAE

Genus of evergreen trees and shrubs, grown mainly for their flower heads. Tender, min. 2°C (35°F). Requires full sun or semi-shade and humus-rich, moist but well-drained, neutral to acid soil. Water containerized plants freely when in full growth, moderately at other times. Propagate by seed in spring or by layering in winter.
T. speciosissima illus. p.142.
T. truncata illus. p.131.

Temple bells. See *Smithiantha cinnabarina.*
Temple juniper. See *Juniperus rigida.*

TEMPLETONIA

LEGUMINOSAE/PAPILIONACEAE

Genus of evergreen shrubs, grown for their flowers. Tender, min. 7°C (45°F). Prefers full light and freely draining, alkaline soil. Water potted specimens moderately, less in winter. Propagate by seed in spring or by semi-ripe cuttings in summer.
T. retusa (Coral bush). Evergreen, erect, irregularly branched shrub. H 2m (6ft), S 1–1.5m (3–5ft). Has oval to elliptic, leathery, bluish-green leaves. Pea-like, red flowers, sometimes pink or cream, appear in spring-summer.

Tenby daffodil. See *Narcissus obvallaris.*
Terebinth tree. See *Pistacia terebinthus.*

TERMINALIA

COMBRETACEAE

Genus of evergreen trees and shrubs, grown for their overall appearance, edible seeds (nuts) and for shade. Tender, min. 16–18°C (61–4°F). Requires full light and well-drained

soil. Water potted specimens moderately, scarcely at all when temperatures are low. Pruning is seldom necessary. Propagate by seed in spring.
T. catappa (Indian almond, Tropical almond). Evergreen, rounded tree. H and S 15m (50ft) or more. Has broadly oval, lustrous, green leaves at stem tips. Small, greenish-white flowers appear in spring, followed by flattened ovoid, keeled, green to red fruits, each with an edible seed.

TERNSTROEMIA

THEACEAE

Genus of evergreen trees and shrubs, grown for their overall appearance. Requires full sun or semi-shade and humus-rich, well-drained, neutral to acid soil. Water containerized specimens copiously when in full growth, moderately at other times. Prune in spring if necessary. Propagate by seed when ripe or in spring or by semi-ripe cuttings in late summer.
T. gymnanthera, syn. *T. japonica.* Evergreen, rounded, dense shrub. H and S 2m (6ft). Oval leaves are lustrous, mid- to deep green. In summer, pendent, 5-petalled, white flowers are borne singly from leaf axils. Pea-sized, berry-like, bright red fruits appear in autumn. Leaves of '**Variegata**' are white-bordered with a pink tinge. Zone 9.
T. japonica. See *T. gymnathera.*

Testudinaria elephantipes. See *Dioscorea elephantipes.*

TETRACENTRON

TETRACENTRACEAE

Genus of one species of deciduous tree, grown for its foliage and catkins. Needs sun or partial shade and fertile, well-drained soil. Propagate by seed in autumn.
T. sinense. Deciduous, spreading tree of graceful habit. H and S 10m (30ft) or more. Bears oval, finely toothed, dark green leaves and long, slender, yellow catkins in early summer. Zone 7.

TETRADIUM,
syn. EUODIA, EVODIA

RUTACEAE

Genus of deciduous trees, grown for their foliage, late flowers and fruits. Needs full sun and fertile, well-drained soil. Propagate by softwood cuttings in summer, by seed in autumn or by root cuttings in late winter.
T. daniellii, syn. *Euodia hupehensis.* Deciduous, spreading tree. H and S 15m (50ft). Ash-like, dark green leaves, with 5–11 oval to oblong leaflets, turn yellow in autumn. Has small, fragrant, 5-petalled, white flower clusters in early autumn, then beaked, red fruits. Zone 6.

TETRANEMA

SCROPHULARIACEAE

Genus of perennials, grown for their flowers. Tender, min. 13°C (55°F).

Grow in a light position, shaded from direct sunlight, and in well-drained soil; avoid waterlogging and a humid atmosphere. Propagate by division, or seed if available, in spring.
T. mexicanum. See *T. roseum.*
T. roseum, syn. *T. mexicanum*, illus. p.303.

TETRAPANAX

ARALIACEAE

Genus of one species of evergreen, summer- to autumn-flowering shrub, grown for its foliage. Requires full sun or partial shade and humus-rich, moist but well-drained soil. Water containerized specimens freely, less in winter. Leggy stems may be cut back to near ground level in winter. Propagate by suckers or seed in early spring.
T. papyrifer, syn. *Fatsia papyrifera*, illus. p.126.

TETRASTIGMA

VITACEAE

Genus of evergreen, woody-stemmed, tendril climbers, grown for their handsome leaves. Tender, min. 15–18°C (59–64°F). Grow in any fertile, well-drained soil, with shade in summer. Water freely while in active growth, less in low temperatures. Provide stems with support; cut out crowded stems in spring. Propagate by layering in spring or by semi-ripe cuttings in summer.
T. voinierianum, syn. *Cissus voinieriana*, illus. p.220.

TEUCRIUM

LABIATAE/LAMIACEAE

Genus of evergreen or deciduous shrubs, sub-shrubs and perennials, grown for their flowers, foliage (sometimes aromatic) or habit. Needs full sun and well-drained soil. Propagate shrubs and sub-shrubs by softwood or semi-ripe cuttings in summer, perennials by seed or division in spring.
T. aroanium. Evergreen, procumbent, much-branched sub-shrub. H 2.5cm (1in), S 10–15cm (4–6in). Has white-haired twigs and oblong to oval, slightly hairy leaves, which are densely hairy below, and, in summer, whorls of small, tubular, 2-lipped, purple flowers. Is good for a trough. Zone 8.
T. fruticans (Shrubby germander, Tree germander). '**Azureum**' is an evergreen, arching shrub. H 2m (6ft), S 4m (12ft). Has oval, aromatic, grey-green leaves, white beneath. Bears tubular, 2-lipped, deep blue flowers with prominent stamens in summer. Cut out dead wood in spring. Zone 9.
T. polium illus. p.379.

Texan walnut. See *Juglans microcarpa*, illus. p.92.

THALIA

MARANTACEAE

Genus of deciduous, perennial, marginal water plants, grown for their foliage and flowers. Tender, min. 7°C (45°F). Needs an open, sunny position

in up to 45cm (18in) depth of water. Some species tolerate cool water. Remove fading foliage regularly. Propagate in spring by division or seed.
T. dealbata. Deciduous, perennial, marginal water plant. H 1.5m (5ft). S 60cm (2ft). Oval, long-stalked, blue-green leaves have a mealy, white covering. Spikes of narrowly tubular, violet flowers in summer are followed by decorative seed heads. Tolerates cool water.
T. geniculata. Deciduous, perennial, marginal water plant. H 2m (6ft), S 60cm (2ft). Has oval, long-stalked, blue-green leaves and, in summer, spikes of narrowly tubular, violet flowers. Needs a warm pool.

THALICTRUM
Meadow rue

RANUNCULACEAE

Genus of perennials, grown for their divided foliage and fluffy flower heads. Flowers lack petals, but each has prominent tufts of stamens and 4 or 5 sepals, which rapidly fall. Does well at edges of woodland gardens. Tall species and cultivars make excellent foils in borders for perennials with bolder leaves and flowers. Requires sun or light shade. Grows in any well-drained soil, although some species prefer cool, moist conditions. Propagate by seed when fresh, in autumn, or by division in spring.
T. aquilegiifolium illus. p.251. '**White Cloud**' illus. p.240.
T. chelidonii. Clump-forming perennial. H 1–1.5m (3–5ft), S 60cm (2ft). Has finely divided, mid-green leaves and, in summer, produces panicles of fluffy, 4- or 5-sepalled, mauve flowers. Prefers cool soil that does not dry out.
T. delavayi, syn. *T. dipterocarpum* of gardens. Elegant, clump-forming perennial. H 1.5–2m (5–6ft), S 60cm (2ft). Has much-divided, mid-green leaves, above which large panicles of nodding, lilac flowers, with 4 or 5 sepals and prominent, yellow stamens, appear from mid- to late summer. **Hewitt's Double**' has double flowers.
T. diffusiflorum. Clump-forming perennial. H 1m (3ft), S 30–60cm (1–2ft). Has much-divided, basal, mid-green leaves. Slender stems produce large sprays of delicate, drooping, mauve flowers in summer. Prefers cool, moist soil.
T. dipterocarpum of gardens. See *T. delavayi.*
T. flavum. Clump-forming perennial. H 1.2m–1.5m (4–5ft), S 60cm (2ft). Has much-divided, glaucous blue-green leaves and, from mid- to late summer, clusters of fluffy, pale yellow flowers on slender stems. '**Illuminator**' is a pale yellow cultivar with bright green foliage.
T. kiusianum. Mat-forming perennial with short runners. H 8cm (3in), S 15cm (6in). Has small, fern-like, 3-lobed leaves and, throughout summer, loose clusters of tiny, purple flowers. Is excellent in a peat bed, rock garden, trough or alpine house. Is difficult to grow in hot, dry areas. Prefers shade and moist, sandy, peaty soil.

T. lucidum illus. p.254.
T. orientale. Spreading perennial with short runners. H 15cm (6in), S 20cm (8in). Leaves are fern-like with oval to rounded, lobed leaflets. Bears small, saucer-shaped, blue-mauve to violet flowers, with yellow stamens and large sepals, in late spring.

Thamnocalamus falconeri. See *Himalayacalamus falconeri.*
Thamnocalamus murieliae. See *Fargesia murieliae.*
Thamnocalamus spathaceus of gardens. See *Fargesia murieliae.*
Thatch-leaf palm. See *Howea forsteriana.*

THELOCACTUS
CACTACEAE

Genus of spherical to columnar, perennial cacti with ribbed or tuberculate stems. Elongated areoles in crowns produce funnel-shaped flowers. Tender, min. 7°C (45°F). Requires sun and well-drained soil. Propagate by seed in spring or summer.
T. bicolor illus. p.472.
T. leucacanthus. Clump-forming, perennial cactus. H 10cm (4in), S 30cm (12in). Spherical to columnar, dark green stem has 8–13 tuberculate ribs. Areoles each bear up to 20 short, golden spines and yellow flowers, 5cm (2in) across, in summer.
T. macdowellii, syn. *Echinomastus macdowellii.* Also sometimes included in *Neolloydia.* Spherical, perennial cactus. H and S 15cm (6in). Has a tuberculate, dark green stem densely covered with white spines, to 3cm (1¼in) long. Violet-red flowers, 4cm (1½in) across, appear in spring-summer.
T. setispinus, syn. *Ferocactus setispinus, Hamatocactus setispinus,* illus. p.467.

THELYPTERIS
THELYPTERIDACEAE

Genus of deciduous ferns. Tolerates sun or semi-shade. Grow in moist or very moist soil. Remove fading fronds regularly. Propagate by division in spring.
T. oreopteris. See *Oreopteris limbosperma.*
T. palustris illus. p.312.
T. phegopteris. See *Phegopteris connectilis.*

THERMOPSIS
LEGUMINOSAE/PAPILIONACEAE

Genus of summer-flowering perennials. Prefers sun and rich, light soil. Propagate by division in spring or by seed in autumn.
T. caroliniana. See *T. villosa.*
T. montana. See *T. rhombifolia.*
T. rhombifolia, syn. *T. montana,* illus. p.256.
T. villosa, syn. *T. caroliniana.* Straggling perennial. H 1m (3ft) or more, S 60cm (2ft). Bears racemes of pea-like, yellow flowers in late summer. Glaucous leaves are divided into 3 oval leaflets.

THESPESIA
MALVACEAE

Genus of evergreen perennials, shrubs and trees, grown for their flowers. Tender, min. 16–18°C (61–4°F). Needs full light and well-drained soil. Water containerized plants freely when in full growth, less at other times. Prune in early spring to maintain as a shrub. Propagate by seed in spring or by semi-ripe cuttings in summer. Whitefly and spider mite may be a nuisance.
T. populnea (Mahoe, Portia oil nut). Evergreen tree, bushy when young, thinning with age. H 12m (40ft) or more, S 3–6m (10–20ft). Leaves are heart-shaped. Intermittently, or all year round if warm enough, produces cup-shaped, yellow flowers, each with a maroon eye, that age to purple. Grows well by the sea.

Theves poplar. See *Populus nigra* 'Thevestina'.

THEVETIA
APOCYNACEAE

Genus of evergreen shrubs and trees, grown for their flowers from winter to summer. Is related to *Frangipani.* Has poisonous, milky sap. Tender, min. 16–18°C (61–4°F). Needs full light and well-drained soil. Water containerized specimens moderately, less in winter. Young stems may be tip pruned in winter to promote branching. Propagate by seed in spring or by semi-ripe cuttings in summer. The seeds are highly toxic if ingested.
T. neriifolia. See *T. peruviana.*
T. peruviana, syn. *T. neriifolia,* illus. p.93.

Thimbleberry. See *Rubus odoratus.*
Thistle. See *Carlina.*
  Alpine. See *Carlina acaulis,* illus. p.375.
  Blessed Mary's. See *Silybum marianum,* illus. p.322.
  Cotton. See *Onopordum acanthium,* illus. p.322.
  Globe. See *Echinops.*
  Mountain sow. See *Cicerbita alpina.*
  Scotch. See *Onopordum acanthium,* illus. p.322.

THLADIANTHA
CUCURBITACEAE

Genus of herbaceous or deciduous, tendril climbers, grown for their bell-shaped, yellow flowers and oval to heart-shaped, mid-green leaves. Requires a sheltered position in full sun and fertile, well-drained soil. Propagate by seed sown under glass in spring or by division in early spring.
T. dubia illus. p.216.

THLASPI
BRASSICACEAE/CRUCIFERAE

Genus of annuals and perennials, some of which are evergreen, grown for their flowers. Small plants may flower themselves to death, so remove buds for 2 years, to encourage a large plant.

Is difficult to grow at low altitudes and may require frequent renewal from seed. Is good for screes and troughs. Needs sun and moist but well-drained soil. Propagate by seed in autumn.
T. alpestre of gardens. See *T. alpinum.*
T. alpinum, syn. *T. alpestre* of gardens (Alpine penny-cress). Evergreen, mat-forming perennial. H 5cm (2in), S 10cm (4in). Has small, oval, mid-green leaves. Produces racemes of small, 4-petalled, white flowers in spring.
T. bulbosum. Clump-forming, tuberous perennial. H 8cm (3in), S 15–20cm (6–8in). Bears broadly oval, glaucous leaves and, in summer, racemes of 4-petalled, dark violet flowers. Suits a rock garden.
T. cepaeifolium subsp. *rotundifolium,* syn. *T. rotundifolium,* illus. p.365.
T. macrophyllum. See *Pachyphragma macrophyllum.*
T. rotundifolium. See *T. cepaeifolium* subsp. *rotundifolium.*

Thorn. See *Crataegus.*
  Chinese box. See *Lycium barbarum.*
  Christ's. See *Paliurus spina-christi,* illus. p.122.
  Cockspur. See *Crataegus crus-galli.*
  Glastonbury. See *Crataegus monogyna* 'Biflora'.
  Jerusalem. See *Paliurus spina-christi,* illus. p.122; *Parkinsonia aculeata.*
  Tansy-leaved. See *Crataegus tanacetifolia.*
  Washington thorn. See *Crataegus phaenopyrum.*
Thornless rose. See *Rosa* 'Zéphirine Drouhin', illus. p.197.
Thread agave. See *Agave filifera,* illus. p.465.
Thread palm. See *Washingtonia robusta,* illus. p.73.
Three birds toadflax. See *Linaria triornithophora,* illus. p.251.
Thrift. See *Armeria maritima.*
Throatwort. See *Trachelium caeruleum,* illus. p.330.

THUJA,
syn. PLATYCLADUS
CUPRESSACEAE

Contact with the foliage may aggravate skin allergies. See also CONIFERS.
T. koraiensis (Korean thuja). Upright conifer, sometimes sprawling and shrubby. H 3–10m (10–30ft), S 3–5m (10–15ft). Scale-like foliage is bright green or yellow-green above, glaucous silver beneath, and smells of almonds when crushed. Contact with the foliage may aggravate skin allergies. Zone 5b.
T. occidentalis (American arbor-vitae, Eastern white cedar, White cedar). Slow-growing conifer with a narrow crown. H 15m (50ft), S 3–5m (10–15ft). Has orange-brown bark and flat sprays of scale-like, yellowish-green leaves, pale or greyish-green beneath, smelling of apples when crushed. Ovoid cones are yellow-green, ripening to brown. 'Caespitosa' (illus. p.110). H 30cm (12in), S 40cm (16in), is a cushion-shaped, dwarf cultivar. 'Fastigiata', H to 15m (50ft), S to 5m (15ft), is broadly columnar, with erect, spreading branches and light green leaves. 'Filiformis' (illus. p.111), H 1.5m

(5ft), S 1.5–2m (5–6ft), forms a mound with pendent, whip-like shoots. 'Hetz Midget', H and S 50cm (20in), growing only 2.5cm (1in) each year, is a globose, dwarf form with blue-green foliage. 'Holmstrup', H 3–4m (10–12ft) S 1m (3ft), is slow-growing, dense and conical, with rich green foliage. 'Little Champion', H and S 50cm (20in) or more, is a globose, dwarf form, conical when young, with foliage turning brown in winter. 'Lutea Nana', H 2m (6ft) S 1–2m (3–6ft), is a dwarf form with golden-yellow foliage. 'Rheingold', H 3–4m (10–12ft), S 2–4m (6–12ft), is slow-growing, with golden-yellow foliage that becomes bronze in winter. 'Smaragd', H 2–2.5m (6–8ft), S 60–75cm (2–2½ft), is slow-growing and conical, with erect sprays of bright green leaves. 'Spiralis', H 10–15m (30–50ft), S 2–3m (6–10ft), produces foliage in twisted, fern-like sprays. 'Woodwardii', H 2.5m (8ft), S to 5m (15ft), is very slow-growing and globose, with mid-green foliage. All zone 3.
T. orientalis, syn. *Biota orientalis* (Biota, Chinese arbor-vitae, Chinese thuja). Conifer with an irregularly rounded crown. H 10–15m (30–50ft), S 5m (15ft). Has fibrous bark and flattened, vertical sprays of scale-like, scentless, dark green leaves. Egg-shaped cones are glaucous grey. 'Aurea Nana' (illus. p.111), H and S 60cm (24in), is a dwarf cultivar with yellow-green foliage that turns bronze in winter. 'Semperaurea' (illus. p.111), H 3m (10ft), S 2m (6ft), is compact, with golden leaves. All zone 6.
T. plicata (Western red cedar). Fast-growing, conical conifer that has great, curving branches low down. H 20–30m (70–100ft), S 5–8m (15–25ft), greater if lower branches self-layer. Has red-brown bark, scale-like, glossy, dark green leaves, which have a pineapple aroma when crushed, and erect, ovoid, green cones, ripening to brown. 'Atrovirens' has darker green foliage. 'Aurea' has golden-yellow foliage. 'Collyer's Gold' (illus. p.111), H to 2m (6ft), S 1m (3ft), is a dwarf form with yellow, young foliage turning light green. 'Cuprea', H 1m (3ft), S 75cm–1m (2½–3ft), is a conical shrub with copper- to bronze-yellow leaves. 'Hillieri' (illus. p.111), H and S to 1m (3ft), is a slow-growing, dense, rounded, dwarf shrub with moss-like, rich green foliage. 'Stoneham Gold' (illus. p.111), H 1–2m (3–6ft), S 1m (3ft), is a conical, dwarf form with bright gold foliage. 'Zebrina', H 15m (50ft), has leaves banded with yellowish-white. All zone 5b.

Thuja
  Chinese. See *Thuja orientalis.*
  Korean. See *Thuja koraiensis.*

THUJOPSIS
CUPRESSACEAE

See also CONIFERS.
T. dolabrata (Hiba). Conical or bushy conifer with a mass of stems.

H 10–20m (30–70ft), S 8–10m (25–30ft). Produces heavy, flat sprays of scale-like leaves, glossy, bright green above, silvery-white beneath. Small, rounded cones are blue-grey. Zone 6. **'Variegata'** illus. p.109.

THUNBERGIA

ACANTHACEAE

Genus of annual or mainly evergreen, perennial, twining climbers, perennials and shrubs, grown for their flowers. Tender, min. 7–15°C (45–59°F). Any fertile, well-drained soil is suitable, with full sun or light shade in summer. Water freely when in full growth, less at other times. Requires support. Thin out crowded stems in early spring. Propagate by seed in spring or by softwood or semi-ripe cuttings in summer.

T. alata illus. p.216.
T. coccinea. Evergreen, woody-stemmed, perennial, twining climber with narrowly oval leaves. H 6m (20ft) or more. Min. 15°C (59°F). Pendent racemes of tubular, scarlet flowers are produced in winter-spring.
T. gibsonii. See *T. gregorii.*
T. grandiflora (Blue trumpet vine). Evergreen, woody-stemmed, perennial, twining climber. H 6–10m (20–30ft). Tender, min. 10°C (50°F). Oval leaves, 10–20cm (4–8in) long, have a few tooth-like lobes. In summer has trumpet-shaped, pale to deep violet-blue flowers.
T. gregorii, syn. *T. gibsonii,* illus. p.217.
T. mysorensis illus. p.207.

Thyme. See *Thymus.*
  Caraway. See *Thymus herba-barona,* illus. p.381.

THYMUS
Thyme

LABIATAE/LAMIACEAE

Genus of evergreen, mat-forming and dome-shaped shrubs, sub-shrubs and woody-based perennials with aromatic leaves. Is useful for growing on banks and in rock gardens, troughs and paving. Requires sun and moist but well-drained soil. Propagate by softwood or semi-ripe cuttings in summer.

T. azoricus. See *T. caespititius.*
T. caespititius, syn. *T. azoricus, T. micans,* illus. p.375.
T. carnosus, syn. *T. nitidus* of gardens. Evergreen, spreading shrub. H and S 20cm (8in). Has tiny, narrowly oval, aromatic leaves. Erect flowering stems bear whorls of small, 2-lipped, white flowers in summer. Needs a sheltered position. Zone 7.
T. x *citriodorus* **'Aureus'.** Evergreen, spreading shrub. H 10cm (4in), S 10–25cm (4–10in). Tiny, rounded to oval, golden-yellow leaves are very fragrant when crushed. Produces terminal clusters of small, 2-lipped, lilac flowers in summer. Cut back in spring. Zone 7. **'Silver Queen'** bears silvery-white foliage.
T. herba-barona illus. p.381.
T. leucotrichus illus. p.381.
T. micans. See *T. caespititius.*

T. nitidus of gardens. See *T. carnosus.*
T. 'Porlock'. Evergreen, dome-shaped perennial. H 8cm (3in), S 20cm (8in). Thin stems are covered in small, rounded to oval, very aromatic, glossy, green leaves. In summer produces clusters of small, 2-lipped, pink flowers.
T. pseudolanuginosus. Evergreen, prostrate shrub. H 2.5–5cm (1–2in), S 20cm (8in) or more. Has dense mats of very hairy stems bearing tiny, aromatic, grey leaves. Produces 2-lipped, pinkish-lilac flowers in leaf axils in summer. Zone 5.
T. serpyllum. Evergreen, mat-forming sub-shrub. H 25cm (10in), S 45cm (18in). Finely hairy, trailing stems bear linear to elliptic to oval, mid-green leaves. Whorls of two-lipped, purple flowers are borne in summer. **'Annie Hall'**, H 5cm (2in), S 20cm (8in), has pale purple-pink flowers and light green leaves. **'Elfin'**, H 5cm (2in), S 10cm (4in), produces emerald-green leaves in dense hummocks; occasionally bears purple flowers. All zone 4.

Ti tree. See *Cordyline fruticosa.*

TIARELLA
Foamflower

SAXIFRAGACEAE

Genus of perennials, some of which are evergreen, that spread by runners. Is excellent as ground cover. Tolerates deep shade and prefers moist but well-drained soil. Propagate by division in spring.

T. cordifolia illus. p.347. var. *collina* see *T. wherryi.*
T. wherryi, syn. *T. cordifolia* var. *collina.* Slow-growing, clump-forming perennial. H 10cm (4in), S 15cm (6in). Triangular, lobed, hairy, basal, green leaves are stained dark red, with heart-shaped bases. Bears racemes of tiny, star-shaped, soft pink or white flowers from late spring to early summer.

TIBOUCHINA

MELASTOMATACEAE

Genus of evergreen perennials, sub-shrubs, shrubs and scandent climbers, grown for their flowers and leaves. Tender, min. 5–7°C (41–5°F). Prefers full sun and fertile, well-drained, neutral to acid soil. Water potted specimens freely when in full growth, moderately at other times. Cut back flowered stems, each to 2 pairs of buds, in spring. Tip prune young plants to promote branching. Propagate by greenwood or semi-ripe cuttings in late spring or summer.

T. semidecandra of gardens. See *T. urvilleana.*
T. urvilleana, syn. *T. semidecandra* of gardens, illus. p.122.

Tickseed. See *Coreopsis.*
Tidy tips. See *Layia platyglossa.*
Tiger flower. See *Tigridia pavonia,* illus. p.423.
Tiger lily. See *Lilium lancifolium.*
Tiger-jaws. See *Faucaria tigrina,* illus. p.479.

TIGRIDIA

IRIDACEAE

Genus of summer-flowering bulbs, grown for their highly colourful but short-lived flowers, rather iris-like in shape, with 3 large, outer petals. Needs sun and well-drained soil, with ample water in summer. Plant in spring. Lift in autumn; then partially dry bulbs and store in peat or sand at 8–12°C (46–54°F). Propagate by seed in spring.

T. pavonia illus. p.423.

TILIA
Lime, Linden

TILIACEAE

Genus of deciduous trees, grown for their small, fragrant, cup-shaped flowers and stately habit. Flowers attract bees, but are toxic to them in some cases. Requires sun or semi-shade and fertile, well-drained soil. Propagate species by seed in autumn, selected forms and hybrids by grafting in late summer. Except for *T.* x *euchlora,* trees are usually attacked by aphids, which cover growth and ground beneath with sticky honeydew. The nectar of *T.* 'Petiolaris' and *T. tomentosa* and may be toxic, especially to bumblebees.

T. americana (American linden, Basswood). Deciduous, spreading tree. H 25m (80ft), S 12m (40ft). Has large, rounded, sharply toothed, glossy, dark green leaves. Small, yellowish-white flowers appear in summer. Zone 2b.
T. cordata (Small-leaved linden). Deciduous, spreading tree. H 30m (100ft), S 12m (40ft). In mid-summer has small, glossy, dark green leaves and small, yellowish-white flowers. Zone 3. **'Greenspire'**, S 8m (25ft), is very vigorous and pyramidal in habit, even when young. **'Rancho'** illus. p.80.
T. x *euchlora* (Crimean linden). Deciduous, spreading tree with lower branches that droop with age. H 20m (70ft), S 10m (30ft). Rounded, very glossy, deep green leaves turn yellow in autumn. Bears small, yellowish-white flowers, toxic to bees, in summer. Is relatively pest-free. Zone 3.
T. x *europaea,* syn. *T.* x *vulgaris.* (European linden). Vigorous, deciduous, spreading tree. H 35m (120ft), S 15m (50ft). Trunk develops many burs. Has rounded, dark green leaves. Small, yellowish-white flowers, toxic to bees, appear in summer. Periodically remove shoots from burs at base. Zone 5.
T. henryana. Deciduous, spreading tree. H and S 10m (30ft). Broadly heart-shaped, glossy, bright green leaves, fringed with long teeth, are often tinged red when young. Has masses of small, creamy-white flowers in autumn. Zone 7.
T. mongolica (Mongolian linden). Deciduous, spreading, graceful tree. H 15m (50ft), S 12m (40ft). Young shoots are red. Heart-shaped, coarsely toothed, glossy, dark green leaves turn yellow in autumn. Small, yellowish-white flowers appear in summer. Zone 3b.
T. oliveri illus. p.67.
T. petiolaris. See *T.* 'Petiolaris'.
T. 'Petiolaris', syn. *T. petiolaris,* illus. p.68.

T. platyphyllos (Large-leaved linden). Deciduous, spreading tree. H 30m (100ft), S 20m (70ft). Has rounded, dark green leaves and small, dull yellowish-white flowers in mid-summer. **'Prince's Street'** is upright, with bright red shoots in winter. Zone 4.
T. tomentosa (European white linden, Silver linden). Deciduous, spreading tree. H 25m (80ft), S 20m (70ft). Leaves are large, rounded, sharply toothed, dark green above and white beneath. Very fragrant, small, dull white flowers, toxic to bees, are borne in late summer. Zone 4.
T. x *vulgaris.* See *T.* x *europaea.*

TILLANDSIA

BROMELIACEAE

Genus of evergreen, epiphytic perennials, often rosette-forming, some with branching stems and spirally arranged leaves, all grown for their flowers or overall appearance. Tender, min. 7–10°C (45–50°F). Requires semi-shade. Provide a rooting medium of equal parts humus-rich soil and either sphagnum moss or bark or plastic chips used for orchid culture. May also be grown on slabs of bark or sections of trees. Using soft water, water moderately in summer, sparingly at other times; spray plants grown on bark or tree sections with water several times a week from mid-spring to mid-autumn. Propagate by offsets or division in spring.

T. argentea (illus. p.265). Evergreen, basal-rosetted, epiphytic perennial. H and S 10–15cm (4–6in). Very narrow, almost thread-like leaves, covered with white scales, are produced in dense, near-spherical rosettes, each with a fleshy, bulb-like base. In summer, small, loose racemes of tubular, red flowers are produced.
T. caput-medusae (illus. p.265). Evergreen, basal-rosetted, epiphytic perennial. H and S 15cm (6in) or more. Linear, channelled, twisted and rolled, incurved leaves, covered in grey scales, develop in loose rosettes that have hollow, bulb-like bases. In summer, spikes of tubular, violet-blue flowers appear above foliage.
T. cyanea (illus. p.265). Evergreen, basal-rosetted, epiphytic perennial. H and S 25cm (10in). Forms dense rosettes of linear, pointed, channelled, arching, usually deep green leaves. In summer, broadly oval, blade-like spikes of pansy-shaped, deep purple-blue flowers, emerging from pink or red bracts, are produced among foliage.
T. fasciculata (illus. p.265). Evergreen, basal-rosetted, epiphytic perennial. H and S 30cm (12in) or more. Has dense rosettes of narrowly triangular, tapering, arching, mid-green leaves. In summer, flat spikes of tubular, purple-blue flowers emerge from red or reddish-yellow bracts, just above leaf tips. Bracts require strong light to develop reddish tones.
T. ionantha (Sky plant). Evergreen, clump-forming, basal-rosetted, epiphytic perennial. H and S 12cm (5in). Linear, incurved, arching leaves, covered in grey scales, are produced in dense rosettes; the inner leaves turn red at flowering time. Spikes of tubular,

699

violet-blue flowers, emerging in summer from narrow, white bracts, are borne just above foliage.

T. lindenii (Blue-flowered torch; illus. p.265). Evergreen, basal-rosetted, epiphytic perennial. H and S 40cm (16in). Linear, pointed, channelled, arching, mid-green leaves, with red-brown lines, form dense rosettes. In summer, produces blade-like spikes of widely pansy-shaped, deep blue flowers, emerging from sometimes pink-tinted, green bracts, which are borne just above leaves.

T. recurvata. Evergreen, basal-rosetted, epiphytic perennial. H and S 10–20cm (4–8in). Has long, loose, stem-like rosettes of linear, arching to recurved leaves, densely covered in silvery-grey scales. In summer produces short, dense spikes of small, tubular, pale blue or pale green flowers, which appear above the leaves.

T. stricta (illus. p.265). Evergreen, clump-forming, basal-rosetted, epiphytic perennial. H and S 20–30cm (8–12in). Narrowly triangular, tapering, arching, mid-green leaves, usually with grey scales, are produced in dense rosettes. Large, tubular, blue flowers emerge from drooping, cone-like spikes of bright red bracts, usually in summer.

T. usneoides (Spanish moss; illus. p.265). Evergreen, pendent, epiphytic perennial. H 1m (3ft) or more, S 10–20cm (4–8in). Slender, branched, drooping stems bear linear, incurved leaves densely covered in silvery-white scales. Inconspicuous, tubular, greenish-yellow or pale blue flowers, hidden among foliage, are produced in summer.

Timber bamboo. See *Phyllostachys bambusoides*, illus. p.308.
Tingiringi gum. See *Eucalyptus glaucescens*.
Tipa tree. See *Tipuana tipu*.
Tipu tree. See *Tipuana tipu*.

TIPUANA

LEGUMINOSAE/PAPILIONACEAE

Genus of one species of evergreen, spring-flowering tree, grown for its flowers and overall appearance when mature and for shade. In certain conditions, may be deciduous. Tender, min. 10–13°C (50–55°F). Requires full light and fertile, well-drained soil. Container-grown plants will not produce flowers. Young specimens may be pruned in winter. Propagate by seed in spring.

T. speciosa. See *T. tipu.*
T. tipu, syn. *T. speciosa* (Pride of Bolivia, Tipa tree, Tipu tree). Fast-growing, mainly evergreen, bushy tree. H 10m (30ft), S 8–10m (25–30ft). Bears leaves, 25cm (10in) long, with 11–25 oval leaflets. Produces pea-like, orange-yellow flowers, 3cm (1¼in) wide, in spring, followed by short, woody, winged, brownish pods in autumn-winter.

TITANOPSIS

AIZOACEAE

Genus of basal-rosetted, perennial succulents eventually forming small,

dense clumps. Produces 6–8 opposite pairs of fleshy, triangular leaves, 2–3cm (¾–1¼in) long, narrow at stems and expanding to straight tips. Tender, min. 8°C (46°F). Requires a position in sun and well-drained soil. Propagate by seed in spring or summer.

T. calcarea illus. p.479.
T. schwantesii. Clump-forming, perennial succulent. H 3cm (1¼in), S 10cm (4in). Has a basal rosette of triangular, grey-blue leaves, covered with small, wart-like, yellow-brown tubercles. Carries daisy-like, light yellow flowers, 2cm (¾in) wide, in summer-autumn.

TITHONIA

ASTERACEAE/COMPOSITAE

Genus of annuals. Grow in sun and in fertile, well-drained soil. Provide support and dead-head regularly. Propagate by seed sown under glass in late winter or early spring.

T. rotundifolia (Mexican sunflower). 'Torch' illus. p.340.

Toad lily. See *Tricyrtis.*
Toadflax. See *Linaria.*
  Alpine. See *Linaria alpina.*
  Dalmatian. See *Linaria genistifolia var. dalmatica.*
  Ivy-leaved. See *Cymbalaria muralis.*
  Purple. See *Linaria purpurea.*
  Three birds. See *Linaria triornithophora*, illus. p.251.
Toadshade. See *Trillium sessile*, illus. p.269.
Tobacco, Flowering. See *Nicotiana sylvestris*, illus. p.226.

TOLMIEA

SAXIFRAGACEAE

Genus of one species of perennial that is sometimes semi-evergreen and is grown as ground cover. Is suitable for cool woodland gardens. Prefers a position in shade and requires well-drained, neutral to acid soil. Propagate by division in spring or by seed in autumn.

T. menziesii (Pick-a-back-plant, Youth-on-age). Mat-forming perennial, sometimes semi-evergreen. H 45–60cm (18–24in), S 30cm (12in) or more. Young plantlets develop where ivy-shaped, mid-green leaves join stem. Produces spikes of tiny, nodding, tubular to bell-shaped, green and chocolate-brown flowers, which appear in spring.

TOLPIS

ASTERACEAE/COMPOSITAE

Genus of summer-flowering annuals and perennials. Grow in sun and in fertile, well-drained soil. Propagate by seed sown outdoors in spring.

T. barbata. Moderately fast-growing, upright, branching annual. H 45–60cm (1½–2ft), S 30cm (1ft). Has lance-shaped, serrated, mid-green leaves. Daisy-like, bright yellow flower heads, 2.5cm (1in) or more wide, with maroon centres, are produced in summer.

Tomato, Tree. See *Cyphomandra betacea*, illus. p.125.

TOONA

MELIACEAE

Genus of deciduous trees, grown for their foliage, autumn colour and flowers. Prefers full sun; requires fertile, well-drained soil. Propagate by seed in autumn, root cuttings in winter.

T. sinensis, syn. *Cedrela sinensis*, illus. p.79.

Toothwort. See *Lathraea clandestina*, illus. p.271.
Torch.
  Blue-flowered. See *Tillandsia lindenii*, illus. p.265.
  Striped. See *Guzmania monostachya*, illus. p.265.
Torch cactus. See *Echinopsis spachiana*, illus. p.457.
Torch lily. See *Kniphofia.*
Torch plant. See *Aloe aristata*, illus. p.480.
Torch, Striped. See *Guzmania monostachya*, illus. p.265.

TORENIA

SCROPHULARIACEAE

Genus of annuals and perennials. Tender, min. 5°C (41°F). Grow in semi-shade and in a sheltered position in fertile, well-drained soil. Pinch out growing shoots of young plants to encourage a busy habit. Propagate by seed sown under glass in early spring.

T. fournieri illus. p.333.

TORREYA

TAXACEAE

See also CONIFERS.
T. californica illus. p.107.

Totara, Alpine. See *Podocarpus nivalis*, illus. p.110.
Tovara virginiana 'Painter's Palette'. See *Persicaria virginiana* 'Painter's Palette'.

TOWNSENDIA

ASTERACEAE/COMPOSITAE

Genus of evergreen, short-lived perennials and biennials, grown for their daisy-like flower heads. Suits alpine houses as dislikes winter wet. Needs sun and moist soil. Propagate by seed in autumn.

T. grandiflora illus. p.383.
T. parryi. Evergreen, basal-rosetted, short-lived perennial. H 7–15cm (3–6in), S 5cm (2in). In late spring produces daisy-like, lavender or violet-blue flower heads, with bright yellow centres, above spoon-shaped leaves.

Toxicodendron succedaneum. See *Rhus succedanea.*
Toxicodendron verniciflu um. See *Rhus verniciflua.*
Toyon. See *Photinia arbutifolia.*

TRACHELIUM,

syn. DIOSPHAERA

CAMPANULACEAE

Genus of small perennials, useful for rock gardens and mixed borders. Some are good in alpine houses. Flowers of half-hardy species are ideal for cutting. Protect under glass in winter as they resent damp conditions. Grow in a sunny, sheltered position and in fertile, very well-drained soil (*T. asperuloides* prefers lime-rich soil). Propagate by seed in early or mid-spring or by softwood cuttings in spring.

T. asperuloides, syn. *Diosphaera asperuloides*, illus. p.383.
T. caeruleum illus. p.330.

TRACHELOSPERMUM

APOCYNACEAE

Genus of evergreen, woody-stemmed, twining climbers with stems that exude milky sap when cut. Tender, min. 2°C (35°F). Grow in any well-drained soil and in sun or semi-shade. Propagate by seed in spring, by layering in summer or by semi-ripe cuttings in late summer or autumn.

T. asiaticum. Evergreen, woody-stemmed, much-branched, twining climber. H to 6m (20ft). Bears oval, glossy, dark green leaves that are 2.5cm (1in) long. Scented, tubular, cream flowers, with expanded mouths, that age to yellow, are produced in summer. Pairs of long, slender pods, 12–22cm (5–9in) long, contain silky seeds.

T. jasminoides illus. p.207.

TRACHYCARPUS

ARECACEAE/PALMAE

Genus of evergreen, summer-flowering palms, grown for their habit, foliage and flowers. Requires full sun and does best in a position sheltered from strong, cold winds, especially when young. Needs fertile, well-drained soil. Propagate by seed in autumn or spring.

T. fortunei illus. p.84.

TRACHYMENE

APIACEAE/UMBELLIFERAE

Genus of summer-flowering annuals. Grow in a sunny, sheltered position and in fertile, well-drained soil. Support with sticks. Propagate by seed sown under glass in early spring.

T. coerulea, syn. *Didiscus coeruleus* (Blue lace flower). Moderately fast-growing, upright, branching annual. H 45cm (18in), S 20cm (8in). Has deeply divided, pale green leaves. Spherical heads, to 5cm (2in) wide, of tiny, blue flowers are produced in summer. Flowers are excellent for cutting.

TRADESCANTIA

Spiderwort

COMMELINACEAE

Genus of perennials, some of which are evergreen, grown for their flowers or ornamental foliage. Hardy to tender, min. 10–15°C (50–59°F). Grow in fertile, moist to dry soil and in sun or partial shade. Cut back or repropagate trailing species when they become straggly. Propagate hardy species by division, tender species by tip cuttings in spring, summer or autumn. Contact with the foliage may irritate skin.

T. albiflora. See *T. fluminensis*.

T. Andersoniana Group 'J.C. Weguelin', syn. *T.* 'J.C. Weguelin'. Clump-forming perennial. H to 60cm (2ft), S 45cm (1½ft). Has narrowly lance-shaped, fleshy, green leaves, 15–30cm (6–12in) long. In summer produces clusters of 3-petalled, lavender-blue flowers, 2.5cm (1in) or more wide, surrounded by 2 leaf-like bracts. **'Osprey'** (syn. *T.* 'Osprey') illus. p.276. **'Purple Dome'** (syn. *T.* 'Purple Dome') illus. p.284.

T. blossfeldiana. See *T. cerinthoides*.

T. cerinthoides, syn. *T. blossfeldiana*. Evergreen, creeping perennial. H 5cm (2in), S indefinite. Tender. Narrowly oval, fleshy, stem-clasping leaves, to 10cm (4in) long, are glossy, dark green above, purple with long, white hairs below. Intermittently produces clusters of tiny, pink flowers, with white centres, surrounded by 2 leaf-like bracts. Leaves of **'Variegata'** have longitudinal, cream stripes.

T. fluminensis, syn. *T. albiflora* (Wandering Jew). Evergreen perennial with trailing, rooting stems. H 5cm (2in), S to 60cm (24in) or more. Tender. Oval, fleshy leaves, 4cm (1½in) long, that clasp the stem, are glossy and green above, sometimes tinged purple below. Intermittently has clusters of tiny, white flowers enclosed in 2 leaf-like bracts. **'Albovittata'** and **'Variegata'** illus. p.300.

T. 'J.C. Weguelin'. See *T.* Andersoniana Group 'J.C. Weguelin'.

T. navicularis. See *Callisia navicularis*.

T. 'Osprey'. See *T.* Andersoniana Group 'Osprey'.

T. pallida 'Purpurea', syn. *T.p.* 'Purple Heart', *Setcreasea purpurea*, illus. p.303.

T. pexata. See *T. sillamontana*.

T. 'Purple Dome'. See *T.* Andersoniana Group 'Purple Dome'.

T. purpusii. See *T. zebrina* 'Purpusii'.

T. sillamontana, syn. *T. pexata*, *T. velutina*, illus. p.303.

T. spathacea, syn. *Rhoeo discolor*, *R. spathacea* (Boat lily, Moses-in-the-cradle). Evergreen, clump-forming perennial. H 50cm (20in), S 25cm (10in). Tender. Rosette of lance-shaped, fleshy leaves, to 30cm (12in) long, is green above, purple below. Bears tiny, white flowers, enclosed in boat-shaped, leaf-like bracts, year-round. **'Vittata'** has leaves striped longitudinally with pale yellow.

T. velutina. See *T. sillamontana*.

T. zebrina, syn. *Zebrina pendula*, illus. p.301. **'Purpusii'** (syn. *T. purpusii*) is a strong-growing, evergreen, trailing or mat-forming perennial. H 10cm (4in), S indefinite. Tender. Has elliptic, purple-tinged, bluish-green leaves and tiny, shallowly cup-shaped, pink flowers. **'Quadricolor'** has leaves striped green, pink, red and white.

Trailing arbutus. See *Epigaea repens*.
Trailing azalea. See *Loiseleuria procumbens*, illus. p.377.

TRAPA

TRAPACEAE

Genus of deciduous, perennial and annual, floating water plants, grown for their foliage and flowers. Tender, min. 5°C (41°F). Requires sun. Propagate in spring from seed gathered in autumn and stored in water or damp moss.

T. natans illus. p.449.

Traveller's joy. See *Clematis*.
Traveller's tree. See *Ravenala madagascariensis*.
Tree cotoneaster. See *Cotoneaster frigidus*.
Tree fern
   Australian. See *Cyathea australis*, illus. p.100; *Dicksonia antarctica*, illus. p.310.
   Black. See *Cyathea medullaris*.
Tree fuchsia. See *Fuchsia arborescens*, illus. p.164.
Tree germander. See *Teucrium fruticans*.
Tree heath. See *Erica arborea*.
   Spanish. See *Erica australis*.
Tree ivy. See × *Fatshedera lizei*, illus. p.152.
Tree lupin. See *Lupinus arboreus*, illus. p.169.
Tree mallow. See *Lavatera*.
Tree medick. See *Medicago arborea*.
Tree of heaven. See *Ailanthus altissima*.
Tree peony. See *Paeonia potaninii*.
Tree poppy. See *Romneya*.
Tree purslane. See *Atriplex halimus*.
Tree tomato. See *Cyphomandra betacea*, illus. p.125.
Trefoil, Moon. See *Medicago arborea*.
Trichocereus bridgesii. See *Echinopsis lageniformis*.
Trichocereus candicans. See *Echinopsis candicans*.
Trichocereus spachianus. See *Echinopsis spachiana*.

TRICHODIADEMA

AIZOACEAE

Genus of bushy, perennial succulents with woody or tuberous roots and cylindrical to semi-cylindrical leaves. Tender, min. 5°C (41°F). Needs sun and well-drained soil. Propagate by seed or stem cuttings in spring or summer.

T. densum. Tufted, perennial succulent. H 10cm (4in), S 20cm (8in). Cylindrical, pale green leaves are each 1–2cm (½–¾in) long and tipped with clusters of white bristles. Roots and prostrate, green stem are both fleshy and form caudex. Stem tip has daisy-like, cerise flowers, 3cm (1¼in) across, in summer.

T. mirabile illus. p.469.

TRICHOSANTHES

CUCURBITACEAE

Genus of annual and evergreen, perennial, tendril climbers, grown for their fruits and overall appearance.

Tender, min. 15–18°C (59–64°F). Needs full sun or partial shade and humus-rich soil. Water freely in growing season, less in cool weather. Provide support. Propagate by seed in spring at not less than 21°C (70°F).

T. anguina. See *T. cucumerina* var. *anguina*.

T. cucumerina var. **anguina**, syn. *T. anguina* (Snake gourd). Erect to spreading, annual, tendril climber. H 3–5m (10–15ft). Has broadly oval to almost triangular, sometimes shallowly 3- to 5-lobed, mid- to pale green leaves, to 20cm (8in) long. In summer produces 5-petalled, white flowers, 2.5–5cm (1–2in) across, with heavily fringed petals; females are solitary, the males in racemes. Cylindrical fruits, 60cm (2ft) or rarely to 2m (6ft) long, often twisted or coiled, are green-and-white striped and ripen to dull orange.

Trichosma suavis. See *Eria coronaria*.
Tricuspidaria lanceolata. See *Crinodendron hookerianum*.

TRICYRTIS
Toad lily

CONVALLARIACEAE/LILIACEAE

Genus of late summer- and autumn-flowering, rhizomatous perennials. Grows in sun or, in warm areas, in partial shade. Needs humus-rich, moist soil. Propagate by division in spring or by seed in autumn.

T. formosana, syn. *T. stolonifera*, illus. p.259.

T. hirta. Upright, rhizomatous perennial. H 30cm–1m (1–3ft), S 45cm (1½ft). In late summer and early autumn, clusters of large, open bell-shaped, white-spotted, purple flowers appear from axils of uppermost leaves. Leaves are narrowly oval, hairy and dark green and clasp stems. var. **alba** illus. p.294.

T. macrantha. Upright, rhizomatous perennial. H and S 60cm (24in). In early autumn has loose sheaves of open bell-shaped, deep primrose-yellow flowers, spotted light chocolate, at tips of arching stems, and small, oval leaves are dark green.

T. stolonifera. See *T. formosana*.

Trident maple. See *Acer buergerianum*.

TRIFOLIUM
Clover

LEGUMINOSAE/PAPILIONACEAE

Genus of annuals, biennials and perennials, some of which are semi-evergreen, with round, usually 3-lobed leaves and heads of pea-like flowers. Some species are useful in rock gardens or on banks, others in agriculture. Many are invasive. Needs sun and well-drained soil. Propagate by division in spring or by seed in autumn. Self-seeds readily.

T. repens 'Purpurascens' illus. p.388.

Trigger plant. See *Stylidium graminifolium*.

TRILLIUM
Trinity flower, Wood lily, Wakerubin

LILIACEAE/TRILLIACEAE

Genus of perennials with petals, sepals and leaves that are all borne in whorls of 3. Is excellent for woodland gardens. Enjoys partial shade and fertile, moist but well-drained, neutral to acid soil. Propagate by division after foliage has died down in summer or by seed in autumn.

T. cernuum illus. p.267.
T. chloropetalum illus. p.268.
T. erectum illus. p.269.
T. grandiflorum illus. p.268. **'Flore Pleno'** is a clump-forming perennial. H 38cm (15in), S 30cm (12in). Large, double, pure white flowers, are borne singly in spring, turning pink with age. Has large broadly oval, dark green leaves.
T. nivale (Dwarf white wood lily, Snow trillium). Early spring-flowering, rhizomatous perennial. H 7cm (3in), S 10cm (4in). Whorls of 3 oval leaves emerge at same time as outward-facing, slightly nodding, white flowers, each with 3 narrowly oval petals. Thrives in a trough or alpine house. Is difficult to grow.
T. ovatum illus. p.268.
T. rivale illus. p.365.
T. sessile illus. p.269.
T. undulatum (Painted trillium, Painted wood lily). Clump-forming perennial. H 10–20cm (4–8in), S 15–20cm (6–8in). Open funnel-shaped flowers with red-bordered, green sepals and 3 white or pink petals, each with a basal carmine stripe, are borne singly in spring, above broadly oval, basal, blue-green leaves.

Trillium
   Painted. See *Trillium undulatum*.
   Snow. See *Trillium nivale*.
Trinity flower. See *Trillium*.

TRIPETALEIA

ERICACEAE

Genus of one species of deciduous shrub, grown for its flowers; is now often included in *Elliottia*. Needs semi-shade and moist, peaty, neutral to acid soil. Propagate by softwood cuttings in summer or by seed in autumn.

T. paniculata, syn. *Elliottia paniculata*. Deciduous, upright shrub. H and S 1.5m (5ft). Bears upright panicles of pink-tinged, white flowers, each with 3 (or 4 or 5) narrow petals, from mid-summer to early autumn. Lance-shaped, dark green leaves persist well into autumn. Zone 7.

TRIPTERYGIUM

CELASTRACEAE

Genus of deciduous, twining or scrambling climbers, grown for their foliage and fruits. Grow in any fertile, well-drained soil and in full sun or light shade. Water freely while in full growth, less in low temperatures. Provide stems with support. Thin out crowded stems in winter or early spring. Propagate by seed when ripe or in spring or by semi-ripe cuttings in summer.

T. regelii. Deciduous, thin-stemmed,

twining or scrambling climber. H 10m (30ft). Leaves are oval and usually rich green. In late summer produces clusters, 20–25cm (8–10in) long, of small, off-white flowers, followed by 3-winged, pale green fruits. Zone 6.

Tristania conferta. See *Lophostemon confertus.*

TRITELEIA

ALLIACEAE/LILIACEAE

Genus of late spring- and early summer-flowering corms with wiry stems carrying *Allium*-like umbels of funnel-shaped flowers. Long, narrow leaves usually die away by flowering time. Needs an open but sheltered, sunny situation and well-drained soil that dries out to some extent in summer. Dies down in mid- to late summer until winter or spring; plant during dormancy in early autumn. Propagate by seed or offsets in autumn.
T. hyacinthina, syn. *Brodiaea hyacinthina*, *B. lactea*, illus. p.419.
T. ixioides, syn. *Brodiaea ixioides*, *B. lutea*. Early summer-flowering corm. H to 50cm (20in), S 8–10cm (3–4in). Bears semi-erect, basal leaves. Stem has a loose umbel, to 12cm (5in) across, of yellow flowers; petals each have a purple-stripe.
T. laxa, syn. *Brodiaea laxa*, illus. p.422.
T. peduncularis, syn. *Brodiaea peduncularis*. Early summer-flowering corm. H 10–40cm (4–16in), S 10–15cm (4–6in). Bears semi-erect, basal leaves. Stem has a loose umbel, to 35cm (14in) across, of white flowers, each 1.5–3cm (⅝–1¼in) long, faintly tinged blue.

TRITONIA

IRIDACEAE

Genus of corms, with flattish fans of sword-shaped, erect leaves, grown for their spikes of colourful flowers. Needs a sunny, sheltered site and well-drained soil. Plant corms in autumn (*T. disticha* subsp. *rubrolucens* in spring). Dry off once leaves start dying back in summer (winter for *T. disticha* subsp. *rubrolucens*). Propagate by seed in autumn or by offsets at replanting time.
T. crocata, syn. *T. hyalina*. Spring-flowering corm. H 15–35cm (6–14in), S 5–8cm (2–3in). Has erect, basal leaves. Each wiry stem has a loose spike of up to 10 widely cup-shaped, orange or pink flowers, 4–5cm (1½–2in) across, with transparent margins.
T. disticha subsp. *rubrolucens*, syn. *T. rosea*, *T. rubrolucens*, illus. p.420.
T. hyalina. See *T. crocata.*
T. rosea. See *T. disticha* subsp. *rubrolucens.*
T. rubrolucens. See *T. disticha* subsp. *rubrolucens.*

TROCHOCARPA

EPACRIDACEAE

Genus of evergreen shrubs, grown for their nodding flower spikes. Tender, min. 2°C (35°F). Needs sun and moist but well-drained, peaty, sandy soil. Propagate by semi-ripe cuttings in summer.

T. thymifolia. Slow-growing, evergreen, erect shrub. H 30cm (12in), S to 20cm (8in). Stems are covered in minute, thyme-like leaves. Carries 4cm (1½in) long spikes of tiny, bell-shaped, pink flowers in summer-autumn. Suits an alpine house.

TROCHODENDRON

TROCHODENDRACEAE

Genus of one species of evergreen tree, grown for its foliage and flowers. Needs shelter from strong, cold winds. Tolerates a sunny or shady position and requires moist but well-drained soil; dislikes very dry or very shallow, alkaline soil. Propagate by semi-ripe cuttings in summer or by seed in autumn.
T. aralioides illus. p.84.

TROLLIUS
Globeflower

RANUNCULACEAE

Genus of spring- or summer-flowering perennials that thrive beside pools and streams. Tolerates sun or shade. Does best in moist soil. Propagate by division in early autumn or by seed in summer or autumn.
T. × cultorum 'Alabaster' illus. p.274. 'Earliest of All' is a clump-forming perennial. H 60cm (24in), S 45cm (18in). Globular, butter-yellow flowers are borne singly in spring, above rounded, deeply divided, mid-green leaves. 'Goldquelle' has large, rich orange flowers. 'Orange Princess', H 75cm (30in), S 45cm (18in), bears orange-gold flowers.
T. europaeus illus. p.275. 'Canary Bird' is a clump-forming perennial. H 60cm (24in), S 45cm (18in). In spring bears globular, canary-yellow flowers above rounded, deeply divided, mid-green leaves.
T. pumilus illus. p.373.
T. yunnanensis. Clump-forming perennial. H 60cm (2ft), S 30cm (1ft). Has broadly oval leaves with 3–5 deep lobes. Produces buttercup-like, bright yellow flowers in late spring or summer.

Trompetilla, Scarlet. See *Bouvardia ternifolia*, illus. p.173.

TROPAEOLUM
Nasturtium

TROPAEOLACEAE

Genus of annuals, perennials and herbaceous, twining climbers, grown for their brightly coloured flowers. Hardy to tender, min. 5°C (41°F). Most species prefer sun and well-drained soil. Propagate by seed, tubers or basal stem cuttings in spring. Aphids and caterpillars of cabbage white butterfly and its relatives may cause problems.
T. Alaska Series illus. p.339.
T. azureum. Herbaceous, leaf-stalk climber with small tubers. H to 1.2m (4ft). Leaves, to 5cm (2in) across, have 5 narrow lobes. Small, purple-blue flowers, with notched petals, open in late summer.
T. canariense. See *T. peregrinum.*
T. 'Empress of India'. Fast-growing,

bushy annual. H 23cm (12in), S 45cm (18in). Has rounded, purple-green leaves. Trumpet-shaped, spurred, semi-double, rich scarlet flowers, 5cm (2in) wide, are borne from early summer to early autumn.
T. Gleam Series. Fast-growing, semi-trailing annual. H 40cm (16in), S 60cm (24in). Have rounded, mid-green leaves. From early summer to early autumn, bears trumpet-shaped, spurred, semi-double flowers, 5cm (2in) wide, in single colours or in a mixture that includes scarlet, yellow and orange and pastel shades.
T. Jewel Series illus. p.341.
T. majus. Fast-growing, bushy annual. H 1–3m (3–10ft), S 1.5–5m (5–15ft). Has rounded to kidney-shaped, wavy-margined, pale green leaves. From summer to autumn bears long-spurred, red, orange or yellow flowers, 5–6cm (2–2½in) wide. Many cultivars often attributed to *T. majus*, and with similar characteristics to the species, are of hybrid origin, and are described in this book under their cultivar names.
T. 'Peach Melba'. Fast-growing, bushy annual. H to 45cm (18in), S 30cm (12in). Bears rounded, mid-green leaves. Trumpet-shaped, spurred, pale yellow, flowers, 5cm (2in) wide, and blotched with scarlet are produced from early summer to early autumn.
T. peregrinum, syn. *T. canariense* (Canary creeper). Herbaceous, leaf-stalk climber. H to 2m (6ft). Grey-green leaves have 5 broad lobes. Small, bright yellow flowers, the 2 upper petals much larger and fringed, are borne from summer until first frosts. In cool areas is best grown as an annual.
T. polyphyllum illus. p.293.
T. speciosum illus. p.210.
T. tricolor. See *T. tricolorum.*
T. tricolorum, syn. *T. tricolor*, illus. p.205.
T. tuberosum illus. p.218. var. *lineamaculatum* 'Ken Aslet' illus. p.216.
T. Whirlybird Series'. Fast-growing, bushy annual. H 25cm (10in), S 35cm (14in). Have rounded, mid-green leaves. Trumpet-shaped, spurred, single to semi-double flowers, 5cm (2in) wide, are borne in a mixture or in single colours from early summer to early autumn.

Tropical almond. See *Terminalia catappa.*
Trumpet creeper, Chinese. See *Campsis grandiflora.*
Trumpet creeper. See *Campsis radicans.*
Trumpet flower. See *Bignonia capreolata.*
Trumpet gentian. See *Gentiana clusii.*
Trumpet, Golden. See *Allamanda cathartica.*
Trumpet, Herald's. See *Beaumontia grandiflora*, illus. p.205.
Trumpet tree, Golden. See *Tabebuia chrysotricha*, illus. p.97.
Trumpet tree, Pink. See *Tabebuia rosea.*
Trumpet vine. See *Campsis radicans.*
Trumpets. See *Sarracenia flava*, illus. p.290.

TSUGA

PINACEAE

See also CONIFERS.
T. canadensis illus. p.107. 'Aurea' (illus. p.111) is a broadly conical conifer, often with several stems. H 5m (15ft) or more, S 2–3m (6–10ft). Shoots are grey with spirally arranged, needle-like, flattened leaves, golden-yellow when young, ageing to green in second year, those along top inverted to show silver bands. Has ovoid, light brown cones. 'Bennett', H 1–2m (3–6ft), S 2m (6ft), is a compact, dwarf form with arching branches and a nest-shaped, central depression. 'Pendula' (syn. *T.c.* f. *pendula*) has weeping branches that may be trained to create a domed mound, H and S 3–5m (10–15ft), or left to spread at ground level, H 50cm (20in), S 2–5m (6–15ft). All zone 4.
T. caroliniana (Carolina hemlock). Conifer with a conical or ovoid crown. H 10–15m (30–50ft), S 5–8m (15–25ft). Red-brown shoots produce spirally set, needle-like, flattened, glossy, dark green leaves. Bears ovoid, green cones, ripening to brown. Zone 6b.
T. diversifolia (Japanese hemlock, Northern Japanese hemlock). Conifer with a broad, dense crown. H 10–15m (30–50ft), S 8–12m (25–40ft). Has orange shoots and needle-like, flattened, glossy, deep green leaves, banded with white beneath, that are spirally set. Ovoid cones are dark brown. Zone 6.
T. heterophylla (Western hemlock). Vigorous, conical conifer with drooping branchlets. H 20–30m (70–100ft), S 8–10m (25–30ft). Grey shoots bear spirally set, needle-like, flattened, dark green leaves with silvery bands beneath. Bears ovoid, pale green cones that ripen to dark brown. Zone 7.
T. mertensiana (Mountain hemlock). Narrowly conical conifer with short, horizontal branches. H 8–15m (25–50ft), S 3–6m (10–20ft). Red-brown shoots bear needle-like, flattened, glaucous blue-green or grey-green leaves, spirally arranged. Cones are cylindrical and yellow-green to purple, ripening to dark brown. Zone 7. 'Glauca' illus. p.105.
T. sieboldii (Japanese hemlock, Southern Japanese hemlock). Broadly conical conifer. H 15m (50ft), S 8–10m (25–30ft). Has glossy, buff shoots that bear needle-like, flattened, lustrous, dark green leaves, set spirally. Cones are ovoid and dark brown. Zone 7.

TSUSIOPHYLLUM

ERICACEAE

Genus of one species of semi-evergreen shrub, grown for its flowers. Is similar to *Rhododendron* and is suitable for rock gardens and peat beds. Requires shade and well-drained, peaty, sandy soil. Propagate by softwood cuttings in spring or early summer or by seed in autumn or spring.
T. tanakae. Semi-evergreen, spreading shrub. H 15cm (6in) or more, S 25cm (10in). Twiggy, branched stems bear tiny, narrowly oval, hairy leaves. In early summer produces small, tubular, white or pinkish-white flowers at stem tips. Zone 7.

TUBERARIA

CISTACEAE

Genus of annuals. Grow in sun and in any very well-drained soil. Propagate by seed in spring.

T. guttata, syn. *Helianthemum guttatum*. Moderately fast-growing, upright, branching annual. H and S 10–30cm (4–12in). Has lance-shaped, hairy, mid-green leaves and, in summer, yellow flowers, sometimes red-spotted at base of petals, that look like small, single roses.

Tuberose. See *Polianthes tuberosa*.
Tufted hair grass. See *Deschampsia cespitosa*.
Tufted sedge. See *Carex elata*.

TULBAGHIA

ALLIACEAE/LILIACEAE

Genus of semi-evergreen perennials. Needs full sun and well-drained soil. Propagate by division or seed in spring.

T. natalensis. Semi-evergreen, clump-forming perennial. H 12cm (5in), S 10cm (4in). In mid-summer, umbels of delicately fragrant, tubular, yellow-centred, white flowers, with spreading petal lobes, open above fine, grass-like, mid-green foliage.
T. violacea illus. p.283.

Tulip. See *Tulipa*.
　Golden globe. See *Calochortus amabilis*, illus. p.434.
　Horned. See *Tulipa acuminata*, illus. p.411.
　Lady. See *Tulipa clusiana*, illus. p.411.
　Mariposa. See *Calochortus*.
　Water lily. See *Tulipa kaufmanniana*, illus. p.412.
Tulip tree. See *Liriodendron tulipifera*, illus. p.65.
　African. See *Spathodea campanulata*, illus. p.71.
　Chinese. See *Liriodendron chinense*.

TULIPA

Tulip

LILIACEAE

Genus of mainly spring-flowering bulbs, grown for their bright, upward-facing flowers. Each bulb bears a few linear to lance-shaped, green or grey-green leaves on the stem. Flowers bear 6 usually pointed petals (botanically known as perianth segments) and 6 stamens, singly, unless otherwise stated below. Each plant has a spread of up to 20cm (8in). All are hardy unless otherwise stated. Requires a sunny position with well-drained soil and appreciates a summer baking; in cool, wet areas, bulbs may be lifted, when the leaves have died down, and stored in a dry place for replanting in autumn. Propagate by division of bulbs in autumn or for species by seed in spring or autumn. If ingested, all parts may cause mild stomach upset, and contact with any part may aggravate skin allergies.

Horticulturally, tulips are grouped into the following divisions. See also feature panel pp.410–12.

Div.1 Single early – has cup-shaped, single flowers, often opening wide in sun, from early to mid-spring.
Div.2 Double early – double flowers open wide, appear in early and mid-spring and are long-lasting.
Div.3 Triumph – sturdy stems bear rather conical, single flowers, opening to a more rounded shape, in mid- and late spring.
Div.4 Darwin hybrids – large, single flowers of variable shape are borne on strong stems from mid- to late spring.
Div.5 Single late – single flowers, variable in shape but often ovoid or squarish and usually with pointed petals, appear in late spring and very early summer.
Div.6 Lily-flowered – strong stems bear narrow-waisted, single flowers, with long, pointed petals often reflexed at tips, in late spring.
Div.7 Fringed – flowers are similar to those in Div.6, but have fringed petals.
Div.8 Viridiflora – variably shaped, single flowers, with partly greenish petals, are borne in late spring.
Div.9 Rembrandt – comprises mostly very old cultivars, similar to Div.6, but has colours 'broken' into striped or feathered patterns owing to virus. Flowers in late spring.
Div.10 Parrot – large, single flowers of variable shape, with petals frilled or fringed and usually twisted, appear in late spring.
Div.11 Double late (peony-flowered) – double flowers are usually bowl-shaped and appear in late spring.
Div.12 Kaufmanniana hybrids – single flowers are usually bicoloured, open flat in sun and are borne in early spring. Leaves are usually mottled or striped.
Div.13 Fosteriana hybrids – has large, single flowers that open wide in sun from early to mid-spring. Leaves are often mottled or striped.
Div.14 Greigii hybrids – large, single flowers appear in mid- and late spring. Leaves are generally wavy-edged, always mottled or striped.
Div.15 Miscellaneous – a miscellaneous category of other species and their varieties and hybrids. Flowers appear in spring and early summer.

T. acuminata (Horned tulip; illus. p.411). Div.15. Mid-spring-flowering bulb. H 30–45cm (12–18in). Flowers are 7–13cm (3–5in) long, with long-pointed, tapered, pale red or yellow petals, often tinged with red or green outside.
T. 'Ad Rem' (illus. p.411). Div.4. Mid- to late spring-flowering bulb. H 60cm (24in). Flowers are scarlet with black bases and yellow edges. Anthers are yellow.
T. aitchisonii. See *T. clusiana*.
T. 'Ancilla', Div.12. Early spring-flowering bulb. H 15cm (6in). Flowers are pink and reddish outside, white inside, each with a central, red ring.
T. 'Angélique' (illus. p.410), Div.11. Late spring-flowering bulb. H 40cm (16in). Delicately scented, double, pale

pink flowers deepen with age. Each petal has paler streaks and a lighter edge. Is good for bedding.
T. 'Apeldoorn's Elite' (illus. p.411), Div.4. Mid- to late spring-flowering bulb. H 60cm (24in). Has buttercup-yellow flowers feathered with cherry-red and with yellowish-green bases.
T. 'Apricot Beauty' (illus. p.412), Div.1. Early spring-flowering bulb. H 40cm (16in). Flowers are salmon-pink faintly tinged with red.
T. 'Artist' (illus. p.412), Div.8. Late spring-flowering bulb. H 45cm (18in). Flowers are salmon-pink and purple outside, sometimes marked with green, and deep salmon-pink and green inside.
T. 'Attila' (illus. p.411), Div.3. Mid-spring-flowering bulb. H 40cm (16in). Strong stems carry long-lasting, pink flowers. Is good for bedding.
T. aucheriana, Div.15. Early spring-flowering bulb. H to 20cm (8in). Has grey-green leaves. Yellow-centred, pink flowers, 2–5cm (¾–2in) long, each tapered at the base, have oval petals.
T. australis. See *T. sylvestris*.
T. bakeri. See *T. saxatilis*.
T. 'Balalaika' (illus. p.411), Div.5. Late spring-flowering bulb. H 50cm (20in). Bright red flowers each have a yellow base and black stamens.
T. 'Ballade' (illus. p.410), Div.6. Late spring-flowering bulb. H 50cm (20in). Reddish-magenta flowers with a white-edged, yellow base have long petals that are edged with white.
T. batalinii (illus. p.412), Div.15. Early spring-flowering bulb. H 10–30cm (4–12in). Is often included under *T. linifolia*. Leaves are grey-green. Flowers, 2–6cm (¾–2½in) long, have broadly oval petals and are bowl-shaped at the base. Pale yellow petals are darker yellow or brown at bases inside. Several cultivars are hybrids between *T. batalinii* and *T. linifolia*. These include **'Apricot Jewel'** with flowers that are orange-red outside, yellow inside; **'Bright Gem'**, which has yellow flowers flushed with orange; and **'Bronze Charm'**, which bears yellow flowers with bronze feathering.
T. 'Bellona' (illus. p.412), Div.1. Early spring-flowering bulb. H 30cm (12in). Fragrant flowers are deep golden-yellow. Is good for bedding and forcing.
T. biflora, syn. *T. polychroma* (illus. p.410), Div.15. Early spring-flowering bulb. H 5–10cm (2–4in). Has grey-green leaves. Stem bears 1–5 fragrant, yellow-centred, white flowers, 1.5–3.5cm (⅝–1½in) long and tapered at the bases. Narrowly oval petals are flushed outside with greenish-grey or greenish-pink. Suits a rock garden.
T. 'Bing Crosby' (illus. p.411), Div.3. Mid- to late spring-flowering bulb. H 50cm (20in). Has glowing, scarlet flowers.
T. 'Bird of Paradise' (illus. p.411), Div.10. Late spring-flowering bulb. H 45cm (18in). Produces cardinal-red flowers that are edged with orange and have bright yellow bases. Anthers are purple.
T. 'Blue Parrot' (illus. p.412), Div.10. Late spring-flowering bulb. H 60cm (24in). Very large, bright violet flowers, sometimes bronze outside, are borne on strong stems.

T. 'Burgundy Lace', Div.7. Late spring-flowering bulb. H 60cm (24in). Flowers are wine-red, each petal with a fringed edge.
T. 'Candela' (illus. p.412), Div.13. Early to mid-spring-flowering bulb. H 30cm (12in). Large flowers are yellow, with black anthers, and long-lasting.
T. 'Cape Cod' (illus. p.412), Div.14. Mid- to late spring-flowering bulb. H 45cm (18in). Grey-green leaves have reddish stripes. Yellowish-bronze flowers each have a black-and-red base; petals are edged with yellow outside.
T. 'Carnaval de Nice' (illus. p.410), Div.11. Late spring-flowering bulb. H 40cm (16in). Double flowers are white feathered with deep red.
T. 'China Pink' (illus. p.410), Div.6. Late spring-flowering bulb. H 55cm (22in). Flowers are pink, each with a white base, and have slightly reflexed petals.
T. 'Chopin', Div.12. Early spring-flowering bulb. H 20cm (8in). Has brown-mottled, grey-green leaves. Lemon-yellow flowers have black bases.
T. chrysantha. See *Tulipa clusiana* var. *chrysantha*.
T. 'Clara Butt', Div.5. Late spring-flowering bulb. H 60cm (24in). Flowers are salmon-pink. Is particularly good for bedding.
T. clusiana, syn. *T. aitchisonii* (Lady tulip; illus. p.411), Div.15. Mid-spring-flowering bulb. H to 30cm (12in). Has grey-green leaves. Each stem bears 1 or 2 flowers, 2–6.5cm (¾–2½in) long, that are bowl-shaped at the base. Narrowly oval, white petals are purple or crimson at base inside, striped deep pink outside. Stamens are purple. Flowers of var. *chrysantha* (syn. *T. chrysantha*; illus. p.412) are yellow, flushed red or brown outside, with yellow stamens, var. *stellata* has white flowers with yellow bases and yellow stamens.
T. 'Couleur Cardinal'. Div.3. Mid-spring-flowering bulb. H 35cm (14in). Plum-purple flowers are dark crimson-scarlet inside.
T. dasystemon of gardens. See *T. tarda*.
T. 'Dawnglow', Div.4. Mid- to late-spring-flowering bulb. H 60cm (24in). Pale apricot flowers are flushed with deep pink outside and are deep yellow inside. Has purple anthers.
T. 'Diana' (illus. p.410), Div.1. Early spring-flowering bulb. H 28cm (11in). Large, pure white flowers are carried on strong stems.
T. 'Dillenburg' (illus. p.412), Div.5. Late spring-flowering bulb. H 65cm (26in). Flowers are brick-orange and are good for bedding.
T. 'Don Quichotte' (illus. p.410), Div.3. Mid-spring-flowering bulb. H 40cm (16in). Purple-pink flowers are long-lasting.
T. 'Dreamboat' (illus. p.412), Div.14. Mid- to late spring-flowering bulb. H 25cm (10in). Produces grey-green leaves with brown stripes. Urn-shaped, red-tinged, amber-yellow flowers have greenish-bronze bases with red blotches.
T. 'Dreaming Maid' (illus. p.412), Div.3. Mid- to late spring-flowering bulb. H 55cm (22in). Flowers have violet petals edged with white.

T. 'Dreamland' (illus. p.411), Div.5. Late spring-flowering bulb. H 60cm (24in). Flowers are red with white bases and yellow anthers.

T. eichleri. See T. undulatifolia.

T. 'Estella Rijnveld' (illus. p.411), Div.10. Late spring-flowering bulb. H 60cm (24in). Large flowers are red, streaked with white and green.

T. 'Fancy Frills' (illus. p.410), Div.10. Late spring-flowering bulb. H 50cm (20in). Fringed, ivory-white petals are striped and edged with pink outside; inside, base is rose-pink. Anthers are pale yellow.

T. fosteriana, Div.15. Early spring-flowering bulb. H 20–45cm (8–18in). Has a downy stem and grey-green leaves, downy above. Flowers 4.5–10cm (1¾–4in) long, are bowl-shaped at the base with narrowly oval, bright red petals, and each has a purplish-black centre inside, ringed with yellow.

T. 'Fringed Beauty' (illus. p.411), Div.7. Early to mid-spring-flowering bulb. H 32cm (13in). Fringed petals are bright red with yellow edges. Is excellent for forcing.

T. 'Fringed Elegance', Div.7. Late spring-flowering bulb. H 50cm (20in). Has pale yellow flowers dotted with pink outside; inside, bases have bronze-green blotches. Each petal has a yellow fringe. Anthers are purple.

T. 'Gala Beauty', Div.9. Late spring-flowering bulb. H 60cm (24in). Yellow flowers are streaked with crimson.

T. 'Garden Party' (illus. p.411), Div.3. Mid- to late spring-flowering bulb. H 40–45cm (16–18in). Produces white flowers; petals are edged with deep pink outside and inside are streaked with deep pink.

T. 'Glück' (illus. p.411), Div.12. Early spring-flowering bulb. H 15cm (6in). Has reddish-brown-mottled, grey-green leaves. Petals are red, edged with yellow, outside and yellow inside, each with a darker base.

T. 'Golden Apeldoorn'(illus. p.412), Div.4. Mid- to late spring-flowering bulb. H 50–60cm (20–24in). Golden-yellow flowers each have a black base and black stamens.

T. 'Golden Artist' (illus. p.412), Div.8. Late spring-flowering bulb. H 45cm (18in). Flowers are bright golden-yellow.

T. 'Gordon Cooper' (illus. p.411), Div.4. Mid- to late spring-flowering bulb. H 60cm (24in). Petals are deep pink outside, edged with red; inside they are red with blue-and-yellow bases. Has black anthers.

T. 'Greenland'. See T. 'Groenland'.

T. greigii, Div.15. Early spring-flowering bulb. H 20–45cm (8–18in). Has downy stems. Leaves are streaked or mottled with red or purple. Cup-shaped flowers, 3–10cm (1¼–4in) long, with broadly oval, red or yellow petals, have yellow-ringed, black centres.

T. 'Greuze' (illus. p.412), Div.5. Late spring-flowering bulb. H 65cm (26in). Flowers are dark violet-purple and are good for bedding.

T. 'Groenland', syn. T. 'Greenland' (illus. p.410), Div.8. Late spring-flowering bulb. H 50cm (20in). Bears flowers with green petals that are edged with rose-pink. Is a good bedding tulip.

T. hageri (illus. p.411), Div.15. Mid-spring-flowering bulb. H 10–30cm (4–12in). Not as hardy. Stem has 1–4 flowers, 3–6cm (1½–2½in) long, tapered at the base and with oval, dull red petals tinged with green outside.

T. 'Heart's Delight', Div.12. Early spring-flowering bulb. H 20–25cm (8–10in). Has green leaves striped red-brown. Bears deep pinkish-red flowers, edged with pale pink, and pale pink inside with red-blotched, yellow bases.

T. 'Hollywood', Div.8. Late spring-flowering bulb. H 30cm (12in). Red flowers, tinged and streaked with green, have yellow bases. Is good for bedding.

T. humilis (illus. p.412), Div.15. Early spring-flowering bulb. A variable species, often considered to include T. aucheriana, T. pulchella and T. violacea. H to 20cm (8in). Has grey-green leaves. Stem bears usually 1, sometimes 2 or 3, pinkish-magenta flowers, 2–5cm (¾–2in) long, tapered at the base and with a yellow centre inside. Petals are oval. Is suitable for a rock garden.

T. 'Jack Laan', Div.9. Late spring-flowering bulb. H 60cm (24in). Purple flowers are shaded with brown and feathered with white and yellow.

T. 'Juan' (illus. p.411), Div.13. Early to mid-spring-flowering bulb. H 35cm (14in). Flowers are deep orange overlaid with scarlet. Leaves are marked with reddish-brown.

T. kaufmanniana (Water lily tulip; illus. p.412), Div.15. Early spring-flowering bulb. H 10–35cm (4–14in). Leaves are grey-green. Stem has 1–5 often scented flowers, 3–10cm (1½–4in) long and bowl-shaped at the base. Narrowly oval petals are usually either cream or yellow, flushed with pink or grey-green outside; centres are often a different colour. Pink, orange or red forms occasionally occur.

T. 'Keizerskroon' (illus. p.411), Div.1. Early spring-flowering bulb. H 35cm (14in). Flowers have crimson-scarlet petals, with broad, bright yellow margins. Is a good, reliable bedding tulip.

T. 'Kingsblood' (illus. p.411), Div.5. Late spring-flowering bulb. H 60cm (24in). Cherry-red flowers are edged with scarlet.

T. linifolia (illus. p.411), Div.15. Early spring-flowering bulb. H 10–30cm (4–12in). A variable species, often considered to include T. batalinii and T. maximowiczii. Has grey-green leaves. Red flowers, 2–6cm (¾–2in) long, are bowl-shaped at the base and, inside, have blackish-purple centres that are usually ringed with cream or yellow. Petals are broadly oval.

T. 'Lustige Witwe', syn. T. 'Merry Widow'(illus. p.411), Div.3. Mid- to late spring-flowering bulb. Flowers have deep glowing red petals edged with white.

T. 'Madame Lefèber', syn. T. 'Red Emperor' (illus. p.411), Div.13. Early to mid-spring-flowering bulb. H 35–40cm (14–16in). Produces very large, brilliant red flowers.

T. 'Maja' (illus. p.412), Div.7. Late spring-flowering bulb. H 50cm (20in). Produces egg-shaped, pale yellow flowers, with fringed petals, that

are bronze-yellow at the base. Anthers are yellow.

T. 'Margot Fonteyn' (illus. p.411), Div.3. Mid- to late spring-flowering bulb. H 40–45cm (16–18in). Flowers have yellow-edged, bright red petals, each with a yellow base inside. Anthers are black.

T. marjollettii (illus. p.411), Div.15. Mid-spring-flowering bulb. H 40–50cm (16–20in). Produces flowers, 4–6cm (1½–2½in) long and bowl-shaped at the base, with broadly oval, creamy-white petals, edged and marked with deep pink.

T. maximowiczii, Div.15. Early spring-flowering bulb. H 10–30cm (4–12in). Has grey-green leaves. Bright red flowers, 2–6cm (¾–2½in) long, with broadly oval petals, have white-bordered, black centres and are bowl-shaped at the base.

T. 'Menton' (illus. p.410), Div.5. Late spring-flowering bulb. H 60cm (24in). Flowers have rose-pink petals that are edged with light orange, and bright yellow and white bases. Anthers are yellow.

T. 'Merry Widow'. See T. 'Lustige Witwe'.

T. 'Monte Carlo', Div.2. Early spring-flowering bulb. H 40cm (16in). Has double, yellow flowers with sparse, red streaks.

T. 'New Design' (illus. p.410), Div.3. Mid-spring-flowering bulb. H 40cm (16in). Flowers have yellow petals that fade to pinkish-white and are edged with red outside and marked with apricot inside. Leaves have pinkish-white margins.

T. 'Orange Emperor', Div.13. Early to mid-spring-flowering bulb. H 40cm (16in). Flowers are bright orange, each with a yellow base inside and have black anthers.

T. 'Orange Triumph', Div.11. Late spring-flowering bulb. H 50cm (20in). Has double, soft orange-red flowers flushed with brown; each petal has a yellow margin.

T. 'Oranje Nassau' (illus. p.411), Div.2. Early spring-flowering bulb. H 25–30cm (10–12in). Has double, blood-red flowers flushed fiery orange-red. Is good for forcing.

T. 'Oratorio', Div.14. Mid- to late spring-flowering bulb. H 20cm (8in). Has reddish-brown-mottled, grey-green leaves. Broadly urn-shaped flowers are rose-pink outside, apricot-pink inside with black bases.

T. orphanidea (illus. p.412), Div.15. Mid-spring-flowering bulb. H 10–30cm (4–12in). Minimally hardy. Green leaves often have reddish margins. Stem has 1–4 flowers, 3–6cm (1¼–2½in) long and tapered at the base. Oval petals are orange-brown, tinged outside with green and often purple.

T. 'Page Polka' (illus. p.410), Div.3. Mid-spring-flowering bulb. Large, deep red flowers have white bases and are striped with white. Anthers are yellow.

T. 'Palestrina', Div.5. Late spring-flowering bulb. H 45cm (18in). Petals of large, salmon-pink flowers are green outside.

T. 'Peach Blossom', Div.2. Early spring-flowering bulb. H 25–30cm (10–12in). Produces double, silvery-

pink flowers flushed with deep pink.

T. 'Peer Gynt' (illus. p.411), Div.3. Mid- to late spring-flowering bulb. H 50cm (20in). Flowers have fuchsia-red petals with purple edges and white bases spotted with yellow. Anthers are purplish-grey.

T. 'Plaisir' (illus. p.411), Div.14. Mid- to late spring-flowering bulb. H 15–20cm (6–8in). Has grey-green leaves mottled with red-brown. Bears broadly urn-shaped, deep pinkish-red flowers, with petals edged pale yellow and with black-and-yellow bases.

T. polychroma. See T. biflora.

T. praestans 'Fusilier', Div.15. Early spring-flowering bulb. H 10–45cm (4–18in). Has a minutely downy stem and downy, grey-green leaves. Stem bears 3–5 flowers that are 5.5–6.5cm (2¼–2½in) long and bowl-shaped at the base. Oval petals are orange-scarlet. 'Unicum' (illus. p.411) has leaves that are edged with pale yellow. Flowers have bright red petals with yellow bases and blue-black anthers. 'Van Tubergen's Variety' (illus. p.412) produces 2–5 flowers per stem that are often yellow at the base; it increases very freely.

T. 'Prinses Irene' (illus. p.412), Div.1. Early spring-flowering bulb. H 30–35cm (12–14in). Produces orange flowers streaked with purple.

T. pulchella, Div.15. Early spring-flowering bulb. H to 20cm (8in). Has grey-green leaves. Flowers, 2–5cm (¾–2in) long and tapered at the base, have oval, purple petals and yellow or bluish-black centres inside. Is useful for a rock garden.

T. 'Purissima', syn. T. 'White Emperor' (illus. p.410), Div.13. Early to mid-spring-flowering bulb. H 35–40cm (14–16in). Flowers are pure white.

T. 'Queen of Night' (illus. p.412), Div.5. Late spring-flowering bulb. H 60cm (24in). The darkest of all tulips, has long-lasting, very dark maroon-black flowers on sturdy stems. Is useful for bedding.

T. 'Red Emperor'. See T. 'Madame Lefèber'.

T. 'Red Parrot' (illus. p.411), Div.10. Late spring-flowering bulb. H 60cm (24in). Large, raspberry-red flowers are carried on strong stems.

T. 'Red Riding Hood' (illus. p.411), Div.14. Late spring-flowering bulb. H 20cm (8in). Produces vivid, black-based, scarlet flowers amid spreading, dark green leaves that are mottled brownish-purple.

T. saxatilis, syn. T. bakeri (illus. p.410), Div.15. Early spring-flowering bulb. H 15–45cm (6–18in). Only slightly hardy. Has shiny, green leaves. Stem produces 1–4 scented flowers, 4–5.5cm (1½–2¼in) long and tapered at the base. Oval, pink to lilac petals are yellow at the base inside.

T. 'Shakespeare' (illus. p.412), Div.12. Early spring-flowering bulb. H 12–15cm (5–6in). Petals are deep red, edged with salmon, outside and salmon, flushed red with a yellow base, inside.

T. sprengeri (illus. p.411), Div.15. Late spring- and early summer-flowering bulb. H 30–45cm (12–18in). Flowers are 4.5–6.5cm (1¾–2½in) long and tapered at the base. Bears narrowly oval, orange-red petals, the outer 3 with buff-yellow backs. Is the latest-flowering tulip. Increases very rapidly.

T. **'Spring Green'** (illus. p.410), Div.8. Late spring-flowering bulb. H 35–38cm (14–15in). Has white flowers feathered with green. Anthers are pale green.

T. sylvestris, syn. *T. australis* (illus. p.412), Div.15. Early spring-flowering bulb. H 10–45cm (4–18in). Yellow flowers, usually borne singly, are 3.5–6.5cm (1½–2½in) long and tapered at the base. Narrowly oval petals are often tinged with green outside.

T. tarda, syn. *T. dasystemon* of gardens (illus. p.412), Div.15. Early spring-flowering bulb. H to 15cm (6in). Has glossy, green leaves. Flowers, 4–6 per stem, are 3–4cm (1¼–1½in) long and tapered at the base. Oval, white petals have yellow lower halves inside and are tinged with green and sometimes red outside. Suits a rock garden or raised bed.

T. **'Toronto'**, Div.14. Mid- to late spring-flowering bulb. H 30cm (12in). Has mottled leaves and 2 or 3 long-lasting flowers per stem. Open, broadly cup-shaped flowers have pointed, bright red petals each with a brownish-green-yellow base inside. Anthers are bronze.

T. turkestanica (illus. p.410), Div.15. Early spring-flowering bulb. H 10–30cm (4–12in). Has a hairy stem and grey-green leaves. Unpleasant-smelling flowers, up to 12 per stem, are 1.5–3.5cm (⅝–1½in) long and tapered at the base. Oval, white petals are flushed green or pink outside; flowers have yellow or orange centres inside.

T. **'Uncle Tom'** (illus. p.411), Div.11. Late spring-flowering bulb. H 50cm (20in). Double flowers are maroon-red.

T. undulatifolia, syn. *T. eichleri* (illus. p.411), Div.15. Early to mid-spring-flowering bulb. H 15–50cm (6–20in). Has a downy stem and grey-green leaves. Flowers, 3–8cm (1¼–3in) long, are bowl-shaped at the base. Narrowly oval, red or orange-red petals each have a pale red or buff back and a yellow-

bordered, dark green or black blotch at the base inside.

T. **'Union Jack'** (illus. p.411), Div.5. Late spring-flowering bulb. H 60cm (24in). Ivory-white petals, marked with deep pinkish-red 'flames', have blue-edged, white bases.

T. urumiensis (illus. p.412), Div.15. Early spring-flowering bulb. H 10–20cm (4–8in). Stem is mostly below soil level. Leaves are green or greyish-green. Bears 1 or 2 flowers, each 4cm (1½in) long and tapered at the base. Narrowly oval, yellow petals are flushed mauve or red-brown outside. Is useful for a rock garden.

T. violacea (illus. p.412), Div.15. Early spring-flowering bulb. H to 20cm (8in). Has grey-green leaves. Violet-pink flowers, 2–5cm (¾–2in) long, are tapered at the base and have yellow or bluish-black centres inside. Petals are oval. Suits a rock garden or raised bed.

T. **'West Point'** (illus. p.412), Div.6. Late spring-flowering bulb. H 50cm (20in). Primrose-yellow flowers have long-pointed, recurved petals.

T. **'White Dream'** (illus. p.410), Div.3. Mid- to late spring-flowering bulb. H 40–45cm (16–18in). Flowers are white with yellow anthers.

T. **'White Emperor'**. See *T.* 'Purissima'.

T. **'White Parrot'** (illus. p.410), Div.10. Late spring-flowering bulb. H 55cm (22in). Large flowers have ruffled, white petals flecked green near the base. Is good for cutting.

T. **'White Triumphator'** (illus. p.410), Div.6. Late spring-flowering bulb. H 65–70cm (26–28in). White flowers have elegantly reflexed petals.

T. whittallii (illus. p.412), Div.15. Mid-spring-flowering bulb. H 30–35cm (12–14in). Minimally hardy. Stem produces 1–4 flowers, 3–6cm (1¼–2½in) long and tapered at the base. Oval petals are bright brownish-orange.

T. **'Yokohama'** (illus. p.412), Div.1. Early to mid-spring-flowering bulb. H 35cm (14in). Pointed flowers are deep yellow.

Tumbling Ted. See *Saponaria ocymoides*, illus. p.378.

Tunic flower. See *Petrorhagia saxifraga*, illus. p.375.

Tunica saxifraga. See *Petrorhagia saxifraga*.

Tupelo. See *Nyssa*.

Turk's cap. See *Melocactus*.

Turkey oak. See *Quercus cerris*.

Turkish hazel. See *Corylus colurna*.

Turkscap lily. See *Lilium superbum*.

Turpentine, Cyprus. See *Pistacia terebinthus*.

TURRAEA

MELIACEAE

Genus of evergreen trees and shrubs, grown for their flowers and foliage. Tender, min. 12–15°C (54–9°F). Prefers full sun. Needs fertile, well-drained soil. Water freely in full growth, less at other times. Young plants may need growing point removed to promote branching. Prune after flowering if necessary. Propagate by seed in spring or by semi-ripe cuttings in summer.

T. obtusifolia illus. p.172.

Turtle-head. See *Chelone*.

TWEEDIA

ASCLEPIADACEAE

Genus of herbaceous, twining climbers; only one species is in general cultivation. Tender, min. 5°C (41°F). In cool climates may be grown as an annual. Grow in sun and in well-drained soil. Pinch out tips of shoots to encourage branching. Propagate by seed in spring.

T. caerulea, syn. *Oxypetalum caeruleum*, illus. p.215

Twin flower. See *Linnaea*.

Twin-flowered violet. See Viola biflora.

TYLECODON

CRASSULACEAE

Genus of deciduous, bushy, winter-growing, succulent shrubs with very swollen stems. Tender, min. 7°C (45°F). Likes sun and very well-drained soil. Propagate by seed or stem cuttings in summer. The leaves of *T. papillaris* subsp. *wallichii* are highly toxic if ingested.

T. paniculatus, syn. *Cotyledon paniculata* (Butter tree). Deciduous, bushy, succulent shrub. H and S 2m (6ft). Swollen stem and branches have papery, yellow coverings. Leaves are oblong to oval, fleshy and bright green. In summer produces clusters of tubular, green-striped, red flowers at stem tips.

T. papillaris subsp. *wallichii*, syn. *T. wallichii*, *Cotyledon wallichii*. Deciduous, bushy, succulent shrub. H and S 30cm (1ft). Has 3cm (1¼in) thick stems with cylindrical, grooved-topped, green leaves at tips. After leaf fall, stems are neatly covered in raised leaf bases. Bears tubular, yellow-green flowers, 2cm (½in) long, in autumn.

T. reticulatus, syn. *Cotyledon reticulata*, illus. p.465.

T. wallichii. See *T. papillaris* subsp. *wallichii*.

TYPHA

TYPHACEAE

Genus of deciduous, perennial, marginal water plants, grown for their decorative, cylindrical seed heads. Grows in sun or shade. Propagate in spring by seed or division.

T. latifolia illus. p.448. **'Variegata'** is a deciduous, perennial marginal water plant. H 90cm–1.2m (3–4ft), S indefinite. Strap-shaped, mid-green leaves have longitudinal, cream stripes. Spikes of beige flowers in late summer are followed by decorative, cylindrical, dark brown seed heads.

T. minima illus. p.449.

U

UGNI
ULMACEAE ...

MYRTACEAE

Genus of densely leafy, evergreen shrubs or trees. *U. molinae*, the only species usually cultivated, is valued for its foliage, flowers and fruit. Tender, min. 2°C (35°F). Needs full sun or partial shade and moist but well-drained soil. Propagate by semi-ripe cuttings in late summer.

U. molinae, syn. *Eugenia ugni*, *Myrtus ugni*. Evergreen, upright, densely branched shrub. H 1.5m (5ft), S 1m (3ft). Glossy, dark green leaves are oval. Has fragrant, slightly nodding, cup-shaped, white-pink-tinted flowers in late spring, then aromatic, edible, spherical, dark red fruits.

ULEX
LEGUMINOSAE/PAPILIONACEAE/

Genus of leafless, or almost leafless, shrubs that appear evergreen as a result of their year-round, green shoots and spines. Is grown for its flowers in spring. Needs full sun, and prefers poor, well-drained, acid soil. Trim each year after flowering to maintain compact habit. Straggly, old plants may be cut back hard in spring. Propagate by seed in autumn. The seeds may cause mild stomach upset if ingested.

U. europaeus illus. p.157.

'Flore Pleno' is a leafless, or almost leafless, bushy shrub. H 1m (3ft), S 1.2m (4ft). In spring, bears masses of fragrant, pea-like, double, yellow flowers on leafless, dark green shoots. Zone 7.

Ulmo. See *Eucryphia cordifolia*.

ULMUS
Elm

ULMACEAE

Genus of deciduous or, rarely, semi-evergreen trees and shrubs, often large and stately, grown for their foliage and habit. Inconspicuous flowers appear in spring. Requires full sun and fertile, well-drained soil. Propagate by softwood cuttings in summer or by seed or suckers in autumn. Is susceptible to Dutch elm disease, which is quickly fatal, although *U. parvifolia* and *U. pumila* appear more resistant than other species and hybrids.

U. americana (American elm, White elm). Deciduous, spreading tree. H and S 30m (100ft). Has grey bark and drooping branchlets. Large, oval, dark green leaves are sharply toothed and rough-textured. Zone 3.

U. angustifolia. See *U. minor* subsp. *angustifolia*. var. **cornubiensis** see *U. minor* 'Cornubiensis'.

U. 'Camperdownii'. See *U. glabra* 'Camperdownii'.

U. carpinifolia. See *U. minor*.

U. 'Dicksonii'. See *U. minor* 'Dicksonii'.

U. glabra (Wych elm). Deciduous, spreading tree. H 30m (100ft), S 25m (80ft). Has broadly oval, toothed, very rough, dark green leaves, often slightly lobed at tips. From mid- to late spring bears clusters of winged, green fruits on bare branches. **'Camperdownii'** (syn. *U.* 'Camperdownii') illus. p.92. **'Exoniensis'** (Exeter elm), H 15m (50ft), S 5m (15ft), is narrow with upright branches when young, later becoming more spreading. All zone 5.

U. × *hollandica* (Dutch elm). Vigorous, deciduous tree with a short trunk and spreading to arching branches. H 30m (100ft), S 25m (80ft). Has oval, toothed, glossy, dark green leaves. Is very susceptible to Dutch elm disease. **'Jacqueline Hillier'**, H and S 2m (6ft), is slow-growing and suitable for hedging. Small leaves, rough-textured and sharply toothed, form 2 rows on each shoot; they persist into early winter. **'Vegeta'** (Huntingdon elm), H 35m (120ft), has upright, central branches and pendent, outer shoots. Broadly oval leaves turn yellow in autumn. All zone 4b.

U. minor, syn. *U. carpinifolia* (Smooth-leaved elm). Deciduous, spreading tree with arching branches and pendent shoots. H 30m (100ft), S 20m (70ft). Small, oval, toothed, glossy, bright green leaves turn yellow in autumn. subsp. **angustifolia** (syn. *U. angustifolia*; Goodyer's elm) has a rounded canopy and elliptic to oval, double-toothed, mid- to dark green leaves, paler beneath. **'Cornubiensis'** (syn. *U. angustifolia* var. *cornubiensis*; Cornish elm), S 15m (50ft), is conical when young and with a vase-shaped head when mature. **'Dicksonii'** (syn. *U.m.* 'Sarniensis Aurea', *U.* 'Dicksonii', *U.* 'Wheatleyi Aurea') illus. p.81. **'Sarniensis'** (Jersey elm, Wheatley elm), S 10m (30ft), is a conical, dense tree with upright branches. Small, sharply toothed, mid-green leaves are mid-green. **'Sarniensis Aurea'** see *U.m.* 'Dicksonii'. All zone 5b.

U. parvifolia (Chinese elm). Deciduous or semi-evergreen, rounded tree. H and S 15m (50ft). Small, oval, glossy, dark green leaves last well into winter or, in mild areas, may persist until fresh growth appears. Zone 5.

U. procera (English elm). Vigorous, deciduous, spreading tree with a bushy, dense, dome-shaped head. H 35m (120ft), S 15m (50ft). Broadly oval, toothed, rough, dark green leaves turn yellow in autumn. Zone 6.

U. pumila (Siberian elm). Deciduous, spreading, sometimes shrubby tree. H 15m (50ft), S 12m (40ft). Has oval, toothed, dark green leaves. Has some resistance to Dutch elm disease, but seedlings may be susceptible in hot summers. Zone 3b.

U. 'Wheatleyi Aurea'. See *U. minor* 'Dicksonii'.

UMBELLULARIA
Headache tree

LAURACEAE

Genus of evergreen, spring-flowering trees, grown for their aromatic foliage, although the scent of the crushed leaves may induce headaches and nausea in some people. Requires shelter from strong, cold winds when young. Needs sun and fertile, moist but well-drained soil. Propagate by seed in autumn.

U. californica illus. p.74.

Umbrella leaf. See *Diphylleia cymosa*.
Umbrella pine. See *Pinus pinea*, illus. p.109.
  Japanese. See *Sciadopitys verticillata*, illus. p.106
Umbrella plant. See *Darmera*.
Umbrella tree, Queensland. See *Schefflera actinophylla*, illus. p.84.
Unicorn plant. See *Martynia annua*, illus. p.320.
Urceolina peruviana. See *Stenomesson miniatum*.

URGINEA
HYACINTHACEAE/LILIACEAE

Genus of late summer- or early autumn-flowering bulbs, growing on or near soil surface, with spear-shaped flower spikes up to 1.5m (5ft) high. Needs sun and well-drained soil that dries out while bulbs are dormant in summer. Plant in mid- to late summer. Water until leaves die down. Propagate by seed in autumn or by offsets in late summer.

U. maritima (Crusaders' spears, Sea onion, Sea squill). Late summer- or early autumn-flowering bulb. H 1.5m (5ft), S 30–45cm (1–1½ft). Broadly sword-shaped, erect, basal leaves appear in autumn after a long spike of star-shaped, white flowers, each 1–1.5cm (½–⅝in) across, has developed.

Urn plant. See *Aechmea fasciata*, illus. p.265.

URSINIA
ASTERACEAE/COMPOSITAE

Genus of annuals, evergreen perennials and sub-shrubs, grown mainly for their flower heads usually in summer, a few species for their foliage. Marginally hardy to tender, min. 5–7°C (41–5°F). Needs full light and well-drained soil. Water potted plants moderately, less when not in full growth. Requires good ventilation if grown under glass. Propagate by seed or greenwood cuttings in spring. Aphids are sometimes troublesome.

U. anthemoides illus. p.338.

U. chrysanthemoides. Evergreen, bushy perennial. H and S 60cm (2ft) or more. Tender. Narrowly oval, feathery, strongly scented, green leaves are 5cm (2in) long. Has small, long-stalked, daisy-like, yellow flower heads, sometimes coppery below, in summer.

U. sericea. Evergreen, bushy sub-shrub. H and S 25–45cm (10–18in). Tender. Leaves are cut into an elegant filigree of very slender, silver-haired segments. Daisy-like, yellow flower heads, 4cm (1½in) across, in summer. Mainly grown for its foliage.

UTRICULARIA
LENTIBULARIACEAE

Genus of deciduous or evergreen, perennial, carnivorous water plants with bladder-like, modified leaves that trap and digest insects. Most species in cultivation are free-floating. Hardy to tender, min. 7°C (45°F). Some species are suitable only for tropical aquariums; those grown in outdoor pools require full sun. Thin out plants that are overcrowded or become laden with algae. Propagate by division of floating foliage in spring or summer.

U. exoleta. See *U. gibba*.

U. gibba, syn. *U. exoleta*. Deciduous, perennial, free-floating water plant. S 15cm (6in). Tender. Slender stems carry finely divided, mid-green leaves on which small bladders develop. Pouched, bright yellow flowers are borne in summer. Is evergreen in very warm water; suitable only for a tropical aquarium.

U. vulgaris. Deciduous, perennial, free-floating water plant. S 30cm (12in). Much-divided, bronze-green leaves, studded with small bladders, are produced on slender stems. Bears pouched, bright yellow flowers in summer. May be grown in a pool or cold-water aquarium.

UVULARIA
CONVALLARIACEAE/LILIACEAE

Genus of spring-flowering perennials that thrive in moist woodlands. Requires semi-shade and prefers moist but well-drained, peaty soil. Propagate in early spring, before flowering, by division.

U. grandiflora illus. p.274.

U. perfoliata. Clump-forming perennial. H 45cm (18in), S 30cm (12in). In spring, clusters of pendent, bell-shaped, pale yellow flowers with twisted petals appear on numerous slender stems above stem-clasping, narrowly oval, mid-green leaves.

VACCINIUM

ERICACEAE

Genus of deciduous or evergreen sub-shrubs, shrubs and trees, grown for their foliage, their autumn colour (on deciduous species), their flowers and their fruits, which are often edible. Requires a position in sun or semi-shade and moist but well-drained, peaty or sandy, acid soil. Propagate by semi-ripe cuttings in summer or by seed in autumn.
V. angustifolium. var. **laevifolium** illus. p.172.
V. arctostaphylos (Caucasian whortleberry). Deciduous, upright shrub. H 3m (10ft), S 2m (6ft). Has red-brown young shoots and oval, dark green leaves that mature to red and purple in autumn. Bell-shaped, white flowers, tinged with red, are produced in spreading racemes in early summer, followed by spherical, purplish-black fruits. Zone 7.
V. corymbosum (Highbush blueberry) illus. p.160. **'Pioneer'** illus. p.173.
V. glaucoalbum illus. p.176.
V. myrtillus (Bilberry, Whortleberry). Deciduous, usually prostrate shrub. H 15cm (6in) or more, S 30cm (12in) or more. Bears small, heart-shaped, leathery, bright green leaves. Produces pendent, bell-shaped, pale pink flowers in early summer; these are followed by edible, round, blue-black fruits. Zone 6.
V. nummularia. Evergreen, prostrate shrub. H 10cm (4in), S 20cm (8in). Slender stems, covered in red-brown bristles, bear oval, wrinkled, bright green leaves with red-brown bristles at their margins. Produces small racemes of bell-shaped, white to deep pink flowers at stem tips in early summer, followed by small, round, black fruits. Is suitable for growing in a rock garden or peat bed. Needs semi-shade. May also be propagated by division in spring. Zone 8.
V. parvifolium illus. p.173.
V. vitis-idaea (Cowberry). Vigorous, evergreen, prostrate shrub, spreading by underground runners. H 2–25cm (¾–10in), S indefinite. Forms hummocks of oval, hard, leathery leaves. Bell-shaped, white to pink flowers are borne in nodding racemes from early summer to autumn, followed by bright red fruits in autumn-winter. May also be propagated by division in spring. Zone 1. subsp. **minus** (syn. **V.v.-i.** 'Minus') illus. p.366.

Valerian. See **Valeriana**.
  Cat's. See **Valeriana officinalis**, illus. p.241.
  Common. See **Valeriana officinalis**, illus. p.241.
  Red. See **Centranthus ruber**, illus. p.245.

VALERIANA

Valerian

VALERIANACEAE

Genus of summer-flowering perennials that are suitable for growing in borders and rock gardens. Requires a position in sun and well-drained soil. Propagate by division in autumn, but **V. officinalis** is best propagated by seed in spring.
V. officinalis illus. p.241.
V. phu **'Aurea'** illus. p.274.

VALLEA

ELAEOCARPACEAE

Genus of one species of evergreen shrub, grown for its overall appearance. Best at 3–5°C (37–41°F) to prevent foliage being damaged by cold. Prefers a position in full sun and humus-rich, well-drained soil. Containerized plants should be watered freely during the growing season, moderately at other times. Untidy growth may be cut out in early spring. Propagate by seed in spring or by semi-ripe cuttings in summer. Spider mite may be a nuisance.
V. stipularis. Evergreen, erect, then loose and spreading shrub. H and S 2–5m (6–15ft). Leaves are lance-shaped to rounded and lobed, deep green above, grey beneath. Small, cup-shaped flowers, each with 5 deep pink petals that have 3 lobes, are borne in small, terminal and lateral clusters in spring-summer.

VALLISNERIA

HYDROCHARITACEAE

Genus of evergreen, perennial, submerged water plants, grown for their foliage. Is suitable for pools and aquariums. Tender, min. 5°C (41°F). Requires sun or semi-shade and deep, clear water. Remove fading foliage, and thin overcrowded plants as required. Propagate by division in spring or summer.
V. americana, syn. **V. gigantea**. Vigorous, evergreen, perennial, submerged water plant. S indefinite. Quickly grows to form colonies of long, strap-shaped, mid-green leaves. Produces insignificant, greenish flowers all year-round.
V. gigantea. See **V. americana**.
V. spiralis (Eel grass, Tape grass). Vigorous, evergreen, perennial, submerged water plant. S indefinite. Forms a mass of long, strap-shaped, mid-green leaves, but on a smaller scale than **V. americana**. Insignificant, greenish flowers are borne year-round.

Vallota speciosa. See **Cyrtanthus elatus**.
Van Volxem's maple. See **Acer velutinum** var. **vanvolxemii**.

VANCOUVERIA

BERBERIDACEAE

Genus of perennials, some of which are evergreen, suitable for ground cover. Prefers cool, partially shaded positions and moist, peaty soil. Propagate by division in spring.
V. chrysantha. Evergreen, sprawling perennial. H 30cm (12in), S indefinite. Oval, dark green leaves borne on flower stems are divided into rounded diamond-shaped leaflets with thickened, undulating margins. Loose sprays of small, bell-shaped, yellow flowers are borne in spring.
V. hexandra illus. p.347.

VANDA

See also ORCHIDS.
V. Rothschildiana (illus. p.298). Evergreen, epiphytic orchid for a cool or intermediate greenhouse. H 60cm (24in). Sprays of dark-veined, violet-blue flowers, 10cm (4in) across, are borne twice a year in varying seasons. Has narrowly oval, rigid leaves, 10–12cm (4–5in) long. Grow in a hanging basket and provide good light in summer.

Variegated apple mint. See **Mentha suaveolens** 'Variegata', illus. p.276.
Variegated Bishop's weed. See **Aegopodium podagraria** 'Variegatum', illus. p.276.
Variegated creeping soft grass. See **Holcus mollis** 'Albovariegatus', illus. p.306.
Variegated gout weed. See **Aegopodium podagraria** 'Variegatum', illus. p.276.
Variegated ground ivy. See **Glechoma hederacea** 'Variegata', illus. p.300.
Variegated iris. See **Iris variegata**, illus. p.235.
Variegated Leyland cypress. See x **Cupressocyparis leylandii** 'Harlequin', illus. p.104.
Variegated purple moor grass. See **Molinia caerulea** 'Variegata'.
Varnish tree. See **Rhus verniciflua**.
Veitch fir. See **Abies veitchii**, illus. p.102.
Veitch's screw pine. See **Pandanus tectorius** 'Veitchii', illus. p.175.

VELLOZIA

VELLOZIACEAE

Genus of evergreen perennials and shrubs, grown for their showy flowers. Tender, min. 10°C (50°F). Grow in full sun and moderately fertile, sharply drained soil. Propagate by seed or division in spring.
V. elegans, syn. **Barbacenia elegans**, **Talbotia elegans**. Evergreen, mat-forming perennial with slightly woody stems. H to 15cm (6in), S 15–30cm (6–12in). Lance-shaped, leathery, dark green leaves, to 20cm (8in) long, each has a V-shaped keel. In late spring bears solitary small, star-shaped, white flowers on slender stems above leaves.

VELTHEIMIA

HYACINTHACEAE/LILIACEAE

Genus of winter-flowering bulbs with dense spikes of pendent, tubular flowers and rosettes of basal leaves. Tender, min. 10°C (50°F). Requires good light, to keep foliage compact and to develop flower colours fully, and well-drained soil. Plant in autumn with tips above soil surface. Reduce watering in summer. Propagate by seed or offsets in autumn.
V. bracteata, syn. **V. capensis** of gardens, **V. undulata**, **V. viridifolia**, illus. p.425.
V. capensis, syn. **V. glauca**, **V. viridifolia** of gardens. Winter-flowering bulb. H 30–45cm (12–18in), S 20–30cm (8–12in). Has a basal rosette of lance-shaped leaves, usually with very wavy edges. Stem produces a dense spike of pink or red flowers, each 2–3cm (¾–1¼in) long.
V. capensis of gardens. See **V. bracteata**.
V. glauca. See **V. capensis**.
V. undulata. See **V. bracteata**.
V. viridifolia. See **V. bracteata**.
V. viridifolia of gardens. See **V. capensis**.

Velvet plant. See **Gynura aurantiaca**, illus. p.220.
Venetian sumach. See **Cotinus coggygria**.
x **Venidioarctotis.** Reclassified as **Arctotis**, also as **Arctotis** Harlequin Hybrids.
Venus flytrap. See **Dionaea muscipula**, illus. p.305.
Venus's navelwort. See **Omphalodes linifolia**, illus. p.318.

VERATRUM

LILIACEAE/MELANTHIACEAE

Genus of perennials, with poisonous black rhizomes, ideal for woodland gardens. Requires semi-shade and fertile, moist soil. Propagate by division or seed in autumn. All parts are highly toxic if ingested. Contact with the foliage may irritate the skin.
V. album (White false hellebore). Clump-forming perennial. H 2m (6ft), S 60cm (2ft). Basal leaves are pleated, oval and dark green. Stems bear dense, terminal panicles of saucer-shaped, yellowish-white flowers in summer.
V. nigrum illus. p.228.

VERBASCUM

Mullein

SCROPHULARIACEAE

Genus of mainly summer-flowering perennials, some of which are semi-evergreen or evergreen, and evergreen biennials and shrubs. Tolerates shade, but prefers an open, sunny site and well-drained soil. Propagate species by seed in spring or late summer or by root cuttings in winter, selected forms by root cuttings only. Some species self seed freely.

V. bombyciferum. Evergreen, erect biennial. H 1.2–2m (4–6ft), S 60cm (2ft). Oval leaves and stems are covered with silver hairs. Produces upright racemes densely set with 5-lobed, yellow flowers in summer.

V. chaixii. Erect perennial, covered with silvery hairs. H 1m (3ft), S 60cm (2ft). Has oval, toothed, rough, nettle-like leaves. Produces slender spires of 5-lobed, yellow, sometimes white flowers, with purple stamens, in summer.

V. 'Cotswold Queen'. Short-lived, rosette-forming perennial. H 1–1.2m (3–4ft), S 30–60cm (1–2ft). Throughout summer, branched racemes of 5-lobed, apricot-buff flowers are borne on stems that arise from oval, mid-green leaves.

V. densiflorum, syn. *V. thapsiforme.* Fairly slow-growing, semi-evergreen, upright perennial. H 1.2–1.5m (4–5ft), S 60cm (2ft). Has a rosette of large, oval, crinkled, hairy, mid-green leaves. Hairy stems each produce a bold spike of flattish, 5-lobed, yellow flowers in summer.

V. dumulosum illus. p.359.
V. 'Gainsborough' illus. p.254.
V. 'Letitia' illus. p.358.
V. lychnitis (White mullein). Slow-growing, evergreen, upright, branching biennial. H 60cm–1m (2–3ft), S 60cm (2ft). Has lance-shaped, dark grey-green leaves. Flattish, 5-lobed, white flowers are borne on branching stems in summer.

V. nigrum illus. p.256.
V. olympicum illus. p.229.
V. 'Pink Domino'. Short-lived, rosette-forming perennial. H 1.2m (4ft), S 30–60cm (1–2ft). Produces branched racemes of 5-lobed, rose-pink flowers throughout summer above oval, mid-green leaves.
V. thapsiforme. See *V. densiflorum.*

VERBENA

VERBENACEAE

Genus of summer- and autumn-flowering biennials and perennials, some of which are semi-evergreen. Slightly hardy to tender, min. 1˚C (34˚F). Prefers sun and well-drained soil. Propagate by stem cuttings in late summer or autumn or by seed in autumn or spring.

V. alpina of gardens. See *V. × maonettii.*
V. bonariensis, syn. *V. patagonica,* illus. p.228.
V. chamaedrifolia. See *V. peruviana.*
V. chamaedrioides. See *V. peruviana.*
V. × hybrida Derby Series. Erect, bushy perennial, grown as an annual. H 25cm (10in), S 30cm (12in). Has oval, serrated, mid- to deep green leaves. Clusters of small, tubular, lobed flowers, in a wide colour range including red, pink, blue, mauve and white, appear in summer and early

autumn. Cultivars of **Novalis Series** are erect and bushy, with flowers in rose-pink, deep blue, pinkish-red and scarlet, as well as single colours of bright scarlet, white or rose-pink. **'Peaches and Cream'** is spreading and branching, and produces pastel orange-pink flowers, maturing to apricot-yellow, and eventually creamy-yellow. **Romance Series** cultivars are erect and bushy, and has flowers in deep wine-red, intense scarlet, carmine-rose-red and blue-purple, as well as single colours of white, bright scarlet, dark rose or lavender-pink. **Sandy Series** illus. p.328. **'Showtime'** illus. p.326.
V. × maonettii, syn. *V. alpina* of gardens, *V. tenera* var. *maonetti.* Spreading perennial with a slightly woody base. H 8cm (3in), S 15cm (6in). Has oblong to oval leaves, deeply cut into linear, toothed, mid-green segments, and, in summer, terminal clusters of small, tubular, reddish-violet flowers, with white-edged lobes.
V. patagonica. See *V. bonariensis.*
V. peruviana, syn. *V. chamaedrifolia, V. chamaedrioides.* Semi-evergreen, prostrate perennial. H to 8cm (3in), S 1m (3ft). Tender. Heads of small, tubular, brilliant scarlet flowers, with spreading petal lobes, are produced from early summer to early autumn. Oval, toothed leaves are mid-green. Prefers to grow in dry soil that is not too rich.
V. rigida, syn. *V. venosa,* illus. p.284.
V. 'Sissinghurst' illus. p.282.
V. tenera var. **maonettii.** See *V. × maonettii.*
V. venosa. See *V. rigida.*

Verbena, Lemon. See *Aloysia triphylla,* illus. p.143.

VERONICA

SCROPHULARIACEAE

Genus of perennials and sub-shrubs, some of which are semi-evergreen or evergreen, grown for their usually blue flowers. Some need sun and well-drained soil, others prefer a moist site in sun or partial shade. Propagate by division in spring or autumn, by softwood or semi-ripe cuttings in summer or by seed in autumn.

V. austriaca. Mat-forming or upright perennial. H and S 25–50cm (10–20in). Leaves are very variable: from broadly oval to narrowly oblong, and from entire to deeply cut and fern-like. Short, dense or lax racemes of small, saucer-shaped, bright blue flowers appear in early summer. Suits a rock garden or bank. subsp. **teucrium** (syn. *V. teucrium*) illus. p.358. subsp. **teucrium 'Royal Blue'** has deep royal-blue flowers. Propagate by division in spring or by softwood cuttings in summer.
V. cinerea. Spreading, much-branched, woody-based perennial. H 15cm (6in), S 30cm (12in). Has small, linear, occasionally oval, hairy, silvery-white leaves. Trailing flower stems bear saucer-shaped, deep blue to purplish-blue flowers, with white eyes, in early

summer. Is suitable for a sunny rock garden.
V. exaltata. See *V. longifolia.*
V. fruticans (Rock speedwell). Deciduous, upright to procumbent sub-shrub. H 15cm (6in), S 30cm (12in). Leaves are oval and green. Spikes of saucer-shaped, bright blue flowers, each with a red eye, are borne in summer. Is suitable for a rock garden. Zone 6.
V. gentianoides illus. p.287.
V. incana. See *V. spicata* subsp. *incana.*
V. longifolia, syn. *V. exaltata.* Variable, upright perennial. H 1–1.2m (3–4ft), S 30cm (1ft) or more. In late summer and early autumn, long, terminal racemes of star-shaped, lilac-blue flowers are borne on stems clothed with whorls of narrowly oval to lance-shaped, toothed, mid-green leaves.
V. pectinata. Dense, mat-forming perennial that is sometimes semi-erect. H and S 20cm (8in). Has small, narrowly oval, hairy leaves and bears loose sprays of saucer-shaped, soft blue to blue-violet flowers in summer. Is good for a rock garden or bank. **'Rosea'**, H 8cm (3in), has rose-lilac flowers.
V. peduncularis illus. p.287.
V. perfoliata. See *Parahebe perfoliata.*
V. prostrata, syn. *V. rupestris,* illus. p.357. **'Kapitan'** and **'Trehane'** illus. p.357. **'Spode Blue'** is a dense, mat-forming perennial. H to 30cm (12in), S indefinite. Upright spikes of small, saucer-shaped, china-blue flowers appear in early summer. Leaves are narrowly oval and toothed.
V. rupestris. See *V. prostrata.*
V. spicata (Spiked speedwell). Clump-forming perennial. H 30–60cm (12–24in), S 45cm (18in). Spikes of small, star-shaped, bright blue flowers are borne in summer above narrowly oval, toothed, mid-green leaves. subsp. **incana** (syn. *V. incana*) illus. p.287. **'Romiley Purple'** illus. p.251.
V. teucrium. See *V. austriaca* subsp. *teucrium.*
V. virginica. See *Veronicastrum virginicum.* f. **alba** see *Veronicastrum virginicum* f. *album.*

VERONICASTRUM

SCROPHULARIACEAE

Genus of evergreen perennials grown for their elegant, pale blue flowers. Requires a position in sun and moist soil. Propagate by division in spring or autumn, by softwood or semi-ripe cuttings in summer or by seed in autumn.

V. virginicum, syn. *Veronica virginica.* (Culver's root). Upright perennial. H 1.2m (4ft), S 45cm (1½ft). In late summer, racemes of small, star-shaped, purple-blue or pink flowers crown stems clothed with whorls of narrowly lance-shaped, dark green leaves. f. **album** (syn. *Veronica virginica* f. *alba*) illus. p.241.

VESTIA

SOLANACEAE

Genus of one species of evergreen shrub, grown for its flowers and foliage. At the limits of hardiness

is often cut to ground level and is best grown against a south-facing wall. Requires sun and fertile, well-drained soil. Propagate by semi-ripe cuttings in summer or by seed in autumn or spring.
V. foetida, syn. *V. lycioides.* Evergreen, upright shrub. H 2m (6ft), S 1.5m (5ft). Oblong, glossy, dark green leaves have an unpleasant scent. Has pendent, tubular, pale yellow flowers from mid-spring to mid-summer. Zone 9.
V. lycioides. See *V. foetida.*

Vetch. See *Hippocrepis.*
  Horseshoe. See *Hippocrepis comosa,* illus. p.386.

VIBURNUM

CAPRIFOLIACEAE

Genus of deciduous, semi-evergreen or evergreen shrubs and trees, grown for their foliage, autumn colour (in many deciduous species), flowers and, often, fruits. Fruiting is generally most prolific when several plants of different clones are planted together. Grow in sun or semi-shade and in deep, fertile, not too dry soil. To thin out overgrown plants cut out some older shoots after flowering. Propagate by cuttings (softwood for deciduous species, semi-ripe for evergreens) in summer or by seed in autumn. The fruits of viburnums may cause mild stomach upset if ingested.
V. acerifolium illus. p.161.
V. betulifolium illus. p.148.
V. × bodnantense 'Dawn' illus. p.150. **'Deben'** is a deciduous, upright shrub. H 3m (10ft), S 2m (6ft). Oval, toothed, dark green leaves are bronze when young. Clusters of fragrant, tubular, white flowers, tinted with pale pink, open during mild periods from late autumn through to early spring. Both zone 7.
V. × burkwoodii. Semi-evergreen, bushy, open shrub. H and S 2.5m (8ft). Rounded heads of fragrant, tubular, pink, then white flowers are borne amid oval, glossy, dark green leaves from mid- to late spring. **'Anne Russell'**, H and S 1.5m (5ft), is deciduous and has very fragrant, white flowers. **'Park Farm Hybrid'** bears very fragrant, white flowers that are slightly pink in bud, and older leaves turn bright red in autumn. All zone 6.
V. × carlcephalum illus. p.117.
V. carlesii illus. p.154. **'Diana'** is a deciduous, bushy, dense shrub. H and S 2m (6ft). Broadly oval leaves are bronze when young and turn purple-red in autumn. From mid- to late spring bears rounded heads of red buds that open to very fragrant, tubular, pink flowers fading to white. Zone 5b.
V. 'Cayuga'. Upright, slightly spreading, deciduous shrub. H 1.5m (5ft), S 1.2m (4ft). Has scalloped, dark green leaves that turn a dull orange tone in fall. In spring, pink buds open to fragrant white flowers with the outer ones flushed pink. Fruit change through green, red and finally black. Zone 5.
V. dentatum (Arrow-wood). An upright, deciduous shrub with arching branches and straight stems. H and S 9m (10ft). Small white flowers are

borne in dense, flattened corymbs and give rise to blue-black fruit. The coarsely toothed dark green leaves turn orange to red in fall. Zone 3.

V. dilatatum. Deciduous, upright shrub. H 3m (10ft), S 2m (6ft). Oval, sharply toothed dark green leaves sometimes redden in autumn. Flat heads of small, star-shaped, white flowers in late spring and early summer are succeeded by showy, egg-shaped, bright red fruits. Zone 5. **'Catskill'** illus. p.139.

V. farreri, syn. *V. fragrans,* illus. p.147. **'Candidissimum'** is a deciduous, upright shrub. H 3m (10ft), S 2m (6ft). Oval, toothed, dark green leaves are pale green when young. Produces clusters of fragrant, tubular, pure white flowers in late autumn and during mild periods in winter and early spring. Zone 6.

V. foetens, syn. *V. grandiflorum* f. *foetens,* illus. p.149.

V. fragrans. See *V. farreri.*

V. grandiflorum. Deciduous, upright, open shrub. H and S 2m (6ft). Stiff branches bear oblong, dark green leaves that become deep purple in autumn. Dense clusters of fragrant, tubular, white-and-pink flowers open from deep pink buds from mid-winter to early spring. Zone 8. f. *foetens* see *V. foetens.*

V. x *juddii* illus. p.154.

V. lantana (Wayfaring tree). Vigorous, deciduous, upright shrub. H 5m (15ft), S 4m (12ft). Has broadly oval, grey-green leaves that redden in autumn, flattened heads of small, 5-lobed, white flowers in late spring and early summer, then egg-shaped, red fruits that ripen to black. Zone 2b.

V. lentago (Nannyberry). Vigorous, deciduous, upright shrub. H 4m (12ft), S 3m (10ft). Oval, glossy, dark green leaves turn red and purple in autumn. Bears flattened heads of small, fragrant, star-shaped, white flowers in late spring and early summer, then egg-shaped, blue-black fruits. Zone 2.

V. **'Oneida'.** A broadly upright deciduous shrub. H. 3m (10ft), S 2.5m (9ft). Thin, almost circular, dark green, toothed leaves turn yellow to orange-red in autumn. Flat heads of white flowers in lacecap-like heads appear in spring and through the summer and turn into glossy red berries that persist into winter. Zone 6.

V. opulus (Guelder rose). Vigorous, deciduous, bushy shrub. H and S 4m (12ft). Bears broadly oval, lobed, deep green leaves that redden in autumn and, in late spring and early summer, flattened, lace-cap-like heads of white flowers. Produces large bunches of spherical, bright red fruits. Zone 2b. **'Compactum'** illus. p.172. **'Roseum'** (European snowball). Has large globular heads of sterile flowers. Is very prone to aphid damage.

V. plicatum (Japanese snowball tree). Deciduous, bushy, spreading shrub. H 3m (10ft), S 4m (12ft). Leaves are oval, toothed, deeply veined and dark green, turning reddish-purple in autumn. Dense, rounded heads of large, sterile, flattish, white flowers are borne along branches in late spring and early summer. **'Mariesii'** illus. p.116. **'Nanum Semperflorens'** (syn.

V.p. 'Watanabe', *V.p.* 'Watanabei', *V. watanabei*), H 2m (6ft), S 1.5m (5ft), is slow-growing, conical and dense, and produces small flower heads from late spring until early autumn. **'Pink Beauty'** illus. p.130. f. *tomentosum* has tiered branches, flattish, lace-cap-like flower heads and red fruits, ripening to black. **'Summer Snowflake'** has tiered branches and lacecap flower heads in late spring and through the summer. [Fall foliage is purple.] **'Watanabe'** see *V.p.* 'Nanum Semperflorens'. **'Watanabei'** see *V.p.* 'Nanum Semperflorens'. All zone 5b.

V. x *pragense.* See *V.* 'Pragense'.

V. **'Pragense'**, syn. *V.* x *pragense*, illus. p.139.

V. rhytidophylloides **'Alleghany'.** Forms a dense, rounded evergreen shrub. H and S 3m (10ft). The dark green, leathery foliage turns a dull purple in fall and may be deciduous above the snow at the limits of hardiness. Domed heads of creamy-white flowers appear in late spring and give rise to bright red fruit that turn black. Zone 5.

V. rhytidophyllum illus. p.118.

V. sargentii. Deciduous, bushy shrub. H and S 3m (10ft). Maple-like, mid-green foliage often changes to yellow or red in autumn. Broad, flattish, lace-cap-like heads of white flowers in late spring are followed by spherical, bright red fruits. Zone 3b.

'Onondaga', S 2m (6ft), has bronzed-red, young leaves, becoming deep green, then bronze-red again in autumn. Flower buds are pink. Zone 3b.

V. sieboldii. Deciduous, rounded, dense shrub. H 4m (12ft), S 6m (20ft). Has large, oblong to oval, glossy, bright green leaves. Rounded heads of tubular, creamy-white flowers are borne in late spring, followed by egg-shaped, red-stalked, red fruits that ripen to black. Zone 6.

V. tinus (Laurustinus) illus. p.149. **'Gwenllian'** has pale pink flowers and fruits very freely. Zone 7.

V. trilobum (American cranberry bush, high bush-cranberry). An upright, slender deciduous shrub with maple-like leaves that turn reddish in fall. H 5m (15ft), S 3m (10ft). In spring, has flattened lacecap heads of white flowers. Bright red berries persist into winter. **'Alfredo'** is only half this height with brighter autumn colour. **'Wentworth'** has orange-red fall colour and yellow-red fruits that ripen later. All zone 2.

V. watanabei. See *V. plicatum* 'Nanum Semperflorens'.

Victorian box. See *Pittosporum undulatum.*

VIGNA

LEGUMINOSAE/PAPILIONACEAE

Genus of evergreen, annual and perennial, erect or scrambling and twining climbers, grown mainly as crop plants for their leaves, pods and seeds. Tender, min. 13–15°C (55–9°F). Provide full light and humus-rich, well-drained soil. Water freely when in full growth, sparingly at other times. Stems require support. Thin crowded stems or

cut back hard in spring. Propagate by seed in autumn or spring.

V. caracalla, syn. *Phaseolus caracalla* (Snail flower). Evergreen, perennial, fast-growing, twining climber. H 3–5m (10–15ft). Leaves comprise 3 oval leaflets. From summer to early autumn carries pea-like, purple-marked, cream flowers that turn orange-yellow.

Villarsia nymphoides. See *Nymphoides peltata.*

VINCA
Periwinkle

APOCYNACEAE

Genus of evergreen, trailing sub-shrubs and perennials, grown for their foliage and flowers. Flowers are tubular with 5 spreading lobes. Is useful for ground cover in shade, but flowers more freely given some sun. Grows in any soil that is not too dry. Propagate by semi-ripe cuttings in summer or by division from autumn to spring. All parts may cause mild stomach upset if ingested.

V. difformis. Evergreen, prostrate sub-shrub. H 30cm (12in), S indefinite. Slender, trailing stems bear oval, glossy, dark green leaves. Erect flower stems produce pale blue flowers in late autumn and early winter. Zone 9.

V. major (Greater periwinkle, Quater). Evergreen, prostrate, arching sub-shrub. H 45cm (18in), S indefinite. Leaves are broadly oval, glossy and dark green. Large, bright blue flowers are produced from late spring to early autumn. subsp. *hirsuta* see *V.m.* var. *oxyloba.* var. *oxyloba* (syn. *V.m.* subsp. *hirsuta*) has leaves, leaf stalks and calyces edged with long hairs. **'Variegata'** illus. p.175. Zone 6.

V. minor (Lesser periwinkle) illus. p.176. **'Alba Variegata'** is an evergreen, prostrate sub-shrub. H 15cm (6in), S indefinite. Forms extensive mats of small, oval, glossy, dark green leaves, edged with pale yellow, above which white flowers are carried from mid-spring to early summer, then intermittently into autumn. **'Bowles' Blue'** see *V.m.* 'La Grave'. **'Bowles' White'** bears large, white flowers that are pinkish-white in bud. **'Gertrude Jekyll'** is of dense growth and produces a profusion of small, white flowers. Flowers of **'La Grave'** (syn. *V.m.* 'Bowles' Blue') are large and lavender-blue. All zone 3.

V. rosea. See *Catharanthus roseus.*

Vine. See *Vitis.*
  Alleghany. See *Adlumia fungosa.*
  Balloon. See *Cardiospermum halicacabum.*
  Blue trumpet. See *Thunbergia grandiflora.*
  Bower. See *Pandorea jasminoides,* illus. p.208.
  Chestnut. See *Tetrastigma voinierianum,* illus. p.220.
  Chinese trumpet. See *Campsis grandiflora.*
  Chocolate. See *Akebia quinata,* illus. p.206.
  Coral. See *Antigonon.*

Vine (continued)
  Crimson glory. See *Vitis coignetiae,* illus. p.218.
  Cross. See *Bignonia capreolata.*
  Cup-and-saucer. See *Cobaea scandens,* illus. p.214.
  Cypress. See *Ipomoea quamoclit,* illus. p.210.
  Firecracker. See *Manettia cordifolia.*
  Flame. See *Pyrostegia venusta,* illus. p.218.
  Glory. See *Eccremocarpus scaber,* illus. p.217.
  Golden-chalice. See *Solandra maxima,* illus. p.206.
  Grape. See *Vitis vinifera.*
  Heart. See *Ceropegia linearis* subsp. *woodii,* illus. p.462.
  Hearts-and-honey. See *Ipomoea* x *multifida.*
  Jade. See *Strongylodon macrobotrys,* illus. p.206.
  Japanese hydrangea. See *Schizophragma hydrangeoides.*
  Kangaroo. See *Cissus antarctica,* illus. p.220.
  Kudzu. See *Pueraria lobata.*
  Lemon. See *Pereskia aculeata,* illus. p.457.
  Madeira. See *Anredera.*
  Mexican flame. See *Senecio confusus,* illus. p.217.
  Mignonette. See *Anredera.*
  Potato. See *Solanum jasminoides.*
  Rex begonia. See *Cissus discolor.*
  Rosary. See *Ceropegia linearis* subsp. *woodii,* illus. p.462.
  Rubber. See *Cryptostegia grandiflora.*
  Russian. See *Fallopia aubertii; Fallopia baldschuanica,* illus. p.217.
  Silk. See *Periploca graeca.*
  Silver. See *Actinidia polygama; Epipremnum pictum* 'Argyraeum', illus. p.219.
  Staff. See *Celastrus orbiculatus.*
  Teddy-bear. See *Cyanotis kewensis.*
  Trumpet. See *Campsis radicans.*
  Wax. See *Senecio macroglossus.*
  Wonga-wonga. See *Pandorea pandorana.*
Vine lilac. See *Hardenbergia violacea.*
Vine maple. See *Acer circinatum.*

VIOLA
Violet

VIOLACEAE

Genus of annuals, perennials, some of which are semi-evergreen, and deciduous sub-shrubs, grown for their distinctive flowers. Annuals are suitable as summer bedding, perennials and sub-shrubs are good in rock gardens, screes and alpine houses. Grow in sun or shade and well-drained but moisture-retentive soil unless otherwise stated; a few species prefer acid soil. Propagate annuals by seed sown according to flowering season, perennials and sub-shrubs by softwood cuttings in spring unless otherwise stated. Species may also be propagated by seed in spring or autumn.

V. aetolica illus. 371.

V. biflora (Twin-flowered violet). Creeping, rhizomatous perennial. H 5–15cm (2–6in), S 15cm (6in). Flat-faced, deep lemon-yellow flowers, veined dark brown, are borne singly or

in pairs on upright stems in summer. Leaves are kidney-shaped and mid-green. Needs shade. May also be propagated by division.
V. calcarata illus. p.368.
V. cazorlensis. Tufted, woody-based perennial. H to 5cm (2in), S to 8cm (3in). Has small, linear to lance-shaped leaves and in late spring carries small, flat-faced, long-spurred, deep pink flowers, singly on short stems. Suits an alpine house. Is difficult to grow.
V. cenisia. Spreading perennial with runners. H 7cm (3in), S 10cm (4in). Small, flat-faced, bright violet flowers, each with a deep purple line radiating from the centre, are produced on very short stems in summer. Has a deep tap root and tiny, heart-shaped or oblong, dark green leaves. Suits a scree. Propagate by division in spring.
V. cornuta illus. p.349.
V. cucullata. See **V. obliqua**.
V. elatior. Upright, little-branched perennial. H 20–30cm (8–12in), S 15cm (6in). Leaves are broadly lance-shaped and toothed. Produces flat-faced, pale blue flowers, with white centres, in early summer. Prefers semi-shade and moist soil. Propagate in spring by division.
V. glabella. Clump-forming perennial with a scaly, horizontal rootstock. H 10cm (4in), S 20cm (8in). Produces flat-faced, bright yellow flowers, with purplish-veined lower petals, in late spring above toothed, heart-shaped, bright green leaves. Needs shade. Propagate by division in spring.
V. gracilis. Mat-forming perennial. H 12cm (5in), S 15cm (6in) or more. Flat-faced, yellow-centred, violet-blue or sometimes yellow flowers are produced in summer. Has small, dissected leaves with linear or oblong segments. Needs sun.
V. 'Haslemere'. See **V. 'Nellie Britton'**.
V. hederacea, syn. *Erpetion reniforme*, *V. reniforme* (Australian violet, Ivy-leaved violet). Evergreen, creeping, mat-forming perennial. H 2.5–5cm (1–2in), S indefinite. Has tiny, rounded leaves and bears purple or white flowers, with a squashed appearance, on short stems in summer. Suits an alpine house. Prefers semi-shade. Propagate by division in spring.
V. 'Huntercombe Purple' illus. p.382.
V. 'Irish Molly'. Evergreen, clump-forming, short-lived perennial. H 10cm (4in), S 15–20cm (6–8in). Has broadly oval, dissected leaves and, in summer, a succession of flat-faced, old-gold flowers with brown centres. Flowers itself to death. Needs sun.
V. 'Jackanapes' illus. p.372.
V. labradorica 'Purpurea'. See **V. riviniana 'Purpurea'**.
V. lutea (Mountain pansy). Mat-forming, rhizomatous perennial. H 10cm (4in), S 15cm (6in). Has small, oval to lance-shaped leaves. Flat-faced, yellow, violet or bicoloured flowers are produced in spring and summer.
V. 'Nellie Britton', syn. **V. 'Haslemere'**, illus. p.381.
V. obliqua, syn. **V. cucullata**. Variable, spreading perennial with fleshy rhizomes. H 5cm (2in), S 10–15cm (4–6in). Has kidney-shaped, toothed, mid-green leaves. In late spring

produces flat-faced, blue-violet, sometimes white or pale blue flowers. Propagate in spring by division. Self seeds freely.
V. odorata (Sweet violet). Semi-evergreen, spreading, rhizomatous perennial. H 7cm (3in), S15cm (6in) or more. Leaves are heart-shaped and toothed. Long stems each carry a fragrant, flat-faced, violet or white flower from late winter to early spring. Is useful in a wild garden. Self seeds prolifically. May also be propagated by division.
V. palmata. Spreading perennial. H 10cm (4in), S 15cm (6in). Has short-stemmed, flat-faced, pale violet flowers in late spring and deeply dissected leaves. Prefers dry, well-drained soil. Self seeds readily.
V. pedata illus. p.369. var. *bicolor* is a clump-forming perennial with a thick rootstock. H 5cm (2in), S 8cm (3in). Flat-faced, velvety-purple or white flowers are borne singly on slender stems in late spring and early summer. Leaves are finely divided into 5–7 or more, narrow, toothed segments. Suits an alpine house. May be difficult to grow; needs peaty, sandy soil.
V. reniforme. See **V. hederacea**.
V. riviniana 'Purpurea', syn. **V. labradorica 'Purpurea'**, illus. p.369.
V. tricolor illus. p.369. **'Bowles' Black'** illus. p.370.
V. x wittrockiana (Pansy). Group of slow- to moderately fast-growing, mainly bushy perennials, usually grown as annuals or biennials. H 15–20cm (6–8in), S 20cm (8in). Has oval, often serrated, mid-green leaves. Flattish, 5-petalled flowers, 2.5–10cm (1–4in) across, in a very wide colour range, appear throughout summer or in winter-spring. The following are among those available:
'Baby Lucia' (summer-flowering) has small, deep blue flowers.
Clear Crystals Series (summer-flowering) is in a wide range of clear colours (yellow, illus. p.337).
'Clear Sky Primrose' (winter- to spring-flowering) illus p.336.
Crystal Bowl Series (summer-flowering) is in a range of colours (yellow, illus. p.337).
Floral Dance Series (winter-flowering) has a wide range of colours (mixed, illus. p.329; white, illus. p.319).
Forerunner Series (winter- to spring-flowering) illus. p.338.
Imperial Series 'Imperial Frosty Rose' (summer-flowering) illus. p.327.
Imperial Series 'Orange Prince' (summer-flowering) has orange flowers with black blotches.
Imperial Series 'Sky Blue' (summer-flowering) has sky-blue flowers, each with a deeper-coloured blotch.
Joker Series (summer-flowering) illus. p.332.
'Majestic Giants' (summer-flowering) has large flowers in a wide colour range.
Princess Series (spring- to summer-flowering) are neat in habit, and produce small flowers in blue, cream, bicoloured purple and white, dark purple or yellow.

'Silver Princess' (summer-flowering) has white flowers, each with a deep pink blotch.
'Super Chalon Giants' (summer- to autumn-flowering) illus. p.336.
'True Blue' (winter- to summer-flowering) illus p.333.
Ultima Series (winter- to spring-flowering) has medium-sized flowers in a very broad range of colours, including bicolours.
Universal Series (winter- to spring-flowering) produces flowers in an extensive range of separate colours (apricot, illus. p.339) as well as in a mixture of colours.

Violet. See *Viola*.
African. See *Saintpaulia*.
Australian. See *Viola hederacea*.
Bird's-foot. See *Viola pedata*, illus. p.369.
Bush. See *Browallia speciosa*, illus. p.266.
Dame's. See *Hesperis matronalis*, illus. p.239.
Dog's-tooth. See *Erythronium dens-canis*, illus. p.430.
Flame. See *Episcia cupreata*, illus. p.301.
Horned. See *Viola cornuta*, illus. p.349.
Ivy-leaved. See *Viola hederacea*.
Mexican. See *Tetranema roseum*, illus. p.303.
Persian. See *Exacum affine*, illus. p.331.
Philippine. See *Barleria cristata*.
Sweet. See *Viola odorata*.
Twin-flowered. See *Viola biflora*.
Water. See *Hottonia palustris*, illus. p.447.
Violet cress. See *Ionopsidium acaule*.
Violet willow. See *Salix daphnoides*, illus. p.74.

VIRGILIA

LEGUMINOSAE/PAPILIONACEAE

Genus of short-lived, evergreen shrubs and trees, grown for their flowers which are borne in spring and summer. Tender, min. 5°C (41°F). Prefers a position in full light and well-drained soil. Water pot-grown plants freely when in full growth, less at other times. Pruning is usually not required. Propagate in spring by seed, ideally soaked in warm water for 24 hours before sowing.
V. capensis. See **V. oroboides**.
V. oroboides, syn. **V. capensis**. Fast-growing, evergreen, rounded shrub or tree. H and S 6–10m (20–30ft). Has leaves of 11–21 oblong leaflets. Racemes of fragrant, pea-like, bright mauve-pink flowers, sometimes pink, crimson or white, are produced in late spring and summer, usually in great profusion.

Virgin's palm. See *Dioon edule*.
Virginia creeper. See *Parthenocissus quinquefolia*.
Virginia pine. See *Pinus virginiana*, illus. p.107.
Virginian bird cherry. See *Prunus virginiana*.
Virginian pokeweed. See *Phytolacca americana*.

Virginian stock. See *Malcolmia maritima*, illus. p.323.
Virginian witch hazel. See *Hamamelis virginiana*, illus. p.125.
Viscaria alpina. See *Lychnis alpina*.
Viscaria elegans. See *Silene coeli-rosa*.

VITALIANA

PRIMULACEAE

Genus of one species of evergreen, spring-flowering perennial, grown for its flowers. Is often included in *Douglasia* and is useful for rock gardens, screes and alpine houses. Requires sun and moist but well-drained soil. Propagate by softwood cuttings in summer or by seed in autumn.
V. primuliflora, syn. *Douglasia vitaliana*, illus. p.372.

VITEX

VERBENACEAE

Genus of evergreen or deciduous trees and shrubs, grown for their flowers. At limits of hardiness grow against a south- or west-facing wall. Needs full sun and well-drained soil. Propagate by semi-ripe cuttings in summer or by seed in autumn or spring.
V. agnus-castus (Chaste tree). Deciduous, spreading, open, aromatic shrub. H and S 2.5m (8ft). Upright panicles of fragrant, tubular, violet-blue flowers appear in early and mid-autumn. Dark green leaves are each divided into 5 or 7 long, narrowly lance-shaped leaflets. Zone 7.
V. negundo. Deciduous, bushy shrub. H and S 3m (10ft). Mid-green leaves are each composed of 3–7 narrowly oval, sharply toothed leaflets. Produces loose panicles of small, tubular, violet-blue flowers from late summer through to early autumn. Zone 6b.

VITIS
Vine

VITACEAE

Genus of deciduous, woody-stemmed, tendril climbers, grown for their foliage and fruits (grapes), which are produced in bunches. Prefers fertile, well-drained, chalky soil and sun or semi-shade. Produces the best fruits and autumn leaf-colour when planted in a warm situation. Propagate by hardwood cuttings in late autumn.
V. aconitifolia. See *Ampelopsis aconitifolia*.
V. amurensis (Amur grape). Vigorous, deciduous, woody-stemmed, tendril climber. H 6m (20ft). Bears dark green, 3- or 5-lobed leaves, 12–30cm (5–12in) long, that mature to red and purple in autumn. Produces inconspicuous flowers throughout the summer, followed in late summer and autumn, by tiny, black fruits. Zone 3b.
V. 'Brant'. Deciduous, woody-stemmed, tendril climber. H to 7m (22ft) or more. Bears leaves that are lobed, toothed, 10–22cm (4–9in) long and bright green. In autumn they mature to brown-red, except for the veins. Produces inconspicuous flowers in summer, followed by green or purple fruits. Zone 6.

V. coignetiae illus. p.218.
V. davidii. Deciduous, woody-stemmed, tendril climber; young stems are densely covered with short prickles. H to 8m (25ft) or more. Heart-shaped leaves, 10–25cm (4–10in) long, are blue- or grey-green beneath, turning scarlet in autumn. Insignificant, greenish flowers in summer are followed by small, black fruits. Zone 8.
V. henryana. See *Parthenocissus henryana.*
V. heterophylla. See *Ampelopsis brevipedunculata* var. *maximowiczii.*
V. quinquefolia. See *Parthenocissus quinquefolia.*
V. striata. See *Cissus striata.*
V thomsonii. See *Parthenocissus thomsonii.*
V. vinifera. (Grape vine) '**Purpurea**' illus. p.218.

Voodoo lily. See *Sauromatum venosum*, illus. p.413.
Voss's laburnum. See *Laburnum* x *watereri* 'Vossii'.

VRIESEA
BROMELIACEAE
Genus of evergreen, rosette-forming, epiphytic perennials, grown for their flowers and overall appearance. Tender, min. 15°C (59°F). Needs a position in semi-shade and a rooting medium of equal parts humus-rich soil and either sphagnum moss or bark or plastic chips used for orchid culture. Using soft water, water moderately when in growth, sparingly at other times, and from mid-spring to mid-autumn keep rosette centres filled with water. Propagate plants by offsets or seed in spring.
V. fenestralis. Evergreen, epiphytic perennial with dense, funnel-shaped rosettes. H and S 30–40cm (12–16in). Pale green leaves, with dark lines and cross-bands, are very broadly strap-shaped and arching or rolled under at tips. In summer, flat racemes of tubular, yellowish-green flowers, with green bracts, are carried above the foliage.
V. fosteriana. Evergreen, epiphytic perennial with dense, funnel-shaped rosettes. H and S 60cm (24in) or more. Has broadly strap-shaped, arching, yellowish- to deep green leaves, cross-banded with reddish-brown, particularly beneath. In summer-autumn, flat spikes of tubular, pale yellow or greenish-yellow flowers, with brownish-red tips, are produced well above the foliage.
V. hieroglyphica (King of the bromeliads). Evergreen, epiphytic perennial with dense, funnel-shaped rosettes. H and S 60cm–1m (2–3ft). Produces very broadly strap-shaped, arching, yellowish-green leaves, cross-banded and chequered with dark brownish-green. In summer bears panicles of tubular, yellow flowers well above the leaves.
V. platynema. Evergreen, basal-rosetted, epiphytic perennial. H and S 60cm (24in). Broadly strap-shaped, mid- to light green leaves, with purple tips, form dense rosettes. In summer flat racemes of tubular, green-and-yellow flowers, with red or yellow bracts, are produced.
V. psittacina. Evergreen, spreading, basal-rosetted, epiphytic perennial. H and S 40–60cm (16–24in). Has dense rosettes of strap-shaped, arching, pale green leaves. Flat spikes of tubular, yellow flowers with green tips, emerging from red-and-yellow or red-and-green bracts, are borne above foliage in summer-autumn.
V. splendens (Flaming sword; illus. p.265). Evergreen, basal-rosetted, epiphytic perennial. H and S 30cm (12in). Has dense rosettes of strap-shaped, arching, olive-green leaves, with purple to reddish-brown cross-bands. Bears flat, sword-shaped racemes of tubular, yellow flowers, between bright red bracts, in summer and autumn.

x VUYLSTEKEARA
See also ORCHIDS.
x *V. cambria* '**Lensing's Favorite**' (illus. p.297). Evergreen, epiphytic orchid for a cool greenhouse. H 23cm (9in). Has narrowly oval leaves, 10–15cm (4–6in) long. Bears long sprays of wine-red flowers, 10cm (4in) across, heavily marked with white; flowering season varies. Needs shade in summer.

WACHENDORFIA
HAEMODORACEAE

Genus of summer-flowering perennials with deep roots, to guard against frost. Requires full sun and moist soil. Propagate by division in spring or by seed in autumn or spring.

W. thyrsiflora. Clump-forming perennial. H 1.5–2m (5–6ft), S 45cm (1½ft). Shallowly cup-shaped, yellow to orange flowers are produced in dense panicles in early summer. Mid-green leaves are narrowly sword-shaped, pleated and rather coarse.

WAHLENBERGIA
CAMPANULACEAE

Genus of summer-flowering annuals, biennials and short-lived perennials, grown for their bell-shaped flowers. Is useful for alpine houses. Needs a sheltered site, partial shade and well-drained, peaty, sandy soil. Propagate by seed in autumn.

W. albomarginata (New Zealand bluebell). Basal-rosetted, rhizomatous perennial. H and S 15cm (6in) or more. Slender stems each carry a bell-shaped, clear blue flower that opens flat in summer. Has narrowly elliptic to oval, mid-green leaves in tufts. Is good in a rock garden.

W. congesta, syn. **W. saxicola** var. **congesta.** Mat-forming, creeping, rhizomatous perennial. H 7cm (3in), S 10cm (4in). Has small, rounded or spoon-shaped, mid-green leaves and, in summer, bell-shaped, lavender-blue or white flowers held singly on wiry stems.

W. saxicola var. **congesta.** See **W. congesta.**

W. serpyllifolia. See **Edraianthus serpyllifolius.**

Wakerobin. See *Trillium grandiflorum,* illus. p.268; *Trillium sessile,* illus. p.269.

WALDSTEINIA
ROSACEAE

Genus of semi-evergreen, creeping perennials with runners. Makes good ground cover. Needs sun and well-drained soil. Propagate by division in early spring.

W. ternata, syn. **W. trifolia,** illus. p.385.

W. trifolia. See **W. ternata.**

Wall flag. See *Iris tectorum,* illus. p.234.
Wallflower. See *Erysimum.*
  Siberian. See *Erysimum* x *allionii.*
Wallich's wood fern. See *Dryopteris wallichiana.*
Wall-spray. See *Cotoneaster horizontalis,* illus. p.172.
Walnut. See *Juglans.*
  Black. See *Juglans nigra,* illus. p.67.

Walnut (continued)
  Chinese. See *Juglans cathayensis.*
  Japanese. See *Juglans ailantifolia.*
  Little. See *Juglans microcarpa,* illus. p.92.
  Texan. See *Juglans microcarpa,* illus. p.92.
Wandering Jew. See *Tradescantia fluminensis.*
Wandflower. See *Dierama.*
Waratah. See *Telopea speciosissima,* illus. p.142.
  Tasmanian. See *Telopea truncata,* illus. p.131.
Warminster broom. See *Cytisus* x *praecox* 'Warminster', illus. p.156.
Washington. See *Crataegus phaenopyrum.*
Washington thorn. See *Crataegus phaenopyrum.*

WASHINGTONIA
ARECACEAE/PALMAE

Genus of evergreen palms, grown for their stately appearance. Tender, min. 10°C (50°F). Grows in fertile, well-drained soil and in full sun. Water containerized specimens freely in summer, moderately at other times. Remove skirt of persistent, dead leaves regularly as they are a fire risk. Propagate by seed in spring at not less than 24°C (75°F). Spider mite may be a nuisance.

W. filifera (Desert fan palm). Fast-growing, evergreen palm. H and S to 25m (80ft). Has fan-shaped, long-stalked, grey-green leaves, each lobe with a filamentous tip. Long-stalked clusters of tiny, creamy-white flowers are borne in summer and berry-like, black fruits in winter.

W. robusta illus. p.73.

Water chestnut. See *Trapa natans,* illus. p.449.
Water crowfoot. See *Ranunculus aquatilis.*
Water dragon. See *Saururus cernuus,* illus. p.447.
Water fern. See *Azolla filiculoides,* illus. p.448; *Ceratopteris thalictroides.*
Water figwort. See *Scrophularia auriculata* 'Variegata'.
Water forget-me-not. See *Myosotis scorpioides.*
Water fringe. See *Nymphoides peltata,* illus. p.451.
Water hawthorn. See *Aponogeton distachyos,* illus. p.447.
Water hyacinth. See *Eichhornia crassipes,* illus. p.448.
Water lettuce. See *Pistia stratiotes,* illus. p.449.
Water lily. See *Nymphaea.*
  Cape blue. See *Nymphaea capensis.*
  Fringed. See *Nymphoides peltata,* illus. p.451.
  Yellow. See *Nuphar lutea,* illus. p.451.

Water lily tulip. See *Tulipa kaufmanniana,* illus. p.412.
Water moss. See *Fontinalis antipyretica.*
Water oak. See *Quercus nigra,* illus. p.68.
Water plantain. See *Alisma plantago-aquatica,* illus. p.446.
  Floating. See *Luronium natans.*
Water poppy. See *Hydrocleys nymphoides,* illus. p.449.
Water soldier. See *Stratiotes aloides,* illus. p.447.
Water violet. See *Hottonia palustris,* illus. p.447.
Waterer's gold holly. See *Ilex aquifolium* 'Watereriana', illus. p.99.
Watermelon begonia. See *Elatostema repens,* illus. p.303.
Watermelon plant. See *Peperomia argyreia.*

WATSONIA
IRIDACEAE

Genus of clump-forming corms, *Gladiolus*-like in overall appearance, although flowers are more tubular. Requires an open, sunny position and light, well-drained soil. Plant in autumn, 10–15cm (4–6in) deep; protect with bracken, loose peat or similar during first winter, if frost is expected. Feed with slow-acting fertilizer, such as bonemeal, in summer. Corms are best left undisturbed to form clumps. Propagate by seed in autumn.

W. beatricis. See **W. pillansii.**

W. borbonica, syn. **W. pyramidata,** illus. p.400.

W. fourcadei. Clump-forming, summer-flowering corm. H to 1.5m (5ft), S 30–45cm (1–1½ft). Sword-shaped, erect leaves are mostly basal. Has a dense spike of tubular, salmon-red flowers, each 8–9cm (3–3½in) long and with 6 lobes.

W. merianae. Clump-forming, summer-flowering corm. H to 1m (3ft), S 30–45cm (1–1½ft). Has sword-shaped, erect leaves both on stem and at base. Stem carries a loose spike of tubular, pinkish-red flowers, each 5–6cm (2–2½in) long and with 6 spreading lobes.

W. pillansii, syn. **W. beatricis,** illus. p.400.

W. pyramidata. See **W. borbonica.**

Wattakaka sinensis. See *Dregea sinensis.*
Wattle
  Cootamundra. See *Acacia baileyana,* illus. p.97.
  Mount Morgan. See *Acacia podalyriifolia,* illus. p.135.
  Ovens. See *Acacia pravissima,* illus. p.97.
  Queensland silver. See *Acacia podalyriifolia,* illus. p.135.
  Silver. See *Acacia dealbata,* illus. p.83.

Wattle (continued)
  Sydney golden. See *Acacia longifolia.*
Wax flower. See *Stephanotis floribunda,* illus. p.204.
Wax plant. See *Hoya carnosa,* illus. p.208.
Wax privet. See *Peperomia glabella,* illus. p.305.
Wax tree. See *Rhus succedanea.*
Wax vine. See *Senecio macroglossus.*
Waxflower, Geraldton. See *Chamelaucium uncinatum,* illus. pp.149 and 150.
Wayfaring tree. See *Viburnum lantana.*
Wedding-cake tree. See *Cornus controversa* 'Variegata', illus. p.89.
Weeping aspen. See *Populus tremula* 'Pendula', illus. p.79.
Weeping beech. See *Fagus sylvatica* f. *pendula,* illus. p.66.
Weeping birch. See *Betula pendula* 'Tristis', illus. p.73.
Weeping fig. See *Ficus benjamina.*
Weeping silver holly, Perry's. See *Ilex aquifolium* 'Argentea Marginata Pendula', illus. p.98.
Weeping silver linden. See *Tilia* 'Petiolaris', illus. p.68.
Weeping willow. See *Salix babylonica.*
  Golden. See *Salix* x *sepulcralis* var. *chrysocoma,* illus. p.74.

WEIGELA
CAPRIFOLIACEAE

Genus of deciduous shrubs, grown for their showy, funnel-shaped flowers. Prefers sunny, fertile soil. To maintain vigour, prune out a few older branches to ground level, after flowering each year. Straggly, old plants may be pruned hard in spring (though this will lose one season's flowers). Propagate by softwood cuttings in summer.

W. 'Bristol Ruby'. Vigorous, deciduous, upright shrub. H 2.5m (8ft), S 2m (6ft). Deep red flowers open from darker buds amid oval, toothed, mid-green leaves in late spring and early summer. Zone 5.

W. 'Eva Rathke'. Deciduous, upright, dense shrub. H and S 1.5m (5ft). Has oval, toothed, dark green leaves. Broad-mouthed, crimson flowers open from darker buds from late spring to early summer. Zone 5.

W. florida. Deciduous, arching shrub. H and S 2.5m (8ft). Bears deep pink flowers, pale pink to white inside, in late spring and early summer. Oval, toothed leaves are mid-green. Zone 5.
  'Foliis Purpureis' illus. p.163.
  'Variegata' illus. p.160.

W. 'Minuet'. Compact, dwarf, spreading, deciduous shrub. H 75cm (30in), S 1.2m (4ft). Purple-tinged foliage and slightly fragrant, bell-shaped pink blooms that are darker outside and have a yellow throat. Zone 3.

W. 'Red Prince'. Upright, deciduous shrub. H 2m (6ft), S 1.2m (4ft). The

bright red, non-fading flowers are borne in early summer with repeat blooms in late summer. Zone 5.
W. **'Tango'.** Deciduous, compact shrub with purple-tinged foliage. H 60cm (24in), S 75cm (30in). In late spring and early summer has bell-shaped, red flowers with yellow throats. Zone 4.

Weingartia neocumingii. See *Rebutia neocumingii.*

WEINMANNIA

CUNONIACEAE

Genus of evergreen trees and shrubs, grown for their foliage, flowers and overall appearance. Tender, min. 5–7°C (41–5°F). Requires a position in partial shade or full light and humus-rich, well-drained but not dry soil, ideally neutral to acid. Water containerized plants freely when in full growth, moderately at other times. Pruning is tolerated if needed. Propagate by seed in spring or by semi-ripe cuttings in summer.
W. trichosperma. Evergreen, ovoid to round-headed tree. H 12m (40ft) or more, S 8–10m (25–30ft). Glossy, rich green leaves have 9–19 oval, boldly toothed leaflets borne on a winged midrib. Spikes of tiny, fragrant, white flowers, with pink stamens, are produced in early summer.

WELDENIA

COMMELINACEAE

Genus of one species of summer-flowering, tuberous perennial, grown for its flowers. Needs sun and gritty, well-drained soil. Keep dry from autumn until growth restarts in late winter. Is suitable for growing in alpine houses. Propagate by root cuttings in winter or by division in early spring.
W. candida illus. p.362.

Wellingtonia. See *Sequoiadendron giganteum,* illus. p.102.
Welsh poppy. See *Meconopsis cambrica,* illus. p.275.

WELWITSCHIA

WELWITSCHIACEAE

Genus of one species of evergreen, desert-growing perennial with a deep tap root. Has only 2 leaves, which lie on the ground and grow continuously from the base for up to 100 years. Tender, min. 10°C (50°F). Requires sun and sharply drained soil. Requires desert conditions: may succeed in a mixture of stone chippings and leaf mould, in a length of drainpipe to take its long tap root. Propagate by seed when ripe.
W. bainesii. See *W. mirabilis.*
W. mirabilis, syn. *W. bainesii,* illus. p.304.

West Himalayan birch. See *Betula utilis* var. *jacquemontii,* illus. p.83.
West Himalayan spruce. See *Picea smithiana.*
West Indian jasmine. See *Plumeria alba.*
Western balsam poplar. See *Populus trichocarpa.*

Western hemlock. See *Tsuga heterophylla.*
Western prickly Moses. See *Acacia pulchella,* illus. p.157.
Western red cedar. See *Thuja plicata.*
Western tea-myrtle. See *Melaleuca nesophila,* illus. p.145.
Western yellow pine. See *Pinus ponderosa,* illus. p.103.

WESTRINGIA

LABIATAE/LAMIACEAE

Genus of evergreen shrubs, grown for their flowers and overall appearance. Tender, min. 5–7°C (41–5°F). Requires full light and well-drained soil. Water containerized specimens moderately, less when not in full growth. Propagate by seed in spring or by semi-ripe cuttings in late summer.
W. fruticosa, syn. *W. rosmariniformis,* illus. p.158.
W. rosmariniformis. See *W. fruticosa.*

Weymouth pine. See *Pinus strobus,* illus. p.102.
Wheatley elm. See *Ulmus minor* 'Sarniensis'.
White ash. See *Fraxinus americana.*
White asphodel. See *Asphodelus albus,* illus. p.239.
White baneberry. See *Actaea pachypoda,* illus. p.259.
White cedar. See *Thuja occidentalis.*
White Chinese birch. See *Betula albosinensis,* illus. p.74.
White cypress. See *Chamaecyparis thyoides,* illus. p.107.
White elm. See *Ulmus americana.*
White evening primrose. See *Oenothera speciosa.*
White false hellebore. See *Veratrum album.*
White fir. See *Abies concolor.*
White ginger lily. See *Hedychium coronarium.*
White kerria. See *Rhodotypos scandens,* illus. p.158.
White mugwort. See *Artemisia lactiflora,* illus. p.227.
White mulberry. See *Morus alba.*
White mullein. See *Verbascum lychnitis.*
White poplar. See *Populus alba,* illus. p.64.
White rosebay. See *Epilobium angustifolium* f. *album,* illus. p.226.
White sails. See *Spathiphyllum wallisii,* illus. p.300.
White Sally. See *Eucalyptus pauciflora,* illus. p.84.
White snakeroot. See *Eupatorium rugosum,* illus. p.240.
White spruce. See *Picea glauca.*
White trumpet lily. See *Lilium longiflorum,* illus. p.404.
White willow. See *Salix alba.*
White-backed hosta. See *Hosta hypoleuca.*
Whitebeam. See *Sorbus aria.*
  Swedish. See *Sorbus intermedia.*
Whiteywood. See *Melicytus ramiflorus.*
Whorl flower. See *Morina.*
Whorled Solomon's seal. See *Polygonatum verticillatum.*
Whorled water milfoil. See *Myriophyllum verticillatum,* illus. p.449.

Whortleberry. See *Vaccinium myrtillus.*
  Caucasian. See *Vaccinium arctostaphylos.*
Widow iris. See *Hermodactylus tuberosus,* illus. p.414.

WIGANDIA

HYDROPHYLLACEAE

Genus of evergreen perennials and shrubs, grown for their flowers and foliage. Tender, min. 7–10°C (45–50°F). Needs full light and moist but well-drained soil. Water potted plants freely when in full growth, moderately at other times. Cut down flowered stems in spring to prevent plants becoming straggly. Propagate by seed or softwood cuttings in spring. Whitefly is sometimes troublesome. Contact with foliage may aggravate skin allergies.
W. caracasana. Evergreen, erect, sparsely branched shrub. H 2–3m (6–10ft), S 1–2m (3–6ft). Produces oval, wavy-edged, toothed, deep green leaves, 45cm (18in) long and covered with white-hairs beneath. Carries 5-petalled, violet-purple flowers in large, terminal clusters from spring through to autumn. Is often grown annually from seed purely for its handsome leaves.

Wigginsia vorwerkiana. See *Parodia erinacea.*
Wilcoxia albiflora. See *Echinocereus leucanthus.*
Wilcoxia schmollii. See *Echinocereus schmollii.*
Wild buckwheat. See *Eriogonum.*
Wild cherry. See *Prunus avium,* illus. p.71.
Wild coffee. See *Polyscias guilfoylei.*
Wild daffodil. See *Narcissus pseudonarcissus,* illus. p.417.
Wild ginger. See *Asarum.*
Wild iris. See *Iris versicolor,* illus. p.234.
Wild Irishman. See *Discaria toumatou.*
Wild jonquil. See *Narcissus jonquilla,* illus. p.418.
Wild lily-of-the-valley. See *Pyrola rotundifolia.*
Wild marjoram. See *Origanum vulgare.*
Wild pansy. See *Viola tricolor,* illus. p.369.
Wild pineapple. See *Ananas bracteatus.*
Wild rum cherry. See *Prunus serotina,* illus. p.65.
Wild yellow lily. See *Lilium canadense.*
Willow. See *Salix.*
  Bay. See *Salix pentandra.*
  Black. See *Salix gracilistyla* 'Melanostachys'.
  Corkscrew. See *Salix babylonica* var. *pekinensis* 'Tortuosa'.
  Crack. See *Salix fragilis.*
  Creeping. See *Salix repens,* illus. p.156.
  Cricket-bat. See *Salix alba* var. *caerulea.*
  Dragon's-claw. See *Salix babylonica* var. *pekinensis* 'Tortuosa', illus. p.85.
  Dwarf. See *Salix herbacea.*
  Goat. See *Salix caprea.*

Willow (continued)
  Golden. See *Salix alba* var. *vitellina,* illus. p.74.
  Golden weeping. See *Salix* x *sepulcralis* var. *chrysocoma,* illus. p.74.
  Hoary. See *Salix elaeagnos.*
  Kilmarnock. See *Salix caprea* 'Kilmarnock'.
  Laurel. See *Salix pentandra.*
  Least. See *Salix herbacea.*
  Mountain. See *Salix arbuscula.*
  Musk. See *Salix aegyptiaca.*
  Net-veined. See *Salix reticulata,* illus. p.370.
  Pussy. See *Salix caprea.*
  Silver. See *Salix alba* var. *sericea.*
  Violet. See *Salix daphnoides,* illus. p.74.
  Weeping. See *Salix babylonica.*
  White. See *Salix alba.*
  Woolly. See *Salix lanata,* illus. p.156.
Willow gentian. See *Gentiana asclepiadea,* illus. p.263.
Willow herb. See *Epilobium.*
Willow moss. See *Fontinalis antipyretica.*
Willow myrtle. See *Agonis.*
Willow oak. See *Quercus phellos,* illus. p.71.
Willow-leaved magnolia. See *Magnolia salicifolia,* illus. p.75.
Willow-leaved sunflower. See *Helianthus salicifolius.*

x WILSONARA

See also ORCHIDS.
x *W.* **Hambuhren Stern 'Cheam'** (illus. p.297). Evergreen, epiphytic orchid for a cool greenhouse. H 23cm (9in). Narrowly oval leaves are 10cm (4in) long. Bears spikes of deep reddish-brown flowers, 9cm (3½in) across, each with a yellow lip; flowering season varies. Requires shade in summer.

Windflower. See *Anemone; Zephyranthes.*
  Snowdrop. See *Anemone sylvestris,* illus. p.268.
Windmill palm. See *Trachycarpus fortunei,* illus. p.84.
Wine-cup, Lacquered. See *Aechmea* Foster's Favorite Group, illus. p.265.
Winecups. See *Babiana rubrocyanea,* illus. p.431.
Wing nut. See *Pterocarya.*
  Caucasian. See *Pterocarya fraxinifolia.*
  Chinese. See *Pterocarya stenoptera.*
Winged spindle. See *Euonymus alatus,* illus. p.148.
Winged thorn rose. See *Rosa sericea* subsp. *omeiensis* f. *pteracantha.*
Winter aconite. See *Eranthis hyemalis,* illus. p.441.
Winter cherry. See *Cardiospermum halicacabum; Physalis alkekengi; Solanum capsicastrum.*
Winter cress. See *Barbarea vulgaris.*
Winter heath. See *Erica carnea.*
Winter heliotrope. See *Petasites fragrans.*
Winter iris. See *Iris unguicularis.*
Winter jasmine. See *Jasminum nudiflorum,* illus. p.151.

Winter savory. See *Satureja montana*.

Winter's bark. See *Drimys winteri*, illus. p.78.

Wintera aromatica. See *Drimys winteri*.

Winterberry. See *Ilex verticillata*, illus. p.98.

Wintergreen. See *Pyrola*.
  Round-leaved. See *Pyrola rotundifolia*.

Wintergreen fern. See *Polypodium cambricum*.

Wintersweet. See *Acokanthera oblongifolia*, illus. p.150; *Chimonanthus praecox*.

Wire-netting bush. See *Corokia cotoneaster*, illus. p.152.

Wishbone flower. See *Torenia fournieri*, illus. p.333.

WISTERIA

LEGUMINOSAE/PAPILIONACEAE

Genus of deciduous, woody-stemmed, twining climbers, grown for their spectacular flowers and suitable for walls and pergolas and for growing against buildings and trees. Grows in sun and in fertile, well-drained soil. Prune after flowering and again in late winter. Propagate by bench grafting in winter or by seed in autumn or spring. Plants produced from seed may not flower until some years old and often have poor flowers. All parts may cause severe discomfort if ingested.

W. brachybotrys f. *alba*. See *W.b.* 'Shiro Kapitan'. **'Shiro Kapitan'** (syn. *W.b.* f. *alba, W. venusta, W.v.* 'Alba Plena'; Silky wisteria) is a deciduous, woody-stemmed, twining climber. H to 9m (28ft) or more. Leaves are 20–35cm (8–14in) long, each with 9–13 oval leaflets. Produces 10–15cm (4–6in) long racemes of scented, pea-like, white flowers, each with a yellow blotch at base of upper petal, in early summer; sometimes flowers again sparsely in autumn. Zone 7.

W. chinensis. See *W. sinensis*.

W. floribunda (Japanese wisteria). **'Alba'** (syn. *W.f.* 'Shiro Noda') illus. p.207. **'Black Dragon'** see *W.f.* 'Royal Purple'. **'Lawrence'** has blue flowers in early summer. Zone 5. **'Macrobotrys'** (syn. *W.f.* 'Multijuga') is a deciduous, woody-stemmed, twining climber. H to 9m (28ft). Leaves, 25–35cm (10–14in) long, have 11–19 oval leaflets. Scented, pea-like,

lilac flowers, flushed darker, carried in racemes, 1–1.2m (3–4ft) long, are produced in early summer, and may produce oblong, velvety pods in late summer and autumn. **'Multijuga'** see *W.f.* 'Macrobotrys'. **'Royal Purple'** (syn. *W.f.* 'Black Dragon') has double, deep purple flowers, carried in racemes, 12–25cm (5–10in) long, produced in early summer; sometimes flowers again sparsely in autumn. **'Shiro Noda'** see *W.f.* 'Alba'. All zone 6 unless noted.

W. x *formosa* illus. p.215.

W. sinensis, syn. *W. chinensis*, illus. p.215. **'Alba'** illus. p.207. **'Prolific'**, H to 30m (100ft), is vigorous, with masses of single, lilac or pale violet flowers in longer racemes. Zone 6.

W. venusta. See *W. brachybotrys* 'Shiro Kapitan'. **'Alba Plena'** see *W. brachybotrys* 'Shiro Kapitan'

Wisteria
  Chinese. See *Wisteria sinensis*, illus. p.215.
  Japanese. See *Wisteria floribunda*.
  Silky. See *Wisteria brachybotrys* 'Shiro Kapitan'.

Witch alder. See *Fothergilla gardenii*.

Witch hazel. See *Hamamelis*.
  Chinese. See *Hamamelis mollis*.
  Japanese. See *Hamamelis japonica*.
  Virginian. See *Hamamelis virginiana*, illus. p.125.

Woad. See *Isatis tinctoria*.

WOLFFIA

Duckweed

LEMNACEAE

Genus of semi-evergreen, perennial, floating water plants, grown for their curiosity value as the smallest-known flowering plants. Is ideal for cold-water aquariums. Needs a sunny position. Remove excess plantlets as required. Propagate by redistribution of plantlets as required.

W. arrhiza (Least duckweed). Semi-evergreen, perennial, floating water plant. S 1mm (¹⁄₂in). Leaves are rounded and mid-green. Insignificant, greenish flowers appear year-round.

Wolf's bane. See *Aconitum*.

Wonga-wonga vine. See *Pandorea pandorana*.

Wood anemone. See *Anemone nemorosa*.

Wood lily. See *Trillium*. **Wood millet.** See *Milium effusum*.

Wood rose. See *Merremia tuberosa*.

Wood sorrel. See *Oxalis acetosella*.

Wood spurge. See *Euphorbia amygdaloides*.

Woodbine. See *Lonicera periclymenum*.

Woodruff. See *Galium odoratum*, illus. p.275.

Woodrush. See *Luzula*.
  Greater. See *Luzula sylvatica*.
  Snowy. See *Luzula nivea*, illus. p.307.

WOODSIA

DRYOPTERIDACEAE

Genus of deciduous ferns, suitable for rock gardens and alpine houses. Tolerates sun or semi-shade. May be difficult to cultivate: soil must provide constant moisture and also be quick-draining, and crowns of plants must sit above soil to avoid rotting. Propagate by division in early spring.

W. polystichoides (Holly-fern woodsia). Deciduous, tufted fern. H 10–30cm (4–12in), S 20–40cm (8–16in). In early spring, has lance-shaped, divided, pale green fronds, to 35cm (14in) long, softly hairy on both surfaces and scaly beneath; each is composed of 15–30 pairs of narrowly sickle-shaped or oblong pinnae, with slightly toothed margins. May be damaged by late frosts.

Woodsia, Holly-fern. See *Woodsia polystichoides*.

WOODWARDIA

BLECHNACEAE

Genus of evergreen or deciduous ferns. Prefers semi-shade and fibrous, moist, peaty soil. Remove faded fronds regularly. Propagate by division in spring.

W. radicans (Chain fern). Vigorous, evergreen, spreading fern. H 1.2m (4ft), S 60cm (2ft). Large, broadly lance-shaped, coarsely divided, arching fronds, with narrowly oval pinnae, are mid-green.

W. unigemmata (Asian chain fern). Evergreen fern very similar to *W. radicans*. H 1m (3ft), S 3m (10ft).

New foliage emerges brilliant red and fades to brown and then green.

Woolly morning glory. See *Argyreia nervosa*.

Woolly willow. See *Salix lanata*, illus. p.156.

Wormwood. See *Artemisia*.

Wormwood cassia. See *Senna artemisioides*.
  Roman. See *Artemisia pontica*, illus. p.290.

WORSLEYA

Blue amaryllis

AMARYLLIDACEAE

Genus of one species of evergreen, winter-flowering bulb, with a neck up to 75cm (2½ft) high crowned by a tuft of leaves and a 20–30cm (8–12in) leafless flower stem. Tender, min. 15°C (59°F). Needs full sun and well-drained soil, or compost mixed with osmunda fibre, perlite or bark chips and some leaf mould. Soil should never dry out. Propagate by seed in spring.

W. procera. See *W. rayneri*.

W. rayneri, syn. *Hippeastrum procerum, W. procera*. Evergreen, winter-flowering bulb. H 1–1.2m (3–4ft), S 45–60cm (1½–2ft). Bears long, strap-shaped, strongly curved leaves and up to 14 funnel-shaped, lilac-blue flowers, 15cm (6in) long, with wavy-edged petals.

WULFENIA

SCROPHULARIACEAE

Genus of evergreen, summer-flowering perennials with rough-textured leaves. Is suitable for alpine houses as it dislikes winter wet. It needs to have full sun and well-drained soil. Propagate by division in spring or by seed in autumn.

W. amherstiana illus. p.356.

W. carinthiaca. Evergreen, basal-rosetted perennial. H and S 25cm (10in). Has oblong to oval, toothed, dark green leaves, hairy beneath. The top quarter of each flower stem is covered in a dense spike of small, tubular, violet-blue flowers in summer.

Wych elm. See *Ulmus glabra*.

X, Y, Z

XANTHOCERAS

SAPINDACEAE

Genus of one species of deciduous, spring- to summer-flowering shrub or tree, grown for its foliage and flowers. Requires sun and fertile, well-drained soil. Does best in areas with hot summers. Propagate by seed in autumn or by root cuttings or suckers in late winter. Is susceptible to coral spot fungus.

X. sorbifolium illus. p.118.

XANTHOPHTHALMUM

ASTERACEAE/COMPOSITAE

Genus of annuals, grown for their daisy-like flower heads. Prefers full sun and well-drained soil. Propagate by seed in spring.

X. coronarium, syn. *Chrysanthemum coronarium*. Fast-growing, upright, branching annual. H 30cm–90cm (1–3ft), S 38cm (15in). Has feathery, divided, light green leaves. In summer bears single or semi-double, daisy-like, yellow or yellow-and-white flower heads, to 5cm (2in) across.

X. segetum, syn. *Chrysanthemum segetum*, illus. p.337.

XANTHORHIZA

RANUNCULACEAE

Genus of one species of deciduous, spring-flowering shrub, grown for its foliage and flowers. Prefers shade or semi-shade and moist soil. Propagate by division in autumn.

X. apiifolia. See *X. simplicissima*.
X. simplicissima, syn. *X. apiifolia* (Yellow-root). Deciduous, upright shrub that spreads by underground stems. H 60cm (2ft), S 1.5m (5ft). Bright green leaves, each consisting of usually 5 oval to lance-shaped, sharply toothed leaflets, turn bronze or purple in autumn. Bears nodding panicles of tiny, star-shaped, purple flowers from early to mid-spring as foliage emerges. Zone 4.

XANTHORRHOEA

Blackboy, Grass tree

XANTHORRHOEACEAE

Genus of evergreen, long-lived perennials, grown mainly as foliage plants. Tender, min. 10°C (50°F). Needs full sun, well-drained soil and a fairly dry atmosphere. Propagate by basal offsets or seed in spring.

X. australis. Evergreen perennial with a stout, dark trunk. H 60cm–1.2m (2–4ft), S 1.2–1.5m (4–5ft). Very narrow, arching, flattened, silvery-green leaves, 60cm (2ft) or more long, 2mm (1/10in) wide, spread from top of the trunk. In summer may produce small, fragrant, 6-petalled, white flowers, in dense, candle-like spikes, 60cm (2ft) or more long, on stems of similar length.

XANTHOSOMA

ARACEAE

Genus of perennials, with underground tubers or thick stems above ground, grown mainly for their attractive foliage. Many species are cultivated in the tropics for their edible, starchy tubers. Tender, min. 15°C (59°F). Requires a position in partial shade and rich, moist soil. The atmosphere should be kept moist at all times. Propagate by division; alternatively take stem cuttings in spring or summer.

X. sagittifolium illus. p.266.
X. violaceum. Stemless perennial with large, underground tubers and leaves rising from ground level. H and S 1.2m (4ft). Purplish leaf stalks, to over 60cm (2ft) long, carry broadly arrow-shaped leaf blades, 70cm (28in) long, dark green with purple midribs and veins. Intermittently bears greenish-purple spathes, yellower within, surrounding a brownish spadix.

XERANTHEMUM

Immortelle

ASTERACEAE/COMPOSITAE

Genus of summer-flowering annuals. Grow in sun and in fertile, very well-drained soil. Propagate by seed sown outdoors in spring.

X. annuum. Fairly fast-growing, upright annual with branching flower heads. H 60cm (2ft), S 45cm (1½ft). Has lance-shaped, silvery leaves. Daisy-like, papery, purple flower heads are produced in summer. Double forms are available in shades of pink, mauve, purple or white (illus. p.325).

XERONEMA

AGAVACEAE/PHORMIACEAE

Genus of evergreen, robust, tufted perennials, with short, creeping rootstocks, grown for their flowers. Tender, min. 10°C (50°F). Grow in sun or partial shade and in humus-rich, well-drained soil. Propagate by seed or division in spring.

X. callistemon. Evergreen, iris-like, clump-forming perennial. H 60cm–1m (2–3ft), S indefinite. Erect, folded leaves, 60cm–1m (2–3ft) long, are very narrow and hard-textured. In summer, short-stalked, 6-petalled, red flowers, to 3cm (1¼in) wide, are borne on one-sided racemes, 15–30cm (6–12in) long.

XEROPHYLLUM

LILIACEAE/MELANTHIACEAE

Genus of elegant, summer-flowering, rhizomatous perennials. Prefers full sun and moist, peaty soil. May be difficult to cultivate. Propagate by seed in autumn.

X. tenax. Clump-forming perennial. H 1–1.2m (3–4ft), S 30–60cm (1–2ft). Star-shaped, white flowers, with violet anthers, are borne in dense, terminal racemes in summer. Basal leaves are linear and mid-green.

Yam, Ornamental. See *Dioscorea discolor*, illus. p.219.
Yarrow. See *Achillea millefolium*.
Yatay palm. See *Butia*.
Yellow asphodel. See *Asphodeline lutea*, illus. p.238.
Yellow banksia. See *Rosa banksiae* 'Lutea', illus. p.199.
Yellow bells. See *Tecoma stans*, illus. p.96.
Yellow birch. See *Betula alleghaniensis*.
Yellow buckeye. See *Aesculus flava*, illus. p.82.
Yellow elder. See *Tecoma stans*, illus. p.96.
Yellow flag. See *Iris pseudacorus*, illus. p.235.
Yellow flax. See *Linum flavum*; *Reinwardtia indica*, illus. p.170.
Yellow foxglove. See *Digitalis grandiflora*.
Yellow fritillary. See *Fritillaria pudica*, illus. p.434.
Yellow haw. See *Crataegus flava*, illus. p.90.
Yellow jasmine. See *Jasminum humile*, illus. p.146.
Yellow kangaroo paw. See *Anigozanthos flavidus*, illus. p.254.
Yellow lady's slipper orchid. See *Cypripedium calceolus*, illus. p.298.
Yellow mariposa. See *Calochortus luteus*, illus. p.415.
Yellow morning glory. See *Merremia tuberosa*.
Yellow musk. See *Mimulus luteus*, illus. illus. p.292.
Yellow oleander. See *Thevetia peruviana*, illus. p.93.
Yellow ox-eye. See *Buphthalmum salicifolium*.
Yellow palm. See *Dypsis lutescens*, illus. p.100.
Yellow parilla. See *Menispermum canadense*.
Yellow pitcher plant. See *Sarracenia flava*, illus. p.290.
Yellow pond lily. See *Nuphar advena*.
Yellow rocket. See *Barbarea vulgaris*.
Yellow Rose of Texas. See *Rosa* x *harisonii*.
Yellow scabious. See *Cephalaria gigantea*.
Yellow skunk cabbage. See *Lysichiton americanus*, illus. p.451.
Yellow turkscap lily. See *Lilium pyrenaicum*.
Yellow water lily. See *Nuphar lutea*, illus. p.451.
Yellow whitlow grass. See *Draba aizoides*.
Yellow wood. See *Cladrastis kentukea*, illus. p.82.
Yellow-root. See *Xanthorhiza simplicissima*.
Yesterday-today-and-tomorrow. See *Brunfelsia pauciflora*.
Yew. See *Taxus baccata*.

Japanese. See *Taxus cuspidata*, illus. p.109.
Plum. See *Cephalotaxus harringtonii*; *Prumnopitys andina*.
Plum-fruited. See *Prumnopitys andina*.
Prince Albert's. See *Saxegothaea conspicua*.
Yoshino cherry. See *Prunus* x *yedoensis*, illus. p.87.
Young's weeping birch. See *Betula pendula* 'Youngii', illus. p.92.
Youth-on-age. See *Tolmiea menziesii*.

YUCCA,

syn. HESPEROYUCCA

AGAVACEAE

Genus of evergreen shrubs and trees, grown for the architectural value of their bold, sword-shaped, clustered leaves and their showy panicles of usually white flowers. Makes excellent container-grown plants. Hardy to tender, min. 7°C (45°F). Requires a position in full sun and well-drained soil. Water containerized specimens moderately except when they are not in full growth and watering should then be reduced. Regularly remove spent flowering stems. Propagate in spring: frost-tender species by seed or suckers, hardier species by root cuttings or division.

Y. aloifolia illus. p.153.
Y. elephantipes 'Variegata' (illus. p.47). Evergreen, large, upright shrub or small tree. H to 10m (30ft), S 5–8m (15–25ft). Min. 10°C (50°F). Several to many sparsely branched trunks arise near ground level. Leaves are narrowly lance-shaped, stiffly leathery, light to mid-green and creamy-white at the margins. On mature plants, pendent, hemispherical, white to cream flowers are borne in dense, erect panicles from summer to autumn.
Y. filamentosa (Adam's needle). Clump-forming, evergreen, basal-rosetted shrub. H 2m (6ft), S 1.5m (5ft). From mid- through to late summer produces tall panicles of pendulous, tulip-shaped, white flowers, which rise up through low-growing tufts of sword-shaped, deep green leaves, each edged with white threads. Zone 4. 'Golden sword' has foliage with a central yellow band. Zone 4.
Y. filifera 'Ivory'. See *Y. flaccida* 'Ivory'.
Y. flaccida 'Ivory', syn. *Y. filifera* 'Ivory', illus. p.160.
Y. glauca (Spanish bayonet). Evergreen, rosette-forming shrub with sharply tipped, narrow leaves up to 60cm (2ft) long. H and S 1.2m (4ft). When established, will send up 1m (3ft) tall spikes of creamy-white, waxy bell-like flowers in summer. Zone 3.
Y. gloriosa (Spanish dagger) illus. p.137. 'Nobilis' is an evergreen shrub. H and S 2m (6ft). Stem is stout and usually unbranched, and crowned with a large tuft of long, sword-shaped, sharply pointed, blue-green leaves, the

outer ones semi-pendent. Pendulous, tulip-shaped, red-backed, white flowers are borne in long, erect panicles from mid-summer to early autumn. Zone 8.
Y. parviflora. See *Hesperaloe parviflora.*
Y. whipplei illus. p.160.

Yulan. See *Magnolia denudata,* illus. p.75.

YUSHANIA

GRAMINEAE/POACEAE

See also GRASSES, BAMBOOS, RUSHES and SEDGES.
Y. anceps, syn. *Arundinaria anceps, A. jaunsarensis, Sinarundinaria jaunsarensis,* illus. p.308.

ZALUZIANSKYA

SCROPHULARIACEAE

Genus of sticky, low-growing annuals and evergreen perennials and sub-shrubs, grown for their spikes of very fragrant, tubular flowers with spreading petals. Needs full sun and moist but sharply drained, humus-rich soil. Propagate by stem-tip cuttings regularly in summer as plants are short-lived.
Z. ovata. Clump-forming, evergreen perennial. H to 25cm (10in), S to 60cm (24in). Branching, brittle stems bear ovate, toothed, sticky, grey-green leaves. Produces crimson-backed, white flowers over a long period in summer.

ZANTEDESCHIA

ARACEAE

Genus of summer-flowering, tuberous perennials, usually remaining evergreen in a warm climate, grown for their erect, funnel-shaped spathes, each of which encloses a club-shaped spadix. Hardy to tender, min. 10°C (50°F). Requires a position in full sun or partial shade and well-drained soil. *Z. aethiopica,* however, will also grow in 15–30cm (6–12in) of water and therefore is suitable as a marginal water plant. Propagate by offsets in winter. All parts of the plant may cause mild stomach upset if ingested, and contact with the sap may irritate the skin.
Z. aethiopica (Arum lily). **'Crowborough'** illus. p.397. **'Green Goddess'** illus. p.397.
Z. albomaculata, syn. *Z. melanoleuca.* Summer-flowering, tuberous perennial. H 30–40cm (12–16in), S 30cm (12in). Tender. Bears arrow-shaped, semi-erect, basal leaves with transparent spots. Produces a yellow spadix inside a white spathe, 12–20cm (5–8in) long, shading to green at the base and with a deep purple blotch inside.
Z. 'Black-eyed Beauty'. Summer-flowering, tuberous perennial. H 30–40cm (12–16in), S 15cm (6in). Tender. Broadly heart-shaped, semi-erect, mid- to dark green, basal leaves are heavily white spotted. Each flower stem has a golden-yellow spadix, surrounded by a cream spathe, 15cm (6in) long, with a central black mark in the throat.

Z. 'Black Magic'. Summer-flowering, tuberous perennial. H 75cm (30in), S 20cm (8in). Tender. Broadly heart-shaped, semi-erect, mid- to dark green, basal leaves are heavily mottled with white. Each flower stem produces a golden-yellow spadix, surrounded by a black-throated, yellow spathe, 15cm (6in) long.
Z. elliottiana illus. p.402.
Z. melanoleuca. See *Z. albomaculata.*
Z. rehmannii (Pink arum). Summer-flowering, tuberous perennial. H 40cm (16in), S 30cm (12in). Tender. Basal leaves are arrow-shaped, semi-erect, green and generally without marks. Each flower stem produces a yellow spadix, surrounded by a reddish-pink spathe, 7–8cm (3in) long and narrowly tubular at the base.

ZANTHOXYLUM

RUTACEAE

Genus of deciduous or evergreen, spiny shrubs and trees, grown for their aromatic foliage, fruits and habit. Requires a position in sun or semi-shade and in fertile soil. Propagate by seed in autumn or by root cuttings in late winter.
Z. piperitum illus. p.145.
Z. simulans illus. p.148.

ZAUSCHNERIA

ONAGRACEAE

Genus of sub-shrubby, evergreen or deciduous perennials, grown for their mass of flowers. Requires a sunny position and well-drained soil. Propagate by seed or division in spring or by taking side-shoot cuttings in summer.
Z. californica, syn. *Epilobium californicum.* Clump-forming, woody-based, evergreen or semi-evergreen perennial. H and S 45cm (18in). Terminal clusters of tubular, bright scarlet flowers, borne on slender stems, are produced in late summer and early autumn. Bears lance-shaped, rich green leaves. subsp. *cana* (syn. *Epilobium canum, Z. cana),* H 30cm (12in) is deciduous and produces linear, grey leaves and fuchsia-like, brilliant scarlet flowers. Subsp. *cana* **'Dublin'** (syn. *Z.c.* 'Glasnevin') illus. p.355. **'Glasnevin'** see *Z.c.* subsp. *cana* 'Dublin'.
Z. cana. See *Z. californica* subsp. *cana.*
Z. septentrionalis, syn. *Epilobium septentrionale.* Mat-forming, non-woody, deciduous perennial. H 10–20cm (4–8in), S to 20cm (8in). Terminal clusters of numerous, short-stalked, tubular, scarlet flowers are produced in late summer. Has oval to lance-shaped, grey to grey-green leaves.

ZEA

Indian corn, Maize

GRAMINEAE/POACEAE

See also GRASSES, BAMBOOS, RUSHES and SEDGES.
Z. mays (Ornamental maize, Sweet corn). **'Gracillima Variegata'** illus. p.320. **'Harlequin'** is a fairly fast-

growing, upright annual. H 1–2m (3–6ft), S 60cm (2ft). Lance-shaped leaves are 60cm (2ft) long and striped with green, red and white. Feathery, silky flower heads, 15cm (6in) long, borne on long stems, are produced in mid-summer, followed by large, cylindrical, green-sheathed, yellow seed heads, known as cobs, with deep red grains. **'Strawberry Corn',** H 1.2m (4ft), produces seed heads with small, yellow to burgundy-red grains, enclosed within yellow-green spathe-bracts.

Zebra plant. See *Aphelandra squarrosa; Calathea zebrina,* illus. p.266.
Zebrina pendula. See *Tradescantia zebrina.*

ZELKOVA

ULMACEAE

Genus of deciduous trees, grown mainly for their foliage and habit and are best when planted as isolated specimens. Produces insignificant flowers in spring. Hardy, but prefers some shelter. Does best in full sun and requires deep, fertile, moist but well-drained soil. Propagate by seed in autumn.
Z. abelicea, syn. *Z. cretica.* Deciduous, bushy-headed, spreading tree. H 5m (15ft), S 7m (22ft). Produces small leaves which are oval, prominently toothed and glossy, dark green. Zone 9.
Z. carpinifolia (Caucasian elm). Deciduous tree with a short, stout trunk from which many upright branches arise to make an oval, dense crown. H 30m (100ft), S 25m (80ft). Produces oval, sharply toothed, dark green leaves, turning to orange-brown in autumn. Zone 6.
Z. cretica. See *Z. abelicea.*
Z. serrata illus. p.71.

ZENOBIA

ERICACEAE

Genus of one species of deciduous or semi-evergreen, summer-flowering shrub, grown for its flowers. Requires semi-shade and moist, peaty, acid soil. Prune out older, weaker shoots after flowering to maintain vigour. Propagate by semi-ripe cuttings in summer.
Z. pulverulenta illus. p.138.

ZEPHYRANTHES

Rain lily, Windflower

AMARYLLIDACEAE

Genus of clump-forming bulbs with an erect, crocus-like flower on each stem. Needs a sheltered, sunny site and open, well-drained but moist soil. Container-grown bulbs need a dryish, warm period after foliage dies down in summer, followed by copious amounts of water to stimulate flowering. Propagate by seed in autumn or in spring.
Z. atamasco (Atamasco lily). Clump-forming, early summer-flowering bulb. H 15–25cm (6–10in), S 8–10cm (3–4in). Basal leaves are very narrow, grass-like and semi-erect. Each stem produces a widely funnel-shaped,

purple-tinged, white flower, opening to 10cm (4in) wide, in spring or summer.
Z. candida illus. p.437.
Z. carinata. See *Z. grandiflora.*
Z. citrina. Clump-forming, autumn-flowering bulb. H 10–15cm (4–6in), S 5–8cm (2–3in). Has rush-like, erect, basal, green leaves. Stems produce funnel-shaped, bright yellow flowers, opening to 4–5cm (1½–2in) wide, in autumn.
Z. grandiflora, syn. *Z. carinata, Z. rosea* of gardens, illus. p.424.
Z. robusta. See *Habranthus robustus.*
Z. rosea. Clump-forming, autumn-flowering bulb. H 15–20cm (6–8in), S 8–10cm (3–4in). Has semi-erect, grass-like, basal, green leaves. Stems produce short-tubed, funnel-shaped, pink flowers.
Z. rosea of gardens. See *Z. grandiflora.*

ZIGADENUS

LILIACEAE/MELANTHIACEAE

Genus of summer-flowering bulbs with spikes of star-shaped, 6-petalled flowers. It requires a position in sun or partial shade and well-drained soil. Water copiously in spring and summer, when in growth; less at other times. Remains dormant in winter. Propagate by division in early spring or by seed in autumn or spring. All parts are highly toxic if ingested.
Z. elegans. Clump-forming, summer-flowering bulb. H 30–50cm (12–20in), S 10–15cm (4–6in). Bears long, narrowly strap-shaped, semi-erect, basal leaves. Every stem produces a spike of greenish-white flowers, each 1cm (½in) wide and with a yellowish-green nectary near the base of every petal.
Z. fremontii illus. p.420.
Z. nuttallii. Clump-forming, summer-flowering bulb. H 30–60cm (12–24in), S 8cm (3in). Narrowly strap-shaped, semi-erect, basal leaves are mid- to dark green. Produces dense spikes of numerous, tiny, creamy-yellow flowers, each 6–8mm (¼–⅜in) across.

Zigzag bamboo. See *Phyllostachys flexuosa,* illus. p.308.

ZINNIA

ASTERACEAE/COMPOSITAE

Genus of annuals with large, dahlia-like flower heads that are excellent for cutting. Requires a position in sun and in fertile, well-drained soil. Dead flower heads should be removed regularly to promote flowering. Propagate by seed sown under glass in early spring.
Z. angustifolia 'Orange Star'. See *Z. haageana* 'Orange Star'. **'Persian Carpet'** see *Z. haageana* 'Persian Carpet'.
Z. elegans. Moderately fast-growing, upright, sturdy annual. H 60–75cm (2–2½ft), S 30cm (1ft). Bears oval to lance-shaped leaves that are pale or mid-green. Dahlia-like, purple flower heads, over 5cm (2in) wide, are produced in summer and early autumn. Hybrids of *Z. elegans* are available in shades of yellow, red, pink, purple, cream or white.

'Belvedere' illus. p.338.
Cactus-flowered Group,
H 60–90cm (24–36in), have large,
semi-double flower heads, similar to
those of cactus dahlias, with long,
narrow, quilled petals, in a broad range
of colours.

Dreamland Series, H 20–25cm
(8–10in), are compact and suited for
growing in containers or for bedding.
'Envy' illus. p.335.

Hobgoblin Series, H to 45cm (18in),
produce sturdy, bushy plants, with
small, single, weather-resistant flower
heads in a broad range of colours.

Peter Pan Series, H 20cm (8in), are
very dwarf, with double flower heads
in a wide range of colours.

Ruffles Series (mixed) illus. p.329,
(scarlet) illus. p.328.

Short Stuff Series, H 25cm (10in),
are dwarf, with double flower heads in
a broad range of colours.

Small World Series, H to 45cm
(18in), are dwarf and produce long-
lasting, double flower heads in an
extensive range of colours, including
pale pink.

'State Fair', H to 75cm (30in), is
vigorous, and produces large, double,
lavender, rose-pink, orange, purple or
scarlet flower heads.

Thumbelina Series illus. p.322.
Z. haageana **'Classic'.** See
Z.h. 'Orange Star'. **'Orange Star'** (syn.
Z. angustifolia 'Orange Star',
Z. haageana 'Classic') illus p.341.
'Persian Carpet' (syn. *Z. angustifolia*
'Persian Carpet') is a moderately fast-
growing, upright, dwarf annual. H 38cm
(15in), S 30cm (12in). Pale-green leaves
are lance-shaped and hairy. Small,
weather-resistant, dahlia-like, double
flower heads, opening to over 2.5cm
(1in) wide, are produced through the
summer, in a range of colours.

Zinnia, Creeping. See *Sanvitalia
procumbens*, illus. p.336.

ZIZANIA

GRAMINEAE/POACEAE

See also GRASSES, BAMBOOS,
RUSHES and SEDGES.
Z. aquatica (Canada wild rice).
Annual, grass-like, marginal water
plant. H 3m (10ft), S 45cm (18in). Has
grass-like, mid-green leaves and, in
summer, grass-like, pale green flowers,
followed by rice-like seeds that attract
waterfowl. Needs sun; suitable for up to
23cm (9in) deep water. Propagate from
seed stored damp and sown in spring.

Zygocactus truncatus. See
Schlumbergera truncata.

ZYGOPETALUM

See also ORCHIDS.
Z. mackaii, syn. *Z. mackayi* (illus.
p.298). Evergreen, epiphytic orchid for
growing in a cool or intermediate
greenhouse. H 30cm (12in). In autumn
produces long sprays of fragrant,
brown-blotched, green flowers, 8cm
(3in) across, with reddish-indigo veins,
and white lips. Ribbed leaves are
narrowly oval, and 30cm (12in) long.
Requires semi-shade in summer.
Z. mackayi. See *Z. mackaii.*
Z. Perrenoudii (illus. p.298).
Evergreen, epiphytic orchid for a cool
or intermediate greenhouse. H 30cm
(12in). Spikes of fragrant, violet-
purple-lipped, dark brown flowers,
8cm (3in) across, are produced in
winter. Has narrowly oval, ribbed
leaves, 30cm (12in) long. Requires a
position in semi-shade in summer.

Glossary of Terms

Acid [of soil]. With a *pH* value of less than 7; see also *alkaline* and *neutral*.

Adventitious [of roots]. Arising directly from a stem or leaf.

Aerial root. See *root*.

Air-layering. A method of propagation by which a portion of stem is induced to root by enclosing it in a suitable medium such as damp moss and securing it with plastic sheeting; roots will form if the moss is kept moist.

Alkaline [of soil]. With a *pH* value of more than 7; some plants will not tolerate alkaline soils and must be grown in *neutral* or *acid* soil.

Alpine house. An unheated greenhouse, used for the cultivation of mainly alpine and bulbous plants, that provides greater ventilation and usually more light than a conventional greenhouse.

Alternate [of leaves]. Borne singly at each *node*, on either side of a stem.

Annual. A plant that completes its life cycle, from germination through to flowering and seeding and then death, in one growing season.

Anther. The part of a *stamen* that produces pollen; it is usually borne on a *filament*.

Apex. The tip or growing point of an organ such as a leaf or shoot.

Areole. A modified, cushion-like *tubercle*, peculiar to the family Cactaceae, that bears hairs, spines, leaves, side-branches or flowers.

Asclepiad. A member of the family Asclepiadaceae, e.g. *Asclepias, Hoya, Stephanotis*.

Auricle. An ear-like lobe such as is sometimes found at the base of a leaf.

Awn. A stiff, bristle-like projection commonly found on grass seeds and *spikelets*.

Axil. The angle between a leaf and stem where an axillary bud develops.

Bedding plant. A plant that is mass-planted to provide a temporary display.

Biennial. A plant that flowers, seeds and dies in the second season after germination, producing only stems, roots and leaves in the first season.

Blade. The flattened and often broad part of a leaf.

Bloom. 1. A flower or blossom. 2. A fine, waxy, whitish or bluish-white coating on stems, leaves or fruits.

Bog garden. An area where the soil is kept permanently damp but not waterlogged.

Bole. The trunk of a *tree* from ground level to the first major branch.

Bolt. To produce flowers and seed prematurely, particularly in the case of vegetables such as lettuce and beetroot.

Bonsai. A method of producing dwarf trees or shrubs by special techniques that include pruning roots, pinching out shoots, removing growth buds and training branches and stems.

Bract. A modified leaf at the base of a flower or flower cluster. Bracts may resemble normal leaves or be reduced and scale-like in appearance; they are often large and brightly coloured.

Bud. A rudimentary or condensed shoot containing embryonic leaves or flowers.

Bulb. A storage organ consisting mainly of fleshy scales and swollen, modified leaf-bases on a much reduced stem. Bulbs usually, but not always, grow underground.

Bulbil. A small, *bulb*-like organ, often borne in a leaf *axil*, occasionally in a *flower head*; it may be used for propagation.

Bulblet. A small *bulb* produced at the base of a mature one.

Bur. 1. A prickly or spiny *fruit*, or aggregate of fruits. 2. A woody outgrowth on the stems of certain trees.

Cactus (pl. cacti). A member of the family Cactaceae, often *succulent* and spiny.

Calyx (pl. calyces). The outer part of a flower, usually small and green but sometimes showy and brightly coloured, that encloses the petals in bud and is formed from the *sepals*.

Capsule. A dry *fruit* that splits open when ripe to release its seeds.

Carpel. The female portion of a flower, or part of it, consisting of an *ovary, stigma* and *style*.

Catkin. A flower cluster, normally pendulous. Flowers lack petals, are often stalkless, surrounded by scale-like *bracts*, and are usually unisexual.

Caudex (pl. caudices). The stem base of a woody plant such as a *palm* or tree fern.

Cladode. A stem, often flattened, with the function and appearance of a leaf.

Claw. The narrow, basal portion of petals in some genera, e.g. *Dianthus*.

Climber. A plant that climbs using other plants or objects as a support: a **leaf-stalk** climber by coiling its leaf stalks around supports; a **root** climber by producing aerial, supporting roots; a **self-clinging** climber by means of suckering pads; a **tendril** climber by coiling its tendrils; a **twining** climber by coiling stems. **Scandent, scrambling** and **trailing climbers** produce long stems that grow over plants or other supports; they attach themselves only loosely, if at all.

Clone. A group of genetically identical plants, propagated vegetatively.

Compound. Made up of several or many parts, e.g. a leaf divided into 2 or more *leaflets*.

Cone. The clustered flowers or woody, seed-bearing structures of a conifer.

Coppice. To cut back to near ground level each year in order to produce vigorous, ornamental shoots, as is usual with some *Cornus* and *Eucalyptus*.

Cordon. A trained plant restricted in growth to one main stem, occasionally 2–4 stems.

Corm. A *bulb*-like, underground storage organ consisting mainly of a swollen stem base and often surrounded by a papery tunic.

Cormlet. A small *corm* arising at the base of a mature one.

Corolla. The part of a flower formed by the petals.

Corona (crown). A petal-like outgrowth sometimes borne on the *corolla*, e.g. the trumpet or cup of a *Narcissus*.

Corymb. A racemose flower cluster in which the inner flower stalks are shorter than the outer, resulting in a rounded or flat-topped head.

Cotyledon. See *seed leaf*.

Creeper. A plant that grows close to the ground, usually rooting as it spreads.

Crisped. Minutely wavy-edged.

Crown. 1. The part of the plant at or just below the soil surface from which new shoots are produced and to which they die back in autumn. 2. The upper, branched part of a tree above the *bole*. 3. A *corona*.

Culm. The usually hollow stem of a grass or bamboo.

Cutting. A section of a plant that is removed and used for propagation. The various types of cutting are: **basal** – taken from the base of a plant (usually *herbaceous*) as it begins to produce growth in spring; **greenwood** – made from the tip of young growth; **hardwood** – mature wood taken at the end of the growing season; **leaf** – a detached leaf or part of a leaf; **root** – part of a semi-mature or mature root; **semi-ripe** – half-ripened wood taken during the growing season; **softwood** – young growth taken at the beginning of the growing season; **stem** – a greenwood, hardwood, semi-ripe or softwood cutting; **tip** – a greenwood cutting.

Cyme. A flower cluster in which each growing point terminates in a flower.

Dead-head. To remove spent flower heads so as to promote further growth or flowering, prevent seeding or improve appearance.

Deciduous. Losing its leaves annually at the end of the growing season; **semi-deciduous** plants lose only some leaves.

Decumbent. Growing close to the ground but ascending at the tips.

Dentate. With toothed margins.

Die-back. Death of the tips of shoots due to frost or disease.

Dioecious. Bearing male and female flowers on separate plants.

Disbud. To remove surplus buds to promote larger flowers or fruits.

Disc floret, disc flower. A small and often individually inconspicuous, usually tubular flower, one of many that comprise the central portion of a composite flower head such as a daisy.

Division. A method of propagation by which a clump is divided into several parts during dormancy.

Elliptic [of leaves]. Broadening in the centre and narrowing towards each end.

Entire [of leaves]. With untoothed margins.

Epiphyte. A plant that in nature grows on the surface of another without being parasitic.

Evergreen. Retaining its leaves at the end of the growing season although losing some older leaves regularly throughout the year; **semi-evergreen** plants retain only some leaves or lose older leaves only when the new growth is produced.

F1 hybrid. The first generation derived from crossing 2 distinct plants, usually when the parents are pure-bred lines and the offspring are vigorous. Seed from F1 hybrids does not come *true* to type.

Fall. An outer *perianth segment* of an iris, which projects outwards or downwards from the inner segments.

Fan palm. A *palm* with *palmate* rather than *pinnate* leaves.

Farina. A powdery, white, sometimes yellowish deposit naturally occurring on some leaves and flowers.

Fibrous root. A fine, young root, usually one of many.

Filament. The stalk of an *anther*.

Floret. A single flower in a head of many flowers.

Flower. The basic flower forms are: **single**, with one row of usually 4–6 *petals*; **semi-double**, with more petals, usually in 2 rows; **double**, with many petals in several rows and few or no *stamens*; **fully double**, usually rounded in shape, with densely packed petals and the stamens absent or obscured.

Flower head. A mass of small *flowers* or *florets* that together appear as one flower, e.g. a daisy.

Force. To induce artificially the early production of growth, flowers or *fruits*.

Frond. The leaf-like organ of a fern. Some ferns produce both barren and fertile fronds, the fertile fronds bearing *spores*.

Fruit. The structure in plants that bears one or more ripe seeds, e.g. a berry or nut.

Glabrous. Not hairy.

Glaucous. Bluish-white, bluish-green or bluish-grey.

Globose. Spherical.

Glochid. One of the barbed bristles or hairs, usually small, borne on a cactus *areole*.

Grafting. A method of propagation by which an artificial union is made between different parts of individual plants; usually the *shoot* (scion) of one is grafted onto the *rootstock* (stock) of another.

Heel. The small portion of old wood that is retained at the base of a cutting when it is removed from the stem.

Herbaceous. Dying down at the end of the growing season.

Hose-in-hose [of flowers]. With one *corolla* borne inside another, forming a double or semi-double *flower*.

Inflorescence. A cluster of flowers with a distinct arrangement, e.g. *corymb, cyme, panicle, raceme, spike, umbel*.

Insectivorous plant. A plant that traps and digests insects and other small animals to supplement its nutrient intake.

Key. A winged seed such as is produced by the sycamore (*Acer pseudoplatanus*).

Lateral. A side growth that arises from the side of a shoot or root.

Layering. A method of propagation by which a stem is induced to root by being pegged down into the soil while it is still attached to the parent plant. See also *air-layering*.

Leaflet. The subdivision of a compound leaf.

Lenticel. A small, usually corky area on a stem or other part of a plant, which acts as a breathing pore.

Lime. Compounds of calcium; the

amount of lime in soil determines whether it is *alkaline*, *neutral* or *acid*.

Linear [of leaves]. Very narrow with parallel sides.

Lip. A lobe comprising 2 or more flat or sometimes pouched *perianth segments*.

Loam. Well-structured, fertile soil that is moisture-retentive but free-draining.

Marginal water plant. A plant that grows partially submerged in shallow water or in moist soil at the edge of a pond.

Midrib. The main, central vein of a leaf or the central stalk to which the *leaflets* of a *pinnate* leaf are attached.

Monocarpic. Flowering and fruiting only once before dying; such plants may take several years to reach flowering size.

Mulch. A layer of organic matter applied to the soil over or around a plant to conserve moisture, protect the roots from frost, reduce the growth of weeds and enrich the soil.

Naturalize. To establish and grow as if in the wild.

Nectar. A sweet, sugary liquid secreted by the **nectary** – glandular tissue usually found in the flower but sometimes found on the leaves or stems.

Neutral [of soil]. With a *pH* value of 7, the point at which soil is neither *acid* nor *alkaline*.

Node. The point on a stem from which a leaf or leaves arise.

Offset. A small plant that arises by natural vegetative reproduction, usually at the base of the mother plant.

Opposite [of leaves]. Borne 2 to each *node*, one opposite the other.

Ovary. The part of the female portion of the flower, containing embryonic seeds, that will eventually form the *fruit*.

Palm. An evergreen *tree* or *shrub*-like plant, normally single-stemmed, with *palmate* or *pinnate* leaves usually in terminal rosettes; strictly a member of the family Palmae.

Palmate. Lobed in the fashion of a hand, strictly with 5 lobes arising from the same point.

Pan. A shallow, free-draining pot in which alpine plants or bulbs are grown.

Panicle. A branched *raceme*.

Papilla (pl. papillae). A minute protuberance or gland-like structure.

Pea-like [of flowers]. Of the same structure as a pea flower.

Peat bed. A specially constructed area, edged with peat blocks and containing moisture-retentive, acidic, peaty soil.

Pedicel. The stalk of an individual flower.

Peduncle. The stalk of a flower cluster.

Peltate [of leaves]. Shield-shaped, with the stalk inserted towards or at the centre of the blade and not at the margin.

Perennial. Living for at least 3 seasons. In this book the term when used as a noun, and unless qualified, denotes an *herbaceous* perennial. A woody-based perennial dies down only partially, leaving a woody stem at the base.

Perianth. The outer parts of the flower comprising the *calyx* and the *corolla*. The term is often used when the calyx and the corolla are very similar in form.

Perianth segment. One portion of the *perianth*, resembling a *petal* and sometimes known as a tepal.

Petal. One portion of the often showy and coloured part of the *corolla*. In some families, e.g. Liliaceae, the *perianth segments* are petal-like and referred to horticulturally as petals.

Petaloid. Like a petal.

Petiole. The stalk of a *leaf*.

pH. The scale by which the acidity or alkalinity of soil is measured. See also *acid*, *alkaline*, *neutral*.

Phyllode. A flattened leaf stalk, which functions as and resembles a leaf.

Pinch out. To remove the growing tips of a plant to induce the production of side-shoots.

Pinna (pl. pinnae). The primary division of a *pinnate* leaf. The fertile pinnae of ferns produce *spores*, vegetative pinnae do not.

Pinnate [of leaves]. Compound, with *leaflets* arranged on opposite sides of a central stalk.

Pistil. The female part of a flower comprising the *ovary*, *stigma* and *style*.

Pollard [of a tree]. To cut back to its main branches in order to restrict growth.

Pollination. The transfer of pollen from the *anthers* to the *stigma* of the same or different flowers, resulting in the fertilization of the embryonic seeds in the *ovary*.

Procumbent. Prostrate, creeping along the ground.

Raceme. An unbranched flower cluster with several or many stalked flowers borne singly along a main axis, the youngest at the apex.

Ray floret, ray flower. One of the flowers, usually with strap-shaped petals, that together form the outer ring of flowers in a composite *flower head* such as a daisy.

Ray petal. The petal or fused petals, often showy, of a ray *floret*.

Recurved. Curved backwards.

Reflexed. Bent sharply backwards.

Revert. To return to its original state, as when a plain green leaf is produced on a variegated plant.

Rhizome. An underground, creeping stem that acts as a storage organ and bears leafy shoots.

Root. The part of a plant, normally underground, that functions as anchorage and through which water and nutrients are absorbed. An **aerial root** emerges from the stem at some distance above the soil level.

Rootball. The roots and accompanying soil or compost visible when a plant is lifted.

Rootstock. A well-rooted plant onto which a scion is grafted; see *grafting*.

Rosette. A group of leaves radiating from approximately the same point, often borne at ground level at the base of a very short stem.

Runner. A horizontally spreading, usually slender stem that forms roots at each node; often confused with *stolon*.

Scale. 1. A reduced or modified leaf. 2. Part of a conifer *cone*.

Scandent. See *climber*.

Scarify. To scar the coat of a seed by abrasion in order to speed water intake and hence germination.

Scion. See *grafting*.

Scree. An area composed of a deep layer of stone chippings mixed with a small amount of loam. It provides extremely sharp drainage for plants that resent moisture at their base.

Seed head. Any usually dry *fruit* that contains ripe seeds.

Seed leaf (cotyledon). The first leaf, pair of leaves or occasionally group of leaves produced by a seed as it germinates. In some plants they remain below ground.

Self-seed. To produce seedlings around the parent plant.

Sepal. Part of a *calyx*, usually insignificant but sometimes showy.

Series. The name applied to a group of similar but not identical plants, usually annuals, linked by one or more common features.

Sessile. Without a stalk.

Sheath. A cylindrical structure that surrounds or encircles, partially or fully, another plant organ such as a stem.

Shoot. The aerial part of a plant which bears leaves. A **side-shoot** arises from the side of a main shoot.

Shrub. A plant with *woody stems*, usually well-branched from or near the base.

Shy-flowering. Reluctant to flower; producing few flowers.

Simple [of leaves]. Not divided into leaflets.

Soft-stemmed. The opposite of *woody-stemmed*.

Spadix (pl. spadices). A *spike*-like flower cluster that is usually fleshy and bears numerous small flowers. Spadices are characteristic of the family Araceae, e.g. *Arum*.

Spathe. A large *bract*, or sometimes 2, frequently coloured and showy, that surrounds a *spadix* (as in *Arum*) or an individual flower bud (as in *Narcissus*).

Sphagnum. Mosses common to bogs; their moisture-retentive character makes them ideal components of some growing media. They are used particularly for orchid cultivation.

Spike. A racemose flower cluster with several or many unstalked flowers borne along a common axis.

Spikelet. 1. The flowering unit of grasses comprising one or several flowers with basal *bracts*. 2. A small *spike*, part of a branched flower cluster.

Spore. The minute reproductive structure of flowerless plants, e.g. ferns, fungi and mosses.

Sporangium (pl. sporangia). A body that produces *spores*.

Sport. A mutation, caused by an accidental or induced change in the genetic make-up of a plant, which gives rise to a shoot with different characteristics to those of the parent plant.

Spur. 1. A hollow projection from a petal, often producing *nectar*. 2. A short stem bearing a group of flower buds such as is found on fruit trees.

Spur back. To cut back side-shoots to within 2 or 3 buds of the main shoot.

Stamen. The *anther* and *filament*.

Standard. 1. A *tree* or *shrub* with a clear length of bare stem below the first branches. Certain shrubs, e.g. roses and fuchsias, may be trained to form standards. 2. One of the 3 inner and often erect *perianth segments* of the iris flower. 3. The larger, usually upright back petal of a flower in the family Leguminosae, e.g. *Lathyrus*.

Stapeliad. A member of the genus *Stapelia* and closely related genera of the family Asclepiadaceae.

Stem segment. A portion of a jointed stem between 2 *nodes*, most frequently occurring in cacti.

Sterile. Infertile, not bearing *spores*, pollen, seeds etc.

Stigma. The part of the female portion of the flower, borne at the tip of the *style*, that receives pollen.

Stipule. A small scale- or leaf-like appendage, usually one of a pair, mostly borne at a *node* or below a leaf stalk.

Stock. See *rootstock*.

Stolon. A horizontally spreading or arching stem, usually above ground, which roots at its tip to produce a new plant.

Stop. To remove certain growing points of a plant so as to control growth or the size and number of flowers.

Stratify. To break the dormancy of some seeds by exposing them to a period of cold.

Style. The part of the flower on which the *stigma* is borne.

Sub-globose. Almost spherical.

Sub-shrub. A plant that is woody at the base although the terminal shoots die back in winter.

Succulent. A plant with thick, fleshy leaves and/or stems; in this book, it is evergreen unless otherwise stated.

Sucker. A shoot that arises from below ground level, directly from the *root* or *rootstock*.

Summer-deciduous. Losing its leaves naturally in summer.

Taproot. The main, downward-growing root of a plant; it is also applied generally to any strong, downward-growing root.

Tendril. A thread-like structure, used to provide support; see also *climber*.

Tooth. A small, marginal, often pointed lobe on a leaf, *calyx* or *corolla*.

Tepal. See *perianth segment*.

Tree. A woody plant usually having a well-defined trunk or stem with a head of branches above.

Trifoliate. With 3 leaves; loosely, with 3 *leaflets*.

Trifoliolate. With 3 *leaflets*.

True [of seedlings]. Retaining the distinctive characteristics of the parent when raised from seed.

Truss. A compact cluster of flowers, often large and showy, e.g. those of pelargoniums and rhododendrons.

Tuber. A thickened, usually underground, storage organ derived from a stem or root.

Tubercle. A small, rounded protuberance; see also *areole*.

Turion. 1. A bud on a *rhizome*. 2. A fleshy, overwintering bud found on certain water plants.

Umbel. A usually flat-topped or rounded flower cluster in which the individual flower stalks arise from a central point. In a compound umbel each primary stalk ends in an umbel.

Upright [of habit]. With vertical or semi-vertical main branches.

Water bud. See *turion*.

Whorl. The arrangement of 3 or more organs arising from the same point.

Winged [of seeds or fruits]. Having a marginal flange or membrane.

Woody-stemmed. With a stem composed of woody fibres and therefore persistent, as opposed to soft-stemmed and *herbaceous*. A **semi-woody stem** contains some softer tissue and may be only partially persistent.

x The sign used to denote a hybrid plant derived from the crossing of 2 or more botanically distinct plants.

+ The sign used to denote a graft hybrid; see *grafting*.

719

Acknowledgements

The publisher would like to thank the following for their kind permission to reproduce their photographs. Most of the photographs are found in The Plant Catalogue and are referenced by two numbers: the page number is given first, followed by the specific number or numbers of the photographs separated by hyphens. The photograph number is determined by the position of the photograph's caption according to one of two page grids. The twelve grid is shown alongside. The same numbering principle has been used for photographs in the feature panels, with numbers from 1 to 42; illustrations elsewhere in the book use the key: A=above; B=below; C=centre; L=left; R=right; T=top.

1	4	7	10
2	5	8	11
3	6	9	12

Alpine Garden Society Slide Library 288/41, 334/5, 348/4–9, 354/3, 356/11, 362/3, 364/10, 373/9, 375/12, 378/6, 379/5, 383/5, 388/3, 396/10, 400/3, 428/13, 429/2–26, 435/1, 436/9
Jacques Amand Ltd/John Amand 236/5–26, 289/42, 431/24
Aylett Nurseries 406/7
A–Z Botanical Collection 144/26, 175/9, 196/6, 199/10, 218/11, 234/35, 242/35, 282/7, 347/6, 374/2, 404/31, 447/2–10, 448/6; Malcolm Richards 13/Row4/1; A. Young 13/Row5/2
Gillian Beckett 119/1, 123/2–3, 132/21, 140/5, 145/1, 150/5, 154/4, 155/7, 157/12, 168/12, 171/1, 174/11, 219/6, 250/4, 251/4, 254/12, 256/1, 264/1, 273/12, 290/5, 292/3, 311/4, 313/10, 320/1, 348/5, 354/11, 356/12, 360/2, 361/3, 363/1, 367/11, 368/12, 373/1, 374/8–9, 377/6, 378/1, 381/10, 383/2, 385/3, 389/1, 402/9, 405/5–33, 412/3–6, 413/3–6, 414/10, 415/3, 417/21–38, 421/3, 423/6, 431/37, 432/2–3, 433/8, 434/1, 435/7, 439/9–10, 440/3–7, 446/6, 448/7–9
Kenneth A. Beckett 77/4, 206/3, 366/2, 368/4
Biofotos/Heather Angel 205/8, 448/12
Patrick Booth/John Thirkell 230/26–37–38
Ann & Roger Bowden 288/35, 289/15
Christopher Brickell 89/4, 100/1, 131/2–4, 132/17, 133/4–25, 134/6, 135/1, 142/12, 147/4, 148/1–5, 165/22, 205/4
Pat Brindley 136/4, 208/12, 210/7, 215/4, 235/5, 237/20, 242/26, 243/1, 255/1–10, 282/10, 313/9, 320/10, 324/7, 338/7, 324/8–12, 325/1, 326/10, 328/1–12, 329/1, 331/6, 332/3–4, 333/9, 336/4, 341/6, 399/5, 410/23, 411/8–41, 412/13–17–27–31, 429/7–29–37, 448/8
British Iris Society 235/2–14–20
Jonathan Buckley 129/2
Brinsley Burbridge 209/12
Ray Cobb 429/9
Eric Crichton 65/5, 70/4, 71/2, 93/1, 97/3, 99/10, 143/3, 157/9, 168/4, 177/11, 208/10, 215/1, 231/3, 234/7–15–29, 238/3, 243/1, 255/1–10, 282/10, 313/9, 320/10, 324/7, 338/7, 349/9, 354/10, 355/1, 357/9, 358/3, 369/1, 375/3, 379/1, 382/9, 383/3, 387/3, 396/7, 407/9, 410/17, 419/11, 420/1, 429/31, 450/31
Philip Damp 406/33
Kate Donald 416/21–28
Alan M. Edwards 418/2, 428/17
Raymond Evison 212/27–31–32–39, 213/12–13–14–15–17–18–33–35–41
John Fielding 37/BR, 40/BL, 48/TL, 50/TL, 51/TR, 53/TR
Valerie Finnis 354/7
Ron & Christine Foord 272/11
Maureen Foster 235/13
John Galbally 281/10
Garden Picture Library Brian Carter 44/TR; Eric Crichton 442&443; Geoff Dann 44/CR; Ron Evans 112&113, 342&343; John Glover 180&181, 222&223, 248/37, 253/10, 317/BC, 344/TC; Neil Holmes 204/6, 206/4, 237/19; Mayer/Le Scanff 445/BR; Jerry Pavia 314&315, 344&345/T, 452&453; Morley Read 43/TR; Howard Rice 331/12, 395/L; JS Sira 39/BR, 45/TL, 183/TL; Ron Sutherland 345/BL; Brigitte Thomas 40&41/T; Steven Wooster 182/CL, 200&201, 202/BL
John Glover 131/3, 134/27, 158/8, 242/42, 249/9, 286/1, 441/3
Derek Gould 116/11, 124/11, 134/4, 135/4, 144/40, 150/6, 153/6, 157/10, 170/2, 205/10, 208/7, 218/6, 233/7, 236/21, 240/4, 241/3–6–8, 249/1, 253/2, 258/11, 268/12, 272/34, 277/6, 279/8, 290/3, 334/11, 347/2, 359/7, 386/7, 390/4, 397/7, 412/11, 415/8, 427/3, 447/7
Diana Grenfell 257/6–10, 289/18
Christopher Grey–Wilson 10/BL
Peter Harkness 198/3–4
Jerry Harpur 55/BL, 55/TR
The Heather Society Slide Library 13/Row5/3, 178/12
Terry Hewitt 456/9, 472/2, 474/2, 480/1
D. Hewlett 407/23
Muriel Hodgeman 353/11, 359/10, 383/12, 385/1

Hortico 418/15
International Flower Bulb Centre 399/7, 431/35
Mike Ireland 367/2, 374/3, 377/7, 429/4–38
Brita Johansson 179/22
Roy Lancaster 11/C–CR
Andrew Lawson 2, 36/C, 38/T, 49/B, 57/T, 60&61, 114/BR, 182&183/B, 205/9, 324/1, 392&393, 404/11–16, 405/3–30
Sidney Linnegar 234/4 (G.E. Cassidy)–11 (R. Henley)–31 (R. Henley)–37 (G.E. Cassidy), 235/3–34 (G.E. Cassidy)– 40 (G.E. Cassidy)
Brian Mathew 402/3, 414/11, 419/1–4, 421/9, 423/11, 424/3, 426/9, 434/11
S. & O. Mathews 151/7
Dr E. Charles Nelson 13/Row2/2–Row3/1
Oxford Scientific Films/Fredrik Ehrenstrom 449/11
Photos Horticultural 105/3, 204/3, 231/12, 234/10, 237/1, 242/18–21, 277/3, 329/3, 335/5, 405/11, 424/2
Plant Pictures Worldwide 339/2
Collection & Photo Riviere (France, 26 Drôme) 236/19, 237/23–36
Howard Rice 14&15, 34&35, 206/5, 444&445/B
Royal Botanic Gardens, Kew 11/TR
Royal Horticultural Society, Lindley Library 11BL Curtis's Botanical Magazine (CBM), cliv (1928), T.9241; 417 CBM, vii (1794), T.252
A.D. Schilling 83/10, 90/11, 132/4, 166/8, 169/9
Harry Smith Collection 13/Row1/1, 65/6, 69/3–12, 70/1, 71/4–10, 72/7–10, 75/7–22–36, 80/4–11(inset), 81/3, 82/6–8, 83/9, 89/6, 91/1–6, 92/3–12, 93/2–6–7–9, 95/8, 97/4–6, 102/1, 104/3–12, 106/9, 108/8–12, 109/6, 111/33, 116/7, 117/1–6, 118/11, 119/4, 121/11, 123/1, 124/1–7, 125/6, 126/9, 129/26–32, 130/12, 131/5–11, 132/20–22–27–32–35, 133/16, 134/16, 135/2, 141/4, 142/7, 143/5, 145/9, 146/7, 147/2–5–12, 148/10, 149/2, 150/1, 151/11, 154/7, 155/3–6, 158/12, 159/25, 160/6, 164/24–36, 165/12, 167/8–10, 170/10, 171/3, 172/6, 173/5–6–12, 177/7, 196/8, 199/1–2–3, 204/10, 206/7, 207/3, 208/1–9, 209/3–9, 210/1–5–6, 211/2–3–7, 214/2–3–4, 217/2–12, 218/8–10, 219/2–3, 220/12, 221/26, 226/3, 228/9, 230/19–35–40, 231/9, 232/1–5, 235/4–23, 236/15, 237/17–18–37, 238/10, 242/13–19–29, 244/11, 248/33–40, 254/6, 257/16, 258/9, 263/9–10, 266/1, 268/8, 269/7, 270/1–4, 271/8, 273/1–4–18, 275/12, 278/6, 282/1–9, 283/12, 286/4, 287/6, 288/26–38, 293/6–10, 295/19, 319/10–12, 320/4, 321/4–9, 327/1, 329/11, 330/4, 331/3–4–5–7, 332/12, 334/3–4–6–7, 338/10, 339/4–8–9, 340/9, 341/4–8–9, 347/1–5, 349/2–10, 351/9, 352/6, 356/9, 357/6, 360/1–4–7, 361/4, 364/5–12, 365/9, 366/11, 368/10, 369/9–11, 371/6–7–8–10, 373/2, 375/5–9, 380/12, 381/5, 383/1–7, 386/8–9, 387/8–12, 388/4, 391/6, 397/4, 398/2, 399/14–26–32–37, 400/1–2, 401/12, 402/5, 403/12, 404/12–15–17–18–19, 405/10–12–19–40, 408/1–6, 409/6, 411/32, 412/5–38, 413/12, 414/6, 415/6, 420/7, 421/6, 422/7–9, 423/1, 424/9, 425/1–11, 426/7, 427/12, 428/16–28–30–42, 429/8–16–34, 430/10, 432/1–4–11, 434/9, 435/3, 436/1–7–10, 437/11, 438/1–4, 439/4, 440/2–11, 441/4–7–10, 447/3–4–12, 449/7–10, 450/11, 467/7, 475/10
Suttons Seeds 327/4
Thompson & Morgan 333/12, 335/6, 336/1
Unwin Seeds Ltd 322/12, 326/9, 328/9, 331/9, 332/1, 336/3, 340/3
Van Staaveren Aalsmeer BV 425/12
W.B. Wade 260/6–13–29–30–33–38, 261/6–13–16–18–21–22–27–28
Jack Wemyss–Cooke 273/13–14–35
John Wright 164/3, 165/10.

Jacket: **Jerry Harpur** front BR.

Picture research Andrew Brown, Susan Mennel
Picture research for the second edition Anna Lord

The publishers would like to thank all those who generously assisted the photographers and provided plants for photography, in particular the curators, directors and staff of the following organizations and those private individuals listed below. Special thanks are due to those at the Royal Botanic Gardens, Kew, and the Royal Horticultural Society's Garden, Wisley, for their invaluable assistance and support.

African Violet Centre, Terrington St Clement, Norfolk; Ken Akers, Great Saling, Essex; Jacques Amand Ltd, Clamphill, Middx; Anmore Exotics, Havant, Hants; David Austin Roses, Albrighton, Shrops; Avon Bulbs, Bradford-on-Avon, Wilts; Ayletts Nurseries, St Albans, Herts; Steven Bailey Ltd, Sway, Hants; Bill Baker, Tidmarsh, Berks; Batsford Arboretum, Moreton-in-Marsh, Glos; Booker Seeds, Sleaford, Lincs; Rupert Bowlby, Reigate, Surrey; Bressingham Gardens, Diss, Norfolk; Roy Brooks, Newent, Glos; British Orchid Growers' Association; Broadleigh Gardens, Somerset; Burford House Gardens, Tenbury Wells, Shrops; Cambridge Bulbs, Newton, Cambs; Nola Carr, Sydney, Australia; Beth Chatto Gardens, Colchester, Essex; Chelsea Physic Garden, London; Colegrave Seeds, Banbury, Oxon; County Park Nurseries, Hornchurch, Essex; Jill Cowley, Chelmsford, Essex; Mrs Anne Dexter, Oxford; Edrom Nurseries, Coldingham, Berwicks; Dr Jack Elliott, Ashford, Kent; Joe Elliott, Broadwell, Glos; Erdigg (National Trust), Clwyd, Wales; Fibrex Nurseries, Pebworth, Warwicks; Fisk's Clematis Nursery, Westleton, Suffolk; Mr & Mrs Thomas Gibson, Westwell, Oxon; Glasgow Botanic Garden, Glasgow; 'Glazenwood', Braintree, Essex.

R. Harkness & Co. Ltd, Hitchin, Herts; Harry Hay, Lower Kingswood, Surrey; Hazeldene Nurseries, East Farleigh, Kent; Hidcote Manor (National Trust), Chipping Camden, Glos; Hillier Gardens and Arboretum, Romsey, Hants; Hillier Nurseries (Winchester) Ltd, Romsey, Hants; Holly Gate Cactus Nursery, Ashington, Sussex; Hopleys Plants, Much Hadham, Herts; Huntingdon Botanical Gardens, San Marino, California; W.E.Th. Ingwersen Ltd, East Grinstead, Sussex; the late Clive Innes; Kelways Nurseries, Langport, Somerset; Kiftsgate Court Gardens, Chipping Camden, Glos; Lechlade Fuchsia Centre, Lechlade, Glos; The Living Desert, Palm Desert, California; Robin Loder, Leonardslee, Sussex; Los Angeles State and County Arboreta and Botanical Gardens, Los Angeles, California; Lotusland Foundation, Santa Barbara, California; McBeans Orchids, Lewes, Sussex; Merrist Wood Agricultural College, Worplesdon, Surrey; Mrs J.F. Phillips, Westwell, Oxon; Mr & Mrs Richard Purdon, Ramsden, Oxon; Ramparts Nurseries, Colchester, Essex; Ratcliffe Orchids, Didcot, Oxon; Mrs Joyce Robinson, Denmans, Fontwell, Sussex; Peter Q. Rose, Castle Cary, Somerset; Royal Botanic Gardens, Edinburgh; Royal Botanic Gardens, Kew, Surrey; Royal Botanic Gardens, Sydney, Australia; Royal National Rose Society, St Albans, Herts; Royal Horticultural Society's Garden, Wisley, Surrey.

Santa Barbara Botanic Garden, Santa Barbara, California; Savill Garden, Windsor, Berks; Mr & Mrs K. Schoenenberger, Shipton-under-Wychwood, Oxon; Mrs Martin Simmons, Burghclere, Berks; Dr James Smart, Barnstaple, Devon; Arthur Smith, Wigston, Leics; P.J. Smith, Ashington, Sussex; Springfields Gardens, Spalding, Lincs; Staite & Sons, Evesham, Worcs; Stapeley Water Gardens, Nantwich, Cheshire; Strybing Arboreta Society of Golden Gate Park, San Francisco, California; David Stuart, Dunbar, East Lothian; Suffolk Herbs, Sudbury, Suffolk; University Botanic Garden, Cambridge; University of British Columbia Botanical Garden, Vancouver; University of California Arboretum, Davis, California; University of California Arboretum, Santa Cruz, California; University of California Botanic Garden, Berkeley, California; University of California Botanical Gardens, Los Angeles, California; University of Reading Botanic Garden, Reading, Berks; Unwins Seeds Ltd, Histon, Cambridge; Jack Vass, Haywards Heath, Sussex; Rosemary Verey, Barnsley, Glos; Vesutor Air Plants, Ashington, Sussex; Wakehurst Place (Royal Botanic Gardens, Kew), Ardingly, Sussex; Primrose Warburg, Oxford; Waterperry Gardens, Wheatley, Oxon; Westonbirt Arboretum, Westonbirt, Glos; Woolman's Nurseries, Dorridge, West Midlands; Wyld Court Orchids, Newbury, Berks; Eric Young Orchid Foundation, Jersey, Channel Islands.

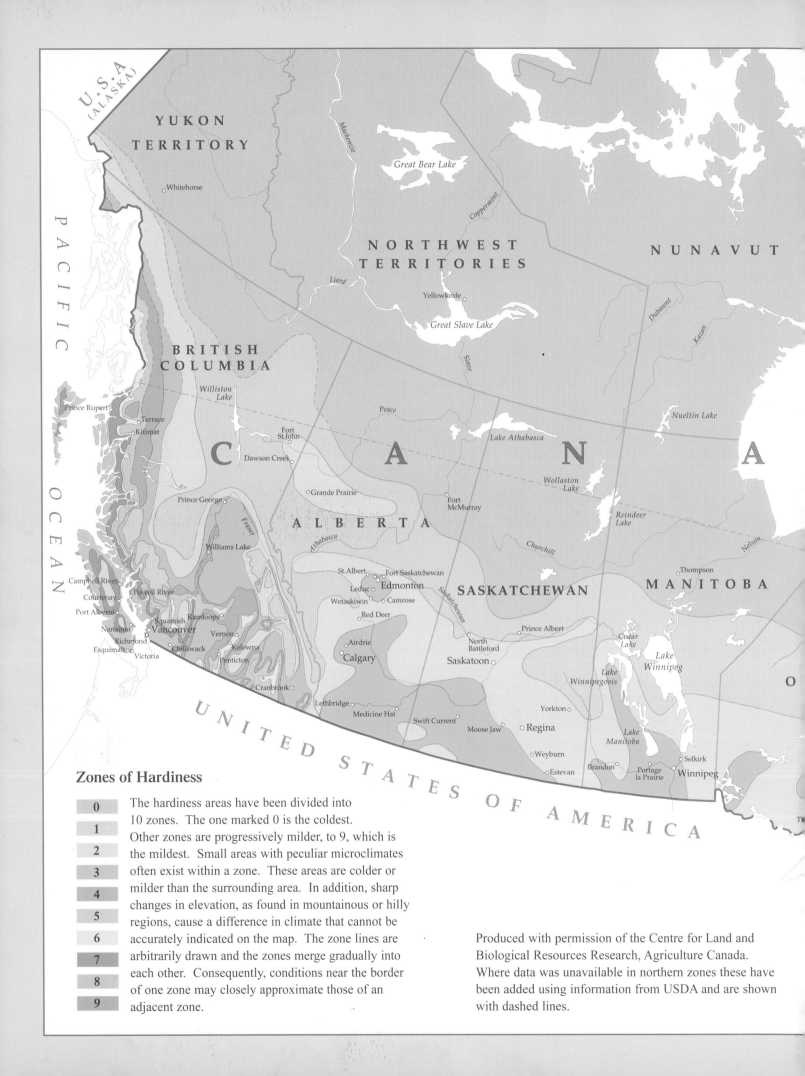

U.S.A
(ALASKA)

PACIFIC OCEAN

YUKON TERRITORY

Whitehorse

Mackenzie

Great Bear Lake

Coppermine

NORTHWEST TERRITORIES

NUNAVUT

Liard

Yellowknife

Great Slave Lake

Slave

Dubawnt

Kazan

BRITISH COLUMBIA

Williston Lake

Peace

Lake Athabasca

Nueltin Lake

Prince Rupert

Terrace
Kitimat

Fort St.John

C

Dawson Creek

A

N

Wollaston Lake

A

Reindeer Lake

Nelson

Grande Prairie

Fort McMurray

Prince George

Fraser

Churchill

ALBERTA

Athabasca

Thompson

Williams Lake

MANITOBA

Campbell River
Courtenay
Port Alberni
Nanaimo
Richmond
Esquimalt
Victoria

Powell River

Squamish
Vancouver
Chilliwack

Kamloops

Vernon

Kelowna
Penticton

St.Albert   Fort Saskatchewan
Leduc   Edmonton
Wetaskiwin   Camrose
Red Deer

Airdrie

Calgary

Saskatchewan

SASKATCHEWAN

North Battleford

Saskatoon

Prince Albert

Cedar Lake

Lake Winnipegosis

Lake Winnipeg

Selkirk

Cranbrook

Lethbridge

Medicine Hat

Swift Current

Moose Jaw

Regina

Weyburn

Estevan

Yorkton

Brandon

Lake Manitoba

Portage la Prairie

Winnipeg

O

UNITED STATES OF AMERICA

Zones of Hardiness

| 0 |
| 1 |
| 2 |
| 3 |
| 4 |
| 5 |
| 6 |
| 7 |
| 8 |
| 9 |

The hardiness areas have been divided into 10 zones. The one marked 0 is the coldest. Other zones are progressively milder, to 9, which is the mildest. Small areas with peculiar microclimates often exist within a zone. These areas are colder or milder than the surrounding area. In addition, sharp changes in elevation, as found in mountainous or hilly regions, cause a difference in climate that cannot be accurately indicated on the map. The zone lines are arbitrarily drawn and the zones merge gradually into each other. Consequently, conditions near the border of one zone may closely approximate those of an adjacent zone.

Produced with permission of the Centre for Land and Biological Resources Research, Agriculture Canada. Where data was unavailable in northern zones these have been added using information from USDA and are shown with dashed lines.